THE OLD TESTAMENT (OT)

Genesis	2 Chronicles	Daniel
Exodus	Ezra	Hosea
Leviticus	Nehemiah	Joel
Numbers	Esther	Amos
Deuteronomy	Job	Obadiah
Joshua	Psalms	Jonah
Judges	Proverbs	Micah
Ruth	Ecclesiastes	Nahum
1 Samuel	Song of Solomon	Habakkuk
2 Samuel	Isaiah	Zephaniah
1 Kings	Jeremiah	Haggai
2 Kings	Lamentations	Zechariah
1 Chronicles	Ezekiel	Malachi

THE NEW TESTAMENT (NT)

Matthew	Ephesians	Hebrews
Mark	Philippians	James
Luke	Colossians	1 Peter
John	1 Thessalonians	2 Peter
Acts	2 Thessalonians	1 John
Romans	1 Timothy	2 John
1 Corinthians	2 Timothy	3 John
2 Corinthians	Titus	Jude
Galatians	Philemon	Revelation

Deuterocanonical Books/Apocrypha: In Roman Catholic Bibles, the OT includes the following deuterocanonical books: (following Nehemiah) Tobit, Judith, Esther with the additions, 1–2 Maccabees; (following Song of Songs) Wisdom, Ecclesiasticus; (following Lamentations) Baruch including the Letter of Jeremiah; (following Ezekiel) Daniel with the additions.

In addition to these books, the Bible of the Greek Orthodox community includes 1 Esdras, the Prayer of Manasseh, Psalm 151, 3 Maccabees, with 4 Maccabees as an appendix.

Protestants regard the deuterocanonical books as not part of the OT canon and either do not include them in their Bibles, or print them in a separate section ("Apocrypha") following the OT or at the end of the Bible.

THE
HARPERCOLLINS
BIBLE
DICTIONARY

REVISED AND UPDATED

THE
HARPERCOLLINS
BIBLE
DICTIONARY

REVISED AND UPDATED

GENERAL EDITOR
MARK ALLAN POWELL

ASSOCIATE EDITORS

Barry L. Bandstra
†Lawrence E. Boadt
Joel S. Kaminsky
Amy-Jill Levine
Eric M. Meyers
Jonathan L. Reed
Marianne Meye Thompson
with the Society of Biblical Literature

PREVIOUS EDITIONS

General Editor: Paul J. Achtemeier
Associate Editors: Roger S. Boraas; Michael Fishbane;
Pheme Perkins; William O. Walker Jr.

HarperOne
An Imprint of HarperCollinsPublishers

Photo Research:
InfoEdit: Leslye Borden, Elizabeth Ely; Interactive Composition Corporation

Color Photograph Insert Design:
Christy Butterfield

Text Illustrations:
Heather Preston, Sally Shimizu

HarperOne

THE HARPERCOLLINS BIBLE DICTIONARY. *Revised and Updated.* Copyright © 2011 by The Society of Biblical Literature. All rights reserved. Printed in the United States of America. No part of this book may be used or reproduced in any manner whatsoever without written permission except in the case of brief quotations embodied in critical articles and reviews. For information, address HarperCollins Publishers, 10 East 53rd Street, New York, NY 10022.

HarperCollins books may be purchased for educational, business, or sales promotional use. For information, please write: Special Markets Department, HarperCollins Publishers, 10 East 53rd Street, New York, NY 10022.

HarperCollins website: http://www.harpercollins.com
HarperCollins®, ✠ ®, and HarperOne™ are trademarks of HarperCollins Publishers

THIRD EDITION

Library of Congress Cataloging-in-Publication Data

The HarperCollins Bible Dictionary. Revised and Updated. — 3rd ed. / general editor, Mark Allan Powell; associate editors, Barry L. Bandstra . . . [et al.].
    p.   cm.
    ISBN 978–0–06–146906–0
    1. Bible—Dictionaries.   I. Powell, Mark Allan.   II. HarperCollins (Firm)
    BS440.H235   2011
    220.3—dc22   2010007897

11 12 13 14 15   RRD (C)   10 9 8 7 6 5 4 3 2 1

Editorial Board

General Editor

Mark Allan Powell
Robert and Phyllis Leatherman Professor of New Testament Studies
Trinity Lutheran Seminary, Columbus, Ohio

Associate Editors

Barry L. Bandstra
Evert J. and Hattie E. Blekkink Professor of Religion
Hope College, Holland, Michigan

†Lawrence E. Boadt
Professor Emeritus of Sacred Scriptures
Washington Theological Union, Washington, D.C.

Joel S. Kaminsky
Professor of Religion and Director of Program in Jewish Studies
Smith College, Northampton, Massachusetts

Amy-Jill Levine
E. Rhodes and Leona B. Carpenter Professor of New Testament Studies
Vanderbilt Divinity School, Nashville, Tennessee

Eric M. Meyers
Bernice and Morton Lerner Professor of Judaic Studies
Duke University, Durham, North Carolina

Jonathan L. Reed
Professor of New Testament
University of La Verne, La Verne, California

Marianne Meye Thompson
George Eldon Ladd Professor of New Testament
Fuller Theological Seminary, Pasadena, California

Contributors

I.T.A. I. Tzvi Abusch
Brandeis University
Waltham, Massachusetts

E.R.A. †Elizabeth Achtemeier

P.J.A. Paul J. Achtemeier
Union Theological Seminary
Richmond, Virginia

P.R.A. †Peter R. Ackroyd

J.E.A. John E. Alsup
Austin Presbyterian Theological
Seminary
Austin, Texas

H.W.A. Harold W. Attridge
Yale Divinity School
New Haven, Connecticut

L.R.B. Lloyd R. Bailey
Mount Olive College
Mount Olive, North Carolina

W.R.B. William Baird
Brite Divinity School, Texas
Christian University
Fort Worth, Texas

D.B. †Denis Baly

B.B. Barry L. Bandstra
Hope College
Holland, Michigan

J.B. †James Barr

S.S.B. S. Scott Bartchy
University of California
Los Angeles, California

J.M.B. Jouette M. Bassler
Perkins School of Theology,
Southern Methodist
University
Dallas, Texas

R.A.B. Richard A. Batey
Rhodes College
Memphis, Tennessee

S.B. Stephen Benko
Sonoma, California

A.B. Adele Berlin
University of Maryland
at College Park
College Park, Maryland

E.B. †Ernest Best

J.W.B. John W. Betlyon
Pennsylvania State University
University Park, Pennsylvania

H.D.B. Hans Dieter Betz
University of Chicago Divinity
School
Chicago, Illinois

P.A.B. Phyllis A. Bird
Garrett-Evangelical Theological
Seminary
Evanston, Illinois

L.E.B. †Lawrence E. Boadt

R.B. †Robert G. Boling

R.S.B. Roger S. Boraas
Philadelphia, Pennsylvania

M.E.B. M. Eugene Boring
Brite Divinity School, Texas
Christian University
Fort Worth, Texas

D.R.B. Dennis R. Bratcher
CRI/Voice Institute
Oklahoma City, Oklahoma

R.G.B. †Robert G. Bratcher

M.Z.B. Marc Z. Brettler
Brandeis University
Waltham, Massachusetts

W.P.B. William P. Brown
Columbia Theological Seminary
Decatur, Georgia

W.B. Walter Brueggemann
Columbia Theological Seminary
Decatur, Georgia

G.W.B. George Wesley Buchanan
Wesley Theological Seminary
Washington, D.C.

Sh.B.	Shlomo Bunimovitz *Tel Aviv University* *Tel Aviv, Israel*	J.L.C.	James L. Crenshaw *Duke University Divinity School* *Durham, North Carolina*
E.F.C.	Edward F. Campbell Jr. *McCormick Theological Seminary* *Chicago, Illinois*	J.D.C.	John Dominic Crossan *DePaul University* *Chicago, Illinois*
C.E.C.	Charles E. Carlston *Andover Newton Theological School* *Newton Centre, Massachusetts*	J.J.D.	John J. Davis *Grace Theological Seminary* *Winona Lake, Indiana*
J.H.C.	James H. Charlesworth *Princeton Theological Seminary* *Princeton, New Jersey*	J.A.D.	J. Andrew Dearman *Austin Presbyterian Theological* *Seminary* *Austin, Texas*
D.L.C.	Duane L. Christensen *Graduate Theological Union* *Berkeley, California*	W.G.D.	William G. Dever *University of Arizona* *Tucson, Arizona*
R.J.C.	Richard J. Clifford *Boston College School of Theology* *and Ministry* *Chestnut Hill, Massachusetts*	J.D.	Joanna Dewey *Episcopal Divinity School* *Cambridge, Massachusetts*
G.W.C.	†George W. Coats Jr.	K.P.D.	Karl Paul Donfried *Smith College* *Northampton, Massachusetts*
M.C.	Mordechai Cogan *Hebrew University* *Jerusalem, Israel*	D.A.D.	David A. Dorsey *Evangelical School of Theology* *Myerstown, Pennsylvania*
R.C.	Richard Coggins *King's College* *London, England*	J.F.D.	Joel F. Drinkard Jr. *Southern Baptist Theological* *Seminary* *Louisville, Kentucky*
A.Y.C.	Adela Yarbro Collins *Yale University* *New Haven, Connecticut*	D.R.E.	Douglas R. Edwards *University of Puget Sound* *Tacoma, Washington*
J.J.C.	John J. Collins *Yale University* *New Haven, Connecticut*	J.M.E.	James M. Efird *Duke University Divinity School* *Durham, North Carolina*

M.D.C.	Michael D. Coogan
	Stonehill College
	North Easton, Massachusetts
		B.L.E.	Barry Lee Eichler
			University of Pennsylvania
			  Museum of Archaeology and
			  Anthropology
			Philadelphia, Pennsylvania

R.A.C.	Robert A. Coughenour *Western Theological Seminary* *Holland, Michigan*		
L.W.C.	L. William Countryman *Church Divinity School of the Pacific* *Berkeley, California*	D.E.	David Ewert *Mennonite Brethren Bible College* *Winnipeg, Manitoba*
F.B.C.	Fred B. Craddock *Candler School of Theology, Emory* *University* *Atlanta, Georgia*	J.C.E.	J. Cheryl Exum *University of Sheffield* *Sheffield, United Kingdom*
P.L.C.	Patricia L. Crawford *Stony Brook University* *Stony Brook, New York*	G.D.F.	Gordon D. Fee *Regent College* *Vancouver, British Columbia*

H.F. †Harold Fisch

M.A.F. Michael Fishbane
University of Chicago Divinity School
Chicago, Illinois

J.A.F. Joseph A. Fitzmyer
Georgetown University
Washington, D.C.

E.L.F. Elisabeth L. Flynn-Chapman
Longwood College
Farmville, Virginia

J.P.F. Jan P. Fokkelman
Leiden, The Netherlands

D.A.F. Daniel A. Foxvog
University of California
Berkeley, California

F.S.F. Frank S. Frick
Albion College
Albion, Michigan

T.S.F. †Tikva S. Frymer-Kensky

R.H.F. †Reginald H. Fuller

V.P.F. Victor Paul Furnish
Perkins School of Theology, Southern
Methodist University
Dallas, Texas

J.G.G. †John G. Gammie

F.O.G. Francisco O. Garcia-Treto
Trinity University
San Antonio, Texas

S.G. †Stanley Gevirtz

Y.G. Yehoshua Gitay
Haifa University
Haifa, Israel

D.A.G. David A. Glatt-Gilad
Ben Gurion University of
the Negev
Beer-Sheva, Israel

R.M.G. †Robert M. Good

F.E.G. Frederick E. Greenspahn
Florida Atlantic University
Boca Raton, Florida

E.L.G. Edward L. Greenstein
Bar-Ilan University
Ramat-Gan, Israel

M.R.G. Michael R. Greenwald
St. Lawrence University
Canton, New York

M.I.G. Mayer I. Gruber
Ben Gurion University of the Negev
Beer-Sheva, Israel

R.H.G. Robert H. Gundry
Westmont College
Santa Barbara, California

P.D.H. Paul D. Hanson
Harvard University
Cambridge, Massachusetts

J.P.H. John Paul Heil, S.S.D.
Catholic University of America
Washington, D.C.

D.C.H. David C. Hester
Louisville Presbyterian Theological
Seminary
Louisville, Kentucky

R.H.H. Richard H. Hiers
University of Florida
Gainesville, Florida

R.F.H. Ronald F. Hock
University of Southern California
Los Angeles, California

C.R.H. Carl R. Holladay
Candler School of Theology, Emory
University
Atlanta, Georgia

H.B.H. Herbert B. Huffmon
Drew University
Madison, New Jersey

F.W.H. Frank W. Hughes
Diocesan School of Theology
Alexandria, Louisiana

A.J.H. Arland J. Hultgren
Luther Seminary
St. Paul, Minnesota

W.L.H. W. Lee Humphreys
University of Tennessee
Knoxville, Tennessee

D.I. David Ilan
Nelson Glueck School of Biblical
Archaeology
Jerusalem, Israel

B.S.J. Bernard S. Jackson
University of Manchester
Manchester, United Kingdom

J.F.J. †John F. Jansen

J.G.J. J. Gerald Janzen
Christian Theological Seminary
Indianapolis, Indiana

W.J.	Waldemar Janzen *Canadian Mennonite University* *Winnipeg, Manitoba*	Z.L.	Zvi Lederman *Tel Aviv University* *Tel Aviv, Israel*
R.J.	Robert Jewett *University of Heidelberg* *Heidelberg, Germany*	W.E.L.	Werner E. Lemke *Colgate Rochester Divinity School* *Rochester, New York*
D.L.J.	Donald L. Jones *University of South Carolina* *Columbia, South Carolina*	A-J.L.	Amy-Jill Levine *Vanderbilt Divinity School* *Nashville, Tennessee*
J.Ka.	John Kaltner *Rhodes College* *Memphis, Tennessee*	B.M.L.	Bernard M. Levinson *University of Minnesota–* *Twin Cities* *Minneapolis, Minnesota*
J.K.	Joel S. Kaminsky *Smith College* *Northampton, Massachusetts*	T.L.	Tom Levy *University of California, San Diego* *San Diego, California*
H.C.K.	Howard C. Kee *University of Pennsylvania* *Philadelphia, Pennsylvania*	B.L.	†Barnabas Lindars
		T.R.W.L.	Thomas R. W. Longstaff
A.D.K.	Anne Draffkorn Kilmer *University of California* *Berkeley, California*		*Colby College* *Waterville, Maine*
P.J.K.	Philip J. King *Boston College* *Chestnut Hill, Massachusetts*	B.M.	Burton MacDonald *St. Francis Xavier University* *Antagonish, Nova Scotia*
J.D.K.	Jack Dean Kingsbury *Union Theological Seminary* *Richmond, Virginia*	D.R.M.	Dennis R. MacDonald *Claremont School of Theology* *Claremont, California*
J.K.	John S. Kloppenborg *University of Toronto* *Toronto, Ontario*	P.B.M.	Peter B. Machinist *Harvard University* *Cambridge, Massachusetts*
D.A.K.	Douglas A. Knight *Vanderbilt Divinity School* *Nashville, Tennessee*	J.A.R.M.	J. A. Ross MacKenzie *Chautauqua Institution* *Chautauqua, New York*
I.U.K.	Ilse U. Köhler-Rollefson *San Diego State University* *San Diego, California*	J.M.	Jodi Magness *University of North Carolina* *Chapel Hill, North Carolina*
J.S.K.	John S. Kselman *St. Patrick's Seminary* *Menlo Park, California*	B.J.M.	Bruce J. Malina *Creighton University* *Omaha, Nebraska*
J.L.K.	James L. Kugel *Harvard University* *Cambridge, Massachusetts*	F.J.M.	Frank J. Matera *The Catholic University* *of America* *Washington, D.C.*
P.L.	Peter Lampe *University of Heidelberg* *Heidelberg, Germany*	G.L.M.	Gerald L. Mattingly *Johnson Bible College* *Knoxville, Tennessee*
N.L.L.	Nancy L. Lapp *Pittsburgh Theological Seminary* *Pittsburgh, Pennsylvania*	P.K.M.	P. Kyle McCarter Jr. *Johns Hopkins University* *Baltimore, Maryland*

T.L.M.	Thomas L. McClellan *University of Melbourne* *Parkville, Australia*	J.M.O.	Julia M. O'Brien *Lancaster Theological Seminary* *Lancaster, Pennsylvania*
F.R.M.	Foster R. McCurley *Mohnton, Pennsylvania*	K.G.O.	Kevin G. O'Connell *Jesuit Center* *Amman, Jordan*
L.C.M.	Lane C. McGaughy *Willamette University* *Salem, Oregon*	S.B.P.	†Simon B. Parker
		L.E.P.	Laurie E. Pearce *University of California at Berkeley* *Berkeley, California*
E.V.M.	Edgar V. McKnight *Furman University* *Greenville, South Carolina*	L.G.P.	Leo G. Perdue *Brite Divinity School, Texas Chris-* *tian University* *Fort Worth, Texas*
A.J.M.	Allan J. McNicol *Institute for Christian Studies* *Austin, Texas*		
J.P.M.	John P. Meier *University of Notre Dame* *Notre Dame, Indiana*	P.P.	Pheme Perkins *Boston College* *Chestnut Hill, Massachusetts*
R.F.M.	†Roy F. Melugin	D.M.P.	Dana M. Pike *Brigham Young University* *Provo, Utah*
B.M.M.	†Bruce M. Metzger		
C.L.M.	Carol L. Meyers *Duke University* *Durham, North Carolina*	J.R.P.	†Joshua R. Porter
		M.A.P.	Mark Allan Powell *Trinity Lutheran Seminary* *Columbus, Ohio*
E.M.M.	Eric M. Meyers *Duke University* *Durham, North Carolina*	J.L.P.	James L. Price Jr. *Duke University* *Durham, North Carolina*
C.H.M.	Charles H. Miller *Rome, Italy*		
J.M.M.	J. Maxwell Miller *Fernbank Museum of Natural* *History* *Atlanta, Georgia*	J.D.P.	James D. Purvis *Boston, Massachusetts*
		C.Q.	Corethia Qualls *Judge Memorial Catholic High* *School* *Salt Lake City, Utah*
M.K.M.	Mary K. Milne *St. Mary's University* *San Antonio, Texas*	A.F.R.	Anson F. Rainey *Tel Aviv University* *Tel Aviv, Israel*
S.C.M.	Stephen C. Mott *Cochesett United Methodist* *Church* *West Bridgewater, Massachusetts*	S.R.	Susan Rattray *Oakland, California*
W.M.	†Winsome Munro	J.R.	Jonathan L. Reed *University of La Verne* *La Verne, California*
R.E.M.	†Roland E. Murphy		
C.A.N.	Carol Ann Newsom *Candler School of Theology, Emory* *University* *Atlanta, Georgia*	S.B.R.	Stephen Breck Reid *George W. Truett Theological* *Seminary* *Waco, Texas*
J.H.N.	Jerome H. Neyrey *University of Notre Dame* *Notre Dame, Indiana*	H.E.R.	Harold E. Remus *Wilfrid Laurier University* *Waterloo, Ontario*

J.H.P.R.   †John H. P. Reumann

S.L.R.   Suzanne L. Richard
Gannon University
Erie, Pennsylvania

K.H.R.   Kent Harold Richards
Society of Biblical Literature
Atlanta, Georgia

J.J.M.R.   J. J. M. Roberts
Princeton Theological Seminary
Princeton, New Jersey

C.J.R.   Calvin J. Roetzel
University of Minnesota–
Twin Cities
Minneapolis, Minnesota

A.R.   Alexander Rofé
Hebrew University
Jerusalem, Israel

J.W.R.   Joel W. Rosenberg
Tufts University
Medford, Massachusetts

A.J.S.   †Anthony J. Saldarini

J.M.S.   Jack M. Sasson
Vanderbilt University
Nashville, Tennessee

M.M.S.   Marilyn M. Schaub
Duquesne University
Pittsburgh, Pennsylvania

B.E.S.   †Bruce E. Schein

L.H.S.   Lawrence H. Schiffman
New York University
New York, New York

J.D.S.   Joe D. Seger
Cobb Institute of Archaeology,
Mississippi State University
Starkville, Mississippi

D.S.   Donald Senior
Catholic Theological Union
Chicago, Illinois

P.L.S.   Philip L. Shuler
McMurry University
Abilene, Texas

D.J.S.   Daniel J. Simundson
Luther Seminary
St. Paul, Minnesota

D.M.S.   D. Moody Smith
The Divinity School, Duke
University
Durham, North Carolina

R.H.S.   Robert H. Stein
Southern Baptist Theological
Seminary
Louisville, Kentucky

D.W.S.   David W. Suter
Saint Martin's College
Lacey, Washington

M.A.S.   Marvin A. Sweeney
School of Theology at Claremont
Claremont, California

C.H.T.   Charles H. Talbert
Baylor University
Waco, Texas

R.C.T.   Robert C. Tannehill
Methodist Theological School in Ohio
Delaware, Ohio

H.M.T.   †Howard M. Teeple

P.Th.   Pamela Thimmes
University of Dayton
Dayton, Ohio

J.W.T.   James W. Thompson
Abilene Christian University
Abilene, Texas

M.M.T.   Marianne Meye Thompson
Fuller Theological Seminary
Pasadena, California

J.H.T.   Jeffrey H. Tigay
University of Pennsylvania
Philadelphia, Pennsylvania

L.E.T.   †Lawrence E. Toombs

W.S.T.   W. Sibley Towner
Union Theological Seminary
Richmond, Virginia

P.T.   Phyllis Trible
Wake Forest University School of
Divinity
Winston-Salem, North Carolina

G.M.T.   Gene M. Tucker
Candler School of Theology, Emory
University
Atlanta, Georgia

J.B.T.   Joseph B. Tyson
Southern Methodist University
Dallas, Texas

J.U.   Jeremiah Unterman
Association of Modern Orthodox
Day Schools and Yeshiva High
Schools
New York, New York

W.W. William O. Walker Jr.
Trinity University
San Antonio, Texas

J.M.W. James M. Weinstein
Cornell University
Ithaca, New York

D.B.W. David B. Weisberg
Hebrew Union College–Jewish
Institute of Religion
Cincinnati, Ohio

J.L.W. John L. White
Loyola University of Chicago
Chicago, Illinois

R.A.W. Robert A. Wild
Marquette University
Milwaukee, Wisconsin

M.M.W. Marsha M. Wilfong
First Presbyterian Church
Bellevue, Iowa

S.K.W. Sam K. Williams
Colorado College
Colorado Springs, Colorado

R.R.W. Robert R. Wilson
Yale Divinity School
New Haven, Connecticut

V.L.W. Vincent L. Wimbush
Claremont Graduate University
Claremont, California

D.P.W. David P. Wright
Brandeis University
Waltham, Massachusetts

Abbreviations

Gk.	Greek	JB	Jerusalem Bible
Heb.	Hebrew	KJV	King James Version
Lat.	Latin	NASB	New American Standard Bible
		NEB	New English Bible
BCE	Before the Common Era (BC in traditional dating)	NIV	New International Version
		NJB	New Jerusalem Bible
CE	Common Era (AD in traditional dating)	NRSV	New Revised Standard Version
		JPS	Tanakh (Jewish Publication Society)
LXX	Septuagint	RSV	Revised Standard Version
NT	New Testament	TEV	Today's English Version
OT	Old Testament		

chap(s). chapter(s)
ms(s). manuscripts(s)
v(v). verse(s)

Books of the Bible

Old Testament

Gen.	Genesis
Exod.	Exodus
Lev.	Leviticus
Num.	Numbers
Deut.	Deuteronomy
Josh.	Joshua
Judg.	Judges
Ruth	Ruth
1 Sam.	1 Samuel
2 Sam.	2 Samuel
1 Kings	1 Kings
2 Kings	2 Kings
1 Chron.	1 Chronicles
2 Chron.	2 Chronicles
Ezra	Ezra
Neh.	Nehemiah
Esther	Esther
Job	Job
Ps. (Pss.)	Psalm(s)
Prov.	Proverbs
Eccles.	Ecclesiastes
Song of Sol.	Song of Solomon
Isa.	Isaiah
Jer.	Jeremiah
Lam.	Lamentations
Ezek.	Ezekiel
Dan.	Daniel
Hos.	Hosea
Joel	Joel
Amos	Amos
Obad.	Obadiah
Jon.	Jonah
Mic.	Micah
Nah.	Nahum
Hab.	Habakkuk
Zeph.	Zephaniah
Hag.	Haggai
Zech.	Zechariah
Mal.	Malachi

Apocrypha/Deuterocanonical Books

1 Esd.	1 Esdras
2 Esd.	2 Esdras
Tob.	Tobit
Jth.	Judith
Add. Esther	Additions to Esther
Wis.	Wisdom of Solomon
Sir.	Sirach
Bar.	Baruch
Let. Jer.	Letter of Jeremiah
Add. Dan.	Additions to Daniel
Song of Three Jews	Song of the Three Jews
Sus.	Susanna
Bel and Dragon	Bel and the Dragon
Pr. of Man.	Prayer of Manasseh
Ps. 151	Psalm 151
1 Macc.	1 Maccabees
2 Macc.	2 Maccabees
3 Macc.	3 Maccabees
4 Macc.	4 Maccabees

New Testament

Matt.	Matthew
Mark	Mark
Luke	Luke
John	John
Acts	Acts of the Apostles
Rom.	Romans
1 Cor.	1 Corinthians
2 Cor.	2 Corinthians
Gal.	Galatians
Eph.	Ephesians
Phil.	Philippians
Col.	Colossians
1 Thess.	1 Thessalonians
2 Thess.	2 Thessalonians
1 Tim.	1 Timothy
2 Tim.	2 Timothy
Titus	Titus
Philem.	Philemon
Heb.	Hebrews
James	James
1 Pet.	1 Peter
2 Pet.	2 Peter
1 John	1 John
2 John	2 John
3 John	3 John
Jude	Jude
Rev.	Revelation

Pseudepigrapha and Early Christian Literature

Adam and Eve	*Books of Adam and Eve*	*Barn.*	*Epistle of Barnabas*
2–3 Bar.	Syriac, Greek Apocalypse	*1–2 Clem.*	*1–2 Clement*
	of *Baruch*	*Did.*	*Didache*
Apoc. Mos.	*Apocalypse of Moses*	*Diogn.*	*Diognetus*
As. Mos.	*Assumption of Moses*	Herm. *Man.*	Shepherd of Hermas,
1–2–3 Enoch	Ethiopic, Slavonic, Hebrew		*Mandate*
	Enoch	Herm. *Sim.*	Shepherd of Hermas,
Let. Arist.	*Letter of Aristeas*		*Similitude*
Jub.	*Jubilees*	Herm. *Vis.*	Shepherd of Hermas, *Vision*
Mart. Isa.	*Martyrdom of Isaiah*	Ign. *Eph.*	Ignatius, *Letter to the*
Odes Sol.	*Odes of Solomon*		*Ephesians*
Pss. Sol.	*Psalms of Solomon*	Ign. *Magn.*	Ignatius, *Letter to the*
Sib. Or.	*Sibylline Oracles*		*Magnesians*
T. 12 Patr.	*Testaments of the Twelve*	Ign. *Phld.*	Ignatius, *Letter to the*
	Patriarchs		*Philadelphians*
T. Levi	*Testament of Levi*	Ign. *Pol.*	Ignatius, *Letter to the*
T. Benj.	*Testament of Benjamin,* etc.		*Polycarp*
Acts Pil.	*Acts of Pilate*	Ign. *Rom.*	Ignatius, *Letter to the*
Apoc. Pet.	*Apocalypse of Peter*		*Romans*
Gos. Eb.	*Gospel of the Ebionites*	Ign. *Smyrn.*	Ignatius, *Letter to the*
Gos. Eg.	*Gospel of the Egyptians*		*Smyrnaeans*
Gos. Heb.	*Gospel of the Hebrews*	Ign. *Trall.*	Ignatius, *Letter to the*
Gos. Naass.	*Gospel of the Naassenes*		*Trallians*
Gos. Pet.	*Gospel of Peter*	Mart. *Pol.*	*Martyrdom of Polycarp*
Gos. Thom.	*Gospel of Thomas*	Pol. *Phil.*	Polycarp, *Letter to the*
Prot. Jas.	*Protevangelium of James*		*Philippians*

Dead Sea Scrolls and Related Texts

CD	Cairo (Genizah text of the) Damascus (Document)	1QSb	*Blessings*, Appendix B to 1QS
Mas	Masada texts	3Q15	*Copper Scroll*
Mird	Khirbet Mird texts	4QpGen^a	*Pesher on Genesis*
Mur	Wadi Murabba'at texts	4QFlor	*Florilegium* (or *Eschatological Midrashim*)
p	Pesher (commentary)	4QMessApoc	*Messianic Apocalypse*
Q	Qumran	4QMess ar	Aramaic "Messianic" text
1Q, 2Q, 3Q, etc.	Numbered caves of Qumran yielding written material, followed by abbreviation of biblical or apocryphal book	4QMMT	*Collection of Works of the Law*
		4QPBless	*Patriarchal Blessings*
		4QPrNab	*Prayer of Nabonidus*
		4QTest	*Testimonia* text
1QapGen	*Genesis Apocryphon*	4QTLevi	*Testament of Levi*
1QH	*Thanksgiving Hymns*	4QPhyl	Phylacteries
1QIsa^{a,b}	First or second copy of Isaiah	4Q159	*Ordinances*
1QpHab	*Pesher on Habakkuk*	11QMelch	*Melchizedek* text
1QM	*War Scroll*	11QPs^a	*Psalms Scroll*^a
1QS	*Rule of the Community*	11QtgJob	*Targum of Job*
1QSa	*Rule of the Congregation*, Appendix A to 1QS	11QT^a	*Temple Scroll*

Targumic Material

Tg. Onq.	*Targum Onqelos*	*Tg. Neof.*	*Targum Neofiti 1*
Tg. Neb.	*Targum of the Prophets*	*Tg. Ps.-J.*	*Targum Pseudo-Jonathan*
Tg. Ket.	*Targum of the Writings*	*Tg. Yer. I*	*Targum Yerushalmi I*
Frg. Tg.	*Fragmentary Targum*	*Tg. Yer. II*	*Targum Yerushalmi II*
Sam. Tg.	*Samaritan Targum*	*Yem. Tg.*	*Yemenite Targum*
Tg. Isa.	*Targum of Isaiah*	*Tg. Esth I.*	*First or Second Targum*
Pal. Tgs.	*Palestinian Targums*		*of Esther*

Mishnaic and Related Literature

m.	Mishnah	*Mo'ed Qat.*	*Mo'ed Qatan*
t.	Tosepta	*Nas.*	*Nasim*
b.	Babylonian Talmud	*Naz.*	*Nazir*
y.	Jerusalem (Palestinian)	*Ned.*	*Nedarim*
	Talmud	*Neg.*	*Nega'im*
'Abod. Zar.	*'Abodah Zarah*	*Nez.*	*Neziqin*
'Abot	*'Abot*	*Nid.*	*Niddah*
'Arak.	*'Arakin*	*'Ohal.*	*'Ohalot*
B. Bat.	*Baba Batra*	*'Or.*	*'Orlah*
B. Mesi'a	*Baba Mesi'a*	*Parah*	*Parah*
B. Qam.	*Baba Qamma*	*Pe'ah*	*Pe'ah*
Bek.	*Bekorot*	*Pesah.*	*Pesahim*
Ber.	*Berakot*	*Qinnim*	*Qinnim*
Besah	*Besah (= Yom Tob)*	*Qidd.*	*Qiddusin*
Bik.	*Bikkurim*	*Qod.*	*Qodasim*
Demai	*Demai*	*Ros. Has.*	*Ros Hassanah*
'Erub.	*'Erubin*	*Sanh.*	*Sanhedrin*
'Ed.	*'Eduyyot*	*Sabb.*	*Sabbat*
Git.	*Gittin*	*Seb.*	*Sebi'it*
Hag.	*Hagigah*	*Sebu.*	*Sebu'ot*
Hal.	*Hallah*	*Seder*	*Seder*
Hor.	*Horayot*	*Seqal*	*Seqalim*
Hul.	*Hullin*	*Sotah*	*Sotah*
Kelim	*Kelim*	*Sukkah*	*Sukkah*
Ker.	*Kerithot*	*Ta'an.*	*Ta'anit*
Ketub.	*Ketubbot*	*Tamid*	*Tamid*
Kil.	*Kil'ayim*	*Tem.*	*Temurah*
Ma'as. S.	*Ma'aser Seni*	*Ter.*	*Terumot*
Ma'as.	*Ma'aserot*	*Tehar.*	*Teharot*
Mak.	*Makkot*	*T. Yom*	*Tebul Yom*
Maks.	*Maksirin*	*'Uq.*	*'Uqsin*
Meg.	*Megillah*	*Yad.*	*Yadayim*
Me'il.	*Me'ilah*	*Yebam.*	*Yebamot*
Menah.	*Menahot*	*Yoma*	*Yoma (= Kippurim)*
Mid.	*Middot*	*Zabim*	*Zabim*
Miqw.	*Miqwa'ot*	*Zebah.*	*Zebahim*
Mo'ed	*Mo'ed*	*Zera.*	*Zera'im*

Other Rabbinic Works

'Abot R. Nat.	*'Abot de Rabbi Nathan*	*Pal.*	*Palestinian I* (used alone)
'Ag. Ber.	*'Aggadat Bereshit*	*Pesiq. R.*	*Pesiqta Rabbati*
Bab.	*Babylonian I* (used alone)	*Pesiq. Rab Kah.*	*Pesiqta de Rab Kahana*
Bar.	*Baraita*	*Pirqe R. El.*	*Pirqe Rabbi Eliezer*
Der. Er. Rab.	*Derek Erets Rabba*	*Rab.*	*Rabbah;* following
Der. Er. Zut.	*Derek Erets Zuta*		abbreviation for biblical
Gem.	*Gemara*		book (e.g., *Gen. Rab.* =
Kalla	*Kalla*		*Genesis Rabbah*)
Mek.	*Mekilta*		
Midr.	*Midrash;* cited with usual	*Sem.*	*Semahot*
	abbreviation for biblical	*Sipra*	*Sipra*
	book (e.g., *Midr. Gen.*	*Sipre*	*Sipre*
	= *Midrash Genesis;* but	*Sop.*	*Soperim*
	Midr. Qoh. = *Midrash*	*S. 'Olam Rab.*	*Seder 'Olam Rabbah*
	Qohelet, Ecclesiastes)	*Tanh.*	*Tanhuma*
		Yal.	*Yalqut*

Nag Hammadi Tractates

Preface

The HarperCollins Bible Dictionary is widely regarded as the most authoritative work of its kind, not least because of the involvement of the Society of Biblical Literature in the production and continual evaluation of its content. This third edition continues in the tradition of excellence of its predecessors, but has been thoroughly updated and revised by a new editorial team. About 50 percent of the content is new, and several dozen charts, tables, and other graphics have been added.

The editorial process has been guided by some key commitments. First, the purpose of the dictionary is to make the results of biblical scholarship available to a wide audience that includes nonspecialists. The individual entries have been written by academic experts, but the material is presented in as nontechnical and reader-friendly a fashion as possible. In many cases, the author of a particular entry is a scholar who has written entire books or monographs on the subject at hand; still, most of the material will be both intelligible and enlightening for general readers who need only a quick summary of basic information.

Second, the focus of the dictionary is on understanding the biblical text itself. For this reason, the number of textual references has been greatly increased in this edition of the dictionary; more examples have been added to the entries, indicating the passages or instances in which particular words, persons, or concepts are featured. Of course, many entries also present background information, including data relevant for understanding the Bible within its historical and literary context. Even then, however, the goal is, not to report everything that can be known about topics pertinent to the ancient world, but to summarize the information scholars find most pertinent for understanding the Bible.

Third, the tone of the dictionary is intended to be descriptive, not argumentative. The field of biblical studies encompasses many schools of thought about which methods of research are most reliable, what sorts of evidence are most conclusive, and so on. Nevertheless, the authors and editors of this dictionary recognize that this book is not the proper forum for advocacy of particular positions or presentation of pet theories. The entries summarize data and, when appropriate, provide some indication of different ways in which that data has been interpreted. There is no attempt to persuade readers to accept one view or reject another.

Finally, this dictionary is an academic reference work that presupposes a scholarly interest in the Bible that transcends devotional or spiritual concerns. That said, it does strive to be considerate of those whose interest in the Bible is informed by religious perspectives. We recognize that faith commitments are often—though not always—what propel people to study the Bible. Our intention has been to avoid privileging skepticism, on the one hand, or promoting any particular religious views, on the other. The editors themselves are a diverse lot, representing different confessional and ideological positions (e.g., Roman Catholic, Jewish, mainline Protestant, evangelical). We identify ourselves as liberals, moderates, and conservatives, and we have often checked each other's work to ensure that material is presented fairly and accurately.

Key features of the dictionary include the following:

- Entries on almost every name (person or place) mentioned in the Bible; the only names of persons or places *not* accorded entries are those for which no substantive information can be provided (e.g., a name found in a list of names without any additional information).

- Entries on every book of the Bible, with outlines, content summaries, historical background information, and discussion of the major themes and interpretive issues relevant for academic study of the book; all of these entries have been newly written for this edition.

- Entries on every one of the deuterocanonical books, which Protestant Christians call the Apocrypha; this edition of the dictionary also pays full attention to these apocryphal/deuterocanonical works throughout, citing appropriate passages from these books whenever they are relevant for any particular entry.

- Entries on all the plants ("fig") and animals ("sheep") mentioned in the Bible.

- Entries on units of money ("denarius") and weights and measures ("cubit").

- Entries on important theological terms used in the Bible (e.g., "justification," "faith").

- Entries on words that are used in the Bible in a distinctive or significant way (e.g., "hallow," "minister").

- Entries on hundreds of everyday phenomena significant for understanding life in the biblical world ("bowl," "lamp," "door," "snare," "phylactery").

- Almost 100 maps.

- Over 50 graphic charts and tables.

- Over 500 photos and drawings.

As noted, this is the only Bible dictionary published in cooperation with the Society of Biblical Literature, a learned academic guild to which most respected and renowned biblical scholars belong. About two hundred members of that society contributed to the entries in this book. Most of the authors offered their time and expertise without financial compensation, so that the book could be offered to the public as inexpensively as possible. All royalties for the sale of this dictionary go to the Society of Biblical Literature to promote continued research and the advancement of biblical scholarship.

Both HarperCollins and the Society of Biblical Literature have a solid track record of commitment to responsible scholarship that allows readers of all persuasions to engage and understand the Bible better. In the case of this book, the cooperative efforts of two persons must be acknowledged: Eric Brandt, Senior Editor at HarperOne, and Bob Buller, Editorial Director for the Society of Biblical Literature. Kent Richards, Executive Director of the Society of Biblical Literature until 2010, also provided wise counsel and significant supervision. Trinity Lutheran Seminary (Columbus, Ohio) granted the General Editor a sabbatical leave to give the project the attention it warranted. Three students helped with a number of potentially thankless tasks, except that we *do* thank them here, now, and in some sense every time this book is opened: Brennan Breed, graduate assistant at Emory University; Jerry O'Neal, graduate assistant at Trinity Lutheran Seminary; and Stephen Shaffer, research assistant at Hope College.

Most of all, however, this book continues to serve as a monument to the massive achievement of Paul J. Achtemeier, General Editor of the original dictionary, and to the work of the numerous Society of Biblical Literature scholars who contributed their time and expertise to researching and writing the various entries.

—Mark Allan Powell

Pronunciation Key

a	cat	ng	sing
ah	father	o	hot
ahr	lard	oh	go
air	care	oi	boy
aw	jaw	oo	foot
ay	pay	*oo*	boot
b	bug	oor	poor
ch	chew	or	for
d	do	ou	how
e, eh	pet	p	pat
ee	seem	r	run
f	fun	s	so
g	good	sh	sure
h	hot	t	toe
hw	whether	th	thin
i	it	*th*	then
i	sky	ts	tsetse
ihr	ear	tw	twin
j	joke	uh	ago
k	king	uhr	her
kh	ch as in German *Buch*	v	vow
ks	vex	w	weather
kw	quill	y	young
l	love	z	zone
m	mat	zh	vision
n	not		

Stress accents are printed after stressed syllables:

ʹprimary stress

ˈsecondary stress

THE
HARPERCOLLINS
BIBLE
DICTIONARY

REVISED AND UPDATED

A

Aaron (air´uhn), a descendant of Levi and the brother of Moses and Miriam (Exod. 6:20; Num. 26:59; 1 Chron. 6:3). The name is of uncertain meaning, but may be Egyptian.

In Mic. 6:4, the only reference to him in the prophetic books, Aaron is said to have been sent by God, together with Moses and Miriam, to lead Israel from Egypt (cf. Josh. 24:5; 1 Sam. 12:6, 8; Pss. 77:20; 105:26), and this conforms to the representation of him in the earliest material found in the Pentateuch. There, he appears as Moses's helper and joint leader in the events of the exodus, and there is no evidence of his having specifically priestly functions. Rather, he is depicted as a prophet (Exod. 7:1), particularly in the sense of one who announces the divine will (4:16; 16:9; Num. 14:26–28). He accompanies Moses and the elders of Israel on important sacrificial occasions (Exod. 18:12; 24:9–11). He and Hur hold up Moses's hands during the battle with Amalek (Exod. 17:12), and these two also act as judges when Moses is absent (24:14). Along with Moses, Aaron receives the report of the spies (Num. 13:26).

These and other references (e.g., Exod. 4:27–31) suggest that Aaron may have played a distinctive, even an independent role in certain exodus traditions; this might also account for the traditions that show Aaron in an unfavorable light, in opposition to Moses (Exod. 32; Num. 12:1–16). In what are thought to be the earliest pentateuchal traditions, however, Aaron is subordinated to Moses and is assimilated to the greater leader. Thus a miraculous rod, which originally belonged to Moses (Exod. 4:2–5, 17), is also attributed to Aaron; with it he causes the Egyptian plagues (7:9–12, 19; 8:5–7, 16–17). Both Aaron and Moses suffer the Israelites' hostility in the wilderness (Num. 16:1–3; 20:2), both are denied entrance to Canaan for the sin of striking the rock (20:12), and both die on a mountain outside the promised land (Deut. 32:48–52).

In the later Priestly source of the Pentateuch (Exod. 25–31; 35–40; Leviticus; Num. 1–10; 15–19; 25–35), Aaron is given greater prominence, for he is presented as the ancestor of the Aaronic priesthood that emerged at Jerusalem after the exile. Only Aaron and his sons are to serve as priests (Exod. 28:1), to offer sacrifices (Num. 8:1–7), and to bless the people (6:22–27). He fathers an everlasting priesthood (Exod. 40:14; Num. 25:13), and his successors in his office are given supreme authority, even over the secular leader (Num. 27:21). In particular, the priestly concern with atonement centers on Aaron, for he and his high-priestly successors are the only ones who are to officiate on the Day of Atonement (Lev. 16:32–34). The postexilic view was that the whole priesthood was descended from Aaron. It was divided into twenty-four families, each serving in the temple for a week, sixteen claiming descent from Aaron's elder son, Eleazar, and eight from his younger son, Ithamar (1 Chron. 24:1–19). The story in the Pentateuch of the budding of Aaron's rod (Num. 17:1–11) may have been intended to establish the

Aaron portrayed as high priest in his robes of office on the west wall of the third-century synagogue at Dura-Europos.

claims of clergy who traced their descent to Aaron over rival claimants.

As an emblem of postexilic high priests, Aaron is ascribed roles associated with preexilic Israelite kings. Thus, Aaron is anointed (Lev. 8:12), as was the Israelite king, and the special vestments he wears are similar to those worn by preexilic monarchs (cf. the breastpiece, Exod. 28:15–30, and the turban with its gold plate, 28:36–38). In Hellenistic texts and deuterocanonical material, the picture of Aaron is developed still further. He appears as the most prominent figure in the list of Israel's great men, ahead of even Moses (Sir. 44–49), and his high-priestly vesture comes to be endowed with symbolic and cosmic significance (Wis. 18:24).

In the NT, Aaron is said to be an ancestor of Elizabeth and, thus, of John the Baptist (Luke 1:5). Reference is also made to his role in the golden calf incident (Acts 7:40), to his call by God (Heb. 5:4), and to the order of his priesthood (Heb. 7:11). *See also* Levites; Leviticus, book of; priests; temple, the.

Bibliography

Cody, Aelred. *A History of Old Testament Priesthood.* Pontifical Biblical Institute, 1969.

Nelson, Richard D. *Raising Up a Faithful Priest: Community and Priesthood in Biblical Theology.* Westminster John Knox, 1993.

Noth, Martin. *A History of Pentateuchal Traditions.* Prentice-Hall, 1972. Pp. 178–82.   J.R.P.

Ab, the fifth month (mid-July to mid-August) in the Jewish religious calendar (equivalent to the eleventh month in the agricultural calendar). The ninth of Ab is the day set aside by tradition for fasting and mourning in commemoration of the destruction of the temple by the Babylonians (587/6 BCE) and the Romans (70 CE). *See also* calendar.

Abaddon (uh-bad'uhn; Heb., "destruction").

1 In the Hebrew Bible, a place of destruction for the dead (Ps. 88:11; Job 26:6; 28:22; 31:12; Prov. 15:11). The term is typically regarded as a synonym for Sheol (cf. Prov. 27:20); if there is any distinction, it might be that people are sometimes said to be "brought up" or rescued from Sheol, but never from Abaddon. *See also* abyss; Sheol.

2 In the NT, the Hebrew name for the ruler of the Abyss, whose Greek name was Apollyon, "the Destroyer" (Rev. 9:11). *See also* abyss; Apollyon.

The Abana River. The Abana descends from Mount Hermon, and in biblical times, as today, it was noted for its clear, plentiful waters.

Abana (ab'un-nuh), a river in ancient Syria. When Elisha told the Syrian commander Naaman that he could be cured of leprosy by washing in the muddy Jordan, he angrily replied, "Are not Abana and Pharpar, the rivers of Damascus, better than all the waters of Israel?" (2 Kings 5:12). The Abana (modern Barada, Hellenistic Chrysorrhoas) is a swift, clean, abundant stream descending from Mount Hermon in the mountainous region called the peaks of Amana (cf. Song of Sol. 4:8). It supplies Damascus through seven branches before finally disappearing in a desert marsh. *See also* Damascus; Elisha; Hermon, Mount; Naaman; Pharpar.   D.B.

Abarim (ab'uh-rim; Heb., "parts beyond"), a mountain range to the east of the Jordan River that probably includes Mount Nebo (Deut. 32:49). The Israelites camped here before descending to the plains of Moab in order to enter the promised land (Num. 33:47–48). Jeremiah later referred to Abarim along with Lebanon and Bashan as places from which the people cry in vain to God for rescue (22:20).

Abba (ah'buh, ab'uh), the definite form of the Aramaic word for "father," typically used in direct address. The word suggests familial intimacy and was used by Jesus and early Christians for addressing God (Mark 14:36; cf. Rom. 8:15; Gal. 4:6). *See also* father; names of God in the New Testament.

Abdiel (ab'dee-uhl; Heb., "servant of El [God]"), the father of Ahi, a leader from the tribe of Gad (1 Chron. 5:15).

Abdon (ab'duhn).

1 A levitical city in Asherite territory (Josh. 21:30; 1 Chron. 6:74), probably modern Khirbet 'Abdeh, nineteen miles south of Tyre and about three miles east of the Mediterranean coast at Achzib.

2 One of the minor judges of Israel (Judg. 12:13–15). The details of his eight-year term are unknown, but his family is described as large and rich: he had forty sons and thirty grandsons who rode on seventy donkeys.

3 A Benjaminite son of Shashak (1 Chron. 8:23–24).

4 The firstborn son of the Gibeonite Jeiel and his wife Maacah, and an ancestor of Saul (1 Chron. 8:30; 9:36).

5 A servant of King Josiah who was commanded to seek the validity of the book of the law found in the temple (2 Chron. 34:20; called Achbor in 2 Kings 22:12).   R.S.B.

Abednego (uh-bed'ni-goh), the new name given to Azariah, one of Daniel's three companions (Dan. 1:7) who were appointed over the province of Babylon (2:40). The name is probably a Hebraic version of an Akkadian name identifying the young man as a servant of Nebo, a Babylonian god of wisdom. According to the book of Daniel, Abednego and his companions remained faithful to the God of Israel and, when they refused to worship an image set up by Nebuchadnezzar, they were thrown into a fiery furnace. They were rescued by a divine deliverer. A lengthy prayer is ascribed to Abednego in the Greek version of Dan. 3. *See also* Azariah; Daniel, Additions to; Meshach; Shadrach.

Abel (ay'buhl; Heb., "breath, vapor"), the second son of Adam and Eve (Gen. 4:1–16). In the biblical narrative, Abel is a shepherd who offers an acceptable sacrifice to God and is thereafter murdered by his jealous brother, Cain. The meaning of his name suggests the fragile quality of his life. In the Hebrew Bible, Abel is not mentioned outside of the Genesis narrative. In the NT, however, there is continuing interest in Abel's innocent blood (Matt. 23:35; Luke 11:51; Heb. 12:24; cf. Gen. 4:9–10), and Abel is listed as an exemplar of faith (Heb. 11:4). *See also* Cain.   W.B.

Abel-beth-maacah (ay'buhl-beth-may'uh-kah), a town in northern Israel probably to be identified with Tell Abil el-Qamh, five miles west of Dan. In 2 Sam. 20:14–15 it is referred to as Abel of Beth-maacah and is associated with Joab's pursuit of Sheba, son of Bichri, through the territory (cf. 1 Sam. 20:18). Later the town (called Abel-beth-maacah in 1 Kings 15:20, but Abel-maim in 2 Chron. 16:4) is listed as one of the cities of Israel conquered by Ben-hadad; still later it is said to have been conquered by Tiglath-pileser of Assyria (2 Kings 15:29).

Abel-maim (ay′buhl-may′im). *See* Abel-beth-maacah.

Abel-meholah (ay′buhl-mi-hoh′luh), a settlement in the Jordan Valley to the south or southeast of Beth-shan. The town's exact location has not been determined, but it is listed as part of Solomon's fifth administrative district, in which Megiddo, Taanach, and Beth-shan were the chief towns (1 Kings 4:12). Abel-meholah was one of the destinations of the Midianites fleeing from the hill of Moreh, where Gideon and his small band had routed (Judg. 7:22). Saul's daughter Merab was married to a man from Abel-meholah, Adriel the Meholathite (1 Sam. 18:19; cf. 2 Sam. 21:8). According to 1 Kings 19:16, Abel-meholah was the hometown of Elisha, and it was here that Elisha was anointed by Elijah to be the latter's successor.
S.B.P.

Abel-shittim (ay′buhl-shi′tim; Heb., "brook of the acacias"), a place of encampment mentioned in Num. 33:49. It is probably to be identified with Shittim. *See also* Shittim.

Abiathar (uh-bi′uh-thahr), the son of Ahimelech who escaped the slaughter of the priests of Nob and joined David's outlaw band (1 Sam. 22:2–23; 23:6–11). After Absalom's revolt, he and Zadok carried the ark back to Jerusalem at David's command (2 Sam. 15:24–29), and he would later be listed as serving with Zadok as a priest under David (20:25). Abiathar was banished by King Solomon, however, for his part in supporting Adonijah, Solomon's rival to the throne (1 Kings 2:26–27). The prophet Jeremiah may have been a descendant of the family of Abiathar (1:1). In the NT, Abiathar is identified as high priest at the time David ate consecrated bread (Mark 2:26), though 1 Sam. 21:1–6 indicates that his father, Ahimelech, was the priest at that time. *See also* priests; Zadok.
M.C.

Abib (ay′bib), the original Canaanite name of the first month (mid-March to mid-April) in the Hebrew religious calendar. It is the month during which the exodus occurred and the Passover was celebrated (Exod. 13:4; 23:15; 34:18; Deut. 16:1). After the exile, it was called Nisan (Neh. 2:1; Esther 3:7). *See also* calendar; Nisan.

Abidan (uh-bi′duhn), a Benjaminite leader, son of Gideoni, who made offerings for the tabernacle and led his people under Moses in the wilderness (Num. 1:11; 2:22; 7:60, 65; 10:24).

Abiel (ay′bee-uhl; Heb., "El [God] is my father").
1 A Benjaminite, the grandfather of both King Saul (1 Sam. 9:1) and Abner, the captain of Saul's army (1 Sam. 14:50–51).

2 One of the group of David's elite warriors known as "the Thirty" (1 Chron. 11:32; he is called "Abialbon" in 2 Sam. 23:31).

Abiezer (ay′bi-ee′zuhr; Heb., "my father is help").
1 A son of Manasseh who received an inheritance in Canaan (Josh. 17:2); his descendants were the Abiezerites, to which Gideon belonged (Judg. 6:11). The name also occurs as Iezer (Num. 26:30).
2 A Benjaminite from Anathoth; one of the group of David's elite warriors known as "the Thirty." He commanded a division of twenty-four thousand men (2 Sam. 23:27; 1 Chron. 27:12).
3 A Manassite, the son of Gilead's sister (1 Chron. 7:18).

Abigail (ab′uh-gayl).
1 The wife of Nabal, a rancher in Carmel. According to 1 Sam. 25:3, she was "clever and beautiful," but her husband was "surly and mean." Nabal refused to acknowledge David's authority, and as a result David determined to have Nabal killed. Abigail arranged a meeting with David, unbeknownst to her husband, and persuaded him not to harm Nabal. Shortly afterward, Nabal died suddenly, and David married Abigail (25:39–42). She and Ahinoam, another wife of David, accompanied him when he sought refuge in the Philistine territories (27:3), and the two were later captured by raiding Amalekites. David tracked down the raiders and rescued his wives (1 Sam. 30). Later, in Hebron, Abigail bore David a son named Chileab (2 Sam. 3:3; 1 Chron. 3:1 records the son's name as Daniel).

Abigail at the deathbed of Nabal; detail from a thirteenth-century French miniature.

2 The daughter of Jesse and sister of David (1 Chron. 2:16). According to 2 Sam. 17:25, she was the mother of Amasa, whom Absalom appointed commander in place of Joab (cf. also 2 Sam. 19:13). She was also the wife of Ithra the Ishmaelite (called Jether the Ishmaelite in 1 Chron. 2:17), the daughter of Nahash, and the sister of Joab's mother, Zeruiah.   A.B.

Abihail (ab´uh-hayl).
  1 The father of Zuriel who is called "head of the ancestral house" of the Merari family groups (Num. 3:35).
  2 Abishur's wife, mother of Ahban and Molid (1 Chron. 2:29).
  3 A Gadite, the son of Huri (1 Chron. 5:14).
  4 A descendant of Jesse and the mother of Rehoboam's wife Mahalath (2 Chron. 11:18).
  5 The father of Esther and uncle of Mordecai (Esther 2:15; 9:29).

Abihu (uh-bi´hyoo; Heb., "he [God] is my father"), a son of Aaron and Elisheba who ascended the mountain of God (Exod. 6:23; 24:1, 9). He later died for offering "unholy fire" before the Lord in a way that had not been commanded (Lev. 10:1). *See also* Nadab.

Abijah (uh-bi´juh; Heb., "the LORD is my father").
  1 The son of Samuel, who served as judge in Beer-sheba (1 Sam. 8:2).
  2 The king of Judah ca. 915–913 BCE, referred to as Abijam in 1 Kings. He was the son of Rehoboam; his mother is variously identified as Maacah, the daughter of Absalom (2 Chron. 11:20) and as Micaiah, the daughter of Uriel (13:2). During his reign the border wars between Judah and Israel continued unabated (1 Kings 15:7). He is described in 1 Kings 15:3–5 as "continuing in the sins of his father," but 2 Chron. 13 portrays him as a pious king who trusted in God, successfully routed his Israelite attackers, and captured Bethel, Jeshana, and Ephron.
  3 The son of Jeroboam, son of Nebat, who failed to recover from a childhood illness; his death was interpreted as a sign of divine displeasure (1 Kings 14).
  4 The head of the eighth division of priests (1 Chron. 4:10), to which Zechariah, the father of John the Baptist, belonged (Luke 1:5).
  5 The son of Becher, grandson of Benjamin (1 Chron. 7:8).
  6 The wife of Ahaz and mother of Hezekiah (2 Chron. 21:9; she is called Abi in 2 Kings 18:2).   M.C./M.A.P.

Abijam (uh-bi´juhm). *See* Abijah.

Abilene (ab´uh-lee´nee), a tetrarchy in the eastern part of the Anti-Lebanon mountain range. Its capital, Abila, was located some nineteen miles northwest of Damascus in the Baroda Valley. According to Luke 3:1 and an inscription at Abila, Abilene was governed by Lysanias at the time of Jesus's public life. In 34 CE it was given to Agrippa I. *See also* Herod; Lysanias.

Abimael (ah-bim´ay-uhl; Heb., "El [God] is my father"), the son of Joktan, a descendant of Noah's son Shem (Gen. 10:28).

Abimelech (uh-bim´uh-lek; Heb., "my father is king").
  1 The king of Gerar (possibly Tell Jemmeh, ten miles south of Gaza), before whom Abraham posed as Sarah's brother (Gen. 20; cf. 12:10–20). Elsewhere, Abimelech is identified as a "king of the Philistines" whom Isaac, living at Gerar, similarly deceives (Gen. 26).
  2 The son of the judge Jerubbaal (Gideon) and a Shechemite concubine (Judg. 8:29–9:57). Abimelech accepted seventy "pieces of silver" from the Shechem temple treasury, slew seventy "brothers," and became local king for three years while commanding a local army. When support collapsed, Abimelech used the troops to destroy Shechem and then moved on to Thebes, where he died when a woman on the city wall dropped a millstone on his head (cf. 2 Sam. 11:21). The story of Abimelech is interpreted as an antidynastic warning: the meaning of his name ("my father is king") is thus ironic. *See also* Shechem.   R.B./M.A.P.

Abinadab (uh-bin´uh-dab; Heb., "father of generosity").
  1 A prominent man from Kireath-jearim, who had custody of the ark after its return from the Philistines until David moved it to Jerusalem (1 Sam. 7:1; 1 Chron. 13:7).
  2 The second son of Jesse (1 Sam. 16:8; 17:13; 1 Chron. 2:13).
  3 The fourth son of Saul (1 Sam. 8:33; 1 Chron. 9:39; omitted from the genealogy of Saul in 1 Sam. 14:49). He was killed on Mount Gilboa with his brothers Jonathan and Malchishua (1 Sam. 31:2; 1 Chron. 10:2).

Abinoam (uh-bin´oh-uhm; Heb., "my father is delight"), the father of Barak, a military leader in the period of the judges (Judg. 4:6; 5:1).

Abiram (uh-bi´ruhm; Heb., "my father is exalted" or "the Exalted One is my father").
  1 A Reubenite who, along with his brother Dathan, a fellow Reubenite named On, and the Levite Korah, conspired with some two hundred and fifty tribal leaders to challenge the authority of Moses and the priestly leadership of Aaron. After Abiram and Dathan defied a summons from Moses, Korah led the rebels in an attempt to offer incense to God. Abiram, along with Korah and Dathan as well as their families and possessions, perished when the ground opened and swallowed them. The rest of the rebels were consumed by fire from God (Num. 16:1–40; Ps. 106:16–18; Sir. 4:18–19; 4 Macc. 2:17). *See also* Korah.
  2 The firstborn son of Hiel the Bethelite (1 Kings 16:34). He died, fulfilling the word of

Joshua (Josh. 6:26), when his father rebuilt the Jericho gates (1 Kings 16:34). *See also* Hiel.

                                   D.R.B.

Abishag (ab′uh-shag), a Shunamite virgin brought to sleep with King David when he was dying in order to keep him warm at night (1 Kings 1:4, 15). Although David did not have sexual relations with her (1:4), Solomon chose to view her as one of David's wives; when Adonijah requested to marry her, Solomon had him executed for treason (2:13–25).

Abishai (uh-bi′shi), the son of Zeruiah, David's sister, and the brother of Joab and Asahel (1 Chron. 2:16). His reputation as a belligerent warrior and defender of David is attested by his desire to kill the sleeping Saul (1 Sam. 26:6–9) and Shimei of Saul's house (2 Sam. 16:9–11), by his killing the Philistine giant Ishbi-benob (21:17), and by his leading a portion of David's army into a battle that resulted in the death of eighteen thousand Edomites in the Valley of Salt (1 Chron. 18:12). He also avenged the death of his brother Asahel by murdering Abner in Hebron (see 2 Sam. 2:12–28; 3:26–30). *See also* Abner; Asahel; Joab; Zeruiah.

                                   F.R.M.

Abishua (ah-bish′oo-uh; Heb., "my father is deliverance").

  1 The son of Phineas and great-grandson of Aaron; he served as a priest (1 Chron. 6:4–5, 50) and was an ancestor of Ezra (Ezra 7:5).

  2 A Benjaminite, the son of Bela (1 Chron. 8:4).

Abner (ab′nuhr), the son of Ner, grandson of Abiel, cousin of Saul, and Saul's army commander (1 Sam. 14:50–51). After the Philistine defeat of Israel at Mount Gilboa, Abner kept the remnant of Saul's kingdom together, ostensibly in the service of Ishbaal, Saul's son (2 Sam. 2:8–9). Abner led operations against David, but eventually abandoned Saul's followers to negotiate a private compact with David for the transfer of the north to him. Nevertheless, Abner was cut down by Joab, his personal rival and the commander of Judah's army; he was buried in Hebron (2 Sam. 3:12–39). *See also* David; Saul.   M.C.

abomination, usually something detestable to a god and, so, to people who are faithful to that god. The Hebrew term recurring in Lev. 11 designates "unclean" creatures that are not to be eaten. The word is used in the NRSV to translate a variety of terms with a range of meanings: foreign gods (1 Kings 11:7; 2 Kings 23:13); improper ways of worshiping God (Deut. 12:31; 17:1); unacceptable or unlawful conduct (e.g., Lev. 18:22; Prov. 20:23; Rev. 21:27); and human wisdom (Luke 16:15). The book of Proverbs includes a few instances of more secular uses, in which something is described not as an abomination to God, but to others (13:9; 16:12; 24:9; 29:7; cf. 8:7). *See also* abomination that makes desolate.   R.H.H./M.A.P.

abomination that makes desolate, an act desecrating the Jerusalem temple, mentioned twice in the book of Daniel (11:31; 12:11; cf. 9:27). Many scholars associate the reference with an altar to Zeus erected by the Syrian ruler Antiochus IV in the temple around 167 BCE. This altar is referred to as "a desolating sacrilege" in Hellenistic deuterocanonical literature (1 Macc. 1:54; cf. 2 Macc. 6:1–5). In any case, the author of Daniel assured his contemporaries that supernatural deliverance would occur within a relatively short time (12:7: "a time, two times, and half a time," probably meaning three and a half years; cf. 12:11–12) from the time the altar was erected. Later, Daniel was read as a book that prophesied events yet to occur, and the abomination that makes desolate was viewed as one of the final signs that must take place before the end (Matt. 24:15; Mark 13:14: "the desolating sacrilege"; cf. also 2 Thess. 2:3–4). The emperor Caligula's plan to erect a statue of himself in the temple (ca. 40 CE) may have been seen by some as a potential fulfillment of this prophecy; the destruction of the temple by the Romans in 70 CE may also have been viewed as such a fulfillment. The Gospels of Matthew and Mark, however, associate the abomination with the events to precede the expected return of Jesus as "Son of Man" and evidently regard the prophecy as yet to be fulfilled at their time of writing (Matt. 24:15–21; Mark 13:14–19). *See also* abomination; Antiochus; apocalyptic literature; Daniel, book of; eschatology; Maccabees; Parousia; temple, the.   R.H.H./M.A.P.

Abraham (ay′bruh-ham; Heb., "father of a multitude"), a Hebrew patriarch and an important figure in three living religions: Judaism, Christianity, and Islam. First known as Abram (Heb., "exalted father"), he became the patriarch of several peoples from the area of the Levant. He is called the "father of many nations" (Gen. 17:5) and the friend of God (2 Chron. 20:7).

  According to the Bible, Abraham moved to the Levant from Mesopotamia. His genealogy (Gen. 11:10–32) places him in Ur when he received divine instructions to leave, along with a promise that he and his descendants would become a great nation and be blessed by God in order to be a blessing to others (12:1–8). He traveled to Egypt with his wife Sarah and his nephew Lot, where Sarah's beauty prompted Abraham to tell people she was his sister, with near disastrous results (12:10–13:1). Then the trio entered the Negev, and Abraham and Sarah settled in the land of Canaan (13:2–18; the story of Abraham and Lot parting ways demonstrates the character and origin of the Moabites and Edomites). Abram subsequently had to rescue Lot from an alliance of eastern kings (14:1–24). Additional stories relate a covenant God made with Abraham and Sarah (15:1–21); the birth of Ishmael, Abraham's son by his wife Hagar, who was Sarah's slave (16:1–6); the origin of circumcision (17:1–27); a visit God paid to Abraham and Sarah (18:1–5); and, Abraham's intercession for Sodom and Gomorrah (18:16–33). Then Abraham

Abraham and the binding of his son Isaac. This illuminated page from a fifteenth-century Armenian Gospel depicts an episode in the story of Abraham told in Genesis 22.

and Sarah traveled to Gerar, where, once again, Abraham presented Sarah as his sister, and the problem they encountered in Egypt was repeated (20:1–18; cf. 12:10–20; also see 26:6–11). Finally, Isaac was born to Sarah, and jealousy prompted Sarah to expel Hagar and Ishmael, who were nevertheless attended by God (21:1–21). Abraham had a dispute with Abimelech, the king of Gerar (21:22–34). Then God tested Abraham by telling him to sacrifice Isaac as a burnt offering (22:1–19). Narratives of Abraham purchasing burial property (23:1–20) and ensuring that Isaac would have a wife from among their relatives (24:1–67) precede an account of his death (25:1–18).

The place of Abraham in the history of the ancient Near East is difficult to assess, depending largely on the model of ancient life used. One model argues the discontinuity of pastoral nomadism and agrarian culture, while a second model maintains the basic continuity of the two. Theories in line with the first model argue that the social context of the Abraham material assumes a nonagrarian nomadic culture and that this would place Abraham in the Early Bronze Age (3000–2000 BCE) or the Middle Bronze Age (2000–1500 BCE). Theories supporting the coexistence of pastoral nomadism and agrarian lifestyles maintain that a later date works just as well: the personal names and social customs described can be found much later, hence the events could be Late Bronze Age (1500–1200 BCE) or Iron Age I (1200–900 BCE). A third position argues that the legendary nature of the stories precludes questions of historicity. Scholars making this proposal often date the "stories of Abraham" to Iron I or later.

In the NT: Abraham is understood as the patriarch of Judaism and, by extension, Christianity, which depends on the traditions of Judaism (Matt. 1:1, 2, 17; 3:9; Luke 13:16; 16:24; 19:9; Acts 13:26). Abraham as patriarch becomes a symbol of compassion (Luke 16:19–31) and the one who legitimates (John 8:33–38). Abraham also functions as a vehicle of the covenant with God (Luke 1:73; Acts 7:5–6; Gal. 4:28; Mark 12:26; Acts 7:32), as one who experienced a special relationship with God (James 2:23), and as one whose company the faithful long to enjoy in the afterlife (Matt. 8:11; Luke 16:22–30). More than all of these, however, the NT describes Abraham as the model of faith and the pioneer of trust in God (Rom. 4:1–25; Gal. 3:1–19; Heb. 6:13–14; 7:1–10; 11:8, 11). *See also* ancestor; Genesis, book of; Isaac; Mari; patriarchs.

Bibliography

Fretheim, Terence. *Abraham: Trials of Family and Faith.* University of South Carolina Press, 2007.   S.B.R.

Abram (ay′bruhm). *See* Abraham.

Absalom (ab′suh-luhm).

1 One of the sons of David who led a rebellion against his father. Because he was handsome and ambitious, Absalom was the most conspicuous of David's sons; his mother was Maacah, princess of the neighboring vassal state of Geshur. The story of Absalom is told in 2 Sam. 13–20. When his half brother Amnon raped his full sister Tamar and David took no action, Absalom killed Amnon and fled, spending three years in exile in Geshur. Laborious mediation on the part of Joab brought Absalom back to court, but David refused to see him for another two years. Once readmitted to full palace life, Absalom began to undermine David's authority (15:1–6). He directed and capitalized on the resistance felt by many people who could not accept the changes in social patterns and values that accompanied the spectacular growth of David's empire, court, and administrative machinery. In his rebellion, Absalom won the support of the royal counselor Ahithophel, whose authority was above all criticism (16:23).

Absalom gave the signal for the revolt from Hebron, the town in central Judah where David himself had risen to national power. His march to Jerusalem forced David to leave the country, and once Absalom had taken the city, he demonstrated his dominance by raping ten of David's concubines in public view. Ahithophel advised Absalom to pursue and isolate David forthwith, but Absalom was deceived by the flattery of Husai, who acted as a spy for David and who gave the opposite advice. Thus, David was able to escape across the Jordan and start the organization of a military comeback. A few weeks later David's experienced regular army, which had remained loyal to him, defeated Absalom's militia in the Transjordan, not far from Mahanaim. Though

David had ordered his generals to spare Absalom, Joab found Absalom entangled by his hair in the branches of an oak and had him slaughtered as an archrebel—a realistic military choice, but one that caused him to lose favor with the mourning father. *See also* David; Joab.

2 The father of Mattathias (1 Macc. 11:70) and Jonathan (13:11), commanders in the Maccabean army. This may be the same person who served as one of two messengers in the negotiations between Judas Maccabeus and Lysias (2 Macc. 11:17).
J.P.F.

abyss, a term employed in the NT for the abode of the dead (Rom. 10:7) and for the place where evil spirits are confined (Luke 8:31). In the book of Revelation, the term is translated "bottomless pit" in the NRSV (9:1–11; 11:7; 17:8; 20:1–3). The word also occurs in Tob. 13:2 and in Sir. 1:3; 16:8; 24:5, 29; 42:18; 4 Esd. 15:67. *See also* antichrist; Hades; heaven; hell; Sheol.   M.A.P.

acacia (uh-kay′shuh), a tree, *Acacia raddiana*, whose wood figures prominently in the exodus narratives. It was used in constructing the tabernacle and its equipment, including the ark of the covenant (Deut. 10:3). Isa. 41:19 lists the tree's presence as evidence that God is restoring the desert. Various parts of the tree were used for tanning leather (bark), the manufacture of rope (fibers), fodder (flowers and fruit), and medicinal salve (gum).

Accad (ak′ad; also Agade, Akkad).

1 A city of Nimrod's kingdom in the land of Shinar (Gen. 10:10). The association with cities in Gen. 10 named Babel and Erech establishes the Mesopotamian location known from numerous extrabiblical textual, artistic, and literary sources. The precise location of the city Accad is not known, but it likely lay somewhere in the terrain around modern Baghdad in Iraq.

2 The territory known as Accad (Akkad), which from 2350 to 2200 BCE constituted the realm of the Akkadian Empire (also known as Old Babylonia). This area began at the narrowest proximity of the Tigris and Euphrates rivers, just north of the confluence of the Diyala tributary to the Tigris. It stretched south to reach ancient Babylon and Kish, a distance of some hundred miles. As with the older Sumerian culture farther south, the city-states composing the Akkadian Empire (Old Babylonia) were sustained by the agriculture and trade provided by the rivers and the flood-nourished agriculture in the plain between the rivers.

Little is known about Akkadian political life. A "Sargon's Chronicle" and a "Sargon of Agade," found on portions of tablets, tell of the expansion by Sargon, king of the city Kish, to the northwest and southeast, establishing an "empire" lasting only four generations. His sons Rimush and Manishtusu succeeded him, but his grandson Naram-sin is better known. The expansion and control of this dynasty was probably established

Stele of Naram-sin, grandson of "Sargon of Agade," commemorating his victory over the Lullubians; third millennium BCE.

primarily to secure supplies of metal and other goods. Ships brought traders from the Indus Valley, and overland connections were made with Iran's plateau. Booty of conquest and trade goods found include metals, timber, and precious stones. An occupation army was stationed at Susa, and construction of storage, temple, and town facilities indicate control of parts of Syria and the upper reaches of the Tigris Valley.

The language known as Akkadian was written in cuneiform script, is Semitic in character, and has been found in a large collection of economic, administrative, legal, and religious texts that give us clues to the nature and location of a third-millennium BCE culture of rich resources and diverse strengths.

Of most interest to biblical students is a rich literary heritage from Akkadian authors, including such works as the *Creation Epic* (*Enuma Elish*), the *Epic of Gilgamesh*, *Descent of Ishtar to the Nether World*, numerous hymns, wisdom speculations, rituals, and law codes. These texts may be found in James B. Pritchard, ed., *Ancient Near Eastern Texts*, 3rd ed. (Princeton University Press, 1974).   R.S.B.

Acco (ak′oh; also Accho, Acre, Tell Acco, Tell el-Fukhhar, Ptolemais), one of the great port cities of antiquity along the Via Maris, on the northern edge of Haifa Bay. There are few direct biblical references to Acco, despite numerous other textual references (e.g., in Execration and Amarna texts, Josephus's histories, and later Crusader and Islamic texts). According to Judg. 1:31, the Israelite tribe Asher attempted to conquer Acco, but was unsuccessful (this is corroborated by characteristic Mycenean pottery associated with the Sea Peoples found at the site—see below). First Maccabees relates political and religious strife during the Hellenistic period between the Maccabeans and the Greek citizens of Acco, then known as Ptolemais (5:14–15, 20–23). The city was clearly hostile to the Jews (1 Macc. 12:45, 48). On his third missionary journey, Paul visited the Christian converts at Ptolemais (Acts 21:7).

Archaeological Excavations: Except for an Early Bronze Age I village and isolated Roman through Crusader remains, the main strata on the tell illuminate an occupational history from the Middle Bronze Age through the Hellenistic period (from about the twentieth through the second centuries BCE). In the Persian and Hellenistic periods, the city had expanded westward from the tell toward Acco Bay, the area of present-day Acre, whose extensive twelfth-century CE remains reflect its importance as the last Crusader capital.

Like other coastal sites, Tell Acco evidences early Middle Bronze Age reurbanization. Defenses are massive, including fortifications, ramparts, a fortress, and a double-chambered sea gate with benches. Imported pottery in tombs and a Hyksos seal attest occupation to the end of the period. In the Late Bronze Age, the urban site was extensive, with numerous large buildings, whose features included silos and a variety of installations suggesting craft working, as well as a purple-dye industry (crushed murex shells). Solid evidence for international trade in the form of Cypriot, Egyptian, and Mycenaean pottery and objects underscores Acco's strategic commercial location. A destruction level ca. 1200 BCE followed by clear Mycenaean pottery points to new occupants—probably the Sherdan, a first wave of Sea Peoples. In decline during the Iron Age until the ninth century, the Phoenician city flourished thereafter until destroyed by Sennacherib in 701 BCE.

On the bay, the city was a great commercial and maritime entrepôt in the Persian and Hellenistic periods. Evidently a Persian administrative center, the city included evidence for Phoenician (inscriptions) and Greek merchants (Attic red-figured ware of the fifth–fourth century BCE), who evidently lived in a separate quarter of the city. Rich finds in the extensive Hellenistic city plan point to continued prosperity. Both the tell and the city center suffered a destruction at the end of the second century CE.   S.R.

Achaia (uh-kay′yuh), the Roman province consisting of the southern half of the Greek peninsula.

The name is derived from the designation for the Greeks in Hittite and Egyptian sources. In the division of provinces in 27 BCE, the Roman province of Achaia comprised the lower half of Greece. In the NT, Paul visits Achaia when he preaches in its two principal cities, Athens (Acts 17:15–34) and Corinth (Acts 18:27; 1 Cor. 16:15; 2 Cor. 1:1). Specific NT references to Achaia include Acts 18:12, 27; Rom. 15:26; 1 Cor. 16:15; 2 Cor. 1:1; 9:2; 11:10; 1 Thess. 1:7–8. *See also* Athens; Corinth.

Achaicus (uh-kay′uh-kuhs), a Christian from Corinth who, with Stephanas and Fortunatus, was with Paul in Ephesus when he wrote 1 Corinthians (16:17). The three apparently brought information to Paul concerning the condition of the church in Corinth and perhaps were the bearers of the letter mentioned in 1 Cor. 7:1. They may also have carried 1 Corinthians back to Corinth. *See also* Fortunatus; Stephanas.

Achan (ay′kan), a Judahite, the son of Carmi, who kept plunder that was supposed to be devoted to God after the victory of Joshua over Jericho (Josh. 7). For this breach, God punished Israel with a military setback at Ai, and Achan and his family were stoned to death. He is called "Achar" in 1 Chron. 2:7. *See also* Ai.

Achbor (ak′bohr; Heb., "mouse").
1 The father of the Edomite king Baal-hanan (Gen. 36:38).
2 The son of Micaiah; he was one of those sent by Josiah to inquire of Hulda the prophetess concerning the significance of the book of the law discovered in the temple (2 Kings 22:12–14). He is possibly the same person mentioned by Jeremiah (26:22; 36:12) as the father of Elnathan, a courtier of Jehoiakim.

Achish (ay′kish), the ruler of the Philistine city of Gath with whom David sought asylum when he fled from Saul. At first David was distrustful of Achish and, after he was recognized as a successful military leader, he feigned madness to escape (1 Sam. 21:10–15). Later Achish accepted David and his men as mercenaries and gave David the city of Ziklag in exchange for his raids on southern tribes hostile to the Philistines (27:1–12). However, because of the suspicions of some of his commanders, Achish excused David from raids on Israel (29:1–11). *See also* David; Philistines.

Achor (ay′kohr; Heb., "trouble"), **Valley of,** part of the northern border of Judah (Josh. 15:7) and the location of the execution of Achan (Josh. 7:24–26) after his profiteering in a holy war. In Hos. 2:15 and Isa. 65:10 its reputation for that former "trouble" is reversed and the prophets use it as a symbol of better times to come. It is probably modern el-Buqei‛ah between Jericho and the north end of the Dead Sea.

Achsah (ak'suh), the daughter of Caleb whom he gave to his nephew Othniel as a wife for capturing the city of Kiriath-sepher (Debir; Josh. 15:16–17; Judg. 1:12–13). She convinced Caleb to give her as a wedding present two springs located near Hebron (Josh. 15:18–19). *See also* Caleb; Debir; Kiriath-sepher.

Achshaph (ak'shaf), an ancient city in northern Canaan along the border of the territory of Asher. The king of Achshaph joined the coalition led by Jabin of Hazor against the Israelites, but the city was eventually captured by Joshua (Josh. 11:1; 12:20). A possible identification of the site is Tel Regev in the southern Acco Plain.

Achzib (ak'zib).
   1 A city in northern Canaan located near the coast north of Acco. Although it was on the border of the territory of Asher, the Canaanites were never totally expelled from the city (Josh. 19:29; Judg. 1:31). It is tentatively identified as the present ez-Zib or Tel Akhziv.
   2 A city in the lowlands of Judah (Josh. 15:44), possibly the same city called Chezib in Gen. 38:5. The site is tentatively identified as Tel el-Beida, northwest of Lachish. *See also* Mic. 1:4.

Acts of the Apostles, the fifth book in the NT. The book deals with the history of the early Christian church and includes a major section on the career of Paul.
   Contents: The book of Acts opens with a preface to Theophilus (1:15), an account of Jesus's ascension (1:6–11), and a brief narrative of how Matthias was chosen to replace Judas as the twelfth apostle (1:12–26). Then, on the day of Pentecost, the Holy Spirit fills 120 believers, who speak in tongues (2:1–13); Peter preaches to the crowd, gaining many new converts (2:37–41). The marks of the early church are described (2:42–47). The healing of a lame man (3:1–10) leads to another sermon by Peter (3:11–26) and to the arrest of Peter and John by Jewish authorities (4:1–31). The Jerusalem church practices communal sharing of possessions and two believers (Ananias and Sapphira) are struck dead by God for trying to take advantage of this arrangement (4:32–5:11). Another account of apostles being arrested relates how they were spared further suffering due to both miraculous intervention and the advice of a tolerant rabbi named Gamaliel (5:12–42). A dispute between Hellenists and Hebrews in the church leads to the appointment of seven men to exercise leadership in the community (6:1–7); one of these, Stephen, is stoned to death by hostile Jews after preaching a sermon accusing them of unfaithfulness (6:8–8:1). Philip, one of the seven, brings the gospel to Samaria (where Peter has a confrontation with Simon Magus); he also leads an Ethiopian eunuch to be baptized into the faith (8:2–40). A persecutor of the church, Saul (also known as Paul), has a vision of Jesus that transforms him into a passionate missionary for

Pentecost: "Divided tongues, as of fire, appeared among them, and a tongue rested on each of them" (Acts 2:3). Detail from the Pala d'Oro, a twelfth-century altar in St. Mark's Cathedral, Venice.

the faith (9:31). Peter heals a man named Aeneas in Lydda (9:32–35), raises a woman named Dorcas (or Tabitha) from the dead (9:36–42), and baptizes a Gentile centurion named Cornelius after receiving a vision about what is clean and unclean (10:1–11:18). Barnabas and Saul become leaders of a Gentile mission at Antioch and take responsibility for a collection on behalf of Jerusalem famine victims (11:19–39; 12:24–25). Meanwhile, Herod kills James, the disciple of Jesus, and has Peter put in prison (12:1–5), but an angel releases Peter (12:6–19). Herod later incurs God's wrath and dies a gruesome death (12:20–23).
   The book of Acts next reports what is called the first missionary journey, of Barnabas and Paul (13:1–14:28); they go to Cyprus and southeastern Asia Minor, preaching in synagogues but enjoying even greater success among Gentiles. Paul strikes a magician named Elymas blind, refuses worship when identified as a god, and is stoned and left for dead. The increasing number of Gentile converts leads to a conference in Jerusalem at which James, the brother of Jesus, proposes terms for the inclusion of Gentiles in the church (15:1–35). Acts then reports a second missionary journey, of Paul and Silas (15:36–18:22); they travel through Asia Minor, Macedonia, and Achaia. They meet a number of significant people (Timothy, Lydia, Aquila, Priscilla); they found churches in Philippi, Thessalonica, Beroea, and Corinth; and they encounter much hostility, including an imprisonment interrupted by an earthquake at Philippi. This section of the book also includes an account of Paul preaching on the Areopagus to philosophers in Athens (17:16–34). The narrative continues with

a third missionary journey, of Paul (18:23–21:15); he travels through Asia Minor and Greece, visiting many places he has been before, but the account focuses on events in Ephesus. There, a powerful preacher named Apollos is instructed by Priscilla and Aquila, Paul brings the gift of the Spirit to former disciples of John the Baptist, seven sons of a priest named Sceva are mauled by a demon, and Paul survives a riot after Demetrius the silversmith convinces people the city's economy and honor are threatened by the Christian affront to the temple of Artemis. On the journey home, Paul preaches a fateful sermon in Troas (during which Eutychus falls out a window and must be revived), and he offers a farewell homily to the Ephesian elders in Miletus. The last part of Acts is devoted to reporting on Paul's life as a prisoner (21:17–28:31). Paul is arrested in Jerusalem (21:17–36) and subsequently moved, first to Caesarea, and then to Rome. He gives his testimony repeatedly, before the Jewish populace (22:1–22), before the council (23:1–10), before the governor Felix (24:1–27), before a later governor Festus (25:1–12), and, finally, before Festus's guests Agrippa and Berenice (25:13–26:32). The adventurous voyage to Rome involves a shipwreck on the island of Malta (27:1–28:10), but Paul is eventually brought to Rome, where he is placed under house arrest and allowed to preach freely for two years (28:11–31).

OUTLINE OF CONTENTS

Acts

J.B.T.

Composition: The book of Acts was written by the same person responsible for the Gospel of Luke (cf. Acts 1:1; Luke 1:1–4). In certain portions of the book (called the "we passages"), the author employs first-person pronouns that seem to indicate he is claiming to be a participant in the events that are being described (see 16:10–17; 20:5–15; 21:1–8; 27:1–28:16). This claim has been questioned by scholars who do not think the author's knowledge of Paul holds up to scrutiny: a number of biographical and theological points are held to conflict with what Paul says in his letters. For example, Paul says in Gal. 1:15–18 that he did not go to Jerusalem to consult with the apostles after his conversion experience; Acts 9:10–30 says that he did. Likewise, in Rom. 1:18–23, Paul says that idol worshipers are without excuse because knowledge

of God has always been evident, but Acts 17:29–30 portrays Paul as saying God will overlook the worship of idols as a consequence of ignorance. Other scholars note these anomalies, but think they can be explained or at least are insufficient to challenge the basic claim that the author of Acts traveled with Paul on certain occasions. In any case, church tradition has typically associated both the Gospel of Luke and the book of Acts with Luke the physician, a companion of Paul mentioned in Col. 4:14; Philem. 24; and 2 Tim. 4:11. Most scholars believe that Acts was written (by Luke or some other part-time associate of Paul) shortly after the Gospel, which would place it in the late 80s. A few scholars (including Pervo) put Acts considerably later, in the second century.

Genre: Acts is usually assigned to the genre of "general history" and compared to other works in the Greco-Roman world that recorded the origins and progress of particular ethnic or national groups. As such, the author would not have been expected to be unbiased in his presentation, for such books blatantly celebrated the accomplishments of their subject group and promoted its ideals. Thus, this "history of the church" reveals a penchant for seeing a positive side to just about everything: the persecution that drives the Christians out of their homeland spreads the gospel to new lands (8:1–4) and the Jews' rejection of Jesus as the Messiah provides incentive for evangelizing Gentiles (13:44–49). The question for modern scholars is whether such an obviously biased work can be viewed as a reliable source for historical reconstruction. Most scholars at least agree that the author has shaped his narrative to highlight his own priorities and perspectives. Thus, the various speeches in the book (e.g., 2:14–36; 3:12–26; 7:2–53; 10:34–43; 13:16–41) are viewed as statements of the author's own theology, and most Pauline scholars would subordinate Acts to Paul's own letters as a source for either reconstructing that apostle's biography or summarizing his ideas.

Major Themes: The book of Acts is deliberate about presenting God as sovereign over history: God determines what will happen, and all things that transpire do so with a strong sense of divine necessity (see, e.g., 1:16; 2:23; 3:18; 10:42; 13:27, 47–48; 14:26; 17:26, 31; 22:10). God also offers people guidance through the Holy Spirit, prophets, angels, and visions. Another notable theme in Acts concerns the relation of Christianity to Judaism. The book makes clear that the Christian movement began in Jerusalem among the Jewish followers of Jesus but, after a period of amazing growth among Jews, the Christian message was taken to Gentiles, among whom it enjoyed even greater success. In many ways, the story in Acts seems to relate how Gentile Christians replaced Israel as the chosen people of God, and the author wants to make clear that this did not involve any anomalies in the divine plan. God is always faithful to promises, but the Israelites' historic rebelliousness caused them to lose their favored status. Not surprisingly, this theme has evoked discussion

PARALLELS BETWEEN LUKE'S GOSPEL AND THE BOOK OF ACTS

Luke's Gospel	*Acts*
Preface to Theophilus (1:1–4)	Preface to Theophilus (1:1–5)
Spirit descends on Jesus as he prays (3:21–23)	Spirit comes to apostles as they pray (2:1–13)
Sermon declares prophecy fulfilled (4:16–30)	Sermon declares prophecy fulfilled (2:14–40)
Jesus heals lame man (5:17–26)	Peter heals lame man (3:1–10)
Religious leaders attack Jesus (5:29–-6:11)	Religious leaders attack apostles (4:1–8:3)
Centurion invites Jesus to his house (7:1–10)	Centurion invites Peter to his house (10:1–23)
Jesus raises widow's son from death (7:11–17)	Peter raises widow from death (9:36–43)
Missionary journey to Gentiles (10:1–12)	Missionary journeys to Gentiles (13:1–19:20)
Jesus travels to Jerusalem (9:51–19:28)	Paul travels to Jerusalem (19:21–21:17)
Jesus is received favorably (19:37)	Paul is received favorably (21:17–20)
Jesus is devoted to the temple (19:45–48)	Paul is devoted to the temple (21:26)
Sadducees oppose Jesus; scribes support him (20:27–39)	Sadducees oppose Paul; Pharisees support him (23:6–9)
Jesus breaks bread and give thanks (22:19)	Paul breaks bread and gives thanks (27:35)
Jesus is seized by an angry mob (22:54)	Paul is seized by an angry mob (21:30)
Jesus is slapped by high priest's aides (22:63–64)	Paul is slapped at high priest's command (23:2)
Jesus is tried four times and declared innocent three times (22:26–23:13)	Paul is tried four times and declared innocent three times (23:1–26:32)
Jesus is rejected by the Jews (23:18)	Paul is rejected by the Jews (21:36)
Jesus is regarded favorably by centurion (23:47)	Paul is regarded favorably by centurion (27:43)
Final confirmation that scriptures have been fulfilled (24:45–47)	Final confirmation that scriptures have been fulfilled (28:23–28)

From Mark Allan Powell, *Introducing the New Testament* (courtesy, Baker Academic); *see also* Charles H. Talbert, *Literary Patterns, Theological Themes, and the Genre of Luke–Acts* (Scholars, 1974)

among modern scholars as to whether Acts promotes supersessionism or even anti-Semitism. In a different vein, Acts is read along with the Gospel of Luke as a book that emphasizes the continuing presence of Jesus in the world (through the Holy Spirit and through the lives of his followers who proclaim his word and act in his name). This presence is particularly realized in acts of healing and other miracles, all of which are presented as manifestations of God's saving power. *See also* Holy Spirit; Luke; Luke, Gospel According to; Paul; Pentecost; Theophilus; tongues, as of fire; tongues, speaking in.

Bibliography

Fitzmyer, Joseph. *The Acts of the Apostles: A New Translation with Introduction and Commentary.* Doubleday, 1998.

Jervell, Jacob. *The Theology of the Acts of the Apostles.* Cambridge University Press, 1996.

Pervo, Richard I. *Acts: A Commentary.* Fortress, 2009.

Powell, Mark Allan. *Introducing the New Testament: A Historical, Literary, and Theological Survey.* Baker Academic, 2009. Pp. 191–213.

———. *What Are They Saying About Acts?* Paulist, 1991.   M.A.P.

Adah (ay'duh; Heb., "ornament").

1 Lamech's first wife, the mother of Jabal and Jubal (Gen. 4:19–20, 23).

2 The Hittite wife of Esau, the mother of Eliphaz (Gen. 36:2, 4; cf. 26:34).

Adaiah (uh-day'yuh; Heb., "the LORD has ornamented himself").

1 The maternal grandfather of King Josiah (2 Kings 22:1).

2 A Levite in the ancestry of Asaph (1 Chron. 6:41).

3 A leader in the tribe of Benjamin (1 Chron. 8:21).

4 The father of the Judean military captain Maaseiah (2 Chron. 23:1).

5 A member of the family of Bani; he divorced his non-Israelite wife in response to Ezra's postexilic proclamation (Ezra 10:29).

6 Another man who also divorced his non-Israelite wife in response to Ezra's postexilic proclamation (Ezra 10:39).

7 A Judahite belonging to the Perez family group who lived in postexilic Jerusalem (Neh. 11:5).

8 A priest who lived in postexilic Jerusalem (1 Chron. 9:12), probably the same one mentioned in Neh. 11:12 as serving in the temple.   D.R.B.

Adam (ad'uhm).

1 The first human being. In Gen. 1:1–2:4a, God creates man and woman in God's own image, separating them from the animals, to rule the earth. In Gen. 2:4b–4:26, God forms Adam (Heb. *'adam,* "human") from the "earth" (*'adamah*), places him in the garden to care for it, and then creates a woman from his side to be his wife. Tranquility rules until Adam and Eve break God's rule, eat the forbidden fruit, and suffer expulsion from the garden and the curse of a life of sweat, pain, and death. The Hebrew Bible pays little attention to Adam outside of Gen. 1–5; he is not mentioned again except for 1 Chron. 1:1. There is, however, considerably more interest in Adam in Hellenistic and deuterocanonical Jewish writings. In some cases, Adam's disobedience is said to have disrupted the cosmos, robbed the earth of fruitfulness, made animals wild and vicious, and stripped humankind of its height, beauty, and immortality (*Jubilees,* Baruch, and *4 Ezra*). Other writings, however, exalt Adam above all creatures (Sir. 49:16) as a wise man, "king," or "angel" (*3 Enoch* 30:11–12) who remained uncompromised even though Eve was seduced (*Vita Adae* 12–15). The first-century Jewish philosopher Philo found two Adams in Gen. 1–2: a "heavenly" Adam in God's image, who was wise, virtuous, and perfect, and an "earthly" Adam, who sinned, becoming the father of all people of a lower nature.

Adam and Eve, from the fourth-century CE sarcophagus of Junius Bassus.

In the NT, Luke carries Jesus's genealogy back to God through Adam (3:38). Most NT references to Adam, however, occur in Paul's letters. Rom. 5:12–21 contrasts the first (earthly) Adam, who was disobedient, with Christ, the last (heavenly) Adam, who was obedient, thus reversing Philo's order. Those who are in the first Adam suffer corruption; those in the last, experience grace and life (see 1 Cor. 15:20–28, 45–49). A possibly pseudepigraphical Pauline letter elevates Adam over Eve because she was deceived (1 Tim. 2:13–14). *See also* creation; Eden; Eve; fall, the; human being, humanity; paradise; serpent; sin.   C.J.R.

2 A city mentioned in Josh. 3:16 where the waters of the Jordan were dammed, allowing the Israelites to cross. Identified as Tell ed-Damiyeh, it stood at the outflow of the biblical Jabbok River (modern Zerqa) into the Jordan River, commanding intersecting travel routes. The "Zarethan" referred to in Josh. 3:16 is identified with Tell es-Sa'idiyeh, some fourteen miles farther up the Jordan River.

Adamah (ad'uh-muh).

1 A city in the region of Naphtali (Josh. 19:33).

2 A Hebrew word that occurs 225 times in the Bible and means arable, cultivable land. That meaning can be seen in the expression "man of the *'adamah*" meaning "farmer" (Gen. 9:20; Zech. 13:5). *'Adamah* is the word used to refer to the material ("dust") from which God forms the first human being (Heb. *'adam;* Gen. 2:7; 3:19; Ps. 90:3; Job 10:9; 34:15); to the "earth" or inhabited world with its many families of people (Gen. 12:3; 28:14; Deut. 7:6; 14:2; Isa. 24:21; Amos 3:2); and to the "land" that God gives to Israel (Deut. 5:6; 7:13; 11:9; 26:10, 15), from which they are exiled (2 Kings

17:23; 25:21) and to which they return (Isa. 14:1; Jer. 16:15; 23:8; Ezek. 28:25).   J.S.K./M.A.P.

Adar (ay'dahr), the twelfth month of the Jewish religious calendar, corresponding to February/March. Adar is referred to in Ezra 6:15 and numerous times in Esther (3:7, 13; 8:12; 9:1, 15, 17, 19, 21). *See also* calendar.

adder, a poisonous snake. The term is often used in poetic passages and in texts conveying symbolic imagery (Pss. 58:4; 91:13; Prov. 23:32; Isa. 14:29).

Additions to Daniel. *See* Daniel, Additions to.

Additions to Esther. *See* Esther, Additions to.

Adiel (ay'dee-uhl; Heb., "El [God] is an ornament").

1 A leader in the tribe of Simeon (1 Chron. 4:36).

2 A priest who lived in postexilic Jerusalem (1 Chron. 9:12).

3 The father of Azmaveth, overseer of the royal storehouses of King David (1 Chron. 27:25).

Adin (ay'din; Heb., meaning uncertain, possibly "luxury" or "delight").

1 The ancestor of a family group who returned with Zerubbabel from the Babylonian exile (Ezra 2:15).

2 The ancestor of another family group (led by Ebed) who returned from the exile with Ezra (Ezra 8:6).

3 A member of the postexilic community in Judah who signed Ezra's covenant to keep the law (Neh. 10:16).

Adlai (ad'li), the father of Shaphat (1 Chron. 27:29); Shaphat served David as a supervising herdsman.

Admah (ad'muh), one of the five "cities of the Plain" in the Valley of Siddim at the southern end of the Dead Sea (Gen. 10:19; 14:2). The city was destroyed, along with Sodom, Gomorrah, and Zeboiim, while the fifth city, Zoar, was spared. Admah and Zeboiim became proverbial examples of God's wrath (Deut. 29:23; Hos. 11:8). The exact site is unknown. *See also* Sodom; Zoar.

Adonijah (ad'uh-ni'juh; Heb., "the LORD is my lord"), the son of David and Haggith and apparent heir to the throne in Jerusalem after the death of Absalom. Though Adonijah was supported by the priest Abiathar and Joab the army commander (1 Kings 1–2), his ambitions were frustrated by the secret anointing of Solomon at the spring of

Gihon by the priest Zadok. Adonijah's subsequent request to marry Abishag, the virgin who had slept with David in his old age to keep him warm, was the occasion of his execution by Solomon.

Adonikam (ad´uh-ni´kuhm; Heb., "my lord has arisen").

1 The ancestor of a family group who returned from the Babylonian exile with Zerubbabel (Ezra 2:13).

2 The ancestor of another, smaller group who returned from the exile with Ezra (Ezra 8:13).

Adoniram (ad´uh-ni´ruhm; Heb., "my lord is exalted"), an official in the service of King Solomon who supervised the conscripted labor force in the construction of the temple (1 Kings 5:13–14). He is probably the same person called Adoram, who served a similar role under King Rehoboam and was stoned to death by the people of the northern kingdom, Israel, when he attempted to enforce the harsh policies of Rehoboam (12:18). He may or may not be the Adoram mentioned in 2 Sam. 20:24. *See also* Adoram.   D.R.B.

Adoni-zedek (uh-doh´ni-zee´dek; Heb., either "my lord is righteous" or "my lord is Zedek"), the Amorite king of Jerusalem who, fearing the strength of the invading Israelites, organized a coalition with four other kings to attack the city of Gibeon because its inhabitants had formed an alliance with Joshua. The attack failed and he and the other kings were put to death by Joshua (Josh. 10:1–26). Some scholars think that Adoni-zedek is the same person referred to as Adoni-bezek in Judg. 1:4–7. *See also* Amorites; Gibeon.

adoption. In the NT, Paul uses adoption as a metaphor for salvation. Paul indicates that people become adopted as heirs of God through faith (by virtue of the mediation of the Son and the Spirit) and are thus enabled to utter "Abba, Father" (Rom. 8:15; Gal. 4:6; cf. Rom. 8:23; 9:4; Eph. 1:5). The image draws meaning from the realities of belonging, connectedness, relationship, and inheritance implied by literal adoption; its scope for Paul is also inclusive of both men and women (cf. Gal. 3:28). As background for this metaphor, Paul may be drawing on adoptive relationships among humans found in the Bible (e.g., Gen. 15:1–3; Exod. 2:10; Esther 2:7, 15), on God's election of Israel (e.g., Hos. 11:1; Exod. 4:22), and on Greco-Roman customs regarding the manumission and subsequent adoption of slaves. *See also* Abba; election; family; father; salvation; slavery in the New Testament; sons of God, children of God.

J.E.A./M.A.P.

Adoraim (ad´uh-ray´im; Heb., possibly "two hills"), one of the fifteen cities in Judah fortified and provisioned by Rehoboam as defensive strongholds (2 Chron. 11:9). Its location has been identified as modern Dura, about six miles west of Hebron in southern Judah.

Adoram (uh-doh´ruhm; a shortened form of Adoniram, Heb., "my lord is exalted"), a name apparently identifying an administrative official who served under both David and Rehoboam, although some scholars believe that there were, in fact, two different persons bearing this name. If so, the first (Adoram, 2 Sam. 20:24) supervised conscripted labor under King David, and the second served a similar role under Solomon and Rehoboam (Adoniram, 1 Kings 4:6; Adoram, 12:18 [but Adoniram in the LXX]). *See also* Adoniram; Hadoram.   D.R.B.

Adrammelech (uh-dram´uh-lek).

1 A deity to whom human sacrifices were offered. He was one of the gods worshiped by the Sepharvites who were resettled in Samaria by the Assyrian ruler Sargon around 720 BCE (2 Kings 17:31). *See also* Molech.

2 One of the sons of the Assyrian ruler Sennacherib who, with the help of his brother Sharezer, assassinated his father in 681 BCE and fled to Ararat (2 Kings 19:37; Isa. 37:38).

Adramyttium (ad´ruh-mit´ee-uhm), modern Edremit, a port on the northwest coast of Turkey opposite Lesbos; in Roman times, it was in the province of Asia. According to Acts 27:2–5, Paul sailed from Caesarea to Myra, en route to Rome, aboard a ship from Adramyttium.

Adria (ay´dree-uh), **Sea of,** in Acts 27:27 the body of water in the central Mediterranean Sea between Crete and Sicily through which Paul's ship, en route to Rome, drifted for fourteen days before breaking up in the surf of Malta. The name derives from the town of Adria on the lower Po River and originally designated the sea between Italy and the Balkan Peninsula, the modern Adriatic. In NT times, it also designated the Ionian Gulf and the waters between the Peloponnesus and Sicily.

Adullam (uh-duhl´uhm), a town in the Judean hills (Josh. 12:15; 15:35; Mic. 1:15; 2 Macc. 12:38). It is probably to be identified with Tell esh-Sheikh Madkur in the Judean hills about five miles south of Beth-shemesh. Nearby is a cave where David and his early followers camped (1 Sam. 22:1). The site was fortified by Rehoboam to strengthen Judah during the early years of the divided kingdom (2 Chron. 11:7). *See also* divided kingdom, divided monarchy.

adultery, illicit sexual relations with someone other than one's marriage partner. Its prohibition is part of the Ten Commandments (Exod. 20:14; Deut. 5:18). In the Bible, the primary referent for adultery seems to be sexual relations between a married (or betrothed) woman and any man other than her husband. Adultery, therefore, was committed against a husband, not against a wife. It was considered a most grievous transgression (Lev. 18:20), to be punished by the death of both parties (Deut. 22:22–24), though there is no record of this punishment ever being carried out. In the teachings of Jesus, the definition of adultery is expanded: first, adultery can be committed in one's "heart" apart from the physical deed (Matt. 5:28); second, a husband can be held responsible for committing adultery against his wife (Matt. 5:32; Mark 10:11; Luke 16:18). The sin of adultery is also mentioned by other NT writers (Rom. 13:9; 1 Cor. 6:10; Gal. 5:19; Heb. 13:4; James 2:11). A story in John 7:53–8:11 indicates that the offense was taken very seriously, though the legitimacy of the prescribed death penalty was a matter for debate. Throughout the Bible, adultery is used as a symbol for the unfaithfulness of people toward God (e.g., Hos. 9:1; Matt. 12:39). *See also* family; fornication; law; marriage; prostitute.   J.M.E./M.A.P.

Adummim (uh-duhm'im), a name referring to both a pass (Josh. 18:17) and an area used to distinguish the border between the tribal inheritance of Benjamin and that of Judah (Josh. 15:7). Following that border constituted the shortest way to go down from Jerusalem to Jericho, and then on to Transjordan.

adversary, in the Bible, anyone (or anything) standing in the way of the completion of God's will or opposing God's people either collectively or individually (e.g., 2 Sam. 19:22; 1 Kings 5:4; 11:25; Ezra 4:1). "Adversary" is the literal meaning of the Hebrew word *satan,* and the idea eventually developed that Satan was *the* adversary (see Job 1:6–2:7). In certain NT passages, the term is also used with this connotation (e.g., 1 Pet. 5:8; cf. 1 Tim. 5:14–15). *See also* devil; Satan.

Advocate. *See* Paraclete.

Aeneas (i-nee'uhs), a paralytic at Lydda who was healed by Peter (Acts 9:33–35).

Aenon (ee'nuhn), a well-watered site that according to John's Gospel was where John the Baptist baptized, in the vicinity of Salim (3:23). The exact location is unknown. A fourth-century reference by Eusebius situated Aenon in the Beth-shan valley, some six miles south of Beth-shan. A mosaic floor map discovered in a sixth-century church in Medeba (modern-day Madaba) in Jordan locates Aenon on the eastern side of the Jordan River. Recent speculation places it near Nablus, not far from the abundant water of Wadi Far'-ah.

Agabus (ag'uh-buhs), a Christian prophet from Jerusalem who, in Antioch, predicted a widespread famine during the reign of the emperor Claudius (Acts 11:27–28); later, at Caesarea, he foresaw Paul's arrest in Jerusalem and subsequent imprisonment by the Gentiles (21:10–11). *See also* prophet.

Agag (ay'gag). The apparent name of two non-Israelite kings, though some scholars speculate that Agag might not be a proper name, but a designation (analogous to "Pharaoh") for all Amalekite rulers.

1 The name of an unknown king referred to in Num. 24:7 (called "Gog" in the LXX). Balaam prophesies that Israel's future king will be more exalted than Agag.

2 The name of the king of the Amalekites whom Saul defeated but spared, contrary to divine command. After rebuking Saul bitterly, Samuel hewed Agag to pieces in Gilgal "before the LORD" (1 Sam. 15). *See also* Agagite; Amalekites; Samuel; Saul.
                                                        M.A.P.

Agagite (ay'guh-git), the ancestry of Haman and his father, Hammedatha, as identified in the book of Esther (3:1, 10; 8:3, 5; 9:24). The usual understanding is that the reference is to descendants of Agag, an Amalekite king defeated by Saul (1 Sam. 15:7–9). This is consistent with the role of Haman as "enemy of the Jews" in the stories in Esther. *See also* Agag.

agapē (ah-gah'pay), the principal Greek word used for "love" in the LXX and in the NT. Because of its prominent use in theological and ethical contexts in these writings, the term has often been taken to imply a sense of unmerited love (such as that of God for human beings) or of selfless and self-giving love (such as humans are urged to exhibit toward God and one another). The word itself, however, need not carry these connotations, and in many instances *agapē* and other words for love (particularly *philos*) are simply used as synonyms (in John 21:15–17 the verb forms appear to be used interchangeably). *See also* love.   M.A.P.

agate, one of the precious stones from which the walls of the heaven-descended new Jerusalem will be composed, according to Rev. 21:19. The stone may correspond to what Pliny calls "chalcedony" (*Natural History* 37, 7, 92), in which case it might be equated with jasper or some kind of emerald. A similar stone was set in the breastpiece worn by Aaron (Exod. 28:19; 39:12).

agora (ag'uh-ruh), the center of the lower part of a Greek town. The usual translation "marketplace" (Matt. 20:3; Luke 7:32; Acts 16:19; 17:17) does not

The agora at Corinth: remains of shops and the temple of Athena.

do justice to its function as the place where people gathered for social and political as well as commercial business. In the early phases of Greek city development, the agora was a natural open space near the main entrance to the acropolis. As the government of Greek cities changed from monarchy to democracy, the citadel, or fortified area, ceded its importance as a vital nucleus of the town to the agora, which served as the place in which the citizens gathered to transact public business.   P.P.

agrapha (ag′ruh-fuh), a term used in NT studies to refer to sayings of Jesus not recorded in the four canonical Gospels. The most obvious examples of agrapha are sayings of Jesus reported in other NT writings (e.g., Acts 20:35; 1 Cor. 11:24–25). More often, however, the term is used with reference to sayings of Jesus reported in noncanonical sources, including apocryphal gospels, writings of early church leaders, and talmudic and Islamic texts. The primary value of the agrapha to scholars is that they provide testimony to the development of the Jesus tradition and to the diversity of religious expressions within which that tradition was considered significant. Very few of the extracanonical agrapha are regarded as citations that can be reliably attributed to Jesus, though certain passages in the *Gospel of Thomas* have been considered worthy of acceptance in that regard. *See also* Thomas, Gospel of.   M.A.P.

agriculture. *See* farming.

Agrippa. *See* Herod.

Ahab (ay′hab).
1 The king of Israel, the northern kingdom, ca. 869–850 BCE; he was the son and successor of Omri. His queen was Jezebel, daughter of Ethbaal, king of Tyre. Ahab inherited his father's military prowess and maintained a strong and stable government. He successfully defended his country against the powerful Aramean kingdom of Damascus, which he defeated in several battles. Ahab was the first king of Israel to come into conflict with Assyria. He was also the first to have his name recorded on extant Assyrian monuments, which indicate that he put two thousand chariots and ten thousand soldiers on the battlefield against Shalmaneser III at Qarqar (ca. 853 BCE). The author of 1 Kings is extremely harsh on Ahab, primarily because he permitted Jezebel to promote the cult of Baal. Excavations at Samaria have revealed the magnificence of his buildings (1 Kings 22:39), and the dominance of Ahab over Judah is shown by his treatment of Jehoshaphat in the campaign of Ramoth-gilead (22:29–31). Ahab's daughter Athaliah was married to Jehoram, king of Judah, and held the throne herself for six years after Jehoram's death.
    In biblical narratives the point of interest lies not in the king himself, but in his four encounters with the prophets, especially Elijah. The first encounter concerns the great drought predicted

by Elijah (1 Kings 17:1), which culminated in the contest between Elijah and the prophets of Baal on Mount Carmel (18:17–40), at which Ahab was present. The second involved two unnamed prophets, one of whom encouraged Ahab in his resistance against Ben-hadad of Damascus (20:22). The third was the episode of Naboth's vineyard. After Naboth had refused Ahab's offer to buy his vineyard, Jezebel had Naboth executed, so that Ahab could take possession of the coveted vineyard. When Ahab did so, he was confronted by Elijah, who threatened the total destruction of his house. As a result Ahab did penance for his part in the crime (1 Kings 21). The fourth narrative found in 1 Kings 22 describes how a war with the Arameans supposedly led to the violent death of Ahab (v. 40, however, describes his death in non-violent language). When Ahab's court prophets predicted success, his ally Jehoshaphat of Judah asked for the word of another prophet of the Lord. The man summoned was Micaiah ben Imlah, who, when pressed, uttered a fateful prediction. *See also* Elijah; Omri; Samaria, city of.
    2 The son of Kolaiah, a false prophet among the Babylonian exiles. Jeremiah accused him of adultery and impiety and threatened him with death by fire at the hands of Nebuchadnezzar (29:21–23).   D.L.C.

Ahasuerus (uh-has′yoo-air′uhs), a Persian king mentioned in the book of Esther, usually identified with Xerxes I (485–464 BCE); the historical Xerxes I ruled over twenty satrapies (Herodotus *History* 3.89), and his queen was Amestris from a noble Persian family (*History* 7.61). Ahasuerus is described in Esther as ruling from India to

King Ahasuerus and Queen Esther (*right*) as depicted in the wall paintings of the third-century CE synagogue at Dura-Europos.

Ethiopia (1:1). After banishing his queen, Vashti, he seeks a replacement, selecting Esther. In the story of Esther and Mordecai, Ahasuerus appears as a ruler who is easily manipulated and prone to extreme actions. The narrative emphasizes his drunkenness, foolishness, and lack of control over his government. He is first manipulated by Haman to allow the destruction of all Jews and then is persuaded by Esther and Mordecai to permit the Jews to defend themselves at the cost of many Gentile lives. According to Dan. 9:1, Ahasuerus was the father of Darius the Mede, and in Tob. 14:15 Ahasuerus joins Nebuchadnezzar in the destruction of Nineveh. Both of these latter notices pose chronological and historical problems. *See also* Persia; Xerxes.   W.L.H.

Ahava (uh-hay´vuh), a river or canal in Babylonia (Ezra 8:15, 21, 31), location unknown; the rallying point for Ezra's journey to Jerusalem, where a preparatory fast was celebrated. In some manuscripts, Ahava is called Thera(s), as it is in 1 Esd. 8:41.

Ahaz (ay´haz; Heb., "he [perhaps God] has grasped"), the son of Jotham and the father of Hezekiah. Ahaz was the eleventh king of Judah, reigning ca. 735–715 BCE. Only twenty years old at his succession, Ahaz is said to have already committed abominable Canaanite practices, including sacrificing his son and worshiping at high places (2 Kings 16:1–4; cf. 2 Chron. 28:22–23). During the reign of Ahaz, the Assyrian Empire advanced to new heights, causing the entire region west of Mesopotamia to fight or pay tribute. Rezin, king of Syria, and Pekah, king of Israel, joined forces to stop the advance of Assyria. When Judah would not join their alliance, those two kings sought ways to replace Ahaz with a man named Tabeel, apparently an Aramean (see 2 Kings 16:5; Isa. 7:1–25). Ahaz sought to rescue himself from this threat by appealing to Assyria's King Tiglath-pileser, even giving him portions of the temple treasury. Perhaps it was this vassalage to Tiglath-pileser that led to Ahaz's replacement of the altar in the Jerusalem temple with one modeled after an altar in Damascus (2 Kings 16:10–16). In the NT, Ahaz is mentioned only once, as an ancestor of Jesus (Matt. 1:9). *See also* Hezekiah; Jotham; Pekah; Rezin; Tabeel.   F.R.M.

Ahaziah (ay´huh-zi´uh; Heb., "the LORD holds firm").
1 The son of Ahab and king of Israel ca. 850–849 BCE. Ahaziah permitted his mother, Jezebel, to maintain and even strengthen the Baal cult (1 Kings 22:52–53). He apparently joined Jehoshaphat of Judah in a naval expedition, which was wrecked at Ezion-geber, the port of departure (2 Chron. 20:35–37; but cf. 2 Kings 22:48–49). The country of Moab rebelled under Ahaziah (2 Kings 1:1), and apparently the Ammonites also gained their freedom at that time (2 Chron. 20:1). In his second year Ahaziah was severely injured in a fall from a window and sent for an oracle from

Baal-zebub, the god of Ekron. He was reproved by Elijah, who threatened him with death, which followed shortly (2 Kings 1:2–18). *See also* Ahab; Elijah; Ezion-geber; Jehu.
2 The son of Jehoram and Athaliah, and king of Judah ca. 843/2 BCE. He was allied with Jehoram of Israel in an unsuccessful campaign to recover Ramoth-gilead from Hazael of Damascus (2 Kings 8:28). When Jehoram was wounded in battle, Ahaziah visited him in Jezreel. Because of their kinship and friendship, Jehu, the king of Israel, assassinated him along with Jehoram (9:27–28). *See also* Jehu.   D.L.C.

Ahiezer (ay´hi-ee´zuhr; Heb., "my brother is help").
1 A leader of the tribe of Dan (Num. 10:25), identified as Ammishaddai's son (1:12). He camped on the north side of the site of the tribe of Dan (2:25), made offerings there (7:66, 71), and led the rear guard (10:25), all to assist Moses.
2 In 1 Chron. 12:3, the chief of the Benjaminite ambidextrous archer-slingers who defended David while he was hiding from Saul.

Ahijah (uh-hi´juh; Heb., "the LORD is my brother").
1 A great-grandson of Eli who was a priest in Shiloh and served in Saul's army, wearing the ephod (1 Sam. 14:3) and taking responsibility for the ark (14:18–19).
2 A prophet from Shiloh who tore his garment into twelve pieces in order to demonstrate visually the coming dissolution of the united monarchy. He also foretold Jeroboam's (ca. 922–901 BCE) rise to power (1 Kings 11:29–31; 12:15; 2 Chron. 10:15) and later predicted the death of Jeroboam's son (1 Kings 14:2–18; 15:29).
3 The father of Baasha, who conspired against Nadab, son of Jeroboam, and reigned in his stead (1 Kings 15:27–33).
4 The son of Jerahmeel, brother of Caleb of the tribe of Judah (1 Chron. 2:25).
5 A Pelonite who was one of David's warriors (1 Chron. 11:36).
6 A Levite, overseer of the treasures of the house of God in David's time (1 Chron. 26:20).
7 A Levite who signed Ezra's covenant-renewal document after the return from the Babylonian exile (Neh. 10:26).   S.B.R.

Ahikam (uh-hi´kuhm; Heb., "my brother has arisen"), the son of Shaphan who served as a courtier of King Josiah. He was among those who went to inquire of Hulda the prophetess concerning the significance of the book of the law found in the temple (2 Kings 22:12–14). He later helped protect Jeremiah from King Jehoiakim (Jer. 26:24) and was the father of Gedaliah (2 Kings 25:22), the governor of Judah appointed by Nebuchadnezzar of Babylon ca. 587 BCE and later assassinated (Jer. 40).

Ahilud (uh-hi´luhd), the father of two royal officials: Jehoshaphat, who served both David and

Solomon as record keeper (1 Chron. 18:15; 1 Kings 4:3), and Baana, who was a district administrator charged with providing Solomon with provisions for one month of every year (1 Kings 4:12).

Ahimaaz (uh-him'ay-az).

1 The father of Ahinoam, wife of Saul (1 Sam. 14:50).

2 The son of Zadok the priest who was active during Absalom's revolt. He was loyal to David and remained in Jerusalem as a spy when David fled the city (2 Sam. 15:27–36; 17:15–22). He later was anxious to inform David about the suppression of the revolt, but he did not report that Absalom had been killed (18:19–32). He may have been King Solomon's son-in-law, married to Basemath, Solomon's daughter (1 Kings 4:15), and stationed in Naphtali as the king's administrator.
J.G.G.

Ahiman (uh-hi'muhn).

1 An associate of She-shai and Talmai (Num. 13:22; Josh. 15:14; Judg. 1:10). All are identified as Anakites located near Hebron, first encountered by the spies Moses sent to assess the promised land of Canaan, then driven out by Caleb (Josh. 15:14) and defeated by Judahites (Judg. 1:10).

2 One of four levitical gatekeepers of the temple precincts in postexilic Judah (1 Chron. 9:17).

Ahimelech (uh-him'uh-lek; Heb., "my brother is king").

1 The son of Ahitub and priest of Nob to whom David fled from the wrath of Saul (1 Sam. 21:1–15). In response to David's claim to being on a secret mission from King Saul, Ahimelech provided David and his men with "holy bread" (see Matt. 12:3–4). He also gave to David the sword of Goliath, whom David had killed years earlier in the valley of Elah (1 Sam. 22:9–10). For so assisting David, Ahimelech and most of his family were killed by Doeg the Edomite at the command of Saul (2 Sam. 22:18–19). *See also* Doeg; Goliath.

2 A Hittite officer in the service of David (1 Sam. 26:6).   F.R.M.

Ahinoam (uh-hin'oh-uhm; Heb.; "my brother is good").

1 The daughter of Ahimaaz who became King Saul's wife (1 Sam. 14:50). She was the mother of Jonathan, Ishvi, Malchishua, Merab, and Michael (14:49).

2 A native of Jezreel of south Judah who was married to David and was the mother of his eldest son, Amnon (2 Sam. 3:2; 1 Chron. 3:1). It is possible that this is the same person as **1**.

Ahio (uh-hi'oh; Heb., "his brother").

1 One of two sons of Abinadab; he drove the cart carrying the ark (2 Sam. 6:3; 1 Chron. 13:7) and walked before it (2 Sam. 6:4).

2 A Benjaminite, son of Elpaal (1 Chron. 8:14).

3 A descendant of Jeiel (1 Chron. 8:29–31; 9:37).

Ahira (uh-hi'ruh), the son of Enan of the tribe of Naphtali (Num. 1:15). Ahira is mentioned four additional times in Numbers as one of Moses's assistants. He helped take the census (2:29), made offerings (7:78, 83), and formed part of the rear guard (10:27) when the tribe moved from Sinai.

Ahiram (uh-hi'ruhm), one of the sons of Benjamin (Num. 26:38); he is sometimes thought to be the person identified as Aher in 1 Chron. 7:12 or the person identified as Aharah in 1 Chron. 8:1. *See also* Gebal.

Ahithophel (uh-hith'uh-fel), one of David's advisers noted for his wisdom (2 Sam. 16:23; 1 Chron. 27:33–34). He proved disloyal to David during the revolt of Absalom (2 Sam. 15:17) and became the latter's chief counselor. When his advice was ignored, he committed suicide (17:23). Bathsheba, David's wife and Solomon's mother, may have been his granddaughter (11:3; 23:34). His house was in Giloh, a town in Judah (15:12). *See also* David.

Ahitub (uh-hi'tuhb).

1 A son of Phinehas (and grandson of Eli) who was the father of Ahijah (1 Sam. 14:3) and Ahimelech (22:9, 11–12, 20).

2 The son of Amariah who was either the father of Zadok (2 Sam. 8:17; 1 Chron. 6:8, 12, 52–53; 18:16; Ezra 7:2) or the grandfather of Zadok (1 Chron. 9:11; Neh. 11:11).

Ahohi (uh-hoh'hi), the father of Dodo and grandfather of the warrior Eleazar, who fought with David against the Philistines. He is mentioned only in 2 Sam. 23:9. *See also* Ahohite.

Ahohite (uh-hoh'hit), a descendant of Ahohi. Four Ahohites are named in the Bible:

1 Eleazar, one of David's warriors, a son of Dodo (1 Chron. 11:12).

2 Zalmon, one of the group of David's elite warriors known as "the Thirty" (2 Sam. 23:28).

3 Ilai, a Davidic warrior (1 Chron. 11:29).

4 Dodai (possibly a variant spelling of Dodo), Eleazar's father (1 Chron. 27:4).

See also Ahohi.

Ai (i, ay'i; Heb., "ruin"), a Canaanite town near and to the east of Bethel (Gen. 12:8; 13:3) generally identified with the modern site of et-Tell. Ai was an important urban center of about twenty-seven and a half acres during the Early Bronze Age from approximately 3100 to about 2400 BCE (biblical Jericho, by way of comparison, was about ten acres).

In the Early Bronze Age, Ai had a temple and a royal quarter. Its inhabitants apparently came originally from Syria and Anatolia. Egyptian influence is evident from the temple of this period and imported alabaster and stone vessels. The city had a massive stone-lined reservoir with a capacity of 480,000 gallons. The Early Bronze Age city was destroyed about 2400 BCE and remained a ruin until about 1200 BCE.

A small unwalled village was established on about two and a half acres of the mound, dating to about 1220 BCE. The inhabitants practiced terrace farming and had sophisticated cistern systems for holding water, suggesting abundant knowledge of agricultural techniques. Their use of pillared houses also suggests a population with a history of settled existence. The village was abandoned a final time about 1050 BCE.

Josh. 8 describes the capture and destruction of Ai by the Israelites. However, at the time commonly accepted for the Israelite conquest of Canaan, about 1250 BCE, Ai was uninhabited. One explanation suggests the account in Josh. 8 is etiological rather than historical, ascribing a well-known ruin to the conquest by Joshua. It has also been proposed that the Israelite capture of Ai came in the Iron Age and can be seen in the two phases of the Iron Age village. The conquest of Ai would then date to about 1125 BCE. An alternative view suggests that the biblical story of Josh. 8 originally referred to the capture of Bethel and was later transferred to the nearby ruins of Ai. However one interprets the archaeological and biblical data, Ai clearly poses difficulties for understanding the Josh. 8 account. *See also* Bethel.   J.F.D.

Aiah (ay'yuh).

1 One of the sons of Zibeon, a Horite in Edomite territory (Gen. 36:24; 1 Chron. 1:40).

2 The father of Rizpah, one of Saul's concubines. His two sons were given to the Gibeonites as compensation for the bloodguilt Saul had incurred through his dealings with them (2 Sam. 3:7; 21:1–11).

Aijalon (ay'juh-lon).

1 The name of a valley and an associated city mostly ascribed to the territory of Dan (Josh. 19:42). It is best remembered as the site where the sun stood still in the stories of Joshua's battles (Josh. 10:12) and where Jonathan defeated the Philistines after the battle at Michmash (1 Sam. 14:31). Part of the second administrative district under Solomon, it was later built up as a defensive center by Rehoboam. The site of the city is usually identified as Yalo at the western end of the valley, but Tell Qoqa, just southeast of Yalo, has also been suggested.

2 The Zebulunite Elon's burial site (Judg. 12:12), possibly referring to a place near Rimmon.

Ain (ah'yin).

1 A village near Riblah on the northern boundary of Canaan (Num. 34:11).

2 A town near Rimmon (Josh. 15:32; 1 Chron. 4:32).

Akeldama (uh-kel'duh-muh). *See* Hakeldama.

Akhenaton (ahk'uh-nah'tuhn), or Amenophis (ah-men'oh-fis), or Amenhotep (ah-men'hoh-tep) IV, the "heretic" king of Egypt ca. 1364–1347 BCE and one of the most controversial figures of antiquity. A pharaoh of the powerful Eighteenth Dynasty (1546–1319 BCE), he is best known for his promotion of the exclusive cult of the sun disk, the Aten. Early in his reign he changed his name from Amenophis, honoring the god Amun of Thebes (and thereby Amun's powerful priesthood), to Akhenaton (Egyptian, "It is well with the Aten"). By the eighth year of his reign he moved the capital from Thebes to the new settlement of Akhetaten (Tell el-Amarna), a site in Middle Egypt unconnected with the cult of any other deity. Under his predecessor Amenophis III (ca. 1402–1364) the Aten had become more prominent, but now the Aten was celebrated as the sole god, creator of all lands and peoples, mother and father of all creation. In many reliefs the Aten is represented as a radiating sun disk whose rays terminate in hands holding out the symbol of life. To some extent Akhenaton and the royal family worshiped the Aten, and the rest of the people worshiped the royal family. His queen, Nefertiti, played an unusually prominent part in the court rituals. Attempts were made to suppress other cults, and the king did not partake in the usual festivals in honor of other gods. It is not clear whether Akhenaton himself or others were the prime movers behind this monotheistic reform. In any case, Akhenaton's successor, the young Tutankhamun, switched his allegiance to Amun and moved the capital back to Thebes. About fifty years later an attempt to eradicate the memory of Akhenaton and his Aten reform was under way. It did not succeed.

Because Egypt was intensively involved politically in the Levant at the time of Akhenaton's rule, historical scholars wonder about the potential influence of Egyptian monotheism on the milieu in which Israel's faith traditions were born. In particular, the "Great Hymn to the Aten" has some striking parallels with Ps. 104. *See also* Amarna, Tell el-; Egypt.   H.B.H.

Akkub (ak'uhb).

1 A son of Elioenai, in the royal line of David; he lived during the postexilic period (1 Chron. 3:24).

2 One of the four gatekeepers of the temple precincts (1 Chron. 9:17; see also Ezra 2:42; Neh. 7:45; 11:19; 12:25).

3 The head of a family of temple servants in postexilic times (Ezra 2:45; cf. 2:43).

4 A Levite who assisted Ezra in expounding and reading the law (Neh. 8:7).

alabaster, compact, translucent gypsum often carved into vases. The NT mentions a globular perfume flask carved from alabaster; made without handles, it had a long neck that was broken to pour

Alabaster vessels from Deir el-Balah, 1500–1200 BCE.

out the perfume (Mark 14:3; Matt. 26:7; cf. Luke 7:37).

Alamoth (al'uh-moth; Heb., "young women"), a musical direction of unknown origin and meaning. Its derivation has led some to suggest it may mean "to be sung by young women" (Ps. 46), but its use as a direction for playing the harp (1 Chron. 15:20) implies a musical theme or rhythm. *See also* Psalms, book of.

Alcimus (al'si-muhs), a Jew installed by the Seleucids as high priest ca. 161–159 BCE in opposition to the Maccabees (1 Macc. 7:5–25; cf. 2 Macc. 14:3–26). He is associated with both a plot that led to the slaughter of sixty Hasideans (1 Macc. 7:12–16) and the atrocities carried out by the Greek general Nicanor (9:1–53). His death is depicted as divine retribution for giving orders to destroy the inner wall of the temple (9:54–57). *See also* Maccabees; Seleucids.

Alemeth (al'uh-meth).
  1 The son of Becher and grandson of Benjamin (1 Chron. 7:8).
  2 A descendant of Saul whose father was Jarah (1 Chron. 9:42) or Jehoaddah (1 Chron. 8:36).
  3 A city in Benjaminite territory (1 Chron. 6:60), also called Almon and identified as Khirbet 'Almit, located just northeast of Anathoth and east of Gibeon.

Alexander (al'ig-zan'duhr).
  1 Alexander III (356–323 BCE), known as "Alexander the Great." In 336 BCE Alexander became king of Macedon and of the Greek city-states conquered by his father, Philip II. In 334, he began the conquest of the Persian Empire in the east. The first phase of his conquest occupied the period 334–330 BCE, during which time the Persian king, Darius III, was still alive and able to offer resistance to Alexander. During the first years of this campaign, Alexander marched through Anatolia, Phoenicia, Judea, Egypt, and Mesopotamia. Though the Greek naval fleet had been disbanded in 334 BCE, Alexander was able to neutralize the

Persian navy by controlling its bases. In 331 the oracle of Amun Re in Egypt proclaimed Alexander divine, and in April of 331 Alexander founded the city of Alexandria on the western edge of Egypt's Nile Delta. Alexander was able to obtain wealth from captured Persian capitals. He burned Persepolis in 330, and in July of that year Darius was murdered. Alexander concluded this phase of his conquest by disbanding his Greek allies.

The second phase of his conquest (330–327 BCE) involved putting down nationalist uprisings in the empire. It saw an increasing orientalization of the court and Alexander's marriage to the Bactrian princess Roxanne. During this period a number of cities called "Alexandria" were founded throughout the empire. In 327 BCE Alexander undertook a famous march through Afghanistan into India. His eastward progress was stopped when the troops refused to go any farther. He marched down the Indus River, but plans to coordinate the army and fleet fell through when the ships were delayed by monsoons. Only 25 percent of the army survived the western crossing of the Gedrosian desert (southern coast of modern Iran and Pakistan). Upon his return, Alexander removed officials whose loyalty had proved questionable while he was in India.

During the final eighteen months of Alexander's life, his Macedonian veterans disbanded and his army and court were increasingly staffed by Persians. Alexander ordered the repatriation of Greek exiles in the empire. He appears to have insisted on being paid divine honors by having those who entered his presence prostrate themselves. While preparing for a campaign into Arabia, Alexander died on June 10, 323. His body was a prize at the funeral games and was won by Ptolemy I, who took it to Egypt.

The primary significance of Alexander for biblical studies is that his conquests and influence ushered in what is called the Hellenistic period

Head of Alexander the Great. Alexander is pictured as a youthful Hercules with lion-skin cap on this silver tetradrachma minted after his death in the second century BCE in Greece.

(ca. 300 BCE–300 CE) throughout the Mediterranean world. Although Alexander had retained the Persian administrative system of satrapies in the lands he conquered, he had also established garrisons and Greek-style cities throughout those areas. Greek culture came to dominate the greater Mediterranean basin, especially among the educated. The results of that dominance include the translation of the Hebrew Bible into Greek (the LXX) and the writing of the NT in that same language. Among the Jewish people, there were pronounced disputes between those who favored adoption of Greek culture and those who opposed it. *See also* Alexandria; Persepolis; Persia.

2 The son of Simon of Cyrene (Mark 15:21).

3 A member of the high-priestly family (Acts 4:6).

4 A Jew from Ephesus who was encouraged to speak when Paul and his companions were dragged into the theater by patrons of Artemis (Acts 19:33).

5 An apostate mentioned in 1 Tim. 1:20.

6 A coppersmith who is said to have done Paul great harm in 2 Tim. 4:14.   P.P.

Alexandra. *See* Salome Alexandra.

Alexandria (al´ig-zan´dree-uh), a city on the Mediterranean coast in Egypt near the Nile Delta founded in 332 BCE by Alexander the Great; under Ptolemy, his successor, it became Egypt's capital. Alexandria was one of the largest cities of the Hellenistic world, a major shipping port (Acts 27:6; 28:11) famed for its 445-foot-high lighthouse, and the focal point of Hellenistic intellectual and cultural life with an unrivaled museum and library housing four hundred thousand volumes.

Alexandria's population of nearly one million included a large Jewish component, which by the first century CE was the largest Dispersion community in the world. Relations between groups in the city were tense, however, erupting into bloody riots and pogroms and producing the first known Jewish ghetto. The violence was quelled in 41 CE by an edict from the Roman emperor Claudius that directly confirmed the religious liberty of the Jews in Alexandria and throughout the empire and indirectly contributed to the period of relative calm that allowed the new Christian church to expand.

The literary flowering in Alexandria had a direct impact on the Bible. There the Greek translation of the Hebrew Bible, the LXX, was made; the Wisdom of Solomon, 3 Maccabees, and perhaps 2 and 4 Maccabees were written; and the allegorical method of interpretation was refined, a method found in the writings of Philo, the Letter to the Hebrews, the *Epistle of Barnabas,* and the later writings of church teachers like Clement of Alexandria and Origen.

Although Alexandria had Jewish inhabitants from its inception, the beginnings of Christianity there are shrouded in mystery. Apollos (Acts 18:24), a co-worker of Paul, was an Alexandrian, but he converted to Christianity only after he left

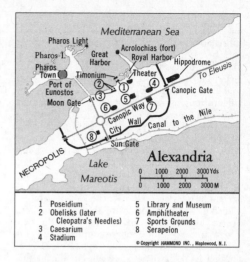

1	Poseidium	5 Library and Museum
2	Obelisks (later Cleopatra's Needles)	6 Amphitheater
3	Caesarium	7 Sports Grounds
4	Stadium	8 Serapeion

© Copyright HAMMOND INC., Maplewood, N.J.

that city. Legend attributes the initial Christian mission there to Mark, but the first firm evidence for Alexandrian Christianity derives from the second century CE. The story of Christianity in Alexandria is intimately bound up with Gnosticism, which flourished on Egyptian soil. *See also* Apollos; Gnosticism; Philo; Septuagint; Wisdom of Solomon.   J.M.B.

algum (al´guhm). *See* almug.

alien, in the Bible, one who is not a member of a particular social group. Accordingly, Abraham was an alien (NRSV: "stranger") among the Hittites at Hebron (Gen. 23:4), as were Moses in Midian (Exod. 2:22) and the Israelites in Egypt (Deut. 23:7; cf. Ruth 1:1). The Hebrew word is *ger,* and it has often been translated "sojourner" in English Bibles. The NRSV is inconsistent, translating it "alien" in some instances and "stranger" in others. After the settlement in Canaan, the term not only designated a temporary guest but also acquired the more specialized meaning of "resident alien," one who lived permanently within Israel (Exod. 22:21; 23:9). No doubt because the Israelites were keenly aware of their own heritage as aliens without rights in a foreign land, they developed specific laws governing the treatment of aliens. Strangers or aliens were to be treated with kindness and generosity (Lev. 19:10, 33–34; 23:22; Deut. 14:29). The basic principle was, "You shall also love the stranger, for you were strangers in the land of Egypt" (Deut. 10:19). And, again, "You shall love the alien as yourself, for you were aliens in the land of Egypt" (Lev. 19:34).

Resident aliens were included in the Israelite legal system (Lev. 24:16, 22; Num. 35:15; Deut. 1:16) and were subject to most of the religious requirements, such as the laws of ritual cleanliness (Lev. 17:8–13; but cf. Deut. 14:21) and the keeping of the sabbath and fast days (Exod. 20:8–10; Lev. 16:29). They could celebrate Passover if they were circumcised (Exod. 12:48–49) and could offer sacrifices (Num. 15:14–16, 29). Ezekiel even envisioned a time when they would be granted an inheritance in the land as a sign of full citizenship (47:22–23). In later Judaism, the laws concerning aliens/strangers developed into the regulations governing the acceptance of Gentile proselytes into Judaism. "Alien" or "stranger" also appears in a figurative sense, usually in appealing to the generosity and mercy of God in dealing with undeserving people (Pss. 39:12; 119:19; 1 Chron. 29:15). The idea of dwelling in a land owned by someone else is also applied theologically to the relationship of the Israelites to the land; it belonged to God and they were the strangers in it (Lev. 25:23).

The NT picks up this concept in two different ways. On one level, the Gentiles, who were excluded by Judaism from being the people of God, are no longer aliens and strangers in the new Christian community, but are counted as full citizens of God's own household (Eph. 2:11–21). On another level, Christians are not citizens of this present world, but citizens of the heavenly kingdom and therefore only strangers or pilgrims in this world (1 Pet. 1:1, 17; 2:11; cf. Heb. 11:13). In a more literal sense, the term "stranger" is used in the NT to refer to someone who is unknown (3 John 5), for example, because the person is from out of town (Luke 24:18). Several NT authors promote the virtue of showing hospitality to such persons (Matt. 25:34–40; Rom. 12:13; Heb. 13:2). *See also* foreigner; hospitality; proselyte.

D.R.B./M.A.P.

almond (*Amagdalus communis*), a fruit tree that grows as high as 25 feet. It flowers toward the end of January, the color of its blooms ranging from pink to pure white. According to Gen. 30:37 Jacob used rods of almond, poplar, and plane in his plan against Laban. In Gen. 43:11 almonds are among the choice fruits of the land. According to Num.

17:8, Aaron's rod put forth buds, blossoms, and ripe almonds, thus demonstrating he was divinely chosen. Jeremiah's vision of the rod of almond (Heb. *shaqed*) signifies that God is watching over (Heb. *shoqed*) God's word (1:11). Ecclesiastes uses the almond blossom to illustrate declining old age (12:5). In Exod. 25:33–34 and 37:19–20, the cups on the six branches and main stand of the lampstand (menorah) were shaped like almonds. *See also* lampstand.   R.J.C.

alms, gifts to the needy. Almsgiving is a common practice in the Bible that recognizes God's blessings and maintains proper community relations. In the Bible, care for the poor is not only recommended as just behavior (Prov. 14:21, 31; Isa. 58:6–8), but is required by the tithe for the poor every three years (Deut. 14:28–29) and by the leaving of fallen produce at harvest for the poor (Deut. 24:19–22). Specific attention to almsgiving is found in the deuterocanonical books of Tobit and Sirach, where the topic receives more attention than anywhere else in the Bible (Tob. 4:7, 16; 12:8–9; 14:2, 8, 10; Sir. 7:10; 12:3; 29:8; 35:4). In the NT, Jesus endorses the traditional Jewish practice of almsgiving, emphasizing that it be done with an integrity that does not merely seek to enhance the honor of the giver (Matt. 6:1–4; cf. 5:42). He also indicates that, in the final judgment, people will be judged according to the care they gave to needy persons (Matt. 25:31–46). The early Christian community also found ways of caring for the needy in ways that did not specifically involve almsgiving (Acts 2:44–45; 4:34–35; 6; 2 Cor. 8–9). *See also* love; poor; poverty.   A.J.S./M.A.P.

almug (al'muhg), a special kind of wood, perhaps red sandalwood (*Pterocarpus santalinus*). Almug was imported from Ophir (southwest Arabia) by Hiram of Tyre and used in the construction of

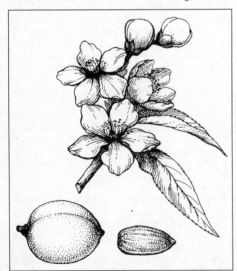

Almond.

Traditional almug.

Solomon's temple and for musical instruments (1 Kings 10:11–12). The parallels in 2 Chron. 2:7 and 9:10–11 have "algum," perhaps by transposition of two letters. The occurrence of a similar word in Ugaritic (*almg*) suggests that the spelling in Kings is preferred.

aloes (al′ohz), any plant of the genus *Aloe*. The aloes mentioned in the Bible are the fragrant wood of either an eaglewood or sandalwood tree used as perfume. Aloes tend to be listed along with other fragrant spices, such as cinnamon, myrrh, and cassia (Ps. 45:8; Prov. 7:17; Song of Sol. 4:14). According to John 19:39, the body of Jesus was wrapped in one hundred pounds of myrrh and aloes before being placed in the tomb.   P.P./M.A.P.

alpha (al′fuh), the first letter of the Greek alphabet. In Revelation, God (1:8; 21:6) and Jesus (22:13) are called "the Alpha and the Omega," meaning the first and the last (omega is the last letter in the Greek alphabet; cf. Isa. 44:6 for God as "first" and "last"). The author of Revelation believes that both God and Jesus have been present from the beginning (cf. Gen. 1:1; John 1:1) and that both God and Jesus will reign in the last days. *See also* creation; eschatology; kingdom of God; millennium; omega; Parousia.

alphabet. *See* writing.

Alphaeus (al-fee′uhs).
  1 The father of James, one of Jesus's twelve disciples. That disciple is called "James the son of Alphaeus" to avoid confusion with another disciple, "James the son of Zebedee" (Matt. 10:3; Mark 3:18; Luke 6:15; Acts 1:13). *See also* James.
  2 The father of Levi (also called Matthew) the tax collector (Mark 2:14; see Matt. 9:9; Luke 5:27). *See also* Levi; Matthew.

altar, any surface upon which any kind of offering to a deity is placed. The actual term for "altar" (Heb. *mizbeakh*) is formed from a verbal root that means "to slaughter" or, more specifically, "to slaughter and cut up for the purpose of sacrifice." Thus, the word must have originally been

Two altars pictured *in situ* in the Holy of Holies of the Israelite temple at Arad, ninth century BCE.

Incense burners from Tel Zafit and Tel Amal and a small altar, first millennium BCE.

connected with the ancient practice of animal sacrifice. However, by the time of its usage in connection with biblical ritual, its meaning had been expanded. In addition to animal sacrifice, altars mentioned in the Bible were used for a variety of foodstuffs, including grain mixed with oil and/or salt and incense, wine, and fruits; they were also used for the burning of incense alone. In animal sacrifice, although the animal parts were deposited on the altar to be burned, the actual slaughtering of sacrificial animals would have normally taken place at a designated spot adjacent to the altar.

The word *mizbeakh* is found approximately four hundred times in the Bible. Many English Bibles also use the word "altar" to render another Hebrew term (*bat har'el*), which literally means "mountain of God" and may refer to Syro-Mesopotamian altar constructions; Ezek. 43:15 probably uses it in reference to an altar built by King Ahaz in emulation of an altar he had seen in Damascus (2 Kings 11:10–16).

Virtually half of the references to altars in the Hebrew Bible appear in the Pentateuch, as might be expected, because of the concentration of priestly texts in that first section of the Bible. Other biblical books with frequent mentions of altars are 1 and 2 Kings, which include the description of the Solomonic temple altar; 2 Chronicles, which has a decidedly priestly interest; and Ezekiel, which reports prophetic visions highly influenced by temple imagery.

In the NT the word for "altar" (Gk. *thysiastērion*) is used in twenty-four places. In one instance, another Greek word (*bōmos*, "high place") is translated "altar" in reference to a pagan structure (Acts 17:23). The NT references exhibit concentrations in Matthew (seven times), with only two mentions in Luke and none in Mark or John, and in Revelation (eight times), as might be expected because of the temple visions of that book.

Because they involved the processing of animal carcasses and the burning of various foodstuffs, altars (except for incense altars) were open-air structures. Therefore, altars could exist and function independently of temple buildings. This fact is especially apparent in the ancestral narratives of Genesis (e.g., 13:18; 33:20). In addition, the somewhat enigmatic shrines known as "high places" were perhaps a category of altar. Temple buildings always had altars in their courtyards, and after the time of Josiah (640–609 BCE) there was increased pressure for all sacrifices to be offered at the temple in Jerusalem.

Types of Altars. Biblical altars can be classified according to the material from which they were fabricated, namely, stone, earth, or metal. The first two kinds of material are associated with altars that could exist apart from sanctuaries. The third type of altar is mentioned only in connection with the central sanctuaries of Israel, the tabernacle and temple. A fourth type of altar, made of brick, is mentioned only once in the Bible, in Isa. 65:3, where a word (*lebenah*) different from the normal Hebrew terms is employed.

Stone Altars: Stone altars consisted of both natural and constructed forms. Evidently any large stone could be used in its original position and condition, as in the story of Gideon's offering of bread and meat upon a rock (Judg. 6:19–23; cf. 13:19–20). In other cases, a large stone might be moved from its existing position into a more convenient place, as for example, when Saul insisted that a stone be brought to where he stood for the slaughter, presumably as an altar sacrifice, of sheep and oxen captured from the Philistines (1 Sam. 14:31–35). Simple stone altars apparently could be enhanced somewhat by the hollowing out of depressions in the rock to contain liquids. The evidence for such altars is archaeological rather than biblical, however, and the identification of large rocks with "cup holes," or shallow depressions, as altars remains tentative. In addition to isolated stones, unhewn stones, as commanded in Exod. 20:25, could be formed into altars, either as irregular heaps (e.g., Gen. 31:46) or as dry-laid masonry structures. The latter seems to be the case for the carefully arranged stones of Elijah's altar on Mount Carmel (1 Kings 18:30–35).

It is obvious that any of these stone altars could be established with relative ease, a consideration no doubt related to the fact that, until Josiah's reform, all slaughtering of animals for meat was to be considered a sacrificial act, at least according to the tradition preserved in Lev. 17:3–5 and altered by the proscriptions in Deut. 12:15–28.

Earthen Altars: Earthen altars could also be erected anywhere, according to Exod. 20:24, for the sacrifice of various kinds of offerings. They were characterized by simplicity and availability to all the people; neither technical competence nor craft specialization was associated with the construction of these altars.

Metal Altars: Altars of metal are mentioned in the Bible only in connection with the central sanctuaries of ancient Israel. Several biblical sources provide descriptive materials: the tabernacle texts of Exodus, the Solomonic temple description in 1 Kings, Ezekiel's temple vision, and to a lesser extent the temple vision in the book of Revelation. These texts contain a number of discrepancies, omissions, or contradictions in their presentation of the altars, but a fairly accurate understanding of the two metal altars of the main cultic center can be acquired from these sources. These were the golden altar of incense and the bronze altar of burnt offerings.

The *altar of incense* was placed inside the sanctuary, directly in front of the inner sanctum and flanked, according to the Exodus texts, by two other appurtenances, the menorah and the table of the bread of the Presence (30:1–10; 37:25–28; cf. 1 Kings 7:20–21, 48). It was made of wood and, like everything within the sanctuary, was covered with the precious metal gold. An upright pillar measuring 1 by 1 by 2 cubits (perhaps 18 by 18 by 36 inches), the incense altar featured horns on its four upper corners. For this reason it has been compared to various horned incense altars recovered from Iron Age levels at such sites as Megiddo and Shechem as well as to small stone altars without horns from Arad, even though these excavated examples are notably different in size and material from the biblical incense altar. Twice daily incense was burned in the tabernacle or temple on the golden altar. In addition, this altar played a central role in the annual purgation rites that maintained or reestablished the sanctity of the entire sacred precinct. In this capacity, it provided a connection between the holiest inner part of the temple and the less holy external zone, the court. Situated on the central axis of the sanctuary, the golden altar united all three zones of temple sanctity.

The *altar of burnt offering* stood in the courtyard of the tabernacle (Exod. 27:1–8; 38:1–7) and occupied a special "holy place," akin to the holiness within the sanctuary, which could be approached only by priests even though nonpriests could be present in the courtyard. The temple description in 1 Kings omits a description of this altar, perhaps because Ahaz had moved it or because Solomon had used one made by David; but 2 Chron. 4:1 does describe a courtyard altar (20 by 20 by 20 cubits, or about 30 by 30 by 30 feet), and 1 Kings 8:64 also mentions it. Thus there can be no doubt that the Jerusalem temple featured a courtyard altar as the focus of its sacrificial cult. Although larger than the tabernacle altar, which was 5 by 5 by 3 cubits (about 7½ by 7½ by 4½ feet), it was also made, or perhaps overlaid, with bronze, like the other courtyard appurtenances. An even larger courtyard altar, in the Syrian style, was introduced by Ahaz and probably continued to be used until the temple was destroyed. The information in Ezekiel emphasizes the altar's great size (12 cubits high and 18 by 18 cubits at its base or about 18 feet high and about 27 by 27 feet at the base) and tiered shape and most likely reflects the altar Ahaz commissioned. Both the tabernacle courtyard altar and that of Ezekiel's vision had horns at their four upper corners, a feature that perhaps can be associated with the large horned altar made of hewn sandstone blocks discovered at Beer-sheba.

In the NT, references to altars are mainly to the courtyard altar of the Jerusalem temple, either in preexilic or postexilic (chiefly Herodian) times. In one significant development of this pattern, the Christian altar of Heb. 13:10 appears to be a metaphor for human self-offering, which brings the offerant close to God. *See also* Bethel; tabernacle; temple, the; temples; worship in the Hebrew Bible.
Bibliography

Haak, Robert D. "Altar." *Anchor Bible Dictionary.* Doubleday, 1992. 1:162–67.

Haran, Menahem. *Temples and Temple Service in Ancient Israel.* Clarendon, 1970.

Meyers, Carol. "Realms of Sanctity: The Case of the 'Misplaced' Incense Altars in the Tabernacle Texts of Exodus." In *Text, Temples, and Traditions: Festschrift for Menahem Haran.* Eisenbrauns, 1996.
C.L.M.

Amalek (uh-mal'uhk).

1 A grandson of Esau (Gen. 36:15–16) and the ancestor of the Amalekites.

2 A shorthand expression for Amalekites (e.g., Exod. 17:8–16; Num. 24:20).

See also Amalekites.

Amalekites (uh-mal'uh-kits), descendants of

Amalek, who was a grandson of Esau (Gen. 36:15–16). As a people, the Amalekites inhabited territory assigned to Israel, Judah, and the Transjordanian states. They were probably nomadic, or at least quite mobile. They are often mentioned as inhabiting desert regions or the fringe of settled territories. The Amalekites attacked Israel on its wilderness journeys from Egypt (Exod. 17:8–16), a report that highlights an antipathy between the two peoples. Other references to them suggest that they were proficient raiders of village and agrarian communities (1 Sam. 30:1–20; Judg. 6:1–6). As Israel solidified its territorial hold during the period of the judges and the united monarchy (ca. 1225–926 BCE), the Amalekite threat gradually lessened (see 2 Sam. 8:12; 1 Chron. 18:11). There are no more references to the Amalekites after the narratives about David, aside from a summary reference in 1 Chron. 4:43. The Amalekites are not mentioned outside the Bible. *See also* Amalek. J.A.D.

Amariah (am'uh-ri'uh; Heb., "the LORD has

spoken" or "the LORD has promised").

1 A Levite, an ancestor of Zadok and Ezra. There are two men in one genealogical list (1 Chron. 6:7, 11) bearing this name: the first is the son of Meraioth, and the second, the son of Azariah. However, other lists omit one of these (1 Chron. 6:52, the first; Ezra 7:3, the second). It is possible that these latter lists were abbreviated or that parts of the longer list were accidently duplicated.

2 A Levite, the second son of Hebron, son of Kohath (1 Chron. 23:19).

3 The chief priest in Jerusalem during the reign of Jehoshaphat (2 Chron. 19:11).

4 A Levite who shared the responsibility for distributing the Levites' portion of the offerings to the levitical cities during the reign of Hezekiah (2 Chron. 31:15).

5 A Levite who returned from the Babylonian exile with Zerubbabel (Neh. 12:2), possibly the same one who signed Ezra's covenant to keep the law (Neh. 10:3) and divorced his non-Israelite wife in response to Ezra's proclamation (Ezra 10:42), although these latter identifications are not certain.

6 A Judahite who lived in postexilic Jerusalem (Neh. 11:4).

7 The ancestor of a family group in postexilic Jerusalem whose leader was Jehohanan (Neh. 12:13).

8 A son of (King?) Hezekiah in the lineage of the prophet Zephaniah (cf. Zeph. 1:1). D.R.B.

Amarna, Tell el- (uh-mahr'nuh, tel' el), the

modern name for the ruins of ancient Akhetaten (Egyptian, "The Horizon of the Sun Disk/Aten"), briefly the capital of Egypt during the later years of Akhenaton (Amenophis IV) and his immediate successors. Settled ca. 1356 BCE, Akhetaten is in middle Egypt, on a wide plain on the east bank of the Nile about midway between Thebes and Memphis. When Akhenaton founded the city, he dedicated it to the cult of the Aten, honored as the sole god. Since the city was abandoned within fifteen to twenty years of its founding—the young Tutankhamun moved the court back to Thebes—it is a unique, one-period city. The city plan features a separate complex for the royal residence and extensive structures for the ceremonial and ritual acts of the royal family. The exaggerated, naturalistic style of the sculptures, reliefs, and paintings, together with the uniquely intimate scenes of Akhenaton, his queen, Nefertiti, and their daughters, has made Amarna art-world famous. From adjacent tombs come the hymns to the sole god, the Aten (or to the Aten and the king), who is also celebrated on the city's boundary stelae. Another major discovery involved tablets in cuneiform Akkadian of both literary

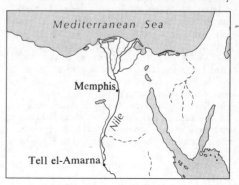

texts and over three hundred and fifty letters exchanged between the Egyptian court and the kings of western Asia Minor. The bulk of these letters came from the Near East, including rulers of Jerusalem, Shechem, and Megiddo among other biblical cities. These texts demonstrate the international character of the age and the socially and politically disturbed situation in the region. Prominent in the letters are the Hapiru, a marginal people reminiscent of the later Hebrews. *See also* Akhenaton; Hebrews; Hapiru.   H.B.H.

Amasa (uh-may'suh; Heb., "to support, defend, protect"; cf. Isa. 46:3).

1 The son of Abigail (sister or half sister of David) and Jether the Ishmaelite (1 Chron. 2:17). He was the cousin of Joab and his successor as military commander-in-chief, despite his defection to the rebelling Absalom (2 Sam. 17:25; 19:14). During the revolt of Sheba, he failed to take prompt action and was therefore murdered by Joab (2 Sam. 20:1–13). He may be the same person called Amasai in 1 Chron. 12:18. *See also* Amasai.

2 The son of Haldai and a prince of Ephraim (2 Chron. 28:12) who helped the prisoners of Judah (2 Chron. 28:12–15).   J.G.G.

Amasai (uh-may'si).

1 The chief of "the Thirty," David's elite fighting force or bodyguard (1 Chron. 12:18). He may be the same person identified in 1 Chron. 2:17 as Amasa the son of Abigail and Jether (which would make him a relative of David). *See also* Amasa.

2 A Levite, son of Elkanah (1 Chron. 6:25) and father of Mahoth (1 Chron. 6:35; 2 Chron. 29:12).

3 A levitical priest who was a trumpeter before the ark in David's time (1 Chron. 15:24).

Amaziah (am'uh-zi'uh; Heb., "the LORD is mighty").

1 The king of Judah ca. 800–783 BCE. Amaziah was the son of Joash; he succeeded his father as king when he was twenty-five years old (see 2 Kings 14:1–20). According to 2 Kings 14:2 he ruled twenty-nine years, but the chronological problems posed by his synchronism with Jehoash, king of Israel (14:17), can only be resolved by supposing that he reigned alone for about eighteen years and was coregent with his son Uzziah for the balance. Ascending the throne when his father was murdered, Amaziah consolidated his power by annihilating the assassins, but sparing their sons. He slaughtered ten thousand Edomites in a battle in the "Valley of Salt" and captured Sela. Emboldened by this success, he challenged his rival Jehoash, king of Israel, who tried to dissuade him with a fable comparing him to a thornbush (14:8–10). Refusing to listen, Amaziah was defeated by Jehoash at the battle of Beth-shemesh, and Judah became a vassal state to Israel (14:11–14). Later a conspiracy was mounted against Amaziah, and he was pursued to Lachish, where he was murdered.

2 A Simeonite, the father of Joshah (1 Chron. 4:34).

3 A Levite of the family of Merari (1 Chron. 6:45).

4 A priest of Bethel (Amos 7:10, 12, 14).   W.G.D.

amen (ah-men', ay'men'), a Hebrew word conveying a sense of certainty, truthfulness, and faithfulness. It is used throughout the Bible as a liturgical response at the end of psalms and doxologies in which the congregation affirms what has been prayed by saying Amen, "So be it" (e.g., Pss. 41:13; 72:19; 89:52). It is also used as an oath conveying the acceptance of a procedure for determining truth (Num. 5:22), commitment to obeying the law (Deut. 27:17–26), or affirmation of a royal decision (1 Kings 1:36). In the Gospels Jesus often prefaces his teachings with "Amen I say to you," a solemn affirmation that the NRSV translates "Truly I tell you." In two NT passages, Jesus is called "the Amen" (2 Cor. 1:20; Rev. 3:14).   M.A.P.

Ami (ay'mi). *See* Amon.

Ammiel (am'ee-uhl).

1 A Danite, son of Amishaddai. He was one of the spies sent by Moses into Canaan (Num. 13:12).

2 The father of Machir, who protected Jonathan's son, Mephibosheth (2 Sam. 9:4–5), and equipped David at Mahanaim (17:27).

3 The father of Bath-shua (variant spelling of Bathsheba; 1 Chron. 3:5).

4 The sixth son of the Korahite temple gatekeeper Obed-edom (1 Chron. 26:5).

Ammihud (uh-mi'huhd).

1 The father of Elishama, an Ephraimite leader (Num. 1:10; 2:18; 7:48, 53; 10:22), and the great-grandfather of Joshua (1 Chron. 7:26).

2 The father of Shemuel, a Simeonite who allotted land for inheritance (Num. 34:20).

3 The father of the Naphtalite leader Pedahel, who also allotted land (Num. 34:28).

4 The father of Talmai, king of Geshur, to whom Absalom fled (2 Sam. 13:37).

5 A Judahite son of Omri and father of Uthai (1 Chron. 9:4).

Amminadab (uh-min'uh-dab; Heb., "my relative is noble").

1 The father of both Elisheba, Aaron's wife (Exod. 6:23), and Nahshan, a tribal leader of Judah during the wilderness wanderings (Num. 2:3). He is named in the lineage of King David (Ruth 4:19–20) and in the ancestry of Jesus (Luke 3:33).

2 A Levite belonging to the Kohath line (1 Chron. 6:22), probably the same one who, as leader of the Uzziel group, helped bring the ark of the covenant from the house of Obed-edom to Jerusalem (15:10).

Ammishaddai (am-i-shad'i; Heb., "my relative is Shaddai"), the father of Ahiezer, leader of the tribe of Dan during the wilderness wanderings (Num. 1:12).

Ammon (am'uhn), an area east of the Jordan River at the headwaters of the river Jabbok, homeland to the Ammonites. According to historical research, the rise of the kingdom of Ammon east of the Jordan River coincided with the rise of several states in the greater Syro-Palestinian area during the Late Bronze Age and Early Iron Age (ca. 1500–1000 BCE). Additional peoples who emerged in that area at that time were the Moabites, the Edomites, Israel, and several Aramean states.

There are no references to the name Ammon in Late Bronze Egyptian sources such as survive for Moab, but the archaeological record is quite clear that there were permanent settlements in the region of modern Amman, Jordan, during that period. In recent years a long-term exploration known as the Medeba Plains Project has made considerable progress in uncovering the Ammonite culture of the Iron Age. Excavations at sites a few kilometers south of Amman (Hesban [perhaps biblical Heshbon], Tell el Umeiri, Tell Jawa) have produced walled settlements, a distinctive pottery profile, and some inscriptional remains. Excavation continues at the large mount of ancient Rabbah, where both Late Bronze and Iron Age remains have been discovered.

The chief deity of Ammon was Milkom. His name is formed from the root word for "king" or "ruler" (*mlk*). According to 1 Kings 11, Solomon built a chapel for Milkom on the hill east of the Temple Mount in Jerusalem. This was likely a response to the needs of a diplomatic marriage between Solomon and an Ammonite princess.

The capital city of Ammon, Rabbah, was rebuilt and enlarged in the third century BCE by Ptolemy Philadelphus, a descendant of one of the generals of Alexander the Great. Ptolemy renamed the new city Philadelphia in his own honor. The eventual reappearance of Ammon in the name of modern Amman (capital of Jordan) is an indication of the long-standing association of the area with that ancient civilization. *See also* Ammonites; Jephthah.

J.A.D.

Ammonites (am'uh-nīts), a people who lived east of the Jordan River, in the area of the modern state of Jordan. The capital city was called Rabbah. Its ancient remains are located in the heart of modern Amman. According to Gen. 19:30–38, a son was born to Lot, Abraham's nephew, named Ben-ammi. This child is reputed to be the ancestor of the Ammonites. His half brother is Moab, ancestor of the Moabites, who lived south of the Ammonite region.

Conflicts between the Ammonites and Israel arose early in their respective political histories. Sometime after the Israelites had entered the land of Canaan, they were defeated by a coalition of Ammonites and Philistines. Jephthah, the son of Gilead and a prostitute, rallied Israel to battle against them (Judg. 10:6–11:40). In later battles, the Ammonites were defeated by Saul at Jabeshgilead (1 Sam. 11) and then by David at Rabbah (2 Sam. 11:14–21). Much that happened to the

Limestone statue of an Ammonite king from the ninth century BCE.

Ammonites after those defeats is obscure, but the defeats by Israel did not subdue them permanently. As the political fortunes of both Israel and Judah waned in the eighth and seventh centuries BCE, Ammonite culture continued to develop, a conclusion substantiated by both epigraphic and artifactual evidence. Ammonites referred to in later biblical literature include Tobiah in the book of Nehemiah (2:10, 19; 4:3) and Achior in the book of Judith (5:5; 6:5; 14:5). See also 1 Macc. 5:6; 2 Macc. 5:7. *See also* Ammon.

J.A.D.

Amnon (am'non; Heb., "faithful").

1 The eldest son of David and Ahinoam and the half brother of Absalom and Tamar. The story of his obsessive desire for Tamar is related in 2 Sam. 13. Amnon "fell in love with her" (13:1). Acting on the advice of his cousin Jonadab, he pretended to be ill and asked David to let Tamar attend him. He raped her when they were alone, then afterward "was seized with a very great loathing for her" (13:15) and threw her out in the street. This action infuriated Absalom, who waited patiently for his revenge. After two years had passed, Absalom arranged with his retainers for the murder of Amnon, which precipitated a rift between David and Absalom. *See also* Absalom; David; Tamar.

2 A Judahite, son of Shimon (1 Chron. 4:20).

M.A.P.

Amon (am'uhn).

1 A governor of the city of Samaria during the reign of Ahab (1 Kings 22:10, 26).

2 A king of Judah, grandson of Hezekiah, son of and successor to Manasseh, and father of Josiah. He became king at age twenty-two and ruled for two years (ca. 642–640 BCE) before being murdered in his palace by servants (2 Kings 21:19–26; 2 Chron. 33:21–25). The conspirators were apparently opponents of his father's pro-Assyrian policies, which he was continuing to endorse.

3 A man listed among those who returned from the exile in Babylon under Zerubbabel and who became one of the ancestors of temple assistants called "Solomon's servants" (Neh. 7:59). He is referred to as Ami in Ezra 2:57.

Amorites (am'uh-rīts), according to biblical tradition one of the primary peoples in the land of Canaan before the rise of Israel; the others were the Canaanites and the Hittites (see Ezek. 16:3). The term "Amorite" can refer to the basic population of the whole area (e.g., Gen. 15:16; Deut. 1:7). In particular, the Amorites are associated with Transjordan and the kingdoms of Sihon, centered at Heshbon, and Og, centered at Ashtaroth and Edrei. These "two kings of the Amorites" appear as opponents of Israel prior to the settlement in Canaan. Og, with his famous "iron bedstead," is cited as the last of the celebrated giants. From the perspective of the Israelites, the Amorites were idolaters and perpetrators of iniquity (e.g., Josh. 24:15; Judg. 6:10). Accordingly, God drove them out of the land.

The Semitic-speaking Amorites appear in cuneiform (and Egyptian) sources as an early population group, associated especially with the west (including areas connected with the ancestors of Israel—Abraham, Isaac, and Jacob), and as politically dominant in Mesopotamia in the early second millennium BCE. There was also a territory of Amurru in western Syria. At times, such as in the two centuries prior to the exodus (fifteenth–fourteenth centuries BCE), there was a specific kingdom of Amurru; in earlier times the area had several kings.

The antiquity of Amorites in the land of Canaan is unclear. Linguistic evidence indicates their presence as a settled population by ca. 1900 BCE, to judge from personal names, but that evidence is not decisive. The archaeological evidence is also unclear. The coming of the Amorites has been correlated by some scholars with the archaeological discontinuity at the end of Early Bronze Age III, ca. 2350 BCE (and a transition to seminomadic pastoralism) or with the emergence of Middle Bronze I, ca. 2000 BCE (and a transition to a more urbanized society). The problem is not settled. The patterns of population shift in the larger area are complex and precise correlations of literary and archaeological evidence are difficult. *See also* Og; Sihon.   H.B.H.

Amos (ay'muhs), **book of,** the third part of the Book of the Twelve in the Prophets section, or Nevi'im, in the Tanakh (Jewish Bible). It is the third book in the Minor Prophets section of the Christian OT.

Contents: The book begins with a superscription, placing the prophet's career during the reigns of Uzziah (Judah) and Jeroboam II (Israel). Verse 1 also identifies Amos as a shepherd in Tekoa two years before a major earthquake (the same earth-

quake mentioned by Zech. 14:5 over 250 years later). The book is easily divided into three sections: oracles against the nations (chaps. 1–2), a collection of Amos's sayings (3–6), and a collection of vision reports (7–9).

The first section presents a series of oracles against nations (1:2–2:16). Each of the oracles begins with a similar phrase "for three transgressions of x and for four, I will not revoke (the punishment)." This formula is used to speak of the many sins of the people of these nations. After identifying a nation's sin, the oracle declares that its leaders will be defeated or destroyed and the people exiled or killed. The series of oracles begins with a judgment upon Damascus (Aram) for its treatment of Gilead (1:3–5). Judgment is then pronounced upon Gaza (Philistia) for exiling communities and handing them over to the Edomites (1:6–8). Tyre is condemned for handing people over to the Edomites and forgetting its covenant with Israel (during the reigns of David and Solomon, 1:9–10). Edom is judged for its anger and wrath against its brother (presumably invoking the image of Jacob and Esau, 1:11–12). The Ammonites are also condemned for their savagery against Gilead for territorial gain (1:13–15). Judgment comes upon the Moabites for their treatment of the leaders of Edom (2:1–3). Up to this point, all of the oracles have been against nations bordering Israel and Judah. Amos then moves to present oracles against Judah for rejecting God's laws and being led astray (2:4–5). Israel is condemned for selling "the righteous for silver and the needy for a pair of sandals" (2:6).

The next section is a collection of the prophet's sayings (3:1–6:14). In this collection, Amos focuses on two main themes: social injustice and condemnation of the sacrificial cult (especially as it is practiced at Bethel). For Amos, to serve the Lord is to practice justice, not offer sacrifices (4:1–3; 6:4–7). The yearly celebrations at Bethel commemorated the exodus from Egypt, an event viewed as establishing a special relationship between the people of Israel and God. Yet Amos argues that this election did not mean they would be spared judgment for their sins and injustices, but that they were called to greater responsibility and would be punished more severely for breaking the covenant. In order to demonstrate this, Amos invokes the imagery of the "day of the LORD" in order to make his point. Many people in Israel understood the "day of the LORD" to be a day of judgment on Israel's enemies, but Amos claims that it will be a day of judgment on Israel and Judah as well. Their special relationship with God will not spare them the coming judgment.

The last section consists of five visions and an interlude. It begins with a vision of locusts devouring the land (7:1–3) and then moves into a vision of fire consuming the land (7:4–6). The next vision is of the Lord with a plumb line (7:7–9). At this point there is an interlude between the prophet Amos and the priest Amaziah (7:10–17). Amaziah accuses Amos of treason, citing prophecies against the king. Amos, however, claims he is not a prophet, but received a call from the Lord (meaning that he is not part of a guild of prophets tied to the king, but has simply been called by God). Amos then prophesies that Amaziah's wife will become a prostitute and that his children will be killed. A fourth vision commences, showing a basket full of fruit, portending the end of Israel (8:1–3). The last vision is of the Lord standing by the altar, prophesying the death and destruction of the people. The book ends with what most scholars believe is an editorial addition, namely, a passage in which the rebirth of the Davidic dynasty is promised (9:11–15).

OUTLINE OF CONTENTS

Amos

I. Superscription (1:1)
II. Judgment oracles against the nations (1:2–2:16)
   A. Damascus (1:3–5)
   B. Gaza (1:6–8)
   C. Tyre (1:9–10)
   D. Edom (1:11–12)
   E. Ammon (1:13–15)
   F. Moab (2:1–3)
   G. Judah (2:4–5)
   H. Israel (2:6–16)
III. Judgment oracles against Israel (3:1–6:14)
IV. Judgment visions (7:1–9:10)
   A. Vision of locusts (7:1–3)
   B. Vision of fire (7:4–6)
   C. Vision of the Lord with a plumb line (7:7–9)
   D. Interlude: Amos and Amaziah (7:10–17)
   E. Vision of summer fruit; prophecies (8:1–14)
   F. Vision of the Lord beside an altar; prophecies (9:1–10)
V. Salvation oracle of the Davidic dynasty (9:11–15)

Background: The prophet Amos is identified in the superscription as one of the "shepherds of Tekoa" (1:1) and in 7:14 as a "herdsman, and a dresser of sycamore trees." There is scholarly disagreement over whether this description means that Amos was an impoverished herder who cared for the rights of his fellow poor or a landowner who pursued the well-being of those less fortunate than himself. Amos was one of the earliest of the writing prophets and was a contemporary of Hosea and Isaiah of Jerusalem. Based on references to the earthquake and the reigns of Uzziah and Jeroboam II, most scholars believe that Amos prophesied between 760 and 740 BCE.

Themes: The most prominent theme of the book of Amos is social justice. Amos took the concepts of justice and righteousness, which were usually used in regard to God's dealings with humanity, and applied them to social interaction. He further privileged responsibility and care of the community over concerns for ritual worship. Simundson claims that the prosperity of Jeroboam's reign had led to an increase in outward piety (acknowledgment that a good God is giving good things), but a lack of social justice.

Interpretive Issues: The major interpretive issue in the book of Amos concerns the book's redaction history and the question of its unity. The superscription is an obvious editorial addition, yet most scholars believe that there are many more. Gottwald claims that over half of the current text is a result of the editorial process. He posits a total of six stages to the editorial process (three of which took place in the eighth century). Other scholars cite three major steps in the editorial process of Amos: oral prophesies of the historical Amos, Deuteronomic additions during the reign of Josiah, and messages of comfort added after the fall of Jerusalem. Peterson connects the prophecy against Judah (for violating Torah) with the work of a Deuteronomistic editor.

Influences: One of the most famous references to the book of Amos in modern times was in Martin Luther King Jr.'s "I Have a Dream" speech in Washington, D.C., in 1963. He quoted Amos 5:24, saying "Let justice roll down like mighty waters, and righteousness like an ever flowing stream."

Bibliography

Bandstra, Barry L. *Reading the Old Testament: Introduction to the Hebrew Bible.* 4th ed. Wadsworth, 2009.

Childs, Brevard S. *Introduction to the Old Testament as Scripture.* Fortress, 1979.

Gottwald, Norman K. *The Hebrew Bible: A Socio-Literary Introduction.* Fortress, 1985.

Peterson, David L. *The Prophetic Literature: An Introduction.* Westminster John Knox, 2002.

Simundson, Daniel J. *Hosea, Joel, Amos, Obadiah, Jonah, Micah.* Abingdon, 2005.

Sweeney, Marvin A. *The Twelve Prophets.* Vol. 1, *Hosea, Joel, Amos, Obadiah, Jonah.* Liturgical, 2000.

Wolff, Hans Walter. *Joel and Amos.* Fortress, 1977.
                    B.B.

Amoz (ay'muhz; Heb., "he is strong"). The father of Isaiah (Isa. 1:1). The name, to be distinguished from Amos, is a shortened form of Amaziah.

Amphipolis (am-fip'uh-lis; Gk., "double city"), a city situated inland above the Gulf of Strymon in northeastern Macedonia. The Strymon River, which formed a loop around part of the city, seems to have been the source of its name ("double city"). In the first century CE, Amphipolis was a military post along the main east–west Roman road from Asia to Italy, the Egnatian Way. After leaving Philippi, Paul passed through Amphipolis on his way to Thessalonica (Acts 17:1).

Amram (am'ram).

1 The grandson of Levi, son of Kohath. He married Jochebed, and they became the parents of

Aaron, Moses, and Miriam (Exod. 6:16–20; Num. 26:58–59). Amram is said to have lived 137 years. He is to be regarded as ancestor of the Amramites (Num. 3:27; 1 Chron. 26:23).

2 A son of Bani (Ezra 10:34).

amulet, a small object believed to be charged with divine potency and thus effective in warding off evil and inviting the protection of beneficial powers. Amulets were integral to belief in magic and derived their efficacy from close physical contact with a holy person or object. *See also* divination; magic.

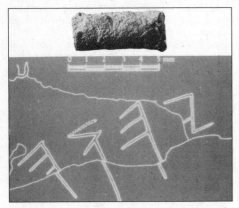

A tiny silver amulet found in Jerusalem inscribed with ancient Hebrew characters that spell out the divine name, YHWH, which are drawn here. Originally the amulet—3.82 inches long, unrolled—was rolled and a string was threaded through it so that a person could wear it around the neck. From the writing, it may be dated to ca. sixth century BCE.

Anah (ay′nuh).

1 One of the eight sons of Seir the Horite; he was a leader of the Horites, ancient inhabitants of the area of Edom (Gen. 36:20; 1 Chron. 1:38). *See also* Horites; Seir.

2 A nephew of 1 above, the son of Zibeon and the father of Oholibamah, who became one of Esau's wives (Gen. 36:2). He was known for his discovery of a hot spring in the desert (36:24).

Anak (ay′nak), eponymous ancestor of a people, the Anakim (Deut. 1:28; 9:2; Josh. 11:21–22), who are also referred to as "Anakites" (Num. 13:22, 33), "descendants of Anak" (Num. 13:28), and "sons of Anak" (Josh. 15:14; Judg. 1:20 cf. 21:11). According to Num. 13:33 the Anakim came from the Nephilim, those of mixed human and divine character (Gen. 6:4). Deut. 9:2 reports that the Anakim were "strong and tall" and reputedly unbeatable. Josh. 15:13 and 21:11 note Arba as the father of Anak. Joshua also reports that Caleb drove out three of Anak's descendants (15:14; *see also* Judg. 1:20). *See also* giants; Nephilim; Rephaim.

Anakim (an′uh-kim). *See* Anak.

Anakites (an′uh-kïts). *See* Anak.

Anani (uh-nay′ni), a postexilic descendant of David (1 Chron. 3:24). He was one of seven sons of Elioeni.

Ananiah (an′uh-ni′uh).

1 One of the rebuilders of Jerusalem's walls under Nehemiah (Neh. 3:23).

2 A postexilic Benjaminite city probably to be identified with Bethany (Neh. 11:32).

Ananias (an′uh-ni′uhs).

1 According to Acts 5:1–11, an early Christian in Jerusalem who, with his wife Sapphira, fell dead shortly after falsely claiming to have given the entire proceeds of the sale of their property to the community's common fund (see 4:32–37). Their death was interpreted as divine judgment, and they were seen as providing a model opposite from that set by the wealthy believer Barnabas (4:36–37).

2 According to Acts 9:10–20; 22:12–16, an early Christian in Damascus who, after a vision from God, reluctantly visited Saul (Paul) after the latter's vision on the road to Damascus, laying his hands upon him and baptizing him.

3 According to the historian Josephus, the son of Nedebaeus and a Jewish high priest ca. 47–58 CE. In Acts 22:30–23:10; 24:1, he is the high priest at the time of Paul's trials in Jerusalem and Caesarea.   A.J.M.

Anat (ah′naht), a Canaanite goddess of fertility and war. Ugaritic literature gives the best evidence of her character and exploits. She is not mentioned as such in the Bible, but place-names (Anathoth, Josh. 21:8; Beth-anath, 19:38) and one personal name (Shamgar ben Anath, Judg. 3:31) indicate that she was known and sometimes revered in the land of Israel. An Anat temple has also been discovered at Beth-shan. There is some speculation among scholars that the "queen of heaven" referred to in Jer. 7:18; 44:17 could be Anat.

anathema (uh-nath′uh-muh; Gk., "something placed or set up"), a term that can refer to a votive offering to God in the temple (Luke 21:5; NRSV: "gifts dedicated to God"), but that, due to association with idolatry (votive offerings to foreign gods in foreign temples), came to mean "something accursed." Paul uses the expression this way in Gal. 1:9, which the NRSV translates, "If anyone proclaims to you a gospel contrary to what you received, let that one be accursed [anathema]." See also Rom. 9:3; 1 Cor. 16:22; Gal. 1:8. *See also* curse.   M.A.P.

Anathoth (an′uh-thoth), a levitical town in the tribal territory of Benjamin (Josh. 21:18; 1 Chron. 6:60). Located less than three miles northeast of Jerusalem along a secondary road connecting the latter with Bethel, Anathoth was the hometown of Jeremiah (Jer. 1:1; cf. 11:21–23; 29:27; 32:7–9). Two of David's warriors, Abiezer (2 Sam. 23:27;

1 Chron. 11:28; 27:12) and Jehu (1 Chron. 12:3), were also from the town, and David's high priest, Abiathar, was banished there by Solomon (1 Kings 2:26). People of Anathoth were among those who returned from the Babylonian exile (Ezra 2:23; Neh. 7:27), at which time the town was resettled (Neh. 11:32). The town's ancient name is preserved in the modern village of Anata; the actual Iron Age ruins of the site are located about a half mile to the southwest, at Ras el Kharuba. *See also* Benjamin; Jeremiah, book of; priests.   D.A.D.

ancestor (Heb. 'ab, "father"), the one from whom a person or group is descended, either literally or figuratively. The Israelites felt a close connection with their ancestors and often thought of their families as including, not only living relatives, but earlier generations as well, all the way back to the founders of the family line. Members of Israel's various social groups often expressed their unity through identification of descent from a common ancestor. Links to the ancestors were typically expressed in segmented or branched genealogies (e.g., Num. 26). The Bible uses the term "ancestor" in a general sense to refer to earlier generations of Israelites (Exod. 3:15; 20:5; Num. 20:15; 1 Kings 14:15; Jer. 7:22; 16:11). Especially important are the founders of the nation: Abraham and Sarah; Isaac and Rebekah; Jacob, Leah, Zilpah, Rachel, and Bilhah. Particularly in Deuteronomy, God's faithfulness to Israel and the gift of the land are linked to divine promises made to these ancestors (1:8; 6:10; 9:5; 29:13; 30:20; cf. Gen. 12:7; 17:1–8; 28:13–15). On the other hand, the sins of the ancestors were sometimes thought to bring God's wrath upon their descendants (Exod. 20:5; 34:7; Num. 14:18). Thus, the destruction of Samaria and Jerusalem could be attributed to accumulated ancestral sin that finally had to be punished (2 Kings 17:7–18; Ezek. 20). Such understandings were explicitly rejected by Jeremiah and Ezekiel, however, who stressed that individuals are punished for their own sin, not the sins of their ancestors (Jer. 31:29–30; Ezek. 18). *See also* child, children; family; genealogy; patriarchs.   R.R.W.

Ancient of Days. *See* Ancient One.

Ancient One, an appellation for God used three times in the NRSV in the account of Daniel's eschatological vision of four beasts (7:9, 13, 22). In many other English versions (e.g., KJV, NIV), it is translated "Ancient of Days." The expression in Aramaic literally means "advanced in days," but it is not intended to suggest that God ages. Instead, it conveys the qualities of wisdom and venerability, which one who is "advanced in days" would possess. *See also* apocalyptic literature; Daniel, book of.

Andrew (an'droo), one of the twelve apostles, identified as the brother of Simon Peter (Matt. 4:18; Mark 1:16; John 1:40). Andrew is among the first persons named in the apostolic lists (Matt. 10:2–4; Mark 3:16–19; Luke 6:14–16; Acts 1:13),

perhaps an indication of his early selection to Jesus's inner circle of disciples; in Mark 13:3, he appears to belong to a select group of four. The Gospels of Matthew and Mark both relate a story in which Andrew and Peter were fishing when called to follow Jesus. In John's account, Andrew is said to be from Bethsaida (1:44) and to have been a disciple of John the Baptist. He ends up following Jesus and then finds his brother, Simon, and brings him to Jesus saying, "We have found the Messiah" (1:35–41). Elsewhere, Andrew appears only in John 6:8–9; 12:20–22. Extracanonical traditions credit him with preaching in Scythia and suffering martyrdom (crucifixion) in Achaia. *See also* apostle; disciple; John the Baptist; Peter; twelve, the.   P.L.S./M.A.P.

angel (Gk. *angelos,* "messenger"), a spiritual being, subordinate to God, who serves at God's command and pleasure to deliver messages, help people, and punish God's enemies. In the Bible, angels appear in the stories of the ancestors (e.g., Gen. 16:7–14; 19:1–22; 22:11, 15–18; 28:12; 31:11–13; 32:1–2) and elsewhere (e.g., Exod. 3:2; 23:20–23; 33:2; Judg. 13:3–5; 1 Kings 19:5–7; 2 Kings 19:35; Isa. 37:36; Pss. 34:7; 35:5–6; 91:11). There is some ambiguity, however, about what form these messengers take, exactly what type of beings they are, and just what their relation to God is, especially in the earlier materials, in which God is often said to confront people directly (making the appearance of angels sporadic). Over time, possibly because God came to be understood as increasingly transcendent, reflection on the identity and role of angels increased. Ideas developed about good and bad angels, a hierarchy of angels before God, and specific duties assigned to each angel or group of angels. Many of these ideas can be found in deuterocanonical (e.g., Tobit, 2 Esdras) and pseudepigraphical (*1 Enoch, Testaments of the Twelve Patriarchs*) writings. By the time of the NT, angels were understood as suprahuman or spiritual beings allied with God in opposition to "the devil and his angels" (Matt. 25:41; Rev. 12:9). In the Bible generally, angels have many functions. They praise God (Ps. 103:20), serve as messengers to the world (Luke 1:11–20, 26–38; 2:9–14), watch over God's people (Ps. 91:11–12), and are sometimes instruments of God's judgment (Matt. 13:49–50). *See also* angel of the Lord; apocalyptic literature; cherubim; demon; devil; Gabriel; God, god; Michael; seraphim.   J.M.E./M.A.P.

angel of the Lord (or "angel of the LORD"), a figure appearing frequently in the Bible (e.g., Gen. 16:7–13; 22:11; Exod. 3:2; Num. 22:22; Judg. 13:3; Zech. 1:11; 3:1; Matt. 1:20, 24; Luke 2:9–15). References to this figure usually occur when something dramatic and meaningful is about to happen, generally with serious consequences, either good or ill, for God's people. The angel of the Lord seems to have been understood as distinct from other angels and serves primarily as a messenger from God to prepare the way for God's appearance and activity. In some passages, the term is probably used with less specificity, to indicate any angel of God (e.g., 1 Kings 19:4–8). *See also* angel.   J.M.E.

anger. *See* wrath.

animals. The Bible makes frequent reference to animals, including domestic animals (providing food, clothing, or transport), game animals, predators, and parasites. Apart from their secular importance, animals figure prominently in Hebrew religious ritual as sacrifices. In addition, the Bible uses references to animals to illustrate various concepts (e.g., the lion symbolizes danger, the horse signifies warfare, and the ass signifies peace). The concept of "animals," however, is not absolutely defined. Sometimes, "animals" can be distinguished from birds, reptiles, and fish; in Gen. 1:24–25 God creates the animals on the sixth day, but fish and birds were created the day before (1:20–23).

Specific Identifications: The specific identification of animal species indicated in various biblical references has always presented a formidable problem, and as a consequence there is great variation in different English translations. For example, one term (Heb. *bat ya'anah*) is translated "ostrich," "owl," and "eagle owl" in various versions of the Bible. There are several reasons for these difficulties. First, the Hebrews did not necessarily distinguish between similar species, and they sometimes lumped two or more together under one term. For example, one word (*nesher*) seems to identify both the eagle and the vulture. Second, early European interpreters of the Bible had little knowledge of zoology and much less of the wildlife of the Levant. As they were unfamiliar with gazelles, they translated the Hebrew for "gazelle" (*tsebi*) as "roedeer," which was better known to Europeans. Matters were further complicated by the fact that many animal species that were common in the Levant when the Bible was written have since become extinct in that location (e.g., lions, ostriches, fallow deer, onagers, and some antelope species). As a consequence, there are still several animal terms in the Bible that cannot be translated with certainty; some of them may refer to animals that no longer exist.

Heron and snake: detail from a floor mosaic in the Church of the Multiplication of Loaves, Tabgah, fifth–sixth century CE.

Clean and Unclean: A crucial distinction is made between ritually clean (and therefore also edible) animals and unclean (inedible) animals. Animals allowed as food are all those that both chew the cud, or ruminate, and have cloven hooves (Lev. 11:2–3; Deut. 14:6). They are enumerated in Deut. 14:4–5 and include cattle, sheep, goats, deer, gazelles, ibex, and antelope. All these species were once extant in or around the Levant, and in zoological terms they are all members of the suborder *Ruminantia* of the order *Artiodactyla*. Specifically mentioned as unclean in Lev. 11:4–7 are the camel, the coney ("rock badger"), the hare, and the pig ("swine"). The first three were all thought to ruminate, but do not have cloven hooves; the swine does have cloven hooves, but does not ruminate. Of all aquatic and marine animals only those that have scales and fins are declared clean (Lev. 11:9–10). Unclean birds are listed in Lev. 11:13–19. Also forbidden as food were all flying insects (with the exception of locusts and the like; see Matt. 3:4), animals that walk on paws (i.e., carnivores), rodents, and lizards (Lev. 11:29–30). Not only was it forbidden to eat unclean animals; they were not even supposed to be touched (Lev. 11:8). In the NT, the Gospel of Mark indicates that provisions for identifying "clean" and "unclean" animals were set aside by Jesus (Mark 7:19; see also Acts 10:10–16).

In Israelite Religious Ritual: As mentioned above, animals also played a fundamental role in Israelite ritual sacrifices, and detailed instructions about the procedures to be followed and the types of animals to be offered are given (Deut. 16:1–4; 17:1; Lev. 1:1–7:38). In general it is the animals "from the herd or from the flock" that are requested for sacrifice (Lev. 1:2)—cattle, goats, and sheep. To the Israelites, whose wealth was measured in numbers of such animals, these were especially precious. All firstborn male animals were to be sacrificed (Deut. 15:19) in an annual ceremonial feast, unless something was wrong with them (15:21). In the NT, animal sacrifices are deemed unnecessary, since Christ's death on the cross is interpreted as an all-sufficient sacrifice for all time (e.g., Heb. 7:27; 9:12; 10:10). *See also* birds.   I.U.K.

Anna (an'uh), a Jewish prophet who, together with the prophet Simeon, witnessed the dedication of the infant Jesus in the temple (Luke 2:22–38). Anna was the daughter of Phanuel, of the tribe of Asher. An aged widow, she had remained celibate following the death of her husband; she lived in the temple, fasting and praying day and night. She praised God when she saw Jesus and spoke of him to all who were looking for the redemption of Israel. *See also* Simeon.   M.A.P.

Annas (an'uhs) or Ananus, son of Seth and high priest installed by Quirinius in 6 CE; he was deposed in 15 CE. Annas's family was wealthy and influential, and five of his sons as well as his son-in-law Joseph Caiaphas attained the office of high priest. Annas is called "high priest" in Luke 3:2

and Acts 4:6, but these references present a historical puzzle not soluble with present evidence (the
indication in Luke 3:2 that Annas and Caiaphas
were joint high priests has not been corroborated
by data elsewhere). In the Gospel of John, Annas
interrogates Jesus at length (18:19–24), and Caiaphas plays only a cursory role (18:24, 28). *See also*
Caiaphas; priests; Quirinius, P. Sulpicius.

anoint, to put oil or ointment upon a body or an
object. In the ancient Near East, anointing oneself
with aromatic oils, usually after bathing, was a
sign of luxury or festivity. For this reason, mourners abstained from anointing (Isa. 61:3). Anointing could also be a means of investing someone
with power, such as the anointing of King Solomon
upon his ascent to the throne (1 Kings 1:39), perhaps to signify divine sanctification and approval.
It could also signify the consecration of someone
or something for a holy purpose. Jacob anointed
a pillar at Bethel, calling the place a house of God
(Gen. 28:18). Aaron was anointed for the priesthood (Exod. 29:7), and, hence, the high priest is
often called the "anointed priest" (Lev. 4:3–15).
The tabernacle and its furnishings were likewise
anointed (Exod. 40:9–15). In the NT, Jesus's disciples anoint the sick with oil as part of a healing ritual (Mark 6:13). Women anoint Jesus's body with
fragrant oils (Luke 7:38; cf. 7:46) and come to the
tomb intending to anoint his dead body on Easter
morning (Mark 16:1). In one instance, a woman
who anoints him the night before his death is said
to have acted proleptically, anointing his body
"beforehand for its burial" (Mark 14:8).

Because of passages like 1 Sam. 24:6, which refers to the king as "the LORD's anointed," the Hebrew (*mashiakh*, "Messiah") and Greek (*christos*,
"Christ") terms for "anointed one" came to signify
a king who would rule in the last days: the Messiah
or the Christ (cf. John 1:41). In this regard, Peter
testifies in the book of Acts to "how God anointed

Jesus of Nazareth with the Holy Spirit and with
power" (10:38). *See also* messiah; priests.

L.H.S./M.A.P.

ant, an insect appearing in the Bible as a homi-
letic model of wisdom and industry (Prov. 6:6;
30:25).

antelope, an animal that may be eaten (Deut.
14:5) and was often caught with nets (Isa. 51:20).
Today the only antelopes in the Near East are gazelles, but the ancient Hebrews also knew the Arabian oryx (*Oryx leucoryx*), a large white antelope
with black markings on legs and face and very
long, nearly straight horns.

anthropomorphism (an'thruh-puh-mor'fiz-
uhm), the description of God in terms that are
literally appropriate for human beings. References
to God's hands or ears or to God taking an evening
walk in a garden (Gen. 3:8) are typical examples
of anthropomorphism. Other references apply
human emotions to God; for example, in 1 Sam.
15:29 God regrets the decision to make Saul king.
Such texts appear to be in tension with passages
that emphasize the great difference between God
and humans (Isa. 55:8–9; Job 38–41) and that
maintain God is utterly consistent and does not
change (Mal. 3:6). Some biblical interpreters and
theologians have addressed the question of anthropomorphism using the concept of the "image
of God": the fact that humans are created in God's
image (Gen. 1:26) implies that God might be humanlike in certain aspects. Other scholars view
anthropomorphism as a consequence of limited
human perception.   J.B./M.A.P.

antichrist (an'tee-krist), the final opponent of
Christ and thus of God. This designation is found
only in the Letters of John. The author supposes
that his audience has heard the term before (1 John

PRECURSORS FOR AN ANTICHRIST

Several NT writings speak of an ultimate enemy
of God who will arise in the last days to deceive
many people and establish himself as an object of
worship. In 2 Thessalonians this person is called
the "lawless one" (2:3–9); elsewhere he is referred
to as the "beast" (Rev. 13:1–18) or the "antichrist"
(1 John 2:18).

Christian teaching about this eschatological foe
has prototypes in biblical and secular history:

The king of Babylon is depicted as God's
archenemy in Isa. 14:12–15.

The prince and king of Tyre are described as
setting themselves against God in Ezek. 28:1–19.

A beast who opposes God is referred to in
the writings of Daniel (7:7–8, 19–27; 8:9–14,

23–25; 9:26–27; 11:21–45; note especially the
abomination in the temple in 11:31; cf. Matt.
24:15; 2 Thess. 2:4).

In 39–41 CE the Roman emperor Caligula decided
to put a statue of himself inside the Jerusalem
temple for the Jews to worship; he died before
actually doing so, but Jews and Christians
remained appalled by the intended abomination.

In the years following Nero's death in 68 CE,
rumors circulated that the emperor would rise
from the dead as a god opposed to the Jewish-
Christian God; this myth of *Nero redivivus* seems
to have inspired some comments about the beast
in Rev. 13.

From Mark Allan Powell, *Introducing the New Testament* (courtesy, Baker Academic)

2:18), and he suggests that it now refers to individuals ("antichrists") whose religious influence is already a danger to the church (1 John 2:18–29; 4:1–6; 2 John 1:7–11). They may be human agents of or precursors to an eschatological enemy who will be revealed in the last days. Such thinking is consistent with a trajectory in early Christianity that depicted God's enemies as individuals or beasts who would be defeated at the Messiah's (Christ's) return. Such opponents included "the lawless one" (2 Thess. 2:8), Belial (2 Cor. 6:15), and Gog and Magog (Rev. 20:8). *See also* apocalyptic literature; Belial, Beliar; John, Letters of; lawless one.   L.R.B.

Anti-Lebanon (an'tee-leb'uh-nuhn), a modern name for the range of mountains running north–south and located east of the Litani Valley in Lebanon, between that valley and the eastern desert. It is parallel to (hence "anti-") the Lebanon range standing west of the valley, between the valley and the Mediterranean Sea. The height of the Anti-Lebanon range is anchored on the south by Mount Hermon (elevation 9,332 feet above sea level) and it drops as the ridge runs northward. Its crevices hold snow well into May on northward slopes. A reference to the region as Antilebanon (without a hyphen) occurs in Jth. 1:7.

Antioch (an'tee-ok), a city in what is now Turkey founded by Seleucus Nicator in 300 BCE and conquered by Rome in 64 BCE. Located on the Orontes River in the northwestern corner of the Roman province of Syria, it was the province's capital, the third largest city of the empire, a center of Greek culture, and a commercial hub. Excavations in the 1930s uncovered some evidence for the city's wealth in the form of exquisite mosaics in houses and baths, but otherwise little archaeological work has been conducted in what is now the sprawling Turkish city of Antakya. Literary evidence indicates that Jews inhabited Antioch from its foundation and enjoyed the right to observe their own customs. The various synagogues of the city sent representatives to a council of elders presided over by a ruler. Apparently, some Antiochene Gentiles were attracted to Jewish worship, including Nicolaus of Antioch, who later became one of the seven Hellenist leaders of the church in Jerusalem (Acts 6:5). Public order, a prosperous urban culture, a Judaism used to contacts with Gentiles, an intellectual and religious milieu open to many currents, fine roads and lines of communication—all these factors favored Antioch as an energetic center for Christian missionary outreach.

Christianity at Antioch: According to Acts, Christianity was brought to Antioch ca. 40 CE by Hellenists who fled from Jerusalem after the martyrdom of Stephen (11:19–20). At Antioch Hellenists from Cyprus and Cyrene made the momentous decision to begin, as a matter of policy, to convert Gentiles without requiring circumcision. This striking difference from Jewish proselytism set these believers apart, and so it was at Antioch

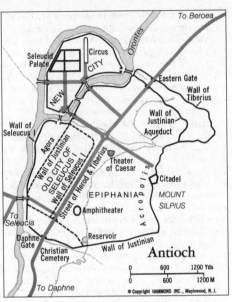

Plan of ancient Antioch that highlights the city in the early Christian period.

that they received a new name, "Christians" (11:26). The Jerusalem church responded by sending Barnabas, a fellow Cypriot, to guide the Antiochene community. To aid him in teaching this "large company" of believers, Barnabas brought Saul (Paul) from Tarsus to Antioch, where "for a whole year they met with the church" (11:22–26). Along with Simeon Niger, Lucius of Cyrene, and Manaen (a member of the court of Herod Antipas), they formed a leadership group of "prophets and teachers" (13:1). This group sent Barnabas and Saul on their first missionary journey (13:2–14:28).

Around 49 CE, objections to Antioch's circumcision-free mission were raised by some Jerusalemite Christians. Paul, Barnabas, and Titus went to Jerusalem for a meeting with church leaders; it was decided that Gentiles did not have to be circumcised (Gal. 2:1–10). Some time after this meeting, Peter visited Antioch. At first he practiced table fellowship with Gentile Christians, but then withdrew under pressure from members of the James party, recently arrived from Jerusalem. Paul publicly rebuked Peter for hypocrisy (Gal. 2:11–21). Since Paul soon left Antioch without Barnabas (who sided with Peter), and since Paul never mentions Antioch again in his letters, returning there only briefly, it may be that Paul lost the argument.

Second Christian Generation: There is practically no source of information for the second Christian generation at Antioch (70–100 CE), with the possible exception of Matthew's Gospel. If, as many think, this Gospel was written in Antioch, then it may be read as evidence that the Antiochene church continued to feel strains between the Jamesian right and the Hellenist left. However, the

Jewish war, the martyrdom of James, the destruction of Jerusalem, and the eventual break with the local synagogue(s) had weakened the conservative Jewish element in the Antiochene church. Meanwhile, the success of the Gentile mission both pointed the way to the church's future and created new problems for the Christian reformation of pagans. It was Matthew's task to reinterpret and synthesize the competing traditions at Antioch to provide a smooth transition from a Jewish past to a Gentile future. Matthew's Gospel takes the form of a "foundation story," to give a pastoral answer to the crisis of identity the Antiochene church faced in the second generation, as it strove to define itself over against both Judaism and paganism. Jewish roots, fulfillment of prophecy, and large blocks of Jewish moral teaching serve to anchor an increasingly Gentile church in the sacred past. But the norm of morality, the center of faith, is now Jesus Christ, who validates a universal, circumcision-free mission at the end of the Gospel (Matt. 28:16–20). This balancing act allows Matthew to preserve both "new and old" (13:52). Hence he extols Peter, Antioch's centrist figure, as the "rock" on which Jesus built his church (16:18–19). Yet, while admitting the need for Christian leaders, Matthew is wary of the trappings of power and titles (23:1–12).

Third Christian Generation: In the third Christian generation (after 100 CE), the new pressures of imperial persecution and gnosticizing tendencies overrode Matthew's dislike of titles. The need for clearer church structures to defend church discipline and teaching called forth the triple hierarchy of one bishop, a council of elders, and deacons. The first testimony we have of this development is from Ignatius of Antioch (d. ca. 117 CE). Like Matthew, Ignatius sought unity through balance. He synthesized strains of Matthean, Pauline, and Johannine traditions to strengthen the emerging "catholic church"—a phrase first used by Ignatius. *See also* Barnabas; James; Matthew, Gospel According to; Paul; Peter.

Bibliography

Brown, Raymond, and John Meier. *Antioch and Rome.* Paulist, 1983.

Downey, Glanville. *A History of Antioch in Syria from Seleucus to the Arab Conquest.* Princeton University Press, 1961.

Meeks, Wayne, and Robert Wilken. *Jews and Christians in Antioch.* Scholars, 1978.

Sandwell, Isabella. *Religious Identity in Late Antiquity: Greeks, Jews, and Christians in Antioch.* Cambridge University Press, 2007.   J.P.M.

Antioch of Pisidia (an'tee-ok, pi-sid'ee-uh), a city located in the east-central region of Asia Minor (modern Turkey), on the banks of the Anthius River. Founded prior to 280 BCE, it was strongly fortified by the Greeks and later by the Romans. Declared a free city by the Romans in 189 BCE and named a Roman colony by Augustus prior to 6 BCE, it served as the center of civil and military administration in the southern portion of the Roman province of Galatia. It was visited by Paul and Barnabas during the first of their missionary journeys recorded in Acts (13:14). Here, they preached first to Jews in the synagogue and then turned their attention to Gentiles, who were more receptive. When leading figures in the city became agitated against the two missionaries, the latter were forced to leave. The city finds no further mention in the NT.

Excavations have uncovered a plaza with an imperial temple dedicated to the emperor Augustus, reached by a broad colonnaded street (*plateia*) leading through a monumental gate (*propylon*) built by Tiberius. The latter is one of only three places where fragments of the *Res Gestae Divi Augusti*, Augustus's autobiography, have been discovered. A Roman-style aqueduct and baths complement Greek statuary and a sanctuary to the indigenous mother goddess Men Ascaenus, indicating the multicultural and polytheistic character of the Roman colony. A few menoroth inscribed in later periods point to a Jewish presence, and in the Byzantine period several churches dominated the cityscape.   J.R.

Antiochus (an-ti'uh-kuhs), a name borne by thirteen rulers or would-be rulers of the Seleucid dynasty (Hellenistic inheritors of Syria, southern Asia Minor, and other portions of the empire of Alexander the Great). The most significant of these was Antiochus IV Epiphanes, who ruled 175–164 BCE, and it is his reign of terror that forms the background for many of the events described in the four books of Maccabees. Many scholars also place the book of Daniel in this time period and believe that its accounts of the Assyrian emperor Nebuchadnezzar are to be read with reference to Antiochus IV Epiphanes. Antiochus sought to promote hellenization at the expense of Jewish distinctiveness: he replaced the Torah with new laws and redefined the temple as a place of worship for foreign deities. The latter action is probably what is referred to as the "desolating sacrilege" in Dan. 11:31; 12:11 (cf. 1 Macc. 1:54). When his reforms met with resistance, Antiochus enacted a program of severe persecution against Jews who practiced their faith. This prompted the Maccabean revolt and led to the eventual establishment of the Hasmonean dynasty. *See also* Alexander; Maccabees; Ptolemy; Seleucids.   M.A.P.

Antipas (an'tee-puhs).
1 A Christian martyr from Pergamum (Rev. 2:13).
2 Antipater. *See* Antipater.
3 Herod Antipas. *See* Herod.

Antipater (an-tip'uh-tuhr), also known as Antipas, an Idumean with strong connections to Rome. He governed most of the Levant (55–43 BCE) and was the father of Phasaelus and Herod the Great. *See also* Herod; Idumea.

Antipatris (an-tip'uh-tris), a town on the coastal plain along the principal international highway of

View of Antipatris (biblical Aphek during the time of the Philistines), rebuilt by Herod the Great in 9 BCE.

the Levant, the Via Maris, guarding the pass between the mountains to the east and the Yarkon River to the west. The site has been identified with Aphek (Josh. 12:18; 1 Sam 4:1; 29:1), where the Philistines were encamped when they captured the ark of the covenant (called Pegae [Gk., "springs"] during the Hellenistic period). The town was rebuilt by Herod the Great in 9 BCE. It was located midway between his new capital, Caesarea, and the old Jewish capital, Jerusalem, and he named it after his father, Antipater. Here Paul stayed overnight during his trip from Jerusalem to Caesarea to stand trial before Felix (Acts 23:31). *See also* Aphek; Herod. M.K.M.

Antonia (an-toh´nee-uh), **Tower of,** a Hasmonean fortress (also known as Baris) on the rocky scarp at the northwest end of the temple in Jerusalem, luxuriously rebuilt in the late first century BCE by Herod the Great and named for his friend Mark Antony. In it were kept the high priest's vestments between festivals, under the seal of Herod and later of the Roman governors. It was taken and destroyed by Titus in the Jewish war with Rome in 70 CE. The Antonia may have been the site of Paul's arrest and imprisonment referred to in Acts 21:34–37; 22:24; and 23:10, 16, 32 (NRSV: "barracks"). *See also* Baris; Herod; temple, the. C.H.M.

Antonius Felix. *See* Felix, Antonius.

Aphek (ay´fek; Heb., "fortress").

1 A city-state on the coastal plain captured by Joshua (Josh. 12:18). Its strategic value was used by the Philistines against hill-based Israelites at both Ebenezer (1 Sam. 4:1) and Jezreel (1 Sam. 29:1). It is modern Ras el 'Ain, some ten miles east of the Mediterranean coast, west and slightly north of Shiloh. The Herodian-Roman city Antipatris was built there as well. *See also* Antipatris.

2 A border town with the Amorites (Josh. 13:4), probably modern Afqa, about fifteen miles east of ancient Byblos in Lebanon.

3 A town of the tribe of Asher (Josh. 19:30), possibly modern Tell Kerdanah, three miles from Haifa and about six miles southeast of Acco. It is called Aphik in Judg. 1:31.

4 A site some three miles from the eastern shore of the Sea of Galilee in the Transjordan, modern Fiq. It marked the location of Ahab's victories against Syria's Ben-hadad (1 Kings 20:26–30) and Joash's defeat of Syria under Elisha's instruction (2 Kings 13:14–25). R.S.B.

Apocalypse (uh-pok´uh-lips). *See* Revelation, book of.

apocalyptic literature, a genre of literature that owes its name to the NT book of Revelation (Gk. *apokalypsis*), though that book is not a completely typical example of the genre. Portions of the book of Daniel are also classed as apocalyptic literature, but the main corpus lies outside the Bible in such books as *1 and 2 Enoch, 4 Ezra, 2 and 3 Baruch, Jubilees,* and the *Apocalypse of Abraham.* These writings have been preserved in various translations—Ethiopic, Latin, Syriac, Greek, Slavonic. Closely related material can be found in the Dead Sea Scrolls, the *Sibylline Oracles,* and the *Testaments of the Twelve Patriarchs.* Fragments of *1 Enoch* discovered in Aramaic among the Dead Sea Scrolls are the oldest extant apocalyptic literature (third century BCE). The genre generally declined in Judaism after the first century CE, but flourished in Christianity down to the Middle Ages. The genre is also attested independently in Persian sources, but the date of the Persian material is notoriously uncertain.

Apocalyptic books report mysterious revelations that are usually mediated by angels and disclose a supernatural world. They are characterized by a focus on eschatology (last times), which may entail cosmic transformation and/or a judgment of the dead. Such books are usually pseudonymous—the revelations are attributed to ancient heroes such as Enoch or Abraham, not to the real authors. A few early Christian apocalypses, notably the book of Revelation and the *Shepherd of Hermas,* are exceptions to this rule.

In general, apocalyptic writings are of two types. The more familiar "historical" apocalypses, exemplified by Daniel and Revelation, are concerned with great historical crises. History is often divided into a set number of periods, and the course of history is "prophesied" from the time of the supposed author down to the actual time of composition. The period before the end is marked by catastrophic upheavals. Salvation involves a transition to a radically different world order. Many themes of the "historical" apocalypses were anticipated in books of the prophets, notably Isa. 24–27. In the other type of apocalypse, exemplified in the *Enoch* books and the *Apocalypse of Abraham,* the visionary ascends through the heavens (usually seven heavens, though three and five are also attested). These journeys, guided by an angel, usually include a vision of the abodes of the dead.

Some apocalyptic books were written in times of distress. Daniel is generally thought to have been written during the persecution of Jews by Antiochus IV Epiphanes ca. 168 BCE; *4 Ezra* and

COMMON FEATURES OF APOCALYPSES

Pseudonymous author

Addressees who are experiencing suffering and persecution

Attempts to motivate faithfulness in a time of crisis

Heavy use of symbolism, including numbers and colors

Engagement with otherworldly beings: angels, demons, etc.

A bizarre menagerie of fantastic creatures

Spiritual or supernatural visions, often interpreted by otherworldly beings

Portentous dreams that must also be interpreted

Mystical journeys from the earthly plane to a heavenly or spiritual realm

A review of history with the ultimate culmination linked to the present era

Revealed secrets about imminent cosmic transformations

A forecast of cosmic catastrophes

Liturgical settings and elements: altars, temples, hymns, etc.

Unveiling of the true but hidden character of present circumstances

A radically dualistic outlook—clear distinction between good and evil with no ambiguity

A deterministic view of history—all proceeds according to a preordained divine plan

A pessimistic forecast for the world as is—things will go from bad to worse

Hope for a favored remnant that lies in radical divine intervention

From Mark Allan Powell, *Introducing the New Testament* (courtesy, Baker Academic)

---

2 Baruch were written in the aftermath of the destruction of Jerusalem; Revelation is typically linked to Roman persecution of Christians, either under Nero or Domitian. Other apocalyptic books responded to less specific problems, but still reflect dissatisfaction with the present world and seek salvation in a new world to come. *See also* Daniel, book of; Dead Sea Scrolls; Enoch; eschatology; Revelation, book of.   J.J.C.

Apocrypha (uh-pok´ruh-fuh) / **deuterocanonical** (dyoo´tuh-roh-kuh-non´i-kuhl) **literature,** those books or parts of books of the Christian OT that are found in the Greek LXX translation of the Hebrew Bible, but not in the Hebrew Bible itself. Their status as scripture is disputed and even the choice of terminology used to refer to them is controversial. For example, most Protestant Christians refer to these writings as "apocryphal" ("set aside" or "withdrawn") to convey that the books, whatever their value, do not have full canonical status as scripture. Roman Catholics generally prefer the term "deuterocanonical," which might indicate books that have a status as "secondary scripture" or, simply, books that were added to the canon later (i.e., secondary only in a chronological sense). Roman Catholics often use the term "Apocrypha" for what Protestants call the "Pseudepigrapha," a group of Jewish writings from the Second Temple period that were not included in either the Hebrew Bible or the LXX.

Listing of Books: In the NRSV, the apocryphal/deuterocanonical books are categorized as follows:

I. Books included in Roman Catholic, Greek Orthodox, and Slavonic Russian Orthodox Bibles:
    Tobit
    Judith
    Additions to Esther
    Wisdom of Solomon
    Sirach (or Wisdom of Jesus son of Sirach)
    Baruch
    Letter of Jeremiah
    Additions to Daniel:
        The Song of the Three Jews (with the Prayer of Azariah)
        Susanna
        Bel and the Dragon
    1 Maccabees
    2 Maccabees

II. Books included in Greek Orthodox and Slavonic Russian Orthodox, but not Roman Catholic Bibles:
    1 Esdras
    Prayer of Manasseh
    Psalm 151
    3 Maccabees

III. Book included in Slavonic Russian Orthodox, but not Roman Catholic or Greek Orthodox Bibles:
    3 Esdras

IV. Book included in an Appendix to the Greek Orthodox and Slavonic Russian Orthodox Bibles:
    4 Maccabees

A few potentially confusing anomalies should be noted: (1) the Additions to Esther is sometimes called the Rest of Esther and the Additions to Daniel is sometimes called the Rest of Daniel; (2) Sirach (or the Wisdom of Jesus son of Sirach) is sometimes called Ecclesiasticus; (3) the Letter to Jeremiah is sometimes incorporated into the book of Baruch, as the final chapter of that book; (4) the three books listed above under Additions to Daniel—the Prayer of Azariah and the Song of the Three Jews, Susanna, and Bel and the Dragon—are sometimes incorporated into the book of Daniel rather than appearing as separate works, and the Additions to Esther may be similarly incorporated into the book of Esther; (5) the Song of the Three Jews is often called the Song of the Three Children; (6) 1 Esdras is sometimes called 3 Ezra, and 2 Esdras is sometimes called 4 Ezra (after their titles in the Vulgate, where Ezra is called 1 Ezra and Nehemiah is called 2 Ezra). For a chart detailing the complex variations of terminology related to this last point, *see* Esdras, First Book of.

Reception: The apocryphal/deuterocanonical books are of Jewish origin, produced for the most part during the period preceding the destruction of the temple by the Romans in 70 CE. Although these books have their source in Hellenistic Judaism, their *status* as scripture among Jews has been less certain. Modern scholars do not agree on which Jewish writings were regarded as scripture by which Jewish groups at which times—quotations of rabbis and other declarations on such matters are often difficult to date. In Christianity, a somewhat more distinct delineation can be seen in the production of influential Bible translations: Jerome's Latin Vulgate (fourth century) included some of the apocryphal/deuterocanonical works, but indicated clearly that they were not a part of the Hebrew canon. Martin Luther's German Bible (sixteenth century) placed the books in a separate section labeled "Apocrypha." He indicated that these books were not of the status of holy scripture, but could be read profitably. The Reformed tradition came to accord an even lower status to the Apocrypha, particularly in England, where, beginning in 1599, editions of the Geneva Bible omitted the works and the Westminster Confession of Faith (1646–48) equated them with secular literature. The Church of England, on the other hand, resisted this tendency and included readings from the Apocrypha in its lectionary. Catholic response to the Protestant treatment of the Apocrypha was to reaffirm the canonical status of most of these books. On April 8, 1546, the Council of Trent declared anathema anyone who did not accept the whole of the Vulgate as canonical, and the edition of the Vulgate intended included all of the disputed works employed in the West except for 1 and 2 Esdras and the Prayer of Manasseh. In later Catholic editions of the Bible, those three books would sometimes be printed in an appendix. Orthodox Christianity has generally shown a greater latitude in its treatment of the OT canon. Bibles approved by the Holy Synod of the Greek Orthodox Church currently include what Catholics term the deuterocanonical books plus 1 Esdras, the Prayer of Manasseh, 3 and 4 Maccabees, and Psalm 151.

Significance: In academic studies, the apocryphal/deuterocanonical books are studied as historical documents on equal footing with works deemed canonical by various confessions. Along with the Pseudepigrapha, the Dead Sea Scrolls, and the writings of Josephus and Philo, the apocryphal/deuterocanonical books are of great value for understanding Jewish faith and practice during the Second Temple period (515 BCE–70 CE). Their content reflects the struggle of the Jewish people to maintain faith as they encountered religious, political, and military oppression under foreign rule and attempted to preserve their way of life in the face of Hellenistic culture both at home and in the Dispersion. Strikingly absent from this body of literature is the prophetic voice, which seems to have been associated with a previous age. The books, on the other hand, give abundant evidence of the continued importance of narrative in Jewish culture. They also reflect the further development of the wisdom tradition and augment the roles of women in scripture: Sarah (in Tobit) and Susanna are examples of vindicated righteous martyrs; Judith is an agent of God's liberation; the mother described in 4 Maccabees is a paradigm of courageous martyrdom; and Wisdom is personified as a woman in Sir. 24 and Wis. 6–12 and as God's agent of liberation for the Jewish people in Judith. *See also* canon; Pseudepigrapha; Septuagint; Vulgate; listings under the individual titles of apocryphal/deuterocanonical books.

Bibliography

De Lange, Nicholas. *Apocrypha: Jewish Literature of the Hellenistic Age*. Viking, 1978.

DeSilva, David A. *Introducing the Apocrypha: Message, Context, and Significance*. Baker, 2002.

Harrington, Daniel J. *An Invitation to the Apocrypha*. Eerdmans, 1999.

Kaiser, Otto. *The Old Testament Apocrypha: An Introduction*. Hendrickson, 2004.

Metzger, Bruce M. *An Introduction to the Apocrypha*. Oxford University Press, 1957.

Nickelsburg, George W. E. *Jewish Literature Between the Bible and the Mishnah: A Historical and Literary Introduction*. Fortress, 1981.

D.W.S./M.A.P.

apocryphal Christian writings, a vast body of early nonbiblical Christian writings that claim to preserve memories of Jesus and the apostles and that frequently imitate the major genres (literary types) of NT literature: gospels, acts, letters, and apocalypses. Most of this literature was written from the second to the ninth centuries CE. The discovery at Nag Hammadi, Egypt, of many previously unknown apocryphal documents revitalized interest in this material.

Even though this literature relates little that is historically reliable regarding the actual words and deeds of Jesus or his disciples, it is indispensable for understanding the piety of Christians in late antiquity and, particularly, the views and attitudes of Christian groups that do not appear to have been related to the mainstream apostolic tradition. Here we find their liturgies, prayers, legends, and theologies in addition to expressions of their attitudes toward the most fundamental issues of their lives: politics, martyrdom, money, sex, and family. Analysis of this literature also reveals much concerning the canonizing of the NT and the theological diversity of the early church.

Gospels: Apocryphal gospels reshaped the memory of Jesus to meet contemporary needs and they satisfied pious imaginations by supplying information about the life of Jesus not found in the NT—most notably, details of his birth, youth, and postresurrection revelations. Unlike the canonical Gospels, few of these books contain stories of Jesus's death. Some of the apocryphal gospels (particularly the *Gospel of Thomas*) have generated much scholarly attention, largely because of the possibility of finding in them dominical *agrapha,* or authentic sayings of Jesus, not found in the Bible. Some of the more important apocryphal gospels are:

Protoevangelium of James

Infancy Gospel of Thomas

Gospel of Peter

Gospel of Nicodemus

Gospel of the Nazoreans

Gospel of the Ebionites

Gospel of the Hebrews

Gospel of the Egyptians

Gospel of Thomas

Gospel of Philip

Gospel of Mary

Acts: Scholars customarily divide the apocryphal acts into two groups: those that were sometimes attributed to Leucius Charinus (a collection of five books used in certain circles) and those outside this group. Of the two, those in the first group have attracted the most attention, in part because of their probable earlier dating and in part because they stimulated considerable opposition from ecclesiastical authors. These five acts, though interrelated, actually seem to have come from different locations and theological circles, some of which were gnostic in orientation. They share a preference for sexual asceticism, a fascination with fantastic tales (e.g., stories about obedient bedbugs, talking colts, and a baptized lion), and a curiosity concerning the apostles' deaths. They also feature women prominently, sometimes in roles otherwise restricted to men. Some of the apocryphal Acts display knowledge of the canonical Acts, but they seldom seem interested in coordinating their information with the latter. In addition to the canonical Acts, the authors of these works were influenced by the Gospels, Greek novels, and, in the case of the *Acts of Andrew,* Homeric epic and Platonic dialogues. The "Leucian Acts" are:

Acts of Paul

Acts of Peter

Acts of John

Acts of Andrew

Acts of Thomas

Other Acts include:

Acts of Andrew and Matthias (originally part of *Acts of Andrew?*)

Acts of Philip

Acts of Thaddaeus

Acts of Peter and Paul

Acts of Peter and Andrew

Slavonic Acts of Peter

Acts of Peter and the Twelve Apostles

Letters: Of the four apocryphal genres discussed here, the pseudonymous letter was apparently the least popular, even though several of the letters that appear in the NT are thought to be pseudonymous by some scholars (e.g., the Pastoral and Petrine Letters). The apocryphal letters include:

Third Corinthians

Epistle to the Laodiceans

Letters of Paul and Seneca

Letters of Jesus and Abgar

Letters of Lentulus

Epistle of Titus

Apocalypses: Unlike the canonical book of Revelation, apocryphal representatives of this genre are pseudonymous; i.e., all of them claim to be divine revelations to a biblical hero. Favorite themes include eschatological events, ethics, and graphic descriptions of heaven and hell. Gnostic apocalypses favor moral instruction and polemics. Apocryphal apocalypses include:

Apocalypse of Peter

Coptic Apocalypse of Peter

Apocalypse of Paul

First Apocalypse of James

Second Apocalypse of James

Apocryphon of John

Sophia of Jesus Christ

Letter of Peter to Philip

Apocalypse of Mary

See also apocalyptic literature; canon; Gnosticism; gospel; Gospels, the; Nag Hammadi; Q; Thomas, Gospel of.

Bibliography

Elliott, J. K. *The Apocryphal New Testament.* Oxford University Press, 1993.

Evans, Craig A., et al. *Nag Hammadi Texts and the Bible: A Synopsis and Index.* Brill, 1993.

Levine, Amy-Jill, ed. *A Feminist Companion to the New Testament Apocrypha.* Pilgrim, 2006.

Meyer, Marvin, ed. *The Nag Hammadi Scriptures: The Definitive International Version.* Harper SanFrancisco, 2006.

Robinson, James M., ed. *The Nag Hammadi Library in English.* 3rd ed. Harper & Row, 1988.

Schneemelcher, W., ed. *New Testament Apocrypha.* Rev. ed. Westminster John Knox, 1991, 1993.

D.R.M

Apollonia (ap'uh-loh'nee-uh) of Macedonia, one among many Greek cities named for the Greek god Apollo. It was a station on the main east–west Roman road from Asia to Italy, the Egnatian Way, and was visited by Paul en route from Philippi to Thessalonica (Acts 17:1).

Apollos (uh-pol'uhs), a Jewish Christian from Alexandria who appears in the narrative of Acts (18:24–19:1) and in 1 Corinthians. According to Acts, he possessed great skills in Greek rhetoric and had already learned much about Jesus when he arrived in Ephesus and began speaking in the synagogue. His abilities soon brought him to the attention of the Christians Priscilla (Prisca) and Aquila, who gave him further instruction in the Christian faith ("he knew only the baptism of John"; 18:25). Apollos then left Ephesus to go to Corinth. While in Corinth, he became acquainted with Paul. When divisions arose in the church at Corinth, Apollos was admired by some Christians as an authority equal to Peter and Paul (1 Cor. 1:11–4:6). Brief mention of Apollos is made in Titus 3:13. *See also* Aquila; John the Baptist; Paul; Prisca, Priscilla. A.J.M.

Apollyon (uh-pol'yuhn; Gk., "the destroyer"), a possible allusion to the Greek god Apollo or, perhaps, to the angel of death (Rev. 9:11). *See also* Abaddon.

apostasy (uh-pos'tuh-see), rebellion against or abandonment of faith. It refers in the Hebrew Bible to Israel's unfaithfulness to God (Jer. 2:19; 5:6; cf. Josh. 22:22; 2 Chron. 33:19) and in the NT to the abandonment of Christian faith (Heb. 6:6). In Acts 21:21, the Greek root of the word "apostasy" is used for Paul's alleged rejection of Moses and, in 2 Thess. 2:3, for an expected rebellion before the end.

apostle, the English transliteration of a Greek word meaning "one who is sent out." An apostle is a personal messenger or envoy, commissioned to transmit the message or otherwise carry out the instructions of the commissioning agent. In the NT Gospels, the term is commonly associated with the inner circle of Jesus's twelve disciples, chosen and commissioned by him to accompany him during his ministry, to receive his teachings and observe his actions, and to follow his instructions. Thus, they are uniquely qualified to both authenticate his message and carry on his work through the ministry of the church. Apostolic lists appear in Matt. 10:2–4; Mark 3:16–19; Luke 6:13–16; and Acts 1:13. Each of the lists contains twelve names, but not always the same twelve. It is possible that some of the persons listed went by more than one name, or that membership among "the twelve" varied over time. The number twelve itself is probably intended to recall God's elect, the twelve tribes of Israel, who settled Canaan after the exodus.

The exact nature of "apostleship" in the early church is obscure. In Acts 1:21–26, the qualification for Matthias, chosen an apostle after Judas's death, is that of being an eyewitness: he was present with Jesus from the time of John the Baptist through the death and resurrection of Jesus. "Peter and the apostles," centered in Jerusalem, are the recognized leaders and guiding force of the development of the church according to the early chapters of Acts. Paul also claims to be an eyewitness to the risen Christ (1 Cor. 9:1; 1 Cor. 15:8), and he claims to be an apostle even though he had not been a follower of Jesus during the time of Jesus's ministry on earth (Gal. 1:1; 11–12; cf. Acts 14:14). The designation of Barnabas (Acts 14:14) and Andronicus and Junias (Rom. 16:7) as apostles seems to use the term in a more general sense that no longer includes being an eyewitness to the ministry and/or resurrection of Jesus as a qualification (see also 1 Cor. 12:28–29). In Heb. 3:1, Jesus is the "apostle," the one sent by God. *See also* Barnabas; church; disciple; John the Baptist; Judas; Junia; Matthias; Paul; Peter; twelve, the. P.L.S.

apothecaries. *See* perfumers.

apparel. *See* dress.

Jesus at the head of a procession of the twelve apostles as depicted in a tenth-century Byzantine illuminated manuscript.

Apphia (af'ee-uh), a Christian woman addressed as "a sister" by Paul in Philemon (Philem. 2), possibly Philemon's wife. *See also* Archippus; Philemon.

Appian (ap'ee-uhn) **Way,** one of the main roads leading in and out of ancient Rome. One branch, the Via Domitiana, led through Cumae to Puteoli, which lay just west of modern Naples. Puteoli was the great port for trade with the east during the first century. The Egyptian grain fleet put in there. It declined after the emperor Trajan built a new harbor for seagoing vessels off the mouth of the Tiber (Ostia). The Forum of Appius mentioned in Acts 28:15 was a market town on the Appian Way south of Rome.

Appius (ap'ee-uhs), **Forum of,** a town about forty miles south of Rome on the Appian Way, where Paul was met by Christians from Rome as he was being led prisoner from the port of Puteoli (Acts 28:15). *See also* Appian Way; Three Taverns.

apple, a tree-grown fruit (*Pyrus malus*) that may not have been originally native to the Levant, although it grows commonly there now. Consequently, many specialists think that the "apples of gold" in Prov. 25:11 were apricots (*Prunus armeniaca*); apricot trees provide both abundant shade and golden fruit, sweet and refreshing to the taste (Song of Sol. 2:3, 5). Other candidates for fruit referred to as "apples" in English Bibles include the citron, orange, and quince. There is some evidence, however, to indicate that apple trees were cultivated in Egypt and Syria in biblical times, which could grant literal accuracy to some apple references. The place-names Beth-tappuah (Josh. 15:33) and the proper name Tappuah (1 Chron. 2:43) both employ the Hebrew word typically used for the fruit designated by the English word "apple" (*tappuakh*). Although the apple has traditionally been considered to be the fruit from the tree of knowledge in the garden of Eden, the biblical text does not mention apples or any other specific fruit in that story (Gen. 2:9, 17; 3:6).   P.L.C.

apron, an outer garment worn over one's clothing. In Luke 17:8, an apron is the garment a slave puts on before serving a meal. In Acts 19:12, Paul's aprons are said to have become endowed with curative properties.

Aqabah (ahk'uh-bah), **Gulf of,** a northern arm of the Red Sea, east of the Sinai Peninsula. At its head were located Ezion-geber (1 Kings 9:26) and Elath (Deut. 2:8). Trade from the south came through the gulf and continued north via the King's Highway. As political fortunes shifted, so did control of the gulf (2 Kings 14:22, 16:6).

Aquila (ak'wi-luh), according to Acts 18:2–3, a Jewish Christian from Pontus in Asia Minor who, like Paul, was a tentmaker (or leather worker) by trade. He and his wife Priscilla (Prisca) were expelled from Rome by the edict of the emperor

Claudius, probably in 49/50 CE. Paul lodged with Aquila and Priscilla during his stay in Corinth, and they became among the most trusted of his co-workers. According to Acts (18:18–19), Aquila and Priscilla left Corinth with Paul, accompanied him to Ephesus, apparently established a house-church there (see 1 Cor. 16:19), and later instructed Apollos when he came to Ephesus (Acts 18:24–26). If Rom. 16 is an integral part of Paul's Letter to the Romans (which is doubted by some), they apparently returned to Rome after the revocation of Claudius's edict in 54 CE; otherwise, they likely remained in Ephesus (Rom. 16:3–5a). *See also* Apollos; Claudius; Paul; Prisca, Priscilla; Romans, Letter of Paul to the.   A.J.M.

Ar (ahr), a city or a region or both. The main references are found in Num. 21:15, 28, both of which relate it to Moabite border territory, and Deut. 2:9 (given to Lot's descendants), 2:18 (marking the Moabite boundary), and 2:29 (settled by Moabites). In Isa. 15:1 its parallel citation with Kir suggests that Ar is a city rather than a regional identification. Num 21:28 celebrates the destruction of Ar by fire (cf. Isa. 15:1). No certain site identification for Ar has appeared to date; one prominent suggestion is Khirbet el-Balu.

Arab (air'uhb).
1 An inhabitant of Arabia. The term is applied to Geshem, who opposed rebuilding Jerusalem, in Neh. 2:19; 6:1. Isa. 13:20 uses the absence of Arab nomadic campsites as a symbol of desolation. Jeremiah refers to an Arab (NRSV: "nomad"; Heb. *'arab*) waiting for lovers in the wilderness as a pejorative description of Judah's infidelity to God and to its covenant obligations (3:2).
2 A town of Judah (Josh. 15:52) near Hebron, most often identified as Khirbet er-Rabiyeh, southwest of Hebron.

Arabah (air'uh-buh; Heb., "desert plain or steppe"), a term variously translated as "plain," "desert," or "wilderness" (Job 24:5; Ps. 68:7; Isa.

The Arabah in modern terminology is the name given to the desert region of the rift valley of the Levant that extends from the Dead Sea to the Red Sea. It has an average annual rainfall of only two inches.

33:9). "The Arabah" refers to the rift valley south of the Lake of Galilee, with three divisions: the Jordan Valley north of the Dead Sea; the area of the Dead Sea, the "Sea of the Arabah" (2 Kings 14:25); and the area from the Dead Sea to the Red Sea, about one hundred miles in length. This last area is "the Arabah" in modern terminology. This area has an average annual rainfall of only 2 inches and rises gradually from 1,298 feet below sea level to 655 feet above sea level in the center before descending gradually to the Gulf of Aqabah. Underground water from the highlands on both sides makes possible a fair amount of desert scrub. A very important north–south route in biblical times, the Arabah contained valuable copper mines at Feinan (biblical Punon). *See also* Dead Sea; Jordan River; Red Sea.   D.B.

Arabia (uh-ray'bee-uh), a vast, largely desert peninsula between Iraq and the Persian Gulf on the east, the Indian Ocean on the south, and the Red Sea on the west. The peninsula is sixteen hundred miles long by nearly fourteen hundred miles wide. The mountainous western escarpment along the Red Sea reaches a height of 12,336 feet in the southeast in Yemen, where the general altitude exceeds 9,840 feet. From the great western wall the plateau slopes gently northeast toward the Persian Gulf, although in Oman, the southeastern corner, a spur of the Iranian mountain chain attains a height of 9,774 feet. The main areas of true sand desert are the vast Ruba 'el-Khali (Arabic, "the Empty Quarter") in the southern part of the peninsula and the smaller Nefud in the northwest. Elsewhere it is largely stony desert, although a great semicircle of sand dunes curving around eastward joins the Nefud to the Ruba 'el-Khali.

The climate is severe. Winters can be bitterly cold on the plateau; frost is common everywhere except in the low-lying coastal areas. Summers are blindingly hot and, near the coast, extremely humid. Except for rare storms, rain is confined to the mountains, occurring in winter in Oman and northwest of Mecca and in summer on the high ranges of Asir and Yemen southeast of Mecca. This alternation of winter and summer rain on the Red Sea mountains made possible the trading caravans between north and south, for the wells were full in the south in summer and autumn and in the north during winter and spring.

As early as 6000 BCE, and perhaps even before, products seem to have been exchanged along this route by means of donkey transport, and after the taming of the camel about 1500 BCE (or possibly as early as 2000) this trade vastly increased. The visit of the queen of Sheba (Saba in the Yemen) was almost certainly concerned with it (1 Kings 10:1–10). The gold the ships of Hiram brought to King Solomon (10:11) may have come from the same source via the port of Jiddah, or perhaps from East Africa, whence came certainly the more exotic "ivory, apes and peacocks" (10:22). This trade became of enormous importance with the development of the vast empires of the Persians,

Alexander and his successors, and the Romans and Parthians; it even included commodities from India and China.

Biblical mention of Arabia is rare and often vague, and for the biblical writers in Jerusalem the name seems to have connoted all the general desert area to the east, including Sinai. Thus, Paul's sojourn in Arabia (Gal. 1:17) was probably in some small settlement east of Damascus, and the Arabians who were present at Pentecost (Acts 2:11) may have come from no farther than eastern Transjordan, although perhaps from a Jewish oasis community such as the one at Medina. "Geshem the Arab" (Neh. 2:19; 6:1) is of uncertain provenance. Some identify him with the ruler of Kedar mentioned in a fifth-century BCE Egyptian inscription and also an Arabian inscription at Dedan (Arabic *el-Ula*), but others believe he was the governor of Edom under the Persians.

Refugees from Assyrian invasions in the eighth century BCE and Babylonian in the sixth century fled to northwestern Arabia (Isa. 21:13–15, where "thickets," Heb. *ya'ar,* may perhaps refer to oasis vegetation). Close to the end of the Babylonian Empire northwest Arabia achieved unusual importance for about ten years when Nabonidus, the last Babylonian ruler, captured Tema (modern Teima) on the Medina-Damascus route, about two hundred and fifty miles southeast of Aqabah, and made it his capital. *See also* Alexander; Damascus; Dedan; Geshem; Hiram; Kedar; Paul; Pentecost; Sheba.   D.B.

Arad (air'ad), a twenty-five-acre site (Tell 'Arad) located about eighteen miles east-northeast of Beer-sheba, in the eastern Negev. Its 130-foot-high mound dominates the surrounding plain. The lower city flourished in the Early Bronze I–II periods (ca. 3100–2650 BCE). On the upper mound, following an Iron I settlement, there were six Israelite citadels dating from the tenth to the early sixth centuries BCE. Later strata show smaller fortresses in the Persian through Roman periods, followed by residential remains from the Arab periods. Strategically, Arad sits at an important crossroads of trade routes running from the Faynan copper mines in Jordan westward to the coast as well as exchange networks through the Negev, Sinai, and northern Egypt.

A *migdal,* or defensive tower, at Arad, ca. 2500 BCE.

Textual References: Aside from an inscription from the Early Bronze I settlement—a Narmer serekh that provides a synchronism between Egypt and Canaan ca. 3100 BCE—the textual evidence regarding Arad refers to the Iron Age Israelite fortress. Of the numerous biblical citations, there are references to the King of Arad defeating (Num. 21:1;14:44–45) and being routed by (21:2–3; 33:40) the Israelites, in particular at nearby Hormah (Tell Malhata). These references suggest that Arad may refer to a district or a region in the Negev. Josh. 12:14 mentions both Hormah and Arad in the list of cities defeated by the Israelites. The lack of Late Bronze Age occupation at Arad raises questions about the conquest; however, at nearby Hormah remains of the period have been found. Elsewhere, a connection is made between Arad and the Kenites (Judg. 4:11). Although Josh. 15:21 places the city in Judah, Eusebius locates the village of Arad rather precisely in relation to Hebron in the Negev (*Onomasticon* 14, 3).

The Arad letters consist of over a hundred Hebrew ostraca found at the site. Dated to about 600 BCE, just before the destruction of Judah by the Babylonians, they provide a rare view of ancient communications, such as that between a commander and his troops (a certain Eliashib ordered rations be given to the mercenaries). There are also references to priestly families, to the city of Beer-sheba, and to the "House of Yahweh." A collection of Aramaic ostraca from the Persian period relates information about mercenaries and the distribution of food.

Archaeological Excavations: Eighteen seasons of excavation in the lower city have revealed the best and most extensive plan known of an Early Bronze Age town, which was destroyed and covered over by a small squatter occupation prior to abandonment. This town had evolved from an unfortified Early Bronze I village, which overlay a Chalcolithic village.

Surrounded by an 8-foot-thick fortification with semicircular towers, the town provides an illuminating look at urban planning in the third millennium BCE. For example, there is a network of streets radiating from a central depression, which served as a natural reservoir for rainwater. Also, there are distinct quarters of the town marked off for residential, public, and cultic activities.

The residential area is characterized by clusters of bench-lined broadroom houses (entered by three descending steps) and by courtyards with silos. A clay model of such a house was found at the site. Near the reservoir was the elite section, i.e., the palace and sacred precinct, as well as a series of large public buildings around the cistern. The sacred precinct comprised large and small twin temples, a stone altar (*bamah*) and basin in the courtyard, a stone stele (*matsebah*), and other buildings. Nearby was another extensive complex of buildings, which has been identified as the palace. A cult stele with incised stick figures possibly representing the myth of the god Tammuz was found in one of its rooms.

Recent petrographic ceramic analysis and archaeo-metallurgical studies of copper objects have clarified the role of Arad as an entrepôt in a three-way exchange network consisting of the Faynan copper mines (not Sinai as earlier believed), satellite outposts in the Negev, and Egypt. The destruction of Arad and other sites in the south marks a decline in overland trade with Egypt and the development of maritime trade between Egypt and the Levantine coast.

In the Iron Age, Arad again dominated the area, as demonstrated by the continuous occupation of large fortresses on the upper mound. The Israelite fortresses included storerooms, dwellings, industrial installations, and a sanctuary. The Arad sanctuary is extremely important, for its continued use from the tenth to sixth centuries BCE shows that the Jerusalem temple was not the sole sanctuary in the land. The sanctuary's tenth-century plan is particularly informative for its tripartite form: a courtyard with sacrificial altar, a sanctuary, and a Holy of Holies that included stelae (*matsebot*) and incense altars. The latter features suggest the worship of two deities, perhaps Yahweh and his Asherah, a view supported by inscriptional evidence from other sites. Two inscribed bowls near the altar indicate priestly offerings. A lion figurine may symbolize Asherah.   S.R.

Arah (air'uh).

1 An Asherite, son of Ulla, who appears in a list of heads of houses, warriors, and chief princes (1 Chron. 7:39).

2 An ancestor of 775 people who returned from the Babylonian exile (Ezra 2:5), though Neh. 7:10 cites a census of his descendants as numbering 652. Some of his descendants were loyal to Tobiah (Neh. 6:18).

Aram (air'uhm).

1 The son of Shem and grandson of Noah (Gen. 10:22–23; 1 Chron. 1:17).

2 The grandson of Nahor, Abraham's brother (Gen. 22:21).

3 A descendant of Asher (1 Chron. 7:34) and an ancestor of Jesus (Matt. 1:3–4).

4 The territory of the Arameans. Aram was a confederation of states that rose to ascendancy during the early first millennium BCE and vied with Israel for control over the Levant. Saul was Israel's first king to clash with the Arameans (1 Sam. 14:47). David defeated Hadadezer, king of Zobah (the Aramean state whose center was north of Damascus) and gained control of Aramean lands from Damascus to Hamath (2 Sam. 8:5–12). Solomon apparently had to crush a revolt in Hamath-zobah early in his reign (2 Chron. 8:3–4); but in the latter part of Solomon's reign Rezon gained control of Damascus and established an Aramean kingdom that was hostile to Solomon (1 Kings 11:23–25). At Rezon's death Hezion seized the throne of Aram and established a dynasty that lasted a century. Members of this dynasty, especially Ben-hadad I and Ben-hadad II, frequently led Aram against the northern kingdom, Israel (e.g., 1 Kings 15:18; 1 Kings 20). In ca. 843 BCE Hazael usurped the Aramean throne and continued the opposition against Israel (2 Kings 8:28–29; 9:15; 10:32–33; 13:22). Jeroboam II of Israel finally overpowered Aram, and the latter declined in importance thereafter, with one short-lived rally during the reign of Ahaz, king of Israel. The kingdom was brought to an end in 732 BCE by Tiglath-pileser III of Assyria. *See also* Aramean; Isaiah, book of.   D.A.D.

Aramaic (air′uh-may′ik), a Semitic language closely related to Hebrew. It has been spoken in the Levant from the ninth century BCE until the present in a variety of dialects. It originated among the Arameans of northern Syria, said to be among the ancestors of Abraham (Gen. 28:2–5; Deut. 26:5). When the Assyrians conquered the Arameans, Aramean scribes within the bureaucracy of the empire made Aramaic into a universal language of the Near East, which endured from the eighth to fourth centuries BCE. Aramaic then continued in widespread use in a number of dialects through the NT period until the Arab conquest (seventh century CE). Several passages in the Jewish Tanakh/Christian OT are written in Aramaic (Ezra 4:8–6:18; 7:12–26; Dan. 2:4–7:28; Jer. 10:10–11; Gen. 31:47). Jesus probably spoke a dialect of Aramaic, and some words in the NT are or come from Aramaic, e.g., "abba," "talitha cum," "maranatha," and "Golgotha." The Dead Sea Scrolls, inscriptions, and many documents show that Aramaic was in common use during the first century CE. In succeeding centuries Aramaic split into several dialects. Syriac, a form of Aramaic, was used by the Christians in Syria. Palestinian Aramaic was used for composition of the Palestinian Talmud, and Babylonian Aramaic for the Babylonian Talmud. Targums are Jewish translations of the Hebrew Bible into Aramaic for the benefit of synagogue worshipers. *See also* Calvary; maranatha; talitha cum; Targums.   A.J.S.

Aramean (air′uh-mee′uhn), designation of a people living in Syria in the second millennium BCE; in Genesis, the people from whom Bethuel and Laban came. Bethuel was the father of Isaac's wife, Rebekah. Laban was her brother (Gen. 25:20). According to an ancient Israelite confession of faith, Abraham was an Aramean: "A wandering Aramean was my ancestor" (Deut. 26:5). Aramean was the ancestry of the concubine of Manasseh, who bore Asriel and Machir, the father of Gilead (1 Chron. 7:14). Subsequent centuries found Israel at war with the Arameans during the Israelite and Judean monarchies. *See also* Aram.

Ararat (air′uh-rat), the biblical name (Assyrian Urartu) for the region around Lake Van (southeast Turkey, extending into northwest Iran) and the people and state established there from the ninth through the early sixth centuries BCE. Best known from Assyrian records, Urartu constantly hindered Assyria's advances northward. The assassins of Sennacherib fled there from Nineveh (2 Kings 19:37; Isa. 37:38). Later, after the collapse of Assyria, Ararat and other northern nations were summoned in Jer. 51:27–28 to attack Babylon. In Gen. 8:4, Noah's ark settled on the mountains of Ararat, evidently considered the highest part of the world. The modern "Mount Ararat" is a later appellation.   S.B.P.

Aratus (air′uh-tuhs), a Stoic poet of the mid-third century BCE whose work *Phainomena* is quoted in Paul's Areopagus speech (Acts 17:28: "for we are indeed his offspring"). *See also* Areopagus; Stoicism.

Araunah (uh-raw′nuh), a Jebusite who sold a threshing floor to David (2 Sam. 24). The man's

ARAMAIC EXPRESSIONS IN THE NEW TESTAMENT

Boanerges	Mark 3:17	"Sons of Thunder"
Talitha cum	Mark 5:41	"Little girl, get up"
Corban	Mark 7:11	"an offering to God"
Ephphatha	Mark 7:34	"Be opened"
Bartimaeus	Mark 10:46	"son of Timaeus"
Abba	Mark 14:36; Rom. 8:15; Gal. 4:6	"Father"
Golgotha	Matt. 27:33; Mark 15:22; John 19:17	"the place of a skull"
Eli, Eli, lema sabachthani or Eloi, Eloi, lema sabachthani	Matt. 27:46; Mark 15:34	"My God, my God, why have you forsaken me?"
Maranatha	1 Cor. 16:22	"Our Lord, come"

From Mark Allan Powell, *Introducing the New Testament* (courtesy, Baker Academic)

name is given as Ornan in 1 Chron. 21, and there is some speculation that Araunah might be a Hurrian title meaning "noble" rather than a personal name. In the biblical narrative, David purchased the threshing floor to set up an altar there after God's plague against the Israelites ceased at that precise location. According to 1 Chron. 22:1 and 2 Chron. 3:1 this was the site on which the temple in Jerusalem would later be built. The man called Araunah in 2 Sam. had offered to donate the threshing floor to David, along with animals to offer as a sacrifice, but David refused, insisting he would not offer sacrifices to God that had cost him nothing (24:24).   M.A.P.

Archelaus. *See* Herod.

archers. Warriors armed with bows and arrows played an important role in ancient Near Eastern warfare, since they could strike accurately from a distance while being protected by a full-length shield. They were so important that in the Bible a bow may metonymically represent general military strength (Hos. 1:5). Although individual archers and even target practice are mentioned in the Bible (e.g., 1 Sam. 20:35–36), no organized Israelite archery corps is ever described. Perhaps Israel lacked the materials needed to produce composite bows and therefore never established a large archery corps. Alternatively, the Bible may never have mentioned an Israelite archery corps even though it existed. Assyrian reliefs of the siege of Lachish portray small groups of Israelite archers trying unsuccessfully to stave off the Assyrian army, which incorporated a large organized corps of archers.   M.Z.B.

Archippus (ahr-kip´uhs), perhaps a member of Philemon's household, greeted by Paul as a "fellow soldier" in Philem. 2, and mentioned in Col. 4:17, where he is urged to complete some unknown task. *See also* Philemon, Letter of Paul to.

Archite (ahr´kit).
  1 Identification given to Hushai, adviser to David (2 Sam. 15:32; 16:16; 17:5, 14; 1 Chron. 27:33). Hushai spied on Absalom and the priests Zadok and Abiathar.
  2 A territory associated with Ataroth, a boundary location between Benjamin and Ephraim (Josh. 16:2), possibly identical with Ataroth-addar (16:5).

architecture. The Bible does not use the term "architecture" as such, but speaks rather of specific constructions, sometimes giving remarkable details, but descriptions are always incidental in narratives composed for other purposes. Furthermore, the archaeological evidence for architecture seldom survives in more than the form of building foundations. Efforts at rebuilding, the redesign of city layouts, damage due to earthquakes, military destruction, or quarrying for reusable stone, and the vagaries of time and weather have all dimin-

Fragment of a sacred pillar from the temple at Shechem, Late Bronze Age (1500–1200 BCE).

ished the evidence drastically. Artistic representations such as the four-column facade of the Roman temple on the Esbus coin found in its proper Roman context at Hesban or the stairway up the mountainside toward Tell er-Ras on a coin found at Shechem are frequently helpful, but usually they are so small that they contain only hints of the architecture represented. An additional problem, shared with all artistic representations, is uncertainty about the accuracy of the artist, whether for reasons of propaganda or artistic license.

With these acknowledged limits one must claim at the outset that the architectural achievements in the ancient Near East were, at their best, relatively minor compared to the massive gates, palaces, ziggurats, and gardens of Mesopotamian centers such as Ur, Babylon, Asshur, and Nineveh. Similarly, examination shows very minor achievement in tombs, temples, canals, and palaces compared to those of Old, Middle, and New Kingdom Egypt, as even a quick glance at the design of the pyramids of Giza, the temples of Luxor and Karnak, and palaces such as Tell el-Amarna will show. It is an elementary but true observation that biblical-period architecture reflects in part the geophysical and geopolitical place of the biblical peoples: they inhabited a narrow corridor on which larger societies played out their histories, often leaving little or no room for truly indigenous development and frequently stifling emerging native life before it had much chance to flower. One result of this situation is a largely eclectic and reflective architecture in many periods. Clear Egyptian influence on temple design and furnishing at Byblos on the Lebanese coast in pre-Phoenician life is paralleled by obvious Canaanite patterns of city defenses, temples, and palaces and later Hellenistic and Roman motifs in everything from city plans (Jerash) to city features (theaters, aqueducts, hippodromes, living quarters, tomb design, temple construction and layout) on both sides of the Jordan Valley.

Canaanite Architecture: The architecture of the Levant during the Middle and Late Bronze Age (2000–1500 BCE) was predominantly Canaanite.

Although the region was nominally under Egyptian control, the Amarna letters from Canaanite city-state monarchs to headquarters in Egypt show that local autonomy was extensive. The main features architecturally were defense walls comprising substantial stone and rubble-filled ramparts, sometimes with an external glacis to increase defensive efficiency. Examples are evident at Hazor and Dan as well as Shechem and Megiddo. Gateways were the most vulnerable point in such constructions and so were reinforced with towers or elaborate entrance routes, putting assaulting forces at an additional disadvantage. All of this was successor to some of the massive mud-brick defense walls and gates of the Early Bronze Age (3000–2000 BCE), such as at Tirzah, though use of stone for major defense construction had been known in the country since Neolithic times in Jericho (ca. 8000 BCE).

Within the defense perimeter, dominant public buildings tended to be the royal residence and a temple for the local Baal. As with the defenses themselves, construction was usually of large uncut stone, yielding the term "Cyclopean" from the assumption that only a giant like the mythical Cyclops could have maneuvered such rock into place. Palaces tended to be multi-roomed with storage and servants' quarters attached. Compared to a structure like the palace at Mari, palaces in Canaan were very modest in size and complexity. Debate over the nature of a structure such as the open-court temple (perhaps really a palace) excavated at Shechem indicates a large degree of diagnostic uncertainty as to function for some of these public buildings.

Temples were similarly elementary and seem to be modeled on north Syria designs. The extensive uncut stone altar of Level XIX at Megiddo was rigged with stairs on the east, presumably to allow priestly access for rites, possibly of sacrifice. The unmortared but carefully built stone walls of the Early Bronze Age temple at Ai (et Tell), its plastered interior wall faces, and the saw-cut pillar bases down the center of the nave for roof support all indicate that construction and decorative technique, while elaborate for Canaan, were yet far removed from the upper reaches of the skills of neighboring lands. The Late Bronze Age temple at Shechem, with its fragment of a sacred pillar and mount, and its use of walls the stone foundations of which were 17 feet thick, attests the utilitarian mind that in later biblical tradition attributed the local use of the building to that of treasury as well as shrine (Judg. 9:4), and possibly even of haven (9:46).

Housing for ordinary folk was modest in most periods. One or two courses of stone used as foundations for single- or two-storied mud-brick structures may have been one-room units or two- to four-room units incorporating an open or partly roofed courtyard in which the cooking hearth, storage vessels for water, and sometimes other goods were placed. Decoration of such dwellings was modest or nonexistent. Roofs were flat layered earth or crude plaster supported by a framework of timbers sometimes with vertical posts of stone or wood for excessively long spans. The walls may have been faced with mud plaster, which, as the roofs, needed annual refacing due to weathering and other wear and tear.

Israelite Achievements: The rise of the Israelites to dominance in the early Iron Age reflects their adoption of Canaanite architecture in reuse of defenses and extremely modest indigenous construction. With the rise of a united monarchy (tenth century BCE) and its brief divided survival prior to invasion by Assyria in the eighth century, the flower of Israelite architectural achievement was reached. Credit for this in the biblical record is given to Solomon. His touted achievements include the construction of store-cities (1 Kings 9:19); rebuilt cities (9:17); chariot cities (9:19); special palaces for his wives (9:24) and for himself (7:1); special units like the House of the Forest of Lebanon (7:2–5), the Hall of Pillars (7:6), and the Hall of the Throne (7:7); fortifications for cities (9:15); and most famously the temple in Jerusalem (6:1–38), reportedly a seven-year project in the construction phase. Of this vast enterprise, nothing has survived archaeologically of the temple or palace materials, but evidences of the fortifications of cities, both those mentioned (Megiddo, Hazor, and Gezer) and others (like Shechem), have been abundant and are impressive.

Solomonic gateways were constructed of cut stone, usually paved, and rigged with interior step barriers, allowing the packing of defenders at each of as many as four internal partitions to keep people from reaching the interior access gate. The gates were flanked with towers allowing three-way crossfire against intruders. The width of the gate was sufficient only to allow one chariot, or in peacetime one cart, abreast. The skilled stonecutting evident in some of these structures suggests that the lessons learned from the Phoenician craftsmen brought in to build the temple were applied well and broadly throughout the construction program.

West guardroom of the gate fortification at Gezer, dating from the time of Solomon.

Painted plaster wall and imitation fluted columns in Herod's northern palace at Masada.

The best example of an Israelite temple is that excavated at Arad. Threefold separation of internal space, an altar of uncut stone and earth, bases of sacred pillars, and two incense altars match numerous biblical descriptions for such design and furnishing.

The palace tradition survived in the facilities built by northern monarchs Omri (ca. 876–869 BCE) and Ahab (ca. 869–850 BCE) at Samaria. Because it was the earliest architecture on the summit and has been overlaid by extensive later construction of Hellenistic and Herodian buildings, little of the palace walls survived. Eloquent testimony to the affluence of the court is given by extensive inlaid ivory decorations, over five hundred fragments of which were recovered. Header-stretcher masonry typical of the Solomonic period was still used extensively, and casemate defense wall foundations illustrate that such a design (found also as widely spread as from Hazor to Tell Beit Mirsim) had been found helpful. It proved insufficient, however, against Assyria's forces at Samaria as well as Hazor and elsewhere.

While the land suffered the ravages of Assyria and then of the Neo-Babylonians under Nebuchadnezzar in the eighth and seventh centuries BCE, architecture declined. The destruction of Jerusalem in 587 BCE was matched by destructions elsewhere in the land (such as depicted on Assyrian reliefs concerning Lachish). Even under Persia's permissive attitudes toward local societies, in the light of which the Jewish return from exile and the efforts to reconstitute both state and national shrines took place (late sixth–early fifth centuries BCE), Israel's struggle was simply to survive.

Herodian Architecture: With the Hellenistic influences brought in first by Alexander's conquests, then under successive domination by the Ptolemies, the Seleucids, and the briefly independent Maccabees, new styles became apparent, felt most firmly under Roman influence by Herod the Great (40–4 BCE) and his successors. Herodian construction can be considered agglutinative, fusing Hellenistic traditions, Hasmonean precedents,

Nabatean aesthetics, and of course Roman materials, techniques, and approaches to space. Herod's initial architectural projects were his fortress-palaces, such as have been excavated at Masada, Jericho, Machaerus, and Herodion. These mixed indigenous palace design with Roman facades and styles: on the one hand, the decorations were principally aniconic and there were always Jewish ritual baths; on the other hand, peristyles and fake fluted columns were accompanied by faux marble frescos, mosaics and opus sectile stone floors, and stuccoed ceilings in geometric designs like those found at Roman luxury villas. These palaces also contained Roman-style baths with rooms heated by underground hypocaust systems, triclinia (dining rooms) with spectacular views of nature or gardens, and the finest imported wares from across the Mediterranean and Nabatea. Herod's cities likewise adopted Roman elements. At Caesarea Maritima he imposed an orthogonal grid, constructed numerous leisure and entertainment structures like the theater and hippodrome, brought water to the city via an aqueduct, and erected a temple dedicated to the goddess Roma and the emperor Augustus. Similar temples were built at Sebaste and near Caesarea Philippi at the site today called Omrit. Herod's most impressive architectural feat, the Temple Mount in Jerusalem, likewise adopted Roman approaches to architecture, though preserving Jewish religious sensibilities and following biblical prescriptions. Like so many Roman temple complexes, Herod imposed his project onto the topography with a massive arch-and-vault foundation, created a series of awe-inspiring facades, and controlled movement through a series of entrances, staircases, and balustrades.

Following the destruction of the temple in 70 CE and the defeat of the Bar Kochba revolt (132–135) by Rome, the latter's architectural dominance in both Judea and the entire Levant became obvious. Particularly during the reign of Hadrian, cities witnessed renovation and expansion along Roman lines. Decapolis cities like Gadara (Umm Qeis in northern Jordan), with a magnificent basalt amphitheater largely intact, and Philadelphia (Amman in central Jordan), with its temple to Jupiter (partly restored) and amphitheater (downtown), match Jerash, with its theaters, colonnaded street, temples, and Hadrian's triple arch, and Baalbek (eastern Lebanon), with its massive pillars of the temple to Jupiter and its better preserved temple to "Bacchus." All show local determination to become part of the Roman Empire by adapting its distinctive architectural visions to local conditions.

The same grandeur is visible in the cities of Asia Minor that figure in Paul's travels, like Ephesus (Acts 18:19, 21), which was marked by structures dedicated to the Roman emperors and later a massive temple complex first built to Domitian but then rededicated to the Flavian dynasty and subsequent emperors. It also boasted a massive theater and even toilets with marble seats that were constantly flushed with running water in the drain below. Prior to the Romans, Pergamum (Rev. 1:11; 2:12) had enjoyed one of largest outdoor altars dedicated to Zeus; in subsequent years under Roman rule that altar was surrounded with additional temples, including one to Trajan and one to Asclepius, along with extensive public baths. These stand as eloquent marks of Rome's adaptations of Greek models, transcended only by some of the monuments in Rome itself. Poignant reminder of the unsuccessful Jewish revolt (60–66 CE) was Rome's Arch of Titus, depicting captured booty from the Jerusalem temple.

A final word pertains to the distinctive architecture of the Nabateans, found not only at their major headquarters of Petra, with the elaborate cave facades, amphitheater, and the distinctive Robinson high-place shrine, but also at other sites. Their mastery of cantilevered roof and stair construction is most evident at modern Umm al-Jimal in the Transjordanian desert, giving vivid proof of a unique interior genius. *See also* house; temple, the; temples.

Bibliography

George, A. R. *House Most High: The Temples of Ancient Mesopotamia.* Eisenbrauns, 1993.

Kempinski, A., and R. Reich, eds. *The Architecture of Ancient Israel from the Prehistoric to the Persian Periods.* Israel Exploration Society, 1992.

Netzer, Ehud. *The Architecture of Herod the Great Builder.* Mohr-Siebeck, 2006.   R.S.B./J.R.

Arcturus (ahrk-toor´uhs), the third brightest star of the Northern Hemisphere. In place of Arcturus (LXX, KJV), NRSV translates "Bear" (Job 9:9; 38:32). It is part of constellation Boötes and is in line with the tail of Ursa Major (Great Bear), whence the associated name.

Ard (ahrd).

1 One of the sons of Benjamin (Gen. 46:21).

2 The son of Bela and grandson of Benjamin (Num. 26:40), called Adar in 1 Chron. 8:3.

Areopagus (air´ee-op´uh-guhs; Gk., "hill of Ares"), a low hill in Athens northwest of the acropolis. The hill had stone seats for the council that met there, the origins of which went back to the advisory council of Athenian kings. In the book of Acts, Paul is brought to the Areopagus by Epicurean and Stoic philosophers who want to know more about the message he is proclaiming (17:16–21). He speaks to them, beginning with an inscription he saw on an idol, "To an unknown god," continuing with reflection on the words of a Greek poet (Epimenides), and concluding with a testimony to God having raised "a man whom he has appointed" from the dead (17:22–31). He loses most of his audience with that last point, but succeeds in converting a few, including a man named Dionysius and a woman named Damaris (17:32–34). *See also* Athens; Damaris; Dionysius; Epicureanism; Stoicism.   M.A.P.

Aretas (air´uh-tuhs) **IV,** Nabatean king who greatly expanded his kingdom (9 BCE–40 CE). His daughter was married to Herod Antipas and was divorced by him when Antipas chose to marry Herodias instead. Aretas took the conflict to the battlefield and won a victory that humiliated Antipas and probably cost him his throne. Despite these intersections with biblical persons and events, Aretas is mentioned by name only once in the Bible, in reference to a completely different matter. Paul says in 2 Cor. 11:32 that, while in Damascus, "the governor under King Aretas" tried to seize him and that he had to escape by being lowered over the city wall in a basket (cf. Acts 9:32–35). The indication that Damascus was under Nabatean jurisdiction at this time illustrates how successful Aretas had been at extending his influence. *See also* Herod; Herodias; John the Baptist; Nabatea, Nabateans.   M.A.P.

Argob (ahr´gob; Heb., "a mound of earth" or possibly "an area of hills").

1 A specified region east of the Jordan, either an area within Bashan or simply another name for Bashan. Its precise location is not known. It was identified as the kingdom of Og, containing sixty cities and captured by the Israelites before crossing the Jordan (Deut. 3:4). The territory was given to the half-tribe of Manasseh whose leader, Jair, renamed it Havvoth-Jair ("settlement of Jair," 3:13–14). *See also* Bashan.

2 A co-conspirator, with Arieh, in Pekah's plan to assassinate King Pekahiah of Samaria (2 Kings 15:25). But since Argob and Arieh are both place-names, they may be misplaced from the listing of territories captured by Tiglath-pileser in the following verses (15:29).   D.R.B.

Ariel (air´ee-uhl; Heb., "altar hearth" or "heroes").

1 One of the leading men summoned by Ezra and sent by him to secure ministers for the temple (Ezra 8:16).

2 According to the NRSV, a Moabite man in 2 Sam. 23:20 (1 Chron. 11:22) whose two sons were slain by David's champion warrior Benaiah. Some English translations, however, take the word in this text as a common noun rather than a proper name: thus, Benaiah might be said to have slain "two ariels" ("two heroes" [KJV: "lionlike men"; NIV: "best men"]) rather than "two men of Ariel" (NRSV: "two sons of Ariel").

3 A poetic designation for Jerusalem ("the city where David encamped" in Isa. 29:1–2). This sense is apparently derived from the presence of the main altar in Jerusalem, since the Hebrew word ´ar´iel can also mean "altar hearth" (e.g., as it is translated in Ezek. 43:14–15). The word is also used (in the plural) in Isa. 29:12 to mean "inhabitants of Ariel (i.e., Jerusalem)"; but cf. 33:7, where the NRSV translates it "the valiant."

          J.J.M.R./M.A.P.

Arimathea (air´uh-muh-thee´uh), a hellenized form of the Hebrew name Ramathaim, Ramoth, or Ramah; home of Joseph, who buried Jesus in his own tomb (Matt. 27:57–60; Mark 15:42–46; Luke 23:50–53; John 19:38–42). Arimathea is variously identified with modern Rentis (fifteen miles east of Jaffa), er-Ram (five miles north of Jerusalem), or el-Birah-Ramallah (eight miles north of Jerusalem). *See also* Joseph.

Arioch (air´ee-ok).

1 The king of Ellasar, who, in alliance with the kings of Shinar, Elam, and Goiim, raided the area around the Dead Sea, including Sodom and the cities of the Plain, and took Lot prisoner. He and the other kings were defeated by Abram and his allies (Gen. 14:1–16).

2 The captain of King Nebuchadnezzar's guard, who was instructed to kill all the wise men of Babylon because they could not interpret the king's dream. He later brought Daniel before the king (Dan. 2:14–15; 24–25).

3 The king of the Elymeans, who rallied to join his forces with those of the Chaldeans when Nebuchadnezzar made war against King Arphaxad of the Medes (Jth. 1:5–6).

Aristarchus (air´is-tahr´kuhs), according to Acts a native of Thessalonica and a companion of Paul in Ephesus, on his final trip to Jerusalem, and on his voyage to Rome (19:29; 20:4–5; 27:2). This is probably the same Aristarchus who is listed as Paul's fellow prisoner in Col. 4:10; Philem. 24.

ark of the covenant, ark of God, a sacred container of indeterminate size. It is most often called the "ark of the covenant" in passages throughout Exodus, Numbers, Deuteronomy, Joshua, Samuel, Kings, and Chronicles, a terminology thought to reflect typical Deuteronomic language. The alternative term "ark of God" (1 Sam. 3:3; 1 Chron. 13:5) and, sometimes, "ark of the LORD" (Josh. 3:3), is found in portions of the books of Joshua, Samuel, and Chronicles; some scholars think this represents an earlier nomenclature. The term "ark of the Testimony" is also employed in some Priestly material (e.g., Num. 4:5), but the NRSV does not recognize that distinction, using "ark of the covenant" in such passages.

According to biblical tradition, the ark contained the two tablets of the law (Deut. 10:2, 5), but the odd Hebrew wording of 1 Kings 8:9 suggests that it may once have held something else, perhaps the two stones that formed the sacred lots, Urim and Thummim. Exod. 16:33–34 and Num. 17:1–11 imply that it also contained a jar of manna and Aaron's miraculous rod (a tradition stated explicitly in Heb. 9:3–5). Originally, the characteristic feature of the ark was that it could be carried about. Thus, the Israelite ark led the people in the desert (Num. 10:33), was carried round the walls of Jericho (Josh. 6), and was brought into the camp during military operations (1 Sam. 4:2–4). It was kept in a tent (2 Sam. 6:17) with an attendant (1 Sam. 7:1) and used for oracular inquiries (1 Sam. 14:18).

Wagon, which may be a depiction of the ark of the covenant, carved in a lintel at a synagogue in Capernaum from the second or early third century CE.

The most striking fact about the ark at an early period was that it was a direct manifestation of God's presence (Num. 10:35–36). The Philistines equated the ark with a god (1 Sam. 4:6–8), and those who desecrated the ark were struck down by its divine power (1 Sam. 6:19; 2 Sam. 6:6–7). When we find the expression "before God" in a sanctuary context, this often seems to refer to the ark. It is possible that at one time various sanctuaries each had their own arks, but the one that became central in Israelite tradition was that of the Shiloh temple, where it had probably already become a national symbol of the tribal confederacy.

A biblical narrative sometimes called the "history of the ark" (1 Sam. 4:1–7:2) recounts the ark's capture by the Philistines, its devastating power in their territory, its triumphant return to Israel, and its concealment at Kiriath-jearim for some twenty years of Philistine occupation. After defeating the Philistines, David brought it from there and installed it in his new capital, Jerusalem, as part of his policy of uniting the tribes under his rule (2 Sam. 6). This event was probably reenacted annually, with Ps. 132 as the liturgy of the festival. The ark was later transferred to the Holy of Holies of Solomon's new temple (1 Kings 8:4–7). From this time on, the ark remained stationary and was viewed as a throne on which God sat as an invisible deity above the two guardian cherubim (2 Kings 19:15). The belief that God resided permanently in the darkness of the Holy of Holies (1 Kings 8:12–13) led to belief in the inviolability of the temple and Jerusalem.

The ark is usually thought to have been destroyed or captured in the Babylonian sack of Jerusalem in 587/6 BCE, though there is no sure report of this. Whether there was an ark in the second temple is uncertain. In Jer. 3:15, which may well be postexilic and is the only reference to the ark in all the prophetic literature, Jerusalem replaces the ark as God's throne. There is also no mention of the ark in the detailed vision of the new temple in Ezek. 40–48. A later Jewish legend, however, tells of its being hidden at the time of the exile until a remote future (2 Macc. 2:4–8). In Rev. 11:19, the Christian prophet John beholds a vision of the ark of the covenant within "God's temple in heaven."

Priestly traditions also took an interest in the gold "mercy seat," or cover, on top of the ark. As indicated, this came to be viewed as God's throne, where God would appear in a cloud (Lev. 16:2) to communicate the divine will (Exod. 25:17–22). As the Hebrew term *kapporet* suggests, this was also the place where atonement was made, supremely by the sprinkling of blood on the Day of Atonement (Lev. 16:14–16). It is this representation of the ark that is found in Heb. 9:3–5 (cf. Rom. 3:25). *See also* cherubim; tabernacle; Urim and Thummim.

Bibliography

De Vaux, Roland. *Ancient Israel: Its Life and Institutions.* McGraw-Hill, 1961. Pp. 297–302.

Von Rad, Gerhard. *Old Testament Theology.* Harper & Row, 1962. Pp. 234–41.

Woudstra, Marten H. *The Ark of the Covenant from Conquest to Kingship.* Presbyterian and Reformed Publishing, 1965.   J.R.P.

ark of Noah. *See* Noah.

Armageddon (ahr´muh-ged´uhn), the location of the final cosmic battle between the forces of good and evil, according to Rev. 16:16. The word is a transliteration into Greek of an unknown Hebrew word (Gk. *har magedon*). The NRSV renders it as Harmagedon, but almost all other English translations use Armageddon. There is, however, no place known to us that was called Armageddon or Harmagedon. One suggestion takes *har magedon* to mean Mount Magedon, though no mountain by that name is known. Thus, many scholars have thought that there has been some corruption of the text (somewhat evident in variant readings found in different manuscripts). If the word was supposed to read *har megiddon,* that could be translated Mount Megiddo. There is no evidence elsewhere of a mountain called Mount Megiddo either, but Mount Carmel is only five miles northeast of the city of Megiddo, so Mount Megiddo could have been an alternative name for Mount Carmel known to the author and readers of Revelation. The city of Megiddo was the site of many well-known ancient battles (Deborah and Barak versus the Canaanite king Sisera, Judg. 5:19; Jehu versus Ahaziah, 2 Kings 9:27; Josiah versus Neco, 23:29). Thus, an area associated with this city (or with this name) may have seemed an appropriate site for the ultimate conflict to occur. It is also possible, however, that the term *har magedon* means something else ("mount of assembly" or "his fruitful mountain"), in which case an association with Megiddo would not be evident and the intended location of "Armageddon" (if, indeed, any literal place was meant) cannot be determined.   R.S.B./M.A.P.

armory, a weapons storage facility, real or metaphorical. King Hezekiah shows his armory in Je-

rusalem to the Babylonian emissaries as part of his psychological warfare (2 Kings 20:13; see also Isa. 39:2). Neh. 3:19 makes incidental reference to a similar, if not the same, facility. Jer. 50:25 metaphorically refers to the Lord opening his armory in the conflict against Babylon.

arms, armor. Biblical references to arms are both literal and metaphorical. In Gen. 14:13–16 there is an account of Abraham's retainers, or "trained men," whose success in battle presupposes their efficient use of arms. In tribal societies like that of early Israel arms consisted of spears, swords, sling stones, and bows and arrows. Armor is known from Egyptian reliefs from the mid-second millennium BCE, but it is first referred to in Israel in Judg. 9:34, which indicates Abimelech had an armor bearer. Later, Jonathan is said to have had an armor bearer as well (1 Sam. 14:1, 6). Saul offered David his armor to use in the upcoming combat with Goliath, but it was too heavy or cumbersome for David to wear (1 Sam. 17:38–39). Goliath's own armor is described: a bronze helmet, a bronze coat of mail, and bronze leglets or greaves. In addition, he carried a sword and a spear and was accompanied by a shield bearer (1 Sam. 17:5–7). All of Goliath's armor except the greaves was paralleled among Israelite forces. Ahab had a coat of scales (mail) according to 1 Kings 22:34, and apparently construction workers rebuilding Jerusalem during Nehemiah's governorship wore protective armor (Neh. 4:16). Bronze armor was used for royalty, but leather shields and body armor were more common for foot soldiers. Armor is also mentioned in figurative contexts: it can be the subject of a proverbial saying (1 Kings 20:11) or the object of God's power (Ps. 46:9). Likewise, arms, transformed, can be the basis for a new social order (Isa. 2:1–4; Mic. 4:1–5).

During the Second Temple period, Antiochus IV Epiphanes is said to have waged war with "companies fully armed with laces and drawn swords . . . brandishing of shields, massing of spears, hurling of missiles, the flash of golden trappings, and armor of all kinds" (2 Macc. 5:2–3). By contrast, Judas and his rebels "did not have armor and swords such as they desired" (1 Macc. 4:6).

Jesus's references to arms are few, but not without surprises, as evidenced by his somber proverb concerning those who wield swords in Matt. 26:52 and the rather different instructions on the bearing of swords in Luke 22:38. Jesus also uses the divisive capability of a sword as a metaphor to describe the nature of his mission (Matt. 10:34). Elsewhere in the NT, the "full armor of God" includes such things as the "breastplate of righteousness" and the "helmet of salvation" (Eph. 6:13–17; cf. 1 Thess. 5:8), and the word of God is declared to be "sharper than any two-edged sword" (Heb. 4:12; cf. Eph. 6:17). In Rev. 1:16 the risen Christ is described as one from whose mouth extends a sword, a metaphor for his role in carrying out divine vengeance and judgment.   J.A.D./M.A.P.

army. Although there was no standing army in ancient Israel until the monarchy, Abraham rallied 318 followers to rescue his relatives who had been captured by a coalition of kings (Gen. 14). Loosely bonded troops drawn from villages or families could also cooperate against a common foe (Exod. 17:8–13). In the tribal federation a people's militia served when called upon by a leader, judge, or field commander. The local muster unit (as few as six men) was, in Hebrew, the '*aleph* (easily confused with the word for "thousand," which has the same spelling). God was commander-in-chief of the army, and the divine will was ascertained by oracles.

Saul added a bodyguard of "three thousand" responsible to himself and Jonathan, and later to Abner, as commander (1 Sam. 13:2; 17:55). Abner's counterpart under the reign of David was Joab. Mercenaries in David's bodyguard (2 Sam. 8:18; 15:19–22) supported the southern throne, in contrast with a tumultuous dynastic sequence in the north. Solomon introduced chariotry. Under the monarchy the army became highly organized, and warfare was greatly routinized.

After the fall of the two kingdoms (Israel ca. 722/1 BCE, Judah in 587/6 BCE), only foreign armies appear in the Bible until Israel achieved national independence under the Maccabees ca. 165 BCE. Then the new standing army included Jewish and non-Jewish soldiers. Later, Herod the Great patterned his organization on Roman models, with mercenaries from as far away as Germany and Gaul. Roman features are also evident in the description of the army found in an apocalyptic text from the Dead Sea sectarians, the so-called *War Scroll* (1QM). Armies mentioned in the NT are either Roman (Luke 21:20; see Acts 23:27) or supernatural (Rev. 9:16; 19:14, 19). Service in the army, however, serves as an apt metaphor for obedience and single-hearted devotion (2 Tim. 2:3–4).   R.B.

Arnon (ahr'nuhn) **River,** a river (modern Wadi el-Mojib), whose water flows from the east into the Dead Sea at about the midpoint of its eastern shore. As a deep gorge, it made north–south travel difficult in Transjordan. The river has a substantial northern tributary that flows southwest and feeds into the main artery of the river just before the main channel empties into the Dead Sea. Dibon, the Moabite capital under Mesha, is located north of the main branch, but south of the northern tributary. On several occasions the Arnon is mentioned as a boundary (Num. 21:24; Judg. 11:18; Deut. 3:8, 16; Josh. 13:16). It is also mentioned in line 26 of the Mesha Inscription. *See also* Mesha; Moabite Stone.   J.A.D.

Aroer (uh-roh'uhr).

1 A fortress on the Arnon River's northern rim, the southern limit of Amorite (Deut. 2:36), Reubenite-Gadite (Deut. 3:12), Davidic (2 Sam. 24:5), and Syrian (2 Kings 10:33) activities in Transjordan. Excavations at modern Khirbet Ara'ir have uncovered fortifications from Mesha's

day (mid-ninth century BCE; cf. Moabite Stone). The last reference to Aroer identifies it as Moabite (Jer. 48:19–20). *See also* Arnon River; Gad; Mesha; Moab; Moabite Stone; Reuben.

2 A town in southern Judah (1 Sam. 30:28), modern Khirbet Ar'areh.

3 An Ammonite settlement near Rabbah (Josh. 13:25).

Arpachshad (ahr-pak'shad), the son of Shem born after the flood, grandfather of Eber, in the line of Abraham (Gen. 10:22–24; 11:10–13; 1 Chron. 1:17–18, 24). He is called Arphaxad in Luke 3:36. The name is probably geographic in origin, referring to a place in Mesopotamia, though the exact reference is not known. *See also* Arphaxad.

Arpad (ahr'pad), a city and small state in northern Syria; the site may be Tell Rifaat, or Tell Erfad, twenty-five miles north of Aleppo. It is linked with Hamath in the question, "Where are the gods of Hamath and Arpad?" (2 Kings 18:34; Isa. 36:19). Similarly, Hamath and Arpad are paired with other cities in a question about the power of their kings (2 Kings 19:13; Isa. 37:13). Their destruction is noted in Isa. 10:9, and in Jer. 49:23 they figure in an oracle concerning the impending destruction of Damascus. Destruction of Arpad's independence came with its fall to Assyria in 740 BCE, after which it never regained power.

Arphaxad (ahr-fak'sad).

1 The son of Shem, listed as an ancestor of Jesus in Luke 3:36. He is called Arpachshad in Genesis and 1 Chronicles. *See also* Arpachshad.

2 The king of the Medes at the time Nebuchadnezzar ruled Assyria. In Jth. 1, Nebuchadnezzar defeats Arphaxad's army in battle, plunders the Medean capital of Ecbatana, and then, capturing the king himself, kills him with spears.   M.A.P.

Artaxerxes (ahr'tuh-zuhrk'seez; Heb. Ar-takh-shast), the name of four known Achaemenid (Persian) kings: Artaxerxes I (Longimanus), 465–424 BCE; Artaxerxes II (Arsakes), 405/4–359/8; Artaxerxes III (Ochos), 359/8–338/7; Artaxerxes IV (Arses), 338/7–336. Identifications of these kings in the biblical text depend on historical probability. The name appears in Ezra 4:7, 8, 11, 23 in a composite passage that is out of chronological context (4:6–23). The usual assumption is that all these refer to Artaxerxes I. Ezra 6:14 adds Artaxerxes after Cyrus and Darius in a list of Persian rulers. Ezra 7:1–8:1 has several references, all to the period of Ezra's activity. Scholarly opinion is divided as to whether these references are to Artaxerxes I or II. Neh. 2:1; 5:14; and 13:6, connected with Nehemiah's two periods as governor, are most often held to refer to Artaxerxes I, though Artaxerxes II cannot be ruled out. Persian desire to control Egypt may have provided the political context for the appointment of both Ezra and Nehemiah regardless of which Persian ruler was responsible. *See also* Ezra; Ezra and Nehemiah, books of.   P.R.A.

Artemas (ahr′tuh-muhs), a companion of Paul mentioned only in Titus 3:12. *See also* Tychicus.

Artemis (ahr′tuh-mis) **of the Ephesians** (i-fee′zhuhnz), a goddess widely worshiped in antiquity throughout the Hellenistic and Roman world. Although identified with the Greek Artemis (and the Roman Diana), the sister of Apollo, the Ephesian Artemis had little in common with those deities of classical mythology. She was more like the ancient Anatolian and Asian mother goddess known also as Cybele, Atargatis, and Ashtoreth— a patroness of nature and fertility. The worship of some sort of mother goddess in this region antedated the settlement of Greeks in the area (ca. 1000 BCE). Acts 19:35 refers to a "sacred stone that fell from the sky," possibly a meteorite, which might have been connected with this ancient cult. The goddess known in NT times, however, has a distinctive image that appears to date only from the fourth century BCE: the upper region of her body is covered with numerous breasts (or possibly eggs), and she wears a turret crown and a long skirt with bands of animals and birds in relief. She is often accompanied by dogs or stags on either side, probably due to syncretism with the original Greek Artemis.

The earliest Greek shrine to Artemis, consisting of two platforms, was eclipsed ca. 600 BCE by the construction of the Archaic Artemision, or temple of Artemis, over the site. The Cretan architect Chersiphron constructed a massive temple (375 by 180 feet) with 60-foot marble columns, which was completed ca. 500 BCE. This temple burned on the night of Alexander the Great's birth in 356 BCE, but a new Artemision was soon begun by the architect Dinocrates and completed ca. 250 BCE. It was regarded as one of the "seven wonders of the world." This temple would be destroyed by the Goths in 263 CE, and practically nothing of it remains today.

The book of Acts tells of Paul visiting Ephesus and preaching so effectively that it was feared interest in Artemis could wane. In particular, the silversmiths (a guild led by a certain Demetrius) were afraid that their trade of making silver shrines of Artemis would be jeopardized (19:23–27). Opinion varies concerning just what these shrines may have been, as nothing quite like this has been found. *See also* Asherah; Demetrius; Ephesus; Paul; shrine; smith.   M.K.M.

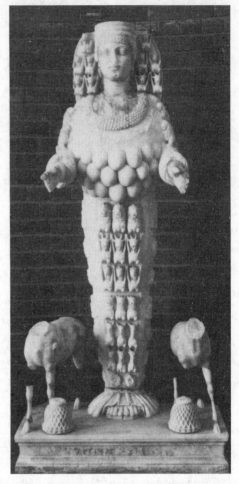

Ancient cultic statue of Artemis of the Ephesians.

Art in the Ancient Near East

THE ARTISTIC INFLUENCE that affected the ancient Near East was fundamentally Eastern, stemming mainly from Egypt and Assyria-Babylonia. Just as those major civilizations dominated the economics and politics of the Levant, so they also provide the backdrop against which Israel's art and that of its neighbors must be seen.

Egyptian Art: Egyptian theology determined the style and content as well as setting for Egyptian art. From the beginning, Egyptian art was characterized by a conceptual rather than a visual approach. The pharaoh, who was both divine and human, was always depicted as larger than any other figure. His shoulders were always seen from the front, because artists had to show the fullness—the completeness—of the pharaoh. Egyptian artists were capable of the necessary technique of foreshortening and could have shown the pharaoh from a side view, but that would not have fulfilled the requirement of indicating the conceptual reality of the god-king. The slate "Palette of King Namur" (ca. 3100 BCE, now in Cairo) shows the pharaoh more than twice the size of his servants and soldiers. This work also gives us the key to the visual analysis of Egyptian art: it is always linear and formal, even when illustrating everyday scenes. Because of this approach, the linear and the conceptual, the Egyptian artists did not need to concern themselves with three-dimensional space. Seen in

Ancient Egyptian banquet scene: female musicians with harp and stringed instruments, from the tomb of Rekhmera, Thebes.

this way, Egyptian art illustrates and explains the continuity of Egyptian civilization.

The major repositories of art from the Old Kingdom (ca. 2700 BCE) to the eve of the Hellenistic period (ca. 350 BCE) are tombs and temples. Art and architecture served the needs of the afterlife, primarily for the pharaoh, the divine king, and his family, but also for nobles and ordinary citizens. The earliest tombs, from which the later step pyramids probably developed, were low, squat mastabas, rectangular brick structures composed of many internal compartments built over the actual subterranean burial chamber. Since these tombs were also temples, the structure provided for a chapel and niche for a statue of the deceased and offering tables upon which gifts for the spirit of the deceased could be placed. The walls of the tomb-temple were covered with bas-reliefs and paintings depicting scenes from the life of the deceased. By the New Kingdom (1550–1100 BCE) rock-cut chambers had been adopted as burial places for kings and commoners, and the kings were buried, for security reasons, at some distance from their mortuary buildings, which were now magnificent temples dedicated to the memory of the divine king and the supreme god, Amon.

Like the buildings, the bas-reliefs and paintings that adorn the New Kingdom tombs had developed from the rather austere scenes of the Old Kingdom, in which the deceased was depicted receiving offerings from the devout who paraded before him on horizontal registers in rather lifeless, frozen form. The New Kingdom scenes depict luxurious living; the offering scene has become a banquet. By contrast with themes painted elsewhere in the ancient Near East, Egyptian artists rendered events from the private and family life of the deceased, including fishing or hunting trips, dances, and games. Boldly the artists projected these scenes of enjoyment and pleasure, drawn from this life, into the next life, so that past and future were fully merged on the tomb walls.

Bust of a monumental statue of the Egyptian pharaoh Akhenaton, from Karnak, fourteenth century BCE.

Statuary, like painting, also served the cause of the next life. In the Old Kingdom, the statues were designed to represent the deceased, providing a perpetual image with which the spirit of the deceased could be identified. This task gave the statuary its distinctive character: it had to offer an ideal representation, since the pharaoh was also a god, and yet the image had to be personal, identifiable with the dead king whose memory it preserved. Egyptian artists succeeded to a remarkable degree in this effort to create individuality and personality within rather rigid formal constraints. By the New Kingdom, statuary had become merely monumental, official memorials to the deceased. Style was basically continuous with the Old Kingdom until the reign of Akhenaton (1369–1353 BCE), whose radical concern for realism broke the tension with the ideal form, resulting in a kind of caricature that went beyond the limits of "realism," exemplified in some thirty statues of this apostate pharaoh found at Karnak. Akhenaton's successors returned to the classical style, yet the effect of the brief revolution in style was not altogether lost. The return to the classical style, however, was more characteristically marked by a penchant for elegance, often devoid of inspiration.

Minor arts from Egypt, of which we have some fine examples, include wood furniture from as early as the Old Kingdom, glassware from the Middle Kingdom onward, and well-modeled bronzes, and fine jewelry.

Assyrian and Babylonian Art: Assyrian art is the heir of Sumerian invention from the third millennium BCE. The sense of struggle against a hostile environment, fraught with threats both natural and supernatural from which protection must be sought by placating the gods and fielding an army, dominates artistic style and content. The confident celebration of life so prominent in Egyptian art is absent from that of Mesopotamia. Here one senses the significant distance between gods and humans. The king is not divine, but can only hope for the favor of the gods, before whom he, as all others, must bow.

Bronze head of a king, possibly Sargon of Akkad, from Nineveh, third millennium BCE.

Ziggurats, or "temple towers," continued in the Assyrian period to exemplify the distance between earth and heaven. They were attached to a number of temples, though not all, and graphically represented the mountain home of the Assyrian storm god. Assyrian architecture seems to have modified the earlier forms by removing the open, external stairways to the top in favor of a less obvious means of approach, in some cases directly from a neighboring temple roof.

At the center of Assyrian cities, however, stood the royal palace. Again developing a Sumerian model, the palaces of the great kings multiplied the courtyards and adjoining buildings enclosed within the complex. The palace at Mari, dated to the beginning of the second millennium BCE, included more than two hundred and sixty rooms and courtyards spread over some six acres. The palace provided the setting for the type of art most characteristic of Assyria: the low relief. Beginning in the ninth century BCE, when Ashurnasirpal II moved the capital from Asshur to Nimrud, Assyrian artists began to fill the walls of the palace rooms with reliefs. Authorities generally regard this innovation as the greatest and most original achievement of Assyrian art. The subject of these carved friezes was the king and his exploits, particularly his victories over ever rebelling vassals. The power of the king was conveyed by the sheer overpowering experience of being completely surrounded by reliefs depicting the unending accomplishments of the monarch. In the beginning, these friezes were usually about 7 feet high, and sometimes the whole surface was covered in a single design. More often, however, the wall was divided into two registers, separated by a band of cuneiform inscriptions. In later buildings (e.g., Sargon's palace at Khorsabad, late eighth century BCE), individual sculptured figures even reach a height of 9 feet. These huge figures are more representational than narrative, as they march in

Ashurbanipal hunting lions from his chariot, bas-relief at Nineveh.

Carved ivory and gold winged sphinx, from Nimrud, eighth–seventh century BCE.

awesome procession—the king and his courtiers—defying any challenge to authority and disparaging any doubt about the stability of the throne. For the most part, however, the wall reliefs were intended to function as narrative art, depicting in stone what the annals attested in writing. The work was highly detailed and skillfully planned, marked by stylistic vitality, especially in the depiction of animals, where musculature and a sense of motion were well developed.

During the reign of Shalmaneser III (858–824 BCE) this new relief style was applied to metal work. The huge doors of a palace near Nimrud were covered with horizontal bands of bronze, each 11 inches in height and 8 feet in length. The subjects of these reliefs, like their stone counterparts, were historical; processional scenes were particularly well suited to the narrow registers.

Not all the themes of the Assyrian mural reliefs were military. From the time of Ashurbanipal (668–627 BCE) we have magnificent hunting scenes vividly portraying dramatic action, with full, sensitive expression of the suffering and death of the victims as well as the power and prowess of the hunter. A comparison of the "Lion Hunt" scenes of Ashurbanipal at the end of the Assyrian period with a similar portrayal of Ashurnasirpal II at the beginning of the period reveals just how well developed and mature the art of relief sculpture had become over two centuries of refinement.

Statuary in Assyria was relatively insignificant, continuing the cylindrical style and impersonal features of Sumerian sculpture. The exception is a kind of statuary that is neither relief nor in the round. Stone slabs, called "orthostats," were set in the entryway to Sargon's palace and the citadel at Khorsabad and carved into winged, human-headed bulls. Those at the citadel were 13 feet high and 14 feet long, and they stared menacingly at all who approached the precincts. They were protective guardians, like their much earlier Hittite predecessors, the lion orthostats at Boghazköy in what is now north-central Turkey.

Among the minor arts represented in Assyria, most notable are cylinder seals, which show the same care for detail and preference for animals and landscape as the reliefs. In the late period, stamps were also molded, but their designs offer nothing new. Cylinder seals remained dominant, providing rich opportunity for personal design and expression. Finally, there are ivories, sculptured and engraved, reflecting exquisite skill and precision. The Nimrud ivories are perhaps the best-known examples. Their style and content, however, raise a difficult question concerning

Ishtar Gate: two mythical creatures. Enameled tile and ceramic brick reconstruction of the processional entrance to Babylon during the time of Nebuchadnezzar, sixth century BCE.

Dying lioness, bas-relief at Nineveh, seventh century BCE.

Lion orthostat from the temple at Hazor, probably Late Bronze Age (1500–1200 BCE).

whether they really represent Assyrian art or, as appears more likely, the distribution throughout the empire of Phoenician ivory.

Babylonian art from the sixth century BCE did not continue the Assyrian style. Instead, it appears to return to the style of pre-Assyrian days, reviving the southern Mesopotamian traditions. Buildings were mudbrick, ornamented with glazed bricks upon which huge bulls and dragons were depicted in bright colors. These beasts, however, by contrast with the gate guardians of the Assyrians, were purely decorative, as their profile images attest, e.g., on the Ishtar Gate. Notably too Babylonians provide us with an example of figures in true profile, as seen on the boundary stone of Marduk-apalaiddina (714 BCE). Finally, we have cylinder seals and a number of rather artless terra-cottas from the period of Nebuchadnezzar.

Near Eastern Art: The style and content encountered in Egypt and Mesopotamia occur again in the Levant. Since the area provided the corridor for trade and warfare between East and West, it should come as no surprise to find that the art of the region betrays the influence of the dominant cultures. To be sure, artistic efforts did not merely ape their sources. For example, figurines are more narrow-shouldered than their Egyptian counterparts and generally less substantial. A stele portraying the weather god found at Ras-Shamra (Ugarit) shows the figure with raised arm in a gesture depicting victory, typical of Egyptian reliefs, yet the god wears typical Syrian garb, including a horned cap symbolic of his divinity.

Large statuary of human figures is rare, but statuettes depicting fertility figures are numerous. These are typically nude female figures with exaggerated breasts and, often, hands raised toward the breasts. The orthostat animal sculptures of the Hittites have already been mentioned. Stone carving of excellent quality has also been found in the Late Bronze Age temple at Hazor. Relief carving is also plentiful, and especially noteworthy is a finely worked golden dish from Ras-Shamra bearing a hammered design of a hunter riding his chariot in pursuit of wild bulls and gazelles.

Israelite Art: Like the rest of the ancient Near East, Israel drew from Egyptian and Mesopotamian models, but, religious conviction determined the character and extent of Israelite artistic enterprise. Since the Torah expressly forbade the shaping of images and idols, the subjects that dominated sculpture and painting among its neighbors were not available to Israel. The only extant items that may be described as Israelite, in fact, are ivories and stamp seals. Seals were particularly numerous and clearly show Egyptian influence in subject matter: griffons, sphinxes, scarabs, and solar disks with wings. These seals were purely decorative, as the frequent inclusion of the owner's name indicates. They were mostly scarab in shape, in imitation of the Egyptian beetle, and made of semiprecious stones. Name seals, without any pictorial representation, have been found almost exclusively in Judah.

Ivories have been found at Megiddo, Samaria, and Hazor. The dominant influence on these pieces too was Egyptian, as the examples from Samaria showing a cherub astride a plant and the child-god Horus crouching upon a lotus indicate. The style of these ivories is Phoenician, and they would have come to Israel through that well-attested channel of trade and technical expertise (see 1 Kings 5–10).

The discovery of Astarte figurines in sites as separated as Megiddo and Hebron confirms the prophets' protest against the popularity of the "Queen of Heaven" as a fertility figure in Israel (Jer. 7:18; 44:17–19, 25). Some statuettes show influence from Egypt in the form of Astarte holding lotus flowers; others reflect a Babylonian style represented by the inclusion of a tiara.

Golden dish from Ras-Shamra: detail of a hunter in his chariot pursuing a wild bull, fourteenth century BCE.

Judean royal stamp-seal impression with symbol of a solar disk with wings, seventh century BCE. At top are the letters *lmlk* and below, the place-name *zp*, "Ziph."

Though nothing remains of Solomon's temple, a detailed description of its floor plan and furniture is provided by biblical tradition. Moreover, the tradition makes no claims to originality in this architectural effort; Solomon relied on Phoenician expertise. The resulting rectangular, tripartite plan was already well known in Egypt.

Bibliography
Frankfort, Henri. *The Art and Architecture of the Ancient Orient.* Penguin, 1969.
Lloyd, Seton. *The Art of the Ancient Near East.* Praeger, 1961.
Moscati, Sabatino. *The Face of the Ancient Orient.* Doubleday, 1962.

D.C.H./E.L.F.

Two winged genii with Horus in the center on a lotus. Ivory plaque from Arslan Tash, northern Syria, eighth century BCE.

Arumah (uh-*roo′*mah), the town where Abimelech, temporary king of Shechem, resided (Judg. 9:31, 41). It was probably modern Khirbet el-Ormeh, about five miles south and slightly east of Shechem and about seven miles north and slightly east of Shiloh.

Arvad (ahr′vad), a north Phoenician island city located 2 miles from shore about 125 miles north of Tyre, known today as Ruad. Its inhabitants are listed among the pre-Israelite descendants of Canaan (Gen. 10:18) and are mentioned in Ezek. 27:8, 11 as having served under Tyre.

Asa (ay′suh), the fifth king of the Davidic dynasty. Asa ruled Judah for a comparatively long period, ca. 913–873 BCE. In the beginning, his grandmother Maaca (a daughter of Absalom) probably acted as regent. The book of Kings presents him as a strict worshiper of God who suppressed the fertility cults of Asherah and Baal (see 1 Kings 15:9–24). Throughout Asa's reign, there were border conflicts between Judah and the northern kingdom, Israel. Asa's main opponent was Baasha, who ruled in Tirzah ca. 900–877. When this king of Israel fortified the strategically situated Ramah (only five miles north of Jerusalem) and thus tried to impose a blockade on the Judean capital, Asa decided to call upon the help of Ben-hadad I, the king of Damascus. The plan succeeded, for Ben-hadad's army invaded Galilee, and Baasha was forced to retreat. In his turn, Asa enlarged the villages of Gebah and Mizpah (a few miles east and north of Ramah, respectively) and rebuilt them as fortifications. A cistern that he built is mentioned later in Jer. 41:9; Ishmael, the killer of Gedelaiah, threw the bodies of eighty would-be worshipers into it. *See also* Baasha; Ramah.   J.P.F.

Asahel (as′uh-hel).
   1 The brother of Joab and nephew of David (1 Chron. 1:13–16). He was one of David's elite troops known as "the Thirty" (2 Sam. 23:24). He relentlessly pursued Abner and was killed by him (2:18–23). He was buried in Bethlehem (2:32).
   2 A Judean Levite who served during the reign of Jehoshaphat (2 Chron. 17:8).
   3 A temple overseer under Hezekiah (2 Chron. 31:13).
   4 The father of Jonathan, who lived during Ezra's administration (Ezra 10:15).

Asaiah (uh-zay′yuh).
   1 A servant of Josiah, commissioned, with others, to inquire of the Lord concerning the book of the law that had been found (2 Kings 22:12, 14; 2 Chron. 34:20), probably an early version of Deuteronomy.
   2 A family leader at the time of King Hezekiah in Judah (1 Chron. 4:36).
   3 A Levite and a member of the Merari family group; the son of Haggiah (1 Chron. 6:30; 15:6, 11).

   4 A Shilonite descendant of one of the men who returned to Judea from the Babylonian exile (1 Chron. 9:5).

Asaph (ay′saf; Heb., "collector").
   1 The father of the Joah who was recorder in the court of King Hezekiah of Judah (715–687/6 BCE; 2 Kings 18:18).
   2 A musician who was among those whom David appointed to oversee music in worship (1 Chron. 6:39) and who sang at the dedication of Solomon's temple (2 Chron. 5:12). A number of psalms were also attributed to him (Pss. 50, 73–83).
   3 A Levite whose descendants lived in Judah after the exile (1 Chron. 9:15).
   4 A Levite whose descendants served as gatekeepers in the temple (1 Chron. 26:1).
   5 The keeper of the forests of King Artaxerxes of Persia, who was commanded by royal letter to furnish timber for Nehemiah's restoration of the temple (mid- to late sixth century BCE; Neh. 2:8).
   6 According to Matthew's Gospel, the son of Abijah and father of Jehoshaphat and, so, an ancestor of Jesus (1:17–18).

ascension of Christ, the risen Jesus's departure into heaven after his final appearance to his disciples. It is described only in Luke 24:50–51 and Acts 1:2–11, although there may be allusions to it elsewhere in the NT (e.g., John 6:62; 20:17; Eph. 4:8–10). In the setting of Acts, the ascension is preparatory to the sending of the Spirit at Pentecost (2:1–4). The setting for the ascension has traditionally been regarded as the Mount of Olives. For possible biblical precedents, note the references to Enoch (Gen. 5:24) and Elijah (2 Kings 2:1–14). *See also* Elijah; Enoch; Holy Spirit; Olives, Mount of; Pentecost; resurrection.   J.M.E.

Asenath (as′uh-nath), the daughter of Potipherah, priest of On (Heliopolis) in Egypt. Pharaoh gave her in marriage to Joseph (Gen. 41:45). Their two sons were Manasseh and Ephraim (41:50–52; 46:20).

Ashan (ay′shuhn), a city in the southern lowlands of Judah, first given to the tribe of Judah (Josh. 15:42) and later reassigned to the tribe of Simeon because the Judahites were unable to conquer the territory originally given to them (19:7). It is possibly the same city listed as a city of refuge and given to the Levites (1 Chron. 6:59), although it is elsewhere called Ain (Josh. 21:16). The site is not known.

Ashbel (ash′bel), the (second?) son of Benjamin (Gen. 46:21; 1 Chron. 8:1).

Ashdod (ash′dod), a town in northern Judah two and a half miles inland from the Mediterranean coast. We know from the Ugaritic material that Ashdod, Accho, and Ashkelon dealt with Ugarit (Ras-Shamra) and hence existed as a city as early as the fourteenth century BCE. The city is supposed to have been allotted to Judah (Josh. 15:47); however, it was also one of the cities in the Philistine Pentapolis (Josh. 11:22; 13:3) and hence may never have come under Judah's control. The ark of the covenant was brought to the temple of Dagon in Ashdod when it was taken by the Philistines. The ark was later sent away (1 Sam. 5:1–8; 6:17).

The city was razed by King Uzziah (ca. 783–742 BCE) of Judah (2 Chron. 26:6). Later, it fell under the control of Sargon, king of Assyria (Isa. 20:1), and when Azuri, the reigning king of Ashdod, rebelled against this domination, he was replaced by his brother Ahimetu (712 BCE). Nevertheless, a year later Sargon had to suppress another Ashdod rebellion, and the town was annexed to the Assyrian Empire. After the conquests of Nebuchadnezzar, Ashdod became part of the Babylonian Empire and, during that period, it was mentioned several times in oracles of prophets (Jer. 25:20; Amos 1:8; 3:9; Zeph. 2:4; Zech. 9:6). At the end of the Babylonian exile, Nehemiah expressed contempt for Jews who had married "women of Ashdod" (Neh. 13:23) and whose children "spoke the language of Ashdod" (13:24). During the Hellenistic period (333–63 BCE) the name was changed to Azotus and Jonathan the Hasmonean destroyed the temple of Dagon (1 Macc. 10:84). Pompey and Galbinius partitioned Azotus from Judea (Josephus *Jewish War* 1.156, 165–66), but Augustus later gave the city to Herod, who in turn gave it to his sister Salome (ca. 38 CE). The evangelist Philip is reported to have passed through Azotus on his missionary travels (Acts 8:40). *See also* Dagon.   S.B.R.

Asher (ash´uhr; Heb., "happy").

1 The son of Jacob and Zilpah (Gen. 30:12–13) and the eponymous ancestor of the tribe Asher. Leah is said to have given him this name, because his birth made her happy and because she knew that women would deem her happy for bearing him. Some scholars have speculated that the name could derive from that of a god, the male counterpart of Asherah, or it may be a variant of Ashar, a divine name evident in Old Akkadian and Amorite lists.

2 The western highlands of Galilee, which constituted the ninth Solomonic district (1 Kings 4:16). The Blessings of Jacob (Gen. 49:20) and of Moses (Deut. 33:24–25) allude to the fertility of Asher's land.

3 One of the twelve tribes of Israel, regarded as descendants of 1 above and as residents of 2. The tribe was rebuked by Joshua for failing to drive out the Canaanites who dwelt in this land (Judg. 1:31), and they were likewise criticized in the Song of Deborah for failing to participate in the battle against Sisera (5:17). They did, however, respond to Gideon's calls to expel the Midianites (6:35; 7:23). In the NT, Anna the prophet is said to be of the tribe of Asher (Luke 2:36). *See also* tribes.

Asherah (uh-shihr´uh).

1 A Canaanite goddess, the wife of El according to Ugaritic tradition, but the consort of Baal in Canaan. In Ugaritic literature she is called "Lady Asherah of the Sea," a title that may signify "she who treads on the sea." Apart from her name, she has other connections with the sea. Her servant is called "fisherman of Lady Asherah of the Sea." A drinking cup from Ras-Shamra seems to portray her under water.

The cult of Asherah was ancient. Tyre seems to have been a major center for her veneration. Her cult was widely diffused, but combinations with the figures Anat and Astarte and other factors have made its identification problematic. She was called, in addition to Asherah, Elat ("Goddess") and Qudshu ("Holy"). Asherah probably stands behind the Punic goddess Tanit (perhaps "she of the Serpent").

Asherah plays an important role in the mythological texts from Ras-Shamra in modern northern Syria. The gods are regarded as the children of Asherah and El. As the wife of El, Asherah is called on to intercede with her husband on behalf of the project of building a palace for Baal. Her relationship with Baal is perplexing. Baal's assault on the offspring of Asherah is once narrated, yet Asherah advocates for Baal the role of king and judge among the gods. A Canaanite myth that survives only in a Hittite version ("El, Ashertu, and the Storm God") reveals that Asherah once sought the storm god (Baal) as a lover, a quest achieved with El's approval but to the eventual

A life-size statue of the Canaanite goddess Asherah, ninth century BCE. The biblical prophets denounced the cult of Asherah, blaming its following in Israel on the influence of Jezebel.

humiliation of Asherah. In the Ugaritic legend of Kirta (Keret), Asherah receives a vow from Kirta, but when he fails to fulfill his vow, she brings sickness upon him. Asherah is a mother figure, and it is announced that the offspring of Kirta will take nourishment at her breasts.

Although the name of Asherah is associated with that of Baal and they were evidently a divine couple, Hebrew jar inscriptions from Kuntillet 'Ajrud raise the problem of the relationship between YHWH (i.e., Israel's God) and Asherah. These inscriptions permit a reading that associates YHWH of Samaria with "his Asherah." If correct, these readings would demonstrate that in popular religion YHWH was associated with a consort, Asherah. But the noun "Asherah" may also signify "sanctuary" or refer to a cult object (see 2 below), and so the interpretation of the Kuntillet 'Ajrud inscriptions can be disputed.

In the Bible Asherah remains a Canaanite goddess whose veneration in Israel is blamed on Jezebel (see 1 Kings 18:19). Jezebel's Asherah had four hundred prophets. Asherah was also worshiped in the south, and 1 Kings praises Asa for destroying a detestable image made for Asherah (15:13). Manasseh, by contrast, is blamed for erecting a statue of Asherah (2 Kings 21:7). Vessels sacred to Asherah were also deposited in the Jerusalem temple (2 Kings 23:4). *See also* Anat; Baal; El; Ras-Shamra.

2 An object or objects (the plural is also spelled "asherah") used in worship, the exact identification of which is unclear. A high place might have an asherah (1 Kings 14:23; 2 Kings 18:4), but an asherah could also be found outside a high place. The Baal temple at Samaria had an asherah (1 Kings 16:33). Some asherah may have been carved from wood (Judg. 6:25); others may have been living trees (Deut. 16:21). Deuteronomy commands the destruction of asherah by burning (12:3). The use of asherah is persistently opposed in Israel's literature (Mic. 5:12–13; Deut. 16:21). *See also* high place.   R.M.G.

ashes, remains of a fire, which in the Bible are often mentioned in conjunction with dust and signify destruction (Ezek. 28:18; Mal. 4:3; Heb. 3:21; 2 Pet. 2:6); they are also contrasted with glory (Isa. 61:3). Sitting on them or putting them on one's head were rituals of mourning and repentance (2 Sam. 13:19; Isa. 58:5; Jer. 6:26). The ashes of a heifer could be used in purification rites (Num. 19:9; Heb. 9:13). Ashes are also mentioned as symbolic of insignificance (Gen. 18:27).

Ashkelon (ash'kuh-lon; also Askalon, Askelon, Eshkalon, Ascalon), a city located about twelve miles north of Gaza. It was loyal to Egypt (Tell el-Amarna texts, ca. 1400–1360 BCE) and was identified as one of the Philistine Pentapolis cities (Josh. 13:3; 1 Sam. 6:4, 17; Judg. 14:19). The Merneptah Stele (ca. 1230 BCE) indicates that Ashkelon, Gezer, and Yanoam were conquered by Pharaoh Merneptah. Ramesses II reconquered

Ashkelon ca. 1280 BCE. Tiglath-pileser III took Ashkelon for Assyria ca. 734 BCE. Hezekiah of Judah and Sidqa of Ashkelon revolted against Assyria, but Sennacherib (701 BCE) reconquered it. Psammetichus I (664–609 BCE) of Egypt took Ashkelon before Nebuchadnezzar of Babylonia destroyed it (609 BCE; Jer. 47:5–7; Zeph. 2:4–7). A Tyrian possession during the Persian period (539–333 BCE), it was a Ptolemaic possession during the Hellenistic period (301–198 BCE).   S.B.R.

Ashkenaz (ash'kuh-naz).
  1 Noah's great-grandson (Gen. 10:3).
  2 A nation near Armenia (Jer. 51:27), generally identified with the Ashkuza, an Indo-European people mentioned in seventh-century Assyrian inscriptions, and with the Scythians mentioned by Herodotus.

Ashtaroth (ash'tuh-roth), the capital city of Og, king of Bashan, whom the Israelites under Moses defeated in battle (Deut. 1:4; cf. Josh. 9:10; 12:4). It is later mentioned as a city of refuge given to the Gershomites, a levitical group, from the territory of the half-tribe of Manasseh (1 Chron. 6:71). It was located to the east of the Sea of Galilee. Because the name is the plural form of Ashtoreth, the Canaanite goddess of fertility, it is probable that the city was once a special place of her worship. *See also* Asherah; Og.

Ashtoreth (ash'tuh-reth), the female consort of the Caananite deity El. *See also* Asherah.

Ashurbanipal (ash'uhr-ban'uh-puhl). *See* Assyria, Empire of.

Ashurnasirpal (ash'uhr-nas'uhr-puhl) **II,** the king of Assyria from 883 to 859 BCE, who by means of regular military campaigns to the four quarters of the Near East forged a new Assyrian Empire. In the West, he reached as far as Betheden (Amos 1:5) and Carchemish (Isa. 10:9). The royal inscriptions depict him as a valiant warrior, mercilessly punishing all resisters. Calah (modern Nimrud), completely rebuilt and repopulated with captives, served as his main administrative center. *See also* Assyria, Empire of.   M.C.

Asia (ay'zhuh), a term occasionally referring to the old Persian Empire, but more generally to the Seleucid kingdoms, whose rulers were called "the kings of Asia" (1 Macc. 8:6). When Attalus III died (133 BCE), he willed his kingdom to Rome, who called the new province "Asia" from the ruler's title. Thus, in the NT, Asia usually refers to a Roman province, one that was evangelized quickly by Christian missionaries (Acts 13–16). Ephesus and Colossae are among the cities located there. Paul reports that he and his companions suffered terrible affliction in Asia, so that they despaired of life itself (2 Cor. 1:8). In Rom. 16:5, he says that Epaenetus was "the first convert in Asia for Christ." A negative report regarding the loyalty of

Paul's Asian converts is offered in 2 Tim. 1:15. The Revelation to John was addressed to "the seven churches of Asia," the coastal cities of Ephesus, Smyrna, Pergamum, Thyatira, Sardis, Philadelphia, and Laodicea (1:4, 11), and some of those to whom 1 Peter was addressed also lived in Asia (1:1). In the early second century, Pliny wrote to Rome about persecuting the Christian churches in Asia.   J.H.N.

Asiarchs (ay'zhee-ahrks), Roman administrative officials selected by a league of cities in the province of Asia. Their duties included overseeing local rituals and ceremonies on behalf of Rome and the emperor. Acts 19:31 represents that some Asiarchs in Ephesus were friendly toward Paul.

asp, a poisonous snake (*Naja haja*). In Isa. 11:18, ultimate peace and security are symbolized by a nursing child playing over the hole of an asp. Elsewhere, people are depicted as having the "venom of asps" within them (Job 20:14; cf. Deut. 32:33).

Asriel (as'ree-uhl), a son of Manasseh by his Aramean concubine (1 Chron. 7:14), probably the same person identified elsewhere as Manasseh's great-grandson (Num. 26:31), although it is possible these are different persons.

ass, a four-footed equine mammal common in both the wild and domesticated state in biblical times. The domestic version is sometimes called a donkey to distinguish it from an ass, which then, by definition, is wild. The NRSV generally preserves this distinction and uses "donkey" for the domestic animal. The wild ass is portrayed most vividly in Job 39:5–8: it enjoys the freedom of the desert and finds its own pasture; thus it can represent the presence of the desert where once there were bustling cities (Isa. 32:14). Ishmael is characterized as a wild ass (Gen. 16:12).

The domesticated ass or donkey appears as a basic item in inventories of a person's property (e.g., Exod. 22:8, 9; 23:4, 5; Job 24:3; Luke 13:15), and the number of donkeys was one of the measures of a person's wealth or of an army's booty. Donkeys are most frequently referred to as a means of transport for goods or people (e.g., 2 Sam. 16:1–2), but occasionally they appear as draft animals (e.g., Isa. 30:24). Issachar is called a donkey because his life is hard labor (Gen. 49:14; cf. Sir. 33:24). Though they usually knew where they were kept (Isa. 1:3), donkeys would not infrequently wander off and get lost (Exod. 23:4; Deut. 22:1–3; 1 Sam. 9–10). Under siege conditions starvation might lead people to pay eighty shekels of silver for a donkey's head, according to 2 Kings 6:25. Normally a dead donkey was simply dragged outside the city and thrown away (Jer. 22:19). Samson used a donkey's jawbone, which he found lying on the ground, to slay a thousand Philistines. Balaam's talking donkey showed greater insight and loyalty than its master (Num. 22:21–35; cf. 2 Pet. 2:16). In the ancient Near East gods

The hunting of wild asses. On the upper register, two men hold a captured wild ass with ropes. On the bottom, two of the animals flee. Bas-reliefs from Ashurbanipal's palace at Nineveh, seventh century BCE.

and kings rode on donkeys. So in the prophecy of Zech. 9:9 the new king of Jerusalem comes to the city riding on a donkey—as then does Jesus (Matt. 21:1–11; Mark 11:1–11; Luke 19:28–38; John 12:12–19).   S.B.P.

assassins (Gk. *sikarioi*; Lat. *sicarii*, from *sica*, "dagger"), the term used in the NRSV for the Sicarii (lit., "dagger men"), a group of Jewish revolutionaries who, according to Josephus, operated surreptitiously against the Romans and their collaborators prior to the revolt of 66 CE. In Acts 21:38, Paul is mistakenly thought to be one of their leaders. *See also* Zealots.

Asshur (ash'uhr), ancient Assyria. In Mesopotamia, Asshur designates the nation and land of Assyria, its oldest capital city, and its god. Originally, the name was associated with just the city and god; its national significance was added in Middle Assyrian times (1500–900 BCE), when the city expanded into a state.

The city itself, modern Qala'at Sharqat (in Iraq) lies on a promontory overlooking the Tigris River. Its history stretches from ca. 3000 to 614 BCE, during which it developed from a satellite of southern Mesopotamia (3000–2000), through an independent city-state (2000–1500), to the capital of the territorial state and empire of Middle Assyria (1500–900), finally to one of several centers—and the primary one for the cultural and religious traditions—of the enlarged Neo-Assyrian Empire (900–614). There was, in addition, a revival in the Parthian period, ca. 100 BCE–250 CE.

Paralleling this history was that of the god Asshur, who is first attested as the patron of the city ca. 2000 BCE and thereafter grew into the principal deity of the Assyrian state and empire, taking on characteristics of many other gods, particularly the Babylonian gods Enlil and Marduk.

In the Bible, Asshur apparently refers only to the nation or land (e.g., Isa. 19:23–25) or, by extension, to its eponymous ancestor (Gen. 10:22; 1 Chron. 1:17). There is no clear mention of the city (Gen. 10:11; Ezek. 27:23 likely indicate the land) or of the god (except obliquely, as an element in the royal name Esarhaddon: 2 Kings 19:37; Isa. 37:38; Ezra 4:2). *See also* Assyria, Empire of.

Bibliography

Harper, P. O., et al. *Discoveries at Ashur on the Tigris.* Metropolitan Museum of Art, 1995.

P.B.M.

Assir (as'uhr; Heb., "captive").

1 The son of Korah and great-grandson of Uzziel (Exod. 6:24).

2 The son of Ebiasaph and great-grandson of 1 (1 Chron. 6:23).

3 The son of a second Ebiasaph and the great-grandson of Izhar the brother of Uzziel (1 Chron. 6:37). *See also* Ebiasaph.

D.R.B.

Assos (as'os), a seaport on the northwest coast of Asia Minor, visited by Paul (Acts 20:13–14).

assurance, as a theological concept, a sense of certainty regarding God and God's utter trustworthiness. The concept is developed most explicitly in Christian theology and with reference to NT texts. For example, the Letter to the Hebrews speaks of "the full assurance of hope" to be realized through diligence (6:11) and also describes faith as "the assurance of things hoped for" (Heb. 11:1; cf. 10:22). In general, the NT authors maintain that assurance is created by God's self-witness and sustained by the experience of God's repeated righteous fidelity (Rom. 5–7; 2 Cor. 1:3–11; 1 Thess. 1; 2:13–16; 2 Tim. 1:12; cf. Isa. 32:17). Above all, the resurrection of Christ is said to offer assurance of God's righteousness, albeit a righteousness that demands repentance and portends judgment (Acts 17:31). *See also* faith; hope; promise.

J.E.A./M.A.P.

Assyria (uh-sihr'ee-uh), **Empire of,** one of the major empires of the ancient Near East. The heartland and original core of Assyria lay in what is now northern Iraq around the upper Tigris River. Its initial development as a territorial state and empire came in the second millennium BCE, in the Old and Middle Assyrian periods. But its greatest period—and the only one involving direct contact with Israel—was its last: the Neo-Assyrian period of the first millennium BCE (934–609). The triumphant achievement of Neo-Assyria was the creation of an empire that went far beyond earlier forms to become the largest political configuration the Near East had yet seen. Four phases marked the course of this achievement.

In the first phase (934–824 BCE), Ashur-dan II, Adad-nirari II, Tukulti-ninurta II, Ashurnasirpal II, and Shalmaneser III halted the Aramean attacks that had plagued Assyria for the preceding three centuries and counterattacked to the west through Syria; the best known of their battles occurred at Qarqar in 853 between Shalmaneser and a Syro-Palestinian coalition that included Ahab of Israel. In these, as in other campaigns to the north,

Ashurbanipal, king of Assyria, carrying a basket for the rebuilding of the temple of Esagila in Babylon, seventh century BCE.

east, and Babylonian south, the Assyrians wanted not so much permanent conquest—although they achieved some of that in territories immediately to their west—as the neutralization of external threats and the acquisition of booty and prisoners. The latter were then put to use, e.g., in building projects like Ashurnasirpal's grandiose reconstruction of the city of Calah.

The death of Shalmaneser III (824) initiated the second phase (824–744 BCE). Its first decades saw more military activity against the Arameans, of which one beneficiary was Israel (2 Kings 13:5). But in the main this was a time of Assyrian retreat, brought on by the growing power of its northern neighbor, Urartu, and by the growing challenge to royal authority by various members of the royal family and other royal officials. With Assyria and the Arameans thus weak, it is no surprise that in the latter years of this phase (770–744 BCE) Israel and Judah were able to expand their territories significantly, under their kings Jeroboam II (2 Kings 14:23–29) and Uzziah (2 Chron. 26).

Assyria's troubles were reversed in the third and climactic phase of the Neo-Assyrian period (744–627), the time of Tiglath-pileser III, Shalmaneser V, Sargon II, Sennacherib, Esar-haddon, and Ashurbanipal. Under the standard set by Tiglath-pileser, they restored and centralized royal power and established a standing army, whose constant campaigning and improved skill and equipment eventually brought under Assyrian sway almost all of the Near East. The aim now was not only spoils, but permanent and organized conquest: an empire of provinces and vassal states backed by an increased use of population resettlement to control the conquered.

To administer this, the bureaucracy became more complex and more dependent on non-Assyrian deportees, especially Arameans, whose language and culture gradually pervaded the whole. In turn, to display the newfound power, the heartland capitals of Asshur, Calah, and Nineveh were made larger and more splendid, and a new, though short-lived, capital was added, Dur-Sharrukin. Nineveh, moreover, became under Ashurbanipal the repository of the largest collection of Mesopotamian literature ever assembled.

This empire had serious flaws, however, largely deriving from overexpansion. Thus, its heartland grew increasingly dependent on tribute and deportees from the conquered areas, who, being increasingly burdened, revolted whenever they could. Israel joined revolts against Tiglath-pileser, Shalmaneser, and Sargon and paid for its "disobedience" by dismemberment into provinces and deportation (732–720 BCE; 2 Kings 17, 18:1–12). Judah, fearing the consequences, remained a loyal vassal through these revolts. Eventually, however, it too yielded, joining the outbreak against Sennacherib, who responded harshly but allowed Judah to resume its vassal status (704–701 BCE; 18:13–20:21).

These recurring revolts, encouraged by peripheral states like Egypt, strained Assyrian resources and organization. They also exacerbated the never absent tensions within the Assyrian ruling elite, which resurfaced especially in the assassination of Sennacherib (681 BCE) and in the civil war between Ashurbanipal and his brother, Shamash-shuma-ukin, who was regent of Babylonia, the most troublesome and complicated of Assyria's vassal states (652–648 BCE). Ashurbanipal won this war, but the ensuing military and political exhaustion began a loosening of imperial authority.

The process accelerated after Ashurbanipal's death (627 BCE), in the fourth and final phase of Neo-Assyrian history (627–609 BCE). Now many subjects openly asserted their independence—e.g., Judah under King Josiah; Babylonia under its new Neo-Babylonian/Chaldean dynasty; the Medes—and conflict broke out again among the Assyrian elite for what power remained. Exploiting this conflict, the Medes and Chaldeans began attacking the Assyrian heartland, and between 614 and 612 BCE the capital cities fell into their hands. The Assyrian army, always a kind of state within the state, held out a little while longer in Harran to the west, apparently with Egyptian support. But in 610–609 BCE, a Chaldean army dislodged the Assyrian forces with help from Josiah of Judah, who at the cost of his life delayed the arrival of Egyptian forces (2 Kings 23:29–30). With that, the Assyrian state disappeared, and the bulk of its territories were taken by the Chaldeans; Assyrian administrative and legal practices, however, continued to be attested for some time afterward in the western part of the former state. *See also* Aram; Babylon; Chaldea; Esar-haddon; Nineveh; Sargon II; Sennacherib; Shalmaneser; Tiglath-pileser III; Uzziah.   P.B.M.

Astarte (as-tahr'tee). *See* Asherah.

astrologer, a person who reads the influence of the stars on human and terrestrial affairs, supposedly foretelling events by the positions of the planets and stars. Clay tablets show that astrology flourished among the ancient Assyrians and Babylonians (ca. 1000–500 BCE). Belief that the stars influence human affairs appears occasionally in the Bible (Judg. 5:20; Job 38:33). It is generally associated with apostasy (Isa. 47:13–14) or with the Gentile nations (Dan. 1:20; 2:2, 10). Combined with Greek mathematics, astrology came into the Greco-Roman world during the Hellenistic period (325–63 BCE). Fragments of what appears to be a horoscope of the messiah have been found among the Dead Sea Scrolls. The magi (Matt. 2:1–12) were led to Jesus by observation of an unusual astronomical phenomenon at the time of his birth. *See also* magi.   P.P.

Atad (ay'tad; from Akkadian *etidu*), either the name of a person who owned a threshing floor mentioned in Gen. 50:10–11 or the name of the place where that threshing floor was found. Jacob's family (returning from Egypt with Joseph) stopped there to mourn his death, and the extent of their mourning led the Canaanites to name (or rename) the place Abel-mizraim, meaning "mourning." The location of this "threshing floor of Atad" is unknown, except that it was in the Transjordan.

Ataroth (at'uh-roth).

1 Khirbet Attarus, eight miles northwest of Dibon (Num. 32:3, 34), associated with the tribe of Gad.

2 Tell el-Mazar, an east border town of Ephraim (Josh. 16:7).

3 Part of the compound name Ataroth-addar (Josh. 16:5; 18:13), a border town between Ephraim and Benjamin, modern-day Kefer 'Aqab.

Ater (ay'tuhr).

1 A family group ("descendants of Ater") who returned with Zerubbabel from the Babylonian exile (Ezra 2:16).

2 A family group of gatekeepers who returned from the Babylonian exile (Ezra 2:42).

3 A member of the postexilic community who signed Ezra's covenant to keep the law (Neh. 10:17); he could be associated with either of the families identified in 1 and 2.

Athaliah (ath'uh-li'uh; Heb., "the LORD is strong"), the only ruling queen of Judah, ca. 843/2–837 BCE. She was the daughter of King Ahab and Jezebel of Israel and was the wife of Jehoram, king of Judah (ca. 849–843/2 BCE). She is said to have introduced Baal worship in Jerusalem during Jehoram's reign (2 Kings 8:16–18); after he was killed, she served as counselor to their son Ahaziah, who reigned for one year (8:25–27). After Jehu murdered Ahaziah, Athaliah instigated a purge of the entire royal family (11:1) and, believing that she had successfully killed all contenders for the throne, she declared herself to be the sovereign. The scheme was ultimately undone, however, when, after seven years, it was revealed that one of the heirs (Ahaziah's infant son Joash) had been saved by his aunt, Jehosheba (Jehoshabeath). Jehoiada the priest then mounted a successful coup against Athaliah: she was executed, and Joash was made king (11:2–20). *See also* Jehoiada; Jehoshabeath; Joash.   M.A.P.

Athens (ath′inz), a major city in ancient Greece and later the Roman provincial capital of Attica (2 Macc. 9:15; Acts 17:15–18; 18:1; 1 Thess. 3:1). The name "Athens" antedates the arrival of the Indo-European peoples in Greece (ca. 2000 BCE). The city stands on a site that has been continuously inhabited since the fourth millennium BCE. In Mycenaean times (ca. 1300–1225 BCE) it was a fortified citadel with a palace and cult sanctuary to Eros Aphrodite. What would later become the agora was at that time a burial site.

The Classical Period: The glory of classical Athens belongs to the fifth century BCE. Tribute money from the vast Athenian empire and its commerce paid for the beautiful buildings erected on the acropolis (454–414 BCE). The Parthenon was built in honor of the goddess Athena. Its architects had mastered the details of perspective and curvature so that they could make its rows of columns appear straight even when viewed along the building's longitudinal axis. The figures sculpted for the processional frieze are completely finished on all sides as though they were to have been viewed straight on and not from 39 feet below. Some four hundred people and two hundred animals are shown participating in the Panathenaic procession, which brought the goddess a new sacred robe every fourth year. The great statue of Athena is known to us from copies. Clothed in a gold robe, the goddess had ivory limbs and an ivory face. She wore gold earrings, necklace, and bracelet, and a military helmet with the sphinx and winged Pegasoi. One hand held a spear. Her shield portrayed the gods and giants. The sacred snake, Erichthonius, was entwined around her left leg while her right hand held an image of a winged victory.

The Hephaisteion temple overlooking the agora is the most perfectly preserved temple of the era. The Erechtheum, built on the site of the Mycenaean palace, was begun in 421 BCE, but interrupted by the Peloponnesian War in 415 and not resumed until 409. It was thought to stand on a holy spot where Poseidon had stuck his trident in the ground and Athena had caused the sacred olive tree to spring up. Its innovative caryatid porch had six maidens, all different, supporting the roof. The Roman emperor Hadrian later had a complete copy made for his villa at Tivoli.

This period also saw considerable building in the agora, including a prison, a council house, a building for semipublic meetings, and several stoa, or colonnaded porches (the Painted Stoa, the Stoa of Zeus, and the long double-aisled stoa to the south). The theater of Dionysus was built on the south slope of the acropolis during the fourth century BCE. The theater as seen today comes from the last part of that century. It seated between fourteen and seventeen thousand. The scene building may have had a temporary stage. The permanent stage was added during the Hellenistic period. The Romans added a marble barrier around the orchestra to protect spectators at beast fights and gladiator shows. In the second century BCE the Stoa of Attalos, which has been reconstructed to house the agora museum, was built.

The Augustan Age and Later: The Augustan age (31 BCE–14 CE) saw some Roman building activity, even though the city as a whole had experienced significant decline after Rome emerged as the dominant political force in the Mediterranean. Julius Caesar had planned a Roman forum for Athens. A small round temple to Rome and the emperor Augustus modeled after the Vesta in Rome was built on the acropolis east of the Parthenon. In the center of the old orchestra in the Greek agora Agrippa built an auditorium for about one thousand persons. The Romans also dismantled and brought to the agora a temple to Ares, which was built in fifth-century BCE style.

There is little evidence of any building in the agora during the first century CE, when Athens was a university town of little political or economic importance. The inscription from an early second-century library reads, "No books circulate. Open 6 A.M. to noon." The middle of the second century saw a new building spree under the hellenophile emperor Hadrian (117–138 CE) including a huge temple to Olympian Zeus, a gymnasium, and a library north of the Roman agora. Agrippa's Odeon, used as a lecture hall, was remodeled in 150 CE to hold five hundred persons and was decorated with pairs of statues representing the various philosophical schools in the city. *See also* agora; Areopagus; theater.

Bibliography

Alcock, Susan E. *Graecia Capta: The Landscapes of Roman Greece.* Cambridge University Press, 1993.

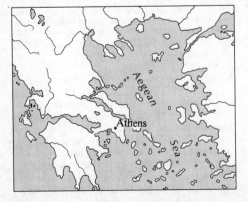

MacKendrick, Paul. *The Greek Stones Speak.* 2nd ed. Norton, 1981.

Wycherley, Richard E. *How the Greeks Built Cities.* 2nd ed. Doubleday, 1969.   P.P.

atonement, the means by which the chain of guilt and punishment produced by violation of God's will is broken and the resulting state of reconciliation ("at-one-ment") with God is achieved. The character of atonement varied greatly in ancient Near Eastern religion, depending on concepts of the deity, human existence, and what constituted violation.

In the NRSV, the word "atonement" appears seventy-nine times in the Hebrew Bible and four times in the NT (Rom 3:25; Heb 2:17; 1 John 2:2; 4:10). The Hebrew word with which the concept of atonement is most often associated in the Bible can also be translated as "purge," "cleanse," "expiate," "purify," "wipe on or off," or "cover."

The Bible associates a number of offerings and sacrifices with atonement. Basic to their development was an understanding of God as the faithful covenant partner to Israel. God did not need appeasement; rather, atonement removed barriers to the covenantal relationship. Through atonement, God provided the means of restoring and continuing the covenant relationship when the sanctuary or the land become defiled or when the people had proven unfaithful. Rites of atonement were carried out by the high priest through prescribed sacrifices in the temple. Covenant renewal and restoration were connected to the Day of Atonement (Lev. 16).

In the NT, atonement is linked conclusively to the ministry, death, and resurrection of Jesus. The Gospels present Jesus as understanding his destiny in atoning terms (Mark 10:45b; 14:24; cf. Isa. 53; Exod. 32:30–32). Early Christian thought developed this and other concepts against biblical backgrounds. Paul identifies the blood of Jesus as "a sacrifice of atonement" (Rom. 3:25). For Hebrews, Jesus's role is likened to that of the high priest (Heb. 2:17; 4:14–5:10; 10:19–21; cf. Lev. 16; Ps. 110:1–4). The concept of atonement as "redemption" (1 Cor. 6:20; 7:23; Gal. 3:13; 4:5) may have its background in other biblical texts (Exod. 4:22–23; 21:30; 30:16; Num. 35:31–33). *See also* Atonement, Day of; blood; covenant; pardon; priests; reconciliation; redemption; sacrifice; salvation; sin.   J.E.A.

Atonement, Day of (Heb. *yom kippur*), a festival observed in Israel ten days after the fall new year (Lev. 16:29; 23:27) to purify the sanctuary and altar and atone for the sins and impurities of the high priest and Israel for the past year (16:1–34; 23:26–32; Num. 29:7–11). The high priest sacrificed a bull for himself and a goat for Israel and used the blood to remove the impurities of the sanctuary and altar. On this day, only the high priest entered the Holy of Holies, the innermost room of the tent or temple. There, he sprinkled blood from the bull and goat on the top and front of the "cover" (or mercy seat) of the ark of the covenant. In a related ritual, the priest symbolically placed the sins of the people upon another goat (the so-called scapegoat) that was then driven into the wilderness, taking the sins and impurities away. Israel observed this festival as a day of fasting on which no work was done. In the NT, Heb. 8–9 draws heavily on the ritual and symbolism of the Day of Atonement as analogies for explaining Christ's atoning sacrifice for sin. *See also* Azazel; tabernacle; temple, the.   A.J.S.

Attai (at'i).

1 The son of Sheshan's daughter and his Egyptian slave, Jarha (1 Chron. 2:35, 36).

2 A Gadite warrior who supported David at Ziklag, representing northern allegiance (1 Chron. 12:11).

3 The second son of King Rehoboam, thus a grandson of Solomon (2 Chron. 11:20).

Attalia (at'uh-li'uh), a seaport on the southern coast of Asia Minor. The city was the harbor for Perga, capital of the province of Pamphylia. From here, Paul and Barnabas sailed to Antioch at the end of their first journey (Acts 14:25).

Augustus (aw-guhs'tuhs; Lat., "august, revered"), a title granted to Octavian (63 BCE– 14 CE), the grand-nephew and adopted heir of Julius Caesar, by the Roman Senate in 27 BCE, when it confirmed his powers to rule (Lat. *imperium*). He was the Roman ruler when Jesus was born (Luke 2:1). Though Augustus was in fact the sole ruler of the empire, he ostensibly contented himself with only the necessary powers of rule, the supreme command of most of the army (*imperium proconsulare*) and the consular powers over the city of Rome (*imperium consulare*). When Augustus ceased to stand for annual election to the consulate, he was granted new tribunician powers. These included powers he already possessed, such as personal immunity from prosecution and appellate jurisdiction and added powers to convene the Senate and popular assembly and to submit measures to either at any time. He could also veto any item of public business or the action of any other magistrate.

Administration of provinces requiring military presence was entrusted to legates who were personal emissaries of the emperor. Augustus created the foundations of Roman imperial power. The title *augustus* implies reverence, honor, and growth and was translated in the Greek East as *sebastos*, the "revered one." This institutionalized the process by which the emperor and his family were deified, which began when Julius Caesar was elevated to a deity after his death; Octavian was then considered the *divi filius*, the "son of a god." *See also* Roman Empire; Rome.   P.P.

Avaris (uh-vahr'is), the capital of the Asiatic Hyksos in the eastern Nile Delta. It was overrun by Egyptian forces in the resurgence beginning the

New Kingdom (ca. 1530 BCE). Avaris may be modern Tell el-Dab'a or possibly San el-Hagar, ancient Tanis, both of which have impressive remains. *See also* Hyksos; Zoan.

Aven (ay'ven; Heb., "evil power").

1 A term used to describe Bethel in Hosea's indictment (10:9). As such, it was an abbreviation for Beth-aven ("house of wickedness"), a pejorative term for Bethel used in Hos. 4:15; 5:8; 10:5. *See also* Beth-aven.

2 A derisive term for a valley mentioned in Amos 1:5. The prophet is probably referring to the Aramean valley between the Lebanon and Anti-Lebanon mountain ranges, calling it the Valley of Aven ("Valley of Wickedness").   M.A.P.

avenger, one who extracts satisfaction from or punishes a wrongdoer. In the ancient Near East, reliance on avengers to ensure justice was evident when strong governmental authority was lacking. In some biblical texts, blood vengeance, the execution of a murderer by the avenger, is recognized as a custom sanctioned by God (Gen. 9:5–6; Num. 35:16–21), although this custom is to be limited by a sense of compassion and mercy (Gen. 4:10–16; Num. 35:9–15, 22–28). Unlimited vengeance is presented as part of the lawlessness that led to the flood (Gen. 4:23–24). In some texts, God's people may be used by God to exercise vengeance against God's enemies (Judg. 12:3–6; 2 Kings 9:7; Jos. 10:13), but they are forbidden to take vengeance upon one another (Lev. 19:18). Elsewhere, God is the avenger (Ps. 94).

In the NT, Jesus taught his followers not to execute vengeance (Matt. 5:38–42; Rom. 12:17–19), but martyrs nevertheless cry out for vengeance (Rev. 10:9). Thus, the concept of vengeance is not rejected, though God is portrayed as one who must avenge the suffering of the faithful (Rev. 19:2) and punish evildoers (1 Thess. 4:6; Rom. 12:19). According to Paul, however, the state can also execute vengeance on God's behalf (Rom. 13:4). *See also* blood; justice; mercy; vengeance.   A.Y.C.

ax, battle-ax. *See* weapons.

Azarel (az'uh-rel; Heb., "God has helped").

1 A Korahite who became one of David's warriors (1 Chron. 12:6, Hebrew v. 7).

2 The son of Jeroham, a Danite leader in the time of David (1 Chron. 27:22).

3 A levitical musician in the time of David (1 Chron. 25:18; often identified with Uzziel in 1 Chron. 25:4).

4 A postexilic Israelite who divorced his foreign wife in response to Ezra's proclamation (Ezra 10:41).

5 A postexilic priest living in Jerusalem (Neh. 11:13).

6 A postexilic priest who participated in the dedication of the wall at the time of Nehemiah (Neh. 12:36, possibly the same as 5).

Azariah (az'uh-ri'uh; Heb., "the LORD has helped"; also Azaryah, Azaryahu).

1 The king of Judah (2 Kings 14:21; 15:1, 7, 17, 23, 27; 1 Chron. 3:12) otherwise known as Uzziah. *See also* Uzziah.

2–3 Two sons of the Judean king Jehoshaphat (2 Chron. 21:2).

4 Azariah son of Nathan, a "high official" under Solomon, placed over other officials (1 Kings 4:5; 2 Chron. 23:1).

5 The son of Oded; a prophet who spoke encouraging words to Asa (2 Chron. 15:1).

6 The son of Zadok; a priest listed as a high official under Solomon (1 Kings 4:2).

7 The original name of Abednego before he was renamed by Nebuchadnezzar (Dan. 1:6–7, 11, 19; 2:17; 1 Macc. 2:59; Song of Three Jews 1:65).
P.B.M.

Azazel (uh-zay'zuhl), a demonic figure to whom the sin-laden scapegoat was sent on the Day of Atonement (Lev. 16:8, 10, 26). *See also* Atonement, Day of.

Azaziah (az'uh-zi'uh; Heb., "the LORD is mighty").

1 A levitical musician during the reign of King David (1 Chron. 15:21).

2 The father of Hoshea, the military commander of the tribe of Benjamin (1 Chron. 27:20).

3 A levitical temple official during the reign of King Hezekiah who helped collect the tithes (2 Chron. 31:13).

Azekah (uh-zee'kuh), a city in Judah a short distance northeast of Lachish, probably to be identified with modern Tell ez-Zahariyeh. Joshua is said to have assaulted Amorite kings at Gibeon and to have pursued them "as far as Azekah" (Josh. 10:10–11; 15:35). The Philistines and Goliath camped between Succoth and Azekah (1 Sam. 17:1). Rehoboam fortified this city (2 Chron. 11:9). When Nebuchadnezzar attacked Jerusalem and the fortified cities of Judah, only Azekah and Lachish were left in the Judean countryside (Jer. 34:7). Azekah is also mentioned along with Lachish in the Lachish letters.   S.B.R.

Azel (ay'zuhl), a Benjaminite, a descendant of Saul's son Jonathan (1 Chron. 8:37).

Azgad (az'gad; Heb., "Gad is mighty").

1 A family group ("descendants of Azgad") who returned with Zerubbabel from the Babylonian exile (Ezra 2:12).

2 Another group who returned with Ezra (Ezra 8:12).

3 A member of the postexilic community in Judah who signed Ezra's covenant to keep the law (Neh. 10:15) and could be associated with either of the families named in 1 and 2.

Azmaveth (az'muh-veth; Heb., "death is strong").

1 One of David's elite troops known as "the Thirty" (2 Sam. 23:31).

2 A Benjaminite descendant of Saul's son Jonathan (1 Chron. 8:36).

3 The father of Jaziel and Pelet, two of Saul's kinsmen from the tribe of Benjamin who joined David at Ziklag (1 Chron. 12:3).

4 The son of Adiel who was overseer of the royal storehouses under King David (1 Chron. 27:25).

5 The ancestor of a small family group who returned to Judea from the Babylonian exile with Zerubbabel (Ezra 2:24). The group is apparently referred to as Beth-azmaveth ("house of Azmaveth") in Neh. 7:28.

6 A village of the postexilic community; identified with the modern Ras-Dhukeir or El-Hizma, about five miles northeast of Jerusalem (Neh. 12:29).   D.R.B.

Azmon (az'mon), a settlement along the southernmost border of the Canaanite land claimed by Israel (Num. 34:4–5) and part of the southern boundary of Judah (Josh. 15:4); it is possibly identical with Ezem (Josh. 15:29). The site is unknown, but is thought to lie slightly northwest of Kadesh-barnea.

Azotus (uh-zoh'tuhs). *See* Ashdod.

Azriel (az'ree-uhl; Heb., "El [God] is my help").

1 The head of a family in the tribe of Manasseh (1 Chron. 5:24).

2 The father of Jeremoth, a military commander of the tribe of Naphtali (1 Chron. 27:19).

3 The father of Seraiah, a courtier of King Jehoiakim (Jer. 36:26).

Azrikam (az'ri-kuhm; Heb., "my help arises").

1 A descendant of Zerubbabel who also belonged to the lineage of the kings of Judah through David (1 Chron. 3:23).

2 The son of Azel and descendant of Saul's son Jonathan (1 Chron. 8:38).

3 A Levite who was the grandfather of Shemaiah, a resident of postexilic Jerusalem (1 Chron. 9:14).

4 The overseer of the royal household of King Ahaz of Judah; he was assassinated along with the king's son and his chief of state by Zichri in conjunction with a coordinated attack against Judah by Pekah, king of the northern kingdom, and Rezin, king of Syria (2 Chron. 28:7). *See also* Pekah.   D.R.B.

Azubah (uh-zoo'buh; Heb., "forsaken").

1 The daughter of Shilhi; she was a wife of King Asa of Judah and the mother of Jehoshaphat (1 Kings 22:42).

2 One of the wives of Caleb, son of Hezron (1 Chron. 2:18).

Azzur (az'uhr; Heb., "helped").

1 A Levite who signed Ezra's postexilic covenant to keep the law (Neh. 10:17).

2 The father of Hananiah, the false prophet who challenged Jeremiah (Jer. 28:1).

3 The father of Jaazariah, a corrupt leader seen by Ezekiel in a vision (Ezek. 11:1).

Baal (bay'uhl, bah-ahl'), a Canaanite god. The Semitic word *ba'al* means "owner," "husband," "lord," or "master." It can be used as a common or proper noun. In the latter case it refers to the god Baal. In the Bible it is not always clear which use is intended. There is an additional complication in using "Baal" as a proper noun. Baal is, in one sense, a specific Canaanite deity with characteristic attributes and functions. But gods other than this specific Baal may also be called baals (gods or lords) and they might even be addressed or referred to as Baal (though this does not mean that they are being identified with the Canaanite deity).

Canaanite Background: These problems notwithstanding, the identity of the Canaanite deity named Baal is clear. Baal was a weather god associated with thunderstorms. Baal was said to appoint the season of rains. Clouds were thought to be part of his entourage. Lightning was his weapon, and it may have been his invention. The windows of Baal's palace were thought to correspond to openings in the clouds through which rain flowed. Rain was important to Canaanite agriculture, and Baal was consequently a god of fertility—a prodigious lover as well as the giver of abundance.

Baal is best known from Ugaritic literature found at Ras-Shamra in Syria (fifteenth century BCE); Philo of Byblos, a Greek historian (ca. 63–141 CE), collected additional valuable information about Baal, whom Philo called Zeus. At Ras-Shamra, Baal was called the son of Dagan. Also known as Hadd (Hadad), Baal was called "the Prince," "the Powerful," "Rider of the Clouds" (an epithet once predicated of Israel's God in the Bible, Ps. 68:4). At Ras-Shamra, Baal's consort, evidently also his sister, was Anat. Ugaritic literature preserves a cycle of myths in which Baal is the protagonist. They link Baal to Mount Zaphon. They tell of his battle against Lotan (Leviathan) and of his struggles against other adversaries called Yamm (Sea) and Mot (Death). The struggle between Baal and Yamm has left its mark on Israelite literature in the form of stories about and allusions to God's encounters with watery enemies (e.g., Isa. 51:9b–10; Ps. 74:13–14). Through his struggles, Baal achieves the first rank among the gods. Along the way Baal perishes and revives, providing the Ugaritic literature with stirring themes and dramatic moments.

The relationship between the god El and Baal in Canaanite mythology has been a matter of dispute. There is some indirect evidence of antagonism between these important gods, inasmuch as they were competitors for the highest position in the pantheon. Yet there is also evidence of concord between them. Philo of Byblos reported an accommodation whereby Baal ruled on earth with the permission of El; many have seen in this arrangement the pattern of relations between the two most important gods of the Canaanites.

Baal and Ancient Israel: The cult of Baal was widespread in the Canaanite world and became the focus of Israelite religious animosity. In Canaan, Baal's consort was not Anat, but Asherah (Judg. 3:7) or Astarte (2:13; 10:6). Syncretism had blurred distinctions between Asherah, Astarte, and Anat, although for Israelite writers such distinctions were not of interest. We hear of the cult of Baal in a number of local manifestations: Baal-berith ("Baal of the Covenant") at Shechem (Judg. 9:4); Baal of Peor at Shittim (Num. 25:3); Baal-zebub ("Baal of the flies") at Philistia (2 Kings 1:2–3); and perhaps Baal-hamon (Song of Sol. 8:11). Jezebel introduced worship of the Baal of Tyre to Samaria (1 Kings 18:19). As indicated above, it is not altogether clear whether these references were to local manifestations of the single great god Baal or whether they were regarded as discrete deities.

Opposition to the worship of Baal is a persistent theme of the Israelite literature. The Deuteronomic perspective from which many of the historical books of Joshua–2 Kings were written repeatedly condemns the veneration of Baal, speaking sometimes of "the Baals" (e.g., Judg. 2:11; 1 Sam. 7:4). Historical narratives applaud the destruction of the Baal temple at Jerusalem in the revolution against Athaliah (2 Kings 11:18) and include stories of conflict between worshipers of "the LORD" and the followers of Baal (Judg. 6:25–32; 1 Kings 18:16–40).

The struggle against Baal worship was carried on forcefully by Israel's prophets, especially in the ninth century BCE and later. The immediate concern was to prohibit outright worship of Baal, but the broader struggle was to prevent the Israelite concept of God from being unduly influenced by Baal theology. In certain respects this may not have been a problem: the majesty of a thunderstorm and the gift of fertility in nature could be construed as the evidence of God's work with no compromise to Israel's traditional faith. But Baal was also a god of sexual congress whose cult sported erotic acts that offended Israelite sensitivities: syncretistic identification of Israel's God and Baal was thus not a possibility. Israel's prophets fought to preserve a vision of Israel's God as a transcendent Creator, over against the Canaanite concept of Baal as a god who was one with nature.

Nevertheless, the worship of Baal appears to have been popular. Many Israelite names were composed with the element "baal" (e.g., Merib-baal, 1 Chron. 8:34). Although the word "baal" in such names could refer to Israel's God as "lord" or "master" in a generic sense, the prevalence of such names could also suggest a somewhat relaxed or accepting attitude toward Baal or baals. Later Israelite scribes sometimes changed biblical names with *baal* in them. The most popular alteration was to substitute *boshet* ("shame") for *baal;* thus, e.g., Ishbaal became Ishbosheth. *See also* Anat; Asherah; Ras-Shamra.   R.M.G.

Baalah (bah'uh-luh), a feminine form of the word *ba'al* ("master"), the name of the Semitic fertility god; it means "the place of Baal."

1 Another name for Kiriath-jearim, a city on the northern border of Judah (Josh. 15:9–10)

where David kept the ark of the covenant before moving it to Jerusalem (1 Chron. 13:6). The site is identified as modern Deir el-Azar or Tel Qiryat Yearim, about eight miles west and slightly north of Jerusalem. Baalah/Kiriath-jearim is called Kiriath-baal (Heb., "the city of Baal") in Josh. 15:60; 18:40 and Baale-Judah in 2 Sam. 6:2. *See also* Kiriath-jearim.

2 A city on the southern border of Judah, possibly the same one elsewhere called Balah (Josh. 19:3) and Bilhah (1 Chron. 4:29) and given to the tribe of Simeon. The site is not known.

3 A mountain on the northern border of Judah near Ekron (Josh. 15:11).   D.R.B.

Baalath (bah´uh-lath), the name of a city in northern Canaan assigned to the tribe of Dan (Josh. 19:44). The site is unknown. A Baalath is also mentioned as one of the cities later rebuilt by Solomon (1 Kings 9:18), but it is not certain that this is the same city. The city rebuilt by Solomon may have been farther south in Judah, perhaps identified with Bealoth (Josh. 15:24) or Baalath-beer (19:8), although these identifications are also questionable. The name Baalath appears to be related to a feminine form of the word *ba'al* (Heb., "master"), the name of a Semitic deity.

Baalath-beer (bah´uh-lath-bee´uhr). A city apportioned to the tribe of Simeon in Josh. 19:8. Also called Ramah of the Negev, it is sometimes equated with Baalath. *See also* Baalath; Ramah.

The temple of Bacchus at Baalbek, a city in the Beqa'a Valley of Lebanon and site of the Roman city of Heliopolis. The architecture is typical of second-century CE Roman design.

Baalbek (bay´uh-bek), a city located in the Beqa'a Valley of Lebanon. It was the site of the Roman Heliopolis cult, and the ruins of temples to Jupiter, Mercury, and Venus have been excavated. The Heliopolitan cult that was centered on those three deities became widespread throughout the Roman Empire. As practiced at Baalbek, the cult was an adaptation of a triad of the older Semitic gods Hadad, Atargatis, and Baal.

Baale-judah (bay´uh-ee-joo´duh). *See* Baalah; Kiriath-jearim.

Baal-gad (bay´uhl-gad´, bah´uhl-gad´), a Canaanite town in the Valley of Lebanon, below Mount Hermon. It is probably to be identified with modern Hasbaiya or modern Banias (Caesarea Philippi of the first century CE). In the book of Joshua, Baal-gad seems to mark the northern limit of Joshua's conquests (11:17; 12:7; 13:5). *See also* Baal-hermon.

Baal-hamon (bay´uhl-hay´muhn, bah´uhl-hay´muhn; Heb., "baal [lord] of abundance, wealth"), a town, location unknown, where Solomon is said to have had a vineyard (Song of Sol. 8:11). Some commentators think the "vineyard" could be a royal harem, in which case Baal-hamon might have been a coy term for the harem quarters in Jerusalem.

Baal-hanan (bay´uhl-hay´nuhn, bah´uhl-hay´nuhn; Heb., "baal [the lord] is gracious").

1 The son of Achbor, and a pre-Israelite king of Edom (Gen. 36:38–39).

2 A Gederite placed in charge of olive and sycamore trees in the Shephelah during the reign of King David (1 Chron. 27:28).

Baal-hazor (bay´uhl-hay´zor, bah´uhl-hay´zor; Heb., "baal [lord] of Hazor"), Absalom's location for shearing sheep (2 Sam. 13:23). It was here that Absalom had his brother Amnon murdered for raping his half sister Tamar. The place should not be confused with the city of Hazor. It was probably modern Tell Azur, some six miles northeast of Bethel and about five miles south and slightly west of Shiloh.

Baal-hermon (bay´uhl-huhr´muhn, bah´uhl-huhr´muhn; Heb., "baal [lord] of Hermon"), a Hivite town (Judg. 3:3) on the north border of Manasseh's tribal land (1 Chron. 5:23). Some scholars consider it identical to Baal-gad (Josh. 11:17; 12:7; 13:5). If so, it was situated somewhere on the western side of Mount Hermon about equidistant from Tyre and Sidon on the Mediterranean coast. The precise location is unknown. *See also* Baal-gad.

Baal-meon (bay´uhl-mee´on, bah´uhl-mee´on; Heb., "baal [lord] of habitation"), an area or town that also appears to be identified as Beon (Num. 32:3), Beth-baal-meon (Josh. 13:17), and Beth-meon (Jer. 48:23). It was assigned to the tribe of Reuben (Num. 32:3, 38; Josh. 13:17; 1 Chron. 5:8), but was under Moabite control in the ninth century BCE when the Moabite king Mesha built a reservoir there (as recorded in the Mesha Inscription). It may have been in Israelite hands again in the eighth century, but it reverted to Moabite control later (Jer. 48:23; Ezek. 25:9). The location was probably that of modern Ma'in, about four miles southwest of Medeba and nine miles southwest of Hesban in central Transjordan. *See also* Mesha.

Baal-peor (bay´uhl-pee´or, bah´uhl-pee´or; Heb., "baal [lord] of Peor"). *See* Peor.

Baal-perazim (bay'uhl-pi-ray'zim, bah'uhl-pi-ray'zim; Heb., "baal [lord] of bursting forth"), the site of David's victory over the Philistine army after he became king (2 Sam. 5:20; 1 Chron. 14:11). David is said to have named the place, because the Lord "burst forth" against his enemies there. The location may be modern Sheikh Bedr northwest of Jerusalem.

Baal-shalisha (bay'uhl-shal'uh-shuh, bah'uhl-shal'uh-shuh), a village in the territory of Ephraim from which a man brought bread to Elijah (2 Kings 4:42–44; cf. 1 Sam. 9:4). The location is modern Kefr Thilth, southwest of Shechem.

Baal-tamar (bay'uhl-tay'muhr, bah'uhl-tay'muhr; Heb., "baal [lord] of the palm"), a town near Gibeah from which the other Israelite tribes launched their successful assault on the Benjaminites to avenge the rape of a Levite's concubine (Judg. 19:1–20:48). Its location is uncertain. One possibility is modern Ras et-Tawil just north of Jerusalem.

Baal-zebub (bay'uhl-zee'buhb, bah'uhl-zee'buhb; also Beelzebub [bee-el'zi-buhb]; Heb., "baal [lord] of flies"), a god worshiped by the Philistines at Ekron (2 Kings 1:2–16). The actual name may have been Baal-zebul, meaning "lord of the lofty abode," but Israelites who considered this god an unworthy rival to Israel's God corrupted it to the word for "lord of flies" (Baal-zebub). During the Second Temple period, when numerous names were used to designate the leader of the forces of evil, one of the names selected was Baal-zebub (or the alternate form Beelzebul). In the Gospels, Jesus denies that he casts out demons by Beelzebul, "the prince of demons" (Matt. 12:24–27; Mark 3:22–26; Luke 11:15–19; cf. Matt. 10:25). *See also* Baal; devil; Satan.   J.M.E.

Baal-zephon (bay'uhl-zee'fon, bah'uhl-zee'fon), possibly Tell Defenneh (Egyptian Tahpanhes) in the eastern Nile Delta; a point on the exodus route (Exod. 14:2; Num. 33:7).

Baana (bay'uh-nuh).
  1 The son of Ahilud and a district administrator under King Solomon. He was responsible for providing the king's household with food for one month of each year. His district included the area around Megiddo and in the Jezreel Valley in north-central Israel (1 Kings 4:12).
  2 The son of Hushai, who was also a district administrator responsible for providing the king's household with food for one month of each year. His district included the coastal area of far northern Israel (1 Kings 4:16).
  3 The father of Zadok, and one who helped repair the Fish Gate in Jerusalem under Nehemiah (Neh. 3:4); he is possibly the same person (called Baanah) listed among those who returned from Babylon with Zerubbabel (Ezra 2:2; Neh. 10:27). *See also* Baanah.   D.R.B.

Baanah (bay'uh-nuh).
  1 A Benjaminite commander of a group of soldiers under Ishbaal, Saul's son. He and his brother Rechab killed Ishbaal and took his head to David, thinking David would be pleased at the removal of this threat to his newly established rule. Instead, David was angry at their treachery and ordered them both killed, mutilated, and publicly displayed (2 Sam. 4). *See also* Ishbaal.
  2 The father of Heleb (Heled), one of David's elite guard known as "the Thirty" (2 Sam. 23:29).
  3 One who returned with Zerubbabel from the Babylonian exile (Neh. 7:7), probably the same one who signed Ezra's covenant to keep the law (10:27); he is possibly the same person elsewhere called Baana, whose son helped rebuild the Fish Gate in Jerusalem (3:4). *See also* Baana.   D.R.B.

Baasha (bay'uh-shuh), the third king of Israel, ca. 900–877 BCE. He gained the throne by murdering his predecessor, Nadab (1 Kings 15:27–28). He later exterminated the house of Jeroboam (15:29). His long rule (twenty-four years) was regarded as wicked by the author of Kings (15:34), and his own house was brought to a violent end when Zimri, an Israelite military commander, murdered Baasha's son Elah, in accordance with the prophecy of Jehu (16:1–4). Baasha's contemporary in Judah was Asa, with whom he battled throughout his reign. The main recorded incident was Baasha's attempt to fortify Raman, resulting in intervention by the Syrian king Ben-hadad at the instigation of Asa (15:16–20).   D.L.C.

Babel (bay'buhl), the Hebrew name for Babylon. It was the site of the episode in Gen. 11:1–9, which recounts the origin of separate languages. Once humankind spoke one language, but when people settled in Shinar (understood by most modern scholars as Sumer), they purposed to make bricks and building materials and build a city and tower "with its top in the heavens, and . . . to make a name for (themselves), lest (they) be scattered abroad upon the face of the whole earth" (Gen. 11:4). God concluded that, with a single common language, people could do anything they wished. Therefore, God confounded human speech, creating linguistic havoc and scattering the people over the earth. The place is called "Babel" because "there the LORD confused [Heb. *balal*] the language of all the earth." This biblical episode has been compared to the building of the Esagila, a temple to Marduk described in the Babylonian creation epic *Enuma Elish* 6.60–62. But whereas the Babylonian tradition reflects deep pride in the building of cities, as an art of civilization, the biblical author characteristically expresses a more negative view. The tower itself may have been of the common spiral or terraced type known in the Akkadian language as a *ziggurat*. A Babylonian ziggurat, the Marduk temple known as Entemenanki, was built in the seventh or sixth century BCE. *See also* Babylon; Mesopotamia; Sumer; ziggurat.   J.W.R.

Babylon (bab'uh-luhn; from Akkadian *bab ili,* "the gate of the god"; Heb. *babel*), in the Bible, both the Mesopotamian region, more properly called Babylonia, and its capital city. The city of Babylon covered over two thousand acres, making it one of the largest ancient Mesopotamian sites. It is located along the Euphrates River in the area where it most closely approaches the Tigris River, in what is now Iraq. Its location at the northern end of the Euphrates floodplain gave Babylon potential control of major trade routes.

Babylonia has supported settled life from as early as the sixth millennium BCE. The name Babylon is first mentioned in an inscription of the Sargonic king Shar-kali-sharri (2217–2193 BCE). By this time, there were already two temples on the site. The city achieved little notoriety, however, until the nineteenth century BCE, when the Amorites, under Sumu-abum, founded their dynasty at Babylon.

Under Hammurabi: The previously weak political position of Babylon strengthened during the reign of the city's most famous king, Hammurabi (1792–1750 BCE). Hammurabi had ambassadors residing at Hazor, indicating Babylonian influence in what would become known as Canaan (and Israel). Hammurabi's political acumen and charismatic personality enabled him to unify Babylonia, which had heretofore been dotted with independent petty states. Several generations later, in 1595 BCE, his successors lost the city of Babylon when the Hittites, under Murshili I, sacked it.

The social and cultural climate in Babylon at the time of the Amorite dynasty laid the foundation for spectacular cultural developments. The law code of Hammurabi, formulated in conditional clauses, contributed the principle of *lex talionis,* the law of exact retributions, found also in the biblical legal material (Exod. 21:23–25). Another legal development in Babylonia at this time was the oral promulgation of acts of justice (Akkadian *mesharum*), which were designed to alleviate short-term social and economic ills. In the Bible this institution is preserved (Heb. *mesharim*) in Pss. 9:9; 58:2; 75:3; 96:10; 98:9; and 99:4.

The scribal school flourished during this Old Babylonian period and gave rise to Babylon's claim to being a literary and scholarly center. Its voluminous output was no less important than the longevity of the school (the latest known cuneiform text, dated to 79 CE, is from Babylon). Scribes in this city, along with those in Uruk, employed the cumbersome cuneiform writing system long after alphabetic scripts had taken hold throughout the Near East. At the end of the first millennium BCE, however, the scribal school at Babylon was producing almost exclusively astronomical and astrological reports. The biblical tradition is aware of this (cf. Isa. 47:13).

Succeeding Dynasties and Kings: During the still poorly understood Kassite dynasty (ca. 1570–1150 BCE), Babylon conducted extensive trade with Egypt during what is called the Amarna Age. Documents treating the relations between these

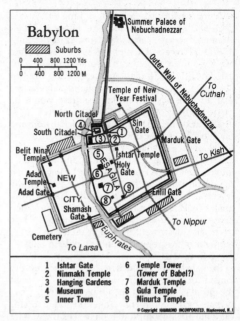

Plan of the ancient city of Babylon as envisioned by a modern mapmaker, highlighting the city of the sixth century BCE.

two regions have been recovered at either end of the Fertile Crescent. Dynastic marriages, such as those between Solomon and Egyptian princesses (1 Kings 9:16), occurred between ruling houses of Egypt and Babylonia.

Babylon did not experience another golden age until the reign of Nabonassar (747–734 BCE). This period was so significant that the Babylonian Chronicle (a contemporary historical record) began its account with it, and later Ptolemaic records assign an exact date and time to its beginning. It is a period marked by a curious blend of cultural achievement and political unrest, a time in which the fortunes of the Israelite nation became intertwined with those of Mesopotamia.

Tiglath-pileser III reigned as king of Assyria 745–727 BCE and simultaneously as regent of Babylonia 728–727 BCE. Known in the Bible as Pul, he collected tribute from Menahem of Israel (2 Kings 15:19) and carried off captives from the tribes of Reuben, Gad, and the half-tribe of Manasseh (1 Chron. 5:26). Isa. 66:19 includes Pul among the rulers to whom God will send a sign of his glory.

During the less glorious reign of his successor, Shalmaneser V (726–722 BCE), events with great ramifications for the biblical world occurred. Shalmaneser V besieged King Hoshea in Samaria after the Israelite king engaged in intrigue with Egypt against the Babylonian king (2 Kings 18:9–10). Shalmaneser died before the siege of Samaria was completed; credit for this task is claimed by his successor, Sargon II (722–705 BCE). Second Kings 18:10–11 records the completion of this siege, although it does not mention Sargon.

Sennacherib, who reigned as king of Assyria (704–681 BCE) and of Babylon (704–703 BCE), attempted to take Jerusalem from Hezekiah, but failed. He received temple treasures as tribute, but was forced to retreat to Nineveh. Merodach-baladan II (721–710 and 703 BCE) sent envoys to Jerusalem, after which the prophet Isaiah warned that all that was in Hezekiah's house would be carried to Babylon (2 Kings 20:12).

The next major contact between Babylon and the biblical kings came during the reign of the Babylonian Nebuchadnezzar II (605–562 BCE). He carried King Jehoiachin of Judah and his family into exile. Records from the palace in Babylon list the rations the Israelite monarch and his family received. Nebuchadnezzar installed Jehoiachin's uncle, Zedekiah, as governor of Jerusalem. When Zedekiah rebelled, Nebuchadnezzar laid siege to the city, destroyed the temple, and carried the remnant of the population off to exile in Babylonia (2 Kings 24:10–25:21).

In Babylonia, the exiled Jewish community longed for their Judean homeland (Ps. 137), but the prophet Jeremiah encouraged them to participate in the commercial, agricultural, and cultural life of Babylonia and even to seek the welfare of the city (29:7). He also depicts the city as the instrument of divine judgment against Judah, while simultaneously indicating that Babylon itself will suffer God's judgment (51:59–64). In

The Chronicle of the Babylonian king Nebuchadnezzar II (605–562 BCE; also spelled Nebuchadrezzar) mentions the removal of Jehoiachin of Judah as king of Israel and the appointment of his uncle, Zedekiah, in his place. It also records the siege and destruction of Jerusalem when Zedekiah rebelled in 586.

the Mesopotamian record, Nebuchadnezzar is remembered for his expansion and restoration of Babylon. Three palaces date to this time period. The Southern Palace, Nebuchadnezzar's principal palace, may have been the site of Belshazzar's feast (Dan. 5). The inner city was divided by a magnificent processional way. At one end stood the Ishtar Gate, decorated with glazed bricks. The hanging gardens of Babylon were also the creation of Nebuchadnezzar. Also notable was the ziggurat to Marduk, who was there called "Entemenanki." Such a stepped tower may have been the prototype for the Tower of Babel (Gen. 11:9).

Political intrigue and domestic unrest plagued Babylonia again. The final Babylonian king, Nabonidus (555–539), absented himself from Babylon at the time of the New Year's feast, making its observance impossible, and sequestered himself for ten years in the Arabian caravan city of Teima. This may have inspired accounts of a seclusion attributed to Nebuchadnezzar in Dan. 4:25, 28–33.

The weakening of Babylonia left the door open for rule by a new, non-Mesopotamian dynasty. The Persian Achaemenid dynasty, of which Cyrus (538–530 BCE) was the first important ruler, restored the fortunes not only of Babylon but of the cities and regions Babylon had conquered. In 538, Cyrus granted permission for the Jews exiled in Babylonia to return to Jerusalem. Among the Jewish community Cyrus enjoyed a good reputation. Isaiah called him God's anointed (45:1). Restoration of the temple was interrupted, however, and not resumed until the reign of the Achaemenid king Darius I (522–486 BCE).

Meanwhile, the increasingly powerful and independent Jewish community of Babylonia (i.e., those who did not return from the exile) separated itself from events in Judea. Babylonia's Jews supported neither the war against Rome (66–70 CE) nor the Bar-Kochba revolt of 132–135 CE. The massive Babylonian Talmud is witness and monument to the legal and biblical issues discussed in the academies, to the theological concerns and formulations of the rabbis, and to the folkways and beliefs of the common people.

The NT has a few references to historical Babylon (Matt. 1:12, 17; Acts 7:43), but also uses the name of the ancient city to depict Rome, since Christian authors found Rome's actions against Christian communities comparable to Babylon's treatment of Israel (1 Pet. 5:13; Rev. 14:8; 16:19; 17:5; 18:2, 10, 21). *See also* astrologer; Babel; Mesopotamia.
L.E.P.

Baca (bay′kuh), an unidentified valley associated with weeping or balsam (Ps. 84:6). The term is derived from the verb "to drip"; hence its association with weeping.

badger, a medium-size burrowing mammal. The Hebrew word (*shaphan*) translated "badger" by the NRSV in Lev. 11:5; Deut. 14:7; Prov. 30:26 is rendered "coney" in Ps. 104:18. It is likely that all four references may actually be to the coney or hyrax (*Procavia capensis*), a rock-dwelling, hare-size ungulate. The true badger (*Meles meles*) also lives in the Near East, but is rarely seen.

bag, a word used in the Bible to refer to a pouch or purse for carrying money (Prov. 1:14; Luke 10:4), a sack for storing or transporting grain (Gen. 42: 35), or a knapsack for carrying goods and provisions. Bags varied in size and material. A small bag of myrrh might lie between a woman's breasts (Song of Sol. 1:3), but a larger sturdier bag would be required for carrying weights (Mic. 6:11; cf. Deut. 25:13; Prov. 16:11). David put five stones in his bag (1 Sam. 17:40), while Judith put the head of Holfornes in hers (Jth. 10:5; 13:10, 15). In the NT, Jesus prohibits his disciples from carrying a bag (Matt. 10:10; Mark 6:8; Luke 9:3; 10:4), but, later, tells them to do so (Luke 22:35–36).

Bahurim (buh-hair'uhm), a town located on the road from Jerusalem to Jericho, probably to be identified with modern Ras et-Tmin east of Mount Scopus. It is mentioned most frequently in the David stories (2 Sam. 3:16; 17:18; 23:31). It was here that Shimei cursed David when the latter fled Absalom (16:5; 19:16; 1 Kings 2:8).

baker. While baking (Heb. *'aphah*) was a normal daily activity of women engaged in the preparation of meals, the specialized profession of baker (*'opheh*) developed in urban centers. Jer. 37:21 speaks of a "street of the bakers," where those engaged in this trade must have had their shops. Baked products included bread (*lekhem*, Lev. 26:26; Isa. 44:15, 19), leavened and unleavened (*matsah*), for ordinary meals (Gen. 19:3; 1 Sam. 28:24) and ritual purposes (Exod. 12:8; Lev. 6:10; 24:5). Several passages in which bakers appear are worthy of note. In Gen. 40, the chief baker and cupbearer of Pharaoh, important functionaries at court, are imprisoned with Joseph, who interprets the dreams that preview their fate. In 1 Sam. 8:13, when Samuel details the abuses of

Woman kneading dough, pottery figurine from a Phoenician cemetery at Achziv, eighth–sixth century BCE.

royal power that will obtain in monarchic Israel, he says, "He [the king] will take your daughters to be perfumers and cooks and bakers." In the futility curse of Lev. 26:26, the scarcity of food is underlined by the statement that ten women will need only one oven for baking bread. A baker also appears in Hos. 7:4, 6.   J.S.K.

Balaam (bay'luhm), a non-Israelite prophet known from both biblical and extrabiblical sources as a person from the region of Transjordan skilled in divination. The biblical material is found mainly in Num. 22–24, but archaeologists have also unearthed a plaster inscription from ca. 700 BCE that refers to "Balaam, seer of the gods" in a language that seems like a hybrid of Canaanite and Aramaic.

The biblical narrative of Balaam in Numbers presents him somewhat ambiguously. In Num. 22:21–35, he is exposed as a prophet who is less gifted in spiritual discernment than his donkey. Moreover, Balaam is held responsible for causing Israel to sin at Baal-peor (Num. 31:8, 16). Certain material preserved in Num. 22–24, however, holds Balaam in a favorable light. When the antagonist, Balak, hires Balaam to curse the armies of Israel so that his defense against the Israelite threat would be manageable, Balaam responds with an appeal to his prophetic virtue. He can offer Balak only the word given him by God for the occasion. Balaam finishes the scene with an affirmation of his prophetic virtue: "Did I not tell your messengers whom you sent to me, 'If Balak should give me his house full of silver and gold, I would not be able to go beyond the word of the LORD, to do either good or bad of my own will; what the LORD speaks, that will I speak'?" (24:12–13). This ambiguous evaluation of Balaam's character is not seen elsewhere in biblical material: he is consistently viewed as exemplary of an evil or false prophet who sells his gift for money (Deut. 23:4, 5; Josh. 13:22; 24:9, 10; Neh. 13:2; Mic. 6:5; 2 Pet. 2:15; Jude 11; Rev. 2:14). *See also* prophet.   G.W.C.

Balak (bay'lak), the son of Zippor and king of Moab who serves as the principal antagonist in the Balaam story (Num. 22–24). His pathetic plea for a curse against Israel casts him as a tragic figure, albeit in a comic light. He is also remembered as one who would try to seduce people into idolatry and immortality (Judg. 11:25; Mic. 6:5; Rev. 2:14). *See also* Balaam.

balances, instruments for weighing. They consisted of a central support and crossbeam from which two equally weighted pans were suspended by cords. From earliest times balances, probably at first handheld, must have been in use for the purpose of commercial transactions. Indeed, the balance is a symbol known from the earliest writing and from many illustrations. The weight of an object was determined by its relationship to an accepted standard, at first grain, then stones of various shapes and sizes. Biblical references to balances are numerous, to both false or deceitful scales (Prov. 11:1; 20:23; Hos. 12:7; Amos 8:5) and just balances (Lev. 19:36; Job 31:6; Prov. 16:11; Ezek. 45:10). Metaphorically the balance was used to judge a person's righteousness (Dan. 5:27; cf. Rev. 6:5).

baldness, in the Bible, a condition that may signify deprivation (Isa. 3:24), defeat (15:2), repentance (22:12), or existence under the threat of destruction (Jer. 47:5; Ezek. 7:18; Amos 8:10). Baldness could result from natural hair loss (Lev. 13:40–41) and, when that was the case, calling attention to a person's baldness was apparently an insult—a group of children who offended the prophet Elisha in this regard were killed by a she-bear (2 Kings 2:23). Shaving one's head could be a sign of mourning (Jer. 16:6; Ezek. 27:31; Mic. 1:16), though prohibitions were placed on the practice (Deut. 14:1; cf. Lev. 21:5; Ezek. 44:20).

balm, the resin or gum of the balsam tree (*Commiphora gileadensis*), which was used as a scent for oils and perfumes as well as a medicine to heal wounds (Jer. 8:22). The resin is collected naturally or by incision, and it hardens into small nodules. Often referred to as a "spice," it was traded throughout the ancient Near East (Ezek. 27:17) and was believed to have been planted originally by King Solomon, who received the trees as gifts from the queen of Sheba (1 Kings 10:10). The balm from Gilead referred to in Gen. 37:25 is probably not from the same plant, but was gathered instead from the mastic tree (*Pistachia lentiscus*). *See also* spices.   P.L.C.

balsam tree, a tree of uncertain species, though a cedarlike conifer appears likely. In David's fight

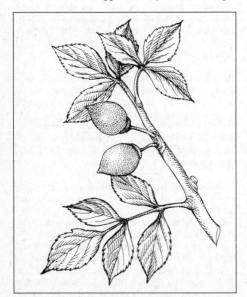

Balsam, the source of balm.

with the Philistines at the Valley of Rephaim, a grove of balsam trees is given both literal and figurative value. God instructs David to mount an attack on Philistine positions from the rear "opposite the balsam trees" (2 Sam. 5:23). He is then to time his attack when he hears "the sound of marching in the tops of the balsam trees" (5:24) as a sign that God has preceded him into battle (cf. 1 Chron. 14:14, 15).

ban (Heb. *kherem*), dedication of persons or materials to God, which typically means destroying those materials (e.g., by fire), so that they will be unavailable for human use. The ban is closely connected to a warfare tactic whose practical consequence is to prohibit warriors taking items as booty (cf. Josh. 8:2, where a partial ban serves to limit the spoils of battle without canceling them altogether). The ban is often commanded by God in a way that calls for warriors to completely annihilate their enemies (Deut. 20:17; Josh. 6:17–18). In other instances, the ban appears to be self-imposed, as a vow of extreme faithfulness (Num. 21:2). Furthermore, distinctions are made between those on whom the ban is to be carried out unconditionally and those on whom it is enacted only if they refuse to accept the Israelite's terms of peace (Deut. 20:10–18).

In the Bible, the ban is exercised most notably in narratives dealing with Israel's postexodus conquest of Canaan; cities placed under the ban include Jericho (Josh. 6), Ai (Josh. 8), Makkedah, Lachish, Eglon, Hebron, Debir (Josh. 10), and Hazor (Josh. 11). In one story, Achan, who violates the ban by taking forbidden items as spoils, is burned with his family and all the goods (Josh. 7). Some historical scholars speculate that the ban might have originated in order to control pestilential disease, especially bubonic plague, in the wake of warfare. Alternatively, the ban may have had its origins in the religious sphere, as part of votary offerings to the Lord of battles, and was later extended in scope. The stated justification for the ban, however, is to prevent potentially sinful influences: the people who must be utterly destroyed are those who might teach Israelites "all the abhorrent things that they do for their gods" (Deut. 20:18). Under the Israelite monarchy, however, royal commands governing distribution of booty were in place (1 Sam. 30:23–25).

Religious policies similar to the ban were known and practiced elsewhere. Some scholars have compared the Israelite *kherem* to the Assyrian *asakkum*, known from cuneiform texts from the city of Mari (eighteenth century BCE). In these documents, the phrase "to eat the *asakkum*" of god or king refers to the violation of a decree regarding spoils of war. Much later, Mesha, king of Moab (ninth century BCE), boasts of imposing the *kherem* on captured Israelites.   R.B./M.A.P.

Bani (bay′ni).
1 One of the group of David's elite warriors known as "the Thirty" (2 Sam. 23:36).

2 A Levite in the line of Ethan who served at the time of David (1 Chron. 6:46).

3 The head of a family of returned exiles (Ezra 2:10; 10:29; Neh. 10:14); he may be the person called Binue in Neh. 7:15. *See also* Binue.

4 A son of Perez and grandson of Judah (1 Chron. 9:4).

5 The father of Rehum, who directed a group of Levites who repaired the walls of Jerusalem at the time of Nehemiah (Neh. 3:17) and who stood with Ezra when he read the law to the people (8:7–8; cf. 9:4). This Bani may have been the father of Uzzi, who was the overseer of Levites chosen by lot to move into Jerusalem (11:22).

6 A Levite who signed Ezra's covenant-renewal document at the time of Nehemiah (Neh. 10:15).

banner, a cloth ensign used for identification of a group (NRSV: "ensign," Num. 2:2; Isa. 62:10; Ezek. 27:7) or as a rallying point that could be easily seen (NRSV: "signal," Isa. 5:26; 11:10; 13:2). Most often used by armies (cf. Song of Sol. 6:4, 10), banners are sometimes mentioned symbolically (Exod. 17:15; Ps. 60:4).

banquet, an elaborate meal, often called a feast. Amos 6:4–6 pictures banquets as ostentatious affairs at which the wealthy recline on ivory beds, drink wine from bowls, and anoint themselves with fine oils while listening to musical entertainment. In the book of Esther, King Ahasuerus gives a banquet for his officials and ministers (1:3; cf. 2:18) and Queen Vashti gives one for the women (1:9); later, Esther gives a couple of banquets for the king, and these become the occasions for exposing Haman's scheme against the Jews (5:4–8; 6:14–7:10). In the NT, Herodias's daughter dances at a birthday banquet for Herod Antipas and his courtiers, with disastrous results for John the Baptist (Mark 6:21–28). Levi throws a banquet at which Jesus eats with tax collectors and sinners (Luke 5:9). Jesus castigates scribes who love places of honor at banquets (Mark 12:39; Luke 20:46), and he refers to banquets in his parables and teaching (Matt. 22:2–14; Luke 12:35–38; 14:8–14).

There are two general types of banquets in the Bible: ceremonial and ritual. A ceremonial banquet is a festive meal at which the inviter and the invited celebrate their mutual solidarity, their belonging to each other, their oneness. Israel's appointed festivals (see Lev. 23:2–44) and the banquets mentioned above in the book of Esther were ceremonial banquets. A ritual banquet is one that marks some personal or interpersonal transition or transformation. As a ritual feature of hospitality, such banquets indicate the transformation of a stranger into a guest (Gen. 19:3–14; Luke 5:29) or of an enemy into a covenant partner (Gen. 26:26–31; 2 Sam. 3:20). Banquets mark important transitional points in a person's life: Isaac's weaning day (Gen. 21:8), the weddings of Jacob (Gen. 29:22) and Samson (Judg. 14:10), the birthday of Pharaoh (Gen. 40:20).

In the NT, special attention focuses on the gathering of Christians for a ritual fellowship meal called the "breaking of bread" in Acts 2:42 and the "Lord's Supper" in 1 Cor. 11:17–33. In addition there is focus on an eschatological banquet to be celebrated at the end of time (Matt. 8:11); in the book of Revelation, this is associated with the "marriage supper of the Lamb" (19:9), an image that probably assumes symbolism of the church as the "bride of Christ (21:9; 22:17; cf. Eph. 5:31–33). *See also* festivals, feasts, and fasts; meals.

B.J.M./M.A.P.

baptism, an initiatory rite involving water. The term is derived from a Greek word meaning "to immerse in or wash with water" (Mark 7:4). In the Bible, baptism is only mentioned as such in the NT, and so it is connected primarily with Christianity or with people like John the Baptist, who came to be regarded as practicing a baptism that, although insufficient (Acts 18:24–25), offered a proleptic foreshadowing of the Christian rite: it provided a prophetic call to repentance and forgiveness of sins (Mark 1:4). Some background for baptism, however, may be found in Jewish purification rituals. In the Bible, rituals that involve washing with water characterize priestly preparation for

A royal banquet at which the king (probably Ashurbanipal) and queen are served in a garden by attendants with fans; from the reliefs at Nineveh, seventh century BCE.

offering sacrifice (Exod. 40:12–15) and are connected with purity concerns in general (Isa. 1:16–17; Jer. 4:14; Ezek. 36:25). The ablutions of the Qumran covenanters described in the Dead Sea Scrolls belong to this tradition of cultic and moral ablutions. Some Jews also apparently performed baptisms of proselytes as part of the purification of new covenant members (*m. Pesah.* 8:7; 'Ed. 5:2).

In the NT, Christian baptism of converts retained some sense of Jewish purification rites (1 Pet. 3:21), but Paul also likens baptism to Jesus's death and resurrection: through baptism, Christians die with Christ and are buried with him; as they rise from baptism in purity, they share the new life brought by Jesus's resurrection (Rom. 6:1–4; cf. Col. 2:12). Those who are baptized into Christ are said to have clothed themselves with Christ (Gal. 3:27). Elsewhere, baptism is compared with Noah's escape from God's wrath (1 Pet. 3:20–21) and to Israel's exodus through the sea (1 Cor. 10:1–4). Baptism in the name of Jesus became the rite of initiation through which people become identified as members of the Christian movement (Acts 2:38; 8:16; 10:48; 19:5; 22:16). Matt. 28:19 presents Jesus (who apparently did not baptize people himself; cf. John 4:2) telling his disciples to "make disciples of all nations, baptizing them in the name of the Father and of the Son and of the Holy Spirit." Baptism is also used metaphorically: individuals' baptism can symbolize their destiny or immersion in suffering (Mark 10:38–39); elsewhere, people are said to be baptized with the Holy Spirit (Acts 1:5) and/or with fire (Luke 3:16). *See also* John the Baptist; proselyte; purity.

J.H.N./M.A.P.

bar, the Aramaic word for "son," equivalent to the Hebrew *ben*, occurring in phrases such as *bar enash* ("son of man," Dan. 7:13; NRSV: "a human being") and *bar elahin* ("divine being," lit., "son of [the] god[s]," Dan. 3:25). It occurs also in personal names, such as Barabbas, Bar-Jesus, Bar-Jona, Barnabas, Barqos, Barsabbas, Bartholomew, and Bartimaeus.

Barabbas (buh-rab´uhs; Heb., "son of abba [father]"), a person mentioned in the Gospels as being released from prison in lieu of Jesus (Matt. 27:15–23; Mark 15:6–14; Luke 23:18–23; John 18:38–40). He is identified as a bandit (John 18:40), "a notorious prisoner" (Matt. 27:16), and as being among a group of rebels who had committed murder during an insurrection (Mark 15:7; cf. Luke 23:18). According to the Gospels, however, Pilate had a custom of releasing a prisoner at Passover (in John 18:39 Pilate refers to this as a Jewish custom). Thus, Pilate gives the crowd a choice of whom he should release, Jesus or Barabbas. The irony of this choice is played up in Matt. 27:16, which says that Barabbas's full name was Jesus Barabbas (i.e., "Jesus son of Abba"). In all four Gospels, the crowd calls for Barabbas to be released and for Jesus to be crucified. Outside of the Gospels, there is no historical evidence for

a Roman or Jewish custom of releasing a prisoner at Passover (or any other Jewish festival). *See also* cross; trial of Jesus.   P.P./M.A.P.

Barak (bair´ak; Heb., "lightning"), the son of Abinoam. Commander of Israelite militia and subordinate to Deborah in Judg. 4–5, Barak was among the deliverers of Israel (1 Sam. 12:11, LXX; cf. Heb. 11:32). The opposition ("kings of Canaan," Judg. 5:19), headed by Jabin "king of Canaan at Hazor" (4:2, 23) and led by the nine hundred chariots of Sisera (a non-Semitic name) from Harosheth "of the nations," represents domination by other newcomers (Sea Peoples). When the people of Israel sought Deborah's judgment concerning this threat, she recalled Barak from Kedesh (in Naphtali) and outlined her strategy, after which she returned to Kedesh with Barak (4:4–9). Barak mustered ten units from Zebulun and Naphtali. Other tribes also responded, according to Judg. 5. At the waters of Megiddo, Barak routed and destroyed the opposition. Sisera fled far north and was slain by the woman Jael (4:17–22). *See also* army; Judges, book of; Sisera.   R.B.

barbarian, a non-Jew who is also not Greek or Roman. In Col. 3:11, the phrase "Greek and barbarian" is used to mean the entire Gentile world. Elsewhere, 2 Macc. 2:21 uses the word pejoratively for the followers of Antiochus IV Epiphanes. *See also* Gentile; Greek, Greeks; nations.

barefoot. Removing one's shoes can be a sign of reverence or, specifically, respect for sacred ground, as in the theophanies to Moses (Exod. 3:5) and Joshua (Josh. 5:15). David's going barefoot is probably part of a ritual of penitence (2 Sam. 15:30). In a prophetic symbolic action, Isaiah goes about naked and barefoot for three years as a sign to Judah of the coming defeat by Assyria of Egypt and Ethiopia, Judah's allies, who will be led away naked and barefoot as prisoners of war and exiles (Isa. 20:2–4).

Baris (bair´is; from Heb. *birah*), name used by Flavius Josephus for the temple fortress of Jerusalem built by Nehemiah (Neh. 2:8; 7:2), later renovated by the Hasmoneans. According to 2 Macc. 4:12, Jason founded a gymnasium "under the citadel." Sostratus was captain of the citadel (4:28), and Menelaus took refuge there during Jason's siege of Jerusalem (5:5). *See also* Antonia, Tower of.

Bar-Jesus (bahr-jee´zuhs). *See* Elymas.

barley, one of the two staple grain crops in the biblical period (wheat was the other). Bread made of barley was the food of lower-income people (Ezek. 4:12; John 6:9). Seven weeks elapsed from the beginning of the barley harvest in late April until the completion of the wheat harvest at the beginning of June (Deut. 16:9–12; Ruth 2:23). The harvest culminated at the feast of Pentecost. Since barley was the staple of the lower classes, failure of the barley harvest or absurdly high prices for barley served as a judgment oracle against the nation (Job 31:40; Rev. 6:6). Ezek. 13:19 may refer to use of barley in connection with divination. Num. 5:15 mandates a barley offering as part of the "test" by which a jealous husband determines the fidelity of his wife. According to John's Gospel, Jesus miraculously fed over five thousand people with five barley loaves (6:3, 9). 　　　P.P.

Barnabas (bahr'nuh-buhs; Heb., "son of encouragement"), according to Acts 4:36–37, a Levite from Cyprus whose cognomen was Joseph and who became a member of the early Christian community in Jerusalem. He was surnamed "Barnabas" by the apostles. A Jew from the Dispersion who had moved to Jerusalem, Barnabas was a cousin of John Mark (Col. 4:10) and soon became a leader in the church. According to Acts, he introduced Saul (Paul) to the apostles in Jerusalem (9:27). Later, he appeared in Antioch, where he was said to be a representative of the Jerusalem church (11:19–26). He affirmed the mission to the Gentiles there and worked with Saul as senior partner or supervisor of a Christian mission in Syria-Cilicia. Acts reports that he and Saul took the famine offering from Antioch to Jerusalem (11:27–30; 12:25). Paul and Barnabas traveled together on a mission tour to Cyprus and to the Iconium region of Asia Minor (13:1–14:28). They also appeared together at the Jerusalem Council (15:1–35), but then disagreed and separated over the question of allowing John Mark to accompany them on a second tour (15:36–41), since he had cut short his participation in an earlier mission (13:13). Barnabas is also mentioned with reference to a dispute in Antioch over whether circumcised and uncircumcised believers should eat together (Gal. 2:11–14). According to Acts 15:1–35, Barnabas was a strong defender of not binding circumcision on Gentile converts, as was Peter, but he and Peter apparently sided against Paul with regard to the related question of mixed table fellowship.

Acts speaks of Barnabas as "a good man, full of the Holy Spirit and of faith" (11:24). Paul refers to him as a fellow apostle (1 Cor. 9:3–6; cf. Acts 14:4, 14). The fact that the second-century *Epistle of Barnabas* was attributed to him further speaks to the high regard in which he was held. *See also* Antioch; apostle; circumcision; Cyprus; Gentile; Hellenists; Levites; Mark; Paul; Peter; Syria. 　　　A.J.M.

barracks. *See* Antonia, Tower of.

Barsabbas (bahr-sab'uhs).

1 According to Acts 1:23–26, "Joseph called Barsabbas, who was also known as Justus." He and Matthias were put forward as candidates to replace Judas Iscariot among the twelve apostles after the latter's death; Matthias was chosen.

2 According to Acts 15:22–34, "Judas called Barsabbas," a prophet and a leader in the Jerusalem church, who was given the task, along with

Silas, of announcing the decision of the Jerusalem Council to the churches in Antioch, Syria, and Cilicia. They accompanied Paul and Barnabas to Antioch, later returning to Jerusalem. *See also* apostle; Judas; Matthias; Paul; Silas, Silvanus. 　　　A.J.M.

Bartholomew (bahr-thol'uh-myoo), one of the twelve apostles about whom little is known. His name appears in all of the NT apostolic lists (Matt. 10:2–4; Mark 3:16–19; Luke 6:14–16; Acts 1:13), but nowhere else in the NT. Because "Bartholomew" follows "Philip" in three of the lists (Matthew, Mark, and Luke), some scholars have identified him with the "Nathanael," whom Philip brings to Jesus in John 1:45–51. Bartholomew is never mentioned in John, nor is Nathanael mentioned in Matthew, Mark, or Luke, but the identification lacks conclusive evidence. Later Christian traditions identify Bartholomew as a missionary in India (Eusebius) and author of an apocryphal gospel (Jerome). *See also* apostle; disciple; Nathanael; Philip; twelve, the. 　　　P.L.S.

Bartimaeus (bahr'tuh-mee'uhs; translated in Mark 10:46 as "son of Timaeus"), a blind beggar healed by Jesus when the latter was leaving Jericho (10:46–52). *See also* blindness; disease; healing; miracles.

Baruch (bair'uhk), Jeremiah's friend and secretary. Baruch, son of Neriah, son of Mahseiah, belonged to a respected Jerusalemite family; his brother, Seraiah, was minister to King Zedekiah (Jer. 51:59). Bullae (seals) of the two brothers, Baruch and Seraiah, have been recently found, and the bulla of Baruch gives his name as *brkyhw*; plausibly, then, the biblical name Baruch (Heb. *brk*)

An Egyptian scribe, from the Fifth Dynasty, ca. 2400 BCE. Baruch's profession was similar; he was a royal clerk, or "scribe."

is a diminutive form of a longer name from which *yhw* (the divine name) has been removed. The bulla further identifies Baruch as a *hspr*, a title also used in Jer. 36:32 that indicates his position was that of a royal clerk, as was that of other people called "scribe" (Heb. *sopher*) at this time (e.g., Jer. 36:10, 20).

Baruch's employment may explain his rather sporadic association with Jeremiah—three times only. First, in the years 605–604 BCE Jeremiah dictated his prophecies to Baruch, who bravely read the scroll to the people in the temple and again to the ministers of Jehoiakim (608–598 BCE). The scroll was then read to the king, who burned it, ordering the seizure of Jeremiah and Baruch. Both went into hiding and rewrote their scroll (Jer. 36). Jeremiah's high opinion of his secretary at that time is illustrated by his dedicating to Baruch a special prophecy that attests to the latter's ambitions either in his professional field or as the prophet's disciple (Jer. 45). Baruch is mentioned a second time when Jeremiah redeemed Hanamel's field in Anathoth (Jer. 32:12–16). The deeds, however, were written by Jeremiah himself; Baruch's role was limited to their proper preservation. It appears that Jeremiah, detained alone in prison, took advantage of a visit by Baruch in order to entrust him with the legal deeds. Baruch is mentioned a third and last time (43:3) when the "commanders of the forces" inquired of the Lord by Jeremiah in Geruth Chimham (cf. 41:17). However, they refused to follow his advice, charging that Baruch had incited the prophet against them. This confirms Baruch's origins from an influential family known for its pro-Babylonian orientation (51:59). For this reason, the captains, having participated in Zedekiah's revolt and not yet having officially submitted to the Chaldeans, were afraid of the acrimony of the sons of Neriah. In spite of Jeremiah's warnings, the commanders opted for fleeing to Egypt and took both Jeremiah and Baruch with them. Nothing more is said about Baruch, but the fact that oracles remain from this late Egyptian period (43:8–13; 44:1–30; 46:13–26) indicate that he survived to continue recording Jeremiah's words.

The story in Jer. 36 attributes to Baruch the first lasting record of Jeremiah's words (27–32). Probably a good deal of the extant original words of Jeremiah were contained in that scroll. Yet internal analysis of the collections of prophecies (chaps. 1–24; 30–31; 33; 46–51) proves that they underwent various transformations before reaching their present form: they were first expanded and reworked by later writers; then they were partly reorganized in collections organized by content. It is thus no longer possible to reconstruct the scroll of Baruch from the book of Jeremiah as it has come down to us. Modern scholars also debate how much of the material in the biographical chapters in Jeremiah is to be attributed to Baruch. This material consists of two distinct parts: a series of nine independent speeches and episodes (25–29; 32; 34–36) and a continuous

story of Jeremiah from the siege of Jerusalem to his captivity in Egypt (37–44). Both portions underwent editorial reworking and expansion, but Baruch may have contributed to the independent episodes, because these do not start with the beginning of the prophet's career in 627 BCE, but rather "in the beginning of the reign of Jehoiakim" (26:1), around the time that Baruch first appeared at Jeremiah's side. Postexilic Judaism elaborated on Baruch's repertoire, attributing to him the composition of one apocryphal book and two apocalypses. *See also* Jeremiah, book of.

Bibliography

Avigad, N. "Baruch the Scribe and Jerahmeel the King's Son." *Israel Exploration Journal* 28 (1978): 52–56.   A.R.

Baruch, book of, a short collection of prayers and poems from diverse sources attributed to Baruch, Jeremiah's scribe (Jer. 36:4), and included in the LXX. It is sometimes termed 1 Baruch to distinguish it from two pseudepigraphical writings, the *Syriac Apocalypse of Baruch* (2 *Baruch*), and the *Greek Apocalypse of Baruch* (3 *Baruch*). Although difficult to date, Baruch seems to have been composed in Hebrew, possibly early in the second century BCE. The occasional affinities to the language of Jeremiah and Deuteronomy are more likely an indication that the authors have steeped themselves in scripture than evidence for composition by the historical Baruch. The book has not survived in Hebrew and seems to have been largely ignored by early Christians. The Latin Vulgate and some manuscripts of the LXX include with it the Letter of Jeremiah, although elsewhere the latter appears as a separate work. Protestants treat Baruch as part of the Apocrypha, while Roman Catholics and Eastern Orthodox Christians classify it as deuterocanonical.

It is composed of four distinct parts. (1) A narrative introduction (1:1–14) sets the writing in Babylonia during the exile. Baruch returns the temple vessels to Jehoiakim, the high priest in Jerusalem, along with funds for burnt and sin offerings and a request that the accompanying prayer of confession be read in the temple on feast days. The introduction also reflects an attitude of accommodation to Gentile authorities in that it requests prayers on behalf of Nebuchadnezzar and Belshazzar, his son. This tradition associating Jeremiah's scribe with preservation of the temple vessels is also reflected in 2 *Baruch* 6 (cf. Ezra 1:7–11). (2) The second part is a prayer of confession (1:15–3:8), a penitential prose prayer on behalf of the inhabitants of Judah as well as the exiles. It addresses God as "Lord" (probably a Greek translation of the divine name) and reflects the point of view of Deut. 28–32 as well as the phraseology of the prayer in Dan. 9:4–19. (3) A hymn to Wisdom personified (3:9–4:4) echoes both Job 28, in speaking of a search for Wisdom, and Sir. 24, in identifying Wisdom as the Torah, the law of God. The personification of Wisdom and the identification with the Torah point to a period late in the development of the wisdom tradition when concern had shifted from practical instruction to revelation as the primary mode of knowledge. This section and the next use the generic term "God" (probably Heb. *'elohim*) rather than "Lord." (4) The concluding section is a psalm of comfort (4:5–5:9) composed primarily of the lament of Zion over her lost children (cf. Lamentations). The tone is one of comfort and hope for the return of the exiles, and in achieving it the psalm frequently echoes Isa. 40–66.

Since the precise date of Baruch is unknown, it is not clear why its writers, who lived long after the sixth century BCE, chose to appropriate the memory of the exile. Most likely, the book is either intended to express a hope for the end of the Dispersion or is related in some way to the desecration of the temple by the Syrian king Antiochus IV Epiphanes. *See also* Apocrypha/deuterocanonical literature; exile; Jeremiah, book of; Letter of Jeremiah.   D.W.S.

Barzillai (bahr-zil′*i*).

1 One of three wealthy individuals from the region of Gilead who sent food and other supplies to David and his followers when they were at Mahanaim during the rebellion of David's son Absalom (2 Sam. 17:27–29). Invited to become a part of David's court at Jerusalem, Barzillai refused the honor because of his advanced age (eighty years; 19:31–40). **2** A Meholathite man whose son Adriel married Merab, the daughter of Saul (2 Sam. 21:8). **3** A priest who married an unnamed daughter of Barzillai the Gileadite (probably **1** above). Thus, he took the name Barzillai for himself. His sons were excluded from the priesthood because their priestly genealogy seemed faulty (Ezra 2:59–63; Neh. 7:61–65).

Basemath (bas′uh-math).

1 A wife of Esau and the mother of Reuel (Gen. 26:34; 36:2–17). She is called the daughter of Elon the Hittite in Gen. 26:34, but is identified as the daughter of Ishmael in 36:3 (the daughter of Elon who married Esau is named Adah in 36:2). **2** The daughter of Solomon and wife of Ahimaaz, Solomon's officer in Naphtali (1 Kings 4:15).

Bashan (bay′shuhn; Heb., "smooth, soft earth"),
the fairly level, very fertile grain-producing plateau of south Syria extending across the Yarmuq to the foothills of Gilead. The name also included the Jebel Druze, the "many-peaked mountain of Bashan" (Ps. 68:15) as far as Salecah (Heb. *Salkah;* Deut. 3:10; Josh. 12:5; 13:11; 1 Chron. 5:11). In pre-Israelite days (prior to 1250 BCE) as the territory of King Og (Num. 21:33; 32:33; Deut. 1:4; 3:4; Josh. 9:10; Neh. 9:22), Bashan included the indeterminate region of Argob (1 Kings 4:13), apparently in the southeast. The fat bulls and cows of Bashan were proverbial (Ps. 22:12; Amos 4:1), as were rams, lambs, and goats, "all of them fatlings of Bashan" (Ezek. 39:18). The great trees of Bashan (Isa. 2:13;

Ezek. 27:6) may have come from the mountain. *See also* Gilead; Og; Salecah.   D.R.B.

basin. Several Hebrew words mean "basin," "bowl," "laver," or the like. One such word (*mizraq*) describes a utensil used in both cultic (Exod. 27:3; Num. 7) and noncultic settings (Amos 6:6; Zech. 9:15). Another common word (*kiyyor*) also identifies a vessel used in both cultic (Exod. 30:18) and secular settings (Zech. 12:6). According to Exod. 30:17–21, a large copper or bronze basin was used for priestly ablutions in the tabernacle; it stood near the altar (Exod. 40:7) and was fashioned from the mirrors of women (Exod. 38:8). Solomon's temple had ten of these basins (1 Kings 7:30, 38, 40) made by Hiram of Tyre. King Ahaz removed them from their stands (2 Kings 16:17; NRSV: "laver"). Other kinds of basins or bowls were used to catch the blood of sacrificial animals (Exod. 12:22; 24:6) or were temple vessels made of gold (1 Chron. 28:17; Ezra 1:10; 8:27). In the NT, Jesus pours water into a basin when he washes his disciples' feet (John 13:5).

bath, a liquid measure, approximately 5 gallons, equal to the ephah of dry measure (Isa. 5:10; Ezek. 45:10–11, 14).

bathing. References in the Bible to bathing as a normal human activity include Pharaoh's daughter bathing in a river (Exod. 2:5), Judith bathing in a spring (Jth. 12:7–8), and Bathsheba bathing in some undisclosed spot where she could be seen from the roof of the king's house (2 Sam. 11:2). Standard birth rituals also included washing the newborn infant (Ezek. 16:4). As a ritual act, bathing to remove ritual uncleanness was part of the priestly consecration ceremony for Aaron and his sons (Exod. 29:4; 30:17–21; 40:30–32; Lev. 8:6; 16:4, 24). Nonpriestly ritual bathings included purification from leprosy (Lev. 14:8–9) and other types of personal uncleanness (Lev. 15; Num. 19). Figuratively, bathing can symbolize moral

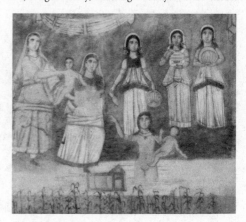

Pharaoh's daughter retrieving the infant Moses from his basket (Exod. 2:5); a panel from the third-century CE synagogue at Dura-Europos.

cleanness, as in the cleansing of the heart (Ps. 51:17; Jer. 4:14). Also to be classed as figurative are the washings associated with healing miracles, such as the curing of Naaman's leprosy (2 Kings 5:10–14) and the restoration of sight to the man born blind (John 9:7). A gruesome example of such figurative usage is the picture in Ps. 58:10 of the victor bathing his feet in the blood of his enemies.   J.S.K./M.A.P.

Bathsheba (bath-shee′buh), the daughter of Eliam, the son of Ahitophel, one of David's advisers (2 Sam. 11:3; 23:34). The wife of Uriah the Hittite, she was coveted, summoned, and impregnated by David while her husband was with Joab, fighting against the Ammonites at Rabbath, east of the Jordan (11:1–5). After David had ordered Uriah sent into the forefront of the battle, where he was killed, he married Bathsheba (11:6–27). The adultery with Bathsheba was rebuked by Nathan the prophet and the child born of that union was struck by God and died (12:1–23). Bathsheba later became the mother of Solomon (12:24), and she and Nathan collaborated to intercede with the elderly David in a way that would ensure Solomon's succession to the throne (1 Kings 1:11–31). In another instance, she appealed (unsuccessfully) to Solomon on behalf of Adonijah, Solomon's half brother and former rival for the throne, when Adonijah asked to marry Abishag the Shunammite (1 Kings 2:13–25). The second portion of her name, "-sheba" ("-shua" in 1 Chron. 3:5), probably refers to a foreign god, which may indicate the family of Bathsheba was of non-Israelite origin. *See also* David.   Y.G.

battering ram, a war engine that usually consisted of a heavy wooden ramrod, probably metal-tipped, suspended within a wooden tower in a fashion that allowed it to be worked back and forth. The tower was wheeled, so it could be moved up an earthen ramp and positioned it at the base of the walls of a city under siege; it was also armored

to afford protection to those within who were operating it. Biblical references to battering rams include possibly 2 Sam. 20:15, which speaks of Joab "battering" the walls of Abel of Beth-maacah (cf. 1 Macc. 1:43). The prophesies of Ezek. 4:2; 21:22; 26:9 depict the siege of Jerusalem and Tyre with a surrounding ramp topped with battering rams (see Isa. 22:5). In 2 Macc. 12:15, God is said to have overthrown Jericho in the days of Joshua "without battering rams or the engines of war."

The earliest examples of battering rams attested in the ancient Near East are ones mentioned in eighteenth-century BCE letters found at Mari, on the Upper Euphrates, and in seventeenth- and sixteenth-century BCE documents from Boghazkoy, the Hittite capital. The massive earthen embankments and plastered slopes (*terre pisé* and glacis) that first appeared in the Middle Bronze II period and that surrounded nearly all of the city-states of the Near East in the eighteenth to sixteenth centuries BCE were probably developed as a defense against these new machines of war. In the Iron Age (1200 BCE on) the Assyrians are known to have used these battering rams against the cities of Israel and Judah. A relief of Tiglath-pileser III (ca. 745–727 BCE) depicts a battering ram working against a tower of the city wall at Gezer (destroyed ca. 734 BCE). Reliefs from the palace of Sennacherib also show Assyrian ramps and battering rams in the depiction of the battle of 701 BCE (cf. 2 Kings 18:13–14). *See also* Assyria, Empire of; Gezer; Lachish; walls; war.   W.G.D.

battle. In the Bible there are many references to battles both on a large scale, where national armies struggle, and in individual combat, where two combatants represent the two groups in the dispute (1 Sam. 17:8–10). Descriptions of battles sometimes offer hints of strategy (Josh. 8:1–25) or the claim that divine activity is more important than the strength of the soldiers (Exod. 15:1–18). Israel's own testimony is that its land was gained and subsequently maintained through

The "Smiting of Dabigu," a city in northern Syria. *Top row:* The town under attack by archers, with a sapper and sealer (*right*). *Bottom row:* The impaled bodies of six vanquished inhabitants. Ornamental gates to a palace of Shalmaneser III (858–824 BCE).

armed struggle. Battles are recorded with various Canaanite cities and with neighboring countries. From a purely political viewpoint some of these battles were offensive (cf. Josh. 1–12) and some were defensive (Judg. 6:1–8:21). Archaeological research has produced evidence of even more battles involving Israel than are mentioned in the Bible. The Moabite Stone narrates various struggles between the Omride dynasty in Israel and Moab (ninth century BCE), and both the annals and palace reliefs of the Assyrian king Sennacherib (ca. 705–681 BCE) depict battles between the Assyrian forces and Judah under Hezekiah's leadership (715–687/6 BCE).

Nations such as Israel or Judah were often forced into battle by complex forces outside their control. One reason for this was geography: the Israelite tribal inheritance lay between the empires of Egypt and Mesopotamia (Assyria, Babylon, Persia). Political tensions between these empires almost always involved Israel as well. Furthermore, two main travel routes passed through the area, a north–south route along the Mediterranean coast known as the Way of the Sea (Lat. Via Maris) and another north–south route in Transjordan known as the King's Highway. These two routes were linked by a road through the Jezreel Valley in northern Israel. The imposing site of Megiddo guarded the western end of the valley and was itself the site of several battles. It is possible that this is the site intended by reference to Armageddon (the ultimate battle at the end of human history) in Rev. 16:16.

In the NT, Paul uses battle as a metaphor for the Christian life (cf. 1 Cor. 14:8). The conflict between God and evil is also depicted as a battle in Rev. 9:7, 9; 16:14; 20:8. *See also* Armageddon; war.

J.A.D.

battle-ax. *See* weapons.

battlement, an ornamentation on a wall that sometimes served as a guardrail to prevent people from falling off of a roof. The NRSV uses "parapet" in Deut. 22:8; Jth. 14:1. According to Deut. 22:8 persons who owned a house without a guardrail were criminally negligent if someone fell from their roof. An ornate example of a porch railing, made from limestone, was found in the excavations at Ramat Rahel, probably the Beth-hacherem of the Bible. Ornamentation is the main point of the figurative reference in Song of Sol. 8:9: "If she [our sister] is a wall, we will build upon her a battlement of silver." Though obscure, the passage may mean that the sister will be decked with jewelry on her wedding day, if she has remained a virgin.

beam, a shaped piece of wood whose length far exceeds its girth. In the Bible, "beam" refers to part of a loom and to timbers for construction of both buildings and gates. The "weaver's beam" was the large bar on which the warp cords were wound. It served as the model for a huge spear handle in biblical tradition (1 Sam. 17:7; 2 Sam. 21:19; 1 Chron. 11:23; 20:5). Any wood could be used, but the best was cedar (1 Kings 6:36; Song of Sol. 1:17). Construction beams were used to support walls and ceilings (1 Kings 6:6, 9) and could level stone courses (6:36). They could also be used in gates (Neh. 2:8; 3:3, 6) either as swing pivots or bars for locking against intrusion. Symbolic beams of God's chambers are mentioned in Ps. 104:3. On Persian authority, a beam from a seditious man's house could be used to impale him (Ezra 6:11) and the beams of his house would cry out against an evildoer (Hab. 2:11). The KJV uses the word "beam" (NRSV: "log") in Jesus's saying about tending to other people's minor faults while ignoring the major weakness in oneself (Matt. 7:3–5; Luke 6:41–42).

R.S.B.

beards. Judging from ancient reliefs, Egyptians were generally clean shaven and Syrians were bearded, while in Mesopotamia the fashion changed several times. The Israelites depicted in the Black Obelisk of Shalmaneser III (mid-ninth century BCE) and the Israelite delegation standing before Sennacherib in the Lachish reliefs (late eighth century BCE) are bearded. This fits with what can be discerned from biblical references. Regulations concerning specific types of beard trim (Lev. 19:27; 21:5) imply that beards were typical for some men in some time periods (cf. 13:29–30; 14:9). David (1 Sam. 21:13), Mephibosheth (2 Sam. 19:24), Amasa (2 Sam. 20:9), and Ezra (Ezra 9:3) are specifically depicted as bearded. The lack of a full beard could be cause for embarrassment (2 Sam. 10:4–5; cf. Isa. 7:20; 15:2; Jer. 48:37), though beardlessness was sometimes a sign of mourning (Jer. 41:5). Beards, like hair, could be treated with oil, and oil running down the beard of Aaron is presented poetically as a paradigmatic symbol of goodness and pleasantness (Ps. 133:1–2). Plucking out the hairs of a beard was a form of torture (Isa. 50:6), but taking a person by the beard was apparently a show of affection (2 Sam. 20:9—though, in this case, the show of affection is duplicitous).

M.Z.B./M.A.P.

beasts, a general term for animals (Gen. 1:24) or, more often, dangerous animals (Rev. 6:8). It is also employed pejoratively for human beings (Titus 1:12). In apocalyptic literature, fantastic beasts are often described in mythical language. Dan. 7 uses four such beasts to symbolize four kingdoms, and in Revelation a beast from the sea symbolizes the Roman Empire (13:1), a beast from the earth represents the leaders of the province of Asia (13:11), and a beast from the abyss portrays the antichrist (11:7; 17:8). *See also* abyss; antichrist; Behemoth; dragon; Leviathan; Rahab; serpent.

Beatitudes (bee-at'uh-tyoodz; Lat., "blesseds"), declarations typically associated with the Sermon on the Mount in Matthew (5:3–12) and the Sermon on the Plain in Luke (6:20–23). They are pronouncements that confer a blessing upon persons who are characterized by what they are (e.g., the poor) or do (e.g., the peacemakers). The blessing assures the addressees of the vindication and reward that attend God's salvation and thus provides encouragement in time of difficulty. Luke has four Beatitudes balanced by four woes (6:20–26), and all take the form of direct address in the second-person plural ("Blessed are you . . ."). Matthew has nine Beatitudes and no woes (5:3–12), and all but the last are in the third-person plural ("Blessed are the . . ." or "Blessed are those who . . ."). Both general (e.g., Jer. 17:7; John 20:9) and specific (e.g., Matt. 17:7; Luke 1:42) beatitudes are also found elsewhere in the Bible. *See also* mercy; peace; persecution; poor, poverty; purity; righteousness; Sermon on the Mount.   J.D.K.

Beautiful Gate. *See* Nicanor.

Bebai (bee′b*i*).
   1 The leader of a family of 623 people who returned to Judea from the Babylonian exile (Ezra 2:11; Neh. 7:16 credits 628 returnees to the family). Specific mention is made of a son named Zechariah (Ezra 8:11) and of four additional descendants, named Jehohanan, Hananiah, Zabbai, and Athlai (10:28).
   2 One of the persons who signed Ezra's sealed document of covenant renewal (Neh. 10:14), possibly the same as 1 or one of his descendants.

Becher (bee′kuhr).
   1 A son of Benjamin (Gen. 46:21; 1 Chron. 7:6, 8).
   2 The ancestor of an Ephraimite family group (Num. 26:35).

bed, a place to recline. In biblical times, most people slept on the floor or on a mud-brick bench (1 Sam. 28:23; Mark 4:21) using garments for mattress and blankets (Exod. 22:27). The well-to-do often had a separate bedchamber (2 Sam. 4:7; 2 Kings 11:2) with elaborate furnishings (Esther 1:6). A wooden bed frame (ninth century BCE) still showing signs of stringing has been found in a tomb in Jericho and is perhaps the type of bed mentioned in 2 Kings 4:10 and 2 Chron. 16:14. King Og of Bashan was famous for having an iron bed of enormous size (Deut. 3:11). Excavations at the palace of Ahab (869–850 BCE) revealed large numbers of small ivory pieces that were probably inlaid in beds and other furniture (1 Kings 22:39); "beds of ivory" were condemned by Amos as symbols of foreign influence and ostentatious wealth (3:15; 6:1–4). According to Luke 11:7, it was common in the NT era for Palestinian families to sleep together in one bed. The bed functions in a number of ways in the Bible: it is a place to sleep or relax (Ps. 132:3; Luke 17:34); a location for dreams and visions (Job 7:13; Dan. 2:28) and for both good and evil meditation (Ps. 63:6; Mic. 2:1); a pallet for the aged, sick, or disabled (Gen. 49:33; 2 Sam. 3:31; Matt. 9:2); and a site for sexual acts,

including lovemaking (Song of Sol. 5:13), adultery (Gen. 49:4), and participation in fertility rites (Isa. 57:7–9). Figuratively, a bed can be a sign of wealth (Song of Sol. 3:7–10), or it can serve as a metaphor for death (Job 17:13; Isa. 57:2), life (Exod. 21:18), apostasy (Ezek. 23:17), or sex (Heb. 13:4). A bed is also an area that can receive or transmit contamination and, as such, is subject to purification (Lev. 15:4, 5, 21–26).   D.R.E.

Beelzebul (bee-el′zi-buhl; Heb., "baal prince"). *See* Baal-zebub.

Beer (bee′uhr; Heb., "well").
   1 A location in the Transjordan where the Israelites dug a well (Num. 21:16–18). Its exact location is unknown.
   2 The place to which Jotham fled for refuge after implicitly attacking the kingship of Abimelech (Judg. 9:21). This was probably modern el-Bireh, north of the Plain of Esdraelon and about ten miles south of the southern tip of the Sea of Galilee.

Beeri (bee′uhr-*i*).
   1 The Hittite father of Esau's wife Judith (Gen. 26:34).
   2 The father of the Israelite prophet Hosea (Hos. 1:1).

Beeroth (bee′uh-roth; Heb., "wells"; cf. Beirut), a Gibeonite city in Benjamin (Josh. 9:17; 18:25). It was the home of the murderers of Ishbaal (2 Sam. 4:2–3), and of Naharai, Joab's armor-bearer and one of David's group of elite warriors known as "the Thirty" (2 Sam. 23:37; 1 Chron. 11:39). Seven hundred and forty-three exiles from Beeroth are included in the census of the first return from Babylon (Ezra 2:25; see also Neh. 7:29; 1 Esd. 5:19). The site has not been conclusively identified, but the most likely location is modern Khirbet el-Burj; note the nearby site Khirbet el-Biyar, which was occupied only in later periods, but which may preserve the name of Beeroth. Other suggestions for its location include Nebi Samwil and el-Bireh (east of Ramallah; this may be Berea or Bereth, 1 Macc. 9:4).   M.D.C.

Beer-sheba (bee′uhr-shee′buh), the major city in the northern Negev desert, in the territory of the tribe of Simeon (Josh. 19:2). The Beer-sheba plain with its ample winter pasturage is well suited for seminomadic living; thus it served as the principal homestead of Israel's ancestors.
   A biblical tradition explains the derivation of the name Beer-sheba. Abraham and Abimelech, king of Gerar, settled their dispute over a well (Heb. *be'er*) by concluding a treaty "sworn" (Heb. *nishbe'u*) ceremoniously with an offering of "seven" (Heb. *sheba'*) ewes; the site was thereafter named Beer-sheba, i.e., "the well of swearing seven" (Gen. 21:22–32). A generation later, renewed contention between the shepherds of Isaac

Reconstructed altar made of hewn stones (cf. Josh. 8:31) found at Beer-sheba, from the eighth century BCE.

and Abimelech was resolved by another oath at Beer-sheba (26:26–33).

An early tradition records that Samuel's two sons were judges at Beer-sheba (1 Sam. 8:2), and it is likely that the city served as a regional administrative center during the monarchy (ca. 1004–587/6 BCE). David's realm stretched "from Dan to Beer-sheba"; this geographic description became the standard term of the limits of Israelite settlement in the promised land (2 Sam. 17:11; 24:2; 1 Kings 5:5).

The prophet Amos makes critical reference to the sanctity of this southern city (5:5; 8:14), which could claim Abraham as the founder of its local religious site. The patriarch had planted a tamarisk and "invoked the name of the LORD, God of the Universe" in Beer-sheba (Gen. 21:33).

The Negev was lost to the Edomites in the late seventh century BCE; Beer-sheba and its environs were temporarily regained during the governorship of Nehemiah (sixth century BCE; Neh. 11:26). Archaeological excavations at the mound of Tell es-Saba', three miles east of the modern city, have uncovered five occupation levels in a walled fortress that date to the Israelite period. A large ashlar stone altar, disassembled and reused in secondary construction, was recovered at the site. The altar's profanation may be evidence for the reform undertaken by King Josiah, who centralized worship in Jerusalem (2 Kings 23:8).   M.C.

beggar, one who is poor and needy, who begs for food or asks for alms. In biblical narratives, beggars are sometimes described as blind (Mark 10:46–52; John 9:8) or lame (Acts 3:10). One parable of Jesus concerns a poor man named Lazarus (probably a beggar) who, upon death, was received into the bosom of Abraham in contrast to a rich man who went to the torments of Hades (Luke 16:19–30). Another character in one of Jesus's parables identifies begging as something he would be too proud to do (Luke 16:3). Likewise, Sir. 40:28 says that it is better to die than to beg (cf. Sir. 18:33). Ps. 109:10 records a curse upon one's enemies: "May his children wander about and beg."   J.G.G.

Behemoth (bi-hee′muhth), a mighty, mortal beast (Job 40:15–16) that served as an object lesson for Job (40:19–24). It may have been the hippopotamus, but some literature from the Second Temple period understands Behemoth to be a mythical animal (1 Enoch 60:7–9; 2 Esd. 6:49–52). *See also* Leviathan.

beka(h) (bee′kuh), a unit of weight averaging 6.2 grams in the inscribed specimens of balance weights recovered to date. Exod. 38:26 identifies it as half a shekel "by the shekel of the sanctuary" (NRSV). See also Gen. 24:22 and Exod. 30:13, 15 for its use as gift and offering. *See also* weights and measures.

Bel, one of the names of Marduk, the leading god of Babylon (Isa. 46:1; Jer. 50:2). In Bel and the Dragon, an addition to Daniel included in the Apocrypha/deuterocanonical literature, Bel is the name of an idol who is fed regularly and supposedly eats the food. Daniel exposes the deception, revealing that the food is actually eaten by the priests.

Bel and the Dragon, one of the Additions to Daniel found at the end of that book in the LXX (and in the Theodotion version of Daniel, a second-century CE Greek translation). It may have been composed in Hebrew and added to some manuscripts of the Hebrew-Aramaic version of Daniel during the course of the second century BCE.

The narrative is a mixture of folklore and Jewish satire directed against idolatry. It centers around the act of eating, becoming more fantastic and humorous as it goes along. The food offered to the "dead" god, Bel, is eaten by his living priests, who are put to death by the king, Cyrus, for their deception after Daniel exposes them as frauds. The dragon, a living god, eats Daniel's concoction and dies. Angered, the Babylonians force the king to cast Daniel into the lions' den. The lions' daily ration of two human bodies and two sheep is suspended, but they do not eat Daniel. In the meantime, God transports the prophet Habakkuk from Judea—suspended by his hair—with boiled pottage and bread to feed Daniel while in the lions' den. After a week, Daniel is discovered alive by the king, who comes to mourn him. He orders Daniel's enemies cast into the den, where they are immediately eaten. Protestants include Bel and the Dragon among the Apocrypha, while Roman Catholic and Eastern Orthodox Christians print it with the canonical text of Daniel. *See also* Apocrypha/deuterocanonical literature; Daniel, Additions to; idol.   D.W.S.

OUTLINE OF CONTENTS

Bel and the Dragon

Belial (bee'lee-uhl), **Beliar** (bee'lee-uhr; Heb., "wickedness," "worthlessness"). Belial appears as a popular name for Satan in the Qumran literature. A variant form of the name, Beliar, appears in Jewish literature from the Second Temple period (*Jubilees, Sibylline Oracles, Testaments of the Twelve Patriarchs*) and, once, in the NT (2 Cor. 6:15: "What has Christ to do with Beliar?"). Following scholarly consensus on the root meaning of the word, the NRSV often translates as "worthless fellows" what the KJV more literally renders as "sons of Belial" (see 1 Sam. 10:27).

bells (Heb. *pa'amon*, "striker"). Bells made of gold were attached to Aaron's vestments (Exod. 28:33–34; 39:25, 26). Another Hebrew word (*metsilot*, "that which tinkles") refers to bells used in equine trappings (Zech. 14:20). *See also* Aaron; tabernacle.

Beloved Disciple, a disciple mentioned only in the Gospel of John and never identified by name. Appearing first at the Last Supper, reclining at Jesus's bosom, at Peter's bidding he asks the identity of Jesus's betrayer (13:23–25). At the crucifixion, standing beneath the cross with Jesus's mother, he is entrusted with her care (19:25–27). On Easter morning, he outruns Peter to Jesus's tomb and finds it empty (20:2–10). Later, in Galilee, he identifies for Peter a figure standing on the shore as the risen Jesus (21:7). Finally, Jesus parries Peter's question about whether the Beloved Disciple will live until Jesus's return (21:20–23). He is also identified as the person responsible for writing down some of the material contained in the Gospel of John (21:24). The Beloved Disciple is probably to be identified with the "other disciple" who gains for Peter admittance to the courtyard of the high priest (18:15–16) and with the trustworthy witness of 19:35 (cf. 21:24). In every case except 19:25–27, 35, the Beloved Disciple appears alongside Peter.

The assumption that the Beloved Disciple must have been one of the twelve led to the traditional view that he was John the son of Zebedee. Yet that identification is never made in the Gospel. Moreover, the Gospel of John contains no accounts of the episodes in which, according to the other Gospels, John the son of Zebedee was a participant (cf. Mark 1:19–20, 29; 3:17; 5:37; 9:2; 10:35–45; 13:3; 14:33). Numerous alternative suggestions have been put forward regarding the identity of this disciple, but none has been able to replace John as the favored candidate. *See also* John the apostle; John, Gospel According to; John, Letters of.

D.M.S.

Belshazzar (bel-shaz'uhr; Neo-Babylonian *bel-shar-utsur,* "Bel protect the king"), the ruler of Babylon in the book of Daniel. He gives a drunken feast at which he, along with his lords, wives, and concubines, drank from the gold and silver vessels taken from the temple in Jerusalem, praising the gods of gold, silver, and other elements (5:1–4). This feast is interrupted by the mysterious appearance of fingers writing on the wall. When the king's wise men are unable to translate the words, the queen informs the king of Daniel's abilities, and he is brought in to interpret the writing. He interprets the words as a proclamation of doom and he denounces Belshazzar, who is slain that very night.

The story raises some historical problems. For instance, the book of Daniel identifies Belshazzar as the son of Nebuchadnezzar (5:2, 11) and as the last king of Babylon (5:30–31); other historical records indicate that Belshazzar was the son of Nabonidus, who was the last king of Babylon (556–539 BCE), Belshazzar being only a regent. *See also* Daniel, book of; Nabonidus; Nebuchadnezzar.

J.J.C.

Belteshazzar (bel'ti-shaz'uhr), the Babylonian name given to Daniel at the royal court (Dan. 1:7). The underlying form was probably Neo-Babylonian *balat-su-utsur,* "protect his life," which in turn was probably abbreviated from *Bel-* (or *Marduk-*) *balat-su-utsur*—an invocation of a Babylonian god for protection. *See also* Daniel, book of.

Benaiah (bi-nay'yuh; Heb., "the LORD has built").
1 The son of Jehoiada, a priest (1 Chron. 27:5) from Kabzeel (2 Sam. 23:20) and one of David's group of elite warriors known as "the Thirty" (1 Chron. 27:6). He supervised the Cherethites and Pelethites (2 Sam. 8:18) and was renowned for his heroic exploits (23:20–23). With Zadok and Nathan, he supported Solomon, whose opponents he executed at Solomon's instruction, after which he was appointed chief of the army (1 Kings 1).
2 An Ephraimite commander in David's army (1 Chron. 27:14).
3 A priest who participated in the celebration of the ark's arrival in Jerusalem during the reign of David (1 Chron. 15:24; 16:6).
4 A levitical musician appointed by David (1 Chron. 15:20; 16:5).
5 The grandfather of Jahaziel, an Asaphite from the time of King Jehoshaphat (2 Chron. 20:14, perhaps to be identified with one of the preceding).
6 A Simeonite leader who settled in rich pastureland near Gedor in the time of Hezekiah (1 Chron. 4:36).
7 A levitical temple official in the time of Hezekiah (2 Chron. 31:13).
8 The father of Pelatiah, a Jerusalemite leader who died after Ezekiel's condemnation (Ezek. 11:1, 13).
9 The name of several postexilic Israelites who divorced their foreign wives in response to Ezra's proclamation (Ezra 10:25, 30, 35, 43; 1 Esd. 9 gives different names). F.E.G.

Ben-ammi (ben-am'i; Heb., "son of my people"), the name given by Lot's daughter to the offspring of her incestuous union with her father; the ancestor of the Ammonites (Gen. 19:38).

benediction, a proclamation of God's blessing on someone. The great priestly blessing of Num.

6:24–26 is a prominent example. Many NT letters close with benedictions (e.g., Rom. 15:13; 2 Cor. 13:14; Heb. 13:20–21).

Benedictus (ben'uh-dik'toos; Lat., "blessed"), a traditional liturgical name for the poetic oracle attributed to Zechariah, the father of John the Baptist, in Luke 1:68–79. It is named for the first word in the Latin translation. According to the biblical account, Zechariah was struck dumb when he disbelieved the angelic promise of John's birth (1:5–25); then, when John was born and Zechariah indicated that his name should be "John," he was filled with the Holy Spirit and prophesied (1:67). The oracle praises God for faithfulness to Israel and indicates that John will go before the Lord to prepare the way for God's salvation. *See also* Elizabeth; hymn; John the Baptist; Zechariah.   J.M.E.

Ben-hadad (ben-hay'dad; Heb., "son of Hadad"). A number of Assyrian kings were named Ben-hadad. Just how many there were—and which exploits are to be attributed to whom—are disputed. The following presents one popular reconstruction of the evidence.

1 Ben-hadad I, son of Tabrimmon and king of Damascus ca. 885–865 BCE. He is referred to in 1 Kings 15:18–21 as a contemporary of King Baasha of Israel and King Asa of Judah. He was bribed by Asa to break his alliance with Israel, after which he conquered several cities and the territory of Naphtali.

2 Ben-hadad II (ca. 865–842 BCE), the king who attacked Israel several times during the reign of Ahab, who was able to defeat him. He was then forced to restore cities he had taken from Ahab's father, Omri, and to grant Ahab commercial privileges in Damascus (1 Kings 20). This might be the same person identified in Assyrian annals as Hadadezer: he is said to have participated with Ahab in a coalition of Syrian kings who resisted the army of the Assyrian emperor Shalmaneser III at Qarqar in 853.

3 Ben-hadad III (ca. 842–797 BCE), the king who besieged Samaria during the time of Elisha (2 Kings 6:24). This Ben-hadad was murdered by Hazael, one of his officers (2 Kings 8:7–15), after receiving a prophecy from Elisha.

4 Ben-hadad IV (ca. 806–?), the son of Hazael; he took several cities from Jehoahaz, king of Israel, which Jehoahaz's son Jehoash recaptured (2 Kings 13:24–25). This is apparently the same person identified in a stela at Zakkur as Mari, who paid tribute to the Assyrian king Adad-nirari III after being besieged in Damascus.   F.E.G.

Benjamin (ben'juh-muhn; Heb., "son of the right hand").

1 Jacob's last son, born after his return to Canaan from Mesopotamia. Benjamin was named Ben-oni (Heb., "son of my suffering") by his mother Rachel, who died in childbirth, but Jacob preferred "Benjamin" (Gen. 35:18). He is mentioned often in association with Joseph, his only full brother. Like Joseph, he becomes his father's favorite son (as "the child of his old age," 44:20). *See also* Joseph; Rachel.

2 One of the twelve tribes of Israel. The tribe of Benjamin, which traced its ancestry back to the son of Jacob and Rachel listed in 1 above, occupied the central ridge between Jerusalem and Bethel (Josh. 18:11–20). It was originally associated with the northern tribes and so, according to some theories, may have been formed as a separate entity relatively late. When a Levite's concubine was raped by a number of men in Benjaminite territory, the other tribes avenged the atrocity in a war that resulted in the death of all the women of Benjamin (Judg. 19–20). As an afterthought, four hundred virgins from Jabesh-gilead were kidnapped to provide the remaining Benjaminites with wives (Judg. 21). The judge Ehud came from the tribe of Benjamin, as did Saul, Israel's first king. The tribe also recognized Saul's son Ishbaal as king instead of David until Abner insisted otherwise (2 Sam. 2:8–9; 3:17–21). The tribe, which constituted one of Solomon's administrative districts (1 Kings 4:18), produced two opponents to the Davidic dynasty, Shimei and Sheba (2 Sam 16:5; 19:16; 20:1), but was incorporated into the southern kingdom of Judah by Solomon's successor. In the NT, the apostle Paul (also known as Saul) was from the tribe of Benjamin (Phil. 3:5). *See also* tribes.   F.E.G./M.A.P.

Beracah (bair'uh-kuh; Heb., "blessed").

1 A relative of Saul from the tribe of Benjamin who joined David's warriors at Ziklag (1 Chron. 12:3).

2 A valley in central Judah near Tekoa. During the reign of Jehoshaphat an alliance was formed by Edom, Ammon, and Moab, and they invaded Judah. But, as promised by the prophet Jahaziel, the army was destroyed when they began fighting among themselves; the people blessed God for the victory, because of the spoils taken and the peace that would follow, and named the site accordingly (2 Chron. 20:26). The location has not been identified. *See also* Jahaziel.   D.R.B.

Berea (bi-ree'uh), a place near Jerusalem (1 Macc. 9:4), not to be confused with Beroea. *See also* Beroea.

Berechiah (bair'uh-ki'uh; Heb., "the LORD has blessed").

1 A son of Zerubbabel (1 Chron. 3:20).

2 The father of Asaph and son of Shimea; a Levite (1 Chron. 6:39; 15:17).

3 A son of Asa; a Levite and a gatekeeper for the ark (1 Chron. 9:16; 15:23).

4 A son of Meshillemoth; an Ephraimite chief (2 Chron. 28:12).

5 The father of Meshullam (Neh. 3:4, 30; 6:18).

6 The father of the prophet Zechariah, a son of Iddo (Zech. 1:1, 7).

7 The full name of Jeremiah's scribe Baruch, occurring on a late seventh-century BCE seal impression from Judah that reads "Belonging to Berechiah son of Neriah the scribe." *See also* Baruch.

8 Beracah, a Benjaminite follower of David (1 Chron. 12:3), whose name is often emended to Berechiah (cf. LXX). M.D.C.

Beriah (bi-ri′uh; Heb., "in misery" or "in misfortune"; see 1 Chron. 7:23).

1 A son of Asher; he was among those who went with Jacob to Egypt at Joseph's invitation (Gen. 46:17). He became the head of a family group (Beriites) who later left Egypt in the exodus with Moses (Num. 26:44).

2 A son of Ephraim, born after two other sons, Ezer and Elead, were killed by the Philistines in a livestock raid against Gath; his name reflects the mourning for those killed (1 Chron. 7:23).

3 A Benjaminite leader who lived at Aijalon and was successful in fighting the Philistines at Gath (1 Chron. 8:13, 16). Some scholars think he may be the same as **2**, reflecting a family group of mixed Ephraimite and Benjaminite origins.

4 A Levite, the son of Shimei of the Gershonite family group (1 Chron. 23:10–11). D.R.B.

Bernice (buhr-nees′), the daughter of Herod Agrippa I and sister of Herod Agrippa II. She was married to Herod of Chalcis, her father's brother. After his death, in 48 CE, she apparently carried on an incestuous relationship with her brother, with whom she listened to Paul while he was a prisoner in Caesarea (Acts 25:13–26:32). In 64 CE, she married Polomon of Cilicia, but then abandoned him to continue her incestuous affair. When the emperor Titus came to Judea, she became his mistress and later followed him to Rome, causing a scandal. *See also* Herod.

Beroea (bi-ree′uh), a Macedonian city located twenty-four miles inland from the Aegean Sea in the plain below Mount Bermion. Springs in the area gave the city its name, "place of many waters." After leaving Thessalonica during the second journey, Paul and Silas probably traveled the main east–west Roman road, the Egnatian Way, to Beroea, where the people were receptive to Paul's message and escorted him safely to Athens (Acts 17:10–15). Later, a man identified as Sopater from Beroea is named among Paul's companions. In 2 Macc. 31:1–7, Menelaus is executed at Beroea according to what is called "the method that is customary in that place": submersion in a tower filled with ashes. Beroea is not to be confused with Berea (1 Macc. 9:4).

beryl, a precious stone of a sea-green color. Emerald and aquamarine are two types of beryl. It was one of the twelve stones on the high priest's breastplate (Exod. 28:20) and one of the jewels worn by the king of Tyre (Ezek. 28:13). Ezekiel had visions of wheels that gleamed like beryl (1:6; 10:9), and

Daniel had a vision of a man whose body was like beryl (10:6). According to the book of Revelation, beryl will be one of the stones used for the foundation of the wall of the heavenly Jerusalem (21:20). *See also* carbuncle.

bet, beth, the second letter of the Hebrew alphabet. It has a numeric value of two. It has been proposed that the letter was originally a crude pictogram of a house. The use of this term as "house" or "dwelling" resulted in its use as a portion of compound place-names such as Bethlehem, Bethel, Bethphage, Bethsaida, and the like. The term can also be used to indicate a dynasty such as the "house of David," a reference to the heirs of the Davidic line.

Bethabara (beth-ab′uh-ruh; Heb., "house of the ford"), where some biblical manuscripts indicate that John was baptizing (John 1:28, KJV; the best manuscripts, however, read "Bethany"). John 1:28 also describes the place of baptizing as "beyond the Jordan" (east of the Jordan), which makes the identification with Bethabara even less likely. There was a Bethany located east of the Jordan, but a sixth-century mosaic floor map discovered in Medeba (modern-day Madaba) in Jordan, shows Bethabara on the west side of that river. *See also* Bethany.

Beth-anath (beth-ay′nath; Heb., "house of Anat [a deity]"), a walled Canaanite city in the territory of Naphtali in Upper Galilee (Josh. 19:38) whose inhabitants the Israelites could not expel but subjugated as servants (Judg. 1:33). Its location is not certain, although it is sometimes identified with modern Safed el-Battikh, about fifteen miles east and slightly south of Tyre.

Bethany (beth′uh-nee).

1 A village on the lower eastern slope of the Mount of Olives (Mark 11:1; Luke 19:29), about two miles east of Jerusalem (John 11:18). According to John's Gospel, it was here that Jesus raised Lazarus, the brother of Mary and Martha, from the dead (11:1–44). Jesus is said to visit the home of Mary and Martha in Luke's Gospel as well, though the location in Bethany is not specified in that account (10:38–42). Other stories associate Bethany with the last week of Jesus's life. Jesus's triumphal entry into Jerusalem began near here (Mark 11:1–11; Luke 19:28–38), and he was anointed here in the home of Simon the Leper (Matt. 26:6–13; Mark 14:3–9) or in the home of Lazarus (John 12:1–8). Finally, Bethany is the site of Jesus's ascension into heaven in Luke 24:50–51. *See also* Lazarus; Martha; Mary.

2 Bethany beyond the Jordan, where John the Baptist baptized (John 1:28); some manuscripts, however, give the location as Bethabara. *See also* Bethabara. M.K.M.

Beth-arabah (beth-air′uh-buh), a town on the northern border of Judah (Josh. 15:6, 61) and the southern border of Benjamin (Josh. 18:18, 22), possibly modern 'Ain el-Gharbah southeast of Jericho.

Beth-aven (beth-ay'vuhn).

1 A location near Ai (Josh. 7:2).

2 A regional designation for the northwest corner of land allotted to Benjamin (Josh. 18:12). In 1 Sam. 13:5 it is placed west of Michmash; Saul's conflict with the Philistines moved "beyond" it into Ephraimite territory (14:23). The prophet Hosea warns against visiting there as a possible idolatrous act (4:15), considers it a site for issuing public warnings (5:8), and associates an idolatrous calf (calves) with it (10:5), the latter a possible designation of Bethel and its shrine.

Bethel (beth'uhl; Heb., "house of God"), an important biblical city (modern Beitin) on the north–south mountain road north of Jerusalem. Bethel had few natural defenses, but it did have plentiful water from nearby springs. It also stood at the intersection of the north–south road that passed through the central hill country and the main east–west road that led from Jericho to the Mediterranean Sea.

W. F. Albright and, later, J. L. Kelso excavated Bethel in 1927, 1934, 1954, 1957, and 1960. Their excavations revealed a thriving town of the Middle Bronze Age (2000–1500 BCE), the period of the biblical patriarchs. Remains included a stone sanctuary with many cultic objects.

Bethel, formerly named Luz (Gen. 28:19), was conquered by the Joseph tribes (late thirteenth century BCE; Judg. 1:22–25) and became a part of the tribe of Ephraim. The religious heritage of Bethel for the Hebrews went back to Jacob (eighteenth century BCE). When Jacob was going to Aram, he spent the night at Bethel and had a dream. As a result he built a shrine there and named the place Bethel (Gen. 28:19; 35:1–7).

Surprisingly, the conquest of Bethel is not mentioned in the book of Joshua, although the men of Bethel are said to have aided the men of Ai against the Hebrews (8:17). This makes the omission of the conquest of Bethel even more striking. The site of Beitin does show a massive destruction by fire at the end of the Late Bronze Age, the time usually ascribed to the conquest (late thirteenth century BCE). W. F. Albright has suggested that the biblical account of the fall of Ai was transferred

from the capture and destruction of Bethel. Ai (modern et-Tell, southeast of Bethel) was not inhabited at the time of the conquest; it was only an impressive ruin.

In addition to the discoveries dating from the Middle Bronze Age, several fine houses were excavated dating to the Late Bronze Age (1500–1200 BCE). Also belonging to this period were flagstone pavements and a drainage system.

In the period of the judges (1200–1000 BCE), Bethel was an important town. The ark of the covenant was located there for a time (Judg. 20:18–28), and it was a center of the tribal confederacy. Samuel made regular visits to Bethel on his annual circuit while he was a judge. But the town was not mentioned during the reigns of David and Solomon, its role as a sanctuary apparently being usurped by Jerusalem, the capital city. With the division of the kingdoms during the reign of Rehoboam, Bethel again rose to prominence (late tenth century BCE). Jeroboam I made it a chief sanctuary and set up a golden calf there (1 Kings 12:26–33). Bethel was a royal sanctuary at the time of Amos (cf. Amos 7:12–13). From the evidence of excavation, Bethel was apparently destroyed by the Assyrians (722/1 BCE). During the resurgence of Judah's power at the time of Josiah (ca. 640–609 BCE), Bethel's sanctuary was destroyed and its priests killed (2 Kings 23:15–20), but the city was spared. Bethel was not destroyed by the Babylonians under Nebuchadnezzar, but was destroyed either by the Babylonian ruler Nabonidus or the Persians.

The town was soon rebuilt and showed continued growth through the Hellenistic and Roman periods (333 BCE–324 CE). The Roman town shows the first use of cisterns, suggesting an increased population or water use beyond the capacity of the springs. *See also* Ai; Luz.   J.F.D.

Bethesda (buh-thez'duh; Heb., "house of mercy"), a name given in some NT manuscripts and used in most English Bibles (including KJV, NIV, NJB) for the pool near the "Sheep Gate" in Jerusalem (John 5:2). Other manuscripts use Bethzatha, which is what appears in the NRSV. *See also* Bethzatha.

Beth-hoglah (beth-hog'luh; Heb., meaning uncertain, possibly "the place of the partridge"), a city on the border between Judah and Benjamin, but assigned to the tribe of Benjamin (Josh. 15:6; 18:21). It is tentatively identified with modern Ein Hajlah, about six miles northwest of the mouth of the Jordan River.

Beth-horon (beth-hor'uhn; Heb., "house of [the god] Horon"), a city assigned to the levitical family of Kohath (Josh. 21:22; 1 Chron. 6:68), near the border of Benjamin (Josh. 18:13, 14). "Upper" and "Lower" Beth-horon are frequently distinguished as two villages built by Sheerah, the daughter of Beraiah and a descendant of Ephraim; she also built a third village, Uzzen-Sheerah, the location

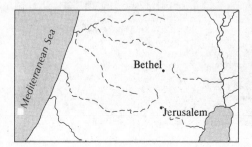

of which is unknown (cf. Josh. 16:3, 5; 1 Chron. 7:24).

Beth-horon guarded a major pass on the road from the coast by way of the Valley of Aijalon to the hill country and Jerusalem (2 Sam. 13:34, LXX); because of its strategic location, Beth-horon was the site of frequent military activity. Joshua chased the Amorite kings from Gibeon "by way of the ascent of Beth-horon" (Josh. 10:10–11; cf. *Jubilees* 34:4). Beth-horon was attacked by Philistine raiders (1 Sam. 13:18) and by Amaziah's northern mercenaries (2 Chron. 25:13). Solomon fortified Beth-horon (1 Kings 9:17; 2 Chron. 8:5), but Pharaoh Shishak captured it ca. 925 BCE. Judas Maccabeus defeated Seron here (1 Macc. 3:16, 24), and Nicanor's army camped here (7:39). Later, Bacchides refortified the city (1 Macc. 9:50; cf. Jth. 4:4). *See also* Shishak.   M.D.C.

Beth-jeshimoth (beth-jes′uh-moth), a settlement east of the Jordan in the plains of Moab opposite Jericho, the area of one of the encampments of the Israelites (Num. 33:49). It was captured by Joshua and assigned to the tribe of Reuben (Josh. 12:3; 13:20), although by the time of the exile it was again under Moabite control (Ezek. 25:9). The site is usually identified as modern Tell el 'Azeima, about two and a half miles northeast of the north end of the Dead Sea. *See also* Jeshimon.

Bethlehem (beth′li-hem; Heb. *bet lekhem,* "house of bread").

1 A small town of over twenty thousand inhabitants, about three miles southwest of Jerusalem. At an elevation of 2,460 feet above sea level, Bethlehem sits along the north–south ridge road of the central highlands. It looks westward to the fertile cultivated slopes around Beit Jala and eastward to the desolate wilderness of Judah. Because of the presence of the modern town, very little systematic archaeological excavation has been possible in

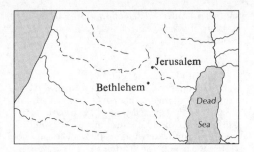

Bethlehem. The limited investigation indicates the site was inhabited sporadically from prehistoric times.

Bethlehem is first mentioned in historical texts in one of the Amarna letters (letters written to Egyptian pharaohs by Canaanite and Syrian kings) from the fourteenth century BCE. In that letter, a Jerusalem ruler complains that Bit-Lahmi has deserted to the side of the Apiru people. In the Bible, Bethlehem is first mentioned as the burial site for Rachel (Gen. 35:19; 48:7; but cf. 1 Sam. 10:2, which locates that burial site north of Jerusalem near Ramah). During the period of the judges, Bethlehem was the home of the Levite who went to act as priest for a man named Micah in Ephraim (Judg. 17:7–13). It was also the home of the family of the concubine whose brutal rape and murder led to a massacre of the people of Gibeah and a war against the tribe of Benjamin (Judg. 19–20). Bethlehem also figures prominently in the story of Ruth, the great-grandmother of David (Ruth 1; 2:4; 4:11). The city is the family home of David (1 Sam. 16:1; 17:12) and the place where he is anointed king (1 Sam. 16:4–13). After the division of the kingdom into Israel (north) and Judah (south) following Solomon's death, Bethlehem became one of the fifteen cities in Benjamin and Judah fortified by Rehoboam (2 Chron. 11:5–12). By the time of

View of modern Bethlehem from the west.

Micah in the eighth century BCE, however, Bethlehem was only a small, insignificant village (Mic. 5:2). Following the murder of Gedaliah, the governor of Judah, under the Babylonians in 582 BCE, some of the Judean refugees stayed near Bethlehem on their way to Egypt. Subsequently, over a hundred Bethlehemites were among those who returned from the exile in Babylon (Ezra 2:21; Neh. 7:26).

Two of the NT Gospels report that Jesus was born in Bethlehem (Matt. 2:1; Luke 2:4–7). Matthew's Gospel connects this birth with fulfillment of prophecy (2:6; cf. Mic. 5:2) and reports that magi from the east came to Bethlehem to worship the "king of the Jews" who had been born there (2:1, 9–11). This Gospel also says that King Herod massacred all of the children in Bethlehem under two years of age in a desperate attempt to kill the baby he assumed would be a rival for his throne (2:16–18; cf. Jer. 31:15). In Luke's Gospel, the baby Jesus is laid in a manger near Bethlehem and shepherds from the surrounding fields respond to an angelic announcement of his birth by coming to worship him (2:4–20). *See also* Benjamin; Gibeah; Judah; Rachel; Ramah.

2 A small town in the hill country of Zebulun (Josh. 19:15) about seven miles northwest of Nazareth, probably (though this is not certain) the home and burial place of Ibzan, one of the minor judges (Judg. 12:8–10).

3 In 1 Chronicles a personal name, once of a descendant of Caleb (2:51, 54), and once of the son of Ephrathah, a descendant of Hur (4:4). Since Ephrath is identified elsewhere with the Bethlehem in Judah (Gen. 35:19; Ruth 4:11; Mic. 5:2), the personal names in 1 Chron. 4:4 are probably tribal designations.   D.B.

Beth-meon (beth-mee'on). *See* Baal-meon.

Beth-millo (beth-mil'loh). *See* millo.

Beth-pelet (beth-pee'lit; Heb., "house of refuge"), a town of the tribe of Judah at the southern extremity of its territory (Josh. 15:27). It remained settled in postexilic times (Neh. 11:26), but its location is still in dispute.

Beth-peor (beth-pee'or; Heb., "house of Peor"). *See* Peor.

Bethphage (beth'fuh-jee; Heb., "house of unripe figs"), a village apparently on the Mount of Olives, near Bethany, where Jesus sent his disciples to procure a donkey for his triumphal entry into Jerusalem (Matt. 21:1; Mark 11:1; Luke 19:29). Its exact location has never been determined.

Bethsaida (beth-say'uh-duh; Heb., "house of the fisherman"), a town situated probably at the northeast corner of the Sea of Galilee near where the Jordan River flows into it. The exact site, however, is uncertain. Apparently a small fishing village, it was raised to the dignity of a "city" by the

tetrarch Philip and renamed "Bethsaida-Julias" in honor of the daughter of Caesar Augustus sometime before 2 BCE. The tetrarch died there in 34 CE. The apostles Peter, Andrew, and Philip were from there (John 1:44; 12:21). Jesus fed the five thousand in the area (Mark 6:45; Luke 9:10–17) and healed a blind man there (Mark 8:22–26). He also cursed the town, however, for not repenting in response to the miracles (NRSV: "deeds of power") he had performed there (Matt. 11:21–22; Luke 10:13–14).

Excavations at the site of et-Tell, the likeliest candidate for the site of Bethsaida, have uncovered an Iron Age city gate in addition to homes and artifacts from the Hellenistic and Roman periods. Although the city might have obtained the status of a *polis* under Philip, the archaeological remains suggest that it was a modest town lacking many of the public urban structures common at larger cities. *See also* Andrew; Bethzatha; Peter; Philip.   C.H.M.

Beth-shan (beth-shan'; also Beth-shean), an important biblical city located between the Jezreel and Jordan valleys. Beth-shan protected the ancient primary highway, a branch of the Via Maris. The archaeological site consists of Tell el-Husn, which excavations reveal was occupied almost continuously from the Chalcolithic period, about 3500 BCE, to the time of the Crusaders.

Some Neolithic pottery similar to that found at Jericho has been excavated at Beth-shan. The first permanent structures belong to the Chalcolithic period. A few houses and copper tools belonging to this era have been recovered.

Two scenes of a dog and lion in combat, from the Amarna period (fourteenth century BCE) at Beth-shan.

The first real town at Beth-shan belongs to the Early Bronze Age (3000–2400 BCE). In addition to private houses, public buildings and intersecting streets of this period have been found. Limited remains also indicate that Beth-shan was inhabited during the Middle Bronze Age (2000–1550 BCE), the period of the biblical patriarchs.

In historical texts, Beth-shan is first mentioned in the list of cities conquered by Pharaoh Thutmose III (1468 BCE). Belonging to this Late Bronze Age city (1550–1200 BCE) is a temple complex close to the city gate. The temple and the city of this time show much Egyptian influence. Among the finds in this level is a cartouche containing the name of Thutmose III. From the Amarna Age at Beth-shan have been found a temple, a granary, and an inner fortress (Heb. *migdal*). Stelae of Seti I and Ramesses II have been found at Beth-shan along with a large statue of Ramesses III. Also belonging to this period is a stele dedicated to Ashtoreth, a Canaanite goddess. The numerous Egyptian artifacts found at the site, including numerous anthropoid coffins, indicate that Beth-shan housed an Egyptian military garrison.

At the time of the Israelite conquest (1250–1200 BCE), Beth-shan was listed among the cities of Manasseh. However, the Israelites were unable to conquer the city because of the strength of the Canaanites living in it (Josh. 17:11–12; Judg. 1:27).

At the beginning of the Iron Age, the plan of the upper city changed completely. Two Canaanite temples of the Iron Age have been found. Both of these temples have a basilica shape, with two rows of columns along the length of the temple and a Holy of Holies of the broadroom type. The two temples are connected by a complex of anterooms and storerooms. The smaller of the two temples is dedicated to the goddess Anat. According to 1 Sam. 31:12, the bodies of Saul and his sons were exposed on the walls of Beth-shan by the Philistines. By implication, Beth-shan was conquered by David, because it appears in a list of towns in the fifth administrative district of Solomon. Beth-shan was destroyed near the end of the eighth century BCE apparently by the Assyrians, perhaps during the campaigns of Tiglath-pileser III. After that the city had only sporadic occupation until the Hellenistic and Roman periods.

In the Hellenistic period (333–63 BCE), a small settlement was built on the tell. This settlement was destroyed by the Hasmoneans. The Romans under Pompey rebuilt the city at the foot of the tell. This thoroughly Hellenistic/Roman city known as Scythopolis prospered during the Roman (63 BCE–324 CE) and Byzantine (324–632 CE) periods. It was frequently mentioned in the literature of the period. Scythopolis was for a time the chief city of the Decapolis and was the only city of the Decapolis west of the Jordan River. The Roman-Byzantine city had typical Roman features such as colonnaded streets with roofed sidewalks, a theater, an amphitheater, temples, and baths. A large civic basilica, the center of commercial activity, early in the Roman period was replaced with

an agora in the later periods. At the foot of the tell on an acropolis stood a temple dedicated to Zeus.
                                                                    J.F.D.

Beth-shean (beth-shee′uhn). *See* Beth-shan.

Beth-shemesh (beth-sheh′mish; Heb., "house of sun"), the name of four cities that appear to have been centers for a sun cult.

1 A city in the Valley of Sorek, sixteen miles southwest of Jerusalem, modern Tell er-Rumeileh (Ain Shems), on the highway to Ashdod and the Mediterranean. The city was established in the Middle Bronze Age (ca. 1750 BCE) and was continuously settled in the Late Bronze Age (1550–1200) and Iron Ages (1200–630 BCE). It is not mentioned in nonbiblical sources. Beth-Shemesh is mentioned as a key point on the northern boundary of the tribe of Judah (Josh. 15:10), listed in the levitical town list (Josh. 21:16; 1 Chron. 6:44), and was part of the allotment for the tribe of Dan (Josh. 19:41). Its location, name, and history would indicate that Beth-shemesh was a community on the Philistine border. When the ark of the covenant was taken by the Philistines, it was finally returned to the people of Beth-shemesh (1 Sam. 6:1–16), but the "lords of the Philistines," following the ark, went only "up to the border of Beth-Shemesh" (6:12).

Recent excavations show that, after a series of flourishing Iron Age I villages (1200–950 BCE), a fortified city was built there at the beginning of Iron Age II, during the days of the established early monarchy. Beth-shemesh is listed as the second of King Solomon's districts (1 Kings 4:10). This city was destroyed violently, a destruction that may have been the result of the conflict between Joash, king of Israel (802–786 BCE), who captured Amaziah, king of Judah, at Beth-shemesh (2 Kings 14:11–14; 2 Chron. 25:21). During the war between Syria and Ephraim, the Philistines were able to get control once again of Beth-shemesh (2 Chron. 28:18). The kings of Israel and Damascus (Syria) put pressure on Ahaz, king of Judah, to join a coalition with them against the Assyrians. Ahaz decided, instead, to become a willing vassal of the Assyrians, and this moment of instability was all that the Philistines needed to make substantial advances into the holdings of Judah, including Beth-shemesh. The city was finally destroyed in 701 BCE, during the military campaign of Sennacherib, king of Assyria. Occupation of the area continued, but Beth-shemesh never regained status as a city. A small-scale attempt to settle again, after some decades of desertion, was made in the twilight of the Assyrian regime (ca. 630 BCE) and was violently terminated. House debris was pushed into the opening of the underground water reservoir, which was blocked and ceased to function.

2 A city mentioned in Josh. 19:22, possibly modern Khirbet Shemsin or el-'Abeidiyeh, south of the Sea of Galilee along the Jordan.

3 A town in the allotment of Naphtali (Josh. 19:38).

4 A center for the sun cult in Egypt, possibly the Egyptian city On (Heliopolis; Jer. 43:13).

S.B.R./S.B./Z.L.

Beth-togarmah (beth-toh-gahr′muh; Heb., "house of Togarmah"), a city mentioned in Ezek. 27:14 as a site that traded horses and mules to Tyre. It may be modern Gürün, located about seventy miles west of Malatya in Asia Minor. The city was apparently associated with descendants of Togarmah, the third son of Gomer and brother of Ashkenaz and Riphath (Gen. 10:3; 1 Chron. 1:6).

Bethuel (bi-thyoo′uhl; Heb., "house of God").
1 The son of Nahor, nephew of Abraham, and father of Laban and Rebekah (Gen. 22:22–23; 24:15, 24, 47, 50). In Gen. 25:20 he is identified as an Aramean of Paddan-aram.
2 A town in Simeonite territory west of the Dead Sea (1 Chron. 4:30; called Bethel in Josh. 19:4).

Bethzatha (beth-zay′thuh; Heb., "house of olives"), a name appearing only in John 5:2 (NRSV; some manuscripts, and thus some English Bibles, read Bethesda ["house of mercy"] or Bethsaida ["house of the fisherman"]. It and its variations all refer to a pool (or twin pools) just north of the temple in Jerusalem, near the district of Bezetha. A reference to Beth Eshdatayin ("house of poured-out waters") in the *Copper Scroll* from Qumran is also probably to these pools. Twin pools separated by a dam were discovered in 1871 near the Church of St. Anne. They had five porticoes, one on each side and one between them. A sophisticated reservoir and sluice system was used to refill the pools, and this may have created the bubbling referred to in John 5:2–9, where Jesus is said to have healed a man who had been sick for thirty-eight years. The area may have been used as a Jewish ritual bath in the first century, but excavations reveal that in the second century it was associated with Asclepius, the god of healing.   C.H.M.

Excavations at the Bethzatha pool (John 5:2) in Jerusalem.

Beth-zur (beth-zuhr′; Heb., "house of the rock"), a town (modern Khirbet et-Tubeiqah) on the Jerusalem road four miles north of Hebron. A Judean town (Josh. 15:58) belonging to the descendants of Caleb (1 Chron. 2:45), it was fortified by Rehoboam as one of fifteen outposts south and west of Jerusalem (2 Chron. 11:5–10). Neh. 3:16 suggests it was a district center in the fifth century.

It changed hands often in the Maccabean struggles as the Hasmoneans and Seleucids both vied for control of the area (1 Macc. 4–11).

Archaeology attests a fortified settlement ca. 1700–1500 BCE abandoned until reoccupied in the eleventh century BCE. There is, however, no town or fortification for Rehoboam's time (tenth century). A succession of citadels and settlements illustrate the strategic importance during the Maccabean clashes. *See also* Maccabees; Rehoboam.

E.F.C.

Beulah (byoo′luh; Heb., "married"; see Gen. 20:3; Deut. 22:22), according to Isa. 62:4 (cf. 54:1), one of the new names to be given to Jerusalem after the exile, when it will be "married" to God. The NRSV simply translates the new name as "Married," but many other English versions (including KJV, NIV) retain Beulah.

Bezai (bee′zi).
1 The ancestor of a family group who returned with Zerubbabel from the Babylonian exile (Ezra 2:17).
2 A leader of the postexilic community in Judah who signed Ezra's covenant to keep the law (Neh. 10:18); he may be the same person as **1**.

Bezalel (bez′uh-lel; Heb., "in the shadow [under the protection] of God").
1 A Judahite, son of Uri and a grandson of Ephrath (1 Chron. 2:20), who was reported to possess divinely given "ability, intelligence, and knowledge in every kind of craft" (Exod. 31:2–3). Along with Oholiab of Dan, he was chosen to work on "the tent of meeting, and the ark of the covenant, and the mercy seat that is on it, and all the furnishings of the tent" (Exod. 31:7; see also 35:30–33; 36:1–2). He constructed the ark (Exod. 37:1) and was remembered for other achievements as well (38:22), including the construction of the bronze altar (2 Chron. 1:5).
2 A descendant of Pahath-moab who returned from the Babylonian exile and divorced his non-Israelite wife in response to Ezra's proclamation (Ezra 10:30).

Bezek (bee′zik).
1 A Canaanite city belonging to the Perizzites, ruled by Adoni-bezek, and conquered by the tribes of Judah and Simeon shortly after Joshua's death (Judg. 1:1–7). It is usually located in north-central Canaan (see **2** below), but that site is in the territory of Manasseh. Since the tribes of Judah and Simeon were allied to take possession of their own lands in the far southern part of Canaan (Judg. 1:3) and the next battles recorded in the biblical account are in the south (Jerusalem, Hebron; Judg. 1:8–10), it seems likely to some that Bezek lay between Shechem and Jerusalem (Judg. 1:7). *See also* Perizzites.
2 A city in north-central Canaan used by Saul as the assembly point for his rally of men to rescue the besieged city of Jabesh gilead from the

Ammonites (1 Sam. 11:8). It is identified as modern Khirbet Ibziq, about twelve miles northeast of Shechem (Nablus) and some sixteen miles west of Jabesh-gilead.   D.R.B.

Bezer (bee'zuhr; Heb., perhaps "gold ore" or "fortress").

1 A descendant of Asher (1 Chron. 7:37).

2 A city of refuge in Reuben, assigned to the levitical family of Merari (Deut. 4:43; Josh. 20:8; 21:36; 1 Chron. 6:63); it is probably the same as Bozrah in Moab (Jer. 48:24). According to the Mesha Stele, it was restored by Mesha, the king of Moab. It was probably located on the site of modern Umm el-Amad, about eight miles northeast of Medeba (modern-day Madaba). *See also* Bozrah; Mesha.

Bichri (bik'ri; Heb., meaning uncertain, either "youthful" or "of [the family of] Becher"; see Gen. 46:21), a Benjaminite, the father of Sheba and the leader of an unsuccessful northern rebellion against the kingship of David (2 Sam. 20:1–22). *See also* Sheba.

Bigvai (big'vi).

1 The ancestor of a large family group who returned with Zerubbabel from the Babylonian exile (Ezra 2:14) and of a smaller group led by Uthai and Zabbud who returned later with Ezra (Ezra 8:14).

2 A leader of the postexilic community who returned from the exile with Zerubbabel (Ezra 2:2); he is possibly the same person who later signed Ezra's covenant to keep the law (Neh. 10:16). He could be the head of the family groups in 1 above or simply a member of one of those groups.

Bildad (bil'dad), one of Job's three friends (Job 2:11) who advises him as to why he is suffering. He is identified as a Shuhite, a possible reference to Shuah, Abraham and Keturah's son who lived in an eastern country (Gen. 25:2, 6; 1 Chron. 1:32). In each of the three cycles of speeches Bildad is the second speaker, offering three separate discourses (Job 8; 18; 25). His explication of retributive justice and claim that no one suffers undeservedly kindles God's wrath (42:7). *See also* Eliphaz; Job, book of; Zophar.

Bilhah (bil'huh).

1 The slave of Laban's daughter Rachel, and the mother of Dan and Naphtali (Gen. 29:29; 30:4–7). Rachel's childlessness led her to give Bilhah as a wife to Jacob (30:4) to bear children for Rachel to claim (30:3). Bilhah bore Dan and Naphtali, leaders of two of the twelve tribes of Israel. Later, Reuben, Jacob's firstborn son (by Leah) committed incest with Bilhah (35:22; cf. 49:4). *See also* Dan; Jacob; Naphtali; Rachel; Reuben; tribes.

2 In 1 Chron. 4:29, a location in Simeonite territory (Balah, Josh. 19:4).

Bilhan (bil'han).

1 The son of Ezer and grandson of Seir the Horite (Gen. 36:27).

2 The son of Jediael and grandson of Benjamin (1 Chron. 7:10).

Binnui (bin'yoo-i; Heb., "built" or "building").

1 The ancestor of a family group who returned with Zerubbabel from the Babylonian exile (Neh. 7:15). Since the names Bani and Binnui are elsewhere associated (Ezra 10:38; see 2 below), it is possible that "descendants of Binnui" (Neh. 7:15) and the "descendants of Bani" (Ezra 2:10) were closely related or identical. *See also* Bani.

2 A member of the family group of Bani who divorced his non-Israelite wife in response to Ezra's postexilic proclamation (Ezra 10:38).

3 A member of the family group of Pahath-moab who also divorced his non-Israelite wife in response to Ezra's postexilic proclamation (Ezra 10:30).

4 A Levite belonging to the family group of Henadad who helped repair the walls of Jerusalem and signed Ezra's covenant to keep the law (Neh. 3:24; 10:9).

5 A Levite who returned from the exile with Zerubbabel (Neh. 12:8). He may be the same as 4.

6 The father of Noradiah, an assistant in the inventory of valuables brought by Ezra from Babylon (Ezra 8:33). He may be the same as 4 and/or 5.
                                                    D.R.B.

birds. Of the three collective terms for birds used in the Bible, one is translated as "flier" (Heb. 'oph), another means literally "owner of a wing" (Heb. ba'al kanaph), and a third means "winged" or "flying" (Gk. peteinon). Furthermore, birds were classified in the Bible as either "screamers" (Heb. 'ayit) or as "twitterers" (tsippor). To the former belonged most of the raptorial birds, such as birds of prey and owl-like birds, and to the latter the passerine (sparrowlike) birds.

In the Bible, birds are created by God on the fifth day along with water creatures (Gen. 1:20–23). In Gen. 2, Adam gives names to all the birds, as he does to the other animals (2:19–20; cf. Hos. 2:18). Birds are likewise removed from creation in the flood (blotted out from the earth, Gen. 6:7), save for those taken aboard the ark for replenishment (6:20; 7:3). In the aftermath of that flood, God makes a covenant with the birds, as with all other living things (Gen. 9:10). The divine threat of ultimate judgment and devastation includes removal of birds from the earth (Zeph. 1:3). Ps. 50:11 says that God knows all the birds of the air, an affirmation echoed by Jesus in using God's attention to birds as an example of providence and compassion (Matt. 6:26; Luke 12:6; cf. Ps. 104:12, 17). Birds are summoned to praise God in Ps. 148:10.

Solomon's great wisdom included knowledge of birds (1 Kings 4:33), and Job says that birds are able to teach wisdom (Job 12:7; but cf. 28:20–21). Birds are often mentioned in proverbs (Prov. 1:17; 6:5; 7:23; 27:8; Eccles. 9:12; 10:20; Amos 3:5), and they can be used to symbolize haste (Ps. 11:1), loneliness (102:7), confusion (Isa. 16:2), protection (31:5), treachery (Jer. 5:27), persecution (Lam.

Mosaic floor depicting various birds. Below the two peacocks are (*from left to right*) a crane, a pheasant, and a goose, and below them, a partridge, a bird of prey, and a quail; sixth century CE, excavated at Beth-govrin.

3:52; Ezek. 13:20), transience (Hos. 9:11), and fearfulness (11:11). In the Gospels, birds are used by Jesus as examples of items of very little value (Luke 12:6–7, 24)—yet even they have a security denied the Son of Man (Matt. 8:20). In Jesus's parable of the mustard seed, the kingdom of heaven is likened to a tree in which all the birds of the earth may nest (Matt. 13:31–32; Mark 4:30–32); similar imagery is employed in Ezek. 17:22–24; 31:2–13; Dan. 4:10–27. Paul differentiates birds as having different types of bodies than do humans, animals, or fish in 1 Cor. 15:39.

Birds are often depicted as creatures that eat the flesh of carcasses, human or otherwise (e.g., Gen. 40:19; 1 Sam. 17:44, 46; 2 Sam. 21:10; 1 Kings 14:11; 16:4; 21:24; Ps. 79:2; Isa. 18:6; Jer. 7:33; 15:3; 16:4; 19:7; 34:20; Ezek. 29:5; 39:4, 17; Rev. 19:17–21). This association may have influenced distinctions between clean and unclean birds—the latter were not to be eaten. There are twenty unclean "birds" listed in Lev. 11:13–19 and Deut. 14:11–20. These are the eagle, metire ("vulture"), osprey, falcon, kite, raven, ostrich, nighthawk, seagull, hawk, owl, cormorant, ibis, marsh hen ("water hen"), pelican, vulture, stork, heron, hoopoe, and bat. Most of these are raptors (though the hoopoe is a vegetarian). The bat of course is not a bird, but a mammal. The clean birds, which are not specifically listed but are mentioned throughout the Bible, include

the pigeon, the partridge, the quail, and the passerines, which are all vegetarians. All of them feature as important sources of food in different circumstances (cf. Matt. 10:29; Luke 12:6). Concerning birds as sacrifices, Lev. 1:14 specifies that turtledoves or young pigeons should be chosen for burnt offerings (see Luke 2:24).   I.U.K./M.A.P.

birth, new. *See* conversion.

birthright (Heb. *bekorah*), or primogeniture, the practice whereby the eldest son receives a larger (double) share of the inheritance than do his younger brothers. This preferential treatment of the eldest son is known throughout the ancient Near East (Mari, Nuzi, Alalakh, Ugarit, Assyria), although the law codes of Lipit-Ishtar (twentieth century BCE) and Hammurabi (eighteenth century BCE) both legislate an equal sharing of the inheritance by all the male heirs. The law of Deut. 21:15–17 protects the birthright of the eldest son, although the sale of the birthright to a younger son is known from Nuzi as well as from the Bible (Gen. 25:27–34). The disregarding of primogeniture through the choice of a younger rather than the eldest son is witnessed in both the Bible (Gen. 48:12–20; 1 Chron. 5:1–2) and texts from Nuzi, Alalakh, and Ugarit.   J.S.K.

bishop (Gk. *episkopos*, "overseer," "guardian"), early Christian office mentioned in Phil. 1:1, qualifications for which are stated in 1 Tim. 3:1–7; Titus 1:5–9 (cf. 1 Tim. 5:17–22). Titus equates bishop and elder (Gk. *presbyteros;* cf. Acts 20:17, 28), but in 1 Tim., bishop, elder, and deacon appear to be distinct offices (or, perhaps, elder is the general term, which includes bishops and deacons). Little is said about a bishop's duties, but 1 Tim. 3:4–5 indicates the bishop is to "take care of God's church" in a manner analogous to managing a household (cf. 1 Tim. 3:15). Titus describes a bishop as "God's steward," implying that bishops are appointed by God to tend to matters on God's behalf (1:7). The duties of a bishop that receive the most attention are proclamation and teaching (1 Tim. 3:1–2; 5:17–18; Titus 1:9). The qualifications of a bishop emphasize character: bishops are to be respectable persons whose lives may be described as "blameless" (Titus 1:7) and "above reproach" (1 Tim. 3:2), persons whose example will reflect favorably on the church in the public eye (1 Tim. 3:7). They must be thoroughly grounded in the faith (1 Tim. 3:6; Titus 1:9) and capable of demonstrating self-restraint with regard to temper and passions (1 Tim. 3:2–3; Titus 1:7–8). In particular, their family life must be in order; parenting skills are a prime indicator of whether one has the competence for church leadership (1 Tim. 3:4–5; Titus 1:5). And they must not be greedy or lovers of money (1 Tim. 3:3; Titus 1:7), since the love of money is a root of all kinds of evil (1 Tim. 6:10). The general advice to Timothy with regard to church leaders is, "Do not ordain anyone hastily" (1 Tim. 5:22); a shortage of leadership in the church is preferable to appointment of leaders who may disgrace the community (cf. 1 Tim. 5:19–20). *See also* elders.   M.A.P.

Bithynia (bi-thin'ee-uh), a Roman province in northwest Asia Minor, the location of the Christian communities to which 1 Peter was written (1:1). The Roman province of Bithynia actually included the area that 1 Peter refers to separately as Pontus; the author of 1 Peter is usually assumed to be calling those regions by their traditional names rather than by the name imposed by Roman rule. Thus, Bithynia in 1 Pet. 1:1 refers to only the southwestern portion of the Roman province that went by that name. The NT records no mission there. According to Acts 16:7, Paul and his companions "attempted to go into Bithynia, but the Spirit of Jesus did not allow them." Around 110 CE, however, Pliny the Younger wrote to the emperor Trajan about the status of Christians in this area. From his letter, it is evident that the Christian movement had prospered in the area, spreading "not only to the cities, but also to the villages and farms" and attracting "many persons of every age, every rank, and also of both sexes."

bitter herbs (Heb. *maror*), vegetables with characteristically bitter taste. The herbs are to be eaten at the Passover seder to represent the bitterness of the lives of the Israelites under Egyptian slavery. Exod. 12:8 states, "They shall eat the lamb that same night; they shall eat it roasted with unleavened bread and bitter herbs." The herbs have been variously identified as certain types of lettuce, endive, and chervil.

bitumen, a type of asphalt or mineral pitch, either occurring naturally or found as a by-product of burning coal or wood. The KJV translates it as "slime." Throughout antiquity this black sticky substance was used as an adhesive or caulk. For example, flint knife blades were set into a sickle haft filled with bitumen as a mortar; likewise bitumen

held in place inlays of shell and stone. It was used for mortar in construction of the Tower of Babel (Gen. 11:3). It could also be used for waterproofing, as in the bulrush basket of Moses (Exod. 2:3; cf. the "pitch," a different word in Hebrew, used for Noah's ark in Gen. 6:14). References are made to bitumen oozing from the earth (Gen. 14:10) near the Dead Sea, where it occurs naturally.   S.R.

blasphemy, a term derived from a Greek word meaning to injure the reputation of another. In the Bible it means showing contempt or a lack of reverence for God (Lev. 24:16; Dan. 3:29; Mark 2:7; Rev. 13:6; cf. Bel and Dragon 1:9) or for something sacred (Neh. 9:18, 26; 1 Macc. 7:33–42; Matt. 26:65; Rev. 13:6). According to the Gospels, this would include claiming divine attributes for oneself (Mark 14:64; Luke 5:21; John 10:33).

blasphemy of the Holy Spirit, an offense that Jesus identifies as an "eternal sin" that can never be forgiven (Mark 3:28–30). In the immediate context for this passage, the works of God performed by Jesus through the Holy Spirit are being attributed to the spirit of Beel-zebul (3:22). Those who identify the saving work of God as something evil commit a sin that is unpardonable because, ironically, the power they reject holds their only hope for pardon. *See also* blasphemy.

S.B./M.A.P.

bless, blessing (Heb. *barak,* "to bless"; *berakah,* "a blessing, good fortune"; the most common form is the passive participle *baruk,* "blessed").

1 When the object is God, a word carrying the sense of "to worship or praise," as in "Bless the Lord" (Ps. 103:1) or "Blessed by the name of the Lord" (Ps. 113:2). *See also* praise; worship in the Hebrew Bible; worship in the New Testament.

2 When humanity or the earth is in view, a word that typically refers to a bestowal of benefits, often from God, but sometimes from other people. As such, the term is counterpoint to "curse," and the two words often occur together, as in Deut. 27:15–26; 28:3–6, which spell out consequences of keeping or not keeping the covenant. Throughout the Bible, the content of what constitutes "blessing" varies, but includes such good things as vitality, health, longevity, fertility, land, prosperity, honor, and numerous progeny ("curse," on the other hand, results in death, illness, childlessness, and such disasters as drought, famine, and war). For the interplay of curse and blessing as an organizing motif in the Bible, *see* curse.

God blesses the first humans, telling them to be fruitful and multiply (Gen. 1:22). Throughout the Bible God continues to bless individuals (Gen. 24:1; Job 42:12; Judg. 13:24), groups (Exod. 32:29; Josh. 17:14), descendants (Isa. 44:3); and nations (Ps. 115:12; Jer. 4:2). God also blesses animals (Gen. 1:22; Deut. 28:4), land (Deut. 26:15), crops (7:13), houses (Prov. 3:33), and special days or times (Gen. 2:3; Exod. 20:11). People also pronounce blessings on others (Gen. 24:60; 47:7; Exod. 39:43; Lev. 9:22–

23; 1 Sam. 2:20; Neh. 11:2): deathbed blessings are particularly noteworthy (Gen. 27–28; 48–49). Abraham is told that all families of the earth will be blessed through him and his descendants (Gen. 12:3). Consecration ceremonies also provide for the blessing of various objects or of animals for a sacrifice (1 Sam. 9:13). Throughout the Bible people pray for God to bless them and those they love (1 Chron. 4:10; cf. Ps. 67:7).

In the NT, Jesus offers a series of blessings called the Beatitudes (Matt. 5:3–11); in Luke's Gospel, these are paired with "woes" in a manner that recalls Deuteronomy's alternation of blessings and curses (6:20–26; cf. Deut. 27:15–26; 28:3–6). Mary (Luke 1:42, 45, 48) and Peter (Matt. 16:17) receive special blessings, and Jesus blesses his disciples when he ascends into heaven (Luke 24:50–51). Jesus also blesses the bread before he feeds the multitude (Mark 6:41; 8:7) and likewise blesses the bread and wine at the Last Supper (Mark 14:22). Jesus taught his disciples, "Bless those who curse you" (Luke 6:28), and these words are echoed in Paul's admonition to the Roman Christians: "Bless those who persecute you" (Rom. 12:14; cf. 1 Cor. 4:12). Paul speaks often of God's blessings (2 Cor. 9:8; Eph. 1:3), referring also to "spiritual blessings" (Rom. 15:27), "the blessing of Christ" (Rom. 15:29), and the blessings of the gospel (1 Cor. 9:23). *See also* Beatitudes; curse.
Bibliography
Westermann, Claus. *Blessing in the Bible and the Life of the Church.* Fortress, 1978.   J.S.K./M.A.P.

blindness. Sightlessness was one of the attributes disqualifying descendants of Aaron from performing sacrifice to God (Lev. 21:16–24). Likewise, Israelites were forbidden to offer blind animals in sacrifice (Lev. 22:22; Deut. 15:21; Mal. 1:8). The blind were to be protected in accord with God's covenantal instructions: no stumbling block was to be placed in their way (Lev. 19:14); and anyone who misled a blind person was cursed (Deut. 21:18). Isaac (Gen. 27:1), Eli (1 Sam. 3:2), and Ahijah (1 Kings 14:4) suffered from blindness when they were old. In the Bible, God has the power to make people blind (Exod. 4:11) as well as to restore their sight (Ps. 146:8). In Gen. 19:11 the angels of God who visited Lot struck the evil men of Sodom with blindness. Through Elisha's prayer God struck the Syrian army with blindness (2 Kings 6:18). In Isa. 42:7 God commissions his servant "to open the eyes that are blind." One of the expectations of the eschatological age was the opening of the eyes of the blind by God (Isa. 29:18; 35:5; LXX 61:1).

In the NT, Jesus's healing of blindness is presented as one of the "deeds of the Christ" that indicates he is the Messiah (Matt. 11:2–6) and the Spirit-anointed servant of the Lord (Luke 4:16–19). There are numerous accounts of Jesus healing the blind (e.g., 15:29–31). In one instance, the faith of two blind men enables them to be healed by Jesus (Matt. 9:27–31); in another, he heals a blind and dumb demoniac through exorcism (12:22). In

Jerusalem, he heals the blind in the temple (Matt. 21:10–17). In the book of Acts, Paul causes Elymas to become temporarily blind (13:11; cf. 9:8–9).

Blindness lends itself easily as a symbol for lack of spiritual perception or insight (Isa. 6:9–10; 42:16–19; 59:10; Matt. 15:14; Acts 28:26–27; Rom. 2:19; 11:8–10). Thus, some of the NT stories of Jesus's healing of the blind carry symbolic meaning. The two-stage healing of the blind man at Bethsaida (Mark 8:22–26) may symbolize progressive levels of revelation; the story leads into a story about Peter, who sees that Jesus is the Christ (8:29), but does not yet see what that means (8:31–33). The long narrative about a man born blind in John 9 particularly emphasizes the irony of people possessing physical sight while remaining spiritually blind (cf. 9:40–41).   J.P.H.

blood. In biblical writings, blood is understood to be the source of life's power. Although the word is sometimes used simply to designate mortal life (usually in conjunction with flesh), blood is often connected with God, the life-giver. Thus, from the time of Noah on, there are injunctions against consuming blood (Gen. 9:4; Lev. 17:10–16; Deut. 12:15–18; 1 Sam. 14:32–35; Acts 15:23–29). Menstruation makes a woman unavailable for sexual intercourse for seven days (Lev. 15:19–24). Spilling blood is forbidden under penalty of death (Gen. 9:4–7; Exod. 20:13; 21:23–24; Lev. 24:20–21; Deut. 19:21; cf. Matt. 5:21–26, 38–42). In Gen. 4:10, Abel's blood is said to cry out to God from the ground. In Matthew's Gospel, Judas is said to betray innocent blood (7:4), and Pilate tries to evade responsibility for Jesus's death by washing his hands "of this man's blood" (27:24).

Blood plays an important role in Israel's worship. The covenant between Israel and God is sealed by a rite involving blood (Exod. 24:3–8). Applied to the altar, blood becomes a powerful expiatory agent as sin offering, especially on the annual Day of Atonement (Lev. 16). The priest, who is himself consecrated through application of blood (Exod. 29:19–21), alone is qualified to apply the blood (Lev. 1–7). The Passover celebration remembers the blood on the doorposts of Hebrew houses in Egypt (Exod. 12:7) and the deliverance accomplished by God (cf. "blood of the covenant" in Exod. 24:6–8; Ps. 50:5; Zech. 9:11). Blood can also symbolize woes and terrors (e.g., 1 Chron. 22:8; 28:3; Exod. 7:14–24; Joel 2:30–31).

The NT writings vary in their use of blood imagery, but where the image does appear it focuses on the atoning character of the shed blood of Jesus: by his blood, believers are justified (Rom. 5:9) and sanctified (Heb. 10:29; 13:12). At the Lord's Supper; the cup is the new covenant in Christ's blood (Mark 14:24; 1 Cor. 11:23–29), which was "poured out for many for the forgiveness of sins" (Matt. 28:20). The significance of Christ's blood for atonement is developed extensively throughout Heb. 9–10 (see also John 6:53–56; 19:34–37; 1 John 5:6–8; Rom. 3:24–25; 1 Cor. 5:6–8; 1 Pet. 1:18–19; Rev. 5:6–14; 7:14; 12:11).

Elsewhere in the Bible, Zipporah calls Moses a "bridegroom of blood" after circumcising their son in a manner that saved Moses's life (Exod. 4:25–26). The Nile river is turned into blood in the first plague before the exodus (Exod. 7:17–21). Jesus heals a woman who suffers from hemorrhages (Mark 5:25–34). Revelation reports a vision of one-third of the sea becoming blood (8:9; cf. 11:6) and says that the judgment of God will involve a slaughter that creates a river of blood two hundred miles long and as high as a horse's bridle (14:20). *See also* atonement; Atonement, Day of; flesh; life; Lord's Supper; Passover; worship in the Hebrew Bible; worship in the New Testament.

J.E.A.

bloodguilt, guilt incurred through an unnecessary shedding of blood (Deut. 19:10). In Exod. 22:2–3, bloodguilt is incurred by killing a thief caught in the act of breaking in after sunrise. Num. 35:27 says that no bloodguilt is incurred when an avenger kills a murderer who has strayed outside an appointed city of refuge. According to Deut. 22:8, bloodguilt can come upon a person who fails to build a parapet around the house roof, if someone falls from that roof and dies. In 1 Sam. 25:23–31, Abigail persuades David to avoid incurring bloodguilt through an act of vengeance against her husband (cf. 25:33). According to 2 Sam. 21:1, Saul's murderous treatment of the Gibeonites brought bloodguilt upon his house.

M.A.P.

Boanerges (boh´uh-nuhr´jeez; Aramaic, "sons of thunder"), the name given by Jesus to James and John, sons of Zebedee (Mark 3:17). The reason for such an appellation is not given; it might have been a reference to their tempestuous dispositions (cf. Luke 9:54). *See also* James; John.

boats. The inland origin of the ancient Hebrews is apparent in the Bible's infrequent references to boats and sailing. Still, the Israelites did know of traders and seafaring (e.g., 2 Chron. 8:17–18; 9:21; Pss. 104:26; 107:23–30; Prov. 31:14; Ezek. 27; 1 Macc. 8:23, 26, 28), and they were acquainted with travel by ship for peaceful purposes (the Egyptian ambassadors, Isa. 18:2; the Chaldeans rejoicing in their ships, Isa. 43:14; Jonah fleeing God's will, Jon. 1) or for making war (the Sea Peoples, Num. 24:24; a galley that cannot attack a town, Isa. 33:21, 23; ships of Kittim, Dan. 11:30; the Egyptian army supported by ships, 1 Macc. 11:1; the Seleucid army landed at Tripoli, 2 Macc. 14:1).

Solomon relied on the expertise of the sailors employed in the commercial fleet of Hiram of Tyre for transporting the materials for the temple (1 Kings 5:9; 2 Chron. 2:16) and on Hiram's sailors for navigating the fleet supplied by him at Ezion-geber near Elath on the Red Sea (1 Kings 9:26–28; 2 Chron. 8:17; 9:21). These seagoing ships traded at faraway Tarshish and Ophir for large amounts of gold for Solomon's treasury. Jehoshaphat's attempt to emulate Solomon's achievement ended disastrously (1 Kings 22:47–49; 2 Chron. 20:35–

37). Inland waters were the home of craft like the ferryboat that carried King David, newly crowned, across the river Jordan at Gilgal (2 Sam. 19:18).

In NT times, fishing and travel across the Sea of Galilee are commonly reported (Matt. 8:23, 9:1; Mark 4:36, 38; Luke 8:22–23; John 6:16, 22, 23; 21:4–14). On one occasion, Jesus used a fishing boat as pulpit (Luke 5:1–11). The Mediterranean travels of Paul were beset by shipwrecks and becalmed seas (2 Cor. 11:25), especially his final voyage to Rome (Acts 27). His trips were made on trading vessels such as the grain boat running between Alexandria, Egypt, and Puteoli, Italy (Acts 28:13).

Evidence from the Ancient World: Artifacts recovered by archaeologists in the area occupied by the ancient Hebrews, and the history of water transport in the ancient Near East, corroborate this picture of the Hebrews as land lovers. Other peoples, however, plied rivers and seas in boats from earliest times. The oldest known model boat, from as early as 5000 BCE, was found broken and left on a floor below a series of seventeen temples at Eridu in southern Mesopotamia. By about 4000 BCE there is evidence from southern Iraq and southwest Iran for cargo-carrying boats, small boats for local passenger traffic with little freight, and an intermediate type that could carry both passengers and some freight; the sail was probably in use and trade by sea was under way. The earliest certain representation of a sail comes from Egypt and belongs to the end of the pre-Dynastic period, ca. 3200 BCE. No doubt the Egyptians did invent their sail quite early, because a boat carried downstream on the Nile could always take advantage of the prevailing wind from the north to sail back upstream.

Whether the Egyptians built the seagoing "Byblos ships" mentioned in their inscriptions is still debated; the phrase could mean that the ships were made in Byblos or that their route was between Egypt and Byblos. Egypt lacked wood suitable for building ships, but wood was plentiful near Byblos. Whether the Egyptians themselves sailed these boats is another question: a sailor in a tomb painting from about 2000 BCE wears a distinctly foreign coiffure. Neither question can be answered definitely on evidence available now.

Inhabitants of coastal cities like Byblos and Ugarit were the chief traders in the eastern Mediterranean after 2000 BCE; eventually the size of the navy of Ugarit far surpassed that of the Greeks at Troy. One Ugaritic boat used for carrying grain had a capacity estimated at 450 metric tons, roughly twice the size of the flagship in which Columbus discovered the New World. Two models recovered from Byblos may depict these ships, as may a Syrian merchant ship in an Egyptian tomb painting. Similar to the models from Byblos is the Egyptian hieroglyph for boat found in inscriptions at Abydos (thirteenth century BCE). The models and the hieroglyph are contemporary with a Syrian boat found off the coast of Turkey. These boats are the direct formal ancestors of the

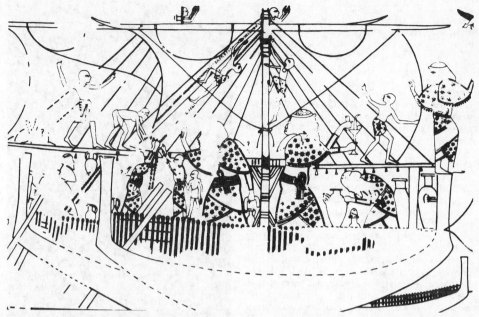

A boat carrying Syrians approaching an Egyptian port. Two Syrians stand in the middle, one giving orders and the other making an offering. Sketch of an ancient Egyptian tomb painting, Thebes.

merchant ships seen in Assyrian reliefs of the late eighth and early seventh centuries BCE, especially those showing the escape of Luli of Tyre from Assyrian troops. The remainder of the ancient history of boats in the eastern Mediterranean is fully documented in Greek and Roman sources.

A Roman-era fishing boat was discovered in the Sea of Galilee in 1986 and has since been displayed as the "Jesus boat." The dilapidated 8-by-26-foot boat would have seated about twelve persons and sheds light on the socioeconomic conditions of Galilean fishermen during the NT period. The boat had been constructed from timbers salvaged from other boats and from inferior or local woods, such as pine, jujube, and willow, which warp in water. The forward keel was a piece of Lebanese cedar that had been used on an earlier boat. At some point, the owner of the boat had apparently decided it was beyond repair and had stripped it of reusable materials (e.g., the anchor, nails, cedar wood) and pushed it out in the lake to sink. *See also* Egypt; Ezion-geber; Hiram; Jonah, book of; Jordan River; Mesopotamia; Noah; Ophir; Ras-Shamra; Red Sea; Solomon; Tyre.

Bibliography

Casson, Lionel. *Ships and Seamanship in the Ancient World.* Princeton University Press, 1971.

Johnstone, Paul. *The Sea-craft of Prehistory.* Routledge, 1980.

Reed, Jonathan L. *The HarperCollins Visual Guide to the New Testament.* HarperOne, 2007.

Rougé, Jean. *Ships and Fleets of the Ancient Mediterranean.* Wesleyan University Press, 1981.

C.Q./J.R.

Boaz (boh′az).

1 A landowner in Bethlehem in Judah who lived "when the judges ruled" Israel (twelfth century BCE) and whose story is told in the book named after his wife, Ruth. Ruth was the Moabite widow of Boaz's relative Mahlon. She had traveled to Bethlehem from Moab with her mother-in-law Naomi (Mahlon's mother), who was also a widow. Naomi encouraged Ruth to seek out Boaz and, when she did, he was kind and receptive to her. When Ruth came to glean wheat left on the ground by the threshers in one of Boaz's fields, Boaz offered her bread and wine and gave her permission to glean from the standing sheaves as well. Later, when Boaz celebrated the conclusion of the harvest with a festive meal at which he became drunk, Ruth came to him, spent the night with him on his threshing floor, and asked him to accept her into his family (probably through a levirate marriage). Boaz was pleased that Ruth came to him rather than going after younger men and, after a legal maneuver at the city gate, he took Ruth as his wife and also obtained the right to redeem Naomi's land. Boaz and Ruth became the parents of Obed, the grandfather of King David (Ruth 4:18–20; 1 Chron. 2:9–15; cf. Matt. 1:3–6; Luke 3:31–33). *See also* Mahlon; Ruth.

2 One of two bronze pillars placed at the entrance to Solomon's temple. *See* Jachin and Boaz.

J.M.S./M.A.P.

body, the physical aspect of human beings and animals. The term can sometimes refer to a corpse or carcass (Lev. 21:11; Deut. 21:1–3; Josh.

8:9; 1 Kings 13:25; Mark 15:43; Luke 17:37; 24:3, 23; Acts 9:40; Heb. 13:11; Jude 9), but it is most often used simply to refer to a person's physical being (e.g., Gen. 25:25; Exod. 4:7; 2 Kings 6:30). The body is that part of a person that is covered by skin (Lev. 13:2), that contains inner organs (Prov. 26:22), and that is composed of such "members" as hands, feet, ears, and eyes (1 Cor. 12:14–16). The body gets sick (Ps. 32:3), becomes weak (109:24), and feels pain (Eccles. 11:10). Offspring are sometimes referred to as the "fruit" of one's body (Mic. 6:7; cf. Deut. 30:9; 2 Sam. 7:12; Ps. 132:11). The body is sometimes mentioned along with the soul and/or the heart (Pss. 16:9; 31:9), but the emphasis in such references seems to be on the totality of the human person rather than on attributes that can be clearly distinguished from one another; "body and heart" (Prov. 15:20) or "body and soul" (16:24) are mentioned in parallel references in much the same way as "body and flesh" (3:8; 5:11). Thus, in Isa. 10:18 "soul and body" is used to refer to the whole person, all that one is. In Matt. 10:28, however, the "soul" seems to be associated with the self that experiences eternal life and the "body" with that which knows only mortal existence. Likewise, Paul speaks of being "absent in body, but present in spirit" (1 Cor. 5:3) and the possibility of being outside the body in a visionary state (2 Cor. 12:2–3).

The Bible maintains that God created the human body (Gen. 2:7), and it generally portrays possession of a body as integral to being human. It does not portray the body unfavorably as a drag on the soul (but cf. Wis. 9:15), but neither does it glorify the body as intrinsically strong or beautiful. In the NT especially, resurrection is explicitly described as involving bodies. To be dead is to be away from the body (2 Cor. 5:6–10; Phil. 1:20–24), but the dead will be given new, immortal bodies when they are raised (1 Cor. 15:3–26). The unity and interdependence of bodily parts becomes a favorite metaphor for the church in the writings of Paul; the church is said to be "the body of Christ" and individual church members are like the various parts that make up a human body (Rom. 12:4–5; 1 Cor. 12:12–31; cf. Eph. 5:23; Col. 1:18). *See also* flesh; flesh and spirit; human being, humanity; mind; resurrection; soul.   R.H.G./M.A.P.

bodyguard. *See* guard, bodyguard.

book. In the Bible, a written document in which events, poems, or prophecies are recorded or in which persons or objects are enumerated. The earliest form of books was the scroll made either of papyrus or animal skins (later vellum or parchment was used). A scroll was made by joining sheets of papyrus or leather together into a continuous strip, which was then rolled. The average size of the scroll was about 10–12 inches high and 20–30 feet long. Although much longer scrolls exist, they were somewhat awkward to use and individual passages could be difficult to find. In the second century CE (and possibly earlier) the scroll

An octagonal prism, used for keeping historical records, from the reign of the Assyrian king Esar-haddon (680–669 BCE).

began to be replaced by the codex, composed of single or folded sheets, stacked and sewn together in the manner of the modern book.

There are books mentioned in the Bible that are not actually contained in the Bible. The majority of these were official court records of the Israelite kings, such as the "Book of the Acts of Solomon" (1 Kings 11:41), the "Chronicles of King David" (1 Chron. 27:24), and other court records of the divided kingdom (1 Kings 14:19; 1 Chron. 9:1; 2 Chron. 16:11; 24:27; Neh. 12:23) as well as of Persia (Esther 2:23; 6:1; 10:2). Historical accounts by the prophets Shemaiah and Iddo are also mentioned (2 Chron. 12:15). Quotations from two books of poetry also occur: David's elegy for Saul and Jonathan (2 Sam. 1:17–27) and the song of Joshua (Josh. 10:12–13) are taken from the "Book of Jashar," and fragments of the victory song (Num. 21:14–15; possibly also 21:17–18, 27–30) are taken from the "Book of the Wars of the Lord." Luke 1:1 might allude to now lost narratives of the life of Jesus.

It is also likely that portions of other books were incorporated into the present biblical books, such as the account of the defeat of the Amalekites (Exod. 17:14), the record of the cities surveyed in Canaan (Josh. 18:9), and various genealogical records (Neh. 7:5). Similarly, the "book of the covenant" (Exod. 24:7) is thought by scholars to refer to the laws attributed to Moses and preserved in Exodus (specifically 20:22–23:33, often called the Covenant Code), and various references to the "book of the law" or the "book of Moses" (Josh. 1:8; 8:34; 2 Chron. 17:9) allude to law codes now contained in the Pentateuch, especially as summarized in Deuteronomy (2 Chron. 25:4; cf. Deut. 28:61). The law book found in the temple by the high priest Hilkiah in the time of Josiah (ca. 622 BCE; 2 Kings 22:8–23:25) was probably a portion of Deuteronomy, while the "book of the law of Moses" read by Ezra after the return from exile was probably a book virtually equivalent to the Pentateuch. An account of the writing of a book of prophecy is recorded in Jeremiah (36:1–32; cf. 25:13; 30:2); there are other references to prophetic books (2 Chron. 12:15; Nah. 1:1; Luke 4:17–20). Furthermore, several examples of ancient books from Israel's neighbors have survived, including the Egyptian "Book of the Dead" and "Pyramid Texts," dealing with the afterlife, and the "Instruction of Amen-em-ope," a collection of proverbial sayings. Books discovered in the ruins of Nineveh include the *Enuma Elish,* a mythical creation epic in which the god Marduk subdues the dragon of chaos, and the *Epic of Gilgamesh,* which tells of a legendary king's quest for immortality and includes an account of a flood sent by the gods to destroy humanity.

The author of Ecclesiastes notes that "of making many books, there is no end" (12:12). In 2 Tim. 4:13, the imprisoned Paul asks Timothy to bring him books. In Acts 19:19, an enormous number of magic books are publicly burned. The concept of a record book kept by God appears several places in the Bible. In it are recorded God's plans (Ps. 139:16) and the record of the sufferings of God's people (Ps. 56:8; cf. Job 19:23). There is also mention of a "Book of Life," God's register from which names of the wicked could be erased, an action that meant death (Exod. 32:32–33; Ps. 69:28). Malachi may fuse these two concepts (a record of deeds and a list of names) by connecting God's "Book of Remembrance" with a future vindication of the righteous (3:16–18). Daniel understands God's book to contain the names of the inhabitants of the coming messianic kingdom (7:10; 12:1). The NT writers understand the "Book of Life" to be both a record of deeds that required judgment (Rev. 20:12–14) and a register of the citizenship of the heavenly kingdom (20:15; cf. Luke 10:20; Phil. 4:3; Rev. 21:27). *See also* clay; codex; Dead Sea Scrolls; papyrus; scroll; writing.

D.R.B.

book of the law, the book found in the temple during the time of Josiah (ca. 620 BCE). According to 2 Kings 22, it was discovered in the temple during a time of renovations in the eighteenth year of Josiah's reign. Its authenticity was validated by the prophet Huldah, the wife of Shallum, who consulted God by means of an oracle (2 Kings 22:13, 18). The book then became the basis for widespread religious reforms that sought to remove all traces of foreign worship from Israel and to centralize worship in Jerusalem. Jewish tradition has typically regarded this "book of the law" (22:8) as the Torah, while Christian tradition has traditionally identified it as the book of Deuteronomy. Modern scholars tend to associate the book with Deuteronomic material that served as one of the sources for the Pentateuch and that probably forms the bulk of what is now contained in Deuteronomy.

booths, temporary shelters built for various purposes. In Gen. 33:17, Jacob builds booths for his cattle at Succoth (which is how the place got its name; *sukkot* is Hebrew for "booths"). Booths were erected on the battlefield for soldiers—Benhadad of Syria and thirty-two other kings drank in them and became drunk (1 Kings 20:12, 16). Job 27:18 mentions booths set up for sentinels of a vineyard (cf. Isa. 1:8). Jonah made a booth for himself outside the city of Nineveh while waiting to see if the city would be destroyed (Jon. 4:5). And in the NT, Levi (or Matthew) the tax collector is called to follow Jesus while sitting in his tax booth (Matt. 9:9; Mark 2:14). The great majority of references to booths in the Bible, however, are to those associated with the Festival of Booths, also called the Festival of Tabernacles. *See* Tabernacles, Festival of.

Booths, Festival of. *See* Tabernacles, Festival of.

bottles, containers for liquids, usually made of goatskin, clay, or glass. God is said to gather the seas as in a bottle (Ps. 33:7). Ps. 56:8 refers to a specific type of bottle, a small "tear vase." These were made of terra-cotta, faience, or highly decorated glass. A number of samples have been found in Egyptian tombs. Jer. 19:1–11 refers to an earthenware jug, employing its fragility as a figure for depicting the destruction of Jerusalem. *See also* skins.

boundary stones, stones erected to delineate boundaries between nations or between individuals; the latter type also served to register status or exemptions with regard to tax laws. The many royal stelae found throughout the ancient Near

Boundary inscription from Gezer, first century BCE–first century CE. It reads, "The boundary of Gezer" on top with the name of the owner of the area, "Alkios," below.

East also served as indications of national boundaries. Although written testimony amply attests to the existence of markings for private property, examples beginning from the Late Bronze Age (1500–1200 BCE) have been excavated almost exclusively in Mesopotamia. In Israel, boundary stones were set up "by former generations" (Deut. 19:14) to guarantee the demarcation of private fields (cf. also Prov. 22:28). Allusions to implicit abuse of such rights are found (cf. Deut. 27:17; Hos. 5:10; Prov. 23:10; Job 24:2).   J.M.S.

bow. *See* archers; weapons.

bowl. Biblical references to bowls are numerous and, on the basis of vocabulary and context, indicate a wide variety of types (Judg. 5:25; 6:38; 2 Kings 2:20; Ezra 1:10; Jer. 52:19). There were large bowls that served as banquet dishes for wine (Amos 6:6) and craters out of which the food of the main meal was apparently lifted by hand (Prov. 19:24; Matt. 26:23). Kneading bowls are mentioned in Exod. 8:3; 12:34; Deut. 28:5, 17. Temple equipment included a wide range of bowls, often of precious metal, for use in sacrifices and offerings (Exod. 25:29; Num. 7:79; Zech. 14:20). Bowls could also be placed on top of lampstands (Zech. 4:2), and they formed the capitals of the temple pillars (1 Kings 7:41). The roundness of a bowl makes it a sensual symbol for a woman's navel (Song of Sol. 7:2). Metaphorically, bowls may hold God's wrath (Isa. 51:22); in Revelation, the contents of seven bowls are poured out upon the earth, bringing devastation and suffering (15:7–16:21).

Archaeological excavation has shown the bowl to be ubiquitous in antiquity, ranging widely in size and in material. Leather, basketry, wood, stone, ceramic, glass, and metal were all used; ceramic was the most common material, and metal and alabaster were the most precious. Except for obvious cases, e.g., cooking pots, lamps, and incense or other cultic equipment, attempts to correlate specific excavated vessel types with terms and usages in the biblical text remain highly speculative.   S.R./M.A.P.

bowstring, the lanyard spanning the two ends of a bow. Delilah used a bowstring to bind Samson, but he broke it easily (Judg. 16:7, 9). The exact composition of that bowstring is not clear from the text.

Bozrah (boz'ruh; Heb., "fortress, enclosure").
1 The chief city of northern Edom, 3,608 feet above sea level, overlooking the Wadi el-Hamayida, eight miles south of modern Tafileh and five miles northwest of the highest point on the plateau. Excavations reveal that it flourished in the seventh and sixth centuries BCE and probably continued into the fourth. As is the case with other Edomite sites, it does not appear to have existed before the eighth century BCE, which raises historical questions concerning the Edomite king lists in

which it is mentioned (Gen. 36:33; 1 Chron. 1:44). Evidently famous for its strong fortifications, Bozrah is used in prophetic oracles to symbolize the whole of Edom (Isa. 34:6; Jer. 49:13, 22; Amos 1:12). Some scholars have speculated, on the basis of Isa. 63:1–3, that it was celebrated for dyeing. *See also* Edom.
2 A town in Moab (Jer. 48:24), perhaps the same as Bezer (Deut. 4:33; Josh. 20:8; 21:36). *See also* Bezer; Moab.
3 A city in Gilead close to the southern frontier of Syria, known today as Busra eski-Sham. According to 1 Macc. 5:26–28, it was captured by Judas Maccabeus (165–160 BCE). A century later, it became the northernmost stronghold of the Nabatean Empire. *See also* Nabatea, Nabateans.
                                                     D.B.

bracelets, a common form of personal adornment in the biblical world. Found with some frequency in archaeological excavations, they were usually made of bronze or precious metals, although iron examples are known and glass bracelets abound in the Roman period. Both men and women wore bracelets, which were placed at or near the wrist, in contrast to armlets, which adorned the upper arm. In addition to being decorative items, bracelets could serve as a repository of wealth (as did jewelry in general). The story of Rebekah (Gen. 24:22, 30, 47) demonstrates the use of bracelets as items of monetary value, as does the fact that bracelets were among the valuables donated to the tent of meeting (Num. 31:50). When Judith ceases mourning, she puts on bracelets and makes herself "very beautiful" (Jth. 10:4). Sirach says that, to the sensible person, education is "like a bracelet on the right arm" (21:21).   C.L.M.

brambles, various spiny bushes often forming impenetrable thickets. In Judg. 9:7–15, Jotham tells a parable of how the bramble ended up being chosen king of the trees. In Song of Sol. 2:2, a maiden is compared to "a lily among brambles." Jesus teaches that people must be evaluated according to their deeds, for "grapes are not picked from a bramble bush" (Luke 6:44). *See also* thorns.

branch, a growth from the main stem or root of a plant. Various Hebrew words are translated as "branch" or "shoot." The most common one (*tsemakh*) can be defined as any sprout of vegetation (Gen. 19:25; Ezek. 16:7; Ps. 85:11). In Gen. 40:10–13, Joseph interprets the cupbearer's dream about three branches on a vine. In 2 Sam. 18:9–15, Absalom is caught by his hair in the branches of a tree and subsequently killed by Joab. Jeremiah had a vision of a branch of an almond tree, which signified that God was watching over God's word, to perform it (1:11–12). The word "branch" or "shoot" is also used in prophecies to refer to the future glory of the Israelites (Isa. 60:21) and, more commonly, to the divinely appointed ruler. In Isa. 11:1–5, the future son of David will be imbued with the divine spirit of wisdom, power, and God's will in order to judge humankind in righteousness. God will establish a "righteous branch" of David whose way will be just (in contradistinction to that of Jeremiah's contemporary, Zedekiah; Jer. 23:5; 33:15; cf. Ps. 132:17). His days will be characterized by security (Jer. 23:6; 33:16), and the Israelites will always be ruled by descendants of David (33:17–26).

In the NT, people spread leafy branches on the road in front of Jesus when he enters Jerusalem on a donkey (Mark 11:8). Jesus says that just as a leafy branch indicates summer is near, so the warnings he has given should be signs that the end is at hand (Mark 13:28). In John's Gospel, he uses the image of a vine and branches to describe his relationship with his followers: as long as they remain connected to him, they will bear fruit (15:1–6). In Rom. 11:16–24, Paul likens Gentile Christians to branches of a wild olive tree that have been grafted onto a cultivated olive tree to become part of the covenant people of God.   J.U./M.A.P.

brass, an alloy of copper and zinc that is malleable and durable. The KJV translates the Hebrew word *nekhoshet* (meaning "copper" or "bronze") as "brass." The NRSV uses "brass" only in Isa. 48:4, rendering the word as "copper" in Lev. 26:19 and as "bronze" in Deut. 28:23. Other translations avoid the word "brass" altogether, since brass was actually unknown in biblical times.

bray, the sound made by the wild ass (Job 6:5) or by social outcasts (30:7).

brazier, a container for fire used for warming a living area. Jehoiakim sat before a fire burning in a brazier and threw in pieces of Jeremiah's scroll of prophecy as it was read to him (Jer. 36:22–23). That brazier was probably made of clay, although in the palace of a king it could possibly have been of metal. *See also* oven.

bread, along with water, one of life's two basic staples (Num. 21:5; Isa. 3:1). Bread is frequently used as a metaphor for food in general (Judg. 13:16; Luke 15:17).

Bread was made primarily from wheat or barley (2 Kings 4:42; John 6:9, 13), the latter eaten primarily by the poor. At times any mixture of grains, such as beans, lentils, millet, etc., might be ground up and made into bread (Ezek. 4:9). Grain was usually ground and used in coarse form (Lev. 2:14, 16), but at times it was ground more finely (Gen. 18:6; Lev. 2:2; 6:15). The best bread was made from wheat in which only the grain, not the bran, was ground (Deut. 32:14; 2 Kings 7:1). After being ground, grain was mixed with water, salt, and old dough. The mixture was then kneaded in a bowl (Exod. 8:3; 12:34), allowed to rise, and baked. Bread was baked either by setting it on hot stones and covering it with hot ashes (1 Kings 19:6; Isa. 44:19), by cooking it on an iron griddle (Lev. 2:5; 6:21; 7:9), or by placing it in an oven (2:4; 7:9; 26:26) that was heated by stubble

(Mal. 4:1), grass (Matt. 6:30), or twigs (1 Kings 17:12). In Deut. 8:3, Moses warns the Israelites that no one lives by bread alone, but also by God's word; Jesus later quotes this when he is tempted by the devil (Matt. 4:4). Bread is associated with key biblical events, including the gift of manna in the wilderness (Exod. 16:14–30) and the instances in which Jesus miraculously feeds multitudes (Mark 6:35–43; 8:4–9). It is also associated with various religious rites: the Passover and Festival of Unleavened Bread (Exod. 12:8, 14–20; 13:3–10); the bread of the Presence (Exod. 25:23–30; 40:22–23; Lev. 24:5–9; Heb. 9:2); various cereal offerings (Exod. 29:2, 23–25; Lev. 2:4–16; 7:9; 1 Sam. 10:3–8); and the Lord's Supper (Matt. 26:26–29; Mark 14:22–25; Luke 22:14–23; 1 Cor. 11:23–26). The Lord's Supper was also called the "breaking of bread" (Acts 2:42, 46; 20:7, 11). In John's Gospel, Jesus identifies himself as the true bread from heaven (6:31–51). *See also* bread of the Presence; Lord's Supper; manna; Passover.

R.H.S.

bread of the Presence, twelve loaves of unleavened bread that were placed on a specially constructed table in the tabernacle and temple as an offering to God. They were to be baked of fine flour and arranged in two rows of six with frankincense in each row. The bread was to be replaced with freshly baked bread every sabbath day, and the old loaves were to be eaten by the priests (Lev. 24:5–9; Exod. 25:23–30; 1 Sam. 21:5–6; cf. Matt. 12:3–4). The bread of the Presence is also referred to as holy bread (1 Sam. 21:4, 6) or as simply "the bread" (Exod. 40:23); in older English translations of the Bible, it was called the "showbread."

The bread of the Presence figures in one biblical narrative related to David (1 Sam. 21:1–6). While fleeing Saul, David and his soldiers came to a sanctuary at Nob and, because there was no other food to give them, the priest Ahimelech allowed them to eat the bread of the Presence. The story emphasizes that David and his men had not had sexual contact with women for some time and thus were in a relative state of holiness, even though they were not priests. This story is cited by Jesus in the Synoptic Gospels as a precedent or analogy for why he does not condemn his disciples for picking grain on the sabbath to satisfy their hunger (Matt. 12:1–8; Mark 2:23–28; Luke 6:1–5).

D.R.B./M.A.P.

breastpiece.
1 An item of Aaron's ceremonial vestments (Exod. 28:15, 22–30; 39:8–21; Lev. 8:8). A kind of pouch, it was a square (about 9 by 9 inches) made by folding in half a rectangular piece of material. It was attached to the ephod by two chains, two frames, and three pairs of rings, all of gold. The breastpiece was like the ephod in that it was made from mixed fabric of linen and wool, woven with gold, using the same brilliant colors (purple, blue, and scarlet), and exhibiting a special kind of workmanship (Heb. *khosheb,* "figured weaving").

These features, like the details of Aaron's robe and diadem, link the breastpiece to the materials and workmanship of the vessels and curtains inside the tabernacle, giving concrete expression to the unique role of Aaron within the sanctuary. The symbolic function of the breastpiece is also evident from the arrangement of precious stones attached to it in four rows of three each: twelve different gemstones, set in gold filigree, were used, each one inscribed with the name of an Israelite tribe. Thus, while only Aaron ministered inside the tabernacle, he symbolically brought all Israel in with him, and the tribal names served as "a reminder before the LORD." In addition, the Urim and Thummim, by means of which Aaron exercised his divinatory function of bearing "the judgment of the people of Israel on his heart" (Exod. 28:30), were attached to the breastpiece. *See also* Aaron; ephod; tabernacle; Urim and Thummim.

2 A military garment, a cuirass or plate of metal or mail worn on the chest (1 Kings 22:34). The metaphoric use of breastpiece in Isa. 59:17 and in the NT (Eph. 6:14; 1 Thess. 5:8; Rev. 9:9, 17) probably stems from this military, protective equipment rather than from the ritual priestly breastpiece.

C.L.M.

breastplate. *See* breastpiece.

Brick makers at work; a wooden model from an ancient Egyptian tomb. The Israelites in Egypt were brick makers (Exod. 5:6–9).

brick, a square or oblong block made of mud or clay used principally for construction of buildings and walls. Mud-brick construction is well known from ancient times in spite of the fact that stones were plentiful in Canaan and Israel and were also used in building projects. Bricks were normally made of a mixture of clay and water, and sometimes straw was included to prevent cracking. Bricks could be sun-dried or fired in a kiln. Mud-brick could be used for either walls or buildings. Good examples of mud-brick architecture have

come from such diverse sites as Jericho, Gezer, and Ezion-geber. In Egypt, the Israelite slaves were forced to make bricks (Exod. 1:13–14; 5:6–9). Bricks are not mentioned in the NT.   J.A.D.

bride, bridegroom. *See* marriage; wedding.

brimstone. *See* sulfur.

broad place, a large and level area, usually with a connotation of goodness. Figuratively, it describes the place to which one is brought by God's deliverance (Job 36:16; 2 Sam. 22:20; Pss. 18:19; 31:8; 118:5). Perhaps the background for the term is to be found in the open spaces in cities used for assemblies; the connotation, then, would include restoration to community.

bronze, an alloy of copper and tin. The Middle Bronze Age (2000–1500 BCE) saw the replacement of copper by bronze in the production of metal weapons, tools, jewelry, and vessels, since bronze was harder than copper, which had been used earlier. Because of its qualities, bronze was used not only for weapons of war, but also for decorations, since it could be burnished to a bright, smooth surface. Both qualities, hardness and brightness, are reflected in the many biblical references to bronze, both literal (e.g., Job 20:24; Exod. 25–38; 1 Kings 7) and figurative (e.g., Job 40:18; Rev. 1:15). Gen. 4:22 identifies Tubal-cain as a maker of bronze and iron tools. Bronze is listed along with gold and silver as precious metals suitable as offerings for the Lord (Exod. 25:3). It was used extensively in the temple (e.g., 1 Kings 7:13–47).   S.R.

Bronze Age, the era spanning the Early Bronze Age, ca. 3600–2000 BCE; the Middle Bronze Age, ca. 2000–1550 BCE; and the Late Bronze Age, ca. 1550–1200 BCE, in the southern Levant, generally the modern areas of Israel (Cisjordan), Jordan (Transjordan), and the Palestinian territories. These eras are roughly coterminous with the Old, Middle, and New Kingdoms in Egypt and the Sumerian, Old Babylonian, and Middle Babylonian periods in Mesopotamia.

Bronze Age civilization witnessed the cyclic rise and collapse of urbanism among the biblical peoples known as the Canaanites. Although the term "Canaan" first appears as a geographic reference in the early second millennium BCE, the archaeological evidence (and ancient place-names) suggests that the Early Bronze Age peoples were Canaanites, a view given further support by a probable reference to Canaan in the Ebla texts of the twenty-fourth century BCE. Newcomers arriving from Syria at the beginning of the Middle Bronze Age, the Amorites ("Martu," "Amu") seem to be related peoples who became part of the mix of the Canaanite population (e.g., Josh. 10). Also, the Hyksos ultimately became pharaohs of the Egyptian Second Intermediate Period. The Amorite cultural milieu (as known from the Mari texts) and the Egyptian context for the Hyksos are thought by some to resonate generally with the ancestral and other biblical narratives. According to the conquest narratives, numerous peoples made up the Canaanite population in the Late Bronze Age on both sides of the Jordan. By 1207 BCE, based on the Merneptah Stele, "Israel" was in the land; the Philistines arrived soon after. The Iron Age ushered in a new era of small kingdoms in Cisjordan and Transjordan.

With few exceptions, attempts to correlate pre-Israelite biblical traditions with Bronze Age civilization have not elicited a consensus of scholarly opinion. For example, dates for the ancestral narratives (e.g., Abraham, Isaac, Jacob) range from the end of the Early Bronze Age through the early Iron Age, although the Middle Bronze Age is cited most often as the probable historical and cultural milieu. The exodus and conquest narratives also lack extrabiblical historical confirmation except for the reference in the Merneptah Stele noted earlier, correlations between Egypt and the Philistines, and clear evidence for twelfth–eleventh century settlement in the central highlands. Growing archaeological and textual evidence for the tenth century suggests that firm historical data for the Israelites begin with the Davidic and Solomonic reigns.

Early Bronze Age: The Early Bronze Age traditionally breaks down into proto-urban Early Bronze I, urban Early Bronze II–III, and post-urban Early Bronze IV periods. Although unlike the advanced primary or "pristine" states of Sumer and Egypt and Syrian city-states, such as Ebla and Mari, it seems that a small-scale type of urbanism was in place in Canaan. Except for writing, the critical elements of an urban culture are apparent. These would be substantial cities surrounded by fortifications, town planning, distinct domestic quarters, monumental public buildings (e.g., palaces and temples), sophisticated water retrieval and storage facilities, an established cult, and an economy based on agriculture, animal husbandry, and trade. Aside from several early fortified sites, the virtual fortification of sites occurs in the Early Bronze II period, e.g., Arad, Lachish, Beth Yerah, Beth-shan, Jericho, Yarmuth, and in Transjordan, Khirbet az-Zeraqun, Bab edh-Dhra, Khirbet Iskander, and Lajjun.

Current research on the copper mines and settlements in the Faynan, Jordan, the location of the largest copper manufactory in the Near East, has uncovered important interconnections with southern Cisjordan (the entrepôt of Arad especially) and Egypt, pointing to a three-way exchange network. Hieroglyphs associated with the Pharaoh Narmer on Early Bronze I Canaanite pottery provide a synchronism with Egypt at about 3100 BCE. It is likely that trade with Egypt was a factor in the emergence of urbanism; metals and other trade are attested with the northern Levant as well. Still enigmatic is the cessation of urban life at the end of Early Bronze III, although climate change was apparently a major factor (documented best for

the First Intermediate Period in Egypt). The Early Bronze IV ("Intermediate Bronze Age") period remains controversial. It is often called a "dark age" or a pastoral-nomadic "interlude," but recent excavations in Transjordan show continuity of tradition and a significant number of agricultural settlements, including central sites, such as Khirbat Iskandar and Bab adh-Dhra. There appears to be more continuity with the preceding and succeeding periods than hitherto believed.

Middle Bronze Age: The Middle Bronze Age marks a return to urban life in Canaan. Textual references in Mesopotamia to "Martu" and in Egypt to the "Amu" strongly suggest new peoples have entered the southern Levant as well as Egypt. The well-known Beni Hasan tomb painting from Middle Egypt illustrates a caravan of "Amu" traders arriving to sell kohl for eye paint. Hammurabi, of the Old Babylonian Period, is the first Amorite king. The period is aptly called the zenith of Canaanite civilization or the dawn of internationalism. Canaan is an integral hub in international trade with Syria to the north (Mari, Ebla, Byblos, Ugarit) and the Egyptian Delta region to the south (Hyksos). Numerous luxury imports from the Mediterranean Littoral, such as from Crete, Cyprus, coastal Syria, Egypt, and Anatolia, reveal the extent of interconnectedness in the period.

The Middle Bronze Age is identified, especially, by its massive and complex ("Hyksos") defenses. These defenses, found from Syria to Egypt, include fortifications, triple-entryway gates, huge towers, and ramparts, the latter probably serving as a defense against the battering ram. Exemplifying monumental defenses in Cisjordan are sites such as Hazor, Shechem, Gezer, Megiddo, and in Transjordan, Tall Dayr Alla, Jawa, Tall al-'Umayri, Tall Rukeis. The impressive and well-preserved remains at Tell Dan (45-foot-tall rampart, stone steps leading to an arched mud-brick gate) are illustrative. Other shared traditions are fortress (Heb. *migdal*) temples, but a variety of cultic expression is evident, e.g., the high place at Gezer and the sanctuary at Nahariya. Sites reveal a new prosperity and wealth in their beautiful, highly burnished wheel-made pottery, tin-bronze weapons and tools, and compelling evidence for elites and a stratified society, given the prestige items found in tombs (unlike the Early Bronze Age). Multitiered settlement patterns point to significant economic and political integration.

There is now documented literacy confirmed by cuneiform texts found at major sites like Hazor and Gezer; there are also numerous references to Canaanite cities, such as those found in the Egyptian Execration texts and the Mari letters. More revolutionary are the proto-Sinaitic/proto-Canaanite inscriptions, which reveal the invention of the (pictographic) alphabet, the forerunner of the later Ugaritic cuneiform and Phoenician linear alphabets. With the collapse of their capital, Avaris, the Hyksos were expelled from Egypt by New Kingdom pharaohs whose campaigns in Canaan ushered in what is often termed the Egyptian Empire.

Late Bronze Age: Despite severe destructions of sites (especially by the Eighteenth Dynasty pharaoh Thutmosis III), there is cultural continuity with the preceding Middle Bronze Age culture, but often in degenerate style, as reflected in the ceramic corpus. Although the cities are rebuilt, the fortifications are not. The garrison city of Beth-shan with its Egyptian temple, stele, and material culture epitomizes the strong foreign presence in the land. In light of such disruption, the high level of prosperity in the land, witnessed by the quantity of luxury imports from Mycenaea, Cyprus, Syria, and Anatolia, is surprising. The city-states attest to glaring wealth differential: extravagant palaces (Megiddo and Hazor), large-scale sacred precincts with bronze statuettes of Astarte and Baal (e.g., Hazor), monumental basalt sculptures (at Megiddo and Hazor), patrician homes (at Tell Beit Mirsim, Tell Batash, Megiddo), luxury items (300-piece ivory hoard from Megiddo), and stone-built (corbelled) graves (at Tell el-Ajjul, Dan, and Megiddo). That the period is rightly termed the "age of internationalism" is evident in the hoard of objects—e.g., 350 copper ingots from Cyprus, Aegean and Levantine pottery, gold, wine amphora, and ebony from Egypt—found in the late fourteenth-century Uluburun and Cape Gelodoniya shipwrecks off the coast of Turkey.

Textual information is more abundant in this period, including both the Ugaritic texts and the Egyptian Amarna letters. The former detail common traditions between Canaanite and later Israelite religion and are written in the first full-fledged alphabet. The Amarna letters describe relations between Canaanite princes urgently requesting help from Akhenaten against the "Habiru." Mentioned in the Nuzi texts as well, these Habiru (comprising various ethnic groups) are depicted as freebooters, plunderers, mercenaries, or people in bondage. They are often equated with the Hebrews. With the invasions of the Sea Peoples, the end of the Late Bronze Age sees sociopolitical collapse and new settlement patterns in the central highlands. It is the breakup of empires, movements of new peoples throughout the Mediterranean area, and general upheaval at the Late Bronze Age/Iron Age transition that provides a context for the first historical appearance of "Israel" (Merneptah Stele) in the land. S.R.

brook (Heb. *nakhal*), the bed of a stream or river (Arabic *wadi*) generally dry or nearly dry during the summer months, but sporadically or continuously filled with water from the rains during the winter. The land of Canaan had numerous such watercourses (Deut. 8:7; 10:7; cf. Lev. 11:9–10). Well-known brooks of the Bible include: the Zered (Num. 21:12), the Arnon (Deut. 2:24), the Jabbok (Deut. 2:37), the Kanah (Josh. 17:9), the Kishon (Judg. 4:7), the Sorek (Judg. 16:4), the Besor (1 Sam. 30:9), the Kidron (1 Kings 2:37; cf. John 18:1), the Cherith (1 Kings 17:3), and the Wadi of Egypt, Canaan's southern boundary (Num. 34:5). All of these are referred to as wadis in the NRSV. *See also* wadi. D.A.D.

broom tree, a species of plant generally agreed to be *Retama raetam*, a shrublike growth usually 4 to 12 feet high, with deep roots suitable for the desert terrain it occupies. It flowers in the spring with small white blooms on twigs with small leaves. A broom tree provided Elijah shade (1 Kings 19:4–5); its roots gave warmth for Job's counselors (Job 30:4). Its power to burn to coals is cited, perhaps figuratively, in Ps. 120:4.

brother, a male blood relative, typically a sibling, but the term may also be used of a close male associate. Cain and Abel are blood brothers (Gen. 4:9), as are Jacob and Esau (Gen. 25:26) and Simon and Andrew (Mark 1:16). Much is made of the pattern of the younger brother superseding the elder; Abel is preferred over Cain, Jacob over Esau, David over Jesse's other sons. In a nonliteral sense, David calls Jonathan his "brother" (2 Sam. 1:26), and Hiram of Tyre addresses Solomon as "brother" (1 Kings 9:13). The term "brother" is also used to express the spiritual relationship of people who share the same faith. Jesus calls his disciples his brothers (Matt. 28:10) and says that all "who hear the word of God and do it" are to be counted as his siblings (Luke 8:21; cf. Matt. 12:50). Paul regularly speaks of the people to whom he writes as his "brothers," typically rendered in the NRSV as "brothers and sisters" (e.g., Rom. 1:13; 1 Cor. 1:10; 1 Thess. 1:4). *See also* sister. J.H.N.

buckler, a small circular shield worn on the forearm. It was usually made of a leather-covered frame (wicker, wood, or metal) and provided more mobile protection than the full-body shield with which it is always associated. Its main function was to deflect projectiles or blows in hand-to-hand combat. Preparation of buckler and shield was preliminary for battle (Jer. 46:3), and bucklers were part of an enemy's armor that was burned subsequent to defeat in battle (Ezek. 39:9; see also 23:24; 38:4). Metaphorical references use the buckler as a symbol of divine armor (Ps. 35:1) or God's faithfulness (91:4). To say that a thousand bucklers could be hung on a person's neck evokes an image of impressive strength and beauty (Song of Sol. 4:4).

Bukki (buhk´*i*).

1 A leader of the tribe of Dan who was in charge of apportioning the land within the tribe (Num. 34:22).

2 A Levite, a descendant of Aaron and ancestor of Ezra (1 Chron. 6:5; Ezra 7:4).

Bul. *See* calendar.

bull, an animal important in ancient Near Eastern religions, including that of Israel. In Egypt, Apis the bull was thought to impart fertility; in one ritual a bull was driven over fields to increase their yield. Apis also came to be the herald of the national god Ptah and occasionally his earthly manifestation, an instance of the Egyptian

Statue of the bull Apis representing
the Egyptian god Ptah.

tendency to ascribe sacral significance to animals.
In Mesopotamia, the bull of heaven was given by
Anu to Inanna to execute wrath against Gilgamesh
and the land of Uruk. "Bull of heaven," "bull,"
and "great bull" are also designations of the storm
god Ishkur/Adad as god of fertility. Among the
Canaanites, El was called Bull for his strength and
procreative power.

One early designation for Israel's God in Genesis, commonly translated "Mighty One of Jacob,"
was originally in Hebrew "Bull of Jacob" (Gen.
49:24). Israel was forbidden to make any image of
God (Exod. 20:4–5; Deut. 4:15–19), so no animal
could be used to represent God. An animal could,
however, be the throne of the Lord, like the cherubim of the Jerusalem temple (cf. 1 Kings 6:23–28);
God was "enthroned upon the cherubim." In the
same way, a sculpture of a bull might be viewed
as a throne for the invisible deity. Still, in Israelite
religion, there was always concern that the animal
throne would itself become the object of worship.
This danger was actually realized, according to
the biblical writers, in the two young bulls that
Jeroboam I set up in Bethel and Dan in the tenth
century BCE. He called to the people, "Behold your
gods, O Israel, who brought you up out of the land
of Egypt" (1 Kings 12:28, cf. Exod. 32:4). Still,
bulls were too much a part of the iconography
of the Near East not to play a part in the temple;
the most famous example was the molten sea, a
huge bowl supported by twelve oxen, three facing
in each direction (1 Kings 7:23–25). Of course,
bulls, like other animals of dignity and value, were
often sacrificed in the temple. *See also* Jeroboam I;
sacrifice.   R.J.C.

bulrush. *See* rush.

Bunni (buhn'*i*).
1 A Levite, an ancestor of some postexilic inhabitants of Jerusalem (Neh. 11:15).
2 A leader of the postexilic community who
signed Ezra's covenant to keep the law (Neh.
10:15).
3 A Levite who participated in the dedication
ceremony of the returning exiles (Neh. 9:4); perhaps he is the same person as **2**, although here the
word may not be a name at all, since there is some
textual evidence to read both Bani and Bunni in
this verse as Hebrew *bene*, "sons of." *See also* Bani.

burden, a heavy load, but also psychological
and spiritual anxiety (Deut. 1:12; Gal. 6:2, 5). In
Jer. 23:33–40, Jeremiah accuses other prophets
of becoming a burden to the deity, although they
claimed to possess the burden of the Lord. In the
NT, Jesus accuses the religious leaders of Israel of
placing heavy burdens on others (Matt. 23:4), and
he describes his burden as light (11:30).   J.L.C.

burial, the disposition of a human corpse to prevent its desecration. The Hebrew word (*qeburah*)
and the Greek word (*entaphiazō*) meaning
"burial" describe either the act of burying (Eccles. 6:3; Isa. 14:20; Jer. 22:19; Matt. 26:12) or the
burial place (Gen. 47:30; Deut. 34:6; 2 Kings 9:28;
21:26: 23:30).

Because of the warm climate of the Near East
and the belief that a dead body was ritually impure,
burial usually took place as soon after death as
possible (Deut. 21:23), usually within twenty-four
hours (Acts 5:5–6, 10). To allow a body to decay
above ground or to become subject to destruction

Cover of a pottery sarcophagus from
Beth shan, twelfth tenth century BCE.

by vultures or dogs was a great dishonor (1 Kings 14:10–14; 2 Kings 9:34–37). Anyone who discovered a corpse by the roadside was required to bury it (2 Sam. 21:10–14).

Although cremation was widely practiced among the Canaanites and later Greeks and Romans, it was the Hebrew custom to inter the body. Embalming was not a part of Hebrew burial practice, but because Jacob and Joseph died in Egypt, they were mummified after the local custom by physicians (Gen. 50:2–3, 26). More often, Semitic tradition favored the ritual of secondary burial, according to which the bones of the deceased were gathered after the body had decomposed for deposit in a pit containing the bones of other family members and previous generations. Thus, in Gen. 49:29 Jacob on his deathbed anticipates being buried with his ancestors, saying "I am about to be gathered to my people."

The most common type of burial arrangement was the simple shaft or trench grave, which was often lined with mats, wood, or stone slabs. These simple graves were sometimes marked by a tree (Gen. 35:8) or by a pile of stones (Josh. 7:26; 2 Sam. 18:17). Caves were frequently utilized for burials either for their convenience or because time or money did not permit the cutting of a tomb from rock. Sarah (Gen. 23:19) and other members of Abraham's family (25:9; 49:31; 50:13) were buried in the cave of Machpelah at Hebron. Both archaeological and biblical data also indicate that individuals of wealth or political rank enjoyed burials with elaborate funerary assemblages that included robes, jewelry, furniture, weapons, and pottery (1 Sam. 28:14; Isa. 14:11; Ezek. 32:27).

During the late Second Temple period, Judean and Galilean Jews built underground shaft tombs designed with secondary burial in mind. Such tombs were room-size chambers that had been cut out of bedrock with a small opening that could be tightly covered to keep out scavenging animals. As the Gospels suggest, it was common to seal such tombs with rolling stones (Matt. 27:60). The Jews would either lay their dead in fingerlike shafts (Heb. *kokhim*) extending 6 feet into the walls or place them on arch-covered ledges (Lat. *arcosolia*) that ran along the walls. Corpses were tied together with a few strips of cloth to keep the jaw shut and the arms and legs together (cf. Matt. 27:59; John 11:44). The body might be washed prior to placement in the tomb (Acts 9:37), and there appears to have been some custom of anointing the body with aromatic ointments (John 12:7; 19:39; Mark 16:1; Luke 24:1). In any case, the family would return to the chamber about a year later, after the body had decomposed, and gather the bones of the deceased for secondary burial.

By the time of the NT, however, Jews did not simply place the bones of their loved ones in a common pit, but stored those bones in stone boxes called ossuaries. The bones of multiple family members would be placed in a single ossuary, which might be elaborately decorated or inscribed with names and other information. Numerous ossuaries have been found by archaeologists and over two hundred of those found in the area around Jerusalem have inscriptions, which sometimes list the home of the deceased. From these inscriptions it becomes clear that many Jews who lived in the Dispersion either came to Jerusalem to die or had their remains interred there. Various Jerusalem ossuaries identify the deceased person as being from North Africa, Italy, Bithynia, or Syria.

Of course, burial conditions would have varied according to a family's status and means. By the time of the NT, the elite might be placed in elaborate tombs with highly visible monuments, such as those that have been found along the western slope of the Kidron Valley. The tombs of the wealthy were frequently located in gardens (2 Kings 21:18, 26; Matt. 27:57; John 19:41–42). Some tombs were marked by monuments or pillars (2 Kings 23:17) or whitewashed on the outside (Matt. 23:27) to prevent Jews from accidently touching them and being rendered ritually unclean.

Simpler graves were inconspicuous and at a distance from the city. A number of such graves were accidentally discovered at Beit Safafa during road construction; they do not appear to have ever been marked by a tombstone or even by a pile of stones. These graves consisted of rectangular vertical shafts that went down 5 to 7 feet with a horizontal shaft at the bottom where bodies were laid. A limestone slab sealed the opening where the vertical and horizontal shafts met, and rock and dirt had been used to fill in the vertical shaft. Most of these tombs contained only a single body. Of the identifiable bones from forty-seven persons, forty-two were from adults and only five were from children. Such statistics are surprising, given the reality of high infant and child mortality; one chilling explanation is that infants and children might not always have been afforded a proper burial. Graves for the very poor have also been found outside Jerusalem: they were shallow, foot-deep depressions cut into bedrock and covered with a stone slab. Interred along with the deceased in these graves were a few coins and glass vials.

Bibliography

Reed, Jonathan L. *The HarperCollins Visual Guide to the New Testament.* HarperOne, 2007.

                                              J.J.D./M.A.P.

burnt offering. *See* sacrifice.

butter. *See* skins.

Byblos (bib′los). *See* Gebal.

Opposite: The Muiredach cross from County Louth, Ireland, ca. 900–925 CE.

C

Caesar (see´zuhr), titular name for the Roman emperor, derived from Gaius Julius Caesar (100–44 BCE). Julius Caesar, as he is usually known, was a Roman general who conquered Gaul (58–51 BCE) and then dispersed the supporters of his rival Pompey and the Roman Senate to emerge as a virtual dictator (49–45 BCE). He was assassinated March 15, 44 BCE. After more civil wars, his grand-nephew and adopted heir, Octavian (Augustus), emerged as sole ruler of Rome. He took the name "Caesar" and became known as Caesar Augustus; the name Caesar was thereafter used as a title for the emperor. Jesus was born under the rule of Caesar Augustus (Luke 2:1), but he conducted his ministry under the rule of a later emperor, Caesar Tiberius (3:1). At one point, he was asked whether it was lawful for Jews to pay taxes to Caesar (NRSV: "the emperor"; Matt. 22:17; Mark 12:14; Luke 20:22; cf. Luke 23:2). He responded, "Give to Caesar the things that are Caesar's, and to God the thing that are God's" (NRSV: "the emperor"; Matt. 22:21; Mark 12:17; Luke 20:25). The Gospel of John also reports that when Jesus stood before Pilate, those who wanted him killed accused him of setting himself against Caesar, proclaimed their own loyalty to Caesar, and told Pilate he would be no friend of Caesar if he let Jesus go (19:12–15). In the book of Acts, Paul and his companions are accused of acting contrary to Caesar's decrees (17:17). Sometime later, after Paul was arrested and held for two years in captivity in Caesarea, he appealed his case to Caesar and, so, was sent to Rome (25:11–12). In 1 Peter, Christians are told to "Honor Caesar" (NRSV: "the emperor"; 2:17) and to respect his authority (2:13). *See also* Augustus; Claudius; emperor cult; Nero; Roman Empire; Tiberius. For a listing of Roman emperors during biblical times, *see* emperor.   M.A.P.

Caesarea (ses´uh-ree´uh), a seaport on the eastern coast of the Mediterranean between the ancient cities of Dor and Jaffa. It was often called Caesarea Maritima to distinguish it from Caesarea Philippi and other cities named in honor of the Roman emperor, but in the NT it is always called simply "Caesarea." It had originally been a small fortified Phoenician anchorage named Strabo's Tower. In 63 BCE, Pompey added the area, together with other towns on the seashore, to the Roman province of Syria. Mark Antony gave it to Cleopatra VII, but when Octavian (Augustus)

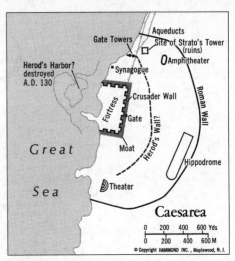

Based on available evidence, this plan of Caesarea highlights the city of Herod the Great and also includes buildings of other periods.

won the battle of Actium, he gave the small town to Herod the Great (30 BCE). Herod built a magnificent new city and port on the site and named it Caesarea in honor of Octavian, now Caesar Augustus. The harbor complex was given the name Limen Sebastos by Herod (Sebastos is the Greek form of Augustus).

According to Acts, Caesarea was visited by both Philip (8:40) and Peter (10:1–11:18). Peter proclaimed the gospel to the Roman centurion Cornelius and baptized him, a precedent that became significant when some Christians from Judea raised the question of whether Gentiles could be brought into the church without first being circumcised (cf. 15:1, 7–9). The city's harbor was also the port of arrival and departure for several of Paul's journeys according to Acts (9:30; 18:22; 21:8; 27:1–2). Paul was brought to Caesarea in custody from Jerusalem (23:23–35) to stand trial before Felix, Festus, and Agrippa II (Acts 24–26).

Caesarea was the capital of Roman government in the Near East for over six hundred years, serving as the seat of the Roman governors of the province of Judea and headquarters for the Roman legions stationed in the province. The great Jewish war against Rome began there with an uprising by the Jews in 66 CE, and "Judaea Capta" coins were minted there to commemorate their defeat. Vespasian (69–79 CE), proclaimed emperor by his legions while at Caesarea, raised the city to the rank of a Roman colony. Many leaders of the early Christian church spent time in Caesarea, including the theologian Origen, who helped establish an extensive library of Christian works there, and the historian Eusebius, who served as the city's bishop.

Extensive excavations at Caesarea since the 1960s reveal the extent to which Herod the Great was inspired by Roman architecture and indebted

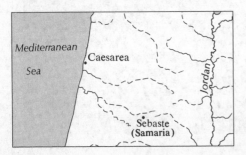

to Roman construction techniques. He built the harbor's massive breakwaters with the latest underwater *pozzolano* cement, and in a manner similar to other Hellenistic cities and Roman colonies, he laid out Caesarea on an orthogonal grid, imposing a sense of order on city life. Public views were focused on the Roman imperial temple to Augustus and Roma, which was raised on a platform and slightly off grid to face ships arriving in the harbor. Further evidence for the imperial cult includes an inscription by Pontius Pilate, which records his dedication of a *tiberium,* a structure to honor the Roman emperor Tiberius. Herod the Great's and later the Roman procurator's seaside villa has also been excavated; it had a large pool and many mosaics. Roman urban amenities in the city included an aqueduct bringing ample freshwater from miles away and a public zone inside the walls with entertainment facilities like a theater and a hippodrome; two amphitheaters outside the city walls have also been discovered.

In later periods, Caesarea thrived as one of the largest port cities in the Levant, and by the Byzantine period the city wall extended to nearly a mile and a half to accommodate the growing population. Several churches have been discovered as well as a civic structure containing a mosaic quoting Rom. 13:3. *See also* Cornelius; Herod; Paul; Peter; Philip.   M.K.M./J.R.

Caesarea Philippi (ses′uh-ree′uh fil-ip′*i*, ses′ uh-ree′uh fil′i-p*i*), the location of Peter's confession of Jesus as the Messiah, Jesus's subsequent blessing of Peter, and Jesus's first passion prediction. Caesarea Philippi was a frontier town located on the southern slope of Mount Hermon at one of the sources of the Jordan River. The site was known in antiquity as a shrine of the Greek and Roman nature god, Pan. According to the Jewish historian Josephus, Caesar Augustus gave the city, under the name of Panion, to Herod the Great. When Herod's son Philip became tetrarch of the region, he rebuilt the city and renamed it after the emperor and himself. The Gospels of Matthew and Mark report that when Jesus and his disciples were in the area around Caesarea Philippi, Jesus asked them, "Who do people say that I am?" (Mark 8:27; cf. Matt. 16:13). After receiving their answers, he asked them, "Who do you say that I am?" (Matt. 16:15; Mark 8:29). In Mark's account,

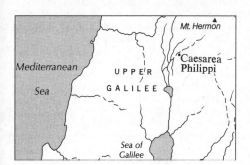

Peter's answer proclaims Jesus to be the Messiah. In Matthew's longer version of this incident, Peter proclaims that Jesus is "the Messiah, the Son of the living God" and is then blessed by Jesus, who identifies him as the rock on which the church will be built and as the one who will be given the keys to the kingdom of heaven (16:16–19). Jesus then predicts for the first time his impending arrest, suffering, crucifixion, and resurrection (Matt. 16:21–28; Mark 8:31–9:1).

Archaeological excavations have uncovered a palatial complex that certainly belonged to the later Herodians as well as evidence for religious activities around the Grotto of Pan. As early as the third century BCE, Syrophoenicians appear to have gathered there for meals and worship in an outdoor setting; later a series of temples were built facing around the grotto, and niches cut into the cliff housed statues of the nymph Echo, who was Pan's consort, and his father, Hermes. The Augusteum, built by Herod to honor his patron and Roman emperor, was likely not one of the temples found at the grotto, but was constructed down the road at the site of Omrit, where a Roman tetrastyle temple has been recently discovered.   M.K.M./M.A.P.

Caesar's household. *See* emperor's household.

Caiaphas (kay′uh-fuhs), Joseph, son-in-law and eventual successor of Annas as high priest, attaining the position in 18 CE under the Roman governor Valerius Gratus and holding it until he was deposed by Vitellius, Pontius Pilate's successor, in 36–37 CE. He would, accordingly, appear to have been the high priest at the time of the trial of Jesus (Matt. 26:3, 57; John 18:13, 24), although Luke 3:2 and Acts 4:6 suggest a more complicated scenario. John's Gospel ascribes to Caiaphas the judgment regarding Jesus that it would be "better . . . to have one man die for the people than to have the whole nation destroyed" (11:50); the author of John's Gospel regards this judgment as an ironic prophecy, by which the high priest (unwittingly) declared that Jesus's death would be for the nation (and for all children of God; cf. 11:51–52).

The discovery of a first-century family tomb in the Peace Forest outside Jerusalem in 1990 yielded a dozen stone ossuaries containing the remains of sixty-three individuals. The most elaborately decorated of the ossuaries is inscribed twice with the name "Yehoseph bar Kayafa" (Aramaic for "Joseph son of Caiaphas"). It contained the bones of four children, an adult woman, and a man of about sixty. Many scholars believe that the last is the high priest Caiaphas. *See also* Annas; ossuaries; Pilate, Pontius; priests; trial of Jesus.   F.O.G.

Cain (kayn; Heb., "metalworker," although Gen. 4:1 connects it with a verb meaning "to acquire" or "create").

1 Adam and Eve's first son, a farmer whose offering God rejected. Angered, Cain killed Abel (whose offering had been accepted) and subsequently denied knowledge of his whereabouts. As a punishment, God withheld the ground's fertility from Cain, who was condemned to a life of wandering. God placed a mark on Cain to warn would-be attackers that he remained under God's protection (Gen. 4:1–16). Cain later built the first city and became the father of Enoch and ancestor of Tubalcain, the first metalworker (4:17). Cain is often regarded as the eponymous ancestor of the Kenites (cf. 15:9; Judg. 4:11). A descendant, Lamech, would claim Cain as a model for vengeance, boasting, "If Cain is avenged sevenfold, truly Lamech seventy-sevenfold" (Gen. 4:24). In the Hebrew Bible, Cain is not mentioned outside of Genesis, but in the NT he is referred to twice as one who should not be emulated (1 John 3:2; Jude 11). *See also* Abel; Kenites; smith.

2 A city in Judah (Josh. 15:57).   F.E.G.

Calah (kay'luh; Akkadian Kalkhu; Arabic Birs Nimrud), a city on the eastern bank of the Tigris River at which significant archaeological excavations have shed light on the Assyrian Empire and Israel's dealings with Assyria. Calah is located in northern Iraq, about twenty miles south of ancient Nineveh (modern Mosul). It is mentioned in the Bible in Gen. 10:11–12. The city was founded in the thirteenth century BCE by Shalmaneser I (1274–1245 BCE) during a period of extensive building and expansion in Assyria. At the beginning of his reign, Ashurnasirpal II (883–859 BCE) moved his capital to Calah from Nineveh. His rebuilding program included a partially subterranean canal, a city wall, a palace of brick faced with stone, and elaborate low-reliefs depicting religious ceremonies and battle and hunting scenes. At this time, the palace covered about six acres. In the northwest section of the palace, excavations have discovered numerous fragments of ivory furniture inlay and decorative plaques carved in the Phoenician style. The Black Obelisk of Shalmaneser III (858–824 BCE), which depicts Jehu, son of Omri, submitting to the Assyrian king, was also found at Calah. Other important records include the governor's archives, dealing with provincial administration during the reign of Tiglath-pileser III (745–727 BCE). The southeast area, called Fort Shalmaneser, also yielded many ivory fragments.   L.E.P.

Caleb (kay'luhb), a leader of Judah who was chosen to be one of the twelve spies sent by Moses to explore the land of Canaan before the Israelites entered (Num. 13:1–16). When the spies returned, ten of them shared a pessimistic report, but Caleb "quieted the people" upset by this report (13:30), and he and Joshua maintained that God would give them the land if they were faithful (14:6–9). In response, "the whole congregation threatened to stone them" (14:10), prompting God to intervene with a display of glory and a threat of divine wrath that was only averted through the intercession of Moses (14:11–24). Nevertheless, the only ones among those who had left Egypt who were allowed to enter the promised land were Caleb and Joshua (14:30; cf. 26:65; 32:12). Caleb is singled out as one whom God says "has a different spirit and has followed me wholeheartedly" (14:24; cf. Deut. 1:36).

Caleb is identified as the son of Jephunneh the Kenizzite, and he is given Hebron as his inheritance (Josh. 14:13–14). He is thereafter regarded as the founding father of the Calebites (who, through Jephunneh, are linked to the Kenizzites). Caleb later gave his daughter Achsah to his brother Othniel as a wife and, at Achsah's request, gave her the two springs known as Upper Gulloth and Lower Gulloth as a wedding present (Josh. 16:15–19; Judg. 1:12–15). *See also* Hebron; Joshua; Judah.   M.A.P.

calendar. The Bible does not contain a complete calendar for ancient Israel, but the one presented in the chart accompanying this entry has been reconstructed from various references, correlated with knowledge of the Babylonian calendar, which Israel seems to have adopted or adapted. It is not absolutely clear whether the year began in the spring or in the fall. On the one hand, Lev. 23:5 seems to indicate that the spring month of Nisan is the first month of the year (since Passover is celebrated on the 14th of the first month); on the other hand, Exod. 23:16 seems to indicate that the year ends in the fall (which would imply a new year begins then as well; cf. 34:22). Scholars have generated the following proposals to explain the apparent discrepancy over when the year began: (1) the agricultural calendar may have begun in the fall and ended each year with the final harvest, while a religious calendar began in the spring; (2) there was a northern vernal calendar and a southern autumnal one; (3) in preexilic times the calendar began in autumn while in postexilic times a spring new year was celebrated.

It is also unclear exactly how many days each month had, or whether this was consistent in all places and times. Although 30 days are alluded to in the Bible as a month's duration, the lunar calendar averaged only 29½ days a month. Since the calendar was also tied to the agricultural or seasonal year, it also had a solar element. The necessity of intercalating the lunar calendar of 354 days a year with the seasonal solar year resulted in the Babylonians' adding a month every two or three years. This system was eventually adopted in Judaism, also—seven out of every nineteen years included an additional month (a "second Adar").

There are no names for months cited in the NT, and if, as seems likely, the figures in Revelation mentioning a specific duration of time refer to the same three and a half years (12:14; 1260 days; 11:3; 12:6; 42 months, 13:5), then it might be surmised that a year was generally thought to have twelve months of thirty days each. *See also* time.   M.A.P.

THE HEBREW CALENDAR

Hebrew Name	Canaanite Name	Equivalent
Nisan (Neh. 2:1; Esther 3:7)	Abib (Exod. 13:4; 23:15; 34:18; Deut. 16:1)	March/April
Iyyar	Ziv (1 Kings 6:1, 37)	April/May
Sivan (Esther 8:9; Bar. 1:8)		May/June
Tammuz		June/July
Ab		July/Aug.
Elul (Neh. 6:15; 1 Macc. 4:7)		Aug./Sept.
Tishri	Ethanim (1 Kings 8:2)	Sept./Oct.
Marchesvan	Bul (1 Kings 6:38)	Oct./Nov.
Chislev (Neh. 1:1; Zech. 7:1; 1 Macc. 1:54; 4:52, 59; 2 Macc. 1:9, 18; 10:5)		Nov./Dec.
Tebeth (Esther 2:16)		Dec./Jan.
Shebat (Zech. 1:7; 1 Macc. 16:4)		Jan./Feb.
Adar (Ezra 6:15; Esther 3:7, 13; 8:12; 9:1, 15, 17, 19, 21)		Feb./March

calf, an animal that could be used as an appropriate sacrifice for a sin offering (Lev. 9:2, 8). A calf might also be used in a sacrifice that sealed a covenant; in Jer. 34:18–19, the prophet declares that those who have not kept God's covenant will be made to be like that calf (split in two and left to be eaten by birds). A calf could also serve as food on special occasions (Gen. 18:7–8; 1 Sam. 28:24; Luke 15:22–24). A psalmist employs the playful skipping of a calf as a positive image for carefree joy (Ps. 29:6), but Jeremiah uses a calf's untrained ways as a symbol for undisciplined behavior (31:18). Isaiah presents the peaceful coexistence of a calf and a lion as a symbol of paradise (6:1). The calf also becomes associated with idol worship, due to the worship of the golden calf in Exod. 32 (cf. Deut. 9:16–21; Neh. 9:18; Ps. 106:19; Acts 17:41). In that story, while Moses was receiving the Ten Commandments on Mount Sinai, the Israelites asked Aaron to provide them with a god to lead them. He collected their gold and shaped it into the form of a calf, mounted on an altar. The people worshiped the calf and sacrificed to it, engaging in wild revelry. Moses, on his return, melted the calf down, ground it to powder, and scattered it on water. He then forced the idolatrous Israelites to drink the water filled with gold dust. In addition, God punished the Israelites with a plague.
I.U.K./M.A.P.

call, a common word acquiring theological significance when God or Christ is the one who calls, implying divine election or commission. Sometimes individuals are called to special vocations: God called Moses (Exod. 3:4), the judges (Judg. 3:9), and the prophets (Jer. 1:5); and Jesus called disciples (Matt. 4:18–22; 9:9). Paul says that he was called by God to proclaim Christ among the Gentiles (Gal. 1:15–16; cf. Rom. 1:1). When the call is a general summons to repentance and salvation, every member of the covenant community is viewed as its recipient, and hence both Israel and the church are designated collectively as God's "called" or "elect" (Isa. 41:9; Heb. 3:1). *See also* apostle; election; Moses; prophet.   J.M.B.

Calneh (kal'neh), a north Syrian city located in the plain of Antioch. Calneh was the capital of the Neo-Hittite state of Unqi. It paid tribute to Assyria in the ninth century BCE and was conquered and annexed to Assyria by Tiglath-pileser III in 738 BCE. The city is referred to in Amos 6:2 and in Isa. 10:9 (where it is called "Calno"). In both cases, it is presented as an example and warning: despite power and self-confidence, Israel's fate will be like that of Calneh. The point is that Israel will not be able to withstand the onslaught of the Assyrian armies.   M.C.

Calno (kal'noh). *See* Calneh.

Calvary (kal'vuh-ree), a name for the site of Jesus's crucifixion derived from a Latin translation (*calvaria*) of Golgotha, which is Aramaic for "Place of the Skull" (cf. Matt. 27:33; Mark 15:22; Luke 23:33; John 19:17). The term is not used in the NRSV. *See also* Golgotha.   J.M.B.

camel (Heb. *gamal*). The camel is frequently mentioned in the Bible as a beast of burden and as a riding animal, often in association with nomadic tribes (e.g., Gen. 37:25; Judg. 7:12; 1 Kings 10:1–2). There are two types of domesticated camels: the one-humped dromedary (*Camelus dromedarius*) and the two-humped Bactrian camel (*Camelus bactrianus*). The dromedary is distributed throughout Arabia, northern Africa, the Near East, Pakistan, and India, whereas the longer-haired and heavier-built Bactrian camel is better adapted to a colder climate and is at home in central Asia, Afghanistan, and Iran. Usually it is the dromedary that is featured in the Bible, but the Bactrian camel may be referred to in Tob. 9:2.

The time and locale of the earliest camel domestication have long been an enigma, but recent finds from Shahr-i Sokhta in Iran and several sites in Turkmenistan suggest that the Bactrian camel came under human control during the third millennium BCE. Archaeological evidence, consisting of camel bones and a reference to a camel on a stele, also indicate that the dromedary was domesticated in Oman and eastern Arabia at about the same time. There is no archaeological corroboration, however, for the camel being known in Egypt or the Near East at the beginning of the second millennium BCE. Still, the book of Genesis offers seventeen references to camels in the area at that time. Abraham is said to have been given camels by Pharaoh (Gen. 12:16) and to have supplied his servant with ten camels to search for Rebekah in Mesopotamia (24:10). Again, Jacob is supposed to have ridden a camel to Canaan (Gen. 31:17) and to have presented Esau with camels (32:15). Genesis also furnishes information on the care of camels, including watering them (24:14, 19–20), feeding them (24:25, 32), and making them kneel (24:11).

In the twelfth or eleventh century BCE, the Levant was invaded by nomadic Arab tribes ("Midianites") riding on camels (Judg. 6:5). At this time, the Israelites started keeping camels themselves and used them (1 Chron. 12:40) to take gifts to King David, who himself employed an Ishmaelite to take care of his camels (27:30). Camels were instrumental for the establishment of long-distance trade; they carried spices and incense all the way from southern Arabia to the Mediterranean and goods from Canaan to Egypt (cf. Gen. 37:25). When the queen of Sheba visited King Solomon, her luggage was transported by camels (1 Kings 10:2). But camels were not only used as beasts of burden; they were also raised as livestock. Thus, the Hagarites are reported to have owned fifty thousand camels (1 Chron. 5:21), and Job first had three thousand camels (Job 1:3) and later six thousand (42:12). In Israel, the camels were raised for their milk (which may be alluded to in Gen. 32:15), hair, and hides, but their meat was forbidden to the Israelites to eat (Lev. 11:4; Deut. 14:7).

In NT times the camel continued to be used as a beast of burden. Jesus focused on their size, using them in proverbial sayings that contrast them with something small: in one instance, he noted that "it is easier for a camel to go through the eye of a needle than for someone who is rich to enter the kingdom of God" (Mark 10:25; cf. Matt. 19:24; Luke 18:25); in another he likened pedantic interpretations of the law to straining out a gnat while swallowing a camel (Matt. 23:24).   I.U.K.

camel's hair, a type of material for clothing mentioned only in Matt. 3:4 and Mark 1:6, which indicate that John the Baptist wore clothing of camel's hair. Because these passages refer to John's austere lifestyle, scholars generally assume that the reference is not to a cloak of camel's hair (though these were commercially available), but to a loincloth or other simple garment that he might have woven himself (cf. Matt. 11:8; Luke 7:25). Some scholars link John's camel's-hair garment with Elijah's "garment of haircloth" (2 Kings 1:8; a sign of his prophetic office according to Zech. 13:4). Specification of John's apparel would then be intended to identify Elijah as his prototype (cf. Matt. 17:10–13). *See also* Elijah; John the Baptist.   P.L.S.

Cana (kay'nuh), a village of Galilee mentioned only in the Gospel of John as the site of Jesus's miracles. First, Jesus attends a wedding feast in Cana and turns water into wine (2:1–11). Later, Jesus is in Cana when a royal official tells him that his son is ill in Capernaum and Jesus heals the boy from a distance (4:46–54; cf. Matt. 8:5–13; Luke

Camel carrying desert raiders in battle against Ashurbanipal's forces, as depicted in the Nineveh reliefs, seventh century BCE.

7:1–10, though there is no mention of Cana in these accounts). Cana is also named as the home of Nathanael (21:2). Latin and Orthodox churches at Kefr Kenna, about four miles northeast of Nazareth, claim to mark the spot of the wedding, but most scholars agree that the more likely site of the ancient village is Khirbet Qana, on a hill about nine miles north-northwest of Nazareth, where excavations have recently been conducted. The discoveries from the Roman period include a series of tombs on the hillside and a public structure that might be a synagogue, but otherwise only modest dwellings indicative of a small Jewish village. By the Byzantine period, the Christian footprint on the site would be prominent: a massive structure might have been a monastery, and a cave appears to have commemorated the miracle of Jesus turning water to wine. *See also* Galilee; Nathanael.

Canaan (kay′nuhn).

1 The son of Ham and the grandson of Noah. He is first encountered in the story of Noah's drunkenness (Gen. 9:18–27). Noah becomes drunk, lies uncovered in a tent, and his son Ham sees him naked. In retribution for this impropriety, Noah curses Ham's son Canaan. Canaan is to be a slave, a curse that may reflect the fate of some elements of the Canaanite population in Israel (Judg. 1:28). Canaan next appears in the "Table of Nations" (Gen. 10:6, 15–20) as brother of Put (Libya), Cush (Ethiopia), and Egypt. He is reckoned the father of Sidon, Heth, the Jebusites, and a host of other peoples living in the land of Israel. This expresses in the form of genealogy the human geography of early Israel: the Canaanites were the recent inhabitants of much of the land that became Israel. Thus, the native inhabitants of the land are sometimes simply called "Canaanites" (12:6).

2 The ancient name of a territory that included parts of what is now Israel and Lebanon. The origin and etymology of the name "Canaan" remain obscure. It is presumably a Semitic term, but the effort to link Canaan with the Akkadian word *kinahhu*, referring to the redness of a wool dye, is problematic. The word "Canaanite" occurs already in third-millennium BCE texts from Ebla.

Sphere of Influence: In proper usage, the term "Canaan" seems to have referred to a discrete region whose precise boundaries cannot at present be determined. At Ugarit on the Syrian coast of the Mediterranean Sea, Canaan was regarded as a region lying to the south. Late Bronze Age letters from the Amarna archives often refer to Canaan, and in some of these Byblos is situated in Canaan and the affairs of Sidon and Hazor are reckoned as Canaanite matters. At other times, however, the Amarna letters use the word "Canaan" broadly; a letter from Tyre implies that Ugarit was a Canaanite city, contradicting the native view at Ugarit itself. Uses of the word "Canaan" in the Bible reflect both the precision and the looseness of the term. In Genesis, the Table of Nations sets the boundaries of Canaan as follows: from Sidon to Gerar near Gaza, and eastward as far as Sodom, Gomor-

Canaanite dignitary with arm raised in salute; bronze plaque from Hazor, fifteenth century BCE.

rah, Admah, and Zeboiim to Lasha (Gen. 10:19). Elsewhere, however, the Bible speaks of Canaan with a less precise referent in view.

Society and Religion: Before the emergence of Israel (late thirteenth century BCE), Canaan was organized into small principalities centered around the major towns of the region. The Amarna correspondence between Egyptian pharaohs and the kings of Canaanite states gives a vivid picture of petty strife and political intrigue in the land. There is little evidence of concerted action of Canaan's rulers, so that the stories in the Bible about Canaanite alliances against the Israelites (Josh. 9:1–2; 10:1–5) appear exceptional. In general, Canaanite rule seems to have been fragmented, as is suggested by the list of kings and kingdoms that fell to Joshua (12:7–24): thirty-one rulers and principalities are accounted for in this small region.

Canaan's major towns were located for the most part in agricultural regions, especially on the fertile plains of the countryside. The Canaanites enjoyed a reputation as traders; in fact, the very word "Canaanite" came to mean "merchant" (Zech. 14:21). Nevertheless, agriculture was a vital preoccupation of Canaan. The religious festivals of Canaan were, insofar as they are known or inferred, devoted to the concerns of farmers and vintners. Israel probably inherited its cycle of harvest festivals from the Canaanite population (Exod. 23:14–17). Canaanite religion seems to have placed emphasis on fertility in the natural world. Sexuality in the cult, a feature of Canaanite religion despised by Israel, may have been linked to the task of maintaining plant and animal fecundity. The gods of the Canaanites were in various ways involved in the life cycles of nature. The powerful storm god Baal was a giver of rain. His adversary, Mot, was a god of death and sterility. The ability of gods and goddesses to mate and their whereabouts in the cosmos were tied directly to the fate of human beings and their crops and animals. Canaanite society was stratified. There was a small advantaged class surrounded by a larger population that was subjected to various controls and placed under the burden of taxes and other impositions. Samuel's description of the ways of a king (1 Sam. 8:11–18) is generally taken as providing a good account of the pattern of Canaanite kingship.

Israel was hostile to Canaan. It loathed much that was associated with Canaanite religion, and its literature urges its eradication, together with the Canaanite people (Deut. 20:16–18). Nevertheless, one can recognize that Israel owed much to the legacy of Canaan. Enclaves of Canaanite people were incorporated into the population of Israel, and Canaanite language and thought influenced the religion of Israel.

In Matt. 15:21–28, Jesus encounters a Canaanite woman, who refers to him as the "Son of David" and begs him to heal her daughter. After initial hesitation and a witty exchange, Jesus praises the woman for her great faith, and her daughter is healed. *See also* Amarna, Tell el-; Baal; Gebal; Hazor; Pentateuch, sources of the; Sidon; Tyre.
Bibliography
Gray, John. *The Legacy of Canaan.* Brill, 1957.
R.M.G.

Cananaean (kay'nuh-nee'uhn; from Aramaic *qan'an,* "zealous"), epithet of the disciple Simon in Mark 3:18 and Matt. 10:4. In Luke 6:15 and Acts 1:13, he is called the Zealot, which might imply association with a faction of Jews opposed to Roman rule or simply indicate that he was notably zealous (e.g., for God or for the Torah). *See also* Zealots.

Candace (kan'duh-see), **the,** a title borne by a woman who is also called the "queen of the Ethiopians" in Acts 8:27. She is mentioned because Philip baptizes her treasury minister, an Ethiopian eunuch. At this time, "Ethiopian" did not designate a specific country, but was used as a generic term for Africans or people with black skin. Ac-

cording to Bion of Soli (*Aethiopica 1,* ca. second century BCE), the head of the government in the Nubian kingdom of Meroe upon the upper Nile (modern Sudan) was called "the Candace." Thus, the "Ethiopian eunuch" in Acts is probably to be regarded as a financial officer in that kingdom. *See also* Philip.

candle. *See* lamp.

candlestick. *See* lampstand.

canon (Gk., "rule" or "standard"), religious writings that are to be regarded as authoritative scripture. Both Jews and Christians have had to consider which books belong to their canon of scripture.

The Jewish Canon: Among Jews, the oldest canon appears to have been the one defining the Torah (the first five books of modern Bibles), which from an early time (sixth to fourth century BCE) became the central document of Jewish faith. To this was added a body of writings called the Nevi'im ("Prophets"), which included what are sometimes called the Former Prophets (Joshua, Judges, Samuel, Kings), the Latter Prophets (Isaiah, Jeremiah, Ezekiel), and the Twelve (Hosea, Joel, Amos, Obadiah, Jonah, Micah, Nahum, Habakkuk, Zephaniah, Haggai, Zechariah, Malachi). A third set of books called Ketuvim ("Writings") included Psalms, Job, Proverbs, Ruth, Song of Solomon, Ecclesiastes, Lamentations, Esther, Daniel, Ezra–Nehemiah, and Chronicles. By the end of the Second Temple period (70 CE), these books appear to have functioned as at least an unofficial canon of Hebrew scripture for most Jewish people (regardless of whether they had been declared such by official proclamations or rabbinic councils, as is sometimes alleged, but impossible to prove). One indication of this is that the Christian church in the next few centuries adopted these writings as its OT, taking over what it clearly thought were the scriptures of Israel. There is some evidence, however, to indicate that the question of canon was in flux during the first century CE: certain comments of Josephus (*Antiquities* 13.297; 18.16–17) have been taken to mean that the Sadducees accepted only the Torah (as did the Samaritans, who had their own version of it). Likewise, the views of the Jewish community at Qumran regarding canon are impossible to determine, since the Dead Sea Scrolls found there include a wide variety of writings with no obvious canonical distinctions. In addition to the Hebrew canon, furthermore, many Greek-speaking Jews at this time would have accepted books included in the LXX, books produced in Greek during the Second Temple period that were not a part of the Hebrew canon. On these, *see* Apocrypha/deuterocanonical literature.

The Christian Canon: Although Christians of the first century CE generally accepted the existing Jewish scriptures, they did not have, at first, any distinctively Christian canon. Early in the second

THE NEW TESTAMENT CANON: EARLY LISTS

The Muratorian Fragment (ca. 170–200)

A list of the books to be regarded as scripture by an unknown author:

Hebrews, James, 1 Peter, 2 Peter, and 3 John: *not* included.

Apocalypse of Peter: included, with the note that "some of us are not willing that it be read in church."

Shepherd of Hermas: approved, but not as scripture; written too recently; ought to be read, but not "publicly to the people in church."

Letter to the Laodiceans and *Letter to the Alexandrians* (unknown to us): two spurious forgeries attributed to Paul, to be rejected.

Origen of Alexandria (ca. 215–250)

The early theologian Origen does not provide a list, but does discuss the books that are disputed:

2 Peter: "Peter left behind one letter that is acknowledged, and possibly a second, but it is disputed."

2 John and 3 John: "Not everyone agrees that they are genuine."

Hebrews: probably not written by Paul, but acceptable anyway, because "the thoughts of the epistle are marvelous and in no way inferior to the acknowledged writings of the apostle."

Eusebius of Caesarea (ca. 311)

The early church historian Eusebius reports the books considered scripture in his day:

James, Jude, 2 Peter, 2 John, and 3 John: "Disputed books which are nonetheless known by many."

Revelation: among *both* the "acknowledged books" *and* the noncanonical books; it is a "book that some reject, but others judge to belong."

Acts of Paul, Shepherd of Hermas, Apocalypse of Peter, Didache, Epistle of Barnabas, and *Gospel of the Hebrews:* listed, but considered noncanonical (the last is only considered noncanonical by "some people" and is "particularly celebrated" by others).

Cyril of Jerusalem (ca. 350)

In his catechism, the Eastern theologian Cyril discusses canon:

All books of current NT listed except Revelation.

No other books should be read in the churches or even privately (as his readers might have heard was acceptable).

Gospel of Thomas: lambasted as a work that, "having been camouflaged by the sweetness of its title, corrupts the souls of the simpler ones."

Mommsen Catalogue, or Cheltenham List (ca. 359)

A list by an unknown author from North Africa:

The NT contains twenty-four books, as symbolized by the twenty-four elders in the book of Revelation (see 4:4).

Hebrews, James, and Jude: not included.

Only one letter of John and one letter of Peter are canonical (but that would throw off the count, which is supposed to be twenty-four).

Athanasius of Alexandria (ca. 367)

Athanasius's letter lists what he regards as "the canon" of Christian scripture:

All twenty-seven books of the NT included.

Didache, Shepherd of Hermas: not included, but "have nonetheless been designated by the fathers as books to be read."

(continued)

THE NEW TESTAMENT CANON: EARLY LISTS (continued)

Amphilochius of Iconium (ca. 375–394)

A poem by the Christian poet Amphilochius teaches the books of the canon in iambic verse:

Hebrews: considered spurious by some, but they are wrong, "for the grace that it imparts is genuine."

2 Peter, 2 John, 3 John, and Jude: books that "some receive," but that should not be received.

Revelation: "Some approve, but most say it is spurious."

Third Synod of Carthage (ca. 393)

A regional meeting of churches—not a churchwide council, but a significant representation:

Athanasius's list (above): ratified; the twenty-seven books of the current NT declared to be the canon of Christian scripture.

---

century, however, they began to treat specifically Christian writings as equal to the Jewish scriptures. Thus 2 Peter (ca. 80–120) refers to letters of Paul as scripture (3:16), and Justin Martyr, writing around the middle of the second century, describes the "memoirs of the apostles" being read alongside the "writings of the prophets" in Christian worship (First Apology 66). Still, no canonical lists appeared until Marcion, around the middle of the second century, proposed that Christians not accept the OT as scripture and that they limit their canon to a collection he produced consisting of an edited version of Luke's Gospel and edited editions of ten Pauline Letters (all but the Pastorals). There is no evidence that Marcion's suggestion had many supporters, but it did raise the issue of canon in a pointed way and, so, additional canon lists began to appear. The lists exhibit some variety in their contents, but the level of consistency is also striking. Twenty of the NT's twenty-seven books appear to have been almost universally accepted (apart from Marcion): the four Gospels, the book of Acts, all thirteen of Paul's letters, 1 Peter (missing only in the "Muratorian fragment"), and 1 John. Another seven books, however, were sometimes questioned: Hebrews, James, 2 Peter, 2 John, 3 John, Jude, and Revelation. Of course, all of these lists reflect views that were preserved by the church, so they might testify only to one prominent strand of Christianity, the one that ultimately prevailed. Most scholars, however, would also see a link between the twenty-seven NT writings that were ultimately deemed canonical and what is called the "apostolic tradition," i.e., books that were written either by apostles (Jesus's twelve disciples plus Paul), by people who had known those apostles, or by those who at least had an early connection to them and thought in similar ways.

Unanimity was never achieved. For example, the Syrian church approved a twenty-three-book NT (missing 2 Peter, 2 John, 3 John, and Revelation) in the fifth century. Still, the Latin Vulgate of Jerome (late fourth century) exerted considerable influence in establishing the twenty-seven-book NT canon as normative in Western Christianity, and there has been only "low-level" discussion of the matter since that time (e.g., in the sixteenth century, Luther distinguished which NT books he considered to be primary and which could be regarded as peripheral, but he did not attempt to remove the peripheral writings from the Bible). The wider field of discussion within Christianity has concerned the question of its OT canon. A few Christian groups have been reluctant to recognize the OT as equivalent with the NT, and Christian groups have continued to espouse different views regarding the scriptural status of the Apocrypha/deuterocanonical literature. See also Apocrypha/deuterocanonical literature; Hagiographa; New Testament; Old Testament; Pentateuch; Septuagint; Tanakh; Torah.

Bibliography

Barton, John. Holy Writings, Sacred Text: The Canon in Early Christianity. Westminster John Knox, 1997.

Bruce, F. F. The Canon of Scripture. InterVarsity, 1988.

McDonald, Lee Martin. The Biblical Canon: Its Origin, Transmission, and Authority. Hendrickson, 2007.

Metzger, Bruce. The Canon of the New Testament: Its Origin, Development, and Significance. Clarendon, 1987.

Miller, John W. How the Bible Came to Be. Paulist, 2004.   M.A.P.

canopy, an open-sided cover giving overhead protection from sun or rain. A canopy stood before the porch pillars in Solomon's Hall of Pillars (1 Kings 7:6), a canopy of wood will stand in front of the envisioned temple vestibule (Ezek. 42:10), and a canopy will shield the throne of Nebuchadnezzar when he occupies Egypt (Jer. 43:10). Joel refers to a bride's canopy (2:16). Holofernes sleeps on a bed under a canopy, and Judith takes the canopy with her after she beheads him; she shows it to the people and presents it as a votive offering to the Lord (Jth. 10:21; 13:9, 15; 16:19). Metaphorically, darkness serves as the Lord's canopy (1 Sam. 22:12), as do thick clouds dark with water (Ps. 18:11), and a canopy over all the Lord's glory will provide shelter (Isa. 4:5).

Canticles (kan'ti-kuhlz). *See* Song of Solomon.

Capernaum (kuh-puhr'nay-uhm; from the Heb. for "village of Nahum"), a town on the northwest shore of the Sea of Galilee, about two and a half miles from the mouth of the Jordan River. Capernaum was the center of Jesus's Galilean ministry (Matt. 4:13). There he healed the son (or servant) of a centurion (Matt. 8:5–13; Luke 7:1–10; cf. John 4:46–54) and engaged in other healing, teaching, and exorcising (Matt. 17:24; Mark 2:1; Luke 4:23, 31; John 2:12; 6:17, 24). In particular, Jesus was active in the synagogue (Mark. 1:21; John 6:59) and in "the house" (perhaps Peter's; Matt. 8:14–17; Mark 1:29–34; 9:33). In spite of all his work there, however, Jesus apparently felt rejected by the people of Capernaum and cursed the town (Matt. 11:23–24; Luke 10:15).

Identified with the site Tell Hum, Capernaum has been extensively excavated beginning in the late nineteenth century. Excavations by the Franciscans have focused on the two most prominent ruins, those of a white limestone synagogue and those of an octagonal church a few yards to the south. Both date in their latest phase to the fifth century CE, when Christian pilgrims brought wealth to the area. Modern stratigraphic excavations show that the limestone for the fifth-century synagogue was quarried and brought from central Galilee to contrast with the local dark basalt stone. Although some earlier walls underneath this structure might be from the first-century synagogue of Jesus's time, the finds are meager and inconclusive.

In the case of the octagonal church, the excavators distinguished three phases: a first-century BCE house from the beginning of settlement in Capernaum, a fourth-century CE *domus-ecclesia,* or "house-church," and finally the fifth century CE church built in concentric octagons centering over one room from the earliest house. Graffiti in several languages dating as early as the second century include what might be Christian phrases (e.g., *amen, maria,* and *petros*), and this has led the Franciscans to conclude that the house was indeed "Peter's House" described in later pilgrim accounts. Whether those responsible for the

second-century graffiti and later church construction were correct in attaching the site as Peter's house is disputed—nevertheless, it is one of the oldest identifiable Christian sites ever discovered.

Excavations on the Greek Orthodox side of the site have uncovered extensive domestic remains from the Byzantine and Arab periods as well as a small bathhouse similar to those excavated along the Roman frontiers and built by legions. The structure cannot, however, be tied to the centurion of the Gospels, since it dates to the second century after the Bar Kochbah Revolt, when Roman legions were permanently stationed in Galilee.

As a whole, the excavations show that Capernaum at the time of Jesus was a simple village of around a thousand inhabitants, mostly peasants and fishermen. Archaeological discoveries like stone vessels show that the inhabitants were Jews who used locally produced pottery with few imports or other signs of wealth like fresco, plaster, or roof tiles. *See also* Peter; synagogue.   C.H.M./J.R.

Caphtor (kaf'tor), a place referred to in Amos 9:7 as the home of the Philistines, who are called the "remnant of the coastland of Caphtor" (Jer. 47:4) and "the Caphtorim" (Deut. 2:23). Scholars have offered various suggestions for its location. The most widely accepted is the island of Crete in the Aegean Sea; some Philistine names suggest an origin in the Aegean basin. Other scholars see a connection between Caphtor and Kafto, an Egyptian designation for the southern coast of Asia Minor, and propose Cilicia on the southeast coast. The LXX translates Caphtor as Cappadocia, a region in Asia Minor, but this is probably not correct. *See also* Caphtorim; Philistines.   D.R.B.

Caphtorim (kaf'tuh-rim), the designation of a group of people described in the Table of Nations (Gen. 10:14; 1 Chron. 1:12) as the "descendants of Egypt" and connected with the descendants of Ham. They are elsewhere identified with the Philistines who inhabited the southern coastland of Canaan north of Egypt (Deut. 3:23; Amos 9:7). *See also* Caphtor; Philistines.

Cappadocia (kap'uh-doh'shee-uh), an isolated interior region of eastern Asia Minor lying north of the Taurus Mountains, east of Lake Tatta, south of Pontus, and west of the Euphrates River. Although possessing urban centers—Mazaca/Caesarea and Tyana were the most important—much of Cappadocia remained rural and was divided as early as Hittite times into immense royal and temple estates. After 585 BCE Cappadocia came under Persian rule, then passed to Seleucid control, and then after ca. 255 BCE was ruled by its own kings. Roman influence in Cappadocian affairs became strong during the late second and first centuries BCE, and Tiberius finally made Cappadocia a Roman province in 17 CE. A Jewish community may have existed in Cappadocia as early as the second century BCE (see 1 Macc. 15:22; Acts 2:9 offers somewhat later evidence). The letter of 1 Peter is

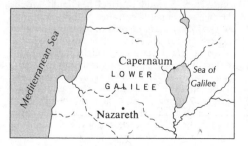

addressed to Christians in Cappadocia and other provinces of Asia Minor (1:1). References in the LXX to Cappadocia probably represent a mistranslation of the name "Caphtor" (Deut. 2:23; Amos 9:7). *See also* Asia; Persia; Peter, First Letter of; Pontus; Seleucids; Tiberius.   R.A.W.

captain, the translation of several different Hebrew and Greek words, which itself reveals little more than that the person to which it refers possessed some degree of authority; people referred to as captains in the Bible include those who are in groups ranging in size from tens to thousands and those with duties in the areas of military authority, civil administration, and judicial responsibility. In Egypt, Potiphar is called the "captain of the guard" (Gen. 37:36; 39:1). When the Israelites complain against Moses in the wilderness, they say, "Let us choose a captain, and go back to Egypt" (Num. 14:4). After David escapes King Achish of Gath, he flees to the cave of Adullam and there becomes captain over the discontented persons who come to him (1 Sam. 2:22). The king of Samaria sends three captains of fifty with their men to menace Elijah—the first two groups are destroyed by fire from heaven, but the captain of the third group of fifty begs Elijah for mercy (2 Kings 1:9–14). Jon. 1:6 refers to the captain of a ship. In the book of Acts, a captain of the temple arrives with police to arrest the apostles when they preach in the temple courts (4:1; 5:24, 26).   M.A.P.

captivity. *See* exile.

caravan, a mixed company of travelers, usually fairly large for the purpose of safety. A caravan might include merchants and their pack animals; merchants regularly traversed the trade routes to oversee the transport of their goods. Gen. 37:25 refers to a caravan of Ishmaelites who purchased Joseph and took him as a slave to Egypt. Judg. 5:6 indicates that instability during the period of the

judges had endangered caravan trade, while Judg. 6:3–5 seems to refer to a situation in which Israel was being overrun by caravans of Midianite and Amalekite traders who "wasted the land as they came in." Judg. 8:11 says that Gideon used a caravan route to overtake the kings of Midian and attack them off guard. Caravan trade is implied in 1 Kings 10:2 as well as in Isaiah's promise of prosperity: "a multitude of camels shall cover you" (60:6). See also Judg. 5:6; Job 6:18–19; Isa. 21:13. *See also* ass; camel; trade; transportation, travel.   F.S.F.

carbuncle, a decorative stone, possibly red, green, or blue, used in liturgical items. In the three places that the term is used in the KJV and RSV (Exod. 28:17; 29:10; Ezek. 28:13), it is translated "emerald" in the NRSV and "beryl" in the NIV. The plural is simply translated "jewels" by both the NRSV and NIV in Isa. 54:12. *See also* beryl; jewels, jewelry.

Carchemish (kahr′kuh-mish), a city on the Euphrates River in northern Syria, about sixty miles northeast of Aleppo. In the eighteenth century BCE, Carchemish was an ally of Shamshi-adad I against Yahdunlim of Mari. In the sixteenth century BCE, Egypt extended its influence into southwestern Asia: Pharaoh Ahmosis (ca. 1565) claimed to have reached the city of Carchemish, and Pharaoh Thutmose III to have conquered it. Later, Carchemish allied itself with the Hittites in the battle against Egypt at Kadesh (1286 BCE). By the end of that century, however, Carchemish had been reduced in size and power by the Sea Peoples. In 717 BCE, Carchemish was taken into the Assyrian Empire by Sargon II, and its leading citizens were deported, an event referred to in Isa. 10:9. Then in 609 BCE Pharaoh Neco encountered Josiah at Carchemish before the two engaged in battle on the plain of Megiddo (2 Chron. 35:20, 22). A few years later, in 605 BCE, Nebuchadnezzar of Babylon defeated the Egyptian forces under Neco and their Assyrian allies in a battle at Carchemish that allowed Babylon to assume control of the region (Jer. 46:2–12; 1 Esd. 1:25).   L.E.P.

Carmel (kahr′muhl; Heb., "garden," "orchard").
1 A range of fertile, forested hills (Amos 1:2; Isa. 33:9; Nah. 1:4) about fifteen miles long on the western border of the land allotted to the tribe of Asher (Josh. 19:26). It extends from the Samaritan hill country west to the Mediterranean and south to the Mount Carmel headland. Mount Carmel, which is the entrance of the Jezreel Valley (Esdraelon), commands an excellent view of the shoreline and rises 556 feet above the harbor of modern Haifa. Because of its height, it provided an important strategic position for the control of the fertile valley land. Mount Carmel was the scene of the contest between Elijah and the four hundred and fifty prophets of Baal and the four hundred prophets of Asherah (1 Kings 18:19). Elijah taunted the prophets, whose gods were unable to send fire from heaven upon their altars, and then,

in response to Elijah's entreaty, the God of Israel consumed waterlogged wood with fire. Poetic references to Mount Carmel are found in Song of Sol. 7:5; Isa. 33:9; 35:2. Jer. 46:18; 50:19; Amos 1:2; 9:3; Nah. 1:4.

2 An ancient city identified as modern Khirbet el-Kirmel (or Kermel) eight miles southeast of Hebron. The city was allotted to the tribe of Judah (Josh. 15:55). It was here that Saul commemorated his victory over the Amalekites by erecting a monument (1 Sam. 15:12). Also, near Carmel the events told in the story of Abigail, David, and Nabal took place. In this story the prosperous but ill-mannered Nabal insulted David, and David's wrath was averted only by the intercession of Abigail on Nabal's behalf. After Nabal died, Abigail was free to marry David, who acquired by that marriage Nabal's wealth, power, and prestige (1 Sam. 25).   S.B.R.

Carmi (kahr´mi).

1 The son of Reuben (Gen. 46:9; Exod. 6:14; 1 Chron. 5:3) who migrated to Egypt with his brothers and was subsequently considered head of the Carmites (Num. 26:6).

2 The father of Achan (Josh. 7:1, 18; Achar in 1 Chron. 2:7), the man who stole spoils dedicated to God after the conquest of Ai. Carmi is listed in 1 Chron. 4:1 as a son of Judah.

Carmites (kahr´mits). The Reubenite family group who traced their descent to Carmi, Reuben's fourth listed son (Num. 26:6). *See also* Carmi.

carnelian, a deep orange-red chalcedony that was used as decoration on the high priest's breastplate (Exod. 28:17; 39:10). It also appears in Ezek. 28:13, where it represents Tyre's lost perfection. In Rev. 21:20 the same term reflects the incomparable glory of the new Jerusalem (cf. 4:3).

carpenter, an artisan skilled in working with wood. Apparently, the Israelites lacked skill in this area in the time of David and Solomon (ca. 1050–975 BCE), since carpenters were imported from Tyre to aid the construction of David's palace (2 Sam. 5:11) and Solomon's temple (1 Kings 5:6). Among the returnees from the exile in the sixth century BCE, however, there were native craftsmen able to aid in the restoration of Jerusalem and the temple (Jer. 24:1; 29:2). A description of a carpenter's tools and procedures is given in Isaiah's account of the manufacture of an idol (44:13–17): a "line" for measuring, a pencil for marking, planes for shaping, and a compass for designing. The carpenter described in that passage also plants, tends, and cuts down the trees with which he works.

In most English translations of the Gospels, Jesus is reported to be a carpenter (Mark 6:3) and the son of a carpenter (Matt. 13:55). The Greek word used in these passages (*tektōn*) simply means "builder" in a generic sense, leaving open the possibility that Jesus and his father worked with stone or other materials.   R.S.B.

Carpus (kahr´puhs), a person in Troas with whom Paul is said to have left his cloak and other items. Timothy is asked to fetch them in 2 Tim. 4:13.

cart, or wagon, a term denoting a two- or four-wheeled vehicle drawn by oxen or other animals (rarely horses). It was used for transporting people and things. In Gen. 45:19, 21, 27; 46:5; Num. 7:3–8 (NRSV: "wagons"); and Jth. 15:11 no special function is indicated. In 1 Sam. 6:7–14; 2 Sam. 6:3; and 1 Chron. 13:7 a cart that had not been used for "secular" purposes and cows that had never been under a yoke are used to transport the ark of the covenant into Jerusalem. Several passages (Isa. 28:27, 28; Amos 2:13) refer to the cart in its agricultural uses. *See also* chariots.   F.S.F.

cassia (kash´uh; *Cinnamomum cassia*), a tree native to India and the Far East whose bark is easily peeled into long hollow rolls. The bark, buds, leaves, and twigs of the cassia tree, having a cinnamon smell, were imported for use in making spices, perfumes, and oils (Ezek. 27:19; Exod. 30:24; Ps. 45:8). The leaves and pods also have medicinal properties. *See also* spices.

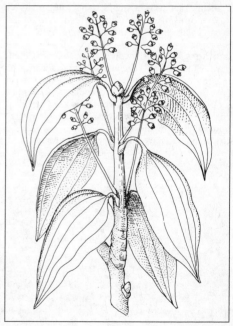

Cassia.

castle. *See* architecture.

Castor and Pollux. *See* Twin Brothers.

caterpillar, the worm-shaped larva of a moth, butterfly, or other insect, considered destructive because of its voracious appetite for growing plants. It is viewed as one of the forms of punishment or judgment God uses (1 Kings 8:37; 2 Chron. 6:28; Ps. 78:46; Isa. 33:4).

Catholic Letters/Epistles, the seven NT letters attributed to James, Peter (2), John (3), and Jude. The letters are written either to general audiences or to multiple churches at large. *See also* epistle; letter; New Testament.

cattle. The Hebrew term *baqar* is used in the Bible for domesticated cattle in general, but a variety of other terms are also used for different kinds of cattle. According to Gen. 1:24–26, God created every kind of cattle on the sixth day, the same day as human beings. Cattle were used by the Israelites in many ways: as a food source (in 1 Kings 4:23; Solomon's daily household ration included thirty cattle and oxen), as sacrificial offerings (Solomon offered twenty-two thousand oxen in 1 Kings 8:63), as pack animals (1 Chron. 12:40), and as work animals used for threshing (Deut. 25:4) and for pulling carts (Num. 7:3). Together with sheep and goats, cattle were valued for producing milk and dung. Possession of large numbers of cattle was a measure of wealth (Gen. 12:16; 13:5). *See also* bull; calf.   I.U.K.

Cauda (kaw′duh), a small island (modern Gavdos) southwest of Crete, by which Paul sailed toward Malta, en route to Rome (Acts 27:16).

caulkers, in the Bible, men from Byblos (Gebal, Ezek. 27:9) or Tyre (Ezek. 27:27) whose work was making ships watertight. Materials used may have been bitumen or pitch, and some type of fiber binder to plug seams between planks. The references to caulkers in the Bible occur in a lamentation over Tyre by the prophet Ezekiel, in which the city is compared to a ship. *See also* bitumen.

cave. Two Hebrew terms designate a cave, *me'arah* and *khor;* the latter term literally means "hole," but is also translated "cavern." Natural caves are abundant in the Near East due to the presence of chalk, limestone, and sandstone formations in the hills and mountains. Because of the soft qualities of these materials, caves were easily constructed as well. The natural caves are frequently massive in size. One cave complex near Damascus in modern Syria was capable of holding four thousand men, according to the late first-century BCE Greek geographer Strabo (cf. 1 Sam. 22:1–2, where a cave in Israel is able to conceal four hundred men).

Caves were utilized in a variety of ways. Archaeological discoveries indicate that one of the earliest and most common uses was as a domestic dwelling. Lot and his daughters lived in a cave after the destruction of Sodom and Gomorrah (Gen. 19:30; see also Num. 24:21; Song of Sol. 2:14; Jer. 49:16; Obad. 3). Caves were also sought out as places of refuge, especially during times of war (Josh. 10:16–27; Judg. 6:2). The cave of Adullam, located in the region of Bethlehem, enabled David and his men to escape from King Saul (1 Sam. 22:1–2). Later, David fled with his men to En-gedi, where they were able to utilize another large cave for protection (23:29; 24:3). It was in this cave that David cut off part of Saul's garment (24:4). Archaeological and biblical data also point to the widespread use of caves as tombs. Abraham purchased the cave of Machpelah from the Hittites in the region of Hebron for that purpose (Gen. 23:1–20); Lazarus was also buried in a cave (John 11:38). At Qumran caves served as places for storing valuable manuscripts (i.e., those now known as the Dead Sea Scrolls).   J.J.D.

cedar (*Cedrus libani*), a tree mentioned frequently in the Bible. It is a deep-rooted coniferous

Caves located in the area of Tel Halif (biblical Rimmon?) were probably created in the third millennium BCE.

tree found in the Middle East, especially Lebanon, where its distinctive pyramidal image adorns the modern flag of that country. The cedar lives to a great age (up to two thousand years), therefore attaining great height and diameter. Consequently, it is often referred to as a symbol of strength and power (Ezek. 31; Ps. 92:12). Its fragrant, gum-exuding wood is red in color and is especially durable and resistant to insects and decay. These properties made it a popular choice for the construction of items such as musical instruments, chests, and various household furnishings. Cedar was also preferred for the construction of buildings, as attested by the numerous references in the book of Kings (1 Kings 6–7). Its superlative qualities made it an important trade item in antiquity. Solomon's temple and palace in Jerusalem had timbers and panels of cedar sent by the king of Tyre (1 Kings 5:6–10; 9:11; 2 Chron. 2:3). The "cedar of Lebanon" (Ps. 37:35) is apparently the laurel (*Lauris nobilis*), whose fragrant evergreen leaves are symbols of prosperity and distinction. The Egyptians are said to have imported cedars of Lebanon for the tall straight masts of their ships and for the durable coffins of their dead. *See also* forest; wood.   P.L.C.

Cenchreae (sen'kruh-ee), a seaport in Achaia, about five miles east of Corinth on the Saronic Gulf. It served as an eastern harbor for Corinth, allowing that city access to the Aegean Sea, Asia Minor, or the eastern Mediterranean in general. Here, prior to sailing to Ephesus during his second journey, Paul shaved his head (Acts 18:18–20). Cenchreae was the home of Phoebe (Rom. 16:1). Excavations have uncovered a sanctuary to the goddess Isis, very likely the one imagined in Apuleius's novel *Metamophoris*. *See also* Phoebe.

censer, a small hand-size vessel containing hot coals on which incense was sprinkled. Brass censers (NRSV: "firepans") were used in the tabernacle (Exod. 27:3) and in the first Jerusalem temple (1 Kings 7:50), while gold censers were among the temple vessels carried off to Babylon when Nebuchadnezzar overthrew Israel, burned the temple, and carried the people into exile in Babylon (2 Kings 25:15). The book of Revelation mentions an angel who stands before God with a censer of incense, then fills it with fire that is thrown upon the earth, causing various disasters (8:3). Several censers have been excavated, suggesting that incense offerings played an important role in popular religion (cf. Ezek. 8:11).

census, a tally that identifies, locates, and numbers the people in a particular group or area, usually for purposes of taxation, but also at times for other ends, such as conscription or forced labor. Several censuses are mentioned in the Bible (e.g., Exod. 30:11–16; Num. 1:1–49; 26; 2 Sam. 24:1–9; cf. 1 Chron. 7:40; 21:1–5; 2 Chron. 2:17; 25:5; Ezra 2:2–67), but the best known may be the one mentioned in Luke 2:1–5 in connection with the birth

of Jesus (cf. Acts 5:37). The association of this latter census with the governorship of Quirinius raises some historical problems with dating, since Roman records date the census about a decade after the death of King Herod, who is said to have ruled Judea at the time Jesus was born (Matt. 2:1; cf. Luke 1:5). *See also* Bethlehem; Quirinius, P. Sulpicius; tax, toll; tribute.

centurion, the commander of a hundred soldiers in a Roman legion, which consisted of six thousand men. Centurions were prestigious members of a relatively small class of military leaders. They received substantial pensions upon retirement and would easily count among the local notables of a town (cf. Luke 7:2; Acts 10:1). In the NT, Jesus heals the son (or possibly the servant) of a centurion at Capernaum (Matt. 8:5–13; Luke 7:1–10; cf. John 4:46–53). A centurion supervises the soldiers who crucify Jesus (Mark 15:19). The centurion Cornelius was baptized by Peter, sparking a controversy over the admission of Gentiles to the church (Acts 10:1–11:18). In Acts, soldiers and centurions intervene when Jerusalem is in an uproar over Paul (21:32), and when Paul is tied with thongs to be beaten, he asks one of the centurions whether it is lawful to flog a Roman citizen without trial (22:25–26). Later two centurions transfer Paul from Jerusalem to Caesarea (23:23) and, still later, a centurion named Julius (of the Augustan Cohort) takes charge of transferring Paul to Rome (27:1, 6, 11, 31, 43). See also Acts 23:17; 24:23.

Cephas (see'fuhs; from Aramaic *kepha'*, "rock"), a surname equivalent to the Greek name "Peter" (John 1:42; cf. Matt. 16:17–18). *See also* Peter.

chaff, the covering of the grain removed during the process of winnowing. Nearly all references in the Bible are to chaff blown in the wind (Job 13:25; 21:18; Pss. 1:4; 35:5; 83:13; Isa. 17:13; 29:5; 33:11; 41:15; Jer. 13:24; Dan. 2:35; Hos. 13:3; Zeph. 2:2). In the NT it is used metaphorically in an image for judgment to be carried out by the one who comes after John the Baptist. This coming one will wield a winnowing fork and the wheat (those judged favorably) will be gathered into the granary, while the chaff (those judged unfavorably) will be burned "with unquenchable fire" (Matt. 3:12; Luke 3:17).

chains. Composed of various metals, both base and precious, chains were used in ancient Israel as jewelry (e.g., Gen. 41:42; Ezek. 16:11), for architectural ornamentation (1 Kings 7:17), and in assembling the priestly vestments (e.g., Exod. 28:14). Apparently, chains were also used to bind prisoners (Ps. 149:8; Lam. 3:7), though these references might refer to temporary leashes, such as are depicted in the Black Obelisk of Shalmaneser III. Later, during the Roman period chains were used to bind people in a more permanent sense (cf. Mark 5:3–4; Acts 12:6–7), replacing the fetters and ropes typically used earlier. The NT makes much of Paul's imprisonment for proclaiming the gospel, referring to him as "an ambassador in chains" (Eph. 6:20; cf. Col. 4:18) who nevertheless maintains that the "word of God" cannot be chained (2 Tim. 2:9; cf. 2 Tim. 1:6). In Rev., Satan is bound with a great chain for a thousand years (20:1). Two NT books also draw on *1 Enoch* 6–19 to indicate that the angels who rebelled against God (the "sons of God" of Gen. 6:1–4) have been chained in darkness until the day of judgment (2 Pet. 2:4; Jude 1:6).

Chalcolithic (kal´koh-lith´ik) **Age.** *See* copper.

Chaldea (kal-dee´uh), a region at the head of the Persian Gulf, home to a loose confederation of Semitic- (possibly Aramaic-) speaking peoples organized along tribal lines. The birthplace and ancestral home of Abraham was in Chaldea (Gen. 11:28, 31; 15:7; cf. Acts 7:34). Because Chaldea overlaps geographically with Babylonia, and because after 626 BCE a Chaldean dynasty ruled Babylon, the term "Chaldea" is often used in the Bible as a synonym for "Babylon." During the eighth century BCE, the Chaldean ruler Merodach-baladan (called the king of Babylon in 2 Kings 20:12; Isa. 39:1) fought against the Assyrians under the successive reigns of Tiglath-pileser III, Sargon II, and Sennacherib. He sought and received support of the Elamites and, according to 2 Kings 20:12–19, sent envoys to Hezekiah in Judah as well. The latter foolishly showed those envoys all the treasures of the royal house, earning a rebuke from Isaiah the prophet (cf. Isa. 39:1–8). A century later, the Chaldean ruler Nabopolassar captured Babylon from the Assyrians in 626 BCE, and his son Nebuchadnezzar ruled Babylon 605–562 BCE. He figures heavily in the Bible as the ruler responsible for the exile (cf. 2 Kings 24–25; 2 Chron. 36). He attacked Jerusalem in 597 BCE, taking leading citizens to Babylon and then, ten years later, destroyed the city, taking even more of its residents to Babylon. The Aramaic sections of the book of Daniel (2:5, 10; 4:4; 5:7, 11) mention Chaldeans among the learned magicians and conjurers. This report is corroborated somewhat by archaeological excavations that have produced Chaldean cuneiform records of detailed astronomical data, suggesting a strong interest in astrology. *See also* Babylon; Merodach-baladan; Nebuchadnezzar; Ur. L.E.P.

chariots, vehicles of various types with two wheels normally drawn by two horses. Horse-drawn chariots were introduced into Canaan by the Hyksos (ca. 1800–1600 BCE), who were major innovators in the technology of warfare. Chariots in Egypt and early Assyria were characteristically operated by two soldiers, a driver (1 Kings 22:34; 2 Chron. 18:33; Jer. 51:21), who did not carry a weapon, and an archer. The Hittites, and later the Assyrians and Syrians, introduced a third person, the shield bearer. The three-warrior chariot seems to have been used by the Hebrews, since the

Assyrian war chariot with armed charioteers; detail from the bas-reliefs at the palace of Ashurbanipal at Nineveh, seventh century BCE.

Hebrew word *shalish*, translated "officers" in the NRSV, literally means "third one" (see Exod. 14:7; 15:4; 1 Kings 9:23; 2 Kings 10:25).

The principal use of the chariot was a military one, especially for rapid flanking movements in open country. As military equipment the chariot was used by the Canaanites against the Israelites (Josh. 17:16; Judg. 1:19). The "chariots of iron" in these passages were probably vehicles on which metal plates (possibly bronze, not iron) were used to reinforce the wooden chariot bodies (Judg. 4:3, 13; Josh. 11:4–9). Similarly, the Philistines employed chariots against the Israelites in the time of Samuel and Saul (1 Sam. 13:5). Since chariots were of limited use in the central highlands, the principal area of early Israelite settlement, they were not used by the Israelites until the time of David (eleventh century BCE), who did use them in his successful campaigns against the Philistines (2 Sam. 8:4; 1 Chron. 18:4). The chariot became a highly developed regular part of the military equipment of the state under Solomon (1 Kings 10:26), under whom there was considerable building activity and trade in connection with horses and chariots (4:26; 9:19; 10:29). The prophet Elijah was taken up to heaven in a whirlwind, just after he and Elisha were separated by a chariot of fire (2 Kings 2:11).

In addition to their use in warfare, chariots were a symbol of power as the vehicle of kings and their court (Gen. 41:43; 2 Sam. 15:1; 1 Kings 1:5). Ps. 20:7 commends taking pride in the name of the Lord, rather than in chariots. The chariot of the

Ethiopian whom Philip addressed (Acts 8:26–38) was a sign of his rank as the queen's minister. *See also* horse; war.   F.S.F.

charity.

1 Acts of kindness typically (but not necessarily) performed on behalf of the poor. In the NRSV, the term is not used in the Hebrew Bible and it occurs only once in the NT, where Tabitha (Dorcas) is said to have been devoted to "acts of charity" (Acts 9:36). In the apocryphal/deuterocanonical literature, Tobit says that he has performed many acts of charity (1:3, 16; cf. 2:14), and Sirach pronounces a blessing on the rich person whose acts of charity will be proclaimed by the assembly (31:11). *See also* alms.

2 The term used in the KJV to translate one of the NT words for "love" (Gk. *agapē*) in 26 of its 116 occurrences. *See also* agapē; love.

Chebar (kee'bahr), a water course in Babylonia, near the city of Nippur. It functioned as an important irrigation channel. It was beside the Chebar canal (called a "river" in the Bible) that Ezekiel received his first vision (1:13; 3:15, 23) as well as later visions or oracles (10:15, 20, 22; 43:3). There was a Jewish settlement there in the sixth century BCE called Tel-abib (Ezek. 3:15). *See also* Ezekiel, book of.

Chedorlaomer (ked'uhr-lay-oh'muhr), "king of Elam" and one of four kings who, according to Gen. 14, joined forces to attack five kings in the Dead Sea valley. The five kings were conquered and remained subject to Chedorlaomer for twelve years. In the thirteenth year they rebelled and in the fourteenth Chedorlaomer and his allies marched against them, conquering widely in Canaan and finally routing the rebels. He plundered Sodom and Gomorrah and took Lot captive. Abraham gave chase and retrieved all the booty and captives. The name "Chedorlaomer" reflects authentic elements of Elamite personal names—*kuter* or *kutir,* as in the royal names Kutir/Kuternakkhunte, and *Lagamar,* the name of a deity—but neither the specific name nor the general events are attested or alluded to elsewhere.   S.B.P.

Chemosh (kee'mosh), the national god of Moab. Although he was worshiped at Ugarit and perhaps also at Ebla, little is known about this god before the first millennium BCE. Biblical evidence is scant: the Moabites were "the people of Chemosh" (Num. 21:29; Jer. 48:46; cf. also Jer. 48:7), and Solomon built a high place for Chemosh, "the abomination of Moab" (1 Kings 11:7; cf. 11:33), which Josiah destroyed (2 Kings 23:13). In Judg. 11:24 he seems to have been the chief Ammonite deity. More information is found in the victory stele of Mesha, the king of Moab (ca. 840 BCE), which speaks of Chemosh in terms similar to those used of the God of Israel: Chemosh becomes angry with his people and, therefore, allows their land to be

taken by a foreign power (Israel); then Chemosh relents and delivers his people. *See also* Mesha; Moab.   M.D.C.

Chenaanah (ki-nay'uh-nuh), a son of the Benjaminite Bilhan (1 Chron. 7:10), and the father of Zedekiah, who is presented as a false prophet during the time of Jehoshaphat (1 Kings 22:11, 24; 2 Chron. 18:10; 19:23).

Chephirah (ki-fi'ruh), one of four cities not attacked by the Israelites under Joshua due to a prior treaty arrangement (Josh. 9:17). It was also one of fourteen towns occupied by the Benjaminites (Josh. 18:26), and it received a portion of 743 resettling Judeans in the postexilic recovery (Ezra 2:25; Neh. 7:29). The site has been identified as Khirbet el-Kefireh, five miles southwest of Gibeon.

Cherethites (kair'uh-thits), a people who lived on the Mediterranean coast to the southeast of Philistia (cf. "the Negev of the Cherethites," 1 Sam. 30:14; "inhabitants of the seacoast," Zeph. 2:5). As mercenaries, they constituted a section of David's personal army under the leadership of Benaiah, son of Jehoiada (2 Sam. 8:18; 20:23).

Cherith (kair'ith), **Wadi,** a brook east of the Jordan, near Jericho. A wadi is a riverbed that fills with water only in the rainy season. The Wadi Cherith has been variously identified with present-day Wadi-Quelt, which empties into the Jabesh River, and with Wadi el-Yubis, in northern Gilead. The Bible says that Elijah sought refuge there from Ahab and Jezebel (1 Kings 17:3, 5). *See also* wadi.   S.B.R.

cherubim (chair'yoo-bim; sing. cherub [chair' uhb]), supernatural, composite beings associated with sacral contexts. Although cherubim are mentioned ninety-two times (ninety-one times in the Hebrew Bible, and once in Heb. 9:5), no single type of creature is referred to in all cases. Rather, the term represents a variety of beings. The only consistent feature in many of the biblical references (particularly in connection with the ark of the covenant and with the visions of Ezekiel) is that the cherubim are winged (Exod. 25:20; 1 Kings 8:6–7; Ezek. 10:5, 16, 19). Otherwise, the ark cherubim apparently have a single face (Exod. 25:20), whereas the cherubim in Ezek. 41:18 have two faces and those in Ezek. 10:14 have four. The character of the faces also ranges from human through bovine, leonine, and aquiline (Ezek. 10:14). Such variations confirm the underlying principle that the cherub was a hybrid creature.

As supernatural beings, cherubim are always connected with the deity. They appear as God's steed (2 Sam. 22:1; Ps. 18:11), as parts of God's chariot (1 Chron. 28:18), or as components of God's throne (1 Sam. 4:4; 2 Sam. 6:2; 1 Chron. 13:6; Pss. 80:1; 99:1; Isa. 37:16). They are indirectly associated with God when they are guardian figures (Gen. 3:24; Ezek. 28:14, 16). *See also* ark of the covenant, ark of God; tabernacle; temple, the.

C.L.M./M.A.P.

child, children, offspring, which were highly valued by Israelites as gracious gifts of God (Pss. 113:9; 127:3; 128:5–6). Having large numbers of children was considered a divine blessing (Gen. 24:60; Ruth 4:11–12), and the multiplication of descendants was part of God's promise to Israel's ancestors (Gen. 12:2; 15:5; 16:10; 17:2; 22:17; 26:4). An inability to conceive was considered at best a vexation (Gen. 16:2; 30:2; 1 Sam. 1:3–8) and at worst a divine punishment (Gen. 20:18). Children often received symbolic names (Gen. 4:1; 25:25–26; 29:32, 35; 30:6, 8, 11, 13, 18, 24; 41:51–52; Isa. 8:3; Hos. 1:2–9) and were educated by their parents, particularly with regard to Israel's faith and tradition (Exod. 12:26–27; Deut. 4:9; 6:7, 20–25; 32:46; Prov. 1:8; 6:20). Children received an inheritance from their parents, the eldest son a double portion (Num. 36; Deut. 21:15–17). Firstborn sons were thought to belong to God, but were to be redeemed (Exod. 13:11–15; 22:29; 34:20; Num. 18:15). However, the Bible also contains many stories of God's blessing going to a younger child (Gen. 28:13–14; cf. 27:1–40; 47:8–20; 49:1–27).

Israel described itself as an extended family (descendants of twelve children who all had Jacob/Israel as their father), so members of the covenant community sometimes called themselves the "children of Israel" (e.g., 1 Kings 6:13; Isa. 17:3, 9; Sir. 51:12; cf. Isa. 29:22–23; Ezek. 37:16; for "children of Abraham," see 4 Macc. 6:17, 22; cf. Matt. 3:9; John 8:39). From their ancestor (Israel) the children inherited both the blessings and obligations of the covenant. In the NT, church members are sometimes addressed as children by church authorities, a practice that the church traced to Jesus (Gal. 4:19; 2 Tim. 1:2; Philem. 10; 1 John 2:1, 12, 18, 28; cf. Matt. 9:2; Mark 2:5; 10:24; John 13:33). Jesus is also remembered as indicating that little children provide a model for recognizing who is the greatest in the kingdom of heaven (Matt. 18:1–5; cf. 19:13–15). *See also* ancestor; daughter; family; son.

R.R.W.

children of God, a term used by Jesus and early Christians to describe those who have a special, favored relationship with God. Jesus says that peacemakers will be called children of God (Matt. 5:9). He also uses the phrase as a synonym for "children of the resurrection" to describe the dead who are raised to new life (Luke 20:36). Paul uses the expression "children of God" to describe those who are adopted as heirs of God's promises (Rom. 8:14–21; 9:8; Gal. 3:26; Phil. 2:15; cf. Gal. 4:4–7). The term may have been the common designation for Christians in the Johannine community (1 John 3:1, 2, 10; 5:2; cf. John 1:12; 11:52).

Chileab (kil'ee-ab), the second son of David, born in Hebron to Abigail, former wife of Nabal

of Carmel (2 Sam. 3:3). In 1 Chron. 3:1, however, David's second son is identified as Daniel.

Chilion (kil'ee-uhn; Heb., "weakness"), the second son born to Elimelech and Naomi, an Ephrathite couple who immigrated to Moab when famine struck the region of Bethlehem (Ruth 1:2; 4:9). As told in the book of Ruth, Chilion married a Moabite woman, Orpah. Upon his death, his widow returned to her own people, unlike his brother's widow, Ruth. According to Ruth 4:9, his estate was later acquired by Ruth's next husband, Boaz.

Chimham (kim'ham), the servant of Barzillai—or possibly his son (cf. 1 Kings 2:7)—whom David took with him to Jerusalem, providing for him there (2 Sam. 19:31–40). Barzillai was a Gileadite who assisted David during Absalom's revolt. He refused David's offer of reward, asking that it be given to Chimham instead. The later mention in Jer. 41:17 of a place called Geruth Chimham near Bethlehem may suggest that David provided Chimham with a tract of land in that region.

Chinnereth (kin'uh-reth; Heb., "harp").

1 A name used in the Hebrew Bible for the lake identified in the NT as the Sea of Galilee (Num. 34:11; Jos. 13:27); the body of water is roughly harp-shaped, which probably accounts for the derivation of this name.

2 A fortified city on the northwest side of the Sea of Chinnereth (Sea of Galilee) in the territory of Naphtali (Josh. 19:35). It has been identified with present-day Khirbet el-Oreime.

Chios (ki'os), a large mountainous island of volcanic origin in the Aegean Sea five miles west of Asia Minor. Paul and his companions passed Chios on the final voyage to Jerusalem (Acts 20:15).

Chislev (kiz'lev), the Hebrew name for the ninth month of the Jewish religious calendar (Neh. 1:1; Zech. 7:1; 1 Macc. 1:54; 4:52, 59; 2 Macc. 1:9, 18; 10:5). Its equivalent in the Gregorian calendar is mid-November to mid-December. The name was borrowed from the Akkadian month name Kisliwu (or Kislimu). *See also* calendar.

Chloe (kloh'ee), a woman from Corinth or Ephesus whose slaves, employees, or household members told Paul, in Ephesus, about problems in the Corinthian church (1 Cor. 1:11). *See also* Corinthians, First Letter of Paul to the; Corinthians, Second Letter of Paul to the.

Chorazin (koh-ray'zin), a first-century CE Jewish town in Upper Galilee two miles north of Capernaum. Along with Bethsaida and Capernaum, Chorazin was reproached by Jesus for failing to repent, even though he had performed deeds of power (miracles) there (Matt. 11:20–24; Luke 10:13–15). Excavations of the now deserted town indicate that it once covered an area of twelve acres

Ruins of a post-NT synagogue at Chorazin, third–sixth centuries CE.

and was built on a series of terraces with the basalt stone local to this mountainous region. A synagogue from a later period was also found.

Christ (Gk. *christos,* "anointed one"). *See* Jesus Christ; messiah.

Christian, a term that eventually became the standard nomenclature for followers of Jesus Christ, but that actually occurs only three times in the NT. The term derives from the word Christ, which means "Anointed One" or "Messiah"; the basic definition of "Christian" is "one who believes in the Messiah" or "one who follows the Messiah." Acts says that "the disciples" (i.e., people who regarded themselves as disciples of Jesus) were first called "Christians" at Antioch in Syria (11:26). The reason for this is not clear, but it is often thought that the new name was given to the movement by those who wanted to distinguish them from Jews (or at least from other Jews, i.e., Jews who did not follow Jesus as their Messiah). The recognition that "Christians" were sufficiently distinctive to merit their own label may have been prompted by the church at Antioch accepting large numbers of uncircumcised Gentiles into its community (cf. Acts 11:20, where some manuscripts read "Hellenists" [Greek-speaking Jews], but others read "Greeks" [Gentiles]). The term is used again in Acts 26:28, where King Agrippa wonders if Paul is trying to persuade him to become a Christian. Finally, 1 Pet. 4:16 speaks of suffering "as a Christian," which means suffering as a consequence of one's faith in Jesus Christ (cf. 4:14).   J.M.E.

Chronicler (kron'i-kluhr), the collective name given to the authors or editors of one of the later portions of the Hebrew Bible, namely, that material contained in the books of 1 and 2 Chronicles

and possibly the books of Ezra and Nehemiah. The inclusion of the latter books, however, is disputed; some scholars note differences in vocabulary between 1 and 2 Chronicles and Ezra–Nehemiah as well as differences in religious outlook. The two books of Chronicles are said to evince a more favorable attitude toward the survivors of the northern kingdom and toward intermarriage than does Ezra–Nehemiah. The Davidic line, so prominent in Chronicles, plays no part in Ezra–Nehemiah. Still some scholars do argue that a single authorial perspective (identified as that of "the Chronicler") informs 1 and 2 Chronicles and Ezra–Nehemiah and that these books were intended to be read as a single continuous work. The matter is complicated still further by a claim that Haggai and Zech. 1–8 reached their present form by being edited in a loosely defined "Chronistic milieu." *See also* Chronicles, First and Second books of; Ezra; Ezra and Nehemiah, books of.   R.C.

Chronicles, First and Second Books of, two books that were originally one volume, known as "Chronicles." In the Writings section, or Ketuvim, of the Tanakh (Jewish Bible), this book is preceded by Ezra and Nehemiah and stands as the last book of the Bible. In the Christian OT, the work is separated into two books, placed directly after 1 and 2 Kings among the "historical books" of the Bible, and followed by Ezra and Nehemiah. In Hebrew, this work was known as the "(book of) the events of the days," and in Greek it was known as the "things left out." It was given the name Chronicles when Jerome translated the book into Latin, entitling it the "chronicle of the complete divine history."

Contents: Chronicles can be easily divided into two sections: material dealing with the premonarchic history (1 Chron. 1–9) and material presenting the history of the Davidic monarchy (1 Chron. 10–2 Chron. 36).

Premonarchic History: The first part of Chronicles retells history from Adam to Saul. Most of this

Unloading timber from a ship. Solomon imported timber from Lebanon for the building of the temple (2 Chron. 2:16). Relief from the palace of Sargon II at Khorsabad, eighth century BCE.

account is presented through lists of names and genealogies. Some of the genealogical lists extend all the way into the postexilic period and include individuals from that time, indicating that this material was finally edited in the postexilic period.

There is very little narrative in this first part of the book. Special attention in the genealogies is given to the names of priests and Levites. The genealogies also focus on the tribe of Judah and its line of David, on the tribe of Benjamin and its line of Saul, and on the tribe of Levi. These three tribes comprised the nucleus of the Persian province of Yehud (Judea) in the postexilic period.

Monarchic History: The second part of Chronicles covers the history of the Davidic monarchy from David to the Babylonian exile. It can be subdivided into three sections: David's reign (1 Chron. 10–29), Solomon's reign (2 Chron. 1–9), and reigns of the kings of Judah from Rehoboam to Cyrus's edict of return from exile (2 Chron. 10–36). The Chronicler used the books of Samuel and Kings from the Deuteronomistic History as the main source in retelling the history of the Judean monarchy. About half of Chronicles comes from the books of Samuel and Kings.

The section on David's reign begins with "all Israel" at Hebron asking David to be their king. This in itself is a recasting of the Samuel account where the tribe of Judah is the first to acclaim David as king at Hebron, followed seven years later by the remainder of the tribes. Also, in Chronicles there is no record of Saul's conflict with David.

The account continues with a description of David's capture of Jerusalem and his moving the ark of the covenant into the city. A comparison of how 2 Samuel and 1 Chronicles tell the story of the ark's trip to Jerusalem demonstrates that the Chronicler reshaped the older account to validate the essential role of the Levites. For example, 2 Sam. 6:1–11 and 1 Chron. 13:1–14 both tell the story of the death of Uzzah (when he touched the ark) and the abandonment of the ark with Obed-edom, but 2 Samuel then moves directly to David's fetching the ark from Obed-edom and taking it to Jerusalem (6:12–19), while 1 Chronicles inserts a lengthy account of the appointment of the Levites to carry the ark to Jerusalem (15:1–24). Also, whereas no lesson was drawn from Uzzah's death in the Deuteronomistic Historian's account, the Chronicler uses this as an occasion to validate the special role of the Levites, drawing the lesson that only the Levites are allowed to handle the ark.

Such deviations from the Deuteronomistic History are generally noteworthy. The Chronicler omits any reference to David's war against Saul or to David's temporary alliance with the Philistines. He omits the story of how David intimidated Nabal and then married Abigail, and he completely ignores David's affair with Bathsheba. In one way or another, all of these stories might reflect negatively on David or tarnish his image, so they are deliberately left out.

On the other hand, the Chronicler adds information not present in Samuel–Kings. David's

extensive preparations for the building of the temple are detailed in 1 Chron. 23–28. This effectively makes David the founder and sponsor of the Jerusalem temple. In contrast, the book of Kings attributes the entire process of planning and building the temple to Solomon.

Most of the section on Solomon's reign is devoted to a description of the building and dedication of the Jerusalem temple, taken almost verbatim from the book of Kings. The Chronicler idealizes Solomon just as he did David by omitting those stories in Kings that show Solomon in a bad light. For example, he deems the bloody political struggle between Adonijah and Solomon that ends with Solomon's triumph (1 Kings 2:13–46a) too violent for inclusion. Also, Solomon's adjudication of the case of the two prostitutes and their babies (1 Kings 3:16–28) was apparently too unseemly. Other instances of the Chronicler's omissions reveal that he may have thought Solomon was too rich (4:22–34), too unholy (11:1–13), and too divisive (11:14–40) in the Kings account.

The Chronicler's account of Solomon in his role as temple builder also includes details not found in the Kings account. In particular, it depicts Solomon as a counterpart to Bezalel, who was the architect of the tabernacle at the time of Moses. Bezalel is mentioned nowhere outside the book of Exodus except in the Solomon narrative of Chronicles. According to the Chronicler, both Bezalel and Solomon came from the tribe of Judah, were designated for their tasks by God, received the spirit of wisdom to complete their tasks, built bronze altars for their sanctuaries, and made sanctuary furnishings. Thus, Solomon, as the new Bezalel and great temple builder, continued in the sanctuary tradition of Moses.

The last section of Chronicles is devoted almost entirely to the kings of Judah after the division of the kingdoms. Virtually no mention is made of the northern kingdom. The Chronicler dwells on the role of the kings of Judah in promoting worship and, proper ritual. When disaster finally comes by way of the Babylonians, it is because certain Judean kings failed in their religious duties.

The Chronicler's account supplements the Deuteronomistic History on a couple of points. The reform program of Hezekiah, not detailed in Kings, is given extended attention in 2 Chron. 29–32.

This includes an account of his temple cleansing and his celebration of the Passover. Also, Josiah's Passover celebration is given increased attention. All this accords with the Chronicler's interest in the right performance of religious ritual.

Background: Very little is known about the author of 1 and 2 Chronicles. Most scholars believe that it was a single author, whom they call the "Chronicler." The Chronicler was arguably less concerned with exact chronology than he was with the theological significance of particular events. The book was written in the context of an almost complete Hebrew canon. Thus, 1 and 2 Chronicles references a myriad of sources from the Bible.

There is no strict consensus on the date of composition for 1 and 2 Chronicles. The earliest possible date is 539 BCE, when Cyrus called the Jewish people to rebuild the temple. However, most scholars date the work between 400 and 250 BCE (most likely between 350 and 300 BCE).

Themes: Genealogies serve different purposes within the biblical world. Within the family, they define privilege and responsibility, as with the firstborn son in relation to later-born children and children of concubines. Within tribes, they establish political and territorial claims, especially land ownership, and might also reflect military conscription lists. Within the religious sphere, they establish membership in the priestly and levitical classes. Membership determines who can and cannot hold priestly offices and who can acquire the privileges and responsibilities associated with them. All of these uses of genealogies are present in Chronicles.

The Jerusalem temple is a main focus of the book of Chronicles. When recounting the reigns of David and Solomon, Chronicles focuses on what they do to secure Jerusalem and to build the temple. The later kings were judged on how well they provided for the worship and services at the temple.

The term "all Israel" is used throughout the book in a broad sense. Under the united kingdom of David and Solomon it could have easily referred to the political nation of Israel. Yet the term is still used after the division between the kingdoms to refer to Judah (the northern kingdom took "Israel" as its political name). Some scholars argue that this illustrates the Chronicler's emphasis on the need for unity among God's people in the postexilic period. Childs thinks that the term "Israel" is used in Chronicles as a religious designation, not a political designation.

The role of the Levites is heightened in 1 and 2 Chronicles. In fact, the term "Levites" occurs more often in 1 and 2 Chronicles than in any other book in the Bible, including Leviticus. The Levites are revered for their commitment to holiness and are seen as an indispensable part of the Jewish community. The Chronicler does not hold the Levites accountable for the fall of Jerusalem, but he does blame the priests for this (see 2 Chron. 36:14).

Interpretive Issues: The most important interpretive issue in the book of Chronicles is its relationship to the book of Ezra–Nehemiah. Scholars have noted thematic similarities and the fact that the beginning of Ezra–Nehemiah is the same as the end of Chronicles. There is currently a divide in the scholarly community over whether these books had the same author or two authors. Some scholars talk of there being a "Chronicler's school" responsible for these books, while others call attention to points of divergence. Childs argues that although the Chronicler played a significant role in the shaping of Ezra–Nehemiah, these books do not have the same author. Eskenazi argues for two authors, claiming that concern for the cult is the only significant similar theme between the two books and other themes demonstrate their dissimilarity. Min argues for separate authorship on literary grounds and holds that the books' ideological differences present even stronger arguments for separate authorship.

Another interpretive issue with the book of Chronicles is its use of sources. Much of the book of Chronicles is drawn from the books of Samuel and Kings, along with selections from the Torah and Psalms. Difficulties have arisen, not only with regard to *which* sources the Chronicler used, but *how* he used them. Although much of the material found in Chronicles can be connected to other biblical passages, there are sections of Chronicles that are not found elsewhere. Some scholars argue that these passages were original to the Chronicler, while others hold that the sources that the Chronicler references had an independent existence. Still others believe that the version of Samuel and Kings that the Chronicler used contained material not present in the final (current) edition. *See also* Ezra and Nehemiah, books of.

Bibliography
Bandstra, Barry L. *Reading the Old Testament: Introduction to the Hebrew Bible.* 4th ed. Wadsworth, 2009.

Childs, Brevard S. *Introduction to the Old Testament as Scripture.* Fortress, 1979.

De Vries, Simon J. *1 and 2 Chronicles.* Eerdmans, 1989.

Eskenazi, Tamara C. *In an Age of Prose: A Literary Approach to Ezra–Nehemiah.* Scholars, 1988.

Japhet, Sara. *The Ideology of the Book of Chronicles and Its Place in Biblical Thought.* P. Lang, 1989.

Knoppers, Gary. *I Chronicles.* 2 vols. Doubleday, 2004.

Min, Kyung-Jin. *The Levitical Authorship of Ezra–Nehemiah.* Clark, 2004.   B.B.

chronology, Hebrew Bible, the historical dating of persons and events in the Hebrew Bible as well as the dating of the books themselves. The biblical books Genesis–2 Kings provide a primary source of information for the history of ancient Israel and Judah, including a continuous chronology of generations, key persons, and events from creation to the return from exile in Babylon (see, e.g., Gen. 5; 11:10–26; 21:5; 25:7, 26; 35:28; 47:9, 28; Exod. 12:40; 1 Kings 6:1; 11:42; 14:21). Further chronological information may be derived from other biblical books, such as 1 and 2 Chronicles, and occasionally from ancient nonbiblical documents. Assyrian and Babylonian records are especially useful in this regard, since they provide actual dates for events that can be recalculated in terms of present-day calendars. Babylonian records, for example, indicate that Jerusalem fell to the Babylonians on March 16, 597 BCE. Theoretically one might begin with this latter "benchmark" date and, utilizing the chronological information provided in Genesis–2 Kings, figure backward to creation. The situation, however, is not that simple.

The most severe difficulties occur with regard to events prior to the divided monarchy. To start with, much of what is provided in Genesis for the beginnings of the universe and human civilization is the sort of information that would not be taken at face value by modern historians (a seven-day creation, people who lived over nine hundred years, etc.—literal acceptance of such accounts depends on a particular religious ideology that cannot be assumed for broader academic study). Beyond this, many of the numbers recorded in Genesis–2 Kings appear to be symbolic or schematic, as could be indicated by the constant recurrence of twenty, forty, and multiples of forty. Further, different manuscripts and versions of the biblical books often provide differing readings, especially where numbers are involved. And, finally, there is no way to verify the biblical chronology or even the historicity of the early biblical characters and events. Abraham, Isaac, Jacob, Joseph, Moses, Joshua, the Israelite sojourn in Egypt, the Israelite conquest of Canaan, Saul, David, Solomon—none of these are mentioned in any extant nonbiblical documents from the ancient world. Indeed, with one exception, nothing has turned up in nonbiblical documents or ancient city ruins that points to a specifically Israelite presence before the ninth century BCE. The exception is an Egyptian inscription from the reign of Merneptah that seems to refer to a group known as "Israel" on the scene in Canaan during the late thirteenth century BCE.

Although the problematic nature of the evidence warns against assigning specific dates to any of the individual characters in the book of Judges, a case can be made for associating the "period of the judges" in general with the opening centuries of the Iron Age, i.e., from roughly 1200 to 1000 BCE. The stories about the judges presuppose village life in the central hill country, a phenomenon more characteristic of the Iron Age than of the preceding Bronze Age. Beginning with chronological information available for later kings (see below) and figuring backward, one arrives at 925 BCE as an approximate date for Solomon's death. Both David and Solomon are credited with forty-year reigns, a number probably not to be taken literally. 1 Sam. 13:1, on the other hand, which reports the length of Saul's reign, is obscure. Thus the most that can be said with any degree of certainty is that Saul, David, and Solomon lived sometime around 1000 BCE.

A higher degree of confidence attends chronologies following the reign of Solomon. The books of 1 and 2 Kings provide for each of the kings of Israel and Judah (the two kingdoms of the divided monarchy) a "synchronism," the year of the king's accession to the throne, dated in terms of the regnal year of his contemporary on the throne of the other kingdom, and a "regnal period," the length of the king's own reign (e.g., 1 Kings 15:1–2, 9–10, 25, 33). Further chronological notations are provided for some kings (e.g., 1 Kings 14:25; 16:23–24; 2 Kings 18:13). Scholars generally believe that these data were derived originally from official records. Occasionally the Chronicler adds similar notations not found in 1 and 2 Kings. Finally, beginning with Omri and Ahab, there are occasional references to Israelite and Judean kings in the royal inscriptions of Moab, Assyria, and Babylon. This abundance of data renders it possible to calculate probable dates for the rulers of the separate kingdoms (ca. 922–587/6 BCE). Such dates are rarely exact, because, as noted, there are variant readings in different manuscripts and versions of 1 and 2 Kings, and because there are sometimes internal discrepancies, synchronisms that do not match. There are also a few crucial unknowns. Did Israel and Judah use the same calendar (e.g., did they begin the year with the same month)? What methods were used for reckoning the length of a king's reign (e.g., when a king died mid-year, was the incomplete year ascribed to his reign, to his successor's reign, or to both)? Were there co-regencies other than the one recorded for Uzziah (Azariah) and Jotham in 2 Kings 15:5? Thus all of the dates provided here for the period prior to the Babylonian conquest of Jerusalem in 597 BCE are to be regarded as approximate.

Both 2 Kings and Jeremiah date certain events associated with the final fall of Jerusalem in terms of the regnal years of both Zedekiah and the contemporary Babylonian rulers (Nebuchadnezzar and Amel-marduk [Evil-merodach]; see 2 Kings 25:8, 27; Jer. 52:12, 31–34). Although there are some minor difficulties in the interpretation of even these passages, it seems clear that Jerusalem fell the second time in 587/6 BCE. Biblical books pertaining to the postexilic period, when Persia dominated the Middle East, often date events in terms of the regnal years of the Persian rulers. Thus the decree that allowed the exiles to return to Judah is recorded in Ezra 1:1 as occurring in Cyrus's first regnal year (538 BCE). Several dates are also provided in connection with the beginning of construction of the second temple, all between Darius's second and sixth year (520–515 BCE; see Ezra 4:24; 6:15, 19; Hag. 1:1, 15; 2:1, 10; Zech. 1:1, 7; 7:1). One tantalizing problem arises with regard to the dating of Ezra and Nehemiah. The Bible says clearly that Ezra returned from exile in the fifth month of the seventh year of Artaxerxes (Ezra 7:1–10) and that Nehemiah returned soon after the month of Nisan in the twentieth year of Artaxerxes (Neh. 1:1). Unfortunately we do not know whether this was Artaxerxes I (464–

CHRONOLOGY OF THE RULERS OF THE DIVIDED KINGDOM

All dates are approximate—the chronological data provided by 1 and 2 Kings can be interpreted in ways that support a variety of schemes. The most disputed dates usually concern the earliest rulers (e.g., Rehoboam's reign may be dated 924–907 BCE; Abijah, 907–906, and Asa, 905–874).

Judah	*Israel*
Rehoboam (922–915 BCE)	Jeroboam I (922–901 BCE)
Abijah (915–913)	
Asa (913–873)	
	Nadab (901–900)
	Baasha (900–877)
	Elah (877–876)
	Zimri (876)
Jehoshaphat (873–849)	Omri (876–869)
	Ahab (869–850)
	Ahaziah (850–849)
Jehoram (Joram; 849–843/2)	Jehoram (Joram; 849–843/2)
Ahaziah (843/2)	
Athaliah (843/2–837)	
Joash (Jehoash; 837–800)	Jehu (843/2–815)
	Jehoahaz (815–802)
Amaziah (800–783)	Joash (802–786)
Uzziah (Azariah; 783–742)	Jeroboam II (786–746)
	Zechariah (746/5)
	Shallum (745)
Jotham (742–735)	Menahem (745–737)
	Pekahiah (737–736)
	Pekah (736–732)
Ahaz (735–715)	Hoshea (732–724)
	Fall of Israel (Samaria; 722/1 BCE)
Hezekiah (715–687/6)	
Manasseh (687/6–642)	
Amon (642–640)	
Josiah (640–609)	
Jehoahaz (609)	
Jehoiakim (608–598)	
Jehoiachin (598/7)	
Babylonian Conquest of Jerusalem (597)	
Zedekiah (597–587/6)	
Destruction of Jerusalem (587/6 BCE)	

423 BCE) or Artaxerxes II (404–358 BCE). Further, it might not have been the same Artaxerxes in both cases.

Bibliography

Barnes, William H. *Studies in the Chronology of the Divided Monarchy of Israel.* Scholars, 1991.

Hayes, John H., and Paul K. Hooker. *A New Chronology for the Kings of Israel.* John Knox, 1988.

Miller, James Maxwell. *The Old Testament and the Historian.* Fortress, 1976.

Shenkel, James D. *Chronology and Recensional Development in the Greek Text of Kings.* Harvard University Press, 1968.

Thiele, Edwin R. *The Mysterious Numbers of the Hebrew Kings: A Reconstruction of the Chronology of the Kingdoms of Israel and Judah.* Eerdmans, 1965.   J.M.M.

chronology, New Testament, the dating of certain events in the NT and of the writings themselves. The principal events of NT history can rarely be dated with certainty. For example, the connection of Jesus's birth to the period of Caesar Augustus (27 BCE–14 CE), the reign of King Herod (37–4 BCE), and the census under Quirinius (6–7 CE) have inspired scholars to date that birth anytime between 12 BCE and 4 CE (though ca. 6 BCE is probably most common). The beginning of Jesus's ministry has been dated between 15 and 32 CE, and the length of his ministry has been estimated as one year (following the Synoptic Gospels) or three years (following the Gospel of John). Likewise, neither Paul's letters nor the book of Acts ever specify any dates for the events they report. Acts is notoriously fond of using imprecise terms with regard to time intervals (cf. "for some time" in 14:28; "for a considerable time" in 18:18), and Paul is also ambiguous with temporal references (e.g., when he says in Gal. 1:18–2:1 that he made his second visit to Jerusalem "after fourteen years," does he mean fourteen years after the first visit, or after his encounter with Christ, or after his return to Damascus?). Still, scholars have found certain promising reference points: 2 Cor. 11:32 places Paul in Damascus at a time when King Aretas had some influence in that city (ca. 37–41 CE), and Acts 18:12 says that Paul was in Corinth when Gallio was the proconsul (51–52 CE). Nevertheless, Pauline chronologies show some variance, placing his conversion between 30 and 35 CE, the Jerusalem Council (Acts 15; possibly Gal. 2:1–10) between 46 and 52 CE, and Paul's execution in Rome between 60 and 67 CE.

As for the writings of the NT, there is general consensus that the Letters of Paul were written before the Gospels, but there is no agreement as to the order in which they were written or, indeed, as to which letters ascribed to Paul were actually written by him. Seven letters (Romans, 1 and 2 Corinthians, Galatians, Philippians, 1 Thessalonians, and Philemon) are typically fit into the time frame ca. 46–64 CE. The six other Pauline letters are typically placed into a similar period (stretching perhaps to 67 CE by some accounts) if they are authentic, but they may be dated to the 80s or 90s if they are deemed pseudepigraphical. As for the Gospels, scholars accepting the priority of Mark usually place it around 70 CE, Matthew and Luke are typically dated ca. 85 CE, and John ca. 90–100 CE (with the Johannine Letters around 100), but the arguments for these dates are not conclusive. Some scholars hold to a scheme of earlier dating that places all four Gospels prior to 70 CE. The book of Acts is usually linked with Luke's Gospel and dated at about the same time as that book, but it has been placed significantly later, even into the second century. The other books of the NT are the most difficult of all to date; proposals often depend upon suppositions regarding authorship and intended readership. Thus, Revelation and 1 Peter might be dated anytime between 64 and 95 CE; James and Hebrews between 55 and 95 CE; and 2 Peter and Jude in the 60s CE when they are

thought to be authentic, but anytime between 100 and 135 CE if deemed pseudepigraphical. *See also* Gallio; Jesus Christ; Paul; Q; Synoptic Problem.

Bibliography

Hoehner, Harold W. *Chronological Aspects of the Life of Christ.* 5th ed. Zondervan, 1981.

Jewett, Robert. *A Chronology of Paul's Life.* Fortress, 1979.

Knox, John. *Chapters in a Life of Paul.* Rev. ed. Mercer, 1987.

Luedemann, Gerd. *Paul, Apostle to the Gentiles: Studies in Chronology.* Fortress, 1984.

R.J./M.A.P.

chrysolite, a magnesium iron silicate usually colored olive green, but it may also be yellow, as in Rev. 21:20. In Ezekiel, it is a gemstone decorating envisioned chariot wheels (NRSV: "beryl" in 1:16; 10:9). It also appears in Ezek. 28:11 in a list of precious stones covering the lamented king of Tyre (and here beryl is included as a separate item). It is the seventh gemstone adorning the wall of the new Jerusalem (Rev. 21:20).

church (from Gk. *ekklēsia,* "assembly" or "gathering"). In the LXX, two main words are used for the people of God: "assembly" (*ekklēsia*) and "synagogue" (*synagogē*). Since Jews in the first century used the latter term, the first Greek-speaking Christians selected the former to distinguish themselves from Jewish congregations while indicating that their roots nevertheless lay in the scriptures. In the NT, the word "church" always denotes a group of people, not a building. It can refer to all Christians in a city (Acts 14:23; 1 Cor. 1:2; 2 Cor. 1:1) or to those who gather for worship in a particular place (Rom. 16:5; 1 Cor. 16:19). Occasionally, it can refer to all Christians everywhere (Eph. 1:22). In the Gospel of Matthew, Jesus is presented as the one who founds the church (calling it "my church"); he refers to it as something that he will build, and he declares

A BASIC CHRONOLOGY OF THE NEW TESTAMENT

Most dates are approximate—and disputed.

63 BCE	Pompey conquers Jerusalem for Rome
ca. 6–4 BCE	Birth of Jesus
ca. 30–33 CE	Crucifixion of Jesus
ca. 32–36 CE	Conversion of Paul
ca. 46–65 CE	Paul's missionary journeys and imprisonment (as recorded in Acts)
	Paul's letters also written during this period
ca. 62–65 CE	Martyrdom of Peter and Paul in Rome
66 CE	Outbreak of Jewish war with Rome
ca. 65–70 CE	Gospel of Mark written
70 CE	Destruction of the Jerusalem temple
73 CE	Fall of Masada—definitive end of the Jewish war
ca. 80–100 CE	Other NT books written: Matthew, Luke, John, Acts, and "second generation" letters by followers of the original apostles

From Mark Allan Powell, *Introducing the New Testament* (courtesy, Baker Academic)

The baptism of a child depicted on a Roman sarcophagus (cf. Mark 10:13–16).

that "the gates of Hades will not prevail against it" (16:18). Elsewhere in Matt., Jesus lays out disciplinary procedures for dealing with unrepentant sin in the church (18:15–18).

If there was continuity between the NT church and Israel, there was also discontinuity brought about by the belief that Jesus was the Messiah, that he was risen from the dead, and, especially, that he was one to be worshiped as the Son of God. Thus, new terms and imagery came to be employed. The church is described as the body of Christ (1 Cor. 12:12, 27; Rom. 12:4–5; Eph. 1:22–23; 4:15–16; Col. 1:18; 2:19) or as a metaphorical building of which Christ is the cornerstone (Eph. 2:20). The church is also called the bride of Christ (Eph. 5:22–33), drawing upon the biblical image in which Israel is presented as the wife or bride of God (Hos. 1–3; Ezek. 16, 23). Another image likens Christ to a vine, of which believers are branches (John 15:1–11).

Throughout the NT, the church is the focal point for fellowship (Gk. *koinōnia*). As a concept related to the Jewish notion of "covenant," fellowship becomes a prominent mark of the church (Acts 2:42; Gal. 2:9; 1 John 1:7) and conveys the basic sense of mutual obligation associated with covenant, but also describes the intimate spiritual relationship believers have with each other and with God through Jesus Christ (1 Cor. 1:9; 1 John 1:6). Through such fellowship, the church participates in the death and resurrection of Christ (Rom. 6:1–11; Phil. 3:8–11) and experiences a unity grounded in the relationship of the Father and the Son (John 17:11, 21–23; 1 John 1:3, 6, 7).

Ministry in the church is described both in general terms (1 Thess. 5:12; Heb. 13:7) and with a variety of more specific titles (e.g., deacons, 1 Tim. 3:8–13; bishops, 3:1–7; elders, 4:17–20; widows, 5:9–12; pastors, Eph. 4:11; teachers, 1 Cor. 12:28; evangelists, Eph. 4:11; and prophets, 1 Cor. 12:28). It is not always clear what function each title implies. Those who held office were believed to be endowed by the Spirit (1 Cor. 12:4–11) and their ministry was a gift from God (Rom. 12:4–8; Eph. 4:7–11). Furthermore, the church as a whole had a ministry. Christians preserved sayings of Jesus that identified his followers as the light of the world, the salt of the earth, and the leaven that leavens the whole lump (Matt. 5:13–16; 13:33). Elsewhere church members are described as a royal priesthood, set to declare to the world the wonderful deeds of God (1 Pet. 2:9).

The NT presents churches as often beset with problems. In 1 Cor., Paul refers to church members who identify themselves divisively with particular human leaders (1:10–17; 3:1–23), who take one another to court (6:1–11), who consider having sex with prostitutes to be a matter of indifference (6:12–20), and who consume all of the food and become drunk at the Lord's Supper (11:21). Early on, one serious problem threatened to split the church: the terms on which Gentiles could become Christians. Did they need to be circumcised or keep the Jewish law (Acts 10:1–11:18; 15:1–35; Gal. 2:1–10)? Further divisions also appeared over what NT authors regarded as "false teaching" and inappropriate behavior (1 John 4:1–6; 2 John 9–11; 1 Tim. 4:1–5; 2 Tim. 3:1–9).

The NT churches often experienced what they regarded as hostility from the world about them (1 Thess. 2:14–16; 1 Pet. 1:6; 3:17; 4:13–14; Heb. 10:32–34; Rev. 2:10; Acts 17:5–9). Their faith forced them to withdraw from many accepted everyday practices connected with the worship of other deities. They became a close-knit group separated from others. At first, according to Acts, believers in Jerusalem shared their possessions (2:44–45; 4:32–5:11), though this practice does not appear to have been repeated elsewhere. There was a concerted attempt to preserve the purity of church life and to discipline those who transgressed or rejected orthodox views (1 Cor. 5:3–5; 2 Cor. 13:2; Acts 5:1–11; 20:29–31; 1 Tim. 1:20; 4:7; 2 Tim. 2:16–17; 3:5; 2 John 10; Rev. 2:14–15).

At the same time, churches were active in preaching Christ to others and sought to draw into their fellowship those outside it. The actual procedures of evangelism are most clear in accounts of Paul, who went to the main centers of population in the northern Mediterranean area. By the early second century, however, strong churches would also be found in Egypt, Babylonia, and North Africa, so other missionaries must have evangelized those areas.

Members of the church were drawn from all levels of society. Some were wealthy enough to own slaves (Philem. 15–16), to have positions of importance in the secular community (Acts 13:12; 17:12,

34; Rom. 16:23), and to have houses large enough for meetings to be held in them (Acts 18:7; Rom. 16:5; 1 Cor. 16:19; Col. 4:15). These, however, appear to have represented a minority (1 Cor. 1:26). Many Christians were slaves (1 Cor. 7:20–24; Col. 3:22–25; Eph. 6:5–9; 1 Pet. 2:18–25). Within the church, social and other distinctions of the ancient world were hypothetically abolished (Gal. 3:28; 1 Cor. 11:5; Philem. 16), although there was apparently no advocacy of the liberation of slaves, and women were given a position below men in at least some of the churches (1 Cor. 14:34; 1 Tim. 2:11–12). *See also* apostle; bishop; deacon; elders; evangelist; fellowship; Lord's Supper; minister; persecution; prophet; teaching; worship in the New Testament.   E.B.

Chuza (kyoo′zuh), a steward (perhaps property manager) of Herod Antipas and the husband of Joanna, one of several women who followed and ministered to Jesus (Luke 8:3). *See also* Antipas; Joanna.

Cilicia (suh-lish′ee-uh), a Roman province along the southeastern coast of Asia Minor, divided into two sections: the mountainous western section ("rugged Cilicia"), into which Cyprus was politically incorporated in 58 BCE, and the fertile, well-watered eastern plain ("level Cilicia"). The province was bounded by the Taurus Mountains on the north. The pass through these mountains to Cappadocia was known as the Cilician Gates. On the east, the Amanus Mountains separated Cilicia from Syria; the ancient pass through these mountains was known as the Syrian Gates. Tarsus, the hometown of Paul (Acts 21:39; 22:3), was located on the eastern plain. Paul says that he spent some time proclaiming Christ in the region even before he became known to the churches of Judea (Gal. 1:21). Acts records that Paul passed through the area during his second journey (15:40–41) and also later when he departed from Antioch for Galatia and Phrygia (18:23). People from Cilicia

are mentioned among those who argued with Stephen in Acts 6:9, and the region is mentioned several times in Hellenistic deuterocanonical writings (Jth. 1:7, 12; 2:21, 25; 1 Macc. 11:14; 2 Macc. 4:36; cf. 4 Macc. 4:2). *See also* Tarsus.   M.K.M.

circumcision, the removal of the foreskin (prepuce) of the penis. In the ancient Near East, the practice varied. Some societies, including the Hebrews, completely amputated the prepuce, while other cultures (e.g., the Egyptians) made dorsal incisions upon the foreskin. According to Jer. 9:25–26, many of Israel's neighbors practiced circumcision, notably the Egyptians, Edomites, Ammonites, Moabites, and Arabs. The Philistines, however, never practiced circumcision (cf. Judg. 14:3; 15:18; 1 Sam. 14:6; 17:26). Ezek. 32:21–30 also names other nations among the uncircumcised.

In ancient Israel and in Judaism, circumcision was routinely performed upon infants of eight days (Gen. 17:12; Lev. 12:3; Luke 1:59; 2:21; Phil. 3:5), though circumstances might permit or require performance upon adolescents (cf. Gen. 17:25) or even upon grooms (cf. Gen. 34:14–24). The Hebrews attributed different aspects of the practice to divine injunctions made to Abraham (Gen. 17:9–27), to Joshua (Josh. 5:2–7), and to Israel (Lev. 12:1–5; cf. Exod. 12:44, 48). In one passage (Exod. 4:24–26), Zipporah, the wife of Moses, is credited with saving her husband's life by circumcising their son.

In Gen. 17:11, circumcision is said to serve as a "sign" of God's covenant with Israel; though this remained the primary meaning, circumcision also acquired a figurative sense. Thus persons who were deemed "to have uncircumcised ears" were considered to be unreceptive, haughty, and proud (Jer. 6:10), while those who had an "uncircumcised heart" were considered to be stubborn (Lev. 26:41; Ezek. 44:7, 9; cf. Deut. 10:16; 30:6; Jer. 4:4; Rom. 2:28–29).

During the Hellenistic period, circumcision became a central issue between assimilationists and nationalists. To avoid scorn (cf., e.g., Horace *Satires* 1.5.95; 9.70; Martial *Epigrams* 7, 72, 5, 6), some hellenized Jews underwent painful surgery to restore the foreskin (1 Macc. 1:15; 1 Cor. 7:18; Josephus *Antiquities* 12.5.1). Probably reflecting this situation, *Jubilees* (15:6) regards circumcision as necessary to distinguish the children of the covenant from those of destruction. Antiochus Epiphanes played into the hands of the more Hellenistic Jews by forbidding circumcision on pain of death (1 Macc. 1:48, 60). During the Hasmonean period (second to mid-first centuries BCE), circumcision was forced upon the Edomites and the Itureans (Josephus *Jewish War* 13.9.1; 13.11.3). Later, the emperor Hadrian once again forbade circumcision, and this helped to trigger the Bar-Kochba revolt (132–35 CE).

In early Christianity, the merits of continuing circumcision were debated, but the rite was ultimately determined unnecessary for those who were baptized into Christ (cf. Acts 15; Rom. 2:29; Col. 2:11; 1 Cor. 7:19; Gal. 6:15). Nevertheless, the church thought it important to remember that Jesus had been circumcised (Luke 2:21), and Paul, who referred to those who argued for the continuance of circumcision as "those who mutilate the flesh" (Phil. 3:2), could nevertheless speak positively of his circumcision as the mark of one whose righteousness under the law was blameless (Phil. 3:5–6). The apparent explanation for this anomaly is that Paul and other early Christians wanted to maintain that circumcision had been a valid (divinely mandated) practice in its time, but that the need for circumcision had been abrogated by Christ's death and resurrection, which initiated a new covenant with God (e.g., 1 Cor. 11:25; 2 Cor. 3:6; Heb. 8:13). Paul also seizes upon the figurative uses of circumcision in the Bible to speak of a circumcision that is of the spirit rather than of the flesh (Phil. 2:3).

Bibliography

De Vaux, Roland. *Ancient Israel.* McGraw-Hill, 1961. Pp. 46–48.

Schauss, Hayyim. *The Lifetime of a Jew.* Union of American Hebrew Congregations, 1950. Pp. 31–76.

            J.M.S.

cisterns, underground chambers for storing water. In the dry climate of the Near East they were used to catch natural rain runoff during rainy seasons and retain it through the months of dry weather. Biblical references to cisterns include declaration of their ritual purity (Lev. 11:36) and mention of normal private use (2 Kings 18:31; Prov. 5:15; Isa. 36:16) and of special construction to allow a city to survive a siege (Jer. 41:9). The Bible mentions specific instances in which a cistern served as a prison (Jer. 38:7), an intended instrument of death (38:6–9), a burial site (41:9), or a hiding place (1 Sam. 13:6). They could symbolize unearned grace (Deut. 6:11), wealth (2 Chron. 26:10), rich booty (Neh. 9:25), or unfaithfulness leading to futility (Jer. 2:13) and destruction (14:3).

Archaeological discovery of cisterns is frequent and varied. In the ancient Near East, most cisterns were cut into rock or adapted from natural cave formations in the rock. The porous nature of the native limestone and chert made a form of waterproofing essential to avoid tragedy (see Jer. 2:13). Use of such waterproofing in the form of a limestone plaster became widespread at the end of the Late Bronze Age (thirteenth century BCE), and the number of cisterns increased substantially thereafter. Most cisterns were protected from unwanted rubbish by being cut in a bottle shape or having a rim that narrowed the mouth, frequently blocked with a cover stone. Water would thus be drawn by lowering a vessel through the mouth by rope, filling it, and raising it for transfer to a carrying vessel or an animal trough. Some cisterns were open by design, and some were even stepped to allow access to water at low levels, as at Qumran. The accumulation of mud in the bottom (Jer. 38:6)

and degeneration of the plaster required periodic cleaning and repair.   R.S.B.

citadel. *See* architecture.

cities. According to Gen. 4:17, Cain built the first city and named it Enoch after his son. Later, the Tower of Babel story relates that God confused the languages of human beings who presumptuously wanted to build a great city for themselves (Gen. 11:4–7). Hundreds of cities are mentioned in the Bible, and archaeological explorations have located and excavated many of these.

In the Bible, the Hebrew terms typically translated "city" (*'ir, qiryah*) and "village" (*hatser*) do not refer directly to size, but to the presence or absence of a defensive wall: cities were walled; villages were unwalled. Villages were generally smaller and less important than cities, but this was not always the case. A number of factors led to the location of a city or village at a particular site; the presence of nearby water was key, along with access to the raw materials for construction and physical features that facilitated defense. Secondary factors such as proximity to trade routes or to sanctuaries and shrines were also considered. The earliest city excavated in the Near East thus far is Jericho (Tell es-Sultan). The initial Neolithic city there dates to between 8000 and 7000 BCE. This walled city was built before the introduction of pottery. It had a strong defensive wall with a huge round watchtower inside the wall. The tower was 28 feet in diameter at its base and still stands 19 feet high. Evidently, even at this early period, enough city organization existed to plan, build, and maintain such defenses.

None of the cities in the Levant compare in size to the great cities of Mesopotamia. Nineveh covered approximately 1,720 acres, or over 2.5 square miles. Calah (ancient Nimrud) covered over 875 acres, or 1.4 square miles. By comparison, Jerusalem at the time of Solomon covered only 33 acres, and even at the time of Jesus covered fewer than 200 acres. Projections suggest that, with regard to population, most cities could support 160 to 200 persons per acre. Thus Jerusalem in Solomon's time could have supported 5,000 to 6,500. Still, the larger Near Eastern cities were often associated with smaller villages around them: the Bible often speaks of cities "with their villages" (Josh. 19:16; Neh. 11:30; cf. Mark 8:27). Given this, most of the trade and commerce for a region would have taken place within the city, which would have sat on or near the main highway and trade route. The chief shrine or sanctuary for the region would also be located in the city. When warfare threatened, the people of the surrounding villages would flee to the walled city for protection.

The walls of cities during the early monarchy were regularly casemates, consisting of two parallel walls reinforced by perpendicular walls at regular intervals. Usually the outer wall was somewhat stronger. The space between the two walls was often used for living space. Later a single massive

The Canaanite moat, tower, and fortification wall at Jericho. Though built before the introduction of pottery (8000–7000 BCE), enough city organization existed to plan, build, and maintain the defenses.

wall, often as thick as 16 feet, replaced the casemates. The development of the battering ram is usually cited as the cause for this new defensive wall. A sloping glacis, or plastered embankment, was frequently added to the outside of the wall to prevent easy access to its foundations and to impede the use of a battering ram. Many cities of the Bible also had an upper city or acropolis. This area was located on the highest part of the tell and often served as an inner citadel with its own defense wall. The aristocracy or royalty usually occupied this area and the sanctuary was most often located here. Houses here were large and made of the finest masonry.

The weakest defense point for an ancient city was the gate. Thus, massive defensive towers usually guarded either side of the gate. The gate opening itself was 12 to 15 feet wide and had two heavy wooden doors that could be shut and braced with bars. The gate complex also had two, four, or six rooms that served as guardrooms. The walls of these inner rooms could support additional wooden doors in time of war. Inside and outside the gate were open squares where much of the business of the city would be conducted. This area, for instance, could serve as a courtroom (Josh. 20:4; Ruth 4:1–6). Public buildings also tended to be located near the city gate (or, if not, they would

often be clustered in one section of the city). A fully preserved gate structure from the Middle Bronze Age has been excavated at Tell Dan. Dating to the eighteenth century BCE, this mud-brick gate was fully preserved, and it features the earliest example of an arch in Canaan. An Early Bronze IV (2500–2000 BCE) entrance gate with stone benches along both sides has also been found at Khirbet Iskander, Jordan.

Cities also had to have a protected water supply that could be reached from within the walls (to allow inhabitants to endure an extensive siege). Most cities were located near springs, and many had cisterns dug in individual houses. The spring was usually at the foot of the tell (mound) outside the city wall. Hezekiah's tunnel in Jerusalem (cf. 2 Kings 20:20) is but one example of a well-developed system for bringing water into the city. At Hazor, Megiddo, and other sites, great water-tunnel and pool systems were constructed by cutting down through the bedrock of the tell to reach the level of the supply.

By the period of the monarchy, Israelite cities had a regular street plan. Immediately inside the city gate was an open court or plaza. From this point, a circular street enclosed the city. A row of houses or public buildings was built between the circular street and the city wall. This street gave easy access to all sections of the city. Other streets branched off this circular street into the core of the city.

Cities changed drastically in the Hellenistic (333–63 BCE) and Roman (63 BCE–324 CE) periods. Following the Greek ideal of the *polis*, cities in the Hellenistic period contained a series of structures that reflected the civic ideal of democracy. Alongside temples and the *agora* (market) could be found a gymnasium and bath complex where wealthy males were educated, and a theater or odeon, where the citizenry could meet. During the Roman period, cities and colonies absorbed most of the Hellenistic elements and added a series of buildings for entertainment and leisure: amphitheaters for bloodsport, hippodromes for races, public bathing complexes with latrines along with sophisticated aqueducts and sewage systems. Like their Hellenistic predecessors, Roman-period cities strove toward a grid pattern while accommodating the topography, with a main north–south road, the *cardo*, and a main east–west road, the *decumanus*. By this time, city walls were less important, and gates had assumed a more ornamental than defensive purpose; the heart of the city moved from the acropolis down into a sprawling level area below, such as at Sythopolis (Bethshan). Only the Roman imperial family could designate a site as a *polis*, with attendant qualifications for taxation rates and political rights; such designations were based less on population size than on personal relations of key citizens and the appropriate urban-architectural aesthetic.

Herod (40–4 BCE) brought many aspects of the Roman city to Judea, Samaria, and Galilee, building and rebuilding cities noted for broad colonnaded streets paved with flagstones and sprinkled with theaters, hippodromes, aqueducts, and at Caesarea and Sebaste even temples dedicated to the emperor Augustus. At Jewish sites like Jerusalem, however, he avoided offending religious sensibilities; thus, no pagan temples, statues, or baths (where nudity might offend) have been found. Similarly, his son Herod Antipas (4 BCE–36 CE) seems to have avoided overtly pagan aspects in his cities of Sepphoris and Tiberias, though a Roman urban aesthetic and set of structures were present.

Excavations in the old Jewish quarter of Jerusalem have uncovered an extensive section of the *cardo* there (although this section of the *cardo* dates to the Byzantine period). This street was 39 feet wide and was flanked by colonnaded, covered sidewalks, each an additional 17 feet wide. The street even had a covered drainage system. From these same excavations, several wealthy houses of the Roman period were discovered overlooking the Temple Mount. Alongside several Jewish ritual baths were found Roman-style heated baths and numerous mosaics, albeit aniconic ones. Decorated with frescoes and plastered walls and ceilings, these houses likely belonged to priestly and aristocratic families. Most of the Levantine cities were reshaped along Roman lines already in the first century CE, when a touch of Rome in the form of mosaics

and frescoes was also apparent inside the wealthy houses. By the second century, these cities had been thoroughly Romanized.

In the Gospels, the Greek term *polis* is frequently used without regard to the required political and urban-aesthetic considerations; even Capernaum receives the designation (Matt. 9:1; 11:20; Mark 1:33; Luke 4:31), as does Nazareth (Matt. 2:23).

Bibliography

Kenyon, Kathleen. *Royal Cities of the Old Testament.* Schocken, 1971.

Reed, Jonathan. *Archaeology and the Galilean Jesus.* Trinity Press International, 2000.

Shiloh, Yigal. "Elements in the Development of Town Planning in the Israelite City." *Israel Exploration Journal* 28 (1978): 36–51.

Yadin, Yigael. *Hazor.* 4 vols. Oxford University Press, 1972.   J.F.D./J.R.

Claudia (klaw'dee-uh), woman sending greetings to Timothy, along with Linus and Pudens (2 Tim. 4:21). *See also* Eubulus; Linus; Pudens.

Claudius (klaw'dee-uhs; 10 BCE–54 CE), the fourth Roman emperor; he assumed power following Gaius Caligula's assassination (41 CE). The Roman historian Suetonius (69–135 CE) reports that Claudius "banished from Rome all the Jews, who were continually making disturbances at the instigation of one Chrestus" (*Life of Claudius* 25). Many scholars think that "Chrestus" could be a mangled spelling of "Christos," Latin for "Christ." It would be possible, then, that the Jews expelled by Claudius were specifically Jews proclaiming Jesus to be the Christ. This would fit with Acts 18:2–3, where the Jews expelled by Claudius include Aquila and Priscilla, who elsewhere appear as Jewish believers in Christ and as co-workers with Paul (Acts 18:18, 26; cf. Rom. 16:3). Claudius is also referred to in Acts 11:28. *See also* Aquila; Caesar; Prisca, Priscilla.

Claudius Lysias. *See* Lysias, Claudius.

clay, a plastic (pliable) material composed of various types of earth combined with moisture. The earliest and most widespread use of clay by human beings appears to have been for the production of pottery. Clay was also formed into brick for the construction of houses and other buildings (e.g., Exod. 5:6–9; Job 4:19). Clay tablets were used in ancient Meosopotamia as the medium on which to preserve writing. Discoveries of libraries of such tablets have added much to our knowledge of ancient cultures. Clay figurines have also been discovered that appear to have served purposes ranging from children's toys to cultic images of idols. The metaphor of humans producing objects out of clay is often applied in scripture to God fashioning humans (Job 10:9; 33:6; Isa. 29:16; 45:9; 64:8; Rom. 9:21). Sometimes clay is used as a symbol for something that is fragile or weak (Job 13:12; Isa. 41:25; 2 Cor. 4:7; Rev. 2:27), malleable (Job 33:14; Jer. 18:4, 6), or plentiful (Job 27:16). In the NT, clay functions as a therapeutic agent in an account of Jesus healing a blind man (John 9:11). *See also* Amarna, Tell el-; cuneiform writing; Ebla; Mari; Nuzi.   P.J.A./M.A.P.

clean. *See* animals; purity.

Clement (klem′uhnt), **letters of,** two letters from the late first and mid-second century CE that early tradition attributed to a Roman bishop (sometimes called Clement of Rome) whom Origen would identify with the Clement mentioned in Phil. 4:3 and Roman Catholic tradition would list as one of the earliest popes. Both letters of Clement were included in Codex Alexandrinus, a fifth-century biblical manuscript, indicating that some quarters of the church at that time must have regarded them as part of the canonical NT. The letters are now recognized to have come from two authors. *1 Clement* was written in the late first or early second century from Rome to the church in Corinth, seeking to quell certain disputes that had arisen there over leadership. Its authorship by a bishop or elder of Rome strikes most scholars as reasonable, though uncertain. *2 Clement* is more of a homily than a letter and appears to have been composed sometime in the mid-second century. Its author cannot be determined (despite the association with Clement), nor is it clear for whom the document was written or from where.
     P.J.A./M.A.P.

Cleopas (klee′oh-puhs), a disciple who with an unnamed companion encountered the resurrected Jesus as they traveled to Emmaus (Luke 24:18–35).

cloak. *See* dress.

Clopas (kloh′puhs), husband of one of the Marys present at Jesus's crucifixion (John 19:25). *See also* Mary.

clothing. *See* dress.

clouds. Because they were seasonally limited harbingers of life-giving rain (Luke 12:54), clouds were often perceived as manifestations of divine power by both Canaanites and Israelites. Ugaritic texts call the storm god Baal "Cloud Rider," and in Ps. 68:5 Israel applies that same title to God. The covenant that God made with Noah is signaled by a bow set in the clouds (Gen. 9:13–16). The book of Exodus reports that a pillar of cloud represented God's presence by day, guiding the Israelites as they traveled through the wilderness (13:21; cf. Num. 12:1, where God comes down in a pillar of cloud to talk with Moses and Aaron). When Moses ascends Mount Sinai, the glory of the Lord descends and a cloud covers the mountain (Exod. 24:15–18). Likewise, a cloud covers the tent of meeting when the glory of the Lord fills the tabernacle (Exod. 40:34–37; cf. Lev. 16:2, 13; Num. 9:15–22). A cloud at the Jerusalem temple similarly manifests divine presence in 1 Kings

8:10–11. In the NT the voice of God comes from a cloud at Jesus's transfiguration (Mark 9:7), and a cloud masks the departure of Jesus from the earth at his ascension (Acts 1:9). The NT expectation of Christ's Parousia is that Jesus is coming on, in, or with clouds (Matt. 24:30; 26:64; Mark 13:26; 14:64; Rev. 1:7) and that believers will be caught up into the clouds to meet him (1 Thess. 4:17). Hebrews speaks of "a great cloud of witnesses" (12:1). Revelation mentions an angel who is wrapped in a cloud (10:1) and describes the Son of Man as seated on a cloud (14:14–16).   R.M.G./M.A.P.

Cnidus (ni′duhs), a city near Cape Krio in southwest Turkey; it received a letter from the Roman consul Lucius (Calpurnius Piso) ca. 140 BCE backing Simon's rule over the Jews (1 Macc. 15:23). Paul's ship sailed past Cnidus en route to Rome, and the ship had to change direction there due to unfavorable winds (Acts 27:7).

coat. *See* dress.

coat of mail, defensive armor consisting of overlapping plates of metal strung on leather or cloth. Cavalry and archers are identified as the warriors who typically wore it (Jer. 46:4; 51:3). Still, Goliath wore a coat of mail that was notably heavy (1 Sam. 17:5), and Saul initially clothed David in a coat of mail that proved too cumbersome for him to use (17:38–39). Aaron's robe was designed with an opening like that of a coat of mail, so that it would not be torn (Exod. 28:32; 39:23).

cock, a rooster (cf. Prov. 30:31). All biblical references are to a cock crowing, a typical signal of daybreak (Mark 13:35; cf. 3 Macc. 5:23). Jesus says that Peter will deny him three times before the cock crows (or crows twice), a prediction that is then fulfilled after Jesus is arrested (Matt. 26:34, 74–75; Mark 14:30, 72; Luke 22:34, 60–61; John 13:38; 18:27). *See also* fowls.

code. *See* law.

codex (pl. codices), one of the two formats in which ancient manuscripts were written; the other is the scroll. A codex was made by placing sheets of papyrus or parchment on top of one another and folding them down the middle, producing a quire. Such a single-quire codex could become cumbersome when a large number of sheets were used, so scribes soon took to developing small quires, each comprising four folded sheets, stitched folded in half three successive times (to make eight pages) and stitching these together at the back.

Some of the most famous parchment codices of the Bible are Codex Alexandrinus, a fifth-century manuscript of the whole Christian Bible, with some lacunae; Codex Vaticanus, dating from the fourth century; Codex Sinaiticus, also from the fourth century; Codex Bezae, a fifth-century manuscript containing the Gospels and Acts in Greek and Latin; Codex Washingtonianus, a fourth- or fifth-century manuscript of the Gospels; the Vienna Genesis, a deluxe purple parchment Greek manuscript of the fifth or sixth century CE with forty-eight watercolor miniatures; and the Khludov Psalter of the ninth century CE, containing more than two hundred miniatures illustrating the LXX text of the Psalms. *See also* papyrus; scroll.   B.M.M.

Coelesyria (see'lee-sihr'ee-uh; Lat., from Gk., lit., "hollow" Syria), a term used in the Apocrypha/deuterocanonical literature for the valley between the Lebanon and Anti-Lebanon ranges, or more precisely for the Seleucid province in that valley, i.e., southwestern Syria (1 Macc. 10:69; 2 Macc. 3:5; 4:4; 8:8; 10:11; 1 Esd. 2:17, 24, 27; 4:48; 6:69; 7:1; 8:67).

coins. *See* money.

collection for the saints, an offering collected by Paul from primarily Gentile Christians for Jewish Christians in Jerusalem. In 1 Cor. 16:1–2, Paul gives instructions to the Corinthian Christians about this fund. His churches in Galatia (1 Cor. 16:1) and Macedonia (2 Cor. 8:1–5; 9:1–2) had also been urged to make contributions, and at least the latter seem to have responded generously (2 Cor. 8:3–5). The Corinthians, while quick to pledge their support, may have been slow to follow through with any gifts (2 Cor. 8:6; 9:1–5). There are hints that opponents of Paul may have caused the Corinthian Christians to suspect Paul's motives in soliciting their money (2 Cor. 12:14–18).

At least two factors account for the high priority Paul seems to have placed on this project over a several-year period. First, he considered it a needed act of charity (Rom. 15:26; 2 Cor. 8:4), perhaps an extension of the relief fund he and Barnabas had delivered to the Jerusalem church on behalf of the Christians in Antioch (Acts 11:27–30). Second, he had committed himself to it as a part of the agreement reached when the Jewish-Christian leaders in Jerusalem approved his mission to the Gentiles (Gal. 2:1–10); it therefore symbolized the partnership of Jews and Gentiles in the gospel. Little information is available, however, concerning the actual completion and delivery of the collection (Rom. 15:25–31; cf. Acts 20:24; 24:17; 1 Cor. 16:3–4). *See also* Paul; poor, poverty.   V.P.F.

Colossae (kuh-los'ee), a small city in Asia Minor located in the upper Lycus River valley about 110 miles east of Ephesus, 10 miles east of Laodicea, and 12 miles southeast of Hierapolis. Although in earlier times Colossae was an important center (Herodotus called it "a large city of Phrygia," and Xenophon described it as "a populous city, large and well off"), by the late first century BCE Colossae had been outstripped by both Laodicea and Hierapolis, and Strabo lists the city as among a group of smaller towns. A severe earthquake in 60 or 61 CE contributed to Colossae's decline. The city was well known for its wool-working and cloth dying industries that made a dark red

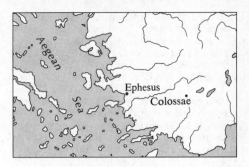

wool cloth known as *colossinum*. A significant number of Jews probably resided at Colossae; a statement made by Cicero (*Pro Flacco* 68) permits the estimate that over ten thousand Jewish males lived in the Laodicea-Hierapolis-Colossae area. A Christian community also existed there by the mid-first century CE, which is mentioned in Philemon and Colossians. The latter letter attributes the church's founding to Epaphras, one of Paul's associates (Col. 1:7–8), though it is not clear that Paul himself had ever been there. Still, the city also appears to have been the hometown of Philemon (since many of the same individuals mentioned in Colossians are also mentioned in Philemon), and Paul's letter to that individual indicates that he is planning to come for a visit when he is released from prison (Philem. 22). After the earthquake in 60 or 61 CE Colossae passed into oblivion, and its structures were heavily quarried in the Byzantine era. The site was rediscovered in 1835, and visible ruins include the acropolis, portions of the city walls, a theater, a nearby necropolis, and a church. Excavations at the site have just begun. *See also* Asia; Colossians, Letter of Paul to the; Epaphras; Ephesus; Hierapolis; Laodicea; Phrygia.   R.A.W./J.R.

Colossians (kuh-losh'uhnz), **Letter of Paul to the,** one of thirteen letters in the NT attributed to Paul, though some scholars believe it is actually a pseudepigraphical composition. Because the letter has many similarities to Ephesians, these two letters are often called "literary siblings." It also names many of the same individuals mentioned in Paul's short letter to Philemon, who, accordingly, is assumed to have lived in Colossae.

Contents: The letter begins with a typical salutation and greeting (1:1–2). A prayer of thanksgiving for the readers' faith and love emphasizes that the gospel they heard from Paul's fellow servant Epaphras has been growing in them and bearing fruit (1:3–8). The authors (identified as Paul and Timothy) continue to pray that the Colossians might be filled with knowledge of God's will, grow in knowledge of God, and be strengthened by God, who is responsible for their current position and status (1:9–14). This opening prayer segues into a liturgical meditation on the magnificence of Christ as the "firstborn of all creation" and the "firstborn from the dead." Christ is the "image of the invisible

God" and the one in whom the "fullness of God was pleased to dwell"; all things were created in him and through him and for him, and in him all things hold together (1:15–20). The letter then presents theological implications of the foregoing exposition of who Christ is and what he has done (1:21–2:23). The Colossians are assured of their perfection before God, provided they continue in the faith, and it is to this end that Paul has been willing to suffer and toil on their behalf, in accord with his commission from God to make known the mystery of "Christ in you, the hope of glory" (1:21–2:7). The Colossians are then warned about being deceived by empty philosophy that suggests their baptism into Christ has been inadequate to secure their position with God or that religious observances or experiences will enable them to grow into the fullness that is found in Christ alone (2:8–23). Such philosophy is denounced as representing mere human tradition (2:8, 22) and as being in accord with spiritual powers that Christ has vanquished (2:8, 15, 20). The letter continues by turning to the ethical implications of the recipients' status in Christ (3:1–4:3). The Colossians should focus completely on the heavenly kingdom to which they now belong, reject practices that marked their life before Christ, and pursue conduct that befits God's chosen ones (3:1–17). A specific table of household duties spells out responsibilities of wives, husbands, children, fathers, slaves, and masters (3:18–4:1). The Colossians should devote themselves to prayer and exercise wisdom in their relations with outsiders (4:2–6). The letter concludes with instructions and greetings (4:7–17) and with a final greeting from Paul in his own hand (4:18).

OUTLINE OF CONTENTS

Colossians

R.A.W.

Authorship: Scholars who believe that Colossians is pseudepigraphical maintain that the letter is different from the undisputed letters of Paul in both style and theology. With regard to style, Colossians uses more long sentences (1:3–8 and 2:8–15 are each just one sentence in Greek); more redundant adjectives (e.g., "holy and blameless and irreproachable," 1:22); far more participles and relative clauses; and far fewer conjunctions. With regard to theology, Colossians is said to evince a higher Christology, a more developed ecclesiology, and a more "realized" view of eschatology (i.e., more emphasis on present benefits than on future hope). Scholars who think the letter is an authentic Pauline composition claim that stylistic distinctiveness may be due to reliance on an amanuensis or attributed to the influence of the letter's coauthors. They also regard the alleged theological differences as developments of Paul's ideas over time or as variations in emphasis necessitated by the letter's particular context.

Historical Setting: The letter is addressed to Christians in Colossae who are said to have been evangelized by Paul's associate Epaphras (1:3–8). Scholars who think the letter is an authentic Pauline composition usually believe that Paul wrote the letter late in his life (to account for the development of ideas), but that he also probably wrote it before 61 CE, when the city of Colossae was destroyed by an earthquake. A popular suggestion is that Paul wrote Colossians and Philemon (and possibly Ephesians) early in his Roman imprisonment (ca. 60 CE). A few scholars suggest composition during an earlier imprisonment (e.g., in Caesarea or Ephesus). If the letter is regarded as pseudepigraphical, it is sometimes attributed to a disciple (e.g., Timothy, the stated coauthor) who might then have written it in the late 60s CE, soon after the apostle's death. Some scholars, however, think that a devoted follower of Paul might have composed Colossians decades after his death, placing the letter in the 80s CE or later.

In any case, the letter seeks to address Christians who are in danger of being deceived by "plausible arguments" (2:4) and taken captive through "philosophy and empty deceit" (2:8). Much attention has been devoted to defining this ideological threat, which scholars refer to as the "Colossian heresy." It appears to have something to do with appeasing or revering the "elemental spirits of the universe" (2:8, 20), and it also seems to involve some variety of Jewish asceticism (2:16, 18, 21). The letter was written (by Paul, one of his disciples, or someone else) to warn believers against such thinking, which is described as a move away from Pauline insistence on the absolute all-sufficiency of Christ.

Major Themes: The letter develops what is sometimes called "a cosmic Christology": Jesus Christ is the Lord of the universe (1:15–17) and the one who reconciles all things in heaven and on earth (1:20). He is also described as the "image of the invisible God" (1:15), the one in whom "all the fullness of God was pleased to dwell" (1:19; cf. 2:9),

DEVELOPMENT OF PAULINE IDEAS IN COLOSSIANS

The Letter to the Colossians seems to expand upon many ideas found in other (undisputed) letters of Paul, taking the points a step farther or to another level:

Romans says that believers have died and been buried with Christ through baptism and will someday be united with him in resurrection (6:4–6); Colossians says that believers have already "been raised with Christ" through baptism (2:12; cf. 3:1; but see also Rom. 6:12).

Romans says that believers have died to sin (6:2); Colossians says that they have "died to the elemental spirits of the universe" (2:20).

Romans says that no spiritual being or power will "be able to separate us from the love of God in Christ"; Colossians says that Christ disarmed the spiritual rulers and authorities and "made a public display of them, triumphing over them" (2:15; cf. 1 Cor. 15:24).

1 Corinthians says that Jesus Christ is the one "through whom are all things, and through whom we exist"; Colossians presents Christ as the one "in whom all things in heaven and on earth were created" (1:16) and in whom "all things hold together" (1:17).

2 Corinthians says that Paul's sufferings manifest the death of Jesus in his body (4:8–12); Colossians says that his sufferings serve the vicarious function of "completing what is lacking in Christ's afflictions for the sake of the church" (1:24).

Philippians refers to Christ as "being in the form of God" (2:6); Colossians refers to Christ as the "image of the invisible God" (1:15) and as the one in whom the "whole fullness of deity dwells bodily" (2:9)

Are these points on which Paul has further developed his own thinking? Or are they instances of a pseudonymous author building on Paul's ideas?

From Mark Allan Powell, *Introducing the New Testament* (courtesy, Baker Academic)

and God's agent in both creation and redemption (1:16). The immediate point of this "high Christology" may be that Christians have no need of other mediators, nor do they have anything to fear from supernatural powers, which Christ has already defeated (2:15). Indeed, the letter maintains that believers need not retreat from the world in order to live upright lives, but have power from Christ through baptism to act morally (3:1–4:1). Furthermore, spiritual growth does not depend on acquisition of new knowledge, but on remaining within the body of Christ (1:18, 22, 24; 2:17, 19; 3:15): growth comes from God (2:19; cf. 1:5–6, 3:10), and one need only remain within the church to come to full maturity. *See also* Colossae; Paul; pseudepigraphy.

Bibliography

Barth, Markus, and Helmut Blanke. *Colossians.* Doubleday, 1994.

Dunn, James D. G. *The Epistles to the Colossians and to Philemon: A Commentary on the Greek Text.* Eerdmans, 1996.

Lincoln, Andrew, and A. J. Wedderburn. *The Theology of the Later Pauline Letters.* Cambridge University Press, 1993.

O'Brien, Peter T. *Colossians, Philemon.* Word, 1982.

Wilson, Robert. *Colossians and Philemon.* Clark, 2005.   M.A.P.

Comforter. *See* Paraclete.

Coming of Christ, Second. *See* eschatology; millennium; Parousia.

commandment (Heb. *mitswah*), a verbal or written requirement or order. This term appears over 180 times in the Hebrew Bible; 90 percent of those references are to God's requirements of Israel as stipulated in the Pentateuch. Such deity-to-human commandments are offered on an analogy to those of king to subject (e.g., 2 Kings 18:36) and parent to child (e.g., Jer. 35:14; Prov. 6:20). The word "commandment" often appears in conjunction with *torah* and laws (e.g., Gen. 26:5; Exod. 24:12; Deut. 6:1). The people are enjoined to "keep" (lit., "guard") the commandments (e.g., Lev. 26:3). Far from being burdensome, the commandments are the psalmist's "delight" (Ps. 119:47, 143) and "love" (119, 127). Indeed, God calls those who observe the commandments "those who love me" (Exod. 20:6; Deut. 5:10).

Jesus specified the two greatest commandments as being love of God and neighbor (Matt. 22:35–40; Mark 12:28–34; Luke 10:25–28, based upon Deut. 6:5 and Lev. 19:18; cf. Rom. 13:9; Gal. 5:14). In John's Gospel, he offers as a "new commandment" the insistence that his followers "love one another" just as he has loved them (13:34; cf. 15:12). Paul speaks of the power of sin using the commandments to bring spiritual death (Rom. 7:8–13). *See also* covenant; law; Ten Commandments.   J.U.

Communion. *See* Lord's Supper.

concubine, a marital associate who bore children for a man and sometimes served as a secondary wife. The Bible frequently mentions men, in the time period up to and including the monarchy, who had children by concubines in addition to the children they fathered with their wife or wives (e.g., Gen. 36:12; 1 Chron. 1:32; 2:46, 48; 3:9; 7:14). In a few prominent stories, a wife (Sarah, Leah, Rachel) gives her slave to her husband as a surrogate to bear children (Gen. 16:1–3; 30:3–13). These surrogate wives (Hagar, Zilpah, Bilhah) are probably to be thought of as concubines, though the word is only applied to one of them on one occasion (to Bilhah in Gen. 35:22). The status of a concubine seems to have varied. Some references clearly indicate that concubines are to be considered wives (1 Kings 11:13). Thus, Hagar is also called Abraham's wife (Gen. 16:3), and Bilhah and Zilpah are called Jacob's wives (30:4, 9). Other texts, however, distinguish concubines from wives. Gideon had many wives and also a concubine (Judg. 8:31); Rehoboam had eighteen wives and sixty concubines. In the latter instance—and in the case of Solomon (a thousand wives, including three hundred concubines, 1 Kings 11:13)— the primary purpose of the (multiple) concubines was not to ensure offspring, but to enhance the man's status. With regard to inheritance and other parental favors, children of concubines are sometimes treated differently than children of the primary wife or wives (Gen. 25:5–6; cf. 21:10–13; 48; 49:22–26). The Torah did guarantee the legal rights of a Hebrew girl sold into concubinage, though it appears that in such an instance to be a concubine was to be a slave (Exod. 21:7–11). The practice of bearing children through concubines was also practiced in ancient Babylonia and laws governing inheritance and other matters are outlined in legal documents contemporaneous with the Bible (*Code of Hammurabi* 144–45, 170–71).

For a man to engage in sexual intercourse with another man's concubine was perceived, not only as adultery, but as a usurpation of the other man's authority (Gen. 35:22; 49:4; 2 Sam. 3:7; 1 Kings 2:13–25). It was for this reason that Absalom lay with his father's concubines "in the sight of all Israel" (2 Sam. 16:20–22). Judg. 19 relates a horrifying account of Benjaminites raping and murdering the concubine of a Levite, who then dismembers her and sends her body parts to the tribes of Israel along with his plea for vengeance. Judg. 20–21 reports how that vengeance was carried out in a way that brought the tribe of Benjamin to near extinction. *See also* marriage.   M.A.P.

conduit, a channel, aqueduct, or trench. The conduits mentioned in the Bible were artificially constructed passageways used to bring water from a spring or stream into a city. Water-conduit systems were varied in their construction. Some were underground tunnels cut through rock, while others consisted of plastered troughs or tiled pipes. Many scholars believe that it was an underground conduit or "water shaft" that David's men used to enter Jerusalem when it was a Jebusite village and to conquer the city for Israel (2 Sam. 5:8). Similar conduits or water tunnels have been discovered at

A water gallery excavated at Megiddo. The narrow tunnel cut through the Solomonic casemate wall (tenth century BCE) carried water to the city from a spring outside the wall.

Gezer, Megiddo, Gibeon, and Hazor. The conduits mentioned most often in the Bible are those from a later period (eighth century BCE) that brought water from the Gihon spring outside Jerusalem to the "upper pool" and, from there, to two lower pools in the city. It was along the conduit of the upper pool in an area called Fuller's Field that garments were washed, and this became a popular meeting place. For example, it was here that Isaiah met Ahaz (Isa. 7:3) and that the officers of Sennacherib taunted Hezekiah (2 Kings 18:17; Isa. 36:2). When it appeared that Sennacherib was about to conquer Jerusalem, Hezekiah ordered that the openings of the conduits be closed, including those associated with the Wadi Kidron (2 Chron. 32:1–4). Later Hezekiah had a 1,780-foot tunnel cut through solid rock to bring water from the Gihon into the city (2 Kings 20:20). During the Roman period, Herod the Great and Pontius Pilate used temple funds to finance the construction of an elaborate system of aqueducts to bring water from pools south of Bethlehem to Jerusalem, a distance of about fifteen miles.   J.J.D.

coney. *See* badger.

congregation, a gathering, usually of people who share common interests or ancestry. Two basically synonymous Hebrew terms denote "congregation": *'edah* (from the root "to appoint") and *qahal* (the corollary verbal root is "to convoke"; Prov. 5:14). The terms can have generic meaning (*'edah* refers to a gathering of animals in Judg. 14:8; Ps. 68:30; and *qahal* is used with a military connotation in Ezek. 17:17; 38:15), but the great majority of references concern the "congregation of Israel" (e.g., Exod. 12:3; Lev. 4:13; Num. 1:2). The latter phrase is used almost as a synonym for the people of Israel or, simply, the Israelites. This concept of Israel as a congregation occurs especially in Exodus–Joshua, but is common also in the Psalms, where the notion of the nation as a worshiping community comes to the fore (e.g., 22:5; 26:12; 35:18; 40:9–10; 68:26; 107:32; 111:1). In the NT, the word is used only four times in the NRSV: twice it translates *ekklēsia* (normally translated "church") in what are either scriptural citations (Heb. 2:12) or references to biblical events (Acts 7:38). The other two times, it translates the word *plēthos*, which is more typically rendered "crowd" or "multitude" (Acts 15:30; 19:9).

J.U./M.A.P.

Coniah (koh-ni′uh; Heb., "the LORD has appointed"), a shortened form of the name Jehoiachin used only in Jer. 22:24, 28; 37:1. The last king of Judah, Coniah (Jehoiachin) was the son of Jehoiakim and the grandson of Josiah. He began his reign as king in Judah about 598 BCE, about a year before the city fell to Babylon in 597, at which point he was deported to Babylon by Nebuchadnezzar. He is also called Jeconiah (Jer. 24:1; Matt. 1:11). *See also* Jehoiachin.

conquest era, a term sometimes applied in biblical studies to the period in which Israel is said to have invaded Canaan and subdued the peoples living there. The biblical accounts of conquest and settlement occur in Num. 13–14; 21:1–3, 21–32; 22–24; 32; Josh. 1–24; Judg. 1:1–2:5. These passages represent somewhat different understandings of what occurred during the thirteenth and twelfth centuries BCE, and the archaeological evidence is similarly diverse. Issues are basically twofold. To what extent was Israel's possession of the promised land sudden and decisive, and to what extent was possession accomplished through a unified effort of all the tribes or of individual tribal efforts? Although the answers to these questions are complicated, the dominant tradition preserved in the Bible is that a unified Israel led by Moses and then Joshua produced sweeping victories that gave Israel unquestioned possession of the land. *See also* Joshua; Joshua, book of; Moses.

K.H.R.

conscience, the English translation of *syneidēsis,* a word that, in classical Greek, referred to knowledge, especially the knowledge derived from reflection on one's past deeds. The appraisal of these deeds determined whether the conscience was "good" or "bad." This is primarily a NT concept: in the Hebrew Bible (where Israel's relationship to God is the focus of attention rather than personal self-reflection), the word "conscience" occurs only in 1 Sam. 25:3. Still, something similar to the concern for a "clear conscience" may be expressed by the desire for a "clean heart" (e.g., Ps. 51:10).

In the NT, the term occurs some thirty times, primarily in writings attributed to Paul (Romans; 1 and 2 Corinthians; the Pastoral Letters). It also occurs twice in Acts (23:1; 24:16, both times on the lips of Paul), five times in Hebrews (9:9, 14; 10:2, 22; 13:18), and three times in 1 Peter (2:19; 3:16, 21), but it is never found in the Gospels. In a few instances, the NRSV does not even use "conscience," because the apparent meaning of *syneidēsis* is something more akin to "consciousness" or "awareness" (Heb. 10:2; 1 Pet. 2:19). Elsewhere, however, the writers speak of a "good" or "bad" conscience (Acts 23:1; 24:16; 1 Tim. 1:5, 19; 3:9; 4:2; 2 Tim. 1:3; Titus 1:15; Heb. 10:22; 13:18; 1 Pet. 3:16, 21) or of "perfecting" or "purifying" the conscience (Heb. 9:9, 14).

Paul's use of the term is more difficult to characterize. In Rom. 2:15; 9:1 and 2 Cor. 1:12, he apparently uses it in the sense of one's knowledge of one's own thoughts, motives, and actions. In 2 Cor. 4:2 and 5:11, it appears to refer to one's judgments concerning the motives and actions of another. The exact meaning in Rom. 13:5 is unclear. Paul's understanding of the role of conscience is most fully expressed in his correspondence with the Corinthians concerning eating food offered to idols (1 Cor. 8–10). Here, he insists that conscience alone is an inadequate guide for Christian ethics. He admonishes believers to submit their consciences to a superior love ethic: their behavior is not to be defined in terms of what conscience allows, but in terms of what love requires. *See also* food offered to idols; heart; love; mind.   R.A.B.

conversion. In the NRSV, the Greek term *prosēlytos* ("convert") first occurs in Acts 13:43, which refers to "Jews and devout converts to Judaism" in a synagogue in Antioch of Pisidia. These "converts" are apparently Gentiles who have become Jews. The word is not used elsewhere in the NT, though it does appear in the LXX with reference to non-Israelites who lived among the Israelites and were expected to observe certain laws (e.g., Lev. 17:8, 10, 13). Later, in Acts 15:3, Paul and Barnabas report "the conversion of the Gentiles," i.e., the acceptance of the Christian gospel by non-Jewish people. The Greek word used here is *epistrophēn,* another term that does not occur elsewhere in the NT (cf. Sir. 18:21; *Pss. Sol.* 16:11) and one that has the basic meaning of changing the focus of one's attention. The NRSV also uses the noun "convert(s)" in Rom. 16:5 and 1 Cor. 16:15, instances where the Greek word (*aparchē*) means "first fruits"; thus, Paul regards those who responded to his preaching by becoming members of the church as the produce of seed that he has sown (see Rom. 1:13; 1 Cor. 3:6; cf. Mark 4:14, 20). Finally, 1 Tim. 3:6 says that a bishop must not be a recent convert (Gk. *neophyton,* from which comes the English word "neophyte"). Notably, the Bible never refers to the Damascus road experience of Paul as a "conversion" (Acts 9:1–19; 22:3–16; 26: 9–18); Paul himself regards it as an experience through which he was "called" by God to the new vocation of proclaiming Christ among Gentiles (Gal. 1:13–17; cf. 1 Cor. 9:1; 15:8). Paul continued to regard himself as a Jew (indeed, as "a Pharisee," Phil. 3:5) so it would not be accurate to construe his experience as a conversion in the sense of the total abandonment of one religious tradition for another. Nevertheless, many of his behaviors, perspectives, and core beliefs were transformed. *See also* Paul; repentance.   M.A.P.

convocation (Heb. *miqra'*, "declaration"), a calling together or a summons to meet. The term appears primarily in the phrase "holy convocation" and signifies the call to assembly at the sanctuary of the Israelite congregation on a holy day. The days decreed as "holy convocation" were the weekly sabbath (Lev. 23:3); the first and seventh days of Passover (Lev. 23:5–8; Num. 28:18–25); the Festival of Weeks (Lev. 23:21; Num. 28:26); the first day of the month Tishrei (Lev. 23:24; Num. 29:1); the Day of Atonement (Lev. 23:27; Num. 29:7); and the first and eighth days of the Festival of Tabernacles (Lev. 23:35–36; Num. 29:12–35). Characteristic of these days was the prohibition of work. The convocation was called by the blowing of special trumpets (Num. 10:2, 10). *See also* festivals, feasts, and fasts.   J.U.

copper, a malleable, metallic element of reddish brown color. The word "copper" (Lat. *cuprum*) derives from "Cyprus," the island renowned in antiquity for its copper industry. In the biblical lands, the discovery of a smelting complex, including remains of ore, slag, and crucibles, at the Chalcolithic site of Tell Abu Matar near Beer-sheba attests a sophisticated copper industry. In one of the more spectacular discoveries of the same period, a hoard of 416 copper objects from the "Cave of the Treasure" came to light in the Nahal Mishmar in the Judean desert. This find comprised a cache of chisels, axes, mace heads, wands or standards, and crowns, all apparently ritual objects. From the Early Bronze Age (3000–2000 BCE) there are copper daggers, pins, awls, axes, spearheads, and jewelry found at nearly every site. About 2000 BCE, the beginning of the Middle Bronze Age, bronze, an alloy of tin and copper, began to supersede copper in the production of metal objects. The area of the Kenites (Gen. 15:19; Num. 24:21; Judg. 1:16), i.e, the Wadi Arabah region south of the Dead Sea, was a principal copper mining area (Deut. 8:9; Job 28:1–5), as is evident from excavations at Fenan and Timna. No evidence, however, has been found thus far of "Solomon's copper mines" at Eziongeber (1 Kings 9:26–28). *See also* metals.   S.R.

 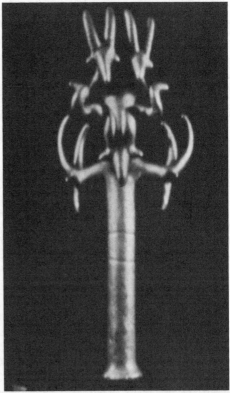

Copper jug with incised zigzag pattern and copper ibex scepter (*right*) from the fourth millennium BCE, found at the "Cave of the Treasure," attest to a sophisticated metallurgy industry.

cor, a measure of capacity. A cor comprised 35 to possibly 60 gallons, wet, or about 14 bushels, dry (Ezek. 45:14). *See also* weights and measures.

coral, saltwater submarine growth composed of the calcareous remains of anthozoan polyps. Pieces of coral were considered precious (Job 28:18). They were considered the epitome of the color red (Lam. 4:7) and were important trade goods (Ezek. 27:16). Found in both Mediterranean and Red Sea coastal waters, coral was a popular material for beads and various forms of jewelry. *See also* jewels, jewelry.

corban (kor'ban), the Hebrew word for an offering dedicated to God (Lev. 1:2; Num. 7:13); it was used of the Nazirites in reference to their lifestyle (Josephus *Antiquities* 4.73). In Mark 7:11–13, Jesus criticizes the notion that property declared to be "corban" did not have to be used in support of one's parents.

coriander (*Coriandrum sativum*), an herb whose leaves and aromatic seeds were used medicinally and for flavoring breads and other dishes. The round white seeds are likened to the manna found in the desert (Exod. 16:31; Num. 11:7).

Coriander.

Corinth

A MAJOR CITY OF ANTIQUITY, occupied at intervals since the fifth millennium BCE, Corinth (kor′inth) acquired its name from pre-Greek inhabitants. During Mycenaean times the area was subject to Argolid powers, but the city known in classical times was effectively founded by Dorian Greeks in about the tenth century BCE. Its first real historical figures seem to be the eighth-century Bacchiads, under whom Corinth established colonies in Corcyra (Corfu) and Syracuse in Sicily. Corinthian sea power was commercial as well as military at the time, and Proto-Corinthian pottery is found around the Mediterranean. Overthrowing the Bacchiads ca. 660 BCE, Kypselos and his son Periander (ca. 625–585 BCE; one of the Seven Sages of Antiquity) established a solid prosperity that flourished for more than a century. The biennial Isthmian games, founded ca. 580 BCE, brought additional prestige and revenues to the city.

After the Persian War, Corinth found itself increasingly squeezed by the expansion of Athens and, more often than not, on the side of Sparta in conflicts between the two major powers. Following the Macedonian victory at Chaironea in 338 BCE, the Synedrion (council) of Corinth ratified Philip II's rule of Greece and later that of his son Alexander. Corinth regained its independence as a member of the Achaean League after 224 BCE, but it was razed by Lucius Mummius's Roman legions in 146 BCE after his defeat of the league. Mummius slaughtered the men, sold the women and children into slavery, and left the city in ruins, a condition it remained in for a century.

The commercially strategic location of the site, however, with its virtually impregnable Acrocorinth (altitude 1,886 feet), begged for rehabitation, and in 44 BCE Julius Caesar established a colony of veterans there under the name Colonia Laus Julia Corinthiensis. It was this settlement, which by 27 BCE had already grown into the flourishing capital of the

The "street" connecting ancient Corinth with the port at Lechaion. In the background is the Acrocorinth.

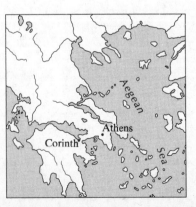

Corinth, located on the isthmus between mainland Greece and the Peloponnesus, had two ports for commerce passing between the Aegean and Adriatic seas.

Roman province of Achaia, that entered biblical history almost a century later with Paul's sojourn in the city.

Situated on the isthmus between the Greek mainland to the north and the Peloponnese to the south, Corinth effectively controlled traffic between the two. The port of Lechaion on the Gulf of Corinth, connected to the city by long walls by 400 BCE, opened to the Adriatic Sea to the west; Cenchreae, only seven miles away on the Saronic Gulf of the Aegean to the east, made of the area a major east–west maritime trade route as well. Periander's *diolkos*, a paved slipway roughly parallel to the modern canal, permitted smaller cargo ships to be carried across the isthmus on wheeled conveyances, thus avoiding the perilous journey around the Peloponnese; larger ships would have to offload their cargo and have it ferried across the isthmus via Corinth.

Having earned renown in Greek antiquity for its wealth and alleged licentiousness, Roman Corinth soon flourished in its own right, and by the time of Paul it was as cosmopolitan as any Mediterranean port. The official language was the Latin of the conquerors, but the common language was the Koine Greek of both the surrounding area and the merchants. The city was rebuilt with Roman institutions over the Greek ruins, the center dominated by upper and lower fora (marketplaces) and the archaic temple of Apollo. It was the relative newness of the city and of its immigrant, cosmopolitan urban working class that gave it both a commercial dynamism and an openness to newer ideas. The imperial cult seems to have been a principal religious institution alongside other temples to the Greek and Roman pantheon. As the largest central market and capital of Achaia, the intellectual and cultural heartland of Greece, Corinth had an immense cultural as well as economic influence on both the surrounding territories and the Greek-speaking provinces of the eastern part of the Roman Empire. Paul's establishment of Christianity there offered opportunities for diffusion of the gospel no other city could provide.

Jewish communities were well established in the Hellenistic world and throughout the Roman Empire by the first century CE, and, according to Acts 18:1–3, Paul encountered the Christians Aquila and Priscilla (Prisca) on his first visit to Corinth ca. 50 CE. Paul remained there, preaching in the synagogue, in spite of a suit brought against him by some Jews before

Part of a colonnade still stands in the agora at the ruins of Corinth.

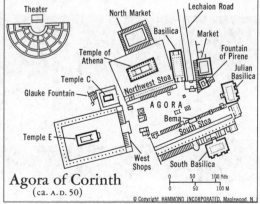

Agora of Corinth
(ca. A.D. 50)

© Copyright HAMMOND INCORPORATED, Maplewood, N.

The *bēma* at Corinth constructed ca. 44 CE. The Roman proconsul Gallio
may have tried Paul from this platform.

the proconsul Gallio, probably in the fall of 51 or the spring of 52 (Acts
18:16). Apollos also visited Corinth (Acts 18:27–19:1; 1 Cor. 1:12; 3:4–9;
4:6), possibly contributing to the factionalism and difficulties Paul addresses in 1 and 2 Corinthians. Paul's Letter to the Romans was probably
written from Corinth (Rom. 15:25–27; cf. Acts 20:3).

The ongoing excavations by the American School of Classical Studies at Athens have revealed much about first-century Corinth. It is clear
that the new Roman inhabitants were keen to absorb and adapt the Greek
legacy and prestige of the city; they carefully negotiated the new grid pattern around earlier landmarks like the archaic temple of Apollo and often
mimicked earlier architectural styles as at the Glauke Fountain. Temples,
buildings, and inscriptions dedicated or related to the imperial family
dominated the forum, which was flanked on the west by the so-called
Temple E built in honor of Augustus's sister Octavia and on the east by
the Julian Basilica.

Several finds are of relevance to the NT. One inscription near the theater
mentions the name of Erastus the aedile, an official in charge of public
works (possibly the "city treasurer" of Rom. 16:23; cf. 2 Tim. 4:20). In
the center of the forum was found a platform (Gk. *bēma*) constructed ca.

An inscription at Corinth (shown here in part) mentioning the name of Erastus,
who may have been the "city treasurer" mentioned in Rom. 16:23.

44 CE, possibly Gallio's "tribunal" at Paul's trial (Acts 18:12, 17). In the Lerna Asclepium and in other temples of the city can be seen the ruins of sacral dining halls that illuminate 1 Cor. 8 and 10. An early first-century Latin inscription refers to a *macellum,* and Paul uses the Greek *makellon* in speaking of the "meat market" (1 Cor. 10:25). A crude, Greek inscription on a broken lintel stone dating centuries after Paul seems to announce the "Synagogue of the Hebrews." Again, in the forum have been excavated rows of shops of the type Paul would have shared with his fellow tent-makers Aquila and Priscilla (Prisca). A contemporary villa gives a good understanding of the limitations on the size of "house-churches," perhaps explaining why factions arose in Corinth (several house-churches) and why there was discrimination in the communal meals of the general assembly (the dining room could only accommodate a select few, according to a Roman custom of ranking guests). ***See also*** Apollos; Aquila; Cenchreae; Corinthians, First Letter of Paul to the; Corinthians, Second Letter of Paul to the; Erastus; food offered to idols; Gallio; Paul; Prisca, Priscilla; tribunal.

Bibliography

Engels, Donald. *Roman Corinth: An Alternative Model for the Classical City.* University of Chicago Press, 1990.

Meeks, Wayne A. *The First Urban Christians: The Social World of the Apostle Paul.* Yale University Press, 1983.

Murphy-O'Connor, Jerome. *St. Paul's Corinth: Texts and Archaeology.* Michael Glazier, 1983.

Schowalter, Daniel, and Steven Friesen, eds. *Urban Religion in Roman Corinth.* Harvard University Press, 2005.   C.H.M.

Corinthians (kuh-rin'thee-uhnz), **First Letter of Paul to the,** one of two letters in the NT addressed to Corinth by the apostle Paul.

Contents: After a customary opening (1:1–3) and thanksgiving (1:4–9), Paul takes up a few matters that have been brought to his attention by some members of the church he calls "Chloe's people" (1:11). The first of these is that there are factions in the church, with different members claiming to follow various human leaders (1:10–4:21). After dealing with this problem at length, Paul touches briefly on three other matters: a man is living in a sexual relationship with his stepmother (5:1–13); members of the church are suing each other in secular courts (6:1–8); and some members evince a promiscuous philosophy of life that justifies visiting prostitutes and other immoral behavior (6:9–20). Paul turns next to questions that the Corinthians have asked him in a letter (7:1). First, he considers the question of whether sexual abstinence might not always be the best policy (even for married people), and he offers some extended teaching on marriage, divorce, and celibacy (7:1–40). Then he takes up the question of whether it is appropriate for Christians to eat food that was dedicated to idols, and this leads into a general discussion of Christian freedom and responsibility (8:1–11:1). Interposed into this latter discussion is a brief excursus in which Paul discusses his own rights as an apostle (9:1–14) and his decision to waive those rights (9:15–27). Finally, he turns his attention to several issues that have arisen with regard to Christian worship: the importance of head coverings for women (11:2–

16), proper conduct at the Lord's Supper (11:17–34), and the role of such spiritual gifts as prophecy and speaking in tongues (12:1–14:39). Embedded in the discussion of spiritual gifts is a poetic ode to love (13:1–13). Having addressed the questions presented to him, Paul continues to instruct the Corinthians regarding what he considers to be matters "of first importance" (15:3): the death, burial, and resurrection of Christ (15:1–58). Then he offers a few words about the collection he is taking for Jerusalem (16:1–4) and concludes the letter with comments on travel plans (16:5–12) and some final exhortations and greetings (16:13–24).

OUTLINE OF CONTENTS

1 Corinthians

V.P.F.

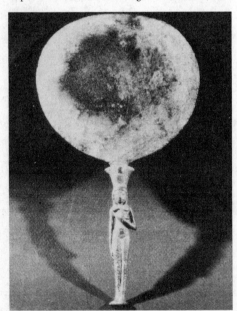

A bronze mirror of Egyptian origin found near Acco. The words of 1 Cor. 13:12, "For now we see in a mirror, dimly," may refer to the imperfect image reflected in the mirrors of polished metal of that time.

Historical Setting: The letter was written by Paul to a Christian church that he founded in the city of Corinth. It is apparently his second letter to that church; an earlier one is mentioned in 1 Cor. 5:9 (some scholars think that a portion of that earlier letter might be found in 2 Cor. 6:14–7:1). According to the book of Acts, Paul had first visited Corinth on his second missionary journey when Gallio was the proconsul there (18:1–17)—this would place his sojourn in the city somewhere between 50 and 53 CE. The congregation he founded was diverse both ethnically and socially; most of Paul's converts were Gentiles, but some, such as Crispus (1 Cor. 1:14; Acts 18:8) and Sosthenes (1 Cor. 1:1; cf. Acts 18:17), had been leaders of Jewish synagogues. Likewise, most of the Corinthian Christians seem to have come from the lower classes (1:26), but Gaius (1:14) had a house big enough to host gatherings of the church (cf. Rom. 16:23), and Erastus was the city treasurer (Rom. 16:23; 2 Tim. 4:20). Paul's correspondence with the church transpires about four years after its founding. He is now in Ephesus (16:8) on what Acts presents as his third missionary journey (18:23–21:15), and he has heard from the congregation in at least two different ways: a visit from some members he calls "Chloe's people" (1:11) and a letter that was probably delivered to him by three church members, Stephanas, Fortunatus, and Achaicus (16:15–18). From these sources, he has learned of a number of problems besetting the church: various groups are competing with one another for status, bolstering their claims by invoking the names of luminaries such as Paul, Apollos, and Cephas (1:11–12); a man in the congregation who is living incestuously with his stepmother has gone undisciplined (5:1–13); celebrations of the Lord's Supper are marred by some members (possibly the wealthy, who do not need to work until dark) consuming most of the available food and even becoming drunk before others arrive (11:17–34); some members need to be told that they should not go to prostitutes (6:15–20), while others apparently claim that celibacy should be practiced even by those who are married (7:1–7); some members claim it is wrong to eat meat that has been sacrificed to idols (8:1–13), which would probably include all meat sold in the Roman marketplace, since animals were typically butchered in homage to a god; some members pride themselves on possessing the spiritual gift of "speaking in tongues" and exercise this gift in ways that others consider disruptive (12:1–14:40). There also seems to have been some uncertainty about the collection of money that Paul had urged the Corinthians to take up for the Jerusalem church (16:1–4). Thus, the letter known as 1 Corinthians represents Paul's response to these and other issues raised by different members of the congregation; it is coauthored by Sosthenes (1:1), who might be the person from Corinth referred to in Acts 18:12–17.

Critical Problems: A few scholars have held that certain passages in 1 Corinthians ought to

be regarded as later, non-Pauline additions (e.g., 11:3–16; 13; 14:34–35). Others have questioned whether the letter as we have it might be a composite of two or more originally distinct Pauline letters: passages such as 6:12–20; 9:1–18; 10:1–22 or 10:1–23; and 11:2–34 are sometimes regarded as intrusive where they stand, and so are suspected of being parts of separate letters addressed by Paul to this church. Most scholars, however, do not find the alleged difficulties serious enough to warrant the kinds of partition hypotheses that are applied with more confidence to 2 Corinthians.

Major Themes: Even though practical issues seem to be uppermost in Paul's mind, interpreters discern broad theological convictions underscoring the way he deals with various issues. First, he believes that the cross of Christ refutes conventional evaluations of wisdom and power. Paul reminds his congregation that God's power and wisdom have been disclosed in the cross, which represents the laying aside of all claims to status (1:18–25; 2:1–5). Second, Paul insists that to belong to Christ is to be a member of the body of Christ, intrinsically connected to all other believers (12:12–27); the Corinthians belong to a believing community that has been formed in the Spirit (12:12–13; cf. 2:12) and that is continually being built up in God's love (chap. 13; cf. 8:1–3). Members of this community will consider all matters according to what is good for others and for the community as a whole. Finally, Paul emphasizes the significance of bodily resurrection (15:35–56), maintaining, against asceticism, that the body is God's good creation (since even the resurrected will have bodies) and also maintaining, against libertinism, that the body is to be respected as God's temple and used in ways that glorify God (6:19–20). *See also* Apollos; church; collection for the saints; Corinth; Corinthians, Second Letter of Paul to the; cross; food offered to idols; fornication; Lord's Supper; love; marriage; Paul; resurrection; spiritual gifts; tongues, speaking in; wisdom; worship in the New Testament.

Bibliography

Conzelmann, Hans. *1 Corinthians.* Fortress, 1975.

Fee, Gordon D. *The First Epistle to the Corinthians.* Eerdmans, 1987.

Furnish, Victor Paul. *The Theology of the First Letter to the Corinthians.* Cambridge University Press, 1999.

Thiselton, Anthony C. *The First Epistle to the Corinthians.* Eerdmans, 2000.   M.A.P.

Corinthians, Second Letter of Paul to the,

one of two letters in the NT addressed to Corinth by the apostle Paul. Some scholars believe it to be a composite of several letters sent to the church at different times and under different circumstances.

Contents: The letter begins with a typical opening (1:1–2) and prayer (1:3–7), to which Paul appends a brief report on how God delivered him and his companions from a terrible ordeal they faced in the Roman province of Asia (1:8–11). After this, he offers a somewhat defensive expla-

PAUL'S CORRESPONDENCE
WITH THE CORINTHIANS

First Visit: Paul founds the church (2 Cor. 1:19; Acts 18:1–18).

Letter One (referred to in 1 Cor. 5:9)

- 2 Cor 6:14–7:1 might be an excerpt from this letter. In its present context, this passage forms an odd interruption in Paul's train of thought; it also deals with the general topic Paul says he addressed in his first letter to the Corinthians (1 Cor 5:9).

Paul receives distressing reports of problems in Corinth via an oral report from Chloe's people (1 Cor. 1:11) and a written letter from the church (1 Cor. 7:1).

Letter Two (1 Corinthians)

Second Visit: a painful confrontation (2 Cor. 2:5; 7:12; 13:2)

Letter Three (referred to in 2 Cor. 2:3–4; 7:12)

- 2 Cor. 10–13 might be from this letter. These four chapters are laced with harsh rebukes and bitter sarcasm that seem out of place in what is otherwise a letter of reconciliation and renewed confidence; they are more characteristic of what we would expect to find in Letter Three, a difficult letter that Paul says he was sorry he had to write (2 Cor. 7:8).

Paul receives Titus's report of goodwill in Corinth (2 Cor. 7:6–7).

Letter Four (2 Corinthians—or *at least* 2 Cor. 1:1–6:13; 7:2–16)

Was there a **Letter Five** (on super-apostles)?

- Some scholars think 2 Cor. 10–13 are from a *fifth* letter Paul wrote to the Corinthians after things turned bad again.

Was there a **Letter Six** (on fund-raising)?

- Some scholars think that 2 Cor. 8–9, which deal with the collection Paul is taking for Jerusalem, should be regarded as an additional fund-raising letter Paul may have written to the church on that subject.

Was there a **Letter Seven** (also on fund-raising)?

- Some scholars think that only 2 Cor. 8 was a fund-raising letter addressed to Corinth (Letter Six) and that 2 Cor. 9 was a different fund-raising letter addressed to the province of Achaia (Letter Seven).

From Mark Allan Powell, *Introducing the New Testament* (courtesy, Baker Academic)

nation for his recent dealings with the Corinthian church, including his rationale for canceling a promised visit and for writing an unusually harsh letter instead (1:12–2:13). This leads to an extended commentary on what Paul considers to be the meaning and value of his ministry among the Corinthians (2:14–6:13). Paul discusses both the character and the content of that ministry, emphasizing what God has accomplished through him and his associates. Then he exhorts the Corinthians to avoid partnerships with unbelievers (6:14–7:1), insists that he has always had their best interests at heart (7:2–4), and returns at last to the subject of his recent relations with the community (7:5–16, picking up from 2:13): he rejoices that the difficult letter he sent did bring them to repentance and he affirms his newfound confidence in them. On a new note, Paul takes up the subject of the collection he is taking for Jerusalem, offering a number of incentives for his readers to contribute generously to this cause (8:1–9:15). Then the tone of the letter changes abruptly as he returns to a defense of his ministry, employing bitter sarcasm as he compares himself to a group of "super-apostles" (11:5; 12:11) who have maligned him in the Corinthian church (10:1–13:10). The letter ends with a few quick exhortations (13:11–12) and a final benediction (13:13).

Historical Setting: According to the book of Acts, Paul evangelized the city of Corinth with help from Timothy and Silas during his second missionary journey (18:1–17). Scholars place the founding of the church somewhere between 50 and 53 CE and believe that Paul's recorded correspondence comes from a time about four years later. The history of that correspondence is complex. First, Paul wrote a letter to the Corinthians that is referred to in 1 Cor. 5:9. Second, Paul received distressing news from the Corinthians via an oral report from "Chloe's people" (1 Cor. 1:11) and a letter sent to him from the church (1 Cor. 7:1). Third, Paul wrote the letter known to us as 1 Corinthians. Fourth, sometime after sending that letter (1 Corinthians), Paul visited the Corinthian church and had a painful confrontation with some members there (2 Cor. 2:5; 7:12; 13:2). Fifth, Paul wrote an angry letter (sometimes called the "Letter of Tears") to the church, a letter he says he regrets having sent (2 Cor. 2:3–4, 7). Sixth, Paul received a good report from Titus—the Corinthians had repented and wanted to repair their relationship with him. Finally, Paul wrote to the church again, and that letter (the one written in response to their desire for reconciliation) is to be equated either with the NT letter called "2 Corinthians" or at least with the main body of 2 Corinthians (at minimum 2 Cor. 1:1–6:13; 7:2–16).

Critical Problems: The primary critical issue raised with regard to 2 Corinthians is the question of whether the letter we possess was in fact one letter sent to the church after Paul received Titus's report of the Corinthians' goodwill or whether it is a composite letter containing a variety of notes, letters, and/or fragments of letters. Numerous versions of the "composite letter" theory have been proposed. Many scholars think that 2 Cor. 6:14–7:1 interrupts the letter in an intrusive way, so they speculate whether it might actually be a piece of the earliest letter Paul is known to have sent to this church (the one mentioned in 1 Cor. 5:9). Many scholars also think that 2 Cor. 10–13 exhibits a harsh and bitter tone that seems out of place for a letter intending to effect reconciliation; accordingly, they wonder whether these chapters of 2 Corinthians might actually come from the "Letter of Tears" that Paul says he wrote when he was angry with the church (2 Cor. 2:3–4; 7:12). Other scholars suggest 2 Cor. 10–13 could represent a letter Paul wrote at a later time when problems with the church had flared up anew. Finally, many scholars have suggested that 2 Cor. 8–9 have little connection with anything else in 2 Corinthians, and they wonder whether these chapters might represent a completely different "fund-raising letter" sent to the church at some point when Paul was taking up his collection for Jerusalem. A variation on this theory suggests that 2 Cor. 8–9 could comprise two similar fund-raising letters, one addressed to the city of Corinth (2 Cor. 8) and the other to the province of Achaia (2 Cor. 9). The assumption behind all of these proposals is that various notes and letters from Paul to Corinth were collected and copied onto a single scroll; in an effort to preserve everything the apostle had written to the church, diverse materials were combined in a way that would confuse later copyists and church leaders. There is, however, no unanimity among scholars on these points. Some hold to certain composite proposals while rejecting others, and others think it best to regard 2 Corinthians as a single, unified document, suggesting that its apparently haphazard character is due to the fact that Paul wrote it over a period of time, returning to the task at times when his mood or interests had changed.

Major Themes: A good deal of 2 Corinthians is devoted to Paul's defense of his ministry and to the related issue of apostolic authority. In the early part of the letter Paul emphasizes the integrity with which his ministry is carried out (7:2; cf. 2:17; 6:4–7), emphasizing that it is God who works through him (2:14, 17; 3:4–6; 4:1, 7; 5:2, 18, 20). Later, he contrasts himself with the so-called "super-apostles" (11:5; 12:11). He lays out the marks of a true apostle (12:12) and suggests an ironic basis of comparison that involves boasting of weakness, through which God's power becomes perfect (2 Cor. 11:30–33; 12:6–10). The important point seems to be not whether one can point to accomplishments or claim to have impressive qualifications or references (such as "letters of recommendation," 3:1), but whether the death and resurrection of Jesus Christ is evident in one's ministry (4:10–12). Thus, Paul lists the hardships he has experienced as an apostle (4:8–9; 6:4b–5; 11:23b–29; 12:10) not in order to boast of the strength with which he has endured them, but because they reveal him to be one who experiences death and resurrection. Finally, as

indicated above, 2 Cor. 8–9 deals at length with a fund-raising appeal on behalf of the poor in Jerusalem (cf. Acts 11:29–30; 24:17; Rom. 15:25–27; 1 Cor. 16:1–4; Gal. 2:10); Paul lays out principles of financial stewardship, including the suggestion that giving be voluntary (9:5) and proportionate to means (8:3, 11–13), and he articulates the notion that the opportunity to give away one's money should be viewed as a privilege or favor from God (8:1–2).

Bibliography

Furnish, Victor Paul. *II Corinthians*. Doubleday, 1984.

Harris, Murray J. *2 Corinthians*. Eerdmans, 2005.

OUTLINE OF CONTENTS

2 Corinthians

If 2 Corinthians is a composite of two or more originally separate letters, then its present structure is due to the work of some early editor. As it stands in its present form, however, it may be outlined as follows:

V.P.F.

Martin, Ralph P. *2 Corinthians*. Word, 1986.

Matera, Frank J. *II Corinthians: A Commentary*. Westminster John Knox, 2003.

Murphy-O'Connor, Jerome. *The Theology of the Second Letter to the Corinthians*. Cambridge University Press, 1991.

Thrall, Margaret E. *A Critical and Exegetical Commentary on the Second Epistle to the Corinthians*. 2 vols. Clark, 1994–2000.   M.A.P.

cormorant, any of about thirty species of birds that live near water and feed mainly on fish. It is listed among birds prohibited as food (Lev. 11:17; Deut. 14:17) for the Israelites. In Isa. 34:11 the kjv uses "cormorant" for a term the nrsv translates "hawk." The kjv also uses it for an uncertain reading in Zeph. 2:14 (nrsv: "desert owl").

corn, a term used generically in the kjv and neb for cereal crops in the Bible (nrsv: "grain"). *See also* grain.

Cornelius (kor-neel′yuhs), a Roman centurion stationed in Caesarea. The story of how he heard the gospel, was filled with the Holy Spirit, and baptized by Peter is told in Acts 10 and then retold, by Peter, in Acts 11:1–18. An additional allusion to him is made in Acts 15:5–7. The repetition of his story indicates its significance for Acts as a model for bringing Gentiles into the church. Before hearing Peter's message about Christ, Cornelius had been associated with the synagogue as a "God-fearer" (possibly a technical term for a Gentile who was a partial convert to the Jewish faith; the nrsv translates this poorly as "a God-fearing man"), and he was spoken well of by the Jews (10:22). He gave alms and dedicated himself to prayer. According to Acts, the fact that the Holy Spirit fell upon Cornelius and his colleagues (causing them to speak in tongues) while Peter was preaching about Christ served as divine attestation that Gentiles should be accepted into the Christian community on the same basis (i.e., faith) as Jews. *See also* Caesarea; Gentile; God-fearers; Peter; proselyte.   A.J.M.

cornerstone, most often the large stone placed in the foundation at the principal corner of a building, but occasionally (e.g., *Testament of Solomon* 22:7–23:4 [ca. 200 ce]) the top or final stone of a building. Most biblical occurrences of this term are metaphorical. Job 38:6 imagines God as creator laying a cornerstone upon which to "construct" the world. The cornerstone of Ps. 118:22 is either Israel or its king, rejected as "insignificant" by the nations, but exalted by God. In Isa. 28:16 God lays a cornerstone in Zion. This much debated image possibly refers to God's announcement of salvation or to the faith of the renewed Israel. In the nt, the Gospels present Jesus as quoting Ps. 118:22 in probable reference to himself (Matt. 21:42; Mark 12:10; Luke 20:17) and, elsewhere, both Ps. 118:22 and Isa. 28:16 are applied to Jesus as the Messiah (Acts 4:11; Rom. 9:33; Eph. 2:20; and 1 Pet. 2:4–8). The pas-

Cornerstone of an unfinished house from the time of the Israelite king Omri, ca. 876–869 bce.

sages from Romans and 1 Peter (also Luke 20:18?) allude as well to the "stone of stumbling" of Isa. 8:14.   R.A.W.

Cos (kohs), an island with a city of the same name in the Aegean Sea, southwest of Asia Minor, where Paul spent one night on his final journey to Jerusalem (Acts 21:1). Known for its ointment, purple dye, and excellent wine, it was a major shipping port. Under Ptolemaic rule in the third century bce, it developed an outstanding library. Several Ptolemaic princes were educated there. A cult of Asclepius as well as hot springs probably influenced Hippocrates, the father of medicine, to found a medical school on Cos. It was a Coan physician who convinced Claudius to grant Cos immunity from taxation. Because it was an important Jewish center (1 Macc. 15:23), Herod the Great gave large sums for building purposes. A dedicatory statue to his son has also been found there.   D.R.E.

cosmetics. Products for dressing the hair or beautifying the skin were used by men and women throughout the ancient Near East, although Egyptian paintings and objects illuminate this practice best. The Egyptians as well as other nations imported a variety of cosmetics, balms, gums, and myrrh from the Levant (Gen. 43:11; Ezek. 27:17). The most common cosmetics were kohl, henna, rouge, powder, ointments, and perfumes. Kohl was used to line the eyes in black, as is clearly illustrated in Egyptian paintings. It appears to have served as protection against light reflected from the bright sun as well as to beautify the eyes. In Israel, women who "painted their eyes" were not held in high regard (2 Kings 9:30; Jer. 4:30; Ezek. 23:40). Henna was used for dying the hair and also for painting the toenails and fingernails. Archaeological finds corroborate the importance of cosmetics in daily life: cosmetic palettes, kohl tubes and sticks, spoons, rods, rouge pots, hairpins, combs, cosmetic dishes, tweezers, ear picks, and mirrors have all been found. In the nt, 1 Pet.

3:3 instructs wives not to adorn themselves outwardly, but using cosmetics is not mentioned among the examples of outward adornment that are specifically cited (braiding hair, wearing gold ornaments or fine clothing). *See also* incense; jewels, jewelry; ointments and perfumes.   S.R.

couch. *See* bed.

council, the, a word used generically in the Bible to refer to various groups or meetings, but also employed in two more specific contexts.

1 The "divine council," a heavenly court at which God presides over "the gods" or "the holy ones," entities that are often equated with angels or other spiritual beings (Pss. 82:1; 89:7; cf. Jer. 23:18, 22).

2 In the NT, a high court among the Jews during the Second Temple period, also known as the Sanhedrin (Gk. *synedrion*). The NT occasionally uses the same expression for local councils of leaders and elders (Matt. 5:22; 10:17; Mark 13:9; Acts 22:5), but most often the reference is to the supreme court of chief priests and elders in Jerusalem that, according to the Synoptic Gospels, judged Jesus (Matt. 26:59; Mark 14:55; Luke 22:56) and, according to the book of Acts, examined and punished Jesus's early followers (4–6; 23–24). Joseph of Arimathea was said to be a member of the council (Mark 15:43; lit., a member of the *boulē*, but context suggests the council elsewhere called *synedrion* is meant).

The Gospels refer to the council without giving its precise composition and powers. In Mark the high priest, chief priests, elders, and scribes (14:54–55; 15:1) are explicitly associated with the council in Jesus's trial. In John the chief priests and Pharisees gather to discuss Jesus, but there is no mention of "the council" as such (11:47). In Acts the council that sits in judgment on the preaching of Peter and John (Acts 4) is composed of the high priest, the high-priestly family, rulers, elders, and scribes. Gamaliel, a Pharisee and "teacher of the law held in honor by all the people" is also a member of the council (5:34). According to Acts 23:6, both Pharisees and Sadducees sit on the council. In evaluating and disciplining Jesus, Peter, John, and Paul the council acts as a judicial court interpreting and guarding Jewish life, custom, and law. According to John 18:31, the Jews in Jerusalem were allowed to judge people according to their law, but they were not permitted to put anyone to death.

The historical precision (and accuracy) of the NT portrayal is questioned, and a variety of theories have been put forward regarding the actual composition and role of the council of Jewish leaders in Jerusalem. The three most prevalent suggestions are that (1) it was composed of political leaders, including some priests and aristocrats; (2) it was composed of religious leaders knowledgeable in the law, including priests, Pharisees, and scribes; and (3) there were two councils, one political and the other religious. All these theories

try to reconcile and harmonize a diverse body of data (including what is found in the NT and what is said in later, hard-to-date rabbinic sources). *See also* Gamaliel.

Bibliography

Mantel, Hugo. *Studies in the History of the Sanhedrin.* Harvard University Press, 1961.   A.J.S.

counselor, in the Bible, usually an adviser to a king, though other counselors are also mentioned: Zechariah, the son of Shelemiah (1 Chron. 26:14); Jonathan, David's uncle (27:32). David's court featured two advisers, but they are differentiated: Ahithophel was David's counselor and Hushai was his friend (1 Sam. 27:33; cf. 2 Sam. 15:12). To his ruin, King Ahaziah of Judah took as counselors his mother (Athaliah) and the "house of Ahab" (2 Chron. 22:3–4). Later, King Amaziah of Judah rebuked a prophet for trying to usurp the role of a royal counselor (2 Chron. 25:16). Other texts mention seven counselors of Artaxerxes (Ezra. 7:14; cf. 7:15, 28; 8:25) and counselors to King Nebuchadnezzar (Dan. 3:2, 3, 24, 27; 4:36; 6:7). Elsewhere, Prov. 11:14; 24:6 recommends "an abundance of counselors," while a psalmist recognizes that God's decrees are counselors (Ps. 119:24). God needs no counselor (Isa. 40:13) and is sometimes portrayed as one who removes counselors (Job 12:17; Isa. 3:3; cf. Isa. 41:28). Isa. 9:6 speaks of the birth of a child whose name is Wonderful Counselor, Mighty God, Everlasting Father, Prince of Peace.   M.A.P.

courage. The Bible contains numerous exhortations for people to "take courage" in a variety of contexts (1 Sam. 4:9; 2 Chron. 15:7; Pss. 21:14; 37:24; Isa. 41:6; Hag. 2:4; cf. 1 Chron. 22:13; 28:20; 2 Chron. 32:7). Examples of those who do this include the Israelites, in their fight against Benjamin (Judg. 20:22); David, in putting forth a daring prayer (2 Sam. 7:27); Asa, in putting away idols (2 Chron. 15:8); Jehoiada, in putting forward Joash as king (2 Chron. 23:1); Amaziah, in leading an army against Seir (2 Chron. 25:11); and Ezra, in bringing exiles in Babylon back to Jerusalem (Ezra 7:28). By contrast, the citizens of Jericho lose courage after they hear how God assists the Israelites (Josh. 2:11), Saul's son Ishbaal's courage fails when he hears Abner has died (2 Sam. 4:1), and the courage of those who go down to the sea in ships melts away when God raises stormy winds (Ps. 107:23–26). In the NT, Jesus tells his disciples, "In the world you will face persecution. But take courage, I have conquered the world" (John 16:33). Paul says he had courage in God to declare the gospel in spite of opposition (1 Thess. 2:2) and, in Acts, Paul inspires sailors to take courage in a storm (27:22–25; cf. 23:11).   M.A.P.

covenant (Heb. *berit*), a formal agreement or treaty between two parties in which each assumes some obligation. In the Bible, a covenant might be a pact of mutuality between two individuals, such as Laban and Jacob (Gen. 31:44–54) or David

Treaty between Esar-haddon of Assyria and Ramataia, a Medean vassal king (672 BCE). A typical suzerain-vassal treaty of the ancient Near East, it ends with a sequence of curses against treaty violators and has affinities with the Sinai covenant.

and Jonathan (1 Sam. 18:3; 23:18), or a covenant between a husband and wife (Ezek. 16:8; Mal. 2:14). More often, a covenant is between political entities or their representatives: Abraham and the Amorites (Gen. 14:13); Abraham and Abimelech, king of Gerar (Gen. 21:22–32); Abner and David (2 Sam. 3:12–13, 21); David and the people (2 Sam. 5:3); Solomon and Hiram (1 Kings 5:26); Asa and Ben-hadad (1 Kings 15:18–19). A covenant also might be imposed by a greater power upon a lesser one. The greater power demands loyalty and obligates itself to the protection of the lesser one, as was the case between Israel and the Gibeonites (Josh. 9). This is also what is reflected in the request by Jabesh-gilead of the king of Ammon (I Sam. 11:1–2). The vast majority of the references to covenant in the Bible, however, are to covenants between God and God's people, especially the covenant that God makes with Israel at Sinai.

The Sinai Covenant: The framework of the Sinai covenant has significant affinities with suzerain-vassal treaties from the ancient Near East, specifically, the Hittite treaties of the fourteenth and thirteenth centuries BCE and the Assyrian treaties of the seventh and sixth centuries BCE. In these documents a suzerain makes a treaty with a lesser king. The main elements of the Hittite treaty are: (1) identification of the treaty maker

(i.e., the great king); (2) historical introduction, listing prior beneficial acts done by the great power on behalf of the lesser one; (3) stipulations (the primary demand is for loyalty); (4) a list of divine witnesses; and (5) blessings and curses to come upon the lesser party as a consequence of keeping or not keeping the treaty. The treaty was recited, a ceremonial meal eaten, and the treaty deposited at the feet of the deity's iconic representation.

The narrative concerning the Sinai covenant in Exod. 19–24 has similar elements: the identification of God, who has performed saving acts for Israel (19:4–6; 20:2); stipulations (20:3–23:33); and treaty recital followed by a ceremonial meal (24:7, 9–11). The other elements appear elsewhere. Deposit of the treaty in the ark of the covenant is mentioned in Exod. 25:16; 40:21; Deut. 10:1–5; 31:25–26 (the ark elsewhere is called the footstool of God, Pss. 99:5; 132:7–8; 1 Chron. 28:2). Witnesses appear in the form of "heaven and earth" (Deut. 4:26; 30:19; 31:28). Blessings and curses are listed in Lev. 26 and Deut. 27:11–28:68 (cf. 29:17–27). This political structure emphasizes the seriousness of the relationship between God and Israel and ipso facto eliminates the possibility of foreign alliances (e.g., Isa. 31:1–3; Jer. 2:18, 36). The Sinai covenant obligates both parties to each other: Israel must keep the stipulations (familial, societal, dietary, ritual, agricultural, etc.) or suffer severe punishment. This, however, does not mean that it is a "conditional covenant"; indeed, the punishment that disobedience brings presumes that the relationship between the parties is still intact.

The judicial element of the Sinai covenant is manifested in the stipulations, which are the law of the nation. Now any crime committed is against God, whether it is ritual, criminal, moral, or civil. Israel was apparently unique in its perception that all its law is divinely given.

Another social element contained in the Sinai covenant is the familial one. The Israelites are called God's children in Deut. 14:1 (see also Exod. 4:22; 19:4; Deut. 32:9–12, 18). Furthermore, the stipulations and even the covenant itself are called *torah* (Deut. 31:25–26), which means "teaching" or "instruction." Within the context of the covenant it is equivalent to law, but if Proverbs (e.g., 3:1; 4:2; 7:2) uses *torah* in its original social context—as parent instructing child—then its usage in the covenant may suggest the analogy of God instructing Israel.

Covenants with Abraham and David: Two other primary divine covenants, those with Abraham (Gen. 15) and David (2 Sam. 7; Ps. 89:1–38), are more unilateral than the Sinai covenant: they speak of what God offers, but not of what God requires in return. Although these proclamations are called covenants, they actually have more in common with promissory royal grants, which also existed in the ancient Near East and which are attested in Hittite and Assyrian documents. According to such a grant, land was given to loyal servants by the king, and the grant required no further action on behalf of the grantee. Gen. 17:1–

14 does demand circumcision of Abraham and his descendants, but this is only a sign of the covenant, not a condition of its validity. The Davidic covenant assures David of a permanent dynasty in which the Davidic king is depicted metaphorically as the son of God (2 Sam. 7:14; Pss. 2:7–8; 89:27–28). Sometimes, however, the Davidic covenant is viewed as conditional and dependent on obedience to the Sinai covenant (1 Kings 2:4; 8:25; 9:4–9; Ps. 132:12). The prophets also tended to view the Sinai covenant as dominant, but they sometimes tried to maintain an ultimate validity of the Davidic covenant by recasting its promises in terms of messianic expectation.

New Covenant: Jer. 31:27–37 (building upon Hos. 2) predicts that God will establish a new covenant with Israel. The uniqueness of this covenant, however, will not lie in its content, which is presumed to be identical to the Sinai covenant (the Torah; 31:33), but in its form—it will be given internally. What the covenant requires will become natural behavior for each individual, so that obedience will be guaranteed (31:34). Thus, the covenant will become unbreakable, and its eternality will be assured (31:35–37; cf. 32:36–44).

In the NT: Influenced by the idea of a new covenant, NT authors saw the death and resurrection of Jesus as instituting such an arrangement (Mark 14:24; 1 Cor. 11:2; cf. 2 Cor. 3:6). Indeed, the coming of Jesus is conceived as providing a fulfillment of God's covenant with Abraham (cf. Luke 1:72–73; Acts 3:35) in that God's salvation is now being offered to all nations of the earth. Although Paul insists that the covenants God made with Israel are "irrevocable" (Rom. 11:27–29; cf. Rom. 9:4; Gal. 3:17), he also avers that "not all Israelites belong to Israel" (Rom. 9:6) and maintains that, with regard to the "old covenant," a veil lies over the minds of Jewish people who do not know Christ (2 Cor. 3:14–15). The most extensive covenant language in the NT is found in Hebrews, where the "new covenant" (8:8, 13; 9:15; 12:24) is also termed a "better covenant" (7:22; 8:6) and the "first covenant" is said to have been flawed (8:7). Indeed, Heb. 8:13 claims that "in speaking of a 'new covenant,' (God) has made the first one obsolete." *See also* Abraham; David; Sinai; Torah.

Bibliography

Hillers, Delbert R. *Covenant: The History of a Biblical Idea.* Johns Hopkins University Press, 1969.

Levenson, Jon D. *Sinai and Zion: An Entry into the Jewish Bible.* Harper & Row, 1987.

McCarthy, D. J. *Treaty and Covenant.* Pontifical Biblical Institute, 1963.   J.U.

covenant, new. *See* covenant; New Testament.

cow. *See* cattle.

crane, a bird of the *Gruidae* family of the *Gruiformes* order. A crane is a tall wading bird similar in appearance to a heron. Isa. 38:14 indicates its noisy character, although the Hebrew is uncertain. Jer. 8:7, similarly uncertain, focuses on its nesting habits.

creation, the act of God by which the universe came into being. The Bible's first account of creation is provided in Gen. 1:1–2:3 (or 2:4a). This text is generally attributed to a sixth-century BCE priestly author (designated by the siglum P), who wanted to challenge other versions of the origin of the cosmos depicted in poetic literature of the ancient Near East (especially the Ugaritic Baal epic and the Babylonian *Enuma Elish*). Instead of describing the world as coming into being as a result of divine combat and a struggle with willful primordial matter, the Gen. 1:1–2:3 account depicts a sole, sovereign master of the universe directing the work of creation by verbal command and a freely determined plan. God is shown making the world in six days and resting on the seventh (cf. Exod. 20:11).

On the first day God creates light and darkness, night and day; on the second, the firmament separating earthly and heavenly waters; on the third, dry land and vegetation; on the fourth, the heavenly luminaries of the sun for ruling the day and the moon for ruling the night; on the fifth, sea creatures and birds; and on the sixth, land creatures and humans. The first three days present frameworks of the cosmos, the last three, their respective inhabitants. God names the works of the first three days; humans presumably name the rest (cf. 2:19–20).

A second, probably older, creation story is found in Gen. 2:4–25 (the first half of the Adam and Eve narrative). The order of creation is here reversed: man appears first (2:7), and plants and

The creation story as depicted in a thirteenth-century mosaic from the dome of St. Mark's Basilica, Venice. The inner circle portrays the creation of light and dark; the next, that of the seas, plants, animals, and Adam; the outer circle (partial view) shows the expulsion from Eden.

animals later (19–20). The woman is created separately (2:22), instead of simultaneously with the man (cf. 1:26–27). The role of humanity in God's creation is also depicted differently. In 2:15–17, the emphasis is on the man being a servant who tills and keeps God's garden, while in 1:26–28, the emphasis is on sovereignty, as humans are to have dominion over all other creatures (cf. Ps. 8:5–9).

God's role as Creator is often mentioned in the Bible, especially in Psalms and Isaiah (e.g., Pss. 8:3–8; 24:1–2; 100:3; 104:24; 143:3 148:5; Isa. 40:28; 42:5; 45:12, 18; cf. Gen. 14:19, 22; Job 4:17; Eccles. 12:1; Amos 4:13; Eph. 3:9; 1 Tim. 4:3–4; 1 Pet. 4:19). In the NT, Paul describes idol worshipers as people who serve "the creature rather than the Creator" (Rom. 1:25). Some NT writers maintain that all things were created through or by Jesus Christ (Col. 1:15–16; cf. John 1:2–3; Heb. 1:2). There is also mention in the Bible of future creation, when God will make new heavens and a new earth (Isa. 65:17); Paul maintains that the new creation has already occurred for one who is in Christ (2 Cor. 5:17; cf. Gal. 6:15). *See also* Genesis, book of; sky.   J.W.R./M.A.P.

creatures, animate beings, whose existence is dependent upon God (Gen. 1:20–24; Ps. 104:24; Rev. 5:13). In the Bible, the term "creatures" usually refers to animals commonly found on the earth, wild or domestic beasts plus, sometimes, birds and/or fish. Occasionally, prophets have visions of fantastic, hybrid creatures unlike anything known on earth (Ezek. 1:5–24; Rev. 4:6–9). Paul describes idol worshipers as people who serve "the creature rather than the Creator" (Rom. 1:25). *See also* creation; life; soul.

creeping things, a general term for various forms of reptile, insect, or worm life. Gen. 1:24–26 uses it as a generic term. It is similarly used in the flood story (Gen. 6:7, 20; 7:14, 23; 8:17, 19). Such creatures are considered unclean (Lev. 22:5), but they join in praise of God (Ps. 148:10). They are associated with corruption and evil (Ezek. 8:10) and express awe at God's wrath (38:20), but they will participate in God's promised covenant (Hos. 2:18). "Creeping things" appears to be a general term for creatures that are neither birds, fish, nor wild or domesticated animals.   R.S.B.

Crescens (kres'uhnz), a person who, when 2 Timothy was written, had left the writer for Galatia (2 Tim. 4:10). Nothing more is known about him.

Crete (kreet), also called Caphtor, the fifth largest Mediterranean island, 152 miles long from west to east, 7.5 to 35 miles wide and 3,189 square miles in area. Crete forms the southern boundary of the Aegean Sea. While maintaining a resolute identity and culture of its own, its primary relationship has been with Greece, rather than with Anatolia, Egypt, or the Levant. Biblical references to Caphtor or Crete are few. The Israelites, who

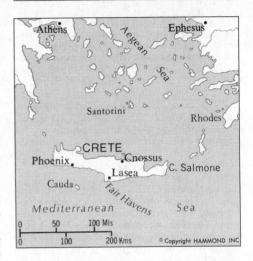

played no active role at all on the Mediterranean Sea, knew the remote island chiefly as the home of the Philistines (Deut. 2:23; Jer. 47:4; Amos 9:7; see also Gen. 10:14; 1 Chron. 1:12), part of the great movement of the Sea Peoples. Among these Philistine immigrants were the Cherethites and Pelethites, who formed an important part of David's army (2 Sam. 8:18; 15:18; 20:23). The island is also mentioned in 1 Macc. 10:67, where it is called Crete, not Caphtor. Crete is mentioned five times in Acts 27, as a boat carrying Paul to Jerusalem navigates around the island but does not land there. The Letter to Titus speaks of a visit to Crete by Paul, who is said to have left Titus in Crete "to put in order what remained to be done" and "appoint elders" (1:5). This letter's derogatory quotation about the Cretans being "always liars, vicious brutes, lazy gluttons" (1:12) comes from the same poem of the Cretan poet Epimenides as that quoted by Paul at Athens in Acts 17:28. *See also* Fair Havens; Pelethites; Philistines.   D.B.

crib. *See* manger.

crime and punishment. *See* law.

Crispus (kris'puhs), according to Acts 18:8, the ruler of a synagogue in Corinth who became a Christian. He was baptized by Paul (1 Cor. 1:14), and his inclusion in the Corinthian church indicates that that congregation was not entirely Gentile. *See also* synagogue.

cross (Gk. *stauros*), an ancient instrument of torture and execution. The use of an upright stake (also *stauros*) to display a corpse or to torture or execute a person was widespread in the first millennium BCE, especially in times of war. The Hebrew Bible does not mention the stake or cross as a mode of execution, but it does refer to the practice of displaying the corpse of an executed person "on a tree" to signify that such a person was accursed by God in Deut. 21:22–23. This text is applied in several of the Dead Sea Scrolls to the act of crucifixion, and Paul also makes that connection in Gal. 3:13.

In the NT, references to "the cross" function primarily as a shorthand way of referring to the death of Jesus and its consequences. Paul says that the "message about the cross" is foolishness to those who are perishing, but the power of God to those who are being saved (1 Cor. 1:18). This message consists of various theological claims. Paul says that by the cross of Jesus Christ, the world has been crucified to him and he to the world (Gal. 6:14). Eph. 2:16 says that God makes peace through the cross, reconciling Jews and Gentiles in one body and putting to death hostility between them. Col. 1:20 indicates that God made peace with all creation through "the blood of (the) cross," so that all things in heaven and on earth have now been reconciled with God. Col. 2:13–14 maintains that God's record of human transgressions of legal demands was nailed to the cross and that the record is now erased and transgressions forgiven. 1 Pet. 2:24 states simply that Christ "bore our sins in his body on the cross." Although some of these claims assume complex theological constructions, they all imply the basic notion that Christ's death on a cross was part of a divine plan intended to bring salvation (variously construed as forgiveness of sins, redemption, reconciliation, or atonement) to humanity (or all creation).

Thus, "the cross" can become a virtual synonym for "the gospel," or the core message of Christian proclamation. People can be persecuted for the cross of Christ (Gal. 6:12) or live as enemies of the cross of Christ (Phil. 3:18). In the latter instances, however, the term assumes an understanding of the gospel that emphasizes a connection with God through grace (as manifested on behalf of humanity through Christ's death) rather than through observance of works of the law. That distinction also informs Paul's refusal to remove the "offense of the cross" (Gal. 5:11) and his insistence that the cross is an ironic source of boasting (6:14), around which he developed a rich theology. The potential offense is not just that "Jesus died a shameful death," but that the consequences of that death relativize the significance of all human endeavors (including, especially, observance of the law). In the same vein, boasting of the cross, for Paul, implies total reliance on what God has done through the death of Jesus rather than reliance on one's own faithfulness in being obedient to the law.

The cross likewise becomes the ultimate symbol of God's love (Rom. 5:8) and, at the same time, the ultimate symbol of Christ's obedience (Phil. 2:8; Heb. 12:2). As such, it becomes a model for Christian existence, which is to be characterized by unselfish concern for others (Phil. 3:18). In the Synoptic Gospels, following Jesus involves "taking up one's cross" through self-denial and service to others (Matt. 10:38; Mark 8:34; Luke 9:23). John's Gospel, on the other hand, uses double entendre to link the raising of Jesus on the cross with his resurrection and exaltation (12:32). *See also* atonement; crucifixion; forgiveness; reconciliation; redemption; salvation. M.A.P.

crown, a headpiece signifying position or honor. The high priest is said to have worn a crown (Exod. 29:6; 39:30; Lev. 8:9; cf. Exod. 28:36–38). Among kings, both Saul (2 Sam. 1:10) and Joash (2 Kings 11:12) are specifically said to have worn crowns, and when David conquered the Ammonite capital Rabbah, he put the Ammonite king's crown on his own head (2 Sam. 12:30). Queen Esther and Mordecai both wore crowns given them by the Persian king (Esther 2:17; 6:8; 8:15). The Hebrew text employs different terms for these crowns, though whatever distinctive meaning might have been implied by each particular term is not evident. The most general Hebrew word for crown (*'atarah*) is found frequently in poetic contexts. Another term (*nezer*) tends to have priestly associations, but this is not always the case and, indeed, royal and priestly authorities were often closely linked (cf. Zech. 6:11–14). A third term (*keter*) appears only in Esther. In the NT the Greek word *diadēma* is used only three times, all in Revelation: the dragon has seven crowns (12:3); the beast from the sea has ten (13:1) and Christ is crowned with many crowns (19:11–13). The more common Greek word in the NT is *stephanos*, which often applies to a wreath or laurel, such as would be bestowed upon a victor in an athletic competition. This is probably the intended sense when it is used to symbolize the final reward of faithful Christians (e.g., 2 Tim. 4:8; James 1:12; 1 Pet. 5:4; Rev. 2:10). Paul twice says that the people to whom he is writing are his "crown" (Phil. 4:1; 1 Thess. 2:19); in these instances the word is used figuratively to mean something similar to the modern expression "badge of honor." Finally, the word is used in the Gospels for the "crown of thorns" placed on Jesus's head (Matt. 27:29; Mark 15:17; John 19:2, 5) and, in this context, it seems intended to invoke ironic images of a royal crown worn by a king.

C.L.M./M.A.P.

Crosses: (*left to right, top*) Greek; St. Andrew's; St. Anthony's; (*bottom*) Latin; Celtic; Slavic or Russian.

crucible, a vessel, usually ceramic, employed for heating substances to high temperatures. It was used mainly for the refining of silver (Prov. 17:3; 27:21). It also designates the bottom of a small furnace where a bloom of metal gathers in the refining process. *See also* refining; silver; smith.

crucifixion, a means of execution that involved fastening a person to a cross so death would be slow and painful. Grisly spectacles involving the crucifixion of sometimes hundreds or even thousands of victims were arranged for the intimidation of besieged cities, the punishment of conquered peoples, or the deterrence of rebellious slaves or troops.

In a rare instance, crucifixion was employed by the Jewish ruler Alexander Jannaeus, a Hasmonean king and high priest (103–76 BCE) noted for his brutality: in a single day, he crucified eight hundred Pharisees who had rebelled against him. Crucifixion is most closely associated, however, with the period of Roman rule. Though the Romans continued the wartime use of mass crucifixions, they also used it as a form of punishment for individuals accused of heinous crimes (e.g., high treason and violent robbery) and for certain classes of people, especially peasants or slaves (cf. the "bandits" crucified with Jesus, Mark 5:27, as well as Jesus himself).

The procedure was subject to wide variation. The upright stake continued to be used, but frequently a crossbar was added across the top of the stake forming a T (later known as the tau cross or St. Anthony's cross). Condemned persons were nailed or tied to the stake or crossbar, sometimes upside down, sometimes with other sadistic touches added at the executioner's whim. Several features became fairly standard. The victim was often flogged and then paraded to the site of execution wearing around the neck a wooden placard proclaiming the crime. The condemned person also carried the crossbar (not the whole cross) to the place of execution, where the upright stake was already in place. Because deterrence was the primary objective, the cross was always erected in a public place. The prisoner was stripped and affixed to the crossbar with nails through the forearms or with ropes. The crossbar was then raised and attached to the upright stake and the victim's feet were tied or nailed to the stake. The weight of the hanging body made breathing difficult, and death came from gradual asphyxiation, usually after a few hours. To prolong the death and thus increase the agony, a small wooden block was sometimes attached to the stake beneath the buttocks or feet to provide some support for the body. Then death came only after several days and resulted from the cumulative impact of thirst, hunger, exhaustion, exposure, and the traumatic effects of the scourging. After death, the body was usually left hanging on the cross. Because of the protracted suffering and the utter degradation of this manner of execution, it was viewed by the Romans as the supreme penalty, the "most wretched of deaths" (Josephus).

Though thousands of persons were put to death in this way, the remains of only one crucified individual have been found, those of a young male Jew named Yehohanan who died in the first century CE and was buried northeast of Jerusalem in an area called Giv'at ha-Mivtar. The physical evidence from his skeleton is scanty—one heel bone penetrated by a nail and bones that show no stress to the hands or forearms, suggesting that in this case the victim's arms were tied to the crossbeam with ropes.

The Crucifixion of Jesus: Jesus's crucifixion is described in Matt. 27, Mark 15, Luke 23, and John 19. According to these accounts, it was decreed by the Roman prefect (Pilate), who alone had the authority to order this form of execution. The wording on the placard ("The King of the Jews") indicates that the crime for which Jesus was condemned was not blasphemy (cf. Matt. 26:65; Mark 14:64), but a political crime of treason, identifying him as one who was perceived as posing a threat to Caesar's sovereignty. Jesus was flogged and led away to a place outside the city called Golgotha, an Aramaic word meaning "Skull." According to the Synoptic Gospels, a bystander named Simon from the North African city of Cyrene was compelled to carry his cross. Two of the Gospels suggest the use of nails through the hands (Luke 24:39; John 20:25), though it was normally the forearms, with their larger bones, that were impaled in order to support the body. According to Mark 15:23, Jesus was offered an opiate (myrrh) to dull the pain, but he rejected it. Death came rather quickly, after only six hours. According to the Gospels, his body was not left on the cross; a disciple, Joseph of Arimathea, appealed to Pilate for permission to remove the body, in accordance with the injunction of Deut. 21:23.

In Theology: When Christians hailed as Messiah and worshiped as Lord one who died on a Roman cross, a central theological problem was posed. How could such status be accorded to one who died a shameful death, condemned as a criminal according to Roman law and cursed by God according to Jewish law (Deut. 21:23)? Paul's Letters reveal how foolish and scandalous this seemed to both Jews and Gentiles (1 Cor. 1:23). *See also* cross; Golgotha; Jesus Christ; Pilate, Pontius; trial of Jesus.

Bibliography

Cousar, Charles B. *A Theology of the Cross.* Fortress, 1990.

Hengel, Martin. *Crucifixion.* Fortress, 1977.

Reed, Jonathan L. *The HarperCollins Visual Guide to the New Testament.* HarperOne, 2007.

Shanks, Hershel. "New Analysis of the Crucified Man." *Biblical Archaeology Review* 11 (1985): 20–21.   J.M.B.

crystal, a form of mineral with flat, symmetrical surfaces. The Greek word can mean ice or rock crystal, namely, pure silica or quartz in a transparent and colorless form (Rev. 4:6; 22:1; cf. Job 28:17; Ezek 1:22).

cubit (kyoo' bit), the standard ancient Near Eastern linear measure. Theoretically it was the distance from the elbow to the tip of the middle finger, about 17.5 to 20 inches. *See also* weights and measures.

cucumber (*Cucumis sativus*), a water-filled vegetable, growing on a vine, that was commonly cultivated in Egypt (Num. 11:5) and throughout the ancient Near East as a staple of the diet. During the growing season, in order to discourage theft, cucumber fields were guarded (Isa. 1:8).

cummin (kuh'min; *Cuminum cyminum*), a cultivated herb whose tiny aromatic seeds were harvested by beating the stalks with a rod (Isa. 28:25, 27). It was used medicinally, as a perfume oil, and as a seasoning for stews and breads. Paying a tithe on cummin symbolizes scrupulous attention to details of the law (Matt. 23:23).

cuneiform writing, a form of written communication done in wedge-shaped marks usually impressed on clay tablets. A massive body of writings in cuneiform script has been unearthed during the past hundred and sixty years. Most of these texts come from Mesopotamia and are written in the Sumerian and Akkadian languages. Writing was first invented in Mesopotamia. The cuneiform ideographic script was devised in the late fourth millennium BCE in order to facilitate the administration of the large economic complexes that the southern Mesopotamian Sumerian temples had become. The formation of the earliest "cuneiform" signs drew upon the system of tokens and upon representation in glyptic art. Originally the script was largely pictographic/ideographic. In-

creasingly, it developed a phonetic dimension, and in addition to representing concepts it could now also represent sounds. Moreover, elements began to be written in the order in which they occurred in speech. Even with phonetization, Mesopotamian cuneiform writing never surrendered its ideographic (some prefer logographic) quality and remained a mixed logographic-syllabic system of linguistic representation.

The Earliest Texts: The earliest texts were administrative accounts and sign lists for scribes. With increased phonetization, the script began to convey complex statements in Sumerian as well as words in a foreign language, namely, Akkadian. Narrations and utterances were now recorded, though initially writing served as an aid to memory rather than a full record. Alongside administrative and lexical texts, votive inscriptions, narratives, incantations, hymns, myths, and proverbial instructions appeared. Accordingly, a distinction may be drawn between two types of texts: those that have no existence except in writing and require writing as their medium (these come into existence alongside and consequent to the invention of writing, e.g., administrative accounts, lexical lists, collections of omens) and texts that exist independently of writing and are set down as the cultural importance of writing is discovered (e.g., epics, incantations, hymns). The recording of this latter type becomes fuller and more explicit in the course of time, and new texts of this type may eventually be composed originally in writing.

With the development of phonetization came the adaptation of the script by Semitic speakers for the representation of Akkadian. The system of writing was eventually adopted and adapted for the rendering of Elamite, Hurrian, Urartian,

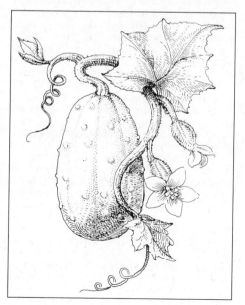

Cucumber.

Cummin.

A ORIGINAL PICTOGRAPH	B PICTOGRAPH IN POSITION OF LATER CUNEIFORM	C EARLY BABYLONIAN	D ASSYRIAN	E ORIGINAL OR DERIVED MEANING
1				BIRD
2				FISH
3				DONKEY
4				OX
5				SUN / DAY
6				GRAIN
7				ORCHARD
8				TO PLOW / TO TILL
9				BOOMERANG / TO THROW / TO THROW DOWN
10				TO STAND / TO GO

Diagram showing pictorial origin of ten early Babylonian and Assyrian cuneiform signs.

Hittite, and others. The Mesopotamian writing system was not borrowed in a vacuum: those who borrowed the writing were themselves influenced by the literary forms and, in turn, became bearers of the culture. In this manner, Mesopotamia influenced biblical literature and Greek mythology, and cuneiform became the point of origin and model for a developed Near Eastern legal tradition.

Writings in Sumerian and Akkadian: The balance of this article focuses on Mesopotamian writings in Sumerian and Akkadian. The classification of texts according to whether they are canonical, archival, or monumental provides a convenient arrangement for purposes of schematic presentation.

Canonical texts include those literary, religious, technical, and scholastic texts that were copied, transmitted, revised, and edited in ancient institutions and private collections. One such institutional collection was the famous library of Ashurbanipal. The discovery of this collection in Nineveh in the mid-nineteenth century served as the starting point for the recovery and reconstruction of Akkadian literature. Although Sumerian texts were also found in the library, it was the discarded remains of the Old Babylonian schools of Nippur that served as the basis for the reconstruction of Sumerian literature. Canonical literature is normally sorted into four major temporal clusters: Sumerian texts from the third

millennium (Fara, Abu-Salabikh, etc.); Sumerian texts from the Ur III and Old Babylonian periods (Nippur, Ur); Akkadian texts from the Old Babylonian period (e.g., *Gilgamesh, Atrahasis, Anzu*); and standard Babylonian Akkadian texts from the end of the second and the first millennium. Prior to ca. 1250 BCE in the post–Old Babylonian period, canonical texts are found mainly outside of Mesopotamia (e.g., Amarna, Ugarit, Boghazkoi). It is often assumed that almost all major works of Akkadian literature were composed and standardized by the latter half of the second millennium, and that the first millennium was relatively impoverished with regard to the creation of traditional religious literature. A more reasoned judgment seems to be that Mesopotamia of the first millennium also was religiously and literarily creative, certainly far more creative than is normally assumed, and that some classics were actually composed during the several centuries prior to their attestation in the libraries and collections of Assyria and Babylonia of the eighth century BCE and later. By the same token, the oft-repeated statement that the religious poetry of the post–Old Babylonian period is characterized in the main by stock phrases combined to create stereotyped forms is to be modified and perhaps disregarded. Given the small number of workers in the field, the pressing need to sort and decipher tablets, to edit texts, and to prepare dictionaries and grammars has resulted in interpretation taking a back seat. Thus, many literary texts still require detailed study and further investigation concerning the creative and editorial activities of literati and theologians in the centers of ancient Babylonia and Assyria.

Key Akkadian texts include the creation epic *Enuma Elish,* the *Epic of Gilgamesh,* prayers of individual suppliants, sequences of incantations and their accompanying rituals, wisdom compositions, and the humorous tale "Poor Man of Nippur." Of no little interest also are the scholarly collections of medical prescriptions, omens, and lexical equations. In these scribal handbooks, both the individual entries and the pattern or arrangement of units merit attention.

The masses of archival texts and numerous monumental texts allow for the study of government administration, international diplomacy, economic enterprises, military organization, and the like. Scholars are not always able to integrate or even harmonize the contemporary evidence of these texts with the information embedded in the traditional canonical literature. Here readers of the Bible may be particularly drawn to examine such diverse bodies of texts as the Akkadian Amarna letters written to Egypt from Canaan in the fourteenth century BCE, collections of laws such as the code of Hammurabi, and Neo-Assyrian and Neo-Babylonian royal inscriptions and historiography. Particularly during these last mentioned periods (from 750 BCE on) there was direct contact between Israelites and Assyrians/Babylonians, and during these periods Mesopotamian literary forms and intellectual life began to have a profound impact on the Bible and Israelite religion.

Bibliography

Cooper, J. C. "Babylonian Beginnings: The Origin of the Cuneiform Writing System in Comparative Perspective," in *The First Writing: Script Invention as History and Process.* Cambridge University Press, 2004. Pp. 71–99.

Foster, B. F. *Before the Muses: An Anthology of Akkadian Literature.* 3rd ed. CDL Press, 2005.

Hallo, W. W., and W. K. Simpson. *The Ancient Near East: A History.* 2nd ed. Harcourt Brace Jovanovich, 1998. Pp. 150–69, 176–81.

Hallo, W. W., and K. L. Younger Jr., eds. *The Context of Scripture: Canonical Compositions, Monumental Inscriptions, and Archival Documents from the Biblical World.* 3 vols. Brill, 1997–2003.

Jakobsen, T. *The Harps That Once . . . : Sumerian Poetry in Translation.* Yale University Press, 1987.

Oppenheim, A. Leo. *Ancient Mesopotamia.* University of Chicago Press, 1977. Pp. 228–87.

Rubio, G. "Sumerian Literature," in *From an Antique Land: An Introduction to Ancient Near Eastern Literature.* Rowman & Littlefield, 2009. Pp. 11–75.   I.T.A.

cup. Cups were usually made of pottery, but were sometimes fashioned of precious metal (Gen. 44:1–34; Jer. 51:7; Rev. 17:4; cf. the cuplike oil holder of the temple lamp, Exod. 25:31–35). They are usually associated with meals (2 Sam. 12:3; Pss. 16:5; 23:5) and are especially connected with drinking wine (Gen. 44:5; Prov. 23:31; Amos 6:6; Matt. 26:7). The term is frequently used metaphorically to refer to the limited and fixed amount of what God allows one to have in life. The wicked's cup may consist of "a scorching wind" (Ps. 11:6); cf. "cup of wrath" (Isa. 51:17) and "cup of staggering or reeling" (Isa. 51:22; cf. Zech. 12:2). A worshiper may give thanks for an overflowing cup (i.e., a life of abundance, Ps. 23:5) or for a cup of salvation (Ps. 111:13) or a cup of consolation (Jer. 16:7). The cup, then, may symbolize a person's lot or fate (Jer. 49:12; Ezek. 23:31–33; Mark 10:38–39; 14:36). At a final meal with his disciples, Jesus identified the cup of wine that they drank with his blood, which in Matthew's Gospel he further identified as "the blood of the covenant, poured out for many for the forgiveness of sins" (26:27–28; cf. Mark 14:23–24; Luke 20:22; 1 Cor. 11: 25). Paul surmised from this that the Corinthians should examine themselves before drinking the cup, since to do so in an unworthy manner would bring judgment upon themselves (1 Cor. 11:27–30).   B.J.M./M.A.P.

cupbearer, a member of a royal court whose full duties are unknown. The first servant of Pharaoh imprisoned with Joseph had apparently been Pharaoh's cupbearer (Gen. 40:11): the description there ("Pharaoh's cup was in my hand") suggests that a cupbearer literally had responsibility for providing food and drink to those in his care.

Nehemiah served as cupbearer to the Persian king Artaxerxes before being granted leave to assist the returning exiles (Neh. 1:11; 2:1). Ahikar was "chief cupbearer" (implying that there might be minor, assistant cupbearers) to King Sennacherib of Assyria (Tob. 1:22). *See also* Ezra and Nehemiah, books of; Joseph.

curse, a pronouncement for harm. Whereas the Hebrew Bible uses only one word for "bless," it employs three different words for "curse." The first (*'alah*) is associated with invoking an oath (Judg. 17:2; Neh. 10:29; also Ps. 10:7, where the context implies false oaths): persons basically request that ill come to them if they fail to carry out what they promise. A second, much more common, term (*'arar*) creates a ban or barrier intended to exclude someone from benefits or to qualify someone for misfortune; pronouncing someone "cursed" in this sense is roughly equivalent to "casting a spell." This is the word employed when God curses both the snake and the land in Gen. 3:14, 17. Cain is likewise cursed by God in Gen. 4:11 and the "angel of the LORD" declares Meroz to be cursed in Judg. 5:23. Noah curses his son Canaan in Gen. 9:25, and Saul pronounces a curse on anyone who eats food before he can be avenged (1 Sam. 14:24, 28). This is also the word used repeatedly in Deut. 27:15–26; 28:16–19, where curses are stipulated for those who fail to keep God's covenant (but *qillel* [see below] is used in Deut. 11:26, 28; Jos. 8:34). The word *'arar* is also used with regard to the "water of bitterness" test to be applied to a woman suspected of adultery in Num. 5:23–27, and it is used throughout the Balaam story in Num. 22–24 (where Balaam is asked to curse Israel, but repeatedly blesses Israel instead). Finally, a third term (*qillel*) describes a wide range of injurious activity, from verbal abuse to material harm. Its basic meaning is "to treat lightly," i.e., to treat with disrespect, to repudiate, to abuse. This word is used, for example, when the law states "whoever curses father or mother shall be put to death" (Exod. 21:17; Lev. 20:9). One who curses God in this sense (Lev. 24:11, 15; cf. Exod. 22:28, where NRSV has "revile") shows a lack of reverence for God or for God's standards. The opposite of curse in this sense is not "bless," but rather "respect" (as exhibited by one who fears God and holds to God's standards). The word is also used without any object to say that someone is "cursing" in general (e.g., Shimei in 2 Sam. 16:5, 7; he is angry at David, but is not said to "curse David" but simply to curse, which might imply a general use of abusive or vulgar language).

A pattern of curse and blessing is sometimes thought to form the basic concept of the book of Genesis. The Priestly author of Gen. 1 places the divine blessing on humankind at the beginning of his work (1:28), but the chapters that follow (attributed to the Yahwist, or J, source) present a narrative dominated by God's curse in response to disobedience (Gen. 3:16–19; 4:11) until, after the flood, there is a renewal of divine blessing (9:1).

The cycle of sin and curse begins again, climaxing in the hubris of the Tower of Babel (11:1–9), but it is countered now by a new act of God, the blessing of Abram (12:1–3). This is the beginning of a history of blessing (22:15–18; 24:60; 26:2–4) that culminates in the blessing of Jacob by Isaac (27:27–29) and by God (32:27). Balancing this history of blessing, however, is the history related in Exodus, Leviticus, and Numbers, until Deuteronomy brings the Torah to a close on the note of covenant, with blessing promised for covenant obedience and curse for covenant breach (Deut. 28). "I have set before you life and death, blessing and curse" (Deut. 30:19); the history that follows (Joshua–2 Kings) demonstrates the tragic consequences of choosing death and curse, a theme fundamental to the preexilic prophets. The relationship between blessing and curse in Deuteronomy and the prophets can be seen by comparing such traditional curses as Deut. 28:30–40; Amos 5:11; Mic. 6:15; Zeph. 1:13; and Hag. 1:6 to corresponding formulations of blessing (Deut. 6:11; Josh. 24:13; Amos 9:14–15; Isa. 62:8–9; 65:21–23).

In the NT, most references to curses or cursing employ some form of the Greek verb *kataraomai* or its related noun *katara* (words typically used to translate both *'alah* and *'arar* in the LXX; *kakologeō* usually translates *qillel*). Jesus curses a fig tree (Matt. 11:21) and instructs his followers, "Bless those who curse you" (Luke 6:28; cf. Rom. 12:14). James 3:9–10 reflects on the inappropriateness of blessing God and cursing people made in God's image. See also Heb. 6:8 and Gal. 3:10, 13 (which quote Deut. 27:26; 28:58). Elsewhere, Peter curses (or perhaps swears an oath) to underscore his denial of Christ: the English word "curse" also translates *katathemtidzō* in Matt. 27:64 and *anathemtidzō* in Mark 14:71, variations on a word meaning something like "anathematize." Paul uses the related noun (*anathema*) in 1 Cor. 12:3 ("No one speaking by the Spirit of God ever says, 'Let Jesus be cursed'"). Finally, Revelation uses the word *blasphēmeō* (usually "to blaspheme") with reference to those who "cursed God" in 16:9, 11, 21. *See also* bless, blessing.

Bibliography

Brichto, Herbert C. *The Problem of "Curse" in the Hebrew Bible.* Society of Biblical Literature, 1963.

Hillers, Delbert R. *Treaty-Curses and the Old Testament Prophets.* Pontifical Biblical Institute, 1964.   J.S.K./M.A.P.

Cush (koosh). *See* Ethiopia.

Cushan-rishathaim (koosh´an-rish´uh-thay´im), the name of a king by whom the Israelites were oppressed until delivered under the leadership of the judge Othniel (twelfth century BCE; Judg. 3:8–10).

cylinder seals. *See* seal.

cymbal. *See* music.

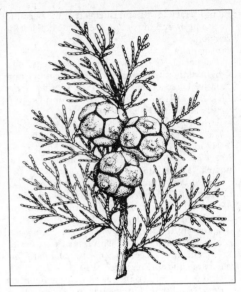
Cypress.

cypress (*Cupressus sempervirens*), a kind of tall evergreen found among stands of cedar and oak. Because of their beauty, cypresses were used as ornamental trees in gardens and cemeteries. The hard fragrant wood was preferred for buildings and furniture (Isa. 44:14, NRSV: "holm tree"). The fir trees supplied by Hiram of Tyre to Solomon for his temple and palace (1 Kings 9:11) were cypress, as was also the wood for Noah's ark (Gen. 6:14; KJV: "gopher wood"). Prophets offer metaphorical references to cypress (Hos. 14:8; Zech. 14:12), and Isaiah uses cypress growth as an image of replenishment and prosperity (41:19; 55:13; 60:13). *See also* fir tree; wood.

Cyprus (si´pruhs), an island in the eastern Mediterranean about sixty miles west of the Syrian coast and about the same distance from the coast of Turkey. Approximately a hundred and forty miles long and sixty miles wide (about the same size as ancient Israel), the island was known as Alashia in the cuneiform literature, and Elishah in the Bible (Ezek. 27:7; cf. Gen. 10:4; 1 Chron. 1:7). Some scholars also equate the island with the biblical name Kittim (Jer. 1:10), although others identify the latter with Crete. By NT times the island was called Cyprus (Greek *Kypros*, related to the word for "copper"). Cyprus was famous throughout the ancient world for its copper, a metal whose importance made the island a center of seafaring commerce. The island's active participation in world trade is evidenced by the discovery of great quantities of Cypriot imports in ancient Mesopotamia, the Levant, Egypt, Asia Minor, and the Aegean world.

Apparently an independent state during the second half of the second millennium BCE, Cy-

prus was colonized and ruled by Phoenicia in the tenth–eighth centuries, then subjugated by the Assyrians in the late eighth and seventh centuries. Cyprus subsequently became part of the Greek and Roman empires. A Jewish population is attested on the island as early as Ptolemy I (cf. 1 Macc. 15:23). Nicanor, the governor of Cyprus, is mentioned in 2 Macc. 12:2 as a ruler who would not allow Jewish farmers to live in peace. By the Roman period (63 BCE–325 CE) the Jewish population was significant. A Jew named Barnabas, an early member of the Jerusalem church, was a native of Cyprus (Acts 4:36), as were some of the other early disciples (Acts 11:19–20; 21:16). Acts reports that Paul and Barnabas traveled across the island, from Salamis to Paphos, on their first missionary journey (13:4–13). At Paphos they encountered the sorcerer Bar-Jesus and the proconsul Sergius Paulus. Barnabas and Mark later returned to Cyprus during Paul's second missionary journey (15:39).   D.A.D.

Cyrene (si-ree'nee), city in Cyrenaica (modern Libya) that had a thriving Jewish community of settlers from Egypt from Ptolemaic times (late fourth century BCE). Jason, the Hellenistic Jewish writer whose history was abbreviated in 2 Mac-

cabees, came from Cyrene. Simon of Cyrene is said to have carried Jesus's cross (Mark 15:21). Cyrenian Christians were also prominent in Antioch (Acts 11:20; 13:1).

Cyrenius (si-ree'nee-uhs). *See* Quirinius, P. Sulpicius.

Cyrus (si'ruhs) **II,** a Persian emperor and founder of the Achaemenid dynasty (ruled Babylonia 539–530 BCE). His name occurs twenty-two times in the Bible, in the books of Daniel, Ezra, 1 and 2 Chronicles, and Isaiah. Extrabiblical evidence comes from the classical Greek authors Herodotus and Xenophon as well as cuneiform records. From the latter we learn that Cyrus's ancestor was Teispes of Anshan. His grandfather was named Cyrus (I). His father was Cambyses (I) and his mother, Mandane, was the daughter of the Median king Astyages. Cyrus is therefore known to modern historians as Cyrus II (or Cyrus the Great). His son, who ruled Babylonia from 530 to 522 BCE, was Cambyses II. Cyrus's capital was Pasargadae, in what is now southern Iran.

Cyrus's military victories eventually put him in possession of the largest empire the world at that time had seen. These began with the conquest of Media (549), followed by Lydia (546) and Babylonia (539). It would seem that the Babylonian provinces of Eber-nari (today's Syria, Lebanon, and Israel) fell to him after the conquest of Babylonia, although no specific mention of them is extant in contemporary records. Cyrus's policy toward the peoples of his empire was one of tolerance and understanding. In the Bible, he is said to have authorized the rebuilding of the Jerusalem temple by returning Judeans (2 Chron. 36:22–23; Ezra 1:1–4), and this accords well with what is known from contemporaneous documents. Isa. 45:1–3 speaks with enthusiasm of Cyrus as the anointed one (messiah) of the Lord. A coregency with his son, Cambyses, ran for a short while in 530 and ended in the same year with the death of Cyrus in battle. Achaemenid rule in Babylonia continued for two hundred years until another major turning point in history, the conquests of Alexander the Great. *See also* Persia.   D.B.W.

D

D, an abbreviation used in biblical studies as a siglum for the Deuteronomist, one of the sources of the Pentateuch. *See also* Deuteronomist; Pentateuch, sources of the.

dagger. *See* sword; weapons.

Dagon (day′gon), an ancient Semitic deity attested in the northern Mesopotamian area from the late third millennium BCE and in Canaan during the time of the Israelite settlement and early monarchy. Texts from Ugarit give no information about the god except that he is the father of Baal Haddu, the major god of fertility at Ugarit; Dagon does have a temple at Ugarit, so he must have been honored in public worship. The place-name Beth-dagon in the tribal territories of both Judah (Josh. 15:41) and Asher (Josh. 19:27) preserve the name of the deity.

The Philistines worshiped Dagon after they settled on the coast of the Levant in the twelfth century BCE. Indeed, the Bible presents Dagon as the chief god of the Philistines, at least as the god to whom thanks were given after a victory. In Judg. 16:23, the imprisoned Samson pulls the temple of Dagon in Gaza down around his head. In 1 Sam. 5:1–7, the Philistines captured the ark of the covenant and placed it in the temple of Dagon at Ashdod (cf. 1 Macc. 10:83; 11:4, which mention a temple of Dagon in Ashdod). God causes the statue of Dagon to fall before the ark; a second fall destroys the statue. According to 1 Chron. 10:10, the Philistines hung up the head of Saul as a trophy

in the temple of Dagon, presumably at Beth-shan (cf. 1 Sam. 31:12). R.J.C.

dainties, delicious sweets, delicacies, and confections generally served at the tables of kings. A sign of ostentatious wealth, they will be lost to those who suffer the judgment of God (Rev. 18:14).

Dalmanutha (dal′muh-*noo*′thuh), an unidentified location to which Jesus sailed across the Sea of Galilee after feeding the four thousand (Mark 8:10). Various manuscripts read "Magadan," "Magedan," or "Magdala" instead of Dalmanutha, and the parallel passage in Matt. 15:39 has "Magadan."

Dalmatia (dal-may′shee-uh), the southwestern part of Illyricum along the modern Yugoslav coast of the Adriatic Sea. Illyricum was established as a Roman province in 9–10 CE. The name Dalmatia dates from the period of the Flavian emperors (ca. 70 CE) and came to be used interchangeably with the name of the province as a whole. In 2 Tim. 4:10 Titus leaves Paul to go to Dalmatia. *See also* Illyricum.

Damaris (dam′uh-ris), a woman who was one of Paul's few converts in Athens (Acts 17:34).

Damascus (duh-mas′kuhs), an ancient (and modern) city in Syria, located about sixty miles east of the Mediterranean coast, east of Sidon. On a plateau about 2,300 feet above sea level, the city

The ark of the covenant being returned by the Philistines (*left;* 1 Sam. 6:7–8) after it caused the statue of Dagon to break in front of his temple (*right;* 1 Sam. 5:2–5). Wall painting from the synagogue at Dura-Europos, third century CE.

had the waters of the oasis Ghuta, which was nourished by the twin rivers draining eastward from the Anti-Lebanon range: the Abana (now called Nahr Barada), which subdivides into numerous branches after a course through a narrow gorge out of the hills, and the Pharpar (now called Nahr el-'Awaj), just south of the town. Naaman compared the quality of these rivers with the Jordan (2 Kings 5:12). The chief deity of the city was the storm god Hadad, as is reflected in the name Ben-hadad ("son of Hadad"), taken by several monarchs.

Damascus is mentioned often in biblical accounts. It is referred to in the story of Abraham rescuing his relatives (Gen. 14:15). David brought it within Israelite control (2 Sam. 8:5–6), but during Solomon's reign the first of a series of Aramean kings made Damascus his capital city; he and his successors continued to intervene in the life of Israel and Judah until the Assyrian conquest in 732 BCE. These kings include Rezon (1 Kings 11:23–25); Tabrimmon, ally of the Judean Abijam against Israel (1 Kings 15:19); his father, Hezion (same verse); his son Ben-hadad, who was allied with Baasha of Israel, but later with Asa of Judah (1 Kings 15:18–19); another Ben-hadad and his son Hadadezer, who fought Ahab of Israel (1 Kings 20); and perhaps yet another Ben-hadad, who was killed by Hazael in accord with a prophecy from Elisha (2 Kings 8:7–15). The deepest Aramean penetration into Israel came under a Ben-hadad, who laid siege to the capital city, Samaria (2 Kings 6:24). Only under Israel's Jeroboam II was Damascus restored to Israel's territory (2 Kings 14:28). When Assyria's pressure worked west, the effort of Rezin of Damascus with Pekah of Israel to bring Judah's king Ahaz into the alliance against Assyria led to the conflict known as the Syro-Ephraimite War. Assyria's success brought the destruction of Damascus in 732 BCE, including Rezin's death. Damascus became an administrative zone under Assyria, but its power did not revive until it was made a Nabatean capital under Roman policy (85 BCE).

In the NT, Paul was traveling from Jerusalem to Damascus when he had the dramatic experience that transformed him from a persecutor of the church to a missionary for the faith (Acts 9:1–8). According to the account in Acts, Paul had letters from the high priest to synagogues in Damascus authorizing him to arrest followers of Jesus there and bring them back to Jerusalem. After his experience on the road, he was baptized in Damascus and spent some days preaching about Jesus in the synagogues (9:10–22). Eventually, he had to escape from the city by being lowered over the wall in a basket (Acts 9:23–25; 2 Cor. 11:3; Gal. 1:17).
R.S.B.

Dan.

1 One of the twelve sons of Jacob, by Bilhah, the slave of Rachel (Gen. 30:1–6); he is the ancestor of the tribe of Dan (see **2**).

2 One of the twelve tribes of Israel assigned a small piece of land west of Benjamin; when the Danites were crowded out, however, they migrated north (Josh. 19:40–48; Judg. 18). *See also* tribes.

3 A city on the northern border of Israel ("Dan to Beer-sheba" expresses the northern and southern limits of Israel; see, e.g., Judg. 20:1; 1 Sam. 3:20). Formerly called Laish, it is mentioned in the Egyptian Execration texts, the eighteenth-century BCE Mari tablets, and the records of the Egyptian pharaoh Thutmose III. It is identified with Tell el-Qadi (Arabic) or Tel Dan (Heb.) covering about fifty acres in the center of a fertile valley near one of the principal springs feeding the Jordan River.

Judges indicates that the city was founded by conquerors who brought a levitical priest named Micah to the site and set up a sanctuary there (18:19-20). Later, Jeroboam set up golden calves at Bethel and at Dan to provide the northern kingdom with sanctuaries in lieu of the temple in Jerusalem (1 Kings 12:26–30). These shrines would be condemned by the prophet Amos (8:14). Tell Dan has been excavated by A. Biran since 1966. The earliest occupation goes back to the Pottery Neolithic period, but its extent is not yet known. The large and prosperous Early Bronze occupation probably covered the full expanse of the mound, dating to about the middle of the third millennium BCE. A Middle Bronze II rampart (1900–1500 BCE) surrounds the city, and at the southeast corner a mud-brick triple arched gate with two towers is preserved to a height of over 20 feet. A large Late Bronze Age (1500–1200 BCE) building and a tomb with quantities of Mycenaean pottery, gold and silver jewelry, bronze swords, and ivory boxes indicate a prosperous fourteenth-thirteenth century occupation in the vicinity.

Occupation was continuous, but a change in the material culture in Iron Age I (1200–950 BCE) indicates the arrival of ethnic groups from both the coastal region of modern-day Lebanon and from the south. This material culture has been interpreted by some as representative of the Danite migration (Judg. 19). Although agriculture was the economic mainstay, a recycling metal industry seems to have been a major enterprise as well.

Archaeologists have uncovered a sacred area dating to Iron Age II (ca. 950–730 BCE), perhaps a *bamah* (Heb., "high place") on the northwest portion of the tell. In three main phases of

A Greek and Aramaic inscription found at Tel Dan from the late third–early second century BCE contains the word "Dan" (second line) and helps to identify the site.

construction (attributed by Biran to Jeroboam I, Ahab, and Jeroboam II, respectively), cultic incense burners and stands, figurines, and a horned altar have been uncovered.

A monumental system of gates and fortifications has been uncovered from this period as well. In the plaza outside the outermost gate, perhaps the most important find from Tell Dan was discovered: an Aramaic "House of David" inscription. This black basalt stele, inscribed in the ninth century BCE, describes the victory of an Aramaean king (probably Hazael) over other kings, among them a king of Israel and a king of the house of David (most often thought to be Jehoram and Ahaziah, respectively). It is evidence for Aramean rule at Tell Dan, but its willful shattering testifies to subsequent regime change, when the area came under Israelite rule.

Tell Dan continued in use down to Hellenistic and Roman times. A bilingual Greek and Aramaic votive inscription of the late third or early second century BCE to the "god who is in Dan" identifies the site. An elaborate water installation existed near the spring in Roman times; the latest coins date to the end of the fourth century CE.   N.L.L./D.I.

dancing, rhythmic bodily movement, often to music. As a sign of rejoicing, dance had a place in the secular and religious life of ancient Israel. Dance could be accompanied by song and instrumental music. Women sometimes greeted the return of victorious soldiers with music and dance (1 Sam. 18:6). Dancing had a role at the old harvest festival at Shiloh (Judg. 21:21). Dance before the golden calf was an expression of idolatry (Exod. 2:19), but dance could also be performed in the worship of God (Ps. 149:3). When David led the ark of the covenant to Jerusalem, he danced before the Lord wearing a linen ephod, a garment usually associated with ceremonial worship (similar to a tunic; cf. Exod. 28:6–10), but that here appears to

be something scant with which David is said to be "girded" (such as a loincloth; 2 Sam. 6:14). His wife Michal claimed that uncovering himself in such a manner was unseemly (2 Sam. 6:20). The Song of Songs celebrates the dance of the Shulammite (6:13). After Judith kills Holofernes, the women perform a dance in her honor (Jth. 15:12), and then she leads women and men alike in a dance of thanksgiving (15:13).

In the NT, dance is part of the celebration of the return of the prodigal son (Luke 15:25). Jesus also refers to children dancing in the marketplace to flute tunes as something that would be an expected or common occurrence (Matt. 11:16–17; Luke 7:31–32; cf. Job 21:11). Dancers were also sometimes engaged for entertainment at royal courts in the Hellenistic and Roman worlds (cf. Matt. 14:6). In Matt. 14:1–2, the daughter of Herodias dances before a drunken Herod Antipas, who is so pleased he offers to grant her whatever she asks. *See also* David; Gebal; Michal; Shiloh.   R.M.G.

Daniel (dan'yuhl).

1 David's second son, according to 1 Chron. 3:1. In 2 Sam. 3:3 his name is given as Chileab.

2 A priest and descendant of Ithamar who returned from the exile with Ezra (Ezra 8:2). He may be the same Daniel listed in Neh. 10:6 as one of the priests who signed Ezra's covenant-renewal document.

3 A hero referred to in Ezek. 14:14, 20; 28:3 about whom nothing else is known. His name may be more accurately rendered Danel and there has been speculation that he could be the Danel referred to in Ugaritic texts (second millennium BCE) as a righteous judge who protected widows and orphans. Ezekiel lists him along with Noah and Job as three persons famous for their exemplary righteousness.

4 The hero of the book of Daniel, represented as a Jew in the Babylonian exile who is skilled

Terra-cotta plate with dancers, musicians, and singers (2000–1600 BCE).

Daniel as depicted in a sixth-century CE mosaic at the Monastery of St. Catherine, Sinai.

in the interpretation of dreams and is miraculously preserved in a lions' den. *See also* Daniel, book of.

Daniel, Additions to,

Daniel, Additions to, several stories, a prayer, and a hymn not found in the Hebrew text of Daniel, but present in both the LXX and Theodotion, two distinct Greek translations of the Hebrew Bible. The passages are called The Song of the Three Jews, Susanna, and Bel and the Dragon. The Song of the Three Jews is included between Dan. 3:23 and 3:24. In Theodotion, Susanna stands at the beginning of Daniel, and Bel and the Dragon at its end, while the LXX version places both additions at the end. Protestants have regarded these passages as part of the Apocrypha, while Roman Catholics and Eastern Orthodox Christians retain them as part of Daniel.

The book of Daniel seems to have grown by accretion, beginning with the stories of Dan. 1–6. The Additions are only the final stage in that process. Susanna and Bel and the Dragon may represent part of a larger cycle of stories associated with Daniel similar to the ones found in Dan. 1–6. The prayer (vv. 1–22) and the hymn (vv. 28–68) in the Song of the Three Jews are probably independent liturgical compositions. All of these passages seem to have been added sometime between the composition of Daniel during the Maccabean revolt (167–164 BCE) and 100 BCE. *See also* Apocrypha/deuterocanonical literature; Bel and the Dragon; Daniel, book of; Song of the Three Jews; Susanna.

D.W.S.

Daniel, book of,

Daniel, book of, a book found in the Ketuvim (Writings) section of the Tanakh (Jewish Bible) and among the Major Prophets in the Christian OT.

Contents: The book of Daniel can be divided into parts either thematically or linguistically. The fact that these divisions do not coincide has been a puzzle to many scholars. A thematic division yields two main parts: Dan. 1–6, containing separate third-person narrative stories about the experiences of Daniel and his friends in the Babylonian and Persian courts, and Dan. 7–12, containing a series of apocalyptic visions in the first-person voice. A linguistic division yields three parts: 1:1–2:3, written in Hebrew; 2:4–7:28, written in Aramaic; and 8:1–12:13, written in Hebrew. A series of Greek additions to the book of Daniel (including Bel and the Dragon and the story of Susanna) are found in the apocryphal/deuterocanonical literature.

Chaps. 1–6 present an account of the trials of Daniel and his friends. The first story focuses on faith in God. Daniel and his friends Hananiah, Mishael, and Azariah are taken to Babylon to be trained as court seers and are given Babylonian names: Belteshazzar, Shadrach, Meshach, and Abednego. They are given royal rations of food, but these violate Jewish dietary laws. Daniel and his friends request to be given vegetables instead and turn out to be healthier than those who ate the royal food.

The second story deals with the coming kingdom of God and depicts one of King Nebuchadnezzar's dreams. The king dreams of a statue of a body made of different metals: the head is gold, the arms are silver, the chest is bronze, the legs are iron, and the feet are iron mixed with clay. A rock comes and destroys the statue and grows to fill the whole earth. Many are called to interpret the dream, but only Daniel is able to do so, because he prayed for God's mercy. The four metals represent four kingdoms, the first of which is Babylon. The rock represents an everlasting kingdom that will arrive once those other kingdoms have come and gone. Although the kingdoms are not named in this passage, scholars believe that they correspond to the Babylonians, Medes, Persians, and Greeks. The rock represents the kingdom of God.

The third story is a story of faith and is the only story that does not involve Daniel. The king builds a large statue and requires all the people to worship it at certain times under penalty of death. Shadrach, Meshach, and Abednego refuse to worship any but God, and the king throws them into a fiery furnace. Yet God saves them through a humanlike figure (possibly an angel).

The fourth story depicts another of Nebuchadnezzar's dreams in which a great tree (representing the king) is cut down. Daniel interprets this dream for him, saying that the king will be sent to the wilderness to eat grass like an animal for seven years. The king boasts later of his glory and power, and Daniel's prediction is fulfilled.

The fifth story depicts a wild party at which the king uses the sacred cups from the temple of Jerusalem, prompting a hand to appear and write four words on the wall. Once again, no one can interpret this omen but Daniel. The four words (*mene, mene, tekel, parsin*) may be read as either monetary units (mina, shekel, half shekel) or as terms related to Hebrew verbs ("number," "weigh," "divide"). Thus, Daniel claims that God has numbered the king's days, weighed his deeds, and will divide his kingdom between the Medes and Persians.

The last story depicts Daniel being accused of breaking the law by praying to God. He is thrown into a lions' den, but is protected by God.

After this series of stories, the book of Daniel moves into a set of four apocalypses (Dan. 7–12). The first involves a vision of four beasts coming out of the ocean: a lion, a bear, a leopard, and a beast with ten horns. These are almost certainly images for four nations: Babylon, Media, Persia, and Greece (though the nations are not named in the text). Then comes one "like a son of man" who is given everlasting kingship over all the other nations. Some scholars believe that the designation "son of man" is used here to depict a humanlike figure (as opposed to the beastly ones), while others believe it refers to an angel. The term clearly took on a messianic connotation by the first century CE, and it would ultimately be used as a designation for Jesus Christ. The second apocalypse depicts a ram and a goat, representing the transition from Persian to Greek rule. The third apoca lypse reinterprets Jeremiah's prophesy of 70 years of captivity (25:11–12) as 490 years (seventy weeks of years). The fourth apocalypse is a depiction of the future history of the world.

Background: There is little consensus in the scholarly community over the identity of the author of the book of Daniel or the historical identity of the prophet by that name. The book of Daniel does not contain a superscription giving authorship to Daniel, but is merely a book *about* Daniel. This fact, in addition to many structural and dating elements, has caused scholars to reject the notion that Daniel should be viewed as the author of the book.

Even if the book is to be regarded as an anonymous writing about someone named Daniel, the identification of that figure is unclear. A Daniel is referenced in Ezekiel in the same breath as Noah and Job, as a paragon of righteousness (14:14, 20). Yet the hero of the book of Daniel would have been an exceedingly young man at this point, not a man whose righteousness was legendary. A figure of Danel is also present in the Ugaritic texts of the fourteenth century BCE. In these texts, Danel is a notably righteous Canaanite king. Most scholars now think that the person named Daniel in the biblical book is a literary character based on a legendary hero of the ancient world. In other words, a historical or semihistorical person named Danel/Daniel served as the model or namesake for development of the character who serves as the protagonist in the prophetic tale related in the biblical book. Other scholars recognize that there is a "Daniel" figure in the legends of the ancient Near East, but deny any connection between that figure and the Daniel in the book of Daniel. McKenzie and Kaltner claim that "Daniel" is merely a pseudonym used by the author to gain validity for the writing. They cite the apocalypses of Adam, Seth, Enoch, Moses, and Abraham as examples of such pseudonymous writing. Hebbard argues that the character Daniel is never presented as someone who is alive during the reading of the text, but as a historical character who offers keys to understanding the present and future.

The story of the book of Daniel is set in the sixth century BCE, during the Babylonian exile, but if this is taken literally, many of the dates and historical references in Daniel present problems. Daniel is said to have been brought to Babylon in 606 BCE, but Jerusalem was not actually besieged until some years after that. In addition, there is no historical evidence of a "Darius the Mede," and Belshazzar was the son of Nabonidus (who temporarily abdicated the throne), not Nebuchadnezzar. The presence of Nabonidus in character, but not name, is confounded by the presence of a "Prayer of Nabonidus" found at Qumran that is closely linked to Daniel 4. These inconsistencies, among others, have led scholars to believe, not only that the book of Daniel was written much later than the time period it portrays, but that it was never intended to be read as a strictly historical book.

Most scholars think that the final composition of Daniel took shape during the Maccabean period, during the reign of Antiochus IV. The great majority of scholars think that Dan. 7–12 was written at this time, and many believe that the entire book was composed during this period. Thus, most interpreters view many of the apocalypses presented in Daniel as thinly veiled allusions to Antiochus IV's anti-Jewish policies and to the tensions that had arisen in Judea as a result of those policies. Although a few scholars do still hold to an earlier date of composition, most date Daniel to around 165 BCE, shortly before Antiochus IV's death in 163 BCE. This date would most likely make Daniel the last book written in the Hebrew Bible.

Although some prophetic books contain apocalyptic elements, the book of Daniel is the only book in the Hebrew Bible that is generally considered apocalyptic in character. In keeping with the genre of apocalyptic literature, Daniel would have been intended to comfort the people of Israel during the crisis of the Maccabean period, not foretell the future.

Interpretive Issues: The most discussed interpretive issues in the book of Daniel concern its dating and unity. Many scholars date Dan. 1–6 to an earlier period than Dan. 7–12. Yet the fact that chaps. 2–7 are in Aramaic has raised a number of questions regarding how the book of Daniel developed into its present form. Childs argues for a unity between chaps. 1–6 and 7–12, because of the common themes of visions and dreams, along with Daniel and his friends fulfilling the call for faithfulness received in the apocalyptic visions.

He also holds that, though the editors did not alter the stories or apocalypses, they did alter the interpretation of Daniel to have it point to the end of the age, which still lay in the future, not with the fall of any particular ruler. Gottwald indicates that the fact that Antiochus IV is not explicitly mentioned in the text allowed Christian and Jewish readers to reinterpret the book with reference to different rulers and empires. Hebbard validates the quest for placing the book of Daniel in its historical context, but argues that one must also read Daniel as a literary work that retains contemporary significance transcending historical particularities.

Influences: The "son of man" apocalypse in chap. 7 has been a significant passage in Daniel, particularly in the Christian tradition. It was seen in the first century CE as a messianic passage and, coupled with Jesus's self-references as the "son of man," was interpreted by the early church as a prophecy about the coming of Christ.

Another point of particular significance in postbiblical history is the reference to resurrection in Dan. 12:2. This is often regarded as the only explicit reference to resurrection in the Hebrew Bible, so it has become important in both Jewish and Christian traditions.

The focus on the end times present in the book of Daniel has led many throughout history to try to read it as a manual for the end of the world. Some Christian groups have worked out dispensationalist schemes that would correlate passages in Daniel with historical and current events in order to discern how close the end times truly are.

Bibliography

Bandstra, Barry L. *Reading the Old Testament: Introduction to the Hebrew Bible.* 4th ed. Wadsworth, 2009.

Childs, Brevard. S. *Introduction to the Old Testament as Scripture.* Fortress, 1979.

Collins, John J. "Current Issues in the Study of Daniel." In *The Book of Daniel: Composition and Reception.* Brill, 2001. Pp. 1–15.

———. *Daniel: With an Introduction to Apocalyptic Literature.* Eerdmans, 1984.

Gottwald, Norman K. *The Hebrew Bible: A Socio-Literary Introduction.* Fortress, 1985.

Hebbard, Aaron B. *Reading Daniel as a Text in Theological Hermeneutics.* Pickwick, 2009.

McKenzie, Stephen L., and John Kaltner. *The Old Testament: Its Background, Growth, and Content.* Abingdon, 2007.   B.B.

Darda (dahr´duh; probably Heb., "thistle"), the son of Mahol, and one of the four sages of 1 Kings 4:31 whose wisdom was exceeded by Solomon.

daric (dair´ik; Heb. *'adarkon*), a gold coin, probably introduced by Darius I. The word "daric" was originally used as an adjective to modify "stater": a "daric stater" (Gk. *dareikos stater*) denotes a stater of the Persian ruler Darius; later, the term was shortened to "daric." It is used of temple building contributions in Ezra 8:27 and also in 1 Chron.

Darics, mentioned in 1 Chron. 29:7, were coins issued by the Persian king Darius I (522–486 BCE). The monarch had his own likeness stamped on the coins showing him running swiftly, holding a spear and bow.

29:7. Another term (Heb. *darkemon*) is used in Ezra 2:69; Neh. 7:70, 72. *See also* Darius; money.

Darius (duh-ri´uhs).

1 Darius I (the Great, 522–486 BCE), the first of three Persian (Achaemenid) rulers. This Darius is intended in Ezra 4–6, Haggai, and Zech. 1–8. He established himself on the throne in a power struggle in the years 522–520 BCE. The account of this struggle appears on the trilingual inscriptions at Behistun in the Zagros Mountains in northern Mesopotamia. Although they contain important information, allowance must be made for Darius's desire to establish his legitimacy as ruler; his relationship to the royal house is not clear. The upheavals of his accession suggest a background to the prophecies of Hag. 2:6–7; 2:21–22, with their reference to the overthrow of kingdoms, and to the complaint in Zech. 1:11–12 that peace has been restored without the expected outcome of the reestablishment of Judah and Jerusalem. However, the precise interpretation of these passages is not certain. Ezra 5–6 shows Darius reaffirming Cyrus's authorization for the rebuilding of the Jerusalem temple, in response to an inquiry by the governor of the province "Beyond the River" and his associates. In 1 Esd. 4:42–5:3 Darius is credited directly with the appointment of Zerubbabel to restore Judah. Darius's conquests, his organization of the Persian Empire, his successful control of it over a period of nearly forty years, and his building achievements, especially at Susa and Persepolis, point to great administrative and military ability. The later years of his reign mark the development of conflict with Greece and his army's defeat at Marathon in 490 BCE. This conflict would dramatically affect subsequent Persian history. The records suggest a mixture of extreme cruelty and generosity. He is credited, probably rightly, with the introduction of the coin known as the daric. *See also* Cyrus II; daric; Persia.

2 Darius II, ruler of Persia 423–405/4 BCE. He is described in the Elephantine papyri as responsible for a rescript to the Persian satrap in Egypt about religious observance at the Jewish shrine there. The reference to Darius the Persian in Neh. 12:22 could be to him or to **3.**

3 Darius III, ruler of Persia 336–330 BCE. He was the last ruler of the empire, murdered shortly after Alexander's final defeat of the Persian army. The reference to Darius the Persian in Neh. 12:22 could be to him or to **2.**

4 Darius the Mede, figure identified as a Median ruler after Belshazzar but before Cyrus (Dan. 5:31; 6; 9:1; 11:1). There is no satisfactory historical explanation for this reference. It might derive from prophecies about the conquest of Babylon by the Medes (e.g., Isa. 13:17), since a Median Empire is placed between the Babylonian and Persian empires (cf. Dan. 8:20; also the interpretation of the dream in Dan. 2:31–45 and of the vision in 7:3–7; 15–18). *See also* Daniel, book of; Medes, Media.

P.R.A.

darkness, the absence of light. According to Genesis, God created light and separated the light from the darkness, calling the light "day" and the darkness "night" (Gen. 1:3–5). In the Bible, darkness often represents destruction, death, or the underworld (Isa. 5:30; 47:5; Ps. 143:3; Job 17:13; cf. Mark 15:33). Conceived as a curse or punishment (Deut. 28:29; Ps. 35:6), darkness characterizes the coming "day of the Lord" (Joel 2:2; Amos 5:18). God's appearance is often accompanied by darkness (1 Kings 8:12), which, according to Gen. 1:2, prevailed prior to creation, although Isa. 45:7 and Ps. 104:20 assert that it too was created by God. The Dead Sea Scrolls contrast light and darkness, which represent the forces of good and evil, both metaphysically and psychologically; a similar view has been noted in the Gospel of John (e.g., 1:5; 8:12; cf. Matt. 5:14).   F.E.G.

dart. *See* weapons.

Dathan (day'thuhn), a Reubenite who, with his brother Abiram, rebelled against Moses, claiming he had led the exodus in order to rule over the Israelites (Num. 16). The earth swallowed Dathan and Abiram alive (Deut. 11:6).

daughter. Most biblical uses of the word "daughter" refer to a female child, though the term can be used more expansively for any female descendant (e.g., 2 Kings 8:26) or as a synonym for "women" (e.g., "daughters of humans" in Gen. 6:4 are human women; "daughters of Jerusalem" in Luke 23:28 are women who live in Jerusalem). Metaphorically, cities may be referred to as daughters (e.g., Ps. 48:11, "daughters of Judah"; NRSV: "towns of Judah").

In many biblical narratives, sons appear to be more celebrated than daughters, perhaps because the family name was usually passed on through the male descendants (cf. Deut. 25:5–6, which expresses concern that a man's name might be "blotted out of Israel" if he dies without a son). The book of Ruth, however, recounts a narrative in which a woman comes to regard her daughter-in-law as her own daughter (e.g. 3:1, 10–11) and, indeed, as a daughter who is more to her "than seven sons" (4:15). Biblical genealogies typically list only sons, but they do sometimes list daughters when no sons were born (Gen. 47:17; Num. 26:46). Daughters were valued and loved, and Israelite law often mandated protection of daughters in ways that surpassed what was required for sons (e.g., Exod. 21:7–11; Lev. 18:9–18; 19:29). The case of Zelophehad's daughters established inheritance rights for women who married within the family group of their tribe (Num. 27:1–11; 36:1–12).

Some biblical stories report treatment of daughters that is probably atypical and recounted for the sake of cautionary shock value. In Sodom, Lot offers his virgin daughters to a mob of potential rapists to dissuade them from attacking his male guests (Gen. 19:8); later, those daughters take advantage of him sexually when he is intoxicated and become pregnant by him (19:30–38). Jephthah offers his daughter as a human sacrifice to fulfill a rash vow (Judg. 11:34–40).

In the NT, Jesus raises the daughter of a synagogue ruler from the dead (Matt. 9:18–26) and heals the demon-possessed daughter of a Canaanite woman (15:21–28). He sometimes addresses adult women as "Daughter" (e.g., Mark 5:34). *See also* Jairus; Jephthah; Lot; son; Zelophehad.   M.A.P.

David

THE MOST POWERFUL KING of biblical Israel, David (day'vid) ruled from ca. 1010 to 970 BCE. The story of David is recorded in 1 Sam. 16:1–1 Kings 2:12.

Path to Kingship: David belonged to the tribe of Judah and was born in Bethlehem as the youngest son of Jesse. He started his career at King Saul's court as player of the lyre and subsequently became his squire. His courage and leadership in regular skirmishes with the Philistines and the immense popularity he gained as a commander soon earned him great notoriety and caused Saul to feel threatened. The old prophet Samuel, who had himself conducted Saul to the first kingship, became disappointed with Saul and anointed David as the new favorite of God.

David survived attempts on his life, made by Saul in bursts of rage, and fled the court. In the south he became a warlord with his own army of outlaws that supported itself through the performance of "protection services." He also fought the enemies of Judah in the west and southwest. Although Saul found no way of eliminating him, the pressure he exerted became so strong that David decided to take refuge in Gath, where he became a vassal of the Philistine king Achish. Playing a double game, David nevertheless managed to maintain good relations with the tribes in the south: Judah, Cain, Jerahmeel, and Simeon. His Philistine sovereign did not call upon him to perform his duties as a vassal in the final war against Saul. Israel was defeated on Mount Gilboa, and Saul and three princes were killed in battle. Saul's tribe, Benjamin, sought to fill the power vacuum by making Saul's remaining son, Ishbaal, king, but the commander of Saul's army, Abner, concluded a pact with David. A short time later, however, both Abner and Ishbaal were murdered in separate incidents (Abner by David's general, Joab, and Ishbaal by two of Saul's former captains who thought, mistakenly, that their treachery would get them in good with David). The upshot of all these events was that the northern tribes of Israel came to David at Hebron and accepted him as their king. Thus, it would be said that David reigned forty years: seven years over Judah (at Hebron) and another thirty-three years over the unified nation of Judah and Israel (2 Sam. 5:4–5). David also conquered Jerusalem and transformed what had been a small Jebusite city-state (hereafter known as the City of David) into a large and impressive new capital for his kingdom. He enhanced the status of the city by bringing the ancient ark to it.

King David playing a harp; from a thirteenth-century Hebrew manuscript.

Israel an Empire: According to the biblical account, David triumphed over nearly all the then neighboring nations in a series of military campaigns. In the north he encountered the Aramaic states, and Damascus, Hamath, and Zobah rendered him tribute; in the east and southeast, David subjected the Ammonites and Moab; in the south he took over Edom; in the southwest he subjected small desert tribes like the Amalekites; and in the west he defeated the Philistines. His success was

David slaying Goliath and cutting off his head (*top*), and Abner bringing David with Goliath's head to Saul (*bottom*). Jonathan, overcome with love for David, gives him his own garments (1 Sam. 17:45–18:4). Page from a thirteenth-century French illumination.

abetted by two factors: (1) the presence of an experienced standing army consisting mainly of mercenaries under the command of the competent military strategist Joab; and (2) the temporary impotence of civilizations along the Nile and between the Euphrates and Tigris. Thus, under David (and Solomon), Israel was for a brief century a powerful empire.

Rebellion: This formation of power, however, had repercussions. David became an absolute ruler, and discontent grew among those who resented the decay of the older tribal order with its theocratical values. This discomfort came to a head during a revolt led by Absalom, one of David's sons. This prince made shrewd use of the mood of resistance and, after thorough preparation, seized power, so that David was forced to leave his own country. When the usurper failed to isolate David at once, however, David gained time to realign himself with those of his standing army who had remained loyal to him. He was able to effect a political reversal through a hard battle in the Transjordan. A later secession of northern tribes under Sheba ben Bichri was dealt with by the quick action of Joab, who eliminated Sheba. David, however, omitted arranging for his succession, so that even before his death a vehement struggle broke out at the court. The group around Solomon, headed by his mother, Bathsheba, and the prophet Nathan, appeared to be the strongest, and shortly after David's death they eliminated the rival prince Adonijah, who was supported by Joab. Joab was subsequently eliminated as well.

Legacy: David was remembered, not only as a very powerful leader and personality, but also as a soldier, statesman, and poet. Numerous stories are recounted of him that had become part of Israel's folklore and were, no doubt, regarded as inspiring or cautionary in addition to being entertaining. The clearest example of an inspirational tale is the narrative of David, when he was but a shepherd boy who trusted in God, killing the giant warrior Goliath (1 Sam. 17). The classic example of a cautionary tale is the story of David's adulterous affair with Bathsheba and his murder of her husband, Uriah, an evil deed exposed by the prophet Nathan in a memorable parable (2 Sam. 11–12). David's ironic friendship with Jonathan, the son of his enemy (King Saul), is also recounted with a mixture of poignant observation and sentimental flourish (1 Sam. 18:1–4; 19:1–7; 20:1–42; 2 Sam. 1:1–27). Likewise the stories of his devoted but

A soldier using a sling similar to the type David used in the story of his encounter with Goliath (1 Sam. 17); relief from an orthostat at the palace at Gozan, tenth–ninth century BCE.

The prophet Samuel anointing David as king of Israel; Byzantine silver plate.

complicated marriage to Saul's daughter Michal are told with a flair for human interest that transcends merely political or religious concerns (1 Sam. 18:20–29; 19:11–17; 2 Sam. 3:12–14; 6:16–23). The account of David's dealings with the curmudgeonly Nabal and his clever wife, Abigail, is told in a way that is both instructive and humorous (1 Sam. 25). In addition to preserving these and many other "David stories," Israel preserved numerous "David poems": the dirge in 2 Sam. 1 and many compositions in the book of Psalms are ascribed to him. Such attributions indicate a strong association of David with liturgy, art, and worship, even if (as most scholars believe) the ascriptions are intended to honor David rather than to indicate literal authorship.

Covenant and Dynasty: The dynasty David founded survived the disruption after Solomon and kept on ruling in Judah until the exile, which began in 587/6 BCE. Despite recounting David's numerous failings in 1 and 2 Samuel, the Deuteronomistic History repeatedly presents David as the role model for Israelite kings in later books (1 Kings 3:14; 9:4; 11:4, 6, 33, 38; 14:8; 15:3, 11; 2 Kings 14:3; 16:2; 22:2). The prestige of the line of David was imbued with a strong sense that God had made an everlasting covenant with David granting his descendants a divine right to rule (2 Sam. 7:1–17; 23:1–15; cf. 1 Kings 11:11–13; 2 Kings 20:4–6; Isa. 9:7; Jer. 33:20–22; 33:15, 17, 25–26; Ezek. 34:23–24; 37:24–25; Hos. 3:5; Amos 9:11; Zech. 12:6–10).

In time, the expectation arose that a messianic deliverer would come from his line (*Pss. Sol.* 17; 4 Ezra). Thus, some NT authors thought it significant to assert that Jesus was a descendant of David, since, in the minds of many, only a Davidic descendant could be the Messiah (Matt. 2:6; 21:9; Luke 3:31; 18:38–39). In several passages, Jesus is called "Son of David," a title that is intended to be virtually synonymous with Christ or Messiah (e.g., Matt. 9:27; 15:22; 20:31–32; 21:9, 15). *See also* Absalom; Abigail; Bathsheba; covenant; Goliath; Jerusalem; Joab; Jonathan; messiah; Michal; Saul; Solomon.

Bibliography

Bright, John. *A History of Israel.* 4th ed. Westminster John Knox, 2000.

Fokkelman, J. P. *Narrative Art and Poetry in the Books of Samuel.* Vol. 1, *King David.* Vol. 2, *The Crossing Fates.* Van Gorsum, 1981, 1985.

Halpern, Baruch. *David's Secret Demons: Messiah, Murderer, Traitor, King.* Eerdmans, 2001.   J.P.F./M.A.P.

David, City of, the name given to the part of Jerusalem that was the Jebusite city, after its capture by David (2 Sam. 5). This oldest part of Jerusalem, which had been an urban site since the early third millennium BCE, was located in the southeastern part of present-day Jerusalem on a land peninsula that is formed by the Kidron Valley on the east and the Tyropoeon Valley (Gk., "Valley of the Cheesemakers") on the west. In area the City of David comprised no more than 7.5 to 10 acres and was thus no more than a medium-size village.

As a fortified city surrounded by valleys, it was vulnerable only at two points: at its principal water source on the east and at the highest part of the ridge on the north, a part of the city's fortifications that received continual attention. The city's principal water source was the Gihon spring, which flowed at the foot of the ridge on the Kidron side, below and outside the city walls. Excavations have shown that the spring was made accessible to the Jebusites by means of a shaft that connected the spring to a point just inside the city walls, about midway down the slope of the valley. The narrative of David's conquest of the city in 2 Sam. 5:7–8 suggests that he took the city by gaining entry to it through this water shaft. Soon after he took the city, David undertook to secure its strategic weak point on the north. He repaired the walls and the Millo (2 Sam. 5:9), which is probably to be identified with the stone retaining walls of the terraces on the slopes, which enabled the expansion of the habitable area of the city. That the spring remained a strategic weak point is attested by the construction of a water tunnel by Hezekiah in the late eighth century BCE. Its purpose was to secure the city's water source against siege by the Assyrians (2 Kings 20:20; 2 Chron. 32:30), a feat recorded in the Siloam Inscription.

David's son and successor, Solomon, expanded the city to the north, where he constructed a large platform on which he built the temple and other elaborate royal buildings (1 Kings 6–7). After Solomon the city grew farther to the north and to the west on the hill today identified as Mount Zion, a hill that is protected on the south and west by the Valley of Hinnom. This identification of Mount Zion, which in 2 Sam. 5:7 is applied to David's city, derives from the Jewish historian Josephus, who identified all of the Jerusalem of his day (the first century CE) with the City of David. *See also* Hezekiah; Jerusalem; Kidron; Siloam Inscription. F.S.F.

day. *See* time.

Day of Atonement. *See* Atonement, Day of.

day of the Lord (or "day of the LORD"). *See* eschatology; judgment, day of.

dayspring, the rising of the sun, used as an image for the coming of the Messiah (Luke 1:78).

Day Star. *See* Lucifer; stars.

deacon (Gk. *diakonos*, "servant" or "table waiter"), an office in the church that could apparently be filled by either men or women, though the qualifications for office and specific function of deacons may have varied from place to place. In the NRSV, the only deacon mentioned by name is Phoebe of Cenchreae, whom Paul commends to the Roman church (Rom. 16:1); it is generally thought that she was the one entrusted by Paul to deliver the letter and, if necessary, explain its contents. "Bishops and deacons" are mentioned together in Phil. 1:1 as leaders to whom that letter is specifically addressed. In 1 Timothy, considerable attention is given to listing qualifications for the office of deacon in the church at Ephesus. Deacons are to be serious-minded people who "hold to the mystery of the faith with a clear conscience"; they are not to be double-tongued, to overindulge in wine, or to be greedy for money (3:8–10). The latter comment suggests that deacons might have been paid for their work. The letter goes on to say that similar qualities should attend either "wives of deacons" or "women deacons" (the Greek can be translated either way; NRSV opts for the latter, but 1 Tim. 2:12 suggests to some that women would not have been permitted to serve as deacons in this setting). Finally, deacons are to be persons who have been married only once, who manage their children and households well, who have a good standing in the community, and who demonstrate boldness in the faith (1 Tim. 3:12–13). Nothing is said about their specific duties.

The seven men appointed to assist the twelve apostles in Acts 6:1–6 are often called deacons in church tradition, though the noun *diakonos* is never applied to them. Their primary responsibility, however, involves waiting (*diakoneō*) on tables, which makes them "deacons" in the original, literal sense of the word (cf. the table waiters in John 2:5, 9, for whom the term *diakonos* is used). There is some question as to whether these seven men (including Stephen and Philip, about whom more is reported in Acts) are to be regarded merely as deacons in a conventional sense (taking care of food allotment) or whether they must also be regarded as "church officers" occupying a position one step below the apostles that apparently did grant them opportunities for public proclamation (cf. Acts 6:8–9; 8:26–38).

The Greek term *diakonos* is used elsewhere in the NT where it is not thought to designate an office in the church and, so, is not translated "deacon" by the NRSV. For example, it is translated "servant" in Matt. 20:26; 23:11, and "attendant" in Matt. 22:13. However, since the office of deacon appears to have been well established in the early church before the Gospels were written, scholars sometimes wonder whether some ecclesiastical connotation might seep through even when the word is used in more secular contexts. Paul also uses the word *diakonos* for himself and for other believers (e.g., 1 Cor. 3:5; 2 Cor. 3:6; 6:4; 11:15, 23), and he calls Christ a deacon (NRSV: "servant") in Rom. 15:8 (cf. Gal. 2:17). *See* bishop; church; elders. M.A.P.

Dead Sea, the lake into which the Jordan River flows. The lake is fifty miles long by ten miles wide. The biblical names vary: "sea of the Arabah" (Deut. 3:17; 4:49; Josh. 3:16; 12:3), "eastern sea" (Ezek. 47:18; Joel 2:20; Zech. 14:8), and "sea of Sodom" (2 Esd. 5:7). The shoreline is 1,294 feet below sea level, with the greatest depth about 1,300 feet below that, and it has a 25 percent mineral content, entirely the result of evaporation. In ancient times it was valued for its salt and for the asphalt that occasionally floats to the surface. The water is usually calm because of its great density, but dangerous storms can develop.

The average annual rainfall is only 2 inches, with occasional severe thunderstorms. The steep, desolate western slopes leave sufficient room for a north–south road, and there are two important springs, one at modern 'Ain Feshka close to Qumran in the north and the other at En-gedi in the center. An important feature of later prophecy is the promise that living water would flow in both summer and winter from the Jerusalem temple down these arid slopes into the Dead Sea, making it fresh and productive (Ezek. 47:1–12; Zech. 14:8). In the extreme southwest is the salt dome of Har Sdom. Most of the eastern shore consists of forbidding sandstone precipices, cleft by the narrow gorges of the Zerqa Ma'in and the Arnon, but in the southeast, behind the Lisan peninsula, there is a coastal plain where winter crops are grown. At the exit of the Kerak wadi (probably the "descent of Horonaim" referred to in Jer. 48:5), is the important Bronze Age site of Bab edh-Dhra'. The whereabouts of Sodom and Gomorrah, which the Bible locates in the region of the Dead Sea (Gen. 13:10; 19:24), remain a total mystery. *See also* En-gedi; Qumran, Khirbet; Sodom.   D.B.

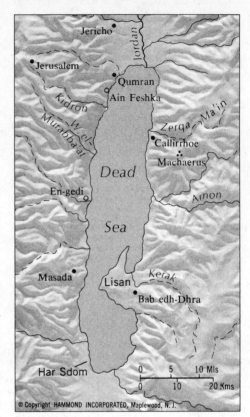

The Dead Sea Scrolls

IN A BROAD SENSE, the Dead Sea Scrolls are scrolls and fragments discovered roughly between 1947 and 1956 at seven sites along the northwest shore of the Dead Sea. In a narrow sense, however, the Dead Sea Scrolls are restricted to the scrolls and fragments found at Wadi Qumran, the most important of the finds.

Major discoveries include the following:

Qumran Cave 1: 7 major scrolls—2 copies of Isaiah, one complete and one fragmentary (1QIsa^a,b); *Rule of the Community* (1QS); *War Scroll* (1QM); *Thanksgiving Hymns* (1QH); *Genesis Apocryphon* (1QapGen); *Pesher* (Heb., "commentary") *on Habakkuk* (1QpHab)—and fragments of 72 other texts (15 biblical and 57 nonbiblical).

Qumran Cave 2: 33 fragmentary texts (18 biblical and 15 nonbiblical).

Qumran Cave 3: 14 fragmentary texts (3 biblical and 11 nonbiblical) and the *Copper Scroll* (3Q15), a record of buried treasure.

Qumran Cave 4: no complete scroll, only fragments (close to 40,000), which have constituted a giant jigsaw puzzle for scholars; to date, 575 texts have been identified (157 biblical texts, 13 *pesharim* ["commentaries"] on quoted parts of the Hebrew scriptures, and 405 nonbiblical documents including some sectarian texts, some Semitic originals of previously known Jewish literature from the Second Temple period, and many previously unknown Hebrew and Aramaic literary texts).

Qumran Cave 5: 25 fragmentary texts (8 biblical and 17 nonbiblical).

Qumran Cave 6: 31 fragmentary texts (7 biblical and 24 nonbiblical).

Qumran Cave 7: 19 fragmentary texts, all written in Greek (2 are identified: Exod. 28:4–7 and Bar. 6:43–44).

Qumran Cave 8: 5 fragmentary texts (4 biblical and 1 nonbiblical).

Qumran Cave 9: a lone papyrus fragment.

Qumran Cave 10: an inscribed potsherd.

Qumran Cave 11: 25 texts (10 biblical, 8 sectarian, 2 apocryphal, and 5 unidentified), all fragmentary, but a few of considerable size; the most important: *Psalms Scroll* (11Ps), *Temple Scroll* (11QTemple), and *Targum of Job* (11QtgJob).

The Qumran texts are dated roughly between the end of the third century BCE and 68 CE (year of the destruction of the community center at Qumran). These dates are palaeographic estimates (with a margin of error of plus or minus fifty years), but a representative sampling of them has been confirmed by radiocarbon dating tests carried out in Zurich in 1991. The Hebrew and Aramaic documents were written in four basic scripts: Archaic Script (last quarter of the third century to 150 BCE); Hasmonean (150–50 BCE); Herodian (50 BCE–40 CE); and Ornamental (from mid-first century CE on), a form also used in the Murabba'at texts. The majority of the Qumran texts have been copied in the Hasmonean and Herodian scripts, as have those of Masada. The Hebrew, Aramaic, and Greek texts of Murabba'at date roughly from between the two Jewish revolts against Rome (66–70 and 132–35 CE).

The Qumran texts are important for the light they shed on four areas: languages of the Near East in the first centuries BCE and CE; Jewish faith and practice in Judea before and at the beginning of the Christian era; the transmission of the text of the Hebrew Bible in the same period; and the Judean Jewish background of NT writings.

Languages of the Near East in the First Centuries BCE and CE: Nineteen Greek texts were found in Cave 7, and a few come from Cave 4 (Greek biblical texts). Apart from these, the remainder of the Qumran texts were composed in Hebrew (the majority) or Aramaic. This newly recovered Qumran Hebrew is related to the late form of postexilic biblical Hebrew; it is not yet the same as Mishnaic Hebrew, but in transition to the latter. Qumran Hebrew is used for the vast majority of the sectarian literature (rule books, prayer books, doctrinal writings) and seemingly represents an attempt on the part of the sect to restore to active use the holy language of a previous era. Before the discovery of the Qumran scrolls, Aramaic, which was probably the language commonly used in the Levant at that time, was poorly documented, being preserved only in a few inscriptions

The first page of the *Thanksgiving Hymns* (1QH) scroll, which is a copy of the Essene community's prayer book.

on ossuaries and tombs. Now it is richly attested, and Qumran Aramaic is regarded as a good example of Middle Aramaic, in transition between the official and biblical Aramaic of the fifth to third centuries BCE and that of the Targums and rabbinic writings of the third to sixth centuries CE. Such Aramaic texts provide good examples of the kind of Aramaic that Jesus of Nazareth and his followers would have spoken.

Jewish Faith and Practice in Judea: The Jewish historian Josephus mentions three kinds or "sects" of Jews in his day: Pharisees, Sadducees, and Essenes (sometimes even adding a fourth, Zealots). He devotes his longest description to the Essenes, a group he admired and whose lifestyle he personally attempted, but eventually renounced. Essenes are also mentioned by the Roman writer Pliny the Elder, the Jewish philosopher Philo of Alexandria, the Greek orator Dio Chrysostom of Prusa, and the Christians Hegesippus and Hippolytus of Rome. Even though what is learned from the Dead Sea Scrolls about the Qumran community does not agree in every detail with such ancient descriptions, especially that of Josephus, most modern scholars have identified the Qumran community with the Essenes. The Qumran scrolls represent, then, the literature either composed by this Jewish sect or used by it, members of which lived in Jerusalem near the "Gate of the Essenes," in towns and villages throughout Judea, and especially in a desert retreat at what is now Khirbet Qumran, the only place that corresponds to Pliny's location of them on the northwest shore of the Dead Sea.

Among the sectarian writings of Qumran there is an almost complete copy of a rule book (1QS) and ten fragmentary copies of it from Cave 4. It bears witness to a mode of communal life that the Essenes and their candidates or novices were to lead. This rule differs from another, previously known, rule book, the *Damascus Document* (CD), found in the Cairo genizah in 1896, extensive fragments of which came to light in Qumran Caves 4, 5, and 6. How to relate these two rule books of the sect is a major problem of interpretation today. The *Damascus Document* may describe the mode of life of Essenes who dwelled elsewhere (not at Qumran), in the "camps" of which it makes frequent mention, and possibly even reflects an earlier state of the sect's development. It contains enigmatic references to the history and prehistory of the sect, which are not easy to interpret. From Cave 1 have also come a copy of the community's prayer book (1QH) and a text describing preparations for an eschatological war (1QM), which reveals the sect's belief that God and the angels would join the "children of light" (the sect) to wipe out the "children of darkness" (its opponents) and all their evil ways. Fragmentary copies of both texts were also found in Cave 4, but are only partially published. From Cave 11 have come the community's psalter (or possibly another prayer book), containing biblical psalms in a different order mixed with nonbiblical writings (some clearly sectarian), and the lengthy *Temple Scroll* (11QTemple). The latter recasts much of pentateuchal legislation in a new form, putting it on the lips of God, who speaks in the first-person singular; it clearly was intended to be a Second Torah. It may, however, stem from a pre-Essene Jewish setting and reflect a stage of thinking among Jews who eventually became part of the Essene movement. The *Temple Scroll* also describes in detail how the Jerusalem temple should be rebuilt.

Fragment of a scroll found at Qumran (1QDanª);
it preserves portions of Dan. 1–2.

This sect's mode of interpreting scripture is seen, not only in its *pesharim* (verse-by-verse "commentaries" on passages from prophets and psalms), but also in isolated citations of the Bible in its sectarian writings. This mode is quite different from anything in the later writings of the rabbis (in the third to fifth centuries CE). We also learn from the Qumran texts of the messianic expectations of this sect; they awaited three figures, a prophet like Moses (cf. Deut. 18:15–18), a Davidic Messiah, and a priestly Messiah from the line of Aaron. A document labeled 4QMMT (*Miqsat Maʿase Hattorah,* "Collection of Works of the Law") is a halakhic letter written by members of the Qumran sect to opponents who did not agree with them, seemingly Pharisees. This text clearly marks off the Qumran group as a special group of Jews. It is important to realize, however, that not all of the Qumran texts are sectarian, i.e., composed by members of the sect and reflecting tenets and practices of the community of Jews who lived at Khirbet Qumran. Many belong to a common Jewish literary heritage often called Second Temple literature and were read and used by members of the Qumran community as well as by other Jews throughout Judea and the Dispersion.

Transmission of the Biblical Text: Prior to the discovery of the Dead Sea Scrolls, the oldest copy of an extended portion of the Hebrew Bible was dated 895 CE (a codex of the Former and Latter Prophets, from the Cairo genizah). In Cave 1, however, a full text of Isaiah was found, dated palaeographically and by radiocarbon to 100 BCE. The differences between the Qumran text and the medieval Hebrew Masoretic Text, separated in date by a thousand years, amounted to little more than a dozen variants and a host of insignificant spelling differences. This illustrates, in general, the care with which the Isaiah text had been transmitted over the centuries.

When Cave 4 was discovered, however, a different picture appeared. For certain books of the Bible, especially Samuel, Jeremiah, and Exodus, there were copies of the Hebrew text from pre-Christian times in a form differing from the medieval Hebrew Masoretic Text. In some cases, these Qumran biblical texts were closer to the Greek LXX; in others, closer to the Samaritan Pentateuch. As a result of these discoveries, the LXX came to be seen, not just as a poor, tendentious translation of the Hebrew, but as a witness to a different pre-Christian Hebrew text form. Moreover, some scholars now hold that there were three local text types in pre-Christian times: a "Proto-Masoretic" form of the Pentateuch known in Babylonia, close to the Masoretic Text; a form known in Judea, close to the Samaritan Pentateuch; and a form known in Egypt, related to the LXX. Eventually (probably between 70 and 132 CE), a process of standardization set in, which preferred one form of the text, a set spelling, and even a definite shape of writing, which developed into the medieval copies of the Masoretic Text.

Judean Jewish Background of the NT: The Dead Sea Scrolls do not appear to make any mention of John the Baptist, Jesus, or early Christians. Many of the tenets and practices of the Qumran community, however, shed interesting light on NT writings and provide firsthand evidence of the Jewish matrix of early Christianity. For example, the mode of quoting scripture to illustrate something in the NT closely resembles the mode of quotation employed in many of the Qumran sectarian texts. Further, the expression "children of light," a designation for Christians (Luke 16:8; John 12:36; 1 Thess. 5:5), has no background in the Hebrew Bible, but does occur in the *Rule of the Community* (1QS 1:9) and the *War Scroll* (1QM 1:1). Also, light has been shed on several titles used for Jesus in the NT ("Son of God," "Son of Man," "Lord," "Prophet," and "Messiah"). Indeed, one passage from the scrolls is remarkably close to Luke 1:32, 35; it reads, "[X, an unknown person] shall also be great upon the earth, [and all peoples sh]all make [peace with him]; and they shall all serve [him, (for)] he shall be called [son of] the [gr]eat [God], and by his name shall he be named. He shall be hailed (as) son of God, and they shall call him son of the Most High" (4Q246 1:7–2:1). A collection of beatitudes is also found in 4Q525, which records five (perhaps more, since the text is fragmentary) macarisms ("blesseds") uttered over the one who pursues wisdom (cf. Matt. 5:3–11; Luke 6:20–22). Moreover, the Essene teaching

Hebrew copper plaques rolled up as scrolls found at Qumran Cave 3.

on justification by God's mercy (1QS 11:2–3, 12–15) may be seen as a transitional mode between teaching in the Hebrew Bible about righteousness and Paul's doctrine of justification by grace through faith. In particular, the Pauline slogan "the works of the law" (Gal. 2:16; Rom. 3:28), a phrase never found in the Hebrew Bible or in later rabbinic writings, is well attested in Qumran texts (4QFlor 1–2 i 7; the title of 4QMMT). *See also* Essenes; messiah; Qumran, Khirbet; Samaritans; Septuagint.

Bibliography

Betz, Otto, and Rainer Riesner. *Jesus, Qumran, and the Vatican: Clarifications.* Crossroad, 1994.

Fitzmyer, Joseph A. *The Dead Sea Scrolls: Major Publications and Tools for Study.* Rev. ed. Scholars, 1990.

———. *Responses to 101 Questions on the Dead Sea Scrolls.* Paulist, 1992.

Vermes, Geza. *The Dead Sea Scrolls in English.* 3rd ed. Penguin, 1987.

———. *The Dead Sea Scrolls: Qumran in Perspective.* World, 1978.   J.A.F.

death. Ancient Israel's official response to mortality was, first, to accept it as God's original design and, second, to forbid worship that was concerned with the dead (Lev. 19:28; 20:1–11). Neighboring cultures believed that the dead lived on in the underworld in a communicative state (Deut. 18:9–14), but Israel tended to regard immortality as a distinguishing characteristic of God (Ps. 90:1–6). Human beings were mortal and *if* they continued to exist after death, they were not, at any rate, to be contacted (1 Sam. 28; Isa. 8:19).

Most references to death in the Bible are essentially biological (e.g., narrative observations that so-and-so died). Such death was typically accepted as natural, but a death that was premature (Isa. 38:1–12) or violent (1 Sam. 15:32) or that left no heir (2 Sam. 18:18) was nevertheless tragic. Some references to death are metaphorical (1 Sam. 2:6–7) and, occasionally, death is personified as a mythological power (Job 18:31; Jer. 9:21). Likewise, death can be described metaphorically as sleep (Job 14:10–12; Ps. 13:3–4). The presence of the dead in Sheol is basically an extended metaphor (though it might have been taken literally): Sheol is a place of darkness and silence (Job 10:21–22; Ps. 94:17; Prov. 2:18; Jon. 2:6) where not even God is remembered (Pss. 6:5; 88:12) or praised (Pss. 30:9; 115:17). Hypothetically, God could bring the dead up from Sheol (1 Sam. 2:6) or wake them from their sleep, but this was not expected to happen (Jer. 51:39, 57). Only on extremely rare occasions are the dead raised (1 Kings 17:17–24), and even then the temporarily restored person remains mortal, destined to die again.

According to Gen. 2–3, the first humans rebelled against their Creator and were denied access to the tree of life. Their status as creatures thus proceeded to its natural conclusion. This is the typical understanding of human destiny in the Hebrew Bible. In some of the later books, however, a belief in resurrection does occur (Isa. 26:19; Dan. 12:2). In the future, furthermore, death would be abolished (Isa. 25:8). Thus, in some literature of the Second Temple period, mortality is decried as the creation of a "devil" rather than as the Creator's design (Wis. 1:12–13; 2:23–24).

The NT writers reflect the later perspective that assumes life beyond death. Paul thus depicts death as an unintended fate unleashed as a consequence of primeval disobedience (Rom. 5:18–19). Furthermore, this situation has been resolved or reversed through the appearance of a second Adam (Christ) who empowers his followers, just as the first Adam affected those who came after him (1 Cor. 15:45–49). His resurrection demonstrated that death has lost its power. In the Synoptic Gospels, little attention is given to mortality. It serves primarily as an incentive to obey Jesus while there is yet time (Matt. 3:1–10; Luke 12:16–20). In the Gospel of John, mortality is overcome by the power of Jesus to give life. Jesus is depicted as mediating "eternal life" to people while they are yet alive (1:4; 3:36; 5:24) and as promising that the dead will be raised as well (5:28–29; 6:39, 54;

11:24). The Bible's final word on the matter is that of apocalypticism: mortality and martyrdom, as the goal of Satan and his instrument, Rome, will shortly come to an end. The paradise the Creator intended will then be restored and "death will be no more" (Rev. 21:4). *See also* devil; eternal life; Hades; resurrection; soul.   L.R.B./M.A.P.

Debir (dee'buhr; Heb., possibly "back part").

1 A king of Eglon who joined the Amorite confederation trying to stop Joshua (Josh. 10:3).

2 Part of the northern border of Judah (Josh. 15:7), probably Thoghret ed-Debr, "pass of Debir," ten miles east of Jerusalem and about eight miles southwest of Jericho.

3 A city of Gad (Josh. 13:26), probably modern Umm el-Dabar, about twelve miles north of Pella. It may be the same as Lo-debar (2 Sam. 9:4–13; 17:27), a refuge for Jonathan's son Mephibosheth, and later a source of assistance to David. Amos uses the name Lo-debar as a sarcastic reference to insignificant business, since the word spelled with these vowels (Debar, not Debir) literally means "a thing of no value" (6:13).

4 A Canaanite city in Judah about eleven miles southwest of Hebron (Josh. 10:36–39; 12:13). Inhabited by Anakim (Josh. 11:21), it was assaulted by Joshua or by Calebites (Josh. 15:15–17; Judg. 1:11–15) or both, and became an administrative district headquarters (Josh. 15:49). It was assigned as a levitical city (Josh. 21:15; 1 Chron. 6:58) and is twice mentioned as having another earlier name: Kiriath-sepher, Heb., "city of the scribe" (Josh. 15:15; Judg. 1:11); Kiriath-sannah (Josh. 15:49) is a probable misspelling of that name. The site location is debated. Proposals have included modern Khirbet Rabud, but the general weight of opinion has favored modern Tell Beit Mirsim over other possible tells in the vicinity. The excavation of Tell Beit Mirsim by W. F. Albright in four seasons (1926–1932) set a new mark in Palestinian archaeology. The separation of strata and their ceramic contents from each other allowed the first development of a decisive ceramic chronology for the periods from Early Bronze (3000–2000 BCE) through Iron Age II (900–600 BCE).

Bibliography

Albright, W. F. *The Excavation of Tell Beit Mirsim.* American Schools of Oriental Research, 1930–31 (vol. 12), 1931–32 (vol. 13), 1936–37 (vol. 17), and 1941–43 (vols. 21–22).   R.S.B.

Deborah (deb'uh-ruh; Heb., "bee").

1 Rebekah's nurse, who was buried near Bethel (Gen. 35:8; 24:59).

2 An Israelite judge and prophet. Though the exact duties of the judges are not clear, some appear to have exercised legal functions, while others were purely military leaders. Deborah combined these two important offices in addition to holding a third one, that of prophet (Judg. 4:4). She rendered legal decisions to Israelites who came to her in the hill country of Ephraim (4:5), and she led an Israelite coalition to victory over the Canaanite forces of Sisera in the plain of Esdraelon. This was a strategic battle in the struggle for control of central and northern Canaan. Deborah's victory is recorded in prose (Judg. 4) and poetry (Judg. 5). In the prose version, her general, Barak, refused to go into battle unless Deborah accompanied him. She agreed, declaring that "the LORD will sell Sisera into the hand of a woman" (4:9). That woman, as it turned out, was not Deborah, but another woman, Jael.

The poem, known as the "Song of Deborah," is one of the oldest examples of biblical literature, dating ca. 1125 BCE and roughly contemporaneous with the events it describes. Vivid and fast-paced, it is widely acclaimed for its literary qualities. It graphically portrays the excitement of the battle in which God comes from the south (Edom, Sinai) with cosmic forces to help the Israelite troops combat the enemy ("From heaven fought the stars / from their courses they fought against Sisera," Judg. 5:20). The poem concludes with a striking juxtaposition of two "domestic" scenes: Jael's assassination of Sisera (5:24–27) and Sisera's mother waiting anxiously for the return of her spoil-laden son (5:28–30). Whereas the prose version mentions only the tribes of Naphtali and Zebulun, the poem praises Ephraim, Benjamin, Machir, Zebulun, Issachar, and Naphtali for their participation in the battle, while censuring Reuben, Gilead, Dan, Asher, and Meroz (otherwise unknown) for not responding to the muster. Though more tribes are mentioned as cooperating in this crucial battle than any other in Judges, the traditional twelve tribes are not all enumerated. Judah, Simeon, and Levi are missing, while Machir and Gilead appear instead of Manasseh and Gad. *See also* Barak; Jael; judge; Judges, book of; poetry.

3 The grandmother of Tobit, who credits her with teaching him to care for widows and orphans in accord with Torah (1:8).   J.C.E.

debt. Israelite law forbade charging fellow Israelites interest on loans (Exod. 22:24; Deut. 23:20; Lev. 25:35–38). The prohibition, however, was not always observed (Prov. 28:8; Ezek. 18:8, 13, 17; 22:12; Matt. 25:27; Luke 19:23). Neh. 5:1–13 speaks of the people as burdened with debts. The annual interest rate among Jews at Elephantine in the fifth century BCE was 12 percent. Movable goods might be taken as a pledge to repay a loan, but the law forbade taking a person's means of livelihood (Deut. 24:6–13). In some cases, the debtor's children would become enslaved to the creditor if the debt was not paid (2 Kings 4:1–7; Neh. 5:2–7; Exod. 22:24; Isa. 50:1). Other persons could intervene as surety on behalf of an insolvent debtor and assume the responsibility for getting the debtor to pay or be liable to seizure themselves (Prov. 6:3–5; 20:16; Sir. 29:14–20). Sabbatical-year legislation requiring that slaves be set free was aimed at the problem of persons who had become enslaved because they were unable to pay debts. Approach of the sabbatical year then became an excuse for the refusal to grant a loan (Exod. 21:2–6; Deut. 15:1–

11). Likewise, although it was considered a good deed to lend money to the poor (Ps. 37:21; Sir. 29:1–2; Matt. 5:42), many refused to do so because they would not be paid back (Sir. 29:3–7).

In the Roman period, high taxes and the vicissitudes of agriculture combined to drive the bulk of the peasant population into extreme debt, a situation that is reflected in certain parables and teachings of Jesus (e.g., Matt. 18:23–35; Luke 7:41–43; 16:1–13). In the Lord's Prayer, Jesus teaches his disciples to pray, "Forgive us our debts as we also have forgiven our debtors" (Matt. 6:12). More literally, he tells his disciples they must not refuse any who want to borrow from them (Matt. 5:42). Paul uses the expression "debtor" figuratively in Rom. 1:14; 8:12. *See also* loan, loans; sabbatical year.   P.P.

Decalogue (dek'uh-log). *See* Ten Commandments.

Decapolis (di-kap'uh-lis), a federation of ten Hellenistic cities in an area east of Samaria and Galilee. The Roman scholar Pliny the Elder (ca. 77 CE) lists them as Damascus, Philadelphia, Raphana, Scythopolis, Gadara, Hippos, Dion, Pella, Gerasa, and Canatha. Great crowds from the Decapolis are said to have come to Galilee to follow Jesus (Matt. 4:25). The man possessed by a legion of demons was apparently from the Decapolis, and after Jesus casts those demons out of him (and into a herd of pigs), he goes home to proclaim Jesus throughout the Decapolis (Mark 5:1–20). Later, Jesus himself travels through the Decapolis, ministering there (Mark 7:31). *See also* cities.

Decision, Valley of, the name given in Joel 3:14 to the place where God will execute judgment on the "day of the LORD" against the nations gathered for the eschatological assault against Jerusalem. The valley is also called "Valley of Jehoshaphat" in Joel 3:2, 12. Traditional interpretation identifies the Valley of Jehoshaphat/Decision with the Kidron Valley, east of Jerusalem, where the pious kings Asa and Josiah are reported to have destroyed pagan idols (1 Kings 15:13; 2 Kings 23:4, 6, 12; 2 Chron. 15:16; 29:16; 30:14).

decrees, in the ancient world, declarations (usually in written form) by rulers or other persons in authority directing the conduct of especially significant matters for communities or individuals. The decree of Cyrus calling for the rebuilding of the temple in Jerusalem (Ezra 5:13, 17) and the decree of Caesar Augustus for a census (Luke 2:1) are but two examples of such decrees mentioned in the Bible (see also, e.g., Isa. 10:1; 2 Chron. 30:5; Ezra 6:1, 3; Esther 1:20; Dan. 3:10; Acts 17:7). Apparently, God's will and purposes were also considered "decrees," although these did not have to be written to be in force. God exercises these decrees in areas of human conduct and destiny (Dan. 4:17, 24), in the development of human history (Ps. 2:7), and in the founding and ordering of the created universe

(Job 28:26). The community of Israel also understood the laws of the covenant, as established initially by Moses, to be God's decrees. Commands of Torah are regularly referred to as "decrees" in Tobit (e.g., 1:6; 6:13; 7:11–13). *See also* commandment; covenant; law.   J.M.E.

Dedan (dee′duhn), the city and kingdom of the Dedanites, an Arabian people of unclear origin (Gen. 10:6–7; 25:1–3). Al-'Ula, an oasis about fifty miles southwest of Tema, was central to Dedan's far-reaching commercial activities, which included trade with Tyre (Ezek. 27:20). The prophets denounced Dedan (Isa. 21:13; Jer. 25:23; 49:8; Ezek. 25:13). *See also* Arabia.

dedication, setting something apart, or marking new use or practice. The Hebrew root *khnk* and its Aramaic cognate appear seventeen times in the Bible, sixteen of which are in the sense of dedication (the one exception is Prov. 22:6, where the verb is used in the sense of instruction or training). According to Num. 7:10–88, the dedication of the sacrificial altar in the desert occurred on the day of its anointing and sanctification (7:1). The dedication consisted of lavish offerings—silver plates, basins, gold spoons full of incense, bulls, rams, lambs with their meal offerings, and goats—all presented by the tribal princes. The dedication of the altar of Solomon's temple took seven days (2 Chron. 7:9). Solomon's temple was dedicated with a multitude of sacrifices (1 Kings 8:63; 2 Chron. 7:5). The relative paucity of offerings at the dedication of the rebuilt temple of the returned exiles from Babylon indicates their meager resources (Ezra 6:16–17). The words "song of dedication of the temple" appear to be an editorial interpolation in Ps. 30:1 that assigns that psalm to the festival of Hanukkah (see *Sop.* 18:2). The dedication of the rebuilt wall of Jerusalem during the days of Ezra and Nehemiah was accompanied by music, song, thanksgiving offerings, and joy (Neh. 12:27–45). The pagan dedication of Nebuchadnezzar's idol was accompanied by music and worship (Dan. 3:2–5).

It appears that a dedication differed from a sanctification (or consecration) in that the community as a whole participated in the former, while the latter was performed only by priests or others responsible for the sanctified object(s). In Deut. 20:5, however, a man who had not dedicated the new house he built was ordered to return home from the mobilized army in order to dedicate it; exactly what dedicating a house (presumably to God) entailed is not clear, because no actual ceremony for this is described. *See also* altar; Dedication, Festival of; temple, the.   J.U.

Dedication, Festival of, also known as Hanukkah (hahn′uh-kuh), a Jewish festival celebrating the purification of the temple in the time of the Maccabean revolt. On the twenty-fifth of Chislev (Nov./Dec.), 167 BCE, during the religious persecution of the Jews by the Seleucid ruler Antiochus Epiphanes, the altar of the temple was polluted with pagan sacrifices. Observant Jews, under the leadership of Mattathias (a priest) and his five sons, rebelled against the Seleucids. Upon Mattathias's death, his son Judas Maccabeus took command of the revolt, won several victories over the Seleucid army, and reconquered Jerusalem. After cleansing the temple and making a new sacrificial altar and holy vessels, "they burned incense on the altar and lighted the lamps on the lampstand, and these gave light in the temple. They placed bread on the table and hung up the curtains" (1 Macc. 4:50–51). Then, on the twenty-fifth of Chislev, 164 BCE, three years to the day after the pollution of the altar, the new altar was dedicated with sacrifices, song, music, and joyous worship (4:52–58). Judas and the people determined that those eight days of dedication should be celebrated annually (4:59). It was apparently the relighting of the temple candelabras that led to the festival also being called the "Festival of Lights" (Josephus *Antiquities* 12.7.7). That name is further associated with a postbiblical story about a small cruse of holy oil discovered at the cleansing of the temple that was miraculously able to light the temple lamp for eight days (*t. Shabb.* 21b). In John 10:22, Jesus attends the Festival of Dedication in Jerusalem. *See also* dedication; Tabernacles, Festival of.   J.U.

deer. The most common deer in the Near East throughout the biblical period appears to have been the fallow deer, a fairly large animal (40 inches high) that traveled in large herds. Bones of two varieties of fallow deer (*Cervus Dama dama* and *Cervus Dama mesopotamica*) have been found for many time periods, especially at Tell Dan and Hesban. In 1 Kings 4:23 two words that are usually translated "deer" (Heb. *'ayyal, yakhmur*) are included in a single list, indicating that two different animals must be meant. The second animal might be a roe deer (*Capreolus capreolus*), a smaller animal that appears to have been somewhat rare (cf. NRSV: "roebuck").

The deer is identified as a clean animal, acceptable for food (Deut. 12:15, 22; 14:5; 15:22). Its need for water is a metaphor for human longing for God (Ps. 42:1), and its jumps are a model of healthy life (Isa. 35:6), but without pasture it symbolizes hopeless confusion (Lam. 1:6). A superscription to Ps. 22 reads, "To the leader: according to The Deer of the Dawn"; the meaning of this phrase is uncertain, but perhaps "The Deer of the Dawn" was the title of a popular song whose tune accompanied this psalm. The terms "hart" (for a male deer) and "hind" (for a female deer) were used throughout the KJV.

defense, public. The requirements for public defense in the ancient world were factors in city planning and national policy. Regarding the former, the "defensibility" of a city and a protected water supply were of paramount importance. One of the oldest known urban structures in the ancient Near East is the Neolithic tower at Jericho. Its purpose was defense against assault, among other things. Major cities from the Early Bronze Age (3000–2000 BCE) had walls; some cities were surrounded by two walls. This pattern continued through the period of the kings in Israel. To protect the water supply at key sites, water tunnels or shafts were dug from inside the city's walls to the water table or spring located outside the walls. Examples of these can be found at the ancient sites of Gibeon, Jerusalem, Hazor, and Megiddo. In terms of *national* defense, Israel's location at a crossroads in the ancient Near East between Mesopotamia to the north and Egypt to the south required strategic policy. This requirement was one reason the kings in Israel and Judah maintained a standing army. According to 2 Chron. 11:5–12, Rehoboam fortified key sites in Judah for defensive purposes, perhaps in response to a campaign in the Levant by Pharaoh Shishak (ca. 922 BCE).

Delaiah (di-lay′yuh; Heb., "the LORD draws up").
1 The head of one of the twenty-four divisions of priests organized by David (1 Chron. 24:18).
2 A royal official who urged Jehoiakim not to burn Jeremiah's scroll (Jer. 36:12, 25).
3 The head of a family who returned from exile with Zerubbabel (Ezra 2:60; Neh. 7:62; 1 Esd. 5:37).
4 A descendant of David through Zerubbabel (1 Chron. 3:24).
5 The father of Shemaiah, the man who tried to persuade Nehemiah to go into the temple in what was actually a plot to discredit him (Neh. 6:10).

Delilah (di-li′luh), a woman who was loved by Samson. Her name (perhaps meaning "loose hair" or "small, slight") is a pun on the Hebrew word for "night" (*laylah*), while Samson's is related to "sun" (*shemesh*). Offered a bribe by some Philistines, Delilah seeks to find out the secret of Samson's strength. He misleads her three times and avoids being overpowered, but then he divulges that his strength is due to his uncut hair. Thus, while Samson sleeps, Delilah shaves his head, binds him, and hands him over to his enemies (Judg. 16:4–22). *See also* Philistines; Samson.

deluge, an excessive amount of rain, which Ezekiel says will fall upon those who say "Peace" when there is no peace (13:10–13). *See also* flood, the.

Demas (dee′muhs), originally one of Paul's "fellow workers" who joins Paul in sending greetings to Philemon, Apphia, and Archippus (Philem. 24; cf. Col. 4:14). According to 2 Tim. 4:10, Demas, "in love with this present world," deserted Paul and went to Thessalonica.

Demetrius (di-mee′tree-uhs).
1 Demetrius I Soter, the son of Seleucus and king of Syria (162–150 BCE). Raised as a hostage in Rome, he escaped, came to Phoenicia, killed

Antiochus V, and established himself as king. He attempted to appease the Hasideans in ways that would undercut the independence movement led by Judas Maccabeus (1 Macc. 7–9; 2 Macc. 14–15).
2 Demetrius II Nicator, the son of Demetrius I and king of Syria for two short periods during tumultuous years following his father's death (145–140, 129–125 BCE). The Hasmoneans sometimes supported him, but switched allegiances back and forth as the political climate changed (1 Macc. 10:67–13:30).
3 A silversmith in Ephesus who instigated a riot against Paul, because Paul's missionary activities threatened the business of making silver statuettes of the goddess Artemis (Acts 19:24–41). *See also* Artemis of the Ephesians.
4 A Christian who was commended by the author of 3 John (v. 12). Scholars often think the main point of that short letter is to provide a reference for Demetrius to a congregational leader named Gaius; the situation is a touchy one, because the Johannine churches are experiencing conflict and another congregational leader, named Diotrephes, is refusing hospitality to people like Demetrius.

demon, the English transliteration of a Greek term (*daimōn*) originally referring to any one of numerous, vaguely defined spirit beings, either good or bad. In the NT the term is reserved for evil spirits who are opposed to God and God's people. Furthermore, in the NT, the expressions "demon," "unclean spirit," and "evil spirit" appear to be interchangeable terms for the same entities. In the KJV, demons are referred to as "devils," but in most other English translations, the word "devil" is used only for Greek *diabolos*, not *daimōn*; thus there is one devil, but multiple demons.

In the ancient world, there was widespread belief in spiritual powers or beings that existed in addition to the well-known gods and goddesses. These beings were not understood as necessarily evil, though some might be. The idea that many or even all such beings were allied with the forces of darkness and wickedness only came into focus during the Second Temple period, probably under the influence of Persian thought. There are traces of the belief in harmful spirits in the earlier biblical writings (e.g., Gen. 6:1–4; Lev. 16:6–10, 26; Isa. 34:14; Job 6:4; Ps. 91:5), but little was made of this idea in Hebrew thought until the late postexilic period. Then the belief developed that there existed not only numerous evil spirits or demons, but also a leader for these evil forces. This leader came to be known by several titles, though the most common designation was Satan (the Greek title *diabolos*, "the devil," was then used as a virtual synonym for Satan, as, e.g., in John 8:44). As a result of this type of thinking, the idea developed that there were armies of demons, under the leadership of Satan or the devil, doing battle with God and God's allies.

Further development led to the idea that demons could invade human bodies and cause mental illness, physical disease, or other specific problems such as deafness or blindness (e.g., Matt. 9:32; Mark 9:5; Luke 6:18; 9:42; 11:14). Some even believed that demons could take control of nature and cause natural calamities and disasters. Such ideology is clearly reflected in the Synoptic Gospels, where Jesus is known as one who characteristically exorcises demons (e.g., Matt. 8:28–34; Mark 5:1–20; Luke 8:26–39; Matt. 12:22–32; Mark 3:22–27; Luke 11:14–23). Likewise, Jesus's disciples are given authority to exorcise demons (Matt. 10:1, 8; Mark 3:14–15; 6:7; Luke 9:1; cf. Mark 9:38–39), the Pharisees are said to exorcise demons (Matt. 12:27), and, in the book of Acts, spirit-filled leaders of the early church exorcise demons (5:16; 8:7; 19:14–16). In John's Gospel, there are no references to exorcism, but Jesus's opponents do claim that he is demon-possessed (7:20; 8:48; cf. 10:19–21); a similar charge was leveled in the Synoptic Gospels with reference to both Jesus (Mark 3:30) and John the Baptist (Matt. 11:18; Luke 7:33).

References to demons occur in numerous contexts. In the Gospel of Mark, Jesus must silence demons or else they will reveal that he is the Son of God (Mark 1:23–25, 34; 3:11–12; cf. Luke 4:41). The reality of Jesus's exorcisms indicate that the kingdom of God has come (Matt. 12:28; Luke 11:20). The claim that Jesus casts out demons by the power of Beelzebul, the prince of demons, is identified as blasphemy of the Holy Spirit, an unforgivable sin (Mark 3:22, 29). Jesus teaches that once a demon goes out of a person, it travels through desert areas and then returns, bringing seven more, if its former home is vacant. Success at casting out demons is not the most appropriate cause for rejoicing (Luke 10:17, 20) and, in fact, many who say they have cast out demons in Jesus's name will be excluded from the kingdom of heaven (Matt. 7:22). Mary Magdalene is named as a person out of whom seven demons were cast—she is the only (former) demoniac named in the Bible. Paul maintains that pagan sacrifices are actually being offered to demons (1 Cor. 10:20–21; cf. Rev. 9:20, which speaks of the worship of demons). Finally, in 1 Tim. 4:1 a different class of demon is mentioned than is referenced elsewhere in the Bible: deceitful spirits who lead people to adopt the "teaching of demons" rather than the orthodox truth of the apostolic tradition. *See also* angel; Belial, Beliar; devil; divination; magic; Satan.   J.M.E./M.A.P.

denarius (di-nair'ee-uhs; pl. denarii), Roman silver coin representing a worker's daily wage (Matt. 18:28; 20:2, 9, 13; 22:19; Mark 6:37; 12:15; 14:5; Luke 7:41; 10:35; 20:24; John 6:7; 12:5; Rev. 6:6). Devaluation under Nero early in the second half of the first century CE cut the value of the denarius in half. *See also* money.

deputy, an official of secondary rank (1 Kings 22:47; Ezra 4:8, 9, 17).

Derbe (duhr'bee), a city in the region of Lycaonia in central Asia Minor where Paul and Barnabas won believers at the end of their first journey through the Roman province of Galatia (Acts 14:20–21). Paul returned here during his second journey (16:1). Paul's companion Gaius was from Derbe (20:4). *See also* Gaius; Lycaonia.

desert, an area inhospitable to human habitation. In the Middle East, "absolute desert," i.e., a region where rain almost never falls, is found only in the Sahara, the peninsula of Arabia, and Iran. The deserts of Israel, Syria, Transjordan, and Sinai are all "tame deserts," with a little rain every winter, often in sudden storms causing dangerous flash floods. Such rain as occurs tends to fall in March and April or even early May, when the high-pressure system over Arabia is breaking up. Occasionally heavy rain can occur more frequently during the winter, and then the desert does indeed "blossom abundantly" (Isa. 35:2).

The character of the desert varies greatly. On the Transjordan plateau it is mainly a level area carpeted with millions of small stones (Arabic *hamada*), and farther east is the formidable and desolate region of black basalt (Arabic *harrah*). In the south the plateau has been broken by a complicated network of geological faults, and the desert here consists of broad sandy corridors between towering cliffs. In the Levant, the southern desert contains much *hamada,* with some sandy areas on the west and precipitous slopes to the rift valley on the east. The Sinai desert is low in the northern basin, but rises to a towering granite massif in the south, reaching 8,671 feet in Jebel Katarina, close to Jebel Musa, the traditional site of Mount Sinai. Sand dunes exist in only very few places, e.g., parts of north Sinai and the extreme south of Transjordan, and are always extremely small and restricted in area.

In the Bible, four Hebrew words are used for "desert": (1) *midbar,* a generic expression for "desolate land"; this is by far the most common; (2) *'arabah,* normally used for the dry plain of the rift valley, especially south of the Dead Sea; (3) *yeshimon,* used especially for the barren dissected slopes of Judah overlooking the Dead Sea; and (4) *khorbah,* for dry, deserted areas. The first three of these terms are regularly translated "wilderness" as well as "desert," so that, in the Bible, the two words become basically interchangeable.

True deserts are nowhere to be found in Jesus's homeland in Galilee. The words in the Greek NT translated "wilderness" (Gk. *erēmos, erēmia*) refer to uninhabited areas (Matt. 4:1; 14:13; 15:33; Mark 1:12–13; 6:31; Luke 4:2), but the writers certainly also had in mind parallels with Israel's testing and feeding in the desert during the exodus. In biblical times, although no longer the case today, the desert was the home of a multitude of wild animals, e.g., gazelles, onagers, wolves, foxes, leopards, hyenas, and ostrich. In the NT period the Transjordan deserts had been largely "tamed" by the Nabateans to promote their far-flung trade, and they managed to cultivate patches of ground that had never been farmed before. *See also* Nabatea, Nabateans; Sinai; Transjordan. D.B.

desolating sacrilege. *See* abomination that makes desolate.

Deuel (doo′uhl), the father of Eliasaph, Moses's assistant from the tribe of Gad (Num. 1:14); he is named in connection with his son's tribal leadership functions: making offerings (7:42, 47) and leading the procession of companies in the wilderness (10:20).

deuterocanonical literature. *See* Apocrypha/ deuterocanonical literature.

Deuteronomist (dyoo′tuh-ron′uh-mist), the term used in biblical studies for the author(s) responsible for one of four principal streams of tradition incorporated into the Pentateuch. The abbreviation employed for this person (or simply for the tradition) is D. According to the dominant version of this hypothesis, the material attributed to D consists of the core of our current book of Deuteronomy and is probably to be equated with the book of the law that was promulgated by King Josiah in 622 BCE (2 Kings 22–23). Further, the theological perspective attributed to D is thought to have been determinative for a later history writer or writers responsible for shaping the material contained in the books of Joshua–2 Kings. That person or persons is referred to as the Deuteronomistic Historian (abbreviated Dtr.). *See also* Deuteronomistic Historian; Deuteronomy, book of; Pentateuch, sources of the. K.H.R.

Deuteronomistic (dyoo′tuh-ron′uh-mis′tik) **Historian,** in biblical studies, the person or persons responsible for shaping the material found in the books of Joshua–2 Kings. The abbreviation employed for this person or group is Dtr. Theories regarding the composition of these books are complicated and diverse, but Dtr. is generally thought to have written or edited the history of Israel's settlement and monarchy from a theological perspective informed by the book of Deuteronomy: one key theme is demonstration that the destruction of the northern kingdom, Israel (by Assyria), and the fall of the southern kingdom, Judah (to Babylon), were acts of divine judgment against a people who had failed to keep the covenant. Certain repetitive patterns (often called "the Deuteronomistic framework") emerge. For example, the stories of the judges repeat a four-part pattern: apostasy; punishment, often in the form of oppression by the enemy; a cry for help or conversion; and deliverance or liberation. This pattern can be observed clearly in the account of Othniel (Judg. 3:7–11). Likewise, accounts of the kings typically introduce the king with a cross-reference to the king ruling in the other Israelite kingdom and with notations of residence, length of reign, age of the king at accession, and occasionally his mother's name. Such accounts usually conclude with an evaluation of the king based upon the degree to which the Deuteronomic laws concerning the centralization of worship in Jerusalem were followed. This may be accompanied by reference to sources where the king's chronicles are recorded, the place of burial, and the name of the successor. A good example for this pattern is the account of Manasseh's reign in 2 Kings 21:1–26. Modern biblical scholars differ regarding the date and number of editions of Dtr.'s work, but there is considerable agreement that it can be studied as a fairly cohesive body of work and that, as such, it can be contrasted with an alternative account of Israel and Judah's history produced by the Chronicler. *See also* Chronicler; Deuteronomist; Deuteronomy, book of; Pentateuch, sources of the.

Deuteronomy (doo′tuh-ron′uh-mee; Gk., "the second law"), **book of,** the fifth of the Five Books of Moses, or the Torah, of the Tanakh (Jewish Bible); the fifth book of the Pentateuch of the Christian OT. Its Hebrew name is *devarim,* meaning "words," from the opening sentence, "These are the words that Moses spoke to all Israel beyond the Jordan." The name Deuteronomy, meaning "second law" or "copy of the law" in Greek, is derived from the title of the book in the Greek LXX, *to deuteronomion* (see Deut. 17:18). The book is presented as Moses's exposition and reapplication of the Mount Sinai laws that were given forty years prior. He revised and adjusted them for their anticipated new setting in the promised land of Canaan.

Contents: The content of Deuteronomy is presented as the addresses of Moses. The first address, in which Moses admonishes the Israelites by recalling their rebellion in the wilderness (1:1–4:42), was probably added to the book at the time of the exile. The earliest portion and core of the book is Moses's second address (4:44–26:19, 28). In it he recalls the delivery of the law on Mount Horeb (called Sinai in Exodus), including a restatement of the Decalogue (5; cf. Exod. 20), and urges the people to remain faithful. He also defines the festivals and rituals that would order the life of the community and lays out the responsibilities of its royal and priestly leaders and the obligations of family members and ordinary citizens. He concludes this address with a series of curses and blessings that will attend disobedience or obedience to the commandments. Chap. 27 anticipates a covenant-renewal ceremony that will take place at Shechem, which is flanked by Mounts Ebal and Gerizim, from which curses and blessings respectively will be announced. A third address (29–30) concludes Moses's speeches in which he renews the covenant and encourages Israel to choose life. Various appendices round out the book, including Joshua's commission (Deut. 31), a poem in praise of the Lord (Deut. 32), a poetic blessing on the tribes (Deut. 33), and a record of Moses's death (Deut. 34). The book situates the farewell speeches of Moses to the Israelites in Moab after their wilderness journey and immediately before they were to enter the land of Canaan. The book often refers to his speeches as *torah* (NRSV: "law"; see, e.g., 1:5), meaning his "teaching." Moses speaks in the first person, and he reports God's words; God does not speak directly to the people. This way of framing the *torah* differs, for example, from Exod. 20:1–2, where God speaks directly: "Then God spoke all these words: I am the LORD your God, who brought you out of the land of Egypt." Compare this with Deut. 5:1–6, where God's words are reported by Moses: Moses convened Israel and said, "Hear, O Israel, the statutes and ordinances that I am addressing to you today. . . . The LORD spoke with you . . . and said: I am the LORD your God, who brought you out of the land of Egypt." In this way Moses's words in Deuteronomy become the divine word.

Background: Deuteronomy had a different compositional history than the Tetrateuch (Genesis–Numbers), which resulted from the editing of Yahwist, Elohist, and Priestly sources. The anonymous writer of Deuteronomy, called the Deuteronomist, made use of preexisting material, including the Decalogue and the Covenant Code from Exod. 20–23, collections of curses and blessings, and poems. The core law code of Deut. 12–26 contains evidence that it was composed from two separate sources. One source addresses the people with singular "you" and the other with plural "you" (evident in the Hebrew text, although not in English translation). For example, chap. 12 on the centralization of worship divides into two parts: vv. 1–12 predominately in the plural and vv. 13–28 in the singular. Arguments have also been made that this grammatical variation is for rhetorical or stylistic effect, rather than being indicative of different sources. When the audience is singular, Moses speaks to the heart of the individual; when plural, Moses appeals to the spirit of the community.

The core of Deuteronomy bears an unmistakable likeness to the description and political effects of the "book of the law" (2 Kings 22:8), which was found in the Jerusalem temple early in the reign of Josiah, as recorded in 2 Kings 22–23. The identification of Deuteronomy with this book has enabled scholars to establish the date of Deuteronomy, and this, in turn, has led to the unraveling of the composition of the Pentateuch and to the eventual identification and description of the work called the Deuteronomistic History, consisting of Joshua, Judges, Samuel and Kings; Deuteronomy is commonly understood as the introduction to this work.

Although there is consensus on the connection between Josiah and Deuteronomy, there is less agreement regarding the profile of the author/editor of Deuteronomy or of the dominant intellectual influences that shaped the views of the book. Based on scribal practice and book content, Van der Toorn identifies four successive stages in the development of Deuteronomy as a document that accumulated material over time: covenant,

torah, history, and wisdom editions. Weinfeld attributes the book mainly to scribes of the royal court in Jerusalem in service to Josiah who were influenced by ancient Near Eastern wisdom traditions. Yet northern Israelite influences also seem to be present: Hosea echoes Deuteronomy's attention to covenant and to the role of love in maintaining the covenant. The many references to levitical priests and the role of Shechem in covenant renewal also indicate northern interests.

OUTLINE OF CONTENTS

Deuteronomy

Deut. 33:9–10 suggests that former levitical priests have attached themselves to the Jerusalem cult.

Themes: Some aspects of the Israelite religion presented in Deuteronomy differ from Israelite beliefs reflected in Genesis–Numbers. Deuteronomy was probably a product of Josiah's new political program in the seventh century BCE, and as such it eliminated provincial religious installations and mandated that the people make sacrificial offerings only in "the place that the LORD your God will choose out of all your tribes" (Deut. 12:5). This place is to be understood as Jerusalem, though the specific place-name could not be specified because the ostensive setting of Deuteronomy predates David's founding of Jerusalem as Israel's capital. The centralizing of all ritual activity at one place had the effect of delocalizing officiated ritual activities, perhaps so the state could better supervise and control the practice of religion. It also had the specific effect of desacralizing the slaughter of animals, with the result that Israelites could now eat meat at any time within any of their towns (12:15).

The notion that the central sanctuary would be "the place where the LORD your God will choose to put the LORD's name" (e.g., Deut. 12:12) changes the notion that the actual being of God dwells in a tabernacle, as the book of Exodus suggests; rather, the name of God resides there, while the being of God resides in heaven (1 Kings 8:27–30). Although early Deuteronomy stops short of asserting strict monotheism—depending on how the Shema of 6:4 is understood—it certainly asserts the superiority of Israel's God (10:17) and demands undivided loyalty to this deity. The late edition of Deuteronomy does move in the direction of monotheism when Moses states, "The LORD is God; there is no other besides (the LORD)" (4:35).

Deuteronomy is framed as the counsel of Moses immediately before the Israelites were to enter the promised land. Above all, Moses commanded them to be loyal to God, as their covenant with God demanded (12:1). If they obeyed God, they would be allowed to remain in the land. Even if they lost the land through disobedience, they would eventually be returned, as promised in 4:26–31 and 30:1–10; both of these are passages added to the early edition sometime during the exile. The Deuteronomist uses the link between obedience and dwelling in the promised land in order to encourage obedience, to explain why the Israelites were exiled, and to offer hope of a return if they would renew their commitment to the covenant.

Influences: Mendenhall was the first to suggest that the structure of Deuteronomy is largely analogous to that of Hittite suzerain-vassal treaties. Each contains the same elements, including the suzerain's titles, a record of the suzerain's past relations with the vassal, the duties of the vassal, blessings and curses sanctioning the vassal's behavior, a list of divine witnesses to the vassal's oath of loyalty, and provisions for the periodic recital of the covenant and for the covenant document's safekeeping. This legal instrument was used to structure the relationship between God as the suzerain and great king of Israel.

Weinfeld suggests that Deuteronomy was in part modeled on the Egyptian testament form of moral instruction whereby kings typically passed on their wisdom to their successors. This is supported by Deut. 17:14–23, which enjoins Israel's king to keep a copy of this law of Moses ready to hand as a manual for office. He also details Deuteronomy's affinities with the covenant setting of royal succession from the Neo-Assyrian world as evidenced in the vassal treaties of Esar-haddon and the ways Deuteronomy was most likely shaped by them. In the treaty setting the king has his subjects pledge loyalty to his successor, as when Esar-haddon enjoined his vassals by oath to devote their allegiance to his son Ashurbanipal (see Wiseman). On this basis he suggests that Deuteronomy does not represent a covenant between two parties so much as a document that commands and structures Israel's loyalty to God. In both the Assyrian treaties and in Deuteronomy the vassal is commanded to love the suzerain, where love combines notions of loyalty, fear, and obedience.

NT writers often draw upon Deuteronomy, making it one of the most quoted books. The "great commandment" affirmed by Jesus (Mark 12:28–30) is none other than the Shema of Deut. 6:4–5. Jesus's wilderness temptation experience (Matt. 4:1–11) mirrors and fulfills Israel's experience as remembered in Deuteronomy, and Jesus is presented as responding to each of Satan's three temptations with an appropriate quote from Deuteronomy. *See also* Pentateuch, sources of the.

Bibliography

Bandstra, Barry L. *Reading the Old Testament: Introduction to the Hebrew Bible*. 4th ed. Wadsworth, 2009.

Mendenhall, George E. *Law and Covenant in Israel and the Ancient Near East*. Biblical Colloquium, 1955.

Tigay, Jeffrey H. *Deuteronomy (Devarim): The Traditional Hebrew Text with the New JPS Translation*. Jewish Publication Society, 1996.

Van der Toorn, Karel. *Scribal Culture and the Making of the Hebrew Bible*. Harvard University Press, 2007.

Weinfeld, Moshe. *Deuteronomy and the Deuteronomic School*. Oxford University Press, 1972.

———. *Deuteronomy 1–11*. Doubleday, 1991.

Wiseman, D. J. *The Vassal-Treaties of Esarhaddon*. British School of Archaeology in Iraq, 1958.   B.B.

devil, the English translation of a Greek word (*diabolos*) meaning "accuser" or "slanderer," used in the LXX to translate the Hebrew "Satan" and in the NT as a virtual synonym for the same term. In the KJV, it is also regularly employed as a translation of another Greek word (*daimōn*), which in the NRSV is transliterated as "demon." Jesus is tempted by the devil in Matt. 4:1–11; Luke 4:1–13. The devil is mentioned in two allegories based on Jesus's parables: in Matt. 13:39, the enemy who sows weeds in a farmer's wheat field is identified with the devil, and in Luke 8:12, the birds that eat seed sown along the path are identified with the devil. In John's Gospel, Judas Iscariot is called "a devil" (6:70; cf. 13:2), and Jesus tells some Jews that their father is the devil (8:44). Likewise, Paul calls the magician Elymas a "son of the devil" in Acts 13:10. The first Johannine letter identifies anyone who commits sin or who fails to love other believers as a child of the devil (3:8, 10). Elsewhere, believers are told to put on spiritual armor that will protect them from the wiles of the devil (Eph. 6:11; cf. 6:16), and they are warned to stay alert because the devil prowls around like a roaring lion seeking someone to devour (1 Pet. 5:8). There is concern that believers, including church leaders, might fall into the "snare of the devil" and be held captive by him to do his will (1 Tim. 3:7; 2 Tim. 2:26). For example, conceit may cause church leaders to fall into the condemnation of the devil (1 Tim. 3:6), and any who let the sun go down on their anger may make room for the devil (Eph. 4:27). James advises, "Resist the devil, and he will flee from you" (4:7). The NT makes clear that Jesus destroys the devil (Heb. 2:14) and his works (1 John 3:8); a lake of fire is reserved for the devil and his assistants (Rev. 20:2; cf. Matt. 25:41), where they will be "tormented day and night forever and ever" (Rev. 20:10). *See also* demon; Satan.

J.M.E./M.A.P.

devoted thing, something irredeemably dedicated to God (Lev. 27:28; cf. Mark 7:11). Such items could be dedicated by an individual (Lev. 27:28), but more commonly they were items proscribed in war. People and cities under the status of a "devoted thing" were destroyed lest they be profaned by human use or contact (Lev. 27:29; Deut. 2:34), while war spoils could become the property of the sanctuary (Josh. 6:24). *See also* ban.

dew. The presence of dew is of prime importance if plants are to survive the hot dry months (May–August) in the Near East when no rain falls. It is thus a sign of blessing (Gen. 27:28), nourishment (Deut. 32:2), peace (Ps. 133:3), royal favor (Prov. 19:12), relief from heat (Isa. 18:4), life for the dead (Isa. 26:19), the environment of animals (Dan. 4:25), short-term loyalty (Hos. 6:4), or the promise of good life (Mic. 5:7).

dial, a flat disk with numbers or other symbols around its edge. Though the sundial was known in antiquity, the word in the story of Hezekiah's healing (2 Kings 20:11; Isa. 38:8) probably refers only to a stairway whose steps were gradually shaded by a nearby object as the day progressed.

Diaspora (di-as′puh-ruh; Gk., "scattered abroad"). *See* Dispersion.

diatribe, a rhetorical style of argumentation developed by Cynic and Stoic philosophers and evident in some NT letters. In essence, this style consists of dialogue with an imaginary partner.

In addition to posing questions for his readers to consider (e.g., Rom. 2:3–4, 21–23; 7:1; 8:31–35; 9:19–21, 30; 10:14–15; 11:34–35), Paul responds to questions he anticipates they might want to ask him. For example, in Rom. 3:1, he asks, "Then what advantage has the Jew? Or what is the value of circumcision?" And, later, he begins a new discussion by asking, "What then are we to say? Should we continue in sin in order that grace may abound?" (Rom. 6:1). In such cases, Paul appears to be anticipating objections that could come up in response to his letter (see also Rom. 3:3, 5, 8; 6:15; 7:7, 13; 11:1, 11). He then demonstrates that he is a step ahead of potentially argumentative readers; he has already thought of the points they will raise and is able to address their concerns.

The Letter of James also employs rhetorical moves associated with diatribe. James engages his readers in direct conversation, addressing them as "you," with an occasional switch to "we" for the purpose of contrast (3:1) or to describe universal tendencies (3:3, 9). He makes ample use of rhetorical questions (2:14, 21; 3:13; 4:1–5) and, at times, also appears to be dialoguing with an imaginary opponent, refuting claims that such a person might make (1:13; 2:18; 4:13).   M.A.P.

Dibon (di′bon).

1 An important Moabite settlement and imposing archaeological site located in central Jordan, situated on the King's Highway, three miles north of the Arnon River and thirteen miles east of the Dead Sea. The ruins of ancient Dibon sit, for the most part, immediately north of the modern village of Dhiban. According to Num. 21:26, the Amorite king Sihon took possession of northern Moab (i.e., north of the Arnon), which included Dibon, before the Hebrews arrived in this region. According to Num. 21:21–31, the Israelites captured this part of Moab, including the town of Dibon. Biblical texts assign the territory around Dibon to Reuben and/or Gad (Num. 32:2–5, 34; Josh. 13:15–23), and Num. 33:45–46 refers to the town as "Dibon-gad."

The Moabite Stone (also called the Mesha Inscription or Mesha Stele), discovered at Dhiban in 1868, describes and celebrates a successful Moabite rebellion against Israel (ca. 840 BCE). Line 1 of this 34-line inscription refers to Mesha as "the Dibonite." The text also mentions a place called "Qarhoh"; most scholars believe this refers to Dibon's royal quarter or citadel, a section of the town where Mesha completed major building projects. Several scholars have suggested that "Dibon" referred originally to a tribe and eventually replaced the older place-name of Qarhoh. Like Numbers, the Mesha Stele also refers to the long-term occupation of the "land of Ataroth" (located near Dibon) by the "men of Gad." At any rate, this famous monument indicates that ninth-century Dibon was important for military, political, and religious reasons. References to Dibon in Isa. 15:2 and Jer. 48:18, 22 illustrate the town's continuing importance.

Between 1950 and 1965, scholars affiliated with the American Schools of Oriental Research conducted a series of excavations at Dhiban. This early phase of investigation recovered material from the Early Bronze, Iron I–II, Nabatean, Roman, Byzantine, and Islamic periods (3000 BCE–1500 CE), but no archaeological evidence from the Middle and Late Bronze Ages. The place-name "Dibon" appears in Late Bronze Age Egyptian texts, though some scholars question the assumption that these actually refer to the Dibon in northern Moab. A new research team conducted excavations at Dhiban in 2004, 2005, and 2009, seeking to clarify the occupational history of this important site. *See also* Gad; Mesha; Moabite Stone; Reuben; Sihon.

2 A site in the Judean Negeb reoccupied in postexilic times (Neh. 11:25). The location of this Dibon (probably identical with the Dimonah of Josh. 15:22) remains uncertain.

Bibliography

Dearman, Andrew, ed. *Studies in the Mesha Inscription and Moab*. Scholars, 1989.

Porter, Benjamin, et al. "The Power of Place: The Dhiban Community Through the Ages." In *Crossing Jordan: North American Contributions to the Archaeology of Jordan*. Equinox, 2007. Pp. 315–22.

Tushingham, A. D., and P. H. Pedrette. "Mesha's Citadel Complex (Qarhoh) at Dhiban." In *Studies in the History and Archaeology of Jordan*, Vol. 5. Department of (Jordanian) Antiquities, 1995. Pp. 151–59.   G.L.M.

Didymus (did'uh-muhs), a Greek name for Thomas, which the NRSV renders "twin" (the literal meaning of both "Didymus" and "Thomas"). The name Didymus is used in three verses in John's Gospel in the KJV and NIV (11:16; 20:24; 21:2). *See also* Thomas.

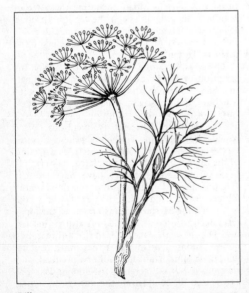

Dill.

dill, an aromatic plant used in cooking as a condiment and medicinally as a carminative and breath freshener. Paying a tithe on dill (Matt. 23:23) symbolizes scrupulous attention to details of ritual law.

Dinah (di'nuh), Jacob's daughter by Leah (Gen. 30:21; 46:15). In an account in Gen. 34, she is raped by Shechem the Hivite, who then falls in love with her and wants to marry her. Her brothers Simeon and Levi are outraged by the assault as well as by the proposed merger of Hebrews and Schechemites, and they exact a terrible revenge. They insist that the Shechemites be circumcised prior to the wedding and, when the Shechemites are weakened, recovering from having undergone circumcision, the Benjaminites enter their city and slaughter them. Dinah's father, Jacob, does not approve of this action, for he thinks it will make him odious to the peoples of the land, who will come against him in time. When challenged, Simeon and Levi respond, "Should our sister be treated like a whore?" The story is recalled by Judith in her prayer to God for help against the Assyrians (Jth. 9:1–4). *See also* Jacob; Shechem.

Dionysius (di'uh-nish'ee-uhs), a member of the Areopagite council in Athens who is said to have been converted by Paul's preaching there (Acts 17:34).

Diotrephes (di-ah'truh-feez), church leader mentioned (unfavorably) only in 3 John 9–10. He "likes to put himself first," rejects the authority of the letter's author, and refuses to receive the latter's emissaries, ejecting from the church those who do. *See also* John, Letters of.

disciple (Gk., "learner"), an apprentice or pupil attached to a teacher or movement; one whose allegiance is to the instruction and commitments of the teacher or movement. Isaiah called his followers disciples (8:16). Most NT references to "disciple" designate followers of Jesus, including both his closest associates (the twelve) and a larger number who also followed him (Luke 6:17); eventually, the term "disciples" was used as a virtual synonym for "Christians" (Acts 6:1). Other people, however, are also said to have had disciples, e.g., John the Baptist (Luke 11:1; John 1:35) and the Pharisees (Matt. 22:16; Mark 2:18). In John 9:28, some Pharisees claim, "We are disciples of Moses." *See also* apostle; twelve, the.   P.L.S.

disciple whom Jesus loved. *See* Beloved Disciple.

disease. The physical illnesses recorded in the Bible are many and varied, but imprecise description of them often makes their identification in modern terms difficult. Since disease could have grave social and economic consequences in the ancient Near Eastern and Greco-Roman worlds, its causes and cures were matters of great moment.

Some passages dealing with disease name no cause (Lev. 13; 1 Kings 17:17; 2 Kings 5:1; Mark 1:30; 5:25). Others specify a cause, whether natural (2 Kings 4:38–40) or, more commonly, divine (1 Sam. 5:6–12; 2 Kings 6:18; Ps. 38), especially when disease is connected with sin (Num. 12; cf. 2 Kings 5:20–27; Num. 16:41–50; 2 Sam. 12:15–18). The Deuteronomic interpretation of disease is the most emphatic and detailed in ascribing it to sin (Deut. 28:22, 27–28, 35, 59–61). Such an interpretation, or its application to specific instances, is questioned in the book of Job and in the account of the healing of the blind man in John 9:1–3. In the NT, disease is frequently attributed to Satan or the devil and his demonic minions (e.g., Mark 1:35; 3:22–26; 7:25; Luke 13:16, 32; cf. 2 Cor. 12:7–8). At the same time the theme of disease as divine retribution is retained (1 Cor. 11:29–30; Acts 12:21–23). *See also* demon; healing; leprosy.

H.E.R.

Dishan (di′shan; an early Semitic, Aramaic, and Arabic spelling of Dishon).

1 A son of the Horite Seir, listed seventh in Gen. 36:21 and 1 Chron. 1:38, and the father of two sons, Uz and Aran (Gen. 36:28; 1 Chron. 1:42).

2 The name of a Horite family group (Gen. 36:30) in the land of Seir.

Dishon (di′shon; an early Northwest Arabic and Canaanite form of Dishan).

1 A son of the Horite Seir, listed fifth in Gen. 36:21 and 1 Chron. 1:38, and father of four sons, Hemdan, Eshban, Ithran, and Cheran (Gen. 36:28; Hamran for Hemdan in 1 Chron. 1:42).

2 The son of Anah (Gen. 36:25; 1 Chron. 1:41), and the brother of Oholibamah (Gen. 36:25).

3 A Horite family group in Seir (Gen. 36:30).

Dispersion (dis-puhr′zhuhn; Gk. *diaspora*, from *diaspeirein*, "scattered abroad"), term referring to the exile or emigration of Jews from Israel to other countries. When the southern kingdom of Judah was conquered in 597 BCE and again in 587 many of its leaders and people were exiled to Babylon, laying the foundation of a community that flourished there until 1000 CE. During the Persian (539–332 BCE) and Hellenistic (332 BCE–63 CE) periods Jews moved to all major population centers in the Mediterranean world, settling especially in upper Egypt and southern Asia Minor. By the first century CE, Jews were a recognized ethnic group with legal rights to practice their religion throughout the Roman Empire. Vigorous communities existed in Rome, Alexandria, Cyprus, the cities of Greece and Asia Minor, Antioch in Syria, and beyond the empire in Mesopotamia. Acts 2:9–11 names the diverse origins of pilgrims to Jerusalem. Greek was the most common language of the eastern Roman Empire, and the LXX served as the primary scriptures for the large Greek-speaking Jewish community. In John 7:35 people speculate whether Jesus will go to the Dispersion to teach the Greeks (i.e., Greek-speaking Jews). The Letter

of James is addressed to the "twelve tribes in the Dispersion," which would literally mean "Jews in the Dispersion," but, given the assumptions of the letter, probably means "Jewish Christians from all twelve tribes" in the Dispersion." First Peter is addressed to the "exiles of the Dispersion," but since it is obviously written to Gentile Christians (1:14, 18; 2:10; 4:3–4), the expression is probably being employed figuratively: the Christians understand themselves to be "aliens" within the present world, in exile or displaced from their true home in heaven. *See also* Babylon; exile.   A.J.S.

distaff. *See* spinning and weaving.

divided kingdom, divided monarchy, the two-hundred-year period in ancient Judah and Israel ca. 922–722/1 BCE. Following Solomon's reign, his son Rehoboam succeeded him as king over Judah (the southern tribes) and, as was the custom (1 Kings 12:1–20), went to Shechem to be confirmed as king over Israel (the northern tribes) as well. There was discontent, however, over Solomon's harsh labor policies, and Rehoboam exacerbated tensions by declaring he would continue and increase his father's demands. As a result, he was unable to retain leadership in the northern state. Israel chose Jeroboam I as king instead, and the era of the divided kingdom began. The kingdom was never reunited. Israel had nineteen kings before being destroyed by Assyria in 722/1 BCE. Judah had thirteen kings during that same period (and then seven more before being devastated by Babylon in 587/6 BCE). The period of the divided kingdom was the era for many of the prophets whose writings are included in the Bible, including such great eighth-century prophets as Amos, Hosea, and Isaiah of Jerusalem (Isa. 1–39). *See also* chronology, Hebrew Bible; Jeroboam I; prophet; Rehoboam; Solomon.   K.H.R.

divination, means through which humans attempt to secure information through spirits, magic, or some other superhuman source. There was great interest in the biblical world in knowing the future, and virtually everyone believed it was sometimes possible to do so; dreams, visions, and other portents could reveal the future, though an interpreter might be needed to know their meaning. Astrology was also widely practiced, offering predictions of the future (and attendant advice for the present) based on the observation of stars, which were believed to be deities affecting earthly events. Professional oracles claimed to have the ability to predict the future for those who sought them out (and performed required services). The most famous of these included the Pythia in Delphi, the oak trees of Dodona, and the Memnon of Thebes. Many people also thought the future could be divined by anyone who knew how to interpret signs sent by God (or the gods); the flight of birds, eating habits of chickens, and condition of the entrails, especially the liver, of sacrificial animals were all deemed relevant at different places and times. The flight of arrows foretold a victory to King Joash (2 Kings 13:14–19).

The Bible contains numerous prohibitions against divination. Deut. 18:10–11 says, "No one shall be found among you who makes a son or daughter pass through fire, or who practices divination, or is a soothsayer, or an augur, or a sorcerer, or one who casts spells, or who consults ghosts or spirits, or who seeks oracles from the dead" (the practice of consulting the dead is called necromancy; cf. Lev. 19:26). Judah and Israel both disobeyed this command, however (2 Kings 17:17), and King Manasseh of Israel is singled out as one who did evil in the eyes of the Lord because he "practiced soothsaying and augury and sorcery, and dealt with mediums and with wizards" (2 Kings 21:6; 2 Chron. 33:6). The story of Saul consulting with the medium of Endor to call up the prophet Samuel from the dead represents an especially egregious example of divination that meets with divine condemnation (1 Sam. 28).

Still, certain types of divination appear to be allowed. During the early history of Israel, it was an accepted practice to "inquire of the LORD" (Judg. 1:1–2; 1 Sam. 10:22). This expression implies an oracle (similar to Delphi in Greece) where a question could be asked and a reply given by God through a medium. The Urim and Thummim (or ephod) were also oracular media, but answers were restricted to yes or no (1 Sam. 23:9–12; 30:7–8; Num. 27:21; Acts 1:26; cf. Jon. 1:7; Esther 9:24–26; Matt. 27:35). Dream interpretation was also legitimate, provided God gave the person that particular gift: Joseph interpreted the dreams of Pharaoh (Gen. 41); and Daniel, those of Nebuchadnezzar (Dan. 2; 4). In the NT, Joseph, husband of Mary, receives messages in dreams (Matt. 1:20–21; 2:13), as do the magi (2:12) and Pilate's wife (27:13). *See also* dreams; magic; Urim and Thummim.

S.B./M.A.P.

divorce. Despite a general disapproval of divorce, Mosaic law did permit divorce to be initiated by the husband (though, apparently, not by the wife). The acceptable grounds for divorce are not stated (cf. Deut. 24:1, "because he finds something objectionable about her") and may have varied over time. The practice was also regulated: the husband had to provide the wife with a written bill of divorce that would permit her to remarry (Deut. 24:1–2). Certain other restrictions were in place as well: divorce was excluded as an option for a man who claimed his bride had not been a virgin when it could be proven that she had been, or for a man who had been forced to marry a woman because he raped her (Deut. 22:19, 29). There were also some legal restrictions placed on those who had been divorced: a divorced woman could not marry a priest (Lev. 21:7, 14; Ezek. 44:22), nor could she remarry a previous husband after having been married to someone else (Deut. 24:3–4). These practices and policies sometimes provided context for prophets to speak of God's troubled relation-

ship with Israel (Isa. 50:1; Jer. 3:1, 8). The insistence in Mal. 2:16 that God "hates divorce" occurs in such a context (God hates the termination of the relationship between God and a nation), but this obviously assumes literal application as well. Thus, divorce appears to have been widely, and perhaps consistently, regarded as an unfortunate occurrence contrary to God's ideal plan for humanity.

Jesus states the latter point explicitly in the NT by distinguishing between allowance for divorce and fulfillment of God's will (Mark 10:2–12; cf. Matt. 5:31–32; 19:3–12; Luke 16:18). His view is that God's plan for humanity was revealed at creation (people were made male and female and joined together by God) and that the subsequent Torah legislation permitting and regulating divorce was given as a necessary concession due to the hardness of human hearts. Therefore, divorce and remarriage should be viewed as tantamount to adultery. In Matthew's Gospel, Jesus's words include an "exception clause": remarriage following divorce on the grounds of unchastity (Gk. *porneia*) does not qualify as adultery (5:32; 19:9). The meaning of this exception clause is disputed: it might refer to marital unfaithfulness on the part of the spouse (which is what the NRSV's "unchastity" suggests) or an illicit or unlawful union (such as incestuous marriage or some other union forbidden by the Torah).

The apostle Paul reiterates as teaching from the Lord that believers should not divorce, and if they do, they should not remarry (1 Cor. 7:10–11). He recognizes, however, that divorces might occur when only one member of a married couple becomes a Christian (7:15). Even so, the believer should not seek a divorce if the unbelieving spouse consents to live with him or her (7:13). Though not ideal, such a relationship allows the believing spouse to sanctify (7:14) and possibly to save (7:16) the unbelieving partner.

In some instances, the Bible recommends or even requires divorce. Thus, Ezra required returning exiles who had married non-Israelite wives in Babylon to "send away" those wives and any children born to them (10:1–19). Joseph intends to divorce Mary when he discovers she is pregnant even though he has not yet had sexual relations with her, and Matthew's Gospel indicates that this is what a "righteous man" would normally do (1:18–19). John the Baptist insists that Herod Antipas divorce his wife Herodias, who had formerly been married to his half brother Philip (Mark 6:17–18). All of these instances seem to assume situations in which the "marriage" to be terminated is viewed as an illegitimate union. Sir. 7:26, by contrast, seems to recommend divorce from a wife whom one detests. *See also* marriage.

M.A.P.

Dodo (doh′doh; Heb., "his beloved").

1 A member of the tribe of Issachar and the grandfather of Tola, one of the judges of Israel (Judg. 10:1).

2 An Ahohite, father of Eleazar (one of the three leaders of David's warriors, 2 Sam. 23:9). He is probably the same person referred to as Dodai the Ahohite (1 Chron. 27:4), although it is probable that due to an inadvertent lacuna in the text it was his son Eleazar who commanded the division of twenty-four thousand men under David and not Dodai himself.

3 A man from Bethlehem, the father of Elhanan, one of David's warriors (2 Sam. 23:9).   D.R.B.

Doeg (doh'ig), "the Edomite," an unscrupulous henchman of Saul (1 Sam. 21–22). He witnessed Ahimelech, a priest in Nob, giving assistance to David. Doeg reported Ahimelech's action to Saul, who, ignoring Ahimelech's protestation of faith in David's loyalty, ordered all the priests of Nob slain. Most of Saul's servants refused to strike God's priests, but Doeg proceeded to kill them, their families, and their livestock. Ps. 52 was inspired by this incident.

dog. In Egypt, dogs were highly esteemed and apparently used as sentinels (cf. Exod. 11:7). They were also popular in Mesopotamia as hunting companions; they are depicted as such on Assyrian reliefs from the seventh century BCE. The Hebrews, however, seem to have viewed dogs with a measure of disgust, as animals that ate their own vomit (Prov. 26:11; cf. 2 Pet. 2:22) and were noted for howling at night and prowling about the city (59:6, 14). In the Bible the dog (Heb. *keleb;* Gk. *kyōn*) is often described as a scavenger. Dogs could be viewed as useful because they cleared away refuse and carcasses (Exod. 22:31; Jer. 15:3), but they are also said to eat human flesh (1 Kings 14:11; 16:4; 21:23–24; 2 Kings 9:10, 36) and to lick human blood (1 Kings 21:19; 22:8; cf. Ps. 68:23; Luke 16:21). In 2 Kings 9:30–36 is the gruesome story of Jezebel, who was eaten by dogs after being thrown over the city wall. Such associations form the background for Jesus's counsel not to give what is holy to dogs or to cast pearls before swine (Matt. 7:6). Dogs did serve as sentinels, however (Isa. 56:10), and occasional references to domesti-

Hunting dog and Assyrian hunter; seventh-century BCE relief from Nineveh.

cated dogs began to appear in the later literature. The book of Job seems to refer to dogs who help with sheepherding (30:1). The book of Tobit refers to a dog that followed at the heels of Tobias (5:16; 11:4). The little dogs (Gk. *kynarion*) that ate the proverbial "crumbs that fall from their master's table" are envisioned as pets that had access to the house (Matt. 15:27; Mark 7:28). When applied to a person, "dog" typically becomes a term of disregard and humiliation. Goliath ridicules David's weapons by saying "Am I a dog, that you come to me with sticks?" (1 Sam. 17:43). Mephibosheth does obeisance to David saying, "What is your servant, that you should look upon a dead dog such as I?" (2 Sam. 9:8; for "dead dog," cf. 1 Sam. 24:14; 2 Sam. 16:9). Likewise, Hazael calls himself "a mere dog" before Elisha (2 Kings 8:13). The term is used generically for enemies in Ps. 22:16, 20. Paul warns the Philippians to "beware of dogs," by which he means those who insist that Christians must be circumcised (3:2). Dogs symbolize those excluded from the new Jerusalem in Rev. 22:15.
                                          I.U.K./M.A.P.

dominion, rule or lordship, referring to political authority exercised by human beings (Gen. 37:8; Judg. 14:4; Ps. 72:8) or the realm in which such authority is exercised (2 Kings 20:13). Oppressive rule is condemned (Lev. 25:43, 53; Matt. 20:25). Ultimate and eternal dominion over all things belongs to God (Pss. 22:28; 145:13; Dan. 4:3; Rev. 1:6). Humanity also rules over creation, though under God (Gen. 1:26, 28; Ps. 8:6). In the NT, dominion may also refer to certain angelic or cosmic powers (Col. 1:16; cf. Rom. 8:38), which, however, are subordinated to the power of God (Eph. 1:21; Col. 2:15). Paul also uses the word "dominion" in constructing his theological arguments throughout Romans: sin and death exercised dominion through the law, but now justification and righteousness exercise dominion through grace unto eternal life in Jesus Christ (5:14–21; 6:9–14).

donkey. *See* ass.

doorkeepers, people who watched or controlled access to important or restricted places. Doorkeepers were appointed in the temple as "keepers of the threshold" to collect money from the people (2 Kings 22:4). A psalmist says, "I would rather be a doorkeeper in the house of my God than to dwell in the tents of wickedness" (Ps. 84:10). Ezra 7:24 mentions doorkeepers of the temple as exempt from taxes and tribute. In a secular context, eunuchs were doorkeepers at the palace of the Persian king (Esther 2:21) and a woman was a doorkeeper at the house of King Ishbaal (2 Sam. 4:6). Mark 13:34 mentions a doorkeeper appointed to keep watch at the house of a rich man (cf. John 18:16–17; Acts 12:13).

doorpost (Heb. *mezuzah*), a supporting beam for a city gate or for the doorway of a sanctuary or

Doorpost.

private house. The Israelites sprinkled the blood of the Passover sacrifice on their doorposts, so that the angel of death would not kill their firstborn (Exod. 12:7, 22–23). The Israelites were enjoined to write divine exhortations upon their doorposts, in addition to reciting and teaching them, and binding them to the hand and forehead (Deut. 6:9; 11:20).

doors. Biblical references to doors are both literal and symbolic. In a literal sense, the Bible refers not only to doors to houses, but also to tents, buildings, and parts of buildings. Applied to tents and to the tabernacle in the wilderness, the English word is slightly misused, referring to a flap or entrance opening that usually had no construction as its support (Gen. 18:1; Exod. 26:36; Lev. 14:11). Elaborate doors were part of the temple, however, with main doors, built of two swinging leaves each (1 Kings 6:34; Ezek. 41:24), and numerous other doors throughout the structure (Ezek. 40:13–47:1). Archaeological evidence in numerous locations supports the suggestion that doors were usually hung from a pivot post set in a socket. They could be bolted shut, both with horizontal and vertical bolt locks. They were sometimes reinforced with iron, carved or otherwise decorated, and, as with gates in city walls, were the most vulnerable point in the building's perimeter when under assault. Stone doors (swinging and rolling types) have been found for both tombs and buildings (cf. Matt. 27:65–28:2).

Symbolically, a door could be a place where sin lay in wait (Gen. 4:7), an aperture through which speech made its exit (Ps. 141:3), a model of sluggish action (Prov. 26:14), an opportunity for proclamation (2 Cor. 2:12), or a passageway to eternal life (Luke 13:24). The Bible also speaks of doors to hope (Hos. 2:15) and to faith (Acts 14:27). In John 10:1, Jesus says, "I am the door," probably meaning that life is found through faith in him (cf. John 20:31). In Rev. 3:20, he stands at the door of a church and knocks, promising to enter and dine with anyone who opens the door by heeding his call to repentance. In Rev. 4:1, John beholds a door standing open in heaven, and he enters to behold the vision recounted in the rest of that book.   R.S.B./M.A.P.

Dor, a well-situated natural seaport on the coast of the Mediterranean Sea south of Mount Carmel. Dor is first mentioned in an Egyptian inscription of the thirteenth century BCE. The king of Dor was part of a coalition of Canaanite kings defeated by Joshua (mid- or late thirteenth century BCE; Josh. 11:2; 12:23). The city was included in the territorial allotment of Manasseh (Josh. 17:7–13; 1 Chron. 7:29), although the Joshua text notes that the Canaanites continued to occupy Dor. This is also known from the Egyptian *Tale of Wen-Amon* (ca. 1100 BCE), which says the city was occupied by the Tjeker, a Sea People related to the Philistines. The city was under Israelite control in the tenth century, however, for at that time Solomon's son-in-law Ben-abinadab was governor of the district of Dor (1 Kings 4:11). Later, it became the center of an Assyrian administrative district in the eighth century (probably the "Way of the Sea" of Isa. 9:1–2). Dor was subsequently controlled by the Persians and the Phoenicians and during the Hellenistic period was a large, well-fortified independent city. The Hasmonean Simon fought against Trypho of Dor in an alliance with Antiochus Sidetes (1 Macc. 15:1–14), and the city was later taken by Alexander Jannaeus. Pompey restored independence to the citizens in 63 BCE. Today, Tel Dor (modern Khirbet el-Burj) is one of the largest tells in Israel (about thirty-five acres), and it has been a rich site for archaeological excavation.   J.D.P.

Dorcas (dor´kuhs; Gk., "gazelle"), a Christian woman in Joppa whose Aramaic name was Tabitha (also, "gazelle"). Well known for her works of generosity and charity, she became ill and died. Two men traveled from Joppa to Lydda, where Peter was staying, and they brought Peter back with them, to the room where Dorcas's body had been washed and laid. There, widows stood beside him, weeping, and showing him the tunics and other clothing she had made. Peter put everyone outside, prayed, and then restored Dorcas to life with the words, "Tabitha, get up!" (see Acts 9:36–42). Dorcas is the only woman in the NT who is specifically called a "disciple" (9:36).   M.A.P.

Dothan (doh´thuhn), the town where Joseph and his brothers pastured their flocks (Gen. 37:17). In antiquity as well as today Dothan was close to the main commercial route and in the midst of pasture lands. It was also here that the king of Syria sought out the prophet Elisha (2 Kings 6:13). Ancient Dothan is identified with modern Tell Dotha, ten miles north of Samaria/Sebaste and near the southern edge of the Esdraelon plain. Excavations reveal rather continuous occupation from Late Chalcolithic times (ca. 3200 BCE) through Iron Age II (to 700 BCE). Widespread Middle Bronze occupation and several Iron Age II levels can be related to the biblical accounts. N.L.L.

dove, a small bird of the Columbidae family. Three varieties of the small species of pigeon identified as turtledoves were known in the ancient Near East. Noah used doves to determine if the flood had subsided (Gen. 8:8–12). Lev. 12:8 prescribes the offering of a pair of doves or two young pigeons to purify a mother after childbirth if the family could not afford a lamb. Doves for such offerings were sold in the temple court (Mark 11:15; John 2:14). Mary made this offering after the birth of Jesus, a sign of the family's poverty (Luke 2:4). In the Song of Solomon, two lovers like to refer to each other as "my dove" (2:14; 5:2, 6:9) and to say that their lover's eyes are "like doves" (1:15; 4:1; 5:12). There are also poetic or figurative references to the moaning of doves (Isa. 38:14; 59:11; Ezek. 7:16; Nah. 2:7) and to the wings of doves (Pss. 55:6; 68:13). To be "like a dove" may mean to be homeless (Jer. 48:28; Ezek. 7:16), to be silly (Hos. 7:11), or to be innocent (Matt. 10:16). The stories of Jesus's baptism all describe the descent of the Holy Spirit being like that of a dove (Matt. 3:16; Mark 1:10; Luke 3:22; John 1:32). P.P.

The dove of the Holy Spirit descends upon Jesus as he is baptized by John the Baptist (John 1:32). Detail from the Florence Baptistery doors by Andrea Pisano, ca. 1336.

dowry. *See* marriage.

drachma (drak'muh). A Greek coin equal in value to a Roman denarius, which was a typical day's wage in NT times (mentioned only in Luke 15:8; Tob. 5:15). *See also* denarius; money.

dragon, a reptilian monster well known in the mythology and iconography of the ancient Near East. In the Babylonian creation myth, *Enuma Elish,* the dragon Tiamat is slain by the god Marduk and her supporters are taken captive. In a Hattic myth, the dragon Illuyankas defeats the storm god but later is slain by him. The Ugaritic myths from Ras-Shamra refer to various monsters defeated by the storm god Baal or his sister, Anat. In the Bible the dragon also appears as the primeval enemy of God, killed or subjected in conjunction with creation (Pss. 74:13–14; 89:10; Isa. 51:9; Job 26:12 13), but appearing again at the end of the world, when God will finally dispose of it (Isa. 27:1). The book of Revelation takes up the latter theme. The dragon (identified now with the devil) and its agents campaign against God, but are finally defeated (12–13; 16:13–14; 20:2–3, 7–10). According to the book of Job, however, the dragon is currently kept under guard (7:12), its supporters lying prostrate beneath God (9:13).

Referred to variously as Tannin, Rahab, or Leviathan, the dragon is often conceived of as a sea monster. Sometimes, however, these terms may refer to literal sea creatures rather than mythological ones—this seems to be the case when the words *tannin* and *leviathan* are used to refer to the monsters of the deep created by God (Gen. 1:21; Ps. 104:26), summoned to praise God (Ps. 148:7), and beyond human capture (Job 41:1). The oracle of Isa. 30:7 gives Egypt the name "Rahab [is] put down," alluding to the dragon's defeat by God. Ps. 87:4 simply assumes Rahab as an accepted name for Egypt. The king of Egypt is portrayed as a sea monster lurking in the Nile, whom God will catch and kill (Ezek. 29:3; 32:2). The story Bel and the Dragon (among the apocryphal/deuterocanonical Additions to Daniel) relates Daniel's unorthodox disposal of a dragon worshiped by the Babylonians. *See also* Leviathan; Rahab. S.B.P.

dreams. In the book of Genesis, God frequently offers guidance through dreams (e.g., Abimelech's dream, 20:3–7; Jacob's dreams, 28:12; 31:9–13; Laban's dream, 31:24; Joseph's dreams, 37:5–10). Joseph is also gifted with the ability to interpret other people's dreams (40:1–41:32). Elsewhere, Gideon is inspired when he overhears a man telling about a dream (Judg. 7:13–15), and God speaks to Solomon in a dream (1 Kings 3:5–15). God is

This composite creature, with the head of a serpent, body of a lion, and hind feet of an eagle, is a reconstruction of the original that decorated the Ishtar Gate at Babylon during the reign of Nebuchadnezzar II, seventh century BCE.

said to speak to prophets in their dreams (Num. 12:6), but concern also arises about false prophets who claim such revelations (Deut. 13:2–6), and a mistrust of dream revelations is expressed in Jeremiah (23:28; 27:9–10; 29:8–9; cf. Zech. 10:2; Sir. 34:1–8). Nevertheless, dreams became a popular mode of revelation in apocalyptic literature. Daniel interprets the dreams of the Gentile king and receives his own revelations in dreams (1:17; 2:1–9, 26–46; 4:5–27; 7:1). Joel prophesies of a day when God's spirit will be poured out on all flesh, with an increase of divinely inspired dreams and visions (2:28; cf. Acts 2:17). In the NT dreams figure most prominently in the nativity story of Matthew (1:20; 2:12, 13, 19, 22). Pilate's wife also has a dream, prompting her to warn Pilate about his dealings with Jesus (Matt. 27:19). *See also* Daniel, book of; divination; Joseph.   J.J.C./M.A.P.

dregs, the residue left in a wine container during fermentation and aging. Wine with the dregs in it was considered a preferable product to new wine (Isa. 25:6), but was also used as a metaphor for sluggish richness (Jer. 48:11; Zeph. 1:12) that deserved to be disturbed. However, when Paul says that Christians are regarded as "the rubbish of the world, the dregs of all things" (1 Cor. 4:13), he is not calling attention to the beneficial effect Christians have on the world, but merely noting that Christians are regarded as worthless or disposable garbage (as were the dregs of wine after the wine itself had been consumed).

dress. The biblical terms for dress, garments, clothes, robes, and various items of garb are general and often interchangeable. Fortunately, artistic representations from the Near East are helpful in providing more detailed information.

The earliest forms of clothing were generally made from animal skins. Linen (from flax) and cotton cloth were apparently distinctively Egyptian developments, whereas the use of wool for fabric seems to have become popular sometime between the Sumerian use of lapped leaves (of leather or metal) for skirts, evident in their statuary, and the draped robes of Gudea, the king of Lagash, in the later Sumerian period. Weaving cloth of wool or hair, stitching fabric pieces together, and dyeing fabric to allow variation in color are known throughout the biblical period.

Biblical styles and materials were those shared throughout the Near East from the Early Bronze Age (3000–2000 BCE) into the Roman period (63 BCE–324 CE). Characteristic references to Israelite garments used by both men and women indicate that the cultural habits in dress changed as different peoples invaded and dominated the Near East.

It is immediately clear that dress was geared to climate and necessities of movement rather than simply to appearance or aesthetic appeal. There were exceptions. The notorious dress of prostitutes (Prov. 7:10) was apparently a public advertisement of their services. Soldiers' dress was geared to battle efficiency. Priestly garments included many symbolic representations.

Men's Clothing: The term translated "clothes" in 1 Sam. 4:12 and Judg. 3:16 was apparently a long robe of some sort, since it could be cut off "in the middle, at their hips" (2 Sam. 10:4). A term for any whole garment could also mean a cover cloth for the ark (Num. 4:6–9) or a bed (1 Sam. 19:13), royal robes (2 Sam. 13:31), war prisoners' clothing (Jer. 52:33), mourning garb (2 Sam. 14:2), and priestly garments (Exod. 28:2). Such clothing might be made of either linen or wool, but in the codes in Deuteronomy and Leviticus they were not to be mixed (Deut. 22:11; Lev. 19:19).

The "wraparound" garment usually called a mantle could cover nakedness (Noah's in Gen. 9:23), a sword (1 Sam. 21:9), or dress clothing while moving incognito (Ruth 3:3). It was the clothing of wanderers (Deut. 8:4), strangers (Deut. 10:18), and the poor (Exod. 22:26–27), who used it as a sleeping cover. For that reason it was not to serve as collateral for more than the part of a day remaining until sundown, when the owner would need it for the night. As with all clothing, it could be ripped (1 Kings 11:30). To be without such garments was the extremity of poverty or neglect (Job 24:7). Ezek. 27:23–24 indicates that clothing was a trading item when it was distinctively rich or finely worked goods. NT language for general clothing items includes reference to an oblong outer garment (Matt. 17:2; 27:31) worn over a coat (Matt. 5:40; Luke 6:29, "shirt").

A long- or half-sleeved, ankle-length shirt in white or colors was used as an undergarment (Gen. 37:3, 31–33). Gen. 3:21 reports that God made such garments for Adam and Eve out of skins. They were usually anchored over one if not both shoulders. The collared tunic of Job 30:18 was usually made of wool, but was to be of linen if worn by priests. The seamless tunic of Jesus (John 19:23) for which the soldiers cast lots was such an item, as was the garment torn by the high priest (Mark 14:63). The young man who lost his "linen cloth" (Mark 14:51–52) in a scuffle was probably dressed only in a wraparound of some sort. The "belt," whether of leather (as Elijah's, 2 Kings 1:8) or cloth (Jer. 13:1), was in effect a loincloth, and although it was loosened at night, it was not necessarily removed. A true belt, sash, or girdle tying one's clothes together at the waist and serving to suspend a soldier's sword was also normal. If made of folded cloth, it could hold money or other valuables (Mark 6:8).

Footwear in the form of sandals or shoes was essential, given the thistle and thorn growth in the countryside. They could be removed in holy places (Exod. 3:5), for mourning, or for repair (Josh. 9:5). Artistic representation shows them attached to the foot by straps around the ankle or, in some periods, even up the calf of the leg.

Head covering was vital for shade from the sun in summer as well as for warmth during the rainy season. A simple cloth might be draped, folded, or wrapped (as a turban) and be held in place by

Ancient Styles of Dress: **1a.** One type of loincloth (Semite, ca. 1800 BCE); **1b.** Animal skin; **2.** Men's tunic or coat; **3.** Men's mantle; **4.** Himation; **5.** First-century cloak or cape; **6.** Women's dress; **7.** High priest's robe; **8.** Type of prayer shawl; **9.** Hebrew royal attire; **10.** Persian attire; **11.** Roman toga; **12.** Roman *stola* and *pallium;* **13.** Egyptian loincloth (ca. 1300 BCE); **14.** Egyptian sheathlike dress (ca. 2000 BCE), **15.** Babylonian attire (ca. 2000 BCE); **16.** Assyrian attire (ca. 900 BCE).

a headband. The use of lightweight cloth was remarkably suited to the climate, providing a shade penetrable by breeze in the heat of the summer, but allowing multiple folds in which to wrap both face and head as protection against cold, wind, or dust. Specific headgear with certain decorations was designated for priests and their ceremonial duties.

Women's Clothing: The same general terms for clothing mentioned above applied to the garments women wore. The same divisions of outerwear, undergarments, belts, footwear, and headgear are appropriate, with the addition of the veil in some situations. Outerwear consisted of a long robe, possibly decorated with fringes or, in later periods, with embroidery. It was fastened at the waist with a belt (Isa. 3:24). Such a mantle or cloak could enfold goods (Ruth 3:15, grain) as well as the wearer. The undergarments of women included the wool or linen shoulder-suspended shift used by men (2 Sam. 13:18), but artistic representations show greater variety of colors than those used by men. For footwear, sandals were normal and might be made especially attractive (Song of Sol. 7:1; Jth. 10:4; 16:9), with special enhancements appropriate at the time of a woman's marriage (Ezek. 16:10). The most distinctive items of dress for women pertain to the head. The "turban" (Isa. 3:23) or "headdress" (Isa. 3:20) was supplemented at least in certain circumstances by a veil for the face (Gen. 24:65; 38:14) or for the body (Isa. 3:23).

Special Occasions: Aside from the special dress for priests in service and soldiers on duty, there was also a customary dress for mourning, whether for the dead, tragedy, or danger from war, usually referred to as sackcloth (a coarse burlap) and ashes (Isa. 58:5; Jer. 6:26; Luke 10:13). Special adornments were also appropriate for weddings, although they may have been unusually ornate garments or headdresses rather than special additional items. Additional jewelry was surely appropriate for any number of celebrations.

Garments were also a symbol of rank and station, especially during the Roman period, when government officials such as kings, legates, prefects, and procurators were each marked by distinctive insignia, much in the way the military uses different uniforms for different units, duties, and stations. As in all societies, the poorest folk were most plainly clothed, the wealthiest most ornately dressed. Pretentiousness could show in dress as in manners. Parades tended to draw finery into public view and to add color, variety, and festivity, whether to religious, civil, or private ceremonies of celebration. Dress could also be a means of protest, as with the shedding of clothes by Isaiah as a warning to Egypt (20:1–6). *See also* jewels, jewelry; priests. R.S.B.

drink. The most significant liquid foods mentioned in the Bible are milk, water, and wine. Physically milk and water are essential; wine gives superabundance and elation. Drinking any of these with another person often connotes fellowship (Job 1:4; cf. Luke 5:30). Offering a drink to another fulfills a common expectation of hospitality (Gen. 24:14–19; 1 Sam. 30:11; 2 Kings 6:21–22; Job 22:1; John 4:7), but may also connote compassion (Ruth 2:9). Finding water to drink was often a problem: the Egyptians could not drink from the Nile when Moses turned the water to blood (Exod. 7:20–21), and the Israelites could not drink the bitter water at Marah until Moses threw a piece of wood into it (15:23–25). The Israelites also had no water to drink at Rephidim until Moses struck a rock with his staff (17:1–6). Not having water to drink was a major concern for a city under siege (2 Kings 18:26–32). Metaphorically, God's wisdom for the exiles is water, milk, and wine (Isa. 55:1–5). People may also drink of God's wrath (Job 21:20; cf. Rev. 14:10) or of God's blessings (cf. Ps. 23:5). Ecclesiastes portrays eating and drinking as emblematic of a good life, to be enjoyed as a gift from God (2:24; 3:13; 5:18; 8:15; 9:7).

Num. 5:1–31 outlines a procedure by which a wife suspected of unfaithfulness is made to drink "water of bitterness," which will cause her uterus to drop if she is guilty. Jael gives Sisera milk to drink (Judg. 4:19). Gideon limits the number of his troops to those who drink water by lapping it like dogs (Judg. 7:5–6). The prophet Nathan told a parable of a man whose pet lamb would drink from his cup (2 Sam. 12:3). David refused to drink water that had been fetched for him at the cost of human blood (2 Sam. 23:15–17).

Drink is also closely connected with Israel's worship life. Israel eats and drinks before God at Sinai (Exod. 24:9–11), but then does the same before the golden calf built by Aaron (32:6). Moses grinds the golden calf to powder, scatters the gold dust on the water, and makes the people drink it (32:20). In time, the presentation of "drink offerings" become a part of Israel's worship life, traced in part to the action of Jacob at Bethel (Gen. 35:14; cf. Exod. 29:40–41; 37:16; Lev. 23:13, 18, 37; Num. 28–29). Aaron and his descendants are commanded not to drink strong wine (Lev. 10:9); likewise, those who make special vows are to abstain from drinking wine or even grape juice (Num. 6:3; cf. Judg. 13:4–14; 1 Sam. 1:11–15). Fasting, furthermore, sometimes involved abstinence from drinking liquids as well as from eating food (Esther 4:16; cf. Luke 5:33; Acts 23:12).

In the NT, Jesus cautions his disciples not to be anxious about what they will drink (Matt. 6:25, 31). He said that those who offer a drink to the thirsty will be judged as having done the same to him (Matt. 25:34–46; cf. 10:42). Jesus also compares what he has to offer a Samaritan woman to living water (John 4:10, 13–14) and speaks of his death on the cross as a "cup" that he must drink (Mark 10:38; 14:36). He shares a final drink with his disciples at the Last Supper and tells them he will not drink again of the "fruit of the vine" until he shares it with them again in God's kingdom (Matt. 26:27). Finally, Jesus is offered wine to drink when he is on the cross, but he refuses to drink it (Matt. 27:34; cf. John 19:29–30). The early church spoke of drinking Jesus's blood through participation in the eucharistic meal (1 Cor. 11:25; cf. John 6:53–56). Paul makes clear, however, that the kingdom of God is not food and drink, but righteousness and peace and joy in the Holy Spirit (Rom. 14:17).   J.G.J.

drunkenness, the state of inebriation induced by the ingestion of wine or of what the Bible calls "strong drink" (e.g., Prov. 20:31). In general, wine was enjoyed in Israel as a divinely given fruit of the ground. Used in cultic meals (Deut. 14:26), it was a figure for divine wisdom (Isa. 55:1–2; Prov. 9:1–6) as well as human love (Song of Sol. 7:9). It bespeaks superabundance, connoting the elative sense of life heightened above the ordinary. Drunkenness is often presented as a natural consequence of enjoying wine, without any evaluative remark one way of the other (Ruth 3:7; 1 Sam. 25:36; 2 Sam. 11:13; Isa. 6:8; John 2:10). Frequently, however, drunkenness is shown to have unfortunate results: Noah is humiliated when he lies uncovered in his tent (Gen. 9:20–27); Lot is essentially raped by his daughters who want to be impregnated by him (19:30–38). King Elah of Israel becomes an easy victim for his assassin (1 Kings 16:8–10; cf. the rout of Ben-hadad in 1 Kings 20:16–20). Thus, while no commandment in the Hebrew scripture prohibits drunkenness, public intoxication does seem to have been regarded as unseemly. The phrase "glutton and drunkard" could be applied to a person who was a disgrace to the family (Deut. 21:20; cf. Prov. 23:21; Luke 7:34). Likewise, when Eli thought (wrongly) that Hannah was drunk, he accused her of making a spectacle of herself (1 Sam. 1:14). People who lack understanding can be said to grope in the dark or to "stagger like a drunkard" (Job 12:25; cf. Ps. 107:27; Isa. 19:14). Elsewhere, drunkards are mentioned along with gossips (Ps. 69:12) and fools (Prov. 26:9–10). Drunkenness is often used as a metaphor for God's judgment (Isa. 19:14; Jer. 48:26; 51:39; Lam. 4:21; Nah. 1:10) or for the offenses that call for such judgment (Rev. 17:2, 6; 18:3). But the symbolism of intoxication can sometimes be used in a positive way, as in "drunk with love" (Song of Sol. 5:1).

The NT is more explicit in its condemnation of drunkenness. Paul equates intoxication with debauchery (Rom. 13:13; Eph. 5:18) and says that drunkards will not inherit the kingdom of God (1 Cor. 5:11; 6:10; Gal. 5:21). Nevertheless, some Christians became drunk at celebrations of the Lord's Supper (1 Cor. 11:21). On the day of Pentecost, when people heard the believers speaking in tongues, they attributed this to drunkenness rather than to the gift of the Holy Spirit (Acts 2:13, 15).
                                                       M.A.P.

Drusilla (droo-sil'uh), the wife of Antonius Felix, who was procurator of Judea (ca. 52–59 CE) while Paul was imprisoned in Caesarea. A Jew, she was the daughter of Herod Agrippa I and great-granddaughter of Herod the Great. In Acts 24:24

27, she is present when Paul speaks about Jesus to her husband. *See also* Felix, Antonius; Herod.
                                                       A.J.M.

Dtr., an abbreviation used in biblical studies as a siglum for the Deuteronomistic Historian, the writer(s) who shaped the material in the books Joshua–2 Kings. *See also* Deuteronomistic Historian.

Dumah (doo'muh; Heb., "silence").

1 A son of Ishmael (Gen. 25:14; 1 Chron. 1:30), possibly resident in south-central Arabia at modern Dumat al-Ghandal (el-Jof).

2 A city in the south-central hills of Canaan, probably modern Khirbet Danmah, six miles southwest of Hebron (Josh. 15:52).

3 The subject of an oracle in Isa. 21:11–12, where it may be a scribal error for Edom, or its meaning, "silence," may indicate the uncertain sense of the oracle.

dung, human or animal feces. Dried bricks of human and animal dung were used in Egypt to fuel ovens, but the Israelite concept of purity made this practice obnoxious to the Hebrews (Ezek. 4:12, 15). Still, dung was used as fertilizer (Isa. 25:10; Luke 13:8). There are several references to the scarcities of a military siege constraining a city's inhabitants to consume their own excrement (2 Kings 18:27; Isa. 36:12; cf. Lev. 26:29; Deut. 28:53–57) or "dove's dung" (2 Kings 6:25), which might designate a plant. Cultic legal texts require that human voiding (Deut. 23:12–14) occur outside of the camp perimeter and the fecal matter in the intestines of sacrificial animals be burned outside of the camp (Exod. 29:14; Lev. 4:11; 8:17; 16:27; Num. 19:5) because of the impurity of excreta (Mal. 2:3). The "Dung Gate" of Jerusalem's south wall (Neh. 2:13; 3:13–14; 12:31) is probably the exit through which the city's refuse was removed. The term "dung" is also used to refer to an unburied human corpse left as offal (2 Kings 9:37; Jer. 8:2; 9:21; 16:4; 25:33; Ps. 83:12) or to the worthless impious (Zeph. 1:17; Job 20:7). Paul regarded all of his religious accomplishments as dung (NRSV: "rubbish") compared to the worth of knowing Christ and being found in him (Phil. 3:8).   B.M.L.

Dura (door'uh), a plain "in the province of Babylon" (Dan. 3:1) where King Nebuchadnezzar set up the golden image for all to worship. Because of the refusal of Daniel and his friends to heed that decree, they were cast into the fiery furnace. The location of the plain is uncertain.

dyeing, the practice of coloring cloth by adding pigment through hot or cold treatment. Dyeing is discussed only by implication in the Bible. Three references occur in one verse related to the defeat of Sisera: the mother of the dead Canaanite king imagines him bringing her the spoils of the victor, which would have included dyed and embroidered cloth, two pieces of which would have been for her neck (Judg. 5:30). Archaeological evidence of a local dyeing industry has been found at Gezer, Beth-zur, Beth-shemesh, Tell en-Nasbeh, and most notably at Tell Beit Mirsim in housed installations numbering about thirty. A 10-by-30-foot room was fitted with two vats with small cover openings and draining rims. Basins and benches were placed near or between the vats. Additional vessels for fixing agents, lime or potash, were nearby. From the vat capacities (cavities about a foot and a half across) and the small openings in the covers, the equipment was apparently intended to dye thread rather than whole cloth. The Hellenistic installation at Gezer included a three-vat room, and vat design was now open-topped in the mode of a tub. A basement furnace here suggested use of hot dyes. *See also* purple.   R.S.B.

Dye vats excavated at Tell Beit Mirsim, seventh century BCE.

Opposite: Head of Ramesses II (1279–1212 BCE), the Egyptian king who may have been the pharaoh of the oppression (Exod. 1–2) or the pharaoh of the exodus (Exod. 5–12).

E

E, in biblical source criticism, an abbreviation used as a siglum for the Elohist, the author or authors of one of the source traditions incorporated into the Pentateuch. The designation Elohist or E derives from the fact that this tradition typically uses Elohim as the name for God. *See also* Elohist; Pentateuch, sources of the.

eagle, a large predatory bird. Several species of eagles are found in Israel and the Near East. In Prov. 23:5, the eagle (Heb. *nesher*) that flies toward heaven is thought to refer to the imperial eagle (*Aquila heliaca*), as this bird was believed to be able to see into the sun. In passages where the same Hebrew word depicts a bird as a symbol for swiftness, it may allude to the golden eagle (*Aquila chrysaetos*), as this bird possesses great speed (Deut. 28:49; 2 Sam. 1:23; Job. 9:26; Jer. 4:13; Lam. 4:19; Hab. 1:8). A number of other eagle species also nest in the area or pass through during migration, such as the booted eagle (*Hieraaetus pennatus*), Bonelli's eagle (*Hieraaetus fasciatus*), and the tawny eagle (*Aquila rapax*), some or all of which may also have been present in biblical times. Eagles were also noted for building their nests in lofty places (Jer. 49:16) and for being protective of their young (Exod. 19:4–6; Deut. 32:11). Isaiah uses the expression "they shall mount up with wings like eagles" to describe the renewed vigor granted to those who wait upon the Lord for strength (40:31). When Ezekiel saw a vision of four cherubim, one of them had the face of an eagle (1:10); likewise the author of Revelation beheld four living creatures before the throne of God, one of which was like an eagle (4:7). That book also refers to a talking eagle who proclaims woe upon the inhabitants of earth (8:13), and the seer beholds a woman who is given the wings of an eagle to flee from the serpent (12:14). The Greek word usually translated eagle (*aetos*) is also used by Jesus in a passage where context suggests the meaning is "vulture" (Matt. 24:28; Luke 17:37).   I.U.K./M.A.P.

earrings. Jewelry for the ear is listed together with brooches, signet rings, and armlets (bracelets) as gifts brought to the tabernacle in the wilderness (Exod. 35:22). They were also offered with beads and other items as atonement for defiling the dead (Num. 31:50), and Ishmaelite men gave them as material from which Gideon could make an ephod

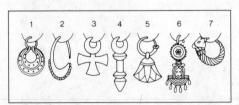

Earrings: **1.** From Tell el-'Ajjul (1600 BCE); **2.** From the period of the judges (1100 BCE), gold; **3–4.** Assyrian (900–800 BCE); **5.** Egyptian (800 BCE); **6.** Egyptian (100 BCE); **7.** Greek (100 BCE).

(Judg. 8:24–26). Ezekiel considered earrings to be part of the garb of an exquisitely clothed woman in an image he uses to describe God's treatment of Jerusalem (16:12). In archaeological evidence, earrings are most commonly found in burials. Both single and multiple pendant designs frequently incorporated a lunar motif. Earrings were often fashioned from silver or gold, as were rings and bracelets. According to 1 Pet. 3:2–3, wives should not adorn themselves with gold ornaments, but with the lasting beauty of a gentle and quiet spirit.
                                                                        R.S.B.

earthquake, a shaking or trembling of the earth's surface, fairly frequent in the Near East. Specific earthquakes within the biblical period include one in 31 BCE reported by the Jewish historian Josephus, which left clear marks in Qumran's ruins, and one in Uzziah's days (ca. 760 BCE) cited in Amos 1:1 and remembered in Zech. 14:5. In biblical narratives, earthquakes relate to the swallowing up of Dathan and Abiram (Num. 16:30–34), to Elijah's experiences at Sinai (1 Kings 19:11–12), to the destruction of Sodom and Gomorrah (Gen. 19:24–29), to the panic among the Philistines at Michmash (1 Sam. 14:15), to both the death (Matt. 27:51) and resurrection (Matt. 28:2) of Jesus, and to Paul's escape from prison in Philippi (Acts 16:26; cf. 4:31). Earthquakes are also projected for the last days (e.g., Isa. 29:6; Matt. 24:7; Rev. 6:12 17).   E.F.C.

east. In the Bible, terminology for "east" is derived chiefly from two sources. First, it is drawn from language associated with sunrise (Heb. *mizrakh,* "rising, shining," Josh. 4:19; Gk. *anatolē,* Matt. 2:1). Second, it is drawn from derivatives of *kdm,* meaning "before" or "in front of" (Gen. 11:2; Ezek. 40:6). Thus, in biblical thought, east was the primary orientation: north could be referred to as being to the left and south as being to the right, on the assumption that east was the default, "straight ahead" position. One common usage of east in the Bible, especially in poetry, is in listings of all four cardinal directions as a way of expressing totality ("everywhere," Joel 2:20; Ps. 75:7; Job 23:8–9; Matt. 8:11; Luke 13:29). Similarly, east is contrasted with west in expressions of immeasurable distance (Isa. 43:5; 59:19); it is in this sense that the psalmist says that God "removes our transgressions from us as far as the east is from the west" (Ps. 103:12). The east is also the source of exotic wisdom, as evidenced by such figures as Job (Job 1:3), Agur (Prov. 30:1), Lemuel (Prov. 31:1), and the magi (Matt. 2:1).   J.S.K.

east wind, a distinctive climactic feature referred to several times in the Bible (Gen. 41:6, 41, 47; Exod. 10:13; 14:21; Job 15:2; 27:21; 38:24; Pss. 48:7; 78:26; Isa. 27:8; Ezek. 17:10; 19:12; 27:26; Hos. 12:1; 13:5; Jon. 4:8). Under normal conditions, the land of Israel is cooled by a westward breeze that blows in from the Mediterranean, but during a short period (about fifty days) in the early fall, a powerful, hot eastward wind (sometimes called a sirocco) can blow suddenly across the land, often destroying crops. When viewed as an instrument of God's judgment, the east wind could also be called the "wind of the LORD" (Isa. 59:19; Hos. 13:15).

Ebal (ee'buhl).
1 The ancestor of a Horite family group in Edom (Gen. 36:23; 1 Chron. 1:40). *See also* Horites.
2 A variant spelling of Obal (1 Chron. 1:22; cf. Gen. 10:28).

Ebal, Mount, the peak, 3,109 feet above sea level, forming the north side of the Shechem pass opposite Mount Gerizim, in the Samaritan hills. On or at Ebal, Joshua was to erect an altar and memorial stones (Josh. 8:30–35; Deut. 27:1–8), features of an ancient covenant ceremony noted in Deut. 11:29; 27:11–26. The altar and stones were probably at what later became the sacred precinct of Shechem on Ebal's lowest slopes, 1,400 feet below the summit near the valley floor. Alternatively they could be identified with structures on the heights such as one that dates to the twelfth century BCE found on the far side of the summit ridge. *See also* Gerizim, Mount; Shechem.   E.F.C.

Ebed (ee'bid; Heb., "servant").
1 The father of Gaal, the leader of a group who settled in Shechem and attempted an ill-fated rebellion against Abimelech (Judg. 9:26–45).
2 The leader of Adin, a family group who returned from exile in Babylon with Ezra (Ezra 8:6).

Ebed-melech (ee'bid-mee'lik; Heb., "servant of the king"), the Ethiopian eunuch and Jerusalem palace official who was responsible for rescuing Jeremiah out of an empty cistern, into which he had been thrown by the Judeans (Jer. 38:1–13).

Ebenezer (eb'uh-nee'zuhr; Heb., "stone of help"), a site near Aphek, four miles south of Gilgal, according to 1 Samuel. In the account of the defeat of the Israelites and capture of the ark by the Philistines (1 Sam. 4:1–11; 5:1), the meaning of the name seems ironic. In 1 Sam. 7:2–12 Samuel names a stone Ebenezer to commemorate God's help in Israel's recovery of the same territory.

Eber (ee'buhr; Heb., "beyond").
1 The great-grandson of Shem, father of Peleg and Joktan (Gen. 10:24–25; 11:14–17; 1 Chron. 1:18–19, 25), ancestor of Abram (Gen. 11:17–26) and Jesus (Luke 3:35). Eber appears to be the eponymous ancestor of the Hebrews (which could be taken as literally meaning "descendants of Eber"), but nothing is made of this beyond placing of the name in Abram's ancestral line.
2 In Num. 24:24, the region and population "beyond" the Euphrates River (cf., e.g., Josh. 24:2, 3, 14, 15).
3 The head of the priestly family of Amok in the generation following that of those who returned

to Jerusalem with Joshua and Zerubbabel (Neh. 12:20).
4 A Gadite whose descendants lived in the land of Bashan (1 Chron. 5:13).
5 A Benjaminite, son of Elpaal (1 Chron. 8:12).
6 A Benjaminite, son of Shashak (1 Chron. 8:22).   S.B.P.

Ebiasaph (i-bi'uh-saf; Heb., "my father has gathered"; more properly Abiasaph, Exod. 6:24).
1 A Levite, the son of Korah through Izhar and either the father (1 Chron. 6:23) or the brother (Exod. 6:24) of Assir.
2 A Levite, the son of Elkanah and great-grandson of a Korah through Uzziel (1 Chron. 6:37), also the father of Assir. If the genealogical lists have become disordered through scribal errors, he may be the same person as 1. *See also* Assir.
3 A Levite, the son of Korah and the father of Shallum, the chief gatekeeper of the Levites (1 Chron. 9:19; also called Asaph, 1 Chron. 26:1). Some scholars understand this passage (1 Chron. 9:17–27) to be a postexilic record (corresponding to Neh. 11:1–19); however, other scholars believe at least part of this chapter is adapted from a record of preexilic Israel, an introduction to the narratives of Saul and David that follow. If it is preexilic, this Ebiasaph may be identified with 1 (and possibly 2) above; otherwise he is a much later descendant of the family group of Korah. *See also* Korah.   D.R.B.

Ebla (eb'luh), modern Tell Mardikh, a large mound of some 140 acres, located in Syria about forty-two miles south of Aleppo, astride major routes of east–west and north–south communication. Systematic excavation of the site began in 1964 under the direction of Paolo Matthiae; and it was those finds that established the identification of the site as ancient Ebla.

The best-known and most widely discussed level dates ca. 2400–2300/2250 BCE, with final destruction by an early Sargonic ruler of Mesopotamia, Sargon or Naram-sin, both of whom claim conquest of Ebla in their inscriptions. The main building so far uncovered is Palace G, sprawling over the west and southwest slopes of the acropolis. Its central element is a large porticoed audience hall, north of which are a massive tower with a stone-inlay stairway, a second stairway, and (storage) rooms; on its east and south are the monumental gateway to the palace and the administrative quarters.

The objects found in this building include wooden furniture decorated with friezes, seal impressions, and small sculptures—all showing local adaptation of Mesopotamian art of the mid-third millennium BCE. Especially important are the tablets: well over seventeen thousand pieces make up perhaps about four thousand whole texts. The tablets come from several places in Palace G, representing different collections or archives; most, however, were found fallen in the debris of two rooms off the audience hall in a way

Cuneiform tablets as they were discovered at Ebla, fallen from their original shelving, ca. 2600–2250 BCE.

that made it possible to reconstruct the original shelving arrangements. All the tablets are in cuneiform script, reflecting the scribal traditions of the northern area of southern Mesopotamia (especially Kish and Abu Salabikh) during the mid-third millennium BCE. They are apparently in two languages: the less frequent is Sumerian, the principal written language of southern Mesopotamia in the third millennium; the more frequent is a hitherto unknown Semitic language, conveniently labeled "Eblaite," whose linguistic affiliations, though still being discussed, seem to be with (Old) Akkadian and Amorite. As for content, the tablets represent roughly four categories, again with Mesopotamian parallels: economic and other administrative records involving the palace (the most numerous); lexical and grammatical texts for the scribes; literary and religious texts; and texts bearing on the events of the day, like a commercial treaty with the city of Abarsal (which a minority of scholars read as Asshur).

Presiding over the city, as over various settlements in its vicinity, were rulers who worked with the city "elders." Under their authority were a variety of officials and workers, who functioned within the "house of the ruler," and other administrative sectors that together made up the city proper, i.e., what physically comprised the acropolis and lower city. They were also active in the outer settlements of the city, supplying separate animal and agricultural farm products to the city. This complex urban structure, which may be called a city-state, was large as well: Pettinato has estimated, from various texts, a population of 260,000 to 300,000.

The religious picture was also complex. Administrative and other texts attest Mesopotamian deities like Enki and Enlil, West Semitic deities like Baal, Dagan, Hadad, Rasap (Resheph), and Sham/pash (written as Sumerian Utu, but female, not male as in Mesopotamia), and various deities representing the local substratum, including Kura, the head of the local pantheon, and his consort, Barama. In distinction from these are names like Damu, Il, and Malik, which never appear alone, but only as elements in personal names, and so may not be separate deities, but appellatives meant to describe deities like Hadad and Kura. Among cultic activities in evidence are an enthronement ritual for the ruler and his consort and texts pointing to the ritual veneration of dead rulers.

The initial enthusiasm about the light the Ebla tablets would shed on the early stages of biblical culture is now seen as exaggerated, even misplaced. Clearly, no biblical personages can be identified in the tablets; and although personal names can be found there similar to those in the Bible (e.g., Ishmael), such names are not exclusive to Ebla, appearing in other areas of the Near East as well. Moreover, Eblaite, though a Semitic language, does not look as close to biblical Hebrew as originally thought; and the proposal to find YHWH (the God of Israel) in the Ebla texts cannot be supported: the supposed form *ya,* which occurs as an element in Eblaite personal names, is ambiguous in reading and interpretation.

The major contribution of the tablets is in understanding Syria and Mesopotamia of the third millennium BCE, especially in showing that the complex city-state system attested in Syria in the second millennium had an honorable precedent in the third.

Bibliography

Biggs, Robert. "Ebla Texts." *Anchor Bible Dictionary.* Doubleday, 1992. 2:263–70.

Gordon, Cyrus H., ed. *Eblaitica* 2. Eisenbrauns, 1990. Pp. 3–29, 31–77.

Matthiae, Paolo. *Ebla: An Empire Rediscovered.* Doubleday, 1981.

———. "New Discoveries at Ebla: The Excavation of the Western Palace and the Royal Necropo-

Large sacrificial basin found at Tell Mardikh (Ebla). The short side shows warriors marching over lions, the long side a banquet scene; Middle Bronze Age.

lis of the Amorite Period." *Biblical Archaeologist* 47 (1984): 18–32.

Pettinato, Giovanni. *Ebla: A New Look at History.* Johns Hopkins University Press, 1991.

P.B.M.

Ecclesiastes (i-klee´zee-as´teez), **book of,** the fourth of the Five Scrolls, or Megilloth, in the Writings section, or Ketuvim, of the Tanakh (Jewish Bible). Each of these scrolls is associated with a particular festival in the Jewish calendar. Ecclesiastes is read at the Festival of Tabernacles (Sukkoth), which celebrates the Israelites' journey from Egypt to the promised land.

The Hebrew name for the book is Qoheleth, stemming from the author's title in 1:1 (often translated "Preacher" or "Teacher" in English). The word derives from the Hebrew term *qahal,* which means "assembly." The Greek word for "assembly" (*ekklēsia*) is used to form the English title Ecclesiastes. Thus, a person called Qoheleth would be one who gathers or assembles, most likely, in this case, students or pupils. Curiously, the title is feminine in form, though it is obviously construed as masculine, since Qoheleth is called "son" (1:1) and "king" (1:12).

Contents: There has been much debate over structure, or lack thereof, in the book of Ecclesiastes. Although much is disputed, there are certain generally recognized sections of the text. Ecclesiastes begins and ends with the admonition "Vanity of vanities! All is vanity" (1:2; 12:8). From this point, it moves quickly into the author's attempts to understand the meaning of life by seeking wisdom (1:12–18) and seeking pleasure (2:1–11). Then a poem claims that there is a "time for everything" (3:1–9). After the disputed middle section, the book concludes with an extended allegory of old age (12:1–8) and an editorial epilogue (12:9–14). Longman argues that Ecclesiastes should be divided into only three sections: Prologue (1:1–11), Monologue (1:12–12:7), and Epilogue (12:8–14).

Eccles. 2:5–6 describes a garden similar to this one with a pond filled with fish, ducks, and plants surrounded by palm and pomegranate trees; Egyptian wall painting, fourteenth century BCE.

He posits a narrator who begins with an introduction, quotes the wisdom of Qoheleth, and then explains the message to readers.

Ecclesiastes also shows evidence of having gone through an editing process. Noticeable editorial additions appear in 1:1; 12:9–12; and 12:13–14. The first gives the author's title and reinforces the appearance of Solomon as author. The second was most likely written by a devoted disciple of Qoheleth praising his effectiveness. The purpose of the third appears to be to bring the text more in line with traditional biblical theology and caution readers not to take what has been said too seriously.

OUTLINE OF CONTENTS

Ecclesiastes

I. Prologue (1:1–11)
   A. Theme (1:1–3)
   B. Cycle of life (1:4–11)
II. Life experiments (1:12–2:26)
III. A time for everything (3:1–9)
IV. Disappointments of life (3:10–4:16)
V. The counsels of wisdom (5:1–12:8)
VI. Epilogue (12:9–14)

Background: The author presents the words of the book in ways that suggest they might be those of Solomon. The introduction says, "The words of the Teacher, the son of David, king in Jerusalem" (1:1; 1:12). In addition, 1 Kings 8 has passages in which Solomon assembles (*qhl,* e.g., 1 Kings 8:1) the people of Israel, suggesting the name Qoheleth can be connected with Solomon. For much of its history, the book of Ecclesiastes has been viewed as a writing of the aged Solomon (repentant of his period of apostasy in 1 Kings 11:1–13). Still, the text does not explicitly name Solomon as the author, nor does the language fit the time of Solomon. Furthermore, there are passages that would be difficult to understand as coming from Solomon (1:12; 1:16a; 4:1–3; 5:7–8; 10:20). As a result, the author remains unknown.

Dating of Ecclesiastes has been difficult. The text shows evidence of Persian influence through the use of such loanwords as *pardes* ("garden," 2:5) and *pitgam* ("response, sentence," 8:11). Thus, the date would not be earlier than the fifth century BCE. Further, the book's reference to the soul's ascension may place the date closer to the third century BCE, when the afterlife had become a more prominent concept within Judaism. The grammar and vocabulary of Ecclesiastes are different from any found in the Hebrew Bible; the book's language has been influenced by Aramaic and has similarities to some forms of Mishnaic Hebrew. Ecclesiastes was therefore most likely written between the fifth and third centuries BCE. There is nothing within the text about the location of its composition.

Ecclesiastes belongs to the category of wisdom literature. Longman has called Ecclesiastes "framed Wisdom autobiography," citing its similarities with Akkadian autobiography and its wisdom sayings. The wisdom tradition in the Hebrew Bible does not appeal to divine revelation for understanding human existence. It does not focus on the Mosaic covenant at Sinai, but relies heavily on the natural order of the cosmos. It presupposes that God has ordered the world at creation, and it seeks to uncover human moral order through examining its likenesses with the created order. History, in wisdom literature, does not have a defined goal. There is no salvation history, for time is often viewed as circular. Books in this genre offer proverbs that are not universal in character, but specific, allowing for exceptions. Ecclesiastes both fits into biblical wisdom literature and critiques it. The author appeals strictly to experience and neglects talk of covenant. Qoheleth is often viewed as critiquing the tradition by questioning the connection between virtue and prosperity. Crenshaw claims the author holds that one cannot secure one's existence through wisdom, that there is no discernable order to the universe, and that there is no divine guarantee of reward for good behavior or punishment for bad behavior.

Themes: One of the most common and important words in Ecclesiastes is the Hebrew word *hebel,* which is often translated as "vanity" or "emptiness." In Hebrew, *hebel* originally meant "mist" or "vapor" and is the name for Abel, the short-lived brother of Cain. The word is used by the author in Ecclesiastes to denote the transitory nature of human existence and knowledge. The author sees vanity in toil (2:17–23), in life (4:1–3), in wisdom (2:12–16), and most clearly of all in the finality of death. Vanity is the only certainty in human experience. Every attempt by humans at permanence is ended by death, for no lifestyle has a "profit" (*yitron,* "that which is left over"). There is nothing that is left over when a person dies. All is ended, according to Qoheleth. The "righteous" and the "sinner" both die. The "wise" and the "fool" both perish. Although life has no "profit," Qoheleth insists it can still be enjoyed. It is often argued that the author does not strictly deny conventional practices, but only relativizes their value and meaning.

The book of Ecclesiastes also centers on the circularity of nature, particularly circles of life and death. Still, this cycle does not lead the author to view the world as self-renewing, but as futile and without purpose. Life moves in cycles from birth to death, and the world continues, but people are forgotten, no matter what their greatness.

The author of Ecclesiastes obtains all of his observations and thoughts from experience. The book does not appeal to divine revelation for insight into human existence, but to experience and to evidence provided by the world. Empirical observation leads to pessimistic conclusions, but what can be known from experience is limited, for no human is able to grasp all that there is to life. In any case, people should not try to transcend humanity's limits, but recognize them and enjoy the good things that God's creation has to offer. The author refers twenty-nine times to "life" and activities done "under the sun." The latter expression could simply mean "on earth," or it might be used to emphasize the limited nature of human understanding.

Although the author of Ecclesiastes has been called an existentialist, a skeptic, and a pessimist, he is not an atheist. In several places, the author refers to God. Crenshaw argues that the author believes God exists, but lacks trust in God and believes that God's actions are as unknowable as God's essence. At no point in the book does the author use the traditional name of God, YHWH ("the Lord"), but always the impersonal "God" (Elohim). Neither the works of God for Israel, the covenant, nor any of the important figures in Israelite history are mentioned. Although the author is clearly a theist, the conception of God in Ecclesiastes is markedly different from that found elsewhere in the Bible.

Interpretive Issues: Ecclesiastes had difficulty making its way into the biblical canon for a number of reasons: lack of focus on Mosaic covenant, no appeal to divine revelation, similarities to contemporary pagan wisdom literature, and the espousal of views at odds with the mainstream of biblical tradition (e.g., Eccles. 11:9, which talks about following the inclinations of one's hearts and eyes, contradicts Num. 15:39, which expressly prohibits going after the lusts of the heart and eyes). Most scholars believe that it was ultimately canonized as a result of both its supposed Solomonic authorship and the editorial revision in 12:13–14, which urges readers to keep the commandments.

An additional critical issue within Ecclesiastes concerns the apparent contradictions within the text (for a commonly identified contradiction, cf. 2:2; 7:3; 8:15). Scholars have offered varied interpretations of the reasoning behind these contradictions. Some have posited that the same editor who added 12:13–14 also added the other more orthodox sayings to help bring the text into line with broader biblical theology. Other scholars have held that these contradictions were intended by the author to display the anomalous nature of human existence. And still others have suggested that these saying are raised only so the author can refute them.

Influences: Ecclesiastes is read every year in the fall by Jewish communities at the Festival of Tabernacles.

Bibliography

Bandstra, Barry L. *Reading the Old Testament: Introduction to the Hebrew Bible.* 4th ed. Wadsworth, 2009.

Crenshaw, James L. *Ecclesiastes.* Westminster, 1987.

———. *Old Testament Wisdom: An Introduction.* Westminster John Knox, 1998.

Fox, Michael V. *A Time to Tear Down and a Time to Build Up: A Rereading of Ecclesiastes.* Eerdmans, 1999.

Longman, Tremper. *The Book of Ecclesiastes.* Eerdmans, 1998.   B.B.

Ecclesiasticus (i-klee´zee-as´ti-kuhs). *See* Sirach.

economics in the Hebrew Bible period.

Economics in the ancient world was a function of three interacting elements: climate and geography, social structures of people living in the land, and historical circumstances affecting the ability of residents to maximize the potential of their locality. Ancient Israel's socioeconomic history reflects three major stages, marked by radical change in response to communal threat: the early settlement period (1250–1020 BCE), the period of the monarchy (1020–587/6 BCE), and the period of restoration (538–416 BCE).

Climate and Geography: The designation of Israel's homeland as a "land flowing with milk and honey" (e.g., Exod. 3:8, 17; Lev. 20:24; Deut. 6:3) offers an idyllic and partial picture of ancient Canaan. Lush, richly producing areas like the central hill country and the eastern hills of the Transjordan provide diverse products, including wheat, barley, grapes, figs, olives, and honey. Here the annual rainfall ranges from 20 to 40 inches. But to the south and east this green belt fades rapidly to desert, where rainfall is fewer than 10 inches per year, and sheep, cattle, and other livestock provide a living. Between the western and eastern hills lies the Rift Valley, stretching from the Orontes River in the far north to the Dead Sea in the south. Through this valley courses the Jordan River, which winds its way from the Sea of Galilee to the Dead Sea, dropping from 695 to 1,285 feet below sea level. Along the narrow floodplain of the valley, called the Ghor, grows the "jungle of the Jordan" (Jer. 12:5), dense thickets of thorn scrub and tamarisk. This "good broad land" (Exod. 3:8) where Israel made a home is a land of sharp geographic contrasts, which mirror equally sharp seasonal changes. The year is divided into two seasons: a rainy winter season and a dry summer season. The winter season begins in autumn with the "early rains" that mark the beginning of the agricultural season and extends to the "latter rains" of March and April, so important for ripening crops. Mean temperatures in January range from 42 degrees in the hill country to 58 degrees on the coastal plain and on the desert's edge. The summer season is virtually rainless, and temperatures rise to an August mean of between 71 and 93 degrees. Available rainfall and temperatures tend to decrease from west to east and from north to south, causing marked differences in the type and amount of agricultural products available to sustain communities.

Early Settlement Period (1250–1020 BCE): In the early period, Israel consisted of a federation of tribes bound together by loyalty to their God, who had delivered them from slavery in Egypt and given them the land in which they now dwelt, thus changing their social status from slaves to settlers. Economically, each tribe was autonomous, consisting, in turn, of a collection of extended families organized into protective associations (usually called "clans" in the NRSV). The land—initially the central hill country and later northern and southern territories—was divided into tribal allotments, which were subdivided for family use. According to the federation's view, the land belonged to God and was granted to the tribes in trust for their use and benefit. The land could be inherited, ordinarily transferred from father to son, but it was not to be sold outside the association of families, since God had given particular land to each tribe in perpetuity. Each family lived off the land, growing or raising what it needed and bartering for the few craft items it could not produce. Life was village-based and agriculture-intensive, producing wine, oil, fruits, and vegetables, supplemented by small cattle herds and larger flocks of sheep and goats. Although pastoral nomadism was sporadically practiced, especially in regions where rainfall and climate varied greatly, necessitating the relocation of animals for winter and summer pasturage, such nomadism does not appear to have played a significant role in the tribal life of ancient Israel. Where it did occur, it seems to have been a specialization of certain people, not the lifestyle of whole tribes, either before or after settlement in the land. In this period, each tribe with its families retained the rights to production from its own land. Tribes were self-governed and largely patriarchal; they were united only by common religious practices and for the purpose of mutual self-defense. By the middle of the twelfth century BCE, however, the incursion of the Philistines from the coast into

The queen of Sheba and Solomon. Her visit may be seen as an effort to establish trade agreements for incense and spices from Arabia; detail from the Gates of Paradise, Florence, ca. 1425.

Israelite territory led to a radical change in Israel's way of life. The tribal federation's increased unification under a single military leader transformed Israelite society into a monarchy.

Monarchy (1020–587/6 BCE): The modest and limited kingship initiated by Saul and David was transformed by Solomon into a complex, bureaucratic, and expansive royal domain. A process of urbanization had begun, focused especially on the royal city, Jerusalem, and on a growing class of courtiers and royal officials, whose increasing wealth and control over the land dominated socioeconomic structures. The royal appetite for expenditures during Solomon's reign was seemingly insatiable, whether for new construction, fortifying towns, or maintaining an increasingly expensive standing army. Solomon resorted to direct taxation for the first time in Israelite history and established a levy of compulsory military and civil service. Population remained largely rural, but socioeconomic power shifted to the cities, favored by royal monopoly over exports and imports. Means of production became state owned or state influenced, as family properties were broken up and taken over by rich landlords. These large estates could be worked either by slave labor or wage labor. The cities became marketplaces where surplus agricultural commodities could be exchanged for urban-based crafts, with various specialties located on specific streets or in specific quarters of the city. Exchange took place "in the gate," where rural and urban population met, together with traders and caravaners passing through the city en route to foreign markets.

Solomon also expanded Israel's participation in foreign trade. Located in the crossroads of trade from Mesopotamia to Egypt or Asia Minor, from Egypt to Asia Minor and Assyria/Babylonia, and from southern Arabia to points north, east, or west, Israel was in a most enviable position to broker goods from all over the region. It is not coincidental that the three cities Solomon is credited with refortifying, Gezer, Megiddo, and Hazor (1 Kings 9:15–18), are all on important trade routes. Indeed, Solomon seems to have established a network of storage cities that enabled him to take full advantage of his control over caravan trade coming overland and maritime trade coming from Phoenicia, Egypt, or southern Arabia. Moreover, he built a fleet of ships to carry goods, including ivory, silver, gold, and apes (1 Kings 10:11, 22), from Ophir to Ezion-geber, whence they continued the journey to market overland. The queen of Sheba's fabled visit to Solomon portends an effort to establish trade agreements for incense and spice from Arabia. Finally, we are told that Solomon imported and exported horses from Cilicia (biblical Kue) and chariots from Egypt, playing the lucrative role of middleman (1 Kings 10:28–29). In all these commercial ventures, Solomon was aided by a close relationship with Tyre, the most important Phoenician port city, which supplied not only building materials for Solomon's projects, but expert technical assistance for the Ezion-geber fleet operations.

A Hebrew inscription on an eighth-century BCE ostracon reads: "gold from Ophir to Beth-horon—30 shekels." Solomon had earlier introduced foreign trade to Israel and built ships to carry goods from Ophir to Israel.

Whatever the economic benefits of Solomon's activity, especially for the new urban aristocracy and merchant class, his reign transformed Israelite society remarkably, imposing a highly structured, bureaucratic, state-monopolized system on a formerly tribal, largely rural, and self-sufficient population. At Solomon's death, the monarchy splintered over the economic demands of the court and the hardships imposed on the people. Nevertheless, the monarchic model stayed in place, both in the northern kingdom, Israel, and the southern kingdom, Judah. These two kingdoms now found themselves dependent on one another, if control of the international trade routes and the export and import efforts initiated under Solomon were to continue. The division of the kingdom ultimately proved disastrous, however, for each kingdom now had to fend for itself in the maelstrom of international politics created by the imperialistic designs of Egypt, Assyria, and Babylonia. Although marked by a few brief periods of prosperity, Israel and Judah's economic history came to be characterized by exploitation at the hands of foreign overlords and by widening disparity at home between the beneficiaries of royal monopolies and the rest of the population. The prophets of Israel addressed these crises, holding up as standard the memory of earlier, more egalitarian social structures and calling for justice for those exploited by the new system.

Restoration (538–416 BCE): With Cyrus of Persia's decree of 538 BCE, Israelites began to return to their land from exile. Those returning found others who had never left living on the land, scraping out a subsistence livelihood much as their ancestors had done when the land was first settled. Still under the tutelage of Persia, for whose economic benefit Israel was expected to labor, those returning attempted to set up a semi-autonomous state, with a priestly class and Judean elite at the helm. Despite the efforts of some of the new leaders, like Ezra and Nehemiah, to establish a more equitable relationship between the upper and lower classes (see Neh. 5:1–13), the egalitarian ideal of earlier days was never realized. Israel's economic welfare remained tied to the vagaries of international politics and the whims successively of Persian, Ptolemaic, Seleucid, and Roman overlords. *See also* ownership; poor, poverty; wealth.

Bibliography

De Vaux, Roland. *Ancient Israel: Social Institutions.* Vol. 1. McGraw-Hill, 1965.

Gottwald, Norman. *The Tribes of Yahweh: A Society of the Religion of Liberated Israel, 1250–1050 BCE.* Orbis Books, 1979.   D.C.H.

economics in the New Testament period.

NT authors maintain that love of money is the root of all kinds of evil (1 Tim. 6:10) and that no one can serve both God and wealth (Matt. 6:24). With such attitudes as these, not to mention the many attacks on the wealthy (e.g., Mark 10:25; Luke 6:24–28; 12:13–21; 16:19–31; 1 Tim. 1:10; 3:3; 6:9–10, 17–19), it might be surprising to find that the NT also provides detailed information about commerce and economic life. Other literary sources from the NT period are also useful. Longus's *Daphnis and Chloe* provides a lengthy and coherent account of the lives of herders and farmers in the countryside; the *Letters* of Alciphron give details about the lives of farmers and fishermen. For the life of hunters at the outermost reaches of the countryside, there is the seventh oration of Dio Chrysostom, and for considerable attention to brigands and their economic roles, Chariton's *Callirhoe* is helpful. Householders, artisans, and other urban characters receive de-

tailed, if humorous, treatment in the satires of Lucian. Further, Apuleius's *Metamorphoses* is an informative source for all dimensions of economic life in NT times. All of these literary sources may be supplemented, furthermore, by documentary evidence detailing virtually every aspect of ancient economic life: papyri and inscriptions that include apprentice contracts, tax receipts, deeds of emancipation, leases of workshops, sales of produce, contracts of all kinds, and records of gifts to temples.

General Introduction: The Roman Empire was characterized by grotesque economic inequality. There was nothing comparable to what would be called a "middle class"; rather, most people were either extremely rich (about 3 percent of the population) or extremely poor (about 90 percent). Most of those who belonged to the latter group lived at or near subsistence level, making just enough to survive, with little hope of saving anything that would allow them to improve their position or provide them with a hedge against calamity. The more fortunate of the impoverished might at least learn a trade (as was apparently the case with both Jesus and the apostle Paul), but for many people in rural areas, "subsistence" meant living off the land, so life was subject to the vicissitudes of agriculture. Thus, for the least fortunate—beggars, widows, orphans, prisoners, unskilled day laborers—survival itself may have been frequently in question. Modern estimates suggest that about 28 percent of the population of the Roman Empire during NT times lived "below subsistence level," meaning they did not know from day to day whether they would be able to obtain the things necessary to sustain life. Given the extremes of such a situation, attitudes toward wealth and poverty were a significant part of the social world. Some religious people at the time of Jesus believed that wealth could be viewed as a sign of God's blessing and that poverty could be understood as a consequence of divine displeasure (such an at-

Overview of the ancient agora in Athens. The agora was a center of economic activity in cities in NT times.

titude might be reflected in the disciples' surprise at Jesus's remark in Mark 10:23–26). It is difficult, however, to know how widespread this notion was. What seems more certain is that virtually everyone in this time period held to what is now called a theory of "limited good." People believed that money and the things that money can buy were in short (or at least finite) supply; the common perception—in stark contrast to modern capitalism—was that acquisition of wealth or resources by some *necessitated* depletion of wealth or resources for others. Simply put, virtually everyone in NT times believed that there was only so much "stuff" to go around and that the reason some people had less than they needed was because other people had more than they needed.

Given this state of affairs, Roman society functioned in accord with strong expectations regarding benefaction and obligation. At the simplest level, the exchange of favors was virtually definitive of friendship (cf. Luke 11:5). At another level, however, almost all people were involved in patron-client relationships with people who were not their social equals. Very few people had money or power, but those who did were expected to serve as benefactors for those who did not; they might, for instance, allow peasants to live on their land, or provide them with food or grain or employment. In sociological terms, such benefactors are called *patrons* and the recipients of the benefits are called *clients*. In such a relationship, the exchange of favors could not be mutual, but clients were expected to offer patrons what they could: gratitude and, above all, loyalty. They were expected to praise their patron, speaking well of him to all and enhancing his social reputation. They were expected to trust their patron to continue providing for them. And, as necessary, they were expected to perform various services the patron might request of them. Such relationships were not constituted legally, but at a basic level they represented how most people thought the world was supposed to work and, indeed, how it usually did work. Patron-client relationships formed a significant backdrop for theological reflection. The term most often used in the Roman world for a patron's bestowal of benefits was *charis* (typically translated "grace" in the NT), and the term most often used for the client's expected attitude of loyalty was *pistis* (often translated "faith" in the NT). Thus the phenomenon of patron-client relationships seems to have served as a rough analogy for divine-human encounters in which the constitutive elements were understood to be grace and faith (cf. Rom. 1:5).

Much more information can be garnered from the NT itself regarding the details of commerce and economic activity. This information is organized in what follows with reference to three geographic divisions of the Greco-Roman world: the city, the countryside, and the wilderness.

Commerce in the City: The city (Gk. *polis*) was the scene of many economic institutions and roles. In the marketplace retailers (2 Cor. 2:17) displayed wares of all sorts: purple cloth (Acts 16:14), swords (Luke 22:36), oil for lamps (Matt. 25:9), linen and spices for burial (Mark 15:46; 16:1), pearls of great price (Matt. 13:45), and even sparrows at five for two pennies (Luke 12:6). The marketplace was also where people gathered early in the morning to be hired for occasional or seasonal labor (Matt. 20:3; cf. Acts 17:5); indeed, such laborers were called *agoraioi*, or "people of the marketplace." In addition, the marketplace was the scene for the sale of slaves (Matt. 18:25; cf. 1 Tim. 1:10). On occasion, one could see in the marketplace a slave girl with a "spirit of divination" bringing in money for her owners (Acts 16:16), young flute players sitting ready to play for a wedding or funeral (Matt. 11:17), or a man carrying water (Mark 14:13). Also in the marketplace and elsewhere in the city were the workshops where artisans crafted innumerable products. Paul was a leather worker, apparently specializing in tents (Acts 18:3; cf. 1 Thess. 2:9; 1 Cor. 4:12; 2 Cor. 11:27), and scattered references identify other artisans as fullers (Mark 9:3), tanners (Acts 9:43), silversmiths (Acts 19:24), potters (Rom. 9:21), and metalworkers (2 Tim. 4:14).

The range of urban economic activity is not limited, however, to retailers and artisans. Port cities were involved in shipping (Acts 21:2–3). Especially important was the Roman grain trade, which receives incidental notice in the course of Paul's journey to Rome for trial (Acts 27:2, 6, 38; 28:11). Grain, of course, was not the only import to Rome. Captains and sailors (Rev. 18:11) brought in merchandise from places as far away as Africa, China, and India, to judge from the long list in Rev. 18:12–13: gold and silver, jewels and pearls, purple cloth, silks and fine linen, scented woods, ivory, cinnamon, incense, perfumes, wine, oil, horses, and slaves. Construction was a ubiquitous urban economic activity. At the time of Jesus, renovations and enlargements of the temple in Jerusalem had been going on for forty-six years (John 2:20), and references to building are quite common (Matt. 7:24; Mark 12:10; Luke 14:28; 1 Cor. 3:10; Eph. 2:20; Heb. 3:3). Equally ubiquitous, though less reputable, were the economic activities of various urban marginals: thieves (Matt. 24:43; Luke 12:33; 1 Thess. 5:2), prostitutes (Luke 15:30), and beggars (Mark 10:46; Luke 16:3, 20; 1 John 3:17).

Economic activity also characterized the temple complex and the culture it maintained. Festivals drew large numbers of pilgrims to Jerusalem, making the temple the focal point of economic life there. The temple complex itself was a site for buying and selling sacrificial animals (Mark 11:15; John 2:14; cf. Luke 2:24) and for the reception of offerings, large and small (Mark 12:41–43; Acts 21:24). When such other economic activities as collecting the temple tax (Matt. 17:24) and money changing (Mark 11:15) are included, Jesus's use of an economic metaphor when denouncing the Jerusalem temple as a "marketplace" (John 2:16) becomes understandable.

The principal locus of the ancient economy, however, was the urban household, especially the "great households" (2 Tim. 2:20). These households were large, complex, and economically central. They included the householder, his wife and children, and also numerous slaves—a social pattern familiar from the household codes of Eph. 5:22–6:9 and Col. 3:18–4:1. But these households might also contain other persons for short or even extended periods of time: other rich friends and neighbors invited in for a banquet (Mark 6:21–28; Luke 14:12; 1 Cor. 11:17–34); more formal groups, or associations, provided with room and resources for religious and social meetings (Rom. 16:1–2, 23; 1 Thess. 5:12; Philem. 22; 3 John 5–8); and still others, such as teachers and workers, admitted into the household for indefinite periods (1 Cor. 9:5; cf. Acts 18:3).

The large numbers of people who belonged to a great household filled a variety of economic roles. Loyal and dependable slaves had positions of responsibility as stewards (Gal. 4:2), overseeing the householder's accounts (Luke 16:1), paying his occasional hired help (Matt. 20:6), or supervising other slaves (Luke 12:42–45). Other tasks assigned to slaves include being in charge of a banquet (John 2:8), preparing food and waiting on tables (Luke 17:8), tutoring the householder's children (1 Cor. 4:15), delivering messages (Luke 14:17), answering the door (Mark 13:34; Acts 12:13), and working as artisans, a role not attested in the NT, but implicit, for example, in Paul's perception of his tentmaking as slavish (1 Cor. 9:1, 19).

A wealthy householder might not need to work (Matt. 13:27, 52; 20:1; 21:33; 24:43; Luke 13:25; 14:21), though there are scattered references to such administrative functions as inspecting a new parcel of land (Luke 14:18), deciding what to do in the wake of sabotaged fields (Matt. 13:27), dealing personally with rebellious tenants (Mark 12:9), dismissing a steward suspected of mismanagement (Luke 16:2), and deciding whether to punish a returning slave who has caused financial loss (Philem. 10–18). As masters, householders could be harsh (Matt. 18:32–34; 1 Pet. 2:18), inflicting both verbal attacks (Luke 19:22) and physical beatings (1 Pet. 2:19–20) on their slaves. The NT counsels against masters making threats toward slaves and advocates fair treatment (Col. 4:1; Eph. 6:9), but slaves are likewise admonished to obey, work hard, and not steal (Col. 3:22; Eph. 6:5–7; Titus 2:9–10). A householder's wife also had economic responsibilities. Her roles in the household are succinctly stated in 1 Tim. 5:14: to marry, bear children, and manage the household (cf. Titus 2:4–5). This third function, managing the household, may have assumed responsibility for the family's internal finances (i.e., the household budget).

Despite their roles in the household economy, the householder and his wife should be viewed as users or consumers of wealth. They typically used their considerable wealth for public display, for impressing others, and for personal enjoyment. Wealth was displayed in jewelry and fine clothing (Luke 7:25; 16:19; James 2:2) as well as at banquets

with gold and silver serving dishes (2 Tim. 2:20), extravagant menus (Luke 16:19), and costly entertainment. The use of wealth for personal enjoyment is also easily documented: the hedonistic motto of one household was "eat, drink, be merry" (Luke 12:19); another householder is depicted as feasting in great magnificence every day (16:19); and the rich are generally characterized as full and sated or otherwise satisfying their many desires (6:25; 1 Thess. 5:6–8; 1 Tim. 6:9–10; James 5:5). Although money-making activities in the city—loans (Matt. 18:23; 25:20–23), savings (Luke 19:23), the sale of slaves (1 Tim. 1:10)—partially supported the aristocratic household and lifestyle, the principal source of the householder's wealth was land, and this wealth came largely from the agricultural produce of extensive and ever expanding (Mark 12:1; Luke 14:18) properties beyond the city walls in the countryside.

Commerce in the Countryside: The word "countryside" (Gk. *chōra*) is a technical term with a decidedly economic meaning. It refers to all agriculturally productive land that surrounded the city. Used quite frequently in the NT in this economic sense (Luke 12:16; John 11:55; Acts 10:39; James 5:4), it refers specifically to fields, vineyards, pastures, orchards, and even woods with their supply of nuts, berries, wood, and game. It is here in the *chōra* that the householders owned land that was worked by tenants (Mark 12:1, 9) or slaves (Luke 17:7), who became rural members of their landlords' already sizable households. On occasion, temporary help in the form of hired laborers (from the city or countryside) was required (Luke 15:15, 17), especially during the harvest of grain (Matt. 9:37; 13:30) or the vintage (Matt. 20:7). After the harvest, a slave manager would pay the temporary laborers (Matt. 20:8) and then take his master's portion of the crop (Luke 21:34), including any surplus (Luke 12:16–18). These tenants and slaves, along with independent farmers (Matt. 21:28; Mark 4:3), lived in villages scattered throughout the countryside. Villages also had carpenters (Mark 6:3), shopkeepers (Luke 9:12; cf. 11:5–6), innkeepers (Luke 10:35; cf. 9:12; 24:28–29), and economic marginals such as beggars (Mark 10:46).

The economic life of the countryside was varied and hence required a variety of agricultural roles, or at least a variety of agricultural tasks. Farming and herding were the basic economic roles. Farmers, of course, grew grain (Matt. 13:24–25; Mark 4:26–29), but they could also take care of a vineyard (Matt. 21:28; Mark 12:1; 1 Cor. 9:7), fig trees (Luke 13:7; James 3:12), olive trees (Rom. 11:17–18), not to mention a garden for planting mustard (Luke 13:19) or vegetables (Matt. 13:32; cf. Rom. 14:2). Likewise, herders obviously tended their livestock, whether cattle (Luke 15:23), sheep (Matt. 18:12; Luke 2:8; 1 Cor. 9:7), goats (Matt. 25:33; Luke 15:29), or pigs (Mark 5:11). In the region of the Sea of Galilee, the fishing industry was especially prominent (Mark 1:16–20; Luke 5:1–11; John 21:1–3). In addition, on occasion, there were other jobs to do: building granaries (Luke 12:18), putting up fencing, making wine presses, building watchtowers (Matt. 21:33), and constructing synagogues (Luke 7:5).

The agricultural tasks can be defined further in order to give a sense of the actual work done in the countryside. Farmers had much to do: plowing the field (Luke 9:62; 17:7; 1 Cor. 9:10), winnowing (Luke 3:17), burning the chaff (Matt. 3:12), and storing the grain in barns (Matt. 6:26; Luke 12:18). In addition, they might set out vines (1 Cor. 9:7) and then cultivate, water, and prune them (Luke 13:7; 1 Cor. 3:8; John 15:2); or they might make olive grafts (Rom. 11:17–18), water the oxen (Luke 13:15), spread manure (Luke 13:8), burn pruned branches (Matt. 7:19), or chop down nonproducing trees (Luke 3:9). Similarly, herders had to watch their flocks (Luke 2:8), which included chasing after strays (Luke 15:4), digging pits to trap marauding wolves (Matt. 12:11), and separating sheep and goats at nightfall (Matt. 25:32). Fishermen could be found throwing their nets into the water (Mark 1:16), hauling in fish (Luke 5:6–7), sorting fish (Matt. 13:48), or washing and mending nets (Luke 17:35). Women in the villages were busy too, spinning and weaving (Matt. 6:28), mending old clothes (Mark 2:21), grinding meal (Matt. 24:41), making bread (Matt. 13:33), sweeping the house (Luke 15:8), or going out to a well for water (John 4:7). On occasion, they might earn some money as mourners for one who had died (Mark 5:38).

Not only the number of tasks but many details about them make clear that the lives of farmers, herders, and fishermen were hard—a far cry from the leisure of the urban landowners. At any rate, many tasks were physically demanding, such as digging (Luke 16:3). There was also the scorching sun (Matt. 20:12; Rev. 7:16) or, in the case of shepherds and fishermen, working the whole night through (Luke 2:8; 5:5; John 21:3). What is more, these workers toiled on diets near subsistence level. At times, the land produced not abundance, but thorns (Heb. 6:8; cf. Matt. 7:16), and fishing nets came up empty (Luke 5:5; John 21:3). Consequently, even sparrows could become a meal (Matt. 10:29), and some might be tempted to eat the pods fed to swine (Luke 15:15). Not surprisingly, famine was always a specter (Luke 15:14; Acts 11:28; Rev. 6:8). Thus, a prayer for "daily bread" was literally appropriate (Matt. 6:11; Luke 11:3).

Agricultural workers, however, had more to face than hard work, long hours, and little food. Herders had to contend with wolves and brigands (Matt. 7:15; John 10:8, 10), fishermen with squalls (Mark 4:37), and everyone with fraudulent tax collectors and their brutal soldiers (Luke 3:11; 19:8). In addition, a householder might withhold the wages of those who had harvested his crops (James 5:4), and when those from the countryside went to the city they could be compelled to do some task (Mark 15:21; cf. Matt. 5:41) or even be misidentified as a brigand (cf. Luke 22:52) and summarily executed (Luke 23:21). Thus, the overall impression is one of most people toiling incessantly in the countryside in order that a few householders and their families in the city might live in ease and extravagance.

Commerce in the Wilderness: The third geographic division for organizing the NT evidence regarding the ancient economic conditions is the wilderness (Gk. *erēmos*). This word is often invested with religious meaning—as a place for repentance and renewal (Mark 1:2–6) or retreat (1:35), but it also has economic significance in connection with the city and the countryside. If the countryside is the productive land that immediately surrounds and supplies the city, then the wilderness is the more distant and nonproductive land that extends beyond the countryside in all directions. As nonproductive land, the wilderness could consist of desert, such as the barren land in the Jordan Valley near the Dead Sea (Mark 1:4; cf. John 11:54) or the Arabian desert (1 Cor. 10:5). Yet the term "wilderness" does not usually imply literal desert; it simply refers to any nonproductive area, such as very hilly, mountainous, or otherwise isolated land (Matt. 15:33; 2 Cor. 11:26). It can even refer to formerly productive and populated areas (Matt. 12:25; Luke 21:20).

Still, to say that wilderness is economically unproductive land is not to deny its economic role. A wilderness might be traversed by roads on which traders and other travelers moved (Luke 10:30–33). Such travelers were exposed to attack by brigands, who seem to have operated at will in these distant and isolated areas (Luke 10:30; 2 Cor. 11:26). Indeed, from the safety of their wilderness hideouts, brigands might make forays into the countryside to attack, say, the flocks of herders (John 10:1) and, if numerous and rapacious enough, they could pose a political threat (Acts 5:36–37; 21:38).

Summary and Conclusion: In NT times, there was considerable commercialization, as reflected in the description of Rome and its merchants presented in Rev. 18. Still, the economy remained fundamentally tied to agriculture. Other than the activities of free artisans and shopkeepers in the cities (and rural villages) and of brigand gangs in the wilderness, the vast majority of people lived as farmers, herders, and fishermen in the countryside surrounding a city and worked on land that was usually owned by the urban aristocracy, who lived—and lived well—off its surplus. The two groups—the producers of wealth and the consumers of it—were related socially through the institution of the household and surrounded geographically by economically marginal hills, mountains, and deserts—the wilderness. *See also* poor, poverty; wealth.

Bibliography

Finley, M. I. *The Ancient Economy.* 2nd ed. University of California Press, 1985.

Holman, Susan R., ed. *Wealth and Poverty in Early Christianity.* Baker Academic, 2008.

MacMullen, Ramsay. *Roman Social Relations 50 B.C. to A.D. 284.* Yale University Press, 1974.

Powell, Mark Allan. *Introducing the New Testament: A Historical, Literary, and Theological Survey.* Baker Academic, 2009. Pp. 41–42.

R.F.H./M.A.P.

Eden (ee′duhn), the garden in which the first man and woman were placed and from which they were driven because of their disobedience to God's command. The name "Eden" might be related to a Hebrew word meaning "luxury, pleasure, delight" (*eden*), or it might be related to a Sumerian word meaning "plain" or "steppe" (*edin*). The location of Eden "in the east" (Gen. 2:8) probably places it, for the author of Gen. 2–3, in the area at the head of the Persian Gulf; this location may relate Eden to Dilmun of Sumerian myth—the idyllic land where old age, sickness, and death are unknown to its blessed inhabitants.

In Gen. 2–3, Eden is a garden created by God for human beings, to provide for human needs. The name is mentioned in 2:8 ("garden in Eden"), 2:10 (simply "Eden"), and 2:14; 3:23–24 ("garden of Eden"). In 2:9, 16 and 3:1–3, it is referred to as "the garden." Eden is said to be the source of four great rivers (Pishon, Gihon, Tigris, Euphrates, 2:10–14) and the site of the tree of life and the tree of the knowledge of good and evil, both of which are "in the midst of the garden" (2:9; 3:3).

After Genesis, the most important references to Eden occur in the book of Ezekiel. In Ezek. 28:11–19, a variant of the Eden story in Genesis, the prophet describes Eden as the "garden of God" (28:13), situated on God's holy mountain from which the first mortal human was expelled by the cherub because of his iniquity. While sharing many motifs with Gen. 2–3 (including the abundance of precious stones in Eden, Gen. 2:12; Ezek. 28:13), Ezek. 28 differs from Genesis in describing Eden as the "garden of God" rather than as a garden created by God for humans to till and keep (Gen. 2:15). The account in Ezek. 28 also differs in that Eden has only one inhabitant. A later passage in Ezek. 31 also treats Eden as the garden of God. This passage offers a complex allegory of a tree that in grandeur and beauty surpassed even the trees in Eden (31:8, 9, 16, 18).

In general, the garden of Eden is used as a metaphor for the renewal of the land of Israel by God after the exile (Ezek. 36:35; Isa. 51:3, where "Eden" is paralleled by "garden of the LORD"). In Joel 2:3, the transformation of the land from garden of Eden to devastated wilderness is part of an oracle forecasting the "day of the LORD." Eden is not referred to by name in the NT, but Jesus's reference to "Paradise" is probably intended as a reference to the garden of Eden (Luke 23:43; cf. Rev. 2:7).

J.S.K.

Eder (ee′duhr; Heb., "flock" or "herd").

1 A Benjaminite ancestor of a family group (1 Chron. 8:15).

2 A levitical leader in the family group of Merari (1 Chron. 25:23).

3 A settlement in southern Judah near the border with Edom, probably in the vicinity of Beersheba (Josh. 15:21); the site is unknown.

4 A site called Migdol-eder (Heb., "the tower of Eder" or "the flock tower") near which Jacob camped following the burial of Rachel in Bethlehem (Gen. 35:21), probably located somewhere between Jerusalem and Hebron.

Edom (ee′duhm; Semitic, "red," ruddy").

1 An alternative name for Esau (Gen. 36:1, 8) He was the brother of Jacob/Israel, and the elder of the twin sons of Isaac and Rebekah (25:19–26). The land of Edom (see **2**) is identified as the region where his descendants lived. Thus, Esau/Edom is the ancestor of the Edomites in the same way that Jacob/Israel is the ancestor of the Israelites. *See also* Esau.

2 The area situated south of the Dead Sea on both sides of Wadi Arabah, so named because of the reddish color of the sandstone of that district. In biblical passages the country of Edom stands in apposition to the land of Seir (Gen. 32:3; 36:8; Judg. 5:4). Edom's northern boundary on the east was the southern boundary of Moab, i.e., Wadi el-Hasa (biblical Zered). West of the Arabah, the northern boundary was the south border of Israel, which was a line running from the Dead Sea southward to the ascent of Akrabbim to Zin and Kadesh-barnea (Num. 34:3–4; Josh. 15:1–3). Num. 20:16 places the latter site on the edge of Edom (Num. 20:23; Josh. 15:1, 21). Edom's eastern border, since it lay in the desert, would not have been clearly defined. Edom extended southward, at least in certain periods, to the shores of the Red Sea at Aqabah (1 Kings 9:26). There was probably no fixed western boundary.

The eastern region of Edom appears more frequently in biblical references. All the kings of Edom listed in Gen. 36:31–43 seem to reside east of the Arabah.

The term "Edom" appears for the first time during the reign of Pharaoh Merneptah (1236–1223 BCE): permission was granted to the Bedouin tribes of Edom to enter the better pastureland of the eastern Nile Delta. Assyria recognized Edom as a clearly identifiable and even important kingdom from the beginning of the eighth century BCE onward.

Archaeological surveys in the eastern segment of Edom have collected evidence of human occupation dating back at least five hundred thousand years. Population appears to have been highest during the Middle Paleolithic (ca. 90,000–45,000 BCE), Iron II (ca. 900–539 BCE), Nabatean (ca. 330 BCE–106 CE), and Byzantine (ca. 324–640 CE) periods.

An important route, the King's Highway (Num. 20:17), passed through the eastern segment of Edom in a north–south direction. Later on, the Roman road Via Nova Triana followed or paralleled this route. It joined Bosra in southern Syria to Aqabah. Other routes traversed the territory in an east–west direction. *See also* Aqabah, Gulf of; Arabah; Edomites; Idumea; Kadesh; Seir.

Bibliography

Bartlett, J. R. *Edom and the Edomites.* Sheffield Academic, 1989.

Bennett, Crystal-M., and Piotr Bienowski. *Excavations at Tawilan in Southern Jordan.* Oxford University Press, 1995.

Bienkowski, Piotr. *Busayra: Excavations by Crystal-M. Bennett 1971-1980.* Oxford University Press, 2002.

———, ed. *Early Edom and Moab: The Beginning of the Iron Age in Southern Jordan.* J. R. Collis, 1992.

Edelman, Diana, ed. *You Shall Not Abhor an Edomite for He Is Your Brother: Seir and Edom in History and Tradition.* Scholars, 1995.

MacDonald, Burton. *Ammon, Moab and Edom: Early States/Nations of Jordan in the Biblical Period (End of the 2nd and During the 1st Millennium B.C.).* Al Kutba, 1994.

Whiting, Charlotte M. *Complexity and Diversity in the Late Iron Age Southern Levant: The Investigation of 'Edomite' Archaeology and Scholarly Discourse.* Archaeopress, 2007.   B.M.

Edomites (ee′duh-mits), the inhabitants of the land of Edom (Seir). The Bible emphasizes the close relationship between the Edomites and Israelites. The Edomite "kings" of Gen. 36:31–39 were probably tribal chiefs, local rulers controlling separate and independent regions. The Edomites refused permission to the group led by Moses to pass through their territory (Num. 20:14–21). Saul fought successfully with the Edomites (1 Sam. 14:47). Doeg, an Edomite, appears among Saul's servants (1 Sam. 21:7; 22:9, 18, 22). David conquered the Edomites (2 Sam. 8:12–14). Solomon appears to have had access to the port of Ezion-geber in the land of Edom (1 Kings 9:26). Pharaoh Shishak's invasion (1 Kings 14:25; 2 Chron. 12:2–9) possibly gave the Edomites a chance to regain their independence. In the time of Jehoshaphat (ca. 873–849 BCE), Judah expanded southward, ruled Edom (1 Kings 22:47), and used the port of Ezion-geber (1 Kings 22:48–49; 2 Chron. 20:35–37). The Edomites successfully revolted when Jehoram was king of Judah (ca. 849–843/2 BCE), set up a king of their own (2 Kings 8:20–22), and maintained their independence for about fifty or sixty years until the middle of Amaziah's reign (ca. 800–783 BCE; 2 Kings 14:7; 2 Chron. 25:11–12). Amaziah's son, Uzziah (Azariah) recaptured Edom and built Elath (2 Kings 14:22; 2 Chron. 26:1–2). At the time of Ahaz (ca. 735–715 BCE), the Edomites defeated Judah (2 Chron. 28:17) and recovered Elath (2 Kings 16:6). From this time onward, Judah was not able to exercise control over them.

It is difficult to say whether the Edomites participated in the destruction of Jerusalem in 587/6 BCE. The Babylonian king Nebuchadnezzar seems to have destroyed the Edomites along with the Judeans (Jer. 27:2–3, 6; 49:7–22). Nabonidus (555–539 BCE), the last Babylonian king, claims that he laid siege to the "town of Edom" in the third year of his reign. The town in question is probably Bozrah, modern Buseirah, the Edomite capital. The oracle of Mal. 1:2–4 indicates that by the time of its writing Edom was in ruin. By the fourth century BCE, the Nabateans replaced the Edomites, many of whom went westward to southern Judea, later to become Idumea, while others were absorbed by the newcomers.

No major monumental Edomite inscription has been found. Explorations and excavations in Edom, however, have uncovered a number of seals, seal impressions (*bullae*), fragments of pottery with inscriptions in ink (ostraca), and one cuneiform tablet. The Edomites used a regional variant of the Northwest Semitic script and language. The Edomites were known for their wisdom (Jer. 49:7; Obad. 1:8; Bar. 3:22). It is believed that they were devoted to the gods and goddesses of fertility. Qaus was their particular deity. Eloah (Hab. 3:3), another divine name, was perhaps also known to them. The Edomite economy was based on a combination of animal herding, crop cultivation, and commerce. Copper was also mined in the Arabah from the Chalcolithic through the Mamluk period. *See also* Bozrah; Edom; Ezion-geber; Seir.

B.M.

Edrei (ed′ree-i).

1 An ancient Transjordanian site, a royal residence of Og, king of Bashan, whose land, following his defeat by the Israelites, was allocated to Manasseh (Num. 21:33; Deut. 1:4; 3:10; Josh. 12:4; 13:12, 31); in Roman times it was called Adraene and today is called Dar'a.

2 A town in Naphtali (Josh. 19:37).

education. Formal processes of instruction are rarely mentioned in the Bible (Dan. 1:5; Sir. 4:24; 10:1; 21:19, 21; 34:9; Acts 22:3), but some formal or informal means of education is frequently assumed. The Israelites are instructed at Sinai to teach their children God's commandments by talking about them in the home (Deut. 11:9); they are also to write words of God (the Shema) on phylacteries and doorposts, a practice that, if taken literally, assumes a general measure of literacy (11:18, 20). Likewise, Judg. 8:3–11 mentions a youth for whom the ability to read and write is simply assumed. The mention of a city named Qiriath Sepher ("City of the Book") in Josh. 15:15–16 and Judg. 1:11–12 has prompted speculation as to whether a formal educational institution or library might have been located there. All of these references are problematic, however, given the fact that the texts in which they occur did not achieve their present written form until well into the First Temple period.

Three texts have often been cited as possible references to formal education in preexilic Israel, but all of them are problematic. Isa. 28:9–13 refers specifically to infants who have just been weaned; Isa. 50:4–9 merely indicates that eloquence was taught somewhere, presumably in the home; Prov. 22:17–21 pertains to a foreign setting, inasmuch as it reflects an indebtedness to the Egyptian

A teacher sits between two students who hold open scrolls; third-century CE tomb relief.

Instruction of Amen-em-opet. Other biblical references that could refer to some system of Israelite education include Isaiah's mention of "disciples" (lit., "students," e.g., 8:16), various references in Proverbs to people buying wisdom (4:5; 17:16), and a reference to the officials of Hezekiah copying proverbs (Prov. 25:1).

The earliest specific reference to an Israelite school comes from the postexilic Second Temple period. Sir. 51:23 invites students to Ben Sira's "house of instruction." As to content, education in Israel during the Second Temple period may have focused on religious traditions and proverbial sayings, if Sirach is regarded as exemplary. Under Hellenistic influence, however, the author of Wisdom of Solomon adopted a much different curriculum: "the structure of the world and the activity of the elements . . . the alternations of the solstices and the changes of the seasons, the cycles of the year and the constellations of the stars, the natures of animals and the tempers of wild animals, the powers of spirits and the thoughts of human beings, the varieties of plants and the virtues of roots" (7:17–22).

Extrabiblical Evidence: The paucity of evidence for schools in the Bible has been supplemented from two sources: ancient Near Eastern parallels and Israelite inscriptions. Knowledge of education in ancient Egypt is quite extensive, thanks to instructional texts that have survived. Similarly, several school texts from Sumer exist today, allowing scholars to paint a reasonably clear picture of education in Mesopotamia. The same is true for Ugarit, where scribes played a significant role in society. It may be possible, therefore, to draw upon this combined picture to clarify the situation in Israel, but such a procedure is risky, given the relative simplicity of the Hebrew language and of Israelite society even during the monarchy. If there were schools in Solomon's

time, one wonders why the list of governmental officials does not include the equivalent of a superintendent of education.

Recent evidence from Israelite inscriptions has elicited differing interpretations. Some critics have used the following data to argue for schools in early Israel: lists, abecedaries (i.e., alphabet lists), transposition of similar letters, repeated words, large letters, poorly formed figures, etc. Such materials are sometimes thought to have been produced by persons learning to write. Some of the features, however, could be attributed to something else: large letters could indicate poor eyesight or an aged writer; less than perfect drawings could suggest a shaky hand. In any case, these materials would only indicate that writing was sometimes acquired by some people (a point that is not under dispute); such instruction could have occurred within individual homes. These materials would only serve as evidence for the existence of formal schools if accumulations of them were found in single sites, which, to date, has not been the case.

Types of Instruction: There is general consensus among scholars that the family was central to education in Israelite society at least up to the Roman period. Indeed, the address "my child" used throughout the book of Proverbs, though usually taken as a metaphorical reference for anyone who wishes to learn wisdom, could be meant literally (e.g., 1:10; 2:1), especially in instances where the mother is mentioned alongside the father as one who is honored or shamed by the child's wisdom or lack thereof (4:3–4; 10:1; 15:20; 23:22). It also seems likely, however, that many young people acquired training in guilds. We hear of prophetic and priestly guilds, and it is probable that other skills like pottery making and metallurgy were acquired in various guilds. A decisive shift in the direction of official bureaucracy may have taken place under King Hezekiah (715–687/6 BCE), if it had not already occurred during Solomon's reign. In any event, young men now received instruction as scribes at the royal court. According to Ecclesiastes, a conscious effort seems to have been made to instruct "the people," if that expression really implies a democratization of learning (12:9). A different sort of teaching is reported in 2 Chron. 17:7–9: official priests, Levites, and princes are said to have instructed the people in the "book of the law."

In the NT: Although no formal education is described in the NT, Jesus is pictured as one who has disciples and who teaches large crowds (Mark 4:1–2; 14:49). Likewise, mention is made of "teachers of the law" (Luke 5:17; cf. 1 Tim. 1:7). The early church believed it had been commissioned by Christ to teach his commandments to all nations (Matt. 28:19–20). Acts reports Paul was educated by the famous teacher Gamaliel (22:3), suggesting that some variety of rabbinic school may have been in existence. There is no evidence in the NT of formal education in the Christian faith; such teaching appears to have occurred within the family (1 Tim. 1:5; cf. Deut. 11:19) and within the church (1 Cor. 12:28; Eph. 4:11). *See also* schools; teaching.   J.L.C.

Eglon (eg′lon).

1 The king of Moab who, together with the Ammonites and Amalekites, invaded Israelite territory during the period of the judges and ruled over the people from the "city of palms" (Jericho) for eighteen years. According to Judg. 3:12–30, Eglon's rule ended when Ehud, the left-handed judge, concealed a dagger under his cloak and assassinated Eglon when they were alone. The story is told with a degree of mockery. Eglon is so foolish that he agrees to a private conference with Ehud, and he is so fat that, when stabbed, the dagger is consumed by his flab; he dies in a latrine, while obtuse guards wait outside.

2 A Canaanite city allied with Jerusalem, Hebron, Jarmuth, and Lachish in an unsuccessful attempt to oppose Joshua's invasion of the land of Canaan (Josh. 10:3–5). Joshua captured the city (10:34–35; cf. 12:12), which was later included among the cities of Judah (15:39). Modern Tell Aitun is currently identified as the site of Eglon.   M.A.S.

Egypt (ee′jipt), one of the great civilizations of the ancient world, centered along the lower reaches of the Nile River in northeast Africa. Egyptian civilization was already ancient by the time of the biblical ancestors, and its Delta settlements reached to within two hundred miles of Israel's territory, yet Egypt's cultural influence on the Near East was considerably less than that of Mesopotamia. For their part, the Egyptians were not very interested in settlement abroad, partly because there were many possibilities for expansion at home. Nonetheless, Egypt did dominate the Near East politically during many periods.

Egypt's influence was greater in the Phoenician coastal cities, with which it had important cultural and commercial ties.

The division into dynasties found in this article follows the Egyptian writer Manetho. Scholars do not quite agree on the absolute chronology or on how to organize the dynasties—some of which are contemporary rather than successive—into larger groupings.

Geographic Setting: Apart from the reach of the waters of the Nile, Egypt is almost entirely desert. The Nile has no tributaries in Egypt proper or for several hundred miles to the south, and the land receives little rainfall. Even the Nile Delta has at best 7–8 inches of rainfall annually, whereas the Nile Valley has virtually none. (The Aswan High Dam has changed the rainfall patterns for southern Egypt.) So the designation of Egypt as the "gift of the Nile" is very apt. The Nile waters define the agricultural, populated realm. The settled area of Egypt therefore resembles a tall flower bending in the breeze. The Nile Delta (Lower Egypt), which spreads out north of Cairo for 100 miles to the Mediterranean and is more than 150 miles wide, is the blossom, and the Nile Valley (Upper Egypt) is the long, slender stalk, between 6 and 9 miles wide and extending 575 miles from Cairo south to Aswan, with its thickest section being the northern portion. The one exception to this image is the Faiyum, an area well watered by a branch of the Nile about 50 miles south of Cairo and reaching some 50 miles into the desert west of the Nile. The few oases in the western desert were not important population centers. Since about two-thirds of the serviceable land is in the Delta, 20 of the traditional 42 nomes, or administrative districts, of ancient Egypt were also in the Delta. Yet, in spite of its great importance, the Delta, for various reasons, is not nearly so well known archaeologically as is the Nile Valley.

Egypt had a strong sense of duality: there were "Two Lands," the delta and the valley, and together they constituted the "Black Land" in contrast to the neighboring desert, the "Red Land." Bordered by the Mediterranean on the north with desert on the remaining sides, Egypt was fairly secure from major movements of people. The overland route into the Levant led through the Sinai wilderness and along the Mediterranean coast before moving up into the hill country and cities such as Hebron and Jerusalem (about 215 miles from the easternmost settlements of the Delta). Accordingly, only relatively small groups of people from Canaan went into Egypt, prompted by drought, commerce, and other concerns (cf. Gen. 12:10; 42–43; Matt. 2:14). Asiatics and Libyans came into the Nile Delta, both hostilely and peacefully, and Nubians into the Nile Valley. Drawing like a magnet from the modest adjacent populations, the Egyptians were a heterogeneous people from early times.

Predynastic and Early Dynastic Periods: Predynastic Egypt featured regional cultures and village society throughout a period of several

An Asiatic tribe in traditional costume asking permission to enter Egypt, as Abraham and Jacob may have done; copy of a mural from the tomb at Beni-Hassan, nineteenth century BCE.

hundred years. Constellations were forming in Upper and Lower Egypt, but with considerable conflict. In the First and Second Dynasties (ca. 2950–2675 BCE), the "Two Lands" experienced the formation and consolidation of a unified government centered at Memphis (Cairo area). Key elements were the development of court culture and royal bureaucracy. An enduring pattern of division into provinces (nomes) was established, provinces that embodied cultural particularities, such as in religious practice, that persevered over the centuries in spite of the subsequent political unification of Egypt.

Old Kingdom Period: The Third through the Sixth Dynasties (ca. 2675–2180 BCE) represented a period of immense cultural and political achievement. Building on the accomplishments of the Early Dynastic period, a remarkable level of culture and organization was reached. The Third Dynasty (ca. 2675–2600) was still a period of some innovation, leading up to the climactic development of the Fourth Dynasty (ca. 2600–2480), whose impressive scale was symbolized by the great pyramids. By this time a distinctive pattern of culture—artistic, political, and religious—had developed that served effectively, with variations and adaptations, for well over two millennia. The central institution was that of the kingship, religiously central in the state cult as the link between the people and the divine powers of the cosmos, and politically central as the embodiment of the unity of the realm. The pharaoh, at the same time both mortal and divine, wielded immense power filtered through an effective bureaucracy. In the Fifth and Sixth Dynasties (ca. 2480–2180), the localized authorities became more prominent. The royal center remained in the Memphis area, where the "Two Lands" joined. During the Old Kingdom, Egypt engaged in extensive commercial interchange with Phoenicia, especially Byblos, and also sent many expeditions to Sinai to obtain materials such as turquoise and copper.

First Intermediate and Middle Kingdom Periods: When the system of the Old Kingdom broke down, it was followed by about a hundred and fifty years of civil war and assertiveness by local provinces (Seventh–Ninth Dynasties, ca. 2180–1939 BCE). During the Eleventh Dynasty, Egypt became unified again (ca. 1970–1939), and during the Twelfth Dynasty (ca. 1939–1756) the central organization was furthered, though the king was less powerful than in the Old King-

dom. Southern Egypt, with its center in Thebes, became more prominent, though the kings still ruled from the Memphis area. During the Middle Kingdom Egypt asserted itself in southern Canaan in more than a commercial relationship. The term "empire" is probably inappropriate, but there was some kind of hegemony. The Execration texts list local rulers and peoples of the area, many specifically from Canaan, Transjordan, and Phoenicia, who owed some kind of allegiance to Egypt. Some of the earlier ancestral traditions of Israel concerning Egypt may relate to this period. Clearly, many Asiatics were now residing in Egypt, especially in the eastern Delta.

Second Intermediate (Hyksos) Period: The forces for decentralization again triumphed (Thirteenth–Seventeenth Dynasties, a group of overlapping dynasties, ca. 1756–1520 BCE), and there were various separatist movements. For the first time pharaonic Egypt experienced a major influx of foreigners, as Asiatic groups, termed Hyksos ("rulers of foreign lands") in Egyptian sources, with superior military technology and organization in spite of their varied backgrounds, gained control in the Delta and, apparently, the northern portion of the Nile Valley (Fifteenth Dynasty, ca. 1630–1522). Also, Nubia had broken away, so traditional Egyptian rulers were restricted to the Nile Valley and were at times under Hyksos domination. This was a period of considerable interchange between Egyptian and Canaanite cultures, though it is not well documented. Many scholars regard this period as the setting for the Joseph story, although there is no specific confirmation from Egyptian sources. The pharaonic traditions endured most effectively in the south, under the domination of Thebes. Eventually the Theban rulers prevailed against the Nubian-Hyksos tandem and their Egyptian allies.

New Kingdom Period: Theban success against the outsiders ushered in the New Kingdom (Eighteenth–Twentieth Dynasties, ca. 1539–1075 BCE). Ahmose I (ca. 1539–1514) captured the Hyksos center of Avaris, drove the Hyksos back into the Levant, subdued Nubia, and unified again the "Two Lands." Indeed, from the time of Thutmose I and II (ca. 1493–1479) to Ramesses II (ca. 1279–1213) Egypt was politically powerful also in much of Canaan as well as in Nubia and, at least by the time of Thutmose III (ca. 1479–1426), it is possible to refer to an Egyptian Empire. Egyptian rulers also maintained diplomatic contact with the major powers of western Asia, including Cyprus and Anatolia. In Egypt, an effective administration endured during the whole of the New Kingdom, surviving crises such as the Amarna revolution and the changes in dynasties. Noteworthy was the power conflict between the royal court and the major priesthoods, especially that of Amun-Re at Thebes. This conflict reached a climax during Amenhotep IV/Akhenaton's reign (ca. 1353–1336), when the king's sacral centrality was reasserted in the Amarna revolution in theology and art. Noteworthy also was the level of cultural interchange with Canaanite and other early civilizations in the Levant. Many Semitic gods had a following in Egypt, and the Asiatic population in Egypt continued to be a significant presence, especially in Lower Egypt. It is most likely that the setting of the exodus tradition is the time of the long-lived and powerful Ramesses II. The Egyptian sources attest to the presence of Asiatic workers, but they make no reference to the flight of a group of Hebrew slaves or of their miraculous escape. In the "Victory Stele" of Merneptah (ca. 1213–1204), the immediate successor of Ramesses II, there occurs the first extrabiblical reference to Israel (with sequential reference to victories over the city-states of Ashkelon, Gezer, Yanoam, and the people Israel). Nevertheless Egypt's power was waning. Though

Ramesses III (ca. 1187–1156) could still repel the Sea Peoples and the Libyans, the effort was the last sign of real strength, as Egypt subsequently entered a period of depression and disorder.

Third Intermediate Period: By the time of the Twenty-First through Twenty-Fifth Dynasties (ca. 1075–656 BCE), Egypt's political greatness and cultural ingenuity were in the past, and the nation was weakened by regionalism and factionalism. According to 1 Kings 9:16, one of the pharaohs of this period even gave a daughter in marriage to a foreign king, namely, Solomon, something formerly unheard of. At times descendants of former Libyan mercenaries and prisoners were in power. One Libyan ruler, Shishak (Shoshenq I, ca. 945–924), gave refuge to the future king of Israel, Jeroboam I, and even campaigned successfully against Israel and Judah, including Jerusalem. Nubian princes succeeded in extending control into Upper Egypt. During the Twenty-Fifth Dynasty (ca. 770–656) Nubian pharaohs came to control a united Nubia and Egypt, partly by allowing Thebes practical independence. But the Nubian kings were not able to restrain Assyria, with whom they had many encounters, and again, in the early seventh century, Asiatic forces found their way into Egypt. The Assyrians sacked Memphis (ca. 671) and even Thebes (ca. 664), but managed only temporary control.

Late Period: The late period covers the Twenty-Sixth through Thirty-First Dynasties (ca. 664–332 BCE). The Twenty-Sixth Dynasty (also called the Saite dynasty, ca. 664–525), based in the western Delta and aided by Greek and Carian mercenaries, led Egypt in its last period of independence and unity. Neco II even campaigned in north Syria—Josiah of Judah died in opposing him—and dominated Judah from 609 to 605. The Saite period formally imitated the artistic style of the Old Kingdom, but did not capture its grandeur. The Saites did enlarge Egypt's commercial contacts and had sizable resident foreign colonies, including many Greeks. They managed to stop the Babylonian army short of Egypt proper, but subsequently Persian strength proved too great. The invasion of Cambyses (525) brought Egypt into the Persian domain. Although Egypt regained some independence from Persia between 404 and 342, it was precariously involved with Greek mercenaries. The Persians enjoyed a brief but troubled period of renewed control (342–332) prior to their collapse in the face of Alexander's forces.

Hellenistic-Roman Period (332 BCE–324 CE): Alexander stayed only about six months in Egypt, spending a good part of that time on an arduous visit to the oracle of Zeus-Ammon (i.e., perhaps Amon) in the Siwah Oasis, some three hundred miles from Memphis into the eastern desert, where he apparently was declared a god. He also arranged the foundation of Alexandria, the most important of the many cities named after him and a major city of the Mediterranean world—much more Hellenistic than Egyptian. Alexander, now regarded as pharaoh, assigned most of the administrative control to Egyptian authorities and

The Egyptian sun god Re; bronze statue, Egypt, first millennium BCE.

Captive Asiatics, with arms upraised in a gesture of submissive greeting to Pharaoh Sahure, being taken by ship to Egypt; stone relief ca. 2446 BCE.

left political matters in Hellenistic hands. Following Alexander's death (323), Ptolemy Soter, one of his generals, gained control of Egypt and soon founded the Ptolemaic dynasty (305–330), of which the famous Cleopatra was the concluding representative. The Ptolemies hellenized the Egyptian administration and exploited the country, while also identifying with the pharaonic traditions and sponsoring major building projects, in the traditional manner, throughout Egypt. For much of the period the Ptolemies contended with other heirs of Alexander, the Seleucid rulers of Syria, for control of the Levant, with Ptolemaic dominance ending in 198. In Egypt, the Ptolemies experienced considerable internal strife and became increasingly subordinate to Rome. Rome assumed direct rule from 30 BCE to 324 CE, but continued the Ptolemaic administrative system. Many originally Egyptian cults, such as that of the goddess Isis, gained a wide following in the Hellenistic-Roman world. The Christian community in Egypt, which began quite early, developed into the Coptic church.

Egypt and the Bible: Egypt's influence on the people and culture of the ancient Near East involved serving as a refuge area or place of exile, exercising political domination, and exerting cultural influence either directly or by way of the Phoenician coastal cities. As the great granary of the eastern Mediterranean, Egypt attracted many people to its abundant agricultural resources and its considerable wealth and grandeur. Individuals and families from the ancestral period on are described as going to Egypt for survival. Similarly, following the fall of Jerusalem to the Babylonians, a group from Judah sought refuge in Egypt. Yet Egypt could also be a place of exile. Israel's model for its self-understanding was the liberating exodus under Moses from state slavery in the Egyptian Delta. Egypt was therefore identified both as the departure point for Israel's liberation from oppression and as the arrival point for threatened divine punishment.

In the few centuries prior to the exodus, Egypt had been a dominant power in the Near East, ruling basically through local princes and strategically located garrisons. During the Israelite monarchy and the subsequent periods of foreign control, Egypt was generally restricted to brief raids and involvements in various alliances against the great Asiatic powers. Significant control by Egypt occurred again only in the time of the Ptolemies. In connection with the military campaigns, many Israelites were taken as captives to Egypt, basically to work for the king and the gods. During the fifth century BCE there was a Jewish military colony—and a Jewish temple—at the southern border of Egypt (Elephantine), and in Ptolemaic times there were many Jewish settlers. From ca. 163 BCE until 71 CE there was even a Jewish temple at Leontopolis in the eastern Delta.

Egypt's cultural influence in the Near East was modest, considering the proximity. Egypt sought raw materials, especially wood and metals, from the area and was not bent on cultural dominance. There are a number of Egyptian loanwords in the Bible (Egyptian and Hebrew are distantly related languages), and indeed Moses and many of the priestly class bore Egyptian names, a pattern that endured for several centuries. According to late tradition Moses was "instructed in all the wisdom of the Egyptians" (Acts 7:22). Moreover, Akhenaton's "monotheism" antedated the time of Moses by almost a century, and some influence is possible. Yet specific influence is difficult to demonstrate, and the contrasts in most areas are considerable; the closest parallel may be that Akhenaton and Moses are similarly entrancing but elusive figures. In spite of some intriguing parallels in details and a plausible initial impetus toward monotheism, Egyptian religion seems to have had little formative influence on that of Israel. The most specific example of literary borrowing is in Prov. 22:17–24:22, which apparently drew upon the Egyptian *Instruction of Amenemope*. Other literary influence is found in novellas, such as the Joseph story, and in love poetry. The political organization under David and Solomon may well have drawn upon Egyptian models, but, if so, presumably through Phoenician intermediaries. For the prophets, Egypt served as an example of idolatry and arrogant power, Israel's redemption from which in the exodus proved to be a lasting, central motif of Israel's faith. *See also* Akhenaton; Amarna, Tell el-; exodus, the; Hyksos; Neco II; Nile; Pharaoh; Sea Peoples.

Bibliography

Bowman, Alan K. *Egypt After the Pharaohs: 332 B.C.–A.D. 642.* University of California Press, 1986.

Grimal, Nicolas. *A History of Ancient Egypt.* Blackwell, 1992.

Kemp, Barry J. *Ancient Egypt: Anatomy of a Civilization.* Routledge, 1989.

Shafer, Byron E., ed. *Religion in Ancient Egypt: Gods, Myths, and Personal Practice.* Cornell University Press, 1991.

Trigger, Bruce G., Barry J. Kemp, David O'Connor, and Alan B. Lloyd. *Ancient Egypt: A Social History.* Cambridge University Press, 1983.   II.B.II.

Egypt, Wadi of. *See* Wadi of Egypt.

Ehud (ee´huhd), a left-handed Benjaminite who by a clever ruse killed the fat Moabite king Eglon and subsequently led the Israelites to victory over the Moabites (Judg. 3:12–4:1). *See also* Eglon.

Ekron (ek´ruhn; Heb., possibly "barren place" or "fertile place"; Gk. Akkaron), the northernmost city of the Philistine Pentapolis. Now identified as Khirbet el Muqanna' (Tel Miqne), it lies about twenty-two miles west of Jerusalem. It was assigned to the territory of Judah (Josh. 15:11) or to Dan (19:43), but was reported to be in Philistine hands when the ark was taken there (1 Sam. 5:10). The town accepted defeated Philistines (1 Sam. 17:52) as David's gains brought compression of Philistine territory. In the last quarter of the tenth century BCE, Ekron was conquered by Egypt's Shishak. The city came back into biblical tradition about a hundred years later when Elijah was called to challenge the authority of Ekron's god, Baal-zebub, during the reign of the Israelite king Amaziah (2 Kings 1:2–16). It was later conquered by Assyria's Sennacherib (ca. 705–681 BCE), but would be referred to in the oracles of certain prophets who denounced Ekron as a symbol of evil power to be destroyed (Jer. 25:20; Zeph. 2:4; Zech. 9:5, 7; cf. Amos 1:8). During the Hasmonean period, the city was given to Jonathan Maccabeus by Alexander Balas (ca. 160–142 BCE; 1 Macc. 10:89).

Excavations of Ekron have revealed occupation from Chalcolithic through Middle Bronze ages. Major development began in the Late Bronze Age with Philistine arrival and expansion (first third of the twelfth century BCE) to the full fifty-acre site. Israelite ascendancy is reflected in shrinkage to ten-acre occupation in the tenth century BCE, but new growth again occurred under Assyrian occupation (eighth century), at which time industrial development as an olive-oil processing center reached its peak. Destruction followed under Babylonian assault (603 BCE campaign of Nebuchadnezzar). Subsequent survival was minimal on evidence to date.

Bibliography

Dothan, Trude. *The Philistines and Their Material Culture.* Israel Exploration Society, 1982.

Dothan, Trude, and Seymour Gitin. "The Rise and Fall of Ekron of the Philistines: Recent Excavations at an Urban Border Site." *Biblical Archaeologist* 50, no. 4 (December 1987): 197–222.

                                  R.S.B.

El, a generic word for "god" in the ancient Semitic languages. The word could be used as either a proper or common noun. As a proper noun, El normally refers to a specific Canaanite god, regarded as the ruler among the gods, but the Bible also speaks of El as "the God of Israel" (Gen. 33:20). In this capacity, El occurs frequently in personal names of persons noted for their fidelity to the God of Israel (e.g., *El*iab, *El*ijah). The plural, Elohim, is also widely used as a name for God in

El, the chief god of the Canaanite pantheon, raises his hand in benediction to a king or high priest before him; relief from Ugarit, thirteenth century BCE.

the Bible, though El is preferred in the book of Job and other works of poetry. The plural form may derive from some original sense of "gods," but in the Bible it is employed as a proper noun that takes singular verbs and is modified by singular adjectives (thus, a word literally meaning "gods" becomes the name of God).

In Ugaritic Literature: Literature produced in the north Canaanite city-state of Ugarit (second millennium BCE) reveals much of what we know about the Canaanite god El. In the assembly of the gods, El holds the highest position. Permission to build a palace for Baal must come from El, and it is El who surrenders Baal to Baal's enemy Yamm. To judge from his epithets, El is a creator. At Ugarit he was called the "Builder of Things Built," and elsewhere he held the title "Creator of the Earth." He is also an aged god, called the "Father of Years." Ugaritic texts refer to his gray beard and speak of his wisdom. El is also called "Compassionate," "The Bull," "Beneficent," and the "Father of Humankind." He lives at the source of two rivers amid the fountains of the (world-encompassing) Deep—a localization that lies beyond the bounds of terrestrial space.

Although he is the titular chief among the gods, El does not always play a forceful role in the Ugaritic myths and legends. His daughter Anat coerces him with threats of violence. His surrender of Baal to Yamm likewise has the character of submission to Yamm. In one short text, El is portrayed as drinking himself into a stupor and wallowing in his own excrement and urine. Such behavior has led to questions concerning El's status in the Ugaritic pantheon. Some have suggested that El at Ugarit was in his twilight, and others believe that Baal was in the process of supplanting El in Ugaritic religion. Yet there are times in the Ugaritic literature when El acts effectively. It is El who brings about the healing of Kirta (Keret) when all other gods fail, and it is the threat of El's intervention that silences a fractious Athtar. It should be noted that although Ugaritic literature presents a variegated picture of El, other sources are more consistently flattering of the god. Philo of Byblos (ca. 64–141 CE), a Greek historian who collected Phoenician lore, identified El with Kronos, told of El's marriage to Astarte, Rhea, and Dione, and reported that Zeus (Baal) ruled the earth with the permission of El.

At Ugarit, El's consort was Asherah, a goddess whom the Bible links with Baal. A Canaanite myth "El, Ashertu, and the Storm God" (surviving in a Hittite version) tells of how Asherah was faithless to her consort El and sought the affection of the storm god (Baal).

In Ancient Israel: The cult of El was widely diffused in the Syro-Palestinian world, and it spread from there to the Phoenician colonies of the central and western Mediterranean basin. El was worshiped in Canaan at an early date, and the Bible reveals many local manifestations of El. At Beer-lahai-roi Hagar encounters El Roi (Heb., "God of Seeing," Gen. 16:7–14). At Beer-sheba Abraham worships El Olam (Heb., "Eternal God," Gen. 21:33). The name El Elyon (Heb., "God Most High") was associated with Jerusalem (Gen. 14:18–20). Jacob has a revelation of El Bethel (NRSV: El-bethel) at Bethel (Gen. 35:7). El Berith (Heb., "God of the Covenant") is linked to Shechem (Judg. 9:46), but the same god appears to be called Baal-berith elsewhere (Judg. 9:4). Many if not all of these local manifestations of El go back to pre-Israelite times (pre–thirteenth century BCE).

The worship of El at local Palestinian sanctuaries provided a setting for the transmission of aspects of the cult of El to the religion of Israel. During its settlement in Canaan, Israel was able to adopt the veneration of El by viewing El as synonymous with the God known to Israel's ancestors. Thus, when Exod. 6:2–3 introduces the divine name, it does so in this way: "I am YHWH [NRSV: "the LORD"]. I appeared to Abraham, Isaac, and Jacob as El Shaddai [NRSV: "God Almighty]." Thus, God, known to Moses and to all subsequent Israelites by the unspeakable name YHWH, was the same God who had been known to the ancestors as El. Throughout the Pentateuch, the name El Shaddai is used for Israel's God, primarily in those portions of the text attributed to P, the Priestly writer(s) or tradition. When it is recognized that the name Israel itself is a compound including the divine name El, the importance of El in the early religion of Israel becomes clear.

The accommodation of El worship by Israel was a remarkable occurrence, for Israel was typically hostile to the cults of Canaanite gods and goddesses. It is, of course, impossible to determine how much integration occurred since, (1) the El known within Israel need not have been synonymous with the El of the Ugaritic literature; and (2) there may have been cross-fertilization in which Israelite tradition influenced El worship among the Canaanites (so it is difficult to tell who influenced whom). Still, the syncretism that allowed aspects of Canaanite El worship to be assumed into Israel's religion may have left some traces within the biblical materials. Thus, "the LORD" (YHWH) could be pictured as occupying the lead role in a council of the gods (Ps. 89:6–7). Application of the title "King" to Israel's God may derive from El worship, as might emphasis on the attributes of mercy and compassion, for which El was especially noted. Affirmations of Israel's God as creator and father are also reminiscent of El, as is the figure of the Ancient of Days in Dan. 7:9–14. *See also* Baal; names of God in the Hebrew Bible; Ras-Shamra.   R.M.G.

Elah (ee′luh).

1 The valley in Judah where David is reported to have killed Goliath (1 Sam. 17:2, 19; 21:9); it was protected by the cities of Libnah and Azekah (modern Wadi es-Sant).

2 The son and successor of Baasha, and king of Israel ca. 877–876 BCE. He ruled for fewer than two years. While intoxicated, he was murdered by Zimri in Tirzah (1 Kings 16:6–14).

3 The father of Hoshea, the last king of Israel (ca. 732–724 BCE; 2 Kings 15:30; 17:1; 18:1, 9).

Elam (ee′luhm), the region east of the Tigris River, in the Fars province of modern-day Iran. Sometimes the term "Elam" also refers to a state or nation located in this region; its capital was Anshan (Tal-i Malyan).

In Ancient History: The region of Elam provided Mesopotamia with a rich source of raw materials; hence there was a continuing Mesopotamian interest in Elam. Three rivers water the region, making it especially fertile. Elamite pictographs first appear around 2900 BCE, whereas writing begins in Mesopotamia around 3100 BCE. A linear Elamite script, known from only eighteen inscriptions, dates from the twenty-third century BCE. Carved seals from the third millennium BCE depict various activities of the Elamite economy: hunting, fishing, herding, and agriculture. A female deity, Pinikir, headed the Elamite pantheon until the middle of the second millennium BCE, when the male Humban replaced her. Contact between Mesopotamia and Elam appears as early as 2550 BCE, when Enmebaragesi of Kish records carrying off "as booty the weapons of the land of Elam." Elam remained under Mesopotamian control until Ibbi-Sin, the last ruler of the Ur III dynasty, was carried off to exile in Elam, where he died. The early Sumerian view of the Elamites as undesirables prevailed throughout the second millennium BCE. Conflict between these two regions continued until the thirteenth century BCE, the high point of Elamite civilization, when Elam freed itself of Babylon's control.

In the Bible: In the Table of Nations, Elam is listed as a descendant of Shem (Gen. 10:22). Then Elam is mentioned in Gen. 14, which details the coalition of several kings, including the Elamite Chedorlaomer, against the kings of the Dead Sea region. This coalition captured Lot, who was then rescued by his uncle, Abram. The Hebrew name Chedorlaomer may reflect an actual Elamite name: Kuter-Lagamar would mean "the goddess Lagamar is protection," a likely name for an Elamite ruler to have, but the name has not yet been found in any native inscriptions. In the eighth and seventh centuries BCE, Elam alternately showed its last independence and joined Chaldean and Aramean coalitions against Assyria. Isaiah records Elamite help in Assyrian attacks on Judah (11:11; 21:2; 22:6). Ezek. 32:24–25 describes the destruction of Elam by Assyria. In all of these instances, Elam is depicted as a fierce nation whose warriors were adept at the use of the bow and arrow as well as chariotry. During the reign of Zedekiah, Jeremiah prophesied God's promise of a total victory over Elam (49:35–39). Jews from Elam are counted among the returnees from the Babylonian exile in Ezra 2:7, 31; 8:7. The chiefs of the Jewish tribes in Elam were among those who set their seals to the reform covenant upon their return (Neh. 10:14). Neh. 12:42 records the participation of a priest named Elam in the rededication of the walls of Jerusalem. The one mention of

Early Elamite writing on a tablet from Susa, ca. 2900 BCE.

Elamites in the NT (Acts 2:9) records their presence in Jerusalem at the feast of Pentecost.

Elsewhere in the Bible, the "people of Susa" are equated with the Elamites (Ezra 4:9), and Susa is called "the capital, in the province of Elam" in Dan. 8:2. Susa is better known as the capital of the Achaemenid empire, where King Ahasuerus ruled; it is mentioned throughout the book of Esther (e.g., 1:2) and provides the setting for the events of that book. The actual capital of Elam, however, was Anshan; Susa was the capital of a neighboring state, Susiana. The references to Susa being Elamite are usually thought to reflect a time when Elam had apparently conquered that area and so counted the capital city of Susiana as a city (though not the capital city) of Elam. *See also* Chedorlaomer.   L.E.P.

Elath (ee'lath). *See* Ezion-geber.

Eldad (el'dad; Heb., possibly "El [God] has loved"), an Israelite elder. With his companion Medad, Eldad was chosen with sixty-eight others to receive God's spirit around the tent of meeting. The two prophesied in the camp. When Joshua learned of their unauthorized activity, he urged Moses to restrain them, but Moses rebuffed the complaint, saying: "Would that all the Lord's people were prophets!" (Num. 11:16, 26–30). *See also* prophet; tabernacle.

elders, senior leaders of Israel, other nations or communities, or, in the NT, the church. Elders are referred to throughout the Hebrew Bible as performing tasks of local government and administering justice. Elders of Egypt are mentioned in Gen. 50:7 and, early in the book of Exodus, Moses is told to assemble "the elders of Israel" that they might accompany him when he goes before Pharaoh (3:16, 18). These "elders of Israel" are mentioned throughout the biblical narratives; aspects of their function and historical importance can be seen in Exod. 24:1–11; Num. 11:16–30; Josh. 7:6; 1 Sam. 8:4–9; and 1 Kings 8:1–3. The exact duties of such leaders is unknown. The phrase "the elders and the heads and the judges and the officers" (Josh. 24:1; cf. 23:2) suggests the position may have been distinct from other leadership roles, at least at certain times in Israel's history (cf. "the elders and the nobles," 1 Kings 21:11; "the elders and the guardians," 2 Kings 10:5; "elders and princes," Isa. 3:14; "elders and dignitaries," Isa. 9:15). Certain texts imply that they were expected to be people capable of exercising discernment and showing wisdom (Job 12:20; Ps. 105:22). A tradition that each tribe had its own elders is reflected in Deut. 31:28 (cf. "elders of Judah," 1 Sam. 30:26; 2 Sam. 19:11). There are also frequent references to the elders of a city or a town (e.g., Deut. 19:12; 21:3, 4, 6, 19–20; Josh. 20:4; cf. Ruth 4:2–11); these leaders could sometimes be called "elders at the gate," since they would sometimes gather in that public area (Deut. 25:7). The mention of elders for specific towns (Israelite and non-Israelite) suggests that some such form of leadership was widespread and not merely a product of Israel's particular religious tradition; see, for instance, elders of Succoth (Judg. 8:14), of Gilead (Judg. 11:5), of Jabesh (1 Sam. 11:3). An individual household may be said to have elders, if it is a large one, such as the royal household of David (2 Sam. 12:17). Lev. 4:15 refers to "elders of the congregation" who play a role in certain sacrificial rites (cf. Judg. 21:16–24). Finally, references to "the elders of the Jews" occur in Ezra 6:7, 8, 14.

The NT also mentions Jewish elders (Luke 7:3), frequently in conjunction with priests and/ or scribes (Matt. 16:21; 26:47, 57; 27:1, 12, 20, 41; 28:12; Acts 4:5, 23; 6:12; 23:14; 25:15); they are sometimes called "the elders of the people" (Matt. 21:23; 26:3, 47; 27:1) and, once, "the elders of Israel" (Acts 5:21). The book of Acts also refers to "a whole council of elders" (22:5), which is said to have issued letters authorizing Saul to arrest Christians in Damascus. The Gospels refer to a "tradition of the elders," an apparently oral body of legal interpretation with which Jesus takes issue (Matt. 15:2; cf. Mark 7:3–5). The book of Acts reveals that elders were also appointed in early Christian churches (11:30; 14:23; 15:2–6, 22–23; 16:4; 20:17; 21:18). The Pastoral Letters refer to a "council of elders" exercising spiritual authority within a congregation (1 Tim. 4:14). Further, the position of "elder" appears in these letters to be an office within the church, though it could also be an umbrella term for various leadership positions, such as "bishops" and "deacons" (Tim. 5:17, 19; Titus 1:5; cf. James 5:14; 1 Pet. 5:1, 5). Two of the Johannine Letters are written by a person who calls himself "the elder" (2 John 1:1; 3 John 1:1). In the book of Revelation, John the Seer beholds a vision of twenty-four elders gathered around the throne of God (e.g., 4:4, 10; 5:8, 14; 11:16; 19:4).   M.A.P.

Elealeh (el'ee-ay'luh), a Moabite city east of the Jordan River that, along with Heshbon and surrounding cities, was given to the tribes of Reuben and Gad after they requested that Moses allow them to settle there (Num. 32:1–5). The city was rebuilt by the Reubenites (Num. 32:33–38), although by the time of Isaiah and Jeremiah it was back in Moabite hands (ca. 700–625 BCE; Isa. 15:4; Jer. 48:34). The city is identified as modern el-Al, a ruin about two miles northeast of Tell Heshban and about fifteen miles east and slightly north of the north end of the Dead Sea.   D.R.B.

Eleasah (el'ee-ay'suh; Heb., "El [God] has made" or "El has acted").

1 A Judahite, the son of Helez from the line of Jerahmeel (1 Chron. 2:39–40).

2 A Benjaminite descendant of Saul's son Jonathan (1 Chron. 8:37).

Eleazar (el'ee-ay'zuhr; Heb., "El [God] has helped"), the third son of Aaron. He became a priest (Exod. 29; Lev. 8) and, later, high priest when Aaron died (Num. 20:25–28). He served as high priest during the remaining years of Moses's leadership and through Joshua's tenure as leader. An Eleazar is also mentioned in the list of Joseph's ancestors in Matt. 1:15.

election, a theological term in the Bible used to convey divine selection or predetermined choice. Election is essentially a NT concept (the term does not appear in the Hebrew Bible), but it is based in part on a Christian reading of the OT (see esp. Rom. 9:10–12). In the Bible, God selects a people (Israel), its king (David), and the city of Jerusalem. These choices reflect divine sovereignty and are not based on the previous accomplishments or natural superiority of those who are chosen. Still, the chosen are under obligation to live by God's will and to be God's servants (e.g., Deut. 7:6–11; 1 Chron. 16:9–13; Jer. 33:19–26; Amos 3:2). The NT authors sought to recognize all of this, while also shifting their focus to Jesus Christ as the elect one through whom God's purposes are ultimately accomplished (e.g., Matt. 12:18; Luke 9:35; 23:35; 1 Pet. 2:4, 6). Through faith and discipleship, Christ's followers are now called "the elect" (e.g., Matt. 22:14; Mark 13:20–27; Titus 1:1; 1 Pet. 1:2; 2:9–10; 2 John 1:1, 13). Although this elect group is now composed of people from all nations, Paul still expects God's election of Israel to be fulfilled (Rom. 11:2, 28). *See also* covenant; grace; predestination; providence.   J.E.A.

Elephantine (el'uh-fan-ti'nee). *See* Egypt; Passover; Syene; temple, the.

Eleusis (i-loo'sis). *See* mystery.

eleven, the, the disciples or apostles of Jesus (originally twelve) during a brief period after the death of Judas Iscariot and before the choice of Matthias (Acts 1:23–26). The eleven are mentioned in Matt. 28:16; Luke 24:9, 33 (and in some manuscripts, Mark 16:14; Acts 1:26; 2:14; 1 Cor. 15:5). *See also* apostle; disciple; Judas; Matthias; twelve, the.

Elhanan (el-hay'nuhn; Heb., "El [God] is gracious").

1 The son of Dodo from Bethlehem; one of the group of David's elite warriors known as "the Thirty" (2 Sam. 23:24).

2 The son of Jair (or Jaareoregim) of Bethlehem, who killed a Philistine warrior at Gob. There is confusion in the biblical record with regard to the name of Elhanan's opponent: 2 Sam. 21:19 says that he killed Goliath (who is elsewhere said to have been slain by David, cf. 1 Sam. 17); 1 Chron. 20:5 says he killed Lahmi, the brother of Goliath.

Eli (ee'li; Heb., "El [God] is exalted"), a judge of Israel (1 Sam. 4:18) and priest in Shiloh, where the ark was located during the period of the judges. On observing Hannah praying silently for children, he first thought she was drunk, but then assured her that her prayer would be fulfilled (1:12–17).

Samuel, the offspring of this promise, was later brought to Shiloh, where he was devoted to divine service (e.g., 3:1–17) and subsequently succeeded Eli, whose sons Hophni and Phinehas were wicked (2:11–12). When Eli learned of their deaths at the battle of Aphek and the loss of the ark, he fell, broke his neck, and died (4:11–18).   F.E.G.

Eli, Eli, lema sabachthani (ee'li, ee'li, lih-mah' suh-bahk'thuh-nee; also "Eloi, Eloi, lema sabachthani"), the Aramaic words attributed to Jesus on the cross (Matt. 27:46; Mark 15:34). The words represent an Aramaic rendering of the first verse of Ps. 22, "My God, my God, why have you forsaken me?" "Eloi" (Mark 15:34) transliterates the most common Aramaic form for "my God"; "Eli" (Matt. 27:46) has sometimes been understood as the transliteration of a Hebrew word, but it has also been found in Aramaic manuscripts among the Dead Sea Scrolls as an alternative form of "my God." According to both Gospels, bystanders who heard Jesus's cry misunderstood it as a call for Elijah (Matt. 27:47–49; Mark 15:35–36). In the Gospel narratives, the citation of Ps. 22:1 communicates Jesus's sense of human separation from God in the face of sin and death; it functions as part of a sharp contrast between his apparent powerlessness and the ultimate victory portrayed in his resurrection. Ps. 22 is actually quoted and alluded to several times in the passion accounts of Mark and Matthew (e.g., Matt. 27:35, 43); it seems to have been a favorite text among the early Christians for interpreting the meaning and manner of Jesus's death. *See also* cross; passion.   A.J.S.

Eliab (i-li'uhb; Heb., "El [God] is father").
1 Reubenite father of Dathan and Abiram who rebelled against Moses (Num. 16:1).
2 Son of Helon, leader of Zebulun in the generation prior to the Israelite settlement in Canaan (Num. 10:16).
3 A Levite in the line of Kohath (1 Chron. 6:27).
4 David's oldest brother (1 Sam. 17:28), whose stature and appearance impressed Samuel when he sought a king from among Jesse's sons (1 Sam. 6:6–7).
5 A Gaddite who served David in the desert (1 Chron. 12:9).
6 A levitical musician in the time of David (1 Chron. 15:18, 20; 16:5).

Eliada (i-li'uh-duh; Heb., "El [God] knows").
1 One of David's sons born in Jerusalem (2 Sam. 5:16), also called Beeliada (Heb., "Baal knows," 1 Chron. 14:7). Although Baal could simply mean "lord," names that contained "baal" were sometimes changed by biblical editors to avoid any association with the Canaanite fertility god of that name.
2 The father of Rezon, the ruler of Syria and enemy of David (1 Kings 11:23).
3 A Benjaminite commander of two hundred thousand bowmen under King Jehoshaphat (2 Chron. 17:17).

Eliakim (i-li'uh-kim; Heb., "El [God] raises up").
1 The son of Hilkiah and royal steward under King Hezekiah. Eliakim had replaced Shebnah (Shebna) in that office in accordance with the prophecy of Isaiah, but he later fell into disfavor with the prophet or his disciples (Isa. 22:20–25). Together with Shebna, now royal secretary, and Joah, royal herald, Eliakim played an important role in the negotiations with the Assyrian Rabshakeh during Sennacherib's siege of Jerusalem (2 Kings 18:18–19:7). *See also* Shebnah.
2 The king of Judah ca. 608–598 BCE; also known as Jehoiakim. When Pharaoh Neco killed Eliakim's father, King Josiah, the Judean people chose a younger son, Jehoahaz, as the new king, but three months later Pharaoh replaced Jehoahaz with Eliakim, whom he renamed Jehoiakim (2 Kings 23:29–34). *See also* Jehoiakim.
3 A priest who took part in the dedication of the wall of Jerusalem rebuilt by Nehemiah (Neh. 12:41).
4 The son of Abiud, listed in Matthew's genealogy of Jesus (1:13).
5 The son of Melea, listed in Luke's genealogy of Jesus (3:30).   J.J.M.R.

Eliam (i-li'uhm; Heb., "El [God] is people").
1 One of David's elite warriors, the son of the Gilonite Ahithophel (2 Sam. 23:34).
2 The father of Bathsheba (2 Sam. 11:3), called Ammiel in 1 Chron. 3:5 (both names include the same components, but in reversed order). *See also* Ammiel.

Eliasaph (i-li'uh-saf; Heb., "El [God] has added").
1 The head of the tribe of Gad during the wilderness wandering (Num. 1:14; 2:14).
2 A Levite, the head of the Gershonite group, which was in charge of carrying the fabrics of the tabernacle (Num. 3:24).

Eliashib (i-li'uh-shib; Heb., "El [God] restores").
1 The head of a priestly division in the time of David (1 Chron. 24:12).
2 The name of three postexilic Israelites, including one levitical singer, who divorced their foreign wives in response to Ezra's proclamation (Ezra 10:24, 27, 36).
3 The father of Jehohanan in whose chamber Ezra spent a night (Ezra 10:6); possibly one of the three persons included in **2**.
4 The Jerusalemite high priest in the time of Nehemiah who assisted in rebuilding a northwest section of the city wall (Neh. 3:1) and whose grandson married the daughter of Sanballat (Neh. 13:28; this may be the same as **2** and/or **3**).
5 A priest responsible for the temple chambers, who permitted an Ammonite to dwell there until he was expelled by Nehemiah (Neh. 13:4–8).
6 A late postexilic descendant of David through the line of Zerubbabel (1 Chron. 3:24).   F.E.G.

Eliel (i-li′uhl; Heb., "El [God] is my god").

1 A Korahite ancestor of Samuel (1 Chron. 6:34, called Elihu in 1 Sam. 1:1 and perhaps Eliab in 1 Chron. 6:27).

2 A Levite from the family of Hebron whom David assigned to assist in bringing the ark to Jerusalem (1 Chron. 15:4–15).

3 A Gaddite who joined David in the desert (1 Chron. 12:11).

4 The name of two of David's elite warriors, one of them a Mahavite (1 Chron. 11:46–47).

5 A temple official who assisted in the supervision of offerings during the reign of Hezekiah (2 Chron. 31:13).

6 The name of two Benjaminites, one the son of Shimei (1 Chron. 8:20), the other of Shashak (1 Chron. 8:22).

7 The head of a Transjordanian Manassite household deported by the Assyrian king Tiglath-pileser III (1 Chron. 5:24).   F.E.G.

Eliezer (el′ee-ee′zuhr; Heb., "El [God] is help").

1 Abraham's servant, who would have been his heir in place of a son (Gen. 15:2). Presumably, it is Eliezer who finds a wife for Isaac in Gen. 24.

2 Moses's second son, the founder of a levitical family (Exod. 18:4; 1 Chron. 23:15–17; 26:25).

3 The son of Do-davahu, and a prophet who spoke against King Jehoshaphat's naval alliance with Ahaziah (2 Chron. 20:35–37).

4 A son of Becher and a Benjaminite "mighty warrior" (1 Chron. 7:8).

5 A priest appointed to blow a trumpet in the procession that brought the ark to Jerusalem (1 Chron. 15:24).

6 The son of Zichri, and a Reubenite chief (1 Chron. 27:16).

7 A leading man sent by Ezra to seek Levites for temple service (Ezra 8:16).

8 The name of three postexilic Israelites who divorced their foreign wives in response to Ezra's proclamation (Ezra 10:18; 10:23; 10:31).

9 The son of Jorim, an ancestor of Jesus (Luke 3:29).   M.A.S.

Elihu (i-li′hyoo).

1 The great-grandfather of Samuel (1 Sam. 1:1). Identified as the son of Tohu and as an Ephraimite, he is called Eliel at 1 Chron. 6:34 and Eliab at 1 Chron. 6:27.

2 A military leader from Manasseh who defected to David when he was in battle against Saul at Ziklag (1 Chron. 12:20).

3 A brother of David, identified as chief officer of the tribe of Issachar (1 Chron. 27:18).

4 A young man who speaks to Job just prior to God's speeches from the whirlwind (Job 32–37). Claiming divine inspiration, Elihu merely repeats in other words the views of Job's three friends. Elihu was angry because he believed Job was justifying himself rather than God (32:2), but he waited to speak last because of his youth (32:4–6). Elihu claims that suffering plays a disciplinary role, purging the heart. Some scholars take Elihu's

speeches as interpolations, since they break the symmetry of the book and since Elihu is mentioned nowhere else. *See also* Job, book of.

Elijah (i-li′juh, Heb., "my God is the LORD"), an Israelite prophet in the time of kings Ahab and Ahaziah, during the first half of the ninth century BCE. Elijah is the protagonist of four stories in the book of Kings. The stories (often called "the Elijah cycle") are thought to have circulated separately for some time prior to being incorporated into the books of 1 and 2 Kings, which scholars regard as a part of the Deuteronomic History. Although theories of composition vary, the stories are generally thought to have been written in the southern kingdom, perhaps under Manasseh, some two hundred years after the time of the events they report. Thus, they would have circulated orally for an extended period of time, making questions of historicity difficult to address. Still, the introduction of the Tyrian Baal cult into Israel during the Omride dynasty (ca. 876–843/2 BCE) is a historical fact; it was brought about by the marriage of Ahab, son of Omri, to the Tyrian princess Jezebel. From its center in Samaria, Baal worship spread out to the provincial towns. As for Elijah himself, he is said to have come from the town of Tosabe in Gilead. His leather attire and his nomadic habits make it plausible that he belonged to a family of shepherds in Transjordan.

Drought, Zarephath, Mounts Carmel and Horeb: In the first story dealing with Elijah (1 Kings 16:29–19:18), King Ahab erects a temple to Baal in Samaria and his Canaanite wife, Jezebel, brings in 450 Baal prophets. Jezebel then begins persecuting and killing prophets of the Lord. Elijah declares a drought to punish the nation for its idolatry. In so doing, he effectively challenges Baal in his very quality as a fertility god. He goes into hiding and is miraculously fed by God, who sends ravens to bring him food. He also goes, at God's direction, to Zarephath and visits a widow; there a jar of meal and a jug of oil remain miraculously full, and the widow's son is raised by Elijah from death. The drought finally ends after a contest between Elijah and the Baal prophets on Mount Carmel; the god who would answer his prophet's call with fire from heaven would be vindicated as the true god. Elijah wins, God is vindicated, and Elijah's Baalite antagonists are slaughtered by Elijah himself with the help of the people who have been convinced that "the LORD indeed is God." Pursued by Queen Jezebel, who seeks vengeance, Elijah flees to Beer-sheba, where he sits under a broom tree and despairs of life. An angel miraculously provides him with food and drink and he is able to travel forty days and nights to Mount Horeb (Sinai), where he experiences a theophany involving wind, earthquake, fire, and silence, followed by the voice of the Lord. He is commanded to anoint Hazael, Jehu, and Elisha as three new protagonists in the fight against Baal. Late composition of this story might be indicated by such features as its adoption of a story from the separate Elisha cycle (17:8–16, cf. 2 Kings 4:1–7),

Elijah (center) receives a dead child from his mourning mother (in black), revives the child, and returns him to his mother (*right*), who is now clad in the bright clothing of happiness (1 Kings 17:17–24); panel from the third-century CE synagogue at Dura-Europos.

its adaptation of the royal annals of Samaria to the present plot (1 Kings 16:29–17:1, to which the end, 19:16–18, corresponds), its incorporation of Isaiah's concept of "the remnant" (19:18), and the probably anachronistic detail about persecution of prophets (18:4, 13, 22; 19:10, 14).

Murder of Naboth: The second story involving Elijah (1 Kings 21) tells about the murder of Naboth. Ahab wants to purchase a vineyard from Naboth the Jezreelite, but Naboth refuses to sell. Noting her husband's depression, Jezebel takes care of the matter by forging letters in Ahab's name and setting Naboth up to be stoned to death on entirely false charges of having "cursed God and the king." Ahab then goes to inherit the vineyard and is confronted by Elijah with a terrible prophecy of doom. It has been suggested that the present form of this story was composed in the postexilic age, on the basis of its late diction and acquaintance with all the legal corpora found in the Torah (cf. Exod. 22:27; Lev. 24:13–16; Num. 36:7–9; Deut. 19:15). An older, more original version of the story may be hinted at in 2 Kings 9:25–26, 36–37.

Ahaziah's Inquiry: In the third story (2 Kings 1:2–2:17) Ahaziah falls ill and inquires of Baal-zebub of Ekron if he will recover. Elijah intervenes and sends the messengers back to the king with a prophecy of doom that he himself reiterates when summoned to the king's presence. The derivative character of this prophetic legend, in which fire twice comes down from heaven in order to save Elijah, although he is in no danger, indicates late composition. This is confirmed by its late diction.

Elijah and Elisha: The fourth story dealing with Elijah (1 Kings 19:19–21; 2 Kings 2:1–18) relates how Elisha becomes Elijah's servant, following him until the day comes when he knows that

God will take him away. Then Elijah is carried up into heaven in a whirlwind, accompanied by a chariot and horses of fire. Elisha inherits a "double share" of Elijah's spirit and takes his mantle upon himself. This story serves primarily to introduce the Elisha cycle and seems aimed at establishing continuity between two great prophets of the past. In many ways, however, the two are quite distinct. Elijah is remembered as a zealot of the Lord fighting against idolatry and injustice, and Elisha is recalled primarily as a wonder worker who saved Israel during the Aramean crisis.

The Legacy of Elijah: Elijah's role as fighter against Baal and injustice is taken up in 2 Chron. 21:12–15. Elijah is also mentioned at the conclusion of the Nevi'im (Prophets) section of the Hebrew canon in Mal. 3:22–24, which identifies him with the Lord's messenger of Mal. 3:1 who would return before the forthcoming "day of the LORD." As such, he is described as both a priest and a teacher of Torah (Mal. 2:7); he is expected to purify the priesthood (3:2–3) and, as supreme teacher, to "reconcile fathers and sons." Likewise, Sir. 48:10 expects him to come from the heavenly chambers and restore the tribes of Jacob. In the NT, Elijah is identified in the popular mind with Jesus (Mark 6:15; 8:28), but Jesus himself identifies John the Baptist as Elijah, who was to return and restore all things (Matt. 17:10–13; cf. Luke 1:17; but see John 1:21, 25). Jesus refers to Elijah and the widow of Zarephath in a sermon at Nazareth, noting God's beneficence to a non-Israelite (Luke 4:25–26). Elijah also appears in glory with Jesus and Moses on the mountain of transfiguration (Mark 9:4–5). When Jesus cries in Aramaic, "Eli, Eli, lema sabachthani" ("My God, my God, why have you forsaken me?"), bystanders think that he is calling for Elijah to rescue him (Matt. 27:47–49). Paul makes reference to Elijah pleading against Israel in Rom. 11:12, and James 5:16–17 cites Elijah as an example of a righteous man who prayed fervently. Probably because of his passage directly into heaven without experiencing death, Elijah also became a popular figure in apocalyptic literature. Two distinct books called the *Apocalypse of Elijah* are known: a Jewish-Christian writing from about 150–275 CE and a much later Jewish writing from the mid-sixth to early seventh centuries CE. *See also* Ahab; Ahaziah; Elisha; Jezebel; Naboth; prophet.   A.R.

Elim (ee′lim), the second stopping place (after Marah) of the Israelites after they crossed the Red Sea (Exod. 15:27; Num. 33:9). This oasis was reported to have twelve springs and seventy palm trees. Because Exod. 15:22–27 and Num. 33:8–9 suggest that the Israelites camped there soon after leaving Egypt but prior to reaching the Wilderness of Sin (Exod. 16:1; Num. 33:10–11), Elim is frequently identified with the Wadi Gharandel, about sixty-three miles southeast of Suez in the western Sinai, which today has fresh water, palm trees, and tamarisks. *See also* exodus, the.   J.M.W.

Elimelech (i-lim′uh-lek, Heb., "El [God] is sovereign," "the divine king," or "my God is Milku"), a member of the Ephrathite family group who immigrated to Moab when a great famine broke out in Bethlehem of Judah during the period of the judges (Ruth 1:2–3; 2:1, 3; 4:3, 9). After his death, his two sons married local women. The ensuing story is narrated in the book named after Ruth, one of Elimelech's daughters-in-law. The story tells how, despite the death of all male members of his family, Elimelech's estate in Bethlehem remained in the family's hands through the maneuvering of Ruth and her mother-in-law, Naomi, Elimelech's widow.   J.M.S.

Elioenai (el′ee-oh-ee′ni; a shortened form of Eliehoenai, Heb., "my eyes are toward El [God]").

1 A descendant of the kings of Judah through David (1 Chron. 3:23–24).

2 A family leader in the tribe of Simeon (1 Chron. 4:36).

3 A Benjaminite belonging to the family group of Becher (1 Chron. 7:8).

4 A Levite belonging to the Pashur group. Upon returning from the Babylonian exile, he divorced his foreign wife in response to Ezra's proclamation (Ezra 10:22). He may be the same priest who served in postexilic Jerusalem (Neh. 12:41).

5 A member of the Zattu group who divorced his foreign wife in response to Ezra's proclamation (Ezra 10:27).

Eliphaz (el′i-faz, Heb., possibly "El [God] is fine gold").

1 The eldest son of Esau and ancestor of several Edomite family groups, including Teman (Gen. 36:15–16).

2 The first and presumably oldest of Job's three friends (Job 2:11; 4:1; 15:1; 22:1; 42:7, 9). Eliphaz's designation, the Temanite, suggests he was from the area settled by the Edomite group mentioned in 1. Assuming Job's basic piety, he urged submission. He maintains that no mortal can be righteous (4:17) and that God not only disciplines, but also heals (5:17–18). In a second speech, he accuses Job of making false claims (15:3–4), and he describes the fate of the wicked (15:20–35). Finally, in a third speech, he presents Job with a list of supposed iniquities (22:5–9). *See also* Job, book of.

Eliphelet (i-lif′uh-let; Heb., possibly "El [God] is deliverance" or "the divine deliverer").

1 David's last son, born in Jerusalem to a nameless wife or concubine (2 Sam. 5:16). His name appears twice in the list of David's sons in 1 Chron. 3:6, 8 (cf. 1 Chron. 14:5, 7).

2 The son of Ahasbai; one of David's elite warriors (2 Sam. 23:34). The author of Chronicles may call him Eliphal, son of Ur (1 Chron. 11:35).

3 A descendant of Saul and Jonathan, the third son of Eshek (1 Chron. 8:39).

4 The son of Adonikam, a leader who returned from the Babylonian exile (Ezra 8:13; 1 Esd. 8:39).

5 The son of Hashum; he divorced his foreign wife in response to Ezra's postexilic proclamation (Ezra 10:33; 1 Esd. 9:33).   J.M.S.

Elisha (i-li′shuh; Heb., "El [God] is salvation"), a prophet of the northern kingdom, Israel, who is presented as being active during the reigns of Joram, Jehu, Jehoahaz, and Jehoash (Joash), a period that would encompass some fifty years (ca. 850–800 BCE). Scholars generally believe that stories concerning him circulated independently for some time before being edited into the Deuteronomistic History (Joshua–2 Kings). Stories relating Elisha as the disciple and successor of Elijah (1 Kings 19:19–21; 2 Kings 2:1–18) were probably not part of the original Elisha material, but were added to the history to create a sense of continuity between two prophets who would otherwise not seem that similar. Whereas Elijah is primarily presented as a zealot of the Lord fighting against idolatry and injustice, Elisha is remembered mainly as a miracle worker who saved Israel during the Aramean crisis (2 Kings 2:19–8:15; 13:14–25). Inserted into this material is a Deuteronomistic account that uses Elisha to legitimate Jehu's purge of the Omride dynasty (2 Kings 9–10).

Elisha is introduced as a farmer who lived with his parents at Abel-meholah (location uncertain; 1 Kings 19:16–21). Since he was plowing with twelve pairs of oxen when Elijah met him, scholars have suggested that his father be envisioned as a wealthy landowner. Elisha offers to follow Elijah after kissing his parents, a proposal that earns him a rebuke for insufficient commitment (1 Kings 16:20–21; cf. Matt. 8:21–22). He then slaughters his oxen, boils them over a fire made with the plowing equipment, gives the food to the people, and becomes Elijah's servant. Elisha is

Elisha, in the dark robe, with Naaman, captain of the king of Aram's army (2 Kings 5); from the Amiens Picture Bible, Spain, 1197.

subsequently present when Elijah is taken up into heaven in a whirlwind; he assumes Elijah's mantle and is gifted with a "double share" of the prophet's spirit (2 Kings 2:1–14). Numerous miracles are subsequently reported. He makes a spring of bad water wholesome (2 Kings 2:19–22); he curses children who call him "Baldhead!" and forty-two of them are immediately mauled by a bear; he multiplies the oil of a disciple's widow (2 Kings 4:1–7); he raises a Shunamite woman's son from the dead (2 Kings 4:8–37); he purifies a pot of stew that had poisonous wild gourds in it (2 Kings 4:38–41); he feeds a hundred people with twenty rolls of bread (2 Kings 4:42–44); he heals Naaman the Aramean commander of leprosy (2 Kings 5:1–19) and causes his own greedy servant Gehazi to become a leper (2 Kings 5:19–27); and he makes an ax head float (2 Kings 6:1–7).

Interspersed with these miracle stories are accounts of Elisha's role in the political sphere. King Mesha of Moab rebels against Jehoram of Israel, and Elisha, out of respect for Jehoshaphat of Judah who had joined Jehoram, makes water appear in the desert for the benefit of Israel's troops (2 Kings 3:4–20). Later, when the king of Aram tries to capture Elisha, the eyes of his troops are opened to see a heavenly army guarding the city of Dothan, where the prophet was staying; then the troops are blinded and led by Elisha inside the walls of Samaria, where they might easily have been slain (2 Kings 6:8–23). Some time later, Ben-hadad of Aram lays siege to Samaria, but his army is routed when God causes them to hear the sound of a great

army in the middle of the night (2 Kings 6:24–7:20). As indicated above, Elisha is also involved in the story of Jehu, calling for him to be anointed king over Israel and sent to slay Ahab, Jezebel, and all of the Omride dynasty (2 Kings 9:1–3, 6–7). Finally, in a story of Elisha's death, one more miracle is reported. Some time after his burial, another corpse was inadvertently thrown into his grave; as soon as the body touched the bones of Elisha, the man came to life (2 Kings 13:20–21).

Unlike Elijah, who lived in caves in the desert, Elisha stayed in the cities (2 Kings 6:13, 19, 32). He was provided comfortable guest quarters by a wealthy woman of Shunem (2 Kings 4:8–10) and apparently maintained his own house at Samaria (2 Kings 6:32; cf. 2:25; 5:3). He often appears in connection with groups of prophets ("the company of the prophets," 2 Kings 2:3–15; 4:1; 5:22; 9:1), and he frequented religious centers such as Bethel (2 Kings 2:23), Gilgal (2:1; 4:38), and Mount Carmel (2:25; 4:25). He sometimes employed his staff in the working of miracles (2 Kings 4:29; cf. Exod. 4:2–5) and he used music to induce a prophetic trance (2 Kings 3:15; cf. 1 Sam. 10:5–7). Many of his miracles demonstrate the power of God over aspects of nature, while others illustrate benevolence for those who suffer material distress. Like Elijah, furthermore, much of his political involvement was directed at bringing the apostate monarchy back to a recognition of God's sovereignty in the world. In the NT, Jesus refers to Elisha's healing of Naaman as an example of God's benevolence to non-Israelites (Luke 4:27). Sirach summarizes the career of Elisha as follows: "He performed twice as many signs [as Elijah], and marvels with every utterance of his mouth. Never in his lifetime did he tremble before any ruler, nor could anyone intimidate him at all" (48:12). *See also* Abel-meholah; Baal; Elijah; Kings, First and Second Books of.   D.R.B./M.A.P.

Elishah (i-li′shuh).

1 The son of Javan (Greece) in Gen. 10:4 and 1 Chron. 1:7.

2 An island producing valuable dyed goods in Ezek. 27:7. This suggests that Elishah is Cyprus, which was known as Alashia in cuneiform (i.e., Babylonian and Assyrian) sources.

Elishama (i-lish′uh-muh; Heb., "El [God] has heard").

1 The son of Ammihud; the leader of the tribe of Ephraim during the wilderness wandering (Num. 1:10; 10:22).

2 A son of David born in Jerusalem (2 Sam. 5:16). Another list of David's sons indicates that he had a second son who was also named Elishama (1 Chron. 3:5–8), but comparison with a third list (1 Chron. 14:4–7) reveals that the repeated name in 1 Chron. 3:6 is probably a scribal error for Elishua, otherwise omitted.

3 A descendant of David and the grandfather of Ishmael, the leader of a group who assassinated Gedeliah (2 Kings 25:25; Jer. 41:1–3).

4 A Judahite, the son of Jekemiah, in the line of Jerahmeel (1 Chron. 2:41).

5 A priest during the reign of Jehoshaphat who taught the people about the law (2 Chron. 17:8).

6 The royal scribe of King Jehoiakim of Judah (Jer. 36:12).   D.R.B.

Elizabeth (i-liz′uh-beth), according to Luke 1:5–80, the wife of Zechariah and mother of John the Baptist. Luke describes her as coming from a priestly family. Her long period of infertility connects her with earlier women in Israel such as Sarah (Gen. 17:15–21; 18:9–15; 21:1–7) and Hannah (1 Sam. 1:1–20), who gave birth to children who would be important for new eras in Israel's history. After Elizabeth's five-month period of seclusion, the news that she would have a child was given to her relative Mary by the angel Gabriel, who also announced Mary's impending pregnancy with the one who would be called Son of God. Mary then visited Elizabeth, who was filled with the Holy Spirit and who proclaimed Mary "blessed among women" (1:41). She further identified Mary as "the mother of my Lord" (1:43). Later, when Elizabeth gave birth, she was the one to insist that the child be named John, in obedience to what an angel had revealed to her husband Zechariah (1:60; cf. 1:13). *See also* Hannah; John the Baptist; Mary, Virgin; Sarah; Zechariah.

A.J.M.

Elizaphan (el′uh-zay′fan; Heb., "El [God] protects").

1 A Levite, the son of Uzziel; a leader of the Kohathites, who were in charge of the utensils of the tabernacle (Num. 3:30); he is probably the same person referred to elsewhere as Elzaphan (Exod. 6:22; Lev. 10:4).

2 The ancestor of a levitical family group headed by Shemaiah who helped bring the ark of the covenant to Jerusalem during the reign of King David (1 Chron. 15:8). The same family group later took part in the cleansing of the temple during the reforms of Hezekiah (2 Chron. 29:13).

3 The son of Parnach; a leader of the tribe of Zebulun who supervised the apportionment of land within the tribe (Num. 34:25).   D.R.B.

Elizur (i-li′zuhr; Heb., "El [God] is rock"), the leader of the tribe of Reuben during the wilderness wanderings (Num. 1:5; 10:18).

Elkanah (el-kay′nuh; Heb., "El [God] created the child").

1 A Levite identified as the son of Assir and grandson of Korah in 1 Chron. 6:23, and as the brother of Assir and son of Korah in Exod. 6:24. He was, at any rate, one of the leaders of the Korahites.

2 The father of Samuel (1 Sam. 1–2). A resident of Ramath-zophim in Ephraim, he favored his infertile wife Hannah over his other wife, Peninnah. He is, notably, the only nonroyal person mentioned in the books of Samuel and Kings as having more than one wife. He took his family on annual pilgrimages to Shiloh and gave Hannah double portions of meat because he loved her (1 Sam. 1:5). God eventually pitied Hannah and allowed her to bear a son; the boy, Samuel, was given to serve the Lord under the priest Eli at Shiloh, and Elkanah would accompany Hannah on annual trips to visit him there. Elkanah and Hannah later had two more sons and three daughters.

3 A royal official in Ahaz's court who was second in authority to the king (2 Chron. 28:7). He is listed among three palace officials killed by Zichri, "a mighty warrior of Ephraim," because they had abandoned God.

Elkosh (el′kosh; Heb., possibly "God gives"), the presumed birthplace of the prophet Nahum (Nah. 1:1). No certain location is known.

Ellasar (el′uh-sahr), the home country or city of King Arioch, who joined a confederation of four kings who attacked the Dead Sea area, captured Lot, and were then pursued and defeated by Abraham (Gen. 14:1–16). The identification of Ellasar is uncertain, but one suggestion is Larsa, a city in southern Babylonia that flourished ca. 2025–1763 BCE. This identification would seem likely if Shinar, the home of Arioch's neighboring king Amraphel (Gen. 14:1, 9), ultimately derives from the nearby Sinjar Mountains of middle Mesopotamia.   J.G.G.

Elnathan (el-nay′thuhn; Heb., "God has given").

1 The son of Achbor who was sent by King Jehoiakim of Judah to capture the prophet Uriah in Egypt (Jer. 26:22). He later protested the king's burning of Jeremiah's scroll (Jer. 36:25).

2 The father of Nehushta, who married King Jehoiakim of Judah and became the mother of King Jehoiachin of Judah (2 Kings 24:8). He could be the same person as **1**.

Elohim (el′oh-him). *See* El; names of God in the Hebrew Bible.

Elohist (el′oh-hist), the name given by modern biblical scholars to the author(s) of material that served as one of the sources for what is now found in the books of Genesis–Numbers. The abbreviation used as a siglum for this source or body of tradition is "E." The designation Elohist (or E) derives from the material's use of the name Elohim for God. Most scholars believe that the Elohistic material was combined with another major tradition called the Yahwistic material (or "J"), which prefers to use the Tetragrammaton, YHWH, as the name for God. Other distinctive features are noted as well. The Elohist prefers to use "Jacob" rather than "Israel," "Jethro" rather than "Reuel," and "Horeb" rather than "Sinai." In the current form of the Pentateuch, Yahwistic material is usually thought to dominate and Elohisitic material to serve primarily as expansions or revisions of Yahwistic passages. The Elohist's work is usually dated sometime in the tenth–eighth century BCE and located within prophetic circles in the north. This fits with the material's emphatic concern with idolatry, worship, and charismatic leadership. Elohistic material begins with the call of Abraham (Gen. 12) and therefore does not have a primeval history. Among passages most prominently mentioned as Elohistic are Gen. 22:1–19 (the binding of Isaac); Gen. 28:10–22 (Jacob's dream at Bethel); Gen. 40:1–23 (the dreams of Joseph's fellow prisoners); Exod. 18:1–27 (Moses's meeting with Jethro); and Exod. 20:1–26 (the giving of the Ten Commandments). *See also* El; Pentateuch, sources of the; Yahweh; Yahwist.   K.H.R.

Eloi, Eloi, lema sabachthani (ee′loh-*i*, ee′ loh-*i*, lah′muh suh-bahk′thuh-nee). *See* Eli, Eli, lema sabachthani.

Elon (ee′lon; Heb., "oak," "terebinth").

1 A Hittite, father of Basemath, a wife of Esau (Gen. 26:34).

2 The father of Adah, a wife of Esau (Gen. 32:6).

3 A "minor judge" for ten years, of the tribe of Zebulun, buried at Aijalon (Judg. 12:11, 12).

4 A town of the tribe of Dan (Josh. 19:43).

5 A son of Zebulun in the lists of Gen. 46:14 and Num. 26:26.

Eloth (ee′loth; Heb., "a grove of large trees," usually terebinth or palm), another name for Elath, an important port city located at the end of the northeast arm of the Red Sea, the modern Gulf of Aqabah. The Israelites passed by Eloth as they left Egypt (Deut. 2:8). Eloth was later expanded by Solomon into a trading port (1 Kings 9:26–28). It was apparently destroyed by Edom (2 Kings 8:20–21), later rebuilt by Uzziah (2 Chron. 26:2), and again lost permanently to Edom (or perhaps Syria) during the reign of Ahaz (2 Kings 16:6). Eloth/ Elath may be a later name for Ezion-geber, or they may be two distinct sites (2 Chron. 8:17). *See also* Ezion-geber.   D.R.B.

El Shaddai (el shad′*i*), a name for God used in stories of Israel's ancestors (Abraham, Sarah, Isaac, Rebekah, Jacob, Leah, Zilpah, Rachel, and Bilhah). It is regularly translated "God Almighty" in the NRSV. Apart from passages dealing with those ancestors (Gen. 17:1; 28:3; 35:11; 43:14; 48:3) it occurs only in Exod. 6:3 and Ezek. 10:5. The first of the latter passages is especially revealing: God reveals the divine name to Moses, a name represented by the Tetragrammaton, YHWH (written "the LORD" in the NRSV, RSV, and KJV), but then God adds, "I appeared to Abraham, Isaac, and Jacob as "El Shaddai" (NRSV: "God Almighty"). El Shaddai is like other Hebrew names of God in Genesis beginning with the element *el*, "God," plus a substantive or adjective, e.g., El Olam ("the Everlasting God"), El Elyon ("God Most High"), El Elohe Yisrael ("El the God of Israel"). The etymology of *shaddai* is not certain; "God, the One of the mountain" is plausible, the mountain being the divine residence. Other suggestions have included, "God who deals might-

ily (or violently) with" and "God of the beasts." The translation "God Almighty" derives from the Vulgate's rendering of what was, by then, an obscure term.   R.J.C.

Elul (ee′luhl), the postexilic (late sixth century BCE on) name of the sixth month of the Jewish year, according to the religious calendar. It would have been the twelfth month of the year in the older agricultural calendar. Mid-August to mid-September, it is the month when vintage begins. For biblical references, see Neh. 6:15; 1 Macc. 4:7. *See also* calendar.

Elymas (el′uh-muhs), a Jewish magician (also called Bar-Jesus, i.e., "son of Jesus"). Elymas was somehow associated with Sergius Paulus, the Roman proconsul of Cyprus. He opposed Paul's preaching, and Paul called him a "son of the devil" and "enemy of all righteousness." At Paul's word, he was temporarily blinded, which led the proconsul to believe (Acts 13:6–12). *See also* divination; magic; Paulus, Sergius.

embalming, a technique used by the Egyptians to preserve the bodies of humans and certain animals. The most important steps in the procedure were removing the visceral organs, dehydrating the body by immersing it for up to seventy days in a "bath" of dry natron salt, applying various spices and unguents, and wrapping the body in clean linen. Both Jacob (Gen. 50:2–3) and Joseph (Gen. 50:26) were embalmed; the treatment for Jacob is said to have taken forty days.

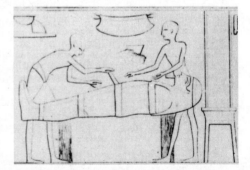

Embalmers wrapping a body in linen bandages; detail from an Egyptian tomb painting, ca. 1350–1200 BCE.

embroidery. *See* needle, needlework.

Emmanuel (i-man′*yoo*-uhl). *See* Immanuel.

Emmaus (i-may′uhs; Heb., "warm wells"), a town of disputed location that figures in the postresurrection story of Luke 24:13–35. After rising from the dead, Jesus joined two of his disciples, Cleopas and an unnamed disciple, who were walking from Jerusalem to their home in Emmaus. Their eyes were kept from recognizing Jesus, who spoke with them about how the events of his own passion had fulfilled the scriptures. When they reached Emmaus, Cleopas and his companion invited Jesus to join them for a meal, and when he took bread and broke it, they recognized him, at which point he vanished from their sight. Most biblical manuscripts say that Emmaus is about seven miles (60 *stadia*) from Jerusalem, but other manuscripts indicate it is about twenty miles (160 *stadia*). A town named Emmaus stood at the latter distance in the Valley of Aijalon during the time of the Maccabees (1 Macc. 3:40, 57; 4:1–15), where Judas defeated Gorgias. Bacchides, a Syrian general, later fortified the site (1 Macc. 9:50).

C.H.M.

emperor, an English word derived from the Latin *imperator* ("one who gives orders"), a title that was originally used of Roman military commanders, but later came to mean the single, chief sovereign. Julius Caesar referred to himself as *imperator,* as did his adopted son, Augustus, although the latter preferred the term *princeps,* "first citizen." Tiberius made this distinction: "I am *dominus* (master) of my slaves, *imperator* of my troops, and *princeps* of the rest," i.e., the free civilian population. Nevertheless, in popular usage, the term "emperor" was used for all supreme leaders of the Roman "empire" from Augustus on—indeed, in deference to Julius Caesar, all of the emperors took the name Caesar, so that "Caesar" and "emperor" became virtual synonyms.

The emperor was expected to make public appearances and dispense justice. He ruled so autocratically that the third-century CE lawyer Ulpian could say, "What has pleased the emperor has the force of law." Below the emperor was the Senate, or council where laws were made. Normally, an emperor nominated his successor and never passed over his son by blood unless it was for an adopted son. The emperor could issue four types of enactments: "edicts" (public policy announcements); "decrees" (judicial decisions); "mandates" (directives to imperial officials); and "rescripts" (written replies conveyed through an elaborate mail system).

Three Roman emperors are named in the Bible. The first is Caesar Augustus (27 BCE–14 CE), who is often credited with establishing the Pax Romana ("Roman peace"), a general absence of war. By assuming tribunician power in 23 BCE, he gained the right to convene the Senate and initiate legislation. He also assumed the titles *pater patriae,* "Father of the Country," and *pontifex maximus,* "High Priest," with control over state religion. Luke 2:1–2 dates Jesus's birth by a Roman census ordered by Caesar Augustus. The Greek translation of Augustus, Sebastos, is used of the emperor in Acts 25:21, 25. The second emperor named in the Bible is Tiberius (14–37 CE), the adopted son of Augustus, who was viewed as more tyrannical than his father. Luke 3:1 dates John the Baptist's preaching and hence the beginning of Jesus's ministry to the fifteenth year of the emperor Tiberius (either 27/28 or 28/29 CE). The coin shown to Jesus

(Matt. 22:15–22; Mark 12:13–17; Luke 20:20–26) was probably a denarius bearing his image. The third emperor named in the NT is Claudius (41–54 CE), who developed the civil service and extended Roman citizenship. He is said to have expelled the Jews from Rome (probably in 49 CE) due to disturbances caused by "Chrestus" (Suetonius *Claudius* 25.4). Many historians think that "Chrestus" is a distortion of "Christos," and that the reported expulsion of Jews was perhaps limited to those Jews and Jewish Christians who were embroiled in disputes over the status to be accorded to Jesus. Acts 18:2 lists Paul's friends Aquila and Priscilla as being among those expelled by Claudius. In addition, Acts 11:28 refers to a famine that occurred during the reign of Claudius.

Two more emperors are noted for their harsh treatments of Christians. Nero (54–68 CE) capped his eccentric reign by attributing a great fire in Rome to the Christians and persecuting them violently in the city of Rome itself. Later, Domitian (81–96 CE) is also reported to have violently persecuted Christians, though the evidence for this is in dispute. Most scholars think that the book of Revelation was written during the reign of Nero or Domitian. Thus the diabolical picture of the Roman Empire offered in Rev. 13 and 17 would be inspired by the policies and practices of one or both of these rulers.

Another two emperors, who ruled in between the times of Nero and Domitian, are significant for their role in the destruction of Jerusalem, which forms a backdrop for some NT writings. Vespasian, founder of what is called the Flavian dynasty, was the first general of Roman troops to lead the assault against the Jewish nation in the revolt of 66–70 CE. He was called back to Rome from the battlefield and became emperor, reigning 69–79 CE. His son Titus finished the job, brutally sacking Jerusalem and destroying the temple, an event commemorated by an arch in Rome. Titus later ruled as emperor for two years (79–81 CE). His destruction of the temple may be the event referred to as the "desolating sacrilege" in Matt. 24:15 (cf. Mark 13:14).

According to the Gospel of John, Jewish opponents of Jesus cited loyalty to the emperor as a rationale for why Pilate should have Jesus crucified (19:12–15). Later, opponents of Paul and Silas claimed that they were "acting contrary to decrees of the emperor, saying there is another king named Jesus" (Acts 17:7). When Paul is arrested at the end of the book of Acts, he exercises his right as a Roman citizen to appeal his case to the emperor (25:9–12; cf. 26:32; 27:24; 28:19). First Peter maintains that the emperor's authority is established by God (2:13), and the author exhorts his Christian readers to "Fear God, honor the emperor" (2:17; the Greek word in both passages is *basileus,* lit., "king"). *See also* Caesar; Roman Empire.

Bibliography

Grant, Michael. *The Roman Emperors: A Biographical Guide to the Rulers of Imperial Rome.* Scribner, 1985.

Millar, Fergus. *The Emperor in the Roman World*. Cornell University Press, 1977.

D.L.J./M.A.P.

emperor cult, or emperor worship, the religious rituals associated with venerating the Roman emperor as a divine being. The emperor cult was basically a means of showing reverence for an emperor, living or dead. The practice had precedence in Greek and Egyptian realms, where such Hellenistic rulers as Alexander the Great and Ptolemy I had been regarded as divine "saviors." In the Roman Empire, beginning with Julius Caesar, emperors were often "consecrated" by a vote of the Senate after they died. Thus, Julius Caesar was posthumously deified in 42 BCE. A praetor swore under oath that he had witnessed Augustus's apotheosis, or ascent into heaven. Likewise, Trajan's apotheosis was attested in several traditions.

Several Roman emperors were reluctant to accept divine honors during their lifetime. Augustus allowed his worship in the provinces only where it was combined with that of the goddess Roma. Tiberius resisted divine honors for himself and his mother, Livia, and forbade the erection of statues. In a letter to Alexandria in 41 CE, Claudius refused the establishment of priests and temples to himself, saying such observances are "only for the gods." Vespasian generally refused divine honors, although on his deathbed he said ironically, "I suppose I am becoming a god." Trajan also rejected divine honors for himself. Nevertheless, in 112 CE Pliny, his legate in Bithynia and Pontus, required Christians, as a test of loyalty, to offer wine and incense before a statue of Trajan, and Trajan approved this action (*Epistles* 10.96–97). A few emperors, furthermore, insisted that they were divine. Caligula demanded that he be wor-

ROMAN EMPERORS OF THE NEW TESTAMENT PERIOD

Dates of Rule	Emperor	Historical Significance and/or Contact with Biblical (NT) Concerns
45–44 BCE	Julius Caesar	Military general who became dictator and was then assassinated; established precedent for position of emperor and gave his name to all later emperors
27 BCE–14 CE	Augustus (Octavian)	Usually regarded as the first Roman emperor; credited with establishing the Pax Romana; birth of Jesus during his reign (Luke 2:1)
14–37 CE	Tiberius	Ministry and death of Jesus during his reign (Luke 3:1); appointed and later removed Pilate as governor of Judea; probably his image on the coin shown to Jesus in Mark 12:14–17 (see also Luke 23:2; John 19:12, 15; Acts 17:7)
37–41 CE	Caligula (Gaius)	Established reputation of emperors for cruelty and decadence; demanded that a statue of himself be placed in Jewish temple, but died before this could be carried out
41–54 CE	Claudius	Installed as a figurehead but turned out to be surprisingly competent; expelled Jews from Rome due to a disturbance over "Chrestus," which brought Priscilla and Aquila into contact with Paul (Acts 18:1–4); made Herod Agrippa I king over the entire Levant (Acts 12:1–3).
54–68 CE	Nero	An exemplary ruler during first five years, then turned self-indulgent and violent; responsible for persecution of Christians in Rome; Peter crucified and Paul beheaded during his reign (ca. 62–64 CE)
69 CE	Galba Otho Vitellius	A time of civil war known as the "Year of Four Emperors"; a quick succession of three emperors before stability restored under Vespasian
69–79 CE	Vespasian	The Roman general in the war with the Jews; returned to Rome to seize power when Nero died
79–81 CE	Titus	Son of Vespasian; took over command of troops when his father became emperor; crushed the Jewish rebellion, destroyed the temple in Jerusalem, and presided over prolonged siege of Masada
81–96 CE	Domitian	Son of Vespasian; reported to have persecuted Christians, but solid evidence for this is lacking; his reign possibly the background for the anti-Roman sentiments in the book of Revelation

From Mark Allan Powell, *Introducing the New Testament* (courtesy, Baker Academic)

shiped, and a temple to him was erected in Rome. He offended the Jews by ordering his Syrian legate Petronius to erect a huge statue of himself in the Jerusalem temple. Fortunately, Petronius's delaying tactics averted a confrontation, and Caligula died before the demand could be carried out. Nero appeared on coins as a "god" wearing the crown of a deified emperor.

In the Roman Empire in NT times, the imperial cult was of greater importance in the provinces than in Rome itself. For example, Ephesus and Pergamum in the province of Asia were rivals for the honor of being named *neokōros* ("temple warden"), the city responsible for overseeing emperor worship for the entire province. On more than one occasion this official designation was withdrawn from one of these two cities and granted to the other, with attendant changes in fortune and prestige. In popular piety, various miracles and divine benefits were often attributed to emperors, living and dead. Furthermore, emperors were frequently referred to by such titles as "Son of God," "Lord," and "Savior," which were an offense to both Jews and Christians (e.g., Rom. 1:4; 4:24; Phil. 3:20). It should be noted, however, that apart from the performance of token rituals and the bestowal of grandiose titles, no real "religion" ever developed around the emperors; the acclamations and actions that Jews and Christians regarded as constituting "worship" of the emperors were viewed by most Romans as simple acts of patriotism (analogous to pledging allegiance to a flag). Thus, the aversion to such acts caused Jews and Christians to be viewed as antisocial and unpatriotic participants in the empire. *See also* Roman Empire.

Bibliography

Fishwick, Duncan. *The Imperial Cult in the Latin West.* 2 vols. Brill, 1987–92.

Price, S. R. F. *Rituals and Power: The Roman Imperial Cult in Asia Minor.* Cambridge University Press, 1984.   D.L.J./M.A.P.

emperor's household, a collective designation for the thousands of slaves and freedpersons of the ruling Roman emperor who performed various governmental functions. In Phil. 4:22, Paul refers to members of the emperor's household in the area where he is in prison. Most scholars think that this would be either at Rome, Caesarea, or Ephesus, but the reference to "emperor's household" does not help to narrow down the location, since people who could be referred to by that designation would have been in all three of those cities. Phil. 1:13 makes a reference to the "imperial guard," but since the governmental workers referred to as the "emperor's household" were typically debarred from military service, this probably refers to a different group of people (i.e., to Roman military personnel in charge of guarding Paul). *See also* Philippians, Letter of Paul to the.   R.A.W./M.A.P.

Enan (ee′nuhn; Heb., possibly "little spring [of water]"), the father of Ahira, the tribal leader of Naphtali. He is mentioned five times in tribal lists (Num. 1:15; 2:29; 7:78, 83; 10:27). Functions of his better-known son included leading tribal participation in the census, presenting offerings, and escorting the tabernacle on marches in the wilderness.

encampment (Heb. *makhaneh,* "bend" or "curve"), a military enclosure. The word itself suggests an encampment's circular form. Thus, Saul can be said to be sleeping "within the encampment," with the army camped around him (1 Sam. 26:5; cf. 25:7). The book of Numbers refers to the "regimental encampment" of four different tribes (2:3, 10, 18, 25). Forces under Joshua set up an encampment between Bethel and Ai (Josh. 8:13), and later David came to an Israelite encampment, where he decided to take on Goliath (1 Sam. 17:20). The Greek word used in the LXX to translate *makhaneh* is *parembolē,* which is used for the Roman garrison in Acts 21:34 (NRSV uses "barracks" rather than "encampment" to indicate that the word here refers to an architectural structure). This same Greek word is used again in Rev. 20:9 (NRSV: "camp"), where it refers to the millennial church in its final battle with Satan.   M.A.P.

enchantment. *See* divination; magic.

Endor or **En-dor** (en′dor; Heb., "spring of circle," "spring of habitation," or "spring of generation"), a Canaanite city belonging to Manasseh (Josh. 17:11–12). It was situated about three miles southwest of Mount Tabor. On the eve of King Saul's fatal defeat by the Philistines at Gilboa, Saul journeys to Endor to enjoin a medium to raise up Samuel from the dead (1 Sam. 28:3–25). En-dor is also mentioned as the site of the defeat of Midian by Gideon (Ps. 83:10). *See also* divination; magic; Saul.   J.U.

En-gannim (en-gan′im; Heb., "fountain of gardens").

1 A town belonging to the allotment of Judah, located in the lowlands (Josh. 15:34). The literary context would indicate that it is in the region near Azekah and Jarmuth.

2 A border town between Issachar and Manasseh (Josh. 19:21; 21:29). It may be the "garden house" of 2 Kings 9:27.

En-gedi (en-ged′i; Heb., "spring of the young goat"), an important oasis, with fresh water and hot springs, on the west shore of the Dead Sea, about eighteen miles southeast of Hebron. It was part of the allotment of Judah (Josh. 15:62). David went to live in the "wilderness of En-gedi" when he was being pursued by Saul (1 Sam. 23:9; 24:1). An alternative name for En-gedi, Hazazon-tamar, is given in 2 Chron. 20:2. In Song of Sol. 1:14, a lover describes his beloved as being like "a cluster of henna blossoms in the vineyards of En-gedi," and in Sir. 24:14, Wisdom says, "I grew like a palm tree in En-gedi." Ezek. 47:10 mentions fishing there. Archaeological excavations at En-gedi have

The spring that feeds the pool at En-gedi, an oasis near the Dead Sea.

revealed an early settlement from the period of Josiah up to the destruction of Jerusalem (ca. 640–587/6 BCE). The settlement was then completely destroyed and a new settlement was built in the Persian period, probably in the time of Zerubbabel (mid-sixth century BCE).   S.B.R.

engines of war, the machinery for warfare, which could be used for either offensive or defensive purposes. Offensively, battering rams were used quite effectively by armies campaigning in the Near East. Graphic examples of fortified battering rams are given in the Assyrian king Sennacherib's palace reliefs depicting the siege of Lachish (701 BCE; 2 Kings 18:13–14). Variations of this siege machine were used by the Babylonians and the Romans. Defensively, catapults were used to hurl stones from battlements on city walls. According to the Chronicler, King Uzziah had catapults in some of his fortified cities for hurling stones and for shooting arrows (2 Chron. 26:15). In open-field warfare chariots were well known and extensively used. Like the battering ram, they required support troops for maximum effectiveness. Engines of war are referred to explicitly in the books of Maccabees (1 Macc. 5:30; 6:20, 31, 51, 52; 11:20; 15:25; 2 Macc. 12:15; cf. 2 Macc. 12:27).   J.A.D.

engraving, incising, the practice of impressing deeply in metal, clay tablets, or stone with an iron tool or stylus. The Bible mentions an engraver

who did work for the temple (2 Chron. 2:7), one Huramabi by name (2 Chron. 2:13–14), though it also prohibits the making of graven "images" (Exod. 20:4). "Holy to the Lord" was engraved on a gold plate for Aaron's turban (Exod. 28:36; 39:30). Cherubim, lions, palm trees, and wreaths were engraved on bronze stands in the temple (1 Kings 7:36; 2 Chron. 3:7). Isa. 8:1 mentions clay tablets, and Jer. 17:1 engraving with a pen of iron with a diamond point. Exod. 28:9, 11 and 39:6, 14 refer to two onyx stones with six Israelite tribal names incised on each. Job 19:24 mentions an incised tablet with lead-filled letters. Zech. 3:9 speaks of a seven-faceted stone engraved with an inscription. Artifacts such as seal cylinders and stamps for impressions on documents are relatively frequent. Inscribed Egyptian and Hyksos scarabs can be used for dating archaeological finds.   R.A.C.

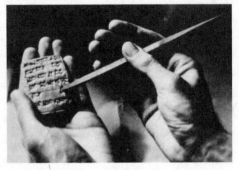

A reed stylus, used to engrave clay tablets throughout the ancient Near East.

Enlil (en'lil; Akkadian, "Lord Wind"), an ancient and important god of Mesopotamia. Though not mentioned in the Bible, he does figure in Mesopotamian accounts of the creation of humankind and human order that are often referred to by biblical scholars (the Atrahasis epic; the Gilgamesh epic). He was the god of the city Nippur and was worshiped there in a temple called Ekur ("House-mountain"). In early Mesopotamia, Enlil was the primary executive of the gods, who bestowed and legitimated divine and human kingship. In a mythological tradition originating in Nippur, Enlil separated heaven from earth, and humankind sprouted forth at the place of the division. Thus, like Ea and the Canaanite El, Enlil was a creator god; like these, he also appears as a patriarchal ruler on whose behalf a young god takes up arms and organizes natural and political structures. In both the Atrahasis epic and the Gilgamesh epic (Tablet XI), Enlil is said to have brought a flood to destroy humankind; the present order emerged as an adjustment necessary to allow humanity to exist without distressing Enlil. In more general terms, Enlil was associated with agriculture and was the god of the wind, of the destructive storm, and of the beneficent breeze of spring. He was also the creator of the primitive farming tool, the hoe, and his wife, Ninlil, was a grain goddess. In a developed form of the pantheon, he shared control of the world with An, Ea, and a mother goddess. Asshur, the god of the Assyrians, was later identified with Enlil. *See also* Nippur.   I.T.A.

Enoch (ee′nuhk), a sixth-generation descendant of Adam mentioned in Gen. 5:18–24; he was the son of Jared and the father of Methuselah. He lived 365 years, walked with God, and God took him. The latter reference has often been interpreted as meaning that Enoch was taken into God's realm without experiencing death. For this reason, he became viewed as one who might be able to disclose secrets of the divine realm. In the Hellenistic age (300 BCE–300 CE) a corpus of apocalyptic writings was attributed to Enoch (*1 Enoch, 2 Enoch;* cf. Jude 1:14, which alludes to *1 Enoch* 1:9). Enoch is also referred to in the NT, as an ancestor of Jesus (Luke 3:37) and as a model of faith (Heb. 11:5; cf. Sir. 44:16; 49:14).   J.J.C./M.A.P.

Enoch, books of. *See* Pseudepigrapha.

Enosh (ee′nosh; Heb., "humanity" or "the human race"), the son of Seth and grandson of Adam through whom genealogies to Noah, Abraham, and eventually Jesus are traced (Gen. 4:26; 1 Chron. 1:1; Luke 3:38). The Bible says that it was during the time of Enosh that "people began to invoke the name of the LORD" (Gen. 4:26). Enosh lived 905 years and was the father of Kenan (Gen. 5:6–11). He is called Enos in the LXX and in Luke 3:38.

En-rogel (en-roh′guhl; Heb., "spring of a treader or fuller"), a spring near Jerusalem that served as the boundary line between the tribes of Judah and Benjamin (Josh. 15:7; 18:16). Its name may derive from its use for laundering clothes, a process that might have involved treading upon the submerged garments with one's feet. During the rebellion of Absalom against his father, David, this spring was the place where information was passed by a maidservant to David's men (2 Sam. 17:17). Later, when David near death, his other son, Adonijah, prematurely declared himself king while sacrificing animals and celebrating with his friends by the Serpent's Stone, which was beside En-rogel (1 Kings 1:5–10). *See also* Absalom; Adonijah.
                                                       F.R.M.

enrollment. *See* census.

En-shemesh (en-shem′ish; Heb., "spring of the sun [god]"), a spring located east of Jerusalem and Bethany. Known today as Ain el-Hod, it is the last spring on the road between Jerusalem and the Jordan Valley. In premonarchic Israel it served as the boundary between Judah and Benjamin (Josh. 15:7; 18:17).

Epaphras (ep′uh-fras), an associate of Paul mentioned in Philem. 23 and Col. 1:7; 4:12–13.

According to Colossians, he was a native of the Lycus Valley in Asia Minor and had worked hard as Paul's representative in Colossae, Laodicea, and Hierapolis. In the Letter to Philemon, Epaphras is identified as being in prison with Paul. *See also* Colossae; Colossians, Letter of Paul to the.

Epaphroditus (i-paf′ruh-di′tuhs), a Philippian Christian who brought gifts from Philippi to Paul in prison (Phil. 4:18). Epaphroditus had become seriously ill, but then recovered. In his Letter to the Philippians, Paul explains that he is sending Epaphroditus back to them, because he knows that they have heard of the man's illness and have been anxious about him (2:25–30). Paul refers to Epaphroditus as his "brother, co-worker, and fellow soldier" (4:25). He also indicates that Epaphroditus "came close to death for the work of Christ," implying that the illness was somehow related to his work on Paul's behalf (4:30). *See also* Philippians, Letter of Paul to the.

ephah (ee′fuh), a dry measure equal to the liquid bath and approximately the equivalent of three-eighths to two-thirds of a U.S. bushel (which is equal to 32 quarts). It may also represent the container for such a quantity (see Zech. 5:6–11). *See also* weights and measures.

Epher (ee′fuhr; Heb., "fawn" or "kid [of a mountain goat]").
   1 A son of Midian and grandson of Abraham and Keturah (Gen. 25:4; 1 Chron. 1:33).
   2 The son of Ezrah, a descendant of Judah (1 Chron. 4:17).
   3 An ancestral family leader of the eastern half-tribe of Manasseh (1 Chron. 5:24).

Ephesians (i-fee′zhuhnz), **Letter of Paul to the,** one of thirteen letters in the NT attributed to Paul. There is some question as to whether the letter was originally (or exclusively) addressed to Christians in Ephesus—and there is also much debate among scholars about whether the letter was actually written by Paul. It is, in any case, similar to Colossians, so that those two letters are often called "literary siblings."
   Contents: After a fairly typical salutation (1:1–2), the author (who identifies himself as "Paul, an apostle of Christ Jesus") presents an elegant blessing of God that serves as a liturgical overture to the letter (1:3–14). He declares that God is bringing to fulfillment a plan to gather all things in Christ. Those who were destined to be God's blameless children have been forgiven their trespasses as a result of the redemption that comes through Christ's blood, and they have been sealed with the Holy Spirit as a pledge of further redemption still to come. The blessing segues into a thanksgiving as the writer acknowledges his recipients' faith and love (1:16–17). He prays that they might be fully enlightened about what God has in store for them and what the power of the risen and exalted Christ will accomplish in and

through the church, which is his body (1:15–23). Once dead in trespasses, they have been saved by grace and exalted with Christ to fulfill their destiny as people created for a life of good works (2:1–10). By reconciling all people to God through the cross, Christ has created a new humanity marked by peace rather than hostility; this is manifest in the church, where Jews and Gentiles alike have access to God and, indeed, compose what is now God's spiritual dwelling place (2:11–22). This new unity of humanity is "the mystery of Christ," revealed to Paul when he was commissioned by God; now, the church's role in the divine drama is to make the mystery known, not only to the world of unbelievers, but also to spiritual powers in heavenly places (3:1–13). The author prays again that his readers might comprehend the immeasurable love of Christ manifested in all of this (3:14–19), and he offers a brief doxology to conclude the first part of the letter (3:20–21).

The second half of the letter explicates practical implications of what was proclaimed in the first part. Readers are urged to live a life worthy of their calling (4:1), which means life with others in a community that functions as a single entity (4:2–16). The specifics of such a life are spelled out with reference to a number of behaviors that will set those in the church apart from others, as imitators of God and children of light (4:17–5:20). A series of household instructions indicate how they are to conduct themselves in family and social relationships (5:21–6:9), and an appeal to guard against the wiles of the devil encourages readers to be dressed in spiritual armor provided by God (6:10–17). The letter concludes with exhortations to prayer (6:18–19), a commendation of Tychicus, the letter carrier (6:20–21), and a double benediction (6:23–24).

OUTLINE OF CONTENTS

Ephesians

E.B.

Authorship: Scholars who think that Ephesians is a pseudepigraphical composition note that the letter is distinct from undisputed Pauline letters with regard to both style and theological concepts. Examples of the former include extremely long sentences, repetitive use of adjectives and synonyms, and distinctive usage of key words: "works" for good works (2:9–10) rather than for works of the law (Gal. 2:16; 3:1, 5, 10, 12), "church" for the universal church (1:22; 3:10, 21; 5:23, 24, 25, 27, 29, 32) rather than for a local congregation (e.g., Rom. 16:23; 1 Cor. 4:17; 14:23; but cf. 1 Cor. 10:32; 15:9). Examples of distinctive concepts include: the church is built on the foundation of the apostles and prophets, with Christ as cornerstone (2:19–20), rather than being built on the foundation of Christ alone (1 Cor. 3:10–11); the Second Coming of Christ has faded in significance, since the power and glory of heaven are experienced now (1:3; 2:4–7; cf. Rom. 8:18–25; 2 Cor. 4:7–18); Jews and Gentiles are merged equally into a new humanity (2:14–16) as opposed to Gentiles being provisionally grafted onto the tree of Israel (Rom. 11:13–21); marriage is highly esteemed (5:21–23) rather than being merely allowed for the sake of controlling lust (1 Cor. 7:8–9); the law is said to have been abolished by Christ (2:15) rather than being described as something that the coming of faith has not overthrown (3:31); the reconciliation of Jews and Gentiles is depicted as an accomplished reality (2:11–18) rather than as a future hope (Rom. 11:25–32); salvation is a present reality (2:7–10) rather than a future hope (Rom. 5:9–10; 10:9, 13; 1 Cor. 3:15; 5:5; but cf. Rom. 8:24; 1 Cor. 1:18; 15:2; 2 Cor. 2:15); and, similarly, the exaltation of believers to heaven is a present reality (2:6) rather than a future hope (1 Cor. 15:23; 1 Thess. 4:16–17). Scholars who think the letter is authentic usually date it late in the Pauline corpus and maintain that it evinces development of Pauline thought, evident also in Colossians. They also claim that stylistic differences can be explained by assuming Paul granted a measure of freedom to his amanuensis or to the letter's coauthors.

Critical Problems: The words "in Ephesus" (1:1) are missing from early manuscripts of Ephesians. Scholars have also noted that the letter is very general in tone, lacking any personal references to the readers. Indeed, certain passages imply that the readers do not actually know the author personally (1:15; 3:2–3; 4:21), though, according to Acts, Paul founded the church in Ephesus and remained there for two and a half years (18:19–20; 19:8–10). Many scholars therefore assume that this letter was intended as a circular tract copied and distributed to different churches—manuscripts that do contain the words "in Ephesus" would simply have been copied from the edition of the letter sent to that particular congregation.

Historical Setting: Given the above, and in recognition of similarities between Ephesians and Colossians, different scenarios emerge. (1) If Paul is regarded as the author of Ephesians, then it could be that he first wrote the Letter to the Colossians to deal with specific issues in that congregation and, while those thoughts were still fresh in his mind, composed what is now called "Ephesians" as a more general letter to be taken to various churches in Asia Minor. In this case, the letter would have been written from prison (6:20), possibly from Rome in the early 60s or from Caesarea or Ephesus itself at an earlier date (mid to late 50s). (2) If the letter is pseudepigraphical, it would have been written after Paul's death by a disciple or admirer who might have used Colossians as a template (unless this pseudepigraphical author is considered to have written Colossians pseudepigraphically as well). According to this scenario, the letter could have been written at almost any point in the latter third of the first century.

In sum, Ephesians is variously regarded as presenting: (1) Paul's most mature developed thinking; (2) Pauline ideas filtered through the mind of a gifted apprentice; or (3) non-Pauline ideas attributed to him by an author who developed Paul's concepts in directions that the apostle himself would not have taken.

Major Themes: The letter reflects on a number of interrelated themes centering on the relationship of the church to Christ and to Christian behavior. The underlying concept is that a mysterious divine plan of God, in God's mind since before the creation of the world (1:4), has now been revealed to the apostles and prophets (3:5) and is being accomplished through the death, resurrection, and ascension of Christ. This plan concerns the unity of all humanity in Christ, who is Lord of all (1:9–10). There is concomitant interest in Christ's defeat of all supernatural "principalities and powers" (1:19–22) and on the elevation of the church as a unified, spiritual entity in which the sanctification of believers becomes a present reality (1:4; 5:27). In a more pragmatic vein, Christian behavior is described as living in a manner appropriate for the household of God (2:7); this includes taking a protected stand against the devil (6:10–17) and following ethical imperatives that recognize "we

PARALLELS BETWEEN EPHESIANS AND COLOSSIANS

Topic	Ephesians	Colossians
Redemption and forgiveness	1:7	1:14–20
All things in heaven, earth are in Christ	1:10	1:20
I have heard of your faith	1:15	1:4
I thank God always for you	1:16	1:3
Pray that God will give you wisdom	1:17	1:9
Riches of a glorious inheritance/mystery	1:18	1:27
God made you alive	2:5	2:13
Aliens reconciled through Christ's death	2:12–13	1:21–22
Christ has abolished the law	2:15	2:14
Paul is suffering for their sake	3:1	1:24
Divine commission given to Paul	3:2	1:25
Divine mystery made known to Paul	3:3	1:26
Paul a servant of the gospel	3:7	1:23, 25
Lead a worthy life	4:1	1:10
Humility, meekness, patience	4:2	3:12
Bear with one another	4:2	3:13
Christ is head of the body	4:15–16	2:19
Put off old nature, put on new nature	4:22–32	3:5–10,12
No immorality among you	5:3–6	3:5–9
Walk wisely and make the most of your time	5:15	4:5
Sing songs, hymns, and spiritual songs	5:19	3:16
Give thanks to God	5:20	3:17
Tables of household duties	5:21–6:9	3:18–4:1
for wives	5:22–24	3:18
for husbands	5:25–33	3:19
for children	6:1–3	3:20
for fathers	6:4	3:21
for slaves	6:5–8	3:22–25
for masters	6:9	4:1
Paul the prisoner exhorts persistence in prayer	6:18–20	4:2–3
Tychicus will inform church about Paul	6:21	4:7
Tychicus sent to encourage their hearts	6:22	4:8

From Mark Allan Powell, *Introducing the New Testament* (courtesy, Baker Academic); see also Charles B. Puskas Jr., *The Letters of Paul: An Introduction* (Liturgical, 1993), pp. 130–31 are members of one another" (4:26; cf. 5:28–30). *See also* Ephesus; Paul; pseudepigraphy.

Bibliography

Barth, Markus. *Ephesians*. 2 vols. Doubleday, 1974.

Best, Ernest. *A Critical and Exegetical Commentary on the Epistle to the Ephesians*. Clark, 1998.

Lincoln, Andrew T. *Ephesians*. Word, 1990.

Lincoln, Andrew, and A. J. Wedderburn. *The Theology of the Later Pauline Letters*. Cambridge University Press, 1993.

Schnackenburg, Rudolf. *The Epistle to the Ephesians: A Commentary*. Clark, 1991.

M.A.P.

Ephesus

A PORT CITY of western Asia Minor at the mouth of the Cayster River, Ephesus (ef'uh-suhs) lay between Smyrna and Miletus. Although the area had a primitive shrine to the Anatolian mother goddess, was visited by Mycenaeans, and was peopled by Carians and Lelegians, it was first colonized by Ionian Greeks under the leadership of Androclus of Athens in the eleventh century BCE. The Greeks identified the deity with their own Artemis, but the attributes remained those of the ancient fertility goddess. A new phase of Ephesus's history began with its conquest ca. 560 BCE by Croesus of Lydia, who contributed columns to the temple to Artemis and reorganized the layout of the city. Lydian influence in Ephesus through the succeeding centuries assured a greater synthesis of Greek and Asiatic culture than anywhere else in Ionia. After Cyrus the Persian defeated Croesus in 547 BCE, Ephesus remained subject to Persian rule until Alexander's arrival in 334 BCE. In the meantime, the temple had burned (356 BCE), and a new temple to Artemis had been begun, the classical structure that came to be known as one of the Seven Wonders of the World, lasting until its destruction by Goths in the third century CE. Only a single reconstructed column and the remains of an altar now mark the spot.

The temple of Artemis, considered one of the Seven Wonders of the World during Hellenistic times. Today only one column of an interior row remains.

Lysimachus led the building of a new city in the third century BCE, with a new five-mile-long wall, a new harbor, and a Hippodamian street plan. From 281 BCE, the Seleucids held Ephesus until Antiochus III's defeat by the Romans left it in possession of the kings of Pergamum. Rome took direct rule at the death of Attalos III in 133 BCE. An abortive revolt, linked to Mithradates VI of Pontus in 88 BCE, was put down by the Roman general

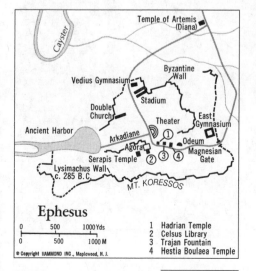

Ephesus

| 0 | 500 | 1000 Yds |
| 0 | 500 | 1000 M |

© Copyright HAMMOND INC., Maplewood, N. J.

1 Hadrian Temple
2 Celsus Library
3 Trajan Fountain
4 Hestia Boulaea Temple

The city plan (*left*) shows buildings and walls over several centuries before, during, and after Paul's time in the mid-first century CE.

Sulla, and the city remained peacefully Roman and then Byzantine for the rest of its history. Having dedicated a sacred precinct to Rome and Julius Caesar in 29 BCE, Ephesus became capital of the Roman province of Asia and enjoyed the height of its prosperity in the first and second centuries CE as the fourth largest city in the empire. As the harbor silted up, the city declined in the Byzantine period (ca. fifth to tenth centuries CE), but a new wall and churches were built. The Turkish town of Seljuk today is the sixth city on the site.

Paul in Ephesus: In the NT, Ephesus and Ephesians are mentioned more than twenty times. According to Acts, Paul sailed from Corinth to Ephesus with Priscilla (Prisca) and Aquila for his first visit there (18:19–21). The latter couple instructed Apollos in Ephesus (18:24–26). Paul returned on his third missionary journey (19:1–20:1) to stay for more than two years, preaching and exorcising. The silversmiths in the commercial agora (marketplace) finally rioted at the threat of Paul's monotheism against their income from miniatures of the Artemis temple and dragged Paul's companions, Gaius and Aristarchus, into the city's theater before the town clerk was able to calm the mob (19:23–41). Later, on his way

Portion of the Ephesus city wall built by Lysimachus, ca. 285 BCE.

Remains of the temple of Hadrian at Ephesus.

The remains of the theater at Ephesus, which may be the one into which Paul's companions Gaius and Aristarchus were dragged, as told in Acts 19:23–41.

back to Jerusalem Paul met with the elders of Ephesus at Miletus (20:16–38). The presence of Paul's companion Trophimus, an Ephesian, was later the reason for a riot of Jews in the Jerusalem temple and the arrest of Paul there (21:27–22:30).

In 1 Cor. 15:32, Paul writes that he "fought with beasts at Ephesus," but whether this is meant figuratively or literally is uncertain. Timothy is charged to remain at Ephesus (1 Tim. 1:3), Onesiphorus rendered service at Ephesus (2 Tim 1:18), and Tychicus was sent there (4:12). The church of Ephesus is the first of the seven churches of Revelation (1:11; 2:1–7). Most (but not all) biblical manuscripts indicate that the NT book titled "Paul's Letter to the Ephesians" was addressed to people in Ephesus (Eph. 1:1).

Austrian and Turkish archaeologists have excavated the site for over a century. Along with spectacular public structures such as a theater seating around twenty-five thousand, the vast commercial agora, and a massive imperial temple complex, an entire neighborhood of private homes of the very wealthy has been excavated. The archaeology gives a clear impression of the city as known by Paul. Already in the Augustan period, a concerted effort was made to fuse the religion and culture of Roman imperialism

A silver denarius depicting the Artemision and the fertility goddess Artemis of the Ephesians, here called Diana, whose adherents had rioted at the threat of Paul's monotheism; from the time of Emperor Hadrian (117–138 CE).

with the indigenous Greek culture, while including foreign influences from across the Mediterranean. An administrative basilica was dedicated to Augustus, Tiberius, Artemis, and the citizenry of Ephesus, and at the state agora the worship of Augustus was coupled with that of Artemis. Over a hundred inscriptions testify to the diversity and tolerance of religious devotion in Ephesus; various associations based on trade networks, professional guilds, neighborhoods, or ethnic origins included in some way patronage by or dedication to a deity. Among them are two from the silversmiths, one recording their devotion to Artemis and the Roman emperor. There has not yet come to light, however, any archaeological evidence of the Jewish community referred to in the NT and the works of the first-century Jewish historian Josephus. The blending of imperial and local culture seems to have been smooth under the Julio-Claudians, though the massive temple complex to the emperor Domitian (81–96 CE) appears intrusive. It did establish the city as the official *neokōros,* or temple warden, of the imperial cult in Asia Minor.

The Hanging Houses at Ephesus built on terraces overlooking the Curetes Street underscore the wealth of Roman Ephesus. Colorful mosaics, artistic frescoes with mythological and philosophical themes, and marble sheeting from across the empire testify to the city's affluence and taste. *See also* Artemis of the Ephesians; Ephesians, Letter of Paul to the; shrine; smith.

Bibliography

Finegan, Jack. *The Archaeology of the New Testament: The Mediterranean World of the Early Christian Apostles.* Westview, 1981.

Koester, Helmut, ed. *Ephesos: Metropolis of Asia.* Trinity Press International, 1995.   C.H.M.

ephod (ee'fod), an article of clothing most often associated with priestly garments, but also mentioned in other contexts. The ephod is one of the elaborate garments described for Aaron and his descendants to wear in the tabernacle (Exod. 28; 39). It appears to be an ornate, sleeveless garment, made of twisted linen and decorated with gold, blue, purple, and scarlet material. It was accompanied by shoulder pieces and a woven belt made of the same materials. The shoulder pieces were adorned with two onyx stones on which were written the names of the sons of Jacob who were regarded as the ancestors of the twelve tribes of Israel. A breastplate was also worn over the ephod, and it was decorated with twelve stones bearing the names of the twelve tribes. A pocket in this breastplate held the Urim and the Thummim, lots that could be cast for divination. The ephod is the only part of the priestly vestments described in the Pentateuch to be mentioned elsewhere in the Bible. A priest can be referred to as one who is chosen by God to wear an ephod (1 Sam. 2:28). Thus, Saul's priest wears an ephod at the battle of Michmash (1 Sam. 14:3), and, at Saul's command, Doeg the Edomite killed "eighty-five who wore the linen ephod" (i.e., eighty-five priests) at the temple of Nob (1 Sam. 22:18).

Elsewhere in the Bible, a "linen ephod" is worn by Samuel (1 Sam. 2:18) and David (2 Sam. 6:14; 1 Chron. 15:27). These latter references could be to some ordinary garment, or they might also suggest some emulation of the ceremonial garb. Samuel wears his ephod while serving in the sanctuary at Shiloh, and David wears his when dancing before the ark. Since David is specifically "girded with a linen ephod" (2 Sam. 6:14), the garment in question appears to be more like a loincloth than a tunic (cf. 6:20). Ephods are also mentioned in several other contexts, including ones that involve idolatrous or inappropriate worship. Gideon made an ephod for himself, and it became a "snare" to him and his family, as "all Israel prostituted themselves to it" (Judg. 8:27). A man named Micah is said to have made a shrine with teraphim and idols in the hill country of Ephraim, and to have also made an ephod and installed one of his sons as the priest (Judg. 17:5; 18:14–20). Finally, in certain passages an "ephod" seems to be an object that one uses for divination (1 Sam. 23:6, 9; 30:7); this might derive from the fact that the breastpiece attached to Aaron's ephod held the Urim and Thummim. *See also* priests; tabernacle; Urim and Thummim.   C.L.M./M.A.P.

ephphatha (ef'uh-thuh), the contraction of an Aramaic verb meaning "Let it be opened." In Mark 7:34 Jesus gives this command while curing a man who is deaf and unable to speak.

Ephraim (ee'fray-im; Heb., probably "fruitful place"; note Gen. 41:52 for a popular etymology).

1 Joseph's younger son born in Egypt to Asenath. Ephraim was blessed by Jacob (Gen. 48:1–20) and favored over his brother Manasseh,

portending the ascendancy of the Ephraimite tribe.

2 An increasingly prominent Israelite tribe. Josh. 16 and 17:14–18 show the tribe and territory of Joseph replaced by two tribes, Ephraim and Manasseh (cf. Josh. 16:4). Josh. 16:5–10 gives Ephraim's boundaries from premonarchic times (prior to tenth century BCE). Josh. 17:7–12 gives the boundaries of Manasseh, showing Shechem with its fertile vale as belonging to Manasseh. But Ephraim's lands had better soil and were more easily protected than those of Manasseh, and eventually Shechem was also listed as part of "the hill country of Ephraim" (Josh. 20:7; 21:15, 20–21), reflecting perhaps the redefinition of districts that occurred under Solomon (1 Kings 4:7–19). Possibly 1 Chron. 7:28–29 retains an authentic memory of the further expansion of Ephraim. By the mid-eighth century BCE, Ephraim became for Isaiah and Hosea a designation for the whole northern kingdom; in Isaiah, it is allied with Syria in the "Syro-Ephraimite war" (7:1–17; cf. 2 Kings 16:5–9), and throughout Hosea it is the disloyal covenant partner of God (e.g., 5:3–14). Ephraim's immensely important role in Israel is indicated in part by the fact that Bethel, Shiloh, and at some point Shechem, all ancient worship centers, were in Ephraim. Joshua was an Ephraimite (Num. 13:8; cf. Deut. 34:9); he and Eleazar, who allotted the land (Num. 34:17; Josh. 14:1), were buried in Ephraimite towns (Josh. 24:29, 33). Other Ephraimites include Samuel (1 Sam. 1:1) and Jeroboam (1 Kings 11:26), men who embodied the northern attitude toward monarchy (i.e., severe limitation in view of and identification of God as Israel's true king). The judges Tola, Abdon, and Deborah were also all connected to Ephraim (Judg. 4:5; 10:1; 12:15). *See also* Bethel; Joseph; Manasseh; Shechem; Shiloh; tribes.

3 A town in 2 Sam. 13:23 where Absalom murdered Amnon, who had raped his sister Tamar. It was most likely located near Bethel in Ephraimite territory (see also John 11:54; 1 Macc. 11:34), but it could have derived its name simply from being a "fruitful place." *See also* Abdon; Absalom; Tamar.

4 A forest in the Transjordan near Mahanaim, where Absalom met his death. As with 3 above, it might have been so named because of its fruitfulness; otherwise its name could be evidence along with Judg. 12:4 that the Ephraimites controlled this portion of Manasseh's eastern holdings at some time.   E.F.C.

Ephraimite (ee'fray-uh-mit), the term for a person of the tribe of Ephraim (translating Heb. *'ephrati* in Judg. 12:5; 1 Sam. 1:1; 1 Kings 11:26, which is elsewhere translated "Ephrathite").

Ephrath (ef'rath).

1 The place where Rachel was buried, after she died while giving birth to Benjamin (Gen. 35:16, 19). It is identified in Genesis as Bethlehem (35:19; 48:7), but there could be a confusion of Ephrath and Ephrathah, which is associated with

Bethlehem in Ruth 4:11 and Mic. 5:1. Elsewhere, Rachel's tomb is said to be at Zelzah in territory of Benjamin (1 Sam. 10:2) near Ramah (Jer. 31:15). Thus, many scholars assume that Ephrath was in southern Benjamin.

2 The wife of Caleb (1 Chron. 2:9), spelled Ephrathah (with feminine endings) in 1 Chron. 2:50 and 4:4. *See also* Ephrathah.

Ephrathah (ef'ruh-thuh; Heb., "fertility").

1 The wife of Caleb, a descendant of Judah; the mother of Hur, the ancestor of Bethlehem, Kiriath-jearim, and Beth-gader (1 Chron. 2:50; 4:4). She is also called Ephrath (1 Chron. 2:19).

2 Another name for Bethlehem or the area immediately surrounding it (Ruth 4:11; Mic. 5:2). Jesse, David's father, is called an Ephrathite of Bethlehem (1 Sam. 17:12), as are Naomi's sons (Ruth 1:2). The identity of Ephrathah in Ps. 132:6, where it is associated with the "field of Jaar," is uncertain. Some scholars understand the field of Jaar to be Kiriath-jearim west of Jerusalem on the border between Judah and Benjamin. Ephrathah would then refer to the district around that field, perhaps including the area around Bethlehem some ten miles to the southeast. Other scholars simply equate Ephrathah here with Bethlehem. *See also* Bethlehem; Ephrath; Kiriath-jearim.

D.R.B.

Ephron (ee'fron).

1 A Hittite, the son of Zohar, who sold Abraham the cave of Machpelah as a burial place for Sarah (Gen. 23; 25:9; 49:30–31; 50:13). *See also* Hittites; Machpelah.

2 A city near Bethel mentioned in 2 Chron. 13:19. The place is not mentioned elsewhere, and there are variant readings in some manuscripts. The Hebrew Masoretic Text has "Ephrain," and other manuscripts identify the city as Ophrah (mentioned elsewhere in Josh. 18:23).

3 A major fortified city east of the Jordan between Karnaim and Beth-shan, captured by Judas Maccabeus (1 Macc. 5:45–51; 2 Macc. 12:27–28; Josephus *Antiquities* 12.8.5).

4 Mount Ephron, a hill on the Judean boundary (Josh. 15:9; 18:15).   G.M.T.

Epicureanism (ep'i-kyoo-ree'uhn-izm), a philosophical school founded by Epicurus (341–270 BCE). Epicureans discussed Paul's religious beliefs with him in Athens, after hearing him preach on the Areopagus (Acts 17:18). Epicurean teaching was expounded in a lengthy poem by the first-century BCE Latin writer Lucretius. Epicureans were often maligned as "atheists," since they held that sense perception was the only basis for knowledge. Everything had come into being out of atoms and the void. A random "swerve" in the path of the atoms caused the world to come into being and provided the material basis for free will, since no god had created or ruled over human beings, according to the Epicureans.

Epicureans argued against fear of death, since in their view death was merely the dissolution of the atoms entangled to make up the human, and they argued against fear of the gods, who enjoyed their own blessedness without concern for human affairs. The Epicureans counseled that people who were free from these fears should seek to live a peaceful life in which the body is free from pain and the mind is undisturbed. Consequently, one should choose a private life, pursuing this ideal in the pleasant company of friends.   P.P.

epistle, a written communication, sometimes considered to be synonymous with a letter and sometimes distinguished from the letter genre. The English word is derived from the Greek *epistolē*, a common word in the NT world for all kinds of letters. In the early twentieth century, the strong tendency was to distinguish letters from epistles: a "letter" was a personal and transitory correspondence, intended only for the person(s) to whom it was addressed; an "epistle" was a literary work intended for circulation. Thus, an epistle was both more impersonal and permanent than a letter, and its letterlike features (salutation, signature, etc.) were regarded as stylistic devices. According to this scheme, all of the undisputed letters of Paul (Romans, 1 and 2 Corinthians, Galatians, Philippians, 1 Thessalonians, and Philemon) as well as 2 and 3 John were considered to be genuine letters. Most, if not all, of the remaining NT documents that are in letter form were to be classified as epistles, viewed more as sermons or theological essays than actual letters. This organizational scheme, however, fell out of favor in the latter part of the twentieth century. There were disputes over which writings fit into which categories: on the one hand, it can be argued that all of the epistles/letters in the NT were intended for specific audiences; on the other hand, it can be argued that all of these writings were intended for some degree of circulation beyond their original recipients. By the end of the twentieth century, most scholars had ceased to distinguish between letters and epistles; the term "letter," furthermore, came to be the preferred term for all NT documents from Romans through Jude. *See also* letter.   J.L.W./M.A.P.

Epistles, Johannine. *See* John, Letters of.

Epistles, Pastoral. *See* Timothy, First Letter of Paul to; Timothy, Second Letter of Paul to; Titus, Letter of Paul to.

Erastus (i-ras'tuhs; Gk., "beloved"), three persons associated with Paul. It is possible that two of more of the following could be the same individual.

1 A city treasurer (or perhaps superintendent of public works), probably of Corinth, among Paul's "fellow workers" sending greetings (Rom. 16:23). A first-century paving stone bearing this name has been found in the ruins of Corinth.

MAJOR PHILOSOPHICAL SCHOOLS OF THE GRECO-ROMAN PERIOD

Epicureanism

- Traces its origins to Epicurus (341–270 BCE).

- Allows for free will, questioning the role of fate (or of the gods) to determine human lives.

- *Pleasure* is the ultimate goal of life, but true pleasure is found through the attainment of tranquility (freedom from anxiety), not through simple gratification of desires.

- Those seeking true pleasure exercise their free will to enjoy good things in moderation and to make responsible choices that improve their lives and the lives of others.

- Those seeking true pleasure avoid those things that lead to disappointment, pain, or grief (romantic love, emotional attachment, political commitments, devotion to material things).

- Rejects any sense of afterlife; what meaning life has is to be found here and now.

- Sometimes degenerated into a notion of freedom from accountability or responsibility (rather than from anxiety); proponents then regarded as "pleasure seekers" in a crass sense and the philosophy viewed as license for self-indulgence.

Stoicism

- Traces its origins to Zeno (333–264 BCE), reshaped by Epictetus in first century CE.

- Everything is predetermined—history is cyclical and happens repeatedly.

- *Virtue* is what matters most in life—and it is attainable through acceptance of fate.

- The person seeking virtue appreciates the logic of the universe (called Logos or Reason) and is indifferent to circumstances ("No reason for joy, still less for grief").

- The moral obligation of virtue accentuated by Epictetus: love and respect for all people, whose merits and station in life lie beyond their control.

Cynicism

- Traces its origins to Diogenes of Sinope (ca. 410–324 BCE).

- More a lifestyle than dogma—emphasized radical *authenticity* and *independence*.

- *Athenticity* attained through repudiation of shame: no embarrassment over bodily features or functions; no concern for reputation or status.

- *Independence* attained through renunciation of what cannot be obtained freely, by embracing simplicity and voluntary poverty and desiring to have only what is natural and necessary.

- *Diatribe* employed for pedagogical instruction—a style of teaching or argument that uses rhetorical questions to engage in conversation with an imaginary partner.

From Mark Allan Powell, *Introducing the New Testament* (courtesy, Baker Academic)

2 Paul's colleague sent with Timothy from Ephesus into Macedonia (Acts 19:22).

3 An associate who remained in Corinth (2 Tim. 4:20).

Erech (ee´rik; Akkadian Uruk), the ancient name of a southern Babylonian city, now known as Warka, situated near the Euphrates River. The Table of Nations in Gen. 10 includes Erech in the kingdom of Nimrod. Ezra 4:9 mentions Ashurbanipal's seventh-century deportation of Erech citizens to Samaria. Archaeological excavations reveal that by the fourth millennium BCE, Erech (or Uruk, as the Babylonians called it) covered approximately two hundred acres; and the first evidence of pictographic writing and numerical notation on clay tablets appeared ca. 3100 BCE. This fits with Babylonian mythology, which identifies "Uruk" as the place where the goddess Inanna brought the arts of civilization to humanity. The city was holy to Inanna and to Anu, head of the Sumerian pantheon. It housed two major temple complexes; Inanna's temple, called Eanna, preserves eighteen archaic levels, and the "white temple" of Anu remains the best example of a Sumerian "high temple" discovered thus far. Another archaeological find, the Uruk Vase, depicts components of Sumerian cultic practices. The city also housed an important cuneiform scribal school and astronomical observatory until the last century of the first millennium BCE.

L.E.P.

Esar-haddon (ee'suhr-had'uhn; Assyrian Assur-aha-iddina), king of Assyria 681–669 BCE. Esar-haddon came to the throne after the murder of his father, Sennacherib, by his brothers. He was not an accomplice to the murder. He rebuilt Babylon and became king of Babylonia; he defended the northern borders against Cimmerian and Scythian incursions; he reasserted and strengthened imperial control, especially in the west, in part for the purposes of controlling mercantile centers (e.g., Phoenicia), and he expanded the borders of the empire into Egypt. Some of the cultural and religious policies of King Manasseh of Judah (2 Kings 21:1–18) may have been due to the constant presence of Assyrians in the west, although the Assyrians did not require vassals to accept Assyrian religious practices. During Esar-haddon's reign, diviners and exorcists exercised particular influence in the Assyrian royal court, in part perhaps because of the king's chronic ailments. It is likely that he suffered from a skin disease, systemic *lupus erythematosus*. A large body of correspondence has survived from the last three or four years of Esar-haddon's reign, and these letters are a rich source of information about Mesopotamian religion and medicine. Around 672 BCE, Esar-haddon established the succession to his throne(s): Ashurbanipal was to be king of Assyria, and Shamashshumukin, king of Babylonia. A treaty binding governors and vassals to abide by and support this succession was drawn up. The vassal treaties show points of similarity to Israelite covenant material in Deuteronomy. *See also* Manasseh.   I.T.A.

Esau (ee'saw), the older son of Isaac and Rebekah (Gen. 25–36). At his birth, Esau was unusually red and hairy in appearance, descriptions that involve puns on his legacy. Esau eventually settled in Seir (related to the Hebrew word for "hair") and his descendants were said to live in Edom (from the Hebrew word for "red"; Esau himself is also sometimes called Edom; cf. Gen. 36:1, 8). His birth was also noteworthy in that he was the first of two twins, and the second born (Jacob) came out of the womb grasping Esau's heel: a portent of usurpation. Esau was "a hunter and a man of the field," while Jacob was "a quiet man, living in tents" (Gen. 25:26); furthermore, "Isaac loved Esau, because he was fond of game, but Rebekah loved Jacob" (25:37). As the firstborn, Esau was entitled to the primary blessing and birthright of his family, but he forfeited both, due to his own foolishness (25:27–34) and the trickery of his mother and Jacob (27:1–45). The Genesis account relates that, after losing this blessing, Esau wanted to kill Jacob (27:41–45), but after some time his anger passed and the two were reconciled (33:44–49; cf. 27:44–45).

Esau would become the paradigm of the rejected elder son displaced by the younger, a recurring motif in the Bible (cf., e.g., Gen. 49:17–19). Although Esau is portrayed in Genesis as gracious (33:1–17), in the ongoing Hebrew tradition he

comes to be mentioned primarily by way of association with the territory of Edom, Israel's rival, and so the motif of his rejection by God becomes dominant (Mal. 1:2–3; Deut. 2:4–29; Jer. 49:8–10; Obad. 6–21). Esau is also mentioned in the NT writings. Heb. 11:20 portrays him as a recipient of blessing, but then 12:16 calls him "an immoral and godless person who sold his birthright for a single meal." Quoting Mal. 1:2–3, Paul cites him as an example of one who was not chosen by God (Rom. 9:13). *See also* Edom; Jacob.   W.B.

eschatology (es'kuh-tol'uh-jee), beliefs or teaching about last things. The word derives from *eschatos,* the Greek word for "last." Biblical writings often distinguish between the present age or eon, the period of history in which life is being lived, and the future, coming age, or period of transformed existence that God will bring at the end of history. The latter age or eon is sometimes also referred to as the age to come, the kingdom of God, the new world, or messianic age. The term "eschatology" is inherently ambiguous, since it may refer to teachings about events expected to take place during the last days (which belong to the present age) or about phenomena associated with the age to come.

In the Hebrew Bible: Many biblical texts suggest that on the "day of the LORD," God will deliver people by overthrowing their enemies (Amos 5:18–20). Some later texts likewise give expression to the hope that, on the "day of the LORD," God will bring judgment against other nations for their offenses (e.g., Isa. 13:1–19:17; Jer. 46–51; Ezek. 25–32; Obad.; Zeph. 2:4–15). Generally, the implication is that after the "day of the LORD" these nations will never again cause Israel or Judah grief. Most of the prophets, however, warned their contemporary Israelites (or Judahites) that God would bring disasters upon them as well because they had violated the covenant relationship. Such violations consisted of worshiping other deities, failing to practice justice and mercy, or otherwise neglecting to observe God's commandments or walk according to God's ways (e.g., Jer. 2–8; Hos. 4–10; Amos 4–8; Mic. 1–7).

Most of the prophets also promised that God would make a new beginning with the people. In many texts, such promises give expression to the hope that God will transform the conditions of historical existence, bringing about a new or messianic age (e.g., Isa. 2:2–4; 11; 35; Jer. 31:1–37; Ezek. 16:53–63; Hos. 2:14–23). These texts often look for the appearance of David, or one of his descendants, who will rule over the newly transformed world on God's behalf (e.g., Isa. 11:1–5; Jer. 30:9; Ezek. 37:24–25; Zech. 3:8; 9:9). Other texts describe transformed conditions, but without mentioning any Davidic or other human king (e.g., Isa. 2:2–4; Jer. 31:1–37; Zech. 14:1–21). A few prophetic visions look for the creation of a "new heaven" and a "new earth" (Isa. 65:17; 66:22).

Among the eschatological events that would mark the beginning of, or life in, this new age were the return of Elijah (Mal. 4:5–6); certain cosmic signs or phenomena (Joel 2:30–32); the reunification of Israel and Judah (Ezek. 37:15–22); the establishment of a new covenant (Jer. 31:31–34; Ezek. 11:19–20; 34:25–31; Hos. 2:18–23); and peace among all nations (Isa. 2:2–4; Mic. 4:1–4), whose people, in some visions, would join in honoring and worshiping God (e.g., Isa. 2:2–3; 19:23–25; 66:18–19; 23; Zech. 14:16–19; Tob. 13:11). Some prophets also looked for the new age as a time of peace and harmony among all creatures, human and animal alike (e.g., Isa. 11:6–9; 65:25; Hos. 2:18). It would be a time when the earth would yield preternatural crops of grain and fruit—perhaps signifying that the ground was no longer "cursed" because of human disobedience (Isa. 25:6; Ezek. 47:6–12; Joel 2:21–26; 3:18; Amos 9:13; cf. Gen. 3:17–19; 4:12). Some texts visualize the new age as one in which Israel or the Jewish people will rule over other nations or one in which other nations will no longer exist (e.g., Joel 3:19–21; Obad.; Zeph. 2:4–15). A few passages in Ezekiel anticipate that wild beasts that threaten human life will be removed (34:25–28). Ezekiel and Zechariah picture a magnificent new temple at the center of the transformed, messianic world (Ezek. 40–48; Zech. 1–8).

Jewish Writings from the Second Temple Period: Additional eschatological themes begin to appear in the apocryphal/deuterocanonical writings as well as in the Pseudepigrapha and in the Dead Sea Scrolls. There are references to holy angels or "watchers" who function as divine emissaries or viceroys (e.g., Dan. 10:13–14; Tob. 12:15) and also to Belial (or Beliar), the devil, Satan, demons, or other evil, cosmic, quasi-supernatural beings bent upon causing harm (e.g., Tob. 3:7–8; Wis. 2:24; *Jub.* 10:5–9; *1 Enoch* 15:11–16:1). At some point in the future, God and the angels will fight these evil powers and, after a time of terrible tribulation, prevail over them (Add. to Esther 11:5–9; Qumran *War Scroll;* 2 Esd. 13:31–34; cf. Ezek. 38:1–39:20; Dan. 12:1; Joel 3:9–15). There will be a day of judgment, and then God's reign will be established forever on earth as well as in heaven. Jerusalem will be decked with jewels (Tob. 13:16–18). The righteous will enjoy abundant food and drink—sometimes characterized by interpreters as "the messianic banquet" (e.g., *2 Enoch* 8; *2 Bar.* 29:3–8). But the wicked will be condemned to eternal torment or even extinction (e.g., Jth. 16:17; *1 Enoch* 103:7–8; 2 Esd. 7:61; cf. Isa. 66:24). Some of these motifs or expectations also appear in the background in many early Christian texts.

NT Gospels: Different understandings of NT eschatology derive from variant interpretations of Jesus's teaching and preaching about the kingdom of God in the Synoptic Gospels. On the one hand, a number of texts have been viewed as indicating that Jesus expected the kingdom of God to come in the near future (e.g., Matt. 4:17; 6:10; 10:5–23; 16:27–28; Mark 1:14–15; 9:1; 15:43; Luke 9:26–27; 10:1–12; 11:2; 21:31–32). On the other hand, other texts have been interpreted to mean that Jesus believed the kingdom of God was already present, "realized" or actualized in his own person and ministry (many of Jesus's parables are read to this effect, in addition to Matt. 11:11–22; 12:28; Luke 11:20; 17:20–21). Studies in NT eschatology have also focused on Gospel materials dealing with the future coming or appearance of the Son of Man (e.g., Matt. 19:28; 25:31; Mark 8:38; 13:24–27; 14:62; Luke 12:8); some texts appear to link the coming of the Son of Man with that of the kingdom of God (e.g., Matt. 16:24–28; 19:16–30; Luke 17:20–24; 21:25–32).

In recent discussions, most scholars have tended to affirm that the Gospel authors believed the kingdom to be already present *in some sense* in the life and work of Jesus, while also believing that the consummation of the kingdom *in a fuller sense* would not come until the Parousia of the Son of Man. There is discussion in NT studies as to whether the Son of Man sayings and/or the future kingdom sayings ought to be regarded as authentic utterances of Jesus or as latter attributions to him on the part of the early church. Either way, however, some eschatological expectations expressed in the Synoptic Gospels had clearly not been fulfilled at the time those Gospels were written: the world had not yet been transformed; the anticipated final tribulation had not yet occurred (Matt. 6:13; Mark 13:19; 14:38); the resurrection of the dead was still to come (Matt. 12:41–42; Luke 11:30–32); the judgment had not yet taken place (Matt. 11:21–24; 12:38–42; 25:31–46; Mark 9:43–48). Still, it appears that the Gospel writers did believe that some events associated with the eschatological timetable had occurred or were occurring: John the Baptist had come, in the role of Elijah, the final prophet and preacher of repentance before "the great and terrible day of the LORD" (Matt. 11:2–15; 17:10–13; Mark 9:9–13; cf. Mal. 4:5–6); the exorcisms and healings performed by Jesus and his followers were a sign that the strong power of evil had been curtailed (Matt. 12:29–30); the good news of the kingdom was being preached throughout the nations (Matt. 28:19; cf. 24:14); and if Jesus himself was to be the designated Messiah of the new age, then that Messiah could be said to be already present with the community (Matt. 18:20).

The Gospel of John offers a different eschatological focus. There are references to the "last day" (e.g., 6:39–40, 54; 11:24), but there is very little attention to the return or Second Coming of Christ (mentioned only in 21:22). The emphasis, rather, is on the qualitative change in one's life that is effected by knowing the truth revealed by Jesus (cf. 10:10; 8:32; 20:31). Eschatological themes normally associated with the end times are present in the Gospel of John, but they tend to be offered with emphasis on present-day experience. Thus, one can enter the kingdom of God now by being "born from above" (or "born again," 3:3). Likewise, judgment occurs in the present: those who do not believe in the Son have been condemned already (3:18) and those who believe in Jesus have already passed from death to life (5:24). Jesus will come for all individuals at some point, to take them to his Father's house (14:1–3) but, for believers, eternal life has already begun (3:36).

NT Letters: Many NT writers urged readers to look for Jesus's coming "soon" or within their own lifetimes (Rom. 13:11–12; 16:20; 1 Cor. 7:29; Phil. 4:5; Heb. 10:37; James 5:8; 1 Pet. 4:7). At the same time, the NT letters recognize that strategies for mission, leadership, discipline, and ethics have to be developed for living in the interim before that happens. In general, the undisputed letters of Paul (Romans, 1 and 2 Corinthians, Galatians, Philippians, 1 Thessalonians, Philemon) reveal more of an accent on imminent expectation than do many of the other NT letters. Paul assumes that he will be alive to see the Parousia (1 Thess. 4:17), and he even questions the advisability of believers marrying and starting families since "the appointed time is short" and "the present form of this world is passing away" (1 Cor. 7:8, 25–31). Paul does affirm that those "in Christ" are already experiencing "a new creation" that began with Jesus's death and resurrection (2 Cor. 5:17; Gal. 6:15), but when the Parousia comes, the "dead in Christ" will be raised, those still alive will be "changed" or transformed "in the twinkling of an eye," and all will join together "in the air" to enjoy life with Christ forevermore (1 Cor. 15:35–55; Phil. 3:20–21; 1 Thess. 4:13–18; cf. 2 Tim. 4:18). In Ephesians, by contrast, believers who have not yet died are said to be already seated with Christ in the heavenly places (2:6). Indeed, in Colossians, events normally associated with the end times are said to have already occurred: believers have already been rescued from the power of darkness (1:13); they have already been transferred to the kingdom of God's beloved Son (1:13); they have already been raised with Christ (2:12; 3:1); the spiritual powers that might oppose them have already been disarmed and Christ has already made a public display of his triumph over them (2:15). If one asks *when* all these things happened, the answer might be that they have already occurred *in the future*—these letters seem less concerned with temporal chronology than with explicating the absolute certainty of what God has accomplished. Other letters attributed to Paul, especially the Pastoral Letters, are devoted to establishing the church as an institution that will have the stability to endure for generations (if necessary). A few NT books seem intent on explaining why the end has not come as soon as some expected (2 Pet. 3:11–13; Jude 17–21) or, indeed, with explaining why it might still be some time in coming (2 Thess. 1:5–10). Finally, the book of Revelation offers a vivid vision of the end times as a period of intense suffering and apostasy, culminating in God's creation of "new heavens" and a "new earth" in place of the old (21:1; cf. 2 Pet. 3:10–13). *See also* apocalyptic literature; eternal life; heaven; hell; judgment, day of; kingdom of God; messiah; millennium; Parousia; resurrection; son of man, Son of Man.

Bibliography

Allison, Dale C., Jr. *The End of the Ages Has Come.* Fortress, 1985.

Gloer, W. Hulitt, ed. *Eschatology in the New Testament.* Hendrickson, 1988.

Hanson, Paul D., ed. *Visionaries and Their Apocalypses.* Fortress, 1983.

Powell, Mark Allan. *Introducing the New Testament: A Historical, Literary, and Theological Survey.* Baker Academic, 2009.

Sullivan, Clayton. *Rethinking Realized Eschatology.* Mercer University Press, 1988.

R.H.H./M.A.P.

Esdraelon (ez´druh-ee´luhn; Gk. for "Jezreel"). *See* Jezreel.

Esdras (ez´druhs), **First Book of,** an alternative version of 2 Chron. 35:1–36:23, all of Ezra, and Neh. 7:38–8:12. It was included in the LXX and is regarded as canonical scripture by Greek Orthodox and Slavonic Orthodox churches, but is not among the books considered deuterocanonical by Roman Catholics, nor is it listed as part of the Apocrypha by Protestant Christians. It is actually called 2 Esdras in the Slavonic Bible (where the book otherwise known as Ezra is called 1 Esdras). It was also called 3 Ezra in the Vulgate (where Ezra is listed as 1 Ezra and Nehemiah as 2 Ezra). Since the sixteenth century, Roman Catholics have sometimes included 1 Esdras (along with 2 Esdras and the Prayer of Manasseh) in an appendix following the NT.

The work is either the remnant of a Greek translation of Chronicles, Ezra, and Nehemiah or a selection of parts of those books that were edited and translated into Greek sometime late in the second century BCE. The translation reflects

OUTLINE OF CONTENTS

1 Esdras

VARIANT DESIGNATIONS FOR EZRA, NEHEMIAH, 1 ESDRAS, AND 2 ESDRAS

Contemporary English Nomenclature	Greek Orthodox Tradition (LXX)	Latin Tradition (Vulgate)	Slavonic Orthodox Tradition
Ezra	2 Esdras	1 Ezra	1 Esdras
Nehemiah	2 Esdras	2 Ezra	Nehemiah
1 Esdras	1 Esdras	3 Ezra	2 Esdras
2 Esdras	(not included)	4 Ezra*	3 Esdras

*Note: 4 Ezra is sometimes used for chaps. 3–14 only; then chaps. 1–2 are called 5 Ezra, and chaps. 15–16 are called 6 Ezra.

greater freedom than is evident in the individual Greek translations of Chronicles, Ezra, and Nehemiah that appear in the LXX. Along with the Additions to Esther and the Additions to Daniel, the existence of 1 Esdras suggests that the format and content of some late biblical books were still in flux during the second and first centuries BCE.

The purpose of 1 Esdras is not certain, although concentration on the temple, its worship, and leaders who reformed or restored its worship suggests that it may have been intended to make a statement of some sort concerning the temple or its leadership. The book begins with the Passover celebrated at the culmination of Josiah's reform of the temple (ca. 622 BCE), then moves swiftly to the restoration of the temple and its worship under Jeshua and Zerubbabel (516 BCE), and concludes with Ezra's reform a generation or so later. It builds up the role of Zerubbabel at the expense of Sheshbazzar, the leader of the first group of returned exiles in 538 BCE, and minimizes that of Nehemiah in relation to Ezra, whom it calls the "high priest" (9:40, 49). It also contains a unique, fanciful account of three bodyguards in the court of Darius (3:1–5:6), an account told in order to honor the wisdom of Zerubbabel and to explain how Darius came to commission him to return to Jerusalem and restore the temple. The history of the restoration given by 1 Esdras appears to be somewhat confused, but the first-century CE Jewish historian Josephus used this book as his primary source for the period when he wrote his *Antiquities*. *See also* Apocrypha/deuterocanonical literature; exile; Josephus; Septuagint; temple, the.

D.W.S.

Esdras, Second Book of,

a Jewish apocalypse dating from the very end of the first century CE. It is regarded as canonical scripture by the Slavonic Orthodox church, where it is referred to as 3 Esdras (since in the Slavonic church "1 Esdras" is used for the book of Ezra, and "2 Esdras" is used for what is more often called 1 Esdras). It is called 4 Ezra in the Vulgate (where Ezra is listed as 1 Ezra, Nehemiah as 2 Ezra, and 1 Esdras as 3 Ezra). Furthermore, since it is now widely recognized that chaps. 1–2 and 15–16 represent Christian additions to the original book, they are sometimes called 5 Ezra and 6 Ezra, respectively, and the term 4 Ezra is reserved for chaps. 3–14 only. Second Esdras is not one of the books considered deuterocanonical by Roman Catholics, nor is it listed as part of the Apocrypha for Protestant Christians. Since the sixteenth century, however, Roman Catholics have sometimes included 2 Esdras (along with 1 Esdras and the Prayer of Manasseh) in an appendix following the NT. The book was probably written in Hebrew and then translated into Greek, but neither Hebrew nor Greek manuscripts have survived. The only extant copies of 2 Esdras from antiquity are translations made from the Greek, including Latin, Syriac, Ethiopic, and Armenian versions.

The material in 2 Esdras was written under the pseudonym of Ezra in order to use the conquest of Jerusalem by the Babylonians as a means of reflecting upon the intense suffering occasioned by the destruction of Jerusalem by Rome in 70 CE. The apocalypse in chaps. 3–14 is divided into seven visions, some of which contain dialogues between Ezra and the angel Uriel concerning God's justice in permitting the chosen people to suffer at the hands of the unrighteous Babylonians (i.e., the Romans). Other visions deal allegorically with history, the sufferings of the present, and the coming of the messianic age. They are somewhat similar to the visions of Revelation. The seventh vision, chap. 14, parallels Ezra to Moses and has Ezra dictate while in a trance the twenty-four books of the Hebrew Bible lost in the burning of Jerusalem. The book thus reflects a particular definition of the canon of scripture, which implicitly treats Moses and Ezra as the beginning and end of revelation.

Although chaps. 3–14 ultimately conclude that the mysteries of sin and suffering are unfathomable, they do develop a theology of history that claims that the whole of the human race from Adam on is sinful, subject to the evil inclination, and therefore deserving God's punishment. After the fashion of the wisdom tradition, various analogies are drawn from nature and human life to deal with the limits of human knowledge and to justify the suffering of the righteous and God's slow pace in setting things right. The goal of history is a four-hundred-year messianic age, following which the messiah will die and all things will be returned to a seven-day primeval silence. Then will come the resurrection and Last Judgment. The sixth vision of the man from the sea in chap. 13 is remarkable in that it is based on Dan. 7:13–14 and thus plays an important role in scholarly discussions of the christological title "Son of Man" in the NT. *See also* apocalyptic literature; Apocrypha/deuterocanonical literature; eschatology; messiah; pseudonym; son of man, Son of Man.

OUTLINE OF CONTENTS

2 Esdras

I. An apocalypse of Christian composition concerned with the rejection of Israel and the announcement of the rewards of the coming kingdom to all of the nations (chaps. 1–2)

II. A Jewish apocalypse consisting of seven visions (chaps. 3–14)

   A. Vision 1: a dialogue between Ezra and Uriel concerning God's justice and the seed of evil sown in Adam (3:1–5:20)

   B. Vision 2: a dialogue concerning the mystery of God's choice of Israel in light of the people's subsequent suffering (5:21–6:34)

   C. Vision 3: a dialogue concerning creation, the messianic age, and the subsequent judgment (6:35–9:25)

   D. Vision 4: Ezra encounters Zion as a woman mourning for her dead son (9:26–10:59)

   E. Vision 5: an allegorical vision of an eagle (cf. Dan. 7:3–8), representing the Roman Empire (chaps. 11–12)

   F. Vision 6: an allegorical vision of a man from the sea (chap. 13; cf. Dan. 7:13–14)

   G. Vision 7: the legend of Ezra and the restoration of the scriptures (chap. 14)

III. An apocalypse of Christian origin describing the tribulations of the end of history (chaps. 15–16)

D.W.S.

Esh-baal. *See* Ishbaal.

Eshcol (esh′kol; Heb., "cluster").

1 The name of the valley near Hebron, in south-central Judea, from which spies sent by Moses brought back a cluster of grapes and some pomegranates and figs (Num. 13:23–24). Although this fruit indicated a good land, their report of giants discouraged the people of Israel from entering the land (Num. 32:9).

2 The brother of Mamre and Aner, Amorite allies of Abram, who helped him rescue Lot when Lot was taken captive by a coalition of eastern kings (Gen. 14:13, 24). *See also* Mamre.

Eshtaol (esh′tay-uhl), a city in the lowlands of Judah counted as belonging to both Judah and Dan (Josh. 15:33; 19:41). It was originally occupied by Danites (Judg. 13:25; 18:2–11) and then later occupied by Judahites when the Danites were forced to move to the north (Judg. 18:11). Evidence of this is seen in 1 Chron. 2:53, where Eshtaolites are regarded as descendants of Judah. It is also possible that the camp of Dan at Kiriath-jearim (Judg. 18:12) led to a mixing of the two tribes in this region. Eshtaol is tentatively located near modern Ishwa, about fourteen miles west of Jerusalem and about six miles slightly southwest of Kiriath-jearim. D.R.B.

Eshtemoa (esh′tuh-moh′uh).

1 A city in the hill country of Judah that was given to the Levites (Josh. 21:14). David shared his booty with the city following his defeat of the Amalekites (1 Sam. 30:28). It is also called Eshtemoh (Josh. 15:50) and is tentatively identified as modern es-Samu, about ten miles south and slightly east of Hebron.

2 A son of Ishbah, descendant of Simeon (1 Chron. 4:17). It is not clear whether Eshtemoa the Maacathite (4:19) is the same person or of a different family.

Essenes (es′eenz), a sect of Judaism from the middle of the second century BCE until the war with Rome in 66–70 CE. They are described by the first-century CE authors Josephus and Philo and mentioned by some non-Jewish writers. They are usually identified with the inhabitants of Qumran who wrote the Dead Sea Scrolls. The meaning of

Aerial view of Qumran showing Cave 4. Qumran is at the northwest edge of the Dead Sea.

the Greek name "Essenes" is unclear; it may come from the Aramaic for "pious" or "healers."

Archaeological research at Qumran, data from ancient sources, and cryptic allusions to the sect's history in its writings suggest that the group, whose members were probably some of the Hasideans who supported the Maccabees, withdrew from Jerusalem and active participation in the temple, because Jonathan, the brother of Judas Maccabeus, assumed the high-priesthood in 152 BCE, though he was not from the correct, hereditary priestly family. The group was led by a prominent priest whose identity is hidden behind the designation "Teacher of Righteousness." The community built a complex of buildings on the cliffs around the Dead Sea at Qumran, between Jericho and En-gedi, and went through several stages of development there, including a refounding of the community after an earthquake in 31 BCE. The community was persecuted and attacked by Jonathan and survived other pressures, but was finally destroyed by the Romans in 68 CE. Some Essenes also lived in towns and cities, probably in small communities, and a few are mentioned by name in Josephus's works as playing a political role.

The Qumran community was sharply divided into hereditary priests and nonpriests. They were ruled by an elaborate hierarchy of officers and councils and guided by a detailed set of rules based on biblical law. Numerous practices were peculiar to this sect. Property was held in common, celibacy was practiced, a high state of ritual purity was maintained, economic and social relations with nonmembers were greatly restricted, and admission to full membership was preceded by three years' probation. Solemn ritual meals were held regularly, participation in the ritual of the Jerusalem temple was forbidden for as long as the temple was improperly run, and detailed rules of behavior supported a rigorous ethic that was sanctioned by judges and punishments, including excommunication. The Essenes who lived outside the Qumran community seem to have married, had private property, and engaged in some social relations with outsiders.

Besides some biblical books and Jewish pseudepigraphical writings, the Essenes had their own biblical commentaries, hymns, rules, and apocalyptic writings. Though Josephus compares them to the Greco-Roman Stoics, the Essenes were apocalyptic in their thought and orientation, maintaining ritual purity, ethical probity, and spiritual readiness for the intervention of God to destroy evil. No convincing evidence has been produced to demonstrate any dependence on Essene thought by John the Baptist, Jesus, or other early Christian leaders. The similarities that exist are more likely due to their common Jewish background than to any direct relationship. *See also* Dead Sea Scrolls; Qumran, Khirbet.

Bibliography

Vermes, Geza. *The Dead Sea Scrolls: Qumran in Perspective.* Collins, 1977.

———. *The Dead Sea Scrolls in English.* 2nd ed. Penguin, 1975.   A.J.S.

Esther, Additions to, five passages found in the LXX version of Esther, but not in the original Hebrew. Jerome, in making his Vulgate translation of Esther, removed all but one of these passages and placed them at the end of the book, so that chapter and verse numbers in modern editions treat them as though they were an ending to Esther.

The purpose of the additions is to give a more specifically religious cast to the book as well as to the festival of Purim associated with it. Since the Hebrew version of Esther never mentions God, its canonical status among Jews was sometimes a matter of dispute. The additions attribute the deliverance to God through the device of the apocalyptic vision and its interpretation, which now begin and end the book, as well as through the composition of prayers for Mordecai and Esther. Salvation now comes not as a consequence of Esther's courage and beauty, but as a result of her piety, in order to show that God answers prayer and protects God's people. The vision draws upon the genre of the apocalypse current in the Hellenistic age to suggest that God is in control of history. The two decrees of Artaxerxes may have been composed in Greek with the intention of adding authenticity to the

OUTLINE OF CONTENTS

Additions to Esther

The following outline shows the way in which the LXX intersperses the additions (in italic below) with the original text of the book. The LXX also embellishes the passages it translates from the Hebrew version, adding references to God and altering the plot at several points.

story, but the other passages were probably written first in Hebrew. Along with 1 Esdras and the Additions to Daniel, the Additions to Esther suggests the fluidity of the biblical text within the Hellenistic era. The colophon of the Greek version attributes translation of the book to a certain Lysimachus, apparently a Hellenistic Jew, and suggests that it was brought to Egypt in the fourth year of Ptolemy and Cleopatra (either 114 BCE, 77 BCE, or 44 BCE, depending upon which royal pair is intended), possibly in an effort to introduce Purim to the Alexandrian Jewish community. The Additions to Esther is treated as a part of the Apocrypha by Protestant Christians, but is regarded as deuterocanonical by Roman Catholic and Eastern Orthodox Christians. *See also* Apocrypha/deuterocanonical literature; Daniel, Additions to; Esdras, First Book of; Esther, book of; Purim, Festival of.   D.W.S.

Esther, book of, the last of the Five Scrolls, or Megilloth, found in the Writings section, or Ketuvim, of the Tanakh (Jewish Bible). Each of the Five Scrolls is connected with a different holiday or commemoration in the Jewish calendar. Esther is associated with Purim, a festival of freedom, where Jews celebrate a time when they were scattered across the world and yet were respected and allowed to defend their way of life. The Christian OT places Esther at the end of the historical books, after Ezra and Nehemiah.

Contents: The story of Esther revolves around four central characters: Esther (whose Jewish name was Hadassah), Mordecai, King Ahasuerus, and Haman. As the tale begins, the king throws a lavish party at which he summons his wife, Queen Vashti, to come before him and a myriad of drunk men, wearing her crown. There have been various arguments about whether she was called to wear

Events in the story of Esther: Ahasuerus selects Esther, Haman and Mordecai, and Haman hangs from the gallows; nineteenth-century embroidered sheet.

only her crown. The queen regards this request to appear before the drunken mass (clothed or not) as damaging to her honor. She refuses, and this slight enrages the king. He dethrones Vashti and proceeds to hold a contest for the next queen. A young Jewish orphan named Esther wins and becomes queen, but she hides her Jewish identity from the court. Shortly after becoming queen, her cousin and guardian Mordecai discovers a plot to assassinate King Ahasuerus, which Esther reports to the king.

Haman becomes second-in-command of Persia, but is angered when Mordecai refuses to bow before him. Haman then plots to kill not only Mordecai, but all of the Jews. Mordecai learns of this plot and calls upon Esther to appeal to the king to save her people. Esther hesitates because of the danger of coming before the king without being summoned, but is eventually persuaded to do so. She enters, receives an audience, and invites the king to come to a dinner party, where she will tell him her true request. Before the party, Haman is further enraged by Mordecai's lack of deference and has a gallows built in order to hang him. That night, the king is reading through the annals, discovers that Mordecai has gone unrewarded for thwarting the assassination plot, and asks Haman how the king should reward a faithful citizen. Haman, thinking it is he who will receive this honor, talks of a royal procession with elegant robes and a kingly horse. The king then instructs Haman to provide these for Mordecai.

At the party, Esther pleads for the Jewish people, getting the unwitting king to allow her to draft a law to protect her people. When the king steps out for a moment, Haman falls upon the queen's couch to beg for his life and safety. When the king returns, he believes that Haman is making advances toward the queen and has him hanged on the very gallows Haman had made for Mordecai. Esther drafts a bill allowing the Jewish people to protect themselves in case of attack. Then the Jews kill hundreds of their enemies in Susa and thousands throughout the empire.

Background: The book of Esther is set in the Jewish Dispersion during the Achaemenid period of the Persian Empire. The king Ahasuerus is known to historians as Xerxes I (486–465 BCE). The story takes place in the Persian royal courts, fitting within the "court tale" subgenre of the Jewish short story (see Dan. 1–6 and the story of Joseph in Gen. 37–50 for other examples). More specifically, it is often read as a comedy.

Although the story takes place within a historical setting, most scholars argue that it is not a historical narrative. Certain elements, in particular, betray what might be regarded as literary fictions. For example, Mordecai is named as having come over in the exile from Israel, but this would make him well over one hundred years old, given the temporal setting of the story. The extravagant 180-day banquets, the one-year contest for the role of queen, and the excessive number of satraps and provinces mentioned likewise suggest that the narrative is not strictly historical in nature.

The origin of the story of Esther is ambiguous and may have a pagan prehistory. Mordecai could be a type of Marduk, the Persian high god. Esther's name is linguistically connected to the name of Ishtar, a Persian goddess. Yet regardless of its origin, the book now has a historical and biblical setting. The biblical setting is manifest through the use of genealogies. Mordecai is a descendant of Benjamin through Kish (making him a descendant of Saul), and Haman is a descendant of Agag the Amalekite (see 1 Sam. 15). These identifications provide a particular backdrop for the story in biblical history, since Saul is reported to have failed to destroy Agag and the Amalekites as ordered by Samuel. Mordecai's revenge is thus a partial fulfillment of what his ancestor Saul failed to do to Haman's ancestors.

An anonymous book, Esther was most likely written in the eastern Dispersion of the third or fourth century BCE. Gottwald, however, argues that the book was written during the Maccabean period, since the Persians were famously tolerant toward the Jews, and the book of Esther shows an oppressive streak in the ruling authorities, which would have been more characteristic of Jewish life under the Hellenistic regimes.

Themes: The book of Esther is presented as an explanation for the celebration of Purim, which is essentially a festival of self-defense and freedom, core components of Jewish identity. The book cautions Jews not to forget their identity or to think they can be safe by assimilating to society. Survival and prosperity are obtained when Jews stick together. Esther is put forth as a model of faithful women in the history of Israel, because of her courage and devotion to her people.

The book is also full of ironic and dramatic reversals. Vashti, a Persian, is replaced by Esther, a Jew, as queen of Persia. Haman prides himself in his power and dislikes Mordecai's lack of deference, yet it is Mordecai who ends with the power, while Haman is stripped of his power and his life. Although God is not mentioned in the book, many interpreters have read Esther as a book about God's hidden providence. Mordecai's statement that Esther was made queen for "just such a time as this" (4:14) has been seen as a subtle pointer to God's providence. Also, Mordecai's understanding that, if Esther fails, the Jewish people will find deliverance from "another quarter" (4:14) has been viewed as a reference to trust in God. Wyler argues that the book centers around Esther's struggle with her dual identity as a Jew and as queen of Persia. Levenson argues that the book of Esther is a ten-chapter chiasm centered on chap. 6, with parallel events on either side (e.g., anti-Jewish edict in 3:12–15, pro-Jewish edict in 8:9–14). The issue of Esther's Jewish identity is evident in the chiasm as well. She identifies herself as a Gentile by taking the role of the queen (2:10–20), and eventually Gentiles identify themselves as Jews at the end of the story (8:17). Furthermore, Beal holds that the book of Esther destabilizes ethnic and gender identity, allowing for constructive dialogue with the other.

Interpretive Issues: The major issue raised with regard to the book of Esther is its absence of any reference to God. Some interpreters have argued that this makes the book "secular," while Levenson claims that the book's content still shows evidence of providence, of God behind the scenes of history. Fox argues that though readers have claimed they experience Esther as "secular" or "religious," the text itself does not give an explicit interpretation; it can be read either as a sign of God's covenant faithfulness or of the resourcefulness of the Jewish people. Sweeney thinks that the absence of God is the very premise of the book of Esther, which claims that sometimes God does not act in the face of evil and humans must take responsibility for dealing with crises.

The violent ending to Esther has been the source of much controversy. The difficulty here lies in justifying the violence that the Jews perpetrate against their enemies at the end of the book. Levenson claims that the focus of the passage is not on the slaughter, but on the honor and status the Jews receive within the empire. Some have argued that Esther demonstrates the threats God's people face when living in a hostile culture, but also demonstrates God's providential deliverance of the people. Gottwald cites the violent ending in support of a Maccabean date for its composition.

Influences: The story of Esther has been memorialized and given life through the Jewish celebration of Purim. This festival continues to celebrate the gift of freedom and identity that Esther represents. The book of Esther is also the first recorded instance of a Gentile plot to exterminate the Jewish people.

In general, Esther has been appreciated for its humor and optimism. The exaggerated events and stock characters give the story a light-hearted feel, while the plot embodies enduring confidence that goodness will ultimately triumph over evil. This has given the book a broad appeal, despite its controversial ending.

Bibliography

Bandstra, Barry L. *Reading the Old Testament: Introduction to the Hebrew Bible*. 4th ed. Wadsworth, 2009.

Beal, Timothy K. *The Book of Hiding: Gender, Ethnicity, Annihilation and Esther*. Routledge, 1997.

Brenner, Athalya, ed. *Ruth and Esther: A Feminist Companion to the Bible*. Sheffield, 1999.

Fox, Michael V. *Character and Ideology in the Book of Esther*. Eerdmans, 2001.

Gottwald, Norman K. *The Hebrew Bible: A Socio-Literary Introduction*. Fortress, 1985.

Levenson, Jon D. *Esther: A Commentary*. Westminster John Knox, 1997.

Sweeney, Marvin A. "Absence of G-d and Human Responsibility in the Book of Esther." In *Reading the Hebrew Bible for a New Millennium: Form, Concept, and Theological Perspective*. Vol. 2. *Exegetical and Theological Studies*. Trinity, 2000. Pp. 264–75.

Wyler, Bea. "Esther: The Incomplete Emancipation of a Queen." In *A Feminist Companion to Esther, Judith and Susanna*. Sheffield, 1995. Pp. 111–36.   B.B.

Etam (ee'tuhm).

1 The place where Samson defeated the Philistines and was subsequently delivered to them by the people of Judah (Judg. 15:8, 11).

2 A village in the territory of Simeon (1 Chron. 4:32), possibly identified with **3**.

3 A city near Bethlehem fortified by Rehoboam (2 Chron. 11:6).

4 The Israelites' first desert stop before turning back after they had left Succoth (Exod. 13:20). It was located on the edge of the wilderness (Num. 33:6).

eternal life. The idea of an afterlife or of eternal life is not clearly attested in Jewish literature prior to the exile, and its development thereafter is sometimes attributed to contact with Persian doctrines. The first clear biblical reference to an afterlife is found in Dan. 12:2, which announces: "Many of those who sleep in the dust of the earth shall awake, some to everlasting life, and some to shame and everlasting contempt." Most scholars believe this passage was written ca. 175 BCE and, so, was intended to proclaim God's vindication of martyrs who had been victims of the persecutions of Jews under Antiochus IV Epiphanes. Antiochus had ordered Jews to give up their ancestral faith or face death. The same historical background illuminates 2 Macc. 7, where seven brothers die in defense of the Torah, confident that "the King of the universe will raise us up to an everlasting renewal of life, because we have died for his laws"

(7:9). The Wisdom of Solomon, another Hellenistic Jewish book from the Second Temple period, speaks not of resurrection from death, but of the immortality of the soul by which humankind survives after death (3:4); according to this book, the wicked seem to vanish at death, while "the righteous live forever" (5:15).

The notion of life after death, however, does not appear to have been accepted by all Jews in the Second Temple period. In describing the Sadducees and the Pharisees, the Jewish historian Josephus contrasts their views on postmortem existence: the Pharisees believe in "an immortal soul" and so in an afterlife where God rewards the righteous and punishes the wicked, but the Sadducees do not believe in the afterlife—God does not reward or punish and certainly not in an afterlife (*Jewish War* 2.162–66; *Antiquities* 18.11–22). Acts 23:6–9 likewise records a dispute between Sadducees and Pharisees over the resurrection. In Mark 12:18–27, Jesus tells the Sadducees that they are "quite wrong" in saying "there is no resurrection," because the God of Israel is "not God of the dead but of the living."

Afterlife and eternal life become an essential part of Christian preaching in virtue of Jesus's resurrection from the dead. That event, according to Paul, broke the dominion of death, making eternal life available to all through God's grace (Rom. 5:12–21). The Gospel of John describes eternal life as a phenomenon that has already begun for those who have received Jesus Christ and become children of God (3:36; 5:24; cf. 1:12). *See also* death; eschatology; immortality; resurrection; soul.

Bibliography

Nickesburg, George W. E. *Resurrection, Immortality, and Eternal Life in Intertestamental Judaism*. Harvard University Press, 1972.

Stendahl, Krister. *Immortality and Resurrection*. Macmillan, 1965.   J.H.N./M.A.P.

Etham (ee'thuhm), the first stopping place after Succoth used by the Israelite exodus in their escape from Egypt. Its location is not known, but it is said to be "on the edge of the wilderness" (Exod. 13:20; Num. 33:6) and is called an area of wilderness in or near which are located Pi-hahiroth and Baal-zephon (Num. 33:7–8). Recent suggestions include its identity as Pithom, possibly in the Wadi Tumilat lying between the eastern Nile Delta and the Sinai wilderness.

Ethan (ee'thuhn; Heb., "enduring," hence "long-lived").

1 A wise "Ezrahite" (meaning uncertain) credited with Ps. 89 (see 1 Kings 4:31).

2 Grandson of Judah and Tamar through the line of Perez (1 Chron. 2:6–8).

3 A levitical musician from the Merarites in the time of David, possibly to be identified with Jeduthun (1 Chron. 15:17, 19; see 16:41–42; 25:1–2).

4 A levitical attendant from the line of Gershom (1 Chron. 6:42).

Ethanim. *See* calendar; Tishri.

ethics, moral conduct according to principles of what is good or right to do. Ethical concerns occupy a central position throughout the Bible with respect to the actions of individuals as well as the whole community. At points, they are presented in terms of general and absolute norms (as in the Ten Commandments), and in other places they must be discerned in the actions of people and the customs of the society.

In the Hebrew Bible: The people of Israel faced a full range of moral problems related to various spheres. Israelite society was structured on a patriarchal base, with primary power vested in the male as head of the household. This colored marital and familial morality, as is often evident in laws and stories. A woman's legal rights were restricted in areas of ownership, inheritance (Num. 27:1–11), and oath taking (Num. 30); essentially every female was under the protection and authority of some male, first her father and then later her husband. Divorce laws, accordingly, required that a "bill of divorce" be issued, allowing the woman to marry again (Deut. 24:1). Children were also under the authority of their parents, especially the father. A harsh law proscribing death for a stubborn child is mentioned in Deut. 21:18–21 (see also Exod. 21:15, 17), although there is no evidence that such a penalty was ever enforced.

Regulation of sexual conduct in the Hebrew Bible is also affected by the patriarchal nature of Israelite society. Polygyny and concubinage were allowed, and prostitutes appear to have been stigmatized more negatively than the men who went to them (e.g., Gen. 38:12–26). Adultery, which refers to intercourse between a married or betrothed woman and any man who is not her husband or her betrothed, is strictly prohibited and hypothetically punishable by death (Deut. 22:20–27), though, again, there is no mention of this penalty ever being carried out (even in John 8:1–11, the adulterous woman is presented as a test case for a question of legal interpretation, not necessarily as a potential victim of an actual stoning about to occur). All negative and restrictive mandates concerning sexual behavior, furthermore, are presented in light of a fundamentally positive evaluation of human sexuality: Gen. 2:24–25 declares the intimate bond between a husband and wife as fundamentally appropriate and good.

Individuals as well as society were expected to act justly, promoting proper relationships within the community (Mic. 6:8; Ps. 112; Job 31). God's release of the Israelites from slavery in Egypt often serves as the basis for other efforts to overcome oppression and exploitation within the Israelite society. The Bible recognizes that there are persons who are especially vulnerable and defenseless in society, such as the poor, widows, orphans, slaves, and strangers; and protecting them is not just a moral requirement, but also a religious duty as a reflection of God's demand. The problem of social justice became a special focus in the eighth

century BCE when prophets like Amos, Isaiah, and Micah were quick to criticize the wealthy who had no regard for the plight of those suffering economically.

In general, then, the ethics of the Hebrew Bible are geared toward creating and maintaining right relationships—in the family, in the larger society, in business dealings, in government, and in other arenas. The covenant between God and Israel becomes a symbol of proper relations among humans, and because of the covenant, God can command the people to live obediently and responsibly. Thus, to take one example, the book of Hosea is able to apply the marriage bond metaphorically to the relationship between God and Israel, because marriage—like all human relationships—is assumed to be reflective of God's relationship with Israel. The covenant faithfulness/loving-kindness of God (expressed in the Hebrew word *khesed*) provides the foundation for construction of an ethical system that defines just and unjust behavior in terms of relationships that are to be expressive of love (for God, Deut. 6:5; neighbor, Lev. 19:18; stranger, Deut. 10:19; and alien, Lev. 19:34).

In the NT: In preaching the advent of God's kingdom, Jesus underscores both the possibility and the necessity of repentance (Mark 1:14–15). Thus, future hope becomes a motivation for acting mercifully and responsibly in the present. At points it may seem that Jesus is thinking mostly about the future: he makes moral acts a strict requirement for admission to the kingdom (e.g., Matt. 25:31–46; Mark 10:24–25), threatens persons with the final judgment (Matt. 5:22; Mark 9:42–48; 12:40), and promises final rewards to those who act rightly (Matt. 6:19–21; Mark 10:21). It is clear, however, that one's primary motivation for morality should be the desire to live in conformity to God's standards, not simply to obtain eternal life or heavenly rewards (e.g., Matt. 5:45, 48). According to the Gospel of Matthew, Jesus's view of the law of Moses was generally positive and, indeed, he often interpreted that law in terms that would intensify its demands (cf. his teachings on murder, adultery, divorce, oath taking, and retaliation in 5:21–42). Jesus's ethical interpretations of the law are grounded in a belief that the twofold love commandment—to love God and to love one's neighbor (Mark 12:29–31; from Deut. 6:4–5; Lev. 19:18)—expresses God's will in a fundamental, definitive sense. With this as the primary principle Jesus proceeds to indicate concrete ways in which love should affect moral behavior: affirming marriage and discouraging divorce (Mark 10:2–9), using wealth to benefit the poor (Luke 19:8), caring for anyone in need (Luke 10:29–37), avoiding violence (Matt. 26:52), and living a life of service (Luke 22:26–27).

For Paul, ethics are presented in terms of human response to the death and resurrection of Christ. Simply put, those who experience God's salvation through Christ are not to live for themselves, but for Christ, who died and was raised for them (2 Cor. 5:14–15), and "the only thing that counts is faith working through love" (Gal. 5:6). Paul devotes generous portions of his letters to instruction on moral and behavioral matters (e.g., Rom. 14:5–6; 1 Cor. 8:1–13; 12:1–14:40) and lists both virtues to be pursued and vices to be avoided (Rom. 1:29–31; 13:13; 1 Cor. 5:10–11; 6:9–10; 2 Cor. 6:6–7; Gal. 5:19–23). A question arises, however, as to how Paul determines what sort of behavior is appropriate for those who are now in Christ. His ethical positions are clearly informed by the Hebrew Bible—the moral commandments of Torah (1 Cor. 7:19)—but Paul also claims that Christians are no longer "under the law" (Rom. 6:14–15; 1 Cor. 9:20; Gal. 3:23–25). In a few instances, he makes reference to a human "conscience" that may serve as a moral guide (Rom. 2:15; 2 Cor. 1:12; 4:2), but this cannot be absolute, since conscience can be weak and is easily defiled (1 Cor. 8:7–12; 10:25–29).

Ultimately, Paul's ethics are shaped by the expectation that believers will imitate Christ with regard to sacrificial humility: they will seek the good of others rather than what is pleasing or beneficial to themselves (Rom. 15:1–3; Phil. 2:4–8). Thus, for Paul, the cross becomes the emblem, not only of Christian salvation, but also of Christian conduct. Furthermore, for Paul, all ethics are community ethics, for the individual believer is united spiritually with others in such a way that all individual actions have consequences for others (1 Cor. 12:11–26). Paul's ethics are also shaped by an expectation that Christ is coming soon and that the time remaining to do what must be accomplished in this world is short (Rom. 13:11–14; 1 Cor. 7:29–31; 1 Thess. 4:13–5:11). And, finally, Paul is certain that believers have divine assistance in living as God would have them live; they are transformed from within, by a renewing of their minds (Rom. 12:1; cf. 2 Cor. 5:17), and they are imbued with the Holy Spirit, who produces in them the fruit that is pleasing to God (Gal. 5:22–23).

Bibliography

Harrelson, Walter. *The Ten Commandments and Human Rights.* Fortress, 1980.

Hays, Richard B. *The Moral Vision of the New Testament.* HarperSanFrancisco, 1996.

Matera, Frank J. *New Testament Ethics: The Legacies of Jesus and Paul.* Westminster John Knox, 1996.

Zimmerli, Walther. *The Old Testament and the World.* John Knox, 1976.   D.A.K./M.A.P.

Ethiopia (ee´thee-oh´pee-uh; Heb. Cush; Gk. Aithiopia) or Nubia, the ancient name of the Nile Valley region between the first and second cataracts south of Aswan, roughly equivalent with modern Sudan. In Homer's *Odyssey* (sixth century BCE), Ethiopia appears to cover a vast area, including parts of modern Saudi Arabia and Yemen (cf. *Odyssey* 1.22–23), but by the time of Herodotus (fifth century BCE), the territory was more restricted to the area south of Egypt bordering

the Red Sea. In any case, the biblical area called Ethiopia should not be confused with the modern nation of Ethiopia. Sometimes, furthermore, the term "Ethiopian" is used as a generic label for Africans or people with dark skin (Jer. 13:23). This might be the case with any number of Ethiopians mentioned in the Bible: Zipporah, the wife of Moses (Num. 12:1; NRSV: "Cushite"); Cushi, an unfortunate messenger with the Israelite army (2 Sam. 18:21–23; 31–32 NRSV: "Cushite"); and Ebed-melech, the eunuch who rescued Jeremiah from a cistern (Jer. 38:7).

The history of Ethiopia/Nubia is caught up with that of Egypt, its closest neighbor. Egypt appears to have exercised control over Ethiopia/Nubia for about two hundred years ca. 1971–1786 BCE, but then the Egyptian influence waned for at least a couple of centuries. After expelling the Hyksos invaders (ca. 1550), the Egyptians once more gained control but, during the time of the Israelite monarchy, Ethiopia/Nubia became an independent kingdom. Thus, 2 Chron. 14:9–15 reports King Asa of Judah defeating an Ethiopian army in the Valley of Zephathah at Mareshah. Then, for a short period (ca. 715–664 BCE), Ethiopia/Nubia actually gained the upper hand in northeast Africa and dominated Egypt. This period was known as the Twenty-Fifth Ethiopian Dynasty, and the best-known ruler of that dynasty was Tirhakah (690–664 BCE), who appears in both Assyrian and Judean records (Isa. 37:9) as the ally of Hezekiah, despite protestations from the prophet Isaiah (cf. Isa. 18:1–2; 20:1–6). Egypt fell to the Assyrians in 670, but Egypt/Nubia remained independent until it became part of the Persian Empire in the sixth century BCE. After the eventual demise of that empire, Ethiopia remained an independent, but diminished, power with its capital in Meroe. The head of the government was known as "the Candace." In Acts 8:26–40 Philip the evangelist baptizes an "Ethiopian eunuch" who was a high official in the court of the Candace.

In the Bible, Cush, the son of Ham, is identified as the father of the Ethiopians. The nation or region of Ethiopia is mentioned numerous times, often in connection with Egypt (e.g., Ps. 68:31; Isa. 20:3–5; Ezek. 30:4). Other texts mention Ethiopia in conjunction with Libya, its neighbor to the west (2 Chron. 16:8; Ezek. 38:5), and some mention all three countries (Ezek. 30:5; Dan. 11:43; Nah. 3). The "rivers of Ethiopia" mentioned in Isa. 18:1 and Zeph. 3:10 are probably the Blue Nile and the White Nile—at the height of Ethiopia's power in the seventh century BCE, its borders seem to have extended to the conjunction of those rivers at Khartoum. Ethiopia is noted for chrysolite in Job 28:19, for "merchandise" in Isa. 45:14, and for "riches" in Dan. 11:43. Several prophets proclaim oracles of doom or destruction against Ethiopia, noting its arrogance or attempts to obstruct God's plans for Israel (Isa. 20:3–4; Ezek. 30:4, 5, 9; 38:5; Zeph. 2:12). *See also* Candace, the; Gihon; Hezekiah; Philip.   D.B./M.A.P.

ethnarch (eth'nahrk; Gk., "leader/ruler of a people"), a title for a political ruler used during the Hasmonean and Roman periods. The exact meaning remains unclear, but it occurs only in 1 Maccabees, where it is applied to Simon Maccabeus (14:47; 15:1–2). Perhaps it was a title given to rulers over their own people (e.g., the Jews), who nevertheless remained under the overall rule of a foreign power (e.g., Rome). Thus, an ethnarch would rank somewhat lower than a king. The Greek term is also used in 2 Cor. 11:32, where the NRSV and NIV translate it "governor." *See also* governor; tetrarch.

Eubulus (yoo-byoo'luhs), a Christian who, according to 2 Tim. 4:21, was with Paul during one of Paul's imprisonments. *See also* Claudia; Linus; Pudens.

Eucharist (yoo'kuh-rist). *See* Lord's Supper.

Eunice (yoo'nis), Timothy's mother, a Jewish Christian who was married to a Gentile (Acts 16:1). She and her mother, Lois, are said to have evinced a "sincere faith" and to have provided Timothy with religious instruction (2 Tim. 1:5; 3:14–15). *See also* Timothy.

eunuch, a male who lacks testicles, either because he was born that way or because he has been castrated (cf. Matt. 19:12). Eunuchs were in demand as guards of royal harems. Consequently, most biblical references to eunuchs come from narratives about kings and their courts. Although excluded from the sacred assembly (Deut. 23:1), eunuchs often received favorable report: Ebedmelech was an Ethiopian eunuch who rescued Jeremiah from a cistern (Jer. 38:7); much later, in the book of Acts, another Ethiopian eunuch was baptized by Philip the evangelist (8:26–40). Becoming a eunuch for religious reasons is mentioned in Matt. 19:12, although the exact meaning of that verse is unclear. It could be a metaphorical expression for remaining celibate in order to serve God more effectively (cf. 1 Cor. 7:32–34). *See also* Candace, the; Philip.

Euodia (yoo-oh'dee-uh), a woman in the church at Philippi who was urged by Paul to settle her dispute with Syntyche (Phil. 4:2). *See also* Syntyche.

Euphrates (yoo-fray'teez) **River,** the largest river in western Asia. The headwaters of the Euphrates are two branches that originate in Armenia in eastern Turkey. The western branch (Kara Su) and the eastern branch (Murat Suyu) run westward from their sources and then join north of Malatiya, from which the course runs southeast and southwest into the Syrian plain. Main tributaries from the north are the Belikh and the Khabur. Continuing its southeastern course, the river divides just above Babylon. It reunites and then joins the Tigris for the last hundred miles before emptying into the Persian Gulf. The bed

of the river ran somewhat higher than that of the Tigris, and this allowed ancient irrigation canals to carry Euphrates water across the land between the two rivers for agriculture and transport. The lower reaches provided some ten thousand square miles of land for such reclamation, allowing the foundations of cities and city-states in what we know as one of the earliest centers of civilization, Sumer. The Hellenistic city of Somasata was built near an important ford. Farther south, the Euphrates passed Carchemish, where Nebuchadnezzar decisively beat the Egyptian-Assyrian alliance in which Neco of Egypt participated (Jer. 46; 2 Kings 24:7). Still farther downstream were Dura-Europos, famous for a synagogue with Hellenistic painted scenes, and Mari, notable for its palace and library of texts.

In biblical tradition, the Euphrates was one of four rivers flowing from Eden (Gen. 2:14). Josh. 24:2 says that Israel's ancestors came from "beyond the Euphrates." After the exile, during the Persian period, Judah belonged to a Persian province called "Beyond the River" (Ezra 4:10–11; 5:3; 6:6; Neh. 2:7). The latter reference assumes a perspective opposite to that of Josh. 24:2. Whereas Joshua spoke of "beyond the Euphrates" from Israel's perspective to mean an area *east* of the river, the Persians used the phrase "beyond the river" from their own perspective to mean an area *west* of the river (which included the territory that had once belonged to Israel). Most biblical references to the Euphrates, however, fall into one of two categories. First, the Euphrates (often called "the great river") is listed as a boundary for the land that God promises Israel (e.g., Gen. 15:18; Deut. 1:7; 11:24; Josh. 1:4); this promise appears to be fulfilled when the Euphrates serves as the northern boundary of Israelite territory under David (2 Sam. 8:3). Most of the time, however, this area was under Aramean control, so a second group of passages that mention the Euphrates do so in the context of oracles proclaiming judgment on Assyria or Babylon (e.g., Isa. 7:20; 27:12; Jer. 13:4–7; 46:2–10). It is probably the latter sense that determines references to the Euphrates in Revelation, where it is a site for apocalyptic terrors (9:14; 16:12). *See also* Damascus; Tigris River.

R.S.B./M.A.P.

Euroclydon (yoo-rok'li-don). *See* northeaster.

Eutychus (yoo'tuh-kuhs), a youth who dozed during a long discourse by Paul, fell from a third-story window, and was presumed dead; Paul intervened and the youth lived (Acts 20:7–12).

evangelist (Gk., "one who proclaims good news"). The noun "evangelist" occurs only three times in the NT (Acts 21:8; Eph. 4:11; 2 Tim. 4:5), though the idea of proclaiming the good news about God's kingdom and about Jesus the Christ is found throughout the NT writings. The cognate verb "evangelize" (lit., "to proclaim good news"), is frequent, as is the related Greek noun

euangelion, translated "gospel" or "good news." In the earliest days of the church, the work of evangelism, i.e., proclaiming the Christian gospel, was carried out by the apostles and others (Philip is specifically labeled an evangelist in Acts 21:8). Later, as the church grew and spread and as time passed, "evangelist" came to designate a specific office (Eph. 4:11) or ministry (2 Tim. 4:11) within the church. By the third century, the authors of the four canonical Gospels had come to be known as "evangelists," i.e., as people who had written "evangels," accounts of good news. *See also* apostle; church; gospel; Gospels, the; Philip.
                                                    J.M.E.

Eve, the first woman, created by God (Gen. 2:21–22). Her name in Hebrew sounds similar to the Hebrew word "life," an association that pertains in Gen. 3:20, where the primal woman is designated the "mother of all living." In the Genesis creation story, Eve is created so that the man, Adam, will not be alone. Specifically, the man needed a partner who would "correspond" to him as his helper and his partner; thus, Eve was created from the man's own rib rather than from the earth, as had been the case with the animals (and the man himself). The man calls her "bone of my bone and flesh of my flesh" (2:23). The narrative explains that this provides the origin and rationale for marriage: a man leaves his father and mother and "clings to his wife, and they become one flesh." That expression has obvious sexual connotations, but it also conveys the sense of unity in a more general way (e.g., mutual loyalty) and, perhaps most important, a merging of family lines: each child born to a man and woman represents one new line of descent produced from two. Special attention is

Eve spins while Adam digs; thirteenth-century stone relief, Sainte Chapelle, Paris.

drawn to the nakedness of the couple and to their lack of shame at being naked (2:25).

As the narrative continues, Eve is tricked by the "crafty" serpent into eating forbidden fruit (Gen. 3:1–7). In part, she apparently believes that if she does so, she will not die, but will become like God, knowing good and evil (a possible figure of speech for "knowing all things"). She also wants to eat the fruit, however, because she sees that it is good for food and a delight to the eyes. After eating the fruit, she gives some to her husband, who the text says "was with her" (i.e., party to the exchange with the serpent, though silent throughout), and he eats as well. As a consequence of this disobedience, both Adam and Eve are suddenly ashamed of their nakedness, and they create garments of fig leaves for themselves. Then, God expels them from the garden and Eve is specifically punished in two ways: she (and apparently, though not explicitly, all women after her) will have to endure (1) increased pain in childbirth; and, (2) subordination to her husband, whom she will desire but who will rule over her (3:16). It is only at this point in the story that she receives the name "Eve" (having been called simply "the woman" up to now); this serves as notice that, as a mother, she will produce life (albeit painfully); notably, it is the man who names her (just as he had named the animals, 3:20; cf. 2:20). Eve gave birth to Cain, Abel, and Seth as well as other sons and daughters (4:1–2, 25; 5:4). According to one tradition, it is Eve who names the children: Gen. 4:1 says that she named Cain and 4:25 says she named Seth, though nothing similar is said of Abel and 5:3 indicates that it was Adam who named Seth.

Eve is not mentioned again in the Hebrew Bible, but in some of the Hellenistic Jewish literature of the Second Temple period she is referenced as the one who brought sin and death into the world: "From a woman, sin had its beginning, and because of her, we all die" (Sir. 25:24; cf. *2 Enoch* 30:17; *Apoc. Moses* 7:1, 21). This understanding is also evident in the NT, where Eve is mentioned twice. Both 2 Cor. 11:3 and 1 Tim. 2:13–15 refer to her as a person who was "deceived," and the latter text emphasizes that this distinguishes her from the man: "Adam was not deceived, but the woman was deceived and became a transgressor." This observation about who was deceived is intended to legitimate the position that women should "learn in silence" and not be permitted to have authority over men (2 Tim. 2:11–12). Elsewhere in Paul's writings, the captivity of humanity to sin and to a dominion of death is attributed to Adam without mention of Eve (Rom. 5:12–21). Also, though Eve is not mentioned by name, she is referenced along with Adam in Jesus's teaching on the permanence of marriage (Mark 10:6–9; cf. Gen. 2:24). *See also* Adam; fall, the.   M.A.P.

everlasting life. *See* eternal life.

evil, a term with several nuances of meaning (e.g., misfortune, corruption, wickedness) in the biblical writings. All forms of evil are typically regarded as stemming from the disobedience and rebellion of the human race against God and God's will (e.g., Num. 32:13; Deut. 4:25; Judg. 2:11). Evil occurs wherever and whenever God's will is hindered (cf. dozens of references to those who "do what is evil in the sight of the LORD," e.g., 1 Kings 16:7, 19, 25, 30; 21:20, 25; 22:52). Bad situations or natural calamities can be referred to as "evil," since such occurrences are typically interpreted as a consequence of human sin, if not a direct punishment for specific sin (e.g., Deut. 31:17; Ezra 9:13; Prov. 11:21; Jer. 26:19; Amos 3:6). It is only in this sense (evil as calamity as opposed to evil as immorality or wickedness) that God can be portrayed as the cause of evil. God is never presented as wicked or immoral in the Bible, but God does sometimes send evil upon people in the sense of causing misfortune to befall them (Deut. 28:20; 2 Sam. 24:16; Job 42:11; cf. 1 Kings 2:44; 14:10). It is also in this sense that God is sometimes said to send "an evil spirit" (a spirit that produces disease or calamity) upon someone (Judg. 9:23; 1 Sam. 14–16, 23; 18:10; 19:9). The idea that misfortune must always be interpreted as a sign of divine displeasure, however, is sometimes challenged (Job 30:26; Eccles. 7:15; John 9:1–3). God is also portrayed as delivering people from evil, a phrase that connotes deliverance from misfortune rather than deliverance from immorality or sin (Jer. 18:8; 26:3, 13, 19; Jon. 3:10; 4:2; cf. Matt. 6:13, "deliver us from evil" or, as in the NRSV, "rescue us from the evil one").

In a broad sense, anything that is unfair or unfortunate can be understood as "evil," including inevitable vicissitudes of life (e.g., Eccles. 6:1–3; cf. Luke 16:25). People can be "afflicted with evil" (Gen. 44:34; Prov. 15:15), and the world at large appears to be infected with evil (cf. Gal. 1:4) insofar as it is no longer the world that God declared "good" at creation (1:31). For example, the wild animals that God created as good (Gen. 1:25) would come to be viewed as evil (Lev. 26:6), and even the land itself had potential for being viewed as evil (Num. 13:10). If one asks what accounts for this state of affairs, there is no simple answer (i.e., in Hebrew thought, at least, the good world did not suddenly become evil when Adam and Eve ate the forbidden fruit, though some such doctrine of "the fall" is evident in the NT; cf. Rom. 5:12). Still, the "primeval history" narratives of Gen. 1–11 do reflect an overall notion of progressive and recurrent disobedience that moves humanity farther from God. There is a clear sense, then, that the world is not as God intended it to be; there is something wrong with the world, something for which God is not responsible, and this "something" can be termed "evil."

Throughout the Bible, evil often has a moral dimension. Conduct is deemed evil when it violates God's will (Ps. 34:13); such conduct includes evil acts (John 3:19), evil speech (James 3:8), and evil thoughts (Matt. 15:9). By extension, persons can be called evil (or "wicked") if they do, say, or think evil things (1 Sam. 24:13; Prov. 11:21; Pss. 7:9; 28:3; Matt. 12:34). When evil is understood in this sense, it usually derives from within humanity; the human heart or will carries an intrinsic impulse toward evil (Gen. 6:5; 8:21; 1 Sam. 17:28; Prov. 6:14; Eccles. 8:11; Mark 7:20–23). The same point is made when evil is described as a consequence of human desire (e.g., 1 Tim. 6:10, "the love of money is the root of all kinds of evil"). The avoidance of evil or repentance (turning from evil, cf. Amos 5:14–15) therefore calls for a deliberate rejection of such impulses: resisting temptation or choosing what is right over what is wrong (Pss. 34:14; 37:27).

Relatively late in the biblical tradition, evil came to be understood as a separate and pervasive power within the created order. According to this perspective, evil had a leader (e.g., Satan or the devil) who might be called "the evil one" (Matt. 13:19, 38; John 17:15; Eph. 6:16; 2 Thess. 3:3; 1 John 2:13–14). In its most developed form, this view ascribed underlings to the evil one, evil spirits (Luke 7:21; 8:2; Acts 19:11–16; cf. Eph. 6:12) or demons who could sometimes possess human beings and/or cause evil things to happen to them (e.g., Mark 5:1–13). This ideology often accompanies a dualistic worldview that sees people, groups, or nations as clearly "good" or "evil," aligned with God or the devil (Matt. 7:17; 13:24–30, 36–43). Even then, however, God can be seen as transcendent in mercy (e.g., Matt. 5:45, blessing good and evil alike). Further, the power of God and of whatever is good will ultimately triumph over all that is evil (Heb. 2:14–15). *See also* demon; devil; fall, the; Satan; sin.   J.M.E./M.A.P.

Evil-merodach (ee′vuhl-mair′uh-dak), a Neo-Babylonian (Chaldean) king (561–560 BCE) and the immediate successor of Nebuchadnezzar II. Evil-merodach released King Jehoiachin from imprisonment; the Judean king was given an allowance, and for the remainder of his life he dined at the Babylonian king's table (2 Kings 25:27–30; Jer. 52:31–34). Evil-merodach may have been trying to modify his father's policies; he was killed in a revolution organized by his brother-in-law Neriglissar.

evil spirits. *See* demon; devil.

ewe, a female sheep. In Gen. 21:28–30, Abraham gives Abimelech seven ewe lambs as part of a covenant at Beer-sheba. In Gen. 32:14, Jacob presents Esau with two hundred ewes in an effort to effect a reconciliation with a brother he has wronged and now fears. Lev. 14:10 prescribes the sacrifice of a ewe lamb as part of the cleansing ritual for a leper, and Num. 6:14 prescribes a similar sacrifice as a sin offering at the completion of a Nazirite's consecration. Lev. 22:28 prohibits the Israelites from slaughtering a ewe and its lamb on the same day. In 2 Sam. 12:2–4, the prophet Nathan tells David a parable about a man who kept a ewe lamb as a pet. Ps. 78:71 describes David as one who tended nursing ewes before being called by God to shepherd the people of Israel. In the Song of Solomon, a lover's teeth are described as being like a flock of ewes (4:2; 6:6).   M.A.P.

exile, a term synonymous with "captivity," used to refer to the period in the sixth century BCE when the Judean population was removed to Babylonia. Deportation as a policy was practiced by various ancient powers. Assyria deported part of the population of the northern kingdom (Israel) in 722/1 BCE (2 Kings 17:6; 18:11 list places to which they were taken, but their subsequent history is unknown). Sennacherib's siege of Lachish (701 BCE) also resulted in deportation of captives. Similar policies are attested for the Persians and for later Greek and Roman rulers. In biblical studies, however, the term "exile" usually refers to the deportation of Judeans by Babylon, which occurred in two or three stages. First, in 597 BCE, King Nebuchadnezzar of Babylon deported King Jehoiachin and his mother and wives, together with royal officials and the "elite of the land" (2 Kings 24:15–16). A second deportation followed in 587/6 BCE consisting of the "rest of the population" of Jerusalem, namely, Judeans who had deserted to the Babylonian side during the preceding conflict and others who had somehow survived Babylon's conquest of the city and destruction of its walls and temple (2 Kings 25:11). Jer. 52:30 records a third deportation in 582 BCE. The number of the exiles are differently computed: Jer. 52:30 gives the total for all three deportations as 4,600; 2 Kings 25:14 has 10,000 for 597 BCE alone.

The biblical account provides little information about Judah or Jerusalem during the exilic age. Following the deportations, the Babylonians appointed a Judean notable, Gedaliah, to rule over the people who remained in their homeland (2 Kings 25:22–24). According to 2 Kings 24:14; 25:12, these consisted of only "some of the poorest of the land" left to tend crops (cf. Jer. 40:7). Jer. 41–44, however, implies that no population was left in Judah after Gedaliah's death. In 2 Chron. 36:21, which takes up prophecies of total desolation (e.g., Jer. 7:34, cf. Lam. 1:3), a land emptied of population is also envisaged. Theologically, this point would be significant for sustaining the view that the eventual restoration of Judah came only from the exiles taken to Babylon (cf. Jer. 24:5–7; 29:4–14; Ezek. 11). This is generally the view offered by accounts of restoration in Ezra, though hints do appear of local inhabitants in addition to returned exiles (cf. Hag. 2:4).

As for conditions in Babylon itself, Jer. 29:5–6 envisages settlement and some independence of life. Ezek. 8:1; 20:1 refer to elders of the community meeting with the prophet there. Ezek. 1:1, 4; 8:15–17 suggest various settlements at which Jews were to be found, and both Ezek. 11:16 and 8:17 might imply the existence of temples. In any case, Cyrus of Persia, who had subdued the Babylonians, issued an edict in 538 BCE allowing the Jews to return to Judah and rebuild Jerusalem; a rebuilt temple was dedicated in 515 BCE. Thus, the exile is said to have lasted approximately seventy years, from 587/6 to 515 BCE (in Jer. 25:11–12; 29:10, a seventy-year figure is used for the exile; Dan. 9:2, 24–27 reinterprets the seventy-year period as 490 years, seeing the end of exile as sequel to the desecration of the temple in 167 BCE). Many Jews did return (e.g., those who accompanied Ezra), but the fact that many Jews continued to live in Babylon after the edict of Cyrus is clear from the presence of some Jewish names in Babylonian documents of the fifth century BCE and from the later importance of Babylonian Jewry. Impetus to renewed faithfulness to Jewish customs came from Babylonian Jews on more than one occasion.

Theological reflection on the exile is prominent in a number of biblical writings. The sins for which the exile was punishment are variously assessed and preconditions are given for the termination of exile; these include divine grace, human repentance, or a combination of the two (cf. Jer. 24; 31; Ezek. 18; Lam. 5). Indeed, the entire Deuteronomic History (Joshua–2 Kings) is thought to have been written or edited in light of the exilic experience, presenting that tragedy (and the termination of the northern kingdom) as consequences of wickedness, idolatry, and disobedience, especially on the part of monarchs. Ps. 137 offers an interpretation of the exile that includes both desolation and hope. The book of Daniel is set in the Babylonian exile, relating stories of faithfulness among Jews who continued to be persecuted there by King Nebuchadnezzar. Most scholars, however, believe that Daniel was actually written during the Seleucid period, some centuries after the exile, when Antiochus IV Epiphanes was violently persecuting Jews in an attempt to prohibit expressions of their ancestral faith. Thus, the exile was being used as a theological metaphor for trials and tribulations that Jews experienced as recurring and ongoing. The impact of the exile would continue to affect the thinking of NT authors as well. Babylon is employed by these writers as a

Two Judean captives of Sennacherib's conquest of Lachish, 701 BCE, Nineveh.

symbol for powerful evil (1 Pet. 5:13; Rev. 14:8; 17:5; 18:10; cf. Jer. 51). First Peter spiritualizes the event, maintaining that Christians are in exile from their true home in heaven (1:1; 2:11).

Bibliography

Ackroyd, Peter R. *Exile and Restoration*. Westminster, 1968.

Bickermann, Elias. "The Babylonian Captivity." *Cambridge History of Judaism*. Cambridge University Press, 1984. Pp. 342–58.

Klein, Ralph W. *Israel in Exile*. Fortress, 1979.

P.R.A./M.A.P.

exodus, the, the successful escape of the Hebrews/Israelites from hardship and forced labor in northern Egypt. According to Genesis, Jacob (Israel) and his sons settled in Egypt because one of those

sons, Joseph, had achieved a position of power and prestige there (37, 39–50). The book of Exodus, however, opens with the observation that some time later (430 years according to Exod. 12:40; 400 years according to Gen. 15:13), "a new king arose over Egypt who did not know Joseph" (Exod. 1:8). The Israelites, numerous by now, became slaves, enduring bitter lives "with hard service in mortar and brick and every kind of hard labor" (1:14). Eventually, God called Moses to challenge Pharaoh and then to lead the Hebrew slaves to the promised land of Canaan. As told in the books of Exodus and Numbers, the journey began with a dramatic escape through the Red Sea (where the pursuing Egyptian army was destroyed) and then entailed forty years of wandering in the wilderness. The high point of the journey was an early stop at

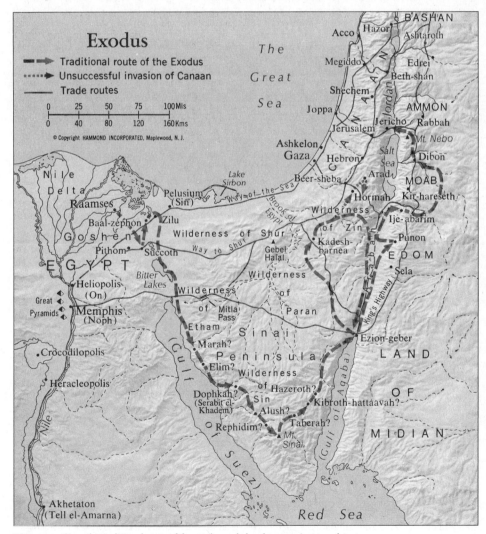

The map outlines the traditional route of the exodus and also shows ancient travel routes across the Sinai that Israelites may have used between Egypt and Canaan.

Mount Sinai, where Moses gave the people the Ten Commandments and, in spite of the people's idolatrous worship of a golden calf, God established an everlasting covenant with them. God guided the Israelites throughout the exodus period, leading them by a pillar of cloud during the day and by a pillar of fire at night. Many miracles occurred along the way: God provided manna from heaven, water from a rock, and quail for meat. The Israelites, however, continually murmured against God and against Moses, necessitating divine rebukes and punishments.

The historical events underlying this narrative are difficult to reconstruct. Some of Israel's ancestors may have entered Egypt as early as the late eighteenth century BCE, at the start of foreign (Hyksos) rule; others may have arrived in the late fourteenth or early thirteenth century, only a few years before the oppression reflected in Exod. 1. Similarly, groups of these ancestors may have left Egypt at different times, separated by many years, and under varied circumstances. The distance in time between even the latest departures from Egypt (thirteenth century BCE) and the composition of the major literary sources for accounts of the exodus (tenth–sixth centuries or later), along with the likelihood that the biblical authors knew little about the geography of the event(s), render all historical conjectures somewhat speculative. That said, most scholars tend to date the (primary or final) exodus from Egypt early in the reign of Pharaoh Ramesses II (ca. 1290 BCE), so that the oppression would have begun not long after the Nineteenth Dynasty took power (ca. 1350 BCE), and the entrance to Canaan would have started some years before the end of Ramesses' reign (ca. 1230 BCE). Another view is that the Hebrew tribes entered Egypt from Canaan at the time of the Hyksos, that the rise of the Eighteenth Dynasty (ca. 1580 BCE) began the oppression, and that the exodus occurred during the reign of Thutmose III (ca. 1450 BCE). This is in harmony with the statement in 1 Kings 6:1 that the construction of Solomon's temple (ca. 970) began 480 years after the Israelites left Egypt, but that figure (twelve generations of forty years) could be symbolic.

Different routes have been proposed for the exodus as well. One route turns south after crossing the line of the modern Suez Canal (near the Bitter Lakes), parallels the eastern coast of the Gulf of Suez to the vicinity of the turquoise mines at Serabit el-Khadem, and continues inland to the traditional site of Mount Sinai at Gebel Musa. After the stay at Sinai, the people would have journeyed in a northeasterly direction to the northern tip of the Gulf of Aqabah, then around Edom and Moab, and on to Transjordan. Although this route locates Mount Sinai at the place accepted since Byzantine times, it lacks earlier support and conflicts with the biblical view that the people first headed for Canaan and were only condemned to wander after they had been at Sinai and had rejected the report of the spies sent into the land from Kadesh in the wilderness of Paran (Num. 13–14). Another proposed route runs north (a little east of the present Suez Canal), turns east along the Mediterranean coast, and follows the narrow strip of land that divides Lake Sirbon from the sea. This allows Lake Sirbon to be identified as the sea where Israel was delivered and the Egyptian pursuers were drowned (Exod. 14–15). Unfortunately, there is neither any obvious route from Lake Sirbon to Kadesh nor any easy access across the sand dunes to Sinai proper. *See also* Exodus, book of.　　　K.G.O./M.A.P.

Exodus, book of, the second of the Five Books of Moses (the Torah) of the Tanakh (Jewish Bible); it is the second book of the Pentateuch of the Christian OT. The name Exodus is taken from the LXX's name for the book, *exodos,* which means "an exit" or "a going out," found in 19:1 and 23:16. The Hebrew name is *'elleh shemot* (or *shemot* for short), meaning "these are the names," which is taken from the first sentence of the book, "These are the names of the sons of Israel who came to Egypt with Jacob." The exodus from Egypt is arguably the most important "event complex" of the Hebrew Bible, and it is narrated in the book of Exodus. The book of Exodus is the second part of a five-part literary work that narrates a history of humanity from creation to Israel's entry into the land of Canaan, which was promised to their ancestors (ca. 1200 BCE). The written text was probably finalized in the late sixth or fifth century BCE.

Contents: The beginning of the book of Exodus connects back to the book of Genesis by specifying the names of Jacob's sons who settled in Egypt with him at the invitation of Joseph. They have multiplied and prospered. But the Egyptians are threatened by this, and a new ruler arises who enslaves the Israelites (Exod. 1). Forced labor fails to curtail the growth of the Hebrew population, and Pharaoh decrees that all male Hebrew infants are to be killed. When Moses is born, his parents hide him temporarily and then put him into a basket and set him afloat on the Nile River (Exod. 2) to save him. Pharaoh's daughter finds Moses, has compassion for him, and raises him as her own son at the royal court.

When Moses reaches adulthood, he rashly attempts to rescue some fellow Hebrews by killing their Egyptian taskmaster. He flees Egypt and takes refuge in the Sinai wilderness. There he marries Zipporah and raises a family. While Moses is shepherding the flocks of his father-in-law, Jethro, God appears to him at a burning bush (Exod. 3–4). God instructs Moses to return to Egypt. Once back in Egypt, he mediates Israel's deliverance from slavery and oppression. With a series of natural and supernatural disasters called the ten plagues (Exod. 5–11), God demonstrates the superior power of Israel's deity. After celebrating the first Passover, the Hebrews escape into the Sinai wilderness (Exod. 12–13). The Egyptian army pursues them and, just when the Hebrews appear doomed, God miraculously opens a pathway through the Reed Sea (NRSV: "Red Sea"). The Hebrews pass through the waters safely, but the Egyptians are drowned when they try to follow (Exod. 14–15). Then Moses leads the people to Mount Sinai (Exod. 16–18), where he had earlier met God at the burning bush.

At Mount Sinai, God reveals the law to the Hebrews and establishes an abiding covenant relationship with them (Exod. 19–24). In addition to making this covenant, he gives them instructions for building worship implements and a portable shrine (Exod. 25–31). Soon after the people agree to the terms of the covenant, they break it by worshiping a golden calf instead of God (Exod. 32–34). Though they deserve to be forsaken, God reestablishes the covenant with them. Then, while still encamped at Mount Sinai, the Hebrews build a tent shrine as the residence for their deity and call it the tabernacle and the tent of meeting (Exod. 35–40).

OUTLINE OF CONTENTS

Exodus

Background: The book of Exodus is organized chronologically, and it narrates the course of events in a linear historical fashion. Yet an analysis of the text reveals that it was compiled from preexisting sources. The Documentary Hypothesis is the standard scholarly explanation of how the Pentateuch was composed and came to have its final shape. Given this theory, the book of Exodus was compiled with material taken from the Old Epic source of Yahwist and Elohist material along with Priestly writings, including the account of the tabernacle. In addition, some material from other sources found its way into the book, including the Song of the Sea (chap. 15) and the Covenant Code (20:22–23:33). The exodus event is recorded only in the Bible, and its historicity cannot be verified

directly on the basis of Egyptian sources. A case can be made, however, for the plausibility of the biblical stories of Joseph, Moses, and the Israelites in Egypt (see Hoffmeier).

Themes: The relationship between God and the Israelites was defined by a legal instrument called a covenant. The notion of covenant comes from the political realm of international relations. A covenant formalized alliances between parties and defined expectations within those relationships. Ancient covenants often took the shape of suzerain-vassal treaties. The covenant established at Mount Sinai between God and Israel took this general form and structured the relationship as a theocracy, with God as sovereign and Israel as the people of God.

Israel's covenant relationship with God was defined by laws, called statutes and ordinances in the text. The entire corpus of regulations derived from God, who articulated them to Moses, who then taught them to the people of Israel. This is the sense of the collective term *torah;* often translated "law," it also has the meaning of "teaching," since Moses was a teacher of God's will. The mode in which Moses received the revelation directly from God became the paradigm of legitimate lawgiving in the biblical world; for any requirement to be legitimate and find acceptance, it had to be issued by God through Moses at Sinai.

The laws contained in the book of Exodus in fact came from various sources, and not all were originally connected with a revelatory event at Mount Sinai. There are two Decalogues in Exodus (20:1–17; 34:11–26) as well as the Covenant Code (20:22–23:33). In addition, the Priestly Code and the Holiness Code in Leviticus were both associated with Mount Sinai, but were written later. There are affinities between legal codes and covenants from the ancient Near East, including the Code of Hammurabi, that suggest Israelite dependency on a prior Mesopotamian legal tradition.

The book of Exodus contains a significant number of divine revelations that serve to characterize God and make God evident to the people through divine appearances, called theophanies. These theophanies typically were associated with storms, clouds, lightning, or fire. The divine name YHWH ("the LORD") was revealed in a burning bush (Exod. 3) and was declared to be the deity's personal name, exclusively revealed to Israel. The crossing of the sea (Exod. 14) revealed God as the warrior god who controlled the sea. The pillar of cloud and fire in the wilderness led the Israelites to their destination. God's presence on Mount Sinai as a prelude to lawgiving took the form of an earthquake and a storm (Exod. 19). When Moses, Aaron, and the elders ascended Mount Sinai for the divine banquet, they beheld the "glory of the LORD" (the divine aura) covering the mountain (Exod. 24). The design plan of the tabernacle (Exod. 25–31) and the construction process (Exod. 35–40) dominate the latter part of the book. The tabernacle was designed to house the "glory of the LORD," and at its dedication a cloud covered it and the "glory of the LORD" filled it (Exod. 40:34–37). A second structure called the tent of meeting is also mentioned frequently. Presumably the references to two different portable dwellings are due to different sources. All together these theophanies portray a powerful deity who cares for and commands the allegiance of the Israelites.

Influences: Exodus is arguably the most influential book of the Hebrew Bible, because it contains the foundational elements of Israel's national story: the revelation of God's name to Israel; the first Passover celebration; Israel's deliverance from Egypt, including crossing the sea to safety in the wilderness; the formal covenant between God and Israel; the divine revelation of the Torah for Israel's life through Moses; and the construction of a structure to house the divine presence among the people. The exodus is an event that demonstrated God's compassion for the oppressed and God's power to deliver people from oppression. In the prophetic literature of the Bible, the exodus becomes a symbol of hope; this is especially true for the book of Jeremiah, written during the Babylonian crisis (see 16:14–15), and for the portion of Isaiah that comes out of the Babylonian exile (cf. 43:16–21; 51:10). Several features in the Gospel of Matthew's account of Jesus (esp. Matt. 1–8), including Herod's killing of Bethlehem's children, the flight of Joseph and Mary with the baby Jesus to Egypt, Satan tempting Jesus for forty days in the wilderness, and Jesus's Sermon on the Mount, find their sequence and inspiration in the book of Exodus.

The exodus was taken up by many people throughout Western history as a source of inspiration and hope. The Puritan flight to freedom in New England, the emancipation struggle of African American slaves, the civil rights movement of the twentieth century, the Christian liberationist movement in Latin America (see Pixley), and the migration of Jews from the Soviet Union to the state of Israel all drew upon the Israelite exodus tradition. The cultural influence of Exodus is no less significant. The ethical Decalogue of Exod. 20 has become the most visible Western symbol of morality and religious devotion, including sabbath observance. The figure of Israel's great lawgiver Moses (see Assmann) was rendered famously in stone by Michelangelo. Cecil B. DeMille's classic film *The Ten Commandments* has iconized Moses and offered a cinematic presentation of how events like the crossing of the sea took place, providing a lens through which the story is sometimes popularly imagined. *See also* exodus, the; Moses; Pentateuch, sources of the.

Bibliography

Assmann, Jan. *Moses the Egyptian: The Memory of Egypt in Western Monotheism.* Harvard University Press, 1997.

Bandstra, Barry L. *Reading the Old Testament: Introduction to the Hebrew Bible.* 4th ed. Wadsworth, 2009.

Childs, Brevard S. *The Book of Exodus: A Critical, Theological Commentary.* Westminster, 1974.

Coats, George W. *Exodus 1–18.* Eerdmans, 1999.

Hoffmeier, James K. *Israel in Egypt: The Evidence for the Authenticity of the Exodus Tradition.* Oxford University Press, 1997.

Pixley, George V. *On Exodus: A Liberation Perspective.* Orbis Books, 1987.

Sarna, Nahum M. *Exodus (Shemot): The Traditional Hebrew Text with the New JPS Translation.* Jewish Publication Society, 1991.   B.B.

exorcism. *See* demon; divination; magic.

expiation. *See* atonement.

eye, in the Bible, usually the literal organ for sight, but the term may also be used to refer to a person's look or appearance (Lev. 13:55) or applied in a variety of metaphorical senses. For example, a person whose eye is "evil" is one consumed with jealousy, envy, or malice toward another (Sir. 14:10; Matt. 6:23; Mark 7:22). "Eye" can also be used in connection with the heart or mind (Sir. 17:8; Eph. 1:18; Luke 19:42). Therefore, those who are without understanding can be described as having their eyes blinded (Isa. 6:10; Matt. 13:15; Mark 8:18; John 12:40; Acts 28:27). The loss of an eye would be a literal tragedy, but may also stand figuratively for calamity in general; thus the law of retaliation permits vengeance that does not surpass "eye for eye and tooth for tooth" (Exod. 21:24; Lev. 24:20; Deut. 19:21). Jesus took issue with that allowance (Matt. 5:38–39), but spoke of plucking out one's own eye if it causes one to sin (Matt. 5:29). God is sometimes pictured as having multiple eyes (Zech. 4:10; cf. Job 1:6).   P.P.

eye of a needle. *See* needle, needlework.

Ezekiel (i-zee'kee-uhl), **book of,** the third book of what is sometimes called the Latter Prophets, a subcollection in the Nevi'im (Prophets) section of the Tanakh (Jewish Bible). It is the third book of the Major Prophets of the Christian OT. The name Ezekiel means "God is strong" or "God will strengthen." Ezekiel the son of Buzi was a Jerusalem priest who was taken to Babylonia in the first deportation of Judeans to Babylonia in 598 BCE. He was married (24:15–18), but there is no mention of children. Along with other Judeans, he was resettled in Tel-abib on the Chebar canal, an offshoot of the Euphrates River. There he had visions of the divine presence in 593. These visions compelled him to communicate to his fellow exiles that the destruction of Jerusalem was a foregone conclusion. He prophesied in exile until 571 (29:17); the forced exile of the Judeans lasted until 538, so he never returned to Judea. Ezekiel's priestly pedigree accounts for the worldview reflected in his visions, his interest in the "glory of the Lord," and his detailed reimagining of the Jerusalem temple.

Contents: Compared to the prophetic books of Isaiah and Jeremiah, Ezekiel is much more linear and logical in composition and structure.

Ezekiel's vision of dry bones; a detail from a panel at the third-century CE synagogue at Dura-Europos. Ezekiel, touched by the hand of the Lord, stands among disjointed human remains; he is told to prophesy that the bones might live again (Ezek. 37:1–14).

The book of Ezekiel hinges on the fact of Jerusalem's destruction in 587. The first half of the book (1–24) consists of Ezekiel's attempts to convince the exilic community that relief from Babylonian domination would not come soon; in fact, Judah's condition would worsen. Thus, any hopes for a swift return to the homeland would not be realized. The second half of the book (25–48) consists of Ezekiel's attempts to bolster the faith of the exiles after Jerusalem's destruction. The oracles against Judah's neighbors and detractors anticipate their demise, which is the necessary precursor to Judah's restoration. The individual components of the book are ordered chronologically with only three segments out of order (cf. 26:1; 29:17; 33:21). Major sections are introduced with a year, month, and day notice; the years are specified in relation to the year of King Jehoiachin's exile and imprisonment in Babylon, 598/7 BCE. Overall, the book displays a deliberate movement from judgment to hope and disaster to salvation.

Themes: Ezekiel is often regarded as the only prophetic book of the Bible that is set in Babylonian exile. (Although much of Daniel is set in Babylon, it is only grouped with the prophetic books in the Christian OT; in the Jewish Bible, it is placed among the Writings, or Ketuvim.) Ezekiel is addressed as "son of man" (Heb. *ben 'adam;* NRSV: "O mortal") consistently throughout the book. Ezekiel introduces divine messages by the clause "The word of the Lord came to me." Ezekiel uses the phrase "glory of the Lord" ten times, more than any other book in the Bible. This phrase is

typically used in the Bible in priestly books to designate God's aura, which made the divine presence evident, usually at the tent of meeting/tabernacle or temple.

In each of his visionary experiences Ezekiel describes how the "hand of the Lord" was upon him, sometimes transporting him to a different place. In Ezekiel's first vision (chaps. 1–3) a flying chariot emerges out of a lightning storm. Ezekiel elaborately describes the cherubim, strange creatures that provide it mobility with wings and wheels. A throne rests upon a dome supported by the creatures, and on it a gleaming and fiery humanlike form resides, which appears to be the "glory of the Lord." A voice commissions Ezekiel to bring advance warning to Israel of the divine plan to destroy Jerusalem as punishment for the sins of the nation. A hand gives him a scroll and tells him to eat it, then speak its words of judgment to God's people in exile. In Ezekiel's second vision (chaps. 8–11) he is transported back to the Jerusalem temple, where he is shown evidence of false worship taking place. This prompts the "glory of the Lord" to leave the temple borne on the wings of cherubim; it hovers, then leaves Jerusalem completely. In Ezekiel's third vision (37:1–14) he is transported to a valley piled high with human bones. God urges him to prophesy to the bones, and by stages the bones become skeletons, then corpses, then by the divine spirit living breathing people, a revived house of Israel. In Ezekiel's fourth vision (chaps. 40–48) the hand of God transports him to a high mountain, and he is shown a new temple and all its implements, along with the precise dimensions of every room and structure. This new temple becomes the centerpiece of a new land. In this last vision the throne-chariot bearing the "glory of the Lord" returns to the temple and fills it (43:1–5).

Ezekiel symbolically depicted the coming destruction of Jerusalem by building a model of the city, then using miniature weapons of war to bring it down. Then he bound himself to the ground one day for each year to depict how long Israel and Judah would be in confinement, all the while subsisting on wretched rations (chap. 4). He shaved his head and beard and then destroyed the cuttings with fire, sword, and wind to symbolize how Jerusalem would meet its end (chap. 5). He packed his bags, dug a hole through a wall of his house, and then took flight in order to symbolize how the people will attempt to get away before the fall of the city (chap. 12). The death of his wife, for which God forbade him to show signs of mourning, served as a sign of the coming desolation of the temple (24:15–27). After the destruction was an accomplished fact, he took two sticks, one standing for Judah and one for Israel, and miraculously joined them into one long stick to symbolize the reconnection of the two into one nation ruled by one king from the house of David (37:15–28).

In what might be called parables or allegories, Ezekiel used a variety of objects as the basis for lessons regarding Jerusalem. Like the people of Jerusalem, the dead wood of a vine is no good for anything except fires (chap. 15). Jerusalem was a helpless infant until God found it and cared for it; then it became beautiful, turned to whoring, and abandoned its God (chap. 16). An eagle and a cedar tree symbolize the power of leaders in Babylon and Egypt (chaps. 17, 31). The proverb "parents have eaten sour grapes and the children's teeth are set on edge" is cited to refute the people's avoidance of direct responsibility for bringing on the disaster of destruction (chap. 18). Two sisters who become prostitutes stand for Israel and Judah gone astray (chap. 23). A pot set to boiling symbolizes the siege and destruction of Jerusalem (chap. 24).

Influences: The vision of the throne-chariot in Ezek. 1 inspired certain esoteric tendencies in Judaism, including *merkavah* ("chariot") mysticism and *hekalot* ("temples") mysticism. In some traditions, because chap. 1 of Ezekiel is mysterious and transcendental, only spiritually mature and learned Jewish teachers were allowed to expound it. Ezekiel's vision of the valley of dry bones (chap. 37) has been used to support expectations of the rebirth of Israel among Jews and Christians, especially dispensationalists, and many have seen its fulfillment in the modern state of Israel. This chapter was also the inspiration for the African American spiritual entitled "Dem Bones."

Bibliography

Bandstra, Barry L. *Reading the Old Testament: Introduction to the Hebrew Bible.* 4th ed. Wadsworth, 2009.

Greenberg, Moshe. *Ezekiel.* 2 vols. Doubleday, 1983–1997.

Levenson, Jon D. *Theology of the Program of Restoration of Ezekiel 40–48.* Harvard University Press, 1976.

Zimmerli, Walter. *Ezekiel.* 2 vols. Fortress, 1979–83.

———. *The Fiery Throne: The Prophets and Old Testament Theology.* Fortress, 2003.   B.B.

Ezem (ee'zuhm; Heb., "bone"), a town in southern Judah counted as belonging to both Judah (Josh. 15:29) and Simeon (19:3). Since the tribe of Simeon was early assimilated into Judah, the town was probably originally assigned to Simeon, but was absorbed into Judah as Simeon lost its identity (note Gen. 49:5–7). The site is unknown.

Ezer (ee'zuhr; Heb. *'ezer,* "help").

1 A descendant of Judah belonging to the Hur family group (1 Chron. 4:4).

2 A Manassite, the son of Ephraim; he was killed with his brother Elead in a raid against Philistine livestock at Gath (1 Chron. 7:21).

3 A Gadite who joined David's warriors at Ziklag (1 Chron. 12:9).

4 The son of Jeshua; he helped rebuild the walls of Jerusalem under Nehemiah (Neh. 3:19).

5 A priest who took part in the dedication of the rebuilt walls in postexilic Jerusalem (Neh. 12:42); he is possibly the same as **4.**

6 A son of Seir and chieftain of the Horites, ancient inhabitants of Edom (Gen. 36:21). In this case, the name Ezer actually translated the Hebrew word *'etser* ("treasure") rather than the word *'ezer* ("help"), as in the first five listings. *See also* Horites.   D.R.B.

Ezion-geber (ee'zee-uhn-gay'buhr), a town in Edom on the Gulf of Aqabah. It is listed in Num. 33:35–36 as a stopping place during the exodus.

Solomon "built a fleet of ships at Ezion-geber" and sent them on profitable journeys to southern Arabia and East Africa (1 Kings 9:26–28; 10:11; 2 Chron. 8:17; 9:10–11). After Solomon's death (ca. 976 BCE) the region reverted to Edomite control. It was reconquered by Jehoshaphat of Judah, who also built a fleet of ships that were subsequently "wrecked at Ezion-geber" (1 Kings 22:48; 2 Chron. 20:36). They may have been destroyed by the Edomites, or by a tempest, for although the average rainfall is only 2 inches, savage winter storms occur along the Arabah.

The exact site of Ezion-geber is far from certain. Some authorities equate it with Elath (Deut. 2:8; 1 Kings 9:26; cf. Eloth, 2 Chron. 8:17), suggesting that Ezion-geber was the Israelite name and Elath the Edomite. The site is then identified with the oasis of Aqabah at the northeast corner of the gulf, an area with a good water supply and easy access to the Edomite plateau via the Wadi Ytem. There is, unfortunately, no evidence of Iron Age (1200–334 BCE) occupation in this area, although it is possible that all vestiges of a settlement could have been washed away by flash floods. Those who believe that there were two distinct settlements usually place Elath at Aqabah and Ezion-geber at modern Tell el-Kheleifeh, which is located almost in the center of the northern tip of the gulf and 550 yards from the shore.

This site was excavated by Nelson Glueck between 1938 and 1940 and revealed five periods of occupation. The earliest structure, probably erected during the reign of Solomon, was a small well-built mud-brick building with a courtyard and massive southern gate. Glueck first equated this with Solomon's copper refinery, but B. Rothenburg has since shown that the nearby copper mines are in fact some centuries earlier, and he suggests that the building was a Solomonic fort or caravanserai. Since the site is completely exposed to the occasional furious winter storms, it can hardly have served as an important anchorage for shipping; a military outpost to guard the south end of the Arabah seems more probable.

The second period had a much stronger building, with a double mud-brick wall and massive four-chambered gate, probably belonging to the time of Jehoshaphat's reign (ca. 873–849 BCE). The last biblical mention of Ezion-geber occurs in connection with Jehoshaphat's rule (1 Kings 22:48), but Elath was recaptured for Judah either by Amaziah (2 Kings 14:22) or more probably by Uzziah (2 Chron. 26:2, NRSV: "Eloth"), whose son Jotham appears to be mentioned on a seal found in the third period of Tell el-Kheleifeh. In about 733 BCE, Elath fell to the Edomites (2 Kings 16:6), who evidently rebuilt Tell el-Kheleifeh, for some Edomite jar handles have been found at the fourth level. The fifth and final occupation was sometime in the sixth century BCE during the Babylonian and early Persian empires, but the site was abandoned in the early fifth century BCE. *See also* Amaziah; Edom; Jehoshaphat; Solomon.

D.B.

Ezra (ez'ruh; Heb., "help"), the priest and scribe whose story appears in Ezra 7–10 and Neh. 8–9. In the biblical tradition, Ezra is commissioned by Artaxerxes to lead the exiles in Babylon back to Judah, and he is vested with authority to impose the Mosaic law there, within the Persian province "Beyond the River." In Jerusalem, Ezra reads the law publicly (Ezra 8:1–12), renews the celebration of festivals (8:13–18), and lends his full support to rededicating the temple and rebuilding the city walls (9–10; 12:36). He also promulgates a strict policy with regard to returnees who have married foreign (non-Israelite) women during the exile. Such people are urged to divorce and banish their wives, along with any children produced from the union (Ezra 9–10). Ezra is also mentioned in Neh. 12:26, 36, and his name appears on lists in Neh. 12:13, 33. In 12:1, 13 he is named as a priestly leader.

Problems arise when trying to fit the biblical accounts of Ezra with known history. First, it is not clear which Persian ruler named Artaxerxes is intended as the ruler who authorizes Ezra's work (Ezra 7:1). Furthermore, as the biblical narratives now stand, the activities of Ezra and Nehemiah overlap, but there is no real contact between them, and it is often believed that the two actually worked separately. This has led to the proposal that Ezra should be placed later than Nehemiah, Nehemiah in the reign of Artaxerxes I and Ezra in that of Artaxerxes II, but there is no certainty in that regard. If Ezra was active under Artaxerxes I, the date of his journey to Jerusalem will have been 458 BCE; if under Artaxerxes II, 398 BCE. A number of scholars, influenced by these uncertainties and the strange lack of reference to Ezra in other sources (e.g., the list of "famous men" in Sir. 44–50), have questioned his very existence. There is also discussion as to whether his mission should be regarded as mainly political (as a trusted servant of the Persian king sent to maintain order in a distant province) or as mainly religious (as the instrument through whom the law of Moses was made available to the Jerusalem community). *See also* Artaxerxes; Ezra and Nehemiah, books of.

R.C.

Ezra and Nehemiah (nee-uh-mi'uh), **books of,** two books of the Christian OT that were originally a single work and are often studied as a combined book (Ezra–Nehemiah). In the Tanakh (Jewish Bible), Ezra–Nehemiah is found in the Writings section, or Ketuvim, immediately before the books of Chronicles. In the Christian OT, they are found as consecutive works, placed among the historical books, right after Chronicles. In the Jewish Tanakh, Ezra–Nehemiah was most likely made part of the canon first, so they were present before Chronicles was added. But in the Christian OT, the chronology of the books' contents determines the order: the events of Chronicles precede those of Ezra–Nehemiah, so Chronicles comes first. The books of Ezra and Nehemiah are the most important source of information about the postexilic restoration of Jewish community life in Judea from 539 to ca. 430 BCE.

Contents: The combined work of Ezra–Nehemiah can be easily divided into three sections: the Book of Zerubbabel (Ezra 1–6), Ezra's memoirs (Ezra 7–10; Neh. 8–9), and Nehemiah's memoirs (Neh. 1–7; 10–13). In addition to the historical material, the presence of Ezra material in Nehemiah has confirmed the link between the two texts for scholars.

Ezra 1–6: The first section of Ezra, termed the Book of Zerubbabel, relates the history of the early returnees from Babylonian exile. It covers the period from the end of exile in 538 to the completion of the rebuilt temple in 515. The book begins with a verbatim record of the decree of Cyrus allowing the Judean refugees to return to Jerusalem. This decree was issued in 538 and authorized the rebuilding of the temple. Cyrus, a Persian, acknowledged that the Lord is the God of Israel, and he attributes to this deity the gift of his own power. The fact that Cyrus authorized the temple rebuilding becomes important later in the book when Samaritans from the north and others oppose rebuilding activities in Jerusalem.

The first group of returned refugees is led by Sheshbazzar, who has been appointed governor of Judea. He may have been the son of Jehoiachin, Judah's king in exile. Sheshbazzar and the first group of returnees succeed in laying the foundations of the temple. For unspecified reasons the work breaks off, and the temple remains unfinished until a subsequent return of Jewish refugees. The most productive return is led by Zerubbabel, another leader from the line of David, in 522 BCE, near the beginning of the reign of Darius I.

The most significant restoration event of this period is the completion of the rebuilding of the temple in Jerusalem. Authorities call this structure the second temple because the one built by Solomon was the first temple. The second temple remained intact until it was destroyed by the Romans in 70 CE. Zerubbabel, the civic leader, is assisted by the high priest Jeshua and by the prophets Haggai and Zechariah. Together they motivate the people to complete the project begun by Sheshbazzar, and it is finished in 515. This section of Ezra ends with an account of the dedication of the temple and the celebration of Passover.

Ezra 7–10; Neh. 8–9: Four chapters of the book of Ezra and two chapters of the book of Nehemiah deal with Ezra the scribe. There is a gap of about sixty years between the events of the Book of Zerubbabel (Ezra 1–6) and those of the Ezra memoirs (Ezra 7–10; Neh. 8–9).

Ezra is a priest descended from the line of Aaron through Zadok. He is also a scribe, which essentially means that he is a royal administrator; he serves under the Persian king Artaxerxes I. He may have returned to Judea from Babylon in 458 with another group of refugees; scholars debate this date of Ezra's mission. The seventh year of Artaxerxes I (Ezra 7:7) would be 458 BCE, the date often used. But the problem is this: Ezra and

Nehemiah do not seem to acknowledge each other, and they seem to work independently of each other, even though the straightforward reckoning of their dates puts them in Jerusalem at the same time. Consequently, some scholars place Ezra after Nehemiah, and they read Ezra 7:7 as indicating the thirty-seventh year of Artaxerxes, rather than seventh, thus placing the beginning of Ezra's mission in 428. Still others place the beginning of Ezra's work in 398 during the reign of Artaxerxes II (404–358). Complicating the matter further, Neh. 8:9 and 12:26, 36 do place Ezra and Nehemiah in Jerusalem at the same time, though these are often judged to be late editorial insertions.

Ezra has authorization from the Persian government to reestablish proper modes for worshiping God and for adherence to the Torah of Moses. In Ezra's analysis, one of the most serious problems among the Judeans is mixed marriages. In the interim of the exile, Judean men have married Canaanite, Hittite, Ammonite, Moabite, and Egyptian women. Ezra sees this as a breach of the injunction to remain separate from non-Israelite people. Intermarriage promotes assimilation and is a threat to Israelite religion and identity. Israel's theological historians had concluded that one of the biggest reasons for Israel's downfall was intermarriage with Canaanites, which led to idolatry. Thus, Ezra requires Jewish men to divorce their non-Jewish wives and to expel them from Judean territory, along with any children from the marriage. It is a time of great anxiety and mourning, but the priests, Levites, and ordinary people who have married foreign women do as Ezra asks.

Ezra also rededicates the people to keeping the Torah (Neh. 8–9). He assembles all Jewish adults in Jerusalem and reads the book of the Torah of Moses to them in Hebrew. However, because Hebrew is no longer their vernacular, having been replaced by Aramaic during the exile, there are translators who interpret the text to the people as he reads. This is the first biblical attestation of the practice of scripture being translated from one language to another. After the Torah is read and interpreted, the people celebrate the Festival of Tabernacles, which is a commemoration of the wilderness-wandering period of early Israelite history. Then Ezra offers a prayer addressed to the Lord, the God of the Jews, citing the manifold ways that the Lord directly intervened in history from creation to that moment.

Neh. 1–7; 10–13: Nehemiah is an official at the court of Artaxerxes I in Susa and is probably a eunuch. He travels to Jerusalem in 445 BCE to be the governor of the Persian Empire's province of Yehud, i.e., Judea. His great accomplishment is rebuilding the enclosure walls of Jerusalem. His work is opposed by Sanballat, leader of the Samaritans, and by Tobiah, leader of the Ammonites. They see his efforts as a threat to their power and influence in the region. On various occasions, they try to stop the work, and they even try to assassinate him. Nehemiah and his crew are able to complete the rebuilding of the walls in fifty-two days despite the opposition. These walls give Jerusalem the protection and security its people need.

Shortly afterward Nehemiah institutes some important social and economic reforms. He closes the city on the sabbath so that no trading can take place. He guarantees that the Levites will receive their proper support and, like Ezra, he forbids mixed marriages. Nehemiah serves twelve years as governor of the province and then returns to Babylon in 433.

OUTLINE OF CONTENTS

Ezra–Nehemiah

Background: It was traditionally thought that both Ezra and Nehemiah were composed by Ezra shortly after the events described in the book. Most modern scholars, however, do not believe that Ezra wrote these books, though it is possible that some of the sections go back to Ezra and Nehemiah. Scholars view Ezra–Nehemiah as a composite work having multiple sources and belonging to several genres. The work shifts from third-person accounts to first-person autobiography at various points. In addition, there are certain sections of Ezra that are written in Aramaic instead of in traditional Hebrew. Although the original order of the chapters and the book's relationship to Chronicles are debated by scholars, most feel that the books were completed around 400 BCE.

Themes: One of the major themes in Ezra–Nehemiah is that God uses foreign rulers to further God's purposes. In the Ezra material, God uses the authority and power of King Cyrus of Persia to instigate a movement to rebuild the temple in Jerusalem. The initiative to begin rebuilding the temple does not come from the people of Israel, but from a foreign ruler. In the Nehemiah material, God uses the authority and power of King Artaxerxes of Persia in order to instigate a movement to rebuild the wall around Jerusalem. The initiative to begin rebuilding comes from Nehemiah, the king's cupbearer, but is authorized by King Artaxerxes.

Another theme found in Ezra–Nehemiah is the opposition of the people of the land. In the Ezra material, this takes the form of opposition to Ezra's reforms. The people who are living in Judah when the people of God return from exile offer to help in the building process, but are denied (4:1–3). As a result, the "people of the land" resist all of the former exiles' attempts to rebuild the temple. In the Nehemiah material, the opposition is to Nehemiah's rebuilding of the wall. Nehemiah is ridiculed by Sanballat, Tobiah, and Geshem for rebuilding the wall (Neh. 2:19, 4:1–7). Even his own people complain of not being able to work their fields (Neh. 5). Nehemiah faces opposition from within and without throughout the process of rebuilding the wall.

The last major theme of Ezra–Nehemiah is the separation of the people of Israel from foreign nations and peoples. First, Ezra's reform calls for those who married foreign wives to divorce them and to expel them along with any children from that marriage. Although this process does encounter resistance, it helps to solidify the cultural and religious identity of the Jewish people. Second, Nehemiah calls the people to build a wall, which will provide security from attack, but also separation from those outside.

Interpretive Issues: The most important interpretive issue in Ezra–Nehemiah studies is its relationship to the book of Chronicles. Scholars have noted thematic similarities and the fact that the beginning of Ezra–Nehemiah is the same as the end of Chronicles. There is currently a divide in the scholarly community over whether these books had the same author or two authors. Some scholars talk of a "Chronicler's school" that was responsible for all of these books, while others call attention to points of divergence between the books. Childs argues that, although the Chronicler played a significant role in the shaping of Ezra–Nehemiah, these books do not have the same author. Eskenazi argues for two authors, claiming that concern for the cult is the only significant similar theme between the two books, while other themes demonstrate their dissimilarity. Min argues for separate authorship on literary grounds and holds that the books' ideological differences present the strongest arguments for separate authorship.

The second major interpretive issue in the book of Ezra–Nehemiah is that of intermarriage. Ezra called the Jewish men to divorce their foreign wives and expel the children from those marriages. This has been viewed as cruel and exclusivist by many modern readers. In particular, it has been noted that Ezra makes no mention of Jewish women marrying foreign men. This is presumably because lineage was traced through the male and the women who married foreign men were no longer considered part of the community.

The last major interpretive issue in the book of Ezra–Nehemiah is the chronological order of the book. The book of Ezra–Nehemiah places the two main figures as rough contemporaries, but they do not refer to each other during the book. In addition, during Nehemiah's second trip to Jerusalem he deals with the same issues of intermarriage that plagued Ezra. The dating of Ezra and Nehemiah's ministries is further complicated by the fact that part of the story of Ezra is in the book of Nehemiah. Gottwald argues that the editor of Ezra–Nehemiah intentionally separated and reordered the sections of Ezra's and Nehemiah's stories in order to draw them closer together thematically. He argues that Nehemiah preceded Ezra and that they worked separately.

Influences: The books of Ezra and Nehemiah drew upon preexisting sources, including personal memoirs, Persian court documents and correspondence, Jewish lists of families and descendants, and narrative records. An Aramaic collection may have been the source behind Ezra 4:7–6:18, which remains in the Aramaic language, while the remainder of Ezra–Nehemiah is in Hebrew. Some scholars believe that it was Ezra who brought what is called the P material, which served as the Priestly source for the Pentateuch, to Jerusalem and helped to integrate it into the existing Pentateuch. Some have argued that Ezra is responsible for the final version of the Pentateuch, though most simply acknowledge that Ezra had some influence on the Pentateuch's formation (cf. Neh. 8).

The combined work of Ezra–Nehemiah and the themes contained therein influenced, not only the Judaism of the Second Temple period, but all of subsequent Jewish life and thought. In particular, the forbidding of marriage to non-Israelites and the imposition of Torah as the civic constitution of Jerusalem and Yehud significantly determined the direction of Judaism after the exile. *See also* Chronicles, First and Second Books of.

Bibliography

Bandstra, Barry L. *Reading the Old Testament: Introduction to the Hebrew Bible*. 4th ed. Wadsworth, 2009.

Berquist, Jon L. *Judaism in Persia's Shadow: A Social and Historical Approach*. Augsburg Fortress, 1996.

Childs, Brevard S. *Introduction to the Old Testament as Scripture*. Fortress, 1979.

Edelman, Diana V. *The Origins of the "Second" Temple: Persian Imperial Policy and the Rebuilding of Jerusalem*. Equinox, 2005.

Eskenazi, Tamara C. *In an Age of Prose: A Literary Approach to Ezra–Nehemiah*. Scholars, 1988.

Gottwald, Norman K. *The Hebrew Bible: A Socio-Literary Introduction*. Fortress, 1985.

Min, Kyung-Jin. *The Levitical Authorship of Ezra–Nehemiah*. Clark, 2004.   B.B.

Opposite: Fisherman with basket of fish; decorated pottery oil lamp, first century CE.

F

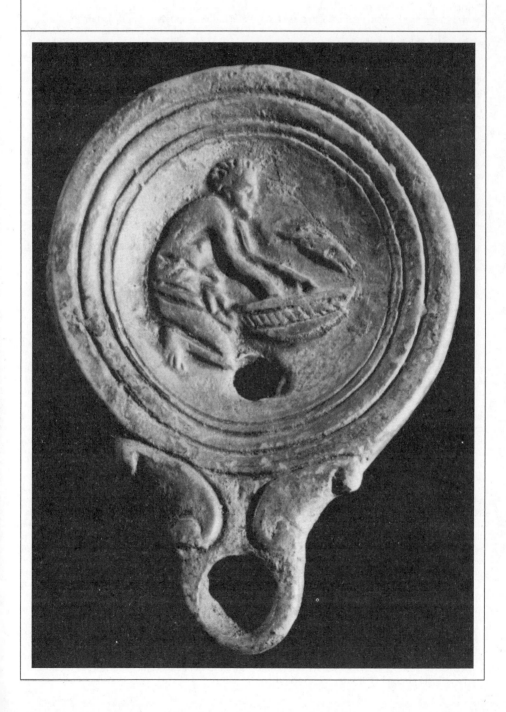

Fair Havens, a bay on the south-central coast of Crete, where Paul's ship put in on his journey to Rome (Acts 27:8); it is still known by the same name in Greek. Weighing anchor there in the fall, Paul's ship (against his advice), made a run for the safer harbor of Phoenix to the west, but was driven off course by a sudden northeast wind (KJV: "Euroclydon"; NRSV: "northeaster"; Acts 27:9–15). *See also* Crete; northeaster; Paul; Phoenix. C.H.M.

faith, in the Bible, trust in or reliance on God, who is trustworthy. The NT and the LXX express the understanding of faith with two terms (*pistis, pisteuein*), which are related to the Hebrew verb "to be true" or "to be trustworthy" (*'aman*).

In the Hebrew Bible: The Hebrew verb *'aman* means, for the most part, "to be true"; lying behind this is the root meaning "solid," "firm." This sense of "to be true" is intensified in the passive form of the verb, so that one can speak of a person as "trustworthy" or "reliable." The causative form of the verb suggests the acceptance of someone as trustworthy or dependable. Thus, one who has faith in God accepts God as trustworthy and believes God's word (Deut. 9:23) and promises. This is the case with Abraham in Gen. 15:1–6; he regards God as trustworthy and God counts this trust as righteousness. The primary nouns derived from the verb "to trust" (*'aman*) are *'emunah* ("firmness, stability"), as in God will be "the stability of your times" (Isa. 33:6), and *'emet* ("truthfulness, fidelity, faithfulness"), as in "I will also praise you with the harp for your faithfulness, O my God" (Ps. 71:22). Stability results in security, and together these are signs of God's fidelity.

God stands at the center of all discussions of faith. Faith comes at God's initiative, for God's faithfulness is shown in creation, in the exodus event, in the covenant, and in the subsequent history of Israel, and faith is in essence a response to this divine fidelity. For example, "Israel saw the great work that the LORD did against the Egyptians. So the people feared the LORD and they believed in the LORD and in his servant Moses" (Exod. 14:31). God's mighty acts evoke fear and trust. The paradoxical relationship between faith and fear owes to the mutuality of obligation that defines the covenant relationship between God and God's people. That covenant results in an exclusive demand (Exod. 20:3; Deut. 6:5; 18:13; 1 Kings 8:61; Isa. 38:3), according to which idols must be totally rejected (Isa. 42:17). In fact, the opposite of faith/faithfulness can be apostasy, as in Deut. 32:20, where the phrase "children in whom there is no faithfulness" is synonymous with idolatry. Thus, the faith of Israel is always reflective of God's fidelity, but it is expressed "fearfully" with equal response to God's demand. This fearful but trusting response takes the form of both obedience (Gen. 6:9, 22; 7:5; 22:1–18; Josh. 1:7–8; 24:22–31; 1 Sam. 15:17–33) and praise (Pss. 5:11; 9:10; 13:5; 18:1–3; 22:1–5; 27:14; 62:1, 5–8; 141:8).

The prophets deepen the meaning of faith in several ways. According to Isa. 7:1–9, security does not rest in political power, but in utter trust in God; in fact, the totality of life must be based on such trust ("If you do not stand firm in faith, you will not stand at all," 7:9). This point is also stressed in Isa. 28:16 ("One who trusts will not panic"). The writings of Second Isaiah (i.e., Isa. 40–55) broaden the concept of faith in the direction of hope and knowledge: faced with difficult predicaments, the energy of faith results, not in despair, but in hope (40:31), and not in speculation, but in certain knowledge of who God is and what God does (43:10). Hab. 2:4 asserts that, unlike those who are proud, "the righteous live by their faith," trusting God to fulfill divine promises.

Finally, the emphasis throughout the Hebrew Bible is, not on the individual, but on the faith relationship of the people of Israel to God. The faith of individual patriarchs, judges, or kings is significant primarily because it determines the status of the people or nation as a whole. It is only in the Psalms, Second Isaiah, and a few other passages that any attention is given to the individual, personal faith of common people.

In the NT: Throughout the NT, the noun and verb denoting faith (*pistis, pisteuein*) appear frequently. In the Synoptic Gospels, faith sometimes means believing or trusting in the gospel (Mark 1:15), but more often faith is related to trusting God to provide extraordinary help in desperate circumstances. Only occasionally does faith have God as its explicit object ("Have faith in God," Mark 11:22), but the same sense is clearly implied in most texts where the word occurs ("Only believe [in God]," Mark 5:36; "All things can be done for the one who believes [in God]," Mark 9:23–24). Accordingly, Jesus often attributes the miraculous works of God done through him to the faith that people have in God (e.g., Matt. 8:13; 9:28; 15:28; Mark 5:34; 10:52; Luke 7:50; 8:12). Lack of faith, on the other hand, can prevent people from experiencing Jesus's miracles (Matt. 13:58; Mark 6:5–6). It prevents Peter from walking on water (Matt. 14:30–31) and other disciples from casting out a demon (Matt. 17:19–20). Lack of faith is sometimes equated with fear (Matt. 14:30–31; Mark 4:40). Jesus's disciples are depicted as people of "little faith" (Matt. 6:30; 8:26; 14:31; 16:8; 17:20; Luke 12:28; cf. Mark 4:40), and yet Jesus maintains that one who has only the tiniest speck of faith ("as a mustard seed") will be able to move mountains (Matt. 17:20; cf. Luke 17:6). In Matthew's Gospel, Jesus lists "justice, mercy, and faith" as the weightier matters of the law (23:23). In the Gospel of John, the word "faith" is never used as a noun, but the verb ("to believe") occurs frequently. The author describes his Gospel as intended to produce faith (20:30–31). The view of faith found in the Fourth Gospel is also closely linked to its understanding of Christology, namely, that Jesus is the one sent by the Father as the revealer ("This is the work of God, that you believe in him whom God has sent," 6:29). In the book of Acts, the term "believer" is used with frequency (e.g., 2:44) and the object of belief is the preaching of the apostles (4:1–4).

The writings of Paul offer the broadest articulation of faith in early Christianity. The object of faith for Paul is not simply God (1 Thess. 1:8), but, specifically, God's salvific manifestation through the death and resurrection of Jesus Christ (1 Thess. 4:14). The proclamation of this act of God produces faith (Rom. 10:17), so that the gospel is received through a faith that rests in "the power of God" (1 Cor. 2:5; cf. Rom. 1:16–17; 3:25). Those who have received the good news of God's act in Christ are therefore called "believers" (1 Thess. 1:7). For Paul, furthermore, the concept of faith is a dynamic one. Thus, he can refer to the "activity of faith" (1 Thess. 1:23), an activity that manifests itself in love (Gal. 5:6). Faith involves "progress" (Phil. 1:25) and "striving" (Phil. 1:27). It increases (2 Cor. 10:15) and is an energy at work in believers (1 Thess. 2:13). Since faith is not a static possession, Paul urges that faith be established (1 Thess. 3:2) and made firm (1 Cor. 16:13; 2 Cor. 1:24), for it is possible, not only to have deficiencies in faith (1 Thess. 3:10; Rom. 14:1), but also to believe in vain (1 Cor. 15:2; Rom. 11:20). Essential for Paul's understanding of faith is the conviction that God assigns to each person a "measure of faith" (Rom. 12:3, 6; 1 Cor. 12:9). Yet no matter what that measure of faith is, it is sufficient both to make the person right with God and also to sanctify that person by producing in him or her "the obedience of faith" (Rom. 1:5; 16:16). In Galatians and Romans Paul links his concept of faith to terms like the "righteousness of God" and "justification" and to a negative attitude toward the "works of the law": people are justified by grace through faith in Jesus Christ *rather than* by doing works of the law (Gal. 2:16; cf. Rom. 10:14). Paul also likes to use formulations that combine the three terms "faith," "love," and "hope" (1 Thess. 1:3; 5:8; 1 Cor. 13:13). On the one hand, as noted above, faith must be active in love; without love faith is empty. On the other hand, faith must be grounded in hope, so that it recognizes that the first fruits of God's promises manifested in the death and resurrection of Christ will be fulfilled on the last day (Rom. 6:8; 15:13; 1 Cor. 15:14, 17; 2 Cor. 4:14; Gal. 5:5). Yet this faith also makes one a part of the body of Christ, the church, which takes the suffering and death of Jesus as its model for behavior. Thus, Paul can say that God "has graciously granted you the privilege not only of believing in Christ but of suffering for him as well" (Phil. 1:29; cf. Rom. 8:18).

Elsewhere in the NT, James 2:14–20 insists that faith without works is useless (probably not a criticism of Paul, but of those who have lost sight of the Pauline relationship between the activity of faith and its expression in and through love). Heb. 11:1 says that faith is "the assurance of things hoped for, the conviction of things not seen," and Heb. 12:2 refers to Jesus as "the pioneer and perfecter" of faith. *See also* hope; justification; love; righteousness.   K.P.D./M.A.P.

fall, the, a Christian doctrine based upon a reading of Gen. 3, a text that narrates the disobedience

Serpent around the forbidden tree, Eve with hand outstretched, and Adam beside her; fifteenth-century relief, Italy.

of Adam and Eve and the results of this disobedience. According to a common Christian interpretation, this disobedience resulted from a desire to be like God and to usurp God's rightful place as Creator. Further, according to the Christian doctrine of the fall, the positive relationship that humans had with God was broken by the disobedience of the first humans, and all evil and tragedy in the created order can be explained as a result of this rebellion and disobedience. As a result of the fall, humanity was trapped in a sinful state, which issued in death, not simply (or primarily) physical death, but rather spiritual separation from God. This idea of a primordial fall is never worked out in the Hebrew Bible (and there is no comparable doctrine in Judaism), but the doctrine is expressed in some Hellenistic Jewish writings as well as in the NT. Sir. 25:24 identifies Eve as the one who brought sin and death into the world: "From a woman, sin had its beginning, and because of her, we all die" (Sir. 25:24; cf. *2 Enoch* 30:17; *Apoc. Moses* 7:1, 21). Paul alludes to Gen. 3, setting up a parallel between the "first Adam," through whose disobedience sin and death achieved dominion, and Christ (the second Adam), whose obedience leads to faith, life, and even a new creation (Rom. 5:12–21; 1 Cor. 15:21–22, 45–49; 2 Cor. 5:17). *See also* Adam; atonement; creation; death; devil; Eden; Eve; redemption; salvation; Satan; serpent; sin.   J.K./M.A.P.

family. The family was the basic social unit in Israel during the biblical period.

The Nuclear Family: The smallest family unit was the nuclear family (Heb. *bayit*), which usually occupied its own dwelling. The nuclear family normally consisted of parents and their unmarried children, although occasionally slaves, long-term visitors, or others also shared the family's living quarters. Archaeological evidence suggests that no more than six or seven people occupied the average house on a regular basis. Within the nuclear family children were socialized by being taught the customs and lore of their people (Prov. 1:8; 6:20), including the story of God's dealings with Israel (Exod. 10:2; 12:26; 13:8; Deut. 4:9; 6:7, 20–25; 32:7, 46). Well into the monarchic period (ca. 1020–587/6 BCE) each nuclear family was also a self-sustaining economic unit. Agricultural products grown by the family were stored in the house, and any animals that the family might own were quartered there. Living arrangements may have been different in the period before Israel's settlement in Canaan (thirteenth–twelfth centuries BCE), but there is little evidence to determine this one way or another.

Most of the authority in the nuclear family belonged to the father, who exercised legal control over his children and wife, although his power was not absolute (Exod. 21:7–11; Deut. 21:15–21). Children were expected to honor and obey their parents, and failure to do so was considered a serious matter (Exod. 20:12; 21:15, 17; Lev. 20:9; Deut. 27:16; Prov. 30:17). The integrity of the family was further protected by harsh laws against adultery and incest (Exod. 20:14; Lev. 18:20; 20:10–21; Deut. 5:18; 22:22). Children remained under their father's control until they were married, when they left home to start a new family unit. Marriages were carefully regulated (Lev. 18). In early Israel polygyny was common (Gen. 4:19; 16:1–2; 22:20–24; 25:1, 6; 29:15–30), but by monarchic times this practice was limited primarily to the royal family. Even after marriage children were expected to honor their parents and were exhorted to care for them in their old age (Prov. 23:22).

The Extended Family: The extended family ("father's house") was composed of two or more nuclear families that claimed descent from the same ancestor. The term employed forty-eight times in the NRSV for such an extended family unit is "father's house," which translates Heb. *bet 'ab* and reflects the patriarchal structure for such units (see, e.g., Gen. 12:1; 24:7; 31:30; Lev. 22:13; Judg. 9:5; 1 Sam. 22:1; Luke 16:27; Acts 17:20). Three times, however, the expression "mother's house(hold)" is used, indicating a female-led counterpart to the normally male-led institution (Gen. 24:28; Ruth 1:8; Song of Sol. 3:4). The story in Genesis about the home to which Rebekah and her brother Laban belong is especially intriguing, for the same social unit is referred to as both the "father's house" (Gen. 24:23) and the "mother's household" (Gen. 24:28). In any case, the bonds of such an extended family unit transcended physical proximity and vocation. Members of an extended family might live together in adjoining houses, but this does not seem to have been common. Likewise, they occasionally worked at the same trade or profession (1 Chron. 4:14, 21, 23), but this was not necessary, or even typical. Still, the extended family acted as a corporate entity and was granted certain legal rights in order to maintain its solidarity. When one of its nuclear families was forced to sell property, the extended family

had the right to redeem the property in order to keep it from leaving the family (Lev. 25:25; Jer. 32:6–15). Individuals threatened with being sold into slavery could be redeemed by a member of their extended family, and, at least in the early period, the family was allowed to avenge a wrong done to one of its members (Lev. 25:47–49). The unit of an extended family also served as a basic military unit for purposes of defense or warfare (cf. Gen. 41:51; 46:31; Judg. 9:5; 1 Sam. 2:27–31; 2 Chron. 25:5). Power in the extended family was exercised by the ancestor from whom all of its constituent nuclear families were descended. If this individual was not living, then questions of authority were negotiated among the heads of the nuclear families.

Clan and Tribe: Several extended families were sometimes linked together to form a larger family group, which the NRSV sometimes calls a "clan" (Heb. *mishpakhah*). In such a group, the families traced their genealogies to a single ancestor, although at the level of the clan factors other than genuine consanguinity often played a role in establishing group unity. Members usually lived in the same geographic area and sometimes made up an entire village (Judg. 18:11–13). Such groups may have helped to protect their members against outside attack, but otherwise seem to have had few social functions. The family metaphor was also extended beyond the clan to include the tribe and the nation of Israel itself, so that the whole people could be seen as one enormous family represented by a complex segmented or branched genealogy (Gen. 46:8–27; Num. 26:5–62; 1 Chron. 1–9). Because of the large numbers of people involved in these groups, it is difficult to know how effectively they functioned as social units.

Although some of the power of the tribes and clans was taken away by the monarchy, the nuclear and extended families seem to have survived intact throughout Israel's history. After the exile caused many changes in Israel's structure, the family played an even greater role in maintaining the people's stability.

In the NT: Biblical views of the family are both adopted and adapted in the NT. On the one hand, Jesus quotes approvingly the command to honor parents and thus supports the traditional Jewish family structure (Matt. 19:16–22; Luke 18:18–30). On the other hand, some of Jesus's sayings subordinate family loyalty to loyalty to the gospel (Matt. 10:34–39; 12:46–50; Mark 3:31–35; Luke 12:49–53). In the early church, support of one's family was seen as a virtue (1 Tim. 5:8), but the traditional view of family was transformed by seeing the Christian community as a new family or "household of faith" (Gal. 6:10; Eph. 2:19; 1 Tim. 3:15; 1 Pet. 4:17). Such imagery may have derived in part from scriptural references to Israel as God's house (Num. 5:7, cited in Heb. 3:2, 5; Jer. 31:31, cited in Heb. 8:8–10; Amos 5:25–27, cited in Acts 7:42–43; Amos 9:11, cited in Acts 15:16). Employment of this metaphor sometimes had literalistic implications: a primary qualification for leadership in the church could be a demonstrated capacity for keeping one's children "submissive and respectful" and in other ways managing one's literal household well (1 Tim. 3:4–5). Several NT letters present "household codes," listing responsibilities associated with different family roles (husbands, wives, parents, children, masters, slaves); see Eph. 5:21–6:9; Col. 3:18–4:1; 1 Tim. 2:8–15; 5:1–2; 6:1–2; Titus 2:1–10; 1 Pet. 2:13–3:7; cf. two letters by other early church leaders, *1 Clement* 1:3; 21:6–9; and Polycarp *Philippians* 4:1–6:2. *See also* genealogy; marriage.   R.R.W.

famine. In Ezek. 14:21, famine is listed as one of God's "four deadly acts of judgment" along with the sword (war), evil beasts, and pestilence. Famine is also mentioned as a divine judgment in Jeremiah, along with the sword (fourteen times) and with the sword and pestilence (fifteen times). In Deut. 28:48, hunger is one of the many curses God will send for disobedience. In the book of Revelation, famine is symbolized by the third horseman of the apocalypse, who announces exorbitant prices for food and precedes the horseman named Death (6:5–8). In the book of Genesis, God enables Joseph to predict a famine by interpreting Pharaoh's dream (41). Other periods of severe famine are recorded during the days of Abraham (Gen. 12:10), Isaac (Gen. 26:1), Elisha (1 Kings 7; 8:16), and Zedekiah (2 Kings 25:3; cf. Lam. 5:10). Philistia was threatened with famine in an oracle from Isaiah (cf. Isa. 14:30). Famine may lead to disease (Jer. 14:18) and, most gruesome, cannibalism of one's own offspring (Deut. 28:47–57). Other attendant judgments may be captivity (Jer. 15:2), exile (Ezek. 5:12), nakedness (Deut. 28:47), and earthquakes (Matt. 24:7). Metaphorically, the prophet Amos speaks of a famine, not as a lack of bread or water, but one "of hearing the words of the Lord" (8:11). The NT refers to a worldwide famine at the time of the Roman emperor Claudius, prompting the church in the Roman world to send help to the Christians in Jerusalem at the hands of Barnabas and Saul (Acts 11:27–30). Paul also affirms that famine will not be able to separate believers from the love of God in Christ (Rom. 8:35–38). In the Gospels, a famine contributes to the plight of a prodigal son in a parable told by Jesus (Luke 15:14).   J.G.G.

farming, the process of cultivating land and raising crops, from soil preparation to the storage and transport of crops to market. No human activity is as prevalent in the Bible as farming. Agricultural pursuits are mentioned in the opening pages of Genesis (2:15; 4:2; 9:20), and farming activities were important enough to be regulated by Mosaic law (e.g., Lev. 19:9; 25:3–5; Deut. 22:9–10). The orderly system used in working the land was attributed to God (Isa. 28:26), and Jesus used figures derived from farming to picture the coming of God's kingdom (Mark 4:3–8, 26–29).

The most important crops were wheat, grapes, and olives (Ps. 104:15; Joel 2:19); other crops in-

A farm near Jerusalem dating to ancient times is still under cultivation.

cluded barley, flax, lentils, chickpeas, cucumbers, onions, melons, dates, figs, and spices. Because of variations in soil productivity, temperature, and rainfall, certain areas of the country were better suited than others for specific crops, but a wide range of crops and trading and pastoral activities enabled farmers to provide for their families. Unlike their Egyptian and Mesopotamian counterparts, Israelite farmers were not dependent upon irrigation to water crops; rainfall and dew usually sufficed (Deut. 11:10–11; 1 Kings 17:1). Naturally, ancient farmers contended with the elements, pests, and warfare, but the major enemy was drought (cf. Jer. 14:1–6).

Farmers were occupied throughout the year with animal husbandry, and heavy field work never ended. Land was marked off with boundary stones (Prov. 22:28); ground was cleared of rocks and thorns (Isa. 5:2); fields, vineyards, and orchards were hedged and walled (Isa. 5:5; cf. Mark 12:1); and hillsides were terraced.

Most farming activities, however, were controlled by the seasons. Plowing for winter crops did not begin until after the "early" or "former" rains of autumn (Prov. 20:4); only then could lightweight plows scratch the surface of sun-baked fields. Once the soil had been broken with a plow and team of draft animals, clods were pulverized and the surface flattened with hoes or harrows (Isa. 28:24–25). Sowing, which was usually accomplished by broadcasting seed, could precede or follow plowing. Fields or individual plants were fertilized with dung (Jer. 9:22; Luke 13:8), and the rain and sun brought different crops to maturity at different times.

Following the winter rains and the "latter" rains of March and April, barley was ready to be harvested in April and May, and wheat matured three or four weeks later. Grain was pulled up by the roots or cut with flint-bladed or iron sickles (Deut. 16:9). The harvested sheaves were spread out on a threshing floor (i.e., a rock outcropping or a hard-packed earthen surface), and the stalk, chaff, and grain were cut apart by animal hooves (Deut. 25:4), flails (Ruth 2:17), or threshing sledges (Isa. 41:15). Grain was separated from the chaff by winnowing (Isa. 41:16), and the kernels were sifted to remove bits of straw (Luke 22:31). After a bumper crop, the threshing and winnowing process could last all summer. The finished product was bagged and hauled away for storage or sale, and the chaff was burned (Matt. 3:12). Meanwhile, summer crops had been planted after the winter rains; these plants were cultivated throughout the dry summer months. The harvesting of fruit, including olives and grapes, began in late summer and continued into fall.

The Bible demonstrates that almost every aspect of agricultural work assumed a figurative meaning in the minds of ancient speakers and writers (e.g., Isa. 21:10; Amos 9:13; Mic. 4:12–13; Matt. 9:37–38; 13:3–32; Luke 9:62; 1 Cor. 9:9–11; Gal. 6:7; Rev. 14:14–20). *See also* plow; sowing; winnowing.   G.L.M.

fasting, abstention from food for intentional, usually religious, reasons. In the Bible, there are two kinds of fasting, private and public. Private fasts were observed as acts of penance (2 Sam. 12:15–23; 1 Kings 21:27; Ps. 69:1–15) or of mourning (Neh. 1:4); fasting could be a means of seeking divine counsel or aid (Ps. 35:13–14; Dan. 9:3), or simply of expressing devotion for God (Luke 18:12). Public fasts were periodically proclaimed for the community as a whole (2 Chron. 20:3; Jer. 36:9). The purposes were essentially the same as with private fasts: to obtain God's help or protection (Judg. 20:26; 1 Sam. 14:24; Joel 1:14; Esther 4:3; Ezra 8:21–23), to express repentance (1 Sam. 7:6; Jon. 3:5–10), or to mourn the death of leaders (1 Sam. 31:13; 2 Sam. 1:12). Fasting was typically accompanied by prayer and supplication and sometimes by wearing sackcloth as a sign of humility, penance, or mourning (Neh. 9:1; Dan. 9:3; 1 Macc. 3:47). "Denying oneself," synonymous with "fasting," was required on the Day of Atonement (Lev. 16:31–34). Public fasts ordinarily lasted a day, and offerings of various sorts were made (Lev. 16:1–5; Judg. 20:26; Jer. 14:11–12). In the tragic days surrounding the fall of Jerusalem, four fast days were proclaimed (Zech. 7:5; 8:19). The prophetic writings contain warnings related to fasting that circumvents what is truly pleasing to God (e.g., sharing bread with the hungry and bringing the homeless poor into one's house, Isa. 58:1–9; Jer. 14:11–12; Zech. 7:3–5; 8:18–19). The prophet Joel, however, unhesitatingly calls for a public fast and communal lamentation (1:8–2:17).

In the NT Jesus stresses that fasting be sincere and not merely for show (Matt. 6:16–18). In one of his parables, he contrasts a self-righteous man who brags of fasting twice a week with a humble sinner who begs God for mercy (Luke 18:9–14).

Jesus himself fasts at the outset of his ministry (Matt. 4:2) but, in contrast to John the Baptist, he later excuses his disciples from fasting on the grounds that his time with them is like a wedding feast (Mark 2:18–19). The Gospels, however, also record Jesus as saying, "The day will come when the bridegroom is taken away from them, and then they will fast" (Mark 2:20). This offers clear indication that the early church thought the physical absence of Jesus marked the time between his resurrection and Parousia as a period when fasting would be appropriate and expected. In the book of Acts, fasting accompanies prayer prior to the consecration of teachers and elders (13:2–3; 14:23) and during times of severe trial (Acts 27:1–38).   J.G.G.

fat, in sacrificial contexts, the greasy tissue of animals burned on the altar as an offering. The Hebrew word for "fat" (*kheleb*) specifically refers to the fat covering and surrounding the entrails and the fat on the kidneys (Lev. 3:3–4), but it also has a more general sense that includes the kidneys, liver appendage, and tail (of a sheep; Lev. 4:31; 7:3–4). The fat of sacrificial animals must not be eaten (Lev. 7:23–25; cf. 3:17).

The same word is also used of human fat (Judg. 3:22, 2 Sam. 1:22) or for "fat" in a more generic or figurative sense: the arrogant have hearts that are fat and gross (Ps. 119:70). Sometimes the term is used to mean "best of," and then it is usually translated as "best" or "finest" in the NRSV (Num. 18:12, 29–32; Pss. 81:16; 147:14). This is also the sense implied by the expression "fat of the land" (Gen. 45:18). In the NT, the word "fat" is used mainly for animals, with a connotation that this makes them desirable for food (Matt. 22:4). In Luke 15:23, a father who is a character in one of Jesus's parables kills the "fatted calf" to celebrate the return of a prodigal son. Elsewhere, James tells the rich, "You have fattened your hearts in a day of slaughter" (5:5).   D.P.W./M.A.P.

father, in the Bible, a designation used, not only for the immediate male progenitor, but also for the head of a people or tribe (Gen. 19:37), or for the founder of a town (1 Chron. 2:41–52), or of some institution (Gen. 4:20–21; NRSV: "ancestor"). The plural, "fathers" (NRSV: "ancestors"), refers to previous generations (Jer. 31:32; Ps. 22:4; Lam. 5:7). "Father" can also be a name for advisers to the king or high governmental officials (Gen. 45:8; Isa. 22:21) or an honorary title given to prophets and priests (Judg. 17:10; 2 Kings 2:11; 6:21; 13:14). And, of course, "father" is an important appellation for the deity (Exod. 4:22; Deut. 14:1; 32:6; Hos. 11:1; Jer. 3:4, 19; 31:9; Ps. 103:13).

A father was permitted to arrange his daughter's marriage and receive her bride-price (Gen. 34:12; 1 Sam. 18:25). The Genesis narratives, however, indicate that it was customary to ask the daughter if she agreed to a marriage (Gen. 24:57–58). The father also had the right to cancel his daughter's vows (Num. 30:4–6). Although the Torah forbade selling one's daughter into prostitution (Lev. 19:29), it did permit the selling of a daughter into servitude on the condition that she become the wife of her master or his son; if the condition was not met, she would be freed (Exod. 21:7–9). As in the ancient Near East, the father apparently could sell his sons into servitude for his debts (Isa. 50:1; cf. 2 Kings 4:1), but this practice was condemned by Nehemiah (5:1–9). Deut. 24:16 decrees that children may not be punished for the sins of the parents (cf. 2 Kings 14:6) and vice versa; this was upheld by the prophets (Jer. 31:29–30; Ezek. 18:20). The father was obligated to circumcise his sons (Gen. 17:12, 23; 21:4; Lev. 12:3), to redeem his firstborn son (Exod. 13:13), and to educate the children in the Torah (Exod. 13:8; Deut. 4:9; 6:7, 20–25; also Prov. 3:12; 4:1). The children were to revere and obey the father equally with the mother (Exod. 20:12; Lev. 19:3; Deut. 21:18, 20; cf. Exod. 21:15; Lev. 20:9).

In the NT, "father" can refer to the male progenitor (e.g., Matt. 1:1–16; Mark 1:20; Acts 28:8), but in most instances it is used to refer to God. This Christian practice probably derives from the fact that "Father" was a favorite term that Jesus used for God (Heb., Aramaic *abba;* Mark 14:36; cf. Rom. 8:15; Gal. 4:6). *See also* family.   J.U.

father's house. *See* family.

fear of the Lord (or "fear of the LORD"), the awe that a person ought to have before God (Pss. 33:8; 34:11; Prov. 5:7; Eccles. 12:13). Sometimes such fear is appropriately demonstrated by those who have displeased God: Adam and Eve were afraid of God after they ate the forbidden fruit (Gen. 3:8–10). The threat of judgment ought to produce fear (Amos 3:7), but in a more general sense fear of God can be engendered by a simple awareness of God's magnificence (Jer. 5:22, 24). In this sense it frequently accompanies theophanies, the appearance of angels, or the occurrence of miraculous events: Moses hid his face and was afraid to look at God when God spoke to him out of the burning bush (Exod. 3:6; cf. Matt. 28:8; Luke 1:30). In wisdom literature, the "fear of the LORD" is presented as a prerequisite for obtaining wisdom or understanding (Ps. 111:10; Prov. 1:7; 9:10; Sir. 1:20); indeed, it can be virtually equated with possession of wisdom or understanding (Job 28:28; Sir. 19:20). It can be taught (Ps. 34:11) or chosen (Prov. 1:29). It is also closely connected to obedience to God's commandments (Job 25:21; Ps. 19:9; Eccles. 12:13), to hating evil (Prov. 8:13), to trusting God (Ps. 40:3), to enjoying friendship with God (Ps. 25:14), to obtaining deliverance and other benefits from God (Pss. 33:18; 34:7; 145:19; Prov. 10:27; 22:4), and to experiencing life in its fullest (Prov. 19:23). In the NT, Jesus contrasts fearing God, who can destroy body and soul in hell, with fearing humans, who can kill the body only (Matt. 10:25). Fear is also represented by the "fear and trembling" with which Paul exhorts the

Philippians to work out their salvation (2:12). It describes the piety of the growing church (Acts 9:31; cf. 5:11; 13:26) and accords with recognition that people will be held accountable by God in the judgment (2 Cor. 5:10–11; 1 Pet. 1:17).   M.A.P.

Felix, Antonius (fee′liks, an-tohn′ee-uhs), Roman procurator of Judea ca. 52–59 CE. According to the historians Josephus, Suetonius, and Tacitus, he was brutal in his rule, instigating the murder of the high priest Jonathan and allowing a violent pogrom against Jews in Caesarea. He owed his position to his influential brother Pallas, but, because of immorality and incompetence, he was eventually replaced. According to Acts 23:23–24:27, Felix became involved with Paul when the apostle was sent to Caesarea for trial upon recommendation of Claudius Lysias, the tribune in Jerusalem. The writer of Acts indicates that Felix followed appropriate judicial procedure during Paul's hearing. After listening to Paul speak on matters pertaining to faith in Jesus Christ, however, he is pictured in unfavorable terms. Hoping for a bribe, which was not forthcoming, and "desiring to do the Jews a favor," he allowed Paul to languish in prison for the remainder of his term in office. *See also* Lysias, Claudius; Paul.   A.J.M.

fellowship, communal association for the mutual benefit of those involved. In the NRSV, the word "fellowship" (Gk. *koinōnia*) is used only in the NT, as a mark of the early church (Acts 2:42; Gal. 2:9; 1 John 1:7) and as a description of the intimate relationship that believers have with God through Jesus Christ (1 Cor. 1:9; 1 John 1:6). In some respects, this becomes a Christian version of the Jewish concept of "covenant." In the Bible, the Sinai covenant bound all Israelites together into what was, ideally, a grand fellowship of mutual obligation and concern. Furthermore, covenant images clearly suggest a kind of fellowship between God and the people. For example, Israel is the wife of God (Hos. 1–3; Jer. 2:2; Ezek. 16); God has "known" (chosen) Israel (Amos 3:2); and Israel is to "know" (acknowledge, obey) God. God's election of Israel is motivated by love (Deut. 7:7), and Israel is to be God's own possession among all peoples (Exod. 19:5). Such relational language sometimes applies to individuals: Enoch "walked with God" (Gen. 5:24); Abraham is called the "friend" of God (2 Chron. 20:7; Isa. 41:8); and Moses talks with God "face to face" (Exod. 33:11; cf. Deut. 34:10). The prophets' experience of being commissioned by God suggests a special bond (Isa. 6; Jer. 1; Ezek. 1), and the Davidic king is called God's son (2 Sam. 7:14; Ps. 2:7).

In Paul's letters, fellowship is the bond among Christians created by their common confession that Jesus is Lord. In Paul's letters this fellowship is marked by the spiritual oneness effected by baptism and bestowal of the Spirit (Gal. 3:27–28; 1 Cor. 12). It is manifested by the gathered community at the Lord's Supper (1 Cor. 11:17–34) and characterized above all by self-giving love

(1 Cor. 13). This fellowship of believers is dependent on—and an expression of—their fellowship with Christ. Fellowship with Christ means that believers share his death and experience the new life that corresponds to his resurrection (Rom. 6:1–11; Phil. 3:8–11), sustained by the hope that at his coming they will forever be with him (1 Thess. 4:13–17). The apostle stresses, further, that communion with Christ excludes other types of fellowship, e.g., with prostitutes or demons (1 Cor. 6:15–17; 10:19–21). Paul's letter to the Philippians is especially imbued with a sense of commonality: the word *koinōnia* (translated "sharing" in the NRSV) is used in Phil. 1:5; 2:1; 3:10, and the letter exhibits a prevalence of Greek words that begin with the prefix *syn-* (meaning "together" or "with," similar to the English prefix "co-"). Paul emphasizes that he and the Philippians have had common experiences (1:29–30) and that, as fellow citizens of heaven, they share a common hope and destiny (3:20); his joy will only be complete when they come to experience the same level of accord with one another that they have experienced up to now with him (2:2).

In the Johannine writings, Christian fellowship is characterized by a perfect oneness grounded in the closest of relationships with the Father and the Son (17:11, 21–23; see also 1 John 1:3, 6, 7). Jesus is the true vine in which believers must "abide" if they would bear fruit. Those who have fellowship with God walk in the light and love one another (John 15:12–13; 1 John 1:6–7). *See also* church; covenant; friend, friendship; Lord's Supper.

S.K.W./M.A.P.

festivals, feasts, and fasts, activities that, in the Bible, are observed to commemorate or emphasize events in the relationship between God and human beings.

Festivals and Feasts: Most religious festivals were occasions of joy. They were times for thanking God for blessings and granting relief to the poor and oppressed. They were often accompanied by singing, instrumental music, dancing, elaborate meals, and sacrifices. Depending on the nature and the requirements of the occasion, they were celebrated either at a sanctuary or at a person's home. The Pentateuch prescribes the observance of several recurring festivals. On the first day of each lunar month, a special series of sacrifices was to be made (Num. 28:11–15; cf. Ezek. 46:6–7). These new-moon festivals were days of feasting (1 Sam. 20:5, 18, 24, 27) and apparently days of rest (Amos 8:5). Of the new-moon festivals, that in the seventh month (the Festival of Trumpets) was the most important (Lev. 23:23–25; Num. 29:1–6). Three festivals, called pilgrimage festivals, required the participation of Israelite males at the sanctuary (Exod. 23:14, 17; 34:23; Deut. 16:16–17): (1) Passover and the Festival of Unleavened Bread, which were celebrated from the sunset of the fourteenth to the twenty-first day of the first month (Exod. 12; 23:15; 34:18, 25; Lev. 23:5–8; Num. 9:1–14; 28:16–25; Deut. 16:1–8; Ezek. 45:21–24); (2) the Festival of Weeks, which occurred at the beginning of the wheat harvest seven weeks after the presentation of the barley omer (Exod. 23:16; 34:22; Lev. 23:15–21; Num. 28:26–31; Deut. 16:9–10); and (3) the Festival of

The joyous festivities marking the occasion when David brought the ark of the covenant to Jerusalem; from a thirteenth-century French miniature.

Tabernacles (Booths), which was celebrated on the fifteenth through the twenty-second days of the seventh month when the harvest and produce were gathered in (Exod. 23:16; 34:22; Lev. 23:33–36; Num. 28:12–39; Deut. 16:13–18; Ezek. 45:25). Later festivals not prescribed in the Pentateuch include the Festival of Dedication (Hanukkah), which commemorates the rededication of the temple altar by Judas Maccabeus on the 25th of Chislev (Nov./Dec.) in 164 BCE (1 Macc. 4:36–59; 2 Macc. 10:6–8; cf. John 10:22); and Purim, celebrated on the fourteenth and fifteenth of Adar (Feb./March), which commemorates the deliverance from the persecutions of Haman as described in the book of Esther (9:19–28).

Besides the foregoing prescribed festivals, there are descriptions of other types of festivals and feasts in ancient Israel. Judg. 21:19–24 tells of a yearly festival in Shiloh. This may have been Shiloh's version of the Festival of Tabernacles (Booths) or it may have been a separate festival celebrating the new vintage. According to 1 Sam. 1–2, Elkanah and his family made yearly visits to the sanctuary at Shiloh to offer sacrifice and worship God. These visits may have been connected with the yearly festival mentioned in Judg. 21, but it seems more likely that they were separate family celebrations in the sanctuary city (cf. 1 Sam. 20:5–6, 24–39).

Public celebrations also accompanied dedication or renovation of temples (1 Kings 8; 2 Chron. 29) and the coronation of kings (1 Kings 1:39–40; 2 Kings 11:12, 13, 20). Military victories were occasions for celebration (1 Sam. 18:6–7; cf. 30:16). Families also celebrated major events in the lives of their members, such as the weaning of children (Gen. 21:8) or marriages (Gen. 29:22; Judg. 14:10–11; Tob. 10:7; Mark 2:19; John 2:1–2). Sheepherders, with families and friends, held festivals when flocks were sheared (1 Sam. 25; 2 Sam. 13:23–29; cf. Gen. 31:19; 38:12). Finally, sharing the sacrifice or offering of well-being with invited guests was a joyful festive occasion (cf. Lev. 3; 7:11–18; Deut. 12:6–7, 11–12, 17–18; 1 Sam. 9:22–24; 16:2–5; Job 1:4).

Fasts: In contrast to feasts and festivals, fasts were times of mourning and self-denial arising from misfortune and sin. The only prescribed annual fast is that on the Day of Atonement (Lev. 16:29–34; 23:26–32; Num. 29:7). It occurred on the tenth day of the seventh month. The people were to "afflict themselves," meaning they were to abstain from food and drink and other bodily gratifications (cf. 2 Sam. 12:16–20; Dan. 10:2–3). After the destruction of Jerusalem and the temple by the Babylonians (587/6 BCE), fasts were annually held in the fourth, fifth, seventh, and tenth months to mourn this calamity (Zech. 7:3, 5; 8:19). A public fast preceded the festival of Purim on the thirteenth of Adar; Esther 9:31 apparently refers to this (cf. 4:16).

In the NT: The Gospels report that Jesus observed Jewish festivals (Matt. 26:17–18; John 5:1; 7:2, 10). Aside from that, however, the NT contains few regulations pertaining either to fasts (cf. Mark 2:20) or to festivals. *See also* Atonement, Day of; fasting; jubilee; Passover; Pentecost; Purim, Festival of; Tabernacles, Festival of; worship in the Hebrew Bible.

Bibliography

De Vaux, Roland. *Ancient Israel.* McGraw-Hill, 1965. Pp. 468–517.   D.P.W.

Festus, Porcius (fes'tuhs, pohr'shuhs), the Roman procurator over Judea who replaced Antonius Felix (ca. 59 CE). According to the historian Josephus, he was a competent public official. He died in office several years after his appointment. According to Acts 25:1–26:32, Festus encountered Paul, a prisoner in Caesarea, when he arrived as procurator. He was bewildered by Paul's religious convictions. After Paul appealed his case to Caesar in Rome, Festus arranged for a hearing in the presence of the visiting King Agrippa II and Bernice, where Paul gave a defense of his belief in Jesus. Although Festus was incapable of perceiving anything worthwhile in Paul's preaching and declared him mad, he also averred that "this man is doing nothing to deserve death or imprisonment" (26:30–32). Nevertheless, because Paul had appealed to Caesar, he was sent, under guard, to Rome (Acts 27–28). *See also* Bernice; Felix, Antonius; Herod; Paul.   A.J.M.

fig (*Ficus carica*), a fruit tree common in both wild and cultivated forms throughout the Near East since ancient times. It is a beautiful shade tree whose large palm-shaped leaves were said to have been used to cover the nakedness of Adam and Eve in the garden of Eden (Gen. 3:7). The pear-shaped fruit, which is produced more than once during the year, has a high sugar content and is very sweet when ripe. It is eaten fresh or dried into

Fig.

cakes, which, like those made from dates, are storable and thus an ideal food for travelers (1 Sam. 25:18). The fertilization of the fruit is dependent on a tiny wasp, which carries pollen into the inner parts by boring into the center of the fruit. The fig tree therefore will not bear mature fruit if the wasp is absent and may even require hand fertilization by incision. The fig also has medicinal properties as a poultice applied to wounds and boils (2 Kings 20:7; Isa. 38:21). A fig tree that failed in its purpose of bearing figs was cursed by Jesus (Matt. 21:18–19), perhaps as a metaphor for the temple, which he thought had failed to bear proper religious fruit (cf. Mark 11:12–25). *See also* mulberry; palm; sycamore.　　　　　　　　　　　　　　P.L.C.

fire. Besides normal domestic uses (cooking, heating, lighting), fire was used in the refining of metals, in various crafts, in the waging of war, and in sending messages. Fire also had specialized uses in worship. A perpetual fire burned in the temple (Lev. 6:12), and fire was used both for roasting sacrifices for human consumption and for burning incense. Fire is a common symbol of holiness and in some cases of protection (cf. Zech. 2:5). It represents divine action: God is called "a consuming fire" (Heb. 12:29; cf. Deut. 4:24). Fire is God's servant (Ps. 104:4; Heb. 1:7), and God's word is like fire (Jer. 23:29). In reference to God's action, fire is often a symbol of destruction associated with divine wrath (Gen. 19:24; Exod. 9:23; Lev. 10:2; Num. 16:35; 2 Kings 1:10–16). This theme is developed prominently in the NT, where it is said that on the coming day of God, the heavens will be set ablaze and "the elements will melt with fire" (2 Pet. 2:12). But fire can also signify a purging or purifying function: the Babylonian exile is described as purification by fire (Ps. 66:12; Isa. 43:2), and the "day of the LORD" will purify Israel (Zech. 13:9; cf. 1 Cor. 3:13–15). Again, this theme is developed in the NT with regard to the sufferings of Christians: their various trials allow the genuineness of their faith to be tested like gold in a refiner's fire (1 Pet. 1:6–7).

Fire is a central element of theophany throughout biblical literature, e.g., the smoking pot and flaming torch that make a covenant with Abraham (Gen. 15:17), the burning bush that appears to Moses (Exod. 3:2), the pillar of fire that leads Israel by night (Exod. 13:21–22), and the appearance of God in fire on Mount Sinai (Exod. 19:18). Such fiery theophanies continue in the NT as well: Christ's appearance in the vision of John is with "eyes of fire" (Rev. 1:14; 2:18), and the descent of the Holy Spirit is accompanied by "tongues, as of fire" (Acts 2:3). *See also* theophany.　　D.L.C.

fire, tongues of. *See* tongues, as of fire.

firebrands, usually pieces of wood set on fire. They were used by Samson in his revenge against the Philistines (Judg. 15:4), and they were sometimes tossed over a city wall in time of military siege. Prov. 26:18 says that one who deceives a

neighbor is "like a maniac who shoots deadly firebrands." Amos 4:11 describes individuals rescued by God as being like "a brand snatched from the fire."

firepan, a portable metal pan for carrying hot coals on which incense was placed as an offering. Firepans were made for use with the lampstand and the burnt offering altar (Exod. 25:38; 38:3; Num. 4:14).

firmament. *See* sky.

firstborn, firstling, the first male child born to a father (Exod. 13:12–15; Num. 18:15–16) and the first offspring of domesticated pure and impure animals (Exod. 13:12–13; Lev. 27:26–27; Num. 18:16–18; Deut. 15:19–23). The firstborn male of humans and beasts in Israel was dedicated to God, because God saved the Israelites' firstborn during the slaughter of the tenth plague in Egypt (Exod. 13:12–15). This plague, in turn, was brought upon the Egyptians for enslaving Israel, God's own appointed firstborn (Exod. 4:22; cf. Jer. 2:3; 31:9). The firstborn son inherits a double portion of his father's estate (Deut. 21:15–17; Isa. 61:7), the paternal blessing (Gen. 27), and succession to authority (Gen. 27:29, 37; 37:21–22; 2 Kings 2:9). The Davidic king is also viewed metaphorically as God's firstborn (Ps. 89:28), an appellation the NT applies to Jesus (Heb. 1:6). *See also* bless, blessing; curse; priests; sacrifice.　　　　　　J.U.

first fruits, the seasonal initial produce of agriculture (Exod. 23:19; Lev. 23:10; Num. 15:20–21; Deut. 26:1–11) and food products (Num. 18:12–13; Deut. 18:4; Ezek. 44:30). The first fruits of agriculture are given to God in religious ritual in acknowledgment of God's ownership of the earth (Ps. 24:1), upon which humans are tenants. This transfer invokes God's blessing on the rest of the produce (Lev. 19:24–25; Prov. 3:9–10). *See also* sacrifice.

fir tree, as a general term, coniferous evergreens such as the cypress, juniper, and pine. The NRSV tends to use those more specific designations rather than "fir," which was used in other English translations in passages such as Isa. 60:13; 2 Sam. 6:5; 2 Kings 5:10; 19:23; 2 Chron. 2:8. Where the NRSV does keep "fir tree," the reference is probably to the Aleppo pine (*Pinus halepensis*). This tree is said to have provided branches for nesting storks (Ps. 104:17) and to have sometimes been cut into planks for shipbuilding (Ezek. 27:5). It was regarded as stately and beautiful but, in the imagery of Ezekiel, could not compare with the "cedar of Lebanon" (31:8). *See also* cypress; forest; pine; wood.　　　　　　　　　　　　　　P.L.C.

fish. The Bible takes fish and fishing for granted and makes no distinction between fresh- and saltwater fish, both of which were readily available. The major saltwater fish sources were the

Fir (Aleppo pine).

became a model for the work of Jesus's disciples, who were called to "fish for people" (Matt. 4:19; Mark 1:17).   R.S.B.

flagon, a vessel for storing and/or serving liquids. The word appears five times in the Bible, in three instances paired with bowls, thus suggesting complete service for food and drink in ritual contexts (Exod. 25:29; 37:16; Num. 4:7). In Esther 1:8, flagons of wine illustrate the lavish nature of the banquets thrown by King Ahasuerus. In Isa. 22:24, flagons are referred to metaphorically for the weight of the responsibility placed on Eliakim as royal vizier to his ancestral house, a house that will perish with his downfall.

flax (*Linum usitatissimum*), a delicate plant with blue flowers. It has been known since prehistoric times in the Near East. It is the earliest known cultivated fiber plant and was used to make linen of varying quality for temple vestments (Exod. 25:4) as well as for ordinary garments, sails, nets, and even twine. It was also the wrapping cloth used for the dead (Matt. 27:59). The harvested flax plants were soaked in water to separate the fibers and were then spread to dry, often on hot exposed rooftops (Josh. 2:6). Linseed oil is extracted from flax seeds, and the dregs are then given to the animals as fodder. In the Bible, the plague of hail ruined the flax in Egypt (Exod. 9:31), and Isaiah speaks of how workers in flax will despair when the waters of the Nile dry up (19:9). When Samson was delivered to the Philistines, the cords that bound him melted off his hands like flax that has caught fire (Judg. 15:14). Prov. 31:13 describes a capable wife as seeking wool and flax and working with both; Hosea condemns an unfaithful woman who knows not from whom her wool and flax come (2:5–9). *See also* linen.   P.L.C.

long coast of the Mediterranean Sea (Ezek. 47:10) and the waters of the Gulf of Aqabah. The primary source of freshwater fish was the Sea of Galilee (Luke 5:1–11) and some of the reaches of the Jordan River. Archaeological recovery of both salt- and freshwater fish bones indicates that fish were shipped considerable distances. For instance, both Mediterranean and Red Sea (Gulf of Aqabah) species have been recovered at Tell Hesban in Moabite Transjordan, east of the Dead Sea. The main freshwater species available in the Sea of Galilee included the mouth-breeding *Cichlidae*, of which two varieties of tilapia (*Tilapia galilaea* and *Tilapia nilotoca*) were common: *Cypinidae*, including two common carp (*Barbus canis* and *Barbus longiceps*); and *Siluridae*, a catfish (*Clarias lazera*).

According to Gen. 1:20–23, God created fish and other sea creatures on the fifth day of creation and blessed them. But, like other living creatures, the "fish of the sea" were placed under human dominion (Gen. 1:26). The primary use of fish was for food (Luke 11:11; Mark 6:41), preparation of which included broiling (John 21:9). Levitical law deemed fish with fins and scales to be clean, but others unclean (Lev. 11:9–12). Catfish were thus prohibited among the freshwater species, as were saltwater eels, sharks, rays, and lampreys. Methods of catching fish included the dragnet (John 21:8), angling with hook (Job 41:1; Amos 4:2; Matt. 17:27), harpoons and spears (Job 41:7), and thrown hand nets (Matt. 4:18). The presence of fish could symbolize the end of drought (Isa. 50:2). The catching of fish could symbolize untimely death (Eccles. 9:12) or the helplessness of humans before the power of God (Hab. 1:14–16). In the NT, however, the techniques of fishing

Flax.

flesh, the soft material of the body (Job 10:11). More narrowly, it can refer to the penis (Exod. 28:42), foreskin (Gen. 17:9–14), and hence sexual union (Gen. 2:24) and generation (John 1:13). More broadly, it refers to a human person as represented by a physical body (John 1:14), to one's relatives (Rom. 9:3), to humanity (Isa. 40:5; Phil. 3:3–4), or to human and animal life (Gen. 6:17–20). Animal flesh is "meat" (Dan. 10:3) or the meaty part of a sacrifice (Lev. 6:24–27). "Flesh" also connotes sensitivity (Ezek. 11:19), superficiality (John 8:15; NRSV: "human standards"), weakness (2 Chron. 32:8), and mortality (Ps. 78:39). Paul also uses "flesh" for the urge to sin (Gal. 5:19–21). *See also* body; flesh and spirit; human being, humanity. R.H.G.

flesh and spirit, complementary and contrastive terms whose meaning must be derived from the context in which they are used. In Hebrew thought (which generally informs both the Hebrew Bible and the NT, even though the latter was written in Greek), flesh and spirit were understood holistically, as different aspects of a human being, which was essentially a single entity; neither could exist apart from the other. In Greek thought, which sometimes influences some of the NT writings, "flesh" and "spirit" were understood dualistically, as separate entities that could be opposed to each other. Indeed, some Greek philosophers (e.g., Plato) even imagined that the spirit (or soul) was immortal and would continue to live after the flesh died.

In the Bible, the phrase "the spirits of all flesh" (Num. 16:22; 27:16) refers to human beings as animated physical bodies. Their spirit, or breath, comes from God, who can withdraw spirit (breath) from flesh so as to produce death (Gen. 6:3) or grant it to flesh so as to produce life (Gen. 2:7), even life after death (Ezek. 37:1–14). Since flesh connotes weakness (Ps. 56:4; Rom. 8:3) and spirit connotes power (Zech. 4:6; Luke 24:49; Acts 1:8), the two stand side by side for the contrast between weak human beings and Almighty God (Isa. 31:3). Similarly, acceptable worship of God in the Spirit contrasts with unacceptable attempts to please God in the flesh (Phil. 3:3). The weakness of flesh (e.g., simple tiredness) can prove ironically strong, however, when it conflicts with the spirit's willingness to pray or to obey God (Mark 14:38). According to 2 Cor. 7:1, sin may defile both the flesh (in the sense of "body," as in the NRSV) and the spirit. One can be absent in flesh (again in the sense of "body," as in the NRSV), but present in spirit (Col. 2:5). At the last day, the spirit may be saved even though the flesh (presumably the present mortal body, though some think the sinful urge) has to be destroyed prematurely in punishment for a heinous and unrepented sin (1 Cor. 5:5).

In Paul's writings, the contrast between the Holy Spirit and flesh (often as the sinful urge) looms larger than the distinction between the human spirit and the physical flesh it animates (in some Pauline passages, however, it is unclear whether God's Spirit or the human spirit is intended). Paul associates the Spirit favorably with faith and the flesh unfavorably with the works of the law (Gal. 3:2–3). In Galatians, Isaac, freeborn according to the Spirit, represents God's gracious promise; Ishmael, slaveborn according to the flesh, represents the law, which brings a curse (4:21–31). The spiritual person lives in a way determined by God's Spirit; the fleshly person behaves like unbelievers, who do not have the Spirit of God (1 Cor. 2:12–3:4). Vices (nonphysical as well as physical) are the works of the flesh; virtues are the fruit of the Spirit (Gal. 5:16–25). Fleshly behavior leads to death; behavior according to the Spirit leads to eternal life (Gal. 6:7–8; Rom. 8:1–17). The contrast between divine Spirit and human flesh is present in the Gospel of John as well; here the gift of the divine Spirit makes up for what is lacking in merely human (but not evil) flesh (3:3–8; 6:52–63). *See also* flesh; Holy Spirit; human being, humanity. R.H.G.

flint, an impure quartz rock, usually gray, brown, or black, abundant in the Near East. It fractures on conchoidal lines and holds an extremely sharp edge, either smooth or serrated. It was used for a variety of tools, such as awls, axes, knives, picks, scrapers, sickles, and weapons (arrowheads and spear points). Knives used for circumcision were made of flint (Exod. 4:25; Josh. 5:2, 3). It can be manipulated by humans (Job 28:9). Flint serves as a metaphor for sharp-cutting destructive power (Isa. 5:28) and stubborn faithfulness (Isa. 50:7) and is a dubious source of water (Ps. 114:8; Deut. 8:15) or nourishment (Deut. 32:13). It describes Judah's sinful heart (Zech. 7:12). In Ezek. 3:9, the prophet's forehead of flint is said to be harder than the people of Israel; i.e., the prophet's persistence will outlast Israel's stubbornness. R.S.B.

flock. See sheep.

flood, the, the catastrophic excess of water described in Gen. 6–8. The biblical story of the flood relates how God destroyed the existing world, but saved Noah and his family and representatives of each animal species in an ark. After the waters subsided and the ark rested on Mount Ararat (8:4), Noah sent out a raven and then a dove (which brought back an olive branch); seven days later he sent out another dove, which did not return (8:6–12). Noah disembarked, offered sacrifices, and formally re-began the world by making a covenant (contract) with God in which God promised not to bring a flood again (8:13–22; 9:8–17), a promise signaled by the appearance of a rainbow (a symbol of God's "bow" now hung in the sky). The Hebrew word for the cosmic flood is *mabbul,* which also refers to the heavenly ocean (cf., e.g., Ps. 29:10). The flood was an undoing of creation: the cosmic waters overwhelmed the earth, coming through the windows of the sky and the fountains of the great deep beneath the earth (7:11; cf. 8:2). Thus, return to the primeval watery

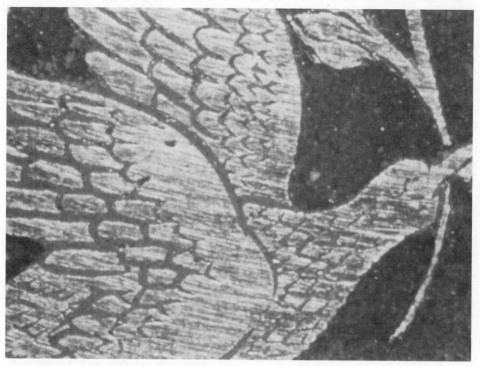

Dove with olive leaf, which indicated to Noah that the waters had subsided from the earth (Gen. 8:11); panel from the Verdun Altar, 1180.

condition set the stage for a new beginning for the world (cf. Gen. 1:2, 9).

Mesopotamian Flood Stories: The meaning of the flood story is illuminated by examination of the many parallels between the biblical account and other Mesopotamian flood stories. There are three major cuneiform retellings of the flood: the Sumerian flood story (which is somewhat fragmentary), the Gilgamesh epic, and the Atrahasis epic. These epics feature, first, an interest in immortality. In the Gilgamesh epic, the survivor of the flood, Utnapishtim, tells Gilgamesh about the flood to show him how his own attainment of immortality was unique. In the Gilgamesh epic and the Sumerian flood story (Atrahasis is broken at this point), the hero/survivor is rewarded with immortality. In the Bible, by contrast, Noah has a more human fate: he becomes drunk, is sexually embarrassed, and ultimately dies (9:20–28). Second, the Atrahasis Epic seems to present the flood as a divine response to overpopulation. In this story, the spread of humanity prompted Enlil and the gods to send plague, drought, saline soil, famine, and ultimately a flood to destroy humankind. One god, Enki, helped people escape the early problems and then had Atrahasis build an ark; after the flood Enki created barrenness, miscarriage, and stillbirth, in addition to celibate women, in order to solve the problem of over-

population without resorting to natural disasters. The biblical story, by contrast, is emphatically not about overpopulation, for people are commanded to be fruitful, multiply, and fill the earth (Gen. 8:1). As in the Atrahasis Epic, however, the biblical flood was a divine attempt to deal with a problem for which God provided an alternative remedy after the flood. In the Bible, the problem was the progressive corruption of the human race (Gen. 6:5–7). Immediately after the flood, therefore, God gave Noah and his sons several laws. The difference between the ante- and postdiluvian worlds is in these laws, for laws are considered the sine qua non of humanity's ability to continue to live on the earth (Gen. 9:2–7).

The Meaning of the Biblical Story: The flood is presented as a means of getting rid of a defiled world and starting again with a well-washed one. The idea that moral misdeeds can defile the earth is an important idea in biblical thought, for Israel believed that it had inherited the land after the previous inhabitants had defiled it and the land had "vomited" them out; Israel could lose the land for the same reason (Lev. 18:24–28). Israel worried that it could defile the land through unsolved murders (Deut. 21:7–8), through failure to execute murderers (Num. 35:31–34), or through sexual impropriety (Jer. 3:1). Ultimately, the prophets came to believe that Israel had indeed defiled its land (Jer. 2:7) and was therefore exiled (Ezek. 36:18). Thus, Israel's retelling of the flood story showed a cosmic parallel to this pattern of corruption, purgation, and ultimate restoration. There are several allusive references to the flood in the first nine chapters of Ezekiel, which portray Israel just before the Babylonian exile, and one finds another striking allusion in Zeph. 1:2–3. The one explicit reference to the flood in the Hebrew Bible outside of Genesis (Isa. 54:9) promises that Israel's exile, like the flood, was a unique occurrence, not to be repeated. In the NT, Jesus says that the coming of the Son of Man will be like the days before the flood when people carried on with life, oblivious to the disaster about to befall them (Matt. 24:37–39). In 2 Pet. 2:5 the flood is referred to as one among many examples that prove destruction comes to those deserving God's judgment.

Despite numerous attempts to find archaeological evidence for a universal deluge, no evidence for such an occurrence has been found. Localized flood levels, however, have been discovered in various Mesopotamian cities.

Bibliography

Dundes, Alan, ed. *The Flood Myth*. University of California Press, 1988.

Lambert, Wilfred G., and A. Millard. *Atrahasis: The Babylonian Story of the Flood*. Oxford University Press, 1969.   T.S.F.

floor, in biblical usage primarily the "threshing floor" (Gen. 50:10; Judg. 6:37; Ruth 3:14; 2 Sam. 24:21; Hos. 13:3; Matt. 3:12; Luke 3:17). This was usually a flat rock surface large enough to accommodate piles of grain from individual farmers with sufficient space to allow each farmer to drive a threshing sledge over the grain at the edge of a harvested pile in order to shred it prior to winnowing. It was usually a communal installation, although individual farmers may have had their own spots for personal operations.

In the more common sense of the word, floors of structures mentioned in the Bible include the tabernacle (Num. 5:17, evidently an earthen floor), a roof chamber (Judg. 3:25, possibly a rolled earthen or plastered floor), Solomon's temple (1 Kings 6:15, described as partly overlaid with gold [6:30]), and the floor of the temple in Ezekiel's specifications (41:16, 20). Archaeological evidence indicates that floors were built of various materials, from plain tamped or rolled earth, to pebble, cobble, and slab stone paving (see John 19:13); in terms of design, they varied from plain to geometric and elaborately decorated or inscribed mosaic tile. Floors and the artifacts associated with their construction and use form part of the data most helpful to archaeologists for dating the construction and use of a building.   R.S.B.

flour. *See* bread; mill.

flowers. In modern Israel, flowers may be found throughout most of the year, and this was probably the case in biblical times as well. The pink,

white, and lilac blossoms of the cyclamen appear as early as January. By spring, various shades of red and pink of the crown anemones, poppies, and mountain tulips successively dominate the landscape. Next to appear are the diverse tuberous plants of the lily family. As the summer progresses, the short-lived blossoms of spring are replaced by fields of yellow and white daisylike flowers of chamomile and chrysanthemums. The less showy yellow, blue, white, pink, and purple flowers of various thorny shrubs and plants remain throughout the summer to decorate the dry hills, rocky terrain, and waste places (Hos. 10:8).

Since flowers are referred to in general terms in the Bible, the specific identity of individual species is difficult to ascertain. Although context may sometimes elucidate which general type of flower is indicated, such information is not usually sufficient to identify a specific species. Furthermore, references in the Bible to such flowers as lilies or roses are not botanically precise and may not correspond to the sense in which such terms are used today. In general, the term "lily" applies to the family of plants that have bulbs, tubers, or rhizomes as roots (*Liliaceae*). Such plants commonly found in the Near East include the true lilies, such as the white Madonna lily and the deep red Martagon lily. The tulip, asphodel, Star of Bethlehem, hyacinth, and related narcissus, daffodil, crocus, and iris inhabit the rocky ground and dry places of the hill country. Lilies are mentioned in 1 Kings 7:26; Ps. 60:1; Hos. 14:5; and Sir. 39:14. The "lily of the valleys" of the Song of Sol. 2:1–2 is probably the blue hyacinth. The "lilies of the field" of Matt. 6:28–30 are probably not true lilies, but one of the numerous showy spring flowers such as the crown anemone.

True roses of the region, such as the wild Phoenician rose, may be referred to in Sir. 24:14 (the "rose plants in Jericho"). Otherwise, the term "rose" is used as a generic word for any showy, colorful flower. These would include the flowers found on such fruit-bearing shrubs as raspberry and blackberry, which blossom along watercourses, and on such fruit trees as apple, plum, cherry, apricot, and almond. The "rose of Sharon" (Song of Sol. 2:1) may have been one of these; or one of the more common flowers such as the tulip or narcissus, both of which grow profusely on the plains of Sharon; or one of the roselike flowers of the woody shrubs of the "rock rose" family (*Cistaceae*), which adorn the rocky and dry areas in the spring and early summer.

Flowers figured in many aspects of life in biblical times. The flowering trees and shrubs, the flowers of the fields, and the less showy blossoms of various herbaceous plants such as mints and mustards provided nectar for bees (Isa. 7:22; Num. 13:37). The fragrances of many flowers were extracted as essential oils for perfumes and unguents. The form or shape of flowers provided inspiration for decorative motifs: the columns of King Solomon's temple were capped by lilies (1 Kings 7:19, 26).

Some biblical references to flowers are symbolic. The flowers of spring signify renewal (Song of Sol.

2:12) as well as the fragility and transience of life (Job 14:2; Ps. 103:16; Isa. 40:6–7; James 1:10–11; 1 Pet. 1:24). The qualities of beauty, purity, and sweetness are also likened to flowers (Song of Sol. 2:1–5; 5:13; Isa. 28:4). In Matt. 6:28–30, Jesus refers to fields of wildflowers (lilies) as signs of God's care for creation: the God who clothes the grasses of the field can be trusted to care for people as well. *See also* almond; fig; flax; lily; mustard; rose.   P.L.C.

flute. *See* music.

fly. Many species of flies are known in the Near East. In the Bible two Hebrew words are translated "fly" or "flies" in the NRSV. First, *'arob* is used for the flies visited on the Egyptians as the fourth plague (Exod. 8:20–32; alluded to in Pss. 78:45; 105:31). The species of fly intended in these references is uncertain; it may have been the Tabanid fly (*Stomoxys calcitrans*). A second word, *zebub,* probably refers to the ordinary housefly (*Musca domestica*); this is the word used in Eccles. 10:1; Isa. 7:18. Baal-zebub, "lord of flies," was a deity worshiped at Ekron, whom King Ahaziah wanted to ask about recovery from his final illness (2 Kings 1:2–6, 16). It is not certain, however, that he was called Baal-zebub by his followers; that name might be an intentional corruption of Baal-zebul, meaning "lord of the lofty abode." *See also* plagues.   J.M.W.

food. The chief staple in biblical times was bread, as suggested by the fact that the Hebrew word for bread (*lekhem*) can also designate food in general (e.g., Gen. 3:19). Barley, wheat, and emmer were the most common varieties of grain from which bread was made. Besides their use in flour, these cereals were also eaten in roasted form, either whole or crushed (Josh. 5:11; Lev. 2:14). Fruits, vegetables, and dairy products were also important staples of the Israelite diet. Common fruits were grapes, olives (used mostly in the form of oil), figs, dates, apples, and pomegranates. Among the vegetables, beans, cucumbers, lentils, onions, leeks, and garlic were commonly grown. Dairy products, derived more from goats than cows, were consumed chiefly in the form of cheese, curds, and butter. Meat was also part of the diet, but for ordinary Israelites only on special occasions, since it was too expensive for daily fare. Both domesticated and wild animals, such as deer, gazelle, fish, and fowl, were used for food. Boiling or roasting were the preferred methods of preparing meat, from which all blood had to be drained carefully, since blood was considered sacred as the seat of life and it belonged to God alone (Gen. 9:4–6; Lev. 17:10–11; Deut. 12:23–25; Acts 15:19). Certain animals considered ritually unclean could not be consumed (see Lev. 11:1–47). The Israelite diet was rounded out by spices and other natural products such as salt and honey.

Although the food supply was generally adequate, famines, caused either by natural calamities, such as drought and locusts, or by human warfare, were not infrequent in biblical times (Gen. 26:1; 43:1; Amos 4:6–9; Luke 15:14; Acts 11:28). Some regions of the country were more fertile and productive than others. Thus, for instance, the tribe of Asher, situated on the northern coast, was known for its abundance of food (Gen. 49:20); and the Transjordanian region of Bashan was blessed with very fertile soil, which made possible the raising of herds of cattle known for their sleekness (Amos 4:1). The adequacy of one's diet also depended to a large extent upon one's wealth and social status. Kings and nobles usually ate better than peasants. The quantity of food consumed at Solomon's court was enormous, as suggested by the following list of daily provisions: "And Solomon's provision for one day was thirty cors [ca. 330 bushels] of fine flour, and sixty cors [ca. 660 bushels] of meal, ten fat oxen, and twenty

Geese being presented, possibly as payment of taxes; ivory from Megiddo, thirteenth–twelfth century BCE.

pasture-fed cattle, a hundred sheep, besides harts, gazelles, roebucks, and fatted fowl" (1 Kings 4:22–23). Divine or miraculous provision of food is also a common motif in the Bible: God provides the Israelites with manna and quail in the wilderness (Exod. 16:13–14, 31); both Elijah and Elisha enable a cruse of oil to endure long after it should have run out (1 Kings 17:14–16; 2 Kings 4:1–7); Jesus feeds multitudes with a pittance of provisions (Mark 6:35–44; 8:1–9) and facilitates an abundant catch of fish (Luke 5:1–11; cf. John 21:4–14).

Besides its obvious function for the maintenance of physical life, food had other functions and uses in the Bible. It was offered as a gift or as tribute (Gen. 32:13–18; 1 Sam. 25:18; 2 Sam. 16:1; 1 Kings 14:1–3). It was also used for making loans (Deut. 23:19) or as wages or payments for goods and services rendered (1 Sam. 2:5; 1 Kings 5:9–11; Ezra 3:7; Matt. 10:10). Scant rations were a means of punishment (1 Kings 22:27; Amos 4:6), and feasting on an abundance of food was a sign of joy and celebration (Isa. 25:6; Luke 15:23). Food was also used for religious purposes, such as the bringing of offerings (Lev. 1–7; 1 Sam. 2:12–17; 1 Cor. 8) and in sacred communal meals (Exod. 12; 1 Sam. 1:4–5; Matt. 26:17–29; Acts 2:46). Meals were often a means of cementing social relationships and, due to their social significance, Jesus was criticized for eating with tax collectors and sinners (Mark 2:15–17; Luke 15:2). Likewise, the early Christian church became embroiled in controversies over whether Jewish and Gentile believers could share community meals at the same table (Gal. 2:11–14).

Because food was of such fundamental significance, it could easily be misused or given undue importance. Consequently, the Bible says that God is the ultimate source of all food (Pss. 104:14; 136:25; 147:9; cf. 2 Cor. 9:10) and that human beings do not live by bread alone (Deut. 8:3; Luke 4:1–4). The absence of God's life-giving word may cause a famine as severe as any lack of food (Amos 8:11–12). Fasting or abstention from eating for religious reasons (e.g., prayer, repentance) was common. Jesus taught his disciples that life consists of more than food (Matt. 6:25) and that God can be trusted to provide food (Matt. 6:25–28). Paul maintains that the kingdom of God does not consist of food and drink, but of righteousness and peace and joy in the Holy Spirit (Rom. 14:17).

Numerous symbolic references to food are also found. Ps. 19:10 says the "law of the LORD" is "sweeter than honey." In John's Gospel, Jesus says that his food is to do the will of God (4:34; 6:27), and he compares himself to the "living bread" come down from heaven (6:35, 41, 51). He frequently uses banquets as a favorite image for the kingdom of God (Matt. 22:2–14; 25:1–10; cf. 8:11–12). Spiritual teaching is sometimes likened to food: basic teaching is like milk for newborn infants (1 Pet. 2:2), while deeper teaching is like solid food for mature disciples (1 Cor. 3:2; Heb. 5:12–14). See also bread; festivals, feasts, and fasts; meals.   W.E.L.

food offered to idols, meat from animals used in pagan cultic observances. In sacrificial offerings, only a portion of the animal was burned on the altar; what was left was sold in the public market. Many Jews would refuse to purchase or consume this meat; some Christians also refused to partake of it, but others did not.

According to Acts, when a special Jerusalem meeting of apostles and elders agreed to admit Gentiles to the church without requiring them to be circumcised, several restrictive provisions were laid down. One was that the Gentile Christians should abstain from eating anything that had been offered in sacrifice to idols (15:29; cf. 21:25). In Revelation, the Nicolaitans (2:14–15; cf. Num. 25:1–2; 31:16) and a female Christian prophet (perhaps their leader, 2:20) are accused of laxity in exactly this regard. The issue also comes up in Paul's letters. Some members of Paul's Corinthian congregation saw nothing wrong with Christians eating such food. They apparently reasoned that, because the only true God is the one known in Jesus Christ, other "so-called gods" had no real existence and sacrifices made to them had no real significance (1 Cor. 8:4–6). Perhaps these people occasionally ate the sacrificial food in pagan temples (see 1 Cor. 8:10), at the quasi-religious dinners of fraternal associations, or at meals hosted by pagan friends or relatives who had offered some special sacrifice. Whatever the particular setting, they seem to have participated with a certain bravado, alleging their possession of a superior "knowledge" (1 Cor. 8:1) and criticizing those brothers and sisters who declined to participate in such meals as "weak" in conscience (1 Cor. 8:7).

In 1 Cor. 8:1–11:1, Paul responds to this situation without mentioning the prohibition reported in Acts 15:29 (though Acts 15:22–35 says that he was one of the ones entrusted with the responsibility of promulgating that decision). Instead, Paul insists that neither eating nor abstaining from food offered to idols is in itself consequential (8:8). Thus, he thinks it unnecessary that Christians inquire about the origin of the meat they purchase in the market or that pagan friends serve at a private dinner (10:25–27). Paul also insists, however, that this Christian freedom must always be exercised in love (1 Cor. 8:1; 10:23–24) and in a manner that does not endanger one's partnership in the body of Christ (cf. 1 Cor. 10:18–22). He understands this to exclude a Christian's participation in any pagan sacrificial meals (10:14–22) and to require abstention from "food offered to idols" whenever eating that food might be injurious to other Christians or confusing to nonbelievers (8:7–13; 10:28–29a). It may be that Rom. 14 refers to the same problem, although the reference to "meat" in that chapter is more general.   V.P.F.

foolishness, folly, a lack of wisdom. Since wisdom, however, has many different nuances in the Bible, folly also takes on a number of different connotations. In a fundamental sense, folly or foolishness is a failure to recognize the significance of God and God's will. A "fool" is virtually by definition a person who lives life as though God and God's will were of no consequence (Pss. 14:1; 53:1; cf. Prov. 1:7). Any number of specific characteristics might exemplify this: lack of knowledge or understanding (Prov. 12:15; Eccles. 5:1); an inability to be cautious in speech (Prov. 18:6–7); a tendency to be indiscreet (Prov. 1:23; 13:16) or hot-tempered (Prov. 14:29; 17:12) or obtuse (Prov. 2:2) or gullible (2 Sam. 3:31–33); a predilection for pursuing conduct that proves harmful (2 Sam. 24:10); deliberate disregard for God's laws (Jer. 29:23; Deut. 22:21; 2 Sam. 13:11–14). Thus, Balaam is a fool when he beats his donkey (ironically claiming that it is making a fool of him) for refusing to take him on a path that would bring him certain death (Num. 22:29). Saul repents (momentarily) of trying to kill David and says, "I have been a fool, and made a great mistake" (1 Sam. 26:21). Joab takes Abner aside for a private conversation, then murders him, prompting David to lament, "Should Abner die as a fool dies?" (2 Sam. 3:33). A man identified as a fool by Jesus plans to build bigger barns to store his crops, not knowing that he will die that very night (Luke 12:20). In Matt. 5:22, however, Jesus expands upon the commandment against murder to warn that anyone who calls a brother or sister a "fool" is in danger of eternal punishment.

In the NT, the concept of foolishness is developed by the apostle Paul in a very different sense: what the world at large calls foolishness may accord with the wisdom of God; God's foolishness is wiser than human wisdom (1 Cor. 1:25). In articulating this point, Paul draws heavily on the prophets who insisted on the inscrutability of God's ways and lamented the arrogance of human claims (e.g., Isa. 29:14, cited in 1 Cor. 1:19; Isa. 40:13, cited in 1 Cor. 2:16; cf. Isa. 55:8–9; Ps. 33:10). But Paul develops the point in specifically christological terms: the "foolishness" of God is displayed in the cross of Jesus Christ (1 Cor. 1:18). Thus, Paul says that he and his companions are "fools for the sake of Christ" (1 Cor. 4:10). In a somewhat different vein, Paul engages opponents (whom he calls "the super-apostles," 2 Cor. 12:11) at Corinth by speaking to them "as a fool," that is, on their own terms, comparing notes as to which of them is the greatest and ironically concluding that inadequacies and failings determine who is truly being used of God (2 Cor. 11:16–12:10). *See also* wisdom.   J.M.E./M.A.P.

foot, a body part used in a variety of figurative ways in the Bible. God required Moses to go barefoot on the holy ground of Horeb (Exod. 3:5). Barefootedness was part of David's mourning (2 Sam. 15:30). God commanded Isaiah to walk barefoot as a symbol of future exile (Isa. 20:2–4). Placing the foot on the neck of the vanquished enemy indicated victory (Josh. 10:24; Ps. 110:1; Matt. 22:44); God's placing all things "under the feet" expresses absolute dominion (Ps. 8:7; 1 Cor. 15:27; Eph. 1:22; Heb. 2:8). Listeners and

pupils sat at their master's feet; Mary sat at Jesus's feet (Luke 10:39); Paul, at Gamaliel's (Acts 22:3). Love is shown Jesus by the washing, kissing, and anointing of his feet (Luke 7:38, 44–47; John 12:3). Jesus washed his disciples' feet as an example of humble service (John 13:5–17). Homage is shown Jesus by falling down at his feet (Mark 5:22; Luke 8:41). Jesus heals those placed at his feet (Matt. 15:30). The disciples are to shake the dust from their feet to reject inhospitality (Matt. 10:14; Mark 6:11; Luke 9:5; 10:11).   J.P.H.

footstool. The only literal footstool in the Bible is part of a royal throne: Solomon's ivory throne had "six steps and a footstool of gold, which were attached to the throne" (see 2 Chron. 9:18). The term is usually used figuratively. Thus, God promises to make vanquished enemies the "footstool" of a king (Ps. 110:1; cf. Matt. 22:44; Acts 2:35; Heb. 10:13). Elsewhere, the ark (1 Chron. 28:2), the temple (Isa. 60:13), or even Zion (Lam. 2:1) is identified as God's footstool, i.e., as part of God's royal throne. To emphasize God's sovereignty, the entire earth may be described as God's footstool (Isa. 66:1; cf. Matt. 5:35; Acts 7:49).

forbearance, restraint with regard to punishment or vengeance. Though this could be a human virtue (akin to showing mercy), in the NRSV forbearance is attributed only to God. In Jer. 15:15 it describes God's allowing a prophet added life to complete his mission. In Rom. 2:4, Paul says that God's forbearance, patience, and kindness are intended to lead to repentance. In Rom. 3:25, he specifies that Christ's atoning work is the result of divine forbearance, according to which God has passed over former human sins.

ford, shallow crossing place in a marsh, river, or stream where firm footing is available. Until Roman occupiers built the first bridges in the Levant, all crossings of water were by boat or through available fords. Bridges and fords had been constructed by the Persians in much of Asia Minor in their control of territories from the sixth through the fourth centuries BCE. Such ford crossing points mentioned in the biblical stories include one on the Jabbok, an eastern tributary of the Jordan (Gen. 32:22), crossed by Jacob and his family. There were also fords on the Jordan itself, crossed by various groups (Josh. 2:7; Judg. 3:28; 12:5, 6; 1 Sam. 13:7); fords "of the wilderness" (2 Sam. 15:28; 17:16); the ford of the Anion, an eastern river draining into the Dead Sea (Isa. 16:2); and fords leading to Babylon (presumably through the Euphrates River; Jer. 51:32).
                                        R.S.B.

forehead, the portion of the face between eyebrows and hairline. The Bible depicts the forehead or brow as a significant spot due to its location and visibility. As represented in ancient Near Eastern art, the upper portion of the forehead was often covered by hair, a headband, or some type of head covering; but the lower portion was generally

Armed Lagashite warriors wearing tight-fitting helmets that nearly cover, but reveal the shape of, their foreheads; detail from Eannatum's stele, ca. 2450 BCE.

visible. Even soldiers' helmets sometimes left the lower brow somewhat vulnerable (which is evident from the story of Goliath, 1 Sam. 17:49). The following passages illustrate the visual prominence of the forehead. The phrase "Holy to the Lord" was to appear over the high priest's forehead (Exod. 28:36–38). God struck Uzziah with leprosy on his forehead (2 Chron. 26:19, 20; cf. Lev. 13:41–43). A frontlet or phylactery was to be worn "between the eyes," a phrase referring to the forehead (Exod. 13:9, 16; Deut. 6:8). In visions of the future, allegiance to God was often represented by a mark or seal on the forehead (Ezek. 9:4; Rev. 7:3; 9:4; 14:1; 22:4); association with "the beast" in the end times was likewise depicted in such a manner (Rev. 13:16; 14:9; cf. 20:4). The term "forehead" was also used figuratively to represent persistent obstinacy: to have a "hard forehead" was synonymous with having a "stubborn heart" (Isa. 48:4; Ezek. 3:7–9). Jeremiah uses a different figure, telling Judah that she has "the forehead of a whore" (3:3); this probably refers to some sort of jewelry worn as an identifying sign by prostitutes (cf. Rev. 17:5). *See also* phylacteries.   D.M.P.

foreigner, in the Hebrew Bible, any non-Israelite having temporary contact with Israel; if friendly, foreigners were entitled to hospitable treatment. In contrast, "resident aliens" enjoyed some social and religious privileges (Exod. 12:49). Israelites were frequently warned that extended contact with foreigners would lead to religious corruption (Exod. 23:31–33; Isa. 2:6–8); thus the directive against foreign wives (1 Kings 11:1–4; Neh. 13:26–27). Also, foreigners were not permitted to participate in ritual festivities (Exod. 12:43; Neh. 9:1–3), nor could their animals be used for Israelite sacrifices (Lev. 22:25). In economic dealings, interest was chargeable on loans to foreigners, but not on those to fellow Israelites (Deut. 23:19, 20), and a foreigner's debt was not remitted in a year of release (Deut. 15:2, 3). References to foreigners as enemies occur in passages such as Obad. 11 and Lam. 5:2 (NRSV: "aliens"; NEB and NIV: "foreigners"). The NT writings make occasional references to foreigners (the Samaritan leper in Luke 17:18; cf. Matt. 27:7), but, as the church spread out into the Mediterranean world, the term lost its primary reference to "non-Israelites"; thus there are "foreigners" in Athens, who were probably non-Athenians (Acts 17:21). The concept of being a foreigner, stranger, or sojourner was also employed with figurative and theological meaning. On the one hand, Eph. 2:19 states that those accepting Jesus as Christ are "no longer strangers and sojourners, but . . . fellow citizens with the saints"; on the other hand, Heb. 11:13 identifies saints as people who confess that they are "strangers and foreigners on the earth." *See also* alien; Gentile; stranger.   D.M.P.

forerunner, in antiquity a military term for soldiers who ran ahead of the regular army either as scouts or to announce or prepare for its arrival (Wis. 12:8). The image of a forerunner (though not the actual term) seems to be applied to John the Baptist in the Gospels: he comes in advance of Jesus to announce and prepare the way for the Lord (Matt. 3:1–12; 11:10; Mark 1:2–8; Luke 3:1–18; 7:27; John 1:6–8, 19–34; cf. Isa. 40:3–11; Mal. 3:1). Elsewhere, Heb. 6:20 refers to Jesus entering the Holy of Holies as forerunner, thereby preparing for others to have access to God's presence. *See also* John the Baptist.

foreskin, a portion of loose skin, also called the prepuce, located at the end of the human male penis. Hebrew ritual law specified that it should be surgically removed from every male child belonging to the covenant people of Israel, normally on the eighth day after birth (Lev. 12:3). This act of circumcision was first practiced by Abraham (Gen. 17:11, 14, 24–25). When God intended to kill Moses, Zipporah, his wife, saved his life by cutting off their son's foreskin and touching her husband's feet with it, proclaiming "Truly, you are a bridegroom of blood to me!" (Exod. 4:24–26). When arranging David's marriage to his daughter Michal, King Saul demanded a bride price of a hundred Philistine foreskins, which was delivered (1 Sam. 18:25, 27; 2 Sam. 3:14). Removal of the foreskin can be viewed symbolically, as when the people are admonished to circumcise the foreskin of their heart (Deut. 10:16; Jer. 4:4); likewise, those whose devotion to God is superficial are said to be "circumcised only in the foreskin" (Jer. 9:25). *See also* circumcision.   R.S.B

forest. In Israel, forests were a source of timber for both local use and foreign export. Wood was important for a wide range of uses, such as domestic and industrial fuels, the construction of buildings, and the manufacture of furniture and household items. The highlands of Lebanon boasted forests of majestic cedars, while oak and pistachio, the characteristic trees of the Mediterranean region, were especially common in the northern hill country. Stands of Aleppo pine, mixed with components of the oak forest, existed in Galilee, Samaria, and Judea. Scrub forests in the foothills, composed of mixed evergreens, once provided shelter for wild animals such as boar and lions (Ps. 80:13; Amos 3:4). Biblical references to specific stands of trees such as the forest of Hereth (1 Sam. 22:5), the forests of the south (Negev; Ezek. 20:46–47), the forests of Arabia (Isa. 21:13), the king's forest (Neh. 2:8), and the forest (wood) of Ephraim (2 Sam. 18:6) indicate the importance of these natural resource areas. *See also* wood.   P.L.C.

forgiveness. The Bible develops the motif of forgiveness through a variety of terms and images: sins or debts or transgressions may be sent away, wiped clean, covered, removed, released, or passed over. In Genesis, God agrees with Abraham's request to forgive the entire city of Sodom if ten righteous people can be found there (18:20–32). The book of Leviticus explicates a system of sacrifices for expiating the guilt of those who have sinned unwittingly or who have repented of their sins (Lev. 4–5), but sacrifice must always be accompanied by a proper disposition (1 Sam. 15:22; Hos. 6:6). Joshua tells the people at Shechem that God is a holy and jealous God who will not forgive their transgressions if they serve foreign gods (Josh. 24:1), but King Solomon later expounds in prayer upon God's willingness to forgive those who pray in or toward the temple as the seat of God's dwelling with Israel (1 Kings 8:30–50). Many of the psalms contain prayers for forgiveness (Pss. 25:18; 51:1–17; 65:3; 79:9) or testimonies to God as the one who forgives (Pss. 103:3; 130:4). The prophets testify repeatedly that God desires to forgive human sins, but asks for repentance as a prerequisite for a renewed relationship between God and Israel (Isa. 1:18–19; Hos. 12:2–3; Joel 2:13). The book of Nehemiah describes God as "ready to forgive, gracious and merciful, slow to anger and abounding in steadfast love" (9:17). Although most references in the Hebrew Bible are to divine forgiveness, there are also occasional references to forgiveness between human beings. Thus, Abigail intercedes for her foolish husband, Nabal, begging David to forgive him for his churlish behavior (1 Sam. 25:14–28). The story of the reconciliation of Esau and Jacob (Gen. 32–33) also testifies to human forgiveness, although the term is not used.

The NT continues the tradition of God's mercy shown in forgiveness of sins. God initiates contact with humans (Rom. 9:23–26; 2 Cor. 5:19; Gal. 1:4) and forgives sins through the death of Jesus (Acts 13:38; Rom. 3:21–26; 4:25; Gal. 1:4). God's forgiveness is variously described as justification, salvation, and reconciliation. It is associated with the celebration of the Lord's Supper (Matt. 26:28), and in some passages Jesus himself forgives sins (Mark 2:5–6; Acts 5:31). This offer of divine forgiveness, however, is emphatically connected with the need

for humans to forgive each other. Jesus teaches his disciples to pray, "Forgive us our debts, as we have forgiven our debtors" (Matt. 6:12), adding, "If you do not forgive others, neither will your Father forgive your trespasses" (Matt. 6:15). This latter point is underscored in his parable of the Unforgiving Servant (Matt. 18:23–35). Such forgiveness, furthermore, is to be limitless: not seven times, but "seventy-seven times" (Matt. 18:22). Indeed, members of the community are told to confess their sins to one another (James 5:15–16), and spirit-filled leaders are authorized to forgive or retain sins on Christ's behalf (John 20:23). *See also* justification; mercy; repentance; salvation; sin.

A.J.S.

forks, implements used by priests for sacrifices (Num. 4:14; 1 Sam. 2:13–14, which speak of them as having three prongs). Those in use at the Jerusalem temple were made of gold (1 Chron. 28:17) and bronze (2 Chron. 4:16).

fornication, a generic term for illicit sexual activity. In the Hebrew Bible, sexual misconduct includes seduction of a virgin, rape, sodomy, bestiality, incest, prostitution, and homosexual acts (cf. Lev. 18; 19:20–22, 29; 20:10–21). The specific sin of adultery tends to be treated separately from these offenses, perhaps because it related to marriage and was considered more serious, or at least in need of special legislation. Similarly, in the NT, almost any form of sexual activity outside the marriage relationship can be designated as fornication or "immorality" (cf. 1 Cor. 6:9; 2 Cor. 12:21; Eph. 5:5; Col. 3:5; 1 Thess. 4:3; 1 Tim. 1:10; Heb. 13:4; Jude 7). *See also* adultery; homosexuality; marriage; prostitute.   J.M.E.

fortification. *See* cities; defense, public; fort, fortress; walls.

fort, fortress. In biblical times, forts were often constructed along borders or trade routes, and cities were typically walled so as to become fortresses themselves (cf. the expression "fortress city" in Neh. 9:5). Already at the time of the exodus, Deut. 3:5 mentions "fortress towns with high walls, double gates and bars" in the kingdom of Og. At the time of David, a "fortress of Tyre" is mentioned (2 Sam. 24:7). David is also said to have garrisoned troops in outlying areas to ensure his political control (2 Sam. 8:6). Solomon likewise had cities for his chariots (1 Kings 9:19). Rehoboam is said to have built fifteen fortified cities and to have made their fortresses strong (2 Chron. 11:11). Jehoshaphat (2 Chron. 17:12) and Jotham (2 Chron. 27:4) are likewise credited with building forts and towers. Nahum calls sarcastically for Assyria to strengthen its forts in preparation for the siege and devastation to come (3:14; cf. 3:12). Isaiah refers to fortresses in Tarshish and Sidon (23:1, 4, 14). Nehemiah makes reference to a "temple fortress" (2:8). The term "fortress" is also used metaphorically for God in prayers and

Battered brick tower of ancient fortification system excavated at
Tell el-Hesi, biblical Eglon (?), in the district of Lachish.

hymns of praise (2 Sam. 22:2; Pss. 18:2; 31:3; 59:9;
62:2; 71:3; 91:2; 144:2).

Archaeological investigations have dated several forts to the period of the monarchy. The fortress of Arad, constructed at the time of Solomon's
rule, guarded the southern approach to Jerusalem
and was used for regional control and administration. An imposing fortress at Lachish guarded an
approach into the Judean hill country from the
southwest. The northern kingdom, Israel, also
possessed several highly fortified sites, including
Megiddo and Hazor. Megiddo guarded the western entrance into the Jezreel Valley, and Hazor
guarded the approach from southern Syria into
Israelite territory. In the Transjordanian kingdoms
of Ammon, Moab, and Edom, archaeologists have
discovered various fort systems ranging from
watchtowers and what could be termed police
outposts to regional garrisons and even double-
walled fortresses. Because of the trade routes running north–south through these kingdoms and
the agrarian, pastoral nature of their economies,
these different types of forts were necessary for
what little security they could ensure. During the
Roman period, Herod the Great is noted for building a number of fortresses throughout Judea (including Masada, Machaerus, and the Herodium).
None of these are mentioned in the NT. Paul was
probably kept in the fortress (NRSV: "barracks") of
the Antonia (Acts 21:34–37; 22:24; 23:10), but it is
not mentioned as such either.   J.A.D./M.A.P.

Fortunatus (for´chuh-nay´tuhs), one of the
three men who brought information to Paul in
Ephesus about troubles in the church at Corinth
(1 Cor. 16:17). The three individuals (Fortunatus,
Achaicus, and Stephanas) may have been emissaries, bearing a letter from some in the Corinthian
church (1 Cor. 7:1). *See also* Achaicus; Stephanas.

forum. *See* architecture.

foundations, a base for construction of any
superstructure. Translating a variety of biblical
terms, the word is used both literally and figuratively. It refers to both natural formations (Deut.
32:32) and humanly prepared anchorages for
different kinds of structures (Solomon's temple,
1 Kings 5:17; the second temple, Ezra 3:10; a house,
Luke 6:48; a prison, Acts 16:26; the new Jerusalem,
Heb. 11:10; Rev. 21:19). Such foundations could be
elaborate and costly (1 Kings 7:10–11). Archaeological evidence shows that bedrock was preferred
for major construction, but if such was not available the next best foundation was a solid stone
platform constructed of layers of blocks of closely
fitted stone. Such a foundation could be leveled by
the use of trenches filled with gravel or small rock.

A cornerstone was important to all wall foundations and frequently served as a repository for
inscriptions or other commemorative goods. To
improve a foundation's stability, the cornerstone
would frequently be a worked stone, even in a wall

of unworked stone. For storage buildings, foundations were made rodent tight by use of plaster in the chinks. For more modest housing, stone foundations one course high and one or two courses thick were minimal.

The image of a foundation lent itself to a variety of metaphorical applications. God, as Creator, is often identified as one who laid the foundations of the earth (2 Sam. 22:16; Job 38:4; Pss. 18:15; 82:5); for this reason the phrase "the foundation of the world" refers to the moment of Creation or to the beginning of all things (Matt. 13:35; John 17:44; Eph. 1:4; Heb. 4:3; 9:26; 1 Pet. 1:20; Rev. 13:8; 17:8). The righteousness and justice of God (Ps. 89:14) and God's redemption (Isa. 28:16) form a stable foundation for life. Similarly, in one of his parables, Jesus likens the person who obeys his teaching to a wise man who builds his house upon a rock (cf. 1 Tim. 6:19), while the person who does not keep his words is like a foolish man who builds a house upon the sand (Matt. 7:24–27; cf. Job 4:19; 22:16). Paul speaks of initial missionary activity as laying a foundation and says that he does not build upon another's foundation (i.e., work in areas where people have already heard the gospel from other missionaries), but prefers to go where Christ has not yet been named (Rom. 15:20; cf. 1 Cor. 3:10). Sticking with this basic metaphor, he also insists that though the missionary lays the foundation, the foundation itself is Jesus Christ (1 Cor. 3:11; cf. Eph. 2:20, where it is "the apostles and prophets," with Christ Jesus as the cornerstone). See also 2 Tim. 2:19; Heb. 11:10. *See also* cornerstone.   R.S.B./M.A.P.

fountain, a spring or source of flowing water. The NRSV uses "spring" and "fountain" to translate a number of Hebrew and Greek terms without distinguishing between a natural outflow of water, an artificial water-storage system (i.e., cisterns and reservoirs), or a well dug by human hands. Though all of these were common, the Levant's geological structure is conducive to the formation of natural springs (Deut. 8:7), and settlements were often located in close proximity to such springs. This reality is sometimes reflected in place-names that begin with the syllable *en*, a prefix derived from a Hebrew word for "fountain" or "spring" (e.g., En-gedi). Natural springs represent divinely bestowed security and bounty (Ps. 104:10–13; Isa. 41:17–18; Ezek. 34:13), especially when the water is taken as symbolic of eschatological blessings (e.g., Ezek. 47:1–12; Joel 3:18; Zech. 14:8; Rev. 21:6; 22:1–2). Thus, the "fountain [or source] of life" may be variously identified as the "fear of the LORD" (Prov. 14:27), the mouth of the righteous (10:11), the teaching of the wise (13:14), or wisdom itself (16:22). God is praised as the "fountain of life" (Ps. 36:9). God is also described as a "fountain of living waters" (Jer. 2:13), a symbol that Jesus later applied to himself (John 4:10–15).The image of a fountain is also used to symbolize an abundant source of things besides water, e.g., descendants (Deut. 33:28), wisdom (Prov. 18:4), or

forgiveness (Zech. 13:1). In love poetry, a fountain (like a garden) is sometimes used as a euphemistic image for feminine sexuality (Prov. 5:15–17; Song of Sol. 4:12–15). *See also* cisterns; water.   G.L.M.

Fountain Gate, a city gate in the southeast sector of Jerusalem opening either to Gihon or to the En-rogel spring (Neh. 2:14; 3:15; 12:47). It was repaired by Nehemiah. It may be identical to the "gate between the two walls" (2 Kings 25:4).

fowler, a person who hunts birds. Such hunting was done by bait, lure, or snare, and it was done for food or sport. Biblical usage sees it as a metaphor for danger (Prov. 6:5; Pss. 91:3; 124:7), even from fellow humans (Jer. 5:26).

A seal found in a grave at Tell en-Nasbeh depicts a fighting cock; sixth century BCE.

fowls, a collective term for edible birds. In the NRSV, the word is used only in 1 Kings 4:23 and Neh. 5:18, though fowlers, who hunted such birds, are mentioned in Pss. 91:3; 124:7; Prov. 6:5; Jer. 5:26; Hos. 9:8. Domesticated poultry are more common in the NT, where Jesus refers to a hen gathering her young (Matt. 23:37) and to the crowing of a cock (Mark 13:35; 14:30, 68, 72). When the chicken first appeared in the Near East is unknown, but a Hebrew seal from Tell en Nasbeh from the sixth century BCE depicts a fighting cock. Prov. 30:31 refers to a strutting rooster.

fox. Three species of fox live in the Near East: the European fox (*Vulpes vulpes*) dwells in temperate zones, and the desert fox (*Vulpes rüppeli*) and the fenek (*Fennecus zerda*) are desert-adapted species; any one or all three may have been there in biblical times as well. Samson tied torches to the tails of three hundred foxes and turned them loose in

Philistine grain fields (Judg. 15:4–5). Tobiah the Ammonite mocked the Jews who were rebuilding their walls by saying, "That stone wall they are building—any fox going up on it would break it down!" (Neh. 4:3). In the NT the fox is mentioned in connection with its habit of burrowing holes (Matt. 8:20; Luke 9:58): foxes have holes, but the Son of Man has nowhere to lay his head. Figurative references to foxes are also found, though their meaning is somewhat elusive. The Song of Solomon refers to catching little foxes that ruin the vineyards that are in blossom (2:15)—perhaps the foxes are lusty youth and the blossoming vineyards nubile girls. Jesus calls Herod Antipas, the ruler of Galilee, a fox (Luke 13:32)—perhaps the reference draws upon a reputation for foxes as rapacious animals given to indiscriminate violence (particularly against chickens, cf. Luke 13:34–35).

frankincense, a fragrant gum resin exuded in large, light yellowish brown tears from boswellia trees (*Boswellia carterii, Boswellia papyrifera, Boswellia thurifera*). These grow in South Arabia, Ethiopia, Somalia, and India. Frankincense was imported into Judah by camel caravan from Sheba (Isa. 60:6; Jer. 6:20), a trade connection illustrated by the queen of Sheba's visit to Jerusalem during the reign of Solomon (1 Kings 10:10; 2 Chron. 9:9). Frankincense could be used for secular purposes as a perfume (Song of Sol. 3:6; 4:6, 14), but in the Bible it usually appears in religious contexts. Exod. 30:34–38 contains the recipe for a frankincense-based incense dedicated for ritual use. No other incense was permitted on the altar (Exod. 30:9), and secular use of the sacred recipe

Boswellia thurifera, a source of frankincense.

was absolutely forbidden (30:38). Frankincense was set beside the bread of the Presence (Lev. 24:7), and it accompanied cereal offerings (Lev. 2:1–2, 14–16; 6:14–18), but was prohibited with a sin offering (Lev. 5:11) or a cereal offering in the case of a suspected impurity (Num. 5:15). Offerings of frankincense were made at the temple (Isa. 43:23; 66:3; Jer. 17:26; 41:5) and stored for later use (Neh. 13:5, 9; 1 Chron. 9:29). Frankincense was among the gifts offered to the infant Jesus by the magi (Matt. 2:11). Rev. 18:13 lists frankincense as part of the cargo of the merchants who weep for the fallen city. *See also* Sheba, queen of; worship in the Hebrew Bible.   M.A.S.

freedman, freedwoman, a person in the Greco-Roman world who had been a slave, but had secured release from that status by purchasing freedom or working to achieve it. Freedmen and -women remained bound to their former masters in certain respects (see 1 Cor. 7:22). For example, if they died without an heir, their property was given to the master. They were not eligible for the higher ranks in the army, nor were they free to embark upon an official career of public office. A synagogue in Jerusalem had apparently been established for or by former slaves; Acts 6:9 reports that "some of those who belonged to the synagogue of the Freedmen" argued with Stephen. *See also* freeman, freewoman; liberation; slavery in the New Testament; Stephen.

freeman, freewoman, a person who had been born free. One of the fundamental distinctions of status in the Roman world was that of slave or free. Free persons might be either free by birth (Lat. *ingenui*), i.e., freemen or freewomen, or free because they had received a grant of freedom from slavery, i.e., freedmen or freedwomen (*liberati*). Children born after a slave had been freed were considered to be freeborn. Paul declared that in Christ the significance of such differences was nullified (Gal. 3:28), but he did not challenge the institution of slavery as such (1 Cor. 7:21–24). *See also* freedman, freedwoman.   P.P.

freewill offering. *See* sacrifice.

friend, friendship. In the Bible, friendship is primarily a relationship of mutual trust and congeniality. In many instances, friends are simply people who are allies, supporting each other in areas of mutual interest. Thus the "elders of Judah" and King Hiram of Tyre are listed among David's friends (1 Sam. 30:26; 1 Kings 5:1; cf. 1 Chron. 12:7). In other cases, however, friendship seems to imply a more intimate bond, such as that exemplified by David and Jonathan (cf. 1 Sam. 18:1; 19:1; 20:17; 2 Sam. 1:26). Deut. 13:6–8 recognizes the danger of an "intimate friend" enticing one to worship foreign gods, implying that such an associate might have at least as much influence as one's closest family members. Judah had a friend called Hirah the Adullamite, who was his only confidante in dealing with a potentially embarrassing sexual exploit (Gen. 38:12, 20). Amnon had a crafty friend named Jonadab, who, when he learned Amnon was in love with Tamar, arranged a way for him to seduce (or, as it turned out, rape) her. In a more positive vein, David's friend Hushai the Archite remained loyal to him after Absalom's rebellion and risked his own life to obtain information that would help David escape (2 Sam. 16:16–18; 17:5–22).

The benefits and requirements of friendship are among the subjects addressed in Proverbs and Sirach. Loyalty and steadfastness are marks of the true friend (Prov. 17:17; 18:24; Sir. 6:14–16), but poverty or adversity often reveals people to be friends in name only (Prov. 19:4, 6–7; Sir. 12:9; 13:21; 37:4–5). To be shunned or betrayed by one's friends is a cause for shame and a mark of deep tragedy (Pss. 38:11; 41:9; 88:18; cf. Luke 21:16). One irony of the book of Job, however, is that his concerned friends, in frenetic attempts to effect his repentance, intensify rather than relieve his suffering. Friends are often depicted as people with whom one celebrates (Luke 15:5, 9, 29). Typically, friends are also expected to do favors for each other (Luke 11:5–8), so Jesus taught that instead of inviting one's friends to a luncheon or banquet, one should invite those who will not be able to return the favor—the poor, crippled, lame, or blind (Luke 14:12–14).

The special bond between God and a person chosen as God's instrument is occasionally described as friendship. God spoke to Moses face-to-face, "as one speaks to a friend" (Exod. 33:11), and Abraham is called God's friend (2 Chron. 20:7; Isa. 41:8). Ps. 25:14 speaks of "friendship with the LORD" as an option for all who fear God (cf. James 2:23). In the NT, Jesus's effort to demonstrate God's mercy for social outcasts earns him the epithet "friend of tax collectors and sinners" (Matt. 11:19; Luke 7:34). In the Gospel of John, two persons, Lazarus and the unnamed Beloved Disciple, are listed as persons for whom Jesus has special affection (11:3, 36; 13:23; 19:26; 20:2; 21:7, 20). Jesus says that his disciples are his friends if they do what he commands; he calls them friends because he has revealed to them what he heard from his Father (15:14–15), and he tells them that the supreme manifestation of love is a person's willingness to give his life for his friends (15:13).

S.K.W. /M.A.P.

fringes, or tassels, a common decoration on ancient Near Eastern garments. Deut. 22:12 states simply: "You shall make tassels on the four corners of the cloak with which you cover yourself." This is elaborated in Num. 15:38–40, which says that the tassels—now called fringes—shall be of blue cord and function as a reminder to obey the commandments. In the Synoptic Gospels a woman with a hemorrhage touches the fringe of Jesus's garment (Matt. 9:20; Luke 8:44), and other sick people wish to do likewise (Matt. 14:36; Mark 6:56). Jesus criticizes Pharisees for hypocrisy in wearing what he regards as ostentatious fringes (Matt. 23:5).

A.J.S.

frog. Although frogs were common in the lands of the Bible, they are only mentioned in the Hebrew Bible in one particular context: as a plague upon the Egyptians. God sent hoards of frogs out of the water and into their homes, even into Pharaoh's bedroom (Exod. 8:1–15; alluded to in Pss. 78:45; 105:30). Pharaoh appealed to Moses and Aaron and promised to let the Israelite slaves go if the frogs were removed. However, after the frogs died, Pharaoh refused to let the Israelites leave. In the NT, frogs are mentioned in the book of Revelation: John sees "three foul spirits like frogs coming from the mouth of the dragon, from the mouth of the beast, and from the mouth of the false prophet" (16:13). *See also* plagues.

frontlet. *See* phylacteries.

fruit. According to Genesis, God created fruit trees on the third day (1:11). The Bible mentions grapes, figs, pomegranates, and olives as favorable produce of the promised land (Deut. 8:8). Melons, peaches, apricots, dates, and berries were also available to the Israelites. All of these may have been found in the wild, but orchards were also planted for the cultivation of popular fruit. Fruit could also be offered as a sacrifice to God (Lev. 27:30). *See also* apple; fig; food; pomegranate.

fuels, materials used to start and maintain fires. Wood and charcoal were the most common fuels in antiquity, the latter of which became more important with the advent of metallurgy and other crafts because of its higher burning temperature. Other fuels were thorny shrubs (Nah. 1:10), sticks, twigs, straw or stubble from the fields (Exod. 15:7), fat remains, date kernels, dung of cattle, bones of fishes, birds, and animals (Ezek. 24:5–10), logs (Gen. 22:3; Lev. 1:7), and chips from the carpenter's shop (Wis. 13:12). Isaiah graphically describes the wrath of God and the horrors of an impending battle by indicating that blood-soaked boots and garments—and even people—will be used as fuel for the fires (9:5, 19). Ezekiel can likewise describe Israel as fuel for the fire (21:32) and compare the inhabitants of Jerusalem to a vine that has been used for fuel and is now charred and worthless (15:2–6). Elsewhere, Isaiah notes the irony of a person using half of a tree for fuel and worshiping an idol made from the other half (44:13–17). The NT knows braziers with charcoal or charcoal fires on the ground (John 18:18; 21:9). R.A.C.

fuller, a person whose occupation it is to clean, whiten, bleach, thicken, shrink, or dye cloth. The fuller cared for newly shorn wool or woven garments. The process varied but generally included washing with lye ("fuller's soap," Mal. 3:2) and cleansing by pressure, usually the treading of feet (Exod. 19:10; 2 Sam. 19:24). The cloth was then spread out on the ground to be bleached by the sun. There was an area outside Jerusalem called the Fuller's Field (2 Kings 18:17; Isa. 7:3; 36:2), designated for these professional laundering and cleaning services. Biblical writers found the fuller's profession to be an apt metaphor for purity (Ps. 51:7; Jer. 2:22; 4:14; Zech. 3:3; Rev. 4:4). When Jesus was transfigured, his garments were whiter than anyone on earth could bleach them (Mark 9:3).

S.R.

funeral. *See* burial.

furnace, an installation for containing fire, whether for domestic or industrial purposes. The word is used in the Bible for various installations employed in daily life. The most common term for a furnace in the Bible is the Hebrew word *tannur*, which refers to an oven, used most often for baking bread (Ps. 21:9; Dan. 3:6). Other terms refer to a pottery or lime kiln (Gen. 19:28; Exod. 9:8; 18:18) or a smelter or refining installation for metals (Prov. 17:3; 27:21; Ezek. 22:20). Archaeological and metallurgical researchers in the Near East have uncovered numerous furnaces from the Chalcolithic period (fourth millennium BCE) at Teleilat et-Ghassul in the southeast Jordan rift, across the valley from Jericho, and at Abu Matar near Beersheba (ca. 3500 BCE), to the late medieval period (1450 CE) at Mugharat Warden in the Gilead mountains (Ajlun district) of Jordan. Perhaps the best examples of early copper furnaces are from Timna in the southern Negev. Iron-smelting furnaces were used in the Near East in the twelfth and eleventh centuries BCE. The furnace site at modern Tell el-Kheleifeh excavated by Nelson Glueck and once thought to be "the Pittsburgh of ancient Palestine" is now known to have been used as early as the Chalcolithic period (4000–3000 BCE) and as late as the Roman (63 BCE–324 CE), but is not likely to be Solomonic in origin. A number of smithing furnaces dating from twelfth century to 870 BCE were found at Gerar (modern Tell Jemmeh).

After Sodom and Gomorrah were destroyed by God, Abraham saw smoke rising from the land like a furnace (Gen. 19:28). In Dan. 3, King Nebuchadnezzar has three Jews who will not worship a golden statue thrown into a furnace of blazing fire; they are not burned, however, because they are protected by a fourth person in the fire who "has the appearance of a god" (3:25). Figuratively, furnaces are used with regard to two themes: destruction and refinement. With regard to the first, furnaces often symbolize God's judgment (Ps. 21:9; Isa. 31:9; 33:14). In this sense, in the NT, they may represent the fires of hell (Matt. 13:42, 50; Rev. 9:2). In other contexts, though, furnace imagery is used to describe something that is pure or the process of purification itself. God tests the heart in the same way that a refiner purifies precious metals in a furnace (Prov. 17:3). Ps. 12:6 describes God's promises as pure, like silver refined in a furnace. Likewise, 1 Pet. 1:7 likens faith that has been tested through suffering to gold that has been refined in a fire, picking up, perhaps, on Isaiah's reference to the "furnace of adversity" (28:10; according to Prov. 27:21, being praised can have the same effect). A vision of Christ in Revelation describes his feet as being like burnished bronze refined in a furnace (1:15). *See also* metals. R.A.C.

furnishings. *See* furniture.

furniture. In the Bible, references to furniture usually describe what the NRSV also calls the "equipment" or "furnishings" of the tabernacle (Exod. 25:9; 40:9; Num. 1:50; 3:8; 4:15, 26, 32; 7:1). These include "the table and its utensils, and the pure lampstand with all its utensils, and the altar of incense, and the altar of burnt offering with all its utensils, and the basin with its stand" (Exod. 31:8–9; cf. 35:14). In a similar vein, 1 Chron. 9:29 refers to the furniture of the temple.

Biblical references to furniture for private dwellings, however, are scant. Num. 19:18 notes that when a person becomes unclean through contact with a corpse or grave, all the furnishings of that person's tent are to be sprinkled with water from the purification offering. Nehemiah says that when he became angry, he threw all the household furniture of Tobiah out of the room (Neh. 13:8), but he does not say what items of furniture this entailed. Likewise, Judith plundered the tent of Holofernes and took "all his silver dinnerware, his beds, his bowls, and all his furniture," but the items of furniture are not mentioned (Jth. 15:11).

Archaeological and artistic evidence indicates that the most common furnishings in wealthy homes were tables, beds, chairs, and storage chests. Royal tomb fittings from Ur in Mesopotamia and from Egypt show that such items of wood were frequently inlaid, carved, gilded, and otherwise embellished with ivory, precious metal, and precious stones. That such opulence was imitated by Solomon may be reflected in the records concerning his palace (1 Kings 7:1–11; see also Amos

Clay model of a bed; found at Gezer, from ca. 3000 BCE.

6:4a). The ordinary family furniture that would have been found in a typical home is less evident. Such a room as Jesus directed the disciples to locate (Mark 14:15; Luke 22:12) may have had a table and some stools, or it may have had only mats for seating, a lamp, and serving vessels for bread and wine. Other contexts suggest that furnishings in such a home included sleeping mats or rolls (Mark 2:9) and a niche or stand for a lamp (Matt. 5:15). Special accommodations for a guest might include a bed, table, chair, and lamp (2 Kings 4:10). R.S.B.

future life. *See* eschatology; eternal life; Hades; heaven; hell.

G

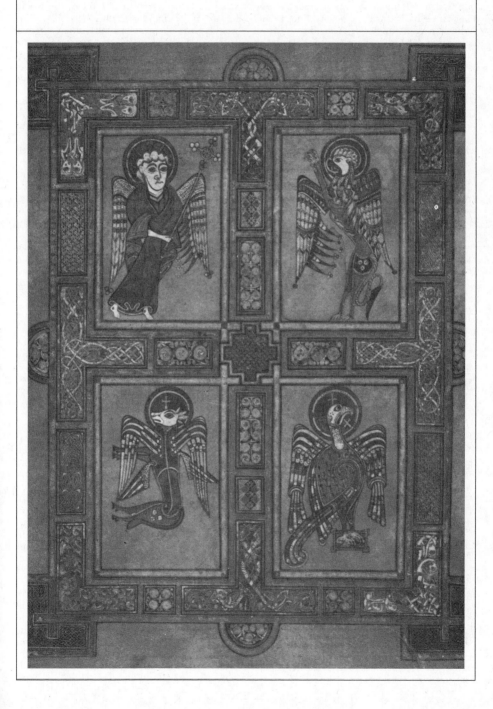

Gaal (gay´uhl; Heb., possibly "beetle"), the son of Ebed who lived in Shechem and usurped leadership from Abimelech (Judg. 9:26–33). This usurpation caused Abimelech to retaliate in force, destroying the city (9:34–49) before further expanding his conquests (9:50–57). Gaal was apparently a Canaanite and may have been a native of Shechem, although the action above is said to occur on his "return" to the city. Both he and Abimelech offer competing credentials for royal political leadership. Within the full narrative of Judges, the account of Gaal and Abimelech is intended to demonstrate the futility of life under a king: both Gaal and Abimelech lead the Israelites to disaster.   R.S.B.

Gaash (gay´ash), a mountain in the territory of Ephraim. Joshua is said to have been buried at Timnath-heres, "north of Mount Gaash" (Josh. 24:30; Judg. 2:9). The "torrents of Gaash" are also identified as the home of Hiddai, one of the group of David's elite troops known as "the Thirty" (2 Sam. 23:30). Elsewhere, the "wadis of Gaash" are given as the home of Hurai, another of David's warriors (1 Chron. 11:32), but the name Hurai could simply be a variant for Hiddai. No certain location is known for Mount Gaash. Speculation locates it some twenty miles southwest of Shechem. The torrents and wadis are probably runoff features of the mountain, water rushing through gullies in heavy rainstorms.   R.S.B.

Gabbatha (gab´uh-thuh), a term that appears only once in the NT, in John 19:13 as the Hebrew (actually Aramaic) equivalent of the Greek term

A gaming board scratched into the flagstone pavement of the courtyard of Herod's Antonia fortress, excavated in Jerusalem.

lithostrōton, "the pavement" where the hearing of Jesus before Pontius Pilate was held. Attempts to locate the Gabbatha have been frustrating. Two sites that still vie for the attention of tourists have been largely discounted by scholars. First, the first-century Jewish historian Josephus refers to a paved yard adjacent to Herod's palace where court was held (*Jewish War* 2.14.8). Today, this would be part of the citadel adjacent to Jaffa Gate. This would seem a likely spot for the location of Jesus's trial, but to date no paved court has been discovered to corroborate the information in Josephus. Second, a possible location for the Gabbatha that was once considered very promising was the area that would have constituted the courtyard of the fortress Antonia, a garrison Herod constructed on the northwest corner of the Temple Mount. Today, this site is found in the basement of the Convent of the Sisters of Zion on the Via Dolorosa. Some 2500 square yards of pavement have been excavated there. This pavement consists of large flagstones averaging 4 feet by 3.5 feet by 2 feet thick with incised treads to prevent animals from slipping. One of the stones displays a Roman gaming board, suggestive of the sort of activity ("casting lots") the soldiers responsible for Jesus's execution are mentioned as doing (Matt. 27:35). This pavement did seem like a promising candidate for the Gabbatha, but it has now been dated to the time of Hadrian in the second century CE. A third possibility has arisen only recently: the foundation of a podium measuring 2200 square feet has been discovered in the Armenian quarter of Jerusalem. *See also* Antonia, Tower of.   F.S.F.

Gabriel (gay´bree-uhl), an archangel. In the Hebrew Bible, Gabriel appears only in Dan. 8:15–26; 9:21–27, and in the NT only in Luke 1:11–20, 26–38. In these passages, Gabriel appears as a messenger ("angel") from God and an interpreter for the people to whom he is sent. In Daniel, he interprets dreams and visions for the prophet, revealing mysteries about the last days. In Luke's Gospel, he appears first to the priest Zechariah to tell him that he and his wife, Elizabeth, will give birth to a son (John the Baptist). Then he appears to the virgin Mary to announce the birth of Jesus. Gabriel is not explicitly called an "archangel" in the Bible (where that term is used only in 1 Thess. 4:16; Jude 9). The concept of archangels is developed in certain deuterocanonical and pseudepigraphical writings, where angels are organized into categories with specific duties and status before God. The most frequently named archangels are Michael (Dan. 10:13; Jude 9) and Gabriel; others include Raphael (*1 Enoch* 20:3; 40:2, 8–9) and Jeremiel (4 Esd. 3:6; called Remiel in *1 Enoch* 20:8 and Ramiel in *2 Bar.* 55:3). In *1 Enoch* 40, Gabriel is considered one of these top four archangels, perhaps second only to Michael. In that writing, Gabriel's duties include intercession on behalf of God's people (*1 Enoch* 9:1; 40:6) as well as being the instrument for destruction of the wicked (*1 Enoch* 9:9–10). Tradition has associated Gabriel with the archangel whose trumpet blast would announce the return of Christ, though this is not actually stated in the Bible. (cf. 1 Thess. 4:16; Matt. 24:31). *See also* angel; Michael.   J.M.E.

Gad (Heb., "luck").

1 The Canaanite god of fortune (Isa. 65:11).

2 The son of Jacob and Zilpah (Gen. 30:9–11) and the eponymous ancestor of the Israelite tribe of that name (see **3**).

3 The tribe of Gad, which occupied territory between the Jabbok and Arnon rivers. At times, this territory seems to have overlapped with that allotted to Reuben. The Jabbok served as the boundary between Gad and the half-tribe of Manasseh. In the Blessing of Jacob (Gen. 49:19), by means of an alliterative play on the name "Gad," the poet alludes to military tactics of the tribe. In the Blessing of Moses (Deut. 33:20–21) Gad is described as a lioness who tears both arm and head and is praised for having performed the righteous ordinances of the Lord. In the Song of Deborah (Judg. 5:17), Gad, under the designation Gilead (cf. Judg. 12:7), is listed among those tribes that failed to participate in the war against Sisera and is chided for having remained across the Jordan. Mesha, king of Moab, ca. 830 BCE, conquered Ataroth, which "the men of Gad inhabited from of old." Some time afterward, the territory of Gad was overrun by Hazael of Damascus (2 Kings 10:32–33). The region may have been restored to Israel by Jeroboam II (2 Kings 14:25), but it was lost again to the Assyrian conqueror Tiglath-pileser, who deported its population (1 Chron. 5:26). *See also* Mesha; tribes.

4 A prophet-seer of David (2 Sam. 24:11).   S.G.

Gadara (gad´uh-ruh), **Gadarenes** (gad´uh-reenz). Some biblical manuscripts mention the "country of the Gadarenes" as the site of a dramatic exorcism performed by Jesus (Matt. 8:28–34; Mark 5:1–10; Luke 8:26–39). The account is remarkable in that it involves a large number of demons being cast into a herd of pigs, who rush into the water to drown. There is considerable confusion in the manuscript tradition, however, with regard to where this occurred: some ancient authorities read "Gadarenes," some read "Gerasenes," and some read "Gergesenes," all of which were actual (though distinct) locations in the Decapolis. The NRSV accepts "Gerasenes" as the preferred reading in Mark and Luke, but accepts "Gadarenes" in Matthew. The country of the Gadarenes would be the area around the city of Gadara (modern Umm Qeis). Gadara was one of the cities of the Decapolis that Jesus is reported to have visited (Matt. 4:23–25; Mark 7:31). It lies about six miles southeast of the Sea of Galilee. The city appears to have been thoroughly hellenized, with only a small Jewish population. In one inscription from the Hellenistic period, Gadara refers to itself proudly as a "cultivator of the arts." A number of Cynic philosophers, orators, and poets are associated with the city, including the Greek poet Meleager of Gadara (first century BCE),

who mentions the Jewish sabbath in one of his love poems: "If your love is a 'sabbath-keeper,' no great wonder. Not even love burns on cold sabbaths." *See also* Gerasa, Gerasenes.   P.P./M.A.P.

Gaius (gay´uhs).

1 A person in Corinth baptized by Paul (1 Cor. 1:14); he likely was partial to Paul's position in the church disputes in Corinth. He may be the same Gaius identified as "host to me and to the whole church" in Rom. 16:23.

2 A traveling companion, with Aristarchus, of Paul mentioned in Acts 19:29. Coming from Macedonia, they were caught up in a riot provoked by Paul's missionary work in Ephesus. *See also* Aristarchus.

3 A traveling companion of Paul in Acts 20:4, identified as being from Derbe (in Asia Minor).

4 A recipient of 3 John (v. 1). His leadership is favored over that of a certain Diotrephes (vv. 9–10). *See also* Diotrephes.   A.J.M.

Galatia (guh-lay´shuh), a geographic term used for both a territory in north-central Asia Minor and (after the first century BCE) a Roman province that included that territory plus portions of other ethnic regions to the south. The region or territory traditionally called Galatia was named for the Gauls, who migrated there in the third century BCE. Their central city was Ancyra (modern Ankara), but after a period of independence, they became a client state of Rome in 64 BCE. After the "Galatian" king Amyntas died in 25 BCE, the Romans created a province that included Galatia and territories south almost to the Mediterranean Sea. They called this province "Galatia." Because "Galatia" can refer to either the specific territory or the larger province, references in the NT are often ambiguous. 1 Pet. 1:1 and 2 Tim. 4:10 (if one prefers the reading "Galatia" to the variant "Gaul") surely refer to the province, but there remains doubt concerning the other four references

(Acts 16:6; 18:23; 1 Cor. 16:1; Gal. 1:2), all of which relate to Paul's ministry. Some think they refer to the province, in which case Paul is believed to have traveled through the southern part of this province and to have written his letter "to the Galatians" to persons in that part of the province (i.e., to people who were not ethnically Galatians, but who were residents of the province of Galatia). In biblical studies, this view is called the "south Galatian theory." Supporters of this view point out that Acts records no mission to north-central Asia Minor, but does record visits by Paul to Antioch, Iconium, Lystra, and Derbe, cities in the southern part of the province, outside the ethnic Galatian territory. An alternative view, the "north Galatian theory," holds that the specific references to Galatia are to the ethnic territory in the northern part of the Roman province, the only part of the province in which the people who were normally called "Galatians" lived. Those who hold to this view maintain that Paul would not have used the term "Galatians" when writing to people who were not ethnically Galatians but merely lived in an area that had been incorporated into a province the Romans called "Galatia." Resolution of this argument affects the dating of Paul's Letter to the Galatians and has implications for the question of whether that letter was written before or after the Jerusalem Council described in Acts 15. *See also* Galatians, Letter of Paul to the.   D.R.M.

Galatians (guh-lay'shuhnz), **Letter of Paul to the,** the ninth book in the NT and one of thirteen letters attributed to Paul. Galatians is typically regarded as Paul's most intense and combative letter, written in anger to believers who are considering options he thinks are contrary to the gospel.

Contents: After a customary salutation (1:1–4), Paul immediately declares his astonishment that the Galatians are deserting God and embracing a false message that perverts the gospel of Christ (1:6–9). He then turns defensive, responding to charges that he is a people pleaser (1:10). He recounts segments of his autobiography to counter allegations that he picked up the gospel message secondhand and that he does not proclaim the gospel in a manner approved by other apostles (1:11–2:10). Continuing in the autobiographical mode, he relates an incident at Antioch that set him at odds with Peter (called Cephas—his Aramaic name) and other respected church leaders (2:11–14). Reporting that incident serves as a segue to discussion of matters at hand, for it brings into sharp focus a question that the Galatians themselves need to consider: whether one is made right with God by doing works of the law or by trusting in Jesus Christ (2:15–21). Seizing the offensive, Paul tells the Galatians they are fools for allowing anyone to convince them the crucified Christ is insufficient for them. With a number of arguments—many drawn from scripture—he reiterates his point that trusting in Christ is incompatible with relying on works of the law as a means to receiving God's Spirit or being declared righteous by God (3:1–18). He considers the true purpose of the law (3:19–4:11) and then turns conciliatory, appealing to the Galatians as his children in the faith and calling them to turn back from a course that will lead them into bondage (4:12–5:1). He warns them against accepting circumcision as a qualification for belonging to God and vents his anger against those who urge them to do so (5:2–12). Finally, Paul launches into a soaring treatise on the meaning of freedom, emphasizing its paradoxical fulfillment in loving service rather than in self-indulgence. He identifies the outcome and evidence of true freedom with the fruit that the Holy Spirit bears in people whose lives have been transformed by God's grace (5:13–25). He then concludes the letter with a quick series of exhortations (5:26–6:10) and a summary paragraph written in his own hand, exalting the cross of Jesus (6:11–18).

Historical Setting: The Letter to the Galatians was written by Paul to a number of churches in a Roman province located in modern-day Turkey.

GALATIAN THEORIES: SEQUENCE OF EVENTS

"North Galatian Theory"	*"South Galatian Theory"*
Paul evangelizes cities in south Galatia (Acts 13:14–15; 14:1)	Paul evangelizes cities in south Galatia (Acts 13:14–15; 14:1)
Jerusalem Council (Gal. 2:1–10; Acts 15)	Paul meets with church leaders in Jerusalem (Gal. 2:1–10)
Paul evangelizes Galatian tribes in north Galatia (Acts 16:6, 18:5)	Paul writes the letter of Galatians to churches in south Galatia
Paul writes the letter of Galatians to churches in north Galatia	Jerusalem Council (Acts 15)
The "north Galatian theory" recognizes that the people usually known as "the Galatians" lived in the northern part of the province visited by Paul after the Jerusalem Council.	The "south Galatian theory" resolves what would be inconsistencies between Gal. 2:1–10 and Acts 15 if these were viewed as describing the same event.

From Mark Allan Powell, *Introducing the New Testament* (courtesy, Baker Academic)

The dating of the letter depends on more precise suppositions about where these Galatians were located: the people who called themselves "Galatians" were a group who lived in the northern part of the province, which Paul does not appear to have visited until at least the early 50s (cf. Acts 16:6; 18:23); if, however, the term "Galatians" was used less precisely to mean "residents of Galatia," then the people addressed could be inhabitants of the southern part of the province visited by Paul in the mid to late 40s. The attraction of this latter view (called the "south Galatian theory") for some scholars is that it allows the Letter to the Galatians to have been written early (indeed, to be the earliest of all Paul's letters), and this helps to resolve historical discrepancies that otherwise arise (e.g., if Paul is writing the letter early—before the Jerusalem Council mentioned in Acts 15—then Gal. 2:1–10 can be taken as referring to meetings and other events not recounted in Acts rather than to events that are recounted in Acts in ways that contradict Paul's report). Most scholars nevertheless hold to the first option mentioned above, the "north Galatian theory." Then the letter is usually dated to the mid-50s, around the same time that Paul wrote Romans.

In any case, the impetus for this letter is that the Gentile Christians in Galatia have been persuaded by certain Jewish Christians that they ought to be circumcised, keep the Jewish law, and, in effect, become Jews (albeit Jews committed to Jesus Christ). It is possible that these teachers had told the Galatians that the salvation brought by Jesus the Jewish Messiah was only available to Jewish people, or it is possible that they simply proclaimed circumcision and Torah observance as the appropriate "next step" for Gentile Christians who wanted to experience the fullness of faith. Either way, they have also belittled Paul, claiming that his law-free gospel was acquired secondhand (since Paul had not known the earthly Jesus) and did not meet with the approval of disciples and family members of Jesus who had a closer link to the Lord.

Paul writes to the Galatians to settle two related matters. First, he responds to the personal charges made against him by claiming that his understanding of the gospel *does* have the endorsement of James, Peter, John, and others (2:1–10) and that he *was* an eyewitness to the risen Jesus and received his gospel directly from Jesus Christ. Second, he rebukes the Galatians for listening to teachers who proclaim a false gospel, insisting that any reliance on the law as a means to obtaining a right (or better) relationship with God is incompatible with the gospel of grace and faith in Christ.

Major Themes: The letter reveals a good deal about Paul's own biography, providing his account of his transformation from persecutor of Christians to proclaimer of the gospel (1:13–24). He also gives an account of an incident at Antioch in which he rebuked Peter for hypocrisy after the latter apparently changed his position on the question of whether Jewish and Gentile Christians

should eat the community meal at one table or at separate tables (2:11–14). Apart from the biographical material, however, the primary theological theme of Galatians is the relationship of Christ and the law. Paul makes at least four points in defense of his claim that Gentile believers do not need to keep the Jewish law. First, he argues that justification is by faith, not works (2:16–17). Second, he maintains that God's favor is universal in scope, and that Jews and Gentiles alike are now recipients of the grace of God manifested through Christ (3:28). Third, Paul claims that the "fullness of time" has now come in a way that marks a radical shift in God's plan (4:4–5). The law belongs to a bygone era "before faith came" (3:23; cf. 3:25); for people of faith to live under the law would be inappropriate, analogous to adults continuing to live under the authority of a servant who had charge of them when they were children (4:1–7). Finally, Paul maintains that God gives the Holy Spirit to believers (3:2) and that this obviates the need for the law; the Spirit produces in believers a righteousness that the law could only describe but not effect (5:22–23). *See also* circumcision; faith; flesh and spirit; Galatia; Gentile; Holy Spirit; justification; kingdom of God; law; Paul.

Bibliography

Betz, Hans Dieter. *Galatians: A Commentary on Paul's Letter to the Churches in Galatia.* Fortress, 1979.

Dunn, James D. G. *The Theology of Paul's Letter to the Galatians.* Cambridge University Press, 1993.

Longenecker, Richard N. *Galatians.* Word, 1990.

Lührmann, Dieter. *Galatians.* Augsburg, 1992.

Martyn, J. Louis. *Galatians.* Doubleday, 1997.

Powell, Mark Allan. *Introducing the New Testament: A Historical, Literary, and Theological Survey.* Baker Academic, 2009. Pp. 307–21.   M.A.P.

galbanum (gal'buh-nuhm), a gum resin derived from several plants (such as *Ferula galbaniflua*). It is an ingredient in incense (Exod. 30:34) for use in worship. Yellow or greenish brown, it has a prominent aroma and, though regularly called a "sweet spice," it has a bitter taste. In Sir. 24:15 galbanum appears on a list of spices that symbolize wisdom.

Galilean (gal'uh-lee'uhn), inhabitant of Galilee (Matt. 26:69; Acts 1:11; 2:7; Mark 14:70; Luke 13:1, 22:59; 23:6; John 4:45; 7:52). The term appears as an epithet for the insurrectionist Judas (Acts 5:37). The regional accent of Galilean speech apparently enabled others to identify origin by it (Matt. 26:73).

Galilee (gal'uh-lee; Heb. Galil), the region of the Levant that is situated between the Litani River in modern Lebanon and the Jezreel Valley in modern Israel. The designation "Galilee" first occurs as a proper name in Joshua (20:7; 21:32) and in Chronicles (1 Chron. 6:76) in reference to the site of Qadesh of Naphtali. It occurs with the definite article in 1 Kings 9:11, "in the land of Galilee." From Isa. 9:1 we learn it was known as a land surrounded by foreigners. The proper name occurs regularly in the writings of the first-century historian Josephus and the NT (Gk. Galilaia).

This tiny region, approximately forty-five miles long north to south, is first mentioned by Pharaoh Thutmose III in 1468 BCE when he captured twenty-three Canaanite cities there. From the time of the Israelite settlement (late thirteenth–early twelfth century BCE) Galilee is associated with the tribes of Naphtali, Asher, Issachar, and Zebulun; the tribe of Dan eventually moved there. The reorganization into administrative districts under King David saw a consolidation of Israelite presence there. King Solomon, however, returned some twenty Galilean cities to Hiram, king of Tyre, in payment for building materials (1 Kings 9:10–11).

During the period of the divided monarchy (ca. 922–587/6 BCE) Galilee was invaded by Pharaoh Shishak during the time of Rehoboam. In ca. 885 during the reign of Israel's King Baasha, Ben-hadad of Damascus captured Ijon, Dan, Able-beth-

maacah, and "all the land of Naphtali" (1 Kings 15:18–20). The confrontation of Ahab, king of Israel, with Shahnaneser III of Assyria at Qarqar in 853 BCE ultimately led to the confrontation at Mount Carmel in 841. Tiglath-pileser III, also of Assyria, however, took much of Galilee in 732 BCE when he captured thirteen of its cities (2 Kings 15:29), depopulated much of the area, and united it to Assyria as a province. From then on Galilee as a region became known as the Assyrian province of Megiddo. Galilee's history remains obscure until the Greek conquest by Alexander the Great in 332 BCE.

Jewish settlement in Galilee followed the Maccabean revolt in 164 BCE. Galilee was annexed by Judah Aristobolus I in 104 BCE. His brother and successor, Alexander Jannaeus, further extended the borders of Galilee during his reign. With the Roman conquest in 63 BCE, Pompey recaptured many Galilean cities and incorporated them into a new Roman administration. Under Herod the Great (40–4 BCE), Galilee, together with Judea and Perea, formed a large portion of a new province. Upon Herod's death in 4 BCE, Galilee and Perea were made part of the tetrarchy of Herod Antipas, his son.

Galilee constitutes the area in which Jesus conducted the major part of his ministry. His youth and early ministry took place in Nazareth in Lower Galilee; much of his public ministry was located at the northwestern end of the Sea of Galilee, at Capernaum, which was known as Jesus's own city (Matt. 9:1).

The first-century historian Josephus (*Life* 45.235) maintains that there were 204 villages in Galilee. Archaeology has shown that that figure is not improbable. In Lower Galilee the major centers in the first centuries CE were Tiberias and Sepphoris. In Upper Galilee, called Tetracomia ("Four Villages") by Josephus, Gush Halav (Gischala) and Meiron were certainly among the largest villages. The population in both areas of Galilee was Jewish, but it was not until after the two devastating wars with Rome in 66–73 and 132–135 CE that the population accelerated. It was in the aftermath of those debacles that Jews from Judea relocated themselves there en masse.   E.M.M.

Galilee, Sea of, a freshwater lake in the district of Galilee, given various names throughout history: "Sea of Chinnereth" (or "Chinneroth"), from the Hebrew word for a harplike instrument (Num. 34:11; Josh. 12:3; 13:27); "Sea of Tiberias" (John 6:1; 21:1); "Lake of Gennesaret" (Luke 5:1); and "waters of Gennesaret" (1 Macc. 11:67). Elsewhere, it is referred to simply as "the lake" (Luke 5:2; 8:22–33) or "the sea" (John 6:16–25). It appears as the "Sea of Galilee" in Matt. 4:18; 15:29; Mark 1:16; 7:31.

Along with the Jordan River and the Dead Sea, this body of water is an integral part of the Syro-African rift, a geological fault that extends from Syria in the north to the northeastern part of Africa in the south. The lake is approximately 700

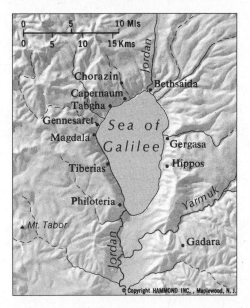

feet below sea level and has a maximum depth of 150 feet. The Jordan River, carrying the melted snows of Mount Hermon, enters the lake from the north, flows through its thirteen-mile length, and continues its course after leaving the lake along the southwestern shoreline. The water surface of the lake varies according to the season and the amount of rainfall. At its widest part, the lake measures about eight miles, and its circumference is about thirty-two miles.

Due to the height of the hills (1200 to 1500 feet) surrounding the below sea-level lake, abrupt temperature shifts occur, causing sudden and violent storms, as the NT accounts indicate (Matt. 8:23–27; Mark 4:35–41; Luke 8:22–25; Matt. 14:22–33; Mark 6:45–52; John 6:16–21). The northern end of the lake has little protection and remains subject to strong winds. Nevertheless, the natural features of climate, fertile soil, and abundance of water attracted inhabitants from prehistoric times to the present day to settle along the shores of the lake.

An offshoot of the international highway known as the Via Maris followed a portion of the western coast of the lake, helping the area to develop as one of the larger population centers in the first century CE. Fishing, agriculture, and fruit growing added to the attraction of the area. Some forty different species of fish inhabit the waters, and salted fish were exported widely throughout the Roman Empire. A Roman-era fishing boat was discovered in 1986. Some of the towns and areas near the Sea of Galilee that are mentioned in the Gospels are Bethsaida, Capernaum, Chorazin, Gadara, Gennesaret, Magdala, and Tiberias. Numerous hot mineral springs near Tiberias, Gadara, and Tabgha, combined with the tropical climate around the lake, made the area a natural health spa. *See also* Bethsaida; Capernaum; Chorazin; Gadara, Gadarenes; Galilee; Magdala; Tiberias.   M.K.M.

gall. When "gall" is used to translate Hebrew *merorah,* the reference is to a bodily organ—the gall bladder or, possibly, the liver (Job 20:25)—and the bile that it produces (Job 16:13). The NRSV also translates a different word (Heb. *rosh*) as "gall" in Lam. 3:19, though it renders that same word as "poison" in Ps. 69:21. This latter word (*rosh*) refers to some unknown herb (possibly, though not certainly, hemlock); in Lam. 3:19, it is paired with wormwood in a metaphorical description of the bitterness of life. The LXX uses Greek *cholē* in both Lam. 3:19 and Ps. 69:21, and that is also the Greek word that the NRSV translates "gall" in Matt. 27:34 and Acts 8:23. In the Matthew reference, Jesus is given wine mixed with gall to drink on the cross. In Acts, the term is again used metaphorically to describe the bitter or poisonous character of Simon Magus. The term "gall" (*cholē*) is also used several times in Tobit, where it refers to an inner organ of a fish believed to have medicinal properties (6:5–9; 11:4, 8, 11).   M.A.P.

Gallio (gal'ee-oh), the son of the Roman rhetorician Seneca, brother of Seneca the philosopher, and holder of several important civil positions in the Roman Empire. His full name was Lucius Junius Gallio Annaeus. According to Acts 18:12–17, Paul was brought before Gallio's judgment seat in Corinth (discovered in recent times in the old city) when Gallio was proconsul in Achaia. After a perfunctory hearing, Gallio perceived that the dispute between Paul and his Jewish accusers was over an internal religious matter, and he refused to continue with the case, even when the Jews proceeded to beat Sosthenes, a synagogue official sympathetic to Paul (Acts 18:17; cf. 1 Cor. 1:1) in front of the tribunal. There are no further references to Gallio in the NT. Roman sources, however, indicate that, after spending time in Achaia and Egypt, he returned to Rome to take an official position. After his brother Seneca's death in a conspiracy against Nero in the early 60s, Gallio fell into disgrace and ultimately committed suicide.

An inscription discovered at Delphi mentioning Gallio as proconsul of Achaia during the reign of the emperor Claudius, important extrabiblical evidence for establishing the date of Paul's presence in Corinth.

The mention of Gallio in Acts is important to biblical studies, because it provides a key piece of evidence for establishing the chronology of Paul's activities. An inscription discovered at Delphi mentions Gallio as proconsul of Achaia at the time of the twenty-sixth accolade (an honor given to Roman officials) of the emperor Claudius. It is not clear whether this was 52/53 or 51/52 CE, but most scholars prefer the earlier date. Thus, according to Acts 18:12–17, the inscription, and Paul's own writings (1 Cor. 3:5–15), it would appear that Paul was in Corinth ca. 51/52 CE and that this was when he founded the church there. Most Pauline biographies start with this piece of information as a relatively firm date and then work forward and backward to determine dates for the rest of Paul's career. *See also* chronology, New Testament; Corinth; Paul; tribunal.   A.J.M.

gallows, a device for execution by hanging. Most gallows comprised a platform from which a vertical support ascended to anchor a horizontal arm from which the strangling rope descended. Biblical law made no provision for such a form of execution, and gallows are mentioned only in the book of Esther, where they are employed by the Persians. In that account, Bigthan and Teresh, who had plotted to assassinate the Persian king, were hanged once their threat was found to be true (2:23). A gallows "fifty cubits high" was also built for the execution of Mordecai at the instigation of Haman (5:14). Thanks to Esther, however, the conspiracy against Mordecai was averted, and Haman and his sons were hung on the gallows instead (7:9–10; cf. 8:7; 9:13, 25). *See also* hanging.

Gamaliel (guh-may′lee-uhl; Heb., "recompense of God").

1 The son of Pedahzur, a prince of Manasseh on the march through the wilderness (Num. 1:10; 2:20; 7:54, 59; 10:23).

2 A Pharisee in the Jewish council, honored by all the people, who, according to Acts 5:34–39, counseled tolerance of the apostles proclaiming Jesus's resurrection and messiahship. He reasoned that, if the movement was not of God, it would die on its own, and if it was of God, the Jewish authorities should not oppose it. He is probably the same person referred to in Acts 22:3 as a teacher of the law at whose feet Paul claims to have been instructed in Jerusalem. In rabbinic literature, this Gamaliel is identified as Gamaliel I or the Elder. He was prominent in the mid-first century CE, but very little reliable information about him is available. The list of princes or patriarchs of Judaism in *Pirqe 'Abot* (part of the Mishnah) lists him after Hillel. He is not to be confused with another Jewish leader known as Gamaliel II, the leader of the rabbinic assembly that gathered after the destruction of the temple in 70 CE.   A.J.S.

games. Categories of games in biblical times include mental exercises, sporting events, and board games. The riddle proposed by Samson (Judg. 14:12–14) is a mental exercise. Riddles were widely known in the ancient Near East, but (unlike the tricky riddle posed by Samson) were supposed to deal with common experience or knowledge.

One reference to a sporting event in the Bible, described in 2 Sam. 2:12–17, set twelve of Joab's men against twelve of Abner's men. The contest, which was probably intended to be wrestling, had, however, a fatal outcome. By Hellenistic times, major sporting festivals such as the Olympian games were held in various cities. In 2 Macc. 4:18 reference is made to the "quadrennial games" held

A game board decorated with shells found in a tomb at Ur. Although not specifically mentioned in the Bible, game boards date as far back as the twenty-sixth century BCE.

at Tyre. NT letters shows the influence of these Greek games through the employment of sporting metaphors (1 Cor. 9:24–27). Specifically, Paul speaks of running a race in several passages (1 Cor. 9:24; Gal. 2:2; 5:7; Phil. 3:14), and he refers to boxing in 1 Cor. 9:26. The Pastoral Letters use the image of fighting a good fight (1 Tim. 1:18; 2 Tim. 4:7) with connotations that seem more athletic than military.

Board games, though not mentioned specifically in the Bible, have been found in a number of archaeological excavations. In the NT, the soldiers cast lots for Jesus's garments, probably gambling with dice (Matt. 27:35). Inlaid game boards were known from Ur as early as the twenty-sixth century BCE. Likewise, game boards and boxes have been uncovered from Egypt dating to the third and second millennia BCE. One Egyptian set is fully preserved. Of the ten ivory playing pieces five were carved with dogs' heads and five with jackals' heads. These pieces were apparently moved around a playing board with numerous holes for the pieces. Three astragali (animal knuckle bones) served as the dice to determine moves. Game boards have also been found in the Near East. An ivory board from Megiddo is largely circular with fifty-eight holes for pieces to move along. A limestone game board from Tell Beit Mirsim has fifteen ruled squares and ten playing pieces of blue faience, five cone-shaped pieces and five tetrahedrons. It also has a small die in the shape of a truncated pyramid, with numbers on the four sides. Unfortunately, no evidence remains to indicate how these games were played. *See also* riddle.
J.F.D.

garden, a plot of cultivated land, often enclosed by walls made of stones, mud-brick, or hedges. Entrance was normally through a gate, which could be locked (Song of Sol. 4:12; 2 Kings 25:4). Located near ample supplies of water, gardens were lush and desirable pieces of property used for both decorative and utilitarian purposes (Gen. 13:10; Num. 24:6; Jer. 31:12). Vegetables, spices, fruit trees, and flowers were grown in them (1 Kings 21:2; Jer. 29:5; Song of Sol. 4:12–16; Luke 13:19). Gardens were also used as meeting places for social occasions and for meditation and prayer (Esther 1:5; John 18:1). Occasionally, idolatrous religious practices were carried on in gardens (Isa. 65:3; 66:17). Ancestral tombs were often located in gardens. Thus, many Judean kings were buried in garden tombs (2 Kings 21:18, 26), and the body of Jesus was laid to rest in a garden tomb belonging to Joseph of Arimathea (John 19:41–42). The care of gardens might require the employ of a gardener (John 20:15).

The word "garden" is also used metaphorically and symbolically in the Bible. Thus, in the Song of Solomon, the word refers to the young woman or bride whom the lover comes to court (4:12; 5:1; 6:2). Elsewhere, the word refers to the "garden of God" or "garden of the LORD," also known as "Eden," where God walked among the trees in the cool of the day and from which the primordial human beings were banished (Gen. 2:15; 3:1, 2, 3, 8, 10, 23, 24; Ezek. 28:13; 31:8–9). In this latter sense it is also used as a simile to describe the eschatological restoration of the land of Israel (Isa. 51:3; 58:11; Ezek. 36:35). *See also* Eden; paradise.
W.E.L.

garment. *See* dress.

gate. *See* walls.

Gate, Beautiful. *See* Nicanor.

Gath, one of the Philistine Pentapolis cities located on the coastal plain in the southern Levant (Josh. 13:3). Like Ashdod, it was one of the remaining homes of the Anakim (giants; see Josh. 11:22; 2 Sam. 21:22). The city is mentioned twice in conjunction with the stories about the ark of the covenant (1 Sam. 4–6; 2 Sam. 6). The Philistine inhabitants of Ashdod sent the ark to Gath (1 Sam. 5:8; 6:17; 7:14). Gath was also the home of Goliath the Philistine (1 Sam. 17:4, 23). David befriended Achish, the king of Gath, during his time as an outlaw (1 Sam. 27:2–11). However, Gath continued as a center of opposition to the Hebrews, and it provided warriors who opposed the Hebrews (2 Sam. 15:18; 21:20). During the reign of Joash (ca. 802–786 BCE) Hazael, king of Damascus/Syria, took the city (2 Kings 12:17). According to 2 Chron. 26:6, the city was captured by David and then recaptured by Uzziah (ca. 783–742 BCE). There is no mention, however, of those conquests in the Deuteronomistic History (Joshua–2 Kings). Ancient Near Eastern sources indicate that Sargon II of Assyria destroyed Gath ca. 712 BCE.
S.B.R.

Gath-rimmon (gath-rim′uhn; Heb., "the wine press of Rimmon"), a city originally assigned to Dan, but later given to the Levites (Josh. 19:45; 21:24). In a parallel account it is listed as being given to the Levites from the tribe of Ephraim (1 Chron. 6:69), but that account omits a verse preserved in Joshua (21:23) that specifies the city belonged to Dan. A second Gath-rimmon given to the Levites from the half-tribe of Manasseh is also recorded (Josh. 21:25), but in the parallel account (1 Chron. 6:70) that city is called Bileam. Most scholars think there was only one Gath-rimmon and that scribal errors led to the multiple and conflicting references in these accounts. The city is thought to have been located northeast of Joppa, although the exact site is unknown. Perhaps the fact that this area is near the borders of Dan, Ephraim, and Manasseh contributed to the confusion in the accounts.
D.R.B.

Gaza (gay′zuh), a settlement about three miles from the Mediterranean coast, marking the southern border of Canaan. It was captured by Pharaoh Thutmose III (ca. 1469 BCE) and is mentioned in the Tell el-Amarna tablets and Taanach tablets as an Egyptian administrative center. It was later conquered by Israelites from the tribe of Judah (Judg. 1:18) and was included in the allotment given to that tribe (Josh. 15:47). Gaza eventually became part of the Philistine Pentapolis, the southernmost city in that league of five cities (Josh. 13:3; 1 Sam. 6:17; Jer. 25:20); it remained an independent Philistine stronghold ca. 1200–600 BCE (though it did fall briefly to the Assyrians in the eighth century). As quintessential Philistine territory, Gaza figured prominently in the Samson narratives. It was here that Samson, while visiting a prostitute, eluded capture by the Philistines and, seizing the Gaza city gates, carried them to Hebron (Judg. 16:1–3). Later, after he was betrayed by Delilah, Samson was taken as a prisoner to Gaza, where he was tortured and confined (16:21–25). Eventually, however, he regained his strength and pulled down the pillars of the temple of Dagon in Gaza (16:28–30).

King Hezekiah of Judah waged war against the Philistines "as far as Gaza" in the eighth century BCE (2 Kings 18:8), and the city was later conquered by Sennacherib of Assyria (734 BCE). Still later, Pharaoh Neco II occupied Gaza briefly in 609 BCE, and Nebuchadnezzar of Babylon conquered the city in 604 BCE, an event referred to in Jer. 47:1–2. According to the Greek historian Herodotus (2.159), Gaza became a royal fortress under Persian control of the area and was then called Kadytis. It was also the only city in its area to oppose Alexander the Great (332 BCE). Later on, it became an outpost of the Ptolemies, who were the ruling power in Egypt during the Hellenistic period, until its capture in 198 BCE by Antiochus III, the Seleucid king in control of Syria. The Seleucid city was subsequently attacked by Jonathan the Hasmonean (145 BCE; cf. 1 Macc. 11:61–62). During the Hasmonean civil war, Gaza was taken by Alexander Jannaeus in 96 BCE. The Roman Pompey restored the city, and Galbinius, also a Roman official, rebuilt it (ca. 57 BCE). King Herod the Great held Gaza for a short time, but after his death it came under the authority of the Roman proconsul of Syria. It flourished as a Roman city and remained a center for the Jewish community and the emerging Christian community throughout the Roman era (63 BCE–324 CE) and continuing into the Byzantine period (324–1453 CE).

Modern Tell Harube has been identified as ancient Gaza. Excavations there have revealed a mosaic pavement, and a synagogue from the sixth century CE. There appears to have been continuous occupation from the Late Bronze era until the Byzantine period (ca. 1500 BCE–632 CE).   S.B.R.

gazelle. Three species of gazelles lived in the Near East during the biblical period: the Dorcas gazelle (*Gazella dorcas*) in the deserts, the mountain gazelle (*Gazella gazella*) in the hillier areas, and the goitred gazelle (*Gazella subgutturosa*) east of the Jordan. They were symbols of love and beauty for the Hebrews (Song of Sol. 2:9, 17). They were also a major game animal, regularly supplied

A gazelle tended by a western Asiatic; detail of a wall painting from a tomb at Beni-Hasan, Egypt, second millennium BCE.

at Solomon's table (1 Kings 4:23), though they were difficult to catch because of their swiftness (2 Sam. 2:18; 1 Chron. 12:8).

Geba (gee′buh), a town to the northwest of the Dead Sea given to the Levites from the tribe of Benjamin (Josh. 21:17). It guarded the Michmash pass and was the scene of Israelite battles with the Philistines (1 Sam. 13:3). It is sometimes confused with Gibeah and Gibeon in the Hebrew text, thus, "from Geba to Gezer" in 1 Sam. 5:25 should probably read, "from Gibeon to Gezer" (cf. 1 Chron. 14:16), and the reference to Geba in Judg. 20:33 should probably be to Gibeah (cf. Judg. 20:20, 34). Geba was later fortified by Asa (1 Kings 15:22) and was repopulated in the postexilic period, after the mid-sixth century BCE (Neh. 11:31). *See also* Gibeah; Gibeon; Michmash; Philistines.

Gebal (gee′buhl; Heb., "mountain").

1 A Canaanite and Phoenician port city about twenty miles north of Beirut, known to the Greeks as Byblos and today called Jebail. Mentioned in Josh. 13:5 as part of the land that still remained to be conquered, it was famous for its skilled laborers. These would include stonemasons and carpenters who helped construct Solomon's temple (1 Kings 5:18) as well as shipwrights (Ezek. 27:9), who used cedar, spruce, and cypress from the high mountains immediately east of the city.

Archaeological excavations at Gebal reveal a long and fascinating history. First settled in the Pre-Pottery Neolithic period as early as ca. 8000 BCE, it was already a major site during the Chalcolithic period (ca. 3500–3100 BCE). In the Bronze Age (ca. 3000–1200 BCE) Gebal traded as far afield as Anatolia, Mesopotamia, and the Sudan, not only in lumber, but also in such goods as wine, leather, and oil. Egypt, which had little wood of its own, sought to control Gebal, but between ca. 1800 and 1500 BCE Gebal was fortified as a city of the Hyksos. Egypt regained control after 1500, but never attained its earlier level of authority. For example, an account of how an Egyptian official, Wen-Amon, was rudely received in ca. 1000 BCE vividly reveals Gebal's complete freedom of action at that time (corresponding to the beginnings of the Israelite monarchy). Specific archaeological finds include the sarcophagus of King Ahiram (tenth century BCE), which bears the earliest known Phoenician alphabetic inscription. In fact, almost all early Phoenician inscriptions that have been discovered thus far come from Gebal.

2 A tribal area south of the Dead Sea mentioned in Ps. 83:7 in connection with Moab and Edom; some modern scholars equate it with 1 above.

D.B.

Geber (gee'buhr; Heb., "vigorous"), the son of Uri; he was Solomon's officer in charge of procuring provisions in Gilead (1 Kings 4:19).

Gedaliah (ged'uh-li'uh).

1 The son of Ahikam son of Shaphan, who was appointed by King Nebuchadnezzar of Babylon to be governor of Judah after Jerusalem fell to the Babylonians in 587/6 BCE (1 Kings 25:22). Gedaliah was a member of a prominent Jerusalem family; his father and grandfather had served in Josiah's court (2 Kings 22:3, 14). He too may have been a royal official, if he is identical with "Gedaliah, the royal steward," whose name appears on a stamp seal discovered at Lachish. Though viewed with suspicion as a Babylonian collaborator by his contemporaries, Gedaliah succeeded in restoring order to the countryside with the support of former army officers and the prophet Jeremiah. His tenure at Mizpah, the provincial capital, was cut short by a conspiracy led by Ishmael, son of Nataniah, of the royal line. Gedaliah and his entourage were slaughtered, and the conspirators escaped across the Jordan to Ammon (Jer. 40–41). A national day of fasting and mourning was inaugurated among the exiles to mark his murder (Zech. 7:5). *See also* Nebuzaradan.

2 The grandfather of the prophet Zephaniah (cf. Zeph. 1:1). M.C.

Gederah (gi-dee'ruh; Heb., "a wall"), a city in the lowlands of Judah noted for its royal potters (Josh. 15:36; 1 Chron. 4:23). It was also the home of Jozabad, one of David's warriors (1 Chron. 12:4), and of Baal-hanan, an agricultural official under David (1 Chron. 27:28). The site is unknown.

Gedor (gee'dor; Heb., possibly "stone pile").

1 The name of a town inherited by Judah (Josh. 15:58), possibly Khirbet Jedur southwest of Bethlehem and northwest of Hebron.

2 A son of the Judahite Penuel (1 Chron. 4:4) who may have been the founder of the town inherited by Judah.

3 A son of the Judahite Jered (1 Chron. 4:18).

4 The name of the entrance to some rich grazing land (1 Chron. 4:39); possibly the intended reference here is to "Gerar."

5 A son of the Benjaminite Jeiel and Maacah (1 Chron. 8:31; 9:37).

6 The residence of Jehoram (1 Chron. 12:7).

Gehazi (gi-hay'zi; Heb., "valley of vision"), the servant or younger associate of Elisha the prophet. In the story of the wealthy Shunammite woman (2 Kings 4:8–37), Gehazi is portrayed as Elisha's faithful messenger and perhaps overzealous protector (4:27). Some time later Gehazi is in conversation with the king of Israel, when this same woman appears seeking recovery of her property after a sojourn in Philistia (2 Kings 8:1–6). In the story of Naaman (2 Kings 5), however, Gehazi is portrayed as greedy and deceitful; he is cursed by Elisha and contracts leprosy. D.L.C.

Gemariah (gem'uh-ri'uh).

1 The son of Shaphan, of an influential Jerusalem family of scribes in the early sixth century BCE. The scroll of Jeremiah's collected prophecies was first read in Gemariah's chamber in the temple precinct (Jer. 36:10). Later, Gemariah appears among the prophet's supporters at the court of Jehoiakim.

2 The son of Hilkiah, who carried Jeremiah's letter to the exiles in Babylonia (Jer. 29:3).

gematria (gay-mah'tree-uh), the practice of assigning a numerical value to proper names or to related words and expressions. This was easily done in the ancient world because, in both Hebrew and Greek, letters of the alphabet were also used as numerals. It became commonplace for people to add up the numerical value of the letters that were used to spell any person's name and to regard the sum of those numbers as "the number of (that) person's name" (cf. Rev. 13:17–18). For example, if gematria were practiced with the modern-day English alphabet, an A would be equal to 1, a B would be equal to 2, and so forth. After the tenth letter, the eleventh (K) would be equal to 20, the twelfth (L) would be equal to 30, and so on until, with the twenty-first letter (U), multiples of 100 would be used. The proper name "Mark" would end up consisting of four letters with these numerical values: M = 40; A = 1; R = 90; K = 20. The sum of these numbers (40 + 1 + 90 + 20) would be 151, so in modern-day gematria, it could be said that the number of Mark's name is 151. Today, this would seem like a code, but the whole process would have been less mysterious in the biblical world, when everyone already knew the numerical value of

GEMATRIA

The practice of *gematria* consists of assigning a numerical value to a word or phrase by adding together the values of the individual letters. This works in Hebrew and Greek, where the letters of the alphabet can also serve as numerals. In Greek, the marks signifying 6 and 90 were not used as letters in New Testament times.

Hebrew Letters

א = 1	ה = 5	ט = 9	מ = 40	פ = 80	ש = 300
ב = 2	ו = 6	י = 10	נ = 50	צ = 90	ת = 400
ג = 3	ז = 7	כ = 20	ס = 60	ק = 100	
ד = 4	ח = 8	ל = 30	ע = 70	ר = 200	

Greek Letters

A α = 1	F Ϝ = 6	K κ = 20	O o = 70	T τ = 300	Ω ω = 800
B β = 2	Z ζ = 7	Λ λ = 30	Π π = 80	Y υ = 400	
Γ γ = 3	H η = 8	M μ = 40	Ϙ ϙ = 90	Φ φ = 500	
Δ δ = 4	Θ θ = 9	N ν = 50	P ρ = 100	X χ = 600	
E ε = 5	I ι = 10	Ξ ξ = 60	Σ σ = 200	Ψ ψ = 700	

In the Roman world, gematria became a basis for riddles, jokes, and games:

- Graffiti on a wall in Pompeii reads, "I love her whose number is 545."

- As a political joke, Suetonius (*Nero* 39) indicates that the name "Nero" (Νέρων) and the phrase "killed his own mother" (ἰδίαν μητέρα ἀπέκτεινε) have the same numerical value (1,005) when written in Greek. This was pertinent because the emperor was rumored to have murdered his mother.

In Christianity and Judaism, gematria could provide a basis for religious symbolism:

- Rabbis noted that "Eliezer" (אליעזר), the name of Abraham's favored servant (Gen. 15:2), has a numerical value of 318, which is the total number of servants mentioned in Gen. 14:14. Thus, Eliezer was equal to all the rest of the servants combined.

- The Hebrew letters in the name "David" (דוד) add up to 14, so that number could be accorded messianic significance: the messiah was to be the Son of David. This is probably why Matthew's Gospel emphasizes that the genealogy of Jesus can be divided into three sets of 14 generations (Matt. 1:17).

- The Greek letters in the name "Jesus" (Ἰησογυς) add up to 888, which some early Christians found significant: 8 surpasses 7 (the number for perfection) and heralds a "new creation" beyond what God did in the first 7 days (Gen. 1:1–2:3).

Many scholars think that gematria holds the clue to resolving the puzzle of 666, the number attributed to the beast in Rev. 13:18:

- A popular spelling for the name of the emperor Nero adds up to 666 when written in Hebrew (קסרנרון = Caesar Neron). An alternate spelling (קסרנרו = Caesar Nero) adds up to 616, a variant reading for the number of the beast found in some manuscripts of Revelation.

- A designation for the emperor Domitian that sometimes appeared on Greek coins also adds up to 666: A. Kai. Domet. Seb. Ge. (an abbreviation for *Autokratōr Kaisar Dometianos Sebastos Germanikos* = Emperor Caesar Domitian Augustus Germanicus).

Over time, most Jewish and Christian groups abandoned the practice of gematria, perhaps because certain groups used numerology in connection with magic and the occult. The practice still features prominently in kabbalah and other mystical traditions.

each individual letter. In any case, gematria became very popular in certain times and places. In the Greco-Roman world, during NT times, it often became the basis for jokes and riddles; for these to have functioned as they did at a popular level, most people would have to have known the numbers of their own names, as well as the numbers to be associated with other prominent people. Most Jews would have known that the letters in the name "David" (in Hebrew) added to 14 and most Christians would have known that the letters in the name "Jesus" (in Greek) added to 888. Likewise, the first readers of the book of Revelation probably knew that the letters in the name "Caesar Nero" (in Hebrew) added to either 666 or 616, depending on how it was spelled. Accordingly, Rev. 13:18 reveals the number of the beast to be 666 in some manuscripts and 616 in others.   M.A.P.

genealogy. The Hebrew Bible contains contains about two dozen genealogical lists. The first is at Gen. 4:17–22 (from Cain through seven generations). Other prominent lists are the generations from Adam to Noah (Gen. 5:1–32), the descendants of Noah (10:1–32), the generations from Shem to Abraham (11:10–26), the descendants of Jacob (46:8–27) and Levi (Exod. 6:16–25), and the list of persons and families of the postexilic community who continue the line from preexilic times (Ezra 2:2b–61). The most extensive genealogy is in 1 Chron. 1:1–9:44 (Adam to the descendants of Saul). These genealogies vary with regard to historical value and purpose. The aim of constructing genealogies was not necessarily to be comprehensive, but to establish descent and thereby to define identity. Accordingly, certain generations and individuals could be omitted. For example, Exod. 6:16–20 appears to identify Moses as the great-grandson of Levi, which is hardly possible in a strict sense, since the time span is over four hundred years (cf. Exod. 12:40). The impetus for genealogies arose after the Deuteronomic reform (seventh century BCE), which stressed purity of the community (Deut. 7:1–4; 23:1–8). This was intensified in the postexilic era when there was some pressure to document ethnic purity (Ezra 2:59–63; 10:9–44; Neh. 13:23–28). Moreover, genealogies were constructed for the Aaronic priesthood (restricted to descendants of Levi; Exod. 28:1–29:44). Furthermore, since royal succession in the southern kingdom was determined by Davidic descent, a royal genealogical record had to be kept. It was expected in some circles that a Messiah would arise from among the descendants of David (Isa. 11:1–5; cf. 2 Sam. 7:16; Ps. 89:3–4), but the persistence and prevalence of that expectation is cast into some doubt by the fact that the Hebrew Bible offers no genealogies for Davidic descendants after Zerubbabel.

The NT genealogies of Jesus in Matt. 1:1–17 and Luke 3:23–38 seek to establish above all his Davidic descent (Matt. 1:1, 6, 17; Luke 3:31). Matthew also demonstrates Jesus's descent from Abraham (1:1–2, 17), while Luke traces his descent all the way back to "Adam, the son of God" (3:38). Both genealogies, therefore, cover the span from Abraham to Jesus, but they differ in detail. Matthew computes three groups of fourteen generations each for this span (1:17), although only forty-one (not forty-two) names actually appear (inclusive of Abraham and Jesus), while Luke lists fifty-seven names for the same period. The names are mostly the same from Abraham to David in both (Luke 3:33 adds Arni and Admin), but thereafter only three names appear in common (Shealtiel, Zerubbabel, and Joseph). The significance of the number "fourteen" for Matthew's genealogy is probably tied to an interest in gematria, according to which the number fourteen was associated with David and thus acquired messianic connotations. Matthew's genealogy is also significant in that it includes four women (Tamar, Rahab, Ruth, and "the wife of Uriah" [Bathsheba]" cf. Matt. 1:3, 5, 6). The mention of women in a genealogy was highly irregular, and Matthew's reason for naming these four women is not certain; it may be because all four were considered to be Gentiles, or because all four (like Mary, the virgin mother of Jesus) were considered to have had irregular sexual unions that nevertheless proved important for God's plan. *See also* David; king; messiah; priests.   A.J.H./M.A.P.

General Letters/Epistles. *See* Catholic Letters/ Epistles.

generation (Heb. *dor*), the period of time between the birth of parents and the birth of their children, or all of the people alive during such a time period. The Bible uses the term "generation" only loosely as a measure of time, so such references do not allow for precise chronological calculations. Although a generation sometimes covers up to a hundred years (Gen. 15:13, 16; Exod. 12:40), most biblical writers seem to consider thirty to forty years to be a normal generation (Deut. 2:14; Job 42:16; Ps. 95:10). Usually "generation" simply refers to the people who are alive at any given time (Gen. 6:9; Pss. 14:5; 24:6; 49:19; 24:6; 112:2; Jer. 2:3). Jesus uses the term this way in the NT when he speaks of judgment to come upon "this generation" (Matt. 12:41–45; cf. 23:36) or when he says, "An evil adulterous generation seeks a sign" (Matt. 12:39; 16:4; cf. 17:17). In Matt. 24:34, after delineating what will happen in the end times before the coming of the Son of Man, Jesus says, "This generation will not pass away until all these things take place" (cf. Mark 13:30; Luke 21:32).   R.R.W.

Genesis (jen'uh-sis), **book of,** the first of the Five Books of Moses (the Torah) of the Tanakh (Jewish Bible); it is the first book of the Pentateuch of the Christian OT. The Hebrew name of the book is *bereshit,* meaning "in the beginning," which is the first Hebrew phrase of the book. The English name Genesis comes from the Greek word *genesis* in the LXX, which translates the Hebrew word *toledot,* meaning "generations." The book consists of two parts, a narrative of the creation of the world and early world events called the primeval story (chaps. 1–11) and a narrative of Israel's forebears Abraham, Isaac, and Jacob called the ancestral story (chaps. 12–50).

Contents: The primeval story begins with an account of creation painted in broad strokes. It accounts for the emergence of entire realms of material reality in short paragraphs full of formulaic repetitions; light, sky, earth, sun, moon, stars, birds, fish, animals, and humans all come into being within six days (Gen. 1). A second rendering of creation follows, which revolves entirely around the first human male, whose creation is followed by the creation of animals and a woman to meet his needs (Gen. 2). The next incident describes how the human–divine relationship becomes broken when Adam and Eve, the first couple, transgress the bounds of allowed behavior by eating the forbidden fruit (Gen. 3). Expulsion from the garden of Eden is shortly followed by the first murder, when Cain kills his brother, Abel (Gen. 4). The text notes how seminal cultural inventions, including the emergence of the city, arts, animal husbandry, and metallurgy, track alongside a growing trend in human violence. These developments prompt a destructive flood in the time of Noah that allows the world the opportunity to start afresh (Gen. 6–9). But human character has not changed, and humans are still driven to make a name for themselves apart from the deity.

The frontispiece to Genesis from the first Bible of Charles the Bald (ninth century) shows (*top*) the creation of man and woman, (*middle*) eating the fruit of the forbidden tree, and (*bottom*) the banishment of Adam and Eve from the garden of Eden.

This effort is frustrated by God at Babel, and God focuses attention on one man, Abram (later renamed Abraham), and his offspring, who become the object of divine blessing (Gen. 11).

The ancestral story is constructed of three narrative cycles that are collections of material revolving around Abraham, Jacob, and Joseph, respectively, with genealogical interludes devoted to Ishmael and Esau. In the Abraham cycle Abraham is guided by God to journey to Canaan and settle there, with the promise of divine blessing and offspring (Gen. 12). Arriving at their destination, Abraham and his wife, Sarah, find the land to be rife with disappointment and danger, from famine to threats to personal safety, to infertility. Eventually Abraham and Sarah have a son, Isaac, but the bestowing deity demands him back, as told in the wrenching episode called the Akedah, or binding of Isaac (Gen. 22). Surviving these challenges, Isaac marries Rebekah, and they have twin sons, Esau and Jacob (Gen. 25). The Jacob cycle is dominated by Jacob's relentless efforts to win blessing and prosperity, acquiring them by dubious and devious methods. He steals the firstborn's rights from Esau (Gen. 25) as well as the paternal blessing (Gen. 27) and then acquires considerable wealth from his uncle Laban (Gen. 29–31). Last, he wrestles a blessing from God at the Jabbok River and receives the name Israel (Gen. 32). Jacob has twelve sons by his four wives (Leah, Zilpah, Rachel, and Bilhah), and they begin the twelve tribes that later constitute Israel. The final cycle is focused on Joseph, son of Jacob, and takes the form of a short story. Driven by jealousy, Joseph's brothers sell him into slavery in Egypt (Gen. 37). While there he rises to a position of power as head of food resources (Gen. 39). When his brothers come to buy food due to a famine in Canaan, he takes revenge on them by imprisoning Simeon and threatening Benjamin (Gen. 40–44). He finally reveals his true identity, to their great shame and relief, and the entire extended family moves to Goshen in Egypt so that he can provide for them (Gen. 45–50). This positions the sons of Israel in Egypt, from which they will later escape, as told in the book of Exodus.

Structure: The book of Genesis has an overall structure that is defined by the occurrence of ten topic sentences that use the word *toledot* (Heb., "generations"), e.g., Gen. 2:4: "These are the generations of the heavens and the earth when they were created." A *toledot* topic sentence introduces a new section that grabs hold of the central figure of the preceding section and describes what it has generated. For example, the creation of the heavens and the earth is told in Gen. 1:1–2:3; then comes the heavens and earth *toledot* topic sentence in 2:4, which introduces the narrative of what the heavens and earth become, as told in the Adam and Eve episodes. A similar pattern recurs in the remaining nine *toledot* sections. On the basis of content and structure, these ten *toledot* sections can be clustered into two groups of five each: the primeval story and the ancestral story.

Background: Genesis combines a variety of materials including genealogies, narrative episodes, and reports such as the creation narratives. Although some of the episodes are prehistorical and could not have been based on eyewitness reporting, many others are vivid and history-like rather than fantastical. Historians and archaeologists have sought evidence to reconstruct a viable context for the events of the primeval and ancestral stories. Late nineteenth-century and early twentieth-century finds in Mesopotamia, Egypt, and Turkey seemed to support the historicity of some of the figures in these stories (see Kitchen); other approaches, however, seem to support a monarchic or postexilic context for the written accounts, rendering the authenticity of the Genesis narratives suspect (see Van Seters, Finkelstein).

Although the book of Genesis does not identify its author, the Torah, including Genesis, was traditionally assumed to contain the writings of Moses. Close attention to details in the text reveals that Genesis was not written by one person, and it is not a book of history in the modern sense of the genre. It is more a chronologically structured book

OUTLINE OF CONTENTS

Genesis

of cultural and family memories. The book was constructed out of a variety of preexisting oral and written material, and it developed in stages over hundreds of years, from the era of the Israelite monarchy to the postexilic period. The consensus of modern scholarship posits multiple authors and a long and involved process of composition. The prevailing Documentary Hypothesis identifies four main source texts for the Pentateuch: the Yahwist, Elohist, Priestly, and Deuteronomic documents. Elements of the Yahwist (J), Elohist (E), and Priestly (P) sources have been identified in Genesis.

According to most reconstructions of the compositional history of Genesis, the Yahwist narrative was an epic containing the episodes that formed the backbone of Genesis: the garden of Eden, Cain and Abel, the flood, the Tower of Babel, Abraham and Sarah (Gen. 12–13), etc. YHWH ("the Lord") is the deity of these texts and is portrayed as very humanlike. Elohist texts include the covenant with Abraham (Gen. 15), the sacrifice of Isaac (Gen. 22), and portions of the Joseph cycle; they were combined with the Yahwist narrative to form the JE "old epic." A Priestly group added narrative episodes and genealogies in the fifth century BCE to complete Genesis; these P additions include the first creation account (1:1–2:3), a version of the flood (interwoven with the J version in Gen. 6–9), and an account of the covenant of circumcision (Gen. 17). This P material refers to the deity as God (Elohim) or God Almighty (El Shaddai).

Themes: Genesis posits that the world came into existence by divine word and action. The creation of humans in the image and likeness of God (1:27) and out of the dust of the ground (2:7) accounts for their unique place within God's world. Genesis also accounts for the origin of the nation of Israel (especially in the accounts of Abraham and Jacob) and grants possession of Canaan to the ancestors of Israel. The core assertion of Genesis is that Israel's deity was responsible for the acts that brought everything into being: the creation of a world, the creation of all living things including humankind, the flood, which demonstrated the vulnerability of creation, and the creation of a divinely chosen people who would become God's special nation. Related themes of blessing and covenant follow from creation and express the potential of the created world.

The words "bless" and "blessing" occur eighty-six times in Genesis. Blessing someone is a speech act that designates someone or something as an object of divine favor leading to its prosperity. It is an act of recognition and affirmation and entails the promise of a good future. Genesis mainly works out this notion in narratives with spoken promises and by the use of genealogies. Promises are so frequent in Genesis (12:2–3; 13:14–17; 18:17–19; 22:15–18; 24:7; 26:3b–5; 28:14; 32:13) and are so similar in vocabulary that Westermann posits a promise source, in addition to the JEP sources, that contributed to the book. The primeval story is largely a demonstration that blessing flows from

being created in the image of God, but blessing is jeopardized when humans attempt to be like the deity by deciding for themselves what is good and evil (3:4, 22), by having intercourse with the gods (6:1–4), or by building a tower to access heaven (11:1–9).

The genealogies of Genesis, in addition to contributing to the chronological structure and flow of the book, give concrete evidence that the creation blessing to "be fruitful and multiply, and fill the earth and subdue it" (1:28) had become a reality. The genealogies also progressively narrow the trajectory of biblical history, so that by the end of the book Israel, represented by the twelve sons of Jacob, has taken center stage. The three ancestral cycles relate how Abraham and his offspring come to experience blessing. The Abraham cycle works out the struggle for blessing primarily in relation to offspring. First, there is Sarah's struggle to have any children at all (Gen. 15), which prompts Abraham and Sarah to use Hagar as a surrogate (Gen. 16). After the birth of Ishmael, Sarah has a child by Abraham, but God demands that Abraham sacrifice this son, Isaac (Gen. 22), delivering the child only at the last moment. The Jacob cycle is presented as a battle for blessing, one that Jacob wins at every juncture. He secures the family birthright (Gen. 25) and blessing (Gen. 27) from Esau, wives and livestock from Laban (Gen. 29–31), and blessing from God at the river (Gen. 32). The Joseph cycle is not focused on blessing to the same extent as the Jacob cycle, but it does work out how Joseph becomes the facilitator of blessing in a time of great famine, and thereby becomes a blessing to the nations, as promised to Abram (12:3).

The Priestly source, P, employs a sequence of three covenants to track the development of the deity's relationship with the world. The first two of these are found in Genesis and the third in Exodus. Each covenant is associated with a stage in the sequential revelation of the identity of the biblical deity, as acknowledged in Exod. 6:2–3. The first is the covenant of God (Elohim) with all creatures after the flood, which is marked by the sign of the rainbow (Gen. 9). The second is the covenant of God Almighty (El Shaddai) beginning with Abraham, which is marked by the sign of circumcision (Gen. 17). The third is the covenant of YHWH ("the Lord") with all Israel as described in the book of Exodus, which is marked by the sign of the sabbath.

Influences: Genesis, more than any other book of the Hebrew Bible, was influenced by the ancient conceptual and literary contexts of Mesopotamia, Canaan, and Egypt in which it arose. For example, the sea monsters of creation (1:21), the image of God (1:26–27), the garden of God (Gen. 2–3), the cherubim (3:24), and the "sons of God" (6:1–4) all draw from Mesopotamian cosmology. Significant portions of Genesis bear more than passing similarity to ancient literary works that have survived. The *Enuma Elish,* a Babylonian creation story, relates how the material world was created from primeval water, with parallels to Gen. 1. Humans were denied immortality (Gen. 3) in *Adapa* and the Gilgamesh epic. In the flood text of Gilgamesh the hero builds an ark, sends birds to find dry land, and offers a sacrifice after landing.

Going in the other direction of influence, Genesis has had a significant impact on art, literature, music, politics, and science in the Western world. The central figures of Genesis and the stories about them, such as Adam and Eve, Noah, Abraham and Sarah, Isaac, Jacob, and Joseph, have been the subject of countless works. To cite just a few examples of the profound influence of Genesis, note the ceiling frescos of Michelangelo in the Sistine Chapel, Caravaggio and Rembrandt's depictions of the sacrifice of Isaac, Milton's "Paradise Lost," and the current discussion of creationism and evolution in political and educational contexts. *See also* ancestor; Pentateuch, sources of the.

Bibliography

Alter, Robert. *Genesis: Translation and Commentary.* Norton, 1996.

Bandstra, Barry L. *Reading the Old Testament: Introduction to the Hebrew Bible.* 4th ed. Wadsworth, 2009.

Campbell, Anthony F., and Mark A. O'Brien. *The Sources of the Pentateuch: Texts, Introductions, Annotations.* Augsburg Fortress, 1993.

Finkelstein, Israel, and Neil A. Silberman. *The Bible Unearthed: Archaeology's New Vision of Ancient Israel and the Origin of Its Sacred Texts.* Free Press, 2001.

Kitchen, Kenneth A. *On the Reliability of the Old Testament.* Eerdmans, 2003.

Sarna, Nahum M. *Genesis (Bereshit): The Traditional Hebrew Text with New JPS Translation.* Jewish Publication Society, 1989.

Van Seters, John. *Prologue to History: The Yahwist as Historian in Genesis.* Westminster John Knox, 1992.

Westermann, Claus. *The Promises to the Fathers: Studies on the Patriarchal Narratives.* Fortress, 1980.   B.B.

Gennesaret (gi-nes'uh-ret). *See* Galilee, Sea of.

Gentile (from Lat. *gens*, "nation"), a non-Jew. The distinction has its roots in the biblical account of seven nations (Heb. *goyim*) not driven completely from the land (Josh. 24:11). According to several traditions, the Israelites were enjoined to maintain separation from the people of these nations in matters of religion, marriage, and politics (Exod. 23:28–33; Deut. 7:1–5; Josh. 23:4–13). Historically speaking, the amount of interchange between the Israelites and the peoples of the land seems to have been considerable, and it was only in postexilic times that individuals were referred to as *goyim* or Gentiles; even then, however, the primary reference seemed to be to nations. Theologically, Israel understood God as creator of all peoples of the earth. The Isaianic tradition, in particular, spoke of Israel as "a light to the nations" (42:6; cf. 60:3) and indicated that, in the latter days, the nations would flow to Jerusalem to learn Torah (2.2–4) or

An inscription forbidding non-Jews (i.e., Gentiles) from entering the temple in Jerusalem; cast of the original stone, which dates to 20 BCE.

to participate in the coming reign of God (45:22–24; 51:4–5). Still, in order for Israel to fulfill its role as a "light to the nations," it was necessary for Israel to remain distinct from those nations, not to be shut off from them, but not to assimilate completely with them either. In the wake of the exile, a renewed emphasis on preserving culture and tradition led many to favor stricter separation of Jews and non-Jews (particularly with regard to marriage and religious observations). Thus, Ezra and Nehemiah commanded Jews in Jerusalem to divorce their non-Jewish wives (Ezra 9–10; Neh. 10:30; 13:23–31). The books of Ruth, Esther, and Jonah, however, give evidence to a countertradition that presented Gentiles more favorably.

Hellenistic Jewish literature from the Second Temple period (e.g., deuterocanonical and pseudepigraphical writings) gives evidence of different attitudes about Israel and the nations (or Jews and Gentiles). A reference in 2 Macc. 14:38 refers wistfully to "former times, when there was no mingling with the Gentiles." Sir. 11:34 warns against receiving a stranger (probably, a non-Jew) into one's household, lest one's way of life become alienated. Thus, mixed marriages continued to be a concern (Tob. 4:12–13; *T. Levi* 9:10; 14:6), and Jews were urged to remain distinctive through diet (Tob. 1:10–12; cf. Dan. 1:8–15), the practice of circumcision (1 Macc. 1:11–15), and, above all, avoidance of the idolatry characteristic of Gentile society (1 Macc. 3:48). The alternative is depicted starkly in 1 Macc. 1:11–15, which reports that "certain renegades came out from Israel and misled many, saying, 'Let us go and make a covenant with the Gentiles around us, for since we separated from them many disasters have come upon us.'. . . So they built a gymnasium in Jerusalem, according to Gentile custom, and removed the marks of circumcision, and abandoned the holy covenant." By NT times, there was resentment among most Jews toward those Gentiles who ruled over them (the Romans), but in general most Jews seem to have been oriented toward peaceful coexistence with Gentiles—and, indeed, toward cooperation and friendship with them at levels that did not compromise their own faith or traditions. Thus, there was a "court of the Gentiles" in the temple at Jerusalem, and many Gentiles became "God-fearers" and worshiped in the Jewish synagogues. These "God-fearers" appear to have been "half converts": Gentiles who accepted much Jewish theology and morality, but who did not undergo circumcision or keep the food laws required of full converts. A number of God-fearers are referred to in the NT, where they are often presented as receptive to the gospel of Christ (cf. Acts 10:22; 13:16, 26; 17:4, 17).

In the NT itself, the term "Gentile" (Gk. *ethnos*) is used with a range of meanings. The basic meaning seems to be "non-Jew," as is apparent from the instances in which Jews and Gentiles (or Jews and Greeks) are referred to in a sense that seems to connote "all humanity" (Acts 14:1, 5; 19:10, 17; 1 Cor. 1:22–24). In other instances, however, the word *ethnos* seems to mean "nation"—and it is usually translated that way in the NRSV (e.g., when Rom. 4:18 calls Abraham the father of many *ethnoi*, he is obviously the father of "nations," not "Gentiles"). But in certain passages. the meaning is ambiguous. In Matt. 28:19, does Jesus commission his followers to make disciples of all nations (as in the NRSV) or of all Gentiles? Another meaning of "Gentile" is found most prominently in the teachings of Jesus, where the term does not seem to indicate an ethnic identification so much as a "pagan" or a person who does not believe in or worship God (cf. Matt. 5:47; 6:7, 32; 18:17; 20:25; cf. Eph. 4:17; 1 Thess. 4:5). Even more striking, perhaps, is a peculiar usage of the term in 1 Peter, a letter written to non-Jewish Christians (evident from 1:14, 18; 2:10; 4:3–4). In this letter, believers in Christ are identified spiritually as the new chosen people of God, heirs to all the promises of Israel (2:9), so the term "Gentile" is used to mean "non-Christians" (2:12; 4:3).

The development of Christianity, which began as a Jewish movement, was profoundly affected by the success of the Gentile mission undertaken by the apostle Paul and others. The Jerusalem Council ca. 49 CE determined that Gentile converts to Christianity did not have to become Jewish proselytes (Acts 15:1–35), thus opening membership in the church to those who might otherwise have remained "half converts" similar to the "God-fearers" in the synagogues. Paul fought efforts to make distinctions between Jew and Gentile in the Christian community (Rom. 3:29–30; Gal. 2:11–21; 3:26–29). He was opposed by Christians who insisted that Gentile converts become Jewish proselytes (he refers to people who hold this view as the "circumcision faction" in Gal. 2:12 and as "those who mutilate the flesh" in Phil. 3:2). His rationale for regarding Jews and Gentiles as "one in Christ Jesus" (Gal. 3:28) was closely associated with his doctrine of justification by grace through faith, an understanding that because of the death and resurrection of Christ, Jews and Gentiles alike could be put right with God through faith, apart from works of the law (Rom. 1:16–17; 3:28; 5:1; Gal. 2:15–17; 3:24–26).

As a result of the controversy over the role of Gentiles in the church, it is difficult to determine the attitude of Jesus himself, since both sides seem to have affected the preservation of the Jesus tradition. There is material in the Gospels that suggests Jesus understood the activity of the Messiah as directed primarily toward the Jewish people with, perhaps, some ultimate inclusion of the Gentiles only at the last (Matt. 10:5–6; 15:24). On the other hand, a number of sayings attributed to Jesus seem to suggest divine favor for Gentiles even at the expense of some in Israel (Matt. 8:10–12; 21:28–32, 43; Mark 11:15–17; Luke 4:23–27). *See also* God-fearers; proselyte.   D.W.S./M.A.P.

Gentiles, court of the. *See* temple, the.

Gera (gee′ruh).

    1 A son of Benjamin (Gen. 46:21).

    2 A son of Bela and grandson of Benjamin (1 Chron. 8:3).

    3 A second son of Bela and grandson of Benjamin (1 Chron. 8:5).

    4 A Benjaminite, the father of Ehud (Judg. 3:15).

    5 A Benjaminite, a son of Ehud (1 Chron. 8:7).

It is difficult to separate these names (**1–5**) and assign them to specific persons. They may all represent the same person whose ancestry has become confused in the records; or the name may represent an ancient family group within the tribe of Benjamin whose exact genealogy was not known.

    6 A member of Saul's family and father of Shimei, the man who pronounced a curse on David (2 Sam. 16:5; 19:16).   D.R.B.

gerah (gee′ruh), a measure of weight equal to $\frac{1}{20}$ of a shekel (Exod. 30:13; Lev. 27:25; Num. 3:47; 18:16; Ezek. 45:12). Recovered samples to date indicate an average weight of 0.565 grams. *See also* weights and measures.

Gerar (gee′rahr), a town in the Negev. Abraham visited the town and entered into some type of agreement with the Philistine king of Gerar, Abimelech (Gen. 20:1–2). However, the bulk of episodes involving Gerar are in the Isaac stories: Isaac and Rebekah settle at Gerar (Gen. 26:2) but, like his father before him, Isaac tells Abimelech that his wife is his sister, because he fears someone will kill him to obtain her. The ruse is exposed when Abimelech looks out a window and sees Isaac fondling Rebekah (26:8). Isaac is guaranteed Abimelech's protection and he subsequently sows seed in the land and becomes rich, with so many flocks and herds and such a great household that the Philistines envy him. Isaac then moves to the valley of Gerar, where he digs wells that become a source of contention with herders in the area (26:17–21). The only other references to Gerar in the Bible are in 2 Chron. 14:9–14, which presents a story of Asa's defeat of Zerah, an invading

Ethiopian (905–874 BCE). Despite several proposals, the location of Gerar remains undetermined.

                                        S.B.R.

Gerasa (gair´uh-suh), **Gerasenes** (gair´uh-seenz). Some biblical manuscripts mention the "country of the Gerasenes" as the site of a dramatic exorcism performed by Jesus (Matt. 8:28–34; Mark 5:1–10; Luke 8:26–39). If this is the correct reading, then the exorcism would have occurred in the area around the city of Gerasa (modern Jerash), one of the three greatest cities of Roman Arabia. There is, however, considerable confusion in the manuscript tradition: some manuscripts read "Gadarenes" or "Gergesenes" rather than "Gerasenes." The NRSV accepts "country of the Gadarenes" as the best reading in Matt. 8:28, but it uses "Gerasenes" in Mark 5:1 and Luke 8:26, 37. Thus, in the NRSV the same exorcism (which involves a large number of demons being cast into a herd of pigs, who run into the sea and drown) is set in two sites, depending on which Gospel is consulted. The location for Mark and Luke, however, is near Gerasa, thirty-three miles southeast of the Sea of Galilee in the mountains of Gilead. This city was administered by an appointee of the legate of Syria and officially known as "Antioch on the Chrysorrhoas." Excavations have revealed extensive remains of public buildings from the first and second centuries CE. The city wall, gates, and towers, several main streets, and the forum as well as remains of the hippodrome, theaters, triumphal arch, and temples of Zeus and Artemis have been found. A coin from the reign of Commodus attests that the city was founded by Alexander the Great. Josephus reports that the Jews living in Gerasa were spared by the Gentile population when the city was attacked by Jewish rebels during the Jewish revolt (*Jewish War* 2.480).   P.P./M.A.P.

Gergesenes (guhr´guh-seenz). *See* Gadara, Gadarenes; Gerasa, Gerasenes.

Gerizim (gair´uh-zim), **Mount,** the mountain (summit 2800 feet above sea level) opposite Mount Ebal in the central Samaritan highlands. Shechem lies in the pass between Mount Ebal and Mount Gerizim, at the intersection of main north–south and east–west roads. Deut. 11:29; 27:12; and Josh. 8:33 portray a ceremony in which the people gathered at Shechem and heard blessings shouted from Mount Gerizim and curses shouted from Mount Ebal. These blessings and curses conveyed the consequences of covenantal loyalty or disloyalty. Elsewhere, in Judg. 9:7, Jotham tells his parable of the Trees at Mount Gerizim, perhaps from the seventeenth- or sixteenth-century BCE sanctuary that has been found on the knoll called Tananir, a quarter mile southeast of Shechem. Judg. 9:37 mentions Tabbur-erez, the "navel" of the land, suggesting that Mount Gerizim was for some the mythic meeting place of heaven and earth. For Samaritans, Mount Gerizim was the site of the Samaritan temple, the place to worship God (John 4:20). Josephus, the first-century CE Jewish

Remains of public buildings from the first and second centuries CE excavated at Gerasa, one of the three greatest cities of Roman Arabia.

historian, reports that this temple was built in the fourth century BCE. During the Hasmonean period, John Hyrcanus reportedly destroyed the Samaritan temple at Mount Gerizim, but Herod the Great later rebuilt it. *See also* Ebal; Samaritans; Shechem.   E.F.C.

Gershom (guhr'shuhm).

1 The eldest son born to Moses and Zipporah in Midian (e.g., Exod. 2:22). His name is popularly explained within the narrative as meaning "sojourner there" (supposedly from Heb. *ger sham*), but this may be a later guess based on a phonetic pun. Gershom was the father of Jonathan, who served as priest to the Danites (Judg. 18:30).

2 A son of Levi, whose descendants were called "Gershomites" (1 Chron. 16:6, 62, 71), but this may be a scribal error for "Gershon," the name that appears to be used for the same person elsewhere. *See also* Gershon.

3 A descendant of Phinehas (Ezra 8:2).   K.G.O.

Gershon (guhr'shuhn),

the first son of Levi, followed by Kohath and Merari (e.g., Gen. 46:11). The name appears as Gershom several times in 1 Chron. 6 (cf. 15:7), but this appears to be a scribal error. Num. 4 and Josh. 21 list Gershon's descendants between Kohath's and Merari's, while 1 Chron. 15:5–7 and 2 Chron. 29:12 put them third. Num. 7:7–9 allocates two wagons to Gershon's sons and four to Merari's (for carrying sections of the tabernacle), but none to the sons of Kohath (for the smaller tabernacle furnishings). Gershon's two sons were named Shimei and either Libni (Exod. 6:17; Num. 3:18) or Ladan (1 Chron. 23:7; 26:21). *See also* Gershom.   K.G.O.

Geshem (gesh'uhm),

an opponent of Nehemiah who ridiculed the plan to rebuild Jerusalem's walls and subsequently plotted against him (Neh. 2:19; 6:1–9). Identified as "an Arab," he is apparently the same person identified in nonbiblical sources as the king of Kedar, an Arabian province just south of Judah. That position may explain his motivation to interfere in Judah's domestic affairs.

Geshur (gesh'uhr).

1 A small ancient kingdom whose territory formed part of southern Golan, east of the Sea of Galilee (Josh. 12:5; 13:11, 13). It was one of the areas that Israel was unable to occupy during the period of conquest and settlement (late thirteenth to early twelfth centuries BCE). Thus, Geshur remained an independent Aramean kingdom into the time of David. Seeking to establish political relationships with this kingdom, David married Maacah, the daughter of Geshur's king, Talmai (2 Sam. 3:3). She bore him Absalom, who, many years later, fled to his grandfather's territory after killing Amnon, who had raped his sister (and Maacah's daughter), Tamar (2 Sam. 13:37–38).

2 A region in the south of Canaan, mentioned in Josh. 13:2 as yet to be won by the Israelites, and

in 1 Sam. 27:8–11 as conquered by David while he was with the Philistines.   Y.G.

gestures, postures, and facial expressions.

The Bible often refers to physical postures, gestures, or facial expressions as indicative of cultural customs and of the ways through which people consciously or unconsciously express their attitudes or emotions.

Prayer: Bowing or bending over is the posture for worship prescribed for one who presents the first fruits of the harvest in Deut. 26:10 and for one who approaches any of the gates of the temple in Ezek. 46, but bowing is also associated with idolatrous worship in Lev. 26:1 and Ezek. 8:16. Other references to bowing as a posture for worship include 2 Kings 18:22; Pss. 5:8; 22:28; 86:9; 132:7; 138:2; and Isa. 66:23. Other postures of worship mentioned in the Bible include stooping (1 Kings 8:54; 19:18; 2 Chron. 29:29; Ezra 9:5; Ps. 22:30; Isa. 45:23), falling on the face (Gen. 24:26, 48; Exod. 4:31; 12:27; 34:8; 2 Chron. 29:30; Neh. 8:6; Ezek. 44:4; Matt. 26:39; Mark 14:35; Rev. 1:17), throwing oneself down (Deut. 9:18, 25; Ezra 10:1), and bowing the head (Isa. 58:5; Mic. 6:6). Kneeling, to be distinguished from stooping, is mentioned as a posture for prayer in 2 Chron. 6:13; Ps. 95:6; Dan. 6:11; and Luke 22:41. Standing is attested as a posture for prayer to God in Neh. 9:2; Ps. 106:30; Jer. 18:20; Matt. 6:5; and Mark 11:25 and as a posture for idolatrous worship in Dan. 2:3. King David is portrayed as praying to God in a

Kneeling figure, probably Hammurabi, in a gesture of prayer; from Larsa, ca. 1750 BCE.

A courtier kisses the ground in a gesture of obeisance; bas-relief from Hermopolis, Egypt.

seated position in 2 Sam. 7:18, and a psalmist prays while lying in bed (Ps. 63:5–6). The prayer gesture most frequently mentioned in the Bible is "spreading the palms" (Exod. 9:29, 33; 1 Kings 8:22, 38, 54; 2 Chron. 6:12, 13, 29; Ezra 9:5; Job 11:13; Ps. 44:21; Isa. 1:15; Jer. 4:31). Apparently this gesture was employed with prayers of petition to suggest that God fill the hands of the petitioner with the requested benefit. This gesture is probably to be distinguished from "lifting up the hands" toward the holy place or sanctuary, possibly as a salute to God in the heavenly temple (Pss. 28:2; 63:4; 134:2; 141:2; 1 Tim. 2:8).

Judicial Proceedings: Because one lifted one's hand, thereby pointing to God's heavenly throne, when taking an oath (Deut. 32:40), swearing came to be referred to as simply "lifting the hand" (see Gen. 14:22; Exod. 6:8; Ezek. 20:5, 6, 15, 23, 28, 42). That the judge was seated while hearing cases is reflected in Exod. 18:13, which also says that the litigants stood during the legal proceeding (see also Judg. 4:4; Ruth 4:2; Ps. 9:8; John 19:13).

Reading and Teaching Scripture: Although no specific posture is prescribed for the reading of Torah in Deut. 31:10–13, Neh. 8–9 states that, when Ezra read from the Torah, both he and the congregation were standing. Luke 4:17–20 informs us that Jesus stood to read from the book of Isaiah in the synagogue at Nazareth, but that he afterward sat down to teach. According to Matt. 5:1, Jesus was seated while preaching the Sermon on the Mount (but cf. Luke 6:17). Matt. 26:55 refers to Jesus's sitting while teaching in the temple. He is perhaps seated in a chair in Luke 10:39, but in any case that verse says that Mary sat at his feet to listen to his word.

Obeisance or Supplication: Throughout the Bible, people bow down (Gen. 23:7, 12; 33:3, 6, 7; 37:10; 2 Sam. 9:6; 14:22; Isa. 49:23), stoop (Esther 3:2, 5), or fall down (Gen. 50:18; Esther 6:13) before sovereigns or social superiors in order to acknowledge the difference in rank. Against that background, two postures are repeatedly mentioned in the Gospels when people come to Jesus to request healing: kneeling and prostration (i.e., lying down in front of him with one's face to the ground). According to Matt. 8:2 and Mark 1:40 a person with leprosy kneels in supplication before Jesus; in Luke 5:12, this person prostrates himself. According to Matt. 15:25 the Canaanite woman kneels when asking Jesus to exorcise the demon from her daughter; in Mark 7:25, she prostrates herself. Entreating Jesus for healing in a kneeling posture is attested also in Matt. 17:14 and 20:20, while prostration is mentioned in Mark 5:22; and Luke 8:28, 41.

Greeting and Farewell: Lev. 19:32 prescribes that when younger persons encounter their elders, the former should stand. In 1 Kings 2:19 King Solomon stands up to greet his mother. Job reports that before disaster befell him, he was so highly esteemed in the community that even the elderly stood up when encountering him (Job 29:8). Another posture for greeting high-status persons is bowing or bending over (Gen. 19:1; 43:28; 1 Sam. 25:41; 2 Kings 2:15). Kissing is also associated with greeting close relatives or friends (Gen. 29:11, 13; 33:4; 45:15; 48:10; Exod. 4:27) and with taking leave of loved ones (Gen. 31:28; 32:1; 50:1; 1 Sam. 20:41; 2 Sam. 19:40; Ruth 1:9, 14; cf. Acts 20:37). An ironic kiss of betrayal, attested in 2 Sam. 20:9 and Matt. 26:49, is treasonous precisely because the gesture is supposed to convey trust, affection, or at least hospitality (cf. Luke 7:45). In the NT, the "holy kiss" or "kiss of love" becomes a greeting exchanged between Christians, possibly as a liturgical act in their worship services (see Rom. 16:16; 1 Cor. 16:20; 2 Cor. 13:12; 1 Thess. 5:26; 1 Pet. 5:14). The erotic kiss between lovers, incidentally, is mentioned in the Bible only in Prov. 7:13 and Song of Sol. 1:2; 8:1.

Facial Expressions: *Sadness* is expressed primarily by a downcast appearance of the face or countenance (Gen. 4:5–6; 40:7; Neh. 2:2; Eccles. 7:3; Mark 10:22). Sometimes, a person is known to be sad simply because the countenance has changed (Job 14:20; Eccles. 8:1; Dan. 5:6, 9, 10; 7:28). Dim (i.e., darkened) eyes (Lam. 5:17) and weeping (Gen. 27:38; 42:24; 50:17; Ezra 3:12; Ps. 126:6) also show sadness. *Happiness* is associated with bright or shining eyes (1 Sam. 14:27, 29; Pss. 13:4; 19:9; Prov. 29:13; Ezek. 9:8), with one's face being lit up (Job 29:24; Isa. 60:1), or with one's head (Pss. 3:3; 110:7) or face (Num. 6:26; Deut. 28:50) being lifted up. *Anger* is often indicated by a reddening of the face. This is applied to persons (Gen. 39:19; Judg. 9:30; 14:19; 1 Sam. 11:6) and also to God (Exod. 4:14; Num. 11:10; 12:9; 25:3; 32:10, 13; Deut. 29:26; 2 Sam. 6:7). Fuming in anger is referred to in 2 Sam. 22:9; Ps. 74:1; and Isa. 65:5. *See also* dancing; mourning rites; prayer.

Bibliography

Gruber, Mayer I. *Aspects of Nonverbal Communication in the Ancient Near East.* 2 vols. Biblical Institute Press, 1980.   M.I.G.

Gethsemane (geth-sem′uh-nee; Heb., "oil press"), the site where Jesus prayed in lonely anguish just before his public betrayal and subsequent arrest (Matt. 26:36, Mark 14:32). Its precise location is not known. Matthew and Mark refer to a "place" called Gethsemane and imply it was near the Mount of Olives. *See also* Jerusalem; Olives, Mount of.

Gezer (gee′zuhr; Arabic Tell el-Jazari; Assyrian Gazru), an ancient city located eighteen miles northwest of Jerusalem and five miles south-southeast of Ramleh. It is first mentioned in the Bible in Josh. 10:33 and 12:12, where, while aiding Japhia king of Lachish, its king Horam is vanquished by Joshua's forces "on the day the sun stood still." Gezer subsequently became part of Ephraim's allotment and was given over to the Levites (Josh. 21:21; 1 Chron. 6:67). However, Canaanites remained in the city as servants (Josh. 16:3–10; Judg. 1:29). The city was later captured by the pharaoh of Egypt and given to Solomon as a dowry for his daughter (1 Kings 9:15–17). Solomon in turn rebuilt it as one of his principal store-cities along with Hazor and Megiddo.

Archaeological Excavations: The mound at Gezer covers 33 acres and is one of the largest Bronze and Iron Age archaeological sites in the ancient Near East. It is located strategically on the edge of the western foothills overlooking the north-central Shephelah. It guards the crossroads where the trunk road up the Valley of Aijalon to Jerusalem branches off from the Via Maris. The site was identified with biblical Gezer by C. Claremont-Ganneau in 1873, when he discovered the first of a series of inscriptions on bedrock in the hills to the southwest of the mound, which read in Hebrew "boundary of Gezer."

Settlement at Gezer began ca. 3500 BCE in the Chalcolithic period, and the occupation contin-

ued as a modest village throughout most of the Early Bronze Age until ca. 2400 BCE. Then, following a prolonged gap, occupation resumed after 2000 BCE in the Middle Bronze Age. Through the ensuing centuries the city grew, ultimately becoming one of the most massively fortified sites in the area. Its defenses included a towering three-entryway gate and a wall system linking intermittent towers fronted by a sloping rampart faced with chalk plaster. The largest tower, overlooking the southwest flank of the gateway, was more than 100 feet long and over 50 feet wide. In the north central part of the city was an outdoor alignment of ten large stelae. This may have been a Canaanite high place of the type recalled in 2 Kings 18:4 and Jer. 32:35. The Middle Bronze city was finally destroyed in the late sixteenth or early fifteenth century BCE by one of the resurgent Eighteenth Dynasty Egyptian pharaohs, either Amenophis I (ca. 1510 BCE) or Thutmose III (ca. 1482 BCE). Thutmose's claim to a victory at the site is recorded on the walls of the temple complex at Karnak.

In the Late Bronze Age between 1550 and 1200 BCE, Gezer remained largely under Egyptian domination. Evidence shows that by the late fifteenth century BCE, trade with Egypt and throughout the eastern Mediterranean flourished. The excavators maintain that a new outer city wall enclosing an area considerably larger than the Middle Bronze limits was built in the fourteenth century BCE. Also dating to this period were ten letters to the pharaohs of Egypt from three successive kings of Gezer. These were found in the archives at el-Amarna in Egypt. However, harassed by internecine conflicts in the region, Gezer declined toward

The six-chambered gate at Gezer, with the entrance at the far end. Solomon similarly fortified Hazor and Megiddo (1 Kings 9:15–17).

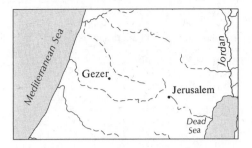

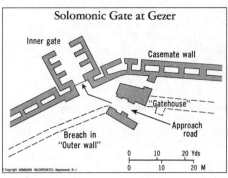

Solomonic Gate at Gezer

Inner gate

Casemate wall

"Gatehouse"

Approach road

Breach in "Outer wall"

0   10   20 Yds
0   10   20 M

the end of the thirteenth century BCE, and it seems to have been partially destroyed in 1208 BCE by Pharaoh Merneptah, whose victory stele mentions both Israel and Gezer.

In the twelfth and eleventh centuries BCE, Gezer remained a Canaanite outpost. Its king Horam may have perished in the battle of Lachish (Josh 10:31), but full control was not taken by the incoming Israelites. The presence of Philistines, possibly Egyptian mercenaries, is attested by Philistine-style bichrome pottery, a granary, and several patrician houses. Several local destructions helped define these Philistine phases, and a more general destruction was presumably the result of an Egyptian punitive raid ca. 950 BCE, after which the city was ceded to King Solomon as dowry in his marriage to Pharaoh's daughter. Remains from the late tenth century BCE dramatically confirm the biblical note in 1 Kings 9:15-17, which reports these events and records Solomon's subsequent fortification of the site along with Jerusalem, Hazor, and Megiddo. Excavations revealed a classic four-entryway city gate with an associated casemate (i.e., double) wall identical to gate and wall systems found at Megiddo and Hazor.

During the period of the Hebrew monarchy into the eight century BCE, Gezer remained an Israelite site. But in 734 BCE it was destroyed by invading Assyrians. This is attested by both archaeological remains and a relief at Nimrud from the reign of Tiglath-pileser III (biblical Pul, ca. 745–727 BCE), which depicts the siege and refers to the city by name (i.e., Gazru). The site recovered under Assyrian hegemony, as the presence of several Neo-Assyrian cuneiform inscriptions indicate, but it was destroyed again a century and a half later by the Babylonians ca. 587 BCE.

The Persian period in the fifth and fourth centuries BCE is represented only by scant remains, but the site became a prominent settlement again in the Hellenistic era. According to 1 Macc. 9:52, the city was fortified by Bacchides, the general of the Syrian army during the Maccabean wars of the second century BCE. This is attested archaeologically by evidence of the renovation and reuse of the erstwhile Solomonic gate and by the addition of towers with sloping bastions along the outer city wall. After 143 BCE Gezer (i.e., Gazara), became the residence of Simon Maccabeus (1 Macc. 13:43, 48), and trash heaps found down the north slope

confirm the text's claim that the city was purged of Gentile remains at that time. Subsequent occupation is represented primarily by domestic houses along with some repairs of the city gate and walls. Coin evidence dated to the reign of Antiochus VII (138–129 BCE) suggests that Jewish settlement was disrupted around 134 BCE, when Antiochus invaded the area, but coins from the reign of Alexander Jannaeus (103–76 BCE) may attest to some recovery at the close of the century. In any case, occupation on the mound ceases by the mid-first century BCE. By this time or in the following century its lands had apparently become the private holding of a certain Alkios.

Bibliography

Dever, William G., et al. *Gezer I. Preliminary Report of the 1964–66 Seasons.* Hebrew Union College, 1974.

————. *Gezer IV. The 1969–71 Seasons in Field VI, the Acropolis.* Hebrew Union College, 1985.

Seger, J. D. *Gezer V. The Field I Caves 1969–1971.* Hebrew Union College, 1989.   J.D.S.

Ghor (gor), **the.** *See* Jordan River.

ghost. Widespread belief in disembodied "shades" is attested in both biblical writings and their cultural contexts. These shades (Heb. *repha'im*) were regarded as spirits of persons who had died and were sometimes represented as inhabiting Sheol (Job 26:5; Ps. 88:10; Prov. 2:18; 9:18; 21:16; Isa. 14:9; 26:19). Although the Israelites acknowledged the tenuous existence of such spirits, they believed that they should be left alone. Deut. 18:10–11 teaches: "No one shall be found among you who . . . consults ghosts or spirits, or who seeks oracles from the dead" (cf. Isa. 8:19). King Saul completely disobeys this injunction when he hires a medium to summon the ghost or shade of the prophet Samuel to speak to him (1 Sam. 28:12–14). Elsewhere, Isaiah refers to a voice of moaning and lamentation being "like the voice of a ghost" (29:2–4). In the Gospels, Jesus's disciples think that he might be a ghost (Gk. *phantasma*) when they see him walk on water (Matt. 14:26; Mark 6:49) and when they behold him risen (Luke 24:37). In the latter instance, Jesus indicates that he cannot be a ghost because "a ghost does not have flesh and bones as you see that I have" (Luke 24:29). *See also* death; divination; magic; Sheol.

giants, a race of people rumored to have lived in Gath, from whom were descended four Philistine warriors killed by David's troops (2 Sam. 21:16–22; 1 Chron. 20:4–8). According to 2 Samuel, the four warriors descended from giants were: (1) Ishbi-benob, killed by Abishai son of Zeruaiah (he is not mentioned in 1 Chron. 20); (2) Saph (called Sibbai in 1 Chron. 20), killed by Sibbecai the Hushathite; (3) Goliath the Gittite, killed by Elhanan son of Jaare-oregim (in 1 Chron. 20:5 Elhanan is said to have killed Lahmi the brother of Goliath, probably because Goliath is said to have been killed by David, when he was a shepherd boy, in a variant tradition; cf. 1 Sam. 17:20–51); and (4) an unnamed warrior with six fingers on each hand and six toes on each foot, killed by Jonathan, the son of David's brother Shimei (Shimea in 1 Chron.).

The Hebrew word often rendered "giants" in these texts is *repha'im*. The precise meaning of that word is uncertain; it has been suggested that it means "the hale ones" and was used in Canaanite mythology to describe a group of gods, and sometimes humans, related to El, the high god of Canaanite mythology. It is probably in this context that the word is sometimes translated "shades" in the NRSV, referring to the spirits of those who have died, lingering perhaps in Sheol (Job 26:5; Ps. 88:10; Prov. 2:18; 9:18; 21:16; Isa. 14:9; 26:19). It has also been suggested that, based on this mythology, an elite group of warriors may have called themselves the *repha'im*, in which case the term would refer to a Canaanite or Philistine military guild composed of men with sufficient wealth to provide chariots and other weapons of war for themselves; there is some evidence that such a group of *repha'im* met together for feasting. Thus, the four warriors encountered by David's troops may have been descended from people who had belonged to that guild. Those warriors, however, are specifically noted for their size and strength: Ishbi-benob wielded a spear that weighed "three hundred shekels of bronze," Goliath (or Lahmi) had a spear the size of a weaver's beam, and the warrior with twenty-four digits was "a man of great size." Other passages also speak of the Rephaim (Gen. 14:5; 15:20; Deut. 2:11, 20; 3:11, 13; Josh. 12:4; 13:12; 15:8; 17:15; 18:16). In these instances, the term is taken by the NRSV to be an ethnic or tribal designation for Transjordanian inhabitants of Canaan about whom almost nothing is known. Great size, however, is sometimes an attribute: Og of Bashan, the last of the Rephaim, had a bed that was 9 cubits long and 4 cubits wide (Deut. 3:11). The Rephaim were called the Emim by the Moabites (Deut. 2:10–11) and the Zamzum-mim by the Amonites (Deut. 2:20–21). A Valley of Rephaim is also mentioned (2 Sam. 5:18, 22; 23:13; 1 Chron. 11:14; 14:9; Isa. 17:5).

Another Hebrew word, *nephilim*, has often been translated "giants" in English Bibles, though the NRSV simply transliterates it in its only two occurrences (Gen. 6:4; Num. 13:33). In Gen. 6:4 the Nephilim are the offspring of the sons of God and the daughters of humans, part of a formidable race of people that is said to have existed on the earth before the flood. Num. 13:33 says that the Anakites come from the Nephilim of old and that these inhabitants of Canaan were so huge that the Israelite spies felt like grasshoppers in comparison. The Anakites are elsewhere called the Anakim, and they are often noted for being especially tall (Deut. 1:28; 2:10, 11, 21; 9:2; cf. Josh. 11:21–22; 14:12–15). In Deut. 2:11, the Emim (Rephaim?) are said to have been as tall as the Anakim. A strong tradition seems to have been passed on within Israel that there had once been giants on the earth—a race of people, probably to be associated with the Nephilim, whose very existence was associated with disobedience and revolt against God (cf. Sir. 16:7; Bar. 3:26; 3 Macc. 2:4).   R.J.C./M.A.P.

Gibbethon (gib'uh-thon; Heb., "mound" or "height"), a city originally assigned to Dan and later given to the Levites (Josh. 19:44; 21:23), although by the time of King Asa of Judah (ca. 900 BCE) it was in Philistine hands (1 Kings 15:27). It was the site of the assassination of Nadab, king of Israel (northern kingdom) by his general Baasha during an attempt to take the city from the Philistines (1 Kings 15:27). It was also the site twenty-four years later of a revolt against Zimri by his general Omni during another siege of the city (1 Kings 16:15). It is identified with modern Tel el-Malat, about four miles northeast of Joppa, although the location is not certain.   D.R.B.

Gibeah (gib'ee-uh; Heb., "hill"), a site in Benjamin, five miles north of Jerusalem. In biblical tradition, Gibeah is where an Ephraimite received inhospitable treatment, including the rape and murder of his concubine; this led to a war between Israel and Benjamin (Judg. 19–20). Later, Gibeah was the home of Saul and center for his career as king (1 Sam. 10:26). It was here that Saul was first associated with a band of prophets (1 Sam. 10:1–10), an event related to his selection as king. From here, Saul engineered a liberation of Jabesh-gilead from the Ammonites (1 Sam. 11:1–11) as well as a contest of strength with the Philistines (1 Sam. 14). He also later sought help from Gibeah in his search for David though, ironically, some of David's associates were from Gibeah (2 Sam. 23:29). Another reference is also possible: 2 Sam. 6:3 says that David discovered the ark at the house of Abinadab, which was either "in Gibeah" or "on the hill" (NRSV prefers the latter).

Ancient Gibeah has been identified with the modern site of Tell el Ful. Excavations there reveal a succession of occupations that, at least in part, correspond with the Bible's account of Saul's career. The earliest relevant level, destroyed by fire in the twelfth century BCE, provides context for a more extensive and fortified construction from the Early Iron Age. The most important building from this level is an eleventh-century structure, a fortress with a casemate wall and corner tower; this could perhaps be the palace of King Saul. Successive constructions suggest that some violent destruction of the fortress/palace occurred, and subsequent rebuilding reflected more modest effort or quality.   G.W.C.

Gibeon (gib′ee-uhn), a town, five and a half miles northwest of Jerusalem. Other towns associated with Gibeon include Chephirah, Beeroth, and Kiriath-jearim (Josh. 9:17). Gibeon has been identified with modern el-Jib, and archaeological excavations have been conducted there.

Gibeon first enters the biblical tradition in narratives relating the Israelite conquest of Canaan. The Gibeonites, who are also described as Hivites (Josh. 9:7) or Amorites (2 Sam. 21:2), tricked the Israelites into making a treaty not to harm them. This treaty was upheld, but the Gibeonites were reduced to becoming hewers of wood and drawers of water (Josh. 9:3–27). In an ensuing battle near Gibeon (Josh. 10:1–14), the Israelites defeated a coalition of Canaanite kings led by Adoni-zedek of Jerusalem. Most scholars would date this period of Israel's history to the thirteenth century BCE, but no evidence for a settlement at el-Jib during that period has been found.

During the tenth century BCE, a famine in the time of King David is associated with bloodguilt incurred by King Saul, who reportedly broke the ancestral treaty and tried to annihilate the Gibeonites. Thus, David allowed the Gibeonites to gain revenge for such mistreatment by impaling seven of Saul's sons on a mountain (2 Sam. 21:1–15), possibly at the high place at Gibeon mentioned later in 1 Kings 3:4. Also during this time of David, young warriors led by Joab and Abner fought on the edge of a pool at Gibeon (2 Sam. 2:12–17). That pool was still a landmark in the area almost five hundred years later, for it is mentioned in Jer. 41:12 (from the early sixth century BCE). Archaeologists at el-Jib have found this pool. It consisted of a circular shaft cut into bedrock at a point immediately inside the city wall. It was approximately 36 feet in diameter and 36 feet deep. A stairway was cut along the edge of the shaft, spiraling down to the bottom. Thereafter,

The spiral staircase cut along the edge of the shaft of the pool of Gibeon became a tunnel at the bottom and provided access to the water table during times of siege.

the stairway continued to descend in the form of a tunnel, to a room whose floor is 1.5 feet below the water level. The purpose of such shafts was to provide access to the water table from inside the city during times of siege.

Gibeon is also mentioned in 1 Kings 3:4–15, where Solomon at the beginning of his reign traveled to the "principal high place" at Gibeon to sacrifice there (this high place is perhaps to be associated with the "large stone that is in Gibeon" mentioned in 2 Sam. 20:8). While there, Solomon had a dream in which God offered to give him anything he asked; he asked for "an understanding mind" with which to govern the people, a request God was pleased to grant. Nothing more is said of Gibeon in the Bible, but during the eighth–sixth centuries BCE there was a winery there, as is attested by inscribed and stamped handles of wine jars and clusters of rock-cut pits that functioned as wine cellars.   T.L.M.

Giddel (gid′uhl).
1 The ancestor of a family of temple servants (Ezra 2:47; Neh. 7:49).
2 The name of an ancestor of a family of Solomon's servants (Ezra 2:56; Neh. 7:58).

Gideon (gid′ee-uhn; from the Heb. root meaning "to cut off"), the son of Joash the Abiezrite of the town of Ophrah in the tribal area of Manasseh. He is called Jerubbaal in Judg. 6:32. At a time of dire circumstances and impoverishment (6:2, 6, 11), Gideon is called by an angel to deliver Israel from the hand of Midian (6:11–23). His hesitancy (6:15–21) is reminiscent of the call to Moses (Exod. 3–4), and he requests a sign that proves God will be with him: meat placed on a rock is consumed by fire. At this point, he recognizes that he has seen an angel of the Lord face-to-face (Judg. 6:22); he builds an altar to the Lord and follows the angel's instructions to take down an altar of Baal (6:24–32). Before proceeding further, however, Gideon requires two more signs that he is the one to deliver Israel, as God has said: first, a fleece placed on the ground overnight is to be damp with dew, though the ground is dry; then the fleece is to be dry, while on the ground there is dew. After these signs have been granted to him, Gideon prepares for battle.

Gideon's battle against the Midianites occupies the main body of the story (6:34–8:21). He gathers men from the tribes of Manasseh, Asher, Zebulun, and Naphtali (6:36–40). In order to emphasize that the victory will be won through the might of God (and not by the people's own might), Gideon follows God's instructions to pare his army down from thirty-three thousand (7:3) to a much smaller force of only three hundred (7:2–8). That night Gideon and a servant gather information (by way of dream interpretation, 7:8–15) at the Midianite camp at Endor between the hill of Moreh and Mount Tabor (7:1; Ps. 83:11). That same night, using psychological warfare, surprise, and darkness, Gideon and his band attack the Midianites with maximum effect, causing them to flee toward the Jordan Valley (7:16–22). Soldiers from the tribes of Naphtali, Ephraim, Asher, and Manasseh (possibly the thousands sent back when the attack force was pared down in size) ambush the Midianites at the Jordan fords, and two Midianite princes, Oreb and Zeeb, are killed (7:23–25; Ps. 83:12–13). After calming the Ephraimites who complain about not being included in this phase of the conflict (8:1–3), Gideon and his three hundred pursue the kings of Midian, Zebah, and Zalmunna beyond the Jordan. On the way, he requests food for his men from Succoth and Penuel, but is rebuffed (8:4–9). At Karkor, once again using stealth and surprise, Gideon falls upon the remnants of the Midianites (8:10, fifteen thousand out of a hundred and twenty thousand) and captures the two kings (8:10–13). After exacting punishment upon Succoth and Penuel (8:14–17), Gideon, acting as the blood-avenger for his brothers' deaths, kills Zebah and Zalmunna (8:15–21). This victory would come to be viewed as heroic, as attested by references elsewhere in the Bible (Isa. 9:3; 10:26; Ps. 83:10–12; cf. 1 Sam. 12:11; Heb. 11:12).

Gideon's humility (cf. 6:15) and religious piety are evinced by his refusal to accept hereditary rulership over Israel. He says, "I will not rule over you, and my son will not rule over you; the LORD will rule over you" (8:23). Thus, he becomes a spokesperson for the antimonarchic perspective that governs the entire book of Judges and most of the Deuteronomistic History (Joshua–2 Kings). Despite Gideon's rejection of kingship, however, his son Abimelech tried to take the kingship for himself after Gideon had died (Judg. 9).

One aspect of Gideon's piety is criticized in the biblical tradition. He is said to have fashioned an ephod out of golden earrings that his soldiers had taken as booty and to have placed it in Ophrah, his town (8:24–27; cf. Exod. 32:2–3). The author or editor of Judges comments that "all Israel prostituted themselves" before this ephod, such that it "became a snare to Gideon and to his family" (8:27). Gideon is said to have had many wives and seventy sons (in addition to Abimelech, born to a concubine in Shechem; Judg. 8:29–32). *See also* Abimelech; Jotham; Judges, book of; Midian; Midianites.   J.U./M.A.P.

Gideoni (gid´ee-oh´ni), the Benjaminite father of Abidan. His son was appointed to assist Moses in the wilderness as head of the Benjaminite family group (Num. 1:11; 2:22; 7:60, 65; 10:24).

gifts of the Spirit. *See* spiritual gifts.

Gihon (gi´hon; Heb., "a bursting forth").
1 The second of the four rivers flowing "out of Eden to water the garden"; it is the one said to flow around the whole land of Cush (Gen. 2:10, 13). Gihon was once equated with the Nile on the assumption that Cush meant Abyssinia (modern

Ethiopia), but it is now thought to refer to an unidentifiable irrigation channel in southern Iraq, "Cush" being the land of the Kassites.

2 A pulsating spring in Jerusalem, south of the temple area on the west side of the Kidron Valley. Because of the steepness of the slope, the spring was outside the town walls at the summit, and although water was normally obtained by carrying jars down to it, perhaps using donkeys, in times of siege the jars could apparently be lowered down a vertical shaft. According to 2 Sam. 5:8, it was by means of this shaft that David was able to gain entrance to Jerusalem when he conquered the city. This shaft has been discovered and is now called "Warren's Shaft" after the person who excavated it. Another, less deep, shaft also exists and was perhaps used at an earlier date when the water table may have been higher. Gihon is Jerusalem's only immediate source of water, and it could support a population of about twenty-five hundred. The Gihon fountain was evidently a sacred place, and for this reason Solomon (and probably also later rulers) was anointed king there (1 Kings 1:32–40). That anointing was accomplished to thwart Adonijah, who had offered a sacrifice at En-rogel, a spring somewhat farther down the valley (1 Kings 1:9–10). Later in the monarchy the supply of water from Gihon seems to have been supplemented by water brought from a greater distance along a conduit, perhaps to the "upper pool," where Isaiah met and rebuked King Ahaz (cf. Isa. 7:3).

Hezekiah, who succeeded Ahaz, was confronted by the danger of Assyrian invasion and therefore sought, not only to prevent the invaders from obtaining water in the vicinity of Jerusalem (2 Chron. 32:4), but to ensure the security of the city's own supply. This he did by digging a tunnel 1,750 feet long from Gihon to the Pool of Solomon, which at that time was probably an underground cistern. The tunnel was carved from both ends simultaneously, and it followed a curiously winding course, perhaps to permit cutting a vertical shaft from inside the city to reach the water in a crisis. D.B.

Gilboa (gil-boh´uh), modern Jebel Fuqu´ah, a hill opposite the Hill of Moreh. Together Gilboa and Moreh guarded the eastern pass from the Plain of Esdraelon into the Valley of Jezreel, the main access from the coastal plain to the Jordan Valley. Gilboa rises to a height of 1,696 feet above sea level, but plunges abruptly 2,000 feet below on the east to the Jordan. Its more gradual western slopes are probably where Saul fought his last battle with the Philistines; his three sons were killed and Saul took his own life after he was seriously wounded (1 Sam. 31). When told of this, David lamented the deaths of Saul and of his son Jonathan (David's close friend) and pronounced a curse on Gilboa: "Let there be no dew or rain upon you, nor bounteous fields" (2 Sam. 1:22). *See also* Jezreel; Moreh. N.L.L.

Gilead (gil´ee-uhd; Heb., "rugged"), a region in the Transjordan (modern-day Jordan) from the Arnon to the Yarmuk rivers, located between Bashan and Moab. Its name describes it well, for Gilead is indeed rugged, mountainous territory, and in antiquity it was densely forested (see Jer. 22:6). The major trade route in the Transjordan, the King's Highway, passed through Gilead on its way from the Gulf of Aqabah to Damascus, and inhabitants of this region thus controlled an important thoroughfare.

Southern Gilead (from the Arnon to the Jabbok) was under the control of Sihon, the king of the Amorites in the Mosaic period (thirteenth century BCE). This area would be assigned to the Israelite tribes of Reuben and Gad in the division of the land, but Israel did not gain or maintain control of the territory, and it would later correspond approximately to the kingdoms of the Moabites and the Ammonites, with their capital at Rabbath-ammon (modern Amman). Southern Gilead was especially well suited for herding (Num. 32:1; Song of Sol. 6:5). Northern Gilead (from the Jabbok to the Yarmuk) was assigned to Manasseh, and remained under Israelite control until the Assyrian conquest (722/1 BCE), although both the Ammonites to the south and the Arameans to the north occupied it at times (see Judg. 10:8; 1 Kings 22:3; Amos 1:3).

During the Persian period (ca. 538–333 BCE) Gilead became its own province, and in the Roman period Gilead was subdivided into Perea and the Decapolis. Major cities in Gilead include Heshbon and Rabbath-ammon (later Philadelphia) in the south, and Pella, Gerasa, Gadara, Abila, Jabesh-gilead, and Ramoth-gilead in the north. The exact composition of the proverbial "balm of Gilead" (Jer. 8:22; cf. Gen. 37:25) has not been established, but it is presumed to have been some sort of salve made from the sap of mountain trees. *See also* Decapolis; Perea.   M.D.C.

Gilgal (gil′gal; Heb., "circle," probably of stones). 1 A town located between Jericho and the Jordan. This Gilgal served as the Israelites' first encampment after crossing the Jordan (Josh. 3–4), and it became Joshua's base of operations. It is probably to be identified with modern Khirbet el-Mafjir, about one and a quarter miles from ancient Jericho, or possibly Khirbet en-Nitleh, about two miles southeast of Jericho. In the tribal period and the early monarchy (thirteenth–eleventh centuries BCE) this city became an important political, religious, and military center, especially for the tribe of Benjamin. It was one of the places visited by Samuel on his yearly circuit (1 Sam. 7:16). A number of the early traditions about Saul are also set here. Gilgal was a rallying point in Saul's campaigns against the Philistines (1 Sam. 13:4–7); it was here that he was affirmed by the people as king (1 Sam. 11:14–15); and it was also here that the kingship was taken from him for presuming on Samuel's priestly prerogatives (1 Sam. 13:8–15). This Gilgal was denounced by the eighth-century prophets as the site of a national sanctuary with a corrupt sacrificial cult (Hos. 4:15; 9:15; 12:11; Amos 4:4; 5:5; Mic. 6:5).

2 Another town that figures in the narratives of Elijah and Elisha (2 Kings 2:1–4; 4:38), probably the present village of Khirbet 'Alyata, about seven miles north of Bethel.

3 Possibly, a third town near Dor mentioned in a list of conquered Canaanite kings in Josh. 12:23 (NRSV reads "Galilee," following the LXX, but the Hebrew text reads "Gilgal"); if this is a reference to a town, it is probably to be identified with the modern village of Jiljulieh, about five miles north of Antipatris.   F.S.F.

girdle. *See* apron; dress.

Girgashites (guhr′guh-shīts), one of the peoples whom God displaced from the land of Canaan for the Israelites at the time of Joshua (Gen. 15:21; Josh. 3:10; cf. Gen. 10:16). According to the genealogy in Gen. 10:16 these nations are the offspring of Canaan. The name could be related to the Gergesenes mentioned in certain NT manuscripts at Matt. 8:28; Mark 5:1; and Luke 8:26.

Gittite (git′it), someone who lives in or is from Gath, one of the five major cities of the Philistines located in the coastal plain of southwestern Judah. The giant Goliath and his brother Lahmi were Gittites (2 Sam. 21:19; 1 Chron. 20:5), as were Obed-edom, whose house was the temporary resting place of the ark of the covenant (2 Sam. 6:10–11; 1 Chron. 13:13), and Ittai, the refugee who joined David and became one of his military commanders (2 Sam. 15:19–22; 18:2). *See also* Gath; Philistines.

Gittith (git′ith), a Hebrew word that appears in the superscriptions to Pss. 8; 81; and 84. Because its meaning is uncertain, it is often left untranslated ("according to the Gittith"). Some translators have sought to explain the term via the Hebrew *gath*, "(wine) press" or through some reference to the Philistine city of Gath. Whatever its precise meaning, the phrase is usually assumed to refer to a musical mode, possibly the name of a well-known song to whose tune the psalm could be sung, or possibly to some variety of musical instrument deemed appropriate for accompaniment when the psalm was sung.   J.L.K.

glass. *See* mirrors.

glory, a human or divine atttribute indicating significance, importance, or presence. The most important Hebrew word for "glory," *kabod*, means "weight" or "importance." Thus, to have glory is to be weighty or important to oneself or others. In this sense, glory may be applied to humans, showing their significance in the world (Job 19:9; Prov. 16:31; 20:29; Isa. 8:7), but more often "glory" is applied to God. The glory of God is sometimes said to appear to people, indicating that God's worth and significance has become particularly manifest (Num. 16:19, 42; Ps. 102:16; Ezek. 10:4). In some such instances, God's "glory" seems to serve as a virtual synonym for God's presence or being: at Mount Sinai, God's glory appears as a cloud and as fire (Exod. 16:10; 24:16–17). God's glory is likewise associated with the tabernacle and with the temple (Exod. 40:34; Num. 20:6; Pss. 24:7–10; 78:60–61). God's glory frequently appears in Ezekiel's visions (10:4; 28:22; 43:2–5) and, in Isaiah, is particularly connected to God's future eschatological appearance (4:5; 60:1–2). Most biblical references to glory, however, occur within contexts of worship: the appropriate human response to God is to ascribe glory to God (Pss. 22:23; 29:2; 86:9; Isa. 66:5).

The NT idea of glory (Gk. *doxa*) continues in the same vein. Occasionally, glory is applied to humans (Luke 12:27; John 7:18), but it is usually applied to God; God's glory is seen (Luke 2:9; John 11:40; Acts 7:55; Rev. 15:8), and people are to give glory to God (Acts 12:23; 1 Cor. 10:31). However, the NT is distinctive in applying glory (in the sense of divine glory, normally an attribute of God alone) to the risen Christ (1 Cor. 2:8; Heb. 2:7, 9; 1 Pet. 1:11; Rev. 5:12–13). The Gospel of John develops this notion even further, attributing glory to Christ during his human existence on earth (1:14). God's glory appears in Jesus (13:31; 17:5) and is revealed through his miracles (2:11; 11:4). It is also closely associated with his death, which is now called his hour of glorification (12:23; 17:1). Finally, both the Gospel of John and Paul speak of the eschatological glory of God, not only as something to be beheld, but as something in which believers may participate (John 17:22; Rom. 5:2).

J.D.

glossolalia (glos'uh-lay'lee-uh). *See* tongues, speaking in.

gnat, a nonspecific term referring to small insects such as gnats, lice, mosquitoes, or sand flies. It probably includes all such blood-sucking, two-winged insects. In Exod. 8:16–18 gnats are the third plague upon the Egyptians. In Matt. 23:24, Jesus accuses certain scribes and Pharisees of straining out a gnat and swallowing a camel, i.e., scrutinizing details of the law while neglecting the weightier matters of justice, mercy, and faith.

Gnosticism (nos'tuh-siz-uhm), a generic term for a variety of religious movements that flourished during the second to fourth centuries CE. Although the theology, ritual practice, and ethics of these groups differed, all purported to offer salvation from the oppressive bonds of material existence through *gnōsis*, or "knowledge." Such knowledge consisted of privileged, esoteric understanding of the relationship between one's true spiritual self and the transcendent source of all being. Typically, this knowledge could only be conveyed to humans by a revealer figure. What is known about Gnosticism must be gathered from two sources: reports in the writings of early church leaders—Irenaeus, Hippolytus, Tertullian, Origen, and Epiphanius—who were opponents of Christian gnostic teaching,

condemning it as a heresy; and a number of ancient works produced by gnostics themselves—Codex Askew, Codex Bruce, the Berlin Gnostic Codex and, especially, works contained in the library found at Nag Hammadi. Both sources of information are problematic. The antignostic Christian writings often provide a fairly clear description of ideas and practices, but since these writings are highly polemical, these descriptions may not be ones that gnostics themselves would have used. The gnostic materials themselves, however, are often highly esoteric, intended for readers who knew much that is not contained in the writings themselves.

All the various expressions of gnostic thought appear to have evinced a radically dualistic attitude that identified "spirit" as fundamentally good and "matter" as fundamentally "evil." Thus, the physical world in general and individual human bodies in particular were understood to be material prisons in which divine souls or spirits had been trapped. The most prevalent form of Gnosticism known to us held that the world was created by an evil god called the Demiurge. Human beings are basically eternal spirits that were captured by the Demiurge and confined in bodies of flesh and in a world of matter. Gnostic Christians believed that Christ had come as a spiritual redeemer (disguised as a human being) to enable the enlightened to be liberated from their material existence and to realize their true identities as spiritual beings. The implications of such a belief system for life in this world varied dramatically. Many (probably most) gnostics held that such liberation from the flesh involved renunciation of bodily pleasures and material concerns; they encouraged virginity, celibacy, fasting, strict diets, and other aspects of an acetic and austere lifestyle that would enable them to become more spiritual. Other gnostics appear to have drawn the opposite conclusion (or so certain Christian authors hold); they engaged freely in all manner of wanton excesses on the grounds that, since the spirit is all that matters, what one does with the flesh is irrelevant.

In any case, although Gnosticism is clearly related to the development of early Christianity, its significance for interpretation of the NT remains highly controversial. There was a period around the middle of the twentieth century when many NT writings (especially the Gospel and Letters of John) were interpreted as a response to Gnosticism. Some passages were even read as potentially supportive of Gnosticism. By the end of the twentieth century, however, it was generally recognized that such interpretations were anachronistic: at the time of these writings (first century CE), Gnosticism did not exist as any developed system that NT authors would have been supporting or denouncing. Nevertheless, historical scholars do not think that Gnosticism would have simply emerged fully formed in the middle of the second century without a considerable period of predevelopment; the ideas and tendencies that would later define Gnosticism must have been present earlier. Thus, it has become common for NT scholars to speak of an almost invisible and largely unidentified "proto-Gnosticism" as part of the milieu in which NT writings were produced. The apostle Paul writes about the distinction between "what is of the flesh" and "what is of the spirit" (Rom. 8:4–13; Gal. 5:16–26; 6:8). The Gospel of John and the Johannine Letters emphasize that Jesus was not *just* a spiritual being, but a man with a body of actual flesh (John 1:14; 1 John 4:2). Such passages seem to indicate that Gnosticism was "on the horizon"; people were already thinking about the kinds of things that Gnosticism would seek to address, sometimes in ways that were compatible with the NT documents and sometimes in ways that were radically distinct from those writings. *See also* Thomas, Gospel of; Nag Hammadi.

Bibliography

Pearson, Birger A. *Ancient Gnosticism: Traditions and Literature.* Fortress, 2007.

King, Karen L. *What Is Gnosticism?* Harvard University Press, 2003.

Makschies, Christoph. *Gnosis: An Introduction.* Clark, 2003.

Perkins, Pheme. *Gnosticism and the New Testament.* Augsburg Fortress, 1993.

Powell, Mark Allan. *Introducing the New Testament: A Historical, Literary, and Theological Survey.* Baker Academic, 2009. Pp. 39–41.

Roukema, Reimer. *Gnosis and Faith in Early Christianity: An Introduction to Gnosticism.* Trinity Press International, 1999.   H.W.A./M.A.P.

goad, an implement used to control oxen (1 Sam. 13:21). Shamgar, one of Israel's early judges, is reputed to have used an ox goad as a weapon (Judg. 3:31). Metaphorically, the sayings of the wise could be called "goads," because they could stimulate thought in others (Eccles. 12:11). Paul is accused of "kicking against the goads" when he persecutes believers in Christ, implying perhaps that he is resisting the obvious leading or direction of God (Acts 26:14).

goat. The goat (*Capra hircus*) is one of the most versatile of domestic livestock animals and has always been of special importance in the Near East, to whose arid climate it is excellently adapted. Goats are hardy beasts that can live off shrubs and the scanty vegetation of the desert, thereby utilizing areas that are useless for agriculture. Goat bones attributed to domesticated animals are the most frequently found faunal remains on the Early Neolithic sites of the southern Levant, as at Jericho, Beidha, and Ain Ghazal. They testify that humans started herding goats in this area about nine thousand years ago. At first, goats were kept mainly for their meat, but by the Chalcolithic period (ca. 4000 BCE) they were also used for milk and products made from the hair and skin.

Numerous references are made in the Bible to the various uses of the goat. Lev. 7:23 and Deut. 14:4 mention its meat, while Deut. 32:14 and Prov. 27:27 report that it provided milk. Gen. 21:14 and Josh. 9:4 refer to goatskin bottles. Goats'

hair was apparently processed into fabric (1 Sam. 19:13), and the roof of the tabernacle was made of goats' hair (Exod. 26:7; 36:14–15). The goat was also of importance as a sacrificial animal. Male animals were preferred (Lev. 1:10; 22:19), but sometimes female goats were demanded (Lev. 4:28; 5:6). In another ritual related to atonement, the priest would symbolically place the sins of the people upon a goat (the so-called scapegoat), which would be driven into the wilderness, taking the sins and impurities away (Lev. 16:7–10). Daniel beheld a vision of a goat and a ram, which portended the conquest of the Persian Empire by the Macedonians under Alexander the Great (Dan. 8). Jesus refers to goats in an eschatological discourse in which he says that, when the Son of Man comes for the final judgment, he will separate the nations of the world as a shepherd separates sheep from goats (Matt. 25:32–33).   I.U.K.

God, god. In English Bibles, the word "God" (capitalized) is used to refer to the deity worshiped by Jews and Christians, and the word "god" (lowercase), to any deity worshiped by other peoples. In the Hebrew Bible, the word "God" usually translates the Hebrew word *el* or its plural form, *'elohim.* The latter form is a plural of majesty (magnitude) and a sign of honor paid to the deity; when applied to the God of Israel, it carries no implication of multiple deities. This is clear from the fact that Elohim (when it refers to the God of Israel) takes a singular verb and is modified by singular adjectives, even though it is technically a plural noun.

The authors of the Bible do not concern themselves with abstract questions of definition (i.e., concerning the existence or nature of God), but rather portray God with images and, above all, through narratives in which God is the subject of action or speech rather than an object of thought. Thus, in the Hebrew Bible, God is presented as the Creator and Sustainer of the world, who enters into covenantal relationship with a chosen people, Israel, and who guides the history of that people toward a redemptive goal. God gives commandments and holds people responsible for obedience to them; the nation as a whole, and sometimes individuals, suffer negative consequences of disobedience to God's commands. God also desires and demands worship and God's jealousy and anger can be aroused when Israel worships other gods. God provides the people of Israel with means of atoning for iniquities, of purifying themselves, and of either retaining or restoring the covenant relationship.

In the NT, the word "God" translates the Greek word *theos,* also a general term for deity and the word used in the LXX to translate *el* and *'elohim.* The characteristics of God in the NT are generally consistent with those ascribed to God in the Hebrew Bible, for even Gentile Christians believed that they were worshiping the God of Israel. The essential difference is that, for most NT authors, the primary locus of God's self-revelation no longer lies in the history of a people, but rather in the person of Jesus Christ (e.g., Matt. 1:23; John 14:9; 20:28–29). Jesus is even called "God" or regarded as equivalent to God in a number of texts (John 1:1, 18; 20:28; Rom. 9:5; Titus 2:13; Heb. 1:8–9; 2 Pet. 1:1; 1 John 5:20). *See also* Abba; El; El Shaddai; Holy Spirit; incarnation; Jesus Christ; names of God in the Hebrew Bible; names of God in the New Testament.   T.R.W.L.

God, kingdom of. *See* kingdom of God.

God-fearers, Gentiles who, during the Second Temple period, embraced Jewish theology, worship, and morality, but who did not follow purity laws, which they regarded as specific for ethnic Jews. According to the dominant theory, they attended synagogues, but were normally not circumcised (which would have constituted a full conversion and made them "Jews"). Eventually, these God-fearers became prime candidates for conversion to Christianity (cf. Acts 10:22; 13:16, 26; 17:4, 17). No direct evidence exists for such an institutional class of "God-fearers," however, apart from a third-century CE inscription from Asia Minor. Some interpreters think that the references in Acts to Gentiles who were God-fearers are simply meant to imply that those Gentiles had an appropriate respect for the Jews and for the Jewish God. *See also* Cornelius; Gentile; proselyte.   M.A.P.

godlessness, a mode of thinking or being that excludes God from life and ignores or perhaps deliberately violates God's laws and commandments. The godlessness of a person is often associated with such characteristics as worthlessness, ruthlessness, wickedness, pride, impiety, and the like. Basically, godless or ungodly persons are those who live, act, and think as though God can be ignored or spurned. For illustrations of godlessness, see Deut. 8:11–20; Job 8:13; Ps. 119:51; Rom. 1:18–32; 4:5; 5:6; 1 Tim. 1:9; 4:7; 6:20; 2 Tim. 2:16; 2 Pet. 2:5–6; Jude 4, 15. *See also* foolishness, folly.   J.M.E.

godliness, godly, a life or attribute that is pleasing to God. Almost all references to "godliness" in the Bible occur in the Pastoral Letters and in 2 Peter (1 Tim. 2:2; 4:7–8; 6:3, 5–6, 11; 2 Tim. 3:5; Titus 1:1; 2 Pet. 1:3, 6, 7; 3:11). The term translates a Greek word (*eusebeia*; also used in Acts 3:12, NRSV: "piety") that was commonly used in the Roman world to describe respect for the Greek and Roman gods and for the orders of society. This may explain why it is not more common in the LXX or in the NT; biblical writers generally prefer such words as "righteousness," "faith," "steadfastness," or "holiness" to describe a faith and life pleasing to God. As an adjective, the related term "godly" (Gk. *eusebōs*), however, is used in the LXX (where it translates Hebrew *khasid*): "There is no longer anyone who is godly" (Ps. 12:1); the mighty ones boast of mischief done against "the godly" (Ps. 52:1); God desires "godly offspring" (Mal. 2:15); see also Ps. 4:3 (NRSV: "the faithful"). The expres-

sion is employed frequently in Sirach (16:13; 23:12; 27:11, 29; 28:22; 33:14; 37:12; 39:27; 43:33; 44:10, 23). In the NT, "godly" modifies behavior and attitudes: "godly sincerity" (2 Cor. 1:12); "godly grief" (2 Cor. 7:9–11); godly lives (2 Tim. 3:12; Titus 2:12). Reference to "the godly" is found only in 2 Pet. 2:9. *See also* religion, religious; worship in the New Testament.   J.F.J.

Gog, a king who, in Ezek. 38–39, is described as an apocalyptic figure who marches from the north (38:6, 15; 39:2) and ravages Israel before being destroyed by God (38:19–22; 39:3–5). This mythical or eschatological ruler is probably based on the historical figure of Gyges, a seventh-century BCE king of Lydia. In describing his activities, Ezekiel is thought to draw upon Jeremiah's writings about an "enemy from the north" (1:14; 4:6; 6:1, 22; 10:22; 13:20) as well as on Isaiah's motif of the destruction of Israel's foes on the mountains of Israel (14:24–25; 17:12–14; 31:8–9). Gog reappears in the NT, paired with Magog (Rev. 20:18–20); in Ezek. 38:2 Magog is probably not a ruler, but a phrase from the Akkadian language (*mat Gog*) meaning "land of Gog."   J.S.K.

Golan (goh'luhn; Heb., possibly "circuit").
1 Part of the plateau of Bashan between Mount Hermon and the Wadi el-Yarmuk east of the Jordan River. It was called Gaulanitis by the historian Josephus. *See also* Bashan.
2 A city of refuge in Manasseh assigned to the levitical family of Gershon (Deut. 4:43; Josh. 20:8; 21:27; 1 Chron. 6:71). This city was located in the Golan region indicated by 1.

gold, the precious metal named more frequently than any other in the Bible (385 times). It was imported from Uphaz (Jer. 10:9), Raamah (Ezek. 27:22), Sheba (1 Kings 10:2), Havilah (Gen. 2:11), and Ophir (1 Chron. 29:4; 2 Chron. 8:18), all sites that have not yet been located. Occasionally gold was acquired as booty (Exod. 12:35; Judg. 8:26), but more often it was obtained through commercial enterprises (1 Kings 10:14–24).

People of ancient sites outside Canaan knew of gold and learned to work it beautifully. At Ebla in Syria (modern Tell Mardikh; ca. 3200 BCE) excavators found objects of gold, such as a ceremonial hammer, and wooden frames overlaid with gold. Also at Ebla commercial texts report a caste or guild of smiths including goldsmiths. Precious metals measured in bars with specific weights given in minas (a mina equaled 47 grams) were held in an Eblaite storehouse. One text showed the tribute paid by the kingdom of Mari to include 134.26 minas of gold. At Ur in Sumer (ca. 2500 BCE), excavations uncovered fluted vases, bowls of pure gold, intricately fashioned ornaments, and 9 yards of gold ribbon in a headdress. Much later (ca. 1350 BCE), the golden treasure of Egypt's Tutankhamen would testify to the prominence and significance of gold in the very area where the Hebrews were perhaps serving as slaves.

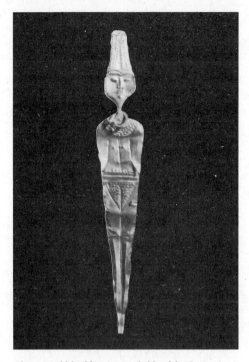

Above: A gold-leaf figurine, probably of the Canaanite goddess Astarte, found at the excavations at Gezer, sixteenth century BCE. *Below:* Gold cup from the royal tomb at Ur, third millennium BCE.

The Bible employs thirteen different words for gold that describe the metal in a variety of forms and usages. Most prominently, perhaps, gold was used for jewelry, including necklaces (Song of Sol. 1:11), rings (James 2:2), and other unspecified items (Exod. 3:22). Gold also played a part in public worship. When the Israelites turned idolatrous, they worshiped a golden calf fashioned by Aaron (Exod. 32:2–4; cf. Deut. 29:17; 1 Kings 12:28; Isa. 2:20; Rev. 9:20), but later gold was employed in both the tabernacle and the temple. The ark of the covenant was covered with gold (Exod. 25:11). Most of the furniture of the tabernacle was gold-plated, and the high priest's clothing, crown, ephod, and breastplate were either adorned with gold or fashioned from pure gold (Exod. 39:2–30). In Solomon's temple the entire inner sanctuary was overlaid with gold, as were the cherubim, carved palm trees, and flowers (1 Kings 6:14–31). Likewise, the book of Revelation indicates, in heaven, the elders wear golden crowns (4:4) and the new Jerusalem will be constructed of pure gold (21:18).

Gold can be used as a standard of importance (Isa. 60:17; Hos. 2:8; 1 Pet. 1:18), referred to as a symbol of spiritual wealth (Rev. 3:18), or contrasted with what is of greater, lasting value. Gold is said to be less worthy than wisdom (Job 28:15, 17; Prov. 3:14; 8:10; 16:16), faith (1 Pet. 1:7), or knowledge (Pss. 19:10; 119:72; Prov. 20:15). One should not put one's trust in gold (Job 31:24), for it can become a stumbling block (Ezek. 7:19), and ultimately it will be of no value at all (Isa. 46:6; Ps. 135:15; 1 Tim. 6:9). Nevertheless, the Bible recognizes its value: the magi bring gold to the infant Jesus (Matt. 2:11).   R.A.C.

Golden Rule, a modern term used for a saying of Jesus regarded as being of inestimable and universal importance: "In everything do to others as you would have them do to you" (Matt. 7:12; cf. Luke 6:31). Jesus maintains, furthermore, that "this is the law and the prophets." Within the context of Matthew's Gospel, the latter comment would not mean that the "Golden Rule" replaces Torah and prophets for Jesus's followers (who are to keep every detail of the law; cf. Matt. 5:17–19), but that it underscores the value of Torah and prophets by summarizing their intent and providing a convenient guide to their application. The Golden Rule basically restates Lev. 19:18 ("Love your neighbor as yourself") in a way that makes explicit the already implied directive for behavior and conduct. Similar statements are found elsewhere in Jewish literature, e.g., Tob. 4:15 ("Do to no one what you would not want done to you") and Sir. 31:15 ("Judge your neighbor's feelings by your own").

Golgotha (gol'guh-thuh; Aramaic, "Place of the Skull"; cf. Matt. 27:33; Mark 15:22; Luke 23:33; John 19:17), the site of Jesus's crucifixion. In Christian tradition, it is also known as Calvary, after the Latin translation for Golgotha used in the Vulgate (*calvaria*). The place may owe its name to a distinctive physical appearance (a hill that, at that time, resembled a skull), or it may have been called this simply because of its habitual use as a site for executions. Apart from the name very little is known about Golgotha/Calvary. John 19:20 indicates that it was located outside Jerusalem's city walls, which would concur with Jewish and Roman execution customs. A reference to passersby (Matt. 27:39) suggests it was near a thoroughfare, while the fact that the cross was visible from afar (Matt. 27:55) could indicate an elevated location. Nevertheless its precise location remains in dispute. Since the fourth century the site now marked by the Church of the Holy Sepulchre has been revered as the location of Golgotha/Calvary. Objections that this church is *inside* the presumed location of the ancient city walls, and thus incompatible with the Gospel account, have been challenged by recent archaeological excavations defining more clearly the location of the walls. A rival hypothesis, first espoused in the nineteenth century, locates Golgotha/Calvary on a vaguely skull-shaped rise northeast of the Damascus Gate (called "Gordon's Calvary," named after the original proponent of this theory). *See also* cross; crucifixion; Jerusalem.

Goliath (guh-li'uhht), a Philistine champion from Gath. According to 1 Sam. 17, he was killed by David in single combat in the Valley of Elah. In that narrative, the might of the seasoned Philistine warrior is contrasted with the vulnerability of the Israelite shepherd boy, who fells his heavily armed opponent with a sling stone. The story is recalled in Sir. 47:4. According to 2 Sam. 21:19, however, Goliath was killed by Elhanan, one of David's warriors. Apparently noting the discrepancy, the Chronicler indicates that Elhanan's victim was Lahmi, the brother of Goliath (1 Chron. 20:5). Some interpreters have suggested another explanation: perhaps the name of the Philistine slain by David was not given in the original, oldest tradition, so the name of Elhanan's victim was substituted for that anonymous adversary of the better-known David. In any case, according to an old textual tradition of 1 Sam. 17:4 (preserved at Qumran, in Josephus, and some LXX versions), Goliath was a giant "four cubits and a span" (6 feet, 9 inches) in height. A different figure is found in the Hebrew text, where Goliath's height is recorded as "six cubits and a span" (9 feet, 9 inches). *See also* David.   P.K.M.

Gomer (goh'muhr).
 1 A son of Japheth (Gen. 10:2) and the ancestor of a people from southern Russia called Gimirrai by the Assyrians and Cimmerians.
 2 A promiscuous woman who became the wife of Hosea and bore him three children. Although she has traditionally been identified as a prostitute, the Hebrew text never names her as such (NRSV: "a wife of whoredom" in 1:2 is thus misleading). The command of God was for Hosea to marry a woman who would be unfaithful to him in order

to dramatize the relationship of God to unfaithful Israel (1:2), whose infidelity was evident through rampant worship of Baal (2:8; cf. 2:16–17). The prophet then gave symbolic names to the children that Gomer bore to him: Jezreel ("God sows"), Lo-ruhamah ("not pitied"), and Lo-ammi ("not my people"). Gomer was the daughter of Diblaim, but nothing else is known of her.

Gomorrah (guh-mor'uh). *See* Sodom.

Good Samaritan, parable of the, a story told by Jesus about a Samaritan who demonstrates love for neighbor by helping a Jewish man who has been wounded by thieves (Luke 10:29–37). A "good Samaritan" would have been a contradiction in terms for most Jews of Jesus's day, because of centuries-long mutual hostility between Jews and Samaritans. Jesus, as a Jewish teacher, tells the parable to an expert in Jewish law to illustrate what is meant by the commandment of Torah, "Love your neighbor as yourself" (cf. Lev. 19:18). In the parable, the unlikely "good Samaritan," who does what the law commends, is contrasted with Jewish leaders (a priest and a Levite), who do not. The point of the parable was clearly not to exalt Samaritans at the expense of Jews, but to indicate that Torah expresses God's will even when those who keep it are not those for whom it was intended. Further, the concept of "neighbor" is given a broad interpretation by Jesus, as is evident elsewhere by his claim that love of neighbor implies love for enemies as well (cf. Matt. 5:43–44; Luke 6:27, 35). *See also* Samaritans.   M.A.P.

gopher wood, the term used in the KJV and RSV for the material that Noah was instructed to use in building the ark (Gen. 6:14). The NRSV and NIV have "cypress wood." The meaning of the Hebrew (*nopher*) is uncertain.

Goshen (goh'shuhn).
 1 The fertile region in the eastern Nile Delta of Egypt (modern Wadi Tumi-lat), where the family of Jacob was allowed to settle (Gen. 47:28–29, 34). Also known as "the land of Rameses" (47:11), this territory was well suited for grazing (47:3–6). Goshen (evidently not called by that name except in the Bible) was apparently something of a hinterland to the Egyptians, perhaps because of its distance from the network of Nile irrigation canals (cf. 46:34). The Hebrews were still dwelling in the region at the time of the plagues (Exod. 8:22; 9:26). From this territory Moses led the Israelites out of Egypt (Exod. 4–13). *See also* Egypt; exodus, the; patriarchs.
 2 A geographic region between the southern hill country of Judah and the Negev, mentioned only in Josh. 10:41; 11:16. Its precise delineations are unknown. It is possibly related to 3.
 3 A city in the southern hill country of Judah, in the same district as Debir (modern Khirbet Rabud), Anab, Socoh, and Eshtamoh (Josh. 15:41). Its identification is unknown. Proposals in-

clude such modern locations as Tell Beit Mirsim, Dhahariya, and, more recently, Tell el-Kheleifeh, all sites near the southeast edge of the Judean hill country.   D.A.D.

gospel (Gk. *euangelion,* "good news"). The noun "gospel" (often but not always rendered as "good news" in the NRSV) is used only in the NT, but background for understanding the concept is found in the LXX, where the verb *euangelizein* ("to bring good news") is used in Isa. 40:9; 41:27; 52:7; 61:1–2 (on the last passage especially, cf. Luke 4:18–19; 7:22). In all of these passages, a messenger is said to announce the good news of Israel's redemption from exile. The NT understanding of gospel also reflects Hellenistic usage of the term, evident in the language of Roman decrees. The Roman proconsul Paulus Fabius Maximus honored Caesar Augustus by declaring the day of Caesar's birth to be "good news" (*euangelion*) for the whole world. Against this background, the word "gospel" came to have at least four different connotations in the NT and the early Christian church.

First, gospel was used to describe the content of Jesus's preaching: "Jesus came into Galilee, proclaiming the good news of God" (Mark 1:14). Here the use of "gospel" is similar to the one in Isaiah: Jesus is announcing what God is about to do, and this message of impending salvation is called "gospel" or "good news." Thus, the term could be employed almost as a synonym for "what Jesus said about God."

Second, gospel was used to describe the content of early Christian preaching, which focused on the death and resurrection of Christ, and on the benefits that faith in Christ has for believers. Paul speaks of "my gospel" (Rom. 2:16; 16:25) and "our gospel" (2 Cor. 4:3), indicating who it is who proclaims this good news (Paul himself) and for whom it is good news (Paul and his readers). He also uses the term "gospel" without any other modifier (Rom. 10:16; 11:28; 1 Cor. 4:15; 9:14, 18). In all of these cases ("my gospel," "our gospel," or simply "gospel") the readers are assumed to understand the *content* of the gospel, i.e., the message Paul and the readers considered to be "good news." At other times, however, Paul speaks of the "gospel of God" (Rom. 1:1; 15:16; cf. 2 Cor. 11:7), the "gospel (or good news) of Christ" (Rom. 15:19; 1 Cor. 9:12; 2 Cor. 2:12; 9:13; 10:14; Phil. 1:27; 1 Thess. 3:2), or the "gospel concerning [God's] Son" (Rom. 1:9). The first of these expressions ("gospel of God") seems only to indicate that the gospel Paul preaches has its origin in God; but the latter two phrases ("gospel of Christ" or "gospel concerning [God's] Son") seem to indicate what the content of Paul's gospel message was: just as Jesus preached good news about God's kingdom ("the good news of the kingdom," cf. Matt. 4:23; 9:35), so Paul preached good news about Christ, the Son of God (the "gospel of Christ" or the "gospel concerning [God's] Son"). In Rom. 1:1–6 and 1 Cor. 15:1–8, Paul describes this gospel further: it comes from God; it was promised through the prophets;

its content is Jesus, a descendant of David according to the flesh, designated Son of God in power by the resurrection. Thus, for Paul, the "gospel" was no longer a message proclaimed *by* Jesus *about* God, but a message proclaimed *by* Christians *about* Jesus (or at least about what God had done in or through Jesus). At a content level, the gospel was now less about the "coming of God's kingdom" and more about the death and resurrection of Christ. The significance of this gospel for Paul can hardly be overstated. It was disclosed to Paul by God (Gal. 1:16) and so was no human affair (Gal. 1:11–12). It contained or conveyed the power of God for salvation to all who believed (Rom. 1:16). Paul also affirms that there is no other gospel (Gal. 1:7), and he strives constantly to prevent anyone from turning his audience toward false versions of the gospel (2 Cor. 11:4; Gal. 1:6). The true gospel demands obedience (Rom. 10:16), and Paul does everything for its sake (1 Cor. 9:23), even surrendering his legitimate rights so that the gospel can be preached free of charge (1 Cor. 9:18).

Third, as a combination of the above, gospel came to refer to preaching that summarized the ministry of Jesus in a way that included both what Jesus had said was the good news about God and what Christians had said was the good news about Jesus. A summary of such "gospel preaching" is found in Acts 10:34–43. Likewise, Mark 14:9 indicates that preaching the gospel in the early church included telling anecdotes about the life and ministry of Jesus. In Mark 8:35 and 10:29, the word "gospel" (NRSV: "good news") seems to refer to the ministry of Jesus as a whole—and perhaps even to the ongoing ministry of his followers on his behalf. Again, there is a subtle shift in focus and content. When the apostle Paul says that he preached the "gospel of God" (Rom. 1:1–5), he does not mean that he repeated what Jesus had said about God or that he told people stories about Jesus—parables he had taught, miracles he had performed, other anecdotes about his life on earth. Still, in NT books written after the time of Paul (including Matthew, Mark, Luke, John, and Acts) the gospel has come to be understood as a message that includes such matters. Indeed, the book that is now called the Gospel of Mark describes its entire contents as "the good news (gospel) of Jesus Christ, the Son of God."

Fourth, gospel came to be used for books that offer in written form what had previously been proclaimed orally. This was a natural outgrowth of the use of the term as just described: a comprehensive message that includes what Jesus himself considered to be the gospel of God, what people like Paul considered to be the gospel about Christ (especially his death and resurrection), and numerous anecdotes and stories about Jesus as the Messiah and Son of God active on earth.

Bibliography

Powell, Mark Allan. *Fortress Introduction to the Gospels.* Fortress, 1998.

Stuhlmacher, Peter, ed. *The Gospel and the Gospels.* Eerdmans, 1991.   M.A.P.

The Gospels

THE FIRST FOUR BOOKS of the NT are called the Gospels of Matthew, Mark, Luke, and John, respectively, and, by extension, other books that were probably written in emulation of these writings are sometimes called "Gospels" as well. The term derives from the Greek word *euangelion*, which means "good news." This term was applied first to preaching about God's redemptive activity (cf. Isa. 61:1–2), then to Jesus's preaching about the kingdom of God (Mark 1:14–15), then to the message that early Christians proclaimed about what God had done in and through Jesus (Rom. 1:9), and finally to the whole story of Jesus: his life, ministry, death, and resurrection (cf. Mark 1:1).

Genre: Because the "Gospel" was not a known literary genre at the time the first four books of the NT were written, the actual literary genre of those books has been a matter of intense debate. Some scholars have maintained that the authors of those books—or one of the authors (probably Mark)—created an entirely new genre of literature that the world had not seen before. Others, without denying that these books are not exactly like anything that preceded them, have focused on identifying analogues in both Jewish literature (apocalypse, biography of righteous individuals, biography of prophets) and Greco-Roman literature (popular biography, laudatory biography, aretalogy, tragedy).

Although there is no consensus on this matter, most recent scholars have concluded that the Gospels can be placed loosely into the genre of

The four evangelists as represented by their symbols in one of two evangelist pages from the eighth-century *Book of Kells*.

ancient biography. Books belonging to that genre were especially popular in the Roman world, and many of them have survived to the present day. The Greek historian Plutarch (45–125 CE) wrote more than fifty biographies of prominent Greeks and Romans. Suetonius and Tacitus recounted the lives of the Roman emperors. There were biographies of generals and military heroes and also of philosophers and religious leaders. Thus, it is sometimes said (with a hint of anachronism) that a Roman library would probably have put the NT Gospels on the same shelf as *Lives of Eminent Philosophers* by Diogenes Laertius and *Life of Apollonius of Tyana* by Philostratus. This understanding of the Gospels, however, is qualified by at least five additional considerations:

1. The NT Gospels are compilations. Although the Gospels as finished products may be identified as ancient biographies, they include other genres of literature within their pages: genealogies, hymns, parables, miracle stories, speeches, pronouncement stories, etc.

2. They were influenced by Jewish literature. All four of the Gospels are written in Greek, the language of the Greco-Roman world, but they are written by persons well versed in the scriptures of Israel. Those scriptures contain semibiographical narratives of people like Abraham, Moses, and Elijah. Even though the Gospels were written for the Greco-Roman world, their authors knew these Jewish stories and were influenced by them.

3. They are ancient biographies, not modern ones. The Gospels make no pretense of offering objective or balanced perspectives on Jesus's life. They do not reveal their sources or offer any way for readers to check the reliability of what they report. Their treatment is far from comprehensive: they offer little insight into Jesus's personality or motivation; they provide almost no information about his early life; they do not even bother to describe his physical appearance. They also lack the sort of data—references to names, dates, and places—that would be standard for any modern biography. The Gospel of Mark reports that Jesus healed a man in a synagogue (3:1–6), but it does not give the man's name or say when this happened or what happened next. (Was the healing permanent? Did the man become a follower of Jesus? Did he continue to attend the synagogue?) Though these lapses may seem strange to modern readers, such questions were not usually expected to be addressed in biographies of the ancient world. The point of ancient biographies was to relate accounts that portrayed the essential *character* of the person who was the subject of the work. Indeed, the purpose of the biography was to define that person's character in a manner that would invite emulation. The anecdotal style of ancient biographies, furthermore, allowed events to be related without much concern for chronology. Events were not necessarily reported in the order in which they happened; rather, they were recounted in a sequence likely to have a particular rhetorical effect on the book's readers. This characteristic may explain why the NT Gospels often relate events in different sequences (e.g., the account of Jesus overturning tables in the

Jerusalem temple is found near the beginning of John's Gospel, but comes near the end of the Gospel of Mark).

4. They employ a fictive ("fictionlike") style of narrative. In many ways, the literary style of the NT Gospels is closer to that of modern fiction than it is to modern historical reporting. The Gospel authors knew the art of storytelling, and they employ such literary devices as irony, symbolism, and foreshadowing. They solicit readers' empathy so that, as their stories unfold, the reader feels drawn into the drama. The genre of ancient biography allows for such analysis, because biographies in the ancient world tended to treat history as a story and to relate events with a flair that modern readers associate with fiction.

5. They are overtly evangelistic. Most biographies of the ancient world were evangelistic in a broad sense. They did not simply pass on information about interesting individuals; they reported on extraordinary lives with an obvious hope that readers would be inspired by what was presented and motivated to change their values or behaviors accordingly. The NT Gospels exhibit this tendency to an extreme. Their authors tell the story of Jesus in a way that may inspire people to accept his teaching or practice his way of life. Beyond that, the claim of these books is that what has happened in and through Jesus altered the very nature of human existence. These authors are telling a story of ultimate significance, recounting things they claim will affect the lives of all people, whether they believe in Jesus or not.

CHARACTERISTICS OF ANCIENT BIOGRAPHIES

- No pretense of detached objectivity
- No concern for establishing facts (e.g., by citing evidence or sources)
- Not much attention to historical data (names, dates, places)
- Little attention to chronology of events or development of the person's thought
- No psychological interest in the subject's inner motivations
- Anecdotal style of narration
- Emphasis on the subject's character and defining traits
- Consistent focus on the subject's philosophy of life
- Strong interest in the subject's death as consistent with the subject's philosophy of life
- Presentation of the subject as a model worthy of emulation
- Depiction of subject as superior to competitors or rivals
- Overall concern with the subject's legacy, evident in followers who carry on the tradition

From Mark Allan Powell, *Introducing the New Testament* (courtesy, Baker Academic)

Types of Material in the Gospels: As indicated, the NT Gospels must be understood as compilations of various types of material. Some of these are specific to particular Gospels: hymns are found only in Luke and John; genealogies only in Matthew and Luke. Other types of material, however, are found in most or all of the Gospels.

Parables: More than forty parables of Jesus are included in the Gospels of Matthew, Mark, and Luke. No parables are found in John, but even there one finds instances of figurative speech not too far removed from the parable genre (4:35–37; 8:35; 10:1–5; 12:24; 16:21). *See also* parables.

Miracle stories: All four Gospels contain multiple accounts of Jesus working miracles. The preferred term for miracles in the Synoptic Gospels (Matthew, Mark, Luke) is the Greek word *dynamis,* which means "power" or "deeds of power" (e.g., Matt. 11:20–23; Mark 6:2, 5). In John's Gospel, the miracles are often called *semeia,* or "signs" (e.g., 2:11; 12:37), because they point beyond themselves to the truth about God that Jesus has come to reveal. *See also* miracles.

Pronouncement Stories: All four of the NT Gospels contain numerous examples of what scholars call "pronouncement stories," anecdotes that preserve the memory of something Jesus said. In such a story, everything leads up to a climactic and provocative pronouncement—the saying, which usually comes at the end, is the whole point of the anecdote (just as a punch line is the whole point of a joke). Thus, a story about Jesus's opponents trying to trap him serves to set up his memorable saying, "Give to the emperor the things that are the emperor's, and to God the things that are God's" (Matt. 22:15–22; Mark 12:13–17; Luke 20:20–26). *See also* pronouncement stories.

Individual Sayings: The Gospels also contain numerous sayings of Jesus that lack narrative context. Sometimes these sayings are strung together to make what appear to be speeches of Jesus given on some particular occasion. Sometimes they are linked together by no more than what appear to be "catchword" connections (e.g., Mark 9:49 follows 9:47–48 only because of the word "fire," and then 9:50a and 9:50b each follow 9:49 only because of the word "salt").

Passion and Resurrection Narratives: All four Gospels conclude with an extended account of Jesus's arrest, trial, crucifixion, burial, and resurrection. In each Gospel, this portion of the story is treated with more intense detail than any other portion, and the pace of the narrative slows to the point that readers receive an almost hour-by-hour account of what is happening. Scholars have noted similarities between these accounts and the death scenes of other famous men in ancient Greco-Roman biographies. These accounts also show an especially strong degree of interaction with the scriptures of Israel; they appear to be written by people who have already thought deeply about the meaning of Jesus's death and resurrection and reflected on those events in light of passages from the Psalms, the Prophets, and other portions of scripture. Thus, the death and resurrection of Jesus is not just one more episode in a series of remarkable occurrences; for each of the four Gospels, it is treated as the climax of the story, the goal toward which everything has been moving all along. Indeed, each of the Gospels prepares its readers for this capstone event

SAYINGS OF JESUS IN THE GOSPELS: SOME EXAMPLES

Wisdom Sayings provide insight into how life really works:

"Where your treasure is, there your heart will be also"
(Luke 12:34).

"If a kingdom is divided against itself, that kingdom cannot stand"
(Mark 3:24).

Prophetic Sayings proclaim the activity or judgment of God:

"The kingdom of God has come near; repent and believe"
(Mark 1:15).

Eschatological Sayings reflect the view that the future is of primary importance:

"The Son of Man is to come with his angels in the glory of his Father, and then he will repay everyone for what has been done" (Matt. 16:27).

Legal Sayings interpret Torah or the will of God:

"In everything do to others, as you would have them do to you, for this is the law and the prophets" (Matt. 7:12).

"I" Sayings are autobiographical:

"I came not to call the righteous but sinners" (Mark 2:17).

"I came that they may have life and have it abundantly" (John 10:10).

From Mark Allan Powell, *Introducing the New Testament* (courtesy, Baker Academic)

by having Jesus predict exactly what will occur (e.g., Mark 8:31–32; 9:31; 10:33–34) and/or offering allusions that readers are expected to understand in a manner that characters in the story do not (see Mark 2:20; John 2:19–22; 3:14; 8:28; 12:32–34). Furthermore, each Gospel tells the story of Jesus's death and resurrection in a distinctive way that pulls together certain threads and fulfills important themes of that particular work. In Matthew's Gospel, Jesus dies as the Messiah of Israel, fulfilling prophecies that indicated he would be the one to save his people from their sin (cf. 1:21). In Mark, he gives his life as a ransom for many, demonstrating the sacrificial way of self-denial that is to mark all of his followers (cf. 8:34–35; 10:43–45). In Luke, he dies as a noble martyr, a victim of injustice, who will overcome death in a way that promises an end to oppression (cf. 4:18). In John, he dies triumphantly, as one who is glorified and exalted in an ultimate expression of God's love (cf. 12:23; 15:13). In these and other ways, each of the passion and resurrection stories serves as the narrative and theological climax of the Gospel in which it appears.

Composition and Sources: The author of Luke's Gospel says that he has done some research and that his intent is to provide an orderly account of what has been handed on "from the beginning" (1:1–4). As this comment implies, the Gospel authors did not have to start from scratch. They were able to rely upon "oral sources" (nuggets of material that had been told from memory), and they probably also had written sources (materials that people had put into writing a generation before the Gospels themselves were produced). A potentially complicating factor with regard to composition of the Gospels concerns the question of whether the evangelists operated independently of each other. Did each of the Gospel authors produce his biography of Jesus without any clue that others were doing (or had done) the same thing? Or did they consult each other? More to the point, did the ones who wrote last have copies of the Gospel or Gospels that were written first? Three of the four Gospels—Matthew, Mark, and Luke—are called the "Synoptic Gospels" because they appear to be related to each other in a way that the fourth one, John, is not. The word "synoptic" literally means "seeing together," and it came to be applied to the first three Gospels, because their contents could be set in parallel columns that allowed them to be read and interpreted side by side. The amount of overlapping material is remarkable, as are the similarities in structure, style, perspective, and overall tone. The question of exactly how these three Gospels should be related to each other is called the "Synoptic Problem." Various solutions to this problem have been proposed. The dominant hypothesis holds that Mark wrote his Gospel first, that Matthew and Luke each used Mark's Gospel as a source, that Matthew and Luke also used a now lost collection of sayings attributed to Jesus (called the "Q source"), and that Matthew and Luke operated independently of each other. Every aspect of this proposal can be and has been challenged. *See also* Synoptic Problem.

With regard to the Gospel of John, the principal question becomes whether the author of this Gospel knew of or had access to Matthew, Mark, or Luke. Scholars are somewhat evenly divided over this issue. In addition, a number of other possible sources for John's Gospel have been proposed, including a now lost "Signs Gospel" that included numbered miracle stories (cf. references to "the first of his signs" in 2:11 and "the second sign" in 4:54) and concluded with what is now 20:30–31. *See also* John, Gospel According to.

In addition to the four NT Gospels, other early Christian writings are sometimes called gospels, mainly because they are assumed to have been written in emulation of these documents. Of the numerous apocryphal gospels produced in the first few centuries CE, the *Gospel of Thomas* has been of most interest to NT scholars, because some think that it might have been written in the first century and so provide a variant tradition for sayings of Jesus that can be compared and contrasted with what is found in the NT Gospels. Despite its name, the *Gospel of Thomas* does not belong to the same literary genre as the NT Gospels, for it contains only sayings attributed to Jesus, not narratives concerning him. The *Gospel of Peter* has also attracted some attention in biblical studies, because a handful of scholars believe it may have drawn upon an early account of Jesus's resurrection that also served as a source for some of the NT Gospels. Other apocryphal gospels are studied for what they reveal concerning the diversity and development of Christianity in the second, third, and fourth centuries, but have no direct impact on NT studies. *See also* gospel; John, Gospel According to; Luke, Gospel According to; Mark, Gospel According to; Matthew, Gospel According to.

Bibliography

Aune, E. David. *The New Testament in Its Literary Environment.* Westminster, 1987.

Powell, Mark Allan. *Fortress Introduction to the Gospels.* Fortress, 1998.

———. *Introducing the New Testament: A Historical, Literary, and Theological Survey.* Baker Academic, 2009.

Stuhlmacher, Peter, ed. *The Gospel and the Gospels.* Eerdmans, 1991.　　M.A.P.

gourd, a hard-rinded inedible fruit of the genus *Lagenaria* (large) or of the species *Cucurbita pepo* (small), used both as utensils (dippers, cups, storage vessels) and for ornamentation. In Jon. 4:4–10 the KJV has "gourd" where the NRSV has "bush" due to uncertain identification. Gourd motifs decorated the temple interior (1 Kings 6:18) and the bronze sea in the temple (1 Kings 7:24; 2 Chron. 4:3). A "wild gourd" referred to in 2 Kings 4:39 had poisonous fruit—just what that gourd might have been remains unknown.

government, the administration of society by those in power. The form of government in the Bible varies: village assemblies, heads of familial and tribal associations, intertribal judges, theocratic kings, and emperors with their representatives (prefect or procurator or subordinate king) or local councils (e.g., the Sanhedrin). The purpose and dangers of government receive attention throughout the Hebrew Bible, particularly with regard to the monarchy. God is the ultimate ruler, and the responsibility of the king is to execute justice, particularly for the weak (1 Kings 10:9; Prov. 31:8–9; Ezek. 34:1–6, 23); this is true even for foreign governments (Dan. 4:27). Ps. 72:1–4 contains a prayer for God to enable and empower the earthly ruler, and Ps. 101 conveys a pledge on the part of such a ruler to show integrity and justice. Government needs limits; rule is a function, not a status or class (Deut. 17:14–20). The people are not mere subjects but are also participants, even in the covenantal aspects of kingship (2 Kings 11:17; 23:1–3). In the NT, different attitudes toward the government can be discerned. First, the government may be understood as divinely established to encourage and maintain what is beneficial and to discourage what is harmful and disruptive; according to this view, believers should honor and obey governing authorities as instituted by God (Rom. 13:1–7; Titus 3:1–2; 1 Pet. 2:13–17). Second, governing authorities may be viewed as lackeys of the devil (Luke 4:6) in control of a world that is intrinsically opposed to Jesus and hostile to his followers; according to this view, believers should seek to withdraw from society, avoid any compromise with worldly powers, and strive to implement what is godly in direct opposition to what the demonic instruments of injustice will seek to produce (John 15:18–19; 1 John 2:15–17; and the book of Revelation, esp. chaps. 13, 17–18). Finally, a mediating position is evident in the teaching of Jesus, who counsels acceptance of the powers that be, while also critiquing them and insisting on a transcendent commitment to God alone (Mark 10:42–44; 12:13–17; cf. Acts 5:29). *See also* council, the; king; law; prefect.
Bibliography
    Pilgrim, Walter J. *Uneasy Neighbors: Church and State in the New Testament.* Fortress, 1999.
S.C.M./M.A.P.

governor, a ruler of a city, territory, or province. In the Bible, governors are not elected officials, nor are they supreme rulers. They are appointed by a king or emperor; while exercising considerable local authority, they only rule at the pleasure of the one who appointed them. In Genesis, Pharaoh appoints Joseph governor of all Egypt (42:6; 45:26). At the time of Ahab, a number of district governors are mentioned who have military responsibilities (1 Kings 20:14–19). During the Babylonian and Persian periods, governors were appointed by emperors. Dan. 3:2 mentions satraps, prefects, governors, counselors, treasurers, justices, and magistrates under King Nebuchadnezzar (if this list implies a hierarchy, governors would seem to occupy a mid-level position of power). After the exile, Tattenai is appointed governor of the Persian province "Beyond the River," which from a Persian perspective would include Judah (Ezra 5:6). Zerubbabel and Nehemiah are listed as local governors appointed by the Persian ruler (Hag. 1:1; Neh. 5:14). In the NT, Quirinius is named as the governor of Syria at the time of Jesus's birth (Luke 2:2), and Pontius Pilate is referred to as the governor of Judea at the time of Jesus's ministry (Luke 3:1) and crucifixion (Matt. 27:2). More precise terminology usually identifies Pilate as a Roman prefect. Felix (Acts 23:24) and Porcius Festus (Acts 24:27; cf. 26:30) are also called governors. Jesus told his disciples that they would be dragged before governors and kings because of him (Matt. 10:18; Mark 13:9; Luke 21:12). First Peter teaches that Christians should "accept the authority of every human institution, whether of the emperor as supreme, or of governors as sent by (God) to punish those who do wrong and to praise those who do right" (2:13–14).   M.A.P.

Gozan (goh´zan; Akkadian Guzana), a city (modern Tell Halaf) on the Habor (Heb. Khabur) River; the city and its surrounding region became part of the Assyrian Empire in the ninth century BCE (alluded to in 2 Kings 19:12; see Isa. 37:12). Gozan was one of the places to which the Israelites were deported after the capture of Samaria (2 Kings 17:6; 18:11; 1 Chron. 5:26); texts from Tell Halaf mention some of the exiles' descendants. *See also* Habor.

grace, as a theological concept, the unmerited favor of God, closely associated with mercy and forgiveness. The noun "grace" (Heb. *khen;* Gk. *charis*) is used only 3 times in the Hebrew Bible (Ps. 45:2; Jer. 31:2; Zech. 4:7), but occurs 115 times in the NT. These statistics, however, can be misleading, for the concept of God's unmerited favor is expressed throughout the Bible. God's choice of Israel to be God's people was not based on prior accomplishments or qualifications (Gen. 12:1–3; cf. Wis. 3:9; 4:15, where "grace and mercy" are connected with election). God loved Israel in spite of puny numbers (Deut. 7:6–9) and rescued the community from the wilderness, encircling them with care (Deut. 32:10). God kept covenant with Israel even when the covenant was violated by the people (Jer. 31:31–34; Ezek. 16:8) and brought the captives home from Babylon (Isa. 49:14–18). Furthermore, the Hebrew verb *khanan,* "to be gracious," is frequently used with God as the subject, and the adjective *khannun,* "gracious," is often applied to God. Thus, God declares, "I will be gracious to whom I will be gracious, and will show mercy on whom I will show mercy" (Exod. 33:19). The seemingly arbitrary nature of that declaration becomes cause for celebration as biblical writers discover that God is frequently, typically, and perhaps intrinsically "gracious and merciful, slow to anger, and abounding in steadfast love" (Exod. 34:6). The psalmists show confidence in asking God to be gracious in hearing prayers (4:1), healing sickness (6:2; 41:4), rescuing the oppressed (9:13), forgiving sin (41:4), etc. Still, grace is not something that can be taken for granted, especially when one has aroused God's wrath (2 Sam. 12:22).

In the NT, the focus of God's grace shifts decisively to the person of Jesus Christ. Divine grace rests on the infant Jesus (Luke 2:40), who subsequently grows in grace (2:52; NRSV: "favor") and speaks gracious words (4:22). Paul regards his apostleship as a gift of grace. Above all, however, Paul associates God's grace with God's unmerited favor shown to sinners through Jesus Christ and expressed supremely though Christ's death and resurrection. Jews and Gentiles alike gain entrance to the messianic community through the "gift" (Rom. 3:24) or "free gift" (Rom. 5:15) of grace (Gal. 2:17–21; Rom. 4:16). People have been justified or put right with God by grace, which is received through faith—and even that comes as a free gift of God (Eph. 2:8). Still, Paul cautions against using grace as a license to sin, lest believers "accept the grace of God in vain" (2 Cor. 6:1). Paul also uses the word "grace" (combined with "peace") as a salutation in the opening of his letters (e.g., Rom. 1:7; 1 Cor. 1:3). *See also* covenant; forgiveness; love; mercy; promise.   C.J.R./M.A.P.

gracious, the quality of showing favor and mercy. The term is usually applied to a person of superior position and power who is kindly disposed toward a person of inferior position and power. Thus, Potiphar dealt graciously with Joseph (Gen. 39:4), Ruth found favor in the eyes of Boaz (Ruth 2:10), and Esther was treated graciously by King Ahasuerus (Esther 2:17; 5:2). In the Bible, it is above all God who is gracious toward human beings, as stated in an ancient liturgical affirmation that calls God "gracious and merciful, slow to anger, and abounding in steadfast love" (Exod. 34:6; cf. Pss. 86:15; 103:8; 145:8). *See also* grace; mercy.   W.E.L.

graft. *See* olive.

grain, a general term used throughout the Bible to indicate the seed of cultivated cereal grasses such as wheat, barley, millet, and sorghum. The term the NRSV regularly translates as "grain" is translated "corn" in the KJV and NEB. Ground into flour, grain was the major component of breads and other cooked foods. An ancient poem

Harvesting grain with sickles; from the tomb of Mennah, scribe of Thutmose IV, ca. 1390 BCE.

designates the promised land a place of "grain and new wine" (Deut. 33:28). The phrase "grain, wine, and oil" occurs repeatedly (Deut. 28:51; 2 Chron. 32:28; Neh. 5:11; 10:39; 13:5, 12; Joel 2:19), denoting the range of native agricultural produce: cereal farming, viticulture, and olive cultivation. The development of cereal agriculture antedated the settlement of Israel's tribes (beginning in the thirteenth century BCE). Israel inherited from Canaan the techniques of farming and a cycle of agricultural festivals: Unleavened Bread (Passover); Weeks (Pentecost); and Ingathering (Tabernacles). *See also* barley; millet; Passover; Pentecost; spelt; Tabernacles, Festival of; Unleavened Bread, Festival of; wheat.   R.M.G.

granary, a storage facility for threshed and winnowed grains such as wheat and barley. The facility ranged in size and format from an entire building of rooms or compartments, to plastered or unplastered pits or silos, to individual jars or containers. The presence of large granary structures in the ancient Near East implies a surplus production of wheat to guard against famine years as well as some type of organized system for redistribution of the grain (see Jer. 50:26; Joel 1:17; Matt. 3:12; Luke 3:17).

grape. *See* vine.

grasshopper. *See* locust.

grave. *See* architecture; burial.

graven images. *See* idol.

greave, armor protecting the lower leg. The ones Goliath wore were made of bronze (1 Sam. 17:6).

Greece (grees), a country that lies at the terminus of the central mountain structure of southern Europe. Between 750 and 500 BCE Greeks, pressed for land, founded numerous colonies in the Aegean, along the Black Sea, in Cyrenaica, Sicily, and southern Italy as well as Asia Minor. By 500 BCE the city-state Sparta had united most of the Peloponnesus. Meanwhile, the Athenians united most of the Greeks in the Aegean area as well as those along the coast of Asia Minor. Athens's defeat by Sparta ended this league, though attempts would be made to form new leagues around prominent cities. In the north, Greece had remained divided into weak tribal monarchies until Philip II of Macedon consolidated power in the region. Philip defeated Athens and a weak coalition of cities at Chaeronea in 338 BCE. The Romans gained control of Greece in 146 BCE.

In the Hebrew Bible, Greece is mentioned only in two of the later books (Dan. 8:21; 10:20; 11:2; Zech. 9:13). It figures much more prominently in the NT, though not by name. During the NT period, the area now known as Greece was divided into two Roman provinces, Achaia (in the south) and Macedonia (in the north). Corinth and

THE GREEK ALPHABET

| Greek Form | | | Translit- | Approximate |
Capital	Small	Name	eration	Pronunciation
A	α	alpha	a	drama
B	β	beta	b	bike
Γ	γ	gamma	g	good
Δ	δ	delta	d	dog
E	ε	epsilon	e	ego
Z	ζ	zeta	z	Zeus
H	η	eta	ē	they
Θ	θ	theta	th	thin
I	ι	iota	i	it
K	κ	kappa	k	kite
Λ	λ	lambda	l	logic
M	μ	mu	m	mother
N	ν	nu	n	not
Ξ	ξ	xsi	xs	axiom
O	o	omicron	o	hot
Π	π	pi	p	poet
P	ρ	rho	r	road
Σ	σ, ς	sigma	s	side
T	τ	tau	t	topic
Y	υ	upsilon	u, y	*tu* (French) *Tür* (German)
Φ	φ	phi	ph	phone
X	χ	chi	ch	chasm
Ψ	ψ	psi	ps	apse
Ω	ω	omega	ō	ode

Athens were in Achaia; Philippi and Thessalonica were in Macedonia. Thus, Paul wrote letters to three churches in Greece (Corinth, Philippi, Thessalonica), and he visited other cities there as well (see Acts 16:9–18:18; 2 Cor. 2:12). When Paul is said to arrive in Greece in Acts 20:2, he is actually arriving in Macedonia (cf. Acts 20:1, 3).   P.P.

Greek, Greeks.

1 As a substantive adjective, the word "Greek" sometimes refers to the Greek language (Acts 9:36; 21:37; Rev. 9:11). The inscription attached to Jesus's cross was written in Hebrew, Latin, and Greek (John 19:20). *See also* Greek language.

2 As a substantive adjective referring to *people,* the term "Greek" or "Greeks" would literally refer to people from the land of Greece. It might mean this in certain passages, such as John 12:20. In the great majority of cases, however, the NT uses "Greek/Greeks" as a synonym for "Gentile/Gentiles," i.e., for persons who are not Jewish. Titus is "a Greek" because he is not a Jew (Gal. 2:3). When Paul says in Rom. 3:9 that "Jews and Greeks" are under the power of sin, he means that all people are under the power of sin, Jews and non-Jews alike.   M.A.P.

Greek language.

All the books of the NT were written in Greek, or more precisely in a dialect called Koine ("common") Greek or Hellenistic Greek. Koine Greek was a "common" dialect in two senses of the word. First, it became the most commonly used language of late antiquity, serving as the *lingua franca* of the Mediterranean world for over a millennium (fourth century BCE–sixth century CE). Second, it represented the language of the "common people"; it was a simplified, colloquial version of the language spoken (and sometimes written) by the less educated classes. A major boon to the study of Koine Greek has been the discovery during the past century of tens of thousands of papyrus documents, mainly in Egypt, in addition to inscriptions and ostraca unearthed by archaeological excavations. Scholars now possess a wide spectrum of written materials from late antiquity, thus permitting a comparative analysis of NT Greek with secular Koine Greek documents of the time. As a result, most scholars now view NT Greek as closely related to the Koine vernacular of the first century CE, though NT Greek does differ somewhat due to the influence of Hebrew and Aramaic patterns on the NT authors (called "Semitisms") and also to the new connotations of Greek words generated by the process of community formation in early Christianity. Moreover, NT Greek varies from book to book as a result of each author's educational level and familiarity with Koine Greek.   L.C.M.

grinding stone, a stone, known as a quern, with a flat or slightly concave surface used for grinding grain into meal by hand. Most samples are basalt or limestone in the Near East, and the grain was pulverized by being crushed with a handheld stone repeatedly kneaded over the grain against the quern surface. Such an activity is probably presumed in Jesus's saying in Matt. 24:41.

groves, clusters of trees such as might be found in an orchard or oasis. Palm groves (Num. 24:6) and olive groves (Deut. 6:11; Judg. 15:5) are specifically mentioned. Jth. 3:8 mentions sacred groves destroyed by Holofernes. In 2 Esdras it is said that neither thick groves nor the clefts of rocks will prove to be effective hiding places from the wrath of God (16:28). *See also* oak; trees; wood.

grudge, a feeling of anger, prohibited by Lev. 19:18. Likewise, God does not maintain anger forever (Jer. 3:5, 12; Ps. 103:9). In Gen. 50:15, Joseph's brothers wonder whether he might bear a grudge against them for selling him into slavery in Egypt. Mark 6:19 says that Herodias bore a grudge against John the Baptist. Ungrudging behavior is encouraged in Deut. 15:10 and 1 Pet. 4:9.

guard, bodyguard, a person or persons assigned to the protection of a individual, place, or thing. Cherubim guard the entrance to the garden of Eden to prevent human access to the tree of life (Gen. 3:24). Various royal figures are depicted as having guards (Gen. 37:36; Dan. 2:14; 2 Kings 25:8–21). David had an elite troop of Cherethites and Pelethites who served as his bodyguard under the leadership of Benaiah, the son of Jehoiada

(2 Sam. 23:22–3; cf. 8:18). As "foreigners" these soldiers would have had personal loyalty to their employer and would have been less influenced by competing internal political factions. The temple area in Jerusalem also required guards (1 Kings 14:27–28; 2 Kings 11:19). Prison guards are mentioned in Gen. 40:3–4; Acts 5:23; 12:6. During the Roman occupation of Judea, the temple area had at least two sets of guards. One set of Roman soldiers was stationed in the fortress of Antonia (see Acts 21:30–34), and the priestly officials had levitical "security officers" as well. Roman guards watched the tomb of Jesus (Matt. 27:65–28:4) and supervised the house arrest of the apostle Paul (Acts 28:16).   J.A.D.

guest, one invited to a feast (1 Kings 1:41; Matt. 22:10–11; Mark 6:22–26) or to lodge overnight (Luke 19:7). In the ancient Mediterranean world, people were often expected to lodge travelers and strangers and to ensure the safety and welfare of their guests, even at extreme inconvenience to themselves or to their family (Judg. 19:15–24; 2 Sam. 12:4; cf. Luke 11:5–6; Heb. 13:2). Some houses were equipped with guest rooms (Luke 22:11; Philem. 22). The practice of such hospitality implied a social bond and could lead to aspersions being cast on either party: Jesus is criticized for going to be the guest of a sinner (Luke 19:7), and a Thessalonian named Jason is attacked for entertaining Paul and Silas as guests in his home (Acts 17:7).

guest chamber. *See* house.

guilt. For the biblical writers, guilt is not primarily an inward feeling of remorse or a bad conscience, but rather a situation that has arisen because of sin committed against God or one's neighbor; a clear presupposition is that human beings are responsible and accountable for their actions, thoughts, and attitudes. The latter notion of responsibility is so great that people can be guilty without even being aware that they have done anything wrong (e.g., Lev. 5:17–19). Guilt, furthermore, can be collective as well as individual. Ps. 51 testifies to a situation in which an individual has sinned and brought guilt upon himself, but what one person does can also cause guilt to come upon an entire group of people (cf. the story of Achan in Josh. 7). In the Bible, guilt brings serious consequences, including separation from God and one's neighbors. Guilt is depicted as a burden or weight that can crush a person (e.g., Ps. 38:4, 6), as a disease that can destroy a person from within (e.g., Ps. 32:3–4), or as a debt that must be paid (e.g., Lev. 5:1–6:7; Num. 5:5–8). When speaking of guilt, NT writers use the Greek word *enochos*, which usually means "deserving of punishment" (e.g., Matt. 26:66; 1 Cor. 11:27; James 2:10). According to Paul, all human beings are guilty before God (e.g., Rom. 1:18–3:20).

Throughout the Bible, guilt can only be removed or set aside because of God's grace, which allows for forgiveness. In Israel, this grace was manifest in a system of sacrifices and rituals designed to cleanse and purify people. Such rituals were not designed primarily to relieve the conscience of the guilty party, but rather to remove the "status" of guilt and so to restore the broken relationship caused by that status. The system was designed, then, to effect reconciliation between the guilty and offended parties. In the NT, Paul makes frequent use of this idea, interpreting the death and resurrection of Jesus Christ as a once-for-all act that effects reconciliation between God and sinful humanity (e.g., Rom. 5:6–11; 2 Cor. 5:16–21; cf. Col. 1:19–20). Although the NT never says that God's action in Christ removes guilt, it does say that it makes available the forgiveness of sins (Matt. 26:28; Luke 24:47; Acts 5:31; 10:43; 13:38; 26:18; Col. 1:14). Likewise, Paul says that people are justified or put right with God through faith in Jesus Christ (Rom. 3:28; 5:1; Gal. 2:16; 3:24). *See also* atonement; evil; justification; reconciliation; sanctification; sacrifice; sin.   J.M.E.

guilt offering. *See* sacrifice.

Guni (gyoo′ni).

1 A son of Naphtali who settled with Jacob's family in Egypt (Gen. 46:24) and became the head of the Gunite group (Num. 26:48).

2 A descendant of Gad (1 Chron. 5:15).

H

Habakkuk (huh-bak´uhk), **book of,** the eighth part of the Book of the Twelve in the Prophets section, or Nevi'im, of the Tanakh (Jewish Bible). In the Christian OT, it is the eighth of the Minor Prophets. The book of Habakkuk has two primary units: chaps. 1–2 are "the oracle that the prophet Habakkuk saw" (1:1), and chap. 3 is "a prayer of the prophet Habakkuk" (3:1). The bulk of chaps. 1–2 (after the introduction) is further divided into two parts: a dialogue between Habakkuk and God and a series of woes.

Contents: The prophet begins by complaining about the problem of injustice toward God's people. The wicked are victorious, and the righteous (though not without fault) are downtrodden and oppressed. After Habakkuk's complaint, God responds by rousing the Chaldeans (1:6). Habakkuk then exclaims that these are not a solution to the oppression, but simply another oppressor. To this, God responds that Habakkuk must trust and wait upon the Lord. At this point, the prophet sets forth a series of five "woes." Last, Habakkuk recounts a "prayer," which is seen as a theophany of God the divine warrior coming to vindicate the people. God's presence shakes the foundations of the cosmos. The book ends with a note to the choirmaster, indicating that it was possibly used liturgically.

OUTLINE OF CONTENTS

Habakkuk

For an alternate chiastic outline of Nahum–Habakkuk read as one book, *see* Nahum, book of.

Background: Not much is definitively known about the prophet Habakkuk. Not even the origin of his name is certain. Most scholars believe it is connected with the Hebrew word for "embrace," while some argue that it is connected to an Akkadian name for a plant. The text gives neither Habakkuk's familial or geographic origins, simply that he was a prophet who saw an oracle and prayed a prayer.

Most scholars believe that Habakkuk prophesied during the rise of the Neo-Babylonian Empire in the last quarter of the seventh century BCE. The only historical reference in the book is to the "Chaldeans" (1:6), who are most likely connected with the Neo-Babylonian Empire, which came to prominence after destroying Nineveh in 612 BCE and fell to the Persians in 539. There are no references or allusions to the capture of Jerusalem or to the exile, which leads scholars to date Habakkuk's career before 587. Sweeney argues that the book focuses on the Neo-Babylonian threat to Jerusalem that arose after their defeat of Egypt in 605.

Themes: Habakkuk offers a sustained reflection upon a problem of injustice. The book has been compared to Job and other wisdom writings in that it questions why the righteous suffer. Yet the coming "day of the LORD," which is present in Habakkuk, is consistent with the theme present throughout the Book of the Twelve. God will come in the future, and God's coming will vindicate Judah and Israel. For Habakkuk, this future coming of God resolves the present problem of injustice.

Interpretive Issues: The greatest difficulty in reading Habakkuk is trying to date it and place its historical references. There is considerable disagreement in the academic community over the identity of the "wicked" in 1:4. Some scholars claim that it refers to the Chaldeans of 1:6, while others hold that God is rousing the Chaldeans in response to the "wicked" Assyrians. Still others hold that the "wicked" are rich Judeans who are oppressing the common people.

Another debated issue concerns the relationship of Habakkuk to the worshiping community. Some scholars hold that the liturgical language used in various places in the book suggests that Habakkuk was connected to the temple. Sweeney argues that Habakkuk was a prophet stationed at or near the temple. Gottwald thinks that liturgical passages in Habakkuk are later additions to the text.

There has also been much discussion about the nature of the hymn in chap. 3. Some have argued that the hymn is integral to the book, while others have argued against this. Childs holds that the hymn may or may not have had an independent life before becoming appropriated for the book of Habakkuk, but that it has been integrated into the book so well that the book now reads as a literary unity.

Influences: Habakkuk is listed among the prophets in 2 Esd. 1:40. He is also mentioned in the story of Bel and the Dragon (part of the apocryphal/deuterocanonical Additions to Daniel). In the first-century CE book "The Lives of the Prophets," his journey to and from Babylon (as recounted in Bel and the Dragon) is seen as a sign of the return of the exiles. A copy of Habakkuk was found among the Dead Sea Scrolls, along with a *pesher* (verse-by-verse commentary) on the book.

Hab. 2:4 had a profound influence on Christian thought. The concept of the righteous living by faith is found throughout the NT and is particularly strong in Paul's thought. In Hebrew, the phrase "the righteous live by their (its) faith" could either refer to the reliability of the vision that God gives or the faithfulness of the righteous person. Most scholars believe that Habakkuk affirms both readings and that either or both would be affirmed by Paul as well.

Bibliography

Bandstra, Barry L. *Reading the Old Testament: Introduction to the Hebrew Bible.* 4th ed. Wadsworth, 2009.

Childs, Brevard S. *Introduction to the Old Testament as Scripture.* Fortress, 1979.

Gottwald, Norman K. *The Hebrew Bible: A Socio-Literary Introduction.* Fortress, 1985.

O'Brien, Julia M. *Nahum, Habakkuk, Zephaniah, Haggai, Zechariah, Malachi.* Abingdon, 2004.

Peterson, David L. *The Prophetic Literature: An Introduction.* Westminster John Knox, 2002.

Sweeney, Marvin A. *The Twelve Prophets.* Vol. 2, *Micah, Nahum, Habakkuk, Zephaniah, Haggai, Zechariah, Malachi.* Liturgical, 2000.   B.B.

Habiru (hah-bee´roo). *See* Hapiru.

Habor (hay´bor), a major tributary of the Euphrates River, which it enters from the northeast below modern Deir ez-Zor in northeast Syria. The Habor was a major route in antiquity and was densely settled, as the many tells that dot its banks show. In the Bible, the Habor is called the river of Gozan and is named as one of the places to which the Israelites were exiled in 722/1 BCE (see 2 Kings 17:6; 18:11; 1 Chron. 5:26). *See also* Gozan.

Hachilah (huh-ki´luh), an unidentified hill in southern Judah in the wilderness of Ziph not far from Hebron. David hid there from Saul (1 Sam. 23:19; 26:1) and, without knowing this, Saul encamped on the hill in his search for David (26:3). *See also* Ziph.

Hadad (hay´dad).

1 A Semitic storm god, also known as Haddu, Adad, and Addu. The meaning of the name is unclear, but it may be connected with the noise of a storm. The veneration of Hadad is attested by some of the earliest Mesopotamian texts. Apparently of West Semitic origin, the god found a special following in Assyria (both early and late) and among the Arameans. In the Ugaritic literature from Ras-Shamra, Hadad (Haddu) is identified with the storm deity Baal and is once called "the shepherd." An Aramaic inscription from Zinjirli dedicates a statue of the god, to whom the local king Panammuwa owed personal thanks. Lucian, a Greek author of the second century CE (or Pseudo-Lucian), treats the cult of Hadad in his work on the Syrian goddess Atargatis; at Hierapolis Hadad was coupled with Atargatis (perhaps Anat), just as earlier at Ras-Shamra Baal (Haddu) was coupled with Anat. In the Bible, "Hadad" survives chiefly in personal names (cf. 2–5 below). The name Ben-hadad (king of Aram at the time of Ahab; cf. 1 Kings 20) literally means "son of Hadad." The book of Zechariah refers to the practice of offering lamentations for Hadad-rimmon (12:11). Rimmon is possibly another name—or perhaps a

title—for Hadad (see 2 Kings 5:18) and, if so, the name Hadad-Rimmon could simply be an exalted way of referring to this god. *See also* Anat; Baal; Ras-Shamra; Rimmon.

2 A son of Ishmael and grandson of Abraham (Gen. 23:15; 1 Chron. 1:30).

3 A king of Edom who defeated the Midianites (Gen. 36:35–36; 1 Chron. 1:46–47). He was the son of Bedad and ruled at Avith.

4 Another king of Edom mentioned in 1 Chron. 1:50–51 (cf. Gen. 36:39, "Hadar"). He was from the city of Pai (or Pau in Gen. 36:39).

5 A third king of Edom who was an adversary of Solomon throughout his entire reign (1 Kings 11:14–25). David had previously killed Edomite males, but Hadad escaped to Egypt, only to return when David was gone.   R.M.G.

Hadadezer (hay´dad-ee´zuhr; Heb., "Hadad is help"), the king of Zobah who was defeated by David in various campaigns against Aramean resistance (2 Sam. 8:3–12; 10:15–19; 1 Chron. 18:3–11; 19:16–19). David's victory consolidated his control over both southern Syria and the Transjordan. His tactics included hamstringing his enemy's horses to cripple their defensive power (1 Chron. 18:4).

Hadad-rimmon (hay´dad-rim´uhn; Akkadian, "Hadad the Thunderer"), probably another name for the Canaanite storm god, Hadad. Rimmon (which means "thunderer" in Akkadian, but "pomegranate" in Hebrew) appears to have been used as another name for Hadad in Damascus (2 Kings 5:18). This observation has led to the theory that Rimmon might have been a title for the deity and Hadad the god's proper name. The construction Hadad-rimmon occurs only in Zech. 12:11, where the prophet compares the mourning to come in Jerusalem to the ritual mourning for Hadad-rimmon at Megiddo. *See also* Baal; Hadad; Ras-Shamra; Rimmon.

Hadar (hay´dahr). *See* Hadad.

Hadassah (huh-das´uh; Heb., "myrtle"), another name for Esther (Esther 2:7), probably her given Hebrew name. "Esther" is a Babylonian or Persian name meaning either "Ishtar" (a goddess) or "star," which may have been the name given her in the royal court (see 2:8–9) or a name adopted in conformity with Persian style.

Hades (hay´deez), in Greek mythology, the god of the underworld, which was the abode of the dead. By extension, Hades came to refer to the realm of the dead itself. In the LXX, the word "Hades" is used to translate Hebrew *sheol* as well as other Hebrew words and phrases that refer to "the pit," "stillness," "death," and "deep darkness." In the NT likewise, Hades appears as both a place (Acts 2:31) and a being (Rev. 6:8). As a place it is the abode of the dead (Acts 2:27, 31), identical with Sheol (since the references are actually quotes from the LXX).

The relationship between Hades and hell in NT thought has been the subject of some reflection. The concepts of Sheol, Hades, and hell all seem to overlap in the NT. In a strict sense, "Hades" (like Sheol) refers simply to a place where the dead dwell, whereas "hell" (Gk. *gehenna*) connotes a place of torment and punishment. Further, the dead enter Hades (or Sheol) immediately, while entrance to hell is reserved for those who fare poorly in a final judgment at the end of time. These distinctions, however, do not always hold up in actual NT passages. First, when Jesus curses Capernaum, his declaration that the city will be "brought down to Hades" accompanies his claim that "on the day of judgment it will be more tolerable for Sodom than for you" (Matt. 11:23; cf. Luke 10:15). Thus entering Hades is associated with being condemned at the final judgment, imagery normally associated with hell. Elsewhere, Jesus tells Peter, "On this rock I will build my church and the gates of Hades will not prevail against it" (Matt. 16:18; cf. Rev. 1:18). The meaning here is somewhat ambiguous, but the sense seems to be that the church's mission will be to release people from the dominion of death, which could fit with a traditional understanding of Hades. But in Jesus's parable of the Rich Man and Lazarus (Luke 16:19–31, esp. 16:23–24), the concepts of Hades and hell seem once again to merge. The rich man does enter Hades prior to any final judgment or general resurrection expected to occur in the last days, but he is specifically said to be tormented there, indeed to suffer agony in flames, an image strongly associated with hell. *See also* abyss; death; heaven; hell; Sheol.   A.Y.C./M.A.P.

Hadoram (huh-dor′uhm).

1 A son of Joktan, descendant of Shem (Gen. 10:27).

2 The son of Tou (Toi), king of Hamath; he was sent with gifts to congratulate David on his victory over Hadadezer (1 Chron. 18:10). He is also called Joram (2 Sam. 8:10).

3 An official of King Rehoboam (926–910 BCE) of Judah; he supervised the conscripted labor force and was stoned to death by the people of Israel (the northern kingdom) when he attempted to enforce the harsh policies of Rehoboam (2 Chron. 10:18). In 1 Kings 12:18, he is called Adoram in the Hebrew text and Adoniram in the LXX. It is possible that persons by either or both of those names mentioned elsewhere (1 Kings 4:6; 5:13–14) are the same individual called Hadoram in 2 Chron. 10:18. *See also* Adoniram; Adoram.   D.R.B.

Hagar (hay′gahr), the Egyptian slave-girl whom

Sarah gave to Abraham as a wife; she bore him Ishmael and became the matriarch of the Ishmaelites. There are two stories concerning Hagar in the Bible, both of which reveal rivalry between her and Sarah. In the first (Gen. 16:1–16) Sarai (Sarah) has borne no children and so, in accordance with custom, gives her slave to her husband so that she can bear a child to him instead. When Hagar becomes pregnant, she acts arrogantly toward Sarah; Sarah then, with Abraham's permission, deals so harshly with Hagar that she flees into the Wilderness of Shur. There she meets an angel who announces that she should return to her mistress and that she will bear a son, to be named Ishmael (Heb., "God hears"), from whom will spring many descendants. Hagar gives a name to God, whose angel spoke to her: El-roi ("God sees").

In Gen. 21:8–21 Hagar is back in Abraham's household. Some time has passed, and Hagar has given birth to Ishmael, but Sarah has also given birth to a son, Isaac. Sarah feels that Ishmael threatens Isaac's position as heir, so she urges Abraham to expel Hagar and Ishmael. Abraham acquiesces only after God assures him that he should heed Sarah, for Abraham's main line of descent is to be through Isaac, although God will also make a nation from Ishmael's descendants. Hagar is sent away into the region of Beer-sheba with some bread and water and her child. When the provisions are used up and the child's death seems imminent, she places the child under a bush and departs to weep where she will not have to "look upon the death of the child." An angel comes to her, however, assuring her that God has heard the voice of the boy and that she is to take him in her hands. The angel repeats the promise to Hagar that her child will produce a great nation. A well of water appears and Hagar gives her son water to drink. Ishmael grows up to become an archer in the Wilderness of Paran and marries an Egyptian woman.

These stories are usually interpreted as explaining that Ishmael's descendants, the people who lived in northern Arabia, south of the Israelites, were of the same lineage as the Hebrews. Some preservers of Israel's traditions and history believed it was significant to remember that, even if Israel had a special and unique covenant with God, the Ishmaelites were their neighbors and God had made promises to them as well.

Although Hagar is not mentioned outside of Genesis in the Hebrew Bible, her story is given an allegorical treatment by the apostle Paul in Gal. 4:21–31. Paul suggests that Hagar (whose offspring was Abraham's offspring, but not his heir) and Sarah (whose son is Abraham's heir) represent, respectively, a covenant based on the law and a covenant based on faith. People who trust in the covenant of the law (given by Moses on Sinai) are like the child of Hagar—they are physically descended from Abraham, but are not heirs to the promise (received only through Jesus Christ); indeed they are enslaved to the law (4:25; cf. 2:4; 5:1). But those who trust in Christ are children of a new covenant, based on faith, not works of the law—they are like Isaac, the true heirs for whom God's promises to Abraham are being fulfilled. *See also* Hagrites; Ishmaelites.   A.B./M.A.P.

Haggadah (huh-gah'duh), the interpretation of nonlegal historical and religious passages of Jewish scripture. Haggadic texts often interpret the biblical narrative by retelling and supplementing the stories contained therein. Some scholars regard the books of Chronicles as Haggadah on the earlier historical writings (1 Samuel–2 Kings). But most examples of Haggadah are found outside the Bible, in apocryphal/deuterocanonical books, the Pseudepigrapha, and the writings of such Hellenistic Jewish historians as Josephus and Philo. These books contain stories and legends about such central figures in Israel's history as Adam, Enoch, Abraham, Joseph, and Moses.

Some NT references indicate that early Christian authors were familiar with such traditions. In 2 Tim. 3:8 the names of the Egyptian sorcerers defeated by Moses are given as Jannes and Jambres—these names are not found in the book of Genesis itself and must have been derived from oral or written Haggadah (the names do appear in the *Damascus Document,* a writing found among the Dead Sea Scrolls, CD 5:18–19). Several writers refer to a tradition that the law was given by angels rather than God (Gal. 3:19; Acts 7:53; Heb. 2:2), a likely haggadic tradition not contained in the Bible itself. In 1 Cor. 10:4, Paul indicates that he believes the water-giving rock accompanied the children of Israel on their journey, a nonbiblical tradition that also appears in rabbinic tradition, drawing on oral Haggadah. Jude 9 refers to a legend that the archangel Michael and Satan struggled over the body of Moses; that story also is not found in the Bible but, according to Clement of Alexandria (150–215 CE), it was contained in a now lost Jewish work called the *Assumption of Moses. See also* Halakah.
P.P./M.A.P.

Haggai (hag'i), **book of,** the tenth part of the Book of the Twelve in the Prophets section, or Nevi'im, of the Tanakh (Jewish Bible). In the Christian OT, it is the tenth book of the Minor Prophets.

Contents: In 520 BCE, Haggai began delivering a series of four oracles, directed primarily to Zerubbabel (the governor) and Joshua (the high priest). For the past eighteen years, no progress had been made on the rebuilding of the temple, while many of the community's leaders had raised their own standard of living. There was a famine in the land and the majority of people were not prospering, but suffering. Haggai accuses the people of having poor priorities. They were looking for their own safety, security, and success, while neglecting God's dwelling place. Haggai calls Israel to look to rebuilding the temple first, insisting that until they do so, they cannot expect to have any prosperity of their own. Thus, Haggai closely connects the presence of the temple with the promise of prosperity for the people. God has no dwelling place and thus, they cannot expect God's blessing. The people respond with obedience and begin the reconstruction of the temple. The prophet proceeds to remind the people of God's promise to be

with them and that this presence is the only true guarantee of prosperity. Then the author moves into an oracle on the relationship between ritual cleanliness and the temple. Uncleanness is contagious, and without the temple everything that the people of Israel touch becomes unclean and withers. The last oracle of Haggai portrays God's defeat of kingdoms and nations, while God exalts Zerubbabel. Zerubbabel is depicted as the Lord's signet ring, which places him in the role of a medium of God's authority. Some scholars argue that this prophecy is implicitly giving Zerubbabel, a Davidic descendant, the title of king or messiah. Others argue that it simply states that Zerubbabel will rule under divine protection. All of this was prophesied between August and December of 520 BCE.

OUTLINE OF CONTENTS

Haggai

I. First oracle: the call to rebuild the temple (1:1–11)
   A. A rebuke of wrong priorities (1:1–6)
   B. Call to rebuild the temple (1:7–11)
II. Interlude: positive response of obedience (1:12–15a)
III. Second oracle: God's past and future presence (1:15b–2:9)
   A. God's presence during the exodus (1:15b–2:5)
   B. God's promise of future glory (2:6–9)
IV. Third oracle: cleanliness (2:10–19)
   A. Contagiousness of uncleanness (2:10–14)
   B. Future blessings (2:15–19)
V. Fourth oracle: God's defeat of the nations and restoration of Judah (2:20–23)
   A. Nations overthrown (2:20–22)
   B. Zerubbabel exalted (2:23)

Background: Very little is known about the prophet Haggai. His name means "festival," causing some scholars to argue that he was born at the time of a festival in the preexilic period, though most scholars think the name merely emphasizes the connection between the observance of festivals and the temple, which was central to Haggai's prophetic career. Scholars disagree over Haggai's age at the time of his prophecy. Baldwin thinks that he was most likely an elderly man who had lived through the entire exile, had seen the first temple destroyed, and vowed to see it rebuilt before his death. Others argue that he must have been quite young, since he is not included on the list of names in Ezra 2. A prophet named Haggai is mentioned in the book of Ezra (5:1–2, 6:14), however, and the majority of scholars attribute the oracles in this book to that prophet, albeit with some allowance for later editing.

The book's superscription mentions the second year of the rule of Darius I, which would place Haggai's oracles in 520 BCE. There is little argument regarding this date as the time for the situation addressed by the oracles, though many scholars date the compilation of the oracles somewhat later (possibly in 516/5 BCE along with Zech. 1–8 for the dedication of the completed temple).

Like many prophets, Haggai is viewed as an intermediary between God and the people and his oracles are directed at the leaders and nobility. Still, he differs from Amos, Micah, and Jeremiah because of his lack of skepticism concerning the value of sacrifice and ritual worship.

Themes: The major theme of Haggai is the rebuilding of the Jerusalem temple. It was the dwelling place of God and must be rebuilt. Its neglect led to famine, and its rebuilding will lead to prosperity. Many scholars connect this theme with the marked emphasis on the temple in postexilic Judaism. The Persians who funded the temple rebuilding project wanted to use this place of religious significance to solidify their political power. O'Brien argues that it was designed to become the focal point of Judean society, which would allow the Persians to use the temple to levy taxes and perform other administrative acts.

Interpretive Issues: Although most scholars hold that the majority of Haggai is original to the prophet, there is marked disagreement over how to interpret 2:10–19. Many scholars feel that the chronology and themes of that passage are difficult, suggesting the possibility of multiple sources. Gottwald argues that 2:11–14 was a separate oracle against ritual defilement that urged the Israelites not to allow the Samaritans to help rebuild the temple. Childs holds that the unity of 2:10–19 is secondary (independent oracles), but that it shows no hint of Samaritan exclusion.

Many scholars think that Haggai, while promoting the building of the second temple, ends in a failed prophecy. The prosperity and glory that was promised to Israel once it rebuilt the temple was never realized. Zerubbabel did not become king, nor were the nations overthrown. For this reason, many scholars call Haggai a failed or false prophecy based upon history. Peterson, however, argues that Haggai was a successful prophet because the temple was rebuilt as a result of his urging. O'Brien claims that the emphasis on Haggai as a prophet (1:1, 3, 12; 2:1, 10) was designed to legitimate Haggai's prophecies once the temple was built. Childs argues that one should not allow history to shape how prophecy is viewed, but let prophecy shape how history is viewed.

Bibliography

Baldwin, Joyce. *Haggai, Zechariah, Malachi.* InterVarsity, 1972.

Bandstra, Barry L. *Reading the Old Testament: Introduction to the Hebrew Bible.* 4th ed. Wadsworth, 2009.

Childs, Brevard S. *Introduction to the Old Testament as Scripture.* Fortress, 1979.

Gottwald, Norman K. *The Hebrew Bible: A Socio-Literary Introduction.* Fortress, 1985.

O'Brien, Julia M. *Nahum, Habakkuk, Zephaniah, Haggai, Zechariah, Malachi.* Abingdon, 2004.

Peterson, David L. *The Prophetic Literature: An Introduction.* Westminster John Knox, 2002.

Sweeney, Marvin A. *The Twelve Prophets.* Vol. 2, *Micah, Nahum, Habakkuk, Zephaniah, Haggai, Zechariah, Malachi.* Liturgical, 2000.

Wolff, Hans Walter. *Haggai: A Commentary.* Augsburg, 1988.   B.B.

Haggith (hag'ith; Heb., "festive"), one of David's wives and the mother of his fourth son, Adonijah (2 Sam. 3:4).

Hagiographa (hag'ee-og'ruh-fuh; Gk., "sacred writings"), another name for "the Writings," the final section of the Jewish canon, which is divided into three parts: Torah, Prophets, and Writings (Hagiographa). Jews typically use the Hebrew terms for these divisions: Torah, Nevi'im, and Ketuvim. The Hagiographa (or Writings or Ketuvim) includes the poetic/wisdom books of Psalms, Proverbs and Job, plus five books that are sometimes called the Megilloth ("five scrolls")— Song of Songs, Ruth, Lamentations, Ecclesiastes, Esther—and the historical-narrative books of Daniel, Ezra–Nehemiah, and 1 and 2 Chronicles.   F.E.G.

Hagrites (hag'rits), the name of a tribe with whom the eastern Israelite tribes of Reuben, Gad, and the eastern half-tribe of Manasseh fought and whom they eventually defeated in the time of Saul (ca. 1000 BCE). Their territory lay east of the Jordan beyond Gilead in northern Arabia (1 Chron. 5:10, 19–20). The similarity of "Hagrite" and "Hagar," the name of Sarah's slave who became the wife of Abraham and mother of Ishmael (Gen. 16:1, 15), suggests a possible connection between the Hagrites and the Ishmaelites, but that is not certain. The Hagrites are listed with the traditional enemies of Israel, including the Ishmaelites (Ps. 83:6), although Jaziz the Hagrite was the overseer of the royal flocks under David (1 Chron. 27:30), and another Hagrite may have fought with David (1 Chron. 11:38, cf. "Gadite" in 2 Sam. 23:36). *See also* Ishmaelites.   D.R.B.

hail. Usually destructive to plants, hail is connected with violent storms in the Bible (Pss. 78: 47–48; 105:32; 148:8; cf. Rev. 8:7; 11:19). It is seen as a plague (Exod. 9:18–34; 10:5–15), as divine judgment (Hag. 2:17), and as a destroying power (Isa. 28:2, 17).

hair. Knowledge about hair and hairstyles in the biblical world may sometimes be derived from references in the biblical texts themselves as well as from artwork, illustrations, and extrabiblical sources. In general, the Israelites and Canaanites seem to have favored long hair and beards

From left to right: **1.** Head of one of the Sea Peoples (Philistines) captured by Ramesses III. He is beardless and wears a tall feathered helmet; Medinet Habu, twelfth century BCE. **2.** Life-size head of the Persian king Darius. His elaborately curled beard extends to his chest, his hair is arranged in ringlets in front and hangs in a bun at the back, and his mustache is curled at the tip; Behistun, fifth century BCE. **3.** The Assyrian king Tiglath-pileser III with long flowing hair and beard; copy of a wall painting from Tell 'Ahmar, eighth century BCE. **4.** Head of a Mede with pointed beard, mustache, and hair bunched at the neck—all elaborately curled; Persepolis, fifth century BCE.

on men, in contrast to the Egyptians who often shaved their heads. By the Roman period, however, this seems to have changed, for the preference of Greeks and Romans was for shorter hair on men, who were frequently clean-shaven. Less is known about hairstyles for women, but long hair (i.e., longer than on men) seems to have been the preferences in all times and places. Isa. 18–24 mentions headbands, headdresses and "well-set hair" as marks of beauty (which are, however, associated with haughtiness). The beautiful woman described in the Song of Solomon had hair "like a flock of goats" (4:1; 6:5), an image that suggests wavy tresses cascading over her shoulders and down her chest. In terms of color, black hair was typical (cf. Matt. 5:36), but gray hair was considered to be more beautiful, a "crown of glory" attained with age as compensation for the loss of strength (Prov. 20:29; 23:7).

Several men in the Bible are known for having long hair or a prevalence of body hair. With regard to the latter, Esau's hirsuteness (Gen. 25:25; 27:11) contrasts with Jacob's smoothness and also links him phonetically with the place in which he ultimately settled: Se'ir (36:8) has the same Hebrew consonants as *se'ar,* "hair." Likewise, the prophet Elijah is identified as "a hairy man" (2 Kings 1:8), although he was apparently bald (2 Kings 2:23). Otherwise, Absalom's long, thick hair is a mark of handsomeness (2 Sam. 14:26), but it also figures in his death—he gets caught by the "head" in a terebinth tree while fleeing opponents in a battle (2 Sam. 18:9). Samson's long hair was the source of his strength: when it was shaved, he became helpless (Judg. 16:17), but when it grew back (16:22), he was able to pull the temple of Dagon down upon the Philistines.

The cutting or treatment of hair was sometimes linked to religious rituals or legislation. Samson had long hair because he was a Nazirite (Judg. 13:5). Nazirites' vows included an injunction that they would not shave or cut their hair (Num. 6:5; cf. 1 Sam. 1:11); once the vow was fulfilled, or if a Nazirite was inadvertently defiled through contact

with a corpse, the head would be shaved and the hair offered as a sacrifice (Num. 6:9–18; cf. Acts 18:18 for an instance in which the apostle Paul has taken a similar vow). Shaving of the body was part of the purification of Levites (Num. 8:5–7), but a priest was not to make his head bald or shave the corners of his beard (Lev. 21:5). Priests in Ezekiel's description of the temple were not to shave their heads or let their hair grow long (44:20). According to another priestly rule, lay Israelites were forbidden to cut the hair of their temples or beard (Lev. 19:27). Shaving was also connected with the diagnosis and treatment of leprosy (Lev. 13:33; 14:8–9).

Disheveled hair was a sign of public shame. Thus the leper's hair was loosened (Lev. 13:45), as was the hair of a woman accused of infidelity (Num. 5:18); a priest's hair could not be let loose (Lev. 21:10; cf. 10:6). Shaving one's head, by contrast, was a sign of mourning (Job 1:20; Isa. 15:2; Jer. 41:5; 47:5; 48:37; Ezek. 7:18; Amos 8:10). When the Israelites captured women in battle, they were commanded to shave the heads of those women, and thus allow them to mourn the loss of their families (Deut. 21:12–13). Pulling out a person's hair was an acceptable means of coercive punishment (Neh. 13:25); to pull out one's own hair could be a sign that one was truly appalled by something (Ezra 9:3).

In the NT, two women show devotion to Jesus by wiping his feet with their hair (Luke 7:38; John 12:3). The apostle Paul argues for the appropriateness of veils for women by comparing an unveiled woman to a woman who has had her hair cut, something that he can assume his readers would regard as disgraceful and degrading (1 Cor. 11:6). He continues by saying, "Does not nature itself teach you that if a man wears long hair, it is degrading to him, but if a woman has long hair, it is her glory? For her hair is given to her for a covering" (11:14–15). Here, Paul seems to associate a woman's long hair with her being under the authority and protection of a man. Elsewhere in the NT, women are discouraged from braiding their hair, a practice associated with vanity and misplaced values that prioritize outward adornment over the cultivation of inner spiritual beauty (1 Tim. 2:9; 1 Pet. 3:3).

One from whose head not one hair shall fall is one who is safe from harm (1 Sam. 14:45; 2 Sam. 14:11; 1 Kings 1:52; cf. Luke 21:18; Acts 27:34). The hairs of the head may be used to represent a large number (Pss. 40:13; 69:5); that their number is known to God is a sign of God's meticulous concern for every person (Matt. 10:30; Luke 12:7). The fact that one cannot change one's hair color exemplifies human limitation or the inability for people to determine outcomes, which Jesus cites as his rationale for prohibiting the swearing of oaths (Matt. 5:36).   A.B./M.A.P.

Hakeldama (huh-kel′duh-muh; "field of blood"), the Aramaic name given in Acts 1:18–19 for the field that Judas Iscariot is said to have purchased with the money he received for betraying Jesus. The name of the field is said to derive from the gory death that Judas suffered there. In a different account, Matthew's Gospel says that the field was purchased by the chief priests of Jerusalem with the money that Judas had returned to them—and that it came to be called the "Field of Blood," because it was bought with blood money (cf. Matt. 27:3–10). *See also* Judas; potter's field.

Hakkoz (hak′oz; Heb., "the thorn"; possibly also Koz, Accos).

1 The seventh priest chosen by lot in David's time, reported in postexilic records (1 Chron. 24:10).

2 The ancestor of some postexilic priests who could not prove their Israelite ancestry (Ezra 2:61; Neh. 7:63).

3 The grandfather of Meremoth who made repairs near the Fish Gate in rebuilding Jerusalem (Neh. 3:4, 21). He is possibly the same person as **2**.

Halah (hay′luh), a region in Assyria to which Israelite exiles were deported by the triumphant Assyrian kings (Pul, Tilgath-pilneser, 1 Chron. 5:26) who overthrew Samaria in 722/1 BCE (2 Kings 17:6; 18.11; Obad. 20). Its exact location in Mesopotamia is still a matter of dispute among scholars, though a location in the north, near Nineveh, seems most likely.

Halakah (hah-lah-kah′; from Heb. *halak*, "to walk, go, follow"), in Jewish tradition, the teaching one is to follow or the rules or statutes that are to guide a person's life. Halakah and Haggadah are often cited as two modes of midrash (biblical interpretation). Halakah focuses on commandments and legislation for life, while Haggadah focuses on the meaning and significance of narrative material. Halakah is concerned with clarifying ambiguities and discerning contemporary relevance and application of texts intended for an ancient context. Examples of halakic debate between Jesus and the Pharisees are found in such NT passages as the story of plucking grain on the sabbath (Matt. 12:1–8), the healing of the man with the withered hand (Matt. 12:9–12), and Jesus's teaching about divorce (Matt. 19:1–9). *See also* Haggadah.   P.P.

hallel (hal′el; Heb., "praise"), a litany of praise. Certain psalms are specified as Hallel Psalms and are specified for liturgical use on certain occasions. Pss. 113–18 make up the "Egyptian Hallel" used for the Festival of Tabernacles, the Festival of Dedication (Hanukkah), and the first day of Passover. At the Passover, it is sung in two parts, Pss. 113–14 before the seder and Pss. 115–18 after. This may have been the "hymn" that Jesus and his disciples are said to have sung at the Last Supper (Matt. 26:30; Mark 14:26). Ps. 136 is called the "Great Hallel" and is used in morning prayers on the sabbath and at numerous festivals. Pss. 146–50 also make up a Hallel that is used in the synagogues. *See* hallelujah; Psalms, book of.

hallelujah (hal′uh-loo′yuh; Heb., "praise the LORD"). In the Bible, the word "hallelujah" occurs only in Psalms and Revelation. It is used twenty-three times in Pss. 104–50 as the introduction or conclusion of a psalm. Both the LXX and Vulgate transliterate the word rather than translate it. The author of Revelation likewise uses a Greek transliteration of the Hebrew word in describing the praises of God in heaven (19:1–6; cf. Tob. 13:17). Curiously, the NRSV renders the word as "Praise the LORD!" in the OT, but as "Hallelujah" in the NT. The term probably arose as a liturgical exhortation, used to encourage congregational participation in worship. Later, it seems to have become a stereotypical cry of joy; the Jews of Alexandria sang "Hallelujah!" after being saved from annihilation by the Egyptians (3 Macc. 7:13).   M.Z.B.

hallow, to make holy or to set apart for special service. In the Bible, the term translates a form of the Hebrew word *qadesh*, the primary meaning of which is "separation" or "setting apart." In its various forms this Hebrew word is also translated as "holy," "holiness," "consecrate," "sanctify," "dedicate," or "purify." Thus, a "hallowed thing" was something set apart for a special use or purpose: the sabbath is a day hallowed by God (Gen. 2:3; cf. Ezek. 20:20; Sir. 33:9; 2 Macc. 15:2); the altar in the tent of meeting is hallowed for sacred purposes only; and Israel is told to hallow the jubilee year (Lev. 25:10). Jesus applies the term to God's name in the Lord's Prayer (Matt. 6:9; Luke 11:2), indicating the sanctity of that name, which is therefore deserving of special reverence. *See also* holiness; sanctification.   D.R.B./M.A.P.

Ham.

1 In Gen. 5–10, Noah's second son (between Shem and Japheth) and the father of Cush, Egypt, Put, and Canaan. Ham was rescued from the flood aboard the ark Noah built and, afterward, received God's blessing (Gen. 9:1). Some days later, however, Ham "saw the nakedness of his father" when Noah, drunk, lay uncovered in his tent. It is widely believed (though not absolutely certain) that the phrase "saw the nakedness of his father" is a euphemism signifying that Ham performed a sexual act on his father (cf. Lev. 18:7–19; 20:11–21). Shem and Japheth, by contrast, show respect for Noah by walking backward into the tent (so as not to see him) and covering him. When Noah awakes and realizes what Ham has done, he pronounces a curse upon Ham's son Canaan, indicating that Canaanites will be slaves of Noah's descendants through Shem and Japheth. Within the Bible, this story serves to legitimate Israel's domination of the Canaanites. In the history of Western Christianity, the curse on Canaan was often misinterpreted to legitimate the African slave trade.

2 A city of the Zuzim in Transjordan (Gen. 14:5).

Haman (hay'muhn), the villain in the book of Esther. He is called "Haman, son of Hammedatha the Agagite, the enemy of the Jews" (Esther 3:10). His primary opponent is a Jew named Mordecai, who is identified as being in the line of Kish (2:5). Thus, their enmity was prefigured by that of Agag and Saul (son of Kish) in 1 Sam. 15. In the Esther narrative, Haman has been appointed prime minister by the Persian ruler Ahasuerus, and he comes into conflict with Mordecai when the latter refuses to bow down to him. Encouraged by his wife Zeresh (Esther 5:10, 14; 6:13), Haman plots to have Mordecai hanged and to destroy all Jews. Rather than tell the king this outright, however, he manipulates Ahasuerus by claiming that "a certain people" in the kingdom do not keep the king's laws (3:8). Mordecai, however, has a relative, Esther, who belongs to the king's harem. Through some subtle maneuvering on the part of Mordecai and Esther, Haman is first humiliated by being forced to honor Mordecai publicly, leading him through the city, robed and crowned, on a horse only the king had ridden. Then, in a second and more serious phase of the story, the tables are completely turned on Haman, and he is hanged on the very gallows that he had erected for Mordecai; Mordecai then assumes Haman's office and estate. Haman's ten sons are also killed by the Jews and subsequently hanged on the gallows as a warning to others who might seek to attack Jews (9:6–14). *See also* Esther, book of; Mordecai; Purim, Festival of.   W.L.H./M.A.P.

Hamath (hay'math), a city (modern Hama) on the Orontes River in Syria between Damascus and Aleppo; it also designated the district of which Hamath was the capital. Excavations have shown that the city has been inhabited almost continually from the Neolithic period (ca. 8000 BCE) to the present. Because of its strategic location and political importance, it is mentioned frequently in extrabiblical sources (including a number found at Hamath itself) beginning in the first millennium as well as in the Bible. The first known

ruler of Hamath was King Toi, who is mentioned in 2 Sam. 8:9 as sending gifts to David after the latter's victory over Zobah. According to 2 Chron. 8:3–4 Solomon captured Hamath-zobah and built store-cities in Hamath. According to 2 Kings 14:28, Jeroboam "recovered for Israel Damascus and Hamath, which had belonged to Judah." Later, inhabitants of Hamath were deported to Samaria after its capture by the Assyrians (2 Kings 17:24) and, apparently, Israelites were exiled to Hamath (Isa. 11:11). This period is documented in Assyrian annals, where Sargon II (ca. 722–705 BCE) describes himself as the "destroyer of Hamath." The name Lebo-hamath refers to a town (modern Lebweh) within the jurisdiction of Hamath, but considerably to the south of the city of Hamath. *See also* Lebo-hamath; Zobah.   M.D.C.

Hammath (ham'ath).

1 A town on the west shore of the Sea of Galilee, a mile south of Tiberias, where there are hot springs. It was part of Naphtali (Josh. 19:35) and is perhaps the same site called Hammoth-dor (Josh. 21:32) and Hammon (1 Chron. 6:76). These springs were the earliest known thermal baths in the Near East; Herod Antipas is known to have made use of them.

2 The proper name of the father of the house of Rechab (1 Chron. 2:55).

Hammedatha (ham'uh-day'thuh), the father of Haman, the Persian official of King Ahasuerus who attempted to exterminate the Jews (early fifth century BCE; Esther 3:1; 8:5).

hammer. Archaeological excavations have found stone hammers from the earliest time of Israelite settlement: they consist of a simple stone or rock with a hole bored for a wood handle. In the building of Solomon's temple, however, iron hammers were used (1 Kings 6:7). Hammered gold was used for the mercy seat and other items featured in the tabernacle (Exod. 25:18, 31, 36). Elsewhere, hammers are used for stonecutting (1 Kings 6:7), jewel working (Isa. 41:7), woodworking (Jer. 10:4), and breaking rocks (Jer. 23:29). In Judg. 4:21, Jael uses a hammer to drive a tent peg into the temple of Sisera, killing him. A hammer can be a symbol of power (Jer. 51:20); when broken, it becomes a figure for helplessness or weakness (50:23). The Jewish rebels who instituted the Hasmonean line were called "the Maccabees" probably through a play on the Hebrew word for "hammer" (*maqqebet*).

Hammon (ham'uhn).

1 An Asherite town (Josh. 19:28), probably modern Umm el-'Awamid near the Mediterranean coast fifteen miles north of Acco.

2 A yet unidentified levitical town of the Gershomites (1 Chron. 6:76) in Naphtali, possibly the same place elsewhere called Hammath (Josh. 19:35) or Hammoth-Dor (Josh. 21:32)

Hammoth-dor (ham'uhht-dor). *See* Hammath.

Hammurabi (ham´uh-rah´bee; also Hammurapi), the most famous member of the first dynasty of Babylon. The members of the dynasty were of Amorite lineage. Under this Old Babylonian dynasty (1894–1595 BCE) the once unimportant city of Babylon became a major center for the first time and started taking on the appearance of a national capital. Hammurabi ruled for forty-three years (1792–1750 BCE) and eventually unified the country under the rule of Babylon. Though his military and diplomatic achievements do not seem to have lasted much beyond his reign, he transformed a small city-state into a large territorial state, created the prototype or even the pattern of the country of Babylonia with its capital in Babylon, and shifted the balance of activity and power to the north. Babylon now began to gain the power and prestige that allowed it to eclipse the southern centers as well as Nippur; in later periods of Assyrian domination, the Assyrian conquerors found themselves compelled to work out various plans of accommodation with the city and the political, cultural, and religious forces that it came to represent.

Hammurabi's activities and times are known to us from year names, royal inscriptions, administrative and legal texts, literary texts, and, most of all, numerous letters and the famous "Code of Hammurabi." The letters and the code have become the standard for what is now treated as the classic form of the Akkadian language.

Letters from Mari provide information regarding diplomatic and political events; letters from such centers as Larsa reveal the intricacies of local administration under Hammurabi. He seems to have devoted much attention and energy to administrative and judicial details. His style of government was similar to that of other successful contemporaries. His involvement in the execution of justice and matters of routine administration seems to indicate a concern for an effective and just governance and for the public perception of such concern. His concerns conform to and continue the earlier tradition and ideal of the king as the one responsible for the peace, well-being, and justice of the land and its inhabitants.

Hammurabi's concern for justice finds its finest expression in what is the single most important document of his period, the Code of Hammurabi. Written near the end of his reign, the code is attested on stelae and tablets from the Old Babylonian and later periods. The most important witness is the stele found in Susa, where it had been moved by Elamites in the twelfth century BCE. The code consists of a prologue that catalogues Hammurabi's conquests of the various cities and his care of their cults, 282 paragraphs—the paragraph divisions are modern—presenting the laws in casuistic or case form, and an epilogue emphasizing the significance of this promulgation of justice. The term "code," however, is something of a misnomer; the document is neither a code in the usual sense of the word nor even a collection of actual laws. The format of the document derives from what are called "misharum edicts" promul-

Hammurabi (*left*), king of Babylon (1792–1750 BCE), worships the god Shamash; detail from the upper part of Hammurabi's stele found at Susa. (A full view is included with the color photographs.)

gated at the beginning of a ruler's reign to alleviate distress and create a new socioeconomic balance (e.g., through adjustment of prices and wages or remission of debts and obligations). Still, the Code of Hammurabi is a literary document whose publication was intended to mark Hammurabi as a good shepherd of his people and a model of a just king, for his generation and for generations to come. In part, the text takes the form of a royal inscription encasing laws rather than campaigns. Incorporating misharum materials as well as legal formulations of earlier collections, the code may perhaps also include examples of customary law, outstanding precedents, and innovations.

Most of all, however, the Code of Hammurabi is a work of legal and literary scholarship. It is fuller and more elegantly articulated and arranged than earlier texts, a monument to the legal speculation of the period. Scribal scholarship is here seen at work: the legal mind behind the text plays out various possibilities, including theoretical and/or unlikely scenarios that present logical alternatives to previously stipulated rulings in order to explore, exemplify, and even invent principles. The code is not binding and does not necessarily reflect actual practice; it is, however, a literary and intellectual construct that gives expression to legal thinking and moral values. The importance of the Code of Hammurabi for the interpretation of such biblical collections as the Covenant Code (Exod. 21–23) can hardly be exaggerated. *See also* Babylon.

Bibliography

Abusch, Tzvi. "'He Should Continue to Bear the Penalty of That Case': Some Observations on *Codex Hammurabi* parags. 3–4 and parag. 13." In *From Ancient Israel to Modern Judaism: Essays in Honor of Marvin Fox.* Scholars, 1989. Pp. 77–96.

Driver, G. R., and John C. Miles. *The Babylonian Laws.* Vols. 1–2. Clarendon, 1952–55.

Frayne, Douglas. *Old Babylonian Period (2013–1595 BC).* University of Toronto Press, 1990.

Roth, Martha T., Harry Hoffner, and Piotr Michalowski. *Law Collections from Mesopotamia and Asia Minor.* 2nd ed. Scholars, 1997.

Van de Mieroop, Marc. *King Hammurabi of Babylon: A Biography.* Blackwell, 2005.

Wright, David P. *Inventing God's Law: How the Covenant Code of the Bible Used and Revised the Laws of Hammurabi.* Oxford University Press, 2009.   I.T.A.

Hamor (hay'mor), the Hivite ruler of Shechem (Gen. 34:2) from whom Jacob bought a piece of land (Gen. 33:19) where Joseph's remains would later be buried (Josh. 24:32; cf. Acts 7:16). Trouble arose when Hamor's son Shechem raped Dinah, the daughter of Jacob and Leah, and then wanted her for a wife. Hamor appealed to Jacob, offering to pay any bride-price for her. Jacob's sons acted deceitfully, saying they would approve the marriage if all the men of Shechem were circumcised. Hamor advocated for this, telling his people, "These people are friendly with us; let them live in the land and trade in it, for the land is large enough for them; let us take their daughters in marriage, and let us give them our daughters. . . . Let us agree with them, and they will live among us" (Gen. 34:21–23). The men of Shechem took Hamor's advice and Dinah's brothers avenged her rape by killing Hamor, his son Shechem, and the other men while they were recovering from being circumcised. Centuries later, the story was recalled by Judith in her prayer for God's help against the Assyrians (Jth. 9:1–4).

hamstring, to cut the tarsal joint tendons, preventing an animal from being able to walk (Josh. 11:6, 9; 2 Sam. 8:4; 1 Chron. 18:4).

Hamul (hay'muhl; Heb., "spared"), the son of Perez and grandson of Judah (Gen. 46:12); he was the head of the Hamulites (Num. 26:21).

Hanamel (han'uh-mel), the son of Shallum and the cousin of the prophet Jeremiah. Hanamel sold a field to Jeremiah. Its purchase at the time the Babylonians were laying siege to Jerusalem (ca. 588 BCE) became a symbol to Jeremiah of God's promised restoration of Israel (32:7–15).

Hanan (hay'nuhn).

1 One of David's warriors (1 Chron. 11:43).

2 A Benjaminite who was the son of Shashak (1 Chron. 8:23).

3 A descendant of Saul who was the son of Azel (1 Chron. 8:38; 9:44).

4 The head of a prophetic guild in the time of Jeremiah (Jer. 35:4).

5 The head of one of the families of "temple servants" after the exile (Ezra 2:49; Neh. 7:49).

6 A Levite who interpreted the law (Neh. 8:7) and signed Ezra's covenant-renewal document (Neh. 10:10).

7 The assistant to the levitical temple treasurers appointed by Nehemiah (Neh. 13:13).

8–9 Two of "the chiefs of the people" who signed Ezra's covenant-renewal document (Neh. 10:22, 26).

Some of the individuals listed in 5–9 could be the same persons.   P.K.M.

Hananel (han'uh-nel; Heb., "God is gracious"), a tower repaired by Nehemiah (Neh. 3:1; 12:39) in the north wall around Jerusalem near the northeast corner (Jer. 31:38; Zech. 14:10). It flanked an approach to the temple and is named for an unknown person.

Hanani (huh-nay'ni; a shortened form of Hananiah; Heb., "the LORD has favored me").

1 A musician, the son of Heman, a contemporary of David (1 Chron. 25:4).

2 A prophet who rebuked the Judean kings Asa (2 Chron. 16:7) and Jehoshaphat (2 Chron. 19:2) and whose son Jehu rebuked the northern king Baasha (1 Kings 16:1).

3 A postexilic priest who divorced his non-Israelite wife in response to Ezra's proclamation (Ezra 10:20).

4 Nehemiah's brother or relative (Neh. 1:2).

5 A musician who helped Nehemiah restore Jerusalem's wall (Neh. 12:36).   M.Z.B.

Hananiah (han'uh-ni'uh; Heb., "the LORD has favored me").

1 The son of Azur, who died for falsely prophesying against Jeremiah (Jer. 28).

2 One of Daniel's three friends, also called Shadrach, who was miraculously saved from the fiery furnace (Dan. 1–3). He was given the name Shadrach by the palace master or chief eunuch serving King Nebuchadnezzar. *See also* Shadrach.

hand (Heb. *yad;* Gk. *cheir*). The word "hand" occurs approximately fifteen hundred times in the Bible, sometimes with metaphorical or figurative meaning. Offering one's hand indicates acceptance, sincerity, and a willingness to help (2 Kings 10:15; cf. Gal. 2:9). Conversely, the hand can be an instrument for murder (Gen. 4:11) or retaliation (Exod. 21:24; Deut. 25:11). The hand's ability to seize, control, or manipulate explains its association with strength or power. When Job is placed in Satan's hand, he is put in his domain and under his authority (Job 2:6; cf. Jer. 22:3; Matt. 26:45). The hand's equation with power or strength helps explain Hebrew passages that are literally translated "the hand of the tongue" (Prov. 18:21;

NRSV: "power of the tongue"). Likewise, "to raise the hand" signifies revolutionary uprising (1 Kings 11:26). The hand of God, therefore, symbolizes God's sovereign power (Deut. 3:24; Job 19:21; Heb. 10:31; 1 Pet. 5:6). God's hand governs the forces of history (Exod. 13:3, 14; 1 Sam. 5:9; Ps. 8:7) and strengthens believers (Mark 6:2; Acts 5:12). The NT places Jesus at the right hand of God, the side of authority and power (Mark 12:36; Acts 2:25; Heb. 1:3; cf. Ps. 110:1, 5; Dan. 7:13). As a ritual the "laying on of hands" occurs frequently with reference to sacrifices (Lev. 16; Num. 8) and also in rites of ordination (Num. 27:18; Deut. 34:9; 1 Tim. 4:14). It may likewise impart a blessing (Gen. 48:18; Isa. 44:3; Matt. 19:13) and, in the NT, it is closely connected with healing, indicating a transference of spiritual and physical wholeness (Mark 1:31; 5:23; Luke 13:13). To eat with "defiled hands" is to partake of food without first performing a ritual act of purification (Mark 7:1–5); in a similar way, a symbolic washing of hands may symbolize innocence (Deut. 21:6; Matt. 27:24). Uplifted hands signify worship (1 Kings 8:22, 54; 1 Tim. 2:8), and the clapping of hands is a form of praise (Ps. 47:1).   D.R.E.

handkerchief, a small piece of cloth used during the Roman period for wiping the face or hands. Several examples in the NT show that the cloth could serve other functions as well. In Luke 19:20, this word is used for a cloth in which money is stored (NRSV: "piece of cloth"). In John 11:44 and 20:7, the same word refers to a cloth that is placed over the face of a dead person. In a different vein, handkerchiefs that had come into contact with Paul were said to have healing power (Acts 19:11–12).   J.M.E.

hanging. In the Bible, hanging is not normally a method of execution; rather, people who have been previously executed are hung after death as a display that renders them disgraced or accursed (cf. Deut. 21:22–23; Gal. 3:10–14). This was permitted, with a proviso that the corpse be taken down before evening to avoid contaminating the land (cf. the removal of Jesus from the cross, Matt. 27:57). Thus Joshua hangs the corpse of the king of Ai (Josh. 8:29) and of the five anti-Gibeonite kings (Josh. 10:26), and David hangs the corpses of Rechab and Baanah (2 Sam. 4:12). The custom was also known among the Egyptians, for Joseph predicted that Pharaoh would hang the baker (Gen. 40:19). It was also practiced by the Philistines (1 Sam. 31:10), although here, since the body is hung on a wall rather than on a tree, it might have been impaled. Likewise, the bodies of Saul's sons are hung on a mountain by the Gibeonites (2 Sam. 21:10–14; NRSV: "impaled"). In the book of Esther, there is frequent reference to bodies being hung on a gallows (2:23; 5:14; 7:9, 10; 9:13–14); this could mean either hung by a rope or impaled on spikes, but it is clear that the ten sons of Haman that were hung on the gallows were already dead (9:7–14). It is only in the Hellenistic period that hanging comes up as a way of executing those who are still alive, and then the practice is not hanging by the neck to produce a quick death, but hanging by limbs so that the person might die slowly. This is the essence of crucifixion, for which "hanging" is sometimes a synonym (cf. Luke 23:39). That Jesus was impaled on a cross with nails rather than tied with ropes (as was also done) is derived mainly from John 20:25 (which mentions nail marks in the hands of the risen Christ; cf. Luke 24:40). The only references in the Bible to hanging as a means of producing a quick death are those in which it is associated with suicide. In Tobit, Sarah, the daughter of Raguel, considers hanging herself in shame over having had seven husbands and still no offspring. In Matthew's Gospel, Judas Iscariot regrets his betrayal of Jesus and hangs himself (27:5).   T.S.F./M.A.P.

hangings, the usual translation of a Hebrew term for the fabric forming the walls of the tabernacle court (Exod. 27:9–18; 35:9; 38:12–18; 39:40). Stretched along the perimeter of the 100-by-50-cubit enclosure (about 150 by 75 feet), the hangings were attached at intervals to pillars 5 cubits (about 7.5 feet) in height. Additional hangings flanked the courtyard gate. Like the material enclosing the tabernacle itself and that of the embroidered "screens" (NRSV) at the door of the tent and at the courtyard gate, the hangings were made of a fine-twined linen (Heb. *shesh*) which suggests an Egyptian origin; but the brilliant colors (blue, purple, and scarlet) of the hangings are more in keeping with what was typical of the Syro-Mesopotamian world. Esther 1:6 also describes blue hangings at the Persian court, adorning the royal garden for a magnificent banquet. *See also* tabernacle.   C.L.M.

Hannah (han'uh; Heb., "grace"), the wife of Elkanah and mother of the prophet Samuel (1 Sam. 1:2, 20). Hannah was the first of Elkanah's two wives and, though she was his favorite, she was childless. Her jealous co-wife Peninnah had borne many children and made her life miserable (1:2–8). On an annual pilgrimage to God's shrine at Shiloh, Hannah vowed that if she bore a son, she would dedicate him to God as a Nazirite (1:9–11). As she was praying, the priest Eli mistakenly thought that she was drunk and initially accused her of making a spectacle of herself; she assured him that she had been pouring out her soul, speaking out of anxiety and great vexation (1:12–18). A short time later God remembered Hannah. She bore a son and named him Samuel; when he was weaned, she fulfilled her vow and brought him to Shiloh to stay with Eli. Hannah later bore three more sons and two daughters (2:21). To Hannah is attributed a prayer (2:1–10), the words of which constitute a song of praise to God, who metes out justice to all the world in accordance with his unique wisdom: abasement of the mighty and exaltation of the lowly. God alone dispenses death and life; God's enemies are doomed, but God's faithful ones are protected. The theme of this song, the reversal of human fortunes, is encountered in other psalms and in wisdom literature (e.g., Ps. 113:5–9; Eccles. 10:5–7). The song of Hannah may have provided inspiration for the Magnificat, attributed to Mary (Luke 1:46–55; esp. vv. 51–53).   S.G./M.A.P.

Hanoch (hay'nok).

1 The son of Midian and grandson of Keturah and Abraham (Gen. 25:4; 1 Chron. 1:33).

2 The son of Reuben who went with Jacob to Egypt (Gen. 46:9; Exod. 6:14).

3 The head of the Hanochites, who left Egypt with Moses (Num. 26:5).

Hanukkah. *See* Dedication, Festival of.

Hanun (hay'nuhn; Heb., "gracious").

1 An Ammonite king whose insult to David's servants led to war and defeat resulting in slavery (2 Sam. 10:1–19; 1 Chron. 19:1–19; 2 Sam. 11:1; 12:26–31). Hanun was the son and successor of Nahash, who David believed had dealt loyally with him. Thus, when Nahash died, David sent envoys to express condolences and establish relations with Hanun. The latter, however, suspected the envoys of being spies. He shaved off half their beards, cut off half their garments, and sent them back to David humiliated. In the ensuing war, Hanun was defeated and the Ammonites were forced into slavery.

2 A man of Zanoah who repaired the Jerusalem city wall and gate (Neh. 3:13, 30).

Hapiru (hah-pee'roo), a term meaning "outcast," once thought to be the source of the word "Hebrew." It is sometimes also written as Apiru, Habiru, Khabiru, or Khapiru. The word "hapiru" appears as a pejorative social term in cuneiform texts from the Ur III period (end of the third millennium BCE) through the Late Bronze Age. These hapiru are variously described as outlaws, displaced persons, and renegades. They appear to have been from many races and ethnic groups, and they had no tribal social organization. At Nuzi on the Tigris, the hapiru are said to have sold themselves into servitude. In the Hittite Empire and elsewhere they are said to have been mercenaries or hired troops. The hapiru often sought refuge in hilly regions away from the urban Canaanite centers, and they were recruited by Canaanite leaders who were seeking to seize neighboring territories. The dynastic state of Amurru is said to have been founded with the help of hapiru troops. According to the Amarna tablets (fourteenth century BCE), Lab'ayu and his sons, rulers of Shechem, used hapiru when trying to conquer the principal towns on the main caravan route. Many theories have been promulgated that would view the hapiru as proto-Israelites, thus establishing extrabiblical references to the people of the Bible prior to the postexodus settlement of Israelites in Canaan. First, some scholars have attempted to

show that the word "Hebrew" (*'ibri*) could derive from *'apiru*. Though this is not impossible, it now seems less likely than was once thought. Second, some scholars have noted that the word "Hebrew" in the Bible is often applied to the Israelites by other people, in contexts where they might have been regarded by those people as displaced persons or renegades. Recent scholarship, however, has moved increasingly away from such connections. *See also* Hebrews.   A.F.R./M.A.P

Haran (hair'uhn).

1 The son of Terah and brother of Abraham and Nahor. He was the father of Lot and also had two daughters, Milcah and Iscah (Gen. 11:27–29). He died in the Chaldean city of Ur.

2 A city located in northern Mesopotamia about sixty miles above the confluence of the Balikh and Euphrates rivers. Haran was an important center of religious and political activity for the Hurrians, who dominated this region in the middle of the second millennium BCE. The city is well attested in the archives from Nuzi, which provide an ample picture of Hurrian life at this time. In the Bible, Haran figures prominently in the narratives of Israel's ancestors. Terah, Abraham's father, takes his household to Haran after leaving Ur of the Chaldees (Gen. 11:31–32) and he dies in Haran. Abram (i.e., Abraham) is living in Haran when he receives the call from God to depart and go to Canaan (Gen. 12:1). He does so, taking with him a sizable household and considerable wealth, amassed while in Haran (12:4–5). Notably, a number of personal names of Abram's relatives are also names of cities or towns in the region of Haran: Peleg, a distant ancestor (11:18); Serug, Abram's great-grandfather; Nahor, his grandfather and his brother; and Terah, his father (11:22–29). And, of course, Abram's brother is named Haran (see **1** above). Later, Abraham sends his servant back to the region of Haran to procure a wife for his son Isaac (24:10). Still later, Abraham's grandson Jacob is instructed by Rebekah to return to Haran as a place of refuge following his appropriation of Esau's birthright (27:43; 28:10). Thus, it is in Haran that the sons of Jacob who become the eponymous ancestors of Israel's tribes are all born.

Haran became an important commercial center in the first millennium BCE (cf. Ezek. 27:23). During the time of the Assyrian Empire, the governor of Haran was a powerful official. He was the commander-in-chief of the Assyrian forces and was appointed by the king; indeed, the city may have been the king's residence in the last decades of Assyrian rule. Following the fall of Nineveh in 612 BCE, Assyrians fled to Haran for refuge. In spite of support from the advancing forces of Pharaoh Neco, however, the Assyrians, under Ashuruballit (611–610 BCE), were unable to stave off the attack from a coalition of Medes, Scyths, and Babylonians, who were under the leadership of Nabopolassar. The destruction of Haran by this coalition is mentioned in 2 Kings 19:12.

Haran was an important center for the worship of the moon god, Sin. Two dedicatory stelae report the rebuilding of the Sin temple, Ehulhul, by Nabonidus (555–539 BCE), the last native Babylonian king. This follows Nabonidus's ten-year absence from Babylon, reported in these stelae, at the command of Sin after the god decimated the populations of urban centers that had sinned against him. At the order of Sin, Nabonidus installed the cult figures of Sin and other lunar deities in Haran on a permanent dais. The biographical text of Adad-guppi, Nabonidus's mother, reports how Sin abandoned Haran. Her report includes a record of her devotion to the moon god's cult, in spite of his decline, and of her procurement for Nabonidus of the right and distinction to return Ehulhul to its former glory and to restore the cult images to their proper places.

The biblical association of Haran with Ur of the Chaldees has also fueled scholarly debate about the actual location of Ur. Some locate Ur in the region of Haran, arguing that the site traditionally identified as Ur in southern Mesopotamia did not become a Chaldean outpost until the late first millennium BCE, long after the time of Abraham, and that it is too far from Haran for the ease of movement from Ur to Haran described in Genesis. However, as an important urban center in Sumerian times, Ur in southern Mesopotamia was the center for worship of the moon god. Its ziggurat (temple with each higher level stepped in from the lower) to the moon god was built at the end of the third millennium BCE. The destruction of Ur by the Elamites in the early second millennium BCE could have provided impetus for Terah's departure for Haran around this time along an established trade route. All of these arguments, of course, assume a historical core for the ancestral narratives that many scholars are reluctant to recognize. *See also* Abraham; Ur.   L.E.P.

Hararite (hair′uh-rit), the name of either a family group or a place from which some of David's elite guard ("the Thirty") came: Shammah, third of the three closest of David's bodyguards (2 Sam. 23:11); Jonathan, son of Shammah (23:33), and Ahiam, son of Sharar (23:33). These last two are probably identical to the persons the Chronicler calls Jonathan, son of Shagee, and Ahiam, son of Sachar (1 Chron. 11:34–35).

hare, any herbivorous rodent of the family Leporidae. Two varieties are especially attested in the Near East: the *Lepus syriacus,* which inhabits wooded areas, especially in the Esdraelon Valley, and the *Lepus aegyptus,* a smaller, sandy-colored animal found in the Negev and the Jordan Valley. The hare is classified as unclean because "even though it chews the cud, it does not have divided hoofs" (Lev. 11:6; Deut. 14:7). Hares are not actually ruminants (i.e., they do not literally "chew the cud"), but they do exhibit an excessive chewing behavior, which (along with not having split

hoofs) apparently qualified them for the list of prohibited animals.

Harim (hair′im; Heb., "consecrated" or "dedicated").
1 A priest, descendant of Aaron and head of a major line of priests (1 Chron. 24:8). Any of the following could belong to this line.
2 The ancestor of a family group who returned from the Babylonian exile with Zerubbabel (Ezra 2:32); eight members of this family group divorced their foreign wives in response to Ezra's proclamation (10:31).
3 The ancestor of another, larger, family group who returned from the exile with Zerubbabel (Ezra 2:39); five members of this family group divorced their foreign wives in response to Ezra's proclamation (10:21). The group headed by Adna could be this group or 2 above (Neh. 12:15).
4 A member of the postexilic community who signed Ezra's covenant to keep the law (Neh. 10:5).
5 A leader of the people who also signed Ezra's covenant to keep the law (Neh. 10:27).
6 The father (or perhaps ancestor) of Malchijah, one who helped repair the walls of postexilic Jerusalem (Neh. 3:11). He could be either 4 or 5 above, or the designation of Malchijah as a "son of Harim" may simply indicate that he belonged to one of the family groups associated with 2 or 3.   D.R.B.

harlot. *See* prostitute.

Harmagedon. *See* Armageddon.

Harod (hair′uhd).
1 A rushing, copious spring (modern 'Ain Jalud), on the northwest spur of Mount Gilboa where the Jezreel Plain narrows to run down to Beth-shan and the Jordan—a crucial military location. Here Gideon's militia camped opposite the Midianites under Mount Moreh (Judg. 7:1). It is also the "spring in Jezreel," where Saul camped (1 Sam. 29:1). *See also* Gilboa; Jezreel; Moreh.
2 The home of Shammah and Elika, two members of David's elite fighting force known as "the Thirty" (2 Sam. 23:25; "Harorite" in 1 Chron. 11:27 is probably a corruption of "Harodite").
          E.F.C.

Harosheth-ha-goiim (huh-roh′shith-huh-goi′im; Heb., "Harosheth of the Gentiles"), the home base of Sisera, the commander of the army of the Canaanite king Jabin (Judg. 4:2). Sisera gathered his men and chariots here and was defeated by Barak and Deborah (4:13–16). Harosheth-ha-goiim was strategically located near the Plain of Esdraelon southeast of Mount Carmel, but its exact location remains unknown. It has been identified with modern Tell Amr or Tell Harbaj on the Kishon River, or with that general region, on the assumption that the name is related to the Hebrew root *khrsh* ("wooded height").

harp. *See* music.

hart. *See* deer.

harvest. *See* farming.

Hashabiah (hash'uh-bi'uh; Heb., "the LORD has considered/regarded").

1 A Merarite Levite who was the son of Amaziah and the father of Malluch (1 Chron. 6:45). He was also an ancestor of Ethan, a temple musician at the time of David.

2 Another Merarite Levite, the son of Bunni (Neh. 11:15) and father of Azrikan (1 Chron. 9:14).

3 A son of Jeduthun whom David set apart for "prophesying with the lyre in thanksgiving and praise to the LORD" (1 Chron. 25:3).

4 A Hebronite official under David in charge of Israel west of the Jordan. He and his brothers led a family of seventeen hundred members (1 Chron. 26:30).

5 A son of Kemuel who was a levitical official (1 Chron. 27:17).

6 A leader of the Levites at the time of Josiah (2 Chron. 35:9).

7 A Levite who accompanied Ezra and the other exiles on the return to Jerusalem (Ezra 8:19).

8 One of twelve priests appointed by Ezra to take charge of items donated to God (Ezra 8:24).

9 A Levite who made repairs on the walls of Jerusalem; he is said to have been ruler of half the tribe of Keilah (Neh. 3:17).   M.A.P.

Hashum (hay'shuhm).

1 The ancestor of a family group who returned to Jerusalem after the Babylonian exile. The group numbered either 223 (Ezra 2:19) or 328 (Neh. 7:22); 7 members of this family group divorced their foreign wives in response to Ezra's proclamation (Ezra 10:33).

2 An individual who stood with Ezra at the reading of the law (Neh. 8:4).

3 A person who signed Ezra's covenant to keep the law (Neh. 10:18).

Hasmoneans (haz'muh-nee'uhnz; Heb., "descendants of Hashmon"), a Jewish family that included the Maccabees and the high priests and kings who ruled Judea from 142 to 63 BCE. The term is not used in the Bible. *See also* Maccabees.

Hasshub (hash'uhb).

1 The father of Shemaiah, a Levite who returned to Judah after the Babylonian exile (1 Chron. 9:14; Neh. 11:15).

2 The son of Pahath-moab who repaired a section of the wall of Jerusalem and the Tower of the Ovens (Neh. 3:11) as well as a section opposite his house (3:23).

3 A person who signed Ezra's covenant to keep the law (Neh. 10:23). He could be the same person as 1 or 2.

Hathach (hay'thak), the name of a royal eunuch appointed to attend Queen Esther. She dispatched him to Mordecai to find out what was happen-

ing and why (Esther 4:5), which he did (4:6). He then reported to Esther (4:9) and subsequently returned with her message for Mordecai (4:10).

Hattin (hah-teen'), **Horns of,** a prominent hill about five miles west of the Sea of Galilee, called in modern parlance the "Mount of the Beatitudes." The site controls a strategic segment of the ancient road from Egypt to northern Syria, near the point where the highway begins its descent to the Sea of Galilee. The remains of the important Canaanite city found on top of the hill have been identified with biblical Adamah (Josh. 19:36) or Madon (11:1; 12:19). There is no way of determining whether it is the site of Jesus's Sermon on the Mount, though that identification has been made for the benefit of Christian pilgrims and tourists since Crusader times.

Hattush (hat'uhsh).

1 A son of Shemaiah, and a descendant of David (1 Chron. 3:22).

2 The head of a household who accompanied Ezra on the return from the Babylonian exile, perhaps the same person as 1 (Ezra 8:2).

3 A son of Hashabneiah, who took part in restoring the walls of Jerusalem (Neh. 3:10).

4 One of the priests who signed Ezra's covenant to keep the law (Neh. 10:4).

5 A prominent priest who returned from the exile in Babylon with Zerubbabel (Neh. 12:2).

Hauran (haw'ruhn), an area basically coterminous with Bashan, encompassing the broad Syrian plateau country south of Damascus, east of Jaulan (Golan Heights), west of the Jebel Druze, and north of the Yarmuk River. Ancient Egyptian texts speak of it as Huruna, and Assyrian records call it Haurana. Easily invaded from the north, Hauran was devastated by the Assyrian kings more than once: by Shalmaneser III in 842 BCE, by Tiglath-pileser III ten years later; and by Ashurbanipal about two hundred years after that. Ezekiel mentions Hauran as the northeast limit of what he envisions will be the restored Israel (47:16, 18). The Maccabees conquered the area in the second century BCE, but in 90 BCE it became part of the Nabatean Empire. During the NT period, the fertile southern region of Hauran was called Auranitis; it was under the jurisdiction, successively, of Herod the Great, Herod Philip, Agrippa I, and Agrippa II. *See also* Bashan; Nabatea, Nabateans; Syria.   D.B.

Havilah (hav'uh-luh; Heb., perhaps "sandy area"), a district east of the Levant. Various traditions locate Havilah in different areas. Gen. 2:11 places Havilah in Eden, surrounded by the river Pishon. Gen. 10:7 and 1 Chron. 1:9 relate Havilah to Cush, suggesting a region in southern Mesopotamia. In Gen. 10:26–29 and 1 Chron. 1:20–23 Hazarmaveth, Sheba, Ophir, and Havilah are closely related as descendants of Shem, indicating a location somewhere in the east or southeast of Arabia. Gen. 25:18 places Havilah in northeast Arabia, saying the Ishmaelites "dwelt from Havilah to Shur, which is opposite Egypt." In 1 Sam. 15:7 "Havilah" should probably read "Hachilah." *See also* Ethiopia; Hachilah; Ophir; Sheba. D.B.

Havvoth-jair (hav′oth-jay′uhr; Heb., "villages of Jair"), a collective reference to sixty (Deut. 3:14) or thirty (Judg. 10:4) villages in Bashan in Gilead.

hawk, a common bird of prey in the Near East. The Hebrew term *nets* probably refers to the sparrow hawk or the small but swift kestrel. Hawks were considered unclean and therefore inedible for the Hebrews (Deut. 14:11–18). Their raptorial habits made them valuable hunters of rodents and other small pests. They are known to frequent desolate areas, nesting in the rocky crags and cliffs of gorges. Thus, Isaiah speaks of a land laid waste as inhabited by hawks, hedgehogs, owls, and ravens (34:11). In Job, the hawk is cited as a symbol of speed and freedom, soaring through the sky and spreading its wings toward the Jordan Valley, the route of its southward migration (39:26). P.L.C.

Hazael (hay′zay-uhl; Heb., "God has seen"), an Aramean king of Damascus during the latter half of the eighth century BCE. An officer of King Ben-hadad, he was sent to learn from Elisha whether his master would recover from an illness, at which time the prophet foresaw the troubles Hazael would bring to Israel (2 Kings 8). Hazael returned and murdered Ben-hadad, then ascended the throne (v. 15). Assyrian sources, which call him "son of nobody" because of his nonroyal background, note his unsuccessful confrontations with Shalmaneser III in 841 and 837. He was able to conquer Ramoth-gilead in the Transjordan (2 Kings 10:32; see also Amos 1:3), leaving the son of Israel's King Jehu with only limited forces (2 Kings 13:7). After conquering Gath, his attention turned to Jerusalem, which bought its freedom with tribute (2 Kings 12:17–18). He was succeeded by his son Ben-hadad, who lost to Israel's King Joash the cities Hazael had conquered (2 Kings 13:25). *See also* Aram; Ben-hadad. F.E.G.

Hazarshual (hay′zuhr-shoo′uhl; Heb., possibly "the haunt of the fox"), a settlement in southern Judah counted as belonging to the tribes of both Judah (Josh. 15:28) and Simeon (Josh. 19:3). It was probably occupied by Simeon first and then later by Judah, as the tribe of Simeon lost its identity and was absorbed into Judah (1 Chron. 4:28–31; note Gen. 49:5–7). It was later occupied by returning exiles (Neh. 11:27). Its exact location is unknown.

Hazeroth (huh-zihr′oth), one of the camping places of the Israelites as they left Egypt. The biblical narrative locates Kibroth-hattaavah and Rithmah in the Wilderness of Paran (Num. 11:35; 33:17–18). At this site Aaron and Miriam criticized Moses's actions and leadership; as a result

Miriam was struck with leprosy (Num. 12:1–16). The site is unknown although several locations in the northeastern Sinai have been suggested.

Hazor (hay′zor; Heb., "enclosed").

1 A city in the northern reaches of Canaan. The main city had two components: an upper tell and a lower rectangular plateau (modern Tell el-Qedah or Tell Waqqas), both located four miles southwest of Lake Huleh, ten miles north of the Sea of Galilee, and covering 175 acres. It was a major fortified Canaanite city that first figures in biblical stories of Joshua's battles. According to Josh. 11, Jabin, king of Hazor, responded to news of the Israelite presence by marshaling allies to meet the intruders. By hamstringing the horses and burning the chariots of the allies, Joshua defeated Jabin and burned the city of Hazor as well as defeating the allies (Josh. 11:6–15; 12:19). Later, according to Judg. 4:2–24, Jabin's commander, Sisera, fought Israelites under Deborah and Barak, but was defeated by them (see Judg. 5 for a poetic version of that battle). Solomon fortified Hazor (1 Kings 9:15), but Assyria captured it under Tiglath-pileser III (ca. 745–727 BCE; 2 Kings 15:29), an event vividly evident in the destroyed brick blocking the doors in the casemate defense walls of the upper city. In Babylonian times (sixth century BCE), Hazor became the subject of Jeremiah's oracle of doom (49:28–33); the prophet declared, "Hazor shall become a lair of jackals, an everlasting waste; no one shall live there, nor shall anyone settle in it."

Hazor has been excavated extensively. Although the city was occupied first in the Early Bronze Age (3000–2000 BCE), sparse architecture survives until the Middle (2000–1500 BCE) and Late Bronze periods (1500–1200 BCE). Then a thirteenth-century BCE destruction by fire is attested. Minor construction marked the early Iron Age city (after 1200 BCE), but construction of defenses (both walls and gates) from the time of Solomon was massive, as at Gezer and Megiddo. Following another destruction by fire, major building again occurred. Public structures built in Iron Age II (900–600 BCE) subsequently became living quarters that were rebuilt after destruction by earthquake. The fiery destruction of this rebuilt city is attributed by Yadin to Assyria's Tiglath-pileser. A major water system comprising an en-

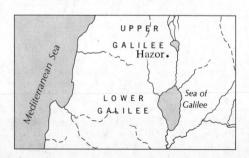

Reconstruction of the citadel gate at Hazor from the time of King Ahab, ninth century BCE.

trance pit and horizontal tunnel to the source was dated as a ninth-century BCE construction.

The significance of Hazor for trade and politics in the ancient Near East is also attested in numerous extrabiblical literary records: nineteenth-century Execration texts; eighteenth-century Mari letters; fourteenth-century Amarna letters; and thirteenth-century Papyrus Anastasi I. *See also* Assyria, Empire of; Solomon.

2 A city in the territory of Judah, modern el-Jebariyeh (Josh. 15:23).

3 A city in the territory of Benjamin, modern Khirbet Hazzur, some four miles north and slightly west of Jerusalem (Neh. 11:33).   R.S.B.

head. Most occurrences of the word "head" (Heb. *rosh;* Gk. *kephalē*) in the Bible are literal, referring to the anatomical part of the body (e.g., Israel laid his hand "on the head of Ephraim," Gen. 48:14). Even then, however, actions involving the head have figurative meaning. Either covering one's head (2 Sam. 15:30) or putting dirt on one's head (15:32; cf. 13:19; Lam. 2:10; Ezek. 27:30) can be a sign of mourning. Shaving the head signifies mourning as well (Deut. 21:12–13; Job 1:20; Isa. 15:2; Jer. 41:5; 47:5; 48:37; Ezek. 7:18; Amos 8:10). Wagging the head signifies scorn or derision (Ps. 109:25; cf. Mark 15:29). Anointing the head with oil (Ps. 23:5) can have a royal connotation (as in, the anointing of a king) or simply convey a pleasant experience of one who is satisfied and blessed (cf. Matt. 6:17).

The Bible also uses the word "head" to refer to a leader, such as the head of a family (Josh. 22:14) or province (Neh. 11:3) or kingdom (Josh. 11:10).

In Eph. 4:15, Jesus is described as the head of the church (cf. Eph. 1:22–23; Col. 1:18; 2:19). In a number of other contexts the words usually translated "head" are often rendered differently in the NRSV: the "top" of the hill (Exod. 17:9; cf. Is. 2:2); the psalmist's "highest" joy (Ps. 137:6). Likewise, "head of the corner" becomes in NRSV simply "cornerstone" (Mark 12:10). Sometimes, "head" is used with an opposite noun to designate a limit: "from the sole of the foot even to the head" (Isa. 1:6); "from the beginning (Heb. *rosh*) to the end" (Eccles. 3:11). *See also* anoint; beards; gestures, postures, and facial expressions; hair.

D.B.W./M.A.P.

healing. In the biblical writings, as well as in ancient Near Eastern and Greco-Roman sources generally, diseased persons are seen as having recourse to several means of treatment. One is folk medicine (balm, Jer. 8:22; 46:11; 51:8; wine, 2 Tim. 5:23; oil and wine, Luke 10:34; music, 2 Sam. 16:23). The sick might also turn to physicians for help (2 Chron. 16:12; Mark 5:25–26; note the mention of physicians in Job 13:4; Jer. 8:22; Sir. 38:1–15; Matt. 9:12; Mark 2:17; Luke 4:23; 5:31; Col. 4:14), or they might appeal to a deity. These various means of healing were not sharply distinguished and might be conjoined: a fig cake was applied to Hezekiah's boil at the command of the prophet Isaiah (2 Kings 20:7); oil was used by early Christian elders in a healing ritual (James 5:14; cf. Mark 6:13). Biblical portraits of certain holy men as healers (Elijah, Elisha, Jesus, Paul, Peter) sometimes involve the use of gestures, physical contact, citation of foreign words, and/or application of oil, mud, saliva, or other material substances (1 Kings 17:21; 2 Kings 5:10–11; Mark 5:41; 6:13; 7:33–34; 8:23, 25; John 9:11; Acts 19:12; 28:8).

In the NT Gospels, the "healing story" becomes a recognized literary genre that exhibits the same essential characteristics wherever it occurs: (1) the presence of a person (or representative of that person) in need of healing, including details that heighten the miraculous deed, e.g., the great length of the illness, previous failures at being healed, the horrible condition of the afflicted person, or various effects the sickness has on members of the community or household; (2) the powerful words and/or actions of the healer, including various bodily manipulations such as touching the ears, washing the eyes, commands to walk, or dialogue with demons; and (3) the confirmation of the sudden healing, which often includes such details as a raised person eating again, the astonishment of those witnessing the event, a visible sign that demons have left a person, a return to previously impossible activity, etc. *See also* disease; magic; miracles.

Bibliography

Howard, J. Keir. *Disease and Healing in the New Testament.* University Press of America, 2001.

Kee, Howard Clark. *Medicine, Miracle and Magic in New Testament Times.* Cambridge University Press, 1986.   H.E.R./J.P.H.

heart. Literally, the word "heart" in the Bible (Heb. *leb, lebab;* Gk. *kardia*) refers to the center or the middle of something (cf. Matt. 12:34, "heart of the earth"); figuratively, it tends to connote the "essence" of that of which it is the center. Most references to the heart are to the "human heart" (in the Hebrew Bible, there are 814 references to the human heart, 26 to the "heart of God," and 11 to the "heart of the sea"), but very few of these have the biological organ in mind. There is occasional recognition that the heart sustains life (2 Sam. 18:14), but when Nabal's heart dies within him (1 Sam. 25:37) he does not die physically—he merely loses the will to live. Eating food is said to strengthen one's heart but, again, that can be meant in the sense of refreshed vigor and renewed determination rather than physical health; the NRSV translates "strengthen your heart" as "refresh yourselves" in Gen. 18:5 and as "be cheerful" in 1 Kings 21:7.

The "heart" in biblical thought is not to be equated with a more godly inner self. Jesus, for example, indicates that men commit adultery in their hearts (Matt. 5:27–28). Likewise, he claims that "the good person out of the good treasure of the heart produces good, and the evil person . . . produces evil" (Luke 6:45). People may love God with all their heart (Matt. 22:37; cf. Deut. 6:5) but, on the other hand, "out of the heart come evil intentions, murder, adultery, fornication, theft, false witness, slander" (Matt. 15:19). The point, then, is that the heart seems to represent the "true self," what one is apart from pretense or hypocrisy. To believe in one's heart is to believe truly (Rom. 10:10; cf. Mark 11:23; to forgive from the heart is to forgive truly (Matt. 18:35); to obey from the heart is to be truly obedient (Rom. 6:17). Thus, references to God knowing the human heart (e.g., Acts 15:8) refer to God's awareness of an individual's essence. This is strongly attested by the "moral" of the story of God's unlikely selection of David in 1 Samuel: "The LORD does not see as mortals see; they look on the outward appearance, but the LORD looks on the heart" (16:7).

The heart represents the essence of a person, which, among other things, includes emotion, volition, and understanding: (1) *Emotion.* Feelings, moods, and passions derive from the heart. Equated with the heart are joy (Deut. 28:47; Acts 2:26), grief (Ps. 13:2; Lam. 2:11), ill-temper (Deut. 15:10), love (Phil. 1:7), courage (2 Sam. 17:10; Ps. 27:14), and fear (Gen. 42:28). A swollen heart breeds arrogance (Isa. 9:9), which is in marked contrast to the gentle and lowly heart of Jesus (Matt. 11:29). The heart is closely connected with desire; where one's treasure is, there one's heart will be (Matt. 6:21). It is the seat of affection; to hold someone in one's heart is to be deeply committed to them in a positive and affectionate manner (Phil. 1:7). (2) *Volition.* The heart also represents the idea of the will, of human choice and conscience (1 Sam. 24:5; 2 Sam. 24:10; 1 Cor. 4:5). The request for a pure heart is the desire for a new and more perfect conscience (Ps.

51:10; Matt. 5:8; 1 Tim. 1:5). Since the heart is the center for decisions (2 Sam. 7:21), it is where people receive God's word (1 Sam. 12:24; Jer. 32:40) and where conversion takes place (Ps. 51:10; Joel 2:12; John 12:40; Acts 2:37). (3) *Understanding.* The heart's function as the source of thought and reflection highlights its intellectual capacities (Isa. 6:10; Mark 7:21–23). To hold a truth in one's heart is to understand it fully in a way that will impact one's life (Deut. 8:5). Conversely, when people do not take something to heart, they fail to understand it in a manner that actually makes a difference in their life (Isa. 42:25). The heart provides wisdom to rule justly and wisely (1 Kings 3:12; 10:24), and it discerns good and evil (2:49). In Luke's story of the birth of Jesus, Mary treasures all the things that are happening in her heart, pondering them there (2:19, 51); this is an indication that she is intent on understanding these things in a profound and significant way. As the seat of understanding, furthermore, the heart is the locus for one's imagination (1 Cor. 2:9).

Numerous expressions and images make reference to the heart. The inaccessibility of the heart helps explain "heart of the sea" (Ezek. 27:25–27) and "heart of heaven" (Deut. 4:11); those areas are incapable of exploration. To "take heart" is to be brave (Matt. 14:27; Mark 6:50; 10:49); to lose heart is to become discouraged (Luke 18:1). To be "hard of heart" or "slow of heart" is to be stubborn or obtuse (Mark 3:5; 10:5; Luke 24:25; John 12:40), but since God hardens hearts (Exod. 4:21; Rom. 9:18), this can also be a sign of judgment (i.e., that one has been rejected by God or is not among the elect). To be "cut to the heart" is to feel convicted (Acts 2:37). A "matter of the heart" is a spiritual matter, not a physical or literal one (Rom. 2:29). In Jesus's parable of the Sower, the word of God is sown in the heart (Matt. 13:19; Luke 8:15). He says in John that "out of the believer's heart shall flow rivers of living water" (7:38). Eph. 3:17 speaks of Christ dwelling in the hearts of believers through faith.   D.R.E./M.A.P.

heaven, the firmament. In the worldview of the ancient Hebrews, heaven was a massive transparent dome that covered the earth. The blue color of the sky was attributed to the chaotic waters that the firmament separated from the earth (Gen. 1:7). The earth was thus surrounded by waters above and below (Deut. 5:8). The firmament was thought to be substantial; it had pillars (Job 26:11) and foundations (2 Sam. 22:8). When the windows of the firmament were opened, rain fell (Gen. 7:11–12). Heaven was the place of the stars, sun, and moon (Gen. 1:14–16) and of the birds (Gen. 1:20; Deut. 4:17). It was also the abode of God (1 Kings 8:30) and where God was enthroned (Isa. 66:1; Exod. 24:9–11).

Heaven and earth are sometimes included in lists of divine witnesses. Heaven was apparently called upon to witness the covenant between God and the Israelites (Deut. 32:1). When the covenant was broken, God accused Israel before heaven (Isa. 2:1; Jer. 2:12).

In biblical Hebrew the word for heaven (*shamayim*) is always plural. Under that influence, the Greek word for heaven in the NT (*ouranos*) also frequently appears in the plural. The use of the plural probably does not mean that the ancient Hebrews conceived of more than one heaven (different heavens located in different places). By the Second Temple period, however, it was common to conceive of heaven as having multiple levels or layers. The Pseudepigrapha in particular contains many references to multiple heavens, seven being the most common notion (*2 Enoch, Ascension of Isaiah*). In the NT, Paul says that he knows someone (though many scholars suspect he is speaking of himself) who was "caught up to the third heaven" (2 Cor. 12:2). Such writings also reflect interest in eyewitness accounts of what transpired in heaven. The earliest prophets of Israel had claimed some degree of access to the heavenly court (1 Kings 22:19–23), but Ezek. 1–3 and Dan. 7–12 report numerous dreams and visions of the heavenly realm. In the NT book of Revelation, an open door appears in heaven, so that the early Christian prophet John may see heavenly secrets (4:1).

In the NT especially, "heaven" sometimes becomes a circumlocution for "God," a way of speaking of God without using the divine name. Thus, "kingdom of heaven" (Matt. 4:17) is simply another expression for "kingdom of God" (Mark 1:15). A "sign from heaven" is a sign from God (Mark 8:11). To say that something "comes from heaven" is to say that it comes from God (Mark 11:30–31). To "sin against heaven" is to sin against God (Luke 15:18). "Heaven forbid!" means "God forbid!" (Luke 20:16). Still, at some level, heaven is known to be part of creation (cf. Gen. 1:1) and, like the earth, it will pass away (Mark 13:31). There will be new heavens and a new earth (Rev. 21:1, 27; 22:3). For the present, however, Christians are urged to view heaven, not only as the abode of God (Matt. 6:9) and angels (Mark 12:25; Luke 2:15), but also as the realm from which Jesus came (John 6:38), to which he has gone (Acts 1:2), in which he now dwells (1 Pet. 3:22), and from which he will return (Acts 1:11). The NT expectation is that believers will be gathered by Jesus into heaven to live with him forevermore (1 Thess. 4:16–17); their reward in heaven will be great (Luke 6:23). Thus, heaven is the true home of those who believe in Christ—they are aliens on the earth (1 Pet. 2:11); their citizenship is in heaven (Phil. 3:20). *See also* eternal life; hell; sky.   A.Y.C.

heaven, kingdom of. *See* kingdom of God.

Heber (hee'buhr; Heb., "enclave").

1 The ancestor of a family group who entered Egypt at the time of Joseph and later took part in the exodus under Moses (Gen. 46:17; Num. 26:45; 1 Chron. 7:31–32).

2 A Judahite, the son of Mered and the father of Soco (1 Chron. 4:18).

3 The ancestor of a Benjaminite family group (1 Chron. 8:17; cf. Eber in 8:12).

4 The husband of Jael, the woman who killed Sisera in her tent after offering him refuge during his flight from Deborah and Barak (Judg. 4:11–21; 5:24). He is called Heber the Kenite and, according to Judg. 4:11, he "had separated from the other Kenites, i.e., the descendants of Hobab the father-in-law of Moses, and had encamped as far away as Elon-bezaanannim, which is near Kedesh." Further, according to Judg. 4:17, "there was peace between King Jabin of Hazor and the clan of Heber the Kenite." This explains why the tent of Heber's wife, Jael, was in the vicinity and why Sisera (Jabin's commander) would trust her. Still, all references to Heber serve merely to set up the encounter between Jael and Sisera; Heber himself is never mentioned as a character in the story. *See also* Barak; Deborah; Jael; Sisera. R.B./M.A.P.

Hebrew language, the tongue spoken by the ancient Israelites and the language in which the Jewish scriptures, also known as the Christian OT, are written. Ironically, the Hebrew scriptures themselves do not make reference to the "Hebrew language." There is a reference to the "language of Canaan" in Isa. 19:18 and a reference to the

THE HEBREW ALPHABET

Form	Name	Transliteration	Approximate Pronunciation
א	aleph	'	(silent)
ב	beth	b	boat
ג	gimel	g	go
ד	daleth	d	dog
ה	he	h	house
ו	waw	w	wide
ז	zayin	z	zebra
ח	heth	kh	Bach
ט	teth	t	tide
י	yod	y	yard
כ	kaph	k	kite
ל	lamed	l	lamp
מ	mem	m	man
נ	nun	n	now
ס	samekh	s	side
ע	ayin	'	(silent)
פ	pe	p, ph	pay, find
צ	tsadhe	ts	mats
ק	qoph	q	kite
ר	resh	r	road
שׂ	sin	s	since
שׁ	shin	sh	ship
ת	taw	t	tide

The forms shown here are those of Hebrew square script, which is the script used in printing today. The Old Hebrew of the biblical period can be seen on ancient inscriptions (*see* Siloam Inscription).

"language of Judah" in 2 Chron. 32:18. These could refer to what is now called "Hebrew." Other passages that refer to a language spoken by the Hebrew people (2 Kings 18:26, 28; Isa. 36:11, 13) probably refer to Aramaic, as is reflected in the NRSV. The first known reference to Hebrew as a language is found in the prologue to the book of Sirach (written in Greek). The grandson of Ben Sira says that he has translated the teachings of his grandfather for Greek readers, and he begs those readers to "be indulgent in cases where, despite our diligent labor in translating, we may seem to have rendered some phrases imperfectly. For what was originally expressed in Hebrew does not have exactly the same sense when translated into another language. Not only this book, but even the Law itself, the Prophecies, and the rest of the books differ not a little when read in the original." Several references to the Hebrew language are found in the NT (John 5:2; 19:13, 17, 20; 20:16; Acts 21:40; 22:2; 26:14; Rev. 9:11; 16:16) and a couple of references are found in 4 Maccabees (12:7; 16:15), but it is possible that some of these passages actually refer to Aramaic (the Greek word *hebrais* was used to mean both "Hebrew" and "Aramaic"). *See also* Aramaic; Hebrews.   A.F.R.

Hebrews (hee'brooz), an alternate designation for the people of Israel, the descendants of Abraham. The Hebrew word translated "Hebrew" is *'ibri,* grammatically an adjective formed from the root *'eber,* a word that is in fact the personal name Eber, an ancestor of several Semitic peoples (Gen. 10:24–25; 11:14–15; 1 Chron. 1:18–19). If the term "Hebrew" is derived from Eber, then one might expect it to be applied to some of the other peoples descended from him, e.g., the Arameans, but this does not necessarily follow from the biblical genealogies in which Eber is mentioned. Other suggestions have been based on the assumption that the root word *'eber* goes back to a form meaning "one who has passed over." Such is the reasoning behind the LXX rendering of "Abram the Hebrew" in Gen. 14:13. The Greek translation is, literally, "Abram, the one who crossed over." Some scholars in modern times have linked the term to the statement that Abraham came from across the Euphrates (Josh. 24:2–3).

Whatever the etymological derivation, the term "Hebrews" was clearly meant to be the designation of an ethnic or national group. This is seen, first, by its usage in juxtaposition to such ethnic/national designations as Egyptians: "The Egyptians might not eat bread with the Hebrews" (Gen. 43:32); Moses "saw an Egyptian beating a Hebrew" (Exod. 2:11); it was reported to Pharaoh that "the Hebrew women are not like the Egyptian women" (1:19). The term is likewise employed in parallelism with "Israel": the "God of Israel" (Exod. 5:1) is equated with the "God of the Hebrews" (Exod. 5:3); also cf. "Hebrews" in 1 Sam. 13:19 with "Israelites" in 1 Sam. 3:20. Finally, Israelites or their ancestors refer to themselves as Hebrews in discussions with foreigners (Joseph, in Gen. 40:15; Jonah, in Jon.

1:9), and the same nuance prevails in the speech of foreigners referring to Israelites (Egyptians, in speaking of Joseph, Gen. 39:14, 17; 41:12). Thus, the biblical writers use the term "Hebrews" to designate the direct ethnic progenitors of the people who later came to be called "Israel" or the "children of Israel." The most striking example of this usage is its application to Abram. It was necessary to give him an ethnic designation to distinguish him from the other persons mentioned in the same context. Thus, we find "Abram the Hebrew" together with "Mamre the Amorite" (Gen. 14:13).

The term becomes a virtual synonym for "Jews" in literature from the Second Temple period. Foreigners speak of Jews as Hebrews (Jth. 12:11; 14:18); Jews describe themselves as Hebrews when speaking to non-Jews (Jth. 10:12; 2 Macc. 10:31); and Jews are called Hebrews to distinguish them from foreigners in third-person narration (2 Macc. 11:13; 15:37). In the NT, the term "Hebrew" may also be used as a synonym for Jew. Thus, Paul maintains that he is "a Hebrew born of Hebrews" (Phil. 3:5), and he clearly uses the term as a synonym for "Israelites" in 2 Cor. 11:22: "Are they Hebrews? So am I. Are they Israelites? So am I. Are they descendants of Abraham? So am I." In the book of Acts, however, "Hebrews" and "Hellenists" are mentioned as two distinct types of Jews (or Jewish Christians). The distinction is probably linguistic: Hebrew Jews used the Hebrew language, while Hellenist Jews used the Greek language.   A.F.R.

Hebrews, Letter to the, an anonymous book appearing in the NT after the letters attributed to Paul. The book sometimes came to be included among letters of Paul in the ancient church and is listed as a Pauline letter in the KJV, but virtually all modern scholars regard that attribution as mistaken. Indeed, contemporary reference to the work as "a letter" is somewhat suspect, since the document lacks any customary epistolary introduction. The author refers to it as a "word of exhortation" (13:22), an expression used elsewhere in the NT for a sermon (cf. Acts 13:15).

Contents: The letter or sermon opens with an eloquent prologue that presents God's Son as the definitive revelation of God (1:1–4). The author proposes that the Son is superior to angels (1:4–13) and then issues a plea for the readers not to drift away from the truth they have received (2:1–4). Returning to the theme of the Son's superiority, the author explains that the temporary humiliation of Jesus was necessary for human salvation and led to his glorious exaltation (2:5–18). He argues that Jesus is also superior to Moses (3:1–6), which leads to a warning not to rebel and fail to enter into God's rest, as did some of those who were delivered from Egypt under Moses (3:7–19). Readers should make every effort to enter God's sabbath rest (4:1–11). This exhortation is punctuated by a reminder of the piercing power of God's word to reveal secret intentions of the heart (4:12–13). The letter then launches into a long exposition on the role of Jesus as high priest (4:14–10:39). First, the author shows that Jesus possesses two qualifications for being such a priest (4:14–5:10): he is able to sympathize with humans and he has been appointed by God to be a priest after the order of Melchizedek. This gives way to another excursus: the author rebukes the readers for their spiritual immaturity, urges them to press on toward perfection, and expresses confidence that they will persevere (5:11–6:20). Returning to the main theme, the author expounds upon what is meant by identifying Jesus as a priest according to the order of Melchizedek (7:1–28). He then spells out the implications of what he has been saying: the earthly sanctuary where priests offer sacrifices is only a sketch or shadow of the heavenly one, and the old covenant has been made obsolete by the new and better covenant in Jesus (8:1–13). These points are elaborated through a treatise on the many ways in which the sacrifice of Christ is superior to the sacrifices of the levitical priests (9:1–10:18). The author then concludes his theological homily on Christ's high-priesthood by exhorting his readers to respond appropriately (10:19–39). He offers a roll call of biblical heroes whose lives have testified to faith as "the assurance of things hoped for" (11:1–40). They constitute a great cloud of witnesses, to which Jesus may be added as the *ultimate* example of one who proved faithful in suffering and prepared the way for others to follow (12:1–3).

The author urges his readers to endure their trials and reflects briefly on the positive role that suffering can play when viewed as discipline from a loving God (12:4–11). These exhortations to faithfulness give way to a contrast between the covenants of Mount Sinai and Mount Zion: readers are receiving a kingdom that cannot be shaken, but those who fail to obtain the grace of God offered through this new covenant will not escape God's judgment (12:12–29). The book then draws to a close with numerous admonitions (13:1–17): readers ought to follow the example of former leaders; they need to keep themselves from strange doctrines; they should be willing to suffer ostracism for their faith; they are to worship God with praise and good works; and they should submit to their current leaders. The book closes in the typical style of a letter, with prayer requests, benedictions, and personal greetings (13:18–25).

Historical Situation: There has been much speculation as to who the author of Hebrews might be (suggestions have included Apollos, Barnabas, Luke, and Priscilla), but current scholarship has reached a virtual consensus that this cannot be determined. The book was probably composed by a person of some prominence in the church who knew the readers personally and assumed a mandate to speak to them authoritatively. This author was well educated with regard to both Greek rhetoric and Jewish scriptures. The presumed audience for the work includes second-generation (2:3) Christians who have a strong interest in sacrificial practices and other matters of Jewish faith. Their geographic location cannot be determined, but prominent sug-

gestions include Jerusalem or Rome (the dominant theory). With regard to date, Hebrews could have been written almost anytime between 50 and 90 CE, but the main question is whether it was written before or after the destruction of the Jerusalem temple in 70 CE. Scholars are divided over this. On the one hand, some passages seem to suggest that sacrifices are still being offered at the time the letter is written (7:8; 8:3; 9:6–7, 9, 13; 13:11); on the other hand, the book never actually mentions the temple, using the ancient Israelite tabernacle for all of its sacrificial imagery. In any case, this letter or sermon appears to be directed to Christians who are considering conversion to Judaism—or at least who want to embrace what the author regards as outmoded aspects of Jewish religion.

Major Themes: Hebrews seeks to establish the superiority of faith in Christ over all other faith traditions, especially Jewish ones. It claims that Jesus Christ is superior to prophets (1:1–3), to angels (1:4–11; 2:15–18), and to all figures from Israel's history (e.g., Moses, 3:1–6; Joshua, 4:1–11; Aaron, 4:14–5:10; Levi, 7:1–22). Furthermore, the salvation Jesus brings is superior to anything attainable within Israel under the old covenant (8:1–13; cf. 7:25; 9:1–28; 10:1–18). In Christian theology, Hebrews is often prized for its Christology, since it offers one of the clearest statements in the NT of the "two natures of Christ": Jesus Christ is presented as fully human (2:11, 14, 17–18; 4:15; 5:7–8; 12:1–3) and yet also as divine (1:2–3, 6; 2:11; 9:27–28; 10:5, 37). Hebrews also develops an image of Jesus as a "high priest" (2:17; 3:1; 4:14; 5:5, 10; 6:20; 7:26; 8:1; 9:11; 10:21), drawing on the biblical figure of Melchizedek (cf. Gen. 14:18–20; Ps. 110:4). With regard to discipleship, Hebrews employs a distinctive pilgrimage motif, according to which believers follow heroes of faith (11:1–12:1) and their pioneer Jesus (12:2–3) on a journey to a heavenly country (11:16). *See also* angel; canon; letter; Melchizedek; priests; worship in the New Testament.

Bibliography

Attridge, Harold W. *The Epistle to the Hebrews.* Fortress, 1989.

Harrington, Daniel J. *What Are They Saying About the Letter to the Hebrews?* Paulist, 2005.

HEBREWS AND PAUL: SOME PARALLELS

Although modern scholars do not believe Paul wrote Hebrews, they do recognize that some parallel expressions and ideas can be found in both Paul's letters and the Letter to the Hebrews. Both:

exalt Christ above angelic spirits (Heb. 1:5–14; 2:2; cf. Gal. 4:9; Col. 1:16; 2:18);

indicate the gospel was confirmed through "signs and wonders" and miracles (Heb. 2:4; cf. Rom. 15:18–19; 2 Cor. 12:12; Gal. 3:2–5);

refer to Christ taking on the likeness of humanity (Heb. 2:14–18; cf. Phil. 2:7–8);

describe Christ as having greater glory than Moses (Heb. 3:2–3; cf. 2 Cor. 3:7–8);

read Israel's desert wanderings as a warning against laxity (Heb. 3:7–4:13; cf. 1 Cor. 10:1–13);

claim that Christ has granted believers access to God and to divine blessings (Heb. 4:16; 10:19–22; cf. Rom. 5:1–2);

say the recipients are infants needing milk, not solid food (Heb. 5:12–13; cf. 1 Cor. 3:1–2);

refer to the Hebrew scriptures as the "oracles of God" (Heb. 5:12; cf. Rom. 3:2);

refer to Christ's death as an expiation (Gk. *hilastērion;* Heb. 9:5; cf. Rom. 3:25) and as an act of obedience (Heb. 5:8; cf. Rom. 5:19; Phil. 2:8);

refer to Christ as one who has been sacrificed (Heb. 9:26, 28; cf. 1 Cor. 5:7);

cite Abraham as an example of faith (Heb. 11:8; cf. Gal. 3:6–9);

refer to perseverance in the Christian life as running a race (Heb. 12:1; cf. 1 Cor. 9:24); and

call the recipients "saints" (Heb. 13:24; cf. Rom. 1:7).

From Mark Allan Powell, *Introducing the New Testament* (courtesy, Baker Academic)

Johnson, Luke Timothy. *Hebrews.* Westminster John Knox, 2006.

Koester, Craig R. *Hebrews.* Doubleday, 2001.

Lindars, Barnabas. *The Theology of the Letter to the Hebrews.* Cambridge University Press, 1991.

Powell, Mark Allan. *Introducing the New Testament: A Historical, Literary, and Theological Survey.* Baker Academic, 2009. Pp. 427–443.   M.A.P.

Hebron (hee′bruhn), one of the central cities (modern el-Khalil) in the southern hill country of Judah some twenty miles south-southwest of Jerusalem. Hebron is situated at one of the highest points (about 3,040 feet above sea level) on the central mountainous ridge and is one of the oldest continually inhabited cities in the Near East. It is in an area with an abundant water supply in the form of wells and springs and is a regional center of grape and olive production. A reference to its antiquity is found in Num. 13:22, where it is said to have been founded seven years before Zoan (later called Rameses) in Egypt, probably in the seventeenth century BCE. Hebron's original name (Gen. 23:2; Josh. 20:7) was Kiriath-arba (Heb., "fourfold city").

In biblical tradition, Hebron has close connections with the traditions of Abraham (Gen. 13:18; 18:1). It was at Hebron that Sarah died, and it was there that Abraham purchased the cave of Machpelah from Hittites in the area for use as a family tomb (Gen. 23:7–16). At the time of the entry of the Israelites, Hebron was controlled by three Anakites (Ahiman, Sheshai, and Talmai, probably to be associated with the legendary giants also known as Anakim; Num. 13:22; cf. Deut. 1:28; 9:2; Josh. 14:12). After falling to Joshua (Josh. 10:1–27, 36–39; 11:21–23) and having been secured again by Caleb (15:13–14), Hebron was allotted to Caleb (14:12) and subsequently became a city of the Kohathite Levites and one of the six cities of refuge (20:7). Hebron also played a prominent role in the early years of David (ca. 1004–998 BCE). It was one of the cities that aided him in his refugee years (1 Sam. 30:31), and it was there that he was anointed "king of Judah" (2 Sam. 2:11) and reigned for seven and a half years (5:5), while Saul's son Ishbaal ruled in the north. David's son Absalom began his revolt against his father at Hebron (2 Sam. 15:7–10). In the period of the divided kingdom (ca. 922–587/6 BCE), Rehoboam strengthened Hebron's defenses (2 Chron. 11:5, 10). A number of stamped jar handles from storage jars of uniform capacity (2 baths, equal to about 10 gallons) dating to the eighth century BCE bear the name of Hebron, where these jars were apparently made in a royal pottery. Later, at the time of the exile (587/6–ca. 538 BCE), Hebron was occupied by the Edomites (Idumeans) until it was recaptured in 164 BCE by Judas Maccabeus (1 Macc. 5:65). *See also* David; Machpelah; Mamre.   F.S.F.

Hebronites (hee′bruh-nɪts), name of a family group belonging to the Kohath line of Levites (Num. 3:27; 26:58). The group was a source of treasury guards (1 Chron. 26:23) and supervised territory west of the Jordan through Hashabiah (26:30) under the leadership of Jerijah (26:31). The name is associated with the Judean city of Hebron and its people, nineteen miles southeast of Jerusalem. *See also* Hebron.

hedge, a barrier or boundary, sometimes composed of live plants such as thorny bush (Mic. 7:4; Hos. 2:6) and used to protect vineyards (Isa. 5:5; cf. Mark 12:1; Matt. 21:33). A hedge can also symbolize God's protection (Job 1:10; NRSV: "fence") or divine restriction (Job 3:23; NRSV: "fence").

hedgehog, a small mammal, also designated as a "porcupine." The Hebrew word (*qippod*) is used for the hedgehogs *Erinaceus auritus* or *Erinaceus sacer*. In Isa. 14:23 and 34:11, the desolation of divine judgment is symbolized by the image of a city becoming the possession of such an animal.

heel. Literal references to a heel include a likely zone of snakebite (Gen. 3:15; 49:17), anatomical contact of twins at birth (Gen. 25:26), and appropriate vulnerability to traps (Job 18:9). Idiomatic expressions to "lifting the heel" against someone convey an act of treacherous betrayal (Ps. 41:9; John 13:18). To march or rush at someone's heels implies proximity in pursuit (Deut. 33:3; Judg. 5:15; cf. Job 18:11).

Hegai (heg'i), a eunuch of King Ahasuerus of Persia; he was in charge of the royal harem, and Esther was placed in his custody before she was called before the king (Esther 2:3, 8, 15).

heifer, a young cow. In ancient Israel, the heifer was used for plowing (Judg. 14:18), trained to thresh grain (Hos. 10:11; Jer. 50:11; Deut. 21:3), and valued for its milk (Isa. 7:21). It was also a sacrificial animal (1 Sam. 16:2) and appears in three significant rites: it was divided to ratify a covenant (Gen. 15:9); it was killed to expiate murder by an unknown person (Deut. 21:1–9); and a "red heifer" was burned and its ashes used to counteract uncleanness caused by contact with a corpse (Num. 19:1–22; cf. Heb. 9:13). The heifer's beauty was much appreciated, so the word could be used figuratively for the splendor of Egypt (Jer. 46:20); in Judg. 14:18, "heifer" refers to a woman, perhaps with connotation of "a beautiful woman" (cf. 14:15). Obedient Ephraim is compared to a trained heifer (Hos. 10:11), disobedient Israel to a stubborn heifer (4:16).   J.R.P.

heir. *See* inheritance.

Heldai (hel'di).
1 David's captain for the twelfth month of each year (1 Chron. 27:15).
2 An Israelite who returned to Jerusalem from the exile in Babylon (Zech. 6:10).

Helez (hee'liz; Heb., "vigor," "strength").
1 An Ephraimite, one of David's warriors who later served him as the commander of a division of twenty-four thousand men (2 Sam. 23:26; 1 Chron. 27:10).
2 A descendant of Judah (1 Chron. 2:39).

Heli (hee'li; Gk. form of Heb. Eli), the father of Joseph in Luke's genealogy of Jesus (3:23). *See also* Eli.

Heliopolis (hee'lee-op'uh-lis). *See* On.

hell, a place of eternal punishment for the wicked. In the NRSV, the word "hell" is only used in the NT, where it translates Greek *gehenna*. It is thus distinct from Sheol and Hades, names for the realm of the dead that the NRSV simply transliterates from Hebrew and Greek respectively. Some English translations, including the KJV, use "hell" to translate *sheol* and *hadēs* as well as *gehenna*.

The Greek word *gehenna* is derived from Hebrew *gehinnom*, meaning "valley of Hinnom," also known as the "valley of the son of Hinnom" (2 Chron. 28:3; 33:6; Neh. 11:30; Jer. 7:31–32; 19:2, 6; 32:35). Located west and south of Jerusalem and running into the Kidron Valley at a point opposite the modern village of Silwan, the valley of Hinnom once formed part of the boundary between the tribes of Judah and Benjamin (Josh. 15:8; 18:16; Neh. 11:30). During the monarchic period, it became the site of an infamous high place (called "Topheth" and derived from an Aramaic word meaning "fire place"), where some of the kings of Judah engaged in forbidden religious practices, including human sacrifice by fire (2 Chron. 28:3; 33:6; Jer. 7:31; 32:35). Because of this, Jeremiah spoke of its impending judgment and destruction (7:32; 19:6). King Josiah put an end to these practices by destroying and defiling the high place in the valley of Hinnom (2 Kings 23:10). Probably because of these associations with fiery destruction and judgment, the word "Gehenna" came to be used metaphorically during the Second Temple period to refer to a place of punishment by fire for evil spirits and the wicked dead (*1 Enoch* 18:11–16; 108:3–7, 15; 2 Esd. 7:36–38).

The concept of hell is different from Sheol (in the Hebrew Bible) and from Hades (in most Greek literature) in three ways: (1) only the wicked enter hell, whereas good and bad alike occupy Sheol and Hades; (2) the wicked are sent to hell after a final judgment at the end of time, whereas people were thought to enter Sheol or Hades immediately upon death; and (3) hell involves eternal torment, whereas Sheol and Hades were characterized only by absence of life, not enhanced suffering. In the NT, however, some references to Hades appear to have been influenced by the concept of hell, so that Hades also can be described as a place of torment reserved only for the wicked or those condemned in the judgment (Matt. 11:23; Luke 16:23).

In the NT, virtually all references to hell (*gehenna*) occur on the lips of Jesus in the Synoptic Gospels.

Hell is variously described as a fiery furnace (Matt. 13:42, 50), an unquenchable fire (Mark 9:43), or an eternal fire prepared for the devil and his angels (Matt. 25:41). The book of Revelation likewise describes a lake that burns with fire and brimstone in which the wicked will be eternally punished (19:20; 20:14–15; 21:8). Jesus warns his disciples about committing sins that will lead to hell (Matt. 5:22, 29–30; 23:33; Mark 9:45; Luke 12:5). They should fear God, who can destroy body and soul in hell rather than people who can kill only the body (Matt. 10:28; Luke 12:5). They should take drastic measures to get rid of anything that causes them to sin, for it is better to go through life maimed or blind than to be thrown into the fires of hell (Matt. 18:7–9; Mark 9:43–47). The scribes and the Pharisees will not escape being sentenced to hell (Matt. 23:33), and those they convert become twice the children of hell that they are (Matt. 23:15).

Aside from these references, the word *gehenna* is used only once in the Bible. James decries the human tongue's potential for causing hurt by saying it is "set on fire by hell" (3:6); here "hell" seems to be a circumlocution for "the devil," much as "heaven" is elsewhere a circumlocution for "God" (cf. Mark 8:11; 11:30–31; Luke 15:18; 20:16). The NRSV also uses "hell" in 2 Pet. 2:4, where the actual reference is to Tartaros, another name for the realm of the dead in Greek mythology. Here the author seems to have merged that concept with the Christian notion of hell, so that angels who rebelled against God (Gen. 6:6–8; 8:18) have been cast into Tartaros, where they are chained in deepest darkness awaiting judgment. Thus, Tartaros, like Hades, is a waiting room, but one into which the wicked are cast and, in some sense, punished (darkness, chains). *See also* Hades; Hinnom, Valley of; punishment, everlasting; Sheol.

W.E.L./M.A.P.

Hellenists (hel′uh-nists), Greek-speaking Jews who were part of the early church in Jerusalem (Acts 6:1; 9:29, 11:20). The book of Acts contrasts "Hellenists" with the "Hebrews," but since at this point all members of the church are Jewish, the distinction must refer to different Jewish groups or synagogues in Jerusalem from which the church members had come. Scholars sometimes speculate that success among Hellenists may have served as a transition for the Christian movement in its eventual spread to the Greek-speaking Gentile world, but the NT writings do not make that point explicitly. *See also* Greek, Greeks; Hebrews.

helmet, a leather or metal protective covering for the head worn by soldiers. Foreigners attacking Israel are often reported as wearing helmets (Goliath, 1 Sam. 17:5; Jer. 46:4; Ezek. 23:24). Later, Israel's armies are similarly equipped (2 Chron. 26:14). A helmet is worn by God in Isa. 59:17, and a helmet is part of the spiritual armor given to Christians in Eph. 6:17 and 1 Thess. 5:8.

Bronze helmet of the type worn by Roman soldiers stationed in Judea, first century CE.

Helon (hee′lon; Heb., possibly "strong"), the father of the Zebulunite leader Eliab. Helon is mentioned in Numbers (1:9; 2:7; 7:24, 29; 10:16) in connection with his son's status and activities.

hem, the edge, border, or "skirts" of a garment. Blue, purple, and scarlet decorations shaped like pomegranates were placed between bells of pure gold around the hem of the blue priestly robe of Aaron (Exod. 28:31–35; 39:22–26). Saul grabbed the hem of Samuel's robe in desperation after the latter informed him that he had been rejected by God as king over Israel. Isaiah saw a vision of the Lord seated on a throne with the hem of the Lord's robe filling the temple (Isa. 6:1). *See also* fringes.

Heman (hee′muhn; Heb., "faithful").
1 A grandson of Jacob and son of Zerah (1 Chron. 2:6).
2 A wise man in the time of Solomon (1 Kings 4:31).
3 A grandson of Samuel and son of Joel whom David put in charge of the service of song (1 Chron. 6:31–33). He is identified as the "singer" and, as the first in the list of three appointed by David, he may have been the chief musician. Ps. 88 is probably attributed to him.

hen.
1 A bird referred to as a "water hen" in Lev. 11:18; Deut. 14:16. It is declared unclean and prohibited for food.

2 A mother of chicks mentioned by Jesus in Matt. 23:37; Luke 13:34. Jesus compares his concern for Jerusalem to a hen who wishes to gather her brood under her wings. *See also* fowls.

Henadad (hen'uh-dad; a shortened form of Henhadad; Heb., "Hadad [a deity] is gracious."

1 The ancestral head of a levitical family group (called the "sons of Henadad"). This group helped to supervise workers in the rebuilding of the temple after the exile (Ezra 3:9).

2 The father of Binnui, a postexilic inhabitant of Jerusalem who helped repair the city walls (Neh. 3:18, 24; 10:9). It is possible that this person is identical to **1**. Another possibility is that Binnui might not be a literal son of Henadad, but a member of the ancestral group who called themselves "sons (descendants) of Henadad."

Hepher (hee'fuhr).

1 A town west of the Jordan (Josh. 12:17).

2 A son of Gilead (Num. 26:32; 27:1; Josh. 17:2, 3).

3 A Judahite, the son of Ashhur and Narah (1 Chron. 4:6).

4 A Mecherathite who became one of David's warriors (1 Chron. 11:36).

Hephzibah (hef'zi-buh; Heb., "my delight rests in her").

1 A wife of Hezekiah, king of Judah (ca. 715–687/6 BCE), and the mother of Manasseh (687/6–642 BCE; 2 Kings 21:1).

2 The name given by God to restored Jerusalem in Isa. 62:4.

herald, one who announces messages on behalf of another (2 Chron. 36:22; Ezra 1:1). In Isa. 40:9; 41:27 the herald is sent by God is to bring "good tidings" to Zion and Jerusalem. In Dan. 3:4 a herald announces the demands for allegiance to the golden statue on behalf of Babylon's king Nebuchadnezzar. In 2 Pet. 2:5 Noah is characterized as a "herald of righteousness," and in the Pastoral Letters Paul is described as a herald (1 Tim. 2:7; 2 Tim. 1:11).

herbs, plants gathered for flavor, aroma, or medicinal value (2 Kings 4:39). Bitter herbs were used at Passover as a symbol of suffering (Exod. 12:8; Num. 9:11). Jesus commends the Pharisees for paying scrupulous attention to tithes on "mint and rue and herbs of all kind," but he attacks them for neglecting matters he deems more essential (Luke 11:42).

herd. *See* cattle; sheep.

Hermas (huhr'muhs), a Christian to whom, along with others, Paul sends greetings in Rom. 16:14. Perhaps the added words "and the brothers and sisters who are with them" refer to a small house-church.

Hermes (huhr'meez).

1 The divine messenger of the Greek gods. Paul and Barnabas are mistaken for Hermes and Zeus when they visit Lystra and Paul heals a cripple there (Acts 14:12).

2 A Christian greeted in Rom. 16:14.

Hermogenes (huhr-moj'uh-neez), an Asian Christian known only as one who deserted Paul (2 Tim. 1:15). *See also* Phygelus.

Mount Hermon rises 9,230 feet above sea level and towers above the upper Jordan Valley.

Hermon (huhr'muhn; Heb., "sacred" or "forbidden"), **Mount,** the three-peaked summit at the southern end of the Anti-Lebanon mountain range. Mount Hermon rises 9,230 feet above sea level and is the highest point in the entire Levant, 1,968 feet higher than any part of the Lebanon mountains and towering above the Bashan plateau and upper Jordan Valley. According to Deut. 3:9, "the Sidonians call Hermon Sirion, while the Amorites call it Senir," and these three names are sometimes used together in the Bible (Deut. 4:48; 1 Chron. 5:23). The Hebrew text of Ps. 42:6 speaks literally of the "Hermons," which may refer to the three peaks.

Heavy precipitation, well over 40 inches, mainly in the form of snow, falls on the summit and western slopes and sinks through the porous sandstone to supply the powerful sources of the Jordan and Litani rivers and the oasis of Damascus. Snow covers the upper regions during the entire winter and early spring and in sheltered crevices may persist even as late as the end of October. Villages with vineyards and orchards are plentiful on the western slope up to about 3,300 feet. Its slopes were thickly forested (Ezek. 27:5) and were the home of lions and leopards (Song of Sol. 4:8). Evidently a sacred mountain (Judg. 3:3 calls it "Baal-hermon"), Mount Hermon formed the northernmost limit of Joshua's conquests (Josh. 11:3, 17; 12:1, 5; 13:5, 11). *See also* Anti-Lebanon. D.B.

Herod (hair'uhd), name of a family of Idumean origin with strong connections to the Roman government. Members of the family, under a variety of titles, governed Judea, Galilee, and adjacent

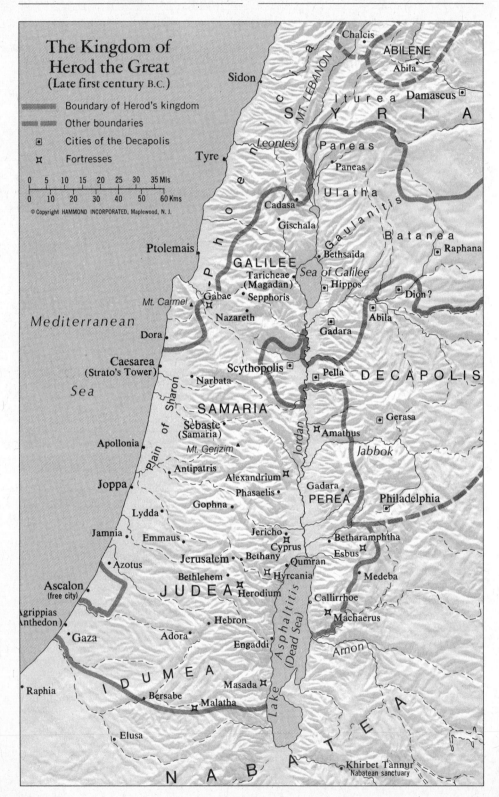

The Kingdom of Herod the Great
(Late first century B.C.)

Boundary of Herod's kingdom

Other boundaries

⊡ Cities of the Decapolis

⤳ Fortresses

0 5 10 15 20 25 30 35 Mls
0 10 20 30 40 50 60 Kms
© Copyright HAMMOND INCORPORATED, Maplewood, N.J.

Chalcis

ABILENE

Abila

Sidon

I t u r e a   Damascus ⊡

P h o e n i c i a

MT. LEBANON

S Y R I A

P a n e a s

Paneas

U l a t h a

Tyre

Leontes

Cadasa

Gischala

Bethsaida

B a t a n e a

Raphana ⊡

Ptolemais

GALILEE

Taricheae (Magadan)

Sea of Galilee

Hippos ⊡

Dion ? ⊡

Gàbae ⤳

Sepphoris

Mt. Carmel ▲

Nazareth

Abila ⊡

Mediterranean

Dora

Gadara ⊡

Caesarea (Strato's Tower)

Scythopolis ⊡

Pella ⊡

D E C A P O L I S

Sea

Narbata

S A M A R I A

Gerasa ⊡

Apollonia

Sebaste (Samaria)

Mt. Gerizim ▲

Amathus ⤳

Jabbok

Antipatris

Jordan

Joppa

Alexandrium ⤳

Gadara ⤳

Lydda

Phasaelis

Gophna

PEREA

Philadelphia

Jamnia

Emmaus

Jericho

Betharamphtha

Cyprus ⤳

Esbus ⤳

Azotus

Jerusalem

Bethany

Qumran

Medeba

Ascalon (free city)

Bethlehem

Hyrcania ⤳

Callirrhoe

Agrippias (Anthedon)

J U D E A

Herodium ⤳

Machaerus ⤳

Gaza

Hebron

Adora

Engaddi

Asphaltitis (Dead Sea)

N A B A T E A

Raphia

Masada ⤳

Bersabe

Malatha ⤳

Arnon

Elusa

I D U M E A

Khirbet Tannur
Nabatean sanctuary

areas from ca. 55 BCE until near the close of the first century CE. The name "Herod" is Greek and originated with a shadowy ancestor about whom little was known even in antiquity. Two ancient traditions make him either a descendant of a notable Jewish family with a lineage traceable to the Babylonian exile or a slave in the temple of Apollo in the Philistine city of Ashkelon. Neither can be proven.

Antipater, the grandfather of Herod the Great, rose to the position of military commander of his native Idumea under the Hasmonean rulers Alexander Jannaeus (103–76 BCE) and Alexandra (76–67 BCE). The Idumeans had been forcibly converted to Judaism by John Hyrcanus (134–104 BCE), and thus the family of Herod was in some sense Jewish, though the Jewish population in the lands they ruled seem to have regarded them as foreigners. Herod's father, also named Antipater (or Antipas), was by all accounts a skilled soldier as well as a shrewd politician and diplomat. His successful intervention in favor of Hyrcanus II in the latter's struggle for supremacy against his brother Aristobulus, coupled with the outstanding services he rendered to Pompey and Julius Caesar in their campaigns, earned him Roman citizenship and the post of governor of Judea, granted by Caesar in 47 BCE. Antipater and his Nabatean wife, Cypros, had four sons and a daughter, and the two eldest, Phasaelus and Herod, were nominated by their father as governors (Gk. *stratēgoi*), the former of Judea and the latter of Galilee.

The following members of the Herodian family appear in the NT:

1 Herod I (Herod the Great), king of the Jews. He was probably about twenty-five years old when, as governor of Galilee, he successfully campaigned against Galilean bandits, executing the leaders and coming out of the subsequent showdown with the Jewish Sanhedrin in Jerusalem, not only politically stronger, but also with enhanced status in the eyes of Rome. When, in 40 BCE, the Roman Senate appointed Herod king of the Jews, he was given a prize still requiring conquest, for on the throne of Judea sat Antigonus II, the last of the Hasmonean rulers, newly placed there by Rome's enemies, the Parthians. Herod succeeded, with the backing provided by his friend Mark Antony, in taking Jerusalem in 37 BCE. Antigonus was executed by the Romans at Herod's request, and in the same year Herod married Mariamne I, a Hasmonean (she was one of ten wives). From 37 until his death in 4 BCE, Herod ruled as king of the Jews, a reign marked by his total loyalty to Rome, his grandiose and sometimes magnificent building programs, his family strife, and his harsh repression of any opposition. Herod showed an uncanny ability to maintain favor with the Roman leadership, managing, for example, to switch his allegiance from Antony to Octavian (later Augustus) after the Battle of Actium in 31 BCE.

In honor of Augustus, Herod rebuilt ancient Samaria into the Hellenistic city of Sebaste (Gk., "Augustus"), and he constructed, on the site of

THE HERODS: A SIMPLIFIED FAMILY TREE

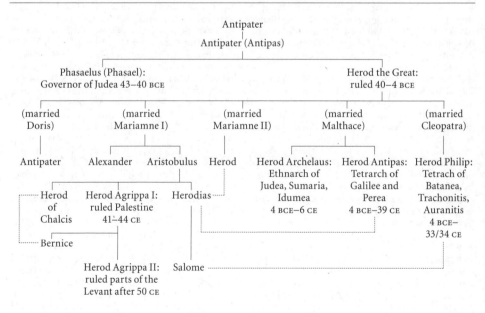

------ represents marriage

a minor anchorage on the Mediterranean coast called Strato's Tower, the magnificently planned city of Caesarea Maritima, a major port and Roman administrative center. The crown of Herod's constructions, however, was the temple in Jerusalem, which he rebuilt on a grandiose scale. The project, begun in 20 BCE, was not completed until 62 CE, but it was noted for its magnificence at the time of Jesus (cf. Mark 13:1). Herod also fortified his realm with a string of impressive wilderness fortress-palaces, the major ones being Masada, Machaerus, the Herodium in Perea, the Alexandrium, Cypros, Hyrcania, and the Herodium southeast of Bethlehem (the only one built on a previously unfortified site and also the place where Herod was buried). These fortresses served also as palaces and often as prisons—given the internal strife that marked Herod's relations with his family, occasionally as places of imprisonment and execution for members of his family. Eventually, Herod ordered the execution of his Hasmonean wife, Mariamne, of their two sons, Alexander and Aristobulus, of other members of the Hasmonean family, and of his son Antipater. According to Matt. 2:1–18 (cf. Luke 1:5), the birth of Jesus occurred while Herod was king. The king's well-known ruthlessness in defending his throne against any threat forms the background for the story of the massacre of Bethlehem's children (Matt. 2:16–17).

After Herod's death in 4 BCE, Augustus Caesar resolved the dispute that broke out among three of Herod's surviving sons by dividing the kingdom, but withholding the royal title of "king" from all of the heirs. To Archelaus, son of Malthace, went the title "ethnarch" and half of the territory (Judea, Idumea, and Samaria). The other half was split into two tetrarchies: Antipas, younger brother of Archelaus, received Galilee and Perea; Philip, son of Cleopatra, received Batanea, Trachonitis, and Auranitis. *See also* Caesarea; Samaria, city of; temple, the.

2 Herod Archelaus (ahr´kuh-lay´uhs), son of Herod the Great and ethnarch of Judea, Samaria, and Idumea (4 BCE–6 CE). According to Matt. 2:22, Joseph and Mary settled in Galilee because, after returning from Egypt (to which they had fled to escape Herod the Great), they heard Archelaus was "ruling Judea in place of his father." His rule was relatively short and disastrous. Both Jews and Samaritans petitioned Rome for his removal because of his brutal and insensitive rule. Augustus banished him to Gaul in 6 CE, and his territory became a Roman province under the prefect Coponius. *See also* ethnarch.

3 Herod Philip, son of Herod the Great and tetrarch of Batanea, Trachonitis, and Auranitis (4 BCE–33/34 CE). He ruled uneventfully and apparently successfully in his northern domains. His name is remembered in that of the city Caesarea Philippi (see Matt. 16:33; Mark 8:27), which was his rebuilding of ancient Panias near the springs of the Jordan River. Philip apparently married his niece Salome, daughter of Herodias and of Philip's

A coin of Herod Agrippa I, ruler over Judea from 41 to 44 CE, with the ruler's image. A human image on a Jewish coin, in light of the biblical prohibition against images (Exod. 20:4), is unusual.

half brother Herod, the son of Mariamne. *See also* Caesarea Philippi; Herodias; Salome.

4 Herod Antipas (an´tee-puhs), son of Herod the Great and tetrarch of Galilee and Perea (4 BCE–39 CE). He is the Herod most frequently mentioned in the NT. Both Jesus and John the Baptist were his subjects and carried out their public careers mostly in his territories (Matt. 14:1–12; Mark 6:14–29; 8:15; Luke 3:19–20; 9:7–9; 13:31–32; 23:6–16; Acts 4:27). Jesus refers to him as a "fox," probably in reference to his penchant for perpetrating seemingly indiscriminate violence. Herod Antipas's career was dominated by his relationship to Herodias, whom he married in spite of the fact that she was his niece and married to his half brother when they met. In choosing to marry her, he also elected to dismiss as his wife a woman who was the daughter of Aretas, the powerful king of the Nabateans. According to both Josephus and the Gospels, John the Baptist criticized Herod Antipas's marriage to Herodias and, on this account, was imprisoned and later executed at Machaerus (Matt. 14:1–12; Mark 6:14–29; Luke 3:19–20; 9:7–9). According to the Gospel of Luke, Antipas also played a role in the trial of Jesus (23:6–16; cf. Acts 4:27).

Antipas's first capital was Sepphoris, which he rebuilt in 4 BCE; later he moved his capital to Tiberias on the shore of the Sea of Galilee, a newly built city characteristically named after the Roman emperor; both later played a central role in the history of rabbinic Judaism. Antipas's downfall came shortly after Gaius Caligula became emperor. Caligula granted the former territories of Herod Philip to Antipas's brother-in-law Herod Agrippa and also bestowed upon him the title "king." Prompted by Herodias, Antipas went to Rome to seek equivalent royal status for himself. Not only did he fail in this endeavor, but the agents of Agrippa accused him of crimes against Rome;

he was deported to Gaul and his territories given to Agrippa. Herodias followed him into exile. *See also* Herodias; John the Baptist; Tiberias.

5 Herod Agrippa (uh-grip′uh) I, son of Aristobulus and Bernice and grandson of Herod the Great. He was born ca. 10 BCE and sent to Rome when he was six, shortly before the death of his grandfather, to be educated in the company of Drusus, son of the emperor Tiberius, and Claudius. Herod Agrippa (or, as he styled himself later, Julius Agrippa) became a close associate of Gaius, who was to become the emperor Caligula. Grown accustomed to luxury and extravagance, Agrippa became a notorious spendthrift, constantly in debt for ever increasing amounts. At the urging of his sister Herodias, his brother-in-law Herod Antipas helped him with money and a position in Tiberias, but they soon quarreled and Agrippa found himself back in Rome, where he remained in debt. His incautious speech led to a brief imprisonment by Tiberius. When Tiberius died, only months later, and Caligula became emperor, Agrippa's fortunes suddenly improved. Caligula bestowed many honors and much wealth upon him and, in 37 CE, granted him the former tetrarchies of Philip and Lysanias. In 40 CE, he added to these the territories of the exiled Herod Antipas. When Caligula was assassinated in 41 CE, Claudius, his successor, also rewarded his old friend, giving him Judea and Samaria, so that Agrippa's territory now included the kingdom formerly ruled by Herod the Great. From 41 to 44 CE, Agrippa ruled with a pious, scrupulous, and apparently sincere adherence to the Jewish law. According to Acts 12, he persecuted the early Christians and was responsible for the beheading of James the son of Zebedee and the imprisonment of Peter (12:1–4). Agrippa's death in 44 CE was sudden and unexpected; Acts and Josephus agree that it came at Caesarea and that he suffered an attack while dressed in splendid robes after having been acclaimed by the crowd (Acts 12:20–23).

6 Herod Agrippa II or Marcus Julius Agrippa, the last of the Herodian house to hold a kingdom. When his father, Agrippa I, died suddenly in 44 CE, Agrippa II was only seventeen and was being educated in Rome. The emperor Claudius, though well disposed toward him, did not immediately grant him the rights of succession because of his youth. By 50 CE, however, he had been given the small territory of his deceased uncle, Herod of Chalcis, and in 53 CE he was permitted to exchange this for rule over the former tetrarchy of Philip and certain territories in the Lebanon. Nero added parts of Galilee and Perea to this realm, and Agrippa renamed his capital, Caesarea Philippi, Neronia in the emperor's honor. Agrippa's sister, Bernice, had been the wife of Herod of Chalcis, and she came to live with her brother after her husband's death. Their relationship became notorious as an incestuous affair, which apparently lasted throughout their lives in spite of her brief marriage to Polemon of Cilicia and her scandalous affair with Titus. In Acts 25:13–26:32, Paul appears before Agrippa and Bernice as a prisoner. Agrippa was directly involved in the completion of the Jerusalem temple and the subsequent paving of the streets of Jerusalem with white marble. His true loyalty to Rome never wavered, however, even when put to the ultimate test provided by the Jewish revolt of 66 CE and its subsequent suppression by the Romans. Agrippa, after futile efforts to forestall revolt, joined the Roman side and not only regained his kingdom with Roman help, but was closely associated with Titus, the conqueror of Jerusalem. Agrippa moved to Rome, and there he died after 93 CE.   F.O.G.

Herodians (hi-roh′dee-uhnz), a group who, together with the Pharisees, are said to have opposed Jesus. The term is found only in the Gospels of Mark (3:6; 12:13; also 8:15 in some manuscripts) and Matthew (22:16). If the name refers to an actual party or faction, the Herodians may have been the supporters of the rule and policies of Herod Antipas. They are described as asking Jesus the difficult question regarding payment of taxes to Caesar (Matt. 22:15–22; Mark 12:13–17). The question is actually posed by both Herodians and Pharisees in order to place Jesus in a no-win situation: he will either offend Jewish religious leaders by supporting the tax or offend supporters of the Roman political regime by denouncing it. Thus, Jesus's clever response is presented as an answer with which neither Herodians nor Pharisees could find fault. *See also* Herod; Pharisees.

Herodias (hi-roh′dee-uhs), the daughter of Aristobulus and Bernice and thus a granddaughter of Herod the Great and sister of Herod Agrippa I. She was married twice: first, to her paternal half uncle Herod (called Philip in Matt. 14:3; Mark 6:17), to whom she bore a daughter, Salome; then once again to a half uncle, Herod Antipas. The second marriage, carried out after she left her first husband and Antipas divorced his royal Nabatean wife, was publicly condemned by John the Baptist. According to the Gospels, Herod Antipas had John arrested for this, but was afraid to execute him. Finally, Herodias got her revenge by having her daughter (who had pleased Antipas with a dance) ask for John's head as a prize (Matt. 14:3–12; Mark 6:17–29; cf. Luke 3:19–20; 9:7–9). Antipas was eventually exiled to Gaul and Herodias followed him into exile. *See also* Herod; John the Baptist; Salome.   F.O.G.

heron, any of the family *Ardeidae* of wading birds, with long thin legs and necks, that feed on fish and other marine life. The Hebrews considered them unclean, so they were not to be eaten (Lev. 11:19; Deut. 14:18).

Heshbon (hesh′bon), a city of northern Moab captured by the Amorite king Sihon, who made it his capital (Num. 21:26–30). The Israelites defeated Sihon in their first battle in the Transjordan (Num. 21:21–24; Josh. 12:2) and distributed his territory to Reuben and Gad, assigning Heshbon to Reuben (Num. 32:37). Later, Heshbon was considered Gad's inheritance (Josh. 13:27) and was allotted to the Levites (Josh. 21:39). Prophetic oracles against Moab mention Heshbon (probably restored to Moab by Mesha, ca. 830 BCE). Heshbon reappears (as Esbus) in documents of the Hellenistic and Roman periods, but it is not mentioned in the NT.

Excavations at a tell near the modern Jordanian village of Hesban reveal successive occupations from the early Iron Age through Late Mamluk (ca. 1200 BCE–1456 CE) with a gap from ca. 500 to 250 BCE. Lack of Bronze Age remains and sparse evidence for early Iron Age settlement suggest necessary reassessment either of the site identification (whether this is biblical Heshbon) or of the historical reliability of the Sihon tradition. *See also* Gad; Moab; Reuben; Sihon.   P.A.B.

Heth, in the Table of Nations (Gen. 10:15; 1 Chron. 1:13) the son of Canaan and great-grandson of Noah, and the eponymous ancestor of the Hittites. The "descendants of Heth" (NRSV: "Hittites") witnessed Abraham's purchase of the cave of Machpelah from Ephron (Gen. 23:6, 16, 18). Rebekah was annoyed by Esau's marriage to a "daughter of Heth" (Gen. 27:46; NRSV: "Hittite woman"). Ezekiel describes Jerusalem's ancestry with the words "your father was an Amorite, and your mother a Hittite" (16:3, 45). *See also* Canaan; Hittites; Noah.

Hexateuch (hek'suh-took), a term sometimes used in biblical studies for the first six books of the Bible (Genesis–Joshua). The term connotes a theological unity that some scholars see in these writings in contrast to the canonical unity called the Pentateuch (the first five books of the Bible). Scholars who prefer Hexateuch to Pentateuch believe the books can be structured according to a series of brief, credolike speeches set in a context of worship (e.g., Deut. 26:5–11; Josh. 24:1–28). These speeches recite God's acts on behalf of Israel in four units: promise for progeny and land to the ancestors, exodus from oppression in Egypt, leadership through the dangers of the wilderness, and conquest of the land in Canaan. Notably, these four units highlighted by the credo speeches exclude reference to God's gift of the law at Sinai, suggesting that the Sinai traditions were originally distinct from the credo traditions. *See also* Pentateuch, sources of the.   G.W.C.

Hezekiah (hez'uh-ki'uh; Heb., "God strengthens"), the son of Ahaz and king of Judah ca. 715–687/6 BCE. He was considered by the author of the book of Kings to have been utterly loyal to the Lord, God of Israel: "There was no one like him among all the kings of Judah after him, or among those who were before him" (2 Kings 18:5). This commendation is based on Hezekiah's attention to matters related to religious practice. He closed down all of the "high places" throughout Judah,

thereby centralizing sacrifice at the altar of the temple in Jerusalem (cf. 2 Kings 18:22). He also banned many practices that had become common: the use of sacred pillars and trees (asherah) and the reverencing of the "bronze serpent" (Heb. *nekhushtan*) associated with miraculous healing (cf. Num. 21:4–10).

Hezekiah's Reign: Hezekiah's reign fell during the age of major Assyrian military and commercial activity in Phoenicia and the Philistian coast. Shalmaneser V campaigned twice in the area and in 722/1 BCE conquered Samaria, the capital of the northern kingdom, Israel. Sargon II reconquered Samaria in 720 BCE and marched as far as Rapiah, where he engaged an Egyptian force supporting local rulers in their rebellion against Assyria. Four years later, Sargon appeared again, this time founding a trading colony south of Gaza, based in part on cooperation with local Arab tribes of the western Negev. The rebellion in Gaza in 713 BCE was quelled by Sargon's commander-in-chief ("Tartan," Isa. 20:1) in 712 BCE, and the city was annexed to the Assyrian Empire. Throughout this decade, Hezekiah remained a vassal of Assyria, a status he inherited from his father, Ahaz. At some point, however, Hezekiah received the Babylonian delegation of Merodach-baladan (2 Kings 18:13; 20:12–13), and this diplomatic dealing with the sworn enemy of Sargon is indicative that there must have been an anti-Assyrian undercurrent

A section of the tunnel that brought water from the Gihon spring to the Pool of Siloam, built during the reign of King Hezekiah (715–687/6 BCE) to ensure Jerusalem's water supply during a siege.

in Judah. Hezekiah was likely involved in the political stirrings in Philistia. Although Sargon does not claim in Assyrian records to have engaged Judah outright, several fortresses in the Judean Shephelah (Ekron, Gibbethon, and perhaps Azekah) did fall to the Assyrian armies.

Rebellion Against Assyria: Hezekiah openly broke with Assyria in 705 BCE, after the death of Sargon. In the west, Hezekiah became the driving force behind a military coalition that was to face the new monarch, Sennacherib. Hezekiah moved into the coastal plain with force (2 Kings 18:8) and ousted rulers who were hostile to his policies. In preparation for a possible siege, Hezekiah secured Jerusalem's water supply by drilling a 1,780-foot tunnel through solid rock to bring water from the Gihon spring into the city (2 Kings 20:20; 2 Chron. 32:3–4). A feat of ancient engineering, this tunnel was dug from both ends simultaneously, to meet in the middle. It follows a somewhat twisting route, probably to enable shafts to be dug down to the tunnel from places that at that time would have been within the city walls. Despite such preparations, Hezekiah's efforts were no match for Sennacherib's superior forces. In 701 BCE, Sennacherib campaigned in the west; the Phoenician cities succumbed quickly and Hezekiah's allies in Philistia were defeated, despite the support lent them by an Egyptian expeditionary force (2 Kings 19:9). The Bible then reports: "Sennacherib king of Assyria came up against all the fortified cities of Judah and took them" (2 Kings 18:13). Assyrian records provide Sennacherib's own account of these conquests: "As for Hezekiah of Judah, who did not submit to my yoke, I laid siege to 46 of his strong cities, walled forts and to the countless small villages in their vicinity, and conquered them. . . . I drove out 200,150 people, young and old, male and female, horses, mules, donkeys, camels, big and small cattle, beyond counting and considered them booty."

Jerusalem then came under siege, and negotiations were conducted between a high-level Assyrian team and Hezekiah's advisers for Hezekiah's total surrender. Sennacherib claims that he made Hezekiah "a prisoner in Jerusalem, his royal residence, like a bird in a cage." Though the prophet Isaiah counseled holding out, for the Lord "will defend this city to save it" (2 Kings 19:34), Hezekiah submitted to the Assyrian demands and paid a heavy indemnity (2 Kings 18:14–16). Jerusalem did not, however, become prey to the Assyrians, and biblical accounts credit this to divine intervention: "That very night an angel of the LORD set out and struck down one hundred and eighty-five thousand in the camp of the Assyrians; when morning dawned, these were all dead bodies" (2 Kings 19:35). Nevertheless, much of Judah's territory was transferred to the coastal city-states loyal to Assyria, and Hezekiah resumed his vassal status as king of Jerusalem and its immediate environs.

Hezekiah's reign overlapped with the time of two Judean prophets, Micah and Isaiah of Jeru-

salem. According to Jer. 26:18–19, he was tolerant of Micah, even when the latter prophesied against him. The relationship with Isaiah was more complicated. Isaiah seems to have initially counseled Hezekiah not to rebel against Assyria (30:1–17; 31:1–5). Later, however, Isaiah speaks words of encouragement during the siege (2 Kings 19:2–7, 20–34; cf. Isa. 37:2–7, 21–35). In 2 Kings 20:1–11, Isaiah prophesies healing when he is ill and makes the shadow on a sundial retreat backward as a sign that the deliverance is from God. But then Isaiah sharply rebukes Hezekiah for displaying treasures to Babylonian envoys (2 Kings 20:11–20); the strong implication is that, by doing this, Hezekiah set in motion the events that would lead to the Babylonian exile. Hezekiah, however, is not bothered by the prospect of disaster for his children and descendants as long as there are peace and security in his days. Hezekiah was succeeded as king of Judah by Manasseh. In the NT, he is listed in the genealogy of Jesus (Matt. 1:9–10). *See also* Isaiah, book of; Kings, First and Second Books of; Sennacherib.

M.C.

Hezron (hez'ruhn).

1 The third son of Reuben and an ancestor of the Hezronites, a family group belonging to the Reubenite tribe (Gen. 49:6; Exod. 6:14; Num. 26:6; 1 Chron. 5:3).

2 The son of Perez and grandson of Judah; he was an ancestor of a Hezronite family group who belonged to the tribe of Judah (Gen. 46:12). He is also listed as ancestor of David (Ruth 4:18–19) and of Jesus (Matt. 1:3; Luke 3:33).

3 A city on the southern border of Judah (Josh. 15:3).

Hiel (hi'uhl; Heb., "God is brother"), a man from Bethel who is said to have rebuilt Jericho during the days of Ahab and to have lost two sons in the process (1 Kings 16:34). According to the Bible, he laid the city's foundation "at the cost of Abiram his firstborn, and set up its gates at the cost of his youngest son Segub." This has been interpreted in two ways. One suggestion holds that Hiel offered his two sons as human sacrifices at key stages during the building process. A different proposal suggests that Hiel's two sons simply died during the construction and that their deaths were attributed to Hiel's building activities because of a curse Joshua had pronounced on anyone who rebuilt the city (Josh. 6:26).

Hierapolis (hi'uh-rap'uh-lis), a city of Asia Minor located in the upper Lycus Valley close to the hot springs of Pamukkale. It is one hundred miles east of Ephesus, twelve miles from Colossae, and six miles from Laodicea. Although originating as the village center of a temple estate dedicated to the Phrygian mother goddess, Hierapolis grew and finally received formal status as a city from the king of Pergamum in the early second century BCE. In 133 BCE Rome took control of Hierapolis and made it part of the province of Asia.

Its subsequent prosperity was largely based on its textile and cloth-dyeing industry. Both grave inscriptions and literary evidence (Cicero *Pro Flacco* 68; Josephus *Antiquities* 12.147–53) indicate a substantial Jewish presence around Hierapolis. The only biblical reference to the city is Col. 4:13, which reports that Paul's colleague Epaphras "labored much" for the Christians in Colossae, Laodicea, and Hierapolis. Hierapolis's extensive remains include a Roman theater, baths, city walls, and a necropolis. *See also* Colossae; Epaphras; Ephesus; Laodicea; Pergamum.   R.A.W.

Higgaion (hi-gay'yon), a Hebrew word that is transliterated by the NRSV in Ps. 9:16. Its meaning is unknown, but it occurs in combination with Selah, another transliterated Hebrew word of uncertain meaning. The term probably specified some sort of musical or liturgical notation. The word actually appears in two other psalms as well, but in those instances the NRSV translates it "melody" in Ps. 92:3 and "meditation" in Ps. 19:14.

high place, an elevated location used for religious rites. In the NRSV, "high place" typically translates Hebrew *bamah* (pl. *bamot*). In certain contexts, this word can refer to geographic features without any religious or cultic connotation (e.g., "high mountains" in Deut. 12:2; "heights (of the earth)" in Deut. 32:13; Isa. 58:14; Amos 4:13). But there were also *bamot* within towns (2 Kings 17:9) and in valleys (Jer. 7:31; 32:35; Ezek. 6:3), and they are commonly spoken of as being "built" (e.g., 1 Kings 14:23) and, when removed, "broken down" (e.g., 2 Chron. 31:1). In such cases, the term seems to refer to an artificially constructed platform on which sacrifices could be offered or on which cultic objects might be placed. All such high places seem to have been in the open air.

The high place was a common feature in the religions of the small states surrounding Israel, including Ammon (1 Kings 11:7) and Moab (Jer. 49:35). In fact, the word has been found on a victory stele of the ninth-century BCE Moabite king Mesha. In the Bible, high places are often associated with Canaanite fertility religion and the worship of Baal (Jer. 19:5; 32:35); thus, they are strongly condemned, especially in Deuteronomic passages in the book of Kings, in Chronicles, and in the Prophets. Reforming kings are often praised for destroying high places (2 Kings 18:4; 23:8, 13, 15, 19). The rites practiced at high places (as reconstructed from biblical data, extrabiblical references, and cult objects recovered in archaeological excavations) seem to have included ritual prostitution (1 Kings 14:23–24; Ezek. 16:16), child sacrifice (Jer. 7:31; 19:5; 32:35; Ezek. 16:20), and the burning of incense (1 Kings 22:43; 2 Kings 12:3). The stone pillar symbolizing Baal and a wooden pole possibly symbolizing the goddess Asherah were set up at high places (1 Kings 14:23; 2 Kings 17:10).

Role in Israelite Religion: Despite the biblical denunciations just noted, high places were considered a legitimate feature of Israelite religion prior to the centralization of worship in Jerusalem. In 1 Sam. 9:12–24, the prophet Samuel is portrayed as sacrificing and presiding at the attendant meal at the high place of Ramah. In 1 Sam. 10:5 a band of prophets is said to have been worshiping at the high place of Gibeath-elohim. Cultic platforms used for sacrifices have been uncovered by archaeologists at several sites from the period of Israelite occupation, among them Hazor and Arad; the one discovered at Dan was almost certainly built by Jeroboam I (1 Kings 13:32).

The word *bamah*, furthermore, is also used in the Bible to denote the whole of a sanctuary or shrine, such as the "hall" at Ramah (1 Sam. 9:22). Before the Deuteronomic reform (ca. 630 BCE), a number of these local sanctuaries, including ones at Shechem, Bethel, Gilgal, Shiloh, and Jerusalem, were significant for Israel's religion. Abraham founded Hebron (Gen. 13:18); both he and Isaac are said to have founded Beer-sheba (Gen. 21:33; 26:23–25); Jacob founded Bethel (28:18–22; 35:7, 14–15) and Shechem (33:18–20), with which Joshua is also associated (Josh. 8:30–35). Joshua erected twelve stones marking a shrine at Gilgal (Josh. 4:20–24), and David inaugurated worship in Jerusalem before there was any temple there (2 Sam. 24). Another reason for the importance of

A bronze model of an Elamite sanctuary, or "high place," found at Susa, twelfth century BCE.

Ten large stelae at Gezer may have been a Canaanite "high place" (cf. 2 Kings 18:4); Middle Bronze Age.

certain high places was that they were the sanctuaries of particular tribes, as may be seen in the case of the one founded by the tribe of Dan, though again on an old Canaanite site (Judg. 18:27–31).

Scholars often suppose that such sanctuaries were erected in important Canaanite centers, and that the stories connecting the sites to Israelite heroes served to legitimize adoption of these places for worship by Israel. The details of Gen. 28:10–22, especially v. 19, show that Bethel was not a deserted spot, but an ancient Canaanite city and sanctuary. Shechem remained Canaanite long after the time of Jacob and was a center of non-Israelite religion (Judg. 9:4, 27, 46); the pillar and the tree said to have been erected in the sanctuary there would be regular features of a Canaanite high place (Josh. 24:26; Judg. 9:6). The patriarchs are also regularly depicted as invoking Israel's God by titles associated with the Canaanite deity El, in combination with different sanctuary names (El Elyon, Gen. 14:22; El Olam, 21:33; El Bethel, 31:13; cf. Jer. 48:13). Inevitably, such practices would have brought about a degree of fusion between Israelite and Canaanite religion, and such syncretism is what may have incurred the condemnation of Israel's prophets (e.g., Hos. 2:2–20) and provided incentive for centralized religion at one temple, where the incursion of Canaanite elements could be curtailed. The great prestige of Jerusalem enabled implementation of a Deuteronomic reform program by Josiah, who destroyed all the numerous high places in both the south and north (2 Kings 23:4–20) and left the temple at Jerusalem as the sole place where God could be worshiped. The Babylonian invasion a few years later (early sixth century BCE) probably brought about the destruction of any high places that had survived. From that time on, nothing further is heard of high places and, after the return from exile, only the Jerusalem sanctuary was reestablished (Ezra 3). *See also* ark of the covenant, ark of God; tabernacle; temple, the.

Bibliography
De Vaux, Roland. *Ancient Israel: Its Life and Institutions.* McGraw-Hill, 1961. Pp. 284–311.

Kraus, Hans-Joachim. *Worship in Israel.* Blackwell, 1966. Pp. 134–178.

Vaughan, Patrick H. *The Meaning of "Bama" in the Old Testament.* Cambridge University Press, 1974.   J.R.P.

high priests. *See* priests.

Hilkiah (hil-ki′uh; Heb., "the LORD is my portion").

1 A Levite from the line of Merari (1 Chron. 6:45).

2 The son of Hosah, a Merarite Levite in the time of David (1 Chron. 26:11).

3 The father of Eliakim, a royal official in the time of King Hezekiah (2 Kings 18:18; see Isa. 22:20).

4 The father of Jeremiah, a priest (Jer. 1:1).

5 A high priest in the late seventh century BCE who reported that a book of the law had been found at the temple (2 Kings 22–23; see 2 Chron. 35:8). He appears to have been an ancestor of Ezra (Ezra 7:1, see 1 Chron. 6:13–15).   F.E.G.

hill country,
a general designation in the Bible for areas that are hilly rather than flat. Since the Levant has a mountainous spine running its length between the Jordan River to the east and the Mediterranean Sea to the west, any area along that spine can be designated hill country. In addition, the hills found along the east bank of the Jordan River also constitute an upland area, any part of which can be termed hill country. Among the areas identified as hill country in the Bible are parts of Seir, south of the Dead Sea (Gen. 36:8); the area of the Jebusites (Josh. 11:3); the dwelling place of the Anakim (11:21); areas in both Judah and Israel (11:21); and the tribal areas of Naphtali and Ephraim (20:7). Indeed, hill country could be identified from as far south as the Wilderness of Ziph (1 Sam. 23:14) to as far north as the land of the Amorites, near the head of the Euphrates River (Num. 13:29). In the NT, the home of Zechariah and Elizabeth (the parents of John the Baptist) is located in the hill country of Judah (Luke 1:39, 65).   D.B.

hin,
a unit of capacity equal to the amount of liquid that would fill a common household pot. *See also* weights and measures.

hind. *See* deer.

Hinnom (hin′uhm), Valley of,
a valley known also as the Valley of the Son of Hinnom. It was probably the Wadi er-Rababi, beginning west of Jerusalem, near the present Jaffa Gate, and curving round south of the Old City to join the Kidron Valley. It was entered from the Potsherd Gate (Jer. 19:2, 6) and formed part of the boundary between Judah and Benjamin (Josh. 15:8; 18:16; Neh. 11:30). The Valley of Hinnom is notorious in the Bible as a site for idolatry, including the human sacrifice of children under Ahaz and Manasseh

(mid-eighth to mid-seventh century BCE; 2 Chron. 28:3; 33:6) and again in Jeremiah's day (7:30–34; 32:35), despite the abolition of such practices by Josiah (2 Kings 23:10). Such evil associations caused its name (Heb. *gehinnom;* Gk. *gehenna*) to be identified with hell (e.g., Matt. 5:22, 29; 23:15, 33; Mark 9:43, 47; James 3:6). *See also* Ahaz; hell; Josiah; Manasseh.   D.B.

Hiram (hi'ruhm; a short form of Ahiram, Heb., "my brother is exalted" or "brother of the exalted one"; rendered as Huram in 1 and 2 Chronicles).

1 Hiram I, the king of Tyre, and a contemporary of David and Solomon. The son of Abibaal, Hiram I was nineteen years old when he ascended the throne, and he reigned thirty-four years (ca. 969–935 BCE). The kingdom he established is vividly pictured in Ezek. 26–27. Under Hiram's rule Tyre became the leading city of Phoenicia, which launched a colonial empire that spread over the whole of the Mediterranean. He enlarged the island city of Tyre by uniting it with a smaller island and undertook extensive building programs. David traded with Hiram for materials and workers to build his royal palace in Jerusalem (2 Sam. 5:11; 1 Chron. 14:1). He established a treaty with Hiram that was renewed by Solomon, who also traded with him for materials and workers for the building of the temple in Jerusalem (1 Kings 5:12–18; 2 Chron. 2:3–12). Hiram supplied cedar and other building materials in exchange for wheat and olive oil. Some years later Hiram gave Solomon gold and another larger shipment of cedar and other woods and received in exchange twenty towns in Galilee known collectively as Cabul (1 Kings 9:10–13). Hiram also aided Solomon in his commercial ventures by supplying both ships and sailors for a merchant fleet that operated out of the port of Ezion-geber (1 Kings 9:26–28). Some scholars have suggested this Hiram of Tyre should be identified with the famous King Ahiram of Phoenician Byblos (ca. 1000 BCE). There was also an eighth-century King Hiram of Tyre mentioned in an inscription of Tiglath-pileser III. *See also* David; Solomon; Tyre.

2 An artisan sent by King Hiram of Tyre to do the bronze work for the temple in Jerusalem (1 Kings 7:13–14). The son of a woman of the tribe of Naphtali (1 Kings 7:14) or of Dan (2 Chron. 2:14) and a man of Tyre, he was responsible for casting the bronze pillars, the molten sea, and other temple furnishings in a specially suited clay that was found between Succoth and Zarethan (1 Kings 7:40–46).   D.L.C.

hired hand, servant, worker, a free person who worked for a wage (Heb. *sakir;* Gk. *misthōtos*). Some hired workers might have been day laborers (cf. Matt. 20:1–16), but there seems to have been a class of hired servants whose terms were at least a year or more in length (Lev. 25:53). The law protected the rights of such persons (Deut. 24:14–15), though they were not to be invited to eat the Passover (Exod. 12:45). Their jobs might include

such tasks as farm work (Lev. 25:6), fishing (Mark 1:20), shepherding (John 10:12–13), or even serving as mercenary soldiers (2 Chron. 25:26). Job 7:1–2 describes the hard life of a hired worker (NRSV: "laborer"), and Mal. 3:5 prophesies divine judgment on those who "oppress hired workers in their wages" (cf. James 5:4). The prophet Isaiah twice refers to years as they would be reckoned by "a hired worker" (16:14; 21:16); this probably means "not one day more than the specified time." When Jesus called James and John to be his disciples, they left their father, Zebedee, in the boat with the hired men (Mark 1:20). In Jesus's parable of the Prodigal Son, the boy who has come to dire straits in a far country determines to return home, asking his father to treat him as one of his father's hired hands (Luke 15:15–17). In John 10:12–13, Jesus contrasts the cowardice of a hired shepherd with the owner's concern for the sheep. In a telling passage that refers to different social classes in Israel during the Second Temple period, the book of Judith refers to a time of repentance when all the men of Israel and "their wives and their children and their cattle and every resident alien and hired laborer and purchased slave" put on sackcloth (4:10); if this list is hierarchical, hired laborers would be esteemed above slaves but below resident aliens and cattle. But Sir. 7:20 counsels against the abuse of "slaves who work faithfully or hired laborers who devote themselves to their task."   M.A.P.

Hittites (hit'tits). In the Bible, the Hittites are a pervasive tribe among the pre-Israelite inhabitants of Canaan (e.g., Gen. 10:15; 15:20; Exod. 23:28). By contrast, historians identify Hittites primarily with an Indo-European people who established a strong kingdom in east-central Anatolia in the second millennium BCE. There is no evidence, however, that the Hittites associated with this Anatolian empire ever penetrated as far south as the Levant. Biblical references to the land of the Hittites (Judg. 1:26) and the kings of the Hittites (1 Kings 10:29; 2 Kings 7:6) probably refer specifically to the Neo-Hittite states of Hamath and northern Syria.

The historical, Anatolian Hittites appear to have been named after the non-Indo-European Hattians, whom they displaced. They spoke several Indo-European languages, but the official language of the Hittite kingdom, written in a cuneiform (i.e., wedge-shaped) script adapted from Akkadian, is called Cuneiform Hittite. In the outlying regions a hieroglyphic system was used to write a related language, referred to as Hieroglyphic Hittite. Luwian, which is very close to Hieroglyphic Hittite, and Palaic were also spoken within the kingdom.

History: The history of the Hittites can be divided into three periods: the Old Kingdom, the New Kingdom, and the Neo-Hittite kingdoms. Sometime around 1650 BCE Hattusilis I pushed out of Anatolia into north Syria and captured Aleppo, and his successor, Mursilis I, sacked Babylon. Following these two great rulers of the Old Kingdom, the Hittite Empire declined, due to both internal difficulties and the growing power of the Hurrians under the rulers of Mitanni.

The revival of the New Kingdom began in the fifteenth century BCE, but it was Suppiluliuma (1375–1335 BCE) who made it a major power by his conquest of Mitanni and northern Syria. All the small states of north and central Syria, including most of Lebanon, became vassals of the Hittites. This area became a battleground between the Egyptians and the Hittites until the peace treaty between Ramesses II and Hattusilis III (ca. 1280 BCE), but the Hittites remained in control of the region. After this treaty, the main threat to Hittite hegemony in Syria came from Assyria, and Carchemish, the capital of the Hittite vice-regent in the east, gained in importance. It was the Sea Peoples (i.e., people from the Greek islands, including Crete) from the west, however, who destroyed the Hittite Empire. The Hittite homeland collapsed first, and then the coastal areas under its control, from Ugarit to Amurru, fell to these invaders about 1200 BCE.

The devastation did not reach too far inland, however, and the remnants of the Hittite Empire formed Neo-Hittite kingdoms in Carchemish, Hamath, and a number of other inland sites, particularly in the Taurus region and in northern Syria. Hieroglyphic Hittite and Neo-Hittite culture continued in many of these sites even after the Aramean influx at the end of the second millennium led to an increase in power for Aramean dynasties.

The Assyrians continued to refer to the inhabitants of these new kingdoms as Hittites. From the time of Tiglath-pileser I (1115–1070 BCE) onward, the Assyrians called all the territory between the Euphrates and northern Lebanon the Land of Hatti. With Assyrian expansion into the Levant, the term "Hittite" was expanded to include the people of those regions. Shalmaneser III (858–824 BCE) lists Ahab among the Hittite kings, and Esar-haddon (680–669 BCE) includes the kings of Judah, Edom, Moab, Ammon, and a couple of Philistine rulers among the kings of Hatti. The term "Hatti" continued to be used into the Neo-Babylonian period (sixth century BCE) as a geographic designation that included the Levant.

In the Bible: The biblical use of the term "Hittite" is probably dependent, at least in part, on cuneiform usage. Canaan is listed as the father of Heth in the Table of Nations (Gen. 10:15), and many texts (e.g., Gen. 15:20; Exod. 23:28) list the Hittites among the pre-Israelite inhabitants of Canaan, though there is no evidence that the Anatolian Hittites ever settled there. Ezekiel refers to the mother of Jerusalem as a Hittite (16:3, 45), and Genesis mentions Hittites in accounts of Israel's ancestors (23; 25:9; 26:34; 27:46); in both of these cases, however, the biblical writer is probably just following the Neo-Babylonian geographical terminology. The references to the land of the Hittites (Judg. 1:26) and the kings of the

Hittites (1 Kings 10:29; 2 Kings 7:6) probably refer specifically to the Neo-Hittite states of Hamath and northern Syria, and thus also reflect an earlier usage than that of the Priestly writer or Ezekiel (sixth century BCE).

All of the Hittites mentioned by name in the Bible—Ephron, Zohar, Beeri, Elon, Ahimelech, and Uriah—bear Semitic, not Hittite, names. Ahimelech (1 Sam. 26:6) and Uriah (2 Sam. 11:3), however, are both designated Hittites in written sources that antedate strong Assyrian influence on Judah. That suggests that they may indeed have been assimilated descendants of Hittite or, more likely, Neo-Hittite lineage. *See also* Horites; Mitanni.   J.J.M.R.

Hivites (hiv′its). *See* Horites.

Hobab (hoh′bab), one of three names for Moses's father-in-law (Judg. 4:11). With Jethro (Exod. 3:1; 18:1) and Reuel (2:18), the name belongs to a complex tradition about Moses's family. Num. 10:29 defines Hobab as the son of Reuel, the founding father of the Kenites. *See also* Jethro.

Hodaviah (hod′uh-vi′uh; Heb., "praise the LORD").

1 A son of Elioenai; a descendant of Judah and of Zerubbabel (1 Chron. 3:24).

2 The leader of a family group belonging to the eastern half-tribe of Manasseh (1 Chron. 5:24).

3 The son of Hassenuah and a member of the tribe of Benjamin (1 Chron. 9:7).

4 The ancestor of a levitical family group who returned from the Babylonian exile with Zerubbabel (Ezra 2:40); he is called Hodevah in Neh. 7:43.

Hodiah (hoh-di′uh; Heb., "the LORD is my splendor").

1 A descendant of Judah who became the brother-in-law of Naham (1 Chron. 4:19).

2 A Levite who helped explain the law read by Ezra to the people (Neh. 8:7); this is probably the same Levite who took part in the covenant-renewal ceremonies and signed Ezra's covenant to keep the law (Neh. 9:5; 10:10).

3 Another Levite who signed Ezra's covenant-renewal document (Neh. 10:13).

4 A leader of the people who also signed Ezra's covenant-renewal document (Neh. 10:18).

Hoglah (hog′luh; Heb., "partridge").

1 The third-named daughter of Zelophehad (Num. 26:33; 27:1; 36:11; Josh. 17:3), a member of the tribe of Manasseh. *See also* law; Mahlah; Zelophehad.

2 A name that occurs as part of the compound place-name Beth-hoglah (Heb., "house of Hoglah"; Josh. 15:6). The name Hoglah also appears as a place-name in ostraca inscriptions from Samaria (eighth century BCE). The territory of Hoglah or Beth-Hoglah was probably located north and east of Samaria and was claimed by

people who regarded themselves as the descendants of 1.

holiness, a biblical concept associated with separation from the ordinary or the profane, on the one hand, and connection with God or the divine, on the other. God is supremely or definitively holy and people, things, and actions may be considered holy through association with God. Holiness may also include the ideas of consecration to God and of purity from what is evil or improper.

In the Hebrew Bible: Israel's earliest hymn praises God as "majestic in holiness" (Exod. 15:11). Both Psalms and Isaiah frequently refer to God as the Holy One (1:4; 5:19; cf. Ps. 99), and in Isaiah's vision of the heavenly court the angels sing praise to God as "Holy, holy, holy" (6:3). Places where God had appeared to people were usually regarded as holy. At the burning bush (Exod. 3:5) Moses is instructed to remove his shoes, because he stands on holy ground. After Jacob receives a vision at Bethel, he consecrates the site as a holy place (Gen. 28:11–22). The temple in Jerusalem was the most holy place in Israel, because God's presence dwelt there (1 Kings 8:10–11). Equipment used in the temple, including the jars, altars, candleholders, musical instruments, and vestments, was set aside for sacred use and was thus holy. Sacrificial animals and other foods used in worship had to meet stringent requirements and, once designated holy, could not be returned to secular use. Such food would either be burned on the altar or consumed by the priests in the temple. The priests and other personnel of the temple were holy, and only they could enter certain parts of the temple and perform the sacrifices and other ritual acts. Holiness also extended to the name of God (Lev. 20:3), the sabbath (Gen. 2:3), and appointed festivals (Lev. 23). Israel itself is to be a holy nation (Exod. 19:4; Deut. 7:6). Israel's holiness depends on its adherence to God's commandments and avoidance of sin. The Holiness Code, a comprehensive series of ethical and ritual laws in Lev. 17–26, demands observance because of Israel's holiness: "You shall be holy; for I the Lord your God am holy" (Lev. 19:2).

In the NT: The NT reaffirms traditional Jewish ideas of holiness. God, the temple, and the law are all holy. God is addressed as "Holy Father" by Jesus (John 17:11) and is designated as such in the Lord's Prayer ("Hallowed be your name"; Matt. 6:9). Jesus is also called holy on numerous occasions because of his closeness to God. An unclean spirit recognizes Jesus as the Holy One of God (Mark 1:24), as does Peter (John 6:69). The angel announcing Jesus's birth to Mary says that the Holy Spirit and God's power will make the child holy (Luke 1:35), and the disciples' preaching after Jesus's death refers to him as holy (Acts 3:14; 4:27, 30), as does the book of Revelation (3:7). Just as Israel is portrayed as holy in the Hebrew Bible, so the Christian community is portrayed as holy in the NT. Paul addresses his communities as "the saints," i.e., "the holy ones" (Rom. 1:7; 1 Cor. 1:2),

and argues that believers consecrate one another as holy (1 Cor. 7:14). In 1 Peter the phrase "holy nation" (a traditional designation for Israel) is applied to the community (2:9); believers are to be holy because God is holy (1:16). Ephesians depicts the community as a holy temple in which God dwells in the Spirit (2:19–22). Consequently, the community must avoid sin and evil and anything that would compromise its holiness and closeness to God. Finally, mention must be made of the Holy Spirit, who plays a special role in the NT. The Spirit of God in the OT guided the prophets and other servants of God and was a manifestation of God's active power. In the NT, however, the Holy Spirit acts as the continuing power and presence of Jesus, filling those who have believed in Jesus as a sign of God's power (a theme especially emphasized in the book of Acts). In Paul's letters the Holy Spirit manifests God's presence, which sanctifies and teaches (Rom. 15:13, 16; 1 Cor. 2:13). In John, the Holy Spirit (called the "Paraclete" or "Helper/Advocate") plays a special role in strengthening and guiding the community in times of trouble (14:26). *See also* Holy Spirit; purity; sanctification; worship in the Hebrew Bible; worship in the New Testament.   A.J.S.

Holofernes (hol´uh-fuhr´neez; possibly from Gk., "to be crafty"), the chief antagonist in the book of Judith. As the chief general of Nebuchadnezzar (Jth. 2:4), Holofernes carries out various campaigns against Nebuchadnezzar's enemies (Jth. 2), including Israel (Jth. 5–12). Achior, a leader of the Ammonites, warns Holofernes about attacking the Israelites, insisting that their God would defend them, but Holofernes despises this counsel (5:5–6:9). He lays siege to Bethulia, Judith's hometown, cutting off its water supply. Leaving the town, Judith is taken captive, but manages to deceive Holofernes, who is captivated by her great beauty. She promises to show him a way of defeating Bethulia without losing any men, so he invites her to stay with him. After some days, she beheads the drunk general, thus earning her status as a heroic figure of Israel (chaps. 13–16).

Holy of Holies. *See* tabernacle; temple, the.

Holy One of Israel, the, a term for God. In the Bible the phrase is used frequently by the Hebrew prophets, especially Isaiah, as a title for Israel's God (Isa. 1:4; 5:19, 24; 10:17, 20; 40:25; 41:14, 16, 20; 43:3, 14–15). The phrase also appears in the Psalms (71:22; 78:41; 89:18). In the NT, "Holy One of God" is applied to Jesus in Mark 1:24; Luke 4:34; and Acts 3:14 (cf. 1 John 2:20). *See also* names of God in the Hebrew Bible; names of God in the New Testament.

Holy Spirit, the mysterious power or presence of God that operates within individuals and communities, inspiring or empowering them with qualities they would not otherwise possess. The term "spirit" translates Hebrew *ruakh* and Greek *pneuma,* words denoting "wind," "breath," and, by extension, a life-giving element. With the adjective "holy," the reference is to the divine spirit, i.e., the Spirit of God.

In the Hebrew Bible: The Hebrew Bible rarely employs the designation "Holy Spirit" as such (only in Ps. 51:11; Isa. 63:10–11; Wis. 1:5), but equivalent expressions like "Spirit of God" or "Spirit of the LORD" are common. From these, we may discern three emphases. First, the Spirit is an agent in creation, a fact masked somewhat by the NRSV's idiosyncratic translation of Gen. 1:1–2: "In the beginning when God created the heavens and the earth . . . a wind from God swept over the face of the waters." The phrase "wind from God" (*ruakh 'elohim*) would normally be translated "God's Spirit" (as it is virtually everywhere else in the NRSV). Still, the representation of God's Spirit here is somewhat impersonal, almost synonymous with God's power to give life (cf. references to the "breath" [*ruakh*] of God in Ps. 33:6; Ezek. 37:1–10). Second, a more prominent emphasis is the Spirit's role as a source of inspiration and power for leaders, judges (Judg. 3:10; 6:34), kings (1 Sam. 10:1–13; 16:13), and prophets (Isa. 42:1). Beginning with Moses, Israel's leaders typically receive their wisdom, courage, and power as gifts received from the Spirit of the Lord, enacted when the Spirit of God comes upon them. Likewise, Israel's prophets either possess or are possessed by God's Spirit and, so, speak and act with an authority not their own (Num. 24:2; 1 Sam. 10:10; Ezek. 2:2; 3:24; Hos. 9:7; Mic. 3:8). This is sometimes illustrated by ecstatic phenomena (cf. 1 Sam. 10:9–13). In this connection, the Spirit can be conveyed from one person to another, as from Moses to Joshua or from Elijah to Elisha. Third, the Hebrew Bible emphasizes the Spirit as God's presence in the covenantal community (Ezek. 11:14–21; 36:22–32; cf. Isa. 32:15; Joel 2:28).

In the NT: A more diverse range of meaning for the Holy Spirit is seen in the NT. The earlier usage does continue: the Spirit of God comes upon Jesus at his baptism (Matt. 3:13–17; 12:28; Mark 1:9–11; Luke 3:21–22; 4:16–21) and empowers the church/community for its mission (Acts 2). Beyond this, however, an appreciation for the close relationship of Jesus to God expands and significantly transforms the understanding of the Holy Spirit, so that the Spirit is related to God and Jesus simultaneously (cf. the related expressions "Spirit of Christ," "Spirit of the Lord," "Spirit of Jesus," and passages such as Gal. 4:6, where God sends "the Spirit of his Son" into the hearts of those who believe in Jesus). Indeed, a number of NT passages suggest that the Holy Spirit is sent jointly from God and the risen Christ (i.e., from the Father and the Son; cf. Acts 2:33). Believers become disciples by being baptized in the name of the Father, Son, and Holy Spirit (Matt. 28:19). In keeping with this, the Holy Spirit comes to manifest and demonstrate the presence and activity of God and of Jesus Christ in the church. This idea is expressed in the Gospel of John, where the Holy Spirit is described as an Advocate who provides divine presence and guidance for the disciples (14:16, 26; 15:26; 16:7; cf. 1 John 2:1), who testifies on behalf of Jesus Christ (15:26), and who glorifies Jesus Christ (16:14).

Since the Holy Spirit is mentioned in almost every book of the NT, other nuances can be mentioned. In Acts, there is a close connection among four elements: the proclamation of the gospel, baptism, the laying on of hands, and the reception of the Holy Spirit (4:28–31; 8:15–17; 10:44; 19:6). In Paul's letters, reception of the Holy Spirit brings "gifts" (Gk. *charismata*) needed for Christian ministry (1 Cor. 12–14). Paul also contrasts life lived according to the "flesh" with life in or by the "Spirit" (Gal. 5:16–26; cf. Rom. 7:6; 8:11; 2 Cor. 3:6). The Spirit makes believers one "in Christ" (1 Cor. 12:13) and empowers them, not only for the mission of the church, but also for the moral and ethical life appropriate to those who understand themselves to be people of the new age (Gal. 5:22–23). *See also* flesh and spirit; inspiration; Paraclete; Pentecost; spiritual gifts; tongues, speaking in.   T.R.W.L.

holy war. The Bible does not present Israel as fighting to spread or defend its religious beliefs; "holy war" in that sense of the term is absent from biblical teaching or narrative. In another sense, however, the Bible often presents war as a means through which God acts as deliverer, protector, and judge of Israel, often fighting and slaying enemies on Israel's behalf. Up to the time of the monarchy (tenth century BCE) all wars involving the Israelites could be called "wars of the LORD" (Num. 21:14). Throughout this period, the Bible consistently presents God as fighting for Israel. For example, in the biblical narrative of the exodus, the Egyptian army pursues Israel and is destroyed by God's action (Exod. 14). Deut. 20 deals specifically with rules for conducting holy war (see also 21:10–14, which gives the protocol for taking a female captive from among the conquered population). This concept of holy war flourished during the settlement of the land when Israel encountered repeated foreign invasions of its territory, but the concept changed considerably under the monarchy, when it was the king who instigated wars to serve national policy. The prophets often criticized such wars, because they were not in keeping with the divine will, and Israel's losses or suffering as a result of war were frequently attributed to Israel's failure to obey God and keep the covenant. The notion of holy war became an increasingly eschatological concept, associated with a decisive struggle between good and evil that would take place at the end of time. This concept continues to inform apocalyptic sections of the NT (e.g., Rev. 19:11–15).   M.M.S.

home. *See* house.

homer. *See* weights and measures.

homosexuality, a word for which there is no specific equivalent in the Hebrew Bible or in the Greek NT, since the concept of homosexuality as a "sexual orientation" originated only in the nineteenth century. Nevertheless, there are a few biblical references to people who engage in sexual acts with persons of the same sex.

In the Hebrew Bible, the most explicit references to sexual acts between men are in the Holiness Code of Leviticus, where, under penalty of death, a male is strictly prohibited from lying with another male as he would with a woman (18:22; 20:13). In addition to these passages, the Bible contains two narratives in which men desire to have sexual relations with other men. The first of these is set in the city of Sodom and provides the derivation for the term "sodomy," which in modern English is sometimes used as a pejorative term for "homosexual sex acts." In the biblical account, the men of Sodom intend to rape two male visitors who have come to the house of Lot, not knowing that the visitors are actually angels of God (Gen. 19:1–11). In a similar story, the men of Gibeah want to rape a Levite who is staying as a guest in a local home (Judg. 19:16–26). Both of these stories are intended to expose crass immorality, but most interpreters regard that immorality as being evinced more through the intention of violent rape than through the intended intercourse with a same-sex partner. Indeed, in the Judg. 19 narrative, the rape is carried out upon a woman, and it is nevertheless harshly condemned, with severe consequences. As for the incident in Gen. 19, other references to Sodom in the Hebrew Bible view that city as a symbol of immorality in general, not specifically of homosexual desire (cf. Ezek. 16:49–50, where the sins of Sodom are gluttony and various instances of social injustice). In the NT, however, Jude 7 equates the sin of Sodom with "unnatural lust" (lit., "pursuing other flesh"). This could be a reference to the desire of men to have sexual relations with other men, or it could refer to the unnatural lust of mortals for angels.

The texts from Leviticus seem to inform two references in the NT in which the Greek term *arsenokoitai* is included on lists of persons whose behavior is condemned: in 1 Cor. 6:9, the *arsenokoitai* are listed as wrongdoers who will not inherit the kingdom of God; in 1 Tim. 1:10, they are named as people who do "what is contrary to the sound teaching" and, accordingly, as people who are lawless, disobedient, godless, sinful, unholy, and profane (cf. 1 Tim. 1:9). The precise meaning of the word *arsenokoitai* is uncertain: in 1 Cor. 1:9, it has been translated as "sodomites" (NRSV, NJB), "homosexual offenders" (NIV), and abusers of themselves with mankind (KJV); in 1 Tim. 1:9, it has been rendered "sodomites" (NRSV, RSV), "perverts" (NIV), "homosexuals" (NJB), and "them that defile themselves with mankind" (KJV). Although the word *arsenokoitai* does not occur anywhere else in Greek literature, it is an obvious combination of *arsen* ("male") and *koitai* ("to lie with [i.e., to have sex with]"); accordingly, most scholars maintain that Paul probably had the aforementioned texts from Lev. 18:22; 20:13 in mind when he used (or possibly coined) this term. The *arsenokoitai* condemned in the NT are men who lie with males in a manner prohibited in the Leviticus Holiness Code, though the question of whether such men should be called "homosexuals" and of whether their activity should be deemed an example of "homosexuality" remains in dispute (often owing to what those English terms are thought to imply or convey). This discussion is complicated somewhat by the occurrence of another term in the "vice list" of 1 Cor. 6:9. The word immediately preceding *arsenokoitai* is *malakoi,* which literally means "soft people" and which has also been translated in a variety of ways: "male prostitutes" (NRSV, NIV), "the self-indulgent" (NJB), and the effeminate (KJV). A common view among modern scholars is that the two words *malakoi* and *arsenokoitai* should be taken together as describing the passive and the active partners in a sexual act between two males; both participants, then, are condemned.

The most extensive biblical reference to sexual acts between same-sex partners (and the only biblical reference to such acts between women) is found in Rom. 1:26–27. There, such activity is mentioned as an example of the perversions that follow when humankind refuses to give glory and thanks to the one sovereign God (see Rom. 1:18–25, 28–32). Paul views such activity as evidence that God's judgment is in effect; because people did not honor God as God but worshiped images, God gave them up to "degrading passions." Specifically, "their women exchanged natural intercourse for unnatural and in the same way also the men, giving up natural intercourse with women, were consumed with passion for one another" (Rom. 1:26–27). Paul views such sexual behavior as "shameful acts" and as the products of "a debased mind" (Rom. 1:27, 28). Again, whether the people described by Paul in this text should be called "homosexuals"—and whether the actions described should be regarded as instances of "homosexuality"—is in dispute, depending to some extent on what is meant by those terms. *See also* law; Leviticus, book of; prostitute.   V.P.F./M.A.P.

honey. Biblical references to honey include mention of domestic or cultivated honey (2 Chron. 31:5) and to wild honey recovered from among rocks (Deut. 32:13), from trees (1 Sam. 14:25–26), and, in one instance, from an animal carcass (Judg. 14:8–9). Honey was basic fare in the wilderness ("locusts and wild honey," Mark 1:6), it symbolized rich, productive land (Exod. 3:17), deceitful enticement (Prov. 5:3), and something that was delightful and desirable (Ps. 119:103). Though frequently used in sacrifices, it was forbidden as part of burnt offerings (Lev. 2:11).

honor and shame. According to many cultural anthropologists, the pivotal social value of the biblical world was honor, i.e., the status that one has in the eyes of those whose opinions one considers to be significant. To some extent, honor was ascribed through factors beyond an individual's control: age, gender, nationality, race, height, physical health, economic class, and the like all defined the limits of how much honor one could hope to attain. Within those parameters, however, there were many things that might increase one's honor (religious piety, courage, virtuous behavior, a congenial or charitable disposition, etc.), and there were many things that might precipitate a loss of honor or even bring its opposite, shame. The language of honor and shame is noticeably prominent throughout the NT. Some voices in the NT seize upon the language to present Christianity as a path to achieving honor and avoiding shame (1 Pet. 1:7; 2:6). Other voices seek to overturn the conventional wisdom regarding how those values are applied, claiming that it is *more* honorable to behave like a slave than to lord over others as a person of power and privilege (Mark 10:42–43; cf. Luke 14:7–11). And some NT documents repudiate the fixation with honor altogether, calling on readers to develop a new value system defined by Christ, who did not seek honor or fame or glory but bore the shame of the cross (Heb. 12:2).

M.A.P.

hope. In the Bible, hope is not normally expressed as desire (something good that one would like to have happen), but as expectation (something good that one knows is going to happen and, so, anticipates). In a religious sense, hope is the expectation of a favorable future under God's direction.

In the Hebrew Bible: The most frequent expression of hope in the Hebrew Bible may be associated with the verbs "to wait, to expect" (*qawah*) and "to be full of confidence, to trust" (*batakh*). The prophet Jeremiah speaks for much of the Israelite tradition when he utters: "O hope of Israel! Oh Lord! All who forsake you shall be put to shame" (17:13; cf. 14:8). This text asserts that God is not only the hope of the nation, but of the individual, a thought echoed in Ps. 71:5: "For you, O Lord, are my hope, my trust, O Lord, from my youth." God's loving-kindness (Heb. *khesed*), revealed in repeated deeds of fidelity (Exod. 6:4–8), gives the people of Israel confidence that God will fulfill promises in the future. Thus, God is the basis of all hope. God will continue to pour out loving-kindness as long as Israel places its hope in God (Ps. 33:18). False hope, i.e., hope in anyone or anything other than God, leads to chaos and disaster. Neither weapons of war (Hos. 10:13), wealth (Ps. 49:5–9), nor idols (Isa. 44:9–11) provide basis for hope, for these things cannot give lasting security.

Crises of hope occurred when Israel was destroyed by the Assyrians in 722/1 BCE and when Judah was destroyed by the Babylonians in 587 BCE. There were a variety of prophetic responses to these disasters. Amos warned the people that their hope was misguided (5:18). Isaiah sternly warned against foreign alliances as an avenue of hope (31:1–9), and Ezekiel described

a vision in which those who say, "Our hope is lost" (37:11) find themselves miraculously restored. This positive vision of restoration and hope in God despite anticipated destruction is found in Hosea under the theme of the new covenant (2:17–20). It is also articulated by Jeremiah: "Surely I know the plans I have for you, says the LORD, plans for your welfare and not for harm, to give you a future with hope" (29:11).

In the NT: The Greek words for "hope" (*elpis*) and "to hope" (*elpizein*) have no unique significance in the Gospels. Only the verb occurs and it is only used in a secular sense (Luke 6:34; 23:8), in quotations of scripture (Matt. 12:41; cf. Isa. 42:1–2), or with specific regard to Israel (Luke 24:21). In John 5:45 Jesus replies to the Jews that "it is Moses who accuses you, on whom you set your hope." Likewise, in Acts the word "hope" is used in a purely secular sense (16:19; 24:26; 27:20) or refers to the hope of Israel as culminating in the "resurrection of the Christ" (2:26; 23:6; 24:15; 26:6, 7; 28:20). In the Letters of Paul, however, the term is used more broadly. Already in Paul's brief and probably earliest letter, 1 Thessalonians, hope is referred to four times (1:3; 2:19; 4:13; 5:8), twice in the triadic formula of "faith, love, and hope" (1:3; 5:8). Paul regards the community itself as a basis for hope, as evidence that he will receive a heavenly reward: "For what is our hope or joy or crown of boasting before our Lord Jesus at his coming? Is it not you?" (1 Thess. 2:19). In addressing the Thessalonians' concern over those who have died, he warns them not to grieve "as others do who have no hope" (1 Thess. 4:13; cf. Eph. 2:12).

The fact that hope appears in association with faith and love, not only in 1 Thessalonians, but also in 1 Cor. 13:13 and somewhat more loosely in Gal. 5:5–6, suggests that, for Paul, it is an essential characteristic of new life in Christ. Fundamental for Paul's concept of hope is the differentiation between justification (already a present reality) and salvation (to be received in the future). In Rom. 5:1–3, he indicates that what the Christian has obtained in this life is "access," not completed entrance, to God's grace, and the apostle rejoices in the "hope of sharing the glory of God" at the future consummation. The sign that "this hope will not disappoint us" is that "God's love has been poured into our hearts through the Holy Spirit that has been given to us" (Rom. 5:5). Thus Paul can assert, "In hope we were saved" (Rom. 8:23–24), although salvation always has a future orientation for Paul and is not yet complete (see Rom. 5:9–10; Phil. 3:7–14). Further, God's revelation in Jesus Christ affects both individuals and creation itself, which God has subjected in hope, meaning that it will be set free from its bondage to decay (Rom. 8:19–21).

For Paul, strong hope leads to strong faith. In Rom. 4:18–21, he cites Abraham as an example of faith because "hoping against hope, he believed. . . . No distrust made him waver concerning the promise of God, but he grew strong in his faith as he gave glory to God, being fully convinced that God was able to do what (God) had promised" (cf. Col. 1:23). This is in keeping with Paul's belief that the scriptures of Israel ultimately testify to the hope that is found in Christ: "Whatever was written in former days was written for our instruction, so that by steadfastness and by the encouragement of the scriptures we might have hope" (Rom. 15:4). Paul also can point to his understanding of hope by using a number of shorter formulations, such as "the God of hope" (Rom. 15:13), "abound in hope" (15:13), and "rejoice in hope" (12:12). Elsewhere he simply declares, "Since, then, we have such a hope, we act with great boldness" (2 Cor. 3:12–17; cf. Heb. 7:19).

Elsewhere in the NT, the Letter to the Hebrews develops its concept of hope in keeping with its presentation of the church as the wandering people of God, in sojourn between their earthly and heavenly homes. Christians must hold fast to their confidence until the end (3:6; 6:11; 10:23). Heb. 11:1 summarizes in a broader way the statements on hope in that writing, and Heb. 6:19 refers to hope as "a sure and steadfast anchor of the soul." The theme of confidence in relationship to hope also appears in 1 Pet. 1:21, where the author urges those who live in the midst of enormous difficulty and persecution to "set all your hope on the grace that Jesus Christ will bring you when he is revealed" (1:13). In the midst of their difficulties they should not fear their persecutors or be troubled by them, but should always "be ready to make your defense to anyone who demands from you an accounting for the hope that is in you" (3:15). *See also* faith; love.   K.P.D.

Hophni (hof′ni; Egyptian, "tadpole"), the brother of Phinehas, and the son of Eli, the priest at the tabernacle of the Lord in Shiloh in the days of Samuel. Hophni and his brother also served as priests at Shiloh, but they disgraced themselves, eating the meat from sacrifices before the fat had burned off (1 Sam. 2:12–17). Hophni thus came under God's judgment (1 Sam. 2:27–36; 3:11–18) and was killed along with Phinehas at the battle of Aphek, when the Philistines captured the ark of the covenant (1 Sam. 4:1–18). Their deaths allowed Samuel to assume leadership upon the death of Eli, which was forthcoming; Eli fell over and broke his neck when he heard the news about his sons and the ark (1 Sam. 4:18). *See also* Eli; Phinehas; Samuel.

Hor, Mount, the mountain on which Aaron died and on which the Israelites gathered and camped on the border of Edom (Num. 20:22–29; 33:37–39). Traditionally it has been identified with modern Jebel Haran, overlooking Petra. This is questionable, however, because Jebel Harun is in the midst of Edom, and its high peaks are not conducive to the gathering of people. Mount Hor is also identified as the northern boundary of Israel's inheritance (Num. 34:7, 8), which suggests it might be identical with Mount Hermon.

Horeb (hor′eb), **Mount,** the name for Mount Sinai used in some portions of the Pentateuch, namely, those that scholars identify as the Elohist (or E) material. This material exhibits certain distinctive tendencies: "Elohim" for God rather than the Tetragrammaton, YHWH (rendered "the LORD" in the NRSV); "Jacob" rather than "Israel"; "Jethro" rather than "Reuel"; and "Horeb" rather than "Sinai." Notably, the book of Deuteronomy uses Horeb exclusively for the mountain of God except in one verse (Deut. 33:2). It was at Horeb (Sinai) that Moses was called in the incident involving the burning bush (Exod. 3:1–12), and it was here that he obtained water from the rock (17:6–7). Here too the Israelites made a covenant with God (Deut. 5:2), and from here they set out for Kadesh-barnea and Canaan (Deut. 1:19). Later, Elijah fled to Horeb because of Jezebel's wrath. *See also* Elohist; mount, mountain; Pentateuch, sources of the; Sinai.   N.L.L.

Horesh (hor′esh; Heb., "forest"), a place in the Wilderness of Ziph used by David as a hiding place when fleeing from Saul (1 Sam. 23:15–16, 18–19). Jonathan sought David out to reassure him, but some Ziphites reported David's presence to Saul, forcing David to move on. Ziph is located in the Judean wilderness southeast of Hebron. Some claim a specific site identification for Horesh, but others think its meaning ("forest") suggests a small region in the Ziph wilderness.

Horites (hor′its), in the Bible the pre-Edomite inhabitants of Seir (Gen. 14:6; 36:20–30; Deut. 2:12, 22), the chief mountain of Edom. The name was traditionally derived from Hebrew *khor*, "hole," and interpreted as meaning "cave dwellers," though there is little archaeological evidence for cave dwelling in Edom. Thus when nonbiblical texts revealed the important role the Hurrians played in Syria during the second millennium BCE, scholars attempted to connect the biblical Horites with the Hurrians referred to in Akkadian, Hittite, and Egyptian texts. Phonetically the names are identical, but two difficulties make the equation doubtful: first, the names of the Horites listed in Gen. 36 are all Semitic, not Hurrian; and, second, while the Hurrians did expand into Cisjordan (i.e., the land west of the Jordan River), where there were Hurrian garrisons in the early fifteenth century BCE, they did not enter southern Transjordan (i.e., the land east of the Jordan River).

The Hivites, however, do appear in regions where the nonbiblical texts make the presence of Hurrians plausible—at Shechem (Gen. 34:2), at Gibeon (Josh. 9:7, 19), at the foot of Mount Hermon (Josh. 11:3), and on Mount Lebanon (Judg. 3:3)—and there is some evidence for the identification of Hivites and Horites. Zibeon the Hivite (Gen. 36:2) is listed among the Horites in Gen. 36:20, 29, and some texts of the LXX read "Horite" for "Hivite" in Gen. 34:2 and Josh. 9:7. Thus some scholars suggest that the biblical tradition has simply switched the terms "Horite" and "Hivite."

Others identify the Hivites with the Hurrians of Cisjordan, assume there was a distinct people in Edom with a homophonous name, and explain the use of "Hivite" to designate the Hurrians of Cisjordan as a gradual development to avoid confusion between the two Hurrian peoples. *See also* Mitanni.   J.J.M.R.

Hormah (hor′muh; Heb., "destruction" or "accursed"), a city in the region of Judea, close to the border with Edom. In their first attempt to take the city the Israelites were defeated by the Canaanites and Amalekites (Num. 14:45; Deut. 1:44). It was later subdued by Joshua and was initially allotted to the tribe of Judah (Josh. 15:30). Later it was considered the land of the tribe of Simeon (Josh. 19:4; 1 Chron. 4:30). It was a center of Davidic sympathizers and thus received some of the spoils of his activity (1 Sam. 30:30). The location of the site remains uncertain.   S.B.R.

horn.
1 The bony projection from the head of various animals, e.g., of a ram (Gen. 22:13) or of a bull (Ps. 69:31).
2 A musical instrument made from a ram's horn (Heb. *shophar*); it was used in worship (e.g., 2 Chron. 15:14) as well as in war (e.g., Josh. 6:5, 13).
3 The projection at each of the four corners of an altar (Exod. 27:2; Rev. 9:13); the precise significance of the symbolism here is not known. The instruction to put some blood of a sacrificed bull on the altar horns (Lev. 4:7) attests to their importance in Israel's religious ritual of animal sacrifice. People desiring asylum symbolized that desire by clinging to the altar's horns (1 Kings 1:50–51; 2:28–34). Persons accused of manslaughter may have sought such asylum at the altar (Exod. 21:14 says it is to be denied), but specific provision for such places of safety was made by means of cities of refuge (e.g., Num. 35:9–28) rather than by means of altars. Altars as places of sanctuary are nowhere specifically mentioned.
4 A receptacle for liquids: for the oil kept in the shrine (1 Kings 1:39) and used for anointing kings (1 Sam. 16:1, 13); perhaps for eye makeup ("horn of paint" is the literal meaning of Karen-happuch, the name of Job's third daughter, Job 42:14); and for ink (Ezek. 9:2–11).
5 A symbol of power, whether in animals (e.g., wild ox, Num. 23:22; Deut. 33:17) or human beings (iron horns symbolize a king's victory in war, 1 Kings 22:11). The term "horn of salvation" denotes royal saving power (e.g., Ps. 18:2; Sir. 49:5; cf. Luke 1:69). A further development of this theme is found in the use of "horn" for "king" in the visions in Dan. 7–8, where the horns refer to specific rulers. In Revelation, "horn" signifies supernatural power: the power of the lamb (5:6), the dragon (12:13), the beast from the sea (13:1), the beast from the earth (13:11), and the scarlet beast upon which a woman sits (17:3–16). Moses's shining face when he descended from Sinai and the presence of God (Exod. 34:29–35) is described in

Hab. 3:4 ("rays of light") with a word (Heb. *qeren*) that could be connected with the word for "horn" (i.e., something that projects outward, as horns do). The Latin Vulgate translated this "horns of light," which led to overly literal interpretations by generations of Christians who assumed Moses had horns after descending the mountain. He is portrayed thus in a famous statue by Michelangelo.
6 The crown of a hill, or the hill itself (e.g., Isa. 5:1).   P.R.A.

hornet, an insect of the order *Hymenoptera*, larger and more dangerous than a wasp, probably *Vespa orientalis*. Hornets were known for having an especially painful sting that would continue to be felt for several days. Worse, they could cause vast damage to trees and fruit when conditions allowed them to reproduce and swarm in large numbers. Indeed, the Hebrew term for "hornet" (*tsir'ah*) also means "depression, discouragement," though it is not clear whether the insect was named for the condition or vice versa. In Josh. 24:12, God reminds Israel, "I sent the hornet ahead of you, which drove out before you the two kings of the Amorites." This could imply a literal plague of hornets or it may be meant symbolically, as a figurative reference to God having preceded the Israelite forces in ways that terrorized or antagonized their opponents. The word is used in a similar way in Exod. 23:28 and Deut. 7:20, where the NRSV opts for symbolic meaning and translates it "pestilence."   M.A.P.

Horonaim (hor′uh-nay′im), a Moabite city mentioned by both Isaiah (15:5) and Jeremiah (48:3, 5, 34). The Isaiah passage refers specifically to "the road to Horonaim" and 2 Sam. 13:34 also mentions "the Horonaim road," which was by the side of a mountain; Jer. 5:34 speaks of "the ascent of Luhith" and the "descent of Horonaim." From these clues, interpreters surmise that Horonaim was a destination along a highway that led down from the Moabite plateau to the Dead Sea. It was probably located in the southern part of Moab and has been identified by some scholars as modern el-Iraq, about nine miles east of the southeast corner of the Dead Sea, although this identification is questionable. Jer. 48:3 cites the devastation and destruction of Horonaim as emblematic of the defeat of Moab in general. The city appears in the Mesha Inscription on the Moabite Stone, which indicates that it was recaptured by King Mesha of Moab from some unidentified enemy—probably the Israelites who are mentioned elsewhere in the inscription (see 1 Kings 3:4). *See also* Mesha; Moab; Moabite Stone.   D.R.B.

horse. The horse (*Equus caballus*) was first domesticated in the Eurasian steppes around 3000 BCE, and horses were introduced into the Near East by the Hyksos in the first half of the second millennium BCE. With horse-drawn chariots, the Hyksos managed to besiege the whole Near East. Horse burials—probably sacrificial rites— dating to this period have been found at Tell el-'Ajjul, some four miles southwest of Gaza.

The first biblical reference to the horse is in Gen. 47:17, where Joseph accepts horses and other livestock as trade for food from starving people in Egypt. But in the Bible the horse is mainly a symbol of power and is most often associated with war: the Philistines mustered thirty thousand chariots and six thousand horsemen against King Saul (1 Sam. 13:5). Even heavenly armies are equipped with warhorses (2 Kings 6:17; Rev. 19:11, 14). In contrast, the donkey or ass may have signified peace (Zech. 9:9; Matt. 21:1–7). It appears that for this reason the Hebrews were forbidden to keep horses on a large scale. In Deut. 17:14–16 Moses tells the Israelites that if they elect a king, they should make sure that he does not "multiply horses for himself" or buy horses from Egypt, i.e., build up an army. Samuel (1 Sam. 8:11–17) repeats this warning and impresses upon the people that, should they insist on a king, their sons will be needed to equip the war chariots. For a while this warning seems to have been observed, as Joshua killed the horses he took from the Canaanites (Josh. 11:9) and David disposed of the horses he captured, except for a hundred chariot teams (2 Sam. 8:4). King Solomon, on the other hand, is reported to have had stables for four thousand horses (2 Chron. 9:25) or even forty thousand (1 Kings 4:26). He also imported horses from Egypt and other places (2 Chron. 9:28) and fed them on straw and barley (1 Kings 4:28). Later King Hezekiah was offered two thousand horses by the general of the Assyrian king Sennacherib (2 Kings 18:23). A vivid description of how the horse acts on the battlefield is given in Job 39:19–25. By the time of the exile, horses must have been quite common, for a Horse Gate existed in Jerusalem and the royal palace was equipped with a special entrance for horses (2 Chron. 23:15). On their return from Babylon, the exiles brought with them 736 horses (Neh. 7:68), and according to Ezek. 27:14 horses were also imported from Togarmah (Armenia).

Horse-drawn chariots were used not only for warfare, but also as a noble and honorable means of transport. Joseph was provided with a chariot by Pharaoh as a special sign of honor (Gen. 41:43), and Jacob's dead body was brought back to Canaan accompanied by horses and chariots (50:9). Similarly the body of King Amaziah of Judah was returned to Jerusalem in a war chariot (2 Kings 14:20), and Elijah was taken alive up to heaven in a whirlwind accompanied by horses and chariots of fire (1 Kings 2:11). Naaman the leper came with horses and chariots to the home of Elisha, apparently hoping to impress the prophet with his wealth or importance. In the book of Esther, Mordecai is honored by being paraded about the town on a horse that no one but the king had ever ridden (6:6–11). In the book of Acts, the Ethiopian eunuch, a royal minister with whom Philip spoke, was traveling by chariot (8:27–28).

Equines other than the horse are also featured in the Bible. The donkey or domesticated ass (*Equus asinus*) was brought to Canaan from Egypt in the fourth millennium BCE. It was used as a riding animal not only for the poor, but also for the well-to-do (Judg. 1:14) and even kings (Zech. 9:9; cf. Matt. 21:5). The onager (*Equus hemionus*), or wild ass, roamed the Syrian steppes until the nineteenth century. The Sumerians used these animals to pull four-wheeled chariots without actually domesticating them (as depicted in a standard from the third millennium BCE found at the royal cemetery at Ur). The mule, a cross between a horse mare and a donkey stallion, was the beast of burden par excellence. The Hebrews were forbidden to crossbreed animals themselves (Lev. 19:19), but they were allowed to use mules, which they probably imported.

As noted, horses are often referred to as symbols of strength or military might (Prov. 21:31; Isa. 2:7). They also may symbolize sure-footedness (Isa. 65:13) or speed (Jer. 4:13). Occasionally the horse is used as an image of something difficult but not impossible to control (Prov. 26:3). Thus, Ps. 32:9 counsels, "Do not be like a horse or a mule, without understanding, whose temper must be curbed with bit and bridle." The Letter of James notes that, ironically, people "put bits into the mouths of horses to make them obey us" and yet no one is able to control the human tongue (3:3, 8).   I.U.K.

Hosah (hoh´suh; Heb., "refuge" or "protection").

1 A porter (gatekeeper) in the time of David (1 Chron. 16:38; 26:10).

2 A village of Asher (Josh. 19:29), possibly the same as Uzu near Tyre.

hosanna (hoh-zan´uh), a Hebrew exclamation meaning "Save, I [we] pray." It is simply transliterated in most English Bibles. The NRSV is oddly inconsistent, translating the word as "Save us" where it occurs in the Hebrew Bible, but translit-

A galloping horse bearing a Scythian rider served as a handle on the lid of a copper jar dating to the fifth century BCE.

erating the Greek equivalent (i.e., the Greek transliteration of the Hebrew) where it occurs in the NT. Thus, a psalmist proclaims, "Save us, we beseech you, O LORD!" (118:25), but in the Gospels the crowds who welcome Jesus into Jerusalem shout "Hosanna!" (Matt. 21:9, 15; Mark 11:9–10; John 12:13). This inconsistency may mask the fact that the crowds in the Gospel stories were probably quoting from Ps. 118:25. The latter psalm was recited once daily for six days during the Festival of Tabernacles, and seven times on the seventh day as branches were waved (*m. Sukk.* 4:5); by the time of Jesus, it had become associated with messianic expectations. *See also* festivals, feasts, and fasts; Tabernacles, Festival of.   A.J.H.

Hosea (hoh-zay´uh), **book of,** the first part of the Book of the Twelve in the Prophets section, or Nevi'im, in the Tanakh (Jewish Bible). It is the first book of the Minor Prophets in the Christian OT.

Contents: There are two basic parts to the book of Hosea. Chaps. 1–3 focus on Hosea's marriage, and chaps. 4–14 consist largely of oracles for which no context is provided. The book begins with a superscription identifying the prophet as "Hosea son of Beeri" and placing his prophetic career during the reigns of one Israelite king and four Judean kings. A third-person account of Hosea's marriage to and relationship with Gomer follows. God commands Hosea to take a promiscuous wife ("of whoredom" in the NRSV is misleading; the Hebrew never refers to her as being a prostitute) and have children with her. Hosea complies and marries Gomer, who has three children, each of which has a symbolic name. The first is named Jezreel ("God sows") after the place where Jehu slaughtered the family of Ahab and claimed kingship and where God promised that the monarchy would be punished. The second is called Lo-ruhamah ("not pitied"), because God will not show mercy and have pity upon the people of Israel. The third child is named Lo-ammi ("not my people"), for God is reversing the covenant that originally contained the promise, "I will be your God and you will be my people." After the children are born, God promises to restore Israel. The prophet then connects the unfaithfulness of his promiscuous wife with the unfaithfulness of Israel in its relationship with God. The people of Israel are accused of either worshiping Baal instead of the Lord or simply worshiping Baal alongside the Lord. The people have turned to other gods, believing them able to provide for Israel, when it is the Lord who is the provider for the people. Chap. 3 is a first-person account either retelling the episode in chap. 1 or telling of Hosea taking back Gomer in spite of her unfaithfulness. In the same way, God will take back unfaithful Israel. However, neither Gomer nor Israel will avoid punishment for unfaithfulness.

Chap. 4 begins with a "covenant lawsuit" in the form of divorce proceedings between God and Israel. The entire book contains alternating sections of judgment and salvation. Israel is accused

of sinning by abandoning its relationship with God, but God continues to promise to restore Israel. Metaphors of God's relationship with Israel are developed in chaps. 4–14. The people are compared to grapes that have grown wild and unruly (9:10–17), a fertile vine that has gone after other gods and rejected God (10:1–10), and a trained heifer that is self-reliant and plows where it wills (10:11–15). The creature in each metaphor requires progressively more care than the one before it. The book ends with a promise that God will restore the people of Israel if they will be faithful. The last verse is clearly influenced by wisdom literature and calls readers to discern the ways of God, which are clearly right, but not always obvious.

OUTLINE OF CONTENTS

Hosea

<table>
<tr><td colspan="2">I. Hosea's family (1:1–3:5)</td></tr>
<tr><td></td><td>A. Hosea marries Gomer, names their children (1:1–11)</td></tr>
<tr><td></td><td>B. Symbolic interpretation of Hosea's marriage (2:1–23)</td></tr>
<tr><td></td><td>C. Restoration of Gomer (3:1–5)</td></tr>
<tr><td colspan="2">II. Judgment against Israel (4:1–14:9)</td></tr>
<tr><td></td><td>A. Covenant lawsuit (4:1–5:7)</td></tr>
<tr><td></td><td>B. Warning and lament (5:8–6:6)</td></tr>
<tr><td></td><td>C. Judgment (6:7–9:9)</td></tr>
<tr><td></td><td>D. Historical review (9:10–13:16)</td></tr>
<tr><td></td><td>E. Salvation (14:1–9)</td></tr>
</table>

Background: The prophet Hosea (whose name means "the LORD saves") is thought by many scholars to be directly or indirectly the source of the majority of the book of Hosea. The first-person section in chap. 3 is thought to be original to Hosea, while parts of the third-person sections and certain collections of sayings may have been compiled by a group of Hosea's disciples within a generation of his death. The prophet Hosea is said in the superscription (1:1) to have prophesied during the reigns of Uzziah, Jotham, Ahaz, and Hezekiah, kings of Judah, along with Jeroboam II, king of Israel. The first four figures span almost the entire eighth century BCE, whereas Jeroboam reigned for forty years in the northern kingdom. Most scholars believe Hosea to be from the northern kingdom (the only literary prophet other than Jeremiah to be from Israel), and they take the reference to Jeroboam most seriously, citing the Judean references as the work of a later editor. Scholars date Hosea's career anywhere between 780 BCE to 721 BCE, when Samaria was conquered, though most scholars place his career between 750 and 725 BCE. Hosea is considered a younger contemporary of Amos, having prophesied slightly later than Amos.

There has been some discussion among scholars over the literary background of Hosea. Simundson argues that Hosea borrowed from both the legal tradition and the wisdom tradition and reshaped them for his distinctive use. There is a possibility that Hosea was connected to both the Elohist and Elijah traditions (both from the northern kingdom), because of his frequent allusions to the Decalogue and the covenant at Sinai. Peterson cites the presence of these elements as definitive markers of Hosea being an Israelite. Although most Judean prophets talked of the Davidic line and Zion, these were not northern sensibilities and are not found prominently in Hosea. Other scholars have also noted a connection with the Deuteronomic tradition (condemnation of high places, references to the exodus, emphasis on the love of God), though that is usually seen as the result of later editors. In addition, Hosea stands within the mythological framework of the Near East at that time, which viewed Baal as the fertility god who brought rain, wheat, wine, and oil to the people; for Hosea, however, it is God who provides these things.

Themes: The central theme of Hosea is that the relationship between God and Israel has deteriorated as a result of Israel's unfaithfulness. God does not abandon, but pursues Israel in its unfaithfulness. These passages were a call to Israel to come back to God and a warning to Judah not to follow in the pattern of Israel. Hosea connects the concept of covenant closely to loyalty and faithfulness. He is critical of the priests (4:4–14) because they encourage people to sacrifice and give offerings (which supplies the livelihood of the priests) instead of helping the people to truly serve God. Hosea opposed the unjust distribution of wealth and the oppression of the lower classes. He was also critical of the monarchy, even seeing the monarchy as an example of the people's lack of trust in God.

Interpretive Issues: One of the major interpretive issues with the book of Hosea is how to understand the sections concerning Hosea's marriage to Gomer. There are three main interpretations of this passage. (1) God ordered Hosea to marry a known prostitute. (2) Hosea saw the providential workings of God as he discovered his wife's promiscuity. Or (3) Gomer was a Baalite and was unfaithful in that sense. Some scholars combine two of these categories and claim that Gomer was a Baalite temple prostitute. Some scholars do not even think the marriage actually happened, but view it as an allegorical story or parable. There are, however, other examples in the Bible of prophets using their family life as illustrations of God's relationship with people (Jer. 16:1–2; Ezek. 24:15–27).

A number of critical problems related to the interpretation of the book of Hosea arise from the status of the Hebrew text. The Hebrew version of the book of Hosea is one of the poorest in the Bible. There is no consensus on why the text is in such poor condition, though some scholars think that it might have been damaged during the fall of Samaria before it was transported to Judah for safekeeping. It has also been suggested that differences between northern Israelite and southern Judean Hebrew might have made the translation and transmission difficult.

Critical issues also arise with regard to the book's redactional history. Hosea shows obvious signs of editing with the presence of third-person accounts of events in Hosea's life, but it is difficult to determine how much of the text can be traced back to Hosea, how much can be assumed to be the product of Hosea's disciples, and how much represents still later editorial additions. Some scholars follow a pattern that finds the oldest material in the first-person accounts of Hosea in chaps. 1–3. Next, the third-person account of Hosea's marriage was recorded by a disciple. Chaps. 4–11 were Hosea's oracles collected by the prophet's disciples within a generation of his death. Last, chaps. 12–14 come from a circle of Hosea's disciples, but are not original to the prophet. Yet this formulation is not undisputed. Some scholars place chaps. 4–11 and 12–14 as additions that took place at a much later date, possibly after the fall of Jerusalem (587 BCE).

Bibliography

Bandstra, Barry L. *Reading the Old Testament: Introduction to the Hebrew Bible.* 4th ed. Wadsworth, 2009.

Childs, Brevard S. *Introduction to the Old Testament as Scripture.* Fortress, 1979.

Gottwald, Norman K. *The Hebrew Bible: A Socio-Literary Introduction.* Fortress, 1985.

McKenzie, Steven L., and John Kaltner. *The Old Testament: Its Background, Growth, and Content.* Abingdon, 2007.

Peterson, David L. *The Prophetic Literature: An Introduction.* Westminster John Knox, 2002.

Simundson, Daniel J. *Hosea, Joel, Amos, Obadiah, Jonah, Micah.* Abingdon, 2005.

Sweeney, Marvin A. *The Twelve Prophets.* Vol. 1, *Hosea, Joel, Amos, Obadiah, Jonah.* Liturgical, 2000.

Wolff, Hans Walter. *Hosea.* Fortress, 1974.

B.B.

Hoshea (hoh-shee'uh; Heb., "salvation").

1 The original name of Joshua (Num. 13:8; cf. Deut. 32:44). Moses changed his name from Hoshea to Joshua (Num. 13:16).

2 The last king of Israel (ca. 732–724 BCE), the son of Elah (2 Kings 15:30), and a contemporary of Ahaz and Hezekiah. Hoshea usurped the throne by murdering Pekah. He served as a vassal ruler to the successive Assyrian rulers Tiglath-pileser III and Shalmaneser V. The latter ruler, however, "found treachery" in Hoshea when he withheld tribute and turned for aid to the Egyptian king "So" (probably Tefnakhte I; 2 Kings 17:4). Egyptian aid never materialized, and Samaria was taken by Sargon II after a siege of three years. The ultimate fate of Hoshea is not known.

3 An alternative spelling for the name of the prophet Hosea.

4 An Ephraimite chief in David's bureaucracy (1 Chron. 27:20).

5 A Levite who signed Ezra's covenant-renewal document during the time of Nehemiah (Neh. 10:23).

D.L.C.

hospitality, the act of extending welcome and providing food, drink, lodging, or other amenities to visitors. Hospitality in the Near East was tightly bound up with social customs and expectations. According to biblical narratives, travelers would often go to a public place in a town and wait for someone to offer them hospitality, such as lodging or food (Gen. 19:1–3; Judg. 19:15–21). Abraham prepared a meal for the three strangers who visited him and stood to the side while they ate (Gen. 18:1–15). Rebekah distinguished herself when the servant of Abraham asked her for water by offering to draw water for his camels as well (Gen. 24:10–20).

In general, hospitality involved the process of "receiving" outsiders and changing them from strangers to guests. Hospitality thus differed from entertaining family and friends. Certain rituals, such as foot washing, could mark the acceptance of the stranger and signal transition of that person's status from stranger to guest (see Gen. 18:4; 19:2; 24:32; cf. Luke 7:36–50, where the absence of this ritual is noted). Since transient strangers lacked customary or legal standing within the visited community, it was imperative that they be placed under the protection of a patron or host who was an established community member. Through a personal bond with the host (something inns could not offer), strangers were incorporated into the community as guests or clients/protégés. To offend the stranger-turned-guest was to offend the host, who was protector and patron of the guest (poignantly underscored in the case of Lot, Gen. 19:1–10).

Given the cultural expectations for hospitality, a host could infringe upon the requirements of hospitality by insulting the guests, by any show of hostility or rivalry, or by neglecting to protect the guests and their honor (Luke 7:36–50). A host's infringing upon these requirements assures that a stranger will rarely, if ever, reciprocate hospitality (cf. Matt. 10:11–15; 25:43, where the failure to show hospitality has eschatological consequences). But a guest could also infringe upon the requirements of hospitality by insulting the host or by any show of hostility or rivalry either toward the host or other guests; a guest must honor the host. Guests must not usurp the role of the host, e.g., make themselves at home when not yet invited to do so, take precedence (cf. Luke 14:8), give orders to the dependents of the host, or take what is not offered.

Hospitality entails reciprocity between individuals, but it can also be viewed as a reciprocal relationship between communities. Hospitality to traveling Christians was both urged (1 Pet. 4:9) and practiced (Acts 17:7; 21:17; 28:7; Rom. 16:23). Paul tells the Romans, "Extend hospitality to strangers" (12:13). Good works performed by widows include showing hospitality and washing the feet of saints (1 Tim. 5:10). Heb. 13:2 says, "Do not neglect to show hospitality to strangers, for by doing that some have entertained angels without knowing it." The latter text offers a twist on the story of Sodom, where gross inhospitality to strangers who turned out to be angels brought divine wrath upon a community (Gen. 10:12–29); the implication is that appropriate hospitality shown unwittingly to strangers who turn out to be angels will bring divine rewards. Numerous other texts also promise rewards for those who show hospitality. Jesus says those who show hospitality to a prophet or a righteous person will be rewarded as though they were prophets or righteous persons (Matt. 10:41–42); likewise, unbelievers who show hospitality to Jesus's followers will be allowed to share in the eschatological salvation enjoyed by those followers (Matt. 25:31–40, 46).

B.J.M./M.A.P.

host, heavenly. The term "host" refers to a multitude or army, but in the Bible it is used almost exclusively for heavenly beings. The title "LORD of hosts" is given the God of Israel (1 Sam. 1:3, 11; 4:4; 15:2; 17:45; 2 Sam. 6:2, 18; 7:8, 26–27; 1 Kings 18:15); a slight variation is "the LORD, the God of hosts" (2 Sam. 5:10; 1 Kings 19:10, 14; 2 Kings 3:14; 19:31). This nomenclature is found throughout Psalms (e.g., Pss. 24:10; 46:7, 11) and was especially popular with Isaiah (e.g., 1:24; 3:1; 5:16), Jeremiah (e.g., 7:1; 9:16), and Zechariah (e.g., 1:4; 3:7). The title implies that God is the leader of a multitude or an army, which could in some instances be the military troops of Israel, but more often appears to be the "hosts of heaven," angels and other beings depicted as part of God's retinue or court (Deut. 4:19; 17:3; 33:2; 1 Kings 22:19; Isa. 6:1–5). The "hosts of heaven" are sometimes associated celestial phenomena, such as stars or planets, which may have been regarded as supernatural beings (Deut. 4:19; 2 Kings 23:5; cf. Judg. 5:20). Sometimes, "the hosts of heaven" are worshiped in lieu of God by those who reject God's commandments or worship Baal (2 Kings 17:16; 21:3, 5; cf. 23:4–5; Acts 7:42). But Ezra says the hosts of heaven were made by God and worship God (Neh. 9:6; cf. Ps. 33:6; Luke 2:13). In the NT, the expression "Lord of hosts" is used only in Rom. 9:29 (which quotes Isa. 1:9) and in James 5:4 (the cries of defrauded harvesters have reached the ears of the Lord of hosts).   M.A.P.

hour. *See* time.

house.

1 The ordinary dwelling unit of the settled population. The Bible offers numerous references to specific parts of houses, such as roofs, upper rooms, doors, and courtyards, but it gives no full description of a typical house. Supplementary evidence provided by archaeology, however, makes it possible to identify general characteristics of houses in Canaan/Israel, although information is not complete for every period and is based mainly upon preserved foundations and partial walls. Differences in style were influenced by a combination of factors: environment, which determined availability of both materials and space; trade relations, which determined from whom new ideas or techniques might be acquired; and patterns of migration, which also determined from whom new skills, habits, and customs would be introduced.

In the Early Bronze Age (3000–2000 BCE) distinctive types of houses appear. The earlier ones feature solid walls and rooms with one rounded or apsidal end. The form that came to dominate this period, however, was a rectangular house with the entrance on one of the longer sides. Stone benches, the "furnishings" of the house, extended around the length of the walls, and there was usually a flat stone slab serving as a table in the center. The size of the houses varied considerably, however, and it is difficult to ascertain the overall appearance of houses since usually only the foundations remain. A terra-cotta model of a rectangular house discovered at Arad (about thirty-five miles south of Jerusalem) therefore has special value. It shows a structure with no windows, indicating that the door was the only source of light; that doorway, furthermore, reaches almost to the roof, suggesting that the height of the house was about equal to that of a person.

The prosperity of the Middle Bronze Age (2000–1500 BCE) is reflected in its architecture. Courtyard houses appear, ranging from single-room, one-story houses to multiple-room, two-story houses with an outer stairway rising to the second floor. All faced a courtyard, which contained a baking oven and a well. The courtyard house with its various arrangements of rooms seems to have continued throughout the Late Bronze Age (1500–1200 BCE).

The nomadic Israelite tribes who settled in Canaan in the thirteenth and twelfth centuries BCE at first copied this type of construction, but in the course of time they developed a distinctive Israelite style of building. This is known as the four-room house. Its principal feature was a back room the width of the building with three long rooms stemming forward from it. This form, with varied expansions and elaborations, continued from the end of the eleventh century BCE to the destruction of Judah (587/6 BCE). It has been found at numerous sites, including Tell Beit Mirsim, Ai,

Four-room house discovered in the Iron Age II (1000–701 BCE) ruins at Beer-sheba.

Hazor, and Beer-sheba. Most houses were two stories high, although two- and three-room, one-story houses are also found. The lower part of the wall was constructed of stone and the upper part of adobe brick or wood and was plastered with lime. The flat roofs were made of wooden beams filled in with dried mud and brushwood and, in the larger houses, roofs were supported by rows of stone columns. The inhabitants generally lived in the upper story, although in the hot weather, roofs were used for sleeping. According to Deut. 22:8, a parapet was to be built around the roof as a safety precaution.

The growing social inequality between rich and poor that was denounced by eighth-century prophets (e.g., Amos 6:4–6) seems to receive archaeological confirmation in certain excavations such as Tell el-Farah. In the tenth century BCE all the houses there were of the same size and arrangement, but in the eighth century, some houses were larger, better built, spaced farther apart, and located in a different quarter of the town than smaller, simpler houses, which were huddled together.

In the Hellenistic (333–63 BCE) and Roman (63 BCE–324 CE) periods, marked changes in architecture occurred. As yet there is little information about the houses of the common people, but excavations in Jerusalem have provided a good picture of how the wealthy lived during the days of Herod the Great (37–4 BCE); their homes resemble the magnificent mansions well known from the ruins in Pompeii (destroyed 79 CE). One huge house, covering over 2000 square feet, had a series of rooms arranged around a central courtyard that contained four sunken ovens. Some houses had frescoed walls with ornamentation done in the decorative style of Pompeii. All of the excavated houses contain at least one cistern hewn into the bedrock; the larger ones had many such water installations. *See also* towns.

Bibliography

Beebe, H. K. "Ancient Palestinian Dwellings." *Biblical Archaeologist* 31 (1968): 38–58.

2 A family line or a tribal group, e.g., "house of Levi" (Exod. 2:1; cf. Num. 1:2). The term "house" (Heb. *bet;* Gk. *oikos, oikia*) is also used in a wider sense in expressions like "house of slavery" (Egypt, Exod. 13:3). A place of worship may be called the "house of God" (Mark 2:26) or "house of prayer" (Mark 11:17). In Heb. 3:3–6, the expression "house of God" is applied to the Christian community. *See also* family.   M.M.S.

household gods (Heb. *teraphim*), small carved or molded figures that were probably small representations of divinities (Gen. 31:19, 34; Lev. 26:1). Such items have been found in almost every era of occupation in a number of archaeological sites. In Gen. 31, Rachel steals "household gods" from her brother Laban when she flees his house with her husband, Jacob. Laban catches up with them in Gilead and searches for his gods, but Rachel conceals them by sitting on them and saying she cannot get up because the "way of women" is upon her.

Huldah (huhl′duh), a woman from Jerusalem who was a prophet. She was the wife of Shallum, keeper of the (king's) wardrobes during the reign of Josiah (640–609 BCE). Consulted by Josiah's officials after discovery of a "scroll of Moses" in the temple, Huldah prophesied the destruction of Jerusalem, adding that Josiah would die before the catastrophe. Huldah's prophecy helped spur vast religious reforms (2 Kings 22; 2 Chron. 34). *See also* Josiah; prophet.

human being, humanity. The biblical creation accounts in Gen. 1 and Gen. 2–3 portray humans as part of the natural world, but also as specially related to God (Ps. 8:3–5). Humankind is of two types: male and female, both made in the image of God (Gen. 1:26; 5:1–2). As created beings, humans are not divine, but stand under God's authority. As uniquely created in God's image, however, they are God's agents in ruling other creatures and caring for the earth (Gen. 1:26; 2:15). Thus, throughout the Bible, the term "humans" is often used in contrast to divine beings (humans are distinct from God and the angels; e.g., Gen. 32:38; Matt. 15:9; 16:23; John 10:33) as well as in contrast to animals (humans are distinct from the beasts; e.g., Exod. 8:17–18; Matt. 12:12; but see Eccles. 3:18–21). Humans are also portrayed as disobedient to God in a way that damages their relationship with God and necessitates their punishment. Still, the life of a human being is sacred, because humankind was made in God's image (Gen. 9:6).

The Bible offers no systematic view of the human constitution, but there is a general sense that humans have visible and invisible properties. Thus, the visible or physical aspect of humans may be described with such terms as "flesh," "body," "members," and "outer person" or with references to individual body parts or organs. The invisible aspect of humanity is often described by references to the "soul," "spirit," "mind," or "inner person"; for the most part, these terms are interchangeable and do not indicate separate aspects. Furthermore, such terminology is not consistent; the "heart," for example, can be a physical organ (the one that pumps blood), but most of the time it refers to the inner person and is essentially synonymous with "spirit," "mind," or "soul." When the breath of life departs a human body, that body returns to dust and the person survives only as an unsubstantial shade. The hope of resurrection as portrayed in the NT involves the creation of new bodies for those who have died (as opposed to the Greek concept of the dead continuing to survive as immortal souls; cf. 1 Cor. 15:35–55). Paul also speaks of Christ as creating a "new humanity" in which former divisions will be done away with (Gal. 2:15; 3:28). *See also* body; conscience; flesh; flesh and spirit; heart; mind; soul.

Bibliography

Eichrodt, Walter. *Man in the Old Testament.* SCM, 1951.

Jewett, Robert. *Paul's Anthropological Terms.* Brill, 1971.

Wolff, Hans Walter. *Anthropology in the Old Testament.* Fortress, 1974.   R.H.G./M.A.P.

humility, in the biblical world a value that directs persons to stay within their inherited social status by not presuming on or lording over others. Humble persons do not threaten or challenge another's rights, nor do they claim more for themselves than has been duly allotted them in life. They even stay a step below or behind their rightful status (e.g., the "unworthy" John the Baptist, Mark 1:7). Conversely, to attempt to better oneself at the expense of others, to acquire more than others, and to strive for honor that others currently enjoy are all instances of proud and arrogant behavior. God humbles such proud people (Matt. 23:12; Luke 18:14; see Deut. 8:2, 16), but exalts those who humble themselves (Matt. 23:11–12; Luke 14:11; 18:14; James 4:10; 1 Pet. 5:6). To humble oneself is to declare oneself powerless to defend one's status (Phil. 2:9) and then to act accordingly—either by becoming literally powerless or by symbolically demonstrating that one's use of power has been set aside (e.g., by fasting, rending garments, weeping, lamenting, or confessing sins; cf. Lev. 26:41; 1 Kings 21:29; 2 Kings 22:8–20; Ps. 69:10).

Humility in general is highly valued (Eph. 4:2; Col. 3:12) and, according to many scholars, is treated as a "prime virtue" in Paul's Letter to the Philippians. There, Paul urges the Philippians to do nothing out of selfish ambition, but to place the interests of others ahead of their own (2:3–4). He associates this self-effacing attitude with having the "mind of Christ" (2:5; cf. Rom. 12:2; 1 Cor. 2:16), and he either quotes or composes a hymn that demonstrates how Jesus Christ provides them with the all-time best example for humility. Jesus did not exploit his prerogatives as one who was equal with God, but "emptied himself" and "humbled himself" by becoming human and becoming obedient unto death—even "death on a cross" (2:6–8). Many scholars have noted that what Paul calls "humility" in Philippians is similar to what he calls "love" in other letters (Rom. 12:10; 14:15; 1 Cor. 13:4–7; Gal. 5:13; cf. Phil. 1:9, 16; 2:1–2).   B.J.M./M.A.P.

hunting, an activity seldom mentioned in the Bible and apparently not a common occupation among the Israelites. Neither of the two men specifically designated as hunters, Nimrod (Gen. 10:9) and Esau (Gen. 25:27), were Israelites. Much more common for the Hebrews was the killing of game encountered by chance (Judg. 14:6) or the killing of wild animals that attacked a shepherd's flocks (lions and bears are mentioned specifically in 1 Sam. 17:34–37). The typical weapons used for hunting included bow and arrow (Gen. 27:3), the sling and sling stone (1 Sam. 17:40, 49–50), and the shepherd's staff (1 Sam. 17:40). Egyptian paintings depict the use of hunting dogs, while Assyrian reliefs show nobles in chariots hunting lions. The first century CE Jewish historian

Spear hunting desert animals, including a lion and an ostrich, as depicted on an Assyrian cylinder seal, twelfth–tenth century BCE.

Josephus tells us that Herod the Great enjoyed hunting on horseback (*Jewish War* 1.21.13). Wild animals considered acceptable for food and thus apparently hunted included the hart, the gazelle, the roebuck, the wild goat, the ibex, the antelope, and the mountain sheep (all listed in Deut. 14:5). Forbidden to the Hebrews, but apparently acceptable to the Canaanites, were the hare and the wild pig (Lev. 11:6–7). Along with hunting, fishing (Isa. 19:8) and trapping birds with nets (Amos 3:5; Prov. 6:5; Pss. 91:3; 124:7) are mentioned. Fishing plays a big part in the NT, where some of Jesus's disciples were fishermen (Matt. 4:18–19; 17:27; Luke 5:1–9; John 21:3–11). *See also* animals; fish.
                                                    J.F.D.

Hur (huhr), a name of uncertain derivation.
   1 One of Israel's leaders, during the wilderness sojourn, who helped govern the people at Sinai in Moses's absence (Exod. 24:14) and supported Moses's arms during the battle with the Amalekites (Exod. 17:10, 12). He evidently was the same Hur who was a descendant of Judah and grandfather of Bezalel, the craftsman who built the tabernacle (Exod. 31:2; 1 Chron. 2:19).
   2 One of the five Midianite kings killed by Moses in Transjordan (Num. 31:8).
   3 The father of Rephaiah, an official contemporary with Nehemiah (Neh. 3:9).

Huram (hyoor'uhm). *See* Hiram.

Hurrians (hoor'ree-uhnz). *See* Horites.

husband. *See* family.

Hushai (hoosh'i), an Archite who is called the "friend of David" (2 Sam. 15:32; 1 Chron. 23:33). The latter designation is a technical term for an official of the king who served as a personal adviser (the same word is used in 1 Kings 4:5). He remained loyal to David during Absalom's attempt to seize the throne and was sent by David back to Absalom as a spy (2 Sam. 15:32–37). He convinced Absalom of his loyalty and persuaded Absalom to take his counsel over the advice of Ahithophel,

another adviser of David's who had joined Absalom's conspiracy. He then sent word to David of Absalom's plans, allowing David and his men to escape (2 Sam. 16:16–18; 17:5–22). He is probably the same person mentioned as the father of Baana, an official of King Solomon (1 Kings 4:16). *See also* Absalom; Ahithophel; David.   D.R.B.

Husham (hoosh'uhm), a pre-Israelite king of Edom, either from the area or the tribe of Teman (Gen. 36:34–35).

Hushathite (hoosh'uh-thit), a resident of the home village of two of David's warriors, Sibbecai (1 Chron. 11:29; 20:4; 27:11; 2 Sam. 21:18) and Mebunnai (2 Sam. 23:27). The location has been identified as Hushah, west of Bethlehem and in the path of Philistine invasion into the hill country. Such a location would involve David's conflicts with the Philistines in which the two warriors performed with distinction.

Hushim (hoosh'im).
   1 A son of Dan who went to Egypt with Jacob (Gen. 46:23), although by a reversal of letters the name is Shuham in Num. 26:42 and the family group of which he is the ancestral head is called the Shuhamites. *See also* Shuham.
   2 The son of Aher; a descendant of Benjamin (1 Chron. 7:12).
   3 The wife of Shaharaim, a Benjaminite, and mother of Ahitub and Elpaal (1 Chron. 8:8, 11).

Hyksos (hik'sohs), the Greek name given by the third-century BCE Egyptian priest Manetho to the Asiatic princes who ruled in Egypt as the Fifteenth and Sixteenth Dynasties (ca. 1667–1559 BCE). The contemporary Egyptians called them *Heqau khasut*, "rulers of foreign hill countries." The Hyksos were largely Semitic in origin, and they were evidently sufficiently well organized to be able to take advantage of a period of weakness in Egypt to gain control of much of the Nile Valley. They had previously consolidated their power in the eastern Delta, where their ancestors had been living since the early second millennium BCE. Their principal deity was the Egyptian god Seth, whom they equated with one of their own Semitic deities. In 1667 BCE the Hyksos captured the Egyptian administrative capital of Memphis, an event that inaugurated the Fifteenth Dynasty. Eventually the Hyksos were defeated and thrown out of Egypt by King Kamose (ca. 1576–1570 BCE) and his successor, King Ahmose (ca. 1570–1546 BCE).

Some scholars connect the Hyksos with narratives in the Pentateuch about the migration of Israel's ancestors to Egypt for a period of time before departing to settle in the land of Canaan. The story of Joseph and his rise to authority in Egypt would be more understandable during a period when Asiatics were in power in Egypt. Moreover, Josephus, a first-century CE Jewish historian, actually equates the expulsion of the Hyksos from Egypt with the exodus of the Hebrews, but this may be an attempt to give a great antiquity to the Jews. This theory remains highly speculative, and nothing in the biblical narratives must necessarily be dated to the Hyksos period in Egypt.

The two principal cities associated with the Hyksos were Avaris and Sharuhen. Avaris, their Egyptian capital, is identified with Tell el-Dabaa in the area of Khatana-Qantir in the eastern Nile Delta. Extensive remains have been found there that date to the Second Intermediate Period (Thirteenth–Seventeenth Dynasties, ca. 1786–1570 BCE). The finds at Tell el-Dabaa include a series of temples as well as tombs. Tell el-'Ajjul, an enormous mound about four miles southwest of modern Gaza, is the most probable site for Sharuhen. A large number of royal-name scarabs have been found there—beetle-shaped semiprecious stones bearing the names of Hyksos rulers. *See also* Sharuhen.   J.M.W.

Hymenaeus (hi′muh-nee′uhs), a person named in two of the Pastoral Letters as an opponent of Paul. In Tim. 1:18–20, he is associated with somebody named Alexander (cf. 2 Tim. 4:14) and is cited as an example of someone who has "rejected conscience" and, so, suffered "shipwreck in the faith." The letter also says that Hymenaeus and Alexander were "turned over to Satan," so that they might "learn not to blaspheme." Some sort of discipline is implied by such language—probably expulsion from the church. In 2 Tim. 2:14–18, Hymenaeus is mentioned in conjunction with someone called Philetus. The two of them taught that the "resurrection has already taken place" (cf. 2 Thess. 2:1–2). The exact content of their teaching is difficult to determine; perhaps they claimed that resurrection was a spiritual reality to be experienced in the present, rather than a bodily or more literal reality to be experienced at the end of time. In any case, their teaching is characterized as "profane chatter" that leads people to more and more impiety that spreads like gangrene. *See also* Alexander; Philetus.

hymn, broadly speaking, any poetical composition in honor of God or suitable for use in a liturgical setting, i.e., in worship. Such poetic pieces could be sung or chanted or recited antiphonally (i.e., in a responsive reading). With this understanding, many of the Psalms in the Bible would fall into the category of "hymn," but there are also numerous passages incorporated into other parts of the Bible that could be understood as hymns. Three classic examples would be the Song of Moses (Exod. 15:1–18), the Song of Miriam (Exod. 15:21), and the Song of Hannah (1 Sam. 2:1–10).

The early Christian church incorporated hymns in its liturgies (e.g., Acts 16:25; 1 Cor. 14:26; Col. 3:16). Some of the best-known poetic compositions in the Gospels are found in Luke: the Benedictus (1:68–79), the Magnificat (1:46–55), the Gloria (2:10–14), and the Nunc Dimittis (2:29–32). There is discussion as to whether Luke himself composed these or whether he simply incorporated into his narrative hymns that were being used in the church.

Likewise, Phil. 2:6–11 is widely recognized as a hymn in honor of Christ; most scholars think that it was a pre-Pauline liturgical work, adapted and used by Paul because it was appropriate to the exhortation he wished to offer the Philippians. Another possible hymn in honor of Christ may be found in Col. 1:15–20, and the prologue to John's Gospel (1:1–18) may have been structured around a Christ hymn. Some scholars affirm that there may also be fragments from early Christian hymnody embodied in Eph. 5:14; 1 Tim. 1:17; 3:16; 6:16; 2 Tim. 4:18; and Rev. 4:11; 5:9–10; 11:17–18; 15:3–4. One collection of early Christian hymns has survived outside the traditional NT canon, the *Odes of Solomon.* *See also* Benedictus; Magnificat; music; Nunc Dimittis; poetry; Psalms, book of; worship in the Hebrew Bible; worship in the New Testament.   J.M.E.

hypocrisy, in the Bible, a term and notion primarily associated with the teaching of Jesus. In the Hebrew Bible, the word is found only in Ps. 26:4, and outside the Gospels it occurs in the NT only in Gal. 2:13; 1 Tim. 4:2; and James 3:17. The Greek word *hypokritēs* (transliterated into English as "hypocrite") was used to denote an actor, one who performed behind a mask. Thus the basic connotation of "hypocrisy" involved pretense or insincerity (putting forward an outward appearance that does not comport with one's true self). The meaning of the word, however, need not be constrained by its derivation. In James 3:17, hypocrites are people who show partiality; in Luke 12:56, they are people lacking in spiritual perception; and in other cases, they simply seem to be people who are wicked or evil in some generic sense (e.g., Matt. 24:51). Jesus, however, uses it primarily for people whom he regards as self-righteous, i.e., for people whose evil might not be apparent to all (or, perhaps, even to themselves). In Matt. 23, Jesus repeatedly applies the term to the scribes and Pharisees, suggesting that they are like "whitewashed tombs," which on the outside look beautiful but are actually full of filth (Matt. 23:27; cf. 23:13, 15, 23, 25, 38, 39; other references involving accusations against the religious leaders of Israel include Matt. 15:7; 22:18; Luke 12:56; 13:15). In Matt. 7:5, Jesus indicates that his own disciples are hypocrites when they are concerned with correcting the faults of others. but oblivious to their own failings (cf. Luke 6:42). Elsewhere, he indicates that hypocrites may pray, fast, or give alms simply to make a good impression on others (Matt. 6:2, 5, 16). In Gal. 2:13, Paul accuses Peter, Barnabas, and other Christians in Antioch of hypocrisy when they quit eating with Gentiles after representatives from the Jerusalem church came to visit. Warnings against hypocrisy are also found in Sir. 1:29; 32:15; 33:2.   J.M.E./M.A.P.

Hyrcanus (hihr-kay′nuhs).
1 Hyrcanus son of Tobias, a wealthy depositor to the temple treasury (2 Macc. 3:11). According to Josephus, his magnanimity was recognized

by Ptolemy (*Antiquities* 12.219), but he committed suicide when the Seleucid ruler Antiochus IV Epiphanes came to power (*Antiquities* 12.236).

2 John Hyrcanus I, son of Simon Maccabeus, who inherited the offices of high priest and ethnarch when his father and two brothers were murdered in an attempted coup staged by his brother-in-law (Ptolemy). He ruled for thirty years (135/34–104 BCE), during which time he consolidated the territorial and political status of Judea, forced the conversion to Judaism of the Idumeans, and destroyed the rival Samaritan temple on Mount Gerizim.

3 Hyrcanus II, son of Alexander Jannaeus and Alexandra Salome, who, as a pawn of Antipater the Idumean, fought with his brother Aristobulus II for the kingship. He served as high priest during his mother's reign (76–66 BCE) and after the Roman conquest (63–40 BCE) and was eventually executed by Herod the Great in 30 BCE.　　F.O.G.

hyssop (*Origanum Syriacum*), a small shrub about 27 inches high with small white flowers in bunches at the end of the stem. A bunch of hyssop was used to apply blood to doorposts at Passover (Exod. 12:22). Hyssop was also used to sprinkle a blood-and-water mixture on a person healed of leprosy or on a renovated house (Lev. 14:4, 6, 49, 51–52). According to Heb. 9:19, Moses sprinkled blood on the people in the ceremony of Exod. 24:6–8 using hyssop. The use of hyssop in purification rituals is referenced in Ps. 51:7. John 19:29 says that hyssop was used to put a vinegar-soaked sponge to Jesus's lips (cf. Matt. 27:48; Mark 15:36).　　D.P.W.

Hyssop.

Ibleam (ib'lee-uhm), a strongly fortified town near one of the southern passes into the Esdraelon Plain. It is to be identified with modern Khirbet Bel'ameh located a quarter mile south of Jenin. Ibleam is mentioned in a fifteenth-century list of Canaanite towns that Pharaoh Thutmose III claims to have brought under his control. During the period of Israelite settlement, the tribe of Manasseh was unable to drive the Canaanites out of Ibleam (Josh. 17:11, 12; Judg. 1:27), and it probably remained in Canaanite hands until the time of David. Bileam of 1 Chron. 6:70 is probably identical with Ibleam; it is listed there as a levitical town of Manasseh, while the LXX version of the parallel passage, Josh. 21:25, lists Ibleam. Ahaziah, king of Judah, was wounded by Jehu near Ibleam (2 Kings 9:27), and according to one LXX manuscript it was at Ibleam that Shallum murdered Zechariah, king of Israel (2 Kings 15:10; the NRSV follows the Hebrew text, which reads "in public" instead of "at Ibleam"). *See also* Jezreel.   N.L.L.

Ichabod (ik'uh-bod; Heb., "Alas, the glory"), a child born to the wife of Phinehas, son of Eli, the priest of Shiloh, at the time of the battle of Ebenezer. According to 1 Sam. 4:19–21 Ichabod's mother gave him the name in grief over hearing that her father-in-law and her husband had been killed in the battle and that the ark of the covenant had been captured by the Philistines. She gave the boy his name as she was about to die (apparently from a difficult labor), explaining that "the glory has departed from Israel, for the ark of God has been captured" (4:22). The appellation belongs to a category of names expressing mourning for an absent deity (cf. the name Jezebel, which means "Where is Baal?" or "Where is the prince?").

Iconium (i-koh'nee-uhm), a city (modern Konya) in south-central Asia Minor in a rich oasis at the edge of the central Anatolian plain. According to Greek mythology, Perseus decapitated Medusa here. The area was apparently settled by Phrygians who spoke an Indo-European language and who came from Thrace or Macedonia ca. 1200 BCE, following the collapse of the Hittite Empire. In an area of shifting political boundaries, however, Iconium was sometimes considered part of Phrygia to the west and sometimes of Lycaonia to the east. Xenophon's *Anabasis* (ca. 399 BCE) mentions the Persian king Cyrus's march eastward through Iconium as the last city of Phrygia, but Cicero, Strabo, and Pliny refer to Iconium as being in Lycaonia. Linguistically and ethnically, Iconium nevertheless remained Phrygian. Iconium was rarely independent, being subject to Lydia and Persia before its hellenization under the Seleucids in the third century BCE. It came under the sway of the invading Gauls after 278 BCE, when the entire central region of Asia Minor became known as Galatia and was ruled by them until ceded to Pontus in 129 BCE. In 36 BCE, Mark Antony returned control of Iconium to the Galatian king Antymas, upon whose death in 25 BCE all of Galatia (including Ico-

nium) became a Roman province. Under Claudius (41–54 CE), Iconium received the honorary name of Claudiconium.

At the time of Paul's first missionary journey as reported in Acts 13:1–14:26 (ca. 47–48 CE), Iconium, Lystra, Pisidian Antioch, and Derbe were all considered part of Galatia. Coming from Cyprus to Antioch, Paul and Barnabas were driven from the city by members of the local Jewish community. They moved on to Iconium, where they remained for some time preaching successfully, but causing division among the inhabitants, both Jews and Gentiles (13:51–14:7). Paul and Barnabas fled Iconium when they heard about a plot to mistreat and stone them and went on to Lystra, some eighteen miles south, but were hounded even there by Antiochian and Iconian Jews. They managed, nonetheless, to return to Iconium in order to encourage the fledgling church they had begun there (14:21–23). On his second missionary journey as reported in Acts 15:40–18:21 (ca. 49–51 CE), Paul visited Iconium again (16:1–6), when he recruited as his companion Timothy of Lystra, who was well known and respected in Iconium. A third journey (ca. 51–54 CE) to Galatia and Phrygia (18:23) may well have included a stop in Iconium. The church in Iconium may have been among the addressees of Paul's Letter to the Galatians and of 1 Peter (Gal. 1:2; 3:1; 1 Pet. 1:1). The persecutions of Paul's first visit to the city are later recalled in 2 Tim. 3:11.

In the second century, Iconium was raised to the status of a Roman colony, and it provided the setting for the apocryphal novel *Acts of Paul and Thecla*. *See also* Antioch; Derbe; Galatia; Lycaonia; Lystra; Phrygia.   C.H.M.

Iddo (id'oh).

1 The father of Abinadab, one of Solomon's twelve district administrators (1 Kings 4:14).

2 The fifth-named son of Gershom, son of Levi (1 Chron. 6:21).

3 An officer responsible for the Gileadite half of Manasseh under David (1 Chron. 27:21).

4 A prophet and writer recording activities of Solomon, Rehoboam, and Abijah (2 Chron. 9:29; 12:15; 13:22).

5 The father (Ezra 5:1; 6:14) or grandfather (Zech. 1:1, 7) of the prophet Zechariah.

6 One of the priests and Levites who returned to Jerusalem with Zerubbabel and Joshua (Neh. 12:4, 16).

7 The head of a Jewish settlement in Casiphia, to whom Ezra sent for ministers to serve in the temple.

8 One of the Jews who returned from the Babylonian exile and then divorced his non-Israelite wife in response to Ezra's proclamation (Ezra 10:43).   S.B.P.

idol, an image or statue of a deity fashioned to be an object of worship. The English word, which has a pejorative meaning, reflects several different Hebrew words. Some of these are neutral terms, e.g., *pasil* or *pesel*, "(carved) image," and *massekah*, "(cast) image." For these the pejorative "idol" is not always appropriate; "image" or "statue" is sometimes better. Other Hebrew words for statues of deities are intentionally contemptuous and therefore are appropriately translated "idols," e.g., *'elilim*, "powerless ones," *gillulim*, "pellets of dung," and *shiqqutsim*, "shameful things." Statues of deities are a common feature of ancient Near Eastern religions. Exactly how the ancients imagined their gods to be present in the statues is not easy to discern. They did not necessarily believe that the image itself was the god. Rather, they may have believed that the image made it possible for the god to encounter the worshiper.

Prohibition Against Idols: Statues of God were strictly forbidden to Israel, a prohibition that sets Israel apart from its neighbors. The aniconic tradition appears to be ancient and effective. No male image identified as the God of Israel has ever been found at an Israelite site. The Decalogue, generally considered to be early, connects the prohibition against images with monotheism: "You shall have no other gods before me. You shall not make for yourself a graven image . . . for I the LORD your God am a jealous God" (Exod. 20:3–5; cf. Deut. 5:7–9). The prohibition against idols is also stated decisively in the book of Exodus. God liberates the Hebrews from slavery to Pharaoh in Egypt, and Israel agrees to worship God alone (Exod. 19–24, esp. 19:1–8). Still, the people's apostasy from this fundamental commitment is depicted in their worship of a golden calf (Exod. 32), which the text interprets as an idol (32:8). Many scholars believe that the calf in the exodus passage would have been intended as a throne for the deity rather than as a deity itself. Statues have been excavated from West Semitic sites, some of which show a god astride an animal and some of which show the animal only. In the latter case, the god was imagined as invisibly enthroned upon the animal. The Exodus passage may have interpreted the animal as a god rather than as a throne in order to make the point that the worship was false. Likewise, 1 Kings 12:28 relates Jeroboam's founding of countershrines outside Jerusalem to the apostasy of Israel worshiping the idol of a calf at Sinai.

Upon settlement in the land of Canaan, Joshua exhorts all Israel to "put away the gods which your fathers served beyond the river, and in Egypt, and serve the LORD" (Josh. 24:14). Much of the power of biblical preaching from Moses to the time of the exile comes from its stark either-or choice between "the LORD" (i.e., Israel's God, known by the Tetragrammaton or unpronounceable divine name YHWH) and the "other gods." The great ninth-century BCE contest at Carmel in 1 Kings 18 between the Lord and Baal regarding control of the rain contains the challenge of Elijah: "If the LORD is God, follow him, but if Baal, then follow him" (v. 21). To choose the other gods would have meant embracing an idol. In the great period of apostasy in Judah under Manasseh in the seventh century, 2 Kings 21:7 mentions a graven Asherah,

Clay idol from the second millennium BCE found in northern Syria.

a sacred pole by the altar, which the king put up in the sanctuary.

During and After the Exile: The exile of the sixth century BCE seems to mark a turning point in the biblical attitude toward idols, a result perhaps of the Babylonian Jewish community's ability to distance itself from the Babylonian culture and worship system. The exilic prophet whose oracles are collected in Isa. 40–55 parodies the idols of Babylon (40:18–20; 41:5–7, 21–29; 44:6–20; 46; cf. Jer. 10:1–16; Pss. 115; 135). In his eyes the idols represented the deities only too well. A passive and inert statue cannot move, nor can it hear, speak, or act; the god is correspondingly lifeless and helpless. This prophet's chief interest in the idols is to contrast them with the God of Israel; Israel by its faithful action witnesses to the vitality of its God. Another text from the same period, Gen. 1:26–27, speaks of humans in their divinely ordained activity as the image and likeness of God. With the exile, the theoretical foundation of monotheism seems sure; postexilic literature does not show the same concern with idolatry as an urgent problem or temptation, as do the earlier, preexilic sources.

Early Christianity inherited the prohibition of idols from Jewish religion. Paul identifies idolatry as the cause of the disintegration of sexual and social morality (Rom. 1:22–29), and he forbids

Christians to take part in rites honoring other gods; civic feasts in the Roman Empire could be so interpreted (1 Cor. 10:14). On the other hand, Paul does not see anything intrinsically wrong with "eating food offered to idols"; people who know that the idols are empty symbols for gods that do not actually exist may consume meat slaughtered in honor of such gods with a clear conscience—the only caveat being that one must be aware of how one's actions affect others (8:1–11:1).

Pauline theology also branded excessive concern with the wealth of this age as idolatry (Col. 3:5). An admonition at the end of 1 John says, "Little children, keep yourselves from idols" (5:21).
R.J.C.

Idumea (id'yoo-mee'uh), the Greek name for Edom as found in the LXX. After the exile (587/6 BCE) the name designated the region in Judea from Beth-zur to south of Beer-sheba, an area occupied in part by Edomites (Idumeans, Ezek. 36:5). Throughout the Seleucid, Hasmonean, and Herodian periods (ca. 198 BCE–44 CE) Idumea changed hands frequently. Herod the Great was an Idumean, and people from Idumea came to hear Jesus (Mark 3:8). Idumea is mentioned several times in 1 Maccabees (4:15, 29, 61; 5:3; 6:31; cf. 2 Macc. 12:32). *See also* Beer-sheba; Beth-zur; Edom; Edomites; Hasmoneans; Herodians; Judea; Seleucids.

Igal (i'gal; Heb., "[God] redeems").
1 The spy from Issachar sent by Moses to scout the promised land (Num. 13:7).
2 One of David's warriors from Zobah (2 Sam. 23:36); apparently named Joel in 1 Chron. 11:38.
3 A son of Shemmaiah and a descendant of both David and Zerubbabel (1 Chron. 3:22).

Illyricum (i-lihr'i-kuhm), land of the Illyrians, a Roman province on the eastern coast of the Adriatic corresponding to modern Yugoslavia and Albania. Ancient writers speak of the Illyrians as wild and given to piracy. It took the Romans about two hundred and fifty years to subjugate the area completely and to integrate it fully into the empire early in the first century CE under Tiberius (14–37 CE). Paul speaks of having preached from Jerusalem to Illyricum in Rom. 15:19, but it is not clear whether he was actually in Illyricum or merely considered it the eastern boundary of his apostolic activity up to the time of writing Romans. There were Christian communities in Illyricum by the second century, and Jerome, translator of the Bible into Latin (the Vulgate), was born there ca. 342. *See also* Dalmatia.
C.H.M.

image. *See* idol.

image of God, a key term for understanding the divine–human relationship in biblical thought. The exact meaning of the phrase in Gen. 1:26–27 and 9:6 is uncertain, and numerous suggestions have been proposed. To speak of human beings ("Adam") as created in the image of God apparently refers primarily to the bodily form (the Hebrew term for "image" usually carries the connotation of similarity in appearance or form; cf. Gen. 5:3), though this may include the spiritual attributes associated with the beings who bear this physical form. The plural pronouns of Gen. 1:27–28 indicate that male and female share equally in the image of God and connect this idea to the twofold commandment ("Be fruitful and multiply . . . and have dominion over . . ."), so that in both nature and function human beings are understood to reflect their Creator. They bring new life into being (though the animals do this also), and they rule over creation, with responsibility to care for it. The occurrence of the phrase in Gen. 9:6 emphasizes that human life is especially sacred: human blood is not to be shed because humans are created in the image of God. In the NT, vestiges of this meaning survive (1 Cor. 11:7–12; James 3:9), but a shift in emphasis identifies Christ as the one who embodies the image of God (2 Cor. 4:4; Phil. 2:6; Col. 1:15). This reflects the Christian view (most evident in John 14–15) in which Christ becomes the mediator between God and human beings.
T.R.W.L./M.A.P.

Imlah (im'luh; Heb., "he fills"), the father of Micaiah the prophet. Micaiah challenged four hundred other prophets and predicted the defeat of King Ahab (1 Kings 22:8–29). *See also* Micaiah.

Immanuel (i-man' yoo-uhl; Heb., "God is with us"), the name of a child whose birth is symbolic of God's guiding and protecting presence (Isa. 7:14; 8:8; Matt. 1:23). The name was first used by the prophet Isaiah as a sign given to King Ahaz of Judah during the Syro-Ephraimite war (ca. 734 BCE). At that time, Syria and Israel declared war on Judah because of its refusal to join their alliance against Assyria. Ahaz in turn appealed to Assyria for help. During his preparations for the impending conflict, Ahaz was warned by Isaiah, not to rely upon the military might of Assyria, but instead to put his trust in the Lord (7:1–9). Ahaz, however, did not heed Isaiah's advice. Shortly after, Isaiah encouraged Ahaz to ask a sign of the Lord that would assure him of God's presence and protection. Ahaz refused, taking recourse in a religious subterfuge in order to mask his lack of faith (7:12). Despite that refusal, the prophet Isaiah gave him a sign in the form of the Immanuel prophecy (7:13–17). A young woman, who either already was or soon would be pregnant, would give birth to a son who would be named Immanuel. Before the child was old enough to know the difference between good and evil, the two nations of whom Ahaz was afraid would be destroyed. But in their stead, a much more formidable threat against Judah would materialize in the rising power of Assyria.

In the NT, Isa. 7:14 was used by Matthew to interpret the meaning of the virginal conception of Jesus. This association was facilitated by two things: (1) the LXX had used the Greek word *parthenos* ("virgin") to translate the Hebrew word *'almah* ("a young woman of marriageable age") in Isa. 7:14; and (2) a tradition in the early church (cf. Luke 1:34–35) held that Mary, the mother of Jesus, had been a virgin at the time that Jesus was conceived. The association of the name "Immanuel" with Jesus is important for Matthew, who presents Christ as the one through whom God dwells with God's people. For Matthew, however, this promise is ultimately fulfilled through the abiding presence of Jesus in the community of his followers (Matt. 18:20; 28:20). *See also* Virgin Birth.

W.E.L./M.A.P.

Immer (im′uhr; Heb., "lamb").
1 The father of a line of priests that numbered 1,052 (Ezra 2:37; Neh. 7:40). One of these descendants of Immer was Jeremiah's opponent, Pashhur (1 Chron. 9:12; Jer. 20:1; cf. 1 Chron. 24:14). In postexilic times, Immer's descendants could not prove their priestly descent (Ezra 2:59; Neh. 7:61); two of them were among those who divorced their foreign wives in response to Ezra's proclamation (Ezra 10:20). One of the postexilic descendants of Immer was Zadok, who repaired part of the Jerusalem wall opposite his house (Neh. 3:29).
2 The father of a line of warriors, including Meshillemoth (Neh. 11:13). He may be identical with **1**.
3 A city in Babylon from which some priests emigrated when they returned to Jerusalem after the exile (Ezra 2:59; Neh. 7:61). The site identification of such a place is unknown.

immortality, immunity to death, endless existence. Two Greek words express the idea of immortality, *aphtharsia* and *athanasia;* they occur together in 1 Cor. 15:53, where the former is translated "imperishability" (cf. Rom. 2:7, where it is rendered "immortality"). It is significant that the only passages in the LXX that contain these two words are in the apocryphal/deuterocanonical Wisdom of Solomon (3:4; 4:1; 6:18–19; 8:13, 17; 15:3). They are also found in two other Greek Jewish writings produced during the Second Temple period, 4 Esdras (7:13, 96; 8:54) and 4 Maccabees (9:22; 14:5, 12; 16:13). Thus, the notion of immortality is a Hellenistic idea. Prior to the Hellenistic period, the Hebrews were inclined to accept death as a limit ordained by God (Gen. 3:19). Blessedness consisted in a peaceful death at an old age and in having posterity to carry on in one's place (Gen. 15). Certain elements in the Hebrew Bible, however, press beyond the notion of death as a limit. For example, the Song of Hannah proclaims, "The LORD kills and brings to life; (the LORD) brings down to Sheol and raises up" (1 Sam. 2:6). Here, however, "bringing to life" probably refers to granting new life through conception and birth rather than raising those who have died, and the reference to God as one who "brings down to Sheol and raises up" is probably not meant literally, but as an image of God's dual

ability to bring both catastrophe and well-being. Still, the vivid language of overcoming death in such passages may have played a role in the later development of the idea of resurrection and to have provided biblical warrant for such an idea when it was encountered in Hellenism (see also Pss. 16:10–11; 49:15; 73:24).

The people of Israel were also familiar with myths in neighboring cultures about dying and rising gods, such as Baal and Osiris. These myths reflect the rhythms of night and day, summer and winter, dormancy and fertility. Though the Israelites did not conceive of their God as dying and rising, they apparently made use of these myths to understand their destiny as a people (Hos. 6:1–3; Ezek. 37:1–14). This language about the people rising from death to life as a nation may have influenced the emergence of the notion of individual resurrection. In the Bible, the idea of individual resurrection appears first in Dan. 12:2–3, which was probably written ca. 167 BCE. According to Daniel, many, but not all, people will rise from the dead. The wise will rise, not to bodily existence on earth, but to a new form of life, "like the stars." Thus, resurrection in Daniel seems to imply some sort of celestial, perhaps angelic, existence (for the wise). The wicked, however, will rise to shame and everlasting contempt. During the Hellenistic and early Roman periods (325 BCE–325 CE) some Jews held to the old idea of death as a limit (Sir. 30:4–6; 1 Macc. 2:49–70). Some looked forward to resurrection (*Pss. Sol.* 3:16; 2 Macc. 7:9). Others believed in the immortality of the soul (*Jub.* 23:31; Wis. 3:1–4).

In the Gospels, Jesus is pictured as sharing the Hebrew notion of resurrection, rather than the notion of an immortal soul (e.g., John 11:23–25; cf. Mark 12:18–27). Indeed, the word "immortal" does not appear in the Gospels. In the Fourth Gospel, "eternal life" describes an unending life that has already begun, since such eternal life can be enjoyed prior to death (e.g., 3:16). Elsewhere in the NT, Paul speaks of a personal afterlife apart from and prior to resurrection (2 Cor. 5:1–15; Phil. 1:23). Still, resurrection is the more common image in his letters; immortality for Paul is not the continuing existence of the soul apart from the body, but rather the new heavenly existence of those who, clothed in "spiritual bodies," share in Jesus's resurrection in the new age (1 Cor. 15:42–50, 53–54). *See also* eternal life; flesh and spirit; resurrection; soul.

A.Y.C.

Imnah (im′nuh; Heb., either "right-hand" or "south" [i.e., on the right, when one is facing east]).
1 A son of Asher who went with Jacob to Egypt (Gen. 46:17); he is considered the ancestor of the Imnites (Num. 26:44).
2 A Levite, the father of Kore, a temple official during the reign of Hezekiah (2 Chron. 31:14).

incarnation (in′kahr-nay′shuhn; Lat. *incarnatio*), a term meaning "to enter into or become flesh." It refers to the Christian doctrine that the preexistent Son of God became human in Jesus. The term does not appear in the NT, but elements of the doctrine are present in different stages of development.

The idea of incarnation is closely connected with "preexistence," i.e., the thought that the person who became known as Jesus Christ existed prior to becoming a human being who lived on the earth. This idea is found in John 1:1–3, where the preexistent being is called "the Word" (Gk. *logos*). John says that the Word was "in the beginning" with God and, in fact, "was God." All things came into being through the Word, and in the Word was life (cf. Col. 1:15–20). Later, at a specific point in human history, "the Word became flesh" in the person of Jesus Christ and lived among humans (1:14). This event of the preexistent being becoming a human is called "incarnation" by Christian theologians. The Gospel of John also speaks elsewhere of Jesus's prior existence (6:62; 8:38), his descent from heaven (3:13; 6:33), his coming from God (16:27; 17:8), and his coming into the world (10:36; 12:46). Moreover, Jesus says, "Before Abraham was, I am" (8:58). From all of these verses, one might surmise that John thought the divine *logos* simply took on flesh and became a fully formed adult human being—but this is almost certainly not what he believed. Although the Fourth Gospel never mentions the birth of Jesus, it does refer to Jesus as having a mother (e.g., 2:1; 19:26), which implies that he was born and raised in a manner typical of human beings. For John, then, incarnation probably took place through a seemingly ordinary process of human birth.

Certain passages in Paul's writings also seem to imply a preexistence of God's Son. Paul speaks of God as one who "sent forth his Son" (Gal. 4:4; Rom. 8:3) and of Jesus Christ as the Lord "through whom are all things and through whom we exist" (1 Cor. 8:6). If Paul believed that the Son of God had somehow existed prior to the historical life of Jesus on earth, then some concept of incarnation might be assumed. When Jesus was "born of a woman" (Gal. 4:4), the Son of God through whom all things exist came into the world through a natural human process with a human body of flesh and blood. The classic Pauline text for understanding preexistence and incarnation, however, is the "Christ hymn" of Phil. 2:6–11. This passage describes the career of Christ Jesus in three stages: (1) he was in "the form of God" (2:6); (2) he was born in human likeness and lived and died as a human being (2:7–8); and (3) he was exalted by God to be Lord of all (2:9–11). It is difficult to know how literally the poetic language of such a hymn would have been taken, but the assumption of the text seems to be that Jesus Christ existed somewhere, somehow (in the form of God) before he became the man Jesus who lived and died on earth. Thus, "being born in human likeness" and "being found in human form" (Phil. 2:7) may be taken as references to the "idea" of incarnation (without implying a fully developed doctrine, such as would be reflected in later Christianity).

Some notion of preexistence and incarnation also seems to be found in the Letter to the Hebrews (1:2; 2:14–18; 10:5–7). The Synoptic Gospels, however, offer no indication of preexistence—and so no real concept of incarnation—though the Gospels of Matthew and Luke do insist that Jesus was conceived by an act of the Holy Spirit and, so, was the Son of God from birth (Matt. 1:18–23; Luke 1:26–38). This perhaps hints at the idea of incarnation in a less developed or explicit sense. *See also* lord; savior; son of God, Son of God; son of man, Son of Man; wisdom; word.   F.J.M./M.A.P.

incense, a compound of aromatic gums and spices. It had a secular use as a costly adornment (Song of Sol. 3:6; 4:6, 14), but is especially associated with worship in both negative and positive ways. Incense was regularly offered in Canaanite religion (Jer. 7:9; 44:17) and is frequently condemned as intrinsic to the worship of other gods (Jer. 1:16; Ezek. 8:11). But the burning of incense also had a part in Israelite religion. The golden altar in Solomon's temple (1 Kings 7:48) was probably for the burning of incense, and two incense altars stood in the Israelite shrine at Arad, which was in use from the tenth to the eighth centuries BCE. Such incense (for use in Israel's worship) was of unique composition and was considered especially holy (Exod. 30:37–38). It was to be made by skilled perfumers (37:29); the ingredients are detailed in 30:34–35. Originally it was burned in portable censers (Lev. 10:1; 16:12; Num. 16:17–18) but, later, was also burned on the altar of incense that stood before the veil of the Holy of Holies in the temple (Exod. 40:26). Because of its sacred character, the offering of incense was confined to the high priest, who burned it morning and evening (30:7–8), although Luke 1:8–9 indicates that this duty may have eventually been transferred to ordinary priests. Those not duly authorized (Num. 16:1–35, 40; 2 Chron. 26:16–21) or those who offered incense improperly made (Lev. 10:1–2) were struck down. In Num. 16:46–48, the burning of incense is

Incense burner (bowl and stand), found in a house at Tell Qiri, twelfth–eleventh century BCE.

associated with propitiating divine wrath; cf. also the high priest's bringing of incense into the Holy of Holies on the Day of Atonement (Lev. 16:12–13). Incense was also added to the cereal offering (2:1), to make the propitiatory "pleasing odor" that was otherwise provided by the burning fat in the case of animal sacrifices (1:9). The offering of incense can also be paralleled to the offering of prayer (Ps. 141:2), a link that is developed in the NT (Luke 1:10; Rev. 5:8; 8:3–4). *See also* altar; worship in the Hebrew Bible.   J.R.P.

India (in'dee-uh). The subcontinent to the east of Africa is mentioned in the Bible when the book of Esther indicates that the boundary of the Persian Empire under Ahasuerus (fifth century BCE) was "from India to Ethiopia" (1:1; 8:9). Elsewhere, 1 Macc. 6:37 indicates that each war elephant of Antiochus (second century BCE) had an "Indian driver." India is not otherwise attested in the biblical record. Nevertheless, widespread trade between ancient Mesopotamia and Indus Valley civilizations did exist, as indicated by an Aramaic inscription from Taxila (near Rawalpindi, Pakistan) from the third century BCE.   D.B.W.

inheritance. Most of the biblical legislation governing inheritance concerns the passing on of land, not personal wealth or other property. Some basic rules are provided in Num. 27:8–11. Normally, the land would pass to a man's sons, but if a man died without leaving a son, his property was transferred to his daughter(s). If he had no daughter, his property was assigned to his brothers. If he had no brothers, it was assigned to his father's brothers. If there were none of these, the property was assigned to the nearest relative in his own family group. A supplementary rule requires a daughter who inherits property to marry into a family of her father's tribe, preferably into the family of her father's brothers (36:6, 11). Thus the primary aim of the legislation was to preserve the territorial integrity of the family groups and tribes established at the time of the settlement of Canaan (cf. 36:7); there was to be no transfer of real property to another family or tribe. This right to inherit and transmit one's patrimony was strongly advocated in the monarchic period (ca. 1025–587/6 BCE; 1 Kings 21:3).

Biblical legislation also established the right of the firstborn son to inherit a double portion of the father's possessions, i.e., twice as much as that received by each of his brothers (Deut. 21:17). It further prohibited the father from conferring the right of the firstborn upon a younger son (21:16), though there is recognition that this had occurred during the period of the ancestors (Gen. 27:37; 48:18–20; cf. 1 Chron. 5:1). It is not clear how the status of the mother affected her son's right to inherit: on the one hand, there is evidence that the sons of a concubine or secondary wife did not inherit (Gen. 25:5–6; cf. Judg. 11:1–2); but, on the other hand, such sons sometimes do seem to have been considered equal to

the sons of the primary wife (Gen. 35:23–26). Perhaps this was not regulated by law, but was dependent upon the wishes of the father (cf. Gen. 21:10, where Sarah appeals to Abraham not to let Hagar's son, Ishmael, inherit along with her son, Isaac). Such a policy would accord well with the Laws of Hammurabi (170–71), which state that if a father legally recognizes the children borne by a slave-girl to be his sons, they are to be counted among his heirs; but if he fails to acknowledge them, they have no claim to his estate. The right of daughters to inherit along with their brothers is mentioned only in the book of Job (42:15), whose setting is non-Israelite.

In addition to legal usage, the term "inheritance" is employed in theological contexts to affirm the relationship between God and people (Deut. 9:26, 29; Jer. 10:16; Ps. 28:9). A number of NT texts speak of God's kingdom or of salvation as inheritance (Gal. 3:7–14; Eph. 5:5; Col. 3:24; Heb. 9:15; 1 Pet. 1:4). Jesus's reference to the meek inheriting the earth (Matt. 5:5) probably means that, when God's will is done, those who have been deprived of their fair share of the earth's resources (or specifically of the land promised to Israel) will receive what is rightfully theirs. Elsewhere in the NT, Jesus refuses to judge the rectitude of a disputed inheritance (Luke 12:13), and Jesus tells parables involving such bequests (Matt. 21:38). In one of his parables, a son asks for his share of the inheritance while the father is still living—a peculiar request that is otherwise unattested (Luke 15:12). *See also* law; marriage.   B.L.E./M.A.P.

iniquity. *See* sin.

ink, in antiquity a liquid material made from soot, gum arabic, and water, used for writing on papyrus. Since this kind of ink does not stick well to leather or parchment, scribes also employed ink made with tannic acid derived from nut galls (oak galls). These were pulverized and then mixed with sulfate of iron and water. The ingredients for making ink were kept in an inkhorn, made of metal or wood, which the scribe carried at his belt (Ezek. 9:2–3; 11). Most ink was black, but other colors were sometimes used. Titles might be written with red ink, which was made from either cinnabar or miniam. Purple ink was made from a liquid secreted by two kinds of gastropods, the murex and the purpura. For deluxe parchment or vellum manuscripts, scribes occasionally employed silver and gold inks. The Bible refers to the use of ink in Jer. 36:18; 2 Cor. 3:3; 2 John 12; and 3 John 13. *See also* writing.   B.M.M.

inn. *See* architecture; caravan.

inspiration, the filling with or domination by spirit. This concept first appears in biblical materials as a way of describing and understanding certain types of oral discourse. In ancient Israel, prophecy was understood as being uttered under the influence of God's Spirit (Num. 24:2; cf.

1 Kings 22:19–23). Sometimes this was evident in peculiar behavior by the prophets (1 Sam. 10:6); at other times, it appears simply as a claim to divine authorization (Isa. 61:1). Likewise, in the early Christian church, the Spirit of God was thought to inspire prophecy in addition to endowing believers with other gifts appropriate for edification of the community (1 Cor. 12:4–11; cf. 1 John 4:1–3). The concept of inspiration is applied to written documents in 2 Tim. 3:16. The same idea may also be implied in Heb. 3:7; 9:8, which describe the Spirit as speaking through the words or provisions of scripture. *See also* Holy Spirit; prophet; revelation; spiritual gifts.   L.W.C.

instruction. *See* education; rabbi, rabbouni; schools; synagogue; Torah; wisdom literature.

intercalation, a literary pattern according to which a narrative or coherent section of material is interrupted by another, seemingly unrelated, story or section of material. The material is thus arranged in an ABA' pattern, with the A material providing a frame around the B material. This pattern is used repeatedly in the Gospel of Mark, and in at least one instance Matthew and Luke seem to have taken over such a pattern from Mark, so that the intercalated material is found in all three Synoptic Gospels (Matt. 9:18–26; Mark 5:21–43; Luke 8:40–56). That instance is the story of

INTERCALATION IN
THE GOSPEL OF MARK

A. Jesus's family sets out to seize him (3:21).
B. Religious leaders accuse Jesus of using the power of Beelzebul (3:22–30).
A'. Jesus's family arrives and is rebuffed by him (3:31–35).

A. Jesus goes to heal the daughter of Jairus, a synagogue leader (5:22–24).
B. A woman with hemorrhages is healed by touching Jesus's garment (5:25–34).
A'. Jesus raises Jairus's daughter from the dead (5:35–43).

A. Jesus sends his disciples out on a mission (6:7–13).
B. We hear an account of how Herod killed John the Baptist (6:14–29).
A'. The disciples return with a report of their mission (6:30).

A. Jesus curses a fig tree for not bearing fruit (11:12–14).
B. Jesus attacks the temple, calling it a "den of robbers" (11:15–19).
A'. The fig tree Jesus cursed has withered and died (11:20–21).

From Mark Allan Powell, *Introducing the New Testament* (courtesy, Baker Academic)

Jesus healing Jairus's daughter, which is wrapped around the account of his healing a woman with a hemorrhage. In its current arrangement, Jairus, a leader of the synagogue, comes to Jesus to tell him that his daughter is ill. Jesus agrees to go with him to heal his daughter, but on the way Jesus is accosted by a woman with a hemorrhage who, in faith, touches his cloak and is healed. He stops to identify who received healing from him and has a brief conversation with her about faith. This interruption, however, delays his mission of healing Jairus's daughter, and he is told that the daughter has died. Jesus proceeds with Jairus to his home all the same and performs a miracle even greater than the intended healing: he raises the girl from the dead. Intercalation may serve the literary purposes of adding suspense, dramatic tension, or an element of irony. Some scholars also think that, in certain instances, intercalated stories are intended to interpret each other. For example, in Mark 11:12–21, the fig tree that is withered because it bears no fruit may serve as a symbol of the temple that Jesus denounces.   M.A.P.

intercession. *See* prayer.

iota (*i*-oh'tuh), ninth (and smallest) letter in the Greek alphabet, frequently equivalent to the English letter *i*. It is mentioned in Matt. 5:18 as a symbol of a very minor matter in the law; Jesus declares that not one iota will pass from the law until all is accomplished. The NRSV translates the word as "letter" but includes a footnote indicating that the literal translation would be "one iota."

Ira (*i*'ruh; Heb., "a male ass").
1 A Manassite (and therefore nonlevitical) priest at the time of David (2 Sam. 20:26). It is possible that he served in some special capacity as a royal official or private priest to the king (cf. 2 Sam. 8:18; 1 Chron. 18:17). He was from Jattir and is possibly to be associated with **2.**
2 One of the group of David's elite warriors known as "the Thirty" (2 Sam. 23:38; 1 Chron. 11:40). Some biblical manuscripts identify him as "a Jattirite," suggesting that he might be the same person as the priest mentioned in **1.**
3 Another warrior who also belonged to "the Thirty" (2 Sam. 23:26; 1 Chron. 11:28). He was the son of Ikkesh from Tekoa and was captain of the division that served in the sixth month of every year (1 Chron. 27:9).

iron, a metal whose hardness and malleability made it ideal for implements of war and agricultural tools.
Biblical References: Biblical references to iron occur in all parts of the Hebrew Bible. Pentateuchal references include the attribution of iron working to Tubal-cain (Gen. 4:22), the traditional "father of metallurgy." Moses uses iron in a simile, stressing its hard and unyielding property (Lev. 26:19). Iron taken as booty in the defeat of Midian was

Dagger with iron blade and other implements from ca. 1200 BCE, found at Tell el-Fardah (Tirzah) and Beth-shan.

required to be purified (Num. 31:22). Og, king of Bashan, had an iron bedstead (Deut. 3:11). Captivity in Egypt is likened to being in an iron furnace (4:20). The land of Canaan is described as a land whose "stones are iron" (8:9). Moses threatens the disobedient with a "yoke of iron" (28:48).

The historical books reflect the use of iron by Israel and its enemies. Canaanites had chariots of iron (Josh. 17:16). The Canaanite Sisera is said to have had nine hundred war chariots plated or studded with iron. Goliath's spear is described as weighing six hundred shekels of iron (1 Sam. 17:7), and the Philistines are said to have had a two-hundred-year local monopoly on the metal industry (1 Sam. 13:19–21), which was broken only when David came to power. In preparation for building, David gathered materials including "great stores of iron for nails for the doors of the gates and for clamps" (1 Chron. 22:3), but iron was prohibited in the temple (1 Kings 6:7). After David's farewell speech, heads of households gave freewill offerings that included "a hundred thousand talents of iron" (1 Chron. 29:7). Solomon also had iron workers (2 Chron. 2:7), and by the reign of Joash (802–786 BCE), the northern kingdom had its own iron workers (2 Kings 24:14; see also 2 Chron. 24:12). The floating ax head recovered by Elisha (2 Kings 6:6) is one specific example of a ninth-century iron implement.

Prophetic references to iron include the most descriptive passages of the ironsmith's craft (Isa. 44:12; 54:16) as well as the metaphoric use of iron as a symbol of strength and toughness (Isa. 48:4; Jer. 1:18); servitude (Jer. 28:13–14; see also Deut. 4:20); and judgment (Isa. 1:25; Jer. 6:29–30; Ezek. 22:20–31). In Psalms, Proverbs, and Daniel, iron is referred to in historical allusion (Ps. 105:18 tells that Joseph's neck was put in an iron collar when he was sold as a slave), proverbially (Prov. 27:17, "iron sharpens iron, and one man sharpens another"), and in apocalyptic dream and vision (Dan. 2:35, where the image of Nebuchadnezzar's dream had

feet of iron and clay; and 2:40–45, where one of the successive kingdoms is of iron).

The NT mentions iron once in Acts and five times in the Revelation to John. These references describe objects made of iron (e.g., an iron gate, Acts 12:10; breastplates of iron, Rev. 9:9; and vessels of iron, Rev. 18:12) and someone ruling "with a rod of iron" (Rev. 2:27; 12:5; 19:15).

Historical and Archaeological Data: The beginnings of iron metallurgy (smelting and forging) are linked generally to the Hittites of Asia Minor, ca. 1400 BCE. The Iron Age in the ancient Near East is separated into three time periods: Iron I (1200–900 BCE, biblically the time of judges and the united monarchy); Iron II (900–600 BCE, the time of the divided monarchy); and Iron III (or Persian, ca. 600–300 BCE, the time of the exile and restoration).

Iron ore sources were very limited. Minor deposits are detected in the area southwest of the Dead Sea, in Galilee, and in the Arabah, south of the Dead Sea. The largest ore source of antiquity was a mine at modern Mugharat Wardeh in the Southern Ajlun mountains (biblical Gilead), a site about twenty-two miles north-northwest of Amman, Jordan, about two miles north of the Zerqa (biblical Jabbok) River. The hypothesis of Philistine and Israelite use of this mine has strong circumstantial evidence, but to date no material evidence of Iron Age use has been found at the site.

Numerous ancient literary texts yield evidence of iron. Documents from Mesopotamia's eighteenth century BCE (the time of Hammurabi) mention iron implements. The Hittite king Hattusilis (1289–1265 BCE) shows Hittite territory as the source of Assyrian iron in the thirteenth century BCE. Papyrus Anastasi I, ca. 1250 BCE in Jaffa, tells of Canaanite craftsmen repairing iron chariots. Assyrian texts from Sargon II (722–705 BCE) mention tribute in iron bars received from various vassals.

Some archaeological artifacts of Near Eastern antiquity are an iron dagger found in Tutankhamen's tomb (ca. 1350 BCE), some 160 tons of iron bars from Sargon II's palace at Khorsabad, an ax head from Ugarit (ca. 1300 BCE), a miner's pick from the eleventh century BCE in Israel, and an iron-tipped plow point from Gibeah of Saul (modern Tell el-Ful). The Philistine sites of modern Tell el Far'ah (Sharuhen), Tell Jemmeh, Tell Qasileh, and Ashdod yielded furnaces and implements; Gezer produced wedge-shaped lumps of iron; and Beth-shemesh (Ain Shems) had forges.

Bibliography

Wertime, T. A., and J. D. Muhly, eds. *The Coming of the Iron Age*. Yale University Press, 1980.

                                        R.A.C.

Iron Age, the designation of an archaeological period during which iron artifacts began to come into common use. In the Levant, the Iron Age began around 1200 BCE. Iron had been utilized as early as 2700 BCE in Mesopotamia and Egypt, but only came into Israel at this later period because of the slower development of the necessary technology there. Biblical references to iron in Josh. 6:24; 17:16; 22:8; 1 Sam. 13:19–22; and 1 Sam. 17 tend to corroborate the archaeological evidence of the relatively late entry of Israel into the Iron Age. The Iron Age is normally broken into these subdivisions: Iron I, or Early Iron, 1200–900 BCE; Iron II, or Middle Iron, 900–600 BCE; Iron III, Late Iron, or Persian, 600–300 BCE. *See also* Egypt; iron; Levant, the; Mesopotamia.   K.H.R.

irrigation. *See* farming; water.

Isaac (*i´zik*; Heb., "laughter"), the son of Abraham and Sarah who is often listed as the second of the three male ancestors of the Israelites: Abraham, Isaac, and Jacob (Exod. 2:24; 3:6; Jer. 33:26). Isaac was born to aged parents (Abraham was one hundred according to Gen. 21:5; and Sarah was ninety according to 17:17). His birth came as the fulfillment of a divine promise that Abraham would have an heir whose descendants would become the specially chosen people of God, bound to God through a covenant that would make them a blessing to all the nations of the earth (17:15–21; 18:10–15; 26:2–5, 24). The boy was named Isaac ("laughter") because both Abraham and Sarah laughed when they initially heard the prediction that Sarah would bear a son when she was well past the age of childbearing (17:17–19; 18:1–15; cf. 21:3, 6–7). Sarah thus provides the Bible's first example of the motif of the infertile woman who bears a son due to divine intervention (see also Rebekah, Gen. 25:21–26; Rachel, Gen. 30:22–24; Samson's mother, Judg. 13:2–25; Hannah, 1 Sam. 1:1–20; and Elizabeth, Luke 1:5–25, 60). Isaac is also the first person to be circumcised at eight days as commanded by God (Gen. 21:4; cf. 17:12). After he is born, Sarah demands that Abraham expel Ishmael along with Hagar, a demand that God reinforces. This is accomplished after the feast of Isaac's weaning, at Sarah's insistence, because she perceives Ishmael to be a threat to Isaac's future as Abraham's heir (21:8–14).

In Gen. 22, Abraham's loyalty to God is tested by a divine command to sacrifice Isaac on a mountain in the land of Moriah. At the time, Isaac is depicted as a lad of indeterminate age. After leaving the servants and donkey behind, Abraham gives the wood for the sacrifice to Isaac to carry, while he himself takes the firestone and knife. Isaac, surprised at the lack of a sacrificial animal, asks his father, "Where is the lamb for a burnt offering?" (22:7). Abraham replies enigmatically, "God will provide the lamb for a burnt offering, my son" (22:8), and the two walk on together. In the rest of the story, Isaac plays a passive role—he is bound and placed upon the altar Abraham makes, and only when Abraham has already taken hold of the knife to slaughter him is his fate resolved. An angel cries out from heaven, and a ram is substituted for Isaac.

Isaac is also presented in a notably passive role in another narrative in Genesis, that in which

The angel staying Abraham's hand as he is about to sacrifice Isaac (Gen. 22); detail from the twelfth-century Lambeth Bible.

Rebekah is chosen to be his wife (Gen. 24). Even though he is forty years old, he does not appear to be consulted on the matter (25:20). Notably, Isaac is the only one of the triad "Abraham, Isaac, and Jacob" who is monogamous and without concubines. Further, of all the husbands of infertile wives in the Bible, only Isaac is presented as one whose prayer for a child is said to have been answered by God (25:21). In his old age, Isaac is tricked by Rebekah and her favorite son Jacob into giving Jacob the blessing that he had intended to bestow upon his favorite son, Esau (Gen. 27).

Thus, in biblical narratives, Isaac often seems to be the passive, naive innocent who is unaware of the intention of others. He is, however, protected by God, and all his doings are blessed by God, so that he attains great wealth and power (26:1–33). Isaac dies at the age of one hundred and eighty, attended by his sons (35:27–29).

There is far less biblical material concerning Isaac than either Abraham or Jacob (or, for that matter, Joseph), which may indicate that some traditions concerning him have been lost. For instance, the origin of the phrase "fear of Isaac" (Gen. 31:42, 53) is unknown. His individual importance is attested by Amos (7:9, 16), who equates the name "Isaac" with the northern state of Israel. Isaac is frequently mentioned in the NT along with Abraham and Jacob (e.g., Matt. 1:2; Luke 3:39; Acts 7:8). The story of the (potential) sacrifice of Isaac is mentioned in James 2:21, and Paul emphasizes his wondrous birth (Rom. 9:7, 10) and the promise of God associated with him (Gal. 4:28). *See also* ancestor; patriarchs.   J.U.

Isaiah (*i*-zay´uh), **book of,** the first book of what is sometimes called the Latter Prophets, a sub-collection in the Nevi'im (Prophets) section of the Tanakh (Jewish Bible). It is the first book of the Major Prophets of the Christian OT. The book is named after Isaiah son of Amoz, who is also called Isaiah of Jerusalem. He was a prophet in Judah at the time when the Neo-Assyrian Empire extended its power westward, first into Aram/Syria (734–732 BCE), then into Israel (722 BCE), and finally dominating Judah beginning in 701 BCE. Although the memoirs of Isaiah of Jerusalem date

An inscription quoting Isa. 66:14 carved on the western wall of the Temple Mount in Jerusalem during the reign of the Roman emperor Julian, who, in the fourth century, promised the resettlement of Jerusalem by Jews.

OUTLINE OF CONTENTS

Isaiah

to the second half of the eighth century, the book itself was not composed until much later. Furthermore, most modern scholars detect material that can be traced to at least three different prophets speaking to three different contexts: the material associated with Isaiah of Jerusalem is called First Isaiah, and the material associated with the other two anonymous prophets is called Second Isaiah and Third Isaiah.

Contents: First Isaiah (chaps. 1–39) offers a mix of different speech types, including first-person divine speeches to Judah (1, 13) and oracles of doom addressed to Judah's neighbors (12–19), accusations in which Isaiah calls Israel to repentance (2, 10) or offers hope (11), and first-person reports of Isaiah's personal experience (6, 8). There are also narratives about Isaiah in the third person (7). First Isaiah contains a section called the Isaiah Apocalypse (24–27), which is of uncertain date (opinions range from the eighth to the second century) and is eschatological in character, focused on universal cosmic destruction followed by a final glorious restoration. First Isaiah also contains four chapters (36–39) that are a virtual duplicate of the account of the Judean king Hezekiah in his encounter with the Assyrian king Sennacherib found in 2 Kings 18–20. This account reinforces the theme of God's support for the Davidic line of Judean kings and the divine protection of Jerusalem.

Second Isaiah (chaps. 40–55) appears to be a collection of poems on various topics, some of which are framed as God's words and others as the prophet's words. The lack of introductions and conclusions to the poems makes for difficult reading with abrupt changes in ideas. The overall mood is one of comfort, encouragement, hope, and renewal. The writer cites the divine work of creation and deliverance from Egypt as cause for hope. Second Isaiah speaks of an unnamed servant of God who suffers on behalf of the people. Cyrus the Persian king, called the Lord's anointed, will initiate the rebuilding of Jerusalem.

Cyrus's clay cylinder text, 538 BCE, recording that he "liberated those who dwelt in Babylon from the yoke that chafed them."

Third Isaiah (chaps. 56–66) is likewise a collection of poems, but they are set after the return to Judah. They look forward to a time when Judah/Israel's power will be restored when God resumes divine rule from Zion/Jerusalem.

Background: In a basic sense, the material in First Isaiah (chaps. 1–39) concerns the kingdom of Judah and its capital Jerusalem in the days of four kings of Judah (cf. 1:1) whose combined reigns stretch from 783 to 687 BCE. The earliest datable passage is Isaiah's temple vision (chap. 6) in 742 BCE. Material in Second Isaiah (40–55) relates to events of the sixth century, particularly the Babylonian exile. The references to the Persian king Cyrus in 44:28 and 45:1 place Second Isaiah within his reign (559–530 BCE). Material in Third Isaiah (56–66) concerns the late fifth- or early fourth-century restoration of Judah during the Persian period. Some scholars today question whether continuing to recognize a Third Isaiah (56–66) is warranted, but there is little question that there are at least two Isaiahs. In actuality, however, the compositional history of the book of Isaiah is even more complex than might be suggested by these subdivisions. For example, chaps. 13–14 and 24–27 in First Isaiah date to the sixth century BCE or later (while most of First Isaiah is from the eighth century BCE).

Sweeney presents a counterproposal to the three Isaiahs by dividing Isaiah into two parts, chaps. 1–33 and 34–66. He claims the focus of the book is on Jerusalem's central role in God's plan to save the world. The first part of the book lays out the grounds for the judgment and eventual restoration of Jerusalem, while the second part assumes this judgment has happened and that the time for restoration is imminent. He identifies four stages in the growth of the book: (1) an eighth-century edition of Isaiah ben Amoz during the Assyrian crisis; (2) a late seventh-century edition to support Josiah's program of religious reform and kingdom expansion; (3) a sixth-century exilic edition by an anonymous prophet; and (4) a fifth-century edition calling for covenant obedience so that God's reign can be realized.

Although the precise break between the first and second parts of Isaiah is open for discussion, there is consensus among scholars that the current book of Isaiah contains material from at least two different prophets that has been joined together into one composition. There is, however, no indication that this material ever circulated as scripture in anything but the unified format. The author of Sirach seems to know a single book of Isaiah that contains material from the different prophets (48:20, 24–25), and the large scroll of Isaiah found among the Dead Sea Scrolls is a manuscript of the full, unified composition.

Critical Issues: Academic study of the book of Isaiah has sometimes hinged on the question of whether the material should be analyzed separately, as the words of different prophets addressing different contexts, or as a unified work in which material drawn from diverse sources has been combined to produce a book that has its own integrity. For example, Clements and Childs suggest that Second Isaiah's "former things" are the words of First Isaiah and represent their fulfillment.

Themes: Israel's covenant relationship with God is based on the leadership of the royal house of David. Zion is to be the capital of the kingdom of the Lord, which will include all of creation. The messianic leadership of Hezekiah and Josiah give way to the kingship of God, and the people at large are related to God, as David used to be (55:3). Isaiah's support of the royal house in Jerusalem also entails God's protection of Jerusalem, called

Zion (used forty-five times in Isaiah) and the holy city. The name Isaiah means "the LORD is salvation," which fits with the overall message of the book. Jerusalem will ultimately find deliverance, and Zion will be the salvation of all people.

On the basis of the term "servant," scholars have isolated four poems in Second Isaiah and have used them to draw a picture of an otherwise anonymous figure called the "servant of the LORD" (42:1–6, 49:1–6, 50:4–9; 52:13–53:12). This figure brings justice to the nations and becomes a light to the nations. Yet this figure suffers greatly for his work. The fourth poem, put in the mouth of those he saved, describes how they first considered his suffering to be for personal wrongs, but then came to see that he suffered for their sins. Scholars have suggested that the figure might have been modeled on Jeremiah, Jehoiachin, the prophet himself, or Israel. A number of NT writers identify the figure in these poems with Jesus.

The phrase "the holy one of Israel" is found twenty-five times in Isaiah (but almost nowhere else). It is found in all three parts of the book. This way of referring to Israel's deity highlights the otherness of God in the Isaiah tradition, exemplified also in Isaiah's vision of the temple's throne room with God as king and the divine council pronouncing "holy, holy, holy" (6:3). Isaiah also draws upon the exodus tradition: God will once again be the warrior-redeemer of Israel, the one who will make a path through the sea to bring people home to Zion (43:16–19, 51:9–11).

Influences: The book of Isaiah is quoted more often in the NT than any other book of the Christian OT. Many of its figures and images were interpreted in a Christian messianic way, including the Immanuel figure of chap. 7 and the "suffering servant" of chap. 53. The book was a major source for the text of Handel's *The Messiah*.

Bibliography

Bandstra, Barry L. *Reading the Old Testament: Introduction to the Hebrew Bible*. 4th ed. Wadsworth, 2009.

Brueggemann, Walter. *Isaiah*. Westminster John Knox, 1998.

Childs, Brevard S. *The Struggle to Understand Isaiah as Christian Scripture*. Eerdmans, 2004.

———. *Isaiah*. Westminster John Knox, 2001.

Clements, Ronald E. *Old Testament Prophecy: From Oracles to Canon*. Westminster John Knox, 1996.

Sawyer, John F. A. *The Fifth Gospel: Isaiah in the History of Christianity*. Cambridge University Press, 1996.

Sweeney, Marvin A. *Isaiah 1–39*. Eerdmans, 1996.
                                                                              B.B.

Iscariot (is-kair´ee-uht), the surname of Judas, the disciple who betrayed Jesus (Matt. 26:14–16; 47–49). Various interpretations of the name have been suggested, including "the assassin" (from Lat. *sicarius*, a term applied to Judean rebels who used daggers to kill Romans and their sympathizers). This seems unlikely, however, because John 6:71 indicates that Iscariot was a family name: Judas Iscariot was the son of Simon Iscariot. More often, the name is thought to identify a location or tribe with which Judas and his family might have been associated. Both "man of Sychar" and "man of Issachar" have been suggested as possibilities, but the most support has been for "man of Kerioth." *See also* Judas; Kerioth.

Ishbaal (ish-bay´uhl; Heb., "man of Baal"). The fourth son of Saul (2 Sam. 3:14–15). He is actually referred to as Ishbosheth in Hebrew manuscripts of 2 Samuel, but most modern scholars think this is a theologically corrected reading of the original name (changing "man of Baal" to "man of shame"). This view is reflected in the NRSV, which uses Ishbaal throughout 2 Samuel. Ishbaal is also called Esh-baal (a different spelling of the same word) in 1 Chron. 8:33; 9:39. Upon the death of Saul, Ishbaal attempted to rule all of the twelve tribes, but the tribe of Judah refused allegiance to him. With Abner as general, Ishbaal set up his capital east of the Jordan River at Mahanaim (2 Sam. 2:8–10). After a stormy career, during which Abner deserted him, Ishbaal was murdered by two of his own henchmen, Rechab and Baanah, who took his head to David at Hebron, expecting a reward. However, David's sense of justice led to the execution of the two criminals and the burial of the head of Ishbaal at Hebron (2 Sam. 4). This event marked the end of Saul's brief dynasty. *See also* Abner; David.   M.A.F.

Ishbosheth (ish-boh´shith; Heb., "man of shame"). *See* Ishbaal.

Ishi (ish´i; Heb., "[God has] saved [me]").
1 A Judahite, the father of Zoheth and Benzoheth (1 Chron. 4:20).
2 A Simeonite whose sons or descendants defeated the Amalekites at Mount Seir (1 Chron. 4:42–43).
3 The son of Appaim, a Jerahmeelite (1 Chron. 2:31).
4 A leader of the Transjordanian Manassites (1 Chron. 5:24).

Ishmael (ish´may-uhl; Heb., "God has heard").
1 The son of Abraham and Hagar, the Egyptian slave-girl of Sarah (Gen. 16; 17; 21:1–21). Sarah gave Hagar to Abraham as a wife when she herself seemed to be infertile. Hagar bore Ishmael to Abraham, but Sarah later also bore a son, Isaac. After Sarah saw Ishmael playing with Isaac at the latter's weaning ceremony (21:9), she pleaded with Abraham to expel both Hagar and Ishmael, so that the two would not share the inheritance. God approved this, but subsequently protected Ishmael and his mother (21:15–21). God promised to make Ishmael "a great nation" (21:18; cf. 16:10). Indeed, God promised Abraham that Ishmael would become the father of twelve princes (a parallel to the twelve tribes of Israel that would descend from Isaac [through Jacob], 17:20; cf.

25:12–16). Ishmael is described as "a wild ass" (16:12), a possibly complimentary reference to his ability to survive in the wilderness. At Abraham's death, Ishmael and Isaac reunited to bury their father (25:9). Ishmael's daughter Mahalath (or Basemath) married Esau, the son of Isaac (28:9; 36:3). Ishmael is said to have lived to be 137 years old (25:7), a further indication that he is to be regarded as someone favored by God and worthy of honor within Israelite tradition. Despite the close connections between Ishmael and Isaac, however, the two would sometimes be viewed as progenitors of competing traditions—and in that sense Ishmael would always be cast in the inferior light. For instance, although Ishmael was circumcised at the age of thirteen and so brought into the covenant of circumcision (17:25; cf. 17:10), he was not included in the "everlasting covenant," as was Isaac (17:19). The latter covenant evidently pertained to possession of the land (17:8). In the NT, Paul refers to Ishmael in an allegory that tries to show how people can be descended from Abraham "according to the flesh," but still miss out on promises that must be received through faith (Gal. 4:21–28). *See also* Hagar; Ishmaelites.

2 The son of Nethananiah, a man of royal blood and the assassin of Gedaliah, whom the Babylonians appointed ruler of Judah after the fall of Jerusalem (2 Kings 25:25).   J.G.G.

Ishmaelites (ish´may-uh-lits), the descendants of Ishmael, son of Abraham and Hagar. They are named as twelve princes or "sons of Ishmael" in Gen. 25:13–16 and 1 Chron. 1:28–31. They are said to have settled in northern Arabia, from Havilah to Shur, opposite Egypt in the direction of Assyria (Gen. 25:18). The names contained in the Gen. 25 genealogy have affinities with the Edomites (see Gen. 36) with whom the Ishmaelites are said to have intermarried (28:9) and with the descendants of Keturah (25:1–4; 1 Chron. 1:32–33). Elsewhere, the caravan of traders who carry Joseph to Egypt are referred to as both Ishmaelites and Midianites, suggesting that those two groups might overlap or that the designations might be synonymous (Gen. 37:25–28; 39:1). In Judg. 8:24–26, "kings of Midian" seem to be included among a group of Ishmaelites defeated by Gideon. In Ps. 83:6, the Ishmaelites are listed among Israel's enemies, and so it must be surmised that they sometimes competed with Israelite tribes for such things as land, pasture, and water rights. Still, the Ishmaelites often seem to have been on friendly terms with Israelites. Amasa, a commander in David's army, was an Ishmaelite (2 Sam. 17:25), as was Obil, the keeper of his camels (1 Chron. 27:30). *See also* Ishmael.

         J.G.G.

Ishtar (ish´tahr), a goddess in the Akkadian pantheon. Ishtar was widely worshiped in Mesopotamia from earliest times until at least the first century BCE. She is related to other Semitic goddesses, including Astarte. In the Akkadian language, "Ishtar" came to mean "goddess" and could be used as a common noun. Ishtar was celebrated as a goddess of war, but at the same time she was vitally involved in the realm of sexuality and fecundity; in Mesopotamian mythology, mating and procreation would cease whenever Ishtar descended to the nether world. The cult of Ishtar was prominent at Nineveh, Arbela, and especially at Uruk (biblical Erech). Ishtar's most famous temple, the Eanna, stood in Uruk, and because the Mesopotamian *Epic of Gilgamesh* was set in that city, she plays an important role in that narrative. Her role in that story, however, is undignified, and she is taunted by the hero Gilgamesh as a faithless lover. Otherwise, Ishtar was associated with the planet Venus and reckoned to be the child of the moon god Sin; her brother was the sun god Shamash, and she had as her consort the sky god Anu, although she was sometimes reckoned the paramour of Tammuz. It is often assumed that the "queen of heaven" mentioned in certain biblical passages (Jer. 7:18; 44:17–19) refers to Ishtar. *See also* Erech; Tammuz.   R.M.G.

Ishvi (ish´vi).

1 A son of Asher who went with Jacob to Egypt (Gen. 46:17); he is considered the ancestral head of the Ishvite group (Num. 26:44). The name Ishvah, which is given for another son of Asher (Gen. 46:17; 1 Chron. 7:30; but omitted in Num. 26:44),

Stele of Ishtar of Arbela standing on a lion. She is armed with a sword and quiver, and her right hand is extended in benediction; from Tell 'Ahmar, eighth century BCE.

probably identifies the same person and is simply a variant spelling of Ishvi.

2 A son of King Saul and brother of Jonathan (1 Sam. 14:49); he is probably the same person elsewhere called Esh-baal (1 Chron. 8:33) and Ishbaal (2 Sam. 2:8). *See also* Ishbaal.   D.R.B.

island. A number of specific islands are referred to in the Bible.

1 Arvad, in northern Phoenicia, an island-city located two miles offshore (Ezek. 27:8, 11).

2 Cauda, a small island south of Crete where, according to Acts, Paul took refuge during a storm (27:13–17).

3 Chios, an island off the northern coast of Ionia (Acts 20:15).

4 Cos, an island off the southwest coast of Asia Minor, fifty miles northwest of Rhodes, to which Paul sailed on his way back to Jerusalem (Acts 21:1).

5 Caphtor, modern Crete, an island 160 miles long, reputed to be the place of origin of the Philistines (Jer. 47:4; Amos 9:7). It is called Crete in the NT. Paul sailed along its coast (Acts 27:7–21) and Titus is said to have supervised ministry there (Titus 1:5–14).

6 Cyprus, a large island located seventy-five miles off the northern Levant coast (Jer. 2:10; Ezek. 27:6; Acts 4:36; 11:19–20; 13:4; 15:39; 21:3, 16; 27:4).

7 Malta, a small island fifty miles south of Sicily, on which Paul, according to Acts, was shipwrecked (27:39–28:10).

8 Patmos, a small island off the Ionian coast, west of the island of Samos, on which John received his revelation (Rev. 1:9).

9 Rhodes, an island off the southwest coast of Asia Minor, visited in the course of Paul's return to Jerusalem (Acts 21:1).

10 Samos, located off the Ionian coast, twelve miles southwest of ancient Ephesus (Acts 20:14).

11 Sicily, the largest of the Mediterranean islands. It was visited by Paul when he landed and stayed for three days at Syracuse, its leading city (Acts 28:12).

12 Tarshish, possibly Sardinia (Ps. 72:10; Ezek. 27:25).

13 Tyre, an island-city of the Phoenicians that was famous for its trade and wealth (Ezek. 26–28). It was conquered by Alexander the Great after he built a half-mile mole from the coast to the island. Thereafter it remained connected to the mainland.   J.G.G.

Israel (iz´ray-uhl; Heb., "may God contend" or possibly "may God rule").

1 The name given by God to Jacob, an ancestor of the people who would thereafter be known as the Israelites. In Gen. 32:28 Jacob is given the name "Israel" after a struggle with a divine being on the bank of the Jabbok (the name *yisra'el* is there understood to mean "he strives [*yisra*] with God [*'el*]" [cf. Hos. 12:4]). A different account of the renaming of Jacob is provided in Gen. 35:10.

The stele of the Egyptian king Merneptah (ca. 1230 BCE) contains the earliest mention of the name "Israel" (*detail, bottom*) outside the Bible. As used on the stele, the name signifies a "foreign people" rather than a "foreign land."

2 The collective name of the twelve tribes descended from Jacob (Israel). In the Bible the people who are understood to be descendants of Jacob are often called the "children of Israel" (NRSV: "people of Israel") or simply "Israel." But the term is also used as a political designation: it may refer to the nation that achieved a particular identity at the time of the monarchy or, during the period of the divided monarchy (ca. 922–722/1 BCE), it may refer to the northern kingdom in particular, as distinct from Judah, the southern kingdom.

The People of Israel: The earliest occurrence of the name Israel outside the Bible is in a hymn celebrating the victories of the Egyptian king Merneptah, composed about 1230 BCE. The poem, which lists numerous enemies defeated in the Near East, contains the boast that "Israel has perished: its seed is no more." In the Egyptian text "Israel" is marked with a hieroglyphic signifying "foreign people," not "foreign land." This is often taken to mean that a group called Israel was present in Canaan at this time, but that they had not yet settled in the land or claimed territory for themselves. Exactly who this group might have been, however, is impossible to determine. It is not likely that it was the fully developed twelve-tribe entity of biblical tradition. Although the Bible presents "all Israel" as a unified people, comprising the ancestors of all later Israelites, who acted in concert from the earliest times, it is improbable that any such unification was achieved before the time of David. This is not to say, however, that Israel had no formal organization before the establishment of the kingdom. The biblical account of the premonarchic period and the rise of kingship (thirteenth–eleventh centuries BCE) suggests that the monarchy was imposed on some kind of antecedent tribal order, which modern scholars have attempted to reconstruct from the biblical evidence on the basis of analogies with other tribal organizations. Intertribal associations united by treaties and bonds of kinship were characteristic of Near Eastern nomadic society, as attested, for example, by the Mari archive, which provides information about the nomadic tribes of northwestern Mesopotamia in the second millennium BCE.

Thus the "Israel" of the Song of Deborah (Judg. 5), an ancient song celebrating a victory over the forces of Canaanite Hazor, was probably a loose confederation of tribes, perhaps ten in number (cf. Judg. 5:14–18) and including some of the later tribes (Benjamin, Zebulun, Issachar, Reuben, Dan, Asher, Naphtali, and Ephraim) along with others (Machir, Gilead). The account of Joshua's covenant ceremony in Josh. 24 is often thought to preserve a memory of the establishment of this institution. It is impossible, however, to trace its history in the premonarchic period with any confidence. The various episodes of the book of Judges have been set in an "all Israel" framework by their editors, as if the ancestors of all the later Israelites were involved in every event, but a careful reading of the stories shows that they were originally local in character. A plausible historical reconstruction holds that some kind of intertribal organization called "Israel" existed in Canaan from at least the last half of the thirteenth century BCE until the time of the early monarchy, when the full twelve-tribe structure became the established ideal. Thereafter Israel's memories of its own premonarchic history were interpreted in light of this ideal structure, which was reinforced by the development of a genealogical scheme linking the twelve tribes together in a tradition of common origin.

The Nation of Israel: Sometime near the end of the first millennium BCE, Israel became a nation. The political ties that had previously bound the tribes together were routinized, and the group as a whole came to recognize the authority of a king. The concept of the people Israel, however, remained as viable as ever during the monarchy and, indeed, provided the starting point for a new understanding of Israel after the fall of the state.

Saul's Kingdom: Saul was Israel's first king, and it was under his rule that the old tribal alliance became a nation (late eleventh century BCE). Saul came from a prominent family in Gibeah of Benjamin (1 Sam. 9:1–2), and after demonstrating his military leadership by a victory over the Ammonites (1 Sam. 11), he was able to command the allegiance of a fairly extensive region in the central hills and Transjordan.

The United Monarchy: Before David became king of Israel, he was king of his native Judah (2 Sam. 2:4). His former alliance to the house of Saul, however, gave him a claim to Saul's throne, and eventually he united the two kingdoms under his rule (late eleventh century BCE; 2 Sam. 5:1–3). It was the personal achievement of David, therefore, that joined Judah with Israel, creating the basis for the biblical view of a greater Israel. According to this view, which the biblical writers retrojected to the time of the conquest, Israel extended "from Dan to Beer-sheba," i.e., from the southern wash of Mount Hermon in the north to the northern Negev in the south.

The Divided Monarchy: In fact, however, the historical Israel attained to the boundaries of the ideal Israel only for a brief period. The union of Israel and Judah did not survive the death of David's son Solomon (ca. 922 BCE). The northern tribes refused to acknowledge the sovereignty of the king in Jerusalem, and Judah was left as a separate state. Nor were the two kingdoms together as extensive as the united kingdom that preceded them. For only two short periods, during the reigns of Omri and Ahab in the first half of the ninth century BCE and Jeroboam II a century later, did Israel expand to its Davidic-Solomonic borders to the north and east.

This history accounts for the ambivalence of the term "Israel" as a political designation in the historical books of the Bible. In the stories of the reigns of David and Solomon, when Israel and Judah were united under a single king, "Israel" is often used to refer to the larger nation (2 Sam. 8:15; 1 Kings 4:1). In the same materials, however, it can be used to designate the northern tribes as distinct from Judah (2 Sam. 19:41). In the account of the divided monarchy in 1 and 2 Kings "Israel" is ordinarily the northern kingdom as distinct from "Judah," the southern kingdom. Nevertheless, the ideal of a greater Israel persists in the literature after the account of the secession of the northern tribes. In 1 Kings 12:17 is a reference to "the people of Israel who dwelt in the cities of Judah." Even before the fall of Samaria (722/1 BCE), therefore, "Israel" is sometimes used in reference to Judah (Isa. 1:3; 8:18), and after the destruction of the northern kingdom this usage becomes common (Ezek. 2:3).

The Idea of Israel: "Israel" is not only an ethnic and political designation in the Bible; it is also a central theological term. The idea of Israel as the chosen people of God pervaded the religious thought, not only of the ancient Israelite community, but of early Judaism and Christianity as well. Two major phases in the development of this idea are discernible.

First, there was the concept of Israel as the people chosen to live in the promised land. Fundamental to this concept was the notion that the land inhabited by the Israelite nation belonged to God. This concept receives its primary articulation in the biblical narrative in Genesis–Joshua. There, God summons Abram to Canaan, promising that his descendants will take possession of the land and become a great nation. Twelve tribes descend from Abram's grandson Jacob (whose name was also Israel), and these "children of Israel" become enslaved in Egypt. God rescues them, guides them through the desert, and brings them into Canaan. They conquer the land, eliminating its previous inhabitants, and settle in it, growing eventually into the great nation promised to Abram. This concept of Israel seems to have been a basic component of the theology of the preexilic community. Its most conspicuous feature is the centrality of the land.

Second, there was the concept of Israel as the people chosen to receive the Torah. This concept is expressed in the same biblical narrative, but in this case the climax of the story is the gift of the Torah at Sinai rather than the conquest of the land. The primary narrative is Genesis–Numbers, especially the Priestly materials ("P") within that narrative: God (Elohim) is the universal creator, and God wills that human creatures should be blessed (Gen. 1:28). Because of their inclination toward error, however, it seems impossible for human beings to live safely in the divinely created world. They tend to pervert the blessing into a curse. The divine solution is the election of one people through whom the other "families of the earth" can receive their blessing (cf. Gen. 12:3). God gives this people a set of instructions by which it will be possible for them to live safely in the world and receive the divine blessing as intended. This concept of Israel probably reflects the theology of the exilic (mid-sixth century BCE) and postexilic (late sixth century and later) communities. Emphasis on the land, the chief characteristic of the preexilic concept (pre–587/6 BCE), has been replaced by emphasis on the Torah.

In later Judaism the biblical concept of Israel as a people chosen by God to receive the Torah was combined with the apocalyptic expectation of the advent of the universal rule of God. The belief was that only when Israel was truly living according to the precepts of the Torah could the kingdom of God arrive. Apocalyptic groups dissented from the authority of those in power in Jerusalem, whom they regarded as corrupt and illegitimate. They believed themselves to be the true Israel and structured their lives accordingly in the convic-

tion that by doing so they would make possible the final realization of the divine plan. One such group was the community at Qumran that kept the Dead Sea Scrolls. They understood themselves as the "precious cornerstone" of Isa. 28:16, laid by God as "a sure foundation" (1QS 8.7–8). Their community organization into twelve tribes led by twelve tribal chiefs (1QSa 1.27–2.1), including both laity and priests, shows that they regarded themselves as the true Israel.

Likewise the early church, which also emerged from apocalyptic Judaism, understood itself as the legitimate heir to the ancient promises. Paul argued that the Jews who did not accept Christ were in danger of forfeiting these promises, which had come to Abraham through faith, not the law (Rom. 4:13). According to Paul, "those who believe (in Christ) are the (true) descendants of Abraham" (Gal. 3:7). It follows that the early Christian community, like the Qumran community, regarded itself as the true Israel, i.e., "the Israel of God" (6:16). Other NT writers refer to the church as the "twelve tribes in the Dispersion" (James 1:1; cf. 1 Pet. 1:1). Appropriating language applicable to ancient Israel, the author of 1 Peter addresses his Gentile Christian audience as "a chosen race, a royal priesthood, a holy nation, God's own people" (2:9). *See also* Hebrews.

Bibliography

Danell, G. A. *Studies in the Name of Israel in the Old Testament.* Appelbergs boktryckeri, 1946.

De Vaux, Roland. *The Early History of Israel.* Westminster, 1978.

Sandmel, Samuel. *The Several Israels.* Ktav, 1971.

P.K.M.

Israel, kingdom of. *See* Samaria, district of.

Israelites (iz´ray-uh-lits), descendants of Jacob. Before the Davidic empire split into two separate kingdoms in the tenth century BCE, the term "Israelites" signified those who traced their ancestry to Jacob (Israel), the son of Isaac and Rebekah, grandson of Abraham and Sarah. After that event, it properly connoted only those Hebrews who traced their ancestry to the ten tribes that constituted the northern kingdom, Israel, as opposed to the tribes inhabiting the southern kingdom, Judah. The Israelite (i.e., the northern) kingdom had its capital at Shechem, then at Tirzah, and finally at Samaria. The latter was destroyed by the Assyrians in 722/1 BCE, and Israelites were deported, only to become assimilated into the alien culture. After the demise of the northern kingdom, the term "Israelite" appears to have again been taken up in its original sense. In postexilic Judaism, the term "Israelites" was virtually synonymous with "Hebrews" or "Jews."

In the NT, Paul claims that "not all Israelites truly belong to Israel" (Rom. 9:6), implying that, for him, the term "Israelites" refers to physical lineage only: "Israelites" are people descended from Jacob, but belonging to "Israel" requires faith in God (and perhaps acceptance of Jesus as the Messiah). The Gospel of John seems to make a subtle distinction between "Israelites" and "Jews"; the term "Jews" is typically used for people who are regarded negatively (5:18–47; 8:31–59; but cf. 4:9), but "Israelites" is applied to those who are viewed positively (1:47).   J.L.C./M.A.P.

Issachar (is'uh-kahr'; Heb., "hire").

1 The ninth son of Jacob, his fifth by Leah (Gen. 30:14–18), and the eponymous ancestor of one of the twelve tribes of Israel. Issachar and his four sons immigrated to Egypt with Jacob's family (Gen. 46:13; Exod. 1:3; Num. 26:23–24; 1 Chron. 7:1). Jacob's blessing of Issachar seems to imply that the tribe would hire itself out to bear the burdens of others (Gen. 49:14–15).

2 The tribe of Issachar, ostensibly descended from 1. They were allotted the fertile territory between the eastern Jezreel Valley and the Jordan Valley (Josh. 19:17–23), i.e., the region known today as the Heights of Issachar. Its allotment extended from Mount Tabor on the north to the edge of the hill country of Samaria on the south and included such towns as Jezreel (the winter palace of Ahab and Jezebel), Kesullot (modern Iksal, in the Jezreel Valley below Nazareth), Shunem (modern Solem; the home of the elderly couple who were hospitable to the prophet Elisha, 2 Kings 4), and En-gannim (evidently the Beth-haggan of 2 Kings 9:27 and the Gina of the Amarna letters; modern Jenin). Issachar was an important factor in the battle of Deborah and Barak (Judg. 5:15). In fact, the territory of Issachar was the scene of a number of battles in ancient times, including those of Gideon (Judg. 7) and Saul (1 Sam. 28). *See also* tribes.

3 The son of Obed-edom, a Korahite gatekeeper during the reign of David (1 Chron. 26:5).   D.A.D.

Isshiah (i-shi'uh).

1 A son of Izahiah and a descendant of Uzzi, from the tribe of Issachar (1 Chron. 7:3).

2 One of the "mighty warriors" who came to David at Ziklag and helped him in battle (1 Chron. 12:6).

3 A Levite who was one of the leading members of the descendants of Rehabiah, possibly descended from Moses (1 Chron. 24:21; see 23:15–17).

4 A son of Uzziel from the tribe of Levi (1 Chron. 24:25).

5 A postexilic Israelite who divorced his foreign wife in response to Ezra's proclamation (Ezra 10:31).

Italy (it'uh-lee), the boot-shaped peninsula extending about 750 miles from the Alps into the western part of the Mediterranean Sea. The name, according to ancient Greek writers, derives from a King Italos, who ruled the southern part in the late second millennium BCE. By the first century CE, it had come to designate the entire peninsula. Settled in remote antiquity by various tribes, Italy was in contact with Mycenaean traders in the second millennium BCE. By the middle of the first millennium, the north was organized into Etruscan city-states, while the south was so heavily colonized by Greeks that it eventually became known to the Romans as Magna Graecia ("Great Greece"). Through the three Punic Wars (264–146 BCE), Rome mastered the entire peninsula and began expanding throughout the Mediterranean.

The earliest account of Jews in Italy is 1 Macc. 8, which recounts the accomplishments of the Romans and a treaty with Rome made by Judas Maccabeus ca. 160 BCE. His brother Jonathan renewed the treaty some years later (1 Macc. 12:1–4), and Simon sent a third delegation in 139 BCE after Jonathan's death (14:16–19, 24). After 63 BCE, Judea was under either direct or indirect control of Rome.

By NT times, there were Jews living in Rome and elsewhere in Italy. Among those banished by a decree of Claudius (ca. 49 CE) were Aquila and Priscilla (Acts 18:2). On his way to Rome, Paul sailed up the west coast from Rhegium to Puteoli, where he encountered fellow Christians, and others came out from Rome to welcome him along the Appian Way in Italy (27:1; 28:13–16).

In Acts 10:1, Cornelius is identified as a centurion of the "Italian Cohort," stationed in Caesarea. In Heb. 13:24, the author tells readers that "those from Italy send greetings," implying that some Italian Christians are with the author, and possibly implying that the letter is being sent to Italy (if the Italian Christians are presumed to be greeting their compatriots). *See also* Aquila; Claudius; Cornelius; Maccabees; Paul; Prisca; Priscilla; Puteoli; Rhegium; Roman Empire; Rome.   C.H.M.

Ithai (ith'i; abbreviation of Heb., "God is with me" or "God exists"), the son of the Benjaminite Ribai and one of David's warriors who belonged to the fighting force known as "the Thirty" (1 Chron. 11:31). His name is given as Ittai in 2 Sam. 23:29. *See also* Ittai.

Ithamar (ith'uh-mahr), the fourth and youngest son of Aaron and Elisheba (Exod. 6:23). The two elder sons of Aaron died when presumptuously offering incense before the Lord, and the priestly succession thus devolved upon Eleazar and Ithamar (Lev. 10:1–7). Kohathites who carried the ark were subservient to Eleazar; Gershonites and Merarites who performed more menial duties were subservient to Ithamar (Num. 4:1–33). The line of Eleazar is traced through Zadok, the line of Ithamar through Abiathar of Shiloh. Ezekiel recognized only the succession through Zadok, but the Chronicler recognized the validity of both lines. *See also* Aaron; Zadok.   J.G.G.

Ithmah (ith'muh), a Moabite mercenary in David's employ (1 Chron. 11:46), one of the sixteen warriors added by the Chronicler to a list of those who constituted David's elite fighting force known as "the Thirty" (cf. 2 Sam. 23:24–38).

Ithnan (ith′nan), a city in the list of Canaanite cities assigned to Judah whose site in the south (Josh. 15:23) is as yet unidentified.

Ithra (ith′ruh), the father of Joab's cousin Amasa who served as chief of staff for Absalom in his rebellion against his father, David. Ithra is called an Israelite in 2 Sam. 17:25 (see NRSV note), but an Ishmaelite in 1 Chron. 2:17, where the NRSV translates his name as "Jether." *See also* Jether.

Ithran (ith′ran).
1 The son of Dishon and descendant of Seir the Horite (Gen. 36:26; 1 Chron. 1:41).
2 The son of Zophah; a descendant of Asher (1 Chron. 7:37).

Ithream (ith′ree-uhm; Heb., "the relative is abundance"), the sixth son of David, born to his wife Eglah at Hebron (2 Sam. 3:5; 1 Chron. 3:3).

Ithrite (ith′rit), a designation applied to Ira and Gareb, two soldiers in David's elite group known as "the Thirty" (2 Sam. 23:38; 1 Chron. 11:40). The word occurs as the name of a family listed in a genealogy and located in the town of Kiriath-jearim (1 Chron. 2:53). However, the name originally may have signified that David's two heroes were from the town of Jattir in the hill country of Judah (Josh. 15:48; 21:14).

Ittai (it′i; Heb., perhaps "with God").
1 The Gittite who swore an oath of loyalty to David during Absalom's revolt (2 Sam. 15:19–23). He was a commander of one-third of David's army, thus ranking with Joab and his brother Abishai (18:2–12). The epithet "the Gittite" indicates that he was from the Philistine city of Gath. *See also* Philistines.
2 The son of Ribai of Gibeah in the territory of the tribe of Benjamin; he was one of David's soldiers who belonged to "the Thirty" (2 Sam. 23:29; 1 Chron. 11:31).

Ituraea (it′yoor-ee′uh), an area northeast of the Sea of Galilee. In Luke 3:1, it is identified, together with Trachonitis, as belonging to the territory ruled by Philip, son of Herod the Great and brother of Herod Antipas. Ituraea was the region occupied by the tribe descended from Jetur, son of Ishmael (Gen. 25:13–16; 1 Chron. 1:31). In 1 Chron. 5:9–10 that tribe is described as the enemy of Reuben, Gad, and Manasseh, as seeking to penetrate Bashan and north Transjordan.

D.B.

ivory, a costly material in ancient times, derived from the tusks of elephants (or sometimes hippopotami) and used for jewelry and various other luxury items. The Hebrew name, *shen,* means "tooth." Ivory is mentioned a number of times in the Bible. Solomon's fleet of ships, on its three-year voyages, brought back ivory along with gold, apes, peacocks, and other exotic items (1 Kings 10:22; 2 Chron. 9:21). Solomon had his "great throne" inlaid with ivory (1 Kings 10:18). "Palaces adorned with ivory" are mentioned in Ps. 45:8; and in Song of Sol. 5:14 the exquisite body of the lover is compared to polished ivory. Amos prophesies against the "palaces of ivory" of the northern kingdom (3:15); and he scornfully refers to the "beds of ivory" (i.e., beds inlaid with ivory) upon which the aristocratic women of Samaria lie (6:4). In the book of Revelation, "articles of ivory" are listed among the precious cargo of Babylon that no one will buy when judgment falls (18:12).

The ivory used in the land of Canaan may have come from elephants of Syria, the so-called Asiatic elephant, which was well known in the upper Euphrates area until it became extinct in the first millennium BCE. At Ugarit ivories were discovered in the royal palace, including both figurines and ivory plaques carved in relief. At Megiddo similar ivories were found in the city's palace. In addition, 380 items of ivory were found in a storeroom adjacent to the palace. One of the most famous pieces is an ivory knife engraved with a scene

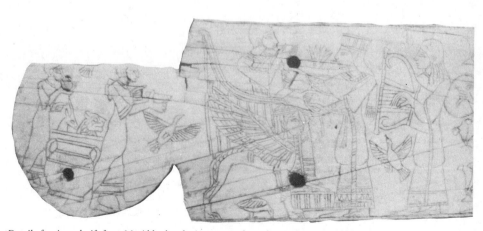

Detail of an ivory knife from Megiddo that depicts a scene from the royal court, twelfth century BCE.

from the royal court, portraying the king seated on his throne, which is supported by cherubim. He is drinking from a cup while one girl (perhaps a princess) presents him with a lotus flower and another girl serenades him with a harp. A procession is approaching the throne, headed by a soldier followed by two naked male captives and a horse-drawn chariot. From behind the throne two cupbearers are bringing refreshments to the king. Such ivories aid in reconstructing everyday life in ancient Canaanite palaces.

During the Iron Age (1200–587/6 BCE) ivory continued to enjoy popularity as a material for luxury items. The Assyrian kings often list ivory alongside the precious metals and stones received as tribute. Sennacherib (ca. 705–681 BCE) mentions tribute that included beds of ivory, chairs of ivory, and tusks. Collections of ivories from this period have been found in Egypt, Samaria, Syria, and Mesopotamia. The Samaritan ivories are carved in high relief and exhibit a decorative repertoire taken from Egyptian art. They were probably carved by Phoenician or Syrian artisans. On the back they are inscribed with Hebrew letters, presumably to facilitate their mounting on furniture.   D.A.D.

Izhar (iz′hahr; Heb., "fresh [olive] oil").

1 The son of Kohath and grandson of Levi (Exod. 6:18). He became the ancestral head of the Izharites, one of the major subdivisions of the Kohathite line of Levites (Num. 3:27). He was the father of Korah, the leader of the wilderness rebellion against Moses and Aaron (16:1).

2 The son of Ashur and Helah; a descendant of Judah (1 Chron. 4:7).

Opposite: Judas's kiss of betrayal (Matt. 26:49); fresco at the fourteenth-century St. Clement Church, Ohrid, in the Macedonia region of former Yugoslavia.

J

J, the siglum for the Yahwist (from the German form *Jahvist*), one of the sources of the material in the Pentateuch. *See also* Pentateuch, sources of the; Yahwist.

Jaazaniah (jay-az´uh-ni´uh; Heb., "the LORD hears").

1 The son of Maacath; he remained with Gedaliah, the governor of Judah, after the destruction of Jerusalem by the Babylonians (2 Kings 25:23; Jer. 40:8).

2 The son of Jeremiah (not the prophet) who was head of the Rechabites during the time of King Jehoiakim. The prophet Jeremiah tested his religious principles and declared the Rechabites to be a model of faithfulness and obedience (35:3).

3 The son of Shaphan; he appears in Ezekiel's vision of elders committing apostasy in the temple (8:11). Apparently Jaazaniah was committing idolatrous acts in the dark, in his "room of images (idols)," maintaining, "The LORD does not see us, the LORD has forsaken the land."

4 The son of Azzur; one of the twenty-five evil leaders in another of Ezekiel's visions (11:1).

Jabal (jay´buhl), the first son of Lamech and Adah, born in the seventh generation after Adam. According to the tradition preserved in Gen. 4:20, Jabal is credited with being the "ancestor of those who live in tents and have livestock." With his brothers, Jubal and Tubal-cain, he was thus considered an originator of ancient social patterns, in his case, nomadism.

Jabbok (jab´uhk), modern Nahr es-Zerqa (Arabic, "the blue river"), one of the four major eastern tributaries of the Jordan. The Jabbok rises in Amman, flows northeast to modern Zerqa, and then west until it joins the Jordan twenty-five miles north of the Dead Sea. In Gen. 32:22–32, Jacob fights with his divine adversary at Penuel on the Jabbok; there is wordplay here on the names: Jacob (Heb. *ya'aqob*) wrestled at the Jabbok (*yabboq*). The Jabbok was a natural boundary, forming a border for the territories of Sihon (Num. 21:24; Josh. 12:2; Judg. 11:13, 22), of the Ammonites (Num. 21:24; Deut. 2:37; 3:16; Josh. 12:2), and of Reuben and Gad (Deut. 3:16). It was a thoroughfare from the Jordan Valley to the Transjordanian plateau; in Judg. 8:4–9, Gideon pursues the Midianites up the Jabbok, passing Succoth and Penuel. Other sites on the Jabbok and its tributaries are Gerasa (modern Jerash), Adam, and Tulul edh-Dhahab. M.D.C.

Jabesh (jay´bish; Heb., "dried").

1 The father of King Shallum of Israel (2 Kings 15:10, 13–14). The name may, however, represent a place rather than a person, meaning that Shallum's family lived at Jabesh.

2 The town otherwise known as Jabesh-gilead. *See also* Jabesh-gilead.

Jabesh-gilead (jay´bish-gil´ee-uhd), a town east of the Jordan River, sometimes called simply Jabesh (cf. 1 Sam. 11:1). The name is evidently related to that of the Wadi Yabis, rising at Mihna north of Ajlun in the Gilead highlands. Jabesh-gilead first appears in Israelite history in the story of how all the men and married women were killed, because no one from the town had come to the assembly at Mizpah; four hundred young virgins were spared and given to the men of Benjamin (Judg. 21:8–15). Later, when Nahash the Ammonite threatened to gouge out the right eye of every man in Jabesh-gilead, Saul, who had only recently been anointed king, came to their rescue and utterly routed the Ammonites. This victory is said to have convinced even his detractors that he was fit to rule Israel (1 Sam. 11). The people of Jabesh-gilead remained profoundly grateful and when, some years later, Saul and his sons died fighting against the Philistines on Mount Gilboa, the men of Jabesh-gilead went to rescue their bodies from the walls of Beth-shan, where the victorious Philistines had triumphantly hung them. The bodies were then ceremonially burned and the bones buried under a tamarisk tree (1 Sam. 31:8–13). As soon as King David heard of this, he sent messengers praising the men of Jabesh for what they had done for his erstwhile enemy (2 Sam. 2:4–7).

Scholars usually identify ancient Jabesh-gilead with the modern joint site of Tell el-Meqbereh (apparently the residential area) and Tell Abu Kharaz (a powerful fortress overlooking it). This places the city on the north bank of the *wadi* where it enters the Jordan Valley, about five miles south of Pella. Others, however, place it at Tell el-Maqlub somewhat farther up the valley on the basis of Eusebius's statement that in the early fourth century CE Jabesh-gilead was still a great city "at the sixth milestone from the city of Pella" on the road to Gerasa. *See also* Abner; Ammonites; Benjamin; David; Gerasa, Gerasenes; Gilboa; Mizpah, Mizpeh; Nahash; Pella; Philistines; Saul. D.B.

Jabin (jay´bin).

1 The Canaanite king of Hazor (ca. 1100 BCE), who led a coalition of Canaanite petty princes against the Israelites. He was defeated at the waters of Merom and apparently executed (Josh. 11:10).

2 The "king of Canaan who reigned in Hazor" (Judg. 4:2) whose army commander Sisera was defeated by the Hebrew leaders Deborah and Barak near the Wadi Kishon (cf. Ps. 83:9). Scholars debate whether this Jabin was in fact a historical king of Hazor ruling a century later than the Jabin mentioned in **1**, or whether that king's name became attached to the Sisera tradition in some way (since Jabin does not actually figure in any of the conflicts between Sisera and Deborah and Barak).

Jabneel (jab´nee-uhl; Heb., "God is builder").

1 A city in northwest Judah (Josh. 15:11). Throughout much of biblical history, control over Jabneel fluctuated between Judah and Philistia.

Jabneel is called Jabneh in 2 Chron. 26:6 and Jamnia in 1 Macc. 4:15; 5:58; 2 Macc. 12:8–9. According to some (questionable) traditions, a Jewish council met in Jamnia ca. 90 CE to establish a canon of Hebrew scriptures.

2 A northern border city of the tribal allotment of Naphtali, west of the south end of the Sea of Galilee (Josh. 19:33).   S.B.R.

Jachin (jay´kin; Heb., "he establishes").

1 The son of Simeon (Gen. 46:10; Exod. 6:15) and ancestor of the "Jachinite family" (Num. 26:12).

2 The leader of the twenty-first division of priests at the time of David (1 Chron. 24:17; cf. 9:10; Neh. 11:10).

3 The name of a pillar at the entrance of the temple. *See also* Jachin and Boaz.

Jachin (jay´kin) **and Boaz** (boh´az), the names of the pillars standing to the right and left of the entrance to the temple in Jerusalem (1 Kings 7:21; 2 Chron. 3:15–17). The meaning of the name "Jachin" is "he establishes," but that of Boaz, which is the same as that of David's great-grandfather (Ruth 4:17, 21–22), is unknown. These pillars were cast of bronze. According to 1 Kings 7:15 and Jer. 52:21 each pillar stood 18 cubits high (26.5 feet), had a circumference of 12 cubits (17.5 feet), and was hollow, with a thickness of 4 fingers (3 inches). Each was surmounted by a bowl-shaped capital 5 cubits high (7.5 feet), ornamented with checker work, wreathed with chain work, and bedecked with lily leaves 4 cubits high (roughly 6 feet). Varying dimensions for the height of the pillars and of the capitals are provided in 2 Chron. 3:15 and 2 Kings 25:17. The location of the pillars is not entirely clear in 1 Kings 7:21, but according to 2 Chron. 3:15 they were freestanding at the temple's entrance. Similar items flanking temple entrances have been noted at Khorsabad. Such pillars are also graphically depicted on coins from Cyprus, Sardis, Pergamum, and Sidon as well as on a clay model of a temple from Idalion (Cyprus) and on a relief from Quyunjiq. Herodotus describes similar pillars as flanking the entrance to the sanctuary of Herakles at Tyre. The presence of such pillars may also be indicated by pillar bases at the entrances of the temples at Canaanite Hazor and Tell Tainat. The function these pillars may have served is uncertain. One suggestion is that they may have been fire altars: the bowl-shaped capitals could have served as cressets in which the fat of sacrificial animals was burned. At the time of the destruction of Jerusalem in 587/6 BCE, the pillars were dismantled, and, along with other metal objects from the temple, removed as booty to Babylon (2 Kings 25:13).   S.G.

jackal (*Canis aureus;* Heb. *tan*), a member of the dog family similar in appearance to the wolf, though considerably smaller in size, with a relatively short tail and small ears. A nocturnal carrion eater, the jackal also devours fruit and crops and kills chickens and other small animals. Its distribution range includes southeast Europe, southern Asia, and northern Africa, and it is still fairly common in Israel and Jordan today. Its preference for a dry habitat is alluded to in Isa. 35:7; 43:20. Numerous passages in the Bible refer to the jackal prowling around settlements, and in Mic. 1:8 its characteristic wailing howl is mentioned. According to Neh. 2:13 a well named after the jackal existed outside Jerusalem. Its lair could symbolize a destroyed or deserted settlement (Jer. 9:11).   I.U.K.

Jacob (jay´kuhb; Heb., "heel grabber" [Gen. 25:26] or "supplanter" [27:36]).

1 A prominent figure in the book of Genesis, remembered among the ancestors of Israel; indeed, he came to be called "Israel" (32:28; 35:10), so in a certain sense "Israelites" are, by definition, descendants of Jacob. He is the son of Isaac and Rebekah, the brother of Esau, and the father of twelve sons who become the eponymous ancestors of the "twelve tribes of Israel."

In the biblical account, Jacob is the second-born son, coming out of the womb moments after his twin brother, Esau, and clinging to the latter's heel (Gen. 25:19–26). Esau grows up to be a hunter and his father's favorite son, while Jacob is a quiet man, living in tents, and especially beloved by his mother (25:27). Jacob persuades Esau to sell him his birthright for a pot of stew (25:29–34), and then Jacob conspires with his mother to trick Isaac into giving his deathbed blessing to him rather than to Esau (27:1–40). Fearing his brother will seek vengeance, Jacob flees to stay with Rebekah's brother Laban in Haran

In a dream Jacob sees angels ascending and descending a ladder to heaven (Gen. 28:12); from the twelfth-century Lambeth Bible. (The binding of Isaac appears on the right.)

(27:41–28:5). On the way there, he has a dream of angels at Beer-sheba and names that place Bethel (28:10–22). Jacob and Laban end up having a relationship marked by mutual trickery. Jacob works for Laban seven years in order to marry

CHIASTIC ARRANGEMENT
OF JACOB TRADITIONS

Genealogical framework (Gen. 25:1–11)

A. Death of Abraham; burial by two sons (Isaac, Ishmael); genealogy and death of Ishmael; birth and youth of Esau and Jacob (25:12–34)

  B. Regional strife (in southern Israel): Isaac vs. the Philistines; honorable covenant (26:1–35)

    C. Beginnings of fraternal strife in Cisjordan (Jacob vs. Esau: settler-farmer vs. hunter); Isaac blesses Jacob, not Esau (27:1–46)

      D. Departure of Jacob alone to northeast with theophany en route at Bethel (28:1–22)

        E. Arrival alone in the northeast Haran in Upper Mesopotamia); marriage to Leah and Rachel; acquisition and naming of sons by Leah; commencement of strife with Laban (29:1–35)

          F. Acquisition and naming of sons by wives' maids and of first son (Joseph) by Rachel (30:1–24)

          F'. Preparation to leave the northeast; acquisition of herds (30:25–43)

        E'. Departure from the northeast with flocks, progeny, and two wives; conclusion of strife with Laban in a covenant in Gilead (31:1–32:2)

      D'. Return from the northeast with theophany en route at Penuel; change of name to Israel (32:3–32)

    C'. Conclusion of fraternal strife in Transjordan (Jacob vs. Esau: herder vs. herder); Jacob blesses Esau (33:1–17)

  B'. Regional strife (in northern Israel): Jacob's sons vs. Shechemites; deceitful covenant; putting away of foreign gods (33:18–35:5); theophany at Bethel; change of name to Israel (35:6–7, 9–15); combines parts of E and E'

A'. Birth of second son by Rachel (Benjamin); death of Rachel; genealogy of Israel; death of Isaac; burial by two sons (Esau, Jacob; 35:8, 16–29)

Genealogical framework (36:1–43)

his daughter Rachel, but is tricked into marrying her sister Leah instead; he must work another seven years as payment for Rachel. But Jacob tricks Laban with a scheme that allows him to receive the stronger and more numerous offspring from among their flocks (30:25–43). Jacob eventually flees Laban (31:1–42), then makes a covenant with him (31:43–32:2), and is subsequently reconciled with his brother, Esau (32:3–33:17). He wrestles with either God or an angel at the Jabbok River (32:22–32). In addition to his twelve sons, Jacob has a number of daughters, including Dinah, who is raped by Shechem the Hivite, leading her brothers to wreak a terrible revenge (34:1–31). Later, Jacob is tricked by his older sons into believing the favored boy Joseph has been killed, when in reality he was sold into slavery in Egypt by his brothers (37:12–36). Eventually, Jacob and all of his sons are reunited with Joseph in Egypt, where Joseph has become prominent and is able to provide them with refuge from a famine (46:1–47:12). Before Jacob dies, he blesses all of his sons, with predictions relevant for the tribes that would take their names (48:1–49:28). His body is embalmed by Egyptian physicians (50:1–3), and many years later his bones are returned to the land of Canaan to be buried at Shechem by the Israelites following the exodus (Josh. 24:32)

Jacob, like Abraham and Isaac, is the recipient of the divine promise of land and plentiful progeny (Gen. 28:13–15). Divine manifestations are made to Jacob (28:10–22; 32:3–22) despite the fact that he engages in deception (27:1–40). Throughout the Bible, Jacob is often named in the triad "Abraham, Isaac, and Jacob" as a shorthand reference for the ancestors of the Hebrew people. Likewise, the God of the Hebrew people is called "the God of Abraham, the God of Isaac, and the God of Jacob" (Exod. 3:6; cf. 3:15–16; 4:5; Matt. 22:32; Acts 3:13) and sometimes simply "the God of Jacob" (2 Sam. 23:1; Pss. 20:1; 24:6; Isa. 2:3). There is frequent mention of the covenant that God made with Abraham, Isaac, and Jacob (Exod. 2:24; cf. Lev. 26:42). The people of Israel can call themselves the "children of Jacob" (2 Kings 17:34) or "the house of Jacob" (Isa. 2:5–6). In the NT, Jesus describes eschatological salvation as eating with Abraham, Isaac, and Jacob in the kingdom of heaven (Matt. 8:11; cf. Luke 13:28). John's Gospel tells of Jesus meeting with a Samaritan woman at "Jacob's well" in Sychar (Shechem); the question arises as to whether Jesus is "greater than our ancestor Jacob" (4:12). Paul uses the story of Jacob and Esau as an illustration of divine election (Rom. 9:10–16). Jacob is also cited as a model of faith in Heb. 11:20–21.

The Historical Jacob: No mention is made of Jacob outside of the biblical narratives, so his historical existence cannot be confirmed. Some scholars regard him as a legendary figure. Those who believe there was a historical person to which the traditions bear witness note that the stories concerning Jacob feature sites in northern Israel (Bethel, Shechem) and in northern Transjordan

(Mahanaim, Penuel), suggesting that he was a northerner. Some authorities favor placing Jacob in the Middle Bronze Age (ca. 1950–1550 BCE) and see an association between Jacob and the Hyksos movement in Egypt (ca. 1720–1570 BCE). Because of the Aramean presence in northern Mesopotamia, other authorities are inclined to place the historical Jacob at the beginning of the early Iron Age (ca. 1200–900 BCE), when a sizable incursion of Arameans into northern Mesopotamia took place. Regardless of date, the diversity of style in the traditions about Jacob gives evidence that they have evolved over a long period of time.

Pattern of Arrangement of the Jacob Traditions: Literary analysis of the Jacob stories reveals that these traditions have been arranged with a degree of order and sophistication in a concentric, mirrorlike, or chiastic pattern (the first element corresponds to the last, the second element to the second from last, etc.).

Because the material in Gen. 35:6–7, 9–15 would be disruptive of the chiastic pattern, it is usually thought that it was inserted into the narrative at a later time. The Jacob tradition, in its chiastic arrangement, is typically attributed to the editor who combined the Yahwistic and Elohistic sources of the Pentateuch; Gen. 35:6–7, 9–15 are usually credited to the Priestly source. *See also* ancestor; Esau; Genesis, book of; Isaac; Israel; patriarchs; Pentateuch, sources of the.

Bibliography

Brueggemann, Walter. *Genesis.* John Knox, 1982.

Kaminsky, Joel. *Yet I Loved Jacob: Reclaiming the Biblical Concept of Election.* Abingdon, 2007. Pp. 43–57.

Gammie, John G. "Theological Interpretation by Way of Literary and Tradition Analysis: Gen. 25–36." In *Encounter with the Text.* Fortress, 1979. Pp. 117–34.

2 The father of Joseph, the husband of Mary (Matt. 1:15–16).   J.G.G./M.A.P.

Jacob, Blessing of, a traditional title for the series of poems in Gen. 49:1–27; it derives from the unit's postscript, 49:28b. Ostensibly the deathbed observations of Jacob (Israel) regarding his sons, the Blessing of Jacob actually offers evaluations of the Israelite tribes from a much later period (49:28a). The figure through whom the poet speaks, the patriarch Jacob, now at the point of death, is the eponymous ancestor of the federated tribes of Israel. Of the component poems, those concerning Judah (49:8–12) and Joseph (49:22–26) predominate and pertain to the kingdoms of Judah and Israel. The Blessing of Jacob, then, appears to have been composed sometime after the inauguration of the divided monarchy; Jacob's observations regarding his sons offer evaluation of the tribes with regard to their roles in the disintegration of the federation. Because Joseph alone is unequivocally blessed, the perspective of the poet is clearly sympathetic to the northern kingdom. *See also* poetry.   S.G.

Jacob's Well, the setting for Jesus's encounter with a Samaritan woman in John 4. Of considerable depth, its still waters are contrasted with the "living water" that Jesus can offer: "a spring of water gushing up to eternal life" (4:14; cf. 4:10). Although no such well is ever mentioned in the OT, its location is fixed in John's Gospel by references to the mountain revered by the Samaritans (4:20), i.e., Mount Gerizim, and by an explicit indication that the well was in Sychar (Shechem), near "the plot of ground that Jacob had given to his son Joseph" (4:5; cf. Gen. 33:18–20; 48:22; see NRSV note c). Early Christian tradition connected Jacob's Well to one a quarter mile southeast of ancient Shechem's edge, now sheltered in the old crypt beneath the Greek Orthodox church in modern Balatah. Measurements of its depth to the water table fluctuate between 105 and 75 feet. *See also* Gerizim, Mount; Samaritans; Shechem; Sychar.   E.F.C.

Jael (jay´uhl; Heb., "mountain goat"), a Kenite woman who killed the Canaanite general Sisera. Jael is called the wife of Heber, though her husband never appears in the biblical accounts, which provide both a prose (Judg. 4) and a poetic (Judg. 5) version of the story. The Kenites were apparently on good terms with the chief Canaanite king in the north, Jabin of Hazor (4:17). Thus, after the Canaanite general Sisera was routed by Israelite forces under Deborah and Barak, he sought refuge among the Kenites, believing he could trust Jael. She offered him refreshment and then, probably while he was resting, killed him with a tent peg. Deborah had earlier predicted that Sisera would be undone at the hand of a woman (4:9); this prediction is fulfilled in an unexpected manner when Sisera's killer turns out to be, not Deborah, but another woman, the Kenite Jael. In this way, Jael becomes an illustration of how unlikely figures may serve the Israelite cause. Her motivation in killing Sisera is never given. The story of Jael and Sisera prefigures the later tale of Judith and Holofernes (Jth. 13:2–8). *See also* Deborah.
                     C.L.M./M.A.P.

Jahath (jay´hath).

1 A Levite, the son of Gershom and father of Shimei (1 Chron. 6:43).

2 A Levite, the son of Libni (Ladan) and grandson of Gershom (1 Chron. 6:20); but elsewhere called Jehiel (23:7).

3 A Levite, the son of Shimei and grandson of Gershom (1 Chron. 23:10–11).

It is possible that the above names have become disordered through scribal errors and that **1–3** all represent the same person.

4 A Levite member of the Shelomoth family of the Izharite group (1 Chron. 24:22).

5 A Levite belonging to the Merari group who helped repair the temple during King Josiah's reforms (ca. 622 BCE; 2 Chron. 34:12).

6 A descendant of Judah who belonged to the Zorathite group (1 Chron. 4:2).   D.R.B.

Jahaz (jay′haz), a Moabite city that had been taken by the Amorite king Sihon and made a part of his kingdom. It was the site of the battle between the Amorites and the Israelites in which Sihon was killed and the Israelites took possession of a large part of the land east of the Jordan (Num. 21:23–26). The city was among those assigned to the tribe of Reuben and later given to the Merarite group of Levites (Josh. 13:18; 21:36; called Jahzah in 1 Chron. 6:78). Jahaz appears in the Mesha inscription on the Moabite Stone. The reference there indicates that it was fortified by Israel, but then captured by the Moabite king Mesha and two hundred men (ca. 850 BCE; see 2 Kings 3:4–5). Jahaz was still in Moabite hands at the time of Isaiah (ca. 742–701 BCE; Isa. 15:4; Jer. 48:34). From the place-names that occur with Jahaz, one can infer that it was located in the vicinity of Heshbon northeast of the Dead Sea. It has sometimes been identified as modern Khirbet el-Medeiyina, about eleven miles northeast of Heshbon, although the site is not certain. *See also* Amorites; Moab; Moabite Stone.   D.R.B.

Jahaziel (juh-hay′zee-uhl; Heb., "El [God] sees").
1 One of Saul's relatives who joined David's warriors at Ziklag (1 Chron. 12:4).
2 A priest who was appointed by King David as a musician to celebrate the arrival of the ark of the covenant at the tabernacle in Jerusalem (1 Chron. 16:6).
3 A Levite belonging to the Kohath priestly line; he was the third son of Hebron (1 Chron. 23:19).
4 A Levite who was a descendant of Asaph. He prophesied to King Jehoshaphat (ca. 873–849 BCE) that he would not need to fight the invading allied armies of Edom, Moab, and Ammon, because God would fight for him. The armies were destroyed in the Valley of Beracah after they began fighting with each other (2 Chron. 20:1–30). *See also* Beracah.
5 The father of an unnamed member of the Shecaniah family group, who returned with Ezra from the Babylonian exile (Ezra 8:5).   D.R.B.

Jair (jay′uhr).
1 A son of the tribe of Manasseh who conquered the region of Argob in Gilead (Num. 32:41; Deut. 3:14). He captured sixty cities, which he called Havvoth-jair (Josh. 13:30; 1 Kings 4:13). In 1 Chron. 2:22, Segub of Judah is the father of Jair, and his mother is from Manasseh.
2 One of the judges, also of Gilead, whose thirty sons rode thirty donkeys and possessed thirty cities. Those cities were called Havvoth-jair. This tradition is sometimes thought to be a variant on that regarding the Jair in **1.** In any case, the judge named Jair is said to have been buried in Kamon (Judg. 10:5).
3 The father of Mordecai, a descendant of King Saul (Esther 2:5; see 1 Sam. 9:1).
4 An otherwise unknown person whose descendant Ira was one of David's priests (2 Sam. 20:26).

5 The father of Elhanan (2 Sam. 21:19; 1 Chron. 20:5).   J.U./M.A.P.

Jairus (jay-i′ruhs), the synagogue leader who fell before the feet of Jesus and begged him to heal his only daughter who was at the point of death. When it was learned that the daughter had already died, Jairus was advised not to trouble Jesus further. Jesus encouraged Jairus with the words, "Do not fear, only believe." By raising the young girl, Jesus manifested his power to overcome death (Mark 5:21–43; Luke 8:40–56; the story is also told in Matt. 9:18–26, though the girl's father is not identified there by name or by profession). In all three of the Synoptic Gospels, this story is intercalated with an account of Jesus healing a woman with a hemorrhage who, in faith, touches his garment as he is en route to Jairus's house.

Jesus raising Jairus's daughter (Mark 5:21–43); from a fourth-century sarcophagus, Rome.

Jalam (jay′luhm), the son of Esau and Oholi-bamah the Hivite. He was the leader of an Edomite family group (Gen. 36:5, 18).

James (jaymz), the English equivalent of the Greek Jacobus, a common name in the first century.
1 James, the son of Zebedee (Matt. 4:21; 10:2; Mark 1:19; 3:17) and brother of John (Matt. 17:1; Mark 3:17; 5:37; Acts 12:2), with whom he is called by Jesus to be one of the twelve (Matt. 4:21; Mark 1:19–20; Luke 5:10–11). Jesus nicknamed James and John "Boanerges," meaning "sons of thunder" (Mark 3:17). The two are prominent in the various lists of the twelve (Matt. 10:2–4; Mark 3:16–19; Luke 6:14–16; Acts 1:13). With Peter, they were present when Jesus raised Jairus's daughter (Mark 5:37; Luke 8:51), at the transfiguration (Matt. 17:1; Mark 9:2; Luke 9:28), and in Gethsemane (Matt. 26:37; Mark 14:33). The brothers (or their mother) request special places beside Jesus at the time of the messianic kingdom (Matt. 20:20–23; Mark 10:35–40). Acts 12:2 reports James's martyrdom by decapitation at the command of Herod Agrippa I. *See also* apostle; Boanerges; disciple; John the apostle; twelve, the; Zebedee.

2 James, the son of Alphaeus. He is identified in the apostolic lists as one of the twelve (Matt. 10:3; Mark 3:18; Luke 6:15; Acts 1:13), but little else is known about him. He is sometimes identified with "James the younger" mentioned in Mark 15:40. If so, he had a brother named Joses, and his mother, Mary, was a witness to the crucifixion and the empty tomb (cf. Mark 16:1–8). *See also* Alphaeus; apostle; disciple; twelve, the.

3 James, the brother of Jesus. Jesus is reported to have had four brothers in addition to a number of sisters (1 Cor. 9:5; cf. Matt. 13:55; Mark 6:3; Acts 1:14; Gal. 1:19). Although they were not followers of Jesus during the time of his life on earth (Matt. 12:46–50; Mark 3:31–35; Luke 8:19–21; John 7:3–5), the brothers are reported as being with the twelve and others after Jesus's resurrection and ascension (Acts 1:14), and James is specifically identified as one to whom the risen Jesus appeared (1 Cor. 15:7). Eventually, James emerged as the leader of the Jerusalem church. Paul acknowledges James's role of leadership (Gal. 2:1–12), and Acts 15 reports his persuasive defense of the Gentile mission. Both the Jewish historian Josephus and the Christian Hegesippus (according to the fourth-century church historian Eusebius) report that James was put to death by the priestly authorities in Jerusalem a few years before the destruction of the temple in 70 CE. The Letter of James in the NT is attributed to him.

4 James, the father of Judas. His son was one of the twelve, distinct from Judas Iscariot (Luke 6:16).   P.L.S.

James, Letter of, the first of what are sometimes called the Catholic, or General, Letters in the NT. Addressed to the "twelve tribes in the Dispersion" (1:1), the letter is intended for the church at large. It is attributed to "James, a servant of God and of the Lord Jesus Christ," an ascription that is usually thought to refer to James, the brother of Jesus, who led the church in Jerusalem for some thirty years after Easter (cf. Acts 12:17; 15:19–29; 21:18; cf. 1 Cor. 15:7; Gal. 1:19; 2:6, 9). Many scholars, however, consider the letter to be pseudepigraphical.

Contents: The letter opens with a salutation identifying it as correspondence from James to the "twelve tribes in the Dispersion" (1:1). It then offers some quick evangelical counsel or advice on different subjects: trials that test one's faith (1:2–4); divine guidance (1:5–8); the value of poverty and the ephemeral character of riches (1:9–11); resisting temptation (1:12–16); God's generosity (1:17–18); anger (1:19–21); acting on God's word (1:22–25); controlling one's tongue (1:26); and the marks of pure religion (1:27). The letter then presents a series of short essays on various topics, some of which have already been mentioned. First, James discusses how attitudes and practices that show partiality to the rich violate the royal command to "love your neighbor as yourself" (2:1–13). Next, he maintains that faith must be revealed or demonstrated in action, for "faith without works is dead" (2:14–26). He issues a warning to

those who wish to be teachers (3:1), which leads to a homily on the power of speech and the need for all people to control what they say (3:2–12). He then reflects upon two types of wisdom—one that is of God and one that is of the world—and he calls his readers to repent of being double-minded with regard to these incompatible philosophies (3:14–4:10). The letter concludes with another series of evangelical counsels on various topics: speaking evil against one's neighbor (4:11–12); the arrogance of human planning (4:13–16); sins of omission (4:17); condemnation of the wealthy (5:1–6); patience and endurance (5:7–11); swearing oaths (5:12); prayer (5:13–18); and restoration of backslidden sinners (5:19–20).

OUTLINE OF CONTENTS

James

Authorship: The primary reason this letter has been regarded as pseudepigraphical is that scholars do not think it reads like a work produced by a Galilean peasant. It is written in elegant Greek, employing concepts and rhetoric derived from Hellenistic philosophy (e.g., the diatribe). In recent years, however, a growing number of scholars have concluded that the work can be ascribed to James the brother of Jesus, if it is allowed that he relied upon a scribe or amanuensis to put his thoughts into words. Other scholars continue to regard the letter as pseudepigraphical, in part because it makes no reference to the personal life of Jesus (odd for a work by Jesus's own brother), and in part because it doesn't display the concern for adherence to Torah (including dietary regulations) by Jewish Christians associated with James elsewhere in the NT (Gal. 2:11–14). Further, some scholars think that a letter actually written by

James the brother of Jesus would have achieved more widespread acceptance in the early church than this one did; the letter was sometimes unknown, its authorship was sometimes questioned (which James?), and its canonicity was sometimes challenged.

Historical Setting: The letter is addressed to the "twelve tribes in the Dispersion," which would typically refer to Jews living outside of the region associated with the historical boundaries of Israel.

In fact, however, it is intended for Christians (2:1). Thus, if the letter is authentic, it would have been sent by James from Jerusalem to Jewish Christians who lived outside of Judea, probably in the mid-50s, but certainly no later than 62, when, according to Josephus, James was murdered (*Antiquities* 20.199–201). If the letter is pseudepigraphical, then the "twelve tribes in the Dispersion" might refer metaphorically to all Christians, who are to be regarded as the new Israel, displaced from their

PARALLELS BETWEEN JAMES AND THE SERMON ON THE MOUNT

The Letter of James	Sermon on the Mount (Gospel of Matthew)
"Whenever you face trials of any kind, consider it nothing but joy." (1:2)	"When people revile you and persecute you and utter all kinds of evil against you . . . rejoice and be glad." (5:11–12)
". . . so that you may be mature (*teleioi*) and complete, lacking in nothing." (1:4)	"Be perfect (*teleioi*) . . . as your heavenly Father is perfect." (5:48)
"Ask God . . . and it will be given you." (1:5)	"Ask, and it will be given you." (7:7)
"Be doers of the word, and not merely hearers." (1:22)	"Everyone then who hears these words . . . and acts on them . . ." (7:24)
"Has not God chosen the poor in the world . . . to be heirs of the kingdom?" (2:5)	"Blessed are the poor in spirit, for theirs is the kingdom of heaven." (5:3)
"Whoever keeps the whole law but fails in one point has become accountable for all of it." (2:10)	"Whoever breaks one of the least of these commandments . . . will be called least in the kingdom of heaven." (5:19)
"Judgment will be without mercy to anyone who has shown no mercy." (2:13)	"Blessed are the merciful, for they will receive mercy." (5:7)
"What good is it . . . if you say you have faith, but do not have works? Can faith save you?" (2:14)	"Not everyone who says to me, 'Lord, Lord,' will enter the kingdom of heaven, but only the one who does the will of my Father." (7:21)
"Can a fig tree . . . yield olives, or a grapevine figs?" (3:12)	"Are grapes gathered from thorns, or figs from thistles?" (7:16)
"A harvest of righteousness is sown in peace for those who make peace." (3:18)	"Blessed are the peacemakers, for they will be called children of God." (5:9)
"Friendship with the world is enmity with God." (4:4)	"You cannot serve God and wealth." (6:24)
"Purify your hearts." (4:8)	"Blessed are the pure in heart." (5:8)
"Who, then, are you to judge your neighbor?" (4:12)	"Do not judge, so that you may not be judged." (7:1)
"Your riches have rotted, and your clothes are moth-eaten. Your gold and silver have rusted." (5:2–3)	"Do not store up for yourselves treasures on earth, where moth and rust consume and where thieves break in and steal." (6:19)
"Do not grumble against one another, so that you may not be judged." (5:9)	"Do not judge, so that you may not be judged." (7:1)
"Do not swear, either by heaven or by earth or by any other oath, but let your "Yes" be yes and your "No" be no." (5:12)	"Do not swear at all, either by heaven . . . or by the earth. . . . Let your word be 'Yes, Yes' or 'No, No.'" (5:34–37)

Other passages in James that parallel sayings of Jesus include 1:6 (cf. Matt. 21:21); 1:9 and 4:10 (cf. Matt. 23:12); 1:12 (cf. Matt. 10:22); 1:21 (cf. Mark 4:14); 4:9 (cf. Luke 6:21, 25); 4:17 (Luke 12:47); 5:1–6 (cf. Luke 6:24); 5:9 (cf. Matt. 24:33); 5:17 (cf. Luke 4:25).

From Mark Allan Powell, *Introducing the New Testament* (courtesy, Baker Academic)

home in heaven. In this case, it could have been written at almost any time in the latter part of the first century. Its primary purpose seems to be moral instruction, and in offering such teaching it draws heavily upon both Greek philosophy and the Jewish wisdom tradition. It also alludes to sayings of Jesus more prominently than any other NT letter (c.f., e.g., James 1:6; Matt. 7:7; James 1:22; Matt. 7:21; James 4:11; Matt. 7:1; James 5:12; Matt. 5:34–37), but, curiously, never attributes any of that material to Jesus.

Major Themes: The Letter of James presents trials and even temptations to sin as occasions for growth and, therefore, as causes for joy (1:2–4). It also draws upon the Jewish wisdom tradition to contrast the "wisdom from above" that leads to godliness (3:17) with conventional thinking that encourages friendship with the world (4:4). The letter also evinces pronounced concern for the poor, whom God has chosen to be rich in faith (2:5; cf. 1:9, 27; 2:2–9, 2:14–17; 5:4), and hostility toward the rich, who are destined for condemnation (5:1–5; cf. 1:10; 2:2–3, 6–7; 4:13–14). Most notably, however, James argues that "faith without works is dead" (2:17, 26) and does so in ways that appear to contradict remarks in Paul's letters (cf. James 2:22; Rom. 4:3; Gal. 3:5; James 2:24; Rom. 3:28; Gal. 2:16). Most scholars conclude that there is no substantive argument between James and Paul; rather, James is countering an understanding of Paul that the latter apostle would have also rejected (i.e., an understanding of "faith" as intellectual assent that does not transform one's life or actions; cf. Rom. 2:13; Gal. 5:6; 1 Cor. 13:2). *See also* faith; Catholic Letters/Epistles; James; poor, poverty; tongue; wealth; wisdom.

Bibliography

Adamson, James B. *James: The Man and His Message*. Eerdmans, 1989.

Chester Andrew, and Ralph P. Martin. *The Theology of James, Peter, and Jude*. Cambridge University Press, 1994.

Johnson, Luke Timothy. *The Letter of James*. Doubleday, 1995.

Laws, Sophie. *The Epistle of James*. Harper & Row, 1980.

Martin, Ralph P. *James*. Word, 1988.   M.A.P.

Jamin (jay′min; Heb., either "right-hand" or "south" [on the right facing east]).

1 A son of Simeon who went with Jacob to Egypt (Gen. 46:10; 1 Chron. 4:24); he became the ancestor of the Jaminites, who left Egypt with Moses (Exod. 6:15; Num. 26:12).

2 The son of Ram, a descendant of Jerahmeel from the tribe of Judah (1 Chron. 2:27).

3 A Levite who explained the law read by Ezra to the people, probably translating it from Hebrew into Aramaic (Neh. 8:7).

Jannes (jan′iz) **and Jambres** (jam′briz), according to Jewish tradition, the names of the Egyptian magicians who opposed Moses in Exod. 7:11–23. Their names are not given in the biblical narrative of the exodus, but they are referred to in 2 Tim. 3:8, which draws on the popular extrabiblical tradition. They appear often in later Jewish and Christian traditions. A pseudepigraphic work attributed to Jannes and Jambres (ca. first–third centuries CE) survives only in fragments, though it is also mentioned in Origen's commentary on the Gospel of Matthew.

Japheth (jay′fith).

1 One of the three sons of Noah (Gen. 5:32; 6:10; 7:13; 9:18, 23, 27; 1 Chron. 1:4), evidently either the youngest (he is normally listed third) or the second son (cf. Gen. 9:22, 24). According to the Table of Nations in Gen. 10, Japheth was the ancestor of a number of widespread ethnic groups known to ancient Israel, including: Gomer (the Cimmerians, who inhabited the Black Sea region, and later, Asia Minor; perhaps related to the Scythians); Magog (possibly the Scythians); Madai (the Medes of the Iranian Plateau); Javan (the Ionians, representing the Hellenic group); Tubal and Meshech (two peoples of Asia Minor); Tiras (often identified with the Etruscans, though this is uncertain); Ashkenaz (the Ashguza of Assyrian inscriptions, a Scythian country); Riphath (unknown); Togarmah (between Asia Minor and the Upper Euphrates); Elishah (Cyprus); Tarshish (identification disputed); Kittim (the Cretians, or a Hellenic people on Cyprus); and the Dodamin (possibly to be read "Rodanim," referring to the inhabitants of Rhodes).

2 A region north of Arabia mentioned in Jth. 2:25. Here Holofernes is said to have routed the Midianites.   D.A.D.

Japhia (juh-fi′uh).

1 A king of Lachish in southern Judea, allied against Gibeon (Josh. 10:3), and executed by Joshua at a Makkedah cave (10:22–26).

2 A son of David born in Jerusalem to an unnamed mother (2 Sam. 5:15; 1 Chron. 3:7; 14:6).

3 A town on the southern edge of the territory of Zebulun (Josh. 19:12), a short distance southwest of where Nazareth would have been in Jesus's day.

Jared (jair′id), antediluvian son of Mahalalel (Gen. 5:15–16) and father of Enoch (5:18–19); he lived a legendary 962 years (5:20). Listed as the fifth person following Adam in the preflood genealogy (1 Chron. 1:2), he is sixth from the beginning in the genealogy cited in Luke 3:37.

Jarmuth (jahr′muhth; Heb., "a height").

1 A city belonging to the tribe of Judah formerly controlled by the Amorites; Joshua killed its king and took the city (Josh. 10:3–23; 12:11; 15:35; Neh. 11:29). It is probably modern Khirbet Yarmuk, about eight miles from Beit Jibrin, south of Beth-shemesh.

2 A levitical city located in the tribal area of Issachar (Josh. 21:29). The archaeological remains from this site are predominantly Early Bronze Age (ca. 3000–2000 BCE).

Jashar (jay'shuhr; Heb., "upright, righteous"), **book of,** a source apparently containing heroic songs, cited twice in the Bible: in the account of Joshua's battle at Gibeon, when "the sun stood still" (Josh. 10:13), and again in David's lamentation for Saul and Jonathan (2 Sam. 1:18). A third possible citation from this source is 1 Kings 8:12–13, where the LXX adds, "is it not written in the book of songs." The Book of Jashar was apparently a collection of archaic poetry that, though well known in ancient Israel, has not survived.   D.L.C.

Jashobeam (juh-shoh'bee-uhm; Heb., "the people will return").

1 The son of Zabdiel the Hachmonite. He was the commander of David's elite group of warriors known as "the Thirty" (1 Chron. 11:11), a position apparently also held at one time by Abishai and Amasai (11:20; 12:18). Jashobeam is credited with killing three hundred men in one battle, and he later became the commander of a division of twenty-four thousand men under King David (27:2). Some scholars understand Josheb-basshebeth the Tahchemonite as a textual variant of the same name (2 Sam. 23:8), while others think the latter reference is to an entirely different member of David's group.

2 A Levite who belonged to the Korah group who joined David's warriors at Ziklag (1 Chron. 12:6); he may be the same as 1.   D.R.B.

Jason (jay'suhn), a Greek name often utilized by Hellenistic (i.e., Greek-speaking) Jews as a Greek alternative to such Hebrew names as Joshua or Jeshua.

1 A Jewish high priest, ca. 174–171 BCE, who obtained the priesthood by bribery and fostered a policy of hellenization. According to the author of 2 Maccabees, he promoted the establishment of a gymnasium in Jerusalem and sent envoys to the Olympic games with money for sacrifices to Hercules. He was eventually deposed, but later attacked Jerusalem in an unsuccessful attempt to regain the high-priesthood. He died in exile (2 Macc. 4:7–5:10).

2 Paul's host while he was establishing a Christian community in Thessalonica (Acts 17:5–9). He was arrested due to his association with the missionaries, but was later released.

3 A companion of Paul who sends greetings to the church in Rome (Rom. 16:21). This could be the same person as 2.   A.J.M./M.A.P.

jasper. *See* breastpiece; jewels, jewelry.

Jattir (jat'uhr), a hill-country village assigned to the tribe of Judah (Josh. 15:48) and allocated to levitical descendants of Aaron (Josh. 21:14; 1 Chron. 6:57). Residents received part of the war spoils from David after his victory over the Amalekites at Ziklag (1 Sam. 30:27). Consensus identifies the site as Khirbet 'Attir, southwest of Hebron and northeast of Beer-sheba, although no specific evidence for occupation during David's time has yet been found.

Javan (jay'vuhn).

1 The fourth son of Japheth (Gen. 10:2; 1 Chron. 1:15). His name, like the names of the fifth son (Tubal) and the sixth son (Meshech), also became the name for the area he settled.

2 A region in southwest Asia Minor mentioned in Isa. 66:19 and Ezek. 27:13. In the Isaiah passage, Javan and Tubal are specifically referred to as "coastlands." In Ezekiel, Javan, Tubal, and Meshech are said to have trafficked with Tyre in slaves and vessels of bronze. During the Hellenistic period, Javan came to be called Ionia. It was situated between Aeolia and Doria, and included the cities of Miletus, Ephesus, Smyrna, and Magnesia.

3 A name used occasionally in the Bible for Greece as a whole. Thus, the Hebrew text has "descendants of Javan" (NRSV: "the Greeks") in Joel 3:6 and "king of Javan" (NRSV: "king of Greece") in Dan. 8:21. See also Zech. 9:13; Dan. 10:20; and 11:2.   J.G.G.

javelin. *See* weapons.

Jazer (jay'zer), an Amorite town in the central Transjordan conquered by Moses and the Israelites prior to their settlement in Canaan (Num. 32:1–3). It was later allotted to the tribe of Gad (Josh. 13:25; cf. Num. 32:34–35; 2 Sam. 24:5). The city was subsequently assigned to the Merarite Levites (Josh. 21:39; 1 Chron. 6:81). It eventually came under control of the Moabites (Isa. 16:8; Jer. 48:32; 1 Macc. 5:8). It was probably located a few kilometers west of present-day Amman, though the precise location is unknown. Biblical references indicate that the land around Jazer was good for grazing (Num. 32:1, 3–4) and wine production (Isa. 16:8–9; Jer. 48:32).

jealousy. When attributed to God, "jealousy" describes God's desire for a relationship with people that is not compromised by infidelity or idolatry (Exod. 20:5; Deut. 5:9; Josh. 24:19; 1 Kings 14:22). The God of Israel is called a "jealous God," because the covenant with Israel is predicated on the notion of God and Israel making mutual but exclusive commitments to each other (Deut. 32:16; 1 Cor. 10:22).

When attributed to humans, "jealousy" can refer to zeal or ardor (2 Cor. 11:2; cf. Rom. 10:2; 2 Cor. 9:2; NRSV: "zeal"). Sometimes, "jealousy" also refers to what is regarded as a normal and appropriate reaction of people who have been betrayed by the infidelity of a spouse or loved one. This concept seems to form the basis for the ritual outlined in Num. 5:14–31, to be followed when "a spirit of jealousy" comes upon a man and he suspects his wife of having been unfaithful to him. More often, though, when the word "jealousy" is applied to humans, it refers to envy, a petty and negative quality that harms relationships and causes distress (Gen. 37:11; Sir. 30:24; Rom. 13:13; 1 Cor. 3:3; 2 Cor. 12:20; Gal. 5:20).   M.A.P.

Jebus (jee′buhs), a village in central Canaan. The Jebusites were children of Canaan (Gen. 10:16). Jebus is not mentioned in ancient Near Eastern texts outside the Bible and the origin of the city remains obscure. Nevertheless, it is clear from the references to the Jebusites that they were a powerful force in the hill country (see Exod. 3:8; 13:5; 23:23; 33:2; 34:11; Josh. 12:8; 24:11; Judg. 1:21). Three passages equate Jebus with Jerusalem (Josh. 15:8; 18:28; Judg. 19:10), which at one time led to a common assumption that Jebus was the original name for the city that would become known as Jerusalem after David conquered it and transformed it into the capital of his kingdom (2 Sam. 5:6–9; 24:18–25). Jerusalem, however, is also mentioned in the Egyptian Execration texts (nineteenth–eighteenth centuries BCE) and in the Tell el-Amarna tablets (fourteenth century BCE). Thus, if Jebus and Jerusalem are to be identified, they should probably be regarded as two different names for the same city used simultaneously rather than as names employed successively by Canaanites and Israelites. Some scholars, however, suggest that Jebus and Jerusalem were two different sites. Jebus is then identified with modern Sha‘fat, north of Jerusalem, which works better for such passages as Josh. 15:5b–11 (ignoring 5:8); 18:15–19; and Judg. 19–21. Whether one accepts Jerusalem or Sha‘fat as the site of Jebus, it is clear that the Jebusites were in control of Jerusalem in the period just prior to David's conquest of it as his royal city (2 Sam. 5:6–9). The Jebusite control of Jerusalem is presupposed in the story of David's purchase of land for the Jerusalem temple; David bought the land from the absentee landlord, who was a Jebusite (24:18–25).   S.B.R.

Jeconiah (jek′uh-ni′uh). *See* Jehoiachin.

Jedaiah (ji-day′yuh; Heb. *yeda‘yah,* "the LORD knows," or *yedayah,* possibly "the LORD is praise").
1 A descendant of Aaron and head of the second group of priests (1 Chron. 24:7); he was probably the ancestral head of one or more of the family groups below.
2 A priest and postexilic inhabitant of Jerusalem; he is called the "son of Joiarib" in Neh. 11:10.
3 A Levite who returned from the Babylonian exile with Zerubbabel (Neh. 12:6); he was the ancestor of a family group led by Uzzi (12:19).
4 A second Levite who returned with Zerubbabel (Neh. 12:7); he was the ancestor of a family group led by Nethanel (12:21).
5 The ancestor of a family group, led by Jeshua, who returned from the exile with Zerubbabel (Ezra 2:36; Neh. 7:39). This group could be related to either **3** or **4**.
6 One of the representative exiles named in a prophecy of Zechariah (6:10, 14).
7 The son of Shimri; a descendant of Simeon (1 Chron. 4:37).

8 One of the men who helped repair the walls of postexilic Jerusalem (Neh. 3:10).   D.R.B.

Jediael (ji-di′ay-uhl; Heb., possibly "El [God] knows").
1 A son of Benjamin and head of a large family group (1 Chron. 7:6, 10–11).
2 The son of Shimri; he and his brother Joha were members of David's fighting band (1 Chron. 11:45); he may be the same person who defected to David at Ziklag from the tribe of Manasseh (12:20).
3 A Levite from the line of Korah, the second son of the eastern gatekeeper Meshelemiah (Shelemiah; 1 Chron. 26:2).

Jeduthun (ji-dyoo′thuhn). A member of a levitical family whose descendants were gatekeepers at the temple in Jerusalem (1 Chron. 1:16; 16:42). Along with Heman, Jeduthun is mentioned also as a musician who served in the tabernacle under David (16:41–42; 25:6) and in the Jerusalem temple at the time of Solomon (2 Chron. 5:12); the latter passage specifies their fine linen garments and their station to the east of the altar. The Jeduthun family appears among the Levites who consecrated themselves and cleansed the temple in Hezekiah's reform (29:13–15; cf. a similar list in Neh. 11:15–17). He and his family also seem to have been associated with prophetic activity (1 Chron. 25:1–6; 2 Chron. 35:15); in the account of Josiah's reform, Jeduthun is described as "the king's seer" (2 Chron. 35:15). The name Jeduthun also appears in superscriptions for Pss. 39; 62; and 77, perhaps indicating a musical or liturgical setting that had become associated with his name. *See also* music; Psalms, book of.   P.R.A.

Jehiel (ji-hi′uhl; Heb., "El [God] lives").
1 The son of Ladan (1 Chron. 23:8). He founded a priestly family called the Jehieli (26:21–22) and had charge of the temple treasury under King David (29:8).
2 A levitical musician who served before the ark (1 Chron. 15:18, 20; 16:5).
3 An attendant of King David's sons (1 Chron. 27:32).
4 A son of King Jehoshaphat (2 Chron. 21:2).
5–6 Two temple officers (2 Chron. 31:13; 35:8).
7 The father of Obadiah who returned from the Babylonian exile with Ezra (Ezra 8:9).
8 The father of Shecaniah, who divorced his non-Israelite wife in compliance with Ezra's postexilic proclamation (Ezra 10:2).
9–10 Two other men who divorced their non-Israelite wives in response to Ezra's postexilic proclamation (Ezra 10:21, 26).

Jehoahaz (ji-hoh′uh-haz; Heb., "the LORD has grasped").
1 The son of Jehu and eleventh king of Israel (ca. 815–802 BCE). His rule was marked by subjugation to Syria, first under King Hazael and then under Hazael's son Ben-hadad (2 Kings 13:3). This was

attributed to divine wrath against Israel due to the worship of Asherah practiced in Samaria (2 Kings 13:6). Jehoahaz sought deliverance from God, who sent an unnamed savior (13:4–5); still, most of Jehoahaz's army was destroyed by Ben-hadad. Jehoahaz was succeeded by his son, Joash.

2 The son of Josiah and Hamutal and the seventeenth king of Judah (ca. 609 BCE). He reigned for a short time, perhaps only three months (2 Kings 23:31). After his father's death at the hands of Pharaoh Neco at the battle of Megiddo, Jehoahaz was made king by the people even though he was not the oldest son of Josiah. Pharaoh Neco deposed him in favor of his brother Eliakim, whom Neco renamed Jehoiakim (23:34). Jehoahaz was taken to Egypt as a captive and died there. Although he is called an evil king in 23:32, neither Jeremiah (who calls him Shallum; 22:10–12) nor Ezekiel refers to him in such terms (19:2–4).

3 The twelfth king of Judah, who is better known as Ahaz. *See* Ahaz.   P.J.A./M.A.P.

Jehoash (ji-hoh´ash). *See* Joash.

Jehohanan (jee´hoh-hay´nuhn; Heb., "the LORD is gracious").

1 A Levite from the line of Korah who was one of the gatekeepers in David's tabernacle (1 Chron. 26:3).

2 A captain under the Judean king Jehoshaphat (2 Chron. 17:15).

3 The son of Bebai; he divorced his foreign wife in response to Ezra's postexilic proclamation (Ezra 10:28).

4 A son of Eliashib (Ezra 10:6). Ezra retreated to Jehohanan's chamber for fasting.

5 A son of Tobiah who married the daughter of Meshullam son of Berechiah (Neh. 6:18).

6 A head of the priestly house of Amariah during the time of the Judean king Jehoiakim (Neh. 12:13).

7 A priest who officiated at the dedication of the rebuilt Jerusalem walls during the time of Nehemiah (Neh. 12:42).

Jehoiachin (ji-hoi´uh-kin; Heb., "the LORD has established"; also called Joiachin, Jeconiah, Jechoniah, and Coniah), one of the last two kings of Judah. His father was King Jehoiakim and his mother was Nehushta, the daughter of Onathan, a high court official. Jehoiachin came to the throne in 598/7 BCE at the age of eighteen after the death of his father (2 Kings 24:8). At that time, Babylon besieged Jerusalem, and, after he had reigned only three months, he, his mother, wives, servants, princes, and officers surrendered themselves to Nebuchadnezzar (24:12; reflected in the prophecy of Jer. 22:24–30). The Babylonians also looted the temple and palace treasures and carried into exile ten thousand soldiers, officers, workers, and smiths, leaving the land impoverished of skilled labor and administrators (2 Kings 24:14, 16; Jer. 24:1; 29:2). Hananiah the son of Azzur predicted an immediate

Babylonian cuneiform text that refers to Nebuchadnezzar's siege of Jerusalem and the exile of Jehoiachin to Babylon in 597 BCE.

return for Jehoiachin and the exiles (28:1–4), but Jeremiah said the divine redemption of the Babylonian captives would only come after a hiatus of seventy years (Jer. 24:4–7; 29:1–14). Several Babylonian food-rationing lists mention Jehoiachin's name or call him "King of Judah." Since he apparently surrendered quickly (2 Kings 24:12), he may have been treated fairly well. The Bible tells us (2 Kings 25:27–30; Jer. 52:31–34) that in the thirty-seventh year of Jehoiachin's captivity (ca. 561 BCE), Nebuchadnezzar's successor, Evil-merodach, raised his status to that of a valued court retainer. He was allowed to put away his prison clothes and to dine regularly in the king's presence (2 Kings 25:27–30; Jer. 52:31–34). For a people then wholly exiled, this fact served to provide hope that the tide had turned and that the promised redemption would eventually come.   J.U.

Jehoiada (ji-hoi´uh-duh).

1 The chief priest in the days of Athaliah and Joash of Judah (early eighth century BCE). His wife was Jehosheba, daughter of King Jehoram and sister of King Ahaziah, Jehoram's son (2 Chron. 22:11). After Ahaziah died, his mother, Athaliah (Ahab's daughter), took the throne and had Ahaziah's children murdered. Jehosheba saved the youngest, Joash, and, with Jehoiada, hid him in the temple for six years. In the seventh year Jehoiada formed a conspiracy of the commanders of the royal guard, the Levites, and the leaders of key family groups to restore the crown to the house of David (2 Chron. 23:1–7, 20). With the citizenry in attendance, Jehoiada crowned and anointed Joash and had Athaliah killed (23:8–15). He then renewed the covenant between God, the king, and the people, which resulted in the destruction of the Tyrian Baal cult (23:16–17). Jehoiada restored proper administration in the temple (23:18–19) and exerted significant influence over Joash (24:2–3). With the king's avid cooperation, Jehoiada collected a tax for the temple's maintenance and effected repairs (24:4–14). The Chronicler relates that he lived to be 130 and that he was buried in the tombs of the kings in the city of David—a sign of the great respect in which he was held (24:15–16). Jehoiada's fame may be remembered in Jer. 29:26. He was the father of Zechariah, who prophesied against Judah's apostasy.

2 A chief priest (1 Chron. 12:27; 27:5), the father of Benaiah, the chief of David's elite mercenaries (2 Sam. 8:18) and the head of the army under Solomon (1 Kings 2:35).

3 A high priest in the time of Nehemiah (Neh. 13:28).   J.U.

Jehoiakim (ji-hoi´uh-kim), king of Judah ca. 608–598 BCE (2 Kings 23:36). He was installed as king at age twenty-five by Pharaoh Neco after Neco had deposed his younger brother Jehoahaz (23:33–35). The son of Josiah and Zebidah, Jehoiakim's given name was Eliakim before Neco changed it. The pharaoh exacted a tribute of a hundred talents of silver and a talent of gold upon Judah, which Jehoiakim raised by tax. Any prophet who dared to oppose Jehoiakim risked his life: Jehoiakim had the prophet Uriah killed and Jeremiah put on trial (Jer. 26).

In 605 BCE, Babylon defeated Egypt decisively at Carchemish (Jer. 46:2; cf. 2 Kings 24:7) and captured Syria and the land of Israel (cf. Jer. 36:9). This had been predicted by the prophet Jeremiah, but when the king's officers and princes had tried to present the scroll of Jeremiah's prophecies to Jehoiakim, he had burned it (Jer. 36:29). Jehoiakim subsequently became Babylon's vassal for three years and then rebelled (2 Kings 24:1). Nebuchadnezzar responded with an invasion of troops from Moab, Ammon, and Aram (24:2; cf. Jer. 35:11), but Judah was able to maintain its sovereignty for a few more years. Although Jeremiah predicted that Jehoiakim would die an undignified death due to his murderous behavior (Jer. 22:17–19; cf. 2 Kings 24:4), 2 Kings 24:6 makes no mention of this; a somewhat different tradition may be reflected in 2 Chron. 36:5–8, where Jehoiakim appears to have spent his final years as a prisoner in Babylon (cf. 1 Esd. 1:39–40). He was succeeded by his son Jehoiachin. *See also* Josiah; Nebuchadnezzar.   J.U.

Jehonadab (ji-hoh´nuh-dab). *See* Jonadab.

Jehonathan (ji-hon´uh-thuhn). *See* Jonathan.

Jehoram (ji-hor´uhm; Heb., "the LORD is exalted"), also Joram, the name of two contemporary kings in Judah and Israel who were also brothers-in-law.

1 The king of Judah ca. 849–843/2 BCE, son and successor of Jehoshaphat, and husband of the Omride princess Athaliah. According to the account in 2 Chron. 21, he murdered his six brothers upon succession to the throne. There was a close alliance between Judah and Israel during his reign and the subsequent reign of Athaliah. Edom rebelled during Jehoram's reign, thus gaining its independence from Judah. According to the Chronicler, the Philistines also attacked Judah, and Libnah was taken (2 Chron. 21:16–17; 2 Kings 8:22). The Chronicler also reports that Jehoram suffered from an incurable disease, predicted by Elijah, and that he was not buried in the tombs of the kings.

2 A king of Israel (ca. 849–843/2 BCE) and brother and successor of Ahaziah. He was unable to put down the rebellion of King Mesha of Moab. The prophet Elisha accompanied the armies of Jehoram when Mesha, in desperate straits, "offered up his eldest son as a burnt offering" on the city wall in full view of the attackers. Israel and Aram were apparently allies early in Jehoram's reign, while Ben-hadad II was alive. In the reign of Ben-hadad's successor Hazael, however, Jehoram was wounded in battle against Aram. He was subsequently assassinated in Jezreel by his commander-in-chief, Jehu, who cast Jehoram's body into the field of Naboth, thus destroying the Omride dynasty (2 Kings 9:23–24).   D.L.C.

Jehoshabeath (jee´hoh-shab´ee-ath; Heb., "the LORD is an oath"; called Jehosheba in 2 Kings 11:2), the daughter of King Jehoram, and the wife of the priest Jehoiada. She saved her young nephew Joash (Jehoash), the youngest son of King Ahaziah, from Athaliah, the king's mother. When King Ahaziah was killed, his mother seized the throne and attempted to murder all of Ahaziah's sons, who would have been deemed rightful heirs to the throne. Jehoshabeath and Jehoiada kept Joash hidden for six years (2 Chron. 22:10–12). Then Jehoiada anointed the boy king and had Athaliah killed (23:8–15).

Jehoshaphat (ji-hosh´uh-fat; Heb., "the LORD establishes justice").

1 The son of Ahilud, "recorder" under David (2 Sam. 8:16; 20:24; 1 Chron. 18:15) and Solomon (1 Kings 4:3).

2 The son of Paruah, an officer in Issachar under Solomon (1 Kings 4:17).

3 The king of Judah ca. 873–849 BCE (1 Kings 15:24; 22:41–46; cf. 1 Chron. 3:10; Matt. 1:8). He was the son of Asa and Azubah. He succeeded his father, Asa, on the throne at the age of thirty-five. He is shown in 1 Kings 22 to be a subordinate ally of the Israelite king Ahab (22:20; 2 Chron. 18:1–3), but Jehoshaphat is distinguished from Ahab in that he insists on consulting the prophets, specifically Micaiah. The latter pronounces an oracle of doom, but Jehoshaphat is delivered in battle, and Ahab (who went into battle disguised) ends up being killed. Something similar happens again in 2 Kings 3:4–27. This time Jehoshophat is allied with Jehoram of Israel and the king of Edom. The prophet Elisha promises victory, but the eventual outcome is disaster for Israel.

According to 2 Chron. 17, Jehoshaphat strengthened the position of Judah against Israel, and also was obedient to God. Priests and Levites were sent to teach the law in the cities of Judah (cf. also 19:4–11). The surrounding nations honored Jehoshaphat and some sent tribute. Details are given of fortresses, store-cities, and military forces. In 2 Chron. 19:1–13, however, there appears a prophetic judgment against Jehoshaphat by Jehu, son of Hanani the seer, because it is said that he allied himself with the wicked apostates of the northern kingdom. Still, this judgment is ameliorated somewhat by notation of Jehoshaphat's pious actions: he responded to an attack by Moabites, Ammonites, and others with fasting and prayer (20:1–30). The specific prayer of Jehoshaphat, set out in 20:6–12, expresses the powerlessness of Judah and its absolute trust in God. In response to these actions, a Levite preacher proclaims divine help and coming victory. An act of praise follows, led by the Levites. Before the ensuing battle, Jehoshaphat further exhorts the people, using words close to those of Isa. 7:9. The singers offer praise, and the result is a divinely arranged victory that leaves the Judean army only the task of despoiling the totally destroyed enemy forces. Peace and prosperity are restored. This story could represent a reworking of 2 Kings 3. A supplement in 2 Chron. 20:35–37 elaborates on 1 Kings 22:47–49, showing another alliance with the Israelite king Ahaziah; a trading expedition to Tarshish is condemned by the prophet Eliezer, and the ships are wrecked.

4 The father of Jehu, king of Israel (2 Kings 9:2, 14), and son of Nimshi, elsewhere described as Jehu's father (1 Kings 19:16; 2 Kings 9:20; 2 Chron. 22:7).   P.R.A.

Jehoshaphat, Valley of, the site where the nations surrounding Israel will be judged by God for transgressions committed against Israel according to Joel 3:2, 12. Some scholars claim that the Valley of Jehoshaphat was known before Joel's time and that it was named for Jehoshaphat, king of Judah. Most scholars, however, believe that it was Joel who symbolically named a valley in Jerusalem (possibly the Kidron Valley or Gehinom) Jehoshaphat, meaning "the LORD judges." It is the place where God "will enter into judgment" (Joel 3:2) and "will sit to judge" (3:12), a place also called "the valley of decision" (3:14).   M.Z.B.

Jehovah (ji-hoh′vuh), an English spelling of the name of God used four times in the KJV (Exod. 6:3; Ps. 83:18; Isa. 12:2; 26:4). The word is formed by adding vowels to an English transliteration of the Hebrew Tetragrammaton, or four consonants that stand for God's name, which is not to be pronounced aloud. Those consonants are usually rendered as YHWH in modern transliterations of Hebrew, but JHVH was used at the time of the KJV. Likewise, in modern biblical studies the Tetragrammaton is sometimes vocalized to produce the name "Yahweh," which is a modern equivalent to "Jehovah." This was used in the JB and NJB. The most common practice in English translation, however, has been to use the expression "the LORD" wherever the Hebrew Tetragrammaton is found. This convention was followed by the KJV in all but the four verses just cited, and it has been followed in almost all English Bibles since, including RSV, NIV, and NRSV. *See also* Tetragrammaton; Yahweh.   M.A.P.

Jehozabad (ji-hoh′zuh-bad; Heb., "the LORD is a gift" or "the LORD has given").

1 A retainer of King Joash of Judah who, with another retainer, Jozacar, assassinated the king (2 Kings 12:21); he was executed by Joash's son Amaziah shortly after Amaziah took the throne (ca. 800 BCE; 14:5). According to 2 Chron. 24:26, Jehozabad had Moabite connections, being the son of Shimrith, a Moabite.

2 The son of Obed-edom; a Levite belonging to the line of Korah who shared responsibility for the southern storehouse of the temple during the reign of King David (1 Chron. 26:4, 16).

3 A Benjaminite commander of a hundred and eighty thousand troops under King Jehoshaphat (2 Chron. 17:18).

Jehozadak (ji-hoh′zuh-dak; Heb., "the LORD is righteous"), a priestly descendant of Aaron who was exiled to Babylon by Nebuchadnezzar (1 Chron. 6:14–15). He was the father of Joshua (Jeshua) who was the high priest in Jerusalem following the exile (587/6–490 BCE; Hag. 1:1; Zech. 6:11). He is also called Jozadak, a shortened form of the same name (Ezra 3:8; 5:2). In some versions the name also occurs as Josedech. *See also* Jozadak.

Jehu (jee′hyoo).

1 The king of Israel for twenty-eight years, ca. 843/2–815 BCE, and founder of a dynasty that lasted five generations, or about ninety years (2 Kings 9–10; 15:12). Jehu was probably the son of Jehoshaphat and grandson of Nimshi (9:2, 14), though he is also listed as the "son of Nimshi" (1 Kings 19:16; 2 Kings 9:20; 2 Chron. 22:7). It is possible that "son of Nimshi" in these passages has the sense of "descendant of Nimshi." The Assyrian inscriptions of Shalmaneser III refer to Jehu as "son of Omri," which contradicts the biblical presentation of Jehu as the one who destroyed the Omride dynasty by seizing power and usurping the throne in a bloody coup that included the murder of the Omride king Joram the son of Ahab. The Assyrian records are sometimes dismissed as

erroneous, but there has been some speculation that Jehu could have been a descendant of Omri, albeit as a member of a family group estranged from that of Ahab. It is noted that the Bible only speaks of Jehu as destroying the house of Ahab (2 Kings 9:7–9; 10:10–11), not the house of Omri.

Jehu's reign and his war against the worship of Baal were set forth in God's speech to the prophet Elijah on Mount Horeb (1 Kings 19:16–18). Although Elijah was given the task of anointing Jehu as king, this was actually carried out by a member of a prophetic band at the command of Elisha (2 Kings 9:1–6). The context for that religious legitimation, however, was a military debacle. During a border conflict between Israel and Aram at Ramoth-gilead, King Joram of Israel was wounded and had to return to Jezreel to recuperate. Jehu was one of the commanders of Israel's army. Thus, Elisha sent the prophet, not only to anoint Jehu king, but also to deliver a divine oracle to him: he was to strike down the house of his master (2 Kings 9:6–8). Jehu received support from his military officers and moved against the incapacitated monarch. He killed King Joram and then directed the killing of King Ahaziah of Judah, who had gone to Jezreel to visit Joram (9:27). He then moved against the families of those rulers, slaughtering Jezebel (the wife of Ahab, Joram's mother, and Ahaziah's grandmother), Ahab's seventy sons, all members and associates of the house of Ahab, Ahaziah's forty-two brothers, and, finally, all the worshipers of Baal in Israel (2 Kings 9:30–10:25). Jehu also ordered the destruction of the temple and the idols of Baal (10:26–28).

Thus, for a time, Jehu is said to have eliminated worship of Baal and to have ended a dynasty of rulers that the biblical authors repeatedly judged to be wicked. Nevertheless, the accounts of Jehu's actions present him as a calculating killer who was skilled at treachery: he ignored Joram's inquiries for peace, shooting him in the back as he fled, shouting, "Treason!" (2 Kings 9:17–24); he calmly went in to eat and drink after trampling the body of Jezebel with horses (9:34–35); he promised to support and accept Baal worshipers so that they would trust him enough to gather in one place, where he massacred them (10:18–25). The bloodiness of his coup was still remembered a hundred years later by Hosea, who maintained that God would punish the Jehu dynasty for what had happened at Jezreel (where the coup began). Indeed, Hosea maintained that it was because of what Jehu had done that God would put an end to the northern kingdom (Hos. 1:4–5).

In order to counter the Arameans, Jehu made himself vassal to the king of Assyria in 841 BCE. In a panel of the Black Obelisk of Shalmaneser III, Jehu is depicted as bowing before the Assyrian ruler and offering him tribute. This arrangement seems to have bought Israel peace for a time, but eventually the Arameans reasserted their military supremacy and conquered all of Ramoth-gilead (2 Kings 10:32–33). *See also* Elijah; Jehoshaphat; Jezebel; Omri; Shalmaneser.

2 The son of Hanani, and a prophet who prophesied against Baasha (ca. 900–877 BCE), king of Israel (1 Kings 16:1–4, 7, 12), and both rebuked and praised Jehoshaphat (ca. 873–849 BCE), king of Judah (2 Chron. 19:2–3). In 2 Chron. 20:34 authorship of the history of Jehoshaphat is attributed to him.

3 The son of Joshibiah, and a prince of the tribe of Simeon (1 Chron. 4:35).

4 One of David's warriors from Anathoth (1 Chron. 12:3).

5 A Judahite who was a descendant of Jarha, an Egyptian slave (1 Chron. 2:38).   J.U./M.A.P.

Jehudi (ji-hyoo´di), a servant of the court of Jehoiakim. He was sent by the nobles to order Baruch to bring them the scroll of Jeremiah's prophecies and then was ordered by the king to read the scroll before the court (Jer. 36:14, 21–23).

Jeiel (ji-i´uhl; Heb., "El [God] takes away").

1 A family chief in the tribe of Reuben (1 Chron. 5:7).

2 A Benjaminite, the father of Gibeon and great-grandfather of Saul (1 Chron. 8:29; 9:35).

3 The son of Hotham the Aroerite; one of David's warriors (1 Chron. 11:44).

4 A levitical musician of the Merarite group who helped celebrate the transfer of the ark of the covenant to Jerusalem (1 Chron. 15:18, 21). A second Jeiel is also listed among the group of musicians (16:5), but he is elsewhere called Jaaziel (15:18) or Aziel (15:20). It is possible that Jeuel, a variant spelling of Jeiel, refers to the same person (2 Chron. 29:13), although he is from the Elizaphan family group.

5 A Levite associated with the musical guild of Asaph; an ancestor of Jehaziel, the prophesier of deliverance for King Jehoshaphat (2 Chron. 20:14), he is possibly the same as **4.**

6 A scribe during the reign of Uzziah (Azariah) in Judah (2 Chron. 26:11).

7 A leader of the Levites who contributed animals for the celebration of the Passover reinstated by Josiah (2 Chron. 35:9).

8 A member of the family of Nebo who divorced his foreign wife in response to Ezra's proclamation (Ezra 10:43).   D.R.B.

Jemimah (ji-mi´muh), the first of Job's three daughters born when God restored his fortunes. All of these daughters were exceptional for their beauty. Job gave them an inheritance along with their brothers, whose names are curiously not given (Job 42:13–15).

Jephthah (jef´thuh; Heb., "the LORD opens"), a Gileadite who delivered Israel from Ammonite domination. Jephthah sacrificed his daughter to fulfill a vow, suppressed an Ephraimite force in Gilead, and judged Israel six years (Judg. 10:6–12:7).

Jephthah was the son of Gilead and a prostitute, but he was apparently raised in the household of

Gilead alongside two sons born to Gilead's wife. When the latter sons were grown, however, they drove Jephthah away, because they did not want to share their inheritance with him. In the district of Tob, near the modern Jordan-Syria border, he gathered a band of mercenaries and was later recalled by the elders of Gilead. Ammonite forces had invaded Gilead and penetrated across the Jordan into Judah, Benjamin, and Ephraim, and the elders of Gilead wanted Jephthah to lead them in their fight against the Ammonites and become their ruler.

Jephthah entered into extended negotiations with the Ammonite king, laying out Israel's position on the territorial dispute that had precipitated the conflict. The land in question had belonged to the Amorite kingdoms north of the Arnon River, which were defeated by Israel under Moses (Judg. 11:14–28; Num. 21). The territory was subsequently taken by Moab (Judg. 3:12–30), and the Ammonites thought this gave them a claim upon it, due to their relationship with the Moabites. Jephthah's point seems to be that Israel's claim is older and has precedence. Ultimately, however, the matter had to be decided by holy war. Jephthah said, "Should you not possess what your god Chemosh gives you to possess? And should we not be the ones to possess everything that the LORD our God has conquered for our benefit?" (Judg. 11:24). After these negotiations failed, Jephthah toured Gilead and Manasseh, presumably to muster the army, and then returned to Mizpeh (in the vicinity of Jebel Jal'ad, south of the River Jabbok).

Upon leaving for battle, Jephthah made a vow that if he returned victorious, he would sacrifice whatever (NRSV: "whoever") emerged first from his house (Judg. 11:30–31). Jephthah did defeat the Ammonites along a line from southern Aroer (the northern edge of the Arnon gorge) to Abelkeramim (probably Tell el-Umeiri at the northern end of the Medeba plain). As a result, the territory of Ammon was pushed back to the desert fringe. But then, when Jephthah returned home, the first creature to emerge from his dwelling was his only child, a daughter who came out to meet him with

timbrels and dance. Jephthah lamented his vow, but knew he had to keep it, as his daughter also insisted. She requested two months to wander the hills with her dear friends, lamenting her virginity (including the fact that she would die childless; 11:39–40). Then she was offered as a human sacrifice by her father. The event served to establish a ritual according to which "for four days every year the daughters of Israel would go out to lament the daughter of Jephthah the Gileadite" (11:40).

The story of Jephthah and his daughter has been regarded as something of a curiosity in the Bible. It bears some similarities to the tale of Abraham and Isaac (Gen. 22), though in that case the sacrifice of the child is, on the one hand, explicitly ordered by God and, on the other, averted by last-minute divine intervention. Otherwise, the Bible portrays human sacrifice as a pagan practice that is an abomination to Israel (Deut. 18:10; 2 Kings 16:3; Ps. 106:37; Jer. 7:31). It is clear from the story that Jephthah had not anticipated sacrificing his child, but it is not clear whether he had intended to offer a human sacrifice (e.g., of the first household servant who emerged upon his return). Iron Age dwellings did incorporate space for livestock, so many interpreters think the assumption behind the story (contra NRSV: "whoever," Judg. 11:38) would be that Jephthah expected to see a goat, cow, or other animal emerge from the dwelling as he drew near. In any case, the sacrifice that does occur is not specifically condoned, but neither is it condemned; it is only lamented. Some interpreters think the story speaks well of Jephthah, because he demonstrated extreme commitment to the irrevocability of a vow; others think the story is intended as a warning against the making of rash or inappropriate vows. In the Bible itself, Jephthah is only mentioned twice outside the cycle of stories concerning him in Judges, and both references portray him as a heroic deliverer (1 Sam. 12:11) and model of faith (Heb. 11:32), without mention of the unfortunate incident concerning his daughter.

As an epilogue to the story of Jephthah, the Ephraimites crossed into Gilead, complaining that Jephthah had not summoned them to the

Jephthah, returning home from battle victorious (*left*), first sees his daughter (*center*), whom he must therefore sacrifice according to his vow to God (*right;* Judg. 11:30–31); from a thirteenth-century French miniature.

Ammonite war and threatening to burn his house (Judg. 12:1). Again negotiations failed, and Jephthah was victorious in fighting, but many Ephraimite fugitives had to be hunted down, which was problematic since they were not obviously identifiable by dress or appearance. The Gileadites, however, recognized that there was a difference in dialect: Ephraimites were not able to pronounce the word *shibboleth;* they said "sibboleth" instead. Thus *shibboleth* was established as a password for leaving the region, and many Ephraimites were slain at the Jordan fords, because they were unable to pronounce the word properly (Judg. 12:5–6). *See also* Judges, book of; shibboleth.   R.B./M.A.P.

Jephunneh (ji-fuhn'uh).

1 A Kenizzite, the father of Caleb, one of the twelve spies sent to Canaan by Moses (Num. 13:6; 32:12).

2 The son of Jether; descendant of Asher (1 Chron. 7:38).

Jerah (jihr'uh; Heb., "moon"),

a son of Joktan (Gen. 10:26; 1 Chron. 1:20), and a member of a tribe whose territories were probably located in the south Arabian coastland.

Jerahmeel (ji-rah'mee-uhl; Heb., "may El [God] have compassion").

1 The ancestor of the Jerahmeelites, a group of non-Israelites who lived in the extreme southern part of the land of Judah. David came into contact with them there after his flight from Saul (1 Sam. 27:10; 30:29).

2 The son of Kish, and a Levite (1 Chron. 24:29).

3 One of the three men sent by the Judean king Jehoiakim to arrest Jeremiah and Baruch (Jer. 36:26). Although Jerahmeel is called "the king's son," that may be an official title rather than an indication that he was Jehoiakim's literal son.   M.A.F.

Jerash (jair'ash). *See* Gerasa, Gerasenes.

Jeremiah (jair-uh-mi'ah), book of,

the second book of what is sometimes called the Latter Prophets, a subcollection in the Nevi'im (Prophets) section of the Tanakh (Jewish Bible). It is the second book of the Major Prophets of the Christian OT. The book of Jeremiah is followed by the book of Ezekiel in the Tanakh and by Lamentations in the OT. Most of the book presents the oracles of the prophet Jeremiah, identified as the son of Hilkiah. Like his father, he was a priest in the town of Anathoth in the tribe of Benjamin, north of Jerusalem. Some portions of the book are autobiographical and some are biographical. Portions of Jer. 26–35 are from the memoirs of Baruch, Jeremiah's secretary and friend. Baruch was instrumental in bringing the written message of Jeremiah to the royal administration of Jerusalem and to the people.

Jeremiah is said to have received the divine word of the Lord beginning in 627 BCE during the reign of Josiah and to have continued receiving and recording God's word until the end of the monarchy and the destruction of Jerusalem in 587 BCE (1:1–3). This forty-year period encompasses most of what is said and done in the book, except for chaps. 40–44, which account for events up to 582 BCE and include Jeremiah's release from prison and his flight to Egypt.

Contents: The book of Jeremiah is a mixture of prose and poetic material. Chaps. 1–25 and 46–51 are mostly Jeremiah's autobiographical poetic reports of what God said to him, and they are mostly denunciations of Judah and surrounding nations, along with predictions of their demise. Included in the first block of autobiographical material are Jeremiah's complaints (11:18–12:6; 15:10–21; 17:14–18; 18:18–23; 20:7–18). These are personal reflections addressed to God in which Jeremiah laments his ill treatment at the hands of his compatriots. He feels that he was seduced by God into believing he would be protected, but instead he was "like a gentle lamb led to the slaughter" (11:19).

Biographical sketches about Jeremiah's professional life include his symbolic destruction of Judah and Jerusalem by breaking a clay jar and his subsequent arrest by Pashhur, a temple official (19:1–20:6); his temple sermon (chap. 26);

OUTLINE OF CONTENTS

Jeremiah

his confrontation of Hananiah over the yoke of Babylon (chaps. 27–28); his letter to Judean exiles in Babylon encouraging them to settle down there (29); his scroll, dictated to his secretary Baruch and read to king Jehoiakim (36, 45); his dire words and ill treatment in Jerusalem during the last days of Zedekiah (37–39); and his involvement with Gedaliah and eventual flight to Egypt after the destruction of Jerusalem (40–44). Many of these biographical narratives are explicitly dated to the reigns of Judah's kings, enabling scholars to build a precise timetable of Jeremiah's experience.

In addition to autobiography and biography, various prose sermons are scattered throughout the first half of the book. Jeremiah is instructed to preach the demands of covenant throughout Judah (11:1–17). His sermons include the sermon in the temple (chap. 7), the sermon in the potter's workshop (18), his sermon to Zedekiah (21), and his sermon to all Judah to submit to Babylon (25). These sermons contain vocabulary and concepts that are quite similar to Deuteronomy and the Deuteronomistic History. This similarity has given rise to claims that these sermons derive from Deuteronomistic circles as early as the exile or as late as the Persian period.

Background: The fact that Jeremiah came from the village of Anathoth is key for reconstructing the probable source of Jeremiah's disposition toward the Davidic monarchs and the temple in Jerusalem. Anathoth was the place to which Solomon banished the priest Abiathar in favor of the priesthood of Zadok, because Zadok had supported Solomon's claim to the throne of David, while Abiathar supported Adonijah (1 Kings 2:26). Given this history, it is no surprise that Jeremiah was critical of the royal line and the temple institution in Jerusalem. Thus, there is a significant political component to most of what Jeremiah says. Jeremiah's call for northern Israelites to return to God and to Davidic rule (Jer. 2–6; 30–31) may reflect support for Josiah's program of expansion to the north to re-create an "all Israel" entity. But after the death of Josiah, Jeremiah had a consistently pro-Babylonian message and was opposed to Jehoiakim and his policies, which were pro-Egyptian.

Themes: Jeremiah comes into conflict with Hananiah in Jerusalem over the stance Judah should take with regard to Babylon. Should Judah expect God to deliver it from the power of Babylon, or would Judah be wiser to capitulate and accept Babylon's hegemony? The conflict arises in part from differing appropriations of Israel's theological tradition. In the David-Zion tradition, God guaranteed the protection and inviolability of a Jerusalem that would eternally be ruled by someone from the line of David. This was promoted by Hananiah. In the Mosaic tradition, the covenant demanded obedience, which was the precondition for the blessing of peace and prosperity. This was promoted by Jeremiah. Prophetic ambiguity arose because both could lay claim to tradition and precedent, and both spoke for God

using the same conventional language of "thus says the LORD." Genuine prophecy then becomes evident only after the fact, when the politics on the ground vindicates one position or the other, or as the Deuteronomic tradition of Moses claims, "If a prophet speaks in the name of the LORD but the thing does not take place or prove true, it is a word that the LORD has not spoken" (Deut. 18:22).

Jeremiah was commissioned to be "a prophet to the nations" (1:5), and he was placed "over nations and over kingdoms, to pluck up and to pull down, to destroy and to overthrow, to build and to plant" (1:10). To that end the divine word in his mouth exposed the destinies not only of Judah, but also its neighbors. Chaps. 46–51 contain judgment oracles against Egypt, Philistia, Moab, Ammon, Edom, Damascus, Elam, and Babylon. This likens Jeremiah to Amos (1–2), Isaiah (13–23), Ezekiel (25–32), Nahum, and Obadiah, who all pronounced the judgment of God upon Israel's detractors. Such proclamations affirm that the Lord is not just Israel and Judah's patron deity, but is also the one who shapes the future of all nations.

Jer. 30–31 have been called the "book of consolation." This section of the book anticipates Israel's return to the land after the exile. Presumably these chapters were written after the destruction of Jerusalem in 587 BCE. Jeremiah declares that God will cut a new covenant with Israel and Judah and make it effective, because it will be written on the hearts of the people (31:31–34). This is the only place the phrase "new covenant" is found in the Hebrew Bible; it would inspire the title of the Christian "New Testament" ("testament" being another word for "covenant").

Interpretive Issues: The book of Jeremiah does not have a clear chronological or topical organization. This becomes clear from a comparison of the Hebrew Masoretic Text with the Greek LXX. The latter is approximately 12 percent shorter and arranges sections differently. For example, the oracles against the nations are found in chaps. 46–51 of the Hebrew text, but in chaps. 25–31 of the Greek text. These two variations are present among the multiple Dead Sea Scrolls; both the Masoretic Text and the LXX orders of books are attested. Apparently the Jeremiah materials were edited differently in Judea and Babylon, where the Hebrew Masoretic Text was used, than in Egypt, where the LXX, based on a differently edited Hebrew text, had been compiled. English translations typically follow the Masoretic Text.

Influences: Early postbiblical tradition attributed the book of Lamentations to Jeremiah based on the tone and topic of its poetic laments on the destruction of Jerusalem. The Christian OT places Lamentations after Jeremiah, and the Roman Catholic version of the OT places Baruch, the pseudonymous deuterocanonical book, after Lamentations. The LXX adds, after Baruch, another pseudonymous deuterocanonical book related to Jeremiah called the Letter of Jeremiah, which is presented as the letter Jeremiah sent to the exiles that is described in Jer. 29.

Bibliography

Bandstra, Barry L. *Reading the Old Testament: Introduction to the Hebrew Bible.* 4th ed. Wadsworth, 2009.

Carroll, Robert P. *From Chaos to Covenant: Prophecy in the Book of Jeremiah.* Crossroad, 1981.

Holladay, William L. *Jeremiah 1: A Commentary on the Book of the Prophet Jeremiah, Chapters 1–25.* Fortress, 1986.

———. *Jeremiah 2: A Commentary on the Book of the Prophet Jeremiah, Chapters 26–52.* Fortress, 1989.

Seitz, C. "The Prophet Moses and the Canonical Shape of Jeremiah." *Zeitschrift für die alttestamentliche Wissenschaft* 101 (1989): 3–27.   B.B.

Jeremiah, Letter of. *See* Letter of Jeremiah.

Jeremoth (jair´uh-moth).

1 A son of Becher and grandson of Benjamin (1 Chron. 7:8).

2 A descendant of Benjamin who belonged to the family group of Elpaal (1 Chron. 8:14).

3 A Levite, the son of Mushai of the Merari group (1 Chron. 23:23); he is also called Jerimoth (24:30).

4 A Levite, head of the fifteenth course of musicians (1 Chron. 25:22); he is probably the same person called Jerimoth in 25:4.

5 The son of Azriel, head of the tribe of Naphtali during the reign of David (1 Chron. 27:19).

6 A member of the family of Elam who divorced his foreign wife in response to Ezra's postexilic proclamation (Ezra 10:26).

7 A member of the family of Zattu who divorced his foreign wife in response to Ezra's postexilic proclamation (Ezra 10:27).

8 A member of the family of Bani who divorced his foreign wife in response to Ezra's postexilic proclamation (Ezra 10:29).

See also Jerimoth.   D.R.B.

Jericho (jair´uh-koh), a city in the Jordan Valley six miles north of the Dead Sea. Its broad plain, irrigated from the copious spring of modern 'Ein es-Sultan, just east of the ancient city, is extremely fertile. A ford near the city carries an important east–west road and makes Jericho a strategic entrance point from Transjordan into the highlands of Judah. The city of OT times is represented today

A human skull molded in plaster excavated at Jericho, from the Pre-Pottery Neolithic period (ca. 7000–4000 BCE).

by a mound 70 feet high and 10 acres in area. The tropical climate and vegetation of the Jordan Valley earned Jericho the title "city of palm trees" (Deut. 34:3).

After the Babylonian invasions (early sixth century BCE) the mound was abandoned and settlement concentrated in the irrigated oasis where modern Jericho is located. During the Hasmonean (167–63 BCE) and Herodian (40 BCE–44 CE) periods a complex of royal buildings grew up on the banks of the Wadi Qelt one and a quarter miles south of the ancient city. This site (modern Tulel Abu el-Alaiq) is commonly called New Testament Jericho.

The earliest occupation at Jericho (ca. 9000 BCE) was a small Mesolithic shrine near the spring. The next phase (the Neolithic, ca. 8000–4000 BCE) has given Jericho the description "the oldest walled town in the world." In the earliest Pre-Pottery Neolithic phase (ca. 8000–7000 BCE), the town, which was then as large as at any later time, was surrounded by a stone wall into which was set a circular stone tower 25 feet high. The second Pre-Pottery Neolithic phase yielded ten human skulls molded over with plaster to produce portrait heads. The city then passed through two pottery-bearing Neolithic phases and, after a period of in-occupancy, a Proto-Urban phase, represented only by rock-cut tombs (ca. 4000–3000 BCE).

With the urbanization of the Levant in the Early Bronze Age (ca. 3200–2000 BCE) Jericho again became a walled city. It flourished for several centuries before being destroyed by nomadic intruders. Little trace of their occupation (Middle Bronze I, ca. 2000–1900 BCE) remains on the mound itself. The culture is known principally by its distinctive shaft tombs, which often contain the remains of only one individual.

The Middle Bronze Age (ca. 1900–1500 BCE), the era of the biblical ancestors, saw Jericho a flourishing city, defended by powerful walls mounted on a high earthen embankment. A feature of this period of special interest to students of the Bible is a series of burial caves in which much of the grave furniture was preserved. The mats, baskets, tables, stools, beds, boxes, bowls, combs, and beads give a sampling of the objects in daily use during the time of the ancestors.

Jericho first appears in the biblical record in connection with the Israelite conquest of Canaan at the end of the Late Bronze Age (ca. 1500–1200 BCE). The wide plain on both sides of the Jordan near Jericho provided an ideal campground from which to launch an attack on Canaan. According to the Priestly document, the invading tribes were encamped in the Transjordanian portion of the plain when they defeated Sihon, Og (Num. 22:1), and the forces of Midian (31:12). At the camp a census was taken (26:3, 63), and the main provisions for the division and settlement of Canaan were made (chaps. 33–36). When two spies, who were saved from death in Jericho by Rahab (Josh. 2), reported favorably, Joshua's army crossed the river, aided by a miraculous division of its waters (Josh. 3:14–17), and laid siege to Jericho.

If it could be established archaeologically, the date of the fall of Jericho would fix the beginning of the Israelite invasion of Canaan. This would require the identification of a layer of destruction debris that could reasonably be attributed to Joshua's total devastation of the city and the identification of the city walls that, according to biblical tradition, collapsed under the spectacular conditions described in Josh. 6. J. Garstang believed that the ruin of a massive mud-brick wall, the destruction of which he dated to about 1400 BCE, was the wall in question. Kenyon's later excavation, however, showed that this "wall" was in fact part of two Early Bronze Age walls many centuries older than the time of Joshua. Kenyon found no trace of Late Bronze Age city walls and only one fragment of a house floor belonging to the period. The forces of erosion had removed all the vital evidence. Principally on the basis of the pottery from five Late Bronze Age tombs, Kenyon suggested a date in the last half of the fourteenth century BCE for the Israelite conquest of Jericho, but the more commonly accepted date of around 1200 BCE cannot be ruled out.

After its destruction by the Israelites, Jericho lay unoccupied for about four centuries. It was uninhabited during the time of the prophets Elijah and Elisha, who were both active in the region (2 Kings 2:4). The long period of abandonment accounts for the almost complete erosion of the

Clay oven, with a juglet nearby (*foreground*), inside a house wall at Jericho; ca. 1350 BCE.

Late Bronze Age walls and buildings. Jericho was rebuilt by Hiel of Bethel during the reign of Ahab (ca. 869–850 BCE). In the loss of his eldest and youngest sons (1 Kings 16:35) Hiel suffered the consequences predicted in the curse that Joshua laid on anyone who reestablished the city (Josh. 6:26).

Archaeologically, little is known about Israelite Jericho. Its remains have been completely eroded from the summit of the mound. It probably began as a small-scale settlement, but by the seventh century BCE it had expanded so that impressive buildings occupied the slopes of the mound outside the line of the earlier walls. After the Babylonian invasions, the site of the ancient city was abandoned.

In the NT Period: Jericho figured in a minor way in the ministry of Jesus. At Jericho Jesus healed blind Bartimaeus (Mark 10:46–52), had his encounter with the tax collector Zacchaeus (Luke 19:1–11), and told the parable of the Pounds (19:12–28).

Herod the Great built a magnificent winter capital on the banks of the Wadi Qelt, where archaeological excavations have produced spectacular results. The Hasmonean structures, all on the north side of the wadi, were probably built by Alexander Jannaeus (103–76 BCE). They consist in part of a palatial building (164 by 230 feet) and a swimming pool (65 by 115 feet) associated with a large courtyard. Herod, who saw himself as successor of the Hasmonean dynasty, renovated and extended the site on a grand scale in three stages and with aspects of the latest Roman architectural styles. Some walls were made in opus reticulatum technique (square stones set diagonally into a concrete core), large floors were paved in opus sectile technique with marble and local stone, and fresco was painted using Roman technique and ingredients. It is likely that Roman architects participated in the palace's construction.

The first palace, south of the wadi, had a large peristyle courtyard and contained an elaborate Roman-style bathhouse with a caldarium (hot room) heated from beneath a floor raised on hypocaust ceramic tiles. The second palace, north of the wadi, incorporated parts of the Hasmonean structures and included a massive pool, a grand triclinium (dining room) with exquisite frescoes, another bathhouse, and spectacular views of the gardens and natural scenery. The third palace was built on both sides of the wadi and was connected by a bridge. Among the halls were one with Ionic columns and another with Corinthian columns; all were painted and stuccoed in the latest styles. The six-room bathhouse took advantage of Roman arch and dome techniques and had a sauna alongside the caldarium. A large sunken garden punctuated the feel of a contemporary palace, though Herod made sure it was sufficiently unique to defy simple categorization as another Roman villa. Its decoration—geometric and floral (aniconic)—and occasional ritual baths and stone vessels punctuate the ruler's Jewishness. *See also* Joshua; Zacchaeus.

Bibliography

Bienkowski, Piotr. *Jericho in the Late Bronze Age.* Warminster: Ars and Phillips, 1986.

Holland, T. A., and Ehud Netzer. "Jericho (Place)." *Anchor Bible Dictionary.* Doubleday, 1992. 3:723–40.

Kenyon, Kathleen M. *Digging up Jericho.* Praeger, 1957.

Kenyon, K. M., G. Foerster, G. Bacchi, and E. Nezer. "Jericho." In *Encyclopedia of Archaeological Excavations in the Holy Land.* Vol. 2. Masada, 1970. Pp. 550–75.

Netzer, Ehud. *The Architecture of Herod, the Great Builder.* Mohr-Siebeck, 2006.   L.E.T.

Jerimoth (jair'i-moth).

1 A son of Bela and grandson of Benjamin (1 Chron. 7:7).

2 A Benjaminite who joined David's warriors at Ziklag (1 Chron. 12:5).

3 A Levite, son of Mushai of the Merari group (1 Chron. 24:30); he is also called Jeremoth (a variant spelling; 23:23).

4 A levitical musician belonging to the Heman group (1 Chron. 25:4); probably the same person also called Jeremoth who was head of the fifteenth course of musicians (25:22).

5 A son of King David and father of Mahalath, a wife of King Rehoboam (2 Chron. 11:18).

6 A levitical temple official during the reign of King Hezekiah (2 Chron. 31:13).

See also Jeremoth.   D.R.B.

Jeroboam (jair'uh-boh'uhm; meaning uncertain; Heb., possibly "may the people multiply" or "he who contends for the people") **I,** the first king of the northern kingdom (Israel), who reigned ca. 922–901 BCE. Jeroboam, the son of Nebat and Zeruah, was an Ephraimite from Zeredah who began his rise to power when Solomon appointed him to oversee the forced labor in Ephraim and Manasseh (1 Kings 11:26–28). Jeroboam rebelled against Solomon and was promised kingship over the northern tribes by the prophet Ahijah of Shiloh, who interpreted the revolt of the north as a judgment on the house of David due to the sins of Solomon (11:29–39). Solomon then sought to kill Jeroboam, who was forced to flee to Egypt, where he was protected by Pharaoh Shishak until Solomon's death (11:40). Jeroboam returned at an opportune time, when Rehoboam, Solomon's successor, gathered an assembly of the tribes at Shechem and sternly rejected all requests for a more lenient rule than Solomon had provided (12:13–14). Thus, the northern tribes of Israel chose Jeroboam to be their king instead; only the southern tribe of Judah pledged allegiance to Rehoboam (12:20).

The LXX text of 1 Kings differs significantly from the Hebrew Masoretic Text in ways that amplify the picture of Jeroboam's rebellion; the legitimacy of those readings (which are not adopted by the NRSV) and their value for historical reconstruction remain a matter of dispute. Lengthy additions to the biblical account found only in the LXX indicate that, prior to Solomon's death, Jeroboam fortified the city of Sarira and gathered three hundred chariots in an effort to overthrow Solomon. He is also said to have married into the royal family in Egypt. Further, he returned to Israel and fortified Sarira again, but was unable to pursue the revolt further because his son became ill.

After becoming king, Jeroboam fortified Shechem and Penuel (1 Kings 12:25) and may have used them as his capital before he established his residence in Tirzah (14:17). In order to discourage his Ephraimite subjects from traveling to Jerusalem for worship, he set up gold bull images ("calves") at Bethel and Dan, an act he probably understood as a revival of an older form of the worship of God, according to which the God of Israel would be understood to be an invisible deity astride the bulls (i.e., the bulls were not representations of gods, but thrones for the God of Israel analogous to the ark of the covenant in the Jerusalem temple). Nevertheless, the Deuteronomistic Historian, who wrote or edited the books of Kings, interpreted Jeroboam's bulls as idolatrous (12:28–30). Obvious connections could be drawn to the golden calf incident at Sinai (Exod. 32:1–6), though some interpreters believe the story of that idolatrous moment in Israel's history was inspired by later objections to Jeroboam's bulls. In any case, Jeroboam is said to have also revised the religious calendar, instituted a nonlevitical priesthood, built shrines on the high places, and served as a priest himself, at least on certain occasions (1 Kings 12:26–33).

These religious reforms earned him the condemnation of the writers of the books of Kings. According to their interpretation of Israelite history, Jeroboam's cultic sins lead to the condemnation of the altar at Bethel by an unnamed prophet from Judah (1 Kings 13:1–10). Later, when Abijah the son of Jeroboam fell ill, Jeroboam sent his wife in disguise to Ahijah, the prophet who had first proclaimed Jeroboam king. God inspired Ahijah to see through this disguise and to bring "heavy tidings" to Jeroboam's wife concerning her son and family: not only would the boy die before she returned home, but the entire royal line of Jeroboam would be destroyed (14:1–9). The evil of idolatry had provoked God to anger and now, God says, "I will consume the house of Jeroboam, just as one burns up dung until it is all gone. Anyone belonging to Jeroboam who dies in the city, the dogs shall eat; and anyone who dies in the open country, the birds of the air shall eat" (14:10–11; this would not be fulfilled until a generation later; cf. 15:27–30). Indeed, Jeroboam became the biblical paradigm of "an evil king"; throughout the account of the history of the northern kingdom, the writers of Kings repeatedly claim that other rulers "did what was evil in the sight of the LORD and walked in the way of Jeroboam" (e.g., 15:26). This pattern of sin and judgment continued until the northern kingdom itself was finally destroyed (2 Kings 17:21–23).

Jeroboam's reign was beset by ongoing conflict with Judah (1 Kings 14:30; 15:6–7; 2 Chron. 12:15; 13:2–20). Perhaps even more devastating, the Egyptian pharaoh Shishak invaded Israel ca. 918 BCE and destroyed a number of cities, though this is barely mentioned in the Bible (1 Kings 14:25–26). This incursion may have weakened Jeroboam's control over his kingdom and encouraged the neighboring Philistines and Arameans to seize Israelite territory. When Jeroboam died (struck by God, according to 2 Chron. 13:20), he was succeeded by his son, Nadab (1 Kings 14:20).
R.R.W./M.A.P.

Jeroboam II, the son of Joash and his successor as king of Israel. Although the writers of the books of Kings say little about Jeroboam II's forty-one-year reign (ca. 786–746 BCE) except that "he did what was evil in the sight of the LORD; he did not depart from all the sins of Jeroboam son of Nebat" (2 Kings 14:24), a more complete account of his relatively prosperous kingship can be reconstructed from extrabiblical sources.

As the penultimate king of the Jehu dynasty, Jeroboam II inherited a more favorable set of political circumstances than any of his predecessors. Effective Assyrian intervention in the region had ended with the campaigns of Adad-nirari III (809–782 BCE), who at the end of the ninth century moved west and defeated the Arameans of Damascus, who had been harassing Israel since the end of Jehu's reign (ca. 815 BCE; cf. 2 Kings 13:5). The Assyrian king exacted tribute from several rulers in the area, including Jeroboam's father, Joash, but the heaviest blows fell on the Arameans, whose political power was severely restricted. In any case, during the first half of the eighth century Adad-nirari III and his successors were occupied with internal strife at home, and the resulting power vacuum in the Near East allowed Jeroboam to expand his borders from the Sea of the Arabah (the Dead Sea) to the "entrance of Hamath" (2 Kings 14:25) and to reclaim territory lost during the reigns of Jehu and Jehoahaz (10:32–33; 13:1–9). He may also have moved into the Transjordan

Bronze copy of a seal inscribed, "Belonging to Shema, the servant of Jeroboam"; Megiddo, from the reign of Jeroboam II, 786–746 BCE.

and gained control over Damascus, thus restoring the boundaries of the old Davidic empire (2 Kings 14:28; Amos 6:13). The texts that describe these events, however, are difficult to interpret.

Jeroboam's expansionist activities, which were supported by the prophet Jonah, the son of Amite (2 Kings 14:25), brought prosperity to Israel, particularly in the larger cities. The new land was presumably assigned to the king's supporters, who became part of a new class of wealthy landowners. Increased agriculture and trade brought more tax revenue into the royal court. This redistribution of land and money increased the number of poor people in the land and created a class of servants and slaves, who were exploited by the rich. These social and economic abuses provoked sharp judgment oracles from the prophet Amos, whose words dramatize the negative aspects of Jeroboam's economic prosperity (2:6–8; 4:1–3; 5:10–12; 6:4–7, 11–14; 8:4–6). R.R.W.

Jeroham (ji-roh´ham; Heb., "may he be loved" or "may he have compassion").

1 A Levite, the father of Elkanah and grandfather of Samuel (1 Sam. 1:1; 1 Chron. 6:34).

2 A family group ("sons of Jeroham") in the tribe of Benjamin (1 Chron. 8:27).

3 A Benjaminite, the father of Benaiah, an inhabitant of postexilic Jerusalem (1 Chron. 9:8).

4 A priest, the father of Adaiah, another inhabitant of postexilic Jerusalem (1 Chron. 9:12; Neh. 11:12).

5 A man from Gedor whose two sons, Jerah and Zebidah, joined David's warriors at Ziklag (1 Chron. 12:7).

6 The father of Azarel, the leader of the tribe of Dan during David's reign (1 Chron. 27:22).

7 The father of Azariah, a military leader under the high priest Jehoiada (2 Chron. 23:1). D.R.B.

Jerubbaal (ji´ruhb-bay´uhl). *See* Gideon.

Jerusalem

Topography: Situated on the crest of the Judean mountains some twenty miles west of the Dead Sea's northern end and thirty miles east of the Mediterranean Sea, the biblical city of Jerusalem (ji-*roo*'suh-luhm) was built over two hills ranging from 2,300 to 2,500 feet above sea level and surrounded by valleys. The earliest walled settlement, which spanned the second millennium BCE, was founded on about fifteen acres of the low southern spur of the eastern hill, the area known today as the City of David. It was bounded on the east by the north–south Kidron Valley, on the west and south by the north–south Central (Tyropoeon) Valley, and on the north by the hump of the Ophel; the population was probably between one and two thousand. Solomon's construction of the first temple doubled the city's size to the north, incorporating the Ophel and what may have been a Jebusite holy place on the highest point of the eastern hill, up to the east–west Bethzatha Valley. Following the split of the two kingdoms and the growth of Assyrian pressure on the north, with a consequent migration of refugees to the south, the early population of Jerusalem grew beyond the capacity of the walled enclosure, spreading through the Central Valley to the southwestern hill now known as Mount Zion. The latter is circled on the west and south by the Hinnom Valley (Heb. *gehinnom,* "Gehenna"), which begins near the Jaffa Gate and descends to meet the Kidron south of Siloam. On the north, Mount Zion is limited by the east–west Transversal Valley, which descends from today's Jaffa Gate along David Street and the Street of the Chain to meet the Central Valley at El-Wad Street. In Roman times, the city was extended again to the north and northwest, essentially to its modern walls. (But see below for discussion of "Third Wall.") The southern third of the biblical city is outside the confines of the walls of today's Old City.

Only two major springs are to be found in the neighborhood, both in the Kidron Valley. Ain Sitti Maryam ("Lady Mary's Spring"), biblical Gihon (1 Kings 1:38), is at the foot of the slope of the City of David, always a key water source for the city; the other, Bir el-Ayyub ("Job's Well"), probably to be identified with the biblical En-rogel (1:9), is a

The word "Jerusalem" incised on a wall of a rock-cut burial cave near Lachish; early sixth century BCE.

Situated in the central hill country, Jerusalem became, under David, the key city of ancient Israel, and thus it remained. (In addition to the three plans of Jerusalem included later in this article, three plans of the city at different historical periods are included in the section of color maps [14–16].)

Aerial view of Jerusalem showing the site of the ancient city (*center*). The Dome of the Rock stands in the area that was the Temple Mount, to the right of which is the Kidron Valley, which continues into the foreground. Above the steep slope of the Kidron is the Ophel hill, site of the City of David.

short distance to the southeast, just beyond the confluence of the Kidron and Hinnom valleys.

The shallow soil of the region makes for meager agriculture, but the underlying Cenomanian limestone provides excellent building material, weathering to a beautiful golden hue in the evening sun. The area was heavily treed in biblical times, but suffered severe deforestation during the first-century Roman siege of the city, and again in the Islamic period with the overgrazing by herds of black goats.

Name: Although some Chalcolithic evidence for settlement about 3200 BCE has been found, the earliest literary references to the city (called Rushalimum) appear in Egyptian Execration texts of the twentieth and nineteenth centuries BCE. The fourteenth-century BCE Amarna letters speak of Urusalim. *Yerushalem* was probably the original pronunciation in Hebrew, later modified to the dual form *yerushalayyim*. The name seems to mean "foundation of [the god] Shalem." Shalem and his twin, Shahar, are known from Ugaritic texts as the gods of twilight and dawn, respectively. Scholarly opinion is divided over the identification of Melchizedek's "Salem" with Jerusalem (Gen. 14:18; Ps. 76:2; Heb. 7:1; see also John 3:23).

Jebus, the city of the Jebusites, is known only from the Bible and seems to be identified with Jerusalem of the immediate pre-Israelite period through the time of David's capture of the city ca. 1000 BCE. Some problems exist in this attribution, however. Zion is first mentioned as the citadel captured by David and renamed "City of David" (2 Sam. 5:6–7). It seems to have been extended in later parlance to refer to the Temple Mount and then to the entire city, particularly in a poetic sense. The erroneous attribution of the name to the western hill dates only from the Byzantine period.

History: A glimpse of the city's actual history is first provided by the Amarna letters, six of which were written by the king of Jerusalem to the Egyptian pharaoh, attesting to his loyalty and begging for help against other Canaanite kings, Hapiru, and even the pharaoh's Nubian garrison in the region. Pottery of the Middle and Late Bronze periods found in the surroundings shows commercial contacts with Egypt, Cyprus, and the Aegean.

Entrance to Hezekiah's tunnel cut beneath the City of David in the eighth century BCE. It brought water from the Gihon spring to the west side of the Ophel hill.

The ethnic composition of Jerusalem of the Bronze Age is not totally clear. The king of the Amarna letters bears a Hurrian theophoric name, Abdi-hepa ("Servant of Hipa"), and writes in the Akkadian lingua franca of the day, but he betrays a West Semitic mother tongue akin to Hebrew. Josh. 10:5 refers to Adonizedek of Jerusalem as one of the "kings of the Amorites," but 18:28 assigns *hayyebusi* ("the Jebusite city"), which is Jerusalem, to the tribe of Benjamin, an identification maintained in Judg. 19:10. Judg. 1:8 attributes an early total conquest and destruction of Jerusalem to the tribe of Judah, but the city reappears again as "Jebusite" in the days of David. The Jebusites survived in Jerusalem with Benjamin, intermarrying with Israelites (Judg. 1:21; 3:6). Ezek. 16:3 charges the city with mongrelized parentage: "Your father was an Amorite, and your mother a Hittite"; these sixth-century references may be pejorative reminiscences of fallen peoples, or they could represent genuine recollections of the origins of the Jerusalem population. When David conquered the city, he set aside the threshing floor of "the Araunah," possibly the former Hurrian or Hittite ruler of the city (2 Sam. 24:16). Thus, the Jerusalem taken by David may have represented an enclave of Hittites/Hurrians remaining from the long-past Hittite Empire, who were ruling over a local Amorite population, increasingly isolated among the surrounding Israelites.

Jerusalem was taken for David by his uncle, Joab (2 Sam. 5:6–8; 1 Chron. 11:4–6), winning for the latter the position of commanding general of David's armies from that time on. Seven years later, David transferred his capital from the Judahite town of Hebron to the more tribally neutral Jerusalem, whose citadel became known as the "City of David." He engaged in rebuilding the Millo (possibly the terraces of the eastern slope) and constructed for himself a palace of Lebanon cedar.

Recognizing the need to centralize the Israelite identity of the fractious tribes around the monarchy, David brought to Jerusalem the ark of the covenant, the central pilgrimage shrine object and symbol of unity of all Israel. The city thus became the cultic as well as the political and military administrative center of the nation. As the royal court developed, it attracted the best talent from throughout the country for royal service as well as non-Israelite mercenaries (such as Uriah the Hittite), who owed their loyalty to David alone, not to a particular tribe. Indeed, it appears that the Jebusite urban establishment may have remained largely in place under David, with Zadok continuing as priest alongside the Aaronite Abiathar.

Solomon continued David's policies, enjoying a time of relative international peace to consolidate his central power in Jerusalem. He undertook massive building projects in Jerusalem, concentrating for the first seven years on the temple north of the City of David and extending the acropolis to include the rise of the hill under today's Haram es-Sharif. The next thirteen years saw the erection of his own palace complex between the new temple and the older City of David to the south as well as pagan temples across the Kidron for his wives. But the royal taxation and centralization of power in Jerusalem offended tribal sensibilities in the north, and the division of the kingdom after Solomon's death (ca. 920 BCE) saw the city reduced to being the capital of only two tribal territories, Judah and Benjamin.

The temple remained the principal (and eventually exclusive) site of approved worship. Jehoshaphat established a royal court system centered in the city, and fortifications were strengthened repeatedly throughout the next three centuries. The Assyrian threat and actual destruction of the northern kingdom drove many refugees south in the eighth century BCE, leaving Hezekiah's expanding Jerusalem effectively once again the capital of the remnants of the entire Israelite nation. For a short time Hezekiah was able to develop new strength in trade relations, but Sennacherib's hostile approach (701 BCE) required new fortifications for the southwestern hill, strengthening of the Millo, and diversion of the Bilhon waters through a 1,700-foot tunnel under the City of David. Sennacherib took Lachish and most of the rest of Judah and laid siege to Jerusalem, but he apparently did not invade the latter city. Instead, he withdrew to Assyria, strengthening the idea of the divinely guaranteed impregnability of Jerusalem. Nonetheless, the city remained under Assyrian hegemony for

Ahaz, Hezekiah, Manasseh, Josiah, and Jehoiakim are among the kings of Judah who reigned in Jerusalem in the eighth to sixth centuries BCE. The prophets Isaiah of Jerusalem and Jeremiah were active in this period.

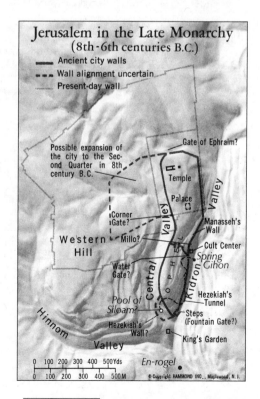

Jerusalem in the Late Monarchy
(8th - 6th centuries B.C.)
— Ancient city walls
- - - Wall alignment uncertain
— Present-day wall

Possible expansion of the city to the Second Quarter in 8th century B.C.

Gate of Ephraim?

Temple

Palace

Manasseh's Wall

Corner Gate?

Western Hill

Millo?

Cult Center

Spring Gihon

Water Gate?

Pool of Siloam?

Hezekiah's Tunnel

Steps (Fountain Gate?)

Hezekiah's Wall?

King's Garden

Hinnom Valley

Central Valley

Kidron

OPHEL

En-rogel

0 100 200 300 400 500 Yds
0 100 200 300 400 500 M   © Copyright HAMMOND INC., Maplewood, N. J.

almost another century, symbolized by the worship of Assyrian gods in the temple.

In the mid-seventh century, Manasseh again reinforced the citadel and built a new outer wall (2 Chron. 33:14). Josiah threw off the weakening Assyrian yoke, purged and renovated the temple, and purified the cult on the basis of a scroll (probably much of Deuteronomy) found in 622 BCE. Josiah was killed at Megiddo in a confrontation between Egypt and Babylon as they attempted to take advantage of the power vacuum following the collapse of Assyria. His successors were unable to keep the Babylonians at bay, however, and the city was destroyed and depopulated by Nebuchadnezzar in 587/6 BCE; for the next half century it lay in the desolation described so vividly in Lamentations.

With the fall of Babylon to the Persians in 539 BCE, Cyrus opened the way for exiles, including the Jews, to return to their various homelands, and small contingents of returnees began to move back into the ruins of the City of David. The first group, led by Prince Sheshbazzar, reestablished worship in 538 BCE. A second group, under Prince Zerubbabel and the high priest Joshua, and spurred on by the prophets Zechariah and Haggai, completed a modest rebuilding of the temple between 521 and 515 BCE.

The next light on the city comes with the arrival of Ezra the scribe and his returnees, probably in 458 BCE, and then with a new governor, Nehemiah, in 445 BCE. Although abortive attempts to repair the walls had been made since the original return, opposition from the surrounding peoples had prevented the Jerusalemites from achieving this symbol of independence. Nehemiah, however, completed walls around the much

The huge retaining wall at the southwestern corner of the Temple Mount from the time of Herod the Great.

Herod the Great (40–4 BCE) undertook a massive building program in Jerusalem that included extending the Temple Mount to the south and constructing a new temple edifice.

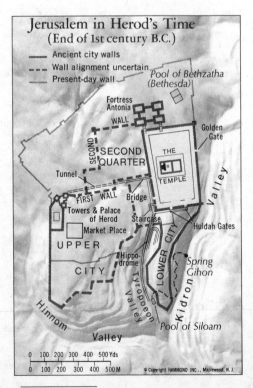

Jerusalem in Herod's Time
(End of 1st century B.C.)

— Ancient city walls
- - - Wall alignment uncertain
— Present-day wall

Pool of Bethzatha (Bethesda)

Fortress Antonia

WALL

SECOND

SECOND QUARTER

THE TEMPLE

Golden Gate

Tunnel

FIRST WALL Bridge

Towers & Palace of Herod Staircase

Market Place

UPPER CITY

Hippodrome

LOWER CITY

Huldah Gates

Spring Gihon

Tyropoeon Valley

Kidron Valley

Hinnom Valley

Pool of Siloam

0 100 200 300 400 500 Yds
0 100 200 300 400 500 M

© Copyright HAMMOND INC., Maplewood, N. J.

restricted area of the crest of the City of David and the temple in fifty-two days. His reform of Jewish marriages and enforced resettlement (Neh. 11:1) of one-tenth of the population inside the walls brought more economic and military security to the city. A number of structures and city gates are mentioned in Nehemiah, but only a few can be located with certainty. Nothing else is known of the city's history for the next century, and the population must have been quite small.

In 332 BCE, Alexander the Great conquered Judah and Jerusalem as he moved through the Levant toward Egypt. With the division of Alexander's empire among his generals, Jerusalem lay under generally benign Ptolemaic rule from 301 to 198 BCE. Political stability seems to have led to economic development and a significant increase in population. Nonetheless, the Jews welcomed the Seleucid Antiochus III after his conquest of the area, and a hellenization of the city began to gain momentum. The construction of a gymnasium in 175 BCE moved the city closer to becoming a Greek *polis*. Repairs to the temple and walls were aided by the authorities, and Jewish traditions were respected at first. But the royal appointment of Menelaus as high priest in 171 BCE, the looting of the temple by Antiochus IV Epiphanes, establishment of a foreign garrison in the Acra in 168 BCE, and the attempt to impose Greco-Syrian pagan worship in the temple incited a rebellion led by the priestly Hasmonean

Persian marble head, perhaps of Cyrus II, sixth century BCE.

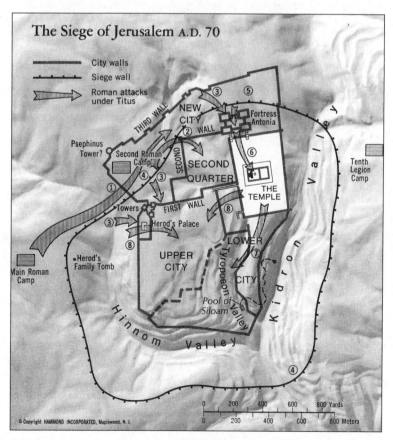

The Siege of Jerusalem A.D. 70

— City walls
— Siege wall
▷ Roman attacks under Titus

KEY TO EVENTS OF SIEGE: **1.** Romans breach Third Wall, May 25, and capture New City. **2.** Romans enter Second Quarter. Jews withdraw behind First Wall, May 30–June 2. **3.** Titus's divided attack on First Wall. The Antonia fails. **4.** Romans build siege wall around city. **5.** Romans renew assault on the Antonia. Fortress falls to Titus, July 22. **6.** Romans burn gates and enter temple courtyards. Temple destroyed by fire, August 29. **7.** Romans burn Lower City, September 2? **8.** Romans assault Herod's Palace and enter the Upper City. Resistance ends on September 26.

Excavations in front of the southern wall of the Temple Mount have revealed significant remains from the Umayyad, Byzantine, Herodian, Hasmonean, and First Temple periods.

family. Judas Maccabeus took the city and cleansed the temple in 164 BCE (an event commemorated by the festival of Hanukkah), but was unable to dislodge the Syrian garrison in the Acra. Nonetheless, the city's fortifications were strengthened under Judas and his brothers, and Simon finally expelled the Syrians and razed the hated Acra in 141 BCE.

Jerusalem prospered under the Hasmoneans (who assumed both high-priestly and royal prerogatives), growing in population and spreading again to the southwestern hill, which was enclosed within the "First Wall" by Simon and John Hyrcanus I. A treaty with Antiochus VII Sidetes traded the demolition of part of the fortifications for Seleucid recognition of the now sizable Hasmonean kingdom under John Hyrcanus I. The city began to grow rapidly, and a new section to the north was encircled by the "second wall" (although some scholars date this wall to the time of Herod the Great). A new aqueduct brought in water from the southern hills to meet the population's increasing needs. A royal palace was constructed in the Upper City on a spur of the southwestern hill overlooking the Temple Mount. After the death of Queen Salome Alexandra in 67 BCE, a period of internecine warfare among the Hasmoneans permitted the Romans under Pompey to conquer Jerusalem in 63 BCE as they consolidated their control of the former Seleucid kingdom of Syria.

The Roman governor, Antipater the Idumean, repaired the walls in 48 BCE, and in 43 BCE named his sons Phasael and Herod, respectively, tetrarchs of Jerusalem and of Galilee. A Parthian invasion in 40 BCE incited a last Hasmonean revolt under Mattathias Antigonus. Phasael died, but Herod sought and obtained Roman sanction for his ambitions; the Senate named Herod king of the Jews and provided the military assistance necessary for the reconquest of the former Hasmonean territories by 37 BCE. Called "the Great" because of his many building projects both throughout his kingdom and elsewhere in the empire, Herod completely changed the face of Jerusalem into that of a typical classical city. This in-

The Mount of Olives (*upper left*) and the traditional site of the
Garden of Gethsemane (*center, to the left of the church*).

volved the adaptation of an older Hasmonean fortress into the Antonia
(named for Herod's patron, Marc Antony), the reconstruction of three
massive towers in the Citadel (named "Phasael" for his brother, "Mariamne" for his wife, and "Hippicus" for a friend), the building of a royal
palace on the southwestern hill adjacent to the present Jerusalem citadel,
and, above all, the massive renovation and expansion of the temple. An
improved water supply system included aqueducts from the higher hills
to the south and reservoirs within and around the city. Herod seems to
have followed, at least in part, a Hippodamian grid for his extensions of
the city; and the historian Josephus speaks of a hippodrome and theater,
but their locations have not yet been discovered. The beautification of the
city made it that much more appealing to pilgrims, who came in tens of
thousands for the major holy days.

After Herod's death in 4 BCE, rule of Judea and Jerusalem passed to his
son, the ethnarch Archelaus, but ten years later, he was exiled to Gaul by
the Romans, and governors (procurators or prefects) were assigned to the
province. The Gospels record the trial and crucifixion of Jesus in Jerusalem under Pontius Pilate (Matt. 27; Mark 15; Luke 23; John 18–19). The
first few chapters of the book of Acts record the life of the early Christian
church in Jerusalem under the leadership of James, the brother of Jesus.
The Gospel of Luke and the book of Acts display particular interest in
Jerusalem: in the Gospel of Luke, the city is the goal of a ten-chapter journey of Jesus and his disciples (9:51–19:44); and in Acts, the Christian mission to the ends of the earth begins in Jerusalem (1:8; cf. Matt. 28:16–20,
where the mission to all nations appears to begin in Galilee). It is only
John's Gospel, however, that portrays Jesus as traveling to Jerusalem multiple times during his adult ministry (cf. 2:13; 5:1; 10:22–23; 12:12).

The relationship between Jews and Roman authorities always carried
a degree of tension. Under Gessius Florus, that tension exploded in
Caesarea Maritima in 66 CE and then spread to Jerusalem. After the

Roman Twelfth Legion and its auxiliaries were severely defeated by the Jews, the "Third Wall," well to the north of the city, was hastily erected in anticipation of a siege by Vespasian's Romans. Vespasian had been named emperor after his successful campaign in Galilee, so it was his son Titus who arrived in early 70 CE to lay siege to Jerusalem. The Romans breached the new north wall in May and took the Antonia in July, the temple area in August, and the remainder of the city in September. Titus destroyed most of the city, sparing only the three towers of the Citadel area to provide protection for the Tenth Legion, which remained stationed there for the next several centuries. The city was largely abandoned, and even the Sanhedrin moved to Jamnia near the coast.

News that the emperor Hadrian planned to settle a Roman colony on the site of Jerusalem provoked a second revolt of the Jews, this time under Bar Kochba in 131 CE. The uprising was put down in 135 CE, and Hadrian proceeded to rebuild the city as Aelia Capitolina, named for his own family and for Jupiter Capitolinus. A Roman temple was built on the Temple Mount. "All circumcised persons" (i.e., principally Jews) were forbidden even to enter the territory of Aelia Capitolina.

The later history of the city is beyond the scope of this article, but a short outline may be given:

135–323	Roman pagan rule of the small town Aelia Capitolina
323–638	Byzantine Christian rule: significant development
(614–628	Persian invasion and interregnum)
638–1099	Early Islamic period: economic decline
1099–1187	Latin Kingdom of Jerusalem under the Crusaders
1187–1291	Alternating Crusader and Muslim rule
1291–1517	Ayyubid/Mamluk rule: Islamic construction
1517–1917	Ottoman Turkish rule: return of Jews
1917–1948	British Mandate from League of Nations: growth
1948–1967	City divided between Israel and Jordan
1967–	City reunited under Israel: significant growth

Archaeology: Modern systematic study of Jerusalem began in the nineteenth century with the observations of the American scholar Edward Robinson. Robinson's reports inspired two expeditions sponsored by the British Palestine Exploration Fund, those under Charles Wilson and Charles Warren. Construction projects brought to light various ancient remains over the next several decades, such as the so-called Lithostratos under the convent of the Sisters of Zion (now identified as pavement of a Hadrianic forum). Systematic excavations were undertaken on the southeastern spur by the Parker and Macalister expeditions early in the twentieth century, and there and elsewhere by Kathleen Kenyon in the 1960s. But the real explosion of archaeological work came after the Six-Day War in 1967 left the Old City under Israeli control. Possibly no other city in the world has been excavated so extensively as Jerusalem since 1967. Only the Haram

The base of the "Tower of David" dates to the time of Herod the Great, when it was part of the Phaesalis tower.

es-Sharif (the Herodian Temple Mount platform) remains untouched by archaeologists.

South and southwest of the Temple Mount, Benjamin Mazar uncovered massive Umayyad palaces and hostels built over Byzantine-period homes. Below these were the Herodian structures associated with the construction and situating of the temple platform: the Huldah Gates, the stairway from "Robinson's Arch," the paved street descending the Tyropoeon Valley, shops, etc. A clear image of this part of Herodian Jerusalem has been pieced together. Ninth-century BCE tombs, a plastered cistern, and a large building bear witness to Judahite Jerusalem. A structure just to the south of the Huldah Gates may be the Syrian Acra built by Antiochus IV Epiphanes, although this is still disputed by many scholars.

On the western hill, Nachman Avigad excavated the old Jewish Quarter, abandoned from 1948 to 1967, discovering the colonnaded Byzantine *cardo maximus* (main north–south street) and the foundations and cistern of Justinian's Nea church, just as depicted in the Medeba Map. Several affluent homes of Herodian Jerusalem were found. A "broad wall," other structures, and pottery bear witness to the expansion of the walls of Jerusalem in the eighth century BCE under the Assyrian threat. Hasmonean engineers had later worked their fortifications into the remnants of the earlier walls.

Yigal Shiloh picked up where Kenyon had left off in the City of David, establishing more accurate dating for earlier discoveries and discerning some twenty-five occupational strata from the Chalcolithic through the medieval periods. The Gihon water systems were clarified, remains of monarchy-period houses were found, and a large stepped-stone structure was reinterpreted as part of the retaining wall/platform of a tenth-century BCE acropolis—David's stronghold.

Other excavations in the Jerusalem Citadel near the Jaffa Gate have confirmed the Iron Age II expansion of the city to the western hill. First Temple period tombs have been found in Silwan, a village across the Kidron Valley from the City of David, in the Valley of Hinnom, and north of the Damascus Gate. Second Temple period tombs and those of later periods have long been known on the Mount of Olives and elsewhere around Jerusalem. Excavations under the Church of the Holy Sepulchre have confirmed that the area was an ancient quarry reused as a cemetery

The twin arches of the now walled-up Golden Gate in the eastern wall of Jerusalem's old city, originally built in the Byzantine period.

THE CENTRALITY OF JERUSALEM IN LUKE-ACTS

Gospel of Luke

1:5–8	The story opens in Jerusalem (in the temple).
2:22–38	Jesus brought to Jerusalem as a baby.
2:41–50	Jesus in Jerusalem at age twelve.
9:51–19:40	Ten-chapter journey to Jerusalem (9:51, 53; 13:22; 17:11; 18:31; 19:11, 28).
19:41–44	Jesus weeps over Jerusalem (also 13:33–35).
24:41–43	Resurrection appearances in and around Jerusalem (24:13, 18, 33).
24:47	Mission to all nations begins with Jerusalem.
24:49	Jesus tells disciples, "Stay in Jerusalem."
24:52–53	Story closes in Jerusalem (in the temple).

See also 5:17; 6:17; 9:31; 10:30; 13:4; 21:20, 24; 23:28.

Acts of the Apostles

1:4	Jesus orders disciples not to leave Jerusalem.
1:8	Mission to ends of the earth begins in Jerusalem.
1:12–26	Believers gather for prayer and planning in Jerusalem.
2:1–4	Holy Spirit comes to 120 believers in Jerusalem.
2:4–47	The Jerusalem church is an ideal community (also 4:32–37).
2:5–41	Peter preaches to residents of Jerusalem; 3,000 are saved.
3:1–8:1	Five chapters on church in Jerusalem (4:5, 16; 5:16, 28; 6:7).
8:14–25	Samaritan mission receives endorsement of Jerusalem church.
9:27–30	Conversion of Paul recognized by the Jerusalem church.
11:1–18	Peter reports to Jerusalem concerning baptism of Gentiles.
11:19–26	Jerusalem church sends Barnabas to check on Gentile mission in Antioch.
11:27–30	Antioch Christians fund relief ministry for Jerusalem (also 12:25).
15:1–29	Jerusalem Council decides controversy over Gentile conversions.
16:4	Paul promulgates decision of Jerusalem Council.
18:22	Paul reports back to Jerusalem after second missionary journey.
21:17	Paul reports back to Jerusalem after third missionary journey.
21:27–23:11	Paul arrested and put on trial in Jerusalem.

See also 8:27; 9:2, 13, 21; 10:39; 13:13, 27, 31; 19:21; 20:16, 22; 21:4–13; 25:1, 3, 7, 9, 15, 20, 24; 26:4, 10, 20; 28:17.

From Mark Allan Powell, *Introducing the New Testament*
(courtesy, Baker Academic)

in the first century CE. To the south of Jerusalem, an ossuary in a burial cave of the first century CE was found in 1990 with two inscriptions reading *jehosef bar ca(i)fa,* "Joseph son of Caiaphas," quite possibly the high priest at the time of Jesus's crucifixion. Work along the "Third Wall" north of the Old City has brought a growing consensus that recognizes its correspondence to the description by Josephus.

As a Symbol: From the time of David's construction of the altar on the threshing floor and Solomon's building of the temple, Jerusalem has been the primary center of the religious universe of the Jewish people. The destruction of the first temple by the Babylonians in 587/6 BCE evoked a national consciousness among the exiles that centered on restoration of the temple and renewal of Jewish life in the city and the land. The book of Ezekiel idealized a rebuilt temple as the place of God's presence to his people. The sanctity of the site was enhanced by its identification in 2 Chron. 3:1 with the mountain of "the Moriah," the site of Abraham's abortive sacrifice of Isaac. Defilement of the temple by Antiochus IV Epiphanes led to the successful Maccabean revolt. Herod rebuilt it to be the most magnificent structure in the Roman world, and even Titus deliberated on how to save it from destruction in his siege. Hadrian's plans for a pagan temple on the site (intended to obliterate the memories and hopes of Jewish worship there) provoked Bar Kochba's unsuccessful revolt, but even the ensuing exclusion of Jews from the city and surroundings did not diminish its importance to them. The Mishnah preserved real and idealized descriptions of the temple and its ceremonies, and the orientation of synagogues always allowed the congregation to face toward Jerusalem during prayer.

Idealization of the city of Jerusalem as such occurs in the exilic and postexilic prophets (e.g., Isa. 44:26–28; 62:1–12). The apocalyptic mindset, increasingly frustrated with the cognitive dissonance between prophetic idealism and reality, began to make a distinction between an earthly Jerusalem and a heavenly one. In Gal. 4:22–31, Paul develops an allegory, equating the slave woman Hagar with Mount Sinai (i.e., the law) and the contemporary Jerusalem, but the free woman, mother of Christians, with the Jerusalem above. The author of Rev. 21:9–22:5 draws heavily upon the new temple imagery in Ezek. 40–48 to describe the "holy city Jerusalem coming down out of heaven from God." The "New Jerusalem" has ever since remained a Christian symbol of God's ultimate saving power.

See also Assyria, Empire of; Babylon; Cyrus II; David, City of; Gihon; Herod; Hezekiah; Hinnom, Valley of; Jebus; Kidron; Maccabees; Moriah; Olives, Mount of; Ophel; Siloam Inscription; temple, the; Zion.

Bibliography

Asali, A. J., ed. *Jerusalem in History.* Olive Branch, 1990.

Purvis, James D. Jerusalem, *The Holy City: A Bibliography.* 2 vols. American Theological Library Association/Scarecrow, 1988–91.

Stern, Ephraim, ed. "Jerusalem." *The New Encyclopedia of Archaeological Excavations in the Holy Land.* Vol. 2. Israel Exploration Society and Carta, 1993.

C.H.M.

Jerusalem Council, also called the apostolic council, a meeting of early Christian leaders to discuss the proposal that Gentile converts to the faith should become circumcised and keep Jewish law if they wish to be saved (Acts 15:1–35). The council appears to have been prompted by the success converting Gentiles that marked Paul and Barnabas's first missionary journey (13:1–14:28). At the council, Peter gave a report concerning the conversion of the Gentile Cornelius (15:7–11), and James the brother of Jesus proposed that Gentile converts should not have to be circumcised, but should agree to keep certain aspects of the law that would facilitate fellowship with Jewish believers (15:13–21). The council agreed with this proposal and drafted a letter to be distributed to all of the churches (15:22–29; cf. 21:25). The contents of that letter, however, do not appear to have remained determinative for the church's ongoing mission; neither the letter nor its stipulations concerning Gentile behavior are mentioned in any other NT document. There has been considerable discussion, however, as to whether Paul's description of a Jerusalem meeting in his letter to the Galatians should be understood as a reference to the Jerusalem Council (1:18–19; 2:1–10). If so, there appear to be numerous discrepancies between Paul's firsthand account of the meeting and the account provided in the book of Acts. Some scholars, accordingly, believe that Galatians was written prior to the Jerusalem Council and that Paul was referring to some earlier meeting.   M.A.P.

Jeshaiah (ji-shay'yuh; Heb., "the LORD saves").
1 A Judahite, the grandson of Zerubbabel; he belonged to the royal lineage of the kings of Judah (1 Chron. 3:21).
2 A levitical musician belonging to the Jeduthun group; head of the eighth course of musicians (1 Chron. 25:3, 15).
3 A Levite who shared the responsibility of keeping the temple treasures (1 Chron. 26:25).
4 The son of Athaliah; a leader of the Elam group who returned from the Babylonian exile with Ezra (Ezra 8:7).
5 A Levite of the Merarite group who joined Ezra at the Ahava River to return to Jerusalem from Babylon (Ezra 8:19).
6 A descendant of Benjamin who moved to Jerusalem during the time of Nehemiah (Neh. 11:7).   D.R.B.

Jeshanah (jesh'uh-nuh; Heb., "old"), a city on the border of Judah and Israel, probably modern Burj el-Isaneh about six miles southeast of Shiloh. Its capture by Abijah in his war with Jeroboam I is related in 2 Chron. 13:19.

Jeshimon (ji-shi'mon; Heb., "desert," "barren waste"). The Hebrew word that is sometimes rendered as the proper name Jeshimon is also sometimes translated "a barren wilderness" (cf. Deut. 32:10; Ps. 107:4). Indeed, that seems to be

the meaning in the majority of uses, but there are a few instances in the Bible where the word does appear to indicate a specific geographic location. Thus, the NRSV use Jeshimon as a place-name in 1 Sam. 23:19, 24; 26:1–3. It refers here to a region in the hill country of Judah into which David fled from Saul. Other locations mentioned in this account (Maon, Ziph, En-gedi) indicate that Jeshimon should be identified with the eastern section of the Judean hill country, an area between Hebron and the Dead Sea, elsewhere called the Wilderness of Judah (e.g., Josh. 1:16). The KJV also uses Jeshimon in Num. 21:20; 23:28 (NRSV: "the wasteland") to refer to an area of the Jordan Valley northeast of the Dead Sea (the Plains of Moab) overlooked by Mount Pisgah (perhaps Nebo) and Mount Peor. There may be some connection between this latter area and the Moabite settlement of Beth-jeshimoth (Num. 33:49). *See also* Beth-jeshimoth; Maon.

Jeshua (jesh'yoo-uh; Heb., "the LORD is salvation"), the Aramaic form of Joshua.
1 A Levite, the head of the ninth division of priests (1 Chron. 24:11).
2 A priest who shared the responsibility for distributing the Levites' portion of the offerings to the levitical cities during the reign of Hezekiah (2 Chron. 31:15).
3 The son of Jozadak (Jehozadak) and a priest and family leader who, along with Zerubbabel, led the return of a group of exiles from the Babylonian exile (ca. 521 BCE; Ezra 2:2; Neh. 7:7). He worked closely with Zerubbabel in reestablishing the worship of God in Jerusalem, first building an altar and reinstating sacrificial worship (Ezra 3:1–5) and then, with the encouragement of the prophet Haggai (1:1–11), helping to organize the rebuilding of the temple (3:8–9; 5:2). He is referred to as the high priest by Haggai (1:1) and Zechariah (6:11), both of whom call him Joshua. He was the father of Joiakim, who probably succeeded him as high priest (Neh. 12:10–12). In Zeh. 3:1–10, Jeshua (called Joshua) is the representative of Israel whose exchange of "filthy garments" for "rich apparel" symbolizes, not only the cleansing and reinstatement of the priesthood (3:7), but also atonement for the people's sins through the suffering of the exile (3:4; cf. Jer. 32:36–44). To him was given the announcement of the coming of God's servant, "the Branch," and of God's intention to remove the guilt from the land (3:8–9). In another vision (Zeh. 6:10–15), he is given a crown and is equated with the Branch; however, most scholars recognize a textual error here (in 6:11) and think that Zerubbabel should be read in place of Joshua (i.e., Jeshua).
4 The ancestor of a group known as the "house of Jeshua" to which belonged the family group of Jedaiah who returned from the exile with Zerubbabel (Ezra 2:36).
5 The ancestor of a family belonging to the Pahath-moab group who also returned from exile (Ezra 2:6).

6 The ancestor of a family of Levites who returned from exile (Ezra 2:40).

7 A Levite, the father of Jozabad, and one who helped inventory the valuables brought back by the returning exiles (Ezra 8:33).

8 An official of the district of Mizpah who helped rebuild the walls of postexilic Jerusalem (Neh. 3:19).

9 A Levite who helped explain the law read by Ezra to the people (Neh. 8:7); he is probably the same Levite who returned from the exile with Zerubbabel (12:8), took part in the covenant-renewal ceremonies (9:4–5), and signed the covenant (10:9). He is possibly also the same as the son of Kadmiel who was a levitical leader under the priest Joiakim (12:24).

10 A name occurring once for Joshua the son of Nun (Neh. 8:17).

11 A town settled by Judahites following the exile (Neh. 11:26). Its location is suggested by some as modern Tel es-Sawa, about nine miles east of Beer-sheba.

Jeshurun (jesh'uh-ruhn), a poetic title in Hebrew for the people of Israel (Deut. 32:15; 33:5, 26), with the symbolic meaning of "upright one" (Isa. 44:2).

Jesse (jes'ee), the father of King David. According to the tradition of the book of Ruth (4:17–22). Jesse was the grandson of Boaz and Ruth. He was a prosperous farmer who could afford to send gifts to Saul (1 Sam. 16:20). Jesse is also mentioned in the prophecies of Isaiah, which refer to the house of David (11:1, 10). He is listed in the NT as an ancestor of Jesus (Matt. 1:5–6; Luke 3:22).

Jesus Christ

JESUS CHRIST is the central figure of the NT: every book is written because of him and, in some sense, about him. Within the NT itself, he is spoken of in two distinct ways.

(1) The NT describes and reflects upon a man named Jesus who lived in Galilee and was eventually crucified in Jerusalem; although this person seems to have been called simply "Jesus" or "Jesus of Nazareth" during his life on earth, he came to be called Jesus Christ by Christians who placed their faith in him. He was revered by NT authors, not only because his life and teaching were thought to present a supreme revelation of God's will (or indeed of God's very being), but also because his death and resurrection were held to represent God's saving act for sinful humanity. His name (Jesus) and his title (Christ) bear witness to that saving act. The name "Jesus" is derived from a Hebrew word that means "savior" (see Matt. 1:21), and the title "Christ" (Heb., "messiah") means "anointed" and refers to one commissioned by God for a special task.

(2) The NT also speaks of Jesus Christ as an exalted, eternal figure who existed prior to creation and who now continues to reign from heaven, seated at the right hand of God and dwelling also in the hearts of those who believe in him. The NT authors would have maintained the unity of this figure with the earthly one; they would have insisted that the earthly and exalted figures were the *same* Jesus. Still, a distinction is often evident. In Matthew's Gospel, Jesus tells his disciples in one passage that he will not always be with them (26:20) and in another passage tells these same disciples, "I will be with you always" (28:20). Scholars say that the author of Matthew's Gospel believed the eternal, exalted Jesus (sometimes called the "post-Easter Jesus") would remain present in a way that the earthly, historical figure (the "pre-Easter Jesus") would not.

The Earthly (Pre-Easter) Jesus in the NT: The NT Gospels refer to Jesus consistently as being a Jew from Nazareth, a small village in the province of Galilee. He is also said, however, to have been born in Bethlehem, and his birth is described as a miraculous occurrence. His mother, Mary, conceived him in her womb while she was yet a virgin, betrothed or engaged to Joseph, who nevertheless took her as his wife. He was thus raised as the son of Joseph and Mary and is said to have had several brothers and sisters. Jesus is depicted as a Jewish peasant (or possibly an artisan) who worked as a *tektōn,* some sort of carpenter, builder, or construction worker. Almost nothing is said about his early life, though some process of education is implied by the fact that, as an adult, he is described as being able to read and familiar with the scriptures. Nothing is said of his marital status, which probably means that he is to be regarded as a single adult, committed (possibly for religious reasons) to a life of celibacy (cf. Matt. 19:12).

Jesus's face as depicted in a sixth-century mosaic at the Monastery of St. Catherine, Sinai.

The NT focuses primarily on the last year or years of Jesus's life. He was baptized by John the Baptist, a preacher of repentance who is presented as someone who modeled his ministry after prophets like Elijah. Then Jesus began a public ministry of his own, traveling throughout the villages of Galilee, teaching, preaching, and healing. He called disciples to follow him and chose twelve of those disciples to constitute an inner circle of followers patterned after the twelve tribes of Israel. Certain facets of his ministry are especially noteworthy. (1) It was an *itinerant* ministry. Whereas John the Baptist preached in the wilderness, expecting the crowds to come out to hear him, Jesus preached on the road, taking his message to different groups as he and his disciples moved from place to place (cf. Matt. 8:20). (2) It was a *rural* ministry. Although there were large cities in Galilee (Caesarea, Sepphoris, Tiberias), Jesus is never said to visit any of these; the focus of his ministry was villages and market towns, places like Bethsaida and Capernaum. He is often pictured as ministering to people in outdoor settings (e.g., beside the Sea of Galilee). (3) It was a *Jewish* ministry. Despite occasional encounters with Gentiles or Samaritans, the ministry of Jesus was primarily directed to Jews and conducted in terms that would be meaningful to Jewish people. He frequently taught in synagogues, he quoted from the Jewish scriptures, and he discussed such topics as how the Torah might be best observed and how the writings of Hebrew prophets were fulfilled. Thus, the NT presents Jesus as a Jewish peasant who assumed the roles of rabbi and prophet on behalf of other Jewish peasants in Galilee during the rule of Herod Antipas. The most prominent phase of his ministry, furthermore, occurred just after Herod had John the Baptist arrested (see Mark 1:14).

The slaughter of the innocents—part of the account of Jesus's birth in Matthew—as portrayed by P. Brueghel (1525–69).

With regard to *content,* the most prominent topic addressed by Jesus in the NT is the imminence and certainty of God's rule. Jesus often uses the phrase "kingdom of God" to describe the sphere of God's influence and power, a phenomenon that cannot be restricted by time and space. According to Jesus, the kingdom of God (which might also be translated "rule of God" or "reign of God") is not just in heaven or in the future; it is a reality to be experienced here and now. When Jesus says, "the kingdom of God has come near" (Mark 1:15), he means something like, "God is ready and willing to rule people's lives—right here, right now." But that is not all there is to it; the kingdom also has a future dimension, and the NT

Galilee, the region where Jesus's ministry began and was centered.

Rugged hillside in the vicinity of Nazareth.

presents Jesus as speaking of this as well. There will be a final judgment at which Jesus himself will preside and human beings will either be granted access to eternal bliss or condemned to everlasting punishment depending on their status relative to God and to Jesus himself. Jesus indicates that the blessings of the future kingdom are for those who believe in him and who are faithful to him in word and deed.

The overall emphasis on God's presence and power has numerous implications. Thus, other prominent themes in Jesus's teaching and preaching include: (1) a call to uncompromising allegiance to God and absolute trust in God; (2) a promise of forgiveness that leads to the reconciliation of sinners and the inclusion of those who are easily marginalized or rejected by society; (3) a reassessment of certain legal interpretations, particularly those deemed burdensome or viewed as fostering elitism; (4) a radical "love ethic" that declares love for God and neighbor to be a synopsis of all God's demands and that urges people to love everyone, even their enemies; and (5) a reversal of conventional value judgments that insists God favors the poor over the rich and the meek over the powerful, with the obvious corollary that those who wish to please God should humble themselves through voluntary poverty and service.

The NT also presents Jesus as teaching about himself—about his identity as one who has a unique relationship with God—and as speaking proleptically about matters that would be of concern to Christians in the life of the early church (e.g., Matt. 18:15–18). He often refers to himself in the third person as the "Son of Man," and he also wants to be identified (at least privately) as the Messiah and the Son of God. In general, he seems

The Samaritan woman meeting Jesus at the well (John 4:1–42); sixth-century mosaic at San Apollinare in Classe, Ravenna, Italy.

to indicate that the possibility and necessity of living under God's rule is a *new* reality, one that is now available because of him: he is the mediator through whom people experience the power and presence of God's rule.

The *style* or *conduct* of Jesus's ministry is also noteworthy. He is especially fond of telling parables, though he also uses proverbs, aphorisms, and other memorable forms of speech associated with the Jewish wisdom tradition. In addition, he is depicted as performing what might be called "prophetic acts" (unconventional public displays intended to make a particular point). Isaiah walked about naked for three years to illustrate the shame that would come upon Israel when the nation was taken into exile (Isa. 20:3); Jeremiah wore a yoke (Jer. 27:1–7) and broke a pot (19:1–3). Prophetic acts attributed to Jesus include dining with tax collectors (Mark 2:15–17), riding into Jerusalem on a donkey (11:1–10), and overturning tables of money changers in the temple court (11:15–17).

Christ as Pantocrator: a fourteenth-century mosaic in the Kariye Church, Istanbul, attempts to represent the resurrected and glorified Christ of faith.

Aramaic inscription in the floor mosaic of the late third- to early fourth-century synagogue at Hammath-Tiberias. It reads, in part, "Peace be upon everyone who has fulfilled the commandment in this holy place."

Another prominent aspect of Jesus's ministry in the NT is his regular practice of healing the sick. He cleanses lepers; he makes the mute speak, the deaf hear, and the blind see; he enables the lame or paralyzed to walk. Often these healings are performed through acts of exorcism. People suffer various afflictions because they are possessed by demons, but when Jesus forces the evil spirits to leave, the people are instantly cured. Jesus says that he is able to do this because the kingdom of God has come (Matt. 12:28); thus his healings and exorcisms also become prophetic acts, illustrating his central message about the presence and power of God's rule. In a few cases, he even restores dead people to life. He also works what are sometimes called "nature miracles," doing things that would typically be impossible for a human being: he walks on water, he multiplies a limited quantity of food, he changes water into wine, he controls the weather, he withers a fig tree. To the extent that these miracles are prophetic acts, they serve to illustrate the power of faith in God (see Matt. 14:28–31; Mark 11:21–24); sometimes they also seem to carry symbolic meaning (e.g., water being changed to wine symbolizes a transformation from mundane life to abundant life).

In any case, Jesus's ministry brings him into conflict with the religious leaders of Israel. They are described as disagreeing with him over matters related to legal interpretation (e.g., sabbath regulations; criteria for divorce) and the appropriate practice of piety (e.g., fasting, ritual handwashings, almsgiving, the wearing of phylacteries). According to the NT, these leaders are jealous of Jesus's popularity with the people, and they are scandalized by his public fellowship with sinners; they are also offended by his claim to speak with a divine authority that trumps their judgments. But Jesus finds *them* offensive as well: he regards them as casuistic fools, insincere hypocrites, or pompous paragons of self-righteousness—and he denounces them publicly in precisely those terms.

The career of the earthly Jesus comes to a climax when he is arrested in Jerusalem on what the NT presents as trumped-up charges. He seeks to prepare his disciples for this trauma by displaying foreknowledge of what is going to occur, predicting exactly what will happen, and observing a final meal with his followers replete with last words and advice for them to follow in the days to come. His death is presented in the NT as a result of collaborative evil: high-ranking Jewish opponents want him out of the way, and they manipulate a predictably unjust Roman ruler, Pontius

Pilate, into commanding the torture and execution of a man he knows to be innocent. Even Jesus's disciples contribute to his disgraceful demise, as one of them betrays him, all of them desert him, and his right-hand man (Peter) denies that he even knows who Jesus is. Nailed to a cross, Jesus suffers and dies; his body is placed in a tomb donated by a sympathetic member of the Jewish elite. Then, just as he predicted, he rises from the dead and appears to a number of his followers.

The Earthly (Pre-Easter) Jesus in Individual Books: No one book of the NT contains all of the data pertinent to Jesus provided in the foregoing sketch, and it is unlikely that any one NT author would have known or believed everything about Jesus that is offered there. Each individual author presents a distinctive portrait of the earthly Jesus; thus it is customary for NT scholars to speak of "Matthew's Jesus" (or the "Matthean Jesus"), "Mark's Jesus" or (the "Markan Jesus"), etc. For example, in the Gospel of Matthew, Jesus does not ask for information from his disciples or other people. In Mark's Gospel, Jesus asks his disciples things like: "How many loaves have you?" (6:38) and "What are you arguing about?" (9:16). The stories in which these questions occur are found in Matthew's Gospel also (see 14:16–18; 17:14–16), but in Matthew the stories are told in such a way that no questions are asked (Matthew also omits the questions that Jesus asks in Mark 5:9, 30; 8:23; 9:12, 21, 33; 10:3; 14:14). This is probably because the author of Matthew's Gospel had an understanding of Jesus as a man so possessed with divine insight and knowledge that he would not need to ask such questions—but the author of Mark's Gospel clearly did not think of Jesus in those terms. Likewise, the author of Mark's Gospel often attributes emotions to Jesus ("pity" in 1:41; "anger" in 3:5; "sadness"

The healed paralytic walks away with his bed (Matt. 9:2–8); seventh-century ivory.

in 3:5; "wonder" in 6:6; "indignation" in 10:14; "love" in 10:21), but these are characteristically absent from parallel stories in both Matthew and Luke. Mark has no problem portraying the earthly Jesus as unable to do certain things (6:5), but such statements are never made about Jesus in Matthew or Luke (cf. Matt. 13:58; Luke 4:16–30). Both Matthew and Luke avoid stories about Jesus in which his healings employ techniques associated with folk magic (cf. Mark 7:31–37; 8:22–26), and Luke seems to shy away from stories that depict Jesus as behaving in a capriciously angry or violent manner (cf. 19:45–46; Mark 11:12–25). Matthew portrays Jesus as defending the eternal validity of Torah (5:17–19), while Mark presents Jesus as abolishing dietary regulations by declaring all foods to be clean (7:19; cf. Matt. 15:17). In Matthew and Luke, Jesus is miraculously born to a virgin, but there is no hint of that in the Gospel of Mark.

Jesus entering Jerusalem (the traditional Palm Sunday); enamel panel from the Pala d'Oro, twelfth century.

The Gospel of John presents a portrait of the earthly Jesus noticeably different from that of all three Synoptic Gospels. Here there are no stories of Jesus's birth or baptism, no mention of his being tempted by Satan, and no account of his transfiguration. He is not said to eat with tax collectors and sinners, nor does he offer any condemnations of the rich or words about helping the poor. He says nothing about loving one's neighbor (or one's enemy), nor does he call people to repent or instruct his disciples to deny themselves or renounce their possessions. He does not predict the downfall of Jerusalem (but cf. 2:19–22), and he almost never mentions the kingdom of God (only in 3:3–5; cf. 18:36) or his Second Coming (only once, in 21:22–23). He tells no parables and performs no exorcisms. There is no mention of him instituting the Lord's Supper (but cf. 6:53–56). Instead, John's Gospel portrays Jesus as the Word of God come to earth in human form (1:1, 18), as the divine Son sent by the Father to reveal God to humanity. His teaching takes the form of lengthy philosophical discourses, and the main topic of his speech is his own person and mission.

The Historical Jesus: It is generally recognized that the NT documents were written "from faith for faith"; i.e., these documents were written by people who believed in Jesus Christ and who wanted to promote the faith they had in him. Scholars, however, often want to use the NT documents (especially the Gospels) as historical resources for determining what can be affirmed about Jesus apart from any particular religious conviction. Such an enterprise involves patient analysis of the Gospel traditions that seeks to determine which portions of what is reported might be the earliest (and least developed) material and which might be the most free of theological bias. In addition, a historical understanding of Jesus involves comprehension of archaeological data and of nonbiblical writings that illuminate the world in which Jesus lived, the Jewish milieu within which he operated, and the culture of the early Christian movement that preserved traditions concerning him.

This historical approach to Jesus is by nature skeptical. Historians generally recognize that Jesus said and did many things (including matters that might be mentioned in the NT) that cannot be confirmed through historical science. For example, historians are not usually willing to accept allegations that people performed miracles or other supernatural feats that would defy known laws of science. In addition, they are cautious

The Last Supper (Matt. 26:20–29, Mark 14:17–25, Luke 22:14–38),
from the twelfth-century *Four Gospels* illuminated manuscript.

about accepting unsubstantiated reports from authors who are reporting
things that would have helped to promote their particular cause. Thus,
when the Gospels of Matthew and Luke both report that Jesus (who was
usually said to be from Nazareth) was actually born in Bethlehem, this is
regarded as historically suspect, because Christians would have wanted
people to believe this about Jesus—a birth in Bethlehem would help to
boost his credentials as the Jewish Messiah, who was expected to be born
there (see Matt. 2:4–6; cf. Mic. 5:2).

The outcome of historical study on Jesus varies broadly from one scholar
to another, but the most widely accepted version of a historically reasonable portrait of Jesus derives from the account of Jesus's life and ministry
as presented in the Gospel of Mark (stripped of supernatural elements),
combined with the tradition of sayings attributed to Jesus in material assigned to the Q source (i.e., material that is almost identical in Matthew
and Luke, but that is *not* found in Mark; on this, see Q; Synoptic Problem). Some scholars are much more generous than others in recognizing
the historical plausibility of material found elsewhere (e.g., the Gospel of
John), but even the portrait built from material in Mark and Q is subject
to intense scrutiny. There are three often disputed aspects regarding the
historicity of this "Mark and Q based Jesus." The first is the question of

IMAGES AND TITLES FOR JESUS CHRIST

Advocate	1 John 2:1
Alpha and Omega	Rev. 21:6
Apostle	Heb. 3:1
Author of Life	Acts 3:15
Bread of Life	John 5:35
Bridegroom	Mark 2:19–20
Brother	Matt. 25:40
Chief Cornerstone	Eph. 2:20
Chief Shepherd	1 Pet. 5:4
Christ (Messiah)	Mark 8:29
Emmanuel	Matt. 1:23
Firstborn from the dead	Col. 1:18
Firstborn of creation	Col. 1:15
Friend	John 15:13–15
The Gate	John 10:7
God	Titus 2:13
Good Shepherd	John 10:11
Guarantee	Heb. 7:22
Head of the body	Col. 1:18
Heir	Heb. 1:2
High Priest	Heb. 3:1
Holy One of God	Mark 1:24
Image of God	Col. 1:15
Judge	Acts 10:42
King	Matt. 25:40
King of Kings	Rev. 19:16
Lamb of God	John 1:29
The Life	John 14:6
Light of the World	John 9:5
Lion of Judah	Rev. 5:5
Lord	Rom. 10:9
Lord of Glory	1 Cor. 2:8
Lord of Lords	Rev. 19:16
Master	Luke 17:13
Mediator	1 Tim. 2:5
Minister	Heb. 8:2
Morning Star	Rev. 22:16
Perfecter of faith	Heb. 12:2
Our peace	Eph. 2:14
Pioneer	Heb. 12:2
Prophet	Luke 13:33
Rabbi	John 3:2
The Resurrection	John 11:25
Root of David	Rev. 5:5
Root of Jesse	Rom. 18:8–12
Sanctifier	Heb. 2:11
Savior	Luke 2:11
Savior of the World	John 4:42
Second Adam	Rom. 12:5–19
Servant	Mark 10:45
Spirit	Acts 16:7
Son of Abraham	Matt. 1:1
Son of David	Matt. 9:27
Son of God	John 20:31
Son of Man	Matt. 20:28
Teacher	John 13:13
The Truth	John 14:6
The Vine	John 15:5
The Way	John 14:6
The Word	John 1:1

From Mark Allan Powell, *Introducing the New Testament*
(courtesy, Baker Academic)

Jesus's self-understanding. Did he think he was the Messiah, Son of Man, or Son of God, or are his self-claims to such status retrojections of the early church? The second is the question of Jesus's eschatology, or vision of the future. Did he believe the end of the world was imminent or that the kingdom of God was about to come in some dramatic, climactic fashion? Had he spiritualized this notion into an ethical recognition of God's influence in the present? Do the seemingly contradictory NT texts on this matter derive from Jesus's own inconsistent or paradoxical perspective, or does one set of texts (the "present kingdom" ones or the "future kingdom" ones) derive from Jesus and the other set from his later followers? And the third aspect is the question of Jesus's political understanding and goals. What did he hope to accomplish *for Israel,* and what was his stance toward Roman imperialism?

The Exalted (Post-Easter) Jesus in the NT: All of the above is concerned with the earthly figure of Jesus, the man who lived in Galilee (and, so, is subject to historical investigation). But, as indicated at the outset of this entry, the NT also devotes a great deal of attention to Jesus as a figure who continues to be active in human lives, even though he is no longer physically present on earth. In fact, the NT generally presents "being a Christian" as a matter of being in a living relationship with Jesus Christ, a relationship that must be construed as different from the one that human beings once had with the earthly Jesus. Sometimes, Jesus is envisioned as dwelling within the individual believer (Gal. 2:19–20). More often, the metaphor is reversed, so that the believer is found in Christ (Phil. 3:9), i.e., as one part of the corporate entity that now makes up Christ's body on earth (1 Cor. 12:27). In any event, the relationship is mutual: believers abide in Jesus Christ, and Jesus Christ abides in them (John 15:5). But there is considerable variation in such imagery. The exalted Jesus can be identified as the Bridegroom of the church (Mark 2:19) or as a great high priest who serves God in a heavenly sanctuary (Heb. 4:18). Indeed, the exalted Jesus is often located in heaven (Col. 3:1), though he remains active on earth, especially through the words and deeds of those who speak and act in his name (Acts 4:30). He is sometimes identified as a spirit that continues to inspire and direct affairs on earth (Acts 16:7). He communicates with people through visions (2 Cor. 12:1) and prophecies (1 Cor. 14:29–31). His presence is sometimes experienced by way of interaction with other people, especially the disadvantaged (Matt. 25:40), vulnerable (Mark 9:37), or persecuted (Acts 9:5). The realization or manifestation of his presence is sometimes linked to baptism (Gal. 3:27) or to participation in a ritual reenactment of his Last Supper (1 Cor. 11:23–26). He answers prayers (John 14:14) and also offers prayers for his followers (Rom. 8:34). Furthermore, the NT insists that Jesus Christ is coming again: he will return to the earth in a tangible way at the end of time, coming on the clouds of heaven to preside at the final judgment (Matt. 24:30; 25:31–32). Until then he remains an object of devotion: Christians can almost be defined as people "who call on the name of the Lord Jesus Christ" (1 Cor. 1:2), as people who believe in Jesus without physical evidence of his existence (John 20:29), or as people who love Jesus Christ even though they have not seen him (1 Pet. 1:8). Indeed, they are people who regard Jesus Christ as worthy of worship and praise (Rev. 5:6–14).

The Crucifixion, by Hubert and Jan Van Eyck, early fifteenth century.

Biblical scholars seek to define the NT's presentation of the exalted or eternal figure of Jesus Christ with specificity, distinguishing between the perspectives of individual authors or books. For some writers, the exalted Jesus is virtually equated with God (Titus 2:13; 2 Pet. 1:1); others strive to maintain some distinction between the exalted Jesus and God, who exalted him and to whom he remains subordinate or obedient (Phil. 2:6–9). Some books or writers emphasize certain aspects of the exalted Jesus's identity or ministry and do not pay much attention to others. For example, the Letter to the Hebrews is largely constructed around an exposition of the exalted Jesus as high priest, an image that does not figure very prominently (if at all) in other NT books. The image of the exalted Jesus being manifest in a body of believers on earth is especially prominent in the Letters of Paul.

See also cross; healing; gospel; Gospels, the; John the Baptist; kingdom of God; messiah; miracles; parables; Q; son of God, Son of God; son of man, Son of Man; Synoptic Problem; trial of Jesus.

Bibliography

Powell, Mark Allan. *Introducing the New Testament: A Historical, Literary, and Theological Survey.* Baker Academic, 2009. Pp. 63–79.

———. *Jesus as a Figure in History.* 2nd ed. Westminster John Knox, 2010.

Tuckett, Christopher M. *Christology and the New Testament: Jesus and His Earliest Followers* Westminster John Knox, 2001. M.A.P.

Jether (jee'thuhr; also Ithra).

1 The father of Amasa (1 Kings 2:5, 32; 1 Chron. 2:17; he is called Ithra in 2 Sam. 17:25).

2 The son of Jeder; he died childless (1 Chron. 2:32).

3 One of the four sons of Ezrah (1 Chron. 4:17).

4 A member of the tribe of Asher, and the father of Jephunneh, Pispa, and Ara (1 Chron. 7:38).

See also Ithra.

Jethro (jeth'roh), Moses's father-in-law, "the priest of Midian" (Exod. 3:1). He is also called Jether (4:18 in the Hebrew Masoretic Text, which is not followed in the NRSV) and appears to be identified elsewhere as Reuel (2:18) and Hobab (Num. 10:9; Judg. 1:16; 4:11). Moses made his acquaintance when he was fleeing from Pharaoh after it became known that he had killed an Egyptian. While in Midian, Moses came to the defense of seven women when they were accosted by shepherds at a well. The father of those women (identified as Reuel) gave his daughter Zipporah to Moses in marriage (Exod. 2:15–22). Later, during the exodus, Moses's father-in-law (called Jethro) cared for Zipporah and for the sons, Gershom and Eliezer, she had borne to Moses (18:1–6); then he suggested a more effective structure for Moses's governance of the people (18:15–27).

The reason for the name confusion (Jethro, Reuel, Hobab) is unclear. Many scholars believe that the distinction between Jethro and Reuel may derive from different source traditions (Jethro may represent the E, or Elohist, source, and Reuel the J, or Yahwist, source). It is also possible that all three persons were relatives of Moses's wife Zipporah (e.g., Reuel, her grandfather; Jethro, her father; Hobab, her uncle), but that their names became confused or the terms describing their relationship to her were misunderstood at some point in the text's transmission. This theory receives partial support from Num. 10:29, which identifies Reuel as the father of Hobab.   K.G.O./M.A.P.

Jeush (jee'ush; Heb., "the LORD will come to help").

1 The son of Esau and Oholibama; he was a chief of the Edomites (Gen. 36:5; 1 Chron. 1:35).

2 The son of Bilhan; he was a descendant of Benjamin (1 Chron. 7:10).

3 A Benjaminite, son of Eshek and descendant of Saul (1 Chron. 8:39).

4 A son of Shemei, of the Gershonite family of Levites (1 Chron. 23:10–11).

5 The son of King Rehoboam and David's granddaughter Mahalath (2 Chron. 11:19).

jewels, jewelry. General references to jewelry in the Bible have both literal and figurative applications. The former often occur in constructions that indicate something else is more valuable: wisdom is "more precious than jewels" (Prov. 3:13–15); a capable wife is "far more precious than jewels" (31:10). Figurative references imply that something is valued or, occasionally, beautiful: "Lips informed by knowledge are a precious jewel" (20:15); a lover's

Gold jewelry found at Tell el-'Ajjul dates to the second millennium BCE.

"rounded thighs" are "like jewels, the work of a master hand" (Song of Sol. 7:1).

Items of jewelry specifically mentioned include the necklace (Song of Sol. 4:9), ring (Hos. 2:13), strings of jewels (Song of Sol. 1:10), and gold and pearls (Rev. 17:4; 18:16). Specific materials from which jewelry was made include silver and gold (Gen. 24:53) and (emphatically) fine gold (Job 28:17).

Certain passages are especially helpful in identifying particular types of jewelry characteristic of the biblical period. One of these is Exod. 35:22, which describes gifts brought for the equipping of the shrine. Included here are brooches, earrings, signet rings, and pendants. In addition, Num. 31:50 mentions "articles of gold, armlets and bracelets, signet rings, earrings, and pendants." Ezekiel's description of the exquisitely garbed woman (metaphoric of Jerusalem) mentions bracelets on the arms, a chain on the neck, a ring in the nose, earrings, and a crown on the head (16:11–12). Ezekiel also describes some of the stones found on royal garb (28:13): "carnelian, chrysolite, and moonstone, beryl, onyx, and jasper, sapphire, turquoise, and emerald," in addition to gold settings. Although this description gives his sense of the royal garb of the king of Tyre, the similarities to the stones used as jewels in the garb of the high priest are striking. In Exod. 28:17–21 twelve stones for Aaron's breastpiece are specified: carnelian, chrysolite, and emerald (first row); turquoise, sapphire and moonstone (second row); jacinth, agate, and amethyst (third row); and beryl, onyx, and jasper (fourth row); all set in gold filigree. The difficulties in matching the ancient names for these precious stones with accurate modern equivalents are considerable, leading some to suggest that what the translations reflect are the stones precious to the translators. There is some of the same uncertainty about additional items considered precious in Job 28:12–19: glass, coral, and crystal are mentioned along with gold, silver, onyx, sapphire, and pearls. Eschatological visions see the holy city of Jerusalem embellished with precious metals and stones (Isa. 54:12; Rev. 21:19–21) and often involve highly imaginative speculations (a city gate made from a single pearl, Rev. 21:21).

A gold bracelet inset with glass, pearls, and semiprecious stones, first century BCE.

Archaeological investigations have recovered samples of all forms of personal jewelry mentioned from a variety of periods in Near Eastern history. Furthermore, they are amply represented in the art of Egypt, Mesopotamia, Persia, Greece, and Rome, giving further evidence that they were commonly used throughout the biblical period. On the other hand, the finds pertaining to Israelite history are remarkably restrained. They include finger rings; seals and scarabs; bracelets of copper, bronze, silver, and gold; bracelets and necklaces of drilled beads in a dozen shapes; earrings of single- and multiple-pendant designs; inscribed and carved brooches; multilayered necklaces; leg bracelets and carved plaques; decorative pins of bone or ivory; amulets rigged for pendant use; and shell and carved bone pendants. But the level of craftsmanship, intricacy of designs, and volume of precious materials discovered at Israelite sites suggest modest economic means rather than extravagant wealth.

A glimpse of the jeweler's craft is given in Exod. 28:9–11, where the names of the Israelite tribal ancestors are to be inscribed on two onyx stones. The phrase "as a gem-cutter engraves signets" describes one of the most distinctive achievements of the Near East: inscribing stones as stamp or cylinder-seal signature devices. The practice of using a small stone cylinder, drilled through the long axis to allow suspension on a cord from one's arm or neck, was first developed into fine art in Mesopotamia. From the older, simpler models, the art developed some of the most exquisite miniature representations of figures, animals, trees, and action scenes (from hunting to votive offerings) ever crafted. Their small size and durability have allowed their survival in archaeological debris to a remarkable extent.   R.S.B.

Jews (jooz), a national-ethnic and, subsequently, religious designation for the people of the Judean state or province living in the homeland or in the Dispersion. In the Hebrew Bible, the term "Jews" is used only in Zech. 8:23 and in the books of Ezra, Nehemiah, Esther, and Daniel. It did not become common until after the Babylonian exile (587/6 BCE), but seems to have become the dominant nomenclature during the Second Temple period (515 BCE–70 CE). It is employed constantly throughout 1, 2, and 3 Maccabees (also note 4 Macc. 5:7, "the religion of the Jews") and 1 Esdras. The term seems to be virtually synonymous with "Hebrews" and "Israelites," designations common in the Hebrew Bible, but used more sparingly in literature of the Second Temple period (1 Maccabees seems to prefer "Israelites" as a synonym for "Jews," while 2 Maccabees prefers "Hebrews," but "Jews" is the favorite term in both of those writings). If there is any distinction in meaning between these terms, it may be a chronological one. The Jews of the Second Temple period typically referred to their ancestors as "Israelites" or "Hebrews" when reflecting upon their history prior to the exile (e.g., they don't normally speak of "Jews" accompanying Moses at the exodus or inhabiting the kingdom of Israel at the time of David). Thus, the various terms might be viewed as coterminous: either "Israelites" or "Hebrews" applied to the people from the time of the ancestors to the present, while "Jews" applied from the exile to the present (and, post-exile, "Jews" increasingly became the dominant designation).

It must be recognized that "the Jews" were a diverse group of people throughout the Second Temple period; that there was no single, unified system of beliefs or practices is evident from the development of various parties and movements (e.g., Hasmoneans, Hasideans, Pharisees, Sadducees, Essenes). Still, there were certain things that all people who called themselves Jews would have typically believed: there was only one God, and this God had chosen them to be an elect and holy people, distinct from all other peoples or nations on earth; God had made a covenant with them and given them the Torah; accordingly, they lived in ways that set them apart from other peoples of the earth—they practiced circumcision, kept the sabbath, observed dietary restrictions, and committed themselves to certain standards of morality (e.g., the Ten Commandments). Most Jews seem to have oriented their religious life around the two institutions of temple and synagogue, though sectarian groups (such as the community at Qumran) may have rejected the legitimacy of one or both of those establishments.

In the NT, the term "Jews" is used frequently, though with different connotations. The ambiguity is perhaps best illustrated in the writings of Paul, which are probably the earliest NT documents. Paul does use the term to refer to the ancestral people of God (Rom. 3:2), those who might just as well be called Hebrews or Israelites (2 Cor. 11:22). But he also uses the word with a more specific connotation, to specify people who are *not* Gentiles (1 Cor. 1:24; cf. Rom. 3:29; 1 Cor. 1:22–23; 10:32; 12:13). Thus, Paul uses the phrase "Jews and Greeks" as a way of referencing "all humanity" (Rom. 3:9; 9:24). What is most interesting, perhaps, is the question of whether Paul, as an apostle of Jesus Christ, regards himself as a Jew. In Galatians, it is clear that he does: "We ourselves are Jews" (2:15; likewise, "the other Jews" referred to in 2:13 are people who believe in Jesus Christ). But in a few places, he refers to "the Jews" as his enemies, a group to which he does not belong and which, in fact, he condemns (2 Cor. 11:24; 1 Thess. 2:14). The overall sense is that, for Paul, the meaning of the word is evolving from "non-Gentile" to "non-Christian" (i.e., a particular subset of non-Christians), and Paul is able to use it with either meaning.

Most references to Jews in the Synoptic Gospels are ones in which Jesus is identified as the "King of the Jews" (Matt. 2:2; 27:11, 29, 37; Mark 15:9, 12, 18, 26; Luke 23:3, 37, 38); the term in those instances seems to refer to an identifiable sociological entity (an ethnic/national group bound by common religious values, traditions, and beliefs). Thus Jews can be distinguished from Gentiles (Mark 7:3, which describes customs of "the Jews") or from Samaritans (John 4:9). In Matt. 28:15, however "the Jews" are a different group of people than the circle of Jesus's followers (though the latter would all have been Jews in the sociological sense); here, the word again seems to be employed in the sense of "non-Christians." This sense becomes primary in the book of Acts and in the Gospel of John. The term "Jews" is used sixty-four times in the book of Acts, and all references seem to fall into one of two categories: Jews are either potential (or actual) converts to the Christian movement (e.g., 2:5, 10; 11:19; 13:43) or they are enemies of Jesus's followers who seek to restrict that movement (e.g., 9:22–23; 12:3; 13:45, 50).

The term "Jews" is used sixty-three times in the Gospel of John, and its employment there has been the subject of much discussion. This Gospel acknowledges that Jesus and his disciples were Jews (4:9), but in the great majority of cases this Gospel uses the phrase "the Jews" to refer to a group of people that does not include Jesus or anyone associated with him. In the world of John's Gospel, people must choose whether they are going to be disciples of Jesus or Moses (9:28), and confessing faith in Jesus is grounds for expulsion from the synagogue (9:22; 12:42; 16:2). Against this background, furthermore, the portrayal of Jews in John is harsh and polemical: the Jews are people who do not believe their own scriptures (5:39–47) and whose basic allegiance to God has been sorely compromised (19:15); they have lost their status as the people of God and are children of the devil (8:39–47). Some scholars think that the English term "Jews" may not be the best translation for Greek *ioudaioi* in these Johannine passages. They claim that the author of John's Gospel did not mean to condemn an entire race, nation, or religion (all Jewish people everywhere), but was launching a specific attack on a rival religious movement (first-century Jewish synagogue religion). Thus, some scholars now translate *ioudaioi* in John as "Judeans" or some other term intended to indicate that the reference was to a specific group of people who should not be simply equated with people to whom the English word "Jews" would usually refer.

Finally, the book of Revelation offers two references to "those who say that they are Jews when they are not" (2:9; 3:9). The meaning here is unclear, but it probably reflects a perspective of Christians who have come to believe that they are the true chosen people of God and who want to deny that status to those to whom the term "Jews" was traditionally applied.   M.A.P.

Jezebel (jez'uh-bel; Heb., "where is the prince?"). An influential, though notorious, queen of Israel. Jezebel was a Phoenician princess (daughter of Ethbaal, king of Sidon), who married King Ahab of Israel. She is regarded negatively in the Bible for inciting Ahab and others to sin (1 Kings 16:31; 21:25). A devotee of the Phoenician god Baal and a zealous missionary, Jezebel supported some 850 prophets of Baal and Asherah (18:19) and sought to suppress worship of the Lord (18:4, 13). Thus she became the formidable adversary of the prophet Elijah, able to instill fear even in him (19:1–3). Her influence in Israel was strong, not only during the reign of Ahab, but also during the reigns of her two sons Ahaziah and Jehoram. Furthermore, her influence extended to the southern kingdom, Judah, where her daughter Athaliah became queen (2 Kings 8:18). The story in 1 Kings 21 of the appropriation of Naboth's vineyard illustrates both Jezebel's disregard for Israelite custom and her ruthless use of royal power.

Elijah's prophecy, "The dogs shall eat Jezebel within the bounds of Jezreel" (1 Kings 21:23), was fulfilled when Jehu seized power (2 Kings 9–10). Jezebel met her death with characteristic audacity: she painted her eyes, adorned her head, and greeted Jehu from her window with a caustic insult (9:30–31). Jezebel was pushed out the window at Jehu's command and trampled by horses so that, when Jehu sent people to bury her (noting that she was, after all, a king's daughter), only her skull, feet, and palms remained. In the NT, her name is used symbolically to refer to someone who is beguiling the congregation at Thyatira to "practice fornication and eat food sacrificed to idols" (Rev. 2:20). *See also* Ahab; Asherah; Baal; Elijah; Jehu.   J.C.E.

Jezreel (jez'ree-uhl; Heb., "God sows").

1 A town on the southern border of Issachar, commanding the Valley of Jezreel, identified with modern Zer'in at the foot of Mount Gilboa. Here the Israelites encamped before battling the Philistines (1 Sam. 29). It was also one of the towns over which Ishbaal, son of Saul, briefly reigned (2 Sam. 2:9). Ahab had a royal residence here (1 Kings 18:45, 46), and Naboth's vineyard, which Jezebel plotted to obtain, was beside the palace (1 Kings 21). At Jezreel, Jehu murdered Jezebel (2 Kings 9:30–37) and the rest of the house of Ahab, putting an end to the Omride dynasty (10:1–11). *See also* Gilboa.

2 The Valley of Jezreel, the eastern section of the broad valley separating Galilee from Samaria. From the pass between the Hill of Moreh and Mount Gilboa, where the town of Jezreel

The fertile valley of Jezreel. A modern highway marks the route of the Via Maris, which ran through the Levant, connecting Egypt and Syria.

was located, the valley descends eastward along the Jalud River to the Jordan, with Beth-shan commanding its eastern entrance. The broader plain to the west, known as Esdraelon (Jth. 1:8; 3:9; 4:6; 7:3), is sometimes counted as a part of the Valley of Jezreel, as is the plain of Megiddo. A fertile growing area, the Valley of Jezreel provided one of the few ways of access to the Jordan Valley and the east. From Beth-shan and the Jordan a road passed through the Yarmuk Valley to Damascus to the north and east. The "way of the sea" referred to in Isa. 9:1 also passed through the Valley of Jezreel, connecting Egypt with the north by way of the Philistine coast. Traders and armies from Egypt as well as invaders from the east used this road from earliest times. The Canaanites controlled the valley with chariots of iron when the Israelites entered the land (Josh. 17:16), and here Gideon met the Midianites and Amalekites in battle (Judg. 6:33–7:23). According to Hos. 1:5, this valley would be the site of a battle that would bring an end to the kingdom of Israel, as punishment for Jehu's purge of the Omride dynasty (see 1). Notably, Megiddo was also located in the Jezreel Valley, guarding the Carmel pass. This was a strategic site, controlled by the Canaanites until the time of David (1:27). Nevertheless, Taanach and the Kishon River, on the plain of Megiddo in the Jezreel Valley, was the site of Deborah's victory over Sisera (4:7; 5:19). *See also* Beth-shan; Megiddo.

3 A town of Judah, location unknown, but probably southwest of Hebron in the vicinity of Ziph and Juttah (Josh. 15:56). Ahinoam, one of David's wives, was from there.

4 The son of Etam, a descendant of Judah (1 Chron. 4:3).

5 The first son of Hosea (cf. Hos. 1:4), named symbolically for the acts that were to befall Israel because of the blood shed by Jehu at Jezreel (see **1**).   N.L.L.

Joab (joh'ab).

1 A Kenizzite, the son of Seraiah, and ancestor of a group of craftsmen called Geharashim (1 Chron. 4:14).

2 The second and most prominent of the three sons of David's sister Zeruiah (1 Chron. 2:16). Joab was the commander of David's army during much of his reign (2 Sam. 8:16; 20:23; 1 Chron. 18:15). He seems to have already held this position at the time of the struggle for power between David and Saul's son Ishbaal (cf. 2 Sam. 2:13), but according to 1 Chron. 11:6 he was awarded his command in consequence of his valor and leadership during David's conquest of Jerusalem. He led the army to its first victory in the war against the Ammonite-Aramean coalition (2 Sam. 10:7–14), and he was in charge of the subsequent siege of Rabbath-ammon, the Ammonite capital (11:1, 26–31). He conducted the census described in 2 Sam. 24. Everywhere he is presented as a skilled and courageous soldier and as a shrewd politician, fiercely loyal to his king and people. At the same time, however, he is shown to be unscrupulous, calculating, and occasionally brutal. He was complicit with David in the plot to kill Uriah the Hittite, so that David might have Uriah's wife, Bathsheba (1 Sam. 11:14–17). In that instance, he might be regarded as merely following the king's orders, but in other instances his determination to do whatever is in the king's (or his own) interest surpasses David's own commitments to do whatever seems politically advantageous (cf. 2 Sam. 3:39, where David says that Joab and his brothers are "too violent" for his tastes; he thinks that they act "wickedly," but also disparages himself as a weak ruler by comparison). On occasions when David's compassion or sentimentality seemed to threaten the stability of his throne, Joab's cold pragmatism proved beneficial. He arranged a reconciliation between David and Absalom after the murder of Amnon (2 Sam. 14:1–24), and he intervened when David's extreme grief at the death of Absalom provoked a crisis in the army (19:1–8). More often, though, he is portrayed as a violent, disruptive force. He assassinated Abner, the strongman of Ishbaal's rump government in Gilead (3:27) who had slain Asahel, Joab's youngest brother (2:18–23), and he ordered the execution of Absalom during the civil war (18:9–15). Both of these killings were without David's knowledge, and the second was against his explicit orders (18:5; cf. 18:12). Joab also slew Amasa (20:8), whom Absalom had set over the army in place of Joab during his revolt (17:25). In the contest over the succession to David's throne Joab sided with Adonijah against Solomon (1 Kings 1:7), a mistake that cost him his life. Solomon charged him with the deaths of Abner and Amasa, and he was executed by Benaiah (2:38–44), who became commander of the army under Solomon (2:35). *See also* Abner; Absalom; Adonijah; Amasa; David.

3 The ancestor of a group of Israelites from the Pahath-moab group listed in the census of the first return from exile (late sixth century BCE) in the time of Zerubbabel (Ezra 2:6; 8:9; Neh. 7:11).

P.K.M.

Joah (joh'uh; Heb., "the LORD is a brother").

1 The son of Asaph; he was the record keeper of King Hezekiah who, with Eliakim the palace steward and Shebnah the scribe, met with the envoy of the Assyrian ruler Sennacherib, who was demanding the surrender of Jerusalem (2 Kings 18:17–37; Isa. 36).

2 A Levite belonging to the Gershonite family group (1 Chron. 6:21).

3 The son of Obed-edom, of the Korahite line of gatekeepers (1 Chron. 26:4).

4 The son of Zimmnah; he was a Levite of the Gershonite group who, with his son Eden, participated in the cleansing of the temple during Hezekiah's reforms (2 Chron. 29:12).

5 The son of Joahaz; he was sent by King Josiah to effect repairs on the temple (2 Chron. 34:8).

D.R.B.

Joanan (joh-an'uhn), one of the ancestors of Jesus in Luke 3:27.

Joanna (joh-an'uh), according to Luke 8:3, the wife of Chuza, Herod Antipas's steward, and one of the women who accompanied Jesus and gave assistance ("out of their resources") to Jesus and the twelve. In Luke 24:10, she is one of the women (with Mary Magdalene, Mary the mother of James, and others) who, having gone to anoint Jesus's body, find the tomb empty. *See also* Chuza; Mary; Susanna.

P.L.S.

Joash (joh'ash; also Jehoash).

1 The father of Gideon (Judg. 6:11, 29–31). He was a member of the Azierite group from the tribe of Manasseh. He was the owner of the "oak at Ophrah," which appears to have been associated with worship of Baal and Asherah. Gideon pulled down an altar of Baal at this site and cut down a sacred pole, prompting the local populace to demand his execution. Joash refused to bring his son out for them, maintaining, "If (Baal) is a god, let him contend for himself, because his altar has been pulled down" (Judg. 6:31).

2 The youngest son of Ahaziah and king of Judah ca. 837–800 BCE. After Ahaziah's death, his mother, Athaliah, had all his children killed. However, Joash, an infant, was saved by Jehosheba, Ahaziah's sister and the wife of the chief priest Jehoiada (2 Kings 11:2), who hid Joash in the temple for six years (v. 3; 2 Chron. 22:11–12). In the seventh year, Jehoiada conspired against Athaliah, crowned and anointed Joash, and had Athaliah slain (2 Chron. 23:1–15). Next Jehoiada renewed the covenant of God with the king and the people, which resulted in the destruction of the Tyrian Baal cult in Judah (2 Kings 11:17–18) as well as the repair of the temple (12:7–17). Afterward, Hazael, king of Aram, attacked Israel, taking Gath, and threatened Jerusalem. Joash was forced to buy him off with the gold of the temple and palace and other gifts (11:19).

The later narrative of 2 Chron. 24:15–27 relates that after Jehoiada's death, Judah lapsed into paganism, provoking a prophecy by Jehoiada's son Zechariah, who was killed at the command of Joash. Another Aramean campaign despoiled Judah, wounding Joash in the battle. Joash was murdered by two of his servants. He was succeeded on the throne by his son Amaziah.

3 The son of Jehoahaz and king of Israel ca. 802–786 BCE. During his reign, Assyria, under Adad-nirari III, resumed its domination of Aram by attacking Damascus and defeating its armies. This allowed Israel to regain its captured cities (2 Kings 13:25). These events are reflected in the prophecy to Joash of the dying Elisha (13:14–19). An Assyrian inscription names Joash as one of those paying tribute to Adad-nirari and includes Israel as one of the countries subdued in the campaign. The later narrative of 2 Chron. 25:6–13 relates that Joash's contemporary, Amaziah, king of Judah, hired one hundred thousand soldiers of Israel for one hundred talents of silver to help him against Edom. However, after a prophecy condemning this hiring, Amaziah sent them home before the battle was joined. On the way back, the Israelites raided Judean cities. These raids may have been the reason for Amaziah's challenging Joash to battle, which ended disastrously for Judah—Amaziah was captured, although not killed, and "the wall of Jerusalem for four hundred cubits from the Ephraim Gate to the Corner Gate" was dismantled, and the temple and palace treasures were looted (2 Kings 14:8–14).

4 The son of Ahab, king of Israel, in whose co-custody the prophet Micaiah's imprisonment was entrusted (1 Kings 22:26).

5 A son of Shelah, the son of Judah (1 Chron. 4:21–22).

6 The brother of Ahiezer and son of Shemah or Gibeah; one of David's warriors, ambidextrous with bow or sling. They were among the relatives of Saul who came to David at Ziklag (1 Chron. 12:1–3). J.U.

Job (johb), **book of,** the third book of the Writings section, or Ketuvim, of the Tanakh (Jewish Bible), where it is placed after Proverbs; it is the first poetic book of the Christian OT, found after Esther and before Psalms. The book is anonymous. It is named after the main character of the book, a wealthy and devout family man. Curiously, he hails from the land of Uz, an Edomite territory, so he was not Israelite or Jewish. Outside the book itself Job was cited twice by the prophet Ezekiel as a legendary righteous person whose righteousness would not have been sufficient to deliver Judah from destruction (14:14, 20). Dating the book is speculative, and claims have been made ranging from the ancestral period, because Job is depicted in ways similar to Israel's ancestors, to the Babylonian exile or later, because Job's story resonates with the plight of the Jews.

Contents: The book of Job tells its story in a linear way, yet it appears to be a composite of different pieces. Between a prose prologue and a prose epilogue, a lengthy poetic section consists of a series of dialogues between Job and his friends in which they attempt to find an explanation for what happened to him.

The prose portion of the book is essentially a folktale about righteous Job who has considerable wealth and a large family. He is described as a morally upstanding individual, a man who "feared God and turned away from evil" (1:1). When the divine council meets in heaven, God expresses pride in Job, but is challenged by one called the adversary, or in Hebrew *hassatan* ("the satan"). This is not the proper name of an individual being, but a designation for a role played by one member of the council whose function was to challenge God. So, in the story, God asks the satan, "From where have you come?" and the satan answers, "From going here and there on the earth, and from walking up and down on it." God says to the satan, "Have you considered my servant Job? There is none like him on the earth, a blameless and upright man, one who fears God (Elohim) and turns away from evil?" Then the satan answers God, "Does Job fear God for nothing?" (1:7–9).

The satan plays the "devil's advocate" by giving God a skeptical explanation of Job's goodness. He implies that Job is calculating, manipulative, and self-serving, and his apparent devotion to God is designed merely to get the best treatment he can manage. Thus, the satan challenges God to take everything away from Job in order to see what his reaction will be. God gives the satan permission first to remove all of Job's wealth and family and then his physical health. Job becomes a suffering social outcast. His wife urges him to "Curse God and die!" (2:9), but Job persists in believing that "the LORD gave, and the LORD has taken away; blessed be the name of the LORD!" (1:21; cf. 2:10).

After this prologue, the poetic section of the book begins as Job's three friends Eliphaz, Bildad,

"The Torment of Job" (*lying on his back in the center*) as imagined by the twelfth-century artists of Chartres Cathedral.

and Zophar appear at his side to give him counsel. In conversation with Job, they attempt to make sense of his plight, but neither Job nor his friends resolve the conundrum of Job's suffering. The friends try various moral strategies. Eliphaz affirms the principle of retribution and claims that no one is ever completely sinless. Likewise, Bildad affirms that God never gets things wrong, and people always get what they deserve; because Job is not yet dead, he must not be too bad a sinner. Zophar claims that Job is not as upright as he seems and must have done something wrong, even if he will not admit to it. Finally, in chap. 32, Elihu, a fourth comforter-friend, appears, but he does not seem to further the moral argument. And then God comes to Job in a terrifying theophany and commands Job's attention. Job is so overcome that he essentially gives up all moral claims and submits himself to the power of the divine. God never really answers Job's questions directly. Instead, he questions Job in a severely intimidating way, seemingly belittling Job because he has presumed to question divine wisdom.

Finally, the book returns to the prose folktale. In what is essentially an epilogue to the story, God vindicates Job by reprimanding his friends and then provides Job with a new family and even greater wealth than he had possessed before. The names of Job's new daughters are provided (though the names of his sons are not). They are Jemimah, Keziah, and Keren-happuch; they are the most beautiful women in the land and Job gives them an inheritance along with their brothers.

Background: The book of Job is typically classified as wisdom literature, a category of ancient Near Eastern texts that address issues such as morality in society, social and personal responsibility, and the role of religion in life. Wisdom literature employs an intellectual orientation that applies reasoning and analysis to human experience in order to grasp the meaning of life. The books of the Hebrew Bible that fall into this category of wisdom literature, in addition to Job, are Proverbs and Ecclesiastes; from the Christian OT, the apocryphal/deuterocanonical books Sirach and the Wisdom of Solomon can be added. A wisdom frame of mind is discernible also in the Mesopotamian texts "A Man and his God," "I Will Praise the Lord of Wisdom," and "The Babylonian Theodicy." The last has the closest affinity to the book of Job. As wisdom literature, the book of Job probes the standard assertion that deity promotes the cause of righteousness by rewarding proper behavior and punishing wrong. The biblical book of Proverbs serves to explain what constitutes righteousness in a person, but the book of Job implicitly takes issue with the assumed relationship between right behavior and blessing. Job suffers in spite of his righteousness, and arguably even because of it. All the while, as he observes, wicked people have been known to live into old age, rich and satisfied: "They spend their days in prosperity, and in peace they go down to Sheol" (21:13). Understandably this calls into question the presump-

tive principle of retributive justice. The cognitive dissonance of moral principle and actual experience drives the book to explore the role of deity in upholding moral order in the world, an issue usually labeled "theodicy" in moral discourse, but the book's conclusions in this regard are ambiguous.

Insofar as Job and his friends argue over the cause of his suffering, the book may be classed as a "symposium," a genre in the classical world that highlighted debate. It also has an affinity with the classical form of the philosophical diatribe, because of the intensity with which the argument is engaged. The dialogic style of argument also characterizes Mesopotamian wisdom literature, and this may have provided a model.

Themes: The obvious theme of the book is the apparent undeserved suffering of the righteous. Scholars debate exactly what point or points the book wishes to make regarding this issue. Suggestions include: (1) human suffering does not necessarily happen with cause or reason, even though it is natural for people to look for such a cause or reason; (2) the role of deity in relation to suffering is not necessarily discernible, even though people presume deity must play a role; and (3) extreme suffering leads people to question the integrity of the victim or the deity, but such judgments are questionable at best and likely to distort or oversimplify the realities of life. All readers know by the end of the book is that Job did nothing wrong to instigate suffering as punishment, the satan figure of the divine council provoked God into allowing Job's suffering, and God vindicated Job in the end. Still, God does not explain to Job the reason for his tragedy.

Interpretive Issues: The relationship of the poetic core to the prose folktale is often discussed. The dialogues offered in the poetic portion of the book are different from the folktale in spirit as well as in style. Job is said to be without fault in the folktale, but he is upbraided and ridiculed by God in the poetic portion. The deity is referred to as "the LORD" in the folktale and in the theophany at the conclusion of the poetic section, but is called El, Eloah, or Shaddai throughout most of the poetic dialogues (except for 28:28). The figure of the satan, who is so prominent in the first two chapters, is never mentioned in the dialogues or in the epilogue; likewise, Job's wife is prominent in the prologue of the book, but does not come up again in the dialogues or in the epilogue. All these idiosyncrasies lead scholars to believe that the book has had a complicated editorial history; the poetic dialogues and the prosaic folktale, at least, seem to have come from different sources and to have been joined together in a manner that does not quite work.

The difficulties of arriving at a satisfying understanding of the book have given rise to a variety of alternate proposals. Whedbee interprets the book through the lenses of comedy and irony. Westermann reads it as if it were a biblical lament. Habel reads it as an allegory of Israelites in the postexilic period; like Job, they were a people who experienced disorienting suffering and alienation from their God.

Influences: Job gained the reputation of being the stereotype of patience in suffering, as attested in the NT book of James, "You have heard of the endurance of Job" (5:11), even though he seems so impatient in the dialogues. Modern theatrical appropriations of the book include *J.B.: A Play in Verse* by Archibald MacLeish (1958) and *God's Favorite* by Neil Simon (1975).

Bibliography

Bandstra, Barry L. *Reading the Old Testament: Introduction to the Hebrew Bible.* 4th ed. Wadsworth, 2009.

Habel, Norman C. *The Book of Job: A Commentary.* Westminster, 1985.

Good, Edwin M. *In Turns of Tempest: A Rereading of Job, with a Translation.* Stanford University Press, 1990.

Pope, Marvin H. *Job.* Doubleday, 1965.

Westermann, Claus. *The Structure of the Book of Job.* Westminster, 1977.

Whedbee, J. William *The Bible and the Comic Vision.* Cambridge University Press, 1998.

Zuckerman, Bruce. *Job the Silent: A Study in Historical Counterpoint.* Oxford University Press, 1991.   B.B.

Jobab (joh´bab).

1 A "son" of Joktan, descendant of Shem, and representative of an Arabian tribe (Gen. 10:29; 1 Chron. 1:23).

2 An Edomite king (Gen. 36:33–34; 1 Chron. 1:44–45).

3 A king allied with Jabin of Canaanite Hazor who fought against Joshua (Josh. 11:1).

4 The son of Shaharim, a Benjaminite (1 Chron. 8:9).

5 The son of Elpaal, a Benjaminite (1 Chron. 8:18).

Jochebed (jok´uh-bed), the mother of Moses, Aaron, and Miriam. She was the daughter of Levi, born to him in Egypt, and she was married to Amram, her nephew (Exod. 6:20; Num. 26:59). According to the story in Exod. 2:1–10, the mother of Moses (here unnamed) hid her baby for three months after he was born, because Pharaoh had ordered the killing of Hebrew children. Then, when she could hide him no longer, she put the baby Moses in a papyrus basket plastered with bitumen and pitch and placed it among the reeds on the bank of the river. Her sister kept watch until he was found by the daughter of Pharaoh, who took pity on him. Then the sister arranged for Moses's mother to be brought to Pharaoh's daughter to nurse the child. Thus, Moses was raised by Pharaoh's daughter with his mother as his nurse.

Joda (joh´duh), an ancestor of Jesus (Luke 3:26).

Joel (joh´uhl; Heb., "the LORD is God"), the inverse form of the name Elijah ("God is the LORD").

1 One of the sons of Samuel who became a judge, but perverted justice (1 Sam. 8:2).

2 A Simeonite whose name appears in early genealogical records (1 Chron. 4:35).

3 A member of the tribe of Reuben, and the father of Shemaiah (1 Chron. 5:8).

4 The father of Shema (1 Chron. 5:12); he may be the same person mentioned in 3.

5 The father of Heman, a Kohathite singer (1 Chron. 6:33).

6 The son of Azariah and the father of Elkanah (1 Chron. 6:36).

7 One of the five sons of Izrahiah, all of whom were leaders (1 Chron. 7:3). He may be the same person as 6.

8 The brother of Nathan and one of David's warriors (1 Chron. 11:38).

9 The chief of 130 Levites, descendants of Gershom; he was included among the Levites appointed by David to accompany the ark to Jerusalem (1 Chron. 15:7, 11).

10 The father of one of the Levites, Heman, appointed by David to sing as the ark was brought to Jerusalem (1 Chron. 15:17). He may be the same as 5.

11 One of the three sons of the Levite Ladan (1 Chron. 23:8).

12 One of the two sons of Jehieli who were in charge of the temple treasuries (1 Chron. 26:22).

13 The son of Pedaiah; he was one of the officers from the half-tribe of Manasseh in David's kingdom (1 Chron. 27:20).

14 A Levite in the reign of King Hezekiah (ca. 715–687/6 BCE); he helped in the resanctification of the temple (2 Chron. 29:12).

15 One of seven sons of Nebo; he divorced his foreign wife in response to Ezra's postexilic proclamation (Ezra 10:43).

16 A Benjaminite, the son of Zichri, who was a leader among those who lived in Jerusalem at the time of its restoration under Nehemiah (sixth century BCE; Neh. 11:9).

17 The son of Pethuel and the prophet of the book of Joel (Joel 1:1; cf. Acts 2:16). *See also* Joel, book of.   M.Z.B.

Joel, book of, the second part of the Book of the Twelve in the Prophets section, or Nevi'im, in the Tanakh (Jewish Bible). It is the second book of the Minor Prophets in the OT. There is slightly different versification between the Hebrew and English versions of Joel. What is 2:28–32 in the English version is 3:1–5 in the Hebrew text. Chap. 3 in the English version corresponds to chap. 4 in the Hebrew version.

Contents: The book of Joel is generally divided into two sections: 1:1–2:27 and 2:28–3:21. The first part centers around a plague of locusts and its meaning for the people of Judah and for their relationship with God. It begins with a short superscription (1:1) followed by a description of a locust plague that has ravaged the countryside. The locusts are compared to an invading army (though some scholars argue it is an actual army that is being compared to locusts). They have left the land desolate. The prophet laments the situation, yet points to it as a foreshadowing of greater judgment upon Judah, if the people do not repent of their sins. Joel declares that the "day of the LORD" is coming; the divine intervention that was sought by the people of Judah will not be what they had hoped for. It will be a dark day of judgment. The land is made truly desolate, while an army ravages the land. The army comes with God at its head. Yet God promises to deliver all those who repent of their sins. The first section ends with a promise that God will come and have pity on the people, delivering, restoring, and blessing them. Where their land was once desolate and barren, the people will now eat and be satisfied.

The second section of the book of Joel has often been characterized as having apocalyptic themes (particularly 2:30–31). The section begins with a promise that God will pour out the divine spirit on "all flesh" (2:28–32). Scholars disagree on whether "all flesh" refers to all Israel or to all people, including those outside of Israel. This prophetic anointing will be universal in scope, not discriminate based upon age or gender. From there, blessings and restoration are promised for Judah and Jerusalem. Judgment is pronounced upon the nations, such as Tyre, Sidon, and Philistia. The book ends with the promise that God will care for and protect Judah, conquering its enemies.

Background: Very little is known about the prophet Joel except that his father's name was

Pethuel (1:1) and he was a prophet of the southern kingdom. Joel has sometimes been called a "cult prophet," because of his positive portrayal of the priesthood and temple. Some scholars have even suggested that Joel was a priest himself. Peterson argues for a priestly Joel, because the prophet calls the people not to ethical reform, but to proper rituals of lamentation and repentance (1:14; 2:16). Others have questioned whether there was a historical prophet Joel. They cite that Joel's name ("the LORD is God") reflects the theme within the book that God is in control of all situations.

There have been many difficulties in dating the composition of Joel. A preexilic date is argued on the basis of its position between Hosea and Amos along with the lack of any mention of the fall of Jerusalem. Those who argue for a postexilic date counter that Joel was placed between Hosea and Amos for thematic reasons: there are similarities between Joel 3:16 and Amos 1:2 and between Joel 3:18 and Amos 9:13; the "day of the LORD" is also a key theme in both books. Those who hold to a postexilic date also point out that there are no references to a king, to the Assyrians, or to the Babylonians in the text, indicating that these phenomena were not relevant to the current political scene. (There is, however, reference to trade with Greece, which drastically increased during the postexilic period). McKenzie and Kaltner place the first section of Joel in the 600s BCE and the second section in the 400s BCE. Peterson argues that the references to "Zion" (2:1) and the temple (1:13; 2:17) place Joel at a time when the temple stood in Jerusalem, most likely the second temple (after 515 BCE) because of the talk of the restoration of Judah's fortunes. Yilpet, however, argues for an earlier date, suggesting that the book could have been written when Joash was still a child during the ninth century BCE (explaining the lack of reference to a king). The locust plague, which creates the setting for the book, cannot be dated and, so, is of no help in this regard.

Themes: The major theme of the book of Joel is the "day of the LORD." This is an eschatological concept that was most likely borrowed from

Amos. The perception of the people was that when God came to intervene, it would be a time for rejoicing, because all of Israel's enemies would be destroyed. The book of Joel portrays it as a day when judgment will also be brought upon Judah for their sins. The nations will be punished for their sins, but so will Judah.

Interpretive Issues: Questions arise concerning the unity of the book of Joel. The differences between the first and second parts of Joel on the nature of the "day of the LORD" have caused many scholars to believe that the second section was added at a later date and is not original to Joel. However, a strong minority of scholars do argue for the unity of the two sections. McKenzie and Kaltner argue that both 1:1–2:27 and 2:28–3:21 are postexilic, but that 2:28–3:21 dates much later than 1:1–2:27. Childs argues for a unity of the book of Joel, but thinks that the unity is a result of redaction, not necessarily origin. How one treats the unity of the book affects interpretation. Those scholars who hold that the book is a single unit often interpret the "day of the LORD" as a judgment upon the nations, but salvation for Israel. On the contrary, those who view Joel as two units see the first as portraying the "day of the LORD" as judgment upon Judah and the second unit portraying the "day of the LORD" as salvation for Judah.

There has been some disagreement among scholars over the nature of the "locusts" in Joel. Simundson believes the locust swarm to be a historical event that triggered Joel's prophesy. Gottwald claims that the locusts were meant to represent invading armies, which ravaged Israel every time they moved through.

Influences: The book of Joel was influential on much of the apocalyptic literature found in the Hebrew Bible. Yet it has also been particularly influential within the Christian tradition. Joel 2:28–32 is quoted in Acts 2 during Pentecost. In that account, the "spirit" that was promised by God in Joel is interpreted as the Holy Spirit, which comes upon the disciples in the upper room.

Bibliography

Bandstra, Barry L. *Reading the Old Testament: Introduction to the Hebrew Bible.* 4th ed. Wadsworth, 2009.

Childs, Brevard S. *Introduction to the Old Testament as Scripture.* Fortress, 1979.

Gottwald, Norman K. *The Hebrew Bible: A Socio-Literary Introduction.* Fortress, 1985.

McKenzie, Steven L., and John Kaltner. *The Old Testament: Its Background, Growth, and Content.* Abingdon, 2007.

Peterson, David L. *The Prophetic Literature: An Introduction.* Westminster John Knox, 2002.

Simundson, Daniel J. *Hosea, Joel, Amos, Obadiah, Jonah, Micah.* Abingdon, 2005.

Sweeney, Marvin A. *The Twelve Prophets.* Vol. 1, *Hosea, Joel, Amos, Obadiah, Jonah.* Liturgical, 2000.

Wolff, Hans Walter. *Joel and Amos.* Fortress, 1977.

Yilpet, Yoilah. "Joel." In *Africa Bible Commentary.* Zondervan, 2006. Pp. 1027–32.   B.B.

Johanan (joh-hay′nuhn; Heb., "the LORD shows favor"; cf. John).

1 The eldest son of Josiah (1 Chron. 3:15).

2 A descendant of the Davidic family, the son of Elioenai (1 Chron. 3:24).

3 A member of the priestly line of Zadok (1 Chron. 6:9–10).

4 One of David's warriors (1 Chron. 12:4), possibly the same as a Gadite in 12:12.

5 Father of an Ephraimite chief, Azariah, in the time of King Ahaz (2 Chron. 28:12).

6 The son of Kareah (2 Kings 25:23; Jer. 40:8–43:5) and a leader in Judah after the destruction of Jerusalem (587 BCE) under Gedaliah, who refused him permission to kill Ishmael, who subsequently assassinated Gedaliah. He was a leader in rescuing the captives taken by Ishmael and in asking for divine guidance from Jeremiah. But Jeremiah's message to stay in Judah was repudiated by Johanan and his associates, and they took refuge in Egypt. *See also* Gedaliah.

7 The son of Hakkatan of the Azgad family who brought 110 men to Ezra's company (Ezra 8:12).

8 The son (possibly grandson) of Eliashib, priest or high priest contemporary with Nehemiah (Neh. 12:22–23; cf. Jonathan in 12:11).   P.R.A.

Johannine (joh-han′in) **Letters.** *See* John, Letters of.

Johannine literature, a name given by modern scholars to the four or sometimes five books of the NT attributed to an author named John. Only one of these books, Revelation, actually carries the name of its author in the text (1:4), and, perhaps ironically, this is the book that is not always included among what scholars mean by "Johannine literature." The other four books are the Gospel of John and the three Letters of John (1 John, 2 John, 3 John). Although the name "John" is not explicitly attached to any of them (in the texts of the books themselves), they were all attributed to John the apostle in early post-NT tradition. The book of Revelation was sometimes attributed to John the apostle as well, but even in the early church the "John" to whom it is attributed was often thought to be a different person. Authorship of all these writings is disputed among modern scholars, but most interpreters do believe that the Gospel of John and the three letters all come from the same community (usually called the "Johannine community," regardless of whether the scholar thinks that anyone named John had anything to do with them). Quite a few scholars allow that John the apostle may have been the founder—or at least a prominent member—of that community and that he contributed to the traditions and influenced the perspective that informs the "Johannine literature." Most modern scholars think the connection of Revelation to that body of literature is more tenuous, though Revelation and the other four Jo-

REVELATION AND OTHER JOHANNINE WRITINGS:
SIMILARITIES AND DIFFERENCES

Similarities	Differences
Jesus is "the Word" (John 1:1, 14; 1 John 1:1; Rev. 19:13).	Vastly different literary styles: Revelation is much less refined with regard to vocabulary, grammar, and syntax.
Jesus is the "lamb of God" (John 1:29; Rev. 5:6–14).	Theme discrepancies: key themes from the Gospel—"new birth," "eternal life," "knowing the truth," "abiding in Christ," and even "believing"—are completely absent in Revelation.
Zech. 2:10 applied to Jesus (John 19:10; Rev. 1:7).	
Jesus is the "faithful witness" (John 5:32; 8:14; 1 John 5:9; Rev. 1:5; 3:14; 19:11).	
"I am" sayings (John 6:35, 51; 8:12; 9:5; 10:7, 9, 11, 14; 11:25; 14:6; 15:1, 5; Rev. 1:8, 17; 21:6; 22:13, 16).	Different ways of using scripture: the Gospel often quotes from the Jewish scriptures; Revelation is rich in biblical imagery, but never cites scripture as such.
Jesus present with God from the beginning (John 1:1–2; 1 John 1:1; Rev. 3:14).	Very different overall theological emphases: the Gospel of John shows little interest in such future events as the final judgment or Second Coming of Christ.
Jesus refers to God as "my God" (John 20:17; Rev. 3:2, 12) and "my Father" (John 5:17, 43; 14:2; Rev. 2:28; 3:5, 21).	
Jesus gives living water (John 4:14; 7:37–39; Rev. 7:17; 21:6; 22:1).	
Jesus is the lamp or light (John 8:12; 1 John 2:8; Rev. 21:23–24).	
Jewish opponents are false Jews who serve Satan (John 8:39–47; Rev. 2:9; 3:9).	

From Mark Allan Powell, *Introducing the New Testament* (courtesy, Baker Academic)

hannine books have a number of features in common. Revelation is said to be written from Patmos, while church tradition associates the Johannine community with nearby Ephesus. Thus, it is possible that the author of Revelation had been influenced by the Johannine milieu, even if he is not to be equated with the author of the Gospel or Letters of John.   M.A.P.

John (jahn).

1 The father of Mattathias and grandfather of Judas Maccabeus (1 Macc. 2:1).

2 The oldest son of Mattathias and brother of Judas Maccabeus (1 Macc. 2:2; 9:35–42).

3 John the Baptist (Matt. 3:1). *See* John the Baptist.

4 John the son of Zebedee, also called John the apostle (Mark 10:35). *See* John the apostle.

5 John Mark (Acts 16:37). *See* Mark.

6 The father of Peter (John 1:42; 21:15–17). *See also* Peter.

7 A member of the high-priestly family (Acts 4:6).

8 The author of Revelation (Rev. 1:1, 4, 9; 22:8). *See* Revelation, book of.

John, Gospel According to, the fourth Gospel in the NT.

Contents: The Gospel of John opens with a poetic prologue describing Jesus as the Word of God made flesh (1:1–18). It continues with an account of how John the Baptist testified to Jesus as the "Lamb of God" (1:19–34) and how his first disciples proclaimed him to be the Messiah, Son of God, and King of Israel (1:35–51). Jesus changes water into wine at a wedding in Cana (2:1–12) and launches an assault on the temple in Jerusalem (2:13–25). He speaks with a Pharisee named Nicodemus about spiritual matters (3:1–21), and John the Baptist offers further testimony to him (3:22–36). Then Jesus speaks with a Samaritan woman at a well, and many Samaritans come to believe he is the "Savior of the world." (4:1–42). A royal official asks Jesus to come to Capernaum to heal his son, but Jesus performs the healing from a distance simply by speaking the word (4:43–54). On a sabbath day, Jesus heals a lame man by the pool of Bethzatha, which leads to a hostile confrontation with Jews (5:1–47). At Passover time, Jesus feeds five thousand people, walks on water, and delivers a long discourse on the "bread of life" (6:1–71). When the Festival of Tabernacles draws near, he goes to Jerusalem and engages in an extended disputation with Jews concerning his claims and origin (7:1–52; 8:12–59). He halts the stoning of an adulterous woman (8:1 11), heals a man born blind (9:1–41), and delivers a discourse on his role as the Good Shepherd who brings abundant life (10:1–18). At the Festival of Dedication, Jesus continues to argue with the Jews, who are divided in their opinions about his identity and authority (10:19–42). Jesus next visits the home of Mary and Martha and raises their brother Lazarus from the dead; the miracle attracts so

OUTLINE OF CONTENTS

John

D.M.S.

much attention that priests decide both Jesus and Lazarus must die (11:1–57; 12:9–10). Mary is criticized by Judas for anointing Jesus with costly perfume (12:1–8). Jesus rides into Jerusalem on a donkey and speaks at length about his mission and impending death, prompting an audible response from God in heaven (12:12–50). Jesus and his disciples gather for a final evening together, and Jesus washes the feet of his disciples (13:1–17) and predicts his betrayal (13:17–30). Then he delivers a long "farewell discourse (13:31–16:33) and offers an extended prayer to the Father for his followers, pleading that they might be one, just as he and the Father are one (17:1–26). The Gospel concludes by recounting Jesus's passion and resurrection (18:1–20:29): he is betrayed by Judas, denied by Peter, and interrogated by both Annas and Pilate; he is crucified and placed in a tomb; he rises from the dead and appears to Mary Magdalene and the other disciples, including Thomas who had refused to believe without seeing him. The Gospel appears to close (20:30–31), but an epilogue relates another incident in which Jesus has private words for Peter and for the disciple he loves (21:1–25).

Composition: The Gospel of John is traditionally ascribed to John, the son of Zebedee, one of Jesus's twelve disciples. The origin of this tradition is tied up with the Gospel's claim that some of its content was based on material put in writing by an associate of Jesus identified as the "disciple whom Jesus loved" (21:20–24; cf. 19:35). But this beloved disciple is not identified as "John" in the Gospel itself, and he is mentioned as present with Jesus only in Jerusalem during the last week of Jesus's life. Thus, interpreters throughout history have ques-

John the evangelist with his symbol, the eagle, behind him; page from the seventh-century *Lindisfarne Gospels*.

COMPARISON OF JOHN'S GOSPEL WITH THE SYNOPTICS

Material Unique to John	Material Not Found in John
Calling of Andrew, Philip, and Nathanael (1:35–51).	No stories of Jesus's birth.
Miracle of changing water to wine at Cana (2:1–12).	No mention of his baptism.
	No temptation by Satan.
Conversation with Nicodemus (3:1–21).	No eating with tax collectors and sinners.
Conversation with Samaritan woman at the well (4:7–26).	No transfiguration.
	No parables.
Healing of man at pool of Bethzatha (5:1–18).	No exorcisms.
Question of stoning adulterous woman (7:53–8:11).	No condemnations of the rich or words about helping the poor.
Healing of the man born blind (9:1–41).	No commandment to love one's neighbor (or one's enemy).
Raising of Lazarus (11:1–44).	No call for people to repent (from either John the Baptist or Jesus).
Washing of the disciples' feet (13:1–20).	No call for disciples to deny themselves or renounce their possessions.
Prayer for followers to be one (17:1–26).	
Resurrection appearance to Thomas (20:24–29).	No predictions of Jerusalem's downfall (but cf. 2:19–22).
	No institution of the Lord's Supper (but cf. 6:53–56).
	Almost no mention of the kingdom of God (only in 3:3–5; cf. 18:36).
	Almost no references to a Second Coming (just once, in 21:22–23).

From Mark Allan Powell, *Introducing the New Testament* (courtesy, Baker Academic)

tioned the identification and proposed other candidates for the beloved disciple. In any case, most scholars believe that this Gospel was produced in stages: the beloved disciple (whether John the son of Zebedee or someone else) may have written an initial testimony to Jesus, but later editors added more content as years went by.

The form of the Gospel we now possess is usually thought to have taken shape toward the end of the first century. Scholars remain divided over what sources the authors/editors of John's Gospel had at their disposal. Particularly controversial is the question of whether those responsible for the Gospel of John were familiar with any of the Synoptic Gospels. Other suggestions include the proposal that John drew upon an early work called the "Signs Gospel," containing several miracle stories. In any case, the Gospel appears to have been intended to meet the needs of a particular community of Christians—probably the same group of churches connected with the three Johannine Letters (1 John, 2 John, 3 John). Wherever this community was located (tradition suggests Ephesus), the believers there seem to have been engaged in the task of defining themselves with regard to other Christians, Jews, and the world at large. There are signals that the community has been driven to adopt a defensive and competitive posture; believers in Jesus may be expelled from synagogues (9:22; 12:42; 16:2) or hated by a world that is hostile to anything that is of God (15:18–25; 16:33; 17:14).

Distinctive Features: The Gospel of John contains many stories not found elsewhere, but even the stories that are paralleled in other Gospels are often told quite differently. For instance, the story of Jesus's crucifixion contains three sayings from the cross not reported in any other Gospel (19:26–27, 28, 30). Also notable is the material *not* found in John. Jesus tells no parables, heals no lepers, performs no exorcisms, and provides no instructions to his disciples for praying the Lord's Prayer or celebrating the Lord's Supper. There is no mention of his birth or transfiguration, nor are there any accounts of his eating with outcasts or calling people to renounce their earthly possessions. John's Gospel is also distinctive in its chronology. The ministry of Jesus extends over three years (compared to what would appear to be one year in the other Gospels) and certain events occur at different junctures. The "cleansing of the temple" comes at the beginning rather than at the end of Jesus's ministry (cf. Mark 11:15–19; John 2:13–25); the great catch of fish comes after his resurrection rather than at the time Jesus first calls his disciples (cf. Luke 5:1–11; John 21:1–8). The language and style of John's Gospel are unique in a number of ways. In John the miracles of Jesus are often called "signs" (2:11; 4:54; 6:2, 14; 12:18), whereas in the Synoptic Gospels "signs" are associated with the work of false prophets (Mark 13:22). John's Gospel also uses distinctive expressions for referring to Jesus ("Word," "Lamb of God"), the Holy Spirit ("Advocate," "Spirit of truth"), and the experience of salvation (being children of God, knowing the truth, having life, being set free, or being born "from above"). John's Gospel makes abundant use of symbolism and develops a related motif of misunderstanding (i.e., characters in the Gospel story misunderstand Jesus, because they take him literally when he is speaking symbolically; cf. 2:19–22; 11:12). Finally, the style and content of Jesus's teaching are distinctive in John. Instead of employing aphorisms and parables, Jesus speaks in long, philosophical discourses, and instead of speaking about the kingdom of God, the Jewish law, wealth and poverty, and various matters of morality, Jesus talks primarily about himself— he speaks about his identity as the one who came to reveal the Father and about what it means for people to believe in him, love him, obey him, and abide in him.

Major Themes: John's Gospel presents Jesus as the true revelation of God. Jesus is the Word of God made flesh (1:14), and so his words and deeds present people with an actual encounter with God's self-revelation. Indeed, Jesus may be called "God" in this Gospel (1:1; 20:28). At the same time, this Gospel is adamant about emphasizing the humanity of Jesus: he feels grief (11:33– 35), fatigue (4:6), and anguish (12:27; 13:21); he gets suspicious (2:24–25) and irritable (2:4; 6:26; 7:6–8; 8:25); he experiences thirst (19:28) and, most important, death (19:30, 33). Jesus also claims to be subordinate to the Father and completely dependent upon God for everything (5:19, 30). Nevertheless, Jesus is God, for John's Gospel is able to speak of God in a twofold sense: God the Father and "God, the Son" (1:18). John's Gospel further presents Jesus's death as his glorification, referring ironically to the brutal act of crucifixion as a "lifting up from the earth" by which Jesus is exalted (3:14; 8:28; 12:32–34) and the will of God is accomplished (20:30). John's Gospel presents salvation as eternal life, but emphasizes the present reality of this phenomenon; the life of faith is not just eternally long but eternally rich, and the bliss of such a life is experienced in the Christian community, where believers abide in Christ and love each other. Finally, much scholarly attention has focused on the hostility evident in John's Gospel with regard to "the Jews." The latter are implacable opponents of Jesus and his followers, and they are no longer regarded as God's people, but as children of the devil, who rules the world (8:39, 42, 44, 47; cf. 12:31; 14:30). The tenor of these comments is usually thought to reflect circumstances specific to the composition of this Gospel, and many scholars suspect that the term "Jews" is being used to refer to a specific group of people (perhaps "Judeans") rather than to Jewish people in general. *See also* Beloved Disciple; gospel; Gospels, the; Holy Spirit; Johannine literature; John, Letters of; John the apostle; logos; Paraclete; Philo; sign.

Bibliography

Beasley-Murray, George R. *John.* 2nd ed. Nelson, 1999.

Brown, Raymond E. *The Gospel According to John.* 2 vols. Doubleday, 1966–70.

Keener, Craig S. *The Gospel of John: A Commentary.* 2 vols. Hendrickson, 2003.

Koester, Craig R. *The Word of Life: A Theology of John's Gospel.* Eerdmans, 2008.

Köstenberger, Andreas J. *John.* Baker, 2004.

Kysar, Robert. *John, the Maverick Gospel.* Rev. ed. Westminster John Knox, 1993.

Powell, Mark Allan. *Introducing the New Testament: A Historical, Literary, and Theological Survey.* Baker Academic, 2009. Pp. 168–89.

Smith, D. Moody, Jr. *The Theology of the Gospel of John.* Cambridge University Press, 1995.

M.A.P.

John, Letters of, three brief writings at the end of the NT situated before Jude and Revelation. They are classed among the seven Catholic or General Letters and are usually interpreted together as a group.

Contents: First John opens with a prologue grounding the word of life that it offers in the personal experiences of the author or authors (1:1–4). The Letter's message is introduced with a contrast between walking in darkness and walking in the light of God (1:5–2:2). The love of God is made perfect in those who obey God's commandments, especially the command to love one another (2:3–11). After a poetic oracle to various groups in the community (2:12–14), the letter offers an impassioned plea for its readers not to love the world (2:15–17). The author distinguishes his readers, who know the truth, from "antichrists" who have left the community (2:18–27). Readers are encouraged to fix their hope on the coming of Jesus (2:28–3:3). A clear delineation is made between those who are children of God and children of the devil (3:4–11) and between people who hate fellow believers and people who have God's love in them (3:16, 12, 24). The author proposes two tests for identifying false prophets: they do not confess that Jesus came in the flesh, and they do not heed the tradition preserved from the beginning (4:1–6). Then the author returns to his main point: love is the sign and source of a true relationship with God (4:7–21). He emphasizes that victorious faith accepts various testimonies to Jesus and leads to a life that is lived in him (5:1–12). In conclusion, the author urges readers to pray confidently for others (5:14–17), and then he offers a series of concluding proclamations (5:18–20) and a final warning against idolatry (5:21).

Second John opens with a salutation that identifies the letter as being from "the elder" to "the elect lady and her children" (vv. 1–2). The elder begins by highlighting faithfulness that has been exhibited by some (v. 4). He urges his readers to love one another and to keep God's commandments (vv. 5–6). Then he warns them to be on guard against deceitful antichrists and urges them not to welcome anyone who promotes the false teaching to which he refers (vv. 7–11). He expresses hope to visit the readers soon, and sends greetings from their "elect sister" (vv. 12–13).

Third John opens with a salutation from "the elder" to a person named Gaius (v. 1). The elder offers a prayer for Gaius's health (v. 2) and commends him for providing hospitality for missionaries (vv. 3–8). He refers to a church leader named Diotrephes, who has aggressively opposed support for these missionaries, rejecting the elder's authority (vv. 9–10). He offers a brief testimony on behalf of someone named Demetrius and concludes with travel plans and greetings (vv. 11–15).

Authorship: The first Johannine letter is anonymous, and the second and third are credited to someone who calls himself "the elder." Similarities in language, style, and outlook lead most scholars to regard the letters as having a common author and also to identify them as coming from the same milieu as the Gospel of John. Popular church tradition has usually ascribed all three letters to John the apostle, who is also traditionally regarded as the author of John's Gospel. A view more commonly accepted by scholars is that the letters may have been written by someone known as John the elder, who Eusebius says was a disciple of John the apostle and a leader in the same community (*Ecclesiastical History* 3.39.4). Many scholars also suggest that the individual responsible for the Johannine Letters (John the elder or some other unknown individual) was one of the people responsible for editing the Gospel of John and putting that book into its penultimate (almost final) form.

Historical Setting: The occasion for all three letters is the outbreak of conflict and schism in a particular network of churches. The letters speak of "deceivers" (2 John 7), "liars" (1 John 2:4, 22; 4:20), "false prophets" (1 John 4:1), and "antichrists" (1 John 2:18, 22; 4:3; 2 John 7), at least some of whom are to be identified with former church members who have left the dominant community (1 John 2:19). The nature of the schism is difficult to determine, but it seems to have involved controversy over christological concerns: whether Jesus is to be identified as Christ (2:22) or Son of God (4:15; 5:5, 10, 13) and, specifically, whether he came "in the flesh" (2 John 7). The latter concern suggests some affiliation with the notions of second-century Gnosticism, which viewed Jesus as a divine being who only appeared to have a human or physical nature. In any case, the three letters are addressed to different settings in which the dynamics of the schism are being felt. First John is directed to those who have remained within the community, encouraging them to strengthen their internal unity by practicing mutual love and limiting their contacts with outsiders. Second John is addressed to a church (called "the elect lady") some distance from the elder's home community, warning the congregation that missionaries from the schismatic faction may come to them and advising them not to grant hospitality to such persons. Third John is a letter of recommendation from the elder to a church leader

OUTLINE OF CONTENTS

1 John

I. Prologue: the grounds of the testimony (1:1–4)
II. The true message of Jesus (1:5–3:24)
   A. Fellowship, obedience, and forgiveness (1:5–2:17)
   B. Warnings against false teachings (2:18–28)
   C. The marks of life in the community (3:1–24)
III. Testing the claims of those who testify (4:1–5:12)
   A. Testing the spirits (4:1–6)
   B. Love as the essential test (4:7–21)
   C. Obedience to the commandments (5:1–5)
   D. The true testimony (5:6–12)
IV. Postscript: sins, forgiveness, and certain knowledge (5:13–21)

2 John

I. Salutation (1–3)
II. The love commandment and the true doctrine of Christ (4–11)
III. Conclusion (12–13)

3 John

I. Salutation (1–4)
II. Hospitality to emissaries (5–12)
III. Conclusion (13–15)

D.M.S.

named Gaius on behalf of a missionary named Demetrius—the elder wants Gaius to grant hospitality to Demetrius, even though another church leader (Diotrephes) is trying to prohibit this.

Major Themes: The Johannine Letters emphasize the reality and significance of Jesus's humanity (1 John 1:1–3; 2:7, 24; 3:11; 4:2–3) and, in particular, the significance of his death for atonement (2:2; 3:16; 4:10; cf. 1:9). The letters also resound with exhortations for believers to "love one another" (3:11, 14, 23; 4:7, 11, 12; 2 John 5; cf. 1 John 3:10, 18; 4:8, 19, 20–21; 5:2). They are frequently analyzed for what they reveal about conflict and schism; a doctrinal dispute may lie at the heart of the crisis addressed in these letters (2 John 9), but power struggles and personal dysfunctions are involved as well (3 John 9). *See also* Beloved Disciple; Catholic Letters/Epistles; Diotrephes; Johannine literature; John, Gospel According to; John the apostle.

SIMILARITIES BETWEEN THE JOHANNINE LETTERS AND THE GOSPEL OF JOHN

Images of light and darkness (1 John 1:5–7; 2:9–11; cf. John 8:12; 12:46)

Unity of Father and Son (1 John 1:3; 2:22–24; 2 John 9; cf. John 5:20; 10:30, 38; 14:10)

References to "the truth" (1 John 2:21; 3:19; 2 John 1; 3 John 3, 8; cf. John 8:32; 18:37)

Use of term "Paraclete" (1 John 2:1; John 14:16, 26; 15:26; 16:7)

Being hated by the world (1 John 3:13; cf. John 15:18–19; 17:13–16)

God sends Christ into the world out of love (1 John 4:9; cf. John 3:16)

Jesus comes in the flesh (1 John 4:2; 2 John 7; cf. John 1:14)

Christ lays down his life for others (1 John 3:16; cf. John 10:11, 15, 17–18; 15:12–13)

Being born of God (1 John 2:29; 3:9; cf. John 1:13; 3:3–8)

Knowing God (1 John 2:3–5, 13–14; 3:1, 6; 4:6–8; cf. John 1:10; 8:55; 14:7; 16:3)

Abiding in God/Christ (1 John 2:6, 27–28; 3:6, 24; 4:13–16; cf. John 6:56; 15:4–10)

New and old commandments (1 John 2:7; 2 John 5; cf. John 13:34)

Love one another (1 John 2:27–28; 3:11, 23; 2 John 5; cf. John 13:34; 15:12)

Water and blood (1 John 5:6–8; cf. John 19:34–35)

That joy may be complete (1 John 1:4; 2 John 12; cf. John 15:11; 16:24; 17:13)

From Mark Allan Powell, *Introducing the New Testament* (courtesy, Baker Academic)

Bibliography

Brown, Raymond E. *The Epistles of John.* Doubleday, 1982.

Powell, Mark Allan. *Introducing the New Testament: A Historical, Literary, and Theological Survey.* Baker Academic, 2009. Pp. 492–507.

Rensberger, David. *The Epistles of John.* Westminster John Knox, 2001.

Schnackenburg, Rudolf. *The Johannine Epistles: A Commentary.* Crossroad, 1992.

Strecker, Georg. *The Johannine Letters.* Fortress, 1996 (German original, 1989).

Witherington, Ben, III. *Letters and Homilies for Hellenized Christians.* Vol. 1, *A Socio-Rhetorical Commentary on Titus, 1–2 Timothy and 1–3 John.* InterVarsity, 2006.   M.A.P.

John the apostle, the son of Zebedee and brother of James. Along with James, John was called by Jesus to be one of the twelve (Matt. 4:21–22; Mark 1:19–20; Luke 5:10–11) while they were fishing. His name appears in each of the apostolic lists (Matt. 10:2; Mark 3:17; Luke 6:14; Acts 1:13). Some think that Mark's reference to "hired servants" indicates a prosperous family background (Mark 1:20). John and James received from Jesus the nickname "Boanerges," meaning "sons of thunder" (3:17). Their prominence among the twelve is indicated by their presence, along with Peter, at the raising of Jairus's daughter by Jesus (Mark 5:37; Luke 8:51), at the transfiguration of Jesus (Matt. 17:1; Mark 9:2; Luke 9:28), and with Jesus in Gethsemane (Matt. 26:37; Mark 14:33). According to Luke 22:8, John and Peter were instructed by Jesus to make the preparations for the Passover that was to serve as his final meal with his followers. All of this indicates that John was close to Jesus. Perhaps for this reason, a number of texts present him as saying or doing things that warrant correction or that earn him a rebuke from Jesus. It is John who complains about an exorcist who does not belong to their circle (Mark 9:38; Luke 9:49), and it is James and John who request that the unresponsive Samaritan village be destroyed (Luke 9:54). James and John (or their mother) ask for special consideration upon the advent of the messianic kingdom (Matt. 20:20–23; Mark 10:35–40). Paul attests to John's prominence by referring to him as one of the "pillars" of the Jerusalem church (Gal. 2:6–10). In spite of these and a few other references to John in the NT, the data necessary for a fuller sketch of his life, character, and activities do not exist.

Further attestation to John's prominence among the apostles is evidenced by the fact that he is traditionally regarded as the author of the Fourth Gospel, the three canonical letters bearing his name, and (sometimes) the book of Revelation. Though widely attested in the early church, that association of John the apostle with the Gospel of John seems to be based mainly on the assumption that John is to be identified as the "beloved disciple" mentioned in 13:23; 19:26; 20:2; 21:7, 20–24. This is possible, but remains conjectural. The Letters of John are apparently attributed to John the apostle, because they bear similarities to the Gospel (which had already been attributed to him). The book of Revelation has some features in common with the Gospel and letters and was written by someone named John, but most scholars think Revelation had a different author than the Gospel (or letters) and that the John who wrote it should be regarded as someone else by that name. *See also* Beloved Disciple; Boanerges; James; Johannine literature; John, Gospel According to; John, Letters of; Revelation, book of; twelve, the; Zebedee.   P.L.S./M.A.P.

John the Baptist, or John the Baptizer, an important figure in each of the four NT Gospels. He is identified with the beginning of Jesus's minis-

John the Baptist; ninth-century mosaic from Hagia Sophia, Istanbul.

try and understood to be the forerunner of Jesus the Messiah. Reference to John is the first point of convergence among the canonical Gospels, all of which give a somewhat similar account of his person, preaching, and activity, albeit with some significant differences of detail. John is also mentioned in the writings of Josephus (*Antiquities* 18.116–19). He is called "John the Baptist" there as well, indicating that this was not simply a sobriquet intended to distinguish him from other people in Christian tradition named John.

The portrayal of John in the canonical Gospels is that of a prophet who appeared in the wilderness, proclaiming the advent of the kingdom of God and issuing a call to repentance (Matt. 3:1–12; Mark 1:4–8; Luke 3:1–20). According to Luke, he was of priestly descent, the son of Zechariah and Elizabeth; his birth was announced by an angel of the Lord and was the consequence of a miraculous conception to a woman beyond the age of childbearing (1:5–80; 3:2). His name was divinely chosen (1:13, 60, 63). Also, according to Luke, the mothers of John and Jesus were relatives who knew each other (1:36), though John's Gospel indicates that Jesus was a stranger to John (1:31, 33). Luke fixes the beginning of his minis-

try with some specificity: "In the fifteenth year of the reign of Emperor Tiberius, when Pontius Pilate was governor of Judea, and Herod was ruler of Galilee, and his brother Philip ruler of the region of Iturea and Trachonitis, and Lysanias ruler of Abilene, during the high priesthood of Annas and Caiaphas, the word of God came to John son of Zechariah in the wilderness" (3:1–2). Matthew and Mark describe John's appearance and diet: he wore a camel's-hair cloak with a waist belt made of leather, and he dined on locusts and wild honey (Matt. 3:4; Mark 1:6). Thus, John is cast in a role like that of Elijah (Matt. 11:7–15; 17:10–13; Mark 9:11–13; cf. Mal. 4:5–6; Sir. 48:10). He baptized those who repented in the Jordan River and announced the coming of one who would be greater than he and would baptize with the Spirit (Matt. 3:11–12; Mark 1:7–8; Luke 3:16–17; John 1:26–27). Jesus was among those baptized by John, and in the Synoptic Gospels that baptism is associated with the Holy Spirit coming upon Jesus and with the inauguration of Jesus's ministry (Matt. 3:13–17; Mark 1:9–11; Luke 3:21–22; cf. John 1:31–34). The Synoptic Gospels also report that John was arrested by Herod Antipas because he opposed Herod's marriage to Herodias, the wife of his brother (Matt. 14:1–12; Mark 6:14–29; cf. Luke 9:7–9). Herodias wanted John killed, and when Herod was so pleased by a dance performed by Herodias's daughter that he promised to give the girl anything she wanted, Herodias told her to ask for the head of John the Baptist on a platter. Thus, John was beheaded in prison, and his disciples buried his body. Josephus also reports the execution of John by Herod Antipas, noting that many Jews thought the defeat of Herod's army by the Nabatean ruler Aretas IV (ca. 36 CE) was divine vengeance for the killing.

Both the Gospels and Josephus indicate that John carried on an effective and successful ministry (Matt. 3:5–6; Mark 1:5). In the Gospels, however, considerable care is taken both to maintain the importance of John and to distinguish him from Jesus. Notably, Luke's Gospel presents stories of the annunciation and birth of John in a manner that parallels stories of the annunciation and birth of Jesus (1:5–32). Thus, similarities between the two agents of God are highlighted, but Jesus is clearly the prominent one (e.g., born to a virgin, not just a woman advanced in years; called "Son of the Most High," 1:32, not just "prophet of the Most High," 1:76). The story of Jesus being baptized by John might allow for the perception that Jesus was John's disciple or follower, a perception the Gospels clearly want to avoid. In Matt. 3:13–15, John is reluctant to baptize Jesus and must be encouraged by Jesus to do so, to "fulfill all righteousness." Basically, all four Gospels start with the fact that John's ministry had temporal priority over that of Jesus and construe this as meaning not that Jesus was John's successor, but that John was a forerunner to Jesus, sent by God to prepare the way for him. Thus, in all four Gospels, Jesus is to be identified with the "greater one" who John himself said would come after him.

PARALLEL STORIES OF JESUS AND JOHN THE BAPTIST

Luke's Gospel tells the infancy stories of John the Baptist and Jesus through a series of parallel segments:

	John the Baptist	Jesus
Luke introduces the parents of the child-to-be.	1:5–7	1:26–27
An angel announces the child's birth.	1:8–23	1:28–38
The mother responds to God's announced plan.	1:24–25	1:39–56
The baby is born.	1:57–58	2:1–20
The baby is circumcised and named.	1:59–66	2:21–24
Prophecy is offered concerning the child.	1:67–79	2:25–39
The child grows and matures.	1:80	2:40–52

From Mark Allan Powell, *Introducing the New Testament* (courtesy, Baker Academic)

While seeking to establish Jesus's prominence over John, however, the Gospels also take care not to present John and Jesus as rivals. Thus, in the Synoptic Gospels, John is arrested and imprisoned before Jesus's public ministry begins (Matt. 4:12; Mark 1:14; Luke 3:20). That is not the case in the Fourth Gospel, but there the issue of rivalry is addressed head-on: when John is informed regarding the success of Jesus's ministry, he responds with joy, comparing himself to the "friend of the bridegroom," i.e., as one who is happy to play a supporting role (3:25–30; cf. 4:1). With regard to Jesus, John's philosophy is, "He must increase, but I must decrease" (3:30). John's Gospel also records that two of John's disciples followed Jesus after hearing John declare Jesus to be the "Lamb of God" (1:35–39); Andrew the brother of Peter also became a disciple of Jesus after hearing John's testimony concerning Jesus (1:40). Scholars are unsure why the Gospels sought to include such stories, but there is speculation that the movement begun by John may have continued until late in the first century CE, and these accounts may have supported evangelistic efforts to bring John's disciples into the Christian fold (cf. Acts 18:24–28; 19:1–7). Or perhaps the early Christians simply wanted to present testimonies to Jesus by someone well regarded among Jews of that period (cf. John 5:33; 10:41).

Elsewhere in the Gospels, disciples of John ask Jesus why his disciples do not fast (Matt. 9:14). John himself hears in prison about what Jesus is doing and sends messengers to ask him, "Are you the one who is to come or are we to wait for another?" Jesus replies by listing works of healing that he has been performing, with allusions to the prophecies of Isaiah (Matt. 11:3–5; Luke 7:18–22; cf. Isa. 29:18–19; 35:5–6; 61:1). Jesus also speaks to the crowds about John (Matt. 11:7; Luke 7:24), claiming that "among those born of women no one has arisen greater than John the Baptist; yet the least in the kingdom of heaven is greater than he" (Matt. 11:11; cf. Luke 7:28). Thus the coming of John seems to mark a transition from a time of the law and prophets to a period marked by the advent of the kingdom (Matt. 11:12–13; Luke 16:16). Further, the coming of John fulfills the prophecy

of Malachi that Elijah would return before the "day of the LORD" would dawn (Matt. 11:14; cf. Mal. 4:5; also Matt. 17:10–13; Luke 1:17; but see John 1:21). Jesus contrasts himself with John, indicating that John is more ascetic with regard to food and drink, but he also notes that they have been equally rejected by those who spurn wisdom (Matt. 11:18–19; cf. Luke 7:33). In Luke's Gospel, the teaching of the Lord's Prayer is prefaced by a request from Jesus's disciples that he teach them to pray "as John taught his disciples" (11:1). A number of NT texts also indicate that, after John was killed, various parties speculated that Jesus might be John raised from the dead (Matt. 16:14; Mark 6:14–16; 8:28; Luke 9:7–9, 19). Finally, when Jesus's authority is challenged in Jerusalem, he asks his opponents to tell him whether the baptism of John was from heaven or of human origin. They do not want to answer, because a denunciation of John would cause them to lose support of people who regarded John as a prophet, while endorsement of John would raise the question of why they had not obeyed him (Matt. 21:25–27; Mark 11:30–32; Luke 20:1–8). Jesus says they compare unfavorably to tax collectors and prostitutes, because "John came to you in the way of righteousness and you did not believe him, but the tax collectors and the prostitutes believed him" (Matt. 21:31–32; cf. Luke 7:29–30)

In the NT John is not mentioned outside the Gospels except briefly in the book of Acts. His ministry is recalled in 1:5 and, when a new apostle needs to be chosen for the church, candidates are limited to those who were witnesses to all that happened from the time of John's baptism to the day of Jesus's ascension (1:22). Later, Apollos is mentioned as a believer who knows "only the baptism of John" and, so, must be more fully instructed in the faith by Priscilla and Aquila before he can become a dynamic teacher of the gospel (18:24–28). Paul encounters disciples of John the Baptist who, after being rebaptized in the name of Jesus, are filled with the Holy Spirit and speak in tongues (19:1–7).

Scholars have noted the possibility that John knew of and perhaps was even associated with the Qumran community (which produced the Dead Sea Scrolls). The location of his ministry in the wilderness, his practice of water purification, and his austere lifestyle are all cited as similarities between John and this group, but the hint of any actual association remains speculative. Most scholars credit the similarities to a pervasiveness of such concepts among diverse Jewish groups during the Second Temple period. *See also* Elizabeth; Herod; wilderness; Zechariah.   M.A.P.

Joiada (joi'uh-duh; Heb., "the LORD knows").

1 The son of Paseah and one of the builders of the wall of Jerusalem under Nehemiah (Neh. 3:6).

2 A postexilic high priest, the son of Eliashib and the father of Jonathan (Neh. 12:10–11, 22), also called Jehoiada in Neh. 13:28.

Joiakim (joi'uh-kim; a shortened form of Jehoiakim; Heb., "the LORD will raise up"), the son of Jeshua, the high priest in Jerusalem following the return from the exile; he succeeded his father as high priest (ca. 500–450 BCE?; Neh. 12:10, 12, 26).

Joiarib (joi'uh-rib; a shortened form of Jehoiarib; Heb., "the LORD will contend").

1 A Levite teacher who met Ezra at the Ahava River and was commanded to return to Jerusalem from Babylon (Ezra 8:16).

2 A Judahite ancestor of Maaseiah, a postexilic inhabitant of Jerusalem (Neh. 11:5).

3 Apparently the father of Jedaiah, a priest who lived in postexilic Jerusalem (Neh. 11:10). However, a parallel passage (1 Chron. 9:10) omits "son of" and lists Joiarib (Jehoiarib) as one of the priests along with Jedaiah.

4 A priest who returned from the Babylonian exile with Zerubbabel (Neh. 12:6); possibly the same as 3 above.

5 A postexilic family group headed by Mattenai (Neh. 12:19).   D.R.B.

Jokneam (jok'nee-uhm), a Canaanite city in Carmel (Josh. 12:22). It was located in the territory of Zebulun and marked its limits (Josh. 19:11). It was assigned to the Levites from among the cities in Zebulun according to Josh. 21:34; according to 1 Chron. 6:68, where it is spelled Jokmeam, it was among the cities in Ephraim. The toponym Jokmeam also occurs in 1 Kings 4:12. It is located six miles northwest of Megiddo at modern Tel Qaimun.

Jokshan (jok'shan), the second child of Abraham and his second wife, Keturah (Gen. 25:2; 1 Chron. 1:32), and the father of Sheba and Dedan (Gen. 25:3; 1 Chron. 1:32; but cf. Gen. 10:7, 28). According to Gen. 25:5–6, Jokshan received no inheritance; Abraham gave all he had to Isaac, sending the sons of his concubines away (with gifts).

Joktan (jok'tan), a descendant of Shem and the brother of Peleg; his thirteen sons are generally

to be identified with various Arabian tribes (Gen. 10:25–30).

Jonadab (joh'nuh-dab; Heb., meaning uncertain, perhaps "the LORD is noble"; a shortened form of Jehonadab, 2 Kings 10:15, 23).

1 The son of David's brother Shimeah (Shimea); he was the cousin of David's son Amnon. He gave Amnon the plan that led to Amnon's rape of his half sister Tamar (2 Sam. 13:3–5). It is possible that he is the same nephew of David elsewhere called Jonathan (2 Sam. 21:21; 1 Chron. 20:7). *See also* Amnon.

2 The son of Rechab, the founder of the Rechabites, a strict religious sect characterized as abstaining from wine, as living in tents rather than building houses, and as not sowing seeds or planting vineyards. Since Jonadab is referred to as the authority for the rules of this group (Jer. 35:6), he probably effectively organized the sect. Jeremiah praised the strictness with which the later descendants of the group followed the traditions established by Jonadab in contrast to the infidelity that Judah and Jerusalem had shown to God (35:1–19). The religious zeal characteristic of the group is perhaps reflected in the fact that Jonadab (here Jehonadab) accompanied Jehu in his chariot as he killed those loyal to the apostate Ahab (2 Kings 10:15–17) and then attempted to exterminate the worshipers of Baal (10:18–25). *See also* Jehu; Jonathan; Rechab.   D.R.B.

Jonah, book of, the fifth part of the Book of the Twelve within the Prophets section, or Nevi'im, in the Tanakh (Jewish Bible). It is the fifth book in the Minor Prophets in the Christian OT. It is different from any other prophetic book in the Bible in that it is not primarily a collection of utterances *by* a prophet, but a tale *about* a prophet.

Contents: God directs Jonah to go to Nineveh, the capital of the Assyrian Empire. Instead, Jonah goes by boat in the opposite direction, so God sends a storm to stop him. The sailors ultimately determine that Jonah was the cause of the storm and, after some deliberation and moral anxiety, they throw him overboard, thus calming the sea. Jonah is swallowed by a large fish and spends three days and nights inside it. During this time, Jonah offers up a hymn of thanksgiving for deliverance. The fish vomits Jonah on the shore, where God again appeals to Jonah to go to Nineveh. Jonah proceeds to Nineveh and, upon arriving, prophesies its doom. The people (and even the animals) repent, and God relents and does not destroy the city. Jonah is resentful of God's mercy and heads out of the city to sulk. God gives Jonah a bush for shade, then takes it away the next day. Jonah is further angered, wishing he would simply die. At the book's end, God asks Jonah why he is more concerned for a single bush than for the 120,000 people (plus animals) in Nineveh.

Background: The book of Jonah centers around the character of Jonah himself, but there is only one reference to a prophet named Jonah elsewhere in the Bible. According to 2 Kings 14:25, a prophet named Jonah was the son of Amittai from Gath-hepher in the region of Galilee. He was a prophet during the reign of Jeroboam II in the mid-700s BCE and a contemporary of Amos who prophesied about the restoration of Israel's boundaries. Nineveh was not a prominent city until the 600s BCE. Most scholars think that the "Jonah" of the book of Jonah was, at best, only loosely based on the prophet of Gath-hepher.

There is no definitive information about the author, date, or location of composition of the book of Jonah. There are, however, a few clues within the text that help with the dating process. First, it is said that Nineveh *was* a great city (3:3), which means that the book was most likely written after the destruction of the city in 621 BCE. Second, the universalist message of the book is often seen as suggesting a postexilic context (such as polemic against the particularism of Ezra–Nehemiah). Thus, the book of Jonah was probably written between the fourth and sixth century BCE.

Themes: The book of Jonah has been interpreted in many different ways: as a satire on prophetic calling and the refusal of prophets to follow God's call; as a criticism of Israelite prophets who were insincere in preaching repentance (because they really wanted to see destruction); as a criticism of the Jewish community's unwillingness to respond to prophetic calls to repentance (in contrast with Nineveh); as a criticism of an exclusive view of divine election (God only cares about "chosen people"); as an assertion of God's freedom to change God's mind over and against prophets who would limit that freedom; as emphasizing the problem with true and false prophecy (even true prophets have words that do not come true); or as an allegory of Israel in exile (both Jonah and Judah look to God for destruction of an evil empire). De La Torre argues for an interpretation of the book that views Jonah as a marginalized person frustrated with God for not punishing those who have brutally oppressed people. Person reads the book of Jonah as a conversation between author and reader, focusing on the implied verbal rejection of God's command by Jonah in 1:3.

Although Jonah is never explicitly called a prophet (he makes only one prophecy in the book, 3:4), his character is commonly considered as a caricature or criticism of the prophetic office. Jonah is an "antiprophet" in that he does the opposite of what is expected of a prophet. Jonah runs when God calls him to prophecy, is never seen as repenting for running, and only desires the destruction of the city of Nineveh. In a satirical vein, Jonah's desire for the destruction of Nineveh may be seen to parallel Israel's desire for the destruction of its foes. Likewise, Jonah's refusal to heed God's call highlights Israel's stubbornness.

The behavior of the people of Nineveh is also important for the interpretive process. At the one prophetic word of Jonah, the entire city of Nineveh fasts and repents in sackcloth and ashes, even its animals. This dramatic repentance of a foreign nation is seen as indicative of God's care for those outside of the covenant and as a warning to Israel against prejudging Gentiles. Furthermore, the repentance of Nineveh is seen as contrasting with Israel's stubbornness in repenting.

Interpretive Issues: The literary genre of Jonah has been a source of some debate. Some interpreters have argued that the book is a purely historical narrative, but the majority of scholars place it within the realm of novella, short story, or satire. The loose nature of the connection between the historical person Jonah (mentioned in 2 Kings 14:25) and the character of Jonah portrayed in the book of Jonah has been said to underscore the nonhistorical nature of the text. Furthermore, the frequent use of the word "great" to describe objects and the exaggerated measurements (Nineveh as a city that it takes three days to cross, when the ruins are only three miles across at the widest point) have been said to give the story a "larger than life" quality. These factors lead many scholars to believe that the story fits better within the realm of short story than historical narrative. However, Jenson argues that the category "short story" is too narrow and does not capture the complexity and depth of the book of Jonah.

Another pressing issue concerns the origin and nature of the poem in Jon. 2:2–9. Most (but not all) scholars argue that the psalm does not fit the context. First, the psalm is one of thanksgiving for deliverance, but Jonah has not been delivered at the time he prays these words, and he continues to be obstinate after being delivered from the belly of the fish (the counterargument runs that his thanksgiving is an expression of faith that God will deliver him; God's future deliverance is so sure that it could be described in the past tense). Second, the psalm talks of waters closing over Jonah (Jon. 2:5, similar to Ps. 69:2), but makes no mention of the ship, sailors, or the very fish in whose stomach he sits. Third, Jon. 2:7 talks of being in God's holy temple, yet the temple resided in Jerusalem (in Judah), while Jonah was from Israel. Accordingly, most scholars think that the psalm was composed on another occasion and borrowed for Jonah's situation, though some argue that the book was composed around the poem, which was original to Jonah.

Influences: The book of Jonah has taken on a different meaning within the Christian tradition than it had in the Hebrew Bible. The three days and nights that Jonah spends within the large fish were seen to prefigure the resurrection of Christ (Matt. 12:39–41). For this reason, Jonah became a symbol of resurrection in early Christian art.

Bibliography

Bandstra, Barry L. *Reading the Old Testament: Introduction to the Hebrew Bible.* 4th ed. Wadsworth, 2009.

Ben Zvi, Ehud. *Signs of Jonah: Reading and Rereading in Ancient Yehud.* JSOT, 2003.

Craig, Kenneth M. *A Poetics of Jonah: Art in the Service of Ideology.* Mercer University Press, 1999.

De La Torre, Miguel A. *Liberating Jonah: Forming an Ethics of Reconciliation.* Orbis Books, 2007.

Jenson, Philip P. *Obadiah, Jonah, Micah: A Theological Commentary.* Clark, 2008.

Person, Raymond F. *In Conversation with Jonah: Conversation Analysis, Literary Criticism, and the Book of Jonah.* JSOT, 1996.

Sweeney, Marvin A. *The Twelve Prophets.* Vol. 1, *Hosea, Joel, Amos, Obadiah, Jonah.* Liturgical, 2000.

Wolff, Hans Walter. *Obadiah and Jonah: A Commentary.* Augsburg, 1986.   B.B.

Jonathan (jon'uh-thuhn), the firstborn son of Saul and Ahinoam. He became the most important prince of King Saul (the first king of Israel) and a close friend to David, his father's rival and successor. He was the father of Merib-baal/Mephibosheth (2 Sam. 9; 1 Chron. 8:34). Jonathan lived in the second half of the eleventh century BCE. He figures in 1 Sam. 13–31, where he first appears as commander-in-chief of Israel's military forces. In this capacity, Jonathan led the army against the Philistines, whose monopoly on forged iron made them a formidable opponent. At Michmash, Jonathan managed to climb what was considered an impregnable rocky mount and eliminate a Philistine watchpost, and the shock of this success sent a panic through the enemy troops that brought a reversal in battle. Saul, however, became jealous, forfeited the victory, and made a scapegoat of his son Jonathan, who had severely criticized him. Saul hoped to have his son executed; but at the last moment the soldiers intervened to save Jonathan.

Later, Jonathan saw the military prowess of David (who slew Goliath) and acknowledged him as his peer. The two became close friends and swore a pact of loyalty (1 Sam. 18:1–4). Jonathan further demonstrated his devotion to David by attempting to mediate on his behalf with Saul and by seeking to warn or protect David against his father's jealous anger (19:1–7; 20:1–34, 41–42). Thus, when David was forced to flee the court, Jonathan met with him at Ziph, and the two of them concluded a renewed covenant according to which Jonathan acknowledged David to be the one God had chosen to rule (23:16–18).

In the final battle on Mount Gilboa, where the Philistines settled accounts with Saul's army, Jonathan died with his father (1 Sam. 31:1–2). David honored him as a hero and celebrated his noble character and selfless behavior by dedicating the climax of his dirge in 2 Sam. 1:19–27 to his friend: "Your love to me was wonderful, / passing the love of women" (1:26). According to 2 Sam. 9, David wanted to show kindness to someone from Jonathan's family, and so he brought his son Mephibosheth, who was crippled in both feet, to Jerusalem to eat at the king's table every day. *See also* David; Saul.   J.P.F./M.A.P.

Joppa (jop'uh; Heb., "beauty"), an important harbor in the ancient Near East. Today it is a suburb of modern Tel Aviv. According to the Bible, this city was allotted to the tribe of Dan (Josh. 19:46). It was also the port through which the cedars of Lebanon came for the construction of both the first and second temples (2 Chron. 2:16; Ezra 3:7). It was from this port that the prophet Jonah sailed in his attempt to evade God's command (Jon. 1:3). It was also in Joppa that Peter raised the widow Dorcas from the dead (Acts 9:36–43).

Archaeological excavations reveal that occupation at Joppa began as early as the Middle Bronze Age (1900–1500 BCE), with a large fortified enclosure with a beaten earth rampart found on the site. The city is first mentioned in the victory list of Pharaoh Thutmose III (ca. 1468 BCE). It is subsequently characterized as an Egyptian stronghold in the Tell el-Amarna tablets. During excavations, a thirteenth-century BCE citadel gate was uncovered, which had dressed stones with titles and an inscription mentioning Pharaoh Rameses II (ca. 1304–1237 BCE). Joppa is also mentioned along with Azor, Bene-berak, and Beth-dagon as having been under the influence of Sennacherib in the "prism stele" (701 BCE). Later, an inscription of Eshmunazar of Sidon (probably fifth century BCE) seems to indicate that the city was under the control of the king of Persia at that time. Joppa was colonized by the Greeks in the Hellenistic period (333–63 BCE). The Zenon papyri, a travel diary of an Egyptian treasury official who visited the Levant (ca. 259/8 BCE) during the reign of Pharaoh Ptolemy II, makes reference to the city. The Seleucids captured Joppa during the Hasmonean period (ca. 175–63 BCE). It was later destroyed by the Romans on more than one occasion, first by Cestius Gallus and then by Vespasian.   S.B.R.

Joram (jor′uhm; Heb., "the Lord is high"; a short form of Jehoram).

1 The son of King Toi of Hamath (2 Sam. 8:10).

2 A Levite who was a descendant of Eliezer the son of Moses (1 Chron. 26:5).

See also Jehoram.

Jordan (johr′duhn) **River** (Heb. *ha-yarden*), a river that runs from north of the Sea of Galilee to the Dead Sea. Occupying two-thirds of the deep rift valley between Israel and Jordan, i.e., a section of the rift valley system that extends from southern Turkey about thirty-five hundred miles to the Zambesi in southeast Africa, it is the world's lowest river, flowing mainly well below sea level. Except just north of the Sea of Galilee, the valley is enclosed between steep mountain walls; the eastern side is usually higher and more precipitous and provides most of the tributaries, since the plateau edge receives heavier rainfall than the highlands. The whole valley is in a rain shadow, since the rain-bearing westerly winds in winter are warmed and dried by their rapid descent. Average annual rainfall at Dan in the north is 24 inches, at the Sea of Galilee 16 inches, and at Jericho 5 inches. Heavy rain can sometimes occur, even far south, causing the desolate wastes to blossom amazingly.

The major headwaters come from the slopes of Mount Hermon; the Hasbani is the most northerly, and the Liddani, near Dan (modern Tell el-Qadi), is the strongest. The smallest, the Bareighit, rises just north of modern Metullah. These streams once meandered through a papyrus marsh to the shallow Lake Huleh, 250 feet above sea level. All this, however, is now drained. Crossing was possible only just south of the lake, where the Damascus road came to join the north–south route that passed farther to the west. Guarding the junction was the great Bronze Age city of Hazor (Josh. 11:10), destroyed by Joshua, but fortified again by Solomon (1 Kings 9:15) and even more strongly by Ahab.

Waterfall at the headwaters of the Jordan River.

South of Lake Huleh the river descends 945 feet through a narrow gorge, sometimes 1,000 feet deep, cut through a basalt outflow. Beyond the basalt is the Sea of Galilee (Lake Tiberias), 695 feet below sea level, roughly heart-shaped and 12 miles long by 7 wide. The encircling hills leave room for a shoreline track, widest at the little plain of Gennesaret in the northwest.

The Jordan then meanders for about two hundred miles to the Dead Sea, though the direct distance is only sixty-five miles. Twenty miles south of the Sea of Galilee, the mountains close in from both sides, creating a narrow "waist" to the valley. The river is joined by the Yarmuq, as large as the Jordan, from the east. Then, farther south, the 'Arab, the Taiyebeh, the Ziqlab, and the Yabis flow into the Jordan. Jabesh-gilead, famous in the saga of Saul (1 Sam. 11:1–11; 31:8–13), was either at the entrance to the Wadi Yabis or farther upstream. At the narrow waist the Kufrinje descends from the Ajlun mountains, towering 4,000 feet above the valley. Westward the Harod comes from Jezreel, the entrance guarded by Beth-shan (Arabic Beit Shean), later called Scythopolis.

Immediately south of the waist, the 'Faria joins the Jordan from the west, and the much larger Jabbok (Gen. 32:22; modern Zerqa) from the east. Close to the confluence is Adam (modern Tell ed-Damiyeh; Josh. 3:16). A desert climate now prevails, and the river wanders in a thick jungle of tamarisk and other shrubs through the Zor, the "thickets" of Jordan (Jer. 12:5; Zech. 11:3). On either side are the gray, desolate badlands of the Qattara, and beyond them the downward sloping plain of the Ghor. The base of the highlands was intensely cultivated wherever there were springs. On the west was Jericho and also the Roman settlement of Phasaelis. On the eastern springline were the well-watered "plains of Moab" (Num. 22:1). The "waters of Nimrim" (Isa. 15:6) flow down the Wadi Shu'eib. The Wadi Kufrein supplied Abel-shittim (modern Tell el-Hammam; Num. 33:49; Josh. 2:1 [Shittim]; Mic. 6:5), and the Wadi Hesban fed Bath-peor (or Baal-peor; Deut. 3:29; Josh. 13:20; Hos. 9:10). *See also* wadi. D.B.

Joseph (joh′sif).

1 The older son of Rachel, who was the favorite wife of Jacob (Israel), ancestor of the Israelites. Thus, Joseph's descendants form one of the original twelve tribes of Israel (Gen. 49:22–26), but the tribe of Joseph divided into Ephraim and Manasseh after Levi left the tribal structure (48:8–22). Joseph plays the central role in a collection of narrative traditions preserved in 37:1–50:26. His story provides a bridge between the traditions about the ancestors (Abraham, Isaac, and Jacob) in Gen. 12–36 and the traditions about Moses in Exodus. In one sense, this narrative link is simply geographic: the Joseph story explains how the children of Israel ended up in Egypt (where the Moses story begins) rather than in Canaan (where the ancestor stories are mostly set).

As is typical for the ancestor traditions, the basic plot of the Joseph story is built around a problem created by family strife. Rachel was infertile for a long time, but she finally gave birth to Joseph (Gen. 29:31–30:21), whom Jacob regarded as the son of his old age and, thus, his favorite son (37:3). He demonstrated such favoritism by giving Joseph a long robe with sleeves (37:3; the same sort of garment is described as a robe of princes in 2 Sam. 13:18). This triggered jealousy on the part of his brothers (37:4). Joseph is also said to have brought his father bad reports about his brothers' behavior (37:4), and he related dreams that portrayed his brothers as well as his parents as someday bowing down to him (37:5–7, 9).

Joseph's brothers conspired to kill him, but at the suggestion of Reuben (who hoped to rescue him) they sold him to slave traders, and he was carried off to Egypt (Gen. 37:22–28). They then tricked Jacob into thinking he was dead. God blessed Joseph in Egypt, where he became a steward to Potiphar, but when he rebuffed the advances of Potiphar's wife, she made false charges against him and he ended up in prison (39:1–20). God was still with him, however, so that he was able to interpret the divine meaning of dreams (Gen. 40). After two years, this gift came to the attention of Pharaoh; Joseph accurately interpreted one of Pharaoh's dreams as meaning that seven years of plentiful harvest would be followed by seven years of famine (41:1–36). Pharaoh made Joseph overseer of all Egypt, in charge of storing food during the years of plenty and selling it during the lean years (41:37–57). This situation provided the context for Jacob's sons to come to Egypt in search of grain. Joseph played an elaborate hoax upon them, requiring them to return to Canaan and bring back Benjamin, his younger brother (and Jacob's new pride and joy), then accusing the latter of theft. At last, all was revealed and Jacob came to Egypt with his entire household. Jacob was reunited with Joseph, and the family settled in the land of Goshen.

The themes of this story are multiple, including the exaltation of wisdom (Joseph is presented as the wisest man in Egypt); the divine reward for moral virtue (God rewards Joseph for resisting the advances of Potiphar's wife, even though his virtue goes unrecognized by others); the insidiousness of jealousy and the nobility of showing mercy (Joseph forgives his brothers); and the political lesson that a royal court needs effective administrators who plan ahead. The main point of the story seems to be that the God of Israel is working behind the scenes of historical events to ensure the preservation of the chosen people. It was actually God's plan for Joseph to be brought to Egypt and into a place of power, so that the family of Israel might survive the famine. Joseph tells his brothers, "It was not you who sent me here, but God" (Gen. 45:8) and, "God sent me before you to preserve life . . . to preserve for you a remnant on earth, and to keep alive for you many survivors" (45:5, 7).

Bibliography

Coats, George W. *Genesis.* Vol. 1 of *Forms of Old Testament Literature.* Eerdmans, 1983. Pp. 259–66.

Kaminsky, Joel S. "Reclaiming a Theology of Election: Favoritism and the Joseph Story." *Perspectives in Religious Studies* 31.2 (2004): 135–52.

Von Rad, Gerhard. "The Joseph Narrative and Ancient Wisdom." In *The Problem of the Hexateuch and Other Essays.* Oliver and Boyd, 1966. Pp. 292–300.

2 The father of Igal, who was one of the spies Moses sent into Canaan (Num. 13:7).

3 A musician in the service of David (1 Chron. 25:2, 9).

4 A priest in the time of Joiakim (Neh. 12:14).

5 A son of one of the priests who divorced their foreign wives in response to Ezra's postexilic proclamation (Ezra 10:42).

6 The son of Jacob (Matt. 1:16) or Heli (Luke 3:23); he was the husband of Mary (Matt. 1:16) and the earthly father of Jesus (Luke 4:22; John 1:45; 6:42). A descendant of David (Matt. 1:20), he decided to divorce his pregnant betrothed "quietly" without exposing her to public disgrace, which showed him to be a righteous man (1:19). He was dissuaded from doing even this by an angel who spoke to him in a dream, telling him that the child was conceived from the Holy Spirit (1:20–24). After Jesus was born, Joseph was again warned by an angel in a dream that Herod planned to kill the baby, and he fled by night to Egypt with Mary and Jesus (2:13–15). After Herod died, an angel told Joseph to bring his family back to Israel, but he settled in Nazareth, because Archelaus, the son of Herod, was ruling in Judea (2:19–23). These accounts of Joseph being guided by dreams and rescuing his family by bringing them to Egypt seem to have affinity with the biblical stories of Joseph, the son of Jacob, reported in Gen. 37–50 (see **1** above).

In Luke's Gospel, the story is told somewhat differently. Joseph took his pregnant wife from Nazareth (where they apparently already lived) to Bethlehem on account of a census (2:1–4). After Jesus was born, he and Mary brought the child to Jerusalem to "present him to the Lord" (2:22–23). According to Luke 2:41, Jesus's parents went to Jerusalem every year for the Passover, and so Joseph is mentioned again (though not by name) in 2:41–51, the story in which the twelve-year-old Jesus visited Jerusalem for the Passover and stayed behind in the temple. Joseph is not mentioned in any Gospel accounts after this and, since the adult Jesus is called the "son of Mary" in one passage (Mark 6:32), most interpreters assume that Joseph died before Jesus began his adult ministry.

7 A Jewish man from Arimathea who wrapped the body of the crucified Jesus in a linen shroud and buried him in a tomb newly cut from rock (Luke 23:53), perhaps the tomb intended for his own family members (Matt. 27:60). Luke 23:50–51 calls him a "good and righteous man" who was waiting expectantly for the kingdom of God (cf. Mark 15:43). Matthew says that he was rich (27:57), and Mark calls him bold (Mark 15:43). Joseph is also identified as a disciple of Jesus (Matt. 27:57), though John's Gospel indicates that he kept this a secret out of fear of his compatriots (19:38). He is further said to have been a respected member of the council that had opposed or condemned Jesus, though Joseph did not agree with their plan or action (Mark 15:43; Luke 23:51).

8 The name of three ancestors of Jesus (Luke 3:26, 30, 34).

9 A follower of Jesus, also called Barsabbas, surnamed Justus, who was not chosen to replace Judas as one of the twelve disciples when he and Matthias were put forward for that position (Acts 1:23).

10 An early Christian, surnamed Barnabas (Acts 4:36), who along with Saul (Paul) was sent on a missionary journey by the church in Antioch (13:2). A later dispute regarding whether John Mark should accompany them on a second voyage (after he turned back without completing an earlier trip) led them to go their separate ways (15:36–39). *See also* Barnabas.

11 One of the sons of Joseph and Mary and a brother of Jesus (Matt. 13:55) who bore the Greek rather than the Hebrew form of the name (Joses; Mark 6:3).

12 A brother of James the younger (Mark 15:40, 47, "Joses"; cf. Matt. 27:56, "Joseph"), perhaps identical with **11**. G.W.C./M.A.P.

Josephus (joh-see′fuhs), Flavius Josephus or Joseph ben Matthias, the single most important Jewish historian in the early Roman period. He was born of a priestly family in the first year of the emperor Gaius (37–38 CE) and also claimed descent from the Hasmoneans. In his twenty-sixth year (63–64 CE) he served on an embassy to Rome. During the revolt against Rome that began in 66, he led the revolutionary forces in Galilee until he was captured by the Roman general Vespasian at Jotapata (67 CE). After his capture, he predicted that Vespasian would become emperor. When the prophecy was fulfilled, he was released. For the remainder of the war he served as an interpreter for the Romans. He spent the rest of his life in Rome, engaged in literary activity under imperial patronage. He died ca. 100 CE.

While in Rome, Josephus produced works, four of which have survived. *The Jewish War* is an account in seven books of the Jewish revolt, prefaced with a brief survey of Jewish history from the second century BCE. *The Antiquities of the Jews* is a twenty-volume work, the first half of which paraphrases historical accounts from the Jewish scriptures, while the second half records, in greater detail than in the *War,* the history of the Jews in the Second Temple period. *Against Apion* is an apologetic work in two books refuting slanders leveled against the Jews during the Hellenistic period. The brief *Life,* an appendix to the *Antiquities,* provides general autobiographical information about Josephus, with a focus on his period of revolutionary leadership in Galilee. Josephus also composed an Aramaic account of the Jewish revolt, which has not survived. Throughout his works, Josephus strove to elicit sympathy for his people and to make Jewish traditions comprehensible to the Greco-Roman world. At the same time he attempted to blame the revolt on a fanatical minority of the Jewish people.

Josephus is of interest to biblical interpreters because his writings provide a wealth of information about the world of Second Temple Judaism, including numerous matters that overlap with what is reported in the books of Maccabees or the NT. His perspective is that of a Hellenistic Jew who wishes to appease or favor the Romans, and everything he says must be evaluated by scholars in that light. Still, his writings offer detailed descriptions of the various Jewish parties (Pharisees, Sadducees, Essenes) and provide information about Pontius Pilate and the various Herodian rulers. His books even include a few references to John the Baptist and Jesus. The latter references are particularly intriguing, because they were written about the same time as the Gospels and offer by far the most extensive comments on Jesus by any non-Christian writer from this period. Unfortunately, the text of his comments was embellished by later Christians who kept the manuscripts and added whole phrases to them, making Josephus an advocate of Christian faith and theology. Nevertheless, scholars are fairly confident that Josephus's original comments can be distinguished from the later additions. One widely accepted reconstruction of his remarks (prepared by John P. Meier) is offered here, with probable embellishments listed at the end:

At this time there appeared Jesus a wise man.[a] For he was a doer of startling deeds, a teacher of people who receive the truth with pleasure. And he gained a following both among Jews and among many of Greek origin.[b] And when Pilate, because of an accusation made by the leading men among us, condemned him to the cross, those who had loved him previously did not cease to do so.[c] And up until this very day the tribe of Christians (named after him) has not died out (*Antiquities* 18.3.3).

Probable embellishments:

[a]if indeed one should call him a man
[b]He was the Messiah.
[c]For he appeared to them on the third day, living again, just as the divine prophets had spoken of these and countless other wondrous things about him.

Bibliography

Meier, John P. *A Marginal Jew: Rethinking the Historical Jesus.* Vol. 2, *Mentor, Message, and Miracles.* Doubleday, 1994.   H.W.A./M.A.P.

Joses (joh′siz; Gk., "Joseph"). *See* Joseph.

Joshaphat (josh′uh-fat). *See* Jehoshaphat.

Joshua (josh′yoo-uh; Heb., "the LORD saves").

1 The dominant figure in the book of Joshua, the successor of Moses and the supervisor of Israel's conquest of Canaan and of the allotment of the land to the tribes. According to Num. 13:8, 16, Joshua was an Ephraimite, originally called Hoshea and renamed by Moses. An Ephraimite genealogy is provided for him in 1 Chron. 7:20–27. Moses appointed him to lead the battle against Amalek, which he did successfully (Exod. 17:8–13). As a young man he served as Moses's assistant in the tent of meeting (33:11). He urged Moses to restrict spirit-inspired behavior, but was overruled by Moses (Num. 11:28–29). As one of the twelve spies sent to reconnoiter Canaan, he agreed with Caleb; Joshua and Caleb constituted the minority who recommended confidence in God and a direct assault (Num. 14:6–10). For this God exempted them from the general condemnation of that

Joshua leads the Israelites as the walls of Jericho fall. Mosaic scene from Santa Maria Maggiore in Rome, early fifth century.

generation to death in the wilderness. God then told Moses to lay his hands on Joshua and designate him a leader like himself, who would be obeyed fully by all the people (27:18–23; cf. Deut. 34:9). Joshua, along with Eleazar and an officer from each tribe, would be responsible for allotting the land to the people (Num. 34:17). Moses publicly encouraged Joshua and recognized his future role (Deut. 31:7–8; cf. 3:28; 31:3). Joshua was also commissioned directly by God (Deut. 31:14, 23; Josh. 1:1–9). The book of Joshua then relates how Joshua fulfilled his dual role as conqueror and distributor of the promised land, concluding with a notice of Joshua's death at age 110 and his burial in his allotted territory (24:29–30; cf. Judg. 2:8–9).

Many of Joshua's deeds are analogous to those of Moses; the text says that God was with Joshua as with Moses (Josh. 3:9) and that the Israelites revered Joshua as they had Moses (4:14). As with Moses, there is no historical evidence for the existence of Joshua outside of the Bible, but whatever the historical antecedents for the Joshua stories may have been, the figure of Joshua as presented in the Bible is an archetypal leader who by his faith and obedience to God accomplishes his mission effectively and completely. He has some of the characteristics of a monarch, especially Josiah. In later tradition Joshua was remembered for his great deeds (Sir. 46:1–8) and cited specifically for his obedience to the law (1 Macc. 2:55) and his intercession for Israel (2 Esd. 7:107). In the NT, Stephen cites Joshua as one who continued the tradition of worship at a tent of meeting rather than a temple (which he considers unnecessary, Acts 7:44–48). The Letter to the Hebrews indicates that for all Joshua's accomplishments, he did not bring the people into the promised "sabbath rest" of God, which is attainable only through faith in Jesus Christ (4:3–8). *See also* Joshua, book of.

2 A resident of Beth-shemesh on whose land the cows bringing the ark from its Philistine captivity came to a standstill (1 Sam. 6:14, 18).

3 A governor of Jerusalem after whom a gate was named during the late monarchic period (2 Kings 23:8).

4 The son of Eliezer and father of Er, listed in Luke's Gospel as an ancestor of Jesus (3:28–29).

S.B.P.

Joshua, book of, the sixth book of the Tanakh (Jewish Bible) and of the Christian OT; it is the first book of what is sometimes called the Former Prophets, a subcollection in the Prophets, or Nevi'im, section of the Tanakh. The books of Joshua, Judges, Samuel and Kings constitute the Deuteronomistic History. This work constitutes the primary history of the kingdom of Israel from the conquest of Canaan to the Babylonian exile. The book of Joshua picks up the story line where Deuteronomy left off and provides an account of the conquest and distribution of the land among the Israelite tribes. The book's author is unknown, but came from scribal circles that wrote history based on the principles of covenant, blessing, reward, and punishment as presented in the book of Deuteronomy. The namesake of the book is Joshua, who was the successor of Moses (Num. 27:12–23, Deut. 31:14–15, 23; 34:9). He was a hero of the battle against the Amalekites (Exod. 17), and he along with Caleb encouraged the invasion of Canaan from the south when the ten other spies discouraged it (Num. 13–14). Only these two men from the first generation of Israelites were allowed to enter the promised land.

Contents: The book of Joshua begins by citing the death of Moses. God speaks to Joshua, Moses's successor, and encourages him to lead Israel into the land of Canaan (Josh. 1). Joshua sends two spies to Jericho to provide intelligence before the battle. There they meet Rahab, a Canaanite, who assists them (2). The Israelites cross the Jordan River and get to Gilgal, where all the males are circumcised (3–5). They attack Jericho and are victorious (6). But Achan steals some property in the process, so the Israelites lose the battle of Ai the first time; they succeed the second (7–8). The Gibeonites become allies, but Israel attacks other cities, including Hazor (9–12). Although many territories are not taken (13), Joshua divides the conquered areas among the tribes (14–19) and designates cities of refuge (20). The Levites are given towns, but no tribal lands (21). The tribes

settle in their territories (22), and Joshua gathers the people to Shechem for his final address and for covenant renewal (23–24).

OUTLINE OF CONTENTS

Joshua

I. Military campaigns (chaps. 1–12)
   A. God commissions Joshua (1)
   B. Spying the land (2)
   C. Crossing the Jordan (3–4)
   D. Events at Gilgal (5)
   E. Military victories (6–12)
     1. Jericho (6)
     2. Ai (7–8)
     3. Southern city-states (9–10)
     4. Hazor (11)
     5. List of conquests (12)
II. Tribal territories (13–21)
   A. Settlement of claims (13–17)
   B. Remainder of tribes (18–19)
   C. Cities of refuge (20)
   D. Levitical cities (21)
III. Covenant considerations (22–24)
   A. Worship in Transjordan (22)
   B. Covenant address to leaders (23)
   C. Covenant renewal at Shechem (24)

Background: The book of Joshua is organized logically insofar as it begins by legitimizing Joshua as the successor of Moses. He takes the Israelites from Moab, which was where they were at the end of Deuteronomy, and gets them across the Jordan River with a miraculous crossing. From there, Joshua initiates three military campaigns to secure Canaan: against Jericho and Ai in the central hill country, against a coalition of southwestern city-states, and against Hazor in the northern region of Upper Galilee.

The events of conquest presumably would have taken place in the Iron I period (1200–1050 BCE). The generally accepted time of the exodus from Egypt is approximately 1250 BCE, and allowing time for the wilderness sojourn, the conquest would have begun around 1200 BCE. This aligns with a general time of upheaval and incursion into Canaan that was a result of the invasion of the Sea Peoples from the Aegean region of the Mediterranean basin.

Themes: The book of Joshua is the official record of how the Israelites took possession of the land of Canaan and divided the territory and its existing cities among the twelve tribes. The approach to conquest mandated in the book of Joshua is termed holy war and is defined by the ban (Heb. *kherem*), where everything and everyone is "devoted to the LORD for destruction" (6:17, 21). Failure to secure possession of the land is traced to Israel's failure to carry through on the ban, epitomized by the sin of Achan (Josh. 7). In the twentieth century, archaeology was thought to confirm unambiguously the course of military conquest described in Joshua at such cities as Jericho and Hazor. The more recent finds, however, do not support an Israelite military invasion and occupation of Canaan, and other models of the emergence of Israel and the literary formation of the biblical account are now preferred (see Finkelstein and Silberman).

The book of Joshua contains two stories of Canaanite people who found acceptance within Israel in spite of the holy-war injunction to eliminate all indigenous people. Rahab was a Jericho prostitute who acknowledged God and aided the Israelite spies. The people of Gibeon deceived Joshua and secured a nonaggression pact with the Israelites; in this way they survived the conquest. Both stories served as explanations for how Canaanites came to live among the Israelites. These stories, along with the results of archaeology, have prompted new views of the literature of the exodus from Egypt and the conquest of Canaan in relation to the identity of the Israelites. The people who came to be called Israel hailed from a variety of backgrounds: some from Egypt, some from Mesopotamia, and some from Canaan itself. For various political and religious reasons they identified as one people and eventually became the kingdom of Israel. Rahab in particular achieved status within Israel and, according to the NT, became a node in the royal messianic line (Matt. 1:5).

The figure of Joshua, whose name means "the LORD saves," is notable as the successor to Moses and the civic leader and military commander who established Israel in Canaan. The book of Joshua is both a literary creation and a historical record of the twelfth century BCE written by the Deuteronomistic Historian during the time of Josiah in the seventh century BCE. The literary presentation of Joshua may have been shaped in the image of Josiah, whose name also means "the LORD saves," in order to promote the military and political program of King Josiah. He sought to recover the northern territories of Israel that had been controlled by the Neo-Assyrian Empire, whose influence in his time was evaporating. He sought to do this within an all-Israel covenant framework of the kind Joshua used to unify the tribes around God in his day (Josh. 24).

Bibliography

Auld, A. Graeme. *Joshua Retold: Synoptic Perspectives.* Clark, 1998.

Bandstra, Barry L. *Reading the Old Testament: Introduction to the Hebrew Bible.* 4th ed. Wadsworth, 2009.

Dever, William G. *Who Were the Early Israelites, and Where Did They Come From?* Eerdmans, 2003.

Finkelstein, Israel, and Neil A. Silberman. *The Bible Unearthed: Archaeology's New Vision of Ancient Israel and the Origin of Its Sacred Texts.* Free Press, 2001.

Rad, Gerhard von, *Holy War in Ancient Israel.* Eerdmans, 1991.   B.B.

Josiah (joh-si'uh; Heb., "the LORD saves").

1 The king of Judah ca. 640–609 BCE. Josiah was the son of Amon and Jedidah, and he was made king at age eight when his father, King Amon, was assassinated (639 BCE). His reign during the last half of the seventh century BCE lasted thirty-one years. The Assyrian Empire, which had previously dominated the region, was in its final decline, making the expansion and religious reform that characterized Josiah's reign possible.

Josiah's religious actions included the removal of all traces of foreign worship and the elimination of all outlying places of worship, including those in Assyrian-controlled sections of what had been the northern kingdom; he removed shrines in Samaria (2 Kings 23:19) and Galilee (2 Chron. 34:6) as foretold in 1 Kings 13:2. The effect of these reforms was to centralize all officially sanctioned religious practice in Jerusalem. In addition, the worship of any deity other than the Lord was made a capital offense. According to 2 Kings 23, his reform movement (ca. 620 BCE) was motivated by the discovery of a "book of the law" in the temple during the eighteenth year of his reign. Jewish tradition has typically regarded this book as the Torah, while Christian tradition has regarded it as the book of Deuteronomy. Modern scholars tend to associate the book with Deuteronomic material that served as one of the sources for the Pentateuch; thus, the shaping of Torah (including Deuteronomy) into its current form may have been a consequence of Josiah's reform.

Second Chronicles pays little attention to Josiah's reform (cf. 34:33), concentrating more on the report of a Passover that he observed (chap. 35). This may be because the Chronicler had already reported on similar reforms being instituted by Hezekiah (chap. 31) and Manasseh (33:15–16). The relationship of Josiah's reform to that of Hezekiah is uncertain.

Josiah's political accomplishments are manifest in the evidence of the kingdom's expansion, perhaps the result of an attempt to re-create the kingdom of David, an attempt made possible by Assyria's weakened condition. His success at expanding the kingdom is attested by a Hebrew letter from this period discovered at Yavneh Yam, a Judean fort on the Philistine coast of the Mediterranean Sea. Josiah was killed in 609 BCE at Megiddo while trying to block Pharaoh Neco II from helping the last remnant of the Assyrian Empire against the rising power of Babylonia (2 Kings 23:29). Whether this action was coordinated with Babylonia or undertaken on Josiah's own initiative is unknown. According to 1 Chron. 35:20–24, he was merely wounded at Megiddo and taken from there to Jerusalem, where he died. He was succeeded by his sons Jehoahaz (2 Kings 23:30, called Shallum in Jer. 22:11), who was installed by the people, and Jehoiakim (Jer. 22:18, previously Eliakim according to 2 Kings 23:34), who was installed by Neco. Later his son Zedekiah (or grandson according to 2 Chron. 36:10), whose original name was Mattaniah, became Judah's last king (2 Kings 24:17).

Josiah's reign was a time of Judean national resurgence. The king was highly regarded by Jeremiah (cf. Jer. 22:15), who lived during his reign, as did the prophet Zephaniah (Zeph. 1:1; cf. Jer. 1:2; 25:3; 36:2). Josiah was considered by the author of Kings to have been Judah's outstanding monarch (2 Kings 23:25).

2 The son of Zephaniah, a Jerusalemite homeowner who lived immediately after the exile (mid-sixth century BCE; Zech. 6:10).   F.E.G./M.A.P.

Jotham (joh'thuhm; Heb., "the LORD is perfect").
1 The youngest of seventy sons of Jerubbaal (Gideon). He alone escaped when his brother Abimelech conspired to be crowned king at Shechem and killed the remaining sons of Jerubbaal (Judg. 8:29–9:5). After hearing that the men of Shechem had made Abimelech king (9:6), Jotham went to the top of Mount Gerizim near Shechem and, speaking loudly enough to be heard in the valley below, denounced the selection of Abimelech as king by telling a parable about trees who foolishly select a thorn bush to be their king instead of a more worthy tree (9:7–21). The curse pronounced against the city of Shechem and Abimelech was fulfilled three years later by a civil war in which Shechem was leveled. At this time, Abimelech was killed when a woman threw a millstone on his head from a wall (9:22–57).

2 The son of Uzziah (Azariah), and king of Judah ca. 742–735 BCE. The sixteen years of his reign included about eight years in which he served as regent for his father, who was struck with leprosy (2 Kings 15:5, 7; 2 Chron. 26:16–27:1). Jotham was given a rather mediocre evaluation as king by the writer of the book of Kings and a slightly better rating by the Chronicler. He is credited with several building projects as well as subjugating the Ammonites, and he prospered because "he ordered his ways before the LORD" (2 Chron. 27:4–6; cf. 2 Kings 15:34). However, he failed to remove the high places where the people offered sacrifice to Baal (2 Kings 15:35; cf. 2 Chron. 27:2). Late in his reign an alliance of Pekah of Israel (the northern kingdom) and Rezin of Syria threatened Judah with invasion, but Jotham died before the threat could be carried out. His son Ahaz bore the force of the invasion (2 Kings 15:37; 16:5). Jotham was contemporary with the prophets Hosea (1:1), Isaiah (1:1), and Micah (1:1).

3 The son of Jahdai, a Judahite belonging to the Caleb family group (1 Chron. 2:47).   D.R.B.

journey, sabbath. *See* sabbath day's journey.

joy. The Bible contains scattered references to happiness derived from sexual love (Song of Sol. 1:4), married life (Prov. 5:18), the birth of children (Ps. 113:9), and especially the pleasures of harvest (Deut. 26:1–11; 1 Chron. 12:40; Isa. 9:3) and feasting (Ezra 6:22; Eccles. 8:15). These, however, merely form the backdrop for a far more pervasive emphasis on joy associated with the experience of God's presence and benefits (1 Chron.

16:27; 29:22; Neh. 8:10; 12:43; Pss. 16:11; 21:6; 43:4; 51:12; 105:43). Nature itself joins this joyous mood of thanksgiving (1 Chron. 16:33; Job 38:7; Pss. 65:12–13; 96:12; 98:8; Isa. 49:13), which is also closely connected with worship, as Israel celebrates God in feasts and liturgy. Joy is expressed by singing (1 Sam. 8:6; Pss. 5:11; 63:7; 84:2; 92:4; 107:22; 149:5; Isa. 24:14; 26:19; 35:6), dancing (Ps. 30:11; Jer. 31:13), shouting (Ezra 3:12; Job 8:21; Pss. 20:5; 27:6; 32:11; 35:27; 65:8; 71:23; 81:1; 126:2, 5–6; 132:9, 16; Isa. 48:20), clapping hands (Ps. 47:1); and playing musical instruments (1 Kings 1:40; 1 Chron. 15:16). The righteous are expected to rejoice in justice (Prov. 21:15), which includes rejoicing when the wicked receive just recompense for their deeds (Ps. 58:10; cf. 2 Chron. 20:27; in the NT, this theme is taken up with regard to the final judgment in Rev. 18:20). In a similar vein, the wise person rejoices in the law, which leads Israel in the paths of obedience and righteousness that are pleasing to God (Pss. 1; 119:11). Under circumstances of oppression, however, the mood of joy becomes more anticipatory, as Israel looks ahead to the joy that will accompany future deliverance by God (Isa. 55:12; 65:17–19; Zech. 8:9). Such joy shall be "everlasting" (Isa. 35:10; 51:11; 61:7), from "age to age" (60:15). God's joy over this event is also anticipated (Zeph. 3:17), and thus joy emerges as a dominant aspect of Israel's eschatological hope.

In the NT, the eschatological joy that Israel had anticipated becomes associated with Jesus Christ. The birth of the infant Jesus occasions an outpouring of human and heavenly joy (Matt. 2:10; Luke 1:14, 44; 2:10), and his ministry (Luke 10:17) and resurrection (Matt. 28:8; Luke 24:41, 52) evoke the same response. The discovery of God's kingdom, in particular, is an occasion for joy (Matt. 13:44), and there is rejoicing in heaven when sinners repent (Luke 15:7, 10). John's Gospel employs the familiar metaphors of marriage and harvest joy to suggest the exultant mood accompanying Jesus's ministry of salvation (3:29; 4:36). Even more characteristic of the Fourth Gospel, however, is the explicit association of joy with the person of Jesus and an emphasis on the perfect (or completed) joy of those secure in their loving relationship with him and one another (15:7–11; 17:13). The book of Acts describes the early church sustaining a mood of rejoicing and spreading joy beyond the borders of Judea (8:8). The NT also strongly associates joy with heavenly rewards and with the bliss of eternal life that awaits the faithful after death (Matt. 25:21, 23; Luke 6:23). On the other hand, the Synoptic Gospels do indicate that joy can be shallow: in Jesus's parable of the Sower, the seed that falls on rocky ground is likened to those who receive the word with joy, but have no root and, so, do not grow or bear fruit (Matt. 13:20; Mark 4:14; Luke 8:13).

The Pauline Letters are filled with the mood of rejoicing (Phil. 4:4), for eschatological joy, closely linked with the Holy Spirit (Rom. 14:17; 15:13), is both the impetus (1 Thess. 2:19–20) and the goal

(2 Cor. 1:24) of Paul's apostolic ministry. Paul, however, also stresses the paradox that this joy can be experienced in the midst of temporal afflictions (Rom. 5:3). Paul further suggests that affliction, even martyrdom, could be viewed as a reflection of Jesus's suffering, and thus it becomes a sign of the true disciple or apostle and an additional basis for rejoicing (2 Cor. 11:23–12:10). Thus Paul's Letter to the Philippians, written under circumstances of severe apostolic suffering, is also the most joyous of all his letters. The author of 1 Peter also affirms the view that sharing Christ's suffering is to be a cause of joy (4:13; 1:6; cf. James 1:2).

J.M.B./M.A.P.

Jozabad (joh′zuh-bad; a shortened form of Jehozabad; Heb., "the LORD is a gift" or "the LORD has given").

1 A Gederathite who joined David's warriors at Ziklag (1 Chron. 12:4).

2 A Manassite who defected from Saul to join David (1 Chron. 12:20).

3 A Levite who helped oversee the collection of the temple offerings during the reign of Hezekiah (2 Chron. 31:13).

4 A levitical leader who contributed animals for the Passover celebration during King Josiah's reforms (2 Chron. 35:9).

5 A Levite who helped inventory the valuables brought back by the exiles who returned with Ezra (Ezra 8:33).

6 A priest belonging to the family group of Pashur who divorced his foreign wife in response to Ezra's postexilic proclamation (Ezra 10:22).

7 A Levite who divorced his foreign wife in response to Ezra's postexilic proclamation (Ezra 10:23).

8 A man, probably a Levite, who helped explain the law to people when it was read by Ezra (Neh. 8:7).

9 A levitical leader who helped supervise the rebuilding of the temple following the return from the exile (Neh. 11:16). He may be the same as **8** above. D.R.B.

Jozadak (joh′zuh-dak; a shortened form of Jehozadak; Heb., "the LORD is righteous"), a priest, the father of Jeshua, the high priest in Jerusalem following the return from the Babylonian exile (Ezra 3:2; 10:18). He is most often called Jehozadak (1 Chron. 16:14; Hag. 1:12). *See also* Jehozadak.

Jubal (joo′buhl), the ancestor of musicians who play the lyre and pipe (Gen. 4:21). The reference might be meant to indicate that he invented these instruments, that he was the first to play them, or that he was the first to play them professionally or competently in a manner that inspired others to do so as well. Jubal was one of two sons of Lamech by Adah; his older brother, Jabal, is identified as the ancestor of people who live in tents and have livestock (4:20). Taken together, the two are intended to symbolize a fraternity of farmers and musicians, or simply of labor and the arts. M.A.P.

jubilee (joo′buh-lee; from Heb. *yobel*, a ram's horn), the fiftieth year occurring at the end of seven sabbatical cycles of seven years each, in which all land was returned to its ancestral owners and all Israelite slaves were freed. The jubilee is described in Lev. 25:8–17, 23–55; 27:16–25; and Num. 36:4. It was proclaimed with the blowing of the shofar (a trumpet made from a ram's horn) on the Day of Atonement. The land was also left fallow in the jubilee year. The jubilee was observed in the seventh sabbatical in Second Temple times, so that there was a forty-nine-year cycle. *See also* festivals, feasts, and fasts; sabbatical year; shofar.

L.H.S.

Jubilees (joo′buh-leez), **book of.** *See* Pseudepigrapha.

Judaea (joo-dee′uh). *See* Judea.

Judah (joo′duh).

1 One of the twelve sons of Jacob (Israel), the fourth born to Jacob and Leah (Gen. 29:35). He assumes a prominent role among the brothers in the Joseph story. He is the one who proposes that Joseph be sold into slavery rather than killed (Gen. 37:26–27); he negotiates with Jacob to bring Benjamin to Egypt, pledging to be personally accountable for the youngest boy's safety (43:1–10); and he offers himself as a slave to Joseph in place of Benjamin, in order that the latter might be allowed to return to Jacob (44:14–34). Another lengthy story about Judah is recorded in Gen. 38. After his son Er dies childless, he fails to make the appropriate levirate marriage provisions for his daughter-in-law Tamar (Deut. 25:5–10). So Tamar disguises herself as a prostitute and is impregnated by Judah himself; when Judah realizes what has happened, he declares that she was more in the right than he (Gen. 38:6).

2 The tribe of Judah, ostensibly consisting of the descendants of **1.** This tribe is said to have occupied the highlands between Jerusalem and Hebron (i.e., the mountains of Judah), the greater part of the southern Levant. The twelve-tribe scheme includes, under Judah, a number of other groups that settled in the area from Hebron southward into the Negev: Calebites (in the territory around Hebron; Josh. 14:13–15; Judg. 1:20), Kenites (in the area around Arad; Judg. 1:16), Kenizzites (in the environs of Debir; Josh. 15:15–19; Judg. 1:11–15), and Jerahmeelites (1 Sam. 27:10; 30:29). The Simeonites are also said to have occupied this area (near Zepath/Hormah; Judg. 1:17), though Simeon is also listed as one of the official twelve tribes with land of its own. The fact that Judah is not mentioned in the ancient Song of Deborah (Judg. 5) is probably due to its firm association with the south from a very early period (the Song of Deborah is concerned with a victory of the tribes in the north). Judah's position in the Blessing of Moses (Deut. 33:7), which stems from a relatively early period, is that of a rather insignificant tribe. The Blessing of Jacob (Gen. 49:8–12), however, indicates that Judah will rule and displace the older Reuben. This probably reflects the situation of the tribes at the time of David (late eleventh century BCE). In Hebron, the capital of Judah, David was anointed king "over the house of Judah" by the "people of Judah" (2 Sam. 2:4). Eventually, David and his son Solomon would rule a kingdom composed of all twelve tribes, but in the division of the monarchy after Solomon, Judah would become an independent nation: the kingdom of Judah, distinct from the kingdom of Israel.

In the NT, Judah is listed first among the twelve tribes in an account of those sealed for salvation (Rev. 7:5), and Jesus is described as the "Lion from the tribe of Judah" who is worthy to open the seven seals of a heavenly scroll (5:5). Jesus's descent from Judah is also noted in Gospel genealogies (Matt. 1:2–3; Luke 3:33); that this was a nonpriestly tribe is noted in Heb. 7:14. *See also* Judah, kingdom of; tribes.   F.S.F./M.A.P.

Judah, kingdom of, a kingdom in the southern Levant consisting of the tribal areas of Judah and Benjamin. It was created by the dissolution of the united monarchy at the death of Solomon (ca. 922 BCE). Following this division there was a period of civil war between Judah (the southern kingdom) and Israel (the northern kingdom) that finally terminated in the time of Jehoshaphat, king of Judah (ca. 873–849 BCE). Although Judah was considerably less populous than Israel, it enjoyed greater political stability due to the presence of Jerusalem and the influence of the Davidic monarchy. Because of its relatively secluded geographic location, it was somewhat less vulnerable to external aggression.

The population of Judah, from the time of David on, had incorporated considerable numbers of non-Israelites, leading to an alternation between pro-Canaanite religious policies on the part of some kings and the reversal of such policies in periodic religious reforms enacted by other rulers. Thus, Rehoboam (ca. 922–915 BCE), the first king of Judah, adopted pro-Canaanite policies (1 Kings 14:21–24), but his policies were reversed by his grandson Asa (ca. 913–873 BCE; 15:9–13). Asa's reforms were continued by his son Jehoshaphat, but they were again reversed by the extremely pro-Canaanite policies of Queen Athaliah (843/2–837 BCE; 2 Kings 8:26; 11:2; 2 Chron. 24:7), a daughter or sister of Ahab of Israel, who seized the throne violently, causing a break in what had been a pattern of orderly succession. Athaliah ruled as Judah's only queen until she was ousted by the Jerusalem priesthood acting in concert with the Judean rural nobility. The Davidic succession was renewed with the installation of the seven-year-old Joash (837–800 BCE) on the throne.

Joash's son Amaziah (ca. 800–783 BCE) campaigned against Edom (2 Kings 14:7) and was involved in costly hostilities with Joash of Israel (14:8–14). He fell victim to a conspiracy mounted by Jehu, who assassinated him and placed his sixteen-year-old son, Uzziah (ca. 783–742 BCE),

on the throne. The reign of Uzziah (or Azariah in 14:21; 15:1, 6, 7, 8) was marked by territorial expansion, an increase in population, strengthening of defenses, advancement of agriculture with the cultivation of semiarid areas, and the development of commerce. Uzziah was afflicted with leprosy, and the Chronicler blamed his illness on the fact that he had usurped a priestly prerogative by sacrificing incense in the temple (2 Chron. 26:16–21). His son Jotham (ca. 742–735 BCE), who began his reign before his father's death, continued Uzziah's successful policies, but Judah suffered losses under Jotham's son, Ahaz (ca. 735–715 BCE), losing territory to the Philistines and Edom and being attacked by an Israel-Syrian alliance. These losses drove Ahaz to Assyria for help, and he instituted pro-Assyrian practices.

Early in the reign of Ahaz's son Hezekiah (ca. 715–687/6 BCE), the Assyrians conquered Israel, leaving Judah as the sole surviving independent state in the area. The Judean state was one of the few that avoided the catastrophe that befell the other states of the area in the latter part of the eighth century during the reigns of the Assyrian kings Tiglath-pileser III (745–727 BCE) and Sargon II (722–705 BCE). The fall of the northern kingdom encouraged Judean kings to pursue nationalistic policies aimed at recovering a united Davidic monarchy. Accordingly, Hezekiah pursued thoroughgoing religious reforms (2 Kings 18; 2 Chron. 29–31). He revolted against the Assyrians after the death of Sargon II in 705 BCE, and Sargon's successor, Sennacherib, responded with an invasion in 701, in which he conquered the fortified cities of Judah and besieged Jerusalem (2 Kings 19). Jerusalem, however, escaped destruction, most likely because Hezekiah capitulated (18:13–16; but cf. the more pious account given in 19:35–36).

In a now familiar pattern, the extensive religious reforms of Hezekiah were completely reversed by his son Manasseh (ca. 687/6–642 BCE; 2 Kings 21:1–18; 2 Chron. 33:1–20), who submitted to the Assyrians and "misled them to do more evil than the nations . . . that the LORD had destroyed" (2 Kings 21:9). His son Amon (ca. 642–640 BCE) was assassinated by nationalist elements, who installed his eight-year-old son Josiah on the throne (ca. 640–609 BCE; 21:24). When he came of age, Josiah instituted strongly nationalist policies in a time when Assyria had begun to be severely threatened by the Babylonians and the Medes (22:3–20; 23:8, 15, 19). He also purified religious practices and centralized them in Jerusalem, outlawing the worship of any god but the Lord. After the Assyrian capital Nineveh fell in 612 BCE, Josiah exploited the situation by seeking to expand his territory. The Egyptian pharaoh Neco, at the same time, sought to go to the aid of the Assyrians. Josiah attempted to stop Neco in 609 BCE at the pass of Megiddo and lost his life in the failed attempt (23:29). The disastrous death of such a reformer king put to rest any visions of a restored Davidic empire and marked the end of an independent Judean state. Josiah's son Jehoahaz reigned for only three months and was then deposed by Neco and deported to Egypt. The Egyptians installed Jehoiakim (Eliakim) on the throne of Judah (608–598 BCE); Jehoiakim was hated by his people, both because of his pro-Egyptian policies and because of the heavy tribute he exacted from them to send to Egypt. There was also a religious decline under his rule (24:2–4).

The last years of Judah saw a struggle between Egypt and Babylon for hegemony over the area. The Babylonians, under the leadership of Nebuchadnezzar (or Nebuchadrezzar), decisively defeated the Egyptians at Carchemish in 605 BCE (2 Kings 24:1). It was this Nebuchadnezzar, as king of the newly ascendant Babylonian Empire, whom Jehoiakim rebelled against three years later. Responding to this rebellion, Nebuchadnezzar moved against Judah (24:2). Thus Jerusalem fell into Babylonian hands on March 15/16, 598/7 BCE, as reported in the Babylonian Chronicles. Jehoiakim died during the siege of Jerusalem and was succeeded by his son Jehoiachin, who surrendered to Nebuchadnezzar (24:12). The upper classes, including many priests, nobles, and skilled artisans, were exiled to Babylon (2 Kings 24:14–16). The Babylonians took Jehoiachin to Babylon as a hostage and appointed Zedekiah as their puppet on the throne. After nine years he rebelled against the Babylonians, bringing Nebuchadnezzar to Jerusalem again, which suffered under a two-year siege. Jerusalem fell in 587/6 BCE, and more people were sent into exile (25:11). Thus, the kingdom of Judah outlasted the kingdom of Israel by some 135 years, but it too fell to a foreign power, bringing to an end a period of national independence that had lasted nearly a half millennium. *See also* Ahaz; Hezekiah; Josiah; Manasseh; Rehoboam.
F.S.F.

Judaism (joo'duh-iz-uhm), the religion of the Jewish people. The term itself is never found in the Hebrew Bible, which was written in a context in which Israelite faith and tradition was not yet conceived as a "religion." The term first occurs in 2 Macc. 2:21, where Judas Maccabeus and his supporters are said to have "fought bravely for Judaism, so that though few in number they seized the whole land and pursued the barbarian hordes" of Antiochus IV Epiphanes. Later in that book, an elder of Jerusalem named Razis is described as a man who had "zealously risked body and life for Judaism" (14:38); he is "accused of Judaism" (possibly of espousing the Jewish faith or practicing rituals associated with Jewish faith traditions) and dies as a martyr. In the NT, the term "Judaism" is used three times. Paul refers to his "earlier life in Judaism" (Gal. 1:13) and says that prior to becoming a missionary for Christ he "advanced in Judaism" beyond many of his peers (1:14). The book of Acts distinguishes "converts to Judaism" from Jews (14:93). The implication here seems to be that the term "Jews" refers to a particular sociological (religious/national/ethnic) group, while "converts to Judaism" are Gentiles who have adopted the Jewish faith (or religion) in a way that did not make them "Jews" in a national or ethnic sense.   M.A.P.

Judas (joo'duhs; Gk. for Heb. Judah).
1 Judas Maccabeus, the third of the five sons of Mattathias. The nickname Maccabeus, which was also used for his followers (the Maccabees), probably derives from a word for "hammer." After Antiochus IV Epiphanes polluted the temple in 167 BCE, Mattathias moved with his family to Modein (1 Macc. 2:1–14). When officers of Antiochus sought to force Mattathias and his family to commit apostasy, Mattathias rose up in defense of the law and the covenant, killed an officer, and led his sons into the wilderness in revolt (2:15–48). Upon the death of his father, Judas successfully led Israel in numerous battles against the Syrians. He defeated a combined army of Syrians and Samaritans (2:49–4:35), the Syrians led by Seron, the Syrians led by Gorgias, and the Syrians led by Lysias, after which the temple was purified (4:36–61; cf. John 10:22). Judas continued to lead Israel in battle with great success, liberating Jews from surrounding territories and even making a treaty with Rome. Finally, against a Syrian army led by Bacchides, Judas fell in battle in 160 BCE (1 Macc. 9:1–18). *See also* Hasmoneans; Maccabees.
2 The son of Chalphi, an officer of Jonathan Maccabeus (1 Macc. 11:70). He and Jonathan remained with Mattathias when all others fled in an ambush at Hazor.
3 The son of Simon Maccabeus and nephew of Judas Maccabeus who with his brother John Hyrcanus successfully led the forces of Israel against Candebeus (1 Macc. 16:2–10).
4 One of the senders of a letter to Aristobolus (2 Macc. 1:10). He was apparently a person of high standing in Jerusalem. Some have speculated that the person intended here could be **1**.
5 Judas of Galilee, a Jewish leader who led a revolt against Rome ca. 6–7 CE, during the census of Quirinius (Acts 5:37). Josephus also mentions him

Judas kisses Jesus, identifying him for Roman soldiers; from the *Winchester Psalter*, ca. 1160.

and credits him with founding the revolutionary group called the Zealots.

6 A brother of Jesus mentioned in Matt. 13:55 and Mark 6:3. He has traditionally been identified as author of the Letter of Jude.

7 One of Jesus's twelve disciples, to be distinguished from Judas Iscariot (cf. John 14:22, where he is called "Judas, not Iscariot"). He is also identified as the son (or possibly the brother) of James (Luke 6:16; Acts 1:13). Virtually nothing else is known of him, though he is sometimes equated in church tradition with Thaddaeus, a disciple mentioned in Matt. 10:3; Mark 3:18.

8 Judas Iscariot, another of Jesus's twelve disciples, who became famous for betraying him (Matt. 10:4; Mark 3:19; Luke 6:16; John 6:71). The origin of the name Iscariot is debated. Some suggestions are man (Heb. *'ish*) from Kerioth; man from Sychar; man from (the tribe of) Issachar; or the assassin (from Gk. *sikarios*). The latter suggestion seems unlikely because John 6:71 indicates that Iscariot was a family name: Judas Iscariot was the son of Simon Iscariot. Judas is said to have possessed a privileged position among the twelve as treasurer of the group (John 13:29), though John's Gospel also claims that he was a thief who would steal from the common purse (12:6). His motivation in betraying Jesus is not given, aside from the suggestions that he did it to obtain thirty pieces of silver (Matt. 26:14–16) or because Satan had entered into him (Luke 22:3; cf. John 13:2, 27). Jesus predicted this betrayal at the last meal that he shared with his disciples (Matt. 26:19–25). Jesus said that it would be better for him if he had never been born (26:24). The betrayal itself seems to have involved leading authorities to Jesus when he was in a private location, apart from the crowds (cf. Mark 14:1–2; John 18:2–3). He did this in Gethsemane, where he identified Jesus specifically as the one to whom he gave a kiss (Matt. 26:48–49; Mark 14:43–45; Luke 22:47–48). After reflecting on what he had done, Judas experienced remorse and returned the money to the authorities who had paid him (Matt. 27:3–4). In sorrow he hanged himself (27:5). According to Acts, he fell headlong, his body split open, and his bowels fell out (1:18).

9 A man who lived in Damascus, into whose home Saul was brought after he was temporarily blinded by his vision of Christ (Acts 9:11).

10 Judas Barsabbas, a leader in the Jerusalem church chosen along with Silas to accompany Paul and Barnabas back to Antioch in order to announce the apostolic decree (Acts 15:22–23). It is possible that he and Joseph (1:23) were brothers.
R.H.S./M.A.P.

Jude, a shortened form of Judas, the ostensible author of the Letter of Jude. He describes himself as "a servant of Jesus Christ and brother of James" (Jude 1). Most interpreters believe this is a reference to the Judas who is elsewhere listed as a brother of Jesus (Matt. 13:55; Mark 6:3; cf. Acts 1:14; 1 Cor. 9:5). It is entirely possible that he would have identified himself as a brother of James, because after Jesus's crucifixion Jesus's brother James was the eldest surviving sibling. A minority view has sometimes identified him with the Judas who is called the son (or possibly brother) of James in Luke 6:16 and Acts 1:13. In this case, he would not be one of Jesus's brothers, but one of his twelve disciples. *See also* Judas; Jude, Letter of; Thaddaeus; twelve, the. M.A.P.

Jude, Letter of, one of the seven Catholic, or General, Letters in the NT. The letter is traditionally ascribed to Jude, the brother of Jesus (though many scholars think it is pseudepigraphical), and it is closely related in content to 2 Peter.

Contents: The letter opens with a salutation and blessing that identify it as a message from Jude, the brother of James, to those who are "kept safe for Jesus Christ" (vv. 1–2). The author explains that the intrusion of ungodly people who pervert the grace of God into licentiousness has made necessary a letter that champions orthodox faith (vv. 3–4). He recites a list of occasions in which God punished the wicked in the past (vv. 5–7) and promises that the current "dreamers" who "slander the glorious ones" will likewise be destroyed (vv. 8–10). He pronounces a prophetic "woe" or curse upon them in language filled with invective and illustrated by allusions to various Jewish writings (vv. 11–16). The letter concludes with exhortations to faithfulness (vv. 17–23) and a doxology to God, who is able to keep people from falling (vv. 24–25).

OUTLINE OF CONTENTS

Jude

J.W.T.

Authorship: The author of the letter identifies himself as Jude "the brother of James," a reference that is almost certainly to James the brother of Jesus; thus, this letter is traditionally ascribed to the Jude who is also identified in the Gospels (along with James) as one of Jesus's brothers (Matt. 13:55; Mark 6:5). The Letter of Jude has often been identified as a pseudepigraphical writing simply because the author's command of Greek surpasses what scholars have thought a Galilean peasant would be capable of producing. This argument has carried less force in recent years, however, as there has been growing recognition that a prominent person in the church would likely have been aided by a trained scribe or amanuensis when composing an official document. Many scholars continue to regard Jude as a pseudepigraphical letter nonetheless, often attributing it to a second-generation Christian who wanted his words to be regarded as part of the legacy of the Holy Family.

Historical Situation: Hypothetically, this letter could have been written at almost any point during the last half of the first century. Certain factors are cited in favor of a date near the beginning of that period (especially if the letter is authentic): the author believes he is living in the last days (v. 18); and he draws upon nonbiblical Jewish traditions (vv. 6, 9, 14–15), which would have ceased to have much relevance for Christians as the church continued to develop. Other factors point to a later date (and contribute to suspicion that the letter is pseudepigraphical): the author refers to "the faith that was once for all entrusted to the saints" (v. 3), suggesting a body of tradition that can be passed from one generation to the next; he also urges his readers to "remember the predictions of the apostles" (v. 17), which suggests he is looking back on the apostolic age as a bygone era. In any case, the Letter of Jude is addressed to a readership that is identified theologically rather than geographically (v. 1), though the extensive use of Jewish traditions suggests an intended audience of Jewish Christians. The purpose of the composition is clear: to expose and condemn false Christians (called "intruders" in v. 4) who are wreaking havoc in the church. The content of the false teaching is difficult to determine, but the troublemakers might be libertine Christians who view the availability of forgiveness as an excuse for permissiveness (v. 4; cf. Rom. 6:1). Other references to the intruders as "dreamers" (v. 8) who reject authority (v. 8) and who slander what they do not understand (vv. 8–10) indicate that they could be hyper-spiritual Christians who place more value on their own ecstatic and visionary experiences than they do on recognized sources of religious authority (e.g., scripture, apostolic tradition, community consensus, decisions of elders).

Major Themes: The Letter of Jude is studied as a paradigm of rhetorical polemic, rife with colorful insults (e.g., "irrational animals," v. 10; "waterless clouds," v. 12; "wandering stars," v. 13; "autumn trees without fruit," v. 12; "wild waves of the sea," v. 13). Much of this language was later taken over by the author of 2 Peter, who reapplied the polemic to different offenders in his context. Perhaps the dominant theme of Jude is simply the certainty of judgment: the fate of the false believers is sealed, for they were designated long ago for condemnation (vv. 4, 13–15). There is also positive affirmation for readers to cling to apostolic tradition and avoid innovation (vv. 3, 5, 17, 22). Finally, discussions of the letter from the early church to the present have focused upon its reliance on nonbiblical traditions. Jude 6 alludes to a story in *1 Enoch* 6–8; Jude 14–15 quotes directly from *1 Enoch* 1:9; and Jude 9 refers to a story that was apparently reported in a now lost work called the *Assumption of Moses*. Jude's reliance on these books is usually viewed as a holdover from a time when the concept of canon was still in flux.

GREAT SINNERS OF THE PAST

The Letter of Jude associates the intruders who have stolen into the church with six notorious examples of wrongdoers from Jewish tradition:

Israelites in the wilderness (v. 5; cf. Num. 14; 1 Cor. 10:1–11; Heb. 3:7–19)

Angels who mated with earthly women (v. 6; cf. Gen. 6:1–4; *1 Enoch* 6–8)

Citizens of Sodom and Gomorrah (v. 7; cf. Gen. 19)

Cain (v. 11; cf. Gen. 4:1–16; Heb. 11:4; 1 John 3:12)

Balaam (v. 11; cf. Num. 22–24; Rev. 2:14)

Korah (v. 11; cf. Num. 16)

See also apocalyptic literature; Catholic Letters/ Epistles; Peter, Second Letter of.

Bibliography

Bauckham, Richard J. *Jude, 2 Peter*. Word, 1983.

Chester, Andrew, and Ralph P. Martin. *The Theology of James, Peter, and Jude*. Cambridge University Press, 1994.

Davids, Peter H. *2 Peter and Jude*. Eerdmans, 2006.

Neyrey, Jerome. *2 Peter, Jude*. Doubleday, 1993.

M.A.P.

Judea (joo-dee′uh), the Greco-Latin form of "Judah." As a geographic term, "Judea" first occurs in Ezra 9:9 to designate the area of the Jewish state ruled by the Persians. It included only a relatively small area around Jerusalem, smaller in extent than the former kingdom of Judah. It extended from Bethel in the north to Beth-zur in the south, and from Emmaus in the west to the Jordan River in the east. After the Persian period (ca. 538–333 BCE), Judea was spoken of during the Maccabean era (ca. 167–63 BCE) as a greatly expanded, independent Jewish state (1 Macc. 5:45; 7:10; 11:28, 34; 12:38). In its most comprehensive political sense, Judea came to include the regions of Galilee, Samaria, Idumea, and Perea. The first-century CE Jewish historian Josephus often uses the term "Judea" in this broad political sense, as does the NT (Matt. 19:1; Luke 1:5; 4:44; 7:17; 23:5; Acts 10:37; 11:1, 29; 26:20). But in other instances, it is used in the more restricted sense, to designate an area around Jerusalem roughly coterminous with the Persian province. Thus, many NT references to Judea might be said to refer to "Judea proper," to the specific territory around Jerusalem that is to be distinguished from Galilee, Samaria, Idumea, or Perea (cf. Matt. 2:22; 4:25; Mark 3:8; Luke 2:4; 3:1; John 4:3–4).

Herod the Great (37–4 BCE) was called king of Judea (Luke 1:5), though he ruled the entire political area (Judea, Galilee, Samaria, Idumea,

Perea). His son Archelaus (4 BCE–6 CE) was called ethnarch of Judea, but he ruled the more limited area of Judea, Idumea, and Samaria (not Galilee or Perea). After Archelaus, this area became part of the Roman province of Syria, and Judea was ruled by prefects or procurators appointed by Rome. These individuals were governors who presided over the same area as Archelaus (Judea, Idumea, Samaria), but they ruled from Caesarea rather than from Jerusalem, as had Archelaus. Throughout Jesus's lifetime (after the banishment of Archelaus in 6 CE), Judea (in this sense) continued to be ruled by a Roman prefect who served under the proconsul, or president, of Syria, who resided in Antioch (Luke 3:1; Josephus *Antiquities* 17.13.5; 18.1.1).

"Judea proper" was not traversed by major trade routes. The land included a sizable desert area in the Wilderness of Judea and had a pastoral economy supplemented by olives and grapes, the principal crops of the highlands. Economically, however, Judea was always dependent upon the revenues generated by Jerusalem, and its population tended to be concentrated around Jerusalem. *See also* Jerusalem; Judah; Judah, kingdom of.   F.S.F.

judge, a person who has the authority to settle disputes and to restore justice. Judges in Israel always ruled with authority delegated to them by God, who was "the Judge of all the earth" (Gen. 18:25). That said, the manner in which judges operated seems to have varied over time. In the early period of Israelite history those who acted in this official capacity were often heads of families or elders of particular tribes. Lot is accused of trying to "play the judge" in Sodom when he defends his visitors (19:9). Judah deigns to exercise such a position as the head of his family in 38:24. Later, the institution of an actual office of judge would be attributed to Moses, whose father-in-law, Jethro, suggested to him that he should attend only to great matters and appoint judges to deal with small matters (18:22). Those selected to be judges were to be capable and God-fearing persons who were trustworthy and incorruptible (Exod. 18:21). Codes for the conduct of judges stress the importance of absolute fairness and impartial judgment (23:1–3, 6–9; Lev. 19:15–16, 35–36; Deut. 16:19–20; 17:8–13). Judges were to protect widows, orphans, and strangers (Deut. 24:17).

In what is called the book of Judges, the term is used in a more discrete sense. The people called "judges" in this book are charismatic leaders upon whom the Spirit of the God falls (3:9). They do not necessarily fulfill a judicial role but, more often, lead armies or in other ways deliver the Israelites from oppressors (2:16; 3:10). Twelve such champions are mentioned: Othniel, Ehud, Shamgar, Deborah, Gideon, Tola, Jair, Jephthah, Ibzan, Elon, Abdon, and Samson. Later, the prophet Samuel is said to have traveled as a judge from city to city, and by this time the role of a judge seems once again to have been more in line with the traditional sense of one who settles disputes (1 Sam. 7:15–16). The book of Ruth also recalls an incident in which elders of the city served as judges (4:2; cf. Judg. 8:16; Job 29:7–8). After the institution of the monarchy, however, the king would serve as the supreme judge (2 Sam. 2–3), though it may be assumed that local magistrates were still appointed (in accord with the model proposed by Jethro in the Pentateuch) and that priests might serve as judges in certain religious matters (Deut. 17:12). In Hellenistic times, the high priest seems to have assumed the role of principal judge (2 Chron. 19:4–11), and by NT times there was some sort of council of priests and other authorities that exercised judicial authority for many matters pertaining to the Jews (Matt. 26:59; Mark 14:55; 15:1; Luke 22:66; John 11:47; Acts 4:15; 5:21, 27, 34, 41; 6:12; 22:5, 30; 23:1, 6, 15, 20, 28; 24:20; cf. Matt. 5:22). Jesus himself refuses to fulfill the role of judge in a personal dispute (Luke 12:14), and he tells a parable about an unjust judge whose yielding to the request of a persistent widow teaches a lesson about prayer (18:2–7).   M.M.S./M.A.P.

Judges, book of, the seventh book of the Tanakh (Jewish Bible) and the Christian OT; it is the second book of the Former Prophets, a subcollection in the Nevi'im, or Prophets section, of the Tanakh. It is preceded by the book of Joshua and followed by the book of 1 Samuel in the Tanakh, but it is followed by the book of Ruth in the OT. The book is anonymous; scholars view it as the second book of the Deuteronomistic History (Joshua–2 Kings), which presents the primary history of the kingdom of Israel from the conquest of Canaan to the Babylonian exile. The book of Judges continues the linear story line of the book of Joshua, but in a rather contradictory way. While the book of Joshua concludes on a note of fulfillment with the full possession of the land (21:43–45), the introduction of the book of Judges contains an inventory of territories that the Israelites did *not* control (1:27–36), and many of the judge stories themselves indicate that the Israelites were at risk from various non-Israelite parties.

The book is entitled *shophetim* in Hebrew, meaning "judges," but the name can be misleading. None of the figures are actually identified as having a formal judicial role as magistrates or legal advocates, except for Deborah (see Judg. 4:4). However, these figures are said to "judge" Israel in a sense associated with advocacy for disadvantaged persons. The notion of justice (Heb. *mishpat*, which is related to *shophet*, "judge") involves standing up for widows, orphans, and strangers (Deut. 10:18, 27:19). A better name than "judges" might have been "defenders" or "protectors."

Contents: After the death of Joshua, the Israelites are attacked by various forces in and around Canaan (Judg. 1). The narrator explains that this happens because the Israelites continue to serve Baal rather than God (2–3). A series of leaders arise to deliver the Israelites. Particularly notable ones are Ehud (3), Deborah (4–5), Gideon (6–8),

Jephthah (Judg. 10–12), and Samson (13–16). Each of these judges has a character flaw or birth defect that is central to the story. Ehud is a left-handed man from Benjamin, which means "son of the right." Because of this aberration he is able to hide his weapon and assassinate the Moabite king Eglon, who is oppressing Israel. Deborah, being a woman, is not a conventional warrior, but she fills a leadership void and leads the charge against Sisera and the Canaanites. Gideon lacks courage, yet he manages to deliver Israel from the Midianites. Jephthah is the son of a prostitute, and he offers his own daughter as a thanksgiving sacrifice after he gains victory over the Ammonites. Samson is a womanizer with a weakness for Philistines; he shows extremely poor judgment and as such serves as the ultimate mirror of Israel during the period of the judges. The remaining chapters of Judges tell of Israelite intertribal conflicts. Micah has a shrine and hires a Levite to be its priest; Danites attack the shrine and take the Levite with them (17–18). The concubine of another Levite is raped and murdered in the town of Gibeah in the territory of Benjamin; this provokes a devastating attack on Benjamin by the other tribes (19–21).

OUTLINE OF CONTENTS

Judges

B.B.

Interpretive Issues: The book of Judges has been the object of considerable analysis using a variety of critical methods (Yee), especially feminist criticism (Bal, Brenner). Women play a remarkable role in the book of Judges, and the way each woman functions within the book reveals something about Israel's attitudes. Ackerman examines the stories of the eleven women in the book of Judges (Achsah, Deborah, Jael, Sisera's mother, the woman of Thebez, Jephthah's daughter,

Manoah's wife [who bears Samson], the Timnite bride of Samson, Delilah, Micah's mother, and the Levite's concubine) and identifies female character "types" within the practice of ancient Israelite religion. Note also that the story of Ruth is set within the period of the judges. The varied roles of the women in Judges reflect both the moral subjection of women and their empowerment at a time of social deterioration.

The core of the book of Judges is the collection of stories about Israel's deliverers. The book was shaped by the Deuteronomistic Historian around the Deuteronomic principle of retribution. Israel had bound itself in a covenant relationship with God that demanded total loyalty to God (Josh. 24) and strict adherence to the terms of the covenant, as laid out in the book of Deuteronomy. But once the Israelites found themselves in Canaan, they strayed from this commitment by worshiping the indigenous deity of that region, Baal, and his female counterpart, Asherah (Judg. 2). Their Canaanite neighbors then overpowered them, and they were at risk of assimilation or worse, annihilation. With Israel in dire straits, God raised up judges and saved the people from certain doom. This state of affairs is repeated regularly in the book and serves as the editorial framework for the account of each judge. The account of the first judge, Othniel (Judg. 3:7–11), typifies the pattern: (1) the Israelites do evil by worshiping Baal; (2) in anger God sends an enemy to oppress them; (3) when Israel begs for help, God sends a judge to deliver them; (4) the judge is victorious over the enemy, and the Israelites find security.

The hand of the Deuteronomistic Historian is especially evident in the way the tales of individual judges are used to create a general picture of Israel during the time period between the initial conquest under Joshua and the founding of the Israelite monarchy. During this period there was apostasy and widespread defection to Canaanite Baalism, the priority of tribalism over tribal unity, and threats from indigenous Canaanites and Canaan's immediate neighbors. The historian uses these pressures to expose the liabilities of the loose tribal federation and the need for structures of kingship in Israel. Occasional local and charismatic leadership was inadequate to the task. The writer concludes the book: "In those days there was no king in Israel; all the people did what was right in their own eyes" (21:25). Webb says the book was structured to address God's nonfulfillment of the land promise made to Israel's ancestors, explained in the book by Israel's repeated apostasy. Klein explains the overall tension between the promise of land and its nonfulfillment in terms of the literary device of irony, which is worked out in the individual stories of the judges.

Bibliography

Ackerman, Susan. *Warrior, Dancer, Seductress, Queen: Women in Judges and Biblical Israel.* Doubleday, 1998

Amit, Yairah. *The Book of Judges: The Art of Editing.* Brill, 1999.

Bal, Mieke. *Death and Dissymmetry: The Politics of Coherence in the Book of Judges*. University of Chicago Press, 1988.

——. *Murder and Difference: Gender, Genre, and Scholarship on Sisera's Death*. Indiana University Press, 1988.

Bandstra, Barry L. *Reading the Old Testament: Introduction to the Hebrew Bible*. 4th ed. Wadsworth, 2009.

Brenner, Athalya, ed. *A Feminist Companion to Judges*. JSOT, 1994.

Klein, Lillian R. *The Triumph of Irony in the Book of Judges*. Sheffield Academic, 1988.

Webb, Barry G. *The Book of the Judges: An Integrated Reading*. JSOT, 1987.

Yee, Gale A. *Judges and Method: New Approaches in Biblical Studies*. 2nd ed. Fortress, 2007.   B.B.

judgment, day of, a term found mainly in the NT referring to the time when God or the Messiah (or the Son of Man) will punish the wicked and redeem the righteous. The background for this concept may be found in the Hebrew Bible, where God is regarded as the Judge of all the earth (Gen. 18:25; Ps. 9:7–8). God's judgment is often invoked on individuals (Gen. 16:5) or nations (Judg. 11:27). Psalm writers, particularly, looked for God to reward the righteous, whether individuals (1:5–6), nations (110:6), the needy and oppressed (72:2–4; 103:6), or the whole world (96:13). Many prophets also spoke of the "day of the LORD," when God would punish nations for their wickedness (e.g., Obad. 15). Such judgment would also come upon Israel (Amos 5:18–20), Judah (Joel 1:15), and all the inhabitants of the earth (Zeph. 1:14–18). Elsewhere, Joel 2:30–32 and Mal. 4:5–6 suggest that those who repent beforehand may be spared. Specific expressions that might be taken as implying a judgment day include "on that day" (Isa. 24:21), "the days are surely coming" (Jer. 9:25–26; cf. Amos 4:2), or simply "then" (Mal. 3:5). Notably, these and similar phrases sometimes point to a time of redemption: "on that day" (Amos 9:11), "in those days" (Jer. 33:16), and, again, "the days are surely coming" (Jer. 23:7–8; cf. Amos 9:13).

Generally speaking, the Hebrew Bible points to God's judgment as occurring within history. Only a few passages hint that the righteous might hope for redemption beyond this life or this world (Job 19:25–27; Isa. 26:19; Ezek. 37:1–14). Dan. 12:1–3 promises that many who have died will awake, some to everlasting life, some to everlasting contempt. Isa. 66:24 contemplates the eternal torment of the wicked. This notion of both punishment and redemption extending beyond human history or life in this world is developed more fully in some Greek texts from the Second Temple period (Jth. 16:17; Wis. 3:1–9; 4 Esd. 14:34–35). It is in those writings that the actual term "day of judgment" first appears (Jth. 16:17; Wis. 3:18; 4 Esd. 7:38, 102, 104, 113; 12:34). The emerging idea is that people will be judged individually in the new age, or perhaps after death, and consigned to their respective destinies. This concept of the "day of

Christ as judge; sixth-century mosaic in San Apollinare Nuovo, Ravenna, Italy.

judgment" has many affinities with what is found in the NT.

According to the first three Gospels, Jesus spoke frequently of the coming judgment. The term "day of judgment" appears in Matt. 10:15; 11:22, 24; 12:36. Often, reference is simply to "the judgment" (Matt. 12:41, 42; Luke 10:14). Related expressions include "that day" (Luke 21:34–35), "on that day" (Matt. 7:22; Luke 17:31), and "in those days" (Mark 13:17, 19, 24). Sometimes, these terms also refer to the expected time of tribulation. Many of Jesus's parables (Matt. 18:23–35) and other sayings (Mark 10:17–25) call his hearers to repentance, so that they might, at the judgment, be found fit to enter the kingdom of God. The classic passage is Matt. 25:31–46, where the Son of Man or "king" sits in judgment, judging the nations of the world as a shepherd separates sheep from goats. According to Matt. 19:28, the twelve disciples of Jesus are to join in judging Israel. In John's Gospel, Jesus speaks of a future judgment (5:28–29; 12:48), but more often emphasizes his own authority as judge (5:22, 30) and suggests that judgment is already taking place (9:39; 12:31).

The term "day of judgment" also appears in 2 Pet. 2:9; 3:7; and 1 John 4:17. That God will judge the world on a certain future day, often designated as "that day" or the "day of the Lord," is also stated (Acts 17:31; Rom. 2:16; 1 Thess. 5:2–4; 2 Thess. 2:2; 2 Tim. 1:18; 4:1–8; 2 Pet. 3:10–12; Jude 6). Paul refers to the coming "day of our Lord Jesus Christ" (1 Cor. 1:8), "the day of the Lord Jesus" (2 Cor. 1:14), "the day of Jesus Christ" (Phil. 1:6), "the day of Christ" (Phil. 1:10; 2:16), and on occasion, "the day of wrath" (Rom. 2:5). Rev. 14:7 looks for the "hour" of God's judgment. In some of these passages, God is the expected judge; in others, it is Christ. Paul thought that "the saints" (faithful Christians) would also judge the world (1 Cor. 6:2; cf. Matt. 19:28). Only those who lived rightly could hope for a favorable decision at the judgment (Rom. 2:1–8; 2 Cor. 5:6–10; cf. Gal. 5:16–21; see also Rev. 20:12–13). Exactly how Paul's ideas about the coming judgment are to be reconciled with his doctrine of "justification through faith" (e.g., Gal. 2:15–16; 3:1–14; Rom. 3:21–4:25) is not completely clear (but cf. 1 Cor. 3:10–15).

Many NT traditions urge that the time of judgment, along with the coming of the kingdom of God (or the Son of Man), is so near that it may happen at any time (e.g., 1 Thess. 5:1–3; James 5:8–9; 1 Pet. 4:5, 7, 17). Paul had to oppose certain enthusiasts who thought the day of the Lord already present (2 Thess. 2:1–12; cf. 1 Cor. 4:5). A few NT passages hint that judgment takes place directly after death (Luke 16:1–9, 19–31; Heb. 9:27; cf. 2 Esd. 14:34–35). *See also* apocalyptic literature; eschatology; heaven; hell; Parousia; resurrection; son of man, Son of Man.   R.H.H.

judgment hall. *See* architecture; Gabbatha.

judgment seat, one translation of the Greek word *bēma*, which refers to the judicial bench of a city court in the Roman Empire. This word is also translated "tribunal" in Acts 18:12, 16, 17; 25:6, 10, 17. Jesus was put on trial before Pilate, who was "sitting on the judgment seat" (Matt. 27:19). The Gospel of John locates this judgment bench "at a place called The Stone Pavement or in Hebrew, Gabbatha" (19:13). Since the Middle Ages, the trial of Jesus was thought to have been at the Tower of Antonia, a belief reinforced in the nineteenth century by the discovery of a Roman pavement under the convent of the Sisters of Zion in the Via Dolorosa section of Jerusalem. That pavement, however, is now known to be from the second century CE, and most scholars would place Jesus's trial before Pilate at the site of Herod's palace, the Citadel of Jerusalem. The term "judgment seat" is used as an eschatological symbol by Paul in Rom. 14:10 ("the judgment seat of God") and 2 Cor. 5:10 ("the judgment seat of Christ"). *See also* Antonia, Tower of; Gabbatha; judgment, day of; tribunal.   C.H.M.

Judith (joo′dith; Heb., "female Judean" or "Jewish woman").
    1 The daughter of Beeri the Hittite (despite her Hebrew name) and wife of Esau (Gen. 26:34).
    2 The heroine of the book of Judith, a widow of Bethulia, who killed the Assyrian Holofernes and saved her city from destruction. *See also* Judith, book of.

Judith, book of, a Greek book found in the LXX, but not in the Hebrew Bible. Roman Catholic and Orthodox Christians include Judith among the deuterocanonical books of the Bible, while Protestants place the book in the Apocrypha. The book relates a tale of faith and horror in which Judith, a beautiful and pious widow, entices and brutally assassinates Holofernes, the Assyrian general besieging her hometown, Bethulia. The story may have been written in Hebrew in the Maccabean era and possibly reflects the defeat of

OUTLINE OF CONTENTS

Judith

I. Holofernes's invasion (chaps. 1–7)
  A. The western nations, including the Jews, refuse to help Nebuchadnezzar, king of the "Assyrians," in defeating Arphaxad, king of the Medes (1)
  B. Nebuchadnezzar commissions Holofernes to invade the western nations (2)
  C. Except for the Jews, all sue for peace and are accepted as vassals (3)
  D. The Jews are alarmed and cry out to God (4)
  E. Holofernes prepares to invade Judea; Achior the Ammonite is turned over to the Jews; he is not to see Holofernes' face again until the general has dealt with them (5–6)
  F. Holofernes besieges Bethulia, and its terrified leaders prepare to surrender (7)
II. The story of Judith (8–16)
  A. Judith is introduced as a beautiful, virtuous, and pious widow with a plan to deliver her people; she asks the leaders to postpone surrender, noting that, in addition to their town, the sanctuary in Jerusalem is in danger (8)
  B. Judith's prayer (9)
  C. She arrays herself in beautiful clothes, provisions herself with kosher foods, and with her maidservant seeks asylum in Holofernes' camp; he is captivated by her great beauty (10–11)
  D. For three nights, Judith goes out to pray and bathe in a spring; on the fourth evening, Holofernes throws a banquet at which he plans to seduce her (12)
  E. Alone in the chambers with the general, Judith decapitates him and, pretending to go out again to bathe, carries his head away to Bethulia in her food bag (13)
  F. Achior looks upon Holofernes' face and becomes a proselyte, as the Assyrians discover Holofernes' body (14)
  G. The Assyrians flee while Judith is honored by the high priest (15)
  H. The song of Judith (16:1–17)
  I. The spoil is dedicated to the temple and Judith returns home (16:18–25)

the Seleucid general Nicanor by Judah the Maccabee (161 BCE). The deliberate confusion of names and events from the Persian, Babylonian, and Assyrian eras, however, is probably a device on the part of the author to indicate that the work is intended as fiction. The name "Judith" means

Judith with the head of the Assyrian general Holofernes, as portrayed by Bernardo Cavallino (1616–56 CE).

"Jewish woman," and, like a good hero from the period of the judges, she returns to her home after delivering her people from the enemy (cf. 16:21). In this way she is contrasted with Judas Maccabeus and his brothers, who continue to seek and attain political power. Like its prototype, the story and song of Deborah (Judg. 4–5), Judith portrays the deliverance of God's people in the face of political and military oppression. The point, furthermore, does not seem to be that God chooses a woman to prove divine strength—Judith is no weakling—but that a woman is the appropriate instrument of a God who is the helper of the oppressed (9:11). Judith may be also a personification of "Judea" and, in her final song of triumph, she speaks as the mother of the Jewish people. The story has had an influence on Western literature and art. It was one of the two apocryphal/deuterocanonical books with sufficient popularity in the West to convince Jerome to include it in his Vulgate translation of the Bible. *See also* Apocrypha/deuterocanonical literature.   D.W.S.

Julia (joo′lee-uh), a woman to whom Paul sends greetings in Rom. 16:15. Philologus, mentioned first in the verse, is perhaps her husband, and "Nereus and his sister" are possibly their children. "All the saints who are with them" may have formed a house-church in their home.

Julius (joo′lee-uhs), a Roman centurion mentioned by name only in Acts 27:1, 3. He is probably the same centurion who was helpful to Paul throughout his eventful sea voyage as a prisoner from Caesarea to Rome (Acts 27:6, 11, 31, 43). According to Acts 27:1, Julius was a member of the "Augustan Cohort." This may have been an honorary title (named after the emperor Augustus) given to Julius's regiment.   A.J.M.

Junia (joo′nee-uh), a Christian to whom Paul sends greetings in Rom. 16:7. It is unclear whether a masculine name (NIV, RSV: Junias) or a feminine name (KJV, NRSV: Junia) is intended, since some Greek manuscripts read the one and other manuscripts read the other. The masculine form, however, is not found elsewhere and may not have existed as a proper name. If a woman, Junia may be the wife of Andronicus. It is significant that the two are perhaps referred to as "apostles." *See also* apostle.

Junias (joo′nee-uhs). *See* Junia.

justice, the standard by which the benefits and penalties of living in society are distributed. The same basic meaning of justice is found throughout the different books and writings of the Bible despite the differing spheres to which it is applied. The pervasiveness of the concept, however, can sometimes be veiled from English readers, because terms approximating justice are often translated in English as "righteousness" or "judgment."

Justice is a chief attribute of God, who is just (Ezra 9:15; Neh. 9:33; Ps. 145:17; Isa. 26:7; cf. Gen. 18:25; Ezek. 33:17, 20). Justice is also fundamentally a relational concept: it exists when things are in their right or proper relationship. This concept underlies the affirmation that Abraham believed the Lord, and "the LORD reckoned it to him as righteousness [justice]." When Abraham trusted in God's promise, his relationship with God was as it should have been, and when relationships are as they should be, there is righteousness or justice.

Specifically, God is the sure defender of the poor and the oppressed (Jer. 9:23–24; Ps. 10:17–18). This care of God is universal (Pss. 76:8–9; 103:6). The Psalms ground justice in God's role as the sovereign creator of the universe (99:1–4). Since the justice of God is characterized by special regard for the poor and the weak, a corresponding quality is demanded of God's people (Deut. 10:18–19). When they properly carry out justice, they are agents of the divine will (Isa. 59:15–16). In the NT, Paul presents God's justice as grace flowing into and through the believers to the needy (2 Cor. 9:8–10). The demand of God for justice is so central that other responses to God are empty or diminished if justice is lacking (Amos 5:21–24; Mic. 6:6–8; Matt. 23:23). Justice is demanded of all people, but particularly of political authorities (Jer. 21:11–12; Isa. 1:10, 17). Furthermore, because God is sovereign over all, the demands of God's justice extend beyond the nation of Israel (Ps. 9:7–9; cf. Dan. 4:27).

Justice is closely related to love and grace (Deut. 10:18–19; Hos. 10:12). Justice thus provides vindication, deliverance, and creation of community in addition to retribution. "Need" becomes the criterion for distributing benefits; particular attention is given to the needy, including the poor, widows, the fatherless, slaves, resident aliens, wage earners, and those with physical infirmities (Job 29:12–17; Ps. 146:7–9; Mal. 3:5). Justice is associated with the basic requirements of life in community. Basic needs become basic rights. Thus, what is literally called "the justice belonging to the needy" is properly translated as "the rights of the needy" (Jer. 5:28, NRSV). These rights include land (Ezek. 45:9), food and clothing (Deut. 10:18), and shelter (Job 8:6). The context for administration of justice is the creation of community and the preservation of people in it (Lev. 25:35–36; Job 24:5; Ps. 107:36; Luke 7:29–30). But justice is obtained by rectifying inequities of the disadvantaged (Ps. 76:9) and eliminating conditions that produce injustice (10:18), and such redress will not be to the advantage of everyone in the community. Those of low degree are exalted, but those of high degree are brought down (1 Sam. 2:7–10; cf. Luke 1:51–53; 6:20–26). *See also* justification; righteousness.

Bibliography

Mott, Stephen Charles. *Biblical Ethics and Social Change.* Oxford University Press, 1982. Chap. 4.

Snaith, Norman H. *The Distinctive Ideas of the Old Testament.* Epworth, 1944. Chap. 3.   S.C.M.

justification, the exculpation of guilt or the demonstration of the correctness of an act or statement. The English word "justification" and its related terms "just," "justly," "justify" are all used to render the Hebrew *tsdq* and the Greek *dikaioō* (all together the two words occur in the Bible about 750 times). These concepts are also frequently expressed in English Bibles by the term "righteousness" and its related forms. Thus, in Rom. 3:26 the death of Christ demonstrates both that God is righteous and that God justifies those who believe in Jesus.

The Hebrew Bible sometimes speaks of a human desire to justify oneself (Job 32:2; 33:32; Isa. 43:9) or to show that one is "in the right." When applied to God (Job 32:2; Ps. 51:4), these same terms can express a response to theodicy, i.e., justifying the ways of God to human beings. The Bible insists that God *is* just (Ezra 9:15; Neh. 9:33; Ps. 145:17; Isa. 26:7) regardless of whether this is apparent to human beings (Ezek. 18:25, 29; 33:17, 20; cf. Gen. 18:25). The more significant question is whether human beings can be justified before God (Job 9:2). The eventual answer is, not that love or mercy triumphs over righteousness, but that righteousness is seen as having a saving dimension (Isa. 51:1, 5, 6, 8; NRSV: "deliverance"). It is an aspect of God's righteousness to save or justify or vindicate human beings (Isa. 50:8; cf. Rom. 8:33).

Early Christians confessed that Jesus was put to death "for our trespasses" and raised "for our justification" (Rom. 4:25). They claimed to be "justified . . . in Christ Jesus . . . by his blood" (3:24–25).

MODELS FOR JUSTIFICATION IN PAUL

In Romans and in his other letters, Paul draws on different images for explaining how the death and resurrection of Jesus Christ can justify people, or make them right with God (Rom. 3:24–26, 30; 4:24–5:1; 5:9, 16–21; cf. 1 Cor. 6:11; Gal. 2:21; 3:11–14).

Substitution: All people are guilty of not living as God requires and the penalty is (eternal) death; Jesus was completely innocent, but died on the cross to take the penalty for everyone else. See Rom. 3:23–24; 5:6–8; 6:23.

Redemption: People are like slaves, owned by some hostile power (sin, death, the devil); the purchase price for freedom is the blood of Christ, and God pays this so that people can now belong to God. See Rom. 3:24; 8:23; 1 Cor. 1:30; 5:20; 7:23.

Reconciliation: People have been unfaithful to God in ways that have severely damaged the divine-human relationship; Jesus comes as the mediator and offers his own life to restore the broken relationship. See Rom. 5:10; 2 Cor. 5:18–20.

Atonement: People have sinned against God, who demands sacrifices of blood to nullify the consequences of sin; Jesus died on a cross to offer one supreme sacrifice for the sins of all. See Rom. 3:25.

Participation: People live under the power of sin and death and the only way out is to die and rise to new life; through baptism, people are united with Christ, participating in his death and (ultimately) in his resurrection. See Rom. 6:1–11; Gal. 2:19–20.

From Mark Allan Powell, *Introducing the New Testament* (courtesy, Baker Academic)

As these passages indicate, the concept was worked out most deliberately by Paul, who also taught that justification through faith "apart from works of the law" (3:28) applied equally to both Jews (3:30) and non-Jews (Gal. 3:8). This universality of justification could be demonstrated by comparing Christ with Adam; Adam's trespass brought condemnation for all, whereas Christ's act of "righteousness" brought justification or acquittal and life to all. Thus sinners are "made [declared, established as] righteous" (Rom. 5:16–21). God "justifies the ungodly" who trust God (4:5); they receive peace and life in the Spirit (5:1; 8:4). The Letter of James also speaks of justification (2:24–25), not in opposition to Paul, but against people who fail to understand that faith includes obedience to God as opposed to mere creedal assent (Rom. 1:5). *See also* righteousness.

Bibliography

Ehrman, Bart D. *The New Testament: A Historical Introduction to the Early Christian Writings,* 3rd ed. Oxford University Press, 2004. Pp. 353–59.

Reumann, John. *Righteousness in the New Testament.* Fortress, 1982.   J.H.P.R.

Justus (juhs′tuhs).

1 The Latin name of Joseph Barsabbas, one of two disciples put forward to be chosen as a replacement for Judas Iscariot. Even though he is not mentioned in any of the Gospels, Acts 1:22–23 indicates that he had been with Jesus and the others from the time of John's baptism through the time of Jesus's ascension. He did not end up becoming one of the twelve, however, because the replacement for Judas was chosen by lot, and the lot fell on another otherwise unknown disciple, Matthias.

2 Titius (tish′ee-uhs) Justus, a "worshiper of God" (perhaps a Gentile attracted to Judaism) in Corinth who, according to Acts 18:7, offered hospitality to Paul after the latter was forced to leave the synagogue. He probably hosted a house-church composed of early followers of Jesus in Corinth.

3 A Jewish-Christian co-worker with Paul mentioned in Col. 4:11. He is actually referred to as "Jesus called Justus," indicating that Jesus was his real name.   A.J.M.

Opposite: Samuel anoints David (*far right*) king (1 Sam. 16:11–13); from a panel at the third-century CE synagogue at Dura-Europos.

K̄

kab, a measure of capacity in 2 Kings 6:25. From rabbinic information it was ⅟₁₈ of an ephah, which is 1¹⁄₁₆ of a quart. *See also* weights and measures.

Kabzeel (kab′zee-uhl; Heb., "may God gather"), a town of Judah near the Edomite border (Josh. 15:21), the home of Benaiah (2 Sam. 23:20; 1 Chron. 11:22). It has been possibly identified as modern Khirbet Hora, about ten miles northeast of Beer-sheba. The city is called Jekabzeel in Neh. 11:25.

Kadesh (kay′dish).

1 Kadesh-barnea (kay′desh-bahr-nee′ah), a place in the wilderness of Paran between Shur and Edom, or alternately in the Wilderness of Zin, where it formed the south border of Canaan and the west border with Edom. In one passage it is called En-mishpat (Gen. 14:7). Abraham dwelt in the area (20:1). It was the camp for the failed invasion of Canaan from the south (Num. 13–14), after which the Israelites left the area. At this time Kadesh became an important symbol in the early history of Israel (see Num. 32:8; 33:36–37; Deut. 1:2, 19, 46; 2:14; 9:23; 32:51; Josh. 10:41; 14:6–7; 15:3; Judg. 11:16–17). Miriam died at Kadesh (Num. 20:1). It was there that the Hebrews were camped when they were denied permission to traverse Edom by the king of Edom (20:14–21). The site is probably to be identified with modern 'Ain-Gedeirat, which has a tenth-century BCE fortress as well as a reservoir 75 feet square and 9 feet deep dating from the pre-Roman era.

The oasis at 'Ain-Gedeirat in southern Israel, the location of the biblical Kadesh-barnea.

2 Kadesh-on-the-Orontes, where Rameses II fought with the Hittites (ca. 1286 BCE). Although the Hittites were able to prevail in the battle, they were unable to press the advantage.   S.B.R.

Kadmiel (kad′mee-uhl; Heb., "God is of old" or "God goes before"), the father of a Levite family (Ezra 2:40; Neh. 7:43) who supervised reconstruction of the Jerusalem temple in the late sixth century BCE (Ezra 3:9) and participated in various services there (repentance, Neh. 9:4, 5; sealing the covenant, 10:9; thanksgiving, 12:8; praise and thanks, 12:24).

Kadmonites (kad′muh-nits; Heb., "easterners"), a tribe or people living in terrain west of the Euphrates River. In Gen. 15:19 they are paired with other nomadic people, the Kenites and Kenizzites, whose lands were promised to Abraham's descendants. The name may simply reflect the direction of their territory from the standpoint of the biblical writer. *See also* Kedemah.

Kain (kayn).

1 Another name for the family group otherwise called Kenites (Num. 24:22).

2 A city of Judah (Josh. 15:57), whose location may be modern Khirbet Yaqin, about seven miles southeast of Hebron, traditionally viewed as a Kenite city.

Kallai (kal′i), the head of a priestly family in postexilic Judah under the high priest Joiakim (Neh. 12:20).

Kanah (kay′nuh; Heb., "reed").

1 The Wadi Kanah, a small brook that filled with water only during the rainy season. Identified with modern Wadi Qanah, it formed part of the boundary between the tribes of Ephraim and Manasseh (Josh. 16:8; 17:9). It flowed generally west and southwest, joining the Yarkon before emptying into the Mediterranean Sea north of present-day Arsuf.

2 The north border town of the tribe of Asher (Josh. 19:28), modern Qana (not NT Cana) about six miles southeast of Tyre.

Kareah (kuh-ree′uh; Heb., "bald"), the father of Johanan, a military commander in Judah at the beginning of the exile (2 Kings 25:23; Jer. 40:8).

Kartah (kar′tuh), a city in Zebulun mentioned in Josh. 21:34. *See also* Athlit.

Kattath (kat′uhth), a town of the tribe of Zebulun (Josh. 19:15) whose location is unknown. It may be identical to Kitron (Judg. 1:30).

Kedar (kee′duhr; Heb., "dark"), a confederation of Arab tribes based in the north Arabian desert. In Gen. 25:13 and 1 Chron. 1:29, Kedar is one of the twelve sons of Ishmael. The Kedarites were a major force from the late eighth century BCE until the rise of the Nabateans in the fourth century BCE and are frequently mentioned in Assyrian and Neo-Babylonian sources. They raided lands on their eastern and western borders and controlled the eastern trade route from Arabia to the Fertile Crescent. Thus, although they dwelt in the eastern desert in dark tents (Isa. 42:11; Jer. 2:10; 49:28; Ps. 120:5; Song of Sol. 1:5) and were herders (Isa. 60:7; Jer. 49:29), their "princes" traded with Tyre, which lay on the coast of the Mediterranean Sea far to the north and east (Ezek. 27:21). The later extent of their influence is illustrated by a silver bowl dated to the fifth century BCE from modern Tell el-Maskhuta in the eastern Nile Delta dedicated to the goddess Han-Ilat by "Qaynu the son of Gashmu the king of Kedar"; this Gashmu is the same as "Geshem the Arab" of Neh. 2:19; 6:1. In the Bible the military might of the Kedarites is indicated by reference to their archers and warriors (Isa. 21:16–17). *See also* Geshem.   M.D.C.

Kedemah (ked′uh-muh; Heb., "easterner"), one of Ishmael's sons (Gen. 25:15; 1 Chron. 1:31). He was probably the ancestor of the Kadmonites (Gen. 15:19). The name derives from the Hebrew root *qdm,* which literally means "front"; it receives the added sense of "easterner" because the "front," or beginning, of the day is in the east. *See also* Kadmonites.

Kedemoth (ked′uh-moth), the wilderness area east of Jordan from which Moses sent a message to Sihon requesting permission to pass through his land (Deut. 2:26). Later Kedemoth appears as a levitical city within the territory of Reuben (Josh. 13:18) assigned to the Merarite families (Josh. 21:37; 1 Chron. 6:79). *See also* Dibon; levitical cities; Merari; Reuben; Sihon.

Kedesh (kee′dish; Heb., "to be holy"), a name for several places with ancient sanctuaries; they are often difficult to distinguish from one another.

1 Kedesh in Naphtali (Josh. 19:37); it is the town from which Barak was called (Judg. 4:6) and where he gathered his forces (4:10). Modern Khirbet Qedish in southeastern Galilee is a more likely site for the Israelite forces to assemble than **2** below.

2 Kedesh in Galilee, a site identified with modern Tell Qadis northwest of Lake Huleh. It was set apart as a city of refuge and as a levitical city (Josh. 20:7; 21:32; 1 Chron. 6:76). The Kedesh where Heber pitched his tent and Sisera escaped (Judg. 4:11, 17) was probably this northern site, near Canaanite Hazor and away from the center of Israelite strength. It was captured by Tiglath-pileser III in the reign of Pekah (ca. 736–732 BCE), king of Israel (2 Kings 15:29).

3 Kedesh in Issachar, the levitical city of Issachar according to 1 Chron. 6:72, although the parallel passage in Josh. 21:28 identifies it as Kishion, as does 19:20. This may be the town listed after Taanach and Megiddo, whose king was taken by Joshua (12:22); perhaps it is to be identified with

modern Tell Abu Qudeis, which lies between the two sites.

4 Kedesh in Judah, a city near the southern border (Josh. 15:23).

See also Kadesh; levitical cities.   N.L.L.

Keilah (kee-i′luh), a town of Judah (Josh. 15:44; 1 Chron. 4:19) identified as modern Khirbet Qila, located eight and a half miles northwest of Hebron. It was repaired by postexilic Levites (Neh. 3:17–18), but it is more prominent as a town rescued by David from Philistine assault during threshing season (1 Sam. 23:1–5) and used by David as a haven from Saul until fear of betrayal by the local people moved him to seek safety in the hills (23:6–14).

Kemuel (kem′yoo-uhl).

1 A cousin of Abraham and ancestor of the Arameans (Gen. 22:21).

2 A leader of the tribe of Ephraim, appointed by Moses to assist in dividing the land of Canaan into tribal territories (Num. 34:24).

3 A Levite whose son was the tribe of Levi's official representative in David's government (1 Chron. 27:17).

Kenan (kee′nuhn), an early Israelite ancestor from the days before the flood. He is listed as the son of Enosh (Gen. 5:9; 1 Chron. 1:2) and the father of Mahalalel (Gen. 5:12; 1 Chron. 1:2) and others (Gen. 5:13), and he is said to have lived 910 years (5:14). Some suggest the name is an alternative form of Cain, since it is sometimes found as Cainan (Luke 3:37). *See also* Kenites.

Kenath (kee′nath), an important city of Bashan guarding the desert highway from Rabbath-ammon to Damascus, located about fifty miles southsoutheast of the latter. Mentioned in the Egyptian Execration texts, the annals of Thutmose II, and the Amarna correspondence, the city was conquered by Nobah of Manasseh, who renamed it Nobah after himself (Num. 32:42). Subsequently the city fell under Aramean control (1 Chron. 2:23), and by NT times it was one of the cities of the Decapolis, called Canatha (but not mentioned in the Bible). It has been identified with the extensive ruins of Qanawat.

Kenaz (kee′naz).

1 The son of Eliphaz, who was the firstborn son of Esau and Adah (Gen. 36:11; 1 Chron. 1:36). As the grandson of Esau, he became a chief of the Edomites. He may be the eponymous ancestor of the Kenizzites, a group known to have later inhabited the Negev (assuming migration from Edom). *See also* Kenizzites.

2 The father of Othniel and younger brother of Caleb (Josh. 15:17; Judg. 1:13; 3:9; 1 Chron. 4:13).

3 The grandson of Caleb (1 Chron. 4:15).

Kenites (ken′its), an ethnic group listed among the pre-Israelite inhabitants of the land of Canaan

(Gen. 15:19). Their name is popularly derived from "smith" (Heb. *qayin*), a theory supported, but not proven, by the fact that the Kenites lived in northern Sinai, a region of copper mining and smelting in ancient times (cf. Num. 24:17–22). Moses's father-in-law, Jethro (also called Reuel and Hobab), a priest of Midian (Exod. 2:15–16; 3:1; 18:1; Num. 10:29), is identified in Judg. 1:16; 4:11 as a Kenite. Some Kenite families evidently accompanied the Israelites to the Plains of Moab, for Judg. 1:16 reports that "the descendants of Hobab the Kenite, Moses's father-in-law, went up with the people of Judah from the city of palms [probably Jericho] into the wilderness of Judah, which lies in the Negev near Arad . . . and settled with the Amalekites." One Kenite family from this Negev community, Heber and his wife Jael, migrated north to settle in Zaanannim, near Kedesh (probably just northeast of Mount Tabor), where Jael subsequently killed Israel's enemy Sisera in her tent (Judg. 4:11, 17–22; 5:24–27). Later, in Saul's campaign against the Amalekites of northern Sinai, he sent word to the Kenites to separate themselves from the Amalekites; Saul wanted to spare the Kenites, since they had shown "kindness to all the people' of Israel when they came up out of Egypt" (1 Sam. 15:6). During Saul's reign (late eleventh century BCE) a section of the Negev, evidently in the Arad area (cf. Judg. 1:16), was known as "the Negev of the Kenites" (1 Sam. 27:10). David, while living in Ziklag, sent gifts of spoil to some of the "cities of the Kenites" in southern Judah (30:29). The Chronicler also mentions scribes who came from three families of Kenites who lived at Jabez: the Tirathites, the Shimeathites, and the Sucathites, all of whom are said to have come from Hammath, ancestor of the tent-dwelling Rechabites (1 Chron. 2:55; cf. Jer. 35). *See also* Cain; Jethro.   D.A.D.

Kenizzites (ken'uh-zits), an ethnic group mentioned among the pre-Israelite peoples of Canaan in Gen. 15:19. Caleb is referred to as "Caleb the son of Jephunah the Kenizzite" (Num. 32:12; Josh. 14:6, 14). Whether the Kenizzites should be connected with the Kenaz of Gen. 36:11 is uncertain. As the grandson of Esau, Kenaz is more obviously associated with the Edomites, but there is some speculation that a group of Edomites may have migrated to the Negev, perhaps early in the Late Bronze Age. In any case, the Kenizzites came to be associated with the Israelite tribe of Judah and appear to have been absorbed by them. *See also* Kenaz.

Keren-happuch (kair'uhn-hap'uhk; Heb., "horn of antimony" [black eye shadow]), the third of Job's daughters, born after his trials had ended (Job 42:14). Although three earlier daughters, lost in a catastrophe, are unnamed, the three new daughters born to Job at the end of the book are named (Jemimah, Keren-happuch, and Keziah). This seems especially noteworthy, since none of his sons are named at either the beginning or

ending of the book (cf. 1:18). Keren-happuch and her sisters are said to be the three most beautiful women in the land, and they receive inheritances along with their brothers (42:15).

Kerioth (kair'ee-oth). A city in Moab (Jer. 48:24, 41). Numerous sites have been proposed by modern archaeologists. It may have been a royal city of some sort, as Amos 2:2 refers to its royal palaces. Line 13 of the Moabite Stone refers to its having a principal sanctuary of the god Chemosh. The word "Iscariot" is sometimes taken to mean "man of Kerioth," indicating that Judas Iscariot might have been from this city. *See also* Iscariot; Kerioth-hezron.

Kerioth-hezron (kair'ee-oth hez'-ron), a town in the mountains of Idumea, west of the southern shore of the Dead Sea. It is mentioned only in Josh. 15:25, which indicates that the place was also known as Hazor. Still, it is not to be confused with the Canaanite city of Hazor in the Huleh Plain north of the Sea of Galilee (11:1–14). This Hazor has been tentatively identified with modern Khirbet el-Quaryatein, about four and a half miles south of Maon. Some scholars, however, think that the reference in 15:25 is to Kerioth and Hezron, two separate cities. If that is the case, Kerioth would be a different (otherwise unknown) city than the Kerioth of Moab (Jer. 48:24; Amos 2:2) and Hezron would perhaps be a border settlement near Kadesh-barnea (Josh. 15:3).

Keturah (ki-tyoor'uh), a wife (Gen. 25:1) or concubine (1 Chron. 1:32) of Abraham who bore him six sons after the death of Sarah: Zimran, Jokshan, Medan, Midian, Ishbak, and Shuah (Gen. 25:1–6; 1 Chron. 1:32–33). The biblical genealogies that list the descendants of Abraham and Keturah link various groups of people who settled to the south and east of the Hebrews with the Israelites, indicating that they too were descendants of Abraham. This identification, however, is muted somewhat in that these nations are consistently referred to as the "children of Keturah" rather than as the "children of Abraham" (Gen. 25:4; cf. 1 Chron. 1:33). In another sense, however, the descendants of Abraham and Keturah provide partial fulfillment of God's promise that Abraham's offspring would be like the "stars of the sky" (Gen. 15:5).

key. In the Bible, a key is often a symbol of a servant's authority over the master's household; the one who holds the key has access to the master's property and presence (cf. Judg. 3:25). Thus, God promises to raise up a new servant within Israel and to give him the "key of the house of David," so that what he opens no one will shut and what he shuts no one will open (Isa. 22:22). Picking up on this, the author of Revelation presents Jesus as the one who possesses the "key of David" (3:7). Elsewhere, Revelation indicates that Jesus possesses keys to open the realms of Hades and death (1:18), while heavenly angels wield keys to the abyss from

Peter receiving the "keys of the kingdom of heaven" (Matt. 16:19), as depicted on an eleventh-century enamel plaque.

which a plague of locusts is released (9:1) and in which Satan is to be bound (20:1). In the Gospel of Matthew, Peter is given the keys to the kingdom of heaven, an authority that is specifically exercised by binding and loosing commandments of the law in a way that unlocks the will of God (16:19; cf. 18:19). In Luke's Gospel, Jesus accuses lawyers of taking away the "key of knowledge": they do not enter into knowledge themselves and they hinder others who would enter (11:52).   P.P./M.A.P.

Keziah (ki-zi′uh). *See* Keren-happuch.

Kibroth-hattaavah (kib′roth-huh-tay′uh-vuh; Heb., "graves of lust"), a locale between Mount Sinai and Hazeroth (identified with modern Rueis el-Ebeirij). It was there that the Israelites died by plague as they consumed quail that God rained down upon them in answer to their complaints. The plague punished their lusting after the meat, fish, and other delicacies they had enjoyed in Egypt (Num. 11:31–34; cf. 1–6; 33:16–17; Deut. 9:22).

kid, a young goat, regarded as savory when prepared for food (Gen. 27:9; cf. Luke 15:29). The animal was used for ritual meals (Judg. 6:19) and sacrifices (Num. 5:11; Judg. 13:15–19; 2 Chron. 35:7). The Israelites were forbidden to boil a kid in its mother's milk (Exod. 23:19; 34:26; Deut. 14:21). A few passages mention someone bringing a kid to someone else as a gift or as payment for services (Gen. 38:17, 20, 23; Judg. 15:1; 1 Sam. 16:20)—perhaps because it was considered a delicacy or simply because it was an animal easy to carry. Apparently, kids also became proverbial examples of weak and helpless animals; when the spirit of the Lord came upon Samson, he tore apart a lion barehanded, as "one might tear apart a kid" (Judg. 14:6). Thus, the paradisal kingdom of God was pictured as a realm in which even a kid would be safe from its natural enemies (Isa. 11:6). *See also* goat.   M.A.P.

kidneys (Heb. *kelayot;* Gk. *nephroi*), part of the group of fat pieces burned on the altar in sacrifi-

cial offerings (Exod. 29:22; Lev. 3:4; 4:9; 7:4). In the NRSV, the term "kidneys" is used only once with reference to the human organ (Job 16:13). The Hebrew and Greek terms, however, are used elsewhere, in two different contexts. First, the Hebrews sometimes used the term "kidneys" as a generic reference to one's inner organs (cf. Ps. 139:13, NRSV: "inward parts"; Lam. 3:13, NRSV: "vitals"). Second, the ancient Hebrews seem to have thought of the kidneys as the seat of emotion or conscience (similar to the role assigned to the heart in modern Western thought). Thus, the Bible refers to God as, literally, searching the kidneys of people to know their true self (Jer. 11:20; 20:12; Ps. 73:21); likewise people may be "upright in kidneys" (Ps. 7:10), and when their speech is insincere, they may be said to have God near to their mouths but far from their kidneys (Jer. 12:2). Their kidneys may rejoice with gladness (Prov. 23:16) or faint with fear (Job 19:27). The NRSV uses "heart" or "hearts" in all of these passages, except Prov. 23:16, where it uses "soul." *See also* fat; heart.   M.A.P.

Kidron (kid′ruhn), the valley that lies east of Jerusalem between the Temple Mount and the Mount of Olives. The valley runs on a north–south axis, joining the Tyropoeon and Hinnom valleys south of the Jebusite and Davidic city of Jerusalem. Originally the Gihon spring flowed into the Kidron, but Hezekiah's tunnel brought the water of Gihon to the Pool of Siloam inside the city. From Jerusalem, the Kidron Valley extends southeastward through the Wilderness of Judah to the Dead Sea.

The Kidron Valley lay just beyond the eastern boundary of Jerusalem during the monarchy (1025–587/6 BCE). David fled from Jerusalem across the Kidron during Absalom's rebellion (2 Sam. 15:23). Nearly a thousand years later, Jesus, with his disciples, crossed the Kidron after the Last Supper on the way to Gethsemane (John 18:1).

The Kidron was also the place where idols and cult objects from pagan shrines were destroyed by the reformer kings Asa (1 Kings 15:13), Hezekiah (2 Chron. 29:16; 30:14), and Josiah (2 Kings 23:4–6). Kidron may have been chosen because it was just outside the boundaries of the city and convenient to the temple.

Aerial view of the Kidron Valley, which separates the Temple Mount area in Jerusalem from the Mount of Olives to the east (*left*).

On the east side of Kidron are a number of ancient tombs along with a modern Jewish cemetery. Most notable of the ancient tombs are the Pillar of Absalom, the Cave of Jehoshaphat, the Tomb of Bene Hezir, and the Tomb of Zachariah. Each of these monuments appears to belong to the Hellenistic period of the third and second centuries BCE.

The Gihon spring is on the west side of the Kidron. Excavations there have uncovered a Jebusite water shaft that led to this spring centuries before Hezekiah constructed his famous tunnel. Remains of a water channel, cut into the bedrock of the hillside, have also been recovered. This water channel brought water from Kidron to the Pool of Shelah, below the Pool of Siloam, during the early monarchy (eleventh–tenth centuries BCE).

Kidron is often identified as the site of the king's garden (Neh. 3:15). Similarly Kidron is frequently identified with the "King's Valley," where Absalom built his monument, which later became his tomb (2 Sam. 18:18). Despite these popular identifications of Kidron, however, there is no definite evidence linking it either to the King's Valley or to the king's garden. The tombs popularly ascribed to Absalom and other kings also belong to a later era. *See also* Gihon; Jerusalem; Olives, Mount of.

J.F.D.

king. In biblical times a king generally held office for life, and monarchies were usually hereditary. In the Bible, the Israelite king is sometimes referred to as a "son of God" (Ps. 2:7; cf. Isa. 9:6–7) and, so, may sometimes be called a "prince" (1 Sam. 9:16; 13:14), since God is the true king. Also, in Israel, the king was sometimes called the "anointed one" (1 Sam. 2:35; Ps. 132:17), a designation from which the term "messiah" is derived.

In the Hebrew Bible: The concept of kingship in ancient Israel was different from that of the monarch in Egypt and Mesopotamia, where kingship was regarded as a divinely ordained political order that had existed from nearly the beginning of time. In Israel, by contrast, kingship was reckoned to be a relatively late institution. Even at the height of the monarchy, the Israelites cherished traditions of a past time when they were ruled directly by God, who raised up champions and deliverers (such as Moses, Joshua, and various charismatic judges) as needed. Their own tradition maintained that the need for kingship developed in response to internal pressures and external threats, especially the need to counter the increasing might of the Philistines (1 Sam. 13:19–21). Kingship was not instituted, however, without serious reservations and misgivings, as the role and function of the king had to be assessed with regard to divine authority. Jotham's fable (Judg. 9:7–15) reflects opposition to the institution of kingship in Israel; the moral is that only a useless person (symbolized by the bramble) would ever accept the office.

Thus, the accounts of the institution of the monarchy in 1 Sam. 1–12 evidence both anti-

and promonarchic tendencies. Samuel warns the people of the "ways of the king" (8:10–19) in a passage that lists monarchic excesses. Still, Samuel, as God's prophet, takes the initiative in finding and anointing Saul as the first king, who is said to be possessed by the "spirit of God" (9:1–10:16; 11). Even when objections to the monarchy waned in Israel, the king's power was not unrestrained and was repeatedly checked by the terms of God's covenant as articulated by influential priests and prophets. Further, the king in Israel (including David, who was later regarded as the ideal king) was never an absolute lord. He could not expropriate land with impunity (2 Sam. 24:24; 1 Kings 16:24; 21:4), nor was he exempt from moral and civil law (Deut. 17:14–20). Even with these restraints, however, Israel did know some despotic monarchs who were guilty of apostasy and lawlessness, chief among them being Manasseh (2 Kings 21:1–18). Excesses in monarchic power were one of the main things to call forth prophetic rebuke, and the Hebrew scriptures record a whole series of prophet-king encounters, beginning with Nathan's challenge to David (2 Sam. 12:1–15) and continuing until the dissolution of the monarchy with the fall of the two nation-states of Israel and Judah.

The prophetic critique of kingship was based upon the conviction that God was the original and only king of Israel and, later by extension, of all peoples (Jer. 10:7–10). The formula introducing a prophetic oracle, "Thus says the LORD," was in fact originally a formula announcing a message from a monarch (i.e., "Thus says the lord . . ."). Therefore, the form of God's covenant with Israel resembles that of a suzerainty treaty between king and people. The king in Israel ruled over the people, but he was God's vassal. A mythically enlarged or spiritualized conception of kingship is found in the Psalms (47; 96–99). For all people to know and worship God, who was "a great King above all gods" (Ps. 95:3), became a goal of Jewish apocalyptic thought.

In the NT: Kings mentioned in the NT include Herod the Great (Matt. 2:1; Luke 1:5), Herod Antipas (Matt. 14:9; Mark 6:14), Herod Agrippa I (Acts 12:1), Herod Agrippa II (Acts 25:13), and Aretas of the Nabateans (2 Cor. 11:32). All of these persons ruled at the pleasure of Caesar and, in some cases, the term "king" seems to be applied imprecisely (Antipas was technically a tetrarch). Jesus tells parables about kings (Matt. 18:23–35; 22:2–14; Luke 14:31–42; 19:12–27); he also refers to God as a king (Matt. 5:35) and both teaches and preaches about the "kingdom of God" (e.g., Mark 1:14–15; John 3:3). The latter concept is also prevalent in the teaching of Paul (e.g., Rom. 14:17; 1 Cor. 4:20).

John's Gospel recalls an incident in which Jesus had to escape from people who wanted to make him king by force (6:15). Jesus' entry to Jerusalem was interpreted as a claim to be a king of some sort (Matt. 21:5; Luke 19:38; John 12:13–15; cf. Zech. 9:9), and Jesus was both suspected and accused of claiming to be the "King of Israel" or the "King of the Jews" (Matt. 2:1; 27:11, 29, 37, 42; Mark 15:2, 9, 12, 18, 26, 32; Luke 23:2–3, 37–38; John 12:13; 18:33, 39; 19:3, 19, 21; cf. Acts 17:17). This designation is treated with special ambiguity in John's Gospel, in which the designation seems to be a confessional title applied to Jesus by those with faith in him (1:49; 12:13), although Jesus himself denies that his kingdom is of this world (18:36–37). In Matthew's Gospel, the Son of Man who returns for the final judgment is designated king (25:31–46).

Later NT literature refers to God as the "King of the ages" (1 Tim. 1:17) and "king of the nations" (Rev. 15:3) as well as to Jesus Christ as "King of kings and Lord of lords" (1 Tim. 6:15; Rev. 19:16; cf. 17:14). The book of Revelation also refers to Abaddon/Apollyon, the king of the bottomless pit, whence comes an army of monstrous locusts (9:11). *See also* kingdom of God; messiah; prince.

F.S.F./M.A.P.

kingdom of God,

kingdom of God, the phenomenon of God's rule, or the realm over which God rules or will rule. The phrase is not used as such in the Hebrew Bible, but occurs first in the apocryphal/ deuterocanonical book Wisdom of Solomon, where Wisdom declares the kingdom of God to the righteous (10:10). The phrase is used repeatedly in the NT, especially in the Synoptic Gospels.

In the Hebrew Bible: Although it does not employ the exact phrase "kingdom of God," the Hebrew Bible does have much to say about God's present and future reign. First, many biblical passages affirm that God rules over creation, caring for people and other creatures, bringing about divine purposes through them or on their behalf (e.g., Job 38–39; Pss. 104; 145; 147; Isa. 45:1–13; Dan. 4:17; Jon. 1–4; Tob. 13:1–2). That God reigns or rules in history, over the affairs of Israel and other nations, is also often affirmed, especially in Psalms (e.g., 22:27–28; 47; 95–99; see also Dan. 4:3, 34–35). God's reign also takes the form of judgment against Israel, Judah, or other nations (e.g., Jer. 1–11; Ezek. 12–16; Amos 1:3–4:13). It is also recognized, however, that other forces are at work, preventing the fulfillment of God's purposes, most notably the perversity of God's own people (e.g., Isa. 1; 3; 5; Jer. 2–8; Hos. 4–10; Amos 2:26–6:13; 8:4–7) and hostile enemy nations (e.g., Isa. 13:1–19:15; Amos 1:3–2:3). Fate and chance are other factors (Eccles. 9:11–12). Thus, the prophetic writings often look forward to a future time when God's rule or reign will be established on earth (e.g., Obad. 21; Hag. 2:21–23; Zech. 14:9). Then God's people will no longer suffer oppression at the hands of other nations. In some prophetic passages, the new era is visualized as one in which Israel, Judah, or the Jewish people will gain the advantage over their erstwhile enemies (e.g., Obad.; Joel 3:19–21). In other texts, the new era is seen as one in which all nations will live at peace, acknowledging, if not also worshiping, the Lord as their sovereign (e.g., Isa. 2:2–4; 19:19–24;

Mic. 4:1–3; Tob. 13:11; cf. Zech. 14:16–19). And in some, the new era will be one of peace and blessing for all creation: humans and other animate beings will enjoy life together without hurting or destroying one another in a transformed world (e.g., Isa. 11:6–9; 65:17–25; Hos. 2:18; cf. Ezek. 34:25–28). Several prophetic texts look specifically for the coming of David—or a "branch" or descendant of David—to rule as king or messiah in that new age (e.g., Isa. 9:7; 11:1–5; Jer. 30:9; Ezek. 34:23–24; 37:24–26; Amos 9:11; cf. Hag. 2:20–23). Many other texts express hope for the coming of the new age, but without mentioning a new king or messiah (e.g., Isa. 2:2–4; Jer. 31:31–34; Dan. 2:44; 7:13–27; Hos. 2:16–23; Obad. 21; Zech. 14:9; Tob. 13:15–18).

In the NT: According to the Synoptic Gospels, the phrase "kingdom of God" was a central feature of Jesus's proclamation. In Matthew's Gospel, the phrase "kingdom of heaven" is often (though not always) used as a circumlocution for "kingdom of God," probably as a way to avoid using the divine name. The meaning is the same. In John's Gospel, Jesus speaks of the kingdom of God in only one passage (3:3, 5). Outside the Gospels, the phrase is mentioned in Acts (1:3; 8:12; 14:22; 19:8; 28:23, 31), and it is used in letters attributed to Paul (Rom. 14:17; 1 Cor. 4:20; 6:9–10; 15:50; Gal. 5:21; Col. 4:11; 2 Thess. 1:5), but nowhere else in the NT.

The references to the kingdom of God in the Synoptic Gospels receive the most attention, because the concept seems so central to Jesus's message and because the phrase encompasses an ambiguity that has intrigued interpreters. Jesus's sayings about the kingdom of God seem to fall into at least three different categories. First, Jesus talks about the kingdom of God as a *reality that is already present.* He points to his exorcisms as signs that the kingdom of God has come, i.e., that it is already present through his ministry (Matt. 12:28). He tells people who want to know when the kingdom of God is coming that it is already among them (Luke 17:21). Second, Jesus also talks about the kingdom of God as an *imminent future reality.* Its arrival is at hand (Mark 1:15; NRSV: "has come near"), and he insists that some people who are currently alive will not die until they see that the kingdom has come with power (9:1). And, third, Jesus sometimes speaks of the kingdom of God as the *culmination of all human history,* as something that comes into existence only when heaven and earth pass away. He urges people to pray for God's kingdom to come (Matt. 6:10) and tells them to watch for signs of its coming (Luke 21:31). They must beware of those who say "The time is near" (21:8), for there will be wars and disasters and tribulations galore before the kingdom is finally revealed (Matt. 24:3–18). Often, Jesus speaks of the kingdom in ways that do not make clear whether he is describing God's present, imminent, or ultimate reign (e.g., Luke 4:43; 9:11).

Many scholars have noted that the English phrase "kingdom of God" does not do justice to the Greek *basileia tou theou* that is employed throughout the NT. The English phrase connotes a physical space or location (the place where God rules), whereas the Greek can refer to an action (i.e., the phenomenon of God ruling). Many scholars suggest "reign of God" or "rule of God" as more appropriate translations for *basileia tou theou* than "kingdom of God" (which is used in the NRSV and almost all other English Bibles). In

THE KINGDOM OF GOD IN THE TEACHING OF JESUS: SAMPLE PASSAGES

"Strive first for the kingdom of God and [God's] righteousness" (Matt. 6:33).

"If it is by the Spirit of God that I cast out demons, then the kingdom of God has come to you" (Matt. 12:28).

"The time is fulfilled, and the kingdom of God has come near; repent, and believe in the good news" (Mark 1:15).

"The kingdom of God is as if someone would scatter seed on the ground, and would sleep and rise night and day, and the seed would sprout and grow, he does not know how" (Mark 4:26–27).

"There are some standing here who will not taste death until they see that the kingdom of God has come with power" (Mark 9:1).

"It is better to enter the kingdom of God with one eye than to have two eyes and be thrown into hell" (Mark 9:47).

"Let the little children come to me; do not stop them, for it is to such as these that the kingdom of God belongs" (Mark 10:14).

"Whoever does not receive the kingdom of God as a little child will never enter it" (Mark 10:15).

"How hard it will be for those who have wealth to enter the kingdom of God" (Mark 10:23).

"I will never again drink of the fruit of the vine until that day when I drink it new in the kingdom of God" (Mark 14:25).

"Blessed are you who are poor, for yours is the kingdom of God" (Luke 6:20).

"There will be weeping and gnashing of teeth when you see Abraham and Isaac and Jacob and all the prophets in the kingdom of God, and you yourselves thrown out" (Luke 13:28).

"The kingdom of God is not coming with things that can be observed; nor will they say, 'Look, here it is!' or 'There it is!' For, in fact, the kingdom of God is among you" (Luke 17:20–21).

"No one can see the kingdom of God without being born from above" (John 3:3).

some cases, Jesus certainly does seem to be referring to a location (Mark 14:25; Luke 13:28). But in other cases he seems to be speaking of something more experiential; people strive for the kingdom of God when they seek to have lives ruled by God (i.e., to live in accord with God's will, Matt. 6:33). Jesus often speaks of "entering" the kingdom, without making clear whether doing so was understood to be a present possibility or something that would only become possible in the future. To enter God's kingdom might mean to enter a realm of life beyond death or it might mean to enter into the sphere of God's present-day power and influence—or it might mean some combination of the two (since these thoughts are not mutually exclusive). When a crucified thief pleads with Jesus, "Remember me when you come into your kingdom," and Jesus responds, "Today, you will be with me in Paradise," the kingdom that is mentioned obviously seems to be a realm beyond death (Luke 23:43). In John's Gospel, however, entering the kingdom definitely seems to be a present possibility, albeit one that involves a transformation of life analogous to a new birth (3:3–5).

Interpreters have dealt with the ambiguity of Jesus's "kingdom of God" sayings in manifold ways. Some stress the authenticity of the "imminent future" sayings and attribute the other material to apologetic tendencies of the early church (since Jesus's predictions of an imminent event did not come to pass). Others insist that Jesus spoke only of the kingdom as a present, ethical experience and maintain that it was a generation of later followers who imposed their apocalyptic mind-set onto the Jesus tradition. The majority of scholars today steer a more moderate course between these extremes, allowing for Jesus to have embodied the ambiguity that is currently manifest in the NT itself. In any case, the cumulative witness of the NT documents is a close association of the rule/reign/kingdom of God with the person of Jesus Christ. The NT authors seem to believe that (1) the kingdom of God was present on earth in an unprecedented manner when Jesus himself was present on earth, for God's presence and power were manifest in his very person and in his ministry; (2) the kingdom of God is still present in some sense in exactly the same way that Jesus Christ is still present, i.e., it is experienced in the community of his followers (the church) and through the Holy Spirit, whom he has given; and (3) the kingdom of God will not be fully present until Jesus comes again and then, at his Parousia, the reality of God's presence and power will be realized in an absolute and ultimate sense, with eternal consequences. *See also* apocalyptic literature; eschatology; eternal life; Jesus Christ; judgment, day of; Parousia; resurrection; son of man, Son of Man.

M.A.P.

kingdom of heaven. *See* kingdom of God.

Kings, First and Second Books of, biblical writings that follow the books of Samuel in the Tanakh (Jewish Bible) and in the Christian

Elijah, with raised arm, as the fire of the Lord falls upon the bull offering, in the contest with the prophets of Baal (1 Kings 18:30–39); panel at the third-century CE synagogue at Dura-Europos.

OT; they are found in the Prophets, or Nevi'im, section of the Tanakh and are the fifth and sixth books of its Former Prophets subcollection. Originally, 1 and 2 Kings were one book, but it was divided into two parts in the LXX, where the books of Samuel and Kings are divided into four books called 1 Kingdoms, 2 Kingdoms, 3 Kingdoms, and 4 Kingdoms. Jewish tradition identifies the prophet Jeremiah as the author of 1 and 2 Kings, though the books themselves are anonymous; scholars view the books as part of the Deuteronomistic History (Joshua–2 Kings), which presents the primary history of the kingdom of Israel from the conquest of Canaan to the Babylonian exile. In 1 and 2 Kings the narrative of Israel is taken up where 2 Samuel leaves off and extended from the death of David and reign of Solomon to the Babylonian exile. The scope of the content of Kings is approximately the same as that of 2 Chronicles, which uses the two-volume work as a source.

Contents: The books of Kings divide into three sections based on historical content. The first section deals with the kingdom of Solomon and the united monarchy, the second with the civil conflict that led to national division and the resulting parallel histories of Israel and Judah, and the third with the history of Judah down to the Babylonian exile.

After David died, Solomon gained control of the monarchy in Jerusalem by eliminating his rivals Adonijah, another son of David, and Adonijah's lieutenant Joab (1 Kings 1–2). Solomon was recognized for his wisdom (3–4) and effectively made Jerusalem the religious capital of Israel by building the temple there (5–8). Solomon lost popular and divine support due to his excesses—too much public debt and too many foreign wives who worshiped their homeland deities (9–11). After Solomon died, Jeroboam led the northern territories in rebellion against Solomon's son Rehoboam, and they established their own independent kingdom, which continued the name Israel, while the kingdom of David's line assumed the name Judah (12–14). Israel's monarchy was less stable than Judah's until Omri took the throne (15–16). Omri's son Ahab promoted Canaanite Baal practices in Israel and was challenged by the prophet Elijah and others (17–22). The prophet Elisha followed Elijah in opposition to Omri's Israelite dynasty (2 Kings 2–9). Jehu violently eliminated the house of Omri and established his own dynasty.

All told, Israel and Judah coexisted for about two hundred years (2 Kings 9–16). Then Assyria conquered and destroyed Israel (17) and attacked Judah, but Hezekiah's Judah survived (18–20). The evil king Manasseh (21) was followed by the good king Josiah, who reestablished worship of the Lord in Judah (22–23). But Judah stood helpless before Nebuchadnezzar of Babylon, who twice invaded Judah and ultimately destroyed Jerusalem and deported influential Judeans to Babylon (24–25).

Thus, 1 and 2 Kings begins with the united kingdom, relates the origin of Israel as a separate kingdom alongside Judah down to its demise, and then traces the history of the two separate kingdoms, concluding with the demise of Judah and the exile of its people.

Background: The Deuteronomistic Historian cites a variety of written sources, such as the "Book of the Acts of Solomon" (1 Kings 11:41) and the "Book of the Annals of the Kings of Israel" (14:19), indicating that written documents from the royal court were available. Portions of Kings found their way into other books: 2 Kings 18:13–20:19 is duplicated in Isa. 36–39, and 2 Kings 24:18–25:30 is mostly duplicated in Jer. 52. The first edition of Kings probably was written during the reign of Josiah (late seventh century BCE). A second edition written during the Babylonian exile added coverage of the last kings of Judah (Jehoiachin, Jehoiakim, and Zedekiah), the destruction of Jerusalem and the temple, and the governorship of Gedaliah. It implies that the long descent and final destruction of Judah were due to the apostasy of Manasseh, the most notable king who reigned between the pious kings Hezekiah and Josiah. The final edition of Kings ends with a touch of optimism by noting that the king of Babylon had released the exiled Jehoiachin from prison. Kings reflects the general outlook of the larger Deuteronomistic Historian that favors Judah over Israel, because

Israel rebelled against the leadership of the house of David and refused to honor the Lord in Jerusalem. The retribution theology of Deuteronomy, which connects apostasy with punishment, is employed to explain the division of the kingdom after the death of Solomon, the destruction of Israel by the Assyrians, and the destruction of Judah and Jerusalem by the Babylonians.

The history of the Israelite and Judean monarchies as told in Kings has numerous points of contact with documents outside the Bible and with the results of archaeological work throughout the Near East. To identify just a few connections: the Mesha Inscription, also called the Moabite Stone, mentions "Omri, king of Israel" and Mesha, king of Moab, who rebelled against Ahab (2 Kings 3:4–5); the Tel Dan "house of David" inscription in Aramaic relates to the coup of Jehu (1 Kings 19:16–17; 2 Kings 9–10); the Black Obelisk of Shalmaneser III pictures Jehu bowing to the Assyrian king; and the Siloam tunnel inscription in Hebrew commemorates the completion of its construction during the reign of Hezekiah (2 Kings 20:20). Various texts from the Assyrian and Babylonian royal archives relate to the history of Israel in Kings, including the Assyrian king Sargon II's destruction of Samaria; the Assyrian king Sennacherib's siege of Hezekiah's Jerusalem (in which Sennacherib brags he locked Hezekiah up "like a bird in a cage"); and the Babylonian king Nebuchadnezzar's siege of Jerusalem in 598 BCE.

Interpretive Issues: The books of Kings relate a history of the Israelite monarchies from a theological perspective. Although the Christian canon identifies the books of Kings as historical works, the Hebrew canon classifies them as prophetic books. They present events in a chronological sequence, but they do not deliver a comprehensive documentary history of Israel in a way comparable to modern historiographic research and writing. Instead, they deliver a prophetic analysis of Israel's kings using the principles of Deuteronomic theology. Kings are presented as the guardians of religion and its institutions. Kings are judged good or evil on the basis of their roles, respectively, in promoting the exclusive worship of the Lord or supporting the worship of other deities. Certain Judean kings are the only ones who receive approval, notably Hezekiah and Josiah, and only because they were from the lineage of David and only insofar as they kept the worship of the Lord exclusive and pure in Jerusalem.

Influences: The books of Kings function as the primary history of the time when the nation of Israel was ruled by kings. Within the Bible itself, these books served as a source upon which other books appear to have drawn. The books of Isaiah and Jeremiah utilize portions of Kings, and Kings was the major source for the revisionist history found in 2 Chronicles. Crucial figures and institutions in 1 and 2 Kings that would prove to be particularly influential on religious, literary, and cultural history include the figure of Solomon, who established the perspectives and practices of wisdom in Israel; the temple in Jerusalem and its related institutions that were foundational for Israel's religion; Elijah, who was the prototype of the courageous and countercultural prophet of the Lord; and Josiah the reformer, who retrieved true Israelite religion and restored faith in Jerusalem.

Bibliography

Bandstra, Barry L. *Reading the Old Testament: Introduction to the Hebrew Bible.* 4th ed. Wadsworth, 2009.

Campbell, Anthony F., and Mark A. O'Brien. *Unfolding the Deuteronomistic History: Origins, Upgrades, Present Text.* Fortress, 2000.

Cogan, Mordechai. *1 Kings.* Doubleday, 2001.

Cogan, Mordechai, and Hayim Tadmor. *2 Kings.* Doubleday, 1988.

Finkelstein, Israel, and Neil A. Silberman. *The Bible Unearthed: Archaeology's New Vision of Ancient Israel and the Origin of Its Sacred Texts.* Free Press, 2001.

Provan, Iain W., V. Philips Long, and Tremper Longman III. *A Biblical History of Israel.* Westminster John Knox, 2003.

Sparks, Kenton L. *Ancient Texts for the Study of the Hebrew Bible: A Guide to the Background Literature.* Hendrickson, 2005.   B.B.

king's garden, the royal gardens in Jerusalem, situated in the tract before the confluence of the Kidron and Hinnom valleys and irrigated by the Siloam Pool and En-rogel. From the City of David, the gardens were reached by descending the steps from the Fountain Gate (Neh. 3:15). Through this exit, King Zedekiah fled besieged Jerusalem in 587/6 BCE (2 Kings 25:4).

King's Highway (Heb. *derek hammelek,* "the royal way"), in the Bible, the route by which Moses sought to lead the Hebrews through Edom and Moab (Num. 20:17; 21:22; cf. Deut. 2:17). Although it is possible that *derek hammelek* was nothing more than the common designation for a public road that ran through a particular region (as in the use of *harran sarri* for a number of roads in Mesopotamia), most scholars use "King's Highway" as a proper name for the major international route that traversed the entire length of Transjordan's plateau. Specifically, this roadway ran from Damascus to the Gulf of Aqabah, connecting many important towns in between (e.g., Ashtaroth, Rabbath-ammon, Dibon, Kir-hareseth, Bozra, Ezion-geber). Known later in Arabic as Tariq es-Sultani, the "Sultan's Highway," an actual roadway was repaired by King Mesha of Moab in the ninth century BCE (cf. Mesha Inscription, line 26). The antiquity of this route is evident in the itinerary recorded in Gen. 14:5–6, though King's Highway is modern nomenclature. The Romans called it the Via Nova after the Roman emperor Trajan (98–117 CE) had his legions construct a road early in the second century CE, and modern Jordan's major highway follows closely the line of the ancient route.

Bibliography

Aharoni, Yohanan. *The Land of the Bible: A Historical Geography.* Rev. ed. Westminster, 1979.

Beitzel, Barry J. "Roads and Highways." *Anchor Bible Dictionary.* Doubleday, 1992. 5:776–82.

Dorsey, David A. *The Roads and Highways of Ancient Israel.* Johns Hopkins University Press, 1991.

Glueck, Nelson. *The Other Side of the Jordan.* Rev. ed. American School of Oriental Research, 1970.   G.L.M.

kings of Israel and Judah. *See* chronology, Hebrew Bible.

King's Pool, a reservoir in the royal gardens at Jerusalem (Neh. 2:14), probably the Pool of Shelah receiving water from the Gihon spring. It may be identical with the Upper Pool (Isa. 7:3).

King's Valley, the valley of Shaveh (Gen. 14:17–18), where Abraham met the king of Sodom and also Melchizedek. In 2 Sam. 18:18 it is the location of Absalom's monument near Jerusalem. It is probably the Kidron Valley just east of that city.

Kir (kihr).

1 The place to which Assyria's king Tiglath-pileser (ca. 745–727 BCE) took his Damascus captives (2 Kings 16:9). It was remembered by Amos (9:7) as the ancestral home of the Syrians, to which they were condemned to return (1:5). It may also have been the source of allies in the action Isaiah anticipated against Judah (22:6). The precise location is unknown.

2 The Moabite city Kir-hareseth, a Moabite capital mentioned in Isa. 15:1. The site has been identified with modern el-Kerak (the site of a magnificent Crusader castle). It is located on a promontory eleven miles east of the Dead Sea and about seventeen miles south of the Arnon gorge. The site was protected by 300-foot drops on all sides of its 2,500-foot-long salient, and it stood 3,110 feet above sea level, 4,400 feet above the surface of the Dead Sea.   R.S.B.

Kiriath (kihr´ee-ath; Heb., "city of"), a frequently used prefix of compound names for places, such as Kiriath-arba, Kiriath-arim, Kiriath-baal, Kiriath-huzzoth, Kiriath-jearim, Kiriath-sannah, and Kiriath-sepher.

Kiriathaim (kihr´ee-uh-thay´im; Heb., "two cities").

1 A city in Moab assigned to the tribe of Reuben (Num. 32:37; Josh. 13:19). It is thought to have been located in the area of modern el-Qereiyat in the Transjordan, five and a half miles northwest of Dibon. Kiriathaim is mentioned in the Moabite Stone inscription (early ninth century BCE), and it was in Moabite hands at the time of the exile three hundred years later (Jer. 48:1, 23; Ezek. 25:9).

2 A levitical city in the territory of Naphtali (1 Chron. 6:76) given to Gershomites, probably modern Khirbet el-Qureiyeh, likely identical with Kartan (Josh. 21:32).

Kiriath-baal (kihr´ee-ath-bay´uhl) *See* Baalah; Kiriath-jearim.

Kiriath-jearim (kihr´ee-ath-jee´uh-rim; Heb., "city of forests"), a city of the tribe of Judah (Josh. 18:14), also called Baalah (Josh. 15:9–10; 1 Chron. 13:6), Kiriath-baal (Josh. 15:60; 18:40), and Baale-Judah (2 Sam. 6:2). The location is modern Deir al ʻAzhar, about eight miles north of Jerusalem and just west of Abu Ghosh. It was the subject of an Israelite treaty with Gibeonites (Josh. 9:17), and its alternative names testify to Caananite influence (e.g., Baalah, "place of Baal"; Kiriath-baal, "city of Baal"). It was a border town of the tribes of Judah, Dan, and Benjamin (18:14), and it had excellent water, for which it was sought as a bivouac (18:12). The Philistines returned the ark to this city (1 Sam. 7:2), where it remained until David moved it to Jerusalem (1 Chron. 13:5–14). The prophet Uriah (Jeremiah's contemporary) came from this city (Jer. 26:20–23), and some of the city's citizens returned to it from exile in Babylon (Neh. 7:29; cf. Ezra 2:25, Kiriath-arim). *See also* Baalah. R.S.B.

Kiriath-sepher (kihr´ee-ath-see´fuhr), an early name for Debir (Josh. 15:15; Judg. 1:11). *See also* Debir.

Kish.

1 A Benjaminite from Gibeah who was the son of Abiel and the father of Saul (1 Sam. 9:1, 3; 10:11, 21; 14:51; 2 Sam. 21:14; 1 Chron. 12:1; 26:28). He is described as a man of wealth. He was buried at Zela in Benjamin, where Saul and his son Jonathan were also buried after their bodies were recovered from the Philistines (2 Sam. 21:14).

2 A son of Jeiel and Maacah (1 Chron. 8:30; 9:36); he may be the same person as **1** if 1 Chronicles is regarded as preserving a corrupted or variant genealogy.

3 A Levite of the Merarite family who was the son of Mahli and the father of Jerahmeel (1 Chron. 23:21–22; 24:29). His sons married the daughters of his brother Eliezer.

4 Another Levite of the Merarite family who was the son of Abdi and who was involved in cleansing the temple during Hezekiah's reforms (2 Chron. 29:12).

5 A Benjaminite ancestor of Mordecai (Esther 2:5).

6 A Mesopotamian city, eight miles east of Babylon, that dominated the history of the first Early Dynastic period (2900–2700 BCE). Excavations reveal extensive remains of the first palace known from this time. Although fragmentary, remains of two ziggurats are visible. According to the Sumerian King List, Kish is the place where kingship was restored following the flood. The Babylonian story *Gilgamesh and Agga* reflects tensions between the kings of Uruk and Kish, respectively.

The title "King of Kish" appears to have indicated hegemony over Sumer and Akkad throughout this time period. Kish declined in political importance with the northward shift of power under Sargon of Akkad, ca. 2350 BCE. L.E.P.

Kishon (ki´shon), **Wadi,** a stream bed in which much of the year water flows westward through the Esdraelon (Megiddo) Plain. One major source rises in the springs west of Mount Tabor and the Galilean hills south of Nazareth and flows to the south. The other major source rises in several springs in the vicinity of Megiddo and flows to the north from near Mount Gilboa. They join in the Esdraelon Plain, and from there the river winds its way northwestward through the narrow pass between Mount Carmel and the Galilean hills and enters the Plain of Acco. It empties into the Mediterranean by the excavated site of modern Tell Abu Hawam. Most of the year the Kishon is a sluggish brook. During the rainy season it can be swampy through the Megiddo Plain. Thus, Judg. 5:21 reports that, during Deborah's defeat of the Canaanites, "the torrent Kishon" swept away the forces of Sisera. Although the exact location of that battle cannot be determined, Sisera's chariots and troops were drawn out to meet Barak at the river Kishon (4:7), and the Song of Deborah suggests a place near Taanach (5:19). This victory at the river Kishon is also recalled in Ps. 83:9. Later, it was near the Wadi Kishon that Elijah killed the prophets of Baal when they could not call down fire on their offering on Mount Carmel (1 Kings 18:40). *See also* Jezreel; Taanach. N.L.L.

kiss. In the Bible, kissing has little to do with eroticism or romance. Kissing between lovers is mentioned only three times: in Prov. 7:13 (where it is the act of a "loose woman"; cf. 7:5) and in Song of Sol. 1:2; 8:1. More often, kissing is associated with greeting relatives or friends (Exod. 4:27; 18:7; 29:11, 13) and with taking leave of loved ones (Gen. 31:28, 55; 32:1; 2 Sam. 19:40; 1 Kings 19:20; Ruth 1:9, 14; cf. Acts 20:37). A kiss could express favor (2 Sam. 15:5), blessing (Gen. 27:26–27; 48:9–10; 2 Sam. 19:39), grief (Gen. 50:1; Acts 20:37), devotion (Luke 7:38), or reconciliation (Gen. 33:4; 45:15; Luke 15:20). In a negative sense, kissing the hand of a creditor is a humiliating example of fawning behavior (Sir. 29:5), while "kissing calves," i.e., idols, is a ridiculous display of misplaced devotion (Hos. 13:2). Kisses from enemies were not uncommon (Prov. 27:6), but they expressed betrayal with cruel irony (2 Sam. 20:9; Matt. 26:49) precisely because a kiss was supposed to convey trust, affection, or at least hospitality (cf. Luke 7:45).

In the NT, the "holy kiss" or "kiss of love" became a greeting exchanged between Christians, possibly as a liturgical act in their worship services. Paul closes a number of his letters with an admonition for the recipients to greet one another with "a holy kiss" (see Rom. 16:16; 1 Cor. 16:20; 2 Cor. 13:12; 1 Thess. 5:26; cf. 1 Pet. 5:14, "Greet one another with a kiss of love"). If, as many think, this practice included men and women kissing each other, then the practice would appear to be a somewhat novel development. Whereas it may have been common in the biblical world for men to kiss men (1 Sam. 20:41; 2 Sam. 20:9) and for women to kiss women (Ruth 1:9, 14), there does not appear to have been widespread precedent in Jewish or Greco-Roman society for cross-gender kisses between men and women who were neither relatives (Gen. 29:11–12) nor lovers (Song of Sol. 1:2; 8:1). Some scholars trace the practice of Christian men and women kissing each other to the teaching of Jesus that identified his followers as family members (Mark 3:35). Based on this idea, a greeting shared between literal brothers and sisters may have become a symbolic act expressing the spiritual relationship between those who considered themselves to be one family in Christ. By the second century, the ritual exchange of a "kiss of peace" became a standard component of the Sunday morning liturgy (see Justin Martyr *First Apology* 66).

Bibliography

Penn, Michael Philip. *Kissing Christians: Ritual and Community in the Late Ancient Church*. University of Pennsylvania Press, 2005.   M.A.P.

Kittim (kit′im).

1 The descendant of Javan, the fourth son of Japheth who was a son of Noah, and Elishah's brother (Gen. 10:4; 1 Chron. 1:7).

2 An island in the Mediterranean Sea, possibly Cyprus. Both Num. 24:24 and Dan. 11:30 refer to "ships from Kittim." The first-century CE historian Josephus (*Antiquities* 1.28) identifies Kittim with Kition, or Kitti, a Phoenician city on the island of Cyprus, later known as Larnaka. It is possible that the biblical texts use the word for this city or for the entire island of Cyprus, or even as a generic reference to all islands of the Aegean Sea. In Jer. 2:10 and Ezek. 27:6, the NRSV simply translates Kittim as Cyprus. First Maccabees, however, says that Philip of Macedon was from Kittim (1:1), indicating the name might refer to Greece (or at least to Macedonia).

3 A people mentioned briefly in the pseudepigraphical books *Testament of Simeon* (6:3) and *Jubilees* (24:28).

4 A people who are described in the Dead Sea Scrolls as the last Gentile world power to oppress the people of God. In the Habakkuk commentary (1QpHab) the "Chaldeans," sent by God to execute divine judgment, were understood to be the Kittim. In a fragmentary commentary on Isaiah (4Q161–165) the downfall of the Assyrians was interpreted as the war of the Kittim. The war of the Kittim is described in the *War Scroll;* the children of light take the field against the enemy of Israel, the Kittim, "those who deal wickedly against the covenant" (1QM 1:2; 15:2). The author of the scroll believed that Isaiah's prophecy against Assyria (31:8) would be fulfilled after the victory over the Kittim. Many scholars identify the Kittim

in these passages with the Syrians, but others associate them with the Romans.   Y.G.

kneading bowl, a container for mixing ingredients in preparing bread (Exod. 8:3; 12:34; Deut. 28:5, 17). It could be made of wood, bronze, or pottery and was important enough to be taken along when traveling (Exod. 12:34). While shallow, it could be round or irregularly shaped. Kneading was usually done by hand, but it could be done by foot also.

kneel. *See* gestures, postures, and facial expressions.

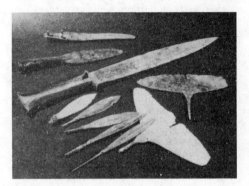

Bronze implements, including a knife, from a fourteenth-century BCE cemetery near Acre.

knife. There is some overlap in biblical references to knives and swords, the former being shorter and used more often for everyday purposes than military ones. Still, the account of Joab's murder of Amasa, where the latter was stabbed as the two men embraced, probably presupposes a knife (or dagger) being used in a military fashion. Knives also played a ceremonial role in the ancient world, as did other implements of war. Archaeological excavations have found a number of them from different historical periods partially constructed with inlaid ivory or with precious metals. The royal treasury of Judah had sufficiently fine ceremonial knives for Nebuchadnezzar to confiscate them when Jerusalem fell to his siege (Ezra 1:9). Specifically, knives were used in the ritual slaughter of animals for sacrifice (cf. Gen. 22:9–14). They were also used for the circumcision ceremony, where at least some of the knives were made of flint rather than metal (Josh. 5:2–3). Yet another ritual use is recorded by the prophets of Baal, who cut themselves to receive their god's attention (1 Kings 18:28). Such activity is forbidden in the levitical law (Lev. 19:28). Knives were also used as razors, for shaving or trimming a beard or other body hair (Ezek. 5:1; Isa. 7:20).   J.A.D.

knowledge. The Hebrew term for knowledge (*yada'*) carries a sense of experience, emotion, and personal relationship along with intellectual understanding. The Greek term (*gnōsis*) refers primarily to intelligent apprehension, but the NT tends to use the word in a manner influenced by the biblical (Hebrew) context. Individual books of the Bible, however, develop particular meanings of "knowledge."

There is a basic sense in which knowledge implies awareness and insight (Eccles. 1:16). Most of the time, however, there is a strong experiential and relational aspect to knowledge. The pharaoh who does not know Joseph (Exod. 1:8) has had no personal relationship with him. The "suffering servant" knows grief (Isa. 53:3; NRSV: "is acquainted with"), because he has experienced it firsthand. Indeed, "knowing" a person can be a euphemism for having sexual relations with that person (Gen. 4:1; Luke 1:34). This concept of intimate experience even applies to self-knowledge; in Gen. 3:1–7, Adam and Eve eat of the tree of the knowledge of good and evil (2:9) and become aware of shame (their nakedness). Thus, Isaiah says that sinners do not know the way of peace, because they do not walk in the ways of justice; their actions or lifestyles reveal what they know or don't know (59:8). In the same vein, wisdom literature (e.g., the book of Proverbs) uses the term "knowledge" as a synonym for "wisdom" or "understanding" and connects knowledge closely with the "fear of the LORD" and obedience to God's commandments (e.g., Prov. 1:7; 2:6). As for knowledge of God, the Bible indicates that God is only known through self-revelation; Israel knows God by acknowledging and accepting God's revelation (Deut. 11:2–7; Isa. 11:2; 41:20; Jer. 2:8; 9:6). The nations do not know God (Jer. 10:25), but God's saving acts on behalf of Israel cause them to know God's power (Isa. 37:20). Conversely, God knows humans completely; for example, God knew Jeremiah before he was born (Jer. 1:5) and appointed him to be a prophet.

The NT also understands knowledge in terms of relational experience. In the Gospel of John both God and Jesus are known through signs, and humans come to know the Father through the sign par excellence, Jesus (8:14; 14:7–9). Jesus knows the Father (16:30; 17:25; cf. 1:18), and the disciples know God through him (17:7–8, 26). This view is also presumed by the thanksgiving formula in Matt. 11:25–27, in which Jesus asserts that the Father and Son know each other, along with those to whom the Son reveals the Father. In the NT, knowledge of God comes through Jesus and concerns the saving work that God does in Jesus. Knowledge assumes faith in God and Jesus as well as obedience to them: "And by this we may be sure that we know him [Christ], if we keep his commandments" (1 John 2:3). Jesus also tells those who believe in him, "You will know the truth, and the truth will make you free" (John 8:32).

Perhaps the most developed view of "knowledge" in the Bible is found in the writings of Paul. According to Paul believers who know God are known by God (Gal. 4:9; 1 Cor. 8:3). God can only be known by the Spirit and believers who have the Spirit (1 Cor. 2:11). God reveals the mystery of salvation in Jesus Christ (1 Cor. 2:7, 12–13; cf. Col. 2:2–3). Both the value and scope of knowledge, however, are limited. Knowledge by itself is not useful. Paul maintains that "knowledge puffs up," i.e., makes people arrogant, "but love builds up" (1 Cor. 8:1). The one who knows all things but does not have love is nothing (13:2). Furthermore, the scope of human knowledge is limited, for there is much that cannot be known in this life. People know only in part, like those who look in a mirror, dimly, but someday knowledge will come to an end and then, ironically, people will know God as fully as they have been known (13:8, 12). This irony seems to depend on a double use of the word. The knowledge that is inferior in value and scope—and the knowledge that will come to an end—is knowledge in the Greek sense of the word (theoretical understanding, awareness of facts, intellectual apprehension), but the "full knowledge" that will then be granted is knowledge in the Hebrew sense, a sense in which "knowing God" is essentially synonymous with "loving God" (cf. Ps. 91:14). But Paul can regard knowledge of mere information as an asset as well. In fact, it is one of the things that qualifies him to be an apostle; he might be untrained in speech, but he does not lack knowledge of the things that his congregations need to know (2 Cor. 11:6). *See also* faith; revelation; wisdom.   A.J.S./M.A.P.

Kohath (koh´hath), the second of Levi's three sons (Gen. 46:11), grandfather of Moses and Aaron (Exod. 6:16–20), and, according to 1 Chron. 6:22–28, the ancestor of Samuel. Although Gershon was Levi's firstborn, the narrative sections of the Pentateuch (e.g., Num. 3–4) sometimes treat Kohath and his descendants as the most important levitical family. At times, Kohath's descendants are even mentioned before Gershon's descendants (Num. 4:34–45; 1 Chron. 15:5). The Kohathites had the most important function in the tabernacle—disassembling and transporting the Holy of Holies (Num. 4:4–20). According to 1 Chronicles, they also prepared the sabbath bread (9:32), and their descendants included Asaph and Heman, two important temple singers (6:31–43).   M.Z.B.

Korah (kor´uh).

1 The leader of an Edomite family group (Gen. 36:16, 18). He is listed as both the son of Esau (Gen. 36:5, 14; 1 Chron. 1:35) and the grandson of Esau, son of Eliphaz (Gen. 36:16).

2 A son of Hebron (1 Chron. 2:43) who may have given his name to a Judean geographic site or family group (cf. 1 Chron. 12:6).

3 A Levite who was the ancestor of a family group belonging to the Kohath line (Exod. 6:21, 24; 1 Chron. 6:22; cf. Heb. 6:7). Num. 16 reports that Korah, the eponymous ancestor of the family, together with 250 leaders of the people, led a revolt against Moses and Aaron in the wilderness. Korah's revolt seems to have involved a conflict between priestly houses over Aaron's exclusive right

to offer incense before the Lord. To settle the dispute, Moses proposed that Korah and his rebels appear before the tent of meeting with censers to see whose incense the Lord would accept. When they did this, the earth opened up and swallowed Korah, Dothan, and Abiram and their families, and fire came forth from the Lord, consuming the 250 rebels. The Korahites, descendants of Korah, later became one of the major guilds of temple singers (2 Chron. 20:19), and their name appears in the superscriptions of Pss. 42; 44–49; 84–85; 87–88. They were also temple gatekeepers (1 Chron. 9:19; 26:1, 19) and bakers (1 Chron. 9:31). *See also* Abiram; Dothan; Levites.   M.A.S.

Kore (kor′ee).

1 A bird, alternatively identified with *Ammoperdix heyi* or the slightly larger *Alectoris graeca;* both are types of partridge.

2 The father of Shallum, a member of the tabernacle gatekeepers' guild (1 Chron. 9:19).

3 A Levite, the son of Imnah, who was appointed by Hezekiah to be keeper of the east gate of the temple (2 Chron. 31:14).

Kue (kyoo′ee), a source of horses for King Solomon's armies. Cited along with Egypt as a place Solomon could buy horses (1 Kings 10:28; 2 Chron. 1:16), it has been identified as a probable ancient name for eastern Cilicia in Asia Minor. If so, it refers to the southeastern portion of modern Turkey between the Taurus and Amanus mountain ranges and the Mediterranean Sea. In Solomon's time it would have been a relatively independent Neo-Hittite community.

L

L, a symbol designating material found only in the Gospel of Luke. Biblical scholars often analyze the "L material" as one step in determining the distinctive perspective or unique contributions of Luke's Gospel. In addition, some scholars regard L as representing one source stratum upon which Luke might have drawn when composing his Gospel. According to one prominent theory, the author of Luke's Gospel had three principal sources: the Gospel of Mark, the Q source, and L. An even more prominent variation of this view holds that Luke used only two written sources (Mark and Q) and that L consists of material Luke himself put into writing based on what he had heard through oral tradition or gathered from any number of miscellaneous sources. The L material includes the entire first two chapters of Luke's Gospel (presenting the annunciation and birth of both John the Baptist and Jesus), five miracle stories and seventeen parables not recounted elsewhere in the Bible, stories of Jesus's postresurrection appearances in Jerusalem, and a brief narrative of Jesus's ascension. Those who study this material note several recurring topics or motifs: women are prominent (1:26–56; 2:36–38; 7:11–17, 36–50; 8:1–3; 10:38–42; 13:10–17; 18:1–8); Samaritans are mentioned repeatedly (9:51–56; 10:29–37; 17:11–19); Jerusalem is a frequent setting or focus (1:5–23; 2:21–38, 41–52; 9:51–56; 19:41–44; 24:13–53); and there is considerable attention to riches and poverty (1:52–53; 3:10–14; 4:14–30; 12:13–21; 14:12–14; 16:1–12, 19–31; 19:1–10). *See also* Luke, Gospel According to; Q; Synoptic Problem.   M.A.P.

Laban (lay'buhn; Heb., "white" or "pale").

1 An unknown location east of the Jordan connected with the Israelites' wilderness wandering (Deut. 1:1); some scholars identify it with Libnah (Num. 33:20).

2 A member of Abraham's ancestral family through Nahor, Abraham's brother; he was the brother of Rebekah and father of Leah and Rachel (Gen. 24:24, 29; 29:16). His home was near Haran in Paddan-aram (or Aram-naharaim, "the river country"), the upper region of the land lying between the Tigris and Euphrates rivers (upper Mesopotamia); he and his father are both called Arameans (24:10; 25:20; 27:43).

Laban's ultimate role in the ancestor narratives is foreshadowed in the first episode in which he plays a part: he shows hospitality to Abraham's servant (Gen. 4:32), but the text hints that he was enthused by the sight of the gifts the servant had bestowed upon his sister, Rebekah

---

THE L SOURCE: MATERIAL UNIQUE TO LUKE

Dedication to Theophilus	1:1–4	Parable of Barren Tree	13:1–9
Promised birth of John	1:5–25	Healing of crippled woman	13:10–17
Announcement of Jesus's birth to Mary	1:26–38	Healing of man with dropsy	14:1–6
Mary's visit to Elizabeth	1:39–56	Two parables for guests and hosts	14:7–14
Birth of John the Baptist	1:57–80	Counting the cost (two parables)	14:28–33
Birth of Jesus (with shepherds, manger)	2:1–20	Parable of Lost Coin	15:8–10
Presentation in the temple	2:21–38	Parable of Prodigal Son	15:11–32
Childhood visit to Jerusalem	2:41–52	Parable of Shrewd Manager	16:1–12
John's reply to questions	3:10–14	Parable of Rich Man and Lazarus	16:19–31
Genealogy of Jesus (to Adam)	3:23–38		
Good news to the poor	4:14–23, 25–30	Cleansing of ten lepers	17:11–19
Miraculous catch of fish	5:1–11	Parable of Widow and Judge	18:1–8
Raising of widow's son at Nain	7:11–17	Parable of Pharisee and Tax Collector	18:9–14
Encounter with homeless woman	7:36–50	Story of Zacchaeus	19:1–10
		Jesus weeps over Jerusalem	19:41–44
Parable of two debtors	7:40–43	The reason for Peter's denial	22:31–32
The ministering women	8:1–3	The two swords	22:35–38
Rejection by Samaritan village	9:51–56	Jesus before Herod	23:6–12
Return of the seventy	10:17–20	Pilate declares Jesus innocent	23:13–16
Parable of Good Samaritan	10:29–37	Sayings associated with Jesus's death	23:28–31, 34, 43, 46
Mary and Martha	10:38–42		
Parable of Friend at Midnight	11:5–8	Appearance on the road to Emmaus	24:13–35
Parable of Rich Fool	12:13–21		
Parable of Severe and Light Beatings	12:47–48	Appearance to the disciples	24:36–49
		The ascension	24:50–53

From Mark Allan Powell, *Introducing the New Testament* (courtesy, Baker Academic)

(24:29–32). Rebekah leaves to become the wife of Isaac, but Laban is encountered again a generation later when Rebekah sends her son Jacob to her brother Laban's house to escape the anger of Esau and to find a wife from among the family group (27:43–28:5). Laban's covetous nature is now fully revealed, as he first agrees to let Jacob marry his daughter Rachel in exchange for seven years of labor and then tricks Jacob into another seven years of labor by substituting his daughter Leah at the wedding and insisting that fourteen years labor is the bride-price for both daughters (29:1–30). Laban himself is outwitted, however, when Jacob strikes a deal with him regarding the livestock. Laban agrees to give Jacob the oddly marked livestock, thinking to take advantage of Jacob again, but Jacob exploits the situation in ways that cause his own herds to increase while Laban's dwindle (30:25–43). Finally, Jacob and his wives leave in the middle of the night, and Rachel steals her father's household gods (*teraphim*). Laban pursues them in anger but is unable to find the gods, since Rachel sits upon them and maintains she cannot get up because the "way of women" is upon her (31:22–35).

Laban is thus presented in the biblical narrative as a trickster who tries to exploit others to his own advantage, but who is outdone by his daughter and son-in-law, who prove to be craftier than he. Many scholars see the characterization of Laban in this account as satirical, and they interpret the story as a satire aimed specifically at the Arameans. Read in that light, the story seems to imply both acknowledgment of exploitation and justification of the same (since it was mutual); the Hebrews sometimes took advantage of the Arameans, but when they did so, the latter were only getting what they had coming to them. Indeed, God is said to have supported and protected Jacob throughout his somewhat devious dealings with his less than trustworthy father-in-law (Gen. 31:5, 9, 13, 24, 42). The final parting of Laban and Jacob at Mizpah symbolizes the break between the Hebrews and their ancestral homeland in Aram and may also reflect an ancient treaty of nonaggression between the two peoples (31:43–55). *See also* Aram; Jacob; Mizpah, Mizpeh; Nuzi; Rachel; teraphim.

D.R.B./M.A.P.

labor. Ancient Near Eastern society knew several varieties of manual labor. Herding, fishing, and various tasks associated with farming (plowing, planting or sowing, harvesting, winnowing, storing in barns) come up especially often. Women were often in charge of the family home, but they worked in the fields as well (Prov. 31:10–31). For more on types of labor, *see* economics in the Hebrew Bible period; economics in the NT period.

The overall biblical perspective on labor is that physical work is natural for humans (Gen. 2:15) and is to be honored and appreciated (Prov. 10:4; 22:29; Eccles. 2:24). God is pictured as working at creation (Gen. 1–2) and as blessing the labor of human beings (Gen. 26:12; Isa. 65:21–23). The hardship or toil of labor, however, is presented as a consequence of human disobedience (Gen. 3:17–19), as are the labor pains of women in childbirth (3:16). In both cases, the onerous aspect of something that is basically good is acknowledged as a wearisome part of the human condition (Eccles. 2:18–20). Ultimately, though, it is "anxious toil" and "labor in vain" that is truly unfortunate (Ps. 127:1–2); those who "eat the fruit of [their] labor" are deemed happy and blessed (128:2). In this regard, many biblical laws were intended to protect laborers from anything that would deprive them of receiving the just reward for their work (Lev. 19:13; Deut. 24:14–15). Furthermore, although diligence and hard work are encouraged (Prov. 10:4; 18:9), rest is also commended—and, indeed, commanded on the sabbath (Exod. 20:9–11).

In the NT Paul speaks the most often about labor. He himself worked as a tentmaker or leather worker (Acts 18:3). Although maintaining that preachers have a right to be supported financially by those to whom they minister (1 Cor. 9:4–18; Mark 6:10–11), Paul himself chose to forgo that right and earn his living through practicing a trade in addition to preaching the gospel (1 Cor. 4:12; 1 Thess. 2:9). He also speaks of work as a normative expectation, condemning those who seek to avoid it either because they are sufficiently wealthy that they do not need to labor for money or because they have found a way to live off the largesse of others (1 Thess. 4:12; 2 Thess. 3:10–12). *See also* sabbath.

A.J.S./M.A.P.

Lachish

A PROMINENT CANAANITE and Israelite city, and in fact the most important Judahite city after Jerusalem, Lachish (lay'kish) is mentioned in both biblical and nonbiblical texts. Indicative of Lachish's importance as a city-state, its name appears in the Amarna cuneiform correspondence (fourteenth century BCE) of Pharaoh Amenophis IV (Akhenaton) as well as in Assyrian records. The Bible contains many references to Lachish. When Japhia, king of Lachish, joined an anti-Gibeonite coalition to resist the Israelite invasion, Joshua put him to death and captured Lachish (Josh. 10:1–32). King Amaziah of Judah (ca. 800–783 BCE) was killed at Lachish, where he had taken refuge from a palace revolt in Jerusalem (2 Kings 14:17–20).

History: The location of Lachish was uncertain until the archaeologist William F. Albright in 1929 proposed Tell ed-Duweir as the site of Lachish, an identification generally accepted today. In modern Israel, it is commonly known as Tel Lachish. An imposing mound in the foothills of Judah, Tell ed-Duweir lies about twenty-five miles southwest of Jerusalem and fifteen miles west of Hebron. This nearly rectangular tell is relatively large, measuring eighteen acres at the summit and thirty acres at the base. A deep well supplied adequate water. The site was occupied with some

Tell ed-Duweir; aerial view from the southwest. This mound has been identified as the site of ancient Lachish.

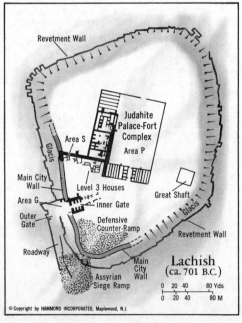

© Copyright by HAMMOND INCORPORATED, Maplewood, N.J.

The Assyrian king Sennacherib conquered most of Judah, including the fortress-city of
Lachish, in 701 BCE. The victory was commemorated in a group of reliefs at his palace at
Nineveh. In this detail, according to the inscription, "Sennacherib, king of the world, king of
Assyria, sat upon a throne and passed in review the booty [taken] from Lachish [La-ki-su]."

interruptions from Chalcolithic times (fourth millennium), when the inhabitants lived in caves, to the Persian period (ca. 538–333 BCE); Tell ed-
Duweir was abandoned finally about 150 BCE. The mound is secured by
deep valleys all around except on the southwestern side, where the city's
only gate, a double gateway complex, was located. This vulnerable access
required strong fortifications to ward off enemy attacks.

Lachish was deserted and lay partially in ruins from the twelfth to
the tenth centuries BCE; this period is often correlated with the time of
Israelite settlement in Canaan, when Joshua is said to have conquered the
city (Josh. 10:1–32). Then Lachish was rebuilt as a garrison city and became second in importance to Jerusalem. According to 2 Chron. 11:5–12,
King Rehoboam of Judah (ca. 922–915 BCE) fortified Lachish to protect
his southern border against Egyptian and Philistine attack.

In 705 BCE Sennacherib acceded to the imperial throne of Assyria.
At that time Egypt, some Philistine cities, and Judah formed an alliance against Assyria; Sennacherib responded by invading the Levant in
701 BCE. After demolishing the Egyptian forces and the Philistines, he
conquered most of Judah, including the fortress-city of Lachish; only
Jerusalem was spared. According to Sennacherib's annals, forty-six of

(*Right*) The towns-people of Lachish defending a tower in the city wall against the invading Assyrians. (*Far right*) Vanquished Lachishites impaled outside the city by Assyrian soldiers.

(*Above*) Judahite families with baggage and cattle are deported after their defeat. (*Left*) Assyrian soldiers carrying away booty from their victory.

King Hezekiah's fortified cities were conquered. Despite its strong defenses—two massive city walls and a gate complex composed of an outer and inner gate—Lachish succumbed to Sennacherib, who was personally present in the city at the time of its demise. The Assyrians (and later the Babylonians) made their assault on the vulnerable gate complex near the southwest corner of the city. There they threw up a fan-shaped siege ramp (measuring about 200 feet at the bottom and 80 feet at the top) against the outer side of the wall to mobilize their siege machines equipped with battering rams. Constructed from tons of boulders bonded with lime plaster, this ramp was topped by a platform for the siege machines. The Judahites countered with a ramp of their own, laid against the inner face of the city wall, but to no avail. After his stunning victory Sennacherib reestablished his imperial rule in the area.

Sennacherib's devastation of Lachish is documented in the Bible (2 Kings 18:13) and is also memorialized in stone relief on the palace walls of the Assyrian royal city of Nineveh (modern Kuyunjik) opposite modern Mosul in northern Iraq. These elaborate bas-reliefs, housed today in the British Museum, depict realistically the siege and conquest of Lachish. Their detail and prominence suggest that Sennacherib viewed his conquest of Lachish as especially significant.

Archaeological Excavations: James L. Starkey began a long-term systematic excavation of Tell ed-Duweir in 1932. Starkey distinguished six occupational levels, but the project ended abruptly in 1938 when Starkey was killed in an ambush.

An ivory head from Lachish, ca. sixteenth–fifteenth century BCE.

Among the outstanding epigraphical discoveries at Tell ed-Duweir are twenty-one Hebrew ostraca, or storage-jar fragments, inscribed in black ink. Known as the Lachish letters (most were letters, others were lists of names), these ostraca date to ca. 590 BCE (Level II), during the reign of Zedekiah, the last king of Judah. Eighteen of the inscribed potsherds, found in 1935, lay on the floor among the ashes in a guardroom adjacent to the city gate. The remaining three, unearthed in 1938, were in the vicinity of the palace-fort. According to many scholars, Hoshaiah, who was stationed in a garrison somewhere between Lachish and Jerusalem, had sent these letters to Yaosh, the military commander of Lachish. Written in classical Hebrew prose, these ostraca shed light on Hebrew philology and epigraphy, and they also provide valuable information about the times of the prophet Jeremiah, who was speaking to King Zedekiah "when the army of the king of Babylon was fighting against Jerusalem and against all the cities of Judah that were left, Lachish and Azekah, for these were the only fortified cities of Judah that remained" (Jer. 34:7).

To complete the unfinished work of Starkey and to study the history of Lachish and its material culture in greater depth, David Ussishkin undertook a long-term project at Lachish from 1973 to 1990. Ussishkin excavated the palace-fort as well as the monumental Canaanite buildings beneath it. The excavators uncovered portions of three superimposed city walls. Ussishkin's most critical undertaking was the Judahite city-gate complex, consisting of several superimposed gates. Ussishkin concurs

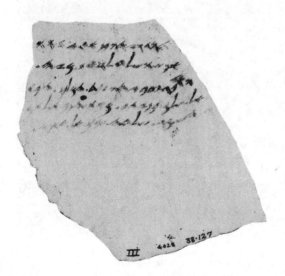

One of the ostraca, or Lachish letters, from Hoshaiah to the Lachish military commander Yaosh, dating to ca. 590 BCE.

(*Top*) Ivory figurine of a crouching cat. From the excavations of the temple at Lachish, dating to ca. the fifteenth century BCE. (*Bottom*) Ivory stopper carved in the shape of a male ibex, found in a house at Lachish. It is perforated so that liquid, possibly perfume, could be poured through the mouth of the ibex.

with Starkey that six strata lay between the Late Bronze Age (1500–1200 BCE) and the Persian-Hellenistic period (ca. 538–63 BCE) at Tell ed-Duweir. The levels are the following:

Level VI, the final Canaanite city level, marks the conflagration of the last Late Bronze Age III city in the twelfth century, perhaps about 1150 BCE. Canaanite Lachish was under Egyptian control at the time of the Israelite settlement. In the Late Bronze Age Lachish was a large Canaanite city-state. Level V pertains to the late tenth century, the period of the united monarchy, when Judahites began to resettle Lachish. This level was destroyed by fire. Level IV, dating from the ninth century, represents the royal Judahite fortified city, composed of two massive city walls (outer and inner), the gate complex, and the palace-fort situated at the center of the city. An earthquake may have been responsible for destroying this level.

Level III may mark the Assyrian conquest of Lachish in 701 BCE. Ussishkin was confident in dating Level III to Sennacherib's conquest in 701 BCE, but other archaeologists disagree, allowing for a variance of more than a hundred years. At the time of the Level III conflagration Lachish was a densely populated city. In this same period the palace-fort complex had been rebuilt and enlarged. Level II (smaller than Level III) represents the Babylonian destruction by fire of Lachish in 588/6 BCE. The city at this level may have been built and fortified by King Josiah (640–609 BCE). The Lachish letters date from this period. Level I dates from the postexilic era,

Moundlike formation that was probably part of the Assyrian siege ramp thrown up against the Lachish city wall. A depiction of an Assyrian siege machine is with the color photographs.

including the Babylonian, Persian, and Hellenistic periods (sixth–first centuries BCE). In the time of Nehemiah, following the Babylonian exile (587/6–538 BCE), Jews settled in Lachish.

In addition to the excavated areas of Tell ed-Duweir already described, two other structures were investigated: the fosse temple (with three phases) and the solar shrine. The fosse temple, so named because it was constructed within a *fosse* (moat) that had been part of the Middle Bronze Age II fortifications, is situated near the northwest corner of the mound, outside the city. The original building was constructed of unhewn stone in the sixteenth century. Rebuilt and enlarged more than once, this temple was destroyed by fire about 1200 BCE. The fosse temple was in use throughout the Late Bronze Age. The nature of the temple's cult is unknown. A new temple (Level VI), probably replacing the fosse temple, was built on the acropolis in the center of the tell. It consisted mainly of an antechamber, main hall, and "holy of holies" (*cella*). The remains of this temple lay under the late Judahite palace-fort.

The solar shrine, so named by Starkey because of its orientation and the presence of an altar with an adoring human figure, is situated in the eastern sector of Tell ed-Duweir. This solar shrine, composed of two main rooms and a court, dates from about 200 BCE.

Bibliography

Ussishkin, David. "Excavations at Tel Lachish: 1973–1977, Preliminary Report." *Tel Aviv* 5 (1978): 1–97.

———. "The 'Lachish Reliefs' and the City of Lachish." *Israel Exploration Journal* 30 (1980): 1744–95.

———. "Excavations at Tel Lachish: 1978–1983, Second Preliminary Report." *Tel Aviv* 10 (1983): 97–175.

———. "The Assyrian Attack on Lachish: The Archaeological Evidence from the Southwest Corner of the Site." *Tel Aviv* 17 (1990): 53–86.   P.J.K.

Ladan (lay´duhn).

1 An Ephraimite, the father of Ammihud and ancestor of Joshua (1 Chron. 7:26).

2 The head of the Gershonite group of Levites (1 Chron. 23:7–9; 26:21); he is also called Libni (Exod. 6:17; Num. 3:18). *See also* Libni.

ladder. In the ancient Near East, ladders might be composed of wood, metal, or rope. The most frequent uses of constructed ladders were to gain access to rooftops or to storerooms that, for reasons of security, had no openings at ground level. The Hebrew word most often translated "ladder" (*sullam*) could also refer to a rock-cut staircase or steps. In Gen. 28:12, Jacob dreams of angels ascending and descending on a ladder set up from earth to heaven. Most interpreters think the intended image is of a winding stair-case similar to a Babylonian ziggurat, a tower with winding steps leading to a small temple at the top. In John 1:51, Jesus applies the image to himself, suggesting that the Son of Man is the "ladder" that facilitates passage between heaven and earth (cf. 3:13).

Ladder of Tyre, a geographic feature on the Phoenician coastline, referred to in 1 Macc. 11:59. The Ladder of Tyre was probably the ridge that extends the coastline out to a point about halfway between Ptolemais and Tyre. Antiochus VI appointed Simon Maccabeus to be governor from the Ladder of Tyre to the borders of Egypt.

Lagash (lah´gash; Arabic Telloh, "tablet hill"), a Sumerian city about fifty miles north of Ur whose ruins have yielded the largest number of cuneiform tablets of the third-millennium Sumerian cities. Lagash flourished in the Early Dynastic III

Diorite statue of Gudea, ruler of Lagash, seated; ca. 2168 BCE.

period (2500–2300 BCE). Just prior to this time, Enhegal bought several parcels of land and asserted Lagashite independence at a time when all other city governors were subject to the ruler claiming hegemony over Sumer. Lagash and Umma, its neighbor and rival, served as political buffers as well as vehicles of cultural transmission between Sumer and Elam. Tensions developed between these two cities over the question of control of a rich stretch of agricultural land called the *edin*. Eannatum of Lagash commissioned the monument "The Stele of Vultures" to commemorate his campaign for this land. He also subdued Elam. Urukagina of Lagash promulgated the first legal reforms, but they were short-lived, as was his reign. The city was already deteriorating under the weight of administrative excesses and was soon conquered by Lugalzagesi of Umma. As city governor, Gudea ruled Lagash during the Gutian domination following the collapse of the Akkadian Empire around 2168 BCE. The Ur III period of Sumerian renaissance produced artistic and textual witnesses to the final flowering of Lagashite power. Among the surviving texts are those that record the instructions Gudea received in a dream for building a temple to the city gods.   L.E.P.

Lahmi (lah´mi), a brother of Goliath, who, according to 1 Chron. 20:5, was slain by David's hero Elhanan. According to 2 Sam. 21:19, however, Elhanan killed Goliath himself. Thus, the reference in 1 Chron. 20:5 is often read as a later editorial attempt to harmonize 2 Sam. 21:19 with 1 Sam. 17:4, which says that David killed Goliath.

Laish (lay´ish; Heb., "lion").

1 The father of Palti(el), to whom Saul gave his daughter Michal, although she was already married to David (1 Sam. 25:44), and for whose return David bargained (2 Sam. 3:12–16).

2 A Canaanite city, modern Tell el-Qadi, which was subsequently occupied by Israelites and named Dan (Judg. 18:7–31). It is located ten and a half miles north of Lake Huleh. *See also* Dan.

lamb. *See* sheep.

Lamb of God, the title with which John the Baptist twice greets Jesus at the beginning of the Gospel of John (1:29, 35). In Revelation, the lamb also appears a number of times as a symbol for Christ, although a different Greek word is used in Revelation (*arnion*) than is found in John's Gospel (*amnos*). In Revelation, the lamb is specifically referred to as the "Lamb that was slaughtered," invoking sacrificial imagery and implying that Christ's death provided atonement for sin (5:6–14). This is probably the idea behind the phrase "Lamb of God" in John's Gospel as well (cf. 1 John 1:7). It seems likely that the "suffering servant" of Isa. 53, who is likened to "a lamb that is led to slaughter," has influenced this description of Jesus (cf. 1 Pet. 1:18–19). Notably, in the Gospel of John, Jesus dies on the afternoon before the Festival of

Passover begins, at the hour when the Passover lambs were slain. *See also* atonement; sacrifice.

D.M.S.

Lamech (lay'mik).

1 The son of Methushael, husband of Adah and Zillah, and father of three sons (Jabal, Jubal, and Tubal-cain, the ancestors, respectively, of nomads, musicians, and smiths) and a daughter (Naamah; Gen. 4:18–22). The Song of Lamech (4:23–24) is composed of three couplets. In the first Lamech exhorts his wives to attend to his words; in the second he vaunts his prowess in having slain a man/boy for merely wounding/bruising him; and in the third he boasts: "If Cain is avenged sevenfold, truly Lamech seventy-sevenfold." Lamech thus expresses disdain for the law of retaliation, according to which a wound may be avenged with a wound or a bruise with a bruise, but nothing more (Exod. 21:25). He boasts that he has instead exacted the penalty of death for minor hurt done to him. The parallelism of the numbers, "sevenfold" (lit., "twice seven," i.e., fourteen) and "seventy-seven," is unique, but it finds explanation in the numeral construction based upon the sum of three consecutive squared numbers; thus, $14 = 1^2 + 2^2 + 3^2$, and $77 = 4^2 + 5^2 + 6^2$.

2 The son of Methuselah and father of Noah. He lived 777 years (Gen. 5:25–29).

S.G.

lameness. Physical defects that inhibited walking were viewed as quite serious in the biblical world (Prov. 26:7). At times, the "lame" are cited as illustrative of people who are weak or useless (2 Sam. 5:8), but more often lame or limping people are looked upon with pity and regarded as persons to be accorded help or charity (2 Sam. 19:16; Luke 14:13–14). Thus, when Job says, "I was eyes to the blind and feet to the lame" (Job 29:15), he is claiming that he has been a righteous and charitable person. Mephibosheth, the son of Jonathan and grandson of Saul, was crippled in both feet (2 Sam. 4:4); David showed kindness to him (and respect for his father) by allowing him to eat at the king's table every day (2 Sam. 9). God cares for the lame, and when the glory of God is revealed in its fullness, "the lame will leap like a deer" (Isa. 35:6; cf. Jer. 31:7–8; Mic. 4:6–7; Zeph. 3:19). Lameness was, however, considered an imperfection that disqualified descendants of Aaron from offering sacrifices to God (Lev. 21:16–24). Likewise, it was not appropriate to sacrifice lame animals to God (Deut. 15:21; Mal. 1:8, 13). In the NT, Jesus is often portrayed as healing the lame, and those healings are cited as evidence that he is the Messiah (Matt. 11:2–6; 15:29–31; 21:10–17; Luke 7:18–23). The book of Acts indicates that such healings were also performed by Peter and John in the temple (3:2–13) and by Philip in Samaria (8:4–8).

Lamentations (lam-en-tay'shuhns), **book of,**

the third of the Five Scrolls, or Megilloth, which are found in the Writings section, or Ketuvim, of the Tanakh (Jewish Bible). The Five Scrolls were used in the Jewish liturgy to commemorate particular events in the history of the Jewish people. The book of Lamentations was read on Tisha B'av (usually in late July or August), the day to remember the fall of Jerusalem and the destruction of the temple in 587 BCE. The Hebrew name of the book is *'ekah*, "woe," after the first word of the book, which is rendered *threnoi*, "dirges," in the Greek LXX. Lamentations is found after the book of Jeremiah in the Christian OT, because tradition attributed its authorship to Jeremiah; for this reason the book is sometimes called the Lamentations of Jeremiah.

Contents: Lamentations consists of five separate poems, each representing a single chapter in most English translations. The first four poems are acrostics (each line beginning with a successive letter of the Hebrew alphabet; the fifth poem is simply a twenty-two-line nonacrostic poem. The first poem is a single-line acrostic presenting Zion as a woman; the first half is an observation of her suffering, and the last half, a personal lament of Zion. The second poem is a single-line acrostic reflecting on God's destruction of Israel and Judah and disowning of his sanctuary. Pham argues that both poems contain two speakers appealing to God, one being Jerusalem herself. The third poem is a triplet acrostic from the perspective of a "man who has seen affliction" who views suffering as punishment, yet believes that God will be steadfast in his love. The poem's author calls the people to examine themselves and return to God. The fourth poem is a couplet acrostic crying out that Jerusalem's suffering is even greater than that of Sodom. The last poem calls out to God to remember his people and restore them, emphasizing the innocent suffering of the people of Zion.

OUTLINE OF CONTENTS

Lamentations

Background: The book of Lamentations is anonymous, though it has been traditionally ascribed to Jeremiah. References to Jeremiah writing laments (2 Chron. 35:25) and his concern over the fate of Jerusalem (Jer. 9:1) have reinforced this assumption. Lamentations, however, differs from the book of Jeremiah, not only in style, but also with regard to the view of the religious and political leadership of Jerusalem; Lamentations is appreciative of that leadership, but Jeremiah is critical of it. The five distinct poems in Lamentations also suggest the possibility of multiple authors. The book probably was written by an observer of Jerusalem's fall who wrote in the wake of that tragedy. This would place the date of composition between 587/6 and 520 BCE, when the temple was rebuilt.

The form and content of Lamentations is that of a complaint psalm. Complaint psalms make up the majority of the Psalter, though the nature of Lamentations' complaint (that of an entire city to its deity) is more in line with other sources from the ancient Near East, including the "Lament over the Destruction of Ur." Hillers notes that much of the book's form as a lament is shaped by its Mesopotamian influences. Lamentations contains both individual and communal laments over the fall and destruction of Jerusalem by the Babylonians in 587 BCE. All expression in Lamentations is from a human perspective; God either remains silent or the divine responses go unrecorded. The book is consistent with the biblical view that the suffering that Jerusalem endured was deserved punishment. Gottwald argues that the purpose of the book was, not simply to express communal grief, but also to help bring the people of Judah to trust and confidence in God once more. Mandolfo argues that Lamentations is a cry of the suffering against both God and the authorities that led them into that suffering. Linafelt highlights that, although Christian interpreters have often focused on the hope seen in chap. 3, the history of Jewish interpretation has been in wrestling and responding to chaps. 1–2.

Influences: Lamentations has been used in mourning rituals since early after its composition. Its laments have been read in response to tragedies throughout the history of the Jewish people, including the destruction of the second temple and the defeat of Bar Kochba. In Christian liturgical traditions, Lamentations is read during the Matins of Holy Week. Its poetic expression of unspeakable horror has been used by many throughout history in recurring tragic situations.

Bibliography

Bandstra, Barry L. *Reading the Old Testament: Introduction to the Hebrew Bible.* 4th ed. Wadsworth, 2009.

Gottwald, Norman K. *The Hebrew Bible: A Socio-Literary Introduction.* Fortress, 1985.

Hillers, Delbert R. *Lamentations.* Doubleday, 1992.

Linafelt, Tod. *Surviving Lamentations.* University of Chicago Press, 2000.

Mandolfo, Carleen. *Daughter Zion Talks Back to the Prophets: A Dialogic Theology of the Book of Lamentations.* Society of Biblical Literature, 2007.

Pham, Xuan Huong Thi. *Mourning in the Ancient Near East and the Hebrew Bible.* JSOT, 1999.
B.B.

lamp, a vessel used to keep and control fire as a source of light. The development of such a vessel was a major achievement of early human history. This vessel, known as the oil lamp, had two basic parts: a receptacle for the oil and a wick inserted into the oil whose protruding end would burn. Olives provided the main source of oil in the Near

Five terra-cotta oil lamps that date to the first century BCE.

East; various materials, including flax, served as wicks. Because the oil lamp was in everyday use and has been found in abundance in excavated sites, its typological and historical development is relatively easy to establish and indicates that most lamps used in the Near East were similar to those in use all over the Mediterranean world.

In the Neolithic period (prior to fourth millennium BCE) ordinary stone bowls were used to contain and burn oil; in the fourth millennium BCE ordinary pottery bowls were used. Early in the third millennium the first adaptations were made for the specific placement of the wick. This vessel, a round saucer with four slight depressions on its rim, eventually developed into a square saucer with four pronounced open spouts at the corners. In the second millennium the dominant shape became a saucer with only one pinched corner. This single-spouted, open form remained in use for over fifteen hundred years, while undergoing only slight utilitarian improvements affecting the base, spout, and rim. By the Late Bronze Age (1500–1200 BCE) the oil lamp had generally assumed a triangular shape. In the Iron Age I period (1200–900 BCE) variations on this basic form included multispouted saucers and lamps with tall pedestal bases. In the Iron Age II period (900–600 BCE) the form of the oil lamp developed somewhat differently in the two politically and culturally divided areas of Israel and Judah. In Israel the tradition of the single-spouted, open shape continued with only slight modifications, but in Judah marked changes occurred as the base became high and heavy and the rim wide. The Israel-type lamp has frequently been found in Judah, but the Judah-type rarely in Israel. With the Babylonian conquest (597 BCE) the Judah-type lamp disappeared, and a broad shallow lamp with wide rim came into use, the last in the long line of open oil lamps that had originated in the second millennium.

The Hellenistic lamp, which developed from a fifth-century BCE Greek form, was a closed vessel with a long nozzle for the wick and a broad circular opening in the cover to receive the oil. Many such lamps were imported into Judea during Hellenistic times (332–63 BCE), but most lamps in use were made locally. These were generally of the closed type, although the older open-type saucer was also made. During the early Roman period (63 BCE–135 CE) Hellenistic forms continued to be used, and the Roman round discus lamp was introduced and copied. However, new and distinctive forms also appeared. One, the "Herodian" lamp, had a round, wheel-made body, a flat base, a large filling hole, and a separately attached nozzle. Unlike the highly decorated Roman lamps, which featured scenes from mythology, most "Herodian" lamps were unadorned, although some had simple incision marks. Sometime in the first century CE a different type evolved, influenced by a technical innovation already common in the Roman world—the mold-made lamp. It had a handle, and its rim and nozzle were decorated with geometric and floral designs, with or without Jewish symbols. Both forms have most commonly been found in southern portions of the Levant.

In houses and public buildings lamps were placed in niches, on shelves jutting out from the walls, or on lampstands; in later times, they were hung from the ceiling. In addition to their chief function of illumination, lamps played a central role in religious practices. The tending of the "eternal light" in the Jerusalem temple was a sacred duty. The abundance of oil lamps found in tombs suggests that, besides illuminating the dark interiors, they may have been used as a symbolic rekindling of the spirit of the deceased, as a remedy against "evil spirits," and as subsequent memorial offerings.

An easily understandable and powerful symbol of the importance of light, the oil lamp (Heb. *nir;* Gk. *lychnos, lampas*) is referred to frequently in the Bible in a wide range of contexts. In the Hebrew Bible, it conveys, for example, the illuminating power of God (2 Sam. 22:29; Job 29:3) and God's precepts (Ps. 119:105); a father's instructions to his dutiful son (Prov. 6:23); and the lasting existence of the Davidic dynasty (1 Kings 11:36; 15:4). In the NT it is a symbol of the eye of the body (Matt. 6:22); the vigilance of the faithful servant (Luke 12:35); and the function of the disciples in the world (Matt. 5:14–16). *See also* lampstand.

Bibliography

Smith, Robert Houston. "The Household Lamps of Palestine in Old Testament Times." *Biblical Archaeologist* 27 (1964): 1–31.

———. "The Household Lamps of Palestine in Intertestamental Times." *Biblical Archaeologist* 27 (1964): 101–24.

———. "The Household Lamps of Palestine in New Testament Times." *Biblical Archaeologist* 29 (1966): 2–27.

Sussman, Varda. *Ornamented Jewish Oil-Lamps.* Aris and Phillips, 1982. Chap. 1.　　　M.M.S.

lampstand (Heb. *menorah*), an object that supported one or more oil lamps. Although such stands could be made of stone, pottery, or wood, the biblical passages dealing with lampstands for usage in worship all refer to golden lampstands,

Menorah, shofar, and other traditional Jewish sacred objects; third-century pottery shard from Beit Natif.

with just one exception (2 Kings 4:10). Four successive lampstand traditions can be identified.

First, the tabernacle texts describe a single golden lampstand composed of a central, cylindrical stand with three pairs of branches and elaborate floral decorations (Exod. 25:31–40; 37:17–24). The unattached lamp or lamps were apparently grouped on the central stand rather than on the ends of the branches (cf. Lev. 24:1–4). The origins of the tabernacle lampstand in the premonarchic period can be discerned in the floral and technical vocabulary used to describe it; this vocabulary also suggests the symbolic value of the lampstand as a sacred tree representing God's unseen presence in the earthly shrine.

Second, ten golden lampstands (1 Kings 7:49), for which no branches are specified, stood in the Solomonic temple. These were probably cylindrical stands holding multispouted lamps similar to those known, archaeologically, from cultic contexts spanning the Middle Bronze and the Iron ages.

Third, the rebuilt temple of the late sixth century, using the tabernacle texts as a guide, evidently resumed the single lampstand tradition, as Zechariah's fourth vision indicates (4:1–6, 11–14). This second temple was repeatedly looted and restored or rebuilt (cf. 1 Macc. 1:21; 4:49) and by the end of its existence, the single temple lampstand with branches was fashioned according to techniques and traditions current in the Roman world. It is the last temple lampstand, of the first century CE, with its characteristic seven lamp-holding branches and tripodal or stepped base, that appears in the earliest artistic renderings of the holy lampstand and dominates its use as a paramount Jewish symbol, representing light and life eternal.

Fourth, the apocalyptic vision in the book of Revelation expands the single golden lampstand to seven (1:12–13), although in Rev. 11:4 two lampstands are suggested to match the two trees that flank the stands in Zech. 4:11. *See also* lamp; temple, the.   C.L.M.

land (Heb. *'erets;* also "earth," "country"; less often *'adamah,* also "ground," "soil," in contrast to "wilderness"), a term occurring in the Hebrew Bible nearly 1,750 times (NRSV). When it refers to a specific geographic region, it is usually phrased in possessive relation to the people inhabiting it. So one reads of the land of the Philistines (Gen. 21:32), the Hittites (Josh. 1:4), Amorites (Josh. 12:8), Ammonites (Josh. 13:25), and Chaldeans/Babylonians (Jer. 51:24). By contrast, it may also be phrased as the possession of a nation: the land of Canaan (Gen. 11:31; 13:12), of Egypt (Gen. 21:21), Edom (Gen 36:17), Moab (Judg. 11:18), Midian (Acts 7:29), Israel (2 Chron. 2:17), Judah (2 Chron. 15:8), Cyprus (Isa. 23:1), and Assyria (Isa. 27:13), to cite the most frequently mentioned.

In connection with a city, "land" most often refers to the city and its surrounding agricultural acreage; this is the case with the lands of the cities of Hebron (Josh. 21:11), Dan (Josh. 21:23), Gezer (Josh. 21:21), Taanach (Josh. 21:25), Aijalon (Josh. 21:24), Mahanaim (Josh. 21:38), Heshbon (Josh. 21:39), Anathoth (1 Chron. 6:60), Debir (1 Chron. 6:58), and Sodom and Gomorrah (Matt. 10:15), to cite the most prominent.

Other expressions indicate regions or geographic units, such as the land of the north (Zech. 2:6), of Goshen (eastern Nile Delta region; Gen. 46:28), or of the Negev (desert; Judg. 1:15).

In most instances, however, the land referred to is the land promised to and occupied by Israel (e.g., Gen. 12:1; Josh. 13:1–7). Only exceptionally, however, is it called the "land of Israel" (esp. in Ezekiel, e.g., 7:2). On the contrary, throughout Israel's long association with the "promised land" (cf. Exod. 32:13; Deut. 6:23; 8:1) or the "holy land" (Zech. 2:12; Wis. 12:3; 2 Macc. 1:7), Israel kept alive the memory that it had originally been the "land of the Canaanites, the Hittites, the Amorites, the Perizzites, the Hivites, and the Jebusites" (Exod. 3:17).

Although the members in this list may vary, it reflects the Bible's land theology. God, sole owner of the whole earth/land (Lev. 25:23; Ps. 24:1), had given the land to Israel as a fulfillment of a promise to Abraham and his descendants (e.g., Exod. 6:1–4; Deut. 6:10, 18). In God's strength alone, Israel, redeemed from slavery in Egypt, had been able to defeat and displace nations greater and stronger, a feat never to be forgotten (e.g., Deut. 7:17–26; 9:1–3). Deuteronomy in particular emphasizes the land as gift (e.g., 8:7–9; 9:4–6), but also warns Israel of its calling to lead a new life marked by obedience to God's covenant law in the newly given land. Failing that, Israel would forfeit the land, as the nations before it had done (e.g., 8:19–20; 9:5), to be cast out into exile again (28:64–68). The Deuteronomistic History (Joshua–2 Kings) and many prophetic texts treat the story of Israel as an interplay between faithfulness to God and

security in the land, on the one hand, and unfaithfulness threatening that security, on the other. Even beyond the loss of the land to the Assyrians (fall of Samaria, 722/1 BCE) and the Babylonians (fall of Jerusalem, 587 BCE), prophets proclaimed God's grace for the future in terms of promises of return to the land.

That the land had not originally belonged to Israel is also reflected in three theologically important designations referring to the land. It is Israel's "inheritance" from God (e.g., Num. 26:52–56; Josh. 11:23), "possession" (from a verbal root meaning "seize," "grasp," "take hold"; e.g., Lev. 14:34; Deut. 32:49), and "rest" after Israel's wanderings (e.g., Deut. 12:9–10; Josh. 1:13, 15; Ps. 95:11).

Israel's heartland extended from the Jordan to the Mediterranean Sea, and from the Wadi of Egypt to the "entrance of Hamath" (Num. 34:1–12). Sometimes, however, a much larger area is included, extending from the Euphrates to the Mediterranean (Deut. 11:24), perhaps reflecting the extent of the Davidic-Solomonic empire. This freedom of the texts in defining the land suggests that the land's significance lay in its symbolic-theological meaning as God's gift and Israel's responsibility rather than in any precise geographical delimitation.

In the NT: "Land" (usually Gk. *gē,* also "earth") appears much less frequently (NRSV, about fifty times) in the NT. Certain continuities with the Hebrew Bible's rich land theology are preserved not only in quotations (e.g., Mic. 5:2 in Matt. 2:6; Gen. 12:1 in Acts 7:3), but also elsewhere. Thus, Jesus's return from Egypt parallels Israel's exodus (Matt. 2:14–15; cf. Hos. 11:1), and the third Beatitude calls the meek blessed, "for they shall inherit the earth/land" (Matt. 5:5).

A certain spiritualization of land motifs in the NT is evident, especially in the Letter to the Hebrews (e.g., 11:8–16, 38–40). Sometimes, the reality of God's gifts, expressed in the Hebrew Bible through the gift of the land, is transferred to the person of Jesus. Thus, he, not Jacob's well, is the source of living water (John 4:7–15); he, not the land, is the believer's inheritance (Gal. 3:29–4:7), in whom the promise of Abraham is fulfilled (Gal. 3:15–18). *See also* Canaan; conquest era; Israel; Levant, the.

Bibliography

Brueggemann, Walter. *The Land: Place as Gift, Promise, and Challenge in Biblical Faith.* Philadelphia: Fortress, 1977.

Davies, W. D. *The Gospel and the Land: Early Christianity and Jewish Territorial Doctrine.* Berkeley and Los Angeles: University of California Press, 1974.

Janzen, Waldemar. "Land." *Anchor Bible Dictionary.* New York: Doubleday, 1992. 4:143–54.

W.J./R.S.B.

landmarks, indications of property boundaries, whether erected (as boundary stones) or natural formations recognized by mutual agreement. They were not to be moved (Deut. 19:14; 27:17), and doing so was a symbol of irresponsible deceit (Hos. 5:10), greed (Job 24:2), or abuse (Prov. 23:10). This concern for recognition of property rights is also present in Babylonian, Egyptian, and, later, Greek and Roman law. International markers were frequently elaborately inscribed stones.

Laodicea (lay-od'i-see'uh), a prosperous commercial city in the region of Phrygia in northwest Asia Minor. It was named by Antiochus II of the Seleucid dynasty, which ruled Syria after the death of Alexander the Great. He named the city for his wife, Laodice. Situated on a plateau in the south of the Lycus River valley, Laodicea was adjacent to one of the ancient trade routes from the east. Two neighboring cities, Colossae and Hierapolis, were in this same river valley, and the three locations are often referenced together (Col. 2:1; 4:13–16). Epaphras, portrayed as one of Paul's companions, apparently worked as a missionary for the Christian gospel in all three cities (4:12–13). According to 4:16, Laodicea received a letter from Paul, and it was to exchange letters with the neighboring community at Colossae. The Laodicean letter is no longer extant unless, as some think, it is to be equated with the work that appears in the NT as Paul's Letter to the Ephesians; many scholars think the latter was sent to multiple churches and, so, may have existed in variant forms (as both the "Letter to the Ephesians" and the "Letter to the Laodiceans"). The church of Laodicea was one of seven congregations rebuked in Revelation (3:14–22); specifically, the believers there are called "lukewarm" (3:15–16). This image may have been chosen with reference to a natural feature of the city. Excavations reveal that Laodicea received its water through an aqueduct coming from a spring four miles to the south; the waters of neighboring Hierapolis, however, were famous as hot springs and would have provided a contrast with the tepid aqueduct water in Laodicea. Among the ruins are visible a large stadium, several theaters cut into the hillsides, and portions of the city wall. The main colonnaded thoroughfare and adjacent buildings have recently been excavated. *See also* Colossae; Epaphras; Hierapolis; Phrygia.   M.K.M.

Lappidoth (lap'i-doth; Heb., "torches" or "lightning"), the husband of the prophetess Deborah

(Judg. 4:4). He is mentioned only once in the narrative. Interpreters have noted that the meaning of the name is essentially the same as that of Barak (Heb., "lightning"), who serves as the commander of Deborah's troops—though what to make of this similarity is not clear. Some interpreters have suggested that the word *lappidot* should not be read as a proper name for a person, but as an adjectival description of Deborah; thus Judg. 4:4 would not describe Deborah as "wife of Lappidoth," but as a "woman of lightning" or something similar. In that case, the description could be a deliberate play on the name of her commander, attributing to Deborah the same quality that is attributed to Barak by virtue of his name. *See also* Barak.

Lasea (luh-see'uh), a city on the south coast of Crete. It is mentioned in Acts 27:8 as a point beyond which the dangers of proceeding by sea increased dramatically, especially in winter. The coast turns sharply north at that point, bringing open sea winds to bear full force, heightening danger. Lasea is near Fair Havens, modern Limenes Kali.

Last Judgment. *See* judgment, day of.

Last Supper. *See* Lord's Supper.

Latin. The primary language used among the educated populace in the western part of the Roman Empire. The term "Latin" originally referred to a group of people who lived in the area of Latium, surrounding Rome. In the second century BCE, Rome's Latin allies had a citizenship of sorts, though they might become full citizens of Rome upon moving to the city. The Latin language was the one spoken by these people, but it had developed considerable flexibility under the influence of Greek. Even in NT times, furthermore, Greek remained the primary language for the eastern part of the empire, even among educated Romans. Latin was used primarily by the military, many of whom had come from the western part of the empire. According to John 19:20, the official reason for Jesus's crucifixion was written in Latin as well as in Hebrew and Greek.   P.P.

laughter, an expression of rejoicing (Ps. 126:2), contrasted with weeping (Eccles. 3:4; Luke 6:21) or mourning (James 4:9) or both (Luke 6:25). Though laughter is generically associated with pleasure, merrymaking, fun, and enjoyment, the contexts of Exod. 32:6 and 1 Sam. 18:7 suggest specifically religious celebrations. Laughter is also used for the play of children (Gen. 21:9; Zech. 8:5). A reference in Gen. 26:8 seems to be explicitly sexual: King Abimelech of the Philistines looks out a window and sees Isaac (whose name means "laughter") laughing with his wife; the NRSV translates this "fondling his wife," which seems to be what the context demands (Abimelech had thought Rebekah was Isaac's sister, but when he sees them "laughing" together, he realizes she must be his wife). The story involves a double play on words. To put the Hebrew into English idiom, Abimelech sees Isaac "isaacing" with his wife—and readers are expected to know that "Isaac" means "laughter" *and* that this can be a euphemism for sex play.

Laughter may also denote mockery, ridicule, or derision. Job complains that his juniors laugh at him (Job 30:1), and Jerusalem recalls how its enemies laughed at its downfall (Lam. 1:7). Prov. 26:19 condemns one who tries to justify an act of deception by claiming it was done for a laugh (NRSV: "joking"). God laughs at the futile presumptions of earthly rulers (Ps. 2:4). Laughter at God, however, is reprimanded. Both Abraham and Sarah laugh in response to God's promise that a son will be born to them in their old age (Gen. 17:17; 18:12), which is why God directs them to call the boy "Isaac" (Heb. *yitskhaq,* Gen. 17:19). Laughter at threats or dangers is an expression of confidence and security (Job 5:22; 39:22; 41:29). Sirach tends to deprecate laughter (21:20; 31:10), while recognizing that one's laughter may reveal one's character (19:30). Rarely mentioned in the NT, laughter may express either joy (Luke 6:21) or derision (Matt. 9:24).   M.A.P.

laver. *See* basin.

law. In the Bible the word "law" can have a wide range of meaning, referring to commandments, to a particular genre of literature (legal codes), or simply to the Torah, or first five books of the Bible. Jewish tradition divides the Bible into Torah (Law), Nevi'im (Prophets), and Ketuvim (Writings). But the Hebrew word *torah* connotes "instruction or teaching" in a broader sense than would be implied by "legislation." There is little evidence, furthermore, that the biblical Torah was the law applied by courts before the Babylonian exile. Prior to that time, "law" was not identified with the idea of a statutory text. The same is true elsewhere; even in Babylonia, where there is considerable evidence of court practice, the ancient "law codes" of Hammurabi, Ur Nammu, Lipit Ishtar, and Eshnunna are never quoted in the judicial records. Rather, they seem to be regarded as royal statements of ideal justice.

A similar pattern is evidenced from the Bible. When courts were instituted, they were charged simply to apply justice and avoid corruption (Deut. 16:18–20); in cases of difficulty they were to resort to higher authority (17:8–13). Jehoshaphat's reform charged the judges in similar fashion (2 Chron. 19:5–11). Quite separately, Jehoshaphat sent officers to teach from the "book of the law of the LORD" in the cities of Judah (17:7–9)—a practice also found in Assyrian sources. The particular association of the book of the law (Heb. *sepher torah*) with the king, and with didactic rather than judicial functions, is found also in Deut. 17:18–20. The actual administration of justice was largely conducted by city elders sitting at the city gate, on the basis of customary rules tempered by occasional royal ordinances and determined in cases of

Moses receiving a scroll from God that contains the law by which the ancient Israelites are to live; a mosaic at the Monastery of St. Catherine, Sinai, sixth century CE.

difficulty by recourse to oracular procedures conducted in local shrines. With the centralization of the worship of God, such difficult cases were transferred to Jerusalem.

The Role of the King: The role of the king in law is much disputed. Some scholars deny him any genuine legislative role. But the legal powers he claims are characteristic of kings in states where central authority is only beginning to consolidate: he could require conscription; establish military, judicial, and administrative structures; commandeer labor for his estates, the production of munitions, and the servicing of his household; confiscate land; and levy taxation (1 Sam. 8:11–17). In the last days of the kingdom of Judah, King Zedekiah (597–587/6 BCE) is said to have enforced an economic reform to relieve debt slavery (Jer. 34), but there is reason to believe that the motivation was more concerned with recruitment into the army than the regulation of private legal matters. Such practical ordinances as these, unlike the *torah* whose teaching the king sponsored, were not designed to establish rules that would continue in force unless repealed. Nevertheless, there is one royal ordinance that is reported to have subsisted: David's law on the distribution of booty, which the author of 1 Sam. 30:25 tells us remained "a statute and an ordinance for Israel." By contrast, God's instructions to Moses regarding the distribution of the booty taken from the Midianites are not presented as establishing a general or permanent rule (Num. 31).

Moses, though not given the title of a king, frequently acted like one. On occasion, he issued commands for which no divine mandate was claimed. For example, he organized the judicial system along military lines (Exod. 18). He dictated the monuments to be raised and the ceremonies to be performed after the crossing of the Jordan (Deut. 27). He required a septennial reading of the law at the Festival of Sukkoth (Tabernacles; Deut. 31:10–13)—but the law of Sukkoth was itself neglected from the time of Joshua until it was rediscovered in the written law by Ezra (Neh. 8:13). At Marah, before the Israelites reached Sinai, Moses issued a "statute and an ordinance" (Heb. *khoq umishpat,* Exod. 15:25, the same term as is used of David's booty law).

Some law was produced in the course of adjudication; here too there are parallels between the narratives of Moses and later kings. In the wilderness, the case of the daughters of Zelophehad (Num. 27; 36) is presented as a dispute; its resolution by Moses is through an oracular consultation with God, and there is a statement of general rules (going beyond the situation of the dispute) that are to have abiding force. David's booty law is the product of a similar sequence; in this case, it follows a dispute between sections of the army regarding the distribution of booty after the campaign. But not all adjudication produced precedents for the future (e.g., Solomon's judgment, 1 Kings 3:16–28); a precedent usually required a new act of authoritative enunciation.

Narrative sources present a picture of piecemeal lawgiving often springing from concrete events. Given the central role of the king in both the promulgation of law and ordinances and the king's capacity to act as supreme judge, it is not appropriate to differentiate strictly between precedent and legislation. The king's power over and responsibility for the cult as well as his patronage of court prophets and court scribes contributed to the institutionalization of divine law and its consolidation into the codes we find in the Pentateuch.

The Institutionalization of Divine Law: When Samuel was asked to authorize the appointment of a king, he acted as a prophet under divine command to issue a formulation of royal privileges, which he wrote in a "book" (Heb. *sepher*) that he deposited in a sanctuary. If the account in 1 Sam. 8 is a guide to its length, the text cannot have been extensive. More substantial was the text God commanded Jeremiah to have read in the temple (Jer. 36:23), a scroll that was then deposited in the temple with the connivance of temple officials. The latter story may cast light on the circumstances leading to the discovery of the "book of the law" found in the temple in the time of Josiah (ca. 622 BCE; 2 Kings 23), a text whose authenticity is validated by a prophet, Huldah, who consults God, probably by means of an oracle (2 Kings 22:13, 18). We have no means of identifying positively the text found on that occasion, although scholarly opinion commonly takes it to have included material now found in the book of Deuteronomy. After the exile (late sixth century BCE), Ezra was sent to Jerusalem with the author-

ity of King Artaxerxes to guide the restoration of Israel in its own land. He is described as a scribe learned in the *torah* of Moses, and he came prepared to "study the law of the LORD, and to do it, and to teach his statutes and ordinances in Israel" (Ezra 7:10). The two traditions kept separate by Jehoshaphat are here combined: the teaching of divine law is now to be implemented through measures characteristic of royal ordinance. At the same time, the text of the *torah* comes to acquire the force of legal statutes, so that verbal interpretation becomes necessary (Neh. 8:7–8).

The Covenant and Priestly Codes: It is not easy to ascertain the place of the pentateuchal laws in the history of the legal institutions of ancient Israel. The Covenant Code (Exod. 21–23, deriving its conventional title from 24:7) is generally regarded as the oldest. It falls into two halves, the first of which (21:1–22:17) is formulated mainly in conditional sentences (known as the "casuistic form"), in which the protasis ("if" clause) states circumstances and the apodosis ("then" clause), the legal consequences. This is also the predominant (though not exclusive) form used in the ancient Near Eastern codes. The subject matter and tone (secular and without rhetorical ornamentation) also make it the most similar to its ancient counterpart. Parallels in content are found between all the biblical codes and those of the ancient Near East—e.g., the law of retaliation ("an eye for an eye") is found in the Code of Hammurabi—but the Covenant Code includes one parallel that is particularly striking in both form and content (Exod. 21:35; cf. *Laws of Eshnunna* 53), despite the impossibility of any direct literary connection. It perhaps serves as indirect evidence of the existence of Canaanite codes (thus far undiscovered), which may have served as intermediaries before the Israelites became familiar with the legal traditions of Babylon and Assyria. The Covenant Code contains rules on slavery, homicide, various types of assault, death caused by animals, cattle theft, agricultural damage, deposit of property, shepherding, loan of animals, and seduction of a virgin.

The second half of the Covenant Code (Exod. 22:18–23:19), expressed largely in the apodictic form (direct, second-person commands, unaccompanied by any statement of sanction), combines sacral offenses; humanitarian injunctions; standards for the administration of justice; laws governing the sabbath, the sabbath year, and the three pilgrimage festivals (see 23:14–17); and regulations regarding sacrifice. It is likely that the code as a whole was compiled from discrete sources, and it is widely believed not to have formed an original part of the Sinaitic narrative, to which it now belongs.

Much of the rest of Exodus, Leviticus, and Numbers is called the Priestly Code, associated with the literary source "P" of traditional biblical criticism. There is increasing recognition of the existence within this corpus of early materials, and some scholars date the source earlier than

Deuteronomy, thus well before the exile. The Priestly Code generally emphasizes religious and ritual concerns, while the Covenant Code deals more with civil law, and Deuteronomy shows special interest in matters of public law. But such characteristics are by no means exclusive; all three codes deal with slavery and homicide. Within the Priestly corpus, there is also a distinguishable text in Lev. 17–26, known as the Holiness Code in view of the reiterated motive for obedience to its laws: "Be holy."

Later Interpretations of Biblical Law: In the Persian, Hellenistic, and Roman periods (539 BCE–325 CE), biblical law was the object of increasing restatement and elaboration. Deuteronomy itself had indicated the continuation of prophetic revelation of the law in promising the coming of a prophet like Moses, who would perform the same function as Moses in mediating the transmission of divine commands (18:15–22). This Deuteronomic tradition was used by the Qumran community to validate its restatement of scriptural rules. There is evidence of a similar association of Jesus with the prophet like Moses in the NT (cf. Acts 7:37). Thus, the Sermon on the Mount (where Jesus claims not to abolish an iota of the law, Matt. 5:18) may be viewed as a compilation of teachings claiming this status of revealed restatement.

In the NT, Jesus clashes repeatedly with the Pharisees over matters of legal interpretation. Although these writings are polemical in their presentation of the Pharisees, they do depict the latter as concerned about faithfulness to Torah and scrupulous in their interpretations. They are also said to have assigned authoritative status to an oral body of material called the "tradition of the elders" (cf. Matt. 15:2), which might be illustrative of the sort of legal interpretations that would eventually be codified within Judaism as the Mishnah. From what can be discerned from the NT texts, the Pharisees' interpretations of the law seem to have been driven by a conviction that all of God's people should live with the utmost sanctity. Thus the Pharisees are portrayed as urging laypeople to follow some of the same purity regulations in their daily lives that priests were expected to follow when serving in the temple (the idea perhaps being that every house was in some sense a temple for God, every table an altar, and every man a priest). Thus, the Pharisees and their followers are said to have practiced hand washings originally designated for temple service before eating *any* meal (see Matt. 15:2; cf. Mark 7:3–4). Their disagreements with Jesus concern such matters as sabbath regulations, criteria for divorce, fasting, almsgiving, and the wearing of phylacteries.

The specifics of these conflicts are hard to determine (since we have only one side of the argument), but it appears that Jesus employed a hermeneutic of interpreting the entire law in light of the "love commandments" (Mark 12:28–34): the command to love God (Deut. 6:4–5) and to love one's neighbor (Lev. 19:18) became the lens through which all other commandments were to be interpreted. This is also articulated in what is the Golden Rule, ascribed to Jesus: "In everything do to others as you would have them do to you; for this is the law and the prophets" (Matt. 7:12). Likewise, in Matt. 23:23 he acknowledges (and even commends) the Pharisees for having been scrupulous in details of legal observance, but chastises them for failing with regard to the "weightier matters" of justice, love, and mercy (cf. Luke 11:42). None of this, however, would have been completely radical for the time; a version of the Golden Rule has even been attributed to Hillel, an influential rabbi whose teaching preceded that of Jesus by about fifty years. To some extent the disputes may have been over details of application—and even moreover the question of who had the authority to make such decisions. Most Jewish teachers would have agreed with Jesus that the commandments of the law must sometimes be "bound" as applying to matters they do not specifically address (e.g., Jesus binds the law prohibiting murder as applicable to anger and insults [Matt. 5:21–23] and the law prohibiting adultery as applicable to lust [5:27–28]). And they would have agreed that commandments must sometimes be "loosed," so that they are not applied in ways that pose an unreasonable burden (thus Jesus relaxes sabbath laws for some specific contexts; 12:5–8, 11–12). In such cases, the commandments themselves remain valid, and the dispute concerns their arena of application. The NT portrays Jesus as having the authority from God to make such determinations (12:8) and as passing that authority to the community of the church with whom he will remain eternally present (16:19; 18:18–20).

There is no hint of an antithesis between law and grace in the teachings of Jesus, but in some of the Pauline writings the matter become more complicated. Even Paul, however, was not an opponent of the law as such (e.g., Rom. 7:12), and in fact he maintains that he observed the Jewish law in a manner that was "blameless" (Phil. 3:4–6). But Paul also claims that Christians are no longer "under the law" (Rom. 6:14–15; 1 Cor. 9:20; Gal. 3:23–25), and interpreters struggle to determine exactly what he means by that. He seems to make at least four points. (1) Paul insists that people are justified or made right with God through faith in Jesus Christ—or through the faith(fulness) of Jesus Christ (the phrase Paul uses can be translated either way)—and not by doing works of the law (Gal. 2:16–17). (2) Paul insists that God's favor is universal in scope and objects to "works of the law" that make a distinction between Jews and Gentiles. God's action in Jesus Christ has effectively removed such distinctions, so that all are now equally children of God through faith (3:26). (3) Paul believes that a radical shift in history has coincided with the coming of Christ, and a new phase in the great plan of God is now in effect. The law governed relationships with God before the "fullness of time had come" (4:4–5), but "now that faith has come" (3:25), people do not relate to God through the law as they once did. (4) Paul also believes that the Spirit produces what the law cannot effect. God has given the Holy Spirit to those who have faith in Jesus Christ (3:2), so that Christ may be formed in them (4:19), and the benefits of receiving the Spirit exceed anything that could be accomplished through human efforts at keeping the Jewish law. When a person belongs to Christ Jesus, the desires and passions of the flesh are "crucified" (5:24), and Christ now lives in and through that person (2:20). The Spirit takes over and produces a rich harvest of virtuous fruit: love, joy, peace, patience, kindness, generosity, faithfulness, gentleness, and self-control (5:22–23). The result is nothing short of "a new creation" (6:15; cf. 2 Cor. 5:17).

This proclamation of a "law-free gospel" seems to have been misunderstood and to have gotten Paul in trouble. In 1 Corinthians, for example, he notes that some people in this congregation are exclaiming "All things are lawful for me!" as a mantra for justifying behavior of which Paul does not approve (6:12; cf. 10:23). In responding, Paul offers some significant caveats to his position. The question a Christian should ask is not, "Am I allowed to do this?" but "Is this a good thing to do?" Even if all things are lawful (allowed), the true Christian only *wants* to do those things that are beneficial (6:12), that build up the community (10:23), and that bring glory to God (6:20). Paul also notes with some irony that the Corinthian concept of freedom leads to what is actually bondage; those who adopt a "do as you please" attitude toward life end up becoming slaves to their own passions, dominated by compulsive desires that are neither fulfilling nor healthy (6:12). *See also* covenant; Moses; Paul; Pentateuch, sources of the.

Bibliography

Blenkinsopp, Joseph. *Wisdom and Law in the Old Testament.* Oxford University Press, 1983.

Boecker, Hans Jochen. *Law and the Administration of Justice in the Old Testament and Ancient Near East.* SPCK, 1980.

Carmichael, Calum M. *The Laws of Deuteronomy.* Cornell University Press, 1974.

Crüsemann, Frank. *The Torah: Theology and Social History of Old Testament Law.* Fortress, 1996.

Das, A. Andrew. *Paul, the Law, and the Covenant.* Hendrickson, 2001.

Falk, Ze'ev W. *Hebrew Law in Biblical Times.* Wahrmann, 1964.

Kaye, Bruce N., and Gordon J. Wenham, eds. *Law, Morality and the Bible.* InterVarsity, 1978.

B.S.J./P.J.A./M.A.P.

lawgiver. *See* Moses.

lawless one, an enigmatic phrase found in 2 Thess. 2:3. Of the many possible interpretations given in the scholarly literature, one plausible suggestion is that the lawless one is an eschatological and representational figure who is to be manifested in the future and whose arrival will signify the culmination of the past, present, and future hostile forces standing in opposition to the apostolic ministry of the church and, thus, of God. His appearance will climax the process the author of 2 Thessalonians refers to as the "mystery of rebellion" (2:7). But since this moment has not yet arrived and the Lord Jesus has not yet destroyed him (2:8), those who argue that "the day of the Lord is already here" (2:2) are in error. *See also* antichrist; Thessalonians, Second Letter of Paul to the.   K.P.D.

lawyer, an expert in the law. Titus 3:13 refers to Zenas, who is apparently an expert in Roman civil law, roughly analogous to a professional who might be called a lawyer today. Otherwise, the term refers to experts in Torah, i.e., the law of God, or simply the scriptures. The "lawyers" Jesus engages in conversation are essentially Bible scholars. They appear in three contexts. First, the person who asks Jesus about which commandment in the law is the greatest is called a "lawyer" in Matt. 22:34–40 and in Luke 10:25–37 (he is called a "scribe" in Mark 12:24–40). Second, Luke 7:30 indicates that "the Pharisees and lawyers rejected God's purpose for themselves" by refusing to be baptized by John the Baptist. Finally, in Luke 11:45–52, Jesus expands upon his caustic condemnations of the Pharisees by indicating that lawyers are condemned in similar terms; in Matthew's Gospel these same condemnations are leveled against the "scribes and Pharisees" (23:13–36; cf. Luke 11:53). As these citations indicate, the NT does not seem to distinguish greatly between "lawyers" and "scribes." Historically, there probably was a difference, but the precise nature of the distinction may no longer be discernible. *See also* Pharisees; scribe.   M.A.P.

laying on of hands, concretely, the activity of exerting force or doing physical violence (e.g., Gen. 22:12; Exod. 7:9; Luke 20:19; 21:12; Acts 21:17). Because of this concrete usage, however, the placing of one's hands on someone or something also became a symbol for the transfer of force. Thus, by laying hands on the head of an animal to be sacrificed, people transfer their past deeds and the effects of those deeds onto the beast to have them annihilated and/or transformed with the destruction of the animal (e.g., Exod. 29:10, 15, 19; Lev. 3:2, 8, 13; Num. 8:12). Laying hands on the sick effects the transference of the power of the healer to those who are ill (Mark 5:23; 7:23; Acts 9:12, 17); laying hands on children serves as a conduit for blessing (Gen. 48:14; Mark 10:16). Finally, people can hand over their power and have another exercise it on their behalf, effecting this by the laying on of hands (Num. 8:10; Acts 6:6; 8:17; 1 Tim. 4:14). Those wielding power or authority within a group may symbolically pass that authority to others through the laying on of hands (Num. 27:23; Deut. 34:9; 1 Tim. 5:22; 2 Tim. 1:6).   B.J.M.

Lazarus (laz'uh-ruhs).

1 A character in a parable told by Jesus in Luke 16:19–31. The mere fact that he has a name is notable, since he is the only character in any

Jesus raises Lazarus from the dead (John 11:1–44); sixth-century mosaic at San Apollinare in Classe, Ravenna, Italy.

of Jesus's parables to be named. In the parable, Lazarus is a poor man who dies outside the gate of a rich man and is carried by angels to Abraham's bosom. The rich man also dies and is tormented in Hades. The rich man asks Abraham to allow Lazarus to come to him to relieve his suffering in some small way, but this request cannot be granted. Then the rich man asks Abraham to send Lazarus back to warn his five brothers, lest they meet a similar fate. But Abraham replies, "If they do not listen to Moses and the prophets, neither will they be convinced even if someone rises from the dead" (16:31).

2 A friend of Jesus who dies and is then raised by Jesus from the dead (John 11). Lazarus is the brother of Mary and Martha, who live in Bethany, a village near Jerusalem (11:1–2; cf. Luke 10:38–42). The Gospel story emphasizes that Jesus loves him and reports that Jesus wept upon arriving at his tomb (John 11:3, 5, 11, 35–36). This point led Martin Luther to propose that Lazarus should be identified as the "disciple whom Jesus loved," who is mentioned at key points in the Gospel after the Lazarus narrative (e.g., 13:23–25; 18:15–16; 20:4, 8; 21:7, 21–23) and who is said to have been responsible for writing things down that are now a part of that Gospel (19:35; 21:24). This view is still taken seriously by many biblical scholars, though the traditional (and still dominant) view is that the "disciple whom Jesus loved" should be identified with John, the son of Zebedee; John was one of Jesus's twelve disciples. In any case, John's Gospel goes on to report that the raising of Lazarus caused many people to believe in Jesus and provided the immediate motivation for religious authorities to seek his death (11:45–57). Jesus later returned to Bethany to visit Lazarus and his sisters; Jesus and his disciples shared a meal with Lazarus, at which Martha served and after which Mary anointed Jesus with perfume (12:1–8). John's Gospel then reports that the religious authorities planned to put Lazarus to death as well, since it was because of him that many people were believing in Jesus in a way that led many people to desert their traditional faith (12:9–11).   D.M.S./M.A.P.

lead, a heavy, malleable, bluish-gray metal. It was Midianite booty (Num. 31:22), and it was used for weights (Zech. 5:7) and for sinkers on fishing lines. Ezek. 22:18–20 mentions lead with other metals; 27:12 indicates the existence of Israelite trade in lead with Tarshish. Job 19:24 describes engraved tablets whose letters are lead-filled for reading clarity and permanence. Exod. 15:10 refers to lead figuratively: Pharaoh's armies sink "as lead" into the waters. Sirach says that Solomon amassed silver as though it were lead (47:18), but also claims that a fool is heavier (i.e., harder to bear) than lead (22:14–15).

leader. The Hebrew Bible makes numerous references to leaders of the people (Heb. *nasi'*). Twelve individuals are called this in Num. 2 (e.g., Nahshon, "leader of the people of Judah," Num. 2:3). Twelve leaders who presented offerings are likewise named in Num. 7 (cf. also 34:18–28). Exod. 22:28 commands, "You shall not curse a leader of your people" and indicates that to do so is parallel with reviling God. Other Hebrew words are also translated "leader" by the NRSV: Rezin becomes leader (*sar*) of a marauding band (1 Kings 11:24), and God makes Jeroboam leader (*nagid*) over Israel (14:7). In the NT, Jesus is termed a "Leader" in Acts 5:31, and the same Greek word translated "leader" in that verse (*archēgon*) is also used for Jesus in Acts 3:1 (NRSV: "author") and in Heb. 2:10; 12:2 (NRSV: "pioneer"). Elsewhere, the Greek word *archōn* is used to refer to someone who is called "a leader of the Pharisees" (Luke 14:1) or "a leader of the Jews" (John 3:1). *See also* captain; pioneer.

Leah (lee'uh; Heb., "cow"), the daughter of Laban, one of the two wives of Jacob, and ancestor of many of the tribes of Israel. Little is known of her, except that she was not Jacob's first choice. He wanted to marry her younger sister Rachel, for whom he contracted to work seven years for Laban as a bride-price (Gen. 29:18). At the end of that time, however, he was tricked into marrying Leah instead. Jacob then married Rachel a week later and worked for Laban for another seven years (29:23–30). The only personal detail about Leah revealed in the Bible is an ambiguous one. Gen. 29:17 says that her eyes were, literally, "tender" (Heb. *rakkot*). The traditional interpretation of this passage, reflected in most English translations, is that Leah had weak eyes, meaning perhaps that she was nearsighted; this defect might help to explain why Jacob preferred her sister. The NRSV, however, takes the ambiguous Hebrew word as a compliment—"Leah had lovely eyes"—but Jacob preferred Rachel in spite of this.

Gen. 29:31 says that God saw that Leah was unloved and opened her womb. She bore Jacob's first four children, Reuben, Simeon, Levi, and Judah (29:31–35). Then childless Rachel gave her slave Bilhah to Jacob as surrogate mother, so that she might have children through her. Leah gave her own slave Zilpah to Jacob, and each of the surrogate wives bore two sons—Bilhah bore Dan and Naphtali, and Zilpah bore Gad and Asher. Rachel, nevertheless, seems to have remained Jacob's favorite wife, for Leah accused Rachel of having taken her husband from her and she had to give Rachel mandrakes (a fertility charm) in return for sleeping with Jacob (30:14–16). Nevertheless, Leah bore two more sons, Issachar and Zebulun, and a daughter, Dinah. Upon the birth of the sixth son, she hoped that now at last her husband might honor her (30:20; cf. 29:34). Rachel and Leah both agreed to accompany Jacob back to his homeland (31:4–15), and they cooperated with him in humbling themselves to seek reconciliation with his brother Esau (33:1–7). Leah was ultimately buried in the cave of Machpelah (49:31).

In Ruth 4:11 Leah and Rachel are mentioned together as matriarchs "who together built up the house of Israel"; their names were apparently invoked in blessings upon women ("May the LORD make the woman who is coming into your house like Rachel and Leah"). Notably, Leah named all six of the sons whom she bore as well as the two sons of Zilpah. Thus, she was responsible for coming up with the names for eight of the twelve tribes of Israel. Interpreters have also noted that the name Leah means "cow" and Rachel means "ewe," a curious observation for which there is no obvious rationale (beyond the suggestion that the story of their rivalry could reflect the jockeying for position of sheepherders and cattle herders in the early tribes of Israel). *See also* Jacob; Rachel.   T.S.F.

leather, processed animal hides suitable as rough clothing (Elijah's belt, 2 Kings 1:8; John the Baptist's belt, Matt. 3:4; Mark 1:6) or as fine accoutrements (the shoes of Ezek. 16:10). Leather was also employed in covering the tabernacle (Exod. 25:5; NRSV: "fine leather"). Although the variety of animal hides usable was large, preparation involved scraping the hair and flesh from the material, then treating it for durability, flexibility, and even watertightness. It degenerates readily once discarded, so finds of intact ancient leather are archaeologically rare and important. Some of the Dead Sea Scrolls were written on leather. Acts 9:3 mentions that Simon Peter stayed with someone called "Simon the tanner," probably a person who processed animal skins for the production of leather.   R.S.B.

leaven, a fermenting agent that in biblical times was normally added to a batch of bread dough by using an unbaked portion of dough from the previous batch. However, the custom of nomads was to eat unleavened bread, and evidence of this is found in the Bible (Gen. 19:3; Judg. 6:19; 1 Sam. 28:24).

Leavened bread was prohibited in sacrifices that went on the altar (Lev. 2:4), because leaven should not be burned (2:11). Leaven caused fermentation and thus appeared to have a life of its own. That caused it to be considered the vital force of the vegetable world, as blood was of the animal world,

both of which were not to be destroyed by burning. Leavened bread was permitted, however, for the thank offering (7:13) and for the first fruits of the wheat harvest (23:7), because these were not burned on the altar (7:14).

The Festival of Unleavened Bread owes its name to the fact that all leaven was avoided during its seven days (Exod. 12:15). Many scholars believe that this festival was originally distinct from Passover. It was an agricultural celebration, first observed in Canaan (Josh. 5:11–12) and possibly adopted from the Canaanites. It marked the gathering of the first crop and so a new beginning. Therefore, only the newly reaped grain was eaten, with no leaven from the previous year's harvest in it. Later, however, when Passover and the Festival of Unleavened Bread had been combined, the eating of unleavened bread was interpreted as a memorial of what had happened at the exodus, when the Israelites had to leave Egypt in such haste that they did not have time to wait for the bread to rise (Exod. 13:7–8).

In the NT, Jesus refers to leaven (NRSV: "yeast") as symbolic of something small that has great influence. The kingdom of heaven is like leaven that a woman mixes with flour until the dough rises (Matt. 13:33; cf. Luke 13:20–21). But the same symbol can apply to "negative influences": Jesus cautions his disciples to beware of the yeast or leaven of the Pharisees, Sadducees, and Herod (Matt. 16:6; Mark 8:15; Luke 12:1). Likewise, Paul compares the potential influence of an immoral person in the Corinthian congregation to that of leaven on a batch of dough (1 Cor. 5:1–7), and then perhaps through mere word association—or perhaps because the Passover was near—he encourages the Corinthians not to eat (figurative) bread leavened by evil and malice, but to eat "the unleavened bread of sincerity and truth" (5:8). In Gal. 5:9, he cites the same proverb quoted in 1 Cor. 5:6 ("A little yeast leavens the whole batch of dough") in reference to the bad influence of those who are telling the Galatians they should get circumcised. *See also* festivals, feasts, and fasts; Passover.   J.R.P.

Lebanon (leb'uh-nuhn), a mountain range parallel to the eastern Mediterranean coast. It has also given its name to the modern Republic of Lebanon, created during the French mandate of Syria between World Wars I and II. In antiquity Lebanon was populated by Canaanites and was the homeland of the Phoenicians. The name derives from a Hebrew word for "white" and refers to the snow-capped peaks of the range (Jer. 18:14). The Lebanon Mountains begin at the northern border of the Levant and extend northward approximately a hundred miles. The highest peak of this rugged range is over 9,850 feet high. On the western slope of the range the coastal zone is narrow and the mountains make communications inland difficult. Narrow, steep valleys and small rivers run down to the sea. The northernmost river is Nahr el-Kabir, in antiquity the Eleutherus, and in the

The cedars of the Lebanon mountain range provided abundant timber for the ancient Near East; few remain today.

south is the Litani River. These and others are fed by heavy annual precipitation (between 40 and 60 inches in the mountains).

The Lebanon Mountains were famous for their beautiful white peaks and also for their cedar forests (1 Kings 4:33; 2 Kings 14:9; Pss. 92:12; 104:16). These tall and beautiful trees were sought by many peoples in the ancient world. The Egyptians imported cedar wood as early as the third millennium BCE, and Byblos became the primary port where timber was obtained. Consequently it was under strong Egyptian cultural influence during the third and second millennia BCE. Rulers from Mesopotamia also took timber from Lebanon for their temples. King Solomon used cedars of Lebanon in the construction of the temple in Jerusalem (1 Kings 5:6–10; 6:15–20) and his palace (7:2–3).

To the east, running parallel to the Lebanon Mountains, is the Beqa'a Valley, classical Coelesyria (Lat., "hollow Syria"), and beyond that, the Anti-Lebanon mountain range, dominated by Mount Hermon at its southern end. The high Beqa'a is a fertile and well-watered river valley drained by two main streams: the Orontes, which runs from Baalbek to northern Syria, and the Litani, which flows down the center of the southern Beqa'a and then cuts westward to empty into the Mediterranean Sea.

In antiquity the two main areas of human settlement were the coastal plain and the Beqa'a Valley. Numerous cities along the coast from the Bronze and Iron ages (ca. 3000–333 BCE) are known from ancient texts and archaeological excavations. Byblos is the best known, and other port cities include Tyre, Zarephath, Sidon, Beirut, Batrum, and Tripoli. At the beginning of the Iron Age the population became known as Phoenicians, and their cities emerged as the leading maritime centers of the Mediterranean. The coastal cities, however, never successfully united, except when Tyre controlled Sidon and southern Phoenicia in the ninth and eighth centuries BCE.

Two cities known from Egyptian sources were Kadesh in the north and Kumidi in the south. Kadesh, identified as modern Tell Nebi Mend, is on the bank of the Orontes River and was the site of a famous battle between Rameses II and the Hittites in the thirteenth century BCE. Kumidi is modern Kamid el-Loz, located a few miles east of the Litani River. Cuneiform tablets and public buildings from the Late Bronze Age have been discovered there. In Roman times Baalbek was the important sanctuary of Heliopolis in the Beqa'a.

Bibliography

Brown, J. P. *The Lebanon and Phoenicia.* Vol. 1, *The Physical Setting and the Forest.* American University of Beirut, 1969.

Marfoe, L. "The Integrative Transformation: Patterns of Sociopolitical Organization in Southern Syria." *Bulletin of the American Schools of Oriental Research* 234 (1979): 1–42.   T.L.M.

Lebbaeus (li-bee′uhs), the name for one of Jesus's twelve disciples found in some NT manuscripts in place of Thaddaeus (Matt. 10:3). *See also* Thaddaeus.

Lebo-hamath (li-bo-hay′math), a town in the district of Hamath, but far to the south of the city of Hamath (Num. 13:21; Josh. 13:5). Identified with modern Lebweh, Libo-hamath marked the traditional northern limit of Israel's territory (see Num. 34:8; Ezek. 47:15). *See also* Hamath.

leech, a bloodsucking parasite of the class *Hirudinea,* of which several varieties are common in the Near East. It is used as a symbol of insatiable appetite in Prov. 30:15.

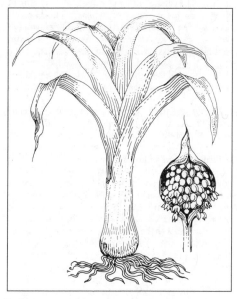

Leek.

leeks, the biennial herb *Allium porrum,* similar to garlic and onion. A staple in the ancient Near Eastern diet, leeks were reportedly yearned for by the Hebrews while in the wilderness (Num. 11:5) as a symbol of more abundant life.

lees. *See* dregs.

legion.

1 A large unit of soldiers in the Roman army. With Augustus's reorganization of the Roman army a legion was composed of 5,400 to 6,000 men and a like number of auxiliary troops. The standing army consisted of twenty-eight legions until 9 CE, when it decreased to twenty-five. This reduction remained in effect until two new legions were

raised at the end of Caligula's reign (37–41 CE) in preparation for the invasion of Britain. Tacitus (*Annals* 4.5) gives the following deployment of the legions for 23 CE: eight along the Rhine; six in the Balkans and along the Danube; three in Spain; two in Africa; and two in Egypt and four in Syria to watch over the eastern frontiers. The auxiliary regiments consisted of infantry cohorts and cavalry recruited from among the subject peoples. Sometimes they were commanded by Roman officers and sometimes by their own tribal leaders. Trajan increased the strength of the Roman army to thirty legions in 98–117 CE. When Jesus was arrested, he claimed God would send more than twelve legions of angels to rescue him if he so desired (Matt. 26:53).

2 The name of a demon or group of demons exorcised by Jesus in Mark 5:1–19. The demon or group of demons indicates that it is called "Legion" because "we are many" (5:9). The man possessed by Legion lives in a cemetery and possesses superhuman strength, breaking the shackles and chains with which he is restrained. At Legion's request, Jesus casts Legion out of the man and into a herd of pigs (rather than into the abyss); the pigs then run into the sea and are drowned. This story is also reported in Luke 8:26–39 and Matt. 28:28–34, though in the latter version, two men are possessed by demons and the name "Legion" is not given.   P.P.

Lehi (lee′hi; Heb., "jawbone"), the site where the Philistines camped as they sought Samson after he had burned their grain (Judg. 15:9). Samson was bound and brought to the Philistines at Lehi, but broke free and killed a thousand Philistines with the jawbone of a donkey. To mark the occasion, the place was named Ramath-lehi, meaning the "height, or high place, of the jawbone" (15:14–17). The name probably refers more to the area where the exploit occurred, including the spring named En-hakkore, rather than to a specific settlement (note 15:9, 19). It was probably located somewhere in the lowlands of southwestern Judah. The occurrence of the name in 2 Sam. 23:11 is textually uncertain and, following different manuscripts, some translations (including KJV) read "in a troop" instead of "Lehi." *See also* Samson. D.R.B.

Lemuel (lem′yoo-uhl; Heb., "belonging to God"), a king mentioned in Prov. 31:1–9 as being the addressee of his mother's wisdom. Two different readings of 31:1 are possible. Following the Hebrew Masoretic Text, Lemuel may be regarded as the king of Massa. This is the reading adopted by the RSV and NJB, although no one knows where Massa would have been. The LXX does not regard "Massa" as a place-name, but translates the Hebrew word with a Greek word meaning "oracle." Thus, following the LXX, the reading would be that of the NRSV ("The words of King Lemuel. An oracle that his mother taught him"). In this case, however, there is no indication of the land over which Lemuel was king.

Lentil.

lentil (*Lens culinaris*), a plant of the legume family cultivated widely in the Near East since prehistoric times. The small lens-shaped seeds are an especially nutritious food, providing both protein and carbohydrates. It was a common component of soups and stews (Gen. 25:34) as well as a flour base for breads (Ezek. 4:9). Lentils are listed among crops in 2 Sam. 17:28; 23:11.

leopard (*Panthera pardus*). Leopards were at home in mountainous terrain of biblical lands, especially Mount Hermon and Lebanon (Song of Sol. 4:8). As a predator, the leopard represented a great danger to shepherds and their flocks as well as to travelers (Jer. 5:6; Sir. 28:23). The prophet Isaiah indicates that cessation of such predatory activity will characterize the time of God's final peace (11:6). One of the beasts seen in Daniel's apocalyptic vision had the appearance of a leopard (7:6), and a beast envisioned in Revelation was part leopard (13:2).

leprosy, in the Bible a disorder affecting humans, fabrics, and houses. Though it is not clear what all of these disorders were, it is certain that they were not modern leprosy (Hansen's disease), which did not exist in the ancient Near East. The "leprosy" that occurred in fabrics and houses is described as displaying greenish or reddish spots (Lev. 13:49; 14:37), indicating a type of mold or mildew. The ailment affecting humans may have included a wide variety of skin diseases.

Persons or objects afflicted with leprosy were deemed unclean, and contact with them could render others unclean as well. The Bible offers various instructions for treating clothing, houses, and persons with leprosy. Fabrics incorrigibly infected with leprosy are to be burned (Lev. 13:52, 55, 57), and building materials so infected must be discarded outside the habitation (14:40, 41, 45). Anyone who enters a leprous house must bathe. If a person tarries there by eating or lying down, both bathing and laundering are necessary (14:46–47). A person with leprosy is, accordingly, to be excluded from habitations (13:45–46; cf. Num. 12:15; 2 Kings 7:3–4). When the person recovers from the affliction, purification rites are performed (Lev. 14:2–20, 21–32). Similar rites are performed for a renovated house (14:48–53). These purification rites are not for the removal of leprosy, but only for the removal of the state of ritual impurity that the leprosy brought (cf. Mark 1:44). There is some evidence that leprosy was sometimes considered a punishment from God for sin (cf. Num. 12:10–15; 2 Kings 5:27; 15:5; 2 Chron. 26:20–21).

In Num. 12, Miriam is afflicted with leprosy as punishment for criticizing Moses's marriage to a Cushite woman. In 2 Kings 5, Naaman, the Syrian army commander, is healed of leprosy by the prophet Elisha, and 2 Chron. 26:16–21 tells of King Uzziah's contracting leprosy. The Gospels likewise report that Jesus healed people afflicted with leprosy (e.g., Matt. 8:1–4; Luke 17:11–19) and that he commissioned his disciples to do the same (Matt. 10:8). Jesus is also reported to have visited the home of Simon the leper (Mark 14:3), perhaps one of those he had healed.   D.P.W.

letter, a form of literary communication. The number of letters discovered in the Middle East and the Mediterranean basin within the past century shows that the letter was one of the most common forms of communication in the ancient world. As abundant as they are, however, such discoveries cannot adequately reflect how extensive letter writing was, because only letters written on decay-resistant materials or those preserved by a dry climate have survived. Although many letters were written by professional scribes, the percentage written by common people indicates that illiteracy was not as prevalent in the Hellenistic culture as scholars once imagined. There was an organized postal system as early as the Persian Empire (sixth century BCE), but it existed only for government business and not for private correspondence. Wealthy families used slaves or couriers, and common people relied on caravans, friends, or passing strangers who were traveling in the direction of the recipient of the letter. This was still the case in the Roman period, when letters from Paul and other Christian leaders were delivered by personal acquaintances or assistants of the letter writer.

Clay tablets from such sites as Ras-Shamra, El-Amarna, Lachish, Babylon, and Mari shed light on letter writing during the time of ancient Israel. Jewish letters found at Elephantine, an island in the Nile River near the first cataract on which there was a Jewish colony in the fifth century BCE, as well as other Aramaic letters on skins and potsherds show what letter writing was like during the Second Temple period. Greek papyrus letters, which have been discovered in great number in Egypt, provide understanding for the conventions of Greek letter writing at the time of the NT.

In the Hebrew Bible, no document is written in letter form, even though letters are referred to and their messages are sometimes summarized (e.g., 2 Sam. 11:15; 2 Kings 5:5–6; 10:6; 2 Chron. 2:11; 21:12–15; Ezra 4:7–23). In the NT, the letter became the largest literary category: twenty-one of the twenty-seven documents are written in epistolary form. A partial explanation for the prominence of letters in the NT is that this was the way in which Christian leaders such as Paul instructed communities under their supervision when they could not be present in person.

In NT Times: People would write on almost anything. Copies of letters have been found written on clay tablets (called cuneiform), shards of pottery (called ostraca), and pieces of wood or animal skin. The most common writing material, however, was papyrus, a reedy plant that grew abundantly in the delta of the Nile River. The core or pith of this plant could be cut into very thin strips; a horizontal row of strips would be laid on top of a vertical row and the two layers pressed together to form a sheet that was laid in the sun to dry. A typical sheet of papyrus measured about 9½ by 11½ inches (close to the size of a modern sheet of paper) and would hold approximately 200 words. Pens for writing were typically made from sharpened reeds or sticks (pens from feather quills appear to have come along later). Ink was made from a combination of chimney soot and tree gum. It would be kept in a dried cake, but would liquefy slightly when touched with the moistened tip of the reed pen. Erasure was difficult—the ink had to be washed away—so mistakes would usually be blotched out in a rather unattractive manner. If the document was an important one, a mistake meant starting over.

The task of composing a letter was sufficiently cumbersome that it was often delegated to persons trained in the craft—a secretary or scribe known as an amanuensis. Thus, Paul's Letter to the Romans identifies Tertius as the one who was actually putting the words on paper (16:22). At other places, Paul specifies that he is writing concluding words in his own hand (1 Cor. 16:21; Gal. 6:11; 2 Thess. 3:17; Col. 4:18; cf. Philem. 19). This suggests that the rest of the letter had been written by someone else. The exact task of an amanuensis varied. Sometimes the amanuensis took dictation, recording what the sender wanted to say by writing the words quickly with a stylus on a wax tablet (a form of shorthand was even in use for this purpose) and, later, copying the words more painstakingly in ink on papyrus. At other times, however, the amanuensis may have been given more freedom with regard to composition; the author of the letter would explain what was to be conveyed in broad terms and allow the amanuensis to come up with the actual wording.

In any case, once a letter was written, it had to be conveyed to the appropriate destination and, in the case of NT letters, the person entrusted with responsibility for transporting the letter was also expected to see that it was read as intended (e.g., aloud to the entire congregation; see 1 Thess. 5:27). In addition, the letter bearer may have been expected to explain various points in the letter that were unclear, respond to objections raised, and return to the sender with a report of how the letter was received. Paul seems to have entrusted Phoebe (a deacon in the church at Corinth) with the important job of delivering his Letter to the Romans (Rom. 16:1–2). Titus (2 Cor. 8:16–18), Tychicus (Eph. 6:21; Col. 4:7–8), and Epaphroditus (Phil. 2:25–28) are similarly identified as bearers of other letters.

Format: The ancient world had stereotypical patterns for letters, to which most NT letters conform in a general sense, albeit with notable idiosyncrasies. In general, a letter exhibited four main parts:

Salutation: A letter would typically open with a salutation identifying the author and the recipient, followed by the word "Greetings!" (cf. Acts 15:23; James 1:1). The NT letters exhibit a strong tendency for substituting the word "Grace!" for "Greetings!" This may have been a play on words, since the words look and sound similar in Greek (*chaire,* "greetings"; *charis,* "grace"). In any case, this use of "Grace!" instead of "Greetings!" seems to have been a peculiarity of Christian writing, and it may have served as an indicator to those in the know that what followed was written by a Christian. It is often thought that Paul originated the practice, since his letters are the earliest ones exhibiting this feature. Jewish letters from this period exhibit a similar tendency, substituting the word "Peace!" (Heb. *shalom;* Gk. *eirēnē*) for "Greetings!" Indeed, the single most common pattern for Christian writers seems to have been to use both "grace" and "peace," combining the traditional Jewish greeting with a transformed version of the Roman greeting. All of the NT letters attributed to Paul open with some form of this "Grace and peace" greeting, as do 1 Peter, 2 Peter, and 2 John. The NT letters also display the tendency of authors to expand the salutation with phrases that describe the sender and/or recipient in particular ways. Paul does not usually identify himself simply as "Paul" (1 Thess. 1:1); more often he is "Paul an apostle of Christ Jesus by the will of God" (2 Cor. 1:1) or something even more elaborate (cf. Gal. 1:1). Likewise, he does not just write to the "church of God in Corinth," but more precisely to "those who are sanctified in Christ Jesus, called to be saints . . ." (1 Cor. 1:2). Hebrews and 1 John do not have opening salutations, which suggests to some that they are more like sermons or homilies than actual letters.

Thanksgiving: Letters in the Greco-Roman world often included a brief word of thanksgiving to the gods for good health, deliverance from calamity, or some other beneficence. Paul retains this feature in his letters, though it undergoes considerable development. The thanksgiving is

TYPES OF LETTERS IN
THE GRECO-ROMAN WORLD

Handbooks from the Greco-Roman world include instructions for writing different types of letters to accomplish different goals:

Friendship: to share memories and provide news between friends who are separated

Prayer: to express the content of prayers said on the recipient's behalf

Congratulations: to applaud the recipient for some accomplishment or honor

Consolation: to express sympathy for one who has experienced suffering or loss

Recommendation: to testify to someone's abilities and/or character

Inquiry: to request information from the recipient

Response: to respond to a letter of inquiry by supplying requested information

Report: to inform the recipient of news that the sender deems relevant

Supplication: to ask the recipient for some sort of favor

Thanks: to express gratitude for a favor that has been promised or performed

Excuse: to explain why the sender will not be able to do something the recipient requested

Instruction: to teach the recipient about some topic

Advice: to recommend one course of action over another

Encouragement: to urge the recipient to be bold in pursuing some course of action

Exhortation: to urge the recipient to avoid immorality and exhibit virtuous behavior

Accusation: to claim the recipient has an improper attitude or behavior

Threat: to inform the recipient of consequences for behavior (especially if it continues)

Defense: to seek to defuse charges made against sender by the recipient or someone else

Praise: to commend the recipient for exemplary behavior

NT letters are longer than the letters that would exemplify one or another of these types (but see Acts 15:23–29; 23:26–30). Thus, they are usually thought to represent "mixed types" for which there was no specific category in the handbooks. Still, all of the NT letters incorporate aspects of these various letter types into their contents, as they seek to accomplish the various functions those types were intended to serve.

From Mark Allan Powell, *Introducing the New Testament* (courtesy, Baker Academic). See also David deSilva, *An Introduction to the New Testament* (InterVarsity, 2004), pp. 533–34.

offered to God in specifically Christian terms (e.g., "through Jesus Christ," Rom. 1:8), and the reason for the thanksgiving is also distinctive; Paul typically gives thanks for the faithfulness of the congregation to which he is writing and for what God has done, is doing, and will continue to do for that congregation. Sometimes matters mentioned in the thanksgiving hint at topics that will be taken up in more detail later (1 Cor. 1:4–7; 12:1–30). Thus, as with the salutations, Paul's prayers of thanksgiving tend to segue into preaching, and it is not always easy to tell when Paul is addressing God or the congregation on God's behalf. Some scholars think that the "thanksgiving" portion of 1 Thessalonians extends all the way to 3:13, taking up more than half the letter. Paul's Letter to the Galatians, however, contains no thanksgiving—most likely because he was angry and disappointed with that church.

Main Body: The main body of a letter had few fixed features, because its structure was determined by what was appropriate for the particular content. Letters served a variety of purposes in the ancient world, and a considerable variety is evident among letters found in the NT as well. Galatians is a defensive letter written to rebuke its recipients, while Philippians is a letter of friendship written to thank a community for its faithfulness and support. The NT letters also employ a variety of rhetorical styles, and many of them incorporate various subgenres of literature into their contents: hymns (Phil. 2:6–11; Col. 1:15–20); liturgical formulas (1 Cor. 6:11; Gal. 3:28; 4:6; Eph. 5:14); church traditions (1 Cor. 11:23–25; 15:1–7); creeds (1 Tim. 3:16; 2 Tim. 2:11–13); virtue and vice lists (Gal. 5:19–23; Eph. 4:31–32; Titus 1:7–10); household codes (Eph. 5:21–6:9; Col. 3:18–4:1; 1 Pet. 3:1–7); autobiography (Gal. 1:10–2:21; 1 Thess. 2:1–3:13); travelogues (Rom. 15:14–33); topical discussions (Rom. 13:1–7; 1 Cor. 7:1–40); chiasms (Rom. 5:12–21; Gal. 5:13–6:2); and prayers (Phil. 1:9–11; 1 Thess. 3:11–13).

Closing: The two most common conventions in the closing of Greco-Roman letters were a wish for good health (cf. 3 John 2) and an expression of "Farewell!" (cf. Acts 15:29). The NT letters do not adhere to these conventions with any sort of regularity. Paul's letters tend to close somewhat haphazardly with mention of travel plans (e.g. 1 Cor. 16:5–9), greetings to specific individuals (e.g., Rom. 16:3–16), miscellaneous exhortations (1 Thess. 5:12–28), a recap of some significant point (e.g., Rom. 16:17–20; Gal. 6:15–16), or a personal signature (e.g., Gal. 6:11) and then, finally, a doxology (Rom. 16:25–27), benediction (Philem. 25), or closing prayer (2 Cor. 13:13). The non-Pauline letters tend to close more quickly, sometimes with brief greetings (Heb. 13:24; 1 Pet. 5:14; 2 John 13; 3 John 13) and a benediction or doxology (Heb. 13:20–21, 25; 1 Pet. 5:14; 2 Pet. 3:18; Jude 24–25).

Finally, the single most distinctive feature of the NT letters may be their length. The typical length of personal letters from this period is around 90 words, but the *shortest* of the NT letters are 2 John and 3 John, which run 245 words and 219 words, respectively. The letters attributed to Paul average about 1,300 words in length, an incredible figure considering that the learned letters of the Roman orator Cicero average no more than 295 words. Paul's Letter to the Romans is 7,101 words long, quite a production considering the time and trouble involved in creating such written correspondences in the ancient world. *See also* epistle; writing.

Bibliography

Aune, David E. *The New Testament in Its Literary Environment.* Westminster, 1987.

Klauck, Hans-Josef. *Ancient Letters and the New Testament: A Guide to Context and Exegesis.* Baylor University Press, 2006.

Malherbe, Abraham J. *Ancient Epistolary Theorists.* Scholars, 1973.

Murphy-O'Connor, Jerome. *Paul the Letter-Writer: His World, His Options, His Skills.* Liturgical, 1995.

Powell, Mark Allan. *Introducing the New Testament: A Historical, Literary, and Theological Survey.* Baker Academic, 2009. Pp. 215–29.

Stowers, Stanley K. *Letter Writing in Greco-Roman Antiquity.* Westminster, 1986.   M.A.P.

Letter of Jeremiah, a writing attributed to Jeremiah (late seventh–early sixth centuries BCE), but composed most likely in the fourth century BCE in order to provide Jews with arguments to counter their Gentile neighbors' belief in the reality of idols. It is more a homily than a letter, arising from Jeremiah's advice to the exiles concerning idolatry—"Thus shall you say to them: 'The gods who did not make the heavens and the earth shall perish from the earth and from under the heavens' " (Jer. 10:11)—as well as from his correspondence with them in Jer. 29. The work defies organization or outline. It is punctuated with the refrain, "Since you know by these things that they are not gods, do not fear them" (see vv. 16, 23, 29, 40, 44, 52, 56, 65, 69), and includes the typical polemics that Jews directed against idols (cf. Jer. 10:2–16; Pss. 115:4–8; 135:15–18; Isa. 40:18–20; 41:6–7; 46:1–7; Bel and the Dragon): idols are helpless; fabricated by human beings out of wood, stone, and metal; subject to decay, rust, and rot; powerless to deliver anyone from danger; and served by impure and dishonest priests and priestesses who engage in immoral activities like cultic prostitution and theft of offerings.

The letter was probably composed in Hebrew, but it has been preserved only in Greek. Its place of composition may have been Babylonia, since it is well informed concerning Mesopotamian religious practices. Some manuscripts of the LXX treat it as a separate book following Lamentations, while others, along with the Vulgate, include it at the end of Baruch. Protestant Christians regard the Letter to Jeremiah as part of the Apocrypha, while Roman Catholics and Orthodox Christians include it among the deuterocanonical books as a part of Baruch. *See also* Apocrypha/deuterocanonical literature; Baruch; idol.   D.W.S.

Letters, Johannine. *See* John, Letters of.

Letters, Pastoral. *See* Timothy, First Letter of Paul to; Timothy, Second Letter of Paul to; Titus, Letter of Paul to.

Levant (luh-vant'), **the,** a term used in geologic discussions to designate the lands of the eastern Mediterranean, especially the region that corresponds to modern-day Israel, Syria, and Lebanon. The term is actually short for Levant Rift Valley, sometimes referred to as the Jordan Rift, which is part of an extensive fault system that was formed over a long period of time. In a broad sense, "the Levant" includes all Mediterranean lands from Greece to Egypt, but biblical and historical scholars tend to use the term in a restricted sense, as a politically neutral synonym for what has popularly been called "Palestine."

Geography: Throughout history the political frontiers of the Levant have fluctuated considerably. Broadly described, the Levant is bounded on the north by the foothills of the Anatolian plateau, on the south by the Sinai desert, on the east by the Syrian desert and the Euphrates ("the great river" in the Bible), and on the west by the Mediterranean ("the great sea" in the Bible). These boundaries include the modern states of Israel, Jordan, Syria, and Lebanon. In round figures the Levant is no more than five hundred miles long and ninety-five miles wide. In accord with the traditional biblical formula "from Dan to Beer-sheba," ancient Israel would have been much smaller, about the size of Vermont. Natural boundaries surrounded Israel on three sides: the desert on the east and south, and the Mediterranean on the west. In biblical times the cities were more like villages,

Aerial view of the Jordan River, which meanders for two hundred miles between the Sea of Galilee and the Dead Sea, three times the distance as the crow flies.

small in size and population. During the time of the divided monarchy, the population of either of the two capitals, Samaria and Jerusalem, probably never exceeded thirty thousand inhabitants. According to scholarly estimates, in the first half of the eighth century BCE the population of the northern kingdom was about eight hundred thousand and of the southern kingdom about three hundred thousand.

Although the Levant was lacking in natural resources, its strategic—and at the same time vulnerable—location as a land bridge made it a vital region. It was situated at the crossroads of the ancient world, with Mesopotamia to the northeast and Egypt to the southwest. Armies and caravans traversed the Levant for centuries. Its geographic position immersed it in the political, commercial, cultural, and military activities of the whole region. The area was ruled by a succession of conquerors: Egypt, Assyria, Babylonia, Persia, Greece, Rome, Byzantium, the Muslim caliphates, the Crusaders, the Ottoman Turks, and the British.

Climate: The climate of the Levant is subtropical, characterized by dry summers and rainy winters. Seventy percent of the annual rainfall occurs between November and February. Precipitation varies greatly in different parts of the country; most of the rain falls along the coastal plain.

The annual rainfall in Upper Galilee to the north is about 45 inches; in the Negev to the south about 8 inches. Vegetation is greatly dependent upon the rainfall. Indicative of the vital importance of rainfall, Hebrew has several words for rain, distinguishing the "early" rain in the autumn, which softens the ground, preparing the soil for plowing and sowing, and the "latter" spring rain, which fosters the growth of the cereal grains. Dew, abundant along the coastal plain, is also vital for vegetation, as it provides moisture where there is no rain (Deut. 33:28).

Westerly winds prevail, but there is also an unpleasant east wind from the desert to the south and southeast; known as the *sirocco* (Italian), the *hamsin* (Arabic), and the *sharab* (Heb.), it is the "east wind" of the Bible (e.g., Gen. 41:6; Exod. 14:21; Isa. 27:8). This oppressive, dust-laden wind blows in the early autumn and late spring and often persists for several days.

Economy: Deuteronomy describes Canaan as "a land of wheat and barley, of vines and fig trees and pomegranates . . . a land whose stones are iron, and out of whose hills you can dig copper" (8:8–9). The economy of this area was basically agricultural and pastoral. Agriculture was conducted primarily in the north, where the chief crops were wheat, barley, olives, grapes, and figs; the breeding

To the north, past the summit of Mount Gerizim in the central foreground, lies Mount Ebal, across the Shechem-Neapolis pass. The site of ancient Shechem lies in the center of the photograph.

of sheep and goats was done mostly in the south. In addition to domestic animals, there were foxes, jackals, hyenas, lizards, snakes, and scorpions.

The Levant is not rich in raw materials, except for the iron mines in Transjordan and the copper mines of the Arabah in the south. The mineral products are limestone, basalt, and clay. There is gypsum in the mountains of Galilee, sulfur in the environs of Gaza, bitumen from the Dead Sea, and glass sand near Beer-sheba.

Limestone, sedimentary rock consisting mostly of calcium carbonate, was the common building stone. Nari, a soft limestone easily quarried and dressed, was used to prepare ashlars and capitals in the construction of monumental buildings. Cenomanian limestone, the bedrock stone of the Levant, is impermeable; depending upon local geological conditions, waterproofing cisterns with plaster was often not necessary. Porous limestone traps water, and the resultant wells and springs were a boon for agriculture. Basalt, a dense volcanic rock, is common in Galilee, the Golan, and Bashan. Its water-resistant quality made it excellent for constructing steps, thresholds, and orthostats. Basalt was also used for grindstones.

Natural Zones: Between the Mediterranean Sea to the west and the Syrian desert to the east, the Levant is divided into five natural zones, or topographical regions, running longitudinally and clearly evident on a relief map; they are, from west to east, the coastal plain, the Shephelah, the central mountain range, the Jordan Valley, and the Transjordan plateau.

Coastal Plain: The coastal plain, rich in vegetation, is divided into the northern, central, and southern sections, a strip a hundred and thirty miles long, with Phoenician Tyre in the north and Philistine Gaza in the south. The main features of the coastal plain, narrow in the north and wider in the south, were (from north to south) the Plain of Acco, the Jezreel Valley, the Sharon, the Philistine coast, and the western Negev. The great international highway, the Via Maris (Lat., "the way of the sea"), ran the length of the coastline. This commercial route originated in Egypt, ran west to the Sea of Galilee, veered north to Hazor, and terminated in Damascus.

Jezreel, or Esdraelon, was the broad and inviting valley connecting the coastal area and the Jordan Valley. This rich agricultural region is excellent for farming. The Plain of Sharon, the central portion of the coastal plain, extended for a distance of about forty-five miles from the Carmel range to Joppa. Forested in antiquity, the Sharon was not heavily inhabited in biblical times. Chariots operated in the valleys and the plains, whereas the infantry fought in the hills. The Philistine coast encompassed the fertile land between Joppa and the Wadi Ghazzeh (located about six miles south of Gaza). The Philistine Pentapolis consisted of Gaza, Ashkelon, and Ashdod along the coast, Ekron six miles inland, and Gath (perhaps Tel Haror). Although natural harbors were lacking in this area, Ashkelon was one of the greatest

To the east, from the caves at Qumran, ancient home of the Essenes, lies the northern end of the Dead Sea, the lowest depression on earth.

Mediterranean seaports from the Early Bronze to the Crusader period.

The western Negev lay at the southern end of the coastal plain. In biblical studies, the area called "the Negev" is the east–west zone that stretches from Gaza to the Dead Sea (technically, the northern Negev). The two prominent biblical sites located in the Negev are Kadesh-barnea, where Moses and the Israelites spent thirty-eight years on their trek from Sinai to Transjordan, and Beer-sheba, where the ancestors of Israel worshiped.

Shephelah: The Shephelah, meaning "lowlands," was the range of limestone hills between the Philistine plain and the Judean mountains. These narrow foothills (twenty-eight miles long, nine miles wide) were "lowlands" from the vantage point of the Israelites living in the higher hill country to the east. Thickly settled in biblical times, the Shephelah was a fertile region. The principal cities in the Shephelah were Gezer in the north and Lachish in the south. As a buffer zone between the coastal plain and the mountains, the Shephelah was strategic in the defense of the Levant.

Central Mountain Range: The hill country, situated between the Shephelah and the Jordan Valley, was the geographic backbone of the Levant and supported the pastoral economy. The principal regions of the hill country were Galilee, Samaria, and Judah. Galilee, bounded on the north by the Litani River and on the south by the Jezreel Valley, was the principal focus of Jesus's public ministry. The highest mountain regions (4,000 feet above the Mediterranean) in the Levant were in Upper Galilee, a terrain not conducive to agriculture; rolling hills and fertile soil characterized Lower Galilee.

The most prosperous part of this hill country was the geographic center, which formed the northern kingdom, Israel (with Samaria as its capital city), during the time of the divided monarchy. This region was rich in agriculture, especially grain, olives, and vines. Mount Ebal and Mount Gerizim were the two most conspicuous peaks among the hills of the northern kingdom. In biblical times these mountains had both military importance and religious significance. Shechem (Nablus) was strategically located in the narrow pass between Mount Ebal and Mount Gerizim.

Judah designated the southern kingdom ruled by the Davidic kings; in Greek and Roman times (ca. 333 BCE–324 CE), this region was called Judea (and the regions to the north were called Samaria and Galilee). The boundaries of Judah/Judea fluctuated throughout history. David made Jerusalem, "the holy mountain," the capital city of the united kingdom. With an elevation of 2,460 feet above sea level, Jerusalem was secured on either side by valleys: on the east by the Kidron Valley and on the west by the Valley of Hinnom. The Tyropoeon Valley is a central valley dividing the mount of Jerusalem into the more affluent Upper City (the western hill) and the Lower City (the City of David and the Temple Mount). Surrounded by hills, off the beaten track, and with only a limited water supply, Jerusalem was an unlikely capital.

Jordan Valley: The unique feature of the Levant's geography is the Rift Valley (Ghor). Splitting the country down the middle, it extends from the foot of Mount Hermon to the Gulf of Aqabah. The Levant straddles this fissure, which has an average width of about ten miles and is the largest geological fault on earth. The Rift, as well as the area's hilly topography and wadi system, militated against political unity or centralized rule; the terrain fragmented the country into separate tribes and other political entities.

The Jordan River flows down the middle of the Rift, which encompasses the Huleh Valley, the Sea of Galilee (Chinnereth), the Jordan Valley, the Dead Sea, the Arabah plain, and the Gulf of Aqabah (Elath). The Huleh Valley lies between the Litani River and Mount Hermon, ten miles north of the Sea of Galilee. Thirteen miles long and seven miles wide, the Sea of Galilee is about 700 feet below sea level. The earliest name for this freshwater lake was Chinnereth (Heb., "lyre-shaped"); it was also known in NT times as the "Lake of Tiberias." The Jordan meanders for an additional two hundred miles between the Sea of Galilee and the Dead Sea, three times the distance as the crow flies. In its southerly course between the Sea of Galilee and the Dead Sea the Jordan drops about 600 feet. The Yarmuk and Jabbok rivers are important tributaries of the Jordan from the east; there are no significant tributaries from the west.

The Dead Sea is another novel geographic feature of the Levant. It is so called because its high mineral content prevents the survival of marine life. In view of its concentration of sodium chloride (six times the oceans' salt content), the Bible refers to this body of water as the Salt Sea (e.g., Gen. 14:3, KJV, RSV, NIV). However, the Dead Sea contains such useful minerals and natural resources as potash, bromine, phosphate, magnesium, calcium, and potassium. The Dead Sea, which has no outlet, extended fifty-five miles (though today it extends only thirty miles) from north to south and was

about ten miles wide. Thirteen hundred feet below sea level at its surface, the Dead Sea is the lowest depression on earth.

The term "Arabah" is used in the Bible to designate the Rift Valley extending from the Sea of Galilee to the Dead Sea; today the term is usually used in a more limited sense to refer only to that portion of the Rift between the Dead Sea and the Gulf of Aqabah (Elath), a distance of about a hundred and ten miles. Covered with alluvial sand and gravel, the Arabah has always been rich in copper deposits.

Transjordan Plateau: The easternmost zone is the Transjordan, coterminous with the modern Kingdom of Jordan. The term "Transjordan" embraces the whole easterly region between the Jordan Rift eastward to the Syrian desert, with an elevation of 2,000 feet in the highlands. Four main east–west tributaries cut the Transjordan highlands: the Yarmuk, the Jabbok, the Arnon, and the Zered. These bodies of water also serve as boundaries dividing Transjordan into discrete geopolitical regions: Bashan (north of the Yarmuk), Gilead (south of the Yarmuk), Ammon (between the Jabbok and Arnon), Moab (between the Arnon and the Zered), and Edom (south of the Zered). To the south of Edom lies the southern desert of Jordan.

The Yarmuk, the largest river in Jordan and the northernmost, is not mentioned in the Bible. The Jabbok is the modern Nahr ez-Zerqa, "the blue river"; Jacob wrestled with an "angel" at the ford of the Jabbok near Penuel (Gen. 32:24–30). Wadi Mojib, the modern name of the Arnon, is a precipitous canyon associated with Moab. The Zered is identified with the Wadi el-Hesa, which divided Moab and Edom. On their way to Jericho, at the end of their sojourn in the wilderness, the Israelites crossed the Wadi Zered (Num. 21:12; Deut 2:13–14).

The King's Highway, a famous international trade and caravan route, extended from Damascus to the Gulf of Aqabah; it ran the length of Transjordan, passing through Bashan, Gilead, Ammon, Moab, and Edom.

Bashan in the northern district of Transjordan parallels the Sea of Galilee; it is good pastureland. Several biblical authors commented on natural features of Bashan, suggesting prosperity and luxury (1 Chron. 6:71: Ezek. 39:18; Mic. 7:14). The black basalt so abundantly available in Bashan is used for building stones today as it was in biblical times.

The mountainous region of Gilead was well known for its excellent pasture. Gilead was also forested in antiquity, and its trees may have produced the balm to which Jeremiah alluded (8:22). David fled to Gilead when Absalom attempted to usurp his throne (2 Sam. 17:21–26). The prophet Elijah was a native of Gilead (1 Kings 17:1).

Ammon, Moab, and Edom constituted the three nation-states of Transjordan. The boundaries of Ammon in the north-central part of the country were never clearly defined. The citadel in modern Amman is the site of the ancient capital of Ammon.

The territory of Moab in central Transjordan lay east of the Dead Sea. Both Kerak and Dhiban (Dibon) served as the capital cities of Moab. This region is known for wheat, barley, sheep, goats, and camels. The Israelites had a strong antipathy toward the Moabites, with whom they often contended.

Edom was the region in the rugged highland of Seir located in southern Transjordan. The biblical kingdom of Edom, also known as Seir, was situated on a high plateau 3,500 feet above sea level. The characteristic shrub forests covering the mountains of Edom may have accounted for the name "Mount Seir," meaning "hairy mountain" in Hebrew. The Edomite territory extended south of the Dead Sea on both sides of the Arabah, as far as the Gulf of Aqabah. Controlling the King's Highway, which brought trade from India and South Arabia to Egypt, the Edomites acquired great wealth. The abiding hostility between Edom and Judah is all too evident in the Bible, especially in writings of the prophets. After the fall of Jerusalem in 587/6 BCE, the Edomites incurred the fury of the Judahites by occupying their land. Their encroachment westward into the land of Judah may have been occasioned by the invading Nabateans, an Arabic-speaking people from the desert who settled in Edomite territory, making Petra their capital. The Edomites of south Judah became the Idumeans of Hellenistic and Roman times. Herod the Great (Luke 1:5) was an Idumean.

P.J.K./M.A.P.

Levi (lee′vi; Heb., "joined").

1 The third son of Jacob and Leah. Leah gave him the name Levi, because when he was born, she said, "Now my husband will be joined to me, for I have borne him three sons" (Gen. 29:34; cf. 29:20).

2 The tribe descended from **1** above. The connection with Leah associated the tribe with five others: Reuben, Simeon, Judah, Issachar, and Zebulun. Levi is the only one of the twelve Israelite tribes that received no allocation of territory (Josh. 13–19). Its members were to have no share in the land, because they had been chosen by God to serve as priests (18:7). Thus, instead of land, the Levites were given a number of towns in which to live (chap. 21). A different (or supplemental) explanation for the scattering of the Levites among the tribes is provided in the story of the rape of Dinah (Gen. 34; recalled in Jth. 9:1–4). When Dinah, the daughter of Jacob and Leah, was raped by a Shechemite, who then wished to marry her, Simeon and Levi exacted a terrible vengeance upon the man and his entire town. They agreed to the marriage on the condition that the men of Shechem circumcise themselves. Then, when those men were incapacitated from the circumcision, they killed them and plundered their city. Jacob said that because Simeon and Levi were so violent and filled with cruel wrath, their tribes would be scattered throughout Israel (Gen. 49:5–7). Later, when the Israelites worshiped the golden

calf at Sinai, Moses spoke to the sons of Levi and said. "Put your sword on your side, each of you! Go back and forth from gate to gate throughout the camp, and each of you kill your brother, your friend, and your neighbor" (Exod. 32:27). They carried out these directions and, so, were told, "Today you have ordained yourselves for the service of the LORD, each one at the cost of a son or a brother, and so have brought a blessing on yourselves this day" (32:29). *See also* Levites; tribes.

3 A tax collector called to follow Jesus in Mark 2:14 (cf. Luke 5:27). He is called Matthew in the Gospel of Matthew (9:9), which allows him to be identified with one of Jesus's twelve disciples (Matt. 10:3; Mark 3:18; Luke 6:16; Acts 1:13). *See also* Matthew; tax collectors.   M.A.P.

Leviathan (li-vi′uh-thuhn), a great, mythological monster. In Ugaritic mythology, Leviathan (appearing by the name Lothan) is one of the primeval sea monsters who battles against Baal on the side of Mot (the god of the underworld) and who is ultimately defeated. This mythological tradition is referenced in the Bible where God appears as the victor over the sea monsters: "You divided the sea by your might; you broke the heads of the dragons in the waters. You crushed the heads of Leviathan; you gave him as food for the creatures of the wilderness (Ps. 74:13–14; cf. Job 3:8; 26:12–13; Ps. 104:26). Job 41 is devoted in its entirety to Leviathan. Most of the chapter describes the might and terror of this monster: its hide is a double coat of mail (41:14); its back is made of shields, joined so closely together that no air can escape (41:15); its sneezes flash forth light, and its mouth, flaming torches (41:18–19); it makes the ocean to boil like a pot (41:31); neither spear, dart, javelin, arrow, sling stones, nor clubs will avail against it (41:26–29); it is a creature without fear that has no equal on earth (41:33); even the gods are overwhelmed at the sight of it, and beside themselves with fear when it raises up or crashes (41:41:9, 25). Still, the main point of Job 41 is that the God who addresses Job from out of a whirlwind views Leviathan as no more than a plaything; God can draw Leviathan out with a hook (41:1), play with it as with a bird, or put it on a leash (41:1, 5). Leviathan speaks soft words to this God, making many supplications and desiring a covenant to become a servant forever (41:3–4). The prophet Isaiah treats the future and final destruction of Leviathan as a symbol for the death of the wicked (Isa. 27:1), to be succeeded by the redemption of Israel (26:20–21; 27:2–13). *See also* Baal; Tiamat; Ugarit.   J.U.

levirate law. *See* marriage.

Levites (lee′vits), generally, those belonging to the tribe of Levi. In some passages, however, "Levite" seems to be a description rather than a tribal name. For example, in Judg. 17:7, a Levite is mentioned who was a Judahite (i.e., a member of the tribe of Judah, not Levi); he may be designated a Levite because he is some kind of priest (17:13).

Thus, there is considerable overlap between "Levites" and the "tribe of Levi," but the two expressions may not be completely synonymous.

In any case, wherever the Levites appear, they are priests. The exact origins of such a "tribe of priests" are shrouded somewhat in mystery. According to Gen. 49:5–7, the descendants of Levi (and Simeon) were especially noted for their violent temper (cf. Gen. 34). But according to Exod. 32:26–29, that tendency could be turned into zeal for the Lord and, indeed it led Moses to proclaim that the Levites were ordained "for the service of the LORD" (32:29). In the book of Joshua, the tribe of Levi is not accorded land, because its members are to serve as priests (18:8). The book of Deuteronomy reflects this also, indicating that the Levites' function will be to perform sacrifices and also to teach the divine law (17:18; 33:10). In Deuteronomy, Levites seem to comprise the entire priesthood; they live in various towns in the country (cf. Josh. 21:1–42), but are to come to the central sanctuary and join the priesthood there (18:5–8).

The role of Levites becomes somewhat confused insofar as they are sometimes distinguished from "descendants of Aaron" and, later, from "descendants of Zadok." Various genealogies indicate that both Aaron (Exod. 6:16–20; Num. 26:58–59; 1 Chron. 6:1–3) and Zadok (1 Chron. 6:1–8; 24:1–3) were descended from Levi, so that Aaronites and Zadokites could technically be regarded as subsets of Levites, but, in fact, distinctions are made. Thus, in the book of Numbers, priestly material that is usually regarded as a fairly late addition to the Pentateuch indicates that the Levites are to serve the descendants of Aaron (3:6; 18:2). They are to lead services at the tabernacle and be in charge of furnishings for the tent of meeting, but they are not to approach the altar; only descendants of Aaron are to offer sacrifices at the altar (Num. 3:7–10; 18:1–8). Other duties prescribed for Levites include carrying the tabernacle and setting it up and taking it down (1:50–51), slaughtering animals for sacrifice (8:19), and collecting tithes (18:26, 28).

The writings of the prophet Ezekiel offer a picture of the situation at the time of the exile. Ezek. 44:10–16 distinguishes between the Levites and the "descendants of Zadok." The Levites are to have a limited role in the new temple, as punishment for straying from God and worshiping idols. They are to be gatekeepers and temple servants, but only the descendants of Zadok (who are called "levitical priests" in 44:15) are to serve as priests at the altar. The Levites may slaughter animals for sacrifice (44:11), but only the descendants of Zadok are to present that sacrifice before the Lord. The historical rationale for these distinctions is not absolutely clear. Despite the harmonizing genealogies, many scholars believe that the order of Zadok represented a new line of priests, possibly instituted by David (2 Sam. 8:17), that became closely attached to temple worship in Jerusalem during the era of the divided monarchy. A prominent theory, then, is that the Levites continued to serve in the northern kingdom, but after the dissolution of that kingdom, some Levites made their way to Jerusalem, where they were accepted as a "second-class priesthood," as servants of Zadok. The tradition of Levites serving Aaron in the wilderness would have developed as a reflection of this new reality.

In any case, 1 and 2 Chronicles offer a fairly detailed account of Levites in the postexilic period. The role of the Levites now seemed to have increased, and much of their former importance had been restored. First, as indicated by the genealogies that developed, all priests who served in the Second Temple period were regarded as descendants of Levi (and, thus, as Levites in a broad sense of the term). The people who were usually called Levites, however, were not priests, but the levitical order was now construed as including all temple personnel other than the priests, and the high position and important duties of such persons were emphasized, sometimes even against the priests (2 Chron. 29:34). For example, only the Levites were allowed to carry the ark, the temple's holiest object (1 Chron. 15:11–15). In addition, they provided the music for the services (16:4–37), and two collections of psalms in the Psalter were attributed to groups into which the Levites were divided: Asaph (50; 70–83) and Korah (42–49). They also retained their ancient functions of administering the law (1 Chron. 23:4; 2 Chron. 19:8–11) and of teaching it to the people (17:7–9; 35:3); many of the speeches in 1 and 2 Chronicles may reflect levitical sermons.

The only mention of a Levite in the NT occurs in Jesus's parable of the Good Samaritan. A Levite traveling from Jerusalem to Jericho sees an injured man by the side of the road, but passes by without helping him (Luke 10:32). The assumption of the story is not that this would be typical behavior for a Levite, but that even those expected to do God's will sometimes fail, while those not expected to do God's will (a Samaritan) may do the right thing. *See also* Aaron; Levi; priests; Zadok.

J.R.P./M.A.P.

levitical cities, forty-eight cities allotted to the Levites. They were spread throughout all of the territories allotted to the other tribes. According to Josh. 13–19, Levi was the only one of the twelve tribes not to be allocated any land. The Levites were to be priests, and their services would be needed in all of the tribal areas; therefore they lived in designated cities in all regions. The names of the cities are given in Josh 21:1–42; 1 Chron. 6:54–81. Archaeological evidence, however, indicates that most of the cities named on these lists were not occupied during the time of the monarchy. Accordingly, some scholars regard the notion of levitical cities as a theological construct, reflecting postexilic reflection on worship in ancient Israel.

Leviticus (li-vit′i-kuhs), **book of,** the third of the Five Books of Moses, or the Torah section, of the Tanakh (Jewish Bible); it is the third book of the Pentateuch of the Christian OT. Leviticus immediately follows Exodus and is followed by Numbers. Leviticus continues the record of the Israelites' experiences in the Sinai wilderness that began in the book of Exodus. Most of Leviticus is devoted to ritual legislation and cultic rules, with a few narrative descriptions of events in the wilderness. The Hebrew name of the book is *wayyiqra'* from its first Hebrew word, "and he called," and its rabbinic designation is *torat kohanim*, "priests' teaching." Since priests came from the tribe of Levi, the book came to be called Leviticus, the book of the Levites, by way of the titles used in the Greek LXX and the Latin Vulgate versions of the OT.

Contents: Leviticus consists of subcollections of priestly teachings organized by topic: offerings, ordination to priestly office, dietary regulations, and human behavior. Leviticus is one portion of the larger collection of priestly material, or P, that also includes the tabernacle design and construction (cf. Exod. 25–31; 35–40) and the tribal stories related to worship in Num. 1–10. The Holiness Code of Lev. 17–26 is a self-contained unit within Leviticus that was added to the other priestly material of the book, which is usually called the Priestly Code (Lev. 1–16). All these legal teachings are projected as speeches communicated by God to Moses, who then delivered them to the people in the wilderness. The sections of teaching are typically introduced with the line: "The LORD spoke to Moses, saying, 'Speak to the people of Israel saying . . .'" or "'Command Aaron and his sons saying . . .'" in order to establish the divine authority of Moses's words.

With regard to sources, the material is associated with the Priestly writer, an editor or school that collected and redacted texts and added them to the older epic material of the Yahwist and Elohist narratives found in Genesis–Numbers. Since the material is associated with the Priestly writer, it reflects the state of understanding of the priestly community of the exilic or postexilic period, though much of the material may have been traditional, with roots in the era of Israel's monarchic kingdoms.

Themes: The system of food and hygiene teachings laid out in Leviticus defines a world where every dimension of community and personal life is regulated and where material reality is categorized in relation to the absolute holiness of God. Because all dimensions of daily life were brought into relationship with deity, people had a high level of awareness that God held them accountable for living properly. If the divine-human relationship became disrupted in some way, the sacrificial system stood ready to repair the brokenness. Various types of sacrifices compensated for various types of sins, and even in the absence of sin other sacrifices would keep the Israelites in good standing with their God.

The categories of clean versus unclean and sacred versus profane are a priestly system that

OUTLINE OF CONTENTS

Leviticus

I. Priestly Code (1:1–16:34)
   A. Laws of sacrifices (1:1–7:38)
      1. Whole burnt offering (1:1–17)
      2. Cereal offering (2:1–16)
      3. Peace offering (3:1–17)
      4. Sin offering (4:1–5:13)
      5. Guilt offering (5:14–6:7)
      6. Priests' sacrificial dues (6:8–7:38)
   B. Ordination rites of the priests (8:1–10:20)
   C. Laws of purity (11:1–15:33)
      1. Clean and unclean animals (11:1–47)
      2. Childbirth (12:1–8)
      3. Skin diseases (13:1–14:57)
      4. Genital discharges (15:1–33)
   D. Day of Atonement (16:1–34)
II. Holiness Code (17:1–26:46)
   A. Teaching on blood (17:1–16)
   B. Sexual relations (18:1–30)
   C. Miscellaneous holiness laws (19:1–22:33)
   D. Festivals (23:1–44)
   E. Ritual objects and blasphemy (24:1–23)
   F. Sabbath and jubilee years (25:1–55)
   G. Blessings and curses (26:1–46)
III. Appendix on religious vows (27:1–34)

served to place material objects and human behaviors within categories. Jenson relates the categories to a priestly worldview of the natural created order; items that align with the prototype of living things as created good by God are clean, and those that are deviations from the natural prototypes are unclean. Diseases and deformities are likewise deviations from normal and, so, render a creature unclean.

The Holiness Code of Lev. 17–26 existed as a separate document before it was included in the Priestly Code. It specifies how God's people could maintain a state of ritual purity. Its foundational rule is, "You shall be holy, for I the LORD your God am holy" (19:2). The notion of holiness is founded on distinction, uniqueness, and separation. The holy is "otherness"; a holy thing is separate from and should have no contact with ordinary and unholy things.

The Holiness Code established a calendar that ordered the life of Israel (chap. 23). It defined the week, which culminated in the sabbath day of rest, and the yearly festivals of Passover (*pesakh*) and Unleavened Bread, First Fruits, Weeks (*shebu'ot*), Trumpets (*teru'ah*), Tabernacles (*sukkot*), and the Day of Atonement (*yom kippur*). Most of these were associated originally with agricultural seasons and later served to memorialize important moments of Israel's history, e.g., Passover with the exodus from Egypt, and Tabernacles with the wilderness sojourn.

Aaron was a brother to Moses, and they were descendants of Levi. Leviticus uses narrative to indicate that the family of Aaron had been divinely designated to supply priests to the community and which of his sons would inherit the rights of office (chaps. 8–10). Moses performs the ordination ritual on Aaron and his sons. But when two of them, Nadab and Abihu, offer "unholy fire" before the Lord, fire from heaven comes down and kills them. Ultimately, another of Aaron's sons, Eleazar, and his son Phinehas became the line of priests (see Num. 25). Non-Aaronic families from the tribe of Levi were later given other responsibilities connected to the tabernacle and later the temple.

Influences: The dietary laws laid out in the book of Leviticus became the foundation of the Jewish system of *kashrut*, which defines which foods Jews may and may not eat. The practice of offering sacrifices to God in order to make amends for wrongdoing is a foundational concept in Judaism as well as in Christianity, where it is the conceptual basis of the crucifixion of Jesus of Nazareth. Carmichael says that the rules laid out in Leviticus were inspired by incidents in the biblical narratives of Genesis–Kings and should be seen to have their origin there. *See also* law; Pentateuch, sources of the.

Bibliography

Bandstra, Barry L. *Reading the Old Testament: Introduction to the Hebrew Bible.* 4th ed. Wadsworth, 2009.

Carmichael, Calum M. *Illuminating Leviticus: A Study of Its Laws and Institutions in the Light of Biblical Narratives.* Johns Hopkins University Press, 2006.

Douglas, Mary. *Leviticus as Literature.* Oxford University Press, 1999.

Jenson, Philip P. *Graded Holiness: A Key to the Priestly Conception of the World.* JSOT, 1992.

Levine, Baruch A. *Leviticus (Va-yikra): The Traditional Hebrew Text with the New JPS Translation.* Jewish Publication Society, 1989.

Milgrom, Jacob. *Leviticus.* 3 vols. Doubleday, 1991–2001.

Watts, James W. *Ritual and Rhetoric in Leviticus: From Sacrifice to Scripture.* Cambridge University Press, 2007.   B.B.

liberation. God's liberation of the people of Israel from Egyptian slavery is a central feature of the Bible; likewise, during the exile, the language of political liberation became normative for describing God's saving purposes for Israel, especially in Isaiah (e.g., 61:1). Liberation from slavery also shaped the social consciousness of the people through laws insisting that Israel translate its own experience into a concern for the poor, the oppressed, the weak, and the enslaved (Deut. 15:12–18). This concern was formalized in the concept of the sabbatical year (Exod. 21:2–6) and later in the jubilee year (Ezek. 46:17). Though perhaps only a theoretical ideal, liberty was to be proclaimed throughout the land every fiftieth year (Lev. 25:10), and enslaved people and foreclosed property emancipated from masters and creditors. The concept of liberty becomes more individualized in the psalms of lament, where God is called on to liberate the psalmist from the tyranny of oppression (Ps. 69) or sin (Ps. 51). A sense of religious or spiritual liberation is also seen in Ps. 119:45, where liberty is obtained through seeking to obey God's precepts, and in Isa. 42:6–7, where Israel is commissioned to liberate those whose imprisonment consists of ignorance of the one true God.

In the NT, John's Gospel often describes salvation in terms of freedom (8:32), but it is in the Pauline Letters that liberation becomes a central theological motif. For Paul, the human predicament is defined by slavery to sin (Rom. 6:20) and consequently by slavery to the law (7:6) and to decay (8:21). Human nature is so corrupt that when the law is embraced as a means of escaping from sin and achieving salvation, the effort is doomed to fail (7:7–20). But through the atoning death of Christ on the cross, sin is remitted and liberation from sin and death is obtained.

This new liberty, however, is not merely freedom *from* past masters; it is also freedom *for* new obedience to God. Thus Paul can say, paradoxically, "Those who have been set free from sin have become slaves of righteousness . . . enslaved to God" (Rom. 6:18–22). This new bondage, however, has as its consequence life, not death. Elsewhere Paul uses a different metaphor, suggesting that the gift of the Holy Spirit indicates that the believer is no longer a slave, but fully a child of God, and the law can be fulfilled out of responsive love instead of enslaving necessity (Gal. 4:1–7). Thus the Spirit becomes a sign of liberty (2 Cor. 3:17).   J.M.B.

Libnah (lib'nuh; Heb., "white").

1 One of the Israelite camps in the wilderness after the Israelites left Egypt (Num. 33:20–21). Its location is unknown.

2 A city of Judah that Joshua took during his southern campaign when he besieged Lachish, Eglon, Hebron, and Debir (Josh. 10:29–39; 12:15). It was named as one of the levitical cities (Josh. 21:13; 1 Chron. 6:57). Hamutal, one of Josiah's wives and the mother of Jehoahaz (2 Kings 23:31) and Zedekiah (2 Kings 24:18; Jer. 52:1), was the daughter of Jeremiah of Libnah. The city has been identified with the northwestern Judean site Tell es-Safi, and with modern Tell Bornat. Its position near the western border may have made possible a revolt against King Jehoram while he was dealing with the rebellious Edomites to the east (2 Kings 8:22; 2 Chron. 21:10). Tell Bornat lies about five miles north of the most important city in the area, Lachish, and the Assyrian king Sennacherib turned to Libnah after the siege of Lachish in 701 BCE (2 Kings 19:8; Isa. 37:8).   N.L.L.

Libni (lib′ni; Heb., "white").

1 The son of Gershon (Gershom) and the grandson of Levi (Exod. 6:17; 1 Chron. 6:20); he was the ancestral head of a major subdivision of the Gershonite group of Levites, the Libnites (Num. 3:21; 26:58). He is also called Ladan (1 Chron. 23:7–9). *See also* Ladan.

2 A Levite, the son of Mahli and the grandson of Merari (1 Chron. 6:29).

Libya (lib′ee-uh), an area on the north African coast of the Mediterranean Sea just west of Egypt. Its people participated in the invasion of Judah led by Pharaoh Shishak of Egypt against Rehoboam (2 Chron. 2:12). Similar forces were later defeated by Asa of Judah (16:8). Daniel saw Libyans serving the "king of the north" together with Egyptians and Ethiopians (11:43), and Nahum recalled their alliance with Egypt against Assyria's invasion (3:9). Frequently associated with Put, Lud, Ethiopia, and Egypt, Libyans figured directly in the defense against the Sea Peoples mounted by Egypt and were at times a dominant influence in Egyptian politics. Ezekiel expected its destruction together with Egypt and its neighbors (30:5). Its language was heard at Pentecost (Acts 2:10). *See also* Lubim; Sea Peoples.   R.S.B.

life. Most references to life in the Hebrew Bible refer to life on this earth. God is the living God (Jer. 10:10), who alone creates human existence on earth and brings life and death to individuals (Gen. 2:7; 1 Sam. 2:6). Life is God's basic blessing (Deut. 30:19). The word "life" frequently refers to one's life span (Deut. 4:9; Jer. 52:33) and is often contrasted with death (Gen. 47:19). Death is understood as the end of life, and life after death is mentioned only rarely in the Hebrew Bible (e.g., Dan. 12:2). Sometimes life means, not only survival, but health and well-being (Prov. 3:13–18). In Deuteronomy and wisdom literature, life is associated with keeping the commandments of God (Deut. 30:15–20; Prov. 4:4).

In the NT, life often means life after death, eternal life. In the Synoptic Gospels, eternal life is associated with following Jesus (Mark 10:28–31) and with living a moral life and helping those in need (Matt. 19:16–19; 25:31–46). Receiving eternal life is not easy and may cost a great deal (Matt. 7:14; Mark 9:42–48). The term "life" occurs with particular frequency in the Gospel of John. God has granted Jesus to have life in himself (5:26) and to bring life to humanity (6:33, 51; 10:10). Jesus is "the bread of life," "the light of life," "the resurrection and the life," "the way, and the truth, and the life" (6:48; 8:12; 11:25; 14:6). The one believing in Jesus receives eternal life in both the present (5:24) and the future (6:40). Indeed, John's Gospel says that it has been written so that readers may come to believe that Jesus is the Messiah, the Son of God, and, through believing, have life in his name (20:31). The first of the Johannine Letters indicates simply that "whoever

has the Son has life; whoever does not have the Son does not have life" (5:12). For Paul too eternal life comes through Christ; baptism into Christ's death and resurrection enables the Christian to walk in newness of life (Rom. 6:4). In Gal. 2:20 Paul says, "I have been crucified with Christ; it is no longer I who live, but Christ who lives in me." *See also* death; eternal life; immortality; resurrection.

J.D.

Life, Book of, a roster of names kept in heaven. It is a list of those who will survive the manifestation of God's wrath (Mal. 3:16–4:3). According to the book of Revelation (21:27), only those whose names are in the Book of Life will enter the new Jerusalem.

life, eternal. *See* eternal life.

light. Light is the first thing created by God in the book of Genesis; before God said "Let there be light" there was only darkness (1:1–3). The sun, the moon, and the stars are specifically mentioned as the lights of the firmament and as sources of light for all who dwell on earth (1:14–18). In the Bible, the word "light" often refers to the light generated from these spheres (usually the sun, as in references to "daylight" or dawn), but it is also used to refer to the light that comes from a fire or a lamp (Exod. 25:37; Num. 4:16; Neh. 9:12, 19). Also, in the Bible, light is frequently a symbol for God, godliness, or illumination. God is described as "wrapped in light as with a garment" (Ps. 104:2). God's countenance is light (Ps. 4:6). At the end of Revelation, the Lord God is said to be the light of the heavenly city (22:5). Inasmuch as walking is used as a metaphor for life (Pss. 1:1; 15:2; 23:3–4; Prov. 4:11–14), God is fittingly implored to provide light (Ps. 43:3). God says, "I will turn the darkness before them into light" (Isa. 42:16). It follows that the law of God is described by a psalmist as "a lamp to my feet and a light to my path" (Ps. 119:105). The longed-for "day of the Lord" is expected to be light (Zech. 14:7); thus, the prophet Amos can astound his hearers by announcing it will be darkness instead (5:18, 20).

The NT use of "light" is also both literal (Matt. 17:2) and symbolic (4:16, quoting Isa. 9:2). In view of the Christian gospel, however, the imagery of light in the NT tends to center on Jesus. Paul speaks of "the light of the gospel of the glory of Christ" with reference to the language of the Genesis creation narrative (2 Cor. 4:4–6). Jesus Christ is called the light of the world (John 8:12; cf. 1:4–5, 9), for he is the emissary of God, who is light (1 John 1:5) and who calls people "out of darkness into his marvelous light" (1 Pet. 2:9). Thus, the disciples of Jesus may also be identified as "the light of the world" (Matt. 5:14). In some NT writings, the image of light is used in a way that tends toward dualism, a perspective that treats the realms of "light" and "darkness" as starkly drawn categories and sees everyone and everything as belonging to one or the other (John 1:5; 3:19; 8:12; 12:35, 46; 1 John 1:5–7). A more extreme version of this perspective is evident in many of the writings from Qumran (the Dead Sea Scrolls), where the children of light are portrayed as locked in conflict with the children of darkness.   D.M.S.

lightning. The frightening and potentially destructive phenomenon of lightning is associated solely with God in the Hebrew Bible. It is routinely associated with theophanies (appearances of God), e.g., at Mount Sinai (Exod. 19:16; 20:18) and in Ezekiel's inaugural vision (1:13–14; cf. Dan. 10:6). Lightning is also a mark of God's wisdom as the creator and the giver of life (Pss. 77:18; 97:4; Jer. 10:13; 51:16; Job 28:26; 37:3; 38:25, 35). In poetic descriptions of God as the divine warrior, lightning is presented as one of the weapons God uses against both earthly foes (2 Sam. 22:15; cf. Neh. 2:4) and the powers of chaos itself (cf. Pss. 18:14; 77:18; 144:6; also Zech. 9:14 for a setting in the future).

In the NT, lightning is mainly referenced as a feature of the end times (see Matt. 24:27; Luke 17:24; esp. Rev. 4:5; 8:5; 11:19; 16:18), though the association with theophany is also present (Matt. 28:3). Only once is it used with reference to a power other than that of God. When the disciples joyously recount their discovery that they possessed power to exorcise demons in Jesus's name, Jesus cryptically remarks, "I watched Satan fall from heaven like a flash of lightning" (Luke 10:18; cf. Isa. 14:12–15; Rev. 12:7–9).   W.S.T.

Lights, Festival of. *See* Dedication, Festival of.

lily, a flower such as the hyacinth or tulip that grows from a bulb (true lily). Similar groups include the iris, crocus, and narcissus. The reference to "lilies of the field" in Matt. 6:28–30 and Luke 12:27–28 implies an impressive showing of blossoms and variety of colors and therefore may be identified as the common crown anemone, or windflower (*Anemone coronaria*). This poppylike flower, which is not a true lily, blooms brightly and profusely in the spring throughout the hilly country of Bible lands. The lilies mentioned in Song of Sol. 2:1–2; 5:13 are referred to as symbols of beauty. The "lily of the valleys" of 2:1–2 is probably the sweet-smelling blue hyacinth (*Hyacinth orientalis*) common in fields and rocky places. The lilies gathered in the gardens (6:2) may be true lilies such as the distinctive white Madonna lily (*Lilium candidum*) and the scarlet Martagon lily (*Lilium chalcedonicum*), both of which are native to the Near East. The lilies that form the decorative floral motif of Solomon's temple (1 Kings 7:19, 26) are probably water lilies or the lotus (*genus Nymphaea*). This flower is commonly represented in Egyptian architecture as well. *See also* flowers.   P.L.C.

limestone, sedimentary rock formed from large concentrations of marine shell life, hence composed largely of calcium carbonate or magnesium carbonate. It is the dominant rock in the central hills of Israel and in the heights of Transjordan. The Hebrews knew the treatment of heating it (Isa. 33:12). When treated with heat and water, the resulting slaked (hydrated) lime could be used for plaster, providing a smooth base for decoration. In its natural state, limestone was the primary construction material for stone walls, foundations, door sockets, lintels, and even decorative work such as stelae, friezes, bas-reliefs, and statuary. Only basalt was in sufficient supply in some sectors to rival limestone's popularity. Most of the frequent biblical references to stone are thus to limestone (e.g., 1 Kings 5:5; 6:36; 2 Kings 12:12; Amos 5:11; Matt. 24:2).   R.S.B.

linen, a fabric woven from yarn made of flax. Flax appears to have been the first vegetable fiber cultivated by early agriculturalists. Flax was also cultivated for its seeds, called linseeds, which contain oil and protein. Flax plants require a great amount of moisture and thus are best suited to areas with fertile clay, rich in silt, as in Egypt, where they grew abundantly. Elsewhere in dryer climates irrigation was necessary for cultivation.

Of exceptional interest and significance are the remains of linen cloth recovered at Bab edh-Dhra, for they are the earliest dated occurrence of flax fiber in the ancient Near Eastern region (ca. 3100 BCE), and they reflect a local industry and a commodity that could have been a trade item even at this early period. The cloth was of a simple weave, consisting of single warps and wefts, clear evidence of loom-weaving technology. Later biblical tradition documents the cultivation of flax and the production of linen cloth (Josh. 2:6; Judg.

Martagon lily.

15:14; Prov. 31:13; Isa. 15:9). Also, the tenth-century BCE Gezer Calendar mentions the "month of the harvest of flax." Lamp wicks were made of flax (Isa. 42:3; Matt. 12:20). The Dead Sea Scrolls were wrapped in linen.

Egyptian linen was considered to be the finest and most desirable; the words "fine linen" usually referred to Egyptian cloth. The fine linen of Egypt was produced by soaking or steeping the flax in water to loosen the fibers of the woody stem, a process called retting; compare Rahab's method of spreading flax on the roof to be moistened by the dew (Josh. 2:6), a method rendering rough, coarse fibers. Once cleaned, the stems were beaten and combed into strands, a process called hackling, then sent to the spinner. Fine linen was a symbol of purity, so it was particularly fitting for Egyptian, Greek, and Jewish priests. Thus, it is again fine Egyptian linen that is called for in instructions concerning the construction of the tabernacle and the proper priestly vestments. Items to be made of fine linen included: the tabernacle curtains (Exod. 26:1); the veil (26:31); the screen (26:36); the court hangings (27:9); and the priestly garments, which included the ephod (28:6), the girdle (28:8), the breastpiece of judgment (28:15), the coat and turban (28:39), and the breeches (28:42). Garments made of linen and wool ("two different materials") were prohibited (Lev. 19:19; Deut. 22:11; Ezek. 44:17–18).

The coolness, luster, and strength of linen made it a luxury item (Isa. 3:23), graphically illustrated by Samson's wager of thirty linen garments (Judg. 14:12–13). The long fiber of Egyptian flax lent itself to the weaver's art. Pharaoh dressed Joseph in garments of "fine linen" (Gen. 41:42); Ezekiel describes the sail of a ship of Tyre as made "of fine embroidered linen from Egypt" (27:7); Lazarus wore "fine linen" and royal purple in the afterlife (Luke 16:19); and a prostitute possessed "colored spreads of Egyptian linen" as bed coverings (Prov. 7:16). Extant pieces of linen from royal Egyptian burials also testify to its superior quality. There, linen was used to wrap mummies in bandages sometimes hundreds of yards long. The body of Jesus was likewise wrapped in a "linen shroud" (Matt. 27:59; Mark 15:46; Luke 23:53; cf. John 19:39).   S.R.

lintel, any solid beam, whether wood or stone, set horizontally over a doorway. Anchored on both ends, the lintel supports the construction above the doorway and prevents its collapse into the doorway's open space. Biblical usage prescribed that blood be placed on both doorposts and the lintel as part of the first Passover ritual (Exod. 12:7, 22–23). According to 1 Kings 6:31, the lintel and doorposts at the entrance to the inner sanctuary of Solomon's temple were five-sided; the Hebrew is a bit obscure, but this might mean that the lintel over the door was shaped like an inverted "V." Archaeological evidence of lintels of stone, sometimes elaborately decorated, is extensive, while the more easily degenerated wooden beams that were often used as lintels are found less frequently.
                                                                R.S.B.

Linus (li'nuhs), a person who sends greetings to Timothy in 2 Tim. 4:21. According to later church traditions, he was the son of the Claudia mentioned in that verse, and he later became bishop of Rome (Irenaeus *Against Heresies* 3.3.3; Eusebius *Ecclesiastical History* 3.2, 13).

lion. Lions are currently restricted to Africa, but an Asian subspecies, *Panthera leo persica,* once inhabited the Near East. The Asian lion is distinguishable from its African cousin by its scantier mane, thicker coat, and longer tail tassel. The lion's preference for river thickets is mentioned in Jer. 50:44. In antiquity lion hunting was a sport favored by nobility, as is mentioned in the Assyrian records and evidenced by a lion hunt relief at Ashurbanipal's palace in Nineveh. Lions

A monolith lintel from the synagogue at Horvat Shema', ca. 284–306 CE, bearing a menorah relief almost a meter wide, the largest such depiction from an ancient synagogue.

A dying lion, part of Assyrian ruler Ashurbanipal's "Lion Hunt" relief from his palace at Nineveh, seventh century BCE.

were also kept in captivity. The Egyptian pharaoh Rameses II is said to have owned a pet lion, and Ashurnasirpal II of Assyria even succeeded in breeding them at Nimrud.

The Bible mentions numerous encounters between humans and lions. The beasts are described as savage killers (1 Kings 13:24, 26). Still, Benaiah (2 Sam. 23:20), David (1 Sam. 17:34–36), and Samson (Judg. 14:6) managed to overcome their aggressors, and Daniel escaped unharmed (Dan. 6:16–24). Amos 3:12 describes how a shepherd rescued a lamb from the mouth of a lion. Some biblical proverbs deal with the lion. In Eccles. 9:4 "a living dog is better than a dead lion," and in Judg. 14:18 Samson is asked, "What is stronger than a lion?" Prov. 26:13 tells the story of the lazy man who does not want to go to work, because there "is a lion in the road! . . . a lion in the streets!" In the NT, the ferocity of the predatory lion makes it an apt simile for Satan (1 Pet. 5:8), and the fearsome nature of the apocalyptic beasts is due in large part to the resemblance of some of their characteristics to those of the lion: teeth (Rev. 9:8), head (9:17), mouth (13:2), and roar (10:3). A reference to Paul being rescued from the lion's mouth (2 Tim. 4:17) alludes to the use of such beasts being turned loose on prisoners in spectacles at the Roman Colosseum.   I.U.K./M.A.P.

lizard. Lev. 11:29–30 lists six types of lizards or reptiles as unclean animals: (1) the "great lizard"

(*tsab*), probably to be identified with the Negev dabb lizard (*Uromastyx*); (2) the "gecko" (*'anaqah*, from a word meaning "groaning" or "crying"), a wide variety of which are found in the area; (3) the "land crocodile" (*koakh*), probably the large carnivorous desert monitor or varan; (4) the "lizard" (*leta'ah*), possibly all of the numerous lacertids (sometimes called "European lizards"); (5) the "sand lizard" (*khomet*), perhaps the burrowing skink; and, (6) the "chameleon" (*tinshemet*), which might refer to what is popularly called a chameleon (as they are quite common throughout the Near East), though the same word is used elsewhere to refer to various kinds of birds (Lev. 11:18; Deut. 14:6). None of these lizards is mentioned anywhere else in the Bible, and nothing more is ever said of them, except that they are unclean. In Prov. 30:28, another type of lizard might be mentioned, though the word used there (*semamit*) is also used in some literature for a poisonous spider. The context here ("the lizard can be grasped in the hand") suggests that some sort of generic lizard is intended.

loan, loans. Biblical legislation concerning lending must be understood against the background of a noncommercial agricultural society with strong tribal roots. The primary motivation of borrowers was to obtain relief from need rather than to further their economic enterprises. Furthermore, the poor and needy were deemed neighbors of all

Israelites (Deut. 15:11). Hence, biblical law considers lending to be a philanthropic act and thus severely restricts the rights of the lender. Jesus ordered his followers, "Do not refuse anyone who wants to borrow from you" (Matt. 5:42).

Interest: According to the Mesopotamian law codes and private contracts to which biblical law may be compared, Mesopotamian creditors commonly charged an annual interest rate of 20 percent for loans of silver and 33⅓ percent for loans of grain. Biblical law, however, prohibits creditors from charging interest to their needy fellow Israelites (Exod. 22:25; Lev. 25:35–37; Deut. 23:20), although it does allow the taking of interest from non-Israelites (Deut. 23:21). The nonlegal biblical references depicting the difficult plight of debtors in ancient Israel (e.g., 1 Sam. 22:2; Jer. 15:10) would seem to attest to the violation of this prohibition. Ezekiel brands creditors who take interest as wicked, while praising those who refrain as pious (18:8, 13, 17; 22:12; cf. Ps. 15:5). Wisdom literature further cautions that wealth augmented by interest is fleeting (Prov. 28:8). In the NT, Jesus cautions his followers against storing up treasure on earth (Matt. 6:19), but indicates in his parable of the Talents that it was possible (if not common) in his day for people to invest money with bankers for the sake of receiving interest (Matt. 25:27; Luke 19:23). "Interest" is the translation given in the NRSV for two biblical Hebrew terms, *neshek* (derived from the verb "to bite") and *tarbit* (lit., "increase"). Some scholars view the terms as a fixed pair denoting a single concept. Others attempt to distinguish them as referring to two different types of interest: advanced interest, which is "bitten" off the principal at the onset of the loan, and accrued interest, resulting in an "increase" at the time of repaying the loan.

Pledges and Surety: Ancient Near Eastern law acknowledges the right of lenders to take a pledge, according to which chattel, real estate, or persons were surrendered as security for a loan. A pledge was a bailment of property to be in the physical possession of the pledgee, who did not thereby have legal title to that property. The law, however, also places restrictions upon creditors: they may not enter the debtor's home to seize a pledge, but must wait outside (Deut. 24:10–11); they may not seize what is needed for one's daily living (24:6; cf. Job 24:3); they may not seize the garment of a widow (Deut. 24:17); and the pledged garment of the poor must be returned by nightfall (24:12–13; Exod. 22:25–26; cf. Amos 2:8). The nonlegal literature of the Bible attests to the seizing of members of the defaulting debtor's family and to the taking of real estate to secure and satisfy a loan (2 Kings 4:1; Isa. 50:1; Neh. 5:3–5; cf. Matt. 18:25, which does not necessarily describe Jewish practice).

Laws governing surety (whereby a person assumes liability for the obligation of the borrower) do not occur in the corpus of biblical law. References to surety, however, are found in the nonlegal literature of the Bible, especially in wisdom litera-ture. The book of Proverbs is replete with advice against standing surety for another (6:1; 11:15; 17:18; 22:26–27; 27:13). The references reveal that the assumption of surety was accompanied by the symbolic gesture of "giving one's hand," perhaps as a type of handshake (6:1; 17:18; Job 17:3). Judah's assumption of surety for Benjamin (Gen. 44:32) seems to indicate that at times a surety would only ensure the physical presence of the debtor for personal prosecution by the creditor, while Prov. 22:26–27 clearly indicates that one who stands surety for another could became a co-debtor. The concept of surety is used also metaphorically in prayer (Isa. 38:14; Ps. 119:122; Job 17:3; cf. Heb. 7:22).

Remission of Debt: Mesopotamian kings are known to have issued edicts designed to restore some measure of equilibrium in the economic life of the society. These edicts entailed cancellation of certain types of debts, release from certain kinds of tenant obligations, and freedom from debt servitude. Biblical law also instituted a cyclical cancellation of debts by decreeing the remission of all outstanding loans in the sabbatical (i.e., seventh) year (Deut. 15:1–11). *See also* debt; law; ownership.   B.L.E.

loaves. *See* baker; bread; miracles.

locks.

1 Devices on doors (Song of Sol. 5:5; Neh. 3:3, 13–15; see also Judg. 3:23–24).

2 Strands of hair, mentioned with regard to Nazirites (Num. 6:5), Samson (Judg. 16:13, 19), and levitical priests (Ezek. 44:20), all of whom were not to have their hair cut (see also Ezek. 8:3; Song of Sol. 5:2, 11).

locust, a small insect resembling a cricket that seasonally migrates in great swarms, causing damage to all vegetation in its path. This insect is therefore a serious pest, especially to crops (Joel 1:4; 2:25). The migrating swarms of locusts were one of the plagues imposed by God on the people of Egypt when Pharaoh refused to release the Israelites from slavery (Exod. 10:12–20). Locusts are edible and are deemed acceptable for the Israelites to eat (Lev. 11:22); they would provide a cheap, though time-costly, form of protein that might be exploited during a swarming event. In the NT, John the Baptist is said to have eaten locusts in the wilderness (Matt. 3:4; Mark 1:6). Some interpreters have suggested that the term "locust" here may also refer to a carob, an edible beanlike pod produced by the carob tree (*Ceratonia siliqua*), which is common in the Near East. It is not impossible that this carob (popularly called a locust) was John's diet, though, without any signal that this is what was meant, readers would probably be expected to assume the locusts he ate were insects.   P.L.C.

Lod. *See* Lydda.

Lo-debar (loh-dee´buhr), a city in Gilead, east of the Jordan, where Jonathan's son Mephibosheth lived after his father's death (2 Sam. 9:4–5). Machir of Lo-debar gave aid to David during his flight from Absalom (17:27). Amos speaks a word against arrogant residents of Lo-debar in (6:13).

log.
1 The smallest Hebrew measure of capacity, about two-thirds of a pint. *See also* weights and measures.
2 A piece of wood, usually the trunk portion of a tree (cf. Matt. 7:3). *See also* beam.

logos (loh´gohs), the Greek term usually translated "word" when it occurs in the NT (especially in reference to the "word of God"). *Logos* has a wide range of meaning, e.g., reckoning or accounting, explanation or reason, statement or discourse. In English, it frequently appears in the names of scientific or other disciplines, e.g., bio*logy*, psycho*logy*, the*ology*.
Originally employed as a technical philosophical term by the Greek philosopher Heraclitus (sixth century BCE), *logos* became a particularly important concept for the Stoics (third century BCE and later). In Stoicism, *logos* was the principle and pattern that gave the world or cosmos its character and coherence. The term was taken over by Philo, the Alexandrian philosophical theologian of Judaism, who was roughly a contemporary of the apostle Paul. By means of the *logos,* Philo sought to reconcile Greek philosophical theories about the universe (cosmology) with the biblical accounts of God's creating the world by the divine spoken word. God's *logos* became a clearly identifiable entity, mediating between God and the world, the mode of the divine creativity and revelation. Already before Philo, *logos* had been used in the LXX to render the Hebrew term *dabar* (usually translated into English as "word")—a term frequently used for the speech (word) of God. At the same time, in writings of the Second Temple period, including some of the apocryphal/deuterocanonical books, "wisdom" (Gk. *sophia*) was beginning to play a mediatorial role between God and creation not unlike that which *logos* would later have for Philo (cf. Prov. 8:22–31; Wis. 9:1–?).
In the NT, Jesus is described as preaching the word (*logos,* Mark 2:2) or word of God (*logos theou,* Luke 5:1). The gospel message about Jesus can also be described as the word or word of God (Acts 4:31; 8:4; 1 Cor. 14:36). In Jesus's parable of the Sower, the seed that is sown is identified with the "word" (Mark 4:14), the "word of the kingdom" (Matt. 13:19), or the "word of God" (Luke 8:11). In the Johannine literature, Jesus himself is called *logos,* "the Word": "In the beginning was the Word (*logos*) and the Word was with God and the Word was God" (John 1:1). In language that recalls both the Greek concept of *sophia* and Philo's concept of *logos,* John insists that this Logos was in the beginning with God and that all things came into being

through the Logos (1:2–3). Then John says, "the Word became flesh and lived among us" (1:14). Elsewhere Jesus is referred to as the "word of life" (1 John 1:1) and "Word of God" (*logos* of God; Rev. 19:13).
The role in creation assigned to the *logos* is particularly significant, especially since that Logos is then said to have become incarnate in Jesus (John 1:14). It is not immediately obvious why a man sent from God, even the Messiah of Israel, should have played a preexistent role in creation itself. Yet Jesus Christ figures as the mediator of creation, not only in John, but also in such NT books as 1 Corinthians (8:6), Colossians (1:15–17), and Hebrews (1:2), although the term *logos* is not used with reference to him in those instances. In 1 Cor. 1:24, Paul calls Christ the "wisdom of God," using the Greek term *sophia,* which has close connections with *logos.* The basic doctrinal idea of the *logos* as God's creating and revealing mediator is intelligible in light of Philo and the role played by "wisdom" in ancient Jewish wisdom literature. Yet an unprecedented step is taken by NT writers, especially the fourth evangelist, when it is claimed that the one who played this role can be identified with a specific historical figure, Jesus of Nazareth.
D.M.S.

loincloth, a minimal item of clothing, perhaps an undergarment, probably formed by wrapping material around the lower trunk. In the Eden story, the couple fashions such garments from fig leaves as the first human apparel (Gen. 3:7). Elsewhere the term (*'ezor*) denotes a sash wrapped over the tunic or outer garment, sometimes serving a decorative as well as a functional purpose (Jer. 13:1–11; cf. Isa. 5:27).

Lois (loh´is). Timothy's maternal grandmother, a Jewish-Christian woman of faith (2 Tim. 1:5). Her daughter, Eunice (Timothy's mother), was also a person of faith, though Timothy's father was a Gentile and, apparently, not a believer in Christ (Acts 16:3). *See also* Eunice; Timothy.

loom. *See* spinning and weaving.

lord (Heb. *'adon;* Gk. *kyrios*), a title of dignity and honor acknowledging the power and authority of the one so addressed.
1 When used to address an individual and not as a title for God or Christ, a term conveying esteem for a male ruler on behalf of his subjects (e.g., Num. 32:25; cf. Acts 25:26), or for a master on behalf of a slave (so the brothers to Joseph, Gen. 44:6–17; see also Jesus's parable of the Wicked Servant, Matt. 18:23–35). It can refer to secular heads of tribes or nations (e.g., the "five lords of the Philistines," Judg. 3:3; 1 Sam. 5:8; Isa. 16:8) or even to an entire class of nobles (Dan. 1:10). In Dan. 5:1, Belshazzar gives a feast for a thousand of his lords or courtiers. That lordship can be demonstrated even against the corrupt elite of Judah (cf. Jer. 22:8; 25:35; 34:5). As a verb ("to lord over")

the term is used occasionally to describe high-handed behavior (Neh. 5:15; Eccles. 8:9), the very antithesis of what Jesus demands of his followers (Luke 22:24–27; cf. 2 Cor. 1:24). W.S.T.

2 A title for God. In the Hebrew Bible, the formulation "my lord" (Heb. *'adonay*) occurs only in reference to God and essentially becomes a name for God. In the LXX, the Greek word for "lord," *kyrios,* was used to translate both *'adonay* and YHWH (i.e., the Tetragrammaton or four consonants that stood for the unpronounceable name of God). In the NT, *kyrios* becomes a standard title for Jesus, though the word is often used in its secular sense as well. In Phil. 2:9–11, Paul maintains that Jesus has been exalted by God, so that at the name of Jesus every knee will bow and every tongue confess that Jesus Christ is Lord. In Rom. 10:9, he says that those who confess with their lips that Jesus is Lord and believe in their heart that God raised him from the dead will be saved. He is acclaimed "King of kings and Lord of lords" (1 Tim. 6:15; Rev. 19:16; cf. Deut. 10:17; Ps. 136:3; Dan. 2:47). The application of this title to Jesus seems to be made within two different but compatible contexts. On the one hand, the application to Jesus of a designation for the God of Israel carried an essential claim to divinity (cf. John 20:28). On the other, the title "Lord" (*kyrios*) was also used in the Roman Empire for the emperor (Acts 25:26, here with the possessive pronoun, "my Lord"); thus the assertion that "Jesus is Lord" would carry an inevitable polemical connotation that "Caesar is not" (cf. Luke 2:11, where the acclamation of Jesus being "Lord" at his birth echoes similar declarations made about Augustus).

As indicated by some of the texts cited above, Paul is the one NT author to develop the theme of Christ's lordship most intentionally. For example, Paul uses the title "Lord" when he appeals to the teaching of the earthly Jesus (1 Cor. 7:10; 9:14; 11:21); thus, the authority of Jesus is projected into the present life of the believing community. Likewise, those who have been justified through faith in Christ have been brought under the authority of the Lord Jesus and are now committed to obedience to him (Rom. 14:8; cf. 6:3–11; 7:4–6). For Paul, to be "in the Lord" is much the same as to be "in Christ," though the emphasis in the formula "in Christ" is primarily soteriological (having to do with salvation), whereas the emphasis of being "in the Lord" is primarily ethical (having to do with obedience). Thus, Christians are to marry "in the Lord" (1 Cor. 7:39), meaning that they are to marry someone whom the Lord Jesus would direct them to marry (a believer in Christ, at the very least). The expression "in the Lord" is also used in contexts concerned with ministerial activity; the phrase occurs repeatedly in Rom. 16, where Paul is greeting those who shared his apostolic labors (Rom. 16:2). Finally, Paul uses "Lord" in contexts that speak of Christ's second coming. Those who are still alive at that time will be caught up in the air to meet "the Lord" (1 Thess. 4:17). That will happen "on the day of the Lord," an ex-pression familiar from the LXX (e.g., Ezek. 30:3; Joel 2:1), but now used with specific reference to the Lord Jesus Christ (1 Thess. 5:12).

Bibliography

Fitzmyer, J. A. "New Testament *Kyrios* and *Maranatha* and Their Aramaic Background." *To Advance the Gospel.* Crossroad, 1981. Pp. 218–35.

Fuller, R., and P. Perkins. *Who Is This Christ? Gospel Christology and Contemporary Faith.* Fortress, 1983. Pp. 41–52.

Kramer, W. *Christ, Lord, Son of God.* SCM, 1966.
R.H.F./M.A.P.

Lord of hosts ("LORD of hosts"), a term describing God in command of all the forces that operate throughout creation (e.g., Ps. 89:6–8). It is an ancient title for God, who, in the role of divine warrior, was the leader of either the armies of Israel, the celestial armies of supernatural warriors, or both. In the NT, the term occurs in Rom. 9:29 and James 5:4. *See also* names of God in the Hebrew Bible. M.A.F.

Lord of Sabaoth (sab'ay-oth). *See* names of God in the Hebrew Bible.

Lord's day, the day of Jesus's resurrection, the first day of the week, Sunday. The term appears in the NT only in Rev. 1:10. A similar phrase appears in the *Didache,* a work written toward the end of the first century, probably in Syria. The readers of this work are instructed to gather on the Lord's day to break bread and to give thanks (14:1). A similar practice seems to be presupposed in Acts 20:7, where the Christians gather "to break bread" on the first day of the week. Likewise, when Paul instructs the Corinthians to contribute to the collection for the saints in Judea on the first day of every week, he presupposes a gathering of the community on that day (1 Cor. 16:2). Each of the Gospels emphasizes the tradition that Jesus was raised on the first day of the week, and Luke's Gospel relates a story in which the first day of the week, Jesus's resurrection, the teaching and interpretation of scripture, and the breaking of bread are all associated (24:13–35). Thus, it seems that fairly early in the Christian movement, people who believed in Jesus Christ began to regard the first day of the week (Sunday) as a special day that would ultimately by called the "Lord's day." It seems likely that the earliest believers in Christ, from the Jewish community, would have observed both the traditional sabbath (the seventh day of the week, Saturday) and the Lord's day (cf. Acts 13:14; 16:13). Paul, however, may have objected to Gentile Christians being required to adopt sabbath observance (Gal. 4:10). Indeed, the Letter to the Colossians instructs its readers that sabbath observance is not required (2:16). At any rate, the latter half of the first century saw a transition for followers of Jesus Christ from sabbath observance on Saturday to observance of the Lord's day on Sunday. Ignatius, bishop of Antioch, explicitly says in the early part of the second century that the Lord's day should be observed in place of the sabbath (*Ign. Magn.* 9:1). *See also* sabbath.

Bibliography

Carson, D. A., ed. *From Sabbath to Lord's Day.* Eerdmans, 1982.   A.Y.C.

Lord's Prayer, a prayer given by Jesus to his followers. It is found in different versions in Matt. 6:9–13 and Luke 11:2–4. The version in Matthew is longer, consisting of an address and seven petitions. In Luke, it consists of an address and only five petitions.

In Matthew, the Lord's Prayer is embedded in the Sermon on the Mount (5:1–7:29), where Jesus instructs his followers (5:3–16) in doing the "greater" righteousness (5:20). Jesus maintains that acts of piety, including prayer, are to be performed out of sincere worship for God rather than for mere show (6:1–18). As an example of how his disciples should pray (6:9a), Jesus teaches the Lord's Prayer, which is devoid of the "empty phrases" and "many words" that characterize the prayers of Gentiles (6:7). Thus, the Lord's Prayer is presented as a model that the disciples are to approximate in formulating their prayers.

In Luke, Jesus is on his way to Jerusalem in the company of his disciples (9:51; 13:22). Having observed Jesus at prayer, one of his disciples asks him to teach them to pray, just as John the Baptist taught his disciples (11:1). In response, Jesus teaches them the Lord's Prayer (11:2–4). Here too it is a model prayer, but probably one intended to be memorized and used habitually by the disciples (11:2a).

In its original form, the Lord's Prayer probably came from the earthly Jesus. One indication of this is that the two versions are quite similar, probably deriving from the Q source, which is generally held to contain the most primitive elements of the Jesus tradition. Another is the thoroughly Jewish character of the prayer (i.e., if it had been composed within the early church and retrojected onto the lips of Jesus, one would expect more distinctively Christian ideas or language). Furthermore, the Greek versions of the prayer found in the NT convey language commonly used for translating Aramaic, the language Jesus and his disciples spoke. For example, the Greek word "Father" as applied to God would translate Aramaic *abba,* which Jesus is known to have used (cf. Mark 14:36). The Greek words for both "debts" (in Matthew) and "sins" (in Luke) would be suitable translations of the single Aramaic word *choba;* thus, that one difference in the two versions of the prayer could stem from the Gospel authors translating the Aramaic original in slightly different ways.

In either version, the Lord's Prayer divides into three parts: the address, the "you" petitions, and the "us" petitions. In the address, Jesus instructs his disciples to call upon God as "Father." In the Hebrew Bible as well as in Hellenistic Jewish literature from the Second Temple period, God is described variously as Father of the covenant people Israel (Deut. 32:6), of the Davidic king (2 Sam. 7:14; Ps. 89:26), and of righteous Israelites (Ps. 103:13; Sir. 51:10; *Jub.* 1:24). As Father, God is the one who will act in the future to deliver those who are God's children (Isa. 63:16; Mal. 3:17). The identification of God as Father, however, becomes far more prominent in the Gospels than in any other previous literature. In Matthew's Gospel it occurs ten times in 6:1–18 alone (with only one of those being the occurrence here in the Lord's Prayer; see also 5:16, 45, 48; 6:26, 32; 7:11, 21; 10:32, 33; 12:50; 15:31; 16:17; 18:10, 14, 19, 35; 20:23; 25:34, 41; 26:29, 42, 53; 28:19). For Jesus and for the Gospel writers, this image seemed to present God as both a caring parent and an authority figure, as the one whose unilateral decisions are to be respected by the whole family of believers (cf. Matt. 23:9). Thus, by encouraging his followers to call God "Father," Jesus urges them both to respect God's authority and to trust in God's generosity and providential wisdom. In a broader sense, Jesus's address of God as Father is sometimes thought to give expression to awareness of his unique filial relationship to God (i.e., as the unique Son of God, Mark 14:36). Jesus is presented in the Gospels as the Son through whom the Father is revealed (Matt. 11:27; Luke 10:22). This sense, however, does not seem to be operative (or at least

THE LORD'S PRAYER IN MATTHEW AND LUKE

Boldface indicates parallels

Matthew 6:9–13	Luke 11:2–4
Our **Father** in heaven,	**Father,**
hallowed be your name.	**hallowed be your name.**
Your kingdom come.	**Your kingdom come.**
Your will be done, on earth as it is in heaven.	
Give us this **day our daily bread.**	**Give us** each **day our daily bread.**
And forgive us our debts, as we also have forgiven our debtors.	**And forgive us our** sins, for we ourselves forgive everyone indebted to us.
And do not bring us to the time of trial, but rescue us from the evil one.	**And do not bring us to the time of trial.**

not emphatically so) in this passage. The point of the prayer is that the *disciples* are to regard God as Father, and their relationship to God is distinct (in the mind of the Gospel authors) from that of Jesus. The point, perhaps, is that through Jesus, who is uniquely the Son of God, the disciples are given to know God as Father as well. The words, "in heaven," found only in Matthew, characterize God as the heavenly Father of the disciples in contradistinction to their earthly fathers.

The "you" petitions of the Lord's Prayer focus on God and implore God to act so that God's purposes might be achieved in the world. The prayers for God's name to be hallowed, for God's kingdom to come, and for God's will to be done are parallel petitions that state the same basic request three times in slightly different words. For either Matthew or Luke, the essential request would be understood as a plea for God to bring to fulfillment what has begun with Jesus. The kingdom has already drawn near (Matt. 4:17; Luke 4:43; cf. Luke 4:18–21); Jesus and his followers are bringing God's will to accomplishment, and God's name is being glorified on account of them (Matt. 5:16; Luke 7:16). Jesus's followers are to pray for the work of Christ to continue. The longer phrase in Matthew's version ("on earth as in heaven") makes explicit what is no doubt implied in the Lukan version as well: God is asked to reign on earth with as much freedom from opposition as is presently the case in the heavenly abode.

The "us" petitions focus on the physical and spiritual needs of the disciples. They offer simple requests of God, ones that Jesus deems appropriate for people to make at any time. The request for "daily bread" flows from an assumption that all followers of Jesus will embrace a simple lifestyle. Bread serves as a metaphor for life's necessities; Jesus's followers are to ask that God provide them with what they need, no more, but also no less. The Greek word that is rendered "daily" (*epiousion*) in this verse is completely obscure and there is no certainty with regard to how it should be translated; "daily" is simply a guess. Other interpreters have suggested "tomorrow," so that the petition would read, "Give us today our bread for tomorrow."

The request for forgiveness of debts or sins is traditional in Judaism. Jesus attaches to it a reminder that those who seek such forgiveness ought also to forgive others. To emphasize this point, Matthew quotes another saying of Jesus on this subject at the conclusion of the Lord's Prayer (6:14–15) and, elsewhere, records a parable Jesus told to illustrate the lesson (18:23–35). It is sometimes noted that, of all the moral precepts Jesus offers in the Sermon on the Mount (or, for Luke, on the "journey to Jerusalem," a central teaching section of that Gospel), the need to forgive others is the only facet of his teaching deemed so important that his followers are to remind themselves of it every time they pray.

The next petition, "Do not bring us to the time of trial," has often been misunderstood in Christian tradition due to the translation made popular through the KJV, "Lead us not into temptation." Neither Matthew nor Luke (nor Jesus) would have wanted to imply the possibility that God might tempt people to sin. Rather, the request is for God to guide Jesus's followers in such a way that they will not experience trials that could test their faith (cf. Matt. 26:41; Luke 22:40). According to the parable of the Sower (Matt. 13:2–9, 18–23; cf. Luke 8:4–18) such trials might take the form of hardship ("trouble or persecution") or distraction ("the cares of the world and the lure of wealth"). Elsewhere, Jesus indicates that some trials are inevitable (Matt. 18:7; 24:9–13; Luke 17:1; 21:12–17). Thus, the request will not always be granted in its most literal sense. Jesus's disciples *will* sometimes be brought to the time of trial; it is God's will that this happen, for it gives them an opportunity to testify (Luke 21:13) and it provides a means of determining who will fall away and who will endure to the end and be saved (Matt. 24:10, 13). Still, Jesus's followers are encouraged to pray that they be spared trials whenever possible and—when this is not possible—that they be protected from the potentially destructive consequences of such experiences (cf. James 1:2–4; 1 Pet. 1:6–7). The latter point is, again, spelled out more explicitly in the Matthean version of the prayer: "rescue us from evil" (or "the evil one").

A well-known conclusion to the Lord's Prayer ("Yours is the kingdom and the power and the glory forever and ever, Amen") was not originally in the Bible. It was written by early Christians when the prayer came to be used in liturgical worship. Later, some copyists began adding the conclusion to manuscripts of the NT with the result that the phrase ended up in a few English translations of the Bible (including the KJV). *See also* prayer; Sermon on the Mount; sin.

Bibliography
Cullman, Oscar. *Prayer in the New Testament.* Fortress, 1995.

Karris, Robert J. *Prayer and the New Testament: Jesus and His Communities at Worship.* Crossroad, 2000.

Longenecker, Richard N. *Into God's Presence: Prayer in the New Testament.* Eerdmans, 2001.

Stevenson, Kenneth W. *The Lord's Prayer: A Text in Tradition.* Fortress, 2004.   J.D.K./M.A.P.

Lord's Supper, an early Christian celebration modeled on the last meal Jesus shared with his disciples prior to his death; it receives this name from Paul's reference in 1 Cor. 11:20. The Synoptic Gospels describe the Last Supper as a Passover meal, but in John it is eaten *before* Passover. The words "after supper" in the tradition quoted by Paul in 1 Cor. 11:23–25 indicate that the Lord's Supper was originally a full meal, introduced by the blessing and breaking of the bread and concluded by the blessing and passing of the cup. In earliest Christianity the Lord's Supper was pervaded by intense eschatological expectation. Fervent hope for the new age, to be inaugurated by the risen and exalted Jesus upon his return to earth, is obvious in Mark 14:25 and Luke 22:18 and is echoed in 1 Cor. 11:26.

Most scholars think that the words spoken over bread and cup were a crucial part of the Lord's Supper liturgy from the beginning. Nevertheless, it is not possible to determine what the original "words of institution" were, for even a cursory comparison shows that the different versions are by no means identical in their details (Matt. 26:26–29; Mark 14:22–25; Luke 22:14–22; 1 Cor. 11:23–26; cf. John 6:35–59). In all the Gospels, as in 1 Corinthians, the bread and wine are connected with Jesus's redemptive death, but the different writings reflect distinctive understandings of the Lord's Supper.

The earliest Christian references to the Lord's Supper are not those found in the Gospels, but those contained in Paul's First Letter to the Corinthians. This is the only NT letter in which the Lord's Supper is ever mentioned and it probably would not have come up here except that problems have arisen in Corinth with regard to its observance. In fact, interpreters believe that there might be two distinct sets of problems that occasion Paul's comments. The most obvious, explicit discussion of the Lord's Supper, comes in 1 Cor. 11, but that meal seems to lie in the background for comments he makes in 1 Cor. 10 as well. The background for those comments concerns the issue of Corinthian Christians participating in pagan banquets at which Paul claims they are partaking of the cup of demons (10:6–22, esp. v. 21). The latter reference seems to draw a parallel between the fellowship that believers share with Jesus Christ through the Lord's Supper and the fellowship they will share with pagan deities through seemingly innocent secular rites. Further, Paul draws a parallel between the eucharistic bread and wine and the spir-

Jesus's last meal with his disciples, as depicted by Nicholas of Verdun on a panel from the altar at Klosterneuberg Abbey, 1180.

itual food and drink (manna and water from the rock) that nourished the Israelite ancestors in the wilderness (10:1–4). The point seems to be that, just as the spiritual food and drink did not protect the ancestors from God's judgment when they committed idolatry, so the Lord's Supper will not magically protect Christians who participate in pagan rites. In driving this point home, however, Paul reveals something that he and the Corinthians believe about the Lord's Supper: the cup of blessing is a "sharing [Gk. *koinōnia*] of the blood of Christ"; the bread is a "sharing [*koinōnia*] of the body of Christ" (10:16) The Greek word *koinōnia* might be translated "fellowship," "communion," or "sharing." Some think that Paul's emphasis is that partaking of the bread and wine is a means of communing with the crucified and risen Lord; others see the partaking as a means of securing the benefits of Jesus's saving death. In either case, playing on a second sense of "body of Christ" (cf. 1 Cor. 12), Paul affirms that those who share bread and cup are bound together with each other: the many are made one by partaking of the one loaf (10:17).

The apostle's emphasis is similar in 1 Cor. 11, where he excoriates the Corinthians for the class consciousness and insensitivity to the poor that keep their common meal from being the *Lord's* Supper. The problem now is that the food for the supper is not getting distributed equitably (11:23). Why not? There could be many reasons, but since Paul says the Corinthians should "wait for one another" (11:33), many interpreters think the problem arose from people arriving at different times and eating in shifts. Possibly, the wealthier members of the church would come early and share with each other whatever they had brought.

Jesus and the disciples at the Last Supper, which is regarded by Christians as the basis for the sacrament of the Eucharist; embroidered gold wire on purple silk, fourteenth century.

Members of the lower classes, who labored until dark, would come later, bringing whatever meager contributions they could afford. They would arrive to find the elite had already enjoyed a nice banquet and were sated with expensive food and sometimes drunk on fine liquor (11:21). There might be some leftovers, but the second-shift meal for late arrivers (probably the great majority of the congregation) would be a decidedly lower-class affair. This may have seemed appropriate to those familiar with Greco-Roman banquets, at which servants always ate separately and considered it a privilege to receive scraps from the feast as a supplement to what they would have had otherwise. Paul, however, thinks that replicating such inequities at this meal shows "contempt for the church of God" (11:22). He is appalled that a meal to be eaten in remembrance of Jesus (11:24) has become an occasion for humiliating the poor (11:22). In dealing with the issue, Paul quotes the tradition that he says he received from the Lord, "that the Lord Jesus on the night when he was betrayed took a loaf of bread, and when he had given thanks, he broke it and said, 'This is my body that is for you. Do this in remembrance of me'. In the same way he took the cup also, after supper, saying, 'This cup is the new covenant in my blood. Do this, as often as you drink it, in remembrance of me'" (11:23–25). Notably, this tradition reminds the Corinthians of the meaning of Christ's death: the bread re-presents the body "for you" and the shared cup actualizes the "new covenant" effected through Jesus's death (see Jer. 31:31–34). Further, Paul adds that the supper is intended to "proclaim the Lord's death until he comes," and in order to do this it must be marked by loving concern for every member of the body. Therefore, to eat and drink without "discerning the body" is to incur divine judgment (1 Cor. 11:29).

In the Gospel of Mark, Jesus offers the cup to his disciples saying, "This is my blood of the covenant, which is poured out for many" (15:24). The phrase "my blood of the covenant" probably echoes Exod. 24:8, and the expression "poured out for many" stresses the atoning efficacy of Jesus's death. Matthew makes the point even more explicit by adding that Jesus's blood is shed "for the forgiveness of sins" (26:28). Among all biblical accounts of the Lord's Supper, the version in Luke's Gospel is unique in that Jesus offers a cup, then bread, and then another cup (22:17–20). Some scholars think this is a conflation of sources: Luke combined the account from Mark's Gospel with a tradition similar to that quoted by Paul.

In the Gospel of John Jesus does not institute the Lord's Supper during the last meal with his disciples, but the "bread of life" discourse in 6:25–59 likely reflects the understanding of the Lord's Supper in the Johannine community. Jesus speaks of eating his flesh and drinking his blood as the means of attaining eternal life (6:53–58). At least three interpretations of these words are possible. First, the language is sacramental; when believers eat the bread and drink the wine, they are partaking of sacred food and drink that give eternal life. Second, the language of eating Jesus's flesh and drinking his blood dramatically suggests that one must *appropriate* God's salvation, made available through Jesus's death, by being spiritually united with the crucified and risen Lord. Third, in light of the emphasis at 6:63, the shocking and offensive language in John 6 (e.g., 6:51, 52–57; cf. 6:60) points to the scandal of the incarnation: to have eternal life one must commit oneself to Jesus as the revealer sent from God, the Word become flesh (1:14).

Bibliography

Jeremias, Joachim. *The Eucharistic Words of Jesus*. Scribner, 1966.

Powell, Mark Allan. *Introducing the New Testament: A Historical, Literary, and Theological Survey*. Baker Academic, 2009.

Schweizer, Eduard. *The Lord's Supper According to the New Testament*. Fortress, 1967.

S.K.W. /M.A.P.

Lot, the son of Abraham's brother Haran. Lot is first mentioned in Gen. 11:31 as migrating with his uncle Abraham and grandfather Terah from Ur of the Chaldeans toward Canaan. After Terah's death in the Syrian locale of Haran, Lot accompanies Abraham on his journey into Canaan (12:1–9) and to and from Egypt (12:10–20; 13:1). Upon their return, a quarrel between Lot's and Abraham's herdsmen (13:7) prompts Abraham to propose an amicable separation, offering Lot his choice of where to settle. Lot prefers the well-watered Jordan plain and its prosperous towns, and Abraham settles in Hebron. Lot appears again in Gen. 14 as a captive in a battle between five kings of the Jordan plain and four invading Mesopotamian kings. Abraham, with only 318 men, pursues the invaders beyond Damascus, recovering Lot and his possessions. Abraham indirectly aids Lot a second time (18:23–33) when he pleads with God to spare Sodom and Gomorrah from destruction, because of the few righteous among its inhabitants. God sends divine emissaries to determine if ten righteous persons can be found in the cities (19:1–29). The emissaries appear to be wayfarers, and Lot offers them hospitality. But then rowdy townspeople desire to rape the newcomers, and Lot pleads with them, offering them his virgin daughters instead. The emissaries blind the mob and, with some difficulty, persuade Lot, his wife, and his daughters to leave. Lot pleads for a refuge in the nearby town of Zoar, which the emissaries grant. On departing Sodom, however, Lot's wife looks back at the destruction and turns into a pillar of salt (cf. Luke 17:32). Lot's daughters, possibly believing themselves to be the world's sole survivors, ply Lot with liquor and have sex with him, conceiving Moab (Heb., "of the same father") and Ben-ammi (Heb., "son of paternal kin"). These children of the incestuous unions are identified as ancestors of Israel's Transjordanian neighbors, the Moabites and Ammonites (Gen. 19:30–38). *See also* Abraham; Ammonites; Moab; Sodom. J.W.R.

Lots found at Masada, a mountaintop fortress on the western shore of the Dead Sea and final holdout of Jews in the rebellion against Rome, 66–73 CE. They are each inscribed with a name and may have been used to determine who would slay the others in order to avoid capture by the Romans.

lot, lots, objects that could be cast or drawn as a means of determining the divine will. References to the use of lots abound, and the legitimacy of this means of determining the divine will is never questioned. Still no detailed description of the actual procedures involved or of the precise nature of the instrument(s) used is offered in the Bible. The usual Hebrew word for "lot" (*goral*) has the additional meaning of "destiny" in certain biblical texts (Isa. 17:14; Jer. 13:25; Dan. 12:13), and in the Dead Sea Scrolls this word is used to mean "fate." In Esther 3:7, a different word, the noun *pur* (NRSV: "the Pur"), is used to denote the instrument Haman uses to fix the day for a pogrom of the Jewish people. This explains the name of the Festival of Purim (*purim* is the plural of *pur*), which celebrates the Jews' deliverance from that intended pogrom.

Several notable events in the Bible are determined by the choosing or casting of lots. Saul, Israel's first king, was selected in this manner (1 Sam. 10:16–26). The land was apportioned among the tribes by lot (Num. 26:55; Josh. 14:2). The identity of Achan as the thief of the spoil from Jericho was discovered by lot (Josh. 7:14). Jonathan was found to be the (unwitting) violator of his father's oath through the casting of lots (1 Sam. 14:42). The ranks of temple personnel were determined by lot (1 Chron. 24:5; 25:8; 26:13; cf. Luke 1:9). The soldiers who crucified Jesus divided up his possessions by lot (Matt. 27:35; Mark 15:24; Luke 23:34; John 19:24), and Matthias was chosen by lot to replace Judas among the twelve apostles (Acts 1:26). *See also* Purim, Festival of; Saul; Urim and Thummim.   W.L.H.

Lotan (loh´tan), a son of Seir the Horite and chieftain of the Horites who inhabited the hill country of Seir (Edom) in ancestral times (Gen. 36:20, 29). *See also* Horites; Seir.

love, usually an inner quality that expresses itself through unselfish behavior. The word, however, has a wide range of meanings that must be determined from context.

In the Hebrew Bible: The verb "to love" (Heb. *'ahab*) and its cognates cover the full range of meanings of the English word "love." It can be used to describe sexual attraction or lust (Gen. 34:3; Judg. 16:4, 15; 2 Sam. 13:4, 15; Prov. 5:18–20; Song of Sol. 8:6–7), but it is also used for love between the sexes that involves something more than just physical desire (e.g., Gen. 24:67; 29:20). The word can also refer to devotion within a family (Gen. 22:2; 25:28; 44:20; Ruth 4:15) or among friends (1 Sam. 18:1–4; 20:17; 2 Sam. 1:26; Ps. 38:12; Jer. 20:4–6). Especially significant are the twin commands, "Love your neighbor as yourself" (Lev. 19:18) and "Love the alien as yourself" (19:34). Transcending all these references, however, is the far-ranging expectation that Israel is to love God (Exod. 20:6; Deut. 6:4–6; Ps. 40:17). Likewise, God's love for Israel is stressed throughout the Bible (Deut. 7:13; Hos. 3:1). This latter sense of God's love for God's people is often stressed in covenant terms through use of the Hebrew word *khesed* (usually translated "steadfast love" or "loving-kindness"). In Deuteronomy, the essential function of divine love is to undergird the concepts of election and covenant (7:12–13). In covenant terms, loving God may be defined as obedience (to love God is to keep God's commandments, 5:10; 7:9; 11:1), and God's love for Israel may be defined in terms of blessing (7:13). Moreover, God's blessings on Israel include the "circumcision of hearts," which is what enables Israel to love God (30:6). Furthermore,

Love as a virtue personified; bronze relief by Andrea Pisano, South Doors, Baptistry, Florence, 1336.

the Hebrew Bible also makes clear that God loves not only Israel, but others as well; the reason for the selection of Israel is that God wishes to form a people who will be a source of blessing to all nations (Gen. 12:2–3). The will of God is for everlasting peace throughout all the earth (Isa. 2:2–4).

With the prophecy of Hosea (mid-eighth century BCE), a profound theological conception of love was introduced into the literature of Israel. Hosea was speaking prior to the fall of Samaria to the Assyrians in 722/1 BCE, and he used the imagery of love and marriage to describe the faithlessness of Israel to its God. The problem is described in Hos. 6:4–6: "What shall I do with you, O Ephraim? What shall I do with you, O Judah? Your love is like a morning cloud, like the dew that goes away early. . . . For I desire steadfast love and not sacrifice" (see also 9:15; 11:1–7). The depth of God's compassionate love is manifested in a directive to Hosea to buy back his adulterous wife, a directive that broke with legal custom (3:1). In the same manner, God continues to love unfaithful Israel: "How can I give you up, O Ephraim! How can I hand you over, O Israel! My heart recoils within me, my compassion grows warm and tender" (11:8). God is said to have initiated the covenant out of love for Israel (11:1; cf. Deut. 4:31–37), and now God invites Israel to respond to the depth of that divine love. Similar language is found occasionally in Jeremiah (2:2; 3:2) and in Second Isaiah (i.e., Isa. 40–55). Isaiah can describe God as Israel's "husband" who takes delight in her (54:5–8; 62:1–5) or as Israel's mother whose love surpasses that of any human mother for her infant child (49:15).

In the NT: The primary Greek words used to express the concept of love are *agapē* and *philia*. Although the NT much prefers the use of *agapē*, the two terms can be used synonymously. In the Synoptic Gospels, one notes that the primary use of "love" is with regard to the great commandment (Matt. 22:34–40; Mark 12:28–34; Luke 20:39–40). Jesus indicates that the most important of all God's commands are, first, the command to love God with all one's being, and, second, the command to love one's neighbor as oneself. All other biblical commands are to be understood in light of these. Jesus also emphasizes that his followers are to love their enemies (Matt. 5:43–46; Luke 6:27–35). Although this concept is not foreign to the Hebrew Bible (cf. Exod. 23:4–5; Prov. 25:21–22; note Paul's expansion of this in Rom. 12:16–21), Jesus clearly intensifies the motif. Jesus also insists that loving God involves a total commitment that annuls devotion to competing concerns; no one can serve "two masters" without despising one and loving the other (Matt. 6:24; Luke 16:13). Although the emphasis in the Synoptic Gospels is mainly on loving God, Luke's Gospel contains a story in which the focus shifts to love for Jesus: a woman from the streets who weeps at Jesus's feet demonstrates that she loves him in a way that Simon the Pharisee does not (7:36–50). In this context, Jesus tells a parable that illustrates the principle that those who are forgiven much love much, while those who are forgiven only a little do not. Matthew's Gospel contains a unique reference to love in an eschatological context, where Jesus says that "because of the increase of lawlessness, the love of many will grow cold" (24:12). That theme seems to be echoed in one passage from the book of Revelation. Jesus addresses the church of Ephesus and says, "I have this against you, that you have abandoned the love you had at first" (2:4).

In John's Gospel (and also in the Letters of John), the importance of love is stressed repeatedly. A number of recurring motifs may be noted. First, the Johannine writings emphasize that God is love (1 John 4:8) and that God loves the world (John 3:16). Jesus has come into the world as a manifestation of the Father's love, and everything he does, particularly his death on the cross, is intended to demonstrate the extent of God's great love (15:13). Second, the Gospel of John emphasizes "love for Jesus" (not just love for God) as an expectation of disciples. In a postresurrection commissioning story, Jesus asks Peter three times, "Do you love me?" (21:15–17; cf. 8:42). Indeed, this Gospel also emphasizes how much God loves Jesus (or how much the Father loves the Son; cf. 3:35; 5:20; 10:17; 17:26). Finally, the Johannine writings emphasize a "new commandment" according to which Jesus's followers are to love one another, just as Jesus has loved them (John 14:15, 21, 23, 24; 15:9, 12, 17; cf. 1 John 2:7; 3:23; 2 John 6); indeed, this will be the defining characteristic of the Christian community (John 13:34–35). Interpreters have often noticed that, despite the emphasis on these themes, the Johannine writings (which speak of love far more often than any other books of the Bible) make no mention of loving people outside the community of faith (i.e., one's neighbors or enemies or simply humanity in general).

The apostle Paul often links love with faith and hope (1 Cor. 13:13; Gal. 5:5–6; 1 Thess. 1:3; 5:8; Gal. 5:5–6). Virtually everything that Paul says about love is linked to his belief that the love of God has been supremely manifest through Jesus Christ (Rom. 5:8), and that the "love of Christ" continues to be a reality experienced by believers through faith and hope. Thus, Paul says, "I am convinced that neither death, nor life, nor angels, nor rulers, nor things present, nor things to come, nor powers, nor height, nor depth, nor anything else in all creation, will be able to separate us from the love of God in Christ Jesus our Lord" (Rom. 8:38–39). Paul also regards the ability of humans to love as a divine gift of the Holy Spirit (Gal. 5:22). Thus, for Paul love becomes the primary term describing the result of faith for both the believer and the community in Christ. He says, "The love of Christ urges us on" (2 Cor. 5:14) and, "The only thing that counts is faith working through love" (Gal. 5:6). Paul is emphatic that love does not originate in the human heart. It is not a human possibility; it is a divine gift. It derives from Christ, who now lives in the believer (Gal. 2:20). Still, the one in Christ must walk in love (Rom. 14:15) and, for this reason, Paul gives priority to love over all other human expressions, virtues, or phenomena (1 Cor. 13:13). In particular, love is preferable to knowledge, for knowledge "puffs up," while love "builds up" (8:1). As Paul's most extensive treatment of love in chap. 13 makes clear, love is not to be understood in terms of emotion, feelings, or sentiment, but in terms of attitude, behavior, and conduct. For example, to love others means to treat them in ways that are patient and kind rather than envious, boastful, arrogant, or rude (13:4). Above all, love means not insisting on one's own way (13:5), a theme that informs much of Paul's ethical counsel to his congregations. An ethic informed by love recasts questions with a view toward, not what is permissible or desirable for oneself, but what will be most beneficial to others (e.g., Rom. 14:15).   K.P.D./M.A.P.

loving-kindness, an attribute of God, according to one traditional translation of the Hebrew word *khesed*. That word, which can probably not be rendered faithfully in English, contains the idea of love, devotion, loyalty, and covenant faithfulness (cf. Exod. 34:6; Neh. 9:32). In the KJV, the word is rendered "loving-kindness" (30 times), "kindness" (38 times), and "mercy" (145 times). This preference for translating *khesed* as "mercy" was influenced by the LXX, which in 168 instances translates *khesed* with the Greek word *eleos* ("mercy" or "compassion"). The NRSV does not use "loving-kindness" as a translation for *khesed* (but cf. Titus 3:4). Rather, it translates that term "steadfast love" (172 times), "kindness" (17 times), "great kindness" (Gen. 19:19), and "faithful love" (1 Sam. 20:14).   J.G.G.

Lucifer (loo´si-fuhr), the English translation in the KJV (Isa. 14:12) of the Hebrew word meaning "light bringer" or "shining one," sometimes designating the morning (or day) star, i.e, Venus (cf. NRSV: "Day Star"). The English word "Lucifer" comes from the Latin for "light bearer." In Isa. 14:12, the king of Babylon, in an apparent reference to Canaanite mythology, is tauntingly called "Day Star, son of Dawn," because he has fallen from his lofty but temporary position of power. In the Christian church, this passage from Isaiah came to be connected with Jesus's saying in Luke 10:18: "I saw Satan fall like lightning from heaven." Thus a connection was made between Lucifer and Satan, and Lucifer came to be understood as another name for Satan. *See also* devil; Satan; stars.   J.M.E.

Lucius (loo´shuhs).

1 A Roman consul who sent a letter supporting Simon Maccabeus in his struggle against the Seleucids (1 Macc. 15:15–24).

2 A prophet and teacher from Cyrene in the church at Antioch (Acts 13:1).

3 An associate of Paul who sends greetings in Rom. 16:21.

Lud (luhd).

1 A name given to the son of Shem (Gen. 10:22; 1 Chron. 1:17).

2 A designation for a group of people (Isa. 66:19; Ezek. 27:10; 30:5). Their identification is difficult, and various proposals have been made, including the suggestion that two different groups were known by this name. In some cases, the people so designated were in Asia Minor (Isa. 66:19; possibly also Ezek. 27:10). In other cases, the people called Lud appear to be centered in North Africa (Ezek. 30:5); here, they are probably to be connected with the Ludim (Gen. 10:13; Jer. 46:9), who are said to be descendants of Mizraim (Egypt). It is possible that these two groups are of the same origin and settled in various places.   D.R.B.

Ludim (loo´dim). *See* Lud.

Luke (look), the transliteration of the Greek Loukas, probably an affectionate form of the Latin name Lucius (Gk. Loukios). The name appears three times in the NT, all in letters attributed to Paul: Philem. 24; Col. 4:14; 2 Tim. 4:11.

In Philem. 23–24, Luke, along with Epaphras, Mark, Aristarchus, and Demas, is said to be with Paul, and they join him in sending greetings to Philemon, Apphia, and Archippus (Philem. 2). Epaphras is called Paul's fellow prisoner (Philem. 23), while Luke and the others are called his co-

Evangelist page of the Gospel According to Luke from the *Lindisfarne Gospels* (ca. 700 CE) shows Luke writing. Behind him is his symbol, the winged ox.

workers, as is Philemon (v. 2). In Col. 4:10–14, Luke, along with Demas, Aristarchus, Mark, Epaphras, and others, joins Paul in sending greetings. Here, Luke is called the "beloved physician." In 2 Tim. 4:10–12, all of Paul's companions except Luke are said either to have deserted him or to have been sent by him to other places; thus only Luke is with him as he awaits his execution. Paul asks Timothy to join him with Mark. All three of the foregoing passages are probably intended to refer to the same person. It is also possible that the Lucius referred to in Rom. 16:21 is this same person, but in this instance Lucius is called one of Paul's "relatives" and he is distinguished from Timothy, who is called his "co-worker." Another Lucius is mentioned in Acts 13:1 as one of the prophets in the church at Antioch, but there is no reason to suspect that this is the person referred to in Paul's letters.

Irenaeus (late second-century bishop of Lyons) appears to have been the first to identify the author of the third Gospel and the book of Acts as Luke, the "companion of Paul." The Muratorian Canon, a late second-century list of authoritative Christian writings, also says this and adds that this Luke was not an eyewitness of the events narrated in the Gospel, but a participant in some of the events reported in Acts (presumably a reference to passages in Acts in which the author uses the first-person plural pronoun, thus appearing to identify himself as a participant in the narrative). In keeping with these traditions, Luke, the companion of Paul, has traditionally been identified as the author of both the Gospel of Luke and the book of Acts. Modern critical scholars agree that the same author wrote both books and that it is likely (though not certain) that this person had been an acquaintance of Paul. They are cautious, however, about identifying that person by name, since both the Gospel and the book of Acts are actually anonymous. *See also* Acts of the Apostles; Lucius; Luke, Gospel According to.   J.B.T.

Luke, Gospel According to, the third Gospel in the NT.

Contents: Luke's Gospel opens with a dedication to Theophilus (1:1–4), followed by a long account of events related to the birth and childhood of Jesus, interspersed with hymns and parallel accounts of events related to the birth of John the Baptist (1:5–2:52). Then the Gospel reports Jesus's baptism by John (3:1–22), provides a genealogy for Jesus (3:23–28), and recounts Jesus's temptation by Satan (4:1–13). Jesus begins his ministry with an inaugural sermon at Nazareth (4:14–30). The Gospel then reports a number of miracle stories interspersed with accounts of Jesus calling disciples and engaging religious leaders in various controversies (4:31–6:16). Next, Jesus preaches the Sermon on the Plain (6:17–49), heals a centurion's servant (7:1–10), raises a widow's son from the dead (7:11–17), engages a question from John the Baptist (7:18–35), and responds positively to the devotion of a sinful woman who weeps at his feet in a Pharisee's house (7:36–50). The Gospel notes that Jesus had a number of women followers (8:1–3) and then relates a few parables of Jesus (8:4–18) and some words about his family (8:19–21). The account of Jesus's ministry continues with four miracle stories: calming a storm at sea, healing the Gerasene demoniac, healing a woman with a hemorrhage, and raising Jairus's daughter from the dead (8:22–56). Jesus then sends the twelve apostles out on a mission (9:1–9) and miraculously feeds five thousand people (9:10–17). After Peter confesses Jesus to be the "Messiah of God" (9:18–20), Jesus tells the disciples about his passion and instructs them regarding self-denial and service (9:21–50); at the same time, he reveals his glory through the transfiguration (9:28–36) and the healing of a boy with a demon (9:37–43). This Gospel then devotes a long section to recounting a journey of Jesus and his disciples to Jerusalem (9:51–19:27). Along the way, Jesus is rejected by a Samaritan village (9:51–56), sends seventy followers out on a mission (10:1–12, 17–20), and visits the homes of Mary and Martha (10:38–42) and Zacchaeus (19:1–10). He performs numerous healings (a crippled woman, a man with dropsy, ten lepers, a blind man). This section of the Gospel also contains a great deal of Jesus's teaching, including the Lord's Prayer (11:1–4), instruction on proper behavior at banquets (14:7–14), and many parables. Finally, Jesus enters Jerusalem (19:28–38) and weeps as he predicts the city's destruction (19:39–44). After a series of conflicts with the religious leaders of Israel (19:45–21:4), he predicts the destruction of the temple and offers a discourse on the end times (21:5–38). The Gospel of Luke concludes with an account of Jesus's passion and resurrection (22:1–24:49): he shares a last meal with his followers, prays in the garden, is arrested, and is crucified after being examined by both Jewish and Roman authorities. After his burial, he is raised from the dead, and he appears to women at the empty tomb, to two men on the road to Emmaus, and to his assembled disciples in Jerusalem. Finally, he blesses his disciples and ascends into heaven (24:50–53).

OUTLINE OF CONTENTS

Luke

                                     J.B.T.

LUKE'S REDACTION OF MARK

Most scholars believe that the author of Luke's Gospel had a copy of the Gospel of Mark and used it as a source. But Luke preserves only a little more than half of the Gospel of Mark, and he edits what he does preserve in accord with certain principles:

Organization

Some Markan material is moved about. *Examples:*

The story of Jesus preaching in Nazareth is moved forward so that it can provide the occasion for his inaugural sermon (Luke 4:16–30; cf. Mark 6:1–6).

The disciples' dispute over who is the greatest is moved to take place at the Last Supper (Luke 22:24–27; cf. Mark 10:41–45).

Abbreviation

Luke omits from Mark's Gospel stories that he considers to be insignificant or inappropriate. *Examples*:

A comment on the incompetence of physicians (Luke 8:42–48; Mark 5:26).

A conversation between Jesus and father of demoniac child (Luke 9:37–43; Mark 9:21–24).

The naked young man in the garden (Luke 22:47–53; Mark 14:43–52).

Note: Matthew's Gospel also omits all of these passages (9:20–22; 17:14–18; 26:47–56).

Sophistication

Casual or colloquial expressions are rewritten in the more polished Greek of the educated class. *Examples:*

Instances of the "historical present" tense are changed (150 out of 151; he missed Mark 5:35 at Luke 8:49).

Mark's repetitive use of words like "and" and "immediately" is reduced.

Pronouns lacking clear antecedents are provided with them.

Use of syntactical constructions such as genitive absolutes and articular infinitives is increased (these portend a "higher class" of Greek).

Accuracy

Instances of questionable accuracy are corrected. *Examples:*

"King Herod" (Mark 6:14) becomes "Herod the Tetrarch" (Luke 9:7).

Reference to Abiathar as high priest in Mark 2:26 is omitted (Luke 6:4; cf. 1 Sam 21:1–6).

Contextual Relevance

Changes are made to make the narrative more relevant to Luke's intended audience. *Examples*:

All eight of Mark's Aramaic expressions are eliminated ("Boanerges" in Mark 3:17; "Talitha cum" in 5:41; "Corban" in 7:11; "Ephphatha" in 7:34; "Bartimaeus" in 10:46; "Abba" in 14:36; "Golgotha" in 15:22; "Eloi, eloi, lema sebachthani" in 15:34), probably because Luke is writing for a culturally diverse audience throughout the Roman Empire.

Notations providing broad historical or cultural context are introduced (cf. Luke 3:1–3; Mark 1:4), because Luke wants the story he tells to be received as a work of "world history" with implications for all humanity.

The word "village" (*kōmē*) is often changed to "city" (*polis*) to give the story a more urban feel that transcends its setting in rural areas.

The monetary value of coins is increased to keep the story relevant for those who live in more prosperous circumstances than did Jesus and his original followers (cf. "silver," Luke 9:3; "copper," Mark 6:8).

LUKE'S REDACTION OF MARK *(continued)*

Character Portrayal

Luke changes the way major characters are portrayed in the Gospel story, including Jesus, his disciples, and the family of Jesus.

Jesus

Statements that imply a lack of ability or authority on Jesus's part are omitted (comment in Mark 6:5 not found in Luke 4:16–30).

References to human emotions are dropped: "pity" (Mark 1:41), "anger" (3:5), "sadness" (3:5); "wonder" (6:6); "compassion" (6:34); "indignation" (10:14); "love" (10:21).

Some stories or parts of stories in which Jesus acts in a somewhat violent way are omitted (cursing of fig tree, Mark 11:12–14, 20–25; overturning tables, 11:15).

Stories that might seem to portray Jesus as a magician are dropped (Mark 7:31–37; 8:22–26).

Disciples

Stories of Jesus rebuking Peter (Mark 8:33), of James and John's presumptuous request (10:35–40), and of the disciples' flight at Jesus's arrest are eliminated.

Peter's denial (Luke 22:31–34; Mark 14:29–31) and the disciples' sleep in Gethsemane (Luke 22:45–46; Mark 14:37–41) are muted and explained.

Lack of understanding is attributed, not to the disciples unperceptive nature, but to divine concealment (Luke 9:45; Mark 9:32; cf. Luke 18:34).

Jesus's Family

Reference to Jesus's family "coming to seize him" is dropped (Mark 3:21).

The story of Jesus designating his "true family" is reworded to lessen the contrast with his earthly family (Luke 8:19–21; Mark 3:31–35).

From Mark Allan Powell, *Introducing the New Testament* (courtesy, Baker Academic)

Composition: Although the Gospel is anonymous, it has traditionally been ascribed to Luke, a physician who is mentioned as being with Paul in Col. 4:14; Philem. 24; and 2 Tim. 4:11. Although this cannot be proven, modern scholars do recognize that the author of Luke's Gospel also wrote the book of Acts (cf. Acts 1:1, which refers to this Gospel as that author's "first book"), and it is usually granted that certain first-person references ("we passages") in Acts are meant to identify that author as a traveling companion of Paul (16:10–17; 20:5–15; 21:1–18; 27:1–28:16). Some scholars question the veracity of that claim, given what they take to be discrepancies between the portrayal of Paul in Acts and what Paul says in his letters; others allow that the books could be written by Luke, a "sometimes" companion of Paul, who did not always think like the apostle or know everything about him. In any case, the Gospel of Luke is thought by most scholars to have employed both Mark's Gospel and the now lost Q document (a collection of Jesus's sayings) as sources. According to this hypothesis, Luke combined Mark and Q, editing both sources and adding a great deal of new content, referred to in NT scholarship as "L material." Minority propos-

als suggest that Luke had a copy of Matthew's Gospel (or copies of both Matthew and Mark). In any case, the Gospel is typically dated around 85 CE. The place of writing cannot be determined, but the Gospel seems to be written for a broad audience, including Gentile Christians dispersed throughout the Greco-Roman world.

Distinctive Features: Luke's Gospel contains a great deal of material that is not paralleled elsewhere in the NT. Particularly noteworthy in this regard are the stories surrounding Jesus's infancy and the large number of parables found only in this Gospel. In addition, women seem to figure more prominently in Luke's Gospel than in the other Synoptic Gospels (1:26–56; 2:36–38; 7:11–17, 36–50; 8:1–3; 10:38–42; 13:10–17; 18:1–8), Samaritans are mentioned repeatedly (9:51–56; 10:29–37; 17:11–19), Jerusalem is a frequent setting or focus (1:5–23; 2:21–38, 41–52; 9:51–56; 19:41–44; 24:13–53), and there is considerable attention to riches and poverty (1:52–53; 3:10–14; 4:14–30; 12:13–21; 14:12–14; 16:1–12, 19–31; 19:1–10). Luke's Gospel also contains more liturgical material (e.g., prayers and hymns) than the others, and many interpreters have noted a curious "food motif" according to which banquets and meals are particularly emphasized (nineteen meals are mentioned, thirteen of which are peculiar to this Gospel). Scholars who believe Luke used Mark's Gospel as a source note that he edited the Markan material by adding historical or chronological notes (3:1–2; 4:23; cf. 2:1–2) and by eliminating or revising material that reflected negatively on Jesus's disciples (8:33; 10:35–41 have no parallel in Luke) or family members (cf. 3:31–35; Luke 8:19–21). Luke has also structured his Gospel so that the whole story begins with a grand overture, presenting the birth of Jesus in a liturgically rich opus that sounds many key themes of the Gospel story (Luke 1–2). Further, his incorporation of the teaching of Jesus into a journey framework (9:51–19:40) is said to capitalize on a pilgrimage image for discipleship. Most significant, perhaps, many scholars believe that Luke intended his Gospel as "part one" of a two-volume work, making his entire story of Jesus preparatory for the life and mission of the Christian church.

Major Themes: Luke's Gospel emphasizes a theme of divine necessity, according to which God is working out a plan of salvation within world history. Its depiction of Jesus, furthermore, seems to draw on a diversity of Jewish and Gentile images. On the one hand, Jesus may be identified with such traditional Jewish figures as the messiah (9:20), the Son of Man (22:69; cf. Acts 7:56), and the servant of the Lord promised by Isaiah (22:37; Acts 8:30–35; cf. Isa. 53:7–8, 12); on the other, he sometimes seems to be portrayed with imagery that Gentile readers would have associated with Greek philosophers, Roman benefactors, or mythological immortal beings. Against this background, Luke's Gospel emphasizes that the salvation Jesus brings has a present-day orientation to it: Jesus has come to seek and save those who are lost (19:10) and to liberate people from things that prevent them from experiencing life as God intends (4:16–21). The Gospel also has a strong emphasis on Jesus's ministry to those who are excluded or disadvantaged, especially the poor, and this theme is developed with concomitant interest in condemnation of the wealthy (1:53; 6:24–25; 12:20–21; 16:19–31). *See also* Acts of the Apostles; gospel; Gospels, the; L (esp. "Material Unique to Luke"); Luke; Q; Synoptic Problem; Theophilus.

Bibliography

Borgman, Paul. *The Way According to Luke: Hearing the Whole Story of Luke–Acts.* Eerdmans, 2006.

Fitzmyer, Joseph. *The Gospel According to Luke.* Doubleday, 1981–85.

Green, Joel B. *The Gospel of Luke.* Eerdmans, 1997.

———. *The Theology of the Gospel of Luke.* Cambridge University Press, 1995.

Marshall, I. Howard. *The Gospel of Luke: A Commentary on the Greek Text.* Eerdmans, 1978.

Nolland, John. *Luke.* 3 vols. Word, 1989–93.

Powell, Mark Allan. *Introducing the New Testament: A Historical, Literary, and Theological Survey.* Baker Academic, 2009. Pp. 147–67.

———. *What Are They Saying About Luke?* Paulist, 1989.   M.A.P.

lute. *See* music.

Luz (luhz).

1 The Canaanite name of the city that was renamed Bethel by Jacob (Gen. 28:19; 35:6). Luz/Bethel was on the border between Benjamin and Ephraim (Josh. 16:2; 18:13; Judg. 1:23). Josh. 16:2 implies that Luz and Bethel are distinct places. Nevertheless, on the basis of all other references, Luz and Bethel are more likely two names for the same place. *See also* Bethel.

2 The name of a town in the land of the Hittites built by a refugee from the Canaanite town of Luz (Judg. 1:22–26).   J.F.D.

LXX, the symbol for the Septuagint, the early Greek translation of the Hebrew Bible, which also included several books that are now included among the apocryphal/deuterocanonical writings. *See also* Septuagint.

Lycaonia (lik′uh-oh′nee-uh), a district in central Asia Minor located on a plateau north of the Taurus Mountains and bounded by the districts of Cappadocia, Cilicia, Pisidia, Phrygia, and Galatia. Annexed to the district of Galatia ca. 35 BCE, it became, with Galatia, part of the Roman Empire ca. 25 BCE. Three cities of Lycaonia were visited by Paul during his first and second missionary journeys, Lystra, Derbe, and Iconium (Acts 13:51–14:21; 16:1–3). Paul's Letter to the Galatians, which reflects the conflict between Gentile and Jewish Christians, may have been addressed to the people residing in the district of Lycaonia. *See also* Derbe; Galatia; Galatians, Letter of Paul to the; Iconium; Lystra.   M.K.M.

Lycia (lish′uh), a coastal district in southwestern Asia Minor, bounded to the west by Lydia, to the north by Pisidia, and to the east by Pamphylia. Its principal city, Xanthus (modern Günük), headed a federation of cities and towns populated by a people possibly of Hittite origin, at least from the

sixth century BCE. The central sanctuary of the federation was the Letoön, sacred to Apollo. Ruled successively by the Persians, Alexander the Great, the Seleucids, the Ptolemies, and the Romans, the area progressively abandoned the Lycian language and merged into the general Hellenistic culture of the times. According to 1 Macc. 15:23, Lycia was among the recipients of the letter concerning the Romans' alliance with the Jews sent out by the consul Lucius Calpurnius Piso in the second century BCE. The Roman generals Brutus and Cassius sacked Xanthus for money in 42 BCE, but the Roman emperor Claudius made Lycia a province in 43 CE, and the emperor Vespasian joined it to Pamphylia in 74 CE. Paul changed ships at the Lycian port of Patara en route to Jerusalem (Acts 21:1) and again at Myra on his final journey to Rome (27:5–6). *See also* Myra; Paul.

C.H.M.

Lydda (lid'uh), a town in the fertile Plain of Sharon along an eastern branch of the ancient international highway, the Via Maris. This location gave Lydda a certain strategic and commercial importance. First mentioned as Lydda in a Late Bronze Age list of towns in Canaan conquered by Thutmose III of Egypt (1490–1435 BCE), the town is called Lod in the OT. Lod/Lydda was rebuilt by the Benjaminites (1 Chron. 8:12), and after the exile it became one of the places resettled by Jews who returned to their homeland (Ezra 2:33; Neh. 7:37; 11:35). At first outside the boundaries of Judea in the Hellenistic period, it was given to Jonathan the Hasmonean as a purely Jewish town ca. 145 BCE (1 Macc. 11:34). An early Christian community lived in Lydda, and there Peter healed the paralyzed man Aeneas (Acts 9:32–35). Later, during the 66–70 CE war of the Jews against the Romans, the city was burned by Cestius Gallus's contingent on its way to attack and destroy Jerusalem. *See also* Aeneas.

M.K.M.

Lydia (lid'ee-uh).
1 An area in south-central Asia Minor, whose most famous king was Croesus (sixth century BCE). Successively occupied by the Persians, Alexander the Great, and his successors, the Romans finally incorporated Lydia into the province of Asia. It is mentioned in 1 Macc. 8:8. Thyatira, Sardis, and Philadelphia (see Rev. 2:18–3:13) were located in Lydia.
2 A woman from Thyatira who, according to Acts 16:12–15, was Paul's first convert in Europe (at Philippi in Macedonia). Paul and his companions met her in a place outside the city gate, by a river, where they had correctly assumed there would be a place for prayer. They went there on the sabbath day and talked with a group of women, including Lydia, who is called "a worshiper of God." Some interpreters take the latter reference to mean that she was a Gentile who had been attracted to the Jewish faith (cf. Acts 10:2, where the Gentile Cornelius is called "a devout man who feared God"). Lydia is also said to be "a dealer in purple

cloth," a reference that is usually taken as implying some wealth on her part, since purple cloth was an expensive luxury item. After she and her household were baptized, she prevailed upon Paul and his companions to stay in her home, suggesting a large domicile befitting a wealthy person. *See also* Paul; Philippi; purple; Thyatira.

A.J.M.

lying. In the Ten Commandments, Israel is exhorted against using God's name for false oaths and against bearing false witness (Exod. 20:7, 16; Deut. 5:11, 20). Elsewhere, it is said that witnesses who testify falsely will receive the punishment that would have been meted out to their accused (Deut. 19:15–21). Indeed, all falsehoods are prohibited by the Torah (Exod. 23:7; Lev. 19:11). Persons who lie, and thereby defraud their neighbor, must pay restitution for the property loss plus a fine to the owner, and they must bring a sacrificial offering before they are forgiven by God (Lev. 6:1–7). Lying is thus an abomination to God (Prov. 12:22; Ps. 119:163), for God never lies (Num. 23:19; 1 Sam. 15:29). False prophets are singled out for particular condemnation (Isa. 9:15; Jer. 23:9–32; Ezek. 13), since their lies may influence the people to oppose God's will. The penalty for false prophecy is death (Deut. 18:20–22; Jer. 28). In the NT, Jesus says that the devil is the "father of lies" (John 8:44), and Paul condemns those who worship idols, because they have exchanged the truth about God for a lie (Rom. 1:25).

J.U.

lyre. *See* music.

Lysanias (li-say'nee-uhs), the tetrarch of Abilene in the days of John the Baptist, according to Luke 3:1. Luke gives the date as the fifteenth year of Tiberius (i.e., 28 or 29 CE), but the only Lysanias otherwise known as a ruler in the region died in 36 BCE. *See also* Abilene.

Lysias (lis'ee-uhs), **Claudius** (klaw'dee-uhs), according to Acts 21:30–23:35, the military tribune who commanded the Roman garrison at the fortress (probably the Tower of Antonia) adjacent to the Jerusalem temple. He arrested Paul when a rumor that Paul had brought a Gentile into the temple created a disturbance among the populace. Afterward, he sent Paul to Caesarea with a letter to Felix, the procurator of Judea, telling about the circumstances of Paul's problems in Jerusalem. The cognomen Lysias indicates that Claudius was of Greek birth. His Roman name would probably have been obtained after he purchased Roman citizenship (Acts 22:28). *See also* Antonia, Tower of; Felix, Antonius.

A.J.M.

Lystra (lis'truh), a city in the region of Lycaonia, about twenty-five miles south-by-southwest of Iconium in central Asia Minor. Paul and Barnabas stopped here during the first journey and were mistaken for gods (Acts 14:6–23), and

Paul returned later with Silas, when he recruited Timothy as a companion (15:40–16:4). Its location was unknown until 1885, when a Roman altar was found, still in place, inscribed with the city's Latin name (Lustra), indicating that it was a Roman colony. Lystra remains unexcavated, but surface finds indicate settlement as early as 3000 BCE. Augustus made the city a Roman stronghold ca. 6 BCE. The Lycaonians had a district language, and a temple to Zeus graced the city of Lystra (14:11–13). *See also* Lycaonia; Timothy.   M.K.M.

Opposite: The Virgin Mary and Child; Greek icon, ca. 1600.

M

M, a symbol designating material found only in the Gospel of Matthew. Biblical scholars often analyze the "M material" as one step in determining the distinctive perspective or unique contributions of Matthew's Gospel. In addition, some scholars regard M as representing one source strata upon which Matthew might have drawn when composing his Gospel. According to one prominent theory, the author of Matthew's Gospel had three principal sources: the Gospel of Mark, the Q source, and M. An even more prominent variation of this view holds that Matthew used only two written sources (Mark and Q) and that M consists of material Matthew himself put into writing based on what he had learned through oral tradition or gathered from any number of miscellaneous sources. For example, scholars note that the only two instances in the NT where Jesus talks about the "church" occur in passages assigned to the M material (16:17–19; 18:15–20); Jesus says that he intends to build a church and he offers advice for how that church should make decisions and regulate its membership. Likewise, a number of stories in the M material are ones in which Peter figures prominently (14:28–31; 16:17–19; 17:24–27; 18:21–22). If, in fact, Matthew's Gospel was written in Antioch, then it would have been produced in a community where Peter had actually lived (see Gal. 2:11–14). *See also* Synoptic Problem.   M.A.P.

Maacah (may´uh-kuh).

1 A small state south of Mount Hermon, apparently encompassing the northern half of the Golan Heights, bounded by the other non-Israelite state of the Golan, Geshur, on its south. The Transjordanian tribes of Israel (Reuben, Gad, the half-tribe of Manasseh) failed to conquer Maacah and Geshur (Josh. 13:11, 13; cf. 12:5; Deut. 3:14). Subsequently, the king of Maacah joined the Ammonites and Arameans in their unsuccessful war against David (2 Sam. 10:6, 8; 1 Chron. 19:7). Following its defeat, Maacah probably became a tributary to David (2 Sam. 10:19). Maacah and Geshur were evidently absorbed into the expanding Aramean kingdom of Damascus after the time of Solomon.

2 The concubine of Caleb (1 Chron. 2:48).

3 The wife of Machir, Manasseh's son (1 Chron. 7:15–16).

4 The wife of Gibeon, or Jehiel, one of Saul's ancestors (1 Chron. 8:29; 9:35).

5 A princess of Geshur who married David and was the mother of Absalom and Tamar (2 Sam. 3:3).

6 The daughter of Absalom, who became the favorite wife of King Rehoboam and mother of Abijah (1 Kings 15:2; 2 Chron. 11:20–22). She is called Micaiah, the daughter of Uriel, in 2 Chron. 13:2. She was deposed by Asa from her position of queen mother because of her involvement in idolatry (2 Chron. 15:16).

7 A son of Nahor, Abraham's brother (Gen. 22:24).

8 The father of Achish, king of Gath (1 Kings 2:39).

9 The father of Hanun who was one of David's warriors (1 Chron. 11:43).

10 The father of Shephatiah, one of David's officials (1 Chron. 27:16).   D.A.D.

Maaseiah (may´uh-see´yah; Heb., "the work of the Lord").

1 One of David's levitical musicians (1 Chron. 15:18, 20).

2 A commander who joined Jehoiada's temple conspiracy to make Joash king (2 Chron. 23:1).

3 An officer under King Uzziah (2 Chron. 26:11).

4 King Ahaz's son who was killed in the war with Israel (2 Chron. 28:7).

5 The governor of Jerusalem commissioned by Josiah to repair the temple (2 Chron. 28:7).

THE M SOURCE: MATERIAL UNIQUE TO MATTHEW

Genealogy of Jesus (from Abraham)	1:2–17	Peter pays the temple tax	17:24–27
Birth of Jesus (with focus on Joseph)	1:18–25	Recovering the sinful member	18:15–20
Visit of the magi	2:1–12	Peter asks about forgiveness	18:21–22
Flight to Egypt	2:13–21	Parable of Unforgiving Servant	18:23–35
On fulfilling the law	5:17–20	Parable of Laborers in Vineyard	20:1–16
The antitheses	5:21–24,	Parable of Two Sons	21:28–32
	27–28,	Prohibition of titles	23:2–5,
	33–38, 43		7–12
On practicing piety	6:1–15,	Denunciations of Pharisees	23:15–22
	16–18	Parable of Bridesmaids	25:1–13
Pearls before swine	7:6	Description of Last Judgment	25:31–46
Mission limited to Israel	10:5–6	Death of Judas	27:3–10
Invitation to rest	11:28–30	Pilate washes his hands	27:24–25
Parables: Weeds, Treasure, Pearl, Net	13:24–30,	Resuscitation of saints	27:52–53
	36–52	Guard at the tomb	27:62–66;
Peter tries to walk on water	14:28–31		28:11–15
Blessing of Peter	16:17–19	Great Commission	28:16–20

From Mark Allan Powell, *Introducing the New Testament* (courtesy, Baker Academic)

---

6 The father of the priest Zephaniah (Jer. 21:1; 29:25; 37:3); he may be the same as **5.**

7 The father of the false prophet Zedekiah (Jer. 29:21); he may be the same as **5.**

8 The son of Shallum and keeper of the threshold (Jer. 35:4).

9 A name that occurs frequently in lists from the postexilic time. Four persons named Maaseiah are listed as being among those who agreed to divorce their foreign wives in response to Ezra's proclamation (Ezra 10:18, 21, 22, 30). Two of these are probably priests who participated in the dedication of Nehemiah's wall (Neh. 12:41–42). Six persons named Maaseiah are also mentioned elsewhere in Nehemiah, though some of these could be the same person occurring in more than one context (Neh. 3:23; 8:4, 7; 10:25; 11:5, 7).   J.J.M.R.

Maccabees (mak'uh-beez), a family (also known as the Hasmoneans) who provided military, political, and religious leaders for Judea during much of the second and first centuries BCE. The events leading to their rise to prominence are related to the attempt of Antiochus IV Epiphanes, Seleucid king of Syria, to foster Hellenism in Judea by tyrannically suppressing Judaism (see 1 Macc. 1–2; 2 Macc. 5–7). Although some Jews, primarily members of the urban upper classes and including members of the temple priesthood, supported hellenization, many others opposed it, and some, such as the "Hasideans" (1 Macc. 2:42; 7:13; 2 Macc. 14:6), fought actively against it.

Antiochus decreed that sacrifice to the Greek deities be offered in every Judean city and village, and, on the fifteenth day of the month Chislev (Nov./Dec.) in 167 BCE, he caused a pagan altar to be built on the temple altar at Jerusalem, where, on the twenty-fifth of the same month, the first sacrifice to Zeus was made. (This was probably the "abomination that makes desolate" in Dan. 11:31; 12:11; see also 1 Macc. 1:54; 2 Macc. 6:1–5.) A spontaneous revolt against his policies broke out at Modein, a small village eighteen miles northwest of Jerusalem (modern As Medieh). An aged priest named Mattathias lived there with his five sons: John ("Gaddi"), Simon ("Thassi"), Judas ("Maccabeus"), Eleazar ("Avaran"), and Jonathan ("Apphus"). Officials from Antiochus arrived in Modein with orders that everyone was to eat swine flesh and offer a sacrifice to Zeus. Mattathias, in anger, killed both the first Jew who approached the pagan altar to comply and the royal official who was presiding over the required sacrifices. Thus, he and his sons were forced to flee to the hills. They became the nucleus of a growing band of rebels united against Antiochus. Mattathias died soon after the beginning of the revolt, leaving military leadership in the hands of Judas, whose surname "Maccabeus" (probably from the Aramaic word *maqqabah*, meaning "hammer") became the source of the popular name "Maccabees," given to the family and its followers.

Under Judas's leadership, what had begun as a guerrilla war turned into full scale military engagements in which smaller Jewish forces managed to defeat much more powerful Syrian armies. Among Judas's most notable achievements were the recapture of Jerusalem (except for the Akra fortress, where the Syrian garrison continued to hold out) and the rededication of the temple. The date of the rededication, 25 Chislev, 164 BCE, with the attendant eight-day festivities, has since that time been celebrated as Hanukkah, or the Festival of Dedication (see John 10:22). Antiochus Epiphanes died in 164, and for a time Judas continued successfully to press what was now a war for independence. His last great victory was over the forces of the Seleucid commander Nicanor at Beth-horon, on 13 Adar (Feb./March), 161 BCE. In the autumn of that same year, Judas was killed in battle against the vastly superior army of the Syrian general Bacchides, under whose occupation the "pro-Greek" party gained ascendancy in Jerusalem.

The Maccabees, although set back by Judas's defeat and death, continued to fight under Jonathan, who sided with one Seleucid ruler (Alexander Balas) against another (Demetrius) in the ongoing struggle for succession to the Seleucid throne. Although Jonathan succeeded for a time in reestablishing the ascendancy of his party in Judea, he was captured and later murdered by Trypho, the Seleucid ruler of Syria, in 143 or 142 BCE. After his death, he was succeeded by Simon, who was now the only remaining son of Mattathias.

From the Syrians, Simon gained de jure recognition of the de facto independence of Judea achieved by his brothers. From the Jews, he received legitimation of the Hasmonean house as their political and religious leaders. On 18 Elul (Sept.), 140 BCE, in decrees that were publicly displayed on bronze tablets in the temple, Simon was granted the hereditary titles of high priest, commander-in-chief, and ethnarch of the Jews. The Hasmonean dynasty had officially begun. In 134 BCE, Simon was murdered, along with his sons Judas and Mattathias, in a bid for power by his

The earliest known representation of the Jewish menorah is depicted on a bronze coin minted during the reign of the Maccabean king Antigonus II, 40–37 BCE.

THE MACCABEES: A FAMILY TREE

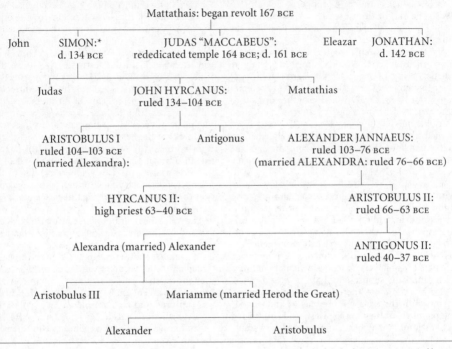

Leaders'/Rulers' names are in capital letters.

son-in-law Ptolemy. Simon's remaining son, John Hyrcanus, after foiling Ptolemy's plan, was confirmed as high priest and ruled with distinction for thirty years (134–104 BCE). During his rule, the Hasmonean state achieved its greatest territorial expansion and political power. At this time, the names "Pharisees" and "Sadducees" make their first appearance, designating rival parties within the Jewish community, and Hyrcanus's break with the former and support of the latter caused much acrimony.

Apparently, the first of the dynasty to assume the title of king was Aristobulus I (104–103 BCE), who is reported, upon the death of John Hyrcanus, his father, to have imprisoned three of his brothers, allowed his mother to starve in prison, and, later, to have caused the death of another brother. All of this was in order that he might assume sole power, contrary to the wishes of his father.

After the death of Aristobulus of a painful illness, his widow, Alexandra, freed the brothers and married one of them, Alexander Jannaeus, whose twenty-seven years of rule (103–76 BCE) were marred externally by war and internally by conflict. Alexandra took the throne in 76 BCE, making her son Hyrcanus II high priest. Reversing the position of her husbands and father-in-law, she was favorable to the Pharisees, who now gained the upper hand over the Sadducees.

After Alexandra's death in 66 BCE, her sons, Aristobulus II and Hyrcanus II, became engaged in a struggle for power, in which Antipater, the military commander of Idumea, played a central role. Rome finally intervened in 63 BCE, when Pompey's legions captured Jerusalem. Aristobulus was taken to Rome as a prisoner to be paraded in Pompey's triumph, and Hyrcanus was left to rule in Jerusalem, no longer as king but as high priest, over a reduced territory (63–40 BCE).

THE MACCABEES: CHRONOLOGY OF LEADERS

Mattathias	167–166 BCE
Judas Maccabeus	166–161 BCE
Jonathan Maccabeus	161–142 BCE
Simon Maccabeus	142–134 BCE
John Hyrcanus	134–104 BCE
Aristobulus	104–103 BCE
Alexander Jannaeus	103–76 BCE
Alexandra Salome	76–66 BCE
Hyrcanus II	66–63 BCE
vs.	
Aristobulus II	66–63 BCE
Hyrcanus II	63–40 BCE
Antigonus	40–37 BCE

In a period of frequent intrigues and political upheavals, in which Antipater the Idumean and his son Herod played major roles, the Maccabean family came to an end with the execution of Antigonus II, who had ruled briefly (40–37 BCE) with Parthian support. The future was with Rome and with Herod, who married Mariamne (granddaughter of both of Alexandra's sons), but who later put her sons, other members of the family, and even Mariamne to death. *See also* Antiochus; Antipater; Hasmoneans; Herod; Seleucids.

F.O.G.

Maccabees, First Book of, a volume that relates the history of the Maccabean revolt from the accession of Antiochus IV Epiphanes to the Seleucid (Syrian) throne in 175 BCE until the death of Simon, one of the leaders of the Jewish resistance and then high priest and ethnarch, in 132 BCE. The book was apparently composed sometime after the death of John Hyrcanus, Simon's son, in 104 BCE, but before the beginning of Roman rule in Judea in 63 BCE. It is the primary source for the history of the period. It may have been originally written in Hebrew; though, if so, that text is no longer extant. The book is, however, preserved in Greek as a part of the LXX. It is considered part of the Apocrypha by Protestant Christians, while Roman Catholic and Orthodox Christians classify it as one of the deuterocanonical writings.

The purpose of 1 Maccabees seems to be to legitimate the Hasmoneans (Maccabees) as rulers of Judea in consequence of the contribution made to the liberation of Judea from Seleucid rule by the founders of the dynasty, Judas, Jonathan, and Simon, the sons of Mattathias. The name "Maccabee" probably comes from the Hebrew or Aramaic word for "hammer"; it was a nickname for Judas, possibly because of the hammerlike blows he dealt the enemy. Eventually, the name came to be applied to the brothers of Judas, as well as to the revolt they led.

The story begins with the Hellenistic "reforms" instituted by the Hellenizers, members of the Jewish aristocracy (the "lawless men" of 1 Maccabees), in association with Antiochus IV. These reforms were intended to turn Jerusalem into a Greek city-state under Greek law, and they led to opposition by a large segment of the Jewish population. Antiochus responds by desecrating the temple and instituting statutes that would essentially abolish the Jewish religion. Circumcision is forbidden, and all Jews would be forced, on pain of death, to consume swine's flesh and offer sacrifices to Zeus. At the forefront of the initial opposition to these policies are the Hasideans, but the focus soon shifts to the revolution led by the Maccabees, who seek, not only religious freedom, but, ultimately, political independence and power.

First Mattathias, and then his sons, one after another, lead the resistance to the Syrians with their Greek ways. The temple is liberated and cleansed in 164 BCE under Judas, and Jonathan later becomes high priest. Simon finally secures liberty and be-

comes both high priest and ethnarch before his assassination by Ptolemy, the governor of Jericho, in 132 BCE. Aiding in the fight for independence is a protracted power struggle within the Seleucid Empire after the death of Antiochus IV in 163 BCE as well as the emergence of Rome as a major power in the Near East. *See also* Apocrypha/deuterocanonical literature; Maccabees; Maccabees, Second Book of.

D.W.S.

Maccabees, Second Book of, an alternative history of the Maccabean revolt, written from a different perspective than 1 Maccabees. Where the latter is concerned to praise Judas, Jonathan, and Simon for their role in the liberation of the Jewish people from Seleucid oppression, 2 Maccabees focuses upon the insult to the temple and its cult, for which it holds the Jewish Hellenizers primarily responsible. Judas Maccabeus is honored as the sole leader of the resistance. The narrative concludes with his defeat of Nicanor, the Syrian governor of Judea (14:12), ending a major threat to the sanctity of the rededicated temple. Judas is even described at one point as a leader of the Hasideans (Hasidim), in curious contrast to 1 Maccabees, where the Hasideans are a separate group focused only on religious freedom and the Maccabees are also intent on achieving political power. The period covered by 2 Maccabees is ca. 180–161 BCE.

Although 1 Maccabees is generally considered to be more reliable historically than 2 Maccabees, the latter book is of value because it describes in greater detail the Hellenistic reform and the origin of the revolt prior to the emergence of the Maccabees, and because it provides greater insight into the history of the Jewish religion. It represents an epitome, or condensation, of a five-volume history written by an otherwise unknown Jason of Cyrene probably sometime after 110 BCE. The original language was probably Greek, and the condensation survived as a part of the LXX. Protestant Christians treat 2 Maccabees as a part of the Apocrypha, while Roman Catholics and Orthodox Christians classify it as one of the deuterocanonical books.

Second Maccabees is generally termed a "pathetic" history (from Gk. *pathos,* "emotion" or "feeling"), because it presents the righteous martyrs or the wicked king in a manner designed to evoke pity or contempt in readers (6:10–11, 18–31; 7:1–42). The writer develops a theology of history in 6:12–17, which echoes the point of view of the Deuteronomistic school (see Judg. 2:11–23). This view holds that, because the Jews themselves profaned the temple when the Hellenizers Jason and Menelaus used its treasure and vessels to buy the high-priesthood from Antiochus, God disciplines them by permitting Antiochus to desecrate the temple (throughout the book God's punishment tends to fit the crime; see 4:38; 9:5–6; 13:8). Repentance, however, ensures that God will protect the Jews from their enemies by sending a leader like Judas and by responding from heaven with a manifestation of supernatural power in defense of temple or people (2:21; 3:22–40; 5:18; 9:5; 10:29–31; 15:22–27). The righteous who perish in the process can expect the resurrection of the dead (7:9–11; 12:44; 14:46), and they are able to intercede on behalf of the living (15:12). Sin offerings on the part of the dead are also possible (12:39–45). Thus, 2 Maccabees is an important piece of evidence for the development of the idea of the resurrection of the dead in the period between the composition of the Hebrew Bible (where it is just barely mentioned in such passages as Isa. 26:19; Dan. 12:2) and the origin of Christianity. *See also* Apocrypha/deuterocanonical literature; Maccabees; Maccabees, First Book of.   D.W.S.

Maccabees, Third Book of, a book that, despite its name, recounts the persecution of the Jews in the era *prior* to the Maccabees. It concerns attempts by the Egyptian ruler Ptolemy IV Philopator (221–203 BCE) to persecute Jews throughout his realm, first through registration and enslavement enforced by threats of death, and finally by transporting them to the hippodrome at Alexandria to be slaughtered by a herd of enraged elephants (cf. Josephus *Against Apion* 2:53–56, for a version of the same story set a century later). God intervenes through two angels (cf. 2 Macc. 3:25–26), and the elephants trample the king's army, leading to Ptolemy's repentance. The Jews of Alexandria then establish an annual festival to celebrate their deliverance in a manner reminiscent of the institution of Purim after the attempted pogrom of Jews in the book of Esther. The narrative reaches its high points in the prayers of two

priests, which evoke Solomon's temple prayer in 1 Kings 8, emphasizing the centrality of the temple and the efficacy of priestly prayers.

Third Maccabees was composed in pseudo-classical Greek, probably by a Jew living in Egypt. The concern for the citizenship status of Egyptian Jews suggests a date in the late first century BCE or, possibly, a later date during the reign of the Roman emperor Gaius Caligula (37–41 CE), during which a threat to the temple also coincided with a crisis for Alexandrian Jews (cf. Philo *Embassy to Gaius*). The book has not been regarded as scripture (not even as part of the Apocrypha or deuterocanonical writings) by Jews or Christians in the West. It was, however, included in some (but not all) manuscripts of the LXX, and it is regarded as canonical by Eastern Orthodox Christians. *See also* Apocrypha/deuterocanonical literature; Septuagint.   D.W.S.

of her gender and even her maternal affection (14:11–16:25). She then commits suicide to avoid being touched by the soldiers in any way that would compromise her lifelong devotion to purity, demonstrating that in women as well as men reason and courage are capable of triumphing over emotions (17:1–4). The martyrs are presented as anticipating the eternal life of their souls in the presence of God (cf. Wis. 3–5), in contrast to 2 Maccabees, where they anticipate the resurrection of their bodies and the restoration of physical life.

Composed in a florid Asiatic style of Greek, 4 Maccabees may come from the middle of the first century CE, perhaps from the time of the Roman emperor Gaius Caligula (37–41 CE). Its place of composition is uncertain, but could have been Alexandria, Jerusalem, or Antioch. The book has not been regarded as scripture (not even as part of the Apocrypha or deuterocanonical writings) by Jews or Christians in the West. It was, however, included in some (but not all) manuscripts of the LXX and out of respect for its piety and antiquity it is sometimes printed as an appendix to 3 Maccabees in Greek Orthodox Bibles. *See also* Apocrypha/deuterocanonical literature; Maccabees; Septuagint. D.W.S.

Maccabees, Fourth Book of, a work composed in memory of the martyrs mentioned in 2 Macc. 6–7. Its theme is the rule of religious reason and the four cardinal virtues—prudence, temperance, courage, and justice—over the emotions. The priest Eleazar and the seven brothers who are tortured and killed along with their mother in 2 Macc. 6–7 are shown to be prime examples of these virtues. Although the discussion of reason and the virtues reflects Stoic philosophy, the argument in favor of reason and virtue is decidedly Jewish, substituting for the Stoic emphasis on the rule of nature (4 Macc. 5:8–9) obedience to the Mosaic law, which becomes the essence of true wisdom (cf. Sir. 24:23), which is defended as consistent with nature (4 Macc. 5:25–26).

After a discussion of reason and the emotions, illustrated with biblical examples, 4 Maccabees turns to the story of the violation of the temple from 2 Macc. 3. The stories of the martyrdoms follow, and they are told in longer and more graphic versions than in 2 Maccabees. In an allusion to Isa. 53:8–12, Eleazar prays that his death may atone for the sins of others (4 Macc. 6:28–29; cf. Mark 10:45). In the climax to 4 Maccabees, the mother, who has watched her seven sons being tortured to death before her, delivers a long speech on how commitment to religion and to the law has enabled her to triumph, overcoming the weakness

Macedonia (mas'uh-doh'nee-uh), a region in the northeastern part of the Greek peninsula. In the English Bible, it is referred to only in the NT. The cities of Neapolis, Philippi, Thessalonica, and Beroea were all part of the Roman province of Macedonia during the NT era. Paul made his first European converts to Christianity in Macedonia (Acts 16:9–17:14). According to the book of Acts, he had intended to go to Bithynia in Asia, but the Spirit of Jesus would not allow it (16:7). Then he had a vision of a man from Macedonia, calling to him, "Come over here." He set sail from Troas, landed at Neapolis and traveled up to Philippi (16:9–12). Paul mentions in his letters his initial journey (ca. 50 CE) from Philippi to Thessalonica

and then south to Athens, which was part of the province of Greece (1 Thess. 2:2; 2:17–3:2; Phil. 4:15–16). He also mentions a second visit to Macedonia (ca. 55 CE; 2 Cor. 2:13; 7:5; see also Acts 20:1–6). His reference in 1 Thess. 4:10 to "brothers and sisters throughout Macedonia" seems to presuppose the existence of other early Christian communities besides Philippi and Thessalonica; on the founding of a church in Beroea see Acts 17:10–12.

History of the Region: The name Macedonia originally designated only the great river plain at the head of the Thermaic Gulf. Here invaders of Dorian extraction established a united kingdom about 640 BCE. In the following three centuries this kingdom contended against its immediate neighbors (Illyrians, Thracians, and northern tribal groups) and against outside powers such as Persia, Athens, and Sparta. Although strongly influenced by Hellenic culture especially after 450 BCE, it retained its independence and slowly expanded, especially into the mountainous north. In the fourth century BCE Philip II (359–336 BCE) annexed these contested northern areas and added the Strymon Valley and the Chalcidicean Peninsula to his kingdom to form the most powerful state in Greece. His son, Alexander III ("the Great"), used this in turn as a base from which to conquer a vast empire stretching to Egypt and India (cf. 1 Macc. 1:1; 6:2). After Alexander's death (323 BCE) this empire broke apart, and Macedonia itself experienced considerable dynastic strife during the next century and a half. Rome decisively defeated the Macedonian army at Pydna (168 BCE) and in 148 BCE established Macedonia as a province with its capital at Thessalonica. Roman engineers began immediately (146 BCE) to construct an arterial military and commercial road, the Via Egnatia, from the Adriatic coast through Pella, Thessalonica, Amphipolis, Philippi, and Neapolis in Macedonia to Byzantium in Asia Minor; portions of this still survive. The apostle

Paul probably traveled the Neapolis–Thessalonica segment of this road (Acts 16:11–17:1). During the struggle for power at the end of the Roman Republic, Macedonia suffered much devastation from the armies that traversed it, and major battles were fought at nearby Pharsalus (48 BCE) and at Philippi (42 BCE). Economic recovery began under Emperor Augustus (27 BCE–14 CE), and by 44 CE Macedonia no longer required direct imperial rule. It was then governed by a senatorial proconsul. *See also* Alexander; Beroea; Neapolis; Philippi; Thessalonica.   R.A.W.

Machaerus (muh-kee'ruhs), a fortress-palace some 3,600 feet above the Dead Sea, about fifteen miles southeast of the mouth of the Jordan River. A fortress built on the site by Alexander Jannaeus (103–76 BCE) was destroyed by Pompey's general Gabinius; it was then extensively rebuilt by Herod the Great to include a palace within the fortress. Because of its proximity to Arabia and its location above the north–south road from the Red Sea to Damascus, the site was regarded as strategically important by Herod Antipas, tetrarch of Galilee and Perea (4 BCE–39 CE). According to the Jewish historian Josephus, Machaerus was the site of the imprisonment and death of John the Baptist (Matt. 14:3–12; Mark 6:17–29). *See also* John the Baptist.   M.K.M.

Machir (may'kihr; Heb., possibly "property [of God]").

1 The son of Ammiel from Lo-debar who harbored Mephibosheth, Saul's grandson (2 Sam. 9:4–5), and was an ally of David (2 Sam. 17:27).

2 Either the oldest (Josh. 17:1–2) or only (Num. 26:29) son of Manasseh. His mother was Aramean (1 Chron. 7:16), and his wife was named Maacah (1 Chron. 7:16). Some traditions claim that his sons conquered the Transjordan region of Gilead (Num. 32:39–40; Deut. 3:15) or even both Gilead and Bashan (Josh. 17:1), while other traditions suggest that they lived west of the Jordan (Judg. 5:14, 17).   M.Z.B.

Machpelah (mak-pee'luh; Heb., perhaps "double"), the burial place of Sarah, Abraham, Isaac, Rebekah, Jacob, and Leah. Both the "cave of Machpelah" (Gen. 23:9; 25:9) and the "field of Machpelah" (23:17, 19; 49:30; 50:13) are mentioned. Abraham purchased the site from Ephron the Hittite for four hundred shekels of silver. The account of the purchase is given in meticulous detail in Gen. 23, emphasizing that their burial place was the only land that the patriarchs owned in Canaan. According to the biblical tradition, the field with its cave was located east of Mamre (23:17), a city identified with Hebron (23:19).

The tradition concerning Machpelah is mentioned in the *Testaments of the Twelve Patriarchs*, *Jubilees* (46:4–10), and in Josephus's *Antiquities* (1.21.1; 2.8.2). Elsewhere, Josephus reports that there were in his time impressive monuments to Abraham and the other ancestors in the town of Hebron (*Jewish War* 4.9.7). Herod had built a wall around the traditional burial place and probably had set up the monuments that Josephus describes. Acts 7:15–16, however, places the tomb "that Abraham had bought," not in Hebron, but in Shechem. *See also* Hebron.   G.M.T.

madness, a state of irrationality or temporary insanity. In biblical times, madness was generally attributed to some spirit or power that took over a person's mind. Deut. 28:28 lists it among the curses that will come upon people who do not keep the covenant: "The LORD will afflict you with madness, blindness, and confusion of mind." Likewise, in Zech. 2:14, God says that, on the day of judgment coming for Jerusalem, "I will strike every horse with panic, and its rider with madness." In biblical narrative, Saul is a primary example of someone afflicted with madness. When God's spirit left King Saul to rest on David, Saul was "tormented by an evil spirit from the LORD" (1 Sam. 16:14–17). This spirit caused outbreaks of violence in which Saul attempted to kill David (18:10–11; 19:9). David himself later feigned madness before the Philistine ruler Achish (21:10–15; cf. the superscription to Ps. 34, which mistakenly reads Ahimelech in place of Achish). In the NT, madness takes the form of demonic possession (e.g., Mark 5:1–13; 9:14–29), but it is also brought up as a charge against John the Baptist (Matt. 11:18), Jesus (Mark 3:21–22; John 8:48), and the apostle Paul (Acts 26:24).   P.P./M.A.P.

Magadan (mag'uh-dan), an unknown region referred to in Matt. 15:39 as the area in which Jesus fed the four thousand. Some manuscripts read Magdala or Magdalan; but Mark 8:10 has Dalmanutha.

Magdala (mag'duh-luh), a fishing town (modern Migdal, called Tarichaeae in Josephus) on the western shore of the Sea of Galilee between Capernaum to the north and Tiberias to the south. It appears to have been larger than nearby Capernaum. Excavations have uncovered fishing implements like hooks, anchors, and net weights as well as a small synagogue, whose date is disputed. The site appears to have followed a more regular grid pattern than most villages, and construction techniques indicate a somewhat wealthier town than Capernaum or Chorazin. Mary "from Magdala" figures among Jesus's women disciples (Luke 8:2) and is reported to have been one of the first witnesses to his resurrection (Matt. 27:56, 61; 28:1; Mark 15:40, 47; 16:1; Luke 24:10; John 19:25; 20:1, 18).

Magdalene, Mary. *See* Mary.

magi (may'ji).
1 Sorcerers who, according to Matt. 2, traveled to honor the infant Jesus when he was born. The NRSV's "wise men" is an inaccurate translation for the Greek *magoi* (Lat. *magi*), which comes from a root meaning "magic." The notice in Matthew that

these magi were "from the East" (2:1) could refer to Arabia, Mesopotamia, or elsewhere. They are portrayed as astrologers, since they are guided by the star (2:2). They are probably assumed to be Gentiles (though the text does not explicitly say this) and, as such, their early homage to Jesus foreshadows the later commission to make disciples of Gentiles with which Matthew's Gospel closes. Thus, it is somewhat ironic that the magi are the first people in the narrative to call Jesus the "king of the Jews" (2:2), a title that comes up again in Matthew's passion narrative (27:11, 29, 37). When the magi arrive in Judea, making inquiries as to the newborn king's whereabouts, they attract the attention of Herod, who sends them to Bethlehem (where, according to his religious scholars, the scriptures say the Messiah will be born). Herod is only helping the magi because, once they have found the infant Jesus, he wants them to tell him where the child is, so he can dispose of the potential threat to his throne (2:3–8, 16). The story, however, emphasizes God's guidance of the magi; the star goes ahead of them in a way that recalls the two pillars, of cloud and of fire, that led the Israelites in the wilderness (2:9; Exod. 13:21). Finally, it stops over the place where the child is, indicating the very house in which the infant Jesus is to be found (2:10–11). The magi become the first people to worship Jesus, kneeling before the child and Mary, his mother (2:12). They open their treasures to him (cf. 6:19–21), giving him gifts of gold, frankincense, and myrrh. They continue to be guided by God, who sends an angel to warn them in a dream not to return to Herod, who had wanted them to tell him where Jesus had been born.

Nonbiblical sources reveal that magi were associated primarily with Persia, where they were members of a priestly class learned in astrology and other magical arts, including divination, dream interpretation, and the concoction of potions. Strabo says, "They attend the Persian kings . . . guiding them in their relations with the

The three magi of the Matthean account of Jesus's birth (2:1–18) as depicted in the mosaics at San Apollinaire in Classe, Ravenna, Italy, sixth century.

gods" (15.1.68). In a more popular sense, however, magi had come to be associated with magicians and sorcerers in general. Thus, it was common by the time Matthew's Gospel was written to identify Pharaoh's sorcerers in the exodus narrative as magi (cf. Exod. 7:11, 22; 8:6, 18; 9:11) and also to identify Balaam, the hapless prophet who is hired to curse Israel in Num. 22–24, as a magus (the singular form of the word). Those identifications are made explicit in the writings of Philo of Alexandria (*Life of Moses I* 16.92; 50.276) as well as in Jewish midrashes that are likely to be reflective of this period (*b. Sanh.* 101a; *Sota* 11a; *Midr. Exod.* I. 9, 18). Furthermore, the LXX actually uses the Greek word *magoi* for the Chaldean sorcerers in Dan. 2:2, 10; thus, the Babylonian magicians at the court of Nebuchadnezzar are called by the same term used for the magi referred to in Matt. 2. It is uncertain how much Matthew or his intended readers would have known about the priestly class of magi in Persia or about the specifics of magian lore that constituted their beliefs and practices, but they certainly would have thought of magi as practitioners of sorcery and astrology in a more generic and popular sense of the word.

How such persons were regarded in the world of the NT is a matter of some ambiguity. Cicero refers to magi as "wise and learned among the Persians" (*Concerning Divination I* 23.47), while Tacitus denounces their arts as "absurdities" (*Annals II* 27–33). Magi seem sometimes to be regarded as learned sages (something akin to ancient scientists) or as holy men who possessed access to supernatural powers. But in any number of instances, they are also dismissed as seducers, deceivers, and experts in nonsense. Suetonius reports that Tiberius banished astrologers from Rome in 19 CE, apparently because he considered their so-called arts to be worthless (*Tiberius* 36). The Jewish perspective tended toward negative evaluation: the magi in Dan. 2 (LXX) are incompetent sorcerers, unable to interpret the king's dream, the meaning of which must be revealed (to Daniel) by God. Philo of Alexandria presents the magus Balaam as a supposedly wise man who is actually the "most foolish of all men" (*Life of Moses I* 293), stupider than his donkey. Once he experiences true prophetic inspiration from the Lord, he comes to despise the "lore of knowledge on which he had once prided himself" (*Life of Moses I* 292). Against such a background, it seems likely that the author and original readers of Matthew's Gospel would have been more inclined to read the story of the magi as an account of God's gracious revelation of sacred truth to pagan fools rather than as an endorsement of astrological lore through which wise men find Christ (while those who study the scriptures do not). *See also* astrologer; stars.

2 Elymas Bar-Jesus (Acts 13:6–12), identified as a magus in the Greek text of the NT (NRSV: "magician," 13:6, 8). He is presented as a servant to Sergius Paulus, proconsul of Cyprus. The book of Acts calls him a "Jewish false prophet," but his role as a magician-counselor to a political ruler is analogous to the role of the magi proper, magician-priests who served Persian kings (see in 1 above). Josephus relates a similar story about a magus named Atomos who served Felix, the governor of Judea, and used his arts to secure the latter's marriage to Drusilla (*Antiquities* 20.142; cf. Acts 24–25). *See also* Elymas.

3 The man popularly known as Simon Magus (Acts 8:9–24), although he is not actually called a magus in the NRSV or in the Greek text of the NT. Rather, he is identified as a worker of magic (*mageuōn;* 8:9; cf. 8:11, *mageia*). Accordingly, he is not to be considered a member of the official class of magi (i.e., the Persian priests), but is simply a magician or sorcerer in some unidentified or generic sense. The same, however, is probably true also of Elymas in 2 above (who is called a magus), and possibly also of the magi in 1. *See also* Simon.

Bibliography

Powell, Mark Allan. *Chasing the Eastern Star.* Westminster John Knox, 2001.

Trexler, Richard C. *The Journey of the Magi.* Princeton University Press, 1997. M.A.P.

magic, means by which humans attempt to secure for themselves some action from superhuman powers. Magic is an attempt by human beings to compel a divinity to do what they wish that divinity to do. Divination is an attempt to secure information about matters and events that are currently hidden or that lie in the future. The word "magus," from which the word "magic" is derived, came originally from Persia, where it designated a priestly class. From there, it spread to all nations in the Mediterranean world. Magical practices are as old as the written records of humanity, and, in the world of the Bible, they can be found in ancient Mesopotamian, Egyptian, and Greek documents. Although a systematic presentation of the theory of magic did not appear in Greco-Roman literature until the third and fourth centuries CE, the general principles upon which the practice of magic was based were more or less accepted by all. These principles may be summarized briefly as follows. A host of intermediary spiritual beings exist between gods and humans. Depending on their proximity to the gods, these spirits possess divine power in diminishing measures. Those closest to the gods have bodies of air; those closest to humans, bodies of steam or water. Because of this descending order, the unity of the cosmos can be preserved. Otherwise, human and divine would be irreparably separated and no communication between the two would be possible. Everything is connected through the spirits who mediate between the divine and material realms. Magic rests upon the belief that by controlling the spirits that inhabit physical objects, the gods can be influenced. The magician's art is to find out which material (metal, herb, animal, etc.) contains which spirits, the degree to which they can be controlled, and how. The connection established might be either sympathetic or antipathetic. Thus magic can achieve either blessing or curse.

Magic could be practiced on various levels. At a fairly high level, there were professional court magicians, such as the sorcerers at Pharaoh's court in Egypt with whom Moses and Aaron had to compete (Exod. 8:5–9:12), the Babylonian sorcerers at the court of King Nebuchadnezzar mentioned in Dan. 1–2; Elymas Bar-Jesus, the magus who served the Roman proconsul Sergius Paulus (Acts 13:6–12), and possibly the magi who came to the infant Jesus in Matt. 2:1–12. At the opposite end of the scale were the "impostors" (2 Tim. 3:13) who relied on tricks to deceive people into thinking they had magical powers when they did not. Between these would be any number of sorcerers, enchanters, and charmers who could cast spells and who knew how to use herbs, potions, and drugs. Simon the magician mentioned in Acts 8:9–14 is perhaps best thought of in this category. Likewise, Acts 19:17–19 says that after many Jews and Greeks came to believe in Jesus in Ephesus, "a number of those who practiced magic collected their books and burned them publicly." It is possible that some of these book burners are to be regarded as professional magicians who were abandoning their trade (since the cost of their books was considerable, computed as fifty thousand silver coins). But it is also possible that some of the Ephesians who "practiced magic" were amateur enthusiasts, for magical lore and writings were widely available to the general public. It is well established, for instance, that protective amulets were often worn by people from all social classes during the NT period; such items are often found in archaeological excavations.

Deut. 18:10–11 makes clear that the practice of magic and divination is forbidden among the Israelites: "No one shall be found among you who makes a son or daughter pass through fire, or who practices divination, or is a soothsayer, or an augur, or a sorcerer, or one who casts spells, or who consults ghosts or spirits, or who seeks oracles from the dead." King Manasseh of Israel is said to have done evil in the eyes of the Lord, because he "practiced soothsaying and augury, and dealt with mediums and with wizards" (2 Kings 21:6). The apostle Paul lists works of sorcery among the despicable works of the flesh that are to be contrasted with the appealing fruit of God's Holy Spirit (Gal. 5:20). (See also Isa. 8:19; 44:25; 47:12–15; Rev. 21:8; 22:15)

Nevertheless, religious and historical scholars often note that terms like "sorcery" (Heb. *kesheph*, 2 Chron. 33:6; Nah. 3:4; Gk. *pharmakeia*, Wis. 12:4; Gal. 5:20; Rev. 18:23) and "magic" (Gk. *mageia*, Wis. 17:7; 18:13; Acts 8:9, 11, 19) can be used in a polemical vein to denounce acts associated with rival or foreign religions, without disparagement of comparable practices within one's own faith system. The Romans accused early Christians of practicing magic, and some of the practices of ancient Israel might have been polemically regarded as magical arts by adherents to other religions. For example, the bronze serpent made by Moses and placed on a pole could have

been easily understood as a magical totem (Num. 21:4–9; 2 Kings 18:4; cf. John 3:14–15). In magic rituals, physical contact with an empowered person could have beneficial consequences. In the Bible, Elijah healed the son of the widow of Zarephath by stretching "himself upon the child three times" (1 Kings 17:17–24). The same miracle was repeated by Elisha with the son of the Shunamite (2 Kings 4:31–37). Further, physical items connected with magicians or wizards were believed to absorb and sometimes transmit the person's power. So Elijah's mantle parted the waters of the Jordan, and when Elisha put it on Elijah's spirit rested on him (2 Kings 2:8–15). Likewise, in the NT, the garment of Jesus transmits healing power (Mark 5:28–29), as do the handkerchiefs and aprons that people carried away from the body of Paul (Acts 19:11–12). Some believers even attributed beneficial properties to the shadow of Peter (Acts 5:15). And in Acts, the Holy Spirit is given through the laying on of the apostles' hands, a phenomenon that Simon the magician seems to think is a work of magic—and one that he would like to add to his own repertoire (8:9–24). The Gospel of Mark contains a number of stories in which Jesus heals people with the aid of physical properties (e.g., spit or dirt) or in which he speaks foreign-sounding words like "Ephphatha!" (Aramaic for "Be opened!"); such tales may have struck some early readers as presenting Jesus in a manner similar to magicians, who often applied salves and ointments or spoke secret words that people believed to be imbued with spiritual power (cf. Mark 5:41; 6:13; 7:33–34; 8:23, 25); scholars who think that Matthew and Luke used Mark's Gospel as a source often note that they removed these features of the healing stories from their accounts, perhaps because they wanted to avoid giving readers this impression.

The Bible does, however, exhibit one particularly strong indication that appeals to the God of Israel are not to be construed as magic. Perhaps the single greatest source of magical power for most practitioners of the arts was possession of a god's name, which could then be used to manipulate or control that deity. This might stand behind the prohibition against taking God's name in vain in the Ten Commandments (Exod. 20:7; Deut. 5:11). At any rate, the Israelites decided early on that the name of their God was not to be pronounced aloud; thus, the name was written as the Tetragrammaton, the four consonants YHWH (Exod. 3:13–15). In the NT, the name of Jesus is invoked for baptisms, healings, and exorcisms, but a story in Acts 19:13–16 sends a warning against the use of his name as a magical formula. Further, according to Rev. 19:12, Jesus "has a name inscribed which no one knows but himself." *See also* amulet; divination; miracles; Urim and Thummim.

Bibliography

Dickie, Matthew W. *Magic and Magicians in the Greco-Roman World*. Routledge, 2003.

Graf, Fritz. *Magic in the Ancient World*. Harvard University Press, 1998.

Janowitz, Naomi. *Magic in the Roman World: Pagans, Jews, and Christians.* Routledge, 2001.

Labahn, Michael. *A Kind of Magic: Understanding Magic in the New Testament and Its Religious Environment.* Clark, 2000.

Luck, Georg. *Arcana Mundi: Magic and the Occult in the Greek and Roman Worlds: A Collection of Ancient Texts.* 2nd ed. Johns Hopkins University Press, 1985.   S.B./M.A.P.

magicians. *See* magic.

magistrate, an official who exercised certain administrative functions in cities of the Roman Empire. Magistrates were elected annually and were typically the highest state officials in an individual city or town. They were responsible for maintenance of public works and the preservation of civil order. Magistrates quieted sedition (Luke 12:11), settled various disputes (Acts 16:20–22), and jailed troublemakers or debtors (Luke 12:58; Acts 16:35–38).

Magnificat (mag-nif'uh-kat; from Lat., "to magnify"), a traditional name for the psalm spoken by Mary, the soon to be mother of Jesus, when she visited her relative Elizabeth, who would soon become the mother of John the Baptist (Luke 1:46–55). The psalm begins, "My soul magnifies the Lord, and my spirit rejoices in God my Savior." It is modeled on the Song of Hannah (1 Sam. 2:1–10) and expresses praise to God for selecting Mary to be a participant in the mighty divine act, for God's care for the lowly, poor, and powerless (a strong Lukan theme and emphasis), and for God's bringing to fulfillment the promise made to Abraham in and through the coming of Mary's son. *See also* Elizabeth; Hannah; Mary, Virgin.   J.M.E.

Magog (may'gog). *See* Gog.

Magus (may'guhs), **Simon.** *See* Simon.

Mahalalel (muh-hal'uh-luhl; Heb., "praise of El [God]").
1 The son of Kenan and descendant of Seth (Gen. 5:12); the Greek form of the name is Mahalaleel (Luke 3:37).
2 A descendant of Judah belonging to the Perez line (Neh. 11:4).

Mahalath (may'huh-lath; Heb., "mild").
1 The granddaughter of Abraham, the daughter of Ishmael, and one of the wives of Esau (Gen. 28:9).
2 The wife of King Rehoboam of Judah (ca. 922–915 BCE) and the granddaughter of David (2 Chron. 11:18).
3 A term of unknown significance that occurs in the titles of Pss. 53 and 88. It may be a musical notation, referring to a melody or rhythm pattern. *See also* Psalms, book of.

Mahanaim (may'huh-nay'im; Heb., "the camp"), a city in Gilead, in the tribal territory of Gad near its border with Manasseh (Josh. 13:26, 30). It is first mentioned in Gen. 32:2 as the place where Jacob stayed before his encounter with Esau; when the "messengers of God" met him there Jacob said, "This is God's camp!" (cf. 32:10). Later, Mahanaim was a levitical city assigned to the family of Merari (Josh. 21:38; 1 Chron. 6:80) and the capital of a Solomonic district (1 Kings 4:14). Strategically situated near the confluence of the Jordan and the Jabbok, Mahanaim was the city in which Ishbaal and his supporters were based when David became king of Judah after Saul's death (2 Sam. 2:8, 12, 29). Ironically, David himself fled there during Absalom's revolt (2 Sam. 17:24, 27; 19:33; 1 Kings 2:18). The exact location of the site is uncertain. *See also* Jabbok.   M.D.C.

Mahaneh-dan (may'hun-uh-dan'; Heb., "camp of Dan"), the location in Judah where the Spirit of the Lord began to stir Samson (Judg. 13:25), and where the Danites encamped when they were en route to Ephraim (18:12). The exact location is unknown, but it was in the area of Zorah and Eshtaol (13:25), west of Kiriath-jearim.

Mahath (may'hath), a Levite, the father of Elkanah. He participated in the cleansing of the temple during Hezekiah's reforms (2 Chron. 29:12) and later shared the responsibility of collecting the temple offerings (31:13). He may be the same Levite who belonged to the Kohath line (1 Chron. 6:35). Some writers suggest that he is identical with Ahimoth, the son of Elkanah (6:25). Such identifications are complicated by the fact that several different men called Elkanah are apparently grouped together in the latter text (cf. 1 Chron. 6:23–26, 34–36). *See also* Elkanah.

Maher-shalal-hash-baz (may'huhr-shal'al-hash'baz; Heb., "the spoil speeds, the prey hastens"), the second or third son of Isaiah to receive a symbolic name. His name assured Judah that it need not fear Damascus and Samaria, since they would soon be plundered (8:1–4).

Mahlah (mah'luh).
1 One of the daughters of Zelophehad of the tribe of Manasseh. She and her sisters appealed to Moses and won the right to inherit their father's property, since he had died with no male heirs (Num. 27:1–5; Josh. 17:3). Their appeal led to a statutory ordinance that allowed women the right of inheritance (Num. 27:7–11). A later appeal by other Manassites who feared this law would result in the dispersal of tribal lands brought a modification of the law that required the daughters to marry within the family group of their tribe to be eligible for the inheritance (Num. 36:1–12). That the names of Zelophehad's five daughters also designated territories has been suggested by Samarian ostraca ca. 775–750 BCE. Mahlah is not named on

these ostraca, but Noah and Hoglah, the names of two other daughters of Zelophehad, are. The people regarded as descendants of Mahlah and who may have called their territory by that name would have lived north and east of Samaria. *See also* law; Zelophehad.

2 A descendant of Manasseh (1 Chron. 7:18).

D.R.B.

Mahli (mah′li).

1 A Levite who was the son of Merari and brother of Mushi. He is mentioned in the genealogy of Exod. 6:19 as well as in various lists of levitical families (cf. 1 Chron. 6:19, 29; 23:21; 24:26; Ezra 8:18). He was the ancestor of the Mahlites, who had specific responsibilities in the operation of the tabernacle (Num. 3:20, 33–36).

2 A Levite who was the son of Mushi (thus, the nephew of **1**) and grandson of Merari (1 Chron. 6:47; 23:23; 24:30).

Mahlon (mah′lon; Heb., possibly "sickly, diseased"), the son of Elimelech and Naomi, with whom he immigrated to Moab during the period of the judges (Ruth 1:1–2, 5; 4:9–10). He married Ruth, a Moabite woman, but died childless. The book named after his widow, Ruth, tells how she ultimately bore a son who was regarded as heir to Mahlon's estate as well as to that of Boaz, Ruth's new husband.

Mahol (may′hol; Heb., "dance"), the father of the wise men Heman, Calcol, and Darda (1 Kings 4:31). These children are among those to whom the wisdom of Solomon is compared, when it is asserted that Solomon was wiser than anyone else.

maid, a female servant, usually a slave. In the NRSV, the female in charge of a maid is called her "mistress" (Ps. 123:2; Prov. 30:23; Isa. 24:2). In Genesis, Laban gives his maid Zilpah to Leah to be her maid, and his maid Bilhah to Rachel to be her maid (29:24, 29). Both Leah and Rachel subsequently give their maids to their husband, Jacob, as surrogate wives, so they end up becoming ancestors of four of the twelve tribes of Israel (30:3–18; 35:25–26). In Egypt, the daughter of Pharaoh has her maid fetch the basket containing the baby Moses from among the reeds at the river (Exod. 2:5). In the book of Acts a maid named Rhoda comes to open the outer gate at the home of John Mark's mother, but she is so surprised to realize Peter is there (thinking him in prison or dead) that she leaves him outside knocking while reporting his presence to those within the house (12:13–16).

mail. *See* dress.

Makkedah (muh-kee′duh), one of sixteen cities in the Shephelah (an area southwest of Jerusalem) assigned to the tribe of Judah (Josh. 15:41). Its precise location is not known. Mentioned alongside Azekah (about twelve miles west of Jerusalem) as

the end of Joshua's rout of the five kings attacking Gibeon, Makkedah is the place where those kings were found hiding in a cave and then slain. Joshua subsequently took the city of Makkedah and killed its king (10:16–28). *See also* Azekah; Gibeon.

Malachi (mal′uh-ki), **book of,** the last section of the Book of the Twelve in the Prophets section, or Nevi'im, in the Tanakh (Jewish Bible). In the Christian OT, it is both the last of the Minor Prophets and the last book of the OT. In the Tanakh, there are fifty-five verses spanning three chapters, whereas the OT makes a chapter break after v. 18 of chap. 3 to make a fourth chapter.

Contents: The book of Malachi begins with a superscription identifying it as an oracle of the word of the Lord that came by way of Malachi (Heb., "my messenger"). A series of six oracles follows. The first oracle (1:2–5) compares Israel (Jacob) and Edom (Esau), proclaiming God's love of Israel in contrast to Edom. The second oracle (1:6–2:9) shows God's contempt for the inferior animals that the priests and people are offering. The third oracle (2:10–16) is a rebuke of Jewish husbands for divorcing their wives in order to marry foreign women. The fourth oracle (2:17–3:5) is a promise that God will send a messenger to purify the priests and people. The fifth oracle (3:6–12) condemns the withholding of tithes and offerings. The last oracle is a promise that God will remember the righteous in Israel and save them from the wicked (3:13–4:3). Most scholars believe that 4:4–6 contains two editorial appendices. The first is an appeal to hold to the law given to Moses, while the second is an identification of the messenger of 3:1 with the prophet Elijah. Thus, these appendices contain references to both the greatest

OUTLINE OF CONTENTS

Malachi

harbinger of the law (Moses) and the ideal prophet (Elijah). Some scholars hold they were intended to be additions to the book of Malachi, while others hold that these were added as an appendix to the Book of the Twelve as a whole in order to close the collection of prophetic writings with an allusion to Elijah and Moses.

Background: Very little information is known about the author of the book of Malachi. The book is identified as "the word of the LORD to Israel by Malachi" (1:1), though scholars disagree over the meaning of that phrase. Malachi means "my messenger" in Hebrew and is not necessarily a proper name. Although the superscription in 1:1 gives no information relevant for dating, most scholars confidently place the book of Malachi between the completion of the second temple (515 BCE) and the time of Ezra and Nehemiah (445 BCE). The prophet complains about the abuses in Jerusalem's second temple and is concerned about foreign marriages (2:10–12), major issues of Ezra's time period.

The major literary convention used in the book of Malachi is the "disputation format." This involves: (1) statement of a principle or norm; (2) expressions of protest and rebuttal by the priests or people; (3) defense of the original statement; and, (4) rebuke and threat of judgment.

Themes: The oracles in Malachi are less concerned with foreign nations than with the spiritual condition of the priesthood and people of Israel. Therefore, priests are accused of breaking a covenant with Levi by sacrificing inferior animals (1:6–8, 2:4); although no covenant with Levi explicitly mentioned in the Torah, such a covenant may have been implied from various events and passages. Although the author is critical of the priesthood, he is sympathetic to the Levites, who had become marginalized.

Attention to covenants is also evident elsewhere. Malachi says that a covenant with the ancestors was broken by the faithlessness of Judah (2:10–11). Likewise, the covenant of marriage is violated when Jewish husbands divorce their wives to marry foreign women (2:10–16). Yet the most prominent of the covenants in the book of Malachi is the covenant between the Lord and Israel, even if it is not explicitly mentioned. Baldwin argues that this is seen when God is referred to as father and Israel as son (1:6, 3:17). The sins highlighted in the book are violations of covenant, and yet God promises to send a messenger to purify the priesthood and the people.

Interpretive Issues: The most significant issue for understanding the book of Malachi is the identity and role of the author. Some argue that the book is anonymous and that "my messenger" is simply a generic way of designating a prophet. Others contend that "my messenger" refers to some specific individual, related to the one who will prepare the way for the Lord in 3:1. Some think that the author of the book is the messenger in 3:1, while others hold that the name Malachi is merely a wordplay upon the theme of the messenger expressed in 3:1.

A related issue concerns the independent nature of the book of Malachi. The superscription of the book ("An oracle. The word of the LORD to Israel by Malachi," 1:1) has often been connected with similar superscriptions in Zech. 9:1 and 12:1. These types of superscriptions begin the last three prophetic sections of the Bible, causing many scholars to argue that these passages were independent, anonymous prophecies that were placed at the end of the Nevi'im (the collection of prophetic books in the Bible) and that they only later became associated with Zechariah and Malachi.

Influences: The expectation of Elijah's return (4:4–6) has had continuing significance for the Jewish community in the celebration of the Passover. A seat is sometimes left vacant at the table in anticipation of Elijah's return. In the NT, the question of why Elijah must come first (i.e., before the Messiah appears or the kingdom of God dawns) is raised by Jesus's disciples (Matt. 17:10; Mark 9:11). In Matthew's Gospel, Jesus responds to this question in a way that identifies John the Baptist as the returned Elijah (Matt. 17:11–13; cf. Mark 9:12–13). This is consistent with earlier quotations in the Gospels that identify John the Baptist with the messenger mentioned in Mal. 3:1 (cf. Matt. 3:1–3; Mark 1:2–4; but see John 1:21–23).

The different ordering of books in the Jewish Tanakh and in the Christian OT has proved significant. Although both canons place the book of Malachi as the last of the prophets (Book of the Twelve, or Minor Prophets), the Tanakh places the entire Writings section (Ketuvim) after Malachi. As a result, Chronicles is the last book in the Hebrew Bible. Chronicles ends with Cyrus freeing the Israelites and commissioning them to rebuild the temple. This ending has created a specific sensibility among the Jewish people. However, in the OT Malachi is the last book, making the expectation of Elijah's return as the Lord's messenger the last words of the OT. This has affected the Christian community's interpretation of Malachi, heightening the understanding of the book as foretelling the coming of John the Baptist, with whom the NT story begins.

Bibliography

Bandstra, Barry L. *Reading the Old Testament: Introduction to the Hebrew Bible*. 4th ed. Wadsworth, 2009.

Childs, Brevard S. *Introduction to the Old Testament as Scripture*. Fortress, 1979.

Gottwald, Norman K. *The Hebrew Bible: A Socio-Literary Introduction*. Fortress, 1985.

O'Brien, Julia M. *Nahum, Habakkuk, Zephaniah, Haggai, Zechariah, Malachi*. Abingdon, 2004.

Peterson, David L. *The Prophetic Literature: An Introduction*. Westminster John Knox, 2002.

Sweeney, Marvin A. *The Twelve Prophets*. Vol. 2, *Micah, Nahum, Habakkuk, Zephaniah, Haggai, Zechariah, Malachi*. Liturgical, 2000.   B.B.

Malchiah (mal-ki′uh; Heb., "my king is the LORD"; also Malchijah).

1 A descendant of Gershom who served in the temple (1 Chron. 6:40).

2 A descendant of Aaron and head of the fifth priestly division (1 Chron. 9:12); he was the ancestor of Adaiah, who settled in Jerusalem after the exile (24:9).

3 A descendant of Parosh who divorced his non-Israelite wife in compliance with Ezra's postexilic reforms (Ezra 10:25).

4 A descendant of Harim who divorced his non-Israelite wife in compliance with Ezra's postexilic reforms (Ezra 10:31).

5 The son of Harim, who repaired a section of the wall and the Tower of the Ovens (Neh. 3:11). He may be the same as **4.**

6 The son of Recchab who rebuilt the Jerusalem Dung Gate (Neh. 3:14).

7 A jeweler who helped rebuild the Jerusalem wall (Neh. 3:31).

8 One of the thirteen men who stood with Ezra when he read the law to the people (Neh. 8:4).

9 A priest who signed Ezra's covenant-renewal document during the time of Nehemiah (Neh. 10:3).

10 A priest who participated in the ceremony of the wall dedication (Neh. 12:42). He may be the same as **9.** M.A.F./M.A.P.

Malchishua (mal′ki-shoo′uh; Heb., "the king is noble" or "help of the king"), the third son of Saul and Ahinoam (1 Sam. 14:49; 1 Chron. 8:33; 9:39). Nothing is known of his life other than that he was killed with his brothers by Philistines at the battle of Gilboa while in military service for his father (1 Sam. 31:2; 1 Chron. 10:2).

Malchus (mal′kuhs), in John 18:10, the high priest's slave whose right ear was severed by Peter when Jesus was arrested; he is not named in the other Gospels. According to Luke 22:51, Jesus healed his ear.

mallow, a plant mentioned twice in the book of Job. It has been identified as a variety of saltwort (*Atriplex halimus*), which grows in shallow, sandy soil. Job 24:24 refers to the color of the plant withering. In 30:1–8, the poor are said to eat mallow and other plant leaves when they are desperate for food.

Malluch (mal′uhk).

1 An ancestor of the levitical temple musician Ethan (1 Chron. 6:44).

2 The son of Bani who married a foreigner (Ezra 10:29).

3 The son of Harim; he divorced his non-Israelite wife in compliance with Ezra's postexilic proclamation (Ezra 10:32).

4 A priest who signed Ezra's postexilic covenant-renewal document under Nehemiah (Neh. 10:4).

5 One of the chiefs of the people who signed Ezra's postexilic covenant-renewal document under Nehemiah (Neh. 10:27).

6 A priest who accompanied Zerubbabel (Neh. 12:2) in the return from Babylonian exile (ca. 530 BCE).

Malta (mawl′tuh), ancient Melita, an island sixty miles south of Sicily, today making up, with two smaller islands to the northwest, the nation of Malta. First occupied in Neolithic times (ca. 8000–4500 BCE), it began to be colonized by Phoenicians in the early first millennium BCE and passed under the control of Carthage from the sixth to the third centuries BCE. Although taken by the Romans in 218 BCE, Maltese culture apparently retained its Phoenician identity, so that Acts 28:2 refers to the people as "natives" (NRSV; Gk. *barbaroi,* "barbarians," perhaps indicating that they did not speak Greek). According to Acts 27:27–28:11, Paul was shipwrecked in a bay of Malta en route to Rome and spent three winter months there. Roman inscriptions mention the principal local official as the "first man" or "leading man" (NRSV), as Publius is called in Acts 28:7. *See also* Paul; Publius. C.H.M.

mammon (mam′uhn), an Aramaic word referring to material possessions. The word is transliterated into Greek in the NT and has been accordingly transliterated into English in many versions (KJV, RSV). The NRSV translates it "wealth" in Matt. 6:24 and Luke 16:9, 11, 13. This translation does not seem justified and is potentially misleading. Mammon refers to money and the things that money can buy. When Jesus says, "You cannot serve God and mammon" (Matt. 6:24), he does not mean to imply that materialism is only or primarily a problem for those who are wealthy (NRSV: "You cannot serve God and

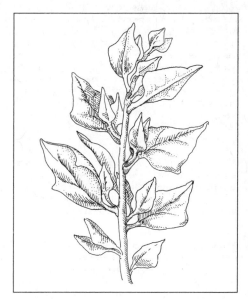

Mallow.

wealth"). Indeed, he is explicitly talking to poor people who have to be warned not to be anxious about having food to eat or clothing to wear (Matt. 6:25–31). This point is less obvious in Luke 16:13, where the wealthy may be in view, but in Luke 16:11 being faithful with mammon is parallel to "being faithful with little" (cf. 16:10). The point of the parable of the Unjust Steward in Luke 16:1–9 is probably not that *rich* people should use their "wealth" to make friends with those who can welcome them in more significant ways, but that *all* people should use mammon (money, material possessions) in this way. The expression "unrighteous mammon" used in Luke 16:9, 11 (NRSV: "dishonest wealth") is curious, but it is probably not intended to designate one type of money in distinction from another (i.e., money dishonestly gained as opposed to money obtained honestly). More likely, "unrighteous mammon" is a denigrating term for all money (similar to the idiom "filthy lucre" in modern English). In Luke's view, mammon or money, regardless of how it is obtained or how much is possessed, falls into the category of things that are worldly (and so unrighteous) and of less value than spiritual things.

M.A.P.

Mamre (mam′ree), an ancient Semitic name.

1 An Amorite ally of Abraham in his battle against Chedorlaomer and the coalition of four eastern kings (Gen. 14:13–24). Mamre was the brother of Eshcol and Aner (14:13, 24).

2 A focal place in Abraham's movements in the southern Levant. Mamre is usually identified with modern Ramet el-Khalil, just north of Hebron. According to biblical tradition, Abraham built an altar at Mamre (Gen. 13:18). Such a shrine would explain Abraham's repeated return to Mamre and his many theophanic experiences there. Abraham purchased the nearby cave of Machpelah for a family tomb. Mamre was apparently named for Abraham's ally in battle (see **1** above). Perhaps this Mamre owned the land or had previously had a shrine there. At Mamre God told Abraham that Sarah would have a son (18:1–15). There, Abraham pleaded for Sodom and Gomorrah to be spared (18:16–33). In the nearby cave of Machpelah, Sarah, Abraham, Isaac, Rebekah, Jacob, and Leah were buried (23:17–20; 25:7–10; 35:27–29; 49:28–33; 50:12–13). *See also* Machpelah.   J.F.D.

Manaen (man′ee-uhn), a Christian prophet and teacher in Antioch who was present when Paul and Barnabas were commissioned to be missionaries (Acts 13:1). Manaen is further identified as a member of the court of Herod. *See also* Antioch; Herod; prophet.

Manasseh (muh-nas′uh).

1 Joseph's elder son, born in Egypt to him and Asenath, the daughter of Potiphera, priest of On (Gen. 41:50–51). His younger brother, Ephraim, receives a superior blessing from his grandfather Jacob and is destined to become preeminent over Manasseh (48:17–20).

2 The tribe Manasseh, which traced its descent from **1**. Its borders are given in Josh. 17; Manasseh occupied much of the heartland of the kingdom of Israel: the territory south of the Jezreel Valley plus Gilead in the Transjordan. All three capitals of the northern kingdom were part of Manasseh's territory: Samaria, Shechem, and Tirzah. Other cities in Manasseh included Megiddo, Taanach, Jezreel, Dor, and Beth-shan. Since Manasseh (and Ephraim) were sons of Joseph rather than of Jacob/Israel, Manasseh is not included among early lists of the twelve tribes. Although such listings are complicated and varied, there are two major types of lists: (1) lists in which Joseph and Levi are included among the twelve tribes, but Ephraim and Manasseh are not mentioned; and (2) lists in which Joseph and Levi are not mentioned, but Ephraim and Manasseh are. The rationale for these latter lists is twofold. Levi ceased to be counted as a tribe, because the Levites became priests, distributed throughout all regions, and the tribe of Joseph split into two, forming Ephraim and Manasseh. Whatever the details behind such configurations, it seems that the biblical authors wanted to preserve the number "twelve" in association with listings of tribes. In one list (Judg. 5, part of the Song of Deborah), a tribe of Machir is listed, but Manasseh is not, leading some interpreters to suggest that Machir was either another name for Manasseh or an early tribe that was eventually absorbed by Manasseh.

The story of Jacob giving a blessing to both Ephraim and Manasseh in Gen. 48:17–20 prefigures the history of those tribes in certain ways. The mere fact that he gave such blessings to his grandchildren indicated that they would have positions equivalent to those of his sons (as ancestors of major tribes). Beyond that, Jacob insisted that Ephraim would have preeminence over Manasseh, even though Manasseh was the firstborn. In subsequent history, the leader of the northern kingdom is chosen from Ephraim (Jeroboam I), not from Manasseh, as one might have expected from the latter's geographic prominence. Eventually, Ephraim became a virtual synonym for the northern kingdom, Israel (e.g., Isa. 7:2). *See also* tribes.

3 The son of Hezekiah and king of Judah ca. 687/6–642 BCE; he reigned longer than any other king of the house of David, fifty-five years. Manasseh is roundly condemned in the book of 2 Kings. The author accuses Manasseh of cancelling the religious reforms of his father, allowing local "high places" to be rebuilt, and fostering the reintroduction of foreign cultic practices (2 Kings 21:3–6). This abandonment of Israel's law was not limited to the royal court; through Manasseh's example, idolatry spread abroad to the people of Judah and Jerusalem (21:9). Furthermore, according to the religious perspective of the book of Kings, according to which loyalty to the Lord is rewarded and apostasy punished, Manasseh was directly to blame for the destruction of Jerusalem and the exile of Judah, so great was his sin (21:12–15; 22:16–17).

As for the political history of Manasseh's age, little is reported in biblical sources. Assyrian sources refer to Manasseh as a loyal vassal for the better part of his reign. Thus the Assyrian king Esar-haddon reports that "the 22 kings of the western countries, the seashore and the islands," among them "Manasseh of Judah," furnished building materials for the reconstruction of the royal palace in Nineveh. This same monarch called upon his western vassals to construct the port town of Kar-Esarhaddon on the Phoenician coast after the destruction of Sidon in 676 BCE. Some years later, during an early campaign of Ashurbanipal of Assyria to Egypt, Manasseh mobilized a Judean contingent to fight alongside other national units who had been enlisted for service in the Assyrian army. Vassal dues included military service as well as steep payments in money and in kind. A fragmentary tradition in 2 Chronicles preserves references to Manasseh's imprisonment by the king of Assyria, who took him captive "with hooks and bound him with fetters of bronze and brought him to Babylon." There, Manasseh prayed to the Lord and was subsequently returned to his former position (33:10–13). That Manasseh was suspected of disloyalty at least once during his long reign is very likely, and this episode may be related to the unrest in the west in 671 BCE at the end of Esar-haddon's rule in Assyria.

Judah's status as a vassal to the Assyrian Empire, which in the seventh century BCE stretched from the Nile to the Taurus Mountains and eastward to the Iranian plateau, can best account for the rampant idolatry recorded in the book of Kings for the reign of Manasseh. It is often suggested that Assyria required the adoption of imperial cults as part of the vassal service due the overlord. But Assyrian imperial policy made no such demands; on the contrary, foreign local cults flourished and were sometimes encouraged by the conqueror. Note the account of the "restoration" of the Israelite cult in Bethel by the king of Assyria for the well-being of the settlers of the province (2 Kings 17:24–34). The repeated commercial and military contacts by Judeans with the admixture of peoples in the empire was the seedbed out of which grew the cultic entanglements decried by biblical writers. Thus, the diminutive kingdom of Judah succumbed to the wave of a new general culture composed of Aramaic and Canaanite elements that united the entire Near East.

The relentlessly negative account of Manasseh's reign in 2 Kings is somewhat in tension with the story of Manasseh's repentance in 2 Chron. 33:10–16, which would seem to obviate the need for the reform of King Josiah (2 Kings 22–23; 2 Chron. 34–35). In the NT, Manasseh appears in the genealogy of Jesus (Matt. 1:10).

4 A descendant of Pahath-moab who divorced his foreign wife in response to Ezra's postexilic proclamation (Ezra 10:30).

5 A descendant of Hashum, who divorced his foreign wife in response to Ezra's postexilic proclamation (Ezra 10:33).   M.C.

Manasseh, Prayer of. *See* Prayer of Manasseh.

mandrake (*Mandragora officinarium*), a plant of the nightshade family that spreads large spinach-shaped leaves in a rosette pattern. The flowers that form in the middle of the rosettes later become yellow-red fruits resembling tomatoes. It was considered a delicacy and was also noted for its fragrance (Song of Sol. 7:13). Sometimes called a "love apple," it was purported to be an aphrodisiac and enhancer of fertility. This identification (evident in ancient Egyptian love poetry and probably also in Song of Sol. 7:13) lies in the background for the story of the birth of Issachar in Gen. 30:14–18. Reuben finds some mandrakes in the field and gives them to his mother, Leah, but Rachel, her sister, who is Jacob's favorite wife, asks for some of them (probably in hope of curing her infertility). Leah responds, "Is it a small matter that you have taken away my husband? Would you take away my son's mandrakes also?" Rachel agrees that Leah may lie with Jacob one night in exchange for the mandrakes, and when Jacob comes from the field in the evening, Leah goes to meet him, saying, "You must come in to me; for I have hired you with my son's mandrakes." Issachar is conceived as a result of that night's union.   P.L.C./M.A.P.

Mandrake.

manger, a box or trough, usually carved from stone, used for the feeding of animals (cf. Luke 13:15). Mangers could be found wherever animals were kept, either in a lower portion of a house, a cave near a house, or even beneath a house. In caves, the manger was frequently carved out of the wall. According to Luke 2:7, 12, 16, a manger was used as the bed for the infant Jesus after his birth in Bethlehem.   J.M.E.

manna (man´uh; from Heb. *man,* Gk. *manna*), a food God provided for the Hebrews in the wilderness (Exod. 16:1–36; Num. 11:4–9). The manna was found each morning on the ground and is described as "a fine, flaky substance, fine as hoarfrost" (Exod. 16:14). It is further described as being white (16:31), like coriander seed (a small, globular, grayish-colored seed, 16:31), and like bdellium (a sticky resinous gum, Num. 11:7). Each Hebrew was to gather one omer (approximately two quarts) of manna each day, but two omers on the day preceding the sabbath (Exod. 16:16, 22). The manna could be boiled in pots or ground into a meal and baked into cakes (Num. 11:8). Manna that was left on the ground after the sun warmed the earth quickly disappeared. A jar of manna was kept, along with Aaron's budding almond branch, in the Holy of Holies beside the ark of the covenant (Exod. 16:33–34; cf. Heb. 9:4). The gift of manna is remembered in Neh. 9:20 as a symbol of God's providence. In the NT, Jesus compares himself to manna, the "bread of life" come down from heaven (John 6:25–35). Similarly, in Rev. 2:17 Jesus promises to give "hidden manna" to the faithful. J.F.D.

Manoah (muh-noh´uh), Samson's father, a Danite from Zorah. The narrative of the events surrounding Samson's birth (Judg. 13:2–25) depicts Manoah as incredulous and slow-witted in comparison to his wife. An angel announces the impending birth of Samson to Manoah's infertile wife, and she tells him the news. He wants the angel's revelation repeated (13:8), he questions the angel to test his wife's truthfulness (13:11), and he peppers the angel with suggestions and questions that are not completely appropriate (13:15–18). Finally, when the angel ascends in fire at the altar, Manoah is afraid that he and his wife will die, prompting her to reassure him with the reasonable conclusion that God would not have told them all these things, or accepted their sacrifice, in order to kill them (13:20–23). According to the Bible, Manoah's tomb lies between Zorah and Eshtaol (16:31), some fifteen miles east of Jerusalem. J.U.

man of lawlessness. *See* lawless one.

mantle. *See* dress; tunic.

Maon (may´on; Heb., "dwelling," "refuge").

1 One of several descendants of Caleb whose names are also place-names; the others are Mareshah, Ziph, Hebron, and Bethzur (1 Chron. 2:42–50).

2 A town in the vicinity of Hebron mentioned in Josh. 15:55. Also, in 1 Sam. 23:24–25, Saul pursues David into the wilderness of Maon. In 1 Sam. 25:2 Maon is identified as the home of Nabal and Abigail. Some scholars identify biblical Maon with modern Khirbet el Main, located twenty-five miles west-northwest of Beersheba, but the majority identify it with Tel Main, which is located eight and a half miles south of Hebron. J.G.G.

Mara (mair´uh; Heb., "bitter"), the name Naomi applied to herself to describe her fate (Ruth 1:19–21). Her name Naomi meant "my pleasant one," but when she returned to her home in Bethlehem after losing her husband and two sons in Moab, she told the people there, "Call me no longer Naomi, call me Mara, for the Almighty has dealt bitterly with me." *See also* Naomi; Ruth.

Marah (mair´uh; Heb., "bitterness"), the unpalatably bitter pools of water (whence the name) reached by the Israelites after they crossed the Red Sea and entered the Wilderness of Shur (Exod. 15:22; the Wilderness of Etham, Num. 33:8). Thirsty and angry, the Israelites slandered Moses, who was then directed by God to turn the waters sweet by throwing wood into the brackish pools. In the exodus narrative, this incident serves to illustrate Israel's tendency to doubt God in spite of the mighty deliverance wrought at the sea (Exod. 15:24). It also illustrates God's propensity to test Israel (15:25). Despite the many locations proposed as the site of Marah, none has gained the complete confidence of scholars. J.M.S.

Three Israelites complain to Moses that the water at Marah is bitter; Moses then turns to God, who shows him a tree that will sweeten the water; detail from a thirteenth-century French illuminated Bible.

maranatha (mair´uh-nath´uh, mahr´uh-nath´uh), an Aramaic expression transliterated into Greek (1 Cor. 16:22) meaning "Our Lord has come" (*maran atha*) or "Our Lord, come" (*murana tha*). The prayer, "Come, Lord Jesus" (Rev. 22:20), which is a Greek translation of this expression, favors the latter. The use of *maranatha* in 1 Cor. 16:22 indicates that this was an early prayer and that Jesus already in earliest times was probably referred to as *mar,* or "Lord."

marble, a metamorphic rock composed of extremely compact crystallized limestone. Its veined and varicolored appearance made it highly desirable for architectural decoration and artistic use. Biblical use attests its functions in architecture ("marble pillars" and marble floors in the palace of Ahasuerus, Esther 1:6) and decoration (material gathered by David for use in the temple, 1 Chron. 29:2). In the seer's vision of the destruction of "Babylon" (Rev. 18:12) marble was part of the precious goods no longer salable by merchants. In archaeological evidence, marble fragments attest its use in statuary during the Greco-Roman period (333 BCE–324 CE) in addition to the more common uses in architectural decoration and construction from various periods.   R.S.B.

Marduk. *See* Merodach.

Mareshah (muh-ree'shuh).
1 An important town in the Judean Shephelah, identified with modern Tell Sandahannah, located about twenty-five miles southwest of Jerusalem. Josh. 15:44 names Mareshah as one of Judah's settlements. According to 2 Chron. 11:5–12, Rehoboam fortified this town, ca. 920 BCE. Near the end of the tenth century BCE, the armies of King Asa and Zerah the Ethiopian "drew up their lines of battle in the valley of Zephathah at Mareshah," a conflict that ended with a Judean victory (2 Chron. 14:9–15). Eliezer, the prophet who spoke against the alliance between Jehoshaphat and Ahaziah, came from Mareshah (20:37). Micah prophesied this town's conquest at the hands of Assyria (1:15). During the exilic and postexilic periods (sixth–fourth centuries BCE), southern Judah became part of Edomite (or Idumean) territory, and Marisa (Mareshah's Greek name) became an important political, economic, and cultural center. Its cosmopolitan population came under the successive control of Seleucid, Ptolemaic, Hasmonean, and Roman conquerors, and the Parthians destroyed Marisa in 40 BCE (cf. 1 Macc. 5:66; 2 Macc. 12:35). The Zenon papyri, which date to the mid-third century BCE, mention this town and point to its commercial importance.

On the basis of texts in the Bible, Josephus, and Eusebius, Edward Robinson identified Sandahannah as ancient Mareshah/Marisa. The site includes a high mound in the center (upper city), an extensive lower city, numerous cave complexes, and several major groups of elaborate tombs. Bliss and Macalister conducted the first excavations at this site in 1900 and recovered evidence of Iron Age and Hellenistic occupation. Under the auspices of the Israel Antiquities Authority, Amos Kloner directed a major series of excavations at Mareshah/Marisa from 1989 until 2000, and fieldwork on a much smaller scale continued until 2008. This more recent project recovered material from the Iron Age and the Persian period, but focused pri-

marily on the Hellenistic remains and layout of the lower city, subterranean complexes (which were used for a variety of industrial, agricultural, and domestic purposes), and tombs. In addition to a full repertoire of Hellenistic pottery (including over three hundred stamped Rhodian amphora handles), terracotta figurines, coins, and inscriptions, the site boasts some of the world's finest examples of rock-cut, elaborately painted tombs.

Bibliography
Erlich, Adi, and Amos Kloner. *Maresha Excavations Final Report II: Hellenistic Terracotta Figurines from the 1989-1996 Seasons.* Israel Antiquities Authority, 2008.

Kloner, Amos. *Maresha Excavations Final Report I: Subterranean Complexes 21, 44, 70.* Israel Antiquities Authority, 2003.

2 The firstborn son of Caleb and the father of Ziph and Hebron (1 Chron. 2:42). In this verse, the LXX uses Marisa for the name of Caleb's first son.

3 A son of Laadah, a descendant of Judah (1 Chron. 4:21).   G.L.M.

Mari (mah'ree), the name of an ancient city uncovered by French archaeologists at modern Tell el-Hariri, located on the right bank of the Euphrates River, just north of the modern Syro-Iraqi border. Since the first expedition of 1933–34, dozens of campaigns have unearthed major

Inscribed statue of Ishtup-ilum, "governor" of Mari, second millennium BCE.

palaces and temples dating from the mid-third millennium to the early eighteenth century BCE. Mari was likely dismantled by Hammurabi of Babylon around 1765 BCE, and it never again rose to prominence.

History: Mari's location midway between the great powers of Sumer (Kish, Uruk, Eridu, Agade, Ur) and those of Syria (Ebla) allowed it to be a center for trade during the third millennium. References to Mari as a major political power are therefore found in the archives recovered from these city-states. The documents from Mari of this period have not been fully published.

When, at the turn of the millennium, Sumerian culture began to give way to that of the West Semitic Amorites, Mari was ruled by *shakkanakku* (governors). These brought prosperity to the city, and it was during their time that the foundation of the great palace was laid that was to last until Mari's fall. A chronology for these governors and a transition to the later Lim dynasty are not yet in full focus.

The largest archives (over 20,000 tablets) come from the palace of the early eighteenth century BCE (1815–1760 BCE). Over 2,500 tablets came to light in new (1998–2000) excavations at a private home, including Sumerian literary texts for scribal education. They tell of Yakdun-Lim, son of the obscure Yaggid-Lim, who fortified cities all along the Middle Euphrates and who even led a military expedition to the Mediterranean; of one who was perhaps his son, Sumu-Yamam, who was assassinated within two years of rule, leaving Mari to the mercy of an ever scheming king, Samsi-Addu (later recalled as Shamshi-Adad of Assyria); of Yasmakh-Addu, son of the latter, who stayed in power for about twenty years, losing it at his father's death; and of Zimri-Lim, scion of Yakhdun-Lim, who occupied the throne. In their days, Mesopotamia was an unstable region, with rulers jockeying for power in search of tribute-bearing vassals, and with usurpers rising and falling at fast clips. Zimri-Lim was a victim of his time, ruling for about fourteen years (1775–1760 BCE). He was the last king of Amorite Mari.

Palace Life and Government: Zimri-Lim's reign, albeit brief, is the most heavily documented of ancient times. We have hundreds of letters from him, his family, and his administrators as well as dozens of documents dated to each month of his reign. From these we can reconstruct life in the palace of a major city-state during peace and war. During those years, the king and his retainers had two meals a day, consisting of a variety of breads, legumes, meats, fish, wine spiked with honey, beer, and dried fruits. Seasonal food included locusts, truffles, and fresh fruits. Ice was available, year-round, stored in underground buildings.

Spoken languages included Akkadian, Amorite, and, in some areas, Hurrian. Sumerian was acquired knowledge. For entertainment, the king hunted lions, listened to recitals in many languages, and watched elaborate ballets. Festivals were many, with elaborate ceremonies that included ritualized processions and acrobatics. Future musicians and dancers were selected from captive women and given instruction by courtiers. Yasmakh-Addu knew only Akkadian and was especially sensitive to the musical arts; he was criticized by his father on both accounts. It is likely that the courtiers also listened to the reading of literary texts, but the examples recovered from Mari have not yet been published. It is possible to reconstruct a voyage that Zimri-Lim took when visiting Halab (Aleppo), where his father-in-law, king Yarim-Lim of Yamkhad, lived. Very likely, he also went to Ugarit. The trip took at least four months and was punctuated by many stops at the courts of allies and vassals as well as by visits to local shrines. A few years later, Zimri-Lim purchased distant Alakhtum (possibly Alalakh, by the Mediterranean coast), giving him a place of escape, should he need it. He never made it to this sanctuary, however, but likely perished near his capital. Hammurabi occupied Mari and then dismantled it, moving its population elsewhere.

The king had many wives and concubines at each of his four palaces along the Euphrates and Khabur rivers. First among these wives was Shiptu of Yamkhad, whom Zimri-Lim married early in his reign. We cannot be sure whether Shiptu bore him any of the three sons he had (one died young); but we know of many daughters from other wives and concubines. We can reconstruct the fate of at least a dozen of these daughters. Some married prominent court functionaries; others became priestesses, in Mari itself as well as in Sippar, where they became "daughters-in-law" of the god Shamash. Most, however, were given as wives to allies and vassals. Especially dramatic were the fates of Shimatum and Kirum. Sisters, they were married to Khaya-Sumu of Ilansura, with tragic consequences for Kirum, who seems to have lost her mind and had to be brought back home.

Government: The king was the main administrator of Mari and its territories. He was helped by a private secretary, who accompanied him on his frequent trips, and, until his death, by a diviner, who was also a brother-in-law. There were countless bureaucrats, male as well as female, in the palace and in the provinces. The more highly placed a functionary, the more diverse were the assigned duties, and we know of court musicians who were also given diplomatic assignments. Major officials were granted homes, fields, and personnel that may have reverted to the crown after their deaths. Conquered land was dispensed to *suqaqu* (mayors) for regular payment of fees. In the provinces, the king's authority was communicated by, among others, the *shapitum* (governor), the *merkhum* (commander of tribal troops), and the *khazannum* (the king's delegates to vassal courts). Noteworthy is the large number of messengers and diplomats, one text citing respectively sixty-four and one hundred of them. Tribal elements constantly needed the king's attention, for some of these, in particular the Benjaminites, were constantly fomenting troubles. More difficult to control were such roaming groups as the Sutu and Turukku, both with unenviable reputations.

The palace archives reveal that trade was largely confined to a heavily codified exchange of gifts between rulers, some of them coming from as far west as Hazor and Byblos. Transport was mostly by water, but by donkey or oxen when by land. Kings, however, could own homes in foreign territory, staffed by officials acting as bankers and purchasing agents. Military campaigns could take place at any time of the year, although the more civilized ones were launched in the spring. The king usually delegated responsibility to a *rab amurrim* (general), but he also went to the front. Zimri-Lim could summon a standing army of four thousand men, but he was likely to raise more from allies and vassals. There are reports of some engagements that pitted tens of thousands, from all levels of the citizenry and tribal elements, but it is difficult to assess whether such reports employ exaggeration. Heavy weaponry included battering rams, towers, and breach-mines. Common soldiers used bows, javelins, swords, knives, and throw-sticks. They were protected by helmets, shields, codpieces, and in some cases hauberks. The defeated were parceled out among the victors, with the king receiving the major share. Prisoners could be redeemed by their own communities, or else they served at the victor's pleasure. The harem of a defeated king was simply taken over by the winning ruler.

Religion: Mari worshiped as many as twenty-five gods, which are listed in a Zimri-Lim period document. The priesthood included men and women, the last frequently kin to the king with such titles as "wife/sister of god." The temples of Mari also housed the gods of surrounding cities; these could be released to their own shrines seasonally or by appeal to the king. Dagan seems to be the god of regional Mari; Itur-Mer of the city itself. Each king had his own protective god, but also venerated the gods of his ancestors. One god, however, did not dominate the others; rather, individuals gravitated to the worship of one deity, and certain deities were better approached for specific requests. It is certain, for example, that the goddess Belet-ekallim was favored by palace women. When Zimri-Lim asked a favor from heaven, he wrote a brief but poignant letter to the river god Naru. Gifts to the gods were many, including baetyls (cut stones, Heb. *matsebot*) for the festival of Ishtar. Sacrifices took place daily. Ceremonies recalling dead ancestors (*kispum*) were regular, requiring the king to move among shrines. The slaughter of sheep, whose innards were used to read omens, was frequent, up to six hundred animals per month. But in this way, (sanctified) meat was made available to members of the palace.

The Divine Will: Gods were unpredictable in communicating their message to the king. They could approach priestly as well as secular figures; they could choose males as well as females as media, young or old. They could relay their message through a trance, a dream, or a vision. The king rarely received messages from them, but intermediaries would write the gist of a message on a clay tablet. Likely, an accompanying oral version gave a fuller account. The settings of one enigmatic divine message betray the individual concerns of three officials relaying it. One prophecy proves to be a splicing of fragments from two others. To verify the authorship of the message as well as the reliability of the medium, the king's diviners turned to various examinations of the entrails of sacrificial animals.

Mari and the Bible: Mari's direct bearing on Hebrew society as reconstructed from the Bible is slight. It is possible that some family groups from tribes that are better known thanks to the Mari documents (particularly Benjamin) eventually found their way to the area around Jericho, but the links for such a migration are broken. It is no longer prudent, therefore, to formulate a second millennium context for the patriarchal period on the basis of Mari's archives. However, Mari does provide a rich repertoire of West Semitic names, along with information on the procedures for census taking, the procurement and installation of baetyls, prophecy and dreams, and legal procedures in adoption and inheritance. Most strikingly, the language of the Mari letters provides the closest parallel to the prose narrative that is found in the Bible. Furthermore, the Mari archives allow for the reconstruction of an ancient Near Eastern society in all of its diversity and uniqueness Scholars can therefore turn to Mari, rather than to contemporary paradigms, for models with which to judge the social and religious experiment that came to be known as Israel.

A rich synthesis of Mari archaeology, history, and culture as well as a good bibliographic source is in fascicles 77–78 of the *Supplément* to the *Dictionnaire de la Bible* (Letouzey & Ané, 2008). The three-volume *Littératures anciennes du Proche-Orient* (LAPO 16–18) of Jean-Marie Durand, *Documents épistolaires du palais de Mari, 1-3* (Editions du Cerf, 1997–2000), gives an invaluable overview of Mari in the Amorite period, with translations of hundreds of letters.

Bibliography

Heimpel, W. *Letters to the King of Mari*. Eisenbrauns, 2003.

Sasson, Jack M. *Civilizations of the Ancient Near East*. Hendrickson, 2000.   J.M.S.

mark, an artificially inflicted sign on the body in the form of incision, tattoo, brand, or stamp. In the Bible, several kinds of distinguishing marks are mentioned.

1 The mark of Cain (Gen. 4:15), given as a protection, marking the person of Cain inviolable.

2 Circumcision (Gen. 17:14; 1 Cor. 7:18), the most prominent mark identifying the Hebrews as people of the covenant (cf. Isa. 44:5; 49:16), though other people practiced circumcision as well.

3 The mark of a slave who did not wish to leave his master—the earlobe was pierced by an awl (Exod. 21:6; Deut. 15:17).

4 The "marks of Jesus" that Paul says he bore (Gal. 6:17); these could have been scars from his sufferings for Christ (Acts 14:19; 2 Cor. 11:23–27). Paul, who called himself a "slave of Jesus" (Rom. 1:1), may also have had in mind the custom of branding a slave.

5 The "mark of the beast," which will be placed on the hand and forehead of those who worship the beast in the end times. The mark will consist of the "name of the beast" or the "number of its name," which is 666 (Rev. 13:16–18). Those who receive this mark will end up drinking the wine of God's wrath, being tormented with fire and sulfur in the presence of the lamb and the angels forever and ever (14:9–11; cf. 16:2). Those who do not receive the mark will be brought back to life to reign with Christ for a thousand years (19:20). John's inspiration for this symbol may have been the mark of an imperial seal, necessary to conduct business in some portions of the Roman Empire. It is likely that the number 666 was a symbol (via gematria) for Nero, the Roman emperor who persecuted Christians violently. In contrast to the mark of the beast, true Christians were marked with God's name upon their forehead (3:12; 7:3; 14:1; 22:4; cf. Ezek. 9:4). *See also* gematria.   S.B.

Mark the evangelist, from the *Lindisfarne Gospels* (ca. 700). Over his head is his symbol, the winged lion.

Mark (mahrk; Lat. Marcus; Gk. Markos).

1 John Mark, the son of a woman named Mary in whose house Christians in Jerusalem met for prayer; Peter went there, apparently as a matter of course, after his miraculous release from prison (Acts 12:12). This same Mark accompanied Saul (Paul) and Barnabas on a journey from Antioch to Jerusalem with famine relief aid (12:25), but his untimely abandonment of a later missionary journey on which he accompanied Barnabas and Paul (13:5, 13) precipitated a dispute when Barnabas proposed taking Mark on another such journey. Paul's opposition to that course of action led to independent missionary journeys undertaken by Barnabas with Mark, and Paul with Silas (15:36–40).

2 A person mentioned as one of five named associates of Paul in Philem. 23–24 and Col. 4:10–14; in the latter passage Mark is identified as the "cousin of Barnabas." If this is the same Mark as **1,**

it indicates a reconciliation with Paul beyond the dispute alluded to in Acts 13:5, 13.

3 A person identified as being with Paul in 2 Tim. 4:11. This person is often assumed to be the same person as **1** and/or **2.**

4 A person called "my son" in a letter whose author is identified as the apostle Peter (1 Pet. 5:13). This person is sometimes, though not always, identified with **1** and, less often, with **2** and/or **3.**

5 The author of the Gospel of Mark, who was assumed by Christian tradition to be the person referred to in all NT references, **1–4** above.   P.J.A.

Mark, Gospel According to, the second Gospel in the NT.

Contents: The Gospel opens with an account of John the Baptist (1:1–8). When Jesus is baptized by John, a voice from heaven calls Jesus the Beloved

The earliest extant manuscript fragment of the Gospel of Mark (8:34–9:1); Chester Beatty papyrus fragment, third century CE.

Son of God (1:9–11). After being tempted by Satan, Jesus begins preaching the gospel of the kingdom of God (1:12–15) and calling disciples (1:16–20). Mark describes an initial day in his ministry, with a focus on teaching and healing (1:21–40). Jesus then becomes involved in a series of controversies (2:1–3:6). Continuing his ministry, he appoints twelve of his followers to be apostles (3:7–19), but tensions mount as his own family tries to restrain him and the Pharisees accuse him of using the power of Beelzebul (3:20–35). Jesus tells a series of parables, including that of the Sower (4:1–34) and then works four miracles: he stills a storm at sea, casts a legion of demons into a herd of pigs, heals a woman with a hemorrhage, and raises Jairus's daughter from the dead (4:35–5:43). Jesus sends his disciples out on a mission and, while they are gone, Mark provides a retrospective report of the death of John the Baptist (6:7–33). Jesus miraculously feeds five thousand people and walks on water (6:34–52). Then, after a controversy with the Pharisees over purification rites and what constitutes purity (7:1–23), he is accosted by a Syrophoenician woman whose surprising faith obtains healing for her child (7:24–30). Jesus expands his ministry into Gentile territory, going throughout the Decapolis (7:31–37) and feeding four thousand people (8:1–9). A tense discussion with his disciples reflects on the significance of the two feedings (8:10–21). Jesus heals a blind man (8:22–26), and Peter confesses at Caesarea Philippi that Jesus is the Messiah (8:27–30). This introduces a new phase of the narrative, in which Jesus instructs his disciples about his upcoming passion and its meaning for their vocation as his followers (8:27–10:52); interspersed with this material are accounts of Jesus's transfiguration (9:2–13), the healing of a boy with a demon (9:14–29), and anecdotes that provide teaching on such matters as tolerance, radical faithfulness, divorce, and material possessions (9:38–10:31). The section concludes with Jesus healing another blind man (10:46–52). Jesus enters Jerusalem on a donkey (11:1–11), curses a fig tree, and assaults the temple (11:12–25). His authority is challenged in a series of encounters with religious leaders (11:27–12:37), against whom he tells the parable of Wicked Tenants (11:27–12:1). He castigates the scribes, but praises a widow who gives all she has to the temple (12:38–44). Then he gives a long discourse on the end times and his Second Coming (13:1–37). Mark concludes his Gospel with an account of Jesus's passion and resurrection. Jesus is anointed by an unnamed woman (14:1–11), and he shares a last meal with his disciples (14:17–25). Then he is betrayed, denied, and deserted by those disciples, as he is arrested and put on trial, first before the Jewish Sanhedrin and then before Pilate (14:26–15:20). When he is crucified, he speaks only once from the cross, to say, "My God, My God, why have you forsaken me?" On Sunday morning, some women come to the tomb in which his body was placed, and they are told that he has been raised from the dead (16:1–8).

OUTLINE OF CONTENTS

Mark

P.J.A.

Composition: Most scholars believe the Gospel of Mark to be the earliest of the four NT Gospels. Thus, it was probably one of the sources used by the authors of the Gospel of Matthew and the Gospel of Luke (cf. Luke 1:1). Although the book is anonymous, early church tradition assigned it to Mark, a companion of the disciple Peter, who reportedly wrote down, in Rome, what he heard from Peter (cf. 1 Pet. 5:13). Further, this Mark has typically been assumed to be the same person who is referred to in other NT writings that mention someone named Mark (Acts 12:12, 25; 15:37, 39; Col. 4:10; 2 Tim. 4:11; Philem. 24). Modern scholarship is skeptical of these traditions, in part because Mark was a common name in the Roman world, and in part because the Gospel itself seems to draw upon oral tradition that would not

DISTINCTIVE CHARACTERISTICS OF MARK'S GOSPEL

Sparse and brief (compared to the other Gospels):

No genealogy or stories about Jesus's birth.

No Beatitudes, Lord's Prayer, or Golden Rule.

No resurrection appearances.

Ends abruptly:

"So they went out and fled from the tomb; for terror and astonishment had seized them; and they said nothing to anyone, for they were afraid" (16:8).

Unrefined linguistic style:

Use of "historical present" verbs (present tense used for past action).

Pronouns frequently lack clear antecedents.

Employs literary patterns:

Two-step progressions (purpose: guide readers to take a second look, which clarifies and emphasizes; cf. 8:22–26):

"Jesus Christ, the Son of God" (1:1).

"The time is fulfilled, and the kingdom of God has come near" (1:14–15).

"What is this? A new teaching?" (1:27).

"The leprosy left him, and he was made clean" (1:42).

"Why are you afraid? Have you still no faith?" (4:40).

"Do not fear! Only believe!" (5:36).

"Keep awake and pray that you may not come into the time of trial" (14:38).

Threefold patterns (purpose: create suspense for readers, who come to anticipate a buildup to a dramatic climax):

Three episodes of conflict in a boat (4:35–41; 6:45–52; 8:14–21).

Three bread stories (6:35–44; 8:1–10, 14–21).

Jesus predicts his death three times (8:32; 9:31; 10:33–34).

Jesus enters the temple three times (11:11, 15, 27).

Disciples fall asleep three times (14:37, 40, 41).

Peter denies Jesus three times (14:66–72).

Pilate asks three questions (15:9, 12, 14).

Crucifixion narrated in three three-hour intervals (15:25, 33, 34).

Intercalation (purpose: creates suspense and adds commentary; the related stories interpret and illuminate each other):

Jairus's daughter and the woman with the hemorrhage (5:21–43).

Mission of disciples and death of John the Baptist (6:7–30).

Cursing of fig tree and cleansing of temple (11:12–20).

Jesus's confession and Peter's denial (14:15–15:5).

Emphasizes Jesus's deeds over his words (compared to the other Gospels):

Miracle stories take up a greater part of the total Gospel and are told in greater detail.

Jesus's teaching takes up a smaller part of the total Gospel and is told in less detail.

Story dominated by Jesus's passion:

Already in 3:6 the plot to kill Jesus is formed (cf. to Matt. 12:14; Luke 19:47).

Three predictions of the passion (8:31; 9:31; 10:33–34).

Marked by a sense of eschatological urgency:

"The time is fulfilled, and the kingdom of God has come near" (1:14).

"This generation will not pass away until all these things have taken place" (13:30; cf. 9:1).

Use of the "historical present" and the repeated use of "immediately" throughout the narrative.

DISTINCTIVE CHARACTERISTICS OF MARK'S GOSPEL *(continued)*

A special interest in Galilee (cf. Luke's emphasis on Jerusalem):

The first half of the Gospel is devoted to Jesus's ministry in Galilee.

Jesus predicts a postresurrection reunion with his disciples in Galilee (14:28; 16:7).

Explains Jewish but not Roman matters:

Jewish custom of purification explained (7:3–4).

Knowledge of Roman divorce law assumed (10:12).

Defines Aramaic words (*Boanerges,* 3:17; *talitha cum,* 5:41; *corban,* 7:11; *ephphatha,* 7:34; *Bartimaeus,* 10:46; Abba, 14:36; Golgotha, 15:22; *Eloi, eloi, lema sebachthani,* 15:34).

Does not define Latin words (*legion,* 5:9, 15; *denarius,* 12:15; *praetorium,* 15:16; *centurion,* 15:39).

Assumes readers already have a basic knowledge of Christian tradition and that they know:

What the term "gospel" means (1:1, 14–15; 10:29; 13:10; 14:9).

The scriptures of Israel as the word of God (cf. 7:8).

What it means to say that Jesus is the Messiah (8:29) or that he gives his life as a ransom (10:45).

Otherwise unidentified characters such as John the Baptist (1:4) and Simon and Andrew (1:16).

Imbued with a motif of secrecy:

Jesus's own disciples do not understand who he is (4:41; 6:51–52).

Jesus commands others to keep his identity or miraculous deeds a secret (1:23–25, 43–44; 3:11–12; 5:43; 7:36; 8:30; 9:9).

Jesus speaks in parables *so that* people will not understand what he says (4:10–12).

Offers a very human portrait of Jesus:

Jesus becomes hungry (11:12) and tired (6:31).

Jesus exhibits a full range of human emotions, including pity (1:41), anger (3:5), sadness (3:5), wonder (6:6), compassion (6:34), indignation (10:14), love (10:21), and anguish (14:34).

Jesus does not know everything (13:32), and his power is limited (6:5).

Highlights the failures of Jesus's disciples:

They are unperceptive (4:41; 6:51–52; 8:14–21).

They are self-interested (8:32; 9:32–34; 10:35–41).

They betray, deny, and forsake Jesus (14:10–11, 17–21, 26–31, 37–38, 44–45, 50, 66–72).

Mark's Gospel ends without recording any redress of the disciples' faithlessness, such as the remorse of Judas (Matt. 27:3–10), the recovery of Peter (John 20:15–19), or the reconciliation of the eleven with Jesus (Matt. 28:18–20, Luke 24:36–53, John 20:19–21:14).

From Mark Allan Powell, *Introducing the New Testament* (courtesy, Baker Academic)

---

necessarily be associated with Peter; indeed, there are fewer stories about Peter in this Gospel than in any of the others, and Peter is portrayed in a less flattering light than in any of the other Gospels. Further, the book's theology is thought to reflect concerns more heavily associated with Paul's priorities than with Peter's. Many scholars, however, recognize some connection between this book and the person sometimes called John Mark, whom biblical tradition associates with both Paul (Acts 12:25; 15:37–39; cf. Col. 4:10; Philem. 24) and Peter (Acts 12:11–12)—thus, a loose connection to the apostolic tradition might be maintained without actually regarding the author as Peter's secretary. The book is usually dated close to the destruction of Jerusalem in 70 CE; its readers are directed to note the significance of events associated with this destruction (13:2). The fact that the Gospel of Mark translates Aramaic phrases (5:41; 7:34; 15:34) and explains Jewish customs (7:3–4) suggests that its intended readers were Gentiles.

Distinctive Features: Mark's Gospel only contains a few passages that are without parallel in the other Gospels. Still, Mark's Gospel is said to be written in a more casual or colloquial style than the other Gospels, and this story of Jesus is told with a particular urgency, marked by repeated use of the word "immediately." The Gospel of Mark employs the literary device of intercalation more frequently than any other biblical book; the device involves wrapping one story around another in a way that begs comparison of the two accounts (e.g., the story of Jesus cursing a fig tree in 11:12–14, 20–21 surrounds the story of Jesus

MATERIAL UNIQUE TO MARK

Parable of seed growing secretly	4:26–29
Healing of deaf and dumb man	7:31–37
Healing of blind man of Bethsaida	8:22–26
Sayings on salt	9:49, 50b
Flight of young man in the garden	14:51–52

attacking the temple in 11:15–19). The ending of Mark's Gospel is also distinctive; the oldest Greek manuscripts conclude with 16:8, a notice that the women informed of Jesus's resurrection "said nothing to anyone, for they were afraid." This ending apparently caused some consternation in the early church, for a variety of later manuscripts reveal that different conclusions to the Gospel were composed in various quarters; one of these is printed as Mark 16:9–20 in modern Bibles. Some scholars believe that the original ending for Mark's Gospel was lost, but the majority think that Mark intentionally ended the work as he did (at 16:8) to achieve a particular rhetorical effect.

Major Themes: The Gospel of Mark emphasizes that the message of Jesus was, in essence, a proclamation that God's reign was imminent: the time was fulfilled and the kingdom had drawn near (1:15). Mark's Gospel is also said to offer the most human portrait of Jesus in the NT. Although Jesus is clearly a divine being, the Son of God (1:1, 11; 9:7; 15:39), he does distinguish himself from God (10:18) and is subject to human limitations and frailty (6:5, 31; 11:12; 13:32); he sometimes struggles to know God's will (14:36). Mark's Gospel seems to place a greater emphasis on the story of Jesus's death than the other Synoptic Gospels, in part because that material is treated in full in a book that is otherwise much shorter. Thus, there is less attention to Jesus's teaching in Mark than in Matthew and Luke, and the importance of his death "as a ransom for many" (10:45) is more obviously central to the narrative. Much scholarly attention has also focused on the "secrecy motif" in Mark's Gospel, according to which Jesus's true identity seems shielded from all non-supernatural beings, including his own disciples (1:27; 2:7; 4:41; 6:2–3, 14–16; 8:27–28). In this Gospel, Jesus tells people not to make known the miracles or healings he performs (1:43–44; 5:43; 7:36; 8:26) or to inform others that he is the Messiah (8:30); he likewise silences the demons who would otherwise announce that he is the Son of God (1:23–25, 34; 3:11–12; cf. 5:7). The motif seems to have something to do with Mark's theological vision of Jesus's identity being revealed through the cross (15:39) and as belonging to the content of post-Easter proclamation (13:9–13). In addition, studies on Mark's Gospel have focused on the portrayal of the disciples in this book. Mark's presentation highlights their failures and apostasy, perhaps in an effort to emphasize the grace of a Lord who chooses unworthy follow-ers or as a means of offering hope to struggling Christians by showing them that even the revered apostles could sometimes be cowards and fools. *See also* Gospels, the; Mark; Synoptic Problem.

Bibliography

Boring, Eugene M. *Mark: A Commentary*. Westminster John Knox, 2006.

Collins, Adela Yarbro. *Mark*. Fortress, 2007.

France, R. T. *The Gospel of Mark: A Commentary on the Greek Text*. Eerdmans, 2002.

Harrington, Daniel J. *What Are They Saying About Mark?* Paulist, 2005.

Powell, Mark Allan. *Introducing the New Testament: A Historical, Literary, and Theological Survey*. Baker Academic, 2009. Pp. 125–45.

Telford, W. R. *The Theology of the Gospel of Mark*. Cambridge University Press, 1999.   M.A.P.

marketplace. *See* agora; architecture; Athens; Corinth.

marriage, a social, economic, political, and sexual unit formed through a public and legally recognized relationship of a man and at least one woman. Marriage customs and expectations varied throughout the biblical period, but all marriage systems appear to have been mainly patriarchal institutions, which defined the domain of a man's responsibility and sovereignty, though some limits were placed upon both.

Monogamous marriage evolved as the ideal within Israel, but the biblical traditions clearly recall times and circumstances when this was not the case. The ancestors practiced polygamy (Gen. 29:15–30). They also took concubines, especially in cases in which the wife had difficulty conceiving children (16:1–2). In the legislation of the Torah, it is sometimes taken for granted that a man might have multiple wives and that relationships would not always be harmonious between his multiple spouses (Deut. 21:15). Even in the period of the monarchy, when the prevailing form of marriage was monogamy, the kings of Israel and Judah were known to have had large harems. Nevertheless, the story of Adam and Eve, preserved in Gen. 2:21–24, expresses what would become the ultimate ideal of monogamous marriage (cf. Mark 10:6–9).

Rules and traditions reflected in the Pentateuch do not necessarily represent practices throughout the history of Israel. Nevertheless, that portion of Israel's scripture indicates that an unmarried woman, living in her father's house, would be transferred into a husband's jurisdiction when the latter paid a "bride-price" (Heb. *mohar*) to her father (Gen. 34:12). Other gifts might also be presented by the groom's family to the bride's family. When the family of Rebekah accepted the terms of her marriage, Abraham's servant responded by presenting costly gifts to her, her mother, and her brother (24:53).

If a man seduced a woman so that she lost her virginity to him, he had to pay the bride-price as a penalty and make her his legal wife (Exod. 22:16). Likewise, according to written law, a man who raped a woman had to take her as his wife (Deut. 22:28–29); there is no recorded instance, however, of the latter ruling actually being enforced or carried out. When a man from Shechem raped Dinah, the daughter of Jacob, he had to plead (through his father) to be *allowed* to marry her; her brothers did not seem to think that the law indicated he *ought* to do so (and indeed they decided the consequence of rape was murder, not marriage; Gen. 34). Likewise, Absalom was not forced to marry Tamar after he raped her (2 Sam. 13; if the law in Deut. 22:28–29 was literally practiced, the change in his feelings for her reported in 2 Sam. 13:15 would have been irrelevant).

The Bible says nothing about the age at which men or women typically entered into marriage. Anthropologists speculate that women would have married young, perhaps soon after menarche, while men may have had to wait some years past puberty until they had the financial means to assume responsibility for a household. But this is not known for certain, and the custom may have varied over time or been affected by such factors as family size or social class. There is some indication that marriages were arranged by parents, but also that the groom and bride were consulted on the matter (Gen. 24:58). The ancestral traditions indicate that it was common (at least at that time) to marry within the extended family or tribal group; first cousins were suitable partners (24:4; 28:2). The Bible, however, prohibits consanguineous marriage (Lev. 18). Priests were subject to even more stringent marriage regulations than ordinary Israelites, such as the prohibition of marriage with a divorcée (21:7).

No marriage ceremonies are recorded in the Bible, and information about such ceremonies must be gathered piecemeal from documents that cover several centuries, often with a focus on the habits of royalty or the well-to-do. Song of Sol. 3:11 describes King Solomon as wearing a special wedding crown given to him by his mother. In Isa. 61:10, the bridegroom wears a garland and the bride is decked with jewels. When Samson was married during the period of the judges, the Bible says that he "made a feast as the young men were accustomed to do," and this feast lasted seven days (Judg. 14:10, 12). The book of Tobit, written during the Second Temple period, refers to a "wedding celebration" that lasted fourteen days (including a seven-day feast), and it indicates that this was an occasion for many gifts to be given to the groom (9:2, 5–6; 10:7; 11:18; 12:1). Another description from the Second Temple period tells of a bride being escorted to meet the groom as the groom came out with his friends, accompanied by musicians and the sound of tambourines (1 Macc. 9:37–39). Likewise, the NT makes frequent reference to banquets that accompanied weddings (e.g., Matt. 22:2–12; Luke 12:36; 14:8). Jesus's parable in Matt. 25:1–13 assumes a custom in which bridesmaids would go out to meet the bridegroom and then accompany him to a wedding banquet. The story of Jesus changing water to wine at Cana

is set at a wedding party (perhaps a reception following the ceremony); the context assumes that even peasants could expect to drink their fill of wine on such an occasion.

It is not clear, however, that such ceremonies were always held, especially in the early period; sometimes a father may simply have brought his daughter to the man's tent or dwelling place (Gen. 29:23–25). The transfer of the woman from the domain of her father to that of her husband does seem to have been the central feature that initiated the marriage event. Sometimes there was a period of betrothal prior to such transfer (Deut. 22:23). David was promised the oldest daughter of Saul, Merab, but when the time of the marriage came, she was given to Adriel (1 Sam. 18:17–19). In the NT, Mary was betrothed to Joseph in a relationship that could only be ended by divorce (Matt. 1:18–19). Such an arrangement appears to have carried stronger legal obligation than modern-day engagement (public announcement of intent), but the betrothed couple typically did not cohabit; the woman might be termed the man's "wife," but she remained under the authority of her father throughout the period of betrothal (probably until the bride-price was paid).

It is not certain if written marriage contracts were employed in ancient Israel, as they are not mentioned until Tob. 7:14. According to Deut. 24:1–4, however, divorce certificates were issued from an early time. Such a certificate allowed a woman to remarry. Notably, a man who had given his wife a certificate of divorce was not allowed to remarry her if she had been married to someone else in the meantime. Also, according to these ancient law codes, if a man was required to marry a woman because he had intercourse with her when she was a virgin, he would never be allowed to divorce her (Deut. 22:29). Likewise, he could not divorce a wife whom he had falsely accused of not being a virgin at the time they married (22:19). There is no stated biblical law that would allow an Israelite woman to initiate divorce (but see Mark 10:12).

In Mark 10:2–9, Jesus distinguishes the allowance of divorce from obedience to God's will. Jesus denounces divorce for any reason as contrary to God's original intent for humanity. The author of Matthew's Gospel seemed to read this as a prohibition of divorce for any reason rather than as a simple statement of God's will, so he adds a caveat to Jesus's comment: divorce is permissible in cases of *porne* (NRSV: "unchastity," but the meaning of the term is disputed). Likewise, the apostle Paul recognizes that divorce may sometimes be necessary when a Christian is married to an unbeliever, but even then, the Christian should remain in the marriage if their spouse is willing (1 Cor. 7:13–16).

The levirate law is specified in Deut. 25:5–10. The brother of a man who dies without a son had an obligation to marry the wife who was left, and "the first son whom she bears shall succeed to the name of his brother who is dead." Tamar, daughter in law of Judah, tried to force Judah to fulfill his obligation to provide a levirate marriage for her (Gen. 38), and the marriage of Boaz to Ruth was intended in some way to fulfill this same custom (Ruth 4:10). The institution of levirate marriage forms the background that the Sadducees put to Jesus in Mark 12:18–23.

Throughout the Bible, marital faithfulness is presented as a strong ideal (Prov. 5:18–29) and as the absolute commandment of God. The prohibition of adultery is one of the Ten Commandments, central to the moral code of the Torah (Exod. 20:14; Deut. 5:18). Although it was certainly considered a wrong against one's neighbor and spouse, it was also a sin against God. Marriage, therefore, became an ideal metaphor for describing the covenant between God and Israel (Hos. 3). Prostitution was condemned and often appears as a metaphor for sins associated with idolatry (e.g., Exod. 34:15; Deut. 31:16; Judg. 2:17; Hos. 9:1). In the NT, this traditional ethic is stated positively in the Letter to the Hebrews: "Let marriage be held in honor by all, and let the marriage bed be kept undefiled" (13:4).

Elsewhere in the NT, there is discussion of whether celibacy is actually preferable to marriage. In 1 Cor. 7, Paul promotes this view not because virginity is intrinsically more holy, but because those who marry experience distress that the unmarried are spared (7:28). Paul says, "The unmarried man is anxious about the affairs of the Lord, how to please the Lord; but the married man is anxious about the affairs of the world, how to please his wife, and his interests are divided. And the unmarried woman and the virgin are anxious about the affairs of the Lord, so that they may be holy in body and spirit; but the married woman is anxious about the affairs of the world, how to

please her husband" (7:32–34). Interpreters generally note that this view is informed by Paul's expectation that the end of the age is at hand, making family responsibilities a lesser priority than the "impending crisis" (7:26; cf. 7:29, 31). Further, Paul notes, realistically, that those who cannot remain celibate without being tempted to sin should not try to do so (7:28, 36). A similar point might be made by Jesus in his somewhat obscure comment about those who make themselves eunuchs for the kingdom of heaven in Matt. 19:11–12. In 1 Tim. 4:3, those who forbid marriage are declared to be false teachers.

Several NT letters offer household codes that lay out the expectations of husbands and wives and other family members (Eph. 5:21–6:9; Col. 3:18–4:1; 1 Tim. 2:8–15; 5:1–2; 6:1–2; Titus 2:1–10; and 1 Pet. 2:13–3:7). Such codes were common in Greco-Roman writings, but the NT examples are distinctive in that they include directives to the more powerful members of the household as well as to the less powerful members; the instructions are for, not just wives, but also husbands; not just children, but also fathers; not just slaves, but also masters. Thus, in Eph. 5:21–6:9, a traditional Greco-Roman household code is transformed within a context of *mutual* submission (5:21), and the overall focus is shifted toward responsibilities of the more powerful party. This would seem to be in keeping with the servant ethic encouraged by Jesus in the Gospels (Mark 10:41–45; John 13:1–7). Most notable, perhaps, is the notion that husbands are to love their wives in the same way that Christ loved the church: they are to put their wives' wants and needs ahead of their own, giving of themselves in selfless service.

Martha and her sister, Mary of Bethany; from a fifth-century ivory of the two watching the raising of their brother Lazarus from the dead (John 11:17–44).

In the NT, marriage is often used figuratively in connection with the kingdom of God (e.g., Matt. 25:1–13; Luke 14:16–24; Rev. 19:7, 9), but it is an institution for the present rather than the future age. The angels of God apparently do not marry, and in the kingdom of heaven men and women will be like them, no longer thinking of themselves as the spouses of particular individuals (Matt. 22:30; Mark 12:25; Luke 20:35).

Bibliography

Perdue, Leo G., Joseph Belenkinsopp, John J. Collins, and Carol Meyers. *Families in Ancient Israel*. Westminster John Knox, 1997.

L.H.S./P.J.A./M.A.P.

Martha (mahr'thuh; Aramaic, "lady" or "mistress"; feminine of *mar*, "lord"), a close friend and follower of Jesus as attested by Luke and John. According to Luke 10:38–42 Martha invited Jesus into her home, where she appeared to be the head of the household. She is described as "distracted by her many tasks" (Gk. *diakonia*), while her sister Mary sits at Jesus's feet and listens to his teaching. Martha asks Jesus to tell Mary to help her, but Jesus replies that Mary has chosen the better part, which will not be taken from her. Martha is "worried and distracted by many things," but "there is need of only one thing." Elsewhere, in John's Gospel, Martha appears in the story of the raising of Lazarus (her brother) in Bethany (11:1–44). Martha is named, along with Mary and Lazarus, as people loved by Jesus (11:5). When she encounters Jesus, she expresses disappointment that he has arrived late, saying, "Lord, if you had been here, my brother would not have died." He tells her that her brother will rise again and then tells her, "I am the resurrection and the life. Those who believe in me, even though they die, will live" (11:23–25). She confesses faith in him as "the Christ, the Son of God" (11:27), but is concerned that if they open the tomb, there will be a stench from the body (11:39). In a later story, Martha is portrayed as serving dinner to Jesus, his disciples, and Lazarus; her sister anoints him with perfume (12:1–8). *See also* Bethany; Mary.   W.M.

martyr (Gk. *martys*), typically, a person who dies as a result of faith and/or allegiance to God or Christ. In a broad sense, the Greek word *martys* simply means "witness" and may refer to any who testify to their faith (e.g., in word and deed, in life as well as in death), but the English word "martyr" is usually reserved for those whose death was understood as a testimony to their faith. The NRSV does not use the word "martyr," but speaks of witnesses instead. The strongest biblical accounts of martyrdom are found in the books of Maccabees, especially 2 Macc. 6, which reports the martyrdom of Eleazar, a scribe, and 2 Macc. 7, which tells of the martyrdoms of seven brothers and their mother. The entire book of 4 Maccabees was composed as an encomium in honor of the latter martyrs. In the NT, Jesus warns his disciples that many of his followers will be put to death be-

cause of their devotion to him (Luke 21:16). He tells James and John that they will "drink his cup," a probable reference to martyrdom (Mark 10:39; cf. 14:36), and he speaks to Peter in a manner that foreshadows his martyrdom by crucifixion (John 21:18–19). The book of Acts reports the martyrdoms of Stephen (22:20) and James the apostle (12:1–2). Paul is said to have persecuted the earliest Christians with "threats and murder" (Acts 9:1), implying that he may have been responsible for the martyrdom of some Christians. After he became a missionary for Christ, he faced the prospect of martyrdom himself (Phil. 1:21–24). Eventually, Paul and Peter and many other Christians died as martyrs in a persecution enacted by the emperor Nero in Rome. Although the authorship of both letters is disputed, 2 Timothy ostensibly presents Paul's words from prison as he awaits his execution, and 2 Peter presents a final testament from Peter as the time of his martyrdom approaches. The book of Revelation also contains references to Christians who suffered death on account of their faith (2:13; 17:6).   M.A.P.

Mary (mair'ee; Gk. Maria or Mariam; Heb. *marah*, "bitter" or "grieved," or *miryam*, "rebellion"), a name borne by seven women in the NT, unless two or more are identical.

1 Mary, the mother of Jesus. *See* Mary, Virgin.

2 Mary of Bethany, the sister of Martha and Lazarus (Luke 10:38–39; John 11:1). She appears once in Luke, sitting at Jesus's feet and listening as a disciple to his teaching (10:38–42). Martha objects that Mary has left her to serve alone, but Jesus commends Mary's choice as "the better part, which will not be taken away from her" (10:42). In John's Gospel, Mary anoints Jesus's feet with costly ointment and wipes them with her hair (12:1–3). Jesus defends her against Judas Iscariot's objection that the ointment could have been sold and the money given to the poor (12:4–8). This story is also told in Mark 14:3–9 and Matt. 26:6–13, though Mary is not mentioned by name in those accounts; a different but similar story of a woman from the streets anointing Jesus is found in Luke 7:36–50. John's Gospel also mentions Mary as present with Martha at the death and raising of Lazarus (11:19, 20, 28–32). Others follow her when she goes out to Jesus (11:31), and her grief moves him deeply (11:33).

3 Mary Magdalene, or "of Magdala," mentioned first in every listing of Jesus's female disciples (Matt. 27:55–56, 61; 28:1; Mark 15:40–41, 47; 16:1; Luke 8:2–3; 24:10). She therefore seems to have been prominent among a group of women who "followed" and "served" Jesus constantly from the outset of his ministry in Galilee to his death and beyond. Matthew and Mark acknowledge these women only immediately after Jesus's death, but Luke mentions their presence with the twelve during Jesus's ministry in Galilee (8:1–3). Here Mary is included among the many women who provided for Jesus's ministry "out of their own resources," suggesting that these women were persons of some financial means who served as patrons for Jesus and his male disciples. Mary is also said to have been healed by Jesus of some unnamed infirmity; the healing involved an exorcism of seven demons (Luke 8:2). Mary is presented in all four Gospels as a witness to Jesus's death (Matt. 27:55–56, 61; Mark 15:40–41, 47; Luke 23:49, 55–56; John 19:25) and to the empty tomb (Matt. 28:1, 6; Mark 16:1–6; Luke 24:1–3, 10; John 20:1–2). In the Synoptic Gospels, she receives a divine commission to tell the male disciples about the resurrection (Matt. 28:5–9; Mark 16:6–7; Luke 24:4–10). According to Luke, her testimony (and that of the other women) was not at first believed, but was later vindicated (24:11, 22–48). According to John 20:11–18 the risen Jesus appeared first to Mary and he talked with her about his coming ascension (20:17). Despite her prominence in the Gospel stories, Mary Magdalene is not mentioned elsewhere in the NT, although it is possible that she would be assumed to be among the "certain women" mentioned in Acts 1:14. She is conspicuous by absence in the list of witnesses to the resurrection provided by Paul in 1 Cor. 15:3–8 The nonhistorical tradition that Mary Magdalene had once been a prostitute derived from confusion of her with the unnamed woman in Luke 7:36–50.

4 Mary, the mother of James, or of James and Joses or Joseph, or "the other Mary." She is among the women disciples at the cross (Matt. 27:55–56; Mark 15:40), and she appears with Mary Magdalene at the burial of Jesus (Matt. 27:61; 28:1; Mark 15:47; 16:1). Later, she is present to behold the first appearance of the risen Christ (Matt. 28:9).

5 Mary, the wife of Clopas, one of the women at the cross in John 19:25. She is often taken to be the same as Mary the mother of James and Joses (see **4** above).

6 Mary of Jerusalem, whose home was used as a meeting place for Jesus's followers after his death. Many were praying there when Peter arrived after his escape from prison to leave a message for James and the brothers and sisters (Acts 12:11–17). That no husband is mentioned may mean that she is the head of the household and so perhaps leader of one of the house-churches mentioned in Acts 2:46. Rhoda, the "maid" who went to the door (v. 13), could be a slave, indicating that Mary was a person of some means. Mary's son John, also known as Mark, accompanied her nephew Barnabas (Col. 4:10) and also Paul on some of their missionary travels (Acts 12:25; 13:5, 13; 15:37–39).

7 A woman greeted by Paul in Rom. 16:6 and described as having "worked hard among you."

W.M.

Mary, Virgin, the wife of Joseph, known as "the Virgin" because of her reported virginal conception

The Virgin enthroned as Queen of Heaven and Earth. Beside her, emperors Justinian (*left*) and Constantine (*right*) offer her the Hagia Sophia church that each built during his reign; tenth century.

of Jesus. She is portrayed somewhat negatively in Mark, less so in Matthew, and positively in Luke. She is not mentioned by name in the Gospel of John, though there are several references there to the "mother of Jesus."

Matt. 1:18–25 and Luke 1:26–56; 2:1–38 give differing birth stories, but both include the virginal conception. In Matt. 1:18–25, Jesus's birth is announced to Joseph in a dream; in Luke 1:26–38, it is announced to Mary herself by the angel Gabriel. In Luke's account, Mary accepts the angel's announcement, humbling herself as God's servant (1:38). She travels from Nazareth to Judea to visit her pregnant relative Elizabeth, who hails her as "blessed among women" and as the "mother of my Lord" (1:39–45). Mary responds with a hymn of praise (1:46–55, the Magnificat). The latter hymn presents Mary in parallel to the biblical figure of Hannah, the mother of Samuel (cf. 1 Sam. 2:1–10). It has strong political overtones, praising God as the one who brings down the powerful from their thrones and lifts up the lowly, who fills the hungry with good things and sends the rich away empty (1:52–53). Thus, Luke's Gospel is unique in presenting Jesus's mother as one who espouses ideals similar to those that will later be typical of her grown son Jesus (cf. 4:16–21; 6:20–26).

Matthew and Luke also tell of the birth of Jesus, which in both accounts occurs in Bethlehem. In Matthew, Mary and the baby Jesus are said to be living in a house in Bethlehem sometime after the latter is born. They are visited by magi from the east, who bring them precious gifts (2:1–11). Joseph then takes Mary and Jesus to Egypt to escape Herod's slaughter of children; later, after Herod dies, they return and settle in Nazareth (2:12–23). In Luke's Gospel, Nazareth appears to be Mary's hometown. Joseph and Mary travel from Nazareth to Bethlehem for a Roman census, and she gives birth while they are there (2:1–7); the baby is laid in a manger, and angels and shepherds pay homage (2:8–20). Luke then reports that Mary and Joseph went to the temple to consecrate the child and to perform post-birth purification rites (2:21–24). While there, the aged Simeon and Anna prophesy over Jesus, testifying that the Messiah has been born (2:25–38). Simeon has a word of prophecy for Mary as well: "A sword will pierce your soul too" (2:35). Luke also reports that Jesus's family went to Jerusalem every year for the Passover celebration (2:41), and he recounts an episode in which Jesus, at age twelve, remains behind in the temple and his parents become distraught when they cannot find him. He explains that they should have known he would be in his "Father's house" (2:49). Still, Luke concludes with a note that Jesus was obedient to Mary and Joseph (2:51).

Overall, Luke's presentation of Mary in these stories of Jesus's infancy is as a dedicated servant of the Lord who treasures all that she hears and sees, pondering such things in her heart (2:19, 51).

All four Gospels make reference to Jesus's mother during the time of Jesus's adult life. The Synoptic Gospels tell of a time when Jesus's mother and brothers came to visit him. In Mark, the motivation for this visit is that Jesus's family apparently accept the verdict of the crowd that he is deranged or that of the Jerusalem scribes that he is possessed by demons (3:21–30). In any case, when they come to seize him (apparently to take him home), Jesus seems to reject them as his family, characterizing instead his followers, who do God's will, as his true family (3:33–35). In Matt. 12:46–50 and Luke 8:19–21, the visit of Jesus's family members is not said to be prompted by an attempt to seize him, nor is anything said there about his mother and brothers thinking he is deranged. In Matthew's Gospel, nevertheless, Jesus still seems to contrast his literal mother and brothers with true family: "Pointing to his disciples, he said, 'Here are my mother and my brothers!'" (12:49). In Luke's Gospel, however, Jesus simply expands the concept of family rather than implying that his disciples are his true family in a way that Mary and his brothers are not. The words, "My mother and brothers are those who hear the word of God and do it" (8:21) includes Mary and the brothers, and in fact seems to affirm their faithfulness. Likewise, later in Luke's Gospel, a woman in the crowd cries out, "Blessed is the womb that bore you and the breasts that gave you suck"; Jesus responds, "Blessed rather are those who hear the word of God and keep it" (11:27–28). In the context of Luke's Gospel, where Mary has been explicitly presented as one who hears and trusts God's word (1:38, 45), the meaning of Jesus's remark is not to contrast those who hear and trust God's word with his mother Mary; the point, rather, is that Mary is blessed not because she is his mother, but because she is faithful to the word.

Mary is also mentioned in Mark 6:1–6, where the people of Nazareth take offense at Jesus, calling him "the carpenter, the son of Mary" (a possible indication that his father Joseph has died). Jesus's response, "Prophets are not without honor, except in their hometown, and among their own kin, and in their own house" again picks up on the Markan theme that Jesus's family (including, perhaps, his mother Mary) do not honor him or believe in him. Matthew's version is similar (13:54–58), but Luke's account is quite different, exposing Jesus to rejection only by citizens of Nazareth, not by members of his own family—and the reference to a prophet lacking honor among his own relatives or in his own house is completely lacking. Luke later includes Mary among the women praying in the upper room with the twelve (Acts 1:14) and so also as one who receives the Holy Spirit at Pentecost (2:1–4).

Jesus's mother is unnamed in John's Gospel. Her belief in Jesus's power is demonstrated at the wedding in Cana (2:1–11), though he initially resists her appeal for him to be of assistance (2:4). She and his brothers accompany him to Capernaum (2:13). Later, John mentions that Jesus's *brothers* did not believe in him (7:1–10), but nothing like that is said of his mother. Finally, in John's Gospel, she appears at the cross with the Beloved Disciple, whom Jesus commends to his mother as her son, and this "son" to her as "mother." She is then taken into his home (19:25–27).

It is possible that Mary is also depicted as being among the women at the empty tomb in the Synoptic Gospels. A woman known as Mary the mother of James the younger and/or Joses (Mark 15:40, 47; 16:2) is said to have witnessed Jesus's crucifixion from afar, seen the place where Jesus was buried, and then accompanied Mary Magdalene and Salome to the tomb on Sunday morning, where they found it empty and were commissioned to tell Jesus's disciples that he had risen (cf. Matt. 27:56, 61; 28:1; Luke 24:10). Since Jesus had brothers named James and Joses (Mark 6:3), it has often been thought that this woman is to be identified with the Mary who was also the mother of Jesus. There is no clear rationale, however, for her being specified here as the mother of James and/or Joses, when she is identified as Jesus's mother everywhere else in these writings.

Mary is not mentioned in any other book of the Bible, aside from the Gospels and Acts. Paul does make one oblique reference to Jesus being "born of woman" in Gal. 4:2, but the point there is simply that he was sent by God into the world through the natural process of childbirth; Paul does not seem to regard the specific woman or mother through whom Jesus was born (much less the miraculous character of that birth) as a point of significance or relevance. The woman who gives birth to the Messiah in Rev. 12:2, 5 is not taken to be Mary, but as a symbol of God's people (Israel and the church) who bring forth the Christ. *See also* Magnificat; Virgin Birth.

Bibliography

Brown, Raymond E., Karl A. Donfried, Joseph A. Fitzmyer, and John Reumann, eds. *Mary in the New Testament*. Fortress, 1978.

Gaventa, Beverly R. *Mary: Glimpses of the Mother of Jesus*. Fortress, 1999.   W.M./M.A.P.

Masada (muh-sah′duh; Heb. *mesadah*, "stronghold"), a rock forming a massive natural stronghold that stands in the Judean desert near the western shore of the Dead Sea, some twelve miles south of En-gedi. The site was probably first fortified by Alexander Jannaeus (103–76 BCE), whose coins have been found in abundance. Remains of Hasmonean buildings were not found, perhaps because they were completely engulfed by the much more extensive construction carried out by Herod the Great (ruled 40–4 BCE). Herod the Great's military architects turned the entire top of the 1,300-foot-tall rock into a walled citadel, abundantly provided with food- and water-storage facilities, not only for a strong garrison, but also for palaces for the king and his family. Masada was the place where the last group of Zealots held out in the first Jewish war, falling in 73 CE to a Roman attack made possible by the construction of a still extant ramp leading to the top. Josephus offers a long and detailed account of the siege of Masada, which he says ended with mass suicide; just before the Romans broke through the fort's defense, the 960 Zealots within killed themselves, and only two women and five children survived (*Jewish War* 7.389–400). *See also* Herod; Maccabees; Zealots.

F.O.G.

maskil (mas'kil), a Hebrew word of uncertain significance that appears in the headings of some thirteen psalms (Pss. 32; 42; 44; 45; 52; 53; 54; 55; 74; 78; 88; 89; 142). Some current versions of the Bible leave the word untranslated, while others, in accordance with its apparent root meaning of "understand" or "ponder," translate it as "instruction" or the like. Scholars have suggested that *maskil* is possibly a technical term relating to the manner of a psalm's performance or a class of composition. The latter hypothesis is supported by the Psalter's use of other apparent class names in parallel fashion as well as by the appearance of the word in Amos 5:13, where it may designate such a class.   J.L.K.

masons, craftsmen who build with stone. They were brought from Tyre to build a house for David (2 Sam. 5:11; 1 Chron. 14:1) and to build the Jerusalem temple under Solomon (1 Chron. 22:15). Later, they came to repair that temple (2 Kings 12:12; 22:6; 2 Chron. 24:12) and, still later, they came again to rebuild it (Ezra 3:7). It is unclear precisely when local talent could fully displace the imported expertise.

In the Bible, masons are only mentioned in association with David's palace and the Jerusalem temple, but masons were employed in many lands mentioned in the Bible throughout the entire biblical period. In Egypt, stone that had been quarried and shaped into geometrical blocks was used for the building of temples, monuments, and, notably, the pyramids. In Israel, the excavated palaces of Omri and Ahab (in Samaria) exhibit a high quality of stonecutting, as does Hezekiah's tunnel in Jerusalem; the latter was cut by masons who started at opposite ends and carved through solid rock to meet in the middle. During the Second Temple period, Herod the Great was particularly known for his promotion of masonry projects, including the building of numerous palaces and forts and renovation of the temple.

Masorah (muh-sor'uh; Heb., "transmission"), detailed notes and annotations added to manuscripts of the Hebrew text of the Bible in order to maintain that text intact. The Hebrew text of the Bible was preserved ca. 600–950 CE by rabbinic scholars called the Masoretes. Most of the Masorah, or notes that they made in the manuscripts, consist of numbers or abbreviations. For example, a type of note called Masorah Parva (Mp) provides a numeral in the margin matched to a word or phrase in the text (indicated by a small circle); the number indicates how many times that word or phrase occurs. Another type of note, the Masorah Magna (Mm) lists the verses enumerated in the Mp notes, citing them by short identifying excerpts at the top or bottom of a page. In addition, notes called Masorah Finalis (Mf) provide summary lists of data at the conclusion of books or sections of the text. *See also* Masoretic Text.

Masoretic (maz-uh-ret'ik) **Text,** the standard or traditional Hebrew text of the Bible, as preserved by the Masoretes, a group of rabbinic scholars active ca. 600–950 CE. There is, however, more than one version of the Masoretic Text. First, there were three major groups of Masoretes: Palestinian, Babylonian, and Tiberian. Of these, Tiberian Masoretes gained prominence, so the Tiberian version of the Hebrew Bible is usually associated with what is called the Masoretic Text today. Beyond this, however, the Tiberian Masoretes differed on minor matters and produced a number of slightly different texts. Those produced by the family of Aaron ben Asher came to be regarded as the best, and these are preserved today in two frequently consulted manuscripts: the Aleppo Codex and the Leningrad Codex. Both of these contain, not only the text of the Bible written out in Hebrew consonants, but also vowels and accent signs determined to be appropriate by the Masoretes. Further, both the Aleppo Codex and the Leningrad Codex contain numerous Masorah, numbers and abbreviations that occur as notes in the margins and other key points in the text. The Masoretic Text of the Bible (as preserved especially in the Leningrad Codex) forms the primary basis for most English Bible translations, including the NRSV, although manuscripts of the LXX are also consulted and sometimes given preference when the reading preserved there is believed to represent a more ancient tradition.   B.M.M.

Massa (mas'uh), the seventh son of Ishmael (Gen. 25:14; 1 Chron. 1:30) and an ancestor of a north Arabian tribe (associated with Tema). The attribution of the words of Agur (Prov. 30:1) and Lemuel (Prov. 31:1) to the region of Massa suggests Arabian sources for that material.

Massah (mas'uh) **and Meribah** (mair'i-bah), according to Exod. 17:7 the spring in the wilderness where Israel tested the Lord. Following the gift of manna to the people in the wilderness, the people of Israel complained against Moses about the need for water. The Lord instructed Moses to strike a rock with his rod in order to provide for their needs. Moses named the place Massah ("Test") and Meribah ("Quarrel"), because there the Hebrews tested and quarreled with the Lord. See also Deut. 6:16; 9:22; 33:8; Ps. 95:8.

master.

1 An owner of property, as in the expression "master of the house" (Judg. 19:22; cf. Esther 19:4; Isa. 22:18).

2 An owner of an animal, e.g., the master of a donkey (Isa. 1:3) or of dogs (Matt. 15:27).

3 An employer (Luke 16:3) or, more often, an owner of a slave. Abraham was a master of slaves (Gen. 24:9); Joseph had a master when he was a slave (39:2). Moses gives instructions for how a master is to treat his slaves (Exod. 21:1–8). Nabal insults David by implying he is a slave who has rebelled against his master (1 Sam. 25:10; cf. 2 Sam. 12:8). See also Judg. 19:11–12; 1 Sam. 20:38; 30:15; Job 3:19; Ps. 123:2; Prov. 30:10; Isa. 24:2. In the NT, Jesus tells numerous parables about masters and slaves (e.g., Matt. 13:24–30; 24:45–51; 25:14–30; Mark 13:33–37; Luke 12:35–48; 14:16–24). The responsibilities of slaves to obey their masters is expressed in a number of NT "household codes" (Eph. 6:5–8; Col. 3:22–25); some of these codes also remind the masters that they have a "Master in heaven" (Eph. 6:9; Col. 4:1; 1 Tim. 6:1–2; Titus 2:9; 1 Pet. 2:18) to whom they will have to answer for their treatment of their slaves.

4 A person who exercises political authority; thus a king is master of his court and of all his subjects (2 Sam. 12:8; 1 Kings 11:23; 12:27; 2 Kings 5:1; 6:22; 8:14; 9:7; 18:23; 19:4; cf. 1 Kings 22:17); a "palace master" has authority over many, but rules under the king (Dan. 1:3–18).

5 A teacher or prophet who has disciples. Elijah is called the master of Elisha (2 Kings 2:3), and Elisha the master of Gehazi (5:20; cf. 6:5, 15). Jesus is frequently addressed as "Master" in the Gospel of Luke (5:5; 8:24, 45; 9:33, 49; 17:13). See also Jude 4 and, probably, 2 Pet. 2:1.

6 God, as the master of human beings (Jer. 3:14). In Malachi, the Lord asks, "If I am a master, where is the respect due me? (1:6). It is in this context that Jesus says, "No one can serve two masters; for a slave will either hate the one and love the other, or be devoted to the one and despise the other" (Matt. 6:24); the point of the proverb is that God alone should be one's master. Paul tells believers, "You have been bought with a price," implying that they now belong to God and not to any human master (1 Cor. 7:23). Simeon the prophet addresses God as "Master" in Luke 2:29.

7 Anything that might control a person: "People are slaves to whatever masters them" (2 Pet. 2:19). Jesus refers to "mammon" (NRSV: "wealth") as a potential master, an influence controlling a person's life and choices (Matt. 6:24).   M.A.P.

Mattaniah (mat'uh-ni'uh; Heb., "the LORD's gift").

1 A levitical musician from the sons of Heman who was appointed to the temple by David (1 Chron. 25:4).

2 An Asaphite Levite who participated in Hezekiah's reform (2 Chron. 29:13).

3 The last king of Judah, renamed Zedekiah by Nebuchadnezzar, who appointed him to succeed his exiled uncle (or brother; 2 Kings 24:17–25:7). *See also* Zedekiah.

4 A Levite, son of Mica, who returned to Jerusalem after the exile (1 Chron. 9:15).

5 The name of four different Israelites who divorced their foreign wives in response to Ezra's proclamation (Ezra 10:26, 27, 30, 37).

6 The name of four postexilic figures whose relationship to one another (or to the persons in **5**) cannot be determined: a Levite who returned from the Babylonian exile with Zerubbabel (Neh. 12:8); a guard of the gates (12:25); a priest (12:35); and the father of Zaccur (13:13).   F.E.G.

Mattathias (mat'uh-thi'uhs; Heb., "gift of the LORD").

1 A priest of the family of Joarib (1 Macc. 2:1) or Jehoiarib (see 1 Chron. 24:7) who, with his five sons, called "Maccabees," began the revolt against Seleucid rule in 167 BCE in their Judean village of Modein.

2 Mattathias the son of Simon, the grandson of **1.** He was murdered at the same time as his father (1 Macc. 16:14–17).

3 Mattathias the son of Absalom, one of the army commanders under Jonathan (1 Macc. 11:70).

4 One of the envoys sent by Nicanor to Judas Maccabeus (2 Macc. 14:19).

5 A name included twice in Luke's genealogy of Jesus (3:25–26).   F.O.G.

Matthew (math'yoo), one of the original twelve disciples called by Jesus. Matthew appears in all four of the apostolic lists (Matt. 10:2–4; Mark 3:16–19; Luke 6:14–16; Acts 1:13). The tradition of the "call" of Matthew is found in Matt. 9:9, where his occupation at the time of the call is identified as that of tax collector (cf. Matt. 10:3). In the parallel accounts (Mark 2:13–14; Luke 5:27–28), however, the name of the tax collector is Levi (the son of Alphaeus according to Mark), and no Levi is subsequently included among the twelve. The use of the different names in these parallel passages has given rise to long-standing debate as to whether "Matthew" and "Levi" are actually the same person. The traditional view is that "Matthew" and "Levi" are simply two names for the same person (like "Simon, who is called Peter," Matt. 4:18, or "John whose other name was Mark," Acts 12:12). If this is the case, then the Matthew who is listed among the twelve was "the son of Alphaeus" (Mark 2:14) and thus perhaps the brother of "James son of Alphaeus" (not to be confused with James the brother of John and son of Zebedee), who is also one of the twelve (Matt. 10:3; Mark 3:18; Luke 6:15; Acts 1:13). Tradition credits Matthew with having composed the Gospel of Matthew, though modern scholarship recognizes the final form of that book as produced at a later time by someone who had not been one of Jesus's twelve disciples.

See also Alphaeus; apostle; disciple; Matthew, Gospel According to; tax collectors; twelve, the.
P.L.S./M.A.P.

Matthew, Gospel According to, the first Gospel in the NT.

Contents: Matthew's Gospel opens with a genealogy that traces Jesus's descent from Abraham (1:1–17), followed by an account of Jesus's virgin birth and such related events as the visit of the magi (1:18–2:23). Then the narrative shifts to recount the beginning of Jesus's ministry as an adult: he is baptized by John (3:1–17) and tempted by Satan in the wilderness (4:1–11); he begins to call disciples and to go throughout Galilee preaching, teaching, and healing (4:12–25). He preaches the Sermon on the Mount (5:1–7:28), which focuses primarily on discipleship (i.e., the life expected of those who are faithful to God). Matthew continues the story of Jesus's ministry by relating

MATTHEW'S USE OF MARK

Matthew preserves about 90 percent of the stories and passages found in Mark's Gospel, but he edits this material in accord with certain principles.

Organization

Some Markan material is moved about. *Examples:*

Five miracle stories are moved to Matt. 8–9, where other miracle stories occur.

Mission charge is given to the disciples as soon as they are selected (Matt. 10:1–42; cf. Mark 3:14–19; 6:7–13).

Abbreviation

Details not directly relevant are pruned away. *Examples:*

The demoniac's chains and behavior (Matt. 8:28; Mark 5:2–5).

Removing the roof tiles for the paralytic (Matt. 9:2; Mark 2:2–5).

"Extra" characters, the crowd and the disciples, in story of woman's healing (Matt. 9:20–22; Mark 5:24b–34).

Sophistication

Casual or colloquial expressions are rewritten in the more polished Greek of the educated class. *Examples:*

Many instances of "historical present" tense are changed (130 out of 151).

Mark's repetitious use of words like "and" and "immediately" is reduced.

Pronouns lacking clear antecedents are provided with them.

Accuracy

Instances of questionable accuracy are corrected. *Examples:*

"King Herod" (Mark 6:14) becomes "Herod the Tetrarch" (Matt. 14:1).

The reference to Abiathar as high priest (Mark 2:26) is omitted (Matt. 12:4; cf. 1 Sam. 21:1–6).

Contextual Relevance

Some changes make the narrative more relevant to Matthew's community. *Examples:*

Mark's explanation of Jewish customs (Mark 7:3–4; cf. Matt. 15:1–2) is omitted, because Matthew's audience is Christians who are either ethnically Jewish or well acquainted with matters of Jewish tradition.

The phrase "kingdom of God" is frequently replaced with "kingdom of heaven" (e.g., Matt. 4:17; Mark 1:15), because some Jews tried to avoid saying "God" out of respect for the sanctity of God's name.

Mark's "village" (*kōmē*) frequently becomes "city" (*polis*), because Matthew's is an urban community removed from rural settings.

"Silver" and "gold" are added to Jesus's injunction for the disciples to take no "copper" with them on their travels (Matt. 10:9; Mark 6:8), because in a more prosperous community the renunciation of "copper" might seem insignificant.

a series of healing stories, interspersed with anecdotes in which Jesus responds to questions that clarify or challenge the nature of his ministry (8:1–9:38). Jesus then appoints twelve of his followers to be apostles and sends them out on a mission similar to his, instructing them with regard to persecution and the need for radical faithfulness (10:1–11:1). Opposition to Jesus begins to mount, as he encounters doubt, apathy, and outright hostility from diverse parties: John the Baptist, the crowds, the Pharisees, and even his family (11:2–12:50). He tells seven parables about the kingdom of heaven (13:1–53) and then meets with rejection in his hometown (13:54–58). His ministry also attracts the attention of Herod, who has had John the Baptist put to death (14:1–12). The Gospel continues with an accent on miraculous deeds interspersed with accounts that portray the Pharisees as blind guides who stand under God's judgment and accounts that show Jesus's disciples to be people of little faith (14:1–16:12). But then Peter receives Jesus's blessing when he confesses Jesus to be the Messiah and Son of God (16:13–20). After that, the narrative shifts into a long section that emphasizes Jesus's instruction of his disciples regarding his destiny, community life, and other matters pertinent for those being prepared to live

in the kingdom of heaven (16:21–20:34). Jesus enters Jerusalem and challenges the religious leaders there (21:1–23:39). Then he retires to the Mount of Olives with his disciples and offers them private teaching regarding the last days, including information about his Second Coming and a series of parables regarding the final judgment (24:1–25:46). Matthew's Gospel concludes with an account of Jesus's passion and resurrection (26:1–28:20): he is anointed by an unnamed woman and shares a last meal with his disciples, who will betray, deny, and desert him; he is arrested, tried before Jewish and Gentile leaders, crucified, and laid in a tomb; on the third day, he rises from the dead, appears to a group of women, and then commissions his disciples to baptize and teach people from all nations.

Composition: Church tradition attributes the Gospel to Matthew, a tax collector who was one of Jesus's twelve disciples (Matt. 9:9; 10:3). Most scholars now believe the book was put together by an unknown Jewish Christian sometime after the destruction of Jerusalem in 70 CE. Antioch of Syria is often suggested as a likely place of writing, because the social conditions reflected in Matthew's Gospel correspond with those that seem to have prevailed there; it was a prosperous,

---

MATTHEW'S USE OF MARK *(continued)*

Character Portrayal

Matthew changes the way major characters are portrayed in the Gospel story. Examples:

Jesus

Questions that might imply a lack of knowledge on Jesus's part are omitted (Mark 5:9, 30; 6:38; 8:23; 9:12, 16, 21, 33; 10:3; 14:14).

Statements that could imply a lack of ability or authority on Jesus's part are modified (cf. Matt. 13:58; Mark 6:5).

References to Jesus exhibiting human emotions are often dropped: "pity" (Mark 1:41), "anger" (Mark 3:5), "sadness" (Mark 3:5), "wonder" (Mark 6:6), "indignation" (Mark 10:14), "love" (Mark 10:21).

Stories that might seem to portray Jesus as a magician are dropped (Mark 7:31–37; 8:22–26).

The Disciples of Jesus

"No faith" is changed to "little faith" (cf. Matt 8:26; Mark 4:40).w

The theme of not understanding Jesus is amended, so they are merely slow to understand (cf. Matt. 16:12; Mark 8:21; Matt. 17:9–13; Mark 9:9–13).

Unseemly ambition is ascribed to James and John's mother rather than to the disciples themselves (Matt. 20:20; Mark 10:35).

References to the disciples "worshiping" Jesus and calling him "Lord" or "Son of God" are added to stories taken from Mark (cf. Matt. 14:32–33; Mark 6:51–52).

The Religious Leaders of Israel

A scribe whom Jesus praises in Mark (12:28–34) is depicted as an opponent who puts Jesus to the test in Matthew (22:34–40).

Friendly religious leaders like Jairus (Mark 5:22) and Joseph of Arimathea (Mark 15:43) are no longer identified as religious leaders in Matthew (Matt. 9:18; 27:57).

From Mark Allan Powell, *Introducing the New Testament* (courtesy, Baker Academic)

Matthew the evangelist, from the *Lindisfarne Gospels* (ca. 700). His symbol, an angel, is behind him.

urban, Greek-speaking area with a large population of both Jews and Gentiles (5:10–12; 10:17–18; 24:9–14). The dominant theory among scholars holds that the author of Matthew possessed a copy of Mark's Gospel as well as a copy of a now lost document that scholars refer to as the Q source. Sometime around 85 CE, these two documents were edited and combined with other materials (referred to by scholars as "M material") into the work that is now called the Gospel of Matthew. Alternative views hold that Matthew expanded Mark without any reliance on a Q source, or that Matthew's Gospel was written first of the four by someone who possessed sources unknown to us.

Distinctive Features: Matthew's Gospel contains numerous passages and stories not found elsewhere (for a list, see M). In addition, Matthew's Gospel treats certain matters differently than the other Synoptic Gospels (Mark and Luke). In general, Matthew takes a more straightforward approach to narrative, presenting material with less lively or colorful detail (e.g., cf. Matt. 8:28; Mark 5:2–5; and Matt. 9:2; Mark 2:2–5). Matthew is thought to have edited the material he took from Mark's Gospel in ways that present a less colloquial, more sophisticated style of Greek. He also appears to have eliminated or changed passages that imply a lack of knowledge or ability on the part of Jesus (cf. Matt. 13:58; Mark 6:5). In general, the disciples of Jesus exhibit more potential for growth and leadership in Matthew than in Mark, while the religious leaders of Israel come off worse in Matthew than in either Mark or Luke. With regard to structure, Matthew may have organized his Gospel by beginning with an extended section focusing on the identity of Jesus (1:1–4:16), followed by a section devoted primarily to his ministry (4:17–16:20), followed by another section focusing on his rejection, passion, and resurrection (16:21–28:20). Another distinctive feature, however, is the presentation of Jesus's teaching in five great discourses, each of which deals with a particular topic: discipleship (chaps. 5–7); mission (10); parables of the kingdom (13); community life (18), and the end times (24–25).

Major Themes: Matthew's story of Jesus emphasizes the abiding presence of God with humanity (1:23). This presence is manifested through Jesus Christ, who continues to be present on earth in and through the community of his followers (18:20; 28:20). This Gospel also seems to place

1

2

3

1 In 701 B.C. Assyrian king Sennacherib conquered most of Judah including the fortress-city of Lachish. The victory was recorded in remarkable detail on bas-reliefs at his Nineveh palace. This scene is poignant testimony to the plight of his victims, who were deported with only what they could carry on their backs.

2 Tell ed-Duweir, the site of ancient Lachish viewed from the air, appears as an imposing mound in the foothills of Judah. The Judahite palace-fort, razed by Sennacherib, is the rectangular raised area on the far side of the top of the mound. **3** The storming of the Lachish gate-tower. On a track of logs a siege engine

equipped with a spearlike beam batters the city gate. One of the Assyrian soldiers within the engine pours water on its front from a long-handled ladle to extinguish firebrands thrown by the Lachish defenders atop the walls. From a door in the tower emerge men and women fleeing the doomed city.

1 The Black Obelisk of Shalmaneser III (858–824 B.C.). This detail shows King Jehu of Omri—the name the Assyrians gave to ancient Israel—prostrate in obeisance before Shalmaneser. **2** A copper crown, one of 416 copper objects found in the "Cave of the Treasure," in the Nahal Mishmar in southern Palestine; fourth millennium B.C. **3** Hill of Shemer. Strategically located beside major routes to Jerusalem on the south, Megiddo and the Jezreel Valley on the north, the Mediterranean Sea and coastal plain on the west, and Shechem and the Jordan Valley on the east, it is here that King Omri built the city of Samaria, capital of the northern kingdom of Israel, in the early ninth century B.C.

1

2

3

1 The stele of Hammurabi. From the reign of the Babylonian king, 1728–1686 B.C., it is inscribed with the "Code of Hammurabi," a prologue, 282 laws, and an epilogue, which parallels in some respects the ancient Hebrew Covenant Code. In the scene at top, Hammurabi worships the enthroned sun god Shamash.
2 Statue head of Gudea, *ensi* or local governor of the city-state of Lagash from 2141 to 2122 B.C. Lagash was close to Ur, traditional home of the biblical Abraham.
3 Section of the wall of the Old City of Jerusalem. The tower, today called the Tower of David, rises from the foundations of the original Phasael Tower, constructed by Herod the Great after 40 B.C. to protect his palace at the vulnerable northwestern corner of the city.

1

2a

1, 2a, 2b Fresco paintings from the western wall of the third-century A.D. synagogue at Dura-Europos, a city on the Euphrates River in Syria. The top panel, "The Consecration of the Tabernacle and Its Priests," is dominated by the figure of Aaron, portrayed as high priest in his robes of office. Beside him is a templelike structure, the Tabernacle, with the *menorah*, an altar, and incense burners aflame in front. At his feet is a stone wall representing the synagogue courtyard with its three entrances (cf. Exod. 40:2–8). To his left are two trumpeters (cf. Num. 10:2–3) and sacrificial animals—a humped bullock and a white, fat-tailed ram. The bottom "Exodus" panel, which begins its narrative at the right (2b), depicts Moses three times, from far right to left: Moses strides toward the Red Sea with staff upraised leading the ancient Israelites out of Egypt, represented by the wall with the red and black columns in front, which symbolize the pillars of fire and cloud that led the Israelites through the wilderness by

(Continued on facing page)

1

2b

(Continued from previous page) night and day (Exod. 13:21–22). In the middle Moses holds back the sea while the people cross. Finally, on the left side, under the protective hands and forearms of God appearing at the top of the panel, Moses holds his staff down to touch the pool of Marah (Exod. 15:23–25a). The twelve figures to his right repre-sent the numbering of the tribes of Israel (Num. 1).

1 Part of the limestone gable of the oldest known Holy Ark (third century A.D.), which sheltered a wooden Torah shrine at the syna-gogue of Nabratein in Upper Gal-ilee. Shows two rampant lions surmounting the decorated gable. A hole is pierced in the center for a chain from which to hang the eternal light. The pediment weighs one thousand pounds and was toppled to the ground by an earthquake; it was reused, upside down and unrecognized by ex-cavators until 1981, in the foun-dation of a later synagogue prayer platform.

1

2

1 Jesus washing Peter's feet (John 13:3–11). Manuscript page from *The Four Gospels*, twelfth century. 2 White limestone remains of the synagogue at Capernaum, late second to fifth century A.D. Beneath it has been excavated an earlier synagogue of black basalt —contemporaneous with the ruins of the first-century houses seen in the foreground—in which Jesus may have preached (cf. Mark 1:21; John 6:59).

1

2

3

1 Jesus as the Good Shepherd was a favorite symbol in the catacombs and on the sarcophagi of early Christians (cf. Ps. 23; Luke 15:4 – 6). This wall painting is from the third-century catacomb of St. Priscilla, Rome. **2** Jerusalem, view of the Temple Mount (site of the ancient Temple) from the Mount of Olives. From the time of its capture by the Israelites under David nearly three thousand years ago, Jerusalem was the key city in biblical history. According to the NT, Jesus entered Jerusalem from the Mount of Olives in the climactic final week of his ministry. **3** The river Jordan just above where it empties into the Dead Sea. The Moabite hills rise in the background. The NT tells that Jesus was baptized by John in the Jordan (Mark 1:9).

1

2

3

1 Aerial view of ancient Ephesus from the southwest. The agora (foreground) and theater seating twenty-four thousand behind it date from the first and second centuries A.D. when Ephesus was the fourth largest city of the Roman Empire. In this or an earlier theater, Paul's opponents in Ephesus gathered to defend their worship of Artemis (Acts 19:28–41). **2** Corinth, first founded in the tenth century B.C., was an important city in the NT. In the foreground is the *bema,* or platform, situated in the center of the city forum and probably Gallio's "tribunal" before which Paul was brought (Acts 18:12–17). Behind the *bema* rises the Acrocorinth. **3** Paul, as depicted in the sepulcher of the child Asellus, ca. 313, Rome.

1 Painted ceramic horse from a tomb near the Philistine city of Gaza, sixth century B.C. **2** Marble sarcophagus of the Roman prefect Junius Bassus, Rome, A.D. 359. The subject matter, depicting scenes from the OT and the NT, represents a newfound freedom of expression for Christians under the emperor Constantine and the Edict of 325. **3** Sumerian bull-lyre, an ancient musical instrument found in a royal burial pit at Ur from the third millennium B.C.. This detail shows the bull's head with its original gold overlay and lapis lazuli beard and hair. **4** Head of an ancient Near Eastern man as depicted on a glazed terra-cotta tile from the Temple of Ramesses III, twelfth century B.C. **5** Statues, from left to right, of Melchizedek, Abraham holding Isaac, Moses, Samuel, and David line the jambs of the Royal Portal at Chartres Cathedral (ca. 1145–1155).

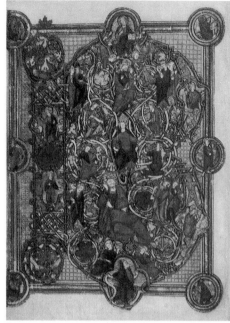

1

2

3

4

1 Carpet page with a double-armed cross and eight medallions from the *Book of Kells*, an illuminated Bible manuscript from the eighth century. **2** Initial B from the *Windmill Psalter*, thirteenth century. Within this letter is a depiction of the Tree of Jesse showing Jesse reclining in the lower loop, David crowned in the middle, and the Virgin and

Child in the upper loop. Also shown are the figure of God at the very top, the creation story interwoven in the foliage, the four major and twelve minor prophets, and the symbols of the four Evangelists in the corner medallions **3** Prism of Sennacherib. It records Sennacherib's conquest of Judah in 701 B.C. and reads in part, "[Hezekiah] I shut

up like a caged bird in his royal city of Jerusalem." **4** The so-called Marzeah Tablet, showing the wedge-shaped marks of cuneiform script, in this case Ugaritic from the fourteenth century B.C.

1

2   **3**

1 Isaiah Scroll "A," one of the Dead Sea Scrolls from the Qumran caves, open to columns 32 (right) and 33. Isa. 38:8–40:28. The Hebrew is in a Hasmonean script, ca. 100 B.C. The break in the second line of the left-hand column may have been to emphasize what follows: "A voice cries: 'In the wilderness prepare the way of the LORD, make straight in the desert a highway for our God' " (Isa. 40:3). **2** A section of the *Pesher* or commentary on the book of Habakkuk found at Qumran. It is written in Hebrew using the Jewish square script, probably of the Herodian type (50 B.C.–A.D. 40). **3** A facsimile of a page from Codex Sinaiticus, showing the opening of the Gospel According to Matthew. This parchment manuscript of the Bible, written in Greek and dating from the fourth century A.D., was found at the Monastery of St. Catherine, Sinai, in the nineteenth century.

1 Columns that lined a main street in Herod's city of Caesarea, first century B.C., lie in ruins at the edge of the Mediterranean Sea. **2** Aerial view, from 570 miles above the earth, of Israel and surrounding area shows the Dead Sea, the Sea of Galilee, mountains, deserts, and (at upper left) the Mediterranean Sea.
3 The Sea of Galilee, variously referred to in the Bible as the Sea of Tiberias, Lake of Genessaret, or the Sea of Chinnereth, is a harp-shaped freshwater lake about thirty-two miles around, located in northern Palestine.
4 The Dead Sea—also called by various names in the OT and not mentioned in the NT—is actually a lake into which the river Jordan flows. Because of its high mineral content (25 percent) the Dead Sea does not support marine life.
5 The Wilderness of Judea, west of the Dead Sea, was not traversed by major trade routes due to its inimical terrain. This is the kind of countryside envisioned by the Evangelists when they describe the temptations of Jesus (e.g., Luke 4:1–2).

1 Ancient Egyptians winnowing with wooden scoops, much as the ancient Israelites did with shallow baskets and as is still done in many places in the Near East. A mural from the Tomb of Mennah, scribe of Thutmose IV (fourteenth century B.C.).
2 Ceramic "pilgrim flasks" from the cemetery of Deir el-Ballah, thirteenth century B.C. 3 A Hellenistic terra-cotta lamp dates to the Maccabean era (167–63 B.C.). Its typical Greek form, with a long nozzle for the wick and a broad opening in the cover to receive the oil, indicates it was probably imported into ancient Israel. 4 Flowers blossoming in the countryside of Galilee along the way to Safed. 5 Terraced rows of olive trees near Antipa- tris along the road from Jerusa- lem to Caesarea. Hardy enough to grow almost anywhere, the olive tree was ubiquitous in the bibli- cal landscape. Its fruit was eaten and the oil derived from it had many uses: in cooking, for lamps, as a medicine, for anointing, and in sacrifices.

1 The paralytic brought by his friends to Jesus to be healed (Luke 5:18). Crowds around the house prevented them from entering, so they went up on the roof and lowered the man on his mat into the room. Manuscript page from *The Four Gospels*, twelfth century. 2 Noah, who according to Gen. 8:8–12 released a dove on three occasions "to see if the waters had subsided from the face of the ground." A detail from the mosaics, begun in the eleventh century, in St. Mark's Cathedral in Venice. 3 Jonah being cast overboard into the mouth of a great fish. Detail of an altarpiece triptych with fifty-one enamel and gold scenes from the OT and NT that was originally part of an ambo, or raised pulpit; from 1181, by Nicholas of Verdun. 4 Stained glass windows at Reims Cathedral depicting the crucifixion were designed by the twentieth-century Russian Jewish artist Marc Chagall in 1974, to replace those destroyed by bombs during World War II.

1 Interior of Hagia Sophia in present-day Istanbul. One of the most imposing structures in the history of architecture, the building was constructed in the sixth century as a Christian church by the Byzantine emperor Justinian. With the Turkish conquest of Constantinople (the older name of the city) in 1453, Hagia Sophia became a mosque; today it is a museum. **2** Elijah. Detail of the Transfiguration mosaic pictured below. **3** Christ rises above the figures of Moses on the right, Elijah on the left, and John, Peter, and James below. Medallions surrounding the scene depict the other nine apostles and major and minor prophets of the OT. The prominence of Moses and Elijah, along with Peter, James, and John, suggests the mosaic takes its theme from Christ's transfiguration (Matt. 17:1–8). The mosaic is in the apse of the Church of St. Catherine, Sinai, also built by Justinian in the sixth century.

1

2   3

1 The annunciation to Mary by the angel Gabriel. The book in Mary's hand is open to the passage from Isaiah, "Behold, a young woman shall conceive and bear a son" (7:14). Detail of a painting by Masolino da Panicale ca. 1430. **2** Sarah and Abraham. Sarah's remarkable conception of a son in her old age (Gen. 17:15–

19) was a continuation of God's promise to Abraham, regarded as the father of the Israelite people, that his descendants would be a blessing for the world. Detail of a Russian icon. **3** Abigail intercepts King David and persuades him not to harm her husband, Nabal, whom he has come to kill for refusing to recognize his au-

thority (1 Sam. 25). Detail from a thirteenth-century French miniature.

special emphasis on the identity of Jesus as the Son of God: (3:17; 17:5) and on the revelation of his identity to humanity (14:33; 16:16–17; 27:54; cf. 11:27). The moral teaching of Jesus receives particular emphasis in this Gospel, in part because of the prominence of the Sermon on the Mount (chaps. 5–7), which emphasizes the eternal validity of God's laws (5:17–18) and the need for Jesus's followers to exhibit a greater righteousness than is associated with either Gentiles or Jews (5:20, 47–48). In recent years, much scholarly attention has also focused on the hostility to Jewish leaders evinced in Matthew's Gospel: Pharisees and other religious leaders of Israel are depicted as an evil "brood of vipers" (3:7; 12:34; 23:33) destined for God's condemnation (15:13; 23:33); passages such as 21:43 and 27:25 have been used historically to justify anti-Semitism. *See also* Antioch; gospel; Gospels, the; kingdom of God; M; Matthew; Q; Sermon on the Mount; Synoptic Problem.

Bibliography

Davies, W. D., and Dale C. Allison. *A Critical and Exegetical Commentary on the Gospel According to Matthew.* 3 vols. Clark, 1988–97.

Hagner, Donald. *Matthew.* 2 vols. Word, 1993.

Keener, Craig S. *A Commentary on the Gospel of Matthew.* Eerdmans, 1999.

Luz, Ulrich. *Matthew.* 3 vols. Augsburg Fortress, 1989–2007.

———. *The Theology of the Gospel of Matthew.* Cambridge University Press, 1995.

Nolland, John. *The Gospel of Matthew: A Commentary on the Greek Text.* Eerdmans, 2005.

Powell, Mark Allan. *Introducing the New Testament: A Historical, Literary, and Theological Survey.* Baker Academic, 2009. Pp. 103–23.   M.A.P.

Matthias (muh-thi′uhs), according to Acts 1:15–26, the successor among the twelve apostles to Judas Iscariot. After prayer, Matthias was chosen by lot over another candidate, Joseph called Barsabbas. According to Acts, both men had been with Jesus from the beginning of his ministry until his ascension. The NT contains no other reference to Matthias. *See also* apostle; Barsabbas; twelve, the.

Mattithiah (mat′uh-thi′uh; Heb., "gift of the Lord").

1 A Levite who was in charge of baked goods in the temple (1 Chron. 9:31).

2 A gatekeeper from the Merari group of Levites during the reign of King David (1 Chron. 15:18).

3 A levitical musician during the time of David (1 Chron. 15:21); he is probably the same musician chosen to help celebrate the transfer of the ark of the covenant to Jerusalem (16:5); and he is possibly also the same Levite from the Jeduthun group who was head of the fourteenth course of musicians (25:3; 21).

4 A postexilic priest from the Nebo family group who divorced his foreign wife in response to Ezra's proclamation (Ezra 10:43).

5 A man, probably a Levite, who was with Ezra at the reading of the law (Neh. 8:4).   D.R.B.

mattock, an agricultural tool with a double-bladed metal head, often made with one blade attached at a hoelike angle and the other in an axlike position. Farmers used the mattock to loosen soil and dig weeds in fields and terraced vineyards (cf. Isa. 5:6; 7:5). The NRSV uses mattock only in 1 Sam. 13:20–21, a passage that says the Hebrews were obliged to take their farm implements to the Philistines for sharpening. The tool might also be referenced in 2 Chron. 34:6 and Isa. 7:25. *See also* farming; metals; tools.

meal offering. *See* sacrifice.

meals. The ancient Israelites usually ate two meals a day, a light meal in late morning or at midday and a more substantial meal in the evening, around sunset. In ancient Israel, the normal diet might include the following: bread, cooked or parched grain (wheat, barley, millet), wine, cheese and curds (primarily from goats' milk), figs or fig cakes, grapes and raisins, dates, olives, wild honey, beans and lentils, melons, and cucumbers. Onions, leeks, and garlic supplied seasoning; olive oil was used for cooking. Poultry and eggs became common only relatively late in Israelite history. The NT indicates that fish was a common food in the first century. Except among the wealthy, meat was not part of the daily diet, but was reserved for special occasions such as feasts or sacrifices (see Lev. 7:11–18). The Torah emphatically distinguishes between living creatures that may be eaten and those that may not be (Lev. 11; Deut. 14). The Torah also stresses that meat to be eaten must be entirely drained of blood, for "the blood is the life" (Deut. 12:23; see Gen. 9:4; Lev. 17:14). Sheep and goats were the main sources of meat, and the tail of the sheep was considered a special delicacy.

In Israel, meals could be more than occasions for satisfying hunger; they were also events through which persons were bound to one another in friendship and mutual obligation. Moreover, a meal could be intensely symbolic when it was eaten in conjunction with the making of a covenant between persons (e.g., Gen. 26:28–30; 31:43–54) or with God (Exod. 24:9–11). The Israelite experience of eating "before the Lord" when one brought sacrifices and offerings (e.g., Deut. 12:6–7; 14:22–26) perhaps reflects the ancient view that through a sacred meal human beings can commune with the deity. Especially when accompanied by wine or music and dancing (Isa. 5:12; Sir. 32:3–6; Luke 15:22–25), meals were fitting occasions for celebration and rejoicing (cf. Amos 8:10), and feasts often marked events of special significance, such as a sheep shearing (2 Sam. 13:23–28), a wedding (Judg. 14:10), or the return of an absent family member (Luke 15:22–24). The feasts prescribed by Torah (e.g., Festival of Weeks) or tradition (e.g., Purim) were celebrations of God's beneficence; the most important of these was the Passover (Exod. 12; Num. 28:16–25; Deut. 16:1–8). During the Roman period, the Jewish sectarians at Qumran observed a daily communal meal, which began with a priestly blessing of the bread and wine. As described in the Dead Sea Scrolls, this bore special religious significance, possibly because it anticipated the banquet of the new age when the two messiahs, priestly and royal, would be present (1QS 6:2–5; 1QSa 2:11–22). This expectation is reminiscent of Isa. 25:6–8, where a "feast of fat things" symbolizes God's eschatological salvation.

Scattered clues in NT documents provide a glimpse into the social etiquette that prevailed at banquets given by the well-to-do at this time. There are references to the proper clothing to be worn by guests (Matt. 22:11–12), the expectation that a host might greet his guests with a kiss and provide for the washing of their feet (Luke 7:44–45; cf. Judg. 19:21), and arrangements for seating in accord with status or rank (Luke 14:7–11). Likewise, Sir. 32:1–2 mentions responsibilities of the banquet master. In Jesus's day it was apparently customary to issue two invitations to a banquet—the first some days ahead of time and the second when the meal was ready (Luke 14:16–17). In describing meals at which Jesus was present, the Gospels sometimes state that he reclined at table (John 13:23, 25; cf. Tob. 2:1; 7:9; 9:6; 1 Esd. 4:10). This indicates that the Greco-Roman custom of reclining at formal meals had become widespread (cf. Amos 6:4–6). Lying on couches placed around a large table (or three tables placed to form an open-ended rectangle), guests and host would rest on their left elbows and eat with their right hands, bodies diagonal to the couch and feet extending off the back. Usually three persons reclined on one couch. This reclining posture at table would explain how Luke could describe the woman with the ointment as standing behind Jesus while anointing his feet (7:36–38). It also explains how, in the Gospel of John, Jesus could wash the disciples' feet as they ate (13:5) and how the Beloved Disciple could recline on Jesus's breast (13:23). By NT times the blessing of the food at the beginning of a meal had become a common practice in Judaism; when wine was drunk, a prayer of thanksgiving over the cup concluded the meal. The Pharisees, in addition, insisted on a ritual washing of hands. Although Jesus blessed the food before eating (Mark 6:41; John 6:11), he and his disciples did not adopt the practice of hand washing (Mark 7:1–5; Luke 11:37–38).

Jesus's table fellowship with his followers was an important feature of his ministry, and according to the Gospels his dining practices drew criticism from his detractors. Their accusation that he was a "glutton and a drunkard" (Matt. 11:18–19; Luke 7:33–34) suggests that he did not practice asceticism with regard to eating and drinking, as did John the Baptist (who was apparently noted for fasting and abstinence from wine). Jesus's disciples also were criticized for not fasting, a lacuna he justified by comparing his time on earth

with them to the celebration of a marriage feast (Mark 2:18–20). Further, Jesus was criticized for his choice of table companions: he became known for eating with "tax collectors and sinners" (Matt. 9:9–10; Luke 15:1–2).

The Gospels also tell stories of Jesus miraculously providing meals for people (Mark 6:30–44; 8:1–9 cf. John 6:1–14). Several appearances of the risen Jesus to his disciples also occur in the setting of a meal. It was only when Jesus blessed and broke the bread that the eyes of Cleopas and his companion at Emmaus were opened, so that they recognized him (Luke 24:30–31). In John's Gospel, the risen Jesus gives his disciples bread and fish to eat beside the Sea of Galilee (21:9–13; cf. Luke 24:41–43).

Several times in the Gospels, especially in Luke, a meal is the setting for important teachings of Jesus (e.g., Luke 7; 11:37–52; 14:1–24; cf. Matt. 9:10–13), and some of Jesus's parables have to do with a feast or with feasting (Matt. 22:1–13; Luke 14:16–24; 15:11–32; cf. Matt. 25:10; Luke 16:19–21). The end-time salvation that God offers the world is symbolized as a great banquet (Matt. 8:11; cf. Matt. 22:1–13; Luke 14:16–24); likewise in the book of Revelation faithful believers will be invited to the "marriage supper of the Lamb" (19:9), but at the "great supper of God" the birds of the air will feed on the flesh of the world's kings, captains, and warriors (19:17–18; cf. Ezek. 39:17–20).

Meals continued to be important in early Christianity. The book of Acts describes the Christians in Jerusalem after Pentecost as breaking bread in their homes and partaking of food "with glad and generous hearts" (2:46); this is probably a reference to observance of the ritual meal that Paul refers to as the "Lord's Supper" (1 Cor. 11:20); in Jude 12, these meals are referred to as "love feasts." There were controversies, however, in the early church regarding joint participation of Jewish and Gentile believers in such common meals. Paul clashed with Barnabas and Peter over this question at the church in Antioch (Gal. 2:11–14). The book of Acts records that an initial compromise involved Gentile Christians adopting certain dietary restrictions that had been traditional for Jews (15:19–29), but there is no evidence that this policy was instituted in a widespread or long-term sense. Paul also discusses the question of whether Christians ought to take part in pagan banquets to which they might be invited (1 Cor. 10:14–22); he maintains that doing so involves partaking of fellowship with demons. In a different vein, however, he sees nothing wrong with Christians eating food offered to idols (i.e., meat that was butchered in dedication to some foreign god), so long as the Christian does so in a way that does not offend or harm the conscience of others (1 Cor. 10:27–33). *See also* fasting; festivals, feasts, and fasts; food; food offered to idols; Lord's Supper; Passover.

S.K.W.

measure. *See* weights and measures.

meat. *See* food; meals; sacrifice; worship in the Hebrew Bible; worship in the New Testament.

meat offered to idols. *See* food offered to idols.

Medan (mee´dan), the third son of Abraham by Keturah (Gen. 25:2; 1 Chron. 1:32); the term may also be a reference to the inhabitants of Midian.

Medeba (med´uh-buh), a city and surrounding territory located on a fertile plateau approximately six miles south of Heshbon and twenty-five miles south of Amman. The modern city of Madaba in Jordan appears to have been built on the ruins of ancient Medeba. In the Bible, Medeba is mentioned along with Heshbon and Dibon (Num. 21:30) in the account of the land taken by the Israelites from Sihon. The tableland of Medeba is part of the inheritance of Reuben (Josh. 13:9, 16). In a battle between Joab and an Ammonite-Syrian coalition, the Syrians encamped before Medeba (1 Chron. 19:7). An inscription on the Moabite Stone indicates that the Israelites had occupied the land of Medeba for forty years. Mesha, king of Moab, claims to have recaptured and rebuilt it. It is included in Isaiah's oracle against Moab (15:2). John, the oldest son of Mattathias, was ambushed by the sons of Jambri from Medeba during the Maccabean revolt against Syria, begun in 167 BCE (1 Macc. 9:36). Jonathan and Simon, his brothers, took revenge by annihilating a wedding party of their enemies (9:37–42). The Jewish historian Josephus relates that John Hyrcanus, Simon's son, captured Medeba after a six-month siege. He also says that Alexander Jannaeus took it along with other towns and that Hyrcanus II promised to restore those towns to Aretas, king of the Nabateans. The most impressive archaeological remains at Medeba are the mosaics, which date from the Byzantine period. The chief mosaic, the Medeba Map, dates from the sixth century CE and displays Jerusalem and other biblical sites.   B.M.

Medes (meeds), **Media** (mee´dee-uh), a people and place often associated with Persia (especially in the books of Esther and Daniel). Media became a province of the Persian Empire in 549 BCE when the Medan overlord was conquered by Cyrus the Great. The cities of the Medes are listed among the areas to which deportees from the northern kingdom were taken in 722/1 BCE (2 Kings 17:6; 18:11). Ecbatana (Agbatana), the Medan capital, located some four hundred miles north of the Persian Gulf, became one of the administrative centers of the Persian Empire (Ezra 6:2). In the stories recounted in Esther and in Dan. 5–6, the laws of Medes and Persians are described by the Medan officials as unalterable (e.g., Esther 1:19; Dan. 5:28), a description that recalls Israelite prohibitions regarding the altering of biblical laws (cf. Deut. 4:2; 12:32; Ezra 6:11). The Medes appear as the divine instrument of judgment on Babylon in Isa. 13:17; Jer. 51:11, 28; also with Elam in Isa. 21:2 (cf. Jer. 25:25, a picture

Median nobles march up a stairway at Persepolis, bringing gifts to the Persian king Darius I (521–486 BCE).

of total judgment on Babylon at the hands of all the nations). Dan. 5:31; 9:1; and 11:1 mention a "kingdom of the Medes" (unknown in history) that existed between the fall of the Babylonians and the rise of the Persians. Media is mentioned frequently in the apocryphal/deuterocanonical books of Tobit (1:14–15; 3:7; 4:1, 20; 5:2–4, 5–6, 10; 6:6, 10; 9:5; 14:4, 12–13, 15) and 1 Maccabees (6:56; 8:8; 14:1–2). Acts 2:9 includes Media as one of the areas from which Jewish pilgrims have come to Jerusalem.

The history of the Medes before their empire was taken over by Cyrus is obscure at many points. They appear in numerous Assyrian inscriptions from the mid-ninth century BCE onwards, established in the area of modern Iran and penetrating the Zagros Mountains. Herodotus, the fifth-century BCE Greek historian, has an account of their history, but appears to have no real knowledge of the chronology. The extent of their empire is a matter of debate; it was evidently fully developed in the seventh century BCE. The Medes took a major part in the eventual overthrow of the Assyrians, capturing Nineveh in 612 BCE and sacking Harran in 610. In the early sixth century, the Medes came into conflict with the Lydians in Asia Minor, a conflict that was brought to a successful conclusion by Cyrus. Under the Persians, Media was a large province. It appears probable that the administrative title "satrap," associated particularly with the organization of the Persian Empire by Darius I, was of Medan origin. *See also* Cyrus II; Darius; Persia.

Bibliography

Cook, J. M. *The Persian Empire.* Dent, 1983.

P.R.A.

mediator, in religious studies, a person who represents the community in worship and other contexts though which contact is made with divine beings. In the Hebrew Bible, various figures in Israel's history mediate between God and humans in a variety of different contexts; in the NT, Jesus is the unique mediator who reconciles sinful humans to God.

In the Hebrew Bible: In Israelite history, a number of leaders are described as mediating between God and people. Abraham sacrificed and prayed to God in the name of his family (Gen. 12:7–8); he also interceded on behalf of Sodom and Gomorrah (18:22–33). Jacob sacrificed to God and received God's blessing on all his descendants in Israel (35:1–15). Moses mediated between God and the Hebrews in Egypt, during the wandering in the desert, at Sinai, and when Israel sinned by worshiping the golden calf (Exod. 32:30–34). Joshua mediated between God and the people in the making of the covenant in Israel (Josh. 24:14–28), Samuel mediated the appointment of the first king (1 Sam. 8–12), and Solomon prayed in the people's name at the dedication of the temple (1 Kings 8:22–53). The prophets who acted as messengers in bringing God's word to the people also functioned as mediators in effecting reconciliation between the people and God (Jer. 14:1–9). Finally, the "suffering servant" of Isa. 53 atones for the sins of Israel and effects a reconciliation between God and Israel.

In a more regularized role, priests are described as religious mediators between humans and God. Their functions include offering community and private sacrifices, praying and singing in the temple, protecting the integrity of the holy places and rituals, and maintaining themselves in a state of ritual purity. All the religious regulations concerning priests, holy places, worship, and the temple were designed to render humans holy, so they could relate to a God, who is holy. The priests themselves were consecrated to their special office (Exod. 29; Lev. 8) as mediators between the profane and the holy. Priests also blessed the people (Num. 6:22–27) and offered the first fruits brought to the temple by the people (Deut. 26:1–10). The mediating function of the priesthood can be seen most clearly on the Day of Atonement, when the high priest alone entered the Holy of Holies, the inner chamber of the temple, to offer incense in atonement for all the sins of the people during the past year (Num. 16).

In the NT: Jesus is explicitly called a mediator in only four passages. First, 1 Tim. 2:5–6 says that there is "one mediator between God and humankind, Christ Jesus, himself human, who gave himself a ransom for all." The other three references are all in Hebrews, where Christ is said to mediate the new covenant between God and humans (8:6; 9:15; 12:24). In other passages, however, Jesus is portrayed as filling the role of a mediator by praying for his disciples (John 17; Matt. 11:25–27). Believers are also instructed to pray in Jesus's name to God (John 14:13). Many Pauline and Gospel passages also say or imply that contact with God is "through Jesus Christ" (e.g., John 1:17; Rom. 1:8; 5:21; Gal. 1:1; Eph. 1:5; Phil. 1:11; Titus 3:6; Heb. 13:21; 1 Pet. 2:5; 4:11) and this implies mediation by Jesus.   A.J.S.

Mediterranean (med´i-tuh-ray´nee-uhn) **Sea,** the large sea enclosed by the coasts of Europe, North Africa, Asia Minor, and the Levant. Its islands and coastal borders formed the basis for trade and the exchange of cultures as well as colonization and conquest from the second millennium BCE on. Although there are occasional references to the Mediterranean Sea in the Hebrew Bible (e.g., Josh. 5:12; Ps. 104:25–26), lack of seaports kept the Hebrews from becoming seafarers. It seems to have remained, in general, a mysterious and forbidding part of their world. Jonah is one of the few characters in the narratives of the Hebrew Bible said to have booked passage on a ship setting sail in this sea (Jon. 1:3).

Surveys of shipwrecks in the Mediterranean show that the major period of trade extended from 300 BCE to 300 CE, with a peak in the middle of this period. Ships hugged the coast of the Mediterranean, sailing from one place to another. Roman ships could carry as many as three thousand amphorae (large jars used for storing grain, etc.). Ignoring risks from storms, it was possible to ship grain from one end of the Mediterranean to another for less than it would cost to cart the same amount seventy-five miles over land. Hence bulk goods were generally transported by sea. In the NT, the apostle Paul frequently traveled the Mediterranean on such ships (Acts 16:11; 20:6; 21:1–3), and he was on one such ship that was wrecked by a storm (27:13–44). *See also* sea.   P.P.

meek, a quality with different meaning in Jewish and Greek contexts. In the Hebrew tradition, "the meek" (*'anawim*) are virtually synonymous with "the oppressed"; the term is generally descriptive of a social condition (lack of power) rather than a virtue. In Greco-Roman literature, however, "meekness" is comparable to humility and is often listed as a virtue of slaves and others who do not try to rise above their station. Most references to "the meek" in the Hebrew Bible should be understood in the former sense. In Isa. 11:4, the meek are equated with "the poor," and in 29:19 they are equated with "the neediest people" of the earth. Thus, the promise in Ps. 37:11 that "the meek shall inherit the earth" should be read as a reversal of social conditions, rather than as a reward for an appealing attitude. When God's will is done, the meek (i.e., the oppressed of the earth) will get what they had coming to them all along (an inheritance, not a reward); they will receive their share of the promised land, of which they had been unjustly deprived. The Greek equivalent (used in the LXX of Ps. 37:11) is *praeis*, and in the NT, there is some question as to whether that word is used in the Jewish sense to mean "the oppressed" or in the Greco-Roman sense of "those who accept their station in life." Most interpreters think that 1 Pet. 3:4 uses the word with the latter meaning, which may be why the NRSV translates it "gentle"; the point seems to be that women should adorn themselves with the spirit of a submissive, quiet person who does not put on airs or act with a sense of self-importance. The same Greek word (*praeis*) is applied to Jesus in Matt. 11:29 and 21:5 (cf. Zech. 9:9), where the NRSV translates it "humble." *See also* humility.

Bibliography

Wengst, Klaus. *Humility: Solidarity of the Humiliated.* Fortress, 1988. M.A.P.

Megiddo (mi-gid′oh), an important city in antiquity located in the Plain of Esdraelon in the northwestern region of the Levant, now identified with modern Tell el-Mutesellim, about twenty miles southeast of Haifa and ten miles northwest of Jenin.

Strategic Location: Megiddo owes its importance to its strategic location, good water supply, and the fertile valley. Two important routes for armies and trade passed at its foot. From Jerusalem in the south, one passed through Shechem and then Megiddo alongside the Carmel range to Acco on the coast and north to Phoenicia. The second linked Egypt with Damascus and Mesopotamia along the coast by way of the Philistine and Sharon plains, passing through the Carmel range by way of Megiddo and then the Plain of Esdraelon (or Megiddo Plain). This was the easiest pass through the Carmel ridge, and throughout history Megiddo's location made control of the city a matter of strategic importance.

In the Bible and Other Ancient Texts: Megiddo is mentioned in a number of Egyptian and Assyrian texts as well as in the Bible. One of the most important is the fifteenth-century BCE annals of Thutmose III inscribed on the wall of the temple of Karnak in Upper Egypt. Megiddo's defeat is described in detail, elaborating the battle plan, the booty of prisoners, chariots, and household goods, and the tribute of gold, silver, grain, and wine. The Barkal Stele erected at the Fourth Cataract of the Nile gives more details of this campaign.

Egypt's domination of Megiddo is attested in the later fifteenth century BCE by two texts. In one of the Taanach letters the king was ordered to send tribute to Megiddo. An Egyptian papyrus, Hermitage 116A, gives lists of emissaries who were supplied with provisions. Amarna letter 244 was written by the prince of Megiddo concerning the threats to his town, and five other letters from Prince Biridiya to Pharaoh are known. An Egyptian letter of the Nineteenth Dynasty (end of the thirteenth century BCE) describes the road from Megiddo to the coastal plain.

According to the Bible, Joshua defeated a king of Megiddo (Josh. 12:21), and although the town was given to the tribe of Manasseh (17:11; 1 Chron.

Part of the defensive wall overlooking the Jezreel Valley, built by Jeroboam II at Megiddo in the eighth century BCE.

7:29), the Canaanites were not driven out (Josh. 17:12; Judg. 1:27). Deborah and Barak are said to have met the Canaanites "at Taanach, by the waters of Megiddo" (Judg. 5:19), but it may have been the time of David before the city was firmly in Israelite hands. Megiddo was in one of Solomon's administrative districts (1 Kings 4:12), and he fortified Megiddo along with Jerusalem, Hazor, and Gezer (9:15).

Although Megiddo is not mentioned in the Bible's description of Pharaoh Shishak's conquest in 918 BCE (1 Kings 14:25, 26), it is listed among his conquests on the walls of the Amun temple at Karnak, and a fragment of a stele bearing Shishak's name was found at Megiddo. Ahaziah, the king of Judah, died at Megiddo during Jehu's revolt (2 Kings 9:27). According to the annals of Tiglath-pileser III the northern part of Israel was captured in 733/2 BCE and Megiddo was made the capital of one of the three Assyrian provinces. Finally, Josiah met his death at the hands of Pharaoh Neco near Megiddo in 609 BCE (2 Kings 23:29; 2 Chron. 35:22). This was probably the end of Megiddo's prosperity, as the town is not mentioned again in ancient texts. Its importance as a battleground, however, may be remembered in the NT; the place of the final victory of God over all the forces of the world is given as Armageddon (Rev. 16:16), which some scholars take to mean the "mound of Megiddo" (Heb. *har megiddon*).

Archaeological Excavations: Segments of mud-brick dwellings, pits, ovens, and mixed pottery date various Chalcolithic settlements from the early fourth millennium to about 3200 BCE. To the Early Bronze Age (3200–2000 BCE) belongs the first of several sanctuaries in the eastern sector of the town, where there was a sacred area for hundreds of years. This temple was of the usual Early Bronze type, rectangular with the entrance

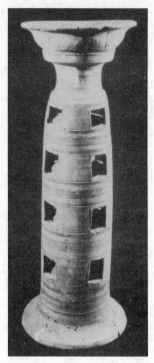

A painted stand with bowl from Megiddo, ca. 1200–1000 BCE.

on the long wall and an altar directly opposite. A courtyard to the east was paved with flagstones, several layers of which had incised figures, mainly of hunting scenes, which are some of the earliest examples of local art in the ancient Near East. The largest city wall in Megiddo's history belongs

A Canaanite "high place" at Megiddo, ca. 2600–2300 BCE.

Egyptian pharaoh Shishak I listed the names of vanquished towns in Canaan—
including Megiddo—within the "walls" depicted below the torso of each fettered
prisoner on these reliefs at Karnak, tenth century BCE.

to this period also; it was 26 feet thick with stone foundations 13 feet deep. During Early Bronze III, a large round altar, more than 26 feet in diameter and 4.5 feet high, was erected in the area of the earlier shrine. A flight of steps ascended the altar on the east, and it was surrounded by a wall, within which were found a great quantity of animal bones indicating cultic sacrifice. Later in Early Bronze III, three new temples were erected, all of the broadroom type with the entrance in the long south side and the square altar opposite.

The Middle Bronze Age (nineteenth–sixteenth centuries BCE) offers indications of Hyksos rulers, perhaps Canaanite, who extended their control to Egypt, ca. 1720–1550 BCE. In the sacred area, stelae and bronze statuettes and large buildings suggest a *bamah* (Heb., "high place") with nearby temples. The earliest city gate comes from this period. The city wall was strengthened, with modifications of the usual Hyksos rampart-and-glacis type.

A relative continuity in plan indicates rather peaceful and prosperous times extending through the Late Bronze Age. With the expulsion of the Hyksos, Megiddo came under Egyptian domination, and even Thutmose III's destruction of the city about 1468 BCE did not lead to decline. Excavations from the second half of the fifteenth century BCE to the first half of the fourteenth show great material wealth with the expansion of the palace and its rich treasures of ivory plaques, jewelry, and beads. A fortified temple is now on the site of the earlier altars. This is the Amarna Age and the Amarna tablets portray weak control exercised

Top: Ivory bull's head, found in the excavations of the palace at Megiddo, ca. twelfth century BCE. *Above:* Ivory duck's head; fourteenth century BCE.

by Egypt. A fragment of a clay tablet containing part of the *Epic of Gilgamesh* (a Babylonian story concerning the origins of the cosmos) found in the vicinity of the gate probably belongs to this time. A cartouche of Ramesses III was found on one of the carved plaques from a great cache of ivories, originally used as inlay decorations for palace furniture. This occupation ended in a great destruction, probably about 1130 BCE.

In the Iron Age, the settlement was much poorer. However, extensive new building activity and late Philistine pottery may indicate Philistine presence. Destruction at the end of the eleventh century may be attributed to David's conquests.

Haphazard constructions may belong to the Israelites under David before the centralized planning of the royal cities of Solomon (tenth century BCE). Recent excavations and research have done much to clarify the confused results of the early excavations for the Solomonic and later periods, but scholars differ widely on the stratigraphic and chronological conclusions. Most scholars assign a six-chamber gateway and casemate city walls similar to those at Hazor and Gezer (1 Kings 9:15) to the time of Solomon (others date the six-chamber gate to the following period with the offset-inset wall). These were contemporary with a palace or fortress that lay beneath the north stables and the offset-inset wall (formerly attributed to Solomon) and a "palace" in the south and a nearby building beneath the south stables. In addition, the gallery (which was the earliest part of the city's water sys-

Above: This box carved from a single piece of ivory and decorated with lions and sphinxes represents part of a hoard found in a twelfth-century BCE palace.

Above: Horn-shaped ivory vessel encircled with a gold band; fourteenth century BCE.

Above: Stairs leading up the side of a storage pit that had a capacity of approximately 12,800 bushels, from the eighth century BCE.
Left: A Philistine pottery "pilgrim flask" found at Megiddo dating to 1100 BCE may indicate Philistine presence during that period.

Left: Eighth-century BCE limestone manger *in situ;* from Megiddo.

tem, a narrow passageway lined with ashlar masonry leading down the southwest slope of the mound to a spring) has been shown stratigraphically to belong to the Solomonic constructions. Solomon's city met destruction at the hands of Pharaoh Shishak in 918 BCE.

Prosperity continued during the Omride dynasty in the first part of the ninth century BCE. To it belong the offset-inset wall with the four-chamber gate (the consensus of most scholars), the stable complexes (considered by some to be storerooms or barracks), and the subterranean water system with a vertical shaft and horizontal tunnel to the spring at the foot of the mound. Alterations and additions to the building complexes indicate continuous occupation down to the time of the Assyrian conquest in 733 BCE.

During the time of Assyrian dominance, there were numerous spacious private dwellings showing Eastern influence. The city gate had two chambers. Later, during the time of Josiah (640–609 BCE) and during the Persian period (ca. 538–333 BCE), the city was unfortified. *See also* Jezreel; Hazor; Taanach.

Bibliography

"Megiddo." In *The New Encyclopedia of Archaeological Excavations in the Holy Land.* Israel Exploration Society, 1993. 3:1003–24.

Davies, Graham. *Megiddo.* Lutterworth, 1986.

Ussishkin, David. "Megiddo." *Anchor Bible Dictionary.* Doubleday, 1992. 4:666–79.   N.L.L.

Melchizedek (mel-kiz'uh-dek; Heb., "king of righteousness"), the king of Salem (Jerusalem) and priest of "God Most High" who blessed Abraham as the latter returned from battle (Gen. 14:17–20). According to this account, Melchizedek and the king of Sodom met Abraham at the Valley of Shaveh (also called the King's Valley). Melchizedek brought out bread and wine and blessed Abraham, who then gave him one-tenth of everything he had gained in the battle. This incident is recalled in Ps. 110:4, where God addresses the Hebrew king as "a priest forever according to the order of Melchizedek." In later literature, Melchizedek is regarded as an ideal priest-king and, in the Dead Sea Scrolls, as a heavenly judge. The fascination with Melchizedek during the Second Temple period focused on the fact that he is identified in the Bible as a priest centuries before the hereditary order of the levitical priesthood was established; thus, in the NT, the author of Hebrews declares that Jesus is a nonhereditary priest "according to the order of Melchizedek" (5:6, 10; 6:20; 7:17). Indeed, since Melchizedek came first chronologically, he should be deemed greater than the later levitical priests and, by this reasoning, such preeminence may also be bestowed upon Jesus. Furthermore, Abraham paid tithes to Melchizedek, which effectively means that all of Abraham's descendants (including Levi and all of the levitical priests) paid homage to Melchizedek as well (7:9–10). The fact that neither the genealogy nor the death of Melchizedek is reported in the Bible is taken in Hebrews as a sign that the superior priesthood (represented now by Jesus) is an eternal one that has neither beginning nor end (7:3).   J.W.T./M.A.P.

Melita (mel'i-tuh). *See* Malta.

memorials, various physical and abstract entities in the Bible such as stones, words, and days intended to serve as reminders to people and to God of some word or event. Physical memorials are set up to commemorate theophanies (Gen. 28:18–22; cf. Exod. 24:4), miracles (Josh. 4:4–24), and times of judgment (Num. 16:40). In another sense, the celebration of the Passover is a memorial to recall God's deliverance of Israel from slavery (Exod. 12:14). Graves also serve as memorials to human lives (Gen. 35:20), and the significance of such memorials seems to be augmented when a person dies childless (2 Sam. 18:18; Isa. 56:5). Written words may also serve as memorials, e.g., through their use in phylacteries (Exod. 13:9; cf. also Exod. 17:14). Memorials to remind God of the covenant with Israel are also mentioned: the written word may serve this purpose (Mal. 3:16); visual cues, such as the shoulder pieces of the ephod of the priestly breastplate (Exod. 28:12, 29), and aural cues, such as the blasting trumpet (Num. 10:10), are also used. In the NT, prayer and alms can serve as a memorial (Acts 10:4), and Luke and Paul claim that the Lord's Supper is a meal intended to be repeated as a remembrance of Jesus (Luke 22:19; 1 Cor. 11:24).   M.Z.B.

Memphis (mem'fis), an ancient (Old Kingdom, ca. 2700–2200 BCE) capital of Egypt, located on the west bank of the Nile about fifteen miles south of modern Cairo, and a prominent political and religious city throughout the pharaonic period (to 605 BCE). The Hebrew form of the name is *nop* (once *mop*), from Egyptian *mennufer*. Traditionally, Memphis was founded by Menes, the first king, as the political center of a united Egypt. Memphis served also as a cult center of Ptah, a creator and artificer god. He not only created the world and all other gods; he also made things useful for human beings, such as shrines, cities, arts, and crafts. The Memphite theology, known from

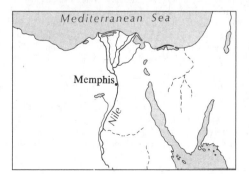

a relatively late text (ca. 700 BCE), emphasizes Ptah's creative word. Memphis is mentioned in the prophetic books as symbolic of Egyptian power and idolatry, to be overthrown (Isa. 19:13; Ezek. 30:13), and as a place of exile or retreat for Israel (Jer. 2:16–18; Hos. 9:6). Indeed, the Egyptians settled many foreigners there. Although extensive remains existed as late as the medieval period, very little survives today. *See also* Egypt; Pyramid Texts.   H.B.H.

Menahem (men'uh-hem), king of Israel ca. 745–737 BCE. The son of Gadi, he was a usurper from the former capital, Tirzah (2 Kings 15:14). He assassinated Shallum, who had slain his own predecessor one month earlier, and ruled in Samaria for ten years. The Assyrian annals indicate that "Menahem of Samaria" paid tribute to King Tiglath-pileser III during his first western campaign (743–738 BCE). The same incident is described in 2 Kings 15:19–20, where Tiglath-pileser is called by his Babylonian throne name, Pul. Menahem raised "a thousand talents of silver" by imposing a levy on the wealthy citizens of Israel. His purpose was to win the favor of Tiglath-pileser "that he might help him to confirm his hold of the royal power." Menahem died soon afterward, and his son, Pekahiah, fell victim to a conspiracy within two years (2 Kings 15:25).   P.K.M.

mene, mene, tekel, parsin (mee'nee, tek'uhl, pahr'sin), the mysterious words written on the wall in Dan. 5:25. These words confound the Babylonian wise men, but are interpreted for Belshazzar by Daniel (5:26–28), who takes them as the Aramaic verbs *mn'*, "to number" ("God has numbered the days of your kingdom"), *tkl*, "to weigh" ("you have been weighed . . . and found wanting"), and *prs*, "to divide" ("your kingdom is divided and given to the Medes and the Persians"). Most scholars think that the original text had only one *mene* and that the reference is to three weights or monetary units—the mina, the shekel (one-fiftieth of a mina), and the half-mina. These in turn may have been intended as a slighting evaluation of successive Babylonian kings with Nabonidus and Belshazzar as the half-minas. Such references are lost in the present text of Daniel, which retains, however, the punning tendency inherent in the riddle (e.g., *parsin* is taken as both "divided" and a reference to the Persians; see v. 28). *See also* Belshazzar; Daniel, book of.   J.J.C.

menorah (muh-nor'uh). *See* lampstand.

Mephaath (mi-fay'ath), a site given to the Reubenites (Josh. 13:18; 21:37; 1 Chron. 6:79), located east of the Jordan, where it is associated with such settlements as Heshbon and Dibon. Jeremiah's oracles against Moab mention Mephaath as having suffered judgment (48:21). Identification of the site is uncertain; modern Umm er-Rasas is one possibility, as the mosaic floor of an eighth-century CE church reads *kastron mefaa* (Gk., "Camp of Mefaa"). It stands twenty miles southeast of Medeba (modern-day Madaba) in Jordan.

Mephibosheth (mi-fib'oh-sheth; Heb., "out of the mouth of shame"), an intentionally distorted form of the original name Mippi-baal (Heb., "out of the mouth of Baal"). Baal, which means "lord," was used as a simple epithet for God, but because the epithet was also used for a major Canaanite deity, later scribes often replaced this element in proper names with the word *boshet*, "shame."

1 A son of Saul whom David handed over to the Gibeonites for execution (2 Sam. 21:8–9).

2 Jonathan's son, the grandson of Saul, whom David spared because of his covenant with Jonathan (2 Sam. 4:4; 21:7; he is called Merib-baal in 1 Chron. 8:34; 9:40). According to 2 Sam. 9, Mephibosheth was crippled in both of his feet and, after the death of his father and grandfather, he stayed at the house of Machir, son of Ammiel, at Lo-debar. When David decided that he wanted to show kindness to someone from Jonathan's family, he was told of Mephibosheth's whereabouts by Ziba, a servant of Saul, and he had Mephibosheth brought to Jerusalem. He promised to restore to Mephibosheth all of the land that belonged to Saul, and he also made provisions for Mephibosheth to eat at the king's table every day. Mephibosheth responded, "What is your servant, that you should look upon a dead dog such as I?" (9:8). Later, however, Mephibosheth did not accompany David when he was forced to flee during Absalom's revolt; Ziba told David that this was because Mephibosheth had switched sides in support of Absalom (16:1–4). This angered David, so that he promised all the lands of Saul would now go to Ziba. Later, however, Mephibosheth welcomed David back to Jerusalem and told him he had been deceived by Ziba. Rather than trying to sort the matter out, David declared that the lands of Saul would be split between Mephibosheth and Ziba (19:24–29). Mephibosheth responded, "Let him take it all, since my lord the king has arrived home safely" (2 Sam. 19:30). Later, when David hands over seven descendants of Saul to the Gibeonites to be executed, he spares Mephibosheth, the son of Jonathan (21:7). *See also* David; Jonathan; Saul.
J.J.M.R./M.A.P.

Merab (mee'rab; Heb., "growth, increase"), the elder of Saul's two daughters (1 Sam. 14:49) whom Saul promised to David for fighting the Philistines, expecting that he would be killed in battle. When David returned, Merab had already been given to Adriel. Later, David gave five sons that Merab bore to Adriel to the Gibeonites for execution as an act of appeasement (2 Sam. 21:8–9).

Meraioth (mi-ray'oth).

1 A descendant of Aaron identified as the son of Zerahiah (1 Chron. 6:6, 52) and the father of Amariah (6:7, 52).

2 The father of Zadok, the son of Ahitub (1 Chron. 9:11), and an ancestor of Azariah the

priest (Ezra 7:3; Neh. 11:11). This could be the same person as 1.

3 An ancestral priestly house (Neh. 12:15) in the days of Joiakim in postexilic Judah, probably the descendants of 1 and/or 2.

Merari (mi-rah'ri).

1 The third son of Levi (Gen. 46:11; Exod. 6:16; Num. 3:17; 1 Chron. 6:1, 16; 23:6) and through his sons, Mahli and Mushi (Exod. 6:19; Num. 3:20; 1 Chron. 6:19; 23:21; 24:26), the eponymous ancestor of the levitical group the Merarites (Num. 3:33–37; 4:29–33; 1 Chron. 6:29, 44). The cities and territories allocated to the Merarites appear in Josh. 21:7, 34–40 and 1 Chron. 6:77–81. Prominent Merarites included Asaiah, who supervised the 220 Merarites whom David selected to help bring the ark to Jerusalem (1 Chron. 15:6); Ethan, who was appointed as a musician for the occasion (1 Chron. 15:17, 19); Kish and Azariah, who assisted in Hezekiah's reform (2 Chron. 29:12); Jahath and Obadiah, who helped supervise Josiah's repair of the temple (2 Chron. 34:12); and Sherebiah, Hashabiah, and Jeshaiah, who led Merarite contingents in the time of Ezra (Ezra 8:18–19). Merarites also served as gatekeepers for the temple (1 Chron. 26:10, 19).

2 The father of Judith (Jth. 8:1; 16:7).   M.A.S.

merchant. *See* agora; trade.

mercy, an attribute of God and a virtue commended for human beings. Hebrew uses several words for "mercy," including *rakham* (Exod. 34:6; Isa. 55:7), *khanan* (Deut. 4:31) and *khesed* (Neh. 9:32; nrsv: "steadfast love"). The most common Greek word for "mercy" is *eleos* (Rom. 9:15–16, 23; Eph. 2:4). The lxx consistently uses Greek *eleos* to translate Hebrew *khesed*, but the nrsv never translates *khesed* as "mercy"; rather, it uses "steadfast love" (172 times), "kindness" (17 times), "great kindness" (in Gen. 19:19), and "faithful love" (in 1 Sam. 20:14). In the Hebrew Bible, *khesed* is closely connected with God's covenant with Israel, though that concept provides the general context for most other references to mercy as well. The book of Exodus associates mercy with the ark of the covenant through explicit references to the "mercy seat" (e.g., 25:17–22). Nevertheless, God's mercy is presented as a divine choice, not an obligation (Exod. 33:19; cf. Rom. 9:15–18); God does not *have* to show mercy to anyone, but elects to do so, in keeping with God's nature; God shows mercy because God *is* "gracious and merciful, slow to anger and abounding in steadfast love" (Exod. 34:6). Psalmists sometimes remind God of this (Pss. 25:6; 51:1; 69:16) or plead with God not to withhold mercy (Ps. 40:11). The author of Ps. 23 is confident: "Surely goodness and mercy will follow me all the days of my life" (23:6). Sir. 51:1–12 offers praise to God for divine mercy. God's instructions to Israel include occasional mandates that they are to show no mercy to the nations that must be rooted out from the land (Deut. 7:2; Josh.

11:20), but the prophets call upon God's people to "show kindness and mercy to one another" (Zech. 7:9; cf. Mic. 6:8).

In the NT, God's merciful faithfulness results in sending John the Baptist and then Jesus to save people (Luke 1:50, 54, 58, 72, 78; Eph. 2:4–5). Individuals who are sick or distressed plead with Jesus to have mercy on them (Matt. 15:22; 17:15; 20:30–31; Luke 17:13; cf. Mark 5:19). Paul emphasizes the salvation of the Gentiles as an ultimate expression of God's mercy (Rom. 11:30–31; 15:9), and in 1 Timothy Paul's own salvation (as a former persecutor of the church) is cited as an illustration of God's mercy (1:13, 16). God's mercy toward the faithful will manifest itself at the final judgment (2 Tim. 1:18; Jude 21; cf. Luke 16:24). References to mercy were incorporated into early Christian benedictions (1 Tim. 1:2; 2 John 3; Jude 2).

Jesus pronounces a beatitude on the merciful (Matt. 5:7), and he tells the parable of the Good Samaritan to illustrate what showing mercy can mean (cf. Luke 10:37). In another parable, he implies that God might withhold mercy from those who do not show mercy to others (Matt. 18:23–35; cf. James 2:13). The concept of mercy also plays a significant role in Jesus's ethical hermeneutic for interpreting the law. He prioritizes the significance of mercy in a way that allows for otherwise legitimate concerns to be ignored. In Matthew's Gospel, Jesus twice quotes from the LXX version of Hos. 6:6, indicating that God prefers mercy to sacrifice (9:13; 12:7). This becomes a principle for relaxing the application of burdensome commandments: it is acceptable to heal on the sabbath or to pick grain to satisfy one's own hunger. The assumed counterargument would seem to be that a sick or disabled person might wait to be healed or the hungry might wait to pick their grain; in either case, one day of unpleasantness would be a sacrifice for God, to ensure the sanctity of Torah. Jesus's vision is that the mercy of God trumps any pleasure that God might find in such sacrifices—God would rather eliminate the distress immediately. The same sort of vision seems to inform Jesus's insistence that mercy is one of "weightier matters of the law" that his opponents ignore while attending to minor affairs (Matt. 23:23). *See also* justice; love.   A.J.S./M.A.P.

mercy seat. *See* ark of the covenant, ark of God.

Meremoth (mair'uh-moth), a name occurring several times in postexilic writings. It is difficult to tell whether these are different people or various references to the same person.

1 A Levite who returned from the Babylonian exile with Zerubbabel (Neh. 12:3).

2 A Levite, the son of Uriah the priest; he inventoried the valuables brought back by exiles returning with Ezra (Ezra 8:33) and helped repair the walls of Jerusalem under Nehemiah (Neh. 3:4, 21).

3 A member of the Bani family group who divorced his foreign wife in compliance with Ezra's postexilic reforms (Ezra 10:36).

4 A person who signed Ezra's covenant to keep the law (Neh. 10:5).   D.R.B.

Meribah. *See* Massah and Meribah.

Merib-baal (mair'ib-bay'uhl). *See* Mephibosheth.

Merneptah (muhr'nep-tah'), the son and successor of the long-lived Ramesses II. He ruled Egypt ca. 1213–1204 BCE. A victory hymn relative to his brief campaign in Canaan and southern Syria between 1212 and 1209 BCE, the Israel Stele, contains the earliest known reference to Israel. On that stele, Merneptah boasts that he has laid waste to the people of Israel and there are no survivors. *See also* Ramesses.

Merodach (mi-roh'dak), also known as Marduk (mahr'dyook), a Mesopotamian god. Merodach is mentioned in Jer. 50:2, where he is also referred to as Bel (cf. Isa. 46:1; Jer. 51:44). Several Babylonian names with Merodach as the theophoric element appear in the Bible: Evil-merodach, Merodach-baladan, and Mordecai. Merodach was the chief god of the city of Babylon and eventually of Babylonia. It appears that originally Merodach was a storm deity, the name Mar-udu-ak probably meaning "Son of the Storm." The biblical reading Merodach seems to be a more correct pronunciation than the conventional Marduk.

According to the Babylonian sources, Merodach was elected to the office of ruler of humankind by the gods An and Enlil (Codex Hammurabi 1.1). This election was a continuation of an old Mesopotamian practice whereby the god of the politically dominant city ruled the land for a time, while ultimate power continued to reside with the divine assembly and its leaders. Merodach, however, did eventually become the chief god of Babylonia, and his rule was absolute and not dependent upon the agreement of the divine council. This seems to have been the case by the latter half of the second millennium BCE. Merodach was thus transformed from a local god into a national or, indeed, universal god. Merodach's rise to absolute kingship among the gods is described in the *Enuma Elish*, the Babylonian epic of creation. This work has been connected with Gen. 1 and to biblical allusions to God's conflicts with a dragon, with the sea, or with chaos. Merodach's cult spread to Assyria, though the Assyrians had some difficulty assimilating it. Apparent threats to the prerogatives of the Merodach cult led the priests of Babylon to welcome and justify Cyrus's conquest (late sixth century BCE). *See also* Merodach-baladan.   I.T.A.

Merodach-baladan (mi-roh'dak-bal'uh-duhn), the name used in the Bible for a ruler otherwise known in history as Marduk-apla-iddina II, twice king of Babylonia (721–710 BCE) and leader of the Chaldean tribe Bit-Yakin in southern Babylonia. The tribal area of Bit-Yakin was in southeastern Babylonia around the great swamp; this tribe lived close to Elam, and during the period of activity of Merodach-baladan, alliances between Bit-Yakin and Elam were forged and stood in opposition to the Assyrians.

Merodach-baladan was already active in the final years of Tiglath-pileser III and even then appears as an important Chaldean chief. Merodach-baladan seems to have been an able political and military strategist and leader. At the death of Shalmaneser V and the accession of Sargon II, Assyria faced serious problems in the west and in Babylonia. Merodach-baladan gained control of the Babylonian throne (721 BCE) and detached Babylonia from the empire. The Assyrians did not achieve victory against the Elamites, allies of Merodach-baladan, at the Battle of Der, 720 BCE, and Merodach-baladan retained the Babylonian throne until 710.

During his reign he held sway over the Babylonian cities along the Euphrates and the Chaldean settlements in the south. He seems to have ruled Babylonia in a relatively efficacious and sympathetic manner and to have created some unity among the Chaldean tribes. Still, in 710 BCE the Assyrian king Sargon was able to defeat Merodach-baladan and conquer Babylonia. Merodach-baladan retreated to the south and the citizens of Babylonia welcomed Sargon. He continued fighting in the south at Dur-Yakin; even here he was defeated, but again escaped. After the accession of Sennacherib to the Assyrian throne, Merodach-baladan again took Babylon

The Babylonian king Merodach-baladan, 721–710 BCE, investing one of his officials with a grant of land; inscribed boundary stone.

in 703 BCE for nine months. The Assyrians under Sennacherib routed Merodach-baladan, though the Chaldeans had drawn the support and assistance of Elamites, Chaldeans, and Babylonians from a number of cities. Merodach-baladan took refuge in the southern swamps. In 700 BCE, Sennacherib directed a campaign against Bit-Yakin. Merodach-baladan fled to Elam, dying there before 694 BCE. Under Sargon and Sennacherib, Merodach-baladan's tribe Bit-Yakin suffered mass deportations by the Assyrians.

In 2 Kings 20:12–19 and Isa. 39:1–8 (cf. 2 Chron. 32:31), Merodach-baladan sends an embassy to King Hezekiah of Judah in order to establish some sort of alliance and coordinate actions against Assyria. Although this text tells of the embassy after recounting events of Sennacherib's campaign against Hezekiah in 701 BCE, the embassy should be dated either to 705 BCE, the year when Sennacherib ascended the Assyrian throne, or even more probably to 714–713 BCE, at the time of the anti-Assyrian rebellion in Ashdod. *See also* Assyria, Empire of; Babylon; Merodach.   I.T.A.

Merom (mee'rom; Heb., "height"), a city in Galilee that was the site of a defeat of the Canaanites by the Israelites (Josh. 11:5, 7). Merom is included in late second-millennium Egyptian lists of captured cities and was taken by Tiglath-pileser III in 733 BCE. Its exact location is not certain. Suggestions include such modern sites as Tell el-Khureibeh and Meiron; in medieval tradition Joshua's victory is associated with the latter. Madon (11:1; 12:19) is often corrected to Merom, following the LXX.   M.D.C.

Merom, Waters of, a major water source or stream near the city of Merom in Galilee. *See also* Merom.

Meroz (mee'roz), a town cursed in the Song of Deborah (Judg. 5:23) for failing to join the Israelites' fight against Sisera. Of uncertain identity, it was most likely somewhere in the Plain of Esdraelon or in the adjacent hills near the battle site.

Mesha (mee'shuh; Heb., "savior").
1 A son of Caleb; the father of Ziph (1 Chron. 2:42; however, LXX: "Maresha").
2 The ninth-century BCE king of Moab who also bred sheep. After a long period of being subject to Israel, as was his father Chemosh-(yat), and paying tribute to Ahab (2 Kings 3:4), he led a revolt (2 Kings 3); a Moabite inscription found at Dibon also describes an extensive building program. Although the accounts differ somewhat, it would appear that Israel's king Jehoram was unable to suppress the revolt, despite assistance from the kings of Judah (Jehoshaphat) and Edom. The Bible ascribes some of Mesha's success to his willingness to sacrifice his son, the crown prince (3:27).
3 A Benjaminite born in Moab; he was the son of Shaharaim and Hodesh (1 Chron. 8:9).

4 A geographic location in the desert of Syria or Arabia; it formed the border of the region inhabited by the Joktanites (Gen. 10:30). Some scholars equate Mesha with Massa (25:14).

F.E.G./M.A.P.

Meshach (mee′shak), the Babylonian name given to Mishael, one of Daniel's three companions (Dan. 1:7). The etymology is uncertain, but a relation to Marduk, the god of Babylon, has been suggested. *See also* Abednego; Daniel; Shadrach.

Meshech (mee′shek).

1 The sixth son of Japheth (Gen. 10:2). His name, like the names of the fourth son (Javan) and fifth son (Tubal), is also the name for an area.

2 A region in Asia Minor. Meshech appears in Assyrian texts as Muski or Musku from 1200 BCE onward. Its people were noted metallurgists and politically aligned with Tubal. The frequent biblical association of Meshech and Tubal reflects this ancient political alliance in mountainous, central Asia Minor (Gen. 10:2; Ezek. 27:13; 32:26; 38:2–3; 39:1; 1 Chron. 1:5). Midas, king of Musku, was an enemy of Sargon II of Assyria.   J.G.G.

Meshelemiah (mi-shel′uh-mi′uh), a Korahite Levite who was the head of a family of gatekeepers in the time of David (1 Chron. 9:21; 26:1–2). He is probably the same person elsewhere called Shallum (9:17, 19; possibly also v. 31) and Shelemiah (26:14). A postexilic family group of gatekeepers were called "descendants of Shallum" and are assumed to be descendants of Meshelemiah (Ezra 2:42; Neh. 7:45). *See also* Shallum.

Meshullam (mi-shool′uhm; Heb., "reconciled, perfected").

1 The grandfather of the scribe Shaphan during the reign of Josiah (2 Kings 22:3).

2 The son of Zerubbabel (1 Chron. 3:19).

3 A Gadite who lived in Bashan (1 Chron. 5:13).

4 A Benjaminite, son of Elpaal (1 Chron. 8:17).

5 A Benjaminite, son of Shephatiah (1 Chron. 9:8).

6 A Benjaminite, father of Sallu (1 Chron. 9:7; Neh. 11:7).

7 A priest, son of Zadok, and father of Hilkiah (1 Chron. 9:11).

8 A priest, son of Meshillemith, and father of Jahzerah (1 Chron. 9:12).

9 A Levite belonging to the Kohathite line who assisted in Josiah's repair of the temple (2 Chron. 34:12).

10 The son of Bani, a man who married a foreign woman in the time of Ezra (Ezra 10:29). He is perhaps the same Meshullam who opposed Ezra's marriage policy (10:15) and sought Levites for temple service (8:6).

11 The son of Berechiah, who helped build the wall of Jerusalem under Nehemiah (Neh. 3:4, 30). His daughter married Jehohanan (6:18).

12 The son of Besodeiah who helped repair the Old Gate in Jerusalem under Nehemiah (Neh. 3:6).

13 A man who stood at Ezra's left hand when he read the Torah (Neh. 8:4).

14 A priest who set his seal to the covenant in Neh. 10:7.

15 A chief of the people who set his seal to the covenant in Neh. 10:20.

16 The head of the priestly house of Ezra in the days of Joiakim (Neh. 12:13).

17 The head of the priestly house of Ginnethon in the days of Joiakim (Neh. 12:16).

18 A gatekeeper who guarded the storehouses during the time of the high priest Joiakim (Neh. 12:25).

19 A prince of Judah who took part in the procession dedicating the rebuilt wall of Jerusalem in the time of Nehemiah (Neh. 12:33).   M.A.S.

Mesopotamia (mes′uh-puh-tay′mee-uh; Gk., "between the rivers"), the region bounded on the east by the Tigris River and on the west by the Euphrates River. The biblical term for Mesopotamia, Aram-naharaim (Gen. 24:10; Judg. 3:8; Ps. 60:1), refers to the land east of the Middle Euphrates. Other terms in the Bible referring to regions of Mesopotamia include Shinar (Gen. 10:10, 11:2; 14:1, 9; Josh. 7:21; Isa. 11:11; Dan. 1:2; Zech. 5:11) and Chaldea (Isa. 47:1, 5; 48:20; Jer. 50:10; 51:24, 35; Ezek. 11:24; 16:29; 23:15–16; Jth. 5:7) as well as the frequently mentioned regions of Assyria and Babylon/Babylonia, which correspond to the northern and southern regions of Mesopotamia, respectively. The peripheral regions, particularly sites such as Mari and Ebla in the west and Nuzi in the north, contributed significantly to cultural and social developments in Mesopotamia proper. Mesopotamia was home to several population groups. The Sumerians entered the southern reaches of the alluvial plain, probably from the east and north. A Semitic group, the Akkadians, developed the first empire in Mesopotamia in the late third millennium BCE. Western Mesopotamia was home to the Amorites, another Semitic population that appears in the Bible. Modern Iraq encompasses much of Mesopotamia.

Geographic conditions range from desert in the central region to forests in the surrounding high country. The combination of natural river levees and seasonally inundated alluvial flats creates the floodplain of the Tigris and Euphrates rivers, a region known as Babylonia in the second millennium BCE. This region supported woodland, consisting predominantly of the date palm. Scarce rainfall and erratic, violent flooding of the rivers made farmers in the region almost entirely dependent upon irrigation for crops. The region is noticeably lacking in natural resources such as stone, wood, and metal ores. Trade for these items developed, with routes following the rivers. The route up the Euphrates would have been the one Abraham's family followed in their travels from Ur to Haran. Control of the river crossings reflected military and political power.

Cultural developments originating in Mesopotamia are numerous. The Neolithic revolution (ca. 8000–4500 BCE), which evidenced the domestication of plants and animals, took place in the eastern, upland reaches of Mesopotamia as well as in the uplands of Anatolia and the Levant. Writing originated in Mesopotamia, as evidenced by pictographic tablets from the southern city of Uruk, which date to the middle of the fourth millennium BCE. Its outgrowth, the cuneiform system of writing the Sumerian and Akkadian languages, flourished in Mesopotamia for three millennia and was adopted for writing Hittite and the West Semitic dialect Ugaritic. Mesopotamia also produced the first compilations of legal writings, including those of Hammurabi, Eshnunna, and Lipit-Ishtar. The literary developments include works such as the *Epic of Gilgamesh.* Numerous historical inscriptions found at sites in ancient Mesopotamia corroborate biblical accounts. The influence of Mesopotamian hymns and prayers can be felt in the later biblical literature. Artistic developments include sculpture, bas-reliefs, monumental architecture, glyptic art (engraving on fine stones), and fine textiles, which were traded as far away as Anatolia (modern Turkey).   L.E.P.

messiah (muh-si′uh; from Heb. *mashiakh,* "anointed one"), an anointed agent of God appointed to a task affecting the lot of God's elect.

Early Usage: Though the Hebrew verb *mashakh* was often used of the anointing of men as kings over Israel (e.g., Saul, 1 Sam. 9:16; David, 2 Sam. 2:4, 7; Ps. 89:20; Solomon, 1 Kings 1:39, 45; Jehu, 1 Kings 19:16) or as priests (Aaron and his sons, Exod. 40:15; 28:41), the title *mashiakh* occurs less often. At first, it was employed for unnamed historic kings of Israel (1 Sam. 2:10; Pss. 2:2; 20:6; 28:8; 84:9) or for specific named kings, including Saul (1 Sam. 12:3, 5; 24:7), David (2 Sam. 19:22; 22:51; 23:1; Pss. 18:50; 89:38, 51; 132:10, 17), Solomon (2 Chron. 6:42), Zedekiah (Lam. 4:20), and even for the pagan king Cyrus (Isa. 45:1). In the postexilic period, when the monarchy was no more, it was used of the high priest (Lev. 4:3, 5, 16; 6:22). Rarely, it was applied to ancestors or prophets (Ps. 105:15; 1 Chron. 16:22); once it may refer to Israel itself (Hab. 3:13).

David, as God's chosen ruler of Israel, was the one after whom the supposed messianic dynasty was named (2 Sam. 7:8–16). Once that dynastic rule was interrupted—when Jehoiakim died, his corpse was given the "burial of an ass" (Jer. 22:19), and his son Jehoiachin was carted off to Babylonian exile—Jeremiah prophesied the restoration of the Davidic dynasty; however, the title *mashiakh* was not associated with the coming of the future king who would effect this restoration. None of the prophetic books of the Bible use *mashiakh* as a title for such a coming king except Daniel (placed not among the Nevi'im, or Prophets, but among the Ketuvim, or Writings, in the Jewish canon).

Dan. 9:25 has the first reference to an anointed one (*mashiakh*), a prince (*nagid*) who is a future, expected leader.

Such expectations are clearer in Hellenistic Jewish literature of the Second Temple period. In the *Psalms of Solomon* (first century BCE) there is expectation of a "righteous king, taught by God," who will be "their king, the Anointed of the Lord" (Gk. *christos kyriou;* 17:32). The author prays that Israel will be purified "for the day of election, for the manifestation of his Anointed" (Gk. *christou autou;* 18:5). This ideal king reflects the current opposition to the non-Davidic Hasmonean dynasty. Similarly, the *Similitudes of Enoch* (*1 Enoch* 37–71), probably dating from the mid-first century BCE, link the day of judgment with an expected heavenly figure, a "Son of Man," also called a "Messiah" (*1 Enoch* 48:10; 52:4).

Within a short time after the final redaction of the book of Daniel, Palestinian Jews. who dwelt at Qumran recorded in their rule books that they were awaiting the coming of three expected figures: "They shall be ruled by the original precepts by which the men of the Community were first instructed, until there comes a prophet, and the Messiahs of Aaron and Israel" (1QS 9:10–11). The "prophet" was the one promised by Moses (Deut. 18:15, 18), the "Messiah of Aaron" was to be a priestly figure, and the "Messiah of Israel," a kingly, probably Davidic, figure. Thus, despite the lack of clear teaching-about the coming of a Messiah in biblical writings prior to the book of Daniel, messianic expectation clearly fed into Jewish belief current at Qumran in the first century CE (see also 1QSa 2:14, 20; CD 12:23–13:1; 14:19; 19:10–11; 20:1; 4QpGen [4Q252] 1:3–4; 4QMessApoc [4Q521] 1:1).

Jesus as Messiah: The Greek term *christos* ("Christ") was used in the LXX to translate Heb. *mashiakh* ("Messiah"; cf. John 1:41). In the earliest writings of the NT it has already become the virtual surname of Jesus: he is called Jesus Christ (Gk. *iēsous christos,* 1 Thess. 1:1, 3; 5:9; Gal. 1:1; 1 Cor. 1:1). Paul sometimes inverts the names as Christ Jesus (*christos iēsous,* 1 Thess. 2:14; 5:18), possibly because he perceived Christ (Messiah) as a title rather than a name. In any case, it identified Jesus as the one who, although he is to be recognized as Lord of all humanity (Phil. 2:9–11), came into the world as the Jewish Messiah, the one who fulfilled God's promises to Israel (Rom. 9:5). The Gospels all portray Jesus as one who claims to be the Christ/Messiah and who is recognized as such by his disciples and others. In Mark's Gospel, particularly, there is some ambiguity surrounding these identifications, because Jesus seems intent on keeping his identity as the Messiah a secret (8:29–30). Mark also wants to connect Jesus's identity as the Messiah with his death on the cross. At his interrogation before a council of Jewish leaders, he is asked point-blank whether he is "the Messiah." He answers, "I am" (14:62), and for this "blasphemy" he is condemned as deserving of death (14:63–64). These themes are also present, though somewhat muted, in Matthew's Gospel, which emphasizes to a much greater extent Jesus's identity as one who fulfills prophecies of scripture (1:22–23; 2:5–6, 15, 17–18, 23; 4:14–16; 8:17; 12:17–21; 13:14–15, 35; 21:4–5; 27:9–10; cf. 3:3–4; 11:10; 15:7–9; 26:54, 56). Such fulfillment of prophecy has the effect of identifying Jesus as the promised one, hence as the Messiah. Luke's Gospel seems intent on emphasizing that Jesus was the Messiah from his birth (2:11, 25–32). Luke also refers to Jesus somewhat distinctively as "God's Messiah" or as the "Lord's Messiah" (2:26; 9:20; 23:35; cf. Acts 3:18) and, in Acts, emphasizes that it is God who has made Jesus Messiah, in spite of human opposition (2:36).

Many of the missionary speeches in Acts seem to reflect arguments between Christians and Jews over the messianic status of Jesus (2:31–32, 36; 3:18; 5:42; cf. 17:3; 18:5, 28), and those debates also seem to lie in the background for what is found in the Gospel of John. There, the woman at the well wonders whether Jesus could be the Messiah, since the latter is supposed "to proclaim all things" and Jesus has told her everything she had ever done (4:25–29). An uncertain crowd of suspicious Jews wonder whether their authorities might not actually know that Jesus is the Messiah and be opposed to him anyway (7:26). The signs (miracles) he works point in this direction (7:31), but there are problems. Jesus comes from Galilee (7:41), and the Messiah is supposed to be from Bethlehem (7:42) or, indeed, be of uncertain origin (7:27). Further, the Messiah is supposed to "remain forever," and Jesus says that he is going to be lifted up or go away (12:34). Such passages seem to reflect the questions and concerns regarding Jesus's identity as the Messiah that might have been current in the community that produced this Gospel, a church where the members also seem to know of people who were expelled from synagogues as a result of confessing Jesus to be the Messiah (9:22). Nevertheless, John also presents people of faith boldly acknowledging that Jesus is the Messiah (1:41; 11:27) and says his Gospel has been written so that readers might believe this as well (20:31).

In the Letters of Paul, the identification of Jesus as Messiah is so firmly established that the word "Christ" in and of itself can be used with clear understanding that "Christ Jesus" is meant. Paul says, "Christ died for our sins in accordance with the scriptures" (1 Cor. 15:3; cf. Rom. 5:6, 8). As Messiah (or Christ), Jesus is believed to be currently in heaven at the right hand of God (Rom. 8:34), to hear the prayers of the church (1 Cor. 1:2), to be present on earth through the church, which is his body (Rom. 12:4–5; 1 Cor. 12:12, 27), and to dwell within individual believers (Rom. 8:10; Gal. 2:20). According to the book of Revelation, as Messiah, Jesus is worthy of worship (5:6–14).

Historical Development of the Concept as Applied to Jesus: Historians debate the question of whether Jesus actually thought of and identified himself as the Messiah during his lifetime. The Gospel record is virtually unanimous that

he did, but it is interesting that the title *christos* is missing from the sayings of Jesus ascribed to the Q material, believed by most scholars to represent the earliest strand of tradition found in the Gospels. Matt. 1:16 and 27:17, 22 refer to Jesus as the one "who is called the Messiah"; it has been suggested that such passages could echo an early tradition that Jesus was first called "Messiah" by others than himself. One theory holds that the title on the cross ("King of the Jews") became the catalyst for the use of Messiah as a title for Jesus (see Mark 15:2, 26). The term "Messiah" did not unambiguously denote a person claiming the political position of "king of Israel," but if Jesus were executed as a political pretender (even ignorantly by a Roman governor who misunderstood his talk about the "kingdom of God"; cf. John 18:33–37; 19:12–15), his followers may subsequently have seized upon the association and read what they took to be messianic prophecies in scripture in a way that caused them to think about his life and mission in new terms.

The claim that Jesus was the Messiah (whether Jesus's self-claim or that of his followers) would have implied for most Jewish people of the day that he was the one anointed by God to restore the fortunes of Israel, delivering God's people from their oppressors (cf. Luke 24:21; Acts 1:6). Or, in an eschatological vein, he might have been expected to execute the final judgment and usher in a messianic age of peace and prosperity (cf. Matt. 3:7–12). The Gospels bear witness to the fact that some who thought Jesus might be the Messiah were confounded by the lack of fulfillment of these expectations (Matt. 11:2–3). Still, by way of application to Jesus, the title and concept of Messiah underwent some transformation. First, the concept of a ruling Messiah was reinterpreted in light of certain psalms (e.g., Ps. 22) and, especially Isaiah's Servant Songs (esp. Isa. 52:13–53:12) to produce the new concept of a suffering Messiah. The Messiah, according to this view, had to suffer before entering into his glory (Luke 24:26; cf. 24:46; Acts 3:18; 17:3; 26:23). It is possible that Jesus himself melded these concepts together, deciding that as the Messiah he was also the servant of the Lord spoken of by Isaiah. Or it is possible that the death of Jesus led those who believed he was the Messiah to search the scriptures for resolution to a paradox (how could the Messiah suffer and die?) and found their answer through reinterpretation of the concept. In any case, for early Christians the concepts of Messiah and servant of the Lord were merged in a manner that they may not have been previously, and the hybrid concept of a suffering Messiah was one that could be applied to Jesus.

The concept also appears to have undergone development in another way. The followers of Jesus developed the novel view that the Messiah was a figure who would come *twice*. A first coming of the Messiah had already been fulfilled in the life, ministry, suffering, and death of Jesus, but the Second Coming of Jesus would constitute a further, ultimate manifestation of the Messiah. This transformation of the concept may have been assisted by a wedding of Messiah with another biblical image, that of the heavenly Son of Man (e.g., Dan. 7; the joining of these two concepts is especially clear in Mark 14:61–62). Again, Jesus himself could have arrived at this understanding of Messiah and applied the new concept to himself, or his followers might have joined the Messiah and Son of Man images through exegetical reflection upon his significance and identity in the years after his death. In any case, the apparently unfulfilled aspects of Jesus's messianic ministry were simply postponed: he *would* execute the final judgment and usher in the era of peace, but not yet. There was to be an interval during which the gospel message would be taken to the nations, giving all people an opportunity to participate in the messianic salvation. Lest this seem like a facetious explanation for why Jesus had not fulfilled the traditional expectations of a Messiah, his followers pointed to evidence that the messianic age had already begun in certain proleptic ways, principal among which was Jesus's resurrection from the dead, attested by reliable eyewitnesses (1 Cor. 15:1–8). Other signs that the new age was already dawning included the outpouring of the Holy Spirit upon Jesus's followers (Acts 2:1–12; Rom. 5:8; 8:9; 1 Cor. 3:16; 2 Cor. 1:21–22; 5:5; Gal. 3:2–5; 4:6), the miracles worked by and through them (e.g., Acts 3:1–4:12), and the character of their lives as a people in whom a new creation was being manifest (2 Cor. 5:17). *See also* Jesus Christ; son of God, Son of God; son of man, Son of Man.

Bibliography

Charlesworth, James H., ed. *The Messiah: Developments in Earliest Judaism and Christianity.* Fortress, 1992.

Fitzmyer, Joseph A. *The One Who Is to Come.* Eerdmans, 2007.

Fredriksen, Paula. *From Jesus to Christ: The Origins of the New Testament Images of Christ.* 2nd ed. Yale University Press, 2000.

Porter, Stanley E., ed. *The Messiah in the Old and New Testaments.* Eerdmans, 2007.

Zetterholm, Magnus, ed. *The Messiah in Early Judaism and Christianity.* Fortress, 2007.

J.A.F./M.A.P.

metals, malleable materials of varying degrees of strength, hardness, and value. Biblical references to metals are frequent but allusive. Tubal-cain (Gen. 4:22) is known as a metalsmith. Canaan is described as "a land whose stones are iron and from whose hills you may mine copper" (Deut. 8:9; cf. Ezra 1:9–11). Tablets from excavations at Ebla in Syria report the transfer of gold and silver in large quantities (ca. 3200 BCE). Judg. 17:3–4; 18:14–18 use the expression "cast metal" (NRSV) in reference to an idol, and Hab. 2:18 contains a similar reference to "cast" (NRSV; cf. RSV: "metal"), also describing an idol made with human hands. Jerusalem's temple reputedly housed 5,469 articles of gold and silver (Ezra 1:11). Palestinian metal-

working sites included numerous mines, smelting and forging operations, and artifacts. In the NT, metal coins are mentioned (Matt. 10:9; Acts 3:6), and the book of Revelation includes bronze and iron along with gold and silver in a list of the precious cargo of merchant ships (18:11–12). Iron was used for construction of gates (Acts 10:12) and breastplates (Rev. 9:9). *See also* brass; copper; gold; iron; lead; refining; silver. R.A.C.

Methuselah (mi-thoo′suh-luh), according to the lineage of Seth, the son of Enoch, the father of Lamech, and the grandfather of Noah (Gen. 5:21–27; 1 Chron. 1:3). Methuselah lived for 969 years, the longest-lived person in the Bible. Cf. Methushael (Gen. 4:18).

Methushael (mi-thoo′shay-uhl), according to the lineage of Cain, the great-grandson of Enoch and father of Lamech (Gen. 4:18). Cf. Methuselah, who is designated the father of Lamech in a different genealogy (5:21–25).

Meunim (myoo′nim), **Meunites** (myoo′nits), an ancient people of disputed and unknown provenance. The Meunim are referred to in 1 Chron. 4:41; Ezra 2:50; and Neh. 7:52. The same people (apparently) are referred to as the Meunites in 2 Chron. 20:1; 26:7. Both Meunim and Meunites are sometimes identified with the people known elsewhere in history as Minaeans, who occupied the region of Main in modern North Yemen. The Minaeans conducted trade throughout the Levant, and numerous Minaean inscriptions, some dated to the early first millennium BCE, have been found, mostly in Arabia, but also as distantly as Memphis in Egypt and Delos. The Meunim of 1 Chron. 4:41 and the Meunites of 2 Chron. 26:7 are explicitly identified as Minaeans in the Greek LXX translation of the Bible, as are the Ammonites in 2 Chron. 20:1 and 26:8, and Zophar in Job 2:11. Such identifications are problematic, however, and may have resulted from the substitution of a more familiar name for a less familiar one. In Ezra 2:50 (cf. Neh. 7:52), the Meunim are temple servants. *See also* Seba, Sabeans. M.D.C.

Mica (mi′kuh; a shortened form of Micaiah; Heb., "who is like the LORD?").

1 The son of Mephibosheth (Merib-baal) and Saul's great-grandson by Jonathan (2 Sam. 9:12); he is also called Micah (1 Chron. 8:34–35). *See also* Micah.

2 A Levite, the son of Zichri and father of Mattaniah, a postexilic inhabitant of Jerusalem (1 Chron. 9:15; Neh. 11:22); he is probably the same Levite who is elsewhere called the son of Zabdiel and father of Mattaniah (1 Chron. 11:17). He may also be the same Levite called Micaiah and the son of Zaccur and father of Mattaniah (Neh. 12:35). It is possible, however, that these represent three different persons.

3 A Levite who signed Ezra's covenant to keep the law (Neh. 10:11); possibly the same as **2** above. *See also* Micaiah. D.R.B.

Micah (mi′kuh; a shortened form of Micaiah; Heb., "who is like the LORD?").

1 The prophet Micah of Moresheth, a town some twenty-five miles southwest of Jerusalem, to whom the book of Micah is attributed. In addition to the information in Mic. 1:1, Jer. 26:18 reports that Micah came to Jerusalem in the time of Hezekiah, i.e., during the last decade or so of the eighth century BCE, and announced the destruction of the city (cf. Mic. 3:12). His exact dates are unknown, but he would have been a contemporary of Isaiah of Jerusalem. *See also* Micah, book of.

2 A man in the hill country of Ephraim, a central but mainly passive figure in the story of the migration of the tribe of Dan (Judg. 17–18). His mother consecrated eleven hundred pieces of silver "to the LORD" (Judg. 17:3) to make a graven image and a molten image, a strange act in light of the biblical prohibitions against images and idols. He established a shrine, made an ephod and teraphim, and set up one of his sons as priest. When a Levite from Bethlehem ("of the family of Judah," 17:7) appeared, Micah hired him as priest at the shrine. When the tribe of Dan, seeking a place to live, sent spies into the hill country of Ephraim, they stayed with Micah, asking the Levite to consult the Lord concerning their journey. Hearing his good report, they completed their exploration to the north and returned to lead the Danites to their new territory. When the five spies (along with six hundred armed Danites) returned through the hill country of Ephraim, they stole Micah's "idol of cast metal, the ephod, and the teraphim" and took the Levite with them to their new territory in the north (18:17). The story, thus, offers a negative account of how the shrine in Dan was established.

3 A Reubenite who was the son of Shimei and the father of Reaiah (1 Chron. 5:5).

4 The son of Merib-baal who was the son of Jonathan (1 Chron. 8:34–35; 9:40), the same as Mica the son of Mephibosheth in 2 Sam. 9:12. *See also* Mica.

5 A Levite in the time of David, one of the sons of Uzziel (1 Chron. 23:20; 24:24–25).

6 The father of Abdon in the time of Josiah (2 Chron. 34:20), named Micaiah in 2 Kings 22:12.
G.M.T.

Micah, book of, the sixth part of the Book of the Twelve contained with the Prophets section, or Nevi'im, in the Tanakh (Jewish Bible). In the Christian OT, it is the sixth book of the Minor Prophets.

Contents: Micah first accuses Israel and Judah of idolatry (1:5–7), but then connects their idolatry with the injustice present in their land. This first oracle also invokes the old tradition of the theophany of the divine warrior, emphasizing the terror of the Lord coming to judge people. Micah is also critical of the prophets and of the "religious." He criticizes prophets who work for wages, particularly those who unreservedly endorsed and legitimated the royal house with their "Zion theology" (3:11–12). In chap. 6, there is criticism of the cultic practices of the "religious," claiming that a life of justice, mercy, and humility is what the Lord wants more than sacrifices. As a result of his many criticisms, Micah came into conflict with the royal administration (King Hezekiah), but he was not executed for treason (this episode becomes important in the book of Jeremiah; cf. Jer. 26).

Though Micah offers many social and religious criticisms, he also prophesies mercy and salvation. He does not completely reject the Davidic ideology, prophesying a good future for Jerusalem (5:2). Yet this good future will come not from the political and economic capital of Jerusalem, but from the small town of Bethlehem, the birthplace of David. Thus, Micah was able to reject the Jerusalem court without rejecting the Davidic line. The Lord will also sustain and renew the community through the faithful remnant (4:7).

OUTLINE OF CONTENTS

Micah

Themes: The structure of the book reveals that Micah is essentially a critic of the economic and political elite in Judah and Jerusalem, and he is an advocate for economic justice. He also balances the themes of judgment and disaster with salvation. His thematic focus is quite similar to that of Isaiah. Both Micah and Isaiah expose issues of justice and both talk of a coming messiah along with a world peace centered on a restored Zion. Sweeney argues that each prophet highlights these themes in different ways and that the present form of the book of Micah was designed as a counterpoint to the theology of Isaiah by emphasizing the exaltation of the remnant of God's people.

Background: Very little is known about the prophet Micah other than his hometown of Moresheth (twenty-three miles southwest of Jerusalem). The prophet's name means "Who is like the LORD?" (a shortened form of Micaiah, used in Jer. 26:18). Some have argued that the name "Micah" is being used as a device (perhaps to hide the true identity of the prophet), because the refrain "Who is like the LORD?" is actually employed in 7:18. However, the majority of scholars believe that a prophet named Micah did live and prophesy in Judah. Micah was a southerner (Judean) and contemporary of Isaiah of Jerusalem. He came from a rural, agrarian background and prophesied in the later half of the eighth century BCE.

Micah was a prophetic critic of the establishment in Judah and Jerusalem. His criticism has often been described as social and hierarchical. He criticizes the aristocrats in Jerusalem who sought more homes and property, but exploited the poor, small-town people. Some have argued that Micah's critique of the upper class demonstrates his humble roots; he may have had firsthand experience with oppression by the elite (either through being oppressed himself or through personally viewing the oppression of his people). Micah even brings a lawsuit against Judah and Israel, on behalf of God (6:1–8), for violating the covenant agreement.

Although there is disagreement over the exact dates of Micah's prophetic career, few scholars doubt the veracity of the book's claim that Micah prophesied during the reigns of Jotham, Ahaz, and Hezekiah. His prediction of the fall of Samaria (1:6–7) would place his first prophetic words some time before 721 BCE. Accordingly, most scholars hold that the allusions to the Babylonian exile (4:10) show the work of editors.

Interpretive Issues: The book of Micah contains a variety of genres, including lament (1:8–16), theophany (1:3–4), prayer (7:14–20), and covenant lawsuit (6:1–8). The majority of scholarship on the book of Micah has investigated the form and genre of the book (and its constituent parts) along with the editorial process that helped to shape the final form of the book. Most form-critical analysis has focused on the presence of a lawsuit (1:27; 6:1–8) and of wisdom-type literature (7:5–6) in the text. In addition, scholars have noted the absence of the conventional introductory and concluding formulas.

Editorial analysis has been less conclusive. Although most scholars agree that an editing process took place, there are innumerable theories about how the prophet Micah's oracles developed into the final version of the text. The majority of scholars hold that the first three chapters of Micah are derived from the prophet, while the last four are editorial additions. Some scholars argue for the unity of the entire book. Gottwald believes that only the first three chapters can be confidently connected to the prophet Micah and that none of the salvation oracles (Mic. 4–5, 7:8–20) were part of the book of Micah even as late as the end of the seventh century. Childs thinks that the oracles of Micah were most likely shaped by the same group of editors who shaped the oracles of Isaiah, who were trying to integrate the oracles of Micah within a larger theological framework. Peterson believes that the final form of the work did not appear until the Persian period of Jewish history.

There is widespread disagreement over how to divide the book. The majority of scholars, however, find there to be three main units within the text, each beginning with the exclamation "Hear!" or "Listen" (1:2; 3:1; 6:1). Most scholars will divide these sections further in order to highlight the alternating pattern of judgment and salvation. The main point of disagreement is over whether there are two sets of judgment and salvation oracles (1:2–3:12 and 4:1–5:15; 6:1–7:7 and 7:8–20) or three sets (1:2–2:11 and 2:12–13; 3:1–12 and 4:1–5:15; 6:1–7:7 and 7:8–20). Mays argues for a twofold division (Mic. 1–5 and 6–7) around the two "Hear" phrases. Except for one message that includes the northern kingdom (1:2–7), all of the prophecies are directed at Judah.

Influences: The life and message of the prophet Micah become important within the Bible outside of the book of Micah itself. In Jer. 26:18–19, Micah is referenced explicitly and quoted (3:12). The book of Jeremiah claims that even though Micah preached the destruction of Jerusalem, Hezekiah did not execute him. For this reason, it is argued that Jehoiakim should not execute Jeremiah, even though he too preached the destruction of Jerusalem.

Some scholars have argued that Micah had a significant effect on the Deuteronomic reform movement in Judah, because Micah's message matches some Deuteronomic material. For example, he advocated land reform, but supported the Davidic monarchy as long as it remained true to Mosaic ideals (Deut. 17:14–20). The long period of editing of the text of Micah has made it difficult to back this claim definitively.

In modern times, the nonviolent restoration portrayed in Mic. 4 became an important part of Martin Luther King Jr.'s understanding of the hope of nonviolent resistance: "beat their swords into plowshares, and their spears into pruning hooks" (4:3).

Passages from Micah are alluded to eleven times in the Christian NT. The location of Bethlehem as the birthplace of the Messiah is highlighted in Matt. 2:6 (cf. Mic. 5:2).

Bibliography

Allen, Leslie C. *The Books of Joel, Obadiah, Jonah and Micah.* Eerdmans, 1976.

Bandstra, Barry L. *Reading the Old Testament: Introduction to the Hebrew Bible.* 4th ed. Wadsworth, 2009.

Childs, Brevard S. *Introduction to the Old Testament as Scripture.* Fortress, 1979.

Gottwald, Norman K. *The Hebrew Bible: A Socio-Literary Introduction.* Fortress, 1985.

Jenson, Philip P. *Obadiah, Jonah, Micah: A Theological Commentary.* Clark, 2008.

Mays, James Luther. *Micah: A Commentary.* Westminster, 1976.

Peterson, David L. *The Prophetic Literature: An Introduction.* Westminster John Knox, 2002.

Simundson, Daniel J. *Hosea, Joel, Amos, Obadiah, Jonah, Micah.* Abingdon, 2005.

Sweeney, Marvin A. *The Twelve Prophets.* Vol. 2, *Micah, Nahum, Habakkuk, Zephaniah, Haggai, Zechariah, Malachi.* Liturgical, 2000.

Wolff, Hans Walter. *Micah: A Commentary.* Augsburg, 1990.   B.B.

Micaiah (mi-kay'uh).

1 King Abijah's mother (2 Chron. 13:2), elsewhere called Maacah (1 King 15:2; 2 Chron. 11:20–22).

2 The son of Imlah, a prophet at Ahab's court (1 Kings 22). Ahab and Jehoshaphat, king of Judah, wanted to liberate Ramoth-gilead from the Arameans. Before going to war they consulted some four hundred prophets, all of whom assured them that God would grant victory. When Micaiah was summoned, however, he reported a vision of the Israelites wandering about the hills like sheep without a shepherd. He described a meeting of the divine council at which God had commissioned "a lying spirit in the mouth of all [the] prophets" (22:22) to "entice Ahab, that he may go up and fall at Ramoth-gilead" (22:20). Ahab ordered Micaiah cast into prison and proceeded with his plan for war. Although he took the precaution of disguising himself before going into battle, he was fatally wounded when "a certain man drew his bow and unknowingly struck the king" (22:34), and the Israelites left the battlefield in disarray, as Micaiah had predicted.

3 One of the princes sent by Jehoshaphat to instruct the cities of Judah in religious matters (2 Chron. 17:7).

4 The father of Achbor, a member of Josiah's delegation to Huldah the prophetess (2 Kings 22:12).

5 The son of Gemariah and grandson of Shaphan, both friends of Jeremiah. When Micaiah heard Baruch read the scroll of Jeremiah's oracles, he reported it to his father and other court officials (Jer. 36:11–13), and they arranged to have it read to King Jehoiakim.

6 The forebear of certain postexilic priests (Neh. 12:35), elsewhere called Mica (11:17, 22).

7 A priest in the time of Nehemiah, one of seven who blew trumpets at the dedication of Jerusalem's rebuilt walls (Neh. 12:41).   P.K.M.

Michael (mi'kay-uhl; Heb., "who is like God?").

1 A man from the tribe of Asher whose son Sethur was one of the twelve spies sent to Canaan (Num. 13:13).

2 A warrior from the tribe of Manasseh who deserted Saul at Ziklag to become a commander in David's army (1 Chron. 12:20).

3 The father of Omri, who served as chief officer for the tribe of Issachar at the time of David.

4 The son of King Jehoshaphat, assassinated when his older brother Jehoram succeeded his father to the throne (2 Chron. 21:2, 4).

5 The father of Zebadiah, who supervised eighty people who returned from the Babylonian exile with Ezra (Ezra 8:8).

6 An archangel, mentioned in the books of Daniel, Jude, and Revelation. He is also mentioned in some nonbiblical Jewish writings of the Second Temple period, including the Qumran *War Scroll*. Dan. 10:13 calls Michael one of the "chief princes" (cf. 10:21) who assisted someone (possibly the angel Gabriel; cf. 8:15–17) in battle against the prince of the kingdom of Persia. Most interpret-

ers think that this is invoking the notion of "patron angels" who represent and defend the people or nation to which they are related. Thus, Michael would be one of the patron angels of Israel, and the vision described in 10:10–21 would imply battle with the patron angel of Persia. Dan. 12:1–3 indicates that at some time in the future (probably during or just after the last days of Antiochus IV Epiphanes), Michael, the great prince who is now called the "protector" of Daniel's people (the Jews), will arise for a time of unprecedented anguish and deliverance. People will be raised from the dead, some to everlasting life and others to everlasting contempt.

In the NT, Michael is mentioned in Jude 9, which seeks to draw a moral lesson from what the author assumes to be a well-known story: "When the archangel Michael contended with the devil and disputed about the body of Moses, he did not dare to bring a condemnation of slander against him, but said 'The Lord rebuke you!'" No such story is recorded in any extant literature, but Clement of Alexandria (ca. 150–215 CE) and a number of other early Christian scholars maintain that it was reported in a Jewish work now called the *Assumption of Moses,* which was extant in their day, but has not survived. Most contemporary scholars think that this writing was probably part of an apocalyptic Jewish work known as the *Testament of Moses;* current manuscripts of the latter work are incomplete and the story to which Jude refers could have been contained in the portion that is missing. Michael is also mentioned in Rev. 12:7–9, where he leads the hosts of heaven in a cosmic battle against Satan: "War broke out in heaven; Michael and his angels fought against the dragon. The dragon and his angels fought back, but they were defeated."   M.A.P.

Michal (mi'kuhl; a shortened form of Michael; Heb., "who is like God?"), Saul's younger daughter (1 Sam. 14:49), who becomes David's wife. Her love for David is exploited by Saul, who hopes to dispose of David by asking an unusual and difficult bride-price: one hundred Philistine foreskins. David is able to meet this price, which leads Saul to realize that God is with David, so Saul fears David even more (18:20–29). Later, Michal becomes aware that Saul is planning to kill David, and she warns him. She helps him to escape from their room by letting him down through a window and then places an idol with a head covering of goat hair in the bed, telling Saul's messengers that David is there, but he is sick. When the ruse is discovered, Saul is upset that his daughter deceived him to save her husband, and she tells him David forced her to do so, threatening to kill her (19:8–17). Subsequently, Saul gives Michal as a wife to Palti, a man from Gallim (25:44), but David later regains her through a political bargain with Saul's son and successor, Ishbaal (2 Sam. 3:12–16; cf. 1 Chron. 15:29). Finally, in the story of the transfer of the ark to Jerusalem, Michal is said to be upset with David for the way he dances in

public before the ark (2 Sam. 6:12–23). She looks out her window, sees him leaping and dancing, and despises him in her heart. In private, she accuses him of "uncovering himself . . . before the eyes of his servants' maids, as any vulgar fellow might shamelessly uncover himself" (6:20). The Bible notes that Michal died childless, perhaps as a divine punishment for her despising David on this occasion (6:23). *See also* David; Saul.   J.C.E.

Michmash (mik'mash), a village located in the rugged hills of the territory of the tribe of Benjamin, about seven miles north of Jerusalem. It was on the north bank of the Wadi Suweinet opposite Geba, and together they guarded the pass to the Jordan Valley. Michmash stood almost 2,000 feet above sea level, and two rocky outcrops called Bozez and Seneh stood nearby on either side of the valley (1 Sam. 14:4–5). In this pass the Philistine power in the eastern hill country was broken (13–14). Saul had gathered troops in the hill country of Bethel (13:2) when Jonathan killed the Philistine governor at Geba. The Philistines rallied their forces at Michmash with greatly superior numbers (13:5) and dispersed raiding parties to the west, north, and east (13:5, 17). But then Jonathan led a surprise attack across the wadi and terrified the Philistines (14:13–15). Saul and Jonathan pursued the Philistines, who had been thrown into confusion (14:15), and drove them from the hill country (14:31). Later, Isa. 10:28 mentions Michmash in a poem describing a northern attack on Jerusalem by the Assyrians. Michmash was also inhabited after the exile according to the lists in Ezra (2:27) and Nehemiah (7:31; 11:31).   N.L.L.

Midian (mid'ee-uhn), **Midianites** (mid'ee-uhn-*its*), a son of Abraham and his concubine Keturah (Gen. 25:1–2), and his descendants. When Abraham expelled Isaac's rivals "to the east country," Midian was included (25:6). Thus, the Midianites were counted among the "people of the east" (Judg. 6:3, 33; 7:12), a general designation for the nomadic inhabitants of the Syrian and Arabian deserts. The "land of Midian" (Exod. 2:15) probably refers to the center of Midianite territory, that part of northwestern Arabia bordering the Gulf of Aqabah's eastern shore (cf. 1 Kings 11:18). The term "Midianite" probably identified a confederation of tribes that roamed far beyond this ancestral homeland, a usage that may explain the biblical references to Midianites in Sinai, Canaan, the Jordan Valley, Moab, and Transjordan's eastern desert. Extrabiblical references to the Midianites are few and ambiguous, making it difficult to associate specific archaeological artifacts with this elusive people. Nevertheless, archaeological surveys have identified ruins of many settlements in the northern Hejaz, with some sites dating back to the Late Bronze/Iron I transition. Especially intriguing is a style of painted pottery that has been tentatively identified as "Midianite."

The first significant reference to the Midianites is a record of their involvement in the sale of Joseph into slavery, an account in which Midianites are closely associated or equated with Ishmaelites (Gen. 37:25–28, 36; 39:1; cf. Judg. 8:24). Later, Moses's sojourn in Midian prior to the exodus is of some significance. Moses goes to Midian as a fugitive from Egyptian justice (Exod. 2:15). He is befriended by Jethro, the priest of Midian (2:16; 3:1), after defending his daughters from some shepherds who drove them away from a well. Moses marries Jethro's daughter Zipporah (2:21), and while still in the general region of Midian, he is commissioned by God (through a burning bush) to lead the Hebrews out of Egypt (3:1–15; 4:19). Later, Moses's Midianite brother-in-law, Hobab, guides the Israelites in the wilderness (Num. 10:29–32). When the Hebrews are encamped in the Plains of Moab, the "elders of Midian" and the Moabite king Balak hire Balaam to curse their new enemies (Num. 22:1–7; cf. Josh. 13:21). The Midianites also lead Israel into idolatry and immorality at Shittim (Num. 25:1–7, 16–18), and Moses is commanded to seek revenge by destroying the Midianite population in this region (31:1–12). Finally, after Israel's settlement in the land, the Hebrew warrior Gideon soundly defeats the camel-riding Midianites, who are said to have oppressed the Israelites for seven years. Many years later, Gideon's victory would be recounted in Ps. 83:9, 11; Isa. 9:4; 10:26. *See also* Amalekites; camel; Horeb, Mount; Ishmaelites; Jethro; Keturah; mount, mountain.

Bibliography

Eph'al, Israel. *The Ancient Arabs*. Brill, 1982.
    G.L.M.

midrash (mid'rash; from Heb., "to search, inquire, and interpret"), a type of biblical interpretation that seeks to explain or elucidate ambiguities in the text, often with reference to other passages. Although midrash is most associated with rabbinic literature (especially the Talmud and various midrashic collections, e.g., *Midrash Genesis*), midrashic interpretation may be found within the Bible itself in instances where relatively late texts are said to offer a midrash on earlier passages. For example, 1 Chron. 5:1 says that Reuben's birthright was given to the sons of Joseph, because Reuben had "defiled his father's bed." This might be described as a midrash that interprets one obscure passage of scripture in light of others. In Gen. 48:5–7, Jacob proclaims that he accepts Joseph's two sons as his own, but the rationale for this is ambiguous (and has nothing to do with Reuben). Elsewhere in Genesis, however, Reuben does lie with Bilhah, his father's concubine (35:22), and he is told by his father that he will no longer excel because of having defiled his father's bed in this way (49:3–4). The author of 1 Chron. 5:1 appears to have connected these two stories, allowing the rejection of Reuben to provide the missing rationale for the elevation of Joseph's sons. *See also* Haggadah.

Migdol (mig′dol; Heb., "tower" or "fortress"), a city in northern Egypt cited in different biblical contexts. The Israelites camped near here on their way out of Egypt (Exod. 14:2; Num. 33:7) in the eastern Delta, possibly near modern Tell el-Maskhutah. When Pharaoh heard that they were camped "between Migdol and the sea," he thought that they were trapped and brought his army of chariots against them. God divided the sea, allowing the Israelites to escape and subsequently drowning the pursuing Egyptians. Migdol is mentioned again, much later, as a Jewish settlement in the time of Jeremiah (late seventh–early sixth century BCE; Jer. 44:1; 46:14). Authorities have differed as to whether this settlement should also be identified with Tell el-Maskhutah or with nearby modern Tell el-Heir. In Ezekiel, the name Migdol seems to be used in combination with Syene (modern Aswan) to designate all of Egypt (29:10; 30:6).

Migron (mig′ron; Heb., perhaps "steep"), a town in the hill country of Judah. According to 1 Sam. 14:2, "Saul was staying in the outskirts of Gibeah under the pomegranate tree that is at Migron." Gibeah in this verse may be a misreading for Geba, across the valley from Michmash (cf. 13:16). In Isa. 10:28 Migron is mentioned in association with Geba and Michmash as a point on the route of the invading Assyrians. The site is probably to be identified with modern Tell Miriam near Michmash. *See also* Geba; Michmash.

Mijamin (mij′uh-min).
1 The ancestral head of the sixth course of priests (1 Chron. 24:9).
2 A Levite who returned with Zerubbabel from the Babylonian exile (Neh. 12:5); he is possibly the same Levite who divorced his foreign wife in response to Ezra's proclamation (Ezra 10:25) and who signed Ezra's covenant to keep the law (Neh. 10:7). Some scholars think the Miniamin mentioned in Neh. 12:17, 41 is also the same person, although that connection is not clear.

Mikloth (mik′loth).
1 A Benjaminite, the father of Shimeah (Shimeam) and son of Gibeon (1 Chron. 8:32; 9:37–38).
2 The chief officer under Dodai who was commander of twenty-four thousand men in King David's army (1 Chron. 27:4).

Miktam (mik′tam), a technical term of uncertain meaning introducing Pss. 16; 56–60; and probably Isa. 38:9 (NRSV: "writing"). All of these poems are laments, so it is possible that the term referred to a particular genre of poetry.

Milcah (mil′kuh).
1 The daughter of Haran and sister of Lot (Gen. 11:29; cf. 11:27). She married Abraham's brother Nahor and they had eight children, one of whom was Bethuel, father of Rebekah (Gen. 22:20–23). *See also* Bethuel; Haran.
2 One of the five daughters of Zelophehad belonging to the tribe of Manasseh (Num. 26:33). They claimed before Moses that, since their father had no sons, his inheritance should belong to them. Their claim was sustained (27:1–7), so long as they married within the tribe (36:1–12). *See also* law; Mahlah; Zelophehad.   F.R.M.

Milcom (mil′kuhm; from the Semitic root *mlk*, "king"), the Ammonite form of Baal, the Northwest Semitic god of fertility and the storm. He was closely related to the Phoenician Baals, Melcart and Molech, to whom human sacrifices, particularly children, were offered. The worship of Milcom was introduced into Jerusalem by Solomon (1 Kings 11:5, 33) and abolished by Josiah (2 Kings 23:13). *See also* Baal; Molech.

mildew (Heb., "yellow" or "pale"), generally a superficial growth on organic matter or plants by fungi of the *Erysiphaceae* or *Peronosporaceae* families. Viewed consistently as divine punishment (Deut. 28:22), it is associated with "blasting" and "fiery heat," which suggests damage in the wake of destructive east winds (sirocco). It is a tool of God's judgment (Hag. 2:17; Amos 4:9), and relief from it is a divine grace (1 Kings 8:37; 2 Chron. 6:28).

mile. *See* weights and measures.

Miletus (mi-lee′tuhs), a large port and commercial center at the ancient mouth of the Meander River on the west coast of Asia Minor. The city was originally founded by the Ionians about the eleventh century BCE. The Persians controlled the port at least twice, but it was freed by Alexander the Great in 334 BCE. The city flourished during the Hellenistic and Roman periods (324 BCE–325 CE), with four harbors and three market areas, one of which was the largest known market of the ancient Greek world. The Roman theater of Miletus, with a seating capacity of fifteen thousand, was situated on a peninsula between two bays and was known as one of the best in all Asia Minor. The temple

The Aegean Sea from the site of ancient Miletus.

of Apollo, the principal deity of the city, stood in front of the northern harbor. Paul stopped in Miletus on his way to Jerusalem and summoned the elders of Ephesus to come for a farewell address (Acts 20:15–38). A reference to another possible visit of Paul to the city can be found in 2 Tim. 4:20.   M.K.M.

mill, any of a variety of installations for grinding food grains (Isa. 47:2; Matt. 24:41) or other foodstuffs (Num. 11:8). The normal domestic form of a mill was a saddle quern of limestone or basalt and a hand-held grinding stone. The grain was placed on the saddle and rubbed with back-and-forth motions of the hand grinder until it reached the desired fineness. Larger communal or industrial installations comprised an upper (movable) and a lower (stable) millstone between which the grain would be placed or fed through a hollow in the upper stone. The upper stone was rotated by human (Judg. 16:21; Lam. 5:13) or animal labor. It pivoted on a small anchoring protrusion of the lower stone's upper surface, working the grain outward toward the edges of the stones as grinding proceeded. Because of the importance of this equipment for everyday survival, Deuteronomic law prevented taking a mill or upper millstone as collateral, since that would be equivalent to "taking a life as a pledge" (Deut. 24:6). Everyday household grinding could be done by servants (Exod. 11:5), though Jesus's casual mention of "two women grinding meal together" (Matt. 24:41; Luke 17:35) suggests that millwork might have typically been done by women. In any case, the use of mills was considered so commonplace that absence of the sound of milling was a symbol of destruction (Rev. 18:22; Jer. 25:10).

The portability of an upper millstone is evident in that it was on occasion used as a weapon (Judg. 9:53; 2 Sam. 11:21). That such a stone could function as a device for execution is also reflected in Jesus's comment about a person being dropped

An olive press, or mill, from Capernaum.

into the sea with a millstone tied about the neck (Matt. 18:6; Mark 9:42; Luke 17:2). The hardness of a millstone is used by Job in a symbolic fashion: the heart of Leviathan is said to be just as hard (Job 41:24). The hurling of a millstone (in this case by an angel) symbolizes violent destruction in Rev. 18:21.   R.S.B.

millennium, a thousand-year period or, generally, an era of permanent peace, joy, and blessings on earth or elsewhere. Ps. 90:4, praising the everlasting God, declares that a thousand years in God's sight "are like yesterday." Possibly on this basis, the author of *Jubilees* (4:30) concluded that Adam did die on the "day" he ate the forbidden fruit (as predicted in Gen. 2:17), because he died within the first thousand years of eating it. Following this clue, the writer of *2 Enoch* speculated that all of history would consist of a week lasting seven thousand years, after which the eighth "day" (i.e., thousand years) would be "endless" (33:1–2). In the NT, 2 Pet. 3:8 likewise suggests that with God a thousand years is the same as a day, which helps to explain why God has not been slow in fulfilling the promise of Christ's return.

The writer of Revelation, vividly portraying the defeat of cosmic evil powers (and of Rome, 17:1–18:24), forecasts a thousand-year epoch within the framework of eschatological events. During this time, Satan will be bound and sealed "in the pit," while those Christians who have withstood persecution and refused to worship the image of the beast will reign with Christ (20:1–6). After a thousand years, Satan will be loosed for a final onslaught, but then, with Death and Hades, he will be forever banished "to the lake of fire and brimstone" (20:7–14). *See also* apocalyptic literature; eschatology; Parousia; Satan.   R.H.H.

millet, a small-seeded annual grass (*Panicum miliaceum*) grown for both grain and stalks. In Ezek. 4:9 it is mixed with other grains and used in making bread. Millet was used for food for both humans and animals.

millo (mil′loh; Heb., "earthen fill"), a type of construction in which a building, a section of a city, or an entire site was elevated on an artificial platform of earth held in place by one or more walls. The earthen platform is the "millo" and the structure built on the platform is the Beth-millo ("house of the millo"). The fortress temple at Shechem was built on an earth filling obtained by cutting down the embankment fortification of the Middle Bronze Age city. This temple is probably the Beth-millo mentioned in Judg. 9:6, 20. Excavations on the eastern slope of the City of David indicate that during the Canaanite period the hill on which Jerusalem stood was too narrow to accommodate a growing population. It was extended by a "millo" construction. Stone walls were built parallel to the line of the hill, and the spaces between them were filled with earth, creating a platform that extended the hill eastward. After his capture of Jerusalem David rebuilt the interior of the city "from the Millo inward" (2 Sam. 5:9). The Jerusalem millo and the walls associated with it required frequent maintenance. Repairs by Solomon (2 Sam. 9:15, 24; 11:27) and Hezekiah (2 Chron. 32:5) are recorded. King Joash was assassinated in one of the structures built on the Jerusalem millo (2 Kings 12:20). *See also* Jerusalem; Shechem.

L.E.T.

mina (min'uh). *See* money; weights and measures.

Minaeans (min-ee'uhnz). *See* Meunim, Meunites.

mind, the English translation of various Hebrew and Greek words denoting the human capacity for contemplation, judgment, and intention. There is little correlation between English and either Hebrew or Greek words in this regard. For example, the NRSV sometimes uses the word "mind" to translate the Hebrew words *leb* (1 Kings 3:9, 12; Isa. 65:17), *nephesh* (1 Sam. 2:35), and *ruakh* (Ezek. 11:5), but it also renders those words as "heart," "soul," and "spirit," respectively, in other passages. With so many possible applications (intellectual capacity, intentions, perception, understanding, perspective) the word "mind" is used throughout the Hebrew Bible, but it occurs with special frequency in Proverbs, where it tends to denote one's inner or true self. Thus, the "mind of the wicked" is of little worth (10:20), the "mind of a fool" broadcasts folly (12:23), the "mind of the wise" makes their speech judicious (15:14), and the "mind of the righteous" ponders how to answer (i.e., seeks wisdom, 15:28). Proverbs also speaks of the "human mind," which is capable of deep thought and elaborate planning, but impotent to establish anything that does not accord with the purposes of God (16:9; 19:21; 20:5).

In the NT, the word "mind" is used to translate the Greek words *dianoia* (Mark 12:30) and *psychē* (Phil. 1:27), which are more often rendered "understanding" and "soul." Still, the most prominent Greek words translated "mind" in the NT (and in the LXX) are terms related to *nous* (Rom. 1:28; 1 Cor. 2 :16) and *phronēma* (Rom. 8:6–7, 27), both of which carry connotations of understanding (e.g., the capacity for mental perception) as well as the sense of attitude, outlook, or perception. In this sense, "mind" may describe one's characteristic point of view or the standards by which one evaluates life and renders judgments. Paul, in particular, is concerned that Christians' minds be transformed by a renewed dedication to the will of God (Rom. 12:2). In fact, Paul speaks of believers having the "mind of Christ," by which he seems to mean that their outlook on all things has been transformed by Christ, so that it is now congruent with Christ's perspective (cf. 1 Cor. 2:16; Phil. 2:5). *See also* conscience; heart.   M.A.P.

minerals, inorganic substances often obtained by mining. The Bible knows both precious and common minerals such as iron (Deut. 8:9; cf. Gen.

4:22; Josh. 6:19; Jer. 28:13; Acts 12:10), copper (Job 28:2; Ezek. 24:11; Matt. 10:9), beryl (Exod. 28:20; Ezek. 28:13; Rev. 21:20), onyx (Gen. 2:2; Exod. 36:9; Job 28:6; Rev. 21:20), and chrysolite (Ezek. 1:16; Rev. 21:20). *See also* flint; jewels; jewelry; marble; metals; refining.

mines, excavations for the extracting of mineral ores. Job 28:1–11 has the most detailed description of mining in the Bible, though the terms employed are of a general rather than technical character. The subject is the inaccessibility of wisdom, which, like precious metal, is hidden and must be diligently sought. Still, the passage mentions an actual mine for silver and a place for gold to be refined. It says that iron is taken out of the earth, that people search underground for ore, cut channels, open shafts in uninhabited valleys, overturn mountains, and put their hands to flinty rock. As descriptive as these procedures are, they show a basic unfamiliarity with technical terms connected with mines and mining. In Deut. 8:9 the verb used for the mining of copper is the same word used elsewhere for digging a cistern or well. The term for a miner is simply "digger." Thus, the verbs "take" or "dig" reveal nothing of the process. Zech. 6:1 refers to "mountains of copper." The lack of specificity about mines and mining is likely due to the paucity of mineral resources in Canaan/Israel. Geological explorations have shown adequate sources of materials for construction purposes generally underlying much of the land, but sources for ore were concentrated in a few locations.

Five centers of ancient mining and metal production have been discovered in Israel and Jordan:

1. The Timna Valley region in the Wadi Arabah, where copper-smelting furnaces were discovered at modern Tell-el-Kheleifeh. These may have been in use during the Solomonic period, though that has been disputed. A copper smelter has also been

The semicircular area extending from the base of the hill marks the perimeter of a smelting camp at Timna from the fourteenth twelfth century BCE.

found, along with a workshop with crushing implements, mining hammers, crushed ore, and pottery from the Middle Bronze I period (just before the time of Abraham in the Bible, ca. 2000 BCE).

2. The 'Amram Valley, south of Timna in the Arabah; it has copper mines and industrial installations.

3. The Wadi Feinan and modern Khirbet e-Nahas at the foot of the Edom mountains in southern Jordan; these have copper and iron mines as well as evidence of smelting sites.

4. The Wadi es-Sabra, in what is now southern Jordan (Edom) about four and a half miles southwest of Petra, the northern capital of the ancient Nabatean kingdom. Copper and iron mines were discovered; deposits of copper and veins of rich iron ore (tested to roughly 63.2 percent iron) were noted.

5. Mugharat Wardeh, about two miles from the Jabbok (Zerqa) River in southern Gilead (Ajlun region of modern Jordan), where the largest iron mine was found.

Bibliography

Glueck, Nelson. *The Other Side of Jordan.* American Schools of Oriental Research, 1970.
Rothenberg, B. *Timna.* Thames & Hudson, 1972.
R.A.C.

minister, a person who serves in either a secular or religious sense. Priests are called "ministers of the LORD" in Joel 1:9, 13 (cf. Num. 3:3; 1 Chron. 16:4; Ezra 8:17), but the same Hebrew word (*shorat*) is also used to describe Joshua as a minister (NRSV: "assistant") to Moses (Exod. 24:13) and Abishag the Shulamite as a minister (NRSV: "attendant") to David (1 Kings 1:4); a different word (*sar*) is used to describe the ministers who were royal officials at the court of King Ahasuerus (Esther 1:3; 2:18; 5:11). Ps. 103:21 refers to angels as God's ministers, and 104:4 says that the forces of nature (wind, fire) are God's ministers as well. In the age to come, all Israelites (Isa. 61:6) and even foreigners (56:6) will be ministers of the LORD (61:6).

In the NT, the English word "minister" is used to translate two Greek terms: *leitourgos* and *diakonos.* Both have a basic sense of "servant," but context must determine whether this is meant in a specifically religious sense. Thus, Heb. 8:2 says that Jesus (as our great high priest) is a minister (*leitourgos*) in the (heavenly) sanctuary of God. Paul uses the same word in saying that he has been given the grace of God to be a minister of Christ to the Gentiles (Rom. 15:16) and in identifying Epaphroditus as a minister to his needs (Phil. 2:25). In the latter instance at least, *leitourgos* does not refer to a leader of a congregation, but to someone who helps another in whatever ways are called for. Likewise, the term *diakonos* is used to describe Paul's assis-

tants Tychicus (Eph. 6:21; Col. 4:7) and Epaphras (Col. 1:7) as faithful ministers "not of letter but of spirit; for the letter kills, but the Spirit gives life" (2 Cor. 3:6). In 2 Cor. 11:15, the term "ministers of Christ" seems to refer to people who devote themselves to work associated with churches in an extraordinary way (either as a full-time commitment or a professional vocation, or at least in a way that causes them to be publicly recognized as "ministers" compared to ordinary believers). The distinction, however, is one of degree: Paul claims that God has made all believers competent to be ministers of the new covenant (2 Cor. 11:5), while also recognizing that some have the gift for ministry that will enable them to excel at it (Rom. 12:7). This gift of ministry is comparable to the gift of being a teacher or a prophet or, for that matter, of being an exhorter, a leader, a compassionate person, or a generous giver (cf. Rom. 12:8). Paul also recognizes that Satan has ministers, who disguise themselves as ministers of righteousness (2 Cor. 11:14–15). *See also* bishop; elders; leader; ordain, ordination; priests; servant.   M.A.P.

Minni (min'i), a state and people mentioned in Jer. 51:27, where they are part of a coalition with Ararat (Urartu) and Ashkenaz (probably Scythians) that opposed Babylon. They are probably to be identified with the people otherwise known as the Manneans. The latter are mentioned in Assyrian royal inscriptions beginning with Shalmaneser III (858–824 BCE). They lived in the eastern Turkish mountain territory south of Lake Urmia, part of modern northern Iraq.

Minnith (min'ith), one of the twenty cities taken from the Ammonites by Jephthah (Judg. 11:33). Its pairing with a southern tribal city, Aroer, as the opposite boundary would suggest a location somewhere in the northern sector, near modern Amman. The precise location is unknown, but probably lies somewhere northeast of modern Hesban.

mint, a strongly scented herb used in cooking, medicinally as a carminative and stomachic, and on floors of synagogues as an air freshener. In Matt. 23:23 and Luke 11:42, Jesus speaks of those who pay tithes on mint and other herbs while neglecting the weightier matters of the law (in Matthew, "justice and mercy and faith"; in Luke, "justice and the love of God"). The point is that such people are scrupulous with regard to matters of little consequence, but lax with regard to what counts most.

miracles, extraordinary events that constitute inexplicable manifestations of God's power. In the Bible miracles can occur through the direct intervention of God in human affairs, or they can be wrought through human intermediaries who function as divinely empowered miracle workers. Miracles are usually (though not always) performed on behalf of humankind, and they always

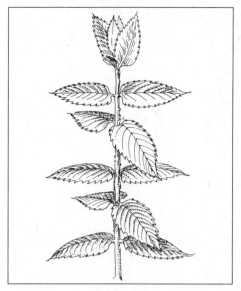

Mint.

The miracle of the healing of the leper by Jesus (Mark 1:40–42) from the *Four Gospels*, a late twelfth-century illuminated manuscript.

serve as exhibitions of divine glory. Miracle stories often strike modern Bible readers as reporting incidents in which known laws of nature are suspended or something is said to occur that scientists would regard as impossible. Such a reading would have been anachronistic in the world of the Bible, where virtually everyone believed that there were spiritual or magical powers at work that could cause things to happen or enable people to do what they could not have done on their own. Thus, the most common response to miracles in the Bible is not disbelief, but astonishment. Miracles are not regarded as supernatural events, but as extraordinary ones. Further, the Bible grants that such extraordinary events may be wrought by powers other than God (e.g., the sorcerers of Egypt in Exod. 7:11–12; 8:7 and the false prophets who will work signs and wonders according to Matt. 24:24; cf. 2 Thess. 2:9). Thus, onlookers who encounter miracles in the biblical world generally recognize that some extraordinary power is at work; the question is *what* power—and *to what end*?

In the Hebrew Bible: The NRSV typically translates the Hebrew word *mophet* as "miracle" (1 Chron. 16:12; Pss. 78:43; 105:5, 27), but it also renders *mophet* as "wonder" (e.g., Exod. 7:3; Deut. 4:34; 6:22; 7:19; 13:1; 26:8; 28:46; 34:11; Neh. 9:10; Isa. 8:18; Jer. 32:20; Dan. 6:27) or as "portent" (Deut. 13:1; 28:46; Isa. 8:18). Likewise, the related Hebrew word *'ot* (NRSV: "sign") often refers to miraculous occurrences. Throughout the biblical narratives of Israel, miracles are closely associated with the creative and salvific deeds of God. Indeed, the very act of creation is presented as a miracle: the heavens and the earth and all they contain are brought into being by the word and spirit of God (Gen. 1:1–2:3). In a certain sense, all other miracles stem from this one, for it is God's

sovereignty as Creator that enables God to do as God wills within creation.

Miracle stories occur at every phase of Israel's history, but are especially concentrated in two parts of the tradition: the account of Israel's exodus and settlement in the land and the traditions associated with Elijah and Elisha. In both of these traditions miracles are worked primarily through chosen intermediaries. In the exodus account, God works astounding miracles through Moses to liberate the Israelites from slavery in Egypt and bring them to the promised land (e.g., guidance by a pillar of cloud and a pillar of fire, Exod. 13:21–22; the dividing of the sea, 14:1–31; the manna in the wilderness, 16:13–31; the water from a rock, 17:1–7). Once the people enter the land, God works through Joshua to miraculously conquer the territory and drive out their enemies (e.g., the fall of Jericho, Josh. 6). Such miracles continue, though perhaps a bit more sporadically, throughout the period of the judges and into the time of the monarchy. Then Elijah and Elisha set a new high point as miracle workers, often demonstrating the power of Israel's God in contrast to Baal or other pagan deities. Elijah provides people with food (1 Kings 17:8–16), raises the dead (17:17–24), and controls the weather (18:1–46); Elisha also provides people with food (2 Kings 4:38–41, 42–44), raises the dead (4:18–37), and heals both infertility (4:11–17) and disease (5:1–27).

Miracles sometimes function as acts of judgment or punishment. The plagues visited upon

MIRACLE STORIES IN THE GOSPELS

	Matthew	Mark	Luke	John
Healings and Exorcisms:				
Demoniac in synagogue		1:23–26	4:33–35	
Peter's mother-in-law	8:14–15	1:30–31	4:38–39	
Man with leprosy	8:2–4	1:40–42	5:12–13	
Paralytic	9:2–7	2:3–12	5:18–25	
Man with withered hand	12:10–13	3:1–5	6:6–10	
Gadarene demoniac(s)	8:28–34	5:1–15	8:27–35	
Woman with hemorrhage	9:20–22	5:25–34	8:43–48	
Gentile woman's daughter	15:21–28	7:24–30		
Deaf-mute		7:31–37		
Blind man at Bethsaida		8:22–26		
Demon-possessed boy	17:14–18	9:17–29		
Blind Bartimaeus (and companion?)	20:29–34 ?	10:46–52		
Centurion's servant	8:5–13		7:1–10	4:46–54
(Blind) Mute demoniac	12:22		11:14	
Two blind men	9:27–31			
Mute demoniac	9:32–33			
Crippled woman			13:11–13	
Man with dropsy			14:1–4	
Ten lepers			17:11–19	
High priest's servant			22:50–51	
Invalid at Pool of Bethesda				5:1–9
Man born blind				9:1–7
Resuscitation:				
Jairus's daughter	9:18–25	5:22–42	8:41–56	
Widow's son at Nain			7:11–15	
Lazarus				11:1–44
Provision:				
5,000 people fed	14:15–21	6:35–44	9:12–17	6:5–13
4,000 people fed	15:32–38	8:1–9		
Catch of fish			5:4–1–11	
Changing water into wine				2:1–11
Post-Easter catch of fish				21:1–11

Egypt are classic examples of such punishment miracles (Exod. 7–11), but God uses miracles to punish Israelites as well. God sends a plague upon those who worship the golden calf (32:35), burns in a fire those who complain about their misfortunes (Num. 11:1–3), and opens the earth to swallow the households of Korah, Dathan, and Abiram (16:23–34).

In the NT: All four Gospels contain multiple accounts of Jesus working miracles. The preferred term for miracles in the Synoptic Gospels (Matthew, Mark, Luke) is the Greek word *dynamis*,

MIRACLE STORIES IN THE GOSPELS (*continued*)

	Matthew	Mark	Luke	John
Miscellaneous:				
Calming the storm at sea	8:23–27	4:37–41	8:22–25	
Walking on water	14:25	6:48–51		6:19–21
Transfiguration	17:1–8	9:2–8	9:28–36	
Withering a fig tree	21:18–22	11:12–25		
Predicting coin in fish's mouth	17:24–27			
Vanishing at Emmaus			24:31	
Appearing in Jerusalem				20:19, 26

From Mark Allan Powell, *Introducing the New Testament* (courtesy, Baker Academic)

which means "power" or "deeds of power" (e.g., Matt. 11:20–23; Mark 6:2, 5). The most common miracle stories in the Gospels are accounts of Jesus healing those who are sick or physically disabled; in a few cases, he is even said to restore dead people to life. Many of these stories exhibit a focus on faith, either that of the afflicted person (Mark 5:34; 10:52; Luke 17:19) or of others (Mark 2:5; 7:29; 9:23). Sometimes the healing stories are intended to be read with a degree of symbolic interpretation; for example, the story of Jesus healing a blind man leads to commentary on his ability to grant spiritual insight (John 9:39). Healing stories overlap considerably with accounts of exorcism. In the Bible, possession by an evil spirit does not cause a person to become sinful or immoral; it causes the person to become blind or deaf, to have seizures or be crippled, or to experience some other sort of physical or emotional distress. The exorcism stories in the NT usually focus on the interaction of Jesus and the unclean spirit; the afflicted person is apparently incapable of independent action or response, which may explain why no one in the NT ever *requests* an exorcism. There are also a handful of miracle stories in the Gospels in which Jesus rescues people from danger (stilling storms at sea) or provides for people's physical needs (multiplying loaves, changing water to wine, effecting a great catch of fish). And, finally, there are a couple of instances of what are sometimes called "epiphany miracles," because they serve to manifest Jesus's divine presence (walking on water, transfiguration).

In the NT, the miracles of Jesus are also presented as one of the ways in which the final, decisive reign of God has come into history. He tells his disciples, "If it is by the Spirit of God that I cast out demons, then the kingdom of God has come to you" (Matt. 12:28). He is plundering the house of Satan, which indicates that Satan has been bound (12:29). Thus the miracles of Jesus, particularly in the Synoptic Gospels, serve as illustrations of Jesus's central message, "The kingdom of heaven has come near" (4:17). But they

are signs of something else as well: they are often depicted as acts of compassion (Matt. 14:14; 15:32–38; 20:34; Luke 7:13–17) and manifestations of divine love. This revelatory aspect of the miracles may account for the distinctive terminology used for them in John's Gospel. There, the miracles are not called *dynamis* ("deeds of power"), but *semeia* ("signs"; e.g. 2:11; 4:54; 6:2, 14; 12:18, 37), because they point beyond themselves to the truth about God that Jesus has come to reveal. In some sense, the miracles are simply signs of legitimation, proving that Jesus has divine power and authority (see 3:2; 7:31; 9:16). Their effectiveness in this regard, however, is mixed: some people believe because of the signs (2:23; 4:53–54; cf. 20:30); others do not (11:47; 12:37; cf. 4:48). In a deeper sense the miracles are signs because, like the metaphors of Jesus's speech, they indicate something symbolic about who God is and what God does; God transforms the ordinary into the extraordinary (2:1–11) and offers people health (4:46–54), sustenance (6:2–14), and life (11:38–44; 12:18).

According to the Gospels, Jesus also gave his disciples the power to work miracles (e.g., Matt. 10:1, 8) and indeed, according to John's Gospel, he indicated that they would do greater works than he had done (14:12). The book of Acts emphasizes the performance of "signs and wonders," spectacular miracles wrought by Jesus's earliest followers, who have been empowered by the Holy Spirit (2:43; 4:30; 5:12; 6:8; 14:3; 15:12). Such actions place the apostles and other followers of Jesus in line with heroes of God like Moses (7:26) and Jesus himself (2:22); they serve to authenticate the word of the gospel, proving that their bold proclamation is endorsed by spiritual powers not subject to human limitation—powers that are usually beneficial, but that are *not* to be offended (Acts 5:1–11; 13:9–12). Paul, indicates that God worked "signs and wonders and mighty works [*dynamesin*]" through him and even seems to suggest that the working of miracles should be regarded as one of the signs that someone is truly an apostle (Rom.

15:19; 2 Cor. 12:12). *See also* apocalyptic literature; devil; divination; eschatology; magic.

Bibliography

Eve, Eric. *The Jewish Context of Jesus's Miracles.* Sheffield Academic, 2002.

Powell, Mark Allan. *Introducing the New Testament: A Historical, Literary, and Theological Survey.* Baker Academic, 2009. Pp. 87–90.

Theissen, Gerd. *Miracle Stories of the Early Christian Tradition.* Clark, 1983.

Twelftree, Graham H. *Jesus the Miracle Worker: A Historical and Theological Study.* InterVarsity, 1999.

Wenham, David, and Craig Blomberg, eds. *The Miracles of Jesus.* JSOT, 1986.   M.A.P.

Miriam (mihr′ee-uhm), the daughter of Amram and Jochebed and sister of Moses and Aaron (Num. 26:59; 1 Chron. 6:3). She is first mentioned when the infant Moses is placed in a basket on the Nile and his sister (not named) watches from a distance; when the baby is discovered by Pharaoh's daughter, the sister offers to find a Hebrew nurse for the baby and fetches Moses's mother (Exod. 2:4–8). After the exodus, Miriam leads the women in a victory song after the events at the Red Sea (15:20–21). She and the women shake tambourines and dance, and she sings to them, "Sing to the LORD, for he has triumphed gloriously; horse and rider he has thrown into the sea" (15:21). Most scholars believe that this brief poem is older than the narrative account of the exodus reported in the preceding chapters. Thus, the Song of Miriam (along with the much longer "Song of Moses" in 15:1–18) is regarded as an especially important passage for reflection on ancient Israelite history—the fact that it is attributed to a female prophet is often noted, since female prophets in the biblical tradition are relatively few in number (cf. Huldah in 2 Kings 22:14; Anna in Luke 2:36).

Miriam is called a prophet in this passage. She later joins Aaron in complaining about the marriage of Moses to a Cushite woman, asking, "Has the LORD spoken only through Moses? Has the LORD not spoken through us also?" (Num. 12:2). God then explains to them that there are different levels of prophets. God speaks to some prophets (like Miriam, presumably) through dreams and visions, but speaks to Moses "face to face," and Moses beholds the form of the Lord (12:5–8). As punishment for having challenged Moses's authority, Miriam is struck with leprosy; Aaron asks Moses to intercede for her, which he does—but God decrees that she must remain outside the camp as a leper for seven days (12:9–15). In later biblical tradition the leprosy of Miriam was presented as a caution to Israel (Deut. 24:9), but Miriam was remembered, together with Moses and Aaron, as a leader sent by God (Mic. 6:4). Her burial at Kadesh is also noted (Num. 20:1).

T.S.F./M.A.P.

Miriam plays a timbrel and sings as other women dance before Moses and the Israelites (Exod. 15:20–21); thirteenth-century French miniature.

mirrors. Archaeological discoveries throughout the Near East attest that during the biblical period mirrors were made not of glass, but of highly polished metal, e.g., silver, gold, copper, or bronze. Textual references also suggest this, since mirrors were sometimes melted down (Exod. 38:8; cf. Job 37:18; Isa. 3:23). The poor quality of a mirror, used metaphorically by Paul to denote a cloudy reflection (1 Cor. 13:12), seems also to suggest metal rather than glass. Excavation has shown a wealthy woman's assemblage of toiletries to include a mirror, garment pins, bead and gold jewelry, fine perfume, and cosmetic dishes. In the Roman period, mirrors became more commonplace. Metal mirrors were round in shape, either of one piece or with a handle of bone, wood, or ivory.

The Wisdom of Solomon refers to wisdom as "a spotless mirror of the working of God, and an image of God's goodness" (7:26). Paul says in 2 Cor. 3:18, "All of us, with unveiled faces, seeing the glory of the Lord as though reflected in a mirror, are being transformed into the same image from one degree of glory to another." The point seems to be that the Holy Spirit is sanctifying believers so that they become Christlike, but that this happens gradually, perhaps because the glory of the Lord is a "reflected glory" and therefore somewhat unclear (1 Cor. 13:12; cf. 1 John 3:1–2). James 1:23–24 says that people who are "hearers of the word and not doers" are like those who look into a mirror and then forget what they were like. The point seems to be that a mirror reveals one's appearance only while one is actually looking into it; likewise, James says, the scripture only speaks to some people while they are actually reading (or hearing) it, but faithful believers should allow the words of scripture to shape their lives and conduct at all times.   S.R./M.A.P.

Mishael (mish'ay-uhl; Heb., "who is what El [God] is?").

1 The son of Uzziel of the Kohathite line of Levites (Exod. 6:22; Lev. 10:4).

2 A man, probably a Levite, who stood with Ezra as he read the law (Neh. 8:4).

3 The Hebrew name of one of the young men taken captive to Babylon by Nebuchadnezzar along with Daniel; he was given the Babylonian name Meshach (Dan. 1:6–7; 2:17). *See also* Meshach.

Mishma (mish'muh; Heb., "a sound").

1 The fifth of the twelve sons of Ishmael (Gen. 25:14).

2 A Simeonite; he was the son of Mibsam and the father of three sons (1 Chron. 4:25–26).

Mitanni (mi-tan'ee), an important empire in northern Mesopotamia from about 1600 to 1330 BCE. It was also called Hanigalbat, Hurri, and Naharina. Its rulers came from a small Indo-Iranian aristocracy, though the population was largely Hurrian. They seem to have been responsible for the introduction of chariot warfare in the Near East. From ca. 1520 to 1420 BCE, Mitanni struggled with Egypt for hegemony over Syria. At one point Mitanni's influence spread as far south as Canaan, contributing to the feudal structure of Canaanite society. Peace came in 1420 BCE, but despite the ensuing good relations with Egypt, Mitanni could not resist the new Hittite power to its west. After a prolonged struggle, the Hittite king Suppiluliuma (ca. 1380–1346 BCE) defeated Tushratta, Mitanni's last great ruler; a century later Assyria destroyed what remained of the once great state.

The significance of the Mitanni for biblical studies lies in the fact that records kept at Nuzi (a Mitannian dependency) provide information about culture and customs relevant for understanding narratives of Israel's ancestors. The Nuzi tablets make reference to such things as adoption of a servant as a son (cf. Abraham's adoption of Eliezer, Gen. 15:2–3), surrogate motherhood (cf. that of Hagar, Bilhah, and Zilpah, Gen. 16:2; 30:3, 9), and the double inheritance of a firstborn son (cf. Deut. 21:17).   J.J.M.R./M.A.P.

mite. *See* money.

Mithredath (mith'ruh-dath; Persian, "gift of Mithra"; also Mithridates, 1 Esd. 2:11, 16).

1 An official at the Persian court, "the treasurer," acting as Cyrus's agent in returning the temple vessels to Sheshbazzar for restoration to Jerusalem (Ezra 1:8).

2 A member of a group that sent a letter to Artaxerxes (Ezra 4:17). This letter appears to be distinct from the one that follows in 4:8–16.

Mitylene (mit'uh-lee'nee), the main city and harbor on the east side of the large island of Lesbos in the Aegean Sea, just off the northwest coast of Asia Minor. The Greek poet Sappho lived there. In the Roman period, it was a popular resort city.

Paul and his companions stopped at Mitylene on their return trip to Jerusalem during the third journey as recorded in Acts 20:14.

Mizar (mi'zahr; Heb., "small"), a hill or small mountain (Ps. 42:6), probably in the region of Mount Hermon and the water sources of the Jordan River. Its precise identity is unknown.

Mizpah, Mizpeh (miz'puh; Heb., "watchtower,"). In addition to being the name of a territory and four cities, the Hebrew word *mizpah* occurs frequently with the definite article to mean "the watchtower." Mizpeh is a variant spelling of Mizpah, occurring four times in the NRSV (Josh. 11:3, 8; 5:38; 18:26).

1 The land of Mizpah (Josh. 11:3, 8); this was in the north of Canaan near Mount Hermon. After Jabin, king of Hazor, was defeated by Joshua, he fled eastward to the valley of Mizpah. It was a dwelling place of the Hivites.

2 Mizpah of Gilead, the name given to the site of the covenant between Laban and Jacob when Jacob returned to Canaan (Gen. 31:49). The popularly named Mizpah Benediction ("The LORD watch between you and me, when we are absent one from the other") derives from Laban's request that God keep Jacob honest while Laban was absent and could not. The location was in Gilead, north of the Jabbok River. At this same Mizpah, the Israelites entered into covenant with Jephthah to be their leader (Judg. 11:11).

3 Mizpeh of Judah, one of the cities in the Shephelah assigned to Judah in the tribal division of the land (Josh. 15:38).

4 Mizpeh of Moab, an unknown site in Moab where David placed his parents under the protection of the king of Moab when Saul was pursuing him (1 Sam. 22:3).

5 Mizpah of Benjamin, a town on the border of Judah and Israel. It was the assembly point for the Israelite tribes going against Gibeah of Benjamin (Judg. 20:1–48). Mizpah was also on the circuit made annually by Samuel when he was judging Israel (1 Sam. 7:16–17). King Asa made Mizpah a fortified city after the heavy fighting between Israel and Judah (1 Kings 15:17–22). After the fall of Jerusalem at the exile (587 BCE), Mizpah became the Babylonian provincial capital. Gedaliah was made provincial governor, but was assassinated at Mizpah by Ishmael and a band of zealots.

This Mizpah has been identified with two modern sites, Nebi Samwil, about five miles north of Jerusalem, and Tell en-Nasbeh, about eight miles north of Jerusalem. Nebi Samwil has not been excavated, but all pottery found in the area comes from periods later than the monarchy (ca. 1025–922 BCE). Tell en-Nasbeh has also been excavated and, although no conclusive evidence proves that it is Mizpah, it does seem to fit well with the biblical and occupational history of Mizpah. The Tell en-Nasbeh mound covers about 7 acres. Its occupation layers extend from the beginning of the Iron Age (1200 BCE) to the Persian period

(539–333 BCE) with only slight evidence for permanent settlement outside these time periods. In fact, Tell en-Nasbeh is one of the few Israelite towns to have been excavated almost completely. It thus provides a good picture of the fortifications, houses, public structures, tools, and utensils of Israel during the monarchy.

One of the most important finds from Tell en-Nasbeh was the city wall. The entire length of about 2,165 feet was excavated. The wall was of the offset-inset type. It had nine or ten towers protecting it. The outer face of the wall ranged up to 40 feet high and averaged 16 feet thick. A fosse (i.e., a ditch) existed along portions of the outside of the wall, the only fosse known from the Iron Age in Canaan/Israel. The wall was also protected by a glacis, material forming an outer downward-sloping abutment at the base of the wall. This wall probably belonged to the fortified city of Asa's time (ca. 913–873 BCE). The city gate belonging to this period was also well preserved. It had an opening nearly 14 feet wide. The massive wooden doors no longer remained; however, the door sockets and the door stop in the middle were found in place. On the inside and outside of the gate were open squares. Stone benches lined the outside of the gate and the inner rooms of the gate complex. Perhaps these benches were used by the elders as they decided the legal matters of the town. J.F.D.

Mnason (nay'suhn), a Christian originally from Cyprus in whose home (either near or in Jerusalem) Paul and his companions lodged at the time of Paul's final visit to Jerusalem (Acts 21:16). Nothing else is known of him, but his description as "an early disciple" suggests that he might have been part of the early Jerusalem church, whose history is recounted in the first half of Acts. This would also make him a Jewish believer.

Moab (moh'ab).

1 Lot's son born from an incestuous relationship with his elder daughter. A similar relationship between Lot and his younger daughter produced Moab's half brother, Ben-ammi (Ammon; Gen. 19:30–38).

2 The people descended from Moab, Lot's son. They were closely linked with their northern neighbors, the Ammonites, with whom they later shared a border. Moab is known from several ancient sources. According to the inscriptions of Pharaoh Ramesses II (ca. 1250 BCE), an Egyptian army passed through Moab and plundered some cities. According to the Bible, contacts between Moab and Israel came in the attempt by Moses to negotiate a safe passage for the Israelites through Moabite territory, i.e., the plateau east of the Dead Sea bordered on the north by the Arnon River and on the south by the Zered (Judg. 11:17). Other sources note that Moab's territory was given to it by God (Deut. 2:9), yet the Moabite king Balak hired a prophet/diviner named Balaam to curse the Israelites (Num. 22–24). Israel camped in the plains of Moab before entering the promised land,

territory north of the Arnon River extending as far north as "opposite Jericho" (Num. 35:1; Deut. 1:5). This brief sojourn was remembered as detrimental to Israelite religion (Num. 25).

Contact between Moab and Israel is mentioned in Judges, where a Moabite king named Eglon had extended his control over Benjaminites in the hill country and valley near the City of Palms (probably Jericho). This account is another indication that Moabite territory extended at times considerably north of the Arnon River. A left-handed Benjaminite assassinated Eglon, providing a period of peace for the region (Judg. 3:12–30). The story of Ruth is also set in the period of the judges and concerns the manner in which this Moabite woman came to Bethlehem, ultimately married, and became King David's great-grandmother. Both Saul and David fought with the Moabites, the latter subduing them (1 Sam. 14:47; 2 Sam. 8:2). Moab's history remains somewhat obscure in the accounts of the divided monarchy, as Moab is mentioned only occasionally (2 Kings 3; 13:20; 24:2). Prophets often spoke against Moab (Isa. 15–16; Jer. 48; Zeph. 2:8–11).

The discovery of the Moabite Stone in 1868 helped illumine Moab's history during the ninth century BCE. It was written at the behest of the Moabite king Mesha, who is mentioned in 2 Kings 3:4. The inscription on the stone reveals that Moab had fallen under the control of the Omride dynasty in Israel, but managed to free itself through armed struggle and the providential care of the national deity Chemosh. Mesha's capital was Dibon, modern Dhiban, about two miles north of the Arnon River.

Moab is also known from Assyrian records, which reveal that Moab paid tribute in the eighth century and that during the reign of Ashurbanipal in the seventh century a Moabite king led a campaign against Arab tribes who opposed Assyrian control of the Transjordan. These records presuppose a subservient but working relationship between the kingdom of Moab and the Assyrian Empire. According to the Jewish historian Josephus, the Babylonian Empire under Nebuchadnezzar ended what little autonomy Moab possessed (sixth century BCE), and although there are no other records from the Persian period to assist historians with recounting Moabite affairs, it seems probable that the Babylonian campaign put a decisive end to the political kingdom of Moab. Of course, the land was still known as Moab for centuries.

Something of Moab's language and culture is known from the Bible and the Moabite Stone. This information is supplemented by the work of modern archaeologists who have made explorations in the region. The chief Moabite deity was named Chemosh, a god known from other texts to have been venerated in northern Syria. The name appears on several seals of upper-class persons from the Iron Age. King Mesha describes Chemosh as angry with Moab and responsible for the nation's subjugation to Israel; however, Chemosh was also responsible for the victory over

Israel. A religious rite of sacrificial dedication, the ban (Heb. *kherem*) was practiced by the Moabites as it was in Israel. The language of Moab was similar to that of its neighbors Israel and Ammon.

The land of Moab is comparatively high in elevation, reaching points over 3,000 feet above sea level, and it is comparatively well watered. Archaeological investigation suggests few large towns existed in ancient Moab, and the economy was based on cultivating wheat and barley, but above all on raising sheep and goats. Several cities are mentioned in either the Bible or the Moabite Stone, some of which can be identified with reasonable certainty. These include Medeba (modern Madaba), Dibon (modern Dhiban), and Kir (Kerak). *See also* Lot; Moabite Stone.   J.A.D.

Moabite (moh´uh-bit) **Stone,** a black basalt stele found at Dhiban, Jordan (biblical Dibon), bearing a thirty-four-line inscription of Mesha,

THE MOABITE STONE: A TRANSLATION OF ITS TEXT

(line 1) I, Mesha, son of Chemosh[yat], king of Moab, the

(2) Dibote (my father reigned over Moab for thirty years and I reigned

(3) after my father)—I made this high place for Chemosh in Karhoh [. . .]

(4) because he saved me from all the kings and caused me to triumph over all who opposed me.

(5) Omri, king of Israel, oppressed Moab for many years, because Chemosh was angry with his land.

(6) When his son succeeded him, he too said, "I shall oppress Moab." In my days he spoke *this way,*

(7) but I triumphed over him and his house, and Israel was utterly destroyed forever. Omri took possession of the entire land

(8) of Medeba, and [Israel] lived there during his days and half the days of his son— forty years; but

(9) Chemosh restored it in my days. I built Baal-meon, making a cistern in it, and I built

(10) Kiryathaim. The men of Gad had lived in the land of Ataroth since ancient times, and the king of Israel had built

(11) Ataroth for them; but I fought against the city and captured it, slaying all the people of

(12) the city *for the satisfaction of* Chemosh and Moab. I brought back from there *the altar-hearth of its beloved* [*god*],

(13) dragging it before Chemosh in Kerioth, and I settled men of Sharon and men of

(14) Maharith there. Then Chemosh said to me, "Go capture Nebo from Israel!"

(15) So I went by night and fought against it from the break of dawn until noon. I captured

(16) it and slew them all—seven thousand men, boys, women, girls,

(17) and maidservants—for I had devoted it to Ashtar-Chemosh. I took from there *the utensils*

(18) of YHWH, dragging them before Chemosh. The king of Israel had built

(19) Jahaz, and he lived there while he was fighting against me. But Chemosh drove him out before me.

(20) I took from Moab two hundred men, all its poor citizens, and exalted them in Jahaz; I took possession of it in order

(21) to annex it to Dibon. It was I who built Karhoh, both the forest wall and

(22) the summit wall; it was I who built its gates and I who built its towers;

(23) it was I who built the palace and I who made both the reservoirs for water inside

(24) the town. There were no cisterns inside the town at Karhoh, so I said to the people, "Each of you make

(25) a cistern for himself and his house!" Also, it was I who cut *beams* for Karhoh using

(26) Israelite captives. It was I who built Aroer; it was I who made the highway in the Arnon;

(27) and it was I who built the high-place temple, for it had been torn down. It was I who built Bezer—for it was in ruins.

(28) [. . .] the men of Dibon armed for battle, for all Dibon is (my) bodyguard. I made

(29) one hundred [. . .] reign as kings in the towns that I annexed to the land. It was I who built

(30) [. . .] Medeba, Beth-diblathaim, and Beth-baal-meon, where I exalted *the herdsmen*

(31) [. . .] *the sheep* of the land. As for Horonaim, [. . .] was living there [. . .]

(32) [. . .]. Then Chemosh said to me, "Go down and fight against Horonaim!" So I went down and [fought against it.

(33) I captured it, and] Chemosh restored it in my days [. . .]

(34) [. . .].

Key: [ ] = restored material at break in the stone; [. . .] = text missing; ( ) = additions for English sense; *italics* = translation of text uncertain.

The Moabite Stone or Stele of Mesha, king of Moab (ninth century BCE), containing an inscription important for study of the language and history of ancient Israel.

the ninth-century BCE king of Moab mentioned in 2 Kings 3:4. After its discovery in 1868 by the Alsatian priest F. A. Klein, the stone was shattered by the local Bedouin, but in subsequent years approximately two-thirds of the fragments were recovered by the French orientalist C. Clermont-Ganneau, who, with the help of an impression taken before the stone was broken, was able to reconstruct the monument, which is now in the Louvre. Because its language is closely related to biblical Hebrew and its script belongs to the same tradition as the earliest Hebrew documents, the Moabite Stone inscription is an important source for the study of the language and writing system of ancient Israel as well as the history of the ninth century BCE.

The stele is dedicated to Chemosh, the god of Moab, in gratitude for Mesha's triumph over his enemies. Speaking in the first person, the king recounts his successes and achievements, beginning with the liberation of Moab from Israelite domination. He boasts of the recovery and rebuilding of the region of Medeba, which had been conquered by Omri, and the capture of nearby Israelite cities. Among the building projects recorded are those in Karhoh, the district of Dibon in which the monument was erected.

A small fragment of a second Moabite stone was found in Kerak, Jordan, in 1958. Its three incomplete lines show that it too was a royal inscription of the mid-ninth century BCE, probably another monument left by Mesha. The complete recoverable text of that second stone reads: (1) [I, Mesha, son of Che]moshyat, king of Moab, the [Dibonite. . . .] (2) Chemosh *for grazing land*, because [. . .] (3) [. . .] him. And behold, I made the [. . .].
P.K.M.

Modein (moh´deen), the home of the Hasmonean family, about twenty-three miles northwest of Jerusalem (1 Macc. 2:1), where the Maccabean revolt began (2:15, 24–35). *See also* Hasmoneans; Maccabees.

Modin (moh´din). *See* Modein.

Moladah (moh´luh-duh), a town assigned to Judah (Josh. 15:26), specifically allocated to Simeon (19:2), and located near Beer-sheba. It was also resettled in postexilic times (Neh. 11:26). Location of the site is unknown. Proposals include Khirbet el-Waten, eight miles east of Beer-sheba, and Tell-Malkhata, located between Arad and Beersheba.

Molech (moh´lek), the epithet of a deity to whom children were offered as sacrifices (Lev. 18:20; 20:3–5). The word *molek*, likely derived from Hebrew *melek*, "king" (cf. Isa. 30:33), was formed by substituting the vowels from the word *boshet* ("shame"). Exactly which god the Israelites dubbed Molech is unclear, however, since the title "king" (*melek*) could be used in many divine names. The names of the gods Adrammelech and Anammelech (2 Kings 17:31), to whom the Sepharvites offered their children by fire, contain the element *melek,* and either or both might be likely candidates for divinities the Israelites called Molech. Milcom, an Ammonite god, is actually called Molech in 1 Kings 11:7, but this could be a textual error (cf. 1 Kings 11: 5, 33; 2 Kings 23:13).

Children were dedicated ("passed over") and burned to Molech at the Tophet in the Valley of Hinnom near Jerusalem. This practice in connection with Molech is specifically mentioned in only four biblical passages (Lev. 18:21; 20:2–5; 2 Kings 23:10; Jer. 32:35), but this type of offering without specific mention of Molech is referred to elsewhere as well (Deut. 12:31; 18:10; 2 Kings 16:3; 17:17, 31; 21:6; Jer. 7:31; 19:5; Ezek. 16:21; 20:26, 31; 23:37; 2 Chron. 28:8; 33:6). Some scholars have suggested that the terms "passing over" children to Molech and "burning in fire" indicate a dedication of the children to the god's service rather than actual sacrifice. Jer. 19:5, however, calls such dedications "burnt offerings"; Ezek. 23:37–39 calls the act "slaughter" and says the children were given to the deity as food. Hence, many scholars conclude that offerings to Molech must be considered actual sacrifices (cf. Ps. 106:37–38).
D.P.W.

molten metal, metal cast by being poured over a form or into a mold. The process was used for several components of Solomon's temple built by Hiram of Tyre, including the pillars, capitals, and basin known as the "molten sea" (1 Kings 7:15, 16, 23). The Bible describes several molten images used as idols (see Judg. 17:3–4; Isa. 40:19; Hos. 13:2), including most prominently the golden calf (Exod. 32). Worship of such objects, which the Bible associates particularly with Canaanite and Assyrian religions (Num. 33:52; Nah. 1:14), is prohibited to Israel (Exod. 20:4; Lev. 19:4; Deut. 27:15).

Money

A COMMODITY used as a medium of exchange or a designation of value. In ancient Israel, goods or livestock were often exchanged as a primitive form of money. Thus, when Abimelech restored Sarah to Abraham, he paid him "sheep and oxen, and male and female slaves," which the Bible says were the equivalent of "a thousand pieces of silver" (Gen. 20:14–16). Likewise, Judah attempted to pay for the services of a prostitute by sending her a kid from his flock (38:17, 23). Over time, however, more standardized and portable commodities were employed (e.g., metal bars, ingots, jewels) and, eventually, coined money, legally authorized by governments, became the standard, especially with regard to payment of taxes.

Bronze coin with name of Agrippa (I); minted in Jerusalem ca. 37–44 CE, obverse.

In the Ancient Near East: The archaeological record in Israel illustrates practices current during the biblical period. Strata at most sites from the period ca. 1300–587 BCE contain little evidence of metal coins used as money. Excavated metal objects include armor, weapons, and jewelry. Each piece of precious metal had monetary value, so that earrings, pins, or other adornments also functioned as money. Money took on many forms, including bar ingots, pieces of cut metal, wire, coils of wire, foil, and rings. Hoards of these items have been found at major sites such as Gaza, Shechem, Megiddo, and Beth-shan. Such items are what Joseph would have collected as payment for grain, when Gen. 47:14–17 says that he "gathered up all the money that was found in the land of Egypt and in the land of Canaan" during the time of famine.

The Hebrew word usually used for "money" (*keseph*) literally means "silver," and silver was generally much more common than gold, which had to be imported from Egypt or Anatolia. The latter, however, is also mentioned, even in the era before coinage (a bar of gold, Josh. 7:21; rings of gold, Job 42:11). The Bible makes many references to silver or gold "shekels" (Gen. 23:15–16; Exod. 21:32; Deut. 22:19, 29), but the term did not originally refer to a coin. Rather, a shekel was a unit of weight that could be applied to silver, gold, or any other solid substance (cf. Gen. 24:22). References to "silver shekels" refer not to minted silver coins but to a given amount of silver (in the form of rings, bars, lumps, or whatever was available). The spoil that Achan took from Jericho included "two hundred shekels of silver and a bar of gold weighing fifty shekels" (Josh. 7:21). Likewise, references to a "talent" in biblical times prior to the exile do not refer to the coin later known by that name, but to a weight; 1 talent was equal to 30,000 shekels (cf. Exod. 25:39; 37:24; 38:27; 2 Sam. 12:30; 1 Kings 30:39; 2 Kings 5:22; 23:33; 1 Chron. 20:22; 2 Chron. 36:3).

Standards for weighing money also varied from place to place (cf. Exod. 30:13). In Gen. 23:16, Abraham is said to have purchased a burying place from Ephron the Hittite for 400 shekels of silver, "according to the weights current among the merchants." This latter reference probably

A Babylonian mina from the reign of Nebuchadnezzar II.

indicates the Babylonian standard, which was the most commonly employed commercial standard in the ancient Near East. This standard set guidelines for transactions between Mesopotamia, Canaan, and Egypt. Specifically, the Babylonian weight standard set 1 silver shekel as equal to 8.25 grams of metal, which supported the following ratio: 1 talent = 60 minas = 3600 shekels. This denominational division lasted into the Hellenistic period.

Ancient texts sometimes include receipts for goods sold in local and international commerce. For example, an ox would commonly cost 1 gold shekel, which was equal to 15 silver shekels or approximately two tons of grain. Solomon dealt in horses and chariots with the kings of the Hittites (Kue) and the kings of Aram (1 Kings 10:28–29); the horses were priced at 150 silver shekels and the chariots at 600 silver shekels. At this rate, four horses would purchase one chariot. Jehoash (Joash), king of Israel in the late ninth century BCE, institutionalized support for the temple by allowing individuals to be assessed a certain amount, while also encouraging "voluntary offerings"; the priests were instructed to use money collected through these means for repairing the temple (2 Kings 12:4–5). The uncoined metals were probably collected, weighed, melted down into small ingots, and measured according to royal standards. The ingots were used to pay the workers.

A bronze coin minted by the Roman emperor Titus ca. 79–81 CE to commemorate the ending of the Jewish revolt; reverse. At the bottom left a mourning Jewish woman is depicted.

Origins of Coinage: The first metal objects coined as money were probably produced in Asia Minor in the late seventh or early sixth century BCE. According to Greek tradition, Croesus, king of Lydia, was the first monarch to strike coins in silver, gold, and electrum (a naturally occurring alloy of silver and gold). The earliest coins bore no inscriptions and did not circulate widely. Their use spread quickly, however, thanks to Persian domination of the entire eastern Mediterranean basin by the late sixth century BCE. The silver *sigloi* of Darius the Great copied coins of eastern Greek manufacture and were used throughout the Persian Empire. Persian gold *darics* were struck by the central government, while the silver *sigloi* were minted by local satrapies and met local monetary needs.

The Greeks quickly adapted to using coined money. Their neighbors, however, were slow to accept coins. Weighed amounts of metal continued to facilitate trade in most large commercial centers. Minted metals initially benefited governing bodies more than merchants or financiers. As trade increased and more wealth was attained, the functions of government changed and became more complex, requiring a greater number and kind of official transactions with the populace. Early minted coins obviously facilitated commerce, but even more they simplified all manner of government transactions, including the payment and receipt of taxes, temple tariffs and maintenance, payment of mercenaries and soldiers, and the construction of public works. Scholars have argued that this conversion from bullion enabled local communities to simplify all of their monetary transactions. Thus, coined metal at first remained near its point of origin and was used for particular government purposes. Soon, however, coins were traded just as any other valuable objects. Differing weight standards among Babylonians, Persians, Phoenicians, and Greeks slowly merged in the fifth and fourth centuries BCE until Alexander the Great established a single standard for all coinage used from Greece to

From left to right: Double shekel from Sidon, late fifth or early fourth century BCE, obverse; gold shekel from Tyre, early fourth century BCE, obverse and reverse; gold coin from Egypt, during the reign of Ptolemy IV, reverse.

India. Foreign trade and internal commerce were greatly enhanced by coined money, but had little to do with its origins.

The use of actual coined money in Israel began under Persian influence after 539 BCE, when Babylon fell to the Persians and Medes and the East came into greater contact with the Greek world. According to Ezra 2:68–69, the Israelites rebuilt Jerusalem after the exile, and families made freewill offerings for the refurbishing of the temple, giving the treasury "sixty-one thousand darics of gold, five thousand minas of silver, and one hundred priests' garments." The *daric* was the principal gold coin at this time, weighing 8.4 grams and punched with a die depicting the Persian king shooting a bow. By the late fifth century BCE, more and more foreign currency appeared in the markets of Gaza, Tyre, Sidon, and Jerusalem. When authorities struck coins, merchants found that they no longer had to weigh the "shekel," because the governmental stamp verified its weight. Coinage made trade simpler and more efficient. The Phoenician cities of Tyre, Sidon, Aradus, and Byblos struck their own coins before 400 BCE, while Gaza produced coins imitating Athenian *tetradrachms* by the early fourth century.

The necessity of coining money was resisted in Israel, especially inland from the port cities, where conservative usage of metal rings and bars persisted. As a transition, Hebrew weights were employed that carried denominational markings regulated by religious authorities to ensure against corruption and fraud (see Prov. 11:1; 16:11). Eventually, as Persian control of the western provinces waned through the fourth century, Jewish authorities in Jerusalem and Samaria also began to strike small coins to supplement larger denominations minted elsewhere. The coins read in Hebrew *yehud* ("Judah"). Most of the *yehud* coins were bronze, struck between 360 and 332 BCE.

The period 375–332 BCE was a time of political upheaval. The Phoenician city-states led two abortive revolts resulting in Persia's imposing severe sanctions upon local rulers, including the revocation of minting privileges. This necessitated the issue of coins with "ethnics" (i.e., phrases identifying the minting authority of the coin) in Aramaic (the Persian diplomatic language) rather than Phoenician or Hebrew, since Persian satrapy officials assumed mint functions. The scenes depicted on these coins assumed nationalistic functions. A war galley with battering ram symbolized the Phoenician city of Sidon. Athenian coinage represented Athens as the center of Greek culture and thought by depicting the head of its patron deity, Pallas Athena, and the owl with an olive branch, symbolic

Silver drachma minted during Persian control of Judea, fourth century BCE. The reverse (*bottom*) bears the Aramaic inscription *yehud*, the Persian name for Judea.

A bronze shekel of Tyre from the Hellenistic period; obverse.

of the Athenian *polis*. One example of a *yehud* coin bears the name of *yehiz-qiyyah*, high priest when Alexander the Great came to Jerusalem in 332 BCE. Another silver coin bears the name of *yohanan*, high priest in Samaria—a coin that may have been struck in defiance of Persia (ca. 340 BCE) during a revolt led by the Phoenicians and Cypriots.

After 332/1 BCE, no coins were struck in the Levant until the Maccabean revolt, except in official mints of Alexander the Great at Acco and Tyre. In 168 BCE, Jews once again won minting privileges. Under Alexander Jannaeus, Maccabean leader from 103 to 76 BCE, coins were struck in Jerusalem with the obverse showing a flower (probably a lily) and the "ethnic" *yehonatan hammelek* ("Jonathan the king"); on the reverse was an anchor with the Greek inscription *basileos alexandrou* ("belonging to Alexander [the] king"). These coins, struck in lead and bronze, were small change and circulated with larger coins produced in other Hellenistic mints. Jonathan later overstruck his coins, altering the title "king" to "high priest and friend of the Jews," for he was not of David's line and some Jews argued that he had no right to the throne. The other Hasmonean rulers continued to issue coins in bronze supplementing Alexandrine issues until Rome seized power in 37 BCE.

A bronze coin minted at Jerusalem ca. 37–34 BCE during the reign of Herod the Great; obverse (*top*) and reverse.

In the NT: Roman coinage was one of the means used by the imperial government to hold the Roman Empire together. Imperial mints were authorized in many regions, because the official mint within the capital city could not meet the monetary needs of such a vast empire. Herod the Great struck coins on Roman standards with the Greek inscription *herodou basileos* ("belonging to Herod [the] king"). He dated his coins and opened mints in Jerusalem and Tiberias on the Sea of Galilee. Concurrently, Roman governors coined money locally to supplement imperial coinage, which came principally from Rome, Alexandria, and Antioch (in Syria). Local denominations were the small change. Their types depicted neutral symbols such as grapes or a cornucopia, i.e., nonreligious symbols that would not anger the Jewish populace, even though Romans preferred images of the gods or other pagan religious symbols on their coins. The mints of Antioch and Caesarea in Cappadocia supplied Judea with the large silver coins such as the *denarius* mentioned in the NT. One *denarius* was the usual salary paid to a laborer for one day's work (Matt. 20:2). It was also used to pay the temple tax in Jesus's time and, since a likeness of the emperor appeared on one side, it was probably the coin referred to in Matt. 22:21 ("Give therefore to the emperor the things that are the emperor's, and to God the things that are God's").

In the later first century, Roman coinage was interrupted by the Jewish revolt in 66–70 CE. Coins were struck with the Hebrew legend *shekel yisra'el* ("shekel of Israel"). Issued on the Athenian standard, the reverse depicted three pomegranates and the words *yerushalayim qadesha* ("Jerusalem [is] holy"). When the Romans put down the revolt, Vespasian and Titus authorized commemorative imperial coins with the Latin inscription *judaea capta* ("Judah [is] captured").

It is impossible to estimate what the value of ancient coins might be in modern terms. The closest equivalents are arrived at first, by realizing that a Roman denarius or a Greek drachma (Luke 15:8) were intended to be equivalent, both equal to a day's wage for an unskilled laborer (e.g., a field hand). Then the values of other coins may be figured relative to these. The following information may thus be obtained, listing units from greatest to least in value:

- *Talent:* a unit of silver equal to 6,000 Greek drachmae or Roman denarii. One talent was roughly equal to what a typical worker could make over a sixteen-year period. Jesus tells one parable (Matt. 25:14–30) in which a wealthy man gives three servants each a different number of talents (1, 2, and 5—in the last case, the amount was more than the servant could hope to earn in a lifetime). In another parable (18:23–35), Jesus uses creative exaggeration to stress the incalculable difference between divine and human mercy. A servant owes his king (God) 10,000 talents (millions of dollars), a debt that is forgiven; but then the first servant does not forgive a fellow servant who owes him 100 denarii.

A shekel of the Bar Kochba revolt, ca. 132–135 CE; reverse.

- *Mina* ("pound"): a silver coin worth 100 drachmae (or denarii); the NRSV uses the word "pound" for a Greek *mina*. The only NT reference comes in a parable told by Jesus in Luke 19:13–26, the parable of the Pounds; another version of the same story appears in Matt. 25:14–30 as the parable of the Talents.

- *Denarius:* a silver Roman coin that would have been the usual day's wage for a typical laborer (plural, *denarii*). This is the most mentioned unit of currency in the NT. Jesus used a denarius as an object lesson for his teaching that one should give to the emperor what belongs to the emperor (Matt. 22:19); his disciples complained that 200 denarii would not buy enough bread for a hungry multitude (Mark 6:37).

- *Drachma:* a silver Greek coin that would have been the usual day's wage for a typical laborer (plural, *drachmae*); the "lost coin" in the parable that Jesus tells in Luke 15:8–10 is a drachma.

- *Shekel:* a term that is not used as such in the NT (but cf. 1 Macc. 10:40, 42), but is considered to be the most likely form of coinage with which Judas was paid for betraying Jesus. The Bible uses an imprecise term in that passage, indicating that Judas was paid thirty "silvers" (Matt. 26:15; Gk. *argyria;* NRSV: "pieces of silver"). Most scholars think that this referred to thirty *shekels.* A shekel was a silver Judean coin (i.e., not Roman or Greek—the priests may have preferred to use local rather than foreign currency). Other interpreters have suggested that the silver pieces might have been shekels from Tyre or Antioch. A shekel was worth about 4 drachmae (or 4 denarii). Thirty pieces (approximately equal to 120 denarii) were considered compensation ("blood money") for an accidentally slain slave (Exod. 21:32).

Silver shekel from the revolt against Rome, with Hebrew inscription. *Top:* "Jerusalem the Holy." *Bottom:* "Shekel of Israel sh[nat] g[imel]" ("year three," i.e., 68 CE).

- *Stater, didrachma:* coins worth 4 and 2 drachmae (denarii), respectively. The temple tax in Matt. 17:24–27 involves two different Roman coins. The amount of the annual temple tax was 2 drachmae (or 2 denarii) per person. In Matt. 17:24, the NRSV uses the English expression "temple tax" to translate a reference to a Greek coin called the *didrachma*, a coin that was worth 2 drachmae—this would be the typical coin an individual would use to pay the tax. Then, in Matt. 17:27, Jesus tells Peter to use the "coin" that he finds in a fish's mouth to pay the tax for both of them. Here, the Greek word translated "coin" in the NRSV is *stater*. A *stater* was a silver Greek coin worth about 4 drachmae—thus, 1 stater could pay the temple tax for two people.

- *Assarion, quadrans, lepton:* small coins of little value; the NRSV uses the English word "penny" for all three of these different Roman coins. An *assarion* was worth one-tenth of a denarius—this is the amount for which Jesus says two sparrows are sold (Matt. 10:29). A *quadrans* (Gk. *kordantēs*) was worth one-fourth of an assarion—this is the amount of the offering that the widow put in the temple treasury (except she used 2 lepta); in Matt. 5:26, Jesus says that those who cannot settle with their accusers will be thrown into prison and not get out until they have paid the last quadrans of their debt. A *lepton* was worth one-eighth of an assarion or one-half a quadrans, the least value of any coin in circulation—the widow put "two *lepta,* which make a *quadrans*" into the temple treasury (Mark 12:42).

See also weights and measures. For money as a *concept* (e.g., how it should be acquired, regarded, managed, or used), **see** mammon; wealth.

J.W.B./M.A.P.

COINS MENTIONED IN THE NEW TESTAMENT

Talent	6,000 drachmae/denarii	Matt. 18:24; 25:14–30; cf. 2 Macc. 8:11
Mina	100 drachmae/denarii	Luke 19:13–26; cf. 1 Macc. 14:24; 15:18
Shekel	4 drachmae/denarii	Matt. 26:15?; cf. 1 Macc. 10:40, 42
Stater	4 drachmae/denarii	Matt. 17:27
Half-shekel	2 drachmae/denarii	
Didrachma	2 drachmae/denarii	Matt. 17:24
Drachma	Greek: a day's wage	Luke 15:8; cf. Tob. 5:15; 2 Macc. 4:19; 10:20; 12:43
Denarius	Roman: a day's wage	Matt. 18:28; 20:1–16; 22:19; Mark 6:37; 14:5; Luke 7:41; 10:35; John 6:17; 12:25; Rev. 6:6
Assarion	1/10 drachma/denarius	Matt. 10:29
Quadrans	1/4 assarion (1/40 drachma/denarius)	Matt. 5:26; Mark 12:42
Lepton	1/2 quadrans (1/80 drachma/denarius)	Mark 12:42; Luke 12:59

From Mark Allan Powell, *Introducing the New Testament* (courtesy, Baker Academic)

money changers. The cosmopolitan nature of a city like Jerusalem made exchange of funds a complex matter. Thus, money changers would often be located at the gate of the city or a building (such as the temple) to perform the exchanges required for commerce. When a money changer exchanged Antiochian tetradrachmas for local shekels, a fee of 4 to 8 percent was exacted. When adult males came to the temple to pay their half-shekel temple tax, rabbinic instruction insisted that it be paid in silver didrachmas; money changers were needed to complete the transaction. In the Synoptic Gospels, Jesus overturns the tables of the money changers in what amounts to an assault on the operation of the temple cult (Matt. 21:12–13; Mark 11:15; John 2:14–15). In the Synoptic accounts, Jesus does not appear to be specifically objecting to anything the money changers are doing. The point, rather, is that since money changers are necessary for the temple transactions (e.g., for animals to be purchased for sacrifices), shutting down the money changers is a way of closing down the temple operation. Jesus's comment about the temple being transformed into "a den of robbers" (Matt. 21:13; Mark 11:17; Luke 19:46; cf. Jer. 7:11) does not imply that the money changers themselves are robbing people; rather, the temple has become a safe refuge for people who commit crimes elsewhere (robbers do not usually rob people in their own den). In John's Gospel, however, Jesus objects that the temple has become "a marketplace" (2:16); thus, commercialization of the institution, which is at least symbolized by the presence of money changers, seems to be in view.   M.A.P.

monogamy. *See* marriage.

monotheism (mon′uh-thee-iz′uhm), the belief that there is only one deity. Most major religions of the biblical world were polytheistic; they had many deities. Israel was exceptional for its emphatic recognition of one God only. This was an essential affirmation of Judaism and part of the foundation of Christianity.

In Ancient Israel: It is not clear how Israel's monotheism originated. Certain trends in Egyptian religion of the second millennium BCE tended to universalize one single deity, and theoretically these could have influenced Moses; but the wide difference in character between these phenomena and the God of Israel counts against the relevance of such parallels. Nor is it easy to see how monotheism could have evolved out of an earlier polytheism by some process of selection and rejection; there are not, at any rate, enough texts available to demonstrate this. It has often been argued that some historical experience, such as deliverance from Egypt, led Israel to recognize "the LORD" as the uniquely active and saving deity. Yet no texts depict this event as a sudden or cataclysmic passage from faith in many gods to faith in one.

What does seem clear is that the belief in the *existence* of only one God developed relatively late in the biblical period. The earlier insistence was that only the one true God of Israel (among many who might exist) was to be worshiped and served. The God of Israel was to be regarded as supreme, not as the only God, but as the "God of gods" (Deut. 10:17). Thus, the biblical record shows that, from the earliest relevant times, there were Israelite groups (tribes) who looked to a single deity as their special God. The Israelites, furthermore, may not have been unique in this regard; the Moabites, at least, also seem to have related to a single deity. Biblical monotheism was therefore practical rather than theoretical. It did not prevent the occasional acknowledgment of other gods as if they existed or had control of other lands or peoples (e.g., Exod. 12:12; Num. 33:4; Josh. 24:15; Judg. 10:6). Elements of their mythology continued to be used. Names and titles used for other gods were sometimes taken over and applied to the God of Israel, but Israelite tradition insisted that the God of their ancestors demanded and deserved exclusive allegiance. This tradition rendered other gods impotent and, eventually, reduced them to nonentities.

Nevertheless, polytheism of some kind, especially perhaps in the form of a female consort for "the LORD" continued to attract many in Israel, as is evident from the biblical polemic against such tendencies (e.g., Judg. 6:30–32; Isa. 27:9). Such notions were attacked as foreign (Jer. 5:19), as a return to the old Canaanite gods (Judg. 10:6–9), as linked to repellent ritual, sexual, or moral practices (Hos. 4:12–13), as associated with the worship of objects of wood and stone (Isa. 44:9–17), and as having brought historical disaster upon the people (Mic. 1:2–7). Above all, the ethical demands of Israelite religion were made to depend on the requirement of monotheism. These elements are given strong character in the Ten Commandments ("You shall have no other gods before me"; cf. Exod. 20:3–6; Deut. 5:6–10) and the Shema (Deut. 6:4–5): "Hear, O Israel: The LORD is our God, the LORD alone. You shall love the LORD your God with all your heart, and with all your soul, and with all your might." Isa. 40–55 combines a strong emphasis on monotheism with a stress on the role of the one God as creator of the world and ruler of all its parts. By the time of the exile and the Second Temple period, polytheism was still continually ridiculed, but in a way that suggests it was no longer felt to be a serious temptation for Israelites.

In the NT: The monotheistic convictions of Second Temple Judaism are taken for granted in the early Christian writings of the NT. The "first of all the commandments" according to Jesus is the Shema, which affirms the oneness of God (Mark 12:29). The NT letters also emphasize the oneness of God (1 Cor. 8:6; Eph. 4:6; 1 Tim. 2:5). The term "God" is applied at times to Jesus (John 1:1, 18; 20:28; Rom. 9:5; Titus 2:13; Heb. 1:8–9; 2 Pet. 1:1; 1 John 5:20), but Jewish opponents are not represented as criticizing Christianity for abandoning monotheism any more than advocates of wisdom theology had been construed as polytheists when they spoke of personified Wisdom as a divine being worthy of devotion and praise (e.g., Prov. 8:22–23; Wis. 7:22–27; 8:1; 9:9). Nevertheless the close association of Jesus with God would point toward a different conception of monotheism than had ever been current within Judaism, a conception wherein the deity has inner distinction (Father, Son, Holy Spirit) as well as unity. The implications of this movement, however, are not yet worked out within the NT itself. *See also* polytheism.   J.B.

months. *See* calendar; time.

moon. Hebrew has two terms for moon, *yareakh* and *lebonah*. The first is a common Semitic term and is the usual word for "month." *Lebonah* is a derivative of "white." In most biblical references, *lebonah* is used in parallelism to *shemesh*, "sun," to describe the brilliant luminosity of the moon (Song of Sol. 6:10; Isa. 30:26). But in Isa. 24:23, lebonah is used in parallelism to *bosh*, "shame," to evoke an image of colorlessness accompanying embarrassment. The Greek term for moon is *selēnē*. In Greco-Roman literature, it can refer, not only to the celestial light visible from earth, but also to the god or heavenly being from which this light supposedly emanated. A vestige of this is seen in Matt. 17:15, where a child brought to Jesus has been literally struck or cursed by the moon (Gk. *selēniazomai*; NRSV: "an epileptic").

Gen. 1:16 records that the moon, called the lesser light, was created by God to shine at night as a counterpart to the greater light, the sun, which shines during the day. Pss. 8:3 and 136:9 describe the moon as part of God's handiwork. The moon is also mentioned in Jer. 31:35 as a marker of the night sky, and the moon's changes as signals of changing seasons is noted in Sir. 43:6–8. Along with the sun and the stars, the moon bows down to Joseph in his dream in Gen. 37:9 (symbolizing, in this instance, his mother Rachel). Joshua commands the sun and moon to stop in their courses during his encounter with the Amorites (Josh. 10:12–13).

Poetic and metaphoric references to the moon abound. It is viewed as a symbol of permanence in Pss. 72:5; 89:38; 121:6; and Heb. 3:11, but Sir. 27:11 takes the constant changes of the moon's phases as emblematic of the conversation of a fool. Wise persons who have much on their mind to express can be called "full, like the full moon" (Sir. 39:12; cf. 50:6). In 1 Cor. 15:40–41, Paul uses the different types of heavenly bodies as an illustration for how the spiritual bodies of those who are raised from the dead will differ from their current physical bodies: "There are both heavenly bodies and earthly bodies, but the glory of the heavenly is one thing, and that of the earthly is another. There is one glory of the sun, and another glory of the moon and another glory of the stars."

Apocalyptic references to the moon are also numerous and speak of it as an object that will darken, because God's light will be everlasting (Isa. 60:19, 20; Job 25:5; Eccles. 12:2; Ezek. 32:7).

Joel 3:4 prophesies that the moon will turn to blood before the coming of the messiah. Similarly, in the Mesopotamian conception, an eclipse of the moon was taken as a portent of evil (cf. Acts 2:16–21). Picking up on this, Jesus cites the darkening of the moon as a portent for the coming of the Son of Man (Mark 13:24; Luke 21:25). In Rev. 21:23, the moon is seen as superfluous, since the Lamb will light Jerusalem.

Worship: The importance of the moon in worship in the ancient world varied in degree and by location. In Mesopotamia, lunar worship was already firmly established by the beginning of recorded history. Records from lunar cult observances taking place in the chapel of the *ursakar*, "new moon crescent," date to 2400 BCE. New-moon festival offerings are attested at pre-Sargonic Lagash and Sargonic Nippur. In the Neo-Sumerian period (2100–2000 BCE), lunar festivals were regularized with observances marking the first, second, and fourth quarters of the moon. A fourth festival occurring on the twenty-fifth day of the month, and not corresponding to a lunar phase, was added in the early second millennium BCE. The lunar festivals survived well into the first millennium BCE, when as many as eight festivals were observed in the course of one lunar cycle.

Two important Mesopotamian centers for moon worship, Ur and Haran, figure prominently in the ancestral narratives. Ur was the homeland of Abraham's father, Terah. After leaving Ur, the family went to Haran, where Terah died (Gen. 11:31, 32). The city god of both Ur and Harran was called Nanna in Sumerian, and Sin (Su'en) in Akkadian. His headdress consisted of four pairs of horns topped by a crescent moon. The crescent resembled a boat, and Nanna was sometimes called the "shining boat of Heaven." His sphere of activity is hard to define. He is seen as a wise god, the originator of life, the leader and guardian of humankind, and the lord of destinies. He is considered the father of the sun god. His consort is known as Ningal, "great lady" in Sumerian, and as Nikkal in Aramaic and Phoenician. The text "Nikkal and the Kathirat" relates the marriage of Nikkal to Yarikh, as the moon god was known in Ugaritic.

Pronouncements against worshiping the moon, decried as pagan practice, are issued in Deut. 4:19; 17:3. Josiah's command to the high priest, Hilkiah, to eliminate worship of the moon is recorded in 2 Kings 23:5. Isa. 1:14 ("Your new moons and your appointed feasts my soul hates") condemns misuse of the cult, including new moon rituals. In spite of these denunciations, evidence for cultic celebration of lunar phases is found in the biblical text. Num. 28:11–15 preserves a ritual calendar that details monthly offerings for the moon. Num. 10:10 and Ps. 81:4 instruct the population to sound the horn at the new moon as a way of offering praise to God. The new moon is celebrated by David and Jonathan (1 Sam. 20). Remnants of lunar celebration are evidenced in the celebrations and gatherings in the historical passages in 1 Chron. 23:31;

2 Chron. 8:13; 31:3; Ezra 3:5; and Neh. 10:33. Most of these include mention of the sabbath. It appears that at the time of the new moon, all commerce was halted (Amos 8:5), and the prophet was not consulted (2 Kings 4:23).

The names of two ancient Israelite cities, Beth Yerakh and Jericho (Heb. *yerikho*) are derived from a word for "moon" and probably indicate the existence of lunar worship at those sites at some early—presumably Canaanite (cf. the god Yarikh)—period. *See also* festivals, feasts, and fasts.   L.E.P

Mordecai (mor´duh-ki; from Akkadian Marduk, Merodach).

1 One of the exiles who returned to Jerusalem with Zerubbabel (Ezra 2:2; Neh. 7:7; 1 Esd. 5:8).

2 The uncle and foster father of Esther, who was the queen of King Ahasuerus of Persia (Esther 2:5, 7). Mordecai aroused the anger of the king's vizier, Haman, by refusing to bow down to him. Encouraged by his wife, Zeresh (Esther 5:10, 14; 6:13), Haman therefore plotted to have Mordecai and all the Jews of Persia killed in revenge. Mordecai prompted Esther to appeal to Ahasuerus to spare her people. Through some subtle maneuvering on the part of Mordecai and Esther, Haman is humiliated by being forced to honor Mordecai publicly for an earlier incident in which Mordecai had uncovered a plot against the king and saved his life. Haman ends up leading Mordecai through the city, robed and crowned and seated on a horse that only the king had ridden. Haman, meanwhile, persists in his plot against the Jews, but Ahasuerus is now outraged to hear of it and orders Haman to be executed on the gallows he had built for Mordecai. Indeed, Mordecai is then allowed to assume Haman's office and estate. This deliverance of the Jews from a potential pogrom would come to be celebrated as the Festival of Purim,

Mordecai, astride a horse, being conducted by Haman through the open square of the city as related in Esther 6:1–11; panel at the third-century CE synagoguc at Dura Europos.

called the "Day of Mordecai" in 2 Macc. 15:36. *See also* Esther, book of; Haman; Purim, Festival of.
                                                        M.A.S.

Moreh (mor´eh; Heb., "teacher, oracle-giver"), a place-name suggesting a location for divine instruction.

1 The Moreh tree, a terebinth (large tree resembling an oak) at the sacred site near Shechem, where Abram built an altar commemorating God's appearance to him (Gen. 12:6–7). In Deut. 11:30, this tree is cited as a landmark for the Gerizim-Ebal pass; in Gen. 35:4, the tree (here: "oak") is where Jacob buried idols near Shechem. Trees in Josh. 24:26 and Judg. 9:6 were inside Shechem; the Moreh tree lay outside. *See also* Ebal; Gerizim; oak; terebinth.

2 Moreh Hill, the extinct volcano opposite Mount Gilboa at the east extremity of the Jezreel plain, where Midian encamped against Gideon's forces (Judg. 7:1). The name suggests that this was also a place associated with reception of oracles or divine instruction.   E.F.C.

Moresheth (mor´uh-sheth), Moresheth-gath (mor´uh-sheth-gath´), the prophet Micah's home village (Jer. 26:18; Mic. 1:1), located near the city of Gath (thus, the compound name in Mic. 1:14). It has been identified with Tell ej-Judeideh, seven miles northeast of Lachish and west of Tekoa.

Moriah (muh-ri´uh).

1 An unidentified site in rugged terrain three days' travel from Beer-sheba where Abraham was to sacrifice Isaac (Gen. 22:2).

2 The rocky hill in Jerusalem where Solomon built the temple (2 Chron. 3:1), a possibly deliberate cross-identification by the Chronicler with David's purchased threshing floor (2 Sam. 24:18–25). In that way the temple, built on land belonging to David, could be associated with him, even if he was not allowed to build it (2 Sam. 7).

morsel, a fragment or piece of bread used for conveying food from bowl to mouth (Ruth 2:14; 1 Sam. 2:36; 28:22; 1 Kings 17:11; Job 31:17; Prov. 17:11). The assumption, often, is that multiple guests use individual morsels to eat from the same bowl; this involved the participants in a covenant-like friendship. To "break bread together" and then betray the friendship was universally acknowledged as contemptible (Ps. 41:9; Matt. 26:23; Mark 14:18–20; John 13:18–30).

mortar.

1 A grinding vessel in which a pestle is the crushing instrument (Prov. 27:22; Num. 11:8). Archaeological examples of stone mortars range from large grain grinders to delicate spice and cosmetic grinders.

2 The sealer between courses of stone or brick, whether a natural material like bitumen (Gen. 11:3) or a prepared compound (Exod. 1:14). A hint of the preparatory process as trampling is reflected in Isaiah's metaphoric reference (41:25). Jeremiah's oracle against Egypt used stones buried under mortar as a figure for the successful Babylonian conquest of the land (43:9). Nah. 3:14 sees treading mortar as a preparation for defense, and Zephaniah refers to "the Mortar wall" as a location in Jerusalem where silver traders functioned (1:11); the precise location of this wall is uncertain, though the upper Tyropoeon Valley has been suggested. Archaeological evidence for mortar includes examples of mud, bitumen, and plaster compounds.   R.S.B.

mortgage. *See* loan, loans.

A mosaic dating to ca. 400 CE on the floor of the church at Tabgha commemorating the miracle of Jesus feeding the multitude (Matt. 15:32–38).

mosaic, a decoration made by inlaying small pieces of different colored materials (such as tile, stone, glass, or marble) to form patterns or pictures. Mosaic inlays can be found on floors, walls, and even furniture. The earliest known mosaics have been found in lower Mesopotamia and date to the fourth millennium BCE. These patterns, called cone mosaics, were formed by placing small painted cone-shaped tiles into mud plaster on walls. Designs of triangles, diagonals, chevrons, and zigzags were formed. These early mosaics may well have been intended to imitate carpets and wall tapestries. The Sumerians from this same region used mosaics also to decorate musical instruments, game boards, and furniture. Apparently the Hebrews in the preexilic period made very little use of mosaics, although some mosaic-like ivory inlay pieces have been recovered from the excavation of Samaria. Mosaics became more prominent in Israel during the Roman period.   J.F.D.

Moses (moh'zis), the first and preeminent leader of the Israelites, who led the people out of Egypt to the threshold of the promised land; he is also the lawgiver and the archetypic prophet. He is the dominant individual character in the biblical narrative from Exodus to Deuteronomy. The text speaks of him in superlatives: "Never since has there arisen a prophet in Israel like Moses, whom the LORD knew face to face" (Deut. 34:10).

Birth and Family Background: The first information readers are given about Moses concerns his birth, in secret, to an unnamed Levite couple (Exod. 2:1–10). Because of the Egyptian decree to kill all newborn Hebrew males, the child was first hidden by his mother and then cast adrift on the Nile in an "ark" (Heb. *tebah;* NRSV: "basket"). As his sister watched from a short distance away, Pharaoh's daughter found him, whereupon the sister stepped forward to suggest an appropriate nurse for the infant—none other than his natural mother. Thus the child was raised by his mother and then returned to Pharaoh's daughter, who adopted him and named him Moses (Heb. *mosheh*), which the Bible explains as meaning "Because I drew [from Heb. *mashah,* 'to draw'] him out of the water" (Exod. 2:10). The name, however, could also be an Egyptian one meaning "is born" (cf. the last component of such Egyptian names as Thutmose and Ahmose).

The story of Moses's birth has similarities with *The Legend of Sargon,* a much older Akkadian text that recounts the birth of Sargon of Agade (ca. 2300 BCE). According to this tale, Sargon's mother bore him in secret, placed him in a basket of rushes sealed with pitch, and floated it down the Euphrates. It was found by Akki, the drawer of water, who raised the child as his own. The goddess Ishtar protected the child, and he grew up to become a great king.

In the folktale-like story of Moses's birth, Moses himself is the only character named. Elsewhere in the Bible, however, his father is identified as Amram, and his mother as Jochebed (Exod. 6:20; cf. Num. 26:59; 1 Chron. 6:3; 23:13). His brother Aaron, older by three years, is mentioned in Exod. 4:14 (cf. 6:20), and his age is given in Exod. 7:7. Miriam, the sister, is omitted from the genealogy in Exod. 6:20, but is named in Num. 26:59; 1 Chron. 6:3.

Nothing is reported of Moses's childhood. He reemerges as a young adult who identifies with his people, the enslaved Israelites. In an attempt to protect one of them, he kills an Egyptian and is forced to flee Egypt (Exod. 3:11–25). He sojourns in Midian, where he defends a group of young women who are being chased away from a well by a group of shepherds. These women are the daughters of a priest of Midian, Jethro (also called Jether, Reuel, and Hobab), who gives his daughter Zipporah to Moses as a wife. Their first son is Gershom (Exod. 2:22); a second son, Eliezer, is mentioned in Exod. 18:3–4 (cf. 1 Chron. 23:15). Zipporah later saves Moses when God decides to kill him (or possibly their son Gershom) for some undisclosed reason. Zipporah circumcises Gershom and touches Moses's feet with the foreskin, proclaiming him to be her "bridegroom of blood" by circumcision. This assuages God's wrath (Exod. 4:24–26).

Moses leading the Israelites safely across the
Red Sea and the Egyptians caught in the water;
page from the tenth-century *Paris Psalter*.

During the Exodus: Beginning with Exod.
3, the biblical narrative recounts Moses's call
by God to liberate the Israelites from slavery
in Egypt. Accompanied by his brother Aaron,
Moses goes to Pharaoh to proclaim this message.
Ten plagues come upon Egypt, culminating with
the death of every firstborn son, a tragedy from
which the Israelites are spared by marking their
doorposts with blood, so that the angel of death
would pass them by (an event commemorated
in the annual Festival of Passover). Then Moses
leads the Israelites on a dramatic escape through
the divided waters of the Red Sea and into the
wilderness of Sinai, where he gives them the Ten
Commandments. For forty years after that, he
leads the people through the wilderness toward
the promised land, providing for them and teaching them the Torah. Throughout these biblical
accounts, which take up much of Exodus and
Numbers (with parallel accounts in Deuteronomy), Moses is presented as a prophet, lawgiver,
and national leader.

Moses's Call: The story of Moses's role in the
exodus begins in Exod. 3. While herding sheep in
Midian, Moses's attention is caught by a burning
bush. Slowly his reaction changes from curiosity
to awe as he realizes that he is in God's presence
(3:1–6). Yet Moses is reluctant to accept the task of
bringing the Israelites out of Egypt, and he gives a
series of excuses, to which God responds, offering
assurances of divine help and appointing Aaron to
be his assistant. Although such initial reluctance
is typical of a number of biblical prophets (e.g.,
Jeremiah and, in an extreme form, Jonah), the
portrait of Moses's response to the divine call provides a classic combination of humility and stubbornness. As a significant part of this call story,
God also reveals the divine name to Moses: "I AM

WHO I AM" (or possibly "I WILL BE WHO I WILL
BE"). Thus, Moses is to tell the Israelites, "I AM (or
I WILL BE) has sent me to you" (3:14–15).

Signs and Wonders: God tells Moses that the
sign that he has truly been commissioned by
God will be the worship that he and the liberated
people will offer to God on the mountain where
the burning bush appeared (Exod. 3:12). In the
meantime, God also enables Moses to works signs
and wonders that will prove to the Israelites and to
the Egyptians that God has sent him. He is enabled
to work a series of wonders: changing a rod into a
serpent and back to a rod again; making leprosy
appear and disappear from his hand; and changing water into blood. The first of these wonders is
also performed before Pharaoh; the last is transformed into the first of the ten plagues. Those
plagues (Exod. 7–11) may also be construed as
signs or wonders, offered as proof to the Egyptians of God's superior power. In another sense,
however, they serve as a form of punishment to
Pharaoh and his people for having dealt harshly
with the Israelites.

Moses is not the only one who performs wonders. Aaron is sometimes the one to set a plague in
motion, as in the first, second, and third plagues
(water turned to blood, frogs, diseased livestock).
Both Moses and Aaron throw soot toward the sky,
bringing the plague of boils. Moses himself brings
the hail, the locusts, and the darkness by stretching his hand or rod upward. The Egyptian magicians are also credited with some degree of power
to work wonders; they can duplicate some of the
early wonders, but apparently cannot undo them.
They can cause a rod to become a serpent, make
water turn to blood, and produce frogs; but their
serpent is swallowed by Aaron's, never to revert to
a rod, and they cannot remove the blood or the
frogs. They recognize God's power, however, when
they are unable to duplicate a wonder—in the
third plague, of the gnats (Exod. 8:16–19).

Moses continues to work signs and wonders
after the Israelites are given leave to go. He divides
the sea (Exod. 14:21–15:21), turns brackish water
into sweet water (15:22–25), and produces water
from a rock (17:1–7). His raised hands ensure victory over the Amalekites (17:11–12). In the book of
Numbers it is recounted that Moses also provided
the people with meat (11:1–35) and with fresh
water (20:2–11).

Spokesperson: A prophet functions mainly as
a spokesperson for God. Ironically it is the ability to speak well that Moses initially claims to
lack, maintaining that he cannot be effective as a
spokesman before Pharaoh. As a concession, God
appoints Aaron to be a spokesman for Moses,
even as Moses was a spokesman for God (Exod.
4:14–16; 7:1). Yet the man who calls himself "slow
of speech" is ultimately credited with the magnificent speeches of Deuteronomy as well as with
all manner of discourse in the Exodus–Numbers
narrative.

Moses speaks for God to the Israelites and to
Pharaoh. His first task is to persuade the Israelites

that he is truly God's representative, and it is to this end that Aaron performs the signs that God had provided. The brothers are successful; the people believe them. Later, however, after the Egyptians have increased their workload and made conditions harsher, the people lose confidence in their leader, and Moses complains to God that he will never be able to convince Pharaoh to do what he requests, if he cannot convince even the Israelites (Exod. 6:12). Despite this weak beginning, Moses and Aaron go again and again to Pharaoh to deliver God's message. But it is really to the Israelites that Moses is sent as prophetic spokesman, and it is to them that he continually conveys God's commands. These range from information about the journey, encouragement, and chastisement, to instructions on how to collect the manna. In fact, everything that Moses says can be viewed as emanating from God. This applies especially to Moses's most important discourse: the giving of the Torah (see below).

Intercessor: The channel of communication operates in both directions. Moses conveys God's words to Pharaoh, but he also relays Pharaoh's wishes to God. When Pharaoh pleads for the removal of the frog plague, Moses entreats God and the frogs are removed. The same occurs in the case of the flies, the hail, and the locusts. Likewise, and to a much greater degree, Moses serves as the link between the Israelites and God; he intercedes with God on behalf of the people. The first of many occurrences of this is in Exod. 5:22–23, after the Israelites' suffering has increased. Such intercession is part of the prophetic aspect of Moses; he is a link between God and human beings. This is brought out clearly in the account at Mount Sinai. Moses has already been commissioned by God to represent God to the people, but at Sinai, the people, fearing direct contact with the divine, commission Moses to represent them before God (Exod. 20:19).

Later, a crucial intercession takes place in the aftermath of the golden calf incident. Here Moses assuages God's anger by suggesting that, if God destroys the people, it will be construed by the Egyptians as a weakness on God's part—an inability to protect the Israelites in the wilderness. This, and a reminder of the promises made to the ancestors, convinces God to withdraw the divine wrath (Exod. 32:11–14). On another occasion God's anger causes fires to break out, burning up the people who are complaining, but the people cry to Moses to plead for them. When he prays on their behalf, they are spared (Num. 11:2). Even when Moses's own position is threatened—when the people want to stone him and appoint a new leader—Moses reacts to God's anger by reminding God, as before, that the other nations will perceive the destruction of Israel as a weakness of God. Once again, Moses is successful in obtaining at least a partial pardon (Num. 14). Other instances of such intercession occur with regard to Miriam's leprosy (Num. 12); Korah's rebellion (Num. 16); and the bronze-serpent incident (Num. 21).

Lawgiver: The law is a central feature of the Pentateuch, and so the role of lawgiver was perhaps regarded as the most important aspect of Moses by the authors and editors of that literature. It is Moses who gives the Torah to the people, the "teaching" that comes directly from God. This, as noted, is part of his prophetic function, as one who speaks for God. Thus Moses brings Israel the Ten Commandments, engraved on tablets, and proclaims the laws and ordinances that constitute a significant part of Exodus, Leviticus, Numbers, and Deuteronomy.

Judge: On a more practical level, Moses serves as judge and arbiter of the people (this is a function of his role as national leader as well as interpreter of God's law). At first he is the sole judge, but at the suggestion of his father-in-law, Jethro, he institutes a system of lower judges for lesser matters; only the difficult cases are brought to Moses (Exod. 18). One such case involves the inheritance rights of Zelophehad's daughters. Since there was no precedent for daughters to inherit land, Moses consults God. The response is that in the event that a man has no sons, his daughters should inherit his land, so that his name and holdings might be perpetuated. God thus rules in favor of the claim of Zelophehad's daughters (Num. 27). But in a sequel to this story (Num. 36) the leaders of the tribe of Manasseh (Zelophehad's tribe) approach Moses with their concern: if the daughters marry men from other tribes, then the land will eventually be passed on to their children and thereby lost to the tribe of Manasseh. Thus the purpose of the original ruling would be thwarted; the land would be alienated from its original owner and tribe. Moses acknowledges the legitimacy of the concern of the Manasseh representatives and rules that, although the daughters can inherit their father's land, they have to marry within their tribe.

National Leader: Moses is sent to lead the people out of Egypt, and there is no question that he is portrayed as a successful leader. He takes a "mixed crowd" (Exod. 12:38) and shapes them under his guidance into a national entity. Moses leads the people from encampment to encampment and directs them when conflicts with other nations arise. He is subjected to complaints and grumblings and even rebellions (e.g., Exod. 16; Num. 12; 16), and he is called upon to provide solutions to problems. At times, he does seem to get discouraged; in Exod. 17:4, after complaints about water, Moses seeks help from God saying, "What shall I do with this people?" Even more vivid is the portrayal of Moses's frame of mind in Num. 11. Displeased with the people's actions and with God's anger, Moses feels that he has been made to appear at fault and that his burden is too heavy for him. At this point God allows the burden of leadership to be shared by seventy elders who also receive a measure of God's spirit.

Death and Burial: Ironically, although Moses is certainly presented as successful in his mission, he himself is not permitted to enjoy the full fruits of this success—he is not granted the privilege of entering the promised land, but can only glimpse it from across the Jordan. At this crucial juncture, a new leader, Joshua, is appointed by God. When it is time for Moses to die, he ascends Mount Nebo, in Moab, and, after viewing the future home of the Israelites, expires. The text suggests that God buried Moses and that no person knows his burial place (Deut. 34:6). The special character of Moses is emphasized through notation of his ideal life span (120 years) and of the fact that he showed no signs of aging.

In Later Israelite Tradition: Moses is referred to fifty-three times in the book of Joshua, mostly in passages that reflect back on the exodus narratives and draw parallels between what happened then and what may happen now: God promises to be with Joshua as God was with Moses (1:2; 3:7); the people agree to obey Joshua as they did Moses (1:17), and they stand in awe of Joshua as they did Moses (4:10). Otherwise, the references to Moses outside the Pentateuch are relatively slight: four in Judges, twelve in the books of Samuel and Kings, twenty-one in 1 and 2 Chronicles, three in Ezra, seven in Nehemiah, eight in the Psalms, two in Daniel, and only five in all of the writings of the prophets combined (Isa. 63:11–12; Jer. 15:1; Mic. 6:4; Mal. 4:4). Many of these references are simply instances of his name occurring in a genealogy; ten involve use of the phrase "the law of Moses." The prophet Samuel does mention Moses's and Aaron's role as leaders sent by God to bring the people out of Egypt (1 Sam. 12:6, 8). The bronze serpent Moses made to save the people from snakebite is mentioned (2 Kings 18:4; cf. Num. 21:4–9); it had since become an object of idolatrous worship and, so, was broken into pieces by King Hezekiah. Ps. 106 recalls the exodus story; Ps. 90 is said to be a "Prayer of Moses"; Ps. 77:20 praises God for leading the people by the hand of Moses (and Aaron); Ps. 103:7 offers thanksgiving that God's ways were made known to Moses. The Second Temple period evinced new interest in Moses. The "book" or "law" of Moses is mentioned frequently in Tobit (e.g., 1:8; 6:13; 7:11–13), and Sirach calls Moses a "holy man," whose "memory is blessed," not least because he ordained his brother Aaron (also a "holy man") as priest (45:1, 6, 15). The time when Moses called down fire from heaven is also remembered (2 Macc. 10–11; cf. Lev. 9:23–24; 2 Chron. 7:1)

In the NT: Because of the towering significance of Moses as the mediator of God's law to Israel, it is not surprising that in the NT Moses is mentioned principally in connection with the law. That is true both in the Gospels (Matt. 19:7; Mark 7:10; Luke 16:31; John 1:17) and in the Letters of Paul (Rom. 9:15; 10:19; 1 Cor. 9:9; 2 Cor. 3:13). He is also cited as exemplary for his faith in God (Heb. 3:2; 11:24) and is regarded as having announced beforehand the coming of Jesus as Messiah (Acts 3:22; 26:22; cf. John 1:45). Moses actually appears in the NT story of the transfiguration of Jesus (Matt. 17:1–8; Mark 9:2–8; Luke 9:28–36), where in Luke's Gospel he and Elijah are said to discuss with Jesus the

Moses before the burning bush, loosening his sandal in response to God's command in Exod. 3:5; from the mosaics at the Monastery of St. Catherine, Sinai, sixth century CE.

"exodus" (Gk. *exodos;* NRSV: "departure") that Jesus is to accomplish at Jerusalem (9:31). The Gospel of Matthew, in particular, seems to present Moses as a prototype of Christ: like Moses, Jesus is endangered by a baby-killing tyrant at birth (2:1–18); he comes out of Egypt (2:13–21); he fasts for forty days and nights (4:2; cf. Exod. 34:28); he interprets the law of God on a mountain (chaps. 5–7); and he miraculously provides people with bread (14:13–21). John's Gospel likewise draws a connection between the saving power of the bronze serpent that Moses lifted up on a pole and the saving power of Christ being lifted up on cross (3:14). In a different vein, however, Jesus is contrasted with Moses as the bringer of a new covenant, which supersedes the Mosaic law. John's Gospel declares, "The law indeed was given through Moses; grace and truth came through Jesus Christ" (1:17). Paul recalls the mention of Moses veiling his face when descending from Sinai and takes this as a poignant image: the old covenant instituted by Moses is covered with a veil, but "when one turns to the Lord [i.e., to Jesus Christ], the veil is removed" (2 Cor. 3:13, 15).

Historicity of Moses: The only source for knowledge about Moses is the Bible. Archaeology has not unearthed any objects bearing his name, nor do ancient Near Eastern documents contain any references to him. By the same token, references to Moses outside of the Pentateuch (especially in prophetic and hymnic literature), even in connection with exodus or Sinai motifs, are relatively few. The poems in Exod. 15:1–18, which are thought to be earlier than any of the narrative accounts of the exodus, do not make any mention of Moses (cf. also 15:21). Some scholars have sought to attribute the various traditions in the Pentateuch narrative to different sources (J, E, D, P); according to this view, the material ascribed to J and E is thought to be the oldest narrative material and may potentially be read as more likely to have been based on historical occurrences than the P and D traditions, which represent later editorial reflection that reinterpret or supplement the earlier material. Another prominent theory suggests that the exodus from Egypt, the revelation at Sinai, the wandering in the wilderness, and the entrance into the promised land were originally four unrelated accounts, preserved as traditions of various tribes. According to this theory, Moses might be a composite figure to whom the exploits of diverse tribal heroes (historical or legendary) have been attributed. It is unlikely that historical scholars will come to a consensus regarding the historicity of Moses or of the events reported concerning him. The Pentateuch, at any rate, presents the view that there was one person who, from the point of view of Israel's literary-religious tradition, played a major role at the crucial point when the nation was born and its religious norms were established. *See also* exodus, the; law; Pentateuch, sources of the; Torah.

Bibliography

Childs, Brevard. *The Book of Exodus.* Westminster, 1974.   A.B./M.A.P.

Moses, Assumption of. *See* apocalyptic literature; Pseudepigrapha.

Most High, the usual translation of a Hebrew adjective meaning "high" or "exalted" when applied to God. Taken from Canaanite culture (cf. Gen. 14:19–20), it became a popular name for God in the Hebrew Bible (e.g., Pss. 7:17; 21:7; 91:1) and, in Greek translation, it appears also in the NT (e.g., Mark 5:7; Luke 1:32; Acts 7:48). *See also* God, god.

moth, a term denoting any small, winged butterfly-like insect; in the Bible it always refers to the insects that eat clothes. As such, it is a symbol of decay and human frailty (Job 4:19; 13:28; Ps. 39:11; Isa. 50:9; 51:8; Hos. 5:12). In the NT, it becomes a more specific symbol for the transitory nature of earthly riches (Matt. 6:19, 20; Luke 12:33; James 5:2).

mother. *See* family; marriage; and such individual entries as Athaliah; Deborah; Elizabeth; Hagar; Hannah; Mary; Rachel; Rebekah; Ruth; Sarah.

mother's house. *See* family.

mount, mountain. Mountains are a dominant feature of the Near Eastern landscape and accordingly have influenced the way of life and beliefs of the ancient peoples inhabiting this land. Mountains have important effects upon the climate, population, economic life, and state of civilization of the region in which they occur; for example, regions on their windward side have greater rainfall, while those on the leeward side are arid.

Mount Gilboa, 1,696 feet above sea level, overlooks the Jezreel Valley.

Mountains are frequently referred to in the biblical text as dwelling places (Gen. 36:8), places of refuge (Gen. 14:10; Judg. 6:2; Matt. 24:16), lookouts (Matt. 4:8), landmarks (Num. 34:7), assembly sites (Josh. 8:30–33; Judg. 9:7), military camps (1 Sam. 17:3), cemeteries (2 Kings 23:16), geographic boundaries (Josh. 15:8), places of ambush (Judg. 9:25), scenes of battle (1 Sam. 23:26), sanctuaries for the animal world (Ps. 11:1), pastures (Luke 8:32), and the habitat of goats (Ps. 104:18) and birds (1 Sam. 26:20).

There are two formidable mountain chains in the Near East: (1) the great western highlands, a chain that runs north–south, west of the Jordan River, as an extension of the mountains of Lebanon and comprises three distinct ranges separated by plains and valleys: the Galilee, Ephraim and Judah, and the Negev; the Carmel mountains near Haifa are an east–west spur of this chain; and (2) the eastern highlands, which rise precipitously above the Rift Valley east of the Jordan River, extending from Mount Hermon in the north through biblical Gilead, Amman, and Moab to Edom in the south. The north–south orientation of these mountains dictated the major routes of communication, i.e., the road system, which likewise, to a large extent, determined settlement patterns. Major trade routes spanned the country north–south forming a land bridge between the great empires of Egypt to the south and Syro-Mesopotamia to the north. This bridge facilitated the movement of trading caravans and invading armies. East–west communication was limited to gaps between the mountain ranges.

The term "mount" is applied to an isolated mountain, a notable peak, or specialized summit within a range, e.g., Mounts Ebal, Seir, Gerizim, Gilboa, Hermon, Nebo, Tabor, Sinai (also called Horeb), Carmel, Olives, and Zion. Two mountains inextricably associated with God are Mount Sinai (Horeb) and Mount Zion. It was on Mount Sinai (Horeb) where the covenant between God and Israel was sealed (Exod. 19:24), where Moses spoke to God (19:3, 10; 24:9), and where God's presence was revealed (19:16, 18). Mount Zion was another favored abode of God (Pss. 68:16; 84:5).

In the NT, Jesus makes it clear that the worship of God was not restricted to any particular mountain (John 4:2–24). Yet mountains figure prominently in contexts of worship, prayer, and events of great religious significance. The Sermon on the Mount exemplifies this continuing tradition (Matt. 5:1–7:29). Jesus's temptation occurred on a very high mountain (Matt. 4:8), as did his transfiguration (Mark 9:2); for his own prayer and devotion, Jesus sought the mountains (Matt. 14:23; Mark 6:46; Luke 6:12; 9:28; John 6:15). The Mount of Olives was the setting for Jesus's encampment with his disciples during his final week in Jerusalem (Mark 11:1; Luke 19:29); his betrayal occurred on the lower slopes at Gethsemane (Matt. 26:30–56; Mark 14:26–50). It is also reported that the Mount of Olives was the site of his ascension (Luke 24:50; Acts 1:9–12). S.R.

Mount, Sermon on the. *See* Sermon on the Mount.

mourning rites. Death was acknowledged by rending the clothes and dressing in sackcloth. Jacob did both when presented with the bloody coat of his son Joseph (Gen. 37:34). Likewise, when Job was informed of the death of his children, he "rent his robe, shaved his head, and fell upon the ground, and worshiped" (1:20); his friends also wept, rent their robes, sprinkled dust upon their heads, and sat on the ground with him for seven days and seven nights (2:12–13; cf. 2 Sam. 13:31). Micah mentions lamentations while naked (1:8) and the cutting off of one's hair (1:16; cf. Ezek. 27:30–31). Jeremiah expects the mourners to make themselves bald and cut themselves (16:16), while Leviticus specifically prohibits shaving, cutting the hair, tattooing, or the making of gashes in the skin on account of the dead (19:27–28).

Ezekiel was commanded by God not to mourn the death of his wife: "Bind on your turban, and put your sandals on your feet; do not cover your upper lip or eat the bread of mourners" (24:17). A contrast between times of mourning and times of joy (Isa. 61:3) enumerates the wearing of ashes and the abstention from anointing oil as signs of mourning. Further, no ornaments were to be worn by those who were mourning (Exod. 33:4). Friends of the mourner might prepare a consolation meal of bread and wine (Jer. 16:7). Formal lamentations or elegies (Heb. *qinot*) were recited, as at the death of Josiah, when "singing men and singing women" performed as professional mourners (2 Chron. 35:25).

Various mourning periods are specified in the narratives ranging from seven days (Gen. 50:10), to three weeks (Dan. 10:2), to "many days" (Gen. 37:34). Although a captive woman is expected to mourn for a month (Deut. 21:13), a definite period of mourning is not commanded anywhere else in the Bible.

There are no specific instructions for mourning in the NT, although the custom of communal mourning for the dead did continue (Mark 5:38; John 11:33). Jesus proclaimed a beatitude on those who mourn, saying that they would be comforted (Matt. 5:4; cf. Luke 6:25). In Matt. 11:17 he associates wailing with mourning, in the same way that flute music would normally be associated with dancing. He tells his disciples that they will "weep and mourn" when he is taken from them, but that their pain will be turned into joy (John 16:20). *See also* sackcloth. L.H.S.

Moza (moh′zuh).

1 The son of Caleb and his concubine (1 Chron. 2:46), a name considered by some to be adapted from a place-name associated with Judah.

2 The son of Zimri (1 Chron. 8:36; 9:42) and the father of Binea (8:37; 9:43), listed as descendants of King Saul.

mulberry, in the Bible, the black mulberry (*Morus nigra*), a long-lived tree whose heart-shaped leaves

Black mulberry.

and dense, spreading branches provide shade (see Isa. 40:20; Luke 17:6). The small blackberry-like fruit produces a dark red juice, which is referred to in 1 Macc. 6:34. The white mulberry tree now found in the Near East is a more recent import from China and Persia.   P.L.C.

mule, the hybrid offspring of a donkey and a horse, normally a jackass and a mare. Although its lack of understanding was proverbial (Ps. 32:9), the mule's strength, endurance, and docility made it ideal for transporting goods (2 Kings 5:17; 1 Chron. 12:40) and riding (Isa. 66:20). From their earliest appearance in the Bible (2 Sam. 13:29), mules were usually associated with royalty (2 Sam. 18:9; 1 Kings 1:33, 38, 44). Since the law prohibited the breeding of hybrids (Lev. 19:19), it is likely that mules were imported into Israel (1 Kings 10:25; Ezra 2:66; Neh. 7:38; cf. Ezek. 27:14). Mules are not mentioned in the NT. *See also* animals; horse; trade; transportation, travel.
                                                          G.L.M.

mummification, an elaborate embalming technique practiced in ancient Egypt, which spread to some extent south and east to Nubia. Early in Egypt's history people observed that bodies buried in the warm, dry sand, and thus dried out, were often well preserved. This experience, coupled with the Egyptian belief in bodily resurrection, prompted the development of intentional, careful means to preserve the body. By the later Old Kingdom (ca. 2300–2200 BCE), there was a well-developed mummification process for wealthy burials, and the techniques were significantly improved by the time of the New Kingdom (sixteenth century BCE).

The expensive, protracted process took about seventy days and involved removing the brain tissue (usually through the nostrils), taking out the major organs, preparing the body interior, and covering the body with natron to help dry it out prior to the final cleansing, padding, and wrapping with many layers of cloth. (The primary organs were separately preserved in special jars or boxes.) There were also less elaborate alternatives. One more modest process involved injecting the body with oil and treating it with natron. The oil was subsequently drained out, bringing with it the dissolved interior organs. In the cheapest style, the embalmers merely cleansed the body and treated it with natron prior to the wrapping. The precise embalming practices varied with time and place as well as in expense. The fully treated body was then placed in a coffin, often rather elaborate, and transported to the tomb for the "Opening of the Mouth" ritual by which the body regained the powers of speech, hearing, and sight, making it ready for new life. Mummification was extended to include the embalming of various animals sacred to particular deities. Sacred animal cemeteries with literally thousands of burials are known from many sites.

Genesis reports that Israel (Jacob), who died in Egypt, was embalmed by the physicians, a process requiring forty days (50:1–4), and that Joseph, who also died in Egypt, was embalmed and placed in a coffin (50:26). The Genesis references reflect the more elaborate process described above. Mummification was not otherwise practiced by the Israelites. *See also* burial; embalming; Jacob; Joseph.   H.B.H.

Muppim (muh′pim). *See* Shephupham.

murder. Protection from murder is a central part of God's covenantal blessing to Noah after the flood; God will seek blood for a human being's blood, whether the latter is shed by an animal or by another human being (Gen. 9:4–6), for human beings were created in God's image. In the Ten Commandments, God forbids killing (Exod. 20:13; Deut. 5:17), which is usually taken to be a prohibition against murder.

Forms of Legal Liability: Causing the death of another rendered one liable to death at the hands of legally recognized avengers (Exod. 21:12), but the possibility of asylum was available in cases where the death had been caused accidentally (Exod. 21:13; Deut. 19:15). Such asylum was not, however, available in cases where there had been premeditation (Exod. 21:13) or even previous animosity (Exod. 21:14; Deut. 4:42; 19:4, 6, 11; Josh. 20:5; Num. 35:20). Direct killing with an instrument liable to cause death also took the offender outside the protection of the asylum laws (Num. 35:17–19). Homicide in the course of a sudden quarrel was viewed as comparable to accidental homicide (35:22–23). Still, the protection afforded through asylum was limited. According to one understanding of Deut. 19:6, it commenced only when the offender reached one of the designated cities of refuge, though Num. 35:12 and Josh. 20:9 also seek to protect the accused en route, which accords with the motive of avoiding the shedding of innocent blood (Deut. 19:10). Once the offender reached the city of refuge, there was an adjudication (Num. 35:24); according to Josh. 20:4, it took place at the city gate, and the fugitive would not be admitted to the city in advance of it. If the offender was found to have acted without premeditation, the avenging relative (Heb. *go'el haddam,* interpreted by some as a public official) would be turned away from the city (Josh. 20:5); if not, the offender would be handed over (Deut. 19:12), to be executed by the relative. Where protection was granted, it extended only within the boundaries of the city of refuge (Num. 35:26–27).

It is likely that this system was designed to monitor and control customary practices in which relatives of the deceased were free to exact blood vengeance or accept a ransom (Exod. 21:30), subject to the offender's recourse to temple sanctuary, probably at the local shrine (21:13). Even then, offenders might be dragged from the altar to their death (21:14), at this stage apparently without any legal proceedings. The later system restricted the rights of relatives, not only by requiring formal adjudication when the accused sought asylum, but also by banning the acceptance of ransom (Num. 35:31–32) and requiring the evidence of two witnesses (35:30). The residual role of the relative as executioner might still lead to abuse (including the acceptance of ransom).

At least by the time of Ezra (mid- to late sixth century BCE), with the loss of autonomy and the territory of most of the cities of refuge, adjudication of murder became entirely a matter of state regulation, to be administered by judges appointed by Ezra under the authority of the Persian king (Ezra 7:25–26). Capital jurisdiction apparently was removed from Jewish courts under the Romans (cf. John 18:31).

Special Situations: The Covenant Code (Exod. 21–23) provides counsel for other special situations that call for consideration of liability in the event of a person's death. When death occurs after the victim has risen from the sickbed and walked outside, the offender is not regarded as the cause of death (21:18–19). Where death has been caused by an ox and the owner had been warned of previous incidents but did not keep the animal restrained, the owner is responsible for the death (21:29). Homicide is justified where a thief is caught breaking in at night (22:2–3). A master is not entitled to kill his slave outright, but if disciplinary measures lead to the slave's death a day or so later, the master is exempt (21:20–21). By contrast, David was held morally, if not legally, accountable for the death of Uriah, although David's personal role was restricted to giving military orders that led to Uriah's death (2 Sam. 11–12).

In the NT, Jesus reiterates the prohibition against murder (Matt. 19:18) and declares that Satan was a murderer from the beginning (John 8:44). To hate another human being is reckoned as a spiritual equivalent to murder by Jesus (Matt. 5:21–22; cf. 1 John 3:15). *See also* law; robbery.

B.S.J./P.J.A.

Mushi (myoo'shi), the son of Merari and grandson of Levi. He was the ancestral head of a major subdivision of the Merarite group of Levites, the Mushites (Exod. 6:19; Num. 3:20; 26:58).

Mushites (myoo'shits). *See* Mushi.

Music

Round-bottomed, silver, stringed harplike instrument found in the royal graves at Ur, ca. 1339 BCE. (It may be incorrectly reconstructed from two different instruments. The sound box from an even earlier lyre is shown in the section of color photographs.)

SECULAR AND SACRED MUSIC played no less a role in the lives of the people of biblical times than it does in the modern era. It added to the pomp of national celebrations, bolstered soldiers' courage, enlivened work and play, lent comfort in times of sadness, and provided inspiration in religious expression. The heptatonic, diatonic scales fundamental to modern Western music existed in antiquity. A number of stringed instruments from ancient times would have produced sounds similar to modern small harps, lyres, and lutes. Other instruments, notably woodwind, percussion, and the simpler stringed instruments, were merely less sophisticated forms of modern orchestral or folk instruments, and some are still in use in the traditional cultures of the contemporary Near East.

Mesopotamian and Egyptian Music: A pictographic sign for a boat-shaped Sumerian harp appears on the earliest Sumerian clay tablets from Uruk (ca. 3000 BCE), and an even earlier depiction of this instrument is found on a seal impression from Chogha Mish (modern southwest Iran, ca. 3200 BCE). An actual example of such a harp, together with nine ornamented lyres and a set of silver pipes, was found at Ur—the traditional home of Abraham—in the royal graves of Queen Pu-Abi and her retinue (ca. 2650 BCE). An inlaid panel that once decorated one of the lyres shows an animal orchestra, a common early folk theme, that included a lyre-playing donkey, a clapping and singing bear, and a jackal keeping time with a sistrum and a percussion instrument. By the end of the third millennium, textual evidence, including collections of divine hymns, hymns to temples, and hymns to and for the kings of the third dynasty of Ur—featuring many musical terms—attests even more directly to a well-developed Sumerian musical tradition.

Even more is known about Assyrian and Babylonian music in the second and first millennia. Illustrations, particularly first-millennium Assyrian reliefs, depict a varied assortment of instruments, and encyclopedic lists of names of instruments were compiled in the scribal schools. A large repertoire of hymns, laments, and liturgical litanies gives some notion of the use of song in religious ritual, especially those that were provided with labels indicating their type or purpose or the nature of their accompaniment or manner of performance.

Mesopotamian sacred and courtly music was apparently performed or directed by families of professional musicians, perhaps not unlike David's levitical guilds of musicians. Professional musicians were trained in the temple schools, and it was probably such musician-scribes who set down on cuneiform tablets dating from ca. 1800 to ca. 500 BCE the Mesopotamian theory of music, whose details have gradually come to light over the past several decades. Assyriological and musicological research has shown that the Mesopotamian musical system knew seven different

Statue of a singer discovered at the royal palace at Mari; third millennium BCE.

A man dances to the music of clappers, pipe, and lute; limestone relief from Carchemish, ninth–eighth century BCE.

heptatonic-diatonic scales, one of them similar to the present-day major scale; the Mesopotamian material therefore provides evidence for the antiquity of Western music some fourteen hundred years before the earliest Greek sources. One complete piece of music whose explicit notation uses technical Akkadian interval names followed by number signs was found at ancient Ugarit in Syria; the piece is a Hurrian hymn to the moon goddess Nikkal and dates to ca. 1400 BCE.

Egyptian music also has a long history, with graphic and written remains stretching from ca. 3000 BCE to Roman times. More important, many instruments depicted in illustrations or mentioned in written documents have actually survived intact and serve as a valuable source of comparative data for the study of both Mesopotamian and biblical instruments. These include several types of lyres, harps, and lutes, a copper and a bronze trumpet from the tomb of Tutankhamen (1347–1338 BCE), true end-blown flutes as well as double-reed pipes of both the clarinet and oboe varieties, and many percussion instruments such as drums, cymbals, sistrums, bells, rattles, and clappers.

Hebrew Secular Music: Biblical references to music begin with the mention of Jubal, "the father of all those who play the lyre and pipe" (Gen. 4:21). It is no coincidence that his name is related to the Hebrew word for "ram" (*yobel*), from whose horns the primitive signal horn (*shophar*) was made.

A blind harpist playing his instrument; detail of a relief from the tomb of Paätenemheb Saqqara, ca. 1212 BCE.

References to the popular enjoyment of music are common in early biblical history. It was always a part of celebrations, whether a farewell party complete with "mirth and songs, with tambourine and lyre" (Gen. 31:27); a joyous homecoming (Judg. 11:34); or the feasts of the idle rich, who spend their days with "lyre and harp, timbrel and flute and wine" (Isa. 5:12). Singing accompanied work as well as play, and many work songs or chants have been recorded, e.g., those of the well diggers (Num. 21:17–18), the watchman (Isa. 21:12), and the pressers of grapes (Jer. 25:30; 48:33).

A pair of bronze cymbals from Megiddo, ca. 1200–1000 BCE.

Warfare gave rise to martial songs. Such heroic ballads were probably set down in the lost "Book of the Wars of the LORD" (Num. 21:14) and the "Book of Jashar" (Josh. 10:13; 2 Sam. 1:18) and were no doubt sung by itinerant minstrels and bards (cf. Num. 21:27–30). Moses and Miriam both sang of God's final defeat of Pharaoh (Exod. 15:1–18, 20–21); and Deborah celebrated Israel's victory over Jabin with a song of triumph (Judg. 5). Samson exulted over his slaying of the Philistines (Judg. 15:16) in a rhythmic victory chant like the one the women sang back and forth at Saul's homecoming (1 Sam. 18:6–7). But Israel was not always victorious, and songs were also composed for fallen heroes, such as David's moving lament for Saul and Jonathan (2 Sam. 1:19–27).

The joy of purely secular music is especially praised in the apocryphal/deuterocanonical book of Sirach. The author says that "a concert of music at a banquet of wine" is like "a ruby seal in a setting of gold" (32:5). Again, "the melody of music with good wine" is like "a seal of emerald in a rich setting of gold" (32:6; cf. 40:20; 49:1). He also opines that such pleasures should be enjoyed without distraction: "Speak, you who are older, for it is your right, but with accurate knowledge, and do not interrupt the music. Where there is entertainment, do not pour out talk; do not display your cleverness at the wrong time" (32:3–4).

Hebrew Sacred Music: Music was not apparently an important part of Israelite religion in the early days of biblical history. With the monarchy (after ca. 1040 BCE), however, and the growth of the temple came professional musicianship both at court (1 Kings 1:34, 39–40; 10:2; Eccles. 2:8) and in religious ritual. The organization of temple ritual and liturgy is described in 1 Chron. 15–16 as the handiwork of David, and the levitical guilds of musicians are said to have been established by him. David himself is presented as a composer of songs and lamentations, a skilled lyre player (1 Sam. 16:16–18), an inventor of instruments (Amos 6:5), a

A seated harpist; Mesopotamian terra-cotta plaque, 1800–1500 BCE.

valued court musician (1 Sam. 19:9), and even a dancer (2 Sam. 6:14–15). The literary record of his many abilities is foreshadowed only by that of the Sumerian king Shulgi of Ur (2093–2045 BCE), who celebrated his own remarkable talents in music, athletics, and statesmanship in a number of finely crafted hymns. In any event, temple music doubtless featured both trumpet calls (cf. Num. 10:10; Ps. 98:6) and the singing of songs of thanksgiving, praise, and petition following the sacrifices (2 Chron. 29:20–30). At the reestablishment of the second temple (late sixth century BCE), the descendants of the original levitical musicians (Ezra 2:41) reassumed responsibility for the music of the liturgy, and the influence of those hereditary guilds can be seen in the references to their founders in the psalm headings. Some idea of how the vocal music may have been performed may be gotten from the structure of many psalms. Refrains and acclamations (e.g., "Hallelujah"), divisions into strophes, and above all the common devices of poetic parallelism all strongly suggest types of responsorial or antiphonal performance.

Musical Instruments: Much of what is known about the instruments of the Bible comes from literary evidence, from the biblical documents themselves and comments on those writings by rabbis, church fathers, and classical authors. Additional evidence has come from archaeological discoveries, both the remains of actual instruments and the abundant pictorial representations of instruments and musical scenes from throughout the entire Near Eastern and Mediterranean world. Even so, identifications are difficult and usually represent the best guesses that scholarship has to offer.

The *shophar,* or ram's horn, is the most frequently mentioned biblical instrument, and the only ancient instrument still in use in the synagogue.

A lyre with twelve strings connected by an oblique crossbar decorates a brown jasper seal (seventh century BCE) from Jerusalem.

A bronze flute player from Byblos; second millennium BCE.

Egyptian crescent-shaped harp (fourth century BCE) with a sphinx head wearing the crowns of Upper and Lower Egypt.

David, the "sweet psalmist of Israel," depicted playing a lyre in a sixth-century floor mosaic at the synagogue at Gaza.

A bronze figurine of a woman playing a long-necked lute (twelfth century BCE); found at Beth-shan.

The word may ultimately have come from the Akkadian name for the ibex, or wild goat, but the instrument was usually made from the horn of a ram, sometimes softened with heat and straightened or shaped. It was a simple instrument that could only produce two or three notes, and it was used mostly for signaling, especially in times of war (Judg. 3:27; 6:34; Neh. 4:18–20) or national celebration (1 Kings 1:34; 2 Kings 9:13).

The trumpet (Heb. *khatsotserah*) was made of metal, either bronze or silver. It was probably a short, straight instrument, with a high, bright tone and a range of only four or five notes. Its early uses are well summarized in Num. 10:2–10. It was played by the priests, usually in pairs, but occasionally in large choirs (2 Chron. 5:12–13), and it numbered among the sacred gold and silver utensils of the temple (2 Kings 12:14; cf. Num. 31:6).

The *kinnor*, David's "harp," was actually a lyre, a portable rectangular or trapezoid-shaped instrument with two arms, often of unequal length and curved, joined at the top by a cross-piece; the strings were of roughly the same length (unlike a harp's). This instrument was popular all throughout the ancient Near East, and the word itself appears in the cuneiform vocabularies of ancient Ebla in Syria (ca. 2400 BCE) and in Assyrian, Hurrian, Hittite, Ugaritic, and Egyptian texts. It was an instrument of joyful celebration, generally used to accompany singing.

Another stringed instrument, always mentioned together with the lyre, was the *nebel*, either a kind of angular harp with a vertical resonator such as is often depicted on first-millennium Assyrian reliefs, or another kind of lyre with an unusual waterskin-shaped sound box known only from depictions on coins from the Bar-Kochba period (132–135 CE). The NRSV usually translates it "harp" (but also "lute" in Ps. 150:3).

The principal biblical wind instrument was the *khalil* (NRSV: "flute" or "pipe"), which consisted of two pipes of reed, metal, or ivory, each with its own mouthpiece containing either a single (clarinet-type) or double (oboe-type) reed. The pipes were played together, one probably acting as a drone accompaniment. The *khalil* was primarily a secular instrument, generally used on joyful occasions (1 Kings 1:39–40; Isa. 5:12), but it was also suitable for mourning (Jer. 48:36; Matt. 9:23).

The *'ugab* is usually considered another kind of pipe, perhaps a true flute, though the LXX considers it a stringed instrument. It is mentioned together with other stringed instruments in Gen. 4:21; Ps. 150:4.

Percussion instruments included the *toph,* a small tambourine without jingles (also called a "timbrel," "tabor," or "tabret"), small bronze cymbals 4 to 6 inches in diameter, which may have been played with an up-and-down motion, and a kind of noisemaker (2 Sam. 6:5), variously translated as "castanets," "rattles," "sistrums," or "clappers." The bells attached to the high priest's robe (Exod. 28:33–34; 39:25–26) are better translated as "metal jingles," since true bells with clappers were unknown in Israel before the ninth century BCE. They served a protective rather than musical function.

A trumpeter from Carchemish, ninth century BCE.

The book of Daniel (3:5, 7, 10, 15) offers a list of instruments reportedly played by the court musicians of the Babylonian king Nebuchadnezzar (604–562 BCE). The names, however, are either Aramaic terms or Aramaic forms of Greek words, and the identification of most of them is still not entirely certain. They probably included a curved horn, a flute or, less likely, a panpipe, a lyre, a small boat-shaped harp, and a second kind of lyre or possibly an early type of zither. The last term (NRSV: "drum") is an Aramaic form of the Greek word *symphonia,* which may simply mean several instruments "sounding together" (thus, "music").

The Psalm Headings: About two-thirds of the psalms designate their authorship in their headings: either David, the "sweet psalmist of Israel" (2 Sam. 23:1), or, with only a few exceptions, founders of families of levitical musicians connected with the original establishment of the temple liturgy. Other terms and expressions in the headings refer more

Pottery rattles found at Tell Beit Mirsim typify those used from the second millennium to the ninth century BCE. They were filled with one or more small pellets to make noise.

directly to musical matters, the nature, purpose, or manner of performance of individual compositions.

Some songs are called "psalms," from the Greek translation of Hebrew *mizmor;* both terms refer to a song with instrumental accompaniment. Other titles include "song" (Heb. *shir,* a word ultimately derived from Akkadian and Sumerian), "song of praise," and the common word for "prayer" (also applied to the misplaced psalm Hab. 3). The meanings of the untranslated terms "Maskil" (Pss. 32; 42; 44–45; 52–55; 74; 78; 88–89; 142) and "Miktam" (16:1; 56–60) are unknown; they come from roots meaning "to have insight" and "to cover, conceal." "Shiggaion" in Ps. 7 (and Hab. 3) is related to the Akkadian word for a kind of lament or cry of woe.

Some comments in the superscriptions of psalms refer to the manner of a psalm's performance, e.g., "upon stringed instruments [*neginot*]" or "for the flutes [*nekhilot*]"—although these translations are not entirely certain. "Alamoth" (Ps. 46) and "Sheminith" (Pss. 6; 12) may refer to a type of harp tuning and the playing of a melody an octave higher. "Mahalath" (Pss. 53; 88) may refer to a type of dance, perhaps to a rhythm. Also found in psalm headings are song cues, the titles or opening words of popular older songs to whose tunes the psalms were to be sung, e.g., "Hind of the Dawn" (Ps. 21), or "Lilies" (Ps. 45).

The frequently occurring word "Selah," which appears within or at the ends of certain psalms, is probably also a kind of performance indication. The word's meaning is unknown, but based upon the translation of the LXX it is thought to indicate a pause in the singing, possibly signaled by the sounding of cymbals. At such points musical interludes may have occurred, or a different group of performers may have taken up the singing.

In the NT: Four different instruments are mentioned in the NT, the double pipe (Matt. 9:23; 11:17; 1 Cor. 14:7; cf. Sir. 40:21; 1 Macc. 3:45; NRSV: "flute"), the lyre (1 Cor. 14:7; Rev. 5:8; cf. Wis. 19:18; Sir. 40:21; 1 Macc. 3:45; NRSV: "harp"), the trumpet (e.g., Matt. 6:2; 24:31; 1 Cor. 15:52; 1 Thess. 4:16; Heb. 12:19; Rev. 8:2–13; cf. Sir. 26:7; 50:16; 1 Macc. 3:54; 5:31), and the cymbals (1 Cor. 13:1; cf. Jth. 15:1; 1 Macc. 4:54; 13:51). The "noisy gong" mentioned by Paul in 1 Cor. 13:1 probably refers to the large brass vases that were placed at the rear of Greek theaters to help amplify the actors' voices. There are also references in the NT to singing in the context of worship (Eph. 5:19; Col. 3:16b), although there is no indication of who did the singing or of when it occurred. The references to heavenly singing in Revelation (e.g., 4:10) and the hymnic fragments cited in that book (e.g., 4:11; 5:9; 7:15–17; 11:17–18) may provide an insight into the kind of music that was used in early Christian worship. The Gospel of Luke also contains some early Christian hymns (1:46–55; 67–79; 2:14, 29–32), and certain NT letters quote passages that may come from hymns (Rom. 11:33–36; 1 Cor. 13; Eph. 1:3–14; 5:14; Phil. 2:6–11; Col. 1:15–20; 1 Tim. 3:16; 2 Tim. 2:11–13). Jesus's parable of the Prodigal Son refers to "music and dancing" as typifying the celebration of the boy's return (Luke 15:25). *See also* Asaph; David; Psalms, book of.

Bibliography
Sendry, Alfred. *Music in Ancient Israel.* Philosophical, 1969.

A.D.K./D.A.F./M.A.P.

Mustard.

Myrrh.

musical instruments. *See* music.

mustard, a common plant used for oil, as a condiment, and as a potherb. Jesus refers to the mustard seed in contexts that emphasize its small size, which is even more notable relative to the size of the plant that grows from it. The kingdom of heaven is like such a seed, because it begins inauspiciously (in the ministry of Jesus himself) but will have earth-shattering consequences (Matt. 13:31; Mark 4:31; Luke 13:19). Elsewhere, Jesus says that if his disciples have "faith the size of a mustard seed" they will be able to move mountains (Matt. 17:20) or tell mulberry trees to be uprooted and planted in the sea (Luke 17:6). The latter comments are offered in the two Gospels in which Jesus's disciples (to whom he is speaking) are explicitly portrayed as "people of little faith" (Matt. 6:30; 8:26; 14:31; 16:8; 17:20; Luke 12:28); rather than increase their faith (cf. Luke 17:5), Jesus assures them that, in spite of their little faith, they will be able to do whatever God requires of them.   M.A.P.

Muth-labben (myooth-lab′ubn), a word in the heading of Ps. 9 that may have served as some sort of notation for its musical performance. *See also* Psalms, book of.

Myra (mi′ruh), a principal city of Lycia in southwestern Asia Minor, where Paul's company changed ships on the way to Rome (Acts 27:5–6), probably at its port of Andriaca. The site, occupied by modern Dembre, has ruins of a theater, tombs, and inscriptions, all from Roman times, attesting to Myra's importance for commercial navigation in antiquity. *See also* Lycia; Paul.

myrrh (muhr), an aromatic gum that grows in Arabia, Abyssinia, and India. Highly prized from earliest times (Gen. 37:25), it was used in incense (Exod. 30:23) and as a perfume for garments (Ps. 45:9) or for a lover's couch (Prov. 7:17). It was part of the cosmetic treatment used to prepare young girls for the king's bed (Esther 2:13), and it was also used in embalming (Mark 15:23; John 19:39). Myrrh appears among the items of luxury trade that exemplify the wealth of Rome (Rev. 18:13). Along with gold and frankincense it exemplifies the rich gifts brought to the infant Christ by the magi from the East (Matt. 2:11).   P.P.

myrtle (*Myrtus communis*), a large ornamental evergreen shrub that grows in dense copses along rivers and streams. Its greens were used to adorn the booths at the Festival of Tabernacles (Neh. 8:15). The fragrant leaves were also used in perfume manufacture. The myrtle is a symbol of peace, joy, generosity, and justice. Esther's Hebrew name was Hadassah, which is derived from the Hebrew word for myrtle, *hadas* (Esther 2:7).

Mysia (mis′ee-uh), the region of northwestern Asia Minor along the Hellespont and the Aegean Sea. Paul passed through two towns in the area, Troas (Acts 16:8, 11) and Assos (20:13). Pergamum was also in this region (Rev. 1:11; 2:12).

mystery, that which is secret, hidden, or beyond normal human understanding, although it may be revealed or disclosed to certain people. The Greek word (*mystērion*) does not usually refer to something puzzling that needs to be figured out. Rather, it refers to something that cannot possibly

Myrtle.

be figured out, unless it is revealed by someone possessing inside information. Thus, Sirach uses the word simply to refer to human secrets: a noble person will not tell such secrets when they have been instructed not to do so (27:16–17, 21). Likewise, 2 Macc. 13:21 refers to a traitor who revealed mysteries (NRSV: "secret information") to the enemy. A divine mystery, however, is something that can only be revealed by God (cf. Eph. 3:5), and this is the primary sense in which the word is used in the Bible.

In the Hebrew Bible: The word "mystery" is not used in the OT portion of the English NRSV except in the book of Daniel, where it translates Hebrew *razah* ("secret meaning") and refers to the hidden meaning of a dream, which God is able to discern and reveal to Daniel (cf. 2:18–19, 27–30; 4:9). Elsewhere, however, God is said to reveal secret knowledge (Isa. 48:3, 6; Amos 3:7). God may deliver

such knowledge in person (Gen. 17:1), through an angel (from heaven, Gen. 22:11; on earth, Num. 22:23), through dreams (Gen. 20:3), or through the "Spirit of the LORD" (2 Sam. 23:2). Divine secrets may also be sealed in books, the contents of which will not be disclosed until the end of this age (Dan. 12:4).

The Israelites believed that divine knowledge was needed to solve human problems; it provided laws for relations with God and among humans, rules for priestly ritual, and explanations of sin, injustice, and foreign domination. Early prophets explained evil as God's punishment of Israel for its sins. With regard to eschatology (beliefs about the end of this age), the secret, divine plan revealed in Daniel and later books is that a new age will come, at which time the wicked will be punished, righteous Jews rewarded, and God will rule permanently over a perfect earth. Even misfortunes fit God's purposes, for they purify the sufferers and ensure their inclusion among the happy righteous. The wicked are blinded to these mysteries of God (Wis. 2:21–22). The Essenes at Qumran believed that God was still revealing mysterious knowledge to them. Numerous Jewish writers retold history to make it fit God's plan.

In the NT: Jesus tells his disciples, "To you has been given the mystery [Gk. *mystērion*, NRSV: 'secret'] of the kingdom of God, but for those outside, everything comes in parables" (Mark 4:11; cf. Matt. 13:11; Luke 8:10). In John 18:20, however, he claims to have said nothing in secret. In other NT writings, God is said to have kept the divine mystery hidden for ages, while revealing it to the ancient prophets and the Christian apostles (Rom. 16:25–26; 1 Cor. 2:7; 4:1; Eph. 3:9; Heb. 1:1–2; 1 Pet. 1:10–12; Rev. 10:7). Thus, the Christian gospel is referred to as "God's mystery" (Col. 2:2; Rev. 10:7); "the mystery of (God's) will" (Eph. 1:9); "the mystery of Christ" (Eph. 3:4; Col. 4:3); "the mystery of the gospel" (Eph. 6:19); "the mystery of the faith" (1 Tim. 3:9); and "the mystery of our religion" (1 Tim. 3:16). In 1 Cor. 2:7, Paul says, "We speak God's wisdom, secret and hidden, which God decreed before the ages for our glory."

The most extensive treatment of mystery in the Bible is found in the Letter to the Ephesians, where the word "mystery" (Gk. *mystērion*) is used six times (1:9; 3:3, 4, 9; 5:32; 6:19), always with reference to something divine. God has commissioned Paul and other "holy apostles and prophets" to disclose the mysterious plan of God to the church (3:1–5, 8–9; 6:19), and God has chosen the church to reveal this mystery to the world and, indeed, to the cosmic powers of the universe (3:9–11). The mystery in question concerns God's plan to unite all things in Christ (1:9–10), including all *people* (e.g., those who have been traditionally identified as "Jews" or "Gentiles," 3:5–6), who will now be identified as a "new humanity" (2:15). The plan is accomplished through the crucifixion and exaltation of Christ, and there are two signs that it is being accomplished: the seal of the Holy Spirit (1:13–14; 4:30) and the unity of the church (4:4–6,

The birth of Mithra, god of light and obedience, whose cult was a major rival in popularity to early Christianity.

11–16), especially the unity of Jews and Gentiles in the church (2:11–21).

Sometimes the word "mystery" is used in a more pedantic sense to refer to something that is simply difficult to understand. Thus, theological puzzles can be called mysteries. Paul refers to the Jewish rejection of Jesus as "a mystery" that he is able to explain: God has hardened part of Israel "until the full number of the Gentiles come in" (Rom. 11:25–26). Other puzzles treated as mysteries include: the nature of the general resurrection (1 Cor. 15:51–55); the time of Jesus's return and the disbelief of many (2 Thess. 2:1–12); and the question of whether salvation is also intended for Gentiles (Eph. 3:4–6; Col. 1:25–27). The meaning of a passage in the Bible can also be a mystery, as is Gen. 2:24 in Eph. 5:31–32. Speaking in tongues is uttering "mysteries in the Spirit" (1 Cor. 14:2).

Mystery Religions: The Roman world also featured a wide variety of cults that were prevalent around the Mediterranean in the late Hellenistic age (ca. 100 BCE–300 CE). They were called "the mysteries" (or mystery religions) because of their secret rites. The Eleusinian and Samothracian mysteries were Greek in origin. Orphism and the cult of Dionysus probably came to Greece from Thrace. The cults of Isis, Mithra, Cybele/Attis, Adonis, and the Syrian goddess originated in the Near East, but became mystery religions after contact with the Greek mysteries. Mystery religions associated with Astarte (Ishtar) and Artemis (Diana) appear to have been particularly popular

in Asia Minor, around the area of Ephesus. The practices of these religions are not mentioned explicitly in the Bible, though Wis. 14:23 does allude to those who "celebrate secret mysteries" and "hold frenzied revels with strange customs."

These religions differed from one another, but always involved participation in secret rites, such as ritual washings, common meals, and sometimes sexual rites related to concerns for fertility (of crops or humans). The secret knowledge that was obtained allowed the devotees to bond with the god or goddess in this life and to establish an intimate connection that would continue in the world beyond death. Concrete knowledge about these religious movements is difficult to obtain precisely because they kept their ideas and practices secret. Most extant reports come from outsiders who debunk and denounce the mystery religions, and it is possible (perhaps likely) that the descriptions they offer are hyperbolic accounts based on speculation and rumor. Christianity was regarded as a mystery religion by some Romans when it first appeared, and early reports concerning Christian worship included allegations of cannibalism and orgies—probably because the Christians called their eucharistic meal a "love feast" and talked about "eating the body of Christ."

Despite the inadequate and untrustworthy character of the data, certain similarities between Christianity and the mysteries are noted, including the offer of personal, eternal salvation and the notion of intimate union with a divine being (cf. John 14:23; Gal. 2:20). Adonis and Osiris were said to have died and returned to life. Mithra ascended into the heavens (in a chariot with the god Sun). Some of the mystery religions appear to have practiced a type of baptism, and most of them practiced some sort of ritual meal. *See also* apocalyptic literature; dreams; Ephesians, Letter of Paul to the; revelation; vision.

Bibliography

Bockmuehl, Markus N. A. *Revelation and Mystery in Ancient Judaism and Pauline Christianity.* Mohr-Siebeck, 1990.

Burkett, Walter. *Ancient Mystery Cults.* Harvard University Press, 1987.

Caragounis, Chrys C. *The Ephesian Mystērion: Meaning and Context.* Gleerup, 1977.

Cosmopoulos, Michael B. *Greek Mysteries: The Archaeology of Ancient Greek Secret Cults.* Routledge, 2003.

Powell, Mark Allan. *Introducing the New Testament: A Historical, Literary, and Theological Survey.* Baker Academic, 2009. Pp. 37–38.

H.M.T./M.A.P.

myth (Gk. *mythos*).

1 In the NT, false and foolish stories that are to be rejected as misleading and dangerous. See 1 Tim. 1:4 ("myths and endless genealogies that promote speculations"); 1 Tim. 4:7 ("profane myths and old wives' tales"); 2 Tim. 4:4 (myths as the opposite of "the truth"); Titus 1:14 ("Jewish myths" parallel with "commandments of those who reject the truth"); and 2 Pet. 1:16 ("cleverly devised myths").

2 In the field of biblical studies, a genre of literature in which the exploits of gods and divine beings are recounted. The term, however, is not used with consistency, and different scholars define the genre of "myth" in very different terms. In the broadest sense, virtually everything in the Bible could be said to reflect a mythical perspective (i.e., one that focuses on interaction of divine and human entities). In practice, however, the term is usually applied to accounts that seem most removed from the realm of ordinary history. For instance, the story of Jesus's temptation in the wilderness in Matt. 4:1–11 might be classed as a myth, because it reports the direct engagement of one who is called the Son of God with Satan; these two supernatural beings converse and interact with each other, traversing the realm of human space to appear suddenly on the pinnacle of the temple and then on a very high mountain from which they can view all the kingdoms of the earth. Biblical scholars generally recognize that this account has literary features in common with stories that are typically classed as myths by literary critics.

M.A.P.

Opposite: An example of Nabatean architecture, carved into a sandstone mountain at Petra. Originally used as a temple to Dushara, the structure was reused by early Christians as a chapel.

N

Naamah (nay'uh-muh).

1 A daughter of Lamech and his wife Zillah, and the sister of Tubal-cain (Gen. 4:22).

2 One of the cities that was included in Judah's "inheritance," i.e., its portion of the promised land (1 Kings 14:21, 31).

3 An Ammonite wife of Solomon and the mother of Rehoboam, who succeeded Solomon to the throne of Judah (1 Kings 14:21, 31; 2 Chron. 12:13).

Naaman (nay'uh-muhn).

1 A son (Gen. 46:21) or grandson (Num. 26:40) of Benjamin; the ancestor of the Naamites.

2 A Syrian army officer cured of leprosy by the prophet Elisha (2 Kings 5). Naaman was the commander of the army of the king of Syria or Aram (Damascus) in the time of Elisha. Having learned of the reputation of the Samarian holy man from a captured Israelite girl who waited on his wife, Naaman resolved to go to Israel to seek a cure for his leprosy. He obtained permission from his king, who gave him a letter for the king of Israel asking that Naaman be healed. The letter, however, alarmed the Israelite king. Knowing that he lacked the power to heal Naaman, he suspected that the Aramean king was trying to provoke a quarrel. Eventually, however, Elisha heard of the king's concern and summoned Naaman to his house. When he arrived, he sent instructions that he should dip himself in the Jordan seven times. At first Naaman, who had expected the prophet to heal him in person, was angry and disappointed, retorting that Damascus had its own rivers, the Abana and Pharpar, that were better than any in Israel. His servants, however, persuaded him to follow Elisha's instructions. He washed in the Jordan and was healed, whereupon he returned to Elisha and vowed to sacrifice only to the Lord from that time on, requesting a load of the local soil so that he could worship the Israelite God in Damascus. Although Elisha explicitly refused any reward from Naaman, his servant Gehazi pursued the departing Aramean and deceitfully procured a gift in his master's name. Elisha, however, was aware of his servant's deceit and proclaimed that Naaman's leprosy would be transferred to Gehazi and his descendants forever.

The healing of Naaman's leprosy is also mentioned in Luke 4:27 in the context of a controversy between Jesus and the people of Nazareth. Jesus, who is regarded with suspicion because he has done great things in Capernaum but not in his hometown, cites "Naaman the Syrian" as an example of a foreigner who received divine help even when persons suffering from leprosy in Israel did not.   P.K.M.

Naamathite (nay'uh-muh-thit), the tribal or geographic identity of Job's "friend" Zophar (Job 2:11; 11:1; 20:1; 42:9). The designation may identify him as being from the town of Naamah. *See also* Naamah.

Naarah (nay'uh-ruh).

1 A city on the border of Ephraim near Jericho (Josh. 16:7); it is probably the same as Naaran (1 Chron. 7:28). It is tentatively identified as modern Tel el-Jisr, about three and a half miles northwest of Jericho.

2 One of the wives of Ashhur, a descendant of Judah (1 Chron. 4:5–6).

Nabal (nay'buhl; Heb., "fool"), a Calebite who acquired much wealth from raising sheep and goats in Carmel and who was married to a beautiful woman named Abigail. He is described as "surly and mean" (1 Sam. 25:3). Shortly after the death of Samuel, when David and his men were outlaws camped in the Wilderness of Paran, David sent messengers to Nabal requesting food for his soldiers (25:6–8). Nabal refused the request and insulted David by referring to him as a runaway slave who had rebelled against his master (25:10). As David gathered his men to avenge this impropriety, Abigail went out to meet David with provisions and with a plea for mercy. This resolved the immediate crisis, and David granted that Abigail's good sense had spared him from incurring bloodguilt through an act of vengeance. When Abigail reported all of this to her husband (the morning after a drunken feast), his "heart died within him" (25:37); ten days later God struck him dead. David blessed God and wooed Abigail (25:38–39). She became his wife and the mother of his son Chileab (25:40–42; 2 Sam. 3:3). *See also* Abigail.

                                                          F.R.M.

Nabatea (nab'uh-tee'uh), **Nabateans** (nab'uh-tee'uhnz), a region and a people east and southwest of the Dead Sea.

Origin and Language: Apparently originating in the northwestern Arabian Desert, the Nabateans seem to have moved into Edom about the sixth century BCE, as the Edomites themselves (later to become known as Idumeans) were migrating into Judah and the Negev. By the fourth

Finely decorated Nabatean "eggshell" pottery found at Moa in the Arabah Valley in modern Israel, first century CE.

century BCE, the Nabateans had occupied the southern part of Transjordan, the Wadi Arabah, and the southern Negev, nominally subject to Persian rule, but asserting their independence after the defeat of Persia by Alexander the Great and warding off a Greek attempt at conquest in 312 BCE.

Although apparently an Arabic people, the Nabateans soon came to speak a dialect of Aramaic, the lingua franca of the Persian Empire, and developed an elongated cursive version of the Aramaic uncial (i.e., capital letter) script. Apparently nomadic people originally, they developed a sedentary lifestyle as they settled into the region that came to be called Nabatea. They built new cities in the desert, including Petra, Acdat, Shivta, and Mamshit, and developed older Edomite and Moabite towns as fortresses to protect their far-flung caravan routes, the principal source of their wealth. To support the population of these desert cities, highly sophisticated water-gathering systems were invented, which allowed the agricultural exploitation of the Negev, in particular, on a scale unmatched until modern times.

Religion and Art: Nabatean religion was dominated by a supreme god, Dushara (perhaps meaning "He of Seir"), later identified with the Hellenistic Dionysus or Zeus, and by el-Uzza, later identified with the mother goddess Atargatis, symbolized by a dolphin. The most significant Nabatean temples have been found at Petra, Khirbet el-Tannur, and in the Wadi Ram in Jordan.

Artistically, the Nabateans excelled in the production of exquisitely painted "eggshell" pottery, the most beautiful of their time in the Levant. Their monumental architecture, a mélange of Greek and Roman classical styles, is remarkable for its scale and is displayed impressively in the city of Petra, carved out of rock in the middle of the Edomite desert.

Political History: Little is known of Nabatean political history from the end of the fourth century BCE until the reign of the first known king, Aretas I (ca. 169 BCE). One of the pretenders to the high-priesthood of Jerusalem, Jason, fled after a revolt by the Jews against the Seleucid (Syrian) king Antiochus IV eastward across the Jordan, where he was imprisoned by "Aretas the ruler of the Arabs" (2 Macc. 5:8). Aretas I is also mentioned in an inscription found at Elousa in the Negev along the Petra-Gaza road. The Nabateans also appear in 1 Macc. 5:25; 9:35 as friendly to Judas Maccabeus and his brother Jonathan.

The names, numbers, and times of reign of the following kings are disputed by scholars, but a possible reconstruction of the series is as follows. Civil war among the Seleucids following the death of Antiochus VII (129 BCE) appears to have allowed the expansion of Nabatean control. A Nabatean Malichus I is known only from coins, but an Erotimus (ca. 110–100 BCE) seems to have warred against both Egypt and Syria. In 96 BCE, Aretas II appears as an ally of Gaza against Alexander Jannaeus of Judea. Obodas I, son of Aretas, and then Rabel I continued hostilities against the Hasmonean and wrested control of parts of Moab and Gilead from him. Aretas III (87?–62 BCE), gained a considerable reputation throughout the area by defeating and killing the Seleucid Antiochus XII in battle. He was invited to become ruler of Coelesyria, and thus beame the first Nabatean to rule over Damascus, where he added to his name the title "Philhellene." In the civil conflict that followed the death of Queen Alexandra in Judah in 68 BCE, Aretas III, at the urging of the Idumean Antipater, entered the fray on behalf of her elder son, Hyrcanus II. Pompey's envoy Scaurus, however, negotiated a solution that sent Aretas back to Nabatea and gave Syria to Rome and Jerusalem to Aristobulus II, Alexandra's younger son. In 62 BCE, Scaurus invaded Nabatea, but, through Antipater's negotiations, retreated after Aretas's payment of three hundred talents in tribute.

Malichus II (47–30 BCE; or Malichus I, 62–30 BCE, by another reckoning) was involved by Antipater on the side of Julius Caesar against Pompey's supporters in 47 BCE in Egypt. Antipater married a Nabatean woman, Kufra or Kypros, who bore him Phasael, Joseph, Pheroras, Herod (the Great), and Salome.

When Herod took over Judea in 40 BCE, he appealed to Malichus for help against the invading Parthians, but was turned down. The Romans did help him and also forced Malichus to pay a tribute to Herod for favoring the Parthians. Cleopatra VII of Egypt, ever conniving, managed to set Herod and Malichus against each other in a way that would weaken them both.

Obodas II (or III; 30–9 BCE) was almost completely overshadowed by his brother Syllaeus, a plotter of the first rank. After Herod turned down Syllaeus's request for the hand of Herod's sister Salome, Syllaeus was sent by Obodas as guide for a disastrous Roman expedition under Aelius Gallus into Arabia and Ethiopia in 25–24 BCE. Later, in 9 BCE, Syllaeus afforded protection for bandits from Trachonitis who raided Herod's kingdom and refused to repay a loan of fifty talents he owed Herod. When Syllaeus departed for Rome, Herod attacked the robbers' stronghold, incurring Caesar's disfavor. When Obodas died, Syllaeus tried in Rome to overturn the succession of Aretas IV in his own favor and simultaneously plotted the assassination of Herod. The latter discovered the plot and sent Nicolaus of Damascus to Rome to plead his case; Syllaeus finished by losing his head.

Aretas IV (9 BCE–40 CE) gave his daughter in marriage to Herod's son Antipas in a mutual effort to heal Jewish–Nabatean relations. It was under the reign of this Aretas that Nabatean commerce and influence attained its peak, with Aretas himself even visiting Rome. About 28 CE, Antipas divorced his Nabatean wife to marry Herodias, eventually occasioning the execution of John the Baptist according to Matt. 14:1–12 and Mark 6:17–29. Aretas attacked Antipas's forces, defeating them in a skirmish, but bringing on the threat of Roman intervention in 37 CE. It was also under this Aretas that Paul's life was endangered in Damascus ca. 34–35 CE (2 Cor. 11:32–33; cf. Acts 9:23–25). During the first Jewish war with Rome, another Malichus (III? 40–70 CE) aided Titus against the Jews with a thousand cavalry and five thousand archers. *See also* Antipater; Arabia; Aretas IV; Herod; Maccabees; Seleucids.

Bibliography

Browning, Iain. *Petra.* Noyes, 1973.

Hammond, P. "New Light on the Nabataeans." *Biblical Archaeology Review* 7, 2 (March/April 1981): 22–41.

Lawlor, John I. *The Nabataeans in Historical Perspective.* Baker, 1974.   M.K.M.

Nablus (nab'luhs). *See* Neapolis.

Nabonidus (nab'uh-ni'duhs; Akkadian Nabuna'id, "Nabu is extolled"), the last of the Chaldean monarchs and last native king to rule Mesopotamia in antiquity. He held the throne from 556 to 539 BCE until displaced by the Achaemenid Cyrus II. Though the cuneiform documentation for Nabonidus is rich, the reconstruction of his personality and rule still lacks many details. He seems to have been at once a military leader of no small merit, a scholar interested in the history of his country, and a deeply religious person. Nabonidus was born in Harran, in northern Mesopotamia. The meaning of his Akkadian name would prove somewhat ironic in that he broke with traditional worship of the Babylonian god Nabu to become a passionate devotee of the moon god, Sin, whose sanctuary, Ehulhul in Harran, was restored by him and his mother, Adad-guppi. A strange fact of his life is his ten-year sojourn in the desert town of Teima, in the Arabian peninsula, while his son, Belshazzar, ruled Babylon in his stead. Nabonidus is not mentioned in the Bible, but Dan. 4, which speaks of the madness of Nebuchadnezzar, is possibly a reflection of a Babylonian propaganda piece against Nabonidus by the priests of Marduk in the city of Babylon objecting to the elevation of Sin of Harran at the expense of their deity. Aramaic scroll fragments from Qumran record a tale of a Jewish adviser to Nabonidus who encouraged him to worship the one Deity rather than the gods fashioned from metal and wood. *See also* Daniel; Daniel, book of; Nabopolassar.   D.B.W.

Nabopolassar (nab'uh-puh-las'uhr; Akkadian Nabû-apli-u'ur, "O Nabu, preserve the heir!"), the Babylonian founder of the Chaldean dynasty (626–539 BCE) and ruler of Babylon for twenty-one years (626–605 BCE). No mention is made of his father's name, which probably indicates that he was not of royal blood. In the early years of his reign, he battled the Assyrian occupiers of Babylonia. Eventually, in league with the Medes and possibly the Scythians, he conquered Nineveh in

612 BCE. Though Nabopolassar's name is not mentioned in the Bible, this defeat of the Assyrians is celebrated in the book of Nahum. Nabopolassar's son, Nebuchadnezzar II, defeated the Egyptians at Carchemish shortly before the death of his father (cf. Jer. 46:2; 2 Chron. 35:20). *See also* Nebuchadnezzar.   D.B.W.

Naboth (nay'both), the owner of a vineyard adjacent to a royal estate in Jezreel. The biblical narrative interprets the fall of King Ahab's dynasty as divine punishment for crimes committed against Naboth. As related in 1 Kings 21, Ahab, the king of Israel, wanted to buy Naboth's vineyard to transform it into a palace vegetable garden, but Naboth refused to sell it. Seeing that Ahab was despondent, Jezebel, his wife, wrote to the elders of Naboth's village demanding that Naboth be charged by two witnesses with cursing "God and the king" (Exod. 22:28; Deut. 17:6; 19:15). Under orders from the queen, the village elders found two "scoundrels" to do this, and Naboth, though fully innocent of the charge, was stoned to death by the villagers in accordance with the prescribed penalty for blasphemy (Lev. 24:16; cf. Deut. 17:2–7). Ahab hurried to Jezreel to confiscate Naboth's property, but there he encountered the prophet Elijah, who he realized had been sent by God. He asked, "Have you found me, O my enemy?" (1 Kings 21:20). Elijah answered, "I have found you," and then pronounced God's judgment: on account of what was done to Naboth, every male in Ahab's house would perish, and his dynasty would come to an end; as for Jezebel, she would be eaten by dogs in the territory of Jezreel (1 Kings 21:20–24). Ahab responded to his condemnation with penitence, so he was spared (21:27–29), but his son Joram was subsequently slain by the usurper Jehu, who cast his body on the plot that had belonged to Naboth and proclaimed Elijah's oracle fulfilled (2 Kings 9:24–26). Shortly afterwards Jezebel was murdered by Jehu and her body trampled by horses and then devoured by dogs, fulfilling Elijah's prediction (9:30–37).

Interpreters sometimes see a clash of monarchic power with traditional tribal values as underlying this story. In wanting to keep his vineyard, Naboth may be seen as upholding the ancient tribal ethos according to which land should remain within a family or tribe (Lev. 25:23; Num. 26:5–9). His reason for not selling is made clear, when he tells Ahab, "The LORD forbid that I should give you my ancestral inheritance!" (1 Kings 21:3). It is also notable that Ahab, though king, could not simply seize the land outright, but had to approach Naboth to buy it; further, he was officially powerless to overturn Naboth's decision not to sell. Jezebel has a different understanding of monarchy; she responds, incredulously, "Do you not govern Israel?" (21:7). Thus, the story seems to reflect debate over the limits of power and prerogative, especially as these applied to royalty during the time of the monarchy.   P.K.M.

Nadab (nay'dab).

1 The firstborn son of Aaron and Elisheba, and the brother of Abihu, Eleazar, and Ithamar (Exod. 6:23). As sons of the priest descended from Levi, the four were trained and ordained to be priests as well (28:1). Nadab and his brother Abihu seem to comprise a pair distinct from the younger pair of brothers (Eleazar and Ithamar). On one occasion, the two eldest brothers were invited to accompany Moses and their father, Aaron, to the summit of Mount Sinai, where, along with seventy elders representing the people, they saw God and ate and drank in God's presence (24:1, 9–11). Later, however, the two sealed their doom when they offered "illicit fire" (i.e., an unauthorized sacrifice) to the Lord during a sojourn at the foot of Mount Sinai. For offering what the Lord did not command, the brothers were consumed by divine fire (Lev. 10:1–2), leaving Eleazar and Ithamar to serve as the only lines of priests descended from their father (Num. 3:4). *See also* Aaron; Abihu.

2 The son of Jeroboam I who served as king of Israel for two years after the death of his father (ca. 901–900 BCE; 1 Kings 14:20; 15:23–31). He was assassinated by Baasha of Issachar, who then took the throne, putting an end to Jeroboam's dynasty (in fulfillment of a prophecy by Ahijah; cf. 14:1–20). During his reign, the Israelites laid siege to Gibbethon (15:27). F.R.M.

Nag Hammadi (nahg' huh-mah'dee), a town in

Upper Egypt near ancient Chenoboskion. In 1945 peasants discovered nearby a collection of texts that have shed important light on the religious history of the first Christian centuries. The find consists of thirteen papyrus volumes or codices, which are bound like modern books. Two codices, XII and XIII, are only partially preserved; the rest are complete, although the texts within them are often fragmentary.

Language and Date of the Texts: The forty-five works in the collection survive in Coptic, the form of late Egyptian written in Greek characters and used in early Christian Egypt. The dialect of most of the texts is Sahidic, although there are frequent deviations from its standard literary form. Two codices, I and X, as well as part of XI, are written in another dialect, Subachmimic. Several of the works are known to be Coptic translations of works that were originally written in Greek (e.g., fragments of Greek manuscripts of two of the texts found here, the *Gospel of Thomas* and the *Sophia of Jesus Christ*, were discovered elsewhere, at Oxyrhynchus, in Egypt). Dates on the papyri used as backing for the leather covers of the codices indicate that the books were transcribed in the fourth century. It is impossible, however, to know when the Greek texts that they translated were originally composed.

Contents: The library contains works of diverse genres, including sayings collections (*Gospel of Thomas* and *Sentences of Sextus*), homilies (*Gospel of Truth*), letters (*Epistle of Peter to Philip* and

Bound papyrus codices found at Nag Hammadi in 1945.

Treatise on the Resurrection), acts (*Acts of Peter and the Twelve Apostles*), expository treatises (*Tripartite Tractate, Marsanes, Allogenes,* and *Valentinian Exposition*), prayers (*Prayer of the Apostle Paul, Prayer of Thanksgiving,* and *Three Steles of Seth*), apocalypses (*Apocalypse of Paul, Apocalypse of Adam, Apocalypse of Peter,* and *First and Second Apocalypses of James*), riddling revelatory proclamations (*Thunder*), dialogues between Jesus and his disciples (*Apocryphon of John, Sophia of Jesus Christ, Dialogue of the Savior*), and an exegetical work (*Exegesis on the Soul*).

Diversity also characterizes the theology of the collection. Many works provide important primary evidence for Gnosticism. Some texts, such as the *Gospel of Truth, Tripartite Tractate,* and *Valentinian Exposition,* are clearly associated with the Christian gnostic school named for the influential second-century teacher Valentinus. Many other works are more difficult to place in the history of Gnosticism. Some texts (e.g., *Eugnostos, Apocalypse of Adam, Thunder*) are clearly gnostic, but not explicitly Christian. Others have only a superficial Christian veneer (e.g., *Sophia of Jesus Christ*). The hypothesis has been advanced that many of the works with little or no Christian content represent an early form of Gnosticism called by modern scholars "Sethian," after the prominence of Seth, the son of Adam, in some of the texts. Still other tractates are not directly related to Gnosticism. Among these are Hermetic works (*Asclepius 21–29, Discourse on the Eighth and the Ninth*), pagan sayings collections (*Sentences of Sextus*), and even a short selection from Plato's *Republic*. The library also includes some nongnostic Christian texts, such as the *Teachings of Silvanus* and possibly the *Authentic Teaching*.

Thus the collection does not represent any single Christian or non-Christian school or sect. Why the texts were assembled remains unclear. The library may have been collected by orthodox Christians for the purpose of combating heresies, although it may be more likely that the tractates represent a collection of works revered by an otherwise unknown group of heterodox fourth-century Christian monks in Upper Egypt.

Significance: The texts from Nag Hammadi have made important contributions to the study of early Christianity, particularly with regard to the development of Gnosticism. Their relevance for study of the NT itself is disputable and has no doubt sometimes been overstated. Works such as the *Gospel of Thomas, Dialogue of the Savior,* and the *Apocryphon of James* do provide new data for exploring early traditions concerning the sayings of Jesus, and in that sense they provide some basis for comparing what is found in the Gospels with streams of tradition that some scholars believe might have been independent of the Synoptic or Johannine traditions. *See also* apocryphal Christian writings; Gnosticism; Thomas, Gospel of.

Bibliography

Layton, Bentley. *The Gnostic Scriptures.* Doubleday, 1987.

Meyer, Marvin, ed. *The Nag Hammadi Scriptures.* HarperOne, 2007.

Perkins, Pheme. *Gnosticism and the New Testament.* Fortress, 1993.

Robinson, James M., ed. *The Nag Hammadi Library in English.* 3rd ed. Harper & Row, 1988.

H.W.A./M.A.P.

Nahalal (nay′huh-lal), a town of Zebulun (Josh. 19:15) assigned to the Levites (21:35), but shared by Canaanite inhabitants (Judg. 1:30; Nahalol) whom Zebulun was unable to expel. The location is uncertain, but it may be modern Tell en-Nahl on the Kishon River near modern Haifa.

Nahaliel (nuh-hay′lee-uhl; Heb., "torrent valley of God"), a stopping point of the Israelites (Num. 21:19) during the wilderness wandering in the Transjordan. It is identified with modern Wadi Zerqa Main, which discharges into the Dead Sea north of the Arnon River.

Nahash (nay′hash; Heb., "serpent"), an Ammonite king who besieged Jabesh-gilead and thus provided the Benjaminite Saul an opportunity to solidify his kingship over Israel (1 Sam. 11). Perhaps this is the same Ammonite king who was kind to David (2 Sam. 10:2) and whose sons Hanun (10:4) and Shobi (17:27–29) had contact with David.

Nahath (nay′hath; Heb., "descent").

1 The son of Reuel and grandson of Esau; he was a chieftain of the Edomites (Gen. 36:13, 17; 1 Chron. 1:37).

2 A Levite belonging to the Kohath line; he was a grandson of Elkanah (1 Chron. 6:26), but elsewhere he seems to be identified as Toah (cf. 6:34) or Tohu (1 Sam. 1:1). *See also* Elkanah.

3 A Levite who shared the responsibility of collecting the temple offering during the reign of Hezekiah (2 Chron. 31:13).   D.R.B.

Nahor (nay′hor).

1 A descendant of Shem, and the son of Serug and father of Terah (Gen. 11:22–25; 1 Chron. 1:26; Luke 3:34).

2 The son of Terah and the brother of Abraham (Gen. 11:26–27; Josh. 24:2) who married Milcah (Gen. 11:29). This Nahor, grandson of 1 above, was the parent of twelve sons born to his wife Milcah and concubine Reumah (Gen. 22:20–24). Those sons became founders of twelve tribes equivalent to the twelve tribes of Israel. The tribes descended from sons born to Milcah were probably the subsequent Aramean tribes living north and east of the Levant. The tribes descended from sons born to Reumah were considered less closely tied to Israel and probably lived north of Damascus. It may have been to this territory that Abraham subsequently sent his servant ("to the city of Nahor," 24:10) to obtain a wife for Isaac. In addition to the marriage of Isaac to Nahor's granddaughter Rebekah (14:15, 24), the relationship of these tribes is further indicated by their worship of a common God (31:53).

3 A city ("the city of Nahor," Gen. 24:10) mentioned frequently in the Mari texts that was located east of the upper reaches of the Balikh River, a northern tributary of the Euphrates. This would put the location in what is now southern Turkey or northern Syria, probably south and east of Haran (Gen. 29:4–5).   R.S.B.

Nahshon (nah′shon), the son of Amminadad and the leader of the tribe of Judah during the wilderness wandering (Num. 1:7; 10:14). His sister Elisheba married Aaron (Exod. 6:23). Nahshon is also an ancestor of David and, so, is listed in the genealogy of Jesus (Ruth 4:20; Matt. 1:4; Luke 3:32).

Nahum (nay′hum), **book of,** the seventh in the Book of the Twelve in the Prophets section, or Nevi'im, of the Tanakh (Jewish Bible), known as the Minor Prophets in the Christian OT. Very little is known about the prophet Nahum or the location of his hometown, Elkosh (1:1). The name Nahum comes from the Hebrew word meaning "to comfort"; hence Nahum is the "comforter." Addressed to the people of Judah, the book of Nahum was seen as a comfort to an oppressed people.

Contents: The main thrust of the book is a series of oracles against Nineveh, the capital of the Assyrian Empire. The Assyrian Empire had dominated the Mesopotamian landscape for over a century. The Assyrians were notorious for being excessively violent in their conquest, using brute strength to dominate. They had destroyed the northern nation of Israel and subjugated Judah. It is from this context that Nahum's prophecy of Nineveh's doom was a comfort to Judah. The book contains passages of encouragement for the oppressed people of Judah, reminding them that God is in control and will not forget those who take refuge in God.

The book begins with the introduction of the prophet (1:1). Nahum is the only book of prophecy in the OT to call itself a "book" or "scroll" (1:1). The book then moves into a psalm of God's wrath, which draws heavily upon imagery of the divine warrior. Most scholars believe this poem to be a fragment of an original acrostic poem (a poem in which the first line begins with first letter of the Hebrew alphabet, second line with second letter, etc.). Nah. 1 finishes with a series of alternating promises of salvation and destruction. Nah. 2 is an oracle directed to Nineveh itself, portraying all the terrors of warfare. Thus, God is responsible for the destruction of Nineveh, even if it is carried out by the Babylonians and Medes. Nah. 3 is a final prophecy in the form of a taunt song pronounced over Nineveh. Like the book of Jonah, Nahum ends in a question, which has been seen by many scholars to connect it thematically with the book of Habakkuk, which follows it. The relationship of these two books has often been seen to be a chiastic pattern.

OUTLINE OF CONTENTS

Nahum

I. Introduction (1:1)
II. The majesty of God in judgment and mercy (1:2–15)
   A. The jealous warrior God (1:2–8)
   B. Tidings of salvation and destruction (1:9–15)
III. The capture and destruction of Nineveh (2:1–13)
IV. The taunt and shame of Nineveh (3:1–19)

Background: Nahum was written after the destruction of Thebes (No Amon) in Egypt by Ashurbanipal in 663 BCE (3:8–10), but before the destruction of Nineveh in 612 BCE by the Babylonians and Medes. This places the approximate date for the book between 663 and 612 BCE. Some scholars argue for an earlier date (around 650 BCE), while others think it was written shortly before the fall of Nineveh.

Themes: The themes of comfort and judgment dominate the book of Nahum. Many scholars believe that the oppressed people of Judah would have been comforted by the knowledge that their oppressor would be destroyed. Ahoga maintains that the book of Nahum shows God's anger at those great powers that oppress; it shows God's control over events and governments and teaches that God will bring down those who destroy others with their power. Many scholars argue that the tone of the book is vengeful and connect it with a surge of nationalism in the late seventh century BCE.

Interpretive Issues: O'Brien thinks that the language and imagery of Nahum create and foster destructive gender roles and even condone rape of the enemy (cf. 2:6–7; 3:5). In addition, it is often remarked that Judah's behavior is never criticized

AN ALTERNATIVE CHIASTIC OUTLINE
FOR TWO BOOKS READ AS ONE

The Books of Nahum and Habakkuk

A   Hymn of theophany (Nah. 1)
B   Taunt song against Nineveh (Nah. 2–3)
C   The problem of theodicy (Hab. 1)
B'   Taunt song against the "wicked one" (Hab. 2)
A'   Hymn of theophany (Hab. 3)

within the book, further connecting it with a nationalist movement against the oppressive Assyrians. Sweeney says that criticizing Nahum for not condemning Judah takes too narrow a view of the prophetic role. Prophets are called to speak on behalf of the Lord, not to simply critique their own people. Gottwald argues that a "nationalistic" interpretation misses the nature of the text and its genre. He claims that Nahum makes moral judgments on Nineveh (3:1, 3:19). Furthermore, he argues that nations such as Assyria stand under God's judgment regardless of the attitude or conduct of other nations, in this case Judah, and that it would be against the nature of prophetic criticism of foreign nations to impose Judah's repentance as a condition for Nineveh's fall.

There is some disagreement over how much of the book is original to Nahum. Most scholars believe that Nahum is the source of most of the book, with the possible exception of the semi-acrostic psalm in 1:2–8. Childs argues that this psalm was placed in the book as an interpretive key to understanding the oracles of destruction that follow. He claims the psalm shows the destruction of Nineveh arises out of God's nature as a jealous God and transforms the particular prophecies about Nineveh into eschatological claims.

Bibliography
Ahoga, C. A. "Nahum." *Africa Bible Commentary.* Zondervan, 2006. Pp. 1059–63.
Bandstra, Barry L. *Reading the Old Testament: Introduction to the Hebrew Bible.* 4th ed. Wadsworth, 2009.
Childs, Brevard S. *Introduction to the Old Testament as Scripture.* Fortress, 1979.
Gottwald, Norman K. *The Hebrew Bible: A Socio-Literary Introduction.* Fortress, 1985.
O'Brien, Julia M. *Nahum.* Sheffield, 2002.
Sweeney, Marvin A. *The Twelve Prophets.* Vol. 2, *Micah, Nahum, Habakkuk, Zephaniah, Haggai, Zechariah, Malachi.* Liturgical, 2000.   B.B.

nails.

1 Fingernails, referred to twice in the Bible. First, Moses instructed the Israelites that if someone captures a beautiful woman in battle and takes her home to be his wife, he should shave her head and pare her nails, then allow her to mourn for her lost family for one month before becoming her husband (Deut. 21:10–13). Second, when Nebuchadnezzar went mad, according to the book of Daniel, he ate grass like an ox and lived apart from human society until his hair grew as long as bird feathers and his nails became like talons (4:33).

2 Iron nails for fastening construction materials together (1 Chron. 22:3). Archaeological studies show that wooden pegs were replaced by copper and bronze nails in construction projects ca. 3000 BCE, but the introduction of iron technology (ca. 1200 BCE) made much harder nails available and opened the possibility of multistoried buildings. Metaphorically, the act of fastening things with nails could be used as an image for security and relative (or supposed) permanence (Eccles. 12:11; Isa. 41:7; Jer. 10:4). Nails were sometimes used for crucifixions, though bodies were often simply tied to the crosses by ropes. Although the Synoptic Gospels do not mention Jesus being nailed to the cross, such an understanding of Jesus's crucifixion underlies Thomas's declaration in John's Gospel about the risen Jesus: "Unless I see the mark of the nails in his hands, and put my finger in the mark of the nails and my hand in his side, I will not believe" (20:25; cf. Luke 24:39).   R.S.B.

Nain (nayn), a village identified with modern Nein, six miles southeast of Nazareth at the foot of Mount Moreh in the Valley of Jezreel (cf. Judg. 7:1). Here Jesus raised a widow's only son from the dead (Luke 7:11–17). According to Luke's Gospel, Jesus encountered the funeral procession as he was entering the city; the boy's body was being carried on a bier out of the city, accompanied by a large crowd. Jesus had compassion on the dead boy's mother, stopped the procession, and raised the boy from the dead. He sat up and began to speak, and Jesus "gave him to his mother" (7:15). News of the event spread throughout all Judea as the people proclaimed, "A great prophet has risen among us!" and "God has looked favorably on (God's) people" (7:16).   M.A.P.

Naioth (nay′yoth), a place in or near Ramah in the tribal area of Benjamin, a short distance north of Jerusalem, where David, fleeing Saul, took refuge with Samuel and the prophets associated with him (1 Sam. 19:18). When Saul's messengers were sent to Naioth to take David, they became imbued with the prophetic spirit and fell into a frenzy. Saul followed, and the same thing happened to him; he fell into a prophetic frenzy, stripped out of his clothes, and lay naked on the ground for a day and a night (19:20–23). This event inspired the coining of a popular saying that may have been used in a variety of contexts: "Is Saul also among the prophets?" (19:24).

name of Jesus, a shorthand expression for the power and presence of the risen Lord Jesus Christ, especially in the book of Acts. At a literal level, the NT records that Jesus is given his name

by an angel. The name means "God saves," and it is deemed especially appropriate for one though whom God will save people from sin (Matt. 1:21). It was actually a common name, however, the Greek equivalent of Joshua. Other people in the NT besides Jesus of Nazareth are said to have been named Jesus (e.g., Jesus Barabbas in Matt. 27:16–17; "Jesus who is called Justus" in Col. 4:11; cf. "Jesus son of Sirach," the author of the book of Sirach).

In the life of the early church, however, the "name of Jesus" took on special significance. First, in the book of Acts, people do things in the name of Jesus that Jesus himself would do, were he still physically present on earth. In the name of Jesus they speak and teach (4:17–18; 5:28, 40; 9:27–28), perform signs and wonders (4:30), exorcize demons (5:41; cf. 9:13–17), and heal the sick (3:6, 16; 4:10). The point of these passages seems to be that the people who speak or act in the name of Jesus do so as his representatives and with his authority. Beyond this, however, readers are expected to believe that it is actually Jesus saying and doing these things through his representatives; there is no real difference in Acts between Peter's pronouncement that someone is healed "in the name of Jesus" (3:6) and his saying, "Jesus Christ heals you" (9:34).

Second, in the book of Acts, people receive divine benefits through the name of Jesus. Salvation is in the name of Jesus (4:12), and forgiveness of sins is received through the name of Jesus (10:43; 22:16). These benefits are received by calling on the name of Jesus (22:16; cf. 2:21), having faith in the name of Jesus (3:16), and being baptized in the name of Jesus (2:38; 8:16; 10:48; 19:5; 22:16).

Finally, in Acts, the name of Jesus seems to stand for the person who bore it and to somehow mediate his presence. The "good news of the name of Jesus" is the good news of Jesus (8:12); to "invoke the name of Jesus" is to invoke Jesus (9:14, 21); to "praise the name of Jesus" is to praise Jesus (19:17); to "oppose the name" is to oppose Jesus (26:9); to "suffer for the name" is to suffer for Jesus (5:41; 9:16). In all of these cases, the *name* is essentially identified with the *person;* the one essential difference is that the name of Jesus remains present and accessible in a way that the literal person Jesus does not (cf. 1:11; 3:20–21). A similar point seems to be made in the Gospels in passages where Jesus uses the expression "my name" to refer to his presence and power in the community (Matt. 10:22; 18:5, 20; 24:5, 9; Mark 9:37, 39; 13:13; Luke 9:48; 21:12, 17; John 14:13, 14; 15:16, 21; 16:23–24, 26; cf. Matt. 19:29; Mark 13:6; Luke 21:8). Acts 9:15–16 quotes the risen Jesus using the expression "my name" in this way as well.

This motif was not altogether novel. In the Hebrew Bible, the name of the Lord can stand for the power and presence of God. Thus, in Exod. 9:16 (quoted in Rom. 9:17), God tells Pharaoh, "I have let you live: to show you my power, and to make my name resound through all the earth." Obedient

Israelites would be "called by the name of the LORD" (Deut. 28:10), and God's messengers spoke in God's name (2 Sam. 12:7). Likewise, representatives of a human authority spoke in that person's name (1 Sam. 25:5; Esther 3:12). It is often thought, however, that early Christianity may have developed this idea with regard to the name of Jesus in a way that surpassed the mere representational aspect—the name mediates Christ's presence in a manner thought to convey real power. Thus, Acts records a story of non-Christians trying to utilize the inherent power of that name without authorization. The sons of Sceva attempt to drive out a demon in the name of "the Jesus whom Paul proclaims" (19:13). This ends disastrously for them, as the demon responds, "Jesus I know, and Paul I know; but who are you?" (19:15). The story seems to represent an effort to encourage Christians to distinguish their belief in the power of the name of Jesus from pagan belief in magical words or formulas; at the very least, the name can only be used by those whom Jesus has authorized to use it.

The Letters of Paul also make some reference to the name of Jesus, though he prefers the expression "the name of our [the] Lord Jesus Christ" (1 Cor. 1:2, 10; 6:11; Eph. 5:20; 2 Thess. 3:6; cf. 1 Cor. 5:4; Col. 3:17; 2 Thess. 1:2). Believers call upon this name (1 Cor. 1:2), give thanks in this name (Eph. 5:20) and are justified in this name (1 Cor. 6:11). Paul passes judgment in this name (1 Cor. 5:3–4) and offers commands in this name (2 Thess. 3:6). Indeed, believers are to do everything in the name of the Lord Jesus (Col. 3:17). Finally, Paul says that the day will come when "at the name of Jesus, every knee should bend, . . . and every tongue should confess that Jesus Christ is Lord" (Phil. 2:10–11).

M.A.P.

names. Biblical narratives preserve a wide variety of personal and geographic names. These are augmented by geographic and genealogical lists in early and late sources, which, when handled critically, can provide much accurate information. Another valuable source of Israelite proper names is the corpus of ancient Israelite inscriptions, preserving hundreds of names, some not attested in the Bible. Most important for the earliest periods are ostraca and stamp seals. Comparative studies of names, furthermore, seek to catalogue those names that are found in ancient Semitic languages most closely related to Hebrew, including Eblaite, Amorite, Ugaritic, Phoenician, Ammonite, Moabite, Edomite, Aramaic, and later Arabian dialects. Akkadian (Semitic) and Egyptian names, although preserved in great numbers, are less similar in style and form to Israelite names, but they have also proven beneficial in understanding difficult and foreign names that occur in the Bible. For the Second Temple period, a number of names have been catalogued as appearing in Aramaic, Hebrew, and Greek inscriptions found on seals, tombs, ossuaries, ostraca, and papyrus documents. These augment the names found in the NT and contemporary Jewish writings.

Personal Names: The majority of Israelite names, and ancient Semitic names in general, had a readily understandable meaning. That parents consciously chose a child's name is implied by the content of these names, many of which are translatable sentences.

Compound names, usually consisting of two elements, are attested in a variety of grammatical constructions, especially statements, which occur in nominal, adjectival, and verbal forms. Interrogative and imperative constructions are infrequent. Most compound proper names (PNs) are theophoric, containing a divine name (DN) or title. The most common DN in Israelite PNs was a form of the Tetragrammaton YHWH (sometimes written with vowels as Yahweh or Jehovah; but rendered in some English Bibles and here as "the LORD"). The next most attested element was the generic 'el, meaning "god" (El was also the DN of the head of the Canaanite pantheon). Titles such as 'adon ("lord"), ba'al ("master," also a Canaanite DN), melek ("king"), zur ("rock") as well as kinship terms like 'ab ("father"), 'akh ("brother"), and 'am ("relative/[paternal] uncle") were sometimes used instead of a DN. Confusion can arise, however, regarding elements used both generically and as DNs, such as ba'al, 'el, and several others; or with kinship terms, which might be associated with a deceased relative rather than a deity.

Different types of compound PNs include: names expressing parents' recognition of divine assistance, such as Mattaniah ("gift of the LORD"), Elnathan/Nathanael ("God has given [this child]"), and Shemaiah ("the LORD has heard [the parents' prayer]"); names expressing parental desires for the child, such as Jeberechiah ("may the LORD bless [this child]"), Ezekiel ("may God strengthen [this child]"), and Jehiel ("may God preserve [this child]"); names expressing parents' convictions, such as Elijah/Joel ("the LORD is [my] God"), Uzziel ("God is my strength"), Adoniram ("my lord is exalted"), and Ahimelek ("my [divine] brother is king"); and names reflecting circumstances at the child's birth, such as Ben-oni ("son of my sorrow," Gen. 35:16–20), and Ichabod ("where is the glory?" 1 Sam. 4:19–22). Names like Menachem ("comforter") and Eliashub ("God restores") may suggest that a newborn was regarded as a substitute for a deceased family member.

The elements of a compound name could also be employed singly, making a shortened (hypocoristic) form, as in Mattan, Nathan, Uzzi, etc. There were other types of simple or one-element PNs too. Some were originally animal or plant names, like Caleb ("dog"), Deborah ("bee"), Jonah ("dove"), Tamar ("palm tree"), and Allon ("oak"). Other PNs reflected circumstances at birth, such as Haggai ("[born on] a festival day"), Becorath ("firstborn"), and Jacob ("heel-grabber"); physical characteristics, as with Esau ("hairy"), Zuar ("little one"), and Laban ("white [fair-skinned]"); or qualities hoped for, as in Amon ("reliable"). Evidence available from the NT and contemporary Jewish writings indicates that these types of simple and compound PNs continued in use, but with a trend toward diminutive, hypocoristic forms of the latter. There was also a greater tendency toward adopting a foreign name or a name showing foreign influence.

The use of patronyms (surnames that serve to distinguish someone from others with the same name) were common among ancient Semites, as is amply attested in the Bible and in Israelite inscriptions. Well-known biblical examples include Joshua son of Nun and Simon Bar-Jona ("son of Jonah"). Other forms of distinct identification included geographical identifications, as in Goliath of Gath and Jesus of Nazareth, as well as professional identifications, such as Simon the tanner and Shimshai the scribe. During the Second Temple period, the phenomenon of "double names" became more common—as Jews interacted with Gentiles, they often had a Hebrew name and another non-Hebrew name for use in Gentile contexts. Thus, Hadassah was known to the Persians as Esther (Esther 2:7), and Saul was known to Gentiles as Paul (Acts 13:9).

Symbolic Meaning of Personal Names in Biblical Narratives: The biblical authors often seize upon meaning inherent in certain PNs and incorporate that into the narrative. At times, one may suspect that the narrative has determined the name, rather than the other way around. It seems unlikely that any parents would have named their child Nabal ("fool"), but the only biblical character said to possess that name lives up to it in the only narrative that has been preserved concerning him (1 Sam. 25; esp. 25:25). On the other hand, there is no doubt that Jesus ("the LORD saves") actually did bear the name attributed to him in the Bible. Still, the NT authors were quick to seize upon that happy coincidence (or, indeed, to maintain it was no coincidence: an angel told Joseph to name him this, because "he will save his people from their sins," Matt. 1:21; cf. Luke 1:31). Names are sometimes allowed to do double duty with both literal and metaphorical application. Jacob was supposedly named "heel-grabber," because he literally was holding his twin brother Esau's heel when he came out of the womb (Gen. 25:26), but subsequent narratives portray him as living up to the connotations of such a name in multiple occurrences (he is often portrayed as manipulative and ambitious, trying to "get the upper hand," to use a comparable modern idiom). Likewise, Moses is named after a word that means "draw out," because he was literally pulled out of the Nile by Pharaoh's daughter (Exod. 2:10), but he lives up to this name in ways she could not have anticipated by becoming the one who draws Israel out of Egypt.

Certain prophets drew upon this tradition of symbolic names by giving names to their children that offered prophetic statements to their audiences. Thus Isaiah named his children Shear-jashub ("A remnant shall return," 7:3); Maher-shalal-hash-baz ("The spoil speeds, the prey hastens," 8:1–4), and possibly Immanuel ("God with us," 7:14).

Hosea likewise named his daughter Lo-ruhama ("Not pitied," 1:6) and his son Lo-ammi ("Not my people," 1:8), because he said God would no longer have pity on the house of Israel and that its people were no longer the people of God.

The Process of Naming: The means through which names are given is sometimes important in and of itself in the Bible. In the garden of Eden, God brings all of the animals to the man "to see what he would call them, and whatever the man called every living creature, that was its name" (Gen. 2:19). This probably implies the special authority and responsibility that human beings will have within God's creation. The fact that Man also names Woman (2:23) and Adam names Eve (3:20) has been taken as an indication of the authority and responsibility that men are to have in ruling over women (cf. 3:16), though it is the woman who subsequently names at least two of their sons (4:1, 25). In fact, there is no consistent pattern in the Bible to which the parent names the child. Out of forty-six instances in which the person who names the child is specified, the father gives the name eighteen times (e.g., Gen. 5:3; Exod. 18:3–4) and the mother gives the name twenty-five times (e.g., Gen. 19:37–38; 1 Sam. 1:20). The remaining instances are anomalies. Pharaoh's daughter names Moses (Exod. 2:10), and the women friends of Naomi name Ruth and Boaz's son Obed (Ruth 4:17). In the case of John the Baptist, the mother declares what the name should be, but this must be confirmed by the father (Luke 1:59–63).

With regard to the process of naming, special significance may be accorded to two phenomena that occur only sporadically. First, in remarkably few instances, God is said to select the name and to communicate it to the parents via an angel or some other medium. God chooses the name Isaac ("laughter"), because both Abraham and Sarah laughed when his miraculous birth was announced. In the NT, God chooses names for John the Baptist (Luke 1:13; cf. 1:59–63) and Jesus (Matt. 1:21; Luke 1:31). A second phenomenon is that of name changes. Changing a person's name displayed the power of the changer and the allegiance owed by the one whose name was changed. Names changed by God include Abram, changed to Abraham (Gen. 17:5); Sarai, to Sarah (17:15); and Jacob, to Israel (32:28). Names changed by a human authority include Eliakim, to Jehoiakim (2 Kings 23:34); Mattaniah, to Zedekiah (24:17); and Daniel, to Belteshazzar (Dan. 1:6, 7). Though Jesus does not change people's names outright, he is said to bestow nicknames on people. According to Mark 3:16–17, Jesus gave the nickname Peter (Gk., "rock") to his disciple Simon and the nickname Boanerges (Aramaic, "sons of thunder") to his disciples James and John. Saul's name is not changed to Paul in the NT, as is sometimes thought; rather, this individual used both names throughout his adult life, Saul in his interactions with Jews, and Paul in his interactions with Gentiles.

Geographic Names: Although many of the features discussed in relation to PNs apply to geographic names (GNS) as well, the GNS are more difficult to treat. Some are very old and their meanings are obscure. The names of many cities, rivers, and mountains preserved in the Bible, though Semitic for the most part, were often in existence before the Israelites entered Canaan and were merely adopted by the Israelites. This probably holds for Jerusalem, Megiddo, Mount Hermon, and the Jordan River. Other GNS were changed by the Israelites, as in the case of Laish becoming Dan (Judg. 18:29), while new sites received new GNS. Inferences from biblical GNS concerning Israelite religion are limited, since Israelite GNS follow the basic typology of pre-Israelite Caananite GNS, making it impossible to discern whether the names were Israelite creations or merely adoptions. The NT similarly reflects the continuation of many GNS, the replacement of others (e.g., Herod's renaming of Samaria as Sebaste), and the formation of entirely new ones.

As with PNS, GNS of both simple and compound form existed. However "sentence" GNS are only infrequently attested in the Bible, as are theophoric GNS. Examples of the latter include Beth-el ("house/temple of God/El"), Beth-dagon ("house/temple of Dagon"), and Baal-hazor ("lord/Baal of Hazor"; this latter type was usually short for a fuller form with "beth" in the first position). "Beth," with the meaning "house/place," also occurred in nontheophoric GNS, as in Beth-marcaboth ("house/place of chariots") and Bethlehem ("house/place of bread/food"). Other compound GNS contain an element referring to the environment, such as *be'er* ("well"), as in Beer-sheba; *'en* ("spring") as in En-gedi; *'abel* ("meadow") as in Abel-meholah; and *'emeq* ("valley") as in Beth-emek.

Many simple GNS also referred to natural features, including Ramah and Ramoth ("height[s]"), Gibeah and Gibeon ("hill"), Horeb and Negev ("dry"). Names based on structures include Mizpah ("watchtower"), Succoth ("booths"), Geder ("wall/enclosure"), and Gath ("wine press"). GNS were also sometimes associated with individuals, as with Nobah (wife of the man who named the city, Num. 32:42) and Dan (ancestor of the tribe that settled in the city, Judg. 18:29), or with an event, as with Bochim ("weepers," Judg. 2:4–5) and Ebenezer ("stone of help," 1 Sam. 7:12). Plant and animal names were employed as GNS too, such as Tamar ("palm tree"), Shimir ("thorn"), En-rimmon ("spring of the pomegranate"), Ephron ("gazelle"), Akrabbim ("scorpions"), and En-gedi ("spring of the goat").

Value of Studying Names: The value of these ancient names for biblical studies is found in the variety of cultural clues they provide. For example, theophoric PNS indicate which deities were important to various societies in the polytheistic ancient Near East. The majority of Israelite theophoric PNS either contained specific reference to "the LORD" or use the more generic *'el* ("god," "God"). Still, the names of Israelites mentioned as living between the exodus and the Babylonian exile (thirteenth

through early sixth centuries BCE, excluding those whose sole attestation occurs in Chronicles, Ezra, or Nehemiah) reveal that only a small percentage of the population of ancient Israel had PNS containing a foreign DN, even during times of proclaimed apostasy. PNS in Israelite epigraphic sources corroborate this point with similar evidence. Theophoric PNS are also a valuable guide to qualities associated with a given deity. PNS containing "the LORD" as the DN depict the deity as strong, glorious, noble, righteous, and gracious; king, father, brother, and light; and as one who creates, gives, strengthens, remembers, knows, blesses, protects, saves, judges, and restores.

Name studies also help to chart various cultural trends, such as preferred grammatical forms of names in different periods; similar categories of GNS used by pre-Israelite Canaanites and Israelites; the small number of theophoric PNS attested for women in the Bible; more frequent use of kinship terms and certain divine titles in PNS through the time of the united monarchy (ca. 1004–926 BCE); the faddish popularity of certain PNS; the increased foreign influence on names by the NT period; the growth in prominence of papponymy (naming a child after his grandfather) from the Persian period (late sixth century BCE) on; and the preference in the Second Temple period for PNS previously borne by biblical or national heroes over ones that had descriptive meaning applicable to the particular child. Luke 1:59–61 suggests a tradition of naming a son after his father or at least some other relative, though this is not widely attested elsewhere.   D.M.P./M.A.P.

names of God in the Hebrew Bible. The names and titles used for God in the Hebrew Bible reflect Israel's setting in the ancient Near East, the theological variety of biblical traditions, and the social settings and institutions that shaped religious life. Some of the names and titles applied to Israel's God are known to have been used for other deities as well. The Israelites believed that the God who had elected them, entered into community with them, and shaped their destiny demanded their undivided obligation and loyalty; nevertheless, Hebrew theologians found justification within that perspective to transform appellations and epithets applied to other deities into designations appropriate for the God of Israel.

YHWH (Yahweh, Jehovah, "the LORD"): The most important name for God in the Hebrew Bible is the Tetragrammaton, a series of the four consonants YHWH, traditionally written without vowels, because God's name is not to be pronounced aloud. This occurs 6,828 times and is found in all writings except Ecclesiastes, Esther, and the Song of Solomon. Its short forms also occur in many personal names (e.g., Isa*iah*, Jerem*iah*, *Jon*athan). Supposedly, the actual pronunciation of the name was known at one time, but was lost during the postexilic period. The typical practice, at any rate, was for those who read from the scriptures aloud to pronounce the word *adonai* (Heb., "my

Lord") wherever the Tetragrammaton was written. Eventually, the vowels for the word Adonai were combined with the consonants YHWH to remind readers to pronounce the word as Adonai. In Christian circles, this gave way to writing and pronouncing the divine name. In the Middle Ages the name was often written and pronounced "Jehovah" (a word that occurs a handful of times in the KJV). In the modern era, "Yahweh" has come to be regarded as the preferred rendering, and this is what appears in the JB and NJB. Most English Bibles, however—including the KJV, RSV, NIV, and NRSV—use the expression "the LORD" (in large and small capital letters) where Hebrew manuscripts have YHWH.

Gen. 4:26 traces use of the name YHWH to primeval times, but other texts present Moses as the first to receive the knowledge of this name (Exod. 3:14; 6:2–3). In these two passages, the deity is specifically identified with the God of the ancestors (3:13, 15; 6:3–4). The meaning of the name probably derives from the imperfect form of the Hebrew verb "to be." In Exod. 3:14, God responds to Moses with the ambiguous statement, "I am who I am" (or, "I will be what I will be"). This connection of the name with the Hebrew root of the verb "to be" appears to connote divine mystery (cf. Gen. 32:22–32) and freedom as well as a sense of God's presence. Another interpretation connects YHWH with the Hebrew Hiphil (causative) verbal stem of the root "to be" and thus understands God's name to mean "The one who causes to be what exists [or happens]"; i.e., YHWH is creator and ruler of history. In any case, the contexts in which the name is revealed (Exod. 3:14; 6:2–3) both involve an anticipation of liberation from slavery and guidance into the land of Canaan.

YHWH Sabaoth ("LORD of Hosts," "LORD Almighty"): This compound name occurs 279 times in the Hebrew Bible. Sabaoth derives from a Hebrew word (sebaot) that may refer to earthly hosts (i.e., armies) or to heavenly hosts comprised of stars, angels, and even deities subordinated to YHWH. Thus, this name may have originated in contexts of holy war and could have expressed a polemic against astral cults: YHWH rules the heavenly armies. The name was eventually understood as a plural of intensity, "LORD Almighty," or an abstract plural, "powerfulness," thus neutralizing the existence of the celestial gods. The LXX captures this more abstract meaning in its translation, "Lord Almighty" (cf. Jth. 4:13; 8:13; 16:5, 17; Bar. 3:1, 4; 2 Cor. 6:18).

Elohim ("God"): The most common generic name for God in the Hebrew Bible, occurring almost 2,600 times is Elohim, a plural form of 'el or 'eloah, Hebrew words for "a god." On occasion, the plural 'elohim can mean "gods" (e.g., Exod. 20:3). When the word is used for Israel's God, however, it is employed as a proper noun that takes singular verbs and is modified by singular adjectives (thus, a word literally meaning "gods" becomes one name for the God of Israel). Unlike the term 'el, 'elohim is not found in other Semitic languages.

Material in the Pentateuch that is ascribed to the E source (i.e., the Elohist) uses this name to refer to God from the time of the ancestors (Gen. 15) to the call of Moses in Exod. 3, at which point Elohim is identified with "the Lord." Material ascribed to P (the Priestly source) uses Elohim for God from creation (Gen. 1) to the covenant of Abraham (Gen. 17). Although the name was used in most traditions, periods, and regions, it was especially favored in northern Israel.

Eloah ("God"): A second generic term for deity in the Bible is the Hebrew word 'eloah, which means simply "a god," but, like 'elohim, is sometimes used as a name for the God of Israel. It is found only fifty-seven times, forty-one of which occur in Job. Because Job and his three "comforters" are non-Israelites, the author of the book may have used this generic word for God to avoid the specific Israelite conceptions of covenant and salvation history associated with the name YHWH ("the LORD"). As an example of wisdom literature, the book of Job speaks of creation in a universal sense and addresses suffering as a problem common to humanity.

El ("God"): A third generic term for deity, the noun 'el (Heb., "a god"), occurs some 238 times in the Bible (including compounds). This was the common Semitic word for deity in ancient Near Eastern cultures. Any divine being might be designated by this generic term. In texts discovered at Ugarit (modern Ras-Shamra), El is also used as the personal name of the head of the pantheon. As creator and father of the gods, El possessed the authority of the divine decree that ordered the world of gods and human beings. The worship of El was, thus, a major component of both Canaanite and Israelite ancestral religions. In the settlement of Canaan, the tribes of Israel began to assimilate Canaanite religious centers and to associate their religious traditions with "the LORD," the one who had liberated them from Egypt. This meant that Israel's God came to assume many characteristics of the Canaanite El and was often called El, especially in the ancestral narratives in Genesis, the Psalter, and Job.

Appellations with El: Various appellations and titles were combined with El, probably in localized traditions associated with particular sanctuaries. Many of these are also applied in the Bible to the God of Israel.

El Shaddai (Heb., "God of the Mountain[s]"; NRSV: "God Almighty") was worshiped by the patriarchs Abraham, Isaac, and Jacob (Gen. 17:1) down to the time of Moses (Exod. 6:3). The combined name occurs thirty-one times in the book of Job, and only seventeen times elsewhere in the Hebrew Bible. In the mythologies of the ancient Near East, gods often resided on a cosmic mountain that was the center of the earth. Thus, Shaddai ("the One on the mountain") came to be identified with El, the head of the Canaanite pantheon, and then, for the Israelites, El Shaddai came to be identified with "the LORD" (Exod. 6:3; Ezek. 1:24). The LXX translated Shaddai as "Almighty." Thus, many English Bibles translate El Shaddai as "God Almighty."

El Elyon (Heb., "God Most High"; NRSV: "God Most High"), originally a compound for the high god El, was worshiped in Jerusalem before David's conquest (ca. 1000 BCE). In Gen. 14:18–22, Melchizedek is the priest-king of Jerusalem who blesses Abraham in the name of "God Most High, maker of heaven and earth," "who delivered Abraham's enemies into his hand." After the Israelite takeover of Jerusalem, the El Elyon tradition is associated with "the LORD" (Ps. 47:2–3).

El Olam (Heb., "God of Eternity"; NRSV: "Everlasting God") may have been the Canaanite god of Beer-sheba. After this religious center was incorporated into Israelite religion, the title would have come to designate "the LORD" (Gen. 21:33).

El Berith (Heb., "God of the Covenant"; NRSV: "El-berith") appears to be the Canaanite god of Shechem (Judg. 9:46). In Josh. 24, a covenant-renewal ceremony for the Israelites is placed at Shechem following their conquest of Canaan and the people pledge to serve only "the LORD" (Josh. 24:21).

El Roi (Heb., "God of Seeing/Divination"; NRSV: "El-Roi"). Gen. 16:13–14 relates a story in which God, called El Roi, promises Hagar a son (Ishmael) who will have many descendants.

In summary, the local Canaanite gods, including El, the head of the pantheon, were worshiped in sanctuaries eventually taken over by Israel. Canaanite religious traditions were eventually applied to "the LORD." In this process, YHWH, the God of liberation from Egyptian slavery, merged with Canaanite gods, especially the high god El, who legitimated a stratified social system of city-states ruled by local dynasts. This combination provided a critical tension—theological, political, and social—that characterized Israelite religion throughout the biblical period.

Social Titles for God: The changing social constructions of Israel also provided important titles for God.

Adonai (Heb., "my Lord"; NRSV: "Lord") is a plural of majesty derived from the singular *'adon* (Heb., "lord"), a title of respect used to address a social superior (e.g., king, husband, or slave owner; e.g., Job 28:8). In the postexilic period, Adonai came to replace the name YHWH ("the LORD") in common worship, because sanctity associated with the latter name discouraged its pronunciation aloud.

Ba'al (Heb., "lord") is also a title designating a social superior (e.g., leader, owner, or husband). In Canaanite religion, Baal was also used as the name of a specific deity, the storm god, god of fertility, who brought rain and military victory. This god rivaled "the LORD" for Israel's devotion, as is especially noted in prophetic literature (e.g., Hosea). Certain theophoric names indicate that some Israelites called their God "baal" in the generic sense of "lord" (e.g., Merib-baal, the son of Jonathan), but the term was usually avoided because of the pagan associations (cf. Hos. 2:16–17).

Royal Titles: Other important titles for God derived from the Israelite family, including father (Deut. 32:6), brother (1 Sam. 14:3; Ahijah [Heb., "brother of the LORD"]), and redeemer (Ps. 19:14). These titles may have originated in ancestral religion, where the personal deity of the family head became protector for the group (cf. Exod. 3:6). The "redeemer" was the closest relative responsible for delivering the relative from hard times (Lev. 25:25). Although God is not explicitly called "mother" or "sister," the Hebrew Bible does use feminine images to speak of God. God is depicted as a mother who conceives, bears, and gives birth to Israel (Num. 11:12; Deut. 32:18) and as a midwife (Ps. 22:9–10). *See also* Baal; El; El Shaddai; father; God, god; Lord of hosts; Pentateuch, sources of the; Yahweh. L.G.P.

names of God in the New Testament.

The names used by NT authors to refer to God reflect the fact that the NT was written in a Greek-speaking culture with tradition and terminology inherited from the LXX. This tradition was significantly modified, furthermore, by the early church's understanding of the teaching of Jesus and by its understanding of the person of Jesus as the definitive expression of God.

God: The most common designation for deity in the NT, used 1,318 times, is the Greek word *theos* ("god"), often used by the LXX as the translation of the Hebrew word *'elohim*. This word, however, was also used by the LXX for the pagan gods, and it was the standard term for the gods of the Greeks and Romans in NT times. The NT writers sometimes also use *theos* for the pagan gods (e.g., 1 Cor. 8:5) and on rare occasions apply it theologically to Christ (e.g., John 20:28). The vast majority of cases, however, refer to the God revealed in the history of Israel. Thus, the expression "the God and Father of our Lord Jesus Christ" (e.g., Rom. 15:6) refers unambiguously to the God of Israel revealed through the Hebrew Bible.

Lord: In the Hebrew Bible, the chief designation for the God of Israel is the Tetragrammaton, YHWH (sometimes written with vowels as "Yahweh" or as "Jehovah"). This is translated *kyrios* (Gk., "Lord") in the LXX and is rendered as "the LORD" in many English versions of the Bible. The name is used in the Hebrew Bible more than 6,000 times, compared to about 2,500 times for Elohim ("God") The NT continues to use *kyrios* for God, about 100 times, primarily in quotations from the LXX (e.g., Mark 1:3; 12:11; Acts 2:34) and in set phrases such as "the hand of the Lord" (Luke 1:66). But the vast majority of the 719 occurrences of *kyrios* ("Lord") in the NT refer to Jesus, usually as the exalted Christ (e.g., Acts 2:36; John 20:28). In some passages, particularly in NT letters where the author refers to "the Lord," it is impossible to tell whether God or Jesus is meant. A much less common word for "Lord" in the LXX, *despotēs* ("lord," "sovereign," "master") is also used in the NT for both God (Luke 2:29; Acts 4:24; Rev. 6:10) and Christ (Jude 4; 2 Pet. 2:1).

Father: Although Father is not a common name for God in the Hebrew Bible, the notion that God was father to Israel is certainly present (e.g., Isa. 63:16). It is, however, extremely common in the NT, becoming the most frequently used designation for God. Hypothetically, the notion of fatherhood applied to God might carry any number of different connotations. The term might serve to identify God, somewhat generically, as the progenitor of all life or of all that exists. This is probably how it is used in James 1:17 ("Father of lights"), but such use is rare in the NT. Rather, the term "Father" is usually used with relational connotations; those who call God "Father" are emphasizing their personal relationship with God. The use of such terminology implies recognition of God's authority, but within a context that appreciates that authority, realizing that God exercises such authority with loving responsibility to protect and provide for those who are identified as God's children. The widespread use of this terminology in early Christianity no doubt owes to the teaching and practice of Jesus, who is consistently portrayed as speaking of God as Father (e.g., Matt. 5:45; 6:9). Jesus appears to have called God by the Aramaic word "Abba," a relational, family term that children would use for their parents (Mark 14:36). This term was also appropriated in the later liturgical practice of the church, employed by people for whom Aramaic would have been an unknown, foreign language (Rom. 8:15; Gal. 4:6). The use of the name "Father" for God implied a metaphorical relationship with numerous implications: those who address God as "Father" acknowledge God as the one to whom absolute obedience is due (Matt. 7:21; 26:42); they identify themselves as siblings of all others who relate to God as Father (1 John 4:20–21); and they claim a privileged position as heirs who will eventually receive a glorious inheritance (Rom. 8:16–17).

The God of Abraham, Isaac, and Jacob: In the NT, "the God of Abraham, Isaac, and Jacob," a significant title for God in the Hebrew Bible, is found only in the Gospels, in a single quotation (Matt. 22:32; Mark 12:26) and in the book of Acts (3:13; 5:30; 7:32; 22:14). It emphasizes the continuity of the faith of Israel and that of the church, that the God of present experience is the same God who was known to Israel's ancestors. In the Letters of Paul and in other NT letters, this title is essentially replaced by "the God and Father of our Lord Jesus Christ" (Rom. 15:6; 2 Cor. 11:31; Eph. 1:3, 17; Col. 1:3; 1 Pet. 1:3).

The Almighty: The LXX used the word *pantokratōr* ("Almighty") to translate two different Hebrew expressions that the NRSV renders "God Almighty" (*'el shaddai*) and "LORD of Hosts" (*YHWH sebaot*). Jesus and the NT authors tend to avoid this appellation, which is found only in 2 Cor. 6:18 and nine times in Revelation, mostly in self-designations of God or in ascriptions of praise in a liturgical context.

Alpha and Omega: Alpha and omega are the first and last letters of the Greek alphabet and thus represent God as the Beginning and the End, the source and goal of all creation, and thus as the *only*

God. Nothing comparable is found in the Hebrew Bible (e.g., God is not called "the aleph and the tav"), but the basic idea of God being the first and the last is found in Isa. 44:6 and 48:12. In the NT, only the author of Revelation uses the name Alpha and Omega for God (1:8; 21:6); he also applies it to Jesus Christ (22:13; cf. 1:17; 2:8).

The Holy One: "The Holy One" as a title for God, used especially in Isaiah, is used in Rev. 16:5. It is used of Jesus in Mark 1:24; Luke 4:34; and John 6:69. In 1 John 2:20, the reference may be either to God or to the exalted Christ.

General Terms: The common impersonal words for God in Greek, *ho theios* ("the deity") and *theotēs* ("deity") are absent from those LXX books derived from the Hebrew canon, and *theotēs* is found only once in the remainder of the LXX (Wis. 18:9). Correspondingly, "Deity" as a term for God is found in the NT only in Paul's address to the Athenians (Acts 17:29) and in Col. 2:9.

The line between explicit names for God and more general designations is sometimes difficult to draw. Among general designations for God found in the LXX and adopted by NT authors are "King" (e.g., Matt. 5:35; 1 Tim. 1:17; 6:15), "Judge" (e.g., John 8:50; Heb. 12:23), and "Savior" (e.g., Luke 1:47; 1 Tim. 1:1; 2:3; 4:10), all of which are applied more frequently to Jesus Christ than they are to God.

During the Second Temple period—or at least in the first century CE—many Jews appear to have expressed reverence for God by avoiding names altogether and finding periphrastic ways to speak of God. This practice is reflected to some extent in the NT. Thus, the high priest refers to God as "the Blessed One" (Mark 14:61), and Jesus refers to God as "the Power" (14:62). See also "the Majestic Glory" (2 Pet. 1:17). The most common periphrastic construction for God, however, is the word "heaven." The prodigal son says, "I have sinned against heaven" (Luke 15:18); throughout Matthew's Gospel, the phrase "kingdom of heaven" is often used in place of "kingdom of God" (cf., e.g., Matt. 13:11 with Mark 4:11). In addition, God is sometimes referred to by using the passive voice (the "divine passive," e.g., Matt. 5:4, 6, 7, 9; Luke 6:38; 12:20, 48). *See also* Abba; alpha; father; God; god; lord; omega.　　　　　　　　M.E.B./M.A.P.

names of God in the Old Testament. *See* names of God in the Hebrew Bible.

Naomi (nay-oh'mee; Heb., "my pleasantness"), the mother-in-law of Ruth, and a prominent character in the book of Ruth. Naomi and her husband, Elimelech of Bethlehem, went to Moab with their two sons during a time of famine (Ruth 1:1–2). The sons married Moabite women, but then Elimelech and both of the sons died (1:4–5). Naomi decided to return to Bethlehem and urged her daughters-in-law to remain with their families in Moab, since she would not be able to bear more sons who, by the time they had grown, would make suitable husbands for them (1:8–14). Ruth refused, vowing loyalty to Naomi, and returned with her to Bethlehem (1:16–17). There, Naomi told the whole town that she should henceforth be called Mara ("bitter") rather than Naomi ("pleasant"), because God had dealt bitterly with her. In the ensuing narrative, Naomi encouraged Ruth to ask protection of Boaz, a relative of Elimelech, telling her, "I need to seek some security for you, that it may be well for you" (3:1). Naomi devised a plan according to which Ruth went to the threshing floor where Boaz was sleeping after a drunken celebration of the harvest and lay down with him. Boaz ended up redeeming Elimelech's property (acquiring it from Naomi, 4:9) and marrying Ruth in accordance with levirate law (4:10; cf. Deut. 25:5–10). Naomi became the nurse for their firstborn son, and the women of the town proclaimed, "A son has been born to Naomi" (4:26–27), because the boy would allow her line (and that of Elimelech) to continue. The women named the child Obed, and he ultimately became the grandfather of King David. Thus, Naomi was remembered as the great-great-grandmother of David. *See also* Ruth.   M.A.S./M.A.P.

Naphtali (naf′tuh-li; Heb., possibly "my wrestling").

1 The second son of Jacob and Bilhah (Gen. 30:7–8). The story of his birth is told against a backdrop of competition between Leah and Rachel, Jacob's two wives. Although Rachel was clearly Jacob's favorite wife, she remained infertile for a time during which Leah bore four sons. Then Rachel gave her slave Bilhah to Jacob as a surrogate wife, and Bilhah bore two sons (Dan and Naphtali). Rachel gave this second boy his name, because she said, "With mighty wrestlings I have wrestled with my sister, and have prevailed" (30:28).

2 The Israelite tribe that traced its descent to 1. Naphtali's territory was bounded on the west by Asher, on the south by Zebulun and Issachar, and on the east by the river Jordan and the Sea of Galilee. This territory Naphtali shared with Canaanites (Judg. 1:33). Its northern location is reflected in the position it occupied along with Dan and Asher on the north side of the tent of meeting (Num. 2:25–31). In the period of the judges, Barak, son of Abinoam, from Qedesh in Naphtali, successfully led a force of ten thousand against the army of Sisera (Judg. 4:6–10, 12–16), and twice the tribe of Naphtali answered the call of Gideon to battle invading Midianites (6:35; 7:23). During Solomon's reign, the administrative officer in charge of Naphtali was son-in-law to the king; and Hiram of Tyre, the son of a widow from the tribe of Naphtali, is credited with the manufacture of the bronze/copper work commissioned by Solomon for the temple (1 Kings 7:13–47; but according to 2 Chron. 2:13–14 it was Huramabi of the tribe of Dan). In the period of the divided monarchy, Naphtali was invaded by Ben-hadad of Syria at the request of Asa of Judah during the course of the war between the latter and Baasha

of Israel (1 Kings 15:16–20). Later, during the reign of Pekah of Israel, Tiglath-pileser III invaded Naphtali and deported its population to Assyria (2 Kings 15:29). In the course of the Maccabean wars, forces of Demetrius of Syria, intent upon removing Jonathan from office, reached Kedesh (Naphtali) in Galilee and were met by Jonathan, who managed to turn a near defeat into victory (1 Macc. 11:63–64, 67–74).

Naphtali is referred to in a number of poetic or literary passages. The Blessing of Jacob (Gen. 49:21) describes Naphtali as "a doe let loose who bears many fawns." The poet thus contrasts Naphtali's prior state of independence with its state of political dependence. The Blessing of Moses (Deut. 33:23) describes Naphtali as "sated with favor, full of the blessing of the LORD" and prophesies that Naphtali will "possess the west and the south [Heb. *darom*]." The final word of this verse is suspect in so early a poem, for it is found otherwise only in the late books of Ezekiel, Job, and Ecclesiastes. It has been suggested that the manuscript may originally have read *marom*, "highland" (cf. Judg. 5:18), in which case the blessing would refer to the tribe's well-favored territory from the Sea of Galilee to the Galilean highlands. The Song of Deborah (Judg. 5:18) lauds Naphtali along with Zebulun for its participation in the war against Sisera. Finally, the book of Tobit presents the tale of the sufferings and healing of a pious member of the tribe of Naphtali (1:1–2, 4–5; 7:3). *See also* tribes.   S.G./M.A.P.

Narcissus (nahr-sis′uhs), person mentioned in the greeting at the conclusion of Paul's Letter to the Romans. Paul says, "Greet those in the Lord who belong to the family of Narcissus" (16:11). Perhaps he was the head of a house-church and his "family" consisted of those who worshiped in his home.

nard, a scented ointment or perfume imported from the Himalayas in alabaster boxes and opened on special occasions. In the Song of Solomon, it is used by a woman to enhance her sexual appeal and, indeed, appears to be employed during the act of lovemaking (1:12; 4:13, 14). In the NT, a woman (unnamed in Mark 14:3–5, but identified as Mary of Bethany in John 12:3–5) breaks open an alabaster jar of nard and pours the ointment on Jesus. The cost of the ointment is estimated as about three hundred denarii, or about a year's wages.

Nathan (nay′thuhn; Heb., "gift").

1 A prophet in the court of David. Three significant events are recorded about him. In 2 Sam. 7 (and 1 Chron. 17), David consults with him regarding his intention to build a temple to house the ark of the covenant. Nathan at first assumes that God approves of this plan, but then is told by God that David's plan will be fulfilled by his son. Nathan explains that the reign of David's heir will be the proof that God has established a permanent relationship with David's line; that reign,

Nard.

not David's, will be the proper symbolic time for the building of a house for God. The assurance in this prophecy of the unconditional eternality of the Davidic dynasty (2 Sam. 7:12–16) became a standard part of Israelite expectation during the First Temple period (ca. 950–587/6 BCE); in some respects, however, Nathan's proclamation of an unconditional Davidic covenant would obstruct attempts of the later prophets to affirm the primacy of the conditional Sinai covenant in order to bring the people to repentance.

Later, after David arranged Uriah's death and committed adultery with Bathsheba (2 Sam. 11), God sent Nathan to rebuke David (2 Sam. 12). Nathan tells David a parable about a poor man who had a pet ewe lamb; a rich man who had plentiful flocks takes the poor man's lamb and prepares it for a meal. David declares that a man who did such a thing deserves to die (12:6; cf. Exod. 22:1), thus unwittingly passing judgment upon himself for what he did to Uriah. Nathan makes this explicit by telling him, "You are the man!" (12:7). David confesses his sin, and Nathan declares his punishment: violence will be a constant family companion (witness Amnon, Tamar, and Absalom); his wives will have public intercourse with another (16:22); and the son of the illicit union with Bathsheba will die (12:18). This story illustrates the unique ability of Israel's prophets to confront a monarch with moral crimes. Unlike other royalty in the ancient Near East, who ruled absolutely and often capriciously, the Israelite king was subservient to the Torah of God.

Finally, in 1 Kings 1, readers are afforded a behind-the-scenes view of the machinations of royal succession. Here, Nathan, without a hint of divine instruction, becomes the kingmaker,

setting the stage and directing dialogue to manipulate David into crowning Solomon as his successor (rather than the eldest son, Adonijah). Nathan elicits Bathsheba's help in his plan, persuading her to "remind" David that he had promised her Solomon would succeed him. Nathan then offers supposedly independent verification of this. The scheme works because David's memory has grown faulty and he trusts Nathan and Bathsheba to deal honestly with him.

Elsewhere in the Bible, the Chronicler mentions the writings of Nathan as part of his source (1 Chron. 29:29; 2 Chron. 9:29) and partly attributes to his authority the musical role of the Levites in the temple (2 Chron. 29:25).

2 A son of David (2 Sam. 5:14; Zech. 12:12; 1 Chron. 3:5; 14:4). He is named as an ancestor of Jesus in Luke 3:31.

3 The father of one of David's warriors (2 Sam. 23:26).

4 The brother of another of David's warriors (1 Chron. 11:38).

5 The father of one of Solomon's officers (1 Kings 4:5). He is sometimes identified with **1**.

6 The father of one of Solomon's priests (1 Kings 4:5; but see 1 Chron. 2:34–36, where the same Nathan is apparently a descendant of an Egyptian servant).

See also Bathsheba; David; prophet; Solomon.
J.U./M.A.P.

Nathanael (nuh-than'ay-uhl; Heb., "gift of God").
1 A priest who divorced his foreign wife in response to Ezra's postexilic proclamation (1 Esd. 9:22).

2 An ancestor of Judith (Jth. 8:1).

3 One of the chosen disciples of Jesus mentioned only in John's Gospel (1:43–51; cf. 21:2). He came from Cana in Galilee and is sought out by Philip, who has already been called by Jesus, and who tells him, "We have found the Messiah . . . Jesus, son of Joseph, from Nazareth." Nathanael is doubtful, responding, "Can anything good come out of Nazareth?" At their first meeting, Jesus describes Nathanael as "an Israelite in whom there is no deceit" and tells him that he "saw" Nathanael when he was under a fig tree before Philip called him. This apparently miraculous insight (having known where Nathanael was when he was apparently alone) prompts Nathanael to declare, "Rabbi, you are the Son of God! You are the King of Israel!" Jesus seems to take this as an overreaction, based on what Nathanael has experienced thus far, but he promises him that greater revelations will come. Indeed, he will see "heaven opened and the angels of God ascending and descending upon the Son of Man." Nathanael apparently remains with Jesus as one of his disciples, though he is not mentioned again until, in the epilogue of John's Gospel, he is among those who encounter the risen Lord on the beach (21:2). Nathanael is not mentioned anywhere else in the NT, and his name is not included in any list of the twelve. This prompted church tradition to identify him with Bartholomew, a member of the twelve not named in John's Gospel. The theory—not impossible, but completely unprovable—is that the same individual was known by both names (Bartholomew and Nathanael). *See also* apostle; Bartholomew; disciple; Philip; twelve, the. M.A.P.

nations. The Hebrew (*goyim*) and Greek (*ethnē*) terms for "nations" do sometimes refer to political entities (in which case Israel might be classed as one of the nations), but more often both terms refer specifically to non-Israelite peoples (e.g., *goyim*, Exod. 34:24; Deut. 11:23; Josh. 23:13; *ethnē*, Acts 7:45; 13:19). Indeed, the Greek word (*ethnē*) is often translated "Gentiles" by the NRSV and most other English Bibles. Thus, the same word is regularly translated "nations" in some instances (Matt. 25:32; Rev. 10:11) and "Gentiles" in others (Matt. 5:47; Mark 10:33); only context can determine whether the political or ethnic sense is intended.

Throughout most of the Bible, the nations exist in an antithetical relationship with Israel. The chief snare of the nations is their gods (Deut. 7:22–26), which are considered to be mere idols (Ps. 96:5) and not true gods (Isa. 44:12–20; 45:14). Further, Israel tests God through its desire to be "like other nations" (1 Sam. 8:5). Still, God's sovereignty over the nations is expressed throughout the Bible in terms that transcend animosity: God appointed the nations (Deut. 32:8) and will be their light (Isa. 42:6; cf. Luke 2:32). In fact, God made Abraham to be a great nation (*goy*) in order that all the nations (*goyim*) of the earth might be blessed in him (Gen. 18:18). In the NT, the gospel of Jesus Christ is to be proclaimed to all nations (Mark 13:10), and Jesus's disciples are to make disciples of all nations (Matt. 28:19). M.A.P.

Nazarenes (naz'uh-reenz), a term used for the early Christian movement in Acts 24:5. Jesus was frequently identified as being a Nazarene (i.e., as being "from Nazareth," Matt. 21:11; Mark 1:9; 14:67; John 1:45) so the term "Nazarenes" (which would have literally meant "people from Nazareth") must have been applied in a way that meant something like "followers of the Nazarene." *See also* Christian; Nazareth; way. J.M.E.

Nazareth (naz'uh-rith), the city from which Jesus's mother came (Luke 1:26) and where Jesus grew up (Matt. 2:23; 13:54; Luke 2:4, 51; 4:16). Nazareth was an insignificant agricultural village nestled in the hills four miles from Sepphoris, the capital of Galilee. It is not mentioned in the Hebrew Bible, in Josephus, or in rabbinic writings. Not surprisingly, Jesus's Nazareth origins are held up to scorn by those skeptical of his mission (John 1:46).

A Hebrew inscription found at Caesarea lists Nazareth as one of the villages in which priestly divisions (cf. Luke 1:8–9) were resident after the Jewish revolt. Some scholars allege that this notice suggests a degree of piety attributed to Nazareth, which has not produced any archaeological

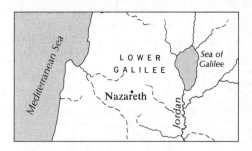

remains with pagan symbolism. Indeed, the few remains found include Jewish stone vessels, simple pottery, and perhaps a ritual bath.

Based on rock-cut tombs surrounding the village and scant remains in the center of the modern city around the Church of the Annunciation, it appears that Nazareth could not have had a population of more than five hundred in Jesus's time. Like most of Galilee, the site was settled by Jews in the second century BCE who were preoccupied with farming. Little evidence of houses has been discovered; no roof tiles, frescoes, mosaics, or even plastered floors have been found from the first century, and luxury items are absent. The typical dwelling probably consisted of a small group of rooms around a central courtyard; some people may have made use of caves in the slopes. Thus, Nazareth was by all indications a simple peasant village, and even the rebuilding of nearby Sepphoris by Herod Antipas does not seem to have elevated its socioeconomic level. P.P./J.R.

Nazirites (naz'uh-rits; Heb., "dedicated/consecrated [ones]"), men or women who entered a consecrated state upon their own or a parent's vow (Num. 6:1–21; 1 Sam. 1:1–11; Judg. 13:1–7). There were three main conditions for entering and remaining in this holy state. First, Nazirites were to refrain from the fruit of the vine and other intoxicants; this was also a distinguishing feature of the Rechabites (Jer. 35). Upon completion of a term, Nazirites could drink wine (Num. 6:20), and some were apparently tempted to do so before (Amos 2:10–11).

Second, Nazirites were not to allow a razor to touch their hair throughout their term as Nazirites. And, finally, Nazirites were not to go near a dead body—not even that of one's own father or mother (Num. 6:1–7). In this last condition the rigor is comparable to that required elsewhere only of the high priest (cf. Lev. 21:10–12 and 21:1–4). The Bible sets forth an elaborate ritual for reconsecration, should a Nazirite become unclean through contact with a dead body (Num. 6:9–12). It also sets out the ritual for bringing the period of consecration to an end (6:13–20).

The Bible mentions two examples of lifelong Nazirites. First, Samson was consecrated as a Nazirite even before he was born. His great strength seems to be linked to his status with God as maintained through obedience to the second condition of Nazirites, i.e., that they leave their hair uncut (Judg. 13:7; 16:17). Second, Hannah pledges that if God grants her a son, he will be "a Nazirite until the day of his death"; this son is the prophet Samuel (1 Sam. 1:11; cf. 1:22).

A reference to Nazirites "who had completed their days" in 1 Macc. 3:49 indicates that the commitment was not always lifelong. Acts 18:18 refers to Paul getting his hair cut because he had been under a vow, which might imply that he was concluding a period of Nazirite observance. Likewise, Acts 21:23–24 refers to a group of Jews completing a vow with a ritual that involves a rite of purification and the shaving of their heads; some interpreters think that such acts may have marked the conclusion of a term as Nazirites.   J.G.G./M.A.P.

Neapolis (nee-ap'uh-lis; Gk., "new city").

1 A seaport for Philippi, which was located ten miles inland (Acts 16:11). The city is to be identified with modern Kevalla and should not be confused with Neapolis in Samaria (see 2) or with numerous other towns in the Roman world that were also named Neapolis. The book of Acts reports that Paul had a vision while in Troas of a Macedonian man summoning him to cross over to Europe. He set sail and landed at Neapolis, then went up the road to found churches in Philippi and Thessalonica. *See also* Philippi.

2 Ancient Shechem in the central hill country of Samaria, refounded by the Roman emperor Vespasian in 72 CE as Neapolis, modern-day Nablus. Extensive ruins, such as the theater and amphitheater, are still visible in the modern city center. *See also* Shechem.   M.A.P.

Nebaioth (ni-bay'oth), the firstborn son of Ishmael (Gen. 25:13; 1 Chron. 1:29) and Esau's brother-in-law (Gen. 28:9; 36:3). As a tribe Nebaioth's descendants were famous for their herds of sheep (Isa. 60:7), and it is possible that they are to be identified with the Nabaiati mentioned in the records of the Assyrian kings Tiglath-pileser III and Ashurbanipal in the eighth and seventh centuries BCE.

Nebat (nee'bat), the name of the father of Israel's king Jeroboam I (ca. 922–901 BCE; 1 Kings 11:26). He is identified as an Ephraimite from Zeredah, modern Deir Ghassaneh, about ten miles west of Shiloh. He is mentioned several times in 1 and 2 Kings and 2 Chronicles.

Nebo (nee'boh).

1 A Babylonian god (Isa. 46:1) considered to be the son of Marduk. His statue was paraded with Marduk's in Babylon at the New Year Festival, setting the context for a taunt by the prophet Isaiah (15:1–9). He was associated with water, writing, and speech. Of the last six kings of Babylon, three carried his name in their personal names, *Nabo*polassar, *Nebu*chadnezzar, and *Nabo*nidus.

2 A Moabite city (Num. 32:3, 38), probably modern Khirbet Mekhayyet, about five miles

southwest of Hesban. It was part of Sihon's kingdom (21:26–30). Assigned to the tribes Reuben and Gad (32:3), it was Moabite under Mesha (mid-ninth century BCE) and it figured in the prophecies of both Isaiah (15:2) and Jeremiah (48:1, 22).

3 A mountain promontory (Deut. 32:49) from which Moses was called to view Canaan at the time of his death, modern Jebel en-Nebu, 2,740 feet above sea level, and about 4,030 feet above the Dead Sea, whose north edge lies below it to the west. As part of the Abarim range (Num. 33:47), the promontory is conspicuously visible from Hesban, but is more accessible from Medeba five miles southeast. The most panoramic view of the Jordan Valley and land to the west is from a lower promontory across a saddle to the northwest, modern Ras es-Siyaghah.

4 The ancestor of some returning exiles (Ezra 2:29; 10:43; and possibly Neh. 7:33) who may have been associated with a town in Judah, Nuba, six miles northwest of Hebron.   R.S.B.

Nebuchadnezzar (neb'uh-kuhd-nez'uhr; Babylonian, "O Nabu, preserve the offspring [lit., 'boundary stone']"), the name of four kings now known to us from ancient Mesopotamia. The first was the king of the Second Dynasty of Isin (southern Mesopotamia), who ruled 1124–1103 BCE. He is known as Nebuchadnezzar I. The king called Nebuchadnezzar in the Bible is known to modern historians as Nebuchadnezzar II. The Behistun inscription of Darius I (522–186 BCE) tells of two contenders for the throne (522 and 521 BCE) who also bore the name Nebuchadnezzar (known to historians as Nebuchadnezzar III and Nebuchadnezzar IV, though some doubt has been raised concerning the existence of the last).

Nebuchadnezzar II ruled Babylonia from 605 to 562 BCE. He was the son of Nabopolassar, founder of the Chaldean dynasty. Nebuchadnezzar II was the most powerful and longest-reigning king of the Neo-Babylonian (625–539 BCE) period. He brought the city of Babylon and the southern Mesopotamian state of Babylonia to the pinnacle of their power and prosperity.

The major competitors for power in the days of Nebuchadnezzar II were Media (northwest Iran) and Egypt, always with great-power ambitions for ports and trade in the Levant (Syria, Lebanon, Israel). Nebuchadnezzar II's marriage to a daughter of the king of the Medes held the alliance with that power secure until after Nebuchadnezzar II's death. As for Egypt, Pharaoh Neco suffered a defeat at the hands of Nebuchadnezzar II at the city of Carchemish in 605 BCE (2 Kings 24:7).

Much information about the early rule of Nebuchadnezzar II comes from the *Chronicles of Chaldean Kings*. However, of the forty-three years of the reign of Nebuchadnezzar II, only those up to 594 BCE are preserved. Other records tell of the conquest of Tyre (571 BCE; cf. Ezek. 27:12) and the invasion of Egypt in Nebuchadnezzar's thirty-seventh year (Ezek. 29:19–21). Accounts indicate

Bulls alternating with serpent-dragons adorn the walls of the Ishtar Gate, built in Babylon by Nebuchadnezzar II (ruled 605–562 BCE) and now reconstructed in the Staatliches Museum, Berlin.

that Nebuchadnezzar was an able but cruel ruler (cf. 2 Kings 25:7) who stopped at nothing to subdue peoples who stood in his path of conquest.

Amel-marduk (Evil-merodach), Nebuchadnezzar's son, ruled from 562 to 560 BCE. According to accounts in 2 Kings 25:27–30 and Jer. 52:31–34 he recognized King Jehoiachin and allocated an allowance for him "all the days of his life." Babylonian clay tablets mentioning the disbursement of oil to Jehoiachin, five sons of the king of Judea, and other Judeans confirm in a dramatic manner this scriptural statement.

Building projects sponsored by Nebuchadnezzar included the beautification of Babylon, his capital, the construction of fortification walls in addition to those already in place, and the improvement of Marduk's temple in Babylon, Esagila. There is extant a list of the personnel of the court of Nebuchadnezzar II, showing the complex infrastructure of the royal palace.

From the perspective of biblical Israel, the events associated with the reign of Nebuchadnezzar II that had the most lasting effect on its destiny were the destruction of Judea, the conquest of Jerusalem, the burning of the temple of Solomon, and the exile to Babylonia (597–581 BCE). The reflection of these events and the events that led up to them can

be seen in the biblical materials in 2 Kings and 1 and 2 Chronicles, taken with Jeremiah. Related materials may be found in Ezra, Nehemiah, and Esther. Dan. 1–5 represents an account of Jews in the court of Nebuchadnezzar, along with apocalyptic visions.

Jeremiah, the great prophet who was an eyewitness to the destruction of the temple, counseled submission to Nebuchadnezzar, whom he viewed as the instrument of the Lord's wrath. In time, Jeremiah wisely foresaw, Nebuchadnezzar's land would face its own day of reckoning (Jer. 27).

It is thought by some scholars that Dan. 4, which records the madness of Nebuchadnezzar, may have incorporated accounts pertaining to the less well-known Babylonian monarch of this same dynasty, Nabonidus. *See also* Daniel; Daniel, book of; Jeremiah, book of; Nabonidus.   D.B.W.

Nebuzaradan (neb´uh-zuh-ray´duhn), a Babylonian high official who, in 587/6 BCE, oversaw the destruction of Jerusalem and its temple (2 Kings 25:8–21). He personally supervised the disposition of the captured property and population in Judah. Vessels used in worship and appurtenances of precious metals were carried off as spoil to Babylon. The poorest people of the land, the refugees behind Jerusalem's walls, were permitted to resume their pursuits as "vinedressers and tillers of the soil." The leaders of the rebellion against Babylon, the high priest and the surviving royal officials, were transferred to Riblah, where they were summarily executed. Nebuzaradan exiled the remainder of the city's populace; an exception was made in the case of the prophet Jeremiah, who was permitted to stay behind as counselor to the new governor, Gedaliah (Jer. 40:1–6). Nebuzaradan's official title, "chief cook," is attested in both Hebrew (*rab tabbakhim*) and Akkadian (*rab nuhatimmu*); in the Bible he is consistently identified as the "captain of the guard" (2 Kings 25:11) or "captain of the bodyguard" (25:8). Nebuzaradan is listed second among the courtiers of King Nebuchadnezzar on a Neo-Babylonian administrative document.   M.C.

Neco (nee'koh) **II** (610–595 BCE), king of Egypt during the Twenty-Sixth (Saite) Dynasty (ca. 664–525 BCE) and successor to the very successful Psammetichus I (664–610 BCE); he established Egyptian control in Philistia during part of his reign. Neco became pharaoh during the last days of the Assyrian Empire, when it was precariously clinging to life in north Syria. As a former Assyrian vassal who now wanted to limit Babylonia's capacity for attaining the sort of dominance Assyria had once held, Neco sent a major expedition to north Syria in 609 BCE to aid Assyria against the Babylonian forces. In doing so, he encountered King Josiah of Judah at Megiddo (2 Kings 23:29); Josiah was presumably acting either for Judean independence or in the interest of Babylonia against Assyria. Josiah died as a result of that encounter, but the Egyptian forces were not successful in their attempt to install the Assyrian remnant in Haran. Nevertheless, Egypt was, for the moment, the dominant power in southern portions of the Levant (Israel, Syria, Lebanon).

On his return from north Syria about three months later, Neco summoned Jehoahaz (Shallum), the king of Judah whom the Hebrew people had anointed as successor to his Josiah, to Riblah, deposed him, put him in bonds, and carried him off to Egypt. Neco then assigned Judah a heavy tribute and installed another son of Josiah, Jehoiakim (formerly Eliakim), in place of Jehoahaz, his younger brother. In 605 BCE Neco again battled Babylonia in north Syria, at Carchemish, losing decisively. Shortly thereafter Jehoiakim switched his allegiance to Babylonia, who came to control all of the Levant.

In addition to his ambitious undertakings in the Levant, Neco expanded the Red Sea trade and tried to reestablish commercial contacts with Punt (Somalia). He sent a major expedition into Nubia, initiated an extensive canal project in the eastern Nile Delta, and successfully resisted the Babylonian attempt to invade Egypt in 601–600 BCE. *See also* Jehoahaz; Jehoiakim; Josiah.   H.B.H.

necromancy. *See* divination.

needle, needlework. Fine needles of bone, copper, and bronze have been found in various archaeological contexts, confirming their widespread use in all periods of biblical history. Nevertheless, needles are mentioned only once in the Bible, when Jesus says, "It is easier for a camel to go through the eye of a needle than for someone who is rich to enter the kingdom of God" (Matt. 19:24; Mark 10:25; Luke 18:25). There is no evidence to support an oft-repeated claim that Jesus was referring to a gate in the city of Jerusalem called "the needle's eye"; rather, he was referring to the literal hole at the end of a sewing needle through which only a fine thread could pass. The point of his saying was to stress the incongruity of being rich and leading a life ruled by God. The saying juxtaposes one of the largest entities that people in his setting would typically encounter (a camel) with one of the smallest (the eye of a needle). His disciples understood the point, realizing that it would therefore be impossible for such a person (and possibly for anyone) to be saved. This prompts Jesus to add a caveat, indicating, perhaps, that he was speaking hyperbolically: "For mortals it is impossible, but for God all things are possible" (Matt. 19:26; cf. Mark 10:27; Luke 18:27).

Needles were used for embroidery or sewing, and such needlework is referred to in the book of Exodus, which describes the needlework used on the screen at the entrance to the tabernacle (26:36). The work was done on blue, purple, and scarlet material with fine twisted linen. The same combination was specified for the screen at the gate of the court (27:16) and Aaron's girdle (28:39; see also 36:37; 38:18; 39:29).   R.S.B./M.A.P.

Negev (neg'ev; Heb. *negeb*, "dry, parched, south country"), the southern part of Judah, and the largest region in the modern state of Israel. The Negev forms an inverted triangle with its base roughly following a line from Gaza past Beer-sheba to the Dead Sea. The line then runs south from the Dead Sea through the Wadi Arabah to the Gulf of Aqabah at Elath, and from there northwestward to Gaza. The Negev is a hot region that receives less than 8 inches of rainfall annually. Although dry, some portions of the Negev can sustain limited agriculture; more usual is the pasturing of flocks.

Some evidence of settlement in the Negev dates back as early as the Paleolithic period (100,000–10,000 BCE). And scattered remains are found from the Neolithic (10,000–4,000 BCE) and Chalcolithic (4,000–3,000 BCE) periods. In the Middle Bronze Age I (2,000–1,800 BCE), hundreds of unwalled settlements are found in the Negev. Several factors seem to have led to the establishment of permanent settlements in the harsh climate of the Negev. First, the presence of sufficient water from springs, wells, oases, or cisterns of sufficient capacity permitted settlement in many areas. Second, the proximity of important trade routes also led to permanent settlement. Towns would naturally be established to meet the needs of travelers and to protect the route. Third, many of the settlements

The Negev, the "dry, parched, south country," where the Israelites spent much of the wilderness wandering period.

or towns on the trade routes of the Negev were established, or at least maintained, as fortresses. Numerous Iron Age fortresses with casemate walls have been discovered.

Several highways went through the Negev. The most important was the Via Maris, the coastal road, which connected Egypt with Mesopotamia and Anatolia. The Via Maris skirted along the western edge of the Negev near Gaza. Three other north–south roads went through the Negev. One ran from Jerusalem and Hebron to Beer-sheba and Nissana, and then connected with the Via Maris. Another road came from Hebron to Arad, Hormah, and then to the oasis at Kadesh-barnea. A third road followed the Wadi Arabah from the Dead Sea to Elath/Aqabah. The main east–west road was the Way to the Arabah, from Kadesh-barnea to Bozrah (modern Bu-seirah) in Edom. Just west of Kadesh, it connected with the Way to Shur, another route to Egypt. A minor road connected Elath with Kadesh; another connected Arad, Hormah and Beer-sheba with the Dead Sea eastward, and the Via Maris westward.

The Hebrews spent much of the wilderness wandering period (ca. 1290–1250 BCE) around the oasis of Kadesh-barnea in the southern Negev (Deut. 1:19, 46). The Amalekites, a seminomadic people, also lived in the Negev (Num. 13:29).

During the period of the monarchy (Iron Age II, 1020–587 BCE), many small villages and fortresses were established in the Negev. The fortresses guarded the southern borders of Judah. The many villages and more intensive agriculture in the region suggest an expanding population during the monarchy, so that marginal land had to be farmed. These farmers knew the technique of terrace farming.

After the fall of Judah and during the exile, the Edomites gained control of the Negev. However, the area had limited population until the arrival of the Nabateans in the last couple of centuries BCE. The Nabateans resettled many sites and built additional villages. They were very adept at farming and pasturing the dry region by careful water conservation. Only during the Byzantine period did the Negev support a larger population. After the Arab conquest, the Negev declined and has supported only limited population until modern times. *See also* Kadesh; wilderness.   J.F.D.

Nehemiah, book of. *See* Ezra and Nehemiah, books of.

Nehushta (ni-hoosh´tuh), the wife of king Jehoiakim of Judah and mother of King Jehoiachin (2 Kings 24:8). As queen mother she played an important role in the royal court; therefore she was exiled to Babylon along with her son (2 Kings 24:12) and the members of other prominent families.

Nehushtan (ni-hoosh'tuhn), the name of the bronze serpent destroyed during the religious reforms of King Hezekiah (715–687/6 BCE; 2 Kings 18:4). It most likely stood in the temple court in Jerusalem for the people who assembled there. The account in Num. 21:8–9 states that its form was that of a "poisonous serpent" (Heb. *saraph*). It appears to have been an apotropaic object, protecting those bitten by serpents (cf. Num. 21:4–9; John 3:14).

neighbor, in the Hebrew Bible, one who lives nearby (Exod. 12:4; Jer. 12:14; Prov. 27:10) or, figuratively, one who is a fellow Israelite (Exod. 2:13; 1 Sam. 28:17). As members of a community united by divine covenant, law, and teaching, the Israelites' obligations to God were reflected in their moral obligations to each other. They were to be "a kingdom of priests and a holy nation" (Exod. 19:6). Thus, they were commanded not to covet their neighbor's wife or possessions (Exod. 20:16–17; Deut. 5:20–21) or to hold a neighbor's garment for pledge past sunset (Exod. 22:25–26). Likewise, they were not to defraud, judge, slander, or reprove their neighbor (Lev. 19:13, 15–17; cf. 25:14–15). Rather, they were commanded, "You shall love your neighbor as yourself" (Lev. 19:18). This involves caring for the poor and needy neighbor in the land (Deut. 15:7–11) and taking positive measures to protect the neighbor's property or livestock (22:1–4). God will destroy those who slander their neighbors (Ps. 101:5; cf. Prov. 11:9). To despise one's neighbor is to be devoid of wisdom (Prov. 11:12) and to sin (14:21). Thus, respect and responsibility for the fellow Israelite receives much attention, but the Hebrew Bible is emphatic in noting that such attention does not imply lack of concern or obligation for others. The Israelites are also to respect and care for the aliens (non-Israelites) who dwell among them. Indeed, the same biblical chapter that contains the commandment, "Love your neighbor as yourself" (Lev. 19:18) also contains the command, "You shall love the alien as yourself" (19:34).

In the NT, Jesus quotes Lev. 19:18 as one of the two greatest commandments in the law, upon which everything else depends (Matt. 22:39; Mark 12:31; Luke 10:27). He also emphasizes that love for neighbor implies love for all human beings, including one's enemies (cf. Matt. 5:44; Luke 6:27, 35). The latter point is illustrated through his parable of the Good Samaritan (Luke 10:27–37), which is told in response to the question, "Who is my neighbor?" Jesus suggests that those who ask this question should place themselves in the position of one who has been beaten, stripped, robbed, and left for dead. Who would they regard as neighbor then? The anticipated answer is "anyone who would help me, even if that were someone I would otherwise have considered my enemy (e.g., a

Samaritan)." Other NT writers also pick up on this concept of loving one's neighbor as implying love for any human being (e.g., Rom. 13:8–9; Gal. 5:14; James 2:8).   J.U./M.A.P.

Nekoda (ni-koh'duh).
1 The ancestor of a family group of temple servants who returned from the Babylonian exile with Zerubbabel (Ezra 2:48; Neh. 7:50). *See also* temple servants.
2 The ancestor of another family group who also returned, but who could not prove their ancestry (Ezra 2:60; Neh. 7:62).

Nemuel (nem'yoo-uhl).
1 A Reubenite belonging to the Pallu family group (Num. 26:9).
2 A son of Simeon and head of the Nemuelites (Num. 26:12; 1 Chron. 4:24). He is also called Jemuel (Gen. 46:10; Exod. 6:15).

Nepheg (nee'fig).
1 One of the sons of Izhar among the descendants of Levi, and brother of Korah and Zichri (Exod. 6:21).
2 One of David's sons born in Jerusalem to his enlarged household of wives and concubines (1 Sam. 5:15; 1 Chron. 3:7; 14:6).

Nephilim (nef'uh-lim), people of the preflood generation, the offspring of human women and divine beings (Gen. 6:1–4). Their generation and their conduct seem to have provoked the flood as punishment (6:5–8:22). In Num. 13:33 the Israelite spies describe the inhabitants of Hebron as Nephilim, so large and powerful that "we seemed like grasshoppers." Since all of the Nephilim supposedly perished in the flood, this latter reference to Nephilim in Hebron is generally taken as figurative; the term "Nephilim" had come to be used as a description for unusually powerful foes. Num. 13:33 also indicates that the Anakites came from the Nephilim (cf. Num. 13:22; also references to the Anakim in Deut. 1:28; 9:2; Josh. 11:21–22; the "descendants of Anak" in Num. 13:28; and the "sons of Anak" in Josh. 15:14; Judg. 1:20; cf. 21:11). These warriors were also described as "strong and tall" and reputedly unbeatable (Deut. 9:2). The meaning of the term "Nephilim" is uncertain, but it has been suggested that it could mean "fallen ones"; thus, it might allude to stories in related cultures of rebellious giants defeated by the gods in olden times (cf. Isa. 14:12). *See also* Anak; giants.

Nephtoah (nef-toh'uh), a water source on the boundary of Judah (Josh. 15:9) with Benjamin (18:15). It is identified as modern Lifta with its spring, three miles northwest of Jerusalem.

Ner (nuhr; Heb., "light"), the name of the Benjaminite father of Abner, Saul's military commander (1 Sam. 14:50–51; 26:5, 14). Nothing else is known of his life, and his relation to Saul is unclear. One passage, 1 Sam. 14:50, may indicate that he was Saul's uncle, but it could also mean that Abner was Saul's uncle. He is called the brother of Kish (Saul's father) in 1 Chron. 9:36, which would indeed make him Saul's uncle, but he is called the *father* of Kish in 1 Chron. 8:33; 9:39, which would make him Saul's grandfather.

Nereus (nee′ri-yoos), a person who, along with his sister, is greeted by Paul in Rom. 16:15. It is possible that Nereus and his unnamed sister are children of Philologus and Julia, mentioned in the same reference. *See also* Julia.

Nergal-sharezer (nuhr′gal-shuh-ree′zuhr; Babylonian Nergal-shar-usur, "O Nergal, preserve the king!"), a Babylonian official. He is listed in the book of Jeremiah as being among the officers present in Jerusalem during and after the siege of 587 BCE. In two passages, he is called Nergal-sharezer the Rabmag (39:3, 13). The meaning of the latter expression is unknown, but contemporary Neo-Assyrian and Babylonian documents do make reference to an official known as a *rab-mugi*. It is also not clear whether this Nergal-sharezer should be identified with the person by that name who later ruled as king of Babylonia (559–556 BCE).   D.B.W.

Neri (nee′ri), an ancestor of Jesus (Luke 3:27).

Neriah (ni-ri′uh; Heb., "light of the LORD" or "the LORD is light"), the father of Baruch, the scribe and associate of Jeremiah (cf. Jer. 32:12; 36:4–32), and also the father of Seraiah, an officer of King Zedekiah (51:59). *See also* Baruch.

Nero (nihr′oh; 37–68 CE), Roman emperor (ruled 54–68 CE), the son of Agrippina, the fourth wife of the emperor Claudius. Nero is reported to have murdered his mother and his wife Octavia in order to marry the beautiful Poppea, whom he also later murdered. The early part of Nero's reign, while Nero was under the influence of the philosopher Seneca, promised a rule of moderation in which the Senate would have restored to it the powers usurped by Claudius. A change in Nero's conduct occurred in 62 CE, after which he tended toward public brutality and sexual licentiousness and demanded public adulation as a god.

Nero came under increasing criticism for his preoccupation with artistic activities such as drawing, painting, and participating in musical and theatrical contests and for his preoccupation with chariot races. He mounted an artistic tour of the Greek East and also portrayed himself as following in the footsteps of Alexander the Great. However, Nero had none of the latter's interest in the conduct of war. He used the wealth of the empire to buy popularity with gifts of money to the praetorians and later to the populace of Rome, whom he kept pacified with cheap or free corn. A fire in Rome in 64 CE enabled Nero to use the land of the burned out area to build a grand palace,

The profile of the Roman emperor Nero portrayed on bronze sestertius (ca. 65 CE).

"the gold house." Nero blamed the fire on Christians (an unpopular new group in Roman society), and he ordered the brutal execution of a number of Christians. Both the apostles Peter and Paul probably lost their lives in this persecution. Nero's relations with Roman aristocracy and the Senate continued to decline. Paranoia about threats to overthrow his rule resulted in his execution of numerous generals and senators as well as persons in the Julio-Claudian line who might have succeeded him as emperor. Revolts broke out in Britain, Gaul, and Spain, and Nero was finally declared a public enemy by the Roman Senate. His suicide in 68 CE marked the end of the Julio-Claudian line of Caesars. Christian hostility to Nero as the epitome of excessive Roman power and brutality is evident in Rev. 13. The number of the beast, "666" (Rev. 13:18), is probably arrived at by way of gematria: in Hebrew, letters also served as numerals and the sum of the letters *qsr nrwn* (Caesar Neron, the typical spelling of his name) is exactly 666. The sum of the letters *qsr nrw* (Caesar Nero, an alternative spelling) is 616, which is given as the number of the beast in some variant manuscripts of Revelation. *See also* Caesar; gematria; Rome.
                                        P.P./M.A.P.

nests. Literal references to nests in the Bible reflect observation of and appreciation for the world of nature. It is forbidden to harm a hen by taking her from her nest (Deut. 22:6); an eagle stirs up her old nest (32:11); doves build nests on the sides of the gorge (Jer. 48:28); the great owl and vulture build nests on deserted sites (Isa. 34:15); and swallows build nests on altars (Ps. 84:3).

In a metaphorical sense, Assyria is likened to one robbing a nest (Isa. 10:14), and the Babylonians are said to have been lulled into a false sense of security by thinking they have set their nests on high, safe from the reach of harm (Hab. 2:9). The term is also used symbolically to refer to the abode of human beings (Job. 27:18; Jer. 22:33). In the NT, Jesus says the kingdom of God is like a mustard seed that grows into a plant so large birds of the air can make nests in its shade (Mark 4:32) or in its branches (Matt. 13:32; Luke 13:19). He also reflects on the irony of his status as one who is supposed to be exalted, but remains homeless: "Foxes have holes, and birds of the air have nests; but the Son of Man has nowhere to lay his head" (Matt. 8:20; Luke 9:58). S.R./M.A.P.

Nethanel (ni-than'uhl; sometimes Nethaneel; Heb. *natanel*, "God gives").

1 The son of Zuar (Num. 1:8) and commander of 54,400 men (2:5; 10:15) who took part in the dedication of the altar of the tabernacle (7:18–23).

2 The fourth son of Jesse, and a brother of David (1 Chron. 2:14).

3 A priest who was to blow the trumpets before the ark (1 Chron. 15:24).

4 A prince of Judah sent by King Jehoshaphat (ca. 873–849 BCE) to instruct all the cities of Judah in the "book of the law of the LORD" (2 Chron. 17:7–9).

5 A Levite, the father of Shemaiah (1 Chron. 24:6).

6 A Levite, the son of Obed-edom, a gatekeeper in the temple (1 Chron. 26:4).

7 One of the Levites who contributed to the Passover offering in the time of Josiah (late seventh century BCE; 2 Chron. 35:9; 1 Esd. 1:9).

8 The son of Pashhur, and a priest who divorced his foreign wife in response to Ezra's postexilic proclamation (Ezra 10:22; 1 Esd. 9:22).

9 The head of the priestly house of Jedaiah in the days of the high priest Joiakim (late sixth–early fifth century BCE; Neh. 12:21).

10 A priest who took part in the dedication of the rebuilt wall of Jerusalem (Neh. 12:36). S.R.

Nethaniah (neth'uh-ni'uh; Heb., "the LORD gives").

1 The father of the man Ishmael who first joined, then attacked and killed Gedaliah, the ruler of Judah appointed by Babylonia (2 Kings 25:23, 25; Jer. 40:8–41:18).

2 A temple musician, the son of Asaph (1 Chron. 25:2, 12).

3 A Levite sent by King Jehoshaphat to teach in Judah (2 Chron. 17:8).

4 The father of Jehudi, a messenger for Jeremiah (Jer. 36:14).

Nethinim (neth'in-im). *See* temple servants.

Netophah (ni-toh'fuh), a Judean hill village near Bethlehem (1 Chron. 2:54; Ezra 2:21–22; Neh. 7:26). It was the home of two of David's warriors, Maharai and Heleb (2 Sam. 23:28–29; 1 Chron. 11:30). It was also the home of Gedaliah's supporter Seraiah, after Jerusalem's fall to Babylon (587/6 BCE; 2 Kings 25:23; Jer. 40:8–9).

Various levitical and other returnees from exile in Babylon counted it their home (Ezra 2:22; Neh. 7:26; 1 Chron. 9:16). It may be modern Khirbet Bedd Faluh, some three and a half miles southeast of Bethlehem. The modern spring 'Ain en-Natuf may reflect the name.

nets. *See* fish.

nettle, any of a group of stinging or thorny plants, usually of the genus *Urtica*. It is a symbol of desolation and inaccessibility (Prov. 24:31; Isa. 34:13; Hos. 9:6; Zeph. 2:9). In Job 30:7 nettles serve as protection for Job's opponents.

new birth. *See* conversion.

new covenant, the term given by Jeremiah to a new arrangement between God and human beings in which the law would be written in their hearts rather than on tablets of stone (31:31–33). It is also a possible translation of the Greek *kainē diathēkē*, which can also be translated "new testament." The early Christians believed that the promise of a new covenant/testament was fulfilled in Christ (see 2 Cor. 3:6; Heb. 8:8, 13; 9:15; 12:24), which gave rise to the designation of their scriptures as the "New Testament." Jesus himself is represented as speaking of a new covenant in his words at the Last Supper (Luke 22:20; 1 Cor. 11:25; the words "new covenant" are missing, however, in the parallel accounts of that meal in Matt. 26:26–29; Mark 14:22–25). *See also* New Testament.

new moon. *See* festivals, feasts, and fasts; moon.

New Testament, the collection of writings making up the second part of the Christian scriptures; the first part is the Old Testament (OT).

Origin of the Name: The words "New Testament" are themselves a variant translation of the "new covenant," a term used in Jer. 31:31–33. The prophet spoke of a time when God would make a new covenant with God's people; according to an early Christian tradition preserved in 1 Cor. 11:25, Jesus alluded to this promise at a final meal with his disciples the night before he was crucified, speaking specifically of the "new covenant in my blood." Accordingly, a number of early Christian writers maintained that the death and resurrection of Christ was the event through which the new covenant/testament had been initiated (2 Cor. 3:6; Heb. 8:8–13; 9:15; 12:24). Thus, the term "new testament" seems first to have referred to this new arrangement by which people might be saved through the act of God in Christ. By extension, the term was later applied to scriptural writings produced within the era of this new arrangement. Christians saw all of God's dealing with humanity as falling into two broad eras—the era of the old covenant/testament and the era of the new covenant/testament. They classed writings they believed to be scripture as Old Testament writings and New Testament writings accordingly.

Contents and Arrangement of the Canon: There is virtual unanimity among Christians regarding the contents of the NT canon, although some branches of the Syriac church do not recognize 2 Peter, 2 and 3 John, Jude, and Revelation. The books are arranged into seven categories.

The Gospels: There are four Gospels (Matthew, Mark, Luke, John), named for the individuals who have traditionally been identified as their authors. All four report on the life, ministry, death, and resurrection of Jesus; thus, they provide four different versions of the same basic story and there is a good deal of overlap in their contents. The first three Gospels, in particular, have so much in common that some sort of literary dependence is generally proposed to account for the often verbatim repetition of material. They are called the Synoptic Gospels, in distinction from the Gospel of John, which is strikingly different in tone and content.

The Book of Acts: Acts probably constitutes "part two" of the Gospel of Luke, but it has been put in its own section in the NT (after all of the Gospels), because it is the only book that relates the history of the early church, i.e., what happened *after* the events reported in the Gospels.

Letters from Paul to Churches: There are nine letters from Paul to churches (Romans, 1 Corinthians, 2 Corinthians, Galatians, Ephesians, Philippians, Colossians, 1 Thessalonians, 2 Thessalonians). The names derive from geographic references, indicating the people in various cities or regions to which the letters were sent (e.g., the Ephesians were people who lived in the city of Ephesus). The designated author of all nine letters is Paul, a missionary who intentionally proclaimed the Christian gospel to Gentiles in the Greco-Roman world, far from the area where Jesus himself had lived. These letters are presented in the NT in order of their length, from Romans (the longest) to 2 Thessalonians (the shortest).

Letters from Paul to Individuals: There are four letters to specific people (1 Timothy, 2 Timothy, Titus, Philemon), named for the individuals to whom they were sent. Again, they are presented in descending order of length. The designated author is the same Paul who is associated with the nine letters to churches, making a total of thirteen letters from Paul.

The Letter to the Hebrews: Hebrews is in a class of its own. It is an anonymous book: both the author and the intended recipients are unknown. Because the book appears to have been written for Jewish Christians (i.e., Hebrew Christians) it is traditionally called the Letter to the Hebrews.

Letters by Others: There are seven other letters (James, 1 Peter, 2 Peter, 1 John, 2 John, 3 John, Jude). Unlike the letters from Paul, they are not named for the people to whom they were sent, but rather for the individuals who have traditionally been identified as their authors. They are often called the General Letters (or Epistles) or the Catholic Letters (or Epistles).

The Book of Revelation: Revelation is also in a class of its own. It offers an account of a visionary experience, as recounted by someone whose name was John. It is sometimes called the Apocalypse of John (the word *apocalypse* means "revelation").

As indicated, then, the books of the NT are *not* arranged in chronological order. To take just one example, the Gospels come first, but they were not the first books to be written. All four of them were probably written after the death of Paul, and thus they must be chronologically later than any letters that Paul wrote.

The Language of the NT: The NT books were all written in what is usually called Hellenistic Greek, with kinship to both Koine Greek (i.e., the Greek spoken in the Mediterranean basin ca. 300 BCE–300 CE) and the Greek of the LXX. This becomes especially significant with regard to the Gospels, because Jesus and his earliest followers probably spoke Aramaic. Thus the Gospels present a translation of Jesus's teaching from original Aramaic to Hellenistic Greek, with accompanying transference of images and context.

Authorship: Nine of the twenty-seven NT books are anonymous (Matthew, Mark, Luke, John, Acts, Hebrews, 1 John, 2 John, 3 John). The titles attached to all of these, with the exception of Hebrews, reflect ancient church traditions regarding the supposed authors, but these claims do not necessarily hold up to the scrutiny of modern scholarship. For example, very few modern scholars think that Matthew (one of Jesus's twelve disciples) wrote the Gospel of Matthew. The remaining eighteen NT books do appear to make claims regarding their authors, but in quite a few cases these claims are suspect as well. Many scholars think that the practice of pseudepigraphy (attributing a writing to someone else) was widely practiced, often in an honorable way (e.g., as a tribute to one whose ideas had inspired the writing in question). This matter is much debated in biblical scholarship, but the only books of the NT for which authorship is undisputed are seven of the letters of Paul (out of the thirteen): Romans, 1 Corinthians, 2 Corinthians, Galatians, Philippians, 1 Thessalonians, Philemon. *See also* Aramaic; canon; covenant; gospel; Gospels, the; Greek language; letter.

Bibliography

Powell, Mark Allan. *Introducing the New Testament: A Historical, Literary, and Theological Survey.* Baker Academic, 2009.   C.H.T./M.A.P.

New Testament chronology. *See* chronology, New Testament.

New Year Festival (Heb. *ro'sh hashanah,* "the beginning [lit., head] of the year"), the festival celebrated on the first day of the month of Tishri (Sept./Oct.), the seventh month of the Jewish calendar. Basic regulations for the observance of the New Year Festival appear in Lev. 23:23–25 and Num. 29:1–6. These texts refer to the festival as "a holy convocation" or "the day of trumpet blasts." It is a day of rest on which no work is to be done. Sacrificial offerings include one young bull, one ram, and seven male lambs together with their respective cereal offerings. In addition, a male goat is to be sacrificed as a sin offering.

There is some confusion in the biblical tradition concerning the New Year Festival. The first of Tishri is nowhere designated as New Year's Day in the Bible. The term *ro'sh hashanah* appears only in Ezek. 40:1, where it refers to the general time of the year, but not specifically to the New Year Festival. According to Exod. 12:2, the month of Abib, later known as Nisan (March/ April), is the first month of the year, but no New Year Festival is prescribed for the first of Nisan. The first of Nisan, however, is the beginning of the eleven-day Babylonian New Year Festival. This has prompted some scholars to suggest that the biblical New Year originally fell on the first of Tishri, but that at some point, probably during the Babylonian exile, the observance shifted to the first of Nisan to conform with Babylonian practice. Others argue that the original New Year was in the spring and later shifted to the autumn. Yet others distinguish two types of New Years. The first of Nisan was the regnal New Year, by which the reigns of kings were reckoned, and the first of Tishri was the religious or agricultural New Year for reckoning the liturgical calendar.

Another issue concerns the relation of the biblical New Year Festival to the Babylonian New Year, or *akitu,* festival. This festival, held in the spring from the first to the eleventh of Nisan, emphasized the renewal of creation and kingship. The celebration featured a liturgical recitation and reenactment of the Babylonian creation epic in which Marduk, the city god of Babylon, defeated the chaos monster Tiamat and set the cosmos in order. The festivities also included a ritual procession around the city, a ritual humiliation of the king, and a ritual marriage of Marduk atop the ziggurat of Babylon. At the end of the festival, the king received the tablets of destiny that assured his rule for another year. Some scholars have attempted to argue that a similar New Year Festival was observed in Jerusalem during the monarchic period. It is likely, however, that the biblical New Year Festival was a harvest celebration associated with the Day of Atonement (Lev. 23:26–32; Num. 29:7–11) and the Festival of Tabernacles (Lev. 23:33–43; Num. 29:12–38; Deut. 16:13–15; cf. Exod. 23:16; 34:22). *See also* Babylon; calendar; Nisan; Tiamat; time; Tishri.   M.A.S.

Nicanor (ni-kay'nuhr).

1 A Syrian general assigned by the Seleucid king Antiochus IV Epiphanes to suppress the Maccabean uprising in Judea. The son of Patroclus, he one of the "king's friends" (1 Macc. 3:38; 2 Macc. 8:9), He was associated with two other high officers, Ptolemy (the son of Dorymenes) and Gorgias. Judas Maccabeus is said to have routed the forces of those officers near Emmaus in 166 BCE (1 Macc. 4; 2 Macc. 8). Nicanor returned later with another army, but was decisively defeated in the battle of Beth-horon on 13 Adar (Feb./March) in 161 BCE. The book of 2 Maccabees ends victoriously with

an account of this defeat (on what would come to be known as "Nicanor Day") and with a description of the mutilation and exposure of Nicanor's remains. In fact, however, swift retaliation by the Syrian commander Bacchides at Beroea a few months later brought Judas's life to an end. *See also* Maccabees; Seleucids.

2 According to Acts 6:1–6, one of the seven appointed by the Jerusalem church to administer the daily distribution of food.   F.O.G.

Nicodemus (nik'uh-dee'muhs), a Pharisee, a teacher of Israel, and a ruler of the Jews as described in the Gospel of John. Nicodemus comes to Jesus by night and engages him in conversation about the need to be born again (or, "from above"), God's love for the world, and Jesus's unique role as the Son of God (3:1–21). Nicodemus is later presented as defending Jesus, objecting that some of his fellow Pharisees are judging him without allowing him a fair hearing (7:50–52). Finally, after the crucifixion, he appears with Joseph of Arimathea, bringing a hundred pounds of myrrh and aloes with which to prepare Jesus's body for entombment (19:39). Mentioned only in the Fourth Gospel, Nicodemus seems to be presented in that Gospel as the personification of a learned Jewish constituency that might be well disposed toward Jesus, but does not understand him adequately or at least does not feel prepared to confess him publicly as the Christ. *See also* Joseph.

     D.M.S.

Nicolaitans (nik'uh-lay'uh-tuhnz), a Christian sect in Ephesus and Pergamum whose members are denounced in Rev. 2:6, 15 for eating food sacrificed to idols and for sexual license. Early church traditions tended to identify the group with followers of Nicolaus of Antioch mentioned in Acts 6:5 and also to associate them with second-century libertine Gnosticism (Irenaeus *Against Heresies* 7.24; Clement of Alexandria *Miscellanies* 2.20). Modern scholarship is skeptical of such connections.

Nicolaus (nik'uh-lay'uhs), one of the seven men selected in the early days of the Jerusalem church to administer the distribution of food to widows (Acts 6:1–6). This appointment was necessitated when disciples among the Hellenists complained against the Hebrews that their widows were being neglected in the daily distribution. The latter two groups appear to have been followers of Jesus associated with different Jewish synagogues or traditions (perhaps distinguished by whether the language used in worship was Greek or Hebrew). Nicolaus is further identified as a proselyte, indicating that he had once been a Gentile, but had fully converted to Judaism. *See also* Hellenists; proselyte.

Nicopolis (ni-kop'uh-lis; Gk., "city of victory"), according to Titus 3:12, the place where Paul hoped to spend the winter and where Titus was to join him. Several towns were named Nicopolis,

but this reference is almost certainly to the town founded in Epirus (west-northwest of Corinth) by Octavian in 31 BCE commemorating his victory over Antony at nearby Actium. It was a Roman colony and the capital of the province of Epirus.

J.L.P.

Niger (ni'guhr), another name for Simeon, a leading prophet or teacher in the church at Antioch (Acts 13:1). *See also* Simeon.

night. In Gen. 1:3–5, God creates light, separates it from darkness, and then names the two phenomena: the light is called Day and the darkness is called Night. Many literal references to night in the Bible refer to it as a time for sleep (thus a night without sleep is unfortunate, Job 7:3–4). Because of the association with sleep, night is also a time for dreams (Gen. 40:5; 41:11; Dan. 7:2, 7, 13; Matt. 2:12). Metaphorically, night may be associated with danger (Ps. 91:5), sadness (Ps. 30:5), secrecy (John 3:2), or the absence of God (9:10; cf. 13:30) and the presence of death (Luke 12:20). *See also* time.

P.J.A.

nighthawk, one of a number of birds listed in the Bible as unclean and, so, as unfit for human consumption (Lev. 11:13–19; Deut. 14:12–18). Its exact identity is unknown; some have conjectured it designates some species of owl.

Nile (nil), the great river of Egypt flowing north from its sources in Lake Victoria in Uganda and in the highlands of Ethiopia, a distance of 4,037 miles, the entire length of the Sudan and Egypt, to the Mediterranean. The two major branches, the White Nile (from Lake Victoria) and the Blue Nile (from Ethiopia), merge at Khartoum, with one modest tributary somewhat farther to the north and none at all in Egypt itself. Beyond Khartoum the Nile flows through several cataracts, inhibiting navigation but not preventing it. The last cataract is at Aswan, the beginning of the Nile Valley proper. (Because the Nile flows from south to north, the southern Nile Valley is referred to as Upper Egypt.) From here on the Nile flows north in a well-developed valley with cliffs on either side almost as far as Cairo, and the river becomes important for its overflow and the hydraulic irrigation of the adjoining floodplain. Within the Nile Valley the river is fairly constant at about six-tenths of a mile in width, whereas the valley varies from six to nine miles across.

Most of the agricultural land is on the west bank, since the river generally flows closer to the eastern cliffs. The wider western floodplain benefits, in a number of areas, from secondary channels of the river. The best known of these is the Bahr Yusuf, which formerly flowed into the Faiyum, a large, well-watered area with a permanent lake somewhat south of Cairo, extending about fifty miles into the western desert. From Cairo (the area of ancient Memphis and On) the river fans out into a great delta, ultimately over one hundred and fifty miles wide. (The Delta is referred to as Lower Egypt.)

Today the Delta has a high water table and extensive areas occupied by lakes and swamps.

Sailing boats in a contemporary photograph of the Nile in front of the Elephantine Island near Aswan, Egypt, the beginning of the Nile Valley proper.

Presumably the situation was similar in antiquity. Following the spring rainfall in the highlands of East Africa, the Nile at Aswan rises over eighteen feet and reaches its peak flow in mid-September, with the low point coming in late April. Prior to the building of the modern dams, the Nile overflow brought a tremendous amount of new sediment and minerals each year (about 185 million tons) and therewith renewal for the agricultural land. But an inundation that was too high, too low, or unseasonal could mean disaster. Nonetheless, almost all the people lived in the Nile Valley or the Delta and owed their very existence to the Nile. Even in the Delta the yearly rainfall is 8 inches or less, and in the southern Nile Valley there is virtually no rain.

The Nile is also the major highway of Egypt. Movement north and south along the floodplain was certainly possible, but on any extensive journey frequent crossings of the Nile were required. Heavy goods of course were transported on the river. Indeed, the great building projects of pharaonic Egypt were dependent on easy movement of massive loads by Nile barges. During the inundation the Nile could deliver great loads to virtually any site along the valley. The importance of Nile transport is indicated by the representations of boats in tombs, the burial of special boats alongside the pyramids, and the provision in the temples of storage places for the boats used by the gods in their journeys. It was the Nile that bound Egypt together.

In biblical times the sources of the Nile were unknown. The Egyptians themselves had practical knowledge of the Nile well into the Sudan, but the Nile was so essential to them and so mysterious that it was also seen in special ways. In some texts the floodwaters of the Nile are described as rising out of caverns at the Aswan cataract. Even the Nile in the Delta area was thought to have a special origin near On (Heliopolis). Special "nilometers" were maintained at strategic points, such as near Memphis in the north and on the island of Elephantine at Aswan, so as to estimate in advance the height of the inundation. As Egyptian power expanded southward into Nubia, additional observation points were established at the second and the fourth cataracts. But even with advance warning a high Nile might prove destructive and a low Nile remain insufficient.

The Nile inundation, the river's dynamic essence, was personified in the god Hapy. Hapy, the Nile's fecundity, was represented as a well-fed figure, apparently both male and female, often colored green or blue, the colors of life. Hapy is a representative of Nun, the primeval water itself. But it is striking that, although Hapy is depicted in most of the temples, Hapy had no special temple. The seasonal festivals recognizing the Nile took place at a number of points along the river, with various offerings, amulets, and figurines. At times there was even human sacrifice to the Nile.

The Nile was well known in biblical tradition and to the biblical writers. There are many references to the Nile and its impressive flooding, unlike any rivers of Israel (e.g., Jer. 46:7–8; Amos 8:8). Punishment of Egypt might mean that God would dry up the Nile (Isa. 19:5), and the ultimate arrogance of Pharaoh was his claim that "my Nile is my own; I made it" (Ezek. 29:3). In the time preceding the exodus, Pharaoh commanded that every Hebrew male child should be cast into the Nile (Exod. 1:22), though Moses was providentially rescued by being placed in a basket of bulrushes (Exod. 2). The signs and wonders wrought by Moses included turning Nile water into blood (Exod. 4:9; 7:14–22). *See also* Egypt.   H.B.H.

Nimrim (nim′rim; Heb., perhaps "leopards"), a desert stream. The waters of Nimrim are said to be desolate (Isa. 15:6; Jer. 48:34). They are identified as those of either Wadi en-Numeira, on the east side of the Dead Sea near its southern end, or the Wadi Shu'eib, seven miles north of the Dead Sea. Based on the context, the former would seem to be the more plausible location. *See also* Dead Sea.

Nimrod (nim′rod), an ancient Mesopotamian king and conqueror mentioned in Gen. 10:8–12 (cf. 1 Chron. 1:10) and Mic. 5:6 (cf. Heb. 5:5). In the latter passage, the "land of Nimrod" is a poetic term for Assyria. Nimrod is called the son of Cush, which in Gen. 10:8 seems to refer to Cossea, the country of the Kassites in Mesopotamia. Nimrod might also be related to "Nimrud," a name used for several places in Mesopotamia, including ancient Calah. The biblical Nimrod is presented as the first powerful king on earth, and the first cities of his kingdom are said to have been Babylon, Erech, and Accad in Babylonia, and Nineveh and Calah in Assyria (v. 10). He was also a mighty hunter "before the LORD."   R.J.C.

Nimrud (nim′rood). *See* Nimrod.

Nimshi (nim′shi), the grandfather of Jehu, king of Israel (i.e., the northern kingdom; 2 Kings 9:2, 14). Although Jehu is called the son of Nimshi in some places (1 Kings 19:16; 2 Kings 9:20), the word "son" may be used broadly in those passages to mean "descendant." *See also* Jehu.

Nineveh (nin′uh-vuh; from Assyrian Nina or Ninua), one of the oldest and greatest cities of Mesopotamia. Nineveh was the capital of Assyria at its height, from the time of Sennacherib, who assumed the throne in 705 BCE, to its fall in 612 BCE. It subsequently became a symbol of Assyria's collapse. The city was located on the east bank of the Tigris River opposite Mosul.

Name and History: The Ninua of cuneiform sources goes back to an earlier form, Ninuwa. In addition to the syllabic spelling, the cuneiform texts also occasionally use a pseudologographic form, Nina, which is the combination of two signs (AB+HA) that represent an enclosure with a fish inside. This reading is of particular interest

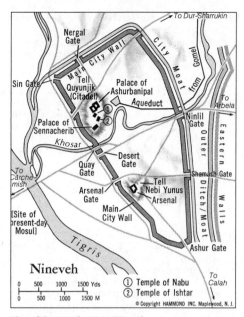

Nineveh

| 0 | 500 | 1000 | 1500 Yds |
| 0 | 500 | 1000 | 1500 M |

① Temple of Nabu
② Temple of Ishtar

© Copyright HAMMOND INC. Maplewood, N.J.

Plan of the site of ancient Nineveh;
a modern mapmaker's reconstruction
based on available evidence.

in light of the biblical story of the prophet Jonah
being swallowed by a large fish after his refusal to
go to Nineveh (Jon. 1:17). Another line of folk interpretation is found in Greek literature, where the
city is called Ninos, after a legendary hero by that
name. It has been suggested that the name of the
city was connected in some way with a goddess associated with fish. From the Akkadian period on,
the city was dedicated to the "Ishtar of Nineveh."

Though the city was occupied from prehistoric
times and rebuilt repeatedly by kings of the Middle Assyrian period, the city reached the height
of its fame at the turn of the eighth century BCE,
when Sennacherib made Nineveh the capital of
the expanding Assyrian Empire. When Assyria
subsequently held sway over Egypt, under Esar-
haddon and Ashurbanipal, Nineveh was the most
powerful city in the world. Nonetheless, its end
was but decades away. In 612 BCE the city fell to
the combined forces of the Babylonians and the
Medes. Some twenty-five centuries later the discovery of the great library of Ashurbanipal in the
ruins of Nineveh would furnish the clues for the
recovery of the intellectual and spiritual treasures
of ancient Mesopotamia.

In the Bible: The earliest biblical mention of
Nineveh is in the Table of Nations (Gen. 10:11),
which claims Nimrod as the city's founder. Parallel passages in 2 Kings 19:36 and Isa. 37:37
mention Nineveh in conjunction with the assassination of Sennacherib by his two sons. The end of
Nineveh is proclaimed by two contemporary biblical prophets, Zephaniah and Nahum. Though
Zephaniah's prophecy is brief and incidental

(2:13–15), the book of Nahum in its entirety is directed against the city, under the title "An Oracle
Concerning Nineveh." Nahum's poetic work
describes the fall of Nineveh in unexcelled imagery and power.

Another biblical work centering on Nineveh
is the book of Jonah. Here, curiously, the people
of Nineveh are unusually responsive to the message of God's prophet. They proclaimed a fast and
put on sackcloth, "from the greatest of them to
the least of them" (3:5), before the news had even
reached the "king of Nineveh," who then followed
suit (3:6). According to the NT, these Ninevites
will arise at the Last Judgment to condemn the unrepentant generation of Jesus (Matt. 12:41; Luke
11:30–32).

Archaeological Excavations: The ruins of
Nineveh consist of a number of small mounds
and two large tells in an 1800-acre enclosure surrounded by a brick wall almost eight miles in circumference. The main focus of excavations has
been the larger of the tells, Quyunjik. The smaller
tell, Nebi Yunus, marks the traditional site of the
tomb of the prophet Jonah and is occupied by a
modern settlement. *See also* Assyria, Empire of;
Jonah, book of; Nahum, book of.   D.L.C.

Nippur (ni-poor′; Sumerian Nibru), a city in
central Babylonia. The city occupied a special
place in the political and religious life of Mesopotamia, especially in the period prior to 1500 BCE.
Its god was Enlil. The god, his priests, the temple,
and the city possessed special political prerogatives; a set of mythological and theological images
and forms developed around the god and temple,
and this Nippur tradition influenced the cultural

A plan of ancient Nippur, indicating the
locations of the temple, city walls, gates, and
canals; clay tablet fragment.

life of the Babylonians and Assyrians. In the sixth century BCE, Nippur served as a major area of settlement for the exiled Judeans.

The core city consists of two main sections: the eastern section (containing the sacred areas of the Enlil complex, Inana temple, and North temple) and Tablet Hill. The city can be traced back almost to the beginning of the Uruk period, ca. 3500 BCE.

Sometime in the early third millennium BCE, Nippur was the central meeting place of a league of cities. Here, under the aegis of Enlil and his priesthood, representatives of major cities met in assembly and decided upon joint actions and offices of the alliance of cities. Located between the cities of the north and south, Nippur was regarded as the seat of the chief god of the Babylonian pantheon, Enlil, and it became an important religious and political center. From this evolved its later role in the monarchy. Thus, during the later Ur III–Isin periods, the ruler of the country was legitimated and charged by Enlil. Regular ritual journeys to Nippur by god (e.g., Nanna) and king were carried out in order to induce Enlil to bestow yearly blessings of abundance and prosperity upon the ruler and the land. The control of Nippur often amounted to legitimacy for a claim of rule over all of Babylonia.

Nippur was a major scribal center. Much of Sumerian literature known to us comes from the remains of scribal schools from the Old Babylonian period. Eventually Babylon attained first political and then religious preeminence, thus replacing Nippur. In the attempt to attain legitimacy and to create connection with earlier traditions, Babylon incorporated and built upon the traditions of Eridu. Assyria, on the other hand, linked up more directly with Nippur; thus the god Asshur is identified with Enlil, Ninlil becomes one of his wives, and Enlil's son Ninurta takes on a significant role in Assyria.

In the late eighth and seventh centuries BCE, Nippur was generally pro-Assyrian (Nippur supported Assyria even when Babylon and other northern cities were antagonistic or indifferent). Nippur served as an Assyrian garrison city in Babylonia during the wars between the Assyrians and Babylonians. It remained loyal even during the ascendancy of Nabopolassar. Eventually taken, the city and region were largely destroyed. Hence the Babylonians settled the Judean exiles in the region of Nippur in order to repopulate and rebuild the area. Autonomous settlement allowed the exiles to retain their ethnic identity and resist assimilation. In the Achaemenid period (seventh–fourth centuries BCE) the business records of the Murashu family found in Nippur mention a considerable number of Jews participating in various economic activities. *See also* Enlil.

Bibliography

Kramer, Samuel Noah. *The Sumerians.* University of Chicago Press, 1963.

Tadmor, H. *A History of the Jewish People.* Harvard University Press, 1976. Pp. 160–64, 173.

I.T.A.

Nisan (ni'san), the first month of the Jewish calendar (Esther 3:7; Neh. 2:1). Nisan is an Akkadian loanword and forms part of the Babylonian system of lunar month names taken over by the Jews sometime after the exile. Akkadian *nisannu,* itself a Sumerian loanword, corresponds to the Sumerian month name Bára.zag.gar, the first month in the Nippur system, which became standard for Babylonia during the Old Babylonian period. Nisan falls in the spring (mid-March to mid-April) and corresponds to the earlier Hebrew designation *'abib* (Exod. 13:4; 23:15; 34:18; Deut. 16:1). The festival of Passover is celebrated in mid-Nisan, and it also marks the time of Jesus's crucifixion (cf. Matt. 26:17–19). *See also* calendar.

No (noh). *See* Thebes.

Noah (noh'uh).

1 The son of Lamech (Gen. 5:28–29), the grandson of Methuselah, and the ninth descendant from Adam via Seth. The story of Noah is found in Gen. 6–9. His birth is the first recorded after Adam's death. Noah and his household are the sole human survivors of the flood, which God brought upon the world to punish human sin. Noah, the sole righteous man of his era (5:9; 7:6; cf. 6:8), was chosen, with his immediate family and his animal entourage, to perpetuate life on earth.

According to Gen. 6:19–20, Noah was commanded to build an ark and take along a male and female of every terrestrial and flying species; according to Gen. 7:2–3, however, he was commanded to take seven pairs of the clean animals and flying species rather than the one pair specified for the unclean species. Scholars view this—and numerous other details—as indications that the story that appears in the Bible has been woven together from two sources. Material that derives from the Yahwistic (J) source prefers the divine name YHWH ("the LORD"), a ready-made ark, a 40-day flood (7:11–23), and an emotionally expressive deity. Other material, derived from the Priestly (P) source, prefers the name Elohim ("God"), Noah's building the ark to specific dimensions, a 150-day flood (7:24), and a

God orders Noah to build the ark (Gen. 6:14–22); ninth-century ivory plaque, Italy.

Noah building the ark; ivory plaque
from Salerno, Italy.

dispassionate, legally minded deity. According to this reckoning, the command to bring just one pair of animals would belong to the P tradition, but the command to bring extra pairs of clean animals would derive from the J tradition. The priests responsible for the P material tended to frown upon traditions that portrayed sacrifices being offered by anyone who was not an authorized priest.

Noah's ark floated for ten months, alighting atop the Armenian mountains of Ararat–Babylonian Urartu (7:14–8:5). After sending a raven (unsuccessfully) and a dove (successfully) to scout the area, Noah emerged with his family onto land, performed sacrifices, and received God's promise not to send more floods (8:15–22). A rainbow appeared as a sign of God's covenant with humankind, symbolizing a bow (i.e., a weapon for shooting arrows) hung in the sky rather than aimed at the earth. Noah also received laws prohibiting bloodshed and consuming of lifeblood (9:1–17), an addendum to the story from the P tradition.

A postflood story about Noah served to justify the Hebrew domination of Canaan and, particularly, the Canaanite people. As the first man to plant a vineyard, Noah became drunk one day, and his son Ham "saw the nakedness of his father," which might imply that he committed some type of sexual offense against him (9:23; in Lev. 18:7–17 the expression "to uncover the nakedness of" is a euphemism for committing sexual violations). Ham's brothers Shem and Japheth averted their eyes and covered their father. When Noah realized what had been done to him, he cursed Ham's son Canaan on account of the indiscretion committed by his father, condemning him to serve his brothers (9:18–27).

An ancient Near Eastern parallel to the story of Noah and the flood is found in the Babylo-

nian Utanapishtim, which recounts Gilgamesh's experiences of a great flood (*Gilgamesh* Tab. 11). Noah is also mentioned alongside Job and Daniel in Ezek. 14:14 as one famed for righteousness. In spite of the seemingly unconditional covenantal promise given in Gen. 9, Zeph. 1:2–3 announces a coming judgment that is harsher than the flood in that even the fish will be killed. Noah is mentioned several times in the NT, especially in passages where Jesus likens the coming day of judgment to what happened in the days of Noah (e.g., Matt. 24:27–28; Luke 3:36; cf. 2 Pet. 2:5). He is also listed as an ancestor of Jesus (Luke 3:36) and as a role model of faith (Heb. 11:7). In 1 Peter Noah's deliverance from floodwaters is compared to salvation through Christian baptism (3:20–21). *See also* flood, the; Genesis, book of.

2 The second named daughter of Zelophehad (Num. 26:33; 27:1; 36:11; Josh. 17:3), a member of the tribe of Manasseh. The name was also used for a region or territory inhabited by people who regarded themselves as descendants of Noah, the daughter of Zelophehad. This is suggested by ostraca from 775–750 BCE, which refer to Noah as a region; these ostraca also refer to a region called Hoglah, the name of another one of Zelophehad's daughters. The settlement of these descendants of Noah (the daughter of Zelophehad) would have been somewhere north and east of Samaria. *See also* law; Mahlah; Zelophehad.   J.W.R.

Nob, a city in the territory of Benjamin (Neh. 11:31–35; Isa. 10:27–32) known as the "city of the priests" (1 Sam. 22:19). Nob developed as a religious center following the destruction of the sanctuary at Shiloh (late eleventh century BCE). David is said to have sought assistance from Ahimelech and the priests of Nob when he was outlawed from Saul's court, receiving some of the holy bread of the Presence for his soldiers and the sword of Goliath for himself (1 Sam. 21:1–9; cf. Matt. 12:1–8; Mark 2:23–28; Luke 6:1–5). When King Saul learned through an informer, Doeg the Edomite, that Ahimelech had "inquired of the Lord" for David, he ordered the death of the priest and of his clergy. The king's guard refused to carry out the order, but Doeg the Edomite complied, slaughtering eighty-five priests and putting all of the city of Nob to the sword (1 Sam. 22:6–23). Abiathar, the son of Ahimelech, was a survivor of this massacre and, thereafter, became the recipient of David's favor. It is evident from Isa. 10:27–32 that Nob was located not far from Jerusalem on the north and within eyesight of that city. *See also* Benjamin; David; Saul.   J.D.P.

Nod, the land of Cain's self-imposed exile, "east of Eden" (Gen. 4:16), otherwise unknown. The Hebrew etymology suggests a "homeless" or "aimless" place.

nomads, people who are without permanent residence, wandering freely with their livestock.

Nomadic life is sometimes imposed by the limitations of climate. In most territory inhabited by nomads there is sparse water and sparse pasture for year-round survival, thus forcing occupants to forage widely to keep flocks and families alive. The tendency is to take the family with the flock for ease of security to both, and living conditions in such times require mobile housing, minimal amounts of baggage, and a grouping of travelers for mutual assistance and security.

As seen in the Bible nomadism is largely pastoral; i.e., people traveled with flocks of sheep and herds of goats, asses (for transport, if not for trade), and camels in search of food and water. By contrast, references to oxen or cattle show clear agricultural settings, where both water and forage were more ample; true nomadic conditions would not have provided a sufficient supply of either for such animals. Even the groups dependent on sheep and goats for life support may have operated in a dimorphic social order, i.e., using settled villages with normal village facilities for part of the year and foraging more broadly for pasture and water during the rest of the year. Pure nomadism is difficult to find in biblical history. The ancestors are depicted as settling for various lengths of time in agricultural and urban centers of Canaan; note Abraham at Shechem (Gen. 12:6) and Hebron (13:8), Isaac at Gerar (26:6), Jacob with Laban's family (29–31), and the move from Canaan to Egypt (46:1–7). Moses's sojourn with the Midianites (2:16–22; 3:1) comes close to presenting nomadic life, except that there is such sparse information that the impression may derive from the simple absence of evidence.   R.S.B.

northeaster, a violent, springtime northeast wind that blew Paul's ship, en route to Rome, south of Crete (Acts 27:14). Some English Bibles transliterate the word from Greek as Euroclydon.

numbers. The Egyptians and the Sumerians had advanced number systems and mathematics by the beginning of the third millennium BCE. The Egyptian system was decimal (based on units of 10). The Sumerian system was a combination of a decimal and a duodecimal (units of 12) or sexagesimal (units of 6) system. Remnants of both the duodecimal and sexagesimal systems are evident in the modern system of marking time (24 hours, 60 minutes, and 60 seconds), the degrees of a circle (360), and in the units of a dozen (12) and a gross (144). The same system originally lay behind the concept of a twelve–month calendar, each with basically 30 days, for a 360-day year.

The Hebrews used the decimal system, but did not develop their own symbols until the postexilic period (539 BCE on). In all preexilic inscriptions, numbers are either represented by Egyptian symbols or are written out. Letters of the Hebrew alphabet began serving double duty as numerals during the Maccabean period (168–40 BCE); this led to interest in gematria, according to which words (especially proper names) could be assigned

An ostracon with numbers written in both Egyptian hieratic script and Hebrew; pieced together from fragments found at the fortress at Kadesh-barnea.

a numerical value based on the sum of the letters that composed the word when those letters were treated as numerals.

Symbolism and Significance: Some numbers in biblical usage had symbolic meaning. Seven probably represented completeness and perfection, as seen in the seven days of creation and the corresponding seven-day week, climaxing with the sabbath (Gen. 1:1–2:4). Even the land was to have a sabbath, lying fallow in the seventh year (Lev. 25:2–7). In Pharaoh's dream, there were seven good years followed by seven years of famine (Gen. 41:1–36). Jacob worked seven years for Rachel; then, when he was given Leah instead, he worked an additional seven (Gen. 29:15–30). The finest-quality silver was described as having been refined seven times (Ps. 12:6).

A similar use of the number seven can be seen in the NT. There are seven churches mentioned in Rev. 2–3 and seven deacons in Acts 6:1–6. To Peter's question concerning forgiveness, Jesus responds that he is to forgive not seven times, but seventy times seven (Matt. 18:21–22, likely reversing Lamech's taunt of vengeance uttered in Gen. 4:23–24).

Multiples of seven were also important. After forty-nine years came a jubilee year, when all Jewish bond servants were released and land that had been sold reverted to its former owner (Lev. 25:8–55). Exodus speaks of seventy elders (24:1, 9), and Jesus appointed seventy disciples to go before him, wherever he intended to go (Luke

10:1–17). Seventy years was to be the length of the exile according to some sources (Jer. 25:12; 29:10; Dan. 9:2). A period of seventy weeks of years was to culminate in the coming of the messianic kingdom (Dan. 9:24).

Three also indicated completeness. The created order has three parts: heaven, earth, and underworld. Three major feasts appear in the religious calendar (Exod. 23:14–19). Prayer was urged three times daily (Dan. 6:10; Ps. 55:17). The sanctuary was divided into three parts: vestibule, nave, and inner sanctuary (1 Kings 6:2–22). Three-year-old animals were prized for special sacrifices (1 Sam. 1:24; Gen. 15:9). Jesus said the Son of Man would be in the grave for three days and three nights (Matt. 12:40).

Four was a significant number, because there were four cardinal directions and, thus, four corners of the earth (Isa. 11:12) and four winds (Jer. 49:36). Four rivers flowed out of Eden to water the world (Gen. 2:10–14). Surrounding God were four living creatures (Ezek. 1:10; Rev. 4:6–7). Forty, a frequently occurring multiple of four, represented a large number or a long period of time. Forty days and nights of rain (Gen. 7:12) flooded the earth. Likewise, Jesus was tempted in the wilderness for forty days (Mark 1:12). During the forty years of Israel's wilderness wandering, all the adults who had rebelled against God died (cf. Num. 14:20–23). At age forty, a person reached maturity (Exod. 2:11; Acts 7:23). One less than forty lashes was the maximum that could be imposed on an offender (Deut. 25:3; cf. 2 Cor. 11:24).

Numbers may also be used in poetic arrangements. The pattern *x*, *x*+1 appears frequently as a device for emphasizing parallels. A good example may be seen in Prov. 30:18–19 with three and four: "Three things are too wonderful for me; four I do not understand: the way of an eagle in the sky, the way of a snake on a rock, the way of a ship on the high seas, and the way of a man with a girl." *See also* gematria. J.F.D

Numbers, book of, the fourth of the Five Books of Moses (Torah) in the Tanakh (Jewish Bible) and the fourth book of the Pentateuch of the Christian OT; it follows Leviticus and precedes Deuteronomy. Its Hebrew name is *bemidbar*, "in the wilderness," taken from the first sentence of the book, "And the LORD spoke to Moses in the wilderness of Sinai. . . ." The name "Numbers" comes by way of the LXX's name for the book *arithmoi* and the Vulgate's name *numeri*. Both reflect the importance of the census of the Israelite tribes in the book that is the basis for the allocation of territory; the phrase "according to the number of names" is found fifteen times in reference to the distribution of land.

Contents: The first portion of the book (1:1–10:10) continues the Priestly Code that also includes the tabernacle sections of Exodus, and Leviticus. The second portion of the book (10:11–21:35) resumes the narrative of Israel's experience in the wilderness. This narrative accounts for the

almost forty years the Israelites sojourned in the wilderness of Sinai. All of the reported episodes happened between the time they left Mount Sinai and the time of their encampment in the plains of Moab near the Jordan opposite the city of Jericho, where they prepared to invade Canaan.

The early chapters of Numbers detail the organization of the Israelite camp. Moses takes a census of the tribes (chap. 1), the tribes array themselves around the tent of meeting (2), and then the Levites were counted (3–4). Moses devises a test for female marital faithfulness (5) and establishes regulations for Nazirite vows (6). Then the tabernacle is dedicated (7), the Levites are

OUTLINE OF CONTENTS

Numbers

purified for tabernacle duty (8), and the Passover is celebrated (9).

The Israelites pack up and leave Mount Sinai to resume their travels (chap. 10). When they complain about their diet, God sends quail (11). When Miriam complains about Moses's marriage to a Cushite woman, she becomes afflicted with leprosy (12). Twelve spies investigate the fortifications of Canaan in preparation for the invasion, but the Israelites refuse to attack after hearing their report (13–14). Because of this the first generation of Israelites is denied entry to the promised land. After more laws of sacrifice (15), Korah, Dathan, and Abiram rebel and are executed (16). Aaron's budding staff proves to the people that he is God's choice (17). More technical instructions are given (18–19), and then Moses gets water from a rock by striking it, thereby incurring God's wrath (20); he too is denied entry into Canaan.

Israel resumes its journey by avoiding Edom, but destroys many other opponents (chap. 21). Moab fears the Israelites and tries to curse them through the prophet Balaam, but this fails miserably (22–24). Then some Israelites sleep with cult prostitutes at Baal-peor, where Aaron's grandson Phinehas executes the offenders and is granted a covenant of perpetual priesthood for his offspring (25). More technicalities, lists, and laws follow (26–36), including the designation of levitical cities and the cities of refuge and the story of the daughters of Zelophehad, who receive the inheritance of their father even though they are not male.

Themes: Numbers contains a collection of episodes that establish lines of authority within Israel. God allocates a portion of the divine spirit given to Moses to the council of seventy elders, including two men, Eldad and Medad, who were not present at the tent of meeting for the distribution of the spirit (chap. 11). Moses's siblings, Aaron and Miriam, challenge his unique authority, but God affirms him (12). The Levites Korah, Dathan, and Abiram lead an insurrection against Moses claiming that all their people are holy, thus qualified to be priests. The ground opens up and swallows them, affirming the unique priestly authority of Moses, Aaron, and Aaron's sons (16). The tribal heads challenge the unique authority of the tribe of Levi, but this matter is settled when Aaron's staff buds and bears ripe almonds, while the others do not (17).

Numbers also contains a collection of episodes that demonstrate the rebellious character of everyone in Israel. The episodes illustrate both challenges to human leaders and resistance to divine leadership. The people grow weary of manna and demand tastier fare, bringing divine wrath upon themselves (chap. 11). Israel's warriors refuse to attack Canaan from the south as they are commanded (13–14). Moses disobeys the directive to speak to a rock for water and instead strikes it, for which he is denied entry to Canaan just like the others of the first generation (20). When the people criticize God and Moses for bringing them

out into the wilderness in the first place, poisonous serpents attack them, and they survive only after they cast their eyes upon the bronze serpent Moses erects in the camp (21). The final affront to the Lord comes when Israel's men have relations with the women of Moab near Shittim at Bethpeor, and the perpetrators are killed (25). The narrative as a whole thus serves to characterize Israel as continually rebellious, unsatisfied, unfaithful, and contentious, hence in need of effective leadership and renewal. Hope is held out for the second generation of Israelites to keep covenant and prosper. They will be led by Joshua, Caleb, and Eleazar, the son of Aaron the priest.

Influences: The wilderness experiences of the Israelites between the Red Sea and Mount Sinai before the revelation of the law to Moses closely mirror the wilderness experiences of the Israelites between Mount Sinai and Moab after the revelation to Moses: murmuring, manna, and quail (Exod. 16; Num. 11); water from the rock at Meribah (Exod. 17; Num. 20); and Moses, his father-in-law, and the elders (Exod. 18; Num. 10:29–32, 11:16–30).

Numbers contains memorable characters, stories, and sayings: Balaam's talking donkey; the bronze serpent that heals the Israelites, later to be found in the temple (2 Kings 18:4); water from the rock, which the apostle Paul would take to be a symbol of Christ (1 Cor. 10:1–5); the Priestly Benediction ("The LORD bless you and keep you . . . ," Num. 6:24–26); and the Nazirite vow as a dedication practice (Num. 6), which plays a notable role in the Samson narrative (Judg. 13–16). *See also* Pentateuch, sources of the.

Bibliography

Bandstra, Barry L. *Reading the Old Testament: Introduction to the Hebrew Bible.* 4th ed. Wadsworth, 2009.

Douglas, Mary. *In the Wilderness: The Doctrine of Defilement in the Book of Numbers.* JSOT, 1993.

Levine, Baruch A. *Numbers.* 2 vols. Doubleday, 1993–2000.

Milgrom, Jacob. *Numbers (Ba-midbar): The Traditional Hebrew Text with the New JPS Translation.* Jewish Publication Society, 1990.

Nimrim, R. P. *Numbers.* Eerdmans, 2005. B.B.

Nun (nuhn), an Ephraimite who was the father of Joshua (Exod. 33:11; Josh. 1:1).

Nunc Dimittis (nuhnk di-mit'tis), a traditional Latin name given to a poem included in Luke's account of the birth of Jesus (2:29–32). It is a hymn of joy and praise attributed to Simeon, a pious man who had been waiting to see God's great act of deliverance on behalf of all people. The poem receives its name from the first words of the Latin version (English: "Now let . . . depart"). This poem centers on one of the major emphases of Luke–Acts, namely, the revelation of God's salvation for all people, Gentiles as well as Jews. It has found a significant place in the liturgies of Christian churches. *See also* hymn; Simeon. J.M.E.

nurse, a woman who breast-feeds a child or one who takes care of another. Hebrew mothers usually nursed their children (Gen. 21:7; 1 Sam. 1:23; 1 Kings 3:21; 2 Macc. 2:27; cf. Song of Sol. 8:1), but wet nurses were sometimes employed, particularly in royal families (Exod. 2:7–9; 2 Kings 11:2; 2 Chron. 22:11). After Pharaoh's daughter found the baby Moses in a basket and decided to raise him, she had to find someone to nurse him and, unwittingly, hired his mother to do this (Exod. 1:15–2:10, esp. 2:7–9). Rebekah had a wet nurse, Deborah, who remained with her all her life (Gen. 24:59; 35:8). The weaning of a child usually occurred about age three and was sometimes accompanied by festivities (Gen. 21:8; 1 Sam. 1:23–24). Distinguishable from the wet nurse (Heb. *meneqet*) is the attendant to whose care the child was entrusted (*'omenet*). Such a nurse had charge of Mephibosheth, Saul's five-year-old grandson (2 Sam. 4:4), and Naomi became Obed's nurse (Ruth 4:16). This role could also be filled by a man (*'omen,* 2 Kings 10:1, 5; Esther 2:7; metaphorically by kings, Isa. 49:23). The role of a nurse became symbolic for nurture, care, and protection. When Moses questions the extent of his responsibilities for Israel, he asks God whether he is to be regarded as the people's mother and nurse (Num. 11:12); the suggestion implied by his rhetorical questions is that God is the one who conceived the people and who is responsible for their nurture (cf. Deut. 32:13–14). The prophet Hosea also describes God as breast-feeding Israel (11:4), and the prophet Isaiah indicates that God's compassion for Israel is even greater than that of a nursing mother for her infant: "Can a woman forget her nursing child, or show no compassion for the child of her womb? Even these may forget, yet I will not forget you" (49:15). The apostle Paul reminds the Thessalonians that when he and his missionary team evangelized the city, "we were gentle among you, like a nurse [Gk. *trophos*] tenderly caring for her own children" (1 Thess. 2:7).   J.C.E.

nuts. Almonds (*Amygdalis communis*), pistachios (*Pistachia vera*), and walnuts (*Juglans regia*) are all native to the Near East, but are rarely mentioned in the Bible. The "nut orchard" referred to in the Song of Sol. 6:11 was probably a walnut orchard. In Gen. 43:11, Jacob sends pistachios and almonds to Egypt as a gift: the nuts were not grown there and would probably have been a somewhat exotic delicacy. *See also* almond.

Nuzi (noo'zee), an ancient city in what is now northeastern Iraq, situated about ten miles southwest of Kirkuk. Excavations at the site (modern Yoghlan Tepe) discovered a number of texts that have been useful for comparative study of biblical history and culture. First, a small body

One of the Nuzi tablets from the second half of the fifteenth century BCE, which help reconstruct Hurrian cultural life during the early biblical period.

of texts date to the late second or early first millennium BCE, at a time when the city was named Gasur. Second, several thousand tablets date from the second half of the fifteenth century BCE, when Nuzi was dominated by Hurrians. These tablets span a period of four generations. Third, additional Nuzi-type tablets were unearthed at Tel al-Fahhar (ancient Kurruhanni), located about nineteen miles southwest of Nuzi. The Nuzi tablets have served as a primary source for knowledge of Hurrian customs and practices, legal matters, and religious mythology. They reveal a thriving economy, marked especially by metalworking and textile industries at the very time that the Israelite ancestors (e.g., Abraham and Sarah) are said to come to Canaan from their homeland in the middle Euphrates Valley (Gen. 12:1–9). A number of practices referred to in the Nuzi tablets are roughly analogous to biblical materials: there is provision for men to father children as heirs to continue a deceased brother's line (cf. Israel's practice of levirate marriage), and for daughters to inherit in the absence of male offspring (cf. Num. 27:1–7). *See also* Mesopotamia.   B.L.E./M.A.P.

Nympha (nim'fuh), a Christian member from Laodicea to whom Paul extends greetings (Col. 4:15). Ancient manuscripts vary as to whether Nympha (feminine) or Nymphas (masculine) is the correct reading. House-churches such as the one that met in the home of Nympha(s) were a common phenomenon in the early stages of Christianity (Philem. 2; Rom. 16:23).

oak. Among the more than three hundred species of oak worldwide are the Palestinian and Tabor oak trees, which grow throughout the Near East. The evergreen Palestinian oak has small leathery leaves edged with tiny thorns, and in biblical times it thrived in the hill country at elevations of 1,000 feet. Forests were also found in Bashan in the northern Transjordan (Ezek. 27:6; Zech. 11:2) as well as in Gilead and parts of Edom, Upper Galilee, and Carmel. The Tabor oak grew at lower altitudes, in the coastal plain, Lower Galilee, and interior valleys. It is a deciduous tree with large leaves. The Plain of Sharon was at one time covered with an impenetrable Tabor oak forest, which was compared with the lush forests of Carmel and the Lebanon (Isa. 33:9; 35:2).

The oak is often a symbol of strength. As a venerable, mighty tree, the oak is associated with worship (Gen. 13:18), with sacrificial offerings (Hos. 4:13), long life (Isa. 6:13), and sanctuaries ("the oak in the sanctuary of the LORD" at Shechem, Josh. 24:26).   S.R.

oath, a statement by which people give assurance that they have spoken the truth or by which they obligate themselves to perform certain actions (Gen. 26:28; Num. 30:2; 2 Kings 11:4). God is usually invoked as guarantor of the oath (Gen. 24:3; 31:53; Deut. 10:20), with the expectation that a broken or false oath will be punished (Ezek. 16:59; Dan. 9:11). Swearing by God's name was most solemn (Matt. 26:63), and to swear falsely was to profane God's name (Exod. 20:7; Lev. 19:12). People also swore by holy things (Matt. 5:36; 23:16–22) or by raising their right hands (Rev. 10:5–6). Covenant ceremonies sometimes demanded the swearing of oaths (Gen. 26:28).

The Hebrew word for "oath" comes from the number seven, and in Gen. 21 seven lambs are used as witnesses to a covenant. Oaths and curses (a related type of statement) are often indicated in the Bible by abbreviated formulas, such as "May God do thus and so if . . ." (1 Sam. 3:17; 14:44) and "As the LORD lives . . ." (19:6). A full oath ritual for a wife suspected of adultery is found in Num. 5. Peter responds to the inquiries of people in the high priest's courtyard with a simple denial, an oath, and a curse (Matt. 26:69–74). According to the NT, Jesus taught that one should not swear oaths (Matt. 5:34; cf. James 5:12). *See also* bless; blessing; covenant; curse; witness.   A.J.S.

Obadiah (oh´buh-di´uh; Heb., "worshiper/servant of the LORD").

1 A Gadite who became a leader in David's army at Ziklag (1 Chron. 12:9).

2 The father of Ishmaiah; he became a leader in the tribe of Zebulon toward the end of David's reign (1 Chron. 27:19).

3 The steward of King Ahab's house (1 Kings 18:3–16); he was in charge of the king's estate.

4 A man commissioned by King Jehoshaphat to teach the law throughout the land of Judah (2 Chron. 17:7–9).

5 A Levite who helped oversee temple repairs during the reign of Josiah (2 Chron. 34:12).

6 A son of Hananiah; he was a postexilic descendant of David (1 Chron. 3:21).

7 The son of Izrahiah; he was a leader of the tribe of Issachar (1 Chron. 7:3).

8 The son of Azel; he was a descendant of Saul (1 Chron. 8:38; 9:44).

9 A Levite who returned to Jerusalem after the exile in Babylon (1 Chron. 9:16); he appears to be called Abda in Neh. 11:17.

10 A descendant of Joab and the ancestor of a family group that returned from Babylon to Jerusalem with Ezra (Ezra 8:9).

11 One of the men who signed Ezra's covenant-renewal document at the time of Nehemiah (Neh. 10:5). He may be the same as **10.**

12 A gatekeeper during the high-priesthood of Jehoiakim (Neh. 12:25).

13 The prophet associated with the biblical book of Obadiah. *See also* Obadiah, book of.
                                                M.A.P.

Obadiah, book of, the shortest book in the Hebrew Bible at twenty-one verses. It is the fourth part of the Book of the Twelve in the Prophets section, or Nevi'im, in the Tanakh (Jewish Bible). Within the Christian OT it is placed as one of the Minor Prophets. Its placement within the canon, following the book of Amos, may be due to thematic connections: the reference to Edom in Amos 9:11–12 and the theme of the "day of the LORD" throughout Amos are matters echoed in Obadiah. Likewise, the book of Jonah follows Obadiah, perhaps because it softens the vengeful spirit of Obadiah, showing that God can be merciful to any nation, even Assyria. Nothing is known of the prophet Obadiah other than his name, which means "servant of the Lord." Some scholars have argued that the name may have been used as a pseudonym by an author who wanted to remain anonymous. Others have postulated that the prophet was the Obadiah who was a disciple of Elijah. Without more information, date and place of composition have been difficult to pinpoint. Most scholars date the book as exilic or postexilic, after the destruction of Jerusalem in 587 BCE. Within the genre of prophetic works, Obadiah is categorized with Nahum as an "oracle against nations."

Contents: The book of Obadiah is a prophecy of condemnation upon Edom, Judah's southern neighbor. The reason for this condemnation is that the Edomites took advantage of the Judeans after the latter were forced to leave Jerusalem, even cooperating with the Babylonians and looting the land. Improper actions of the Edomites upon the fall of Judah are referenced elsewhere in the Bible (Ezek. 25; Ps. 137:7). The book begins with a superscription ("the vision of Obadiah"), then proceeds into an oracle against Edom that shows marked parallels to Jer. 49:7–22. There is disagreement over whether Jeremiah drew from Obadiah or vice versa, or whether both drew from an earlier prophetic source. Musopole argues that these prophetic connections are similar to African oral traditions, stating that visions become the property of the community and are not limited to the original messenger.

The next section (vv. 8–18) contains another oracle against Edom. It begins with grounding Edom's punishment in that nation's betrayal of Judah. The author connects the current strife between Judah and Edom to the ancestral struggles between Jacob and Esau. Thus, when Edom stands aside and allows Babylon to take Jerusalem and then plunders the land, Edom is betraying Judah as its brother. The oracle continues by stating that God's punishment of Edom will be enacted by the people of Judah and Israel. The book finishes (vv. 19–21) with a promise that the exiles will return and overtake Edom.

OUTLINE OF CONTENTS

Obadiah

I. Edom's arrogance and impending fall (vv. 1–7)
II. Judgment against Edom (vv. 8–18)
   A. Overview of oracle (v. 8)
   B. Grounds for Edom's punishment (vv. 9–14)
   C. Process of Edom's punishment (vv. 15–18)
III. Overtaking of Edom and restoration of exiles (vv. 19–21)

Themes: Like most of the Minor Prophets or works contained in the Book of the Twelve, Obadiah makes use of the theme of the "day of the LORD." In Obadiah (particularly in vv. 15–21), the "day of the LORD" is a future day in which the Edomites will be punished. Many scholars point out that the book criticizes and punishes Edom, but makes no mention of the sins of Judah that led to the fall of Jerusalem. Some have dealt with this anomaly by citing the book's genre as an "oracle against nations," claiming that it would not make sense within that genre to criticize Judah as well, putting a condition on Edom's fall.

Interpretive Issues: Scholars disagree on how Obadiah should be divided. Many scholars divide the book after v. 14, placing vv. 15–21 as an addition that universalizes the message of vv. 1–14. McKenzie and Kaltner argue for two sections based upon theme: oracle against Edom (vv. 1–14) and "day of the LORD" (vv. 15–21). According to Gottwald, vv. 1–15 are original and the remainder of the book consists of two separate editorial expansions: vv. 16–18 (promises of destruction of Edom and exaltation of Mount Zion) and vv. 19–21 (affirmation of Mount Zion's coming vindication through possessing Mount Esau). Sweeney argues for two separate oracles (vv. 1–7, 8–18) and an editorial addition (vv. 19–21).

Bibliography

Bandstra, Barry L. *Reading the Old Testament: Introduction to the Hebrew Bible.* 4th ed. Wadsworth, 2009.

Gottwald, Norman K. *The Hebrew Bible: A Socio-Literary Introduction.* Fortress, 1985.

McKenzie, Steven L., and John Kaltner. *The Old Testament: Its Background, Growth, and Content.* Abingdon, 2007.

Musopole, A. "Obadiah." In *Africa Bible Commentary.* Zondervan, 2006. Pp. 1041–44.

Sweeney, Marvin A. *The Twelve Prophets.* Vol. 1, *Hosea, Joel, Amos, Obadiah, Jonah.* Liturgical, 2000.

Wolff, Hans Walter. *Obadiah and Jonah: A Commentary.* Augsburg, 1986.   B.B.

Obed (oh'bid; Heb., "worshiper").

1 The son of Boaz and Ruth who becomes the father of Jesse and grandfather of David (Ruth 4:13–22; 1 Chron. 2:12). Naomi, Ruth's mother-in-law, was his nurse (Ruth 4:16). According to Ruth 4:17, Obed was named by the women of Bethlehem, who proclaimed, "A son has been born to Naomi." Thus, through the laws of levirate marriage (Deut. 25:5–10), Obed was considered to be one who would continue the line of Ruth's first husband Mahlon and, so, of his father, Elimelech, the deceased husband of Naomi. He is also listed in the NT as an ancestor of Jesus (Matt. 1:5; Luke 3:32).

2 The son of Ephlal and the father of Jehu, of the tribe of Judah (1 Chron. 2:37–38).

3 One of the mighty warriors in the list of King David's armies (1 Chron. 11:47).   F.R.M.

Obed-edom (oh'bid-ee'duhm; Heb., "worshiper of Edom").

1 The name of a Gittite in whose house David stored the ark of God for three months. During the transport of the ark from Baale-judah (or Kiriath-jearim) to Jerusalem, Uzzah, one of David's men, touched the ark and died. Unwilling to continue with the ark into Jerusalem, David left it in the house of Obed-edom, who was then blessed because of its presence (2 Sam. 6:6–12; 1 Chron. 13:13–14). *See also* ark of the covenant, ark of God; Kiriath-jearim; Uzzah.

2 One of the levitical gatekeepers at the tent of meeting who, along with others, led with lyres the procession that brought the ark of God from the home of Obed-edom the Gittite to Jerusalem (1 Chron. 15:18, 21). When the ark was set inside the tent in Jerusalem, Obed-edom the Levite was appointed one of the ministers of the ark (16:5). *See also* ark of the covenant, ark of God.   F.R.M.

obedience. The Hebrew Bible has no separate word meaning "obey," but the NRSV often uses "obey" to translate *shama'*, the Hebrew word for "to hear" (Gen. 22:18; Isa. 42:24). The concept is also expressed as "keeping" or "observing" the commandments (Exod. 16:28; 34:11) and "walking" in God's ways (1 Kings 11:33). God punishes disobedience by exile, e.g., from the garden of Eden (Gen. 3:22–24) or the promised land (Deut. 4:25–28), but God forgives and restores (Deut. 30:1–5).

In the NT, the connection between hearing and obedience is made explicit by Jesus in his parable of the Two Builders, which in Matthew's Gospel concludes the Sermon on the Mount. The person who hears Jesus's words and does them is like a wise man who builds his house on a rock, but the person who only hears and does not obey is like a foolish man who builds his house on sand (Matt. 7:21–27). Christ is obedient to God (Rom. 5:19; Phil. 2:8; Heb. 5:8), and Christians are called to obedience of faith (Rom. 1:5; 16:26), obedience to Christ (John 3:36; Heb. 5:9), and obedience to the gospel (Rom. 10:16; 1 Pet. 4:17). The NT also reflects Roman social-political order in calling for obedience to the state (Rom. 13:1–5) and obedience of slaves, children, and wives within the household (Eph. 5:21–6:9; 1 Pet. 2:13–3:7). *See also* commandment; law.   J.D.

obeisance, a gesture made by kneeling and placing one's face to the ground (cf. Josh. 5:14); it may be repeated several times for emphasis (Gen. 33:3; 1 Sam. 20:41). The gesture indicates submission, servitude, and respect to one's superior (1 Sam. 25:41; 2 Sam. 24:20); it can also express gratitude (2 Kings 4:37) and is thus appropriate as an act of worship (2 Sam. 12:20). The verb for obeisance can be used as a metonym for the worship of God and is found in this sense in prohibitions against idolatry (Exod. 20:5; 1 Kings 9:6). Jesus prostrates himself before God in Gethsemane (Matt. 26:39); such obedience is also implied in Matt. 2:11; 20:20, where the NRSV translates the word for prostration as "knelt" or "kneeling."

obelisk, a four-sided free-standing pillar, normally monolithic, tapering inward as it rises, terminating in a small pyramid. Obelisks were produced in Egypt from at least the latter part of the Old Kingdom (Fifth Dynasty, late third millennium BCE) until the Ptolemaic period (late fourth century BCE). Associated especially with the cult of the sun god Re, whose primary worship center was On (Heliopolis), obelisks were apparently seen as resembling the rays of the sun, the podium being the primeval hill over which the sun rose, and became symbolic of royal rejuvenation. Jer. 43:13 refers to the obelisks of Heliopolis, literally "the pillars of the sun temple which is in Egypt." As a pair flanking a temple entrance, obelisks represented the rising and setting sun; as models in tombs they related to resurrection. On, Thebes (center of the cult of Amun-Re), and Pi-Ramesse (a capital of Ramesses II) had major obelisks, products of the Eighteenth–Twentieth Dynasties (ca. 1546–1085 BCE), the tallest of which exceeds 105 feet. The obelisks elsewhere were generally shorter. Some obelisks were themselves objects of worship. Obelisk-type pillars, inspired by Egyptian models, were erected at Byblos

(Phoenicia) and at other Canaanite sites. See also Egypt; On.   H.B.H.

oblation, an evening temple sacrifice referred to in 2 Kings 18:29, 36 (Heb. *minkhah*). *See also* offering; sacrifice; worship in the Hebrew Bible.

Oboth (oh'both; Heb., "fathers"), a place on the Israelite route in the wilderness, associated with Punom and Zalmonah (Num. 33:41, 42), which the Israelites reached after leaving Egypt (21:10, 11). Its location remains uncertain due to debate about the route the Israelites took. Based on a presumed identification of Punon, some have suggested 'Ain el-Weiba, on the western edge of the Arabah Valley.

Ochran (ok'ruhn; Heb., perhaps "trouble"), the father of Pagiel, Moses's assistant from the tribe of Asher (Num. 1:13; 2:27; 7:72, 77; 10:26).

Oded (oh'did).
1 The father of the prophet Azariah (2 Chron. 15:1).
2 A prophet of Israel in the reign of Pekah (736–732 BCE). He persuaded the army of Israel to treat the captives from Judah kindly and to allow them to return home (2 Chron. 28:9–15).

odor, pleasing. Offerings burned on the altar are often described as a "pleasing odor to the LORD." This terminology occurs specifically with the burnt offering (which was entirely burned on the altar; cf. Lev. 1:9, 13, 17), the cereal offering (2:2, 9, 12), the fat parts of the well-being offering (3:5, 16), and the fat parts of the consecration offering and accompanying bread, which was burned on the altar (Exod. 29:25). It is used once of the fat parts of the purification offering (Lev. 4:31). Num. 15:24, however, when describing a burnt offering and purification offering, does not apply the term to the fat parts. This indicates that calling the burning of fat pieces of the purification offering a "pleasing odor" was not originally part of the way that sacrifice was understood. In a few cases "a pleasing odor" is used of the burnt offering plus the cereal offering and libation that accompany it (cf. Num. 15:7; 28:8).

Ezekiel uses the phrase "a pleasing odor" in connection with illicit offerings the Israelites make to idols (6:13; 16:19; 20:28). Once he says God will accept the people as "a pleasing odor," perhaps meaning accept them when they make proper offerings (20:41). *See also* offering; sacrifice; worship in the Hebrew Bible.   D.P.W.

offering, a gift presented to God, usually consisting of a nonliving object in contrast to an animal sacrifice, e.g., meal (Lev. 2:4), first fruits (2:12), or land for the sanctuary (Ezek. 48:9). The prophet Isaiah denounces vain oblations (1:13, 16–17). *See also* sacrifice; worship in the Hebrew Bible.

offering for the saints. *See* collection for the saints.

Og, the king of Bashan, whose territory lay north of the river Jabbok. He was defeated by the Israelites at Edrei before they crossed the Jordan River to enter the land of Canaan (Num. 21:33–35; Deut. 1:4; 3:1–13). Og and another Amorite king, Sihon, were massacred, and the Israelites took control of their land, including sixty walled cities that had formerly belonged to Og's kingdom. This victory became legendary and was celebrated in many subsequent writings (Josh. 12:4; 13:12, 30–31; 1 Kings 4:19; Neh. 9:22; Pss. 135:11; 136:20). Israelite tradition identifies Og as the last remnant of the Rephaim, a race of giants who inhabited Canaan prior to the Israelite settlement. This tradition is supported by mention of his great bed of iron located in Rabbah of the Ammonites (Deut. 3:11). His territory was occupied by the tribe of Manasseh. *See also* giants; Rephaim.   M.A.S.

Oholah (oh-hoh′luh; Heb., "she of the tent"), **Oholibah** (oh-hohl′i-bah; "my tent is in her"), the names of the allegorical sisters spoken of in Ezek. 23; Oholah represents Samaria and Oholibah represents Jerusalem. After a youth of prostitution with the Egyptians, Oholah turned her lust upon the Assyrians and was eventually destroyed by them. Oholibah surpassed the whoring of her sister, defiling herself with the Assyrian and Babylonian lords. Ezekiel says that she too will suffer punishment for her lewd ways, for God will not ignore the faithless idolatry of Samaria and Jerusalem.   A.B.

Oholiab (oh-hoh′lee-ab; Heb., "the father's tent"), a Danite craftworker and designer who worked with Bezalel in the design and construction of the tabernacle (Exod. 31:6; 38:23).

Oholibamah (oh-hoh′li-bah′muh; Heb., "tent of the high place").
1 The daughter of Anah and wife of Esau (Gen. 36:2, 5). She bore three children: Jeush, Jalam, and Korah (Gen. 36:5, 14, 18).
2 A descendant of Esau and a chieftain of the Edomites (Gen. 36:41; 1 Chron. 1:52).

oil, in the Bible, olive oil. Oil of varying qualities was produced at different stages of production. The best oil—beaten oil (cf. 1 Kings 4:11)—was produced by placing olives that had been crushed (e.g., by treading on them, Mic. 6:15) in baskets and letting the oil drip through. An oil of a lesser quality was obtained by beating the olive pulp and applying pressure. The pulp could be ground again and squeezed another time to obtain still more oil.

As a component in bread making, oil was a basic part of the diet. This is illustrated by the fact that the widow at Zarephath had only a jar of flour and a jar of oil (1 Kings 17:12–16). Oil was also a basic component in cereal offerings (cf. Lev. 2). Any type of oil could be used for most of these offer-

A man crushes olives, a source of oil in the biblical world, using a restored ancient stone press. Once crushed, the olives were placed in baskets that allowed the oil to drip out.

ings, but beaten oil was required for a cereal offering that accompanied the daily burnt offering (Exod. 29:40; Num. 28:5). Neither oil nor incense was to be used for certain offerings in which the element of joy was absent (Lev. 5:11; Num. 5:15).

Oil was also used for cosmetic purposes. It could be compounded with perfumes to make aromatic ointments (cf. Esther 2:12; Song of Sol. 1:3; 4:10). Mourners did not use oil on their bodies during their period of sadness (2 Sam. 14:2; Isa. 61:3; Dan. 10:2–3), for its use was an expression of gladness, refreshment, and pleasure (Pss. 23:5; 104:15). Oil was also used as an emollient to soften skin of wounds (Isa. 1:6) or to treat leather shields (21:5).

Oil was used in the religious anointing of objects and persons. Jacob anointed sacred pillars (Gen. 28:18; 31:13; 35:14). A special anointing oil was applied to Aaron, his sons, and various pieces of tabernacle furniture (cf. Exod. 29; 30:22–33). Oil was put on the right ear, thumb, and toe of a person healed of leprosy (Lev. 14:10, 12, 15–18). Kings were anointed (1 Sam. 10:1; 16:13; 1 Kings 1:39). Prophets too apparently received an anointing (1 Kings 19:16). A recipe for the composition of the priestly anointing oil is given in Exod. 30:22–25.

Oil was also used as fuel for lamps. The oil for the lamp in the tabernacle was to be beaten oil (Exod. 27:20; Lev. 24:2). In the NT, Jesus tells a parable about ten bridesmaids waiting for the wedding feast to commence; five are foolish and do not bring enough oil to keep their lamps burning through the night. Also in the NT, people are anointed with oil in healing rites (Mark 6:13; James 5:14).

Oil is used to indicate fertility of land (Deut. 33:24; Job 29:6) and, with wheat and new wine, to indicate agricultural blessing and abundance

(Deut. 7:13; 11:14). *See also* anoint; lamp; ointments and perfumes. D.P.W.

ointments and perfumes, soft unguents or salves and aromatic scents commonly used in the ancient Near East for anointing, for medicinal purposes, for beautification, in incense, and (in Egypt) for embalming. Most ointments contained a base of olive oil, to which aromatic spices, especially myrrh, were added (Exod. 30:23–25). Archaeological excavation has brought to light a great variety of small delicate flasks and jars that undoubtedly served as containers for cosmetics, ointments, and perfumes. The most precious containers were of alabaster (Matt. 26:7) and were often small jars with a lid and pedestal base or vials with a sealed neck. Anointing the head with oil was a common form of hospitality (Pss. 23:5; 92:10; 133:2), though on two occasions in the NT someone anoints Jesus's feet (Luke 7:46; John 12:3). Ointments were a precious commodity and symbolized a sacred consecration. Kings were anointed (1 Sam. 10:1; 2 Kings 9:1; 1 Kings 1:39), as was the tabernacle (Exod. 30:26–29). Similarly well attested are the uses of ointments for healing (Isa. 1:6; Luke 10:34; Jer. 8:22) and for perfume (Ruth 3:3; 2 Sam. 12:20; Song of Sol. 1:3).

Perfumes were likewise regarded as precious and served, not only cosmetic uses, but as a main ingredient of incense and the sacred anointing oil. Often referred to as spices (Exod. 25:6; 35:28), aromatic sources derive from plants such as frankincense, myrrh, cinnamon, and saffron. The spice trade was extremely profitable, and caravans plied the routes between Africa, India, Arabia, and Near Eastern ports (Ezek. 27:22; Gen. 37:25; 1 Kings 10:10). Such perfumes were used to heighten sexual attraction (Esther 2:12), to provide a pleasing scent to clothes and furniture (Song of Sol. 4:11; Ps. 45:8), and to flavor wine (Song of Sol. 8:2). The blending of several perfumes was an important component of formulas for the sacred incense and anointing oil (Exod. 30:22–25, 34–35). S.R.

Old Gate, a gate in the wall of Jerusalem restored by Nehemiah (Neh. 3:6; 12:39), probably in the west, possibly in the north, wall. Its precise location and identification remain unclear.

old prophet, the, an unnamed prophet (1 Kings 13:11) who lived in Bethel during the reign of Jeroboam I (ca. 922–901 BCE). Hearing of a Judean prophet, also unnamed, who had uttered a prophecy against an altar in Bethel, the old prophet went in search of him. When he found him and heard that God had forbidden the Judean prophet to eat or drink in Israel, the old prophet lied to him, claiming an angel had told him to give the Judean prophet food and drink. The Judean prophet believed this and, after he had eaten and drunk, the old prophet proclaimed God's judgment on him for disobedience to God's word. The unnamed Judean prophet went on his way, but was soon killed

by a lion. The old prophet buried him in his own grave, mourned him, and insisted that the word he had spoken against Bethel would come to pass (1 Kings 13).

Old Testament (from Gk. *diathēkē*, "testament" or "covenant"), the first section of the Christian Bible, in its Protestant form identical in contents but not in order to the Tanakh, the Jewish Bible. Some of the earliest Christians thought in terms of an old and a new covenant (2 Cor. 3:14; Heb. 8:7), but it was the church leaders Tertullian (ca. 160–230 CE) and Origen (ca. 185–254 CE) who first used the term "Old Testament" for the pre-Christian scriptures as a whole.

OT Canons: The simplest definition of the OT is that it is part of the Christian canon, a formally recognized list of sacred books. However, whereas all Christian communities accept that definition, its precise application is by no means simple, because various churches include different books in their particular canons of the OT. The Protestant OT includes the same thirty-nine books as the Jewish Tanakh, but in a different order. In addition to these thirty-nine books, the Roman Catholic OT includes other books identified as "deuterocanonical": Tobit, Judith, Additions to Esther, 1 and 2 Maccabees, Wisdom of Solomon, Sirach, Baruch (with the Letter of Jeremiah), and three Additions to Daniel. Bibles of the Orthodox churches include all of these deuterocanonical books, plus 3 Maccabees, 1 Esdras, the Prayer of Manasseh, and Psalm 151, with 4 Maccabees sometimes added as an appendix. In the Protestant Bible, the books that are in the other Christian OT canons but not in the Jewish Tanakh are usually identified as the Apocrypha and are printed in a separate section, either between the OT and the NT or following the NT; in Roman Catholic and Orthodox Bibles, those books occur at various places within the canon itself.

The differences between these OT canons can be explained by the history of the Bible in the different religious communities. The foundation for the development of all these canons was the Hebrew Bible of Judaism (the Tanakh). It consists of three parts, corresponding to the stages of their acceptance as sacred scripture. They are called the Torah, the Nevi'im, and the Ketuvim (the Law, the Prophets, and the Writings). With the exception of a few chapters in Aramaic, all these books were written in Hebrew. In the Hellenistic age (325–63 BCE) these scriptures were translated into Greek and additional writings (mostly composed in Greek) were added to what became a Greek version of the Jewish Bible, called the Septuagint (LXX). It was this Greek LXX version of the Bible, which included the apocryphal/deuterocanonical books, that became the OT of the Roman Catholic and Eastern Orthodox churches. The three-part Protestant Bible (OT, Apocrypha, NT) was the result of the Reformers Martin Luther and John Calvin. During the Reformation of the sixteenth century, as the Reformers called for reliance upon scripture

David (*bottom center*) slaying Goliath (1 Sam. 17); illuminated manuscript, twelfth century.

to their readers. In particular, the biblical writers tended to interpret all events according to their religious convictions. The narrative works of the OT also include short stories, tales, and stories with a lesson, such as Ruth, Esther, and Jonah. Contained within the narrative books are individual stories of different types, such as family sagas, and etiologies, i.e., narratives that explain the origin of places, names, or practices.

The first five books of the OT also contain a significant amount of legal material. Virtually all of ancient Israel's laws were understood to have been revealed by God to Moses at Mount Sinai. This means that they are understood in the framework of the covenant between God and Israel, as the stipulations by which the people continued to be God's people. Moreover, the covenant was established and the law given to a people whom God had brought out of Egypt. Laws are found in collections, such as the Decalogues in Exod. 20; 34 and Deut. 5, the Book of the Covenant in Exod. 20–23, and the Holiness Code in Lev. 17–26. For the most part, the individual laws are of two kinds, casuistic and apodictic. The casuistic is case law in two parts, the statement of a condition and then its legal results, e.g., "If a man borrows anything of his neighbor, and it is hurt or dies . . . he shall make full restitution" (Exod. 22:14). Apodictic laws are different in their inclusive and absolute character. They consist of a single short sentence, either a command or prohibition, e.g., "Honor your father

over church tradition, they returned to what they considered to be the earlier form of the OT, the books held sacred in Judaism.

A comparison of the tables of contents of Jewish and Christian Bibles shows that the order of the books is also different. There are three key differences. (1) The Jewish Tanakh places the Writings last, while the Christian OT places the Writings after the Pentateuch and certain historical books (ones sometimes called the Former Prophets—Joshua, Judges, and the books of Samuel and Kings). (2) The Jewish Tanakh places Ruth, Ezra, Nehemiah, and the books of Chronicles among the Writings, while the Christian OT places these among the historical books. (3) The Jewish Tanakh places Lamentations and Daniel among the Writings, while the Christian OT places these books among the Prophets. Differences in sequence occur between the different Christian canons as well; for example, the Orthodox canon places the twelve "minor prophets" (Hosea–Malachi) ahead of the "major prophets" (Isaiah–Daniel), while Roman Catholic and Protestant Bibles do just the opposite.

Literature: The OT is a veritable library of ancient Israelite literature. In broad terms, the various books and their parts may be identified as narratives, law, poetry, wisdom reflections and proverbs, corporate and personal prayers, and apocalypses.

The Pentateuch and the historical books are mainly narrative, though other types of literature can be found within them. Genesis includes poetry, and Exodus, both poetry and law. Many of the OT narratives must be identified as historical in the sense that they report and interpret public events of the past, but they are also told in ways intended to invoke responses and teach lessons

Moses (*center*), *The Well of Moses,* by Claus Sluter, at Dijon, France, 1395–1406.

and your mother" (Exod. 20:12); "You shall not steal" (20:15).

The OT poetic books include Psalms, Job, Proverbs, Ecclesiastes, and the Song of Solomon. The most characteristic mark of Hebrew poetry is parallelism of lines or phrases, e.g., "Why do the nations conspire // and the peoples plot in vain?" (Ps. 2:1). This is an example of synonymous parallelism, with "nations" in the first line paralleled by "peoples" in the second, and "conspire" paralleled by "plot in vain." Israelite poetry also made use of wordplays, assonance, and other rhetorical devices.

Wisdom literature, whether in the form of short sayings such as those found in Prov. 10–30 or longer compositions such as Job, was written mainly in poetry. One also finds lyrical poetry, i.e., lines meant to be sung, ranging from the love poetry of Song of Solomon to the liturgical songs of the Psalms. Among the liturgical songs are in-

dividual and communal laments or complaints, thanksgiving songs, hymns, and royal psalms.

The prophetic books, Isaiah, Jeremiah, Ezekiel, and the twelve Minor Prophets (called the Book of the Twelve in the Tanakh), contain some of the most distinctively Israelite literature, although prophets and prophecies were known in the ancient Near East generally. Behind the development of the books stand the prophetic figures themselves, individuals who announced the word of God concerning the immediate future, whether that future contained disaster or salvation.

The most common genres in the prophetic books are speeches. As a rule they are short, poetic addresses to the people as a whole, to a group, or even to an individual. When the prophets announced judgment, they usually indicated the reasons for divine punishment, typically the sins of those addressed. Remarkably, the prophets ordinarily present these speeches as the direct word

THE TANAKH AND THE OLD TESTAMENT IN VARIOUS TRADITIONS

Jewish Tanakh	Roman Catholic Old Testament	Eastern Orthodox Old Testament	Protestant Old Testament
Torah (Law)	Pentateuch	Pentateuch	Pentateuch
Genesis	Genesis	Genesis	Genesis
Exodus	Exodus	Exodus	Exodus
Leviticus	Leviticus	Leviticus	Leviticus
Numbers	Numbers	Numbers	Numbers
Deuteronomy	Deuteronomy	Deuteronomy	Deuteronomy
Nevi'im (Prophets)	History	History	History
Joshua	Joshua	Joshua	Joshua
Judges	Judges	Judges	Judges
Samuel (1, 2)	Ruth	Ruth	Ruth
Kings (1, 2)	1 Samuel	1 Kingdoms (1 Samuel)	1 Samuel
Isaiah	2 Samuel	2 Kingdoms (2 Samuel)	2 Samuel
Jeremiah	1 Kings		1 Kings
Ezekiel	2 Kings	3 Kingdoms (1 Kings)	2 Kings
The Twelve:	1 Chronicles	4 Kingdoms (2 Kings)	1 Chronicles
Hosea	2 Chronicles	1 Chronicles	2 Chronicles
Joel	Ezra	2 Chronicles	Ezra
Amos	Nehemiah	1 Esdras	Nehemiah
Obadiah	Tobit	2 Esdras (Ezra, Nehemiah)	Esther
Jonah	Judith		
Micah	Esther	Judith	
Nahum	with Additions	Tobit	
Habakkuk	1 Maccabees	1 Maccabees	
Zephaniah	2 Maccabees	2 Maccabees	
Haggai		3 Maccabees	
Zechariah		Esther	
Malachi		with Additions	

THE TANAKH AND THE OLD TESTAMENT IN VARIOUS TRADITIONS *(continued)*

Jewish Tanakh	*Roman Catholic Old Testament*	*Eastern Orthodox Old Testament*	*Protestant Old Testament*
Ketuvim (Writings)	*Writings*	*Writings*	*Writings*
Psalms	Job	Psalms (with Ps. 151)	Job
Proverbs	Psalms	Prayer of Manasseh	Psalms
Job	Proverbs	Job	Proverbs
Song of Solomon	Ecclesiastes	Proverbs	Ecclesiastes
Ruth	Song of Solomon	Ecclesiastes	Song of Solomon
Lamentations	Wisdom of Solomon	Song of Solomon	
Ecclesiastes	Sirach	Wisdom of Solomon	
Esther		Sirach	
Daniel			
Ezra–Nehemiah			
Chronicles (1, 2)			
	Prophets	*Prophets*	*Prophets*
	Isaiah	Hosea	Isaiah
	Jeremiah	Joel	Jeremiah
	Lamentations	Amos	Lamentations
	Baruch	Obadiah	Ezekiel
	with Letter of Jer.	Jonah	Daniel
	Ezekiel	Micah	Hosea
	Daniel	Nahum	Joel
	with Additions	Habakkuk	Amos
	Hosea	Zephaniah	Obadiah
	Joel	Haggai	Jonah
	Amos	Zechariah	Micah
	Obadiah	Malachi	Nahum
	Jonah	Isaiah	Habakkuk
	Micah	Jeremiah	Zephaniah
	Nahum	Lamentations	Haggai
	Habakkuk	Baruch	Zechariah
	Zephaniah	with Letter of Jer.	Malachi
	Haggai	Ezekiel	
	Zechariah	Daniel	
	Malachi	with Additions	
			Apocrypha
			Tobit
			Judith
			Additions to Esther
			1 Maccabees
			2 Maccabees
			Wisdom of Solomon
			Sirach
			Baruch
			Additions to Daniel

of God as it has been revealed to them. In addition to speeches, most prophetic books also contain shorter or longer narratives and sometimes prayers, words addressed to God.

The apocalypse is a distinctive type of literature that arose in the late OT period. It is represented in the OT only in the book of Daniel, though there are somewhat similar materials in Isa. 24–27 and Zech. 9–14. An apocalypse is a long and elaborate report of a vision of the course of history and its end. It generally is marked by a strong sense of the struggle between the powers of good and evil, belief in angels and demons, and in the resurrection of the dead. Such literature was widespread in the last two centuries BCE and the first century CE.

Origin and Growth: Most of the works of the OT are anonymous and undated. Literary analysis also reveals that many books, including those of the Pentateuch, are composite works; i.e., the words of more than one author have been combined to form the present book. The development of the written literature of the OT spanned more than a thousand years, and even more if one includes the oral traditions that preceded the written material. Some of the earliest works, most likely poetry such as Exod. 15:21, probably arose before 1000 BCE, and the latest works, such as the book of Daniel, were composed in the last century or two BCE. *See also* apocalyptic literature; canon; law; Pentateuch, sources of the; poetry; prophet.

G.M.T.

Old Testament chronology. *See* chronology, Hebrew Bible.

Old Testament quotations in the New Testament.
The Hebrew Bible, regarded as the OT by Christians, is quoted in the four Gospels, Acts, Romans, 1 and 2 Corinthians, Galatians, Ephesians, 1 and 2 Timothy, Hebrews, James, and 1 Peter. It is alluded to in every book of the NT except Philemon and 2 and 3 John. By one count, there are at least two thousand clear citations of the Hebrew Bible in the NT.

The sacred books of the Jews were equally sacred to the first Christians, who were themselves either Jews or Gentiles who became thoroughly familiar with the Bible. The books of the Hebrew Bible are referred to as "the writing(s)" and also as "the oracles (Gk. *ta logia*) of God" (Rom. 3:2; Acts 7:38; 1 Pet. 4:11; Heb. 5:12; *chrēmatismos* in Rom. 11:4). The Pentateuch, the Prophets, and the Psalms (which are often treated as prophecy) are cited most frequently. Isaiah is favored by Paul and the Gospels; Psalms is favored by Hebrews.

Modes of Reference: OT influences on the NT may be found in quotations, allusions, narrative parallels, themes, and language. Explicit quotations are often introduced by a formula such as "it is written" (Mark 7:6; John 2:17) or "it is said" (John 7:42). Some formulas contain and others lack the name of the book or speaker. Sometimes an unnamed prophet is invoked (Matt. 1:22–23; 2:5). In introducing quotations, the NT

authors refer to a variety of speakers, including God (Heb. 1:1, 13), the divine oracle (*chrēmatismos;* Rom. 11:4), biblical figures speaking by the Holy Spirit (Mark 12:36; Acts 28:25), and biblical authors speaking through books attributed to them (Rom. 10:19, 20; 11:9). Other quotations have no introductory formula (Mark 4:12; 8:18) or receive a narrative introduction (12:36). Occasionally an introductory formula is used where no explicit passage is quoted (Matt. 2:23; John 7:38). Frequently more than one passage is blended into a mixed quotation (Matt. 11:10; 27:9; Mark 1:2–3, 11; 13:24–25), or a series of quotations is cited (Heb. 1; Rom. 10; John 12:38–40). A fulfillment formula is a special feature of at least ten quotations in Matthew (1:22–23; 2:15, 17–18, 23; 4:14–16; 8:17; 12:17–21; 13:35; 21:4–5; 27:9). One of these (2:23) is actually followed by a quotation not found in the Bible. Several other passages have also been suggested as fulfillment passages (2:5–6; 3:3; 11:10; 13:14–15; 26:54, 56). In John, five quotations are introduced as fulfillments (12:38; 13:18; 15:25; 19:24, 36), and the fulfillment formula is used three times without an actual quotation (17:12; 18:9, 32).

Allusions, which are difficult to define precisely, are found in many contexts in the NT. Where a biblical passage or theme is the subject of a sustained argument, a writer may include allusions to the passage or its context in the course of the exposition. A good example of this is found in Paul's argument on Abraham in Rom. 4. Often, however, allusions consist of suggestive words and phrases (e.g., Luke 1:25, alluding to Gen. 30:23). In many cases, words, terms, phrases, metaphors, and symbols are used as a natural mode of expression by writers whose minds are thoroughly familiar with the Bible. For example, Luke–Acts is noted for its use of LXX style and phrases; the writer of Revelation never quotes the Bible outright, but draws on it constantly, creating a new composition out of a wealth of biblical allusions, images, metaphors, and symbols; and the author of John draws on many biblical metaphors and symbols such as shepherd/sheep imagery (John 10) and manna (John 6).

Narrative parallels in which the situation and action of NT events match those of the OT may be seen in the infancy narratives (Matt. 1–2; Luke 1–2), which share patterns with the Jacob/Israel stories, the Moses and exodus accounts, and birth stories associated with Israel's ancestors. Luke models stories about Jesus on the Elijah/Elisha cycle (Luke 7), and Mark's passion narrative invokes Ps. 22.

Biblical themes related to creation, Adam, the patriarchs, Moses, the exodus, David, and the like appear frequently in the NT. Prophetic themes concerning God's promises, sin, punishment, restoration, the remnant, salvation, God's servant and Messiah, and the like form the backbone of NT theological reflection on God, Jesus, and Christian life. Themes may be adduced with very little allusion to the actual text (e.g., Cain as an example of hatred in 1 John 3:12). Usually, however, themes and allusions go together, as in Rom. 4 on the faith of Abraham and in Heb. 7 on Melchizedek.

Text Form of Quotations: The biblical manuscripts discovered among the Dead Sea Scrolls testify to multiple textual forms for many biblical books. Such textual variants may account for anomalies found in NT citations of biblical passages. Some quotations adhere closely to one or another Greek version, some to a Hebrew version, and some to both or neither. Specifically, Mark, Luke, and the early Gospel source Q usually adhere to the LXX. Matthew, in reliance on Mark and Q, also uses the LXX, but his fulfillment quotations sometimes evince a mixed text closer to the Hebrew. John contains four quotations that agree fully with the LXX and others that agree only partially. Other quotations agree with the Hebrew, and some agree with neither the Greek nor the Hebrew versions available to us. More often than not, Paul's quotations agree with various versions of the LXX; he seldom quotes Hebrew versions that disagree with the Greek, but he does cite passages in a form that does not agree with either the LXX or the Hebrew. Some apparent anomalies in scripture quotation may be explained by the manner in which NT authors used scripture. They sometimes quoted imprecisely from memory, adapted OT texts to new contexts, or conflated OT texts to produce a passage loosely based on biblical words and phrases.

Uses of Scripture: Biblical quotations, allusions, and language are marshaled by NT authors for a variety of purposes, including apologetics, moral exhortation, and liturgical expression. Of special interest is the relationship of the followers of Jesus to Israel and to OT law.

Many passages are used to explain and validate the special status of Jesus, and certain texts are used repeatedly in different books. The basic resurrection/exaltation text is Ps. 110:1, which is quoted in the Gospels, Acts, the Pauline Letters, and Hebrews. Jesus's relationship with God as son is supported by Ps. 2:7, quoted in Acts 13:33; Heb. 1:5; and 5:5, and alluded to in Rom. 1:4. The same text may lie behind the divine words at the baptism of Jesus in Mark 1:11, though the main reference there is Isa. 42:1. Passages from Ps. 118 are applied to Jesus in Acts 4:11; 1 Pet. 2:7; and on two occasions in the Gospels (Matt. 21:9, 42; Mark 11:9; 12:10–11; Luke 20:17; John 12:13). Jesus's future function as the exalted Messiah is expressed in terms of the "one like a son of man" (Dan. 7:13; NRSV: "one like a human being") in Matt. 24:30; Mark 13:26; and Luke 21:27. In Matt. 26:64; Mark 14:62; and Luke 22:69, Dan. 7:13 is combined with Ps. 110:1; in Rev. 1:7, it is conflated with Zech. 12:10. Dan. 7 is alluded to frequently in the Gospels and Acts. Jesus's suffering and execution are explained and justified with passages from Isaiah, Zechariah, and certain psalms that concern the righteous person who suffers. Almost every verse of Isa. 53 is quoted or alluded to in connection with Jesus's sufferings; this chapter may

also lie behind the pre-Pauline statement in 1 Cor. 15:3 that "Christ died for our sins in accordance with the scriptures" (cf. the passion predictions in, e.g., Mark 8:31). Isa. 53 is also used for ethical teaching. Words from this passage are also used in a description of Christ in 1 Pet. 2:21–25, not to prove that his sufferings accord with God's plan as revealed in scripture, but for the sake of moral example. Zech. 9:9 is applied to Jesus's entry into Jerusalem in Matt. 21:5 and John 12:15, and Zech. 12:10 is applied to the crucifixion in John 19:37. Zech. 13:7 appears in Matt. 26:31 and Mark 14:27. Psalm 41:9 is alluded to in Mark 14:18 and quoted in John 13:18 to account for the treachery of Judas. Ps. 22:1 provides Jesus's cry of dereliction in Matt. 27:46 and Mark 15:34, and Ps. 22:18 is applied to the parting of Jesus's garments in all four Gospels (fully quoted in John 19:24). Ps. 69 is also widely used in connection with the passion, principally in John 2:17; Acts 1:20; and Rom. 15:3 (cf. also Rom. 11:9–10).

The rejection of Jesus's followers by the majority of Jews and Gentiles is mitigated by reference to certain biblical passages. Isa. 6:9–10 is quoted in Matt. 13:14–15; Mark 4:12; John 12:40; and Acts 28:26–27. Similar words in Isa. 29:10 are quoted in Rom. 11:8 along with words from Deut. 29:3. Paul also quotes Isa. 29:14 in 1 Cor. 1:19. From the point of view of faith, Jesus is both the precious cornerstone (Isa. 28:16, quoted in 1 Pet. 2:6) and the rock of offense (Isa. 8:14, quoted in 1 Pet. 2:8). These two quotations are conflated by Paul in Rom. 9:33 and may be alluded to in Matt. 16:18 and 16:23. Both Paul (Rom. 10:6) and John (12:38) quote from Isa. 53:1 in connection with rejection of Jesus. Speeches in Acts that are addressed to Jewish audiences (e.g., 2:14–36; 7:2–53; 13:16–41) are much richer in biblical quotations and allusions than are those addressed to Gentiles and serve an apologetic purpose in the face of Jewish rejection of Jesus's followers. Numerous scriptural quotations also appear in Rom. 9–11, where Paul is concerned with the Jewish rejection of Jesus, and again in 1 Pet. 2. These passages argue that Jewish rejection of Jesus is not a count *against* the Christian proclamation, but is itself a fulfillment of what God made known in scripture. For example, Hab. 1:5 serves as a warning against rejection of Paul's teaching in Acts 13:41. Hab. 2:4 is used as a key affirmation of justification in Paul (Gal. 3:11; Rom. 1:17) and as an exhortation to perseverance and faithfulness in Heb. 10:38.

In relation to the law, biblical quotations occur often in matters of controversy. Disputes concerning the sabbath (Matt. 12), purity laws (Matt. 15), and divorce (Matt. 19) are argued using scriptural laws and examples. The double love commandment is created from two biblical texts (Deut. 6:4; Lev. 19:18) in Mark 12:28–31. The Beatitudes (Matt. 5:3–12) incorporate biblical allusions, but these are not formal quotations. Paul argues for Gentile freedom from the law using a series of intricate interpretations of scriptural quotations (Gal. 3–4).

Sections of the letters devoted to moral teaching show familiarity with the Bible as well. This explains why the same quotation sometimes appears in the work of two authors. Thus, Prov. 10:12 ("love covers all offenses") is found, somewhat revised, in both 1 Pet. 4:8 and James 5:20. Deut. 32:35 ("Vengeance is mine") occurs in Rom. 12:19 and Heb. 10:30. In 1 Pet. 3:10–12, there is an extended quotation of Ps. 34:12–16, which provides the basis for the surrounding exhortation. Paul, in Rom. 12:20, makes similar use of Prov. 25:21–22. Paul also appears to know Jesus's use of Lev. 19:18 to summarize the law (Rom. 13:8–10; cf. James 2:8, where it is quoted with allusions to the wider context of Lev. 19).

Arguments Based on Scripture: Besides the use of scripture as proof texts, the NT contains examples of arguments conducted entirely on the basis of scriptural interpretation, notably in the major Pauline Letters and in Hebrews. Thus, Paul argues justification by faith in Galatians and Romans on the basis of scripture, because his opponents share his respect for scripture and must be defeated on common ground. In Gal. 3 and Rom. 4, direct quotations from Genesis are subjected to detailed analysis, and additional allusions are adduced in the process. An important distinction is made in Gal. 3:16 by pressing the exact meaning of the words. Another example is the allegory of Hagar and Sarah in Gal. 4:21–31, where the main argument depends on allusions to Gen. 16 and 21, but Isa. 54:1 is adduced to support the interpretation. Other instances are the allusions to Israel in the wilderness (1 Cor. 10:1–13) and the highly complex exposition of Exod. 33–34 in 2 Cor. 3, contrasting the old and new dispensations by means of an *a fortiori* argument. In Hebrews, the argument of the entire letter depends on the contrast between old and new. Quotations and allusions are taken up with regard to Moses (Heb. 3), the promised land (Heb. 4), Melchizedek (Heb. 7), the covenant (Heb. 8), and the sacrificial system (Heb. 9–10). Apocalyptic passages (e.g., Mark 13; Rev.) make a sustained use of images and phrases from the Bible to create a new symbolic presentation of the plan of eschatology on a cosmic scale. Many of the biblical images used in Revelation can be paralleled in Jewish apocalyptic writings. The central figure of the "Lamb that seemed to have been slain" (5:6) as the image of Christ is derived from imaginative use of Isa. 53:7 and other sacrificial passages in connection with the death of Christ.

Sources and Background of OT Interpretation: NT interpretation of the Bible and use of biblical quotations have much in common with the presuppositions, approaches, and techniques found in Qumran *pesher* commentaries and later rabbinic midrashic collections and Targums. Similarities and differences between Jewish and NT interpretations are illuminating. Paul explains one Bible passage by adducing others (Rom. 10:18–21) and uses a very common *a fortiori* argument (Heb. *qal wa-homer*) in 2 Cor. 3:11: "For if what was set aside came through glory, much more has the perma-nent come in glory." In 1 Cor. 10:4 is an allusion to a midrashic tradition that the rock followed Israel in the wilderness, which shows that this tradition was known in the first century.

Some quotations show features found in the Targums, the Aramaic translations of the scriptures used in synagogues where Aramaic was the language of the people. As the translation, originally given orally, followed the reading of the lesson in Hebrew, it is often periphrastic and explanatory, sometimes modernizing the ideas to make them more relevant to the congregation. Paul has examples of this in 1 Cor. 10:1–14 (the theme of Israel in the wilderness applied to temptations of Christians) and Rom. 10:6–8 (Deut. 30:12–14 adapted and applied to Christ).

The Dead Sea Scrolls have presuppositions and procedures in common with NT documents. According to the *Covenant of Damascus* (CD) 6:19, the community regarded itself as the people of the New Covenant, and according to the *Rule of the Community* (1QS), this was specifically to "prepare the way of the Lord" (8:14, quoting Isa. 40:3). Messianic prophecies are applied, not only to the messiah of Israel, who is the legitimate king of the line of David, but also to the community as a whole. Thus, Amos 9:11 is applied to the messiah in the *Florilegium,* or *Eschatological Midrash* (4QFlor 1:12), but refers to the "congregation" in CD 7:6–17. The Psalms are treated as prophecy and so are given an eschatological interpretation. Thus, Ps. 2:1–2, on the raging of the nations against God's anointed one, is interpreted in 4QFlor 1:19 as follows: "Interpreted this saying concerns [the kings of the nations] who shall [rage against] the elect of Israel in the last days." "The elect" is plural, meaning the whole community, not just the messiah, as the psalm ("his anointed one") implies. Behind this method of interpretation is the idea of God's plan, kept secret in past ages, but revealed in a "mystery" (Heb. *raz*) to the prophets and now coming to pass in the last times. There is also a Christian expression of this idea (Col. 1:26). The biblical commentaries found among the Dead Sea Scrolls expound the prophets and psalms through a verse-by-verse exposition of the text in relation to the history and eschatological expectations of the community. Similarly, many of the quotations of the prophets and psalms in the NT are applied to Jesus and the church in relation to the eschatological plan of God, though not in commentary form.

The citation of brief and long quotations from memory and the use of anthologies as well as original texts was common in Greco-Roman literature. Greek and Latin authors adapted texts to the grammar and style of the literary context in which they used them. They freely omitted irrelevant or contradictory phrases and sentences and sometimes added words and interpretive comments. Similar phenomena are found in NT biblical citations. A text may be telescoped so as to concentrate attention on the particular point at issue or to leave out matter that appears unsuitable to the interpretation. Thus, in Matt. 12:18–21, part of Isa. 42:3–4 is omitted from v. 20, because it seems to contradict the quietness of Jesus's ministry. The versions of Isa. 6:9–10 in both Mark 4:12 and John 12:40 are greatly abbreviated in different ways. Conflation (combination and mixture) of texts usually involves some adaptation of the text to make the quotations fit together. Paul does this frequently. Matthew's account of the death of Judas Iscariot (27:9) includes a composite quotation of Zech. 11:12–13 that involves phrases from Jer. 32:6–15 and 18:2–3. This seems to be the reason that it is attributed to Jeremiah in the fulfillment formula. *See also* Dead Sea Scrolls; messiah; midrash; New Testament; Old Testament; Targums.

Bibliography

Carson, D. A., and H. G. M. Williamson, eds. *It Is Written: Scripture Citing Scripture: Essays in Honour of Barnabas Lindars.* Cambridge University Press, 1988.

Evans, Craig A., and James A. Sanders. *Paul and the Scripture of Israel.* JSOT, 1992.

Lindars, Barnabas. *New Testament Apologetic: The Doctrinal Significance of the Old Testament Quotations.* Westminster, 1961.   B.L./A.J.S.

olive, an evergreen tree and its fruit, an oval-shaped oil-bearing drupe. With its characteristic gnarled trunk and bluish green leaves, the olive tree thrives in the Mediterranean climate of hot, dry summers and cool, damp winters. It was ubiquitous to the biblical landscape (Deut. 8:8), even clinging to rocky hillsides. It can survive for a thousand years; some specimens current in Israel are said to date from the Roman period. The tree became a symbol of fertility (Ps. 128:3), beauty (Jer. 11:16; Hos. 14:6), divine blessing (Deut. 7:13), and peace and bountifulness (Gen. 8:11). The olive branch was the first vegetation seen by Noah after the flood (Gen. 8:11).

The tree was propagated through grafting (Rom. 11:17–24; in Ps. 128:3, the shoots at the base of a parent tree are compared to a family blessed with many children). There was hardly a phase of life not touched by the olive tree. Its fruit was used for food (Num. 11:8), and olive oil was used for fuel for lamps, as medicine (Isa. 1:6; Luke 10:34), for anointing (1 Sam. 10:1; 2 Kings 9:3; Isa. 61:1), and in sacrifices (Lev. 2:4; Gen. 28:18). Its wood was used for furniture (1 Kings 6:23, 31–33).

Olive cultivation, well established in the Early Bronze Age (third millennium BCE), had its origins in the preceding proto-urban age. The earliest known domesticated olives have been recovered from fourth-millennium BCE Chalcolithic sites, e.g., at modern Teleilat Ghassul near the northern tip of the Dead Sea. Fruit tree cultivation in this area would necessarily have involved irrigation, a relevant fact supporting domestication. The olive pit is easily identifiable and, despite some overlap, domestic varieties are generally larger than their wild relatives. Besides actual floral remains, evidence for an established olive-oil industry in the

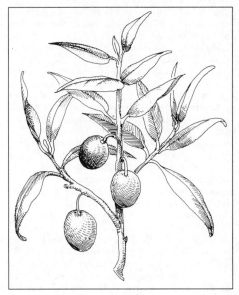

Olive.

Early Bronze Age appears in the form of Egyptian texts that mention imports from Canaan and in the large basins and jars probably used as containers and transport vessels. At Ras-Shamra, ancient Ugarit, similar basins have been found in association with an oil-pressing installation, dated to the Late Bronze Age (ca. 1500–1200 BCE).

Numerous olive-oil installations have been found throughout the biblical lands. The basic technology, with some variation, involved two separate processes: the olives were crushed, then subsequently squeezed. The first process required a huge stone crushing wheel, which was set on edge, pivoted on a vertical beam, and rolled on top of a circular stone basin upon which the olives were placed. A few rotations of the wheel were sufficient to crush the olives. Treading the olives was another method (Mic. 6:15). The crushed olives were then placed into special baskets and set so the oil drained into a basin; this was the "first oil" or "beaten oil," the oil used for lighting lamps (Exod. 27:20). The oil-pressing operation consisted of a beam to which stone weights (average weight: 650 pounds) were attached and a vat that included a deeper depression beside it to collect the oil. Pressure from the beam on the olives in the vat squeezed the oil out of the olives. Eventually the sediment and water settled while the pure oil rose to the surface.   S.R.

Olives, Mount of, a high hill to the east of Jerusalem. It is a relatively good area for growing olives in the poor land surrounding Jerusalem. An area of the mount was appropriately called Gethsemane (Heb., "oil press"), possibly a garden area where the fruit of the mount was processed (John 18:1). Jesus is said to have come here often

(Luke 22:39), and it was here that he gathered his disciples to pray on the night he was arrested (Matt. 26:36; Mark 14:32).

The mile-long Mount of Olives dominates Jerusalem, rising 230 feet above the Temple Mount. This high place was a natural location for the first sanctuary in the Jerusalem area, Nob (1 Sam. 21:1; 2 Sam. 15:32), probably in the area of the present-day Augusta Victoria Hospital. The mount itself is part of a Senonian limestone range of hills protecting Jerusalem that resulted from a bifurcation of the highland ridge dividing two miles north of the city and uniting again just south of it. The Mount of Olives is the central section of the ridge's eastern branch and is separated from the city by the Kidron Valley. The section north of it is called Scopus, "lookout." The southern section begins after the Mount of Olives descends to the level of the Temple Mount. This is known as the Mount of Offense, because Solomon built pagan shrines here (1 Kings 11:7). The Mount of Olives was Jerusalem's watchtower. All approaches from Transjordan as well as from the north and south are visible from it. Jerusalem also communicated to the world from here by signal fires, as when the beginning of each month was announced.

This natural bulwark against attack from the east was further strengthened by two villages at the base of its slope facing the Judean desert, Bahurim, at the junction of Mount Scopus and Mount of Olives on the north, and Anania or Bethany, near the descent to the Mount of Offense on the south. Bethphage fortified the center of the mount. This was the terminal of the Jericho road. From this strategic location Jesus entered Jerusalem at the completion of his ministry (Matt. 21:1; Mark 11:1; Luke 19:29).

As a bulwark whose penetration meant the destruction of Jerusalem, the Mount of Olives became a symbol for the way of defeat. David climbed the mount in humiliation as he fled from Absalom (2 Sam. 15:13–30). Isaiah pictures the Assyrians advancing to Nob, whence the city was cursed (10:32). The way to exile across the mount established this as the way of defeat. Ezekiel pictured Jerusalem's departed glory resting here before it disappeared (11:23). Jesus also used the mount as his podium for pronouncing judgment over the city (Matt. 24:3; Mark 13:3; Luke 19:37–44).

Israelite prophets maintained that the defeat of Jerusalem would be reversed and God would return to the city (Ezek. 43:2; Isa. 40). Zechariah pictures God on that day standing on the mount, which will be divided as God enters the city. Following that entry, the Mount of Olives, a now useless defense work, will be leveled (14:4, 10). Because the mount was associated with the departure and return of God's glory (Ezek. 11:23; 43:2), it became the appropriate setting for the ascension of Jesus and for his promised return (Luke 24:50; Acts 1:12). *See also* Bahurim; Bethphage; Gethsemane; Kidron; Nob.   B.E.S.

Olivet (ol'i-vet). *See* Olives, Mount of.

Olympas (oh-lim'puhs), a man in Rome whom Paul greets along with others, who may be members of the same household (Rom. 16:15).

omega (oh-meg'uh), the last letter in the Greek alphabet. It thus came to mean "last." It is used symbolically with alpha (the first letter in the Greek alphabet) in Revelation to refer to God and Christ (1:8; 21:6; 22:13). *See also* alpha.

The letters alpha (*left*) and omega.

omer (oh'muhr). A dry measure equaling one-tenth of an ephah (roughly three-fifths of a bushel; Exod. 16:36; cf. Exod. 16:16, 18, 32–33). *See also* weights and measures.

Omri (om'ri), the sixth king of Israel (ca. 876–869 BCE), a contemporary of King Asa of Judah and founder of a dynasty that included his son Ahab (ca. 869–850 BCE), Ahaziah (ca. 850–849 BCE), and Jehoram (ca. 849–843/2 BCE). According to 1 Kings 16:23, Omri ruled Israel for twelve years, six of them in Tirzah. The background to his ascent to the throne in Tirzah was the extinction of Baasha's dynasty and the subsequent power struggle among the high officers of the army. When Zimri, an army officer, assassinated Elah, son of Baasha, "all Israel" made Omri the "captain of the host," king of Israel. Omri and "all Israel" with him captured Tirzah, and Zimri took his own life. The power struggle continued between Omri and Tibni, son of Ginath (1 Kings 16:21–22), each supported by "half of the people," but it ended with Omri's death.

Of all Omri's deeds after he became king of Israel, the only one mentioned in the Bible is the founding of a new capital at Samaria, which marked a new chapter in the history of the Israelite kingdom. From a historical point of view, Omri was to the kingdom of Israel what David before him was to the united kingdom. Both brought stability and prosperity to a troubled land by establishing a dynasty in a neutral political center. Archaeology has demonstrated the fact that Samaria was unoccupied until Omri's time, and it has revealed high-quality building and fortification under the reigns of both Omri and Ahab (his son and immediate successor). The name "Omri" became an established term in Assyrian documents to indicate Israelite kings even after the death of Omri and his descendants. Jehu, who founded a new dynasty in Israel, is called by Shalmaneser III "the son of Omri"; and Assyrian annalists continued to refer to Israel as the "land of (the house of) Omri" for a hundred years after the end of Omri's dynasty.

According to the Stele of Mesha, king of Moab, Omri gained possession of Medeba (modern-day Madaba) in Transjordan. Such successes were the result of a policy of mending quarrels and establishing peaceful relations with his neighbors. The prolonged war between Judah and Israel terminated with the kings of the Davidic line accepting (at least temporarily) the existence of the northern kingdom. Omri entered into an alliance with Ethbaal, king of Sidon, which was sealed by the marriage between Ahab, Omri's son, and Jezebel, Ethbaal's daughter. The triple alliance between Israel, Judah, and Phoenicia served as a counterweight to the threat of Aram-Damascus, which continued to influence affairs even in Samaria.

Whatever his political accomplishments, Omri receives a relentlessly negative treatment in the biblical writings, where he becomes the paragon of an evil king who permits or promotes syncretism and apostasy (1 Kings 16:25–26). See also Ahab; Jehu; Mesha; Samaria, city of; Shalmaneser.   D.L.C.

On (Egyptian, "city of the pillar").

1 An ancient city and religious center in northern Egypt whose ruins (modern Tell Hisn and Matariyeh) are located in the suburbs of modern Cairo, seven miles northeast of the center of the city. On, called in Greek Heliopolis ("city of the sun"), was Egypt's center of sun worship, where the solar god Re (Atum) was venerated. The temple of Re in On was the next largest temple in all Egypt, surpassed only by that of Amun in Thebes. The city was famous for its obelisks (thus its name), one of which still stands there today, almost four thousand years old. Two of On's obelisks, erected there by Thutmose III in the sixteenth century BCE, now stand in Western countries, one in Central Park, New York City, the other on the Thames embankment in London.

In the Bible, Joseph marries Asenath, the daughter of Potiphera, priest of On (possibly the high priest there; Gen. 41:45, 50; 46:20). According to the LXX, On (Heliopolis) was one of the cities in Egypt built by the Israelites (Exod. 1:11). Isa. 19:18 may contain a reference to On in its prediction that the "City of the Sun" will be one of the five cities in Egypt where Hebrew-speaking worshipers of the Lord will dwell. In his oracle concerning Egypt, Jeremiah predicts that Nebuchadnezzar will destroy the temples of Egypt and will demolish the "pillars" (i.e., obelisks) of the "temple of the sun," probably referring to the temple of Re in On (43:13). Ezekiel predicts that judgment will befall the city of On (written 'awen, perhaps as a pun; 'awen in Hebrew means "trouble, wickedness") and that the inhabitants will be taken into captivity (30:17). *See also* Egypt; Joseph.

2 The son of Peleth, a leader of the tribe of Reuben who joined the rebellion of Korah against Moses in the wilderness (Num. 16:1).   D.A.D.

Onam (oh′nuhm; Heb., "vigorous").

1 The son of Shobal and grandson of Seir the Horite (Gen. 36:23).

2 The son of Jerahmeel, a descendant of Judah (1 Chron. 2:26, 28).

Onan (oh′nuhn; Heb., "power," "wealth"), the second son of Judah and the daughter of a Canaanite named Shua (Gen. 38:4; 46:12; Num. 26:19). After the death of Er, Judah's firstborn, Judah instructed Onan to perform the levirate marriage rite with Er's wife, Tamar. His duty was to impregnate Tamar and produce offspring for

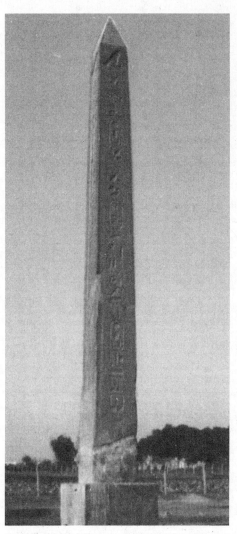

Obelisk of Pharaoh Senwosret I (1971–1926 BCE) at modern Tell Hisn (near Cairo), site of biblical On.

his deceased brother, but since Onan knew the child would not be his, he deliberately spilled his semen on the ground (presumably through coitus interruptus), an act displeasing to God, who slew him (Gen. 38:8–10). *See also* marriage.

Onesimus (oh-nes´uh-muhs; Gk., "useful"), the slave of Philemon for whom Paul made an appeal in his Letter to Philemon. Onesimus, who was alienated from his master, visited Paul apparently to seek his service as a mediator. Paul sent Onesimus back to Philemon with the letter, which urges Philemon to receive Onesimus as "a beloved brother" (Philem. 16), i.e., as a member of the church and "no longer as a slave." Although Onesimus had formerly been "useless" to his master, he had now become "useful" to both Philemon and Paul (Philem. 11, a pun on his name). Onesimus is also referred to in Col. 4:9. That this Onesimus is to be identified with the Onesimus who was bishop of Ephesus some sixty years later seems unlikely, but is not impossible. *See also* Philemon; Philemon, Letter of Paul to.
W.R.B.

Onesiphorus (on´uh-sif´uh-ruhs), a Christian who is commended in 2 Timothy for special kindnesses to Paul, both in Ephesus and during Paul's Roman imprisonment (1:16–18). Specifically, Onesiphorus is mentioned as one who was not ashamed of Paul's "chain," i.e., of his status as a criminal and prisoner. The letter seems to speak of him in past tenses, and it includes a prayer for the Lord to grant mercy to his household (1:16; cf. 4:19); such references may imply that Onesiphorus has died (cf. 1:18).

Ono (oh´noh), a town near the southern end of the Plain of Sharon. It was built by Benjaminites (1 Chron. 8:12), is identified with modern Kefr Ana, and is mentioned in the Karnak list of Pharaoh Thutmose III. Along with Lod it was reoccupied after the exile (Neh. 11:35), and Nehemiah's enemies waited to meet him in the plain of Ono (6:2).

onycha (on´i-kuh; Heb., "nail," "claw," "husk," or "flap"), a spice that was noted for the especially pungent odor it emitted when burned. For this reason, it was an ingredient in the incense used in Israelite worship (Exod. 30:34). This incense was not to be used in secular contexts (30:33, 37–38). Some scholars have suggested that onycha was derived from the resin of the labdanum plant, but the dominant theory is that it was extracted from the muscles of the stromb, a mollusk found in the Red Sea.

onyx, a type of quartz with varicolored bands. Onyx is the usual NRSV translation of a Hebrew word (*shoham*) that designates a precious stone, found in the land of Havilah, according to Gen. 2:12, and ranked with gold of Ophir (Job 28:16). It heads the list of precious stones provided by David

for the temple (1 Chron. 29:2). The two stones on the shoulders of the high priest's ephod were onyx (Exod. 28:9–12), and so was the eleventh stone on his breastpiece (28:20). In Ezek. 28:13 "onyx" translates a different word (Heb. *yashepheh,* called "jasper" in Exod. 28:20), while *shoham* is translated "beryl." Onyx appears in Rev. 21:20 (Gk. *sardonyx*) as one of the twelve jewels adorning the wall of the heavenly Jerusalem.   P.A.B.

Ophel (oh´fel; Heb., "hill"), the ridge extending south between the Kidron and Tyropoeon valleys that was fortified by David after his capture of Jerusalem (2 Chron. 27:3; 33:14). Repaired by Nehemiah after the exile (Neh. 3:26–27), it was also the dwelling of some temple personnel (11:21).

Ophir (oh´fuhr), a people descended from Shem (Gen. 10:29; 1 Chron. 1:23). The land of these people is designated by the same name (1 Kings 9:28; 10:11) and was a famous source of gold (Job 22:24; 28:16; Ps. 45:9; Isa. 13:12). The location of Ophir is uncertain. *See also* Tarshish.   R.S.B.

Ophrah (of´ruh).
  1 A town belonging to the Abiezrite group from the tribe of Manasseh (Judg. 6:11, 15). It was the home of Gideon (chaps. 6–8), and it was here that Gideon built an altar inscribed with the words, "the LORD is peace" to commemorate the appearance of an angel of the Lord to him (6:24). Later, Gideon made an ephod here that ultimately became an object of idolatrous worship (8:22–28). After Gideon's death, his son Abimelech slaughtered seventy of his brothers, an event for which Ophrah would also be remembered (9:5).
  2 A town of Benjamin (Josh. 18:23; cf. 1 Sam. 13:17), identified with modern et-Taiyiba, four miles northeast of Bethel; it is evidently identical with Ephron (2 Chron. 13:19), Aphairema (1 Macc. 11:34), and Ephraim (2 Sam. 13:23; John 11:54).
  3 The son of Meonothai, a descendant of Judah (1 Chron. 4:14).   D.A.D.

oracle.
  1 A message from God delivered through a prophet. This is the primary way in which the word "oracle" (Heb. *massa'*) is used in the Bible. The word derives from a Hebrew word for "burden," implying that it is something placed by God upon the prophet that the prophet must "unload." The divine inspiration for oracles plays into the Balaam narrative, in which Balaam is hired to curse Israel, but discovers that when he opens his mouth, words of blessing come out instead (Num. 23–24); as a prophet, he is only able to speak what the Lord says through him (cf. Num. 24:13). Mic. 3:11, however, mentions prophets who give oracles for money, assuring rulers of what they want to hear. David delivers an oracle, in which the "spirit of the LORD" speaks through him (2 Sam. 23:1–7). Oracles tend to be proclamations of doom or judgment (against the nations, Isa. 13:1; Nah. 1:1; against Israel, Ezek. 12:10; against Judah, Isa.

Ancient site at Delphi, Greece, of one of the best-known oracles of the Greco-Roman world.

22:1). Acts 7:38 says that Moses received "living oracles" from God at Mount Sinai, and Paul says in Rom. 3:2 that "the Jews were entrusted with the oracles of God." Heb. 5:2 uses the same expression ("oracles of God") as a description of basic Christian teaching. *See also* prophet.

2 In the Greco-Roman world, a professional diviner who offered to predict the future or reveal other hidden information. The Hebrew Bible reveals some awareness of such phenomena in the earlier period, for it condemns anyone who "practices divination, or is a soothsayer, or an augur, or a sorcerer, or one who casts spells, or who consults ghosts or spirits, or who seeks oracles from the dead" (Deut. 18:10–11). By the NT era, however, such oracles had become prominent institutions in the pagan world, as is evident from the prestige of the oracle at Delphi in Greece. *See also* divination; lot, lots; magic; Urim and Thummim.

M.A.P.

ordain, ordination.

1 In the Bible, God may be said to ordain that which God establishes, determines, or appoints. For example, God ordains the ruin of Absalom (2 Sam. 17:14) and the downfall of Ahaziah (2 Chron. 22:7). But God may also ordain blessing (Ps. 133:3) or peace (Isa. 26:12). "May the Lord so ordain!" is an appropriate response to a royal edict (1 Kings 1:36). Lam. 2:17 says that the destruction of Jerusalem was ordained by God "long ago," and 3:37 affirms that nothing can come to pass if God has not ordained it. Thus, what accords with God's will may be described as divinely ordained. God ordained the festivals

of Israel (2 Chron. 2:4) and the law was ordained through or by angels (Acts 7:53; Gal. 3:19). Likewise, Heb. 9:20 describes the covenant through the blood of Christ as ordained by God. *See also* predestination.

2 Those who are commissioned or set apart for a particular role (especially a religious one) are said to be ordained to their particular ministry or function. The priests of Israel are often said to have been ordained by God or Moses (Exod. 28:41; 29:9, 22, 35; 32:29; Lev. 8:3; Num. 3:3), but the kings of Judah are also said to have ordained idolatrous priests (2 Kings 23:5). In the NT, the Pastoral Letters deal with the appointment of bishops, deacons, and other church leaders; qualifications for such offices are spelled out, and Timothy is told not to ordain anyone hastily (1 Tim. 5:22). *See also* minister.   F.B.C.

ordeal. *See* divination; magic.

ordination offering. *See* sacrifice.

Oreb (or'eb; Heb., "raven") **and Zeeb** (zee'eb; "wolf"), two Midianite princes who were killed by the Ephraimites in Gideon's battle against the Midianites (Judg. 7:24–8:3). Their deaths were commemorated by "the rock of Oreb" and "the press of Zeeb," and their crushing defeat was invoked by the psalmist in Ps. 83:11.

Orion (oh-ri'uhn), a constellation thought in ancient times to resemble the mythological hunter for whom it is named; it contains two stars of the first magnitude, Betelgeuse and Rigel. The constellation lies south of Gemini and Taurus. God's creation of Orion is cited by Amos (5:8) and Job (9:9; 38:31) as evidence of God's overwhelming majesty. *See also* Pleiades.

ornaments. *See* amulet; breastpiece; divination; dress; jewels, jewelry; magic.

Ornan (or'nuhn). *See* Araunah.

Orontes (or-on'teez), the principal river of western Syria (modern Nahr el-'Asi, "the rebellious river"), which originates on the eastern side of the Lebanon range and flows for two hundred and fifty miles north through Syria into southern Turkey, where it turns southwest and enters the Mediterranean below Antioch-on-the-Orontes (modern Antakya). It thus forms the northern part of the great Rift Valley, which continues south through the Jordan Valley, the Dead Sea, and the Arabah into the Red Sea and east Africa. The Orontes Valley is extremely fertile, a fact that, together with its strategically important geography, accounts for the number of major cities situated in it. These include: Riblah (see 2 Kings 23:33; 25:6, 21); Kadesh-on-the-Orontes (modern Tell Nebi Mend); Emessa (modern Homs); Hamath (modern Hama); Qarqar, where in 853 BCE a coalition of Syrian kings together with Ahab of Israel fought with the Assyrian king Shalmaneser III; Alalakh (Tell 'Atshana); Antioch (Acts 11:19; 13:1); and Seleucia, Antioch's port. *See also* Antioch; Hamath; Riblah.   M.D.C.

Orpah (or'puh), the sister-in-law of Ruth. In the book of Ruth, an Ephrathite named Elimelech migrated to Moab from Bethlehem with his wife, Naomi, and their two sons, Mahlon and Chilion. After Elimelech died, the sons married Moabite women; Mahlon married Ruth, and Chilion married Orpah. Then Mahlon and Chilion also died, leaving Naomi and her two daughters-in-law as widows (1:1–4). Naomi was determined to move back to her home in Bethlehem, and both Ruth and Orpah wanted to return with her (1:10). Naomi tried to dissuade them, pointing out that she would not be able to produce more sons for them (1:11–13). Then "Orpah kissed her mother-in-law, but Ruth clung to her" (1:10); i.e., Orpah remained in Moab as Naomi suggested, but Ruth persisted and returned to Bethlehem with her (1:11–14). Orpah is not heard from again, but Ruth found a husband and ended up becoming the great-grandmother of King David (4:13–17). *See also* Ruth, book of.   M.A.P.

Osnappar (os-nap'uhr), an Assyrian ruler who resettled non-Jewish people "in the cities of Samaria and in the rest of the province Beyond the River" after the fall of Israel in 722/1 BCE (Ezra 4:10). "Beyond the River" was the Persian name for the area that included Judea and Samaria. There was no Assyrian king named Osnapper, so the name either refers to a lesser ruler (a nobleman who exercised authority under a king) or is a corruption of some other name, such as Esar-haddon or Ashurbanipal, both of whom were kings of Assyria in the seventh century BCE.

ossuaries (from Lat. *os* or *ossum*, "bone"), small chests used for gathering human bones after the corpse had decomposed. Ossuaries were usually made from limestone with average dimensions of 20–30 inches by 12–20 inches by 10–16 inches.

The Orontes River with Tell Nebi Mend, biblical Kadesh-on-the-Orontes, in the background.

Limestone ossuaries engraved with decorative motifs such as these were sometimes used for secondary burials in the ancient Near East.

They became popular among Jews especially in Judea in the first century BCE, but fell out of use after the second century CE. Their use during that period may be associated with the burgeoning craft of stone masonry under Herod the Great's temple construction. After death, a corpse was placed in a wall niche of a burial cave and, about

a year later, after the corpse had disintegrated, the bones were gathered into an ossuary, which was placed either in a smaller niche or on the floor. Typically, the bones of several individuals, probably family members, were placed inside a single ossuary. Many ossuaries have been excavated in the tombs of Jerusalem and Jericho; they were sometimes decorated with engravings and identified with the names of the deceased. Although most burials around Jerusalem during the Second Temple period used ossuaries, graves have also been found in which the deceased were simply placed in the ground or interred in shaft tombs without secondary burial. At one point, theories were advanced to suggest that the diversity in burial practices might reflect different conceptions of the afterlife, but most scholars now attribute the variance to practical questions of space and socioeconomic factors (i.e., the very poor could not afford ossuaries). *See also* burial. A.J.S.

Ostia (os'tee-uh), a Roman city at the mouth of the Tiber River. It was the principal harbor for Rome during the first and second centuries CE. Alexandria in Egypt, the source of the grain supply for Rome, was three weeks away by sea. Until the harbor was made deep enough for seagoing ships, they had docked at Puteoli, 138 miles from Rome. Grain then had to be carted overland, an expensive undertaking. The natural harbor at Ostia had filled with silt, so that a large ship there

Remains of the fourth-century CE synagogue at Ostia.

would have had to anchor outside and transfer cargo to barges, a considerable risk in stormy weather. Julius Caesar (100–44 BCE) planned to enlarge Ostia, but the actual project was not undertaken until Claudius (emperor 41–54 CE) constructed a large artificial harbor three miles north at Portus. Trajan (emperor 98–117 CE) completed a second harbor in 104 CE beside that constructed by Claudius, and the following years marked the peak of Ostia's prosperity. Because those harbors had not been completed when Paul was taken to Rome, he landed at Puteoli (Acts 28:13).

Construction of the artificial harbor required dredging 200 acres and constructing concrete breakwaters, lighthouses, wharves, and unloading facilities. In the ancient city itself one could find warehouses, granaries, offices for the imperial administration, banks, stores, eating places, bakeries, bars, and apartment buildings of red and yellow brick. The imports coming into the harbor were grain, fruits, fish, meat, hides, oil, wine, minerals, jewelry, lumber, glass, paper, dyes, clothing, spices, ointment, and perfumes. Ship owners complained that a lack of exports cost them money. They were provided with incentives in the form of special insurance against shipwreck, tax exemptions, and citizenship for anyone who had been in the grain-carrying service for six years. The study of this shipping business at Ostia provides background for understanding the condemnation of merchants who serve Babylon (i.e., Rome) in Rev. 18.

As befits a city with a polyglot population from all over the world, a number of shrines and temples were located in Ostia, the remains of which have been found in addition to those that served the imperial cult. A Serapis temple served sailors from the Levant. A late first-century CE house was refashioned into a synagogue in the second century and some eighteen Mithras shrines dating to the second century and later have been found. The Mithras cult appealed to the merchants and sailors in this port city.   P.P.

ostraca (os′truh-kuh), plural of the Greek *ostrakon,* "potsherd." Potsherds provided a readily available medium on which to make hasty or informal notations in pen and ink during biblical times. Many prophetic oracles may have been preserved originally in the form of ostraca, written by disciples of the prophets. Numerous examples of ostraca have been found by archaeologists. Several hundred ostraca were found at Masada, and over two hundred at Arad. The ostraca from Samaria are receipts for taxes paid to the governor of Samaria during the eighth century BCE. The eighteen Lachish letters from the time of Jeremiah (sixth century BCE) are military correspondence between Yaoush, the commander at Lachish, and a junior officer, Hoshaiah, in charge of a nearby garrison town. Numerous other sites have produced smaller numbers of ostraca. *See also* Arad; Lachish.   L.E.T.

This ostracon, one of two hundred ostraca found at Arad (ca. 600 BCE), reads in part "to Nahum."

ostrich (Heb. *ya'anah*). Although ostriches are now extinct outside of Africa, they inhabited the open steppes of Mesopotamia and Arabia throughout the biblical period. The ostrich (*Struthio camelus*) stands up to 8½ feet high. It has only rudimentary wings and is unable to fly, but its long legs and two-toed feet make it especially adapted to running, and it can reach a speed of forty miles per hour. The cocks are taller than the hens and have a better developed plumage; the feathers were a much sought after item. In antiquity ostrich eggs were eaten and the eggshells used to manufacture containers and ornaments. The meat, however, was forbidden to the Hebrews (Lev. 11:16; Deut. 14:15). Though living mostly on plant food, the ostrich can be considered an omnivore, because it also eats insects and other small animals. The cocks are polygamous, and the hens use a communal nest for the eggs. The cock takes over the incubation of the eggs at night, and the hens take turns during the day.

These peculiar habits have apparently puzzled people for a long time. Detailed references to ostriches are found in Job 39:13–18. Its way of nest building is referenced in 39:14, which notes that the eggs are laid in the sand rather than in a nest in a tree, as with most species of birds. It is also alleged that ostrich eggs are easily crushed (39:15), and a number of biblical references suppose that the ostrich hen is indifferent or cruel to her young (39:13, 16; Lam. 4:3). The ostrich is also accused of stupidity (Job 39:17), but is justifiably acclaimed to be quicker than a horse (39:18).   I.U.K.

Othniel (oth′nee-uhl), one of the judges of Israel mentioned in both Joshua and Judges. The son of Kenaz and brother of Caleb, Othniel won his niece's hand in marriage by capturing the city of Debir (formerly called Kiriath-sepher). This young woman, Achsah, proceeded to request that her father give her a field with ample springs of water. According to the story in Josh. 15:15–19,

Caleb gave his daughter the upper springs and the lower springs (cf. Judg. 1:11–15). The other valiant deed attributed to Othniel was the defeat of Cushan-rishathaim, king of Mesopotamia (Judg. 3:7–11). This account is preserved in a manner typical of Deuteronomistic History (Israel sinned; God sent an enemy against Israel; Israel repented; God sent deliverance). Likewise, a standard formula concludes the story, indicating that the land had rest forty years. Othniel's name occurs in subsequent genealogies that provide information about his descendants (1 Chron. 4:13; 27:15).

J.L.C.

oven. In the biblical world, an oven (Heb. *tannur*; Gk. *klibanos*) was used mainly for baking bread (Lev. 2:4; 7:9; 26:26), though it could also serve as a stove when a large cooking pot was placed upon it. The typical oven consisted of a cylindrical clay structure seldom more than 2½ feet in diameter and open at the top. A hole could be scraped out in the middle, and potsherds were sometimes plastered around the outside to retain the heat. The floor of the oven would be covered with pebbles, on which a fire could be built. When bread was baked, a potsherd or stone could be placed over the top to enclose the oven, and the dough would be placed on hot stones within. Ovens were fired with any available fuel, including cut grass (Matt. 6:30) and animal dung (Ezek. 4:12, 15). Reference to a section of Jerusalem called the Tower of the Ovens (Neh. 3:11; 12:38) may indicate some sort of communal facility or a place where commercial bakers worked (cf. "bakers' street," Jer. 37:21). Ovens were cited metaphorically to designate great heat (Ps. 21:9; Lam. 5:10; Hos. 7:6, 7). Hosea compares the wicked to ovens, for their anger and passions burn within them (7:4–7). Malachi, however, compares the day of judgment to an oven in which the wicked will be burned (4:1); cf. references to what the NRSV calls a "furnace" (*tannur*, the same word it otherwise translates as "oven") as a symbol of God's wrath in Ps. 21:9; Isa. 31:9. The scorched black color of ovens is noted in Lam. 5:10, which uses it as a simile for the "scorching heat of famine." *See also* bread.   N.L.L./M.A.P.

owl, a member of the *Strigidae* family of birds. Several species of owl occur in the Near East, but their correlation with the biblical terms is problematic. Several different Hebrew words occur: (1) The word *kos* is translated in the NRSV as "little owl"; see Lev. 11:17; Deut. 14:16; Ps. 102:6; it probably is the bird popularly called a "little owl" (*Athene noctua*) or another known as a "tawny owl" (*Strix aluco*). (2) The term *yanshuph* probably refers to the "barn owl" (*Tyto alba*), though the NRSV sometimes translates it as "great owl" (Deut. 14:6; Lev. 11:17; also "owl" in Isa. 34:11). (3) The *qa'at* is called a "desert owl" in the NRSV and NIV (Lev. 11:18; Deut. 14:17; Zeph. 2:14), but some English Bibles take it to be a pelican; in Ps. 102:6, however, this word is used in parallel to

kos, the word for "little owl": "I am like an owl (*qa'at*) of the wilderness, like a little owl (*kos*) of the wasteplaces." (4) The word *tinshemet* is translated "water hen" (not an owl) by the RSV and NRSV (Lev. 11:18), but is translated "white owl" in the NIV; this animal has also been identified as a swan (KJV) or an ibis (NJB), and some authorities think the term might not refer to a bird at all, but to a chameleon. (5) The word *qippoz* is translated "owl" in Isa. 34:15 and "screech owl" in Zeph. 2:14.

The Bible has little to say about owls except that they are unclean and forbidden as food for the Israelites (Lev. 11:16–18; Deut. 14:12–17). They are associated with desolate places (Ps. 102:6) and, therefore, the image of owls roosting in a city symbolizes devastation (Isa. 34:11, 15; Zeph. 2:14). Owls are not referred to in the NT.   I.U.K./M.A.P.

ownership, the legal right of possession, which allows the one possessing it complete dominion over property to the exclusion of all others. Theologically, the Bible is consistent in insisting that everything belongs to God (e.g., Job 1:21; Ps. 24:1; 1 Chron. 29:14; 1 Cor. 4:7). In a more mundane sense, however, the Bible does recognize human ownership, as inheritance laws and prohibitions against stealing imply.

The concept of ownership varies in different legal systems. In ancient Near Eastern law, this concept seems to have involved varying degrees of possession and control. Thus, scholars argue that the ancient pledge was purchased or owned by the creditor by virtue of the loan that represented a purchase price. This ownership of the pledge, however, was subject to the debtor's right of redemption upon repayment of the loan. The highest degree of ownership is the one that bestows upon the possessor the legal power to voluntarily relinquish control over the property to a third party. This degree of ownership was achieved—only after the owner had been induced to sever all connection with the property and to relinquish all claims on it—by gifts and money. Thus, the purchase price did not serve merely as an objective sum of money whereby one acquired title to the property, but primarily as the inducement by which the seller's heart was fully satisfied to relinquish rights to the property. Echoes of this necessity to satisfy the seller's heart in order to obtain complete ownership may be found in the biblical account of Abraham's purchase of the Machpelah cave (Gen. 23). Although Ephron pretended to prefer presenting the land to Abraham as a gift, Abraham insisted on a final sale transaction, albeit at an exorbitant price, so that Ephron would be fully satisfied and thereby relinquish all claims to the cave.

Biblical Law: Biblical law does not restrict the transfer of ownership of movable property. It strongly disapproves, however, of the sale of land that would undermine the socioeconomic structure of ancient Israel's tribal and familial holdings, fixed at the time of the settlement of Canaan (thirteenth century BCE and later). In Lev. 25:23, the irrevocable transfer of ownership of land is prohibited. This law is rooted in the religious concept of the divine ownership of the land, and it is safeguarded by the institution of the jubilee year and the law of redemption.

The jubilee year was the final year in a fifty-year cycle consisting of seven sabbatical year periods. It effected the automatic return of land to the original owner. Accordingly, every sale of land was considered to be leased for the number of years remaining until the onset of the jubilee year. Hence the sale price was computed by the number of years for which the land would be leased (Lev. 25:13–17). According to the law of redemption, even before the jubilee year, the seller had the right to redeem the land from the purchaser whenever he could afford to do so. If the seller did not have the means, the closest living relative could redeem the land (Lev. 25:25–28). Hence, an impoverished man would often offer his land first to a relative (Jer. 32:9).

This right of redemption and automatic return in the jubilee year also extended to houses in unwalled villages. However, houses in walled cities had only a one-year redemption period and were not subject to return in the jubilee year (25:29–31). Thus, both the law of the jubilee and the law of redemption limited severely the transfer of ownership of land. This attitude against loss of one's ancestral inheritance is expressed strongly in the monarchic period by Naboth, who refuses to sell his vineyard to King Ahab (ca. 869–850 BCE; 1 Kings 21:3). From this narrative, however, it may be learned that the crown had the right to confiscate and thereby acquire ownership of the property of one who committed treason (1 Kings 21:16).

The nonlegal literature of the Bible records examples of land acquisition through purchase. In addition to the aforementioned story of Abraham purchasing the field and cave of Machpelah (Gen. 23), mention is made of Jacob's purchase of land from Hamor (33:18–20). Elsewhere, Jer. 32:6–16 describes a legal procedure for the transfer of property in preexilic Judah (pre-587/6 BCE); it includes the witnessed signing of a deed of purchase that is then placed in an earthenware jar for safekeeping. In Ruth 4:7–8, there is a terse reference to the symbolic act of removing one's shoe in the ratification of redemption and exchange transactions.

In the NT: There are no comparable regulations concerning ownership in the NT, where possession of goods and real property is simply taken for granted, as is evident in references to the purchase (cf. Matt. 13:34–35) or sale (cf. Acts 4:34–37) of such property. The attempt of hired hands to gain property by eliminating the heir (Mark 12:7) also seems to presume legal arrangements, but no evidence to explain such a practice has been found. It was further assumed that persons had the right to dispose of their possessions as they saw fit (cf. Matt. 20:15). *See also* redemption; sabbatical year.

B.L.E.

ox. *See* bull.

P̄

P, the siglum for the Priestly source, one of the four sources that scholars believe was used for the Pentateuch. It is concerned with religious ritual and exact specifications of time and measurement. *See also* Pentateuch, sources of the; Priestly writer(s).

Paddan-aram (pay′duhn-air′uhm), one of the names for the northwest region of Mesopotamia, between the Khabur and Euphrates rivers (Gen. 25:20; 28:2, 5–7; 31:18; 33:18; 35:9, 26; 46:15). It is also called Aram-naharaim (Heb., "Aram between two rivers"; NRSV: "Mesopotamia") in 24:10. In the Assyrian language, *padana* was a road or garden; Aram refers to the people or land of the Arameans. Haran and perhaps Ur were located in Paddan-aram. Isaac's wife, Rebekah, was from there (25:20), and Isaac sent Jacob back there to Rebekah's brother, Laban, to obtain a wife (28:2–7).

Pagiel (pay′gee-uhl; Heb., "El [God] has met"), the leader of the tribe of Asher during the wilderness wandering (Num. 1:13; 10:26).

Pahath-moab (pay′hath-moh′ab; Heb., "governor of Moab"), a leader of the postexilic community who signed Ezra's covenant to keep the law (Neh. 10:14); he was the ancestor of a family that included at least two groups, descendants of Jeshua and Joab (Ezra 2:6; 8:4; Neh. 7:11). He may also be the father of Hasshub, who worked to repair the walls of Jerusalem under Nehemiah (Neh. 3:11).   D.R.B.

paint, painting. In the Bible, painting is mentioned as a form of cosmetic decoration (e.g., painting the eyes, 2 Kings 9:30; Jer. 4:30; Ezek. 23:40) as well as the practice of decorating a home (Jer. 22:14; 2 Macc. 2:29). Archaeological evidence reveals that paint was also used on pottery and building interiors and exteriors. Israelite mention of painting is sparse, possibly due to the legal prohibition against making images (Exod. 20:4; Deut. 5:8). The Wisdom of Solomon gives a fairly explicit description of painting in precisely this context. A skilled worker takes a cast-off piece of wood and "forms it in the likeness of a human being, or makes it like some worthless animal, giving it a coat of red paint and coloring its surface red and covering every blemish in it with paint," and then he prays to it, for "when he prays about possessions and his marriage and children, he is not ashamed to address a lifeless thing" (13:13–17; cf. 15:4; Sir. 38:27).

palace. The Bible contains numerous references to royal residences (2 Chron. 2:1, 2), their staffs (1 Kings 4:6; 2 Kings 20:18; 24:12), their facilities (Esther 1:5; 5:1; Dan. 4:29; 5:5), and their security forces (Luke 11:21). Archaeological excavations reveal that specific palaces (e.g., at Luxor, Knossos, Mycenae, Persepolis, and Boghazkoy) were elaborate, richly decorated, and heavily fortified. No remains have been found of the palaces of David (2 Sam. 5:9; 7:102) and Solomon (1 Kings 7:1–12), but palaces at Hazor and Megiddo have been dated to the time of Solomon. The palace of Ahab and Omri at Samaria has been found, and the excavations there uncovered furniture inlaid and decorated with ivory (1 Kings 22:39).

Palestine (pal′uh-stin), the territory along the eastern coast of the Mediterranean Sea. Although the name "Palestine" has often been applied to this area in accounts dealing with the biblical period, such use is historically anachronistic. The term is never used in the Bible. Rather, such terms as "Canaan," "Israel," and "Judea" are employed for this region—or for portions of it—depending on the time period. Geographically, the area may be designated as "the Levant," though that term is sometimes also used more broadly with reference to a larger area (including Asia Minor). The area is also called the "Near East," a term that clearly reflects the perspective of Europeans and Americans. Historical references to this land up to the time of the monarchy often employ the phrase "ancient Near East."

The word "Palestine" is derived from the name of the Philistines, who inhabited a southern coastal strip of the territory. The Greek historian Herodotus (fifth century BCE) appears to have been the first to use "Palestine" in reference to the larger area (corresponding to modern Israel, Syria, and Jordan). After the suppression of the Bar-Kochba revolt in 135 CE, the Roman emperor Hadrian expunged the name *provincia judea* and substituted *provincia syria palaestina* or simply *palaestina* (Palestine). *See also* Levant, the.   M.A.P.

Pallu (pal′yoo; Heb., perhaps "conspicuous"), the second son of Reuben (Gen. 46:9; Exod. 6:14; 1 Chron. 5:3) and the father of Eliab (Num. 26:8). He was the ancestor of the Palluites (Num. 26:5). *See also* Eliab.

palm (*Phoenix dactylifera*), a tall, slender tree whose leaves fan out at the top like a plume. The botanical name, *Phoenix*, is derived from "Phoenicia." The palm is especially hardy in arid environments, since it has deep taproots that effectively seek out the water table. This enables it to live a long life, bearing fruit for many years (Ps. 92:12–14). Palms are therefore especially characteristic of water sources and oases; thus the reference to them at the springs of Elim (Num. 33:9) and at Jericho, the oasis city of palms (Deut. 34:3). The upright and stately form of the palm with its array of leaves provided a decorative motif in Solomon's temple (1 Kings 6:29, 32). The leaves were used as roofing for houses and for weaving mats and baskets. According to tradition, the leaves were also gathered and displayed as a symbol of joy and celebration on the arrival of Jesus into Jerusalem (John 12:13; cf. Lev. 23:40; Rev. 7:9).

The variety of palm that grows in the Near East is the date palm, which bears dates as fruit. Since

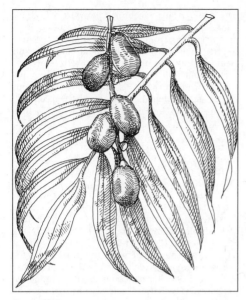

Date palm.

the trees grow as either male or female plants, however, they must be wind- or hand-pollinated, and the dates do not appear until at least five years after the tree reaches maturity. Then they hang in clusters from the top of the trees and are collected when they ripen in the late summer and early fall. Dates are especially valued by desert travelers. They provide a high-energy source of nutrition when fresh, and they also become a storable, easily portable food when dried or made into small cakes. The ground and soaked seeds provide a nutritious fodder for camels and other animals. A sweet wine is made from the fermented juice of the terminal buds. A similar fermented drink was also made from the tree's sap.

The Hebrew word for date palm, *tamar,* is used as a proper name in the Bible. As a place-name, Tamar is referred to in Ezek. 47:18–19 and 48:28. Absalom's sister (2 Sam. 13:1) and daughter (14:27) were both named Tamar.   P.L.C.

Pamphylia (pam-fil′ee-uh), a district about eighty miles long and thirty miles wide in southern Asia Minor, bounded on the north by the Taurus Mountains, on the east by Cilicia, and on the west by Lycia. The Kestros River, which was navigable in the first century, flows through the district to the southern coast of Asia Minor. The climate along the coastal plain was uncomfortable, and malaria was prevalent in that region. During the Maccabean period, Jews were apparently living in the area (1 Macc. 15:23), and Jews from there were reported in Jerusalem at Pentecost (Acts 2:10). In 74 CE, Pamphylia became a Roman province and expanded its boundaries to include the northern highland region (Pisidia). Two cities in Pamphylia, Perga and Attalia, were visited by Paul

and his companions during their first journey. At Perga, just five miles from the Kestros River, John Mark left Paul and Barnabas and returned to Jerusalem (Acts 13:13). A Roman road through the district connected Perga with the main port of Attalia, which Paul and Barnabas used to board a ship bound for Antioch (14:24–26). Paul sailed past Pamphylia en route to Rome (27:5). *See also* Attalia; Perga.   M.K.M.

paper, material upon which writing was done (2 John 12; 3 Macc. 4:20; 4 Esd. 15:2), in antiquity made from the pith of the papyrus plant. *See also* papyrus; writing.

Paphos (pay′fos), a city located on a rocky plateau along the southwestern coast of Cyprus, visited by Paul and Barnabas on their first missionary journey. It was here that they met the Roman proconsul Sergius Paulus and the Jewish prophet Elymas (Bar-Jesus), associated with him (Acts 13:6–12). The city they visited was New Paphos (modern Baffo), a port city about eleven miles from the inland city of Paphos (or Old Paphos, as it came to be called). In antiquity, Old Paphos had been the seat of the kingdom of Paphos, and it was renowned throughout the Greek world for its temple to Aphrodite, who, according to legend, had been born of the sea foam along the nearby coast (near New Paphos, actually). The newer city was built at the end of the fourth century BCE by King Nikokles of Paphos, and it grew in importance as a political capital and commercial center throughout the Ptolemaic and Roman periods. *See also* Cyprus; Elymas; Paulus, Sergius.   M.K.M.

papyrus, an aquatic plant of the sedge family (*Cyperus papyrus*) that grew abundantly in the shallow waters of the Nile in the vicinity of the Delta (Job 8:11). Resembling a stalk of corn (maize), the plant was used in a great variety of ways, not only in making paper, but also for fuel, food, medicine, clothes, rugs, sails, ropes, and even a kind of chewing gum.

Papyrus.

In the manufacture of paper, the stem of the mature plant was cut into sections about 12 to 15 inches in length. After each of these was split open lengthwise, the core of pith was removed and sliced into very thin strips. These were laid lengthwise on a flat surface just overlapping each other and all facing the same direction; then a second layer, placed at right angles, was laid on top. The two layers were pressed or pounded together until they formed one fabric. The resultant sheet, when dried and smoothed with pumice, was light in color, strong, and flexible. If the sheet had been well made, there would be little difference in the smoothness and finish of the two sides. The size and character of these papyrus sheets, however, varied considerably with the quality of the papyrus. About twenty individual sheets would be joined together end to end to form a roll. From such a roll, pieces could then be cut to the size needed for writing a letter, a bill of sale, a deed, or any other record. For a book of some considerable length, several rolls would be glued together. Christians, however, preferred the format of the codex, or leaf-book, in which individual sheets were stitched together in a binding analogous to that used for modern books.

The price paid for a sheet or roll of papyrus was determined by its size and quality. In general, papyrus was relatively expensive, and economically minded people would sometimes write on the back of a sheet or roll already used for other purposes or, indeed, wash the ink off a sheet and reuse it.

Preserved by the dry climate of Egypt, thousands of papyrus documents of all kinds have been found. Among biblical manuscripts, the most noteworthy collections are those acquired by Chester Beatty (Dublin) and Martin Bodmer (Geneva). The Beatty collection includes a fragmentary codex from the second century containing the Greek text of the books of Numbers and Deuteronomy and a codex of ten letters of Paul from about 200 CE; the Bodmer collection includes a codex of the Gospel of John from about 200 CE and another, dating from the third century, containing the Gospels of Luke and John. *See also* codex; writing.   B.M.M.

parables, short sayings or stories with a double meaning. In the Bible, the term "parable" (Gk. *parabolē*) is used broadly to designate a variety of literary forms that convey metaphorical or figurative meaning—not just stories, but aphorisms, proverbs, riddles, dialogues, and discourses. In the Aristotelian tradition, by contrast, the definition of a parable was more detailed and precise. In the *Art of Rhetoric* (2.20) Aristotle divides rhetorical proofs into general statements that can be used for deductive purpose (such as maxims and proverbs) and specific stories that can be used for inductive purposes. These latter stories can be further subdivided as historical or fictional, and the fictional ones can be subdivided again into parables (stories that, while fictional, would be possible) and fables (stories that are both fictional and impossible). For the Aristotelian tradition, then, parables are a very specific type of metaphor: they are realistic but metaphorical narratives.

The Hebrew Bible abounds with material that might be described as "parables" in the NT sense of the word (metaphors, aphorisms, proverbs, riddles, and other figurative discourse), but the NRSV uses the word "parable" only once outside the NT, in Ps. 49:4: "I will open my mouth in a parable; I will utter dark sayings from of old." The Hebrew word *mashal,* translated "parable" in that verse, is actually found many other places in the Bible and is consistently translated *parabolē* in the Greek LXX, which was the primary Bible for most of the NT authors. Thus, it seems fairly certain that when the NT authors represent Jesus as teaching in parables, they mean to associate his teaching with the sort of materials that were designated by that word in the LXX, material for which the term *mashal* is used in the Hebrew Bible. This includes allegories (Ezek. 17:2–10; 24:3–5), proverbs (Jer. 23:28; 1 Sam. 24:13; Ezek. 18:2), and other sayings (Hab. 2:5–6; Mic. 2:4). But the Hebrew Bible also contains a handful of narrative parables more in keeping with the narrower sense of the term. These include the Song of the Vineyard (Isa. 5:1–2; cf. Mark 12:1–11) and the story of the Wise Woman of Tekoa (2 Sam. 14:5–7). Jotham's tale of the Trees and the Bramble in Judg. 9:8–15 may also be cited (though it would be a fable, according to Aristotle's definition). The story that Nathan tells David about the theft of a prized lamb (2 Sam. 12:1–4) is an especially good example of a parable similar in style, tone, and content to many stories of Jesus. Notably Nathan appends an interpretation to the story that applies it directly and explicitly to his audience (12:5–9).

Parables of Jesus: More than forty parables of Jesus are included in the Gospels of Matthew, Mark, and Luke. No parables are found in John, but even there one finds instances of figurative speech not too far removed from the parable genre (4:35–37; 8:35; 10:1–5; 12:24; 16:21). As indicated, however, the stories and sayings that get classed as parables in the Gospels are of many different types. In their simplest form, the parables compare heavenly or spiritual things to mundane realities: the kingdom of God is like a mustard seed (Mark 4:30–32), a pearl (Matt. 13:45–47), or a treasure hidden in a field (Matt. 13:44). A couple of Jesus's better-known parables are explicitly presented as allegories: Jesus explains the parable of the Sower (Mark 4:2–9; cf. 4:13–20) and the parable of the Weeds (Matt. 13:24–30; cf. 13:36–43) by indicating that every element of these stories stands for something else (the seed is the word, the birds are the devil, etc.). Most of the parables, however, are not allegories. Many are short anecdotes that function like sermon illustrations: the parable of the Rich Fool in Luke 12:16–21 illustrates the folly of equating quality of life with the acquisition of possessions. In some cases, however, the parables do not help to clarify a difficult point, but do exactly the opposite—they introduce an element of complication with regard to what would otherwise be clear. The parable of the Pharisee and the Tax Collector challenges the notion that God prefers those who keep Torah to those who do not, by proposing a scenario in which that distinction is in tension with God's desire to exalt those who humble themselves and humble those who exalt themselves (Luke 18:9–18). Indeed, in some instances, the parables pose riddles for people to figure out (Mark 3:23) and in certain cases they function as a sort of code language for speaking of divine matters in terms that the unenlightened will not comprehend (cf. Mark 4:11–12, 33–34; 7:17). In a few cases, sayings or proverbs that are called "parables" actually seem to summarize the basic idea of what could be a more developed

"story parable"; e.g., "If one blind person guides another, both will fall into a pit" (Matt. 15:14; cf. 15:15). In such cases, the narrative aspect of the parable seems to be implied (left to the hearers' imagination), though it is always possible that the Gospel tradition has preserved only the moral or message of the story, absent the story itself.

Literary Characteristics of Parables: Drawing on seminal work by scholar Rudolf Bultmann, a number of interpreters have noted typical characteristics of the narrative parables of Jesus.

Parables are usually concise. Only the persons who are absolutely essential to the story appear. For instance, in the story about the prodigal son (Luke 15:11–32) there is no mention of the lad's mother. In the story of the friend at midnight (11:5–8) there is no mention of the householder's wife. There are never more than three persons or groups in the stories, and no more than two seem to appear at a time.

Parables are usually told from a single perspective. There is one series of events, always told from the point of view of one person. In the parable of the Prodigal Son, for instance, there is no word of the father's mood or actions while the son was away.

Characters are usually presented through a process of "showing" rather than "telling." It is rare that anyone in a parable is described by the narrator. Readers are told that the judge is unjust (Luke 18:2) and that the bridesmaids are wise and foolish (Matt. 25:2), but this kind of description is quite exceptional. Knowledge of the character of the persons involved emerges from their behavior.

Feelings and motives are only described when essential to the point of the story. Readers are told of the distress of the fellow servants of the merciless servant (Matt. 18:31), of the joy of the shepherd who found the lost sheep and the woman who found the lost coin (Luke 15:6, 9), and of the compassion of the good Samaritan (10:33); but in the story of the prodigal son and in the one contrasting a Pharisee with a tax collector, the feelings of the people involved are expressed not through descriptions offered by the narrator, but through the words and the actions of the characters themselves.

There is little interest in motivation. There is no description, for instance, of the prodigal son's motives in leaving home. Nothing is allowed to deflect attention from the point of the story.

There is often no expressed conclusion to the story. Readers are not told, for instance, that the rich fool died (Luke 12:3–31) or whether the good Samaritan had to pay additional money (10:35). The main point is made—and that is the end of the story.

There is usually minimal description of events. Readers are not told what the prodigal son's particular brand of loose living was (Luke 15:13) or what the widow did and said when she "kept coming" to the judge (18:3).

There are often direct speech and soliloquy, which make for simplicity, vividness, and speed of narrative. In a number of parables, the main characters

The Roman road from Jericho to Jerusalem. The parable of the Good Samaritan is set in this region (Luke 10:30–35).

PARABLES IN THE GOSPELS

Parable	Matthew	Mark	Luke
New Patch on an Old Cloak	9:16	2:21	5:36
New Wine in Old Wineskins	9:17	2:22	5:37–38
The Sower	13:3–8	4:3–8	8:5–8
Lamp Under a Bowl	5:14–16	4:21–22	8:16; 11:33
Seed Growing Secretly		4:26–29	
Mustard Seed	13:31–32	4:30–32	13:18–19
Wicked Tenants	21:33–44	12:1–11	20:9–18
Fig Tree	24:32–33	13:28–29	21:29–31
Watchful Slaves		13:33–37	12:35–38
Wise and Foolish Builders	7:24–27		6:47–49
Yeast Leavens Flour	13:33		13:20–21
Lost Sheep	18:12–14		15:4–7
Thief in the Night	24:42–44		12:39–40
Faithful and Wise Slave	24:45–51		12:42–48
The Talents (or The Pounds)	25:14–30		19:12–27
Weeds Among the Wheat	13:24–30		
Treasure Hidden in a Field	13:44		
Pearl of Great Value	13:45–46		
Net Full of Good and Bad Fish	13:47–50		
Treasure New and Old	13:52		
Unmerciful Servant	18:23–34		
Workers in the Vineyard	20:1–16		
Two Sons	21:28–32		
Wedding Banquet	22:2–14		
Ten Bridesmaids	25:1–13		
Two Debtors			7:41–43
Good Samaritan			10:30–37
Friend at Midnight			11:5–8
Rich Fool			12:16–21
Severe and Light Beatings			12:47–48
Barren Tree			13:6–9
Lowest Seat at a Banquet			14:7–14
Excuses for Not Attending a Banquet			14:16–24
Building a Tower			14:28–30
Waging War			14:31–32
Lost Coin			15:8–10
Prodigal Son			15:11–32
Shrewd Manager			16:1–9
Rich Man and Lazarus			16:19–31
Slave Serves the Master			17:7–10

PARABLES IN THE GOSPELS (continued)

Parable	Matthew	Mark	Luke
Widow and Judge			18:2–8
Pharisee and Tax Collector			18:10–14

Summary:
9 parables from Mark (most of which are also in Matthew and Luke)
6 parables from Q (found in Matthew and Luke, but not in Mark)
10 parables unique to Matthew
17 parables unique to Luke
42 parables total

From Mark Allan Powell, *Introducing the New Testament* (courtesy, Baker Academic, 2009)

speak to themselves. For example, see the prodigal son (Luke 15:17–19), the shrewd manager (16:3–5), and the rich fool (12:17–19).

There is often repetition of phrases, which has a kind of underlining effect. In the parable of the talents (Matt. 25:14–30), readers are told repeatedly of servants presenting their accounts to the master (25:20, 22, 24).

Parables often exhibit end stress; the most important point is scored at the end. The emphasis in the parable of the Sower (Mark 4:1–8) is on the fruitful seed, just as the emphasis in the story about the good Samaritan is on the third traveler, the one who does act as neighbor (Luke 10:30–35).

The stories often seek to involve hearers or readers, demanding some sort of decision. The parables lead to a verdict, which is based on antithesis and contrast. Readers are asked to align themselves with one side or the other.

Interpretation: Scholars seek to interpret parables in at least two different contexts. First, the parables are often read as plausible statements of the historical Jesus, and an effort is made to determine what he might have meant in telling the story in its original first-century setting. Second, the parables are often read within the contexts of the Gospels in which they now appear; the effort, then, is to determine how the parable would have been understood by the Gospel writer as it related to the life and mission of the church. For example, the original focus of the parable of the Sower might have been its promise that inauspicious beginnings can yield abundant results (despite setbacks, the seed produces an incredibly rich harvest; in like manner, the kingdom of God has begun to arrive through the apparently inauspicious ministry of Jesus and, despite opposition, will soon come with power). In the Gospels, however, the focus of the parable shifts to the four types of soil in which the seed is cast, and the story teaches moral lessons about what kinds of people bear fruit for God and about what sort of trials and temptations must be avoided to do so.

While recognizing that parables are somewhat open to multiple interpretations, scholars generally try to discern the basic point or points that each parable was expected to make and warn against reading too much into the stories otherwise. In Luke 18:1–5, Jesus tells a parable about prayer using the example of a persistent widow who seeks justice from a corrupt and uncaring judge. The basic point is that persistence is important with regard to spiritual quests; neither Jesus nor Luke wanted people to view God as corrupt and uncaring. Likewise, Jesus tells a parable about laborers all being paid the same wage, although they worked different hours (Matt. 20:1–16). The basic point seems to be that God can be surprisingly generous in a way that offends those who think they are especially deserving; the story was not intended to offer an endorsement of any particular economic system or to argue in favor of some view concerning management and labor relations. *See also* Good Samaritan, parable of the; Jesus Christ; kingdom of God; Prodigal Son, parable of the.

Bibliography

Bultmann, Rudolf, *The History of the Synoptic Tradition*. 3rd ed. Harper & Row, 1963. Pp. 188–92.

Hultgren, Arland. *The Parables of Jesus.* Eerdmans, 2000.

Powell, Mark Allan. *Introducing the New Testament: A Historical, Literary, and Theological Survey.* Baker Academic, 2009.

Scott, Bernard Brandon. *Hear Then the Parable: A Commentary on the Parables of Jesus.* Fortress, 1989.

Snodgrass, Klyne. *Stories with Intent: A Comprehensive Guide to the Parables of Jesus.* Eerdmans, 2008.
M.A.P.

Paraclete (pair′uh-kleet), the transliteration of a Greek term meaning "called to the side of" and hence "advocate" (cf. 1 John 2:1). Jesus uses this as a designation for the Holy Spirit in the Gospel of John (14:16–17, 26; 15:26; 16:7–11; cf. 16:13–15). Some English Bibles translate the term with a variety of words (NRSV and NIV: "Counselor"; KJV: "Comforter"; JB and NEB: "Advocate"), but the word "Paraclete" itself has obtained some use in Christian tradition and liturgy. According to the

Fourth Gospel, the Paraclete is the Spirit of truth (14:17; 15:26). The Paraclete continues the work of Jesus himself (14:16–17), recalling things the earthly Jesus taught or revealing things he was unable to convey (14:26; 16:12–14). This spiritual knowledge or insight, unavailable until after Jesus's death and resurrection, makes Christian faith and understanding fully possible. *See also* Holy Spirit; John, Gospel According to.   D.M.S.

paradise, a location or status of uninterrupted bliss. By the early second century BCE, many Jews had come to believe in life after death. They sought concrete images with which to express that new faith as an extension of traditional ideas. Since God had placed the first couple in an idyllic park (the garden of Eden), it was plausible to assume that a similar location awaited the righteous after death. The LXX referred to the garden of Eden as "Paradise" (Gk. *paradeisos;* Gen. 2:9, 15–16; 3:1, 8, 10; Heb. *gan;* NRSV: "garden"). Thus, the term came to be used for the ultimate destination of the righteous. The word "paradise" is ultimately of Persian origin and denotes a "park" or "forest."

NT writers generally accept the paradise image. Paul speaks of it in connection with his vision of the "third heaven" (2 Cor. 12:1–4), and in Luke's Gospel Jesus assures a crucified thief that they will both be in Paradise that very day (23:43). The book of Revelation suggests that, following the resurrection, the righteous will live in a paradise on earth and will feast from the "tree of life" (2:7; 22:1–2; cf. 4 Esd. 8:52; *2 Enoch* 8). Some passages, however, suggest that the martyrs are immediately taken to the highest of seven heavens, where they await the resurrection at "the altar" (6:9–11; 7:9–17). Passages in other books imply that the dead, righteous and wicked alike, descend to the underworld and await the resurrection in a sleeplike state (Matt. 12:40; 1 Thess. 4:13–16). *See also* death; heaven; resurrection; Sheol.   L.R.B.

parallelism, a rhetorical device involving one or more linguistic repetitions or correspondences (grammatical, lexical, semantic, or phonetic) in adjacent lines or phrases. Although present in prose, parallelism is more prominent in biblical poetry, where it often appears to be a basic structuring device. An example is Ps. 103:10: "He does not deal with us according to our sins // nor requite us according to our iniquities." This is an example of synonymous parallelism, meaning that the two phrases of the verse basically state the same thing. Ps. 1:1 offers an example of threefold synonymous parallelism: "Those who do not follow the advice of the wicked // or take the path that sinners tread // or sit in the seat of scoffers." Although the meaning of the three phrases is not exactly the same, all three phrases offer similar examples of behavior to be avoided, and the phrases are also semantically similar: "follow the advice," "take the path," and "sit in the seat" are parallel expressions, as are "the wicked," "sinners," and "scoffers."

Another type of parallelism, called antithetic parallelism, presents two lines in contrast to one another: "A soft answer turns away wrath," but "a harsh word stirs up anger" (Prov. 15:1). The same sort of contrast is often made in poetic passages where the semantic equivalence is less pronounced, e.g., "My flesh and my heart may fail," but "God is the strength of my heart" (Ps. 73:26).

As a poetic device, the primary purpose of parallelism may be aesthetic: it is appealing and memorable. Beyond this, it creates emphasis. The admonition, "You shall love the LORD your God with all your heart, and with all your soul, and with all your might" (Deut. 6:5) does not indicate that people are to love God with three different parts of their being, but stresses three times that they are to love God with their entire being. In some instances, parallelism is used in a climactic way, piling up synonymous expressions one upon another until finally the significant declaration is made: "Though the fig tree does not blossom, and no fruit is on the vines; // though the produce of the olive fails, and the fields yield no food; // though the flock is cut off from the fold, and there is no herd in the stalls, // yet I will rejoice in the LORD" (Hab. 3:17–18).

In the NT, Jesus makes frequent use of parallelism. Many of his more memorable sayings would have been heard by his contemporaries as poetry. An instance of threefold synonymous parallelism is found in Matt. 7:7: "Ask, and it will be given you; // search, and you will find; // knock, and the door will be opened for you." The Beatitudes (5:3–10) and the Lord's Prayer (6:9–13) should probably also be interpreted in this light.

The accuracy of defining parallelism as a characteristic of Hebrew poetry has been questioned by some scholars, who find the application of such a category to be overly simplistic and anachronistic. The claim is that biblical Hebrew did not sharply distinguish poetry from prose, and modern attention to parallelism has imposed a structure on texts that might not have been discerned by their original authors. For more on this, see the comments regarding parallelism in the entry on poetry. *See also* poetry; Psalms, book of.   M.A.P.

paralysis, one of the afflictions Jesus heals (Matt. 4:24). Three Gospel narratives recount the healing of specific individuals who suffered from paralysis. In Mark 2:1–12, Jesus is teaching in a house, when some men come to him, carrying a paralyzed man. They cannot get to him because of the crowd, so they go up on the roof of the house and lower the paralyzed man down to Jesus through a hole in the ceiling. Seeing their faith, Jesus tells the man his sins are forgiven and then tells him to take up his mat and go home—healed of his paralysis, he does just that, to the amazement of all (cf. Matt. 9:1–8; Luke 5:17–26). In another instance, a centurion comes to Jesus in Capernaum and tells him that his servant is "lying at home paralyzed in terrible distress" (Matt. 8:5). Impressed by the centurion's faith, Jesus heals the servant from a distance (i.e., without actually going to see him); a parallel story is told in Luke 7:1–10, but with no mention of paralysis (cf. also John 4:46–54). Then, John 5:1–9 recounts the story of Jesus healing a paralyzed man at the Beth-zatha pool on a sabbath day during a Jewish festival. His directions to the man, "Take up your mat and walk" are strikingly similar to the words spoken to the paralytic in Galilee in the first narrative mentioned above (Mark 2:11; cf. 2:9). In both stories, Jesus arouses the ire of certain religious leaders: in Mark 2:1–12, because he tells the man his sins are forgiven; and in John 5:1–9, because the healing is performed on a sabbath and because Jesus subsequently calls God his Father in a way that the religious leaders think constitutes a claim to equality with God (5:10–18).

In the book of Acts, Philip heals paralyzed people in Samaria (8:37). Then Peter encounters a bedridden man named Aeneas, who has been paralyzed for eight years. He tells him, "Aeneas, Jesus Christ heals you; get up and make your bed!" and the man is healed immediately (9:34).   M.A.P.

Paran (pay'ruhn), the wilderness site where the Israelites camped after they left Mount Sinai (Num. 10:11–12; 12:16) and from which spies were sent to reconnoiter Canaan (13:3–26). The return of the spies to Kadesh suggests that the location was south of Canaan along the north edge of the Sinai triangle. The association of Kadesh with the Wilderness of Zin (33:36) reinforces this identification. Gen. 21:21 designates Paran as Ishmael's home after his banishment. According to 1 Sam. 25:1, David visited Paran after Samuel's death, and 1 Kings 11:18 reflects the flight of Edomite Hadad from Midian through Paran to Egypt. Poetic references to "Mount Paran" in Deut. 33:2 and Hab. 3:3 speak of God's manifestation in the southern region for battle against Israel's enemies—if any literal mountain is in view, it is probably Mount Sinai.   R.S.B.

parapet. *See* battlement.

parchment, writing material made from the skins of animals. During the Roman period, papyrus (a writing material made from plant fibers) was replaced in many of its uses by parchment, which was much more durable. The word itself is derived from the name of the city where it was invented, Pergamum (cf. Rev. 1:11; 2:12–17). According to Pliny the Elder (*Natural History* 12.21) parchment was first developed in Pergamum around the beginning of the second century BCE during a time when a rivaly between libraries led to an Egyptian embargo on the export of papyrus. It eventually became the preferred material for sacred documents. According to the *Letter of Aristeas* (176 BCE) leather was mandatory for Torah scrolls used in public worship. The Dead Sea Scrolls found at Qumran were written on parchment. Prior to the fourth century CE, however, most NT writings were copied on papyrus, probably because it was cheaper and more readily available. The production of parchment involved washing the skin, scraping the hair off, rubbing it with pumice to make it smooth, and then treating it with chalk. Superior parchment, called vellum, was usually made from the skins of goats, calves, or lambs. *See also* writing.

pardon, in a legal sense, an action by which an empowered authority reverses a sentence imposed under a verdict of guilty. The biblical concept of pardon, however, is primarily a religious or theological one in which God is the empowered authority and human beings are guilty of sin or iniquity. From the biblical perspective, the human creature is subject to the created order and accountable to the Creator for violations of this order; nevertheless, humanity exhibits a strong and consistent tendency to violate God's will (as articulated in both law and covenant), and the condition of humanity would be hopeless if the Creator were not mercifully disposed. Moses prays for God to pardon the "stiff-necked" Israelites (Exod. 34:9; cf. Num. 14:19), but also warns them that such pardon is not something they can take for granted (Deut. 29:20; cf. 2 Kings 39:4). Hezekiah prays, "The good LORD pardon all who set their hearts to seek God" (2 Chron. 30:18–19). Isa. 55:6–7 expresses the same thought, but as a promise rather than a prayer: "Seek the LORD while (the LORD) may be found; . . . let the wicked forsake their way, and the unrighteous their thoughts; let them return to the LORD . . . for (the LORD) will abundantly pardon" (cf. Mic. 7:18).

The concepts of pardon and forgiveness are closely connected, and the two words can be used almost interchangeably: "You forgave [Heb. *nasa'*] the iniquity of your people; you pardoned [*kasah*] all of their sin" (Ps. 85:2). The Hebrew Bible thus describes God as eager to forgive (Neh. 9:17; Pss. 86:5; 130:4; Jer. 36:3; Dan. 9:9), especially in the face of humility and repentance (2 Chron. 7:14; Ps. 86:5) and the will to change (Deut. 30; Num. 14:18; Josh. 24:19–21; 1 Kings 8:36; Ps. 51:12; Jer. 5:1–9). The provision for pardon as atonement/expiation has been made by God to remedy the condition of sin.

The NRSV does not the use the word "pardon" in the NT, though the related themes of forgiveness (e.g., Matt. 6:12; 9:2; Luke 1:77; 23:34; 24:47; Acts 2:38; 5:31; Eph. 1:7; 1 John 1:9) and justification (e.g., Rom. 3:22–4:5; 5:1; 1 Cor. 6:11; Gal. 2:16–17) are prominent there. The NT especially emphasizes the role of the community (and its leaders) in mediating such a pardon (John 20:23; James 5:15) and, accordingly, stresses the responsibility for those who have been pardoned by God to pardon others (Matt. 6:14–15; 18:21–35; 2 Cor. 2:7; Eph. 4:32). *See also* atonement; covenant; forgiveness; guilt; reconciliation; redemption; salvation; sin.   J.E.A./M.A.P.

Parmenas (pahr'muh-nuhs), one of the seven selected in the Jerusalem church to care for the widows and distribute food to the poor (Acts 6:1–6). He was probably a hellenized Jew. *See also* Hellenists.

Parosh (pay'rosh; Heb., "flea").

1 The head of a family returning from exile with Zerubbabel (Ezra 2:5; Neh. 7:8) after being exiled under Artaxerxes (Ezra 8:3). Some members of the family had married foreign women (Ezra 10:26); a descendant, Pedaiah, led repairs near the Water Gate (Neh. 3:25–26).

2 A signatory on the covenant-revenewal document of Ezra during the time of Nehemiah (Neh. 10:14); some conclude that this person is a descendant of the family designated in **1.**

Parousia (puh-roo'zhee-uh), the Second Coming of Jesus Christ. The word is a transliteration of the Greek word *parousia*, which means "coming," "arrival," or "being present." As such, the Greek word *parousia* occurs in the LXX and in the NT in a variety of contexts, often without any particular religious implications. But since the word is used in a number of NT passages that refer specifically to the coming (i.e., Second Coming) of Christ, it has come to be used as a somewhat technical term for that event. Key texts in which the word is used in this regard include Matt. 24:3, 27, 37, 39; 1 Cor. 15:23; 1 Thess. 2:19; 3:13; 4:15; 5:23; 2 Thess. 2:1, 8; James 5:7–8; 2 Pet. 1:16; 3:4, 12; 1 John 2:28. These passages, and others, testify to the Christian belief and expectation that Jesus will appear, in the future, as Son of Man, Christ (Messiah), and Lord. One passage possibly refers to Jesus's previous coming as his "Parousia" (2 Pet. 1:16; NRSV: "coming"). Many other NT passages refer to Jesus's future coming, but without using the Greek word *parousia*. In only one text (John 14:3) does Jesus say that he will come "again," and only Heb. 9:28 refers explicitly to his "second" coming. Jesus's future appearance is described most dramatically in Revelation (19:11–16), which thematically assures readers that Jesus is coming "soon" and that the "time" is now "near" (1:1, 3; 3:11; 22:10, 12, 20). Other NT writings also encourage the expectation that Jesus will come soon (Rom. 13:11–12; 16:20; 1 Cor. 7:29; Phil. 4:5; 1 Pet. 4:7; Heb. 10:37; James 5:8). More directly, the author of 2 Peter attempts to counter "scoffers," who point out that things remain the same as always and that various arguments account for the apparent delay of the Parousia (2 Pet. 3:3–9). A number of synoptic passages suggest that certain "signs" or preliminary phenomena may indicate that Jesus's Parousia or other Parousia events are imminent (Matt. 24:4–34; Mark 13:5–20; Luke 21:8–28; cf. 2 Thess. 2:1–12; 1 John 2:18). Other texts call on readers to be ready, because such events will take place without warning (see, e.g., Matt. 24:43–44; Luke 12:35–40; 1 Thess. 5:2–3; James 5:7–11; 2 Pet. 3:10; Rev. 3:3; 16:15). *See also* apocalyptic literature; eschatology; judgment, day of; kingdom of God; messiah; millennium; Paul; resurrection; Revelation, book of; son of man, Son of Man.

Bibliography

Carroll, John T., ed. *The Return of Jesus in Early Christianity.* Hendrickson, 2000.

Hiers, Richard H. *Jesus and the Future.* John Knox, 1981.

Holman, Charles L. *Till Jesus Comes: Origins of Christian Apocalyptic Expectation.* Hendrickson, 1996.

Moore, A. L. *The Parousia in the New Testament.* Brill, 1966.

Robinson, John A. T. *Jesus and His Coming.* Abingdon, 1957.

Witherington, Ben, III. *Jesus, Paul, and the End of the World.* InterVarsity, 1992.   R.H.H.

Parthians (pahr'thee-uhnz), an Iranian people. The northeastern region of Iran, known as Parthava since at least the seventh century BCE, became prominent when the Parni tribe of central Asia wrested it from the Seleucids in the third century BCE. In the following century, the Parni dynasty, traced to Arsaces I, expanded its empire throughout the Iranian plateau and beyond. The Parthians were strong enough to stop Roman expansion at the Euphrates in 53 BCE, although Trajan did later briefly occupy their capital at Ctesiphon. As a result of their rivalry with western powers, the Parthians became involved in Judean affairs, supporting Antigonus II as king in Jerusalem until Roman assistance enabled Herod to displace him. Luke reports some Parthians were present in Jerusalem at Pentecost (Acts 2:9). The Parthian Empire fell to the Sasanians early in the third century CE.   F.E.G.

partridge, a medium-size, stout-bodied game bird. The most frequent species of the partridge is the chukar partridge (*Alectoris chukar*), a medium-sized game bird with red legs and red beak that lives in rocky terrain. Its typical cackling voice is similar to that of a clucking hen. When chased, it prefers to run, and it only flies short distances. In 1 Sam. 26:20 Saul's pursuit of David is compared to a partridge hunt. Jer. 17:11 refers to partridges as hatching eggs from other birds' nests (something they are not actually known to do). Sir. 11:30 compares "the proud" to "a decoy partridge in a cage," apparently highlighting their insincerity.

paschal (pas'kuhl), a Greek term meaning "pertaining to Passover." It is frequently transliterated into English, especially with reference to the lamb slaughtered for the Passover feast (cf. Exod. 12:3–8, 21). According to the Gospel of John, Jesus was crucified the day before Passover, at the time the paschal lamb was slain (19:14; cf. 1:29, 36). In 1 Cor. 5:7, Paul refers to Christ as "our paschal lamb" who "has been sacrificed."

Paseah (puh-see'uh; Heb., "limper"), the personal name of three people, perhaps because they were all partially disabled.

1 The Judean son of Eshton (1 Chron. 4:12).

2 An ancestor of some temple servants working in postexilic Judah (Ezra 2:49; Neh. 7:51).

3 The father of Joiada who, with Meshullam, repaired the Old Gate (Neh. 3:6).

Pashhur (pash´huhr; Egyptian, "portion of [the god] Horus").

1 A priest, son of Immer, and chief officer in the temple; he opposed Jeremiah's prophecy, beat him, and put him in stocks. Jeremiah renamed him "Terror-all-around," reaffirmed his own word of destruction, and prophesied personal exile to Babylon for Pashhur and his family (Jer. 20).

2 The son of Malchiah, who apparently was King Zedekiah's son. Zedekiah sent Pashhur to "inquire of the LORD" through Jeremiah while Nebuchadnezzar was making war against Judah (Jer. 21). Jeremiah repeated God's word of destruction. The same Pashhur, a high official, accused Jeremiah of treason and recommended his death (Jer. 38). The descendants of Pashhur, distinct from the descendants of Immer (see **1**), made up one of the important priestly families who returned from the exile (1 Chron. 9:12; Ezra 2:38; 10:22; Neh. 7:41; 11:12).

3 The father of the Gedaliah who joined Pashhur, son of Malchiah, in the action against Jeremiah (Jer. 38:1); he was perhaps the same Pashhur as **1** above.

4 A high official who was contemporary with Nehemiah (Neh. 10:3). H.B.H.

The name "Pashhur," written in Hebrew on an ostracon from Arad, ninth–sixth century BCE.

passion.

1 Aroused or inflamed emotions (Prov. 14:30; 1 Cor. 7:9; 1 Thess. 4:5). The biblical attitude toward such powerful feelings is almost relentlessly negative. A lover in the Song of Solomon is proud to proclaim his passion: it rages like a fire and is to be equated with love (8:6). But Proverbs says, "A tranquil mind gives life to the flesh, but passion makes the bones rot" (14:30). The NT has nothing positive to say about passion, which is variously linked with desire, pleasure, sex, lust, and sin. Paul speaks of "degrading passions" that lead people to commit abominable sexual acts

(Rom. 1:26–27); when sin exercises dominion, it forces people to obey the passions of their mortal bodies (6:12). Paul thinks that the law of God only arouses such passions without taming them (7:5); but "those who belong to Jesus Christ have crucified the flesh with its passions and desires" (Gal. 5:24; cf. 2:20). By the same token, believers must practice self-control and take reasonable measures to control their passions; for instance, a believer who would be committed to remaining a virgin should marry if his passions are strong and he is not behaving properly toward his fiancée (1 Cor. 7:26; cf. 7:9). Elsewhere passion is classed as something "earthly" that should be "put to death" (Col. 3:5); the grace of God trains believers to denounce "worldly passions" (Titus 2:12). "Lustful passion" characterizes the Gentiles, who do not know God (1 Thess. 4:5; cf. 1 Pet. 4:3). Timothy is told specifically to shun "youthful passions" (2 Tim. 2:22). Passions and pleasures are things that enslave the foolish (Titus 3:3).

2 The suffering and death of Jesus. The Greek word for passion (pathos) is used once in the Bible to refer to the event of Jesus's suffering and death, in Acts 1:3, though the NRSV and other contemporary English Bibles have chosen to translate the word "suffering" in that one occurrence (KJV, RSV, NJB: "passion"). In any case, the expression "passion narrative" is widely used in biblical studies to refer to the biblical account of Jesus's arrest, trial, and crucifixion in the four Gospels. *See also* cross; passion narratives; trial of Jesus. P.P./M.A.P.

passion narratives, literary accounts of Jesus's suffering and death. All four Gospels conclude with extended stories of Jesus's arrest, trial, crucifixion, burial, and resurrection. In each Gospel, this portion of the story is treated with more intense detail than any other portion of the book, and the pace of the narrative slows to the point that readers receive an almost hour-by-hour account of what is happening. Scholars have also noted similarities between these accounts and death scenes of other famous men in ancient Greco-Roman biographies. Furthermore, the Gospel passion narratives show an especially strong degree of interaction with the scriptures of Israel; they appear to have been written by people who had already thought deeply about the meaning of Jesus's death and resurrection and reflected on those events in light of passages from the Psalms, the Prophets, and other passages of scripture. Thus, the death and resurrection of Jesus is not treated as just one more episode in a series of remarkable occurrences; for each of the four Gospels, it is treated as the climax of the story, the grand conclusion to which everything has been pointing all along. Indeed, each of the Gospels prepares readers for this capstone event by having Jesus predict exactly what will occur (e.g., Mark 8:31–32; 9:31; 10:33–34) or offer vague allusions that readers are expected to understand in a manner that characters in the story do not (see Mark 2:20; John 2:19–22; 3:14;

8:28; 12:32–34). More to the point, each Gospel tells the story of Jesus's death and resurrection in a distinctive way that pulls together certain threads and fulfills important themes of that particular work. In Matthew's Gospel, Jesus dies as the Messiah of Israel, fulfilling prophecies that indicated he would be the one to save his people from their sin (cf. 1:21). In Mark, he gives his life as a ransom for many, demonstrating the sacrificial way of self-denial that is to mark all of his followers (cf. 8:34–35; 10:43–45). In Luke, he dies as a noble martyr, a victim of injustice, who will overcome death in a way that promises an end to oppression (cf. 4:18). In John, he dies triumphantly, as one who is glorified and exalted in an ultimate expression of God's love (cf. 12:23; 15:13). In these and other ways, the passion narratives serve as theological climaxes of the Gospels in which they appear. *See also* cross; trial of Jesus.

Bibliography

Brown, Raymond E. *The Death of the Messiah: From Gethsemane to the Grave.* 2 vols. Doubleday, 1994.

Matera, Frank. *Passion Narratives and Gospel Theologies: Interpreting the Synoptics Through Their Passion Stories.* Paulist, 1986.

Powell, Mark Allan. *Introducing the New Testament: A Historical, Literary, and Theological Survey.* Baker Academic, 2009. Pp. 91–92.   M.A.P.

Passover (pas'oh-vuhr), a religious festival commemorating God's deliverance of the Jews from slavery. The English term translates the Hebrew word *pesakh* as used in Exod. 12:13, "*I will pass over you,* and no plague shall destroy you when I strike the land of Egypt" (see also vv. 23, 27). In the Bible, the noun *pesakh* always refers to the sacrifice (Exod. 12:27) or the attendant festival (2 Kings 23:22).

In the Hebrew Bible: The Hebrew Bible contains references to eight different Passover celebrations. The first relates the Passover of the exodus in Exod. 12:1–13:16. This material is generally thought to derive from a pastiche of sources, the dominant one being what scholars call P, the Priestly source for material in the Pentateuch. Since Exod. 12 starts out with a reference to eating the paschal lamb in the first month of the year (12:2–10), Abib (March/April; 13:4), some scholars think that the Passover was originally a spring New Year festival, similar to the autumnal Festival of Tabernacles. On the tenth of the month each family was to choose a lamb (12:3) to be slaughtered at twilight on the fourteenth (12:6). The blood was to be smeared on the doorposts and lintel of the house (12:7), which God would see and thus spare the inhabitants from the destruction of the Egyptian firstborn (12:12–13). The apotropaic (protective) nature of the rite is thus indicated. The lamb was to be roasted and all of its flesh was to be eaten in the house that night, but only by the Israelites and their circumcised slaves; remnants of the animal were to be burned in the morning (12:8–10, 43–47). The people were to eat the

sacrifice hurriedly, dressed to flee Egypt (12:11). This day was to be a memorial feast in perpetuity (12:14). From the evening of the fourteenth until that of the twenty-first the Israelite houses were to be clean of leaven, and only unleavened bread, *matsot,* was to be eaten (12:14, 18–20). These days were also to be celebrated annually (13:10), although the text is not clear as to whether it was to be celebrated already in the desert (implied in 12:17?) or only upon entering Canaan (13:5–7, which comes from the E source). The first and seventh days of eating the *matsot* were to be shared assemblies, with no work allowed (12:16). The festival of *matsot* was also conceived as a memorial to the exodus (12:17; 13:3, 9). It was incumbent upon parents to explain the significance of these feast days to children (12:26–27; 13:8; cf. 13:14).

The second reference is found in an account of the second year of the exodus (Num. 9:1–14, also identified as P material by most scholars); the Passover sacrifice and its attendant rites were kept in the wilderness of Sinai (9:3, 5). Those who were unclean due to recent contact with a corpse (9:6, 10) or who were too far away to participate (9:10, 13) were to keep the Passover with *matsot* and bitter herbs on the 14th day of the second month. A non-Israelite who dwelled among the tribes was also required to observe the Passover (9:14). The lateness of this passage is evidenced by the reference to the "too distant way" (9:10), which assumes a central sanctuary (cf. Deut. 12:21; 14:24).

The third reference to Passover observance occurs after the Israelites enter Canaan in the days of Joshua (Josh. 5:10–12); at Gilgal on the plains of Jericho, they performed the Passover sacrifice (5:10) and on the following day ate *matsot* and parched corn (5:11; cf. Lev. 2:12).

A fourth reference is set in the time of the judges and Samuel. In the midst of a description of Josiah's Passover, 2 Kings 23:22 and 2 Chron. 35:18 allude to an exemplary Passover of earlier times. A fifth reference, to the time of Solomon, is implied by 1 Kings 9:25 and stated in 2 Chron. 8:13 (the feast of *matsot*) and 30:26.

A sixth reference mentions Passover celebration during the days of Hezekiah (715–687/6 BCE; 2 Chron. 30:1–27, not recorded by Kings). This Passover was kept by royal decree in the second month due to impurity of the priests (30:3); it was observed in Jerusalem by the tribe of Judah and by some of the remnants of the northern tribes (30:11–13). The priests purified the people (30:16), and the Levites oversaw the slaughter of the paschal lamb (30:17). The Passover was followed by the seven-day *matsot* festival accompanied by praise of God and music (30:21). Three factors have led scholars to question the historical authenticity of this report. First, Kings records no such event. Second, the description appears to contain elements of Solomon's dedication and Josiah's Passover (2 Chron. 35:1–18). And, third, Hezekiah is elsewhere presented as one who wished to make reforms in the north (2 Kings 23:15–20; 2 Chron. 34:33). However,

2 Kings 18:4 does depict Hezekiah's broad religious reforms, which would have been consistent with an attempt at a proper Passover celebration.

A seventh reference is to the days of Josiah (640–609 BCE; 2 Kings 23:21–23; 2 Chron. 35:1–19). In the eighteenth year of Josiah's reign, as part of his reforms based upon the newly found book of the law (2 Kings 23:21; cf. 22:8, 11; 23:2–3), he decreed the observance of the Passover in Jerusalem (cf. Deut. 16:2, 5–6), which is presented in 2 Kings as extraordinary (23:22–23). The Chronicler's expanded account (2 Chron. 35:1–19) adds that the Levites slaughtered and flayed the thirty thousand lambs and kids for the *pesakh* given by the king and the twenty-six hundred given by the princes as well as the cattle for the sacrifices (2 Chron. 35:6–11). The *pesakh* was roasted, but the other animals destined for the sacrifices were boiled (35:13): thus, Chronicles reconciles the discrepancies between Exod. 12:8–9, which commands roasting, and Deut. 16:7, which states that the *pesakh* should be boiled. The seven-day feast of *matsot* accompanying the *pesakh* (2 Chron. 35:17) and the uniqueness of the event are reemphasized (35:18).

A final, eighth reference to Passover observance in the Hebrew Bible is set in the days of Zerubbabel (Ezra 6:19–22). After the dedication of the rebuilt temple, during the sixth year of Darius (515 BCE; 6:15–17), the returned exiles from Babylon observed the Passover. The purity of the community is emphasized (6:20–21), in keeping with the concern for reinstituting proper worship after the exile. As in 2 Chron. 35, the Levites slaughtered the *pesakh* (v. 20). The seven-day feast of *matsot* was kept with great joy (v. 22).

The Hebrew Bible also mentions the Passover in Lev. 23:5; Num. 28:16; 33:3; and Ezek. 45:21. Extrabiblical references also make mention of the Passover. Two ostraca and a papyrus refer to the meticulous celebration of the Passover in the Jewish community of Elephantine in Egypt in the fifth century BCE.

Origin and Significance: There has been much discussion among scholars concerning historical reconstruction of the Passover festival's origins. The most widely held position is that the *pesakh* sacrifice originated in a seminomadic ceremony held in spring and fall when feeding grounds for the flock were alternated due to change of seasons. The ceremony thus would have been a petition for the deity's protection and favor during the time of migration. Another view ties the Passover in with a spring New Year's festival. At some point, this event, involving a sacrifice from the flock, was joined with ceremonial offering of the first fruits of the barley harvest, but there is no clear agreement as to when this happened. Eventually, the event came to be associated with historical memory of the escape from Egypt. This is clearly the dominant theme in the P material (Exod. 12:13–16; Num. 9:1–14, the first and second references discussed above), but that material is deemed late by most scholars, reflecting the understanding of the meal at the time of the exile or later. The source and dating for the material in Josh 5:10–12 (third passage discussed above) is uncertain. Those who see it as early contend that it provides evidence for connecting the Passover sacrifice with a historical memorial to the exodus already at Israel's incursion into Canaan. Others think the material itself was composed sometime after Josiah's reforms, and they view the description of early Israelites using the Passover as a commemoration of the exodus as historically anachronistic.

The Bible itself gives no hint of disparate origins for the various aspects of this celebration. The historical aspects (linking it to exodus commemoration) always appear together with those related to agriculture and sheepherding, just as the feast of *matsot* is always joined to the *pesakh*. This fact is taken by many as evidence that all these elements came together at an early stage in Israelite history. Further, it is apparent that the command in Deut. 16:2, 5–7 to observe the *pesakh* "at the place that the LORD your God will choose" indicates a transition from the house ceremony (Exod. 12:46) to that of the temple. Unfortunately, it is impossible to know the date of that transition.

In the life of the Jewish people, Passover became the festival of freedom and redemption par excellence. It served to give people hope in the face of physical and spiritual oppression, highlighting God's acts of liberation and redemption. As a family celebration, the Passover served as a unifying bond from generation to generation.

In the NT: Luke's Gospel reports that Jesus's parents would come to Jerusalem every year to celebrate the Passover (2:41). It was during one such occasion, when Jesus was twelve years old, that Jesus stayed in Jerusalem when the family group departed, causing some anxiety for his parents when they discovered his absence and returned a day later to find him seated among teachers in the temple (2:42–52).

John's Gospel uses references to the Passover as a way of marking time, noting three Passovers during the adult ministry of Jesus. For the first of these, Jesus goes to Jerusalem and assaults money changers in the temple court, driving them out with a whip (2:13–16; cf. 23). For the second, he appears to stay in Galilee, but John notes that his miracle of feeding the multitude occurs when "the Passover, the festival of the Jews, was near" (6:4). Finally, when the Passover is once again said to be near, Jesus defies expectations (11:55) by going to Jerusalem, stopping in Bethany (six days before Passover, 12:1) and then meeting in Jerusalem with his disciples (13). He is arrested and put to death on the day before Passover, i.e., the day when the Passover lamb was slain (19:14; cf. 1:29, 36). In 1 Cor. 5:7, Paul reflects this tradition by referring to Christ as "our paschal lamb" who "has been sacrificed (the word "paschal" means "pertaining to the Passover").

The Synoptic Gospels recount a slightly different tradition in which Jesus actually celebrates the Passover meal with his disciples the night before he is crucified (Matt. 26:19–29; Mark 14:16–25; Luke 22:]3–38). At this meal, he interprets the bread and the wine as representative of his body and blood, which is given for his disciples, for the forgiveness of sins (Matt. 26:20) or to institute a new covenant (Luke 22:20; cf. Mark 14:24). Paul knows this tradition as well, maintaining that a meal based on this observance is to be celebrated regularly by Christians in remembrance of Jesus's death (1 Cor. 11:24–25; cf. Exod. 12:14; Luke 22:19).

The book of Acts reports that when Herod Agrippa I arrested Peter, he intended to bring him out to the people "after the Passover" (1:24). Heb. 11:28 refers to Moses's keeping of the Passover as an exemplary act of faith. *See also* exodus, the; festivals, feasts, and fasts; temple, the; worship in the Hebrew Bible.

Bibliography

Childs, Brevard S. *The Book of Exodus.* Westminster, 1974. Pp. 178–214.

Schauss, Hayyim. *The Jewish Festivals.* Schocken, 1977. Pp. 38–85.

Segal, Judah B. *The Hebrew Passover.* Oxford University Press, 1963.   J.U./M.A.P.

Pastoral Letters, a common designation for three letters attributed to Paul, two of which are addressed to Timothy and one to Titus. These three letters are called "pastoral," because they are written to individuals who are leaders of local congregations. They also deal with what are often considered to be "pastoral matters," i.e., issues related to responsible and orderly care for Christian congregations. *See also* Timothy, First Letter of Paul to; Timothy, Second Letter of Paul to; Titus, Letter of Paul to.

Pathros (path'ros), **Pathrusim** (path-*roo*-seem'), Upper Egypt, the region south of Memphis and the Nile Delta. There were Israelite exiles in Pathros (Isa. 11:11); Jeremiah and Ezekiel cried out against them, accusing them of having abandoned their homeland and of practicing idolatry (Jer. 44:1, 15; Ezek. 29:14; 30:14). The Pathrusim (Gen. 10:14; 1 Chron. 1:12) were the people of Pathros; they are described as descendants of Egypt.

Patmos (pat'muhs), one of the Sporades Islands in the Aegean Sea. It lies about thirty-seven miles southwest of Miletus, a city on the coast of western Asia Minor. It is a small island, about ten miles long from north to south and six miles wide at its broadest point. In Rev. 1:9, a prophet named John says that he was on Patmos "because of the word of God and the testimony of Jesus." Reasonable speculation holds that this may mean that he had been banished to Patmos by the Roman authorities; such banishment was a common punishment during the Imperial period for a variety of offenses, including unauthorized practice of divination, magic, or astrology. Prophecy may have been viewed by the Romans as falling into the same category, and prophecy with political implications, like that expressed by John in the book of Revelation, would have been particularly suspect. Three of the islands in the Sporades are listed in extrabiblical sources as places where political offenders

The island of Patmos, where the author of the book of Revelation received his vision.

were banished (Pliny *Natural History* 4.69–70; Tacitus *Annals* 4.30). Patmos was the scene of at least some of John's visionary experiences and was probably the place where he wrote the book of Revelation. His banishment was what made communication in written form a necessity. *See also* Miletus.   A.Y.C.

patriarchs, a traditional term for referring to the three male figures prominent in the early history of Israel: Abraham (Gen. 12–24), Isaac (25–36), and Jacob (25–36). The strong tendency in modern biblical study is to speak of "ancestors" in order to include the wives of these figures: Sarah and Hagar; Rebekah; and Leah, Zilpah, Rachel, and Bilhah. The term "patriarch" is not used in any modern English translation of the Hebrew Bible (cf. NRSV: "ancestor" for Heb. *'ab* in Gen. 17:4–5; "ancestors" for *'abot* in 31:3). But the NRSV does use the term several times in the NT, where it translates Greek *patēr* ("father"; pl. *patroi,* "fathers"), when that term is used in an obviously nonliteral sense. Thus, Heb. 7:4 refers to "Abraham the patriarch," John 7:22 says that circumcision came from the patriarchs, and in Rom. 15:8 Paul says that Christ confirmed the promises given to the patriarchs (cf. Rom. 9:5). Acts 7:8–9 is somewhat distinctive in that it identifies the twelve sons of Jacob/Israel as the "twelve patriarchs"; more traditionally, it is Abraham, Isaac, and Jacob who are called the patriarchs, not the sons of Jacob.

Although the preference for gender-inclusive references to "ancestors" is well-grounded, the Bible does frequently speak of the three male leaders as a significant triad. For example, when God speaks to Moses in the burning bush, God says, "I am the God of your father, the God of Abraham, the God of Isaac, and the God of Jacob" (Exod. 3:6). Later, God promises the Israelites, "I remember my covenant with Jacob; I will remember also my covenant with Isaac and also my covenant with Abraham" (Lev. 24:42). Similar language is repeated in Exod. 3:6, 15–16; 4:5; Deut. 1:8; 6:10; 9:5, 27; 29:13; 30:20; 34:4; 2 Kings 13:23; Jer. 33:26. The same emphasis continues into the NT, where, for instance, Jesus speaks of people from east and west being gathered to feast with Abraham, Isaac, and Jacob in the kingdom of heaven (Matt. 8:11; cf. Luke 13:38) and Peter tells Jewish religious leaders, "The God of Abraham, the God of Isaac, and the God of Jacob, the God of our ancestors [Gk. *patroi;* elsewhere translated "patriarchs" in the NRSV] has glorified his servant Jesus" (Acts 3:13).

Historical and Literary Reflection: Whether these three individuals were actually historical persons is debated by scholars, for there is no mention of them outside of the Bible, nor is there any archaeological evidence that would lend direct support to the traditions concerning them. At most, archaeological study has proposed a degree of correlation between the patriarchal figures and the data of Mesopotamian culture. That synthesis has linked the patriarchs to various peoples of the Middle Bronze (2000–1500 BCE) and/or Late Bronze (1500–1200 BCE) period, with special reference to the Amorite, Hurrian, and Aramean movements. Such correlations, however, have been increasingly regarded as problematic. Still, the view that the patriarchs are simply literary fictions is a minority opinion. Nevertheless, the materials contained within the book of Genesis have undergone an extensive evolution, or editing process, a process that seems to have moved from early tribal memories to sophisticated and disciplined theological reflection. As a part of the process, the traditions concerning Abraham, Isaac, and Jacob were no doubt subjected to stylization, imagination, and literary construction.

Theological Significance: The religion of the patriarchs cannot be equated with that of later Israel, but it does contrast sharply with the animistic religion that was otherwise dominant in the Mesopotamian world at this time. In particular, the God of the patriarchs is not fixed to a perfect location, but goes with the designated community to lead, guard, and protect. Further, the God of the patriarchs is presented as one who makes promises and keeps them. This promissory character of the narratives figures strongly in later theological reflection, as evidenced, for example, in those portions of the book of Isaiah written during the exile (41:8–10; 43:1–2; 51:2–3; 54:1–8); it also comes to the fore in certain NT texts (Rom. 4; Gal. 3–4; Heb. 11:8–22). *See also* Abraham; ancestor; Genesis, book of; Isaac; Jacob; Pentateuch, sources of the.

Bibliography

Gunkel, Hermann. *The Legends of Genesis.* Schocken, 1964.

Hunt, Ignatius. *The World of the Patriarchs.* Prentice-Hall, 1967.

Von Rad, Gerhard. *Old Testament Theology I.* Harper & Row, 1962. Pp. 165–75.

Westermann, Claus. *The Promises to the Fathers.* Fortress, 1980.   W.B./M.A.P.

Paul

PAUL THE APOSTLE was the most effective missionary of early Christianity and the most prominent of the church's early theologians. Almost half of the books of the NT are attributed to him. Whatever else is said about Paul, he does not appear to have been "typical." He was not "a typical Jew," "a typical Christian," or "a typical citizen of the Greco-Roman world." He was both controversial and persuasive. As is often noted, one reason Paul wrote so many letters is that people argued with him, and yet one reason we still *have* those letters is that his views usually prevailed. It is also worth noting that the letters of Paul are the only extant writings from any Pharisee from the Second Temple period of Judaism (537 BCE–70 CE); thus, despite Paul's ultimate identification with Christianity, he is somewhat important for Jewish studies as well.

Sources for Studying Paul's Life and Thought: Four types of materials might be used for reconstructing Paul's biography and theology: (1) *seven undisputed letters,* acknowledged by all scholars to have been written by Paul (Romans, 1 Corinthians, 2 Corinthians, Galatians, Philippians, 1 Thessalonians, Philemon); (2) *six disputed letters,* believed by some, but not by all, to have been written by Paul (Ephesians, Colossians, 2 Thessalonians, 1 Timothy, 2 Timothy, Titus); (3) the *book of Acts,* much of which was written about Paul a couple of decades after his death; and (4) *traditions from church history,* such as comments in the writings of Eusebius, Tertullian, and Clement of Rome and apocryphal books concerning Paul, such as the *Acts of Paul and Thecla.*

Third-century papyrus fragment of the book of Acts from Oxyrhynchus, Egypt.

Of these, scholars regard the undisputed letters as the most important source, for they present what everyone agrees to be Paul's statements about his life and thought. Still, since these letters are directed to specific occasions, they only deal with topics that needed to be addressed at the time. If the Corinthian church had not experienced problems with regard to its celebration of the Lord's Supper (which Paul has to deal with in 1 Cor. 11), there would be no indication that Paul believed in that ritual or had any opinions about it one way or the other. Thus, scholars realize the possibility of ignorance with regard to significant matters that simply do not come up in the handful of letters that form the primary source for Pauline study. Partly on this account, Pauline scholars also make cautious use of secondary sources. The disputed letters fill out the picture gained from the undisputed ones, but they are used sparingly in academic scholarship, for the simple reason that whatever claims about Paul are made on the basis of these letters may not be accepted by scholars who regard the works as pseudepigraphical. A similar caution holds for use of the book of Acts, since many scholars think that Luke's presentation of Paul in that book is colored by his own priorities and concerns. Church traditions regarding Paul are evaluated on an individual basis; some are taken seriously as preserving probable facts, and others are dismissed as conveying unverifiable legends.

The Life of Paul: Paul alludes to various aspects of his life in key portions of his undisputed letters: his upbringing (Phil. 3:4–6); his calling (Gal. 1:13–17); his trips to Jerusalem (Gal. 1:18–2:14); his ministry (1 Thess. 2:1–12); and his hardships (2 Cor. 11:23–29). In addition, the book of Acts relates numerous narratives of his life (7:58–8:3; 9:1–30; 11:25–30; 12:25–28:31) and presents speeches in which he offers brief summaries of his life (see esp. 22:1–21; 26:2–23). The approach of academic scholarship is to look first at what Paul says in the letters and then

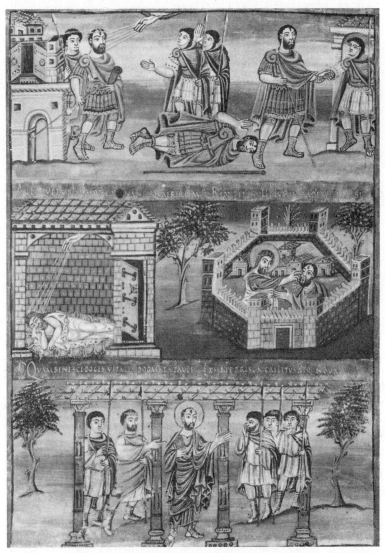

A medieval depiction of the dramatic conversion of Paul according to Acts 9. *Top register, left to right:* The Lord calls Saul, who falls to the ground blinded and then is led to Damascus. *Center:* Ananias, instructed in a vision, heals Saul's blindness. *Bottom:* Saul preaches in the synagogue. Illuminated page from the First Bible of Charles the Bald (846 CE).

to look at the material in Acts, noting what it adds and recognizing when those additions seem to conflict with Paul's testimony.

Early Years in Judaism: Whenever Paul reflects upon his birth and upbringing, he emphasizes his Jewish identity (see Rom. 11:1; 2 Cor. 11:22; Gal. 1:13–14; Phil. 3:4–6). He does not say when or where he was born, but he does say that he was circumcised on the eighth day of his life, as was traditional among devout Jews. He was born and raised as "a member of the people of Israel," as a "descendant of Abraham," and, specifically, as a member of the tribe of Benjamin. He is proud to identify himself as "a Hebrew born of Hebrews" and, indeed, as a Pharisee. He maintains that he observed the Jewish law in a manner that was "blameless" and that he "advanced in Judaism" beyond many of his peers.

The book of Acts provides many more details about Paul's early life than those related in the letters. First, Acts indicates that Paul's Jewish name was actually Saul (7:58–13:9; 22:7; 26:14). This was the name of Israel's first king, who had also belonged to the tribe of Benjamin and who was remembered as one of that tribe's more illustrious members. Saul did not come to be called Paul at the time of his conversion or as a result of that event. Rather, he seems to have had two names: his given Hebrew name, Saul, and a more Roman-sounding name, Paul, for use in the Gentile world (as Silas was likewise called Silvanus).

A portrait of Paul by the Lombard artist Vincenzo Foppa, ca. 1490.

The book of Acts also indicates that Paul was brought up in Jerusalem, where he studied "at the feet of Gamaliel" (22:3), a famous rabbi of the era (cf. 5:34–39). But Acts also indicates Paul was a native of Tarsus, the capital city of Cilicia (22:3; cf. 9:11; 21:39), and that, furthermore, he was a Roman citizen (16:37–38; 22:25–29). Some scholars suspect that this information from Acts could be idealized, providing Paul with perfect pedigrees for both Jewish and Roman audiences. If he really did have such credentials (a student of Gamaliel, a Roman citizen), why doesn't he mention any of this in his letters, particularly in those instances where he lists things of which he could boast if he were so inclined (2 Cor. 11:16–12:13)? Still, there is nothing in Paul's letters that contradicts this information outright, and those letters do seem to be written by someone who is equally at home in Jewish and Gentile environments (1 Cor. 9:19–23).

A Life-Changing Revelation: Paul says in his letters that he persecuted the early Christian church violently and tried to destroy it (1 Cor. 15:9; Gal. 1:13, 23; Phil. 3:6; cf. 1 Tim. 1:13; Acts 22:3–5, 19; 26:9–11). He never says exactly what it was about the new faith that invoked his ire, but he does say that he was driven by zeal for ancestral traditions, which he apparently believed were being challenged. But then Paul received a revelation from God that turned his life around (Gal. 1:15–16). What exactly happened? Paul says that the risen Jesus appeared to him in the same way that he had appeared to many of his followers in the days following his crucifixion (1 Cor. 15:3–8; cf. 9:1). He gives no details regarding what Jesus said or did, but as a result of the experience, Paul's life would be forever changed. Christians traditionally refer to this episode in Paul's life as his "conversion," but Paul himself seems to have regarded it more as the reception of a prophetic call or, simply, as a moment of enlightenment—God corrected his misguided zeal (cf. Rom. 10:2) and gave him a new purpose in life. Paul did not quit one religion to join another (as the word "conversion" might imply), but he did begin proclaiming the faith he had previously tried to destroy, and he always regarded the divine revelation that brought about this change as an act of unmerited grace that God had performed on his behalf (Rom. 1:5; 1 Cor. 15:10).

The book of Acts provides narrative descriptions of these pivotal events in Paul's life. With regard to persecuting the church, Acts says that Paul (called Saul) was present in Jerusalem for the murder of Stephen, the first Christian martyr, holding the coats of those who stoned him and approving of the deed (7:58; 8:1; 22:20). He also ravaged the church, going from house to house and dragging men and women away to prison (8:3). According to Acts, Paul had believers bound and punished (perhaps tortured) in order to force them to deny their faith, and when they would not do so, he voted to have them condemned to death (26:10–11; cf. 22:4, 19). Further, Acts says that Paul wanted to expand this persecution to other areas as well (9:1–2, 13–14, 21; 22:5) and that he was on his way to Damascus to do so when the dramatic conversion experience occurred. The story of that transforming event is recounted three times in Acts with lively and colorful details not mentioned elsewhere (see 9:1–22; 22:6–21; 26:4–23).

Interim Years: Paul indicates in his letters that the first few years following his encounter with Christ were spent in the region of Arabia and in the city of Damascus, in southern Syria (Gal. 1:15–24; cf. 2 Cor. 11:32–33). After three years, he went to Jerusalem and stayed with Peter for fifteen days; he also met James the brother of Jesus at that time. Then he went into the regions of Syria and Cilicia and spent more than a decade there. Those years are often viewed as a time of formation for Paul, a period during which he honed his missionary skills and developed his theological understanding of the gospel. For one thing, he became persuaded that uncircumcised Gentiles could be put right with God through faith in Christ without first becoming Jews. It was this conviction that brought him back to Jerusalem after fourteen years to have a "private meeting" with leaders of the church. He shared the gospel he was proclaiming among Gentiles, and Peter, James, John, and others gave him their support. Sometime after this, however, a controversy erupted in Antioch, focused on whether Gentile and Jewish believers could share table fellowship with each other. Paul took one view, but "people from James," Peter, and Barnabas (Paul's co-worker) took a different view.

The book of Acts also contains some information regarding these interim years of Paul's life. There is mention of his time in Damascus (9:19b–25), a visit to Jerusalem (9:26–30), and time spent in Tarsus and Antioch (9:30; 11:19–30). The information provided in these narratives goes beyond what Paul says in his letters and sometimes seems to be in tension with Paul's account. For example, in Acts, Paul seems to become well known among the believers in Jerusalem (9:26–29), which is not something one would surmise from the letters (cf. Gal. 1:22). More to the point, Acts reports on an apostolic council in Jerusalem at which the question of Gentile inclusion was discussed and a compromise decision reached: no circumcision required, but *other restrictions would apply* (15:1–35). If the meeting of this council is the same event as the "private meeting" Paul says he had with church leaders in Gal. 2:1–10, then the two accounts of that meeting have to be regarded as widely diverse and probably irreconcilable. Some scholars think the accounts refer to two completely different meetings: a private meeting between Paul and a few apostles in Gal. 2:1–10 and a church-wide apostolic council in Acts 15:1–35 (the Jerusalem Council). In any case, most scholars do not think that the account of the council reported in Acts 15 warrants much attention in Pauline biography. Even those who regard the account as historically accurate must admit that Paul does not appear to have taken what transpired there very seriously; there is no evidence in his letters that he ever favored or promulgated the compromise that the book of Acts indicates was reached at that council.

Missionary Work in the Mediterranean World: Paul's letters make clear that he eventually left the areas of Syria and Cilicia in which he had been at home for a considerable period of time and ventured out into the provinces of the Roman Empire north of the Mediterranean Sea. The bulk of this work appears to have occurred in four major areas: Galatia, Asia, Macedonia, and Achaia; the first two of these areas correspond to modern-day Turkey and the latter two to modern-day Greece. Paul also mentions that he proclaimed the gospel in Illyricum (Rom. 15:19), a region far to the north overlapping with what would now be Albania—but nothing else is ever said about that particular evangelistic effort (either in Paul's letters or in the book of Acts).

Paul's letters provide a few clues as to how he went about his mission strategy. First, he appears to have targeted urban, commercial centers as prime locations for founding churches that could help him take the gospel to the world. Four cities are mentioned repeatedly: Ephesus (in Asia), Philippi and Thessalonica (in Macedonia), and Corinth (in Achaia). All four cities were major cosmopolitan centers, situated on important trade routes around the Aegean Sea. Paul's emphasis on urban ministry affects

Paul discoursing with bystanders who become intent listeners; eleventh-century enamel plaque.

his writing. Scholars often note that, although Jesus used agrarian images appropriate to rural life in Galilee (farming, fishing, shepherding), Paul uses images more appropriate to city life: political identification (Phil. 3:20); commerce (Philem. 18); athletic competition (1 Cor. 9:24–27; Phil. 2:16); legal proceedings (Rom. 7:1; Gal. 3:15; 4:1–2); public festivities (1 Thess. 2:19); and even the slave trade (Rom. 7:14; 1 Cor. 7:22).

Second, Paul worked as the leader of a missionary team. Numerous assistants and emissaries are mentioned in his letters, though we are left to imagine just what their job descriptions might have been. In some cases, trusted assistants like Timothy (1 Cor. 4:17; 16:10; Phil. 2:19, 23; 1 Thess. 3:2, 6) and Titus (2 Cor. 7:6–8, 13–15) seem to function as his troubleshooters. He sends them to churches where there are problems, investing them with authority to act on his behalf in negotiating settlements.

Third, Paul indicates in his letters that he often supported himself financially by practicing a trade within the community (1 Cor. 9:14–15; 2 Cor. 11:9; 1 Thess. 2:9). In this way, he took care not to place any financial burden on the fledgling churches, and he avoided giving potential converts any reason to suspect he was after their money (cf. 2 Cor. 2:17; Titus 1:11). Once a church was established, however, he would draw upon its resources to support his ministry in other locales (2 Cor. 11:8–9; Phil. 4:15–16).

The Cilician Gates, a pass through the Taurus Mountains, linked the Roman provinces of Cilicia and Cappadocia in Asia Minor. Acts records that Paul passed through this area on two journeys.

Fourth, Paul insists that his missionary work was independent of any human (ecclesiastical) authority. Although he tries to be respectful of other church leaders (1 Cor. 3:4–6) and is even involved in taking up a collection for the church in Jerusalem (Rom. 15:25–26; 1 Cor. 16:1; 2 Cor. 8–9; Gal. 2:10), he takes orders from no one but Jesus Christ (Gal. 1:1, 11–12). Perhaps for this reason, Paul indicates that his typical goal is to proclaim the gospel in new areas and to found churches in areas where other missionaries have not worked—he does not want to "build upon another's foundation" (Rom. 15:20; cf. 2 Cor. 10:13–16). He then assumes that he has a special relationship with his converts—they are his children in the faith (1 Cor. 4:15; Gal. 4:19) and he has apostolic authority over them (1 Cor. 5:3–5; 2 Cor. 10:8; 13:10). Accordingly, he resents missionaries who come to the churches he established after he has moved on and who undermine his (absent) authority in the community (2 Cor. 11:4; Gal. 1:6–9).

Paul's letters reveal other scattered bits of information that might be useful in reconstructing a biography for this prominent period of his life. We learn, for instance, that he is not currently married and that he regards the single, celibate life as ideal for Christians who are expecting Jesus to return soon (1 Cor. 7:7, 25–40; cf. 9:5). We also learn that he suffers from some sort of affliction that he calls his "thorn in the flesh" (2 Cor. 12:7–9), but despite many guesses no one has ever been able to determine just what that might have been. The letters also contain several references to trials and tribulations that Paul endured while engaged in missionary work. He says that he was shamefully mistreated at Philippi (1 Thess. 2:2), that he fought with (perhaps metaphorical) wild beasts in Ephesus (1 Cor. 15:32), and that he suffered such affliction in Asia as to despair of life itself (2 Cor. 1:8–9). And then, in one startling summary passage, he declares: "Five times I have received from the Jews the forty lashes minus one. Three times I was beaten with rods. Once I received a stoning. Three times I was shipwrecked; for a night and a day I was adrift at sea; on frequent journeys, in danger from rivers, danger from bandits, danger from my own people, danger from Gentiles, danger in the city, danger in the wilderness, danger at sea, danger from false brothers and sisters; in toil and hardship, through many a sleepless night, hungry and thirsty, often without food, cold and naked. And, besides other things, I am under daily pressure because of my anxiety for all the churches" (2 Cor. 11:24–28).

The book of Acts fills out the picture of Paul's missionary work with colorful stories of the adventures he and his colleagues had as they traveled about the Roman world. Most important to scholars, perhaps, Acts provides an itinerary for Paul's travels. It presents his work in such a way that he has been traditionally understood as embarking on three missionary journeys: the First Missionary Journey (13:1–14:28)—to the island of Cyprus and to cities in southern Asia Minor, including Pisidian Antioch, Lystra, Derbe, and Iconium, for a total distance of about 1,400 miles; the Second Missionary Journey (15:36–18:32)—through Asia Minor to Macedonia (especially Philippi, Thessalonica, and Beroea), and then on to Achaia (especially Athens and Corinth), for a total distance of about 2,800 miles; the Third Missionary Journey (18:23–21:15)—through Galatia and Phrygia to Ephesus, then on to Macedonia and Achaia, for a total distance of about 2,700 miles. No such itinerary is discernible from Paul's letters, which make no reference to distinctive trips. Some scholars think the scheme of three missionary journeys is a literary device Luke created to organize the stories he wanted to tell in Acts. More often, however, the itineraries are regarded as inherently plausible, and they are employed as a general outline for making sense of this critical phase of Paul's life. In particular, Acts presents Paul as spending at least eighteen months in Corinth on his Second Journey (18:11; cf. 18:18) and as spending at least twenty-seven months in Ephesus on the Third Journey (19:8–10; cf. 20:31). These "long tenure" stays in key cities fit well with most reconstructions of Paul's life and ministry.

When it comes to mission strategy, the book of Acts also presents Paul as working a trade to support himself while seeking to evangelize certain communities. It indicates, furthermore, that the particular trade Paul practiced was some form of tentmaking, a vocation he shared with his friends and co-workers Priscilla and Aquila (18:3). It is usually thought that such an occupation would have placed Paul among the more fortunate members of the Roman Empire's impoverished population; he was poor, but he may have been a step above those who were living at a mere subsistence level (or worse).

Further, as to his mission strategy, Acts consistently portrays Paul as first going to Jewish synagogues in each area and as turning to the Gentiles only after the Jews had rejected his message (13:5–7, 13, 44–48; 14:1–7; 17:1–2, 10; 18:5–6; 19:8–9). One would never gather from Paul's letters that this was his approach; in the letters, Paul seems to indicate that God called him specifically to proclaim the gospel to Gentiles and that this was one thing that set him apart from other missionaries (Rom. 11:13; Gal. 1:16; 2:7; but cf. 1 Cor. 9:20).

PAUL'S MISSION SITES

This chart lists areas of Paul's missionary work mentioned in his letters. Names in italics are cities mentioned in Paul's "undisputed letters."

Province of Achaia
Rom. 15:26; 1 Cor. 16:5; 2 Cor. 1:1; 9:2; 11:10; 1 Thess. 1:7–8; cf. Acts 18:12; 19:21
Cities in the province of Achaia
Athens: 1 Thess. 3:1; cf. Acts 17:15–16; 18:1
Cenchreae: Rom. 16:1; cf. Acts 18:18
Corinth: 1 Cor. 1:2; 2 Cor. 1:1; 1:23; cf. 2 Tim. 4:20; Acts 18:1

Province of Asia
Rom. 16:5; 1 Cor. 16:9; 2 Cor. 1:8; cf. 2 Tim. 1:15; Acts 16:6; 19:10, 22, 26–27, 31; 20:4, 16, 18; 21:27; 24:19; 27:2
Cities in the province of Asia:
Colossae: Col. 1:2
Ephesus: 1 Cor. 15:32; 16:8; cf. Eph. 1:1; 1 Tim. 1:3; 2 Tim. 1:18; 4:12; Acts 18:19, 21; 19:1, 17, 26; 20:16–17
Hierapolis: Col. 4:13
Laodicea: Col. 2:1; 4:13, 15–16
Miletus: 2 Tim. 4:20; cf. Acts 20:15, 17
Troas: 2 Cor. 2:12; cf. 2 Tim. 4:13; Acts 16:8, 11; 20:5–6

Province of Crete
Titus 1:5

Province of Galatia
1 Cor. 16:1; Gal. 1:2; cf. 2 Tim. 4:10; Acts 16:6; 18:23
Cities in the province of Galatia:
Iconium: 2 Tim. 3:11; cf. Acts 13:51; 14:1, 19, 21; 16:2

Province of Illyricum
Rom. 15:19
Cities in the province of Illyricum:
Dalmatia: 2 Tim. 4:10

Province of Lycaonia
Province not mentioned in Paul's letters; cf. Acts 14:6.
Cities in the province of Lycaonia:
Lystra: 2 Tim. 3:11; cf. Acts 14:6, 8, 21; 16:1–2

Province of Macedonia
Rom. 15:26; 1 Cor. 16:5; 2 Cor. 1:16; 2:13; 7:5; 8:1; 9:2; 11:9; Phil. 4:15; 1 Thess. 1:7–8; 4:10; cf. 1 Tim. 1:3; Acts 16:9–10, 12; 18:5; 19:21–22; 20:1, 3
Cities in the province of Macedonia:
Philippi: Phil. 1:1; 1 Thess. 2:2; cf. Acts 16:12; 20:6
Thessalonica: Phil. 4:16; 1 Thess. 1:1; cf. 2 Thess. 1:1; 2 Tim. 4:10; Acts 17:1, 11, 13; 20:4; 27:2

From Mark Allan Powell, *Introducing the New Testament*
(courtesy, Baker Academic)

Another aspect of Paul's mission work that is especially striking in Acts is the prominence of the miracles that God works through him. The letters do not mention any specific miracles. Paul himself never says that he cast demons out of people (16:16–18) or healed the sick (14:8–10; 28:8), much less that his very handkerchiefs came to possess extraordinary divine power (19:11), or that he could punish opponents with curses that would strike them blind (13:9–11). Paul, does, however, indicate in his letters that God worked "signs and wonders" through him without getting any more specific about just what those signs and wonders entailed (Rom. 15:19; 2 Cor. 12:12; cf. Acts 14:3; 15:12).

Many stories in Acts serve to illustrate the diverse trials and tribulations that Paul refers to in his letters. Paul meets with opposition from local Jewish communities (13:45–50; 14:2, 4, 19; 17:5, 13; 18:12–13; cf. 1 Thess. 2:14–16), but he is also mocked by pagan philosophers (17:32) and attacked by merchants whose economic interests are threatened by the success of his ministry (16:16–24; 19:23–41). Still, when compared with what Paul says in 2 Cor. 11:24–29 (quoted above), the record Acts gives of Paul's trials actually seems a bit slight. There is a story in Acts of Paul receiving a stoning (14:19), but he is beaten with rods only once (16:22–23), not three times, and there is no account of his receiving the thirty-nine lashes that he says were meted out to him on five different occasions. Nor does Acts record any tales of Paul being repeatedly shipwrecked or frequently imprisoned (cf. 2 Cor. 11:23); indeed, apart from one night in jail at Philippi (16:23–26), the only references to imprisonment or shipwreck found in Acts come from a period of Paul's life after the time when 2 Corinthians would have been written. Scholars are left to conclude that either the author of Acts was restrained in reporting on the sufferings Paul endured, that he did not know about many of these incidents, or that Paul himself was exaggerating.

Final Years: Paul's undisputed letters say nothing about what happened after the period of his missionary work in the areas surrounding the Aegean Sea. In one of his later letters he does say that he wants to come to Rome, and he hints that he would like the church there to assist him with a westward missionary journey all the way to Spain (Rom. 15:22–24). But did that happen?

The book of Acts reports that after the period of Paul's great missionary work, he was arrested in Jerusalem, imprisoned for two years in Caesarea, and then, after a perilous sea voyage, was imprisoned for another

Ships in a storm on a third-century Roman relief. Acts 27 recounts a tumultuous storm and shipwreck on Paul's journey to Rome.

two years in Rome (21:17–28:31). This information is generally accepted as a reliable postscript to what can be known about Paul's life from his letters. Some scholars believe that certain of Paul's letters might have been written while he was a prisoner in Rome and, if that is the case, those letters might be read as a witness to Paul's thoughts and priorities at this time. Even then, however, we would obtain few biographical details about his life situation.

For additional information on Paul's final years, the only available sources are extrabiblical ones. Church tradition says that Paul was executed under the emperor Nero (Eusebius *Ecclesiastical History* 2.22.3) and that he was killed in the same manner as John the Baptist, i.e., by beheading (Tertullian *On the Prescription of Heretics* 36). These traditions are generally accepted as reliable. Other traditions, however, suggest that Paul was released for a time between his two-year imprisonment in Rome and his martyrdom under Nero, and that during this period his missionary work continued beyond what is reported in Acts. This idea first appears in the writings of Clement of Rome, about thirty years after Paul's death. Clement says that Paul "traveled to the extreme west" (*1 Clement* 5:7), which suggests to some that Paul actually did make it to Spain as he had intended (Rom. 15:23). A later witness, the *Muratorian Fragment* (ca. 180) explicitly mentions Spain rather than simply referring to the "extreme west." But this notion that Paul had a second career as a missionary between his imprisonment in Rome and martyrdom has not found universal acceptance among scholars. Those who do accept the tradition think that positing a second career for Paul helps to account for anomalies in some of the Pauline Letters that might otherwise cause those letters to be regarded as pseudepigraphical.

Chronology of Paul's Life and Letters: Interpreters note at least four obstacles to developing a chronology for Paul. First, neither Paul's letters nor the book of Acts ever specify any dates for when the things that they report took place. Second, the book of Acts is notoriously fond of using imprecise terms with regard to time intervals (cf. "for some time" in 14:28; "for a considerable time" in 18:18). Third, the book of Acts also uses approximations that frustrate scholars desirous of more precision (e.g., 19:8–10 indicates Paul stayed in Ephesus for two years and three months, but 20:31 seems to round this up to three years). And, finally, Paul himself is ambiguous with temporal references. In Gal. 1:18–2:1, he says that he made his first visit to Jerusalem "after three years" and his second visit "after fourteen years." Does he mean the first visit was three years after his encounter with Christ (1:15–16) or after his return to Damascus (1:17)? And what about the second visit? Was it fourteen years after the first visit? Or fourteen years after the encounter with Christ? Or after the return to Damascus?

Nevertheless, scholars have noted what seem to be promising reference points:

- Acts 22:3 indicates that Paul was educated in Jerusalem under Gamaliel, whose school flourished in that city from 20 to 30 CE.

- Acts 7:58 says that Paul was a "young man" at the time of Stephen's martyrdom.

CHRONOLOGY OF PAUL'S LIFE AND LETTERS

When the dating of a letter is uncertain, the name of that letter is italicized and listed in all of the time periods that have been proposed for it.

Earliest Suggested Date		Latest Suggested Date
32	Conversion to Christ	36
32–35	Initial Time in Arabia and Damascus	36–39
35	First Visit to Jerusalem	39
35–45	Interim Years in Cilicia and Syria	40–45
45	Private Meeting with Church Leaders	46
46–48	First Missionary Journey	
	Galatians—if addressed to "South Galatia"	46–49
48	Jerusalem Council	49
49–51	Second Missionary Journey	50–52
	1 Thessalonians	
	2 Thessalonians—if authentic	
52–57	Third Missionary Journey	54–58
	Galatians—if addressed to "North Galatia"	
	Philemon—if from Ephesus	
	Colossians and/or Ephesians—if authentic	
	Philippians—if from Ephesus	
	1 Corinthians	
	2 Corinthians	
	Romans	
57	Arrested in Jerusalem	58
57–59	Prisoner in Caesarea	58–60
	Philemon—if from Caesarea	
	Colossians and/or Ephesians—if authentic	
	Philippians—if from Caesarea	
59–60	Voyage to Rome	60–61
59–62	Prisoner in Rome	61–63
	Philemon—if from Rome	
	Colossians and/or Ephesians—if authentic	
	Philippians—if from Rome	
62–64	Second Career—not recognized by most scholars	63–67
	1 Timothy, 2 Timothy, and/or Titus—if authentic	
62	Death of Paul	67
62+	The Post-Pauline Era	67+
	2 Thessalonians—if pseudepigraphical	
	Colossians and/or Ephesians—if pseudepigraphical	
	1 Timothy, 2 Timothy, and/or Titus—if pseudepigraphical	

From Mark Allan Powell, *Introducing the New Testament*
(courtesy, Baker Academic)

- 2 Cor. 11:32 places Paul in Damascus at a time when King Aretas had some influence in that city, which would fit well with the political situation in 37–41 CE.

- Acts 18:2 says that Paul arrived in Corinth at a time when Claudius had "recently" expelled the Jews from Rome—Roman records indicate this occurred in 49 CE.

- Acts 18:12 says that Paul was in Corinth when Gallio was the proconsul, a position that Gallio is known to have held from the summer of 51 CE to the summer of 52 CE.

- Acts 24:27 indicates that Paul was a prisoner in Caesarea at the time Festus replaced Felix as the Roman governor there; records indicate this was in 59 or 60 CE.

- Paul calls himself an "old man" in his Letter to Philemon (v. 9).

Of these reference points, the mention of Gallio in Acts 18:12 has turned out to be the most useful. Scholars working out a chronology for Paul typically start with his time in Corinth (51–52 CE) and work forwards and backwards from there. Given this, some broad-ranging conclusions are possible, though many questions remain.

The Seven Undisputed Letters: The greatest degree of clarity attends four of Paul's undisputed letters—1 Thessalonians, 1 Corinthians, 2 Corinthians, and Romans. These appear to have been written in that order during the decade of the 50s CE while Paul was engaged in what Acts presents as his Second and Third Missionary Journeys. First Thessalonians was written from Corinth toward the end of the Second Journey; the two Corinthian letters were written from Ephesus and Macedonia while he was on the Third Journey; and the Letter to Romans was written from Corinth a few months later on that same trip. Two more letters—Philippians and Philemon—were both written from prison, which suggests to many that they were written near the end of Paul's life, when he was imprisoned in Caesarea or, more likely, in Rome. Many scholars, however, think one or both of these letters might have been written earlier, during some imprisonment not mentioned in Acts. The most popular of these alternative suggestions holds that either or both of the letters might have been written during that prolific Third Missionary Journey, assuming that Paul spent some time in prison during his long tenure in Ephesus (cf. 1 Cor. 15:32; 2 Cor. 1:8–11). Discussion of all these options continues, but the best time period for these two letters remains uncertain.

Galatians is the most difficult of the undisputed letters to date. It does not fit obviously or easily into any part of Paul's itinerary narrated in the book of Acts, and whether the letter is addressed to a northern or southern region is uncertain. Scholars who think it is addressed to "South Galatia" tend to date it early, at the conclusion of the First Missionary Journey (making it the earliest of all Paul's extant letters). Those who think it is addressed to "North Galatia" place it later, perhaps around the time of Romans.

The Six Disputed Letters: Chronology of the "disputed letters" depends entirely upon whether those letters are viewed as authentic Pauline compositions or as pseudepigraphical works produced after his death. If 2 Thessalonians is considered to be authentic, it is usually thought to have been written shortly after 1 Thessalonians (i.e., near the end of the Second Missionary Journey). If Ephesians and Colossians are considered to be authentic, they are usually grouped with Philemon and considered to come from a period close to the time when that letter was written (but the date of that letter—during which imprisonment?—remains in dispute). If 1 Timothy, 2 Timothy, and Titus are considered to be authentic, they are often thought to stem from the time of a second career that Paul is presumed to have had following his Roman imprisonment. Second Timothy in particular is seen by those who consider the letter to be authentic as coming from a time close to Paul's execution by the Roman authorities.

When any or all of these disputed letters are considered to be pseudepigraphical, however, they are usually dated to the latter part of the first century CE, to the decade of the 80s or 90s CE.

Paul's Theology: Paul speaks often of the "gospel" (lit., "good news") that has been revealed to him by God. In some sense this gospel is a message that can be conveyed through proclamation (Rom. 10:14–17), but it is also more than that. It is a dynamic force that Paul identifies as the "power of God for salvation to everyone who believes" (Rom. 1:16; cf. 1 Cor. 1:18). He says that it is a "gospel of Jesus Christ" (Rom. 1:3–4).

Paul believes that Jesus Christ has died for people's sins (Rom. 4:25; 5:6–8; Gal. 1:4; 1 Cor. 15:3; 1 Thess. 5:10). Moreover, God raised Jesus from the dead (Rom. 4:24–25; 1 Cor. 15:4; Gal. 1:1; 1 Thess. 4:14). Jesus is now at the right hand of God in heaven, where he intercedes for believers (Rom. 8:24), and he will come again (1 Thess. 4:13–18). Those who confess that Jesus is Lord and place their trust in him will be saved (Rom. 10:9). After death, they will live forever in a glorious realm that renders the troubles of this present life insignificant by comparison (Rom. 8:18). Furthermore, Paul believes that, in some sense, this wondrous new age of God has already begun. Through Jesus Christ, believers are reconciled with God (Rom. 5:8–11; cf. 2 Cor. 5:18–21). They are justified (made right with God) by faith (Rom. 3:24, 26; Gal. 2:16). They become children of God (Rom. 8:14–17; Gal. 4:4–7) and receive the Holy Spirit (Rom. 5:8; 8:9; 1 Cor. 3:16; 2 Cor. 1:21–22; 5:5; Gal. 3:2–5; 4:6). Their lives are transformed in a way that can only be described as "a new creation" (2 Cor. 5:17).

Paul's interest in Jesus seems to have focused especially on the last week of his life—his institution of the Lord's Supper (1 Cor. 11:23–26) and, especially, his death, burial, and resurrection (15:3–7). Since Paul knew disciples of Jesus as well as James the brother of Jesus, he must have known some of the stories about Jesus that we find in our Gospels—and probably other stories as well. He does quote sayings of Jesus in a few places (7:10–11; 9:14; 11:23–25), but for the most part he displays little interest in the details of Jesus's earthly life and ministry. He never mentions that Jesus told parables, worked miracles, or had numerous arguments with the Pharisees over various matters of the law (a striking omission, since Paul is a Pharisee himself!). Paul's focus, rather, is on "Christ crucified" (1:23) and on the risen Christ who is Lord of all (Phil. 2:9–11).

Theologically, Paul understands Jesus Christ to be the image of God (2 Cor. 4:4; cf. Phil. 2:6; Col. 1:15; 1 Cor. 15:49), the one who makes God visible and accessible to human beings. Jesus is the Son of God (Rom. 1:3–4, 8:3) and, so, remains in some sense subordinate to God and distinct from God (1 Cor. 15:27–28). Thus, Paul wants to respect Jewish monotheism; he does not mean to make Jesus into a second God, though at times he comes close to doing this (2 Cor. 8:6). He often quotes scripture passages in which the word "Lord" originally referred to the God of Israel and interprets those passages in such a way that the word "Lord" now refers to Jesus Christ (see, e.g., the treatment of Joel 2:32 in Rom. 10:13; cf. Rom. 10:9). He also speaks of Christ as having been "in the form of God" and as having chosen not to regard "equality with God as something to be exploited" (Phil. 2:6). Paul clearly has an exalted view of Christ as one who is more than just a prophet, messiah, or any other human servant of God.

Paul also speaks of Christ in strongly relational terms, marked by a depth of religious feeling. He doesn't want to think or talk or write about anything else (cf. 2 Cor. 10:3–5). He feels compelled to proclaim the gospel (1 Cor. 9:16), and he accepts his call to do so as a great honor; the gospel is a prized treasure with which he has been entrusted (Gal. 2:7; 1 Thess. 2:4). When he shares the gospel with others, he is fulfilling the purpose for which he was born (Rom. 1:1; Gal. 1:15). Thus, Paul is not simply committed to a cause or to an ideology, but to a person; he *knows* Jesus Christ (Phil. 3:7–10) and can say, "It is no longer I who live, but it is Christ who lives in me" (Gal. 2:20). And he is not claiming to be exceptional in this regard; rather, union with Christ is a reality to be experienced by all believers (Rom. 8:10; 2 Cor. 13:5; cf. Col. 3:3). Paul speaks of Christians as "those who are *in* Christ Jesus" (Rom. 8:1; 16:7; 2 Cor. 5:17) and describes the church as the "body of Christ" (Rom. 12:4–5; 1 Cor. 12:27). Accordingly, Paul's gospel is very much a message for a *community;* it is good news for the church, the new people of God formed in Christ and empowered by the Holy Spirit.

Paul's theology ultimately has practical consequences for how people live in the present world. Those who experience God's salvation through Christ are to live, not for themselves, but for Christ, who died and was raised for them (2 Cor. 5:14–15), and "the only thing that counts is faith working through love" (Gal. 5:6). Thus, Paul devotes generous portions of his letters to instruction on moral and behavioral matters. He addresses controversial issues (e.g., Rom. 14:5–6; 1 Cor. 8:1–13; 12:1–14:40) and lists both virtues to be pursued and vices to be avoided (Rom. 1:29–31; 13:13; 1 Cor. 5:10–11; 6:9–10; 2 Cor. 6:6–7; Gal. 5:19–23). His positions on such matters are often informed by the Hebrew Bible—the moral commandments of Torah—but Paul also claims that Christians are no longer "under the law" (Rom. 6:14–15; 1 Cor. 9:20; Gal. 3:23–25), and many interpreters have struggled to determine exactly what he means by that. In a few instances, Paul makes reference to a human "conscience" that may serve as a moral guide (Rom. 2:15; 2 Cor. 1:12; 4:2), but this cannot be absolute, since conscience can be weak and is easily defiled (1 Cor. 8:7–12; 10:25–29).

Ultimately, Paul's ethics are shaped by the expectation that believers will imitate Christ with regard to sacrificial humility; they will seek the good of others rather than what is pleasing or beneficial to themselves

(Rom. 15:1–3; Phil. 2:4–8). Thus, for Paul, the cross becomes the emblem, not only of Christian salvation, but also of Christian conduct. Furthermore, for Paul, all ethics are community ethics, for the individual believer is united spiritually with others in such a way that all individual actions have consequences for others (1 Cor. 12:11–26). Paul's ethics are also shaped by an expectation that Christ is coming soon and that the time remaining to do what must be accomplished in this world is short (Rom. 13:11–14; 1 Cor. 7:29–31; 1 Thess. 4:13–5:11). And, finally, Paul is certain that believers have divine assistance in living as God would have them live; they are transformed from within, by a renewing of their minds (Rom. 12:1), and they are imbued with the Holy Spirit, who produces in them the fruit that is pleasing to God (Gal. 5:22–23).

Concluding Remarks: Perhaps the best word to describe Paul is "multifaceted." He spoke in tongues (1 Cor. 14:18). He experienced celestial visions in which he believed he had been transported to the heavenly realm (2 Cor. 12:1–7). He received revelations from the Lord (Gal. 2:2) and sometimes expected people to regard his rulings on matters as bearing the mark of divine authority (1 Cor. 14:37–38; cf. 7:12, 39–40). He was a man who prayed much (Rom. 1:9; 1 Thess. 1:2–3; 3:10), sometimes with troubled longing (Rom. 8:26), but often with joyful praise (Phil. 1:3–4). He is often given to unabashed displays of emotion and sentiment (2 Cor. 2:4; Phil. 3:18), speaking openly of his affection for those who are dear to him (2 Cor. 7:2–4; Gal. 4:19–20; Phil. 4:1; 1 Thess. 2:17–20; Philem. 4–7). But he can also be roused to anger and is not shy about expressing that emotion either (1 Cor. 4:19–21; 2 Cor. 11:12–15; Gal. 1:9; 3:1; 5:12). At times Paul seems to embody a confident faith that many would regard as idealistic (Phil. 4:11–13), but at other times he seems remarkably down-to-earth, recognizing a need for dealing with practical concerns in a realistic manner (1 Cor. 7:3–5).

At times Paul can seem to be a morass of contradictions. He can seem a champion of women's rights in one instance (Rom. 16:1–2) and a proponent of patriarchal chauvinism in another (1 Cor. 11:1–16). At one point, he seems to question the validity of all human authority figures (Gal. 2:6), but elsewhere he commends his readers to show respect for those who are over them in the Lord (1 Thess. 5:12–13)—and even to be subject to pagan political rulers, since all authorities have been instituted by God (Rom. 13:1–7). He can adopt a tolerant "agree to disagree" attitude on some controversial issues (Rom. 12:5), but he seeks to lay down the law in an absolute sense on other matters (1 Cor. 7:17; 11:16; 14:33–36). He is capable both of commending gentleness (Gal. 5:23; 6:1; Phil. 4:5) and of threatening people with harsh discipline (1 Cor. 4:21; 5:1–5; 2 Cor. 13:2). He emphasizes grace and forgiveness, but insists that people reap what they sow (Gal. 6:6–10) and says that wrongdoers will not inherit the kingdom of God (1 Cor. 6:9). Unless such seeming inconsistencies are recognized, any understanding of Paul may be one-sided or incomplete.

Bibliography

Dunn, James D. G. *The Theology of Paul the Apostle.* Eerdmans, 1998.

Fitzmyer, Joseph A. *Paul and His Theology.* 2nd ed. Prentice-Hall, 1989.

Powell, Mark Allan. *Introducing the New Testament: A Historical, Literary, and Theological Survey.* Baker Academic, 2009. Pp. 231–53.

Roetzel, Calvin. *Paul: The Man and the Myth.* Fortress, 1999.   M.A.P.

Paulus (paw'luhs), **Sergius** (suhr'jee-uhs), the Roman proconsul when Paul and Barnabas visited Cyprus (Acts 13:5–12). He is pictured as an intelligent Gentile, sympathetic to the Christian gospel. According to Acts, he became a Christian after Paul caused the blindness of the hostile Jewish magician Elymas or Bar-Jesus. He and his family are attested in inscriptions found at Pisidian Antioch and at Rome. *See also* Cyprus; Elymas; proconsul.

pavement. *See* Gabbatha.

peace. The concept of *shalom* (the Hebrew word usually translated "peace" in the Bible) implies much more than mere absence of conflict. At root shalom means wholeness or well-being, and the word can be used in both religious and secular contexts. It is also used as a general greeting (Judg. 6:23; Ezra 5:7; Dan. 4:1) and as a farewell (Exod. 4:18; 2 Sam. 15:9). In those cases, it seems to express good wishes for the people addressed and friendly intentions on the part of the speaker. The term comes to mean peace in the more conventional sense of the English word by extension; *shalom* implies absence of conflict due to an absence of those things that cause conflict. At a political level, for instance, *shalom* connotes peace between nations in a sense that implies those nations would have no cause to wage war (Josh. 10:1, 4; 1 Sam. 7:14; 1 Kings 5:12).

Peace (*shalom*) is often associated with other terms. The Hebrew Bible speaks of "peace and security" (2 Kings 20:19; Ps. 122:7) and "peace and prosperity" (Deut. 23:6; Ezra 9:12). Here, peace is associated with material well-being, good harvests, and safety from wild beasts and enemies (Lev. 26:6–10; Zech. 8:12). Peace is also found in conjunction with moral concepts. It is associated with truth in the sense of faithfulness (Esther 9:30; Zech. 8:16, 19). Above all, it is parallel with righteousness (Ps. 85:10; Isa. 60:17). Righteousness will bring peace (Isa. 32:17), but there is no peace for the wicked (48:22; 57:21).

Peace is described as the gift of God (Lev. 26:6; 1 Kings 2:33; Pss. 29:11; 85:8; Isa. 26:12). False prophets cry, "Peace, peace," at times when true prophets know that God is not sending peace (Jer. 6:14; 8:11; Ezek. 13:10, 16). The Hebrew Bible also speaks of God's covenant of peace in connection with priests (Num. 25:12–13; Mal. 2:4–6) and in connection with God's promises to Israel (Isa. 54:10). In Ezekiel, God's peace is the future or eschatological blessing (34:25–31; 37:26), and, according to Isaiah, the Messiah will be a Prince of Peace (9:6). In all of these instances, the emphasis is on peace as a relational concept: peace exists between people or between people and God. The notion of inner peace as an individual experience is not found in the Hebrew Bible.

In the NT, the Greek word for "peace" (*eirēnē*) acquires much of the range of *shalom*, albeit with specifically Christian understanding. Like *shalom,* the Greek word *eirēnē* is used in the Gospels as a greeting and farewell (Mark 5:34; Luke 7:50; John 20:19, 21, 26). This peace appears to be a concrete blessing the disciples can give to others, but, if the others are unworthy, it returns to the disciples (Matt. 10:13; Luke 10:5, 6). Virtually all of the NT letters include "peace" in their opening greeting, usually paired with "grace" (e.g., Rom. 1:7; 1 Cor. 1:3; 2 Cor. 1:2; Gal. 1:3).

The term "peace" (*eirēnē*) is also used in the NT with reference to absence of strife among individuals or nations (Luke 11:21; 14:32; Rev. 6:4). It is used to express order and concord within the Christian congregation. Paul frequently exhorts Christians to be at peace with one another (Rom. 14:19; 1 Cor. 14:33; 2 Cor. 13:11; 1 Thess. 5:13; cf. also Mark 9:50). Christians should strive for peace with all people, Christian or not (Heb. 12:14). This is probably the sense of Jesus's Beatitude on "the peacemakers" (Matt. 5:9), a message that may seem to be contradicted by his claim to bring not peace but a sword, creating division in families (Matt. 10:34–36; Luke 12:51–53). The point of the latter texts seems to be that hostility to Christ and the gospel will inevitably cause tension and division, but the followers of Jesus will not be the ones who exacerbate this. So, Paul writes, "If possible, so far as it depends upon you, live peaceably with all" (Rom. 12:18–19). Here and in Jesus's commands on not resisting evil and on loving one's enemies (Matt. 5:38–48; Luke 6:27–36), the NT advocates a nonaggressive stance.

The association between peace and material prosperity found in the Hebrew Bible is not stressed in the NT; rather, a connection between peace and spiritual blessing is emphasized. Peace occurs in association with righteousness (Rom. 14:17; Heb. 12:11; James 3:18), grace (Phil. 1:2; Rev. 1:4), mercy (Gal. 6:16; 1 Tim. 1:2), love (Jude 2), joy (Rom. 14:17; 15:13), and life (Rom. 8:6). It is identified as a fruit of the Holy Spirit, produced within believers who trust in Christ (Gal. 5:22). God is called a God of peace (Rom. 15:33; Phil. 4:9; 1 Thess. 5:23; Heb. 13:20), and the gospel can be described as the gospel of peace (Acts 10:36; Eph. 6:15). Christ's death has accomplished peace between God and humanity (Rom. 5:1; Col. 1:20) and peace between Jew and Gentile (Eph. 2:14, 17).

Finally, in the NT, the notion of individual spiritual peace or peace of mind is found in a few passages. The peace of God (Phil. 4:7) or the peace of Christ (Col. 3:15) may rule people's hearts; a mind set on the Spirit is life and peace (Rom. 8:6). The God of hope may fill one with joy and peace (Rom. 15:13). *See also* reconciliation.   J.D.

peace offering. *See* sacrifice.

pearl. Pearls appear to have been more highly valued by Greeks than by Hebrews, for the latter do not seem to have had much awareness of them (or esteem for them) prior to the Hellenistic era. Apart from Job 28:18 ("The price of wisdom is above pearls"), there are no references to pearls in the Hebrew Bible. In the NT, however, pearls are associated with gold and costly attire (1 Tim.

2:9), gold and precious stones (Rev. 17:4; 18:16), or other precious materials (Rev. 18:12). Jesus likens discovering the kingdom of heaven to finding a single pearl of such value that it is worth giving up everything one has to obtain it (Matt. 13:45–46). The book of Revelation indicates that the twelve gates of the new Jerusalem will be formed from twelve individual pearls (21:21). M.A.P.

Pedahzur (pi-dah´zuhr; Heb., "the rock has redeemed"), the father of Gamaliel who was the leader of the tribe of Manasseh during the wilderness wandering (Num. 1:10; 10:23).

Pedaiah (pi-day´yuh; Heb., "the LORD has ransomed").

1 The father of Joel, an officer of King David in charge of the western territory of Manasseh (1 Chron. 27:20).

2 The father of Zebidah, the mother of King Jehoiakim (2 Kings 23:36).

3 The third son of King Jehoiachin (Jeconiah) and father of Zerubbabel and Shimei (1 Chron. 3:18–19). According to Hag. 1:1, 12, 14; 2:2, 23; Ezra 3:2, 8; 5:2; and Neh. 12:1, Shealtiel, the brother of Pedaiah, was the father of Zerubbabel.

4 One of the men who assisted Nehemiah in rebuilding the wall of Jerusalem (Neh. 3:25). He was a son of Parosh, an important postexilic family group (Ezra 8:3; Neh. 7:8).

5 The grandfather of Sallu, a Benjaminite resident of postexilic Jerusalem (Neh. 11:7; cf. 1 Chron. 9:7).

6 A Levite appointed by Nehemiah as treasurer in the storehouse to distribute food to Levites (Neh. 13:13).

7 One of the men who stood at the left hand of Ezra during the reading of the Torah in Jerusalem (Neh. 8:4). M.A.S.

peg. The Hebrew word *yated* is translated as either "peg" or "pin" in the NRSV, depending on context. When it is rendered "peg" the reference is to either a tent peg (normally driven into the ground to help secure a tent) or a hanging peg (normally driven into a wall so that things might be hung from it). In Judg. 4:21–23, Jael drives a tent peg through the temple of the Canaanite commander Sisera's head while he is resting in her tent (cf. 5:26); tent pegs are also mentioned in Zech. 10:4; Sir. 14:24; 26:12. The prophet Isaiah likens the ancestral house of Eliakim to a peg in a wall, seemingly secure and capable of bearing much weight, but it too "will be cut down and fall, and the load that was on it will perish" (22:23–25; cf. Ezek. 15:3). *See also* pin.
M.A.P.

Pekah (pee´kuh, Heb., "the LORD opened [the eyes]"), the king of Israel ca. 736–732 BCE, during the time of the divided monarchy. The name Pekah is actually a shortened form of Pekahiah, but the Bible maintains a distinction between those two forms, because there were two successive kings in Israel who had the same name. The one

usually referred to as Pekah, the son of Remaliah, actually seized the throne of the northern kingdom by murdering its king, Pekahiah, the son of Menaham. In 2 Kings 15:27 Pekah is assigned a twenty-year reign, but he could hardly have ruled in Samaria longer than three years, since contemporary Assyrian records show that Menahem was still on the throne in 737 BCE. One solution is to assume that Pekah had already begun to rule independently in Gilead prior to the murder of Pekahiah.

Pekah was the ally of the Aramean king Rezin of Damascus, who may have supported Pekah's usurpation of the throne. In contrast to Menahem and his son Pekahiah, who had been submissive vassals of Assyria, Pekah supported Rezin's attempt to establish an anti-Assyrian coalition. Tyre and Philistia joined them, but Ahaz of Judah refused. A combined Aramean–Israelite army then attacked Jerusalem in an attempt to replace Ahaz with a certain Tabeel, but the attempt failed (Isa. 7:1–10), and Assyria soon crushed the Aramean–Israelite allies. Pekah himself was murdered by Hoshea, who managed to secure Assyrian confirmation allowing him to rule over what remained of Israel. *See also* Ahaz; Isaiah, book of; Rezin. J.J.M.R.

Pekahiah (pek´uh-hi´uh; Heb., "the LORD opened [the eyes]"), the son of Menahem and king of Israel ca. 737–736 BCE, during its last, unstable period prior to the destruction of the capital, Samaria, in 722/1 BCE. After a brief reign he was assassinated by one of his officers of the same name, Pekah the son of Remaliah, who then took the throne (2 Kings 15:23–26). It is possible that Pekah usurped both the throne and throne name of his predecessor, since the name Pekah is actually a shortened form of Pekahiah. In any case, Pekahiah and his father had both been pro-Assyrian, but after Pekahiah's death the usurper Pekah joined in a doomed alliance with Damascus, Tyre, and Philistia to oppose Assyria (and thereby wage war against Judah, the pro-Assyrian southern kingdom). R.J.C.

Pelaiah (pi-lay´yuh; Heb., "the LORD has performed a wonder").

1 The son of Elioenai, descendant of David and in the royal lineage of the kings of Judah through Zerubbabel (1 Chron. 3:24).

2 A man (probably a Levite) who explained the law read by Ezra to the people (Neh. 8:7).

3 A Levite who signed Ezra's postexilic covenant to keep the law (Neh. 10:10); perhaps the same as **2** above.

Pelatiah (pel´uh-ti´uh; Heb., "the LORD has rescued").

1 A descendant of David and in the royal lineage of the kings of Judah through Zerubbabel (1 Chron. 3:21).

2 One of the leaders of the Simeonite Ishi group, which drove out the Amalekites and settled on Mount Seir (Edom; 1 Chron. 4:42).

3 A leader of the people in postexilic Jerusalem who signed Ezra's covenant to keep the law (Neh. 10:22).

4 A corrupt leader in Jerusalem during the exile seen by Ezekiel in a vision; he symbolized an attitude of arrogant false security and a misunderstanding of God's purposes in the exile. His death represented God's judgment on such a distorted perspective (11:1–13).   D.R.B.

Peleg (pee'lig), the ancestor of the Mesopotamian branch of the sons of Eber ("Hebrews")—those who lived by irrigation (cf. Heb. *peleg,* "canal"). It was though Peleg that Abram (Abraham) was descended from Shem (Gen. 11:16–26). When Gen. 10:25 notes that it was in the days of Peleg that the earth was divided (an allusion to the Tower of Babel story), the text employs a play on words: the Hebrew term for "divide" is *palag.* As an ancestor of Abraham (Gen. 11:16–26), Peleg is also mentioned in the NT as ancestor of Jesus (Luke 3:35).

Peleth (pee'lith).

1 The father of one of the conspirators in Korah's rebellion (Num. 16:1). "Peleth," however, could be a mistake for "Pallu" (cf. Num. 25:6, 8).

2 One of the two sons of Jonathan, a descendant of Jerahmeel (1 Chron. 2:33).

Pelethites (pel'uh-thits), a group of mercenaries who, along with the Cherethites, constituted David's bodyguard (2 Sam. 8:18; 23:23). Though their origins are obscure, the Pelethites probably had Aegean or Anatolian forebears who, like the ancestors of the Cherethites and Philistines, settled on the coastal plain at the time of the invasions of the Sea Peoples. David may have won their allegiance while he was in the service of the Philistine king of Gath (1 Sam. 27).

Pella (pel'ah), a major site in the Transjordan prominent as a city of the Decapolis (Matt. 4:25; Mark 5:20) in Roman times. Modern Tabaqa Fahil, it stands in the lower foothills of the eastern edge of the Jordan Valley about eighteen miles south of the Sea of Galilee and about seven miles southeast

Columns stand at the site of ancient Pella of the Decapolis. In the background is the 400-yard-long, 100-foot-high tell.

of Beth-shan. Nourished by a strong spring at the south foot of the 100-foot-high, 400-yard-long tell, the site has been inhabited at least since Chalcolithic times (3000 BCE). It flourished during the period of Canaanite occupation (Middle and Late Bronze ages, 2000–1200 BCE) and was mentioned in the Tell el-Amarna letters (as Pehel, 1400 BCE). Excavations in 1958 and 1967 brought evidence of occupation in the Iron Age I and Iron Age II periods (1200–600 BCE). Pella was then expanded and revitalized in Hellenistic times (334–63 BCE), being taken from the Ptolemies by the Seleucids in 218 BCE, and captured subsequently by the Hasmonean Alexander Jannaeus (83–82 BCE). The Roman general Pompey took Pella in 63 BCE, launching another period of prosperous expansion. There have been reports that Jerusalem Christians fled to Pella as a refuge during the first Jewish revolt (66–70 CE), but these remain inconclusive. *See also* Maccabees.   R.S.B.

Pelusium (pi-loo'see-uhm), the Greek name for the "stronghold of Egypt," which, according to Ezek. 30:15–16, is one of the places destroyed by the Babylonian king Nebuchadnezzar. Some older English translations render the name as "Sin," which is simply a transliteration of the Egyptian word for "fortress." Pelusium/Sin was an important stronghold protecting Egypt's northeast frontier. The Pyramid Texts of the Old Kingdom mention Sin as the provenience of good wine, and a prince of Sin is mentioned in the Assyrian annals of Ashurbanipal. Pelusium/Sin has been identified with modern Tell Farama, situated in the northeast corner of the Nile Delta about twenty-four miles southeast of Port Said. *See also* Nebuchadnezzar.   J.M.W.

pen. *See* writing.

pendant. *See* amulet; jewels, jewelry.

Peninnah (pi-nin'uh), one of the wives of Elkanah and the rival of Hannah (1 Sam. 1:1–6). Peninnah had children, but Hannah did not. Nevertheless, Elkanah showed Hannah preferential treatment, giving her a double portion of the annual sacrifice at Shiloh. Perhaps for this reason, Peninnah would "provoke (Hannah) severely, to irritate her, because the LORD had closed her womb" (1 Sam. 1:7).

penknife. *See* writing.

penny, a word that occurs four times in the NRSV to indicate a coin of little value. In Matt. 5:26 and Mark 12:42 the term "penny" is used for a Roman *quadrans,* which was worth ¹⁄₄₀ of a denarius (or about ¹⁄₄₀ of a typical day's wage). In Matt. 10:29, the term is used for a Roman *assarion,* which was worth ¹⁄₁₀ of a denarius, and in Luke 12:59 it is used for a Roman *lepton,* which was worth half a quadrans, or ¹⁄₈₀ of a denarius. *See also* money.   M.A.P.

Pentapolis (pen-tap′uh-lis; Gk., "five cities"). Although the term is not employed in the Bible itself, biblical scholars sometimes refer to the league of five Philistine cities mentioned in Josh. 13:3 as the "Philistine Pentapolis." The cities were Gaza, Ashdod, Ashkelon, Gath, and Ekron, and they are said to have been ruled by five lords (cf. 1 Sam. 7:7). Less often, the five "cities of the Plain" mentioned in Gen. 14:2 are called a Pentapolis (cf. Wis. 10:6).

Pentateuch (pen′tuh-took), a traditional name used by Christians for the first five books of the Bible. The books are also known as the "books of Moses" or the "Law of Moses." They represent the Torah, the first portion of the Tanakh, Jewish Bible. *See also* law; Old Testament; Pentateuch, sources of the; Tanakh; Torah.

Pentateuch, Samaritan. *See* Samaritan Pentateuch.

Pentateuch, sources of the, the materials from which the first five books of the Bible were composed. As a very extensive composition that incorporates many diverse genres and discrete units of material, the Pentateuch (Genesis–Deuteronomy) is without parallel in ancient Near Eastern literature. The question of how this unique composition was produced has occupied biblical scholarship for four centuries, and various models accounting

for the composition of the Pentateuch have been propounded. No single model satisfies the evidence conclusively.

There are two broad types of models. One views the Pentateuch as the product of an author who worked earlier traditions and sources into a new, independent composition. The other sees the Pentateuch as a composite work, produced by a redactor who edited parallel literary documents into a single text. Some envision a longer history of oral tradition and literary sources behind the documents the redactor used, some a shorter history. Some reconstruct a series of redactions prior to the final one; others imagine a single redaction. It is also possible to mix the two models.

Critics of all schools agree that behind the text of the Pentateuch lie earlier sources. These are only identifiable, however, as a result of scholarly hypothesis; there are no extant texts of the proposed sources.

Identifying the Sources: The Pentateuch quotes one source. It cites the "Book of the Wars of the LORD" as the source for a border description in Num. 21:14–15. The excerpt to which it refers appears to be in verse form, and the term for "book" (Heb. *sepher*) usually refers to a written record (e.g., Exod. 32:32; Num. 5:23; Deut. 17:18; 24:13). Apart from the intriguing title, however, nothing more is known about the "Book of the Wars of the LORD." Num. 21:27 also attributes a song about the fall of Moab to unidentified "ballad singers"

Detail of page from the Pentateuch of a Hebrew Bible, 1310. The left-hand column is a commentary on the text.

(Heb. *moshelim*). Elsewhere in the Bible, the song at Gibeon (Josh. 10:13), David's lament (2 Sam. 1:18), and Solomon's hymn (1 Kings 8:13) are all said to have been excerpted from a written work called the "Book of Jashar"; thus, it is not impossible that the song found in Num. 21:27–30 was also excerpted from a written source.

The Pentateuch further implies discrete written sources when it delineates specific records that Moses is directed to write down: the indictment of Amalek (Exod. 17:14), the laws of Exod. 20–23 (24:4), the cultic laws of Exod. 34 (34:27–28), the Israelites' itinerary (Num. 33:2), the Deuteronomic law code (Deut. 31:9, 24), and the poem in Deut. 32 (31:22). Exod. 24:12 and Deut. 9:10 attribute a written form of the Decalogue to God, suggesting that it also existed as a discrete writing prior to its incorporation in the narrative account. Likewise, the genealogy of ten generations from Adam to Noah in Gen. 5 probably existed as an independent writing, since it is introduced as a "book" (v. 1).

Identifications of other sources in the Pentateuch are based on less explicit evidence or on more subtle discriminations. The clearest cases are those in which the source of one passage is another text within the Pentateuch itself. Exod. 1:1–5 seems to draw directly on, and abridge, the family tree of Jacob in Gen. 46:8–27. The narrative outline of the Israelites' journey from Egypt to Moab, extending from Exod. 12 through Numbers, directly excerpts the itinerary in Num. 33 (see, e.g., Exod. 12:37; 13:20; 14:1, 8, 22; 15:22–23, 27; 16:1; 17:1; 19:2). One could infer that an author or editor used material from written sources to frame the narrative or provide it with continuity.

On the basis of the distinctive character of genealogical and other lists, and the inference that such lists were excerpted and inserted in passages like Exod. 1:1–5 and the narrative of the wilderness journey, one might also deduce that other lists were incorporated into the Pentateuch. Additional support for that theory may be found in lists that abruptly break off before their anticipated end. An example is the genealogy of the Israelites in Exod. 6:14–27, which stops at Levi, because the text's interest is in tracing the lineage of Moses and Aaron, as the conclusion of the passage states. An even more abrupt case is Gen. 37:2: "This is the history [lit., generations] of the family of Jacob." The expected genealogy of Jacob's twelve sons jumps ahead to Joseph, the focus of the ensuing narrative.

The Num. 33 itinerary, most genealogies, and the list of the kings of Edom (Gen. 36:31–39) all display distinct beginnings and closings and a distinctive style. When critics observe distinct beginnings and closings and a distinctive style in other passages in the Pentateuch, they tend to conclude that these too were incorporated into the present text from earlier sources.

Gen. 2:4a, for example, says: "These are the generations of the heavens and the earth when they were created"—a closing, referring to the account of creation given in the preceding verses. Then Gen. 2:4b says: "In the day that the LORD God made the earth and the heaven . . ."—a beginning, introducing an account of creation different from the one in Gen. 1:1–2:3 in both content (e.g., man was created before vegetation and the other animals) and style (e.g., the former account names God Elohim only, and the latter, YHWH Elohim; the former denotes the act of creation by "create" [Heb. *bara'*], and the latter, by "form" [Heb. *yatsar*]). One could deduce that Gen. 2:4a closes one account of creation and that Gen. 2:4b begins another, partly parallel account of creation, which is not imagined to have followed the previous account chronologically. Rather than reporting two creations, the text preserves two somewhat different accounts of the one creation. Thus, one might deduce that these two accounts derive from two different sources.

Collections of law (esp. Exod. 20:22–23:19; 34:10–27; Lev. 17–26; Deut. 12–26) and archaic poems (e.g., Gen. 4:23–24; 27:27–29, 39–40; 49:2–27; Exod. 15:1–18; Num. 21:14–15, 17–18, 27–30; 23:7–10, 18–24; 24:3–9, 15–24; Deut. 32:1–43; 33:2–29) also stand out in genre, structure, and style and are attributed to independent sources. Most of these law collections and poems are set off by introductory and/or closing formulas.

In passages where divergence in content and style is not accompanied by explicit indications of a distinct source, identifying sources is less certain. Nevertheless two types of sources have been posited and may now be discussed: those that are discerned within the text of the Pentateuch and those that are hypothesized to have existed outside the text.

Source-Critical Analysis: Biblical scholars have attempted to analyze passages into their component parts by segregating units that diverge in content and style. Repetitive duplication, substantive inconsistency or contradiction, abrupt digression, and sustained difference in terminology have been taken to suggest boundaries between sources. Although none of these features would in and of itself indicate a different source, the coincidence of a number of these features may be taken as suggestive of such a source.

A case in point is the flood story in Gen. 6:5–9:19. Here there are repetitions, contradictions, and consistent divergences in style and terminology from passage to passage. The text fluctuates between passages in which God is called "the LORD" (Heb. YHWH) and passages in which God is always called "God" (Heb. *'elohim*). In the first set of passages, "the LORD" commands Noah to take seven pairs of all pure animals and one pair of the impure animals into the ark, and it rains for forty days and nights. In the second set of passages, God commands Noah to take only one pair of each animal, and the flood rises for 150 days. In addition, the former passages are characterized by a more personal deity whose heart is grieved about human behavior (6:6) and who personally shuts Noah in the ark (7:6). The latter passages show more preference for statistics and legal arrangements; they feature a genealogy (6:9–10), details of age and date (7:6, 11; 8:4–5, 13–14), and the terms of a covenant (6:18; 9:8–17).

Scholarly convention assigns the first passages in this example of the flood story to a stream of ancient tradition identified as the J source. The siglum J derives from a German spelling of the name of God, *Jahveh*, used throughout the material. *Jahveh* is typically written as Yahweh in English, but either spelling (*Jahveh* or Yahweh) represents a vocalization of four Hebrew consonants (JHVH or YHWH) that appear in the biblical text as an unpronounceable name for God. The latter passages are ascribed to what is called the P source (the siglum deriving from its association with priestly concerns). The J and P accounts employ distinctive vocabulary, as may be seen in their description of the destruction of life by the flood:

J: Everything on the dry land in whose nostrils was the breath of life died. (7:22)

P: And all flesh died that moved on the earth, birds, domestic animals, wild animals, all swarming creatures that swarm on the earth, and all human beings. (7:21)

The same stylistic difference can also be observed in the two accounts of creation mentioned above, which likewise employ different names for God:

J: Then the LORD God formed man of dust from the ground, and breathed into his nostrils the breath of life. (2:7)

P: And God said to [the humans], Be fruitful and multiply, and fill the earth and subdue it; and have dominion over the fish of the sea and over the birds of the air and over every living thing that moves upon the earth." (1:28)

Thus, scholars have proposed that two written sources lie behind these portions of the book of Genesis, the so-called J source and the so-called P source. Both contained accounts of creation and of the flood, and the present text of Genesis was produced by splicing these two sources together. Further, scholars believe that other materials in Genesis may be reckoned to each of those two sources as well. A common analysis yields the following:

J: Gen. 6:5–8; 7:1–5, 7–10, 12, 16b–17, 22–23; 8:2b–3a, 6–12, 13b, 20–22

P: Gen. 6:9–22; 7:6, 11, 13–16a, 18–21, 24; 8:1–2a, 3b–5; 8:13a, 14–19; 9:1–17

Using similar criteria, scholars have sought to isolate another source, called E, because it refers to God as Elohim and appears to be distinct from both J and P. Although E is difficult to identify outside Genesis, interpreters sometimes assign to it chapters that seem to present a variant version of an episode that occurs in J. Thus, the E material would include Gen. 20:1–17 (which doubles 12:10–20); 21:8–20 (which doubles 16:1–16); and

21:22–34 (which doubles 26:17–33). Characteristic of E is that God appears less immanently than in J, addressing people through messengers (angels) or dreams. Commonly, J and E are understood to be combined in several narratives, such as the story of Joseph (Gen. 37–50). In the portions of that story ascribed to J (where God is referred to as YHWH; NRSV: "the LORD"), the father is called Israel, Judah tries to save Joseph, and the Ishmaelites buy Joseph and take him down to Egypt. In E (where God is referred to as Elohim; NRSV: "God"), the father is called Jacob, Reuben tries to save Joseph, and the Midianites kidnap Joseph. Style and vocabulary also identify the two sources.

Once separated, the hypothetical sources in the flood story, the Joseph narrative, and other texts do not appear complete. Some narrative material was probably omitted (e.g., J's description of the ark). There is also no way of knowing how much material originally in these sources was not included in the Pentateuch. There is no way to determine the original extent or shape of the sources.

Hypothesizing Sources Outside the Text: Because many cultures transmit epics and other literary forms orally, and because the Bible frequently refers to oral performance or transmission of its texts or traditions (e.g., Exod. 13:8; 15:1, 21), oral traditions could lie behind the Pentateuch and its written sources. The postulation of such sources, however, is necessarily speculative. Still, Deut. 26:5–9 presents a formula summarizing Israel's story from the descent of the ancestors from Canaan to Egypt, where the Israelites grew in numbers and then were enslaved, through God's deliverance from Egypt and guidance to the land of Canaan. This "credo," as it has been called, was to be recited by Israelites bringing first-fruit offerings to God. Perhaps, it has been suggested, this credo is a miniature of a large epic, an oral account stretching from the promises made to Israel's ancestors to the arrival of Israel at the promised land. Fragments of what looks like ancient verse (e.g., Exod. 19:3) dot the Pentateuch; they could be vestiges of such an epic.

That prose texts in the Pentateuch may have been transformed from earlier accounts told in epic verse can be argued in two additional ways. First, the prose account of crossing the Red Sea in Exod. 14 seems to adapt parts of the archaic song preserved in Exod. 15. Second, several of the prose episodes in Gen. 1–11 include occasional bursts of archaic verse (e.g., 1:27; 2:23; 3:14–19; 7:11b) and exhibit poetic patterns or diction. The written sources or the redactors or authors of the Pentateuch, then, may have employed an extensive oral epic or a number of smaller works in verse, when composing the present text, just as they drew upon the "Book of the Wars of the LORD" and the "ballad singers."

More remote, and for the most part indirect, sources for sections of the Pentateuch are narratives and laws attested in other works of ancient Near Eastern literature. Among the many possible interrelations are the Mesopotamian flood story in the *Epic of Gilgamesh* (for parallels to Gen. 6–9); the Egyptian "Tale of Two Brothers" (with parallels to Gen. 39); the Akkadian legend of Sargon (with parallels to the birth story of Moses in Exod. 2); the Code of Hammurabi and other ancient Near Eastern law codes (for parallels to Exod. 21–23); and the Assyrian vassal treaties (for parallels to the curses in Deut. 28–30).

The Documentary Hypothesis: The prevailing account of the composition of the Pentateuch in modern scholarship is called the "Documentary Hypothesis." In most versions of this theory, four documents are hypothesized to have been redacted in forming the Pentateuch: J, a southern Judean source from about the tenth century BCE; E, a northern Israelite source from about the eighth century BCE; D, the core of Deuteronomy, which is roughly identified with the "book of the law [*torah*]" promulgated by King Josiah ca. 622 BCE (2 Kings 22–23); and P, a collection of priestly materials variously dated before, during, or after the Babylonian exile of the sixth century BCE. The redaction of these materials is generally understood to have taken place in stages: first JE, then JED, then JEDP. At each stage of redaction, editorial adaptation and reshaping of the prior material is assumed. Most of Exod. 25–Num. 36 is assigned to P, as are the first and last chapters of the Pentateuch, giving the impression that partisans of P were the final redactors. The final redaction would have occurred by the fifth century BCE.

The chronological sequence of the material is reconstructed by relating the other sources to D. Laws in JE seem to precede Deuteronomy. JE (e.g., Exod. 23:19) allows Israelites to bring offerings to God to any sanctuary, but D (e.g., Deut. 12:13–14) restricts their offerings to a single site—this is presumed to represent a later development (reflective of Josiah's centralization of worship in Jerusalem). Several laws in D actually appear to revise laws in JE. For example, Deut. 15:12–28 follows the structure and uses some of the phraseology of the slave law of Exod. 21:2–6 (JE). The D text, however, treats women the same as men, unlike JE, and exhorts the Israelites to be generous toward manumitted slaves. The law concerning rape in Deut. 22:23–27 could likewise be regarded as an expansion of the less comprehensive law in Exod. 22:15–16.

The P material definitely seems to reflect concerns that developed later in Israelite history than would be apparent in the J or E material. For example, in J's flood narrative, Noah offers the excess pure animals he took into the ark as thanksgiving to God after the flood, but in P's version Noah takes no extra animals and makes no offering, because he is not a proper priest authorized to make such sacrifices. *See also* Deuteronomist; Deuteronomy, book of; Elohist; Exodus, book of; Genesis, book of; Leviticus, book of; Numbers, book of; Priestly writer(s); Yahwist.

Bibliography

Blenkinsopp, Joseph. *The Pentateuch.* Doubleday, 1992.

Friedman, Richard E. *Who Wrote the Bible?* Summit, 1987.

Hahn, Herbert F. *The Old Testament in Modern Research.* Fortress, 1966.

Nicholson, Ernest. *The Pentateuch in the Twentieth Century.* Clarendon, 1998.

Rendtorff, Rolf. *The Problem of the Process of Transmission in the Pentateuch.* JSOT, 1990. E.L.G.

Pentecost (pen′ti-kost; from Gk., "fiftieth"), a religious observance that has roots in the Hebrew Bible and continues to be observed in Christianity. The term originated as the Greek name for what is otherwise known as Shavuot, the Festival of Weeks (cf. Exod. 23:14–17; 34:18–24; Deut. 16:16; 2 Chron. 8:13). The term "Pentecost" is used to refer to that festival twice in the LXX (Tob. 2:1; 2 Macc. 12:32) and three times in the NT (Acts 2:1; 20:16; 1 Cor. 16:8). The day, however, came to be invested with new meaning for Christians, due to what the NT reports occurred on one particular Pentecost in Jerusalem when the Holy Spirit came upon a community of Jesus's followers a few days after Jesus's ascension into heaven. In modern parlance, Shavuot usually designates the Jewish festival, and Pentecost, the Christian one (though both are observed on the same day).

Festival of Weeks (Shavuot) in the Hebrew Bible: In Exod. 23:16, the Festival of Weeks is identified as an agricultural observance; it is a time for celebrating "the first fruits of wheat harvest, and the festival of ingathering at the turn of the year." Thus, the focus appears to have been on showing gratitude to God for the early harvest. The dating of this festival also suggests this original agricultural context. Deut. 16:9–10 says that it is to be dated seven weeks "from the time you first put the sickle to the standing grain." Lev. 23:15–16 directs: "And you shall count from the morrow after the sabbath, from the day that you brought the sheaf of the wave offering; seven full weeks shall they be, counting fifty days to the morrow after the seventh sabbath." According to biblical regulations, one was not allowed to work on the day of Shavuot. Deut. 16:16 lists the Festival of Weeks as one of the three principal festivals for the Israelites (cf. 2 Chron. 8:13), the others being Unleavened Bread (Passover) and Tabernacles (Booths). On these three occasions all male Israelites were to appear "before the Lord" at a designated place (later, the Jerusalem temple), and they were not to appear empty-handed; the sacrifice of various animals and bread made from newly harvested grain was required (cf. Lev. 23:15–21; Num. 28:26–31).

During the Hellenistic period (300 BCE–300 CE), however, Shavuot/Pentecost began to lose its association with agriculture and came increasingly to be associated with the religious history of the Hebrew people. The book of *Jubilees* continues to refer to it as "first fruits" (22:1), but identifies the day with the covenant between God and Noah (6:1–21; cf. Gen. 8:20–22; 9:8–17). At some point, the day also became strongly associated with the giving of Torah on Mount Sinai. Exod. 19:1 was interpreted to mean that the interval between Passover and the arrival at Sinai was fifty days. It is not known, however, whether this association had developed at the time of the NT; many scholars see the association with Sinai as a post–70 CE development, which would undermine the notion that Luke wanted to parallel the giving of the Spirit with the giving of the law by locating the former event on a day set aside for observing the latter. Nothing in Acts, at any rate, seems intended to draw attention to such a parallel.

The date of the festival also became standardized at some point roughly contemporary with the NT era. Josephus indicates that the date of Shavuot/Pentecost was fixed in his day (latter part of first century CE) as the fiftieth day after the first day of Passover, but just how established such a "fixed date" would have been at that time (or when and how such dating developed) is not known. In time, however, the "fifty days after the first day of Passover" formula became standard dating for both Jewish Shavuot and Christian Pentecost.

Pentecost in Acts: The book of Acts mentions Pentecost once in connection with Paul's travels (20:16), but of greater interest is the description of the first Pentecost after the death and resurrection of Jesus (2:1–42). In this passage, the apostles and others have convened in Jerusalem on the day of Pentecost. The author of Acts reports that there was a sudden sound "like the rush of a violent wind" (2:2) from heaven, followed by divided tongues of fire that appeared to rest upon each person (2:3). As a result, the apostles began to speak in tongues, i.e., in foreign languages that were understood by the Jews from various nations who were living in the city. The commotion drew a large crowd, some of whom dismissed the spectacle as drunkenness (2:13). The apostle Peter, however, interpreted what was happening as a fulfillment of the prophecy of Joel 2:8–32. He proclaimed that the last days had arrived and that Jesus had been raised from the dead. Then he promised all of the spectators that if they repented and were baptized in the name of Jesus Christ, their sins would be forgiven and they too would receive the gift of the Holy Spirit (Acts 2:38). As a result, about three thousand persons were added to the group of believers.

Within the literary context of Acts, the events associated with Pentecost constitute the fulfillment, not only of the prophecy of Joel, but also of the promise of Jesus. In Acts 1:8, just prior to his ascension, the risen Jesus had said, "You will receive power when the Holy Spirit has come upon you; and you will be my witnesses in Jerusalem, in all Judea and Samaria, and to the ends of the earth" (cf. Luke 24:49; Acts 1:5). Thus, the events of Pentecost are presented in Acts as the fulfillment of this promise—on that day the Holy Spirit did indeed come upon the apostles and empower them to witness to Jesus the Christ.

Pentecost in 1 Corinthians: In 1 Cor. 16:8, the apostle Paul mentions to the Corinthians that he plans to stay in Ephesus until Pentecost. Some interpreters have suggested that since he is writing to Gentile Christians and apparently expects them to understand his meaning, Pentecost might have already become a Christian observance by this time. The book of Acts, however, was probably written three decades or more after Paul's letter to the Corinthians and Paul never displays any knowledge of the events that Luke recounts in Acts 2 (even in passages of his letters that deal extensively with the Spirit, such as Rom. 8; 1 Cor. 12, 14; Gal. 5). Thus, most scholars assume Paul is probably referring to the Jewish Festival of Weeks, without any particular intimation of the day the Spirit descended. *See also* Acts of the Apostles; festivals, feasts, and fasts; spiritual gifts; tongues, as of fire; tongues, speaking in. J.B.T./M.A.P.

Penuel (peh-nyoo′uhl).

1 A city located on the Jabbok (modern River Zerqa), east of the Jordan. Here Jacob wrestled with a "man" who later tells him that he has striven with God (Gen. 32:24–31); in a play on words, Jacob says Penuel should be called Peniel (Heb., "face of God") because here he saw God face-to-face (32:30). Here too Gideon was refused food by the local inhabitants when he was pursuing the Midianites (Judg. 8:8–9); he later took revenge upon them by pulling down a tower and killing the men of the city (8:25). Penuel was rebuilt by Jeroboam I (ca. 922–901 BCE; 1 Kings 12:25). The site has been identified with modern Tulul edh-Dhahab. *See also* Gideon; Jacob; Jeroboam I.

2 A son of Hur and grandson of Judah (1 Chron. 4:4).

3 The son of Shashak, a Benjaminite (1 Chron. 8:25).

people, peoples,

terms used to translate a number of Hebrew and Greek terms referring to different kinds of social, ethnic, or cultural collectivities. Interest in the origins of the various peoples of the world is evident in genealogies (Gen. 5; 10) and in the Tower of Babel story about the development of different languages (Gen. 11). Gen. 10 also reflects an important division between peoples based on language groups. Semitic (derived from the name Shem, a son of Noah) peoples were prominent in the Near East. Some spoke Hebrew and Aramaic; others spoke Akkadian (Assyro-Babylonian) and dialects of Arabic (Minaean, Sabean, and Ethiopic). The Egyptians, for the most part, constituted a Hamitic (from Ham) group. Indo-Aryans (from Japheth) constituted a third major group.

In the Hebrew Bible, however, the term "people" (Heb. ′am) is also used as a designation for the social entity of Israel (Num. 23:9). Israel is often called simply "the people" (ha′am). In several instances, "the people" refers to the community acting with authority in making covenants or declaring war (Judg. 5:2; 21:2, 15; 1 Sam. 4:4; 14:45). "The people" also designates a juridical community (Exod. 22:28; 23:11). Primary subgroups within Israel are also called "a people" (′am; the tribe of Joseph in Josh. 17:14–17; of Zebulun in Judg. 5:18). In the NT, the Greek term *laos* is often used in a way that implies "the people of Israel" (cf. 2 Cor. 6:16; Heb. 7:11), while the word *anthropoi* (also translated "people" in the NRSV) has more of the sense of "human beings." Such distinctions do not always hold, however, and the terms can be applied synonymously.

In an expanded sense Israel is often identified in the Hebrew Bible as "the people of the LORD" (Heb. *'am YHWH*; Judg. 5:11, 13; 1 Sam. 2:24), which makes explicit what is probably implied in most references to Israel as "the people." In the LXX, the phrase "people of the LORD" is translated into Greek as *laos theou* ("people of God"), a phrase that continues to be used in the NT (Heb. 11:25; Matt. 1:21; Luke 1:68; Rom. 11:1–2). More often in the NT, however, it is used as a designation for the church (Rom. 9:25–26; 2 Cor. 6:14; Titus 2:14). The subtle implication seems to be that those who believe in Jesus Christ have become "the people of God" in a way analogous to the identification of Israel in the scriptures (cf. 1 Pet. 2:9–10). *See also* Amorites; Canaan; Hittites; Horites; nations; people of the land; Semites.   F.S.F.

people of the land, a phrase that occurs frequently in the Hebrew Bible (*'am ha'arets*), but assumes different meanings in various periods and contexts. In premonarchic contexts, the term seems to apply to free citizens (i.e., not slaves) who live in a particular place. Thus Pharaoh complains that the Hebrew slaves have become more numerous than the people of the land in Egypt (Exod. 5:5; cf. Gen. 23:7, 12–13; 42:6). Later, after the institution of the monarchy, the term seems to refer to people who are distinguished from the royal or ruling class. Thus the people of the land are said to join in a popular uprising at the time of Queen Athaliah when Joash is crowned king (2 Kings 11:13–20). The exilic prophets Jeremiah and Ezekiel often use the term in this light, though it has been debated among scholars as to whether the phrase was actually a technical term with fairly specific meaning or a more general and ambiguous expression. Further, there is discussion as to whether those referred to as "the people of the land" were those associated with lower classes or, quite differently, the landed elite, or simply the people of Israel in general. In any case, the term takes on a very different connotation in the postexilic texts of Ezra and Nehemiah (Ezra 10:2, 11; Neh. 10:30). Here, the phrase "people of the land" becomes a derogatory term for those who oppose the standards set by Ezra and Nehemiah.

Peor (pee'or; Heb., "opening"), a mountain in Moab, also known as Baal-peor (Hos. 9:10) because there was a sanctuary to Baal here. The latter sanctuary was apparently called Beth-peor, so the latter name is sometimes used for the mountain as well. The location is unknown, although some area in the region of Mount Nebo makes the most sense of the texts. Peor is first mentioned as the moun-

tain to which Balak took Balaam, when he wanted him to curse the wandering Israelites prior to their arrival in Canaan (Num. 23:28). A short time later, the mountain became the scene of an episode in which a plague broke out among Israelites who had begun having sexual relations with Moabite women and, so, yoked themselves with the "Baal of Peor" (25:3–5). This incident would be long remembered (Num. 31:16; Deut. 4:3; Josh. 22:17; Ps. 106:28; Hos. 9:10). Finally, just before their invasion of Canaan, the Israelites camped "in the valley opposite Beth-peor," where Moses recounted their long journey and repeated Israel's covenant obligations (Deut. 3:29; 4:46). Shortly thereafter, Moses viewed the promised land from Mount Pisgah, died, and was buried in the vicinity of Beth-peor (34:1–6).   M.A.P.

Perea (puh-ree'uh; from Gk., "beyond"), an area east of the Jordan River. The name occurs nowhere in the Bible, but is frequent in the writings of the first-century historian Josephus. Such biblical expressions as "beyond the Jordan" and "across the Jordan" appear to be the equivalent of Perea in Matt. 4:15, 25; 19:1; Mark 3:8; 10:1; John 1:28; 3:26; and 10:40. The area was the scene of John's baptizing, and its people flocked to hear Jesus.

Located on the eastern slopes of the Transjordanian plateau, Perea's northern boundary was just south of Pella. Its southern frontier ran from the Dead Sea to Machaerus, the fortress where John the Baptist died, up to the edge of the Moabite Plateau. The eastern boundary ran north–south about fifteen miles east of the Jordan River. The region had been conquered by the Hasmonean (Maccabean) kings in the second century BCE, but it was reorganized as a Roman province by Gabinius, the Roman proconsul of Syria, in 57 BCE. At the time of Jesus, Perea remained predominantly Jewish and belonged, with Galilee, to the tetrarchy of Herod Antipas. Later it became part of the territory ruled by Herod Agrippa II until his death ca. 100 CE. *See also* Herod.   C.H.M.

Perez (pee'riz; Heb., "a breach"), a son of Judah and Tamar; his twin brother was Zerah. Gen. 38:28–30 tells the story of his birth with an accent on the rivalry of the twins within the womb. Zerah put his hand out of the womb first and the midwife bound his wrist with a crimson thread, saying, "This one came out first." But then Zerah drew back his hand, and Perez was born. The midwife exclaimed, "What a breach you have made for yourself," which explains his name. Perez himself does not figure again in biblical narrative, but his descendants were known as the Perezite branch of the Judah tribe (Num. 26:20; 1 Chron. 2:4–5). David was a Perezite and brought prestige to the group (Ruth 4:12, 18–19). Also, through this line, Perez was an ancestor of Jesus (Matt. 1:3; Luke 3:33).   M.A.P.

perfect, perfection, an English word sometimes used to translate Hebrew and Greek words with a range of meaning ("completeness," "wholeness," "blamelessness," "maturity"). In the Bible, God is described as perfect with regard to knowledge, justice, fidelity, and promise keeping (Job 37:16; Deut. 32:4; 2 Sam. 22:31; Ps. 18:30); God's law is also perfect (Ps. 19:7). Human beings are sometimes described as (or urged to become) perfect with regard to observance of the law (Ps. 119:1) or with regard to upright and blameless behavior (Gen. 6:9; Deut. 18:13; Prov. 2:21), which does not imply that they would be "perfect" in other aspects (i.e., they might be "godly" in behavior without becoming gods). In Matt. 5:48, Jesus commands his followers to "be perfect," indicating that their goal should be the attainment of righteousness equal to that of God. Elsewhere, Paul says that the goal of obtaining righteousness or becoming like Christ is something he has not yet attained (Phil. 3:12), but that he strives nevertheless toward what might be realized only in the life to come (3:8–21). The Letter to the Hebrews indicates that Christ became perfect through his sufferings (2:10; 5:9; 7:28) and that perfection is a gift bestowed by Christ (10:14). *See also* justification; righteousness; sanctification.

A.J.H./M.A.P.

perfume. *See* cosmetics; incense; ointments and perfumes.

perfumers, traders who compounded and dispensed a variety of aromatic substances. Perfumers played an important role in ancient Israel, where the aromatic oils and incense they provided were required for religious as well as cosmetic and medicinal use, including embalming (2 Chron. 16:14). The holy anointing oil and the incense used in the tabernacle were the work of such perfumers (Exod. 30:25, 35; 37:29), who constituted a recognized guild in postexilic times (Neh. 3:8), drawn from priestly families (1 Chron. 9:30). Perfumers are also mentioned in the royal household as a class of female servants alongside cooks and bakers (1 Sam. 8:13). *See also* incense; ointments and perfumes; spices. P.A.B.

Perga (puhr´guh), a city near the Kestros River in the district of Pamphylia, about twelve miles inland from the southern coast of Asia Minor. Excavations at the site have brought to light an inscription indicating that the inhabitants considered Greek heroes of the Trojan War to be the founders of their city. Perga was fairly prosperous in NT times, for it had a theater, a stadium, Roman baths, and a gymnasium. Its patron deity was the goddess Artemis. Paul and Barnabas visited Perga on their first missionary journey, traveling from Paphos to Pisidian Antioch, and it was at Perga that John Mark left them to return to Jerusalem (Acts 13:13). Paul and Barnabas preached here at the end of that journey as well (14:24). *See also* Mark; Pamphylia. M.K.M.

Pergamum (puhr´guh-muhm), a city in the region of Mysia in western Asia Minor. The modern

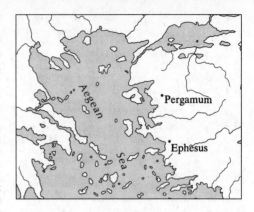

village of Bergama, Turkey, now covers part of the ancient site. One of the seven messages of the book of Revelation was addressed to Pergamum (1:11; 2:12). In Rev. 2:13, Pergamum is described as the place where Satan's throne is located. This has sometimes been identified as the temple of Zeus in the city, but at least two other interpretations have been advanced in light of the connection Revelation makes elsewhere between Satan's power and that of Rome (chaps. 12–13). "Satan's throne" could be an allusion to Pergamum as one of the oldest and most prominent centers for emperor worship. Or the reference could be to the fact that Pergamum was a city in which the imperial governor regularly held court. The governor alone held the right of capital punishment, and the message to Pergamum in Revelation refers to Christ as one who wields a sharp two-edged sword (2:12, 16), which might be intended to contrast Christ's ultimate authority as judge with that exercised by the governor. The message to Pergamum also refers to a Christian named Antipas being put to death, apparently on account of his faith.

The site of Pergamum was occupied from prehistoric times, but became famous only in the Hellenistic period. In the third century BCE, Pergamum became the center of an independent kingdom, and its cultural achievements were notable. King Eumenes II (197–159 BCE) founded a library second only to that of Ptolemy Philadelphus in Alexandria. Pergamum also had a famous school of sculpture. Its wealth was based on agricultural surplus, silver mines, stock breeding, woolen textiles, and the making of parchment (which may have been invented in Pergamum, since the very word "parchment" is derived from the city's name). In 133 BCE the last king to reign in Pergamum, Attalus III, bequeathed his kingdom, which comprised parts of Phrygia, Ionia, and Caria as well as Lydia and Mysia, in his will to the Romans. After his death it was constituted as the Roman province of Asia with Pergamum as its capital. Under Augustus, the province was reconstituted as a senatorial province governed by a proconsul. The capital was probably changed at this time to Ephesus.

Remains of the ancient temple of
Asclepius at Pergamum.

At the time of the NT, Pergamum would have
been one of the most beautiful of the Greek cities.
Its public buildings were built on terraces on a
steep mountain, offering a spectacular view. The
layout of the city is often cited as a magnificent
example of Hellenistic city planning, with particular focus on the palace and fortifications of the
acropolis. During the Roman period, a shrine of
Asclepius, the Greek god of healing, was built in
the lower city. It was a kind of spa at which both
natural and supernatural modes of healing were
employed.   A.Y.C.

Perizzites (pair'i-zits), one of the older population groups of the land of Canaan, usually listed as
one of the six or seven groups inhabiting the land
(Exod. 3:8, 17; 23:23; 33:2; 34:11; Deut. 7:1; 20:17;
Josh. 3:10; 9:1; 11:3; 12:8; 24:11; Judg. 3:5; 1 Kings
9:20; cf. Gen. 15:20). Occasionally the Perizzites
are mentioned with the Canaanites as the two native peoples of Canaan (Gen. 13:7; 34:30; Judg.
1:4–5). They evidently lived in the central highlands, particularly the forested hill country of
Ephraim (cf. Josh. 17:15; Judg. 1:4–5). Their identity is uncertain. Some have connected them with
the Hurrians; others, with the Amorites. *See also*
Canaan.   D.A.D.

persecution, applied broadly, a virtual synonym
for oppression, hostility, or opposition. Thus, in
the Bible, the Israelites were "persecuted and oppressed" by their enemies in the land of Canaan
(Judg. 2:18), and the psalmist complains that
"the wicked persecute the poor" (Ps. 10:2). This
is probably also the sense that should be applied
to the term when Stephen claims that all of God's
prophets were persecuted (Acts 7:52). Prophets
were not regularly hunted down in a systematic
way, but they did frequently meet with opposition
and even severe harassment (Isa. 28:9–10; 50:5–6;
Ezek. 33:32–33; Jer. 26:20–23; cf. 11:8–23; 1 Kings
19:10; 22:26–27). In a more narrow sense, however, "persecution" refers to systematic, targeted
hostility directed against a specific group. In this
sense, Antiochus IV Epiphanes (175–164 BCE) persecuted the Jewish people; he tried to suppress
customs necessary for Jewish identity and condemned to death those who practiced dietary
rules, circumcision, and other matters central to
the Jewish faith (cf. 1 Macc. 1:41–61).

In the Gospels, Jesus speaks of "persecutions"
coming upon his followers, and his words may
have different meanings in different contexts.
First, when he indicates that his followers will be
persecuted in the same way as the prophets, he may
mean no more than that their proclamation of his
message will be met with the same hostility and
opposition that often attended the prophets (cf.
Matt. 5:10–12). Second, Jesus sometimes seems to
refer to persecutions in the generic sense of strife
and suffering that will come to those who follow
him, sometimes as a consequence of their faith.
Thus, in the parable of the Sower, Jesus can speak
of persecution in the same terms as "trouble"
that arises on account of the word (Mark 4:14; cf.
10:30). Likewise, Paul includes "persecutions" on
the same list as "hardship," "calamity," and other
forms of suffering that must be borne in this life
(Rom. 8:35; 2 Cor. 12:10). In a few passages, however, Jesus seems to speak of persecution in the
specific sense of systematic, targeted hostility:
"They will arrest you and persecute you; they will
hand you over to synagogues and prisons, and you
will be brought before kings and governors because of my name" (Luke 21:12).

Paul claims in his letters that he "persecuted"
the church (1 Cor. 15:9; Gal. 1:13; Phil. 3:6; 1 Tim.
1:13; cf. Acts 8:1; 9:1–2) and also that once he became a Christian missionary, he suffered violence
as a result of that conviction (2 Cor. 11:24–25). He
refers to his churches also suffering persecution,
but he does not seem to be referring to organized,
formal attempts to extinguish the Christian faith
(cf. 1 Thess. 1:6; 3:3–4, 7; cf. 2 Thess. 1:4).

The most systematic persecution against Christianity was conducted by the Romans, but it is difficult to know exactly when this became official
policy. The book of Acts reports that Herod Agrippa
I had James the son of Zebedee and Peter thrown in
prison (12:1–3), but the fact that the church continued to operate openly in Jerusalem indicates the
governmental action was not against all Christians
as such. Nero persecuted Christians in Rome after
a fire in the city ca. 64 CE, but this was not apparently a long-term action, nor does it appear to have
been enacted outside of Rome in any official capacity. The book of Revelation makes reference to witnesses who may have been killed through imperial
persecution (2:13; 17:6), though, again, it is not
clear that such harsh measures were enacted against
all Christians everywhere. It is only in the second
century (ca. 110), at the time of Pliny the Younger
(*Letters* 10.96–97), that there is clear evidence of a
formal Roman policy to root out Christian beliefs
throughout the empire. Pliny's letters to Trajan
indicate that those suspected of being Christian
would be tortured and forced to make sacrifices to
the emperor; if they refused they would be put to
death.   J.H.N./M.A.P.

Persepolis (puhr-sep′uh-lis), a Persian city mentioned in 2 Macc. 9:2 as a place whose temples Antiochus IV attempted to rob. This incident demonstrated the impiety evident in Antiochus's attack on the Jewish temple at Jerusalem (ca. 175 BCE).

Excavations at Persepolis have yielded two collections of tablets in Elamite from 509–494 BCE and 492–457 BCE. These records deal with supplies and payments and suggest that Persepolis served as an administrative center for the Persian Empire (ca. 509 BCE at the latest). The massive terrace on which the palatial buildings stand stems from the reign of Darius I (the palace was begun about 520 BCE). Darius, Xerxes, and other Persian kings are buried in the vicinity. However, the city was unknown in the western part of the empire. The Greeks only came to know of the city when it was taken by Alexander the Great (331/0 BCE). Though the city had offered no resistance, Alexander ordered the great palace of Xerxes destroyed, perhaps in revenge for Xerxes' burning the temples on the Acropolis at Athens. The great palace at Persepolis shows no signs of having been inhabited. The only objects revealed by excavators were trophies such as might be captured in war, and the complex did not contain sanitation facilities. Therefore, it would appear that the palace was used for ceremonial purposes only. Diodorus, a historian who wrote in the first century BCE, records a later complaint that the palaces at Persepolis had been built with spoils taken from Egypt (*History* 1.146). Though the tablets found at Persepolis record the presence of magi and offerings to the god Ahura-Mazada, there is no archaeological evidence for the temples mentioned in 2 Maccabees.   P.P.

Persia (puhr′zhuh), an empire that at its height stretched from Greece in the west to India in the east. The Persian Empire came into being with the victories of Cyrus the Great over his Medan overlord (ca. 550 BCE) and lasted until the conquests of Alexander the Great (ca. 330 BCE). The origin and original locality of the ancestors of the Persians remain uncertain; links with Parsua, south of Lake Urmia (some 175 miles west of the southern end of the Caspian Sea), are possible, but more probable are those with Persis, east of the Persian Gulf, where Pasargadai and Persepolis, great centers of the empire, were situated.

Rulers: The rulers of the Persian Empire were: Cyrus (king of Anshan, ca. 560 BCE, d. 530 BCE), Cambyses (530–522 BCE), Darius I (522–486 BCE), Xerxes I (486–465 BCE), Artaxerxes I (465–424 BCE), Xerxes II (424 BCE), Sogdianos (424–423 BCE), Darius II (423–405/4 BCE), Artaxerxes II (405/4–359/8 BCE), Artaxerxes III (359/8–338/7 BCE), Artaxerxes IV (338/7–336), and Darius III (336–330 BCE). Of these, Cyrus is hailed in the Bible as the chosen deliverer of the Jews from Babylon (Isa. 44:28; 45:1)

Opposite: The territory of the ancient Israelites became part of the Persian Empire when it was established in the sixth century BCE. As part of the Persian Empire, Judah was known as "Yehud."

Overview of Persepolis; construction was begun by the Persian king Darius in the sixth century BCE.

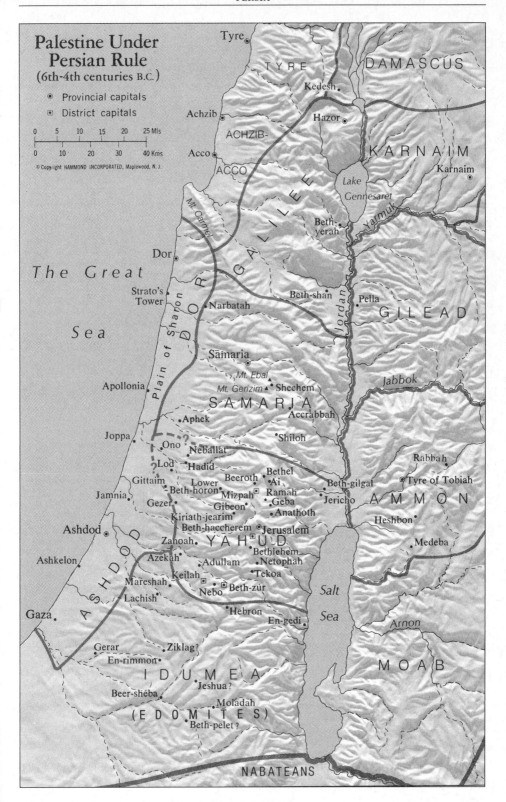

Palestine Under Persian Rule
(6th-4th centuries B.C.)

- ◉ Provincial capitals
- ▣ District capitals

0 5 10 15 20 25 Mls
0 10 20 30 40 Kms

© Copyright HAMMOND INCORPORATED, Maplewood, N. J.

Tyre

TYRE

DAMASCUS

Kedesh

Achzib

Hazor

KARNAIM

ACHZIB-

Acco

Karnaim

ACCO

Lake
Gennesaret

Beth-
yerah

Yarmuk

Mt. Carmel

Dor

The Great

Strato's
Tower

Narbatah

Beth-shan

Pella

GILEAD

Sea

Jabbok

Samaria

Apollonia

Mt. Ebal
Mt. Gerizim   Shechem

SAMARIA

Aphek

Accrabbah

Joppa

Shiloh

Ono

Neballat

Rabbah

Lod

Hadid

Gittaim

Lower
Beth-horon

Beeroth

Bethel
Ai

Tyre of Tobiah

Jamnia

Mizpah

Ramah

Beth-gilgal

AMMON

Gezer

Gibeon

Geba

Jericho

Kiriath-jearim

Anathoth

Heshbon

Ashdod

Beth-haccherem

Jerusalem

Medeba

Zanoah

YAHUD

Ashkelon

Azekah

Adullam

Bethlehem

Netophah

ASHDOD

Keilah

Tekoa

Mareshah

Nebo

Beth-zur

Salt

Lachish

Sea

Gaza

Hebron

En-gedi

Arnon

Gerar

Ziklag?

En-rimmon

IDUMEA

MOAB

Jeshua?

Beer-sheba

Moladah

(EDOMITES)

Beth-pelet?

NABATEANS

and as the one who authorized the rebuilding of the Jerusalem temple (2 Chron. 36:22–23; Ezra 1:1–2; 3:7; 4:3).

The reign of Darius I provides the dating framework for the books of Haggai and Zechariah. Artaxerxes is mentioned in Ezra 6:14; 7:1; 9:9 and in Neh. 2:1; 5:14; 13:6. The story of Esther is set in the reign of Ahasuerus (Xerxes; 1:1–2). A later Darius (II or III) is named in Neh. 12:22.

Both Esther and Daniel refer to Medes and Persians together (Esther 1:3, 18–19; Dan. 5:8; 6:28), particularly to stress the inalterability of their laws. Daniel distinguishes a Medan from a Persian empire (5:31; 6:28; cf. 10:1), but also treats the two as one (8:20). Dan. 10:13, 20–21, dealing with the conflicts of the empires, speaks of a "prince of Persia" against whom the angel Michael represents divine power on behalf of the Jews (cf. also 11:2). In a list of officials in Ezra 4:9–10, Persians and other peoples appear among those who were settled in Samaria and elsewhere by Osnappar (probably Ashurbanipal).

Lack of precision in statements about Persia suggests limited knowledge among the Jews. The impression of benevolent Persian protection is clear in some passages (e.g., Ezra 1:11; 5:5; 7:6, 9, 27; Neh. 2:8), but is not borne out by hostile material in Ezra 4:8–23 or by distress under Persian rule indicated in Ezra 9:9 and Neh. 9:36–37. Persia, like other ancient empires, taxed local populations heavily; imperial policy was dictated by strategic and economic needs, especially in wars against Egypt, which necessarily affected Judah, and against Greece. The empire was skillfully administered, but rebellions were frequent, including those of satraps in the province Beyond the River, to which Judah belonged.

Religion: The nature of Persian religion in this period remains a matter of debate. Although Zoroaster seems to have lived in the seventh century BCE, how far and when the particular emphases and practices of Zoroastrianism spread remains unclear. Nevertheless, influences from Zoroastrianism on Judaism and Christianity are sometimes intimated, and these would be traced to the period of Persian rule over Judea. *See also* Artaxerxes; Cyrus II; Darius; Ezra; Ezra and Nehemiah, books of; Medes, Media.

Bibliography

Boyce, Mary. *Zoroastrians: Their Religious Beliefs and Practices.* Routledge, 1979.

Cook, J. M. *The Persian Empire.* Dent, 1983.

P.R.A.

Persis (puhr´sis), a woman greeted by Paul as "beloved" and as "one who has worked hard in the Lord" (Rom. 16:12). The name Persis is known to have been a common one for slaves.

pestle, a crushing instrument used in a vessel (mortar) to grind grain, spices, or condiments; it was usually short, hand-held, and made of wood or stone. Prov. 27:22 says that if a fool were crushed with a pestle, the folly would not be driven out (because it belongs intrinsically to the fool's very nature).

Peter

PETER WAS A GALILEAN and one of the twelve disciples of Jesus. His given name was Simon, but Jesus bestowed upon him the nickname "Peter" (Gk., "rock"; Matt. 10:2; Mark 3:16; Luke 6:14). He is sometimes referred to as Cephas, the Aramaic version of that name, which Jesus would no doubt have actually used (John 1:42). Peter is variously identified as the "son of Jonah" (Matt. 16:17) and "son of John" (John 1:42), though some interpreters regard the former designation as metaphorical (indicating, perhaps, a relationship to the prophet Jonah; cf. Matt. 16:4).

Overview: The Gospels agree on certain pieces of information about Simon Peter. He had a brother Andrew, who was by trade a fisherman and was called by Jesus as one of his first disciples. The Synoptics further report that Peter was a resident of Capernaum and spoke with the characteristic Galilean accent (Matt. 26:73; Mark 14:70; Luke 22:59). He was married (Matt. 8:14; Mark 1:30; Luke 4:2; 1 Cor. 9:5), and his mother-in-law lived with his family. Jesus called him as a disciple and commissioned him to "fish for people" (Matt. 4:19; Mark 1:17; Luke 5:10). His name appears first on every list of the twelve (Matt. 10:2; Mark 3:16; Luke 6:16; cf. Acts 1:13).

In the Synoptic Gospels, Peter, James, and John often figure as an inner circle among Jesus's disciples, present at events when others are not. They are invited to accompany Jesus when he raises Jairus's daughter from the dead (Mark 5:37; Luke 8:51), when he is transfigured on a mountaintop (Matt. 17:1; Mark 9:2; Luke 9:28), and when he prays in Gethsemane (Matt. 26:37; Mark 14:33). Mark's Gospel reports an incident in which the three of them question Jesus privately (13:3), and Luke indicates that Peter and John were the two disciples selected to prepare Jesus's final Passover meal (22:8). In contrast to the rich man who declined Jesus's invitation to discipleship, Peter speaks for the group about their renunciation of wealth (Matt. 19:27; Mark 10:28; Luke 18:28). Most important of all, perhaps, Peter is portrayed in all three of the Synoptic Gospels as the first of the disciples to confess Jesus to be the Messiah, in response to Jesus's question, "Who do you say that I am?" (Matt. 16:15–16; Mark 8:29; Luke 9:20). But then, in two of the Gospels, he is also the one to receive Jesus's sternest rebuke, "Get behind me, Satan!" on account of his effort to dissuade Jesus from going to the cross (Matt. 16:22–23; Mark 8:32–33). Finally, the Gospels concur that Jesus predicted Peter's denial (Matt. 26:33–35; Mark 14:29–31; Luke 22:36–38; John 13:37–38) and that this prediction was fulfilled (Matt. 26:69–75; Mark 14:66–72; Luke 22:56–62; John 18:15–27).

Peter is singled out as one who will have a distinctive role in the post-Easter church (Matt. 16:17–19; Luke 22:31–32), and various biblical traditions indicate that the risen Lord appeared privately to him (Luke 24:34; 1 Cor. 15:5; cf. John 21:15–19). Peter plays a leading role in the ministry of the early church described in the book of Acts (see 1–5; 8:14–25; 9:32–11:18; 12:1–19), and he is also mentioned as a missionary and "pillar of the church" in Paul's letters (1 Cor. 9:5; Gal. 2:9). Fairly reliable church tradition indicates that Peter was martyred in Rome under the emperor Nero ca. 64–68 CE. Not surprisingly, numerous pseudepigraphical works were produced in his name, including a *Gospel of Peter,* an *Acts of Peter,* and an *Apocalypse of Peter,* none of which appear to bear any connection to the actual apostle or to be expressive of his thoughts. Most scholars also view the NT letter called 2 Peter as pseudepigraphical, and some regard 1 Peter as pseudepigraphical as well.

Distinctive Portraits of Peter in the NT: The various NT authors all present Peter in somewhat distinctive ways.

Peter in Mark: The Gospel of Mark tends to emphasize the failings of Jesus's disciples and this is true of its portrayal of Peter. He rarely says or does anything worthy of approval—even his confession of Jesus as the Messiah is met with a stern warning not to tell anyone (8:30). In general, Peter is no worse than the other disciples in Mark, but he is ultimately no better. When he earns Jesus's "Get behind me, Satan!" rebuke, he does so by expressing aloud what was probably the view of all the disciples (cf. 8:33; "looking at his disciples, he rebuked Peter"). Likewise, Peter's denial of Jesus does not mark him as worse than the others, who deserted Jesus (Mark 14:50). Rather, Peter is presented as the one who holds out the longest, but he ultimately succumbs to apostasy as well.

Peter in Matthew: The Gospel of Matthew is notable for containing several stories about Peter not found anywhere else. First, the story of Jesus walking on water is greatly expanded in Matthew's Gospel to include an account of Peter's also walking on water, though his success is only momentary; his fear and doubt cause him to sink and require rescue by Jesus (14:28–31). Another story presents Jesus instructing Peter to catch a fish that has a coin in its mouth sufficient to pay the temple tax for both of them (17:24–27). And in another instance, Peter is presented

Jesus hands the keys to the kingdom of heaven to Peter (Matt. 16:19) in this fifteenth-century fresco by Perugino in the Sistine Chapel.

as asking Jesus whether it is appropriate to forgive someone as many as seven times, prompting Jesus to respond, "Not seven times, but, I tell you, seventy-seven times," and to tell a parable illustrating the need for forgiveness (18:21–35). Most significant, however, is Matthew's considerable expansion of the story in which Peter confesses Jesus to be the Messiah. In this Gospel, Jesus responds by blessing Peter as one who received this knowledge directly from the Father in heaven (16:17). Further, he identifies Peter as the rock on which he will build his church (16:18), and he promises to give Peter the keys to the kingdom of heaven, so that whatever he binds on earth will be bound in heaven and whatever he looses on earth will be loosed in heaven (16:19). The precise meaning of this latter sentence is unclear, but it probably refers to possessing the authority to unlock or reveal God's will by interpreting Torah, binding commandments in situations where they apply and relaxing them in contexts where they do not apply. Matthew's Gospel indicates that this authority would ultimately be given to all of the apostles and, perhaps, to the whole church (18:17–20), but Peter is nevertheless recognized as possessing a status that was somewhat unique among the twelve.

Peter in Luke: The Gospel of Luke adds three scenes that serve to confirm Peter's status as the leader of the twelve. First, in the story of the miraculously great catch of fish (not reported in Matthew or Mark), Peter's devotion to Jesus is especially highlighted (5:1–11; cf. John 21:1–11). His words, "Go away from me, Lord, for I am a sinful man" (5:8), express the sort of humble confession that Luke's Gospel maintains is especially pleasing to God (cf. 18:13–14). Second, at the Last Supper, Jesus reveals that Peter will be attacked by Satan (22:31), but as a result of Jesus's supportive prayer he will be able to turn and strengthen the others (22:32); thus, the episode that leads to his denial of Jesus is presented as a necessary trial that ultimately serves a beneficial purpose (after he has recovered, he will be stronger and better able to help others). Finally, Luke reports that the risen Jesus appeared uniquely to Peter, though nothing is said about what transpired during that meeting (24:34; cf. 1 Cor. 15:5). Luke's portrayal of Peter is also significant for what it omits—the "Get behind me Satan!" episode is completely missing. Scholars also detect an apologetic element in Luke's portrayal that explains or mutes what might be regarded as failings. For example, he retains the account of Peter and other disciples falling asleep in Gethsemane when Jesus had told them to watch, but he explains that they were tired because of their grief (22:45–46; cf. Mark 14:37–41). Likewise, Luke insists that although Peter denies Jesus, his *faith* does not fail (22:32); the point seems to be that, even though Peter was a coward and told a lie, he never actually quit believing in Jesus as the Messiah.

Peter in Acts: The somewhat sanitized portrait of Peter in Luke's Gospel prepares readers for what follows in the book of Acts. There, Peter appears at once to be in charge of the church, leading the process to find a replacement for Judas (1:15–26). And then, as the narrative unfolds, Peter conducts a spirit-filled ministry as one who speaks and acts as an utterly reliable agent of God. Indeed, scholars have noted that the principal events of Peter's ministry in Acts all seem to parallel key events in the life and ministry of Jesus as related in the Gospel of Luke. (1) *Peter is filled with the Holy Spirit while praying* (2:1–13; cf. 1:14). In the Gospel of Luke, Jesus is filled with the Holy Spirit, not at the moment of his baptism, as in the other Synoptic Gospels, but while praying (3:21–22). (2) *Peter preaches a sermon explaining why this has happened* (2:14–40). In the Gospel of Luke, Jesus preaches a (short) sermon that explains why the Spirit of the Lord has come upon him (4:16–30). He claims that what has happened is the fulfillment of biblical prophecy (from the book of Isaiah), just as Peter claims the Spirit's descent on the apostles is the fulfillment of biblical prophecy (from the book of Joel). (3) *Peter heals a lame man in the name of Jesus and encounters trouble with the religious leaders* (3:1–4:22). In the Gospel of Luke, Jesus gets in trouble with the religious leaders of Israel for the first time when he heals a man who cannot walk (5:17–26). (4) *Peter heals a paralytic, telling him to "Get up and make your bed!"* (9:32–34). In the Gospel of Luke, Jesus heals a paralytic, telling him to "Stand up, take your bed, and go to your home" (5:17–26). (5) *Peter raises a widow from the dead* (9:36–43). In the Gospel of Luke, Jesus raises a widow's *son* from the dead (7:11–17). (6) *Peter ministers to a Gentile centurion* (Acts 10). In the Gospel of Luke, Jesus ministers to a Gentile centurion by healing his servant (7:1–10). In both stories the question of whether it is appropriate for a Jewish man to enter the house of a Gentile poses an obstacle that must be overcome. (7) *Peter is criticized by (Christian) Pharisees for eating with Gentiles* (11:1–18; 15:5). In the Gospel of Luke, Jesus is criticized by Pharisees for eating with sinners (5:50; 7:39; 15:2). (8) *Peter is delivered from prison by an angel* (12:1–9). There is no exact parallel for this regarding Jesus in the Gospel of Luke, but if the tomb of Jesus is something like a prison, then there is an account of Jesus being freed from *that* prison (24:1–11); both stories involve an angel who opens the enclosed space.

Peter represented dictating to Mark, following an early Christian tradition; ivory relief.

The reason for such parallels between Jesus in Luke and Peter in Acts is not absolutely clear, but Luke seems intent on presenting Peter as the representative apostle who continues the ministry of Jesus. In the Gospel of Luke, Jesus implies that when his disciples are "fully taught" they will be like him (6:40). As one instructed by Jesus (Luke 24:44–48) and empowered by the Spirit, Peter demonstrates the potential for such a vision to be fulfilled. In Acts, he sometimes functions as a virtual stand-in for Jesus himself. He can heal people in the name of Jesus (3:6), or he can simply speak for Jesus, as when he tells Aeneas the paralytic, "Jesus Christ heals you" (9:34). Indeed, Peter is so filled with spiritual power that any sick person upon whom his shadow falls is healed of their disease (5:15–16; cf. the power invested in Jesus's garments in Luke 8:43–48). Peter is also able to know the secret thoughts of others (5:3), to discern the hidden meaning of scripture (1:15–22; 2:16–22, 25–32; 4:11, 24–26), to interact freely with angels (5:19–20; 8:26), and to pass authoritative words of judgment upon the wicked (5:1–10; 8:20–23).

Peter in John: The Fourth Gospel presents Peter quite differently. In this account, Andrew is called first (1:40–41), and he brings his brother Peter to Jesus. Most of the other stories about Peter in the Synoptic Gospels are without parallel in John. After Jesus presents some difficult teaching, John notes that many of his disciples deserted him. When Jesus asks the twelve, "Do you also wish to go away?" Peter apparently speaks for them all in saying, "Lord, to whom can we go? You have the words of eternal life. We have come to believe and know that you are the Holy One of God" (6:66–69). This account might be regarded as a rough analogy to the synoptic account of Peter confessing Jesus to be the Messiah at Caesarea Philippi (Matt. 16:15–16; Mark 8:29; Luke 9:20). Peter is not singled out again until the story of Jesus washing his disciples' feet on the night of his arrest. He objects and has to be told that he will understand the meaning of the action later (13:6–10). In the story of that arrest, John's Gospel identifies Peter as the disciple who fights for Jesus with a sword, cutting off the ear of the high priest's servant, which is not pleasing to Jesus (18:10–11; cf. Matt. 26:51–52; Mark 14:47; Luke 22:50–51). Finally, in the concluding chapter of John's Gospel, the risen Jesus confronts Peter three times with the question, "Do you love me?" When Peter responds that he does, Jesus says, "Feed my lambs" or "Feed my sheep" (21:15–17). Then Jesus tells Peter, "When you were younger, you used to fasten your own belt and go wherever you wished. But when you grow old, you will stretch out your hands, and someone else will fasten a belt around you and take you where you do not wish to go" (21:8). According to the author of John's Gospel, this enigmatic saying indicated "the kind of death by which (Peter) would glorify God," i.e., death by crucifixion (21:9).

The most notable aspect of Peter's portrayal in John's Gospel may be the relationship established between Peter and the unnamed disciple called "the disciple whom Jesus loved." The two are often mentioned together in contexts that seem to portend competition or "friendly rivalry." Peter does not know the identity of Jesus's betrayer and must ask this other disciple (who is closer to Jesus at the table) for the information (13:24). Later, Peter and the Beloved Disciple run to the empty tomb, but the latter runs faster and arrives there first; he nevertheless waits for

Peter's threefold denial of Jesus as the rooster crows
(Matt. 26:69–75); fifth-century ivory detail.

Peter, who enters the tomb first, but when the Beloved Disciple enters the tomb behind Peter, he is the one who sees and believes (20:1–9). Still later, when the risen Jesus appears to the disciples when they are fishing, it is the Beloved Disciple who tells Peter, "It is the Lord!" (21:3–7). And then, after Jesus indicates how Peter is going to die, Peter responds by asking what will become of the Beloved Disciple, prompting Jesus to respond, "If it is my will that he remain until I come, what is that to you? Follow me!" (21:22).

Peter in the Letters of Paul: Paul typically refers to Peter as Cephas. In 1 Corinthians, he indicates that some of the members of the church in Corinth identify themselves as belonging to Cephas, while others identify themselves as belonging to Apollos or to Paul (1:12, 22). This might indicate that Peter had been active in Corinth, perhaps baptizing some of the church members (1:13–15). In any case, Paul does not appear to regard Peter as a competitor; rather, he urges the Corinthians not to focus on human leaders, but to view themselves as the body of Christ (1 Cor. 12). In Gal. 2:7–8, however, Paul seems to distinguish between his calling and that of Peter. He was entrusted with the gospel for the uncircumcised (i.e., Gentiles), while Peter was entrusted with the gospel for the circumcised (i.e., Jews). Against the backdrop of this understanding, Paul also relates an incident in which he publicly accused Peter of hypocrisy in the church at Antioch (Gal. 2:11–14). The crisis involved the issue of table fellowship. Representatives of James (brother of Jesus and leader of the Jerusalem church) encouraged the Jewish Christians in that community to observe Jewish dietary laws, even though this required them to separate themselves from the Gentile Christians when the community shared meals together (including, no doubt, celebrations of the Lord's Supper). Paul and Barnabas had instituted a different policy in Antioch, one that involved a common table for Jews and Gentiles alike. Peter apparently went along with this until certain people from James came to the church—then he withdrew and would no longer eat with the Gentiles. Paul maintains that Peter acted out of "fear of the circumcision faction" (2:12) and that he stood "self-condemned" (2:11).

The Petrine Tradition in 1 and 2 Peter: Peter's authorship of the two letters that bear his name is disputed, though a considerable number of scholars are willing to allow that 1 Peter comes either from the apostle himself or from a circle of his followers whose views represent the tradition associated with his name. One intriguing aspect, then, is that 1 Peter appears to have been written from Rome (called "Babylon" in 5:13) to Gentile believers in Asia Minor (1:1; for their status as Gentiles, see 1:14, 18; 4:3–4). The notion of Peter being in Rome is not corroborated by any other biblical data, but it corresponds broadly to the fact that he and his wife traveled as missionaries (1 Cor. 9:5) and with extrabiblical tradition that he died in Rome (see below). The idea that he would be writing to Gentile Christians seems to conflict with Paul's claim that Peter was called to be an apostle "to the circumcised" (Gal. 2:7–8), but it may be corroborated by stories in Acts that portray him as one of the initiators of Gentile missions (Acts 10; cf. 15:7) and by his known activity in such Gentile-heavy areas as Antioch (Gal. 2:11) and Corinth (1 Cor. 1:12; 9:5). When 1 Peter is read as a document expressive of Petrine tradition, however, it is often noted that this tradition seems remarkably indistinctive. There is almost nothing in 1 Peter that stands out as unique; rather, the letter seems expressive of what might be considered mainstream, non-controversial Christian ideas. Some scholars argue that this was precisely what typified Peter and the Petrine tradition.

As indicated, the great majority of scholars do not regard 2 Peter as an authentic composition of the apostle Peter, nor do they think it has any reliable claim to have been produced by persons who had known Peter or worked with him. What this letter does indicate, however, is that, by the early second century, Peter had become a person of considerable stature and, specifically, had come to be regarded as a guarantor of orthodox tradition. Peter is remembered as an elder statesman of Christianity whose views are to be regarded as the antithesis of troubling innovation.

Death of Peter: Christian tradition holds that Peter was martyred in Rome under the emperor Nero, that he was put to death by crucifixion, and, specifically, that he was crucified upside down. As indicated above, John 21:18–19 indicates that Peter would die with outstretched hands; this seems to be an allusion to crucifixion (though not, actually, to upside-down crucifixion). Clement of Rome (ca. 96 CE) says that, "because of jealousy and envy the greatest and most upright pillars were persecuted, and they struggled in the contest even to death. . . . Peter bore up under hardships not just once or twice, but many times; and having thus borne his witness he went to the place of glory that he deserved" (*1 Clement* 5:2–4). Around a hundred years later, Tertullian states that Nero was the one responsible for the apostles' deaths (*Antidote for the Scorpion's Sting* 15). He also refers to Rome as "a fortunate church . . . where Peter had a passion like that of the Lord, where Paul was crowned with the death of John" (*On the Prescription of Heretics* 35). The reference to Peter having a passion "like that of the Lord" probably refers, again, to crucifixion (Paul's death was like that of John the Baptist, because he was beheaded). Peter's death in Rome also receives minor support from archaeological investigations under St. Peter's Basilica in Rome, where an early shrine to Peter, located in an ancient cemetery, was allegedly built over his grave. Although there is no certainty, most scholars regard the tradition that Peter was crucified as relatively secure and see no strong reason to doubt that this would have occurred in Rome during the time of Nero.

The specific idea that Peter was crucified upside down comes from the apocryphal *Acts of Peter,* a fanciful second-century work that is not usually given much credence by religious scholars. In this case, however, the work devotes several paragraphs to explaining why Peter was crucified in this manner: Peter himself requested it and then explained the elaborate and esoteric symbolism of the act (something like birth imagery, recalling Adam). The analogy is sufficiently strained as to seem apologetic. The author of this work would probably not have invented the idea that Peter was crucified upside down in order to make the rather elusive point; more likely, that point would have been developed in an attempt to find meaning in something that was otherwise simply horrifying. In this regard, the Roman historian Josephus does note that soldiers would sometimes amuse themselves by crucifying criminals in humiliating positions, so it is possible that the *Acts of Peter* is attempting to help Christians deal with an awful fact regarding Peter's execution that other ecclesiastical figures thought was best left unsaid. *See also* Acts of the Apostles; Antioch; Capernaum; Peter, First Letter of; Peter, Second Letter of.

Bibliography

Brown, Raymond E., Karl P. Donfried, and John Reumann, eds. *Peter in the New Testament.* Augsburg, 1973.

Lapham, Fred. *Peter: The Myth, the Man, and the Writings: A Study of Early Petrine Text and Traditions.* Sheffield Academic, 2000.

Perkins, Pheme. *Peter: Apostle for the Whole Church.* University of South Carolina Press, 1994.

Powell, Mark Allan. *Introducing the New Testament: A Historical, Literary, and Theological Survey.* Baker Academic, 2009. M.A.P.

Peter, First Letter of, the first of two NT letters attributed to the apostle Peter (1:1) and one of the seven Catholic (or General) Letters.

Contents: The letter opens with a salutation that identifies the author as "Peter, an apostle of Jesus Christ" and designates the readers as "exiles of the Dispersion" who inhabit five regions of Asia Minor (1:1–3). It continues with an eloquent blessing of God that segues into a call for the readers to rejoice in the salvation that God is providing for them (1:3–9); they have received a new birth and await their glorious inheritance with hope, faith, and love that cannot be tarnished by suffering temporary trials. What was predicted by prophets is now a reality, announced through the gospel (1:10–12). Therefore, the readers should discipline themselves for lives appropriate to the gospel, lives marked by obedient holiness, reverent fear, mutual love, and continued spiritual growth rather than by the ignorant desires and futile ways of their former lives (1:13–2:3). Their new identity as God's chosen people allows them to be built into a living house for God to inhabit (2:4–10). The author exhorts the readers as aliens and exiles to abstain from evil and to conduct themselves honorably (2:11–12). They are to honor the emperor, as instituted by God (2:13–17). Further instructions are provided for slaves (2:13–25), wives (3:1–6), and husbands (3:7). In general, they should conduct themselves in ways that do not invite opposition, and they should regard any abuse they suffer for doing good as a blessing (3:8–17). In this way they follow the example of Christ, whose suffering secured salvation for the baptized and led to a vindication over all angels and spiritual powers (3:18–22). In keeping with this, their intention must be to live in a distinctive way, as stewards of God's grace and gifts, ready to give an account of themselves in the final judgment, which is near (4:1–11). The next section of the letter seems to recapitulate previous exhortations regarding the proper response to suffering (4:12–19). The readers should not be surprised by the "fiery ordeal" that tests them; indeed, they should rejoice insofar as they share Christ's suffering and suffer in accordance with God's will. Then the author speaks "as an elder" to encourage church leaders to exercise their office responsibly and to urge others to submit to their leadership (5:1–5). He exhorts everyone to humility and steadfastness, and he assures his readers that, even though their adversary, the devil, is on the prowl, God's deliverance is near (5:6–11). The letter closes with greetings and a benediction (5:12–14).

Authorship: The letter was widely regarded as pseudepigraphical throughout most of the twentieth century for reasons that would eventually be discarded. (1) It is written in relatively refined Greek beyond what would be expected of a Galilean fisherman (but scholars now recognize that Peter probably would have employed an amanuensis to put his thoughts into writing). (2) It refers to widespread suffering of Christians in Asia Minor, and imperial persecutions did not take place there

until decades after Peter's death (but scholars now believe the suffering referenced in this letter to be social discrimination and harassment, not government-sponsored violence). (3) It evinces numerous parallels with other NT books, suggesting a collection of such writings that would not have been available in Peter's lifetime (but most scholars now attribute those parallels to shared traditions, not literary dependence). Although admitting that the case for pseudepigraphy is not as strong as it once seemed, the majority of scholars still regard 1 Peter as pseudepigraphical for other reasons. For example, the use of "Babylon" as an epithet for Rome (5:13) did not become popular among Jews and Christians until after 70 CE. Also, a date toward the end of the first century would allow more time for Christian trajectories to synthesize into the common tradition expressed in the letter and would also allow more time for the churches in Asia Minor to develop into the established institutions that they appear to be. A growing minority of scholars, however, now regard the letter as authentic. A popular theory espoused by many who deem it authentic allows that Peter

OUTLINE OF CONTENTS

1 Peter

J.H.N.

IMAGES FOR THE CHURCH IN 1 PETER

The Dispersion: exiles on earth, separated from the true home in heaven (1:1, 17; 2:11)

The new Israel: a chosen race and a holy nation (2:9; cf. Isa. 43:20; Deut. 7:6; 10:15); God's own people (2:9; cf. Exod. 19:5; Isa. 43:21)

A priesthood of all believers: a holy priesthood (2:5); a royal priesthood (2:9; cf. Exod. 19:6)

A living temple: a spiritual house made of living stones, where spiritual sacrifices are offered (2:5; cf. 1 Cor. 3:16)

A flock of sheep: tended by pastors (shepherds) with Christ as chief shepherd (2:25; 5:3–4; cf. John 10:11; 21:15–19; Acts 20:28; Isa 40:11; Ezek. 34:12)

A woman: "your sister church in Babylon" (5:13), a reference to an individual congregation as a woman (lit., "she who is in Babylon"; cf. 2 John 1).

From Mark Allan Powell, *Introducing the New Testament* (courtesy, Baker Academic)

might have entrusted his stated coauthor, Silas, with much of the letter, and that this could explain the numerous parallels to Pauline writings (assuming this was the same Silas who had been a frequent companion of Paul).

Historical Setting: The letter is addressed to Gentile Christians (1:14, 18; 4:3–4) in Asia Minor who are suffering for their faith (1:6, 2:19). A number of passages seem to assume that the readers are relatively new to the faith (e.g., 2:2–3; cf. 1 Cor. 3:2; Heb. 5:12–13), and this has prompted some interpreters to suggest that the letter may have originated as a baptismal homily (cf. 3:21). If the letter is authentic, it was probably composed in the early to middle 60s CE, after Peter came to Rome but before Nero began his violent attacks on believers (cf. 2:13–14). If it is pseudepigraphical, it could have been written at almost any time in the last three decades of the first century.

Major Themes: The most notable aspect of 1 Peter may be its frequent references to suffering (1:6, 11; 2:19–23; 3:14, 17–18; 4:1, 13, 15–16, 19; 5:1, 9–10). There is an assumption that members of the church are "aliens" on earth, or people lacking the honor and support they would typically derive from family and civic ties (1:1, 17, but cf. 1:2–5). The letter calls for endurance, reflects upon the meaning and value of suffering, and prescribes practical steps the readers might take to make life more bearable (e.g., they should look to the church as a support community and not behave in ways that antagonize the opposition unnecessarily). Another prominent theme in 1 Peter is the depiction of Christians as the new Israel; terminology and categories traditionally employed for Jews are applied to Gentile Christians (1:1, 8–12; 2:9)—and the term "Gentile" is used

as an epithet for pagans or unbelievers (2:12; 4:3). Thus, 1 Peter interprets conversion to God and to Jesus as "a new birth" (1:3, 23) involving a radical change of identity and status. *See also* baptism; Catholic Letters/Epistles; Peter; Rome.

Bibliography

Achtemeier, Paul J. *1 Peter: A Commentary on First Peter.* Fortress, 1996.

Chester, Andrew, and Ralph P. Martin. *The Theology of James, Peter, and Jude.* Cambridge University Press, 1994.

Elliott, John H. *1 Peter.* Doubleday, 2000.

Jobes, Karen. *1 Peter.* Baker Academic, 2005.

Powell, Mark Allan. *Introducing the New Testament: A Historical, Literary, and Theological Survey.* Baker Academic, 2009. Pp. 463–79.   M.A.P.

Peter, Second Letter of, a second letter in the NT collection purported to be from the apostle Peter (3:1) and classified as one of the seven Catholic (or General) Letters. Most scholars regard the letter as pseudepigraphical. Parts of 2 Peter are remarkably similar to Jude.

Contents: The letter opens with a traditional salutation and blessing identifying it as a message from the apostle "Simeon Peter" to all believers who share his faith (1:1–2). The author declares that God has provided believers with everything necessary for a godly life, and he exhorts them to capitalize upon this in fruitful ways that will confirm their election (1:3–11). His own death is near, and he is writing to them so that after he is gone they will be able to recall those things that they know now to be true (1:12–15). He was a witness to the transfiguration of Jesus, which confirms the truth of Christ's power and coming, to which Spirit-inspired prophecies also attest (1:16–21). The author then announces that false teachers will

---

OUTLINE OF CONTENTS

---

2 Peter

                                          J.H.N.

arise in the church, marked by both "destructive opinions" and "licentious ways" (2:1–3a). He provides a brief history of God's judgment upon the wicked to make clear that these false teachers will also be condemned (2:3b–10a). Then he offers a blistering attack on the teachers, describing them as greedy, moral reprobates who promise freedom but deliver slavery (2:10b–22). The author says he is writing to remind the readers to hold fast to the tradition delivered to them by prophets and apostles (3:1–2). Then he turns his attention to the Second Coming of Jesus, dispelling arguments that scoffers use for rejecting its relevance (3:3–9) and exhorting the readers to live in anticipation of the fiery judgment and glorious salvation that

it will bring (3:10–13). The letter concludes with a few final exhortations and a doxology to Jesus Christ (3:14–18).

Authorship: The reasons given for regarding this letter as pseudepigraphical are many. (1) It is very different from 1 Peter in language, theology, and tone. (2) It appears to draw upon the Letter of Jude (written near the end of Peter's life at the earliest) as a source. (3) It is written from a very Hellenistic viewpoint (1:4; 2:4), which is inconsistent with what would be expected of a Galilean known as an apostle to Jews (Gal. 2:7–8). (4) It deals with the problem created by a common perception that the promise of Christ's coming had not been fulfilled (3:4), and this would not

PARALLELS BETWEEN JUDE AND 2 PETER

	Jude		*2 Peter*
v. 4	stole into the community	2:1	bring in opinions secretly
v. 4	long ago designated for condemnation	2:3	condemnation pronounced long ago
v. 4	pervert the grace of God	2:2	way of truth is maligned
v. 4	licentiousness	2:2	licentious ways
v. 4	deny our Master	2:1	even deny the Master
v. 6	angels kept in chains in deepest darkness for judgment	2:4	angels kept in chains in deepest darkness until judgment
v. 7	Sodom and Gomorrah serve as an example	2:6	Sodom and Gomorrah made an example
v. 7	unnatural lust	2:10	depraved lust
v. 8	defile the flesh, reject authority, and slander the glorious ones	2:10	indulge their flesh, despise authority, and slander the glorious ones
v. 9	archangel did not bring a condemnation of slander	2:11	angels do not bring a slanderous judgment
v. 10	slander what they do not understand	2:12	slander what they do not understand
v. 10	like irrational animals, live by instinct, and are destroyed	2:12	like irrational animals, creatures of instinct, will be destroyed
v. 11	"Woe to them!"	2:14	"Accursed children!"
v. 11	abandon themselves to Balaam's error	2:15	follow the way of Balaam
v. 11	error for the sake of gain	2:15	wages of doing wrong
v. 12	blemishes on your love feasts	2:13	blemishes (at your feasts)
v. 12	feast with you without fear	2:13	revel while they feast with you
v. 12	waterless clouds	2:17	waterless springs
v. 12	clouds carried along by the winds	2:17	mists driven by a storm
v. 13	deepest darkness reserved for them	2:17	deepest darkness reserved for them
v. 16	bombastic, flatter people	2:18	bombastic, entice people
v. 17	remember predictions of apostles	3:2	remember commandments spoken through apostles
v. 18	in the last time, scoffers will come, indulging their own lusts	3:3	in last days, scoffers will come, indulging their own lusts

From Mark Allan Powell, *Introducing the New Testament* (courtesy, Baker Academic)

have been an issue while followers of Jesus were still alive. (5) It speaks of apostolic tradition as a norm to be defended (3:2), reflecting the perspective of a postapostolic age. (6) It makes explicit reference to the deaths of "our ancestors" (3:4), which most scholars take to mean the apostles or the first generation of Christians. (7) It refers to Paul's letters as a group of writings that are being studied and interpreted in divergent ways within the church (3:15–16). (8) It shifts back and forth between using the future tense to present Peter predicting things that will happen after his death (2:1–3; 3:1–4) and the present tense to address readers for whom those predictions are apparently coming true (2:10–22; 3:5–7). (9) It had considerable trouble gaining recognition and acceptance within the church, something that would not have happened if there had been confidence that it had actually been written by Peter. Indeed, 2 Peter is never even mentioned in church writings until the third century, and then it is only alluded to in a passage from Origen of Alexandria, who questions its legitimacy. A few scholars do try to respond to these arguments and argue for authenticity of 2 Peter, but the great majority of scholars treat the letter as pseudepigraphical.

Genre: Second Peter is usually thought to belong to the literary genre of "testament," a popular form of writing in which a famous person from the past is presented as giving a fictive "deathbed speech" addressing issues of the day. Second Peter exhibits all of the standard literary conventions of a testament, with the exception that it is cast in the form of a letter (which causes some scholars to question the accuracy of this classification).

Historical Setting: Given the above considerations (regarding authorship and genre), 2 Peter is usually regarded as a second-century writing (100–125 CE) by which some church authority seeks to bring the legacy of Peter to bear on the problem of false teaching in the church. The exact content or form of the teaching that is opposed is difficult to determine. Two prominent suggestions (which are not mutually exclusive) are a variety of Christianity influenced by Gnosticism and a variety of Christianity influenced by Epicureanism. The false teachers are said to exhibit shocking moral laxity (2:10), to lure people into licentiousness (2:2), to disrespect ecclesial authorities (2:15, 21–22), to rely upon idiosyncratic interpretations of scripture (1:20–21; 3:16), and to scoff at the prospect of divine judgment or accountability (3:3–9).

Major Themes: As with the Letter of Jude (upon which 2 Peter seems to draw), there is more concern with condemning false teachers than with articulating why they are wrong. Thus, this letter's major theme is a simple affirmation of the certainty of judgment (2:4–6; 3:5–7, 10–12). It also addresses the faith crisis precipitated by an apparent delay of the Parousia. It says fulfillment of the promise only seems slow from a human perspective (3:8) and, indeed, the delay could be motivated by divine mercy (3:9). There is also strong exhortation to godliness, with regard to both the prospect of growth (1:4) and the avoidance of backsliding (2:20–21). *See also* Catholic Letters/ Epistles; Jude, Letter of; Parousia; Peter; Peter, First Letter of; testament.

Bibliography

Bauckham, Richard J. *Jude, 2 Peter*. Word, 1983.

Chester, Andrew, and Ralph P. Martin. *The Theology of James, Peter, and Jude*. Cambridge University Press, 1994.

Davids, Peter H. *2 Peter and Jude*. Eerdmans, 2006.

Neyrey, Jerome. *2 Peter, Jude*. Doubleday, 1993.

Powell, Mark Allan. *Introducing the New Testament: A Historical, Literary, and Theological Survey*. Baker Academic, 2009. Pp. 281–91.   M.A.P.

Pethahiah (peth´uh-hi´uh).

1 The head of the family to which the nineteenth division of the priesthood was assigned in the time of David (1 Chron. 24:16).

2 A Levite who participated in Ezra's penitential service (Neh. 9:5). He was among those who agreed to divorce their foreign wives in response to Ezra's proclamation (Ezra 10:23).

3 A Judahite of the time of Nehemiah who was "at the king's hand in all matters concerning the people" (Neh. 11:24). This may mean that he served as an adviser on Jewish affairs at the Persian court.

Pethor (pee´thor), a place in Mesopotamia from which Balaam was called by Barak, king of Moab, to curse Israel (Num. 22:5; Deut. 23:4). Pethor is also mentioned in the annals of Pharaoh Thutmose III of Egypt and of King Shalmaneser III of Assyria. It was located a little south of Carchemish, on the west side of the Euphrates on the Sagur River. It may be modern Tell Ahmar.

Phanuel (fuh-nyoo´uhl), a member of the tribe of Asher and the father of Anna, the aged Jewish prophetess who spoke of the future greatness of Jesus (Luke 2:36–38). *See also* Anna.

Pharaoh (fair´oh; Egyptian, "great house"), the Hebrew word for the title held by the king of Egypt. Sometimes the word is used in the Bible without further designation, as though it were the Egyptian ruler's name (e.g., Gen. 12:15–20). At other times it is used with a ruler's name (e.g., "Pharaoh Hophra," Jer. 44:30). The literal meaning of the term ("great house") reflects the fact that it was first used to designate the royal palace; this was the case up until the middle of the second millennium BCE. Starting with the reign of Thutmose III (1504–1450 BCE) in the Eighteenth Dynasty, the term was applied to the ruler himself, and, from the reign of the Twenty-Second Dynasty ruler Shoshenq I (945–924 BCE) on, the term can be found, just as in the Bible, prefixed to the king's name, e.g., "Pharaoh Shoshenq."

The pharaoh of Egypt was considered a god by his subjects. He was the embodiment of the royal falcon god Horus and, from at least the

One of the Colossi of Memnon representing
Amenophis III, 1403–1365 BCE; west bank of
the Nile at Thebes.

Fifth Dynasty (ca. 2494–2345 BCE) on was looked
upon as the son of the great sun god, Re. When
he died, he became the god Osiris and joined the
other divinities in the afterworld. Theoretically,
all of the land of Egypt and its products belonged
to Pharaoh (see Gen. 47:20), and his word was the
law of the land.

Throughout most of the third millennium BCE,
the king ran the government with the aid of members of the royal family. Toward the end of the
third millennium and into the early second, more
and more governmental authority became distributed among the nobles, and with the rise of
the Egyptian empire in the Eighteenth Dynasty
an enormous bureaucracy had to be established to
handle the affairs of government. The chief officer
in this bureaucracy was the vizier (Egyptian *tjaty*).
The description given in Gen. 41–47 of Joseph's
responsibilities under Pharaoh reflects the duties
of a vizier.

The king wore one of several crowns. The
"White Crown" symbolized his dominance of
Upper (southern) Egypt, while the "Red Crown"
symbolized his rulership of Lower (northern)
Egypt, and the "Double Crown" reflected his
control over both Upper and Lower Egypt. The
"Blue Crown," or war crown, was worn by the king
when he went into battle. The king is often depicted holding a shepherd's crook and a flail across
his chest as symbols of authority, while in battle
scenes he usually holds a mace or a short, curved
sword (the scimitar).

At least four, and possibly five, pharaohs are
mentioned by name in the Bible. There are also
many other references to unnamed Egyptian

kings, a few of whom can be identified with more
or less probability. The pharaohs mentioned by
name include:

1 Shishak, the Twenty-Second (Libyan) Dynasty
king Shoshenq I (945–924 BCE), who gave asylum
to Jeroboam (1 Kings 11:40) and later invaded the
Levant (1 Kings 14:25–26; 2 Chron. 12:1–9).

2 Tirhakah, the Twenty-Fifth (Kushite) Dynasty
king Taharqa (690–664 BCE), who is mentioned in
2 Kings 19:9 and Isa. 37:9 as the "king of Ethiopia."
Before he became king, he fought unsuccessfully
against the Assyrian king Sennacherib in 701 BCE.

3 Pharaoh Neco, the Twenty-Sixth (Saite) Dynasty king Neco II (610–595 BCE), who defeated
and killed Josiah at Megiddo in 609 BCE (2 Kings
23:29; 2 Chron. 35:20–24), removed Josiah's son
and successor, Jehoahaz, from the throne, and
put Jehoiakim in his place (2 Kings 23:30–35;
2 Chron. 36:1–4). Neco ultimately lost all of
Egypt's west Asiatic possessions to the Babylonian
king Nebuchadnezzar (2 Kings 24:7).

4 Pharaoh Hophra, the Twenty-Sixth (Saite)
Dynasty king Waibre (Gk. Apries; 589–570 BCE),
who Jeremiah said would be delivered into the
hands of his enemies, just as Zedekiah, king of
Judah, had been delivered into the hands of the
Babylonian king Nebuchadnezzar (Jer. 44:30).
Hophra later had to flee Egypt when a rebellion
broke out; he allied himself with Nebuchadnezzar
in an attempt to retake his throne, but the attack
was repulsed and he was executed.

5 So, the "king of Egypt" (2 Kings 17:4) to
whom King Hoshea sent messengers just before he
revolted against the Assyrians. No pharaoh, however, is known to have borne this name. The word
might refer to the Twenty-Second Dynasty king
Osorkon IV (ca. 727–720 BCE), or it might come
from an Egyptian epithet meaning "the Saite" and
thus refer to all of the kings of the Twenty-Sixth
(Saite) Dynasty (664–525 BCE).

Other, unnamed Egyptian kings who are prominently mentioned in the Bible include:

6 The pharaoh from the time of Abram (Gen.
12:15–20). He took Abram's wife Sarai into his
house after Abram told him she was his sister, but
the ruse was exposed after God afflicted his house
with great plagues.

7 The pharaoh of the Joseph story (Gen. 39–50).
Joseph alone was able to interpret his dreams and
to predict the years of famine that would come
upon the land. Pharaoh appointed Joseph to be
in charge of food distribution, making him the
second most powerful man in all Egypt.

8 The pharaoh of the oppression (Exod. 1–2),
whom many biblical scholars often equate with
either Sety I (1291–1279 BCE) or Ramesses II (1279–
1212 BCE). This was the new king who arose over
Egypt "who did not know Joseph" (Exod. 1:8).
Because the Hebrews had become more numerous and powerful than the Egyptians themselves,
he enslaved them, setting them to harsh labor. He
ordered all male babies born to the Hebrews to be
exterminated, but Moses was rescued from this
fate by Pharaoh's daughter, who raised him in the

palace as her child. The biblical text does not distinguish between this pharaoh and the pharaoh of the exodus, but some interpreters think the span of time is sufficient to allow for two rulers.

9 The pharaoh of the exodus (Exod. 5–12), often identified by biblical scholars as Ramesses II (1279–1212 BCE) or sometimes his son and successor, Merenptah (1212–1202 BCE). The adult Moses is sent before this pharaoh with his brother Aaron to demand the release of the Hebrew slaves. God sent plagues upon the land, but also repeatedly hardened Pharaoh's heart so that he refused to release the Hebrews until, finally, a tenth plague brought the death of every firstborn son in Egypt.

10 The pharaoh(s) who grants asylum to Hadad of Edom and gives Hadad his wife's sister in marriage (1 Kings 11:14–22). The first king (who grants asylum) may be the Twenty-First Dynasty Pharaoh Amenemope (993–984 BCE); the pharaoh responsible for the second action may also be Amenemope or he could be Siamun (978–959 BCE).

11 The pharaoh who takes Gezer and presents the city as a dowry to his daughter when she marries Solomon (1 Kings 9:16). This diplomatic marriage is also mentioned in 1 Kings 3:1; 7:8; 9:24; 11:1. This Pharaoh is probably the Twenty-First Dynasty king Siamun (978–959 BCE), though he could perhaps be Siamun's successor, Psusennes II (959–945 BCE). *See also* Neco II; Ramesses; Shishak; So; Tirhakah.

Bibliography

Frankfort, Henri. *Kingship and the Gods.* University of Chicago Press, 1948.

Gardiner, Alan H. *Egypt of the Pharaohs.* Clarendon, 1961.

Montet, Pierre. *Eternal Egypt.* Weidenfeld and Nicholson, 1964.   J.M.W.

Phares (fair´is), **Pharez** (fair´iz). *See* Perez.

Pharisees (fair´uh-seez), a group of particularly observant and influential Jews, mainly in Judea, from the second century BCE to the first century CE. The meaning of the name itself is obscure. It may mean "separate ones" in Hebrew, referring to their observance of ritual purity laws in ways that separated them from others, or it could mean "interpreters," referring to their penchant for studying and teaching biblical law. In many Gospel stories, the Pharisees function as the opponents of Jesus in Galilee. The apostle Paul, however, was raised a Pharisee and continued to regard himself as a Pharisee even after he became a missionary for Christ (see Phil. 3:5).

As Literary Figures: As characters in the Gospel narratives, the Pharisees play a somewhat stereotypical role as the antagonists of Jesus. In Matthew and Mark, particularly, they tend to be associated with scribes, Sadducees, chief priests, and other Jewish leaders in a way that such historical distinctions become almost irrelevant (cf. Matt. 3:7; 5:20; 16:1, 6–12; 21:45; 27:62; Mark 3:6; 12:13; esp. Mark 7:3); the religious leaders of Israel

in general function as a united front, opposed to Jesus and, perhaps, to God. The Gospel of Mark seems most interested in presenting them as critics of Jesus and his disciples (2:16, 24; 7:5) and as persons who want to put Jesus to the test (8:11; 10:2). Mark does not seem to have much interest in the Pharisees as such; their main function in the story is to set up opportunities for Jesus to say something profound, often at their expense. Mark does note their involvement in a plot to destroy Jesus (3:6), but they are not mentioned in connection with his crucifixion as such.

The Gospel of Matthew goes well beyond Mark in presenting the Pharisees as personifications of evil, as people incapable of speaking or thinking anything good (12:34; cf. 9:4; 12:39, 45; 16:4; 22:18). This quality identifies them closely with Satan, the evil one (13:19, 38–39). Throughout the Gospel they are identified with epithets that characterize them as offspring of the devil rather than as children of God: "brood of vipers" (3:7; 12:34; 23:33); "child of hell" (23:15). The meaning of such an identification becomes clear in a parable Jesus tells. The world is like a field in which God has placed potentially good people and the devil has placed evil people (13:24–30, 36–43). Jesus explicitly identifies the Pharisees as being among those "plants that the heavenly Father did not plant"; they are not God's people and they will be uprooted in time (15:13). Further, this portrayal is presented without exceptions (cf. the mention in other Gospels of Pharisees who are not opposed to Jesus: Luke 13:31; John 3:1–2; probably Mark 12:28–34). Likewise, in Matthew's Gospel (unlike the others) Jesus never summons Pharisees to repentance; he no more attempts to minister to them than he would to the demons he exorcizes. Rather, he counsels his disciples to "leave them alone" (15:14). They provide a paradigmatic example of people who will never enter the kingdom of heaven (5:20), and Jesus promises that they will not escape being sentenced to hell (23:33). Thus, Matthew's portrayal provides a fairly extreme example of the manner in which the Pharisees become literary ciphers who serve to advance the plot and message of the Gospel story. Matthew wants to portray Jesus as the Son of God though whom God overcomes the forces of ultimate evil, so the Pharisees (who may have been historical opponents of Jesus) become emblems of that evil, which must be defeated.

Something similar occurs in the Gospel of Luke, but here the Pharisees do not represent "evil" so much as "self-righteousness." The Pharisees in Luke's story are stereotypically persons who justify themselves in the sight of others (16:15) and who consider themselves righteous while regarding others with contempt (18:9). They proclaim their righteousness, exalting themselves at the expense of others (18:10–14). They are quick to denounce others as sinners (7:39) and to promote ostracism of such individuals (15:2). They think that they themselves need little forgiveness and, as a consequence, show little love (7:40–47). Almost as an aside, it is also noted in Luke that the Pharisees are "lovers of money" (16:14), and so they become foils for this Gospel's polemic against greed and materialism. In the book of Acts, Christian Pharisees become exemplars of believers who have an inadequate understanding of the gospel: they believe that Gentiles must be circumcised and told to keep the law of Moses (15:5). In Luke's writings, however, the Pharisees often seem to be more pitied than despised. Jesus eats with them (Luke 7:36; 11:37; 14:1), tries to correct them through teaching (11:37–41; 14:12–14; 15:1–32; 17:20–21), and tells them the benefits they will receive if they change their ways (11:41; 14:14; possibly 10:28). Further, certain Pharisees seem to be willing to give Jesus and his followers the benefit of the doubt (13:31; cf. Acts 5:34), and the portrait of Paul in Acts serves as an illustration of successful conversion of a Pharisee to the gospel of Christ (cf. 23:6; 25:5–6).

In the Gospel of John, the Pharisees seem to assume the role of persecutors. Though Nicodemus is an honest inquirer (3:1–2), the Pharisees are otherwise portrayed as united with the chief priests in sending temple police to arrest Jesus (7:32) and giving orders that anyone who knew Jesus's whereabouts should let them know so they can arrest him (11:57). Indeed, the Pharisees have the authority in this Gospel to call a meeting of "the council," a group at which the high priest Caiaphas is present (11:46–50). Only John reports that the Pharisees accompanied the chief priests and Judas to arrest Jesus (18:3). Further, the Pharisees are presented as harassing the man whom Jesus healed of blindness—as well as his parents—insisting that people must choose between being disciples of Moses or Jesus (9:13–28). The implications of this policy (9:22) are spelled out clearly in 12:42–43, where it is said that the Pharisees (who loved human glory more than the glory that comes from God) were expelling from synagogues any who confessed faith in Jesus. Thus, in John's Gospel the Pharisees appear to serve as exemplars of Jews who might have opposed the spread of Christianity or who at least wanted to preserve the distinctiveness of Jewish faith against the incursion of Christian ideas. In this way, the Gospel is probably using the historical tensions between Jesus and Pharisees to address (from a Christian perspective) tensions between Christians and Jews in the world in which the Gospel was written (in Asia Minor, toward the end of the first century CE).

What all the Gospel stories have in common is a notable lack of interest in portraying the Pharisees as historical persons who lived in Galilee and Judea at the time of Jesus. The Gospel portraits of the Pharisees are primarily rhetorical. Some Pharisees might have been historical opponents of Jesus (most evident and least developed in the Markan accounts), yet each Gospel writer goes well beyond this bare fact to develop the Pharisees as a personification of something "opposed to Christ," e.g., blatant evil in the case of Matthew,

self-righteousness in the case of Luke, and persecution of Christians in the case of John.

The Historical Pharisees: The Pharisees are described, not only in the NT, but also in writings of the first-century historian Josephus. They are also discussed in rabbinic literature, which is more difficult to date.

It is clear from the NT stories that the Pharisees emphasized faithfulness to Torah, including the study of scripture and obedience to the law. They are also said to have assigned authoritative status to an oral body of material called the "tradition of the elders" (cf. Matt. 15:2), which is often linked to the body of material that would eventually be identified with the Mishnah and become part of the Jewish Talmud. Some theories suggest that Pharisaic interpretations of the law as depicted in the NT (despite the polemical cast) may be understood to have been driven by the conviction that all of God's people should live with the utmost sanctity. Thus, the Pharisees would have urged laypeople to follow the same purity regulations in their daily lives that were expected of priests serving in the temple, the idea being that (in some sense) every house was a temple, every table was an altar, and every man was a priest. This would explain why the Pharisees and their followers might have practiced hand washings originally designated for temple service before eating *any* meal (see Matt. 15:2; cf. Mark 7:3–4).

In the NT, some Pharisees appear to have been scribes, and it is possible that some NT references to "the scribes" are referring to scribes who were Pharisees (cf. Mark 2:16; Luke 5:30; Acts 23:9). The same may be true of the "lawyers" referred to in certain passages (cf. Matt. 22:35; Luke 11:45); they may have been Pharisees who were known to be experts in the law (i.e., Torah). Many Pharisees also appear to have been synagogue leaders, and some are referred to as "rabbis" (i.e., teachers; cf. Matt. 23:6–8). Thus, historically, Jesus (who is also called "rabbi") probably had more in common with the Pharisees than with other Jewish groups of the day (e.g., those connected primarily with the priesthood and the temple in Jerusalem). The NT also contrasts the Pharisees with the Sadducees over belief in resurrection (Acts 23:1–8; Mark 11:18–26).

Josephus refers to the "philosophy" of the Pharisees and gives some general characteristics of the Pharisees in contrast to the Sadducees and Essenes. His description is somewhat anachronistic in that, writing for Romans, he uses the analogy of different Greco-Roman philosophical schools to explain the different Jewish groups. Still, according to Josephus, the Pharisees were the group that was most influential with the general populace, and they were noted for their authoritative interpretations of Jewish law. They had a simple standard of living and cultivated harmonious relations with others. On the issue of free will, a distinguishing factor among Greek philosophies, Josephus places the Pharisees between the Essenes and the Sadducees, because they accepted the influence of both fate (or providence) and free will on human actions. They also believed in life after death, which could be experienced as either eternal reward or everlasting punishment.

Rabbinic literature, which in its present form dates from 200 CE and later, contains three types of data regarding the Pharisees. First, there are records of laws associated with certain pre-70 CE Pharisees, particularly the schools of Shammai and Hillel, who are often seen as first-century Pharisaic leaders. Many of these laws concern ritual purity, tithing, and sabbath observance, concerns that also surface in the Gospels. Second, there are stories about these Pharisaic leaders that present them as authoritative and dominant figures in Jewish society, religion, and politics. Finally, some rabbinic texts speak of the "separatists" (Heb. *perushim*), a group often presumed to be Pharisees, though at times the term appears to refer to dissidents in general or to ascetics. All of this material presents the Pharisees as scholars who accept the written and oral law; they are the leaders who set the law for Jewish society and the judges who enforce it. It is often pointed out, however, that this portrait fits rabbis after 70 CE and might be anachronistic for the Pharisees active during the Second Temple period prior to the fall of Jerusalem. *See also* rabbi, rabbouni; sabbath; Sadducees; scribe.

Bibliography

Neusner, Jacob. *From Politics to Piety*. Prentice-Hall, 1973.

Saldarini, Anthony J. *Pharisees, Scribes, and Sadducees*. Glazier, 1988.   A.J.S./M.A.P.

Pharpar (fahr'pahr), one of the two rivers of Damascus according to 2 Kings 5:12. It is probably to be identified with the modern Nahr el-Awaj, which flows from Mount Hermon in an easterly direction and passes about ten miles south of Damascus. Together with the Abana (modern Nahr el-Barada) it waters the fertile Damascus oasis. *See also* Abana; Damascus.

Phicol (fi'kol), the commander of Abimelech's army. Phicol witnessed the agreement between Abimelech and Abraham at Beer-sheba (Gen. 21: 22) and, later, the agreement between Abimelech and Isaac at Gerar (26:26). *See also* Abimelech.

Philadelphia (fil'uh-del'fee-uh; Gk., "familial love"), an ancient city in the region of Lydia in western Asia Minor, on the site of modern Alashehir, Turkey. It was founded by Attalus II, king of Pergamum (159–138 BCE). Because of its strategic location, it served as a vital link in communication and trade between Sardis and Pergamum to the west and Laodicea and Hierapolis to the east. It was a center of agriculture, leather production, and textile industry. Philadelphia is one of the seven cities addressed in the book of Revelation (1:1; 3:7). The church is praised for having kept Christ's word of "patient endurance," and the congregation is promised that it will be kept "from

the hour of trial that is coming on the whole world to test the inhabitants of the earth" (3:10). *See also* Hierapolis; Laodicea; Lydia; Pergamum; Revelation, book of; Sardis.

Philemon (fi-lee'muhn), a resident of Colossae and owner of the slave Onesimus, for whom Paul makes an appeal in his Letter to Philemon. Philemon had apparently been converted through Paul's ministry (v. 19) and was regarded by Paul as a "dear friend and co-worker" (v. 1). Since he was able to host a congregation (v. 2) and prepare a guest room for Paul (v. 22), he was probably an individual of financial means. *See also* Onesimus; Philemon, Letter of Paul to.   W.R.B.

Philemon, Letter of Paul to, the shortest of Paul's letters. It is a personal letter, though not a private one, addressed to a prominent individual, his household, and congregation.

Contents: After a brief salutation and blessing (vv. 1–3), Paul offers a prayer of thanksgiving for Philemon's faith and for his refreshing the "hearts of the saints" (vv. 4–7). Then he turns to the matter at hand, an appeal on behalf of Philemon's slave, Onesimus (vv. 8–21). Paul says that Onesimus has become like a son to him during his imprisonment (v. 10), but that he is now sending him back (v. 12). He does so reluctantly and hints that Philemon might allow Onesimus to return to him (vv. 13–14). In any case, he wants Onesimus to receive a favorable reception, and he offers to repay any debt that Philemon has incurred because of him, though Philemon also owes a great debt to Paul—his "own self" (vv. 15–19). Paul expresses confidence in Philemon's obedience (v. 21) and asks to have a guest room prepared for when he comes to visit (v. 22). He closes the letter with a series of greetings from his companions (vv. 23–24).

OUTLINE OF CONTENTS

Philemon

I. Letter opening (vv. 1–3)
II. Prayer (vv. 4–7)
III. Appeal concerning Onesimus (vv. 8–22)
  A. Return of Onesimus (vv. 8–14)
  B. Appeal on Onesimus's behalf (vv. 15–22)
IV. Letter closing (vv. 23–25)

          W.R.B.

Historical Situation: Because many of the persons mentioned in this letter are also mentioned in Colossians, Philemon is usually assumed to have lived in the city of Colossae. Paul is in prison, but expects to be released soon. Some scholars think he is imprisoned in nearby Ephesus (ca. 54–55 CE), which would fit well with his request for Philemon to prepare a guest room for him (v. 22). Other scholars prefer to think that Paul is imprisoned in

Caesarea (ca. 58–60 CE) or Rome (ca. 60–63 CE), which would allow a later date for the letter. The primary reason for this is that, if Paul is held to have written Colossians at the same time as Philemon, a later date allows more time for the development of ideas expressed in that letter. In any case, the situation that calls for the Letter to Philemon is clear. A slave named Onesimus, who belongs to Philemon, is now with Paul, but Paul is sending him back to his master with an appeal for Philemon to welcome him graciously and with an implied request that Philemon return Onesi-

SANCTUARY FOR A RUNAWAY SERVANT

A letter from Pliny the Younger written in the late first century offers an appeal to a certain Sabinianus on behalf of a runaway servant. It makes for an interesting comparison to Paul's Letter to Philemon, written on behalf of Onesimus:

> To Sabinianus. Your freedman, whom you lately mentioned as having displeased you, has been with me; he threw himself at my feet and clung there with as much submission as he could have done at yours. He earnestly requested me with many tears, and even with the eloquence of silent sorrow, to intercede for him; in short, he convinced me by his whole behavior that he sincerely repents of his fault. And I am persuaded he is thoroughly reformed, because he seems entirely sensible of his delinquency. I know you are angry with him, and I know too, it is not without reason; but clemency can never exert itself with more applause, than when the cause for resentment is most just. You once had an affection for this man, and, I hope, will have again: in the meanwhile, let me only prevail with you to pardon him. If he should incur your displeasure hereafter, you will have so much the stronger plea in excuse for your anger, as you show yourself more exorable to him now. Allow something to his youth, to his tears, and to your own natural mildness of temper: do not make him uneasy any longer, and I will add too, do not make yourself so; for a man of your benevolence of heart cannot be angry without feeling great uneasiness. I am afraid, were I to join my entreaties with his, I should seem rather to compel than request you to forgive him. Yet I will not scruple to do it; and so much the more fully and freely as I have very sharply and severely reproved him, positively threatening never to interpose again in his behalf. But though it was proper to say this to him, in order to make him more fearful of offending, I do not say it to you. I may, perhaps, again have occasion to entreat you upon his account, and again obtain your forgiveness; supposing, I mean, his errors should be such as may become me to intercede for, and you to pardon. Farewell.

mus to Paul (probably, though not necessarily, as a freedman). It is often thought that Onesimus is a runaway slave who either robbed his master or otherwise caused him financial loss (vv. 18–19), but this is not stated in the letter as such. It is possible that Onesimus was simply a slave who was fearful of his master (perhaps because of having incurred financial loss while representing him in some business transaction) and who had sought sanctuary with Paul, as was provided by Roman law in such situations. In any case, it seems that Paul's ministry had been responsible for Philemon's becoming a Christian, and Paul believes that this justifies his request.

Major Themes: The Letter to Philemon is examined for its rhetoric, with interest in how the apostle employs diverse tactics for persuasion. He makes his request publicly (vv. 2, 25); he plays on Philemon's reputation for generosity (vv. 4–7); he reminds Philemon of his spiritual indebtedness to Paul (v. 19); and he appeals for sympathy by describing himself as an "old man" (v. 9) who is in prison (vv. 1, 9, 23). The letter is also studied to determine Paul's attitude toward slavery. There are differences of opinion on this, but most scholars think that Paul probably did not approve of slavery, though he stopped short of condemning the institution outright or even of prohibiting Christians from owning slaves. *See also* Onesimus; Paul; Philemon.

Bibliography

Donfried, Karl P., and I. Howard Marshall. *The Theology of the Shorter Pauline Letters.* Cambridge University Press, 1993.

Dunn, James D. G. *The Epistles to the Colossians and to Philemon: A Commentary on the Greek Text.* Eerdmans, 1996.

Fitzmyer, Joseph A. *The Letter to Philemon.* Doubleday, 2000.

Petersen, Norman R. *Rediscovering Paul: Philemon and the Sociology of Paul's Narrative World.* Fortress, 1985.

Wilson, Robert. *Colossians and Philemon.* Clark, 2005.   M.A.P.

Philetus (fi-lee´tuhs), a man accused, with Hymenaeus, of upsetting the faith of some by teaching that "the resurrection has already taken place" (2 Tim. 2:16–18). It is unclear exactly what such teaching would have implied, but Hymenaeus and Philetus might have been maintaining that the new era of salvation had dawned in such a way that participation in glorious eternal life was already a present possibility. Thus, resurrection would then be conceived as a spiritual experience rather than as a literal, bodily reality that would occur at the end of time. *See also* Hymenaeus.

Philip (fil´ip).

1 Philip II, king of Macedonia (359–336 BCE) and father of Alexander the Great (1 Macc. 1:1; 6:2). He unified Macedonia and was a major proponent of Hellenistic culture. *See also* Alexander; Macedonia.

2 Philip V, king of Macedonia (220–179 BCE), mentioned in 1 Macc. 8:5. He was decisively defeated by Roman forces at the battle of Cynoscephale (198 BCE), but the Romans allowed him to remain in power as a buffer against Syria.

3 Philip the Phrygian, governor of Jerusalem, appointed by Antiochus IV Epiphanes ca. 179 BCE (2 Macc. 5:22; 6:11; 8:8). After the death of Antiochus IV, Philip became regent over his successor, Antiochus V (1 Macc. 6:14–17, 55; 2 Macc. 9:29). He tried to seize power himself, but was defeated by Lysias at Antioch ca. 164/3 BCE. *See also* Antiochus.

4 Philip, a close associate and foster brother of Antiochus IV Epiphanes (1 Macc. 6:14–15; 2 Macc. 9:29).

5 Herod Philip, the son of Herod the Great and Mariamne II, and half brother of Herod Antipas. He is probably the person intended by Matt. 14:3 and Mark 6:17 (cf. Luke 3:19) as Philip, the brother of Herod (Antipas) and first husband of Herodias. *See also* Herod; Herodias.

6 Philip the Tetrarch, son of Herod the Great and Cleopatra of Jerusalem, not to be confused with **5.** According to the historian Josephus, he was granted rule over a portion of his father's kingdom following the latter's death in 4 BCE. His rule over this non-Jewish territory, stretching from the Sea of Galilee north and east toward Damascus, was apparently a benevolent and prosperous one. He built Caesarea Philippi, named in honor of the emperor (and himself), and rebuilt the city of Bethsaida on the Sea of Galilee. He died ca. 33–34 CE, and his territory became part of the Roman province of Syria. *See also* Caesarea Philippi.

7 Philip the apostle, one of the twelve whose name appears in the four apostolic lists (Matt. 10:3; Mark 3:18; Luke 6:14; Acts 1:13). John's Gospel contains the most references to Philip. According to 1:43–51, Philip was from Bethsaida in Galilee, the home also of Andrew and Peter. When called by Jesus, Philip sought out a skeptical Nathanael, who also responded to Jesus. Philip is also the disciple who responds to Jesus's direct question concerning feeding the multitude, observing that it would take a large amount of money to feed so many (6:1–14). Later, it is Philip whom Greeks approach with their request to meet Jesus (12:20–22). In 14:8–11, it is Philip who says to Jesus, "Lord, show us the Father, and we shall be satisfied." Philip later appears with the other apostles in Jerusalem after Jesus's ascension (Acts 1:13). *See also* Andrew; apostle; Bethsaida; disciple; Nathanael; twelve, the.

8 Philip the evangelist, not to be confused with **7.** This Philip appears only in the book of Acts, where he is appointed (along with Stephen and others) to supervise the daily distribution of food to the widows following the dispute between the "Hellenists" and the "Hebrews" (6:1–6). Thus he is regarded as "one of the seven" (21:8), but not as one of the twelve (cf. 6:2). Later, Philip carries the gospel to Samaria (8:5–13). He proclaims "the good news about the kingdom of God and the name of Jesus Christ" (8:12), and he also works signs and great miracles among the people. Many of them believe and are baptized, including Simon, a magician. The Samaritan converts, however, do not receive the gift of the Holy Spirit until Peter and John come from Jerusalem to lay hands on them and pray for them (8:14–24). Philip is subsequently directed by an angel to go to the road from Jerusalem to Gaza, where he encounters an Ethiopian eunuch reading the scriptures and seeking someone to interpret a passage from Isa. 53:7–8. Starting with this scripture, Philip proclaims the good news about Jesus to the Ethiopian and then baptizes him. The Spirit of the Lord then snatches Philip away and he finds himself at Azotus, from which he travels to Caesarea, proclaiming the gospel in all towns along the way (8:26–39). A final NT reference to this Philip is in 21:8–9, where he and his four daughters are said to be residing in Caesarea. They are visited by Paul, who is on his way to Jerusalem. Philip's daughters are explicitly identified as "virgin [NRSV: 'unmarried'] daughters who have the gift of prophecy."

Several authorities in the early church identified Philip the evangelist with the apostle Philip, in spite of the fact that Luke clearly thought of them as different persons (cf. Eusebius *Ecclesiastical History* 3.31.3; 5.24.2). Indeed, this identification is said by Eusebius to have been made by Papias, a second-century authority who claimed to have actually known Philip's daughters (*Ecclesiastical History* 3.39.9). Most interpreters assume that these identifications stem from confusion in the church regarding two individuals who bore the same name. A minority postion, however, holds that it is Luke's account that is confused. Luke attributes the activities of Philip the apostle to a new character ("one of the seven"), because he is committed to the principle that the twelve remained in Jerusalem (e.g., Acts 8:1, though that principle would be violated in any case by Peter's sojourn in Joppa, Acts 9:43). *See also* apostle; deacon; Ethiopia; eunuch; Stephen.   P.L.S./M.A.P.

Philippi (fi-lip′i, fil′i-pi), an ancient city in northeastern Greece. Its site, dominated by a high acropolis and surrounded by mountains on three sides, lies ten miles inland from the modern port city of Kavalla (ancient Neapolis).

The history of Philippi before the fourth century BCE remains obscure, although there are reports of two older settlements on or near the site, Krenides and Datum. Philip II of Macedonia, particularly interested in the nearby gold and silver mines of Mount Pangaeus, annexed the entire region and in 356 BCE formally established Philippi as a city bearing his name. Although the extensive city wall, which still survives, perhaps originated at this time, Philippi remained insignificant until after the Roman conquest of Macedonia in 168–167 BCE. Included by Aemilius Paulus in the first of the four districts into which Macedonia was then divided (Livy *Roman*

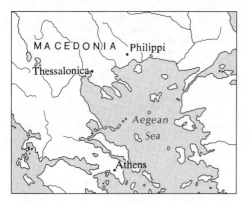

History 45.29; see Acts 16:12), it became a major stopping place on the Via Egnatia, the newly constructed road connecting Byzantium with the Adriatic ports that led to Italy.

In October of 42 BCE Mark Antony and Octavian defeated Roman Republican forces led by Brutus and Cassius in two separate battles just west of Philippi. Shortly afterward, Mark Antony settled many veterans from his army here and refounded Philippi as a Roman colony; its territory included the towns of Neapolis, Oisyme, and Apollonia. After the battle of Actium (31 BCE) more settlers arrived from Italy by order of Octavian (Augustus), and Philippi was founded anew, receiving the formal name that it thenceforth retained, Colonia Julia Augusta Philippensis. These settlers along with some of the previous inhabitants constituted the legal citizen body; and Philippi was governed by "Italian law" (*ius italicum*), the highest privilege attainable for a Roman provincial municipality.

Literary and archaeological evidence suggests that Philippi's population, like that of many Roman colonies on Greek soil, was a mix of Roman, local Greek, and other Mediterranean peoples who blended into the somewhat homogenous urban culture of the empire. Aspects of Philippi's religious life suggest that its inhabitants, noncitizens included, were very mixed in their backgrounds and that diversity was tolerated by Roman political leadership. Roman gods such as Jupiter and Mars had their cults and were worshiped, as was the imperial family, but the Thracian goddess Bendis also remained very popular. Gods from Egypt as well as Cybele, a Phrygian goddess, were also known and their devotees included Roman citizens. According to Acts, a Jewish synagogue was apparently located just outside the city walls (16:13). The apostle Paul came to Philippi ca. 50 CE and founded here his first European Christian community (Acts 16:12–40; 1 Thess. 2:2). This church, apparently one of Paul's favorites, received his Letter to the Philippians ca. 54 CE and one or more additional visits from him ca. 55 CE (1 Cor. 16:5–6; 2 Cor. 2:13; 7:5; Acts 20:1–6). A letter of Polycarp of Smyrna written to the Philippian Christians ca. 125 CE has also survived.

Excavations at the site have uncovered extensive remains on the now uninhabited ancient site. For the most part, they date to the second century CE and after, when the city was extensively renovated and expanded. Among the interesting finds are a portion of the Via Egnatia with deep ruts cut into the stone slabs from years of traffic, an extensive forum with surrounding porticoes, and an ancient theater cut into a hillside that dates back to the fourth century BCE, but that was extensively rebuilt for gladiatorial games in the third century CE. Around the theater were carved numerous niches and reliefs featuring divinities like Isis, Serapis, and Cybele, and the city had shrines and temples for the Latin nature god Silvanus, the Greek protector god Artemis, and the Roman imperial Antonius Pius. After the fourth century, Christianity dominated the landscape, and the ruins of several Byzantine churches are among the prominent structures still visible. A Roman-period cistern that may still be seen has been known since the fifth century as "The Prison of St. Paul" (i.e., the cell where Paul and Silas were kept for a night, according to Acts 16:6–40). This attribution, however, is extremely dubious. *See also* Macedonia; Paul; Philippians, Letter of Paul to the.

R.A.W./J.R.

Philippians (fi-lip'ee-uhnz), **Letter of Paul to the,** one of the thirteen letters in the NT attributed to the apostle Paul. The letter is noted for its strong accents on joy and friendship, and this tone seems all the more remarkable considering it was written from prison (1:7, 13–14, 17) at a time when Paul believed he could be facing execution (1:19–24).

Contents: The letter opens with a customary but brief salutation (1:1–2) and a report of Paul's prayers of thanksgiving for the church (1:3–11). Paul then fills the Philippians in on the circumstances regarding his current imprisonment; it has served to advance the gospel (1:12–18), but he looks forward to being set free in response to their prayers (1:19–26). After these preliminaries, he offers an extended appeal for humility and unity in the church (1:27–2:18): the Philippians are to live in a manner worthy of the gospel, even though this means suffering (1:27–30), and they are to follow the example of Christ Jesus in setting aside personal interests for the sake of others (2:1–2:18). Embedded in this appeal is a poetic account of how Christ "emptied himself" for the sake of humanity and was subsequently exalted by God to become Lord of all (2:6–11). Paul then discusses his hopes for future visits to the church and provides an update on the status of one of their members, Epaphroditus, who became ill while visiting Paul (2:19–30). At this point, the letter seems to be winding down (3:1), but instead of concluding Paul launches into another major appeal, warning the Philippians against false teachers and calling on them to imitate him as one who suffers for Christ in hope of the resurrection (3:1–4:1). Embedded in *this* appeal is a brief autobiographical section in which Paul lists personal attributes and achievements that might typically be considered badges of honor, but that he denounces as "rubbish" for the sake of knowing Christ and obtaining the righteousness of God that comes through faith (3:4–11). Then he offers a series of pastoral exhortations (4:2–9), expresses his thanks to the church for the concern and support they have offered him (4:10–20), and concludes with final greetings (4:21–23).

OUTLINE OF CONTENTS

Philippians

R.A.W.

Historical Setting: Paul is believed to have evangelized the Macedonian city of Philippi around 50–51 CE, establishing what is usually regarded as the first Christian church on European soil (cf. Acts 16:6–40). He enjoyed a particularly good relationship with the church, and the Philippians would prove particularly loyal in supporting him and his missionary projects (Phil. 4:10, 16; 2 Cor. 8:1–4; 9:1–5; 11:8–9). His letter to the church was written from prison, but the precise date and location of its composition cannot be determined. At various points in his career, Paul is thought to have been imprisoned in Ephesus (1 Cor. 15:32), Caesarea (Acts 23:23–26:30), and Rome (Acts 28:16–31). If Philippians were written from Ephesus, it would be one of Paul's earliest letters (ca. 54–56 CE); if from Caesarea (ca. 58–60 CE) or Rome (ca. 61–63 CE), it could be one of his last. All of these options are explored by modern scholars without clear resolution. The im-

mediate occasion for the letter, in any case, seems to be to update his friends on his current situation (1:12–26), to ease their minds regarding Epaphroditus, a member of the church who became ill while visiting Paul (2:25–30), and to thank them for a gift that Epaphroditus delivered (4:10–20).

Critical Problems: Scholars have noted a number of oddities about the letter that sometimes lead them to suspect that the document is actually a composite of different letters written by Paul to the Philippians at different times. (1) Phil. 3:1a, 4:8–9, and 4:21–23 all sound like possible conclusions to letters. (2) Phil. 3:1b–4:3 has a different tone than the rest of the letter (warnings against enemies in a letter that is otherwise upbeat and confident). (3) Phil. 4:10–20 expresses thanksgiving for a gift, which would typically come at the beginning of a letter rather than at the end. (4) Phil. 2:25–30 speaks of Epaphroditus returning to Philippi after a protracted illness, but Phil. 4:18 refers to him as if he has just arrived. A number of proposals have been offered to explain these anomalies. A *two-letter theory* suggests Paul wrote one letter (3:1b–4:20) when Epaphroditus first arrived and another letter (1:1–3:1a; 4:21–23) after Epaphroditus recovered from sickness. A *three-letter theory* suggests he wrote an early thank-you note (4:10–20), a follow-up letter that was hopeful and confident (1:1–3:1a; 4:4–7, 21–23), and a third letter to address problems in the church (3:1b–4:3; 4:8–9). In either case, a later editor is supposed to have woven the different letters together to form the letter that is found in all extant biblical manuscripts. Many scholars, however, think the letter we possess represents a single, unified document that need not be subjected to partition theories.

Major Themes: Interpretation of Philippians has focused especially on the "Christ hymn," a poetic passage in 2:6–11 that is thought to offer early references to the Christian concepts of preexistence (the idea that Christ existed in heaven before the man Jesus lived on earth) and incarnation (the belief that Jesus was God in human flesh). The hymn presents Christ as one who was "in the form of God," but in humble obedience gave up "equality with God" to be "born in human likeness" and subsequently suffer death on a cross (2:6–8). Another major theme in Philippians, related to this theme, is the presentation of humility as a prime virtue; the Philippians are to do nothing out of selfish ambition, but are to place the interests of others ahead of their own (2:3–4). The letter also extols the value and sufficiency of knowing Christ. Paul regards all else as rubbish compared to this (3:8) and assures the Philippians that they do not need circumcision or anything else in addition to Christ (3:2). Other themes include the potential value of suffering (1:29; 3:10) and the experience of Christian fellowship (1:5; 2:1; 3:10). *See also* Epaphroditus; Ephesus; Paul; Philippi; prison.

Bibliography

Donfried, Karl P., and I. Howard Marshall. *The Theology of the Shorter Pauline Letters.* Cambridge University Press, 1993.

Hawthorne, Gerald F. *Philippians*. Rev. ed. Nelson, 2004.

O'Brien, Peter T. *Epistle to the Philippians: A Commentary on the Greek Text*. Eerdmans, 1991.

Reumann, John. *Philippians*. Yale University Press, 2008.   M.A.P.

Philistines (fi-lis′teenz), a warlike people who, with the other Sea Peoples, migrated from the Aegean basin to the southern coast of the Levant in the early twelfth century BCE. They became one of Israel's principal rivals.

Name: The Hebrew name for the Philistines is *pelishtim;* the Bible usually refers to their territory as *'erets pelishtim* ("land of the Philistines") or *peleshet* ("Philistia"). The modern term "Palestine" is derived from the Greek and Latin names given to the descendants of the Philistines.

Origin: Although the exact origin of the Philistines remains uncertain, there is no doubt that they were part of a great ethnic upheaval that occurred in the Aegean area in the final decades of the thirteenth century BCE. During this unsettled period, an unknown combination of social, political, and economic factors caused the displacement of various peoples on the Greek mainland and Aegean islands and in eastern Anatolia. The Sea Peoples, or "foreigners from the Sea," emerged from the hodgepodge of refugees, and their military advance across the eastern Mediterranean brought an end to the Hittite Empire and the city-state of Ugarit. Ultimately, the Sea Peoples reached the coasts of Phoenicia, Egypt, and the Levant. Pharaoh Ramesses III of Egypt is known to have fought two groups of the Sea Peoples, the Tjekker and the Philistines, in the eighth year of his reign (ca. 1190 BCE). Though the battle was fought on land and sea, the Egyptians prevailed; an important written and pictorial description of this episode was carved on the walls of Ramesses' funerary temple at Medinet Habu (Thebes). Following his victory, Ramesses settled the Philistines along the southern coast of Canaan, and this Aegean people claimed a new homeland—the region that came to be known as Philistia.

In agreement with the external sources, the Bible points to an Aegean origin for the Philistines by linking them with Caphtor (Jer. 47:4; Amos 9:7; cf. Gen. 10:14; Deut. 2:23; 1 Chron. 1:12). Caphtor is almost certainly to be identified with Crete (cf. Cherethites; Palethites; Caphtorim).

History: Since nonbiblical texts do not use the term "Philistines" before ca. 1200 BCE, most scholars assume that the appearance of this name in Gen. 21:32, 34; 26:1, 8, 14–18 is anachronistic. Although it is quite possible that there were peoples of Aegean origin in Canaan during the period of Israel's ancestors, it seems likely that a later editor "updated" their ethnic designation by calling them Philistines. If the name "Philistine" was not used until the twelfth century BCE, a similar explanation must be given for its appearance in Gen. 10:14; Exod. 13:17; 23:31; Josh. 13:2–3.

As the Philistines consolidated their claim to the southern coast, roughly in the area between Gaza and modern Tel Aviv, they organized themselves into a league of city-states. The "Philistine Pentapolis" was composed of Gaza, Ashdod, Ashkelon, Gath, and Ekron; these five cities remained important throughout Philistine history. Although this region had great agricultural and commercial potential, the Philistines were not satisfied with

---

TROUBLE IN PHILIPPI

Paul's Letter to the Philippians is not particularly polemical, but references to opponents or enemies do pop up here and there.

Text	Comment	Possible Reference
1:15–18	Some proclaim Christ out of false motives—envy, rivalry, and selfish ambition.	Christian missionaries who compete with Paul and create factions in the church; cf. 1 Cor. 1:11–13.
1:28–29	Opponents cause the Philippians to suffer the same struggles Paul experienced as a missionary in the city.	Nonbelievers who persecute Christians; cf. Acts 16:19–39; 2 Cor. 1:8–9; 6:4–5; 11:23–26.
3:2	Evil-workers (whom Paul calls "dogs") insist on "mutilating the flesh."	Jewish Christians who say all Christians need to be circumcised; cf. Gal. 5:2–12.
3:18–19	Many live as "enemies of the cross," with their god as their belly, their glory in their shame, and their minds set on earthly things.	Christians who seek power and glory apart from suffering and service; cf. 1 Cor. 1:18–2:5; 2 Cor. 10–12.

Note that only the second reference (1:28–29) is to troublemakers who are definitely in Philippi. The first reference (1:15–18) is to people in the area where Paul is in prison. The last two references *could* be to troublemakers who are in Philippi, but it is also possible that Paul is simply warning the Philippians about the kinds of people who have caused trouble elsewhere.

From Mark Allan Powell, *Introducing the New Testament* (courtesy, Baker Academic)

such a narrow strip of land. Their expansion into the hinterland eventually brought them into conflict with the Israelites, who were expanding their territory at about the same time from the opposite side of Canaan. This competition for land and political control produced a fierce rivalry that lasted from the middle of the twelfth century BCE until ca. 965 BCE (i.e., from the time of the Philistine expansion into Israelite territory until their defeat by David).

In agreement with Josh. 13:2–3, Judg. 3:1–3 says that the Philistines were among the nations that God left in Canaan "to test" Israel. Beginning with the book of Judges, the Bible records numerous encounters between the Hebrews and Philistines. The first reference to hostility between these two rivals is Judg. 3:31, a single verse that praises Shamgar for delivering Israel by killing six hundred Philistines with an oxgoad. Strength and military prowess are also acclaimed in the stories of Samson (Judg. 13–16), but those accounts also serve to illustrate Philistine encroachment into Hebrew territory; they mention Philistine presence in Timnah and Lehi, both in the strategic Valley of Sorek. According to Judg. 18, this Philistine expansion worsened the land shortage that eventually forced the Danites to migrate northward.

Shortly after the call of Samuel, Israelite–Philistine tension erupted into all-out war. Israel was defeated at Ebenezer, the ark was captured, and Shiloh was destroyed (1 Sam. 4–6; cf. Pss. 78:56–66; Jer. 7:12–14). After rededicating themselves to God, the Israelites defeated the Philistines at Mizpah (1 Sam. 7:3–14). The balance of power fluctuated, but the establishment of the monarchy and subsequent maintenance of a regular army enabled Saul to defeat his foes (1 Sam. 13–14), in spite of the Philistine superiority in weaponry (cf. 13:19–22). According to the Bible, the acclaim that David received after his victory over Goliath and the resultant rout of the Philistines (17:41–54) provoked Saul to jealousy. David took refuge with the Philistine king of Gath, Achish, and became one of his vassals (27:1–28:2), but David was not present when the Philistines killed Saul and his sons on Mount Gilboa (1 Sam. 31). This Philistine victory led to an even greater expansion of their holdings (cf. 31:7).

The death of Saul caused David to break his alliance with the Philistines and establish his kingship in Hebron (2 Sam. 1:1–2:11). In an effort to crush David's independent state, the Philistines attacked, but David "smote the Philistines from Geba to Gezer" (5:17–25). Ultimately, David's opposition to the Philistines broke their power (8:1; cf. 1 Chron. 18:1). Although the Philistines continued to resist Israel's expansion (cf. 2 Sam. 21:15–22; 23:8–39), they were no longer a major threat to the Hebrews.

When Solomon came to the throne, he received tribute from subordinate kingdoms on the Israelite frontiers, including the city-states of Philistia (1 Kings 4:21). Solomon allied himself with the Egyptian Pharaoh by taking an Egyptian wife and receiving the city of Gezer as dowry (9:16). The passing of this important city from Egyptian to Israelite hands is a good indication of the low ebb of Philistine power at this time.

Nevertheless, intermittent fighting between these two peoples continued throughout the history of the divided monarchy. Judah received tribute from the Philistines during the reign of Jehoshaphat (2 Chron. 17:11), but the Philistines were among those who raided Judah in Jehoram's day (21:16–17). Uzziah made successful incursions into Philistia (26:6–7), but Ahaz lost territory to the Philistines (28:18). According to the biblical record, the last Israelite king who had contact with the Philistines was Hezekiah; he directed successful campaigns against this traditional rival (2 Kings 18:8).

Since much of this fighting took place during the eighth century BCE, reference should be made to oracles of two Hebrew prophets from this era. Amos leveled a severe indictment against Gaza, Ashdod, Ashkelon, and Ekron because of the Philistine involvement in slavery (1:6–8; cf. Zeph. 2:4–7; Joel 3:4–8). Isaiah says that God used the Philistines to punish Israel (9:12), but the prophet also warned Philistia about an approaching enemy who would come "out of the north"—the Assyrians (14:28–31).

Isaiah's warning in 715 BCE (i.e., the year Ahaz died) came long after the Assyrians began interfering with the internal affairs of Philistia. At the end of the ninth century BCE, Adad-nirari III men-

The Philistines began settling along the coast of the Levant in the early twelfth century BCE. When they consolidated their claim to the area, their principal cities were Ashdod, Ashkelon, Ekron, Gath, and Gaza.

Ashdoda, a Philistine cultic object in the shape of a seated woman, from Ashdod, twelfth century BCE.

tioned tribute payments from the Philistines to Assyria. The military power of Tiglath-pileser III, Sargon II, Sennacherib, and Esar-haddon was felt by the often rebellious cities of Philistia between 734 and 676 BCE (cf. Isa. 20). Although the Assyrians exacted tribute from the Philistines and set pro-Assyrian rulers on the thrones of Philistia's city-states, the Assyrian kings allowed this coastal region to retain a measure of autonomy, because Philistia acted as a buffer zone on the Egyptian frontier.

Following the collapse of Assyria, the Philistines joined Egypt in an anti-Babylonian alliance. In response, Nebuchadnezzar deported the rulers and populace of Philistia (cf. Jer. 25:20; 47:2–7; Zech. 9:5–6). Although some of the Philistine cities (e.g., Gaza, Ashdod, Ashkelon) were reoccupied and survived, the Babylonian conquest brought an end to the cultural and political unit known as Philistia.

Archaeology: Our knowledge of the Philistines is based, not only on the Bible and extrabiblical historical sources (including the temple reliefs at Medinet Habu), but on excavated material from numerous archaeological sites. Evidence from these sites, most located in the coastal plain and foothills of the southern Levant, agrees with written sources in placing the Philistine arrival, expansion, and decline between ca. 1200 and 1000 BCE. Even the distinctive, Aegean-influenced Philistine pottery, which is commonly found in strata dating to the twelfth–eleventh centuries BCE, disappears after ca. 1000 BCE, a clear indication of the Philistines' adoption of local culture.

The locations of three cities of the Philistine Pentapolis are certain—Gaza, Ashkelon, and Ashdod. Excavations at modern Khirbet el-Muganna (Tel Miqne) might identify this site as ancient Ekron, but the location of Philistine Gath is still uncertain (perhaps modern Tell es-Safi). Major excavations have been conducted at Ashdod, with the recovery of significant data, while the Philistine evidence from Gaza and Ashkelon is meager. Recent investigations at other sites (e.g., Deir el-Balah, Tell el-Batashi, Tell Gezer, Tell Jemmeh, Tell Qasile) have shed new light on Philistine architecture, burials, pottery, metallurgy, religion, and commerce. For example, Tell Jemmeh, located about seven miles south of Gaza, yielded artifacts from Arabia, Egypt, Phoenicia, Assyria, Cyprus, and Greece; such evidence demonstrates that Philistia was a crossroads for international trade.

Religion: The Bible refers to three Philistine deities—Dagon, Ashtaroth, and Baal-zebub—all of whom had Semitic names; this indicates that the Philistines assimilated the divinities or the names used in local Canaanite religion, a common phenomenon in ancient times. Dagon had temples in Gaza (Judg. 16:21, 23–30), Ashdod (1 Sam. 5:1–7), and probably in Beth-shan (1 Chron. 10:10; cf. 1 Sam. 31:10). Ashtaroth had temples in Ashkelon (Herodotus 1.105) and probably in Beth-shan (1 Sam. 31:10); and Baal-zebub had a temple in Ekron (2 Kings 1:1–16).

Like other ancient peoples, the Philistines offered sacrifices to their gods (Judg. 16:23), sought counsel from priests and diviners (1 Sam. 6:2–9), and developed the art of soothsaying (Isa. 2:6). Apparently, Philistine warriors carried portable idols into battle (2 Sam. 5:21) and had respect for other national deities (cf. 1 Sam. 5:1–6:21).

Prior to the excavations at Tell Qasile, virtually all information about Philistine religion was derived from the biblical passages mentioned above. This situation changed when three superimposed Philistine temples were uncovered at this important site, which is located within the city limits of Tel Aviv. The layout of the latest temple includes both Canaanite and Cypriot-Greek features. Also important was the recovery of a number of cultic vessels from this complex, some of which have Aegean antecedents.

Language: Strangely enough, not one written text can be attributed to the Philistines with certainty. There are several inscriptions in Cypro-Minoan or Cypro-Mycenaean script that might be Philistine (e.g., seals from Ashdod and tablets from Tell Deir Alia), but none of them can be deciphered. Although most Philistine names are Semitic, the names Achish and Goliath find their parallels in Crete and western Anatolia, respectively. Several Hebrew words were probably borrowed from the Philistine language, e.g., *seren*, "lord" (cf. 1 Sam. 5:8); *koba'*, "helmet" (cf. 1 Sam. 17:5); and *'argaz*, "box" (cf. 1 Sam. 6:8). Like the rest of Philistine culture, their language ultimately disappeared and a local Semitic dialect was adopted. The isolation of Philistia's cities, even in postexilic times, produced a language barrier between the Ashdodites and the Judeans (Neh. 13:23–24). *See also* Cherethites; Palestine; Pelethites.

Bibliography

Bierling, Neal. *Giving Goliath His Due: New Archaeological Light on the Philistines.* Baker, 1992.

Dothan, Trude, and Moshe Dothan. *People of the Sea: The Search for the Philistines.* Macmillan, 1992.

Katzenstein, H. J., and Trude Dothan. "Philistines." *Anchor Bible Dictionary.* Doubleday, 1992. 5:326–333.

Kitchen, K. A. "The Philistines." In D. J. Wiseman, ed. *People of Old Testament Times.* Clarendon, 1973. Pp. 53–78.

Mazar, Amihai. *Archaeology of the Land of the Bible: 10,000–586 B.C.E.* Doubleday, 1990. Pp. 300–328.   G.L.M.

A Philistine pottery sarcophagus from Deir el-Balah, twelfth century BCE.

Philo (fi'loh; ca. 20 BCE–50 CE), a wealthy Alexandrian Jew, both statesman and philosopher, who was a prolific author during the time of Hillel, Shammai, Gamaliel, Jesus, and Paul. One of the remarkable aspects of his writings, therefore, is that they betray absolutely no knowledge of those figures or their ideas. This may be an indication of the extent to which Alexandria was isolated from the concerns and events of Judea, or it may simply be a consequence of Philo's fascination with Greek philosophy. His writings combine a fierce loyalty to (Hellenistic) Judaism with a literary defense of the Jewish faith through allegorical interpretation of scripture that renders Jewish traditions consonant with the ideals of Stoic, Pythagorean, and especially Platonic thought.

No NT writing owes a direct debt to Philo, but some books are often compared with his writings when they also seek to interpret Jewish concepts from a perspective informed by Greek philosophy. An example may be seen in the use that both Philo and the NT Letter to the Hebrews make of Plato's notion of "ideas." Plato (fourth century BCE) claimed that the world of "ideas" was the most real and true world and that the physical world in which people live contains only representations of those ideas that are in some sense less real and less true. Thus Philo of Alexandria applied this concept to the two Genesis creation stories, maintaining that 1:26 27 reports the creation of the "idea" (or "ideal form") of humanity and 2:7 reports the creation of a material representation of this idea (a physical man formed from the dust of the earth). The author of Hebrews argues that the Jewish tabernacle described in the Pentateuch was only "a sketch and a shadow" of a heavenly sanctuary in which Jesus exercises his office as high priest (8:5–6; cf. 9:23; 10:1). Thus, the earthly sanctuary made by human hands is only a material representation of the more real heavenly sanctuary that was not made by hands; obviously, a more true and more real salvation is to be obtained in the heavenly sanctuary than in the earthly one. Thus, both Philo and Hebrews (written around the same time) demonstrate divergent ways that Hellenistic Judaism could apply Greek philosophic concepts to the interpretation of Jewish scriptures. *See also* Alexandria.   J.M.B./M.A.P.

Phinehas (fin'ee-huhs).

1 A priest, son of Eleazar, grandson of Aaron (Exod. 6:25; 1 Chron. 6:4, 20), and ancestor of Ezra (Ezra 8:2). Phinehas demonstrated his zeal for God during the wilderness period when Israelite men began having sexual relations with women of Moab and, so, became yoked to the Baal of Peor, the god these women apparently served. A terrible plague broke out among the Israelites, and God demanded that the offenders be impaled. Seeing an Israelite man having intercourse with a Midianite woman, Phinehas killed them both with one thrust of a spear. This stayed the wrath of God against the people and earned a covenant of eternal priesthood for Phinehas and his descendants (Num. 25:1–9; cf. Ps. 106:30–31; Sir. 45:23–24; 1 Macc. 2:26, 54). Phinehas later accompanied Israelite soldiers in a holy war against Midian (Num. 31:6), successfully negotiated a religious dispute between Israel and the Transjordanian tribes (Josh. 22:10–34), and advised the Israelite tribes to attack Benjamin (Judg. 20:27–28). He was in charge of the temple gatekeepers (1 Chron. 9:20). His home was in Gibeah (Josh. 24:33). *See also* Peor; priests.

2 A priest, the son of Eli (1 Sam. 1:3). He and his brother Hophni abused their priestly office at Shiloh and were condemned for doing so (1 Sam. 2:12–36). Both were killed in battle at Aphek by the Philistines who captured the ark (4:11), and Eli himself died when he heard this report. When Phinehas's pregnant wife heard the news that her husband and father-in-law were dead and that the ark had been captured, she immediately gave birth to a son she named Ichabod ("the glory has departed"), saying, "The glory has departed from Israel, for the ark of God has been captured" (4:21). *See also* Eli; Hophni; priests.

3 The father of the priest Eleazar (Ezra 8:33; 1 Esd. 8:63).　　　　　　　　　　　　　M.A.S.

Phlegon (fleg′uhn), a Christian greeted by Paul in Rom. 16:14, perhaps a member of a house-church.

Phoebe (fee′bee), a woman commended by Paul in Rom. 16:1. The commendation is usually thought to mean that Paul entrusted her with the delivery of his letter to the Christians in Rome, a role that might have included taking responsibility for reading the letter, interpreting it as necessary, answering questions it raised, and bringing a response back to Paul. Phoebe is designated by Paul as "sister," a common term used for female Christians, indicating the close familial relationships prevailing in early Christian communities. She is also called a "deacon" of the church in Cenchreae, a community near Corinth. The term "deacon" is used elsewhere by Paul for leaders or officers in the church (Phil. 1:1). Finally, Phoebe is identified as one who has been a benefactor to many, including Paul (Rom. 16:2). The term here rendered "benefactor" (Gk. *prostasis*) is not used elsewhere in the Bible, but is often thought to imply provision of material support. Thus, Phoebe may have been a woman with a certain amount of wealth, capable of leading a Christian community that met in her house. *See also* Cenchreae; Romans, Letter of Paul to the.　　　　　　　　　　　　　P.J.A.

Phoenicia (fi-nish′uh), the name given to a strip of the coastal Levant during the first millennium BCE. It was in that period that the city-states of Tyre, Sidon, Arvad, Byblos, and others engaged in long-distance navigation, maritime commerce, and colonization with Cyprus, North Africa, Sicily, Sardinia, and Iberia.

Name and Origin: The geographic and chronological boundaries for Phoenicia are imprecise,

Phoenician silver coin showing a Phoenician ship and hippocampus (part horse, part sea monster).

in part because neither the Phoenicians nor their Near Eastern neighbors used the term "Phoenician." It is in Homer, probably in a milieu of the ninth–eighth centuries BCE, that the inhabitants of Sidon are called Phoenician, although the term may first occur in Mycenaean texts from the thirteenth century BCE. The Phoenicians were famous for their costly purple dye produced from crushed mollusks; it has long been suggested that the name "Phoenicia" is derived from the Greek word for red-purple, *phoinix*. By the same token, "Canaan," a name for parts of the Levant, may come from a Hurrian word for red-purple, *kinahhu*.

In fact, the Phoenicians of the Iron Age (first millennium BCE) descended from the original Canaanites who dwelt in the region during the earlier Bronze Age (3000–1200 BCE), despite classical tradition to the contrary. There is archaeological evidence for a continuous cultural tradition from the Bronze to the Iron Age (1200–333 BCE) at the cities of Tyre and Zaraphath. In the Amarna age (fourteenth century BCE) many letters to Egypt emanated from kings Rib-addi of Byblos, Abi-milki of Tyre, and Zimrida of Sidon, and in other New Kingdom Egyptian texts there are references to the cities of Beirut, Sidon, Zaraphath, Ushu, Tyre, and Byblos. Additionally there is a thirteenth-century BCE letter from the king of Tyre to Ugarit, and a Ugaritic inscription has turned up at Zaraphath. Despite these facts showing that the coastal cities were occupied without interruption or change in population, the term "Phoenician" is now normally applied to the inhabitants of the area from the Iron Age (beginning about the twelfth century BCE) on. This was the period in which traits that characterize Phoenician culture evolved: long-distance seafaring, trade and colonization, and distinctive elements of the material culture, language, and script.

Principal Cities and Sites: The heartland of Phoenician city-states was the coastal area from Acco in the south to Arvad in the north, which in the main constitutes modern Lebanon. The most

Phoenician porters, in pointed caps and unfringed robes, carry tribute to the Assyrian ruler Shalmaneser III; ninth-century BCE engraved bronze gates.

important cities and sites are the island-city Tyre, with its mainland counterpart Ushu (Old Tyre), and Sidon and its neighbors, Zaraphath and the religious center Eshmun, followed by the other island-city, Arvad, with its mainland settlement of Amrit/Marathus, the ancient port of Byblos that was famous long before the Phoenician period, and Beirut with the small burial ground at Khalde. The roster of Phoenician cities changed during the near millennium-long period beginning in 1200 BCE, reflecting the waxing and waning of their individual fortunes and the impinging historical events of the Near East.

At the beginning of the Iron Age, as part of the invasion of the Sea Peoples (groups from the Greek islands, especially Crete), the Philistines occupied the coastal area south of Mount Carmel, including Dor, Ashdod, Ashkelon, and Gaza. By the eighth century BCE, however, the material culture of the Phoenicians extended southward, and Sidon controlled Dor and Joppa during the Persian period (539–333 BCE). There were no major Phoenician cities north of Arvad, but Phoenician influence extended into Cilicia in the ninth and eighth centuries BCE.

Obscurity surrounds the emergence of Phoenician culture during the twelfth and eleventh centuries BCE. In a foray, the Assyrian king Tiglath-pileser I (1114–1076 BCE) sojourned at Arvad and received tribute from Byblos and Sidon; there are archaeological data from Tyre and Zaraphath for this period. The Egyptian *Tale of Wenamun,* dating to the mid-eleventh century BCE, graphically portrays the decline of Egyptian prestige and power in the Levant. This was due in part to the invasions of the Sea Peoples and the general disruptions of Late Bronze Age cultures throughout the eastern Mediterranean, with the collapse of Mycenaean and Hittite cultures and the destruction of city-states in the Levant. Trade was severely affected. During the fourteenth and thirteenth centuries BCE, Mycenaean and Cypriot imports flowed into the Levant, but they were only a trickle from the twelfth century BCE on.

In the aftermath of the disruptions and the power vacuum a new order emerged in which flourishing Phoenician settlements replaced such destroyed centers as Ugarit on the coast of northern Syria. Instead of the Levant being the recipient of Aegean wares, Phoenician cities began exporting goods and services.

The histories of Tyre and Sidon are intertwined (indeed, they were only twenty-two miles apart). Classical tradition suggests that Sidon was the more powerful at first, but by the tenth century BCE Tyre dominated. Tyre's kings ruled a stretch of the coast that included Sidon, and often they were referred to as kings of the Sidonians (1 Kings 16:31).

By the tenth century BCE Phoenician workers were sent to Israel to assist Solomon in the construction of the temple at Jerusalem. In return Solomon sent grain and olive oil to Hiram, king of Tyre, and even Galilean territory was given to him (1 Kings 5), although it was not to his liking. Tyre's colonization of Cyprus in the tenth century BCE was established, and it controlled the southern coastal city of Kition, where Phoenicians constructed temples for their goddess Astarte.

In the ninth century BCE Tyre strengthened its influence over the northern kingdom, Israel. Phoenician influence is also to be seen in the region of Cilicia at Zinjirli, where King Kilamuwa, probably Aramean in origin, chose the Phoenician language and script for a long inscription at the front of his palace. Other Phoenician inscriptions come from the same region in the following centuries; Azitiwada marked the rebuilding of his city with bilingual inscriptions in Phoenician and hieroglyphic Hittite at Karatepe. The strong Phoenician influence in Cilicia may be due to trading activities in a network including Urartu, the northern rival of Assyria in the ninth and eighth centuries BCE. Phoenician trade and colonization of the western Mediterranean became strong in this period. Classical tradition dates the foundation of Carthage at 814 BCE by Tyrians.

During the earlier centuries Phoenician cities were autonomous for the most part and free from interference from outside political forces, although Assyrian monarchs from time to time demanded tribute. The pace of Assyrian activity in Phoenicia quickened in the ninth century BCE, when Ashurnasirpal II, Shalmaneser III, and Adad-nirari III exacted tribute and taxes from Sidon, Tyre, and other Phoenician cities. Assyria was gradually extending its control over the Levant. As a result of the far-reaching reorganization of the Assyrian Empire by Tiglath-pileser III (745–727 BCE), the nature of the impact on Phoenician areas changed from one of occasional demands by raiding armies to incorporation as vassals into the empire. Many cities lost their autonomy altogether and became part of Assyrian provinces administered by governors; for example, an Assyrian province of Simyra was established by Tiglath-pileser III.

Sennacherib crushed a serious revolt by coastal cities in 701 BCE and forced Luli (Elulaeus), king of Tyre, to flee to Cyprus, where he died. Later Sidon revolted against the Assyrian ruler Esar-haddon (681–669 BCE), who in 676 BCE sacked and destroyed it and in its place built a governor's residence, called Kar-Esarhaddon, for a new Assyrian province. He also made a treaty with Baal, king of Tyre. Ashurbanipal (668–627 BCE) laid siege to Tyre, and Nebuchadnezzar besieged it for thirteen years (587/6–573 BCE; Ezek. 26–28:19).

Sidon reemerged as the dominant city of Phoenicia in the Persian period (539–333 BCE) and led a Phoenician contingent in the Persian wars of the early fifth century BCE, helping bridge the Hellespont and fighting at Salamis. In Phoenicia itself, remains of this period are best represented at a sanctuary near Sidon (dedicated to the god Eshmun), at Byblos, and at Amrit (Marathus). In 332 BCE Tyre finally yielded to military attack, when Alexander built a mole between the island-city and the mainland during his seven-month siege.

Culture and Influence: Phoenicians expanded into the western Mediterranean during the ninth and eighth centuries BCE in Sardinia, Sicily, North Africa, and Iberia. Their trading stations and colonies on the Atlantic and Mediterranean sides of Gibraltar (Tartessos region) exploited the rich silver mines and other raw materials of Iberia. Many causes have been put forward for the impetus for Phoenician expansion: the geographic setting of an inland mountain barrier that naturally turned them seaward; depletion of natural resources (timber); overpopulation; development of a craft industry that demanded raw materials and foreign markets (Ezek. 27–28); and the influence of Assyria. It is debatable whether Phoenician expansion developed internally or was in reaction to growing Assyrian imperialism. If it was in response to Assyrians and Chaldeans, did the Phoenicians flee their homeland to escape oppression (Isa. 23) or did they prosper economically as key middlemen in the empire's trade network (Isa. 23; Ezek. 27–28), which extended the length of the Mediterranean? The greater economic threat

came from competing Greek expansion during the eighth century BCE and later. The Phoenicians extracted from the mollusk *Murex trunculus* a rare and costly purple dye for textiles and garments. Heaps of crushed murex shells have been found at Zaraphath, Sidon, and Tyre.

Solomon turned to skilled Phoenician builders, who helped cut and assemble stone and wood for the temple at Jerusalem (1 Kings 5). Today the best examples of Phoenician sacred architecture are the temple of Astarte at Kition, the sanctuary at Eshmun, and a small shrine at Zaraphath. Phoenicians often constructed stone walls with vertical piers of ashlar blocks laid in an alternating pattern of header and stretcher. The area between the piers was filled with irregular fieldstones. Ivory carving was another Phoenician craft. Their ivories, which were often inlays for furniture, date to the eighth and seventh centuries BCE and have been found at Megiddo, Samaria, and elsewhere in the Near East, in Assyrian cities, on Cyprus and in the western Mediterranean, and in the homeland at Zaraphath and Byblos. The ornate Levantine style exhibits a strong Egyptian influence with motifs of winged sphinxes, lotus flowers, and human figures with Egyptian headdress. Metal bowls with embossed and engraved designs of a central medallion and concentric bands were produced by skilled Cypro-Phoenician workers in bronze, silver, and gold.

Phoenicians spoke a Northwest Semitic language closely related to Ugaritic, Hebrew, and Aramaic. According to the ancient Greek historian Herodotus, the Phoenicians introduced the alphabet to Greece. Alphabetic writing was already well established in the Late Bronze Age at Ugarit, where a cuneiform script was used. The Phoenician alphabetic script is similar to early Hebrew and Aramaic scripts of the first millennium BCE.

Religion: Phoenician religion shared elements with other Canaanite cultures of the Levant in which the pantheon (i.e., the gods who were worshiped) differed from city to city and from one age to the next. Nature and fertility deities predominated. Baal, Astarte, Eshmun, Adonis, and Melqart were the chief deities, while Tanit, most popular in North Africa, was also known in Phoenicia. Baal, the chief god of Tyre and Sidon, was the leading rival to worship of "the Lord" in the northern Israelite kingdom (1 Kings 16:29–32:18). Baal's consort was the goddess Astarte. At Byblos the deities El and Baalat took the place of Baal and Astarte, and nearby the young god Adonis was worshiped at a country shrine of Aphka at the source of the river Nahr Ibrahim. Lucian (second century CE) relates that the death of Adonis was marked by annual rites of mourning when the river became red with the god's blood. At Sidon the god Eshmun was also worshiped at an important country sanctuary near springs for the river Nahr el-Awali. Eshmun, whom the Greeks identified with the healing god Asclepius, was most popular in the Chaldean and Persian periods. Melqart, whose relationship to Baal is ambiguous, was worshiped at Tyre and in the western

Mediterranean. At Carthage the goddess Tanit was propitiated by infamous child immolation by fire. Sacrificial precincts (Heb. *tophet;* 2 Kings 23:10; Jer. 7:31) containing cremation urns have been found at Carthage and on Sicily and Sardinia, but none have turned up in Iberia or Phoenicia. However, a dedicatory inscription from Zarephath for Tanit-Astarte makes it clear that Tanit was worshiped in Phoenicia as early as the seventh century BCE.

In the NT, Jesus journeyed into this region (Mark 7:24; cf. v. 26), and the area was visited by various Christian missionaries (Acts 11:19; 15:3; 21:2). *See also* Hiram; Philistines; Sidon; Solomon; Tyre.

Bibliography

Harden, Donald. *The Phoenicians.* Praeger, 1962.

Moscati, Sabatino. *The World of the Phoenicians.* Weidenfeld & Nicolson, 1968.

Pritchard, James B. *Recovering Sarepta, A Phoenician City.* Princeton University Press, 1978.

T.L.M.

Phoenix (fee′niks).

1 A mythical bird that was said to live an extremely long time (five hundred or sometimes thousands of years), after which it would build itself a funeral pyre and then rise as a small worm from the ashes to begin another long life. The phoenix is used as a symbol of long life in Job 29:18.

2 A seaport (possibly modern Port Loutro) on the southeastern coast of Crete. It was while on board an Alexandrian ship en route from Fair Haven to Phoenix for winter harborage that Paul and his captors were shipwrecked (Acts 27:12).

Phrygia (frij′ee-uh), a large region of interior western Asia Minor. The area itself consisted of a broad plateau that included mountains, pine forests, and river basins. During the NT period, the area of Phrygia was an ethnic territory, not an actual nation or province. It overlapped the Roman provinces of Asia and Galatia, encompassing the eastern portion of the former and the southern portion of the latter. Thus, references to Phrygia at this time can be somewhat ambiguous, but most often they seem to refer to the area around Colossae, Hierapolis, and Laodicea.

The Phrygians had migrated from Thrace around the end of the second millennium BCE. A short-lived Phrygian empire, founded by King Midas, ruled western Asia Minor ca. 725–675 BCE. Phrygians were renowned for worship of the mother goddess Cybele and her consort, Attis. According to Josephus, Jews also inhabited the region as early as the second century BCE. Acts 2:10 mentions Phrygian Jewish pilgrims among those who heard the apostles speaking in tongues at Pentecost.

The book of Acts says that Paul passed through Phrygia twice (16:6; 18:23). Paul never explicitly mentions Phrygia, but he does refer to the provinces of Galatia and Asia as areas in which he and his team worked, and a number of cities that would have been located in the Phrygian territory are mentioned by name: Antioch, Laodicea, Hierapolis, Colossae, and Iconium (Col. 1:2; 2:1; 4:13, 15–16; 2 Tim. 3:11). Philemon, whom Paul knew personally and whom he intended to visit, probably lived in or near Colossae. Some of the churches addressed in the book of Revelation (certainly Laodicea) were also found in the Phrygian territory (Rev. 2–3). *See also* Colossae; Hierapolis; Laodicea.

D.R.M.

Phygelus (fi′juh-luhs), a Christian from the Roman province of Asia who, with Hermogenes and others, is said to have abandoned Paul when he was a prisoner in Rome (2 Tim. 1:15). *See also* Hermogenes.

phylacteries (fi′lak′tuh-reez; Heb. *tephillin*), a pair of small black boxes containing passages from scripture written on parchment. According to ancient Jewish tradition, phylacteries are normally fastened by black straps to the upper left arm and above the forehead. The tradition is based on the biblical commendation to bind the words of Torah "as a sign on your hand" and to let them be "as a frontlet on your forehead" (Deut. 6:8; cf. Exod. 13:9, 16; Deut. 11:18). The passages placed inside the phylacteries were Exod. 13:1–10, 11–16; Deut. 6:4–9; 11:13–21. By the time of the first century CE, other passages, including the Decalogue and the Shema, were also sometimes used, as is evident from phylacteries found among the Dead Sea Scrolls.

Some religious scholars have speculated that phylacteries might have been viewed as apotropaic (i.e., protective), an analogy to magical amulets known as *qemia* that were used in pagan circles. Most interpreters, however, noting the choice of scripture texts that the phylacteries contained, believe the purpose was educational and spiritual; the phylactery was to serve as a constant reminder (to oneself and others) that one was committed to obedience to Torah. A number of other biblical passages refer to ornaments as metaphors for something that is carefully remembered and held dear (Prov. 1:9; Song of Sol. 8:6; Isa. 62:3; Jer. 2:32).

In Matthew's Gospel, Jesus criticizes the Pharisees for wearing what he thought were oversized phylacteries as a way of flaunting their piety (23:5). He does not criticize the wearing of phylacteries in and of itself.   D.A.G./M.A.P.

physicians. The primary term for a professional healer in the Hebrew Bible is *rophe'*, a word that the NRSV translates "physician" in four passages. None of these inspire or encourage confidence in the physician's abilities to assist the sick. In Gen. 50:2, the physicians in question are being employed postmortem, to embalm the body of Jacob; in 2 Chron. 16:12, King Asa of Judah (who is diseased in his feet) is denounced for seeking help from physicians rather than from God. Job compares his counselors to "worthless physicians" (13:4); and the prophet Jeremiah asks, rhetorically, "Is there no balm in Gilead? Is there no physician there? Why then has the health of my poor people not been restored?" (8:22). In the last three of these passages, the LXX translates *rophe'* with Greek *iatros,* a word that is also used in Tobit, Sirach, and the NT. Some of the latter references underscore the motif of inadequacy. Sir. 10:10 states simply that "a long illness baffles the physician." In Tob. 2:10, the author reports that after sparrow droppings fell into his eyes, his vision was obscured; he went to physicians to be healed, but claims that "the more they treated me with ointments the more my vision was obscured by the white films, until I became completely blind." Likewise, Mark 5:26 relates that a woman with a hemorrhage had spent all of her money on physicians who were unable to help her.

A more positive outlook on physicians is presented in Sir. 38:1–15. This long passage implores readers to "honor physicians for their services, for the Lord created them . . . their gift of healing comes from the Most High" (38:1–2). Sirach expresses confidence in the "skill of physicians" (38:3) and assures readers that physicians are able to heal and to take away pain (38:7). This positive view seems to be assumed by Jesus when he justifies his association with sinners by coining or quoting a proverb, "Those who are well have no need of a physician, but those who are sick?" (Matt. 9:12; Mark 2:17; Luke 5:31). Finally, in Col. 1:14, Paul refers to "Luke, the beloved physician" as being among his companions.

As with other ancient cultures, there was no necessary conflict in Israel between belief in divine or demonic causes of illness and the application of natural and practical therapy. Prayer did play a role in some treatments, and miraculous cures were certainly anticipated (1 Kings 17:17–24; 2 Kings 5:1–14). Still, natural factors contributing to illness were recognized and rational diagnoses and treatments coexisted with other approaches.

Practical aids included bandages, salves, poultices, and bone setting (e.g., Isa. 1:6; Jer. 8:22; Ezek. 34:4, 16). Medicine is referred to in Jer. 30:13; 46:11; Tob. 6:5; 11:8, 11 (cf. Sir. 6:16; Prov. 17:22), and Sir. 38:4 insists that "the Lord created medicines out of the earth and the sensible will not despise them." In general, trust in God and in spiritual remedies was not thought to be compromised by reliance on human physicians. Sir. 38:10–12 offers the following advice for the sick: "Give up your faults and direct your hands rightly, and cleanse your heart from all sin. Offer a sweet-smelling sacrifice, and a memorial portion of choice flour, and pour oil on your offering, as much as you can afford. Then give the physician his place, for the Lord created him." This mutual dependence upon divine and human assistance would probably have been typical for Jews during the Second Temple period.

Other medical personnel in biblical times would have included midwives (e.g., Gen. 35:17; 38:28) and, on occasion, priests, prophets, or miracle workers (e.g., 1 Kings 17:17–24; 2 Kings 4:14–37; 5:1–14; 20:1–11; Isa. 38). The passage in Sirach also refers to a "pharmacist" (38:8). In the NT era, exorcists were also viewed as professional healers. *See also* disease; healing.   M.A.P.

Pi-beseth (pi-bee′sith), a city in the Delta in Egypt. Ezek. 30:17 includes it as part of the prophet's oracle against Egypt. Known in Greek as Bubastis, it is modern Tell Basta, on an eastern branch of the delta flow. Its name reflects its identification with the Egyptian cat goddess, Bastet.

Pi-hahiroth (pi′huh-hi′roth), a town mentioned in Exod. 14:2, 9 as an Israelite stopping place on the route from Egypt (see also Num. 33:7). Its associations with Baal-zephon and Migdol suggest an eastern Nile Delta location, but the site is not precisely known.

Pilate (pi′luht), **Pontius** (pon′shuhs), Roman prefect of Judea, the fifth governor of the province, and the second-longest holder of the office (26–36 CE). His term included the time of John the Baptist's activity as well as that of the public ministry and crucifixion of Jesus (see Luke 3:1). Pilate is mentioned several times in the NT in connection with events surrounding the trial and crucifixion of Jesus (Matt. 27:1–2, 11–26; Mark 15:1–15; Luke 23:1–25; John 18:28–19:16; Acts 3:13; 4:27; 13:28; 1 Tim. 6:13). He and his rule are also discussed in the historical writings of Philo (*Embassy to Galus* 299) and Josephus (*Antiquities* 18.2.2; 18.3.1; *Jewish War* 2.9.2), both Jewish writers from the first century CE. The only extant Roman mention of Pilate is in a brief reference in the historian Tacitus to the crucifixion of Jesus. Thus, virtually everything known of him must be reconstructed from the Jewish and Christian writings, both of which view him in a pejorative light. Historians do sometimes note that, since Pilate governed Judea for an unusually long term, the Roman government must not have been too displeased with his performance. Archaeology has added only one piece of information: a Latin inscription, found in Caesarea Maritima in 1961 refers to Pilate as a prefect (not procurator).

In Jewish Sources: Pilate's character is represented very negatively in the Jewish sources. He is presented as insensitive to Jewish religion and all too ready to use brutal force to repress any dissent. He is also charged with incompetence and venality.

Josephus reports that, when Pilate first brought Roman troops to Jerusalem from Caesarea, he committed an unprecedented violation of Jewish sensibilities by allowing the troops to bring into the city their military standards with the busts of the emperor, which were considered idolatrous images by the Jews. This was done in an underhanded manner, though, as the troops brought in and set up the images by night. A massive protest demonstration in Caesarea's stadium forced the removal

Pilate washing his hands at the trial of Jesus (Matt. 27:24); from a fifth-century ivory.

of the standards, but only after the Jews used tactics of nonviolent mass resistance, lying down and baring their necks when Pilate's soldiers, swords in hand, surrounded and attempted to disperse them.

Philo tells of an incident in which Jewish letters of protest to Rome brought the intervention of the emperor himself, who commanded Pilate to remove golden shields with the emperor's name on them that he had placed in his residence in Jerusalem. Similar incidents, however, were not always resolved without bloodshed. Josephus again speaks of protests that broke out when Pilate appropriated temple funds to build an aqueduct for Jerusalem. On this occasion, Pilate had Roman soldiers, dressed as Jewish civilians and armed with hidden clubs, mingle with the shouting crowd and attack the people at a prearranged signal. Many were killed or hurt.

Finally, Josephus also mentions a slaughter of Samaritans in 35 CE, which apparently brought about Pilate's recall. A Samaritan prophet had gathered large numbers of his people to Mount Gerizim with the promise of showing them the holy vessels supposedly hidden there by Moses. Pilate treated the event as an insurrection and attacked the crowd with cavalry and heavy infantry, killing many in the battle and executing the leaders among the captured. Vitellius, the imperial legate to Syria, felt compelled to remove Pilate from office and send him to Rome to render account of his conduct. This Samaritan massacre reported by Josephus is sometimes mentioned as an intriguing parallel to the incident mentioned in Luke 13:1, where Jesus refers to the "Galileans whose blood Pilate had mingled with their sacrifices." Nothing is recorded anywhere else of the latter incident, but scholars note that such a slaughter would fit with the character of Pilate as described by Josephus in recounting the Samaritan incident.

In the Gospel Accounts: Pilate's part in the trial and execution of Jesus is the focus of most later interest in him. In general, the Synoptic Gospels present him as possibly weak and certainly cavalier about the administration of justice. He questions Jesus about the accusation that he claims to be the "King of the Jews" (Mark 15:2; cf. Matt. 27:11; Luke 23:3) and is amazed by Jesus's silence in response to charges brought against him (Mark 15:5; cf. Matt. 27:14). He knows that it is out of jealousy that Jesus's opponents have handed him over (Mark 15:10; cf. Matt. 27:18) and recognizes that there is no valid reason for his execution; still, he capitulates to the will of the people, sending Jesus to the cross (and setting Barabbas free), hoping that this will "satisfy the crowd" (Mark 15:14–15; cf. Luke 23:23–24) or prevent a riot (Matt. 27:24). Later, Pilate gives the body of Jesus to Joseph of Arimathea (Mark 15:43–44; cf. Matt. 27:58; Luke 23:51–52); in Matthew's Gospel he allows for a guard to be placed at the tomb (27:62–65).

Matthew's account also introduces Pilate's wife (not named in the Gospel, but called Procla or Procula in later tradition). She warns Pilate to have nothing to do with "that innocent man," about whom she has had a dream (27:19). In addition, Matthew's Gospel includes an episode in which Pilate washes his hands before the people, maintaining that, though he knows he is sentencing an innocent man to death, he will be free of responsibility for his blood; this prompts the people to respond, "His blood be on us and on our children!" (27:24–25). The meaning of that exchange is debated, but it is part of a motif according to which Judas and the chief priests also attempt to avoid responsibility for Jesus's blood (27:3–7). It seems unlikely that Matthew would have wanted to present Judas, the chief priests, and Pilate as somehow escaping condemnation and having it fall, instead, on the people Jesus supposedly came to save (cf. 1:21). Thus, one prominent interpretation suggests that the attempt to avoid Jesus's blood is ironic: Jesus's blood brings forgiveness of sins (26:20), and Pilate is depicted as foolishly cleansing himself of his only chance for salvation, while the Jewish people in general are depicted as unwittingly praying for forgiveness.

Luke's version of the story has Pilate send Jesus to Herod Antipas, whose soldiers mock him. Furthermore, in Luke's account Pilate actually declares Jesus to be innocent three separate times (23:4, 14, 22). Many interpreters think that Luke wants to emphasize for Roman readers that Jesus was not actually a criminal—the Roman governor himself acknowledged this and, so, acted irresponsibly in having Jesus put to death.

In the Gospel of John, Pilate attempts to engage Jesus in philosophical discussion over the definition of kingship (Jesus says his kingdom is "not from this world," 18:36) and the nature of truth (Pilate asks, "What is truth?" 18:38). Also, according to John, the Jewish opponents of Jesus need Pilate's judgment against Jesus, because they were not permitted to put anyone to death (18:31), and they believed Jesus had committed offenses that merited death, even though those offenses would not be capital crimes under Roman law (19:7). Therefore, they had to manipulate Pilate into passing judgment against Jesus for another reason, namely, that he had set himself against the emperor (19:12; cf. 18:30). In John, Pilate is also said to be afraid of Jesus, who has claimed to be the Son of God (19:7–8). Jesus, further, makes clear that Pilate has no authority over him except that given from above (19:11). Thus, in John, Pilate is depicted as a helpless pawn, but less a pawn of the Jewish authorities who want to manipulate him than a pawn of God, who is determining what must take place. In seeming recognition of this, Pilate has an inscription put on the cross that reads, "Jesus of Nazareth, the King of the Jews," and when the authorities object that it should read, "This man said, I am King of the Jews," Pilate answers defiantly, "What I have written I have written" (19:19–22). *See also* Barabbas; Judea; prefect; trial of Jesus.   F.O.G./M.A.P.

pilgrimage, a journey to a shrine, holy place, or sanctuary for a religious reason. Such journeys are a common feature of religious devotion and are not confined to any particular religious tradition, period of time, or group of people. In the ancient Near East, shrines for worship were often established at sites connected with divine activity, such as an extraordinary event (e.g., Josh. 4:1–7), or at sites revered by tradition as holy (e.g., Gen. 13:18). Shrines often became the goal of pilgrimages, and worshipers would bring offerings to a shrine for petition or thanksgiving.

The earliest pilgrimages recorded in the Bible were to the shrines that existed throughout Israel before the reforms of King Josiah (ca. 622 BCE). At a critical point in Jacob's life (the changing of his name to Israel), he made a pilgrimage to Bethel, the place where he had earlier erected an altar after seeing God in a dream (Gen. 35:1–15; cf. 28:10–22; 12:8). Shiloh became the site for an early annual pilgrimage (Judg. 21:19–21; 1 Sam. 1:3–7, 21), and other sacred places in Israel also attracted worshipers, including Gibeon (1 Kings 3:4), Beer-sheba (Amos 5:5; 8:14), and Gilgal (Hos. 4:15; Amos 4:4–5; 5:5) as well as numerous "high places" (1 Sam. 9:12–19, 25).

Jerusalem: In the time of David (ca. 1000 BCE), Jerusalem was established as a religious center (2 Sam. 6:12–19), and following the completion of the temple under Solomon (1 Kings 8; 2 Chron. 7:8–10) it increasingly became the goal of pilgrimage, a place to which the people could bring their offerings and a place they could celebrate festivals and offer sacrifices to God (Deut. 12:6–7, 11–12, 17–18). After the division of the nation (ca. 922 BCE), Jeroboam I, ruler of the northern kingdom, established sanctuaries at the ancient sites of Bethel and Dan in an attempt to prevent the people from traveling to the temple in Jerusalem in the southern kingdom (1 Kings 12:26–30). The reforms of Hezekiah and Josiah attempted to eliminate the outlying shrines and high places because of the threat of corruption by Baal worship (2 Kings 18:4; 23:4–20), but they continued to exist until the period of the exile (587 BCE).

Israelite religious legislation required pilgrimage to Jerusalem three times a year: at the Festival of Unleavened Bread (Passover), the Festival of Weeks (Pentecost), and the Festival of Tabernacles (Deut. 16:16; cf. Exod. 23:13–17; 34:18–23). In NT times, large crowds of pilgrims are depicted as coming to Jerusalem for such festivals (Luke 2:41–45; John 12:20). According to John's Gospel, Jesus made several pilgrimages to Jerusalem to celebrate festivals (2:13; 5:1; 7:2–10). Those on pilgrimage often traveled in groups (Pss. 42:4; 55:14; Luke 2:44), and the joy of the occasion would be marked by singing and rejoicing (Isa. 30:29). Several pilgrimage songs are preserved in the "Songs of Ascent" collected in the book of Psalms (120–134). In a figurative sense, the NT portrays the Christian life as a journey toward a heavenly city (Heb. 11:13–16; cf. 1 Pet. 1:17; 2:11). *See also*

Bethel; festivals, feasts, and fasts; high place; Passover; Pentecost; Shiloh; Zarephath.   D.R.B.

pillars.

1 Vertical columns of wood or stone used as architectural members to hold up roof supports, whether in temples (1 Kings 7; Judg. 16:25–29), palaces (Esther 1:6), or houses, as archaeological evidence abundantly shows. They were set on firm bases or in sockets for stability and were capped by capitals sometimes elaborately decorated or carved. Pillars could be solid, single-block columns, sometimes fluted, or composite columns built of drum cylinders fitted together in vertical alignment. Pillars were said to support the earth (1 Sam. 2:8; Ps. 75:3) and the heavens (Job 26:11). Symbolically, they also supported the "house" of wisdom (Prov. 9:1). In the NT, the church is described metaphorically as "the pillar and bulwark of the truth" (1 Tim. 3:15)

2 Columns of wood or stone set up as memorials. Pillars were used for marking individual burials (Gen. 35:20, Jacob's memorial to Rachel at her grave), self-commemorations (2 Sam. 18:18, Absalom's monument to himself), and as commemorations of significant events (Gen. 28:22; 31:45; 35:14, aspects of Jacob's life). In Exod. 24:4, Moses is said to have built an altar in the wilderness and to have set up twelve pillars corresponding to the twelve tribes of Israel. Likewise, acacia pillars were part of the tabernacle (Exod. 26:32), and two elaborate bronze pillars named Jachin and Boaz were erected at the front entrance of the temple (1 Kings 7:15–22). It is perhaps in this sense of the term—a pillar as a monument rather than as a support—that provides the best context for the story in which Lot's wife is transformed into a pillar of salt, i.e., a monument to folly (Gen. 19:26). *See also* Jachin and Boaz.

3 The stone pillar representing the male deity and the lush tree or wooden post representing the female deity that were standard parts of Canaanite Baalist shrine equipment. Their presence symbolized the sexual union of the gods necessary to allow agricultural fertility to continue from one year to the next. Israelite religion opposed this point of view vigorously in law (Exod. 23:24; Deut. 7:5; Lev. 26:1) and prophetic declarations (Hos. 3:4; 10:2; Mic. 5:13), but its appeal continued (Amos 2:7–8).

4 Meteorological or volcanic phenomena, such as the pillars of cloud and fire (Exod. 13:21) that guided Israel in the wilderness and marked the door of the tent of meeting (Exod. 33:9, 10; Deut. 31:15). These phenomena were long remembered as acts of God's gracious love (Neh. 9:12–19; Ps. 99:7).

5 Markers of various sorts. According to archaeological evidence from the Near East, pillars were used as boundary markers and milestones. The function of the enigmatic dolmens (usually two vertical slabs of rock capped by a horizontal slab) scattered in fields is still debated.

6 People of importance. Isaiah describes people who are mainstays of society as pillars (19:10).

Likewise, Paul refers to James, Cephas, and John as people reputed to be pillars in the church (Gal. 2:9).   R.S.B.

pillow. Jacob used a stone for a headrest when he slept (Gen. 28:11, 18), but the story in 1 Samuel of Michal disguising an idol to look like David asleep in bed suggests that pillows at that time consisted of a net filled with goats' hair (19:13, 16). Mark 4:38 refers to Jesus being asleep in a boat with his head on a cushion, which was probably a seat pad, but there is no way of knowing of what it consisted. In 1 Esdras 3:1–4:42 three bodyguards write statements concerning wisdom and place them under the pillow of King Darius, so he can determine which is wisest (3:8).   M.A.P.

pim, a weight averaging 7.8 grams in samples found. This makes it equal to three-fifths of a heavy shekel or seven-eighths of a light shekel. In 1 Sam. 13:21, a pim of silver was the Philistine price for sharpening iron implements. *See also* weights and measures.

pin (Heb. *yated*), in Judg. 16:13–14, a short, pointed stick used to beat up the weft in a loom (the Hebrew Masoretic Text is unclear here, and the LXX understands the term to refer to a peg driven into the wall to secure the loom). The same Hebrew word is elsewhere rendered "tent peg" (Exod. 27:19), "peg" (Ezek. 15:3), and "trowel" (Deut. 23:13). *See also* peg.

pine, a tree of the genus *Pinus*, producing edible cones and straight-grained, highly resinous wood. The stone pine (*Pinus pinea*) grew plentifully in the sandy soil near the Mediterranean coast. Its wood was good for construction (Song of Sol. 1:17), fitting ships (Ezek. 27:6), reclamation (Isa. 41:19), decoration (Isa. 60:13), aromatics, and other products. The Aleppo pine (*Pinus halapensis*) was also found throughout the Near East.

pioneer, a term applied to Jesus in the Letter to the Hebrews. The Greek term *archēgos* typically refers to a leader or guide or to a founder of a school or movement. Heb. 12:2 calls Jesus the "pioneer and perfecter" of faith; 2:10 notes that as the "pioneer of salvation," he was made perfect through suffering.

pipe. *See* music.

Piram (pi'ruhm; Heb., perhaps "wild ass"), the king of Jarmuth and one of the Amorite allies who attempted to stop Joshua at Gibeon (Josh. 10:3–11), only to be killed and hung (10:22–26). Jarmuth is probably modern Khirbet Yarmuk, about fifteen miles southwest of Jerusalem.

Pirathon (pihr'uh-thon), a town in the land of Ephraim, probably to be identified with modern Farata, about five miles west and slightly south of Shechem. Pirathon was the home of Hillel the Pirathonite, whose son Abdon was one of the judges of Israel and who was subsequently buried there (Judg. 12:15). It was also the home of Benaiah, one of David's guards (2 Sam. 23:30; 1 Chron. 11:31; 27:14).

Pisgah (piz'guh), a mountain in the area east of the Dead Sea. In the Bible "the top of Pisgah" is mentioned four times. In Num. 21:20, the top of Pisgah is said to be beside the region of Moab and to overlook the desert wastelands. Then, in Num. 23:14, Balak takes Balaam to the field of Zophim, to the top of Pisgah, in the land of Moab, that he might look upon the Israelites below and pronounce a curse on them. The final two references are in Deut. 3:27 and 34:1, where Moses goes up from the plain of Moab to Mount Nebo, to the top of Pisgah, which is opposite Jericho, to view the land.

The "slopes of Pisgah" are also mentioned four times. In Deut. 3:17 and 4:49 the Sea of the Arabah, the Salt Sea, is "under the slopes of Pisgah" to the east. In Josh. 12:3 the territory of the Israelites, beyond the Jordan, is described as extending "to the sea of the Arabah, the Salt Sea, southward to the foot of the slopes of Pisgah." In Josh. 13:20 the Reubenite territory includes "the slopes of Pisgah."

Most interpreters identify Mount Pisgah with modern Ras es-Siyaghah, which is located east of the Dead Sea and northwest of Mount Nebo, separated from the latter by a saddle. *See also* Arabah; Balaam; Balak; Dead Sea; Jericho; Moab; Moses; Nebo.   B.M.

Pishon (pi'shon), one of the rivers in the garden of Eden (Gen. 2:11), though a minor one in the company of the Tigris and the Euphrates. There is no scholarly agreement as to which river might have been meant or whether, perhaps, the intended referent was some larger body of water, such as the Persian Gulf.

Pisidia (pi-sid'ee-uh), a mountainous region just north of Pamphylia in south-central Asia Minor. In 25 BCE, Pisidia became part of the Roman province of Galatia. Paul and Barnabas passed through this region twice during their first journey (Acts 13:14–51; 14:24) and were persecuted in its principal city, Antioch, where there was apparently a sizable Jewish community (13:14–15, 43–45). *See also* Antioch; Galatia.   M.K.M.

Pisidian Antioch (pi-sid'ee-uhn an'tee-ok). *See* Antioch of Pisidia.

pit, a term that translates a variety of Hebrew and Greek words for natural, crafted, or symbolic depressions in the earth. Included are such natural formations as bitumen pits (Gen. 14:10) and miry bogs (Ps. 40:2) in addition to the lairs of animals (2 Sam. 23:20). Many pits, however, were dug intentionally (Ps. 7:15), apparently to be used as traps for animals. There are references to pits that were either dug or found being used to imprison

humans (Gen. 37:22) or to bury a body (2 Sam. 18:17). If not covered over, they could become public hazards (Exod. 21:33), but some pits (possibly large ones, perhaps used as garbage dumps) were sufficiently permanent to be used as landmarks (cf. "the pit at Beth-eked," 2 Kings 10:14). Metaphorically, the "the pit" may refer to the abode of the dead (Job 33:18) or to a bottomless source of scourges and plagues (Rev. 9:1, 2; 11:7). It is also the destination of the devil (20:2–3).

Archaeological evidence of pits is frequently found. Pits include wells, cisterns, lined and unlined storage vaults, graves and shafts dug in soil or cut in rock, and modifications of natural caves for use as cisterns, dry storage, or animal and human shelter. Chalcolithic and some Early Bronze Age houses are partially pits in earth or stone built up with surrounding walls and roofs for shelter.

R.S.B.

pitch, a brown-black, gummy substance used both as an adhesive and for waterproofing. Resinous pitches are derived from conifers such as pine. Tarlike mineral pitches can be derived from natural asphalt or bitumen deposits or as by-products of petroleum processing. The Dead Sea area provides natural deposits of asphalt. Moses's mother waterproofed a rush basket by smearing it with pitch before placing the infant Moses in it and setting it upon the Nile (Exod. 2:3). Noah's ark was likewise caulked with pitch (Gen. 6:14). The burning streams of pitch in Isa. 34:9 refer to the flammable properties of asphalt and bitumen. Pitches were also commonly used as adhesives for hafting tools and weapons as well as for securing inlays.

P.L.C.

pitcher, a ceramic, glass, or stone container, usually with a single vertical loop handle and a molded lip or inserted spout for pouring, the latter sometimes through a set of sieve holes in the vessel just above the pouring lip. Jeremiah was instructed to bring wine to the Rechabites in pitchers (35:5). In Ecclesiastes, a broken pitcher symbolizes death (12:6).

Pithom (pi′thom; from Egyptian *per-atum,* "house of Atum"), an Egyptian store-city mentioned in Exod. 1:11 together with Raamses. It was built by Israelite slave labor not long before the exodus. Apparently the city contained a temple center of the creator god, Atum, of On-Heliopolis. The modern identification is uncertain. Many scholars locate Pithom at modern Tell el-Maskhuta, in the eastern Delta along the Wadi Tumilat, but confirmation is lacking. A location in the general area is likely because Ramesses II (1279–1213 BCE) and his predecessors undertook major building projects in the eastern Delta, and many people from the biblical lands were located there. *See also* exodus, the; On; Raamses, Rameses.   H.B.H.

pity. *See* loving-kindness; mercy.

plagues, in the Bible, typically calamities sent by God. Sometimes, plagues involve contagious or widespread disease (1 Sam. 6:4), but other sorts of disastrous occurrences might be involved as well (cf. 1 Kings 8:37). In Gen. 12:17, God strikes Pharaoh "with great plagues," because he has unwittingly taken Abram's wife into his house. This foreshadows the later punishments inflicted on another pharaoh during the time of Moses (Exod. 7–12). The ten plagues recounted in the story of the exodus involve blood, frogs, gnats, flies, disease among livestock, boils, hail, locusts,

darkness, and death of the firstborn. In the exodus story itself, these calamities are only referred to as plagues in Exod. 8:2; 9:14; 11:1; 12:13. They are also called "signs and wonders" (Exod. 7:3; cf. Deut. 4:34). The tradition of these plagues, which brought about Israel's deliverance from Egypt, is also mentioned elsewhere (Deut. 28:60; 1 Sam. 4:8; Pss. 78:43–51; 105:27–36; 135:8–9; 136:10; cf. Amos 4:10; Hab. 3:5).

Source Analysis of Exod. 7–12: Some scholars believe that the exodus story is a composite of material from different sources. According to this theory, a cycle of tradition from the J material may be seen to include eight episodes: Nile water turning foul (7:14–17a, 18, 20a, 21a, 23–24); frogs swarming out of the Nile into living quarters (7:25–8:4, 8–15a); flies on the Egyptians and their land, but not on the Israelites (8:20–32); a plague on the cattle of the Egyptians, but not on the cattle of the Israelites (9:1–7); thunder and hail to harm cattle in the fields (9:13–21, 23–25a, 26–30, 33–34); locusts to devour crops left after the hail (10:1–11, 13–19); darkness over the land of Egypt for three days, except where the Israelites lived (10:21–26, 28–29); and the death of all the Egyptian firstborn (11:1, 4–8; 12:29–32). If the plague on cattle is secondary within J (since it harmonizes awkwardly with the hail on cattle in the fields), the original J cycle would have had seven episodes.

Moses (*right*) turns Egypt's water into blood, the first of the ten plagues (Exod. 7:14–19), while Aaron (*center*) performs miracles; woodcut from the fifteenth-century Cologne Bible.

According to this same source-critical analysis, the P tradition recast the J material as a contest between Pharaoh and God. The staff that turned into a serpent, originally a sign to authenticate Moses before the people (4:1–5, from J), now begins a contest between Aaron and Pharaoh's magicians (7:8–13, from P), and that contest theme recurs several times. As reconstructed, P's contributions are: all Egypt's water, not just that in the Nile, is turned to blood, and the magicians produce the same effect (7:17b, 19–20a, 21b–22); frogs come up out of all Egypt's waters, not just the Nile, and the magicians also equal that (8:5–7, 15b); the dust of the earth is turned to gnats on humans and animals in all the land, the magicians fail to reproduce that, and they acknowledge God's "finger" at work (8:16–19); ashes from the kiln are thrown into the air and cause boils breaking out in sores on humans and animals throughout all the land, and the magicians cannot stand before Moses because of the boils (9:8–12); hail is brought on all the land, upon humans and animals and plants, and the magicians are not even mentioned (9:22, 25b, 35). Characteristic formulas are also added to the episodes of locusts (10:12, 20) and darkness (10:27) as well as in conclusion (11:9–10). The death of the firstborn is moved outside P's contest cycle to come within the Passover description (12:12–13; cf. 12:17). Thus it inaugurates the actual deliverance from Egyptian slavery.

Elsewhere in the Bible: Plagues are often referred to as potential and generic punishment that will come upon Israel as a result of unfaithfulness (Exod. 30:12; Lev. 26:21; Num. 8:19) or that might be averted through worship or other appropriate measures (2 Sam. 24:21–26). Specifically, God sends plagues upon the Israelites who worshiped the golden calf at Sinai (Exod. 32:35), upon quail eaters who craved meat (Num. 11:33), upon the spies who brought back an unfavorable report regarding the land (14:37), upon the congregation that rebelled over the deaths of Korah, Dathan, and Abiram (16:46–50), and upon the people at Peor who had sexual relations with Moabite women and yoked themselves to the Baal of Peor (Num. 25; cf. 31:16; Josh. 22:17). The prophet Zechariah promises plague will strike the nations who attack Jerusalem (14:12, 15, 18). Finally, in the NT, Luke 7:21 says that Jesus cured people of plagues, and in Luke 21:11 Jesus says that plagues will come upon the earth prior to the end. The book of Revelation details many plagues that accompany the apocalyptic last days (9:18, 20; 11:6; 15:1, 6, 8; 16:9, 21; 18:4, 8) and concludes with a warning that "if anyone adds to (the words of this book), God will add to that person the plagues described in this book" (Rev. 22:18). *See also* exodus, the; Moses; Pentateuch, sources of the.   K.G.O

plains. In the Levant, plains are significant because the level land facilitates trade, conquest, and ease of travel. A number of plains are mentioned by name in the Bible.

The Plain of Megiddo, or Esdraelon Plain, is a fertile valley (Heb. *biqʻah;* 2 Chron. 35:22; Zech. 12:11) linking the coastal plain with the Jordan Valley; this was the main land route from Egypt to Damascus and the east. Megiddo guarded its western entrance, and Taanach and Jezreel were other towns on the plain that were the scenes of biblical events. The Song of Deborah places the defeat of the Canaanites near Taanach (Judg. 5:19), Jezreel was a royal residence during Ahab's kingship (1 Kings 21:1), and Josiah was killed in battle at Megiddo (2 Kings 23:29).

The Plain of Sharon was only eight to twelve miles wide along the Mediterranean coast, but during biblical times it was thick with forests of oak and swampy marshes; it was not fertile or productive. North of the Plain of Sharon, however, were several smaller plains along the coast: the Plain of Dor, south of Mount Carmel; the Plain of Acco, north of Carmel; and the Phoenician plain, with its natural harbors at Tyre, Sidon, and Byblos. South of Sharon was the broad Philistine plain, which often defied Israelite control. The cities of the Philistine Pentapolis were Ashdod, Askelon, Gaza, Gath, and Ekron. Valleys in the hill country formed small plains such as those around Shechem and Dothan.

The Jordan Valley broadens out into a plain particularly around Jericho (Josh. 5:10; 2 Kings 25:5). The Hebrew word most often used to describe the Jordan plain is *ʻarabah,* meaning "wilderness" or "desert plain"; the NRSV often translates *ʻarabah* as a proper name for the plain west of the Jordan River (Josh. 12:8; 2 Sam. 2:29), east of the river (Josh. 12:1), and on both sides (11:2). The term is also used to describe the area east of the Dead Sea opposite Jericho, usually in reference to the "plain [*ʻarabah*] of Moab" (Num. 22:1; 33:48–50; Deut. 34:1; Josh. 13:32).

Five cities believed to be on the southeast shore of the Dead Sea (Sodom, Gomorrah, Admah, Zeboiim, and Zoar) are referred to in the Bible as the "cities of the Plain" (Gen. 13:12; 19:25, 29). Archaeological excavations, however, seem to indicate that occupation of this area was in the first ridge of foothills rather than down in the plain itself. The Hebrew word translated "plain" (or sometimes "valley") is *kikkar* (meaning "round" or "circle"); perhaps it was meant to refer to the cities around (but not in) the Dead Sea plain.

Elsewhere, the Hebrew word *mishor* is used for a plain or level place both literally (1 Kings 20:24; 2 Chron. 26:10) and figuratively (Ps. 27:11; Jer. 21:13; 28:8). When *mishor* refers to a particular plain, the NRSV translates it "tableland" (the Medeba plain, Josh. 13:9, 16).

In the NT, the most prominent reference to a plain is in the Gospel of Luke, where Jesus is said to have "stood on a level place" and preached a sermon to his disciples and a great multitude of people (6:17). Because the content of that sermon closely parallels material found in the Sermon on the Mount in Matthew's Gospel, Jesus's sermon in Luke 6:17–49 is often called the Sermon on the Plain. *See also* Jezreel; Philistines; Sharon, Plain of. N.L.L.

plane, a tree of the genus *Platanus*. Biblical usage associates it with pine (Isa. 41:19; 60:13) and describes its use in controlling the appearance of the offspring of animals (Gen. 30:37–39). Its symbolic value as beauty is also mentioned (Ezek. 31:8). *Platanus orientalis* is most likely a correct identification.

plants. According to the book of Genesis, God created plants on the third day of creation (1:11). The general view throughout the Bible is that plants, like animal, marine, and other forms of life, are gifts of God that should be cherished, used, enjoyed, shared, and processed for the good of all people (1:29, 30; 2:8; 3:18). A tree growing by water (Jer. 17:8; Ps. 1:3) or a rich vineyard (2 Kings 19:29; Prov. 31:16; Amos 9:14) may be a symbol of blessing. Conversely, a failed harvest is a sign of judgment (Isa. 7:10–11). Overgrown, barren, or deserted sites are also used as metaphorical expressions of divine displeasure or judgment (Amos 4:9; 5:11). Levitical law forbade early exploitation of fruit-bearing trees (Lev. 19:23), and it was forbidden to plant a tree as the religious symbol of the Canaanite fertility goddess Asherah (Deut. 16:21). R.S.B.

pleasing odor. *See* odor, pleasing.

pledges. *See* loan, loans.

Pleiades (plee′uh-deez), a constellation mentioned three times in the Bible, along with Orion. Amos 5:8 refers to God as "the one who made Pleiades and Orion" in a passage promising judgment of the unrighteous. Likewise, Job 9:9 refers to God as the creator of these constellations, and in 38:31 God's control of them is cited as evidence of divine sovereignty and grandeur. M.A.P.

plow. Biblical texts include both literal and figurative references to the plow. In the agricultural cycle of the ancient Near East, plowing was a seasonal activity geared to preparation of the soil prior to planting. Practically, it could occur anytime in the rainy season (October–April) or in the dry season before soil hardened too severely (cf. Prov. 20:4; Isa. 28:24). While Israel's acquaintance with agriculture is attested early (Gen. 45:6), the Israelites were sometimes dependent on Canaanite neighbors for the care and maintenance of their plows and other equipment (1 Sam. 13:19–21). Primitive plows were made of forked tree branches with metal points to dig into the earth. Israel's law prohibited plowing with mixed teams (Deut. 22:10). The anticipated time of peace was represented as an era when weapons of war would be transformed into equipment for plowing (Isa. 2:4; Mic. 4:3); by contrast, anticipation that there would be no peace could be expressed by a call to reverse that process (Joel 3:10).

The act of plowing is often referred to as symbolic of something that is preparatory; in this sense it can mean cultivating sin (Job 4:8; Hos. 10:13) or imply preparing for the future in a more positive sense (Hos. 10:11). In 1 Cor. 9:10 it is used as a metaphor for doing something in anticipation of a legitimate reward. To put one's "hand to the plow" implies dedication to a task, while "plowing the sea" is a metaphor for doing something absurd (Amos 6:12). In a different sense, to be plowed by someone summons an image of severe abuse (Ps. 129:3; Jer. 26:18; Mic. 3:12); this may be all that is meant in Judg. 14:18, where Samson accuses the men who threatened his wife with having plowed with his heifer (a "heifer" being a term of endearment for a beautiful woman), but some have speculated that the word may have a more vulgar sexual connotation in this instance. R.S.B./M.A.P.

plowshare, a sharp iron blade attached to the beam of a plow. Lacking rudimentary iron technology, Israelites of the early monarchic period (ca. 1020–1000 BCE) took plowshares for sharpening to the Philistines (1 Sam. 13:19–23). As instruments that can only be used in times of peace, they are contrasted to swords, also made of iron. Turning swords into plowshares demonstrates peace (Isa. 2:4; Mic. 4:3). In Joel 3:10, however, the process is reversed.

plumb line, a length of string or light rope with a weight (Lat. *plumbum*, "lead") attached at one end that, when suspended by the other end, will show a true vertical line. It is used in the construction of a wall or fence that needs to be vertically true. Amos sees a vision of God with a plumb line in hand, indicating that Israel is going to be tested. Thus, the prophet proclaims Israel will be judged and destroyed on account of not being "plumb" with God (7:7–9).

pods, probably the fruit of the carob or locust tree, common in the Middle East and in Egypt. When ripe, these pods were filled with a dark honeylike syrup. They were then collected, ground up, and fed to animals. In the parable of the Prodigal Son, Jesus says that the destitute boy wished that he could eat the pods he fed to pigs (cf. Luke 15:16).

poetry. In the Bible, songs, prayers, proverbs, oracles, and other lofty pronouncements have been identified as "poetry," although there does not appear to be any one biblical term that corresponds to the English word "poetry."

Form: The characteristic feature of Hebrew poetry is a brief, two-part sentence whose second part typically reasserts, strengthens, or otherwise completes what was said in the first: "Happy are those who fear the Lord, who greatly delight in (God's) commandments" (Ps. 112:1). The effect of this sentence form is to provide the whole with a feeling of closure and completeness. Just as, in

Western poetry, a rhyme can pull things together and give a couplet a final "click," so the second part of such a sentence, strengthening and finishing off the first, marks it as complete and polished. The sentence gains an elegant and sometimes emphatic or epigrammatic quality.

Variety in the form is observable in the relationship between the two (or, rarely, three) parts of the sentence. Sometimes the second part seems to repeat the same point in different words, offering an emphatic restatement: "I will praise the LORD as long as I live; I will sing praises to my God all my life long" (Ps. 146:2). More often, however, the second element carries the first part farther and completes it by supplying some grammatically or semantically necessary conclusion (e.g., "Since X . . . then Y . . ." or "by day . . . by night . . ."). Especially in wise sayings such as those in the book of Proverbs, this two-part structure can function almost like a riddle: listeners are invited to figure out the relation between the first and second parts. Such is the statement in Eccles. 7:1: "A good name is better than precious ointment, and the day of death, than the day of birth." Almost everyone would agree with the first part of this statement (that a person's good name is a more precious commodity than any material possession), but the second statement subverts conventional thinking (a day of birth is almost always a happy occasion, and a day of death is normally a time for mourning). Thus, the statement poses a riddle. In what sense is the latter element "better" than the former? In this case, the point seems to be that the human body, like precious ointment, is perishable; eventually it must spoil and die. A good name, however, is quite the opposite; it takes a lifetime to build, but once completed, i.e., on the day of a person's death, it is immutable, imperishable. Thus, the proverb suggests that the day of one's death, when the building of one's reputation is complete, is better than the day of one's birth, when that process is only beginning.

Effects of the Two-Part Form: Although scholars have long been aware of the feeling of regularity and heightened eloquence created by Hebrew poetry, they have had some difficulty in describing its workings. In antiquity, Josephus, and later Eusebius, Jerome, and others, asserted that biblical songs were written in quantitative meters, just like Greek or Latin verse—in fact, in the same meters as these! It was not until the Renaissance that Western scholars began to realize that this assertion was false (and of apologetic intent); yet even afterward scholars have intermittently continued to search for some other sort of metrical system underlying Hebrew sentences—accentual, syllabic, "word rhythm," and so forth. In truth none of the systems proposed can be made to work consistently, for the regularity is only approximate. It seems that an approximate and intermittent regularity was all that this style demanded. One contributing factor to the regularity is the extraordinary terseness and compression characteristic of the Hebrew style. Utterances framed in poetry

frequently dispense with such features as the Hebrew definite article *ha-*, the relative pronoun *'asher* ("which" or "that"), and other common signposts of ordinary discourse. More generally, this same principle of terseness holds clauses to three- or four-word expressions, allowing complex thoughts and images to develop within the confines of the brief, two-part assertions strung one after the other.

Parallelism: The attempt to pin down the workings of Hebrew poetry led the eighteenth-century biblical scholar Robert Lowth to coin the term *parallelismus membrorum* (Lat., "the parallelism of the clauses"), and ever since, the term "parallelism" has enjoyed wide popularity as an explanation of the principle underlying Hebrew poetry. Of late, however, this approach has been seriously questioned, for although some form of paralleling, in meaning or syntax, can be shown to characterize quite a few of the two-part sentences involved, far too many exceptions exist to allow paralleling to be accepted as the generative force behind all such sentences. Moreover, it is clear that the term "parallelism" has been used loosely by biblical scholars. Almost no series of consecutive sentences (in the Bible or anywhere else) can be shown to be utterly devoid of some form of parallelism, so that finding instances of parallelism in this style, in whatever muted or obscure form, proves very little. Moreover, the notion of parallelism has occasionally served to group together very different features and thus cover over important distinctions. For example, parallelism has been used to label such phenomena as actual repetition, or numerical ("Three things . . . four things . . .") or other sequences.

Contemporary scholars have shown that the "principle of parallelism" is shorthand for a complex of phenomena: various forms of ellipsis, especially of subject or verb in the second part (called "gapping" by one writer), and a whole range of semantic equivalences and associations. The basic principle underlying this style might be better described as simply "seconding" or "extending," the process of following up the typically short, spare assertion of Part A with another, subjoined one in Part B: "A is so, and what's more, B"; "Not only A, but B"; "Not A, and certainly not B"; "First A happened, then B"; "If A, then B"; and so forth. This form was sometimes abstracted to include almost any sequence of two or three short clauses. The basic requirement seems only to have been that parts A and B be (syntactically) separated, so that the pause between them is maintained, and that B could be identified, semantically or syntactically, as A's completion rather than as the start of a wholly new thought. It is the necessity of maintaining this delicate balance, i.e., of keeping A and B divided yet related, that generates the frequent recourse to repetition, apposition, ellipsis of subject or verb, word pairs, and other manifestations of parallelism.

Poetry Versus Prose: A particularly vexing problem for scholars has been that of distinguishing biblical "poetry" from "prose." Neither of these terms, derived from other literary traditions, has an equivalent expression in biblical Hebrew, and there is no evidence that ancient Israelites divided their literary corpus into these two camps. Obviously, the terse, two-part sentence form was favored for some types of compositions (songs, proverbs, etc.), where it was used with consistency; but the same sentence form can frequently be found in ordinary narratives, particularly in dialogue, as well as in legal material, blessings and curses, oracles and prayers. Moreover, in various prophetic books, this terse, binary style seems now and again to slip into a looser and less easily identified idiom; it is often hard to say where "poetry" ends and "prose" begins. Even in the Psalms, the contrast between the clipped, binary style of, say, Ps. 94 and the looser style of Pss. 23; 35; and 122 is striking. Some scholars have used statistical analyses (e.g., of the relative presence or absence of the definite article) in order to help distinguish poetry from prose in the Bible. But at present this remains a crude tool (the Song of Solomon ends up in the prose camp by such a measurement). The distinction appears, at any rate, to be more one of degree than of kind.

Historically, the distinction between biblical poetry and prose was at first wholly dependent on literary genre. Those compositions that would have been composed in verse if they had been written in Latin or Greek were declared by early biblical commentators to be the Bible's poetry: the Psalms and various songs such as the hymn of the Israelites at the Red Sea (Exod. 15) and songs of Moses (Deut. 32), Deborah (Judg. 5), and David (2 Sam. 22) as well as Job, Lamentations, and other books. Prophetic books were held to be prose, at least until the scholar Robert Lowth forcefully argued their structural similarity to psalms and songs on the basis of their parallelism. In more recent biblical studies, the term "poetry" has been used to refer to those parts of the Bible in which the terse, seconding style is most apparent (especially Psalms, Proverbs, Job, Song of Solomon, Lamentations, Ecclesiastes, much of the prophetic corpus, and individual songs, oracles, etc., found in biblical narrative); but there is an increasing awareness that in biblical Hebrew, even more than in other languages, the precise distinction between poetry and prose is difficult to draw.

Poetry in the NT: The NT contains a few fragments of poetic lines cited from classical Greek poets (Acts 17:28, citing Aratus *Phaenomena* 5; 1 Cor. 15:33, perhaps Menander *Thais;* Titus 1:12, Callimachus *Hymn to Zeus*). These classical poets wrote in the formal meters of ancient Greek verse. Elsewhere in the NT, however, the poetry that is evinced is of a piece with LXX translations from the Hebrew Bible. Thus, such passages as the Lord's Prayer (Matt. 6:9–13; Luke 11:2–4) and the Magnificat (Luke 1:46–55) seem to conform to the same principles of composition as the prayers and hymns of the Hebrew Bible. *See also* parallelism; Psalms, book of.

Bibliography
Kugel, James L. *The Idea of Biblical Poetry.* Yale University Press, 1981.
O'Connor, Michael. *Hebrew Verse Structure.* Eisenbrauns, 1980.
Watson, Wilfred G. E. *Traditional Techniques in Classical Hebrew Verse.* Sheffield Academic, 1994.
J.L.K.

polygamy. *See* adultery; family; marriage.

polytheism (pol´ee-thee-iz´uhm), the belief in the existence of numerous gods. In the environment of the Bible most societies were polytheistic; there were "many gods and many lords" (1 Cor. 8:5). Different deities had different functions, associations, characters, and mythologies. Some were male, some female, and they had individual personal names. They might be grouped in families and generations; the younger gods might overcome and displace the older. Theomachy, war among the gods, could have an important role, not least in creation stories. In numerous myths, a younger god defeated an older, monstrous deity and from its body fashioned the world. The variety among the gods did not exclude elements of rank and leadership, but leadership did not always mean complete supremacy.

Polytheistic religions are known in detail from ancient Egypt, Mesopotamia, Greece, and Rome. Particularly relevant for the Bible, however, is the Canaanite polytheism of Ugarit (cf. also the later evidence of Philo of Byblos [ca. 63–141 CE]), in which occur divine names known from the Bible: El, Elyon, Baal, Anath, Athirat (cf. Heb. Asherah), Dagon. This Canaanite mythology stressed the elements of conflict, sexuality, fecundity, the mountain of the gods, and the building of the palace.

The biblical writings consistently opposed the ethos of polytheism and its mythologies. Certain echoes of that ethos would nevertheless remain, evident perhaps in the various names employed for Israel's God, in the concept of the "sons of God" (Gen. 6:2, 4) or court of heavenly beings (Job 1:6), in the imagery of battles between God and hostile powers (Ps. 74:14; Isa. 51:9), and in the occasional recognition that another land is the sphere of another god (Judg. 11:24). But for Israel there was only one God, and sole devotion to this one God was a paramount essential; to follow or serve "other gods" was a cardinal offense, emphasized particularly in Deuteronomy and Isa. 40–55. Polemic against polytheism became an internal argument among the Israelites; it reinforced the theology and the ethical demands of the God of Israel. Eventually, rejection of it became a standard constituent of Jewish life, and it ceased to form a real temptation for many Jews.

The NT follows this tradition in taking for granted the established monotheism of Judaism. Within the Greco-Roman world, Christianity appears to have followed the lines of established Jewish apologetic, dismissing the absurdities of polytheism, linking it with moral depravities, and affirming the oneness of true deity as background to the Christian affirmations. *See also* monotheism.   J.B.

pomegranate (*Punica granatum*), a small tree whose bright red fruit resembles an apple. Its hard shiny rind encloses a pulp of fleshy seeds, the juice of which is especially refreshing in a hot environment (Song of Sol. 8:2; Deut. 8:8). The beautiful round fruit was a common decorative motif used on the hems of the robes of the temple priests (Exod. 28:33–34). The same motif was also carved into the timbers and beams of Solomon's temple (1 Kings 7:18, 20). Extract of the rind was used medicinally and as a red dye as well as in tanning leather. The pomegranate was regarded as a symbol of fertility and eternal life.   P.L.C.

Pomegranate.

Pontius Pilate. *See* Pilate, Pontius.

Pontus (pon'tuhs; Gk., "sea"), a Roman province of Asia Minor stretching along the south shore of the Black Sea from Bithynia to Armenia. The name comes from a Greek word for "sea" that is often used without further modification to identify the Black Sea. According to Philo, a first-century Jewish author, Jews lived throughout the province of Pontus. The book of Acts refers to Jews from Pontus who lived in Jerusalem as being among those who heard the followers of Jesus speaking in tongues at Pentecost (2:9). Acts 18:2 mentions a Jewish native of Pontus named Aquila who, with his wife Priscilla, left Rome during Claudius's eviction of Jews and met Paul in Corinth. The NT mentions no mission to Pontus, though 1 Pet. 1:1 addresses Christians there.   D.R.M.

pool. *See* cisterns; reservoir; Solomon's Pools; water.

poor, poverty, lacking in material or spiritual goods.

In the Hebrew Bible: Poverty is treated in two different ways in the Hebrew Bible. In some instances, especially in Proverbs, poverty is the consequence of moral lassitude, such as laziness (13:18; 20:13). Far more often, however, poverty is understood as a consequence of social factors, particularly injustice (Prov. 13:23). The poor are often referred to as needy, without power, and abused by those with greater power. Thus, the expression "fall into difficulty" in Lev. 25:35 literally means to have one's hand (power) waver; likewise the phrase in 14:21 that indicates a poor person "cannot afford" much literally indicates that the hand (power) of such a person is insufficient. The poor are those who do not have the capacity to provide the essentials of life for themselves. Their deficiency in life-supporting power is understood to exist in relation to the rest of the community (as is indicated by such expressions as "the poor among you," Exod. 22:25). Behind such poverty lies economic conflict (Eccles. 4:1). The intensity of the conflict is reflected in the prevalence of slavery (Neh. 7:66–67; Exod. 20:17), since slavery was the lot of the losers in the economic struggle (2 Kings 4:1; Amos 2:6–7; 8:4–6). The condition of the wage earners, vulnerable because they were cut off from a reliable relationship to the land, was as bad (Job 7:1–2) or worse (Deut. 15:16–17).

The extent of poverty increased to a new level in the time of the eighth-century BCE prophets Amos, Isaiah, and Micah. Economic conditions in the preceding two centuries had produced a commercial and landed aristocracy. Inequities increased, and the new elite was able to exploit the poor through sharecropping arrangements (Isa. 3:14–15). Through foreclosures, land became concentrated in fewer hands (Isa. 5:8). The peasants lost their patrimonies in the land (Mic. 2:1–2). From the standpoint of the prophet Amos, a whole class was being wiped out (8:4).

In the NT: The world of the NT was characterized by fairly extreme economic inequality. Most people were either extremely rich (about 3 percent of the population) or extremely poor (about 90 percent); many of those who belonged to the latter group lived at or near subsistence level, living off the land in a manner that made them subject to the vicissitudes of agriculture. Modern estimates suggest that about 28 percent of the population of the Roman Empire during NT times lived "below subsistence level," meaning that they did not know from day to day whether they would be able to obtain what was necessary to sustain life. Persons like Jesus and Paul, who had acquired trades (carpentry, tentmaking) may have been somewhat better off, but given the extremes of the economic situation, attitudes toward wealth and poverty were highly significant. Jesus's condemnations of the wealthy (e.g., Luke 6:24) and beatitudes on the poor (e.g., Luke 6:20) reflect a view stated succinctly in James 2:5, that "God has chosen the poor in the world to be rich in faith and to be heirs of the kingdom." Nevertheless, the early Christians had to be counseled against showing favoritism to the wealthy (2:2–3).

Responsibility to the Poor: The responsibility of redressing the plight of the poor is fundamental to biblical faith. At base is the nature of God as one who hears the cries of the poor (Ps. 12:5). The deliverance from Egypt is presented as one great example of God's justice to the needy (68:5–10; Exod. 2:23–24). As their dilemma is grounded in injustice, their need is for justice (Isa. 10:2). As their condition is loss of power, the response required is empowerment. A literal rendering of "You shall maintain him" in Lev. 25:35 is, "You shall make them strong." This demand is extended outside the chosen people, for almost the same wording is used in condemning Sodom, which did not "make strong the power [hand] of the poor and needy" (Ezek. 16:49).

In biblical law, attention is given to social structures that affect the poor. The land is to be left fallow every seventh year "so that the poor of your people may eat" (Exod. 23:11). In this year the landed means of production are to be given over in their entirety to the poor and the debts of the poor are to be cancelled (Deut. 15:2). That the landless poor have rights in the land is also supported in their claim to immediate sustenance from the fields (23:24–25) and in restrictions on reaping and gleaning so that some harvest is left to them (Lev. 19:9–10). The law also restricts the processes that tear people down. The empowering in Lev. 25 includes a proscription of interest on loans intended to relieve the distress of the recipient (23:36–37). A collateral (pledge) is prohibited if it were one that would further weaken the debtor (Deut. 24:6) or cause the debtor to suffer (Exod. 22:26). Finally, there is to be open-handed sharing with the poor (Deut. 15:11).

The biblical ideal for a ruler in the Bible is to be one who fully assumes the responsibility of delivering the poor and crushing their oppressors (Ps. 72:4). It is part of the messianic expectation (Isa. 11:4) seen to be fulfilled in Jesus (Matt. 11:5; Luke 1:52–53; 4:18–21). The hope for "good news proclaimed to the poor" (Luke 4:18; 7:22) was ancient (Ps. 68:10–11; Isa. 29:18–19; 35:4–6). Jesus taught that, by selling one's possessions and giving the money to the poor, one could obtain treasure in heaven (Matt. 19:21). While affirming that poverty would be a permanent part of the world's social order (Mark 14:5), he also commanded his disciples, "Give to everyone who begs from you, and do not refuse anyone who wants to borrow from you" (Matt. 5:42). A major concern of Paul was to make a collection for the poor in Jerusalem (Rom. 15:26; 2 Cor. 8–9). *See also* economics in the Hebrew Bible period; economics in the New Testament period; justice; ownership; wealth.

Bibliography

Batey, Richard. *Jesus and the Poor.* Harper & Row, 1972.

Boerma, Conrad. *The Rich, the Poor—and the Bible.* Westminster, 1980.

De Vaux, Roland. *Ancient Israel.* McGraw-Hill, 1965. Pp. 65–90, 164–77.   S.C.M./M.A.P.

poplar, a tree of the genus *Populus.* Probably the white poplar (*Populus alba*) or the storax (*Styrax officinalis*) is the tree mentioned in Gen. 30:37, where its color is of consequence. It grew in groves with other trees (Hos. 4:13) and symbolized solid life (14:5).

Poplar (*Populus alba*).

porch, or vestibule.

1 A forecourt or central court of a house (1 Kings 7:6; Mark 14:68) or the pillared hall on a flat roof (Judg. 3:23). Private homes during the Greco-Roman period often had porches that opened onto the street just outside the front door.

2 A colonnaded portico or passageway, often part of a public building or temple (e.g., the stoa at Athens; Solomon's Portico). These frequently provided shelter for travelers or those in ill health (John 5:2) and a forum for religious and philosophical discussions (Acts 17:16–32).

3 An area of the throne from which the king of Israel pronounced judgment (1 Kings 7:6–7).

Porcius Festus. *See* Festus, Porcius.

Portico, Solomon's. *See* Solomon's Portico.

post.

1 A vertical beam, usually of wood, that served as part of a frame from which a door or a gate was hung. When Samson took revenge on the Gazites, he carried off not only the gate but the posts as well (Judg. 16:3), thus leaving the town defenseless until they could be replaced. One not permitted entry could stand at the gatepost and observe what occurred inside (Ezek. 46:2).

2 The position occupied by persons in pursuit of their duties, whether king (1 Kings 20:24), priest (2 Chron. 7:6), or watcher (Isa. 21:8).

postexilic period, the time following the Babylonian exile of Israel (587–539 BCE). The period began with the conquest of Babylon by the Persians in 539. The Persian ruler Cyrus pursued a policy of toleration of diverse religions. This moderate and enlightened practice led to the restoration of the Jewish community in its homeland (cf. Ezra 1:2–4; 6:3–5). Among the most prominent examples of literature from this period are Isa. 40–66, Haggai, Zech. 1–8, Ezra, and Nehemiah. *See also* exile.
K.H.R.

Potiphar (pot'uh-fuhr; Egyptian, "he whom Re has given"), an official of Pharaoh and captain of the guard, who purchased the patriarch Joseph in Egypt from some Midianite (Ishmaelite) merchants, who had themselves purchased him from his brothers (Gen. 37:36; 39:1). His name was actually a shortened form of "Potiphera," which was also the name of Joseph's future father-in-law. Potiphar cast Joseph into prison because of a false accusation against him by Potiphar's wife (39:6–20). *See also* Joseph.

Potiphera (puh-ti'fuh-ruh; Egyptian, "he whom Re has given"), a priest of On whose daughter, Asenath, was given in marriage to Joseph by Pharaoh (Gen. 41:45, 50; 46:20). As priest of On, center of the cult of the sun god Re, Potiphera would have been an important person. The priests of On engaged in a wide variety of commercial, political, and cultic duties. *See also* Asenath; Joseph; On.

potter. *See* pottery.

potter's field, a tract of land near Jerusalem used to bury strangers. According to Matt. 27:1–10, the field was purchased by the chief priests of Jerusalem with the thirty pieces of silver paid to Judas for betraying Jesus; it was thereafter called the Field of Blood, because it had been bought with blood money. Acts 1:18–19 does not mention the designation "potter's field," but indicates that Judas himself bought a field with his money and that this field came to be called the Field of Blood (or Hakeldama in Aramaic), because it is where he fell headlong and burst open. Matthew believed that Judas's return of the money and the purchase of the field fulfilled a prophecy in Zech. 11:12–13 (some association with a potter's field may have been derived from Jer. 18:1–3; 32:6–15). Since the fourth century, the field has been identified with a location near the confluence of the Hinnom and Kidron valleys. *See also* Hakeldama; Judas.
C.H.M.

potter's wheel. *See* pottery.

Pottery

POTTERY IS MADE FROM CLAY and hardened by fire. One who makes pottery is a potter, and the art of pottery making is ceramics.

Significance for Biblical History: Clay has two distinctive traits: it can be fashioned into a particular shape and retain that shape; and when it is fired at a temperature of 700–900 degrees Fahrenheit, it undergoes chemical changes that harden the shape and render it almost impervious to decay or corrosion (although it can be broken by impact).

Because of these characteristics, pottery has become an indispensable tool of archaeologists as they seek to reconstruct the history of the biblical lands. In contrast to Egypt and Mesopotamia, the Levant contains very few stone monuments that record its past and relatively few inscriptions. On the other hand, potsherds, broken bits of ancient pottery, are found in abundance wherever biblical peoples and their predecessors settled. A common pattern of settlement was to build a new city on the ruins of one that had been destroyed. A *tell,* the mound that results from the accumulated layers of the remains of cities, is eloquently described in Josh. 8:28: "So Joshua burned Ai, and made it forever a heap of ruins, as it is to this day." Buried within the tells of the Levant, the broken remnants of the everyday utensils and objects of each successive generation lay unnoticed for their historical importance until 1890, when William Flinders Petrie conducted the first excavation of a tell in the Levant at Tell el-Hesi.

Petrie recognized that pottery unearthed and understood in the light of its proper sequence had enormous chronological value for dating successive occupation layers and thus the other artifacts and architectural features contained within them. This is because the styles and methods of manufacture of pots changed over the centuries, sometimes rapidly, sometimes very slowly. Bases were rounded, flattened, or elongated; handles altered their shape and their point or manner of attachment; variations on rims—wide, narrow, turned-in, turned-out—were almost limitless. If the form of the pottery associated with a particular period could be established, then a simple piece of rim, base, or handle made in this form could be dated. Thousands of whole pots have been found in the tombs from various periods, contributing greatly to the identification of pottery forms. Petrie was able to use his knowledge of pottery from dated Egyptian tombs to suggest dates for comparable wares at Hesi, thus introducing the principle of cross-dating to turn a relative chronology into an approximate absolute chronology. Since this pioneering contribution, the pottery unearthed in the course of every excavation has been the object of critical examination and study, resulting in continuous progress in the identification and dating of pottery forms.

In recent times this emphasis on the changing shape of pottery as a gauge of passing time or new developments has been broadened so as to

Parthian twisted-handled amphora (second–fourth century CE).

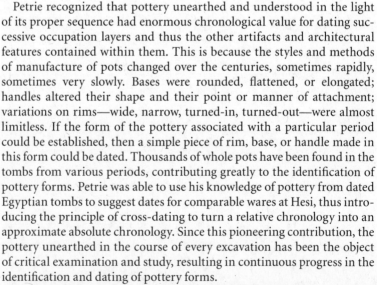

exploit more fully the cultural significance of the ceramic evidence. Pottery industries are now being carefully studied as excellent indicators of the technological achievement and economic structure of any one period. Scientific techniques of examination, such as petrographic and spectrographic analysis, are being applied to thin sections of potsherds to determine the mineral content and composition of the clays and, if possible, their geological source. Furthermore, surface surveys of the broader landscape of which the tells were always an integral part have become a regular feature of archaeological endeavor. In order to provide a fuller picture of the complex political, social, and economic occupational history of the whole land, specialists collect and analyze potsherds from every period that have gradually been exposed on the surface of the soil either through erosion or human activity. Their studies indicate that there were marked regional variations in the pottery forms of any given period.

Manufacturing Techniques: The clay used by the potter in the biblical lands was an earthen clay usually found in the immediate vicinity. It was combined with nonplastic grit and mixed with water. When it had attained the desired consistency, the water was removed, leaving the clay bed or batch. It then had to be de-aired, or wedged, to prevent air pockets from building up and shattering the fired ware. A common method was by treading with the feet (see Isa. 41:25).

Evidence indicates that the earliest vessels were shaped by hand in a variety of ways. One was by molding. Clay was pressed around the inside of a basket, which was then consumed in the firing process, leaving the finished pot. Some small vessels were formed by holding a lump of clay in the palm of one hand while pinching it into the desired shape with the other—the "pinch-pot." Large square or oblong vessels were fashioned from flat slabs of clay joined together with slip (clay diluted with water). Sometimes long rolls of clay were coiled in a circle around a base, layer upon layer, until the desired height and shape were achieved; the walls of the vessel were then thinned and smoothed.

It is impossible to say where and when the potter's wheel was introduced, but it clearly revolutionized the pottery industry. All pots had to be turned or moved in the making, and a wheel greatly facilitated this effort. The earliest form was the tournette, or slow wheel, of which many examples have been found in the Levant. A typical tournette consisted of a lower thick-walled stone bowl that had a conical depression in the center and an upper stone bowl with a flat upper surface and a lower conical projection that fit into the depression. This type of wheel, topped by a turntable, was rotated either by hand or foot and was probably lubricated with olive oil. On the basis of archaeological evidence, we can conclude that the tournette probably remained in use throughout the Israelite period. The fast wheel, introduced later, consisted of a shaft with a horizontal disk on top and a heavy wheel that was turned with the feet until the proper momentum was achieved. A lump of clay was thrown onto the disk with great force so that it would stick, the form was opened with the hand, and the sidewalls drawn up to the desired height, thickness, and shape. A number of small vessels might be made from one large lump of clay, each one being cut off from the top of the column as it was finished. Larger, more sophisticated pieces were often made in segments and later joined

Early Bronze Age (3200–2100 BCE) pottery from Tell Halif has distinctive markings made by the potter, perhaps a personal signature or designation of the customer.

together with slip. This was a common practice for adding necks, handles, and spouts as well.

Newly shaped articles were allowed to dry slowly in the sun until they reached the stage of leatherlike hardness. The earliest vessels were sun-dried but not fired and could only be used for storing dry materials. If they were filled with water, they would absorb it, become soft, and even-

A selection of pottery vessels from the Early Bronze through the Iron II periods. The years (all BCE) below each vessel refer to the approximate date range of construction.

tually collapse. In the early 1960s excavations at a Neolithic settlement at Çatal Hüyük revealed a variety of such unbaked earthenware estimated to date to ca. 6750 BCE. The earliest examples of true pottery, fired clay, in the Levant appeared in Jericho in the late sixth millennium. Although there is no precise evidence concerning the firing techniques in ancient Israel, extrapolation from contemporary Near Eastern methods has proved helpful. In early times pots were simply stacked in a shallow hole in the ground and a heap of combustible material was burned over them. At a later stage the pottery was separated from the fuel by a perforated clay partition, and finally the closed kiln was developed. Firing probably took from two to three days, since the temperature had to be raised and lowered slowly to avoid cracking the vessels. The amount of air in the kiln at the time of firing as well as the composition of the clay body determined the color of the pot. Particularly well-preserved examples of ancient kilns have been found at Seraf and in Lebanon.

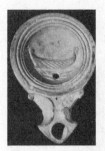

An oil lamp from the first century BCE–first century CE depicts a Roman galley.

Israelite pottery differs from modern pottery in that it was not glazed. The preferred mode of decoration was to coat the whole pot or parts of it with a liquid clay or slip. After the pot had dried but before it was baked, it would be burnished or polished with a rubbing tool of bone, stone, or wood. During the tenth and ninth centuries BCE burnishing was generally done by hand; afterward burnishing was accomplished as the pot was turned on the wheel. Some ware was painted, although this was not a common practice except for an occasional line of red or black around the shoulder or middle of the pot. A third type of decoration seen on much early pottery was incision or puncture along the rim and neck.

The art of the potter was difficult to master. It required knowledge of finding the right raw materials and of the best method of preparing the batch and shaping, decorating, and firing the ware. Traditions of pot making were passed on from generation to generation, and an abrupt change in the tradition indicated newcomers on the scene. Potters and their workshops were familiar scenes in every village and town (see Jer. 18:3–4). Eventually, as cities became larger, guilds of potters were established to meet the needs of increased production (see 1 Chron. 4:23).

Most Canaanite pottery was made for utilitarian purposes. Articles in the home included bowls, cups, cooking pots, lamps, jars, pitchers, and juglets as well as the household oven and huge storage jars. Other items like spindle whorls, buttons, figurines, and toys were also made of pottery. Although essentially functional, the pottery of the biblical period frequently displays high artistic accomplishment.

Even broken vessels had their use. Potsherds were used as note paper on which important messages, such as the Lachish letters, were written. Larger shards were used as braziers to take fire from the hearth or as ladles (see Isa. 30:14). Potsherds may also have been used to scrape oil or dirt from the skin (see Job 2:8). Broken vessels were occasionally repaired in antiquity by drilling holes at the edges of shards and joining them together with some sort of string. Most potsherds, however, were simply discarded and forgotten, providing the archaeologist of today with invaluable historical clues.

Some Distinctive Features of Canaanite Pottery: The pottery of the late Neolithic period (5500–4300 BCE) was handmade, of coarse

Storage jar from
the Jordan Valley,
Chalcolithic Period
(4300–3200 BCE).

ware, and poorly fired. Its types include saucers, bowls, and storage jars decorated with a burnished red slip, painted triangular designs, or incisions. Pottery continued to be handmade in the Chalcolithic period (4300–3200 BCE), but the ware is finer and better fired and the forms more advanced. These include V-shaped bowls, goblets, cornet cups, and "churns," decorated by incision or paint. The largest collection of Chalcolithic pottery has been found in Ghassulian and Beer-sheba cultures. In the Early Bronze Age (3200–2100 BCE) typical of the first phase (Early Bronze I) are forms with ledge handles, high loop handles, or vertical pierced lug handles and wares with gray or red burnish, or band slip or line-group paint. The key diagnostic pottery of the second phase (Early Bronze II) is called "Abydos" ware after the site in Egypt where it was first found in First Dynasty tombs and identified as non-Egyptian. The subsequent association of this pottery with Canaan has been very important for correlating the pottery of Egypt and Canaan. Characteristic vessels are pitchers and jars with burnished red slip on the lower half and brown painted triangles and dots on the upper half. Typical of the third phase (Early Bronze III) is Khirbet Kerak ware, red- or black-burnished vessels decorated with incised lines. New pottery forms, indicating a new culture, appear in the Middle Bronze Age (2100–1500 BCE). By 1900 BCE all pottery was produced on the wheel, which allowed for the development of homogeneous and pleasing forms. Distinctive are the carinated bowls, often burnished over rich dark or cream slip, and graceful large jar forms. The single-spouted open oil lamp came into widespread use at this time. In the Late Bronze Age (1550–1200 BCE) the Levant was under Egyptian control, and its pottery was influenced both by Egypt and by trade connections with Aegean and eastern Mediterranean civilizations. Bichrome painted ware with friezes of birds, fish, and geometric designs appeared. Imports, mainly of Cypriot and Mycenaean origin, became common and were widely imitated.

There is clear continuity between the Canaanite pottery of the Late Bronze Age and the pottery of the Iron Age (1200–587 BCE), including Israelite pottery and the pottery of other groups. However, the profound changes brought about in Canaan by the settlement of the Israelite tribes are reflected in some new ceramic elements that eventually developed into a distinctive Israelite pottery. This reached its highest expression in the days of the divided kingdom (ca. 918–587 BCE) when standardization of ware through mass production resulted in shapes that remained virtually unchanged for three hundred years.

The typical Israelite bowl was covered with slip, usually red, inside and over the rim, and on that a band of burnish was rubbed in spiral fashion, beginning in the center and extending over the rim. This is the well-known "ring-burnished" bowl. Evidence of the high standard of the potter's art is nowhere better seen than in the beautiful shape of the ring-burnished water decanter from the eighth and seventh centuries. A popular perfume juglet with one handle is distinctive because of its black color, which contrasts with the usual "Palestinian red." The large storage jars that could hold about ten gallons each also testify to the expertise of the potter. In the eighth century under the Judean kings royal stamps were pressed into the wet clay of the handles reading *lmlk*, "Belonging to the

"Syrian bottle"
from a burial cave
at Gezer, fourteenth
century BCE.

king." The "Samarian thin bowls" are noteworthy for their eggshell-thin ware and their striking decoration. They had red slip inside and outside or red and yellow slip alternating in bands and were highly burnished.

In sharp contrast to the generally unpainted Israelite pottery was the elaborately decorated Philistine pottery of the early Iron Age. The most characteristic features in the decoration are metopes enclosing stylized birds or geometric patterns like friezes of spirals and groups of interlocking circles. The presence of considerable quantities of this distinctive pottery at particular sites is an indication of Philistine settlement or cultural influence or trade.

The conditions of hardship and privation that followed the Babylonian destruction of Judah in 587 BCE are reflected in the marked decline in the quality of local pottery made during the Persian period (587–332 BCE). This is also true of the Hellenistic period (332–63 BCE), characterized as it was by almost constant warfare. In these periods finer wares were imported from the highly specialized workshops of the Greek world. Most notable were the black-figure, red-figure, and black-glazed vessels. The pottery imported from the West was widely imitated, although the Palestinian pottery generally did not succeed in duplicating the superb quality and carefully wrought decoration of the Hellenistic models. An exception is the Nabatean ware found mainly in southern Transjordan, but also in the Negev. This hard-fired and beautifully decorated pottery reflects high technical skills and is the most outstanding ceramic accomplishment in the history of the Levant. During the early Roman period (63 BCE–135 CE) pottery manufacturing centers all over the Mediterranean began to produce vessels with the same distinctive shapes and glossy red surface treatment. This *terra sigillata* ware is found in abundance in the Near East. Local potters under the Herods also developed some very fine ware of their own design. Recent excavations in Jerusalem have uncovered thin-walled bowls of excellent quality, painted on the inside in stylized floral patterns in red and sometimes in brown or black.

A clay oil lamp from Amka, a town northeast of Acre, is shaped like a schoolmaster unrolling a scroll as he reads; third–second century BCE.

Symbolic References in the Bible: The potter's art provided the biblical writers with many symbols. Perhaps best known is the creation story of Gen. 2:7, which depicts God as a potter fashioning a man from clay. The theme of God as the Master Potter, molding people and nations is a common one (Jer. 18:1–6; Isa. 29:16; 64:8; Rom. 9:20–24). One who argues with God is as foolish as the potsherd who argues with the potter (Isa. 45:9; cf. Rom. 9:20). The smashed vessel symbolizes utter and permanent destruction (Jer. 19:10–11). Human frailty is that of the earthen jar (Lam. 4:2; 2 Cor. 4:7). The pottery oil lamp is a favorite biblical symbol used in a variety of contexts.

See also lamp.

Bibliography

Amiran, R. *Ancient Pottery of the Holy Land.* Masada, 1969.

Homès-Fredericq, D., and H. Franken, eds. *Pottery and Potters—Past and Present.* Attempto, 1986.

Rice, P. M. *Pottery Analysis: A Sourcebook.* University of Chicago Press, 1987.

M.M.S.

pound, the term used by the NRSV for *mina* in a parable of Jesus related in Luke 19:13–26. A mina was equal to 100 denarii, making it equivalent to about a hundred times a typical day's wage. *See* money.

poverty. *See* poor, poverty.

power, the actual or potential capacity to effect something by virtue of inherent excellence or rightful authority. Power is manifested in the reproductive forces of nature (Gen. 4:12; 49:3), in the physical strength and vitality of human beings (Judg. 16:6; Prov. 20:29) and animals (Job 39:11; Prov. 14:4), and more specifically in military prowess (1 Sam. 14:52; 2 Sam. 23:8–10). Natural forces exhibit power (Exod. 14:21; Isa. 43:16), as do emotions like love and greed (Song of Sol. 8:6; Isa. 56:11). Various forms of political authority are also a manifestation of power (Luke 7:8; Acts 26:10, 12; Rom. 13:1).

In the Bible, however, God is the ultimate source of all power (Pss. 66:7; 147:5; Jer. 10:6; Job 36:22). God's power is manifested in nature (Ps. 65:6–7; Jer. 10:12) and in history, especially in God's act of redemption at the exodus (Exod. 15:6, 13; 32:11; Deut. 3:23). Compared to God's power, human power pales in significance (Pss. 33:16–17; 147:10–11). God gives power to the faint (Isa. 40:29), and human beings may take refuge in God's strength (Ps. 28:7–8; Jer. 16:19; Luke 1:49). According to the NT, the power of God was made manifest in the life and deeds of Jesus (Mark 6:2, 5; Luke 4:14, 36; 5:17; 6:19). His followers were empowered by the Holy Spirit (Acts 1:8; 4:33; Rom. 15:19). Even the proclamation of the gospel of Jesus Christ was seen by Paul as a manifestation of divine power (Rom. 1:16; 1 Cor. 1:18). The NT also speaks of cosmic powers at work in the world who stand in opposition to God, but whose power has already been broken and subordinated to the power of God made manifest in Christ (Rom. 8:38; 1 Cor. 15:24; Eph. 1:21; Col. 2:15; 1 Pet. 3:22). The book of Revelation speaks repeatedly of God and the Lamb as ones who are worthy to receive power (e.g., 4:11; 5:12). *See also* dominion.   W.E.L.

Praetorian (pri-tor′ee-uhn) **Guard,** the probable meaning of "imperial guard" in Phil. 1:13 (cf. also "those of Caesar's household" in 4:22). It refers either to a select unit of the Roman army that served as imperial bodyguards or simply to the military (and other) personnel attached to a *praetorium* (the official residence of a Roman official; translated "governor's residence" by the NRSV in Mark 15:16). *See also* architecture; Gabbatha.

praise, in the Bible, the act of glorifying God, frequently in communal worship (Ps. 113; Luke 1:64; Acts 2:47; Rev. 19:5). The Hebrew term for "psalms" literally means "praises." *See also* hallelujah; Psalms, book of; worship in the Hebrew Bible.

prayer, the act of petitioning, praising, giving thanks, or confessing to God; it is expressed by

Jesus praying in the garden at Gethsemane (Luke 22:39–46); sixth-century mosaic at San Apollinare in Classe, Ravenna, Italy.

several different words in both Hebrew and Greek. Prayer can be individual or corporate, audible or silent. It is conditioned by the biblical understanding of God as a personal being who hears prayers (1 Kings 9:3; Pss. 34:15; 65:2; Matt. 7:11; 1 John 5:15). Postures for praying include "standing before the Lord" (Gen. 18:22), being seated (2 Sam. 7:18–29), lying in bed (Ps. 63:5–6), and prostrating oneself, i.e., lying flat on the ground (Mark 14:35). People kneel (Acts 9:40) and bow (Gen. 24:52) and are encouraged to do both (Ps. 95:6–7). People in the Bible often pray with their hands uplifted (Pss. 28:2; 63:4; 134:2; 141:2; 1 Tim. 2:8).

In the Hebrew Bible: The earliest instances of prayer in the Hebrew Bible are conversations between persons and God. Such conversations take place between God and Adam (Gen. 3:9–12), Abraham (15:1–6), and Moses (Exod. 3:1–4:17). It is said that God spoke to Moses "face to face, as one speaks to a friend" (Exod. 33:11). Kings (1 Sam. 23:2–4; 1 Kings 3:5–14) and prophets (1 Sam. 3:4–9; Isa. 6:1–13; Jer. 1:4–19) are portrayed as conversation partners with God.

The forms of prayer in the Hebrew Bible include petitions for guidance, requests for divine help, intercessions, praise and thanksgiving, and confession. Prayers for guidance are offered by Isaac (Gen. 24:12–14), Moses (Num. 11:11–15), and Solomon, who asks for wisdom (1 Kings 3:5–14). Requests include prayers for the necessities of life (1 Kings 8:22–53; Prov. 30:8), deliverance from enemies (Gen. 32:11; Pss. 31:15; 59:1), and retribution (Judg. 16:28; Ps. 137:7; Jer. 17:18). Intercessions are offered by the patriarchs and Moses (Gen. 18:22–32; Exod. 5:22–23; 32:11–13), David (2 Sam. 12:16–17), and various prophets (Amos 7:1–6; Ezek. 9:8; 11:13). Such intercessions are generally for the whole people, but there are instances of intercessions for individuals (1 Kings 17:20–21; 2 Kings 4:32–33) and Gentile governmental authority as well (Jer. 29:7; Ezra 6:10). Praise and thanksgiving are offered to God in response to

God's steadfast love (Pss. 100:4–5; 108:3–4) and God's creation and benevolent rule of the world (Pss. 145–150). Confession is prescribed for the annual Day of Atonement (Lev. 16:21), but it can be made whenever an offense against God has occurred. Confession is usually made by the confessor on behalf of the people (Exod. 32:31–32; Neh. 9:16–37; Dan. 9:20) or by the community (Judg. 10:10), but there are instances of individual confession (2 Sam. 24:17; Ps. 51). Confession is made in the certainty of God's promises to forgive (Lev. 26:40–45; Isa. 1:18; Mic. 7:18–19).

The Hebrew Bible assumes that prayer can be offered at any time and place. There are, however, prescribed times: confession is made on the Day of Atonement; hours are set for daily prayer (Dan. 6:10); and the sabbath and other festivals are days for prayer. The temple was a place of prayer, as was the synagogue in the postexilic era. The prophets taught that prayer was more than a matter of ritual; it must be offered with integrity and pure motives, and by people who have attended to ethical concerns (Isa. 1:15–17; Hos. 6:6; Amos 5:21–24; Mic. 6:8; cf. Ps. 24:3–6).

In the NT: Jesus is portrayed as a model and instructor in prayer, especially in Luke's Gospel, where he prays at decisive moments: at his baptism (3:21), when he selects disciples (6:12), at his transfiguration (9:29), on the night of his arrest in Gethsemane (22:39–46), and from the cross during his crucifixion (23:46). Prominent prayers attributed to Jesus include those that have come to be called the Lord's Prayer (Matt. 6:9–13; cf. Luke 11:2–4) and the High-Priestly Prayer (John 17). Jesus teaches that prayer should not be ostentatious and verbose, but discrete and brief (Matt. 6:5–8). He tells parables encouraging persistence in prayer (Luke 11:5–13; 18:1–5), and he urges his disciples to pray in faith (Mark 11:23–24) and with a forgiving spirit (11:25). He likens prayer to a child making requests of his or her father (Matt. 7:9–11).

Within the early church, prayer was addressed directly to God (1 Cor. 1:4; Col. 1:3) or "through" Christ (Rom. 1:8). That prayer should be directed to God through Christ is based on the prior concept that God's grace and love come through Christ (Rom. 1:5; 5:1; 8:39) and that the reigning Christ is Lord and is accessible as mediator (Rom. 10:9–13; 1 Cor. 1:9). The same concept is expressed through invitations to pray in the name of Jesus (e.g., John 14:13–14; 15:16; 16:24). Further, Christ himself is said to pray as intercessor for the saints (Rom. 8:34; Heb. 7:25).

As in the Hebrew Bible, the prayers of the NT are of several kinds. Paul frequently gives thanks for the faith and witness of those to whom he writes (Rom. 1:8–9; 1 Cor. 1:4; Phil. 1:3–5), and worship regularly includes prayers of thanksgiving (1 Cor. 14:16–17) and praise (Acts 2:47). Prayers are to be offered for daily needs (Matt. 6:11; 7:11; Phil. 4:6) and for the healing of the sick (James 5:13–16). Intercessions are made by Paul for his congregations (Rom. 15:13; Phil. 1:9–11), and he asks for their intercessions (Rom. 15:30–32; 2 Cor. 1:11; 1 Thess. 5:25). Intercessions are to be made for all persons, including rulers, that a peaceable life may be enjoyed by all (1 Tim. 2:1–2). There are prayers for forgiveness (Luke 18:13; cf. Matt. 6:12) and guidance (Acts 1:24–25; 6:6; 13:2–3).

Christ and the Spirit take on special roles in the prayers of the NT. Prayers are offered directly to Christ (Acts 7:59; 1 Cor. 1:2), although not frequently. The liturgical language of the "Kyrie" ("Lord, have mercy") is found in Matt. 17:15 and 20:30–31 (cf. 8:25), and the prayer "Maranatha" ("Our Lord, come!") appears in 1 Cor. 16:22 (cf. Rev. 22:20); both are addressed to Christ. Likewise, the Spirit's role in prayer is manifold. Prayer is "in the Spirit" (1 Cor. 14:15; Gal. 4:6; Phil. 3:3), who prompts and guides believers in prayer. Like Christ, the Spirit intercedes for believers (Rom. 8:26–27), because the Spirit knows their weaknesses and the mind and will of God (Rom. 8:27; 1 Cor. 2:10–11).

Prayer is not always answered in the manner expected. A number of biblical passages, especially in the NT, appear to offer blanket promises that those who pray rightly or with faith will receive what they request (e.g., Mark 11:24; John 14:14), but both Jesus (Mark 14:26) and Paul (2 Cor. 12:7–9) are presented as examples of persons whose requests are not granted. The picture that emerges from a survey of the biblical materials is that prayer is to be made to God in faith and expectation, but also with submissive respect for the divine will. *See also* Atonement, Day of; festivals, feasts, and fasts; Holy Spirit; Lord's Prayer; maranatha; Psalms, book of; worship in the Hebrew Bible; worship in the New Testament.

Bibliography

Cullman, Oscar. *Prayer in the New Testament.* Fortress, 1995.

Karris, Robert J. *Prayer and the New Testament: Jesus and His Communities at Worship.* Crossroad, 2000.

Longenecker, Richard N. *Into God's Presence: Prayer in the New Testament.* Eerdmans, 2001.

A.J.H.

Prayer, Lord's. *See* Lord's Prayer.

Prayer of Manasseh, a penitential prayer composed sometime during the second or first century BCE. It is typical of Jewish prayer during the Second Temple period (ca. 515 BCE–70 CE; cf. Tob. 3:2–6, 11–15; Jth. 9:2–14; Add. Esther 13:9–11; 14:3–19; Song of Three Jews 3–22), yet goes beyond the typical to provide perhaps the finest example of the genre.

The prayer was suggested by 2 Chron. 33:12–13, 18–19, where the idolatrous king, Manasseh, is said to have prayed to God for forgiveness. Its intended audience may have been Jews who had broken the first or second commandment (Exod. 20:1–6) in responding to the lure of Hellenistic culture. The theme is the efficacy of repentance in securing God's pardon for the wicked. In speaking of guilt as a weight or burden (v. 10), the work contains perhaps a hint of the Hellenistic theme of psychological self-punishment (cf. Wis. 17:1–21; Philo *Flaccus* 162–80). The metaphors for this experience of guilt also seem to reflect the details of the punishment of the fallen angels in *1 Enoch* 9:4, 11–12; 13:5; 54:1–5; 56:1–4. The petitioner is weighed down by iron fetters, cannot lift his face to heaven, and asks God not to condemn him to the depths of the earth (vv. 9–10, 13).

The Prayer of Manasseh is not found in the Hebrew Bible, and it appears in only a few LXX manuscripts, generally appended to the Psalms. It was apparently unknown to Jerome, who translated the Latin Vulgate Bible in the fourth century BCE, and so it was not in the edition of the Vulgate declared canonical by the Council of Trent. The Eastern Orthodox church considers it to be canonical and places it in the Bible between Psalms and Job. Protestants include it among the Apocrypha. Roman Catholics sometimes print it along with 1 and 2 Esdras in an appendix to the NT. *See also* Apocrypha/deuterocanonical literature; prayer.   D.W.S.

preaching, a mode of communication with specifically religious content. Preaching is primarily a NT concept, though it has roots in the proclamations of prophets as described in the Hebrew Bible.

A number of Hebrew and Greek words are variously translated in the NRSV as "preach" or "proclaim." Terms in the Hebrew Bible meaning "to announce" or "to make known" are generic and neutral words that are only given religious meaning through context. Jonah is to proclaim (*qara'*) a message of imminent destruction to Nineveh (3:2), and Sanballat accuses Nehemiah of planning to set up prophets to proclaim (*qara'*), "There is a king in Judah" (Neh. 6:7). Isa. 52:7 says, "How beautiful upon the mountains are the feet of the messenger who announces [*shama'*] peace, who brings [*basar*] good news, who announces [*shama'*] salvation, who says to Zion, 'Your God reigns.' " The phrase that means "to bring good tidings" in this passage was translated in the LXX by the Greek word *euangelizō*, which became a favorite word for NT authors, who use it to mean "preaching

the gospel," particularly in contexts where the "gospel" is associated with the announcement of God's reign (as in Isa. 52:7). Thus Luke 8:1 describes Jesus as going through cities and villages "bringing the good news [*euangelizō*] of the kingdom [reign] of God." The same word is used in Matt. 11:5; Acts 10:36; Rom. 1:15; and 1 Cor. 9:18. An even more common word for preaching in the NT, however, is *kēryssō*, meaning "to herald" or "to make an authoritative proclamation" (Matt. 3:1; Acts 10:42; 2 Cor. 4:5). Preaching is also described by more modest words that convey a sense of announcing (Luke 9:60), speaking (Acts 20:7), or simply telling (Mark 2:2). In addition, there are terms that carry a special emphasis: witnessing (Acts 2:40), exhorting (Rom. 12:8), and prophesying (1 Cor. 12:28).

In the NT, both John the Baptist (Mark 1:7) and Jesus (Luke 4:18) are described as preaching. The twelve continue this function (Acts 5:42), and Paul understands his primary task as preaching the gospel (1 Cor. 1:17). At times, the content of preaching is spelled out. In Mark 1:14–15, Jesus proclaims, "The time is fulfilled, and the kingdom of God has come near; repent, and believe in the good news." For Paul, the content of preaching typically concerns reflection on the death, burial, and resurrection of Jesus Christ (1 Cor. 15:3–8). Portions of sermons in Acts (2:16–36; 3:12–26; 13:16–41; 17:22–31) reveal the content of preaching in some early churches. The Letter to the Hebrews, called by the writer a "word of exhortation" (13:22), is essentially a sermon and represents a formal, developed style of preaching (citing a text, interpreting and applying it) that would become widespread after the second century CE. In the NT, however, most references to preaching do not elaborate on the content, but simply refer to the basic subject matter as having to do with the kingdom of God (Luke 9:2), Christ (Phil. 1:15), Christ crucified (1 Cor. 1:23), or the word of God (Acts 13:5).

The purpose of apostolic preaching according to Luke 24:47 is to bring about "repentance and forgiveness of sins." Distinctions between preaching and teaching are sometimes made (Matt. 9:35; Rom. 12:6–8), but preaching could also serve to edify and instruct believers. *See also* gospel; teaching.   F.B.C.

precious stones. *See* breastpiece; jewels, jewelry.

predestination, the theological notion that God has planned history and things take place according to God's predetermined plan. Whereas *providence* emphasizes a divine ordering and regulation of the world and history toward a positive goal, *predestination* emphasizes a divine predetermination of human destiny in conformity with an eternal plan. To use the biblical terms, God foreordains according to God's design and purpose; God chooses and elects according to God's own counsel and will. Nothing can come to pass if God does not ordain it (Lam. 3:37; cf. Prov. 16:4), but

God's plans are for welfare, not evil (Gen. 50:20; Jer. 29:11; Rom. 9:18, 20–24; 11:15). God alone is the Creator and sustainer of all that is, the sovereign Lord who directs all things toward their appointed destiny (e.g., Ps. 115:3; Isa. 45:5–7; 46:8–11; Rom. 9:11, 15; Eph. 1:11).

In the Bible, God chooses the Israelites to be God's covenant people (e.g., Deut. 7:6–10); God chooses individuals to carry out the divine will and purpose (e.g., Judg. 2:16; 1 Kings 18:1); God raises up prophets to proclaim the divine word (Isa. 6:1–13; Jer. 1:1–2; Amos 3:6–8); and, God uses nations and events of history to execute judgment and to accomplish God's goals (Isa. 7:18–19; 45:1–4). The worlds of nature and history are under God's control (Gen. 3:17–18; Isa. 45:5–7).

In the NT, God alone decides when the fullness of time or an appointed time has come (e.g., John 2:4; 7:30; 12:27; 13:1; 17:1; Acts 1:7; Rom. 3:25–26; 9:11; Eph. 1:10; Col. 1:26; 2 Tim. 1:9). Divine necessity is connected with the destiny of the Son of Man figure in the Gospels (e.g., Mark 8:31; 9:31; 10:33–34; cf. also Luke 24:25–27, 44–46). God has appointed a day for fulfillment of the divine plan (e.g., Heb. 4:7; Acts 17:26–31; 2 Tim. 4:8; 1 Thess. 4:13–5:11; 2 Pet. 3:8–10), which God determined before the foundation of the world (1 Cor. 2:7; Eph. 1:4; 1 Pet. 1:20). God decides what is to be granted (Mark 10:40; Rom. 9:11; Eph. 1:6) in accord with divine purposes in Christ (Acts 10:42; Eph. 1:9; 3:11; 2 Thess. 2:13; 1 Pet. 1:2). God's gifts and call are irrevocable (Rom. 11:29); and God's counsels are beyond human scrutiny (11:33–36; 1 Cor. 2:6–13). *See also* covenant; election. J.E.A.

preexilic period, a specifically historical term referring to the period of time in Israelite history prior to the Babylonian exile (587/6 BCE). It typically refers to the time of the united monarchy and the divided kingdom (ca. 1000–587/6 BCE). *See also* divided kingdom, divided monarchy; exile; postexilic period; premonarchic period; united kingdom, united monarchy.

prefect, the title of a Roman governor appointed to administer a Roman province under direct control of the emperor. Judea was one province that was so administered, and Pontius Pilate was prefect of Judea at the time of Jesus. A similar position in Roman administration was that of the procurator, and Pilate has often been identified as a procurator in Christian literature. A Latin inscription found in Caesarea Maritima in 1961, however, refers to Pilate as a prefect. Some sources indicate that Judea came to be ruled by procurators during the time of Claudius (41–54 CE; i.e., after the rule of Herod Agrippa I, who ruled Judea and other areas as king 41–44 CE). If this is correct, then Felix and Festus, who figure in the stories of Paul's Caesarean imprisonment in Acts, would have been procurators, not prefects. In any case, the exact distinction between a prefect and a procurator is not absolutely clear, and most English Bibles do

not employ either term, opting to call all of these individuals "governors" (Pilate, Matt. 27:11; Felix, Acts 23:24; Festus, Acts 24:27). The Greek word in all these cases is *hēgemōn,* a fairly generic term for a leader or ruler.

premonarchic period, in the ancient history of Israel, the period of the judges, the thirteenth and twelfth centuries BCE. It represented a time of transitions for the Israelites: from a seminomadic population to a farming nation; from a highly diverse people to one with common purposes; and from a confederacy of tribes to a monarchy. The book of Judges illustrates the problems in these transitions, yet it also demonstrates the birthing of a determined and resilient people. *See also* Judges, book of.

presbyter, presbytery. *See* elders.

press, a device for crushing olives or grapes. *See also* olive; vine.

priesthood. *See* priests.

Priestly writer(s), the name given to the author(s) of one of the sources found in the books of Genesis–Numbers. The siglum given the source is "P," because the authors appear to have come from priestly circles. In Genesis and Exod. 1–24, the Priestly writers appear to have accepted the narrative of Israel's origins as told in the J and E materials; material ascribed to P in this portion of the Pentateuch consists mainly of editorial additions, such as dates and genealogies that tie the material together. A few longer additions explain the origins of such rituals as the sabbath (Gen. 1), the prohibition against eating meat with blood (Gen. 9), and circumcision (Gen. 17). Many scholars also detect signs that there were separate P narratives of the flood and the crossing of the sea. The core of the P material is usually thought to lie in the corpus of laws and regulations found in Exod. 25–Num. 10 (including the whole book of Leviticus). Here, there are instructions about the tabernacle (Exod. 25–31; 35–40), the sacrificial system (Lev. 1–7); the consecration of priests (Lev. 8–10); purity and impurity (Lev. 11–15); the Day of Atonement (Lev. 16); and holiness (Lev. 17–26). The last section is often called the Holiness Code and has received particular attention as a distinct block of P material dealing with behavior that will serve to distinguish Israel from other nations. *See also* Levites; Pentateuch, sources of the; priests; Sinai.   K.H.R./M.A.P.

priests, the specially designated officials who served in the temple performing ritual functions and conducting the sacrificial services. The Hebrew word *kohen* designates Jewish priests, and also those who served in temples dedicated to other gods. Melchizedek, the king of Salem, was a Canaanite priest (Gen. 14:18); Asenath, the wife of Joseph, was the daughter of an Egyptian priest (41:45); Jehu assembled the priests of Baal (2 Kings 10:19–20). Another term, *kemarim,* is used only rarely in the Bible, but always designates priests who served foreign gods in contexts that the Israelites regarded as idolatrous (cf. 2 Kings 23:5; Zeph. 1:4).

Identity: The Jewish priesthood was limited by pentateuchal law to the Levites, i.e., members of the family of Levi, the son of Jacob. According to Deuteronomy, all the levitical families had a right to the priesthood, since they did not receive an inheritance of land like the other tribes (10:8–9). One particular family of Levites, Aaron and his sons, exclusively received the anointing oil and were attired in special clothing of the priesthood (Exod. 28–29). Still, the families of Eli at the temple of Shiloh (1 Sam. 14:3), Zadok in Jerusalem (Ezek. 40:46), and Amaziah at Bethel (Amos 7:10–17) were not specified as Aaronites, but were of levitical descent.

History: During the period of the ancestors (ca. 2000–1700 BCE) there was no official priesthood. The head of the family performed sacrifices in various holy places (Gen. 31:54). The only priests mentioned at this time are of nations that were not nomadic and had fixed sanctuaries (e.g., Gen. 41:50; Exod. 3:1). As the Israelites developed a more structured society, a special class came to preside over the increasingly complex rituals that their religion entailed.

After the settlement in Canaan (probably late thirteenth to early twelfth centuries), ordinary Israelites often sacrificed at altars (Judg. 13:19–20) or high places (Heb. *bamot;* 1 Kings 3:3–4), but it appears that in the temples, the "houses of God," only priests of levitical lineage were allowed to perform the rites. These temples were constructed

Hittite priestesses holding ritual vessels; relief from Carchemish (ca. 1400–1200 BCE).

from Dan to Beer-sheba. The ark of the desert period (ca. 1300–1250 BCE), under the care of the family of Aaron, came to rest at Shiloh, and the Aaronites then became the officiators at this temple. In the time of Josiah (ca. 640–609 BCE; 2 Kings 23:8), all the priests were brought to serve in the Jerusalem temple, and the outlying temples and sacrificial sites were abolished. This centralization gave control of the entire cult to the priests serving in the Jerusalem temple.

Ezekiel typifies the desire of the Israelites in the Babylonian exile (after 587/6 BCE) to reconstitute the priesthood in all its glory. The building of the second temple (begun in late sixth century BCE) allowed the priests to return to duty. Sacrificial functions were discharged by the descendants of Aaron, while the other Levites held subsidiary roles. The second temple, however, differed from the first; the ark was missing, and certain customs, such as the use of the anointing oil, were no longer practiced. At this time, the ranks of the priesthood swelled, and the temple dues were not sufficient to support them. Many priests, therefore, turned to agriculture. Nehemiah chastises the people for not bringing their obligations (Neh. 12:44–47), and he likewise rebukes priests for deserting the house of God (13:10–11). According to many scholars, it was decided at this time that the priests would be called upon to officiate for only short periods of time each. The various duties were divided, so that all households had an opportunity to serve and no priests were completely dependent on temple duties for their livelihood. The first-century historian Josephus knew of such priestly divisions in his day (see also Luke 1:8–9).

During the Hellenistic period (ca. 333 BCE–70 CE), the priesthood dominated the nation. The priests were many in number, and some enjoyed considerable prestige. The head of the temple, the high priest, was de facto the head of government of Judea. He represented Judea in dealing with the ruling powers, collected taxes, and was responsible for the spiritual welfare of the people. A large number of aristocrats were of priestly lineage. Many priests were scattered throughout the country and came to Jerusalem only to officiate during their terms of temple service. Until the time of Antiochus IV Epiphanes (175–163 BCE), the high priest held his position for life.

The priestly households attained their greatest power during the Hasmonean period (ca. 165–63 BCE), although there was often conflict prompted by acceptance or repudiation of Hellenistic influences. At this time, priests appear to have been leaders among the Sadducees and to have dominated the Sanhedrin, but at the same time the Pharisees became prominent as teachers of the Torah and were viewed by many as spiritual leaders despite their nonpriestly status. When Herod became king (37 BCE), the rule of the nation shifted from the priests to the secular monarchy. He claimed authority to appoint the high priest and reduced the role of that office to a more ceremonial function, deprived of actual political power.

Stone table found in a priest's home in Jerusalem in the Upper City, facing the Temple Mount; ca. 70 CE.

After the rule of Herod the Great, the Roman prefects or procurators who ruled in Judea (6–41, 44–66 CE) appointed high priests, many of whom are said to have bought the office. Thus, wealthy priestly families created an oligarchy of power and prestige, and they were sometimes regarded by the Pharisees as Roman sympathizers. The sect at Qumran rejected the Jerusalem priesthood entirely, but accorded respect to Zadokite priests. They also believed that a priestly messiah would take an exalted role in the reestablished independent state, alongside the Davidic messiah.

Functions: In First Temple times (ca. 950–587/6 BCE) the high priest had the Urim and Thummim attached to his breastplate, which he consulted for a divine reply to an inquiry (Num. 27:21). Lots were often cast, as was the case in the division of the land among the tribes (26:55–56) and the choosing of Saul as king (1 Sam. 10:20–21). In this period, especially, the function of priests overlapped with that of judges (Deut. 17:9; 12; Ezek. 15:1; 24). The priests, for example, administered the ordeal of the suspected adulteress (Num. 5:11–31). Further, in the Blessing of Moses before Moses's death, Levi is charged with teaching Torah to the people of Israel in addition to offering incense and sacrifices upon the altar (Deut. 33:10).

In general, however, the functions of priests involved duties specific to the sanctuaries to which they related. Not only Israelite priests, but priests in the ancient Near East in general were thought to be persons who ministered to the god they served by fulfilling that god's needs and performing divine service in the house in which the god's presence was manifest. Thus, in Ezekiel, the service of God is expressed in terms of taking care of God's needs and feeding God from the sacrifices upon the altar (table). The tribe of Levi is enjoined to "come near to me to minister to me; and they shall attend me to offer me the fat and the blood . . . it is they who shall enter my sanctuary, it is they who shall approach my table, to minister to me, and they shall keep my charge" (44:15–16).

Chief among the duties of the priests was the performance of sacrifices. Only they were allowed to approach the altar, and then only within the context of a complex series of rituals and while wearing specific vestments that symbolized their holiness. The blood of an animal was often sprinkled, and certain portions of meat were burned, depending upon the type of sacrifice. Ordinary priests performed these daily functions, but the high priest was entrusted with the sin offerings, especially that of the Day of Atonement. Priests also pronounced the priestly blessing (Num. 6:22–26) over the people, blew trumpets on festive occasions such as holidays and new moons, and blew the shofar (trumpet made from a ram's horn) on the Day of Atonement to announce the sabbatical year (Lev. 25:9). The Levites who worked in the temple alongside the Aaronic priests were the musicians, gatekeepers, singers, and the like.

In addition to preparing the sacrifices, the priests also were in charge of the maintenance of the temple. They conducted routine inspections of the temple grounds, noting what had to be repaired, and they solicited funds to carry out the work. In connection with donations to the temple, they were often called upon to evaluate property and fix the type of sacrifice permitted for those of limited means by evaluating the ability of a worshiper to pay for a sacrifice (Lev. 12:6–8; cf. Luke 2:22–24). The collection of tithes and other obligatory temple donations was administered by the priests, who were expected to eat their emoluments in a state of ritual purity.

When a person suffered a disease or physical sign of impurity, the purification rites were performed by a priest. The methods of purification included waiting a specific amount of time, bathing, washing one's clothes, being sprinkled with water by the priest, and bringing a sacrifice from which the priest could sprinkle the blood on one's behalf. The priests were charged with diagnosing the disease *tsaraʿat* (usually translated "leprosy," but a term used to designate a number of skin disorders; cf. Lev. 13–14) as well as purifying the persons or objects affected by it (Lev. 14; see Mark 1:44). Contact with the dead (Num. 19:11–19), emissions (Lev. 15), the carcass of an unclean animal (Lev. 11:24–40), even contact with the red heifer, the means by which impurity of the dead was removed (Num. 19:1–10), required these rites of purification.

As a prestigious, elite class the priests were also expected to preserve the holiness of the sanctuary and the uniqueness of the people of Israel. Therefore, they were subject to added restrictions not incumbent upon average Israelites. A priest was forbidden to officiate if he had a physical defect (Lev. 21:17–24), was ritually impure, was under the influence of alcohol, or had married a woman forbidden to a priest. A priest was allowed to marry only a virgin of Israel, not a divorcee, prostitute, convert, or, in the case of the high priest, a widow (21:14). Ezekiel allows an exception to this last rule, if the widow is the widow of a priest (44:22).

A priest could not defile himself by attending a cemetery except for the burial of a close relative (parent, sibling, or child; Lev. 21:1–3). The high priest could not have contact with the dead even if they were his parents (21:11). Upon the death of Aaron's sons, Moses forbade Aaron and his remaining sons to manifest the signs of mourning during the week of their consecration (Lev. 10:6). Although Israel is said to be "a kingdom of priests and a holy nation" (Exod. 19:6), it was the priesthood that embodied the highest levels of sanctity in ancient Israel.

In the NT: The father of John the Baptist, Zechariah, is a priest who receives an angelic announcement of his son's future birth while he is serving in the temple (Luke 1:5–21). The chief priests of Jerusalem are presented in all four Gospels as hostile to Jesus and as conspiring to have him put to death (e.g., Matt. 26:3–4). Jesus tells a person he heals of leprosy to show himself to the priests (8:4). Acts 6:7 indicates that a great many of the priests in Jerusalem came to faith in Jesus. In time, some Christians transferred the role of the priest as mediator between God and humans onto Jesus. The Letter to the Hebrews, in particular, presents Jesus as an eternal high priest (5:1–6) who has supplanted the ancient sacrificial system by his own sacrifice (7:27–28; 9:23–26). Elsewhere, 1 Peter and Revelation identify Christian believers as the true priests of God (1 Pet. 2:5, 9; Rev. 1:6; 5:10; 20:6). *See also* Josiah; purity; temple, the; tithe; worship in the Hebrew Bible.

Bibliography

Cody, Aelred. *A History of the Old Testament Priesthood*. Pontifical Biblical Institute, 1969.

De Vaux, Roland. *Ancient Israel*. McGraw-Hill, 1965. Vol. 2. Pp. 345–405.

Gray, George B. *Sacrifice in the Old Testament*. Ktav, 1971. Pp. 179–270.   L.H.S.

prince, a person of high rank or prestige. The Hebrew terms for "prince" are multiple, but they invariably refer to a person of extraordinary power and authority. The Hittites tell Abraham, "You are a prince among us" (Gen. 23:6). David eulogizes Abner as "a prince and a great man" (2 Sam. 3:38). The term can also refer to a family leader (1 Chron. 2:10) or, for example, to the most prominent brother among a group of siblings (Gen. 33:16). In the NRSV, the word "prince" only occasionally has its conventional English meaning of the "son of a king" and/or "heir to a throne" (Gen. 34:2; 2 Chron. 11:22); more often, it refers to the king himself (e.g., to David as "prince over Israel," 1 Sam. 25:30; 2 Sam. 6:21; 7:8; also Hezekiah in 2 Kings 20:5). This may reflect the notion that the Lord is the true king of Israel and the human ruler is thus the Lord's prince (1 Chron. 29:22). It is also used for the rulers who answer to another king (so the seven princes of Persia and Media whose names are given in Esther 1:14). The prophet Isaiah anticipates that God will send a messianic Prince of Peace (9:6).   M.A.P.

Prisca (pris'kuh), **Priscilla** (pri-sil'uh), a prominent woman in the early Christian church, always mentioned in connection with Aquila, her husband. Paul calls her Prisca (a common Latin name), but Acts prefers Priscilla (18:2–28; cf. Rom. 16:3; 1 Cor. 16:19). The fact that Prisca is often mentioned before Aquila, by both Paul and the writer of Acts, may indicate that Prisca had a higher social status (e.g., through inherited wealth) than her husband, or it could be a consequence of her assuming greater significance in the early church, so that Aquila was remembered primarily as her husband. Prisca and Aquila were driven from Rome by an edict of the emperor Claudius that expelled Jews from the city (49/50 CE). They moved to Corinth, where they came into contact with Paul. Like Paul, they were leatherworkers, and he stayed with them for a time (Acts 18:3). At this time, they were both Christians, but it is not known whether Paul converted them or whether they were already Jewish believers in Jesus by the time he met them. In any case, they left Corinth with Paul and settled in Ephesus, where, according to a story in Acts 18, they had a role in the education of Apollos. The latter was preaching enthusiastically about Jesus, but his knowledge was somehow deficient ("he knew only the baptism of John," 18:25); Priscilla and Aquila "took him aside and explained the Way of God to him more accurately" (18:26). Prisca and Aquila are greeted by Paul in Rom. 16:3; 1 Cor. 16:19; 2 Tim. 4:19. *See also* Aquila; Claudius; decrees; Paul.   A.J.M./M.A.P.

Priscilla. *See* Aquila; Prisca, Priscilla.

prison, a building or other facility used for holding individuals in judicial confinement.

Types of Imprisonment: Various types of imprisonment were known in biblical times. Accused persons were often imprisoned either while their cases were being investigated or to assure their appearance for trial. The Hebrew Bible contains several examples: Gen. 39:19–41:14; 1 Kings 22:26–27; Num. 15:34 (see also Lev. 24:12, "until the decision of the Lord should be made clear to them"). The asylum granted under Israel's law to those who had accidentally killed someone in fact constituted a form of imprisonment, since the individual who left the city of refuge could be slain by the victim's relatives (Num. 35:9–34; see also Deut. 4:41–43; 19:1–10; Josh. 20:1–9). Solomon's confinement of Shimei ben Gera to Jerusalem can be compared to this practice (1 Kings 2:8, 36–46). Although the use of imprisonment as a legal penalty remained uncommon, it may have sometimes been employed. Jeremiah's retention in "the court of the guard" may reflect a judicially imposed penalty (32:2–3; 37:21; 38:13). Ezra 7:26 lists imprisonment as one of several recognized forms of legal punishment.

In the NT, there are no clear references to imprisonment imposed as a legal penalty. This is in keeping with Roman policies, which did not view the purpose of imprisonment as reform or punishment; imprisonment was simply a means of holding on to those awaiting judgment. Prisoners were held *prior* to trial; once a verdict was rendered, they might be executed, beaten, or sent into exile, but they would not normally be sentenced to more time in captivity.

The NT does offer many examples of such pretrial imprisonment: Acts 4:3; 12:3–4; 16:23–24; 23:35; Phil. 1:7–26. The binding or chaining of Jesus before he was brought to Pilate may also reflect some sort of formal arrest procedures (Matt. 27:2; Mark 15:1). Paul's imprisoning of Christians (Acts 8:3) probably refers to his handing them over to the custody of synagogue authorities who would then administer the penalty provided for in Israel's law, a flogging of up to forty lashes (Deut. 25:1–3; 2 Cor. 11:24; Acts 22:19). Pretrial retention, however, could be easily abused and become, in effect, a means of punishment. This appears to have been the case with John the Baptist, for whom no trial was scheduled (Mark 6:17–20), and with Paul, who was held without trial for two years in Caesarea (allegedly because the governor wanted a bribe to release him, or wanted to appease the Jews whom Paul had offended; cf. Acts 24:26–27). Debtors unable to pay their creditors were also imprisoned, sometimes in special debtors' prisons, until their debts were paid. Luke 12:58 makes precise reference to the "officers" who in Roman times had charge of such prisons (see also Matt. 5:25; 18:30).

Prison Conditions: Conditions in ancient prisons were often harsh. Most prisoners wore chains; their feet might be shackled, their hands manacled or even attached to their neck by another chain, and their movements further restricted by a chain fastened to a post. The existence of laws prohibiting chains that were too short or too restrictive indicates that such practices were employed often enough to merit regulation. The very word "chains" became a synonym for imprisonment. Some prisoners were also kept in wooden stocks, devices to restrain the feet, hands, or even the neck of an individual (see Acts 16:24). Prisons were often very dark (see Isa. 42:7); the inner area of the prison mentioned in Acts 16:24 was probably without windows. Although solitary confinement was known, prisoners generally were kept grouped together, accused and condemned, men and women alike. Overcrowding was not infrequent (Isa. 24:22). Prisons often had poor air circulation, a lack of hygienic facilities, rats and vermin, and food of poor quality. Unscrupulous guards might at times use the withholding of food or even outright torture to extort money from prisoners or their relatives. Although various rulers, especially in Roman imperial times, struggled to enact reforms or prevent the most severe abuses, the quality of prison life largely remained the responsibility of local officials, and conditions varied considerably from place to place. Somewhat ominously,

Heb. 13:3 speaks of "those who are in prison" in parallel with "those who are being tortured"; the two groups are apparently assumed to be the same.

Respectable individuals were sometimes accorded a form of house arrest, guarded by soldiers but allowed a relative measure of comfort and freedom. They could, for example, receive visitors and transact business while waiting for their case to come to court or be resolved. According to the book of Acts, something of this nature was the situation Paul experienced in Rome (28:16, 30–31). Paul, however, indicates in 2 Cor. 11:23 that he has been imprisoned multiple times (cf. 2 Cor. 6:5), and that letter was written prior to his imprisonments in Jerusalem, Caesarea, and Rome, as reported in Acts 22–28. The exact circumstances or longevity of those imprisonments is difficult to determine. In Phil. 1:7, 13, Paul says that he is "in chains" (NRSV: "imprisonment"), but it is not known whether he means that literally or in a metaphorical sense (as the NRSV assumes). Elsewhere, 2 Tim. 1:9 presents Paul as complaining that he has been "chained like a criminal."

Whatever the conditions, imprisonment always brought social disgrace, casting aspersions on the person's reputation and generating a significant loss of honor. This is clearly reflected in 2 Tim. 1:16, where Onesiphorus is singled out for praise as one who was not ashamed of Paul's chain. In Philippians, Paul tries to turn the humiliation factor to his own ironic advantage: he will not truly be put to shame if his personal humiliation results in the exaltation of Christ (1:20). Likewise, 2 Tim. 1:9 affirms that, even if Paul is chained, the word of God is not.

All told, five NT letters are said to have been written from prison: Ephesians, Philippians, Colossians, 2 Timothy, and Philemon. All of these are attributed to Paul; they are sometimes called the Captivity Letters and treated as a group.

The NT also contains exhortations to visit those who are in prison (Matt. 25:36; Heb. 13:3). *See also* cities; John the Baptist; Joseph; Paul.
Bibliography
Sherwin-White, A. N. *Roman Society and Roman Law in the New Testament.* Clarendon, 1963.
R.A.W./M.A.P.

prize, either the spoils of war (Jer. 21:9; 38:2; 39:18; 45:5) or something won in an athletic contest. Paul employs the latter as a metaphor for salvation (Phil. 3:14), the imperishable nature of which he contrasts with the perishable wreaths (made of parsley, celery, etc.) coveted by the athletes of Greece and Rome (1 Cor. 9:24–25). *See also* crown; games.

Prochorus (prok'uh-ruhs), one of the seven in the Jerusalem church appointed by the apostles to take care of food distribution to widows among the Hellenists (Acts 6:1–6). *See also* deacon; Hellenists.

proconsul (proh-kon'suhl), a former Roman consul who served a one-year term of office as the governor of a province under administration of the Senate. Under the Roman system, provinces that required a significant military presence to deal with potential insurrections were under the direct control of the emperor, who appointed legates, prefects, or procurators to administer them in his name. Provinces that did not require such military presence (e.g., those in Asia and Africa) were ruled by the Senate, which appointed either praetors or proconsuls to administer them. Two proconsuls are mentioned in the book of Acts: Sergius Paulus, proconsul of Cyprus, became a Christian, after his court magician Elymas was struck blind by a word from Paul (13:7–10); Gallio, proconsul of Achaia, refused to pass judgment on Paul, when opponents brought charges against him that he deemed to be Jewish matters irrelevant to Roman law (18:12–17).

procurator (prok'yuh-ray'tuhr). *See* prefect.

Prodigal Son, parable of the, a story told by Jesus in response to criticism that he was welcoming sinners and eating with them (Luke 15:11–32; cf. 15:1–2). The story concerns a father who has two sons. The younger one (who comes to be known as the titular "prodigal son") asks for his share of

Return of the Prodigal Son, detail,
by Rembrandt, ca. 1668.

the family inheritance and then squanders it in a far land. After falling victim to a famine, he returns home, where he is welcomed by his father. His dutiful elder brother, however, protests the father's actions, apparently believing that his brother's misfortune is a just consequence of irresponsible actions. The father evinces an attitude of unmerited mercy: "We had to celebrate and rejoice, because this brother of yours was dead and has come to life; he was lost and has been found" (15:32). The parable is the third in a series of three stories that deal with joy over the recovery of something that has been lost (cf. 15:3–7, concerning a lost sheep, and 15:8–10, concerning a lost coin).

promise. The concept of promise runs throughout the Bible, with particular attention to promises made by God. For example, God promises innumerable offspring to Abraham and Sarah (Gen. 15:5; 17:6–7; 22:17–18), land to Israel (15:18–21; 50:22–25), perpetual rule to David's descendants (2 Sam. 7:16), and a future, untroubled world to God's chosen ones (e.g., Isa. 11:6–9). In the Psalms, God is praised for being faithful to God's promises (18:30; 105:9, 42). In the NT, Mary proclaims that the birth of her son, Jesus, will be in accord with the promises God "made to our ancestors, to Abraham and to his descendants forever" (Luke 1:55; cf. 1:72). Jesus refers to the Holy Spirit as "the promise of the Father" (Acts 1:4; cf. Luke 24:49; Acts 2:33, 39). Paul finds scriptural authority for his Gentile mission in God's promise that all nations would be blessed through Abraham (Rom. 4:9–25; Gal. 3:6–29). The author of Hebrews sees in Jesus the realization of the promises given to, but not realized by, the ancients (11:39–40). Elsewhere, Paul says that, in Christ, "every one of God's promises is a 'Yes' " (2 Cor. 1:20). Godliness is said to hold promise for both the present life and the life to come (1 Tim. 4:8). James refers to a "crown of life" and a kingdom that God has promised to those who love God (1:12; 2:5), and Titus 1:2 maintains that the hope of eternal life is something that "God, who never lies, promised before the ages began" (cf. 1 John 2:25). Second Peter addresses scoffers who wonder why the promise of Christ's Second Coming has not been fulfilled (3:4, 9) and maintains that "in accordance with (God's) promise, we wait for new heavens and a new earth, where righteousness is at home" (3:13). *See also* Abraham; covenant; eschatology.   C.J.R.

pronouncement stories, also called *chreiai* (sing. *chreia*), a type of anecdotal literature found in the NT Gospels and other narrative writings from the Greco-Roman world. In general, what scholars call "pronouncement stories" are anecdotes that preserve the memory of something Jesus said. In such a story, everything leads up to a climactic and provocative pronouncement. The saying, which usually comes at the end, is the whole point of the anecdote (just as a punch line is the whole point of a joke). Such stories were popular in the ancient world, and entire collections of pronouncement stories have been found that preserve such anecdotes for other ancient figures. For example, an educational textbook called the *Progymnasmata* by Theon preserves the following: "Some people came up to Alexander the Great and asked him, 'Where have you hidden your treasure?' He pointed to his friends and said, 'In them.'"

The NT Gospels recount dozens of stories about Jesus that are stylistically similar to these secular anecdotes. Sometimes the climactic saying of Jesus constitutes a *correction:* Peter offers to forgive his fellow church member seven times; Jesus says, "Not seven times, but seventy-seven times" (Matt. 18:21–22). In other cases, it offers a *commendation:* Jesus praises a poor widow for her sacrificial generosity (Mark 3:31–35). Furthermore, in the Gospels, pronouncement stories frequently assume a context of controversy. Many of Jesus's most memorable sayings are prompted by objections raised to his ministry or by other challenges to his authority. Jesus declares, "The sabbath was made for humankind and not humankind for the sabbath" in response to a conflict with the scribes and Pharisees (2:23–27). He exhorts people to

PRONOUNCEMENT STORIES IN THE GOSPELS: SOME EXAMPLES

Correction Stories

Let the dead bury the dead (Matt. 8:21–22)

Forgive seventy-seven times (Matt. 18:21–22)

Whoever wants to be first (Mark 9:33–35)

Whoever is not against us (Mark 9:38–40)

Who is truly blessed (Luke 11:27–28)

Commendation Stories

The confession of Peter (Matt. 16:13–20)

The generous widow (Mark 12:21–44)

The woman who anoints Jesus (Mark 14:3–9)

Controversy Stories

Eating with sinners (Mark 2:15–17)

Jesus's disciples don't fast (Mark 2:18–22)

Picking grain on the sabbath (Mark 2:23–28)

Eating with defiled hands (Mark 7:1–15)

By what authority? (Mark 11:27–33)

Paying taxes to the emperor (Mark 12:13–17)

Whose wife will she be? (Mark 12:18–27)

From Mark Allan Powell, *Introducing the New Testament* (courtesy, Baker Academic)

"give to the emperor the things that are the emperor's, and to God the things that are God's" in response to an attempt to trap him into incriminating himself (12:13–17).

Bibliography

Powell, Mark Allan. *Introducing the New Testament: A Historical, Literary, and Theological Survey.* Baker Academic, 2009.

Tannehill, Robert C. "The Gospels and Narrative Literature." In *The New Interpreters Bible: New Testament Survey.* Abingdon, 2005. Pp. 1–16.

M.A.P.

property. *See* inheritance; ownership; trade.

prophet (Heb. *nabi'*; Gk. *prophētēs*), a person who serves as a channel of communication between the human and divine worlds. Biblical prophets played a crucial role in the development of Judaism and Christianity. Since their appearance in ancient Israel, prophets have been understood in a number of different ways, by both scholars and general readers of the Bible. In an uncritical sense, prophets have sometimes been regarded as predictors of the future; their words were seen to point to the future course of world history and, in Christian tradition, to the coming of Jesus. Prophets have also been regarded as moral and ethical innovators who brought Israelite religion to a higher level of development than it had previously achieved. Most scholars, however, recognize such understandings as simplistic. Prophets were usually more intent on speaking to present circumstances than to future ones, and they were often more concerned with faithfulness to what was imbedded in Israel's traditions than to the development of new paradigms. Still, portraits of the prophets offered by scholars have been extremely diverse. Israel's prophets have been portrayed in recent literature as great preachers, moral philosophers, raving ecstatics, isolated mystics, cultic officials, political analysts, and keepers of old Israelite traditions.

The variety of ways in which prophets have been described suggests that they were multifaceted figures and that Israelite prophecy was a complex phenomenon. Although it is possible to support almost any given picture of prophets by appealing to limited evidence, no single picture seems to be able to incorporate all of the biblical data. Various types of prophets existed in Israel, and individual prophets also had unique characteristics they did not share with other prophets. Once this diversity is recognized, however, it is possible to make some broad generalizations about the biblical prophets and the roles they played in Israelite religion and society.

Terms: The most common term for a prophet in the Hebrew Bible is *nabi'*, a word usually translated in the LXX by the Greek word *prophētēs* and in English versions by the general term "prophet." The etymology of the title is uncertain, but it may mean "one who calls" or "one who is called." Although this title was used throughout Israel in all

A prophet, as depicted in a sixth-century mosaic at San Apollinare in Classe, Ravenna, Italy.

historical periods, it did not have the same connotation for all writers. In Deuteronomy and in the writings of the Deuteronomistic History (i.e., Joshua, Judges, Samuel, Kings), and in literature influenced by that perspective (e.g., sections of Jeremiah), *nabi'* is the preferred title for people who are considered to be legitimate links between the human and divine worlds, and other titles are used for figures who are not thought to be legitimate. In this literature legitimate prophets are accorded high status and play an authoritative role in Israel's religious life (Deut. 18:9–22).

Other writings (Amos, Micah, Isaiah, Chronicles) use the term *nabi'* less frequently, and it often appears in negative contexts. In this literature the preferred designation for prophetic figures is "seer" (Heb. *khozeh*), a title that refers to the distinctive means by which these individuals received their revelations. Such visionary prophets seem to have been active primarily during the monarchic period (ca. 1004–587/6 BCE), when some of them were members of the royal establishment in Jerusalem (1 Chron. 21:9; 25:5; 29:29; 2 Chron. 9:29; 12:15; 19:2; 29:25, 30). This variant use of terms may be traceable to the distinct socioreligious development of northern versus southern traditions.

In addition to "prophet" (*nabi'*) and "seer" (*khozeh*), the Hebrew Bible uses three other titles that were not in common use. In 1 Sam. 9:9, Samuel is called a *ro'eh* (NRSV: also "seer"). This title was already archaic at the time; it refers to a person who was a specialist at communicating with God through visions, dreams, or divination, a function that was later taken over by either prophets (Deut. 18:9–22) or various diviners and

priests. Although there are some late references to *ro'eh* (2 Chron. 16:7, 10), it is likely that this distinctive class of prophet disappeared from Israel early in the monarchic period.

More frequently used is the title "man of God" (*'ish ha'elohim*), which appears often in stories set during the time of Elijah and Elisha (1 Kings 17–2 Kings 10; cf. 1 Kings 17:18; 20:28). A "man of God" may have originally been someone able to use divine power in miraculous ways, but it is likely that the title was eventually given to anyone who enjoyed a special relationship to God.

Finally, also during the period of Elijah and Elisha, the writers of Kings speak of prophetic groups called "sons of the prophets" (*bene hannebi'im*; e.g., 1 Kings 20:35; 2 Kings 2:3; NRSV: "company of the prophets"). These groups were clearly hierarchically structured prophetic guilds that flourished for a brief time in northern Israel (ca. 869–842 BCE) and played an important role in the overthrow of the dynasty of Omri (1 Kings 17–2 Kings 10).

Origins and Development: For many years historians assumed that prophecy was a uniquely Israelite religious phenomenon that had no parallels elsewhere in the ancient Near East. However, during the past century several archaeological discoveries have shown this assumption to be false. The most important of these finds occurred at the Mesopotamian city of Mari, where excavators uncovered letters written in the eighteenth century BCE. Several of these texts describe the activities and messages of various types of oracle givers whose words and actions resemble those of the later Israelite prophets. Some of those early figures bear special titles, such as "answerer" and "ecstatic." In addition, titles apparently related to the common Hebrew designation *nabi'* ("prophet") are attested at both Mari and the ancient Syrian city of Emar. Archaeologists have also discovered Assyrian texts (ca. 680–627 BCE) that contain collections of oracles from "ecstatics," "shouters," "revealers," and "votaries."

All of this extrabiblical evidence indicates that prophetic activity existed elsewhere in the ancient Near East both before and during the biblical period. Some scholars have therefore suggested that prophecy originated on the periphery of Mesopotamia, in Canaan, or even in Egypt and was subsequently borrowed by the Israelites. At the moment there is no way to prove or disprove this hypothesis, although it is important to note that there is no biblical evidence to indicate that Israel recognized prophecy as an import. In addition, anthropological studies of prophetic phenomena show that prophecy can arise spontaneously in any society where the necessary social and religious conditions are present.

Although the Bible locates most prophetic activity during the period of the monarchy, some biblical traditions place the origins of prophecy at the very beginning of Israel's history. Even if the references to the prophetic activities of Abraham and Moses are treated as retrojections from later times (Gen. 20:7; Num. 12; Deut. 18:9–22), the fact that Miriam, Deborah, and others are identified as prophets may indicate that prophecy had important religious and social functions among some early Israelite groups (Exod. 15:20–21; Judg. 4:4–10; 6:1–10). It is at least clear that in the period just before the rise of the monarchy (eleventh century BCE) prophets were well established at some of Israel's sanctuaries. Samuel played an important role at several Israelite worship centers and was involved in the creation of the new central government (1 Sam. 3–16). Thereafter, prophets were a regular part of Israel's public life, in both Judah in the south and Israel in the north. They related to the government and to the temple in various ways, some supporting the royal establishment or working inside it and some standing outside and advocating radical change. Although prophetic attitudes shifted during the monarchic period, it is difficult to detect major changes in the institution of prophecy itself. The relatively late prophets who wrote books (e.g., Jeremiah) do not seem to have been markedly different from the earlier prophets who did not (e.g., Elijah).

Just as it is difficult to determine when prophecy began in Israel, so also it is difficult to identify the point at which prophecy ceased. Prophetic activity did continue after the exile (sixth century BCE), and prophets such as Zechariah and Haggai helped to shape the restored community in Jerusalem. After the exile, however, prophecy seems to have lost much of its influence, and prophets became much less visible. In spite of the later rabbinic claim that prophecy ceased in the early postexilic period (after Haggai, Zechariah, and Malachi), it seems likely that prophets had minor official du-

The angel carries the prophet "Habakkuk" by the hair from Judea to Babylon, an incident in the deuterocanonical Bel and the Dragon (33–39); seventh-century CE relief.

ties in the worship practices of the Second Temple period (1 Chron. 25). Outside of this officially sanctioned activity, prophecy seems to have continued only in peripheral groups that left no imprint on the biblical record, unless the book of Daniel (probably written ca. 165 BCE) is to be regarded as the writing of a prophet (in the Jewish Bible, Daniel is placed among the Ketuvim, or Writings, rather than among the Prophets, as it is in the Christian OT; and Daniel is called a prophet in Matt. 24:15). Nevertheless, the NT writings produced in the first-century CE maintain that both John the Baptist and Jesus were regarded as prophets by some Jewish people of the day (Matt. 21:11, 26, 46); Josephus likewise thought that God was still sending prophets to the Jews in his day.

Personal Experiences: The prophet's experiences with the divine world were essentially private and difficult to communicate even in the best of circumstances. It is therefore not surprising that the prophets say little about their encounters with God and concentrate instead on the visual or aural messages they received. Only a few of the prophets describe their initial "calls" to prophesy (Amos 7:15; Isa. 6; Jer. 1:4–10; Ezek. 1–3), and still fewer speak in detail of the experience that gave rise to a particular oracle (1 Kings 19:9–18; 22:17–23).

Nevertheless, enough clues have been preserved to suggest that Israelites thought of the prophetic experience as something that occurred when people were possessed by the spirit of God (Judg. 6:34). The "hand of the LORD" would be on them (1 Kings 18:46; 2 Kings 3:15; Jer. 15:17; Ezek. 1:3) or the spirit of God would rest on them (Num. 11:25–26). In this situation they were no longer in control of their own actions and words, but were completely dominated by God. They felt compelled to speak the divine message that had been given to them (Amos 3:8; Jer. 20:9). Because of the feelings of helplessness and terror that accompanied possession by God's spirit, many prophets viewed the vocation negatively and tried unsuccessfully to avoid it (Jer. 1:6; 11:18–12:6; 15:15–21; Ezek. 2:1–3:15).

Behavior and Speech: During their possession experiences, the prophets seem to have exhibited characteristic patterns of behavior and speech that allowed them to be identified as prophets. The details of these patterns are unclear, and may have varied somewhat according to the historical, geographical, and social settings of the prophets' activities. However, the existence of characteristic prophetic behavior is suggested by the fact that the Hebrew verb "to prophesy" sometimes actually means "to act like a prophet" or "to exhibit the behavior that is typical of prophets." Such behavior could be recognized by all Israelites, although some groups evaluated it positively, while others did not. In some instances it was understood as a sign of divine legitimation and favor (Num. 11:11–29; 1 Sam. 10:1–13), while in other cases it was thought to be an indication of madness or of possession by an evil spirit (1 Sam. 18:10–11; 19:18–24; 1 Kings 18:26–29; Jer. 29:24–28).

Some of the prophets were probably ecstatics whose behavior was marked by psychological and physiological symptoms such as reduced sensitivity to outside stimuli, hallucinations or visions, loss of control over speech and actions, and a sense of being out of touch with reality. The intensity of these symptoms and the degree to which the prophets could control them probably varied, but ecstasy was sometimes incapacitating and dangerous (1 Sam. 19:18–24; 1 Kings 18:26–29). Among the writing prophets, however, if ecstasy was a factor at all, it was accompanied by controlled actions and intelligible speech (Jer. 4:19; 23:9; Ezek. 1:1–3:15).

As part of their characteristic behavior, some prophets wore distinctive clothing or bore a special mark that identified them as prophets or as members of prophetic guilds (1 Kings 20:35–41; 2 Kings 1:8; Zech. 13:4). Others sometimes performed symbolic acts, either as dramatic reinforcement for an oracle (Hos. 1:4–9; Isa. 7:3; 8:1–4; 20:1–6; Jer. 19:1–15; 27:1–28:17) or as a way of actually bringing about the state of affairs described in the oracle (2 Kings 13:14–19; Ezek. 4:1–8).

One of the clearest marks of prophetic behavior was the stereotypical way in which the prophets constructed their oracles. Oracles often began with an account of the commissioning of the prophetic messenger, an account that was followed by an accusation against an individual who had violated Israel's covenant law. After the accusation, the prophets delivered an announcement of judgment directly to the accused. The announcement usually began with the "messenger formula" ("thus says the LORD"), which identified the sender of the message and gave the authority for the oracle of judgment (1 Sam. 2:27–36; 13:11–14; 15:10–31; 2 Sam. 12; 1 Kings 11:29–40; 13:1–3; 14:7–14; 17:1; 20:35–43; 21:17–22; 22:13–23; 2 Kings 1:3–4, 6; 20:14–19; 21:10–15; Jer. 20:1–6; 22:10–12, 13–19, 24–27; 28:12–16; 29:24–32; 31:17; 36:29–30). A variation on this speech pattern was used by prophets in Judah and Jerusalem, who sometimes began their oracles with the cry "alas," followed by one or more participles describing the addressee and indicating the crime. This introduction was followed by an announcement of judgment (Amos 5:18–20; 6:1–7; Isa. 5:8–10, 11–14, 18–19, 20, 21, 22–24; 10:1–3; 28:1–4; 29:1–4, 15; 30:1–3; 31:1–4; Mic. 2:1–4).

Social Context and Functions: Prophets did not carry out their activities in isolation, but were an integral part of their society. Because divine possession was not a continuous experience for any of the prophets, they played various social roles in addition to carrying out their prophetic activities. Prophets like Amos prophesied only occasionally and were normally involved in secular occupations (1:1; 7:14–15). Others, such as Jeremiah and Ezekiel, were priests who were occasionally transformed into prophets (Jer. 1:1; Ezek. 1:3). Although some prophets may have had full-time responsibilities in the temple or the royal court, others carried out religious tasks that

did not always involve prophecy (1 Chron. 25:1–8; 2 Chron. 20:1–23; 34:30).

In addition to being involved in normal community activities, prophets had to receive support and legitimation from some quarter. Anyone could claim to have received a message from God, but that person could become a prophet only when a group of people recognized the prophetic claim as genuine and accepted the prophet's authority. Such support could be provided by an organized group of disciples (Isa. 8:16), but usually the process was more informal (Jer. 26). Prophets who could not obtain at least a minimal amount of social support were unable to influence their societies and were in danger of being branded false prophets or lunatics. On the other hand, prophets who were considered authoritative by at least one group were usually tolerated by the rest of Israelite society. Some prophets seem to have had relatively unrestricted access to the king, the royal court, and the temple, and they were not normally harassed unless their messages became overly strident and threatening (26:1–24; 38:1–13). Prophets might be excused from accountability for otherwise inappropriate words or actions, because they were believed to be under the direct control of God (26:12–16).

All prophets shared the common task of delivering to individuals or groups the divine messages they received during their prophetic experiences. Prophets, however, also had various social and religious functions depending on their context. Those prophets who were part of the royal court or who had regular roles in the temple worship were usually concerned to preserve and strengthen the social structure. They were certainly capable of criticizing current institutions, but they did so from a perspective that valued the institutions as such. Prophets who had no regular involvement with Israel's powerful social institutions were more likely to advocate radical change, even at the expense of social stability.

Theology: Prophets were firmly rooted in history, and this fact has important implications for understanding their theology. Because prophets were not all members of the same social or religious group, they inherited different historical and theological traditions. All prophets knew the basic outline of Israel's history and shared the major elements of Israelite faith, but they understood those elements in different ways and used different words to speak about them. In addition, prophets spoke to specific groups of people and directed oracles to particular historical and social situations. These contextual dimensions of prophecy make it difficult to talk about prophetic theology in general. Instead, it is necessary to examine the theologies of individual prophets and to appreciate the unique shape that each of them gave to divine revelation. It is possible, however, to summarize some general theological beliefs that were held by all prophets.

All prophets held the fundamental belief that Israel had been elected by God and enjoyed a special relationship with God by virtue of that election. The mutual obligations involved in this relationship were spelled out in various covenants, particularly the covenant at Sinai (Exod. 19–Num. 10; Deuteronomy) and the covenant made with the house of David (2 Sam. 7). Most of the biblical prophets, however, also believed that the people of Israel and Judah had refused to fulfill their obligations and had rebelled against God. The prophets described this rebellion in various ways (cf. Isa. 1:2–6; Jer. 2:2–37; Ezek. 16), but they seem to have been concerned with all breaches in the divine–human relationship. Deviations in ethical behavior, social injustice, the worship of other gods, and religious abuses were all condemned, because they were considered symptoms of Israel's general religious illness (Isa. 1:9–17). Different prophets, however, focused upon different issues: Amos directs much of his venom at those engaged in social abuses, while Hosea homes in on illicit worship practices.

The biblical prophets also thought that Israel's rebelliousness would be punished, although they did not always agree on the nature of the punishment or on its severity (cf. Isa. 1:7–8; Jer. 7:1–15; 14:1–15:4; Amos 4:6–12). Some, such as Isaiah and Ezekiel, believed that God would punish Israel, but remain faithful to the promises that had been made to David; Israel would remain the elect people of God. Others, such as Jeremiah, at least considered the possibility that God's punishment would involve termination of the special relationship between God and Israel. Prophetic disagreements on this point became particularly sharp during the exile, when the very existence of Israel was in question.

Early Christian Prophets: Prophecy played an important role in Christianity from the very beginning (Acts 2:14–21). The early church used biblical prophecy to interpret the life and teachings of Jesus, who was himself recognized as a prophet (Matt. 13:57; 21:11; Luke 4:24; John 4:19; 9:17). The book of Acts reports on the activities of various prophets among the early Christian believers (11:27; 13:1; 15:32; 21:10). Paul's letters make clear that prophecy was regarded as one of the gifts of the Spirit in the early church and, at least in some congregations, was a normal part of worship (1 Thess. 5:20; 1 Cor. 12:28–29; 14:26–32). Women prophets were active in some quarters, though certain restrictions were sometimes placed upon them (1 Cor. 11:4; 14:34–35; cf. Acts 21:9). Prophets were ranked with apostles and teachers as church leaders (Acts 11:27; 13:1; 15:32; Eph. 2:20; 3:5; 4:11; James 5:10; 1 Pet. 1:10; Rev. 22:6–9). The presence of so many prophets sometimes caused problems and made it necessary to devise tests to determine the validity of prophetic oracles (Matt. 7:15; 24:11, 24; Mark 13:22; Acts 13:6; 2 Pet. 2:1; 1 John 4:1; Rev. 2:20; 19:20; 20:10). *See also* prophetess.

Bibliography

Aune, David E. *Prophecy in Early Christianity.* Eerdmans, 1983.

Blenkinsopp, Joseph. *A History of Prophecy in Israel.* Westminster, 1983.

Heschel, Abraham J. *The Prophets.* Harper & Row, 1962.

Von Rad, Gerhard. *Old Testament Theology.* Vol. 2. Harper & Row, 1965.

Wilson, Robert R. *Prophecy and Society in Ancient Israel.* Fortress, 1980.   R.R.W.

prophetess (Heb. *nebi'ah*), a woman who serves as a channel of communication between the human and divine worlds. In their prophetic behavior and religious functions prophetesses are not distinguished from their male counterparts. The NRSV uses the word "prophetess" in eight passages (Exod. 8:20; Judg. 4:4; 2 Kings 22:14; 2 Chron. 34:22; Neh. 6:14; Isa. 8:3; Luke 2:36; Rev. 2:20), but the strong tendency in contemporary biblical scholarship is to call a woman who prophecies a "prophet."

The prophet Miriam is said to have composed a song to celebrate Israel's crossing of the sea (Exod. 15:20–21), and the prophet Deborah judged Israel and helped to lead the people in battle (Judg. 4:1–10). In a much later period, the prophet Huldah appears as an important religious official to whom King Josiah sends messengers to inquire of God (2 Kings 22:14–20). Nehemiah reports that his work reconstructing Jerusalem was opposed by prophets, including a woman named Noadiah (Neh. 6:10–14). In NT times, the prophet Anna is presented as one of the first to recognize Jesus as the Messiah (Luke 2:36–38). Rev. 2:20 refers metaphorically to a false prophet named Jezebel (cf. 1 Kings 18–19; 2 Kings 9) who beguiles believers into practicing immorality and eating food offered to idols.

Joel 2:28–29 says that in the last days the spirit of God will be poured out on both men and women, and "sons and daughters" will prophesy; in Acts 2:16–18, Peter declares that this prophecy was fulfilled on the day of Pentecost, when women and men alike were filled with the Holy Spirit and spoke about God's deeds of power in languages they had never learned (Acts 1:14; 2:1–4, 11). Later, Philip the evangelist is said to have had four virgin (NRSV: "unmarried") daughters who prophesied (21:9). Women prophets were also active in the church at Corinth, where certain restrictions were apparently placed upon them (1 Cor. 11:4; 14:34–35). *See also* prophet.   R.R.W./M.A.P.

propitiation. *See* atonement.

proselyte (pros'uh-lit), a convert from one religious faith or group to another. In biblical studies this term usually refers to Gentiles who become Jews. In the Hebrew Bible, many laws recognize the rights and place of resident aliens, non-Israelites living permanently in Israel. They had to observe certain laws, could offer sacrifice, and, if circumcised, could take part in Passover. Such open association with Israelites probably led to their assimilation into Israel. The book of Judith tells the story of Achior, leader of all the Ammonites (5:5), who is summoned to see that Judith has slain the

Babylonian general Holofernes. Jth. 14:10 then reports, "When Achior saw all that the God of Israel had done, he believed firmly in God, and was circumcised, and joined the house of Israel, remaining so to this day." From the second century BCE through the fourth century CE some evidence suggests that many Gentiles were attracted to Judaism because of its monotheism, sexual ethics, and sabbath observance.

In NT times, proselytes to Judaism were required to accept one God and Jewish ethical and religious observances; males had to be circumcised. The book of Acts mentions proselytes among those listening to Peter (2:10) and Paul (13:43). Nicolaus, a proselyte who had come to faith in Jesus, was chosen as one of the seven Hellenist leaders to be in charge of distribution of food to the widows (6:5). In Matt. 23:15, Jesus castigates the Pharisees for traversing sea and land to make proselytes who become twice the children of hell that they themselves are. Some interpreters have taken this as an indication that some Jews actively sought converts during this period; others think the reference is to Pharisees attempting to get other Jews to join the Pharisaic movement.

Acts also mentions Gentiles who "fear God" or "reverence God." These expressions could simply indicate non-Jews who evinced a proper attitude toward God, but in some cases (e.g., 13:16, 26) the references are thought to refer to half-converts, uncircumcised Gentiles who did not fully embrace Judaism, but who were attracted to aspects of it (e.g., monotheism, worship, morality, but not purity laws). *See also* conversion; God-fearers.   A.J.S.

prostitute. Several important characters in Israelite history were connected to prostitutes. The Jericho prostitute Rahab sheltered Joshua's spies (Josh. 2; Heb. 11:31; James 2:25), Jephthah was the son of a prostitute (Judg. 11:1), and Tamar pretended to be a prostitute to induce Judah to have sex with her (Gen. 38:14–18). None of these women were stigmatized, but prostitutes in general were considered an underclass. Priests could not marry prostitutes (Lev. 21:7), Israelites should not make their daughters prostitutes (19:29), and a priest's daughter who became a prostitute should be burned (21:9). The payment a prostitute received was considered analogous to the price of a dog; neither could be used to fulfill vows (Deut. 23:18). Like the death of children in battle, the turning of wives into prostitutes was considered a tragedy of destruction (Amos 7:17).

Little is known about how prostitutes actually worked. Tamar waited at a crossroads; Rahab had a house. Tamar was veiled for her meeting with Judah, but this was probably to conceal her identity rather than to indicate that she was a prostitute (note that in Assyria prostitutes were forbidden the veil). The phrases "act like a prostitute" or "treat as a prostitute" are not always literal. When Dinah's brothers complained that Shechem treated Dinah like a prostitute (Gen. 34:31), the reference conveys lack of propriety (he raped her)

rather than an offer of money. Again, the nonvirgin bride who is deemed guilty of having prostituted herself prior to marriage is simply believed to have acted wantonly regardless of whether any exchange of money was involved (Deut. 22:20–21). Likewise, when the personified Israel is called a "prostitute," the point of the allegation is to charge Israel with brazen unfaithfulness, not mercenary behavior (cf. Hos. 1:2). The Hebrew Bible also makes some mention of temple prostitutes, who were associated with the fertility cults that Israel sought to suppress (e.g., Judg. 8:33; Ezek. 16).

In the Roman Empire and in the NT: The cosmopolitan cities of the Roman world featured exotic brothels at which prostitution was openly practiced and considerable money could be made. There is no evidence of such brothels in Judea, Samaria, or Galilee, however, and the prostitutes who worked in those parts of the world were apparently "street prostitutes" who earned little money, lived in squalor, and had short life spans. Further, a strong connection has been documented between prostitution and slavery in the Roman world. Indeed, the general rule for literature of this period is that a prostitute is assumed to be a slave, unless her status as a free- or freedwoman is specifically stated (e.g., in one story by the second-century Greek author Artemidorus the plot depends upon readers assuming that a prostitute is a slave, though nothing is actually said to indicate that she is one [*Oneirocritica* 4.4]). In the NT era, it was relatively common for women to be sold into slavery by fathers desperate for cash. Roman law actually allowed such a sale to include a *ne serva prostituator* clause, which prohibited the buyer (or subsequent buyers) from forcing the slave to be a prostitute. Such a clause, however, greatly reduced the sale price, and the actual attachment of such clauses appears to have been rare. The mere fact that such a law existed indicates that ordinarily a female slave could be forced into prostitution, and the fact that the worth of a female slave was determined by her availability for such use suggests that this was probably one of the more common functions for which female slaves were employed. Accordingly, it is likely that most, if not all, of the prostitutes mentioned in the NT are to be regarded as slaves, and hence as individuals who had not chosen their profession and who could not abandon it. Thus, no ex-prostitutes or former prostitutes are mentioned in the NT or in any other literature of this period. In particular, the tradition that Mary Magdalene was once a prostitute has no foundation in the Bible (and originated through confused identification of Mary, an apparently wealthy supporter of Jesus's ministry [Luke 8:1–3], with the unnamed prostitute in Luke 7:36–50). An assumption of slavery may explain the difference between the words attributed to Jesus when addressing a prostitute ("Your sins are forgiven," Luke 7:48) and an adulteress ("From now on, do not sin again," John 8:11). In the case of a prostitute, abandonment of a (sinful) lifestyle was not an option.

Prostitutes are mentioned in both the Gospels and one of the letters of Paul. The references are sometimes divided into two groups: those that refer to prostitutes within Judea or Galilee, where prostitutes were almost certainly pathetic individuals forced into slavery, and those in the Hellenistic world at large, where prostitutes associated with brothels might be in view (though there is no necessary reason to assume that the prostitutes at brothels would not have been slaves as well).

Luke 7:37 refers to "a woman of the city, who was a sinner," a description that is almost certainly intended to identify her as a street prostitute and therefore a member of the first group. She comes into a house where Jesus is a dinner guest and proceeds to weep at his feet, kissing them, and wiping them with her hair—behavior that scandalizes his host, Simon the Pharisee, who reasons that if Jesus were a prophet, he would know what sort of woman she is (7:39). Jesus praises the woman for showing him great love and tells her that her sins are forgiven (7:44, 47–48). Elsewhere, Jesus tells the Pharisees that tax collectors and prostitutes will enter the kingdom of God ahead of them, because they believed John the Baptist and the Pharisees did not (Matt. 21:31–32).

With regard to prostitutes in areas outside of Israel, the older brother in Jesus's parable of the Prodigal Son accuses his younger sibling of having spent his inheritance on prostitutes while in a far country (Luke 15:30; cf. 15:13); such depletion of wealth may imply the services of expensive brothels. Elsewhere, Paul must deal with a situation in which some of the Christians in Corinth apparently do not think there is anything wrong with going to prostitutes. Paul denounces the behavior in strong language, saying, "Do you not know that your bodies are members of Christ? Shall I therefore take the members of Christ and make them members of a prostitute? Never! Do you not know that he who joins himself to a prostitute becomes one body with her? For, as it is written, 'The two shall become one flesh' " (1 Cor. 6:16; cf. Gen. 2:24). Finally, in the book of Revelation, Rome itself is compared to a "whore" (e.g., 17:1, 15), an image that depicts the city (and probably the empire) as alluring and seductive, but immoral and corrupt.

Bibliography

Fleming, Rebecca. "*Quae Corore Quaestrum Facit:* The Sexual Economy of Female Prostitution in the Roman Empire." *Journal of Roman Studies* 89 (1999): 38–61.

Glancy, Jennifer A. *Slavery in Early Christianity.* Oxford University Press, 2002.

McGinn, Thomas A. J. *Prostitution, Sexuality, and the Law in Ancient Rome.* Oxford University Press, 1998.

Shields, Mary E. *Circumscribing the Prostitute.* Continuum, 2004.   T.S.F./M.A.P.

proverb, a short, popular saying that communicates a familiar truth or observation in an expressive and easily remembered form. The term is applied to a variety of sayings in the Bible. The most common example is the folk saying drawn from human experience and characterized as a picturesque, insightful, witty, or even amusing comment on human behavior or experience (e.g., Prov. 16:18; 27:15; 29:2; Luke 4:23). The majority of these proverbs are composed of two lines in a poetic form that closely links the first line with the second (a couplet). They occur in several distinct forms depending on what they are based on: direct correspondence or association (Judg. 8:21; Prov. 9:10; Gal. 6:7), contrast (Prov. 11–13, 18:23; Jer. 23:28; John 1:46), comparison (Gen. 10:9; Prov. 20:2; Ezek. 16:44; Hos. 4:9), what is futile or absurd (Prov. 1:17; Amos 6:12; Jer. 13:23), the characterization of certain persons (the fool, Prov. 1:7, 32; the adulteress, Prov. 7:6–27; the lazy, Prov. 6:6–11; 24:30–34; 26:15), proper priorities (1 Sam. 25:22; Prov. 22:1; 25:4; 27:5), the consequences of actions (Jer. 31:29; Hos. 8:7; Prov. 26:27), or character (Prov. 15:13; 30:32–33; 2 Pet. 2:22). Many of the biblical proverbs, however, are not simply maxims or truisms, but express religious and ethical interpretations of Israelite faith (e.g., Prov. 3:1–12, 27–35; 6:16–19; 14:12). Even the more humanistic of the proverbs were collected, not simply for their practical value, but to provide instruction in the proper ordering of one's life under God (note Prov. 1:2–7).

The term "proverb" can also refer to a variety of speech and literary forms: a figurative saying that was not easily understood, similar to a parable or allegory (so translated in many versions; Ezek. 17:2; 20:49; cf. John 10:6; 16:25, 29); poetry in ode or ballad form (Num. 21:27–30); a teaching psalm, used with riddle, dealing with a perplexing moral problem (Ps. 49:4); a wisdom discourse (Job 13:12; cf. 27:1); a byword used to taunt or jeer (Deut. 28:37; Jer. 24:9; cf. Isa. 14:4); or a lament (often translated "taunt song" in newer versions; Mic. 2:4; Hab. 2:6). *See also* parables; parallelism; Proverbs, book of; riddles; wisdom.   D.R.B.

Proverbs, book of, the second book of the Writings section, or Ketuvim, of the Tanakh (Jewish Bible), where it is found after Psalms and before Job; these three books make up the section known as the Sifrei Emet, or "Books of Truth." In the Christian OT, it is found after Psalms and before Ecclesiastes.

Contents: The book of Proverbs is an anthology of seven collections. Each consists of a set of short sayings, except for the first, which consists of a collection of wisdom essays. Only the first collection (chaps. 1–9) and the last (chap. 31) have longer subunits with thematic continuity (e.g., chap. 31 is an acrostic poem about the ideal wife). Each collection of sayings is identifiable, because it is introduced with a title.

The first collection, chaps. 1–9, serves as an introduction, or prologue, to the rest of the book by developing themes in brief poetic essays. The topics of these essays include the origin of wisdom, justification for studying wisdom, the contrasting character of wisdom and folly, and the role of wisdom in creating the world.

Chaps. 10–31 are mostly single-couplet proverbs in list form, one after another in almost random order thematically. The proverbs typically articulate a world of moral values and character traits in a binary way using antithetic parallelism. Opposites are contrasted, and the positive virtue is clearly identifiable. The most frequent opposing pairs are:

Laziness and diligence: "A slack hand causes poverty, but the hand of the diligent makes rich" (10:4).

Wealth and poverty: "The wealth of the rich is their fortress; the poverty of the poor is their ruin" (10:15).

Righteousness and wickedness: "The righteous will never be removed, but the wicked will not remain in the land" (10:30).

Pride and humility: "When pride comes, then comes disgrace, but wisdom is with the humble" (11:2).

Wisdom and folly: "Wisdom is a fountain of life to one who has it, but folly is the punishment of fools" (16:22).

The proverbs are presented as observations, yet they are not simply statements of the way things are. Given their instructional setting, they intend to recommend the way things ought to be. The wisdom of Proverbs upholds the traditional values of family, hard work, honesty, humility, and loyalty. The book served as an aid in the socialization of Israel's youth, and probably especially its potential leaders, and as a way to instill the time-honored values of the community.

Proverbial wisdom is also situational, or pragmatic. Although proverbs are framed as universal statements, they need to be applied with discernment.

OUTLINE OF CONTENTS

Proverbs

Themes: A fundamental theme of Israelite wisdom is that the "fear of the Lord" is the beginning of knowledge and wisdom (1:7). The "fear of the Lord" statement serves as the basic postulate of the book. It conditions all that follows and serves as a reminder that even though wisdom's instruction has to do with matters of personal behavior, family responsibility, business ethics, and community loyalty, it is grounded in the fear of God. This notion may have originated in the context of "fear in the face of death," such as the Israelites are said to have experienced before God when they gathered at Mount Sinai after the exodus. But in a wisdom context, fear is probably not to be understood as momentary terror or fright. It refers to the deep awe and reverence for God that brings the realization that one must live properly. One must always be aware that there is a deity and that this deity holds persons responsible for their actions. Knowing that God keeps account of behavior is presented as an incentive to act wisely and properly. The claim that "the fear of the Lord is the beginning of wisdom" is well-nigh universal in biblical wisdom literature. It is found, not only in Proverbs (cf. also 9:10, near the conclusion of the prologue), but also in Job 28:28; Ps. 111:10 (a wisdom psalm); and Sir. 1:14.

The traditional wisdom of Proverbs divides humanity into two groups, the wise (equated with the righteous) and the foolish (the wicked). The characteristics and behaviors of each group are identified. The proverbs indicate what will become of each group; e.g., the wise store up knowledge, but the nonsense of a fool draws ruin near (Prov. 10:14). In this way, community values summed up in the notion of righteousness are given divine sanction; i.e., righteous behavior is recognized and rewarded by God, and folly is punished. Retribution theology maintains that God uncompromisingly and unfailingly punishes the wicked for their evil deeds and rewards the righteous with long life and prosperity. The book of Proverbs affirms retribution theology as intentionally as the Deuteronomistic tradition. It maintains the strict correlation between the practice of wisdom and earthly reward, contrasted with the foolish life that leads inexorably to tragedy and ruin. The righteous will never be removed, but the wicked will not remain in the land (10:30). The book of Proverbs thus projects a vision of the world as an ordered moral universe where truth and justice rule. This basic theological perspective of the proverbial wisdom outlook is challenged and refined in other wisdom literature, including the books of Job and Ecclesiastes.

Background: The book of Proverbs is an anthology and, as such, does not have an identifiable author. The six proverb collections have differing superscriptions. The book as a whole is attributed to King Solomon, but the other superscriptions demonstrate that this is not to be taken too literally. Solomon was revered in Israelite society for his wisdom (1 Kings 4:29–34), and attribution of the book to Solomon was a means of placing it within the wisdom tradition of the people of Israel.

Because all of the proverbs are presented out of context, it is difficult to date any of them with particular clarity. Gottwald argues that the second, third, and fourth subdivisions of the book belong to the preexilic period, while subsections one, five, and six are postexilic. Most scholars do not see any hints of a Hellenistic influence and thus date the book's final composition at around 400 BCE.

Although unaffected by Hellenistic wisdom, the book of Proverbs does show some evidence of being influenced by Egyptian wisdom. Many scholars argue that the compiler of Proverbs drew from such ancient Egyptian sources as the *Maxims of Ptahhotpe* and *The Teaching for Merikare.* Prov. 22:17–23:11 is taken almost verbatim from the *Instruction of Amenemopet.*

Interpretive Issues: One of the major interpretive issues in the book of Proverbs is the relationship of Prov. 1–9 to the rest of the book. These chapters contain the most religious language of the book along with the personification of wisdom (see below). Some scholars have argued that this section must be later, because it contains religious language, which, they argue, would only have been added at a later date by the religious community. Other scholars have raised objections to the assumption that the proverbs were originally secular and that the religious notions were only added later. Some have pointed to personifications of wisdom in ancient Egypt to indicate the possibility of an early date for the expression of that theme. The majority view, however, is that Prov. 1–9 constitutes a relatively late addition, intended to serve as an introduction to the book of Proverbs.

Modern biblical studies have focused attention on the description of the "ideal wife" (or, lit., "woman of power") in Prov. 31. The passage has been read as both a validation of women and as an oppressive text defining the roles of women from a patriarchal perspective. Some scholars have interpreted chap. 31 as referring to the figure of Wisdom of Prov. 1–9.

Another interpretive issue in the book of Proverbs concerns the character of the figure of Wisdom. The woman who is a personification of wisdom speaks to the young man, invites him into her house, and claims to be God's companion. She speaks in the first person (1:20–33; 8:1–36; 9:1–6) and even indentifies herself as the divine's artisan who was the source of order and success in the world (8:15–21). Scholars disagree over the exact nature of this figure. Some hold that she is God's consort, in the same way that Asherah was Baal's consort in Canaanite religion. This connection is drawn from similar images in other biblical and apocryphal sources (Job 28; Wis. 7–9; Sir. 24). Others claim that she is merely a personification of an abstract quality, like Virtue or Justice. Baumann argues that the Wisdom figure is

multifaceted, but can be seen (though not uncritically) as a female image of God.

Bibliography

Bandstra, Barry L. *Reading the Old Testament: Introduction to the Hebrew Bible.* 4th ed. Wadsworth, 2009.

Baumann, Gerlinde. "A Figure with Many Facets: The Literary and Theological Functions of Personified Wisdom in Proverbs 1–9." In *Wisdom and Psalms: A Feminist Companion to the Bible.* Sheffield, 1998. Pp. 44–78.

Camp, Claudia V. *Wisdom and the Feminine in the Book of Proverbs.* Almond, 1985.

Childs, Brevard S. *Introduction to the Old Testament as Scripture.* Fortress, 1979.

Gottwald, Norman K. *The Hebrew Bible: A Socio-Literary Introduction.* Fortress, 1985.

Westermann, Claus. *Roots of Wisdom: The Oldest Proverbs of Israel and Other Peoples.* Westminster John Knox, 1990.   B.B.

providence, the notion that there is a benevolent and purposeful ordering for all events of history. According to a belief in providence, there is a divine or cosmic plan to the universe, a beneficial reason for everything. Philosophically, providence might be seen as one form of "determinism" (sometimes called "fatalism"), the idea that everything is determined by destiny or fate. In Hellenistic thought, providence is related to the positive determinism of the Stoics, who held that "world-reason" permeated the cosmos and could be recognized in all natural and historical phenomena. Stoic philosophy was designed to put one in harmony with this principle of world-reason. The end result was the achievement of perfect serenity through oneness with what is and shall be.

Some authors of the Bible held to a religious view of providence. God the Creator was personally responsible for preserving and regulating the created order. In this context, providence could be related to the notions of "election" and "predestination." So conceived, providence is not a principle of orderliness or reason, but is the will of the Creator, who is actively involved in moving creation toward its goal. History, then, is not a cyclical process of endless repetition, but is moving toward a predetermined end.

In Jewish literature, the book of Job and the Wisdom of Solomon represent two classic locations for this confidence in providence. The Greek term translated "providence" in Wis. 14:3; 17:2 (*pronoia*) means "foresight" (which, indeed, is the etymological meaning of English "providence"). The basic thought is that humans see and judge from the limitations of time and space, but God sees the end from the beginning. Therefore, it is wise for humans to trust in the providential care and goodwill of the Creator (Deut. 32:7–43; Job 10:12; Pss. 74:12–17; 104:27–30; cf. 3 Macc. 4:21; 5:30; 4 Macc. 9:24; 17:22). The earliest Christians proclaimed a christological understanding of providence with a great variety of verbal expressions and human situations (e.g., Matt. 6:25–33; 10:29–31; Rom. 8:28–39; 2 Cor. 4:11–18; 1 Pet. 1:3–9).   J.E.A.

provinces, administrative areas set up within the Roman Empire. The Latin term for "province," *provincia,* originally referred to a definite sphere of action. In the late Republic it was applied to territories such as Asia, Gallia, and Narbonensis. Under Augustus (27 BCE–14 CE) the empire was organized into twenty-eight provinces, some created by dividing larger provinces like Gaul, Spain, and Macedonia. These also included a number of allied states ruled by client kings. Many of the provinces consisted of territory that had been directly annexed through conquest: Sicily, Sardinia, Corsica, Spain, Macedonia, Cyprus, Illyricum, Cilicia (southeast Asia Minor), Syria, Gaul, Egypt, and most of the Danube and German territories. The conquest of Britain and Dacia (modern Romania) was completed by later emperors. Other provinces came into being as bequests from native kings, who sought to ensure a safe transition for their supporters: Asia, Bithynia (northwest Asia Minor), and Cyrene. Judea became a Roman province when Herod the Great's son Archelaus proved unable to govern. The grain-producing area of the Bosporus was unusual in that it remained a client kingdom.

In 27 BCE the Senate made the emperor Augustus responsible for those provinces that were not entirely pacified (called "imperial provinces"). He had supreme command of the army, which was deployed to the imperial provinces. The Senate retained control of provinces in which military presence was not required (called "senatorial provinces"): Sicily, Sardinia and Corsica, Illyricum, Macedonia, Greece, Asia, Bithynia, Crete and Cyrene, and Africa. Legions were, however, stationed in Africa, Illyricum, and Macedonia during the early principate. Proconsuls or propraetors were normally sent to govern senatorial provinces for a one-year term, but the emperor could always overrule a senatorial governor. The emperor also had financial agents in those provinces who took care of the imperial estates and served as a watch on the governor. Since the agents could bring harsh retribution on rapacious officials, these agents could actually be more powerful than the governor. The imperial provinces were governed by legates of consular or praetorian rank. Their appointments lasted as long as the emperor chose to retain them in office, and they were responsible only to the emperor. Egypt, whose grain supply was crucial to the city of Rome, remained the private possession of the emperor. It was governed by a prefect.

A province essentially consisted of the network of cities within its boundaries. Those cities formed the political and social nucleus of each province and were concentrated along the coasts or major rivers. In the eastern provinces urbanization had resulted from the hellenization of the area after Alexander's conquest.

The Romans inherited a dense and ready-made network of cities. In the western provinces the only cities were those of Phoenician and Greek foundation. Under Augustus, urbanization was extended in Gaul and Spain. Towns and cities served to diffuse Greco-Roman culture. In areas such as Germany, where Rome could not build an administrative structure based on cities, its rule was a failure. Most of the thousand or so cities of the empire had populations in the area of ten to fifteen thousand persons. Only a few—Alexandria, Antioch, and Carthage—had populations of several hundred thousand. Inland, there were great stretches with no cities at all.

The areas to which 1 Peter is addressed are the names of Roman provinces (1:1). The book of Acts also makes frequent references to various provinces, though in some cases the author of Acts also uses ethnic designations for various areas rather than the official Roman designation. There is some question as to whether the reference to "Galatia" in Acts 16:6 means the province of that name or the older, more limited area occupied by the Gauls (hence, ethnic Galatia). *See also* Roman Empire.   P.P.

pruning. *See* vine.

Psalm 151, a psalm included at the end of some manuscripts of Psalms in the LXX, where one manuscript, Codex Sinaiticus, numbers it Psalm 151. It is not found in the book of Psalms in the Jewish canon of scripture, which enumerates 150 psalms; however, a version of this psalm in its Hebrew original was found among the Dead Sea Scrolls (in 11QPsa, a manuscript containing both canonical and noncanonical psalms). That original Hebrew version makes clear that the Greek version is actual a summary of two seemingly autobiographical psalms, one telling the story of the anointing of David, the young shepherd, maker of instruments and singer of psalms, and the other telling of David's defeat of Goliath. The psalm is significant, because it reflects the developing role of David in Second Temple Judaism (515 BCE–70 CE) as the founder of temple worship and writer of hymns, as the anointed of God, and even as an inspired "prophet," since the psalms attributed to him became scripture.

The two Hebrew psalms behind Psalm 151 seem to antedate the Qumran community, indicating that they must have originated prior to the second century BCE. The presence of this psalm in both 11QPsa and the LXX suggests that the book of Psalms must have been a somewhat fluid collection up until the first century CE.

Psalm 151 is accepted as canonical scripture by Eastern Orthodox churches, but not by Jews, Roman Catholics, or Protestants. The NRSV now prints it as a book of the Apocrypha out of respect for those who revere Eastern Orthodox canons, but it is not actually regarded as part of the Apocrypha by Protestant Christians (or as deuterocanonical by Roman Catholics). *See also*

Apocrypha/deuterocanonical literature; David; Dead Sea Scrolls; Psalms, book of; Septuagint.

D.W.S.

Psalms (sahlmz), **book of,** the first book of the Ketuvim, or Writings section, of the Tanakh (Jewish Bible), where it is followed by Proverbs; it is the second poetic book of the Christian OT and is found there between Job and Proverbs. The Hebrew tradition calls it *tehillim,* meaning "Praises." The name Psalms is derived from the book's LXX term *psalmos,* "psalm," which is the Greek translation of the Hebrew word *mizmor,* "song." The book is also referred to as the Psalter. Psalms is not a book in the sense of being a cohesive composition; rather, it is an anthology of 150 self-contained poems. Each poem has its own literary structure and can be analyzed for form and content. They were collected together in the postexilic period to serve as a hymnbook for Jewish worship at the rebuilt temple in Jerusalem. Tradition associates David with Psalms, because biblical history includes episodes in which he played the lyre (1 Sam. 16:14–23) and voiced lament (2 Sam. 1:17–27), thanksgiving (2 Sam. 22; Ps. 18), and praise (2 Sam. 23:1–7). But many of the psalms lack anything that would connect them to David.

Many of the psalms (116 out of 150) include a superscription as the first statement; these are not part of the poetic content, but function as notes about the poem. Many contain a phrase that indicates either authorship or a dedication, e.g., the phrase *mizmor le-dawid,* found first on Ps. 3 and on many others. This is translated "A Psalm of David" in the NRSV, though it could also be rendered "A Psalm for David" or "A Psalm About David." Thus the superscriptions might be intended to indicate that the psalm was written by David, that it was dedicated to David, or that it was inspired by David. In addition to David, Asaph (Pss. 50; 73–83), the sons of Korah (Pss. 42–49; 84–88), Ethan the Ezrahite (Ps. 89), Heman the Ezrahite (Ps. 88), Solomon (Ps. 72), Jeduthun (Pss. 39; 62; 77), and Moses (Ps. 90) are cited in superscriptions. Some superscriptions include performance directions; e.g., Ps. 5: "To the leader: for the flutes." Others include reference to an event meant to be the inspiration of the poem; e.g., Ps. 51: "To the leader. A Psalm of David, when the prophet Nathan came to him, after he had gone in to Bathsheba." The Masoretic (Hebrew) Text gives verse numbers to the superscriptions, but English translations do not. Thus, when verses from the book of Psalms are quoted from a Hebrew text, the numbers cited do not correspond to the intended verses as they appear in English Bibles.

Contents: The outline below does not account for every psalm, but only the identifiable subcollections. The editorial process appears to have appropriated various existing collections and organized them along with other self-standing psalms into five books of psalms. The first book (1–41) uses the divine name YHWH ("the LORD") to reference the deity and has been called the

David depicted composing psalms, a role that tradition ascribes to him; page from the *Paris Psalter* (900).

Yahwist Psalter. In contrast, the second book (42–72) uses the divine designation Elohim ("God") almost exclusively and has been called the Elohist Psalter, which may have a northern Israelite origin. Compare Pss. 14 and 53, which come from the Yahwist and Elohist Psalters, respectively, and are virtually identical except for the way they refer to the deity. The Psalms may have been allocated into five books on analogy with the Torah/Pentateuch, or Five Books of Moses. The books of Moses are Israel's record of divine revelation and the covenant that orders its life before God. The five books of Psalms are presented as the revelation of proper prayer responses back to God, serving as the inventory of authorized expressions and attitudes to be used by faithful Israelites. Each of the five books ends with a doxology blessing God (41:13; 72:18–19; 89:52; 106:48; and 150, which closes book five and the entire Psalter).

Interpretive Issues: The psalms were composed in poetic form, and they follow the conventions of ancient Semitic poetry. In the ancient world, however, poetry did not have strict meter, nor did the lines typically manifest end rhyme. The dominant feature of Semitic poetry was the pairing of lines, which were roughly balanced in length and related to each other semantically by repetition, contrast, or logical continuation so as to form a literary unit. This phenomenon is called "parallelism," and analysts typically designate at least three basic types of parallelism. In *synonymous* parallelism, line 2 equals line 1; in *antithetic* parallelism, line 2 contrasts with line 1; and in *formal* or *synthetic* parallelism, line 2 continues line 1. For example, the first couplet of Ps. 23, "The Lord is my shepherd, I shall not want," displays synthetic parallelism;

a cause-and-effect relationship exists between the lines: because the Lord is my shepherd, I shall lack nothing. The second couplet, "He makes me lie down in green pastures; he leads me beside still waters," displays synonymous parallelism, in which both lines express analogous thoughts of peacefulness and sufficiency. In addition to the microstructure of parallelism, some psalms were designed using macrostructures. Refrains are used to define stanzas in Pss. 42–43, which should be seen as one composition. The Hebrew alphabet is used as a macrostructure for Ps. 119, which consists of twenty-two stanzas, one for each letter of the Hebrew alphabet; each of the eight couplets in the first stanza begins with the letter aleph, each of the eight in the second stanza begins with the letter beth, etc. Variations on an alphabet scheme, called an acrostic, can also be found in Pss. 9–10; 25; 34; 37; 111; 112; and 145.

Form-critical analysis of the psalms was pioneered by Gunkel and examines the shape of a psalm's language in order to discern the *Sitz im Leben,* or setting in life, that it was intended to serve. Gunkel identified five primary psalm types and associated each with a worship occasion in the life of Israel: (1) hymns were used in the sanctuary during annual festivals and national celebrations; (2) community laments expressed the needs of the people when they met at the sanctuary during times of national calamity; (3) royal psalms expressed the people's support of the king at his enthronement or on other state occasions; (4) individual laments were used by worshipers when they came to the sanctuary during times of personal distress; and (5) personal thanksgivings were used when worshipers returned to the sanctuary to offer a sacrifice in celebration of deliverance from illness or disaster. Based largely on Gunkel's work, an inventory of types or genres has emerged in biblical studies that is widely used to categorize the individual psalms.

OUTLINE OF CONTENTS

Psalms

The type found most often in the book of Psalms is the *lament,* also called the *complaint.* It can be found as the expression of an individual or a group. A lament psalm typically begins with the psalmist describing a difficult situation and crying out to God for relief. The psalmist often imagines how life will be better, once God intervenes, and promises to give God the credit for deliverance. For example, Ps. 22, an individual lament, begins with an initial cry of desperation: "My God, my God, why have you forsaken me? Why are you so far from helping me, from the words of my groaning?" (22:1). The psalmist goes on to describe feelings of despair: "But I am a worm, and not human; scorned by others, and despised by the people" (22:6). The psalmist cries for help: "Deliver my soul from the sword, my life from the power of the dog!" (22:20). Then, confident that the cry has been heard and deliverance will come, the psalmist vows, "I will tell of your name to my brothers and sisters; in the midst of the congregation I will praise you" (22:22).

The *thanksgiving* psalm type is the reverse of the lament. The psalmist looks back on unfortunate experience from a position of security and health. For example, Ps. 30 recalls that things were dire until God intervened: "O LORD my God, I cried to you for help, and you have healed me. O LORD, you brought up my soul from Sheol, restored me to life from among those gone down to the Pit" (30:2–3). The psalmist then invites everyone to join in giving thanks to God: "Sing praises to the LORD, O you his faithful ones, and give thanks to his holy name" (30:5). The *hymn* psalm type also uses praise language, but does not link the praise to an act of deliverance. Instead, hymns laud something about the character or creativity of God: divine kingship (Pss. 47; 93; 96–99), creation of the world (Pss. 8; 19; 104; 139; 148), Zion (Pss. 46; 48; 76; 84; 87; 122), Torah (Pss. 1; 119), wisdom (Pss. 36; 37; 49; 73; 111; 112; 127; 128; 133), and God's appointed king (Pss. 2; 18; 20; 21; 45; 72; 89; 101; 110).

Influences: Psalms played a role in Jewish worship of the Second Temple period (sixth century BCE to first century CE) and beyond. The *Thanksgiving Hymns* scroll (1QH), discovered among the cache of Dead Sea Scrolls at Qumran, is a unique collection of psalm-type compositions that draw upon the form and language of the biblical psalms and biblical prophetic literature; presumably they were used in worship at Qumran. The Hallel praise psalms (Pss. 113–118) continue to be used in Jewish daily prayers and on all Jewish pilgrim festivals (Passover, Weeks, Tabernacles), and they were recited by Jesus and his disciples at the conclusion of the Passover (see Mark 14:26). The dominant genres of lament, thanksgiving, and hymnic praise are the foundation of prayers and songs in formal community worship and in private devotion.

Bibliography
   Alter, Robert. *The Art of Biblical Poetry.* Basic, 1987.
   Bandstra, Barry L. *Reading the Old Testament: Introduction to the Hebrew Bible.* 4th ed. Wadsworth, 2009.

Berlin, Adele, and Lida Knorina. *The Dynamics of Biblical Parallelism.* Eerdmans, 2007.

Gerstenberger, Erhard. *Psalms.* 2 vols. Eerdmans, 1988–2001.

Gunkel, Hermann. *Introduction to Psalms: The Genres of the Religious Lyric of Israel.* Mercer University Press, 1998.

Whybray, Norman. *Reading the Psalms as a Book.* Sheffield Academic, 1996.   B.B.

Psalter (sawl'tuhr), a name designating the biblical book of Psalms. *See also* Psalms, book of.

Pseudepigrapha (soo'duh-pig'ruh-fuh; Gk., "falsely ascribed writings"), a collection of some sixty-five documents connected with, but not part of, the Jewish Bible (Christian OT) and written ca. 300 BCE–200 CE. They are ostensibly Jewish writings, but some exist only in versions edited by later Christians, and others were actually composed by Christians who wrote from an assumed perspective of ancient Israelites or Jews.

These works came to be called Pseudepigrapha because in many cases the person to whom they are ascribed was not the actual author. As such, the term can have pejorative connotations, but such are not intended by modern scholars, who recognize that many canonical books of the Bible are also ascribed to persons who were not their actual authors. Furthermore, some books included in the Pseudepigrapha lack ascription to any author. Thus the term is employed in modern scholarship without reference to its etymological meaning; it is simply a traditional, internationally and ecumenically accepted word for a group of ancient religious writings.

For clarity of classification, the Pseudepigrapha may be distinguished from:

a. Canonical writings that compose the Tanakh, or Bible, for Jews and the OT for Christians; on these, *see* Old Testament; Tanakh.

b. The books that Protestant Christians place among the Apocrypha and Roman Catholic Christians call "deuterocanonical writings"; on these, *see* Apocrypha/deuterocanonical literature.

c. Apocryphal Christian writings, which are often similar to the later books of the Pseudepigrapha, especially those produced by Christian authors. Indeed, an argument might be made for excluding all Christian writings from the Pseudepigrapha, which would then be, by definition, a collection of noncanonical Jewish writings. Still, this is not usually done; rather, the conventional distinction is drawn on the basis of *ostensive authorship.* Works classed as "apocryphal Christian writings" are written from a blatantly Christian perspective (e.g., a pseudepigraphical work attributed to one of Jesus's twelve disciples), while Christian works listed among the Pseudepigrapha are written from a supposed Jewish perspective (e.g., a pseudepigraphical work by a Christian attributed to a Hebrew patriarch or prophet). *See also* apocryphal Christian writings.

It must also be said, however, that "Pseudepigrapha" is a Western concept. The Eastern Orthodox canon of scripture differs somewhat from that used by Jews and Western Christians (Catholic or Protestant), and there are a handful of writings listed among the Pseudepigrapha that Eastern Orthodox Christians include in the canon. These include the Prayer of Manasseh and 3 Maccabees (and to some extent 4 Maccabees, which Orthodox Bibles often include as an appendix).

Virtually all of the religious writings contained in the Pseudepigrapha offer reflection and meditation on the writings of the Hebrew Bible, drawing the language, symbols, and metaphors from those texts. For example, when the author of the *Testament of Judah* wants to describe the Maccabean wars (chaps. 3–7), he does so by relating an account of how the ancestral tribes of Dan and Judah pretend to be "Amorites" (who function as a literary cipher for the Maccabees) and fight against the "Canaanites" (a cipher for the Seleucids). Indeed, one hindrance in dating these writings is their penchant for referring to contemporary events in terms of past cataclysms; for example, the Roman destruction of Jerusalem in 70 CE is described with prose and poetry borrowed from old descriptions of the sixth-century BCE conquest of Jerusalem by the Babylonians. Thus, the author of *4 Ezra* laments Rome's conquest of Jerusalem with the words: "Are the deeds of those who inhabit Babylon any better? Is that why she has gained dominion over Zion?" (3:28).

Although most of the sixty-five documents of the Pseudepigrapha were written between 300 BCE and 200 CE, one writing, *Ahiqar,* probably predates this period. Some of the writings also postdate 200 CE, at least in their current form, but are

Leather manuscript fragment of the *Sibylline Oracles,* in Greek, ca. the fourteenth century CE.

included because they provide valuable information regarding the development of earlier traditions, contain an edited version of an otherwise lost document, or preserve earlier traditions. There is, accordingly, diversity of contexts. One must be careful to distinguish between a book like *Jubilees*, which certainly dates from the second century BCE, and a work like the *Ascension of Isaiah*, an originally Jewish writing that has been thoroughly reworked by later Christians.

The documents in the Pseudepigrapha can be arranged into five loosely defined genres.

Apocalyptic Literature and Related Works: The first genre of documents in the Pseudepigrapha contains nineteen works:

1 Enoch (Ethiopic *Apocalypse of Enoch*)

2 Enoch (Slavonic *Apocalypse of Enoch*)

3 Enoch (Hebrew *Apocalypse of Enoch*)

Sibylline Oracles

Treatise of Shem

Apocryphon of Ezekiel

Apocalypse of Zephaniah

4 Ezra

Greek Apocalypse of Ezra

Vision of Ezra

Questions of Ezra

Revelation of Ezra

Apocalypse of Sedrach

2 (Syriac Apocalypse of) Baruch

3 (Greek Apocalypse of) Baruch

Apocalypse of Abraham

Apocalypse of Adam

Apocalypse of Elijah

Apocalypse of Daniel

Either the author or a subsequent scribe gave these titles to the documents. In most cases, the only extant manuscripts of works come from a much later time, though in a few cases fragments of some of the documents were discovered among the Qumran literature (Dead Sea Scrolls).

The noun "Apocalypse" comes from the Greek word meaning a "revelation" or "disclosure." Thus, these documents contain a revelation of what is occurring in the heavens above the earth or what is to happen in the impending future. Such disclosures are often graphically illustrated with visions and auditions, and the books often relate cosmic trips by Enoch or other "holy ones" into the hidden reaches of the universe. The interest in relating these visions, however, is not cosmological, but theological. The primary concern is with ramifications that such disclosures regarding the future or the heavens have for choices to be made on earth in the present. Hence, an ethical dimension is always implied and often explicit, as in *1 Enoch* 101:1: "Examine the heaven, you sons of heaven, and all the works of the Most High; and be

ፆዶሰ፡ታለዓበጮፉ፡ገ፡ትሥም፡ሰ.ዳ፯ጮ፡ርተ፡ግ

።.ረ.ዘሥሰ፡በ፦በ፡ሰጮሰ፡ጓልጮ.፡ፍ፡ም.ጮ፡ደ፦ተ

።ሴ፩ፆ።፡ሰ፬.፦)፡ሙ.ጌፉ፡ሙ.፦ሙስጮ።ፈሰኍ፦

'ዶ፡)ግ፻ተጮ።ጓሕፀ።ጋጠ.ኢፍ.ደ፡ለበጼ፬ም

ト.ጮስጮ፡ጌፆሰ፡ተቡስዋሰ፦ተበፈፍ.ደ፡ለበ

ቀፈ፦፡ፉበ፡ቀ.ፆሙ።ሰ.ዘፆሰ.ሙ.ፀፉቡ.ም.ጮ.ደ

።በ።ጮስ፡ሰ.ዳ.ፉጮ፡ም.ቀጌጸሰ፡ኢፍበ.ርጮ.ነ

afraid to do evil in (God's) presence." The moral import of apocalyptic thought is emphasized, e.g., in *2 Enoch* 39–66, where Enoch returns to the earth and instructs his sons regarding righteousness, and in the *Testaments of the Twelve Patriarchs* (see below), where each of the twelve sons of Jacob instructs and admonishes his sons. Some apocalyptic writings lament the present state of the world and are pessimistic, e.g., *4 Ezra:* "O Adam, what have you done? For though it was you who sinned, the fall was not yours alone, but ours also who are your descendants. For what good is it to us, if an eternal age has been promised to us, but we have done deeds that bring death?" (7:48–49). Other apocalypses contain a yearning for a new, glorious age, which seems to be dawning, e.g., *2 Baruch:* "And it will happen that after (God) has brought down everything which is in the world, and has sat down in eternal peace on the throne of the kingdom, then joy will be revealed and rest will appear. And then health will descend in dew, and illness will vanish, and fear and tribulation and lamentation will pass away from among (people), and joy will encompass the earth" (73:1–2).

The character and date of the apocalyptic works already listed may be succinctly suggested. *First Enoch*, a most important apocalypse replete with divine information about the world and history, is a Jewish composition; it is composite and dates from the third century BCE to the first century CE (probably the first half). *Second Enoch*, also a brilliant apocalypse with penetrating insights into our universe and humanity, is extant only in Slavonic; the original Jewish core probably dates from the end of the first century CE. *Third Enoch* is Jewish and in its present form dates from the fifth or sixth century CE. It is not the work of one author, but rather the deposit of many traditions; portions of the writing probably date from the first or second century CE.

The *Sibylline Oracles*, which predict future woes and calamities, comprise both early Jewish and later Christian writings, dating from the second century BCE to the seventh century CE. They usually served as political propaganda. The *Treatise of Shem* clarifies the features of a year according to the house of the zodiac in which the year begins; although difficult to date, the document seems to be an Alexandrian composition from the end of the first century BCE. The *Apocryphon of Ezekiel* is lost, except for quotations and an excerpt in both the writings of the fourth-century church father Epiphanius and the Babylonian Talmud. The original Jewish document dated from sometime around the turn of the era. The *Apocalypse of Zephaniah* is only partly preserved; the original Jewish work probably described Zephaniah's travels to heaven and Hades and was written around the turn of the era.

The fourth book of Ezra (*4 Ezra*) is a Jewish work that postdates the destruction of the temple in 70 CE; a later Christian altered its pessimistic tone by prefixing two chapters (sometimes called *5 Ezra*) and affixing two others (sometimes called *6 Ezra*). The *Greek Apocalypse of Ezra* records Ezra's visions of heaven, hell, and the antichrist; in its present form, this apocalypse is Christian, is rather late (perhaps as late as the ninth century CE), and is a mixture of Jewish and Christian sources. The *Vision of Ezra* is Christian, but is clearly in the cycle of Ezra writings like *4 Ezra* and the *Greek Apocalypse of Ezra;* it dates from between the fourth and the seventh centuries CE. The *Questions of Ezra* is Christian and, like the *Vision of Ezra,* is placed within the Ezra cycle; its date has not yet been determined. The *Revelation of Ezra* concludes the Ezra cycle; somewhat like the *Treatise of Shem,* it describes the nature of the year according to the weekday in which it begins. It is Christian and difficult to date. The *Apocalypse of Sedrach,* in its present form, is Christian and perhaps as late as the fifth century CE, but it obviously preserves material from the early centuries of the present era.

The *Syriac Apocalypse of Baruch* (*2 Baruch*), a Jewish work that is far more optimistic than *4 Ezra* and probably a later reaction to it, dates from around 100 CE. *3 Baruch* is either a Christian work that utilized Jewish traditions or a Jewish work that has been edited by a Christian. The latter possibility seems more probable. The original Jewish work would have dated from the first or second century CE.

The *Apocalypse of Abraham* is extant only in Slavonic; the early Jewish core is dated by most scholars between 70 and 150 CE. The *Apocalypse of Adam,* in its present form, is gnostic, but not Christian gnostic, and several scholars have argued or suggested that it derives from Jewish traditions

Aramaic fragment of *1 Enoch* 22 found among the Dead Sea Scrolls.

or sources that are from the first century CE. The *Apocalypse of Elijah,* a composite work of Jewish and Christian materials, was probably completed between 150 and 275 CE, but the Jewish material was earlier. The *Apocalypse of Daniel,* according to some scholars, contains fourth-century CE sections; the present work, however, dates from the beginning of the ninth century CE.

Testaments: The second genre of documents in the Pseudepigrapha contains the following "Testaments" (often with apocalyptic sections); this group contains the following documents:

> *Testaments of the Twelve Patriarchs*
>
> *Testament of Job*
>
> *Testaments of the Three Patriarchs*
>
> > *Testament of Abraham*
> >
> > *Testament of Isaac*
> >
> > *Testament of Jacob*
>
> *Testament of Moses*
>
> *Testament of Solomon*
>
> *Testament of Adam*

Biblical narratives usually provide the setting for these "Testaments." Although there was no concrete genre to bind the authors, there is a shared structure or format to most of these writings. The biblical hero, on his deathbed, calls his sons and followers around him in order to convey his last words of instruction and perception. These testaments (or last wills) contain moral instruction and are often dramatized by visions of the future. In a certain sense, this genre was influenced by Jacob's testament to his sons (Gen. 49).

The *Testaments of the Twelve Patriarchs,* in its present form, is a Christian work that probably dates from the second half of the second century CE. Most scholars are convinced, however, thanks to the recovery of the testaments of *Levi, Judah,* and *Naphtali* (from the *Testaments of the Twelve Patriarchs*) among the Qumran scrolls, that the work was originally a Jewish composition that dated from the second or first century BCE. This important document is a depository of Jewish ethics, but there are also apocalyptic sections and testimony to a belief in two messiahs (found also in the Qumran literature): "And there shall arise for you from the tribe of Judah and [the tribe of] Levi the Lord's salvation" (*T. Dan* 5:10).

The *Testament of Job* is a Jewish work that urges the embodiment of an endurance like Job's; it was written around the turn of the era. The *Testaments of the Three Patriarchs* is a version of three works that are also found separately: the testaments of *Abraham, Isaac,* and *Jacob.* Of these, the *Testament of Isaac* and the *Testament of Jacob* are Christian writings that evolved from the *Testament of Abraham,* an originally Jewish work that probably dates from around 100 CE. The *Testament of Moses,* which purports to be Moses's farewell exhortation to Joshua, is a Jewish composition that obtained its present form shortly after the turn of the era; it is only partly preserved in one Latin palimpsest (i.e., a manuscript that was washed clean in order to be reused, but from which text is still recoverable).

The *Testament of Solomon* is a folk story about how Solomon built the temple using magic and demons, but fell from God's favor because of his love for an idolatrous Shunammite woman. As extant, it dates from around the third century CE. Although it is possible, as some scholars have argued, that an underlying earlier writing dates from the first century, it is clear that portions of this testament represent first-century Palestinian Jewish ideas. The *Testament of Adam* is a composite work containing the Horarium (Hours of the Day), the Prophecy, and the Hierarchy (of the Heavenly Powers); it reached its present Christian form before the end of the third century CE. In their original form, however, the Jewish portions may have been at least a century earlier.

Expansions of the OT and Other Legends: The third genre of documents in the Pseudepigrapha contains the following works:

Letter of Aristeas

Jubilees

Martyrdom and Ascension of Isaiah

Joseph and Asenath

Life of Adam and Eve

Pseudo-Philo

Lives of the Prophets

Ladder of Jacob

4 Baruch

Jannes and Jambres

History of the Rechabites

Eldad and Modad

History of Joseph

These documents demonstrate the creative force of the Hebrew Bible; with only one exception, they expand upon and embellish biblical narratives and stories.

The *Letter of Aristeas*—the exception just mentioned—is an apology primarily for the LXX, but also for the temple; it dates from the first half of the second century BCE. *Jubilees* is a conservative writing that celebrates the supremacy of the law and the sabbath, directs polemics against a lunar calendar, and extols Jewish distinctiveness. It is a rewriting of Gen. 1:1–Exod. 12:50 and is ostensibly a revelation to Moses by the Angel of the Presence. It was written during the second century BCE. The *Martyrdom and Ascension of Isaiah* (chaps. 1–5) is Jewish and was composed certainly long before the end of the first century CE and probably around 100 BCE. Joined to the *Martyrdom* is the "Vision of Isaiah" (chaps. 6–11), a Christian work, which predates the third century CE. Later interpolated into the *Martyrdom* is another Christian work, the so-called *Testament of Hezekiah* (3:13–4:22), which dates perhaps from the end of the first

century CE. The three sections were combined before the fourth century.

Joseph and Asenath, a romance between Joseph and Potiphera's daughter, is an expansion of Gen. 41:45. Modern scholars date this work ca. 100 CE, if not earlier. The *Life of Adam and Eve,* an expansion of Gen. 1–4, dates from the first century CE, perhaps the first half. *Pseudo-Philo,* a rewriting of Genesis–2 Samuel with legendary expansions, was written either between 70 and 135 CE or just before 70 CE. It contains a memorable lament attributed to Seila, Jephthah's daughter (cf. Judg. 11:30–40), which includes the following lines:

> May my words go forth in the heavens,
> and my tears be written in the firmament!
> That a father did not refuse the daughter
> whom he had sworn to sacrifice. (40:5)

The *Lives of the Prophets,* apart from some Christian accretions, is a deposit of tradition regarding the lives and deaths of twenty-three prophets; the account is enriched with folklore and legends, many undoubtedly popular in and around Jerusalem. It was written in or just before the first century CE. The *Ladder of Jacob,* preserved only in the *Explanatory Palaia,* a medieval Slavonic text, is an expansion on Jacob's dream at Bethel (Gen. 28:11–22). Some scholars have seen behind chaps. 1–6 an early Jewish document, dating perhaps from the late first century CE; chap. 7 is a Christian work, once independent, but now included as an appendix to standard collections of the Pseudepigrapha. *Fourth Baruch,* an expansion on Jeremiah, was written shortly after 100 CE; it is a Jewish writing edited by a Christian. *Jannes and Jambres,* a tale about the pharaonic magicians who opposed Moses (Exod. 7–8; cf. 2 Tim. 3:8–9), derives from many diverse, very early legends. It is Christian in its present edited form, but it certainly goes back to Jewish traditions that predate the first century CE.

The *History of the Rechabites,* a legendary expansion of Jer. 35, as extant, is a Christian work that

Ptolemy IV on a gold coin; on his head is a crown formed of the sun's rays.

predates at least the sixth century, but there are reasons to speculate that portions preserve early Jewish traditions. The core chapters may derive from a Jewish writing that predates 100 CE. *Eldad and Modad* is lost, except for one quotation in the *Shepherd of Hermas;* if a Jewish pseudepigraphon, it would have been very early, offering an expansion of Num. 11:24–30. The *History of Joseph,* an elaborate legend based on Gen. 41:39–42:38, is difficult to date, but may originally have been both early and Jewish.

Wisdom and Philosophical Literature: The fourth genre of documents in the Pseudepigrapha contains the following works:

Ahiqar

3 Maccabees—included in the canon of Eastern Orthodox churches

4 Maccabees—included as an appendix in some Eastern Orthodox Bibles

Pseudo-Phocylides

Sentences of the Syriac Menander

These writings preserve some of the insights of ancient wisdom, not only within early Judaism, but also in surrounding cultures. Here, one confronts universal truths essential for sophisticated and enlightened conduct. The Jewish authors of these works tended to borrow philosophical truths from other cultures, frequently but not always recasting them in light of the Torah.

Ahiqar, an Assyrian composition of the late seventh or sixth century BCE, predates the period covered by the Pseudepigrapha; as such, it is an especially important work for understanding the thought of early Jewish faith. It is cited by the author of Tobit (1:21–22). *Third Maccabees* provides a somewhat humorous account of divine intervention that saved the Jews from persecution by Ptolemy IV Philopator. It was written near the turn of the era, perhaps even as early as the early decades of the first century BCE and is included in the canon of Eastern Orthodox churches. *Fourth Maccabees,* a philosophical diatribe influenced by Stoicism and Greek rhetoric, was composed probably sometime in the century preceding the destruction of Jerusalem in 70 CE. It is often printed as an appendix in Eastern Orthodox Bibles. *Pseudo-Phocylides,* Jewish maxims attributed to an Ionic poet who lived in the sixth century BCE, was compiled perhaps between 50 BCE and 100 CE. The *Sentences of the Syriac Menander* is a collection of old wisdom sayings probably compiled by a Jewish editor around the third century CE. The work is at times strikingly similar to *Ahiqar* and to Sirach.

Prayers, Psalms, and Odes: The fifth, and final, genre of documents in the Pseudepigrapha contains the following writings:

More Psalms of David

Prayer of Manasseh—included in the canon of Eastern Orthodox churches

Psalms of Solomon

Hellenistic Synagogal Prayers

Prayer of Joseph

Prayer of Jacob

Odes of Solomon

Some of these poetic compositions are influenced by the thought and style of the Davidic psalms, while others show the freer developments of poetic style characteristic of early Jewish hymns. *More Psalms of David* contains five additional psalms attributed to David and some verses of a sixth; these were composed over a wide period of time. One dates from the third century BCE, while others date from the second century BCE to the first century CE. Sometimes the reference to David is palpable, e.g., Psalm 151: "I was the smallest among my brothers, and the youngest among the sons of my father; and he made me shepherd of his flocks, and the ruler over his kids" (v. 1). The *Prayer of Manasseh,* included in the Eastern Orthodox canon, is a beautiful and penetrating penitential prayer composed by a Jewish author around the turn of the era. The *Psalms of Solomon* preserves eighteen psalms written by pious Jews near or in Jerusalem during the last half of the first century BCE. *Hellenistic Synagogal Prayers,* Jewish prayers identified behind books 7–8 of the *Apostolic Constitutions,* are difficult to date. They were probably composed during the second and third centuries CE, if not earlier. The *Prayer of Joseph,* as extant, is more typical of the works collected under the category "Expansions of the Old Testament"; it is only partially preserved, but there are reasons to date it to the period between 70 and 135 CE. The *Prayer of Jacob* is lost, except for twenty-six lines preserved in a papyrus fragment. It is a Jewish prayer that is difficult to date. The *Odes of Solomon,* a Christian collection of forty-two odes significantly influenced by the literature of early Judaism, especially the Qumran scrolls, was composed around 100 CE and is strikingly similar to the Gospel of John.

In addition to the works listed above, scholars sometimes include several "supplements" to the Pseudepigrapha, some thirteen Jewish works that have not survived, but that are quoted by the fourth-century bishop and church historian Eusebius, who found them in a now lost work by Alexander Polyhistor (who Eusebius says lived in the first century BCE). Some of the quoted excerpts are fascinating. One, for example, indicates that the Jewish philosopher Aristobulus argued that Pythagoras, Socrates, and Plato all heard God's voice. Another maintains that Artapanus, a Jewish historian who lived in the second century BCE, suggested that all the greatness of Egyptian culture (including idolatry and polytheism) was to be attributed to the influence of Abraham, Joseph, and Moses. ***See also*** apocalyptic literature; Apocrypha/deuterocanonical literature; apocryphal Christian writings; canon; Dead Sea Scrolls; Esdras, Second Book of; Maccabees, Third Book of; Maccabees, Fourth Book of; Old Testament; Prayer of Manasseh; pseudepigraphy; pseudonym; Septuagint; Tanakh; wisdom.

Bibliography

Charlesworth, James H., ed. *The Old Testament Pseudepigrapha*. 2 vols. Doubleday, 1983, 1985.

J.H.C.

pseudepigraphy (Gk., "false ascription"), the practice of attributing a writing to someone who did not actually write it. The word is used with reference to the Pseudepigrapha and apocryphal Christian writings, almost all of which are deemed to be pseudepigraphical (i.e., ascribed to persons who did not actually write them). But the word is also used prominently in NT studies, and it is that usage that will be the focus of this entry.

Ten NT writings are often deemed pseudepigraphical. As noted, the term itself means "false ascription," *not* "false writings," as is sometimes thought. Most scholars who use the term do not mean to imply that the works they call pseudepigraphical are illegitimate or invalid, nor does the term necessarily imply dishonesty or deceit. It is, however, applied only to those books that contain an apparent self-claim to authorship, not to works that have been ascribed to an author by tradition. For example, most modern scholars do not believe the Gospel of Matthew was written by Matthew, the disciple of Jesus, but the work is not called pseudepigraphical, because its attribution to Matthew derives from church tradition, even if that attribution may be inaccurate; the book itself is anonymous. The Letter to the Ephesians, on the other hand, says it is written by Paul the apostle (1:1); thus, if it was not actually written by Paul (i.e., if "Paul" is a pseudonym being employed by some other author), it would be called pseudepigraphical.

Possibly Pseudepigraphical NT Books: The ten NT writings that are sometimes deemed pseudepigraphical are all letters. Of the twenty-one letters in the NT, four are anonymous: Hebrews, 1 John, 2 John, and 3 John—there are church traditions about the authorship of these writings, but the letters themselves do not name their authors. Seven of the remaining seventeen letters are universally regarded as authentic letters of Paul. These are Romans, 1 Corinthians, 2 Corinthians, Galatians, Philippians, 1 Thessalonians, and Philemon. They form a group referred to by Bible scholars as the *undisputed letters of Paul*. Six of the remaining ten letters (the ones often deemed pseudepigraphical) are also ascribed to Paul, but that assertion is questioned: Ephesians, Colossians, 2 Thessalonians, 1 Timothy, 2 Timothy, and Titus. Scholars sometimes refer to these letters as the *deuteropauline letters*, meaning "secondary letters of Paul." That label, however, can be confusing, since those who employ it mean different things by it ("secondary" in a chronological sense—written later than the others by someone after Paul died—or "secondary" with regard to significance or authority, if viewed as scripture).

In any case, the other four letters often deemed to be pseudepigraphical are James (ascribed to James, the brother of Jesus), 1 Peter and 2 Peter (ascribed to the apostle Peter, one of Jesus's twelve disciples), and Jude (ascribed to Jude, the brother of James, and, thus, also a brother of Jesus).

Levels of Authenticity: When scholars talk about authorship and pseudepigraphy, they do so in a way that assumes various constructions that might account for why a letter would be attributed to a prominent church leader like Paul, James, Peter, or Jude. The variety of possibility yields seven recognizable degrees or levels of authenticity:

1. *Literal Authorship:* A church leader writes a letter in his own hand.

2. *Dictation:* A church leader dictates a letter almost word for word to a secretary or amanuensis.

3. *Delegated Authorship:* A church leader describes the basic content of an intended letter to a disciple or an amanuensis, who then writes the letter for him to approve and sign.

4. *Posthumous Authorship:* A church leader dies, and his disciples finish a letter that he had intended to write, sending it posthumously in his name.

5. *Apprentice Authorship:* A church leader dies, and disciples who had been authorized to speak for him while he was alive continue to do so by writing letters in his name years or decades after his death.

6. *Honorable Pseudepigraphy:* A church leader dies, and admirers seek to honor him by writing letters in his name as a tribute to his influence and in a sincere belief that they are responsibly carrying on his tradition.

7. *Forgery:* A church leader obtains sufficient prominence that, either before or after his death, people seek to exploit his legacy by forging letters in his name in which they present him as a supporter of their own ideas.

With regard to the NT letters that are sometimes deemed pseudepigraphical, scholars who argue that those letters are authentic (*not* pseudepigraphical) do not usually try to make a case for either literal authorship (level one) or dictation (level two). They usually grant that there are enough anomalies in the letters to rule out those possibilities. Rather, scholars who want to claim that one of these letters is authentic usually argue for some kind of "delegated authorship" (level three). For example, a scholar who claims that Ephesians or Colossians is an authentic letter of Paul might explain some of the apparent anomalies in those letters by saying that Paul granted disciples latitude in the crafting of these letters. Still, they would say, Paul proposed the main thrust of the letters and approved their content, so it is fair to say the letters were "authored "by Paul.

By the same token, scholars who argue that certain letters are pseudepigraphical do not usually jump all the way to "level seven" and claim that the letters are forgeries. More often, they allege pseudepigraphy at the in-between levels (four, five, six). For example, a few scholars have suggested that 2 Timothy might be an example of "posthumous authorship" (level four); the letter is pseudepigraphical only because Paul died before he could complete it, and one of his followers had to finish the letter or put into words what Paul had intended to say.

The most common scenarios for pseudepigraphy of NT letters, however, are those of "apprentice authorship" (level five) and "honorable pseudepigraphy" (level six). The first of these assumes that the disciples of a deceased church leader would continue to write letters in his name to enable his tradition to continue after death. This appears to have been an established convention in some quarters of the ancient world. Disciples of the Greek philosopher Pythagoras continued to attribute all of their writings to their master long after he had died, because they claimed to have learned so much from him that he should receive credit for all of their insights. The "honorable pseudepigraphy" scenario simply takes this a step farther, allowing that people who had not been literal disciples—who perhaps had never even known the teacher in question—would nevertheless consider themselves to be that person's spiritual disciples in an extended sense of the term. Although such a practice may seem disingenuous to people today, it was definitely practiced with the best of intentions in the early church. A bishop in the second century actually wrote a "Third Letter from Paul to the Corinthians," supplementing the teaching of 1 and 2 Corinthians with what he was sure Paul would want to say about new crises that had arisen (e.g., Gnosticism). Accordingly, many scholars claim that it is not hard to imagine that a well-meaning first-century admirer of Paul could have composed a second letter to the Thessalonians in Paul's name—or that other devout and sincere Christians could have composed letters in the names of Peter, James, or Jude.

Finally, it is also known that outright forgeries were produced. People would present their work under the name of a prominent church leader, so that their ideas might obtain wider acceptance than they would have received otherwise. Second Thessalonians contains an explicit warning about forged letters that might be circulating under Paul's name (2:2), a warning that may seem a bit disingenuous if that letter itself is deemed pseudepigraphical. The Muratorian Canon, a document from the latter half of the second century, also refers to pseudepigraphical writings that it clearly regards as dishonest, illegitimate forgeries: "There is current also an epistle to the Laodiceans and another one to the Alexandrians, both forged in Paul's name to further the heresy of Marcion,

and several others which cannot be received into the catholic church—for it is not fitting that gall be mixed with honey" (63–70). The question regarding the NT letters is whether any of them, if pseudepigraphical, ought to be regarded as forgeries rather than being attributed to categories that preserve some degree of legitimacy. Some scholars do allege that particular writings (2 Thessalonians, 2 Peter) ought to be regarded as outright forgeries, but this is not the dominant view.

Early Church Views on Pseudepigraphy: A significant and controversial point in all discussions of NT pseudepigraphy concerns the question of whether the church would have preserved these writings, if they had been deemed pseudepigraphical in one of modes indicated above. The bishop responsible for producing 3 Corinthians in the second century came under discipline after he confessed to being the actual author of that document. The letter itself was condemned as spurious, and the bishop was required to resign in disgrace for having perpetrated the hoax. The content of the letter was not in question; rather, it was rejected for only one reason: it presented itself as a letter from Paul, but it was not. Likewise, according to the early third-century theologian Tertullian, an Asian church elder who confessed to writing an apocryphal book called *Acts of Paul and Thecla* was deposed, in spite of the fact that he claimed to have done so out of great love for the apostle. Thus, many scholars maintain that no letter known to be pseudepigraphical would ever have been admitted to the NT canon.

Other scholars, however, suggest that the church only developed its hard line against pseudepigraphy, because the practice was being abused. The problem of forgeries led to an eventual rejection of any sort of pseudepigraphy, including varieties that the church might have previously found acceptable. So, some scholars maintain that the *first-century church* would not have had a problem with people, whose thinking was in line with that of Paul, writing works in Paul's name; such books (especially ones written in the first two or three decades after Paul's death) could have been viewed as part of the legitimate Pauline tradition. But this era of "acceptable pseudepigraphy" was fairly short and did not continue into the second century. This theory is widely held among current scholars, but there is no certain evidence to support it; there is no extant record of anyone in the early church ever recognizing that a writing was pseudepigraphical (in any sense of the word) and still regarding it as legitimate.

Decisions About Pseudepigraphy: Discussion as to whether certain writings of the NT are pseudepigraphical or authentic tends to focus on six issues:

Intrinsic Probability: Those who favor authenticity sometimes claim that letters encouraging ethical responsibility and moral virtue are not likely to have been produced by unscrupulous frauds. They insist that some of the NT letters thought to be pseudepigraphical cannot be explained as the products of well-meaning Christians who did not think they were doing anything dishonest. For example, the author of 2 Thessalonians goes out of his way to reassure readers that the letter actually is being written by Paul (3:17; cf. 2:2). Thus, if the letter is pseudepigraphical, it must be viewed as a product of deliberate deceit. The question then becomes, does it seem intrinsically likely that the author of this letter (which promotes high moral standards) would be a person given to such tactics?

Reliability of Church Tradition: Proponents of authenticity often argue that authorities in the early church are far more likely to have known the truth about these matters than people today. Modern scholars should be cautious about second-guessing such decisions unless they have strong evidence to the contrary. Thus, the "conservative" position is that tradition is innocent until proven guilty; the burden of proof is on those who want to establish pseudepigraphy. Many scholars, however, claim that church tradition is known to have been in error about a great many matters (including authorship of the Gospels). Further, those who preserved these traditions were often uncritical, passing on what they wanted to believe was true without possessing the means or the inclination to evaluate the tradition scientifically. Thus, the "liberal" position is that tradition is suspect unless proven viable; the burden of proof is on those who want to claim authenticity.

Language and Style: Scholars who suspect that a given letter is pseudepigraphical often indicate that it is written in a language and style that the author would not have used. Do the letters ascribed to Peter really seem like the work of a Galilean fisherman? Or, with regard to the letters of Paul, literary analysts compare the language and style of possibly pseudepigraphical letters with the language and style of the undisputed letters. As a result, some claim that the person who wrote Romans could not possibly have written Ephesians (or some of the other letters that bear Paul's name). Proponents of authenticity usually claim that linguistic and stylistic differences can be explained by the fact that Paul, Peter, and other church leaders sometimes allowed their amanuenses or co-writers to take responsibility for the actual wording of letters.

Theological Inconsistencies: Scholars sometimes claim that a letter must be pseudepigraphical, because it conveys ideas with which the putative author would not agree. For example, Ephesians presents Paul as saying the Christian church is "built upon the foundation of the apostles" (2:20), a point that some scholars think conflicts sharply with Paul's actual opinion that apostles are nothing special in the eyes of God (Gal. 2:6) and that Jesus Christ alone is the foundation for the church (1 Cor. 3:10). Proponents of authenticity typically minimize such discrepancies (e.g., they might claim that Eph. 2:20 does say that Jesus Christ is the "cornerstone" of the church, so the distinction is more one of imagery than substance). They also question the validity of assuming too much consistency for Paul, who admits he could become "all things to all people" (1 Cor. 9:22) and so (on some matters) may have shaped his ideas to fit particular contexts.

Historical Anachronism: Scholars may argue that letters are pseudepigraphical because they reflect historical ideas or circumstances associated with a time later than the period when the putative author would have lived. For example, letters that reflect a fairly well-developed, hierarchical form of church government are often said to represent a period of the church a generation after the time of the first apostles. Proponents of authenticity tend to regard this as a circular argument. Writings that depict a developed church structure are deemed pseudepigraphical, because there is no evidence that such structure existed during the apostolic period; however, the claim that there is no early evidence for developed church structure during the apostolic period is sustained by ascribing all writings that depict that type of structure to a later period.

Biographical Anachronism: Scholars sometimes argue that certain letters ascribed to Paul might be pseudepigraphical, because the presumed circumstances of their composition do not fit with what is known about Paul's biography from other letters or the book of Acts. This comes up especially in discussions of 1 Timothy and Titus, which presume missionary activity by Paul not reported elsewhere. Proponents of authenticity claim that there are gaps in the available record of Paul's life; specifically, they sometimes claim that Paul may have had a "second career" as a missionary after the events reported in Acts.

Finally, it must be noted that proponents of authenticity often pursue a "divide and conquer" approach to defending letters against allegations of pseudepigraphy; they consider each potential problem one by one. By contrast, those who argue in favor of pseudepigraphy usually do so on the basis of *cumulative evidence.* They agree that explanations for individual considerations can be offered, but maintain that pseudepigraphy provides one simple explanation for multiple anomalies that otherwise need to be accounted for in different and (they think) desperate ways.

Significance: The question of whether the NT letters were actually written by the persons whose names they bear becomes significant when scholars seek to define the historical contexts the letters were intended to address. The issue of authorship is inevitably linked to date of composition. If 1 Peter really was written by the apostle Peter, it may be addressing concerns in the Roman Empire around the time of Nero (just prior to Peter's martyrdom). If the letter is pseudepigraphical, it may be dealing with sociological issues that arose in Roman churches decades later. Thus, decisions about authorship and pseudepigraphy end up affecting how particular passages in NT letters are to be interpreted. Such decisions become even more important for church historians and biblical theologians who want to read the NT letters as a chronological witness to developments in early Christianity. Pauline scholars, in particular, like to develop biographical accounts of Paul's life and thought, and such reconstructions are dependent upon judgments regarding which letters were actually written by Paul and which might have been written by his followers or admirers after his death. *See also* apocryphal Christian writings; Colossians, Letter of Paul to the; Ephesians, Letter of Paul to the; James, Letter of; Jude, Letter of; Peter, First Letter of; Peter, Second Letter of; Pseudepigrapha; pseudonym; Thessalonians, Second Letter of Paul to the; Timothy, First Letter of Paul to; Timothy, Second Letter of Paul to; Titus, Letter of Paul to.

Bibliography

Meade, David G. *Pseudonymity and Canon*. Mohr-Siebeck, 1986.

Powell, Mark Allan. *Introducing the New Testament: A Historical, Literary, and Theological Survey*. Baker Academic, 2009. Pp. 222–28.

Wilder, Terry L. *Pseudonymity, the New Testament, and Deception: An Inquiry into Intention and Reception*. University Press of America, 2004.

M.A.P.

pseudonym, a fictitious or assumed name. During the Second Temple period, many writers would assume the name of a person mentioned in the scriptures (e.g., Adam, Enoch, Moses, Job, Ezra) and produce a work addressing present circumstances from that person's supposed perspective. The book of Daniel is often thought to have been written by an author using a pseudonym. Many scholars also think that numerous NT writings are pseudepigraphical (i.e., ascribed to persons who did not actually write them), though the questions involved in those discussions are more complicated (and controversial), since in those cases the name being employed would not have been that of an ancient hero, but a recently deceased individual who might conceivably have been the true author (and who, indeed, was usually assumed to be the actual author by the communities that preserved those writings). *See also* Apocrypha/deuterocanonical literature; apocryphal Christian writings; Pseudepigrapha; pseudepigraphy.

M.A.P.

Ptolemais (tol'uh-may'uhs). *See* Acco.

Ptolemy (tol'uh-mee), the dynastic name of the kings who ruled Egypt after the death of Alexander the Great.

1 Ptolemy I, "Soter" (d. 283/2 BCE), founder of the dynasty. He established the administrative and military structure of Egypt. He also created a hellenized Egyptian cult around the god Serapis for the Greek populace and established the museum, the library at Alexandria that would make the city the center of learning and research throughout the Hellenistic period.

2 Ptolemy II, "Philadelphus" (ruled 283/2–246 BCE), who adopted the Egyptian custom of marrying his full sister, which scandalized his Greek subjects. Under his reign the hellenization of Egypt and the ascent of Alexandria to intellectual prominence continued. During his reign, translation of the LXX was begun.

3 Ptolemy III, "Euergetes" (ruled 246–222/1 BCE).

4 Ptolemy IV, "Philopator" (ruled 221–204 BCE).

5 Ptolemy V, "Epiphanes" (ruled 204–180 BCE), who was crowned according to ancient Egyptian rites in 197 BCE, an event commemorated on the Rosetta Stone.

6 Ptolemy VI, "Philometor" (ruled 180–145 BCE), who shared rule with his brother, Ptolemy VII.

7 Ptolemy VII, "Neos Philopator" (145–144 BCE).

8 Ptolemy VIII, "Euergetes II" (ruled 140–116 BCE). The second half of the second century was characterized by considerable strife between the brothers and constant wars with various factions in Syria.

9 The children of Ptolemy IX, Cleopatra Bernice (81–80 BCE) and sons Ptolemy X and XI (80 BCE), with whose deaths Ptolemaic rule ended.

10 The illegitimate Ptolemy XII, who took the throne and ruled until 51 BCE. His two sons were killed fighting Julius Caesar and were followed on the throne by their sister Cleopatra VII, who had a child by Julius Caesar and was later married to Mark Antony, from whom she received territory in the Levant. She committed suicide when she and Antony were defeated by Octavian (Augustus) in 31 BCE.

P.P.

Puah (pyoo'uh).

1 One of the midwives of the Hebrews who cleverly disobeyed Pharaoh's orders and spared the male Hebrew children (Exod. 1:15). She is mentioned with Shiprah, another midwife, who assisted her in rescuing babies. It is not clear whether Shiprah and Puah were Hebrews or Egyptians.

2 The son of Issachar and head of the Punites (1 Chron. 7:1). The name also occurs as Puvah (Gen. 46:13; Num. 26:23).

3 The father of Tola, one of the judges of Israel (Judg. 10:1).

publicans. *See* tax collectors.

Publius (puhb'lee-uhs), the chief magistrate of the Island of Malta when Paul was cast ashore there by a shipwreck (Acts 28:1). Paul healed Publius's father of fever and dysentery, and the people of Malta showed Paul and his companions much kindness (28:7–10).

Pudens (pyoo'dinz), a person mentioned in 2 Tim. 4:21 as sending greetings to Timothy. Nothing else is known of him. *See also* Claudia; Eubulus; Linus.

Pul (puhl), a nickname for Tiglath-pileser III, king of Assyria, used in certain documents, including 2 Kings 15:29; 2 Chron. 5:26. Pul may be a shortened and familiar form of the second

Tiglath-pileser III, king of Assyria 745–727 BCE, is also called Pul in the Bible; relief from Susa, eighth century BCE.

element, *-pileser,* a wordplay on the Akkadian word *pulu,* "limestone block."

punishment, everlasting, the concept that after death an individual can be subjected to on-going retribution for evil acts committed during life. The idea developed slowly over a long period of time. The ancient Hebrews, like other Semitic peoples of the ancient Near East, believed that at death the human person lost earthly life, but did not cease to exist entirely. They had no notion of an immortal soul separable from the body, but they did believe that the dead had a shadow-like or phantomlike existence in the realm of the dead. This realm of the dead was usually located under the earth. It was called by various names, most commonly Sheol. This name is related to the verb "to inquire" in Hebrew, which might reflect the practice of seeking oracles from the dead, though that practice was strongly condemned in Israelite law (Deut. 18:10–11; cf. 1 Sam. 28). In the Bible, Sheol is not a place of punishment, though existence there is characterized by weariness and forgetfulness.

The notion of eternal punishment does appear a few times in the Hebrew Bible, though not in explicit association with Sheol. In referring to the wicked, Isa. 66:24 says, "Their worm shall not die, their fire shall not be quenched, and they shall be an abhorrence to all flesh." Dan. 12:2 indicates that some will rise from the dead to shame and everlasting contempt.

In 2 Kings 23:10 the Valley of Hinnom, a ravine south of Jerusalem, is mentioned as a place where children were burned as sacrifices to the god Molech. Perhaps as early as the third century BCE, this valley came to represent the place of eternal punishment (*1 Enoch* 27; 90:26–27; 2 Esd. 7:36). That notion appears in the NT, where the valley is called Gehenna (e.g., Matt. 5:22). In Jewish literature of the Greco-Roman period and in the NT, the punishment envisaged in this valley is a fiery one. The book of Revelation does not use the term "Gehenna," but speaks of a lake of fire in which the wicked will be punished (20:14–15). Likewise, in the Gospel of Matthew Jesus says that at the end of the age "the Son of Man will send his angels, and they will collect out of his kingdom all causes of sin and all evildoers, and they will throw them into the furnace of fire, where there will be weeping and gnashing of teeth" (13:41–42). Elsewhere in that same Gospel, Jesus says that the Son of Man will separate the nations as a shepherd separates sheep from goats, and those who are condemned "will go away into eternal punishment, but the righteous into eternal life" (25:46). *See also* apocalyptic literature; eschatology; heaven; hell; judgment, day of.   A.Y.C.

pur. *See* Purim, Festival of.

purge, to cleanse of impurities. The term appears in a variety of contexts: to cleanse a land of idolatry (2 Chron. 34:3, 8); to atone for sin or purify from iniquity (1 Sam. 3:14; Pss. 65:3; 79:9; Isa. 6:7; Heb. 1:3; 10:2; 2 Tim. 2:21); and to prepare a new altar for use in temple sacrifice (Ezek. 43:20, 26). The purging or refining of metal was used as a metaphor for expiating sin (Isa. 1:25; Mal. 3:3). The removal of undesirable persons could be expressed as an explicit purging of rebels from the land (Ezek. 20:38) or metaphorically as the purging of a threshing floor (Matt. 3:12; Luke 3:17) or the purging of a lump of leaven (1 Cor. 5:7).

purify, purification. *See* purity.

Purim (pyoo´rim), **Festival of,** a minor holiday of the Jewish calendar based upon the account in the book of Esther. King Ahasuerus of Persia was persuaded by his minister, Haman, to destroy all the Jews in his kingdom on a day chosen by the drawing of lots (Heb. *purim*). The king's Jewish wife, Queen Esther, along with her cousin, Mordecai, foiled the plot and saved her people. The book of Esther indicates that "these days should be remembered and kept throughout every generation, in every family, province, and city; and these days of Purim should never fall into disuse among the Jews, nor should the commemoration of these days cease among their descendants" (9:28). *See also* Esther, book of.   L.H.S.

purity, the state of being free of ritual contamination. In the Bible, people may contract ritual impurity by contact with a corpse, certain dead animals, the involuntary flow of fluids from the sexual organs, certain diseases, or the eating of prohibited foods. Certain objects are regarded as pure (*tahor*), but may be rendered impure (*tame'*) as a result of contact with an impure person who has not undergone purification rites. While impure, a person is enjoined from certain actions, primarily contact with the temple or its religious practices. Specific rites of purification were required for various forms of ritual impurity. The process of purification consisted of several stages: a waiting period of from one day to several months, depending upon the nature of the impurity, counting from the time of the cessation of the cause of pollution; a cleansing agent such as water (Lev. 15:16), fire (Num. 31:23), or blood (Lev. 14:25); and the offering of a sacrifice. The duty of the priest was to maintain the ritual purity of Israel and its sanctuary. Thus, laws of purity are found mainly among Priestly materials in such biblical books as Leviticus and Numbers. In the NT, Jesus is depicted as indicating that true purity has to do with moral behavior, determined by the status of one's heart (Mark 7:14–23). *See also* priests; worship in the Hebrew Bible.   L.H.S.

purple, a distinctive dye color associated with royalty and wealth. Such dye was a product of the Syrian and Phoenician coastal zone, whose people maintained a monopoly on the dye through much of history. It derived from a distinctive combination of colors acquired from gastropod mollusks that lived in Mediterranean waters of the region. Various shades were mixed, primarily red to purple. The expression "the purple" came to stand for the color, for cloth dyed this color, for people who wore such cloth, and for classes rich enough to afford such cloth (e.g., royalty). The dye was extracted from the secretion of the hypobranchial gland of the mollusks, and the most popular shades were produced by a double-dyeing treatment. From the middens of shells along the north Mediterranean coast of Lebanon and Syria, the *Murex brandaris* and *Murex trunculus* were the most frequently used sources. The limited habitat and the small amount of dye extractable from each murex made the product especially valuable.

Biblical references to blue and scarlet together with purple are extensive (Exod. 25:4; 36:35), and the colors were prized for priestly vestments in Israel's tradition. Although Israel imported its purple, Solomon specified that men skilled to work in "purple, crimson, and blue fabrics" be included in the Phoenician workforce he obtained from Hiram, king of Tyre (2 Chron. 2:7), in response to which Hiram sent one Huramabi (2:14), and the work was done (3:14). Solomon's palanquin seat was purple (Song of Sol. 3:10), and it was said that a good wife would be clothed in purple (Prov. 31:22). In a parable of Jesus, a rich man's purple clothing is mentioned as a symbol of his wealth (Luke 16:19). Jesus himself was temporarily cloaked in purple during his pre-execution incarceration (Mark 15:17–20; John 19:2–5). Lydia of Thyatira, a convert of Paul in Philippi, was a trader of purple goods (Acts 16:14). In the book of Revelation, purple is mentioned in the eschatological vision of a condemned prostitute, who symbolizes Rome (17:4; 18:12, 16).   R.S.B.

purse, a leather pouch in which money was carried (Prov. 7:20; Hag. 1:6; Luke 22:35–36). Jesus forbade his disciples to carry money in their purses, as evidence of their trust that God would provide for them through the generosity of others (Matt. 10:9). The Gospel of John reports that Judas Iscariot was in charge of the "common purse" (i.e., the communal funds) used by Jesus and his disciples (12:6; 13:29).

Put (poot).
   1 The third son of Ham (Gen. 10:6; 1 Chron. 1:8).
   2 A region in Africa, probably located in Libya. Warriors from Put fought on the side of the Ethiopians and Egyptians when the Assyrians captured No-amon (Thebes) in 663 BCE (Nah. 3:9; Ezek. 30:5).

Puteoli (pyoo-tee'oh-lee; Lat., "small wells" or "stink"), the seaport (modern Pozzuoli) just west of Naples where, according to Acts 28:13–14, Paul landed on his way to Rome and stayed seven days with the local Christian community. Founded in the sixth century BCE by Greek colonists from Samos, Puteoli was originally a port of Cumae named Dicaearchia. In 215 BCE, the Romans garrisoned the town against the Carthaginian general Hannibal and renamed it Puteoli. In 194 BCE, it became a Roman colony. During the first century CE, Puteoli was the major port of Italy, where Alexandrian grain ships (like Paul's) docked to unload cargo for Rome. *See also* Paul.   C.H.M.

Pyramid Texts, a collection of magical spells relating to the rebirth and eternal glory of the king of Egypt. The texts occur in several pyramids of kings and queens from the end of the Fifth Dynasty to the Eighth Dynasty (ca. 2350–2160 BCE). The texts are not found in the earlier, great pyramids of Giza. First discovered by scholars in 1881, the texts are carved on the walls of the burial complexes inside the pyramids. Each pyramid has its own particular collection of spells. The intent of the spells was to affirm—even bring about—the resurrection and ascent to the sky of the deceased ruler. The spells generally predate the pyramids in which they are inscribed and are often quite archaic. They represent the oldest corpus of religious texts from Egypt and underlie the later Coffin Texts and Book of the Dead, in which the afterlife is no longer a prerogative for royalty only. *See also* Egypt; Pharaoh; resurrection.   H.B.H.

Pyrrhus (pihr'uhs), the father of Sopater of Beroea, who accompanied Paul on his last journey to Jerusalem (Acts 20:4).

Opposite: Ancient Romans as depicted in the "Imperial
Procession" portion of a frieze on the *Ara Pacis Augustae*
("Altar of the Peace of Augustus"), 13–9 BCE.

Q R

Q, a hypothetical collection of the sayings of Jesus that was used as a source for the Gospels of Matthew and Luke. According to the Two-Source Hypothesis, Matthew and Luke independently used Mark and another documentary source, consisting largely of sayings of Jesus. Its designation "Q" derives from the German word *Quelle*, meaning "source." The contents of Q can basically be identified with material that Matthew and Luke have in common, but that is not found in the Gospel of Mark. It is generally thought that the original order of the material is preserved better in Luke than in Matthew.

The basic idea that Matthew and Luke made use of a source other than the Gospel of Mark is widely (though not unanimously) accepted. Still, the exact nature of Q is debatable. Some scholars

CONTENTS OF Q

	Luke	Matthew
Preaching of John the Baptist	3:7–9	3:7–10
Temptation of Jesus	4:1–13	4:1–11
Beatitudes	6:20–23	5:3–12
Love for Enemies	6:27–36	5:39–48; 7:12
On Judging Others	6:37–42	7:1–5; 10:24; 15:14
On Bearing Fruit	6:43–45	7:15–20
Parable of Two Builders	6:47–49	7:24–27
Healing of Centurion's Servant	7:1–10	8:5–10, 13
John the Baptist Questions Jesus	7:18–35	11:2–19
The Would-Be Disciples	9:57–60	8:19–22
Jesus's Missionary Discourse	10:2–16	9:37–38; 10:9–15; 11:21–23
Thanksgiving to the Father	10:21–24	11:25–27; 13:16–17
The Lord's Prayer	11:2–4	6:9–13
Asking and Receiving	11:9–13	7:7–11
Jesus Identified with Beelzebul	11:14–23	12:22–30
Return of an Evil Spirit	11:24–26	12:43–45
The Sign of Jonah	11:29–32	12:38–42
On Light	11:33–36	5:15; 6:22–23
Woe to the Pharisees	11:37–52	23:4–7, 13–36
Fear of Humans and God	12:2–12	10:19, 26–33; 12:32
Do Not Worry About Life	12:22–34	6:19–21, 25–33
Be Ready for the Master's Return	12:39–46	24:43–51
Divisions in the Family	12:51–53	10:34–36
Signs of the Times	12:54–56	16:2–3
Settle out of Court	12:57–59	5:25–26
Mustard Seed and Leaven	13:18–21	13:31–33
The Narrow Door	13:23–30	7:13–14, 22–23; 8:11–12
Lament over Jerusalem	13:34–35	23:37–39
Parable of the Banquet	14:15–24	22:1–14
Carrying the Cross	14:26–27	10:37–38
Parable of the Lost Sheep	15:1–7	18:12–14
On Serving Two Masters	16:13	6:24
Role of the Law and Prophets	16:16–17	5:18; 11:13
Rebuking and Forgiving Sin	17:1–6	18:6–7, 15, 20–22
The Day of the Son of Man	17:23–27, 33–37	24:17–18, 26–28, 37–41
Parable of the Talents	19:11–27	25:14–30

From Mark Allan Powell, *Introducing the New Testament* (courtesy, Baker Academic)

have regarded Q as no more than a common body of oral tradition, though the majority assume that it was probably a written document. Evidence for this includes the internal theological consistency expressed throughout the Q passages and the strength of the verbal agreements between these passages as they are reported in Matthew and in Luke, an agreement that frequently extends even to the order in which the passages occur. For many years, scholars thought that Q was originally written in Aramaic and then rendered, independently, by both Matthew and Luke into Greek. Evidence of this was seen in various "Semitisms" or Semitic expressions that Matthew and Luke sometimes evince in material thought to derive from Q. In recent years, however, scholars have tended toward the opinion that Q was composed in Greek and came to both evangelists in that form.

Q consists almost entirely of sayings and, in that regard, resembles the form of the apocryphal *Gospel of Thomas.* The few narrative portions include the story of Jesus's temptation found in Luke 4:1–13 and Matt. 4:1–11 and the healing of the centurion's servant found in Luke 7:1–10 and Matt. 7:24–27, but even here the emphasis is on the sayings of Jesus preserved in those narratives. The Q material contains parables, aphorisms, beatitudes, and pronouncements. There are examples of many different types of sayings associated with Jesus: prophetic sayings, eschatological sayings, legal sayings, and wisdom sayings. Some scholars have suggested that Q might have gone through two or three editions before assuming the form to which Matthew and Luke had access. According to this theory, the wisdom sayings were part of the original version of Q, while the eschatological sayings were not. This theory, however, is regarded as highly speculative.

Scholars sometimes study the Q material apart from other Gospel material to determine what sort of beliefs might have been expressed by followers of Jesus in the early pre-Gospel period. The first thing noted is that there seems to be very little (if any) awareness of theological notions associated with Paul. Thus, the Q material (unlike the finished Gospels) may witness to a context in which Paul's particular take on the gospel (driven, for instance, by ministry to Gentiles) had not yet taken hold.

In the Q material, the death of Jesus is hardly mentioned and seems to be viewed only as a martyrdom, not as an atoning sacrifice for sin. In fact, there is no mention of the cross, only allusions to suffering the fate of the prophets (and of John the Baptist). Jesus saves people, not by dying for them, but by inaugurating God's kingdom and granting fellowship in this kingdom to those who are faithful. This will occur shortly, at the final judgment, over which Jesus himself will preside when he returns, vindicated by God, as the glorified Son of Man.

True discipleship according to the Q sayings consists of being like Jesus (cf. Luke 6:40). This means, among other things, that disciples are ex-pected to forgo domicile, family, and possessions. Just as the Son of Man had nowhere to lay his head (Luke 9:58; Matt. 8:20), so his disciples are called to leave their homes and families, renounce all worldly security, and devote their lives entirely to the kingdom of God.

Some scholars speak loosely of "a community of Q," by which they mean early followers of Jesus who used this document as their primary Christian text. Such people might be characterized as believing that they live at the very end of time, guided by the words of Jesus and totally dependent upon God for sustenance. They view their mission as a continuation of the ministry of Jesus on earth. They have collected the sayings of their coming Judge to serve as a guide for living in the last days. In addition to collecting and repeating these sayings, they continue to proclaim the dawn of God's kingdom through inspired prophets that speak in Jesus's name. *See also* Synoptic Problem.

Bibliography

Catchpole, David R. *The Quest for Q.* Clark, 1993.

Goodacre, Mark. *The Case Against Q: Studies in Markan Priority and the Synoptic Problem.* Trinity Press International, 2001.

Mack, B. L. *The Lost Gospel.* San Francisco: HarperSanFrancisco, 1993.

Piper, Ronald A., ed. *The Gospel Behind the Gospels.* Brill, 1995.

Powell, Mark Allan. *Introducing the New Testament: A Historical, Literary, and Theological Survey.* Baker Academic, 2009. Pp. 96–98.   M.A.P.

Qadisha (kah-dee′shah; Heb., "the holy [river]"), modern Nahr Abụ Ali, a river that flows from the upper slopes of the Lebanon range northwest to the Mediterranean, which it enters at the city of Tripoli. The modern park containing the few remaining cedars of Lebanon is in the upper gorge of the river, but there is no evidence for the conjecture that it was the route used for transporting the cedars sent by Hiram of Tyre to Solomon for the construction of the temple (cf. 1 Kings 5:1–12).

quail. The species of quail (Heb. *selaw*) referred to in the Bible is probably the common quail (*Coturnix coturnix*). Its plumage is of a sandy brown base color with black and pale streaks. This quail breeds in Europe and western Asia and passes through the Levant and Sinai on its way to its winter quarters in Africa. During the exodus large flocks of quail provided the Israelites with the food God had promised them (Exod. 16:13; Num. 11:31; Ps. 105:40). The large numbers so easily collected by the Hebrews (over a hundred bushels per person) can be explained by the fact that the quail, though a strong flyer over short stretches, is dependent on the wind to cover large distances. Changes in the wind direction force it to the ground and make it easy prey.   I.U.K.

quarries, sources of construction stone, whether cut from the sides of outcrops or dug from beneath soil layers. The labor involved in quarrying stone

Quail; Coptic tapestry, third or fourth century CE.

in antiquity was immense (1 Kings 5:13–18) and sometimes proverbially dangerous (Eccles. 10:9). In prosperous times quarried stone was commercially available (2 Kings 12:12; 22:6; 2 Chron. 34:11). Finishing the product was sometimes done at the quarry site (1 Kings 6:7). Labor to quarry stone for some projects could be conscripted by royal command (2 Chron. 2:2, 18).

Quarrying techniques were extensively developed in ancient Egypt, where the blocks for the Old Kingdom pyramids were cut from quarries far up the Nile and floated downstream on barges, sometimes guided by two or three pilot boats to navigate and keep the load under way. Aswan was the site of famous granite quarries, and the techniques used there were similar to ones used for quarrying sandstone or limestone in the Levant. Cuts outlining the blocks were made with picks. Wedges of wood were then inserted and wetted, and the swelling forced the block loose from its setting. The economy of trimming an already available block versus having to quarry a new one was nearly irresistible to ancient builders, so that blocks were frequently reused.   R.S.B.

Quartus (kwor′ tuhs), a companion of Paul who joins him in sending greetings in Rom. 16:23.

queen.

1 A woman sovereign. Israel and Judah, unlike other nations around them, did not have any legitimate female sovereigns during the period of the monarchy. At one point, however Athaliah, the daughter of Ahab and Jezebel of Israel, and wife of King Jehoram of Judah, seized control of the throne upon the death of her son, Ahaziah; she ruled Judah for seven years (ca. 843/2–837 BCE) before being deposed in favor of Joash, who

had narrowly escaped her purge of all legitimate male heirs (2 Kings 8:26; 11:1–4). Later, during the Second Temple period, Salome Alexandra was a Hasmonean queen of Judah (76–67 BCE). Two queens who were the ruling sovereigns of other nations are also mentioned in the Bible: the queen of Sheba (1 Kings 10; 2 Chron. 9); and "the Candace," a term designating the queen of the Ethiopians (Acts 8:27). Although not mentioned in the Bible, Hatshepsut of Egypt was one of the important pharaohs in the Eighteenth Dynasty (ca. 1500 BCE). *See also* Athaliah; Candace, the; Salome Alexandra; Sheba, queen of.

2 A consort or wife of a king. Royal marriages were often contracted to cement alliances with other nations (2 Sam. 3:3; 1 Kings 3:1; 16:31; 2 Kings 8:25–27). The wives of kings are frequently mentioned in the Bible (e.g., Bathsheba, Michal, both wives of David), but they do not appear to have had official functions in the government. Sometimes, however, they exercise considerable influence. Bathsheba conspires with the prophet Nathan to make certain that her son Solomon succeeds David as king (1 Kings 1). The most influential "king's wife" in the Bible, however, is Jezebel, wife of King Ahab of Israel. She dominates the narratives related to that period of Israel's history, extending her influence to the southern kingdom, Judah, as well. Since that "influence" involved propagation of Baal worship, she is given a consistently negative report in the biblical materials (1 Kings 16:31; 18:4, 13, 19; 21:25). Another prominent queen who had little official power, but who was the wife of the king was Esther, the Jewish woman who became queen of Persia and saved her people from genocide (see the book of Esther). *See also* Bathsheba; Esther, book of; Jezebel; Michal.

3 A mother of a king. The "queen mother" actually had a more prominent and important role than the king's wife in both Israel and surrounding nations (1 Kings 2:19; 15:13). Athaliah (2 Kings 8:26; 11:1–4) was a queen mother who actually usurped the throne of Israel for seven years upon the death of her son, Ahaziah. *See also* Athaliah.
         F.S.F./M.A.P.

queen of heaven, a goddess worshiped by some Judeans living in Jerusalem and Egypt in the time of Jeremiah (late seventh–early sixth centuries BCE). Jeremiah depicts the worship of the goddess as a family enterprise: "The children gather wood, the fathers kindle fire, and the women knead dough, to make cakes for the queen of heaven" (7:18). These cakes were pounded out and marked with the image of the goddess (44:19). Such worship is denounced as idolatrous, but the women who participate in it are recalcitrant. They tell the prophet, "We are not going to listen to you" (44:16). They will continue to make offerings to the queen of heaven and pour out libations to her, because this is what they have vowed to do and because it is what their ancestors, kings, and officials "used to do in the towns of Judah and streets of Jerusalem" (44:17). They claim to have the support of their husbands for this defiance (44:19) and even give a pragmatic rationale for continuing (or indeed resuming) the practices Jeremiah condemns: "We used to have plenty of food, and prospered, and saw no misfortune. But from the time we stopped making offerings to the queen of heaven and pouring out libations to her, we have lacked everything and have perished by the sword and by famine" (44:17–18). Thus, Jeremiah's response is equally pragmatic: their continued worship will bring about the fall of Jerusalem and such action will be punished with famine and with war until not one of the idolatrous worshipers is left (44:25–28).

Interpreters have sought to identify the specific deity intended by the expression "queen of heaven." Some of Jeremiah's comments have been thought to associate the goddess with both fertility and war, and the title "queen of *heaven*" has been thought to suggest astral connections. The Canaanite goddess Astarte is often suggested as one who would satisfy all of these criteria, and Phoenician inscriptions sometimes refer to Astarte as "queen." Another prominent candidate is the Mesopotamian goddess Ishtar, who (unlike Astarte) is noted for having large numbers of female devotees, who would weep in empathy for her loss of her lover Tammuz (cf. Ezek. 8:14) and who would apparently bring offerings of cakes as part of the worship rite. Rather than choose between these possible identifications, some scholars suggest that the "queen of heaven" attractive to Judeans could have been a possibly unique amalgam of Canaanite Astarte and Mesopotamian Ishtar.

In the first century CE, the mother goddess of Ephesus, called Artemis by the Greeks, the Syrian goddess Atargatis, and the Egyptian Isis were all worshiped as queen of heaven. *See also* Artemis of the Ephesians; Asherah; Ishtar.   M.A.P.

Quirinius (kwi-rin'ee-uhs), **P. Sulpicius** (suhl-pi'shuhs), the Roman consul who held the position of governor (legate) of Syria for several years, beginning in 6 CE. He is the Quirinius of Luke 2:2, which reports that an "enrollment" took place during his administration, requiring Joseph to travel to Bethlehem with his pregnant wife, Mary, at which point Jesus was born. The historian Josephus also tells of a census carried out under Quirinius's authority in 6 or 7 CE, after the banishment of Archelaus, the ethnarch of Judea, Samaria, and Idumea. There is a historical problem, however, because Jesus is also said to have been born during the reign of Herod the Great (Matt. 2:1–22; Luke 1:5), who died in 4 BCE. A second problem concerns Luke's reference to "all the world" being enrolled (by edict of Caesar Augustus); Josephus limits the census under Quirinius to the former territory of Archelaus. Various possible solutions to these problems have been proposed, but none has received general acceptance. *See also* census; Herod.   F.O.G.

quiver, a container for carrying arrows, usually made of leather and carried on the back or over the

shoulder. The quiver was standard equipment for archers, both hunters (Gen. 27:3) and soldiers (Job 39:23; Isa. 22:6). Figuratively, Lam. 3:13 attributes the distress that accompanied Jerusalem's fall to the arrows of God's quiver (Heb. *bene 'ashpat,* "sons of the quiver"). This connection between arrows and quivers was so well known that biblical writers used these objects as symbols for the relationship between children and parents (Ps. 127:5), between a servant and God (Isa. 49:2), and between war and death (Jer. 5:16). *See also* archers; arms, armor; weapons.   G.L.M.

Qumran (koom'rahn), **Khirbet** (kihr'bet), a sectarian settlement associated with the Dead Sea Scrolls, eight and a half miles south of Jericho, above the west shore of the Dead Sea. The site was excavated 1951–56 by Roland de Vaux of the École Biblique et Archéologique Française de Jerusalem. The sectarian settlement dates from ca. 130–100 BCE to 68 CE. There was also a late Iron Age settlement at Qumran and a brief period of Roman occupation after 68 CE.

Archaeological and literary evidence indicates that Qumran was inhabited by the same Jewish sect that deposited the scrolls in the nearby caves. The Qumran community probably was part of the larger Essene movement described by Josephus, Philo, and Pliny the Elder. The sectarians viewed themselves as a replacement for the temple priesthood, and they extended the temple requirements for priests to all full members. The high degree of ritual purity required for the sectarian lifestyle finds physical expression in the archaeological remains at Qumran. For example, the presence of ten *mikvot* (ritual baths) can be understood in light of references in the Dead Sea Scrolls to purification by immersion in water. Communal meals apparently were held in two dining rooms at Qumran. Bones belonging to sheep, cows, and goats were found under potsherds or inside pots in the open-air spaces outside the dining rooms. These bones apparently represent the remains of animals consumed at the communal meals and perhaps reflect a sectarian belief that these meals were a substitute for participation in the temple sacrifices.

Both dining rooms had adjacent pantries stocked with hundreds of dishes, mainly of plates, cups, and bowls. The large number of dishes probably should be understood in light of the sectarian belief that impurity could be transmitted through

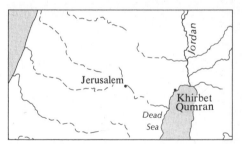

food and drink. For this reason the sectarians were served individual portions instead of dining from common dishes. The sectarian concern with the transmission of impurity also explains the presence of a potters' workshop at Qumran, which enabled the community to assure the purity of the pottery by manufacturing it themselves. The pottery types manufactured at Qumran include the tall cylindrical jars (or "scroll jars") that reportedly contained some of the scrolls found in Cave 1 and that were found in great numbers in other caves around Qumran as well as inside the settlement. These distinctive jars—which are virtually unique to Qumran—may have been used as storage containers for the pure goods of the sect.

Some scholars have suggested that Qumran was not a sectarian settlement, but a villa, manor house, fort, commercial entrepôt, or pottery-manufacturing center, thereby rejecting the association of the scrolls with the site. However, none of the anomalous features at Qumran is paralleled at any other site. These include the large number of *mikvot* (and their large sizes), the animal-bone deposits, the large adjacent cemetery, the communal dining rooms with adjacent pantries of dishes, the numerous workshops, and an unusual ceramic repertoire. *See also* Dead Sea Scrolls; Essenes.

J.M.

Quran (koo'roon) **Hattin** (hah-teen'). *See* Hattin, Horns of.

Raamah (ray'uh-mah; also Raama, 1 Chron. 1:9), the Cushite father of Sheba and Dedan (Gen. 10:7), and the Arabian locale inhabited by people whose ancestry was traced to him. Famous as a spice trading source (Ezek. 27:22), Raamah was probably in southwest Arabia near modern Ma'in, although the location is uncertain.

Raamses, Rameses (ray-am'seez), one of two store-cities (the other was Pithom) built by the Hebrews for Pharaoh (Exod. 1:11). It was from Raamses that the Israelites departed on the exodus (Exod. 12:37; Num. 33:3, 5). The Egyptian name of this city was Piramesse (*per-ramessu*, "house of Ramesses"). Named after Ramesses II (1279–1212 BCE), who is often considered the pharaoh of the exodus, Raamses served as the Delta residence for the succeeding kings of the Nineteenth–Twentieth Dynasties (ca. 1212–1070 BCE). For many years, scholars identified Raamses with Tanis (Heb. Zoan), modern San el-Hagar in the Egyptian Delta, where many monuments inscribed with the name of Ramesses II and his successors were discovered. It was eventually determined, however, that these monuments had been moved to Tanis from somewhere else. It is therefore most probable that Raamses is to be placed in the area of modern Khatana-Qantir on the Pelusiac branch of the Nile, about fifteen miles south of Tanis. Evidence for a palace of Sety I (1291–1279 BCE) and Ramesses II and the houses of high officials of the period have been found there, within what would have been an enormous city stretching more than a mile from Qantir south to Tell el-Dabaa. *See also* Pithom; Ramesses; Zoan. J.M.W.

Rabbah (rab'uh).
1 A city of Judah (Josh. 15:60) in the district with Kiriath-jearim, identified tentatively with modern Khirbet Hamideh. It appears as Rubute in

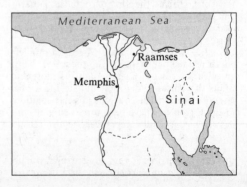

several ancient extrabiblical sources (the Amarna letters, Thutmose IV's topographical list, and Shishak's list).

2 The only town mentioned in the Bible as specifically Ammonite. It is modern Amman, located about twenty-four miles east of the Jordan River and twenty-three miles northeast of the Dead Sea. The name is also given as Rabbat of the Ammonites and as Rabath-ammon (meaning the "great" or "capital" of the Ammonites).

Recent excavations on the citadel of the ancient city indicate at least sporadic occupation throughout the Bronze Age and a fairly heavily fortified town ca. 1750–1550 BCE. The excavations reveal tenth- and ninth-century BCE phases of a defense wall, quite possibly related to David's siege of the city and the later rebuilding (2 Sam. 11:1; 12:26–31). Iron Age II remains date to the eighth and seventh centuries BCE, with evidences of destruction that recall the rebukes of prophets against Rabbah and the Ammonites (Jer. 49:2, 3; Ezek. 25:5; Amos 1:14).

Rabbah was renamed Philadelphia after it was captured by Ptolemy Philadelphus (third century BCE), and it flourished as a Hellenistic city, as fortified walls and structural remains testify. Architecturally, the second-century CE Roman remains are what appear prominent today, especially the Nymphaeum, columned street, and large amphitheater in downtown Amman. *See also* Ammonites.   N.L.L.

rabbi (rab′i), **rabbouni** (ra-booh′ni; Heb., "my great one"), a title that took on a general meaning of respect, "my master," or a specific meaning, "my teacher." In the Hebrew Bible, *rab,* without the possessive, is used to mean "chief" or "officer" of something (2 Kings 18:17; 25:8). In the NT, this term (with the possessive suffix) is transliterated into Greek letters as *rabbi* (Matt. 23:7–8; 26:25, 49; Mark 9:5; 11:21; 14:45; John 1:38, 49; 3:2, 26; 4:31; 6:25; 9:2; 11:8), a word that does not occur in the Hebrew Bible or in any of the apocryphal/deuterocanonical writings of the Second Temple period. The variant form, *rabbouni,* is found only in Mark 10:51 (NRSV: "my teacher") and John 20:16. It probably reflects an Aramaic pronunciation of the word.

Notably the word is used only in the Gospels of Matthew, Mark, and John, and the only person addressed as rabbi is Jesus. Matthew's Gospel, however, seems to offer a distinctive take on the word. In Matthew, Jesus criticizes the scribes and Pharisees as people who like to have people call them "rabbi" (23:7), and then he tells his disciples that they are not to be called rabbi, because they have one teacher (Gk. *didaskalos*) and they are all siblings (23:8; Gk. *adelphoi;* NRSV: "students"). One might suppose from this that Matthew wants to limit the title to Jesus, but application to Jesus seems somewhat suspect as well—in Matthew's Gospel, the only disciple who ever calls Jesus "Rabbi" is Judas (26:25, 49); the other disciples address him as "Lord" (Gk. *kyrie;* 8:21, 25; 14:28, 30; 18:21).   A.J.S.

Rabmag (rab′mag). *See* Nergal-sharezer.

Rabsaris (rab′suh-ris; Akkadian, "chief of the eunuchs").

1 One of three Assyrian officials sent by Sennacherib to convince King Hezekiah to surrender (2 Kings 18:17–37).

2, 3 Two Babylonian officials who appear in Jerusalem in the time of Nebuchadnezzar's destruction of the city (587/6 BCE; Jer. 39:3, 13).

4 An official mentioned as being in charge of the youths in Nebuchadnezzar's palace (Dan. 1:3).
                                                            I.T.A.

Rabshakeh (rab′shuh-kuh), one of the emissaries sent by the Assyrian king Sennacherib (705–681 BCE) to Hezekiah, the king of Judah (ca. 715–687/6 BCE), with a demand for a ransom, which Hezekiah paid out of the temple treasury. When an additional demand for surrender was relayed by Rabshakeh, the prophet Isaiah promised Hezekiah that God would prevent Jerusalem from falling into Sennacherib's hands. A plague subsequently visited on the Assyrian army caused Sennacherib to withdraw from Judah. He was later slain by two of his sons (2 Kings 18:13–19:37; cf. Isa. 36–37). *See also* Sennacherib.

race, racing. The metaphor of the footrace seldom occurs in the Hebrew Bible, probably because competitive sports had no significant place in the social life of ancient Israel. When a gymnasium was erected in Jerusalem by the hellenizing high priest Jason early in the second century BCE, the devout Jews declared that "new customs" were being introduced "contrary to the law" (2 Macc. 4:7–17). Jeremiah, however, reveals a certain awareness of such diversions when he chooses his figures for illustrating how current hard times will only get worse: "If you have raced with footrunners and they have wearied you, how will you compete with horses?" (12:5). Another exception to the usual disinterest in sports is Eccles. 9:11, which observes that "the race is not to the swift, nor the battle to the strong," because so many things in life are determined by "time and chance."

The NT is more attuned to the environment of the Mediterranean world. From prehistoric times, the Greeks had promoted athletic contests in association with their religion. For example, the Olympic games in Athens were held in honor of Zeus, and the Isthmian games in Corinth honored Poseidon. These games included chariot, horse, and foot races. Thus, metaphorical allusions to the footrace are numerous in the writings of Paul, who lived and ministered in these areas. From one perspective, Paul viewed the Christian's life as an intense striving, a combat requiring self-discipline and strenuous training. In running this race, one must exert one's energies to the full, throwing off sin, contending for the faith, and persisting in the race to the finish line (1 Cor. 9:24–27; Phil. 1:27–30; 3:13–14; 1 Thess. 2:2; cf. Col. 1:28–29; 1 Tim. 4:7–10; 2 Tim. 4:7–8; Jude 3). Thus, the author of the Letter to the Hebrews also exhorts his Christian readers to "run with perseverance the race that is set before us" (12:1). The victors in the race are to receive "the crown of righteousness"—an "imperishable wreath," not woven of fading leaves like those so proudly worn by winners in the Greek games (2 Tim. 4:8; cf. 1 Cor. 9:25; Phil. 3:12–16; 1 Tim. 6:11–12). Other NT passages probably also allude to the footrace or athletic contest (Rom. 9:16; 15:30; Gal. 2:2; 5:7; Phil. 2:16; Col. 2:1; Acts 13:25; 20:24; 2 Tim. 2:5). *See also* crown; games.

J.L.P.

Rachel (ray´chuhl), the more favored of the two wives of Jacob. While looking for his relative Laban, Jacob met Rachel at a well, for she was the one who kept her father's sheep. Discovering she was the daughter of his mother's brother, he kissed her, wept aloud, and returned to Laban's household with her. According to Gen. 29:17, Rachel was "graceful and beautiful" and Jacob loved her. He agreed to serve Laban for seven years to pay the bride-price for her. When her elder sister, Leah, was substituted for Rachel at the bridal feast, Jacob married Rachel a week later and agreed to serve another seven years for her (29:9–20). Rachel remained infertile in the early years of her marriage, during which time Leah bore Jacob four sons. To maintain her position vis-à-vis Leah, Rachel offered her slave Bilhah to Jacob as a surrogate mother (30:1–8). Rachel herself named the children born to Bilhah (Dan. 30:6; Naphtali, 30:8). Even while infertile, Rachel appears to have been the dominant wife. When Leah's son Reuben found mandrakes (a fertility symbol), Rachel was

Jacob meets Rachel at the well (*left*) and then bargains to serve her father, Laban, for seven years in exchange for her hand in marriage (Gen. 29:10–20); detail from a thirteenth-century French miniature.

able to offer Leah a night with Jacob in exchange for the mandrakes; even Jacob had little to say about this (30:14–16).

Rachel finally bore a son, Joseph. Her favored position among the wives continued, and during their return to Canaan Jacob placed Rachel and Joseph (Gen. 33:1–2) in the least exposed position. Leah supported Jacob's decision to leave Laban's household, and Rachel took with her the family teraphim (household images). When Laban searched for them, Rachel hid them in her camel cushion and sat on them, pretending that she could not get up because she was menstruating (31:32–35). Rachel later died while giving birth to Benjamin and was buried in what would be the tribal territory of Benjamin (35:16–21). She and Leah are mentioned as the matriarchs of Israel in Ruth 4:11. She is also remembered in a poetic passage in Jer. 31:15, in which the voice that the prophet hears is that of Rachel weeping for her children (i.e., the exiled people of Ephraim, a tribe descended from one of the sons of Joseph and thus from Rachel's grandson). The verse is quoted in Matt. 2:18, where Rachel's children are associated with the Bethlehem infants slaughtered by Herod.

The fact that Leah means "cow" and Rachel means "ewe" has led to speculation that the rivalry between the two sisters reflected rivalry between sheepherders and cattle herders, or that they were projections of totemic symbols of early groups of tribes (the Leah tribes and the Rachel tribes) that joined the tribal federation. *See also* Jacob; Joseph.

T.S.F.

Rahab (ray´hab).

1 The prostitute who sheltered Joshua's men when they came to spy on Jericho (Josh. 2). She defied the orders of the king of Jericho, misdirected the king's men, and then helped Joshua's men escape from Jericho by climbing down a rope from her home, which was built against the city wall. Rahab is portrayed as motivated by a genuine fear of God and a belief that the Israelites would conquer the city; she asked in return that she and her family would be spared when the men returned. Rahab was to indicate to the invaders which home was hers by tying a length of crimson cord to her window (2:18). When the Israelites did conquer Jericho, only Rahab and her father's family were saved (6:25). According to later Jewish legend, Rahab was one of the four most beautiful women in history. She became a righteous convert, married Joshua, and was the ancestor of eight prophets (including Jeremiah) and Huldah the prophetess (*b. Meg.* 15a). In the NT, Rahab is cited as a heroine of faith (Heb. 11:31) and of righteous works (James 2:25). She is listed in the ancestry of Jesus in Matthew's Gospel, which also indicates that she married Joshua (1:5).

2 The mythical chaos dragon whom God killed in battle, making an orderly creation possible (Isa. 51:9; Ps. 89:10).

3 A pejorative name for Egypt (Ps. 87:4; Isa. 30:7).

T.S.F.

The god Asshur using a rainbow as a bow; fragment from a glazed brick, Assyrian, ninth century BCE.

rain. *See* farming; Levant, the.

rainbow, a multicolored arc in the sky caused by refraction of sunlight through droplets of water. First mentioned in Gen. 9:12–13, the rainbow appears as a sign of God's covenant promise never again to destroy the world by flood. Lam. 2:4 and Hab. 3:9–11 speak of God's bow as an instrument of divine wrath, its arrows (e.g., lightning, thunderbolts) released earthward. An ancient illustration of the god Ashur likewise depicts that deity as drawing a rainbow as a weapon. Thus, Gen. 9:12–13 suggests a *spent* bow, one that has been hung in the sky and is no longer aimed at the earth. Ezek. 1:28 associates the rainbow with a manifestation of divine glory (cf. Rev. 10:1). *See also* covenant; flood, the; Noah; sign.   J.W.R.

raisins, sun-dried grapes used for food (Song of Sol. 2:5), gifts (1 Sam. 25:18–31; 2 Sam. 16:1–4), military rations (1 Chron. 12:40), or religious offerings (Hos. 3:1; Isa. 16:7; Jer. 7:18). They were nourishing and traveled well both unprocessed and pressed into cakes.

Ram (Heb., "high, exalted"; cf. Ab*ram*, Ahi*ram*, Am*ram*, Adoni*ram*, Jo*ram*).
1 The son of Hezron, an ancestor of David according to Ruth 4:19 (the LXX reads "Aram," which is followed in Matt. 1:3, 4) and 1 Chron. 2:9.
2 The son of Jerahmeel and grandson of Hezron (1 Chron. 2:25, 27).
3 An ancestor of Elihu's family (Job 32:2).

ram, a male sheep (Heb. *'ayil*), frequently mentioned as a sacrificial offering in Priestly legislation (Lev. 5:15; 8:18–29; Num. 7:15). God provided a ram as a substitute for the sacrifice of Isaac (Gen. 22:13). Rams' skins were used for the covering of the tabernacle (Exod. 36:19), and a ram's horn (Heb. *shophar*) was used to call Israel to battle and to worship. Ps. 114:4 describes mountains "skipping" like rams when God appears. The

two-horned ram of Daniel's vision represented the kings of Media and Persia (cf. Dan. 8). There is no equivalent word in the NT.   P.A.B.

Ramah (ray′muh; Heb., "height").
1 Ramah of Benjamin, which is identified with modern er-Ram, about five miles north of Jerusalem and west of Geba and Michmash on the border of Israel and Judah. It is unexcavated, but surface exploration indicates occupation beginning about the twelfth century BCE. The site can be associated with a number of biblical passages. Deborah judged between Ramah and Bethel (Judg. 4:5). Baasha, king of Israel (ca. 900–877 BCE), fortified Ramah, but, by an alliance with Ben-hadad of Damascus, Asa of Judah (ca. 913–873) tore it down (1 Kings 15:17–22). According to Isa. 10:29, the Assyrians advanced toward Jerusalem through Ramah. Ramah is mentioned in Hosea's cry against Israel (5:8), and Jeremiah was set free there (Jer. 40:1). Ramah is among those towns listed with inhabitants following the exile (Ezra 2:26; Neh. 7:30). Rachel was associated with this town (Jer. 31:15; Matt. 2:18).
2 Ramah of Ephraim. The Ramah that features in the stories of 1 Samuel is probably to be distinguished from Ramah of Benjamin. Elkanah is introduced as "a Zuphite from the hill country of Ephraim" and as "a man of Ramathaim" (1 Sam. 1:1), which is apparently the same place elsewhere

The "Ram in a Thicket" from a royal grave at Ur, third millennium BCE.

called Ramah in this book. Samuel's hometown was Ramah; he returned there periodically, and he was buried there (7:17; 25:1). David was pursued by Saul to Ramah (19:18–24). This may be the Arimathea of the NT (Matt. 27:57; John 19:38) and may be identified with modern Rentis, about eighteen miles east of Joppa. *See also* Samuel; Samuel, First and Second Books of.

3 A border town in Asher (Josh. 19:29); a location to the north in the vicinity of Tyre seems to be indicated. Its identification is unknown, but it is usually associated with modern Ramieh near the southern border of Lebanon.

4 A fortified town in Naphtali (Josh. 19:36), probably located at modern er-Ramah in the Valley of Beth-kerem about twenty miles east of Acco.

5 Ramah of the Negev or Ramath-negeb (Josh. 19:8), in the lands of the tribe of Simeon. Here David sent some of his spoil from the Philistines (1 Sam. 30:27). Ramath-negeb is mentioned in Arad ostraca, where the context suggests it was an outpost against the Edomites; therefore it has been identified with modern Khirbet Ghazzah, southeast of Arad and on the southeast edge of the Negev.

N.L.L.

Rameses (ram′uh-seez). *See* Raamses, Rameses.

Ramesses (ram′uh-seez; Egyptian, "Re [the sun god] is born"; also Ramses, Rameses), the family name of eleven kings of Egypt during the Nineteenth–Twentieth Dynasties (ca. 1293–1070 BCE). This era is often referred to as the Ramesside period. The Ramesside pharaohs were buried in the Valley of the Kings in western Thebes, but they lived in the eastern Delta at Piramesse (see 2). The principal kings of the Ramesside period are the following:

1 Ramesses I (1293–1291 BCE), an army general who founded the Nineteenth Dynasty. His son was Sety I (1291–1279 BCE), whose reign included military campaigns into western Asia in which the Hittites were defeated and various Canaanite cities were conquered.

2 Ramesses II (1279–1212 BCE), son of Sety I, sometimes called "the Great" by early scholars. In the fifth year of his reign, he fought a great battle against the Hittites at Kadesh in Syria. This king was a very active builder throughout Egypt and Nubia; he also liked to have his name inscribed on the monuments of earlier kings. He founded the city of Piramesse (the biblical Raamses) in the eastern Delta as the new royal residence. Many biblical scholars consider Ramesses II the pharaoh of the exodus.

3 Merenptah (1212–1202 BCE), a son of Ramesses II. A stele set up to record some of this king's victories includes the words "Israel is desolated and has no seed"; this is the first documented mention of Israel in the ancient Near East and has led some scholars to suggest that Merenptah was the pharaoh of the exodus (which would make Ramesses II the pharaoh of the oppression).

4 Ramesses III (1182–1151 BCE), the son of the first king of the Twentieth Dynasty, Setnakht. He successfully fought off an invasion of Egypt by the Sea Peoples from the northern Mediterranean region in the eighth year of his reign. One tribe included among the Sea Peoples was the Peleset (the biblical Philistines), who subsequently settled in a southwestern region of the Levant.

5 Ramesses IV–XI (1151–1070 BCE). The later Ramesside kings ruled over a country decaying economically, politically, and militarily. The Egyptian empire probably ended in the reign of Ramesses VI (1141–1134 BCE).

See also exodus, the; Pharaoh.   J.M.W.

Ramoth (ray′moth). *See* Ramoth-gilead.

Ramoth-gilead (ray′muhth-gil′ee-uhd), in the tribal inheritance, a city assigned to Gad that became both a levitical city and a city of refuge (Josh. 21:38; 1 Chron. 6:80; Deut. 4:43; Josh. 20:8). It was located east of the Jordan River in an area that later became the shifting border between Syria and Israel. During Solomon's reign it was a chief town of a tax district (1 Kings 4:13). King Ahab of Israel was killed there (1 Kings 22), and it was here that the prophet Elisha anointed Jehu king of Israel (2 Kings 9:1–16). The precise location is unknown, although two major possibilities are Tell el Husn near Irbid and Tell Ramith. The latter is the more likely location and is situated farther east near the current Jordanian-Syrian border.   J.A.D.

ransom. *See* redemption.

Rapha (ray′fuh; Heb., "[God] has healed"), the son of Benjamin and leader of a family group (1 Chron. 8:2).

Ras-Shamra (rahs-shahm′ruh), the modern Arabic name of the site of the ancient city of Ugarit. Ras-Shamra lies beside the Syrian coast of the Mediterranean Sea at roughly the northern latitude of Cyprus. Inscriptions from the site establish its identification as Ugarit. The name "Ugarit" perhaps means "field" (Ugaritic *ugar*) or the like. The existence of Ugarit was known prior to excavations at Ras-Shamra from reference to the city

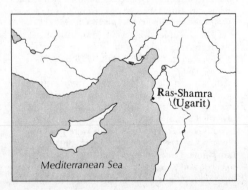

Ras-Shamra
(Ugarit)

Mediterranean Sea

Weight in the form of a human head found
at Ras-Shamra; thirteenth century BCE.

in an Amarna letter, but the importance of the site
could not have been guessed apart from the work of
archaeologists.

The site attracted the attention of archaeologists in 1928 when a peasant happened upon a
thirteenth-century BCE tomb. This discovery occurred at coastal Minet el-Beida (Arabic, "White
Harbor"; Gk. *leukos limēn*) close to Ras-Shamra.
The excavation of both sites began in 1929 under
the direction of the French archaeologist C. F. A.
Schaeffer. The *tell*, or mound, of Ras-Shamra is
trapezoidal, with a maximum length of approximately 3,300 feet and a width of 1,650 feet. A freshwater stream flows to the Mediterranean Sea by
Minet el-Beida.

Five Phases: The excavators of Ras-Shamra
have divided its material remains into five major
phases. The earliest level is assigned the number
V. According to radiocarbon data, its material belongs to the seventh and sixth millennia BCE. The
first inhabitants of the location did not use pottery, although they possessed crude clay figurines
of a sort usually associated with primitive fertility religion. Stone tools and weapons have been
found in this level, and the site may have been surrounded by a crude wall.

Level IV at Ras-Shamra represents what archaeologists call the Chalcolithic Age (in the fifth millennium). The pottery from this level is similar to
pottery found elsewhere in the Mediterranean, at
first to the pottery of Cyprus, later to the pottery
of Tell Halaf on the frontier between Syria and
Turkey.

Level III begins with the decline of the Chalcolithic Age (ca. 3500 BCE) and is followed by an
intrusion of Ubaid culture. The intrusion ends
abruptly. Ubaid culture seems to have spread from
Mesopotamia. This level continues into the Early
Bronze Age (ca. 3000 BCE) and terminates after the
appearance of "Khirbet Kerek" pottery, a type of
pottery known also in early Canaan (ca. 2500 BCE).

Level II encompasses remains dated to ca. 2100–
1600 BCE. Egyptian artifacts are relatively common for this period; city life flourished at Ugarit,
and two monumental temples, for Baal and Dagon,
were built, perhaps on the site of earlier sanctuaries. In the latter part of this phase Ugarit suffered
a decline associated with the era of the Hyksos in
Egypt (ca. 1750–1550).

Level 1, the most recent, includes material
from the Late Bronze Age (1500–1200 BCE). To
this level belong the cuneiform texts of Ras-Shamra as well as the imposing royal palace of
Ugarit. The royal palace was one of the largest
palaces of its day. This was the "golden" age of
the city. It ended abruptly ca. 1200 BCE in conjunction with the general movements of the Sea
Peoples, invaders from Crete and other Greek
islands (the Philistines among them), into the
ancient Near East. No significant habitation occurred at Ras-Shamra after this period.

Cuneiform Texts: By far the most important
discoveries at Ras-Shamra have been the deposits of cuneiform texts recovered from a number
of locations on the tell. "Cuneiform" texts are so
called because they were produced by impressing
wedge-shaped marks (Lat. *cuneus*, "wedge") on
clay. Allowed to harden or baked, these clay texts
are durable and survive long after papyrus and
other writing materials decay. At Ras-Shamra,
a large number of cuneiform texts were written
with symbols for syllables (syllabic cuneiform) in
the Akkadian language. A second variety of text
displayed a previously unknown script that proved
to be alphabetic (alphabetic cuneiform). These
alphabetic texts revealed a previously unknown
Semitic language having affinities with biblical
Hebrew. This language is now called Ugaritic.

Syllabic cuneiform texts have come primarily from the royal palace of Ugarit. They reveal
the history, economy, society, and religion of the
ancient city. Alphabetic texts have come from
scattered spots on the tell including the royal palace and a priestly "library" in the vicinity of the
Dagon and Baal temples. These texts sometimes
treat daily matters, but among the alphabetic
texts have been found fine literary works divisible roughly into the categories "myths" and "legends." The most important Ugaritic texts come
from the fourteenth century BCE, although many
scholars assume that a period of oral transmission preceded commitment of the literary works
to writing. The Ugaritic texts have thrown extraordinary light on the Bible. Composed as poetry, they exhibit stylistic devices known from
the Bible. They tell of the deeds of gods worshiped in Israel's environment (El, Baal, Asherah,
Anat) and even reveal for the first time a legendary patriarch, Danel ("Daniel"), known also in
the Bible (Ezek. 14:14, 20; 28:3).

Ugarit at Its Height: At its height, Ugarit was a
thriving city. The metropolis was the administrative center of a small kingdom that followed political tides and was subject at times to Egypt, at
times to the Hittite Empire. Personal names reveal

a diverse population in the kingdom, with a large Hurrian element. The countryside produced a variety of agricultural products—olive oil, grain, wine. Seafaring was important to the city; votive anchors have been recovered from its Baal temple.

Baal Zaphon was the chief god of the city, although in lists of gods he ranks below others. Alongside El, Baal plays an important role in the myths of Ugarit. Nonmythic texts reveal the veneration of a host of gods and goddesses. Of public ritual, very little is known directly. It is widely assumed that the affairs of the cult at Ugarit were coordinated with the concerns of the farmer. Private religion is still more difficult to reconstruct, although the existence at Ugarit of an institution called the *marzeakh,* a type of funerary observance, is of interest because of a biblical reflection of it (Jer. 16:5). Mortuary concerns may have played an important role in the piety of ancient Ugarit's people. *See also* Amarna, Tell el-; Anat; Asherah; Baal; Dagon; El; writing.
Bibliography
Gray, John. *The Legacy of Canaan.* Leiden: Brill, 1957.   R.M.G.

raven. The Hebrew word for "raven" (*'oreb*) probably refers, not only to the true raven (*Corvus corax*), but also to other members of the crow family (*Corvidae*), including the rook, the jay, the fan-tailed raven, the jackdaw, and the hooded crow. Although an object of God's care (Job 38:41; Ps. 147:9; Luke 12:24), the raven is an unclean bird (Lev. 11:15; Deut. 14:14), mentioned for its habit of picking at the eyes of its prey (Prov. 30:17) and for its tendency to live in ruins (Isa. 34:11). In Gen. 8:7 Noah sends a raven out to look for land, and in 1 Kings 17:4 Elijah is fed by ravens.   I.U.K.

Reaiah (ree-ay'yuh; Heb., "the LORD has seen").
1 A descendant of Judah belonging to the Zorathite family group (1 Chron. 4:2).
2 A descendant of Reuben; he was the son of Micah and belonged to the family group headed by Joel (1 Chron. 5:5).
3 The ancestor of a family group of temple servants (Nethinim) who returned from the Babylonian exile with Zerubbabel (Ezra 2:47; Neh. 7:50).

reaping, the harvesting of grain. The term is used figuratively for the final judgment (Matt. 13:24–30, 36–43; Rev. 14:15–16), evangelism (Matt. 9:37–38; Luke 10:2; John 4:35–36; Rom. 1:13), and recompense for good (Hos. 10:12; 2 Cor. 9:6; Gal. 6:7–8) or evil (Job 4:8; Prov. 22:8; Hos. 8:7; 10:13; Gal. 6:7–8). *See also* farming.

Reba (ree'buh), one of the five kings of Midian killed by the Israelites (Num. 31:8). His territory was assigned later to the tribe of Reuben (Josh. 13:21).

Rebekah (ri-bek'uh), the wife of Isaac, the daughter of Bethuel (Abraham's nephew), the sister of Laban, and the mother of Jacob and Esau.

Gen. 24 recounts how Abraham's servant returned to his homeland to find a wife for Isaac, and how (in response to prayer) he found Rebekah at the well. By giving him a drink and offering to water his camels, she fulfilled the criteria that he had asked for as a sign from God that she was the one to marry Isaac. Thus, he returned with her and offered gifts to her family. The negotiations for Rebekah's marriage were carried out by her mother and her brother Laban, an indication that her father, Bethuel, may have been old or infirm. They asked her if she wished to go with the servant to become Isaac's wife, and she said, "I will" (24:58). Isaac took her as his wife, loved her, and was thus "comforted after the death of his mother" (24:67).

Rebekah remained infertile for twenty years, but then, after Isaac interceded with God, she conceived the twins Jacob and Esau. During her pregnancy the children struggled within her; when asked what it meant, God told her that the twins would be the ancestors of separate nations, and that Jacob would be dominant despite Esau's status as firstborn (Gen. 25:20–26; cf. Rom. 9:10–13). After the boys were born, Isaac favored Esau because he was fond of game, but Rebekah loved Jacob the most (25:27–28).

The next story about Rebekah comes as something of an interlude in the account of the two sons (Gen. 26:6–11). When Isaac settled in Gerar, he told the men of the region that Rebekah was his sister, because he feared they might otherwise kill him, since she was so beautiful. This ruse is detected when Abimelech, the Philistine king of Gerar, looked out a window and saw Isaac "laughing with" Rebecca, an apparent euphemism for sex play (26:8; NRSV: "fondling"). The king was appalled at what might have happened and warned everyone not to touch either Isaac or Rebekah, lest guilt come upon the land. The story appears to be a doublet of the story of Abraham and Sarah in Gerar (Gen. 20).

Rebekah was subsequently responsible for instigating the plot by which Jacob received his father's deathbed blessing. She covered Jacob's arms and neck with goatskins, so that he could take advantage of Isaac's failed eyesight and impersonate Esau when it was time for the blessing to be given (Gen. 27:1–29). She then convinced Isaac to send Jacob to his relatives to find a wife in order to take him out of the path of Esau's anger (27:41–28:5).

Nothing more is known about Rebekah other than the fact that she was buried in the cave at Machpelah (Gen. 49:31). Deborah, her nurse, who accompanied her from her family home, was buried beneath an oak at Bethel (24:59; 35:8). *See also* Esau; Isaac; Jacob; Laban.   T.S.F./M.A.P.

rebirth. *See* conversion.

Rechab (ree'kab).
1 The son of Rimmon who, with his brother Baanah, was a captain of Ishbaal's bands. After Abner's death, the two brothers murdered Ishbaal

and brought his head to David, expecting him to be pleased; instead, David had the brothers executed (2 Sam. 4).

2 An ancestor of Jehonadab (Jonadab), a Kenite (1 Chron. 2:55) who supported Jehu's coup (2 Kings 10:15). Toward the end of Jehu's monarchy (ca. 816 BCE), a group of his followers called "Rechabites" came to Jerusalem to escape Nebuchadnezzar's invasion. They apparently lived in tents, avoided agriculture, and drank no wine in accordance with the principles of Jehonadab. Jeremiah cited them as an example of fidelity to prior commitments, in contrast to the unfaithful Judeans. Although Judah had to be punished for its infidelity, Jeremiah assured the Rechabites that there would always be a descendant of Jonadab (Jer. 35). *See also* Abner; Ishbaal; Nazirites.

F.E.G.

reconciliation (Gk. *katallagē*), a term indicating a repaired relationship between persons or groups who were formerly at enmity with each other. Sirach indicates that reconciliation can follow abusive speech or actions, unless one has betrayed secrets (22:22; 27:21). The NT encourages reconciliation between estranged parties (Matt. 5:24; Luke 12:58) and spouses (1 Cor. 7:11). But the noun and its corresponding verb most often refer to the renewed relationship between God and humanity effected through Christ's redemptive work (Rom. 5:10–11; 11:15; 2 Cor. 5:17–20; Eph. 2:16; Col. 1:20, 22). For Paul the subject of this reconciling activity is always "God through Christ" (2 Cor. 5:18). Paul describes the human condition prior to reconciliation as weak, ungodly, and sinful (Rom. 5:6–8; cf. Eph. 2:12), but maintains that "while we were enemies, we were reconciled to God through the death of his Son" (Rom. 5:10; cf. 2 Cor. 5:19; Col. 1:22). The immediate effect of reconciliation is "peace with God" (Rom. 5:1; cf. Eph. 2:14). Paul also speaks of reconciliation in cosmic terms: the world has been reconciled to God through Christ (2 Cor. 5:19; cf. Rom. 11:15; Col. 1:20). Further, even though the work of reconciliation belongs to God, Paul views his ministry as one of reconciliation and himself as an ambassador for Christ inviting others to receive this reconciliation (2 Cor. 5:18–20). *See also* justification; peace; redemption; salvation.   F.J.M.

red, in biblical usage, the color of the earth from which Adam was made (Gen. 2:7; the letters for "Adam" in Hebrew can also mean "ruby," and "dust" can also mean "reddish in color"); of Esau at birth (25:25); of pottage (25:30); of drunken eyes (49:12), of cattle (Num. 19:2), of blood (2 Kings 3:22), of weeping faces (Job 16:16), of wine (Prov. 23:31), of sin (Isa. 1:18), of clothing (Isa. 63:1–2), of horses (Zech. 1:8; 6:2), of threatening skies (Matt. 16:3), and of the apocalyptic dragon (Rev. 12:3). *See also* scarlet.   R.S.B.

redeemer, one who buys back a property or house that has been sold, or a relative who buys

back a family member who has fallen into slavery (Lev. 25:25–34, 47–55). In the Bible, the term is applied in its latter meaning to God (Job 19:25; Pss. 19:14; 78:35; Prov. 23:11; Isa. 41:14; 43:14; 54:5; 60:16; Jer. 50:34). It is never used in the Bible for Jesus Christ, although the term "redemption" is applied to him (e.g., 1 Cor. 1:30). *See also* redemption.

redemption, the release of an item (or person) in exchange for some type of payment. The contexts of usage in the Bible, however, add important dimensions to this general meaning.

In the Hebrew Bible: Three Hebrew words are used to express different ideas of redemption. The first (*ga'al*) is a technical legal term and is applied to the redemption of inheritance, family members from servitude or difficulties, tithes, or various objects and property (e.g., Lev. 25:25, 47–49; 27:15–20; Ps. 72:4, 14). Of special importance was the question of redemption of land. Israelite legal codes guaranteed the right of Israelite landowners to regain property that had been sold (Lev. 25:23–34). The land was considered as belonging to God and therefore the inheritances granted to the tribes divinely ordained; the laws of redemption were designed to protect the poor by keeping family inheritances intact. Provisions were made for various means through which the land could be reclaimed: a designated relative could purchase the land (cf. Jer. 32:6–15; Ruth 4:1–4), the original owner could buy it back (Lev. 25:26–27; cf. 25:14–16), or it would automatically revert to the previous owner every fifty years (the jubilee year; Lev. 25:10, 13, 28).

Often without great distinction from the first, a second word (*padah*) is used for the redemption of the firstborn among male children or animals (since the firstborn belong to God) by means of some payment or offering (e.g., Num. 3:45–51; 18:15–16). Where offenses and conflicts are involved, redemption can also be achieved through payment of money (e.g., Exod. 21:8, 30). Specialized usage in cases of the shedding of blood (e.g., Num. 35:12, 19) and of God acting in a redemptive manner toward people (e.g., Exod. 6:6; 15:13; Deut. 7:8; 1 Chron. 17:21; Pss. 19:14; 25:22; 106:10; Isa. 41:14; 43:1–4; 44:21–28; Hos. 13:14) or toward individuals in difficult or life-threatening situations (e.g., Gen. 48:16; 2 Sam. 4:9; Job 19:25; Pss. 26:11; 49:15; 69:18; 103:4) can also be found.

These first two Hebrew roots are somewhat synonymous, although the former (*ga'al*) is favored by certain writers (the authors of some of the Psalms and Isa. 40–55, sometimes called Second Isaiah), while the latter (*padah*) is preferred by others (the authors of Deuteronomy and certain other psalms).

A specialized theological notion of redemption tends to be associated with a third root (*kopher*), which is frequently used where God's relationship to people is reestablished or restored after acts of rebellion, disobedience, or infidelity. This third root is often translated as "ransom" (e.g., Ps. 49:7–8; Exod. 21:30), or as "redeem" (Ps. 130:8), or as "bribe" (Amos 5:12) and carries the sense of atonement.

In the NT: The theological sense of redemption is reflected in Christian traditions and appropriated somewhat differently by NT writers. Emphasis is placed on the human need for deliverance and freedom (Rom. 5:9; 6:6; 7:6; 8:2; cf. 1 Cor. 2:6; Gal. 5:4; Heb. 2:14–15). Presupposed is the idea that alienation and bondage (e.g., to sin, death, or the devil) are endemic to the human condition and have far-reaching consequences. Thus, the Creator becomes the Redeemer, and redemption itself is represented as being accomplished through the sacrificial death of Jesus (Rom. 3:23–25a; 8:23; 1 Cor. 1:30; 6:20; 7:23; Gal. 3:13; 4:5; Eph. 1:7, 14; 4:30; Col. 1:14; Heb. 9:15; Rev. 5:9; 14:4) and as being verified by his resurrection from the dead (1 Cor. 15:3–7; 1 Pet. 1:18–21). In the Gospels, Jesus is presented as understanding the significance of his impending death in these terms (Mark 10:45; Matt. 20:28; cf. Mark 8:31). *See also* atonement; forgiveness; pardon; reconciliation; salvation.   J.E.A./D.R.B.

Red Sea, the narrow sea between Africa and Arabia, part of the Great Rift Valley system, about 1,450 miles long and averaging about 150 miles wide. The constricted southern exit through the straits of Bab el-Mandeb opens into the Indian Ocean, and the northern end divides around the Sinai Peninsula, with the Gulf of Aqabah on the east and the Gulf of Suez on the west. Enclosed between hot deserts, the summer water temperature reaches 85 degrees Fahrenheit.

Dangerous coral reefs and powerful north winds make navigation difficult, but trade along the Red Sea was important from a very early date. The Egyptian queen Hatshepsut used it for her expedition to Punt in the mid-fifteenth century BCE. Whether the Edomites used it to supplement their important land trade is uncertain, but King Solomon maintained a fleet at Ezion-geber on the Gulf of Aqabah, a fleet that made triennial journeys to south Arabia and east Africa (1 Kings 9:26–28; 10:11, 22). Jehoshaphat of Judah later attempted to do likewise, but his ships were destroyed (22:48).

It is not certain whether this or some other body of water is meant by references in the exodus story.

The Red Sea, with the tip of the Sinai Peninsula at bottom.

The Hebrew term that is often translated "Red Sea" in English Bibles (including the NRSV) is *yam suph*, literally "Sea of Reeds." Furthermore, the Hebrews did not distinguish between "sea" and "lake" (cf. "Sea of Galilee," which is actually a lake). Three possible routes for the exodus have been suggested: the southern route at, or close to, the Gulf of Suez; the central route across the marshes of Lake Timsah, now part of the Suez Canal; and the northern route, identifying *yam suph* with Lake Bardawil and assuming the Israelites followed the narrow spit of land dividing the lake from the Mediterranean. None of these suggestions, however, has won general acceptance. *See also* Edom; exodus, the; Jehoshaphat; Sinai; Solomon.   D.B.

Common reed.

reed, a general term referring to tall hollow grasses growing in shallow water by streams, rivers, lakes, and marshes throughout Egypt and the Levant. It may be identified as any of several common plants. The giant reed (*Arundo donax*) grows to over 10 feet high, forming dense thickets along lake margins (Job 40:21). Reed mace or cattail (genus *Typha*), topped by a cylindrical brown spike, is often depicted as the mock scepter of Jesus in Matt. 27:29–30. The common reed (*Phragmites communis*) sports dense purple plumes atop its tall stems, which move gracefully in the wind (Matt. 11:7).

The tall, sturdy stems of these grasses had diverse uses. The jagged edges of the broken stems were capable of piercing flesh (2 Kings 18:21) and may have been used as fishing spears. Some were sturdy enough to be used as a walking stick (Ezek. 29:7). Reeds were used as flutes and were also effective as makeshift pens (3 John 13; 3 Macc. 4:20) or rulers (Ezek. 40:3). *See also* rush.   P.L.C.

refining, the process of removing impurities from metal ore by filtering, washing, burning, or smelting. When referring to metalworking, the process is that of melting a solid to a liquid in order to remove the dross or of burning, in which the fire helps in the extraction of metal from an ore by enhancing chemical reactions. Copper smelting was practiced early by the Hebrews using pottery crucibles or by heating ore with charcoal in a furnace. Refining by smelting is known from Timna in the Arabah and other sites, e.g., Gerar, Rumeileh, Tel Qasile near Tel Aviv, and Abu Matar near Beer-sheba. In the Bible, the concept of refining is often employed metaphorically for the cleansing or purifying of persons or things (Ps. 12:6; Isa. 1:25; 48:10; Jer. 6:29; 9:6; Mal. 3:3). In 1 Peter, the refining of gold is used as a metaphor for the manner in which the faith of believers is strengthened when they are persecuted (1:7). *See also* furnace; mines; smith.   R.A.C.

refuge, a place of safety or protection from enemies. Six of the levitical cities were designated as cities of refuge, where one who accidently caused a death might seek asylum from avengers until the case could be judged by the elders of the city (Josh. 20:7–9). If the person was found to be innocent of deliberate murder, that person could continue to live in sanctuary in the city of refuge (Num. 35:6–28; Deut. 19:1–13). God is often portrayed as a refuge or shelter for humanity, most frequently in psalms (Pss. 7:1; 11:1; 46:1; 2 Sam. 22:3; Isa. 25:4; Jer. 16:19; Heb. 6:18). *See also* avenger; levitical cities; priests.   D.R.B.

Rehabiah (ree´huh bi´uh; Heb., "the LORD has enlarged"), the son of Eliezer and grandson of Moses. He became the head of a large family group (1 Chron. 23:17; 24:21).

Rehob (ree´hob; Heb., "broad, wide"; a shortened form of the name Rehabiah).
1 The father of Hadadezer, king of Zobah, an Aramean city-state north of Damascus (2 Sam. 8:3, 12).
2 A Levite who signed Ezra's covenant-renewal document at the time of Nehemiah (Neh. 10:11).
3 A site in Upper Galilee (Num. 13:21). It marked the upper limit of the territory investigated by the spies sent out by Moses.
4 A place in the plain of Acco of the tribe of Asher (Josh. 19:28, 30; 21:31; Judg. 1:31; 1 Chron. 6:75).
5 A place in Beth-shan from which Aramean warriors came to oppose David's troops under Joab (2 Sam. 10:8).

Rehoboam (ree´huh boh´uhm), the son of King Solomon and his wife Naamah, who was an Ammonite princess (1 Kings 14:31). He was successor to his father as the last king of the united monarchy and the first king of Judah after the northern tribes revolted against his rule and made Jeroboam I their king. There is some uncertainty about the chronology for Rehoboam's reign. He is said to have become king when he was forty-one and to have ruled for seventeen years (1 Kings 14:21; 2 Chron. 13:7). His reign has been variously dated as starting in 937, 933, 926, or 922 BCE, the last of which would date Rehoboam's reign as ca. 922–905 BCE. The basic biblical narratives concerning Rehoboam are found in 1 Kings 11:43; 12:1–24; 14:21–31; and 2 Chron. 9:31–12:16.

Rehoboam's accession to the throne came under very difficult political circumstances. Solomon's policies of forced labor and high taxation (necessary to support his greatly expanded court and administrative apparatus) had created a good deal of popular unrest. In addition, Solomon had attempted to break up tribal loyalties by creating twelve administrative districts that basically disregarded the old tribal borders. The growing resentment against such policies erupted after Solomon's death, on the occasion of Rehoboam's aborted coronation at Shechem. Rehoboam rejected the counsel of his older mentors, who advised easing the people's tax burden, and went with the guidance of his contemporaries, who counseled continuing the policies of his father. Thus, he announced to the people at Shechem that he would not only continue his father's policies but intensify them. Upon hearing this, the northern tribes revolted and instituted their own monarchy. Rehoboam unsuccessfully attempted to put down the revolt (1 Kings 12:18, 21–24).

After the division, Rehoboam instigated border warfare against Israel (1 Kings 12:21–24; 14:30; 2 Chron. 12:15), apparently in an attempt to clear the approaches to his capital city. The threatened nature of Rehoboam's kingdom is reflected in his construction of a line of fortresses around Judah (2 Chron. 11:5–10). The line ran south of Jerusalem along the central ridge, turned west south of Hebron, and continued northward through the Shephelah to Aijalon, where it turned back toward Jerusalem. The sixteen stations in the line are little more than three miles apart, and the area enclosed does not include the coastal plain, with its trade routes and access to the Mediterranean, or the plain of Beer-sheba.

Rehoboam's reign saw the campaign of Pharaoh Shishak I (1 Kings 14:25–28; 2 Chron. 12:2–9), founder of the Twenty-Second Dynasty in Egypt. He invaded the hill country, the coastal plain, and the Negev. The biblical account only mentions the assault upon Judah, but Shishak's version, on the wall of the temple at Karnak, shows 156 captives, each representing a Palestinian city, most in Israel. The section of the inscription that apparently lists sites in Judah, however, is very poorly preserved. In any case, the raid illustrates the military weakness caused by the division of the Hebrew kingdom, which resulted in widespread destruction of cities in Judah and Israel only five years after the death of Solomon. This destruction has been confirmed to some extent by the results of archaeology, especially at Tell Beit Mirsim, Lachish, and Beer-sheba. According to 1 Kings 14:25–28,

Shishak came up against Jerusalem, and many of the treasures of the temple and palace had to be handed over as ransom.

From the perspective of the Chronicler (2 Chron. 12:5), Shishak's invasion came as retribution for Rehoboam's infidelity to God. A list of his apostasies, many of which reflect the pagan influences introduced by Solomon, is found in 1 Kings 14:22–24. The Chronicler also includes a section on Rehoboam's family, material without parallel in Kings; he says that Rehoboam had eighteen wives, sixty concubines, twenty-eight sons, and sixty daughters (2 Chron. 11:18–22). *See also* Jeroboam I; Shishak.   F.S.F.

Rehoboth (ri-hoh′both; Heb., "broad places").

1 A well dug by Isaac's servants, named Rehoboth ("broad places"), because they had finally found respite from their quarrel over water rights with the herdsmen of Gerar (Gen. 26:22). The site is most often identified with modern Ruheibeh, southwest of Beer-sheba. *See also* Beer-sheba; Gerar; Isaac.

2 Rehoboth-on-the-River, the home of Shaul (Gen. 36:37; 1 Chron. 1:48), one of the early kings of Edom (Gen. 36:31). The river in question is possibly the Wadi Zered (modern Wadi el-Hasa). The site itself is unidentified. *See also* Zered, Wadi.   B.M.

Rehoboth-ir (ri-hoh′both-ihr′; Heb., "open places of a city" or "city plazas," as, e.g., in Lam. 2:12), a place built by Nimrod (in Gen. 10:11). It might be an otherwise unknown city between Nineveh and Calah or a district of Nineveh.

Rehum (ree′huhm).

1 One of eleven leaders who accompanied Zerubbabel in the return to Judea after the Babylonian exile (Ezra 2:2; Neh. 7:7 has "Nehum").

2 A royal deputy in the Persian province Beyond the River (to which Judea belonged) who wrote a letter to the Persian king Artaxerxes telling him that the Jews were rebuilding Jerusalem and warning him, "If this city is rebuilt and the walls finished, they will not pay tribute, custom, or toll, and the royal revenue will be reduced" (Ezra 4:13). This led Artaxerxes to stop the work, and it remained stopped until the second year of the reign of Darius I (Ezra 4:8–23). This is often assumed to have preceded the activity of Nehemiah. *See also* Artaxerxes; Ezra and Nehemiah, books of; Zerubbabel.

3 A Levite, son of Bani, sharing in the repair of the wall under Nehemiah (Neh. 3:17; perhaps also 10:25), a "chief of the people" and signatory to Ezra's covenant-renewal document (Neh. 9:38).

4 A levitical priest who returned from the Babylonian exile with Zerubbabel and Jeshua (Neh. 12:3; cf. "Harim" in 12:15).   P.R.A.

Rei (ree′i), a member of David's court who remained loyal during the conspiracy of Adonijah (1 Kings 1:8).

Rekem (ree′kuhm).

1 A Midianite king slain with four others by the Israelites on their way to Canaan (Num. 31:8; Josh. 13:21).

2 The son of Hebron; he was the ancestor of a Calebite family group belonging to the tribe of Judah (1 Chron. 2:43–44).

3 The grandson of Machir and Maacah; he was the ancestor of one of the Machir family groups in Gilead (1 Chron. 7:16).

4 A town in the territory of the tribe of Benjamin (Josh. 18:27).

religion, religious. The NRSV uses "religion" or "religious" to translate three different Greek words. The word *deisidaimōnia,* in Acts 25:19, was commonly used in Hellenistic culture for observances offered to a deity; when explaining why Paul has been arrested, Festus tells King Agrippa that the case concerns disagreements between Paul and other Jews regarding "their own religion." Paul uses the adjective form of this word when he tells the Athenians, "I see how extremely religious you are" (Act 17:32), but he uses a different word (*thrēskeia*) when referring to Judaism: "I belonged to the strictest sect of our religion and lived as a Pharisee" (26:5). This word is also used in James 1:26–27: "If any think they are religious and do not bridle their tongue, their religion is in vain." Col. 2:18 uses the word to refer to "religion of angels" (NRSV: "worship of angels"), which might refer to idolatrous religious practices that involve worshiping angels or, possibly, to hyperspiritual experiences in which mortals believe they are practicing the religion angels practice, worshiping God in the court of heaven itself. Finally, the word *eusebeia* (verb form: *eusebeō*) seems to refer to religious devotion and behavior. It is used in a broad sense in 1 Tim. 3:16 ("the mystery of our religion is great"), but more often refers to pious acts or attitudes that derive from faith ("religious duty," 1 Tim. 5:4). This word is fairly common in the NT, but is translated in the NRSV by many different terms: "godliness" or "godly" (1 Tim. 2:2; 4:7, 8; 6:3, 5–6; 2 Tim. 3:5; Titus 1:1; 2:12; 2 Pet. 1:3, 6; 2:9; 3:11), "piety" (Acts 3:12), "devout" (Acts 10:2, 7), and "worship" or "worshiper" (Acts 10:23; John 9:31). *See also* godliness, godly; worship in the Hebrew Bible; worship in the New Testament.   M.A.P.

Remaliah (rem-uh-li′uh), the father of Pekah, an official of King Pekahiah of Israel (i.e., the northern kingdom) who assassinated the king and took the throne (2 Kings 15:25; Isa. 7:1).

remnant, the portion left over after a part has been removed. "Remnant" may refer to vegetation (Exod. 10:5) or human and animal life (Gen. 7:23), but in the Bible it often refers to that portion of a community that has escaped death or exile (Jer. 24:8; Ezra 9:13–15).

The concept of "remnant" is used with reference to postjudgment Israel. It is the obverse of the idea that God will punish the sinning people with total destruction (cf. 1 Kings 19:15–18). Amos speaks of a nonviable or pitiful remnant in his prophecies of rebuke (3:12; 5:3; 6:9; 7:1–6; 9:1; cf. 1:8), but if the people repent, destruction of the "remnant of Joseph" may be avoided (5:14–15). This concept becomes significant in Isaiah, where a penitent remnant will return to God and to the land (7:3; 10:20–22; 11:10–16; 17:5–8; 28:5; 30:17–19; 37:4, 31–32; cf. 6:13). In Micah, the word "remnant" serves as a technical term for "those who will be redeemed" (4:6–7; 5:2–8; cf. 2:12; 7:18–20). This understanding is evident also in Joel 3:5 (cf. Obad. 17). In Zephaniah, the righteous remnant of Israel will be redeemed (3:11–20; cf. 2:3, 7, 9).

Jeremiah's prophecies of rebuke are very harsh; they depict no surviving remnant (6:9; 11:21–23; 15:9) or they sometimes predict a terrible destiny for the survivors (8:3; 24:8–10). In his prophecies of hope, however, Jeremiah assures redemption to the "remnant of my flock" (23:3–4) who were led astray by their rulers (23:1–2). Also, God will save the "remnant of Israel" (31:7), but if the "remnant of Judah" after the Babylonian destruction immigrates to Egypt, they will forfeit God's mercies and be destroyed (42:9–22). Similarly, Ezekiel, indicates that even the remnant of Judah will be destroyed (5:1–4, 8–17; 9:4–10), but then his cry, "Ah, Lord GOD! Will you make a complete end of the remnant of Israel" (11:13) evokes a prophecy of redemption (11:14–22).

The postexilic community identified itself as the remnant (Ezra 9:13–15; Neh. 1:2–3; 7:72; Hag. 1:12, 14; 2:2). Zechariah promises the remnant a life of peace and prosperity (8:1–15), but they must adhere to moral behavior (8:16–17).

Members of the Qumran community saw themselves as the last wave of the returning exiles from Babylon and identified themselves as the "remnant" of Israel (CD 1:4–5; 1QH 6:8). So too the apostle Paul, citing prophecies from Hosea and Isaiah (Rom. 9:25–29), concluded that those Jews who followed Christ would constitute the true remnant, "chosen by grace" (Rom. 11:5).   J.U.

repentance, a word covering several biblical ideas that range from regret to reversal, from changing one's mind about something to a complete moral or ethical conversion. Thus in the Bible, God can repent (Heb. *nakham*) in the sense of regret: God regrets having made Saul king (1 Sam. 15:11). The more profound notion of repentance in the sense of "reversal," however, is expressed through the Hebrew word *shub,* which expresses the idea of turning back or retracing one's steps.

In the early stages of Israelite history, the nation was more conscious of its collective guilt than of its individual guilt. In times of national catastrophe, therefore, it celebrated liturgies of repentance that included an assembly of the people, fasting, lamentation, and confession of sin. The prophets of the eighth century BCE, however, and those who followed leveled strong criticism against repentance

that seemed to be nothing more than a liturgical rite. Amos complains that the people did not turn to God (4:6, 8–11). Hosea, after describing a liturgy of repentance (6:1–3), says that Israel's love "is like a morning cloud, like the dew that goes early away" (6:4). Isaiah pleads for social justice rather than empty ritual (1:10–17; cf. 58:5–7; Amos 5:21–24). The prophets, therefore, insist upon an interior conversion manifested in outward acts of justice, kindness, and humility (Mic. 6:6–8). Jeremiah calls upon Israel to acknowledge its guilt (3:11–14), and Ezekiel brings the notion of individual responsibility to a climax (3:16–21; 18; 33:10–20). For all of their harshness, however, the prophets also hold out hope to Israel. Jeremiah and Ezekiel look to a day when God will place a new heart within people (Jer. 24:7; Ezek. 36:26–31), and Isaiah promises forgiveness to those who will repent (1:18–19).

In the NT the notion of repentance as turning to God (Heb. *shub*) is expressed by the Greek verb *metanoein.* The idea includes the concept of changing one's mind, coming to a new way of thinking. John the Baptist calls the people to repentance and demands proof of authentic conversion (Matt. 3:9–10). Yet John's message differs from that of the prophets in that his call for repentance is connected to the imminent arrival of God's kingdom and the coming of the Messiah (Matt. 3:2, 11–12; Luke 3:15–17). Moreover, John seals this repentance with a baptism of water for the forgiveness of sins (Mark 1:4; Luke 3:3).

Jesus's call to repentance is also closely linked to the arrival of God's kingdom (Mark 1:14–15). His summons to conversion, moreover, is associated with his own person, so that a decision for or against him signifies a choice for or against repentance (Matt. 11:20–24; 12:41–42). He comes to call sinners (Luke 5:32), and he tells parables that promise God's forgiveness to those who recognize their sinfulness (Luke 15; 18:9–14).

The Gospel of John does not use the word "repentance," but speaks of spiritual transformation as a new birth (3:3). Paul likewise employs the term "repentance" only rarely (Rom. 2:4; 2 Cor. 7:9–10), but frequently exhorts his readers to reject vice and practice virtue (Rom. 1:29–31; 13:13; 1 Cor. 5:10–11; 6:9–10; 2 Cor. 6:6–7; Gal. 5:19–23). His emphasis, however, is not on the human commitment to change one's lifestyle, but on the obedience of faith (Rom. 1:5), the transformation of one's mind and actions through the inner working of Christ and the sanctifying power of God's Holy Spirit (Rom. 6:22; 12:1–2; 2 Cor. 5:17; Gal. 2:20; 5:22–23).

The author of Hebrews develops the idiosyncratic notion that there cannot be a second repentance after one's initial conversion (6:4–6; 10:26; 12:16–17). The author of Revelation, however, calls seven churches to renewed repentance (2:5, 16; 3:3, 19).   F.J.M./M.A.P.

Rephaiah (ri-fay′yuh; Heb., "the LORD heals").
1 A descendant of Judah in the royal lineage of the kings of Judah (1 Chron. 3:21); the text is

not clear whether this is an individual or a family group.

2 One of the Simeonite leaders of the Ishi group who drove out the Amalekites and settled on Mount Seir (Edom; 1 Chron. 4:42).

3 The grandson of Issachar and a leader in the family group of Tola (1 Chron. 7:2).

4 A Benjaminite descendant of Saul (1 Chron. 9:43); he is also called Raphah (1 Chron. 8:37).

5 An official of postexilic Jerusalem who helped repair the city walls (Neh. 3:9).   D.R.B.

Rephaim (ref′ay-im).

1 Pre-Israelite inhabitants of Transjordan (Gen. 14:5; 15:20; Deut. 2:11, 20; 3:11, 13; Josh. 12:4; 13:12; 15:8; 17:15; 18:16). Little is known about them, but they are associated with great size. Og of Bashan, the last of the Rephaim, had a bed that was 9 cubits long and 4 cubits wide (Deut. 3:11). The Rephaim were called the Emim by the Moabites (Deut. 2:10–11) and the Zamzummim by the Amonites (Deut. 2:20–21). In Deut. 2:10–11, the Emim (Rephaim) are said to have been as tall as the Anakim, who were descended from the Nephilim, the race of giants produced by the mating of the sons of God and the daughters of humans before the flood (cf. Gen. 6:4). The word "Rephaim" is used in the NRSV only with reference to these pre-Israelite Transjordanians, but the Hebrew word *repha'im* (which "Rephaim" transliterates) is used in two other contexts in the Bible, as indicated by **2** and **3**.

2 The Hebrew word *repha'im* is translated "giants" in 2 Sam. 21:16, 18, 20 (cf. 1 Chron. 20:4, 6, 8). The reference is to four Philistine warriors descended from the "Rephaim," which could mean the pre-Israelite inhabitants of Transjordan (see **1**) or some mythical race of divine men, or a military guild that had taken this name for itself. *See also* giants.

3 The Hebrew word *repha'im* is translated "shades" in a number of passages where it seems to refer to the spirits of people who have died (Job 26:5; Ps. 88:10; Prov. 2:18; 9:18; 21:16; Isa. 14:9; 26:19). *See also* ghost; Sheol.   M.A.P.

Rephaim, Valley of, modern Baqa, the broad
valley or plain southwest of Jerusalem. The boundary between the tribal lands of Judah and Benjamin went up the Hinnom Valley from Jerusalem, passing the northern end of the Valley of Rephaim, to the Waters of Nephtoah (springs of Lifta today), northwest of Jerusalem (Josh. 15:8; 18:16). The Philistines encamped in the Valley of Rephaim, and David met them there in battle (2 Sam. 5:18, 22; 23:13). The valley was known for its fertility (Isa. 17:5).   N.L.L.

Rephidim (ref′i-dim), a stopping place for the
Israelites during the exodus after they left the Wilderness of Sin, but before they reached the Wilderness of Sinai (Exod. 17:1; 19:2; Num. 33:14–15). The people complained because there was no water there, so Moses struck a rock, and water

The miracle at Rephidim, where, according to Exod. 17:1–7, Moses struck a rock and caused water to flow out; wall painting from the catacomb of St. Callixtus, Rome, fourth century CE.

flowed miraculously (Exod. 17:1–7). Afterward, the Israelites fought against the Amalekites at Rephidim and discovered that they could prevail in the fight whenever Moses held up his hand, but not when he lowered it; so Aaron and Hur stood at his side until sunset, holding up his hands, and the Israelites prevailed (17:8–16). The location of Rephidim is uncertain; some identify it with the Wadi Refayid in southwest Sinai.

Resen (ree′suhn), a yet unidentified city in Assyria lying "between Nineveh and Calah" (Gen. 10:12) whose construction is ascribed to Nimrod.

reservoir, a natural or artificial rock-cut storage container for the collection of rainwater. Such installations, variously called reservoirs, pools, or cisterns, were essential for settlements relying almost totally on winter rains for their water source. Even sites located close to a spring augmented their water supply by such collection methods. Early Bronze Age exploitation of water resources is attested at Jawa, Arad, and Ai, but it was not until the second and first millennia BCE that public and private reservoirs multiplied greatly as the use of plaster for waterproofing became widespread. Kings constructed cisterns to hold water for times of siege (2 Kings 20:20) and for agriculture (2 Chron. 26:10), and great rock-cut pools are referred to at Hebron (2 Sam. 4:12), Samaria (1 Kings 22:38), and Gibeon (2 Sam. 2:13). Early Israelite settlement in the less fertile hill country was in large part made possible by means of plastered cisterns.   S.R.

Resheph (ree′shif; Canaanite, possibly "flame").

1 A Canaanite god of pestilence, equated in antiquity with Mesopotamian Nergal and Greek Apollo. The meaning of the name may reflect association with the heat of fever that accompanies sickness. The cult of Resheph is attested from earliest times in Mesopotamian sources (third millennium BCE) and, later, at Ras-Shamra. It penetrated

Egypt, especially during the Eighteenth Dynasty (ca. 1546–1319), where Resheph was thought of as a warrior. Transliteration of the name of this god became a Hebrew word, *resheph,* which the NRSV translates "pestilence" (Deut. 32:24; Ps. 78:48).

2 An Ephraimite who was the son of Rephah and the father of Tela (1 Chron. 7:25). The name in Hebrew means "pestilence" or "disease," but it since it seems unlikely that anyone would name a son this, the name probably reflects the Canaanite meaning of "flame" and may imply some association with the Canaanite deity.

rest.

1 Remainder (the most frequent meaning of the term; Gen. 14:10; 44:10; 1 Kings 11:41; 1 Chron. 11:8; Luke 12:26; Acts 15:17; Rev. 2:24).

2 The condition of repose, cessation of motion, or peaceful restoration. This meaning of the term occurs in a wide variety of biblical applications, translating several words. The model of God's resting on the seventh day (Gen. 2:2) established the sabbath as a day of rest (Lev. 16:31), the sabbatical year (25:3–6) as a year of rest for cultivated land, and the jubilee year as a periodic social restoration of wealth and property (25:8–17). The necessity of daily rest was recognized for animals (Ezek. 34:14) as well as for humans (2 Sam. 4:5). A special rest was often associated with the conclusion of a journey or pilgrimage (Deut. 12:10; Rev. 14:13). Rest is portrayed as a state of peace, contentment, and tranquility, with reference to the individual soul (Ps. 116:7), communities (Jer. 6:16), and the entire earth (Isa. 14:7). Such rest is hindered by distress, pain, or fruitless labor (Ps. 22:2; Eccles. 2:23).

A particular aspect of rest is associated with the cessation of war; a period of rest is a time of peace (Josh. 11:23; Judg. 3:11, 30; 5:31). In 2 Chron. 14:5 a peaceful rule under a king is described as a rest for the kingdom. Lack of international disturbance was viewed as a time of rest for the monarch (2 Chron. 20:30). Deliverance from oppression of enemies even during a siege was viewed as rest (2 Chron. 32:22).

The Bible also speaks of rest as a spiritual quality given by God to those in close harmony and fellowship with their Lord. In Exodus, God says to Moses, as the people set out from Sinai, "My presence will go with you, and I will give you rest" (33:14). In the NT, Jesus says, "Come to me, all you that are weary and are carrying heavy burdens, and I will give you rest. Take my yoke upon you, and learn from me; for I am gentle and humble in heart, and you will find rest for your souls" (Matt. 11:28–29).

The book of Hebrews develops the concept of divine rest as one of its central motifs. In 3:7–4:13, the author uses Ps. 95:7–11 to interpret the meaning of the Moses and Joshua stories, which had promised rest to God's people. He claims that the psalm reveals that the Israelites did not enter God's rest, because they did not listen to God's voice, but were unbelieving (3:12, 19), rebellious (3:16),

disobedient (4:6, 11), and hard of heart (3:13, 15; 4:10). Still, the author of Hebrews maintains that the plea to listen to God's voice "today" (Ps. 95:7) implies that God's rest is still available. Taking the "today" literally, he decides that the available rest can no longer be that associated with the exodus from Egypt or conquest of Canaan; rather, looking to Gen. 2:2, he determines it must be the "sabbath rest" that is now available (Heb. 4:9). Thus, the importance of hearing God's voice is exponentially greater than before, because doing so will bring one into the ultimate sabbath rest of God (4:9–11).   R.S.B./M.A.P.

restitution, a biblical concept closely related to the idea of restoration. Both are involved with sins committed against persons and/or property, either deliberately or inadvertently. Restoration appears to indicate replacement for whatever was taken or destroyed, whereas restitution seems to be repayment over and above the actual loss, analogous to what are today called "punitive" damages (e.g., Exod. 22:1–15; Lev. 6:1–7; Num. 5:5–7). For example, the ancient law found in Exod. 22:1, 4 stipulates that anyone who steals an ox or a sheep must pay restitution to the owner of the animal. If the thief kills or sells the ox, he is required to pay restitution of five oxen; if he kills or sells the sheep, he is required to pay restitution of four sheep (cf. also 2 Sam. 12:6). If, however, the animal has not been harmed and is found safe in the possession of the thief, the culprit is required to pay double. If the thief has no means to pay this fine, he is to be sold into slavery for his theft.

In Leviticus, it is commanded that if someone robs or cheats a neighbor, that person is to restore the amount in full and add a fifth to it (6:1–7). In addition, the guilty party was required to make a guilt offering. This principle is reflected in the NT story of Zacchaeus, who says that he will repay fourfold anyone he has defrauded (Luke 19:1–10). The biblical principle of restitution is in view, but Zacchaeus' offer of fourfold payment goes well beyond the legal requirement. *See also* forgiveness; law; reconciliation.   J.M.E.

Rest of Esther. *See* Esther, Additions to.

resurrection.

1 A rising to life from death. The Bible contains numerous accounts of prophets or other spiritually empowered people restoring life to those who have died. This is typically presented as one of the greatest of all miracles, surpassing mere acts of healing. In the Hebrew Bible, Elijah raises a widow's son from the dead (1 Kings 17:17–24), and Elisha raises a Shunammite woman's son from the dead (2 Kings 4:32–37; see also 2 Kings 13:20–21). In the NT, Jesus raises three people from the dead: Jairus's daughter (Mark 5:22–42; cf. Matt. 9:18–25; Luke 8:41–56); the son of a widow at Nain (Luke 7:11–15); and his friend Lazarus (John 11:1–44). He also mentions the dead being raised as one of the messianic signs that would allow John the Baptist and others to recognize him as the one who was to come (Matt. 11:2–6). Furthermore, Jesus instructs his disciples to raise the dead (Matt. 10:8). The book of Acts reports that Peter raised the widow Dorcas from the dead (9:36–41). Paul is possibly presented as raising Eutychus from the dead, though it is possible Eutychus had only been unconscious (20:9–12; the text does not make clear whether he was presumed dead or actually dead).

2 A restoration from mortal death to a state of immortality. In a theological sense, this is what is usually meant by "resurrection." It is to be distinguished from temporary resuscitation (as depicted in 1). Resurrection in this more profound sense implies that the persons brought back from the dead will never die again. Indeed, they will have spiritual bodies that no longer suffer the limitations of mortal flesh (1 Cor. 15:35–55).

Resurrection in this sense is primarily a NT concept, dependent upon developments in Jewish thinking during the Second Temple period. The only clear reference to resurrection to immortal or eternal life in the Hebrew Bible is Dan. 12:2, which says, "Many of those who sleep in the dust of the earth shall awake, some to everlasting life, and some to shame and everlasting contempt." Another possible reference is Isa. 26:19 ("Your dead shall live, their corpses shall rise"), but it is possible that this was meant metaphorically, and it is not clear that Isaiah envisioned resurrection to eternal life (as opposed to temporary resuscitation). Nevertheless, during the Second Temple period, when the book of Daniel was written, the concept that the mortal dead would be raised to a transformed state of immortal life took hold and

The general resurrection at the end of history as depicted in a panel of the Verdun Altar, 1180.

seems to have been almost taken for granted by NT authors. There is acknowledgment, however, that not all Jews believed this (Mark 12:18).

This concept of resurrection is to be distinguished from the Greek concept of the immortality of the soul. Belief in *resurrection* implies that a person who was truly dead is brought back to life; belief in *immortality of the soul* implies that the person's true self (soul) does not die, which obviates the need for resurrection. Thus the doctrine of resurrection assumes that death is total—the whole person (body, mind, soul, spirit) dies, and no part of that person remains alive. God then brings the whole person (body, mind, soul, spirit) back to life. Biblical materials, however, do evince degrees of acceptance of the notion of immortality. The concept of Sheol in the Bible allowed for some sort of continued existence of the dead, albeit in a shadowy state (Pss. 6:5; 30:9; 88:1–12; 115:17). The widespread belief in ghosts, even in the NT period (Matt. 14:26; Luke 24:37–39; cf. Deut. 8:19; 18:11; 19:3) also indicates that belief in the absolute finality of death may have been somewhat compromised.

Nevertheless, Paul presents the most extensive biblical teaching on resurrection in 1 Cor. 15 and does so in a way that distinguishes the concept from both the Greek idea of immortality of the soul and the traditional Hebrew notion of extended mortal life. Resurrection, for Paul, denotes a complete transformation of the person into a being that now has eternal life (1 Cor. 15:35–55). Just *how* this happens is unclear, but Paul seems to liken future resurrection to a reenactment of creation. Just as God created the person initially, so God will re-create that person, with a body that is no longer made of flesh (1 Cor. 15:35–55). This thinking may also be reflected in Jesus's comment that, in the resurrection, people will be like angels (Mark 12:25).

Resurrection of Jesus: The earliest references to the resurrection of Jesus are not found in the Gospels, but in 1 Cor. 15:3–8, written by Paul ca. 55 CE. He quotes the teaching he says he had delivered to the Corinthians when he founded that community, ca. 50 CE, and indicates that this was already a tradition that he had received (1 Cor. 15:3–7). Thus, the tradition can be traced to a very early time. Notably, this earliest account of the resurrection tradition does not focus on an empty tomb (to which Paul only alludes through mention of Jesus's burial), but on the appearances of the Risen One. The word used for "appeared" (ōphthē), furthermore, is the same Greek word used elsewhere for visionary experiences; thus, Paul makes no distinction between the postresurrection appearances of Jesus to his disciples (he mentions no appearances to Mary Magdalene or to the women at the tomb) and the appearance of Jesus to him (15:8). These visionary encounters with Jesus were sufficient for him to know that Jesus had been raised from the dead and, indeed, that Jesus had been raised to new, immortal life. For Paul, the latter point was most important: the resurrection was viewed as "first fruits" in anticipation of the general resurrection of all people that would follow as a result (1 Cor. 15:20–22). For Paul, the resurrection of Jesus was a proleptic indicator that the new era of eternal salvation had begun.

The story of the empty tomb as found in the Gospels belongs to a slightly later tradition; what is probably the earliest account (in Mark 16:1–8) was written ca. 65–70 CE. This tradition nevertheless appears to rest on an early report of Mary Magdalene and other women who visited the tomb of Jesus after his burial and discovered it empty. In itself, such a discovery would not necessarily establish a resurrection, for an empty tomb would be susceptible to other explanations, some of which are mentioned (and dismissed) in the Gospels (cf. Matt. 28:13; Mark 15:47; John 20:15). Still, the narrative of the empty tomb became an effective vehicle for proclaiming the resurrection faith confirmed by appearances of the Risen Lord to his disciples. The Gospel narratives also emphasize that Jesus appeared to people in a more material way than might have been suggested by Paul's references to such appearances. Jesus walks on earth as he had walked before (Luke 24:15). He talks, eats, drinks, and invites people to touch him (Luke 24:39–43; John 20:27; 21:12–13). *See also* ascension of Christ; death; eternal life; Hades; immortality; Sheol; soul; tomb of Jesus.

Bibliography

Allison, Dale. *Resurrecting Jesus: The Earliest Christian Tradition and Its Interpreters.* Clark, 2005.

Fuller, Reginald H. *The Formation of the Resurrection Narratives.* Fortress, 1980.

Perkins, Pheme. *Resurrection, New Testament Witness and Contemporary Reflection.* Doubleday, 1984.

Sawicki, Marianne. *Seeing the Lord: Resurrection and Early Christian Practices.* Fortress, 1994.

Wright, N. T. *The Resurrection of the Son of God.* Fortress, 2003.   R.H.F./M.A.P.

retribution, the concept of repaying in kind. Retribution as a principle of human law was well established in antiquity, and biblical Israel was no exception. The most famous expression of this principle is the "law of retaliation" (Lat. *lex talionis*) stated in Deuteronomy: "Life for life, eye for eye, tooth for tooth, hand for hand, foot for foot" (19:21). Although this principle is explicitly commended in antithesis to showing pity (which in Deut. 19:21 one is not to do), its articulation and application within the broader corpus of Israelite law demonstrates that the primary function was to limit retaliation (no more than an eye for an eye, etc.). The *lex talionis* served as a guarantee that punishment would not exceed the crime (cf. Exod. 21:23–25; Lev. 24:19–20). Furthermore, in Exod. 21:22, it is not the aggrieved individual who decides how the principle is to be applied in any specific case, but rather judges who make the determination. In broader terms, retribution is presented as the prerogative of God. The prophets

speak of God's just punishments for injustice and idolatry, upon both Israel's enemies and Israel and Judah themselves (Isa. 66:6; Jer. 5:9, 29; 9:9). The "day of the LORD" will be a day of retribution against God's enemies (Jer. 46:10). From this develops the concept that human beings should trust in God to bring just retribution against those who wrong them rather than seeking to effect such retribution themselves. Jeremiah translated this hope into actual prayer: "O LORD . . . bring down retribution for me on my persecutors" (15:15; cf. 20:12; 46:10). This line of thinking is continued in the NT, where Jesus proposes an ethic of nonretaliation in place of the traditional "eye for an eye" (Matt. 5:38–42). Paul echoes the same theme in Rom. 12:17, assuring his readers, however, that "the wrath of God" will provide vengeance where it is due (12:19–21). Thus, both Jesus and Paul discourage humans from seeking retribution, but insist that God effects retribution. Jesus says, "With the judgment you make you will be judged, and the measure you give will be the measure you get" (Matt. 7:2; cf. Mark 4:24; Luke 6:38; Matt. 18:23–35; 25:31–46); Paul warns, "Do not be deceived; God is not mocked, for you reap whatever you sow" (Gal. 6:7–8). *See also* law; vengeance.

                         W.S.T./M.A.P.

Return of Christ. *See* eschatology; Parousia.

Reu (ree′yoo), the son of Peleg; a descendant of Shem and an ancestor of Abraham (Gen. 11:18–21). He figures in the ancestry of Jesus through Joseph (Luke 3:35).

Reuben (roo′bin; Heb., "look, a son!").

1 The firstborn son of Jacob by his wife Leah and the ancestor of the tribe that bears his name (Gen. 29:32; 35:23; 46:8; 49:2–3; Exod. 1:1–2; 6:14; Num. 26:5; 1 Chron. 2:1; 5:1, 3). According to Gen. 29:32, Leah named him at his birth, in hope that the birth of a son would prompt her husband to love her (perhaps more than her sister, Rachel, who was Jacob's favored wife).

Gen. 30:14–15 depicts Reuben as a child who gathers mandrakes (associated with fertility) for his mother and presents them to her; she trades them to Rachel to gain another night with Jacob, which leads to the birth of Issachar (30:16–18). Later (after Rachel's death), Reuben has intercourse with Rachel's slave Bilhah, who was also his father's concubine (35:19–22). Some interpreters have suggested that the purpose of this act might have been to cause his father to return to Leah's tent by "spoiling" the woman whose children would continue to be attributed to Rachel's side of the family. In any case, it was viewed as a usurpation of authority (cf. 2 Sam. 16:21–22) and ultimately led to Reuben's disenfranchisement as the firstborn (Gen. 49:3–4; 1 Chron. 5:1–2). In the meantime, however, Reuben is portrayed as exercising a key role in the Joseph story. When his brothers plan to kill Joseph, he intervenes, suggesting they put him in a pit instead. The brothers do this, but then sell Joseph as a slave to the Ishmaelites, perhaps spoiling Reuben's plan to rescue him (Gen. 37:20–30; cf. 42:21–22). Reuben is also depicted as offering his sons as surety for the life of Benjamin when the latter accompanies the brothers to Egypt (42:37).

Many scholars interpret the information about Reuben in Genesis as reflective of the fortune of the tribe. The Reubenites once enjoyed a prominent role among the Israelites and thus Reuben is the firstborn, but in the course of time the tribe weakened. Reuben's intercourse with Bilhah is then viewed as providing an etiological explanation for the fact that the initial power of the Reuben tribe passed to the tribes of Judah and Joseph (as indicated by the superior influence of Judah and Joseph in the Joseph story; see also Gen. 49:8–12, 22–26; Deut. 33:13–17; 1 Chron. 5:1–2). *See also* Bilhah; Jacob; Leah.

2 The tribe that carried the name of the firstborn of Jacob and Leah, Reuben (Gen. 29:32). As such the tribe is mentioned first in the list of those who leave Egypt (Exod. 6:14), in the list of the tribal leaders in the desert (Num. 1:5), in the census taken there (1:20–21; 26:5–10), in the Blessing of Moses (Deut. 33:6), and in the apportionment of the land by Joshua (Josh. 13:15–23; see also Num. 2:10, 16; 7:30; 18:18; Deut. 13:4; Ezek. 48:31). This placement, however, is not followed by the Chronicler, whose emphasis is on the Davidic dynasty. Chronicles acknowledges Reuben as the first of Jacob/Israel's sons (1 Chron. 2:1; see also 27:16), but proceeds to list the genealogy of the tribe of Judah first (2:1–4:19). The most complete genealogy of Reuben is found in 1 Chron. 5:3–8.

According to Num. 32, Moses granted the Reubenites and the Gadites their request to dwell in Gilead due to the pastureland available there for their cattle. The one agreed condition was that they spearhead the capture of western Canaan (see also Josh. 1:12–18). After Joshua's victories, they were permitted to return to Gilead (Josh. 22:1–9). The sources (Num. 32:33–38; Josh. 13:15–23; 1 Chron. 5:8–10; 6:63–64), although not always consistent, indicate that the Reubenites settled south of Gad in Gilead, north of the Arnon River (but see Josh. 15:6; 18:17, which might indicate a Reubenite settlement west of the Jordan).

Due to the paucity of material, the history of the tribe is difficult to reconstruct. Scholarly conjecture holds that the biblical viewpoint of Reuben as Jacob's firstborn suggests Reuben was once a powerful tribe. However, Jacob's rebuke (Gen. 49:4; cf. 1 Chron. 5:1) and Moses's blessing (Deut. 33:6) indicate that Reuben became weak.

The Song of Deborah (Judg. 5:15–16) testifies to the tribe's refusal to join the battle against Sisera, but 1 Chron. 5:10 witnesses to the Reubenites' strength during the days of Saul (late eleventh century BCE). The captivity of Reubenite families by Tiglath-pileser III of Assyria in 732 BCE (1 Chron. 5:6) is the last historical mention of the tribe. The prophet Ezekiel predicts the ultimate resettlement of the tribe alongside the others (48:6–7, 31). *See also* Gilead; tribes. J.U.

Reuel (roo´uhl; Heb., "friend of God").
1 The son of Esau and Basemath, the daughter of Ishmael, whose descendants show Esau's ties with Edom (Gen. 36).
2 The priest of Midian and father of Hobab, who gave his daughter Zipporah in marriage to Moses (Exod. 2; Num. 10:29). He is probably to be identified with the same individual who is also called Jethro (Exod. 4:18). *See also* Hobab; Jethro; Midian, Midianites; Moses; Zipporah.
3 A Gadite, father of Eliasaph (Num. 2:14).
4 A Benjaminite living in Jerusalem who was the son of Ibnijah and the grandfather of Meshullam (1 Chron. 9:8). H.B.H.

revelation. The concept of revelation in the Bible assumes an unveiling of what was always true, whether as enduring reality, past event, or foreordained future. The term also implies that, although whatever is being revealed was true all along, it has been truth that was concealed or largely unknown.

Human beings may reveal human secrets (Prov. 11:13), but God is the revealer of ultimate truth, and the knowledge that results from such revelation comes as a divine gift. God is said to reveal Torah (i.e., teachings of the law; Deut. 29:29), secrets (Amos 3:7; Dan. 2:29), and prophecies (1 Cor. 14:29–30). In a single breath, Paul speaks of the righteousness of God being revealed through faith (Rom. 1:17) and the wrath of God being revealed against all ungodliness (1:18). He also maintains that the experience through which Christ appeared to him and called him to be an apostle was a revelation from God (Gal. 1:16). The prophet, apostle, or other agent who receives such revelations may be obliged to transmit them to others (Amos 3:7–8; Gal. 1:15–17) or may be instructed to keep some revelations hidden (Rev. 10:4), perhaps because it would be altogether wrong to utter them (2 Cor. 12:1–4) or because they are intended for another era (Dan. 12:9; 2 Esd. 14).

The principal modes by which human beings receive revelations in the biblical documents are visions (e.g., Jer. 1:11–13) and auditions (e.g., Isa. 22:14). These may come while one is awake or in dreams. God may speak directly to a human being or through an angelic intermediary, and sometimes the two modes are difficult to distinguish, as in Moses's encounter with the burning bush (Exod. 3:2–4) and Abraham's meeting with the three travelers (Gen. 18:1–19:1). Revelation may also be made available in the created order itself (Rom. 1:18–23). Revelation is not limited to extraordinary experiences; some texts seem to treat it more as a matter of inner conviction (e.g., Ps. 16:7) or the interpretation of historical events (111:6). *See also* dreams; inspiration; vision.
L.W.C.

Revelation, book of, the last book of the NT, also called the Apocalypse. The term "apocalypse" comes from the Greek word for "revelation," which is used in the preface to characterize the work (1:1).

Contents: After a brief preface (1:1–3) and a salutation similar to those with which many NT letters begin (1:4–8), John reports that he received a revelation while "in the spirit on the Lord's day" (1:10) and that he was directed to write this revelation in a book and send it to seven churches. The first thing he sees is a spectacular image of the Son of Man, who dictates seven letters to him, specific messages for each of the churches (chaps. 2–3). After recording these letters, John sees a door open in heaven, and he is taken up into the heavenly realm itself. There, he beholds the throne of God, angels, and other wondrous creatures (chap. 4). The one seated on the divine throne holds a scroll with seven seals; there is a search to find one who is worthy to open this scroll—the only one worthy is the Lion of Judah, who, as it

The end of the Revelation to John in the Codex Sinaiticus, an outstanding fourth-century CE manuscript of the Greek Bible.

turns out, does not look like a lion, but like a lamb that has been slaughtered (chap. 5). One by one, this Lamb opens the seals of the scroll, and as he does this, catastrophes strike the earth until, with the sixth seal, stars fall from the sky and the sky itself rolls up like a scroll and disappears (chap. 6). Then angels intervene to ensure the safety of God's faithful ones; 144,000 people of Israel are marked for protection, and John sees an innumerable multitude of people, robed in white, from all nations being brought before the Lamb (chap. 7). The Lamb opens the seventh seal, initiating a half hour of silence in heaven (8:1). Seven angels appear, each with a trumpet, and as these trumpets are blown, more disasters strike the earth (chaps. 8–9). But following the sixth trumpet, there is a brief interlude during which an angel appears with a small scroll, shouting with a sound of seven thunders. John is told to seal up what the seven thunders said and not write it down, and he is given the scroll to eat; it tastes sweet, but makes his stomach bitter (chap. 10). He then takes some measurements in heaven and is told about two witnesses who will come to the earth and be martyred, raised, and taken up into heaven. Finally, the seventh angel blows the seventh trumpet, and God's temple in heaven is opened amid loud shouts of praise (chap. 11). Great portents appear in heaven: a cosmic, pregnant woman and a red dragon, who turns out to be Satan. War breaks out as the archangel Michael leads the heavenly forces to defeat Satan (chap. 12). On earth, a series of beasts blaspheme God, oppress the saints, and insist on conformity to idolatrous ways (chap. 13). Angels call for saints to endure this tribulation, and John beholds a vision of the Son of Man reaping the earth with a massive sickle; the wrath of God comes mightily upon the earth, as evidenced by an awful river of blood (chap. 14). Seven angels with seven bowls appear, and each bowl brings a terrible plague upon the earth (chaps. 15–16).

John is invited to witness the judgment of a great whore, who is identified as the city of Babylon. Her downfall is lamented on earth, but celebrated in heaven (chaps. 17–18). Amid great canticles of praise, John then sees heaven opened, and a rider who is called Faithful and True comes on a white horse to wage a final victorious war against all the kings of earth. The flesh of those kings is consumed in a grotesque but spectacular banquet, and the beasts responsible for the tribulation mentioned earlier are thrown into a lake of fire (chaps. 19). Satan is imprisoned, and those who proved faithful in the previous trials are allowed to reign with Christ on earth for one thousand years. After that time, Satan is released for a final battle and then is also thrown into the lake of fire to be tormented forever and ever (chap. 20). Then John sees a new heaven and a new earth, and a new Jerusalem coming down from heaven. He concludes his book with a vision of paradise: gates of pearl and streets of gold, and a city where there is no fear or pain or trouble of any kind (chaps. 21–22).

Genre: The book of Revelation exhibits features of three types of literature: letter (1:4–8; 22:21), prophecy (1:3; 22:7, 10, 18–19), and especially apocalypse. The apocalypse is an ancient genre of heavily symbolic literature that claimed to unveil the truth about the world as viewed from a dualistic and deterministic perspective. Apocalyptic thought, which underlies Revelation and other apocalypses, typically offers a pessimistic forecast for the world at large combined with an optimistic outlook for a favored remnant, who will be rescued out of the evil world through some imminent act of divine intervention.

Three modes of interpretation have been applied to Revelation. (1) In a popular vein, the book is considered from a *futurist* perspective, assuming that its symbols and images will apply to people and events at the end of time. Interpreters who employ this approach usually believe that they *are* living at the end of time and that the meaning of the book is becoming apparent. (2) Virtually all academic scholars analyze Revelation from a *preterist* (or *historical*) perspective, assuming that its symbols and images were meaningful to the people in the first century for whom the book was written. The goal of interpretation, then, is to determine what the book would have meant to its first readers. (3) In between these two approaches lies an *idealist* approach, which grants a more timeless quality to the book's symbols and images, assuming that they may have universal and polyvalent

application. This approach is often combined with one of the other two; it is then viewed as seeking an additional level of meaning supplemental to the primary futurist or historical sense.

Historical Situation: The book recounts a vision received by a Christian prophet named John on the island of Patmos, where he has apparently been exiled on account of his faith (1:9). Popular traditions often identify this "John" with John the apostle, one of Jesus's twelve disciples, but that identification was questioned in the early church, and it is challenged by the great majority of modern scholars. Although it is granted that the author of Revelation could have been associated with the same circle of churches that produced the Gospel of John and the Johannine Letters, he is usually assumed to be a different person from either John the apostle or John the elder, two individuals sometimes associated with those writings. In any case, the report of his vision is intended for seven churches in the Roman province of Asia (1:4). The time of writing is uncertain, but most scholars link the book to one of two crises in first-century Christianity: the persecution of Christians under Nero (ca. 64–68) or that under Domitian (ca. 95). The number of the beast referred to 13:18 (666 in most manuscripts; 616 in others) is gematria for Caesar Nero in Hebrew (666 when spelled *nwrn rsq* or 616 when spelled *wrn rsq*). Still, like many other clues to the book's dating (11:1–2; 17:9–11), this is not conclusive. The identification of Nero as "the beast" could be literal if the book were written during his reign or figurative if it were written later (i.e., Domitian is like "a second Nero"). In any case, the book's stated purpose is to reveal "what must soon take place," and it strives to do this in ways that will inspire confidence in those whose obedience to God may prove costly, stir up indignation toward those who defy God and promote injustice, provoke repentance on the part of those who have been overly accommodating, and inspire praise for God from those who realize the Lord of history is worthy of their trust.

Major Themes: The most obvious theme in this book may be its negative portrayal of human society as corrupt and unjust. For all its splendor, the Roman Empire is pictured as a decadent abomination destined to suffer the condemnation and wrath of God. The book is recognized as a work that takes seriously the power and nature of sin, portraying unrighteousness, not merely as personal immorality, but more profoundly as systemic evil and social injustice. It offers a sustained political critique of an anti-God society, a society that uses its power to dominate or enslave others, that becomes prosperous by making others poor, that revels in self-adulation, that ignores the suffering of the innocent, and that allows or perpetrates violence against the righteous. A second, compatible, theme in Revelation presents God as the one who controls the future; despite present tribulation, an ultimately hopeful outcome for believers is assured. Finally, the book of Revelation is heavily liturgical; it encourages adulation of God and the Lamb (5:12; cf. 4:11) and is threaded with songs of worship and hymns of praise (1:5–6; 4:8, 11; 5:9–14; 7:10–12; 11:15–18; 12:10–12; 15:3–4; 16:5–7; 19:1–8). *See also* apocalyptic literature; Nero; Roman Empire.

Bibliography

Aune, David E. *Revelation*. 3 vols. Thomas Nelson, 1997–98.

Bauckham, Richard J. *The Theology of the Book of Revelation*. Cambridge University Press, 1993.

Beale, G. K. *The Book of Revelation: A Commentary on the Greek Text*. Eerdmans, 1999.

Koester, Craig. *Revelation and the End of All Things*. Eerdmans, 2001.

Mounce, Robert H. *Revelation*. Eerdmans, 1997.

Osborne, Grant R. *Revelation*. Baker Academic, 2002.

Powell, Mark Allan. *Introducing the New Testament: A Historical, Literary, and Theological Survey*. Baker Academic, 2009. Pp. 519–37.   M.A.P.

SYMBOLISM IN REVELATION

Symbols interpreted within the book itself:

Seven lampstands are churches; seven stars are angels (1:20).	Seven heads are seven mountains, but also seven kings (17:9).
Four horses are conquest, slaughter, famine, death (6:1–7).	Ten horns are ten kings yet to receive their kingdoms (17:12).
The red dragon is Satan (12:9).	The woman is "the great city" (17:18).

Colors with symbolic associations:

White: victory or purity (1:14; 2:17; 3:4–5, 18; 4:4; 6:2, 11; 7:9, 13–14; 14:14; 19:11, 14; 20:11).	Scarlet: perverse luxury (17:3–4; 18:12, 16).
Red: destruction (6:4; 12:3), bloodshed (6:12), fire (9:17).	Black: mourning (6:5, 12).
Purple: royalty, luxury (17:4; 18:12, 16).	Pale: death (6:8).

Numbers with symbolic associations:

3: the spiritual realm (8:13; 16:13; 21:3).	10: totality (2:10; 12:3; 31:1; 17:3, 7, 12, 16).
3½: tribulation (11:9; cf. Dan. 7:25; 9:27; 12:7); likewise, 1260 days = 42 thirty-day months or 3½ years (11:3; 12:6).	12: Israel (12:1; 21:12–14, 16, 21; 22:2); likewise, 24 (4:4, 10; 5:8, 14; 11:16; 19:4); and 144 (7:4–8; 14:1–5; 21:17).
4: the earth (4:6–8; 5:6, 8, 14; 6:1–8; 7:1–2, 11; 9:13–15; 14:3; 15:7; 19:4; 20:8; 21:16).	1,000: a very great number; thousands of thousands = unimaginably large (5:11); 144,000 = a large Jewish multitude (7:4–8; 14:1–5); 7,000 = a "complete" large number— as many as necessary (11:13); 1,000 years = a very long time (20:2–7).
6: failure (13:18).	
7: perfection or completion (1:4, 12, 16, 20; 3:1; 4:5; 5:1, 6; 8:2; 10:3; 11:13; 15:1, 7; 17:9); but sometimes 7 appears to signify Rome, which was built on seven hills (12:3; 13:1; 17:3, 7, 9, 11).	

Animals with symbolic associations:

Lamb: sacrifice (5:6–8, 12–13; 6:1, 3, 5, 7, 16; 7:9–10, 14, 17; 8:1; 12:11; 13:8, 11; 14:1, 4, 10; 15:3; 17:14; 19:7, 9; 21:9, 14, 22–23; 22:1, 3).	Lion: might, royalty (5:5; 10:3; 13:2).
	Eagle: perseverance, victory (8:13; 12:14).

Imagery drawn from the Hebrew Bible:

Trumpet blasts (1:10; 4:1; 8:2–11:15): see Gen. 19:16–19; Joel 2:1.	Plagues (8:7–9:20): see Exod. 7:17; 9:18; 10:4, 21.
Blackened sun, moon like blood, falling stars (6:12): see Isa 13:10; 50:3; Joel 2:10.	Hybrid beast (13:2): see Dan. 7:4–6.

Poetic imagery with no specific referent:

"A rainbow that looks like an emerald" (4:3).	"A sea of glass, like crystal" (4:6).

From Mark Allan Powell, *Introducing the New Testament* (courtesy, Baker Academic)

revenge. *See* avenger.

Rezeph (ree′zif), a town cited as having fallen to Assyria (2 Kings 19:12; Isa. 37:12) and symbolizing in part the unstoppable Assyrian force. From Assyrian royal records it is known as Rasappa, and had served as an Assyrian provincial capital after its capture, probably by Shalmaneser III ca. 838 BCE. Possibly it is modern Rezzafeh, about a hundred miles southeast of Aleppo, off the south bank of the Euphrates River.

Rezin (ree′zin; Heb., "pleasant, agreeable").
1 The king of Damascus 738–732 BCE. Upon accession to the throne, Rezin paid tribute to the Assyrian king Tiglath-pileser III, but within three years he had organized an anti-Assyrian coalition consisting of Damascus, Tyre, Philistia, Israel, some Arab tribes, and perhaps Edom. When King Ahaz of Judah refused to join, the allies seized part of his territory, including Elath on the Red Sea. Rezin's attempt to take Jerusalem and depose Ahaz failed (Isa. 7:1–10), however, and Tiglath-pileser soon crushed the allies. After neutralizing Phoenicia and Philistia in 734 BCE, he devastated Rezin's territory in 733. Damascus survived, but the following year, bereft of its allies, the city fell, and Rezin was executed (2 Kings 16:5–9). *See also* Ahaz; Isaiah, book of; Pekah.
2 The ancestor of a group of temple servants in the postexilic period (Ezra 2:48; Neh. 7:50).
J.J.M.R.

Rezon (ree′zuhn; Heb., "potentate"), the son of Eliadah (1 Kings 11:23), one of the adversaries raised by God against Solomon on account of Solomon's sin in taking foreign wives. He is sometimes identified with Hezion (1 Kings 15:18), the Aramean Rezon who mutinied against Hadadezer and established in Damascus an independent fiefdom that broke free of Israelite hegemony.

Rhegium (ree′jee-uhm), a Greek colony (modern Reggio di Calabria) located at the southwestern tip of the Italian boot, opposite Messana in Sicily. Although a Roman ally as early as the Punic Wars, Rhegium maintained a Greek character into the time of the Roman Empire. In spite of numerous earthquakes, it remained well populated throughout the first century CE and was a center for Pythagorean philosophy. Unfavorable winds hindered navigation between the narrow straits, perhaps explaining Paul's delay there (Acts 28:13).

Rhoda (roh′duh), a slave who worked as a "maid" (Acts 12:13; NRSV) in the home of Mary, the mother of John Mark, in Jerusalem. When Peter was miraculously released from prison and came to the house, she answered his knock, but was so overcome at the surprise of seeing him that she ran and announced his presence to the others without first letting him in (Acts 12:12–16). *See also* Mark; Mary; Peter.

Rhodes (rohdz), an island off the southwest tip of Asia Minor (1 Macc. 15:23; Acts 21:1). In the third century BCE the Rhodian navy guarded seaborne trade in the Mediterranean. The city was famous for a colossal statue of Apollo, which was destroyed by an earthquake in 227/6 BCE. Roman conquest of Greek territories after the conclusion of the third Macedonian war in 167 BCE ended the island's prosperity as a commercial center. Rhodes was stripped of its territories in Asia Minor and saw its banking and shipping revenues drop by 90 percent. With Rhodes no longer able to support a navy, the pirates and slave traders of Cilicia and Crete preyed on Mediterranean trade until Pompey rid the area of pirates in the 60s BCE. Rhodes was pillaged by Cassius in 43 BCE, but the island returned to a modicum of prosperity under Roman rule. It was known as a cultural center and as a center of higher education. It was also known for its healthful climate. Paul passed Rhodes on his sea journey from Ephesus to Tyre (Acts 21:1).
P.P.

Riblah (rib′luh).
1 A city in the Lebanese Beqa'a Valley that guarded the important international thoroughfare connecting Egypt with northern Syria and Mesopotamia. Situated about seven miles south of Kedesh on the Orontes at a crossing place of the river, Riblah functioned as a strategic military base during the seventh and sixth centuries BCE. Here, Pharaoh Neco II established the Egyptian headquarters following his defeat of Josiah at Megiddo and the capture of Kedesh in 609 BCE. In the same year Neco summoned Jehoahaz to Riblah, deposed him, put him in chains, and appointed Jehoiakim as Judah's king in his stead (2 Kings 23:31–35). Two decades later, after the Babylonian conquest of Jerusalem, Nebuchadnezzar brought King Zedekiah to Riblah, killed his sons before his eyes, then blinded him and carried him off in chains to Babylon (2 Kings 25:5–7; Jer. 52:9–11). Many of Judah's leading officials were also brought to Riblah and executed at that time (2 Kings 25:19–21). The ruins of the ancient site are near the modern village of Ribleh.
2 According to Num. 34:11, a border city on the northeast corner of the promised land (cf. Ezek. 6:14), but it is uncertain whether this is the same city as 1.   D.A.D.

riddle, in the Bible, a saying with purposely veiled meaning or meaning that is not immediately clear. The clearest example is Samson's riddle of the lion and the honey; the answer was to be guessed by his groomsmen; but they would have to have seen what he had seen in order to know that answer (Judg. 14:12–19). In a different context, the mark of a wise person was the ability to understand riddles (Prov. 1:6; cf. Dan. 5:11–12); thus, the queen of Sheba came to Solomon with "hard questions" (1 Kings 10:1; 1 Chron. 9:1). A riddle could also refer to an allegorical saying in which the meaning was deliberately concealed by symbolism (Ezek. 17:2–24; cf. 24:1–15); riddles might include "dark speech" that required interpretation (Num. 12:8; cf. John 10:6; 16:25, 29). A perplexing moral problem could be termed a riddle (Ps. 49:4), and in this sense the numerical sayings of Prov. 30:15–31 illustrate a riddle form in which things are described as "too wonderful" to be easily understood. The element of "hiddenness" implied in the riddle also allowed the term to be used in a negative sense to describe the shrewdness and deceit of the insolent king in Daniel's vision (8:23–25). *See also* proverb; wisdom.   D.R.B.

righteousness, the state of being right, of being in a right relationship with someone or something, or of being vindicated. "Righteousness" renders an important Hebrew root, *tsdq,* that appears over 500 times in the Bible, and a Greek root, *dikaio-,* that appears over 225 times in the NT. English Bibles translate these terms as "righteousness" (or "right," "righteous," "make right," etc.) in some instances, as "justice" (or "just," etc.) in other instances, and as "justification" (or "justify," etc.) in still other instances. The interrelatedness of such seemingly diverse concepts reflects the richness of the biblical terms and indicates that the English words only approximate the fullness of what was expressed in the original languages (e.g., the noun *dikaiosynē* does not mean "righteousness" in some instances and "justice" in other instances, but always means something that incorporates what is intended by both of those words, and English translators must choose which approximation fits best in each particular context).

In the Hebrew Bible: Righteousness is used of God (Pss. 119:137–38, 144; Isa. 24:16), the king (Pss. 45:4, 7; 72:1–7), the community or nation (Pss. 32:11; 92:11), and individuals (Ezek. 18:5–9; e.g., Noah, Gen. 6:9). Some interpreters stress righteousness as conforming to a norm, the Torah, or "what is right" (Deut. 16:20). Others see the concept as more relational, fitting the situation (Gen. 38:26; 1 Sam. 24:17). Often a law-court setting is involved: the guilty are condemned, the innocent acquitted (Deut. 16:18; 25:1; Isa. 5:23). This forensic (i.e., legal) use extends to God's judgment too (Ps. 7:7–11; Jer. 2:4–13; 12:1; Mic. 6:1–8). God's loyalty to (covenant) promises is likewise part of God's righteousness (Neh. 9:7–8, 33; Dan. 9:14–16).

There is a strong ethical component to righteousness, as seen in righteous or upright conduct (Lev. 19:36; Pss. 1:6; 23:3; Prov. 8:20; 13:6; 16:13; 21:3). For Abraham, believing God's promise was reckoned as righteousness (Gen. 15:6). Habakkuk likewise stresses that the righteous live by their faith (2:4).

The term also refers to God's saving actions, to God's "vindication" (Isa. 62:1–2), "deliverance" (Isa. 46:12–13; 51:5, 6, 8), "victory" (Isa. 41:2), or "triumphs" (Judg. 5:11). "The LORD is our righteousness" refers to God as savior (Jer. 23:6; cf. Isa. 45:21). Hence "the righteous" become those who trust in God's vindication (Ps. 37:12–13; Jer. 20:12). The Dead Sea Scrolls speak often of a "teacher of righteousness" and describe God's righteousness as offering hope for redemption from sin.

In the NT: Jesus sought "sinners," not "the righteous" of the day (Mark 2:17). Jesus called for righteousness (Matt. 5:20), but also spoke of it, like the kingdom, as God's gift (Matt. 5:6; 6:33). The early Christians drew upon "righteousness" language from the scriptures to express the meaning of Jesus's death. Jesus is the "Righteous One" (Acts 3:14; 7:52) whose suffering and resurrection bring the unrighteous to God (1 Pet. 3:18; cf. Rom. 4:25). This saving righteousness means forgiveness, justification, and sanctification (Rom. 3:24–26; 1 Cor. 6:11; cf. 1 Cor. 1:30; 2 Cor. 5:21).

Paul develops both forensic (1 Cor. 4:4) and ethical aspects (1 Thess. 2:10) of righteousness when speaking of salvation (2 Cor. 3:9). How one attains righteousness comes to new prominence in Paul's Letter to the Galatians, where he wishes to stress that righteousness comes by faith, not "works of the law" (3:5; in making this point, he appeals to Gen. 15:6 and Hab. 2:4, cited above). These two ways to righteousness—one based on the law, and one that comes through faith in Christ—are also contrasted in Phil. 3:9–11 and Rom. 10:3–13.

Paul claims that the gospel he preaches reveals the "righteousness of God" (Rom. 1:17; cf. 3:21–22), which many scholars take to be the central theme of his letter to the Romans. In that one letter, he speaks of righteousness as something that God displays (3:25), reckons (4:3, 6), and imparts (10:3). With regard to the first, Paul wants to emphasize that what God does through Jesus Christ demonstrates that God is righteous. Specifically, God displays the righteous qualities of faithfulness and generosity. God is faithful to the covenant God made with Israel, because God gives Jews a means of salvation through faith in their Messiah (3:3–4), and God is generous beyond all measure in offering this same means of salvation to Gentiles (5:6–10). But righteousness is also something that God reckons and imparts, for when Paul says that Christ makes people righteous (Rom. 5:18–19; cf. 2 Cor. 5:21), he means this in a double sense: (1) people can now be counted as righteous even though they continue to struggle and fail to live as God wishes; and (2) people can now be transformed, so that they actually are able to please God in ways that would not be possible otherwise. Both of these elements seem to be a part of what Paul means by the expressions "sanctification" (Rom. 6:19, 22; 15:16) and "obedience of faith" (Rom. 1:5; 16:26); by trusting in what God has done through Jesus Christ, people are reconciled with God and set on a path to godly living. *See also* justice; justification.

Bibliography

Powell, Mark Allan. *Introducing the New Testament: A Historical, Literary, and Theological Survey.* Baker Academic, 2009. Pp. 262–65.

Reumann, John, Joseph Fitzmyer, and Jerome Quinn. *Righteousness in the New Testament.* Fortress, 1982.   J.H.P.R./M.A.P.

A pomegranate-shaped ceramic bowl found at Tell Halif suggests the site may be biblical Rimmon (Heb. *rimmon* means "pomegranate").

Rimmon

Rimmon (rim'uhn; Akkadian, "thunderer"; Heb., "pomegranate").

1 A title borne by the Syrian storm god Hadad, who was worshiped in his temple in Damascus by Naaman, the Syrian army commander (2 Kings 5:18). After Naaman was cured of leprosy by the God of Israel, he asked the prophet Elisha for "two mules' burden of earth" from Israel to take back to Syria; he intended to set up an altar to the God of Israel on the earth in the temple of Rimmon. This temple is thought to have been on the site of the later Roman temple to Zeus and the present Umayyad mosque.

2 A Benjaminite from Beeroth, father of Baanah and Rechab, the men who killed Ishbaal and brought his head to David (2 Sam. 4:2, 5, 9).

3 A town in the south of Judah given to the tribe of Simeon (Josh. 15:32; 19:7; 1 Chron. 4:32). It is called En-rimmonin in Neh. 11:29, which says the town was inhabited by Jews returning from the exile. According to Zech. 14:10, Rimmon was south of Jerusalem. Its exact location is uncertain. Often associated with Khirbet Umm er-Ramamin, about nine miles north of Beer-sheba, Rimmon has recently been connected with the site of Tell Halif (Arabic Tell Khuweilifeh), a few miles to the northwest.

4 A rock to which six hundred Benjaminites fled to escape from the Israelites (Judg. 20:45–47; 21:13); it is identified with a limestone hill about three miles east of Bethel, on which is the modern village of Ramun.

5 A town in Zebulun, given to the Levites (Josh. 19:13). It is called Rimmono in 1 Chron. 6:77 and Dimnah in Josh. 21:35. The town has been identified with modern Rummaneh, about six miles north-northeast of Nazareth. J.M.W.

rings.

1 Circular rings were attached to various furnishings of the tabernacle, so that staves could be placed through the rings and the furnishings could be carried during the wilderness journey: the ark (Exod. 25:12–15; 37:3–4); the table (25:26–28; 37:13–15); the altar of burnt offerings (27:4–7; 38:5–7); and the altar of incense (30:4; 37:27). Such rings were also used to secure the frames of the tabernacle (26:24–30; 36:29–34). *See also* tabernacle.

2 Circular rings attached to the breastplate of the high priest secured the ephod, a decorative linen garment (Exod. 28:23–28). *See also* breastpiece; ephod.

3 Rings were used for adornment and worn on the fingers (Job 42:11; Luke 15:22; James 2:2), ears (Gen. 35:4; Exod. 32:2, 3), or nose (Gen. 24:47; Isa. 3:21; Prov. 11:22). They sometimes served as a symbol of authority, i.e., as a signet ring of a king (Gen. 41:42; Esther 3:10; Jer. 22:24). Such rings were frequently used as official seals (Esther 8:8, 10). *See also* jewels, jewelry. R.H.S.

river of Egypt. *See* Wadi of Egypt.

Rizpah

Rizpah (riz'puh), the daughter of Aiah and concubine of Saul (2 Sam. 3:7). After Saul's death, Ishbaal, Saul's son, accused Abner of having taken her (perhaps as a way of making a bid for the throne); this accusation provided the instigation for Abner to begin negotiations with David, claiming that, since his loyalty to the house of Saul had been unappreciated, he would now devote himself to establishing the throne of David (2 Sam. 3:6–11). Later, when God sent a famine because Saul had brought bloodguilt upon the nation by massacring Gibeonites (2 Sam. 21:1), David agreed to hand seven sons of Saul over to the Gibeonites for expiation. Two were the sons of Rizpah. Her devotion led to a long vigil over her sons' bodies, keeping off the birds by day and the beasts by night, from the beginning of the barley harvest (April/May) until the rains came (October). Finally David's attention was drawn to the matter, and he ordered a public burial for the members of Saul's household (2 Sam. 21:1–14). *See also* Abner. N.L.L.

robbery.

robbery. The basic prohibition of robbery is found in the Ten Commandments: "You shall not steal" (Exod. 20:15). Elsewhere, the Bible contains specific rules regarding theft of domestic animals (Exod. 22:1–4), imposing penalties of multiple restitution in kind. Both the evidence required and the nature of the sanctions suggest the setting of an agricultural community that sought to avoid getting tied up in court proceedings. This is reflected also in the provision for self-defense. If the owner kills a thief who intrudes by night, he is exempt; if he kills a daytime intruder, he is liable. The distinction apparently has to do with the owner's knowledge of the intruder's intentions. Highway robbery was a quite different phenomenon, representing a form of political opposition. The threat from such organized bands was to the central authority's control of the communications network; hence, brigandage was treated by military rather than judicial means. But the Hebrew word for such robbery (*gazal*) came to be used by the prophets for a wide range of economic exploitations (robbing the fatherless, Isa. 10:2; Ezek. 39:10; robbing the poor, Isa. 3:14–15; Prov. 22:22; charging excessive credit terms, Ezek. 18:7–9; 33:15). The NT continues the condemnation of robbery (1 Cor. 6:10; cf. 1 Pet. 4:15), yet

Jesus used the sudden and unexpected intrusion of a robber as a metaphor for the sudden inbreaking of God's kingdom and the consequent need to stay alert (Luke 12:39–40; cf. 1 Thess. 5:2; 2 Pet. 3:10; Rev. 16:15). *See also* law.   B.S.J.

robe. *See* dress.

Robinson's Arch, part of a spring or support for a descending staircase of the complex of buildings constructed on the Temple Mount in Jerusalem by Herod. The remnants of this arch can still be seen near the southwestern corner of the Temple Mount in the Old City of Jerusalem. During the Herodian period (late first century BCE to early first century CE) a stairway descended from the top of the temple complex to the ground, allowing access to this high point of the city for persons who approached from the south. The arch is named after an American clergyman who surmised its ancient function during his investigations of Jerusalem in 1838.   J.A.D.

rock. In lands such as those of the Mediterranean basin, rocks are plentiful. They are a danger to ships when near shore (Acts 27:29), but on land they can be used as places of refuge for both animals (Prov. 30:26) and human beings, to hide from either other human beings (1 Sam. 24:2) or God (Isa. 2:19, 21). Moses used the cleft in a rock to protect himself from seeing God's face, which would have cost him his life (Exod. 33:20–23). It was by striking a rock at God's bidding that Moses provided water for the Israelites in the desert (Exod. 17:6). Paul later identified that rock with Christ (1 Cor. 10:4). In his parable of the Sower, Jesus spoke of rocky soil as having no depth (Mark 4:5–6); in his parable of the Two Builders, he likened those who acted on his teaching to a man who built his house upon a rock foundation rather than upon sand (Matt. 7:24–25). Jesus resisted Satan's temptation to turn rocks into bread to satisfy his own hunger (Matt. 4:2–3) and identified Peter (whose name literally means "rock") as the rock upon which his church would be built (Matt. 16:18). Biblical faith often identified God as a rock (Deut. 32:4; 2 Sam. 22:2; Pss. 18:2; 71:3).   J.A.D.

rod.

1 A walking stick for travelers, usually called a "staff" in the NRSV (Gen. 32:10). When Jesus sent his disciples out on a mission, he told them to take nothing with them for the journey except a staff (Mark 6:8; but in Matt. 10:10 and Luke 9:3, they are not even to take that).

2 An instrument for punishment; it might be used by a parent for beating a child (Prov. 13:24; 22:15) or by an officer for beating a prisoner (Matt. 27:26; see 2 Cor. 11:25).

3 A symbol of authority (Judg. 5:14; Gen. 49:10). Moses's rod was a symbol of his office and evidence of the divine authority for his actions. With this rod Moses performed wonders in Egypt and even instructed Aaron to use his for similar purposes (Exod. 4:1–5; 7:8–24; 14:16). By striking the rock at Horeb with his rod Moses provided water for the Israelites in the wilderness (Exod. 17:1–7). When there was a dispute over the authority to lead the people, Moses took Aaron's rod and placed it in the tabernacle along with others representing the leading families of the nation. Aaron's rod budded and produced almonds, signifying the authority vested in his line (and that of Moses) by God.

4 Something used to measure distances (Ezek. 40:3, NRSV: "reed").

5 A shepherd's rod (Ps. 23:4), a type of club used for defending the flock; by contrast, the staff (in the phrase "rod and staff") was a longer rod or pole upon which the shepherd could lean or with which he could guide the flock (see **1**).   J.A.D.

Rodanim (roh′duh-nim), probably the people of Rhodes (i.e., Rhodians). In 1 Chron. 1:7 the Rodanim are listed among the descendants of Javan, but Gen. 10:4 uses the name Dodanim for the same people (cf. Ezek. 27:15). Since Javan's other descendants lived in the Aegean region, a connection between the Rodanim and the island of Rhodes seems reasonable. *See also* Javan; Rhodes.

roe, roebuck, the roe deer *Capreolus capreolus;* it was considered clean by the Hebrews and therefore edible (Deut. 14:5). It was a delicacy suitable for the royal table of Solomon (1 Kings 4:23). *See also* deer.

Roman Empire, the lands around the Mediterranean Sea and in Europe ruled by Rome. Although events recorded in the Hebrew Bible took place prior to the consolidation of Roman power, Rome's influence was strong by the time of the Maccabean revolt (167 BCE), and from that point until Rome assumed control over the Levant in 63 BCE its power influenced events throughout the eastern Mediterranean world. All events reported in the NT occurred within the Roman Empire (near the height of its power), and that empire provides a context within which all NT writings must be interpreted. The first century CE was dominated by the Julio-Claudian and Flavian dynasties, 27 BCE–68 CE and 69–96 CE, respectively. Sources for this period include Tacitus's *Annals and Histories,* Suetonius's *Lives of the Caesars,* Dio Cassius's *Histories,* and Josephus's *Antiquities* and *Jewish War* as well as papyri, inscriptions, and coinage.

Synopsis: According to first-century BCE antiquarian M. Terentius Varro, Rome was established in 753 by its legendary founder, Romulus. The monarchy lasted from 753 to 509 BCE, when the last of seven kings, Tarquinius Superbus, was defeated. Rome was a Republic from 509 until 33 BCE, when the Republic collapsed in political, economic, and military chaos. Following the battle of Actium in 31 BCE, Octavian took control of military and political affairs in Rome. Four years later the Senate gave him the title "Augustus," and he became the first in a series of Roman emperors until the last

The *Ara Pacis Augustae* ("Altar of the Peace of Augustus"), dedicated by the emperor Augustus in 9 BCE to proclaim a new era of peace in the Roman Empire.

emperor in the West, Romulus Augustulus, was deposed in 476 CE.

The Early Republic: From the mid-third century BCE through the early second century CE the Romans expanded their power over an enormous variety of peoples outside Italy. The granaries of Sicily came under Roman control in 241 BCE, and Sardinia, in 231 BCE. Large areas of Spain were added after the second Punic war (ca. 201 BCE), though the Roman conquest of Spain would take another two centuries to complete. Macedonia (northern Greece) fell to the Romans in 148 CE, and Achaia (southern Greece) in 146 BCE, at which time Corinth was completely destroyed (the Corinth of the NT was a city rebuilt by Julius Caesar). Also in 146 BCE, the destruction of Carthage gave Rome the province of Africa, another grain-growing region. In 133 BCE the last ruler of the Attalid dynasty of Pergamum, which had broken away from the Seleucids (rulers of Syria), bequeathed the heavily populated province of Asia Minor to the Romans. It provided growing cities with textile and other industries as well as agricultural resources. Pergamum, the former royal capital, remained a free city under Roman control. Pompey's campaigns in the east in the 60s BCE abolished the Seleucid monarchy. Judea was annexed to heavily populated Syria, which was intended to serve as a buffer against the Parthians across the Euphrates.

Julius Caesar: In the 50s BCE, Julius Caesar was given command of an army to subdue Illyricum (modern Yugoslavia) and Gaul (modern France and Belgium) on both sides of the Alps. Caesar conquered tribes in France and Belgium and invaded Britain as well. The new territories of north and central France to the Rhine border became a new province, Gallia Comata (Lat., "long-haired Gaul"). This area had a vigorous provincial culture and resources in agriculture, stock breeding, mining, pottery, and glass making. Following these successes, Caesar invaded Italy, where he assumed dictatorial powers. He was assassinated in 44 BCE.

Augustus: The civil wars that followed the assassination of Julius Caesar ended when Augustus (Octavian) defeated Antony and Cleopatra (31 BCE) at the battle of Actium and established himself as sole ruler of the empire (27 BCE–14 CE). Augustus established and maintained peace. During his tenure, the population of the empire is estimated to have been between 70 and 90 million, with 30 to 50 million in Europe, slightly fewer in Asia Minor, and somewhat less than 20 million in Africa. Luke 2:1–2 dates Jesus's birth by a Roman census ordered by Caesar Augustus.

The official transfer of command to Augustus in 27 BCE was an implicit acknowledgment that the Republican system was not able to deal with the problems of such a vast rule. By assuming tribunician power in 23 BCE, he gained the right to convene the Senate and initiate legislation. He also assumed the titles of *pater patriae*, "Father of the Country," and *pontifex maximus*, "High Priest," with control over state religion. He was, however, constrained by the limited number of persons he could call upon to administer the empire. Consequently, the Senate retained as much power as possible. In addition, Rome was reluctant to intervene in the governing structures of provinces at the local level. Augustus, however, did evolve a separate financial system that made the governors of the provinces responsible directly to the emperor for collecting taxes and other revenues.

After Augustus: Tiberius (14–37 CE), the adopted son of Augustus, was more tyrannical than his father. Luke 3:1 dates John the Baptist's preaching and hence the beginning of Jesus's ministry in the fifteenth year of the emperor Tiberius (either 27/28 or 28/29 CE). The coin shown to Jesus (Matt. 22:15–22; Mark 12:13–17; Luke 20:20–26) was probably a denarius bearing his image. The incompetent Gaius (37–41 CE), nicknamed Caligula, "little boots," by soldiers when he was a toddler, was the first autocratic emperor installed with the backing of the Praetorian Guard.

Claudius (41–54 CE) developed the civil service and extended Roman citizenship. He expelled the Jews from Rome, probably in 49 CE, an event apparently precipitated by disturbances over "Chrestus," a possible distortion of "Christ" (Suetonius *Claudius* 25.4). Nero's eccentric reign (54–68 CE) was marked by a great fire, which he attributed to the Christians, precipitating the first overt persecution of Christians in Rome. Following Nero's death, Galba, Otho, and Vitellius fought unsuccessfully for the succession (68–69 CE). The Flavian dynasty was founded by the popular general in the East, Vespasian (69–79 CE), who was called back to Rome from the Jewish revolt of 66–70 CE. His son Titus also reigned for two years (79–81 CE), having brutally sacked Jerusalem and commemorated the event by an arch in Rome. Another son of Vespasian, Domitian (81–96 CE), concluded the rule of the Flavians.

Pax Romana: The Romans saw themselves as the legitimate rulers of the civilized world. Their vast empire had been gained, Cicero wrote, only through just wars (*De Re Publica* 3.35). After the aristocratic misrule in the provinces and the bloody civil wars at home, the imperial order seemed to usher in a new age of peace. It provided permanent military security and high standards of administrative, judicial, and fiscal efficiency. The new era of peace was widely proclaimed in Augustan literature. Augustus's return from campaigns in Gaul and Spain was celebrated by dedication of the *Ara Pacis Augustae* ("Altar of the Peace of Augustus"), in January, 9 BCE. Imperial coinage also celebrated the new age of peace. Even for many of the subject peoples the new Roman order presented an effective and stable rule that transcended local and regional disputes.

The Levant Under Roman Rule: For Jesus and his followers in the Levant, the local Roman rulers had more immediate relevance than the emperors in faraway Rome. When the Romans conquered a country, they typically set up a king, governor, or some other ruler in the land, but they also tried to preserve some institutions of native rule. Thus, according to the NT, a council of Jewish leaders called the Sanhedrin had authority in Jerusalem in some matters (Mark 14:55–64; Acts 5:21–40), but the Roman authorities always had the final say (John 18:31). Judea and Galilee, where most of the events reported in the Gospels took place, were ruled by such delegated authorities as Herod the Great, Herod Antipas, and Pontius Pilate.

What was life like under Roman rule? On the one hand, the Romans were very good at administration, and many things probably ran more smoothly under their control. They cleared the sea

---

ROMAN RULERS IN THE LEVANT: NEW TESTAMENT REFERENCES

37–4 BCE ruled all of the Levant	**Herod the Great** Luke 1:5; Matt. 2:1–19
4 BCE –6 CE ruled Judea, Samaria	**Archelaus**, a son of Herod the Great Matt. 2:2
4 BCE –39 CE ruled Galilee	**Herod Antipas**, a son of Herod the Great Matt. 14:1–12; Mark 6:14–29; Luke 3:19–20; 9:7–9 Luke 13:31–33 Luke 23:6–12
26–36 CE ruled Judea	**Pontius Pilate** Luke 13:1–5 Mark 15:1–5; Matt. 27:1–26; Luke 23; John 18:28–19:16 Acts 3:13; 4:27; 13:28; 1 Tim. 6:13
41–44 CE ruled all of the Levant (certain areas, 37–40 CE)	**Herod Agrippa I**, a grandson of Herod the Great Acts 12:1–23
52–60 CE ruled Judea	**Antonius Felix** Acts 23:23–24:27
60–62 CE ruled Judea	**Porcius Festus** Acts 25–26
44–100 CE ruled Galilee	**Herod Agrippa II**, a son of Herod Agrippa I Acts 25–26

From Mark Allan Powell, *Introducing the New* Testament (courtesy, Baker Academic)

of pirates, built aqueducts and roads, kept crime to a minimum, and provided many opportunities for employment. Trade flowed more freely than ever before, and both travel and communication (e.g., the sending of letters) became relatively easy—a factor that would eventually prove essential to the rapid spread of Christianity. In the Levant, however, these benefits came at a very high price. First, the tax burden appears to have been incredibly oppressive, forcing most people into poverty and keeping them there. Indeed, it has been estimated that in the NT era, between one-fourth and one-third of all people in the Roman Empire were slaves. Second, the people knew that they were not free, and that knowledge was an affront to their national honor and religious sensibilities. There were soldiers everywhere, reminding them that they were a conquered people. The Jews were officially allowed to practice their religion, but Israel had a long-standing tradition of prophets who railed against injustice and exposed dealings of the powerful, and the Romans did not tolerate that (as John the Baptist discovered). What was allowed were expressions of religion that did not upset or challenge the ruling powers.

Examples of Roman Presence in the NT: John the Baptist preached to Roman soldiers, telling them to be content with their wages and not to extort money (Luke 3:14). Jesus drew illustrations in his teaching from the continual presence of occupying Roman troops (Matt. 5:41). He healed the servant (or son) of a Roman centurion (Matt. 8:5–13; Luke 7:1–10), and he was put to death by the order of a Roman governor via a distinctively Roman means of execution (Matt. 27; Mark 15; Luke 23; John 18:28–19:37). Paul carried out his entire mission within the bounds of the eastern portion of the Roman Empire, wrote his most carefully reasoned letter to Christians who lived in its capital, took advantage of his Roman citizenship (Acts 16:37–38), was arrested by Romans in Jerusalem (21:31–33) and escorted by them (23:24) to the Roman governor's residence in Caesarea (23:33), and when he exercised the citizen's right to appeal to Caesar (25:11), he was taken to Rome (Acts 27–28).

The most negative view of the Roman Empire is found in the book of Revelation, where Rome is repeatedly referred to as "Babylon" (14:18; 16:19; 17:5; 18:2, 10, 21). In Rev. 17, the prophet John beholds a vision of a woman who is really "the great city that rules over the kings of the earth" (17:18). Scholars identify this city as Rome. The woman sits on seven mountains (17:9) just as Rome was built on seven hills, and she is also seated on many waters (17:1), just as Rome was fabled for its control of the seas. She is adorned with jewels and clothed in fine linens (17:4) in a manner emblematic of Rome's great prosperity. But although this woman seems rich and powerful, she is not a figure to be envied—she is, in fact, a drunken whore, supported by a monster, covered with blasphemies, sated with the blood of martyrs and saints (17:1–6). A horrible fate awaits her, and

when it comes, the seer avers, she will only be getting her just deserts (17:15–16). Thus, the view of Rome in Revelation is that the powerful and prosperous empire is not what it appears to be; when it is unveiled, it is exposed as a corrupt and horrible reality that those who are faithful to God should renounce and abhor.

This view (which may reflect a response to the persecution of Christians under Nero or another emperor) differs from the perspective of Paul, who urges readers to obey the Roman authorities as instituted by God. Likewise, the author of 1 Peter joins the author of Revelation in calling Rome "Babylon" (5:13), but nevertheless commends his readers to honor the emperor and accept his authority (2:13–17). *See also* Augustus; Caesar; Claudius; emperor; Herod; Nero; Pilate, Pontius; provinces; Rome; Tiberius. For a listing of Roman emperors during biblical times, *see* emperor.

Bibliography

Carter, Warren. *The Roman Empire and the New Testament: An Essential Guide.* Abingdon, 2006.

Cassidy, Richard J. *Christians and Roman Rule in the New Testament: New Perspectives.* Crossroad, 2001.

Jeffers, James S. *The Greco-Roman World of the New Testament Era: Exploring the Background of Early Christianity.* InterVarsity, 1999.

P.J.A./M.A.P.

Romans, Letter of Paul to the, the sixth book of the NT and the first in a series of thirteen letters attributed to Paul. It is the longest of Paul's letters and is often regarded as the most important from a theological standpoint.

Contents: The letter begins with Paul greeting the Romans (1:1–7), giving thanks for their renowned faith (1:8–10), and stating his intention to visit them soon (1:11–15). Then in 1:16–17 he offers what many regard as a sort of "thesis statement" for the letter: the gospel that he preaches conveys the power of God for salvation to everyone who has faith, to Jews first, but also to Gentiles. This thesis is then developed in two stages. First, Paul claims that Gentiles and Jews are both under the wrath of God (1:18–3:20). Next Paul claims that Gentiles and Jews are both the beneficiaries of God's grace (3:21–5:21). The patriarch Abraham becomes an example of how people may be reckoned as righteous because of their faith. Likewise, God's action in Jesus Christ has restored human beings to a right relationship with God, so that they are justified by faith (5:1). Through Jesus Christ both Jews and Gentiles may enjoy peace with God and live in confident hope of eternal life. Having summarized the gospel that he preaches in this way, Paul takes up several questions (or objections) he thinks people might pose. If salvation comes by grace, why shouldn't people just "continue in sin in order that grace may abound" (6:1–7:6)? What now is the role of the law—does it still have a place in the lives of Christians (7:7–8:39)? And what about God's covenant promises to the Jews—are those nullified by a gospel that places Jews and Gentiles on even terms

(9–11)? In answering these questions, Paul develops a number of themes. He maintains that the righteousness of God works an inner transformation in believers so that, through baptism, they die to sin and come alive to Christ (6:11). The law serves to show people their sin, but true obedience to God's will comes with a life that is lived "according to the spirit" rather than "according to the flesh"—the Spirit of God makes possible what mere human effort cannot achieve (8:3–4). And as for the promises to Israel, Paul remains confident that "all Israel will be saved" (11:26) while also maintaining that "not all Israelites truly belong to Israel" (9:6).

Finally, Paul addresses the Roman Christians with a number of exhortations regarding the Christian life, a life marked by inner transformation that yields conformity to the will of God (12:1–2). They are to live in harmony with one another, recognizing the different gifts that various members exercise within the community (12:3–13). They are also to live peacefully with society (12:14–13:10), respecting the authority of the secular government (13:1–7). And with regard to various matters of controversy—particularly those that arise from the clash of Jewish and Gentile traditions—they are to respect divergent

OUTLINE OF CONTENTS

Romans

C.J.R.

opinions (14:5) and avoid passing judgment on one another (14:10). Paul counsels those who accept the full implications of the gospel he preaches (he calls them "the strong in faith") to be patient with those who continue to follow various rules and restrictions that he considers unnecessary (14:1–15:13). The letter concludes with a description of Paul's travel plans (15:14–32), a list of greetings to various individuals (16:1–24), and a final doxology (16:25–27).

Historical Setting: The letter was written by Paul to Christians in Rome toward the end of his missionary career. He is in Corinth at the end of what is sometimes called his third missionary journey (cf. Acts 18:23–21:15, esp. 20:2–3). He is planning to make a trip to Jerusalem to deliver an offering that he has collected for the poor (Rom. 15:25–26), and then he plans to visit the Roman Christians in preparation for a missionary trip to Spain (15:23–24, 28). Paul's relationship to the Roman church is different from that with other churches to which he writes: he did not found this church, so the congregation knows him by reputation only. Scholars surmise that one purpose of the letter may be to introduce himself to these Christians in a manner that prepares for his visit. He may want them to support his trip to Spain, so he may feel it is necessary to summarize the gospel that he preaches and to respond to objections that people sometimes offer (or might offer) to that gospel. In addition, some scholars think that Paul is rehearsing the case that he wants to make in Jerusalem, where the validity of his law-free gospel could be under attack. Paul could also be aware of problems within the Roman church itself and, if that is the case, many of his ostensibly generic remarks in this letter could be intended to address problems between Gentile and Jewish Christians in that community. Most scholars date the Letter to the Romans sometime around 57–58 CE.

Critical Problems: Some scholars have questioned whether Rom. 16:3–20 was originally a part of this letter. Paul greets twenty-six believers by name, a large number for a letter written to a community he has never visited (albeit one in a locale to which people might have relocated). There has been speculation that Rom. 16:3–20 (or 16:3–15, or some other set of verses in this final chapter) was originally an addendum to another letter, or that it might have been an appendix attached to a copy of Romans when it was sent to some other church. There is even more doubt among scholars regarding the last three verses of this letter (16:27–29). Due to a host of manuscript problems, many scholars believe these verses were composed by someone other than Paul and added to a truncated version of the letter to provide a suitable closing.

Major Themes: Paul claims that his gospel reveals the "righteousness of God." This is a rich concept that might entail three somewhat different things: righteousness is something that God displays (3:25), reckons (4:3, 6), and imparts (10:3). First, the gospel reveals that God is righ-

teous; i.e., God behaves righteously by being both faithful to Israel and generous to Gentiles. Second, the gospel proclaims that God reckons righteousness to sinners: those who are unable to live as God wants are put right with God (justified) by faith (3:28; 5:1); their relationship with God is restored. Finally, righteousness is something God imparts, in accord with what Paul calls the "obedience of faith" (1:5): people are not only justified by faith (5:1); they are also sanctified (6:22); they are made righteous by Christ (5:18–19) and through the spirit (8:4), so that they will be able to please God in a manner that would otherwise be impossible. The Letter to the Romans also proclaims a universal availability of salvation (1:16), and it presents a fairly well-developed soteriology that links salvation to the death and resurrection of Jesus Christ and, in some sense, to baptism (6:3–4). For those who question how Jesus's action can benefit others, Paul appeals to the example of Adam. Just as his disobedience determined the destiny of humanity to be an experience of condemnation and death, so the obedience of Christ, the second Adam, determines the destiny of humanity to be an experience of justification and life (5:12–18). *See also* Acts of the Apostles; baptism; collection for the saints; election; flesh and spirit; Gentile; grace; justification; law; Paul; reconciliation; Rome; Spain; spiritual gifts.

Bibliography

Dunn, James D. G. *Romans*. 2 vols. Word, 1988.

Fitzmyer, Joseph A. *Romans*. Doubleday, 1993.

Hacker, Klaus. *The Theology of Paul's Letter to the Romans*. Cambridge University Press, 2003.

Jewett, Robert. *Romans: A Commentary*. Fortress, 2007.

Moo, Douglas J. *The Epistle to the Romans*. Eerdmans, 1996.

Powell, Mark Allan. *Introducing the New Testament: A Historical, Literary, and Theological Survey*. Baker Academic, 2009. Pp. 255–71.

Schreiner, Thomas R. *Romans*. Baker Academic, 1998.   M.A.P.

Rome (rohm), the capital and by far the largest city of the Roman Empire.

The Early City: Several hills of Rome were settled as early as the tenth and ninth centuries BCE. In these pre-Etruscan times, Latins lived on the Palatine and Sabines on the Quirinal hill. The depressions between the hills were swampy. Under Etruscan rule, probably around 650 BCE, the city was founded and named after the Etruscan family Rumlna. The traditional date for the founding of the city, 753 BCE, is based only on legend. Latins and Sabines populated the city. The *pomerium,* the city limit, established in Etruscan times, remained more or less unchanged until the time of the emperor Claudius (41–54 CE). The later fortification walls and urbanized area did not necessarily coincide with the perimeter of the *pomerium,* which was marked by boundary stones. Military commands and certain foreign cults were prohibited within its confines.

During the Etruscan period until around 500 BCE, kings ruled the city. They built the Jupiter temple on the Capitoline hill and the Via Sacra, which ran across the Forum, and started the Cloaca Maxima (sewer), which then was a canalized stream draining the marshy forum area and flowing into the Tiber River south of Tiber Island. Early buildings included the Vesta temple and the Regia. The Regia was the king's residence; it became the office of the Pontifex Maximus in Republican times. The kings also originated the tradition of Roman games and triumphs.

Republican Times: In the Republic, from the fifth century until 31 BCE, the Senate, the patrician magistrates (consul, praetors, etc.), and the tribunes (representatives of the nonpatrician citizens) steered the city's public life. Most dwelling quarters were tangled webs of narrow, winding streets. At the Roman Forum, the city's center of judicial and public business, tradespeople worked in their shops. Nearby, cattle and vegetable markets attracted customers. During the first two Republican centuries, at least eight new temples were erected, among them one on Tiber Island for the Greek god of medicine, Asclepius (291 BCE). After the Gallic invasion in 387 BCE, the so-called Servian Wall was constructed. This included the Aventine hill, although this hill remained outside the *pomerium*. Despite the traumatic experience of 387 BCE, the Roman Republic gradually expanded its influence until it dominated first Italy from Tuscany to the south (272 BCE) and finally the Mediterranean Sea (146 BCE, the fall of Carthage). In the following time, almost all Mediterranean territories became Roman provinces: Asia (129 BCE), Gallia Narbonensis (121 BCE), Cilicia (102 BCE), Gyrene (74 BCE), Bithynia, Pontus, and Syria (64 BCE), Cyprus (58 BCE), Gallia (56 BCE), Africa Nova (46 BCE), and Egypt (30 BCE).

This expansion was accompanied by various social and political crises within the city, but also by a building boom. From 312 BCE on, the first aqueduct supplied running water, and the Appian Way, a road covered with pebbles, led toward southern Italy. Other aqueducts followed (in late Imperial times there were eleven, feeding more than a thousand fountains, the public baths, and even private homes). Additional roads led to various Italian cities. On the Campus Martius, a stadium called Circus Flaminius originated in 221 BCE. Bridges, previously wooden, began to be made with stone piers in 179 BCE (in late Imperial times, Rome had nine bridges). The second century BCE saw the first paved streets. A complex of large boathouses at the Campus Martius was extended. Southwest of the Aventine hill, commercial ships were unloaded and their goods placed in large storehouses. The sewer, the Cloaca Maxima, was repaired (later, in Imperial times, its whole conduit was subterranean). A triumphal arch, porticos, and the novelties of marble statues and basilicas gave second-century Rome a monumental appearance. The basilicas at the Roman Forum served as market halls. Foreign religious movements entered Rome, including cults

Head of the emperor Augustus (ruled 27 BCE–14 CE) on a bronze sestertius minted toward the end of his reign, ca. 10–14 CE.

for Hercules and the Muses and, already in 191 BCE, for the Great Mother (Magna Mater, or Cybele), an Anatolian fertility goddess.

In the first century BCE, many suburbs developed beyond the *pomerium*. More temples were built. On the Campus Martius, Pompey erected the first stone theater in 55 BCE. It became the model of all Roman theaters. Under Julius Caesar (murdered in 44 BCE), many shops in the Roman Forum were replaced by the construction of the Basilica Julia. The adjacent Forum Fulium was also built. Between the Palatine and the Aventine hills, Caesar built anew the Circus Maximus, which had been there since pre-Republican times. Under Augustus (ruled 31 BCE–14 CE), fifty-five to sixty thousand spectators could watch chariot races there, or, according to Ovid, watch for attractive members of the opposite sex. To counterbalance the city's many tall tenement houses and narrow streets, Caesar and other rich contemporaries (Lucullus, Sallust, and Maecenas) had parks built in and near the city. In Imperial times, the number of parks rose to almost thirty. The first public library was founded in 39 BCE.

Imperial Times: Augustus reorganized the city by dividing it into fourteen regions. From this time on, marble and travertine were used for temple buildings. The architectural style followed Greek models. Augustus restored some eighty-two temples that had been damaged or had decayed during the civil wars of the late Republic, and he had new ones built. At the Roman Forum, he completed Caesar's Basilica Julia and constructed the Basilica Aemilia. Following Caesar's example, he erected the Forum of Augustus in the vicinity of the Roman Forum (later emperors—Vespasian, Domitian, and Trajan—continued this tradition by building their own fora). Augustus opened public libraries at the Apollo temple on the Palatine hill and on the Campus Martius. His successors followed his example until Rome had twenty-eight public libraries in the fourth century. On the Campus Martius, Augustus had his own mausoleum built and the monumental *Ara Pacis,* an altar of the "Augustan peace"; here, an obelisk imported from Egypt was raised as the pointer of a monumental sundial. Also on the Campus Martius, a precursor to the Pantheon (built under Hadrian) was finished in 25 BCE by Agrippa, a friend of Augustus and later of Herod, king of the Jews. In the same year, the construction of the adjacent Agrippian public baths was begun. This was the earliest of the huge and architecturally impressive public baths with which emperors such as Nero (54–68 CE), Titus (79–81 CE), and Trajan (98–117 CE) proudly decorated Rome. The public baths were centers of social life where one also enjoyed massages, conversation, playing ball, and other sports. Even libraries were connected with them, and in their neighborhoods restaurants and bordellos flourished. The largest bath remains are those of Caracalla (211–217 CE) and Diocletian (284–305 CE). In addition to the public baths, Rome had hundreds of private bathhouses. In the second century CE, the Christian theologian and philosopher Justin Martyr lived in a rented apartment above the "bath of Myrtinus."

Tiberius (14–37 CE) established the Praetorian Camp. Caligula (37–41 CE) and Claudius installed two new aqueducts. Caligula added a third *circus* (stadium) to the city in the Vatican gardens. Claudius incorporated the Aventine hill and parts of the Campus Martius into the *pomerium.*

Nero completed Caligula's stadium, dedicated a new temple to his deified predecessor Claudius, and opened another large grocery market, the Marcellum Magnum, in the east of the city. His new palace, the "Golden House," stretched from the Palatine to the Esquiline slopes. In 64 CE, a great fire severely damaged ten of the city's fourteen regions. Nero unjustly accused the Christians of arson, crucifying and burning many of them as torches in the Vatican gardens. In the depression between the Palatine and Esquiline hills, where Nero's Golden House complex had contained a pond, Vespasian (69–79 CE) built the Colosseum. This impressive amphitheater provided room for up to fifty thousand spectators watching gladiator fights. At the beginning of his reign, Domitian (81–96 CE) erected the Arch of Titus, commemorating the fall of Jerusalem (70 CE) and the Roman triumph over the Jews. On the Palatine hill, Domitian enjoyed new luxurious palace buildings. His stadium on the Campus Martius can still be seen today (the Piazza Navona coincides with its outline). Domitian's Forum Transitorium was completed by Nerva (96–98 CE). Trajan's huge Forum with its famous column connected the Roman Forum with the Campus Martius. The column shows scenes of Trajan's campaigns against the Dacians. Hadrian (117–38 CE) built the Pantheon we know today. His mausoleum near the Vatican and remains of his temple for Roma and Venus in the Roman Forum can still be seen. Seven years after his death, a temple for him, the Hadrianeum on the Campus Martius, was inaugurated by Antoninus Pius (138–61 CE). This emperor also

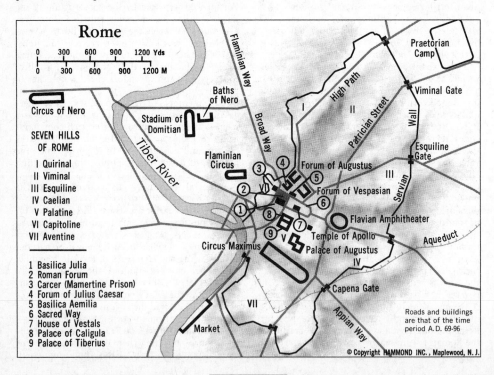

Rome

| 0 | 300 | 600 | 900 | 1200 Yds |
| 0 | 300 | 600 | 900 | 1200 M |

Circus of Nero

SEVEN HILLS OF ROME

I Quirinal
II Viminal
III Esquiline
IV Caelian
V Palatine
VI Capitoline
VII Aventine

1 Basilica Julia
2 Roman Forum
3 Carcer (Mamertine Prison)
4 Forum of Julius Caesar
5 Basilica Aemilia
6 Sacred Way
7 House of Vestals
8 Palace of Caligula
9 Palace of Tiberius

Baths of Nero
Stadium of Domitian
Flaminian Circus
Flaminian Way
Broad Way
High Path
Patrician Street
Wall
Praetorian Camp
Viminal Gate
Esquiline Gate
Tiber River
Forum of Augustus
Forum of Vespasian
Servian
Flavian Amphitheater
Temple of Apollo
Palace of Augustus
Aqueduct
Circus Maximus
Capena Gate
Market
Appian Way

Roads and buildings are that of the time period A.D. 69-96

© Copyright HAMMOND INC., Maplewood, N.J.

Panorama of the Roman Forum.

dedicated a temple to his wife, Faustina, in the Roman Forum in the year of her death (141 CE). In 147 CE, Rome celebrated its nine hundredth birthday. The impressive Aurelian city wall that visitors see today was not begun, however, before 271 CE.

In Imperial times, Rome contained around one million people from all over the empire with different languages, customs, and deities. The wealthier inhabitants lived in villas, which were atrium-style houses with a peristyle section and a garden area in the background, around which were the dining room and bedrooms. Heaters created warm air under the floors. Pipes connected the homes to the water systems and the sewer. Most people, however, were crowded into *insulae* (brick and wooden tenement houses). Rising five to six stories, these buildings were firetraps. Most of them had no water supply or latrines. The ground floors contained shops, workshops, and storerooms. As one went higher in the building, the units became smaller and darker. The *insulae* were crowded and noisy. Even at night, it was difficult to sleep because of the carts that rumbled under the windows (Julius Caesar had banned vehicular traffic from the congested city streets during daytime). In the fourth century CE, more than 44,000 *insulae* were counted in Rome, along with 1,791 villas.

Jews and Christians: Pompey, who conquered Judea in 63 BCE, deported large numbers of Jews to Rome as slaves. Soon, at the latest under Augustus, they were freed. At their manumission, most of them gained Roman citizenship. Thus, when Tiberius expelled many Jews from the city in 19 CE, the freed persons and their offspring could not be forced to leave without individual trials, because they enjoyed citizenship. Tiberius, therefore, drafted four thousand of Rome's Jewish freedmen into armed service to fight Sardinia's bandits. In the first century CE, there were at least three synagogues of Jewish freed persons in Rome (the synagogues of the Augustenses, who were imperial freed persons, and of the Aggrippenses and the Volumnenses). Altogether, the inscriptions mention around fourteen Roman synagogues in Imperial times. The Jewish congregations in Rome were only loosely connected with one another.

Three areas can still be identified where Jews resided in the first century CE. Many lived in Trastevere, a crowded quarter west of the Tiber River across Tiber Island. Others of poor economic means settled on the Appian Way outside the Capena Gate. A synagogue was also founded in the vicinity of the Viminal Gate. All three locations were outside the Republican wall and the *pomerium* (see Acts 16:13 for a similar situation in Philippi). The Egyptian cults, with which Judaism was often associated by the Romans, were also banned from the *pomerium*.

It appears that the Christian faith entered the city in the 40s CE through Jewish Christians who joined one or several Jewish synagogues in town. By preaching about Christ, they stirred up turmoil within the synagogues, attracting the attention of Roman officials. The key persons in this intra-Jewish argument were apparently expelled by Claudius's administration in 49 CE. Among them were Aquila and Prisca/Priscilla (Acts 18:2). Following this disruption, the Christians appear to have assembled on their own. At the latest, Christianity in Rome was separated from the Jewish synagogues at the time of Paul's Letter to the Romans in the second half of the 50s CE. The majority of Roman Christians now were Gentile, although many of these Gentiles may, before their baptism, have been loosely connected with Jewish synagogues as sympathizers with Jewish monotheism. By 64 CE, even Nero could distinguish the Christians from the Jews in the city.

Like the Jews, the early Christians lived at the periphery of the *pomerium:* in Trastevere and in the valley of the Appian Way outside the Capena Gate. Both areas were permeated with immigrants from the provinces who swept into the city on the Appian Way and the Tiber River. People of lower social strata populated these quarters. Other Christians dwelt between these two areas on the Aventine hill, still others on the Campus Martius. Although the lower classes predominated in Roman Christianity, all social strata were soon represented, even the senatorial. In 96 CE, a relative of the emperor Domitian, Flavia Domitilla, was banned to an island, because her faith (probably Christian, but possibly Jewish) did not allow her to acknowledge Domitian as a god.

Early Christianity in Rome consisted of various house-churches (see Rom. 16). These groups met in private homes. There was no local center for Roman Christianity. This factionalism, similar to that of the Jews in the city, facilitated a theological pluralism, which may help to account for the diversity of Christian expression evident in literature produced by nonorthodox groups throughout the second, third, and fourth centuries.

The author of *1 Clement* claimed that both Peter and Paul suffered martyrdom in Rome, probably in connection with Nero's massacre in 64 CE (see also Ign. *Rom.* 4). Both 1 Peter and Revelation refer to Rome as "Babylon" (1 Pet. 5:13; Rev. 14:8; 16:19; 17:5; 18:2, 10, 21). The latter book pictures Rome as a great whore drunk with the blood of martyrs (Rev. 17). *See also* Appian Way; Aquila; Augustus; Caesar; Claudius; emperor; Latin language; Nero; Paul; Peter; Prisca, Priscilla; Roman Empire; Romans, Letter of Paul to the; Tiberius; triumphal arch.

Bibliography

Lampe, Peter. *Christians at Rome in the First Two Centuries.* Continuum, 2006.

Rutgers, Leonard V. *The Jews in Late Ancient Rome.* Brill, 1995.   P.P./P.L.

roofs. In the biblical world, the roof of a building served to give shade, to keep out rain or other foul weather, and to support a variety of activities carried out on rooftops, from sleeping to storage to sounding alarms. Simple roof construction usually consisted of a horizontal bed of branches or beams, sometimes supported by columns, on which layers of earth or limestone plaster were laid. Roofs weathered in the rainy season and needed to be restored in dry weather. Large public buildings had roofs suspended from the side walls or supported by columns or a combination of both, especially where balconies were part of an interior structure. The law required parapets be built around roofs to reduce the hazard of falling (Deut. 22:8). Roofs could provide storage, and they could be used as a hiding place (Josh. 2:6–8), a latrine (Judg. 3:20–25), or an observation platform (Judg. 16:27). From his roof David saw Bathsheba bathing (2 Sam. 11:2), and a roof was used as a guest room for Elisha (2 Kings 4:10).

A palace roof could contain various shrines to foreign gods (2 Kings 23:12), and a house roof could serve as a place to pray (Acts 10:9). In one NT story, a group of men dug through a roof in order to lower a sick man's bed to a room inside (Mark 2:4; Luke 5:19). Roofs needed regular restoration (Eccles. 10:18).   R.S.B.

rope, a twisted or braided line. Rope could be made of cloth, string, leather, vine, or any other strong material. It could be used as a belt (Isa. 3:24), as a means of escape (Josh. 2:15), as a device to trap someone or something (Job 18:10), to lead a beast (Job 41:2), to tie a prisoner (Judg. 15:13), to symbolize submission (1 Kings 20:31–32), to guide a domestic animal (Job 39:10), to pull a vehicle (Isa. 5:18), to lower someone into a pit or cistern (Jer. 38:6, 11), or as marine rigging (Acts 27:32, 40). The archaeological evidence for rope tends to be sparse because of the material's vulnerability to decay. String-cut bases on small jars are common in several periods, and potters often used a "rope" molding for decorative purposes, frequently incising or marking it with fingers. Lug handles were intended to be carried by cord or rope suspension.   R.S.B.

rose, a general term for a colorful flower, the specific identification of which is often dependent on context. The Phoenician rose (*Rosa phoenicia*) is one of the true roses growing wild in the Levant. A thorny bush bearing many blossoms, it grows well at higher altitudes and therefore is probably the rose of the mountains in 2 Esd. 2:19. The rose by the brook (Sir. 39:13) and the rose plants of Jericho (Sir. 24:14) most likely refer to the oleander bush (*Nerium oleander*), a plant with shiny, leathery evergreen leaves and large deep pink or white

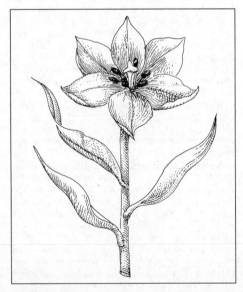

Rose of Sharon.

flowers. Growing along *wadis* (dry riverbeds) and other watercourses, the oleander is an outstanding feature of the otherwise arid countryside. The rose of Sharon (Song of Sol. 2:1) is probably not a true rose either, but rather a bright red tuliplike flower (*Tulipa montana*). It displays a dramatic deep red mat of color in the grass at the beginning of spring, after the winter rains.   P.L.C.

Rosh (Heb., "head"), a son of Benjamin; he is listed as one of those who descended to the Egyptian Delta with the Jacob tribes (Gen. 46:21).

Rosh Hashanah (rosh´ huh-shah´nuh). *See* New Year Festival.

ruby. The true ruby, a transparent red variety of corundum, has not been found in any ancient Near Eastern sites prior to the third century BCE. Earlier biblical translations used the word "ruby" for a Hebrew term, *peninim*, that is now thought to designate pearls (Job 28:18; Prov. 3:15 [NRSV: "jewels"]; 8:11; 20:15; 31:10) or coral (Lam. 4:7). The NRSV continues to use the term "ruby" for Heb. *kadkod* (Isa. 54:12; Ezek. 27:16) and for two Greek terms (*smaragados*, Tob. 13:16; *anthrakos*, Sir. 32:5). The *kadkod* was almost certainly not a ruby, but some other prized red-colored stone. The references in Tobit and Sirach, however, could be to actual rubies, since they come from a period late enough for the authors to be familiar with the gem. *See also* pearl.

rue (roo), an herb, *Ruta graveolens*, used as condiment, medicinal ingredient, and charm component. Paying a tithe on rue (Matt. 23:23) symbolizes scrupulous attention to details of ritual law.

Rufus (roo´fuhs; Lat., "red"), a common name in the Greco-Roman world of the first century.
1 The brother of Alexander and son of Simon of Cyrene, the man who was compelled to carry Jesus's cross (Mark 15:21; neither Rufus nor Alexander appear in parallels, Matt. 27:32; Luke 23:26). Scholars have often wondered why the author of Mark's Gospel would inform his readers that Simon was "the father of Alexander and Rufus" unless, perhaps, Alexander and Rufus were known to those readers—and, if that were the case, then they or their father could have served as sources for Mark's composition of the passion narrative.
2 A recipient, with his mother, of Paul's greeting in Rom. 16:13. If, as some think, Mark's Gospel was written in Rome, it is possible that he could be the same individual as **1.**
See also Alexander; Mark, Gospel According to; Romans, Letter of Paul to the; Simon.

Rule, Golden. *See* Golden Rule.

ruler, a word used to translate several terms that represent various kinds of leadership positions in society. Joseph was made to be a "ruler [Heb.

mashal] over all the land of Egypt" (Gen. 45:8, 26). Later, an Egyptian asks Moses, "Who made you a ruler [Heb. *sar*] and judge over us?" That same word, *sar*, is used elsewhere for overseers of livestock (Gen. 47:6), a director of David's public works projects (1 Chron. 29:6), rulers of Persian satrapies (Esther 8:9), and leaders of cities under Hezekiah (2 Chron. 29:20)—though the NRSV uses a variety of terms to translate the word in those instances. Lev. 4:22 specified the sacrifices to be offered "when a *nasi'* [ruler] sins." David is also anointed to be a *nagid* over Israel, and Solomon is called the *nagid* over Israel and Judah—the NRSV translates this word "ruler" in 1 Sam. 9:16, but "prince" in 1 Sam. 25:30 and 1 Kings 1:35.

In the NT, the most generic term for a ruler is the Greek word *archōn*. It is used for city magistrates (NRSV: "authorities"; Acts 16:19, where the reference is to the local Greek magistrates, rather than to the Roman authorities). It is also used to describe Jairus, the "leader" of the synagogue in Mark 5:22. Likewise, in Luke 18:19, "a certain ruler" asks Jesus, "What must I do to inherit eternal life?" Jesus says that the rulers of the Gentiles are tyrants who lord over people (Matt. 20:25). Satan is called "the ruler of this world" (John 12:31; 14:30; 16:11), and Beelzebul, "the ruler of the demons" (Luke 11:15); and Paul says that the end will come when Jesus Christ "hands over the kingdom to God the Father, after he has destroyed every ruler and every authority and power" (1 Cor. 15:24).   F.S.F.

run, runners, words that are used with different shades of meaning in the Bible. "Run" is, of course, moving quickly from one place to another (cf. 2 Sam. 2:18–23; John 20:2, 4), but it is also used figuratively to denote the struggle of the person of faith to stay the course against evil and remain committed to God in this world (cf. 1 Cor. 9:24–26; Gal. 2:2; 5:7; Heb. 12:1).
Professional runners could be messengers who relayed news (cf. Jer. 51:31; 2 Chron. 30:6, 10; Esther 3:13; Job 9:25), persons assigned to a king to do errands at his bidding (cf. 1 Sam. 8:11; 2 Sam. 15:1), or persons who served as a bodyguard for the king, running in front of the king's chariot (1 Sam. 22:17; 2 Sam. 15:1; 1 Kings 1:5; 2 Kings 10:25; 11:4). The term "runners" was also used for foot soldiers, as contrasted with the cavalry and charioteers. Finally, Paul refers to runners as athletes in a race who compete for a prize (1 Cor. 9:24). *See also* army; chariots; race, racing; soldier.   J.M.E.

rush (or bulrush), a grasslike member of the sedge family, with a pithy or hollow stem, that grows in marshy or wet areas (Job 8:11). Various species of rushes and reeds are common along the rivers of the Middle East, including the Nile and the Jordan, and the Huleh Basin of northern Israel. Since there are several species of this type of plant it is not immediately clear which is referred to in the Bible, but scholars generally agree that

Rush.

papyrus was the rush most often meant. The "bulrushes" of which the infant Moses's basket was woven were probably papyrus (Exod. 2:3), since Isa. 18:2 mentions "papyrus vessels" used by the Ethiopians. These plants were also used as fuel (Job 41:20) and woven into ropes (Job 41:2). Because of their fragile stems and their requirement for a specific environment, they became a symbol of weakness and vulnerability (Job 8:11–14; Isa. 19:6–7; cf. 2 Kings 18:21; Matt. 11:7) or the lowly and insignificant (Isa. 9:14; 19:15; cf. 58:5). In the same manner the flourishing of rushes could be a symbol of abundance and blessing (Isa. 35:7). Various English versions often use the words "rushes," "bulrushes," and "reeds" interchangeably for several Hebrew and Greek words. *See also* papyrus; reed.   D.R.B.

Ruth (rooth; Heb., probably "satiation"), the Moabite woman whose story is told in the book that bears her name. Ruth married a man from Judah, Mahlon, who was the son of Elimelech and Naomi. Both Elimelech and Mahlon died. Widowed and childless, Ruth left her homeland to accompany her mother-in-law, Naomi (also widowed and childless), to Bethlehem. There, with help and advice from Naomi, Ruth gleaned wheat in a field belonging to a relative named Boaz and subsequently went to him as he slept on a threshing floor following a drunken celebration of the harvest. He was impressed that a young woman would take interest in him and determined to fulfill his role as the family redeemer for the line of Elimelech, which otherwise would have come to an end. Boaz married Ruth, and their son, Obed, was the grandfather of King David. The women of Bethlehem exalted Ruth as the loving

daughter-in-law who meant more to Naomi than seven sons (Ruth 4:15). Her name later appears in the Matthean genealogy of Jesus (1:5). *See also* Boaz; Naomi; Orpah; Ruth, book of.   P.T.

Ruth, book of, the second of the Five Scrolls, or Megilloth, which are found in the Ketuvim, or Writings division, of the Tanakh (Jewish Bible). Each of these scrolls is read within the Jewish community on the occasion of a yearly commemoration. The book of Ruth is connected to Shavuot, the Festival of Weeks (later termed Pentecost), which marks the beginning of the barley harvest, for the climax of the book took place during Bethlehem's barley harvest (1:22).

Contents: The book consists of four chapters, and its genre has been compared to that of a modern short story. The first chapter begins with a famine in Bethlehem, literally "house of bread," which prompts the family of Elimelech to move east to Moab. Elimelech died there, his sons married Moabites, and then the sons died too. Naomi, Elimelech's wife, decided to return to Bethlehem, and Ruth, one of her Moabite daughters-in-law, went with her. The second chapter tracks the growing relationship between Ruth and her Judean benefactor and relative Boaz. The third chapter relates Ruth's rendezvous with Boaz at the threshing floor and the plans they make. The fourth chapter describes the legal proceedings at Bethlehem's city gate, which end with Boaz acquiring Ruth as his wife. Ruth bears the male child Obed, who is reckoned as Naomi's son and Elimelech's heir. The concluding genealogy tracks the Judean royal family line beginning with Judah's son Perez by Tamar (Gen. 38:29), going through Obed, and ending with Ruth's great-grandson David.

OUTLINE OF CONTENTS

Ruth

Themes: The plot of the story brings to expression core biblical themes of personal loyalty and commitment to kin. Ruth is determined to support Naomi and refuses to leave her. Naomi is determined, with Ruth's help, to secure a future for her husband's line. And Boaz demonstrates both compassion by the way he treats Ruth and unselfishness by maintaining the lineage of Elimelech through Ruth on behalf of her dead husband, Mahlon. These Israelite virtues are developed within an overall movement from emptiness to fullness. The famine in Judah is the reason Elimelech's family fled Israel, and it provides the context for the deaths of the males, through whom the lineage would be extended. But when food was again available in Judah, Naomi and Ruth return, and Elimelech's future is secured within the context of harvest.

Background: The book of Ruth is anonymous, though the gynocentric character has led some to suggest that the author could have been a woman. Presumably the book had a Judean provenance, because of its setting in Judah and its genealogy, which ends at David; but its date of composition is uncertain. If the genealogy was originally part of the book rather than an appendix, it could not be earlier than the tenth century BCE, the time of David. Certain vocabulary that recalls Aramaic or Mishnaic Hebrew suggests a postexilic date. The redeemer law that governs Boaz's marriage to Ruth and his acquisition of Elimelech's property rights has affinities with the Deuteronomic law of levirate marriage (see Deut. 25:5–10), yet differs from that law because Boaz is not Ruth's brother-in-law; thus, it has been suggested that the book could be earlier than the Deuteronomic writings. In the past scholars have argued that Ruth functioned as a postexilic polemic against Ezra's prohibition of marriage to non-Jewish women, but this premise is not secure, and the date of the book remains an open question.

Interpretive Issues: The LXX took its cue from the book's first clause, "In the days when the judges ruled," and placed Ruth between Judges and 1 Samuel; the Christian OT follows this order of books. But the placement of Ruth among the historical books (LXX, Christian canon) or among the Ketuvim (Megilloth, Jewish canon) affects reader expectations regarding the nature of the book. Is it a story or is it history? Is it a tale of human loss and redemption, "a human comedy" (as Trible labels it) or an episode in the chronicles of the royal house? Scholars continue to work on identifying the precise genre and intent of the book. Sasson finds folklorist forms within Ruth, seeing Ruth as the hero on a "heroic journey." Bal reads the many relationships in Ruth as part of the book's social agenda in the realm of gender and family relations. Dube builds upon the importance of the Moabite identity of Ruth and argues that the book serves to define and maintain Judah-Moab international relations. Fuchs argues against Meyers that Ruth does not represent a women's voice genuinely coming to expression, but rather is a story told by a patriarchal narrator about women who effectively serve a patriarchal agenda.

Bibliography

Bal, Mieke. *Lethal Love: Feminist Literary Readings of Biblical Love Stories.* Indiana University Press, 1987.

Bandstra, Barry L. *Reading the Old Testament: Introduction to the Hebrew Bible.* 4th ed. Wadsworth, 2009.

Brenner, Athalya."Female Social Behavior: Two Descriptive Patterns within the 'Birth of the Hero' Paradigm." *Vetus Testamentum* 36 (1986): 257–73.

Dube, Musa W. "Divining Ruth for International Relations." In *Postmodern Interpretations of the Bible—A Reader.* Chalice, 2001. Pp. 67–79.

Fuchs, Esther. "The History of Women in Ancient Israel: Theory, Method, and the Book of Ruth." In *Her Master's Tools? Feminist and Postcolonial Engagements of Historical-Critical Discourse.* Society of Biblical Literature, 2005. Pp. 211–33.

Hurvitz, Avi. "The Chronological Significance of 'Aramaisms' in Biblical Hebrew." *Israel Exploration Journal* 18 (1968): 234–40.

Meyers, Carol. "Returning Home: Ruth 1.8 and the Gendering of the Book of Ruth." In *A Feminist Companion to Ruth.* Sheffield, 1993. Pp. 85–116.

Sasson, Jack. *Ruth: A New Translation with a Philological Commentary and a Formalist-Folklorist Interpretation.* JSOT, 1989.

Trible, Phyllis. *God and the Rhetoric of Sexuality.* Fortress, 1978.   B.B.

S

Sabaoth (sab′ay-oth), **Lord of.** *See* names of God in the Hebrew Bible.

sabbath (sab′uhth; Heb. *shabbat,* "to cease, desist"), the weekly day of rest and abstention from work enjoined upon the Israelites.

Origin: An etiological origin for the sabbath is supplied in Gen. 2:1–3, which speaks of God ceasing from the work of creation on the seventh day, blessing the day, and declaring it holy. The Bible also credits Moses with instituting specific sabbath laws (e.g., Exod. 16:22–30).

Scholars have looked for parallels between Hebrew sabbath observance and days of rest in other religions or cultures of the ancient Near East. Three similarities with Babylonian rites are intriguing, though they ultimately serve to point up the distinctiveness of Israel's traditions. First, the Babylonian monthly calendar designated certain days on which normal activities of the king and certain professions were restricted. These days, known as "evil days," were determined by the lunar cycle, corresponding with the quarters of the moon. The biblical sabbath, however, was ordained as a weekly institution with no relation whatsoever to the lunar cycle. Moreover, the somber nature of the Babylonian "evil days" stands in stark contrast to the joyous nature of the sabbath.

Second, in Babylonian culture, the full moon on the fifteenth of the month was known as *shapattu,* a term possibly related to *sabbath.* This day was described as a "day of pacifying the heart [of the god]" by certain ceremonies. Apart from the name, however, no significant similarities between this day and the Israelite sabbath have been recognized. Finally, the closest analogy between the biblical sabbath and Babylonian culture is the shared literary motif in Israelite and Babylonian creation stories of the god(s) resting after having created humans (see *Enuma Elish* 7.8, 34). Even here, however, the parallel is distant. The biblical God rests to signify that the work of creation is completed (nothing more needs to be done), while the Babylonian gods rest because, once humans were created to feed them, they no longer needed to labor to feed themselves.

Observance: The sabbath was a cornerstone of Israelite religious practice from earliest times. This can be seen from the consistent mention of the sabbath throughout all the strata of pentateuchal and extrapentateuchal sources, with the exception of wisdom literature. In the Pentateuch, sabbath observance is legislated repeatedly in general terms (Exod. 20:8–11; 23:12; 31:12–17; Lev. 23:3; Deut. 5:12–15), though the types of work prohibited are relatively limited; those mentioned include gathering food, plowing and reaping, kindling a fire, and chopping wood (Exod. 16:29–30; 34:21; 35:3; Num. 15:32–36). The positive specifications of sabbath observance include giving rest to one's servants and animals (Exod. 20:10; 23:12; Deut. 5:14).

Outside the Pentateuch, evidence relating to the practical observance of the sabbath is not overabundant, but it is more extensive than that found for most laws. During the monarchic period (ca. 1050–587/6 BCE), the sabbath (as well as the New Moon) was marked by visits to prophet and temple (2 Kings 4:23; Isa. 1:13). Business activity came to a halt (Amos 8:5). The sabbath was a joyous day, much like the festivals (Hos. 2:13; Lam. 2:6). Its desecration was severely attacked by Jeremiah, who lashed out against those who carried burdens from their houses or through the gates of Jerusalem on the sabbath (17:19–27). During the period of postexilic restoration, Nehemiah enforced observance of the sabbath by locking the city gates of Jerusalem in order to prevent traders from selling their wares (Neh. 13:15–22). Contemporary documents from a Jewish colony in Elephantine, Egypt, likewise mention the sabbath, attesting to its recognition by Jews in the Dispersion (i.e., outside the land of Israel) in the fifth century BCE.

In addition to these features of popular observance of the sabbath, one can piece together a picture of sabbath observance in the temple. The pentateuchal prescriptions of additional sacrifices and changing of the bread of the Presence on the sabbath (Lev. 24:8; Num. 28:9–10) apparently reflect accepted practice (cf. Ezek. 45:17; 46:4–5; 1 Chron. 9:32; 23:31; 2 Chron. 2:3; 8:13; 31:3). The sacrificial service may have been accompanied by a special psalm (Ps. 92:1). There is also a somewhat cryptic reference to the changing of the royal guards at the temple on the sabbath (2 Kings 11:4–12).

Purpose: Two major rationales for sabbath observance are presented in the Pentateuch. The concept of the sabbath as a memorial to God's resting from the work of creation is expressed in Gen. 2:1–3 and repeated in Exod. 20:11; 31:17. The last passage broadens the concept in defining the sabbath as "a sign forever between (God) and the people of Israel." Although God had already sanctified the seventh day at the time of creation, God did not reveal its special status to humankind at large, but only to Israel. Thus, Israel's observance of the sabbath underscored its special relationship with God. This rationale was emphasized by Priestly writers.

Along with the theological rationale, a distinctly humanistic approach is to be found in Exod. 23:12 and Deut. 5:14–15, both of which ground the observance of the sabbath on the need to give servants, strangers, and work animals an opportunity to rest. The added reminder in Deut. 5:15 of Israel's experience in Egypt most likely intends to bolster the owner's feeling of compassion for the weak and destitute (cf. 15:15; 16:12).

Sabbath observance took on an added significance with the prophets active shortly before and during the exilic period. Jeremiah attaches the very fate of Jerusalem to the observance of the sabbath, thereby expressing a radical new conception (17:19–27; cf. Neh. 13:17–18). Ezekiel subscribes to the same line of thought in equating the sabbath with all the other commandments (20:11–24). The prophecies in Isa. 56:2–7 and 58:13–14 likewise single out the sabbath as the primary commandment, observance of which will bring personal as well as national salvation. The mention of the sabbath in the Elephantine papyri and the appearance of the personal name Shabbetai, meaning "born on the sabbath" (Ezra 10:15), likewise attest to its importance in this period.

This unique prophetic idea may stem from the ever growing need for Israel to preserve its own identity in the face of a hostile pagan world. To this end, Ezekiel significantly draws from the Priestly formulation in describing the sabbath as a "sign" between God and Israel (20:12), though his stress on the national consequences of sabbath desecration represents a new application of the Priestly concept. Another explanation for the prominence of the sabbath in the exilic literature is the fact that observance of the sabbath was not dependent on the temple. Although some of the old sabbath practices, such as the additional sacrifices, became impossible with the destruction of the temple, the continued observance of the sabbath on the lay level ensured Israel's steadfastness to its faith.

In addition to the weekly seventh day of rest, the term "sabbath" and its related form *shabbaton* occur in the Pentateuch with reference to festival days and to the "sabbatical" year, during which the land was to lie fallow (Lev. 16:31; 23:24, 32, 39; 25:2–6; 26:34, 35, 43). Each of these occasions shares the chief characteristic of the weekly sabbath, namely, the restriction of work. It has been suggested that the sabbath day and the sabbatical year express the belief that Israel's time and land belong ultimately to God.

In the NT: Jesus appears to have respected and observed the sabbath, but he entered into disputes with the Pharisees over what was or was not permitted on the sabbath. One such dispute was raised by an incident in which his disciples plucked grain on the sabbath (Matt. 12:1–8; Mark 2:23–28); Jesus defends their action as appropriate, claiming that "The sabbath was made for humankind, and not humankind for the sabbath" (Mark 2:23), a perspective paralleled by Jewish traditions later included in the Talmud ("The sabbath is given to you; you are not to be delivered to the sabbath," *Yoma* 85b). But then he also claimed, "The Son of Man is lord even of the sabbath" (Mark 2:28), implying that his legal interpretations were to be accepted on the authority of his person. Other sabbath controversies between Jesus and the Pharisees involved the question of healing on the sabbath (Matt. 12:9–14; Mark 3:1–6; Luke 6:1–11; 13:10–17; 14:1–6; John 5:9–18). Here, the basic points at issue would also have been matters of internal Jewish debate: questions of what constitutes work (Jesus merely speaks a word, without applying medicine, etc.) and whether such activity is justified if it allows the beneficiary to enjoy the sabbath as intended. In any case, Jesus is never presented as opposing sabbath observance as such. Indeed, Matt. 24:20 records his telling people to pray that the coming day of sacrilege will not happen in winter or on a sabbath, since they will have to flee to the mountains and travel would be restricted at either of those times.

In the early Christian community, observance of the sabbath seems to have given way to observance of what the Christians called the "Lord's day" (Rev. 1:10; cf. *Did.* 14:1). This was the first day of the week (rather than the last), and a number of NT passages indicate that it was the special day for gatherings of the community for worship and fellowship (Acts 20:7; 1 Cor. 16:2); the first day of the week was probably chosen because it was the day on which Jesus was said to have risen from the dead (Matt. 28:1). Paul, furthermore, may have objected to Gentile Christians being required to adopt sabbath observance (Gal. 4:10). Indeed, the Letter to the Colossians instructs its readers that sabbath observance is not required (2:16). Thus, by the beginning of the second century, Christians appear to have transitioned from sabbath observance on Saturday to observance of the Lord's day on Sunday.

Bibliography

Carson, D. A., ed. *From Sabbath to Lord's Day.* Eerdmans, 1982.

Greenberg, Moshe. "Sabbath." *Encyclopaedia Judaica.* Vol. 14. Pp. 557–62.

Porten, Bezalel. *Archives from Elephantine.* University of California Press, 1965. Pp. 122–33, 150, 173.   D.A.G./J.H.T./M.A.P.

sabbath day's journey, the distance one is allowed to walk on the sabbath. Work was to be suspended on the sabbath, and extensive walking was regarded as a form of work. Exod. 16:29 legislates, "Do not leave your place on the seventh day." Num. 35:5 defines the levitical pasture lands as extending 2,000 cubits in each direction from the city center. Tannaitic law defined the sabbath day's journey as 2,000 cubits. Acts 1:12 mentions that Jerusalem is a sabbath day's journey from the Mount of Olives. The Zadokite Fragments among the Dead Sea Scrolls (Damascus Document) also counted 2,000 cubits from the city as a sabbath limit for walking after one's animals. Boundary stones marking the sabbath limits (Heb. *tekhum shabbat*) of the city were found in the excavation of Gezer. *See also* sabbath.   L.H.S.

sabbatical (suh-bat'i-kuhl) **year,** the biblical prescription that every seventh year the land must lie uncultivated. This regulation is based on the assumption that the land does not actually belong to any one person to dispose of at will, but to God. Fruit that grows on its own in the sabbatical year is to be left for the poor and the wild animals (Exod. 23:10–11; Lev. 25:1–7). In addition, "every creditor shall remit the claim that is held against a neighbor" (Deut. 15:2). This remission of debts is designed to provide the means to correct social inequities.

The observance of the sabbatical year in Second Temple times (late fifth century BCE–70 CE) is attested in Neh. 10:32 and 1 Macc. 6:49, 53, and Julius Caesar confirmed the Jews' exemption from taxes in the sabbatical year (Josephus *Antiquities* 14.202). *See also* jubilee.   L.H.S.

Sabta (sab'tuh; also Sabtah), a son of Cush (1 Chron. 1:9; Gen. 10:7) and a tribe in southwestern Arabia of uncertain location.

Sabtecha (sab'tuh-kuh), a son of Cush (Gen. 10:7; 1 Chron. 1:9) and a tribal locality in Arabia still unidentified.

Sachar (say'kahr).

1 One of David's bodyguards, a Hararite (1 Chron. 11:35).

2 A levitical gatekeeper of Korahite descent (1 Chron. 26:4).

sackcloth, a dark-colored material of goat or camel hair used for making grain bags and garments. A garment of sackcloth was uncomfortable and was therefore worn by those in mourning. Jacob "put sackcloth upon his loins" when mourning for Joseph (Gen. 37:34). When national calamity threatened the destruction of the Jewish people in the book of Esther, the Jews lay in sackcloth and ashes, fasting, weeping, and lamenting (4:3). The use of sackcloth continued for a long time, as it is still mentioned in 1 Macc. 2:14, 3:47 and the NT (Matt. 11:21) as a sign of distress and repentance. *See also* mourning rites.   L.H.S.

sacrifice. The offering of animal sacrifices was central to worship in Israel until the end of the Second Temple period. Sacrifices were also a constituent part of most other religions in Canaan and the ancient Near East. Israel differed from many in its prohibition of human sacrifice (Deut. 18:10; 2 Kings 16:3; Ps. 106:37; Jer. 7:31), though that prohibition was not always followed (Judg. 11:30–40). The story of Abraham's near sacrifice of Isaac in Gen. 22 may have served as an apologetic account to clarify that Israel's nonperformance of human sacrifice did not stem from a lack of devotion or commitment, but was in keeping with the preferences of its merciful deity.

In general, sacrificial worship was modeled after the service given to human sovereigns; this was especially prominent in pagan religions. In these the deity's image inhabited a palace (temple) and had servants (priests) who supplied food (offered sacrifices), washed and anointed and clothed the image, scented the air with incense, lit lamps at night, and guarded doors to the house. Worshipers brought offerings and tithes to the deity, said prayers, and bowed down, as one might act toward a king. Indeed the very purpose of human existence, in Mesopotamian thought, was to provide the gods with the necessities of life (this was why humans had been created).

Although Israelite worship shared many of these external forms, even to the point of calling sacrifices the "food of God" (e.g., Lev. 21:6), some of the underlying theological assumptions were quite different. As the prophets pointed out, God could not be worshiped through ritual alone. To honor God, it was necessary to obey God's laws, the moral and ethical ones as well as ritual prescriptions. To appear before God with sacrifices while flouting God's demands for justice was to insult God (cf. Isa. 1:11–17; Amos 5:21–22). Furthermore, God certainly did not need the sacrifices for food (Ps. 50:12–13); rather, sacrifice and other forms of worship were offered to honor God. Sacrifices were brought as gifts to God. The Hebrew term for cereal offering (*minkhah*), for instance, is used in other contexts to refer to a gift presented by one person to another (cf. Gen. 32:18, where Jacob offers a large "present" to Esau to win his favor); it is, however, also used for "tribute" paid by vassals or subjects to the superior, conquering power (e.g., 2 Sam. 8:2).

Historical Development: Actual sacrificial practices in Israel developed over time.

Ancestral Period: The practice of the ancestors was simple and informal; they had no priests or temples. Rather, the ancestors themselves offered burnt offerings at temporary altars they built themselves in the open (cf. Gen. 8:20; 12:7–8; 13:18; 22:13; 26:25). Jacob also worshiped by pouring a drink offering on a pillar he set up and by anointing it with oil (28:18; 35:14). In later periods this would probably have been considered idolatrous (Exod. 23:24; Deut. 7:5; 1 Kings 14:22–23).

Period of the Judges: During the time of the judges this type of worship continued to be practiced, but priests and temples were also known. Levites were considered the proper people to act as priests (Judg. 17:13), but individual Israelites continued to offer their own sacrifices on simple outdoor altars (6:24–27; 13:19). There was a shrine at Shiloh during this period, where the ark of God was kept until it was captured by the Philistines. The account in 1 Sam. 1–3 provides a glimpse of worship at this time. Families might go to the shrine for a yearly feast, where they would offer sacrifice, such as a peace offering, and pray, as Hannah did. The priests there took a portion of the meat, whatever "the fork brought up" (2:13–14). As in Leviticus the animal's suet belonged to God. It was to be offered first, after which the priest could take his share. Eli's sons were condemned for disregarding this rule and thereby slighting God (2:15–17).

First and Second Temple Times: Even after Solomon built the temple in Jerusalem and installed the ark there, the people continued to offer sacrifices at "high places" (local outdoor altars). After Solomon's death (ca. 922 BCE), Jeroboam, king of Israel, built two shrines of his own at Bethel and Dan, for fear that the people, by worshiping in Jerusalem, would defect to the Davidic kings there (1 Kings 12:26–29). Jeroboam also appointed non-Levites as priests (12:31) and moved the Festival of Tabernacles to the eighth month (12:32–33). The books of Kings and Chronicles condemn both Jeroboam's shrines and the high places as idolatrous (1 Kings 14:23; 15:14; 2 Kings 12:3; 14:4;

15:4; 2 Chron. 11:14–15; 15:17). These high places were often associated with idolatrous pillars and other pagan practices (1 Kings 14:23–24; 2 Kings 15:3–4), and Jeroboam's shrines were condemned for the calf images he erected at them (1 Kings 12:31; 14:9). Under Josiah these high places were finally eradicated, and sacrificial worship was centralized at the Jerusalem temple (2 Kings 23:5–9), as prescribed in Deuteronomy. The people, however, continued to offer cereal offerings and incense privately, since there was no blood involved (cf. Jer. 41:4–5, where these offerings are brought to a ruined temple). This practice persisted even in Second Temple times.

As Described in Priestly Writings: Ideal sacrificial worship is described in the Priestly instructions (P) of Exodus, Leviticus, and Numbers. Cattle, sheep, goats, doves, and pigeons were the only kinds of animals that could be offered, and vegetable offerings were wheat, barley, olive oil, wine, and frankincense. All offerings were salted (Lev. 2:13; cf. Ezek. 43:24). Sacrificial animals had to be unblemished; i.e., they could not be diseased or injured or castrated (see Lev. 22:17–25).

The most important part of any animal sacrifice was the manipulation of the blood at the altar. Whether it was dashed against its sides or smeared on its horns, this ritual act made the sacrifice valid; in fact, it distinguished sacrifice from mere slaughter. Leviticus requires that all animals eligible as offerings be sacrificed, rather than simply slaughtered (17:3–4). In addition, the animal's suet (the hard fat on the entrails) and kidneys belonged to God and therefore had to be burned on the altar (3:16). Only a priest could perform these essential acts, since only he could officiate at the altar (3:5, 11). In exchange for his services, the priest received some portion of the sacrifice.

Burnt Offering: The burnt offering (Lev. 1) was the most common sacrifice. Appropriate for atonement or thanksgiving, its purpose, basically, was to win God's favor. It was probably the oldest kind of sacrifice (it is mentioned throughout the Bible), and it played a major role in public worship (Num. 28–29) and rites of cleansing (Lev. 12:6, 8; 14:19, 22; 15:15, 30; 16:24). The animal offered normally had to be male (except for birds). The animal was entirely burned on the altar, except for the hide, which went to the priest (Lev. 7:8).

Peace Offering: The peace offering (Lev. 3) was brought when one wished to eat meat. It could be a bull or a cow, or a sheep or a goat (male or female). The officiating priest received the right thigh, while the animal's breast was shared by all the priests (7:31–34). The person bringing the sacrifice received the rest of the animal, which had to be eaten within one or two days (7:15; 19:6–8).

The peace offering was further subdivided, according to purpose, into the *thank offering,* the *freewill offering,* and the *votive offering* (Lev. 7:11–18). Ps. 107 mentions four occasions for which a thank offering would be appropriate: successful passage through the desert, release from prison, recovery from a serious illness, or survival of a storm at sea. The votive offering was given to repay a vow (cf. 2 Sam. 15:7–8), while the freewill offering needed no special occasion. These offerings were distinguished ritually, in that the thank offering required different kinds of breads to accompany it (Lev. 7:12) and had to be eaten in one day, whereas the votive offering and the freewill offering could be left over one night and finished on the following day. Under no circumstances could a sacrifice be eaten after the second day (7:15–18).

The *ordination offering* was a special type of peace offering, the blood of which was used as part of the ritual for ordaining the high priest. Like the thank offering, the ordination offering had a bread accompaniment and had to be eaten on the same day that it was offered (Exod. 29:19–28, 31–34; Lev. 8:22–29, 31–32).

Sin Offering: The term "sin offering" is somewhat misleading. The purpose of this sacrifice (Lev. 4–5:13) was not to atone for any kind of sin, as the name seems to imply. Crimes against other people were dealt with by appropriate punishments that did not involve sacrifice, while deliberate crimes against God (done "with a high hand") could not be sacrificially atoned for at all (Num. 15:30–31). Rather, the sin offering was used to cleanse the sanctuary of impurity. For this reason it was regularly offered at festivals (28:15, 22, 30; 29:5, 11, 16, 19). As a private offering, the sin offering (or, more properly, the purification offering) was brought when a person had unwittingly violated a prohibition (Lev. 4:2) or for rites of cleansing (12:6; 14:19, 22; 15:15, 30; 16:3, 5; Num. 6:14, 16), or for failure to cleanse oneself (Lev. 5:2–3), or to fulfill a vow (5:4), or to respond to a public adjuration (5:1). When both the sin offering and the burnt offering were to be offered, the sin offering always came first; the altar had to be cleansed before other sacrifices could be offered on it (cf. 9:7–21; 14:19).

The animals used for the private sin offering varied with the status of the offender. The high priest or community as a whole offered a bull; a ruler offered a male goat, while a layperson brought a female goat or a ewe. The ritual also varied. When the community (or the high priest, who represented it) had transgressed, the sanctuary itself was defiled; it was cleansed by sprinkling some of the bull's blood in front of the sanctuary veil and smearing it on the horns of the incense altar (Lev. 4:5–7, 16–18). The bull's meat could not be eaten, so it was burned outside the camp (4:12, 21). In the case of an individual, whether ruler or commoner, only the outer altar was defiled. It was cleansed by smearing the blood of the goat or ewe on the altar's horns, and the priest received the meat of the animal. For those who were poor, there was a provision for a less costly sin offering (5:7–13; 12:8; 14:21–22).

Guilt Offering: The guilt offering (Lev. 5:14–6:7) was brought when one had desecrated some holy thing (5:14) or perjured oneself (6:2–5). Its purpose was the reparation of damages. The sacrifice consisted of a ram, offered in a manner similar to the peace offering (7:2–7); also necessary were the offerer's confession of guilt and the repayment of damages, plus a 20 percent fine. The priest who offered it received the meat (7:7). Uniquely, this sacrifice could be paid for in money (5:18; cf. 2 Kings 12:16). It was always a private sacrifice.

In two special cases, cleansing a person healed of leprosy or a person whose Nazirite vow had been compromised through accidental contact with a corpse, the guilt offering was a male lamb (Lev. 14:12, 21; Num. 6:9, 12). For the cleansing of the person healed of leprosy, the blood of the guilt offering was applied to the person's extremities as part of the cleansing ritual (Lev. 14:12–14, 25).

Cereal Offering: The cereal offering (Lev. 2) was a vegetable counterpart to the burnt offerings. It could be raw, in which case frankincense was added, or cooked in various ways (baked, boiled, fried), but it could not be leavened or sweetened (2:11). Oil was present whether the offering was cooked or raw. The flour used was usually wheat (semolina), but barley flour or parched grain could also be used (2:14). A poor person was allowed to substitute a cereal offering for an animal sin offering, and when this occurred, the flour was offered dry, without oil and incense (5:11; cf. also Num. 5:15). Only a handful of the cereal offering (together with all the incense, if present) was burned on the altar; the remainder went to the priest (Lev. 2:2–3; 6:14–16). The sole exception was the priest's cereal offering; it was burned entirely since a priest could not profit from his own offering (6:23).

According to Num. 15 the burnt offering and the peace offering were normally accompanied by cereal offerings (mixed with oil) and drink offerings (wine libations). The amount of grain and wine depended on the type of animal being offered; the larger the species, the more grain and wine.

Temple Ritual: The daily ritual was as follows. Every morning, the ashes on the sacrificial altar were cleared off, the fire was stoked (Lev. 6:10–13), and the daily burnt offering, a yearling male lamb, plus its accompanying cereal and drink offerings, was offered (6:8–13; Exod. 29:38–42; Num. 28:3–8). The high priest, dressed in his priestly garments (Exod. 28:29, 30, 35, 38), entered the sanctuary, trimmed the oil lamps, and offered a specially formulated incense on the incense altar inside (Exod. 30:7–9, 34–36). Outside, he would offer a special cereal offering composed of wheat cakes cooked on a griddle (Lev. 6:19–23). In the evening, a second lamb was offered, and the high priest again entered the sanctuary to trim the oil lamps (24:1–4; cf. 1 Sam. 3:3) and burn incense. He would also offer the second half of the high-priestly cereal offering.

Such was the daily routine. Every sabbath day two additional lambs were offered, like the daily ones (Num. 28:9–10). Also, the high priest would replace the twelve loaves of bread (the bread of Presence), which were arranged in two rows on the table inside the sanctuary, with frankincense on top (Lev. 24:5–9; cf. 1 Sam. 21:1–6). At the beginning of each month (the new moon) and at all the festivals the priests blew trumpets (Num. 10:8, 10), and additional sacrifices were offered, both burnt offerings and a sin offering (which was always a male goat; see Num. 28–29). Festival days (or the beginning and end of weeklong festivals) were days of rest, like the sabbath (Lev. 23:7–8, 21, 24, 27, 35, 36).

On the Day of Atonement the people rested and fasted, and the high priest, wearing special garments for the occasion, performed the Day of Atonement ritual (Lev. 16), which cleansed the sanctuary of all impurity. It consisted of two sin offerings, one for the high priest and one for the people, whose blood was brought, not only into the sanctuary, but into the inner shrine itself, the Holy of Holies, where the ark of God was kept. The high priest entered the Holy of Holies only after placing a pan of burning incense inside, to make a screen of smoke between him and the ark (16:13). After cleansing the sanctuary, the priest laid his hands on a living goat and confessed the people's sins, thereby transferring those sins to the goat, which was then sent away into the wilderness.

It is difficult to ascertain to what extent the rituals performed in Solomon's temple corresponded to the instructions of the Pentateuch. For instance, there may have been only one daily burnt offering (cf. Ezek. 46:13–15) offered every morning, rather than two, with only a cereal offering presented in the evening (2 Kings 16:15; cf. Ezra 9:5; Ps. 141:2; Dan. 9:21; where the "evening sacrifice" is literally the evening cereal offering). In Second Temple times, the pentateuchal instructions were followed in detail in temple worship.

Donations: In addition to public and private sacrifices, offered at regular seasons or at will, the people donated a tenth portion of their produce to the sanctuary. According to P, this tithe was given to the Levites, in exchange for their work in guarding and transporting the tabernacle (Num. 18:21–24; cf. Deut. 14:22–29). The Levites themselves gave a tithe of their tithe to the priests (Num. 18:26). Furthermore, the priests received the first fruits of all produce, including a sheaf of grain at the beginning of the harvest and two loaves of leavened bread at its end (Lev. 23:10–11, 17; cf. Num. 18:11), the firstborn of all livestock (Num. 18:12–13, 15–17), and the first part of the processed produce (flour, wine, oil; cf. 15:17–21; 18:12).

People might also voluntarily donate items to the sanctuary, which would then belong to the priests. If persons or nonsacrificial animals were donated, only the monetary value was paid (Lev. 27:1–8). Land, tithes of vegetable produce, and nonsacrificial animals could also be redeemed from the sanctuary by the donor, by paying the value plus a 20 percent penalty (27:13, 19, 31).

Ritual Purity: Persons participating in sacrificial worship had to be ritually clean. Contact with a corpse (Num. 19) or animal carcass (Lev. 11:8,

24–25, 31, 39), sexual emissions (15), childbirth (12), and leprosy (13) all caused a person to become unclean in various degrees. An unclean person could not eat sacrificial meat (7:20), enter the sanctuary, or even handle tithes or other items belonging to God (12:4). Cleansing was effected by the passing of time accompanied by bathing and washing one's clothes. Certain more severe states of impurity required additional rites of cleansing and might take several days to complete. Although one was excluded from worship, being unclean was not a crime. Failure to cleanse oneself after the period of impurity had passed, however, was sinful and necessitated bringing a sin offering (5:2–3), since (prolonged) impurity defiled the sanctuary (cf. 16:19; Num. 19:20).

To be eligible to officiate in the sanctuary, priests were required to be not only clean, but unblemished (Lev. 21:17–23). Furthermore, they could not officiate while drunk (10:9) or mourning (10:6). They had to be properly dressed (Exod. 28:40–43); and before officiating at either the altar or inside the sanctuary they were to wash their hands and feet (30:18–21; officiating priests did not wear shoes; cf. 3:5; Josh. 5:15).

Other Versions of Sacrificial Procedures: The book of Deuteronomy presents a slightly modified (though much less detailed) version of the system for sacrifices described in Exodus, Leviticus and Numbers. The principal difference lies in Deuteronomy's insistence on a single sanctuary for the entire land of Israel to which all sacrifices were to be brought (cf. 12:5–14). As a result, Deuteronomy permits nonsacrificial slaughter of animals for meat (12:15; cf. Lev. 17:2–4), since for many Israelites the distance to the sanctuary would have been too great for them to travel whenever meat was to be eaten (12:20–21). There are also other differences in detail in Deuteronomy regarding the Passover (16:2; cf. Exod. 12:5; Deut. 16:7; cf. Exod. 12:9), tithes (Deut. 14:22–29; cf. Num. 18), firstborn animals (Deut. 15:19–23), and the priests' share of sacrifices (18:2; cf. Lev. 7:31–32).

Sacrificial practice in Ezekiel's visionary temple (Ezek. 40–48) also differs somewhat from the Priestly system. For instance, Ezekiel calls for a purification of the temple on the first and seventh days of the first month, presumably in preparation for the Passover (45:18–20; cf. v. 21). He also mentions only a single daily burnt offering sacrificed each morning (46:13–15). Ezekiel's system was never actually put into effect, but it may reflect the thinking of certain priests of his time, since Ezekiel himself was a priest (1:3).

Early Christian Interpretation: The NT authors interpret the death of Christ as a sacrifice for sin (John 1:29; Rom. 3:24–25). This one sacrifice was deemed so perfect that no more sacrifices would ever be needed (Heb. 9:11–12, 24–26). Thus, although Christians retained the writings of the Hebrew Bible as scripture, the entire institution of temple, priesthood, sacrifice, and cleansing rituals became obsolete. Frequently, these were spiritualized: e.g., the community itself was a living temple

of God, inhabited by the Holy Spirit (1 Cor. 6:19; cf. Eph. 2:21–22; 1 Pet. 2:9); all believers in Christ were deemed to be priests (1 Pet. 2:5, 9; Rev. 1:6; 5:10); and a life of service and self-denial was construed as sacrificial worship (Mark 8:34; Rom. 12:1–2). *See also* festivals, feasts, and fasts; priests; tabernacle; temple, the; temples.   S.R.

Sadducees (sad'joo-seez), a group in Judaism active from the second century BCE to the first century CE. The name may derive from a Hebrew word meaning "righteous ones" (*tsaddiqim*) or from the name of Zadok, the high priest under David (1 Kings 1:26). The Sadducees are mentioned in the writings of the Jewish historian Josephus, the NT, and rabbinic literature, but no consistent picture emerges. None of their own literature has survived.

According to Josephus: In the writings of Josephus the Sadducees are enumerated, along with the Pharisees and Essenes, as a Jewish philosophical school or way of life (*Antiquities* 10.277–81; 13.173, 294, 297; 18.16–17; 20.199; *Jewish War* 2.164–65). In contrast to the other two groups, the Sadducees are said to reject the immortality of the soul, to attribute all human activity to free will and none to fate (or providence), and to reject other traditions, especially those of the Pharisees. Josephus also says that the Sadducees were influential with only a few wealthy families and not with the general populace, which followed the Pharisees' interpretation of the law. Josephus also describes the Sadducees as boorish in their social interaction; he indicates that they encouraged conflict with teachers rather than respect for them and were more stern than the Pharisees in recommending punishments for crimes. Apart from such references to attributes of the Sadducees, however, Josephus has little to say; he does not describe their origins, indicate how the party was organized, or summarize its actual teaching and agenda.

In the NT: The Gospels and the book of Acts mention the Sadducees occasionally, but no coherent picture emerges. The main point is simply that, like the Pharisees, they were opponents of Jesus. John the Baptist tells them to bear fruit worthy of repentance (Matt. 3:7), and Jesus warns his disciples to beware of their teaching (16:12). A few details, however, differentiate them from the Pharisees. They do not believe in life after death (Mark 12:18; Acts 23:8) or in angels and spirits (Acts 23:8). In the book of Acts, the Sadducees are active in the temple, associated with the priests (4:1; 5:17). They also serve as members of "the council," which is probably to be identified with the Sanhedrin (23:6).

In Rabbinic Literature: In rabbinic literature the Sadducees are treated as opponents of the Pharisees and their heirs, the rabbis. The items on which they disagree with the Pharisees in the Mishnah and Tosefta include purity laws, civil law, temple ritual, and sabbath observance, all matters of great interest for the rabbis. The Babylonian

Talmud also mentions their denial of resurrection. Some texts treat the Sadducees as heretics; in all cases they are set against the rabbinic interpretation of the tradition and used as foils for presenting that tradition.

In consideration of all of this data, many commentators have surmised that the Sadducees were mostly priests and probably wealthy or aristocratic community leaders who sat in the Sanhedrin, were hellenized (i.e., influenced by Greek culture), and interested in cultivating good relationships with the Romans and, in general, preserving the status quo. This common portrait, however, probably tends toward oversimplification. According to the book of Acts some members of the Sanhedrin were Pharisees (23:6–8), and according to Josephus some priests were also Pharisees; and many priests do not appear to have been associated with the Sadducees or the Pharisees. Thus, Sadducees cannot be identified as exclusively priestly, nor can the chief priests of the NT all be assumed to have been Sadducees. It must ultimately be acknowledged that all of the sources for information on the Sadducees are biased against them, so that an accurate picture of their beliefs and practices cannot be fully recovered.

The biblical story in which the Sadducees figure most prominently is one in which Sadducees present Jesus with a hypothetical scenario that, to their thinking, reveals the absurdity of belief in an afterlife. If a woman is married to seven different brothers (in keeping with the law for levirate marriage), whose wife will she be in the resurrection? Jesus says they are wrong, because they "know neither the scriptures nor the power of God." The scenario they propose is not relevant because, in the resurrection people are like angels and "neither marry nor are given in marriage"; this has often been taken to mean that the spiritual bodies people possess in heaven will no longer be male or female, though it could simply mean that all perfected beings will be celibate. In any case, Jesus goes on to defend the notion of resurrection by pointing out that, in the episode of the burning bush, God used the present tense to say, "I am the God of Abraham, the God of Isaac, and the God of Jacob," implying that those long dead ancestors were still living in heaven (Mark 12:18–27; cf. Matt. 22:23–32; Luke 20:27–38). This story is presented as one in a series of challenges put to Jesus by religious authorities. Matt. 22:34 indicates that his answer "silenced the Sadducees," and the Gospels of Mark and Luke both indicate that scribes (possibly Pharisees) were pleased with his comments (Mark 12:28; Luke 20:39). *See also* Essenes; Josephus; Pharisees; Zadok.
A.J.S./M.A.P.

saffron (*Crocus sativus*), the dried styles and stigmas of the crocus used as a flavoring and as a yellow coloring in foods and textiles (Song of Sol. 4:14). Highly valued, it was originally imported from the Far East.

Saffron.

saints, persons distinct because of their relationship to God. The only reference to saints in the Hebrew Bible in the NRSV occurs in Ps. 31:23 ("Love the LORD, all you his saints!"); here, the word translates a Hebrew term (*khasid*) expressive of covenant faithfulness. The same word also occurs in a number of other psalms, where the NRSV translates it "faithful ones" (30:4; 37:28; 149:9) or the "faithful" (85:8; 97:10; 148:14). A similar expression (*'am qaddish*) is rendered "people of the holy ones" in Dan. 7:27; 8:24. In both of the latter cases, the faithful of Israel are in view, and their "sainthood" consists in the relationship they bear to God, who has destined them for righteousness and salvation (cf. Pss. 16:3; 132:9, 16).

The same associations are present in the NT, where "saints" always translates the Greek term for "holy ones" (*hagioi*) and where it refers to those whose relationship with God is maintained through faith in Jesus Christ (e.g., 1 Cor. 6:2). Thus, in Rom. 1:6–7, the phrases "called to belong to Jesus Christ," "God's beloved," and "called to be saints" are virtually synonymous. In Acts and the Pauline Letters, the term most often refers to Christians who live in particular places, such as Jerusalem (e.g., Acts 9:13; Rom. 15:25, 26, 31), Lydda (Acts 9:32), and Corinth (e.g., 1 Cor. 1:2); occasionally, however, Paul gives it a broader reference (e.g., Rom. 16:2), which becomes the normal usage of later writers (e.g., Heb. 6:10; Jude 3). In Revelation, it is a frequent term for the Christian martyrs (e.g., 17:6). *See also* holiness; sanctification. V.P.F.

Salamis (sal'uh-mis), a city on the eastern coast of Cyprus, which, according to Greek mythology, was founded at the end of the Trojan War. Named after the island of Salamis, the city developed around an excellent natural harbor, becoming the main port of Cyprus and a commercial center for the Roman Empire. After leaving Antioch and sailing from the port of Seleucia, Saul, Barnabas, and John Mark stopped in Salamis (Acts 13:1–5). *See also* Cyprus.

Salecah (sal′uh-kuh), a city of Og in Bashan (Deut. 3:10) captured by Israel and assigned to Gad (Josh. 12:5–6; 13:11; 1 Chron. 5:11). Modern Salkhad in the Jebel Druze in Syria is a likely identification.

Salem (say′luhm; Heb., "peace"), the locality over which Melchizedek was king (Gen. 14:18), frequently identified with Jerusalem. The latter identification is specifically made in Ps. 76:2, where Salem is used in parallelism with Zion as the dwelling place of God. Later writers, including Josephus, also connected Salem with Jerusalem, but some ancient writers identified it with other sites. In the Letter to the Hebrews, the author recalls that the root meaning of Salem is "peace" (7:2); thus, Melchizedek is identified as "king of peace." *See also* Jerusalem; Melchizedek; peace; Zion.

Salim (say′lim), a place near Aenon, possibly in the Beth-shan Valley near the northern end of the Jordan River, where John was baptizing (John 3:23). *See also* Aenon.

Sallai (sal′i).

1 A postexilic Benjaminite resident in Jerusalem (Neh. 11:8).

2 A priest in Jerusalem under the high priest Joiakim, possibly of the family Sallu (Neh. 12:20; cf. 12:7).

Sallu (sal′oo).

1 A postexilic Benjaminite resident of Jerusalem (1 Chron. 9:7; Neh. 11:7).

2 A postexilic levitical family in Jerusalem (Neh. 12:7).

Salma (sal′muh).

1 The father of Boaz, also called Salmon (1 Chron. 2:11). *See also* Salmon.

2 A descendant of Judah and the father of Bethlehem (1 Chron. 2:51, 54).

Salmon (sal′muhn), a Judahite, the son of Nahshon and the father of Boaz (Ruth 4:20–21). He is also called Salma (1 Chron. 2:11) and Sala (Luke 3:32). Salmon was an ancestor of David and so, also, of Jesus (Ruth 4:22; Matt. 1:4–5; Luke 3:32). In Matthew's Gospel, his wife's name is given as Rahab (who is thus the mother of Boaz).

Salmone (sal-moh′nee), modern Cape Sidero at Ermoupolis (ancient Itanos) on the northeast extremity of Crete, site of a temple to Athena Salmonia. Paul sailed past here en route to Rome (Acts 27:7).

Salome (suh-loh′mee).

1 The daughter of Herodias who is mentioned, but not named, in the Gospels (Matt. 14:3–11; Mark 6:17–28). She danced at a banquet given by her uncle and stepfather Herod Antipas, who was so pleased that he offered to give her anything she desired. At the instigation of her mother, she requested the head of John the Baptist on a platter. Josephus, who does not recount this incident, gives the location of John's imprisonment and death as the Herodian fortress of Machaerus; he also gives Salome's name and says that she later married her uncle Herod Philip the tetrarch. *See also* Herod; Herodias; John the Baptist.

2 According to Mark 15:40 and 16:1, one of the Galilean women at Jesus's crucifixion and later at the empty tomb. Comparison of Matt. 27:55–56 with Mark 15:40 leads to the plausible suggestion that Salome is to be identified with the woman who is also called "the mother of the sons of Zebedee," i.e., the mother of James and John, two of Jesus's most prominent disciples. This would also make her the wife of Zebedee, who appears to have been a moderately wealthy man, since he employed "hired men" and owned a boat (Mark 1:20).

Along with Mary Magdalene and "Mary the mother of James and Joses" Salome is said to have "provided for Jesus" when he was in Galilee. The latter reference may simply mean that she and the other women assisted with cooking and other domestic chores, but some interpreters have speculated that it might imply financial support; Luke 8:1–3 indicates that women provided for Jesus and his disciples "out of their resources," and one of the women mentioned there (Joanna, the wife of Herod's steward Chuza) may also have been part of an affluent family. It is possible, then, that Zebedee was a patron of Jesus's ministry, and finances from the family's fishing business were

Salome dancing before Herod, twelfth-century illuminated manuscript.

contributed to the work in which Zebedee's own wife and sons took an active part. By contrast, it has been suggested that, since Zebedee himself does not interact with Jesus in any Gospel stories, his wife and sons may have left him to follow Jesus (cf. Mark 1:20), dividing the family in a manner that would exemplify the extreme costs of discipleship Jesus describes in Matt. 10:34–37.

In Matthew's Gospel, Salome (identified as "the mother of James and John") comes to Jesus, worships him, and then asks a favor of him: "Declare that these two sons of mine will sit, one at your right hand and one at your left, in your kingdom" (20:21). The same story is told in Mark 10:35–37, but there the sons make the request themselves (and even in Matthew, Jesus responds directly to James and John rather than to their mother). There is no indication that Salome's request is out of line. Jesus merely indicates that he cannot grant her request, because the ones who are to fill the positions she wishes for her sons have already been chosen (Matt. 20:23). Jesus does query James and John as to whether they are prepared to drink his cup and be baptized with the baptism he must undergo (allusions to suffering and martyrdom), and he explains to all twelve disciples that "whoever wishes to be great among you must be your servant" (20:27), but he never rebukes Salome for wanting this for her sons or for making the request in the humble and worshipful manner that she does.   F.O.G./M.A.P.

Salome (suh-loh′mee) **Alexandra** (al′ig-zan′druh), the wife of the Hasmonean king Alexander Jannaeus. She ruled over the Jewish state from her husband's death in 76 BCE until 67 BCE and, so, became the nation's only legitimate queen (an earlier queen, Athaliah, had seized the throne of Judah and ruled for seven years, ca. 843/2–837 BCE, before being deposed). The Pharisees enjoyed considerable influence during her reign, which was a peaceful time for the Maccabean kingdom. At her death, her two sons, Hyrcanus II (who had served as high priest during his mother's rule) and Aristobulus II, began a bitter struggle for the kingdom. *See also* Hasmoneans; Maccabees; queen.

salt. The preservative powers of salt made it a necessity in the ancient world, and seasoning properties made it most desirable. Job asks, "Can that which is tasteless be eaten without salt?" (6:6). Numerous references to the "Salt Sea" (Josh. 15:5; Deut. 3:17) and the Valley of Salt (2 Kings 14:7; 2 Chron. 25:11) clearly identify the Dead Sea area as the place where supplies of salt were procured. Salt could either be mined in the rock formations along the Dead Sea or obtained by letting water evaporate from pans. Once the salt was removed from sediment, it was rinsed, purified, and crushed until fine.

In Israelite worship, salt was used to season incense (Exod. 30:35), and all offerings had to be seasoned with salt (Lev. 2:13; Ezek. 43:24). Salt was also used in the making of a covenant (Num.

18:19; 2 Chron. 13:5). Because of its preservative properties, salt could be a metaphor for life and sustenance, but because nothing would grow in a field that had been salted (Judg. 9:45), it also became associated with the destruction of life (Deut. 29:23; Job. 39:6; Ps. 107:34; Jer. 17:6; Zeph. 2:9). Lot's wife was turned into a pillar of salt (Gen. 19:26).

In the Sermon on the Mount, Jesus calls the people who listen to him the "salt of the earth" (Matt. 5:13), and in Mark, he tells his disciples, "Have salt in yourselves, and be at peace with one another" (9:50). Similarly, Col. 4:6 says, "Let your speech always be gracious, seasoned with salt." The precise connotation of having salt in one's life, actions, or speech cannot be determined, but the general sense seems to have been cultivation of qualities that are appealing and valuable: good works in Matthew (cf. 5:16), peace in Mark, and graciousness in Colossians. By contrast, Jesus's warning that "everyone will be salted with fire" (Mark 9:49) seems to use the figure in a negative vein, though just what it means to be "salted with fire" remains obscure.   S.R./M.A.P.

Salt, City of, a town assigned to the tribe of Judah (Josh. 15:62) in the wilderness and in association with En-gedi, along the Dead Sea. It is now identified as Khirbet Qumran, the location of the community that produced the Dead Sea Scrolls. *See also* Dead Sea Scrolls; Qumran, Khirbet.

Salt Sea. *See* Dead Sea.

Salt Valley, the valley where David (or Abishai) defeated the Edomites (2 Sam. 8:13; cf. 1 Chron. 18:12). Later, Amaziah defeated the same enemy in the Salt Valley, conquering Sela (2 Kings 14:7; 2 Chron. 25:11). Wadi el-Milk (Arabic, "salt") in southern Judah carries its name today, but most scholars think the biblical Salt Valley was in Edom near the southern end of the Dead Sea.

saltwort. *See* mallow.

salvation, an important term in the Bible with a wide range of meaning. The primary word for salvation in the Hebrew Bible (*yosha*ʿ) has a root meaning of "broadening" or "enlarging" and can connote the creation of space in the community for life and conduct. More often than not, this is done with divine help, particularly in circumstances where God's people face an adversary (e.g., Exod. 14:13–14, 30; 15:2; 1 Sam. 7:8; 2 Sam. 22:28; 1 Chron. 16:35; Neh. 9:27; Pss. 7:1; 17:7; 18:1–3; 54:1; 59:1–2; 106:43–48; 116:1–6; 118:5–14). God rescues and delivers people out of a situation of opposition and peril, placing them into a situation of recovered prosperity and well-being. This meaning of the term is expanded to include deliverance from other forms of conflict, particularly in matters of the people's relationship to God. Such a field of reference draws on such concepts as "redemption," "atonement," "reconciliation," "pardon," and "expiation." The goal of such deliverance is the establishment of God's reign among God's people and other nations of the world (e.g., Isa. 49:25–26; 52:6–10; 55:1–5; Jer. 31:31–34; Ezek. 36:22–32; 37:23–28).

In the NT, God's intent to "save" or "rescue" (the meaning of the Greek root *sōzō*) is identified with the person and ministry of Jesus (e.g., Luke 19:10; also 14:16–24; 15:3–10; 18:10–14; Matt. 10:6–8; 15:22–28; 18:12–14; 21:28–32). The identification of God as Savior and Jesus as Savior become inextricably linked (e.g., Matt. 1:21; Luke 2:11; also John 4:42; Acts 5:31; 13:23; Phil. 3:20; 2 Tim. 1:10; Titus 1:4; 2:13; 3:6; 2 Pet. 1:1, 11; 2:20; 3:2, 18; 1 John 4:14). Specific traditions about Jesus record acts of delivering people from disease and demonic possession, bringing them to a condition of restored wholeness (e.g., Mark 1:40–45; 2:1–12; 5:1–20, 34; 10:52; Luke 7:50; 17:19; John 9; 12:3–7). In the Gospels and in Acts, the Greek word for "saved" is often used for such transformed situations, although the NRSV and other English Bibles often translate the word as "healed" or with similar language (e.g., in Luke 17:19, Jesus tells a person cleansed of leprosy, "Your faith has saved you"; NRSV: "Your faith has made you well").

Still, for the NT writers, the death and resurrection of Jesus is the ultimate focal moment for salvation. Drawing on the sacrificial images and institutions of ancient Israel, these writers associate Jesus's death with "atonement" (John 1:29, 36; 6:51; 1 Cor. 5:7; Heb. 9:24–26) and "reconciliation" (Rom. 5:1–11; 2 Cor. 5:18–20). It affects the whole cosmos (Rom. 8:19–23; Eph. 1:10; Col. 1:19–20), and his resurrection has present significance (Rom. 13:11–14; 1 Cor. 15:1–2), and it also points to future deliverance from impending judgment and wrath (1 Thess. 1:9–10; cf. Rom. 1:18–2:11; 5:9–11; Phil. 3:20; Titus 2:13). Thus, salvation involves life and well-being in the future kingdom of God (Luke 13:28–30; 22:29–30; 23:43; 1 Cor. 2:9–10; 11:26; 1 Thess. 4:16–17; Rev. 21:1–22:5). Some traditions stress the language of inheritance and the certainty of sharing the eternal life of Jesus's resurrection (Rom. 8:12–17; 1 Thess. 5:9; Heb. 1:14; 5:9; 9:28; 1 Pet. 1:5, 9; also John 4:14; 7:37–38; 10:10). *See also* atonement; conversion; eschatology; eternal life; forgiveness; grace; Holy Spirit; justification; kingdom of God; pardon; reconciliation; redemption.   J.E.A.

Samaria (suh-mair'ee-uh), **city of,** the capital of the northern kingdom, Israel, for the greater part of the history of that independent state. Omri built the city in the early ninth century BCE and moved his administrative center there from Tirzah (1 Kings 16:24). It remained the capital until the demise of the kingdom in 721 BCE, when the city was taken by the Assyrians after a long siege (17:1–6, which credits Shalmaneser V with taking the city; cf. the Assyrian annals, in which credit is claimed by Shalmaneser's successor, Sargon II). According to the folk etymology preserved in 16:24, the place-name (Heb. Shomron)

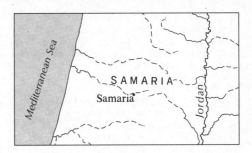

was derived from Shemer, from whom Omri is said to have purchased the hill on which the city was built. The name was also used for the administrative district of which Samaria was the capital, and the gentilic form (Samaritan) was used for the residents of the area. Both usages came into vogue only after the Assyrian conquest, in line with the Assyrian practice of naming a province after its capital city.

The city was well situated defensively on a hill rising about 300 feet above the valleys on the north, west, and south, with a long, sloping ridge to the east. Strategically located beside major roadways, the city gave access to Jerusalem on the south, Megiddo and the Jezreel Valley on the north, the sea and coastal plain on the west, and Shechem and the Jordan Valley on the east. The city, however, lacked an adequate water supply. Thus, in addition to practical considerations, the building of the new capital was clearly a symbolic statement for Omri, expressing the dominance and power of his developing state.

In the Hebrew Bible: Samaria is mentioned frequently in the Hebrew Bible, as would be expected of the seat of political power and, from the perspective of biblical historians and the prophets, a source of corruption. In addition to chronicling events that took place in Samaria, the Deuteronomistic Historian reports that Ahab built an altar and temple for Baal in Samaria (1 Kings 16:32), a

Bronze figurine of a calf, found at a cult center in Samaria from ca. 1200 BCE.

shrine later destroyed by Jehu in the reform that accompanied his coup d'état (ca. 843 BCE). The royal city of the north, Bethel, did not become a cultic pilgrimage center after the model of Jerusalem in the south. Bethel remained the "king's sanctuary" (Amos. 7:13). The reference to "your calf, O Samaria" and "the calf of Samaria" in Hos. 8:4–6 is to the calf (or calves) of Bethel, venerated by the kings of Samaria, as is clear from the parallel oracle in Hos. 10:3–6 (Beth-aven in v. 5 [Heb., "house of falsehood"] is a term of contempt for Bethel). That Bethel was the site of pilgrimage and worship by the nobles of Samaria is seen also in the juxtaposition of oracles against Samaria and Bethel in Amos 4:1–3 and 4:4–5. But Samaria was not regarded as unique in its embrace of idolatry, being compared in this respect to both pagan cities and Jerusalem (Isa. 10:10–11; Ezek. 16:46–55; 23:1–49). Elsewhere in the prophetic oracles, the people of Samaria are condemned for their pride (Isa. 9:8–17), wickedness (Hos. 7:1–7), rebellion (Hos. 13:16), oppression and exploitation of the poor (Amos 3:9–12; 4:1–3), and the indolence and spiritual insensitivity engendered by their wealth (6:1–7).

Archaeological Evidence: The affluence of the people of Samaria so graphically portrayed by Amos 6:4–6 ("those who lie upon beds of ivory") is revealed also in the material remains excavated at the site, including over five hundred ivory fragments used mostly as inlays for wooden paneling, furniture, boxes, and toilet articles. Extensive excavations reveal that the city was built in the ninth century BCE, although pottery from the Early Bronze period (3000–2000 BCE) also indicates earlier, informal settlements. Six periods from the ninth century to the Assyrian conquest have been distinguished and ascribed to the otherwise known activities of Omri, Ahab, Jehu, Jeroboam II, and the Assyrian conquerors.

During the Assyrian and Persian periods Samaria was the capital of the district of the same name. Following conquest by the Macedonians (332 BCE) the city was rebuilt as a Greek *polis* (city). It was destroyed by John Hyrcanus in 108 BCE and rebuilt magnificently by Herod the Great (ca. 30 BCE), who renamed it Sebaste in honor of Augustus (Gk. Sebastos). The Greek name is still preserved in the name of the modern Arab village, Sebastiyeh.

The Gospel of John records a journey of Jesus through Samaria and his conversation with a woman there; the text indicates that many believed in him "from that city," which may refer to the city of Samaria (4:4–42). *See also* Samaria, district of; Samaritans.

Bibliography

Crowfoot, J. W. and G. M., and K. M. Kenyon. *The Objects from Samaria.* Palestine Exploration Fund, 1957.

Crowfoot, J. W., K. M. Kenyon, and E. L. Sukenik. *The Buildings of Samaria.* Palestine Exploration Fund, 1942.

Reisner, George A., C. S. Fisher, and D. G. Lyon. *Harvard Excavations at Samaria.* Harvard University Press, 1924.   J.D.P.

Samaria, district of, an area in the central hill country of Canaan, the natural borders of which were defined by the sea on the west, the Valley of Jezreel or Plain of Esdraelon on the north (with Mount Carmel to the west and Mount Gilboa to the east), the Jordan River on the east, and the Valley of Aijalon on the south. This was the region settled by the Joseph tribes, the half-tribe of Manasseh in the northern half and the tribe of Ephraim in the southern half (to the north and south of the twin mountains Gerizim and Ebal, respectively). Important cities of the region were Beth-shan, Bethel, Dothan, Megiddo, Taanach, Tirzah, and Samaria itself. The area was comparatively more fertile than the southern portion of Canaan in which the tribe of Judah and its family groups settled. Soil and rainfall were conducive to viticulture, the cultivation of fruit and olive trees, vegetable gardening, and wheat farming. It would appear that the use of the name "Samaria" for the region dates from the time of the Assyrian conquest (post–722/1 BCE), in line with the Assyrian practice of naming a province after its capital city.

In the Bible: References to Samaria in biblical literature predating the Assyrian conquest are to the city and not the political district (e.g., Amos

Fragment of an Achaemenid throne found at Samaria, probably from the Persian period (fourth century BCE). The throne may have belonged to a governor of Samaria.

3:9, 12; 4:1; 6:1; 8:14; Hos. 8:6; 10:5–7; 13:16; Isa. 7:9; 8:4; 10:9–11; Mic. 1:5–6). But the later oracle of Jer. 31:5–6 is clearly a reference to the region ("the mountains of Samaria," "the hill country of Ephraim"). The use of the term "Ephraim" for the region and its people was popular with the prophets both before and after the Assyrian conquest—especially the earlier prophets Hosea (about thirty-six times) and Isaiah (about twelve times), where the term is often synonymous with the kingdom of Israel, of which this region was the political and cultural heart. The Deuteronomistic Historian wrote after the time when this region came to be known as Samaria, and this is reflected in use of the term "cities of Samaria" in the account of the settlement of Mesopotamian colonists in the regions by the Assyrians (2 Kings 17:24–28). Still, biblical authors do not refer to the region or to the kingdom of Israel as Samaria, except for two anachronistic slips: one in 1 Kings 21:1, where Ahab is called king of Samaria; the other in 13:32, where "cities of Samaria" is truly an anachronism, inasmuch as the city of Samaria had not yet been built at that point in the narrative.

In addition to Samaria (Assyrian *sa-me-ri-na*), Assyrian texts also refer to the region as the land of the House of Omri (Assyrian *bit hu-um-ri-a*), a term used not only after the fall of that dynasty but also after the fall of that kingdom (722/1 BCE).

History: Following the Assyrian conquest, the character of the local population of Samaria was altered due to the loss of some native Israelites by deportation (2 Kings 17:6; Assyrian records indicate about twenty-seven thousand) and evacuation (many of the evacuees settled in Jerusalem, expanding that city to about four times its previous size) and by the concurrent settlement of foreign colonists in the region (17:24–41). This is said to have resulted in the paganization of the area, of which the judgment in 17:34–41 appears to be an overstatement (cf. Jer. 41:5).

During the time of Josiah (late seventh century BCE) attempts were made by Judah to bring Samaria under political and cultural domination, but this was short-lived. Following the destruction of Jerusalem (587/6 BCE), the Babylonians incorporated Jerusalem and the northern part of Judah into a province of Samaria, but the Persians later separated Jerusalem from Samaria and restored the Judean province. This accounts for the hostility of Sanballat, governor of Samaria, who with his allies, Tobiah of Ammon and Geshem of Arabia, harassed the rebuilders of the Jewish state (Neh. 2:9–20; 4:1–9; 6:1–14). Antipathy between Judah and Samaria was also abetted by the refusal of the leaders of the Jewish community to allow the Yahwists of Samaria to assist in the reconstruction of the Jerusalem temple (Ezra 4:8–24; 1 Esd. 5:64–73).

At the beginning of the Hellenistic period (325–63 BCE), a revolt against Macedonian rule broke out in Samaria and the local population was forced to flee. Samaria was rebuilt as a Hellenistic city, and the ancient city of Shechem was rebuilt by the disenfranchised Samaritans. It was this segment of the Samaritan people who built a temple to the Hebrew God on Mount Gerizim and whose descendants are encountered in the NT and the writings of the first-century historian Josephus as the "Samaritans." During the Hasmonean period (ca. 166–63 BCE), both Samaria and Shechem were destroyed by John Hyrcanus and the territory passed to Judean control. But in 63 BCE Pompey assigned the area to the province of Syria. It was later granted to Herod the Great (30 BCE) and subsequently to Herod's son Archelaus (4 BCE–6 CE). The Romans understood the cultural relationship between Judah and Samaria and did not divide the two into separate governances. Both were ruled by Roman prefects or procurators (and by Herod Agrippa, 41–44 CE) after Archelaus was deposed. In the NT, Samaria is mentioned as the region of the Samaritan religious community (Matt. 10:5; Luke 9:52; John 4:1–42), a territory of early evangelization (Acts 1:8; 8:4–25), the home of Simon Magus (8:9–24), and an area whose churches were supportive of the theological position of Paul (15:1–3). *See also* Samaria, city of; Samaritans.
J.D.P.

Samaritan, the Good. *See* Good Samaritan, parable of the.

Samaritan Pentateuch, a version of the first five books of the Bible preserved by Samaritans and written in Samaritan letters (i.e., in the Hebrew language, but with letters of the Samaritan alphabet). This version of the Pentateuch was apparently produced as a result of conflict between Samaritan and Jewish communities in the fifth century BCE. The Samaritans established their own place of worship at Shechem (now Nablus) and accepted the Pentateuch as their Bible. The Samaritan version of the Pentateuch differs from that preserved by the Hebrews in ways that highlight the significance of Mount Gerizim (rather than Sinai) and in other ways that support Samaritan beliefs. The Samaritan claim is that their version of the Pentateuch is original, while the Jewish version was redacted in a heretical fashion by Ezra after the exile.

Since the Samaritan Pentateuch was prepared long before the Hebrew text became standardized, scholars regard it as an important witness to the early form of the text, and not all of its variant readings would be ideologically motivated. Further, in some places, the reading of the Samaritan Pentateuch agrees with the reading of the Dead Sea Scrolls against the Hebrew Masoretic Text, and in numerous instances, it agrees with the LXX against the Masoretic Text. *See also* Samaritans.

Samaritans (suh-mair′uh-tuhnz).

1 In the Hebrew Bible, an ethnic term for the residents of the district of Samaria. The term

Ruins of a Roman basilica constructed at the hilltop site of the ancient city of Samaria.

appears only once in the account of the settlement of Mesopotamian colonists in the region by
the Assyrians. According to 2 Kings 17:29, these
foreign people made gods of their own, which they
placed "in the shrines of the high places which the
Samaritans had made."

2 In the NT, members of a particular ethno-
religious community based in the area, living for
the most part around Mount Gerizim (John 4:1–
42), but residing also in their own villages throughout the region (Matt. 10:5; Luke 9:52). They might
be encountered in villages neighboring on Samaria
(Luke 17:11–19) or even on the roadway between Jerusalem and Jericho (10:29–37).

From these texts one learns that the Jews and
Samaritans shared a common heritage ("our father Jacob," John 4:12), but differed from one another radically with regard to the relative sanctity
of Jerusalem/Zion and Mount Gerizim (4:20).
They also had different legal traditions regarding the cleanliness of vessels and, in general, they
avoided contact with one another (4:7–10). The
negative attitude of the Jews toward the Samaritans is reflected in Jesus's statement in Matt. 10:5,
in which Samaritans are linked with Gentiles in
contrast to "the house of Israel" (cf. Acts 1:8, in
which Samaria occupies a median position between Jerusalem/Judea and the Gentile world; and
John 8:48, in which the adversaries of Jesus refer
to him contemptuously as "a Samaritan"—and
demon-possessed as well). The itinerary of Jesus in
Mark (10:1; it is followed in Matt. 19:1, but altered
somewhat in Luke) seems to reflect a standard

Jewish practice of avoiding Samaria in pilgrimages
to Jerusalem.

Basically, the Jews regarded the Samaritans
as "foreigners" (Luke 17:18; the Greek word
allogenēs is the same term used in the Jerusalem
temple inscription excluding non-Jews from the
court of Israel). The historian Josephus relates that
the Samaritans were excluded from the Jerusalem
temple by formal edict, not because of nationality,
but due to acts of mischief they allegedly perpetrated there. It was the alien nature of the Samaritans, as commonly perceived, that gave an ironic
sting to the story of the grateful leper (17:11–19;
only one out of ten returned to express thanks,
and "he was a Samaritan") and to the parable of
the Good Samaritan (10:25–37; the Samaritan
stranger was the good neighbor, not the priest or
the Levite).

From the few references to Samaria and the
Samaritans in the NT, one might be left with the
impression that all of the residents of Samaria
were members of this community. This is not so.
There were, in fact, people of various cultural
backgrounds living in the area. Nonetheless, the
Samaritan community was quite large and included a Dispersion; there were Samaritan groups
scattered along the Mediterranean coast (notably
at Gaza and Caesarea), in Lebanon, in Egypt and
Syria, and as far away as Byzantium, Thessalonica,
Rome, and Babylon.

Religious Heritage: As a religious sect, the
Samaritans were a strict, Torah-observant party
with a resolute pride in their religious heritage.

They maintained that they (and not the Jews!) were the bearers of the true faith of ancient Israel as expounded by Moses and as practiced at Mount Gerizim in ancient times. The name by which they called themselves, *shamerim*, meant "observers (of the Torah)." They understood themselves to be the descendants of the Joseph tribes of ancient Israel, just as Jews claimed to be descendants of the tribe of Judah. From the Samartian perspective, Judaism was a heresy, which they traced to the priest Eli, who established a rival sanctuary at Shiloh. The Samaritans accepted only the Pentatuech as scripture, since the other material preserved in the Hebrew Bible was regarded as apostate history. Furthermore, they possessed their own distinctive version of the Pentateuch, claiming that the Jews had edited their version to minimize the importance of Gerizim and to justify the building of a temple in Jerusalem. In particular, the Samaritans cited Ezra as having led the Jews astray, redacting their scriptures in heretical ways after the exile and introducing deviant legal and calendrical interpretations. As a priestly community at odds with Pharisaic interpretations, the Samaritans might be compared with the Sadducees of NT times, or with the Essenes, who are usually credited with having preserved the Dead Sea Scrolls at Qumran. Some studies of early Samaritan traditions reveal early Samaritanism as but one of a greater complex of disparate religious movements and ideologies within Judaism (broadly defined) prior to the destruction of the Jerusalem temple in 70 CE.

Origin: Most scholars have rejected the Samaritans' claim to being the remnant of the Israelite people who had always worshiped the Hebrew God at Shechem. Indeed, they tend to be more inclined toward considering the claims of Samaritan detractors, notably Josephus, whose personal animus against the Samaritans was intense. Josephus claims that the Samaritans were descendants of the foreign colonists from Cutha mentioned in 2 Kings 17:24, an opinion shared by some rabbinic authorities who called the Samaritans *kutim*. They came to have an independent cultic life, Josephus says, as the result of a schism that occurred in the time of Sanballat (i.e., Sanballat II, not the contemporary of Nehemiah) and Alexander the Great

Archaeological remains on Mount Gerizim, where the Samaritan ethno-religious community was centered.

(late fourth century BCE), when a temple was built on Mount Gerizim and staffed with renegade and disenfranchised priests from Jerusalem. This cult was corrupted by hellenization in the time of Antiochus IV (ca. 175 BCE, a date with which 2 Macc. 6:1 agrees) and later destroyed by John Hyrcanus in 128 BCE. Although there seems little doubt that the Samaritan sect of NT times (and of today) was derived from the Gerizim cultic establishment of the Hellenistic period and developed subsequently through Samaritan Torah teachers who produced their own redaction of the sacred text, the account of Josephus presents difficulties in the reconstruction of early Samaritan history (or prehistory). Because it is highly biased and denigrating in its intent, one must view with suspicion his claim that the Samaritan priestly caste derived its sacerdotal authority from the Zadokite line of the Jerusalem temple. Moreover, the story Josephus gives to explain the reason for the exodus of the priests from Jerusalem to Shechem—expulsion due to intermarriage with the family of Sanballat—is problematic (although not impossible). The story is remarkably similar to an earlier incident mentioned in Neh. 13:28–29. This has prompted some scholars to postulate a Samaritan schism as early as the Persian period (sixth century BCE), even though the Bible makes no reference to such and Josephus dates the alleged "schism" to the early Greek period (first century BCE). Ultimately, it seems appropriate to regard the Samaritans as

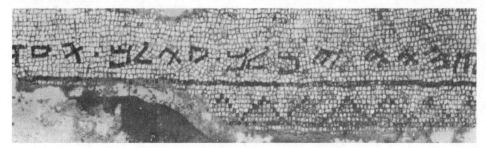

Inscription from a fourth-century CE Samaritan synagogue at Shaalbim reads, "The Lord shall reign for ever and ever" (Exod. 15:18, preserved in the Samaritan version).

NEW TESTAMENT REFERENCES TO SAMARITANS

Matt. 10:5	Jesus instructs his disciples not to take their ministry to any city of the Samaritans.
Luke 9:52–55	Jesus rebukes his disciples after they want to call fire down from heaven to consume a Samaritan village that would not receive them.
Luke 10:30–37	Jesus tells a parable about a Samaritan who demonstrates love for one's neighbor.
Luke 17:11	Jesus passes through Samaria on his way from Galilee to Jerusalem.
Luke 17:12–19	Jesus heals ten lepers, and the only one who returns to give thanks is a Samaritan.
John 4:4–42	Jesus converses with a Samaritan woman at a well; other Samaritans persuade him to stay with them for two days, and they acknowledge him as the Savior of the world.
John 8:48	Some Jews accuse Jesus of being a Samaritan (after he has suggested that they are not the true children of Abraham).
Acts 1:8	Jesus says his disciples are to be his witnesses "in Judea, in Samaria, and to the ends of the earth."
Acts 8:5–25	Many Samaritans, including Simon Magus, accept baptism from Philip the evangelist; Peter and John bring the gift of the Spirit to the Samaritan converts and preach the gospel to many Samaritan villages.

From Mark Allan Powell, *Introducing the New Testament* (courtesy, Baker Academic)

a religious community that developed independently of the spiritual leadership of Jerusalem among a people who were, for cultural and historical reasons, alienated from the Jews and who, in time, found it impossible to maintain fraternal relations. *See also* Samaria, city of; Samaria, district of.

Bibliography

Anderson, Robert T., and Terry Giles. *The Keepers: An Introduction to the History and Culture of the Samaritans*. Hendrickson, 2002.

Chang, Choon Shik. *The Samaritan Origin and Identity*. Pai Chai University Publishers, 2004.

Coggins, R. J. *Samaritans and Jews: The Origins of the Samaritans Reconsidered*. Blackwell, 1975.

Montgomery, J. A. *The Samaritans*. Ktav, 1968.

Purvis, J. D. "The Samaritan Problem." In *Traditions in Transformation: Turning Points in Biblical Faith*. Eisenbrauns, 1982. Pp. 323–50.   J.D.P.

Samgarnebo (sam′gahr-nee′boh), a Babylonian mentioned among Nebuchadnezzar II's officials who took their seats in the Middle Gate of Jerusalem during the siege of 587 BCE (Jer. 39:3). The name Samgarnebo (Babylonian *sin-magir*) is a Babylonian title that can also be used to connote a district.

Samlah (sam′luh), a pre-Israelite king of Edom (Gen. 36:36; 1 Chron. 1:47).

Samos (say′mos), a mountainous island twenty-eight miles long and twelve and a half miles wide, located about a mile and a half from the western coast of Asia Minor, opposite Trogyllium. Greek settlers arrived on Samos ca. 1000 BCE. The Samian fleet was famous throughout various periods of

history. In the third century BCE, the Ptolemies of Egypt used the island as a naval base. During the Maccabean period, there were apparently Jews living on the island (1 Macc. 15:23). In 129 BCE, Samos became part of the Roman province of Asia. Paul and his companions stopped at Samos prior to sailing for the city of Miletus during their final trip to Jerusalem (Acts 20:15).   M.K.M.

Samothrace (sam′uh-thrays), a mountainous island, elliptical in shape, in the northeastern extremity of the Aegean Sea, about twenty miles south of the mainland of Thrace. The rugged coastline leaves the island without a harbor. Before arriving at Neapolis on his second missionary journey, Paul's ship dropped anchor off Samothrace (Acts 16:11).

Samson (sam′suhn), an early Israelite hero. The traditions about Samson depict him as a judge who assisted his tribe, the Danites, in their struggle against the Philistines. The stories present him as a Nazirite from birth, but his passion for foreign women compromised the Nazirite vow, which required him to refrain from cutting his hair and to avoid wine and any unclean food. The tales associate his extraordinary strength with the length of his hair, apparently because unshorn locks evinced faithfulness to that part of his vow, but they also attribute that strength to the spirit of God coming upon Samson in somewhat unpredictable ways (e.g., Judg. 14:19; 15:14). A religious spirit colors the Samson stories from first to last, despite their racy theme.

Samson is born to a previously infertile woman who is the wife of a Danite named Manoah (Judg. 13:1–25). An angel announces the impending birth

Page from a 1310 Pentateuch portrays Samson grappling with the lion (Judg. 14).

to her and tells her that the boy is to be a Nazirite from birth. She shares the news with her husband, who requires the angel's revelation to be repeated, asks various inappropriate questions, and requires reassurance from his (unnamed) wife that God is not going to kill them. The story is told with a touch of humor, presenting Samson's father as slow-witted in comparison with Samson's mother.

Samson's life story is told with reference to his erotic involvement with three women. The first story (Judg. 14–15) is initiated when he deigns to marry an unnamed woman from Timnah, a few miles southeast of Beth-shemesh (located between Jerusalem and Ashdod). At their wedding festivities, he wagers sixty festal garments that the guests will not be able to tell him the meaning of this saying: "Out of the eater came something to eat. Out of the strong came something sweet" (14:14). He explains it to his wife (i.e., that he had killed a lion and bees made honey in its carcass), and she tells the meaning to some of the guests, when they threaten her. Enraged, Samson takes revenge on local Askelonites from whom he steals garments to cover his wager. Then the situation escalates when he returns to his home in Zorah to find that his bride has been given to his companion, the best man, under the mistaken assumption that he had abandoned her. Samson takes further revenge for this by catching three hundred foxes, setting fire to their tails, and releasing them in the grainfields. Angry Philistines retaliate by burning Samson's bride and her father, whereupon Samson kills a large number of them. The Philistines now seek to capture him, intimidating the local tribe of Judah into assisting them. He allows himself to be bound by his countrymen, is turned over to the enemy, and then breaks the bonds and slays a thousand Philistines with the jawbone of an ass. Samson then composes a victory song and prays for water to quench his thirst. Appropriate names are given to the sites of battle and prayer: Hill of the Jawbone and Partridge Spring (14:1–15:20).

The second woman with whom Samson becomes entangled is a prostitute in the Philistine city of Gaza (located near the Mediterranean seacoast). According to the brief story in Judg. 16:1–3, the local residents learn that he is in town with her, and they surround her house, anticipating victory over an exhausted Samson. But he rises early and walks off with the doors of the city gate on his shoulders, depositing them some distance away on a hill opposite Hebron.

Samson's downfall is related in Judg. 16:4–22 in a colorful story involving a third woman, a Philistine named Delilah, with whom he falls in love. The Philistines pressure Delilah to discover the secret of his strength and, though he tricks her with a wrong answer a couple of times, he finally divulges the truth; she then cuts off his hair while he sleeps and delivers him to the Philistines. They put out his eyes and set him to work grinding at a mill in Gaza. In due time they celebrate their good fortune with a victory song and make sport of Samson during a sacrifice to their god, Dagon. Resolving to get revenge once more, Samson asks to be situated by the two pillars holding up the house and prays for renewed strength just once more. God grants his wish and Samson pulls down the Philistine structure upon himself, killing a multitude of Philistines in this final act (16:4–31).

The traditions about Samson have been brought together with great skill; they probably circulated orally for some time before achieving written form. Various motifs combine to enhance their popularity: the infertile wife, terror accompanying a theophany, the powerful man helpless to resist the charms of a woman, the quest for a hidden source of power, loss of charisma, the heroic death wish. The stories also make use of many different literary forms, e.g., three prayers, three riddles, two etiologies (explanations for place-names), two victory songs, a birth story, and five accounts of heroic deeds. The stories reflect the period described in Judges, a period when tribal jealousies divided Israelites and when rivalry existed between the Philistine population and Israelite groups.

Bibliography

Crenshaw, James L. *Samson: A Secret Betrayed, a Vow Ignored.* John Knox, 1978.   J.L.C.

Samuel (sam'yoo-uhl), a prophet who ruled Israel at the end of the period of the judges and who anointed Israel's first two kings. He is the dominant figure in the first few chapters of the first of the two books of the Bible that bear his name.

Samuel's father, Elkanah, was an Ephraimite from the village of Ramathaim-zophim. Samuel's mother, Hannah, was infertile, but prayed for a child during a visit to the shrine at Shiloh, promising to devote her son to the service of God (1 Sam. 1). The young Samuel, therefore, grew up in Shiloh under the tutelage of Eli, the chief priest. One night, he heard the voice of God calling his name, though he did not at first realize it was the Lord.

The men of Israel approach Samuel to request a king (1 Sam. 8); thirteenth-century French miniature.

After some prompting from Eli, he responded to the voice, "Speak, for your servant is listening" (3:10), and he was given his first oracle: a renunciation of the house of Eli, whose sons had corrupted the cult of the Lord (3:11–14; cf. 2:12–17). This marked the beginning of Samuel's career as a prophet (3:19–4:1).

Samuel assumed national leadership after a disastrous battle in which the Israelites were routed by the Philistines (4). Having driven out the enemy and pacified the entire land (7:13–14), he began to make periodic visits to a circuit of cities where he passed judgment on cases brought before him (7:15–17). This pattern continued for most of Samuel's life, but in his old age the men of Israel approached him to request a king (8). Though angered, he acted on God's instructions and, after warning the people of the burdens a king would impose on them (8:11–18), he acceded to the request.

Samuel anointed Saul to be king during a private audience in Samuel's hometown (9:1–10:16). Subsequently, however, he presided over a public ceremony in which Saul was chosen king by casting lots (10:17–27). After Saul's victorious campaign against the Ammonites (11) the kingship was ratified in yet another ceremony conducted by Samuel (11:15). Then, in a final public appearance (12), the prophet admonished the people and their new king to obey the commands of God and promised to continue to act on their behalf.

Samuel was also the agent of Saul's rejection as king. Because Saul did not carry out God's instruc-

tions in the manner that Samuel had conveyed them to him, Samuel prophesied that Saul would be removed from office in favor of a new king (13:7–14; 15:10–29). Then God sent Samuel to Bethlehem, where he anointed David (16:1–13). In that account, Samuel reviews the sons of Jesse, but God rejects each of them, one by one, telling Samuel, "Do not look on his appearance or on the height of his stature . . . for the Lord does not see as mortals see; they look on the outward appearance, but the Lord looks on the heart" (16:11). Samuel must ask Jesse if he has any other sons and only then does he learn about the youngest, who is keeping the sheep. This is David, and Samuel anoints him to be king of Israel.

Although Samuel's death is reported in 25:1, he makes one additional appearance in the biblical story. In chap. 28, Saul asks a medium to conjure up Samuel's ghost, hoping to receive a favorable oracle regarding an upcoming battle with the Philistines. The ghost, however, reminds Saul of the divine rejection of his kingship and correctly predicts a Philistine victory in the battle.

All told, the biblical narrative presents Samuel as the last of the heroes of the premonarchic age and as the first of the prophets who would stand alongside the kings. In one sense, he is a transitional figure, the last of the judges and the first of the prophets. In 1 Sam. 7, he is presented as an ideal judge, a person in whom all types of authority—military, judicial, and sacerdotal—are combined. In subsequent chapters, after the reality of kingship has been acknowledged, Samuel becomes a paradigm for the prophetic office under the monarchy: a prophet who confirms or rejects kings, intercedes with God on Israel's behalf, and guides the conscience of the people (cf. 1 Sam. 12:23). *See also* David; Eli; Hannah; king; prophet; Saul; Shiloh.   P.K.M.

Samuel, First and Second Books of, biblical writings that follow the book of Judges in the Tanakh (Jewish Bible) and the book of Ruth in the Christian OT; they are found in the Prophets, or Nevi'im, section of the Tanakh and are the third and fourth books of its Former Prophets subcollection. Originally, 1 and 2 Samuel were one book, but it was divided into two parts in the LXX, where the books of Samuel and Kings are divided into four books called 1 Kingdoms, 2 Kingdoms, 3 Kingdoms, and 4 Kingdoms. Tradition ascribed the authorship of the books of Samuel to the prophet Samuel, but in fact the author is anonymous; scholars view the books of Samuel as part of the Deuteronomistic History (Joshua–2 Kings), which presents the primary history of Israel from the conquest of Canaan to the Babylonian exile. First and Second Samuel trace that history from the birth of Samuel to the end of the reign of King David. The first book of Chronicles covers approximately the same period of time, but with attention focused on David's role as patron of the temple in Jerusalem (chaps. 10–29).

Contents: The contents of the books of Samuel can be organized into three cycles of episodes revolving around the main characters Samuel, Saul, and David. Samuel exercises leadership in the mode of judge, prophet, and priest. He presides over the transition from charismatic to royal dynastic state leadership. Saul is the first royal figure; he comes from the tribe of Benjamin. He fails to establish a ruling dynasty, and Samuel anoints David to be a new king in his place; David is from the family of Jesse in Bethlehem of Judah.

Samuel's birth is portrayed as a miracle; God enables previously infertile Hannah to conceive him. He distinguishes himself early on as a prophet in Shiloh, where Eli is the high priest and the ark of the covenant is kept in Israel's central sanctuary (1 Sam. 1–3). The Philistines capture the ark of the covenant in battle, but later return it (4–6). They emerge at this time as Israel's most dangerous foe. Samuel secures Israel from the Philistines for a time, but Israel still demands a king (7–8), thereby pitting a theocracatic form of state administration against a monarchic form. Samuel anoints Saul king (9–10), and Saul demonstrates his leadership by rescuing Jabesh-gilead (11). But then Saul breaks the rules of holy war, and Samuel removes Saul's divine endorsement, though Saul still remains in office for a time (12–15). Meanwhile, Samuel anoints David king (16), and David demonstrates his leadership by defeating Goliath and the Philistines (17). This leads to an intense rivalry between Saul and David causing Saul to pursue David to kill him, yet David always eludes Saul's grasp (18–27). Saul faces the Philistines in a final battle in which he and his sons die (28–31).

David, earlier designated king, takes office in Judah, and later all the tribes of Israel accept his authority (1–5). David establishes Jerusalem (formerly Jebus) as his capital and moves the ark of the covenant there (6). Nathan mediates God's eternal endorsement of the Davidic line in the form of a covenant (7). David then defeats Israel's enemies (8–10), but sins with Bathsheba, has her husband killed, and is punished for this (11–12). The punishment takes the form of deadly infighting among his sons as they position themselves in line for the throne (13–14). David's son Absalom actually usurps the throne from his father for a time, but is then assassinated by Joab, David's chief of staff (15–19). Then David consolidates his power and further builds his empire (20–24). The conclusion of the story of David and the transition to the reign of his son Solomon is told in 1 Kings 1–2.

Background: Standing behind the three cycles are stories and story collections that may originally have existed as separate works. Scholars identify an ark narrative (4:1–7:1) within the Samuel cycle that details the Philistine capture of the ark and its return to Israelite territory; the figure of Samuel is

David, by the sculptor Bernini, 1625.

completely absent from this tale. They also identify a history of succession to the Davidic throne (2 Sam. 9–1 Kings 2), also called the court history of David. Further, the psalm that appears as 2 Sam. 22 is also Ps. 18 in the Psalter. Beginning in the nineteenth century scholars hypothesized two sources in Samuel based on how the monarchy was viewed. One source was highly critical of the people's proposal for a king, reflected in Samuel's speeches in 1 Sam. 8 and 12. A pro-monarchy source may be discerned in the material of 1 Sam. 9–11, which views Saul positively. Campbell and O'Brien propose that a Prophetic Record source (1 Sam. 1–2 Kings 10) formed the backbone of the Deuteronomistic History in Samuel and Kings; it features prophets, who represent the authority of God, as the ones who promote and demote kings within Israel.

The books of Samuel deal with the rise of kingship within Israel. They begin with a sketch of Samuel, a prophet and the last judge, who advocates the ideals of the age of the tribal federation, which was dominated by the ideology of theocracy. In this view God and only God could be imagined as the king of Israel. However, the Philistine wars proved that a stable tactical military leader who could organize the tribes for victory was needed. Although Samuel's first choice for king, Saul, proved inadequate, his second choice, David, proved more effective. The Deuteronomistic Historian tells the story in such a way that the complex dimensions of this revolutionary institutional change are brought together. Kings are needed but they can be dangerous, because they are sometimes motivated by self-interest. God favored the tribe of Judah and endorsed its lineage of David by a divine covenant, going so far as to declare Davidic kings to be sons of God (2 Sam. 7:14). When these Davidic kings sinned, God would punish them, but not ultimately abandon them in the manner of Saul.

Interpretive Issues: The books of Samuel portray David in a complex way. He is the youngest of Jesse's sons. He courageously defended Israel against the Philistines by defeating Goliath in single combat. He befriended Saul and remained loyal to him, serving at his court. He conquered Jebus and established it as Jerusalem, the "city of David," and made it both the political and religious capital of the united kingdom of Israel. Yet he committed adultery and murder in the Bathsheba affair. And he was deceptive when he hid among the Philistines when Saul sought to kill him. This picture of David has given rise to various scholarly efforts to understand the text of Samuel as literature and to sort out legend and political propaganda from historical truth (see esp. Finkelstein and Silberstein, Halpern, and McKenzie).

The issue of the historicity of the kingdom of David has been raised at the archaeological level in reference to the city of Jerusalem. Very few remains have been found that are datable to the tenth century BCE, the century of David and Solomon. This suggests that Jerusalem may have been a very small village at that time, rather than the major administrative center of a united kingdom. On the other hand, an Aramaic inscription containing the phrase "house of David" was found at Tel Dan dating to the mid-800s BCE. This attests a ruling dynasty associated with the figure of David.

Influences: The Davidic covenant (2 Sam. 7) is the foundation of Israel's messianic ideal of political leadership. It stipulates that God's commitment to the line of David would be enduring. According to the Deuteronomistic writer of the books of Samuel, legitimate royal leadership could only come out of the line of David. The portrayal of David in this work introduces a complex notion of leadership that binds God and the king together in a covenant, but that also obligates the king to obedience to Torah. The revisionist history of 1 and 2 Chronicles idealized the figure of David in part by omitting the episodes that reflected negatively on him, including his intimidation of Nabal and subsequent marriage to Abigail, and his affair with Bathsheba and the subsequent murder of Uriah.

The NT Gospels of Matthew and Luke trace the lineage of Jesus of Nazareth through the line of David. The prayer of Hannah in 1 Sam. 2 becomes the prototype for the Magnificat of Mary (Luke 1:46–55).

David as poet and singer, boy-warrior who beheaded Goliath, and adulterous lover of Bathsheba became subjects for much artistic and literary imagination within the Western tradition. Sculptures by Michelangelo and Donatello especially idealize the youthful and heroic David.

Bibliography

Bandstra, Barry L. *Reading the Old Testament: Introduction to the Hebrew Bible.* 4th ed. Wadsworth, 2009.

Borgman, Paul. *David, Saul, and God: Rediscovering an Ancient Story.* Oxford University Press, 2008.

Campbell, Anthony F., and Mark A. O'Brien. *Unfolding the Deuteronomistic History: Origins, Upgrades, Present Text.* Fortress, 2000.

Finkelstein, Israel, and Neil A. Silberman. *David and Solomon: In Search of the Bible's Sacred Kings and the Roots of the Western Tradition.* Free Press, 2006.

Halpern, Baruch. *David's Secret Demons: Messiah, Murderer, Traitor, King.* Eerdmans, 2001.

McCarter, P. Kyle. *1 Samuel.* Doubleday, 1980.

———. *2 Samuel.* Doubleday, 1984.

McKenzie, Steven L. *King David: A Biography.* Oxford University Press, 2000.   B.B.

Sanballat (san-bal′at), the governor of Samaria in the latter half of the fifth century BCE and one of the chief opponents of Nehemiah's plan to rebuild Jerusalem. Sanballat conspired with Tobiah, governor of Ammon, and Geshem, king of Kedar, to intimidate the Jews and interrupt the work (Neh. 2:10, 19). As the walls neared completion, Sanballat and Tobiah authorized raids on the city (4:1–2) and, accusing Nehemiah of planning a rebellion against Persian rule, they repeatedly summoned him to account for his actions (6:1–7).

Sanballat's name was Babylonian (Sinuballit), but the names of his sons, Delaiah and Shelemiah (mentioned in the Elephantine papyri), incorporate "the LORD," the divine name for the God of Israel (and Samaria). In Neh. 2:10 he is called "the Horonite," i.e., a native of Beth-horon. The founder of a dynasty was also sometimes referred to in this way, and there is evidence that five of Sanballat's descendants governed Samaria after him, including Sanballat II early in the fourth century and Sanballat III at the time of Alexander the Great. *See also* Ezra and Nehemiah, books of; Samaria, district of.   P.K.M.

sanctification, the concept of setting something apart for holy use or consecrating a place, person, or thing to God. In the Bible, sprinkling with blood and other sacred rites (Lev. 4:5–7, 16–18; Num. 19:9–22) serve to sanctify places, objects, and persons. The people must consecrate or sanctify themselves before they can approach God (Exod. 19:22–24). Sanctification is also associated with obedience to Torah (Lev. 22:31–32): the people are called to be holy, just as God is holy (19:2; 20:26). In postexilic times, the persistent sinfulness of the people led to the image of an eschatological purification of the people (Dan. 7:18–22; Ps. 34:10). God would "sanctify" them and in so doing sanctify the divine name, which had been profaned among the nations by Israel's sinfulness. Ezek. 36:22–27 describes this process in three steps: first, the people are purified from their old sinfulness and idolatry by being sprinkled with clear water; second, the Lord gives them a "new heart" (cf. 11:19; Jer. 31:31–34); and, third, the Spirit of the Lord is put in the human heart. The result of this divine sanctification is a person freed from the "evil inclination" of the human heart and obedient to the will of God.

NT writers sometimes speak of the eschatological sanctification as in the future (Matt. 6:9), but they frequently describe it as something already accomplished for those with faith in Christ (2 Thess. 2:13). Christians, or their communities, are sanctified as temples of the Lord (1 Cor. 6:11, 20; Eph. 2:21; 1 Pet. 2:9). They have been made holy by anointing (1 Cor. 1:30; Eph. 5:26; 1 John 2:20). Jesus's sacrificial death is said to sanctify Christians (Heb. 9:11–14; 10:10; John 17:19). Sanctification, however, is not a passive gift. Christians must live out their lives in a holiness that reflects what they have received (Rom. 6:19; 1 Thess. 4:3, 4:7; 1 Tim. 2:15; Heb. 12:14). *See also* holiness.

P.P.

sanctuary, a holy place where God is present. In the wilderness, this was the tent of meeting or the tabernacle; in the time of Solomon, it was the temple at Jerusalem. There were, however, degrees of holiness in the temple. A few steps up from the court was the holy place, which was separated from the court by a hanging curtain. Only priests were allowed in the holy place. A few more steps and a curtain separated the holy place from the Holy of Holies, where only the high priest was allowed. Sometimes the entire temple is called the sanctuary; at other times "sanctuary" means only the Holy of Holies. *See also* temple, the.   G.W.B.

sand. The vast deserts of the biblical lands and the long stretch of sandy coastal land along the Mediterranean Sea are sources for powerful metaphors in the Bible. The most frequent allusions are to the inestimable number of grains of sand. God promises to make Abraham's "offspring as the sand of the sea, which cannot be counted because of their number" (Gen. 32:12); in Egypt, Joseph stores up grain "as the sand of the sea" (41:49). NT writers also use the metaphor of sand to symbolize great quantities (Rom. 9:27; Heb. 11:12). Elsewhere, the weight of sand is referenced (Prov. 27:3), and the shifting, unstable qualities of sand provide an image for one of Jesus's parables: those who do not keep his words are like a foolish man who builds

his house upon the sand, where wind and rain will cause it to collapse (Matt. 7:26).   S.R.

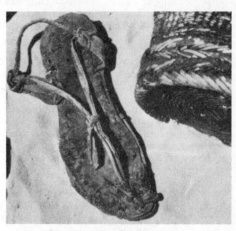

Leather sandal, almost two thousand years old, found at Masada.

sandal, a shoe fastened to the foot with thongs or straps. *See also* shoes.

Sanhedrin (san-hee'druhn; Gk. *synedrion*). *See* council, the.

Sansannah (san-san'uh), a town in the Negev belonging to the tribe of Judah listed in Josh. 15:31. It has been identified by scholars as Khirbet esh-Shamsaniyat, about three miles northwest of Beer-sheba, in southern Judea.

Saph (saf), one of the four Philistines identified as "descendants of the giants" slain by David's soldiers (2 Sam. 21:18; "Sippai," 1 Chron. 20:4).

Sapphira (suh-fi'ruh), the wife of Ananias who, like him, died after misrepresenting a gift to the apostles (Acts 5:1–11). *See also* Ananias.

sapphire, a gem composed of corundum, blue in color. The references in Exod. 24:10; Ezek. 1:26; 10:1 may be to lapis lazuli. *See also* breastpiece; jewels, jewelry.

Sarah (sair'uh; Heb., "princess").

1 Abraham's wife, who shared his journey to the land promised to them by God and lived with him there. She is initially called Sarai, just as Abraham is initially called Abram, but in Gen. 17:15, God declares that she is henceforth to be called Sarah.

God promised Abram numerous descendants, to whom the land of Canaan would belong. For this promise to be fulfilled, his wife would have a necessary and crucial role. But no sooner is the divine promise given than Abram jeopardizes everything by going to Egypt, where he passes Sarai off as his sister, and she is taken into the harem of Pharaoh (Gen. 12). A similar story appears later in Gen. 20, where Sarah is taken by Abimelech, king of Gerar (cf. Gen. 26). In both cases, Abram/Abraham practices this deception for fear of being killed on account of Sarah (Gen. 12 stresses her great beauty).

Another obstacle to the fulfillment of the promise of numerous progeny is Sarah's infertility (Gen. 11:30; 16:1). Her solution to this problem is to give her Egyptian slave Hagar to Abram, a custom according to which Hagar's child would be considered to be Sarai's (Gen. 16). The plan backfires when Hagar bears a son and subsequently regards Sarai with contempt. Asserting her superior status, Sarai deals harshly with Hagar, and Hagar flees to the desert, where God instructs her to return and submit to Sarai.

When Abram and Sarai are too old for childbearing, God reiterates the promise of offspring, changing their names and promising to bless them. Sarah is a variant of Sarai, both of which mean "princess," but the change of names is symbolic, representing a special destiny: "She shall give rise to nations; kings of peoples shall come from her" (Gen. 17:16). Abraham's reaction to this news is laughter (17:17). Sarah also laughs when she later overhears mysterious visitors informing Abraham that she will bear a son (18:1–15). Finally, in Gen. 21, the long-awaited heir is born and, appropriately, is named Isaac, meaning "laughter." Sarah protects Isaac's inheritance by having Hagar and her son, Ishmael, sent away. Though Abraham is displeased with this, God supports Sarah's decision, instructing Abraham, "Whatever Sarah says to you, do as she tells you, for it is through Isaac that offspring shall be named for you" (21:12).

Sarah dies at age 127, and Abraham purchases the cave of Machpelah from the Hittites for her burial place. Later Abraham (Gen. 25:9–10), Isaac (35:27–29), Rebekah (49:31), Jacob (50:13), and Leah (49:31) are also buried there. After Sarah's death, Abraham takes another wife, Keturah (25:1). Isaac is said to find comfort after his mother's death by marrying Rebekah (24:67).

Sarah is mentioned in the NT in three passages that recall Abraham's faith in God's promise (Rom. 4:19; 9:9; Heb. 11:11). The author of 1 Peter presents her as a model of women who accept the authority of their husbands: "It was in this way long ago that the holy women who hoped in God used to adorn themselves by accepting the authority of their husbands. Thus Sarah obeyed Abraham and called him lord" (3:5–6). The most extended treatment of Sarah in the NT, however, comes in Gal 4:21–31, where she is not mentioned by name. In that text, Paul uses Sarah and Hagar as allegorical symbols for two covenants: Sarah (the free woman) stands for the covenant of promise experienced by those who have faith in Jesus Christ; she is contrasted with Hagar (the slave woman), who stands for those who know only the covenant of law at Sinai. *See also* Abimelech; Abraham; Hagar; Isaac; Ishmael.

2 The daughter of Raguel who, after many difficulties, became the wife of Tobias in the book of Tobit. Prior to marrying Tobias, she had been married to seven husbands, each of whom was killed by the demon Asmodeus before the marriage could be consummated. She was reproached by one of her father's maids, who said, "You are the one who kills your husbands." This prompted her to weep and pray for God to take her life. Her prayer was heard and the angel Raphael sent to assist her. Tobias, the son of Tobit, married Sarah and, with Raphael's help, exorcised the demon from her. Thus, Sarah became Tobit's daughter-in-law. *See also* Tobit, book of.   J.C.E.

Sarai (sair'i), a variant spelling of Sarah, the name of Abraham's wife (Gen. 11:29–31; 12:5, 11, 17; 16:1–3, 5–6, 8; 17:15). Her name was changed by God to "Sarah" (17:15) at the time she received a divine blessing, as Abram's name was changed to "Abraham" (17:5). *See also* Sarah.

sarcophagus. *See* burial.

Sardis (sahr'dis), the regional capital of Lydia in the province of Asia Minor and one of the seven churches addressed in Revelation (1:11; 3:1, 4). The city had been founded in 1200 BCE as capital of the kingdom of Lydia, which was conquered by the Persians in the sixth century BCE. After Alexander defeated the Persians (334 BCE), the city was independent for a brief time before becoming a provincial capital of the Seleucid Empire. After Roman occupation (189 BCE), Sardis was placed under the administration of Pergamum. In the first century CE, it was a thoroughly hellenized city that served as the center for emperor worship in the region. There was also an impressive temple to Artemis. Of the seven churches addressed in Revelation, Sardis receives some of the harshest rebukes: "You have a name of being alive, but you are dead" (3:1). But there are still a few persons in the church who have not "soiled their clothes," and they are encouraged to persevere in their faithfulness (3:4).   P.P.

Sarepta (suh-rep'tuh; Heb., "smelting place"), a Phoenician city midway between Tyre and Sidon, where Elijah lodged with a widow during a famine and restored her son to life (1 Kings 17:8–24; cf. Luke 4:26). It is probably present-day Sarfend (Surafend). *See also* Zarephath.

Sargon II (sahr'gon; Akkadian, "the king is legitimate"), king of Assyria 722–705 BCE. Though mentioned by name only in Isa. 20:1, Sargon II has great significance for biblical history, as he was the king of Assyria responsible for the conquest of Samaria and deportation of Israelites in 720 BCE. Sargon II succeeded Shalmaneser V, apparently his brother, whose sudden death may have been due to court intrigue. Some have seen the very name of Sargon ("the king is legitimate") as a hint that he was a usurper. In any case, the death

Cuneiform inscription on a fragment of a stele erected by Sargon II at Ashdod after his conquest in 712 BCE.

of Shalmaneser V provoked massive disruptions in the empire, which took Sargon II two years to quell. His first year (721 BCE) focused on appeasing various groups at home, particularly those in the city of Asshur. In his second year (720 BCE), he attacked the two main rebellious clients: the Chaldean Marduk-apla-iddina II (biblical name: Merodach-baladan) and a Syro-Palestinian coalition led by the city of Hamath with Egyptian support (2 Kings 17:4). The battle against Merodach-baladan and his Elamite ally ended at the Mesopotamian city of Der, leaving Merodach-baladan as Babylonian king for the next decade. The battle against forces in the Levant, however, crushed all resistance (Isa. 10:9–11), even pushing the Egyptians back to their Sinai frontier at Raphia, which was destroyed. In the process, Israelite Samaria was retaken—it had joined the rebellion after an apparently earlier conquest by Shalmaneser V in 722 BCE (2 Kings 17:3–6)—and this time it was converted into an Assyrian province, and its population was largely deported and then replaced with peoples imported from other regions (an Assyrian tactic for dealing with conquered peoples). This action by Sargon II effectively marked the end of Israel as the northern kingdom (2 Kings 17). By contrast, Judah, the southern kingdom, was spared, having remained loyal to Assyria throughout.

These wars of 720 BCE, far from providing a permanent peace, set a pattern for the rest of Sargon II's reign. He spent his remaining years continually fighting to maintain the empire. Thus, in the Levant, several additional, and successful, campaigns were undertaken: in 717 BCE, to conquer Carchemish (Isa. 10:9); in 716 BCE, to force Egypt and the Arabs to yield control of the trade routes (19:23); and in 713–711 BCE, to deal twice with rebellions led by the Philistine city of Ashdod. Judah, however, was again spared, because

it refused to join Ashdod against Assyrian rule (Isa. 20).

In this same period, Sargon II was active in the north, against Urartu and its allies. He seriously weakened this old enemy of Assyria, even as he strengthened the Assyrian presence in southeastern Turkey, building on the base established by his earlier capture of Carchemish. With the Levant thus relatively stable, Sargon II returned, finally, in 710 BCE to Babylonia, intent on removing Merodach-baladan from power and making himself king of Babylonia, like his predecessors Tiglath-pileser III and Shalmaneser V. By 709 BCE, those goals were achieved, and by 707 BCE, Merodach-baladan's capital had been destroyed, although the Chaldean himself remained safe with his ally, the Elamites.

Sargon II's Babylonian triumph was acknowledged by kings far and wide, as was his completion in 706 BCE of a lavish new capital in the Assyrian heartland, where all his triumphs could be celebrated. The new city, Dur-Sharrukin (modern Khorsabad), was under Sargon II's rule for barely a year, however, for in 705 BCE he lost his life against Tabal in southeastern Turkey, where trouble had stirred again. In the wake of Sargon's shocking death (cf. perhaps Isa. 14:4–21), his successors abandoned Dur-Sharrukin as a royal residence, though they retained it as a headquarters for a provincial governor. *See also* Ashdod; Assyria, Empire of; Babylon; Samaria, district of.   P.B.M.

Sarid (sair'id), a town on the southern border of Zebulun (Josh. 19:10, 12), most likely modern Tell Shadud in the Esdraelon Plain about six miles north and slightly east of Megiddo.

Sargon II (*left*) and his vizier on a bas-relief at his Khorsabad palace, eighth century BCE.

Sarsechim (sahr'suh-kim), the name or title of one of the Babylonian princes who took Jerusalem (Jer. 39:3). If it is a title, it means "chief of slaves."

Satan (say'tuhn; Heb., "adversary"). The figure of Satan is found in only three places in the Hebrew Bible and all of these are often thought to be postexilic in date (i.e., after 538 BCE): Job 1–2; Zech. 3:1–2; and 1 Chron. 21:1.

In the first two instances, Satan is depicted as a member of God's court whose basic duty is to accuse human beings before God. He is not presented at this point as an enemy of God or as a leader of evil, demonic forces. In the third instance, Satan (or possibly a *satan*, "an adversary") is said to incite David to take a census (1 Chron. 21:1). There is some question as to whether the word here refers to a specific personality (as indicated by the NRSV) or whether the point might be that David fell victim to some undefined "adversary," such as the general human tendency toward evil; in the Hebrew text no definite article is used with the noun. In any case, the figure in 21:1 is not yet *the* embodiment of evil with whom the figure of Satan would come to be associated.

The idea of Satan evident in the NT writings developed during the Second Temple period, as is witnessed by some of the Hellenistic apocalyptic writings produced during that period. Probably under the influence of Persian ideology, Jewish thought embraced a more radical concept of dualism with regard to the created order—a dualism of good versus evil. There existed already the idea that God had a heavenly host, a group of messengers to carry out God's work and orders. The Persians also believed in a ruler over the powers of evil, who had many servants in this realm known as demons. The Hebrews could easily understand and assimilate such thinking into their already existing ideas: if there are good spiritual beings (angels), there can also be evil spiritual beings (demons). Still, they had no immediate notion that one supernatural being would be the preeminent leader of these forces of evil. Thus, as the religious thinking of the Jewish people developed, several different names were used to designate the leader of forces hostile to God: the devil, Belial (also Beliar), Mastemah, Apollyon (meaning the "Destroyer"), Sammael, Asmodeus, and Beelzebul (also Beelzebub). Satan, however, came to be the most used designation, possibly because in the LXX the name Satan in the passages cited above was rendered as "the devil." Another interesting development took place during this period—the figure of the devil or Satan came to be identified with "the serpent" of Gen. 3, allowing that story to be read in a different way than it had been before.

Satan and his cohorts came to represent the powers of evil in the universe, which, by Jesus's time, were even referred to as the kingdom of Satan. Jesus says that he is plundering this kingdom when he drives out demons in a way that manifests the kingdom of God (Matt. 12:26, 28–

29). The demons were considered to be the cause of sickness, both physical and mental, and of many calamities of nature (e.g., storms, earthquakes); in general, they were the forces responsible for much of human misery, and they were always opposed to God's purposes and God's people.

In the NT writings, Satan appears frequently, especially in the Gospels. The figure is also known by numerous other designations, among which are "devil" (e.g., Matt. 4:1), "tempter" (e.g., Matt. 4:3), "accuser" (e.g., Rev. 12:10), "ruler of demons" (e.g., Luke 11:15), "ruler of this world" (e.g., John 12:31) as well as some of the proper names listed above. One of the most interesting designations is "the evil one." In fact, it is likely that in the Lord's Prayer the petition traditionally rendered "deliver us from evil" would be better translated (as in the NRSV), "rescue us from the evil one" (Matt. 6:13b).

In the Gospels, Jesus confronts Satan before commencing his public ministry. Satan tests him with a series of challenges, and he proves that he is the faithful Son of God (Matt. 4:1–11; cf. Mark 1:12–13; Luke 4:1–13). In Luke's Gospel, Jesus indicates that Peter's denial of Jesus will constitute a similar trial, necessary because Satan demanded to have Peter in order to sift him like wheat (22:31). In his parable of the Sower, Jesus says that just as birds sometimes devour seed before it has a chance to grow, so Satan snatches the word that is sown in people before it can bear fruit (Mark 4:15). Elsewhere he refers to a woman who is crippled as having been "bound by Satan" (Luke 13:16). In Luke 10:18, Jesus says that he saw Satan fall like lightning, which explains why his disciples are able to drive out demons. Nevertheless, Satan would continue to harass believers in the life of the church, seeking to outwit them (2 Cor. 2:11) and tempting them to sin (1 Cor. 7:5). Sometimes, Satan successfully hinders Paul from carrying out his mission (1 Thess. 2:18). But, curiously, Satan can serve useful purposes; when wayward church members need discipline, they can be handed over to Satan for a time (1 Cor. 5:5; cf. 1 Tim. 1:20). Likewise, Paul refers to some physical affliction he suffers (his "thorn in the flesh") as a messenger from Satan that God has deemed he should retain so as not to become too elated (2 Cor. 12:7).

Satan is said to operate through human beings as well as through demons. Jesus refers to Peter as one who speaks for Satan when Peter tries to dissuade him from going to the cross (Matt. 16:23; Mark 8:33). Satan enters into Judas when the latter sets out to betray Jesus (Luke 22:3; John 13:27). In the early church, Satan fills the heart of Ananias to lie to the Holy Spirit about selling his possessions and giving the money to the church (Acts 5:3). Paul says that Satan disguises himself as an angel of light and that his ministers disguise themselves as ministers of righteousness (2 Cor. 11:14–15).

It is also clearly affirmed that, no matter how powerful Satan may appear to be, his final overthrow by the power of God is certain (Rom. 16:20; Rev. 20:1–10). *See also* adversary; angel; apocalyptic literature; Baal-zebub; Belial, Beliar; demon; devil; eschatology; evil; fall, the; Lucifer.

J.M.E./M.A.P.

satrap (say'trap), a provincial governor among the Achaemenid Persians. The word, originally Persian and taken over by the Hebrews and Greeks, occurs in the Bible only in the plural (Esther 3:12; Dan. 3:2). According to Dan. 6:1, "It pleased Darius to set over the kingdom one hundred twenty satraps, stationed throughout the whole kingdom."

Saul (sawl).

1 A Benjaminite from the mountain village of Gibeah who became Israel's first king. According to biblical tradition Saul was divinely appointed in response to a popular demand for a king, but he was not long in favor with God, who rejected him for disobedience. He spent much of his reign in conflict with David, whom God had chosen as his successor.

The story of Saul's selection as Israel's first king is told in 1 Sam. 9–10, where Saul is introduced as the handsome and unusually tall son of a prominent Benjaminite named Kish. One day, while searching for some asses that belonged to his father, he entered a village in the Ephraimite hills to seek the assistance of the local seer. The man turned out to be the prophet Samuel, who anointed his surprised guest as prince, or king-designate, over Israel (1 Sam. 10:1). After this private ceremony Saul was selected in a public lottery and acclaimed king by the people (10:17–27). His kingship would be subsequently confirmed through his prowess as a military leader (cf. 14:47–48). He seems first to have achieved regional prominence by leading a successful march against Nahash, an Ammonite

king who had laid siege to the fortress of Jabesh-gilead (1 Sam. 11). This victory won Saul a base of power extending beyond Benjamin and across the Jordan into Gilead. The summary of his wars in 14:47–48 also mentions campaigns against Moab, Edom, the Aramean state of Zobah, and Amalek (cf. 15). Israel's primary enemy at this time, however, was Philistia. Although Saul never achieved any permanent advantage over the Philistines (cf. 14:52), he did enjoy some success against them, and his kingdom offered the Israelites an alternative to Philistine sovereignty. His son Jonathan attacked the Philistine garrison in Gibeah, provoking an open revolt (13:3–4). The result was a decisive Israelite victory at Michmash (14), and the Philistines were temporarily excluded from the central hill country. It is difficult to determine how much territory Saul actually controlled, but it is unlikely that his kingdom extended beyond the central hills and parts of Gilead. The incorporation of Judah and the outlying territories into Israel was probably the achievement of David.

The biblical account of the latter years of Saul's reign (16:14–31:13) focuses mainly on David's rise to power. Saul serves as a foil, the divinely rejected king (13:7–14; 15:1–35) in contrast to whom the chosen successor is eulogized. Saul brings David into his court at Gibeah as a musician (16:14–23) and warrior (17:1–58), but David soon surpasses the king in military prowess (cf. 18:6–7) and wins the loyalty of all Israel, including Saul's eldest son, Jonathan (18:1–4), and his daughter Michal, who becomes David's wife (18:20–27). Saul, now tormented by "an evil spirit from the LORD" (16:14), becomes increasingly obsessed with jealousy and suspicion. He determines to kill David, who is aided and protected by both Jonathan and

Saul being presented by Samuel to the people, who proclaim him king (1 Sam. 10:17–24); detail from a thirteenth-century French illuminated manuscript.

Michal (19:1–1; 20:1–42). Saul persecutes David relentlessly, driving him into hiding in the desert and slaying eighty-five priests at Nob whom he suspects of having aided David. Still, David twice spares Saul's life when he has the opportunity to kill him. These stories are told with a touch of humor at Saul's expense. First, Saul goes into a cave to relieve himself, not knowing that David is hiding there, and David cuts off a piece of his cloak to display later as proof that he could have killed him (1 Sam. 24). Second, David sneaks into a camp where Saul is sleeping and takes a spear and water jar from his side to show him in the morning that, once again, he had opportunity to kill the king, but didn't (1 Sam. 26).

After Saul abandons his quest to kill David, he seeks out a medium at Endor to summon the ghost of Samuel, hoping for a favorable oracle on the eve of a battle with the Philistines. Instead, Samuel prophesies defeat and death, which then come to pass. On Mount Gilboa, Saul watches as his army is decimated by the Philistines and his sons are killed in battle. Then he kills himself by falling on his own sword (1 Sam. 31:4, but cf. 2 Sam. 1:1–16), thus leaving the way open for David to come to the throne. David offers an eloquent lament over the deaths of Saul and Jonathan. The Philistines cut off Saul's head and impale his body and the bodies of his sons on the walls of Beth-shan, but when the inhabitants of Jabesh-gilead hear this, some men from the city travel all night to take the bodies down and burn and bury them (1 Sam. 31:8–13). For this, David says they will be forever blessed (2 Sam. 1:4–5).

The biblical account of Saul and of the origin of monarchy in Israel reflects a point of view that is suspicious of kingship. Still, the account seems to incorporate material from a tradition that had a more favorable regard for Saul and kingship in general. The presence of doublets (two accounts with a similar theme) offers a strong indication that the story as told in the Bible has been edited from more than one earlier account. The two stories of David sparing Saul's life are one example of such a doublet. Another is the two (or actually three) accounts of Saul's selection as king. The first (1 Sam. 9:1–26) presents Saul very favorably, as a folk hero who did not seek to be king, but accepted his divine selection by the prophet Samuel. In a second story that presents his public selection as king, Samuel openly warns the people that it is sinful for them to want a king (10:17–27). Finally, in what is presented as a renewal of Saul's kingship, he appears as a warrior similar to the judges who delivered Israel in ways that obviated the need for a king (10:27b–11:15). Saul's rejection as king is also told twice. In one account (13:7–14), Saul himself offers a sacrifice that Samuel was supposed to conduct; as a result, Samuel tells him he will have no dynasty (i.e., his sons will not rule after him). In a second account (15:1–35), Saul fails to exterminate the Amalekites according to the ban under which they have been placed by God; thus, Samuel tells him that he has been rejected as king.

Through the interweaving of these traditions, the office of king is shown to be subordinate to the divine will as mediated through the office of prophet. Readers are assured that Samuel supervised all the events that brought Saul to the throne—and also oversaw Samuel's rejection and God's choice of David in his place. *See also* Benjamin; David; Jonathan; king; Samuel.

2 The Jewish name of the NT apostle and missionary also known as Paul (Acts 7:58; 9:1). *See* Paul.   P.K.M./M.A.P.

savior, one who delivers from present or future danger or distress. The primary usage of the word "savior" in the Hebrew Bible is in reference to judges and other leaders raised up by God to bring deliverance to Israel in time of national crisis (e.g., 2 Kings 13:5; Neh. 9:27). The term is also used for God, who employed these human saviors as divine agents. In Isaiah, "Savior" became a recognized title for God (e.g., 43:3; 45:21; 49:26; 60:16) in connection with the deliverance of Israel during the return from the exile. David is also presented as calling God "my savior" in prayer (2 Sam. 22:3) and psalms of praise (Ps. 17:7).

In the NT, Mary refers to God as "my Savior" (Luke 1:47; cf. 1 Tim. 4:10; Titus 1:3; 2:10; 3:4), but most uses of the word in the NT refer to Jesus, who is said to have been born a savior in Luke 2:20 (cf. 1:69). The term also occurs once in Eph. 5:23, six times in Jude and 2 Peter (Jude 25; 2 Pet. 1:1, 11; 2:20; 3:2, 18), and twice in the Johannine writings in the unique phrase "savior of the world" (John 4:42; 1 John 4:14). It is found ten times in the Pastoral Letters (1 Tim. 1:1; 2:3; 4:10; 2 Tim. 1:10; Titus 1:3, 4; 2:10, 13; 3:4, 6). Sometimes, the word refers to Christ in his capacity as the end-time deliverer (Acts 5:31; 13:23; Phil. 3:20), but more often it is used to describe him as the one who brings present, personal benefits such as cleansing from sin.

In the Greco-Roman world the title "savior" was frequently used of gods as the source of present, material benefits such as health, peace, and prosperity. The combined title "god and savior," or "god-savior," was very common. The term also had political connotations. Ptolemy I was called "savior" in the same sense as that of another title, "benefactor" (cf. Luke 22:25). Beginning with Caesar Augustus, the Roman emperors also assumed the title "god and savior." This imperial usage may offer an added reason for the early Christian use of this title: the true savior is not Caesar, but Christ (note the exact phrase "God and Savior" is applied to Jesus Christ in 1 Tim. 1:1; 2:3; Titus 2:13).   R.H.F./M.A.P.

scapegoat. *See* Atonement, Day of; Azazel.

scarlet, a bright red color associated with a dye extracted from an insect, the *Caccus ilicis,* and used for treating fabric and leather. The Hebrew for scarlet was *shani* or *tola'at,* used separately or in combination; the latter's basic meaning is "worm," referring to the insect producing the color. In Isa. 1:18 the two Hebrew words are used in parallel: "scarlet" and "crimson," in this case referring to the blood-red guilt of the sinner as opposed to whiteness of innocence. According to Matt. 27:28, Jesus was draped with a scarlet robe by soldiers mocking him as the "king of the Jews." That the color was associated with royalty, or at least considered to be luxurious, accounts for the references in Revelation, where the whore of Babylon (symbolizing Rome) is dressed in scarlet and sits on a scarlet beast (17:3, 4); condemnation also comes upon wealthy merchants who have dealt in purple and scarlet and various fine gems (18:12, 16). *See also* red.   N.L.L./M.A.P.

scepter, a king's elaborate ceremonial staff (Ps. 45:6). Originally a club that could also be used for digging (Num. 21:18), the scepter appeared frequently in ancient art and in the biblical writings as royal regalia with an established role in protocol (Amos 1:5, 8; Isa. 14:5; Esther 4:11; 5:2; 8:4). Israel in the wilderness period was the scepter (i.e., constituted the sovereignty) of God (Num. 24:17). Judah acquired similar status (Gen. 49:10; Ps. 60:7; Ezek. 19:11) as the origin of the Davidic king, the mighty scepter God sends forth from Zion. By metonymy, "scepter" might stand for any national sovereignty, e.g., Moab (Jer. 48:17) or Egypt (Zech. 10:11). The single NT reference to scepter (Heb. 1:8) is a variation of Ps. 45:6.   R.B.

Sceva (see'vuh), a Jewish high priest and the father of seven Jewish exorcists who attempted to imitate Paul's use of the name of Jesus in their exorcising of evil spirits, according to Acts 19:11–20. This unauthorized use of the name had unanticipated negative consequences when, rather than exorcising a spirit, the exorcists themselves were overcome by the spirit-possessed man. The tale is told with a dose of ribald humor, as the seven men flee the house naked and wounded. The residents of Ephesus, both Jews and Greeks, are awestruck, and many become believers, confessing to their own previous reliance on magical practices. As a result, a number of magic books are collected and burned. The name Sceva does not appear in known lists of Jewish high priests of the era; the designation "high priest" is probably intended only to identify him as a locally prominent priest. *See also* divination; magic.   A.J.M./M.A.P.

schools.

1 Institutions for formal education. In antiquity many wealthy families provided tutors at home for their children, and all families passed on occupational skills, cultural information, and values to their children, but these wider educational processes must be distinguished from what took place in actual schools. The Bible does not mention formal educational institutions, but there is nevertheless some evidence of their existence and function.

Lintel from a third-century school at El-Al, near Golan, with the inscription, "This is the school of Eliezer Ha-Rapad."

Schooling in Ancient Israel: The existence of schools may be deduced from the activities of monarchs, officials, and priests and from Near Eastern parallels. The priests had to preside over a complex ritual, teach Israel's traditions, and instruct the people who came to the temple, so it is highly likely that priests were trained in the temple. Even at an early date (twelfth century BCE), Samuel goes to Eli for an apprenticeship at Shiloh (1 Sam 1:24–28). In a later period Jehoshaphat is pictured as sending the Levites and priests to teach the book of the law in the cities (2 Chron. 17:7–9). The kings, nobles, and high officials of the complex state under the monarchy (1025–587 BCE) also needed training. When Solomon's son Rehoboam became king, he consulted with the young men who had grown up with him (1 Kings 12:8–10), and one of Solomon's enemies, Hadad, married an Egyptian and had his son Genubath raised in Pharaoh's house among the sons of Pharaoh (11:20). The seventy sons of Ahab were raised by elders who were their guardians (2 Kings 10:6). Chronicles attributes to Jonathan, David's uncle, and to Jehiel the care of the king's sons. Though none of these texts speaks directly of an institutional school, they demonstrate the need for organized training of the leaders of Israel.

Israel's position as an active participant in diplomacy and trade in the first millennium BCE demanded that the leaders and numerous officials and bureaucrats be educated to read, write, and carry on business according to law and accepted form. Israel's calendar, taxes, and economics demanded a knowledge of mathematics, and the numerous traditions that were handed on demanded written records, even in a society that still had a strong oral base. In addition, the Bible often refers to writing, to the chronicles that lie behind the books of Kings, to the duty of reading the law yearly (Deut. 31:12–13), and to the duty of every householder to write the law on doorposts of the house (6:9). A good number of people, then, were assumed to be able to read and write: not only royal scribes (2 Kings 22;3), but also an anonymous boy selected apparently at random from among the people of Succoth (Judg. 8:14). Prophets (Elisha, Isaiah, Jeremiah) also had disciples who preserved their traditions orally and in writing; these schools of prophets may have been more like schools of thought and ways of life than institutional schools, but at some point literary training and activity took place. Finally, the Hebrew

Bible itself bears witness to intense literary activity and reflection on previous written traditions from the exile (587/6 BCE) on.

Possible Methods of Instruction: Isa. 28:10 and 13 exhibit a pattern that may match memorization techniques like those that would have been used in schools; some interpreters have likewise claimed that the book of Proverbs was a school text. Archaeological discoveries in the Near East reveal that students learning how to write copied exercises (a calendar found at Gezer with the agricultural seasons on it may be a student's exercise). More advanced students copied classics and documents such as letters and contracts. Students being trained for high office learned diplomacy, economics, and government. It is a reasonable hypothesis that fortified cities and regional capitals had either scribes or priests able to teach the young.

Ezra the scribe (fifth century BCE) was a high official of the Persian government charged to see that the law of God was known and observed. The book of Sirach (early second century BCE) has praise for the scribe who knows God's law and is an adviser to rulers (38:24–39:11). Sir. 51:23 summons the uneducated to "lodge in the house of instruction"; this is probably a metaphorical invitation from Wisdom, but the metaphor itself depends upon familiarity with some sort of physical structure where formal education occurred. The Ptolemaic and Syriac empires, of which Israel was a part from 332 BCE, and the Roman Empire, which succeeded it in 63 BCE, were highly literate and had well-developed institutions for instruction of youth. It is likely, therefore, that Jews of this period were influenced by the cultural milieu and had comparable educational institutions. The community at Qumran, which had a strong priestly component and produced the Dead Sea Scrolls, was highly literate, and Josephus, who was a first-century priest, describes his education (but without mentioning actual schools he attended).

Schooling in the NT: In Luke's Gospel, Jesus is portrayed as reading from scripture in the synagogue (4:16–20), but we have no evidence that Jesus ever wrote anything as part of his teaching. He is portrayed, rather, as an oral teacher par excellence. John 8:6 says that Jesus wrote on the ground as part of his interaction with the crowd that wished him to condemn an adulteress, but it does not say that he wrote letters or words. Paul wrote greetings in his own hand in his letters to his churches (e.g., Gal. 6:11–18; cf. Col. 4:18), and Acts says that he had been educated in Jerusalem at the feet of Gamaliel (22:3), but Paul does not describe the nature of his schooling. Still, the early Christian community quickly set its traditions in writing in a manner that assumes a fairly high degree of literacy. *See also* education; scribe; teaching.

2 Followers of a particular philosophy or lifestyle. In the Greco-Roman world, philosophical systems were often called "schools" (Gk. *hairesis*), since a philosopher would typically recruit disciples (students) and train them in a particular way of thinking marked by a particular way of life. Josephus refers to the Pharisees, Sadducees, and Essenes as "schools," perhaps to assist his Roman readers in understanding these Jewish groups on analogy with Greco-Roman schools of philosophy. Luke also does this in the book of Acts, though the NRSV translates *hairesis* in those references as "sect" (5:17; 15:5; 26:5). Those who do not hold to the Christian faith refer to the followers of Christ as a "school" (NRSV: "sect") as well (24:5, 14; 28:22).
A.J.S.

scorpion, any arachnid of the order Scorpionida, of which a dozen species are known in the Near East, most of which are the yellow variety *Buthus quinquestriatus*. They are mainly nocturnal and carry a stinger at the end of the tail by which they paralyze food and defend themselves. They are symbols of desolate danger (Deut. 8:15), extremely severe treatment (1 Kings 12:11, 14; 2 Chron. 10:11, 14), the most hazardous surroundings (Ezek. 2:6), and excessive pain and torture (Rev. 9:3, 5, 10). They symbolize the powers of evil (Luke 10:19), and Jesus uses them as a symbol of the paternal mistreatment no caring father would offer to his child (Luke 11:12).
R.S.B.

scourge, whip or lash made of leather thongs attached to a handle (John 2:15). As a metaphor, it refers to any punishment (at the hands of enemies or natural disaster) visited on the people by God (Josh. 23:13; Isa. 10:26; 28:15, 18; Job 9:23).

The word often refers to the use of scourging to punish criminals. Legally, a "milder" form of flogging was used by magistrates as a warning to those responsible for disorder. Josephus (*Jewish War* 2.13.7) reports that authorities in Caesarea quelled rioting between Jews and Greeks by catching those responsible and punishing them "with stripes and bonds." Paul says that he endured such punishment on several occasions (2 Cor. 11:24–25; Acts 16:22–25; 21:24). A more severe beating was administered in connection with other punishments. It could sometimes lead to the death of the condemned person. Livy reports that such lashing preceded crucifixion (*History* 22.13.9; 28.37.3). In Luke 23:14–22, Pilate suggests that Jesus be given the lighter beating as a warning. Mark 15:15 and Matt. 27:26 report that Jesus received the severe beating as one who had been condemned to death. *See also* cross; trial of Jesus.
P.P.

scribe, one trained in the formal art of reading and writing, usually with competence in some area such as law, economics, or the like. The word derives from the Latin root for "write" and translates Hebrew and Greek words with similar etymologies. In the ancient Near East the designation "scribe" covered a variety of offices from the local copiers of documents and contracts for ordinary people to government officials invested with serious responsibilities. Like the modern secretary, the scribe was generally concerned with

Egyptian royal scribes, New Kingdom period.

written records, bureaucracy, and administration. Scribes were common to Egypt, Mesopotamia, Israel, and other countries of the Near East. The book of Proverbs contains international wisdom traditions that were developed by the scribal class in many countries.

In the Hebrew Bible, the scribe first appears as a muster officer (Judg. 5:14). In the monarchic period (eleventh–tenth centuries BCE) the scribe was a high cabinet officer concerned with finance, policy, and administration (2 Kings 22; Jer. 36:10). Jeremiah's associate, Baruch, who recorded his words, was also a scribe (Jer. 36:32). In postexilic times (sixth century BCE), Ezra the scribe was sent by the Persian king to instruct and guide the inhabitants of Judea. He was both an official of the Persian Empire and knowledgeable of the laws and customs of Israel (Ezra 7). In the early second century BCE, Ben Sira praises the scribe for his learning and for his involvement in affairs of government (Sir. 38:24–39:11). In the Maccabean period (167–63 BCE) the learned Hasideans who sued Alcimus and Bacchides for peace (1 Macc. 7:12–13) and Eleazar, the prominent leader who was martyred (2 Macc. 6:18), are all called scribes, with the probable implication that they were learned in Mosaic law. The term does not seem to denote a group with particular beliefs or a set political program, but rather learned men of any party or persuasion.

In the NT scribes sometimes appear alone, but they are frequently associated with other Jewish groups. In Matthew and Luke the scribes are also paired with the Pharisees in questioning Jesus; the phrase "scribes and Pharisees" occurs eight times in Matthew (5:20; 12:38; 23:13, 15, 23, 25, 27, 29; cf. 15:1; 23:2). In Mark's Gospel, the scribes typically appear in association with the high priests and elders (11:27), and the bulk of their appearances are in conjunction with the death of Jesus. Similarly, in the early chapters of Acts the scribes and elders are opponents of Christianity (4:5; 6:12). Thus the scribes are seen both as part of the leadership and also as a learned class. Two passages (Mark 2:16; Acts 23:9) use the phrase "scribes of

the Pharisees," indicating that scribes could belong to other groups within Judaism. Scribes are mentioned only once in John ("the scribes and the Pharisees," 8:3) and, apart from 1 Cor. 1:20, they are not mentioned in the NT outside of the Gospels and Acts.

In almost all Gospel references they are opponents of Jesus, but Mark's Gospel has a story in which a scribe agrees with Jesus and extrapolates on Jesus's words in a manner that leads Jesus to tell him, "You are not far from the kingdom of God" (12:28–34). Matthew and Luke also tell of a scribe who wants to follow Jesus, but Jesus responds to him in a way that might imply he does not think the man has the commitment to bear the hardship such discipleship would require. He tells Jesus, "I will follow you wherever you go," and Jesus responds, "Foxes have holes, and birds of the air have nests; but the Son of Man has nowhere to lay his head" (Matt. 8:19–20). In Matt. 13:52, Jesus refers to scribes who have been trained (literally "discipled") for the kingdom of heaven. *See also* education; schools; teaching; town clerk.

A.J.S./M.A.P.

scripture (from the Lat., "writing"), a document or collection of documents containing material that is highly esteemed in a religious community accepting the document(s). Greeks, Romans, Persians, and Egyptians all preserved and valued written documents such as hymns, oracles, myths, and revelations. In Judaism and Christianity, the term "scripture" (Gk. *tais graphais,* lit., "the writings") eventually came to be restricted to those writings included in an approved canon. Jesus refers many times to the scriptures, always invoking writings that are now found in the Christian OT (e.g., Matt. 21:42; 22:29; John 2:22; 7:38; 19:24). In several instances, Jesus speaks of the scriptures being fulfilled though his ministry (Luke 4:21; John 13:8; 17:12) and, especially, through his death on the cross (Matt. 26:54, 56; Mark 14:49; Luke 22:37; cf. Luke 24:27; John 5:39; 19:24, 28, 36–37; Act. 1:16). In the book of Acts, Christian missionaries are depicted as using the scriptures to present their claims about Jesus (8:32, 35; 17:2, 11; 18:24, 28). Paul quotes frequently from the scriptures, again citing texts that are now included in the Christian OT and almost always interpreting those passages in ways that point to Christ (Rom. 4:3; 9:17; 10:11; 11:2; Gal. 3:6; 4:30). Specifically, "Christ died for our sins in accordance with the scriptures, and ... he was buried, and ... raised on the third day in accordance with the scriptures" (1 Cor. 15:3–4). In Rom. 15:4, Paul affirms that "whatever was written in former days was written for our instruction, so that by steadfastness and by the encouragement of the scriptures we might have hope."

Jesus sometimes refers to the scriptures as the "word of God" (Matt. 15:6; Mark 7:13; John 10:35), and he declares that the scripture cannot be annulled (John 10:35). Timothy is told to attend to the public reading of scripture (1 Tim. 5:18) and is reminded, "All scripture is inspired by God and is useful for teaching, for reproof, for correction, and for training in righteousness" (2 Tim. 3:16). In 2 Peter 3:16 Paul's letters seem to be regarded as among the scriptures. *See also* canon; inspiration; New Testament; Old Testament; revelation.

L.W.C./M.A.P.

scroll (Heb. *megillah*), a roll of papyrus or specially prepared leather used for writing (see Jer. 36). Papyrus scrolls were imported from Egypt, where they had been manufactured since at least 3000 BCE. To make a papyrus scroll, evenly sized strips were cut from the pith of the papyrus plant and laid side by side horizontally and vertically, forming two layers that would become the front and back sides of the sheet. Water and pressure were applied to make the strips adhere. After drying, the sheets were rubbed smooth with shells or stones. Leather scrolls were made of sheep, goat, or calf skin that had been de-haired, scraped, washed, stretched on a frame, and dried. The hair side, on which the writing was done, was scraped smooth and rubbed with a pumice stone. Rectangles of prepared leather were stitched together to make a scroll. Vertical and horizontal guide lines were traced with a dry point and a straight edge. Black ink was made from carbon soot mixed with water and gum, red ink from red ocher or iron oxide. Although writing could be erased from papyrus with water (Num. 5:23), errors on leather had to be marked out or scraped off. Scribes wrote with pens made from rushes, frayed at the end, and from the Hellenistic period on (after 63 BCE), with pointed reed pens split at the end. Equipment was carried in a case tied to the scribe's waist (Ezek. 9:2). Whether papyrus or leather scrolls were customarily used for writing biblical books in the preexilic period (prior to 587/6 BCE) is disputed, but at least by the Hellenistic period leather was the preferred material (e.g., the Dead Sea Scrolls). References to scrolls and writing in the Bible include Deut. 28:58; Josh. 1:8; Ps. 45:1; Isa. 8:1; Jer. 8:8; 25:13; Ezek. 2:9–10; Rev. 5:1. *See also* Dead Sea Scrolls; writing.

C.A.N.

sculpture, the art of carving or modeling in relief or in the round. The second commandment's prohibition of graven (carved) images (Exod. 20:4) is thought to have inhibited development of this art among the Hebrews. The sculpture known to us from the Bible and from archaeology attests dependence on foreign (especially Phoenician) models and artisans, e.g., the carved cedar beams and panels of Solomon's temple, with their motifs of palms, pomegranates, and cherubim, and the carved ivory inlays discovered in Samaria (cf. Amos 6:4). Most standing images were understood as idols representing foreign gods, including Aaron's golden calf (Exod. 32) and Jeroboam's calves (1 Kings 12:28–30), but the cherubim in the inner sanctuary of the temple (6:23–28) were a notable exception. The "sculptured stones" near Gilgal (Judg. 3:19, 26) may represent memorial stones

or carved images in an open-air sanctuary (cf. Josh. 2:20). *See also* cherubim; idol; ivory; temple, the.

P.A.B.

Scythians (sith'ee-uhnz), a nomadic people from the Caucasus who threatened the Assyrian Empire and later the Persian Empire from the north. In the Bible they are called Ashkenaz (Gen. 10:3; 1 Chron. 1:6; Jer. 51:27). The fifth-century BCE Greek historian Herodotus describes an unsuccessful campaign by the Scythians against Egypt, in the course of which they looted a temple of Aphrodite in Ashkelon; on the basis of this account the Scythians have sometimes been identified as the unnamed enemy from the north in Jer. 1:14 (cf. Zeph. 1:10), but this is uncertain. The Scythians' cruelty was proverbial in later antiquity (see 2 Macc. 4:47; 3 Macc. 7:5; 4 Macc. 10:7; and also perhaps Col. 3:11). *See also* Ashkenaz.

M.D.C.

Scythopolis (sith-op'uh-lis). *See* Beth-shan.

sea, a term (Heb. *yam*) denoting any large body of water, salt or fresh. In the Bible, "the sea" often designates the Mediterranean Sea. The "bronze sea," sometimes also called simply "the sea," was a great basin in the forecourt of the temple (2 Kings 25:13; Jer. 27:19).

seah (see'uh), a unit of measure for dry volume of uncertain size, probably about one-third of a bushel. It is translated simply as "measure" in the NRSV (Gen. 18:6; Matt. 13:33). *See also* weights and measures.

seal, a device by means of which ownership of objects or origin of documents could be designated. The term is used in two primary senses in the Bible, with secondary meanings developing from them through the use of metaphor. The primary references are to (1) an object, usually a small, semiprecious stone with writing cut into its surface, that makes an impression on clay or wax; and (2) the impression itself made by such an object.

Use and Manufacture: Seals were widely used throughout the ancient Near East from the fourth millennium BCE through the Roman period, because they provided both identification and prestige to the owner. The majority of seals from the biblical period identify the owner, and they often have a title and an emblem or engraved scene as well. Those persons who possessed seals were usually members of the upper classes and were often associated with the workings of government (see below). Their seals performed important functions in their professional activities.

Cylinder seals were popular in antiquity, though less so among Israelites and early Christians than among others. Such seals could be rolled by hand across wet clay in order to produce an intricate scene once the cylinder had made a complete revolution. Scenes of religious activities and depictions of deities or royalty could be executed easily in this fashion and then made public through the distribution of impressions.

The question of a seal's manufacture is an intriguing one, especially because so many of them are quite small (oval in shape, some less than an inch long), yet possessed of exquisite design. Apparently copper and iron were used for drilling, sometimes with an abrasive glued to the implement. That diamonds were occasionally used is a recent conjecture, but the evidence is not conclusive. Water and olive oil were probable lubricants. The lapidary must have possessed keen hand–eye coordination, artistic talent, and the ability to write in reverse so that the impression made by the seal could be read correctly. Some seals were bored through at one end so that they might be fastened to a cord and worn around the neck (see Gen. 38:18). Others were set in a frame and used for rings or necklaces.

There are approximately sixty references to seals and sealing in the Bible. The contexts imply use of seals to render something secure against tampering (Jer. 32:10; Matt. 27:66), demonstrate authority (1 Kings 21:8; John 6:27), seal a letter (1 Kings 21:8; 1 Cor. 9:2), seal a covenant (Neh. 9:38), delegate authority (Esther 8:8; John 6:27), and seal documents (Isa. 8:16; Jer. 32:10; Rev. 5:1). Archaeological research suggests that seals were also used as amulets, heirlooms, gifts, temple or burial deposits, and as tools used to imprint pottery vessels.

The NT usually uses the terms "seal" and "sealing" in their primary senses (e.g., Rev. 5:1), but metaphorical use is made of the terms as well. Paul refers to the circumcision of Abraham as a "seal of the righteousness which he had by faith" (Rom. 4:11). Christians are "sealed with the promised Holy Spirit" (Eph. 1:13). Perhaps most striking of all is the reference in Heb. 1:3 to Christ as the "stamp" of God's nature, where the single Greek word (*charaktēr*) refers to the impression made by a seal.

As Archaeological Evidence: Seals can be of great benefit to the reconstruction of past history and cultures. On numerous occasions Egyptian scarab seals (so named because they resemble the sacred beetle) or cartouches (name-rings used to produce seals) have been found in the Levant. Not only does this illustrate the cultural influence of Egypt in Canaan during the third and second millennia BCE, but a seal found by an archaeologist in a stratified deposit can be very helpful in dating the stratum. Excavations at Tel Lachish have uncovered a seal on one of the ancient gate systems bearing the name of Ramesses III (ca. 1183–1152 BCE). The gate is part of a stratum destroyed by fire. The destruction, therefore, is dated to the reign of Ramesses III and is taken by some scholars to be evidence of early Israelite incursion during the settlement of Canaan (Josh. 10:31–32).

Seal from the reign of Nebuchadnezzar II (605–562 BCE) portrays a man, a woman, and a snake beneath the tree of life.

Recently discovered clay *bullae* (hardened seal impressions) from the postexilic era (i.e., after late sixth century BCE) have shed additional light on an obscure period in biblical history. They have provided names with the title "governor" that supplement the meager evidence of the Bible for reconstructing the succession of leaders of the community. Furthermore, various impressions bear the stamp *yehud,* "Judah," supporting the conclusion that Judah was administered as a separate province in the Persian Empire.

Over a thousand seal impressions on jars have been discovered dating to the late eighth and early seventh centuries BCE. These impressions have in common the inscription "to [belonging to] the king" (Heb. *lmlk*); a scarab figure with either two or four wings; and the name of one of four towns in Judah: Hebron, Ziph, Socoh, or an unknown location (Heb. *mmsht*). Recent investigation has dated these impressions to the reign of Hezekiah (ca. 715–687 BCE) and perhaps to his preparations for war with Assyria. The stamped jars were containers for commodities that may have come from taxation and/or royal landholdings.

Personal Seals: A number of personal seals have been discovered that may shed light on the structure of Israelite society in the preexilic period. They range in date from the ninth to the sixth centuries BCE, with the vast majority coming from the eighth and seventh centuries. Among the titles following the personal name are:

"Who is over the house," probably a title synonymous with majordomo or royal steward. The office is known from several references in the Hebrew Bible.

"Scribe." A recently discovered impression reads: "Barakiah son of Neriah the Scribe." This name and title should be compared with that of Jeremiah's faithful friend of the same name and title in Jer. 36:32 ("Baruch" and "Barakiah" are the shorter and longer forms, respectively, of the same name).

"Servant of the king." A number of seals have been found with this title.

"Son of the king." Several examples have been discovered.

"Daughter of the king." Only one of these has been found, reading in Hebrew *mah adanah.* A beautiful lyre was engraved on the seal.

Bibliography
Gorelick, Leonard, and Elizabeth Williams-Forte. *Ancient Seals and the Bible.* Udena, 1983.

J.A.D.

Sea Peoples, the name given to a group of peoples, apparently from the Greek island of Crete, who began to invade the eastern coastlands of the Mediterranean Sea sometime around the thirteenth century BCE. Their attempt to invade Egypt was repulsed by Ramesses III (ca. 1190 BCE), a victory he commemorated on a monumental frieze. There, the Sea Peoples, called in Egyptian the Perasata (probably the source of the biblical term "Philistines," which designates these people), are depicted as slender warriors wearing tasseled kilts and magnificent helmets. Their subsequent invasion of the plains of Canaan sometime later was more successful, and, since their invasion from the west coincided with the Israelites' invasion from the east, a collision between the two groups was inevitable. That collision, which lasted for many years, is reflected in the conflicts between the Israelites and the Philistines recorded in the books of Judges and 1 and 2 Samuel. *See also* Amarna, Tell el-; Ashdod; Caphtor; Crete; Gaza; Philistines.   K.H.R.

season. There are only two seasons in the Levant, the dry (April–September) and the wet (October–March). The amount and duration of rainfall and the temperatures vary from year to year and place to place. Generally as one goes south or east, rainfall is lighter and the temperatures are warmer. In Hebrew or Greek no particular word designates season, but several words are used for specific periods of time described by such things as weather (the time of rain, Deut. 11:14, the time of heat, Ps. 32:4) or agricultural features (a time of threshing and sowing, Lev. 26:5; the time when a fig tree has fruit, Matt. 24:32) or annual festivals (the time of Unleavened Bread or Passover, Exod. 23:15; Luke 2:41; 22:1). In the Gezer Calendar, a schoolboy's ditty written on a potsherd during the period of the early Israelite monarchy (tenth century BCE), the months of the year are described by agricultural activity: "His two months are olive harvest, His two months are planting grain, . . ." *See also* weather.   N.L.L.

seat, judgment. *See* judgment seat.

Seba (see´buh), **Sabeans** (suh-bee´uhnz), a place mentioned four times and a people mentioned three times in the biblical text. Job 1:15 identifies the destroyers of Job's family as Sabeans. Isaiah sees the Sabeans as one of several nations God gave as a ransom for Israel (43:3); they were also a source of wealth (45:14), together with Egypt and Ethiopia. In Joel 3:8 they are described as a "nation far away," in Joel's threat that they will buy Phoenician and Philistine slaves from Judah. Gen. 10:7 catalogs Seba as a son of Cush, together with Havilah, Sabtah, Raamah, and Sabteca, as does 1 Chron. 1:9. Kings from Seba are mentioned together with those of Sheba and Tarshish as bringing tribute and gifts (Ps. 72:10) to Israel's king. Their definition as a distant source of riches seems clear. The precise location is not evident from biblical sources.

From the evidence of archaeological work, it is clear that the Sabeans occupied the portion of southwest Arabia that is today the land of Yemen. It was comparatively well watered and fertile, but the resources were augmented by extensive irrigation facilities (as at Marib). The Sabeans' location was also fortunate for trade development. They could capitalize on traffic in myrrh and frankincense through the land caravan route running north up the Hijaz, the coastal plain that lies at the eastern shore of the Red Sea. Their extensive trade in gold and precious stones was known to the biblical writers (see also Isa. 60:6; Jer. 6:20; Ezek. 27:22–23, where Sheba occurs as the Hebrew spelling of the South Arabic name Saba). Their territorial controls fluctuated, but included at times the port of Aden, where contacts with shipments of goods from India as well as Africa were made. Sabean ships ranged to Africa and India, contributing both to the variety of trade goods and to the wealth of the exchanges flowing into Sabean resources.

Although Sabean history is not well known, its Semitic inhabitants successfully developed caravan trade by the tenth century BCE, as evidenced by the visit of the queen of Sheba to Solomon (1 Kings 10:1–13; 2 Chron. 9:1–12). Sabean colonization apparently included parts of the adjacent Ethiopian coast. From the ninth to fifth centuries, Sabean kings numbered over twenty, from which archaeological evidence survives in the form of temples, dams, sluices for irrigation, bronze statues, and inscriptions. Saba weakened thereafter, but its successful defense against Rome's initial efforts to subdue it led to importation of Hellenistic art and pottery soon locally imitated. *See also* Sheba; Sheba, queen of.   R.S.B.

Secacah (si-kay´kuh; Heb., "thicket, cover"), a city of Judah (Josh. 15:61), probably modern Khirbet es-Samrah, located about three miles southwest of Khirbet Qumran in the Valley of Achor.

Second Coming of Christ. *See* eschatology; Parousia.

second death, the death of the soul or spirit, the death of a resurrected person, or eternal damnation, referred to in the NT book of Revelation (2:11; 20:6, 14; 21:8). According to this book, all the dead will rise on the day of judgment. Then the wicked will be cast into the lake of fire to suffer their second death. In Matt. 10:28, Jesus alludes to God as one who has the power to destroy both soul and body. A Jewish text written in the second century BCE describes a chaotic wilderness in which fire blazes brightly. In this place the spirits of the wicked will be killed during the last days (1 Enoch 108:3–4). *See also* abyss; Hades; hell; punishment, everlasting.   A.Y.C.

Second Quarter, the western hill of Jerusalem, the part of the city in which Huldah the prophet lived (2 Kings 22:14; 2 Chron. 34:22). *See also* Huldah; Jerusalem.

sect, a term used six times in the NRSV to translate Greek *hairesis* when it refers to such Jewish parties as the Pharisees or Sadducees (Acts 5:17; 15:5; 26:5) or, indeed, to the nascent Christian movement (Acts 24:5, 14; 28:22). That same term is used in Greco-Roman literature to refer to philosophical schools. *See also* Essenes; Pharisees; Sadducees; schools.   A.J.S.

Secundus (si-koon′duhs), a Christian from Thessalonica who accompanied Paul from Macedonia on his last trip to Jerusalem (Acts 20:4–5). He probably helped Paul gather money for his contribution from the Gentile churches to the poor in Jerusalem (see 2 Cor. 8:23). *See also* collection for the saints.

seed.
   1 The grain or ripened ovules of plants in contrast to stems, leaves, and flowers (Gen. 1:11, 12, 29; Deut. 11:10; 14:22). Jesus used seeds as examples in four of his parables: the Seed and Weeds (Matt. 13:24–30); the Sower (Matt. 13:3–9); the Seed Growing Secretly (Mark 4:26–29); and the Mustard Seed (Mark 4:30–32).
   2 Human semen (Lev. 15:16–18; 22:4; Heb. 11:11).
   3 Human offspring or descendants (Gen. 9:9; Lev. 22:4; Mark 12:19–22). In this sense, the term is particularly applied to the physical (Gen. 12:7; 17:7) and spiritual (Gal. 3:29; Rom. 4:11–12, 16) descendants of Abraham. Jesus Christ is also referred to as the seed of Abraham (Gal. 3:15–18) and of David (2 Tim. 2:8).
   4 The divine nature implanted in believers (1 John 3:9; cf. 1 Pet. 1:23).   R.H.S.

seer (Heb. *khozeh* or *ro'eh*), a person who received divine messages in visions or dreams. Visionaries existed in Israel throughout its history and were found particularly in Judah, where they may have been connected with the royal court (2 Sam. 24:11; Amos 7:12; Mic. 3:7; Isa. 29:10; 30:10; 1 Chron. 21:9; 25:5; 29:29; 2 Chron. 9:29; 12:15; 19:2; 29:25, 30). The title "seer" is given especially to Samuel (1 Sam. 9:5–21). *See also* prophet.

Segub (see′guhb).
   1 The youngest son of a Bethelite named Hiel. He died (possibly as a human sacrifice) when his father rebuilt the Jericho gates (1 Kings 16:34), fulfilling the word of Joshua (Josh. 6:26).
   2 The son of Hezron and a daughter of Machir (1 Chron. 2:21, 22).

Seir (see′uhr; Heb., "hairy").
   1 The mountainous region southeast of the land of Canaan inhabited by the Edomites. Also called "Mount Seir," the region may have encompassed, not only the mountains east of the Arabah (the Rift Valley), but also those on the west side. This is suggested by such passages as Num. 20:16, where

Kadesh-barnea (modern Ain el Qudeirat) is said to be a town on the edge of Edom's territory (cf. Num. 20:23; Deut. 1:44; 33:2; Judg. 5:4). The eastern highlands, built mainly of red Nubian sandstone, rise up to over 5,000 feet above sea level and receive enough rainfall for some cultivation and animal husbandry. Perhaps the most important physical advantage of Seir in ancient times was its location, positioned to control the trade routes from Arabia and the Red Sea. The two centers of power in the land were Bozrah and Teman, both of which guarded important caravan routes.
   According to Deut. 2:22, the Horites (Hurrians) had inhabited Seir before they were driven out by the Edomites; these Horite groups are enumerated in Gen. 36:20–29. The Edomites, descendants of Jacob's brother Esau, eventually established a kingdom in the region (36:9–19, 31–43; Josh. 24:4). The Israelites were denied passage through Seir by the Edomites on their journey from Kadesh-barnea to the plains of Moab (Num. 20:14–21; Deut. 2:1–8). The region continued to play a significant role in Israel's history (cf. 2 Sam. 8:13–14; 2 Kings 14:7, 22).
   2 A hill on the northern border of the tribe of Judah, located west of Jerusalem on the western slopes of the Judean highlands, between Kiriath-jearim (modern Deir el Azar) and Chesalon (modern Kesla; Josh. 15:10). Its exact identification is uncertain.   D.A.D.

Seirah (see′uh-ruh), the haven to which Ehud fled (Judg. 3:26). Its location and identity (whether it was a town, region, cave, or some other feature) are unknown.

Sela (see′luh; Heb., "crag").
   1 The fortress city of Edom (2 Kings 14:7), renamed Sela by King Amaziah of Judah. This Sela is modern Umm el-Bayyarah, just above Petra in south Transjordan.
   2 An Amorite border town (Judg. 1:36) whose location is unknown.
   3 An unidentified location mentioned in Isa. 16:1.

Selah (see′luh), a word of uncertain origin and meaning found in certain psalms (e.g., Pss. 3; 4; 52; 88; 143). It also appears in Hab. 3:3, 9, 13, verses that are part of a psalm preserved in that book. There has been much speculation about the meaning of this word—a musical notation, a pause in singing for narration, instructions for choral singers or instrumentalists—but there is no agreement among scholars as to which is to be preferred.

Seleucia (si-loo′shuh), the ancient port city of Antioch in Syria (modern Samandag, Turkey), founded by Seleucus I Nicator in 301 BCE, apparently on an older site called Pieria. In the mid-third century BCE, Ptolemy III Euergetes of Egypt took the city ("fortress" in Dan. 11:7), but it was regained by Antiochus III in 219 BCE. According to 1 Macc. 11:8, Ptolemy VI Philometor again captured Seleucia for Egypt in his coastal campaign of 146 BCE, but the city reverted to Seleucid control in 138 BCE. Granted the status of a free city by Pompey in 63 BCE, Seleucia remained so throughout NT times. According to Acts 13:4, Barnabas and Paul, accompanied by John Mark, sailed from Seleucia to Cyprus at the beginning of their first missionary journey (ca. 49 CE). Other references to voyages to and from Antioch probably imply embarkation and landing at Seleucia as well (14:26; 15:39). Other cities named Seleucia were in Cilicia, Mesopotamia, and Bashan. *See also* Antioch; Paul; Ptolemy; Seleucids.   C.H.M.

Seleucids (si-loo'sidz), a dynasty of Hellenistic kings that ruled an area including, at various times, Bactria, Persia, Babylonia, Syria, and southern Asia Minor. The name originates from Seleucus I Nicator, son of Antiochus, one of the generals of Alexander. In the struggle for power following Alexander's death in 323 BCE, Seleucus was eventually successful in carrying out a series of moves that made him one of the most powerful of the Diadochi ("successor kings"). The rule of the Seleucid dynasty dates from 312 BCE, when Seleucus and Ptolemy I of Egypt joined to defeat Antigonus of Phrygia at the battle of Gaza, thus regaining for Seleucus the satrapy of Babylonia, earlier lost to Antigonus. At the battle of Ipsus in 301 BCE, Seleucus gained much of Asia Minor and Syria, but the area of the Levant, which Seleucus regarded as rightfully his, was appropriated by Ptolemy, his former ally. The struggle for this region was finally settled in 198 BCE, when Antiochus III ("the Great") defeated the Egyptian general Scopus at the battle of Paneas, and Seleucid rule of Judea began.

Antiochus IV Epiphanes is the most important Seleucid ruler for biblical literature. His eleven-year reign was marked by an aggressive attempt to hellenize the Jews, an attempt that led to the

THE SELEUCID DYNASTY

Seleucus I Nicator	312–281 BCE
Antiochus I Soter	281–261 BCE
Antiochus II Theos	261–246 BCE
Seleucus II Callinicus	246–226 BCE
Seleucus III Soter (Ceraunus)	226–223 BCE
Antiochus III ("The Great")	223–187 BCE
Seleucus IV Philopator	187–175 BCE
Antiochus IV Epiphanes	175–164 BCE
Antiochus V Eupator	164–162 BCE
Demetrius I Soter	162–150 BCE
Alexander Balas	150–145 BCE
Demetrius II Nicator	145–139 BCE
(Antiochus VI Epiphanes Dionysus	*145–142 BCE)*
Antiochus VII Sidetes	138–129 BCE
(Hereafter, much internal strife and	
frequently rival claimants.)	

Maccabean war and eventually to Jewish independence from Syria. The first two books of Maccabees reflect this struggle, detailing the offensive actions of Antiochus, who meddled in the appointment of high priests, forced Greek customs upon the Jews, looted the temple, defiled the altar, and cruelly persecuted the pious Jews who wished to observe their religious laws and customs (see 1 Macc. 1:10–62; 2 Macc. 4:7–7:42). The book of Daniel may also reflect the impact of Antiochus Epiphanes upon the Jews. Antiochus is usually identified as the "little horn" and the oppressor of the "holy ones of the Most High" referred to in 7:8, 20–27; 8:9–14, 23–25. The "abomination that makes desolate" of 11:31 is probably a reference to an altar to Zeus that Antiochus caused to be erected on the altar of the Jerusalem temple.

The latter years of the Seleucid dynasty saw much internal strife among princes and, eventually, a conquest of the weakened kingdom by Tigranes of Armenia (83–69 BCE). Eventually, the Romans put an end to Seleucid rule when Pompey made Syria a Roman province in 64 BCE.

The Seleucids founded Antioch in Syria as their capital as well as many other cities that were to become centers for the spread of Hellenism (e.g., Antioch of Pisidia, Apamea, Laodicea, Edessa, Beroea, Seleucia, and Dura-Europos). Hellenized Jews lived in these cities, in part due to the Seleucid practice of rewarding veterans with land in newly colonized areas (Jewish soldiers had fought in the army of Seleucus I, just as other Jews had fought with Ptolemy). *See also* Alexander; Antiochus; Daniel, book of; Maccabees; Maccabees, First Book of; Maccabees, Second Book of; Ptolemy; Seleucia.   F.O.G.

self-control. Although self-control (Gk. *enkrateia*) was deemed a prime virtue in Greek philosophical tradition, the concept is mentioned only rarely in the LXX and in the NT. The Roman procurator Felix was alarmed when Paul "argued about justice and self-control and future judgment" (Acts 24:25). Paul knew that it was difficult for Corinthian Christians to exercise self-control in sexual matters (1 Cor. 7:9). He compared himself with an athlete who "exercises self-control in all things" for the gospel's sake (9:25). For Paul, self-control was not really a human achievement, but one of the manifold manifestations of the "fruit of the spirit" (Gal. 5:22–23). The Pastoral Letters maintain that "God did not give us a spirit of cowardice, but rather a spirit of power and of love and of self-discipline" (2 Tim. 1:7). In particular, a bishop must not be arrogant or quick-tempered or a drunkard, but "a lover of goodness, prudent, upright, devout, and self-controlled" (Titus 1:7–8). Second Peter links self-control with such characteristics as faith, knowledge, and steadfastness (1:6).   J.F.J.

Semites (sem'its), a term used to describe various peoples of the Fertile Crescent in antiquity (i.e., Arabs, Arameans, Assyrians, Babylonians,

Canaanites, Hebrews, and Phoenicians). The word denotes a modern categorization that originated in the eighteenth century CE among Western scholars to describe observable tendencies in language and culture within the peoples of the region from Persia in the east to Africa in the west. The term itself derives from the name Shem, one of Noah's three sons born after the flood. In Gen. 10:21–31 there is a description of Shem's descendants according to the names of nations known to the biblical writer(s). The whole of Gen. 10 has been called by scholars the "Table of Nations," because it presents the then known world of nations in three categories, each tracing its lineage back to one of Noah's three sons, Shem, Ham, and Japheth (10:1).

Linguists and philologists also use the term "Semitic" with regard to groups of languages. There is some disagreement among them concerning the interrelationships among the various Semitic languages, but there is general agreement on the following classifications. *East Semitic* includes various dialects of Assyrian and Babylonian. The term "Akkadian" is sometimes used as a reference to these languages, which were written in cuneiform, impressed on wet clay with a wedge-shaped pen. *Northwest Semitic* includes the various Aramaic and Canaanite dialects. Classical Hebrew, Moabite, and perhaps Ugaritic are some examples. *South Semitic* includes Arabic and Ethiopic. The advance of archaeological work in the past two centuries has made a number of texts written in these languages available to scholars for the first time. This has placed the study of classical Hebrew on firmer historical ground as far as its relationship to other ancient Semitic languages is concerned. The development of an alphabetic language and script among ancient Semites was transmitted by the Phoenicians to the Greek Isles, ultimately to influence many of the world's most widely used languages, including English. Although many details of this transmission remain obscure, the contribution of the alphabet is one of the enduring legacies of Semitic culture.

Religion appears in great variety among the Semites as evidenced by surviving texts. Some scholars point to the early narratives in the book of Genesis concerning Israel's ancestors as one illustration. Yet another example can be found in the texts discovered in Syria at the site called Ras-Shamra (ancient Ugarit). The institution of sacrifice was generally characteristic of Semitic religions.   J.A.D.

Senaah (suh-nay'uh), a city whose people are listed among those returning from exile in Babylon (Ezra 2:35; Neh. 7:38). It may be modern Khirbet 'Auja el-Foqa, about three miles north of Jericho. Its location parallels its identification with Magdalsenna (Heb., "Tower of Sena'a"), a fortress that guarded the road from the Jordan Valley to Baal-hazor in earlier times.

Seneh (see'nuh), the name of one of two rocky crags flanking the pass at Michmash, which

Jonathan used in approaching the Philistines (1 Sam. 14:4). Identity of the crags remains uncertain, but they are probably to be located in the Wadi es-Suweinit, about seven miles northeast of Jerusalem.

Senir (see'nuhr), the Amorite name for Mount Hermon, according to an editorial note in Deut. 3:9. In Ezek. 27:5, Senir supplied fir planking (and Lebanon, a cedar mast) for the metaphorical ship Tyre—here Senir probably designates the entire Anti-Lebanon mountain range. Hermon and Senir appear together, as separate parts of a whole, in Song of Sol. 4:8 and 1 Chron. 5:23. *See also* Hermon, Mount; Lebanon; Tyre.

Sennacherib (suh-nak'uh-rib), king of Assyria 705–681 BCE. He assumed the throne of the vast Assyrian Empire convulsed by uprisings on both its southern and western flanks following the death of his father, Sargon II. Babylon and its sometime ally Elam were perceived as the most immediate threat to his rule, so that Sennacherib undertook a two-year campaign (704–702 BCE) to restore Assyrian suzerainty over the south. In 701 BCE, he turned to the troubled west. Details of this military undertaking are known from two major sources: an Assyrian royal inscription about Sennacherib's "third campaign" and the biblical book of 2 Kings (see 18:7–8 and 18:13–19:37). These sources complement each other and are in agreement as to the main outline of the rebellion and its suppression by the superior Assyrian forces, but only the biblical source reports the miraculous salvation of Jerusalem.

According to these two sources, King Hezekiah of Judah spearheaded an anti-Assyrian coalition of Phoenician, Philistine, and south Syrian states. Though there were several years to prepare for the inevitable Assyrian response—note the drilling of the Siloam tunnel in Jerusalem to supply water to the city in case of siege (2 Kings 20:20; 2 Chron. 32:3–4)—the coalition was no match for Sennacherib. The coastal cities succumbed quickly, so that the full brunt of reprisal was soon directed against Judah. An Egyptian relief force

Sennacherib seated on his throne, receiving booty from Lachish, which he conquered in 701 BCE; Nineveh reliefs.

under the command of Tirhakah engaged Sennacherib at Eltekeh in the Judean Shephelah (cf. 2 Kings 18:21; 19:9), but it suffered heavy losses and withdrew.

During the attack upon Judah's border fortresses, Sennacherib sent a negotiating team led by top Assyrian officers—their titles are recorded in 2 Kings 18:17 (Tartan, Rabsaris, Rabshakeh)—to solicit Hezekiah's surrender. The counsel of the prophet Isaiah not to surrender strengthened Hezekiah's determination to hold out (19:5–7). But "when all the fortified cities of Judah" had fallen to Sennacherib, Hezekiah capitulated. He agreed to pay a heavy indemnity of "three hundred talents of silver and thirty talents of gold" (18:14–16), which he sent to Nineveh with other valuables. Thus, the siege of Jerusalem was lifted and the city spared destruction. According to 2 Kings, that deliverance from destruction was due to the fact that an angel of the Lord killed eighty-five thousand Assyrian soldiers during the night (19:35). Nevertheless, the other territories of the kingdom of Judah were ceded to loyal Assyrian subjects, namely, the rulers of Ashdod, Ekron, Gaza, and Ashkelon, and Hezekiah resumed his former status as Assyrian vassal.

Sennacherib commemorated his victories in Judah with a wall relief in his palace at Nineveh depicting the attack and capture of Lachish. He maintains that he shut up Hezekiah in Jerusalem "like a bird in a cage" and offers this detailed account of his conquests: "I laid siege to 46 of his strong cities, walled forts and to the countless small villages in their vicinity, and conquered them. . . . I drove out 200,150 people, young and old, male and female, horses, mules, donkeys, camels, big and small cattle beyond counting and considered them booty."

Assyrian historical inscriptions indicate that for the next twelve years, Babylonian affairs engaged Sennacherib's attention. Other areas of the empire remained pacified, but at least three campaigns to Babylon were undertaken (700 BCE, 694–693 BCE, and 691–689 BCE).

Sennacherib designated his son Esar-haddon as his heir, even though the latter was not in the direct line of succession. Two of his other sons, Adrammelech and Sarezer, murdered their father and led an unsuccessful rebellion against Esar-haddon (2 Kings 19:37). *See also* Assyria, Empire of; Hezekiah.   M.C.

sentinel, a person stationed on a wall (2 Sam. 18:24; Song of Sol. 5:7) or in a watchtower (2 Chron. 20:24) whose task was to warn of approaching danger (Ezek. 33:2–6; cf. Ps. 127:1). Sentinels also guarded the fields and vineyards, especially during harvest season (Isa. 5:2; cf. Job 27:18). The term is often used in a figurative or symbolic sense, as the prophets identified themselves as sentinels for the house of Israel (e.g., Isa. 62:6; Ezek. 3:17; 33:7–9; Mic. 7:4). *See also* tower; vine; watchtower.

Sephar (see´fuhr), one of the limits of the territory inhabited by the family of Joktan (Gen. 10:30). It may be either a region, a boundary, or a town. The location remains uncertain, although most suggestions place it somewhere in southern Arabia.

Sepharad (sef´uh-rad), the residence of some exiles from Jerusalem mentioned in Obad. 20. It is identified with Sardis (modern Sart) in east central Turkey, the capital city of the ancient Lydian empire. Its standing as a major commercial center is reflected in the archaeological materials uncovered at this site, including a large Jewish synagogue from the later stages of settlement. *See also* Sardis.

Sepharvaim (sef´uhr-vay´im), a city from which the Assyrian government drew settlers to place in Israelite territory after Israel's fall to Assyria ca. 722/1 BCE (2 Kings 17:24, 31). Later references to Sepharvaim as a city whose kings and gods are impotent (18:34; 19:33) may refer to the identical location, but that remains uncertain. A Sepharvaim is likewise mentioned in Isa. 36:19 and 37:13, but the information given there is insufficient for identification of its location.

Sepphoris (sef´uh-ris), a Jewish town in Lower Galilee, about three miles northwest of Nazareth. During the Hasmonean period (152–37 BCE), the town probably became the administrative center for the Galilean area. Sepphoris submitted to Herod the Great, but, after his death in 4 BCE, it was sacked by Varus. While tetrarch of Galilee and Perea, Herod Antipas rebuilt the city and resided there prior to making the city of Tiberias his capital. After the destruction of Jerusalem in 70 CE, Sepphoris was the seat of the Sanhedrin for a time before that body moved to Tiberias. There is no reference to Sepphoris in the Bible, but the inhabitants of nearby Nazareth certainly would have been acquainted with it. It was probably during the second century CE, during Hadrian's reign, that the city's name was changed to Diocaesarea, meaning "City of Zeus and the Emperor."

Sepphoris became the focus of intense scrutiny in the last decades of the twentieth century, because it was believed that analysis of the area might reveal something about the milieu in which Jesus was raised. Since Sepphoris was a large city within walking distance of Nazareth (a small village), it seemed reasonable to assume that residents of Nazareth would have frequented Sepphoris and maybe even worked there. This might have been especially true of persons like Jesus and his father, Joseph, if their trade involved work associated with construction projects (cf. Matt. 13:55; Mark 6:3, where the term *tektōn,* translated "carpenter," literally means "builder"). A prominent theory in the late twentieth century held that Jesus would have had frequent opportunities to encounter Greek philosophers and other attributes of Hellenistic thought during his trips to Sepphoris.

Initial excavations at the city seemed to bear this out. Much of the archaeological work in the 1970s and 1980s revealed extensive building projects. Besides paved, colonnaded streets and large buildings, a public theater was also excavated. Such discoveries did suggest Greek influence, but further work in the 1990s called this into question. Of particular interest was excavation in the domestic quarters, in which virtually no pig bones were found in strata that were prior to the Bar Kochba revolt, compared to the situation in the Late Roman and Byzantine periods, when pig bones came to represent 30 percent of the animal remains. This is taken to suggest that prior to the two Jewish revolts, the population of Sepphoris was overwhelmingly Jewish and observed Jewish laws and customs. Likewise, the prominence of stone vessels points to a Jewish population at Sepphoris prior to 70 CE (stone vessels were preferred by Jews because they cannot easily be made unclean; cf. John 2:6). Furthermore, coins minted at Sepphoris during the pre–70 BCE period do not depict the image of the Roman emperor or pagan deities (as was common in the coinage of this time). And the excavations have not uncovered any structures typically present in a Greco-Roman city (such as pagan temples, gymnasium, odeum, nymphaeum, or shrines and statues). It is only in remains attributable to the post–70 BCE period that pagan art and architecture begin to make their appearance.   M.K.M./M.A.P.

Septuagint (sep′too-uh-jint), the Greek translation of the Hebrew Bible that was begun in the third century BCE in Alexandria, Egypt. "Septuagint" comes from the Greek word for "seventy" and refers to the tradition recounted in the *Letter of Aristeas* that seventy-two Jewish translators were brought to Egypt by Ptolemy II Philadelphus (285–246 BCE) to translate the Pentateuch. Why the number seventy-two was rounded off to seventy is uncertain, but it may have seemed appropriate, since seventy elders had accompanied Moses up the mountain to receive the law (Exod. 24:1, 9). The traditional abbreviation for the Septuagint is LXX (seventy in Roman numerals). The translations of the books differ in style, accuracy, and substance. Manuscripts of the LXX found among the Dead Sea Scrolls at Qumran indicate that revisions were constantly being made. In addition, Hebrew manuscripts found at Qumran differ from the standard Hebrew Masoretic Text, but agree with some of the Greek renderings in the LXX. Thus the LXX often witnesses to a Hebrew manuscript tradition different from and earlier than the Masoretic Text and, so, is valuable in solving textual difficulties. The LXX sometimes arranges material within a book in a different order and it occasionally evinces a shorter or longer version of a book. For example, Jeremiah is one-eighth shorter in the LXX than in the Masoretic Text and may derive from a Hebrew version earlier than the one presently in the Bible. The

order of materials in Psalms and Proverbs differs from all extant Hebrew texts, and the book of Joshua contains numerous additions, omissions, and other changes. Several later Greek translations of the Hebrew Bible were also made (Aquila, Theodotion, Lucian) and parts of these have found their way into extant copies of the LXX.

The LXX was the biblical text from which the NT writers, who wrote in Greek, quoted most often. Moreover, the translation of Hebrew words into Greek resulted in Greek words taking on Hebraic meanings, a fact of great significance for the interpretation of the NT. For example, the Greek word for "grace" (*charis*) came to mean God's benevolence (because it was used to translate Hebrew *khesed*), whereas in Greek literature prior to the LXX it had no particular religious significance, connoting only the human quality of kindness, charm, or pleasantness. *See also* Dead Sea Scrolls; Masorah.   A.J.S.

Serah (sihr′uh), a daughter descended from the Hebrew tribe of Asher (Gen. 46:17). Serah reportedly moved to Egypt. She is subsequently included in the census (Num. 26:46; 1 Chron. 7:30) of settlers in Canaan. This prominence spawned heroine status in later nonbiblical stories.

Seraiah (si-ray′yuh; Heb., probably "the LORD persists"), a name borne by twelve people in the Bible, but for seven of these no biographical data is provided (cf. 1 Chron. 4:13–14, 35; 6:14; Ezra 2:2; 7:1; Neh. 10:2; 11:11; 12:1, 12).

1 David's scribe (2 Sam. 8:17); the same man's name, however, is given as Sheva in 20:25, as Shavsha in 1 Chron. 18:16, and as Shisha in 1 Kings 4:3.

2 The chief priest who had the misfortune of witnessing the burning of the first temple in Jerusalem in 587 BCE before he was personally executed by Nebuchadnezzar (2 Kings 25:18–21; Jer. 52:24–27). He is possibly the same person listed in 1 Chron. 6:14.

3 The son of Tankhumeth who survived the destruction of Jerusalem and brought his militia to swear allegiance to Gedaliah, the Judean governor installed by the Babylonians (2 Kings 25:23; Jer. 40:8).

4 The "quartermaster" who accompanied the defeated Judean king Zedekiah to Babylon, bearing with him the prophet Jeremiah's written curse against that enemy kingdom (Jer. 51:59–64).

5 The son of Azriel, whom King Jehoiakim had earlier sent to arrest Jeremiah and his scribe, Baruch (Jer. 36:26).   W.S.T.

seraphim (ser′uh-fim; Heb., "fiery ones"), fiery beings of supernatural origin. Seraphim appear in Isaiah's vision of God, where they are attendants or guardians before the divine throne, analogous to the cherubim (6:1–7). They praise God, calling "Holy, holy, holy is the Lord of Hosts," and one touches Isaiah's lips with a hot coal from the altar, cleansing him from sin. Seraphim have six wings. Two cover their faces, two cover their feet (a euphemism for genitals), and the other two are used for flying. A flying seraph (Heb. *saraph;* NRSV: "serpent") appears in Isa. 14:29 and 30:6 together with "adders" and "vipers." The same Hebrew word (*saraph*) is used to describe the "fiery serpents" (NRSV: "poisonous serpents") that afflicted Israel in the wilderness (Num. 21:6–9; Deut. 8:15). Thus, seraphim may have had a serpentine form and served, not only as guardians of the divine throne, but also as emissaries of divine judgment. *See also* cherubim.   M.A.S.

Serapis (si-rah′pis), the deity of a cult established by Ptolemy I (d. 383/2 BCE) to serve as a focal point for the Greek population in Egypt. The god was derived from Osor-Hapi, the deified Apis bull, and Osiris, the god of the underworld and consort of the goddess Isis. The cult mixed Egyptian and Greek features and was centered in Alexandria. The temple, called a Serapeum, contained a great cult statue with a gold head and jeweled eyes. Artistic representations of Serapis often present him with a head like Zeus. He is represented as ruler of the fertile earth and was thought, like Isis, to overrule fate. He was also a healing god known for curing blindness. As one of the many deities worshiped in the Roman Empire, Serapis would have been part of the "idolatry" denounced by Paul (Rom. 1:22–23; 1 Cor. 8, 10).   P.P.

Sergius Paulus. *See* Paulus, Sergius.

Sermon on the Mount, the traditional designation for a section of Matthew's Gospel (chaps. 5–7) that presents the teaching of Jesus on matters of discipleship.

Nomenclature: The name "Sermon on the Mount" derives from Matt. 5:1, which indicates that Jesus delivered this teaching to his disciples on a mountain. It has been called this at least since the time of Augustine (354–430 CE), who wrote what is believed to be the first commentary on the Sermon on the Mount ca. 392–394 CE. About half of the material in the Sermon on the Mount finds parallel in a section of Luke's Gospel in which Jesus instructs a multitude of people "on a level place" (6:17); this portion of Luke's Gospel is accordingly called the Sermon on the Plain (6:20–49).

Contents and Theme: The Sermon on the Mount contains material that has been extremely influential on the Christian religion and on secular civilization in areas where Christianity has flourished. It is here that one finds the Beatitudes (5:3–12), the Golden Rule (7:12), and the Lord's Prayer (6:9–13). Here Jesus speaks of the meek inheriting the earth (5:5) and identifies his followers as the "salt of the earth" (5:13). He urges people to "turn the other cheek" and to "go the second mile" (5:39, 41). He refers to "wolves in sheep's clothing" (7:15), to "serving two masters" (6:24), to storing up "treasure in heaven" (6:20), and to

"casting pearls before swine" (7:6). As presented in Matthew's Gospel, the overall theme of the Sermon on the Mount is discipleship or response to the call of Jesus. The sermon follows Jesus's announcement that "the kingdom of heaven is at hand" (4:17) and explains the implications of this announcement for those who repent and follow Jesus. It also provides a compendium of the commands of Jesus that missionaries will teach to their converts when they seek to fulfill the Great Commission given at the end of Matthew's Gospel (28:16–20).

The Sermon on the Mount begins with the Beatitudes, which indicate for whom the advent of the kingdom will be a blessing, and then proceeds to describe the "greater righteousness" that is to mark followers of Jesus. These expectations are detailed with explicit contrast to traditional ethical teachings, including those that this Gospel attributes to the scribes and Pharisees. The sermon then turns to private religious duties (almsgiving, prayer, and fasting) and describes the proper attitude toward wealth and material things that characterizes those who seek God's kingdom above all else. It continues with exhortations commending self-critical humility and trust in God and multiple warnings regarding laxity, false prophets, and evildoers. It concludes with a parable likening obedient and disobedient disciples to wise and foolish builders whose homes are built on rock or sand.

Setting and Audience: Matthew's Gospel specifies the setting for the Sermon on the Mount as "the mountain" and the primary audience for these words as Jesus's disciples (5:1). The reference to an unnamed mountain is ambiguous, and the precise geographical location that Matthew might have intended cannot be determined. It is likely, however, that readers are expected to regard this mountain as the same one to which the risen Jesus summons his disciples at the end of the Gospel to give what is called the Great Commission (28:16–20). Further, the location of his teaching on a mountain recalls the giving of the law to Moses in Exod. 19–31. Just as God gave the law to Moses, who then became the great teacher of Israel, so here Jesus gives divine commandments to his disciples, who will teach them to a church composed of people from all nations (16:18; 28:19–20).

The designation of Jesus's disciples as the intended audience for the Sermon on the Mount indicates that the author of this Gospel understands the words that follow as primarily Christian teaching rather than as an exposition of moral behavior to be expected of or imposed upon the world at large. Baptized persons who want to be "made disciples" (28:19–20) will obey these commandments of Jesus, which call for a greater righteousness than is exhibited by people in general (5:20). At the conclusion of the sermon, however, readers suddenly learn that the words have also been overheard by the crowds, who were astounded at Jesus's teaching, since he taught "as one who had authority, not as their scribes" (7:28–29).

The point of the crowds' astonishment is not simply that Jesus taught in an authoritative style, but that his teaching revealed him to be a person authorized to speak for God in a way that other religious teachers were not (cf. 8:5–13; 9:8; 10:1; 21:23–27; 28:18). In this way, Matthew seems to acknowledge that the Sermon on the Mount possesses an inherent wisdom capable of impressing or challenging those for whom it was not primarily intended. For Matthew's community, "the crowds" may represent the unbelieving world in which their church is situated, those who have not experienced Jesus's call, but who have heard snippets of his message. Although they do not know what to make of Jesus or his message, such people may be astonished at the authority evident in his words. Thus Matthew's Gospel presents the Sermon on the Mount as teaching that is explicitly intended for the church, but it does so with an awareness that people outside the church might find these words stimulating as well.

Sources: Jesus is not likely to have preached the material found in Matt. 5–7 as a single sermon in the form that we now have it; rather, sayings of Jesus that Christians remembered or attributed to him were gathered and compiled in the format of a sermon. Since Matthew's Gospel was composed about fifty years after the time of Jesus's Galilean ministry, it is usually assumed that this material also underwent a process of redaction.

Aramaic sayings of Jesus were translated into Greek and amended in ways that would serve the developing needs of the church. Scholars disagree in their estimates of how extensive this editing may have been.

Most scholars attribute the final composition of the Sermon on the Mount (as we now have it) to the author of Matthew's Gospel, but they believe this evangelist already possessed a similar though less-developed sermon in the pre-Gospel material that is commonly called the Q source. The author of Luke's Gospel is also thought to have had access to this source, so those parts of Matthew's Sermon on the Mount that parallel Luke's Sermon on the Plain are believed to represent material that both evangelists derived from Q. Following this logic, Q appears to have contained a sermon by Jesus that began with the Beatitudes and concluded with the parable of the Two Builders. Other material also occurs in the same sequence in both versions of Jesus's sermon:

Beatitudes, 5:3–12 (Luke 6:20–23)

Love of enemies, 5:38–47 (Luke 6:27–36)

Judge not, 7:1–2 (Luke 6:37–38)

Speck and log, 7:3–5 (Luke 6:41–42)

Tree and its fruit, 7:16–20 (Luke 6:43–45)

Lord, Lord, 7:21 (Luke 6:46)

Parable of Builders, 7:24–27 (Luke 6:47–49)

The Golden Rule (Matt. 7:12; Luke 6:31) also occurs in both the Sermon on the Mount and the Sermon on the Plain, although its placement is slightly out of sequence. A common theory holds that Matthew constructed his Sermon on the Mount by inserting a lengthy central section (including all of Matt. 6) into the sermon that he found already formed in Q.

The matter is complicated by the fact that other parts of the Sermon on the Mount have parallels to material found elsewhere in Luke, including: Matt. 5:13–16 and Luke 14:34–35; Matt. 5:25–26 and Luke 12:57–59; Matt. 6:9–13 and Luke 11:2–4; Matt. 6:19–21 and Luke 12:33–34; Matt. 6:22–23 and Luke 11:34–36; Matt. 6:24 and Luke 16:13; Matt. 6:25–34 and Luke 12:22–31; Matt. 7:7–11 and Luke 11:9–13; Matt. 7:13–14 and Luke 13:23–24; Matt. 7:22–23 and Luke 13:26–27. Such passages are generally thought to derive from the Q source, though not necessarily from a single or coherent sermon of Jesus presented in Q.

All told, 62 of the 106 verses that make up the Sermon on the Mount have close parallels to material in Luke's Gospel. A few additional verses have parallels in Mark's Gospel (Matt. 5:31–32 and Mark 10:11–12; Matt. 6:14–15 and Mark 11:25–26); these could be items that Matthew took from Mark and integrated into the sermon material from Q. The rest of the Sermon on the Mount consists of material not found in the other Gospels (5:17–24, 27–30, 33–37, 48; 6:1–8, 16–18; 7:6, 15); this could be material derived from Q that Luke did not use, or it could be material that Matthew composed himself or took from unknown sources.

Finally, the attention of scholars is often drawn to passages in the Sermon on the Mount that parallel material found in various NT letters:

5:10 (1 Pet. 3:14)

5:11–12 (1 Pet. 4:13–14)

5:16 (1 Pet. 2:12)

5:31–32 (1 Cor. 7:10–11)

5:34–37 (James 5:12)

5:39 (Rom. 12:17; 1 Thess. 5:15; 1 Pet. 3:9)

5:44 (Rom. 12:14; 1 Cor. 4:12)

5:48 (1 Pet. 1:15)

6:19–20 (James 5:1–3)

6:25 (Phil. 4:6)

7:1–2 (Rom. 2:1–3; 14:10)

7:7 (James 1:5; 1 John 5:14–15)

7:16 (James 3:12)

7:21–27 (Rom. 2:13; James 1:22)

Such parallels are striking, because the authors of these letters are not thought to have had access to either Matthew's Gospel or the Q source. The common suggestion, therefore, is that such sayings were attributed to Jesus via oral tradition in various sectors of the church.

This material allows for a spectrum of opinions regarding the composition of the Sermon on the Mount. On the one hand, virtually all of the material can be attributed to Q or to comparable pre-Gospel sources; in this case the contribution of the Matthean author may be regarded as modest, limited primarily to structural organization and the provision of a theological framework for primitive material that had been passed on to him. On the other hand, over a third of the Sermon on the Mount can be attributed to the evangelist himself or to late sources; in this case, the contribution of the Matthean author may be deemed considerable.

Interpretation: The Sermon on the Mount is understood in light of three interpretative contexts: the time and place of Jesus's ministry, the developing era of the early church, and the literary composition of Matthew's Gospel.

The Historical Jesus: Interpreters seek to determine the meaning that individual passages would have had for Jewish peasants in Galilee around 30 CE. They also compare the passages to other sayings of Jesus and try to relate the meaning of particular texts to what appear to have been prominent concerns articulated by Jesus. Such investigation usually involves consideration of whether the passage has undergone redactional development and, if so, whether a reasonable reconstruction of the original content can be sustained. A high degree of confidence has attended much of the Sermon on the Mount material in this regard, making it a focal point for study of the historical Jesus and his earliest followers. Such studies typically interpret the Sermon on the Mount within the context of Galilean Judaism, reading it more as a Jewish document than as a Christian one.

The Early Church: Interpreters seek to determine what various passages would have meant to followers of Jesus in the years between Easter and the composition of the Gospels. The Sermon is often viewed as a valuable resource for gaining access to Jewish-Christian material that may have circulated in the developing church around the same time as the Letters of Paul. Such studies often compare and contrast the views of Paul and the Sermon on the Mount in order to delineate the points of diversity and continuity between two early expressions of what would become the Christian religion.

The Gospel of Matthew: The most prominent approach to the Sermon on the Mount in modern scholarship has sought to interpret the material as a constitutive part of Matthew's Gospel. Scholars emphasize connections between the Sermon on the Mount and other portions of Matthew's Gospel, and they interpret the Sermon on the Mount in light of what appear to have been the theological priorities of this particular evangelist. The Sermon on the Mount is strategically placed in Matthew's Gospel following Jesus's announcement that the kingdom of heaven is near (4:17) and his initial calling of disciples to follow him and "fish for people" (4:18–22). Matthew had earlier established the credentials of Jesus as the Messiah of Israel (1:1, 16) and Son of God (2:15; 3:17). Born of a virgin, Jesus embodies the presence of God among God's people (1:23) and is destined to save his people from their sins (1:21). As the one in whom God is well pleased (3:17), he triumphs over the devil's temptations (4:1–11) and embarks on a public ministry of preaching, teaching, and healing (4:23) that fulfills the prophecies of scripture (4:14–16) and brings him the acclaim of multitudes (4:25). In short, the material in Matthew's Gospel prior to the Sermon on the Mount focuses heavily on the identity and authority of Jesus; the effect of locating the Sermon on the Mount after such material is to accentuate the claim that these are the words of one who possesses divine authority surpassing what might be attributed to any other human being (7:28–29). Matthew's readers are expected to hear and obey the words of Jesus presented in the Sermon on the Mount not simply because they are inherently sensible, but because they are spoken by Jesus the Messiah, the Son of God. *See also* Beatitudes; kingdom of God; Matthew, Gospel According to; Q.

Bibliography

Betz, Hans Dieter. *The Sermon on the Mount.* Fortress, 1995.

Carter, Warren. *What Are They Saying About Matthew's Sermon on the Mount?* Paulist, 1994.

Guelich, Robert A. *The Sermon on the Mount: A Foundation for Understanding.* Word, 1982.

Powell, Mark Allan. "Sermon on the Mount." In *The New Interpreters' Dictionary of the Bible,* vol. 4. Abingdon, 2009.   M.A.P.

serpent. In the ancient world, there was general respect for, revulsion at, and fear of serpents, since many were assumed to be poisonous. The serpent thus came to be understood symbolically with both positive and negative connotations. In some ancient cultures, the serpent was associated with deity and was depicted in statues and paintings with various gods and goddesses. Serpents also played various roles in ancient mythological stories (e.g., the Babylonian *Epic of Gilgamesh*). Some even linked the serpent with the process of healing, as in the case of the Greek god Asclepius. In Canaanite religion, which the early Hebrew people encountered upon their arrival in the area, the serpent was associated with the fertility worship of Baal, since his consort Astarte (also known as Anath or Asherah) was often depicted with a serpent.

In the Bible, serpents usually have a negative connotation. In the story of Adam and Eve (Gen. 2:4–3:24), a serpent functions as a wise but crafty creation of God who leads the first humans into disobedience (note, however, that it is not until much later that the serpent in this story is identified with Satan or the devil). References to Leviathan and Rahab (e.g., Isa. 27:1; 51:9–10a; Pss. 74:14; 104:26; Job 26:12) are vestiges of an ancient Mesopotamian tradition that viewed a great sea serpent as a primordial foe of the gods. The same negative attitude toward serpents is evident in NT passages where religious leaders are called "a brood of vipers" by John the Baptist (Matt. 3:7; cf. Luke 3:7) and by Jesus (Matt. 12:34; 23:33).

In a few instances in the Bible, positive qualities are associated with serpents. First, they symbolize wisdom (Matt. 10:16; cf. Gen. 3:1). Further, Moses

Aaron turning his staff into a serpent in an attempt to persuade Pharaoh to let the Israelites go (Exod. 7:10); from the Alba Bible.

makes a bronze serpent in the wilderness that is believed to have healing properties (Num. 21:4–9; cf. John 3:14–15; note, however, that Hezekiah needs to destroy this bronze serpent later on, because it comes to be associated with idolatrous worship, 2 Kings 18:4).

In several passages, the ultimate victory of God and of God's people over the evil of this age is depicted using serpent imagery. Jesus tells his disciples, "I give you authority to tread on snakes and scorpions" (Luke 10:19). In Revelation, victory over Satan is depicted by the binding of "that ancient serpent" for a thousand years (20:2–10). *See also* dragon; Leviathan; Nehushtan; Rahab.   J.M.E.

Serpent's Stone. *See* Zoheleth.

Serug (sihr′uhg), the son of Reu; he was a descendant of Shem and ancestor of Abraham (Gen. 11:20–23), and he is in the ancestry of Jesus through Joseph (Luke 3:35).

servant. The word "servant" is used over eight hundred times in the Bible (i.e., NRSV), and in the great majority of instances where the application is literal the reference is to a slave rather than to a hired attendant. Both the Hebrew word *'ebed* and the Greek word *doulos* normally have the literal meaning of "slave." Thus, the chief characteristic of a person called a "servant" in the NRSV is usually that they belong to another and so have no legal rights. Both *'ebed* and *doulos*, however, came to be widely used as terms of humble self-designation (2 Kings 8:13). For example, the soldiers of the king's army referred to themselves as his servants, though they were not literally his slaves (2 Sam. 11:24).

It was against this background that a religious sense of the term developed. The Hebrew Bible refers to godly people as "servants" of the Lord, e.g., Moses (Deut. 34:5), Joshua (Judg. 2:8), Samuel (1 Sam. 3:9), David (2 Sam. 7:5), Solomon (1 Kings 3:7), Job (Job 1:8), and the righteous in general (2 Kings 9:7; Pss. 113:1; 134:1; 135:1; Isa. 54:17). In addition, the term became almost a technical term for identifying prophets (2 Kings 17:13, 23; cf. Abijah, 1 Kings 14:18; Elijah, 2 Kings 9:36; Jonah ben Amittai, 2 Kings 14:25).

The most striking usage in the Hebrew Bible, however, occurs in what are called the four Servant Songs found in the latter half of Isaiah (42:1–4; 49:1–6; 50:4–9; 52:13–53:12). The last of these is the longest and the most puzzling of the poems, for it speaks of the servant of the Lord as one who brings redemption through suffering. Most interpreters recognize that the primary referent here is probably Israel (cf. Isa. 44:1, 21; 45:4; 49:3), though some have identified the servant with some historical figure, such as Cyrus of Persia, Hezekiah, the prophet Jeremiah, or Isaiah himself. The NT authors apply this passage to Jesus Christ (e.g., Acts 8:32–35), and Christian interpreters generally accept this application as an additional level of meaning.

In the NT, the concept of service (i.e., slavery) continues to be a way of expressing humankind's relationship to God. Jesus says that "no one can serve two masters" (Matt. 6:24). Jesus tells his disciples that he came "not to be served but to serve" (Mark 10:45), and Matt. 12:18–21 quotes from the first Servant Song (Isa. 42:1–4) to describe Jesus. Christians refer to themselves as "servants of God" (1 Pet. 2:16). Paul describes himself as a "servant of Jesus Christ" (Rom. 1:1; Gal. 1:10; Phil. 1:1), as do the authors of James (1:1), 2 Peter (1:1), and Jude (1). *See also* slavery in the ancient Near East; slavery in the New Testament.   F.J.M.

service, in the Bible, normally something done by a slave, tasks performed by lesser persons for those who controlled their existence. Service with regard to God usually concerned temple worship and its rituals (e.g., Exod. 31:10; 35:19; Luke 1:23), but service to humans often involved forms of bondage (e.g., Gen. 30:26; Exod. 1:14). For Paul, the service a person owed God was to be displayed through service to one's neighbor, which constituted service to Christ (Rom. 12:1–2; 14:17–18; Gal. 5:13; see also 1 Cor. 9:19; 2 Cor. 4:5).   B.J.M.

Seth, the third son of Adam and Eve, according to the genealogy in Gen. 4:25 (cf. 5:3). Eve named him Seth (which is similar to a Hebrew verb meaning "appoint"), because she said, "God has appointed for me another child instead of Abel, because Cain killed him" (4:25). Seth's birth seems intended to contrast with the debauched and violent line of Cain, for Seth later has a son named Enosh and, the Bible notes, "At that time people began to invoke the name of the Lord" (4:26).

seven, seventy. *See* numbers.

seven words from the cross, the seven sentences spoken by Jesus from the cross in the passion stories. Matt. 27:46 and Mark 15:34 have the Hebrew/Aramaic phrase "Eli, Eli, lema sabach-

thani," alluding to Ps. 22. Lukan themes of forgiveness and repentance appear as Jesus forgives his enemies (Luke 23:34; "Father, forgive them; for they do not know what they are doing") and promises salvation to the repentant criminal (23:43; "Truly, I tell you, today you will be with me in Paradise"). In John 19:26–27, Jesus entrusts his mother to the Beloved Disciple. John 19:28, "I thirst," fulfills Ps. 69:21. Finally, Luke 23:46 ("Father, into thy hands I commend my spirit") and John 19:30 ("It is finished") indicate the completion of Jesus's mission as he entrusts himself to God. *See also* Eli, Eli, lema sabachthani; vinegar.   M.A.P.

Shaalbim (shay-al′bim; Heb., "place of foxes"), an Amorite city dominated by Dan (Shaalabbin, Josh. 19:42; Judg. 1:35) and in the jurisdiction of Ben-deker, one of twelve administrative officers under Solomon's jurisdiction (1 Kings 4:9). The site is probably modern Selbit, three miles northwest of Aijalon and about five miles northeast of Gezer.

Shaalim (shay′uh-lim), an area scouted by Saul when he hunted the lost asses of his father, Kish (1 Sam. 9:4). The precise location is unknown, but it was likely in Benjaminite territory.

Shaaraim (shay′uh-ray′im; Heb., "double gate").
1 A town of Judah in the Shephelah (Josh. 15:36); it was somewhere near Azekah in or near the Wadi es-Sant (1 Sam. 17:52).
2 The Simeonite city of 1 Chron. 4:31. It may be the Sharuhen (modern Tell Fa′ra) of Josh. 19:6.

Shaashgaz (shay-ash′gaz), the royal eunuch in charge of concubines at the second harem of King Ahasuerus (Esther 2:14).

Shabbethai (shab′uh-thi), the name of three persons in postexilic Judaism; any two (or all three) could be the same individual.

DYING WORDS OF JESUS

Jesus speaks seven times from the cross—but he does not speak seven times in any one Gospel. The Gospels relate three different stories regarding Jesus's dying words. In one story, Jesus speaks only once; in a second, he speaks three times; and in a third, he speaks another three times. There are no parallels, however, between what is said in any one of these three stories and what is said in the other two stories.

Story A: Matthew and Mark	*Story B: Luke*	*Story C: John*
"My God, my God, why have you forsaken me?" (Matt. 27:46; Mark 15:34)	"Father, forgive them; for they do not know what they are doing" (23:34).	"Woman, here is your son . . . Here is your mother" (19:26–27).
	"Truly, I tell you, today you will be with me in Paradise" (23:43).	"I am thirsty" (19:28).
	"Father, into your hands, I commend my spirit" (23:46).	"It is finished" (19:30).

From Mark Allan Powell, *Introducing the New Testament* (courtesy, Baker Academic)

1 A Levite opposed to Ezra's reform policy of separating from foreign wives (Ezra 10:15).

2 A Levite who stood with Ezra when he read the law, helping to explain it (Neh. 8:7).

3 A Levite who conducted external business in the temple of Jerusalem (Neh. 11:16).

Shaddai (shad′i). *See* El Shaddai.

shades. *See* ghost; Rephaim.

Shadrach (shad′rak), the Babylonian name given to Hananiah, one of Daniel's three companions (Dan. 1:7), subsequently thrown into the fiery furnace. The etymology is uncertain, but the name probably contains some reference to Marduk, god of Babylon. *See also* Abednego; Daniel; Meshach.

Shadrach, Meshach, and Abednego in the "burning fiery furnace" of Nebuchadnezzar; third-century CE fresco from the catacombs of St. Priscilla, Rome.

Shaharaim (shay′huh-ray′im), a descendant of Benjamin who lived in Moab (1 Chron. 8:8). He banished his wives Hushim and Baara for some reason that is not mentioned and subsequently had seven sons by a third wife, Hodesh (8:9).

Shalisha (shuh-li′shuh), one of the regions scouted by Saul while searching for his father's lost asses (1 Sam. 9:4). It was probably located in the region of the tribal lands of Ephraim or Benjamin.

Shallum (shal′uhm).

1 The son of Jabesh, who made himself king of Israel ca. 745 BCE by assassinating Zechariah, son of Jeroboam II, ending the dynasty of Jehu. Shallum was assassinated a month later (2 Kings 15:10–15).

2 The husband of the prophet Huldah (2 Kings 22:14; 2 Chron. 34:22).

3 Jehoahaz, the fourth son of King Josiah (1 Chron. 3:15). He was proclaimed king of Judah ca. 609 BCE, after his father was killed by Neco of Egypt. Three months later Neco made Eliakim (Jehoiakim) king, deporting Shallum to Egypt, where he died (2 Kings 23:30–34), as announced in Jer. 22:10–12.

4 The father of Hanameel, a relative from whom Jeremiah bought family land (Jer. 32:6–10).

5 The father of Maaseiah, a temple official (Jer. 35:4).

6 The chief gatekeeper in the Levites' area of the temple (1 Chron. 9:17–18), whose descendants were also gatekeepers (Ezra 2:42; Neh. 7:45; 1 Esd. 5:28). He was one of those who divorced their foreign wives in compliance with Ezra's reforms (Ezra 10:24; 1 Esd. 9:25). He may be the same person as the father of Mattithiah who was a Korahite official (1 Chron. 9:19, 31).

7 Another man in postexilic Jerusalem who divorced his foreign wife in compliance with Ezra's reforms (Ezra 10:42).

8 A levitical priest (1 Chron. 6:1–15), ancestor of Ezra (Ezra 7:1–2; 1 Esd. 8:1; 2 Esd. 1:1).

9 The son of Hallohesh, governor of half of the district of Jerusalem. He and his daughters helped rebuild part of the city wall (Neh. 3:12).

10 A Judahite of the Jerahmeel branch, the sons of Sismai and the father of Jekamiah (1 Chron. 2:40–41).

11 A Simeonite, the son of Shaul and father of Mibsam (1 Chron. 4:25).

12 A son of Naphtali (1 Chron. 7:13); he is called Shillem in Gen. 46:24; Num. 26:49.

13 The father of Jehizkiah, an Ephraimite leader who opposed the deportation of Judean captives taken in the Syro-Ephraimite war on Jerusalem (2 Chron. 28:12).   S.B.P.

Shalmai (shal′mi), a family of temple servants resettled in Jerusalem after the exile (Neh. 7:48). They are probably the same people referred to as Shamlai in Ezra 2:46; cf. 1 Esd. 5:30.

Shalman (shal′muhn), a ruler mentioned in Hos. 10:14. The name may be an abbreviation for Assyria's king Shalmaneser (IV or V), or it may refer to the Moabite monarch Shalmanu, who invaded Gilead in the late eighth century.

Shalmaneser (shal′muh-nee′zuhr), the name of several Assyrian kings, two of which are important for the history of ancient Israel.

1 Shalmaneser III, the son of Ashurnasirpal II and king of Assyria 858–824 BCE. Though not mentioned in the Bible, two contacts with kings of Israel are recorded in his royal inscriptions. In 853 BCE, Shalmaneser's advance into north Syria was halted at Qarqar on the Orontes River by a coalition of twelve Phoenician and Syrian states, among them "Ahab of Israel," who had sent a contingent of "2,000 chariots and 10,000 foot soldiers." In 841 BCE, following Shalmaneser's defeat of Hazael of Damascus, King Jehu, who had seized the throne in Samaria in a bloody coup the year before (2 Kings 9–10), acknowledged Assyrian hegemony and rendered tribute. A relief on the Black Obelisk of Shalmaneser memorializes this act of submission.

2 Shalmaneser V, the son of Tiglath-pileser III and king of Assyria 727–722 BCE. A picture of his

The Assyrian king Shalmaneser III (*left*), armed with a bow and arrows and accompanied by an attendant and a soldier, receives Sua, the Gilzanite; from the Black Obelisk of Shalmaneser, ninth century BCE.

five-year reign is reconstructable on the basis of 2 Kings 17:1–6 and some passages in the writings of the first-century historian Josephus (*Antiquities* 9.283–87). Shalmaneser undertook two military campaigns to the Mediterranean coast, the area that had been under his governance while he was crown prince. In 726 BCE, Hosea of Israel recognized him as overlord and rendered tribute (17:3). Shortly thereafter, a rebellion against Assyria, with the backing of a Delta chieftain of Egypt, broke out in Phoenicia and Israel; this prompted the second appearance of Shalmaneser in the west. Hosea was imprisoned in 724 BCE, in his ninth and last year as king (for this calculation, cf. 17:5; 18:9–10). Shalmaneser laid siege to Samaria, then ruled by army officers and/or city elders; the city held out for two years, until the autumn of 722/1 BCE. Samaria fell to Shalmaneser (17:6a); this event is recorded in the Babylonian Chronicle (col. 1, line 28): "He destroyed the city of Samaria." Because of Shalmaneser's death, the fate of Samaria was left undetermined; the usual punishments meted out to defeated cities were postponed. The "king of Assyria" who exiled Israelites from Samaria (17:6b) was Sargon II, who reconquered the city in 720 BCE. *See also* Assyria, Empire of.   M.C.

shalom (shah-lohm′), Hebrew spelling of the general Semitic term for "peace, wholeness, well-being." It describes the ideal human state, both individual and communal, the ultimate gift from God. It came to be used as a personal salutation, both for greeting and departing. *See also* peace.

Shama (shay′muh), the son of Hotham, and one of David's warriors (1 Chron. 11:44).

shame, a concept that is expressed in the biblical writings by a variety of Hebrew and Greek terms. In the Hebrew Bible, shame often denotes the guilt a person feels or should feel for having sinned against God (e.g., Jer. 2:26), but it can also connote the disgrace one finds in failure, either by actively having done something wrong or by having failed to do something right (e.g., Prov. 14:34). The biblical writers believed that there should be a natural sense of disgrace and unworthiness when one offended God or one's companions. It was considered appalling when people no longer had any sense of shame (cf. Jer. 6:15; also Job 19:3). In the NT, it is possible to be ashamed (or not ashamed) of Christ and his gospel (e.g., Mark 8:38; Rom. 1:16; cf. Heb. 2:11; 11:16). *See also* conscience; guilt; honor and shame; repentance; sin.   J.M.E.

Shamgar (sham′gahr), a mighty warrior in Israel in the premonarchic period. He was famed for killing a total of six hundred Philistines with an oxgoad (Judg. 3:31). Bearing a non-Semitic name, he is identified as the "son of Anath," perhaps identifying him as a devotee of the Canaanite goddess Anath or possibly indicating his origin from Beth-anath. A second reference to him appears to be only temporal: Judg. 5:6 notes, "In the days of Shamgar son of Anath, in the days of Jael, caravans ceased and travelers kept to the byways."

Shamir (shay′muhr; Heb., "thorn").
1 A Levite, the son of Micah (1 Chron. 24:24).
2 The hometown of Tola, one of the judges about whom little is reported (Judg. 10:1–2).
3 A hill-country village assigned to the territory of the tribe of Judah (Josh. 15:48), probably modern el-Bireh, about twelve miles southwest of Hebron.

Shamma (sham′uh), the name of a family group belonging to the tribe of Asher (1 Chron. 7:37).

Shammah (sham'uh).

1 The son of Reuel, who was the son of Esau and Basemath. Along with his brothers Nahath, Zerah, and Mizzah, Shammah was a chief of the tribe of Reuel in the land of Edom (Gen. 36:13, 17; cf. also Isaac's genealogy in 1 Chron. 1:37). *See also* Basemath; Esau.

2 The third of Jesse's eight sons who passed before Samuel in order to determine who was God's anointed (1 Sam. 16:6–10). He was one of the three eldest sons who followed Saul into battle against the Philistines, and to whom his younger brother David took provisions from Jesse in Bethlehem to the valley of Elah (17:12–54). He is called Shimea in 1 Chron. 2:13. *See also* Jesse; Samuel.

3 The son of Agee the Haraite who is listed as one of "The Three," an inner circle of elite warriors (probably bodyguards) in the army of David. While others fled from the Philistines at Lehi, Shammah took his stand in a plot of lentils and slew the enemy (2 Sam. 23:11–12).   F.R.M.

Shammai (sham'i), the name of three men, all of whom were from Judea.

1 The son of Onam (1 Chron. 2:28, 32).

2 The son of Rekem (1 Chron. 2:44–45).

3 The son of Mered and the Egyptian woman Bithiah (1 Chron. 4:17).

Shammua (sha-myoo'uh; Heb., "heard").

1 The son of Zaccur; he was one of the twelve spies, a representative of the tribe of Reuben, sent by Moses into Canaan (Num. 13:4).

2 One of David's sons born in Jerusalem (2 Sam. 5:14; 1 Chron. 14:4); he is also called Shimea (1 Chron. 3:5). *See also* Shimea.

3 A Levite whose son Abda (Obadiah) was a postexilic inhabitant of Jerusalem (Neh. 11:17); he is elsewhere called Shemaiah (1 Chron. 9:16). *See also* Shemaiah.

4 The head of the family group of Bilgah, which returned to Jerusalem during the period of restoration (Neh. 12:18); he is possibly the same as **3** above, but this is not likely, since he lived in the time of the second high priest after the return from the exile (cf. 12:12).   D.R.B.

Shaphan (shay'fuhn; Heb., "rock badger, coney").

1 The head of a family of Judeans serving the court at the time of King Josiah (ca. 640–609 BCE; 2 Kings 22:3–20; 2 Chron. 34:8–20). He was involved in relaying the book found in the temple to the king, on the basis of which the Josianic reforms were shaped. He was sent to consult the prophet Huldah as part of a royal embassy. His sons and grandsons continued to play roles in the life of the court at the time of the prophet Jeremiah; they saved Jeremiah from those at the court who desired his death (Jer. 26:24), relayed Jeremiah's letter to the exiles in Babylon (29:3), and provided the house in which Baruch could read Jeremiah's dictated scroll (36:10–12).

2 The grandfather of the Gedaliah in whose custody Jeremiah was placed after the fall of Je-

rusalem to Babylonian forces (39:14; 40:5), to assure that Jeremiah was cared for properly. Some scholars think that this Shaphan may be the same person described in **1**.

3 The father of Jaazaniah (Ezek. 8:11) whose apostasy is reviewed in Ezekiel's vision. Apparently Jaazaniah was committing idolatrous acts in the dark, in his "room of images [idols]," maintaining, "The LORD does not see us, the LORD has forsaken the land."   R.S.B.

Shaphat (shay'fat; Heb., "judged").

1 A Simeonite who was one of the twelve spies sent by Moses to check out the land of Canaan (Num. 13:5).

2 The father of the prophet Elisha (1 Kings 19:16, 19; 2 Kings 3:11; 6:31).

3 A Davidic descendant and a grandson of Zerubbabel (1 Chron. 3:22).

4 A Gadite chief living in Bashan, the son of Abihail (1 Chron. 5:12).

5 The son of Adlai who was overseer of David's cattle "in the valleys" (1 Chron. 27:29).

Sharai (shair'i), one of the returned Judean exiles who divorced his foreign women in compliance with Ezra's reforms (Ezra 10:40).

Sharezer (shuh-ree'zuhr).

1 A son of the Assyrian monarch Sennacherib who reportedly helped murder his father (2 Kings 19:37; Isa. 37:38). This act was apparently in response to Sennacherib's declaration that a younger son, Esar-haddon, would be heir to his throne. After a brief dynastic battle, Esar-haddon triumphed and assumed the throne in 681 BCE.

2 One of the two emissaries sent from Bethel in 518 BCE to "inquire of the LORD" whether the people should continue fasting in the fifth month of the year (Zech. 7:2). There is a textual problem in this verse, such that the name might be Bethelsharezer.

Sharon (shair'uhn), **Plain of,** the area where the coastal plain widens south of Mount Carmel. The plain extends about thirty miles south to the Yarkon River north of Joppa. It varies from about eight to twelve miles in width. In biblical times, the dunes of this plain supported an impenetrable oak forest (compared to the thick forests of Lebanon and Carmel in Isa. 35:2) rather than the citrus groves seen today. To speak of fertile Sharon becoming "like a desert" evokes an image of extreme devastation (33:9). By contrast, to say that the majesty of Sharon will be given to a desert conveys abundant rejuvenation (35:2). Still, Sharon was somewhat forbidding jungle with pastureland only on the fringe of the forest (1 Chron. 27:29), so the idea that "Sharon shall become a pasture for flocks" suggested more productive use of the region's fertility (Isa. 65:10). The rose of Sharon was a kind of tulip that grew in the forest as a "lily among brambles" (Song of Sol. 2:1–2).

A major caravan route, called "The Way of the Sea," ran through the Plain of Sharon, hugging the drier foothills of the highland on the east. Along this road were the more permanent settlements, Socoh (modern Wadi Zeimar, 1 Sam. 17:1) and Aphek (modern Ras el-Ain, Josh. 13:4) at the source of the Yarkon.

The coast was without good natural harbors. The Romans under Herod the Great developed the imposing city of Caesarea with its artificial harbor, its aqueducts bringing fresh water from Mount Carmel, and a network of roads to the interior. *See also* plains.   N.L.L.

Sharuhen (shuh-roo′huhn), an important Hyksos stronghold in the southwest Levant in the seventeenth and early sixteenth centuries BCE, captured by the Egyptian king Ahmose (ca. 1560 BCE) after a siege lasting three years. Sharuhen was held by an Egyptian garrison at the time of Thutmose III's great victory at Megiddo in 1482 BCE. In Josh. 19:6 it appears in a list of cities allotted to the tribe of Simeon at the time of the Israelite conquest; parallel lists give its name as Shilhim (Josh. 15:32) and Shaaraim (1 Chron. 4:31).

Sharuhen is probably to be identified with Tell el-ʿAjjul, the largest mound in southern Israel, which is located about four miles southwest of modern Gaza near the principal ancient highway leading up from Egypt. Excavations there indicate that the mound was initially used as a cemetery at the end of the third and beginning of the second millennium BCE. It became a rich and powerful city in the latter part of the Middle Bronze Age (ca. 1750–1550 BCE), when it was protected on three sides by an enormous ditch set in front of a glacis (steep slope). Within this enclosure were several stratified city levels belonging to the Middle Bronze Age and beginning of the Late Bronze Age (ca. 1550–1200 BCE). Evidence for a major destruction (probably due to Ahmose) is also apparent. The excavations also revealed a series of five superimposed palaces, two of which belonged to the Middle Bronze Age, and three of which were evidently Egyptian fortresses dating to the Late Bronze Age. The great wealth of the Hyksos city is attested by the fact that more gold objects were found at Tell el-ʿAjjul than at any other Bronze Age site in the Near East. The end of the Egyptian empire in the twelfth century BCE resulted in the abandonment of the garrison at Sharuhen. There is little evidence of later occupation other than some burials on the mound that belong to the tenth century BCE. *See also* Hyksos.   J.M.W.

Shaul (shawl; Heb., "dedicated" or "asked for").

1 An Edomite king from Rehoboth (Gen. 36:37–38).

2 One of the sons of Simeon, born to a Canaanite woman (Gen. 46:10; Exod. 6:15; 1 Chron. 4:24). He was the founder of the family group known as the Shaulites (Num. 26:13).

3 The son of Uzziah, a Levite of the Kohath line (1 Chron. 6:24).

Shaveh (shay′vuh), **Valley of,** the valley where the king of Sodom and Melchizedek, king of Jerusalem, met Abraham as he returned from his battle with the kings of the north (Gen. 14:17). This valley, also called the King's Valley, was presumably the same as that in which Absalom erected his monument (2 Sam. 18:18). Suggestions as to its location include the Kidron, the western Hinnom, and the Wadi Joz, all valleys in the vicinity of Jerusalem.

Shaveh-kiriathaim (shay′vuh-kihr-ee-uh-thay′im; Heb., "plain of Kiriathaim"), the plain in Moab where the Elamite king Chedorlaomer fought and subdued the Emim (Gen. 14:5). Its location would be somewhere near el-Qereiyat, northwest of Dibon in what is now Jordan.

shaving. Israelite men of the preexilic period wore full beards and shoulder-length hair, as may be seen in their depiction on Assyrian reliefs. The beards were trimmed (2 Sam. 19:24), but under normal circumstances men were ashamed to appear in public without them (10:4–5). When in mourning, however, they shaved their heads and beards (Job 1:20; Jer. 41:5; 48:37). A female prisoner of war was allowed to shave her head and mourn the loss of her parents for one month before her captor could have relations with her (Deut. 21:10–13). There also seems to have been some controversy regarding the association of shaving and mourning, as individual regulations appeared at different times. Deut. 14:1 indicates, "You must not lacerate yourselves or shave your forelocks for the dead," but that law seems little known prior to the exile (Isa. 22:12). The rationale may have had something to do with mourning rites of other Canaanite religions. This could also explain the prohibition against priests shaving parts of their heads or the edges of their beards (Lev. 21:5).

The men or women who consecrated themselves to God as Nazirites could not cut their hair until they fulfilled their vow; then they shaved their heads and offered the hair on the altar for their purification (Num. 6:5–19). The Bible mentions two lifelong Nazirites, Samson (Judg. 13–16) and Samuel (1 Sam. 1:11, 22). Priests were prohibited from taking such vows (Ezek. 44:20).

Shaving also played an important role in certain purification rituals, such as that for the patient who had recovered from serious skin disease (Lev. 13:33; 14:8–9). *See also* Nazirites.   J.J.M.R.

Shavsha (shav′shuh), a scribe in David's court (1 Chron. 18:16). Other forms of the name may include Seraiah (2 Sam. 8:17), Sheva (20:25), or even Shisha (1 Kings 4:3). Because of its non-Hebrew origin, the name may indicate use of foreign scholars at the royal court.

Sheal (shee′uhl), a returning exile who divorced his non-Israelite wife in compliance with Ezra's reforms (Ezra 10:29).

Shealtiel (shee-al'tee-uhl; Heb., "God is a shield" or "God is victor"), a son of the Judean King Jeconiah (also called Jehoiachin; 1 Chron. 3:17; Matt. 1:12). He was the father of Zerubbabel, the leader of postexilic returnees (but 1 Chron. 3:17–19 calls him Zerubbabel's uncle). Shealtiel thus connected the royal family of King Jeconiah with postexilic Judean developments under Zerubbabel.

Sheariah (shee-uh-ri'uh), one of the Benjaminite sons of Azel (1 Chron. 8:38; 9:44) and a descendant of Saul.

Shearjashub (shee-uhr-jay'shuhb; Heb., "a remnant will return"), the eldest of Isaiah's sons (Isa. 7:3). By giving his child this unusual name, Isaiah made Shearjashub a living symbol of the prophet's early message concerning the northern kingdom, Israel (10:21–22). Only a remnant of it would survive.

Sheba (shee'buh).
1 A town included in Simeon's inheritance, along with Beer-sheba and Moladah (Josh. 19:2).
2 A Benjaminite, the son of Bichri, who led a revolt against David after Absalom's rebellion was put down. Hoping to seize northern Israel, he was pursued by Joab and his army and was decapitated at the instigation of a "wise woman" of the town of Abel-beth-maacah (2 Sam. 20).
3 A man of the tribe of Gad (1 Chron. 5:13).
4 A country in southwest Arabia also known as Seba. It was an area known for its wealth (Isa. 60:6; Jer. 6:20; Ezek. 27:22–25). Inhabitants of Seba/Sheba were called Sabeans. *See also* Seba, Sabeans; Sheba, queen of.

Sheba, queen of, a ruler of the Sabeans contemporary with King Solomon (tenth century BCE), whom she visited to test his wisdom. Impressed with his wealth as well as his wisdom, she blessed both Solomon and the God of Israel for such splendor. She gave Solomon 120 talents of gold in addition to other precious items, and Solomon in his turn bestowed rich presents upon her prior to her return to her own land. Her appearance in the narrative of 1 Kings is intended to glorify the figure of Solomon rather than give information about this wealthy queen, who is otherwise unknown in the Hebrew Bible (10:1–10, 13; cf. 2 Chron. 9:1–9, 12). She is mentioned by Jesus (as the "queen of the South") in Matt. 12:42. *See also* Seba, Sabeans.

Shebaniah (sheb-uh-ni'uh; Heb., perhaps "the LORD has restored").
1 A priest appointed by the Levites to blow the trumpet before the ark of God (1 Chron. 15:24).
2 A Levite from Jerusalem who led people in worship at the covenant-renewal ceremony led by Ezra (Neh. 9:4).
3 The ancestor of a family group who settled in postexilic Jerusalem during the high-priesthood of Joiakim (Neh. 12:14). A man named Joseph was head of this group. Three persons named Shebaniah who are said to have signed Ezra's covenant-renewal document under Nehemiah were probably members of this family (10:4, 10, 12).

Shebat (shee'bat), the eleventh month of the Hebrew year (mid-January to mid-February; Zech. 1:7; 1 Macc. 16:14). *See also* calendar.

Shebnah (sheb'nuh), the state secretary of King Hezekiah at the time of Sennacherib's campaign against Judah (2 Kings 18:18–19:2; Isa. 36:3–37:2). Apparently he had been demoted to this position from the higher office of royal steward following a bitter critique of Isaiah (cf. Isa. 22:15–25).

Shebuel (shi-byoo'uhl).
1 The son of Gershom, a Levite and, thus, a descendant of Moses (1 Chron. 23:14–16; 26:24). His duties (assisting the priests in temple services, managing the treasuries, and dividing temple duties) reflect late rather than early temple practice.
2 A levitical musician (1 Chron. 25:4) also called Shubael (25:20).

Shecaniah (shek-uh-ni'uh; Heb., "the LORD has taken up abode").
1 A descendant of David and Zerubbabel (1 Chron. 3:21–22) and head of a family who returned with Ezra from Babylon (Ezra 8:3).
2 The chief of the tenth division of priests in the Davidic order (1 Chron. 24:11).
3 One of the priests in Hezekiah's time who distributed the temple offering to the priests in outlying cities (2 Chron. 31:15).
4 The son of Jahaziel who returned to Judah with Ezra after the exile (Ezra 8:5).
5 A man who had married a foreigner and repented, and who then proposed a covenant for all postexilic Judahites to divorce their foreign wives and disown the children born to those wives (Ezra 10:2–4).
6 The father of one who helped repair the wall of Jerusalem (Neh. 3:29).
7 The father-in-law of Tobiah the Ammonite (Neh. 6:18).
8 A priest who returned from the Babylonian exile to Jerusalem with Zerubbabel (Neh. 12:3).
P.A.B.

Shechem (shek'uhm), a city located forty-one miles north of Jerusalem in the pass between Mount Ebal and Mount Gerizim. It dominated an important trade route and controlled a fertile valley to the east where Jacob's sons pastured their flocks (Gen. 37:12–14). Shechem was a Korathite levitical city of refuge in the territory of Manasseh (Josh. 17:2, 7), although it is also described as being "in the hill country of Ephraim" (20:7).
The Ancestral Period: Shechem was the first city visited by Abraham in his migration from Haran (Gen. 12:6), but it figures most prominently

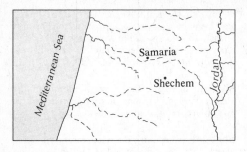

in the traditions associated with Jacob. It was the scene of the rape of Dinah by Shechem, the son of Hamor, king of Shechem (Gen. 34; note that in the narrative of the event the prince and the city have the same name). During excavation in the east gate, the decapitated skeleton of a donkey was found, with what appeared to be the bones of an animal sacrifice nearby. The ass was probably the sacred animal of the city; the name Hamor means "ass" in Hebrew.

Egyptian texts of the nineteenth century BCE indicate that Shechem was an important urban center during the patriarchal period. Archaeological evidence shows that during the nineteenth and eighteenth centuries BCE the city was surrounded by a massive embankment of earth, topped by walls of mud-brick on stone foundations. The highest ground within the walls was occupied by a multiroom palace-temple complex set off from the rest of the city by a stone wall. In the seventeenth century BCE the embankment was replaced by a wall composed of huge stones and entered by impressive gates on the north and east sides. The royal palace was moved to a position directly against the inner face of the new wall, and the palace-temple complex was replaced by a rectangular "fortress temple" with walls 17 feet thick.

While the Israelites were in slavery in Egypt, Shechem continued to flourish. Its king, Lab'ayu, is described in the Amarna letters (fourteenth century BCE) as the most important ruler in the area, controlling a small empire and making inroads into the territory of his neighbors. During this period the fortress-temple was rebuilt and continued in use into the Israelite period. It is the temple of the Lord of the Covenant (NRSV: "Baal-berith," "El-berith") mentioned in Judg. 9:4, 46.

The Israelite Period: When the Israelites entered Canaan (thirteenth century BCE) Shechem passed peacefully into their hands and became the earliest religious center of the tribes. Indeed, they buried the mummified body of Joseph in a tomb near the city (Josh. 24:32). At Shechem Joshua renewed the Sinai covenant with Israel's tribal leaders, probably at the temple of the Lord of the Covenant (Josh. 24). Abimelech, a son of Gideon by a concubine who lived at Shechem, roused the Shechemites to his support and had himself declared king (Judg. 9:1–6), against the spirit and traditions of the old tribal confederacy, which held that the Lord was the only king in Israel (8:22–23). Shechem soon revolted against Abimelech's rule and in reprisal he destroyed the city (9:45).

After a time in which the site was occupied only by crude huts and grain-storage pits, the city was rebuilt. The old Canaanite royal tradition, which had long been associated with Shechem, continued to be attached to the rebuilt city. Rehoboam went there to be crowned king in the northern part of his kingdom (1 Kings 12:1). After the revolt of the northern tribes Jeroboam I rebuilt the city (12:25). Traces of his work survive in the tower of the east gate. For a time Shechem served as Jeroboam's capital, but its population had too many local loyalties, and he moved his capital to Tirzah. Shechem then settled down to a fairly prosperous existence as a provincial center. Typical Israelite four-room houses were built on a series of terraces rising from the east gate to the former sacred area, which was now transformed into a granary, probably for the collection of taxes. The fortifications of the Israelite city followed the plan of its Canaanite predecessor. Israelite Shechem was destroyed by the Assyrian armies in 722/1 BCE. The walls of the

Remains of a high place at the site of ancient Shechem.

Silver coin depicting a temple and altar at the top of a stairway leading up Mount Gerizim, ca. 198–217 CE.

houses were covered by over 4 feet of destruction debris.

Shechem was rebuilt ca. 350 BCE as the religious center of the Samaritans. Their temple stood on Mount Gerizim, and at the foot of the mountain they constructed a city designed to rival Jerusalem. A strong defensive wall enclosed solidly constructed houses and at least one luxurious villa near the old sacred area. The city was destroyed, probably by John Hyrcanus during his conquest of Samaria, in 107 BCE. It was razed to the ground. Its walls were buried beneath deep layers of fill, and it was never rebuilt. *See also* Abimelech; Amarna, Tell el-; Dinah; Rehoboam; Samaritans.

Bibliography

Toombs, Lawrence E. "Shechem (Place)." *Anchor Bible Dictionary.* Doubleday, 1992. 5:1174–86.

Wright, G. Ernest. *Shechem: The Biography of a Biblical City.* Doubleday, 1962.   L.E.T.

Shedeur (shed´ee-uhr; Heb., "Shaddai is light" or "Shaddai is fire"), the father of Elizur who was chosen to be the leader of the Reubenites during the time of Moses (Num. 1:5; 2:10; 7:30, 35; 10:18).

sheep, a ruminant mammal related to the goat. Sheep are mentioned in the Bible more than five hundred times, and a large variety of terms are employed to describe the different breeds, ages, and genders. Although most of the references in the Hebrew Bible are literal, practically all references in the NT are metaphorical, comparing the relationship of Christ and his followers to that of the shepherd and his flock.

The earliest evidence for the domestication of sheep comes from Zawi Chemi Shanidar in northern Iraq and dates back to about 9000 BCE. Sheep were originally domesticated to provide a steady supply of meat. Wild sheep do not have real wool, just a woolly undercoat, and it was probably not until 4000 BCE that the animal's potential in this respect was discovered and sheep were bred especially for wool production. Another domestic trait is the fat tail, which is common to most breeds in the Near East, including the Awassi sheep raised in Israel today. The fat tail is considered a delicacy and was sometimes required as a sacrifice (Exod. 29:22–25).

In contrast to goats, sheep prefer flat or gently rolling grazing grounds and eat plants down to the root, thriving on the stubble left over from the barley and wheat harvest. Both sheep and goats provided most necessities of life: milk (Deut. 32:14; Isa. 7:21, 22), meat (1 Sam. 14:32), hides (Exod. 25:5; Heb. 11:37), and wool (Lev. 13:47–48; Job 31:20). Even their horns were used as containers for oil (1 Sam. 16:1) or as musical instruments (Josh. 6:4). The skins were usually made into clothing, and the inner covering of the tabernacle was made from skins that had been dyed red (Exod. 26:14). Wool was especially prized and was valuable for trade. The Moabite king Mesha had to pay the king of Israel an annual tribute of the wool of a hundred thousand rams (2 Kings 3:4). The shearing of sheep was always a special occasion, and Jacob used it to escape from his uncle Laban,

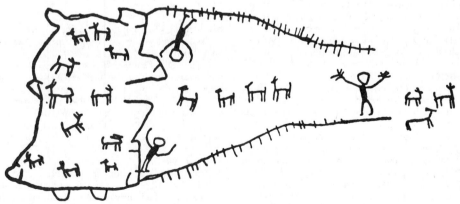

Shepherds driving their flock into a fortified sheepfold erected to protect the animals from marauders. Extended walls shield the narrow entrance; a Safaite rock drawing found in the desert east of Amman, Jordan.

whose attention was on the shearing (Gen. 31:19). This same Jacob is said to have increased his flock through a combination of systematic breeding and folk magic (Gen. 30); he selected the strongest animals for reproduction and managed to induce his ewes to produce offspring of a certain color by placing a similar color in front of them (30:37–39).

Throughout the NT, sheep are used in a figurative sense for human beings. Jesus speaks of "the lost sheep of the house of Israel" (Matt. 10:6; 15:24; cf. Isa. 53:6) and has compassion on a crowd, which he considers to be like sheep without a shepherd (Matt. 9:36). Sheep also play a role in several parables of Jesus (12:11; 18:12; Luke 15:2–6), and the Gospel of John pictures Jesus as a protecting shepherd, willing to give his life for his sheep (10:7–9; cf. Ezek. 37:24; Ps. 23:1; Heb. 13:20). Jesus indicates that at the final judgment the Son of Man will separate the nations of the earth as a shepherd separates sheep from goats (Matt. 25:32). He is himself compared to a sheep led to slaughter (Acts 8:32; cf. Isa. 53:7).   I.U.K.

Sheep Gate, a gate probably located in the north city wall of Jerusalem, on the north side of the temple area. This gate was built after the return from exile by Eliashib and his brothers (Neh. 3:1) as part of Nehemiah's reconstruction of the Jerusalem walls (12:39). Because of its proximity to the temple area and pool of Beth-zatha (John 5:2), it has been surmised that sheep to be sacrificed were brought into the city through this gate.

Sheerah (shee'uh-ruh), the daughter of Ephraim (1 Chron. 7:24), who was credited with building up both Upper and Lower Beth-horon.

Shehariah (shee-huh-ri'uh), a Benjaminite chief and the son of Jehoram (1 Chron. 8:26).

shekel (shek'uhl).
1 A standard unit of weight, approximately 14.5 grams of silver. *See also* weights and measures.
2 In NT times, a common silver coin weighing a shekel (1 Macc. 10:40, 42). It was struck by Jewish authorities and equal to about four denarii (which is to say its value was about four times a typical day's wage). It was the equivalent of a Greek stater (Matt. 17:27). The NRSV avoids the use of both "shekel" and "stater." *See also* money.

Shelah (shee'luh; Heb., "javelin").
1 A Shemite son of Arpachshad (Gen. 10:24) who was the father of Eber (1 Chron. 1:18, 24; Gen. 11:12–15; but see Luke 3:35–36, where he is identified as a son of Cainan).
2 The third son of Judah and Shua (Gen. 38:5, 11, 14, 26; 46:12; 1 Chron. 2:3). He was the ancestor of the Shelanites (Num. 26:20; cf. 1 Chron. 4:21). Judah promised his daughter-in-law Tamar that Shelah would be given to her in marriage when he was grown, since Tamar's husband Er had died and his brother Onan had been killed by God

for failing to fulfill his levirate duty of impregnating her. But when Shelah was grown, Judah did not give him to Tamar, which prompted her to disguise herself as a prostitute and trick Judah into impregnating her himself.

Shelemiah (shel'uh-mi'uh; Heb., "the LORD has recompensed/restored").
1 The son of Cushi and father of Nethaniah. He was sent by Jerusalem officials to tell Baruch to read from the scroll of Jeremiah (Jer. 36:14).
2 The son of Abdeel. He was one of Jehoiakim's men sent to arrest Baruch and Jeremiah (Jer. 36:26).
3 The father of Jehucal (Jer. 37:3). King Zedekiah sent him to ask Jeremiah to pray for the nation. He subsequently recommended that Jeremiah be put to death (38:1)
4 The son of Haniah and father of Irijah, captain of the guard sent to arrest Jeremiah (Jer. 37:13).
5–6 Two men who were descendants of Bani or Binnui and who divorced their foreign wives in compliance with Ezra's postexilic reforms (Ezra 10:39, 41).
7 The father of Hananiah who helped repair the Jerusalem wall (Neh. 3:30).
8 A priest in charge of the storehouses; along with a Levite named Pedaiah and Zadok the scribe, he was found to be trustworthy (Neh. 13:13).
9 A gatekeeper (1 Chron. 26:14); this Shelemiah appears to be the same person called Meshelemiah in 26:1 and Shallum in 9:17, 19, 31. *See also* Shallum.   P.A.B.

Sheleph (shee'lif), a son of Joktan and descendant of Shem (Gen. 10:26; 1 Chron. 1:20). Like his brothers, he is probably to be regarded as the ancestor of an Arabian tribe.

Shelesh (shee'lish; Heb., "third" or "triplet"), a man who headed an Asherite tribe (1 Chron. 7:35).

Shelomi (shi-loh'mi; Heb., perhaps "peace"), the son of Ahihud, who was leader of the tribe of Asher at the time of the division of the land (Num. 34:27).

Shelomith (shi-loh'mith), a name used by both men and women; it is sometimes written as Shelomoth.
1 The Danite mother of a sojourner in the Israelite camp who blasphemed the name of God (Lev. 24:11).
2 A daughter of Zerubbabel and sister of Meshullam and Hananiah (1 Chron. 3:19).
3 A son or daughter of King Rehoboam and Maacah, who was the daughter of Absalom (2 Chron. 11:20).
4 A Levite, the chief son of Izhar (1 Chron. 23:18); he is called Shelomoth in 24:22.
5 The son of Josiphiah, a descendant of Bani. He was head of a family group who returned with Ezra from Babylon (Ezra 8:10).   P.A.B.

Shelomoth (shi-loh'moth).

1 A Gershonite Levite who was a son of Shimei (1 Chron. 23:9). Some manuscripts read as Shelomith.

2 A Levite, the chief son of Izhar (1 Chron. 24:22); he is called Shelomith at 23:18.

Shelumiel (shi-loo'mee-uhl; Heb., perhaps "God is peace"), the Simeonite son of Zurishaddai (Num. 1:6; 2:12; 7:36–41; 10:19) who assisted Moses with the census and led the tribe of Simeon during the wilderness wanderings. Judith's ancestry is traced to him (Jth. 8:1, where he is called Salamiel).

Shem (Heb., "name," "renown"), one of the three sons of Noah. Shem occupies a special place among the sons of Noah because he was the eldest (5:32; 9:18), the recipient of special blessing (9:26, NRSV), and the ancestor of a group of peoples that included the Hebrews (Eber, 10:21, 24). The modern term "Semite" derives from his name ("Shemite"), but the list of Shem's descendants in 10:21–30 includes people (e.g., the Elamites, 10:22) who would not fit modern racial or linguistic classifications of Semitic peoples. Thus, the original basis for the grouping appears to have been geographical or political. In 9:20–27, Shem is the ancestor of Israel and dwells in the land alongside his two brothers, Ham (father of Canaan, representing the original inhabitants of the land) and Japheth (ancestor of the Philistines and other Sea Peoples). Ham is cursed for dishonoring his father when the latter was drunk, but Shem is rewarded by a special relationship with God (9:26, NRSV), and Japheth is promised an enlarged dwelling place "in the tents of Shem" (i.e., in the territory of Israel).   P.A.B.

Shema (shee'muh).

1 One of the four sons of Hebron, who was of the tribe of Judah (1 Chron. 2:43–44).

2 A town in the southern part of Judah (Josh. 15:26). It is probably to be associated with **1** and located in the area of Hebron.

3 The son of Joel of the tribe of Reuben (1 Chron. 5:8). He may be the same person called Shamaiah in 5:4.

4 A son of Elpaal of the tribe of Benjamin (1 Chron. 8:13).

5 One of the men who stood at Ezra's right hand to offer support during the public reading of the law (Neh. 8:4).

Shema (shuh-mah'), **the,** a traditional name given to the classic declaration of faith found in Deut. 6:4, which reads, "Hear, O Israel: The LORD is our God, the LORD alone" (or, in some translations, "... our God, the LORD is one"). The passage continues with the injunction, "You shall love the LORD your God with all your heart, and with all your soul, and with all your might" (6:5). The passage is called the Shema because in Hebrew *shema*'

("Hear, you") is the first word. In the NT, Jesus identified the Shema as the first and greatest commandment in the law (Mark 12:29), though in the Gospels of Matthew and Luke, he quotes only the injunction to love God, omitting the declaration, "The LORD is our God, the LORD alone." Some interpreters have speculated that this omission might have been prompted by the Gospel writers' increasing tendencies to identify Jesus as Lord and God.   J.U.

Shemaah (shi-may'uh), the father of the Benjaminite bowmen Ahiezer and Joash, both of whom joined David to assist him in his battles (1 Chron. 12:1–3).

Shemaiah (shi-may'yuh; Heb., "the LORD has heard").

1 A late tenth-century BCE prophet who warned King Rehoboam of Judah against fighting Israel (1 Kings 12:22; 2 Chron. 11:2). Later, he called Rehoboam and his princes to repent before Pharaoh Shishak invaded Judah from Egypt, an invasion that he claimed was punishment for idolatry. Believing their repentance to be sincere, he declared that the wrath of God would be limited and they would not be destroyed completely (1 Chron. 12:5–12). Shemaiah reportedly kept records concerning Rehoboam's reign, and these were used as sources for the Chronicler's history (2 Chron. 12:15).

2 The father of one of the princes of the court of Jehoiakim who listened to the scroll Baruch read to them (Jer. 26:12–15).

3 The father of Uriah, a prophet from Kiriath-jearim whom King Jehoiakim put to death for his prophecies (Jer. 26:20–23).

4 A Nehelamite who was a false prophet living among the exiles in the days of Jeremiah. He prophesied that a return to Judah was imminent and denounced Jeremiah for saying the exile would continue for many years. He wrote to the priests and people in Jerusalem, encouraging them to reprimand and imprison Jeremiah. Jeremiah responded by declaring that Shemaiah would have no descendants in Judah and would not live to see the return (29:24–32).

5 The son of Shecaniah, a descendant of David (1 Chron. 3:22).

6 A descendant of Simeon who was a leader of that tribe, and the father of Shimri (1 Chron. 4:37).

7 The son of Joel and a leader of the tribe of Reuben (1 Chron. 5:4).   N.L.L.

Shemariah (shem'uh-ri'uh; Heb., "the LORD has kept").

1 One of the Benjaminite men who joined David's troops at Ziklag (1 Chron. 12:5).

2 A son of King Rehoboam of Judah and his wife Mahalath (2 Chron. 11:19).

3 A descendant of Harim who divorced his foreign wife in compliance with Ezra's postexilic reforms (Ezra 10:32).

4 A descendant of Binnui who divorced his foreign wife in compliance with Ezra's postexilic reforms (Ezra 10:41).

Shemeber (shem-ee′buhr), a king of Zeboiim (Gen. 14:2) who was defeated by an alliance of eastern kings.

Shemed (shee′mid), a Benjaminite who, with Eber and Misham, founded the cities of Ono and Lod (1 Chron. 8:12).

Shemer (shee′muhr; Heb., perhaps "watch").
1 The owner of the hill Omri bought and used for his capital city Samaria (1 Kings 16:24).
2 The father of Bani in the lineage of temple musicians (1 Chron. 6:46).
3 An Asherite; he was the son of Heber and the father of four sons (1 Chron. 7:34; "Shomer," 7:32).

Shemida (shi-mi′duh; Heb., perhaps "Eshmun [a Phoenician god] has known"), the Gileadite who headed the family of Shemidaite descendants of Manasseh (Num. 26:32; Josh. 17:2; 1 Chron. 7:19). The name appears on an ostracon from Samaria from the eighth century BCE.

Sheminith (shem′uh-nith; Heb., "on the eighth"), a musical notation that appears in the superscriptions to Pss. 6 and 12, and in 1 Chron. 15:21. The meaning is unknown, but it might have something to do with "an octave" (e.g., to be played an octave lower or higher). Other suggestions are that it indicates the song is to be accompanied by an eight-stringed instrument (cf. "lyre" in 1 Chron. 15:21) or that it is sung according to "the eighth mode," one of several melodic patterns.

Shemiramoth (shi-mihr′uh-moth; Heb., perhaps "name of heights").
1 A levitcal harpist in the group David organized to accompany the ark as it was brought to Jerusalem (1 Chron. 15:18, 20; 16:5).
2 A Levite who was commissioned by King Jehoshaphat (ca. 873–849 BCE) to teach people in Judah the law (2 Chron. 17:8).

Shemuel (shem′yoo-uhl; Heb., "name of God" or "his name is God").
1 The son of Ammihud who represented the tribe of Simeon at the time of the division of the land (Num. 34:20).
2 The son of Tola and head of an ancestral house belonging to the tribe of Issachar (1 Chron. 7:2).

Shenazar (shi-naz′uhr), the fourth son of the exiled Judean king Jehoiachin (Jeconiah), the captive king of Judah (1 Chron. 3:18). He may be the same person known as Sheshbazzar mentioned in Jerusalem after the exile (Ezra 1:8, 11; 5:14, 16).

Sheol (shee′ohl), a biblical term for the netherworld, in some respects the Hebrew counterpart of Hades and Tartarus. The etymology of the word

is still in question, but "Sheol" probably derives from the verb "to ask or inquire" and thus refers to the realm of the dead as the place from which oracles were sought. The seeking of such oracles was forbidden by the Torah (Deut. 18:11), but was apparently practiced (1 Sam. 28:3–25).

Sheol usually refers to a place (Gen. 37:35), namely, the underworld where departed spirits go (Prov. 9:18). The dead in Sheol are referred to as "shades," pale reflections of the men and women they had once been (Isa. 14:10; Eccles. 9:10). Existence in Sheol is characterized by forgetfulness and inactivity (Ps. 88:12; Eccles. 9:10), but Sheol is not a place of punishment in the Bible. Rescue from Sheol is a recurring theme in biblical poetry (Pss. 30:3; 49:15; 86:13; cf. 18:3–16; 116:3–8; Jon. 2:2–9). In some cases, this may indicate deliverance from a near-death experience, but eventually such texts would be read as expressive of hope for resurrection, life beyond death.

A few biblical texts preserve a metaphorical sense in which Sheol is personified as a being or power that can destroy the living (Job 26:6). Sheol is then portrayed as insatiable with an immense, devouring mouth (Isa. 5:14; Prov. 30:15–16).   M.A.F.

Shepham (shee′fuhm), a town on the northeast border of Israelite land (Num. 34:10–11). It is presumed to have been near modern Riblah on the Upper Orontes, but the exact location remains uncertain.

Shephatiah (shef′uh-ti′uh; Heb., "the LORD has judged").
1 The son of David and Abital (2 Sam. 3:4). He was David's fifth son and was born in Hebron.
2 The father of a Benjaminite who resettled in Jerusalem after the exile (1 Chron. 9:8).
3 One of the Benjaminite warriors who went over to David while he was at Ziklag (1 Chron. 12:5).
4 The chief officer of the Simeonites in David's tribal administration (1 Chron. 27:16).
5 One of the sons of King Jehoshaphat of Judah who were slain by their brother Jehoram when he ascended the throne (2 Chron. 21:2).
6 The head of a family group whose members returned to Jerusalem from Babylon with Zerubbabel (Ezra 2:4) and Ezra (8:8).
7 One of Solomon's servants whose descendants returned to Jerusalem with Zerubbabel (Ezra 2:57).
8 A Judahite whose descendants lived in Jerusalem after the exile, during the time of Nehemiah (Neh. 11:4).
9 One of the four princes who demanded that King Zedekiah put Jeremiah to death for his prophecies during the siege of Jerusalem. After Zedekiah handed Jeremiah over to Shaphatiah and the others, they cast him into a dry cistern to die (Jer. 38:1–6).   P.A.B.

Shephelah (shi-fee′luh), an area of the western Levant that consists of low hills separating the coastal plains from the central mountain ridge to the east. It is often called the "Shephelah of Judah." These hills provided a buffer between Judah and Philistia, and both parties sought control of the Shephelah because of its strategic value (Jer. 17:26).

Shepher (shee'fuhr), one of the places where the Israelites camped during their wanderings after the exodus from Egypt (Num. 33:23–24). It is called "Mount Shepher" but its location is unknown.

shepherd, one who pastures or tends a flock of sheep. Since these were the most important domestic animals in the Near East, there are many references to sheep and shepherds throughout the Bible. In addition to being a major sacrificial animal, sheep provided the ancients with meat, milk, fat, wool, skins, and horns. Many important figures in Hebrew history were shepherds, including Abraham, Isaac, Rachel, Jacob, Jacob's sons, Zipporah, Moses, and David. The occupation first appears in Gen. 4:2, when Abel, "a keeper of sheep," comes into conflict with Cain, "a tiller of the ground." The shepherd's humble status can be seen in the contrast drawn between David's pastoral and royal careers (2 Sam. 7:8; cf. Ps. 78:70–71).

The economic value of sheep stands in direct proportion to the amount of supervision (i.e., guidance and protection) these beasts require. Sheep become lost easily; once lost, they are defenseless (Ezek. 34:5–6; Matt. 18:12). The shepherd's work was a livelihood that called for diligence and endurance. The search for pasturage and water sometimes took the herdsman and his flock far from home. This meant that shepherds put up with simple food, harsh weather (cf. Gen. 31:40), and primitive lodging (Song of Sol. 1:8; Isa. 38:12). Such routine hardships were occasionally accompanied by danger from wild animals, e.g., lions, bears, and wolves (1 Sam. 17:34–35; Isa. 31:4; Amos 3:12; Mic. 5:8; John 10:12). Shepherds also had to be on guard against thieves (Gen. 31:39; John 10:1, 8, 10).

Most of the shepherd's work involved a routine of leading the sheep to food and water and returning them to the safety of the fold. The search for greener pastures is a constant task for those who tend sheep (Ps. 23:2; 1 Chron. 4:39–40). The importance of finding adequate shelter for the night is also mentioned (Luke 2:8; Num. 32:24). Sometimes natural caves were used for this purpose (1 Sam. 24:3). The shepherd had to keep alert for strays, counting the sheep as they entered their enclosure for the night (Lev. 27:32; Jer. 33:13; Ezek. 20:37). If animals were missing, the shepherd's duty was to recover them (Ezek. 34:11–12; Matt. 18:11–14). Special attention was given to expectant ewes, newborn lambs, and sick animals (Isa. 40:11; Ezek. 34:15–16).

In addition to fieldstone or brush sheepfolds, shepherds used simple but functionally sound equipment. Protection from the elements was provided by a heavy cloak (cf. Jer. 43:12). A staff was used to control the movement of the flock, and a rod was used to ward off enemies (Ps. 23:4). Also important were a bag for food and a sling (1 Sam. 14:40). Shepherds played reed flutes to calm the flocks and while away the hours (cf. Judg. 5:16). Reference is also made to the use of dogs to help manage the movement of the sheep (Job 30:1).

Shepherd Imagery in the Bible: In numerous biblical passages, the customs of shepherds are used to illustrate spiritual principles; for example, shepherds are compared to spiritual overseers (Num. 27:16–17; Eccles. 12:11; John 21:15–17), and "sheep without a shepherd" symbolize vulnerable people in need of leadership and protection (Matt. 9:36; Mark 6:34).

Descriptions of the shepherd's work are often used to symbolize divine activity (cf. Gen. 48:15; 49:24). The most extended allegories of the shepherd are found in Ps. 23 and Ezek. 34; both passages portray God as one who protects and cares for a helpless flock. The analogy also appears elsewhere, especially in Psalms (e.g., 28:9; 74:1; 77:20; 78:52–53; 80:1; 95:7; 100:3; 121:3–8) and prophetic writings (e.g., Isa. 40:11; 49:9–10; Jer. 23:1–4; 31:10; 49:19–20; 50:17–19; Mic. 4:6–8; 7:14).

Although kings and princes were called shepherds in other ancient Near Eastern literature (cf. Nah. 3:18), the Bible normally applies this title to political leaders in a negative way. Since God was the true shepherd of Israel, other rulers often fell short of God's standards; as such, they were

The "Good Shepherd" depicted on the ceiling of the crypt of Lucina in Rome, second or third century CE.

condemned for their mismanagement of God's flock (e.g., Jer. 10:21; 22:22; 23:1–4; 25:34–38; Ezek. 34:1–10; Zech. 10:3; 11:4–17). There are, however, exceptions to this negative portrayal. David was a shepherd who ruled people with an "upright heart" and a "skillful hand" (Ps. 78:70–72), and Cyrus is also referred to as God's shepherd (Isa. 44:28). Most important was the promise that God would raise up new shepherds (Jer. 3:15; 23:4), a promise that eventually took on messianic significance (Ezek. 34:23; 37:22, 24). Not only would God's shepherd be from the Davidic lineage, but he would also suffer on behalf of the sheep (Zech. 13:7).

The only literal reference to shepherds in the NT is found in Luke 2:8–20; elsewhere they appear in parables and figures of speech, most often in the Gospels. Jesus claimed that his mission was "to the lost sheep of the house of Israel" (Matt. 10:6; 15:24). He told a parable about a shepherd recovering a lost sheep to exemplify God's love (18:12–14; Luke 15:3–7), but he also said that on the day of judgment, the Son of Man would separate the nations as a shepherd separates sheep and goats (Matt. 25:32–33). Jesus also referred to himself as the "good shepherd" who "lays down his life for the sheep" (John 10:1–29; cf. the quotation of Zech. 13:7 in Matt. 26:31 and Mark 14:27). Outside the Gospels, Jesus is called "the great shepherd of the sheep" (Heb. 13:20), "the shepherd and guardian of your souls" (1 Pet. 2.25), and "the chief shepherd" (5:4). Pauline writings apply the word "shepherd" to church leaders. While issuing a warning about fierce wolves (i.e., false teachers), Paul admonishes the Ephesian elders to oversee and care for the flock, which he equates with "the church of God" (Acts 20:28–30). Eph. 4:11 lists shepherds (NRSV: "pastors") among those whom God has gifted to be leaders in the church. *See also* sheep.   G.L.M.

Shephi (shee'fi), an Edomite, the son of the family leader Shobal (1 Chron. 1:40). The name also appears as Shepho (Gen. 36:23).

Shephupham (shi-fyoo'fuhm), a son of Benjamin and ancestor of the Shuphamites (Num. 26:39); Shephuphan (1 Chron. 8:5), Shuppim (1 Chron. 7:12, 15) and Muppim (Gen. 46:21) may be other names for the same family group.

Sherebiah (sher'uh-bi'uh; Heb., perhaps "the LORD has sent severe heat").

1 A Levite among the postexilic Judeans working with Ezra (Ezra 8:24). He is called a "man of discretion" (8:18); he was sent to Jerusalem from Casiphia to serve as a minister for the house of God (8:17).

2 A Levite who explained the law to the people as Ezra read it aloud (Neh. 8:7). He also served as a worship leader during the covenant-renewal ceremony (9:4, 5).

3 A chief of the Levites who returned from the exile with Zerubbabel (Neh. 12:8, 24).

Sheshach (shee'shak), a cryptogram for Babylon found in Jer. 25:26; 51:41. The word is obtained by using a rabbinical cipher called Athbash, in which the last letter of the alphabet is used for the first (tav = aleph), the second from the last is used for the second (shin = beth), etc. Many English versions (including the NRSV) simply replace the word with "Babylon."

Sheshai (shee'shi), one of three descendants of Anak (Num. 13:22; Josh. 15:14; Judg. 1:10) who lived in Canaan when the Israelite spies entered the land. He was defeated by Joshua's forces under Caleb, presumably near his residence, Hebron.

Sheshan (shee'shan), the son of Ishi of the tribe of Judah (1 Chron. 2:31). Because he had no sons, he gave one of his daughters to his Egyptian slave Jahra, so that his family line might continue through her (2:34–35).

Sheshbazzar (shesh-baz'uhr; Babylonian, "Shamash [or Sin] preserve the father"), the "prince of Judah" (Ezra 1:8, 11; 5:14, 16) to whom Cyrus (538 BCE) entrusted the "gold and silver vessels" of the temple to be restored to Jerusalem. He appears to have been the first Babylonian governor of Judah charged with rebuilding the temple, though he did not complete this task (5:15–16). Sheshbazzar may be identical with Shenazzar, a son of King Jehoiachin (also called Jeconiah); this would make him the uncle of Zerubbabel (1 Chron. 3:18).   D.R.B.

Shetharbozenai (shee'thahr-boz'uh-ni), a Persian provincial official who, along with the provincial governor Tattenai, challenged Zerubbabel's right to rebuild the temple (mid-sixth century BCE). He sent an official protest to the Persian king Darius. After a search of the archives in Ecbatana, a copy of the decree of Cyrus allowing the Jews to return and rebuild the temple was found, and Darius ordered Shetharbozenai and Tattenai to cease harassing the Jews and to lend them financial assistance from the provincial treasury (Ezra 5:3, 6; 6:6, 13). *See also* Darius.

Sheva (shee'vuh).

1 The chief scribe or secretary of King David (2 Sam. 20:25), elsewhere called Shavsha (1 Chron. 18:16) and Seraiah (2 Sam. 8:17). He is probably also the same person called Shisha, the father of two scribes in the time of Solomon (1 Kings 4:3). Some scholars suggest that he was a non-Israelite, probably Egyptian, which would account for the variation of the name. *See also* Seraiah; Shavsha.

2 A son of Caleb and Maacah (1 Chron. 2:49).

Shibah (shi'buh; Heb., "oath"), the well dug by Isaac's servants during his time with Abimelech of Gerar (Gen. 26:26–33). It is probably the source for the city named Beer-sheba.

shibboleth (shib′uh-lith; Heb., either "ear of grain" or "flood, torrent"), the password required by Jephthah's Gileadite sentries, employed as a test for detecting Ephraimites who were trying to cross in disguise (Judg. 12:6). The Ephraimites, who spoke a distinct dialect of Hebrew, could only say "sibboleth," and forty-two units were slain.

shield. *See* spear.

Shiggaion (shuh-gay′on), a Hebrew word of uncertain meaning that appears in the heading of Ps. 7. Its plural form appears in Hab. 3:1, which is also a superscription for a psalm. One suggestion is that it indicates the psalm is to be sung as a lament or dirge.

Shihor (shi′hor), a body of water "east of Egypt" (Josh. 13:3) or near the Nile (Isa. 23:3) that served as a reference for the southern edge of Israel (1 Chron. 13:5). The northern parts of the Pelusiac or Bubastite branches of the Nile in the eastern Delta are most likely meant.

Shihor-libnath (shi′hor-lib′nath), a boundary of Asher where it adjoined Carmel (Josh. 19:26). It may be modern Wadi Zerqa, which drains the western slope south of Dor.

Shiloah (shi-loh′uh). *See* Siloam Inscription.

Shiloh (shi′loh), an ancient religious center of Israel. Located about ten miles north of Bethel to the east of the Jerusalem-Nablus road (Judg. 21:19), it is identified with modern Khirbet Seilun. Shiloh was the administrative and religious center for the Israelite tribes during the early settlement period (twelfth century BCE). There the tabernacle was set up (Josh. 18:1), the distribution of the land by lot took place (Josh. 18, 19), the Levites were assigned their cities (Judg. 21), and the ten tribes gathered to consider the apostasy of the east Jordan tribes (Josh. 22).

Shiloh was the central sanctuary and seat of the priesthood (Eleazar, Josh. 21:1, 2; Eli and his sons, 1 Sam. 1:3, 9; Samuel, 1 Sam. 1:24; 3:21) until the ark was captured in the battle with the Philistines at Ebenezer (1 Sam. 4). The ark was not returned to Shiloh, and the city never regained its prestige. Shiloh's destruction by the Philistines is not related in the Bible, but Jeremiah cites its fate in his prophecies (7:12–14; 26:6–9). It did continue as a town to some extent, as is shown by the fact that the wife of Jeroboam sought Ahiah the prophet at Shiloh (1 Kings 14:2–4) and that men of Shiloh came to Mizpah after the murder of Gedaliah (Jer. 4, 5).

Shiloh has been the scene of several excavations.The first Middle Bronze Age settlement was probably a small unfortified village, but it was followed by a town of about four acres surrounded by a massive city wall reinforced by an earthen glacis. The glacis differed in size and construction depending on the need for reinforcement. This city was destroyed in the sixteenth century BCE.

Pottery and bones from the next period on the summit may indicate an isolated cultic place, but there was a period of abandonment before the site was resettled in the twelfth–eleventh centuries BCE. This may have been a settlement of early Israelites who had already developed construction and architectural techniques. Pillared buildings on the west side contained storage jars with "collared rims." The fierce destruction of this settlement was probably the work of the Philistines in the mid-eleventh century BCE.

The site appears to have lain in ruins for some time after this destruction. Scanty architectural and ceramic finds represent village occupation of Iron Age II and Hellenistic times. Roman remains are much more widespread, with evidence of fortification walls. N.L.L.

Shilonite (shi′luh-nit), someone from Shiloh. Ahijah the prophet is so identified five times (1 Kings 11:29; 12:15; 15:29; 2 Chron. 9:29; 10:15), perhaps reflecting his association with the shrine there. See also 1 Chron. 9:5; Neh. 11:5.

Shilshah (shil′shuh), the son of Zophah and a member of the tribe of Asher (1 Chron. 7:37).

Shimea (shim′ee-uh; Heb., "the LORD has heard").

1 The third son of Jesse and, thus, a brother of David (1 Chron. 2:13); he appears to be called Shammah in 1 Sam. 16:9. *See also* Shammah.

2 One of David's sons born in Jerusalem (1 Chron. 3:5). He is called Shammua in 14:4.

3 A Levite from the house of Merari (1 Chron. 6:30).

4 A Gershomite Levite, the father of Berechiah (1 Chron. 6:39).

Shimeath (shim′ee-ath), an Ammonite woman who was the mother of Jozacar/Zabad, one of the murderers of King Joash of Judah (2 Kings 12:21; 2 Chron. 24:26).

Shimeathites (shim′ee-uh-thits), a scribal family living at Jabez (1 Chron. 2:55). They are said to be Kenites and, as such, are associated with the Rechabites.

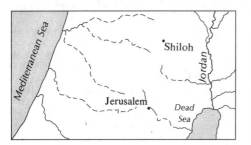

Shimei (shim′ee-*i*; Heb., "[God] has heard").

1 The second son of Gershon, the son of Levi (Exod. 6:17; Num. 3:18; 1 Chron. 6:17; 23:7). The Shimeites were one of the main levitical families after the exile (Num. 3:21; Zech. 12:13).

2 The son of Gera. A Benjaminite of Saul's house in Bahurim, he cursed David as the latter fled Jerusalem during the revolt of Absalom, accusing David publicly of having incurred blood-guilt through his usurpation of the throne of Saul (2 Sam. 16:5–13). When David returned, Shimei met him at the Jordan with a thousand Benjaminites, confessing his sin and pledging his allegiance (19:16–23). David spared Shimei's life on oath, but on his deathbed instructed Solomon to contrive a way to have him put him to death (1 Kings 2:8–9). Solomon initially confined him to Jerusalem but, after three years, when Shimei left the city momentarily to recover two runaway slaves, Solomon maintained that he had violated his confinement and ordered his execution (2:36–46).

3 A member of David's court who did not support Adonijah's attempted usurpation of the throne (1 Kings 1:8). He may be the same Shimei (son of Ela) who wielded authority over Solomon's Benjaminite district (4:18).

4 A Ramathite overseer of David's vineyards (1 Chron. 27:27).

5 The brother of Zerubbabel and grandson of Jehoiachin (1 Chron. 3:19).

6 The grandfather of Mordecai (Esther 2:5).

P.A.B.

Shimeon (shim′ee-uhn), a son of Harim who divorced his foreign wife in compliance with Ezra's postexilic reforms (Ezra 10:31).

Shimon (shi′muhn), a family of the tribe of Judah (1 Chron. 4:20).

Shimrath (shim′rath), the son of Shimei, a Benjaminite, who lived in Jerusalem after the exile (1 Chron. 8:21).

Shimri (shim′ri).

1 The son of Shemaiah and a Simeonite ancestor of Ziza (1 Chron. 4:37).

2 The father of Jediael, one of David's warriors (1 Chron. 11:45).

3 The son of Elizaphan who was among the Levites working to cleanse the temple during the reign of King Hezekiah of Judah (2 Chron. 29:13).

Shimrith (shim′rith; Heb., "God has protected"), a Moabite woman who was the mother of Jehozabad, one of the murderers of King Joash of Judah (2 Chron. 24:26).

Shimron (shim′ron).

1 The fourth son of Issachar and the head of the Shimronites (Gen. 46:13; Num. 26:24; 1 Chron. 7:1).

2 A Canaanite royal town (Josh. 11:1) assigned to the tribe of Zebulun (19:15). The king of Shim-ron joined King Jabin of Hazor in an alliance against the Israelites, but they were defeated by Joshua (cf. 12:19–20, where it is called Shimron-meron). The site is identified with Khirbet Sammuniyeh, five miles west of Nazareth.

Shimshai (shim′shi; Heb., "sun"), an officer of the Persian court on duty in Judea (Ezra 4:8, 9, 17, 23). He endorsed a letter to Artaxerxes, the king of Persia, complaining about Judean postexilic reconstruction work and received official support for its cessation. He maintained, "If this city is rebuilt and the walls finished, they [the Judeans] will not pay tribute, custom, or toll, and the royal revenue will be reduced" (4:13). As a consequence of his complaint, the work in Jerusalem was discontinued until the second year of the reign of King Darius of Persia (4:24).

Shinab (shi′nab; Heb., "Sin [a god] is my father"), the king of Admah, one of the five monarchs in a coalition against the eastern alliance of four other kings (Gen. 14:2). The alliance was defeated in battle and the kings taken captive, only to be subsequently rescued by Abram (14:13–16).

Shinar (shi′nahr), **Plain of,** a district of Babylonia in what is now southern Iraq. According to Gen. 10:10, the Plain of Shinar included Babel (Babylon), Erech (Warka), and Accad or Akkade in central Mesopotamia close to Baghdad. The Tower of Babel is said to have been built on "a plain in the land of Shinar" (Gen. 11:2). Amraphel, king of Shinar, was one of the four kings who, according to Gen. 14, invaded the Dead Sea region and were subsequently pursued and defeated by Abram at Horbah, north of Damascus (Gen. 14:1–16). In later times Shinar was equated with Babylon: Isa. 11:11 speaks of God bringing back a remnant from Shinar (i.e., returning exiles from Babylon); Dan. 1:2 says that Nebuchadnezzar took "Jehoiakim king of Judah . . . with some of the vessels of the house of God" to Shinar; Zech. 5:11 predicts the ephah of wickedness will be taken to a house built for it in Shinar. *See also* Babylon; Nebuchadnezzar.

D.B.

Shion (shi′uhn), a border post of the lands of Issachar (Josh. 19:19). Its location is uncertain.

Shiphi (shi′fi; Heb., "abundance" or "overflow"), the son of Allon and father of Ziza; he was a member of the tribe of Simeon (1 Chron. 4:37).

Shiphrah (shif′ruh), a woman who was one of two midwives approached by Pharaoh to carry out his plan to destroy all Israelite boys when they were born (Exod. 1:15–16). But because Shiphrah and Puah (the other midwife) feared God, they allowed the babies to live. Summoned by Pharaoh to explain why so many babies were surviving, they lied to him, saying, "The Hebrew women are not like the Egyptian women; for they are vigorous and give birth before the midwife comes to them"

(1:19). The text then says God rewarded Shiphrah and Puah by giving them families (1:21), but Pharaoh came up with a new plan, ordering that all of the male Hebrew infants be thrown into the Nile (1:22).

Shiphtan (shif'tan; Heb., perhaps "the god has judged"), the father of Kemuel and a leader of the tribe of Ephraim (Num. 34:24). Shiphtan was one of the men assigned to divide the land among the tribes of Israel.

ships. *See* boats.

Shishak (shi'shak; Heb.), a pharaoh of Egypt whose Egyptian name was Shoshenq I (945–924 BCE). Born in Egypt but descended from a line of Libyan nobles, he was the founder of the Twenty-Second (Libyan) Dynasty (ca. 945–715 BCE), whose capital was at Tanis (Heb. Zoan) in the northeast part of the Delta. A contemporary of Solomon, he gave asylum to Jeroboam (1 Kings 11:40) until the latter returned to take over the northern kingdom after Solomon's death (12:2–3). When the country was divided between Rehoboam and Jeroboam, Shishak, for reasons still unclear, launched a major invasion of Judah and Israel. This campaign, which took place in the fifth year of Rehoboam's reign, is described in 1 Kings 14:25–26 and 2 Chron. 12:1–9. This invasion included the hill country, the coastal plain, and the Negev. The biblical account only mentions the assault upon Judah, but Shishak's depiction of the campaign, inscribed on the wall of the temple at Karnak, shows 156 captives, each representing a Near Eastern city, most of which were in Israel. According to 1 Kings 14:25–28, Shishak came up against Jerusalem, and many of the treasures of the temple and palace had to be handed over as ransom. Rehoboam decided to pay this tribute to Shishak to avoid an Egyptian conquest of the city (2 Chron. 12:5–9). From the perspective of the Chronicler (12:5), Shishak's invasion came as retribution for Rehoboam's infidelity to God. In 1 Kings 14:22–24 are listed his apostasies, many of which reflect the pagan influences introduced by Solomon. Historically, the success of Shishak's campaign against Judah and Israel illustrates the military weakness caused by the division of the Hebrew kingdom, which resulted in widespread destruction of cities in both Judah and Israel only five years after the death of Solomon. This destruction has been confirmed to some extent by the results of archaeology, especially at Tell Beit Mirsim, Lachish, and Beersheba. *See also* Rehoboam; Zoan.   J.M.W.

Shitrai (shit'ri), a Sharonite, one of David's servants. He handled the livestock in the Sharon plain (1 Chron. 27:29).

shittah (shit'uh; "acacia" tree or wood), a transliterated Hebrew term that identifies the tree or wood *Acacia nilotica* or the more substantial *Acacia tortilis*. In the plural form, *shittim* (Exod. 25–38), it is designated as the proper wood to be used in constructing the ark of the covenant (25:10) and the accompanying items like the carrying poles (25:28), bars (26:26), pillars (26:32), tables (25:23), and altars (37:25; cf. Deut. 10:3). In Isa. 41:19 its growth, along with that of other substantial trees, symbolizes the revival of lush life. It was highly resistant to insects and other decay and, being both hard and durable, was suitable for cabinet making.   R.S.B.

Shittim (shi'tim), short for Abel-Shittim (Heb., "meadow of the acacias"), a place in Moab north of Mount Nebo and Heshbon and across the Jordan River from Jericho. Shittim was the place from which Balaam was supposed to curse the Israelites, though he found that he could only bless them instead (Num. 22–24). Later, it was where the Israelites camped just before crossing the Jordan River into Canaan (33:48–9). It was here that the Israelite men engaged in idolatrous and immoral liaisons with Moabite women (25) and it was also here that the Israelites were numbered in a census (26). In addition, Joshua was commissioned to succeed Moses at Shittim (27:23), and Moses delivered his final address to the people at Shittim (Deut. 31–33). From Shittim, spies were sent into the land (Josh. 2:1). The site has been identified with Tell el-Hamman in present-day Jordan.

Shiza (shi'zuh), a member of the tribe of Reuben. He was the father of Adina and one of David's warriors (1 Chron. 11:42).

Shoa (shoh'uh), a people Ezekiel envisioned as joining with Babylonians, Assyrians, and probably Arameans to attack Judah (23:23). The people have not been precisely identified, although they were probably located north of Judah, given the known locations of the associated groups. In the relevant section of Ezekiel, Judah appears as one of two sisters and is named Oholibah. *See also* Oholah, Oholibah.

Shobab (shoh'bab).
   1 A son of Caleb and Azuba (1 Chron. 2:18).
   2 A son of David and Bathsheba born in Jerusalem (2 Sam. 5:14; 1 Chron. 3:5; 14:4).

Shobach (shoh'bak), the commander of the eastern Aramean forces of Hadadezer, who marshaled troops to assault David. In the subsequent fight at Helam in the Transjordan Shobach's forces were beaten decisively, and Shobach himself was mortally wounded. The defeat stymied further Aramean-Ammonite action against David (2 Sam. 10:15–19; Shophach, 1 Chron. 19:16–19).

Shobai (shoh'bi), one of the families of returning exiles who served as gatekeepers in Jerusalem (Ezra 2:42; Neh. 7:45; 1 Esd. 5:28).

Shobal (shoh'buhl; Heb., "basket").

1 The second son of Seir, a Horite chief who lived in Edom (Gen. 36:20, 23, 29; 1 Chron. 1:38, 40).

2 The son of Hur, an ancestor of a Calebite tribe that lived in Kiriath-jearim (1 Chron. 2:50, 52), which was considered part of Judah (4:1–2).

Shobek (shoh'bek), one of the men who signed Ezra's covenant-renewal document in Jerusalem (Neh. 10:24).

Shobi (shoh'b*i*), the Ammonite prince, son of King Nahash, who supplied David with provisions when he and his troops were staying at Mahanaim during the conflict with his son Absalom (2 Sam. 17:27–29). Shobi may have served as successor to his brother Hanun, who had previously treated David insolently, which had ended disastrously for the Ammonites and their Aramean allies (10:1–11:1).

shoes. Sandals were the most common form of foot covering in biblical times, but Assyrian and Roman soldiers wore laced or strapped boots, and Near Eastern women are depicted in ankle-high shoes in an Egyptian tomb painting (cf. Ezek. 16:10). Most people, however, appear barefoot in ancient Egyptian and Mesopotamian art, although sandals are shown on soldiers, travelers, and persons of rank. Footwear may have been more common in northern regions. Sandals consisted basically of a leather, wood, or fiber sole attached to the foot by thongs (Gen. 14:23). Assyrian sandals were characterized by a heel cap.

Putting on sandals was a sign of preparation for a journey (Exod. 12:11; Deut. 29:5; Josh. 9:5, 13) or warfare (Isa. 5:27). Jesus's instructions in sending out the twelve, that they should go barefoot (Matt. 10:10; Luke 10:4), countered normal practice. Sandals belonged to fine dress (Luke 15:22) and full dress (Acts 12:8). Footwear was removed indoors, in sacred precincts (Exod. 3:5; Josh. 5:15), and during mourning (Ezek. 24:17).

Transfer of property was confirmed in Hebrew custom by the symbolic exchange of a sandal (Ruth 4:7, 8; Amos 2:6), arising, probably, from

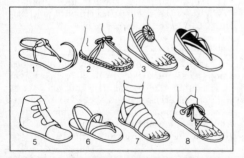

Shoes: 1. Egyptian (1200 BCE); 2. Egyptian;
3. Babylonian; 4. Assyrian (900 BCE); 5. Greek *krepis;*
6. Greek *pediba;* 7. Roman *calceus;* 8. Roman *crepeda.*

the practice of claiming title to land by walking its boundaries or casting a shoe upon it (Ps. 60:8). The public removal of a man's shoe by the woman he has refused to take in levirate marriage was a humiliating gesture (Deut. 25:9–10). During NT times, removing or carrying a master's shoes was a slave's task (cf. Matt. 3:11; Mark 1:7). P.A.B.

shofar (shoh'fahr). *See* trumpet.

Shoham (shoh'ham), a Merarite Levite, the son of Jaaziah (1 Chron. 24:27).

Shomer (shoh'muhr; Heb., "keeper, watcher").

1 A Moabite woman who was the mother of Jehozabad, one of the murderers of Judah's king Joash (2 Kings 12:21; Shimrith in 2 Chron. 24:26).

2 A son of Heber from the tribe of Asher (1 Chron. 7:32; Shemer, 7:34).

shoot. *See* branch.

shovel, altar, an implement for clearing away ashes from the tabernacle's outer altar. The altar shovels were made of copper (Exod. 27:3; 38:3). The ashes were scooped up in them and apparently placed in copper pots (27:3), which were then carried outside the camp and emptied at a specified ash dump (Lev. 6:10–11). Solomon's temple also had copper shovels for its burnt offering altar (1 Kings 7:40, 45; 2 Chron. 4:11, 16). When Jerusalem fell, the Babylonians took these as spoil (2 Kings 25:14; Jer. 52:18).

showbread. *See* bread of the Presence.

shrine, a place in which sacred objects are kept. The NRSV uses the word inconsistently to translate several different Hebrew and Greek words. A prophet named Micah is said to have set up a shrine (lit., "a house of God") in which he placed an idol of cast metal (Judg. 17:4–5). When Saul is looking for his father's donkeys he encounters the prophet Samuel offering a sacrifice at the local shrine (lit., "high place," 1 Sam. 9:11–19). The same word is later used in 10:5, which refers to a company of ecstatic prophets coming from a shrine at Gibeath-elohim. Isaiah writes mockingly about a carpenter making an idol out of wood and putting it in a shrine (lit., "a house") and worshiping it (44:13). In Jer. 17:12, the ark of the covenant is called a shrine (lit., "a place"; cf. Exod. 26:33; 1 Kings 6:19; 8:6). And in the NT, the Letter to the Hebrews refers to the Holy of Holies in the temple as an "inner shrine" (lit., "inner place," 6:19). The word could have been used in numerous other instances also, e.g., with reference to the tent of meeting (Exod. 33:7) or the pagan temple of Artemis (Acts 17:24). *See also* ark of the covenant, ark of God; tabernacle; temple, the; temples; worship in the Hebrew Bible; worship in the New Testament. M.A.P.

Reconstructed shrine house with snake and animal motifs; from Beth-shan, 1000–850 BCE.

Shua (shoo′uh).

1 The Canaanite father of Judah's unnamed wife (Gen. 38:2).

2 The daughter of Heber from the tribe of Asher (1 Chron. 7:32).

Shuah (shoo′uh), a son of Abraham and Keturah (Gen. 25:2). He may be associated with the Shuhites, who according to Assyrian inscriptions, inhabited a land on the Euphrates River in Syria. Bildad, one of Job's counselors, is called a Shuhite (Job 2:11).

Shual (shoo′uhl; Heb., perhaps "fox" or "jackal").

1 A territory against which Philistine raiders moved in the time of King Saul (eleventh century BCE; 1 Sam. 13:17). Its association with Ophrah suggests a northerly location for the Philistine camp at Michmash.

2 A son of Zophah from the tribe of Asher (1 Chron. 7:36). The name was probably used by a family group who regarded him as their ancestor.

Shuham (shoo′ham), the ancestor of a group of people from the tribe of Dan (Num. 26:42–43). In Gen. 46:23, he is called Hushim.

Shuhite (shoo′hit), an identification of Job's counselor Bildad (Job 2:11; 8:1; 18:1; 25:1; 42:9). It may identify him as a descendant of Shuah (a son of Abraham and Keturah), though the main point may be to locate him geographically as being from an area in modern Syria that Assyrian inscriptions indicate was inhabited by Shuhites. *See also* Shuah.

Shunammite (shoo′nuh-mit), a native of the town of Shunem.

1 Abishag, who nursed David in his old age (1 Kings 1:3). *See also* Abishag.

2 A woman whose dead son was revived by Elisha (2 Kings 4:8–37). *See also* Elisha.

Shunem (shoo′nuhm), a town on the southern border of Issachar (Josh. 19:18) guarding the pass to the Valley of Jezreel on the north, opposite the town of Jezreel at the foot of Mount Gilboa. It is identified with modern Solem. Shunem is mentioned in the fifteenth-century BCE conquest lists of the Egyptian pharaoh Thutmose III, the fourteenth-century Amarna letters, and the tenth-century inscription of Pharaoh Shishak at Karnak. The Philistines camped at Shunem before defeating the Israelites at Mount Gilboa (1 Sam. 28:4), and David's nurse in his old age, Abishag, was from Shunem (1 Kings 1:3). Elisha frequently stopped at this town in his travels, and a woman there provided him with quarters; in return Elisha's promise of a son was fulfilled and later Elisha revived him from death (2 Kings 4). Some interpreters have sought to connect Shunem with the Shulammite woman of the Song of Solomon (6:13). *See also* Gilboa; Jezreel.   N.L.L.

Shuni (shoo′ni), the third son of Gad, and grandson of Jacob and Zilpah. He was the ancestor of the Shunites (Gen. 46:16; Num. 26:15).

Shur (shoor), **Wilderness of,** a desert region somewhere in the Sinai Peninsula, east of the present Suez Canal. It was inhabited by Ishmaelites (Gen. 25:18) and was for a time the home of Abraham (20:1). The Israelites during the exodus entered the wilderness of Shur immediately after crossing the sea (Exod. 15:22). Earlier, an angel had met Hagar at a "spring on the way to Shur" (Gen. 16:7), probably the desert track leading southward from Beer-sheba. Along this same pathway, Saul, and later David, pursued the Amalekites "as far as Shur" (1 Sam. 15:7; cf. 27:8). *See also* exodus, the; Hagar; Ishmaelites.   D.B.

Shushan (shoo′shan). *See* Susa.

Shuthelah (shoo′thuh-luh), a son of Ephraim, ancestor of the Shuthelahites (Num. 26:35–36). The Ephraimite mentioned in 1 Chron. 7:21–22 may be the same person.

Sia (si′uh), **Siaha** (si′uh-huh), the head of a family of temple servants who returned from exile in Babylon and worked on the reconstruction of the city of Jerusalem. The servants are identified as descendants of Sia in Ezra 2:44 and descendants of Siaha in Neh. 7:47.

Sibbecai (sib′uh-ki), a Hushamite who killed a giant named Saph (2 Sam. 21:18; Sippai in 1 Chron. 20:4) in the battles against the Philistines at Gob (Gezer in 1 and 2 Chronicles). Identified as a Zerahite (1 Chron. 27:11), he commanded David's forces in the eighth month and was among his elite forces known as "the Thirty" (11:29; possibly Mebunnai, 2 Sam. 23:27).

Sibmah (sib′muh), a place in the rich Moabite plateau allocated to the tribe of Reuben (Num. 32:38; Sebam in 32:3). In later prophetic oracles it was described as Moabite territory (Isa. 16:6–9; Jer. 48:31–32) known for vineyards. It may be modern Qurn el-Kibsh, some five miles southwest of Hesban.

Iron sickle, which represents the type of tools the Philistines manufactured and supplied to the Israelites.

sickle, an instrument with a simple or compound blade set as a small curve and rigged with a handle to allow short horizontal strokes for cutting grass, weeds, or grains. Early models recovered are compound blades of serrated flint segments fastened in a wooden frame with bitumen. Later models include metal blades, but the use of flint continued long into the Bronze and Iron ages. A quick sweeping arc at the stems held by the other hand would provide efficient use of the tool. Biblical references to its use in harvest are numerous (Deut. 16:9; 23:25; Jer. 50:16; Joel 3:13; Mark 4:29), and it appears metaphorically as a tool of the harvest of human life at the Last Judgment (Rev. 14:14–20).

R.S.B.

Siddim (sid′im), **Valley of,** a depression at the south end of the Dead Sea that was the scene of a war in which four eastern kings (of Shinar, Ellasar, Elam, and Goim) defeated the kings of five local cities (Sodom, Gomorrah, Admah, Bela [Zoar], and Zeboiim, Gen. 14:1–10). The valley is said to be filled with bitumen pits, and many of the retreating forces fell into these. The location is most likely the eastern shore of the Lisan projection, from modern Bab edh-Dhra south.

Sidon (si′duhn), one of the two leading cities (with Tyre) of ancient Phoenicia. Sidon is located twenty-two miles north of Tyre on the Mediterranean coast of modern Lebanon. It possesses a port with an inner and outer harbor on the north side and another on the south. Substantial archaeological investigation is not possible because of the modern city on the site. Immediately outside

Sidon, however, stone round houses of the Chalcolithic period (4000–3000 BCE) have been found, and the neighborhood cemeteries of the Babylonian to Late Roman periods (ca. 625 BCE–324 CE) have produced numerous sarcophagi, the most famous of which depicts Alexander the Great in battle and hunting scenes carved in marble.

In the Amarna Age (fourteenth century BCE) King Zimrida of Sidon wrote two letters to the pharaoh of Egypt. In one he professed his loyalty and requested Egyptian aid in regaining territory that had fallen to Hapiru rebels. But in other correspondence the kings of Byblos and Tyre portrayed Zimrida as having joined the rebellion and allied himself with Aziru, king of Amurru, against them and Egypt. At the beginning of the Iron Age (ca. 1200 BCE) Sidonian colonists refounded Tyre, according to classical tradition. The Egyptian *Tale of Wenamun,* dated to the mid-eleventh century BCE, mentions the presence of fifty ships in the port of Sidon. It may have outclassed Tyre during the first centuries (1200–1000 BCE) of the Iron Age, but during most of the Phoenician period Tyre led or controlled Sidon, despite the fact that from the Greek perspective of the Homeric poems the term "Phoenician" was synonymous with "Sidon." For example, the Assyrian king Sennacherib in 701 BCE defeated Luli, whom he called the king of Sidon but who was almost certainly Elulaeus, the king of Tyre. In the seventh century BCE Sidon was besieged by King Esar-haddon of Assyria, who razed the city (677 BCE) and built in its place an Assyrian residence nearby called Kar-Esarhaddon.

Sidon's fortunes improved during the Persian period (539–332 BCE), due in part to the decline of Tyre following a thirteen-year siege (587/6–573 BCE) by the Babylonian king Nebuchadnezzar and in part to the favor bestowed upon Sidon by Persian monarchs. The mainland settlement of Sidon may have been more tractable than the island of Tyre, which submitted but remained unconquered. Phoenician refusal to support the Persian king Cambyses' planned attack on North Africa, where Tyre's chief colonies were located, may have been led by Tyre.

Cambyses conquered Egypt in 526 BCE with the aid of the Phoenicians. King Tabnit of Sidon ruled about this time, and it may be no accident that he was buried in an Egyptian general's reused stone sarcophagus upon which Tabnit left his own inscription. His mummified body revealed him to be a strong man, 5 feet 5 inches tall, with wavy reddish-brown hair tinted with henna. The sarcophagus of his son, King Eshmunazar II, possessed a Phoenician inscription of twenty-two lines, from which we learn that he built several temples for Astarte at Sidon and for Eshmun at a mountain spring and that Sidon was given possession of Dor and Joppa south of Tyre. His father, King Tabnit, was a priest of Astarte, and his mother, Amo′ashtart, was priestess of Astarte, and both were offspring of Eshmunazar I, king of Sidon. The sanctuary of Eshmun on a hillside a few miles away at the river Nahr el-Awali has been excavated by M. Dunand and others, revealing important buildings, inscriptions, and statuary of the Babylonian, Persian, and Hellenistic periods dedicated to Eshmun. He was the god of healing and was equated with the Greek deity Asclepius. In the Persian wars, when Darius and Xerxes attacked Greek city-states, King Tetramnestus and his fleet of three hundred Sidonian triremes (warships with three banks of oars) led the Persian navy.

In 351 BCE, on the enthronement of Artaxerxes III Ochus in Persia, Sidon revolted. King Tennes led Sidon in rebellion, but when the Persians reacted and the cause looked hopeless, Tennes treacherously betrayed Sidon in order to save himself. The city was burned and, although rebuilt, did not regain its former position. Sidon quickly submitted to Alexander the Great in 332 BCE and assisted him in the siege of Tyre. During the Hellenistic and Roman periods Sidon was a prosperous center for commerce and learning.

Sidon is mentioned frequently in the prophetic books of the Bible, often in conjunction with Tyre (e.g., Isa. 23:2, 4, 12; Jer. 25:22; Ezek. 28:21–22; Joel 3:4; Zech. 9:2). The area was also visited by Jesus (Matt. 15:21; Mark 7:24) and Paul (Acts 27:3).

Bibliography

Jidejian, Nina. *Sidon Through the Ages.* Dar el-Machreq, 1971.

Katzenstein, H. Jacob. "Tyre in the Early Persian Period" (539–486 BCE). *Biblical Archeologist* 42:1 (1979): 23–34.   T.L.M.

siege, the military tactic of surrounding a community, cutting off its supplies, and reducing its resistance to the point of surrender or destruction. Less precisely, the word can be used to refer to any prolonged distress or suffering.

Biblical references to siege works, siege towers, and siege mounds indicate common experience with the process. Only unfruitful trees were permitted to be cut for preparing siege works against an enemy city (Deut. 20:20). Babylon built siege works against Jerusalem under Nebuchadnezzar (2 Kings 25:1). Metaphorically, Job speaks of God as placing him under siege (Job 19:12), and the helplessness of siege works in the face of a wise person is touted in Eccles. 9:14. Isa. 29:3 and Ezek. 4:2 portray God as besieging Jerusalem (Ariel) with towers and siege works, and Dan. 11:15 mentions siege tactics used against the forces of the south (the Egyptians).

Countermeasures to defend a siege included securing a water supply that could be accessed from within the city walls. Such constructions have been found at Hazor and Megiddo, in addition to the tunnel Hezekiah dug in anticipation of a siege of Jerusalem. Ezekiel's description is quite graphic and accurate, combining a siege wall (to protect the attackers), a mound or ramp (to scale the walls), camps for the attacking troops, and battering rams (most graphically presented in the bas-reliefs from the palace of Sennacherib at Nineveh showing the Assyrian conquest of Lachish). Siege tactics also included sapping under the defender's walls, ramming the gates, storming the gates and walls with ladders or towers, and setting fire to the wooden materials in the defense system. One of the longest sieges in biblical history occurred at Samaria, the capital of the northern kingdom, Israel. The city held out for three years against the Assyrians before capitulating in 722/1 BCE.

Other references in the Bible include Joshua laying siege to Lachish (Josh. 10:31) and Joab to Beth-maacah (2 Sam. 20:15). Ben-hadad or Aram lays siege to Samaria, and the situation becomes so bad that people resort to cannibalism (2 Kings 6:24–30). Certain passages in the Gospels may betray knowledge of the Roman siege of Jerusalem, which ended with the destruction of that city in 70 CE (e.g., Luke 21:20). *See also* war; weapons.   R.S.B.

sign, a significant event, act, or other manifestation that signifies God's presence or intention. Signs may be miraculous and spectacular, as in the case of those performed by Moses before the people of Israel to demonstrate that God had sent him to them (Exod. 4:1–9, 17, 30) or before Pharaoh for the same purpose (7–11). On the other hand, a natural phenomenon such as a rainbow or a sunset may be called a sign (Gen. 9:13; Ps. 65:8), as may an identifying mark such as circumcision (Gen. 17:11) or even a prophet and his children (Isa. 8:18).

In the NT, signs tend to be apocalyptic or miraculous, but the shepherds are told that the infant Jesus "wrapped in bands of cloth and lying in a manger" (Luke 2:12) will be a sign of God's salvation. When Jesus is asked about a sign indicating the coming destruction of the temple (Mark 13:4), he responds by predicting natural, if catastrophic, events (13:5–13). Still, these phenomena are described in apocalyptic terms and merge with more distinctly supernatural events predicted later on in the same discourse (13:24–27).

In the Synoptic Gospels, when Jesus is asked to perform or manifest a sign, he refuses and denounces the quest for signs as something that an evil and adulterous generation seeks (Matt. 12:38–39; Mark 8:11–12). This is in part because signs are something that false prophets and messiahs work in order to lead people astray (Matt. 24:24; Mark 13:22). In broad terms, Jesus says that the people will be given only one sign, which he calls "sign of Jonah" (Matt. 12:38–40; 16:4), a slightly veiled reference to his resurrection (he will emerge from the tomb after three days, just as Jonah did from the belly of the fish). That one sign will be all that is needed before "the sign of the Son of Man" appears in the skies (24:3, 30) at his Second Coming.

The Gospel of John takes a rather different view. In this Gospel, Jesus's miracles are called "signs" (Gk. *semeia,* 2:11; 4:54; 6:2, 14; 12:18; the preferred term for miracles in the Synoptic Gospels is *dynamis,* which means "power" or "deeds of power," e.g. Matt. 11:20–23; Mark 6:2, 5). Thus, for John, the miracles do function as potential signs of legitimation; they *ought* to demonstrate to people that Jesus has divine power and authority (see 3:2; 7:31; 9:16). Their effectiveness in this regard, however, is mixed; some people believe because of the signs (2:23; 4:53–54; cf. 20:30), but others do not (11:47; 12:37; cf. 4:48). In a deeper sense, then, John seems to present the miracles as signs because, like the metaphors of Jesus's speech, they indicate something symbolic about who God is and what God does. God transforms the ordinary into the extraordinary (2:1–11) and offers people health (4:46–54), sustenance (6:2–14), and life (11:38–44; 12:18). The miracles are "signs," because they are charged with symbolism signifying something more than the fact that some deed of power has occurred. Indeed, one popular theory suggests that the person responsible for producing John's Gospel had a copy of a now lost book that scholars call the "Signs Gospel." This book (if it existed) may have contained several miracle stories presented as numbered "signs" that Jesus performed (cf. 2:11 and 4:54), and it would have concluded with the words now found in 20:30–31, indicating that Jesus also did many other signs not written in the book and claiming that the purpose of the signs is to bring readers "to believe that Jesus is the Messiah, the Son of God," so that readers "may have life in his name" (20:31).

The book of Acts also emphasizes the performance of "signs and wonders," spectacular miracles wrought by those who receive the Spirit's power (2:43; 4:30; 5:12; 6:8; 14:3; 15:12). Such actions place the apostles and other followers of Jesus in line with heroes of God like Moses (7:26) and Jesus himself (2:22); they serve to authenticate the word of the gospel, proving that their bold proclamation is endorsed by spiritual powers not subject to human limitation—powers that are usually beneficial, but that are *not* to be offended (5:1–11; 13:9–12).

Paul indicates in his letters that God worked "signs and wonders" through him (Rom. 15:19), and he even cites miracles as the "signs of a true apostle" (2 Cor. 2:12), but he does not get any more specific about just what those signs and wonders entailed. Furthermore, Paul can be dismissive of the role that signs play with regard to faith: "Jews demand signs and Greeks desire wisdom, but we proclaim Christ crucified, a stumbling block to Jews and foolishness to Gentiles" (1 Cor. 1:22–23). *See also* miracles.   D.M.S./M.A.P.

signet. *See* seal.

Sihon (si'hon), a king of the Amorites whose capital was Heshbon, a city lying east of the northern tip of the Dead Sea. The etymology of his name is obscure, as are the circumstances of his origins. According to the Bible, Sihon opposed the Israelites as they sought to move from the south through the Transjordan. The two forces clashed at Jahaz, resulting in the defeat of Sihon and the incorporation of his territory into the Israelite

tribal holdings (Num. 21:21–30; Deut. 2:24–37; Judg. 11:18–22). Although the Israelites were not to inherit Moabite or Ammonite territory, the area attributed to Sihon's kingdom and claimed by Israel seems to have included some territory also claimed by Ammon and Moab. The memory of this victory continued as a theme in later literature (1 Kings 4:19; Pss. 135:11; 136:19; Neh. 9:22).

Recent archaeological work in the general area attributed to Sihon—essentially the area between the headwaters of the Jabbok and the Arnon—has shown some occupational evidence dating to the Late Bronze Age and earliest Iron Age (fifteenth to twelfth centuries BCE). None of this evidence relates directly to Sihon with the exception of the excavations at Tell Hesban, north of Medeba. Only scattered twelfth-century BCE artifacts have been found there, and they give indication of a very small settlement during the end of the period assigned to Sihon.   J.A.D.

Silas (si'luhs), **Silvanus** (sil-vay'nuhs), a leader in the early church and an associate of Paul. The Letters of Paul and 1 Peter refer to him as Silvanus (a Latinization), but Acts prefers Silas (either a Semitic or a shortened Greek form). According to the book of Acts, Silas and Judas Barsabbas, prophets in the Jerusalem church, were sent along with Paul and Barnabas to take the apostolic decrees from the Jerusalem Council to the church in Antioch (15:22–35). Later, when Paul and Barnabas at Antioch quarreled over Mark (15:36–41), Paul chose Silas to accompany him on a mission tour in Asia Minor and ultimately into Macedonia and Achaia (15:41–18:5). Luke says that Silas (like Paul) was a Roman citizen (16:37–38), and in 1 Thess. 2:7 Paul refers to Silas as an apostle (cf. 1:1). Silvanus (Silas) is mentioned as a coauthor of two Pauline letters (1 Thess. 1:1; 2 Thess. 1:1), and he is listed in a manner that probably indicates he is to be regarded as the secretary or courier of 1 Peter (5:12). In 2 Cor. 1:19, he is mentioned as one who proclaimed the gospel to the Corinthians and assisted in the founding of the church in Corinth.   A.J.M.

Siloam (si-loh'uhm) **Inscription,** a Hebrew inscription recovered from the Siloam tunnel in Jerusalem. The eighth-century text commemorates the excavation of that tunnel, which connected the spring of Gihon, the principal source of water for ancient Jerusalem, with a reservoir within the city known as the pool of Siloam.

The Inscription, now in the Museum of the Ancient Orient in Istanbul, was found in 1880 by two boys wading inside the tunnel some 20 feet above the western reservoir. It consists of six lines incised on the lower part of a prepared surface on the rock wall of the shaft. The blank upper surface has led some scholars to suppose that part of the inscription is missing; others believe that the text was originally intended to be surmounted by a relief. The inscription cannot be dated long before 701 BCE, the year of Sennacherib's siege of Jerusalem. The script is the Hebrew lapidary hand of the

Cast of the Siloam Inscription originally carved on the wall of Hezekiah's tunnel, Jerusalem, describing the construction and completion of the tunnel, which connected the Gihon spring to the Pool of Siloam; eighth century BCE.

eighth century BCE, and the language is comparable to the standard Hebrew prose of the Bible. The text describes the completion of Hezekiah's tunnel by two crews who, having set to work from opposite directions, dug until only 3 cubits (4.5 feet) of rock separated them at a point 100 cubits (150 feet) beneath the streets of the city. From there they were able to guide each other through the remaining rock by shouting. This was possible because of something extending north and south in the rock. Perhaps this was a fissure, as the translation suggests, but the Hebrew word is obscure.   P.K.M.

THE SILOAM INSCRIPTION: TRANSLATION

(line 1) The [ ] of the penetration. This is how the penetration took place. While [the diggers were] still [wielding]

(2) their axes toward each other, with three cubits still to be pen[etrated, they could he]ar each other sho-

(3) uting, for there was a *fissure* in the rock running to the south [and to the nor]th. So at the moment of pene-

(4) tration, the diggers struck toward each other, axe against axe. Then the waters flowed

(5) from the spring to the pool—one thousand two hundred cubits. And one h[un-]

(6) dred cubits was the height of the rock above the heads of the digger[s].

Siloam (si-loh'uhm) **tunnel,** a subterranean water supply system in ancient Jerusalem, also known as Hezekiah's tunnel. The tunnel carried water from the the Gihon spring to the Siloam Pool, located inside the city walls. The tunnel replaced an earlier aqueduct system that is also referred to in the Bible, and various terms are applied to the tunnel and the aqueduct at various stages in history. The final construction of the Siloam tunnel was documented ca. 701 BCE with a plaque containing what is now called the Siloam Inscription.

The Gihon spring arises on the eastern slope of the Ophel, the southeastern hill of Jerusalem, upon which the City of David was located. Originally, therefore, it emptied into the Kidron Valley. After the occupation of the site, however, an open basin was dug at the mouth of the spring to collect the waters. From this basin, known as the "upper pool," the waters were conveyed south along the slope of the city mound by an aqueduct called the "conduit of the upper pool" (2 Kings 18:17; Isa. 7:3). Recent excavation has shown that this aqueduct was in part a tunnel and in part an open canal, so that in addition to receiving the flow from the upper pool it collected rainwater from the slope of the mound. It contained a number of "windows," through which water could be released for the irrigation of the valley below. The reference in Isa. 8:6 to "the waters of Shiloah that flow gently" probably reveals the name for this water system that was in use during the reign of Ahaz. "Siloam" is a later Greek form of "Shiloah." At the mouth of the aqueduct was another reservoir called the "lower pool" (Isa. 22:9), the "Pool of Shelah" (Neh. 3:15), or the "King's Pool" (Neh. 2:14).

Because the original Shiloh or Siloam channel lay outside the fortifications of the city, it was difficult to protect during a siege. As part of his preparations for Sennacherib's attack on Jerusalem, therefore, Hezekiah sealed the old outlet of the upper pool (2 Chron. 32:2–4, 30; cf. Isa. 22:8–11) and devised an underground passage to divert the flow of the Gihon to a reservoir within the fortified precincts of the city (2 Kings 20:20), evidently the "reservoir between the two walls" of Isa. 22:11. The shaft of Hezekiah's tunnel followed a sinuous path through 1,749 feet of bedrock under the City of David to a new pool on the western slope of the Ophel in the valley later known as Tyropoeon. The name of the older aqueduct was transferred to the new system.

The first-century Jewish historian Josephus speaks of a reservoir named Siloam, and John 9:7 refers to the "pool of Siloam." This is likely the lower pool, which was discovered in 2004 by archaeologists. This slightly trapezoidal pool was accessible on three sides by steps and was likely used for bathing by Jewish pilgrims approaching the Temple Mount. Although the masonry appears to be from the Herodian period, an earlier and simpler plastered pool might have been built by the Hasmoneans on the same site. The channel connecting the upper to lower pool is still functional. *See also* Siloam Inscription.   P.K.M.

Silvanus. *See* Silas, Silvanus.

silver (Heb. *keseph*), a pale, precious metal capable of being hammered or drawn out thin, known to people in the Near East as early as 3000 BCE.

Silver mining and metallurgy were known and practiced by craft workers at Ebla (Tell Mardikh in Syria). Some Ebla texts show the value of cattle in silver and list silver as tribute from Mari, recording in one instance 2,188 minas of silver (1 mina equals 47 grams). Silver bars, daggers, adze heads, and small ceremonial shovels are in evidence from biblical times, as are pieces of jewelry and amulets. Silver was used as a standard for business transactions and as a measure of wealth. Excavations at Ur of artifacts from ca. 2500 BCE show Sumerian use of silver for musical instruments, pipes, statuettes, and filigree jewelry. The source of silver in antiquity was probably western Asia Minor and particularly the islands of the Aegean. The Laurion mine near Athens was in use by 1000 BCE as a source of silver. Spain's Rio Tinto silver mines were likely the source of silver for Phoenician and Roman coinage. Among the most recent archaeological findings in Jerusalem is a small silver scroll bearing text that includes God's name in Hebrew. The scroll dates to the sixth century BCE.

The first biblical reference to silver from among the approximately four hundred Bible passages from Genesis to Malachi is Gen. 13:2, where Abraham's possession of silver along with his cattle and gold mark him as a wealthy man. He purchased the burial cave at Machpelah from Ephron the Hittite for four hundred shekels of weighed silver (23:16). Joseph, the Hebrew in Pharaoh's court (ca. 1750 BCE), had a silver cup that

he placed in his brother Benjamin's sack (44:2, 5, 12, 16). Later he gave Benjamin "three hundred shekels of silver" (45:22). As early as the period of the judges (ca. 1200–1000 BCE), the Israelites knew of silver craftsmanship; Judges reports that Micah's mother took eleven hundred pieces of silver to a silversmith for fashioning an idol (17:1–6).

Other passages refer to silver used for foundations, decorations, vessels for worship, and trumpets for the tabernacle (Exod. 26:19; 27:10, 17; 36:24, 26; Num. 7:13, 14; 10:2), and in connection with the Jerusalem temple and its treasury (1 Kings 7:51; 1 Chron. 28:15, 16; 2 Chron. 2:7; Ezra 8:26, 28; Neh. 7:71). Silver was known in the raw state (1 Kings 15:15; Exod. 31:4; 35:24, 32) as well as mined (Job 28:1) and refined (Prov. 10:20; 1 Chron. 29:4; Mal. 3:2, 3; Ezek. 22:20). Long before coinage, silver was known as a standard of wealth (Gen. 13:2; 24:35; Exod. 25:3; Num. 22:18) and was weighed out for payment of an obligation in measures such as the shekel, talent, and mina (Gen. 20:16; Exod. 21:32; Lev. 27:16; Josh. 24:32). Silver was used for special articles of value or prestige, such as a royal crown of silver and gold (Zech. 6:11), jewelry given to Rebekah (Gen. 24:53), booty received from Egyptian women (Exod. 3:22), and silver-studded ornaments for Solomon's bride (Song of Sol. 1:11). By contrast, silver was often a material for idols as early as the exodus and Judges and as decried in the prophets (Exod. 20:23; Judg. 17:4; Isa. 2:20; Jer. 10:4; Dan. 2:32, 33; Hos. 13:2).

The NT also mentions silver idols (Acts 17:29; Rev. 9:20). In the book of Acts, shrines to Artemis of Ephesus were made by Demetrius the silversmith, who feared Paul's preaching in the city would destroy his business (19:23–27). The majority of references to silver in the NT, however, are to silver money. Jesus tells his disciples not to take any silver (or copper or gold) in their belts when they go out as missionaries (Matt. 10:9). In the book of Acts, some magic books burned by Christians at Ephesus are said to have been valued at fifty thousand pieces of silver (19:19). In what is perhaps the Bible's best-known reference to silver, Judas receives thirty pieces of silver for his betrayal of Jesus (Matt. 26:15; 27:3, 5, 6, 9). Most scholars think that this refers to thirty shekels. A shekel was a silver Judean coin minted according to a standard unit of weight. Each coin contained one shekel (approximately 14.5 grams) of silver. Such a coin was worth about four drachmae (or four denarii) and one drachma (or one denarius) was the typical day's wage paid to an average worker. Thirty pieces (approximately equal to 120 drachmae or denarii) was considered the compensation to be paid to the owner of a slave if someone accidentally killed that slave (Exod. 21:32).

Figuratively, silver and the refining process are used to show the testing of people's hearts (Ps. 66:10; Isa. 48:10), great abundance (Zech. 9:3; Isa. 60:17; Job 3:15; 22:25; 27:16), and, either, positively, the brightness of a dove's wings (Ps. 68:13) and the purity of God's word (12:6) or, negatively, the corrosive deterioration of God's people (Jer. 6:30; Isa. 1:22).

The value of silver is often belittled in the NT by way of comparison with what is spiritual. In Acts, Peter tells a man who is lame that he has no silver (or gold), but is able to offer him something much more valuable: healing in the name of Jesus (3:6). The readers of 1 Peter are reminded that they were not ransomed from their futile ways with perishable things like silver or gold, but with the precious blood of Christ (1:18). Wealth measured in silver corrodes and corrupts (James 5:3) and brings only weeping instead of joy (Rev. 18:22). But there is also recognition of the value of silver. Paul refers to different sorts of foundations upon which people might build: gold, silver, precious stones, wood, hay, straw (1 Cor. 3:12)—silver appears to represent the second best of the possibilities. Likewise, 1 Tim. 2:20–21 compares believers who have cleansed themselves from various things to utensils of gold and silver, set aside by God for special use (unlike less-cleansed believers, who are compared to utensils of wood and clay, fit for ordinary use).   R.A.C.

Simeon (sim'ee-uhn; Heb., "to hear").

1 The second son of Jacob and Leah (Gen. 29:33). Simeon and his brother Levi massacred the men of Shechem to avenge the rape of their sister, Dinah (Gen. 34, recalled in Jth. 9:1–4). Simeon was later held hostage in Egypt when Joseph sent the other brothers back to Canaan for Benjamin (Gen. 42:24). Subsequently Simeon and his six sons migrated to Egypt with the entire family of Jacob (Gen. 46:10; Num. 26:12–14; 1 Chron. 4:24). In Jacob's blessing, Simeon was rebuked because of his actions at Shechem and was told his descendants would be divided and scattered (Gen. 49:5–7). *See also* Dinah; Joseph.

2 One of the twelve tribes of Israel, composed of those who traced their descent to **1.** The tribe of Simeon was given an allotment within the tribal territory of Judah in the southernmost region of Canaan. Their cities included Beer-sheba, in the center of the Negev; Ziklag (possibly modern Tell Sheriah) and Sharuhen (perhaps modern Tell el Far'ah) in the western Negev; and Hormah (perhaps modern Tell Malhata) in the eastern Negev (Josh. 19:1–9). Simeon joined forces with the tribe of Judah during the early phase of the Israelite conquest of Canaan (Judg. 1:3–17). During the divided monarchy (tenth–eighth centuries BCE), Simeon was reckoned as one of the ten tribes belonging to the northern kingdom (cf. 1 Kings 11:30–32; 12:20–23; 2 Chron. 15:9), but nothing is said of the tribe during that period except for a note that in the days of Hezekiah (715–687/6 BCE) Simeon achieved a military victory over the Amalekites, the perennial enemy of the inhabitants of the Negev (1 Chron. 4:41–43). The tribe of Simeon is not mentioned again in the Hebrew Bible, but surfaces again in the book of Judith,

written during the Second Temple period. Judith herself is of the tribe of Simeon (6:15), and this becomes significant for her prayer in Jth. 9. She begins, "O Lord God of my ancestor Simeon" (9:2) and then rehearses the account of how God aided Simeon in avenging his sister's rape as a prelude to calling on God for assistance against the Assyrians. *See also* tribes.

3 The grandfather of Mattathias and great-grandfather of Judas Maccabeus and his brothers (1 Macc. 2:1).

4 The Hebrew name of Simon Maccabeus (1 Macc. 2:65). *See also* Simon.

5 An ancestor of Jesus according to Luke's genealogy (3:30).

6 An early, devout man of Jerusalem during the days of Herod who was "looking forward to the consolation of Israel" (Luke 2:25–35). He had been promised by the Holy Spirit that he would see the Messiah before he died. Simeon recognized the infant Jesus as the Messiah when Jesus's parents presented him at the temple. He held the infant in his arms and praised God with a hymn, saying, "My eyes have seen your salvation, which you have prepared in the presence of all peoples, a light for revelation to the Gentiles and for glory to your people Israel" (2:31–32). Then he blessed Jesus's parents, Joseph and Mary, told Mary, "This child is destined for the falling and the rising of many in Israel" (2:34), and added a prophecy regarding her personal suffering: "A sword will pierce your own soul too" (2:35). *See also* Nunc Dimittis.

7 The Hebrew name of Simon Peter (2 Pet. 1:1; possibly Acts 15:14, though this Simeon could be Simon **8** below). *See also* Peter.

8 A Christian at Antioch with prophetic and teaching gifts, who served the church there together with Barnabas and Paul prior to the latter's first missionary journey (Acts 13:1; possibly 15:14, though this Simeon could be **7** above). The note that he was called "Niger" (Lat., "black") indicates that he was probably an African.   D.A.D.

Simon (si'muhn).

1 Simon Maccabeus, the son of Mattathias Hashmon and ruler of Judea 142–134 BCE. Following in the tradition of his brothers Judas Maccabeus and Jonathan, he led the Jewish forces against the Seleucids and won independence for Judea, establishing the Hasmonean dynasty, which would endure until 63 BCE. Simon appears to have been a capable ruler, enlarging the territory and improving the fortunes of the Jews, but he was murdered by his son-in-law Ptolemy. He is eulogized in 1 Macc. 14:4–15. *See also* Maccabees.

2 Simon Peter, one of the twelve disciples of Jesus (Matt. 10:2; Mark 3:16; Luke 6:14). *See also* Peter.

3 Another of the twelve disciples of Jesus, distinguished from Simon Peter by two epithets: "Simon the Cananaean" (Matt. 10:4; Mark 3:18) and "Simon the Zealot" (Luke 6:15; Acts 1:13). The latter expression has provoked interest over the years because the Zealots are often

considered to have been a violent group of Jewish revolutionaries who used terrorist tactics to assassinate Romans and Roman collaborators. Most interpreters think it unlikely that a person associated with this group would have been among the twelve, and they assume that the epithet was simply meant to identify Simon as notably zealous or enthusiastic. By extension, it is sometimes said that the designation of one of Jesus's disciples as a Zealot should prompt consideration of whether the Roman depiction of Zealots as revolutionary terrorists should be taken at face value (since such a depiction is found only in biased, pro-Roman sources). *See also* twelve, the; Zealots.

4 Judas Iscariot's father (John 6:71; 13:2, 26).

5 One of Jesus's brothers (Matt. 13:55; Mark 6:3). The Synoptic Gospels report that Jesus had four brothers—James, Joses, Judas, and Simon—plus an unknown number of sisters, whose names are also unknown (Mark 6:4). The Gospels indicate that the brothers of Jesus did not "believe in him" during the time of his ministry (John 7:5). At one point, they attempt to seize him and take him home for a forced retirement from doing and saying things that are leading people to think he is "beside himself" (Mark 3:21, 31–35). Still, the book of Acts indicates that the brothers of Jesus (all of them?) were part of the early church in Jerusalem (1:14), and Paul also refers to the "brothers of the Lord" (all of them?) as Christian missionaries, noting specifically that they were married and often accompanied by their wives (1 Cor. 9:5). Of the four named brothers of Jesus, however, nothing specific is ever said about Joses or Simon; it is possible that the post-Easter references to brothers of Jesus are to James (who was a leader of the Jerusalem church) and Judas/Jude (to whom a NT letter is ascribed) only, rather than to a larger group that would have included Simon and/or Joses. *See also* James; Jude.

6 "Simon the leper," at whose house in Bethany Jesus was anointed with expensive ointment (Matt. 26:6–13; Mark 14:3–9). John's Gospel seems to tell this same story, but locates the event in the home of Lazarus (also in Bethany) without mentioning Simon; John then identifies the woman doing the anointing as Mary, the sister of Martha and Lazarus (12:1–8). Some scholars identify "Simon the leper" with 7. *See also* anoint; Mary.

7 Simon the Pharisee, at whose house (apparently in Galilee) Jesus was anointed with ointment by a sinful woman who wept at his feet (Luke 7:36–50). Simon takes this as a sign that Jesus cannot be a prophet, because a prophet would realize "what kind of woman" was touching him (7:39). Jesus tells Simon a parable that suggests a causal connection between receiving forgiveness and demonstrating love; he then upbraids Simon for failures to show even moderate devotion to Jesus, maintaining that the sinful woman loves him more because she has received more forgiveness. Many interpreters have wondered whether this Simon should not be identified with 6. In the biblical narratives as we have them, they are two different persons, but the question is posed as to whether a single, original story might have given rise to different accounts of Jesus being anointed by women in the homes of people named Simon. *See also* anoint; prostitute.

8 Simon of Cyrene, a man from North Africa who was compelled to carry Jesus's cross (Matt. 27:32; Mark 15:21; Luke 23:26). The Gospels do not indicate that this man ever became a follower of Jesus or a part of the Christian movement. He is not mentioned again in the Bible, unless he is to be associated in some way with "Simeon who was called Niger," mentioned among prophets in Antioch (Acts 13:1). The only connections supporting this are: (1) the name Simeon is a variant form of Simon; (2) the nickname "Niger" (Lat., "black") may indicate that he was African; and (3) the fact that Mark's Gospel tells readers that Simon of Cyrene was the "father of Alexander and Rufus" (15:21) may imply that his readers knew Alexander and Rufus, indicating that Simon (or at least his sons) did retain associations with the Christian community.

9 Simon the tanner, a leatherworker in Joppa with whom Peter remained "for many days"; during this stay Peter had his vision of the clean and unclean animals (Acts 9:43; 10:5–6, 32) and subsequently went to visit the centurion Cornelius, whom he baptized as one of the first Gentile converts to the faith. *See also* tanning.

10 Simon Magus, a magician from Samaria who became a Christian believer and was baptized as a result of the preaching of Philip (Acts 8:9–24). Subsequently, however, he was excoriated by Peter for attempting to purchase the power of bestowing the Holy Spirit. Peter tells him that his heart is not right and that he is "in the gall of bitterness and the chains of wickedness" (8:23). He responds by pleading with Peter to pray for him, so that he might be spared the consequences Peter had implied could come upon him for his action. This story provides the derivation for the English word "simony," which refers to the use of money to purchase power or influence. *See also* magi.   P.L.S.

sin, that which is in opposition to God's benevolent purposes for creation. The Bible speaks of sin in broad and varied terms. Modern theologians might classify sins as ritual sins, moral sins, spiritual sins, political or social sins, etc.—but no such categories or labels are found within the Bible itself. What is clear is that one may sin by what one says (Prov. 2:12) or thinks (Matt. 9:4) or does (Eccles. 8:12). One may also sin by failing to do what one should have done (e.g., Matt. 25:31–46; Luke 16:19–31). There is even unconscious or inadvertent sin (Lev. 5). Thus, many biblical passages point to the universality and inevitability of sin in human life. The prophets located the source of sin in the "heart," i.e., in the very depth of one's being, the seat of volition and action (e.g., Jer. 5:23; 17:9–10; cf. Ezek. 36:26; Isa. 29:13). In the NT, the author of 1 John says, "If we say we have no sin, we deceive ourselves, and the truth is not in us" (1:8).

Terminology: The Hebrew Bible uses a number of terms associated with the concept of sin, but four are especially prominent. *Khata'* has a basic sense of missing the mark or failing to achieve one's intention; e.g., Prov. 19:2 says that "one who moves too hurriedly misses [*khata'*] the way." But the term takes on an ethical component when divine expectations for humanity are involved; a person who utters a rash oath and later realizes it must "confess the sin [*khata'*]" that he or she has committed (Lev. 5:5).

'Awon carries the connotation of something that incurs guilt, such as a crime (cf. Deut. 19:15, "a single witness shall not suffice to convict a person of any crime [*'awon*]." It is often used in the Bible with reference to disobedience to God's commandments. The NRSV often translates this word "iniquity," as in Exod. 20:5, which indicates that God punishes children for the "iniquities" (*'awon*) of their parents. The word is used in parallel with *khata'* in Isaiah's Servant Song: the servant will "make many righteous" and "bear their iniquities [*'awon*]" (53:11); he will be "numbered with the transgressors," though he "bore the sin [*khata'*] of many" (53:12). This demonstrates that the terms, despite some difference in connotation, can be used as virtual synonyms.

Pesha' conveys the sense of deliberate and rebellious action. The NRSV often translates the word "transgression," as when the psalmist prays, "O God, according to your steadfast love . . . blot out my transgressions" (Ps. 51:1). This word is frequently used in parallel with the other two (e.g. Gen. 31:36; Pss. 32:5; 51:3; Amos 1:3; Mic. 6:7). Ezek. 21:24 manages to use all three terms: "You have brought your guilt [*'awon*] to remembrance . . . your transgressions [*pesha'*] are uncovered . . . your sins [*khata'*] appear."

To'ebot is usually translated "abomination" in the NRSV (e.g., 1 Kings 14:24). It can refer to something impure or unclean (Lev. 7:18; 11:13) or prohibited sexual practices (18:22–30), but it is also frequently used as a generic term for practices of other nations that Israel is to reject (Ezra 9:1, 11, 14).

The primary Greek word for sin, employed throughout the NT and in the LXX is *hamartia*, which has a wide range of meaning (failing, disobedience, rebellion) and can be used to translate any of the first three Hebrew terms cited. Synonyms employed with less frequency include *anomia* ("lawlessness"), *adikia* ("unrighteousness"), and *asebeia* ("ungodliness").

In the Hebrew Bible: The issue of sin in the Hebrew Bible is closely connected to obedience to God's will, especially as expressed through the covenant. Sin is not mentioned in the narrative of Adam and Eve, but comes up for the first time in Gen. 4:7, where God warns Cain, "Sin is lurking at the door; its desire is for you, but you must master it." The failure of humans to master sin, however, is attested in this and other stories, and so God chooses one people from all those of the earth and gives them two things that will keep sin under control. The first is the Torah, which defines God's will in terms that allow sin to be recognized and avoided. The giving of this Torah implies a need for comprehensive ethical instruction and also establishes a basis from which prophets can call for repentance. The second way that God seeks to control sin in the Hebrew Bible is by providing for sins to be forgiven and their effects limited or removed. Although this is expressed most clearly through the priestly system of rituals and sacrifices, the availability of forgiveness of sins in the Hebrew Bible is not to be merely equated with such rites. Many writers in the Hebrew Bible presuppose that God will forgive their sins if they repent and ask for forgiveness quite apart from the offering of sacrifices.

In the NT: The writings of the NT are often said to deal with sin in two distinct ways. First, "sins" are seen as actions, thoughts, or attitudes that violate the will of God. This is essentially the same meaning found in the Hebrew Bible, and it is articulated throughout the teaching of Jesus (e.g., when he says, "If your right eye causes you to sin, tear it out and throw it away," Matt. 5:29). The second sense of sin in the NT, however, is found mainly in the writings of Paul, where sin is conceived as an ever present reality or power that has corrupted God's created order and enslaved the human race. Thus, Paul insists that all people, both Jews and Greeks, are "under the power of sin" (Rom. 3:9; cf. 1:18–3:20; 5:12–21). Sin in both of these aspects is said to have been dealt with through God's action in Christ. For some NT writers, the death of Jesus provided a once-for-all atonement for sins, in a manner analogous to the forgiveness of sins available to Israel through its sacrificial system (Heb. 9:11–12, 24–26; cf. John 1:29; Rom. 3:24–25). But for Paul, the additional and perhaps more important point is that the resurrection of Christ from the dead broke the power of sin, so that people no longer need to be slaves to sin but can be participants in a new creation (Rom. 6:17–18; 2 Cor. 5:17). *See also* atonement; demon; devil; evil; fall, the; forgiveness; grace; guilt; holiness; justification; pardon; reconciliation; redemption; salvation; sanctification; Satan.   J.M.E./M.A.P.

Sin. *See* Pelusium.

Sin, Wilderness of, a desert area "between Elim and Sinai" (Exod. 16:1), where the Israelites "complained against Moses and Aaron" (16:2–3), and where manna was first given to satisfy their hunger (16:13–36). The Israelites crossed the Wilderness of Sin early in the exodus and continued from there to Rephidim via Dophkah and Alush (17:1; Num. 33:11–12). Unfortunately, none of those three places can be clearly identified, which makes location of the Wilderness of Sin difficult as well. The region should not be confused with the Wilderness of Zin, a distinct area. *See also* Elim; Rephidim; Sinai; Zin, Wilderness of.   D.B.

Sinai (*si'ni*; derivation uncertain, perhaps related to the Mesopotamian moon god Sin).

1 The Sinai Peninsula, a large, wedge-shaped block of territory that forms a land bridge between Africa and Asia. Sinai is bounded on the west by the Suez Canal and Gulf of Suez, while the Negev and Gulf of Aqabah form the peninsula's eastern border. Sinai's northern and southern limits are clearly defined by the Mediterranean Sea and the Red Sea, respectively. Its total area is about 24,000 square miles. The southern apex of this inverted triangle is about 240 miles from the Mediterranean shore; the northern base extends from Rapha to the Suez Canal, a distance of about 125 miles.

Since it is actually part of the Sahara-Arabian desert, Sinai's climate is arid. The peninsula's extensive wadi system drains an annual rainfall that seldom exceeds 2.5 inches, except along the Mediterranean coast. More diversity is found in the geology and topography of Sinai's three major regions. The northern region consists of a low, sandy plateau and includes large tracts of sand dunes and some oases; this coastal zone has served as a thoroughfare for many ancient and modern armies. Sinai's central region is a high, limestone plateau that has little water and sparse vegetation. The peninsula's southern region is covered by rugged, granite mountains, some of whose peaks exceed 8,000 feet in elevation and are snow-capped in winter.

Although the Sinai Peninsula may appear to be inhospitable to human occupation, archaeological research demonstrates that this wilderness has been occupied by sedentary and/or nomadic peoples, albeit intermittently and sparsely, for about thirty thousand years.

The Sinai Peninsula appears as an inverted triangle in this photo taken from an orbiting satellite.

Naturally, the prehistoric inhabitants of Sinai had contacts with neighboring regions, but the earliest significant evidence of such connections dates to ca. 2650 BCE. At this early date, the Egyptians began mining Sinai's turquoise, an enterprise that led to later Egyptian activities in the peninsula. Most famous are the turquoise and copper mines at modern Serabit el-Khadem, a site in west-central Sinai that was worked throughout most of the second millennium BCE. The proto-Sinaitic inscriptions from Serabit el-Khadem date to ca. 1500 BCE and represent the earliest stages in the development of a Semitic alphabet.

This script also serves as an example of the kinds of cultural exchanges that occurred in the Sinaitic corridor. Other contacts came through commercial and military activities in this region and, although the Bible notes that Sinai's environment was hostile (Deut. 1:19; 8:15), it also observes that Sinai was not impassable. When Abraham, Jacob, and the family of Jacob made their way between Canaan and Egypt, the trade routes across the peninsula were already well established. Many centuries later, Saul and David fought the Amalekites in northwestern Sinai (1 Sam. 15:7; 27:8), and Elijah made a pilgrimage to this region's famous mountain (1 Kings 19:8). Still later, Joseph, Mary, and Jesus entered the Sinai as they fled from Herod (Matt. 2:13).

Throughout its history, Sinai was crossed or occupied by many other peoples—Assyrians, Babylonians, Persians, Greeks, Nabateans, and Romans—but the most famous sojourn in this wilderness was made by the Hebrews after the exodus. Indeed, Sinai was the setting for some of the most important events in Israelite history. The Bible does not, however, refer to the entire peninsula when it uses the word "Sinai." Instead, the Bible mentions five smaller, distinct tracts of wilderness in this large territory (i.e., Shur, Sin, Sinai, Paran, and Zin).

2 The Wilderness of Sinai, the biblical name for the small, distinct wilderness region in which Mount Sinai was located. Its exact location cannot be ascertained, since its limits are defined in relation to other place-names that also defy accurate pinpointing. In general, the Bible locates this tract of wasteland in between the wildernesses of Sin and Paran and in the vicinity of Elim, Rephidim, and Kibroth-hattaavah (Exod. 16:1; 19:1–2; Num. 10:12; 33:15–16). The traditional location of the Wilderness of Sinai is in the south-central part of the peninsula. It was in this wilderness that the Israelites were encamped when they received the law (e.g., Exod. 19:1–2; Lev. 7:38), were numbered (Num. 1:19; 3:14; 26:64), and celebrated the Passover (9:5). It was also in the wilderness of Mount Sinai that Moses encountered the burning bush (Exod. 3:1–2; Acts 7:30, 38).

3 Mount Sinai, the mountain on which the law was delivered to Moses (Exod. 31:18; 34:29, 32; Lev. 26:46; 27:34; Neh. 9:13). The biblical writers refer to Mount Sinai by various names (e.g., "the mountain," "the mountain of God," "Mount Horeb," "the mountain of Horeb," and "the mountain of God in Horeb"). This mountain played a significant role in the spiritual development of Moses (Exod. 3:1–12), and its sacred character was magnified when Sinai became the locus of divine revelation par excellence (19:18, 20, 23; 24:16; Deut. 33:2; Judg. 5:5; Ps. 68:8). Indeed, the Lord's presence on this peak came to symbolize divine protection (Judg. 5:4–5; Ps. 68:8). In his allegory of the two covenants, Paul uses Sinai to symbolize the old system (Gal. 4:24–25; see Heb. 12:19–21).

Although Exodus and Numbers provide many details concerning the itinerary followed by the Israelites in their trek from Egypt to the plains of Moab, few of these places can be identified with any certainty. In fact, the general direction of the wanderings in Sinai is still debated, although scholars usually choose between three possible routes (i.e., a northern, central, or southern route). Consequently, the location of Mount Sinai is also disputed. As many as a dozen mountains have been identified as this sacred spot, but none of them has been accepted by all scholars. *See also* exodus, the; Horeb, Mount; mount, mountain; Sin, Wilderness of.

Bibliography

Arden, Harvey. "Eternal Sinai." *National Geographic* (April 1982): 90–102.

Beit-Arieh, Itzhaq. "Fifteen Years in Sinai." *Biblical Archaeology Review* (July/August 1984): 26–54.

Bernstein, Burton. *Sinai: The Great and Terrible Wilderness.* Viking, 1979.   G.L.M.

sinew, in biblical usage, a variety of anatomical elements including tendons, ligaments, and possibly muscle and other tissues. It is used figuratively in Isa. 48:4 for stubbornness. In Job 10:11 and Ezek. 37:6, 8 the actual connective human tissues seem to be involved. In Job 40:17 "the sinews of his thighs" in the description of an animal may refer to the penis.

Sinites (sin´its), a Canaanite tribe included in the Table of Nations (Gen. 10:17; 1 Chron. 1:15). They have often been associated with Lebanon or Phoenicia, but nothing about such a location is certain.

sin offering. *See* sacrifice.

Sirach (si´ruhk), or the Wisdom of Jesus the Son of Sirach, or Ecclesiasticus, a book of instruction and proverbs written in Hebrew ca. 180 BCE in Jerusalem by an instructor of wealthy youths. It was translated into Greek in Alexandria by the author's grandson sometime after 132 BCE. The work provides extensive evidence for the character of Jewish faith and society just prior to the Maccabean revolt (167–164 BCE), though the perspective is decidedly that of the upper class. We gain a picture of a social order highly polarized between rich and poor, powerful and weak, male and female,

pious and nonobservant, and Jew and Gentile as well as a look into the development of the way of Torah—life centered around the Mosaic law—which would become the central characteristic of Judaism after the destruction of the temple.

Much of the Hebrew of Sirach has survived in manuscripts found in the Genizah (an attic where badly worn Torah scrolls were "treasured" away when retired from service) of the Ezra Synagogue in Cairo as well as in a few fragments from the Dead Sea Scrolls. Although not considered canonical, the book remained in use within Judaism as late as the eleventh century CE. The complete version has survived in Greek translation as a part of the LXX. In Western Christianity it came to be known as Ecclesiasticus ("the church's Book"), probably because it was considered the most important of the writings not found in the Hebrew Bible to be preserved in the Vulgate. Protestant Christians regard Sirach/Ecclesiasticus as part of the Apocrypha, while Roman Catholic and Greek Orthodox Christians classify the book as deuterocanonical.

Sirach defies outline in any detail, since much of it consists of short passages on a variety of topics from how to give and attend a party to exhortations regarding care for the poor. The predominant types of language are proverb and instruction, the latter of which is characterized by imperatives followed by reasons for fulfilling the command. The outline below gives some idea of the book's contents.

OUTLINE OF CONTENTS

Sirach

In some ways, Sirach reads like an ancient textbook on business ethics, although the author clearly prefers the public sector to the private and assumes that all merchants are corrupt (26:29). His goal is to instruct the young in the art of living well, in the best sense of the phrase. His students will seek careers in public service as scribes, the class from which public administrators, civil servants, and diplomats were drawn (39:1–11). Frugality, hard work, compassion for the poor, honesty, and independence are the true measure of character rather than riches, though wealth is preferable to poverty. The goal of instruction is to learn self-control and correct management techniques in both private and public life in order to enjoy the good life, under the guidance of the law of God. Sirach's comments regarding women are often noted: the wickedness of a wife is the highest of all evil (25:13); sin and death had their origin from a woman (25:24); a good wife keeps silent (26:14); and, a father must remain eternally vigilant to preserve his daughter's purity (26:10–12).

Although Sirach stands within the general wisdom tradition of Proverbs, an important difference between those books can be noted. Whereas Proverbs offers a clear separation between the responsibility of the priest for Torah and the sage for counsel (Jer. 18:18), those two functions have come together in Sirach. Wisdom is now to be found in the temple in Jerusalem (24:10), and it is identified with the "book of the covenant of the Most High God, the law which Moses commanded us" (24:23). Sirach, like Bar. 3:9–4:4, declares that wisdom has been revealed to Israel by God in the moral instruction of the law, rather than being reserved in the heavens where only the specially initiated receive instruction (cf. Wis. 8:15–22; 9:4, 9–10; *1 Enoch* 42). According to Sirach, the sage must be satisfied with the limitations of the human intellect (3:21–24). The marriage of Torah and counsel is also reflected in the models for the good life offered in the praise of the famous in Sir. 44–50. The highest praise is reserved for Moses, Aaron, and Phinehas the son of Eleazar, priestly heroes important for their work as public administrators and leaders of worship, each of whom, in the son of Sirach's eyes, was the recipient of a covenant with God (Sir. 45). Next in rank comes David. He is pictured as an effective ruler concerned for the administration of public worship, who was given a covenant of kingship (45:25; 47:2–11). In his own time, the son of Sirach offers the model of Simon the Just, the high priest who was the theocratic ruler of his people ca. 219–196 BCE and as such combined the offices of priest and king (thus also wedding Torah and counsel). Simon is pictured both as an effective public administrator and leader of worship in a passage important for its information about temple worship in the Second Temple period (50:1–21). Sirach's praise of the famous also makes it clear that by 200 BCE both the Torah and the Prophets were recognized as fixed divisions of scripture. *See also* Apocrypha/deuterocanonical literature; education; proverb; temple, the; Torah; wisdom literature.

Bibliography

Fox, Michael V. *Qoheleth and His Contradictions.* Almond, 1994.   D.W.S.

Sirah (si'rah), **cistern of,** the location from which the rebellious Absalom was called by Joab, who subsequently killed him (2 Sam. 3:26–27). It is probably near Hebron, but its location is not precisely known. *See also* Absalom; Joab.

Sirion (sihr'ee-uhn), the name used for Mount Hermon by the people of Sidon (Deut. 3:9; 4:48). Both Ps. 29:6 and Jer. 18:14 employ the word in a way that is parallel with Lebanon, which is consistent with reading it as a reference to Mount Hermon.

Sisera (sis'uh-ruh).

1 The commander of Canaanite forces defeated by Deborah and Barak. The tale of this epic battle and of Sisera's humiliating defeat at the hand of a woman is told in prose in Judg. 4 and then in poetry in Judg. 5. The war may be dated ca. 1125–1100 BCE, when Megiddo was abandoned and Taanach was violently destroyed.

Sisera is said to have commanded nine hundred chariots, opposing Israel for control of Esdraelon. His headquarters at Harosheth "of the nations" lay somewhere in the Sharon Plain. In Judg. 5:19, Sisera is said to have headed a coalition force of the "kings of Canaan," but in Judg. 4 his specific overlord is identified as "Jabin king of Canaan," who ruled at Hazor (4:2; 23–24; 1 Sam. 12:9; Ps. 83:9). With Israelite strength in the hill country (Judg. 4:5) and Galilee, Barak summoned ten units from Zebulun and Naphtali to muster at Mount Tabor and engaged Sisera in battle at Taanach, by the waters of Megiddo. A cloudburst and an ensuing flash flood gave the advantage to Israel. Sisera's forces were destroyed in retreat, while Sisera himself fled on foot to the tent of the Kenite woman Jael. Feigning hospitality, she received him into her tent and then killed him by driving a tent peg through his head, presumably while he slept (4:17–22). His demise proves an ironic fulfillment of the prediction in Judg. 4:9. At the outset of the story, Deborah had determined to accompany Barak into battle, telling him that the glory of the victory would not come to him, because God was going to deliver Sisera "into the hands of a woman." This prediction was fulfilled, but the woman who proved to be Sisera's downfall was not the warrior Deborah, but Jael.

The humiliation of Sisera's defeat is further emphasized in a brief epilogue concerning his mother. Wondering why he is so long in returning, she and her ladies-in-waiting reason that it must be because there is so much spoil to be divided after what was surely a glorious victory over the Israelites: "A girl or two for every man; spoil of dyed stuffs for Sisera, spoil of dyed stuffs embroidered, two pieces of dyed work embroidered for my neck as spoil?" (Judg. 5:28–30). The narrative ends with this ironic fantasy and an editorial note that after the defeat of Sisera, the land had rest for forty years (5:31). *See also* Barak; Deborah; Jael.

2 The head of an ancestral family of temple servants who returned to Judea from the exile (Ezra 2:53; Neh. 7:55; 1 Esd. 5:32). Interpreters have thought it odd that anyone in Israel would name their son after the defeated Canaanite leader who had been an archenemy of the people. Some have speculated that the "descendants of Sisera" who were temple servants (i.e., slaves) were not Israelites.   R.B.

Sismai (sisʹmi), the son of Eleasah and the father of Shallum (1 Chron. 2:40); he was a descendant of Jerahmeel from the tribe of Judah.

sister, in its literal sense, a female regarded as a sibling or family member. The Bible seldom makes any distinction between a half sister and a full sister, nor is there any interest in whether the relationship is defined by blood or through adoption. Lev. 18:9 does note that a sister might be the daughter of one's father or the daughter of one's mother, but the point is that sexual relations with one's sister are prohibited in either instance (cf. 20:17; Deut. 26:22). Several sisters are mentioned by name, including Miriam, the sister of Aaron and Moses (Num. 26:59; cf. Exod 2:4). Jesus is said to have had sisters, but (unlike his brothers) they are not named (Mark 6:3). Mary and Martha are sisters of each other and of Lazarus (Luke 10:38–42; John 11:1–45; 12:1–8).

Three stories in Genesis relate accounts in which one of Israel's ancestors tells people his wife is really his sister, because he fears someone might kill him in order to obtain her. Abraham does this twice (12:1–20; 20:1–18), and Isaac once (26:1–11). A classic case of sibling rivalry between sisters informs the story of Jacob's marriage to Leah and Rachel, two sisters who compete with each other to bear him children and receive his favor (29:15–30:24). The responsibility of men to protect or (in this case) avenge their sister is dramatically illustrated in the story of Levi and Simeon's massacre of the town of Shechem after a prince from that town raped their sister Dinah and then wanted to marry her (Gen. 34); even their father, Jacob, thought they went too far in doing this, but they responded, "Should our sister be treated like a whore?" (34:31). Later, the rebellion of Absalom against his father, David, began when Absalom killed his brother Amnon, who raped their sister Tamar (2 Sam. 13); the fact that Tamar was Absalom's full sister while Amnon was only a half brother to both Absalom and Tamar may or may not have been a factor in this drama of extreme sibling conflict.

The term "sister" is also used in metaphorical ways. In Song of Sol. 4:9–11 it is used as a term of endearment for one's beloved. Prov. 7:4 counsels, "Say to wisdom, 'You are my sister,' and call insight your intimate friend." Israel and Judah could also be described as sister kingdoms; Jeremiah views Israel as a faithless adulteress and Judah as her "false sister" (3:7–10). Ezekiel claims that Samaria is Jerusalem's elder sister and Sodom is her younger sister (16:44–52); he also develops an extended allegory in chap. 23 of two sisters named Oholah (Samaria) and Oholibah (Jerusalem).

It is only in the NT that the term "sister" comes to be used for a person to whom one feels related through a common bond of faith. Jesus says that whoever does the will of God is his "brother, sister, and mother" (Matt. 12:50). Paul refers to his co-worker Phoebe as his sister (Rom. 16:1); young women in the churches of the Pastoral Letters are also called "sisters" (e.g., 1 Tim. 5:2). *See also* brother; family.   M.A.P.

sit. *See* gestures, postures, and facial expressions.

Sitnah (sitʹnuh; Heb., "hostility"), a well dug by Isaac's servants in the valley of Gerar. The water rights were contested by the servants of Gerar's king Abimelech (Gen. 26:19–21). This well could be near Rehoboth in south-central Judah, but it has not yet been precisely located.

Sivan (siʹvan), the third month of the Hebrew calendar, mid-May to mid-June (Esther 8:9; Bar. 1:8). *See also* calendar.

six, a number that appears occasionally in the Bible without apparent symbolic significance. It appears to have sometimes assumed a negative quality, symbolizing what is evil or wrong. There is no data to indicate how or when this would have come about, but scholars speculate that since seven often symbolized completeness (perhaps due to the seven days of the week) or perfection, six came to symbolize incompleteness or imperfection. Revelation appears to use the number 666 to indicate superlative evil (triple bad), and the author conveys the secret information that this is the number of a name (13:18), probably meaning it is the sum of the letters of a name when those letters are treated as numerals (a practice known as gematria). Interpreters have since discovered that the letters of "Caesar Nero" when written in Hebrew add up to 666. *See also* gematria; numbers.

skins. Animal skins, called simply "skins" in the Bible, were used for three primary purposes: garments, shelter, and drinking vessels. The first of these is referred to at the conclusion of the Adam and Eve story, when God makes "garments of skins for the man and for his wife" and clothes them (Gen. 3:21). Later, Rebekah puts the skins of two kids on Jacob's hands and neck, so that he can fool his aging father, Isaac, into thinking he is Esau, a hairy man (27:16). The best example of skins being used for shelter are the tanned skins of rams used for the wilderness tabernacle or tent of meeting (Exod. 25:5; 26:16; 35:7, 23; 36:19, 34).

For the manufacture of drinking vessels, the dried skins of goats were sewed up with the hair on the outside. Skins filled with milk were hung from trees, then shaken until the contents thickened to the consistency of butter. A related process turned fermented milk into yogurt (Judg. 4:19; 5:25). Similar skins were also used to carry water (Josh. 9:4, 13; Judg. 4:19; 1 Sam. 16:20) or wine (Gen. 21:14–19; 1 Sam. 25:18; Neh. 5:18). In the NT, Jesus speaks parabolically about the inappropriateness of putting new wine into old skins (Matt. 9:17; Mark 2:22; Luke 5:37); skins that have become old and dried out cannot be used for new wine, which produces gas as it ferments and causes the skin to burst (but cf. Job 32:19, which seems to indicate that it is *new* wineskins that are likely to burst).   S.R.

sky, in biblical thought, a sheet or dome used by God to separate cosmic waters from the earth. The Hebrew term *raqia'* (NRSV: "dome," Gen. 1:6) suggests a thin sheet of beaten metal (Job 37:18; Jer. 10:9). Job 26:13 depicts God's breath as the force that calmed (NRSV: "made fair") the heavens. According to Genesis, God created the dome of the heavens on the second day of creation and called it "sky" (1:6–8); then luminaries were set in the dome on the fourth day of creation (1:14–19). Rain was thought to fall through windows or sluices in the surface of this dome (cf. 7:11). During the flood in the days of Noah, the upper waters above the dome joined with the waters of the primordial deep (Heb. *tehom*). In more pacific contexts, the sky (NRSV: "firmament"), or its pattern of luminaries, may be said to declare the praises of God (Ps. 19:1; cf. 150:1). In Ezekiel's chariot vision, a crystal dome supports the divine throne (1:22, 25,

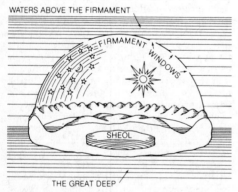

WATERS ABOVE THE FIRMAMENT

FIRMAMENT WINDOWS

SHEOL

THE GREAT DEEP

The Hebrew universe. The ancient Hebrews imagined the world as flat and round, covered by the great solid dome of the firmament, which was held up by mountain pillars (Job 26:11; 37:18). Above the firmament and under the earth was water, divided by God at creation (Gen. 1:6–7; cf. Pss. 24:2; 148:4). The upper waters were joined with the waters of the primordial deep during the flood; the rains were believed to fall through windows in the firmament (Gen. 7:11; 8:2). The sun, moon, and stars moved across or were fixed in the firmament (Gen. 1:14–19; Ps. 19:4, 6). Within the earth lay Sheol, the realm of the dead (Num. 16:30–33; Isa. 14:9, 15).

26), just as something resembling a pavement of lapis lazuli is said to lie at the feet of God's throne in Exod. 24:10. According to Dan. 12:3, those who are wise will shine like the brightness of the sky. *See also* creation.   J.W.R.

slave. *See* servant; slavery in the ancient Near East; slavery in the New Testament.

slavery in the ancient Near East. Aside from crown and temple slavery, slave labor played a minor role in the ancient Near East, since privately owned slaves functioned more as domestic servants than as an agricultural or industrial labor force. Crown and temple slaves were often captives of war (1 Kings 9:21; Num. 31:25–47; Josh. 9:23); private slaves were usually defaulting debtors and their families (Exod. 22:2; 2 Kings 4:1) or indigents who had resorted to voluntary self-sale (Lev. 25:39; Exod. 21:5–6; Deut. 15:16–17).

Ancient Near Eastern law collections tend to treat slaves as property (e.g., in rules assessing reparations to be made if one injures or kills the slave of another person). Most biblical legislation, by contrast, focuses upon matters concerning the relationship between masters and slaves, thus emphasizing the slaves' humanity. Although the Bible does acknowledge the master's ownership of the slave (Exod. 21:32; Lev. 25:46), it seeks to restrict the master's power over the slave. The master was punished for excessive use of force that caused death or permanent maiming (Exod. 21:20, 25–26). The slave was also regarded as part of the master's household (Lev. 22:11) and, so, was allowed or indeed required to rest on the sabbath (Exod. 20:10; Deut. 5:14) and to participate in religious observances (Gen. 17:13; Exod. 12:44; Lev. 22:11; Deut. 12:12, 18; 16:11, 14).

In contrast to ancient Near Eastern treaties providing for the mutual extradition of fugitive slaves, biblical law prohibited such extradition and granted slaves asylum (Deut. 23:16–17; but cf. 1 Kings 2:39–40). The servitude of a Hebrew debt slave was limited to six years (Exod. 21:2; Deut. 15:12; Jer. 34:14). Upon manumission, slaves were to receive gifts (Deut. 15:14) that would enable them to maintain their new freedom economically. The servitude of voluntarily self-enslaved Hebrews ended with the onset of the jubilee year (Lev. 25:13, 40). *See also* law; slavery in the New Testament.   B.L.E.

slavery in the New Testament. Among the many relationships of personal power and submission constituting the patriarchal society of Greco-Roman antiquity, the most extreme form was slavery, the legal ownership of one person by another as property.

The institution of slavery was deeply ingrained in Roman society, as is evident from the prominent reference to slaves as characters in the parables of Jesus (Matt. 18:23–34; 24:45–51; Luke 16:1–13; 17:7–10). Roman conquests often led to the enslavement of resident populations, and slave

Terra-cotta tablet inscribed with a contract for the purchase of a slave by Lugal-Ushumgal, prince of Lagash; Tello, ca. 2300 BCE.

hunters captured victims in provinces not yet taken over by Rome (cf. 1 Tim. 1:10; Rev. 18:13). Individuals could also be sentenced to slavery as punishment for various offenses, and entire families were sold into slavery when someone defaulted on a debt; self-sale was also an option for those who had no other means of providing for themselves or their families (1 Cor. 7:23; *1 Clem.* 55:2). Since children born to slaves were automatically slaves themselves, the passage of generations guaranteed the growth of a large slave population. By the time of the NT, about 30 percent of the population of the Roman Empire is estimated to have been slaves. The keeping of slaves, furthermore, was practiced by Jews as well as by Romans (e.g., Malchus, the high priest's slave, John 18:10). It was likewise practiced by Christians (e.g., Rhoda, the slave [NRSV: "maid"] in the home owned by John Mark's mother, Acts 12:13; Onesimus, the slave owned by Philemon, to whom Paul writes a letter).

To understand NT texts mentioning slavery, one must keep in mind major factors that distinguish first-century slavery from that later practiced in the New World. (1) Race differences played no role, and an enslaved person generally could not be distinguished by appearance. (2) Education was encouraged and enhanced a slave's value (some slaves were better educated than their owners). (3) Many slaves functioned in sensitive and highly responsible positions (see Phil. 4:22: "those of the emperor's household," some of whom were Christians). (4) Persons sometimes sold themselves into slavery to escape poverty, pay debts, climb socially,

and obtain special jobs. (5) Slaves could control property (including owning their own slaves). (6) Slaves' cultural and religious traditions were largely those of the free. (7) No laws prevented public assemblies of slaves. And (8) the majority of urban and domestic slaves could anticipate being set free (manumitted) by age thirty, becoming "freedmen" or "freedwomen" (1 Cor. 7:21–23; Acts 6:9).

Slaves functioned as managers and accountants as well as field hands, dominating large-scale production in both the countryside and the urban areas and providing their owners' primary income. This income, enabling the leisure class to develop high culture, supported in turn the maintenance of large numbers of domestic slaves, including cooks, body attendants, teachers, physicians, and musicians, who not only provided personal services and also displayed the owner's status and prestige.

The life and condition of slaves seems to have varied enormously. Social decorum encouraged humane treatment, and the extreme abuse or killing of slaves was prohibited by law. Still, the welfare of slaves generally depended on the disposition of their masters. In some cases—notably, for slaves who worked in mines or rowed the oars of galley ships—the conditions of life were appalling. Even in the best of circumstances, however, slaves had few legal rights, and they could be beaten at the discretion of their master (cf. Matt. 18:25, 34; 24:48–51; 25:30). They had virtually no autonomy—no ability to make decisions regarding their own lives or destinies—and in a world that valued honor above all else, they occupied the bottom tier of the social pyramid. A slave was a person with no honor, a person who lived in shame.

One other aspect of slavery must also be noted, namely, the extremely high correlation of female slavery and prostitution. In the NT era, it was relatively common for women to be sold into slavery by fathers desperate for cash. Most, if not all, of the prostitutes mentioned in the NT were probably slaves, which helps to explain why there is no mention of ex-prostitutes or former prostitutes in the NT or in any other literature of this period.

Slavery had become such an accepted part of the social fabric that no teachers of morality thought to question its practice, including the Stoic philosopher Epictetus, who was educated while a slave. No plan to abolish slavery motivated the slave revolts that were confined to the period of rapid Roman expansion (140–70 BCE). Only the Essenes at Qumran (see Josephus *Antiquities* 18.18–22) repudiated slavery in principle. Although not rejecting slavery, the NT nowhere seeks to justify it, and Gal. 3:28 makes clear that the distinction between slave and free means nothing "in Christ." There is, furthermore, no evidence that Jesus or any of his immediate followers owned slaves, or that Paul, Barnabas, Timothy, Silas or any other prominent NT missionary did. Jesus's call for his followers to forgive debts (Matt. 6:12) would have undermined the basis for debt slavery.

Slaves gained a new "social life" as "brothers and sisters" in the Corinthian house-churches. Onesimus was probably a managerial slave owned by the house-church patron Philemon. Onesimus had done something that made him fear returning home to his master without first engaging Paul as his advocate. Paul encourages Philemon to treat Onesimus "no longer as a slave but more than a slave, a beloved brother" (Philem. 15–17).

NEW TESTAMENT REFERENCES TO SLAVES AND SLAVERY

Literal References

On two occasions, Jesus heals a slave (Matt. 8:5–13; Luke 22:50–51).

Paul casts a demon out of a slave (Acts 16:16–17).

Slaves have equal status before God (1 Cor. 12:13; Gal. 3:28; Col. 3:11; Rev. 6:15; 13:16; 19:18).

Instructions are given about how slaves should behave—and how their masters should treat them (Eph. 6:1–5; Col. 3:22–4:1; 1 Tim. 6:1–2; Titus 2:9–10; 1 Pet. 2:18–21).

Paul advises slaves about seeking their freedom (1 Cor. 7:20–24).

Slave traders are condemned (1 Tim. 1:10; Rev. 18:13).

Paul returns a runaway slave to his master with a letter (Philemon).

Metaphorical References

Jesus tells parables in which slaves are characters (Matt. 13:24–30; 18:23–35; 22:1–13; 24:45–51; 25:14–30; Mark 12:1–9; 13:34–36; Luke 12:37–48).

Jesus uses slavery as a metaphor for discipleship (Matt. 6:24; 10:24–25; Mark 10:42–44; Luke 17:7–10; cf. John 8:31–36).

Paul uses slavery as a metaphor for devotion to others (1 Cor. 9:19; 2 Cor. 4:5; Gal. 5:13; Phil. 2:7).

Slavery can be a metaphor for controlling influences over one's life (Rom. 6:16–20; 7:6, 14, 25; 8:15; 2 Cor. 11:20; Titus 2:3; 3:3; 2 Pet 2:19; cf. Matt. 6:24).

Slavery can be a more general symbol for a negative spiritual condition, to be contrasted with freedom in Christ (Gal. 4:1–7; 4:22–5:1; Heb. 2:15).

From Mark Allan Powell, *Introducing the New Testament* (courtesy, Baker Academic)

The "household codes" contained in several NT letters (Col. 3:22–4:1; Eph. 6:5–9; 1 Tim. 6:1–2; 1 Pet. 2:18–21) offer fairly standard advice for the duties of slaves, but sometimes also contain words to masters that might transform their attitude toward their slaves (e.g., Col. 4:1, "know that you also have a Master in heaven").

Paul continues the Bible's use of slave metaphors when describing himself and Timothy as "slaves of Christ Jesus" (Rom. 1:1; Phil. 1:1). He also draws a sharp contrast between "slavery" to sin and "slavery" to righteousness or to God (Rom. 6:12–23). *See also* freedman, freedwomen; freeman, freewoman; liberation; Onesimus; prostitute; slavery in the ancient Near East.

Bibliography

Bartchy, S. S. *First-Century Slavery and the Interpretation of 1 Corinthians 7:21.* Scholars, 1985.

Bradley, K. R. *Slavery and Society at Rome.* Cambridge University Press, 1994.

Callahan, Allen Dwight, Richard A. Horsley, and Abraham Smith, eds. *Slavery in Text and Interpretation.* Scholars, 2001.

Combes, I. A. H. *The Metaphor of Slavery in the Writings of the Early Church: From the New Testament to the Beginning of the Fifth Century.* Sheffield Academic, 1998.

Glancy, Jennifer A. *Slavery in Early Christianity.* Oxford University Press, 2002.

Harrill, J. Albert. *Slaves in the New Testament: Literary, Social, and Moral Dimensions.* Fortress, 2006.

———. *The Manumission of Slaves in Early Christianity.* Mohr, 1995.

Martin, D. B. *Slavery as Salvation: The Metaphor of Slavery in Pauline Christianity.* Yale University Press, 1990.

Westermann, William L. *The Slave System of Greek and Roman Antiquity.* American Philosophy Society, 1955.

Wiedemann, Thomas. *Greek and Roman Slavery.* Johns Hopkins University Press, 1981.

S.S.B./M.A.P.

sledge, an instrument for threshing grain. It was made of long, flat pieces of wood, turned up in the front, on which would be placed stones for weight. The underside was studded with sharp stones or pieces of metal (Job 41:30; Isa. 28:27; 41:15). *See also* threshing.

sling, a weapon used to hurl small projectiles at an enemy, human or animal. This simple device was made of a cloth pad (i.e., "the hollow of a sling," 1 Sam. 25:29) and two cords, one attached to each side of the pad. Ammunition consisted of smooth pebbles (17:40), hammer-worked stones, or, in the Greco-Roman period, lead pellets. To "load" the weapon, the warrior placed a projectile on the pad, which was held with one hand; a small pouch was created when the slinger pulled the cords taut with the other hand. While holding the ends of the cords, the sling was whirled in the air, thereby building up centrifugal force. At

Copper foundry workers; detail of an Egyptian wall painting from the tomb of Vizier Rekhmire, fifteenth century BCE.

the proper instant, one cord was released, and the missile was fired at its target.

The sling was long used by shepherds to protect their flocks from predatory animals, but this weapon was also used at an early date in warfare. The story of David's victory over the heavily armed Goliath illustrates the military value of slings (1 Sam. 17). The accuracy of the left-handed slingers from the tribe of Benjamin was famous (Judg. 20:16; 1 Chron. 12:2). From at least the tenth century BCE onward, many ancient Near Eastern armies had regular units of slingers (2 Kings 3:25; 2 Chron. 26:14). Biblical writers also refer to this weapon in symbolic ways (1 Sam. 25:29; Job 41:28; Prov. 26:8; Jer. 10:18; Zech. 9:15). *See also* weapons.   G.L.M.

smith, one who works metal. The first-named smith of the Bible is Tubal-cain in Gen. 4:22. He was the son of Lamech and Zillah and belonged to the eighth generation from Adam. Described as one "who made all kinds of bronze and iron tools," Tubal-cain is known traditionally as the father of metallurgy.

Descriptions of the smith's craft are found in Isa. 44:12 and Sir. 38:28. In Isaiah the term refers to an ironworker laboring over the coals of his forge, shaping the metal with hammers, powered by his strong arm. The passage in Sirach pictures the smith seated at an anvil intent on the pattern of the iron object and its decoration. Sirach also emphasizes the importance of smiths, for "no city can be inhabited without them" (38:32). He considers this to be ironic: "They are not sought out for the council of the people, nor do they attain eminence in the public assembly. They do not sit in the judge's seat, nor do they understand the decisions of the courts; they cannot expound discipline or judgment, and they are not found among the rulers. But they maintain the fabric of the world" (38:32–34).

The Bible knows of smiths for silver (Acts 19:24), gold (Isa. 40:19; 41:7; 46:6), iron (Isa. 44:12), and bronze (1 Kings 7:14). Many processes and techniques of the smith's craft are mentioned in the Bible including forging, casting, beating, overlaying, furnishing, whetting, cutting, and soldering. A significantly large proportion of the exiles (one-tenth of all captives) were smiths and artisans (2 Kings 24:14, 16; Jer. 24:1; 29:2).

The earliest archaeological finds related to the smith's craft come from Tell Mardikh (Ebla) in Syria dating to the Early Bronze Age (ca. 3200 BCE). Here, excavators found a ceremonial hammer of gold and silver and pictures in bas-relief attached to wooden frames with copper pegs. A few of the frames had been overlaid with gold. Texts from Ebla indicate a guild or caste of smiths, and one burial site contained evidences of the goldsmith's art.   R.A.C.

Smyrna (smuhr′nuh), an ancient city (modern Izmir, Turkey) on the west coast of Asia Minor. It is one of the seven cities mentioned in the book of Revelation (1:11). It lay at the end of a major east–west road, possessed an excellent harbor, and was surrounded by rich farmland. The city's leadership was consistently loyal to Rome. A temple dedicated to the worship of Rome (*dea roma;* Lat., "the goddess Rome") was built there in 195 BCE.

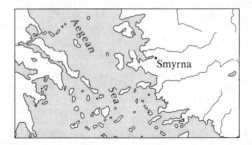

The message addressed to Smyrna in Revelation is remarkable in that it is the only one of the messages to seven churches that contains no words of rebuke or calls to repentance (2:8–11). Rather, the affliction and suffering of the Christians in Smyrna is recognized, and they are called to persist in their present faithfulness. The message predicts that the devil is going to have some members of the church thrown into prison in order that they might be tested; they will suffer affliction for ten days and then apparently be martyred—but if they are faithful until death, they will receive the crown of life (2:10). These words are strongly suggestive of Roman persecution, though it is not known when the book of Revelation was written and what government policies (if any) would have allowed for such violent measures to be enacted. In any case, the message to the church in Smyrna also indicates that the Christians have been slandered by "those who say that they are Jews and are not, but are a synagogue of Satan" (2:9). This seems to suggest conflict between the Christians and their Jewish neighbors regarding which group could lay claim to being the true followers of the God revealed in the Hebrew Bible. *See also* Revelation, book of. A.Y.C./M.A.P.

snail, a gastropod mollusk. Its sole biblical appearance, in Ps. 58:8, is symbolic of impermanence by reference to its slimy trail.

snake. *See* serpent.

snare. Almost all references to snares in the Bible are metaphorical. A literal snare would probably have consisted of a slip-knotted cord or wire pulled tight to wrap and hold the leg(s) of an animal or bird when it stepped into the loop, either by accident or to obtain bait. Biblical references do allude to the catching of birds (Pss. 91:3; 124:7; Prov. 7:23; Amos 3:5), but the word is used more often to refer to such things as foreign influences and idolatrous worship (Exod. 23:33; 34:12; Deut. 7:16; 12:30; Josh. 23:13; Judg. 2:3; Ps. 106:36); death (2 Sam. 22:6; Pss. 18:5; 116:3; Prov. 13:14; 14:27), the actions of wicked people (Ps. 119:110; cf. 9:16), the heart of a woman (Eccles. 7:26); or tricks of the devil (1 Tim. 3:7; 2 Tim. 2:26). The image often implies something that is deceptive (Ps. 64:5), something that takes people by surprise (Eccles. 9:12), or something in which one becomes entangled (Prov. 22:25). A pledge made to a neighbor can become a snare (6:1–2), as might a hasty vow (20:25) or foolish speech in general (18:7). Fearing human beings rather than trusting in God is also a snare (29:25).

Gideon made an ephod and put it in his town, Ophrah, but "all Israel prostituted themselves to it there, and it became a snare to Gideon and to his family" (Judg. 8:27). Saul hopes that his daughter Michal will become a snare for David, who wants to marry her because, Saul thinks, David will surely perish trying to pay her bride-price of a hundred Philistine foreskins (1 Sam. 18:21–25).

The medium at Endor thought that Saul was laying a snare for her when he asked her to summon the ghost of Samuel, a practice he himself had forbidden (28:9). M.A.P.

snow. Although it is relatively rare in biblical lands, the presence of snow in northern reaches and at higher elevations made it sufficiently well known for biblical writers to refer to it (Ps. 148:8; Prov. 25:13; Isa. 55:10; Jer. 18:14; 2 Sam. 23:20). Snow was recognized to be properly seasonal (Ps. 26:1), and its control lay in the hand of God, as with all of nature (Job 37:6; 38:22). Snow also served as a metaphorical standard for whiteness, whether as symptomatic of an illness like leprosy (Exod. 4:6; Num. 12:10; 2 Kings 5:27) or as an image of moral purity (Ps. 51:7; Isa. 1:18). It is probably in association with purity (cf. Lam. 4:7) that divine figures are often described as having garments (Dan. 7:9; Matt. 28:3) or facial features (Rev. 1:14) that are as "white as snow." R.S.B.

So, the king of Egypt to whom King Hoshea sent messengers just before the latter revolted against the Assyrians (2 Kings 17:4). The Assyrians under King Shalmaneser then attacked Samaria (725 BCE). Historical identification of So is uncertain, since no name similar to this appears anywhere in the Egyptian records. The name might refer to the Twenty-Second Dynasty king Osorkon IV, who ruled Egypt ca. 727–720 BCE, or it may be derived from an Egyptian term meaning "the Saite" and, thus, indicate an individual from the city of Sais in the Egyptian Delta. *See also* Pharaoh.

soap. In the Bible, soap is used for cleaning both the body (Jer. 2:22) and clothes (Mal. 3:2). The composition of such soap in biblical times probably included olive oil as the fat and some salt-bearing plants as the alkali source.

Soco, Socoh (soh'koh; Heb., "thorny").
1 A town in Judah between Adullam and Azekah (called Socoh in Josh. 15:35; 1 Sam. 17:1, and Soco in 2 Chron. 11:7; 28:18). It was located in an area of strategic importance in the buffer area between Israel and Philistia; the Philistine army was encamped between Azekah and Socoh when David confronted Goliath. The town was later fortified by King Rehoboam of Judah (11:7), but by the time of Ahaz it was at least temporarily back in Philistine hands (28:18). It was probably modern Khirbet 'Abbad, about two miles south of Azekah.
2 Another town in Judah, distinct from 1, probably modern Khirbet Shuweikeh, about ten miles southwest of Hebron (Josh. 15:48).
3 Socoh, a town in Solomon's third district (1 Kings 4:10). It was probably modern Tell er-Ras, located about ten miles northwest of Samaria.
4 Soco, a descendant of Judah and a son of Heber (1 Chron. 4:18). He may have been the founder of the Socoh mentioned in Josh. 15:48.
R.S.B.

Sodom (sod'uh.n), one of the five cities of the Plain (Gen. 13:12; 19:29). Abraham's nephew, Lot, chose Sodom for his residence, though the people there were wicked, "great sinners before the LORD" (13:8–13). Sometime later, the king of Sodom joined with the kings of the other four cities (Gomorrah, Admah, Bela [Zoar], and Zeboiim) to fight an invading coalition of four eastern kings (of Shinar, Ellasar, Elam, and Goim) in the Valley of Siddim. They were soundly defeated, and Lot was taken captive. Abraham pursued the invading kings and rescued Lot as well as all of the booty taken from Sodom. Upon his return, he was met by the king of Sodom at the Valley of Shaveh. There, the priest Melchizedek blessed him, and the king of Sodom said that Abraham could keep the possessions he had recovered, but Abraham refused (14:1–24).

Sodom is best remembered in the Bible as a thoroughly wicked city destroyed in an act of divine wrath. According to the Genesis narrative, God made the plan to destroy Sodom (and its sister city Gomorrah) plain to Abraham, who then bargained with God for the city's salvation, arguing that the righteous should not perish on account of the unrighteous. God agreed that if ten righteous people could be found there, the city would be spared (Gen. 18:17–32). Two angels then went to the city and stayed at the house of Lot. At nightfall, the men of the city surrounded the house and demanded that Lot turn the visitors over to them, so that they could rape them. Lot refused, even to the point of offering to let them rape his virgin daughters instead. The angels then told Lot and his family to flee the city, and the cities of Sodom and Gomorrah were destroyed when God rained sulfur and fire upon them from heaven (19:1–28).

In later biblical literature, Sodom is cited as a warning of God's wrath and potential judgment (Deut. 29:16–28). The general point is stated succinctly in 2 Pet. 2:6: "By turning the cities of Sodom and Gomorrah to ashes (God) condemned them to extinction and made them an example of what is coming to the ungodly." Isaiah notes that the preservation of a remnant prevents Israel from becoming like Sodom (1:9–10; cf. Amos 4:11; Rom. 9:29), but he says that Babylon will become like Sodom (13:19; Zeph. 2:9 says this of Moab). Jeremiah notes that when a city or nation receives the kind of judgment visited upon Sodom, it becomes totally desolate, so that no one lives there (49:18; 50:40). Lam. 4:6 indicates that the exile of Judea was a worse chastisement than the destruction of Sodom, apparently because the suffering was prolonged, while Sodom "was overthrown in a moment." Ezekiel offers an extended allegory of Jerusalem and her elder sister Samaria and younger sister Sodom (16:44–58). Rev. 11:8 may have this passage in mind when it refers to Jerusalem as the city that is prophetically called Sodom. Elsewhere in the NT, Jesus says that on the day of judgment the people of Sodom will fare better than the residents of towns that do not welcome his followers (Matt. 10:15; Luke 10:12) or, specifically, the

residents of Capernaum, who have not repented in spite of the great miracles he worked there; indeed, he says that Sodom would have remained until this day if his miracles had been performed there (Matt. 11:23–24). He also says that the judgment to come upon the earth on the day the Son of Man is revealed will be just like what befell Sodom in the days of Lot (Luke 17:28–30).

The sin of Sodom is construed differently. In Isa. 3:9, the blatant aspect of its sinfulness is emphasized: people "proclaim their sin like Sodom" when "they do not hide it." Jeremiah likens the prophets of Jerusalem to Sodom, because they "commit adultery and walk in lies" and "strengthen the hands of evildoers, so that no one turns from wickedness" (23:14). In Ezekiel, the "guilt of Sodom" is defined quite specifically: the people of Sodom "had pride, excess of food, and prosperous ease, but did not aid the poor and needy. They were haughty, and did abominable things" (16:49–50). In Jude 7, the people of Sodom are said to have "indulged in sexual immorality and pursued unnatural lust." Most interpreters think that the "unnatural lust" referred to here is an allusion to sex between humans and angels (cf. Jude 6, which alludes to Gen. 6:1–4). If, instead, it refers to a desire for men to have sex with other men, then this would be the only passage in the Bible that calls attention to that aspect of the Sodom story.

A precise location is not given for the city of Sodom, though the general area is associated with the Dead Sea. Archaeological research early in the twentieth century suggested to some that Sodom, along with other cities of the valley, was located under what is now the shallow, southern end of the Dead Sea. Furthermore, this research assigned a date for Sodom early in the second millennium BCE on the basis of observable settlement patterns in the general area and the assumption that the chronological reckoning of the biblical narratives implied such a date. There is, however, no positive evidence that ancient Sodom is submerged under the Dead Sea. More recent investigation has shown that there were urban areas just to the east and south of the Dead Sea during most of the third millennium and perhaps into the early second millennium as well. Indeed, on the basis of the excavations of the Bab ed-Dhra (located on the tongue of land extending into the Dead Sea from its eastern shore) and at Numeira (farther south on the eastern shore), some have proposed that the valley cities of the Genesis narrative should be associated with those two cities. *See also* Abraham; Lot.   J.A.D./M.A.P.

sojourn, an extended stay in one particular place. The word is used twice in Second Temple literature to refer to the time that Israel spent in Egypt prior to the exodus (Wis. 19:10; 1 Esd. 5:7). In the Hebrew Bible, the term is used to indicate a long life span. Joseph tells Pharaoh that his earthly sojourn has been 130 years, but that this does not compare with the long lives of his ancestors (Gen.

47:9). Ps. 5:4 says that evil will not sojourn with God.   M.A.P.

sojourner. *See* alien; foreigner; Gentile.

soldier, a person involved in military activity, one who is trained for war. The word "soldier(s)" appears in the Bible quite frequently, along with a number of synonymous terms such as "troops" or "warriors" (1 Chron. 12:23–38) or "men bearing arms" (Judg. 8:10). During the biblical period, soldiers were equipped with a variety of offensive and defensive weapons. Fully armed soldiers from two distinct eras are described in 1 Sam. 17:5–7 and Eph. 6:11–17; the latter reference compares the panoply of a Roman soldier to the Christian's spiritual armor. Distinction was made between infantrymen, horsemen, and charioteers (Ezek. 26:7; Acts 23:23).

Although other ancient Near Eastern peoples had standing armies at an early date, the Hebrews had no professional soldiers until the establishment of the monarchy (eleventh century BCE). Abram's "trained men" were obviously skilled warriors, but they were recruited from his household (Gen. 14:14). The settlement of the Israelites in Canaan (thirteenth–twelfth centuries BCE) was accomplished by tribal militias of adult males (Num. 1:1–46). Since combat entailed great risk, some men were exempt from military service on the grounds that their death would come at an inopportune time (Deut. 20:5–8). The Levites, likewise, were not counted among those who were "able to go forth to war," but they offered reassurance to soldiers before battles (Num. 1:47–50;

Deut. 20:1–4). In the period of the judges and in the early reign of Saul (twelfth–eleventh centuries BCE), soldiers were mustered to battle by trumpet call or messengers (Judg. 6:34–35; 1 Sam. 11:7–8).

The beginning of a standing army in Israel may be seen in the special force that Saul gathered (1 Sam. 13:1–2; 14:52). David continued this process by developing a bodyguard of elite troops (22:2; 2 Sam. 10:7) and by making a census of the Israelites, a necessary step in the establishment of a national army (2 Sam. 24). Thereafter, the professional soldier became the norm. Mercenaries were also a part of this early Israelite army (2 Sam. 20:23; 2 Chron. 25:6). As in modern armies, the soldier's routine included guard duty (Judg. 7:19).

Rules governing warfare no doubt changed in different settings and time periods, and what is stated for one context ought not be assumed to have applied everywhere or always. That said, materials in the Pentateuch indicate that soldiers typically shared in the loot captured in battle (Num. 31:27; Deut. 21:11), which included a right to keep young women they captured and, if they wished, to make those women their wives after allowing them one month to mourn the loss of their families (Deut. 21:10–13). Judg. 5:28–32 indicates that the soldiers of other nations also looked forward to seizing booty and "a girl or two for every man" from the Israelites (cf. 2 Kings 5:2). The return of soldiers from a battle is often depicted as a cause for celebration (Judg. 11:34; 1 Sam. 18:6–7).

Because the Roman Empire was maintained by military power, the Roman soldier was a common sight in NT times. Soldiers are depicted as listening

Assyrian infantry and cavalry equipped with spears and bows pursuing fleeing desert raiders; from a relief at the palace of the Assyrian king Ashurbanipal at Nineveh, seventh century BCE.

to John the Baptist and asking him what they should do to prepare for the coming judgment; he told them to be content with their wages and not to extort money from any one by force (Luke 3: 14). Jesus healed the slave (or son) of a centurion, i.e., an officer in charge of a hundred soldiers (Matt. 8:5–13; Luke 7:1–10). Soldiers were involved in the arrest and crucifixion of Jesus (John 18:3, 12; 19:2, 23–25, 32, 34). After Paul was arrested in Jerusalem, he was frequently in the company of soldiers; he used the word "soldier" figuratively to describe his co-workers (Phil. 2:25; Philem. 2). In 1 Cor. 9:7, Paul cites military provisions for soldiers as an analogy in making his point that ministers of the gospel should be compensated for their work. In 2 Tim. 2:3–4, Christians are referred to as soldiers of Christ Jesus and, as such, should not become entangled in "civilian affairs," but should seek only to please their "enlisting officer."

Soldiers are also frequently mentioned in the Greek writings of the Second Temple period, especially those that concern the Hasmonean struggles against the Seleucids and other foes (e.g., 1 Macc. 3:13; 6:30, 48; 9:4; 12:49; 14:32; 16:6). Likewise, the book of Judith frequently mentions the Assyrian soldiers associated with Holofernes (2:5, 19; 7:2, 7; 9:7; cf. 15:3). *See also* army; war.

G.L.M./M.A.P.

solemn assembly, the translation generally used for the Hebrew terms 'atseret and 'atsarah. These terms refer to gatherings of the people, in a state of ritual purity, for sacred, religious purposes. These purposes include set festivals, such as the seventh day of the Festival of Unleavened Bread (Deut. 16:8) or the eighth day of the Festival of Tabernacles (Lev. 23:36; Num. 29:35; 2 Chron. 7:9; Neh. 8:18). They might also include special assemblies such as that called by Jehu for Baal (2 Kings 10:20) or for times of emergency (Joel 1:14; 2:15–16). Such assemblies were sometimes criticized by prophets when the people acted unjustly in their everyday lives (Isa. 1:13; Amos 5:21). *See also* worship in the Hebrew Bible; worship in the New Testament.

Solomon (sol'uh-muhn; also known as Jedidiah; Heb., "the LORD's beloved," 2 Sam. 12:25), the son of King David and Bathsheba, and David's successor as king of Israel. He reigned for forty years in the middle of the tenth century BCE. Although 1 Sam. 12 implies that Solomon was Bathsheba's second child by David, born after the child conceived during their adulterous affair had died, 1 Chron. 3:5 may indicate that there were intervening children.

As David grew old, his son Adonijah began to take steps to succeed his father with the support of several court officials, including the general Joab and the priest Abiathar. Another faction gained the support of Bathsheba in approaching David on the claim of a previous promise, not recorded in the Bible, that Solomon would be his successor. David affirmed his commitment to Solomon, who

was immediately installed by the priest Zadok with the assistance of Nathan the prophet and Benaiah from the royal guard. Solomon served as coregent until David's death, at which time Adonijah, who had previously agreed to accept Solomon's succession, sought Bathsheba's support in his request to marry Abishag, a young woman who had been obtained to sleep with David in his old age. Solomon interpreted this request as another attempt by Adonijah to legitimate a claim to the throne and had Adonijah executed, along with his supporter Joab. The priest Abiathar was expelled from Jerusalem, and Shimei, a Benjaminite who had caused problems for David, was restricted from leaving Jerusalem on pain of death, a threat that was later carried out (1 Kings 2).

Reign: Solomon appears to have been responsible for political consolidation, demonstrated by his creation of administrative districts that cut across the old tribal boundaries (1 Kings 4:7–19). His priestly activities also suggest a substantial expansion of the king's role (1 Kings 8; cf. 1 Sam. 13). Solomon's reign was further characterized by vigorous activity in the international sphere. His empire included trade routes linking Africa, Asia, Arabia, and Asia Minor, thus generating substantial revenue while supporting widespread commercial activities, including, apparently, participation in the horse trade based in Asia Minor. His fleet sailed from Ezion-geber in the Gulf of Aqabah to Ophir on the coast of the Red Sea (either in eastern Africa or western Arabia). The Bible ascribes seven hundred wives to him, including Moabite, Edomite, Phoenician, and Hittite women (1 Kings 11:1). Many of these he doubtless married to seal political alliances. Among his wives were an Egyptian princess, whose father (probably Pharaoh Siamon) gave Solomon the city of Gezer, and an Ammonite woman, whose son Rehoboam eventually succeeded to the throne (14:21). Solomon's extensive building program included storecities, fortifications, an elaborate palace complex, and the Jerusalem temple. Such activities brought wealth and a cosmopolitan atmosphere to Solomon's kingdom.

Wisdom: Solomon's wisdom is said to have "surpassed the wisdom of all the people of the east, and all the wisdom of Egypt" (1 Kings 4:30; cf. Heb. 5:10). Such a description reflects the kind of international intellectual activity Solomon's political accomplishments would suggest. According to the Bible, this wisdom was God's gift to him. The Lord had appeared to Solomon in a dream and offered to give him whatever he asked for. Solomon asked for "an understanding mind" and, pleased with this request, the Lord promised to grant him this, and also to give him what he had not asked for, riches and honor so great that no other king would compare with him (1 Kings 3:5–14). The Bible makes much of Solomon's wisdom: he is able to decide which of two prostitutes was a disputed child's mother (3:16–27), and he is able to answer difficult questions posed by the queen of Sheba (10:1–3). He is also noted for creating fables and

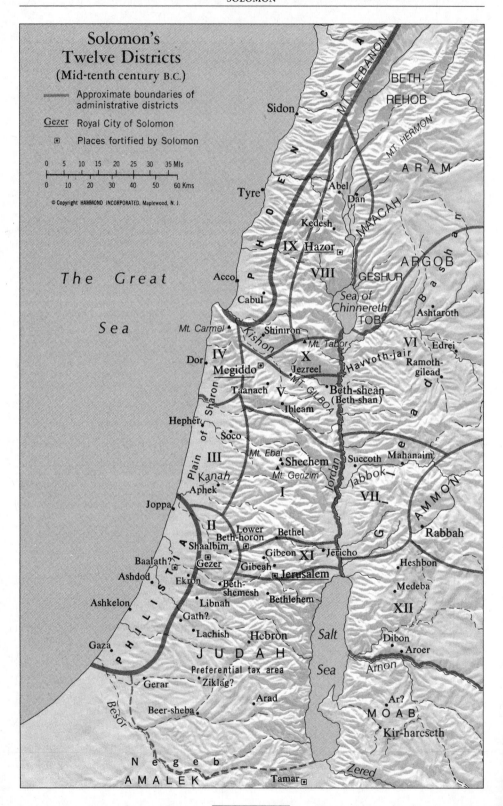

Solomon's Twelve Districts
(Mid-tenth century B.C.)

〰️ Approximate boundaries of administrative districts

<u>Gezer</u> Royal City of Solomon

▣ Places fortified by Solomon

0 5 10 15 20 25 30 35 Mls

0 10 20 30 40 50 60 Kms

© Copyright HAMMOND INCORPORATED. Maplewood, N. J.

The Great

Sea

PHOENICIA
MT. LEBANON
BETH-REHOB
MT. HERMON
ARAM
Sidon
Tyre
Abel
Dan
MAACAH
Kedesh
IX Hazor
VIII
GESHUR
ARGOB
Acco
Cabul
Sea of Chinnereth
TOB
Ashtaroth
Mt. Carmel
Shimron
Mt. Tabor
Havvoth-jair
VI
Edrei
Ramoth-gilead
Dor
IV
Megiddo
X
Jezreel
Kishon
Taanach
V
MT. GILBOA
Beth-shean
(Beth-shan)
Ibleam
Hepher
Plain of Sharon
Soco
Mt. Ebal
Shechem
Succoth
Mahanaim
III
Kanah
Mt. Gerizim
I
Jordan
Jabbok
Aphek
VII
Joppa
AMMON
II
Lower Beth-horon
Bethel
Rabbah
Shaalbim
Gibeon
XI
Jericho
Heshbon
Baalath?
Gezer
Gibeah
Jerusalem
Ashdod
Ekron
Beth-shemesh
Medeba
Ashkelon
Libnah
Bethlehem
XII
Gath?
Lachish
Hebron
Salt
Dibon
Gaza
JUDAH
Sea
Aroer
Preferential tax area
Arnon
Gerar
Ziklag?
Arad
Ar?
MOAB
Beer-sheba
Kir-hareseth
Negeb
AMALEK
Tamar
Zered
PHILISTIA
Besor

Solomon is portrayed as a wise teacher in this late fourteenth-century illustration for the book of Proverbs.

songs (4:32–33, cf. Heb. 5:12–13). This tradition is further reflected in the ascription of several sections of the book of Proverbs to Solomon (see 1:1; 10:1) as well as the book of Ecclesiastes. Solomon's reputation for having had many wives and great wealth probably played a role in the traditional ascription of the Song of Solomon to him (1:1), just as the tradition that he wrote poetry was doubtless important in the ascriptions of Pss. 72 and 127 to him. His impact as the last Davidic king to rule over a united kingdom seems also to have served as an inspiration for the activities of Judah's King Hezekiah in the eighth century BCE (cf. 2 Chron. 30:26; Prov. 25:1).

Policy: The Bible criticizes some of Solomon's activities. The cosmopolitanism resulting from his participation in international affairs brought many foreign religious practices to Jerusalem, things that various biblical authors found unacceptable. He is condemned for building high places for worship outside of Jerusalem and for marrying foreign women (e.g., Neh. 13:26). The book of Kings (e.g., 1 Kings 11:9–25) presents these problematic activities as the reason for God's

decision to split the kingdom, removing ten of the twelve tribes from Davidic control.

Solomon's policies were not only religiously offensive; they also created political enemies. The Bible mentions three opponents: Hadad, an Edomite prince (1 Kings 11:14), Rezon of Zobah (v. 24), and Jeroboam of Israel (v. 26), each of whom sought refuge in Egypt, adding an international dimension to his opposition. Moreover, Solomon's building activities were expensive both economically and in human resources. Indeed, some interpreters consider the warning against royal behavior in 1 Sam. 8:11–17 to have been based on Solomon. In any case, later complaints suggest a high level of taxation and a use of forced labor, limited to non-Israelites according to some sources (1 Kings 9:20–22), but not according to others (5:13). The schism that followed Solomon's death is implicitly ascribed to his heavy-handed policies and burdensome taxation (12:4).

The Bible's view of Solomon is thus ambivalent. On the one hand, his reign clearly marks the peak of Israelite success, both politically and religiously. It is in Solomon's reign that the promises made to the ancestors come to their fulfillment (1 Kings 4:20). On the other hand, syncretism and the influx of foreign practices under Solomon mark the beginning of religious decay, accompanied by growth in internal dissent and the emergence of external enemies.

The proverbial nature of Solomon's glory and his wisdom is reflected in sayings of Jesus (Matt.

Opposite: Solomon's twelve districts. From 1 Kings 4:7–19, an "administrative text," it is possible to derive the approximate territories of Solomon's "district commissioners," but the boundaries between the districts can only be drawn in a general way.

6:29; 12:42). Matthew also lists Solomon as one of Jesus's ancestors (1:6–7). *See also* David; wisdom.

F.E.G.

Solomon, Song of. *See* Song of Solomon.

Solomon, Wisdom of. *See* Wisdom of Solomon.

Solomon's Pools, three reservoirs, one above another, about twelve miles south of Bethlehem, below Qala't el-Burak. They vary in length: 714 feet, 441 feet, and 390 feet. Despite their name, they were constructed no earlier than the second century BCE and repaired by Pontius Pilate. They were used to supply water along two aqueducts to Jerusalem. The identification with Solomon is derived from Josephus, a Jewish historian of the first century CE. *See also* Pilate, Pontius.

Solomon's Portico, a colonnade thought to have been situated along the east side of the temple enclosure built by Herod the Great as part of his restoration of the temple of Jerusalem. If so, the portico would have been directly above the Kidron Valley, facing the Mount of Olives. With the destruction of the temple in 70 CE, nothing from this colonnade remained standing, and there have been no excavations along the east side of the Temple Mount. Jesus was familiar with this porch (John 10:23), and, in the early days of the Christian movement in Jerusalem, the apostles gathered here with the people (Acts 3:11; 5:12). *See also* temple, the.

M.K.M.

Solomon's servants, foreign slaves used for menial tasks in Solomon's temple (Ezra 2:55, 58; Neh. 7:57, 60; 11:3). They were similar in function to the Nethinim (Ezra 8:20), who helped the Levites after the exile (587/6 BCE). *See also* temple servants.

son. The Hebrew word for "son," *ben* (Aramaic *bar;* Gk. *huios*), enjoyed a rich semantic range, although it is used most often in the Bible with reference to actual physical lineage. An adopted son was also referred to by this word. In polite address persons with no actual kinship to the speaker were afforded this title; the one addressed was ordinarily an inferior (cf. the aged priest Eli's use of "my son" in speaking to the child Samuel, 1 Sam. 3:16). In Proverbs and Ecclesiastes "my son" becomes a common expression for a student. In the NT, the apostle Paul uses the word to denote an affectionate relationship with one who shares his faith in Christ: he calls Timothy (1 Cor. 4:17; cf. Phil. 2:22) and Onesimus (Philem. 10) his son (NRSV: "child"). Likewise, Peter refers to his son Mark in a passage that is usually taken as a metaphorical reference to John Mark, though some have suggested it could refer to a literal son about whom nothing else is known (1 Pet. 5:13).

The expression "son of" is used in the Bible in an idiomatic way that is generally ignored by

English translations. It may describe a characteristic feature of something; e.g., "son of fatness" with reference to the land suggests fertile soil (Isa. 5:1; NRSV: "very fertile"), and "son of strength" connotes might.

In the plural, the word "sons" is often used in contexts where gender is irrelevant, and so, the NRSV typically translates the term as "children," as in "children of Israel" (1 Kings 6:13; Isa. 17:3) or "children of Zion (Ps. 149:2; Lam. 4:2). Far more often the plural word is used to mean "descendants," and that is how the NRSV typically translates it, even when only male descendants are indicated (Gen. 6:9; Num. 1:20–43). The biblical prophetic tradition uses the expression "sons of prophets" to describe professional membership in the prophetic guild; the NRSV usually renders this "company of prophets" (1 Kings 20:35; 2 Kings 2:3–15; cf. Amos 7:14).

The expression "sons of God" is somewhat more ambiguous. In some instances, the "sons of God" are divine beings (Gen. 6:2–4), but in other cases the phrase "sons of God" (NRSV: "children of God") is used to refer to people who are loved by God and who acknowledge God's authority (Matt. 5:9; Rom. 8:14). This expression is treated in a separate entry. The expressions "Son of God" and "Son of Man" are special cases, also considered in separate entries. *See also* child, children; daughter; family; inheritance; son of God, Son of God; son of man, Son of Man; sons of God, children of God.

J.L.C.

song. *See* music.

Song of Ascent, a musical piece sung by pilgrims as they climbed the hill to Jerusalem at the time of festivals such as the Festival of Tabernacles, the Festival of Weeks, and the Passover, which were celebrated in the temple. A number of such songs are preserved as Pss. 120–134. *See also* music; Psalms, book of.

Song of Solomon, the first of the Five Scrolls, or Megilloth, in the Ketuvim (Writings section) of the Tanakh (Jewish Bible). Each of the five scrolls is associated with a particular festival in the Jewish calendar. The Song of Solomon is read at Passover. Its Hebrew name is *shir hashirim,* "the Song of songs," which is the book's first phrase. "Song of songs" is a superlative phrase, similar to "King of kings" or "Lord of lords," meaning that the book was considered the best of all songs, hence it is also called "the Song." In the Christian OT, the Song of Solomon is the last of the poetic books, coming after Ecclesiastes and before the Major Prophets.

Contents: The Song of Solomon is a collection of love poems. In English Bibles—and in all Hebrew and Greek manuscripts that have come down to us—it is difficult to tell when one poem ends and another begins or to determine who is speaking at every juncture. Reconstructions have discerned anywhere from five to thirty separate poems within the book. Three distinct voices are generally identified: the male lover, the female lover, and the "daughters of Jerusalem," though additional speakers have been posited as well. The poetry itself is often erotic in nature, using nature metaphors to describe both love itself and the physical appearance of the lovers.

Any outline of contents depends on how the overall book is interpreted. The accompanying general outline is only one of many possible analyses.

Background: The Song of Solomon is so named because of a presumed Solomonic authorship and it is grouped with Proverbs and Ecclesiastes in the Christian OT as books that Solomon supposedly wrote. Solomon had a reputation for writing songs (1 Kings 4:32) and for having a large harem (11:3). In addition, the Song of Solomon contains six references to Solomon (1:1, 5; 3:7, 9, 11; 8:11–12), including a supposed attribution of authorship to Solomon in v. 1 ("The Song of Songs, which is Solomon's"). The phrase translated "which is Solomon's" (Heb. *lishlomo*) could mean either "by Solomon," "to Solomon," or "for Solomon." Thus, the connection of this book to Solomon is similar to the connection between David and many of the psalms. Most scholars do not think Solomon wrote the Song of Solomon, at least in its present form. For one thing, the book is usually dated to a period much later than that of King Solomon. For another, there are passages where the male lover appears to contrast himself with Solomon (8:11–12), and none of the references explicitly portray Solomon as speaking. Therefore, most scholars think that the references to Solomon are meant to associate the book with Solomon's reputation for wisdom, splendor, and love; they are not to be taken as literal attestations of authorship. Longman points to the superscription of *lishlomo* in Proverbs, which is clearly a collection of materials by a variety of authors. He claims that the reference to Solomon in v. 1 is intended to place the book within the Solomonic ("wisdom") tradition. However, Stoop-van Paridon argues that the text can be read in the context of Solomon incorporating a female lover into his harem.

The date and origin of Song of Solomon are highly disputed. Dates range from the tenth century (early monarchic period) to the second century BCE, but most scholars favor a postexilic date between the fourth and second century BCE. The presence of Persian loanwords (*pardes*, "garden") also suggests a later date. Determining the origin of the work, however, is actually a more complicated task than discerning the date of the book as a whole or even of its particular poems; if it is a compilation of love poems, the materials could have been drawn from different time periods and different places.

There are many connections between Song of Solomon and other love poetry within the ancient Near East, particularly Egypt during the twelfth–fourteenth centuries BCE. Gottwald argues that these Egyptian love poems provide various sub-

genres with which to better understand the Song of Solomon: songs of yearning, admiration songs, boasts, teases, erotic poems, descriptive songs (*wasfs*), and travesties (portrayals of lovers in roles outside of their social class, i.e., as a king).

Interpretive Issues: There are five major contemporary interpretations of Song of Solomon: (1) a drama with two or three main characters; (2) a series of wedding songs (either human or divine); (3) a collection of poems highly influenced by fertility cults; (4) a collection of love poems; and, (5) a single love poem. Gottwald holds that the poems are marriage songs that would be read at elaborate ceremonies in which the bride and groom dress up as king and queen or shepherd and shepherdess.

The love between the two characters is generally considered to be reciprocal and egalitarian in nature, though the female voice is dominant. Exum, however, argues that the male lover has a certain freedom and autonomy that the female lover lacks, destroying the illusion of gender equality. The implications of that observation on the perceived social status of the lovers is disputed. Hess argues that the lovers were most likely married, either in actuality or in fantasy. The book's sexual ethic is contrasted sharply with that found elsewhere in the Bible (Deut. 22). The titles given to the lovers throughout the book are ambiguous as well. Some argue that the female lover had multiple suitors wooing her (a king and a shepherd). Others argue that the titles "king" and "shepherd" are fictional imaginative love language, according to which lovers would address each other as "king" and "queen" or as "shepherd" and "shepherdess."

Along with Esther, the Song of Solomon is one of only two books in the Hebrew Bible that do not mention God. This has sometimes caused the book to be demeaned as "secular." The problem is intensified by the erotic nature of the poetry, which has scandalized some readers throughout the history of the book's interpretation. For this reason, many interpreters have held that the book is to be read, not literally as referring to human sexual love, but allegorically as a testimony to the love between God and God's people.

Influences: The Song of Solomon, as part of the Megilloth, is read each year at the Jewish festival of Passover. In Christian circles, due to allegorical readings that interpreted it as communication between Christ and the church, it became the most preached book of the OT in the Middle Ages. St. John of the Cross composed the *Spiritual Canticle* with over twenty references to the Song of Solomon. Pope Gregory the Great wrote a treatise on the book, explaining it as an allegory of the soul's love for God in which common love language is used to stir up the heart for God. Alcuin of York viewed the book as an allegory of faith and the Gospel. St. Thomas Aquinas is reported to have written two commentaries on the book.

Bibliography

Bandstra, Barry L. *Reading the Old Testament: Introduction to the Hebrew Bible.* 4th ed. Wadsworth, 2009.

Exum, J. Cheryl. "Ten Things Every Feminist Should Know about the Song of Songs." In *The Song of Songs: A Feminist Companion to the Bible* (Second Series). Sheffield, 2000. Pp. 24–35.

Gottwald, Norman K. *The Hebrew Bible: A Socio-Literary Introduction.* Fortress, 1985.

Hess, Richard S. *Song of Songs.* Baker Academic, 2005.

Longman, Tremper. *Song of Songs.* Eerdmans, 2001.

Stoop-van Paridon, P. W. T. *The Song of Songs: A Philological Analysis of the Hebrew Book.* Peeters, 2005.

Turner, Denys. *Eros and Allegory: Medieval Exegesis of the Song of Songs.* Cistercian Publications, 1995.   B.B.

Song of Songs. *See* Song of Solomon.

Song of the Three Jews, one of the Additions to Daniel found between Dan. 3:23 and 3:24 in the LXX and Theodotion. It is also called the Song of the Three Children.

The prayer and the hymn are probably independent liturgical compositions done in Hebrew and later adapted sometime during the second century BCE to fit the story in Dan. 3. The addition follows the practice of supplying prayers and songs at appropriate places in stories, but it may also have been intended to shift the emphasis of Dan. 3 away from the tyranny of the king to the piety of the three youths. The prayer is penitential in character and seems to reflect the desecration of the temple by the Syrian king Antiochus IV Epiphanes in 167 BCE. It treats the catastrophe as

OUTLINE OF CONTENTS

Song of the Three Jews

the consequence of "our sins," begs God's mercy for the sake of the divine promise to Abraham, Isaac, and Israel (Jacob), and, in the absence of a physical place to make an offering, it presents the sacrifice of "a contrite heart and a humble spirit" (v. 16). The last suggestion echoes Ps. 51:17, but also anticipates the ultimate transformation of Judaism under the Pharisees into a religion concerned with prayer, acts of mercy, and the way of Torah even in the absence of a temple.

The hymn calls upon God's creatures to bless God, moving from heavenly to earthly things, then from animals to humanity, and finally to Israel. Its order is related to Ps. 148, but it is possible that both the psalm and the hymn are dependent upon a system of cosmic order present in speculative wisdom. In contrast to the prayer, in which the temple seems to be desecrated, the hymn refers to God "in the temple of your holy glory" (v. 31), which might refer to a heavenly rather than an earthly sanctuary—an idea prominent in apocalyptic Judaism (cf. Rev. 11:19).

Protestants include the Song of the Three Jews among the Apocrypha, while Roman Catholics and Eastern Orthodox Christians retain it as part of the book of Daniel. *See also* Apocrypha/deuterocanonical literature; Daniel, Additions to.

D.W.S.

son of God, Son of God, a person with a special relationship to God, often with a special role in salvation history. When used in the plural, the term carries a very different sense. *See* sons of God, children of God.

In the Hebrew Bible: In pre-Christian Judaism there are three notable uses of the term "son of God." First, it is predicated of Israel as a collective role for the nation as a whole. God says to Pharaoh, "Israel is my firstborn son" (Exod. 4:22; cf. Hos. 11:1). Second, it is a title given to the monarch at the time of enthronement (e.g., Ps. 2:7, a coronation psalm). Third, in Wisdom of Solomon, the term is used to mean "a righteous person" (2:18; NRSV: "child").

It is a matter of dispute whether the term "son of God" was already current in pre-Christian Judaism as a messianic title, as Mark 14:16 would seem to suggest. Yet in view of the discovery of Ps. 2:7 with a messianic interpretation in the Dead Sea Scrolls (4QFlor 10–14) it is probably safe to conclude that it was at least beginning to be used in this sense prior to the time of Christian origins.

In the NT: The singular expression "Son of God" takes on new meaning in the NT, where it is applied as a principal title for Jesus Christ, identifying his status and authority based on a unique relationship with God. According to Luke's Gospel, the angel Gabriel told Mary that the child to be born to her would be called the Son of God (1:35; cf. 1:32). The Synoptic Gospels all indicate that, when Jesus was baptized, God spoke from heaven, identifying Jesus as "my Son" (Matt. 3:17; Mark 1:11; Luke 3:22); this affirmation is repeated later at his transfiguration (Matt. 17:5; Mark 9:7;

Luke 9:35). Both Matthew and Luke indicate that Jesus was tempted as the Son of God in the wilderness by the devil (Matt. 4:3, 6; Luke 4:3, 9). During the time of Jesus's ministry, supernatural beings such as demons recognize him as the Son of God, and he encounters them in that capacity (Matt. 8:29; Mark 3:11; 5:7; Luke 4:31; 8:28). The Gospel of Matthew indicates that Jesus's disciples worshiped him as the Son of God after he stilled a storm at sea (14:33), and that Peter identified him as "the Christ, the Son of the living God" when Jesus asked him, "Who do you say that I am?" (16:15–16). The Synoptic Gospels also contain sayings in which Jesus refers to himself as "Son" in relation to God as his Father (Matt. 11:27; 24:36; Mark 13:32; Luke 10:22) and parables in which he likens himself to a son of a figure to be identified with God (Matt. 21:33–39; 22:2; Mark 12:1–8; Luke 20:9–15). Further, Jesus addresses God as his *Abba* (Aramaic, "Father"), an appellation normally used for an earthly father (e.g., Mark 14:36). All three of the Synoptic Gospels record that Jesus was asked by the religious authorities if he was the Son of God and that he answered in a manner they took to be an affirmative response (Matt. 26:63–65; Mark 14:61–63; Luke 22:70–71). Matthew's Gospel also displays Jesus as being mocked on the cross for having claimed to be the Son of God (27:40, 43). Matthew and Mark both recount that at the moment of Jesus's death, the centurion at the foot of the cross proclaimed, "Truly, this man was God's Son!" (Matt. 27:54; Mark 15:39; cf. Luke 23:47). Finally, in Matthew's Gospel, the risen Jesus commissions his followers to make disciples of all nations by baptizing them in the name of the Father, and of the Son, and of the Holy Spirit (28:19).

In the Gospel of John, John the Baptist (1:34), Nathanael (1:49), and Martha (11:27) all identify Jesus as the Son of God, and Jesus refers to himself as the Son of God several times (e.g., 3:18; 5:25; 11:4)—something he does not do in the Synoptic Gospels. The explicit reason that his opponents give for wanting him put to death is that "he claimed to be the Son of God" (19:27). In a concluding passage, the author of John's Gospel says that the book has been written so that readers "may come to believe that Jesus is the Messiah, the Son of God, and that, through believing . . . have life in his name" (20:31). John's Gospel also presents Jesus as referring to himself as "the Son" and to God as "the Father" or as "my Father" who has sent him into the world. For example, "God so loved the world that (God) gave (God's) only Son, so that everyone who believes in him may not perish but may have eternal life" (3:16).

The book of Acts records that after his experience on the Damascus road, Paul began "to proclaim Jesus in the synagogues, saying, 'He is the Son of God'" (9:20; cf. Gal. 1:16). Paul's letters use the phrase "Son of God" only a few times (Rom. 1:4; 2 Cor. 1:19; Gal. 2:20; Eph. 4:13), but he often employs the shorthand version "the Son" when talking about Christ (esp. in Rom. 1–8 and

Galatians). Paul maintains that Jesus was "declared to be Son of God with power" at his resurrection (Rom. 1:4). God's grace is evident in the fact that God's own Son was given up "for all of us" (8:32), sent to redeem those under the law (Gal. 4:4). Further God predestines believers to be conformed to the image of the Son (Rom. 8:29) and sends the Spirit of the Son into human hearts, crying, "Abba! Father!" (Gal. 4:6). Thus, Paul's understanding of what it means for Christ to be the Son of God is closely connected to what it means for him (and for those to whom he writes) to be "in Christ" (or to have Christ in them). Paul says, "The life I now live in the flesh I live by faith in the Son of God, who loved me and gave himself for me" (2:20).

The identification of Jesus as Son of God is also significant for the Letter to the Hebrews (4:13–14; 6:6; 7:3; 10:29) and, especially, for the first of the Johannine Letters (1 John 3:8; 4:15; 5:5, 10, 12–13, 20).

Historical Development of "Son of God Christology": Scholars are uncertain as to whether the historical Jesus referred to himself as "son" in relation to God as his father. At the very least, they usually grant that his use of *Abba* implied a distinctive filial consciousness, so that it seems likely that "Father" was one of his preferred images for God. The use of "Son of God" as a christological title, however, may be distinguished from the employment of Father/Son language as such. The evidence suggests that the phrase was not used prominently as a title for Jesus until after Easter. Rom. 1:4 suggests that application of this title to Jesus was associated with the resurrection event. In the course of time the moment at which Jesus was appointed "Son of God" may have been pushed back to his baptism (Mark 1:11) and then to his conception or birth (Luke 1:32,35).

An additional development in this process of retrojection is the idea of the sending of the Son. This appears in a formula exhibiting a constant pattern: God as subject; a verb of "sending" or its equivalent; the Son as object; and a statement of God's saving purpose in sending the Son (cf. Gal. 4:4–5; Rom. 8:3–4; John 3:17). In the parable of the Vineyard (Mark 12:6) a similar image occurs, though without an explicit statement of saving purpose. The roots of this saving formula could lie in the earlier designation of Jesus as prophet. Jesus had a strong sense of mission (cf. 9:37), a consciousness shared by the Hebrew prophets who believed themselves to be sent by God (e.g., Isa. 6:8). When "Son of God" came to be preferred to "prophet" as an identifier for Jesus, the sending-of-the-Son formula came into being. *See also* Abba; father; messiah; son; wisdom.

Bibliography

Brown, Raymond E. *An Introduction to New Testament Christology.* Paulist, 1994. Pp. 103–52.

Casey, Maurice. *From Jewish Prophet to Gentile God: The Origins and Development of New Testament Christology.* Westminster John Knox, 1991.

De Jonge, Marinus. *Christology in Conflict: The Earliest Christian Response to Jesus.* Westminster, 1988.

Fuller, Reginald H., and Pheme Perkins. *Who Is the Christ? Gospel Christology and Contemporary Faith.* Fortress, 1983. Pp. 41–66, 96–108, 121–34.

Hengel, Martin. *The Son of God.* Fortress, 1976.

Tuckett, Christopher. *Christology and the New Testament: Jesus and His Earliest Followers.* Westminster John Knox, 2001.   R.H.F./M.A.P.

son of man, Son of Man.

1 An idiomatic way of speaking of a human being, or of humanity collectively. The Hebrew phrase is *ben 'adam,* which the NRSV often translates as "mortal(s)." Sometimes, the phrase *ben 'adam* is used in synonymous parallelism with "human being," as when the psalmist asks, "What are human beings that you are mindful of them, mortals that you care for them?" (Ps. 8:4); note that in Hebrew the word translated "mortals" is singular (lit., "the son of man"), though it does seem to be used here in a collective sense (to refer to human beings in general). Likewise, in Ps. 80:17 "the one whom you made strong" is literally "the son of man whom you made strong." In the book of Ezekiel, the prophet is repeatedly addressed by God or by an angelic messenger as "son of man" (NRSV: "mortal"; e.g., 2:1, 6). The point is probably to suggest the prophet's humanity (weakness and finitude) as contrasted with the divine majesty. In Dan. 7:13, the meaning of the phrase, "one like a son of man" (NRSV: "one like a human being") is disputed. It may mean (as the NRSV suggests) that the symbol for God's faithful people is a human being, whereas the symbols for the previous kingdoms described by Daniel were beasts and monsters. Some scholars, however, interpret the phrase in this verse in line with **2** below.

2 An angelic, supernatural figure often associated with apocalyptic scenarios of judgment. This sense of the phrase is clearly evident in some Hellenistic Jewish writings of the Second Temple period (e.g., *1 Enoch* 37–91; *2 Esd.* 13). The son of man figures as God's agent of judgment and salvation. Many scholars read the references to the coming of the son of man in Daniel in this light: "As I watched in the night visions, I saw one like a son of man [NRSV: "one like a human being"] coming with the clouds of heaven. And he came to the Ancient One and was presented before him. To him was given dominion and glory and kingship, that all peoples, nations, and languages should serve him. His dominion is an everlasting dominion that shall not pass away, and his kingship is one that shall never be destroyed" (7:13–14). It is disputed, however, whether the angelic concept of "son of man" had developed before the NT period; if it had not, then the "son of man" reference here would be understood along the lines of **1** above.

3 When spelled "Son of Man" (in the NRSV and other English Bibles), a title for Jesus employed especially in the Synoptic Gospels. With one exception (Acts 7:56) and apart from the cita-

tion of Ps. 8:4 in Heb. 2:6 (NRSV: "mortals") and an allusion to Dan. 7:13 in Rev. 1:13, the term is used exclusively by Jesus in reference to himself. It is customary to classify the references in the Synoptic Gospels under three headings: sayings in which Jesus refers to his present activity during his earthly ministry (e.g., Matt. 8:20; 11:19; Mark 2:10, 28; 10:45a); sayings in which Jesus refers to his impending passion and/or resurrection (Mark 8:31; 9:9, 31; 10:33, 45b); and sayings in which he refers to his future activity as Judge and Savior (e.g., Mark 8:38; cf. Luke 12:8; Mark 13:26; 14:62; Luke 17:22, 24, 26, 30). In John's Gospel, "Son of Man" as a self-referent for Jesus has a more varied usage, the most characteristic being those sayings that speak of the exaltation of the Son of Man, an expression that makes a double allusion to the cross and resurrection/ascension (3:14; 8:28; 12:34). John 1:51 looks like an original Parousia saying (third category above) transferred to the present ministry (first category). John 6:53 speaks of eating the flesh and drinking the blood of the Son of Man, and 9:35 of believing in the Son of Man.

The difficulties begin when scholars inquire about the origin and meaning of the term as it appears in these Gospels. There is some discussion as to whether the historical Jesus actually used the term and, if so, did he mean it as a reference to himself or to a divine deliverer he believed was coming? Or is the term a post-Easter title retrojected by the Gospel authors upon the pre-Easter Jesus? Some would hold that Jesus did use the title as a self-designation, but that he meant it in a self-effacing way, referring to himself as a mortal in contrast with God (cf. Ps. 8:4 and the usage in Ezekiel, as noted in **1** above). A variant of this view is that Jesus used the phrase, but as a generic designation for all humanity; thus, his affirmations that "the Son of Man has authority on earth to forgive sins" (Matt. 9:6) or "the Son of Man is lord of the sabbath" (12:8) were not meant to apply only to himself. Whatever is made of these different theories, most interpreters concur that the Gospels writers intended for the title to apply exclusively to Jesus and to identify him with the apocalyptic deliverer that had come to be associated with the "son of man" image in apocalyptic Jewish writings (and in the interpretation of Dan. 7:13–14 current in first-century CE apocalyptic Jewish circles).

Bibliography

Brown, Raymond E. *An Introduction to New Testament Christology.* Paulist, 1994. Pp. 89–102.

Burkett, Delbert. *The Son of Man Debate: A History and Evaluation.* Cambridge University Press, 2000.

Casey, Maurice. *The Solution to the "Son of Man" Problem.* Clark, 2007.

Hare, Douglas R. A. *The Son of Man Tradition.* Fortress, 1990.

Lindars, Barnabas. *Jesus Son of Man: A Fresh Examination of the Son of Man Sayings in the Gospels in the Light of Recent Research.* Eerdmans, 1983.   R.H.F.

sons of God, children of God, phrases with different meanings in the Hebrew Bible and in the NT. In both cases, the Hebrew or Greek term "sons of God" is probably not to be read with overly literal attention to gender; thus the NRSV and most modern English Bibles render the phrase "children of God" unless the context clearly implies that only male beings are intended.

In the Hebrew Bible: The phrase "sons/children of God" always denotes superhuman beings in the Hebrew Bible. Gen. 6:1–4 gives an account of how sexual union of the "sons of God" with the "daughters of men" produced a race of giants known as the Nephilim. Here the expression clearly refers to male divine beings. The passage is a remnant of ancient Near Eastern mythological tradition. In the Ugaritic texts, the pantheon or the gods as a whole are identified as the children of the chief god, "the totality of the sons/children of El."

There are other biblical texts in which "sons/children of God" refers to divine beings, but in all of the following instances the NRSV translates the phrase "heavenly beings," thereby losing the filial aspect: in Job 38:7, the sons of God are said to have shouted for joy at creation as the morning stars sang together; in Ps. 29:1, the sons of God are called to praise God; in 89:6, God is beyond comparison with the sons of God. In all of these passages the sons of God may represent a heavenly court, though in the last (89:6), the reference could be to other deities (who are not a part of God's court).

Another prominent context reflects a similar use of the term. In Job 1–2, "the satan" is listed as one of the "sons of God" (1:6; 2:1). Here the LXX translates the phrase as "angels" (Gk. *angeloi*), which, again, loses the filial aspect, but makes clear that the "sons of God" represented here are not competing deities, but heavenly beings subordinate to God who function primarily as God's messengers. As one of the sons of God, however, "the satan" has a specific role, that of accusing people before God's throne.

In Dan. 3:25, the fourth figure in the furnace has an appearance "like a son of the gods" (NRSV: "like a god"). In later, mainly apocalyptic, reflection such ideas provided the basis for accounts of the rebellion or fall of the angels (*1 Enoch* 6–36; *Jub.* 5:1–10).

In the NT: The phrase "sons of God" (NRSV: "children of God") is used in the NT in a manner similar to the way that the Hellenistic Jewish writing, Wisdom of Solomon, uses the singular term "son of God" to refer to a righteous person (e.g., 2:18, NRSV: "child"). The determinative factor, however, is not demonstrable righteousness so much as inner purity (Matt. 5:9). In the Letters of Paul, particularly, the sons/children of God are those who have been granted this status through the Holy Spirit (Rom. 8:14–21) on account of their faith in Jesus Christ (Gal. 3:26). Thus, in the NT, the phrase "children of God" refers to human beings who have been put into a right relationship with God through Jesus Christ; the phrase is essentially synonymous with what would later be expressed by the term "Christians" (e.g., John 1:12; Phil. 2:15; Heb. 12:7; 1 John 3:1; 5:2). *See also* angel.   G.M.T./M.A.P.

sons of prophets, a term probably denoting a group of professional prophets (e.g., 1 Sam. 10:5; NRSV: "company of prophets"). When Amos asserts that he is neither a prophet nor a prophet's son, he is probably disclaiming any identification with such a group (7:14). *See also* prophet; son.

sons of thunder. *See* Boanerges.

soothsayer, one who foretells events. The word has a negative connotation in the Bible, where soothsayers are classed with sorcerers (Jer. 27:9) and are associated with magical practices (Deut. 18:10, 14) forbidden to Israel (Mic. 5:12).

Sopater (soh′puh-tuhr). *See* Sosipater.

Sophereth (sof′uh-rith; Heb., "scribe"), one of "Solomon's servants" whose descendants constituted a family of temple servants in postexilic times; they returned to Jerusalem from Babylon with Zerubbabel (Neh. 7:57).

Sophia (soh-fee′uh), the woman who appears as a personification of wisdom in Prov. 1–9; Sir. 24; Wis. 6–12; and Bar. 3:9–4:4. The name does not appear as such in English Bibles, but *sophia* is the Greek word used for "wisdom" in the Greek versions of all these texts (the Hebrew word used in Proverbs is *khokmah,* but *sophia* is used in the LXX translation of Proverbs, and the other texts were written in Greek and appear only in the LXX, not the Hebrew Bible). Thus, Sophia is used as the name of the figure who is sometimes called Woman Wisdom or Dame Wisdom or simply Wisdom (with a capital letter).

According to Prov. 1:20–22, "Wisdom [*sophia*] cries out in the street . . . 'How long, O simple ones, will you love being simple?'" Sophia/Wisdom offers to teach people ways of truth and justice, ways that lead to a prosperous long life. She is contrasted with the smooth-talking "loose woman" (sometimes called Woman Folly), who counsels a way of life that is not pleasing to God and that brings disaster to those who pursue it (Prov. 2:16; 5:3; 7:5; 22:14; cf. Sir. 9:3). In Sirach and Baruch, Sophia appears to be a personification of the Torah (Sir. 24:23; Bar. 4:1) while in the Wisdom of Solomon, she is more a personification of God's image or presence, a reflection of God's glory and a figure who represents the order and reason found in God's creation (7:25–26; 8:1).

In several passages, Sophia/Wisdom speaks almost as a goddess (i.e., as a woman who possesses divine attributes). Sophia/Wisdom is "a spotless mirror of the working of God and an image of (God's) goodness" (Wis. 7:26). Sophia/Wisdom was "before all things" (Sir. 1:4); Sophia/Wisdom was present with God before creation (Prov. 8:22–31). Sophia/Wisdom served as God's agent through whom everything in heaven and earth was made (Prov. 3:19; 8:27–31; Wis. 7:22; 8:4–6; 9:2). Sophia/Wisdom "holds all things together" and "orders all things well" (Wis. 1:7; 8:1). Sophia/Wisdom reconciles people to God, making them be "friends of God" (Wis. 7:14, 27). This is poetic language, and it is not clear how literally readers would have taken it (did they believe that Sophia/Wisdom was an actual divine being?). Some scholars think the figure of personified wisdom evident in these texts evolved from belief in a Hebrew goddess, Sophia, who was the consort of YHWH ("the LORD") in a way analogous to other goddesses in ancient Near Eastern religion (e.g., Ishtar, Isis). Others have sought to interpret the concept against the background of Greco-Roman philosophy, according to which reason, rationality, or "the world of ideas" was sometimes conceived of as a divine essence underlying the realm of physical life.

Significant parallels can be noted between what is said of Sophia/Wisdom in these passages and what is said of Jesus Christ in such NT texts as John 1:1–4 and especially 1:15–20. Thus, some scholars believe that the personification of wisdom as a divine being (whom they call Sophia) set a precedent within Second Temple Judaism for an understanding of Jesus Christ as a personification/incarnation of God's word or will. Texts such as Luke 7:35 are sometimes read as implying that Jesus presented himself as the child or prophet of Sophia. *See also* Apocrypha/deuterocanonical literature; wisdom; wisdom literature.

Bibliography

Camp, Claudia V. *Wisdom and the Feminine in the Book of Proverbs.* Sheffield Academic, 1985.

Collins, John J. *Jewish Wisdom in the Hellenistic Age.* Westminster John Knox, 1997.

Lang, Bernhard. *Wisdom and the Book of Proverbs: A Hebrew Goddess Redefined.* Pilgrim, 1986.

Schüssler Fiorenza, Elisabeth. *Jesus: Miriam's Child, Sophia's Prophet: Critical Issues in Feminist Christology.* Continuum, 1994.   M.A.P.

sorcery. *See* divination; magic.

Sorek (sor'ik), the name of the valley (and its brook) where Delilah lived; it is mentioned only once in the Bible (Judg. 16:4). There Samson was captured by the Philistines and taken to their city Gaza, where he destroyed the temple of Dagon. The story, along with other evidence, indicates that the area, once inhabited by the tribe of Dan and serving as the boundary between Dan and Simeon, was under Philistine control during the period of the judges (1200–1000 BCE).

The valley extends between Ashkelon and Gaza in the southwestern region of the Levant, and the Wadi Sorek runs westward and then northward into the Mediterranean Sea from the area near Beer-shemesh. In biblical times this city served as the guardian of the Sorek Valley, which is known in modern times as Wadi es-Sarar. *See also* Delilah; Samson.   F.R.M.

Sosipater (soh-sip'uh-tuhr), a Jewish Christian who, with Timothy, Lucius, and Jason, joins Paul in sending greetings in Rom. 16:21. Perhaps he was the same person as Sopater of Beroea, who accompanied Paul through Macedonia as he prepared for his last trip to Jerusalem (Acts 20:4). Paul refers to Sosipater, Lucius, and Jason as "my relatives," indicating that he has brought family members into the faith and that they are assisting him in his work.

Sosthenes (sos'thuh-neez).

1 The official of a synagogue in Corinth during the time Paul was there (Acts 18:17). He apparently replaced Crispus as synagogue leader or shared that office with him (18:8). Sosthenes was beaten by a local mob in the presence of Gallio the proconsul, who chose not to intervene in what he regarded as a religious dispute (18:12–17). *See also* Corinth; Crispus; Gallio; Paul; synagogue.

2 The coauthor with Paul of 1 Corinthians (1:1). If he is the same person described in **1,** he became a Christian and possibly went from Corinth to Ephesus to visit Paul with the delegation of Stephanas, Fortunatus, and Achaicus (16:17–18). Otherwise, nothing further is known about him.
                                            A.J.M.

soul. In the Hebrew Bible, the word translated "soul" (*nephesh*) does not have the same meaning that the English word sometimes carries (through the influence of Greek, and especially Platonic, philosophy). The word sometimes simply refers to a "person," though in those instances it is not usually translated "soul" in the NRSV; e.g., Leah was responsible for the existence of sixteen "souls" (NRSV: "persons") who would be counted as descendants of Jacob (Gen. 46:18). It also refers to "life" in the sense of what makes a human being alive: God "breathed the breath of life" into Adam, and he became a "living soul" (2:7; NRSV: "being"). Thus, in the biblical view, Adam does not *have* a soul; Adam *is* a soul (i.e., a person, a living being). It is in this latter sense that people may fear for their souls (Ezek. 32:10; NRSV: "lives"). Judg. 5:18 says, literally, that Zebulon was a people who "risked their souls" (NRSV: "who scorned death"). Thus, to "lose one's soul" means simply "to die" (Gen. 35:18); i.e., it means to lose whatever it is that makes a person alive. Indeed, a corpse can be called "a dead soul" (Lev. 21:11; Num. 6:6; NRSV: "a dead body").

In a related sense *nephesh* refers to the essence of what a person truly is—and it is when the word carries this meaning that the NRSV tends to translate it as "soul." It is in this sense a synonym for the word "heart," and the two words are often used in parallel or interchangeably (e.g., Deut. 4:29; 10:12; Josh. 23:14;). The word still differs from the Platonic sense in that it does not describe one part or aspect of a person (e.g., the soul as distinct from the spirit or the body), but defines the essence or totality of who a person truly is. The accent of such a definition may be on unseen (inner) qualities, but the point is rarely to contrast the inner self with the outer person. For example, to love God with all one's soul (Deut. 6:5) means to love God completely, with one's full being. The same sense is conveyed when the Bible says, "The soul of Jonathan was bound to the soul of David" (1 Sam. 17:55). The depth of their friendship was such that Jonathan found himself completely devoted to David; that devotion was representative of the very essence of who he was as a human being. Such devotion, however, is not always expressed in contexts that are positive. Shechem rapes Dinah, because his soul has been drawn to her, meaning, perhaps, that he was completely obsessed with her (Gen. 34:3). Likewise, Prov. 21:10 indicates that "the soul of the wicked desires evil."

In poetry especially, the soul is often treated as the seat of emotions; e.g., "My soul is satisfied" (Ps. 63:5); "My soul was embittered" (73:21); "My soul refuses to be comforted" (74:2); "My soul is full of troubles" (88:3); "Your consolations cheer my soul" (94:19). In all these expressions, however, the implication is that the emotional state is not superficial, but goes to the depth of one's being. It is also important to recognize that the Greek notion of the "immortality of the soul" was virtually unknown to authors of the Hebrew Bible.

The NT employs a Greek word (*psychē*) for "soul," but the concept generally retains its basic Hebrew field of meaning. "Soul" refers to one's life. Herod sought Jesus's soul (Matt. 2:20; NRSV: "life"). To save a soul (Mark 3:4; NRSV: "life") is the opposite of killing (depriving someone of life). Death occurs when God "requires your soul" (Luke 12:20; NRSV: "life"). Thus, the word "soul" generally refers to the whole person, the self. When the satisfied rich man speaks to himself, he addresses his "soul" (Luke 2:19), because his soul represents his "self," all that he is as a person. Paul argues against the notion of an "immortal soul" in 1 Cor. 15, because the Greek idea that one's soul survived after death would obviate the need for resurrection. Paul's view is that God will bring the dead back to life, meaning that those whose souls are dead will be revived by the power of God (and, incidentally, given new immortal bodies, since in Paul's Hebraic thinking a soul cannot exist apart from a body).

A few NT passages, however, do betray the Greek notion of a soul as the aspect of the person that continues to exist after the body has died. In Matt. 10:28, Jesus says, "Do not fear those who kill the body but cannot kill the soul; rather fear him who can destroy both body and soul in hell." Likewise, in Rev. 6:9, the seer beholds in heaven the souls of those martyrs who were killed on earth. *See also* flesh and spirit; human being, humanity; resurrection.   J.H.N./M.A.P.

sowing, the act of scattering seeds as part of the cultivation of crops. Although the seeds of some crops were planted more carefully, "sowing" typically referred to the wholesale scattering of wheat and barley. Unlike their Mesopotamian counterparts, who sometimes used a seeding device that was attached to the plow, Egyptian and Near Eastern farmers simply carried a container full of seed and broadcast this seed with their free hand. In contrast to Western practice, the farmer would often plow after sowing, thereby working seeds into the soil for protection and germination; this practice is apparently presumed in Jesus's parable of the Sower (Matt. 13:3–8).

Mosaic law contains certain regulations regarding sowing (Lev. 11:37–38; 19:19; Deut. 22:9). The process of sowing also attained metaphorical significance as a figure for speaking of inevitable consequences (Prov. 11:18; 2 Cor. 9:6; Gal. 6:7–8). In Ps. 126:5, however, this image is subverted as the psalmist prays, "May those who sow in tears reap with shouts of joy." *See also* farming; plow; seed.   G.L.M.

Spain (spayn), a large peninsula in southwestern Europe known since Roman times as Hispania. It first received the Ligurerians from Italy, then the Celts (sixth century BCE), who were then challenged by the Iberians (fifth century BCE). Known by the Phoenicians and the Greeks, Spain was invaded by Carthage in 237 BCE, but lost to Rome in 206 BCE. After some two hundred years of stubborn resistance, a "pacified" Spain gave Rome three emperors and many of its best soldiers. Spain is mentioned in the Bible only in Rom. 15:24, 28 as the intended western horizon of Paul's mission. The NT indicates that Paul was arrested in Jerusalem before the planned mission to Spain and sent as a prisoner to Rome, where it is normally thought that he was executed. That execution is not reported in the NT, however, and one early church tradition (ca. 97 CE) suggests that Paul did make it to Spain (1 Clem. 5:6–7). This tradition has become the basis for a proposal by some scholars that Paul was released from his Roman imprisonment and embarked on a continued "second career" as a missionary, doing work not reported in Acts and writing letters otherwise deemed to be pseudepigraphical. Most scholars, however, do not find this proposal convincing, and they assume that the early tradition that Paul went to Spain has been misinterpreted (the passage literally says he went "to the limits of the west") or is simply wrong. *See also* Paul.   C.J.R./M.A.P.

span, a linear measure equal to the distance between extended fingertips, about one-half of a cubit (or approximately 9 to 10 inches). *See* weights and measures.

sparrow. The Hebrew (*tsippor*) and Greek (*strouthion*) words that are sometimes translated "sparrow" in the Bible refer to any small, brown bird that flits and twitters. The NRSV mentions sparrows in only a handful of passages (Ps. 84:3; Prov. 26:2; Tob. 2:10; Matt. 10:29, 31; Luke 12:6–7) and otherwise tends to translate these words with something more generic, such as "bird" (Pss. 11:1; 102:7; 104:17; 124:7; Eccles. 12:4; Lam. 3:52). The birds identified as sparrows (probably members of the weaver family) are mentioned as nesting near the temple altar (Ps. 84:3), and they were sold in the marketplaces as inexpensive food for the poor. Jesus uses them as a symbol for something of minimal value, indicating that if God cares even for sparrows, how much more God will care for humans (Matt. 10:29, 31; Luke 12:6, 7).   M.A.P.

speaking in tongues. *See* tongues, speaking in.

spear, a close-range weapon composed of a long wooden shaft on which was mounted a shorter, pointed blade (i.e., spearhead). During the biblical period, the spearhead was usually made of bronze or iron and attached to the shaft in various ways. Through most of the spear's early history, a blade was inserted into the end of a split shaft, and the juncture was tightly bound. By the middle of the second millennium BCE, the socketed spearhead became almost universal. Artistic representations and excavated examples demonstrate that spearheads were made in different sizes and shapes (e.g., leaf-shaped, triangular, and barbed blades). Since the spear was a major weapon in most ancient

Warrior holding a spear with a triangular spearhead; from a Moabite stele, second millennium BCE.

armies, metallurgical advancements were quickly adapted for the production of stronger and more effective spearheads.

The NRSV uses "spear" to translate several words in the Hebrew Bible; some distinction is made, however, since one of these Hebrew terms (*kidon*) is more frequently rendered "javelin" in the English text (see passages where both weapons are named, e.g., 1 Sam. 17:6–7, 45; Job 39:23; 41:16; Ps. 35:3). Although these two weapons were similar in form, they served different functions in combat. The spear was used primarily for thrusting or stabbing (Num. 25:7–8; 1 Sam. 26:8; 2 Sam. 23:8, 18, 21, as opposed to 1 Sam. 18:11; 19:10; 20:33), but the lighter, shorter javelin was a medium-range weapon designed for throwing.

Although it is not so frequently mentioned as the sword, the spear was a well-known weapon in the biblical period. Deborah lamented the lack of spears in her army (Judg. 5:8; cf. 1 Sam. 13:19–22), thereby acknowledging their importance. To emphasize his trust in God, David belittled Goliath's dependence upon sword, spear, and javelin (1 Sam. 17:45–47). Since spear and shield complemented each other in hand-to-hand combat, they are often mentioned together (2 Kings 11:10; 1 Chron. 12:8; 2 Chron. 11:12; 14:8). Indeed, one's ability "to handle spear and shield" made one "fit for war" (2 Chron. 25:5). Naturally, giants carried very large spears (1 Sam. 17:7; 2 Sam. 21:16). The only reference to a spear in the NT is in John 19:34, where a spear is thrust into the crucified Jesus's body to determine if he has died. The two hundred "spearmen" who escorted Paul to Antipatris (Acts 23:23) might have been javelin throwers.

Figurative references to the spear are rare but potent (Pss. 35:3; 46:9; 57:4). The prophets speak about the future age of peace as a day in which spears would be converted into pruning hooks (Isa. 2:4; Mic. 4:3; cf. Joel 3:10, where the opposite process was envisioned). *See also* soldier; war; weapons.   G.L.M.

speck, a small fragment of chaff, fiber, wood, etc. Wis. 11:22 says that the whole world is like a speck to God. Jesus criticizes judgmental tendencies when he asks, "Why do you see the speck in your neighbor's eye, but do not notice the log in your own eye?" (Matt. 7:3; cf. 7:4–5; Luke 6:41–42).

spelt, a variety of wheat generally known as *Triticum dicoccoides* or more specifically *Triticum aestivum spelta*. In biblical usage it refers to a crop that survived the hail plague because of late germination (Exod. 9:32), a crop used to border the field (Isa. 28:25), and an ingredient for bread (Ezek. 4:9).

spices, salves, perfumes, or aromatic oils. Spices were part of the luxury trade of the ancient world; a "balm," resin of *Pistacia mutica*, was among the gifts sent to Joseph (Gen. 43:11). Balsam oil or perfume in general appears in the catalogue of wealth that flows through Tyre (Ezek. 27:22).

Spices were used in the anointing oil, perhaps a balsam oil (Exod. 35:28; 1 Kings 10:2). "Spices" may also refer to a sweet-smelling cinnamon or a sweet cane (Exod. 30:23). Aromatic oils and perfumes were used for embalming and anointing a corpse (Mark 16:1; Luke 23:56; John 19:40).   P.P.

spies. In the Hebrew Bible, spies are involved in three complexes of material: the dispatch of twelve spies by Moses to reconnoiter the land of Canaan (Num. 13–14; Deut. 1:19–46); the sending of two spies to Jericho by Joshua (Josh. 2); and the mission of the five spies sent to Laish as part of the Danite migration to the north (Judg. 18). All of these occur in narrative contexts prior to the establishment of the monarchy and evince a common theme—Israel's possession of the land God has promised them. The usual form of the spy story includes the selection and dispatch of the spies, their return and report, the announcement that God has given the reconnoitered land to Israel, and the report of the subsequent invasion and conquest. In a very different context, Judas Maccabeus sends men to spy out the enemy during the Hasmonean-led war for independence (1 Macc. 5:38). In the NT, Paul complains that when he first presented his gospel in Jerusalem, false believers were brought in secretly and "slipped in to spy on the freedom we have in Christ Jesus, so that they might enslave us" (Gal. 2:4).   J.S.K./M.A.P.

spinning and weaving, the arts of producing yarn and cloth from fibers of various kinds. Spinning and weaving were traditionally women's arts in the ancient Near East and Greco-Roman world. The distaff represented the female domain, and portraits of noblewomen with spindle in hand show that spinning was common to all classes of women. The woman praised in Prov. 31 "seeks wool and flax and works with willing hands. . . . She puts her hands to the distaff and her hands hold the spindle" (31:13, 19). She is said to clothe her family and also to produce goods for the market (31:21–24). The women of Israel spun the wool, flax, and goats' hair for the tabernacle hangings and coverings (Exod. 35:25–26). Before Josiah's reforms women wove vestments in the temple for

Woman spinning; stone relief, seventh century BCE.

the Asherah cult figure (2 Kings 23:7). Delilah wove Samson's locks in her loom (Judg. 16:13–14).

Textile production was an important industry of both palace and temple in ancient Syria and Mesopotamia, often employing slave labor. Ebla (in modern Syria) was the center of a far-reaching textile trade (ca. 2300 BCE), and Phoenician weaving and dyeing were renowned. Early Egyptian models recovered from tombs show workrooms with women engaged in various operations of cloth production. Men appear as weavers in later texts, working in government factories or at home looms under contract.

Wool and flax were the common textile fibers of the Near East, Mesopotamia, and Greece, while goats' hair was used for tent fabrics, coarse mantles, and sackcloth. Wool was often dyed to produce patterned weaves, including intricate tapestries. Linen, the main textile of Egypt, was usually left white, since it was difficult to dye. Cotton was not used in the Near East until Hellenistic times.

The fiber was prepared for spinning by washing, retting (soaking to separate out the flax), and carding to produce a fluffy mass. It was then secured on a hooked stick (distaff) held under the spinner's left arm and wisps of fiber were drawn out in a continuous strand as they were spun or a lightly twisted rope (rove) was formed with the fingers and coiled in a pot or basket. The drawn-out fibers were attached to a spindle, with which they were twisted and attenuated into a strong thin yarn. The spindle was a rod, 9 to 15 inches long and tapered at both ends, with a notch or hook at one end to catch the yarn and a perforated disk (whorl) of stone, bone, or pottery to weigh it down and steady its rotation. The spindle was twirled in the hand or hands, rolled against the thigh, or suspended after being set in motion. As a length of thread was formed, it was wound onto the spindle and the process was repeated.

Weaving was done by intersecting one set of threads (the warp), attached to a loom, with a running thread or threads (the weft or woof). Several types of looms were used in biblical times. In early times, the common loom consisted of two vertical beams fixed into the ground with a horizontal beam attached at the top (cf. Samson's spear, which was "like a weaver's beam," 1 Sam. 17:7). The warp threads were hung from the crossbeam and secured in bunches with small clay or stone weights. In later times, a lower crossbeam was introduced, and the web was woven up, rather than down as in the warp-weighted loom. The ancient Egyptians used a horizontal loom consisting of two beams held by pegs in the ground, with the warp stretched between them.

The weft was drawn by a shuttle through a "shed" created by separating the warp threads into two series by means of a heddle (today called a warping stick). After each passage of the shuttle the new thread was pressed firmly into the growing fabric with a sword-shaped beater (batten), pin, or (later) comb. Patterns were made by adding or alternating different colors of yarn and by changing the interlacing of warp and weft. Gold and silver "thread" was also used (Exod. 39:3). Simple garments were commonly woven in one piece (cf. Jesus's seamless tunic, John 19:23). Tassels were formed at the lower corners (Num. 15:38) from the free warps left when the garment was cut from the loom (Isa. 38:12). *See also* Asherah; linen; pin; tabernacle; wool.   P.A.B.

spirit. *See* flesh and spirit; Holy Spirit; soul.

Spirit, Holy. *See* Holy Spirit.

Spirit of God. *See* Holy Spirit.

spirits, evil. *See* demon; devil.

spiritual gifts, a concept present only in the NT, primarily in the Pauline Letters, although the idea of being empowered by the Holy Spirit for particular tasks is by no means alien to the Hebrew Bible (e.g., Judg. 3:10; Num. 11:29). Various Greek terms are employed for spiritual gifts, but the most notable are *ta pneumatika,* which emphasizes the spiritual origin of the gifts (*pneuma* means "spirit"; see 1 Cor. 14:1), and *ta charismata,* which emphasizes that they are bestowed as an act of divine grace (*charis* means "grace"; see Rom. 12:6). In distinction from the "fruit of the Spirit," which all Christians are to manifest without variation (Gal. 5:22–23), the gifts of the Spirit are understood to vary from one believer to another (Rom. 12:6; 1 Cor. 12:4–11; cf. 1 Pet. 4:10).

In the letters of undisputed Pauline authorship, there are four separate listings of the Spirit's gifts (Rom. 12:6–8; 1 Cor. 12:8–10; 12:28; 12:29–30), but since no two of the lists are identical, it seems clear that no list is intended to be definitive. The various gifts may be grouped under three general headings: *gifts of utterance* include prophecy (Rom. 12:6; 1 Cor. 12:10, 28; cf. 12:8; 14:6), the ability to distinguish between true and false prophecy (1 Cor. 12:10; cf. 14:29; 1 Thess. 5:19–21); instruction (Rom. 12:7; 1 Cor. 12:28; cf. 14:6); speaking in tongues (1 Cor. 12:10, 28; cf. 14:1–19); and the ability to interpret speaking in tongues (1 Cor. 12:10, 30; cf. 14:5, 13); *gifts of practical ministry* include caring for the needy (Rom. 12:7–8), forms of assistance (1 Cor. 12:28), and leadership (Rom. 12:8; 1 Cor. 12:28); *gifts of wonder-working faith* include healing (1 Cor. 12:9, 28) and performing miracles (12:10, 28). The gift of apostleship, ranked first in 12:28, is active in all three ways: in the ministry of the word (e.g., 1:17; 4:17), in pastoral care (e.g., Rom. 15:25–29; Philemon), and in the working of miracles (e.g., 2 Cor. 12:12; Gal. 3:5). Additional lists of gifts found in Eph. 4:11 and 1 Pet. 4:10–11 refer only to intelligible utterance and practical ministry (not speaking in tongues or miracle working).

Responding to disruptions caused by speaking in tongues in his Corinthian congregation, Paul emphasized that every believer is graced by some gift and that all gifts are bestowed by "the same Spirit" (1 Cor. 12:4–11). Nevertheless, since their purpose is to serve the "common good" (12:7), he concluded that prophecy, intelligible to all, is to be preferred to speaking in tongues, intelligible only to God (unless there is an interpreter; 1 Cor. 14:1–5). *See also* apostle; Corinthians, First Letter of Paul to the; Holy Spirit; miracles; Paul; prophet; teaching; tongues, speaking in.   V.P.F.

spitting. *See* gestures, postures, and facial expressions.

sponge, the porous skeleton of marine animals, whose fibrous connective structure has water-retaining properties that make it useful for bathing. The Gospels report that Jesus was offered a sponge soaked in wine vinegar to drink on the cross (Matt. 27:48; Mark 15:36; John 19:29).

springs. *See* En-gannim; En-gedi; En-rogel; Gihon; Jericho; Siloam Inscription; water.

squad, the English translation of a Greek word designating a group of four soldiers. It is found in Acts 12:4 (cf. John 19:23), where Peter was placed in the custody of four such groups, one for each of the three-hour night watches. Normally, one squad would be sufficient, one person standing guard on each of the watches while the other three slept. Apparently Peter was thought to need especially careful guarding. *See also* guard, bodyguard; prison; soldier.

Stachys (stay′kis), a Christian who received a special greeting from Paul (Rom. 16:9).

stacte (stak′tee), an ingredient to be used in preparing incense (Exod. 30:34; Sir. 24:15). The meaning of the Hebrew root *nataph,* "to drip" or "ooze," has led some to identify it as the sap of the storax tree, *Styrax officinalis,* or the opobalsamum tree, *Commiphora opobalsamum.*

staff. *See* rod.

stairs. Most references to stairs in the Bible are related to the temple built by Solomon, which had stairs to both the second and third stories (1 Kings 6:8). Repairs were made in Jerusalem in postexilic times, using the stairs down from the "City of David" as a zone marker for repair responsibility (Neh. 3:15; see also 12:37). Special stairs for Levites are mentioned in Neh. 9:4. In Ezekiel's vision of the temple the inner court vestibule facing the outer court had a stairway of eight steps on the south, east, and north sides (40:31, 34, 37). In his vision, access to the second and third stories was by a single stairway on the side (41:7).

Stairs were part of normal temple access in Roman architecture, in many instances using the foundation platform as a step or steps (Jerash, Baalbek, Petra, Pergamum). The same was true of the earlier Greek temples. Cities frequently cut elaborate stairways to ensure access to the water supply (Gezer, Megiddo, Gibeon). The Nabateans were noted for building inside and outside stairways in both their public and private buildings. A spectacular example of an ancient staircase is the interior stairs in the great pyramid of Cheops at Giza.   R.S.B.

stall, normally a space for one animal within a stable or barn, but the Bible sometimes uses the term for what would now be called a pen. In Amos 6:4 the "calves from the midst of the stall" reflects the still common practice of isolating animals for special preslaughter fattening, or "finishing." Mal. 4:2 reports the typical exuberance of young animals released from their pen into open pasture. More traditional individual pens may be specified in 1 Kings 4:20, citing Solomon's forty thousand stalls of horses (2 Chron. 9:25), but 2 Chron. 32:28 and Hab. 3:17 may refer to group pens.   R.S.B.

stars. In modern times, the sun is considered a star, but in the ancient world and in the Bible the sun, moon, and stars were distinguished (Gen. 1:16). Moreover, though planets are not considered stars today, biblical writers did consider them such. The "Day Star, son of Dawn" (Isa. 14:12), was most likely Venus, and "the star of your god Rephan" (Acts 7:43) was probably Saturn. The Bible often expresses wonder at the stars as part of the magnificence of God's creation, with particular attention to their quantity: no one can count them (Gen. 15:5; 22:17; 26:4).

In the ancient Near East, the stars were regarded as supernatural beings (divinities) affecting human destiny. The same was true in Greek and Roman culture, particularly after the time of Alexander the Great (fourth century BCE). In the Bible, however, the stars are not thought of as divinities; rather, the stars and constellations were created by God (Gen. 1:16; Pss. 8:3; 136:9; Job 9:9; Amos 5:8). God named them (Ps. 147:4; Isa. 40:26) and set them in their courses (Jer. 31:35; Job 9:7). There is nevertheless evidence that star worship was practiced. Amos condemned it in the northern kingdom in the eighth century BCE (Amos 5:26). Star worship was also introduced in the southern kingdom during the reign of Manasseh (687/6–642 BCE; 2 Kings 21:3–5), but was subsequently suppressed by Josiah (640–609 BCE; 2 Kings 23:4–14). The book of Deuteronomy, which played a major role in Josiah's reform ca. 622 BCE, condemns star worship (4:19; 17:2–5).

Astrology sought to predict coming events through observing the courses of the stars and planets. Although a handful of biblical passages also imply that stars and planets influence human events (Job 38:33; cf. Judg. 5:20), the practice of astrology is routinely rejected as a foreign influence (Jer. 10:2). A lament over Babylonia refers to Babylonian astrologers "who divide the heavens, who gaze at the stars, who at the new moons predict what shall befall you" (Isa. 47:13).

Stars are sometimes associated with angels in the Bible (Job 38:7), though it is not clear whether this was intended as a literal identification. The seven stars of Rev. 1:20 seem to be the seven angels of the churches that receive messages in Rev. 2–3. The star that led the magi in Matt. 2:1–12 is sometimes thought to have been an angel, since it goes before them and stops over the very house where Jesus was.

Stars are also associated with apocalyptic signs attending the end times. When the end comes, stars will fall from the heavens (Mark 13:25; Luke 21:25; cf. Dan. 8:10; Rev. 6:12–13; 8:10, 12; 12:1, 4). The righteous who are granted eternal life will shine like the stars forever (Dan. 12:3; cf. Matt. 13:43). *See also* astrologer; moon; sun.

                     A.J.H./M.A.P.

stater (stay′tuhr), a Greek silver coin worth about four drachmas, equal to wages for four days' work. The stater in Matt. 17:27 (NRSV: "coin") was probably the heavier stater from the mint at Tyre accepted by Jews as a holy shekel. *See also* money.

stealing. *See* robbery.

stele (stee′lee), **stela** (stee′luh; Gk., "standing stone"; pl. stelae), an upright stone slab, usually inscribed, used to commemorate an event, mark a grave, or give a dedication to a deity. Egyptian stelae have been found at several sites in the Near East, including Beth-shan, Timna, and Deir el-Balah. Canaanite stelae are known from Beth-shan, Hazor, and Tell Beit Mirsim. A small piece of an inscribed Hebrew stele was found at

Black limestone stele of Melishipak II, the Cassite king of Babylon; 1200 BCE.

Samaria; this fragment contains only a single word, *'asher* ("who, which"). Several uninscribed stelae were discovered in the Israelite sanctuary at Arad. The most famous stele from the Near East is the Moabite Stone, written ca. 850 BCE on behalf of Mesha, king of Moab, in a language close to Hebrew. This stele, found at Dhiban (biblical Dibon) in 1868, records Mesha's victory over Israel and his building activities at various Moabite sites. *See also* Mesha; Moabite Stone; writing.   J.M.W.

Stephanas (stef'uh-nuhs), the head of a household whose members were Paul's first converts in Corinth (1 Cor. 16:15; cf. 1:16). Apparently he remained loyal to Paul, and when trouble broke out in the Corinthian church he accompanied Fortunatus and Achaicus on a visit to Paul in Ephesus with information about the problems (16:17–18). Some of these problems were also detailed in a letter (7:1), which may have been carried by the trio. They may also have carried the letter known to us as 1 Corinthians back to Corinth. Stephanas is strongly commended by Paul as one worthy of exercising authority in the church (16:16). *See also* Achaicus; Corinth; Corinthians, First Letter of Paul to the; Fortunatus; Paul.   A.J.M.

Stephen (stee'vuhn), a leader in the early Jerusalem church whose story appears in Acts 6:1–8:2. The other references to Stephen in the NT refer to this story (Acts 11:19; 22:20).

According to Acts 6:1–6, a dispute had developed in the Jerusalem church between the "Hellenists" (probably Jewish Christians whose first language was Greek) and the "Hebrews" (Jewish Christians who spoke Hebrew or Aramaic). The dispute concerned daily distributions of food to widows in the community. The apostles did not want to have to take time to deal with such matters, so seven Hellenists were chosen to supervise the distribution and, it would seem, to attend to other matters of community leadership. Stephen was one of these seven Hellenist leaders.

Stephen is portrayed in Acts as a bold man, wise, full of faith, and possessed of the Holy Spirit (6:5, 8, 10). The ecstatic aspect of Stephen's short Christian career is highlighted in the account. It was by the power of the Spirit that Stephen confronted his fellow Hellenists who did not believe in Jesus as Messiah. They, in turn, brought Stephen's activities to the attention of the council of Jewish leaders (6:11–15).

Apparently, the opposition to Stephen was based primarily on a deduction he had made from his messianic faith in Jesus—that, with the vindication of Jesus as Messiah, the religion of the temple had outlived its usefulness and the Mosaic law should now be seen in a new and different light (Acts 6:11–14; cf. Matt. 24:2; Mark 13:2; Luke 21:6). Stephen's opponents recognized that this deduction would undermine the basic legitimacy of the religious practice associated with the temple.

The speech of Stephen in Acts 7:2–53 is presented as Stephen's defense of his position. It can be read as a sample of early Christian apologetic vis-à-vis Hellenistic Judaism. The essential point is that Israel has always been slow to accept any new activity of God. After the promises were given to Abraham (7:2–8), Israel systematically rebelled against the call of its inspired leaders (7:9–43) and was prone to limit the presence and activity of God to local places such as the temple rather than seeing God in crucial historical events such as the resurrection of Jesus in Jerusalem (7:44–53). According to Acts, this message angered Stephen's audience and he was stoned to death (7:54–58).

Although Stephen's speech offers a sample of Christian apologetic, it is almost certainly not intended as a model for such defense of the gospel. Indeed, most interpreters have noted that Stephen's speech makes points that would be at variance with what the author of Luke–Acts believes and presents elsewhere. In particular, Stephen claims that the construction of the temple was a rebellious and ignorant act on the part of people, who did not realize "the Most High does not dwell in houses made with human hands" (Acts 7:48). But the author of Luke–Acts presents Jesus himself as strongly devoted to the temple, which he calls, "my Father's house" (Luke 2:49). The disciples of Jesus also regard the temple as a place where God is to be worshiped (Luke 24:53; Acts 2:46; 3:1).

Nevertheless, Stephen is recognized for his courage, and his death is presented as a noble martyrdom. Indeed, the writer of Acts draws parallels between Stephen's death and that of Jesus, especially with regard to their last words. Jesus says, "Father, forgive them, for they do not know what they are doing" (Luke 24:34), and "Father, into your hands I commend my spirit" (23:46). Stephen says, "Lord, do not hold this sin against them" (Acts 7:60), and "Lord Jesus, receive my spirit" (7:59).

Likewise, the narrative in Acts links the martyrdom of Stephen to the forthcoming ministry of Paul, by mentioning that Saul (i.e., Paul) was present at his stoning, approving of the sentence against Stephen (7:58; cf. 8:1; 22:20). Finally, Acts indicates that Stephen's death ultimately served the purposes of God, because it led to a scattering of his fellow messianic Hellenists, which caused the gospel to be proclaimed elsewhere (8:4). One example of this scattering is related in the mission of Philip in Samaria and elsewhere (8:5–40). *See also* deacon; Hebrews; Hellenists; law; martyr; persecution; temple, the.   A.J.M./M.A.P.

steward, a person who oversees the possessions or interests of an owner or master. Stewardship might involve responsibility for a private household (Gen. 44:1; Luke 12:42; Gal. 4:2), a specific task (1 Chron. 29:6), a palace (Esther 1:8; 1 Kings 18:3; Isa. 36:3; Luke 8:3), business affairs (Matt. 20:8; Luke 16:1–8), or a city treasury (Rom. 16:23). Also, in the NT, the word is used in a metaphorical sense for having responsibility for divine mysteries, such as the gospel (1 Cor. 4:1), a divine commission (1 Cor. 9:17), or a divine gift (1 Pet. 4:10). Bishops or elders are called stewards (Titus 1:5–9) and are expected to possess holy qualities as they manage the household of God. The apostle Paul also saw himself as a steward (1 Cor. 4:1–2) who would have to give an account of his stewardship (4:3–4; cf. 2 Tim. 4:7–8) as the apostle to the Gentiles (Eph. 3:2; Gal. 2:7–8; Rom. 1:5–6; 13–15). There is also a sense in which every Christian is a steward entrusted with a divine gift (1 Pet. 4:10). Faithful and wise stewardship of God's gifts will result in blessing and reward, but unfaithfulness will result in judgment (Luke 12:42–43; Matt. 25:14–30).   R.H.S.

Stoicism (stoh´i-siz-uhm), a philosophical school founded in Athens by Zeno (335–263 BCE). Although the scholars of the school developed theories of physics, cosmology, and logic, it was best known for its emphasis on moral conduct. The school was named for the "Painted Porch," a colonnade (Gk. *stoa*), in which it met at Athens. The Stoics held that the entire universe was a living creature animated by the divine Logos (reason or mind). This Logos was identified with Zeus. Every person was a slave of the ruling Logos.

Since the Logos pervaded everything, whatever happened in the universe was governed by this universal law of nature or providence. All human beings were brothers and sisters in this universal, living body. This imagery was well-suited to the cosmopolitan empires of the period. Since everything that happens to people was determined, the only way in which individuals could control their lives was to control the passions governing how external events affected them. Stoics often claimed that *virtue* was what mattered most in life and that virtue is attainable through acceptance of fate. The person seeking virtue appreciates the logic of the universe and is indifferent to circumstances. A Stoic proverb held, "There is no reason for joy, still less for grief."

In the turbulent world of Roman politics, many leading Romans found the Stoic philosophy to offer consolation and guidance for life. One of the most famous Stoic teachers and writers of the first century, Epictetus, was a lame Phrygian from Hierapolis who had been slave to Nero's freedman Epaphroditus. After gaining freedom, Epictetus lectured to large audiences that they should only be concerned about what was under their control. Epictetus accentuated the moral obligation of virtue, which was to love and respect all people, whose merits and station in life lie beyond their control. Another famous Stoic teacher was Nero's tutor and adviser, Seneca, who retired from the court when Nero's career turned bad and was later forced to commit suicide by the suspicious emperor. In the second century, the emperor Marcus Aurelius, who had studied Epictetus, recorded his meditations while in the field with the army. Stoicism did not hold out hope for life after death, but sought to call

people to identify with the divine reason immanent in the cosmos.

Some Stoic philosophers in Athens discussed Paul's religious views with him (Acts 17:18). Paul also seems to draw on key concepts from Stoic philosophy in some of his letters, particularly the Letter to the Romans. In the first part of that letter he contends that God's invisible nature is discernible through reflection on the natural world (1:20). The idea that certain patterns of behavior are "unnatural" (1:26) also invokes the Stoic tradition of grounding ethics in "natural law," and in 2:15 Paul appeals to "conscience," a word that is never found in the Hebrew Bible, but that figures mightily in Stoic thought (see also 9:1; 13:5; 1 Cor. 8:7, 10, 12; 10:29; 2 Cor. 1:12; 4:2; 5:11).

Stoics are also credited along with Cynics for development of the "diatribe" style of argumentation, which is evident in certain letters of Paul and in the Letter of James. *See also* diatribe. For a comparative chart of philosophical schools, *see* Epicureanism.   P.P.

stone. The main varieties of stone found in the Levant are limestone, sandstone, and the volcanically produced and very hard basalt. These provided for everyday construction needs. Precious and semiprecious stones, however, were frequently imported from various supply points (e.g., turquoise from the Sinai Peninsula). Ore-bearing stone carrying copper and iron was located in the southern reaches of the Levant and in the Transjordan.

Biblical references to stone provide examples of the wide spectrum of uses to which it was put. Stones could serve as memorials, shrines, or pledges (Gen. 28:18–22). They were set up to commemorate significant events (Josh. 4:1–10; 24:26–27) or to mark boundaries (15:6; 18:17). Stone could also serve as a construction material for altars (Exod. 20:25), but idols could be fashioned from stone as well (Ezek. 20:32; Deut. 28:36, 64; 29:17), and stones themselves sometimes became objects of worship (Lev. 26:1). Large stones were used to cover wells (Gen. 29:2–10) and doorways to tombs (Matt. 27:60; Mark 15:46; Luke 11:39). Stone could be worked into bowls, mortars, pestles, sockets for doors, and other implements (Exod. 7:19). Stone jars for water or wine are mentioned in John 2:6–11. Stone was also used as a writing surface for carving such things as a record of binding law (Exod. 24:12), the accomplishments of persons (28:10), or an account of noteworthy events (as with royal stelae). A stone could be used as a seat (17:12) or as a pillow (Gen. 28:18). And stones served as weapons, whether thrown by hand (Exod. 8:26), sling (Judg. 20:16; 1 Sam. 17:49), or catapult. In that capacity, stones were used both in public executions (Lev. 24:14) and by individuals in private fights (Exod. 21:18).

Symbolically, stone stood as the measure of hardness (e.g., for ice, Job 38:30; for the human heart, 41:24). They also symbolized stumbling (Matt. 16:23; cf. Ps. 91:12). Because they sank rapidly in water, stones could be used as symbols for immediate destruction (Exod. 15:5), and their immobility could symbolize death (15:16). The phenomenon of stones crying or shouting out symbolizes the absolute need for such exclamations to be made (Hab. 2:11; Luke 19:40). Another symbolic use of stones is the recurrent idea of fashioning something alive from them: John the Baptist says that God can make children of Abraham from stones (Matt. 3:9). Satan tempts Jesus to "make these stones bread" (4:3). *See also* limestone; stoning.   R.S.B.

stoning, a form of capital punishment. Most of the offenses punished by stoning were crimes against the sovereignty of God. They included blasphemy (Lev. 24:15–16; cf. 1 Kings 21:13; Acts 7:11, 58), incitement to worship other gods (Deut. 13:6–10), worship of other gods (17:2–7), worship of Molech by child sacrifice (Lev. 20:2–5), divination by mediums (20:27), violation of the sabbath (Num. 15:32–36), and violation of the taboo of devoted objects (Josh. 7:25). Stoning is also specified in cases of adultery (Deut. 22:21, 24; cf. John 8:3–7), filial insubordination (Deut. 21:18–21), and homicide by a goring ox (Exod. 21:28–29).

A description of the procedure in judicial stoning may be gleaned from various references. The stoning usually took place outside the city (Lev. 24:14; Num. 15:35; Deut. 17:5; 22:24; 1 Kings 21:13; but cf. Deut. 22:21). The criminal was probably stripped (Ezek. 16:39). The witnesses were the first to cast stones, followed by the entire community (Deut. 13:10; 17:7; cf. John 8:7). Accounts of nonjudicial stoning are recorded in 1 Kings 12:18; 2 Chron. 24:21.

The custom continued into NT times, but there is no sure evidence that it was practiced as an official legal procedure. The book of Acts recounts the stoning of Stephen, who is killed (7:58–60), and of Paul, who is left for dead (14:1–9); Paul mentions the latter incident himself in 2 Cor. 11:25. In both of these cases, however, the stoning is described as more of a spontaneous mob action than the result of a judicial process. John 8:3–11 tells of an occasion when Jesus was asked whether the commandment of Moses requiring the stoning of an adulterous woman should be carried out; he replies, "Let anyone among you who is without sin be the first to throw a stone at her" (8:7). The posing of the question in itself indicates that such a sentence was not automatic. Indeed, Jesus's interlocutors do not actually propose that the woman should be stoned; rather, they seem to be presenting him with a test case for legal interpretation, to determine whether or not he favors strict applications. *See also* law.   B.L.E.

storage, the laying up of supplies for future use. Biblical references to storage focus on the special accommodations of store-cities and storehouses in addition to the routine acts of saving material or, metaphorically, storing up emotions and other human traits.

Store-cities were used in Egypt (Exod. 1:11), where Israelites helped build them. Solomon's construction program included store-cities (1 Kings 9:19; 2 Chron. 8:4–6) in addition to fortifications and other facilities. Store-cities in Naphtali were captured by Ben-hadad of Syria during his invasion of Israel at the time of King Baasha (900–877 BCE; 2 Chron. 16:4). Jehoshaphat built store-cities in Judah during his rule (873–849 BCE; 2 Chron. 17:12). In each of these cases it is likely that the facilities were intended to cache military goods in addition to economic supplies.

We also read of storehouses, which required assigned gatekeepers and watchers (1 Chron. 26:15). Stores could be carried off as booty of war (Isa. 39:6). Royal storehouses could provide equipment for rescuing a person in trouble (Jer. 38:11–13) or supply food in times of famine (Gen. 41:56); empty storehouses at such times were a disaster (Joel 1:17). The temple storehouse retained the tithes of the people (Mal. 3:10), and storehouses were regular parts of the postexilic temple facility (Neh. 10:38). Storehouses were also coupled with barns as routine equipment for rich people (Luke 12:16–19; cf. 12:24). As for materials kept in storage, references include edible food (Gen. 6:21); crops (Luke 12:17); grain (Gen. 41:49); wine (2 Chron. 11:11, 32:28); wheat, barley, and oil (Jer. 41:8); and iron (1 Chron. 22:3). People also stored documents (Ezra 6:1); silver, gold, and sacred vessels (2 Chron. 5:1); and baggage (Isa. 10:28).

According to popular cosmology, God's storehouses held the wind (Ps. 135:7; Jer. 10:13; 51:16), snow and hail (Job 38:22), and the ocean (Ps. 33:7). The very heavens and earth could be stored for the eschatological fire that would judge "the godless" (2 Pet. 3:7). And in a metaphorical sense, people could store up sin (Hos. 13:12), violence (Amos 3:10), and wrath (Rom. 2:5) for days to come, or they could store up wisdom (Prov. 2:7).

Archaeological evidence shows that storage containers ranged from modest jars, bowls, and perfume juglets to large jars. Silver tetradrachmas were found in a jug at Shechem, and Islamic coins in a lamp at Hesban. Jars held some of the Dead Sea Scrolls, and a small juglet retained some dried ink in the desk of the scriptorium at Qumran. Storage chambers varied from dry and wet pits or cisterns, to caves, to elaborate buildings such as those found at the Hittite capital of Boghazkoi, Masada, and Shechem (where the Late Bronze Age temple was adapted for storage in the Iron Age). Some storage chambers could be entered only by ladders, and subterranean storage pits were frequently sealed with stone lids. Material could be stored on house roofs as well.   R.S.B.

stork, a large wading bird. The Hebrew word usually translated as "stork" (*khasidah*) could also appropriately be translated "heron." Two species of stork migrate through the Levant in spring: the white stork (*Ciconia ciconia*) and, less frequently to be seen, the black stork (*Ciconia nigra*). Jer. 8:7 probably refers to the seasonal appearance of the stork, whereas Ps. 104:17 ("has her home in the fir trees") enigmatically refers to storks once nesting in Lebanon. Zech. 5:9 compares the wings of angels to those of a stork, although the stork was considered an unclean animal (Lev. 11:19; Deut. 14:18).   I.U.K.

stove. *See* oven.

stranger. *See* alien.

strangled animals. According to Mosiac law, the flesh of animals killed by strangulation could not be eaten; the Torah calls for slitting the throat and draining the blood. This law also applied to meat eaten by Gentiles who lived among Jews (Lev. 17:10–14). In Acts 15:20, Gentile Christians were enjoined not to eat meat from strangled animals. The motivation for the latter prohibition is not clear. Perhaps it had to do with the partaking of meals in pagan temples, or perhaps it was to help facilitate table fellowship between Gentile and Jewish Christians. In any case, the prohibition of strangled animals among Christians is not mentioned anywhere in the NT except Acts 15:20, and there is no indication that it was in effect for any of the churches to which the Pauline and other letters in the NT were written.

straw, the dried parts of grasses or herbaceous plants often used as fodder for animals (1 Kings 4:28; Gen. 24:25, 32). Straw is also a by-product of the processing of cultivated cereals, either the stubble of the cut grain left in the fields for herds to graze over or the chaff separated from the threshed grain by winnowing (Pss. 1:4; 83:13). In addition to being used as animal food, straw was used as a binder for mud-bricks (Exod. 5:7–18), as a covering for dung (Isa. 25:10) and, when mixed with animal dung, as an efficient fuel for kitchen hearths (Isa. 25:10). Metaphorically, Job 21:28 says that the wicked are often "like straw before the wind," and Nah. 1:10 says that they are "consumed like straw." The great monster Leviathan "counts iron as straw" (Job 41:27). Paradise is imagined as a time when the lion will eat straw like an ox (Isa. 11:7; 65:25). Jeremiah quotes a proverb, "What has straw in common with wheat?" which, judging from the context, might have been intended to contrast worthless and worthwhile things (23:28). *See also* chaff.   M.A.P.

stripes, wounds inflicted by beating with a whip or rods. The NRSV uses the word only in Exod. 21:25, a passage that refers to the punishment of slaves. In other English translations, however, the term is used prominently in Isa. 53:5: "with his stripes, we are healed" (KJV, RSV, JPS; NRSV: "by his bruises we are healed"). The passage refers to the "suffering servant," whom the prophet sees either as a role to be filled by Israel or as one who suffers on behalf of Israel. In 1 Pet. 2:24, this verse is applied to Jesus. *See also* scourge; servant.

stumbling block, any obstacle that may cause someone's downfall, whether literal (Lev. 19:14) or figurative (Matt. 16:23). In Ezekiel the stumbling block is idolatry (e.g., 14:3–4, 7), while in Jer. 6:21 it is left unspecified. According to Isa. 8:14–15, the disobedient stumble over God, and in the NT this thought is applied to the unbelievers who stumble over Christ (Rom. 9:32–33; 1 Pet. 2:8). Paul specifically calls Christ's death a stumbling block, or offense (Gk. *skandalon*), to the world (1 Cor. 1:23; Gal. 5:11), but he also warns that believers who flaunt their newfound freedom in Christ may place a stumbling block (*proskomma*) or hindrance (*skandalon*) in the way of others who do not share their knowledge (Rom. 14:13; 1 Cor. 8:9). Peter became a stumbling block to Jesus when he sought to dissuade him from going to the cross (Matt. 16:21–23). *See also* liberation; rock; snare; stone.   V.P.F.

Succoth (suhk'uhth; Heb., "booths," "tents," or "temporary dwellings").
1 A town in the Jordan Valley on the "Way of the Plain" (2 Sam. 18:23), which connected it with such towns as Adam, Zarethan, and Pella, and on a major route from the central Levant to the Transjordan. Jacob returned from the east to Shechem by way of Succoth after his meeting with Esau (Gen. 33:17). Josh. 13:27 places it in Gad, although its previous control by Sihon, king of Heshbon (Hesban), would locate it farther south, near Medeba on the plateau. When Gideon was driving the Midianites out of Esdraelon to their homeland in eastern Transjordan, he asked the inhabitants of Succoth to give nourishment to his three hundred warriors. Perhaps because they feared reprisals from the Midianites, they refused him scornfully, for which he meted out brutal punishment on Succoth after his victory over the Midianites (Judg. 8:5–16).

The final biblical mention of Succoth concerns the bronze vessels to be used in the temple, which Solomon had cast "in the clay ground between Succoth and Zarethan" (1 Kings 7:46; 2 Chron. 4:17, which has "Zeredah" in place of "Zarethan"). Two parallel passages in the Psalms (60:6; 108:7) celebrate the conquest of the "Vale of Succoth" as well as the territory of Shechem, and, in the following verses, the whole of Transjordan. This celebration evidently belongs to the period of the united monarchy (ca. 1025–922 BCE) and probably to the reign of Solomon rather than that of David, who would have discouraged any idea of "conquering" Shechem.

Taken together, these passages indicate that Succoth was a place of considerable importance, fairly close to the east bank of the Jordan, where there was a ford giving access to both Shechem and Esdraelon, and with easy access to the Transjordan plateau. Unfortunately, neither Succoth itself nor the neighboring towns of Zarethan and Penuel can be identified with any certainty. At present the weight of scholarly opinion seems to favor Tell Deir 'Alla for Succoth, about two miles north of the Jabbok (modern Zerqa); for Zarethan perhaps Tell es-Saʻidiyeh, about two miles farther north; and for Penuel, Tulul edh-Dhahab, one and a half miles up the Jabbok. Some scholars, however, prefer to identify Tell Deir ʻAlla with biblical Gilgal.

In any case, Tell Deir ʻAlla (possibly Succoth) was first occupied in the Late Bronze Age (ca. 1500 BCE) and was evidently at that time an important sanctuary, but it was destroyed by an earthquake at the beginning of the twelfth century. Subsequently itinerant metalworkers occupied the tell in the twelfth century, and they were followed in the period of the united monarchy by new immigrants from farther east, who built a small walled town on the tell. This was captured by Pharaoh Shishak of Egypt during the reign of Jeroboam I of Israel (ca. 926–907 BCE). Deserted for a considerable period, it was reoccupied and the sanctuary rebuilt in the seventh century BCE, but it was once more destroyed at some point in the Persian period and not reoccupied until the Middle Ages.

2 The first stopping place on the exodus route (Exod. 12:37; Num. 33:5–6), often identified with Tel el-Mashkutah, on the eastern edge of the Nile Delta; but this now seems very dubious. The name may perhaps indicate a merely temporary encampment.   D.B.

Succoth-benoth (suhkʼuhth-beeʼnoth; Heb., "booths of daughters"), the name of a god worshiped in Samaria by the Babylonians who had been brought there under Assyria's policy of population displacement. In order to keep conquered areas pacified, Assyria deported native populations and replaced them with foreigners. The policy was implemented when the northern kingdom, Israel, fell to Assyria ca. 722/1 BCE. As a result, 2 Kings 17:29–30 reports that the people of Babylon made images of Succoth-benoth and placed them in shrines located at high places throughout Samaria.

suffering. In the Bible, suffering takes many forms: physical pain, frustrated hopes, depression, isolation, loneliness, grief, anxiety, spiritual crises, and more. The biblical peoples struggled with the presence of suffering and sought ways to understand and cope with it in view of their belief in God's power and goodness. The biblical responses to suffering can be divided into five categories.

The Result of Human Sin: The most common way to understand the presence of suffering in the world is to say that it is the fault of human disobedience. The first three chapters of Genesis state that the world was intended to be a good place, but that the disobedience of the man and woman (with help from the snake) introduced suffering into the world (as demonstrated by the curses in 3:14–19). No longer is the world the way God wanted it to be. All descendants of the first parents now live in a world where there is potential for disaster, and all are vulnerable to the possibility of suffering in

their lives. The mere fact of being human and living in a world where people hurt each other and themselves can thus account for much of what is called suffering.

Other biblical texts push the idea of cause and effect between human sin and human suffering a bit farther. Historians and prophets interpret the meaning of specific calamities in Israel's history. In the time of the judges, all went well for the people when they were obedient to God, but when they turned against God, the Almighty would raise up an enemy to punish them. When they finally cried out to God in desperation, God would raise up a judge to fight on their side and restore their good fortunes. Thus, the ups and downs of Israel's history can be explained (says the Deuteronomistic Historian in Judges—2 Kings) as rewards for fidelity or punishment for idolatry. Similarly, the great catastrophe of the exile was seen as a fit retribution for all of Israel's and Judah's failings (see esp. 2 Kings 17). Such a calamity would not have occurred if God had not allowed it, and God would not have allowed it if it were not just; therefore, the people deserved it.

Such a view, however, does not necessarily imply just retribution in each individual life. Good people as well as evil people suffered and died in the defeat by the Babylonians. Some texts, however, go even farther to indicate that just retribution even for individuals is possible. Ezek. 18 argues that God will deal with each individual, rewarding or punishing every person according to his or her deeds and not because of what their parents (or the nation) might have done. Many of the Proverbs also imply that the one who leads a good life will be more successful and less likely to suffer than the one who defies God. Job's counselors were convinced that a good God would not have allowed such horrible misfortune to have befallen Job, if he had not done something to deserve it. Though Job seemed to be innocent, he must have had a secret sin of which he needed to repent before his good fortunes would return.

This theory of suffering is also critiqued within the Bible. The book of Job shows that his counselors are actually wrong; Job was an innocent sufferer, just as he had said. In Luke 13:1–5 and John 9:1–3, Jesus indicates the mistake of interpreting each example of suffering as if it is the consequence of someone's sins. And from the apocalyptic perspective of many NT books, the righteous are actually more likely to suffer than the evil. So Jesus warns his listeners that if they follow him, they should be prepared to take up their crosses (Mark 8:34–35).

Suffering That Leads to Greater Good: Although suffering is by definition a very undesirable experience, the Bible sometimes indicates that it may lead to some greater good. First, suffering may be of benefit to other people. Joseph suffered greatly at the hands of his brothers, who sold him into slavery. At the end of his life, however, Joseph looked back and saw that many people had benefited because of his suffering (Gen. 50:15–21).

He ended up in the right place to prepare for the famine, and thus God used the wickedness of Joseph's brothers and the suffering of Joseph himself to bring about the salvation of the Israelite ancestors. NT authors likewise believe that the suffering of Jesus Christ is somehow of benefit to all humanity; the suffering of one can, and did, benefit the many (cf. Mark 10:45).

In another sense, the Bible suggests that suffering may also be of benefit to the person who suffers. This point is usually established by viewing adversity or trouble as a test through which the person learns something or improves in character. Eliphaz (Job 5:17) and Elihu (33:15–18; 36:8–12) suggest this possibility to Job. Prov. 3:11–12 likens suffering to the discipline meted out by a loving parent, an idea picked up and expanded by the author of Hebrews (12:3–11). In Rom. 5:1–5, Paul tells his readers to rejoice in their suffering, because it will help produce endurance and character and hope in them. First Peter 1:6–7 uses the analogy of a refiner's fire, suggesting that the genuineness of one's faith is purified by various trials. James tells his readers that whenever they experience trials of any kind, they should "consider it nothing but joy, because you know that the testing of your faith produces endurance" (1:2–3).

Caused by Cosmic Evil Forces: In the NT, suffering is often ascribed to the presence of demons (Luke 9:38–39), evil spirits (Acts 19:11–12), Satan (Luke 13:16), or the devil (Acts 10:38). Psychological, physical, and spiritual suffering may be caused by these evil forces, so such suffering is not due to human sin, nor should it be viewed as God's execution of justice. This view developed relatively late, during the Second Temple period, and it is not articulated with any clarity in the Hebrew Bible. Satan causes the suffering of Job, but he does so with God's authorization. Certain poetic passages, however, refer to the Sea or a sea monster as a personification of superhuman powers of evil (e.g., Isa. 27:1; 51:9–10; Job 7:12; 26:12). Thus, there is some precedent for the later development of this third option, which is an explanation for suffering that does not blame either God or self. This view is also accompanied by assurances that God will ultimately triumph over all hostile forces that cause suffering (e.g., Rom. 8:35–39).

The Mystery of Suffering: A fourth approach taken in some biblical texts involves recognition that human efforts to explain experiences of suffering are doomed to frustration. Answers may be found that are partially satisfying or that apply to certain cases, but fundamental unanswered questions remain. This is generally the view of Ecclesiastes and, ultimately, of the book of Job. In that book, Job and his friends try out all the best explanations for suffering that their tradition has to offer, but every interpretation offered by the counselors is rejected by Job. When God finally speaks in chaps. 38–41, Job is simply told that human beings cannot comprehend the complex wonders of the created order, let alone the mysteries of human suffering.

Lament: Other biblical texts ignore the question of why there is suffering and try, rather, to offer ways for people to cope with the immediate experience. The biblical laments are often said to address, not the "why" questions, but the "how" questions. How can one survive? How can one get through the long nights of pain, the months of loneliness without the loved one, the weeks and months when despair hangs like a heavy weight around one's neck? The laments (e.g., Pss. 3; 5; 10; 17; 38) provide a biblical resource that helps sufferers to keep praying to God even when they are angry with God, doubtful of God's intentions, or uncertain of where God might be found. They also remove the aspect of isolation, letting people know that others have traveled this way before—even great heroes of the faith like David and Jeremiah—and that these persons have had thoughts and feelings similar to their own. Furthermore, there is repeated assurance from biblical writers that God will hear the prayers of those who cry out for help and comfort (e.g., Pss. 65:2; 66:16–20; 102:1–2, 17; Mark 11:24; 2 Cor. 1:8–11; Phil. 1:19–20). *See also* apocalyptic literature; demon; devil; evil; Job, book of; prayer; providence; Satan; sin.

Bibliography

Crenshaw, James L., ed. *Theodicy in the Old Testament.* Fortress, 1983.

Gerstenberger, Erhard S., and Wolfgang Schrage. *Suffering.* Abingdon, 1980.

Simundson, Daniel J. *Faith Under Fire: Biblical Interpretations of Suffering.* Augsburg, 1980.

D.J.S.

Sukkoth (suhk´uhth). *See* Tabernacles, Festival of.

sulfur, a greenish-yellow nonmetallic substance that is highly flammable. It is used in the modern manufacturing of matches and gunpowder. Sulfur is associated with divine punishment, such as when God rained sulfur and fire from the heavens upon Sodom and Gomorrah (Gen. 19:24; cf. Deut. 29:23; Luke 17:29). This particular act of judgment is taken as a template for the wrath to be executed upon the wicked in general. Ps. 11:6 says that God will "rain coals of fire and sulfur" upon the wicked; Ezek. 38:22 says the Lord will do this to the armies of Gog; and Isa. 34:9 indicates that even the soil of the garden of Eden will be turned to sulfur. The book of Revelation speaks of horses who breathe fire and sulfur (9:17–18) and describes a lake of fire and sulfur into which the devil and other adversaries of God will eventually be cast (19:20; 20:10; 21:8; cf. 14:10). Sulfur is referred to as "brimstone" in the KJV. *See also* fire; hell; Sodom.   M.A.P.

Sumer (soo´muhr), an ancient civilization situated in the alluvial plain between the Tigris and Euphrates rivers in the southern part of what is now Iraq. The Sumerians developed the first major civilization of the ancient Near East. Together with Akkad, its neighbor to the north, the country was later known as Babylonia. Major cities of

Sumer included Ur (the birthplace of Abraham, Gen. 11:26–32), Uruk (biblical Erech), Lagash, Nippur, Shuruppak, Eridu, Kish, and Eshnunna. Archaeological excavation of these cities and others has yielded a wealth of information on the culture, history, literature, and religion of Sumer, providing important material for understanding the cultural context of the ancient Near East and the Bible.

The Sumerians were not the original inhabitants of the Tigris-Euphrates plain. They entered the plain approximately 3300 BCE, displacing the native population known to scholars as Ubayids. The Sumerians' original homeland is uncertain, although their non-Semitic, agglutinative language, like that of the Turkic peoples, suggests south-central Asia as a possibility.

Originally, Sumer consisted of a number of city-states, each with its own protective god. Political power was held by the free citizens of the city and a governor, called *ensi*. But as the city-states vied with one another for power and as pressures from outside invaders increased, the institution of kingship (Sumerian *lugal*, "big man") emerged, whereby the ruler of one city-state dominated others.

The first known king of Sumer is Etana of Kish (ca. 3000 BCE). He is described as the "man who stabilized all the lands." His descendant, Enmebarragesi, built a temple in Nippur to Enlil, god of the air and chief of the Sumerian pantheon. This established Nippur as the leading cultural and religious center of all Sumer.

Kish eventually lost its power as the kings of Uruk, Lagash, and other cities established their hegemony over the region. Conflict among the city-states so weakened the country that by 2360 BCE a Semitic king, Sargon I of Agade (biblical Akkad), was able to conquer Sumer. During the rule of the kings of Agade (2360–2180 BCE),

the region became known as Sumer-Akkad, and Akkadian, the Semitic language of Akkad, began to replace the Sumerian language. Sargon's grandson, Naram-sin, plundered the temple of Enlil at Nippur. Later Sumerian writers saw Enlil's anger as the cause of an invasion by the Gutians, who overran Naram-sin's empire and destroyed Agade.

After several generations, Sumer began to recover under the leadership of King Gudea of Lagash. After the last of the Gutians were overcome, Ur-nammu founded the Third Dynasty of Ur (2050–1950 BCE), which saw a renaissance of Sumerian culture. The famed ziggurat of Ur, a stepped-pyramid structure with a temple dedicated to the moon god, Nanna-sin, was built during this period. The law code of Ur-nammu is the earliest law code known in history. Later invasion by Amorites and Elamites resulted in the destruction of Ur, and the following centuries saw continuing struggle between the Sumerian city-states. Finally, around 1750 BCE, the Semitic king Hammurabi of Babylon defeated King Rin-sin of Larsa and became the sole ruler of Sumer-Akkad. This marked the end of Sumer and the beginning of Babylonia.

Invention of Cuneiform Writing: Nevertheless, much of Sumerian culture continued to thrive in Babylonia. Perhaps the most important Sumerian contribution to civilization was the invention of cuneiform writing, a wedge-shaped script formed by pressing a reed stylus into wet clay tablets, which were later dried, baked, and stored in libraries. The Babylonians and other surrounding peoples adapted the cuneiform script to their own languages, so that for centuries cuneiform was the dominant mode of writing in ancient Mesopotamia. Most Sumerian tablets contain economic and administrative records, but others include mythology, history, hymns, wisdom texts, law, and much more. Of special interest to students

Shamash, the Akkadian sun god, stepping through the mountains at dawn with rays springing from his shoulders; cylinder seal impression, ca. 2400 BCE.

of the Bible are the aforementioned law code of Ur-nammu, the Sumerian King List, the flood story of Ziusudra, the *Paradise Myth* of Enki and Ninhursag, early forms of the *Epic of Gilgamesh*, and the *Descent of Inanna to the Underworld*.

Sumerian religion included a large number of gods and goddesses identified with the forces of nature. Prominent among them were the four creating gods who controlled the major elements of the universe: An, the sky god; Ki, the earth goddess, later known as Ninhursag; Enlil, the air god and chief of the Sumerian pantheon; and Enki, the god of water and wisdom. Other important deities included Nanna, the moon god; Utu, the sun god; and Utu's daughter Inanna, the evening star, known to the Babylonians as Ishtar. Inanna's husband was the vegetation god, Dumuzi (Babylonian Tammuz). Dumuzi was conceived of as a dying and rising god. During the dry season when nothing grew, he was in the world of the dead. But in Sumerian mythology, Inanna rescued him for six months of the year, during which time the rains came and the earth bloomed. Their reunion was celebrated at the New Year Festival when the king and a priestess assumed the roles of Dumuzi and Inanna in a sexual sacred marriage rite, thus assuring continued fertility and prosperity for the coming year. *See also* Babylon; Mesopotamia.

Bibliography

Kramer, Samuel Noah. *Sumerian Mythology.* Rev. ed. University of Pennsylvania Press, 1972.

————. *The Sumerians: Their History, Culture, and Character.* University of Chicago Press, 1963.

Pritchard, James B. *Ancient Near Eastern Texts Relating to the Old Testament.* 3rd ed. Princeton University Press, 1969.   M.A.S.

sun. The sun was recognized in the Bible as a beneficent source of light and heat (Deut. 33:14) upon which all life depended, but its power to smite was also known and feared (Isa. 49:10; James 1:11). Created and appointed by God to "rule over the day" (Ps. 136:8), it marked the hours and seasons by its movements (Gen. 1:14–16), and it marked directions by its rising and setting (Isa. 45:6; Deut. 11:30). It surveyed the whole earth from its heavenly course (Ps. 19:6), marking all that occurred below as existence "under the sun" (Eccles. 1:3, 9). It traversed its course like a runner (Ps. 19:4–5) or as drawn by horses and chariot (2 Kings 23:11). It was resplendent as a bridegroom (Ps. 19:5) and as enduring as the ages (72:17). Surrounding peoples worshiped the sun (Babylonian Shamash; Egyptian Re, Aton) and place-names like Beth-shemesh (Heb., "House or Sanctuary of the Sun") attest such worship in pre-Israelite Canaan. Illicit sun worship was also found in Israel (2 Kings 23:5, 11; Ezek. 8:16). The sun's radiance and restorative power served as figures of God's reign; e.g., in Mal. 4:2, God says, "For you who revere my name the sun of righteousness shall rise, with healing in its wings" (cf. Isa. 30:26; Rev. 21:23). Divine intervention in history was signaled by miraculous changes in the sun's course or appearance

(darkening, Isa. 13:10; Mark 13:24; premature setting, Amos 8:9; advance or retreat, Josh. 10:12; Isa. 38:7–8; see also Luke 21:25).

In the NT, Jesus uses the sun as evidence of God's gracious character, which human beings should imitate. His followers should love their enemies and do good to those who hate them, so that they can be like their heavenly Father, who makes the sun to shine on the good and the bad alike (Matt. 5:45). In his parable of the Sower, however, the sun stands for "trouble or persecution," which can cause those who receive the word with joy to fall away as surely as the sun scorches plants with no root (Matt. 13:6, 20–21; cf. James 1:11). At the transfiguration, Jesus's face shone like the sun (Matt. 17:2), and in Matt. 13:43, Jesus says that when the Son of Man returns, "the righteous will shine like the sun in the kingdom of their Father." Imagery involving the sun abounds the book of Revelation, e.g., a woman clothed with the sun (12:1) and an angel whose face is like the sun (10:1). Finally, that book ends with images of the new Jerusalem, a city that has no need of sun, because the Lord God will be its light (21:23; 22:5).

P.A.B./M.A.P.

Supper, Lord's. *See* Lord's Supper.

surety. *See* loan, loans.

Susa (*soo'*sah), a biblical name for the ancient capital of Elam (the southwestern area of modern Iran), which reached its height of importance as the residence and especially the winter capital of the kings of Persia. It is called Susa in the Bible (Ezra 4:9; Neh. 1:1; Esther 1:2; Dan. 8:2), but is otherwise known as Shushan. The book of Esther is set in Susa, and one of Daniel's visions features the court of Belshazzar in that same city.

Archaeological work has determined the outlines of the history of Shushan (Susa) from the fourth millennium BCE until after its capture by Arabian armies in the seventh century CE. Excavation has centered on the impressive remains of the royal palace and city as well as the acropolis. The city was said to be the site of a huge marriage ceremony of about ten thousand men from the army of Alexander the Great with Persian women in 324 BCE. *See also* Esther, book of; Persia.   W.L.H.

Susanna (*soo*-zan'uh).

1 The heroine of the apocryphal/deuterocanonical book who is falsely accused of adultery by two elders whose advances she refuses. In the story she is successfully defended by a wise youth, Daniel. The story either precedes or follows the book of Daniel in manuscripts of the LXX and is included in many Bibles as one of the Additions to Daniel. *See also* Apocrypha/deuterocanonical literature; Susanna, book of.

2 One of the group of women who traveled with Jesus and his disciples and provided for them (Luke 8:3). Nothing more is known of her.

Susanna, book of, one of the Additions to Daniel included in ancient Greek translations of the Hebrew Bible. Different versions of the story are found in the Theodotion Greek translation of Daniel and in the LXX translation. In some manuscripts it precedes the book of Daniel; in others, it appears at the end of the Daniel, following Dan. 12 (and so may be numbered in modern Bibles where it is included as Dan. 13). The story was probably composed sometime between 300 and 100 BCE.

The story of Susanna is essentially a courtroom drama that is sometimes regarded as the world's oldest "detective story." It relates how Daniel rescues a young and beautiful woman who has been falsely condemned to death for adultery as a consequence of a plot by two magistrates to blackmail her into having sex with them. Like the rest of the book of Daniel, the story is set in Babylon, where all of the Hebrew characters are living as a result of the exile. That setting, however, has virtually nothing to do with the story; for example, there are no references to the suffering of the exile or to the trauma the Hebrews experienced in a foreign land (as are evident in the main portions of the book of Daniel).

The story opens with the marriage of Susanna to Joakim, in whose house the local court sits (vv. 1–6). Two of the elders or magistrates of the court become lustfully obsessed with Susanna on account of her great beauty, and they look for an opportunity to find her alone (vv. 7–14). One day, she seals herself in her garden to bathe, and the men, who have hidden themselves in the garden, surprise her and give her the choice of submitting to them or having them accuse her falsely of adultery (vv. 15–21). Susanna refuses their demands (vv. 22–23). She is accused, tried, and condemned to death (vv. 24–41). In response to her prayer for help, God sends the youth Daniel to aid her (vv. 42–46). He interrogates the two elders separately and asks each of them under what tree they saw Susanna being intimate with another man. One of them says, "A mastic tree," and the other says, "An evergreen tree." Thus, their guilt in offering false testimony is proved, and the court sentences them to death in Susanna's place (vv. 47–62). The story concludes with Susanna's parents and husband praising God; a final note indicates that this case first established Daniel's reputation among the people (vv. 63–64).

As with Tobit, Judith, Additions to Esther, and the stories in Dan. 1–6, the story of Susanna is intended to illustrate how God defends the righteous. The difference in the case of Susanna is that the threat comes from within the Hebrew community rather than from outside it.

Protestants include the book of Susanna among the Apocrypha, while Roman Catholics and Eastern Orthodox Christians include it as part of the canonical text of Daniel. *See also* Apocrypha/deuterocanonical literature; Daniel, Additions to.

D.W.S./M.A.P.

swaddling, the practice of wrapping newborn infants in strips of cloth to keep their limbs straight. Ezek. 16:4 indicates the procedure that was followed upon the birth of a child: the umbilical cord was severed, the infant was washed, rubbed with salt, and then wrapped in cloths. According to Luke 2:7, 12, Jesus was wrapped in swaddling cloths after his birth. The Hebrew word of which "swaddling" is the English translation could also denote cloths used in the binding of broken limbs (cf. Ezek. 30:21) and was sometimes used figuratively (cf. Job 38:9).   J.M.E.

swallow, a small bird of the family *Hirundinidae*. It is not certain, however, that either of the two Hebrew words translated "swallow" in the NRSV (*deror, sis*) represents the bird that is now known by that name. The first term (*deror*) appears twice in the Bible: once in Ps. 84:3, where it occurs along with a general term for "bird" to portray the peace and tranquility of the Jerusalem temple; and once in Prov. 26:2, where it is used to compare an unfounded curse to the flight of a bird. The second term (*sis*) is likewise used twice: once as a simile to describe the sound of clamor from the sick Hezekiah (Isa. 38:14); and once as an example of habit in contrast to the fickleness of God's people (Jer. 8:7). In all of these cases, the reference is to a "small bird"; more precise identification than that may have been irrelevant to the biblical writer and, in any case, cannot be determined today.   F.R.M.

swearing. *See* oath.

swine. In the Bible, swine are "unclean animals," because they have cloven hooves but no ruminant stomach (Lev. 11:7; Deut. 14:8). The pig was domesticated in Neolithic times (ca. 9000–4500 BCE) from the wild boar (*Sus scrofa*), which still roams the Jordan Valley and the Jordanian highlands in great numbers today. For many peoples, swine were useful animals, because they converted all kinds of otherwise unusable food, such as leftovers, rodents, acorns, and roots, into meat. They did, however, require higher maintenance than some animals (e.g., sheep) to prevent them from overrunning cultivated areas. By the Second Temple period, the Jewish aversion to pig's flesh was so well established that Antiochus IV Epiphanes seized upon swine as a paradigmatic example of "uncleanness" to be overcome if the Jews were to be thoroughly hellenized. He sacrificed a pig on the altar in the Jerusalem temple (1 Macc. 1:47) and instituted measures requiring Jews to eat pig's flesh, on pain of death (2 Macc. 6:18).

The low estate to which the prodigal son fell is signified by his occupation as a swineherd (Luke 15:15, 16). Pigs also figure in the story in Matt. 8:28–34, in which Jesus heals two men by allowing the demons that had possessed them to occupy a herd of swine that then rushes headlong into the Gadarene Lake. The proverbial foolishness of "casting pearls before swine" has its origin in

Matt. 7:6, while the saying "like a gold ring in a swine's snout" stems from Prov. 11:22. *See also* animals; Maccabees; purity.   I.U.K.

sword, a close-range weapon composed of a metal blade, which was usually bronze or iron in the biblical period, and a wood or bone handle (Judg. 3:22). The sword is distinguished from the dagger on the basis of length; "sword" is normally applied to weapons over 1 foot long. Depending upon its function (i.e., slashing or stabbing), the blade was single- or double-edged (Judg. 3:16; Ps. 149:6), curved or straight, pointed or blunt. Since swords were so common in the ancient world, the biblical writers provided few descriptive details about these weapons. Fortunately, archaeologists have recovered many swords and daggers from virtually every period of antiquity; this makes it possible for readers of the Bible to obtain some understanding of the weapons mentioned in particular biblical episodes.

Between the third millennium BCE and the Greco-Roman period (333 BCE–324 CE), the sword evolved through a variety of shapes, lengths, and levels of durability. The earliest swords were made of bronze and averaged only about 10 inches in length; blades were double-edged, straight, and pointed. Although this daggerlike weapon was used primarily for stabbing, the longer sickle-sword was made for slashing. Through the centuries, numerous changes were made in blade production and in the method of attaching the blade to its hilt, but the major change in the development of swords took place when ironworking became widespread. Archaeological and biblical evidence points to the Philistines' early monopoly on the military use of this superior metal (1 Sam. 13:19–22). With the arrival of the Iron Age ca. 1200 BCE, the straight, long sword was developed as a formidable weapon. Since iron possesses greater hardness and strength than bronze, iron was ideal for the forging of longer blades and more durable cutting edges. The double-edged, pointed sword reached a length of 30 inches, and this weapon was strong enough for thrusting and slashing. Although the long sword was improved and used throughout the Mediterranean region until relatively modern times, Greek and Roman soldiers also used shorter swords. The typical sword of Roman soldiers in NT times was the *gladius*, a lightweight, well-balanced weapon with a blade about 2 feet long (see Eph. 6:17: "sword of the Spirit," Lat. *spiritus gladius*).

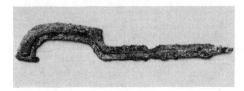

Curved sword from the excavations at Byblos, eighteenth century BCE.

Between the first biblical reference to the sword, the mysterious "flaming sword" in Gen. 3:24, and the final mention of this weapon, the sword of judgment in Rev. 19:21, the term "sword" appears in the Bible well over four hundred times, making the sword the most frequently mentioned weapon in the Bible. References to swords occur in accounts from every biblical period. Most passages refer to the literal weapon of war, but the sword also symbolizes aggression (Jer. 2:30; Matt. 26:52), disharmony (2 Sam. 2:26; Matt. 10:34), deceit (Ps. 55:21), divine assistance (Ezek. 30:21–25), God's word (Eph. 6:17; Heb. 4:12), and divine wrath (Isa. 34:5–6; Jer. 50:35–37; Ezek. 21:9–20; Hos. 11:6). Since the sword was normally kept in a sheath (1 Sam. 17:51), the drawn sword signified war (Judg. 8:10). The prophets allude to swords to symbolize the threat of God's judgment (Jer. 47:6; Ezek. 21:3–5, 28–30). Highly figurative are the book of Revelation's references to the sword that protrudes from the Lord's mouth, a probable reference to the power attributed to Christ's words of judgment (1:16; 2:12, 16; 19:15, 21). Above all of this military terminology stands the hope that an age of peace will eventually eliminate the need for swords (Isa. 2:4; Mic. 4:3; cf. Joel 3:10, where this situation is reversed). *See also* soldier; war; weapons.   G.L.M.

sycamore, a tree mentioned in the Bible that is probably to be identified with the mulberry fig (*Ficus sycomorus*). In the Near East, it thrives in warm lowland areas and produces a small fruit that is a popular food. The wood, though soft and porous, is quite durable and is therefore often used in the manufacture of furniture and the construction of buildings. Amos claimed to be no professional prophet, but a herdsman and a dresser of sycamore trees (7:14). Zacchaeus climbed up in a sycamore tree in order to see Jesus when he passed by (Luke 19:4). See also 1 Kings 10:27; 1 Chron. 27:28; Isa. 9:10.   P.L.C.

Sychar (si'kahr), according to the Gospel of John, a village in Samaria where Jesus spoke with the Samaritan women (4:5–42). It was located near a field reputedly given by Jacob to his son Joseph (4:5), with a well still active in Jesus's time (4:6). The actual site of the village is disputed, but most scholars suggest Tel Balata, ancient Shechem (Lat. and Gk. Sychem; cf. Acts 7:16). Other scholars favor the nearby village of Askar. Both are near what is today called "Jacob's Well," some thirty miles due north of Jerusalem. The solution depends in part on the accuracy of the identification of the site of Jacob's Well. *See also* Jacob; Jacob's Well; Joseph; Samaria, district of; Samaritans.   C.H.M.

Sychem (si'kuhm). *See* Shechem.

Syene (si-ee'nee), a town on the east bank of the Nile just north of the First Cataract. Called *Swn* (modern Aswan) by the Egyptians, it was at the southern border of Egypt; Ezekiel's pronouncement on the forthcoming fate of all Egypt at the hands of the Babylonians speaks of "from Migdol to Syene" (29:10; 30:6). On the island of Elephantine, across from Syene, there was a late sixth- and fifth-century BCE military colony in the service of the Persians. The Elephantine papyri, several groups of Aramaic documents found on the island, show that this colony included many Jews, who had their own temple to God, were permitted to celebrate the Passover festival, and lived both on the island and in Syene. *See also* Passover; temples.

J.M.W.

Symeon (sim′ee-uhn). *See* Simeon.

synagogue (sin′uh-gog; Gk., "a gathering of things" or "an assembly of people"), a congregation of Jews who gather to pray, read scripture, and hear teaching and exhortation based on scripture and the place where such a congregation assembles. Synagogues are not mentioned in the Hebrew Bible or in any of the apocryphal/ deuterocanonical writings produced during the Second Temple period. The NT, however, presents synagogues as prominent throughout Galilee, Judea, and the Mediterranean world.

Jesus is descibed as teaching throughout the synagogues of Galilee (Matt. 4:23; 9:35; Mark 1:21, 39; Luke 4:15, 44; John 6:59; 18:20), including the synagogue in his hometown of Nazareth (Matt. 13:54; Mark 6:1–2; Luke 4:16). The Gospel of Mark recounts an episode in which he exorcises a demon from a man in a synagogue (1:21–27). He also raises a girl from the dead who was the daughter of a synagogue ruler named Jairus (5:22–43). Elsewhere, Jesus enters into disputes with Jewish authorities over questions raised by his healing the sick in synagogues on the sabbath (Mark 3:1–5; Luke 13:10–17). He criticizes hypocrites who blow trumpets when they give alms in the synagogues (Matt. 6:2) or who like to stand and pray in the synagogues in order to be seen by others (6:5). He likewise chastises people who like the best seats in synagogues (23:6). Jesus also warns his disciples that they will be flogged or beaten in synagogues (Matt. 10:17; 23:34; Mark 13:9; cf. Luke 12:11; 21:12; cf. Acts 22:19; 26:11).

The book of Acts mentions a particular synagogue in Jerusalem called the "synagogue of the Freedmen" (6:9). The apostle Paul obtains letters from the high priest addressed to synagogues in Damascus authorizing him to arrest followers of Jesus who might be there (9:2). After his conversion, Paul himself begins proclaiming in the synagogues that Jesus is the Son of God (9:20). The book of Acts tells how Paul and his companions travel throughout the Roman world teaching about Christ in synagogues (13:5, 14–15, 43; 14:1; 17:1, 10, 17; 18:4, 7–8, 17, 19; 19:8; cf. 18:26). The strong impression from this portrait of Paul's ministry in Acts is that he normally goes first to the synagogue to offer the gospel to the Jews, and

only after he meets rejection there does he turn to the Gentiles. This is not, however, the impression one would gain from Paul's letters, in which he never mentions synagogues and maintains that he was called by Christ to be an apostle to the Gentiles from the start (Gal. 1:16).

The stories in the Gospels and Acts often present Jesus or Paul as being in conflict with synagogue leaders or worshipers. The Gospel of John develops this theme by maintaining that the Jews had a policy of expelling people from the synagogues if they confessed Jesus to be the Messiah (9:22; 12:42; 16:2). Such tensions are also reflected polemically in the book of Revelation, which refers to a "synagogue of Satan" in Smyrna (2:9) and in Philadelphia (3:9), both of which are composed of people who "say that they are Jews and are not." Such comments appear to presuppose a situation in which Christians claim to be the true Israel (as faithful followers of the Messiah) and, accordingly, view synagogues as places where unfaithful Jews (who reject the Messiah) worship Satan rather than God.

Despite the polemical cast of the NT materials, certain aspects of synagogues do come to the fore. The texts reveal first-century CE synagogues to be places devoted to prayer, reading of scripture, and teaching of Torah and places where regular worship was held on the sabbath. Josephus, the late first-century Jewish historian, also speaks of synagogues in Galilee, and Philo, the first-century Egyptian Jewish writer, attests to the presence of numerous synagogues in Alexandria.

The origin of the synagogue remains unknown. One suggestion is that synagogues arose during the Babylonian exile as a response to the loss of the temple as the center of Jewish religious life. Though the suggestion is reasonable, no direct evidence for such an origin exists, and the biblical passages cited in support of this theory (Ezek. 11:16; 14:1) are inconclusive. This theory also cannot account for the absence of mention of synagogues in Ezra or Nehemiah or the absence of references to destruction of synagogues during the period of persecution associated with the Maccabean revolt. Accordingly, some scholars suggest that synagogues arose not during the exile, but during the Hellenistic crisis of the second century BCE, in which there was a conflict among Jews over acculturation and fidelity to tradition. If this were the case, then synagogues would not have developed to fill a void created by a temporary absence of the temple; instead, they would have developed as a mode of resistance to Hellenism (the influence of Greek culture).

The earliest structure that has been identified as a synagogue is on the Aegean island of Delos, constructed in the first century BCE. Pre–70 CE synagogues have also been found at Gamla, Masada, and Herodium; the evidence for pre–70 CE structures at Migdol and Capernaum (cf. Luke 7:5) remains inconclusive. It seems likely that most of the synagogues mentioned in the NT were not buildings set apart for exclusive religious use;

rather, the Jews probably met in large rooms that were part of a house or another public building. In some instances, the synagogue may simply have been a gathering place out of doors.

Bibliography

Catto, Stephen K. *Reconstructing the First-Century Synagogue: A Critical Analysis of Current Research*. Clark, 2007.

Fine, Steven. *This Holy Place: On the Sanctity of the Synagogue During the Greco-Roman Period*. Notre Dame University Press, 1998.

Fine, Steven, ed. *Sacred Realm: The Emergence of the Synagogue in the Ancient World*. Oxford University Press, 1996.

Harland, Philip. *Associations, Synagogues, and Congregations: Claiming a Place in Ancient Mediterranean Society*. Fortress, 2003.

Kee, Howard Clark, and Lynn H. Cohick. *Evolution of the Synagogue*. Trinity Press International, 1999. A.J.S./M.A.P.

Synoptic Problem, the problem of accounting for the similarities and differences among the Gospels of Matthew, Mark, and Luke. If the four Gospels are printed in parallel columns with similar materials located alongside each other, it becomes clear that the first three have such similarities in content and order that their materials can be "seen together" (syn-optically). Hence they are called the "Synoptic Gospels," in a manner that distinguishes them from the more independent Gospel of John.

Such an arrangement discloses both extensive and detailed similarities between those first three Gospels as well as significant differences. Many narratives are told in almost the same words (e.g., Matt. 14:13–21 and Mark 13:3–32 and Luke 21:7–33; Matt. 3:7–10 and Luke 3:7–9). The agreements are sometimes among all three Gospels (the "triple tradition"); sometimes they are between only Matthew and Luke (the "double tradition"); and, less frequently, they are between only Matthew and Mark or, rarely, between only Mark and Luke. Significant phenomena involving the order of passages can also be observed, for example, that Matthew and Mark present their material in a rather different order in the first sections of their Gospels (Matt. 1:1–12:21; Mark 1:1–3:21), but never disagree on the order of material thereafter. Virtually all scholars agree that these factors demand some kind of literary interrelationship among the three Synoptic Gospels: one or more of these Gospels used one or more of the other two Gospels as a source. The question of which Gospel(s) used which is the crux of the Synoptic Problem.

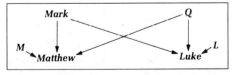

Relationships among the Synoptic Gospels according to the Two-Source Hypothesis.

The earliest proposed solution to this puzzle was that of Augustine (fourth–fifth century CE). He suggested that the Gospels were written in their canonical order (i.e., first Matthew, then Mark, and then Luke), with each of the later evangelists utilizing the work of all his predecessors. This solution was generally accepted until the Enlightenment, when all such issues were examined with the tools of historical and literary methods. During the nineteenth century, every conceivable solution was proposed and tested, and only a few ended up being regarded as viable options.

Today, most scholars consider some form of the Two-Source Hypothesis to be the most adequate solution. Mark was the earliest Gospel and was used independently by Matthew and Luke. But Matthew and Luke also used another source (no longer extant), known as "Q," a work that consisted mostly of sayings of Jesus. In addition, both Matthew and Luke incorporated traditions preserved only by themselves ("M" and "L," respectively), but these are usually regarded as complexes of (possibly oral) tradition rather than unified documents.

Two alternative solutions to the Synoptic Problem are held by a minority of scholars. (1) The Farrer hypothesis holds to the priority of Mark, but without positing a Q, so that the double tradition is accounted for by Luke using Matthew. (2) The Griesbach hypothesis (also called the Two-Gospel Hypothesis) suggests that Matthew was written first, that Luke was dependent on Matthew, and that Mark was written last as a conflation of Matthew and Luke. *See also* L; M; Q. M.E.B.

Syntyche (sin'ti-kee), a Christian woman in Philippi who received urgent exhortations from Paul to resolve her dispute with Euodia, a fellow Christian (Phil. 4:2–3). *See also* Euodia.

Syracuse (sihr'uh-kyooz), a Greek colony on the southeast coast of Sicily, founded by Corinth ca. 734 BCE. It developed into the principal city of the island, with a fifth-century BCE temple of Athena. Phoenician settlers were expelled in 234 BCE, but the city was taken by Rome in 212 BCE. On his voyage to Rome, Paul spent three days there (Acts 28:12).

Syria (sihr'ee-uh), an indeterminate regional term applied to the eastern Mediterranean shore. In ancient history the term "Syria" usually referred to the area surrounding Damascus, the Aram of the Hebrew Bible, which varied in size according to the strength of the rulers. The northern limit of Syria was also the limit of Israelite imperial ambitions (Num. 34:7–9; 2 Kings 14:25; Ezek. 47:15–17).

Geography: Damascus lies in a great oasis east of the Anti-Lebanon Mountains, fed by the river Barada (Abana, 2 Kings 5:12), which also provides a route westward into the elevated rift valley of the Beqa'a. The mountains fan out toward the northeast, and great basalt outflows lie to the southeast, extending far into Arabia. These barriers to movement direct all routes toward the rich oasis, making Damascus a city of major commercial importance. The rainfall is everywhere scant, however; Damascus has an average annual total of only 8.6 inches. The whole area is therefore essentially desert, with settlements confined to the areas surrounding the rare springs. Farther south Syria includes the better-watered region of Bashan, which lies east of Galilee and which in NT times was divided into three areas: (1) Gaulanitis on the west (modern Golan Heights; Geshur and Maacah in the Hebrew Bible), characterized by volcanic cones rising sometimes 1,500 feet above the plateau; (2) the tableland of Batanea (Argobor Bashan in the Hebrew Bible); and (3) the wild volcanic area of Trachonitis, part of the territory of Philip (Luke 3:1). Bashan was famous for fertility and livestock (Ps. 22:12; Ezek. 39:18; Amos 4:1), and in NT times it exported grain to Rome. West of the Anti-Lebanon, in the Beqa'a area, known to the Romans as Coelesyria, the northward-flowing river Orontes and the southward-flowing Litani both rise to about 3,000 feet above sea level. This valley provides an obvious access for invaders from both north and south, but it is not an easy route and the great trading caravans all went through Damascus. Unquestionably Damascus considered the Beqa'a as Syrian, but its control was intermittent.

Relations with Israel and Surrounding Empires: Israelite–Syrian relations were often antagonistic, but at times the two combined for mutual defense, as when King Ahab of Israel joined with Ben-hadad of Damascus and other rulers to resist the Assyrian Shalmaneser III at Qarqar (Tell Qurqur) in 853 BCE. Normally Syria dominated Israel, but David apparently conquered and garrisoned Damascus (2 Sam. 8:3–6), and Ahab gained commercial rights there (1 Kings 20:34). Jeroboam II of Israel (786–746 BCE) is said to have conquered Damascus (2 Kings 14:28) and restored the empire of David and Solomon. The text is unfortunately obscure, but evidently Syria for a time paid tribute to Israel. Later (753–733 BCE) King Pekah of Israel sought the help of Rezin of Syria against King Ahaz of Judah, but he achieved nothing (Isa. 7:1–17). Ahaz appealed for help to Tiglath-pileser III of Assyria, who conquered and ravaged Damascus in 732 BCE, making it part of his empire. Later, in 720 BCE, Sargon II overwhelmed Hamath. Thereafter Syria was a vassal, passing from Assyrian control to Babylonian, and becoming in 333 BCE part of the empire of Alexander the Great. After Alexander's death in 323 BCE Syria was governed by the Seleucids, who in ca. 300 BCE made Antioch their imperial capital. From 64 BCE and throughout the NT period Syria was under Roman control, forming part of a much larger province of that name.

Jesus may have visited the larger province of Syria when he traveled to the region of Tyre and Sidon (Matt. 15:21). After Pentecost the Christian faith spread rapidly into the region, and according to Acts Paul's conversion occurred as he traveled to Damascus to arrest followers of Jesus there (9:1–25). The Nabatean king Aretas in distant Petra is said to have exercised some influence over the governor of Damascus at the time (2 Cor. 11:32–33). *See also* Antioch; Aretas IV; Bashan; Damascus; Hamath; Trachonitis.   D.B.

Syrophoenician (si'roh-fi-nish'uhn), a person from Phoenicia, which in NT times was located in the Roman province of Syria. When Jesus visited the area of Tyre and Sidon (Matt. 15:21), he was accosted by a Syrophoenician woman who sought healing for her daughter (Mark 7:26). The woman is also referred to as a Greek, i.e., as a Gentile, or, as some would say, a "pagan." In the parallel passage (Matt. 15:22), the woman is called a "Canaanite," an ancient geographical designation that would have included this area. *See also* Canaan; Gentile; Greek, Greeks; Phoenicia; Sidon; Syria; Tyre.
                                                            P.L.S.

Syrtis (suhr'tuhs), the ancient name of two bays on the northern coast of Africa south of Sicily, between Cyrene and Carthage. The Greater Syrtis, now the Gulf of Sidra off Libya, was to the east; the Lesser Syrtis, now the Gulf of Gabes, to the west. Both held navigational dangers dreaded by sailors in antiquity (Acts 27:17); the Greater Syrtis was shallow and full of shifting banks of quicksand, and the Lesser had rough winds and surf.

Opposite: The reading of the Torah, perhaps by Ezra; panel from the third-century CE synagogue at Dura-Europos.

Taanach (tay'uh-nak), a site in the Near East occupied for over three thousand years. Ancient Taanach is located at Tel Ta'annak, next to the modern village that still bears the ancient name. It is situated on the southern edge of the Esdraelon Plain five miles southeast of Megiddo. The main route from the southern hill country to Megiddo and the Plain of Acco and a route linking the Plain of Esdraelon with the Sharon Plain through the Carmel Range both passed by Taanach.

The earliest historical text mentioning Taanach is the relief at the temple of Karnak in Upper Egypt of Pharaoh Thutmose III's first Asian campaign in 1468 BCE. The Akkadian tablets found in the excavations at Taanach, some of which are letters to the local king, are dated to about 1450 BCE. According to the biblical tradition Joshua defeated the king of Taanach (Josh. 12:21), and although the town was allotted to Manasseh (17:11; 1 Chron. 7:29) and named a levitical city (Josh. 21:25), the Canaanites were not driven out (Judg. 1:27). Taanach is also mentioned as the place where Deborah and Barak defeated the Canaanites, and the victory is celebrated in the Song of Deborah (5:19). The town may not have been controlled by the Israelites until the period of the monarchy (late eleventh century BCE); then it is listed in one of Solomon's administrative districts (1 Kings 4:12). Taanach

Taanach cultic stand with reliefs of animals and a winged sun disk in the top row; tenth century BCE.

is mentioned in another Karnak relief describing Pharaoh Shishak's victorious campaign in 918 BCE. It does not appear again in a historical source until Eusebius's *Onomasticon* of the fourth century CE.

Taanach was one of the first Near Eastern sites to be excavated. Spectacular early finds included a Bronze Age patrician's house, a large incense stand with reliefs, and several Akkadian cuneiform tablets. Subsequent excavations have allowed for an occupational history of the site to be developed.

Taanach was first inhabited in the Early Bronze Age ca. 2700–2400 BCE. It was a typical city-state of the period, as attested by its fortifications, their rebuilds, and the intricate stratigraphy. The site was then unoccupied for about seven hundred years except for campsite occupation near the beginning of the second millennium BCE. In the Hyksos period of the seventeenth and sixteenth centuries BCE it prospered again. There were massive fortifications of the Hyksos type and one of the earliest casemate constructions found in the ancient Near East. The fine patrician house of the earlier excavation belonged to this period, and about sixty subfloor burials revealed a great variety of intramural burial practices. At the end of the sixteenth century the city suffered a substantial destruction, but revived quickly for a flourishing era in the next half century, attested by a large Late Bronze I building complex with an adjacent cobbled street. This occupation came to an end near the middle of the fifteenth century, probably at the hands of Thutmose III in 1468 BCE.

A modest occupation followed, and it is to this period that the Akkadian tablets may belong. There is little evidence of occupation from the late fifteenth to the late thirteenth century BCE, which suggests that the place-name found in one of the Amarna tablets does not refer to Taanach. Several substantial structures belong to the twelfth century BCE, and a Canaanite cuneiform tablet concerning a shipment of grain was uncovered in one of these. The occupation ended in a violent destruction about 1125 BCE, which may be associated with the victory celebrated in the Song of Deborah (Judg. 5). The light eleventh-century settlement was followed by an important tenth-century occupation revealing an area that contained a mass of cultic material including iron blades, pig astragali (bones), loom weights, three small stelae, about eighty reconstructable vessels, a unique cultic stand, and a complete figurine mold. This ended in major destruction, leaving ceramic evidence suggestive of Shishak's campaign of 918 BCE.

Finds from later occupations were limited to a few Iron Age II remains, a number of stone-lined pits and a building of the Persian period (ca. 538–333 BCE), and scattered Hellenistic shards. *See also* Deborah; Jezreel; Megiddo.

Bibliography

Lapp, P. W. "Taanach by the Waters of Megiddo." *Biblical Archaeologist* 30 (1967): 2–27.   N.L.L.

Tabeel (tab´ee-uhl; Heb., "El [God] is good").

1 The father of an unnamed person whom Pekah, the king of Israel (northern kingdom), and Rezin, the king of Syria, conspired to make king over Judah (southern kingdom), should they succeed in overthrowing Ahaz (Isa. 7:6).

2 A Persian official residing in Samaria; he was one of those who wrote to the Persian king Artaxerxes protesting the rebuilding of the temple in Jerusalem by the returned exiles (Ezra 4:7).

tabernacle (tab´uhr-nak´uhl), the portable sanctuary of the Israelites during the wilderness period, according to the Pentateuch and related texts. The directions for building it are given in Exod. 25–30, and the account of its actual construction follows in Exod. 35–40. It consisted of a rectangular enclosure, hung with curtains supported on poles, some 145 feet long, 72 feet wide, and 7 feet high (Exod. 27:18). Within this, there was another building, also curtained, divided in two by a veil, behind which was the Holy of Holies containing the ark; before the veil stood the altar of incense, the seven-branched lampstand, and the table for the bread of the Presence (25:30). In the courtyard outside this building stood the altar of burnt offering and the laver (30:18). When the Israelites moved about during their wilderness wanderings, the whole tabernacle was dismantled and re-erected by the Levites wherever the tribes pitched camp (Num. 1:51). When the tabernacle was set up, the twelve tribes camped around it in a defined order (2:1–31), with the Levites in its immediate vicinity (1:52–53). The furnishings of the tabernacle were made of the finest and costliest materials (Exod. 25:3–7).

The "tent of meeting" may have been a simple portable shrine similar to the one depicted in this drawing from the temple of Bel at Palmyra and known from Egypt, Mesopotamia, and Canaan.

Tent of Meeting: In addition to the word "tabernacle" (Heb. *mishkan*), the Bible employs the expression "tent of meeting" (Heb. *'ohel mo'ed*), a much simpler type of shrine, described in Exod. 33:7–11. The tent of meeting was a simple tent that one person could pitch, and it was set up outside the camp, unlike the tabernacle, which was in the middle. Looked after by a single officiant, it was not a place of sacrifice, nor is there any evidence that it ever sheltered the ark. Rather, the tent of meeting was a shrine for the receiving of oracles; the divine presence did not reside there permanently, but was only manifested, in the form of a pillar of cloud, when Moses entered the tent to inquire of God.

For the NT writers, the significance of the tabernacle is found in Exod. 25:40, which they interpret as meaning that the earthly tabernacle had a

An ark—which stood within the tabernacle—with draped curtain and flanked by seven-branched lampstands, palm fronds, shofars, and incense shovels; mosaic from the fourth-century synagogue at Hammath-Tiberias.

heavenly counterpart (Heb. 8:2, 5; 9:22). In Acts 7:44–50, the wilderness tabernacle, made according to the pattern of the one in heaven, is contrasted with Solomon's temple made with hands, while in Revelation the only tabernacle envisaged is the one in heaven (13:6; 15:5; 21:3). *See also* ark of the covenant, ark of God; high place; Levites; temple, the.

Bibliography

Clements, Ronald E. *God and Temple.* Fortress, 1965.

Wright, G. Ernest, and David Noel Freedman, eds. *The Biblical Archaeologist Reader I.* Doubleday, 1961. Pp. 201–28.   J.R.P.

Tabernacles, Festival of (or Booths, Ingathering, Heb. *sukkot*), along with Passover and the Festival of Weeks, one of three major pilgrimage festivals of Judaism. Celebrated for eight days from the fifteenth of Tishri (September/ October), it was Israel's joyous harvest festival to mark the ingathering from the threshing floor and the wine press (Exod. 23:16; 34:22; Deut. 16:13–15). Its most distinctive ritual is a requirement to "dwell in booths" in commemoration of God's protection of Israel during the wilderness wanderings (Lev. 23:39–43; Neh. 8:13–18). The preeminent annual festival, called "the festival of God" (Lev. 23:39; Judg. 21:19) or "*the* festival" (1 Kings 8:2, 65; 12:32; Isa. 30:29; Ezek. 45:23, 25; Neh. 8:14; 2 Chron. 5:3, 7–8; John 7:10; cf. John 7:2), it was the occasion for the dedication of Solomon's temple (1 Kings 8) and for the public reading of the Torah (every seven years, Deut. 31:10–11). In the future, it would also be the occasion for the ingathering of all nations to Jerusalem to worship God (Zech. 14:16). *See also* festivals, feasts, and fasts; time.   J.U.

Tabitha (tab'i-thuh; Aramaic, "gazelle"), another name for Dorcas, a highly regarded Christian widow in Joppa whom Peter raised from the dead (Acts 9:36–42). *See also* Dorcas.

tablets of the law, the two stone tablets of the Ten Commandments inscribed by God on Mount Sinai (Exod. 24:12; 31:18; 32:15–16; Deut. 9:10–11; 10:1–6). The first set was broken by Moses in his anger at the sight of the golden calf (Exod. 32:19). The second set was placed in the ark of the covenant.

Tabor (tay'buhr).

1 An isolated mountain rising to a height of 1,843 feet in the northeast portion of the Plain of Esdraelon. On the border of the tribal lands of Issachar (Josh. 19:22), Zebulun (Chisloth-tabor in 19:12, cf. 1 Chron. 6:77), and Naphtali (19:34), it was the central place where Barak gathered his forces (Judg. 4:6, 12), and from there he descended for his battle with the Canaanites (4:14). The north–south road from Hazor and Damascus to the pass of Megiddo and the coastal plain passed around the foot of Mount Tabor, and the east–west route from the Megiddo Plain went between Mount Tabor and the Hill of Moreh to the Sea of Galilee. Here Gideon's brothers were killed by the Midianite kings Zebah and Zalmunna (8:18).

Although it is not actually very high, Mount Tabor's isolation in the plain led the psalmist (Ps. 89:12) and the prophets (Jer. 46:18) to compare it to Mount Carmel and Mount Hermon. It may have been a sacred mountain from early times (cf. Deut. 33:18–19). It is not mentioned in the NT, but since the fourth century CE it has been celebrated as the site of the transfiguration. *See also* Jezreel; transfiguration.

2 The "oak of Tabor," a tree near Bethel that served as a prominent landmark. The prophet Samuel told Saul to meet people here after he was anointed king (1 Sam. 10:3).   N.L.L.

Tadmor (tad'mor), a city (modern Tadmur) in Syria located in a fertile oasis in the Syrian desert a hundred and forty miles northeast of Damascus. Because of its location midway between Mesopotamia and the western arm of the Fertile Crescent, it was an important caravan city. During the height of its prosperity in the Roman period it was called Palmyra (Lat., "palms"). The well-preserved ruins from this era give a detailed picture of a wealthy Syrian metropolis. Its monumental architecture includes temples that were Semitic in plan but that featured classical decorative motifs dedicated to such gods as Bel, Nebo, and Baal Shamin. The excavations have also uncovered a theater, an agora, baths, and numerous ornate tombs with elaborate sarcophagi and statuary. The large number of inscriptions from Palmyra in Greek and Palmyrene (the local Aramaic dialect) reveal its syncretistic religious traditions.

Tadmor is mentioned only once in the Bible. In 2 Chron. 8:4, Solomon is said to have built "Tadmor in the wilderness." The related but not identical passage in 1 Kings 9:18 reports that Solomon built "Tamar in the wilderness, in the land of Judah." Tamar (Heb., "palm") is known from Ezek. 47:19 and 48:28 as a town south of the Dead Sea. Some scholars suspect that "Tamar" (rather than

Aerial view of the well-preserved ruins at Palmyra (Tadmor).

Tadmor) is meant in 2 Chron. 8:4 as well. *See also* Solomon.   M.D.C.

Tahath (tay'hath; Heb., "beneath" or "low").

1 One of the encampments of the Israelites during the journey in the wilderness (Num. 33:26–27); the site is unknown.

2 The son of Assir; he was a Levite from the family group of Kohath (1 Chron. 6:24, 37).

3 An Ephraimite who was the grandfather of **4** below (1 Chron. 7:20). Some scholars understand Tahan (Num. 26:35) to be the same person (or the same as **4**), but Tahan could be a different son (descendant) of Ephraim (see 1 Chron. 7:25).

4 The son of Bered, an Ephraimite (1 Chron. 7:20).

Tahpanhes (tah'puhn-heez), a town mentioned several times in the book of Jeremiah (2:16; 43:7–9; 44:1; 46:14). It was known to the Greeks as Daphnai and has been identified with the modern Tell Defenneh, situated on the Pelusiac branch of the Nile in the northeast Delta. According to Herodotus (*History* 2.30), the Twenty-Sixth Dynasty king Psammetichus I (664–610 BCE) established a garrison of Greek mercenaries at Daphnai to guard against the Assyrians; later, the Persian king Darius I (522–486 BCE) also kept guards there. In about 587/6 BCE, the prophet Jeremiah and other Jews sought refuge at Tahpanhes from the Babylonian king Nebuchadnezzar (Jer. 43:7; 44:1; 46:14). *See also* Jeremiah, book of.   J.M.W.

Tahpenes (tah'puh-neez), the wife of an unnamed Twenty-First Dynasty pharaoh; her sister was given in marriage to Hadad of Edom during the time of David (1 Kings 11:19–20). After David's death, Hadad became Solomon's adversary (11:21). The sister of Tahpenes bore a son named Genubath to Hadad, and this son was weaned by Tahpanes in the house of Pharaoh, where he was brought up in the Egyptian court. The name Tahpenes is not attested in any Egyptian source. It may be a Hebrew transcription of an Egyptian title meaning "the king's wife." *See also* Hadad.

talent. A large unit of money equal to 6,000 drachmae or denarii. Thus, 1 talent was roughly equal to what a typical worker would make over a sixteen-year period. Jesus tells a parable in Matt. 25:14–30 in which a wealthy man gives his slaves different amounts of talents (1, 2, and 5—the last amount was more than an average worker could hope to earn in a lifetime). In another parable (18:23–35) Jesus uses creative exaggeration to stress the incalculable difference between divine and human mercy: a slave owes his king (God) 10,000 talents (equal to millions of dollars), but is upset with a fellow slave who owes him 100 denarii. *See* money; weights and measures.   M.A.P.

talitha cum (tal'uh-thuh koom'), an Aramaic sentence that means "Young girl, arise." It is spoken by Jesus when he raises the daughter of Jairus from the dead. Mark translates it into Greek as "Little girl, get up!" (5:41).

Talmai (tal'mi).

1 One of the sons of Anak (descended from the Nephilim, Gen. 6:4) who lived at Hebron when spies sent by Moses into that region of the Negev returned with reports of giants in the land. The sons of Anak were finally driven away by the military commander Caleb (Josh. 15:14) or by Judahites (Judg. 1:10). *See also* Caleb; Nephilim.

2 The king of Geshur whose daughter, Maacah, was one of David's wives and the mother of Absalom (2 Sam. 3:3; 1 Chron. 3:2). It was to Talmai that Absalom fled after killing his half brother Amnon (2 Sam. 13:37). *See also* Geshur; Maacah.

                                    F.R.M.

Talmon (tal'muhn).

1 A levitical gatekeeper mentioned in 1 Chron. 9:17. It is not clear to scholars whether the passage in which this reference is found (9:17–34) should be seen as applying to postexilic Jerusalem (after 587/6 BCE; cf. Ezra 2:42; Neh. 11:19) or whether it is intended to serve as an introduction to the narratives of Saul and David that follow. In either case, Talmon is to be regarded as the ancestral head of a family group of gatekeepers (see Neh. 7:45), but if the passage is postexilic, he is probably the same person as **2** below.

2 A levitical gatekeeper in postexilic Jerusalem (Neh. 11:19; 12:25).   D.R.B.

Tamar (tay'mahr; Heb., "date palm").

1 The Canaanite daughter-in-law of Judah whose story is told in Gen. 38. Tamar marries Judah's eldest son, Er, but because he is wicked, God kills him while Tamar is still childless. Judah tells his next oldest son, Onan, to do his duty as a brother-in-law and have sex with Tamar in order that she might bear children to continue Er's line. Onan, however, does not like the idea of producing offspring for his deceased brother, so each time he has intercourse with Tamar he spills his semen on the ground. God is angered by this and kills Onan as well. Judah promises Tamar that he will give her his next son, Shelah, when he is old enough, but the boy grows up and Judah does not keep his promise, because he is afraid of losing another son. Finally, Tamar takes matters into her own hands. She puts on a veil and sits by the roadside when Judah, whose wife has died, goes to shear his sheep. Judah mistakes her for a temple prostitute and ends up impregnating her himself. When he learns that she is pregnant, he initially decrees that she is to be burned for having "played the whore" (38:24), but Tamar then produces Judah's own signet, cord, and staff (which she had procured from him as a pledge of payment) and says, "It was the owner of these who made me pregnant" (38:25). Judah declares that she has acted more righteously than he, since he had failed to give her his son Shelah. Tamar subsequently bears twins, Perez and Zerah. Perez was an ancestor of King David (Ruth 4:12, 18–22; 1 Chron. 2:4). Both Tamar and Perez are also listed in the NT as ancestors of Jesus (Matt. 1:3).

2 The daughter of David and Maacah who was a half sister of Amnon and a full sister of Absalom. According to a narrative recounted in 2 Sam. 13:1–29, Amnon became obsessed with Tamar, because she was very beautiful. His friend and cousin Jonadab came up with a plan for getting her alone. Amnon feigned sickness and asked to have Tamar bring him food and feed it to him. Once he got her alone in his bedchamber, he propositioned her. She responded, "No, my brother, do not force me; for such a thing is not done in Israel. . . . As for me, where could I carry my shame? And as for you, you would be as one of the scoundrels in Israel" (13:12–13). Instead, she begged him to ask King David to give her to him as a wife, assuring him that the king would surely grant this. Amnon, however, raped Tamar and then was seized with loathing for her. Indeed, his loathing for her "was even greater than the lust he had felt for her" previously (13:15). She begged him not to send her away, maintaining that this would be an even greater wrong, but Amnon summoned men to cast her out. Tamar put ashes on her head, tore the long robe with sleeves that women wore in that day as a sign of virginity, put her hand on her head, and went about crying loudly until her brother Absalom found her and quieted her. Absalom took her into his household, where she remained a desolate woman. King David, meanwhile, was angered by what had happened, but refused to punish Amnon because he was his firstborn. Thus, Absalom bided his time and eventually murdered Amnon as the first step in mounting a coup against David and, temporarily, seizing control of the kingdom. *See also* Absalom.

3 Absalom's only daughter, "a beautiful woman" (2 Sam. 14:27), and his sister's namesake.

4 A city marking the southeast border point in Ezekiel's description of the restored territory of Israel (47:18–19; 48:28). The site remains unidentified (cf. Hazazon-tamar, Gen. 14:7).

P.A.B./M.A.P.

tamarisk (Heb. *'eshel*), a tree or shrub of the genus *Tamarix*. Tolerating sandy and even saline soils, this drought-resistant tree grows in deserts as well as in watered places, near streams and marshes. It is an evergreen with tiny, jointed, grey-green, needlelike leaves, which give it a feathery appearance. It provides year-round food for goats. Its wood is used for construction and is a good source of charcoal. Its common occurrence in desolate places makes tamarisk an ideal shade tree and a revered spot for burials (1 Sam. 31:13). *See also* trees; wood.

tambourine (also timbrel), a hand-carried percussion instrument. It was associated with religious hymns (Ps. 149:3; 150:4) and was popularly used by women (Exod. 15:20, Miriam; Ps. 68:25,

girls; 89:2; 149:3; 150:4; Jer. 31:4, "virgin Israel"). Jephthah's daughter met her father with timbrels and dancing as he returned victorious from battle (Judg. 11:34). Timbrels or tambourines usually reflected joyous occasions, and the silencing of them was symbolic of despair (Isa. 24:8).

Tammuz (tam'uhz).

1 The fourth month (mid-June to mid-July) of the Hebrew religious calendar. *See also* calendar.

2 The Hebrew form of Dumuzi (Sumerian, "proper son"), a god widely honored from the third millennium BCE in Mesopotamia. The vast and complex Mesopotamian literature about this god shows him to have been a god of vegetation who was also the lover and consort of Inanna/Ishtar. Central to his story, however, is his premature death, which leads to the drying up of vegetation at the onset of winter. The worship of Tammuz involved rites of mourning and lament, all in anticipation of his release from the underworld, which would mark the embodiment of spring. Many laments have been preserved that bewail the "far one" who has disappeared. The cult of Tammuz may have been brought to Israel by the Assyrians in the ninth and eighth centuries BCE. Aspects of Tammuz became synthesized with West Semitic gods of similar characteristics (e.g., Baal Haddu also went down into the underworld and was mourned during his absence). In Ezekiel's vision of four sins being committed in the Jerusalem temple, the third involves a group of women weeping for Tammuz in the north gate (8:14). This is an abomination to Ezekiel, who believes that God does not die and cannot be mourned. *See also* Ezekiel, book of.   R.J.C.

Tanakh (tah'nahk), the Jewish Bible, a collection of twenty-four books originally written in Hebrew (with a few passages in Aramaic). It is divided into three main sections. The Torah (often called "the law," though "instruction" or "teaching" would be a better translation) contains Genesis, Exodus, Leviticus, Numbers, and Deuteronomy. The Nevi'im (Prophets) includes Joshua, Judges, Samuel, Kings, Isaiah, Jeremiah, Ezekiel, and the Book of the Twelve (Hosea, Joel, Amos, Obadiah, Jonah, Micah, Nahum, Habakkuk, Zephaniah, Haggai, Zechariah, Malachi). The Ketuvim (Writings) are Psalms, Job, Proverbs, Ruth, Song of Solomon, Ecclesiastes, Lamentations, Esther, Daniel, Ezra–Nehemiah, and Chronicles. Thus, the Tanakh is equivalent in content to the Christian OT, but the order of the books is different. The word "Tanakh" is formed from an acronym for the three constituent parts: T(orah) + N(evi'im) + K(etuvim). *See also* canon; Old Testament.

M.A.P.

Tanis (tan'is). *See* Raamses, Rameses.

tanning, the process of rendering leather permanently soft and pliable. Because of the many uses to which it could be put, leather was a valuable com-

"Nash Papyrus" (ca. 150 BCE). This portion
of the Tanakh contains the Ten Commandments
and the Shema (Deut. 6:4).

modity. "Tanned rams' skins" were offerings given
by the people of Israel at Mount Sinai (Exod. 25:5;
35:7, 23). These skins were fashioned into the coverings for the tent of meeting and the tabernacle
(26:14; 36:19; 39:34). Skins were used for clothing
and many other products, including leather buck-
ets, waterskins, wineskins, and butter churns (Gen.
21:14; Judg. 4:19; Matt. 9:17). Nevertheless, due to
the nature of the work, tanners were not always held
in high regard. The odors accompanying the process and the contact with unclean animals were re-
pugnant to townspeople. Thus, Simon the tanner is
described as living outside of town (by the seaside,
at Joppa, Acts 10:16). *See also* skins.   S.R.

Taphath (tay'fath), Solomon's daughter who was
married to Ben-abinadab, Solomon's administrator of Naphath-dor (1 Kings 4:11).

Tappuah (tap'yoo-uh).
   1 A town of the Shephelah (Josh. 15:34), perhaps modern Beit Nettif, west of Bethlehem.
   2 Both a territory and a town on the border of
Ephraim and Manasseh (Josh. 16:8). Ephraim
possessed the town, but the territory of Tappuah
was occupied by Manasseh (17:8). The town is
probably to be identified with modern Tell Sheik
Abu Zarad, south of Shechem.

3 An area or town whose king was defeated by
Joshua (Josh. 12:17). It is probably to be identified
with either 1 or 2 above, but there is no way of determining which.

tares. *See* weeds.

Targums (tahr'guhmz), translations of the books
of the Hebrew Bible into Aramaic, made when Aramaic was the common spoken language in Judea.
They were produced between ca. 250 BCE and
300 CE and were usually read in the synagogues.

Tarshish (tahr'shish).
   1 A Benjaminite son of Bilhan (1 Chron. 7:10).
   2 One of seven princes of the Medes and the
Persians (Esther 1:14).
   3 An unknown location famous for its association with sea traffic (1 Kings 10:22; 2 Chron. 9:21;
Isa. 23:1, 14; 60:9; Ezek. 27:25). Isaiah refers to the
numerous and beautiful ships of Tarshish (2:16);
Ezekiel mentions the abundance of the city's great
wealth, for it exported silver, iron, tin, and lead
(27:12). Jonah caught a ship at Tarshish to flee
from God (Jon. 1:3). Despite the numerous references to Tarshish in the Bible, many of which suggest the city was prominent, the location has not
been determined; speculation has favored sites in
both North Africa and Spain.   R.S.B.

Tarsus (tahr'suhs), a large, prosperous commercial city located on the Cydnus River, about
ten miles from the Mediterranean Sea at the foothills of the Taurus Mountains on the southeastern
coast of Asia Minor. Situated 79 feet above sea level
in the fertile eastern plain of the region of Cilicia,
Tarsus became the region's capital under the Romans.
   According to the book of Acts, Paul was born
in Tarsus (21:39; 22:3), and he returned to Tarsus
following his conversion, until at some later point
Barnabas went there to find him and bring him to
Antioch (9:30; 11:25–26). Although Paul himself
does not mention Tarsus in any of his letters, most
scholars do not see any good reason to doubt this
element of Paul's biography; the association with
Tarsus helps to explain his understanding of Gentiles and his ability to relate to them. As a native

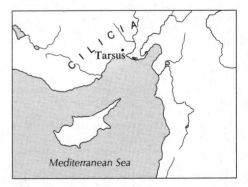

of Tarsus, Paul would have been a Jew of the Dispersion, at home in a non-Jewish environment. In particular, Tarsus had long been a center of Stoic philosophy, and several of its citizens were famous Stoic philosophers: Zeno, Antipater, Athenodorus, and Nestor. Many Pauline scholars have detected what they believe to be Stoic influences on Paul's rhetorical style (e.g., the use of diatribe) and on his thought (e.g., appeal to conscience in Rom. 2:15, and to virtue in Phil. 4:11–12).

According to the Greek geographer Strabo (ca. 63 BCE–23 CE), the Cydnus River had its source from the melting snows of the mountains above the city. The river flowed through the ancient capital into a lake some five miles to the south, which served as a naval station and harbor for Tarsus. It was because of the river that inland Tarsus had the opportunity to develop into a thriving maritime center. This feature gave Tarsus a cosmopolitan nature. Furthermore, the main trade routes passed north through Tarsus to central Asia Minor via the Cilician Gates in the pass through the Taurus Mountains, or east via the Syrian Gates of the Amanus Mountains to Syria. Paul's description of Tarsus as "an important city" in Acts 21:39 was warranted. It was the meeting place of West and East, of the Greek culture and its oriental counterpart.

The date of the foundation of the city is uncertain, but archaeological evidence shows habitation dated back to the Neolithic period (ca. 5000 BCE), and several Bronze Age (ca. 3000–1200 BCE) cities were built successively on the site. In the middle of the tenth century BCE, the Assyrian king Shalmaneser III conquered Tarsus. When the city rebelled during the reign of Sennacherib a century later, it was destroyed. Rebuilt, Tarsus was under Persian control until it was taken in 333 BCE by Alexander the Great, who resided there for a short period. The city passed into the hands of the Seleucid dynasty (312–65 BCE), whose efforts to hellenize the inhabitants provoked an insurrection against Antiochus IV Epiphanes (2 Macc. 4:30). With the advent of the Romans, the region of Cilicia was organized into a Roman province with Tarsus as its capital. Cicero, the Roman orator and statesman, was governor of Tarsus in 50 BCE. Mark Antony gave Tarsus the status of a free city, and it was here that he met Cleopatra in 41 BCE. It was under the rule of Augustus (27 BCE–14 CE) that the city came to its golden age and was renowned as a center of intellectual life, surpassing even Alexandria and Athens. *See also* Cilicia; Paul; Stoicism.

M.K.M.

Tartan (tahr´tan), an official title of rank within the Assyrian military, the commander-in-chief or field marshal second only to the king. An officer of this rank led Sargon's assault against Ashdod (ca. 712 BCE; Isa. 20:1). Another officer of this rank was sent by Sennacherib along with two other officials, the Rabshakeh and the Rabsaris, to demand Hezekiah's surrender of Jerusalem (ca. 701 BCE; 2 Kings 18:17). *See also* Rabsaris; Rabshakeh.

Tattenai (tat´uh-ni), the governor of the Persian province called Beyond the River (Ezra 5:3, 6). In postexilic times, this province included Samaria and Judea, and so the rebuilding of the Jerusalem temple at the time of Zerubbabel came to Tattenai's attention. He checked into the situation and reported to King Darius that the Judeans claimed they had authorization from Cyrus to build the temple. Tattenai recommended a search of the Persian archives to determine if such authorization could be found. The search was made, and a copy of Cyrus' edict was located, after which time Tattenai was instructed not to interfere with the building in progress (6:1–5, 6, 13). *See also* Shetharbozenai.

tax collectors, persons responsible for collecting tolls and taxes on behalf of the Roman government. In areas ruled by the Roman Empire, contracts for collecting taxes in a region were farmed out, usually to wealthy foreigners. These persons, in turn, hired local inhabitants to collect the taxes, such as Zacchaeus, who is called a chief tax collector in Jericho (Luke 19:1). Such individuals would rely on low-level tax-gatherers (often slaves) to do the actual work of collecting the monies, which might involve, for example, examining goods being transported along local roads and assessing tolls accordingly. Goods sold in certain markets were also subject to taxes. Tax collectors were responsible for paying to the government the revenue they had promised in obtaining their contract, but they were generally free to collect extra taxes from the people in order to make a profit. Opportunities for theft, fraud, and corruption abounded, and tax collectors are portrayed negatively in almost all Greco-Roman literature. Thus in the NT, "tax collectors and sinners" are cited together as examples of undesirable types (Matt. 9:11; 11:19; Luke 15:1). In a surprising reversal of cultural norms, Jesus lauds tax collectors and prostitutes over the Jewish leaders, because the tax collectors and prostitutes believed John the Baptist (Matt. 21:31). The chief tax collector Zacchaeus believes in Jesus and says either that he will now repay fourfold those whom he has defrauded or, as a matter of policy, he always repays fourfold anyone whom he inadvertently defrauds (Luke 19:8; the Greek syntax would allow either meaning). Jesus is sharply criticized for associating with tax collectors (Matt. 9:10–13; 11:19; Luke 15:1), and he is even reported to have called a tax collector to be one of his disciples (Matt. 9:9; cf. 10:3). *See also* Matthew; tax, toll; Zacchaeus.

A.J.S./M.A.P.

tax, toll. The most precise information regarding taxation in the biblical world pertains to the Roman period, though taxes were certainly in effect before then.

The institution of the Israelite monarchy probably brought a system of more or less regularized taxation. The census David took when he became king could be related to such a system (2 Sam. 24;

cf. Luke 2:1–2). Solomon imposed taxes that were ultimately deemed oppressive (1 Kings 4; 2 Chron. 9:13–28). In addition, special taxes may have been levied for specific purposes. Jehoash taxed the people for temple repairs (12:14–18), and Jehoiakim taxed them to pay tribute to Pharaoh Neco (2 Kings 23:35). Menahem taxed the wealthy only in order to buy off the king of Assyria (15:20).

In the Roman period, people throughout the empire were required to pay "taxes to the emperor" (12:14). Jesus appears to have given tacit support to this, though his counsel, "Give to the emperor the things that are the emperor's, and to God the things that are God's," allows for some ambiguity (Mark 12:17). Paul was more explicit in telling people to pay taxes to all governing authorities to whom they are due (Rom. 13:6–7).

Taxes were generally of two sorts: direct tax and indirect tax. The direct tax was either a tax on land or on persons, to be paid by everyone of taxable age. This was owed automatically, by virtue of where one lived. In the Roman period, this was used for maintenance of the empire, including such things as the building of roads and aqueducts and sustaining the military. It was collected by the prefects responsible for governing individual provinces.

Indirect taxes were levied on various activities. Merchants had to pay import and export taxes. Heirs paid a 5 percent inheritance tax. Someone who bought the freedom of a slave paid a 5 percent emancipation tax. Someone who sold a slave paid a 4 percent tax. Goods bought at public auctions were subject to a 1 percent tax, which went to a military pension fund. Another very common type of indirect tax consisted of tolls for traveling on roads or using bridges or ferries. Matthew, the "tax collector" who became a disciple of Jesus was apparently a collector of tolls, since he was sitting in a toll booth (NRSV: "tax booth") when Jesus called him (Matt. 9:9; cf. Mark 2:14; Luke 5:27; he is called Levi in Mark and Luke).

Direct taxes were collected by local leaders, but the indirect taxes were collected by hired tax collectors. Josephus reports that the wealth of one of the Jewish leaders at Caesarea, John, came from taxes collected on business at the port (*Jewish War* 2.287). Luke 19:1–10 refers to a wealthy man named Zacchaeus who was a "chief tax collector" at Jericho. Such persons would bid for government contracts granting them the right to collect the indirect taxes for a given region. The actual work of collecting those taxes, however, was assigned to slaves and other low-level employees. The tax collectors with whom Jesus eats controversial meals were probably persons of this stature (Mark 2:15–16; Luke 15:1)—though Jesus does offend the pious by going to the home of Zacchaeus as well.

Taxation and the consequent confiscation of land when taxes could not be paid led to the consolidation of landholdings in the hands of the rich, who then leased the land and employed stewards (often slaves) to supervise their property. Such a situation seems to have been the case during the time of Jesus. The division between wealthy landowners and peasants is reflected in a number of the parables of Jesus (Luke 12:13–21, 42–46; 14:11–27; 16:1–6; Matt. 20:1–16; 21:33–41; 28:23–24).

Another tax mentioned in the NT is the temple tax (Matt. 17:24–27). Every Israelite male was to pay an annual half-shekel offering toward the costs of the temple (17:24; Josephus *Jewish War* 7.218; *Antiquities* 3.194–6; Philo *Special Laws* 1.78), though the sectarians at Qumran appear to have refused to make such an offering (*Ordinances*, 4Q159 11.6–7). After the revolt in 70 CE, Vespasian imposed the "Jewish tax" on Jews up to age sixty-two; it was apparently equal to the amount of the former temple tax, but was now paid to the temple of Jupiter Capitolinus in Rome (Josephus *Jewish War* 7.218; Suetonius *Domitian* 12). *See also* money; tax collectors; tithe; tribute.

Bibliography

Freyne, Sean. *Galilee from Alexander the Great to Hadrian 323 B.C.E. to 135 C.E.* Michael Glazier, 1980.

Safrai, S., and M. Stern, eds. *The Jewish People in the First Century.* Vol. 1. Fortress, 1974.   P.P.

teaching. The Hebrew word for teaching is *torah*, so it is not surprising that from at least the time of Josiah on, the primary focus of teaching in Israel was instruction in the Torah, the stories of Israel's ancestors and the commandments and the covenant (Deut. 33:10; Pss. 78:5; 94:12; 119:29). Little is known of the mode of teaching, except that it would have been through oral presentation, usually conducted within the family, tribe, or village. Such teaching was also a role of priests (cf. 2 Kings 17:27; 2 Chron. 15:3), and, after the exile, Ezra is described as one who "set his heart to study the law of the Lord, and to do it, and to teach the statutes and ordinances in Israel" (Ezra 7:10). The author of Ecclesiastes calls himself "the Teacher" (1:1), marking a shift from oral instruction to written modes of teaching. The book of Proverbs also seems to be a written compilation of teaching, perhaps intended for use as an instruction manual with children. By NT times, synagogues had become prominent institutions for teaching, and "teachers of the law (Torah)" are said to be prevalent in all the villages of Judea and Galilee (Luke 5:17). Gamaliel is named as one such teacher in Jerusalem (Acts 5:34). Teachers are also mentioned as being present in the temple (Luke 2:46).

Jesus is presented as the oral teacher par excellence (John 3:2; 13:13), and he is often addressed as "Teacher" (e.g., Mark 10:17; Luke 12:13), as is John the Baptist (Luke 3:12). The Gospel of Matthew, in particular, focuses on Jesus as a teacher; much of its content is organized into five large blocks of his teachings (chaps. 5–7, 10, 13, 18, 24–25). That Gospel ends with Jesus commissioning his followers to make disciples of all nations by teaching people to obey his commands (28:19–20). The book of Acts presents devotion to the apostles' teaching as one of the ideal marks of the early church (2:42). Some of the NT letters speak of teachers in local congregations (1 Cor. 12:28–29; Eph. 4:11), though they never indicate just how this teaching was carried out. Faithful teaching of apostolic doctrine is emphasized in the Pastoral Letters (1 Tim. 4:6, 11, 16; 6:2, 3). *See also* education; schools; scribe. M.A.P.

Tebeth. *See* calendar.

teeth, a word used of both humans and animals, in both literal and figurative ways in the Bible. References to teeth often denote predators or agents of devastation. God breaks the teeth of young lions (Job 4:10), but can also send the teeth of beasts as a punishment upon those who turn to other gods (Deut. 32:34; cf. 32:21). In Joel, the devastation wrought by the teeth of locusts is taken as a judgment sent by God, calling the people to repentance (1:2–2:27; cf. Rev. 9:8). In addition to the teeth of actual animals or insects, the Bible refers to the teeth of symbolic (Dan. 7:5, 7, 19) and mythic (Job 41:14) creatures. One psalmist prays for God to break the teeth of the predatory and impious (Ps. 58:3–6); another praises God for deliverance from the teeth of enemies (124:1–7; cf. 3:7; Prov. 30:11–14).

To gnash one's teeth typically expresses hostility and intention of harm (Job 16:9; Pss. 35:16; 37:12; 112:10; Lam. 2:16; Acts 7:52), but references to "weeping and gnashing of teeth" convey deep regret and despair, as will be characteristic of those excluded from the kingdom of God (Matt. 8:12; 13:42; Luke 13:28). To have white teeth (Gen. 49:12) or "teeth like ewes" (Song of Sol. 4:2; 6:6) is a sign of blessing and beauty, but "cleanness of teeth" evokes an image of famine (Amos 4:6). The expression "eye for eye, tooth for tooth" conveys a sense of justice equivalent to—but not exceeding—the injury received (Exod. 21:24; Lev. 24:20; Deut. 19:21). "By the skin of my teeth" (Job 19:20) suggests that an escape was as narrow as the film on teeth. One can also "have one's teeth set on

edge" by vinegar (Prov. 10:26) or sour grapes (Jer. 31:30; Ezek. 18:2). J.G.G.

Tekoa (tuh-koh′uh), a name used in reference to a wilderness (2 Chron. 20:20) and to a town. Two persons known to David came from the settlement (2 Sam. 14:1–17; 23:26), and according to the author of Chronicles Rehoboam fortified the site (2 Chron. 11:6). It is located on a ridge about six miles south of Bethlehem. Because of this vantage point, warnings could be given from Tekoa if an enemy threatened Jerusalem from the south (Jer. 6:1). This may be the home of the prophet Amos (cf. Amos 1:1), though some scholars think that Amos's home would have been a Tekoa in Galilee, a site not mentioned in the Bible, but known in postbiblical times. J.A.D.

tell, in archaeological study, an artificial hill composed of the accumulated debris from human occupation. The formation of tells was due to fundamental factors involving human settlement patterns, weather, and the peculiar nature of construction materials in the Near East.

First, settlement by communities was bound by the necessities of a stable freshwater supply, an economic base of support, and the defense potential of a site. A good combination of all three drew people to occupy a single location century after century, and each culture would leave its physical remains at the site, whether by design or accident. Second, weather in the Near East tends to be dry and hot, allowing unusually good preservation of even organic remains. And, third, construction in the Near East favored extensive use of mud-brick, partly because it was easy to produce almost everywhere, and partly because mud-brick walls could be torn down and rebuilt as needed. The remains of such mud-brick covered all material lost or discarded when it was mashed flat, thus preserving layer after layer of human occupation debris over the centuries. The catch-basin effect of major city

Tell el-Milh, located in the Negev near Arad, is typical of the artificial hills of accumulated debris from human occupation common in the ancient Near East.

walls surrounding a town simply increased the cumulative pace.

Tells, then, are the physical record of human occupancy starting with the first inhabitants of the site over bedrock or virgin soil and proceeding to the most recent inhabitants' deposits at the uppermost layer. Reading that record is the archaeological task called stratigraphy. The value of a tell is unpredictable. Huge formations like that at Bethshan (over 100 feet high before excavation) are not necessarily most helpful. Tell el-Harmal in Iraq, a major administrative center, rose only 4 feet over the plain, but contained much useful information.

R.S.B.

Tema (tee′muh).

1 The ninth-named son of Ishmael (Gen. 25:15; 1 Chron. 1:3). He is probably to be regarded as the ancestor of the tribe or people called Tema who are mentioned in Jer. 23:25, and so he would also be associated with **2.**

2 A location in northern Arabia, known for caravan traffic (Job 6:19) and possibly an oasis (Isa. 21:14). There was apparently a tribe or family group called Tema who are likely to have occupied this site (Jer. 25:23). Most scholars agree that it is to be identified with the northern Arabian caravan intersection, Teima, located at the western edge of the Arabian Desert, east of the western mountain ridge. Babylon's last ruler, Nabonidus, lived there for ten years, precipitating Persia's conquest of Babylon.

Teman (tee′muhn).

1 The Edomite son of Eliphaz and grandson of Esau (Gen. 26:9–11; 36:15, 42; 1 Chron. 1:36, 53). He may be the ancestor of the Temanites.

2 A location in Edomite territory (Jer. 49:7, 20; Ezek. 25:13; Amos 1:12; Obad. 1:9). It appears to be a regional designation (as opposed to the name of a city or town), but site identifications are all contested. In some cases, Teman could simply be another name for Edom. The reference to Teman in Hab. 3:3 is sometimes thought to refer to a different location, farther to the south, but also presently unidentified.

Temanite (tee′muh-nit), either a tribal or geographical identification. One of Job's counselors was Eliphaz the Temanite (Job 2:11). Likewise, Hisham, an Edomite king is referred to as a Temanite (Gen. 36:34; 1 Chron. 1:45). If the designation is primarily tribal, it would indicate that such persons were descendants of Teman, the Edomite grandson of Esau (Gen. 26:9–11). If it is primarily geographical, it would indicate that (whatever their tribal identification) they come from the Edomite territory of Teman.

The Temple

THE JERUSALEM TEMPLE was the center of Israelite national life in the biblical period, beginning with the monarchy (tenth century BCE) and continuing until its final destruction by the Roman legions in 70 CE. Despite the fact that the temple's existence for over a millennium was nearly continuous, however, it did undergo major reconstructions. The first temple, built under Solomon in the early tenth century, was destroyed by the Babylonians ca. 587/6 BCE. A second temple was constructed during the time of Nehemiah, beginning in 520 BCE; it underwent major renovation duing the reign of King Herod (37–4 BCE).

Although these major architectural periods for the temple can be identified, many other changes in its ground plan, appurtenances, and decoration took place during the centuries when it stood in the administrative center of the nation in Jerusalem. Some of those changes are recorded in the biblical account of the monarchy; other alterations perhaps were made, but were not included in the biblical record. Because of the continual refurbishing of the temple, the ancient sources that provide the bulk of the information about the temple's appearance and function are sometimes confusing and contradictory. These sources include twenty-three of the books of the Hebrew Bible and eleven NT books in addition to many extrabiblical works, including works found among the Apocrypha/deuterocanonical literature, the Pseudepigrapha, and the Dead Sea Scrolls (especially the *Temple Scroll*). In addition, the writings of Philo and Josephus provide information about the temple, particularly in its final form before the fall of Jerusalem in 70 CE. Archaeological evidence and depictions of the temple on coins are also helpful.

The most common designation for the temple in the Bible is "house of the LORD"—and this indicates that the building was conceived of primarily as a residence for God rather than as a place of public worship and prayer. In fact, the general populace had access only to the temple courts and not to the inside of the structure itself. Even the clergy did not circulate freely within the building; the inner sanctum was off limits to all but the chief priest and to him only on one occasion annually (the Day of Atonement). Still, if the temple was not a public building in the sense of its interior being open to the public, it was very much a public building in a political and economic sense. Because ancient Israel, even during the monarchy, was not a secular state, the temple played an integral role in the organization, legitimation, and administration of the national community.

First Temple: The first temple is known chiefly from the description in 1 Kings 6–8 and the parallel account in 2 Chron. 2–4. Ezekiel also has an extensive temple section (chaps. 40–46). However, because of the visionary nature of Ezekiel's description and because it probably dates from after the destruction of the temple in 587/6 BCE, its reliability as a witness to the first temple, at least as it appeared at the beginning of its history, is minimal. Not a trace of the first Jerusalem temple is available archaeologically; and even if it were, it is doubtful that a razed building of the early first millennium could supply the kind of detail that exists in the biblical sources. Nonetheless, the archaeological recovery of other ancient temples in the Near East provides an important corpus of comparative material.

The basic shape of the Jerusalem temple was a rectangle, which was subdivided laterally into three sections on the same axis, and all of the same interior width, 20 cubits. The building measured 60 cubits long and was 30 cubits high. (For the temple, the royal cubit, 20.9 inches, is probably the intended unit of linear measure; that would make it about 105 feet long, 35 feet wide, and 52 feet high.) These are internal measurements based on the information in 1 Kings 6:2. The dimensions provided in Ezek. 41:13–14 are for a 100-by-50-cubit structure. Ezekiel's data may reflect the external measurements of the temple and include the subsidiary rooms built around it; they also may have been influenced by the proportions of the tabernacle, which was situated within a 100-by-50-cubit precinct. Although the interior decorations of the temple are described in great detail (1 Kings 6), no information is given about its external appearance aside from the specifications about the hewn stone used for the walls. From the outside, the building probably presented a rather stark, formidable appearance.

Entrance to the temple interior was gained by passing through the first of its three sections, the 'ulam, which is related to an Akkadian word meaning "front" and which is translated "vestibule" by the NRSV (1 Kings 6:3; 2 Chron. 3:4). Other versions render it as "porch," "portico," or "entrance hall." None of these translations accurately reflects the function of this 10-cubit-deep section of the temple. The 'ulam, unlike the other two sections, was not flanked by the side chambers of the temple. Directions for paneling its internal walls do not appear, in contrast with the instructions for the inner two rooms, making questionable whether its walls were paneled or decorated at all. Instead, its manner of construction (1 Kings 7:12; cf. 6:36) is identical to the technique described for the

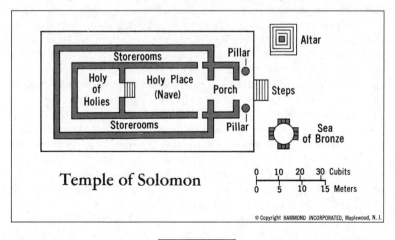

In this plan of the temple of Solomon, the "Sea of Bronze" is placed according to 1 Kings 7:39.

construction of both the public court of the temple and the great court of the adjacent palace area. Furthermore, the doorways to the inner two sections are described in detail, but no doorway to the 'ulam is specified; it apparently had none. The account in the book of Kings also gives no height for the 'ulam. This series of contrasts between the information about the two inner rooms and the details of the first room suggest that it was not an enclosed room at all but, rather, an open-air forecourt through which the divine dwelling was entered; thus, it functioned in a manner analogous to the private courtyard of a Near Eastern house.

The presence of Jachin and Boaz (two hollow, cast-bronze pillars) at the entrance to the temple further suggests that the 'ulam was a forecourt. These great bronzed columns were situated at the top of the ten stairs that, according to Ezek. 41:8, led up to the 6-cubit-high platform on which the temple stood. Each stood 18 cubits high (1 Kings 7:15; cf. 2 Chron. 3:35, which records 35 cubits) and was surmounted by an elaborate capital or double capital of at least 5 additional cubits. The pair of Jerusalem pillars loomed large at the entrance to the temple. They were highly visible elements of the temple's architecture, and consequently they were the visual link for the general public to the unseen grandeur within the building. Furthermore, they were probably freestanding and as such represented the gateposts that were part of the entryway to the temple's private forecourt.

The second section of the temple was its main or largest room, measuring 40 by 20 cubits and reaching a height of 30 cubits. Its name in Hebrew, hekal, is related to Akkadian and Ugaritic terms and ultimately to a Sumerian word, meaning "great house," referring to a palace or any large and imposing dwelling (as in Hos. 8:14; 2 Kings 20:18). The residence of a deity would qualify as a "great house," and in fact this term for the largest chamber of the temple is occasionally used to designate the temple as a whole (e.g., Jer. 7:4; Zech. 8:9). The NRSV calls it the "nave" (1 Kings 7:50; 2 Chron. 3:4–5); other translations include "main room," "temple proper," and "holy place." Like the more common name for the temple, "house of the LORD," this term also signifies the conceptualization of a temple as an earthly dwelling place of the deity. A large and elaborate cypress-wood doorway carved with cherubim and palm trees and overlaid with gold provided entry to the central room.

The size of the hekal and the fact that it had windows indicate that this was the chamber in which most of the activity associated with the building's interior took place. The windows were probably clerestory windows, set in the upper part of the walls above the flanking series of external subsidiary rooms. In addition, the internal temple furniture was situated in this room and required regular attention. A small altar for incense, made of cedar and overlaid with gold, stood in front of the entrance to the third room. Ten golden lampstands, which probably consisted of cylindrical stands surmounted by multispouted lamps (1 Kings 8:49), were situated in two groupings, five on the north and five on the south. The third major appurtenance placed in this chamber was also made of gold, or at least overlaid with gold: the table for the bread of the Presence (8:48). The floors and walls of cypress wood were overlaid with gold, the latter first having been carved with figures of cherubim and with flowers and palm trees. The extensive use of gold in this room and also in the third room is to be contrasted with the use of bronze for the other appurtenances: the huge "molten (or bronze) sea," the ten lavers with their stands, the pillars Jachin and Boaz, and probably the great altar for sacrifice. Made of the less valuable metal, they represented the lower order of sanctity of the outside courtyard in which they stood, to which nonpriests as well as priests had access.

The innermost chamber of the temple is known in Hebrew as the *debir,* which the NRSV translates "inner sanctuary" (1 Kings 6:5; 2 Chron. 4:20; 5:9) and which other versions render "Holy of Holies," "oracle," "shrine," "adytum," or "most holy place." The Hebrew word may be related to the ordinary verb meaning "to speak," in which case the inner chamber would be the place where God speaks, or the "oracle." Entrance to the innermost room was gained through olive-wood doors; like the doors to the *hekal,* they were carved with flowers, palm trees, and cherubim and were overlaid with gold. The carved walls and the floors, also like those of the central chamber, were covered with gold. The internal measurements of the inner chamber, 20 by 20 by 20 cubits, made it a perfect cube. Its height was 10 cubits less than that of the adjacent central chamber, with which it was otherwise so closely associated in construction and decoration. Perhaps a slightly elevated floor and lowered roof accounted for the difference and helped to create an architectural focus on the contents of the inner room. At the same time, its elevated floor may have symbolized its location in cosmological terms over the "rock of foundation," the primordial mound of creation.

The darkness of the *debir* was filled with two enormous olive-wood cherubim, overlaid with gold, each with a 10-cubit spread to its outstretched wings and each 10 cubits high. Under the adjacent wings of the cherubim, which commonly represented the protective quality of supernatural beings (cf. Gen. 3:24) in ancient Near Eastern iconography, stood the "ark of the covenant of the LORD" (1 Kings 6:19). The ark was the most important object in the temple. If the building as a whole was conceived of as the earthly dwelling place of God, with the rich furnishings and decorations suitable for a microcosmic replication of the heavenly abode of the Lord, then the ark was the object within that building that represented

A depiction of the temple of Solomon by T. A. Busink, an authority on ancient architecture.

both the divine presence itself and also the binding covenantal relationship between God and Israel. Although the Israelites did not believe that God's presence could be localized or confined to a particular building, they shared with all peoples the psychological and emotional need for a visible and material indication that God was nearby. Because God was seen as the source of material blessing and national protection for the Israelites, affirmation of God's availability to provide those essentials was communicated by the physical structure that, with all its splendor, symbolized a divine dwelling and assured the people of ready access to their God.

The symbolic nature of the temple as a residence for God went beyond the function of providing assurance to the Israelites that God was with them. Construction of the temple was anticipated by David, who brought the ark to Jerusalem and who, at least according to the Chronicler (1 Chron. 22:2–5), began the task of assembling the raw materials—stone, metal, and wood—from which the temple would be built. Within four years of ascending to the throne, Solomon began the actual construction. Although the biblical sources may exaggerate the scope of the project, it is clear that Solomon gave great priority to its completion. An enormous workforce was assigned to the task (1 Kings 5:27–32; cf. 2 Chron. 2:17–18). Within seven years, a remarkably short span of time for a project of this nature, the work was completed. According to the biblical record, an elaborate, fourteen-day ceremony of dedication was held, with a guest list that included international as well as national dignitaries (1 Kings 8:1–2, 65).

The decision to build the temple coincided with the formation of the monarchy and the emergence of Israel, for the only time in its long history, as a political power that was not only independent, but that also was the dominant force in the Levant for almost a century. During the reigns of David and Solomon, Jerusalem was the capital of a kingdom that appeared to have imperial control over territory that reached from "the entrance of Hamath to the Wadi of Egypt" (1 Kings 8:65). The construction of the temple was integrally related to the formation of the Israelite state and to the imperial claims of its capital in Jerusalem.

The formation of nation-states or city-states in the ancient world involved the concept that the nation's or city's chief deity approved and would support the concentration of power in the hands of the few who controlled the administrative structure of that state. Consequently, the building of a temple nearly always accompanied the establishment of a dynastic power. A temple building, as the visible symbol of a god's presence, was the most effective way for the leaders of a country to communicate the fact that their god favored the political organization that was being established. The building of a temple added the essential note of absolute legitimacy to the formation of a new system of governance. The Davidic monarchy depended upon the existence of the temple as well as upon the skill and charisma of the monarchy's leaders to secure the support and loyalty of the populace.

The legitimizing function of the temple also operated on an international level. Its existence in Jerusalem demonstrated to non-Israelites—ambassadors, merchants, and visitors—who had come to Jerusalem, especially during Solomon's long reign, that the God of Israel was present and had granted to the king his right to exercise dominion over Israel and all the conquered territories. David had established extra-Israelite dominance through his brilliant use of military force; Solomon sustained that dominance through diplomacy. The temple in Jerusalem bore the message that the Israelite domination of nearby states had divine sanction.

Comparative archaeology contributes to this understanding of the political role of the temple. The situation of Jachin and Boaz as gateposts to the temple's inner court (*'ulam*) made them highly visible symbols of the entrance of the invisible God into the temple, just as stone-carved reliefs from ancient Near Eastern sites marked the important event of the bringing of the image of a city's god into its dwelling place. The enigmatic names of the pillars indicate God's cosmic rule and power; Jachin perhaps means that God "has founded" the dynasty and temple, and Boaz refers to the divine "power" emanating from the temple. That the Jerusalem pillars surpassed in size analogous entry columns of other Canaanite temples suggests that the status of the Jerusalem temple was greater than that of the temples of any other contemporary city-state or nation-state. The very size of the temple as a whole presents a similar situation. The interior space of the Jerusalem sanctuary was considerably greater than that of the excavated temples of Syria and Canaan from the centuries closest to the existence of the Israelite empire. The Jerusalem temple with its tripartite plan was part of Near Eastern architectural traditions for temples, but it surpassed similar buildings in size, as befitting its location in a city of international status.

Another indication of the political role of the temple can be seen in the way it incorporated imported materials and artistry into its decoration. Israel's lack of skilled workers and suitable raw materials led Solomon to enlist Phoenician aid. However, with Jerusalem conceived of by the Israelites as the theological center of the ancient world, the use of materials from all parts of that world also helped establish Jerusalem's cosmic centrality. The greatest influence upon the embellishment of the temple can be found in the artistic traditions uncovered in the ruins of the major Syro-Hittite cities of the early Iron Age. Solomon

Hebrew inscription (shown here in part) from the outer wall of the Temple Mount reads, "of the place of trumpeting"; first century BCE.

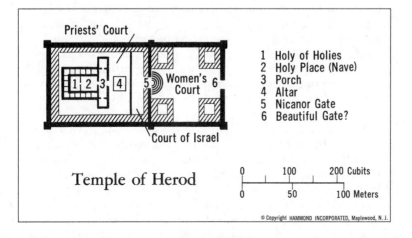

Priests' Court

1 Holy of Holies
2 Holy Place (Nave)
3 Porch
4 Altar
5 Nicanor Gate
6 Beautiful Gate?

Women's Court

Court of Israel

Temple of Herod

| 0 | 100 | 200 Cubits |
| 0 | 50 | 100 Meters |

© Copyright HAMMOND INCORPORATED, Maplewood, N. J.

used the visual embellishments best known to those populations to whom he most needed to communicate the divinely chartered rule and dominance of Jerusalem.

The international role of the temple can also be seen in the elaborate, three-tiered complex of storerooms, thirty rooms to a story, that surrounded the temple on three sides. The storage capacity of these rooms exceeded the needs of the temple's rituals and personnel. Known as the *yatsiʿa* (rendered "galleries," "side rooms," or "side chambers"), this structure housed the temple treasury. It was a storehouse for religious objects as well as for precious items sent to Jerusalem as gifts and tribute or secured as booty or taxes. The fortresslike architecture of the temple is a feature of its economic function, along with the palace, as a repository for the national wealth and even weaponry (cf. 1 Kings 7:51; 14:25–26; 15:18; 2 Kings 11:10; 12:4).

Jesus driving the money changers from the temple (Mark 11:15–19); alabaster relief at the Basilica of St. Mark, Venice, sixth century CE.

Second Temple: The second temple was built between 520 and 515 BCE to replace the temple built by Solomon, which had remained at the center of national life in the southern kingdom of Judah after Solomon's death until the Babylonians conquered Jerusalem. Renovations, repairs, and refurbishings may have altered the first temple somewhat during the centuries of the Judean monarchy (ca. 922–587/6 BCE), but the basic structure had remained the same. The Babylonians destroyed the first temple by carrying away all its precious items and furnishings, dismantling those too large to transport easily, and burning what remained (2 Kings 25:8–17). Since only the roofing and internal paneling of the temple were wooden, however, the stone foundation and much of the superstructure probably remained. There is no indication that the walls were razed. With the prodding of the postexilic prophets Haggai and Zechariah and through the leadership of the high priest Joshua and the Persian-appointed governor Zerubbabel, who was also a Davidic descendant, the work of restoration was carried out. Concern about the lack of splendor in the postexilic building (Hag. 2:3; Ezra 3:12) probably reflects the dearth of precious metals in its decoration rather than any diminution in its size.

Although the restored temple was crucial in representing continuity with both the appearance and the role of the preexilic building and institution, a radical change took place in its traditional balance of religious and political-economic functions. Without a king to sit on the throne of David, the legitimizing role of the temple in national life shifted to the priestly administrators of Judah, which had become the postexilic Persian province of Yehud. The priests had always been important in national life, but their responsibilities were enlarged after the exile as they stepped in to fill the gap left by the absence of the civil authority. The Persians evidently allowed the high priest and his staff to assume much of the internal governance, fiscally and legally, of Yehud (Judah). Zechariah's temple visions continue the age-old concept of the temple as a legitimizing factor for the administrative structure of the community (Zech. 3–4). For Zechariah, the priesthood's role is expanded and the monarchic role becomes a matter of future expectation. The temple stood alone, without the palace, as the center of semi-autonomous national life and as the focus of the dispersed community still in exile.

The form of the temple best known to us physically is the one that existed during the reign of Herod the Great (37 BCE–4 CE). Herod's temple-building project, described in considerable detail by the first-century historian Josephus and referred to extensively in other Jewish sources (especially the Mishnaic tractate *Middoth*) and in the NT, went far beyond any simple task of refurbishing or repairing the sixth-century structure. Herod's struggle to take over the Judean kingdom and his monumental efforts to make it a significant part of the Roman Empire are reflected in the magnitude of his building projects.

Herod, probably the descendant of an Idumean, was in essence a usurper of the throne in Jerusalem. He did not enjoy the traditional Jewish support that had been held by the Hasmonean (Maccabean) rulers who preceded him and who had combined the office of high priest with the kingship acquired as the result of their revolt against the Seleucids in the second century BCE. His grandiose building projects included the construction of an entirely new, gold-covered temple, although the sanctuary itself continued to correspond to the Solomonic dimensions, constructed on an enormous platform (roughly 169,000 square yards) within a broad public area (see Matt. 21:12; Mark 12:15). The temple and its courts were surrounded by a Roman-style double colonnade and entered through monumental gates. Both literary sources and archaeological discoveries affirm that the builders of this vast complex sought to incorporate current Greco-Roman architectural fashions in their design. It is questionable that Herod's intentions arose from religious sensibilities or allegiance to the God of Israel. The political dimension that had always been present in temple building came to dominate Herod's plans. He hoped that his attention to the temple would win over dissident Jewish elements within his kingdom. Furthermore, the scale and style of the temple, as of the other buildings of Herodian conception, were meant to make a visual statement to Rome about the importance of the Jewish kingdom.

The importance of the temple in the religious life of Jews at this time is evident in the NT. There, the birth of John the Baptist is announced in

Romans carrying spoil, including a menorah and trumpets, from the temple; relief on the Arch of Titus, Rome, 81 CE.

the temple (Luke 1:11–20), and a sacrificial offering is presented for Jesus eight days after his birth (2:22–24). His future prominence is announced by Simeon (2:25–35) and Anna (2:36–38) in the temple, and at the age of twelve he makes a notable impression on priests and teachers in the temple (2:42–51). Later, as an adult, he teaches in the temple precincts (Mark 12:35; John 7:14, 28) and turns over the tables of money changers, claiming that the temple has been transformed from a house of prayer into a den of robbers (Mark 11:15–19). Allegations that Jesus threatened to destroy the temple figure prominently in the charges that brought about his death (14:58; 15:29; cf. 13:1–2). Early Christians continued to gather in the temple (Acts 2:46; cf. 3:3; 4:1–2), and Acts records that Paul was arrested there at the instigation of his opponents (21:27).

The Herodian temple turned out to be short-lived. The Roman general Titus and his legions set fire to the Jerusalem temple in 70 CE. Today, the Muslim shrine called the "Dome of the Rock," or the Mosque of Omar, stands on the temple site. *See also* altar; David; Herod; Jachin and Boaz; lampstand; priests; Solomon; tabernacle; temples; worship in the Hebrew Bible; worship in the New Testament; Zerubbabel.

Bibliography

Barker, Margaret. *The Gate of Heaven: The History and Symbolism of the Temple in Jerusalem.* SPCK, 1991.

Haran, Menahem. *Temples and Temple Service in Ancient Israel.* Clarendon, 1978.

Lundquist, John. *The Temple: Meeting Place of Heaven and Earth.* Thames and Hudson, 1993.

Meyers, Carol. "Temple, Jerusalem." *Anchor Bible Dictionary.* Doubleday, 1992. 6:350–69.   C.L.M.

temple servants (Heb. *netinim*), a class of workers known from the books of Ezra, Nehemiah, and Chronicles. According to Ezra 2:43–58 and Neh. 46–60, 320 temple servants returned to Jerusalem after the exile with Zerubbabel, and according to Ezra 8:16–20 another 220 temple servants returned with Ezra. The origin and function of these servants is unclear. Ezra 8:20 mentions them as people "whom David and his officials had set apart to attend the Levites." A number of the personal names given for the servants do not occur elsewhere, suggesting that they might have been non-Israelites pressed into service when taken as prisoners of war. Scholars are divided as to whether the temple servants were actually slaves, property of the temple, or simply servitors like the Levites (cf. 1 Chron. 9:1–2). L.H.S.

temples, religious structures, which were probably the most important and most visible institutions in the biblical world. Their prominence as architectural structures on the ancient landscape is a reflection of their integral role in the political and economic structure of ancient society. We think of temples primarily with regard to their religious dimension, i.e., as relating specifically to deities, but temples were in fact basic components in the political organization and administration of territorial units, from city-states to nation-states or empires, in the ancient Near East.

The English word "temple" is misleading in its usage as a translation of certain terms in the Hebrew Bible. Derived from the Latin word *templum,* which, strictly speaking, denotes a separated or marked-off space, or a holy place, it could theoretically denote any of a number of types of worship places known in the biblical world, including altars, high places, and stelae. English parlance, however, normally uses "temple" to indicate an actual building or structure that partakes of the sacred.

The essential nature of such a building in biblical times is revealed in the two Hebrew terms translated "temple": *bayit,* "house [of God]," and *hekal,* "[the LORD's] palace." These words differ from the two Greek (NT) terms for temple: *naos,* which refers to a sacred building, and *hieron,* which refers to a sacred area or place. Both Hebrew terms are essentially secular in origin, both refer to a structure rather than to a holy place or precinct, and both conceptualize such a structure as a residence or dwelling for the deity. Although neither the Israelites nor their Canaanite neighbors may have adhered to the literal notion of a deity inhabiting an earthly building, that idea undoubtedly underlies the origins of all ancient Near Eastern temples and continued to function symbolically throughout the biblical period. Indeed, the plan, furnishings, personnel, and service associated with temples can be reconstructed rather well on the basis of both archaeological and textual sources. All this information depicts the functioning of an institution intended to provide amply and royally for the needs of its divine inhabitant,

Early Bronze Age (3000–2000 BCE) "broadroom" building at Ai, which may have been a temple.

even if the earthly house was only a pale copy of the deity's real and splendid residence in heaven.

Archaeological Data: The archaeological investigation of temples is not a simple matter. Since the organizing principle of temple building was the construction of a dwelling place for a god, the designs for temples were drawn, at least in the earlier stages, from the typical plans for larger human houses or palaces. Identification of excavated buildings as temples (rather than as houses or palaces) is thus problematic.

Nonetheless, a number of features usually allow certain buildings to be identified as temples. Temples tend to be located in prominent places within a city. As part of the administration of the political unit in which they existed, they were often adjacent to similar, and often larger, royal buildings. Together, the divine and royal residences, which we call temple and palace, constituted a separate precinct in an ancient city. At least in some cases, the temple-palace complex was set off as an acropolis or as a raised and/or walled section of the city. Even if a palace was not included, the temple by itself, since it was technically sacred space, would normally have been separated from the rest of the city by surrounding courtyards and walls, although the dwellings of the city's inhabitants were often built up against the courtyard walls.

In addition to the prominence of their location, temples can often be identified as residences for deities by some architectural divergence from the secular monumental buildings of their time. Size alone is not a criterion since, as noted, palaces might exceed temples in size. However, the thickness of a temple's walls matched or even surpassed that of the walls of adjacent palaces. The temple was in a sense like a fortress, protecting the sanctity of the god, the lavish furnishings of the god's dwelling, and also the precious commodities brought into and stored in the temple storerooms.

Perhaps the most indicative feature of a temple is that its ground plan typically includes, in its innermost part, a special recess or distinct small room meant for the statue of the resident deity. Furthermore, the artifacts recovered in buildings that might be classified as temples include a repertoire of pottery forms and other objects not found in normal domestic settings. Superior artistry, religious symbolism in the decoration, and costly materials characterize such artifacts and allow them to be designated "cultic objects." They constitute the furnishings of the deity's house and the vessels for the provision of all the god's needs. Finally, the courtyard of a temple, if it can be fully excavated, would be expected to reveal an altar. As a place for burnt offerings of all kinds and for animal sacrifice, altars had to be outside the roofed temple building, although small altars might exist inside the building for the burning of incense.

Types of Temples: With these criteria in mind, the existence of temples in many of the major cities occupied by the Canaanites or Philistines, either prior to or contemporary with ancient Israelite settlement, can be established with reasonable certainty. Two major types of temples have been recognized. The oldest is called the *broad-room* building, which was basically a rectangular or roughly square room with the entrance on one of the long sides and a niche or platform for the god opposite the entrance. The orientation is thus along the short axis. Some of the earliest examples, as in Early Bronze Age (3000–2000 BCE) Ai and Megiddo and possibly also at Arad, are clearly derived from typical house architecture. It is to be noted that some scholarly dispute regarding their identification as temples persists. The basic broadroom was expanded in various ways: by the addition of ancillary rooms around the associated courtyard, by the development of the niche into a discrete *cella* (shrine room), or by the construction of a portico at the entrance.

The last two mentioned features extend the short axis of the building and so relate the broad-room sanctuary at least in some instances to the other major temple type, the *long-house* building, in which the orientation is along the long axis. In their more developed forms, these were consisted of a series of rooms, usually two or three, along an axis, so that an officiant would have to pass through each room in succession to reach the innermost room. Usually, the second or middle room in a long-house temple was the largest; it provided the space for the daily rituals carried out in attending the resident deity. The first room served as an anteroom or inner court; it marked the transition from the profane exterior world to the sacred space within. The third room was a *cella,* the place where the deity lived, as marked by a statue. It was the most holy spot in the temple, the place where the divine presence was accessible to humans. Courtyard space, and sometimes annexes or subsidiary rooms for personnel and equipment, often combined within the tripartite building to form a sacred precinct. The basic tripartite arrangement is evident in several Megiddo and Hazor structures as well as, according to the biblical description, in the Jerusalem temple. This type of temple design emerged in the Middle Bronze Age (2000–1500 BCE), with the earliest examples perhaps being the extremely thick-walled fortress temples of Shechem, Hazor, and Megiddo.

This typology does not exhaust the kinds of temples excavated in Canaan. The Philistines, as

at Tel Qasile, evidently had their own variation; and so did those Canaanites strongly influenced by Egyptian (as at Beth-shan) or Syrian (northern) traditions. In addition the so-called square temples, such as the one from the beginning of the Late Bronze Age (1500–1200 BCE) at Amman, are set apart from urban areas; such buildings may not be temples at all, but rather mortuary installations. In short, there is no dominant form, although all types tend to have an inner and outer sanctuary as well as an anteroom. Each example adhering roughly to one of the major types also exhibits its own unique characteristics. Similarly, no dominant pattern of orientation can be discerned, except that orientation tends to remain constant at a given temple site over the duration of its existence, often many hundreds of years. This may indicate that the principle of orientation relates to the layout of the city in which the temple is built and not to any theological concerns.

Further developments in temple architecture appeared, beginning in the Hellenistic period (300 BCE–300 CE), with the introduction of Greco-Roman temples. These imposing structures, along with the older Semitic sanctuaries, helped determine the architectural form of the synagogues and churches that emerged in the early centuries CE. Although early Christians continued to participate in worship at the temple in Jerusalem (Acts 2:46), after its destruction in 70 CE the Christian community did not build its own temple. Worship was held in houses, which owed more to the synagogue than to the temple in Jerusalem.

Biblical Information: The archaeological recovery of Palestinian temples is supplemented by biblical references to temples, or residences for non-Israelite gods, at various places. First Samuel mentions the "house of Dagon" (5:2, 5) and the "house of Ashtaroth" (31:10). Judges refers to the "house of Baal-berith" (9:4) and the "house of El-berith" (9:46). Although the latter two temples are at Shechem, they cannot with certitude be related to any of the excavated buildings at that site. Neither can the "house of El" in the ancestral stories be linked with any remains from Bethel.

The Bible also records the existence of a number of Israelite temples in addition to the major one in Jerusalem. Although the terminology associated with such buildings does not usually include the designation "house," other information indicates that a temple building or an equivalent tent shrine, rather than simply an altar or high place, is to be understood. Except for the northern kingdom sites of Dan and Bethel, these possible Israelite temples (Shiloh, Gilgal, Mizpah, Hebron, Bethlehem, Nob, Micah's shrine in Ephraim, Ophrah, and Gibeah) are mentioned in sources describing the premonarchic or early monarchic periods. None of them have been recovered archaeologically. Furthermore, it is not clear that any of them continued to function once the Jerusalem temple was built. Outside of Jerusalem, the only temple apparently existing in the southern kingdom (Judah) during the monarchy was a cultic building at Arad, which is not mentioned in the Bible. It is known only from excavations, and its very identity as a temple has been questioned.

The apparent disappearance of non-Jerusalem temples from Israelite territory once the Jerusalem temple was built by Solomon is evidence in part of the administrative nature and political role of temples, which served to legitimize the political power responsible for their construction and maintenance. The non-Jerusalem buildings were regional centers servicing the tribal groups. With the centralization of political power in a monarchy, the location of the mechanisms of statecraft in one capital city meant that the complementary cultic institutions likewise shifted to that place, although altars and high places continued to exist throughout Israel. The close connection of the god's dwelling with political administration is further indicated by the fact that temples were not public houses of worship. They were entered only by priests, although the laity could enter the courtyard and worship there. The archaeological evidence of temple size and layout, along with the information from both the Bible and Near Eastern temple texts about temple personnel and ritual, allow for such a conclusion. *See also* temple, the; worship in the Hebrew Bible; worship in the New Testament.

Bibliography

Ahlström, Gosta W. *Royal Administration and National Religion in Ancient Palestine.* Brill, 1982.

Biran, Avraham, ed. *Temples and High Places in Biblical Times.* Hebrew Union College, 1981.

Haran, Menahem. *Temples and Temple Service in Ancient Israel.* Clarendon, 1978.

Ottsson, Magnus. *Temples and Cult Places in Palestine.* Acta Upsaliensis, 1980.

Ward, William A., John F. Robertson, William D. Dever, and Susan G. Cole. "Temples and Sanctuaries." *Anchor Bible Dictionary.* Doubleday, 1992. 6:369–82.   C.L.M.

temptation of Jesus. All three of the Synoptic Gospels have accounts of Jesus's temptation (Matt. 4:1–11; Mark 1:12–13; Luke 4:1–13), although only Matthew and Luke give any details (John's Gospel has no such account). In each Gospel, the temptation takes place immediately after Jesus's baptism, at which he is proclaimed to be the Son of God by a voice from heaven (Matt. 3:13–17; Mark 1:9–11; Luke 3:21–22; cf. Mark 10:45). Further, in each Gospel the temptation occurs prior to the inauguration of Jesus's public ministry and is guided by the Spirit in a manner that indicates it is a necessary step in preparation for that ministry. In Mark's brief version, the mere fact of the temptation seems to be what matters, perhaps because it presents Jesus as one who does not fail or disappoint God in ways associated with Adam (Rom. 5:14, 18) or with Israel as a nation. The extended versions of the temptation in Matthew and Luke present material thought to derive from the Q source. The devil plies Jesus with three successive temptations that seem to be intended as responses

to the baptismal identification of him as God's Son ("If you are the Son of God . . . ," Matt. 4:3, 6; Luke 4:3, 9). The temptation is not for Jesus to prove his divine Sonship; there is no question that Satan knows who he is (cf. the knowledge of demons, Matt. 8:29; Mark 3:11; 5:7; Luke 4:31; 8:28). Rather, the temptation is for Jesus to construe his divine Sonship in terms of privilege, conquest, or power rather than in terms of suffering and service. Thus, for example, he refuses to use his divine power to create bread to satisfy his own hunger (Matt. 4:3–4) but, later, he will use it to create bread for others (14:13–21; 15:32–39).

                                       M.A.P.

temptation, testing. The Hebrew word *nasah* and the Greek word *peirazō* both carry a broad range of meaning that allows them to be translated as either "temptation" or "testing" in the Bible. In the first instance, the word implies enticement to do evil, while, in the second, the connotation is an event or process that proves one's character or determines the depth or integrity of one's commitment to God.

The NRSV displays a strong preference for the latter sense when translating the Hebrew and Greek terms, so that references to "tempt," "tempted," "tempting," "temptation," etc., occur only in the NT, and fewer than a dozen times there. The devil tempts Jesus in the wilderness (Matt. 4:1; Mark 4:13; Luke 4:2) and continues to tempt believers in churches to which NT letters are written. Those who might prove especially susceptible to such temptation include married couples who pledge themselves to a temporary period of sexual abstinence (1 Cor. 7:5), church members who are seeking to restore another who has been detected in some transgression (Gal. 6:1), new believers who are suffering persecution (1 Thess. 3:5), and those who want to be rich (1 Tim. 6:9). Of course, the NT authors are clear that God does not tempt anyone in this sense of the word; rather, people are lured and enticed by their own desires (James 1:13–14).

God does, however, put people to the test. God tests Abraham by commanding him to offer his son Isaac as a sacrifice in Gen. 22:1–19. The trial of Job may also illustrate such a trial (Job 1–2). In the NT, some writers thought of persecution as a "testing" in this manner (e.g., 1 Pet. 1:3–9). The intent of such testing is ultimately to strengthen the person's faith and devotion to God. The author of James even believed that temptation in the sense of enticement to sin could double as a test that would strengthen the faith and resolve of those who resisted it (1:12). The petition in the Lord's Prayer that is popularly translated "Lead us not into temptation" should probably be understood in this light (cf. Matt. 6:13; NRSV: "Do not bring us to the time of trial"). Even so, the NT makes clear that this is one petition that God will not always grant: the followers of Jesus will have to endure trials that test their faith (Matt. 18:7; 24:9–13; Luke 17:1; 21:12–17). In Luke's Gospel, the process

Jesus tempted by the devil to throw himself from the pinnacle of the temple in Jerusalem (Luke 4:9–12); fourteenth-century mosaic depiction at the Kariye Church, Istanbul.

that leads Peter to deny Christ is understood as a trial that will ultimately serve to help him in strengthening others (22:31–32).

In some instances, the NRSV's rather extreme preference for understanding *nasah* and *peirazō* as "testing" rather than "temptation" might be subject to challenge. For example, Heb. 4:15 refers to Jesus as "one who in every respect has been tested as we are, yet without sin" (cf. 2:17). The point of the passage does not seem to be that Jesus proved his character by enduring adversity, but that he experienced mortal enticement to sin and yet did not yield to such temptation.

A quite different aspect of "temptation" or "testing" in the biblical writings is that of human beings attempting to put God to a test, usually for the purpose of testing God's plans or purposes (e.g., Judg. 6; cf. Matt. 12:39) or, even more, to determine whether they can manipulate God (e.g., Ps. 95:8–11). Moses warned the Israelites not to put the Lord to the test as they previously did at Massah, when they said, "Give us water to drink," and asked, "Is the LORD among us or not?" (Exod. 17:2–7). Jesus also refuses to put God to the test in ways that would exploit the status of his divine Sonship (Matt. 4:5–7; Luke 4:9–12). Paul takes this a logical step further by saying, "We must not put Christ to the test" (1 Cor. 10:9). *See also* persecution; sin; suffering.   J.M.E./M.A.P.

ten. *See* numbers.

Ten Commandments, a series of commands from God to Israel, mediated by Moses. The text of the Decalogue (Gk., "ten words"), or Ten Commandments, is given in its entirety twice in the Bible with only slight variations. In Exod. 20:1–17 the setting is Mount Sinai; Moses brings the two tablets of the law written by the very hand of God down to the people (24:12). In Deut. 5:6–21 the text is part of Moses's recitation of the history of salvation with which he prefaces his last will and testament.

Origin and Setting: Everything about the Ten Commandments suggests that it was a text intended to be memorized and publicly recited by the covenant community. A similarity of form pervades most of the list: "You shall not" is followed by a verb. Placed at the very beginning of the lengthy block of legal materials known as the Sinai passage (Exod. 19:11–Num. 10:10), the Decalogue functions as a summary of the covenant tradition suitable for recitation on public occasions of national reaffirmation of loyalty to the sovereign God.

Form: The Ten Commandments are often discussed as examples of "apodictic law" and "categorical law." Both designations imply form distinctions. First, legal material is sometimes said to be either "apodictic" or "casuistic" in form. A casuistic form is illustrated by material found in Exod. 21:1–22:17. The laws there are formulated mainly in conditional sentences, in which an "if-clause" (the protasis) states circumstances and a "then-clause" (the apodosis) states consequences. This is the predominant form used in ancient Near Eastern law codes. The Ten Commandments, however, are expressed in an apodictic form: direct, second-person commands, unaccompanied by any statement of sanction.

Second, describing biblical commandments may use the categories of "categorical law" and "case law." Case law is represented by material in Exod. 20:22–23:33 (a section that is often called the Covenant Code). This material preserves decisions about actual cases reached through the judicial processes of the community. Categorical law, by contrast, does not seem to emerge from actual cases, but sets forth the broad principles of community life. Some scholars have suggested that the Ten Commandments and similar lists of legal sentences (see Deut. 27:15–26; Lev. 19:13–18) amount to something like the constitutional law of ancient Israel. Of all the statutes needed to regulate the life of the community, these ten were given special emphasis.

Enumeration: The commandments are not numbered in the Bible, but three passages do indicate that there are ten of them (Exod. 34:28; Deut. 4:13; 10:4). A traditional system of enumeration has taken "You shall have no other gods before me" and "You shall not make for yourself an idol" as a single commandment (the first one). In the sixteenth century, however, John Calvin proposed treating those declarations as two separate commandments and combining the two commandments that deal with coveting into one. The traditional system is still used by Jews, Roman Catholics, Lutherans, and Anglicans, but Calvin's system is popular among a number of Protestant groups, especially in America. The Eastern Orthodox church also employs a system of enumeration similar to the Calvinist model.

The Commandments in Brief: The commandment "You shall have no other gods before me" (Exod. 20:3; Deut. 5:7) does not deny the existence of other gods, but demands total allegiance on the part of Israel to its own God, the covenant giver. The prohibition against making idols (Exod. 20:4–6; Deut. 5:8–10) may restate this commandment (if the idols are presumed to be other gods), or it may have been aimed at prohibiting images of Israel's own God, in which case it probably ought to be treated as a second, distinct commandment and the RSV translation ("You shall not make for yourself a graven image") preferred over the NRSV ("You shall not make for yourself an idol"). Israel's God is not to be localized in an object (such as a golden calf; cf. Exod. 32:4–6; 1 Kings 12:28). This point is usually made, however, with regard to what would have been the original, unamended commandment; in its current biblical context, the command does not just prohibit images of Israel's God, but images of "anything that is in heaven above, or that is on the earth beneath, or that is in the water under the earth" (Exod. 20:4).

The prohibition against the misuse of the name of God (Exod. 20:7; Deut. 5:11) is directed at a form of manipulation of the deity for personal interest. Magical, imprecatory, and other trivial cultic uses of the sacred name are forbidden.

The commandment to rest on the sabbath is motivated in Exod. 20:11 by the Creator's own sabbath rest. In Deut. 5:12–15 the sabbath is a day of remembrance of liberation from Egyptian slavery. The commandment to set one day apart from all others ("to keep it holy") stands as a

bulwark against the human propensity to forget one's creaturely status.

The command to honor father and mother (Exod. 20:12; Deut. 5:16), the only one accompanied with a promise, promotes a community climate in which the chances of survival are enhanced by a tradition of solicitude shown by the young toward the older generations. The uninterrupted flow of community tradition from one generation to the next is also ensured by the "honor" shown to the father and—in a perfectly equal way—to the mother.

"You shall not kill" (Exod. 20:13; Deut. 5:17) actually prohibits only antisocial killing, done in vulgar self-interest. It forbids killing that poses a threat to the existence of the community, not that necessary to maintain the community. Capital punishment of criminals and the killing of enemies in warfare are not only allowed, but commended elsewhere in the Torah.

"You shall not commit adultery" (Exod. 20:14; Deut. 5:18) guards marriage and family against the intrusion of third parties and the socially disruptive questions of the legitimacy of children and the transfer of the family legacy.

"You shall not steal" (Exod. 20:15; Deut. 5:19) may originally have included, as the object of the verb, the term "a person" inasmuch as the surrounding commandments suggest that the text is dealing with capital crimes (see Exod. 21:16). Thus, the commandment may originally have been a prohibition of kidnapping. As it stands, however, this commandment protects private property from illegal attachment.

The prohibition against bearing false witness (Exod. 2:16; Deut. 5:20) is aimed not so much at lying in general as it is at perjury in court. The

---

NUMBERING THE TEN COMMANDMENTS

Jewish/Catholic/Lutheran Enumeration	Reformed/Orthodox Enumeration
1. You shall have no other gods before me. You shall not make for yourself an idol.	1. You shall have no other gods before me.
	2. You shall not make for yourself an idol.
2. You shall not make wrongful use of the name of the LORD your God.	3. You shall not make wrongful use of the name of the LORD your God.
3. Remember the sabbath day, and keep it holy.	4. Remember the sabbath day, and keep it holy.
4. Honor your father and your mother.	5. Honor your father and your mother.
5. You shall not murder.	6. You shall not murder.
6. You shall not commit adultery.	7. You shall not commit adultery.
7. You shall not steal.	8. You shall not steal.
8. You shall not bear false witness against your neighbor.	9. You shall not bear false witness against your neighbor.
9. You shall not covet your neighbor's house.	10. You shall not covet your neighbor's house. You shall not covet your neighbor's wife, or male or female slave, or ox, or donkey, or anything that belongs to your neighbor.
10. You shall not covet your neighbor's wife, or male or female slave, or ox, or donkey, or anything that belongs to your neighbor.	

very survival of a community is threatened when the weak, disadvantaged, and falsely accused can find no remedy before impartial judges informed by credible witnesses (see 1 Kings 21).

Finally, the double commandment against covetousness (Exod. 20:17; Deut. 5:21) points for the first time beyond public and overt acts to private attitudes. Although unenforceable in a literal sense, it seeks to forestall the inordinate desires that lead to illegal, ruthless seizure of persons and property. Furthermore, like all Hebrew verbs of mental activity, "to covet" includes an element of enactment; it refers not only to what one *thinks,* but also to what one *does* as a result of such thinking.

All of the commandments demonstrated a capacity for evolving in a manner that would expand their meaning beyond the original context of a wilderness community. To take just one prominent example, Jesus's radicalization of the commandment against murder in Matt. 5:21–26 took that proscription as implying a default divine preference for life. Likewise, his comments in 5:27–28 inferred from the prohibition of adultery that God is displeased by exploitative lust as well. *See also* law.   W.S.T./M.A.P.

tent, a portable shelter made of cloth or skins, used by shepherds (Isa. 38:12), nomads, and soldiers. In Israel's experience it covered a shrine (2 Sam. 7:2) and served as storage space (1 Sam. 17:54, armor; 1 Kings 8:4, holy vessels), but it was primarily used as living quarters (Gen. 4:20, 25:27; 2 Sam. 20:1).

Dark in color (Song of Sol. 1:5), tents were likely woven of goat hair (Exod. 36:14) and required purification on occasion (Num. 31:20). Large tents could be constructed piecemeal and fastened by clasping loops at the edges (Exod. 36:15–18). Entrances could be covered by a screen (36:37) or arranged by simply raising the side or a flap of the side. The anchorage to the ground was by pegs (Judg. 4:21) or by tying the line to a large stable boulder when camped on rock. Unless supported by poles and raised by tightly anchoring the fabric over the poles on all sides, a tent would collapse and lie flat (7:13). The stability of a tent depended on well-placed stakes or pegs and strong and durable cords or anchoring lines (Isa. 33:20). The work of raising a tent involved unpacking and unrolling the fabric, anchoring the corner lines, then raising the poles in place, work requiring the spreading of the fabric to place corners, anchorages, and poles (10:20). Only when it was erected could the curtain(s) dividing the interior space be rigged (Jer. 10:20). Failure of the cords to hold provided a metaphor for death (Job 4:21).

As a Dwelling: Households might live in a single tent (Exod. 33:8) or have a group of tents for individuals and servants (Gen. 31:33) of the family. Because of the relatively expensive nature of tents and the need for several animals to transport a group of them, multiple tents signified wealth above average. Tents could also be used to store or

hide precious or forbidden material (Josh. 7:21). Thus guards could be posted at tents (1 Chron. 9:23). Like cities, tents could be besieged (Job 19:12). Care was needed in selecting sites to pitch one's tents (Deut. 1:33), because unwise selection would bring hazards (Hos. 9:6). Royal tents could be palatial (Dan. 11:45), but life in tents could also symbolize the purer style of a nomadic past (Jer. 35:6–10, the Rechabite ideal).

Contact with such a past is most vividly given in Gen. 18, in which Abraham hosts some visitors at his tent camp at Hebron. Set in a grove of trees, the tent was used for shady rest in the hot part of the day. When the visitors approached, Abraham ran out to greet them and extended the hospitality of shade, food, drink, and conversation. Inquiry about Abraham's wife elicited the fact that she was "in the tent" (either her own nearby tent [31:33] or in the divided portion of the tent reserved for women, close enough to overhear the conversation (18:10). Implied in the actions of hospitality was a variety of equipment normal to any household. Some kind of storage and carrying vessel for water to wash the feet of the travelers was available. Bread was provided, implying a facility to grind meal and bake over an open fire or in a small oven (possible in a long-term campsite). Meal storage, a kneading quern, and the necessary metal sheet or rock for baking the cakes was involved. There were tools for butchering the calf and vessels for the curds and milk, for cooking the meat, and for serving the food to the guests. Rest under the tree may have been on the ground, but it would not have been strange for relatively wealthy persons to provide reed mats or cloth pads for guests in that situation. In addition, a tent was normally furnished with some kind of oil lamp for night light.

Where Located and Situated: Tents, like houses, were preferably located close to a good supply of fresh water, on terrain that was secure from unexpected intrusion either because it was hidden or because it was high and afforded good visibility. The ground needed to be reasonably smooth and flat for comfort and stability. A small stone circle or depression in the earth could serve as the location for the cooking fire. Tents were normally set up with one long side to the east, allowing early warmth from the morning sun. The opposite long side facing west could be kept anchored low to keep out the chilling wind or raised in the heat of the day to allow cooling breezes to enter. Domestic animals would have been corralled nearby, but dogs, chickens, or other small livestock were allowed to roam the tent and its environs at will.

Biblical usage includes metaphoric references to tents in addition to the long, detailed descriptions of the sacred tents (e.g., Exod. 26). God was portrayed as living in a tent (Ps. 15:1), and God had provided a tent for the sun (19:4). God's tent provided secure hiding for God's people (27:5), and God stretched out the heavens like a tent (Ps. 104:2). A tent could also serve as a metaphor for life (Prov. 14:11) or, specifically, for the transitory nature of life (2 Cor. 5:1, 4). The writer of Hebrews contrasts the earthly shrine-tent with the "true tent" available in Christ (8:1–6).

The apostle Paul while in Corinth stayed with Aquila and Prisca, Priscilla, recent victims of the Roman emperor Claudius's ban on Jews in Rome, because they, like he, were tentmakers (Acts 18:1–4). It is said that he worked at his trade while in Corinth, presumably engaging in missionary effort and pastoral work as time and opportunity afforded. As a native of Tarsus in Cilicia, he may have learned about *cilicium,* a goat's hair cloth used especially by sailors and soldiers, or he may have been a leatherworker, since in Hellenistic times many tents were constructed of leather.

Tent campsites are notoriously difficult to locate archaeologically, because the occupants seldom stayed long in one place. The result is that little physical evidence remains from their occupation. A small area swept clear of pebbles and stones, a small hearth or fire pit, possibly a broken pot, a lost scraper blade, or a broken grinding stone would be all that was left to be found archaeologically. Recent studies have focused on the dimorphic communities where people used houses in settled towns for part of the year, moving into tents for wider pasturage or simply for cooler accommodation for the other part of the year. These studies may develop better techniques for learning the archaeology of tent sites.   R.S.B.

tent of meeting. *See* tabernacle.

Terah (tair´uh; possibly from Akkadian *turahu,* "ibex," or from Aramaic *yerakh,* "moon"), a descendant of Shem, the son of Nahor; he is the father of Abram, Haran, and Nahor (Gen. 11:24, 26). All three of Terah's sons were born when he was seventy (12:26). In the book of Genesis, a number of narrative cycles are introduced via the repeated formula, "These are the generations of . . ." (cf. 2:4; 5:1; 25:12, 19; 36:1; 37:2). The phrase, "These are the generations of Terah" in 11:27 is used to begin the Abraham cycle. Terah's son Haran died during his father's lifetime, having fathered one child, Lot. After Abram and Nahor married, Terah tried to move the entire family group from Ur-of-the-Chaldees to Canaan, but he got only as far as the north Syrian locale of Haran (the place-name is unrelated to that of the person). He settled there and died at age 205. *See also* Abraham; Ur.
                                                    J.W.R.

teraphim (tair´uh-fim), statues or figurines representing household gods. They were common in Syria and Canaan, even among Israelites, throughout the preexilic period (to 587/6 BCE). In Gen. 31:19, Rachel stole her father's teraphim (NRSV: "household gods"). Laban's angry reaction suggests their importance. Such objects may have had legal significance as indicators of family status.

In Judg. 17:5 and 18:4, 17, 20, teraphim are objects employed in worship and are mentioned as symbols of a private priesthood. The Ephraimite Micaiah had established his own shrine, furnished with a hired Levite, ephod, teraphim, and a silver statue donated by his mother (Micaiah had earlier robbed her, but then confessed and repaid the theft). Some Danites migrating from Judah persuaded the Levite to serve at their intended shrine in Laish, and they took Micaiah's teraphim with them. Micaiah's desolation over the loss (18:24) again reveals the importance of teraphim.

Most teraphim were apparently quite small (Rachel hid Jacob's teraphim in her saddlebag, Gen. 31:34). Archaeologists have found numerous small terra-cotta figurines that are probably to be identified as teraphim. But in 1 Sam. 19:13–16, Michal aids David's escape from Saul by putting a large teraph (NRSV: "an idol") in the bed, disguised as David himself.

Among Israelites, the teraphim may have sometimes served as symbols of Israel's God or been associated with worship of Israel's God. The prophet Hosea seemed to regard them as integral to Israel's royal and priestly institutions (3:4). But teraphim were also associated with divination, which led prophets to inveigh against them as wanton superstition (Zech. 10:2; cf. 1 Sam. 15:23). Josiah's reform sought to ban them from the land (2 Kings 23:24). Ezek. 21:21 portrays the king of Babylon using teraphim for divination prior to his attack on Jerusalem. *See also* idol; Jacob; Laban; Micaiah; priests.   J.W.R.

terebinth (tair´uh-binth; *Pistachia terebinthus,* variety *palaestina*), a tree common to the lower regions of the hills of the Levant. Its broad, spreading branches, great size, and long life make it a tree much venerated. The NRSV only refers to the "terebinth" by name in Isa. 6:13; Hos. 4:13, but in other places the same word is translated "oak" (e.g., Gen. 35:4; 1 Chron. 10:12).

Tertius (tuhr´shee-uhs), Paul's amanuensis or "secretary" who, in Rom. 16:22, sends his own greetings along with those of Paul. *See also* epistle; letter.

Tertullus (tuhr-tuhl´uhs), the prosecutor who represented the Jewish leaders from Jerusalem before the Roman procurator Felix, when charges were brought against Paul in Caesarea (Acts 24:1–8). Tertullus is described as presenting the charges against Paul in classical Roman style. He may have been a Jew or a professional Roman advocate hired by Paul's Jewish opponents to present their case in the Roman setting (the name is Roman). The fact that Felix postponed Paul's trial suggests that Tertullus was not entirely successful in his plea (24:22–23). *See also* Felix, Antonius; Paul. A.J.M.

testament (Gk. *diathēkē*), a term not used in the NRSV, but employed by biblical scholars in four different, though overlapping, contexts.

1 A will or an agreement disposing of a person's property upon death (Gal.3:15).

2 A covenant, such as the Sinai covenant. In Gal. 3:17 Paul likens the testament (NRSV:

"covenant") God made with Abraham to a testament (NRSV: "will") in which a person specifies promises to an heir. The point depends to some extent on a wordplay, because the same Greek word (*diathēkē*) is used for both a covenant and a will. The use of the word "testament" to mean covenant also explains the origin of the terms "Old Testament" and "New Testament," which Christians used to describe the two major portions of their Bible. The OT contains writings associated with God's covenant with Israel, and the NT contains writings associated with a new covenant that God has made with all humanity through Jesus Christ.

3 The blessing given by a father to his children, especially that given to his firstborn son. In keeping with **1,** this blessing was typically given when the father was an old man nearing death (Gen. 27:2; 48:21; 49:1). A prime example of such a testamentary farewell is the blessing of Jacob by Isaac in Gen. 27, although in that case the blessing is acquired through deceit (cf. 28:1–5). In Gen. 48–49, Jacob himself (now called Israel) is presented as offering a parental blessing on the two sons of Joseph and then on his own twelve sons.

4 A literary genre common in Jewish literature during the late Second Temple period (ca. 200 BCE–70 CE). This genre seems to have taken the parental blessing referred to in **3** as its central motif (especially as portrayed in Gen. 49) and developed this into a rhetorical presentation that allowed figures from the past to offer commentary on present events. The central features of the genre are: (1) a heroic person from Israel's past offers a précis of his teaching or ideas; (2) the hero then announces that his death is near; (3) the hero urges those he is addressing to remember his message after he is gone; and (4) the hero predicts what will happen after his death, describing circumstances that have become reality for readers of the testament and offering advice for applying his ideas in those circumstances. Examples of such works include the *Testament of the Twelve Patriarchs,* the *Testament of Levi,* the *Testament of Abraham,* and the *Testament of Moses,* all of which are included among the Pseudepigrapha. Many NT scholars think that aspects of the testament genre influenced the presentation of Jesus's farewell speech to his disciples in John 13–17 as well as the letter known as 2 Peter. *See also* Peter, Second Letter of; Pseudepigrapha.   A.J.S./M.A.P.

Testament, New. *See* New Testament.

Testament, Old. *See* Old Testament.

Testaments of the Twelve Patriarchs. *See* Pseudepigrapha.

testimony.
1 The laws of God as a directive for one's life (1 Kings 2:3; cf. Deut. 4:45; Ps. 119:36, 88; NRSV: "decrees"). In this regard, the tablets containing the law given by God to Moses are sometimes called the "tablets of the testimony" (Exod. 31:18; Num. 17:4; NRSV: "tablets of the covenant").

2 Observations about the world or life based on common perceptions or one's personal experience. Job considers testimony that "the wicked are spared in the day of calamity, and are rescued in the day of wrath"; such is the common perception of those who are well traveled in life (Job 21:29–30). Titus 1:12–13 affirms the truth of the testimony (common perception) that "Cretans are always liars, vicious brutes, lazy gluttons."

3 The claims that a witness makes in court and the evidence that might be cited in support of those claims (Mark 14:55–59). Israelite law did not allow a person to be put to death on the testimony of a single witness (Num. 35:50). A similar meaning might inform the "testimony" that Jesus directed a healed leper to present to the priests (Matt. 8:4). Perhaps, the leper was to give evidence of his healing, so that he could be declared "clean" and reintegrated with society (Lev. 14:1–32)—or maybe this "testimony" is to be construed more polemically as **4.**

4 A symbolic indicator of judgment that might be intended to provoke repentance or to relieve the one who offers the testimony of responsibility for the consequences that befall those who do not respond to the sign appropriately. Thus, Jesus tells his disciples that when a town does not welcome them, they are to shake off the dust of their sandals as a testimony against them (Mark 6:11). Likewise, the disciples will be dragged before governors and kings as a testimony to them and to the Gentiles (Matt. 10:18). This could mean that they will have an opportunity in such forums to offer testimony in the sense of **5,** or it could mean that their forced presence in such setting will itself be a testimonial sign of the divine judgment that is to come.

5 In the NT, God's activity through Jesus in word and deed (John 5:32; 1 John 5:11; Rev. 1:2) and the Christian presentation of God's revelation in Jesus Christ (Acts 4:33; 22:18; 1 Cor. 1:16; 2 Tim. 1:8). In John's Gospel, Jesus gives testimony to God (3:32–33), and others offer testimony to Jesus (1:1:19; 4:39; 8:17–18). Indeed, the very content of that Gospel is referred to as the reliable testimony of a disciple (19:35; 21:24). The word is used repeatedly throughout the book of Revelation to refer to the confession of faith offered by the author of that book (1:2, 9) and others who prove faithful in dire circumstances (6:9; 11:7; 12:11, 17; 20:4). Finally, the book of Revelation itself is described a testimony offered by Jesus to the churches (22:16).   M.A.P.

testing. *See* temptation, testing.

Tetragrammaton (tet′ruh-gram′uh-ton; Gk., "four letters"), the designation for the four Hebrew consonants YHWH, which comprise the name of Israel's God (Exod. 3:15; 7:2). The name itself was considered by the Hebrews as too holy to utter, so the word "Lord" (Heb. *'adonay*) was substituted when the text was read. The word "Jehovah" as a name for God was formed by combining the vowels of "Adonai" with the consonants of the Tetragrammaton (which at one time was written JHVH, a form now considered archaic). *See also* names of God in the Hebrew Bible; Yahweh.

tetrarch (tet'rahrk), originally the title for "a ruler of a fourth" or "one of four rulers." In Hellenistic and Roman times, however, it was applied somewhat loosely to petty rulers of dependent states; a tetrarch is lower in status than an ethnarch, who, in turn, is lower than a king. The term occurs seven times in the NT, but in all instances is translated "ruler" in the NRSV, though that same word is also used to render a number of other titles. Three of the references are in Luke 3:1, where Philip of Iturea, Herod Antipas, and Lysanias of Abilene are all called tetrarchs. The other four occurrences refer to Herod Antipas (Matt. 14:1; Luke 3:19; 9:7; Acts 13:1). *See also* ethnarch; governor; ruler.   F.O.G.

Thaddaeus (thad'ee-uhs), one of the twelve apostles as identified in two of the apostolic lists (Matt. 10:3; Mark 3:18). In the other lists, however, "Judas, the son [or brother] of James," appears instead of "Thaddaeus" (Luke 6:16; Acts 1:13). Some biblical manuscripts have the name "Lebbaeus" in Matt. 10:3. It is possible that Thaddaeus, Judas, and Lebbaeus are all the same person or that the lists in Luke and Acts reflect a change in the apostles over time. *See also* apostle; disciple; twelve, the.   P.L.S.

thank offering. *See* sacrifice.

theater (Gk. *theatron*, a "place for seeing"). The theater developed out of ancient Greek religious rituals involving song and dance. It consisted of a circular section of flat, hard earth, surrounded by stepped seating.

Until Hellenistic times the scene building (Gk. *skēnē*) was a simple tent, booth, or hut that served as a background for the performance. If a stage was added, it was a simple platform. The orchestra might be marked by stone slabs or a water channel. Seating, which went somewhat farther around the orchestra than a semicircle, was created by hollowing out the slope in the middle and banking it up at the ends, which widened out to give those seated a better view and make it easier to exit from the theater. The ends were held up by retaining walls above the passages on either side that led to the auditorium. The seating area was divided by one or two horizontal passages and cut by radiating stairways. Seats were cut out of native rock or made of stone slabs. One or two rows of specially ornamented and carved seats in the front of the theater were reserved for priests and public officials. The audience probably brought cushions to the theater for seating comfort.

Nothing separated the audience from the orchestra, so that the audience might feel included in the action of the tragic drama. In comedy the actors or the chorus could approach the audience across the orchestra and speak directly to individuals.

In Hellenistic times more permanent scene buildings with an added stage were constructed. Pillars or columns and panels might be used in the front of the stage building. The Romans joined the ends of the auditorium to the scene building, which thereby reduced the shape of the auditorium to a semicircle. They also began to replace the hard, flat earth with ornamental stone paving.

The remains of the Greek theater at Gebal, modern Jebail, on the Mediterranean coast of Lebanon.

Having mastered the technique of vaults and arches, the Romans were able to build theaters just about anywhere.

Romans preferred gladiator shows, beast fights, and other spectacles to drama. They added walls around the orchestra in Greek theaters to accommodate such entertainments. Popular performances consisted of comedies or farces with stock characters and mimes or clown burlesques. The more serious comedies and tragedies written during the Roman period, such as those by Nero's mentor Seneca, were not written to be performed, but to be read.

Theaters in Hellenistic cities also served as gathering places for political events or criminal prosecutions. During the riot in Ephesus caused by Paul's Christian preaching, two of his companions were dragged into the theater to be dealt with (Acts 19:28–41).   P.P.

Thebes (theebz). Egypt's magnificent capital city during much of the second and first millennia BCE. Located in Upper Egypt some 330 miles south of modern Cairo, the metropolis included vast monumental temple and palace complexes along both banks of the Nile, much of which is still visible today in the ruins of Luxor, Karnak, Qurneh, and Medinet Habu. After its zenith in the Middle and Late Kingdoms (ca. 1570–1085 BCE) the city continued to enjoy periods of ascendancy until its violent and bloody conquest by the Assyrians ca. 663 BCE. Nah. 3:8–10 alludes to Thebes' conquest, and both Jer. 46:25 and Ezek. 30:14–16 convey pronouncements of doom upon the city.   D.A.D.

Thebez (thee-'biz), a city near Shechem. It was attacked by Abimelech, the son of Gideon, when he decided to make himself king (Judg. 9). Like Shechem, Thebez had a "strong tower" (Heb. *migdal*), a sort of fortress-temple. Abimelech lay siege to this tower when the Israelites sought refuge there, but a woman threw an upper millstone on his head, crushing his skull. He had his

armor bearer run him through with a sword, so that people would not say, "A woman killed him" (Judg. 9:50–54; cf. 2 Sam. 11:21). *See also* Abimelech; Shechem; Tirzah.

theft. *See* robbery.

theophany (thee-ahf'uh-nee), a manifestation of God. The Bible contains a number of narratives and poems that recount revelations of God to men and women. Such theophanies frequently are associated with particular holy places, though the point of the narrative is sometimes to explain how that site came to have sacred associations (Gen. 12:6–7; 13:18; 18:1; 28:1–17; Exod. 40:34–38). The story of the call of Isaiah in the temple records a theophany in a place already deemed holy (6:1–8). Theophanies tend to follow a particular literary form. First, God appears, frequently as a divine warrior or king, surrounded by fire or in splendor (Deut. 33:2; Pss. 18:8; 104:2; Ezek. 1:27–28; Hab. 3:4) or sometimes riding upon the wind and clouds (Pss. 18:10; 68:33; 104:3). Second, there is a notable response to God's appearance: nature trembles (Exod. 19:18; Judg. 5:4–5; Pss. 18:7; 68:8; Hab. 3:6, 10) or the recipient responds with dread (Gen. 15:12; 28:17; Exod. 3:6; Job 42:5–6; Isa. 6:5; Hab. 3:16). Third, the consequence of God's appearance is described: nature becomes fertile (Pss. 68:8–10; 104:10–23; Isa. 35:2, 6–7), God saves and rules (Deut. 33:5; Judg. 5; Pss. 18:16–19; 29:10; 68:19–20; Isa. 35:4–6; Hab. 3:13), or the recipient is given a revelation or call (Gen. 15:12–16; Exod. 3; Isa. 6:8–13; Jer. 1:4–19; Ezek. 1:1–3:15).

Common to many of these passages is an experience of dread before the holy. In the extreme, to see God's face brings death (Gen. 32:30; Exod. 33:20; Isa. 6:5). The account of God *not* speaking to Elijah in earthquake, wind, or fire (1 Kings 19:9–18) may represent a rejection of Canaanite imagery associating God with the forces of nature.

Literature from the Second Temple period was often inspired by Ezek. 1, but the manifestation of God was typically located in heaven rather than upon earth, requiring the seer's ascent to the heavenly realm (see *1 Enoch* 14:8–25). This is also the case in Rev. 4:1–11. Elsewhere in the NT, more traditional echoes of the language of theophany are heard in the narratives of Jesus's baptism (Matt. 3:17) and transfiguration (17:1–8; cf. Exod. 34:35) and in the account of Paul's conversion (Acts 9:1–9).   D.W.S.

Theophilus (thee-ahf'uh-luhs; Gk., "lover of God" or "friend of God"), the person to whom the Gospel of Luke and the book of Acts are addressed (Luke 1:3; Acts 1:1). Hellenistic authors sometimes dedicated their books to patrons, benefactors, or persons who had an interest in the subject matter, and it is probable that the author of Luke–Acts so dedicated his writings. In Luke 1:3, Theophilus is given an honorific title ("most excellent" or "your excellency") that would appear appropriate for a high-ranking government official, but may also have been used for a benefactor or patron. Various suggestions have been made about the identity of Theophilus, but no information about him is available outside the prologues to Luke and Acts.

J.B.T.

Thessalonians (thes'uh-loh'nee-uhnz), **First Letter of Paul to the,** one of thirteen letters in the NT attributed to Paul, and one of two letters said to be written by him to Christians in Thessalonica. Most scholars think that 1 Thessalonians is the earliest Pauline letter included in the NT and, thus, the oldest extant Christian writing.

Contents: After a brief salutation (1:1), Paul and his companions give thanks to God for the Thessalonians' faithfulness (1:2–3). They recall the powerful spiritual transformation that occurred in the lives of the letters' recipients: the Thessalonians responded to the gospel by turning to God from idols and, despite persecution, became an inspiring example to believers everywhere (1:4–10). Paul reminds them of the purity and integrity with which he conducted his ministry among them (2:1–12) and the conviction with which they accepted the gospel as the very word of God (2:13). He tells them that the suffering they have had to endure from Gentiles is analogous to what Christian Jews have had to experience from Jews who reject Christ (2:14–16). Although he regrets not having been able to visit them, he has received word from Timothy of their continuing steadfastness (2:17–3:10). Paul concludes this "thanksgiving" portion of his letter with a threefold benediction (3:11–13). He then offers the Thessalonians advice on a few matters. He reminds them that they must be pure and holy with regard to sexuality (4:1–8). He says they should live quiet, productive lives, marked by mutual love for other believers and commendable behavior toward outsiders (4:9–12). Paul then takes up a topic that has apparently been troubling the Thessalonians: the fate of those who have died. He assures them that the departed will not miss out on the resurrection or even the Parousia (the Second Coming of Christ). When Christ returns, the dead in Christ will rise to meet him in the air—and then believers who are alive will be caught up in the air to join them (4:13–18). Exactly when and how this will occur cannot be known, but the assurance is that both those who live and those who die in Christ are destined for salvation (5:1–11). Having offered this encouragement, Paul concludes the letter with a number of final exhortations, blessings, and greetings (5:12–28).

Historical Setting: The letter was written by Paul to the Thessalonians "a short time" after he founded the church (2:17). Paul is thought to have evangelized the Macedonian cities of Philippi and Thessalonica sometime around 48–51 CE (see Acts 16:9–17:9). Although the account in Acts focuses on his preaching in Jewish synagogues (17:2–4), his ministry there must have had a broader compass, for many of his converts were Gentiles who "turned to God from idols" (1:9). After a few months in the city, furthermore, Paul and his co-workers were forced to leave. Separated from the Thessalonians, they became distraught over what would become of the new believers now facing persecution for their faith (2:14; 3:3–4). Unable to come to them himself (2:18), Paul finally succeeded in sending Timothy to visit them (3:2–3), and he returned with good news: the Thessalonians were standing firm (3:8), and they continued to think well of Paul (3:6). It was in response to this news that Paul wrote the letter that is now called 1 Thessalonians. The primary purpose of the letter seems to be to celebrate and cement the good relationship that Paul has with the believers in this community; the letter has a general tone of "reminding" the Thessalonians of the continued relevance of what they already know to be true (cf. 1:5; 2:1; 3:3, 4; 4:2, 6, 9, 11; 5:1, 2). In addition, however, Paul wants to respond to one new matter that has come up. The Thessalonians are troubled over what will become of members of the community who die prior to Christ's return (4:13). They might have been troubled by this because they were ignorant of basic Christian teaching concerning life after death, but many interpreters think the concern was something else. The Thessalonians may have believed that the dead would be raised to eternal life, but they were nevertheless grieved that their loved ones would miss the Parousia, the spectacular return of Christ that they had longed to behold.

Major Themes: Much of the letter is devoted to explicating the conduct of Paul's ministry. He reminds the Thessalonians of how he and his companions behaved while among them (1:5; 2:1–12),

OUTLINE OF CONTENTS

1 Thessalonians

possibly as a model for them to follow in their own ministries to others. The dominant theme of the letter, however, is articulated in response to the question that helped to prompt it. Paul explains to the Thessalonians that when Christ returns, the dead in Christ will rise first, and then the living and the dead together will be caught up to meet the Lord in the air as he descends (4:13–18). Thus, those who are alive at the time of the Parousia will have no advantage over those who died; the dead will be raised prior to Christ's return, in time to celebrate his coming. *See also* Paul; Thessalonians, Second Letter of Paul to the; Thessalonica.

Bibliography

Collins, Raymond F. *The Thessalonian Correspondence.* Leuven University Press, 1990.

Donfried, Karl P., and I. Howard Marshall. *The Theology of the Shorter Pauline Letters.* Cambridge University Press, 1993.

Jewett, Robert. *The Thessalonian Correspondence: Pauline Rhetoric and Millenarian Piety.* Fortress, 1986.

Malherbe, Abraham J. *The Letters to the Thessalonians.* Doubleday, 2000.

Powell, Mark Allan. *Introducing the New Testament: A Historical, Literary, and Theological Survey.* Baker Academic, 2009. Pp. 371–85.

Wanamaker, Charles A. *The Epistles to the Thessalonians: A Commentary on the Greek Text.* Eerdmans, 1990. M.A.P.

Thessalonians, Second Letter of Paul to the,

one of thirteen letters in the NT attributed to Paul and one of two letters ostensibly addressed to Christians in Thessalonica. About one-third of its contents closely parallels what is said in 1 Thessalonians. Some scholars believe that 2 Thessalonians is pseudepigraphical (attributed to Paul, but actually written by disciples or admirers of Paul after his death).

Contents: A brief salutation (1:1–2) identifies the letter as being from Paul, Silas, and Timothy, who testify to the fact that the Thessalonians' mutual love and faithfulness in persecution have inspired pride and thanksgiving among the churches of God (1:3–4). This is followed by a promise that God will wreak vengeance on those who afflict the Thessalonians, punishing them with eternal destruction on the day of judgment (1:5–12). The mention of that day leads to instruction on a significant issue: some people have been telling the Thessalonians that the "day of the Lord" has already arrived (2:1–2). The authors assure them that this is not the case and that, indeed, that day will not come until after "the lawless one" mounts a final and futile opposition to God (2:3–12). The authors are confident that the Thessalonians will not be among those deceived by this satanic foe, provided they hold fast to what Paul taught them (2:13–15). They offer the Thessalonians their blessing in this regard (2:16–17), ask for their prayers (3:1–2), repeat the affirmation of confidence (3:3–4), and offer another blessing, similar to the first (3:5). Then the letter turns to

another topic, the problem of idleness. The Thessalonians ought to follow the example of productive labor that Paul set for them, and they should avoid association with believers who do not follow this example (3:6–15). The letter closes with two benedictions and some words in Paul's own handwriting by which the readers will be able to recognize the authenticity of this letter as coming from him rather than from someone using his name to mislead them (3:16–17).

OUTLINE OF CONTENTS

2 Thessalonians

Authorship: Scholars who think that 2 Thessalonians is pseudepigraphical often make the following points. (1) It would be odd for Paul to repeat so much of what he said in 1 Thessalonians in another letter written to the same people a few months later. (2) The advice given in 2 Thess. 2:1–12 (the day of the Lord will be preceded by recognizable events) seems to contradict what Paul says in 1 Thess. 5:1–3 (the day will come without warning). (3) The claim in 2 Thess. 2:5 that Paul taught the Thessalonians the end was not yet at hand is hard to reconcile with the fact that the Thessalonians were surprised when some members of the community died before the end arrived (cf. 1 Thess. 4:13–18). (4) The warning in 2 Thess. 2:2 that forged letters from Paul might be circulating is anachronistic for a period early in the apostle's career (when the letter would be dated, if authentic). (5) The letter displays a number of features atypical for Paul, e.g., the use of the term "hope" to mean simply "patience" in 1:3–4 and reference to salvation as a primarily future phenomenon in 1:7–12. Scholars who consider the letter authentic assume that Paul's thinking on a subject as mysterious as the end times could have been inconsistent or paradoxical, and they allow that Paul might have emphasized different aspects of his beliefs at different times, depending on which pastoral concern needed to be addressed. It also seems unlikely that anyone writing after 70 CE would compose a letter in Paul's name claiming that some sort of abomination in the temple (which no longer existed) would precede the day of the Lord (2:4). Finally, many scholars believe that the letter's explicit claim to authenticity in 3:17 combined with the early church's unanimous recognition of the letter's canonicity make pseudepigraphy unlikely; if not authentic, the letter would have to be regarded as an outright forgery, which seems unlikely for a letter that was never challenged in the early church.

Historical Setting: If 2 Thessalonians was actually written by Paul, then it is usually thought to have been composed shortly after 1 Thessalonians (in part because the two letters are so similar). The suggested scenario is that soon after sending that letter Paul received word back from the church that a new crisis had arisen: some members had bought in on a rumor that "the day of the Lord is already here" (2 Thess. 2:12). Some scholars have even suggested that this rumor might have been fed by a misunderstanding of certain comments Paul makes in 1 Thessalonians. In any case, according to this scenario, the letter would have been sent by Paul from Corinth some time between 50 and 53—it would be one of Paul's earliest letters, possibly the second earliest writing among all NT books. If, however, the letter is judged to be pseudepigraphical, its historical circumstances become impossible to determine. It could have been written at almost any time in the last three decades of the first century, and the point would be simply to update or revise Paul's teaching on the Parousia with more specific ideas that had developed in the interim.

Major Themes: Second Thessalonians emphasizes the certainty of judgment for those who do not know God or obey the gospel (1:7–8). The letter also deals with the problem of idleness (3:6–12; cf. 1 Thess. 4:11; 5:14), suggesting that people unwilling to work should be excluded from the community meal. The dominant theme of the letter, however, is its teaching on the Parousia. It maintains the end will not come until after "the rebellion comes" and "the lawless one is revealed" (2:3); for the moment, this lawless one is being restrained by someone or something (2:7–8), but when the restraint is revealed, the lawless one will take his seat in the temple and declare himself to be God (2:4)—and *then* the day of the Lord will come and Jesus will return (2:8). This teaching has proved enigmatic throughout the centuries, and many proposals have been offered regarding its interpretation. *See also* lawless one; Paul; pseudepigraphy; Thessalonians, First Letter of Paul to the.

Bibliography

Collins, Raymond F. *The Thessalonian Correspondence.* Leuven University Press, 1990.

Donfried, Karl P., and I. Howard Marshall. *The Theology of the Shorter Pauline Letters.* Cambridge University Press, 1993.

Jewett, Robert. *The Thessalonian Correspondence: Pauline Rhetoric and Millenarian Piety.* Fortress, 1986.

Malherbe, Abraham J. *The Letters to the Thessalonians.* Doubleday, 2000.

Powell, Mark Allan. *Introducing the New Testament: A Historical, Literary, and Theological Survey.* Baker Academic, 2009. Pp. 387–95.

Wanamaker, Charles A. *The Epistles to the Thessalonians: A Commentary on the Greek Text.* Eerdmans, 1990.   M.A.P.

WHO OR WHAT IS THE RESTRAINER?

Second Thessalonians 2:6–7 indicates that "the lawless one" is currently being restrained by someone or something that will eventually be removed. The Thessalonians knew who or what this restrainer was (2:5–6). Interpreters since then have had some guesses:

God *or* God's power *or* the Holy Spirit

Satan

The angel Apollyon (mentioned in Rev. 9:11)

The archangel Michael (Jude 1:9; Rev. 12:7)

The Christian church

Some prominent Christian leader (Paul himself or James of Jerusalem)

The Gentile mission, which had to be completed first (cf. Mark 13:10)

The Roman empire and/or the emperor (cf. Rom. 13:1–7)

Such ideas are sometimes combined: 2 Thess. 2:6 seems to speak of a restraining force ("what is now restraining him"), while 2:7 seems to speak of a person ("the one who now restrains"). In the fifth century, St. Augustine's comment on 2 Thess. 2:6–7 was: "I must admit that the meaning of this completely escapes me" (*City of God* 20.19). Modern scholars have fared no better than Augustine in their analysis of this puzzle.

From Mark Allan Powell, *Introducing the New Testament* (courtesy, Baker Academic)

Thessalonica (thes̩'uh-luh-ni'kuh), a city in Macedonia (modern Thessaloniki), located at the head of the Thermaic Gulf. In the NT, Thessalonica is referred to exclusively in connection with the missionary activities of the apostle Paul (cf. Acts 17:1–13; 20:4; 27:2; 1 Thess.; 2 Thess.; Phil. 4:16; 2 Tim. 4:10). The city was founded in 316 BCE by Cassander, a general in the army of Alexander the Great, who gave the city its name in honor of his wife, Thessalonikeia, the daughter of Philip II and the half sister of Alexander. The new city included ancient Therme and some thirty-five other towns. When Macedonia became a Roman province in 146 BCE, Thessalonica was made the capital and thus the center of Roman administration. The city supported the victorious Antony and Octavian prior to the battle of Philippi in 42 BCE, an event that ushered in a prosperous new era for Thessalonica. Additionally, the Roman statesman and orator Cicero spent part of his exile in Thessalonica in 58 BCE, the Roman general Pompey took refuge from Julius Caesar in the city in 49 BCE, and such prominent literary figures as Lucian and Polyaenus visited the city. The extensive coinage of Thessalonica underscores its prosperity, certainly due to its status as a free city (i.e., one granted certain tax concessions and other privileges) and its location as a main station on the Via Egnatia, which ran through the city on the east–west axis from the Balkans to Asia Minor.

Religious Life: Among the many deities worshiped at Thessalonica were the traditional Greek gods like Zeus (extensively represented in the city's coinage), Asclepius, Aphrodite, Dionysus, and Demeter. There is also evidence for the cult of the Egyptian god Serapis, the closely associated cult of the goddess Isis, and the cult of the Phyrigian Cabiri, for which we have both literary and numismatic evidence. The Cabiri are also given the name "great gods" (Gk. *megaloi theoi*), and it is possible that the archaeological results in Samothrace may shed new light on these originally Phrygian deities who promoted fertility and protected sailors, a not unimportant fact for a city located at the head of the Thermaic Gulf. The Cabiri are often identified with the Dioscuri (Castor and Pollux, sons of Zeus), who also appear on a coin of

Thessalonica dated 89 BCE. So deeply revered were these Cabiri/Dioscuri in Thessalonica that they are portrayed on two pilaster reliefs on the face of the arched western gate (built no later than the first century BCE) as armed guardians of that gate. The steady growth of their influence is evidenced by coins from the Flavian Age (last third of the first century CE), which depict them as the city's tutelary powers.

In addition, there was a very strong civic cult in the Roman period that regularly expressed gratitude to Roman patrons and Roman client rulers (e.g., a Thracian dynast) in recognition of the fact that the city's well-being was dependent on Roman benefaction. There is also evidence for the granting of divine honors to the goddess Roma in connection with honors bestowed on other Roman benefactors, and for a temple dedicated to Julius Caesar, whom the Thessalonians along with others acclaimed as a god, and his son Augustus, who was deemed the son of god on Thessalonian inscriptions. A group known as "priests of the gods" also had connections to the imperial cult. An interrelationship between the civic cult and the Cabiri/Dioscuri is probable. According to Acts, the pluralistic religious life of Thessalonica included a Jewish component. In Acts 17 (cf. 1 Thess. 2:13–16), Paul encounters unusually bitter opposition from the Jews of the city. But Jews were not the only foreigners who brought their deities to Thessalonica.

Remains of the Ancient City: Little can be excavated in the modern city of Thessaloniki, though one uncovered city block reveals the ruins of the ancient Roman forum, which may have been adjacent to the site of the Hellenistic forum. It is possible that there was a second agora (marketplace) to the south and close to the harbor as, e.g., in Pirene. In the Hellenistic period there was a stadium, a gymnasium, and to the west a serapeum (i.e., a temple of Serapis), which was part of a larger sacred area. From the remains of the Vardar Arch at the western entrance to the city a broken inscription reading "in the time of the politarchs" has been found. This term is identical to the unusual description given in Acts 17:6 for the rulers (*politarchai*) of Thessalonica. *See also* Thessalonians, First Letter of Paul to the; Thessalonians, Second Letter of Paul to the.   K.P.D./J.R.

Theudas (thoo'duhs), the leader of a messianic movement in Judah. According to the Jewish historian Josephus (born ca. 37 CE), Theudas saw himself as a new Joshua figure who would lead his people by God's power across the Jordan to commence a new era for Israel. He was killed by the Romans ca. 44 CE (*Antiquities* 20.97–98). Theudas is also mentioned in the NT (Acts 5:36–37), but he is there placed prior to another revolutionary, one Judas, who led his doomed rebellion about 6 CE. This discrepancy in the date for Theudas (NT: prior to 6 CE; Josephus, 44 CE) remains unresolved. *See also* Judas.

thigh.

1 The right thigh of the animal that constituted the Israelites' well-being offerings was given to priests as a stipend in addition to the animal's breast (Lev. 7:32–34). These portions could be eaten by both the priests and their households outside the sanctuary area (10:14). The custom of giving the thigh to a sacrificial officiant is quite ancient (cf. 1 Sam. 9:24).

2 Oaths were made by placing one's hand "under the thigh" of another (Gen. 24:2, 9; 47:29). Punishment from God for breaking such an oath might include the death of one's offspring or the fate of dying childless. *See also* gestures, postures, and facial expressions; oath.   D.P.W.

thistle. *See* thorns.

Thomas (tom′uhs; Aramaic, "twin"), one of the

twelve disciples of Jesus, called "the Twin" (Gk. Didymus) in the Gospel of John (11:16; 20:24; 21:2). He appears in each of the apostolic lists (Matt. 10:3; Mark 3:18; Luke 6:15; Acts 1:13). Receiving little mention in the Synoptic Gospels, Thomas becomes important in the later portions of John's Gospel. When Jesus announces his intent to go to Judea, Thomas exclaims, "Let us also go that we may die with him!" (11:16); interpreters are not sure whether to take that comment as evocative of pessimism or courage (or both). Thomas appears to be without understanding when, in 14:5, he confesses his ignorance about where Jesus is going and therefore finds it difficult to follow him. Finally, after the resurrection he is the only one of the remaining eleven disciples to be absent when Jesus appears to them, gives them the Holy Spirit, and commissions them for ministry (20:19–23). When the others tell him what has happened, he refuses to believe that Jesus has been raised unless he can see for himself and touch the wounds in his hands and side. Jesus then appears to the disciples again and beckons Thomas to do this; Thomas calls him, "My Lord and my God!" (20:24–29). The latter story is told as a paradigm for all Christians who are called to believe in Christ without having seen him or having been granted tangible proof of his resurrection; Jesus tells Thomas, "Blessed are those who have not seen and yet have come to believe" (20:29). Later, in 21:1–14, Thomas is one of the small group of disciples who go fishing and see the risen Lord again.

Little is known about Thomas's activities after the crucifixion of Jesus. He is mentioned in the book of Acts as among those gathered in the upper room after the ascension (1:13) so he is presumably also among the apostles who receive the Holy Spirit at Pentecost (2:1–4) and among the apostles whose teaching sustained the early community (2:42–43). Thereafter, tradition preserves only legendary stories of little apparent historical value. At least two apocryphal gospels are attributed to him (*Gospel of Thomas, Infancy Gospel of Thomas*). *See also* apostle; disciple; twelve, the.   P.L.S.

Thomas, Gospel of, one of the more signifi-

cant books among a vast collection of apocryphal Christian writings. The *Gospel of Thomas* is not actually a Gospel, but a collection of 114 secret sayings purportedly dictated by the "living Jesus" to Judas Thomas, "the Twin" (i.e., one of Jesus's twelve disciples). A Coptic manuscript of the book was discovered in 1945 as part of the Nag Hammadi library found in northern Egypt. The work contains no narratives about the birth, ministry, life, or passion of Jesus. In outward form it may resemble the lost Q source that most scholars think was a collection of Jesus's sayings used as a source for the Gospels of Matthew and Luke. The Nag Hammadi version is a Coptic translation of a work that was originally written in Greek. Three fragments of a Greek manuscript of the work had been found earlier at Oxyrhynchus in Egypt in 1898 and 1903, but they were not identified as parts of the *Gospel of Thomas* until the complete Coptic version was discovered. The earliest Greek fragment can be dated to the early third century CE. Thus, the *Gospel of Thomas* must have been composed prior to 200 CE, earlier than many of the other apocryphal Christian writings. It may be impossible to determine the date of the original

The closing page of the Coptic *Gospel of Thomas,* with title; second century CE.

composition more precisely than this. A majority of scholars who have examined the work believe that it is probably dependent on the Synoptic Gospels found in the NT, which would place it at the end of the first century at the earliest. Some have deduced what they consider to be evidence that it is dependent on Tatian's *Diatessaron,* which would probably put it in the mid-second century. A few scholars, however, have argued that the *Gospel of Thomas* is independent of any other NT writings and, so, could have been written as early as any of the Gospels that are included in the NT. The place of composition was probably Syria, where traditions about the apostle Judas Thomas, identified as the twin brother of Jesus, were common and where the ascetic and unconventional form of Christianity advocated in the *Gospel* appears to have been at home.

Contents: The sayings that make up the *Gospel of Thomas* are not organized according to any clear thematic pattern, but are loosely strung together with catchword associations, a characteristic of oral transmission. Many of the sayings, parables, proverbs, and brief dialogues presented in the *Gospel of Thomas* parallel sayings attributed to Jesus in the Synoptic Gospels. For example, consider the following version of the parable of the Sower:

Behold, the sower went out, he filled his hand, he sowed the seed. Some seeds fell on the road. The birds came and gathered them up. Others fell on the rock and did not send a root down into the earth, and did not send an ear up to heaven. And others fell among thorns. They choked the seed, and the worm ate it. And others fell upon the good earth; and it brought forth good fruit up to heaven. It bore sixty-fold and one-hundred-and-twenty-fold." (*Gos. Thom.* 9; cf. Matt. 13:1–9; Mark 4:1–9; Luke 8:4–8)

What is intriguing to some scholars is that the *Gospel of Thomas* does not follow the Synoptic Gospels in offering an allegorical explanation that interprets the story somewhat anachronistically as diverse responses to Christian preaching (cf. Matt. 13:18–23; Mark 4:13–20; Luke 8:11–15). Because that explanation is generally regarded as a secondary accretion, a case might be made that *Thomas* preserves a more original (less interpreted) version of this parable.

In other cases, *Thomas* preserves a version of a parable or saying quite different from the version found in the Synoptic Gospels. This is the case with the parable of Hidden Treasure:

The kingdom of the Father is like a person who had a treasure hidden in his field but did not know it. And when he died he left it to his son. The son did not know about it either. He took over the field and sold it. The buyer went plowing, discovered the treasure, and began to lend money at interest to whomever he wished. (109:1–3)

This may be compared with the story as it appears in the Gospel of Matthew: "The kingdom of heaven is like treasure hidden in a field, which someone found and hid; then in his joy he goes and sells all that he has and buys that field." (13:44).

Further, the *Gospel of Thomas* contains parables and sayings that have no parallels at all in the Synoptic Gospels. Among its unique material are the parable of the Jar and the parable of the Assassin:

The kingdom of the Father is like a woman who was carrying a jar full of meal. While she was walking along a distant road, the handle of the jar broke and the meal spilled behind her along the road. She didn't know it; she hadn't noticed a problem. When she reached her house, she put the jar down and discovered that it was empty. (97:104)

The Father's kingdom is like a person who wanted to kill someone powerful. While still at home he drew his sword and thrust it into the wall to find out whether his hand would go in. Then he killed the powerful one. (98:1–3)

These parables, though different in content, are at least similar in form to material associated with Jesus in the Synoptic Gospels.

Much of the material in *Thomas,* however, is of a different order, presented in language that is mysterious, if not baffling: "Jesus said to (his disciples), "When you make the two into one, and when you make the inner like the outer, and the upper like the lower, and when you make male and female into a single one, so that the male will not be male nor the female be female, then you will enter the Father's domain" (22:4–7).

Gnostic Affiliations: The relationship of the *Gospel of Thomas* to the second-century religious movement known as Gnosticism is greatly disputed by scholars. *Thomas* is often thought to betray a gnostic orientation, but it is uncertain whether the work should therefore be regarded as a product of some gnostic Christian group (probably in the second century) or as evidence for protognostic ideology present among some people attracted to Jesus early on.

The book claims to offer an esoteric *gnōsis,* or knowledge, that guarantees immortality (*Gos. Thom.* 1). The contents of this troubling yet marvelous knowledge (2) involve an understanding of one's true self, which is superior to any other knowledge (67). Through this knowledge, one recognizes the origin of the essential self in the world of light (49–50), where the self preexisted (19) and to which it is destined to return (18) to enjoy a state of final rest (60). Recipients of this knowledge thus realize that they are children of the Living Father (4, 50). A sharp dichotomy between flesh and spirit and a sense of alienation from "the world" also characterize this gospel. Without the saving *gnōsis* provided by Jesus, people are in a state of drunken blindness (29), in a world that threatens to devour the true self (7, 60). When one understands the world, it becomes clear that it is a corpse (56). The soul must be freed from bondage in this realm, and any soul content with a state of dependence on the body is wretched (87, 112).

Disciples who achieve internal illumination (*Gos. Thom.* 24) must reject the world. Most concretely, disciples must reject familial ties in favor of the "true Mother" (55, 99, 101) and avoid the involvement in commerce with the "buyers and traders," who will not enter the Father's realm (64). The disciple must be a "passerby" (42), a wandering ascetic who will "fast from the world" (27). Such "fasting" is clearly metaphorical; conventional piety is not recommended (14, 53). More positively, the illuminated disciple, who has "found the self" (111), enters the "bridal chamber" (75) and is able to achieve a unitary state (11), wherein the differentiations of inner and outer or male and female are overcome (22). Most dramatically, Jesus promises that Mary will be "made male" and thus be the equal of the male apostles (114). The ultimate goal of discipleship is to be a *monachos,* or "solitary one" (4, 16, 23, 49). It is the solitary one, in a state of inner harmony, who enters into the kingdom of God. This realm is not an eschatological or heavenly manifestation of divine sovereignty, as it is in the Synoptic Gospels or in Paul (3). Rather, it is a spiritual reality from which the disciples have come, to which they return, and which is present on earth within them (49, 113, 114).

The *Gospel of Thomas* is reticent about the Jesus who provides this illumination. It says nothing about his miracles, death, and resurrection, and these events apparently have no special significance. Only one remark (*Gos. Thom.* 55) refers to the "cross" that a disciple must bear. Jesus is primarily a revealer who has come into a hostile world (28) to set it ablaze (10), presumably with his wisdom. It is his words, not his deeds, that are important (43). He imparts hidden mysteries (17), imaged as a "bubbling wellspring" (13). Those who drink from this spring become his equals (108).

Despite the gnostic flavor of some of this material, the *Gospel of Thomas* incorporates some material likely to have been rejected by second-century gnostics. A saying that exalts the importance of James the Just (12) seems to promote the tradition that emerged from early Jewish-Christian circles in Jerusalem. Many interpreters conclude that the collection developed through various editorial stages that introduced different types of material with different nuances of meaning along the way. *See also* apocryphal Christian writings; Gnosticism; Nag Hammadi.

Bibliography

Meyer, Marvin, ed. *The Nag Hammadi Scriptures: The Definitive International Version.* HarperOne, 2006.

Patterson, Stephen L. *The Gospel of Thomas and Jesus.* Polebridge, 1993.

Robinson, James M. *The Nag Hammadi Library.* 3rd ed. Harper & Row, 1988.   H.W.A./M.A.P.

thorns. Thorns are referred to in the Bible by several different terms such as "brambles," "briers,"

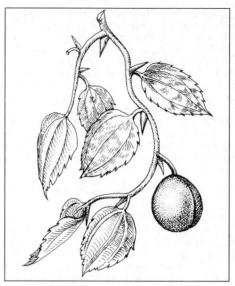

Thorns (*Zizyphus spina-cristi*).

"thistles," and "nettles." They are usually mentioned in a negative sense as irritants, impediments, noxious plants, or indicators of desolate areas. Collectively, the term "thorns" refers to the spine-bearing plants that are especially common in the arid regions of the Near East. The prickly armor of these plants, not only protects them from being destroyed by the indiscriminate grazing of goats, camels, and donkeys, but also reduces transpiration and loss of water during dry periods.

In Judg. 9:7–15, Jotham tells a parable about thorns when he hears that the lords of Shechem have made Abimelech king. In his parable, the trees of the forest decide to choose a king, but all of the fruitful and productive plants are too occupied with important tasks to accept the job; therefore, the trees ask the bramble to reign over them. In the Synoptic Gospels, Jesus tells the parable of the Sower, in which thorns also play a significant role. Seed that falls among the thorns is likened to people who hear the word, but do not bear fruit because "they are choked by the cares and riches and pleasures of life" (Luke 8:14; cf. Matt. 13:22; Mark 4:18–19).

The crown of thorns that was placed on Jesus's head (Matt. 27:29) has been variously identified as Christ thorn (*Zizyphus spina-cristi* or *Zizyphus lotus*), thorny burnet (*Poterium spinosum*), or paliurus (*Paliurus spina-cristi*), all of which are shrubs common in the plains and hill regions of the Levant. The "bramble bush" from which Jesus says one would never gather figs (Luke 6:44) may refer to the fruit-bearing blackberry or raspberry plants (genus *Rubus*) growing on moist stream banks or the spiny burnet dominating the limestone soils. Both plants form impenetrable thickets. Briers, like thorns and brambles, also form woody thickets and spiny hedges (Mic. 7:4; Ezek. 28:24). Many such woody, thorn-bearing shrubs are placed in piles as fencing to keep in animals and to keep out intruders or are used as fuel when dried (Prov. 15:19; Hos. 2:6). *See also* brambles.   P.L.C.

thousand. In addition to being used in a literal sense, the number one thousand is sometimes employed figuratively to express "a large number." This was especially true with multiples of a thousand. Whenever Moses set the ark of the covenant to rest after a day of traveling through the wilderness, he said, "Return, O Lord of the ten thousand thousands of Israel" (Num. 10:36). This tendency can also be observed in the NT (Mark 6:44; 8:9; Acts 2:41; 4:4; Rev. 7:4–8; 21:16). The number was also employed for military units (1 Sam. 8:12; 1 Chron. 13:1); in NT times, a Roman legion was hypothetically composed of 6,000 troops. Thus Jesus could have called 72,000 angels to assist him in Gethsemane if he had so wished (Matt. 26:53). In temporal expressions, "thousand" is often used to mean "a long time" (Pss. 84:10; 90:4; cf. 2 Pet 3:8; Rev. 20:3). In the NT, one thousand years are reckoned in God's time as but a day (2 Pet. 3:8). *See also* legion; millennium; numbers.   J.A.D.

Thrace (thrays), the region east of Macedonia and west of the Black Sea, populated by independent tribes sometimes considered savage. The NT records no mission or church there, though Samothrace, Neapolis, and Philippi lay nearby.

three. *See* numbers.

Three Taverns, a way station on the Appian Way about thirty miles south of Rome and ten miles north of the Forum of Appius. Paul was met here by members of the Christian community of Rome when he traveled as a prisoner from Puteoli to Rome (Acts 28:15). *See also* Appius, Forum of.

threshing, the process by which the seed coverings of ripe cereals such as wheat and barley are removed. After the harvest, the cut grain was spread to dry on flat, open surfaces, or threshing floors (1 Chron. 21:20–23). The dried stalks were then either beaten with flails or crushed by a heavy board in which sharp stones have been imbedded. The board was dragged across the threshing floor by an ox or a donkey (Deut. 25:4; 1 Cor. 9:9). The husks were also loosened from the grain by slow heating, or parching, in an oven. The loosened husks, or·chaff, were then separated from the grain by winnowing before the grain was ground into flour or stored in jars or granaries (see Matt. 3:12). *See also* granary; winnowing.   P.L.C.

threshold, the bottom part of a door frame, over which one steps in entering a building or the gateway to a city. Guards were posted at the threshold (i.e., the entrance) of the temple; these were priests (2 Kings 12:10) or Levites (2 Chron. 34:9). One of their duties was to receive donations from the people entering the temple (2 Kings 22:4). In Ezekiel's visionary temple, the laity were not permitted to enter the gates to the temple; even the lay ruler was allowed to come only as far as the inner threshold of the gate to worship (46:2). Zephaniah condemns those who jump over the threshold of the temple (1:9), possibly because it was an idolatrous practice. The priests of Dagon in Ashdod would not tread on the threshold to Dagon's temple, since the image of Dagon had fallen on it when the captured ark of God had been placed in that temple (see 1 Sam. 5:4–5).   S.R.

throne, a literal seat for a king or queen (Exod. 11:5) and, thus, a symbol of royal power (2 Sam. 3:10; cf. Luke 1:32) and sometimes of the authority to pass judgment (1 Kings 7:7). In a religious sense, the word "throne" may be used to describe the seat of God as king over the earth (Ps. 47:8; cf. Heb. 8:1; Rev. 3:21) and as the judge of the nations (Ps. 9:4; cf. Matt. 19:28; Rev. 20:11). Lesser thrones may be offered to those who sit with God in judgment (Dan. 7:9; cf. Matt. 19:28). In the book of Revelation, the word "throne" appears forty-seven times, far more than in any other book of the Bible, and this is reflective of the conflict of powers portrayed in that book's apocalyptic scenario. Many of the references are to the throne of God in heaven, surrounded by worshiping saints and angels (e.g. 5:1, 6–7, 11, 13). But 2:13 refers to "Satan's throne" in the city of Pergamum, a possible reference to the Roman governor's seat of judgment or, perhaps, to a temple devoted to emperor worship. Likewise, an apocalyptic beast is given a "throne and great authority" by a dragon, which is the devil (13:2; 16:10; cf. 12:9). *See also* antichrist; judgment, day of; messiah; Pergamum; vision.   A.Y.C.

thumb. The right thumb was daubed with sacrificial blood during a priest's ordination, as were the big toe and the right ear lobe (Exod. 29:20; Lev. 8:23, 24). A person healed of leprosy was likewise daubed with blood and then oil on the same members as part of a cleansing ritual (Lev. 14:14, 17, 25, 28). The purpose was primarily to provide protection from forces of evil on the most vulnerable parts of the body—its extremities. Loss of the toes and thumbs was humiliating and disabling. In the book of Judges, King Adonibezek thus mutilated some seventy defeated enemy rulers and was later treated in the same way himself by the conquering Israelites (1:6–7).   S.R.

Thummim. *See* breastpiece; Urim and Thummim.

thunder. In biblical perspectives thunder was often associated with heights (2 Sam. 22:14; Ps. 18:13; Job 36:29), storms (Exod. 9:23; 1 Sam. 12:17; Job 38:25), and other violent natural phenomena

The Assyrian king Shalmaneser III on his throne, receiving the spoils taken from one of the conquered cities; bronze decorations from the great door of the palace, ninth century BCE.

(Isa. 29:6; Rev. 11:19). Used metaphorically it describes the sound of the sea (Isa. 17:12) or roaring streams (Ps. 42:7) and the power and authority of the voice of God (Job 37:2, 5; Ps. 29:3; Exod. 19:19; John 12:28–29). Prophets refer to thunder to express the presence (Ezek. 1:24) and awesomeness of God (Isa. 33:3). R.S.B.

thunder, sons of. *See* Boanerges.

Thutmose (thy*oot*′mohs; Gk. Tuthmosis; Egyptian, "Thoth [The moon god] is born"), the name held by four kings of the Egyptian Eighteenth Dynasty (1570–1293 BCE). The time when these four pharaohs ruled is sometimes referred to as the Thutmoside period. During this time, Egyptian power expanded considerably, especially in Syria and the Levant. Some of the kings and major events of their individual reigns are listed below.

1 Thutmose I (1524–1518 BCE), a military man of nonroyal birth who reached the throne by marrying the daughter of his predecessor (Amenhotep I). He conducted a raid deep into Syria, crossing the Euphrates River and setting up a victory stele on the riverbank near Carchemish.

2 Thutmose II (1518–1504 BCE), a son of Thutmose I, husband of Queen Hatshepsut. His only campaign into the Levant was a minor raid undertaken against a group of Bedouins.

3 Thutmose III (1504–1450 BCE), initially co-ruler of Egypt with his stepmother, Queen Hatshepsut, then sole ruler of Egypt from 1483 BCE on. In the twenty-second year of his reign he led an Egyptian army up to Megiddo, where the prince of the Syrian city of Kadesh had brought together a large army of Syrians and Canaanites under his leadership. Thutmose III's capture of Megiddo in 1482 BCE resulted in the establishment of the great Egyptian empire in western Asia. This king conducted a total of seventeen campaigns in the Levant; his army reached the Euphrates River in the eighth campaign. Thutmose III is often considered the greatest military leader in Egyptian history. Egypt became wealthy and prosperous as a result of all the tribute and trade that reached the Nile Valley from its empire in western Asia and Nubia.

4 Thutmose IV (1419–1386 BCE), a son of Amenhotep II (who was a son of Thutmose III); he sealed Egypt's diplomatic relations with the north Syrian kingdom of Mitanni by marrying the daughter of the Mitannian king. On a stele found in western Thebes, Thutmose IV claims to have conquered the city of Gezer.

See also Gezer; Megiddo. J.M.W.

Thyatira (thi′uh-ti′ruh), a city (modern Akhisar), about fifty-five miles northeast of Izmir (Smyrna), Turkey. It lay on the road between Pergamum and Sardis in Lydia (or at times in Mysia) on the Lycus River. Founded as a Hellenistic city by Seleucus I Nicator in 300 BCE, it had developed many industrial and commercial guilds by the first century CE. According to Acts 16:14–15, Paul's first convert at Philippi was Lydia, "a dealer in purple cloth" from Thyatira. By the late first century, a sufficiently significant Christian community existed in Thyatira to merit the fourth and lon-

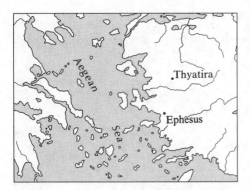

gest of the seven letters of Revelation (2:18–29). That letter contains harsh condemnation of a local woman (possibly a Christian prophet) who is compared to Jezebel, who induced King Ahab to allow the worship of Canaanite deities (2:20; cf. 1 Kings 18–19; 2 Kings 9). She is said to have led church members into practicing fornication, committing adultery, and eating food sacrificed to altars. The accusations regarding sexual indiscretions could be metaphorical descriptions for idolatry, in which case the controversy at Thyatira may have involved Christian participation in pagan celebrations and banquets, at which foreign gods were routinely honored and food dedicated to them was consumed (cf. 1 Cor. 10:14–22). But it is also possible that the Thyatiran prophet was simultaneously involved with the Christian community and a local fertility cult, into which she hoped to draw members of the congregation. *See also* Lydia; Mysia.   C.H.M./M.A.P.

Tiamat (tee-ah'maht; from Akkadian *tamtu,* "sea"), the watery source of life and Marduk's defeated opponent in the *Enuma Elish,* the Babylonian account of the emergence of the gods, the for-

mation of the physical world, and the organization of the pantheon under the rulership of Marduk at Babylon. In the *Enuma Elish,* the goddess Tiamat is either identified with the sea (Persian Gulf, Mediterranean Sea) or subterranean waters. In any case, she is the mother who begot everything, and she is presented with both sympathy and hostility in the *Enuma Elish.* Her slayer, Marduk, divides her body and creates heaven and earth out of its two halves (cf. Gen. 1:6). Tiamat is not referred to as such in the Bible, but references to "the deep" (Heb. *tehom*) would have evoked her memory for any who knew the myth (cf. Gen. 1:2; 7:11; 8:2). *See also* Babylon.
                                                                      I.T.A.

Tiberias (ti-bihr'ee-uhs), a city named for Tiberius Caesar on the west shore of the Sea of Galilee. Herod Antipas, tetrarch of Galilee and Perea (Matt. 14:1–6; Luke 3:19), founded it (ca. 20 CE) to replace Sepphoris as the capital of Galilee. Administration, trade, and fishing became its major industries, while nearby hot springs made Tiberias a popular health resort. Herod Antipas built a palace there, the remains of which might have been uncovered by archaeologists. In addition, a Roman-style theater and a massive city gate have been found from the first century. From later periods, ancient synagogues have been discovered.

According to Josephus, the city was built upon a necropolis (possibly the cemetery for the ancient city of Hammoth; cf. Josh. 19:35) and, so, was ritually unclean according to Jewish law. Still, many were drawn to the site, and perhaps the promise of land and housing attracted the poorer classes. By the second century, it became known as a prominent place for rabbinic learning, and it continued as such for nearly a millennium, in spite of its inauspicious origins.

Tiberias is conspicuous by absence in the NT. John 6:23 records the only biblical reference to the city in a passage that simply mentions "some boats

Remains of walls at Tiberias (founded ca. 18 CE), on the west shore of the Sea of Galilee.

from Tiberias." Jesus is not said to have ever visited the city, although much of his ministry was spent in smaller towns throughout the surrounding area. The Sea of Galilee was sometimes called the Sea of Tiberias (cf. John 6:1; 21:1).   D.R.E.

Tiberias, Sea of, better known as the Sea of Galilee (John 6:1; 21:1). *See also* Galilee, Sea of.

Tiberius (ti-bihr′ee-uhs), Claudius Caesar Augustus, Roman emperor from 14 CE, when he succeeded Augustus, until 37 CE, when he died in Capri, reportedly the victim of his many years of dissipation. He was the reigning emperor during Jesus's public ministry and thus (except in Luke 2:1) is the "Caesar" of the NT Gospels. Luke 3:1 uses his name in fixing the date for John's preaching and the baptism of Jesus ("in the fifteenth year of the reign of Tiberius Caesar," i.e., in 29 CE). Matthew, Mark, and Luke report the incident of the questioning of Jesus concerning the payment of taxes to Caesar (Matt. 22:15–23; Mark 12:13–17; Luke 20:20–26). Jesus's answer centered on the display of a coin of Tiberius, bearing the emperor's portrait. In about 18 CE, Herod Antipas, tetrarch of Galilee, founded the city of Tiberias, named in honor of the emperor, as his capital on the western shore of Lake Chinnereth (the Sea of Galilee). *See also* Caesar; emperor; Roman Empire; Tiberias.   F.O.G.

Silver denarius of Tiberius, Roman emperor 14–37 CE, during Jesus's public ministry.

Tibni (tib′ni), the son of Ginath and leader of a faction in the northern kingdom who struggled with Omri for control of the throne following the suicide of Zimri (ca. 876 BCE). He was unsuccessful, however, and died soon after. The reason for his death is unknown (1 Kings 16:21–22). *See also* Omri.

Tidal (ti′duhl), the king of Goiim who, in alliance with the kings of Shinar, Ellasar, and Elam, raided the area around the Dead Sea, including Sodom and the cities of the Plain, and took Lot prisoner. He and the other kings were defeated by Abram and his allies (Gen. 14:1–16). *See also* Siddim, Valley of; Sodom.

Tiglath-pileser III (king of Assyria, 745–727 BCE) wearing his royal cap with a pointed top; from the palace at Nimrud.

Tiglath-pileser (tig′lath-pi-lee′zuhr) **III,** the king of Assyria 745–727 BCE, also known as Pul (2 Kings 15:19; 1 Chron. 5:26) and referred to as Tilgath-pilneser (1 Chron. 5:6, 26; 2 Chron. 28:20). He reorganized and revitalized the Neo-Assyrian Empire after decades of internal disintegration. He campaigned vigorously in the west, reaching as far as the Wadi of Egypt in the northern Sinai Peninsula. The hegemony of Tiglath-pileser was recognized by the kings of Israel and Judah. Menahem of Israel bought the political support of Assyria for his illegitimate rule with "a thousand talents of silver" (2 Kings 15:19); in Tiglath-pileser's annals at least two tribute payments by Menahem, in 740 and 738 BCE, are recorded. The rebellion of Tyre, Aram-Damascus, and Israel against Assyria was crushed during the three years of war, 734–732 BCE. Tiglath-pileser captured Galilee and Gilead, exiled its populace, and organized the areas as Assyrian provinces (2 Kings 15:29; 1 Chron. 5:26). He installed Hosea as vassal king of a greatly reduced Israel.

Ahaz of Judah came under attack for refusing to join the anti-Assyrian coalition; in order to save his kingdom, he turned to Tiglath-pileser and undertook the obligations of Assyrian vassaldom (2 Kings 16:5, 7–9). Ahaz is mentioned in an Assyrian list of tributaries dated to 734 BCE. His onerous tax payments required stripping the palace and the temple of their treasures (16:17–18). The victorious Tiglath-pileser held court in Damascus in 732 BCE; Ahaz was in attendance as befitting a loyal vassal (16:10). *See also* Assyria, Empire of.   M.C.

Tigris (ti′gris) **River,** one of the two major rivers (the other is the Euphrates) that nourished an extensive floodplain providing the physical basis for the rise of civilization in the ancient Near East. In

Gen. 2:14 it is identified as the third river "which flows east of Assyria" running out of Eden. It was designated also as the location in which Daniel received a major vision (Dan. 10:4).

The headwaters of the river lie in the mountains of southern Armenia, modern eastern Turkey and northern Iraq, just west and south of Lake Van. It runs generally southeastward along the base of the western foothills of the Zagros Mountains. It is joined en route by three major tributaries and several minor ones draining the western slopes of the hills to the northeast. The main tributaries are the Upper Zab, the Lower Zab, and the Diyala.

Important ancient cities built on the Tigris include Assyria's Nineveh (opposite modern Mosul) and Asshur (the original Assyrian capital), modern Qal'at Shergat. Near modern Baghdad lay the Neo-Babylonian commercial center Opis, and farther south at modern Sulman Pak was the Parthian and Sassanian city named Ctesiphon. Its location is still marked by a brick vaulted arch. Across the river on the west bank at modern Tell Umar are the ruins of the Seleucid capital, Seleucia.

Physically the river is fast and rugged in the upper reaches, being navigable only from Mosul southward. Its 1,146-mile length was close enough to the Euphrates from Baghdad south to allow canals to run irrigation water across from the higher western riverbed toward the Tigris. This 10,000-square-mile basin provided the agricultural sustenance for the early city-state and empire. The lower reaches of the river were slow-flowing and meandering, and, in antiquity, they ended in salt marshes. *See also* Asshur; Euphrates River; Nineveh.   R.S.B.

Tilgath-pilneser (til'gath-pil-nee'zuhr). *See* Tiglath-pileser III.

Timaeus (ti-mee'uhs). *See* Bartimaeus.

timbrel (tim'brel). *See* tambourine.

time. There is no general word for "time" in the Hebrew Bible, nor are there specific words for the categories of "past," "present," or "future." The Hebrew word most commonly translated as "time" is *'et*, which really refers to the instant or length of time during which something occurs (1 Sam. 9:16; Eccles. 3:1–8; Ezra 10:13; 2 Chron. 24:11). Another word, *'olam*, refers to immeasurable time, whether past (Eccles. 1:10) or future (Mic. 4:7). Although it does not mean "eternal" in the sense of "time without end," it does point to a length of time beyond human comprehension. Another common word, *mo'ed*, means "fixed time," i.e., a time designated for a specific occurrence, such as a festival (Lev. 23:2, 4). In other words, time in ancient Israel was not perceived as an abstract dimension, but primarily as related to specific happenings, whether of short or long duration.

God is the creator and master of time (Gen. 1:14) and time begins at creation (1:5). There are

The "Gezer Calendar," which describes the months by their particular harvests; cast from a tenth-century BCE inscription.

no clear references to time having an end point, but there are references to the broad sweep of time, as implied by references to things that will always be true or that will never come to pass (9:15–16; Isa. 34:10). The smallest amount of time is called a "moment" (Exod. 33:5; Isa. 54:7–8; Jer. 4:20).

The Hebrew Bible also uses the terms "day," "week," "month," and "year." A "day" was measured as either the time between sunrise and sunset or from sunset to sunset (Gen. 1:5). Ps. 55:17 speaks of three divisions of daylight, "evening, morning, and noon," while Neh. 9:3 refers to four parts of the daylight. The night was divided into three "watches" (Exod. 14:24; Judg. 7:19; Lam. 2:19). That the day started with sunset is probably due to Israel's calendrical system, which was based on the moon. The word "week" in Hebrew comes from the word for "seven" (*shabua'*). Ancient Israel is the first society known to have a seven-day week (Gen. 1:1–2:3). The days are not named, but they are numbered one through six, except for the seventh day, which is called the "sabbath"—from the Hebrew meaning "rest," in reference to God's rest after creation (Gen. 2:2–3; Exod. 20:10–11). As in English, the Hebrew word for "month" is related to the word for moon, *yereakh*, or the "new (moon)," *khodesh*.

In the NT, three words refer to time in its various dimensions. Two words, sometimes translated "times" (Gk. *chronos*) and "seasons" (*kairos;* Acts 1:7; 1 Thess. 5:1), can refer to time under two different aspects. The word *chronos* is typically used when time is thought of as a *quantity* (e.g., "a little time," John 7:33; cf. 1 Cor. 7:39); the word *kairos* tends to be used when time is conceived in terms of *quality* (e.g., as "time for" something, Mark 1:15; John 7:8). That distinction, however, is not always maintained (*chronos* can mean a specific time, Luke 1:57; Acts 7:17; Gal. 4:4; *kairos* can refer broadly to "the present," Rom. 11:5). A third Greek word, *aiōn,* can refer to a broad sweep of time (an era or an age); its usage reflects apocalyptic speculation that divided the world into the present evil age and a coming future age when God would redeem the faithful and transform creation (cf. Matt. 12:32; Eph. 1:21; cf. Luke 20:34; Rom. 12:2; 1 Cor. 2:6 for "present age"; Mark 10:30; Eph. 2:7; Heb. 6:2 for "coming age"). *Aionōs,* the plural of *aiōn* (lit., "ages"), is often translated "forever," although as in the Hebrew Bible, it is questionable whether the implied meaning was "unending time" or simply "time of unimaginable duration" (e.g., Matt. 21:19; John 12:34; Rom. 16:27; Heb. 1:8).

The Gospels presume the Jewish reckoning of a seven-day week, although Christians came to revere the first day in the week (modern Sunday), because it was the day of Christ's resurrection (Acts 20:7; 1 Cor. 16:2; cf. Matt. 28:1; Mark 16:2), rather than the last day of the week (sabbath), when God rested from creation (Gen. 2:2–3; cf. Exod. 20:8–11). It is not certain when this shift in focus occurred, but reference to "the Lord's Day" in Rev. 1:10 indicates the change had probably been made by the end of the first century (cf. *Did.* 14:1).

The Jewish practice of reckoning days as beginning with sunset is presumed in some places (e.g., Mark 1:32, where people waited until the sabbath mentioned in 1:21 came to an end), but in other places the Roman method of dividing the night into four rather than three watches is assumed (e.g., in 6:48, the text literally says, "about the fourth watch of the night"; NRSV: "early in the morning"). *See also* farming; festivals, feasts, and fasts; New Year Festival; sabbath.   J.U./P.J.A.

Timna (tim′nuh).

1 A sister of the Horite chief Lotan (Gen. 36:22; 1 Chron. 1:39); she was given as concubine to Eliphaz (the son of Esau) and became the mother of Amalek (Gen. 36:12).

2 A chief of Edom (Gen. 36:40). He is designated as a son of Eliphaz in 1 Chron. 1:36.

Timnah (tim′nuh; also Timnath, Timnatha; Gk. Thamnath).

1 A town in the southern hill country where Judah pastured sheep (Gen. 38:12–14); perhaps to be identified with the Timnah in the seventh district of Judah (Josh. 15:57).

2 A town on the northern border of Judah, between Beth-shemesh and Ekron (Josh. 15:10), now generally identified with modern Tell-el-Batashi in the Sorek Valley in the western part of southcentral Israel. Once assigned to Dan (19:43), it was Philistine territory at the time Samson married a woman from Timnah (Judg. 14:1–5). It fell again to the Philistines in the time of Ahaz (2 Chron. 28:18) and was captured by Sennacherib in 701 BCE.

3 A town in the hill country of Ephraim, fortified in 160 BCE by the Seleucid general Bacchides (1 Macc. 9:50).   P.A.B.

Timnath-serah (tim′nuhth-sihr′uh), Joshua's inherited city (Josh. 19:50) in which he was buried (24:30). It is probably modern Khirbet Tibneh, about eleven miles southwest of Shiloh.

Timon (ti′muhn), one of the seven Hellenists appointed by the apostles to help in the distribution of food to widows in the early Jerusalem church (Acts 6:1–6). *See also* deacon; Hellenists.

Timothy (tim′uh-thee).

1 A military officer of the Ammonites who joined forces with the Syrians to oppose Judas Maccabeus in the Judean rebellion (ca. 164 BCE); the Ammonites were crushed in several battles and Timothy was slain (1 Macc. 5:6–8; 2 Macc. 8:30–33; 9:1–4; 10:24–38; 12:1–25).

2 Paul's "beloved and faithful child in the Lord" (1 Cor. 4:17; cf. 1 Tim. 1:2). Timothy is associated with Paul in the prescripts of several letters (2 Cor. 1:1; Phil. 1:1; Col. 1:1; 1 Thess. 1:1; 2 Thess. 1:1; Philem. 1; cf. Rom. 16:21), an indication of the extent of their joint endeavors. He is otherwise mentioned as an associate and helper of Paul in four letters (1 Thess. 3:2, 6; 1 Cor. 4:17; 16:10; 2 Cor. 1:19; Phil. 2:19) and appears in Acts in a similar role (16:1–3; 17:14–15; 18:5; 19:22; 20:4). Finally, he is the named addressee of two of the Pastoral Letters, 1 and 2 Timothy (1 Tim. 1:2, 18; 6:20; 2 Tim. 1:2).

In Acts: According to Acts 16:1–3, Timothy was the son of a Gentile man and a Jewish woman who lived in the town of Lystra in southeastern Asia Minor; his mother was a believer (i.e., a Christian), but his father was not. Timothy was also a Christian and was "well spoken of by all of the believers in Lystra and Iconium." Paul recruited him as a companion for his second missionary journey, circumcising him so as not to offend the Jews. When the team encountered trouble in Thessalonica, Timothy and Silas stayed behind, while Paul went on to Athens (17:14–15); they later joined him in Corinth (18:5). Timothy accompanied Paul on his third missionary journey and, so, was with him during his lengthy stay in Ephesus (Acts 19). Paul sent him to Macedonia (19:22), but he later joined up with Paul again and went ahead of him to Troas, where Paul spent a week with him on his way to Jerusalem (20:4–5).

This brief biography seems generally compatible with information about Timothy in Paul's letters, which sometimes supply information that helps to fill in some of the gaps. Some scholars have questioned the claim that Timothy was already a Christian when Paul met him, since Paul refers to Timothy as his "child in the Lord" (1 Cor. 4:17; cf. 1 Tim. 1:2; 2 Tim. 2:2), but others note that the latter reference would not have to imply that Paul had converted him. The accuracy of the report that Paul circumcised Timothy is also challenged, given Paul's strong resistance to those who require circumcision in Gal. 5:2–4. The usual explanation for such an action is that the circumcision of Timothy was appropriate, because he was

Jewish (unlike Titus, Gal. 2:1–5), and Paul was not opposed to circumcision *as such* (1 Cor. 7:19; Gal. 5:6; 6:15); what he resisted was the claim that circumcision was necessary for justification (Gal. 2:15–16, 21). Further, scholars who accept the report that Paul circumcised Timothy sometimes note that he did this early in his career before his understanding that Christ had done away with distinctions between Jews and Greeks was fully developed (cf. 3:28).

In the NT Letters: According to Paul's earlier letters, Timothy was a colleague of Paul and Silvanus (Silas) in missions to the Thessalonians and the Corinthians (1 Thess. 1:1; 3:2, 6; 1 Cor. 4:17; 16:10; 2 Cor. 1:1, 19; cf. Acts 17:14–15; 18:5; 19:22). Shortly after leaving Thessalonica Paul's anxiety about the effects of persecution led him to send emissaries to encourage the Macedonian church in its faith. Paul was then left alone in Athens (1 Thess. 3:1–5; cf. Acts 17:13–16). From 1 Thess. 3:2–3 we learn that a special responsibility for ministry to the beleaguered Thessalonians was entrusted to Timothy, "our brother and co-worker for God in proclaiming the gospel of Christ." Paul sent Timothy to the Thessalonians to "strengthen and encourage" them, and when Timothy rejoined Paul in Corinth, he was the bearer of good news: the Thessalonians remained steadfast in "faith and love," they remembered Paul kindly, and they longed to see him (1 Thess. 3:6). Later, Paul's dealings with the Corinthian church led him to send colleagues there to act on his behalf. It is not clear that Timothy was the bearer of 1 Cor. or that a firm decision had been reached to send him to Corinth, but disturbances there made such a trip likely (1 Cor. 16:10, "if Timothy comes"; cf. 4:17). His inclusion in the prescript to 2 Cor. (1:1) further indicates that he did play a role in dealing with the unruly Corinthians (even though it was Titus, not Timothy, who served as Paul's emissary to the church when one particular crisis arose, 1:23–2:13; 7:5–16).

The later letters of Paul continue to portray Timothy as a trusted associate and useful emissary of the apostle (see Phil. 1:1; Philem. 1; cf. Col. 1:1). According to Phil. 2:19–24, Paul plans to send Timothy to Philippi and writes, "I have no one like him who will be genuinely concerned for your welfare. All of (the others) are seeking their own interests, not those of Jesus Christ. But Timothy's worth you know, how like a son with a father he has served with me in the work of the gospel."

Two problems arise in constructing Timothy's biography from NT letters. First, it is not known for certain whether Paul's "prison letters" to the Philippians and to Philemon (both of which mention Timothy) were written from Ephesus, Rome, or some other location. If they were written from Ephesus, then Timothy would have simply been present with Paul during this phase of his missionary work, as is also attested by Acts. But if either of the letters was written from Rome, then there would be evidence that Timothy was in Rome with

Paul during what was probably the final year of his life.

A second problem concerns the two Pastoral Letters that are actually addressed to Timothy. Many (though certainly not all) scholars believe that these letters are pseudepigraphical and, if they are, it is not clear whether the biographical information should be regarded as well-grounded or legendary. If the information they provide is accepted, then 1 Timothy would indicate that Paul left Timothy in charge of the church in Ephesus, while he was in Macedonia (1:3; a scenario never mentioned elsewhere in the NT). Further, 2 Timothy would indicate that Timothy was *not* in Rome with Paul during the final year of his life, although Paul, believing his execution to be near, summoned Timothy to come to him (4:6, 9, 13). Of course, Timothy may very well have gone to Paul in response to this invitation, but it seems unlikely that he would then have been in Rome with Paul for an extended period, during which other letters from prison were written.

Otherwise, the Pastoral Letters add only minor details to Timothy's biography. Timothy's mother's name was Eunice and his grandmother, also a believer, was named Lois (2 Tim. 1:5); he was young in comparison to Paul (1 Tim. 4:12; 5:1), he suffered from frequent illnesses (5:23), and he had received a spiritual gift through prophecy and the laying on of hands (4:14; 2 Tim. 1:6).

Someone named Timothy is also mentioned as having been "set free" in the anonymous Letter to the Hebrews (13:23). If this is a reference to the same Timothy mentioned in Acts and the Letters of Paul, it would indicate that Timothy himself was a prisoner at some point during his career, but we have no information as to when or where that would have been. *See also* Timothy, First Letter of Paul to; Timothy, Second Letter of Paul to.

J.L.P./M.A.P.

Timothy, First Letter of Paul to,

one of thirteen NT letters attributed to Paul and one of three that are collectively known as the Pastoral Letters (cf. 2 Tim.; Titus). Many scholars regard these letters as pseudepigraphical.

Contents: After an opening salutation and greeting (1:1–2), the author (identified as Paul) urges Timothy to curtail those who teach false doctrines and to promote faithful instruction that recognizes the proper role of the law (1:3–11). Paul's own story as a former blasphemer saved by Christ Jesus is a testimony to the extent of divine mercy (1:12–17). Other persons who have suffered "shipwreck in the faith" exemplify the judgment that comes upon those who reject conscience and continue to blaspheme (1:18–20). The letter encourages fervent prayer, especially for those in authority (2:1–4), and quotes a confession that describes Christ as the "mediator" whose herald and apostle Paul is (2:5–7). It offers gender-specific instructions regarding the roles of men and women, emphasizing that the latter should dress modestly and learn "in silence with full submission" (2:8–

15). It then provides summary qualifications for church leaders (3:1–15), including bishops (3:1–7) and deacons (3:8–13).

After another quote from a Christian confession or hymn (3:16), the letter issues additional warnings about false teachers (4:1–5) along with positive exhortations for Timothy's behavior and ministry (4:6–5:2). This leads to specific advice concerning widows (5:3–16), elders (5:17–20), and slaves (6:1–2), along with more personal exhortations to Timothy (5:21–25). The topic of false teaching is taken up again, with specific attention to the corrupting influence of money (6:3–10). The letter then concludes with charges for Timothy to be faithful (6:11–16), some advice for the wealthy (6:17–19), and a final charge for Timothy to guard what has been entrusted him against what is "falsely called knowledge" (6:20–21).

OUTLINE OF CONTENTS

1 Timothy

W.W.

Authorship: Many scholars believe that the three Pastoral Letters have a common origin (probably written by the same person) and that, when considered together, they must be regarded as pseudepigraphical. The following points are offered to support this contention. (1) The language and style are not typical of Paul's letters. For example, 1 Timothy and Titus lack both a thanksgiving and a formal closing, and the vocabulary of all three letters is strikingly different from that of other letters ascribed to Paul. (2) Certain theological ideas are different. For example, salvation is linked to the epiphany (or appearance) of Christ (1 Tim. 3:16; 2 Tim. 2:9–10; Titus 2:11; 3:4), while the cross and resurrection of Christ are virtually ignored (except for 2 Tim. 2:8), and words like "righteousness" and "faith" are used in a way that accents the human dynamic ("right behavior" or "correct belief") rather than the activity of God. (3) The description of church government seems too developed for Paul's lifetime (1 Tim. 3:1–13; 5:3–22; 2 Tim. 2:2; Titus 1:5–7). (4) The nature of the false teaching that is opposed is distinctive (1 Tim. 1:3–7; 6:3–5; 2 Tim. 2:17–18; 3:6–9; 4:3–4; Titus 1:9–16). The exact nature of this teaching is unclear, but it seems to have certain points in common with Gnosticism, a religious system that posed a serious challenge to Christianity in the second century—but not much before then. (5) The manner of dealing with false teaching is not characteristic of Paul. Rather than seeking to refute the objectionable ideas with cogent arguments, the author of the Pastoral Letters is inclined to call upon church leaders to exercise their authority in promoting what is regarded as sound doctrine and forbidding what is not (1 Tim. 4:1; 6:20; 2 Tim. 1:13–14; 2:2; Titus 2:1; 3:9–11).

In addition to these arguments, which might apply to all of the Pastoral Letters, 1 Timothy seems to presume a situation in which Paul has left Ephesus for Macedonia and is writing back to Timothy, who is now in charge of the Ephesian church (1 Tim. 1:3). According to Acts, however, Timothy had already left Ephesus by the time Paul went to Macedonia (19:21–22).

A growing minority of scholars regard 1 Timothy (and the other Pastoral Letters) as authentic. They usually argue that linguistic differences count for little, if Paul is presumed to have employed an amanuensis for the task of putting his thoughts into words. Other anomalies might be explained by a presumption that both the style and substance of Paul's writing would be different in personal correspondence than in letters to congregations. Scholars who favor authenticity also maintain that current knowledge of first-century Christianity is insufficient for forming strong opinions regarding the development of church polity or for determining when and where certain unorthodox ideas might have flourished. Likewise, they indicate that there are significant gaps in all reconstructions of Paul's biography— the apostle could have left Timothy in charge of Ephesus at some time not otherwise mentioned in the NT. A popular suggestion among some scholars favoring authenticity has been that Paul was not executed ca. 62–64 CE (as is usually thought) but was released from prison to have a "second career" as a missionary, during which time he wrote the Pastoral Letters. This view receives some support from *1 Clement*, a late first-century writing that seems to suggest Paul traveled to Spain (lit., "to the extreme west," *1 Clem.* 5:6–7), a journey not recounted in the NT (cf. Rom. 15:22–24)

Historical Situation: If Paul is thought to be the author of 1 Timothy, then the historical situation presumed by the letter's contents may be taken at face value: the apostle is writing to his colleague to provide advice for appointing leaders and refuting heresy in Ephesus. If one allows that there may be gaps in our record of Paul's life, then the letter to Timothy might be dated sometime around 52–56 CE. As indicated, however, a common assumption by many who argue for authenticity is that Paul wrote the later in the mid-late 60s CE, after the time when he is traditionally (but, according to this view, erroneously) thought to have been executed.

If the letter is considered to be pseudepigraphical (the majority view), then the situation presumed by the letter's contents is regarded as a literary fiction. In reality, the letter was composed by someone who stood within the Pauline tradition in an effort to ensure that this tradition would be carried forward in the face of competing ideas. The date and place of writing would then be unknown. Most interpreters would place it in the late first century (80–100), though some would put the work in the first quarter of the second century.

Major Themes: First Timothy is especially concerned with the appointment of church officers and leaders: bishops, deacons, and widows seem to represent three distinct leadership roles. Qualifications for the first two of these emphasize moral responsibility and social respectability (3:1–13); the third office (mentioned only in this letter in the NT) may have represented an outgrowth of charitable ministry (providing for indigent widows, who in turn support the church with prayer and good works), but enrollment in the program must now be limited (5:3–16). As indicated above, 1 Timothy is also concerned with the correction of false teaching in the church; restrictions must be placed on who is allowed to teach and on what they are allowed to teach (1:3; 2:12). *See also* bishop; church; deacon; elders; Ephesus; letter; Paul; pseudepigraphy; pseudonym; Timothy; Timothy, Second Letter of Paul to; Titus, Letter of Paul to.

Bibliography

Collins, Raymond F. *1 and 2 Timothy and Titus: A Commentary*. Westminster John Knox, 2002.

Harding, Mark. *What Are They Saying About the Pastoral Epistles?* Paulist, 2001.

Johnson, Luke Timothy. *The First and Second Letters to Timothy*. Doubleday, 2000.

Knight, George W., III. *The Pastoral Epistles: A Commentary on the Greek Text*. Eerdmans, 1992.

Marshall, I. Howard. *A Critical and Exegetical Commentary on the Pastoral Epistles*. Clark, 1999.

Mounce, William D. *Pastoral Epistles*. Thomas Nelson, 2000.

Powell, Mark Allan. *Introducing the New Testament: A Historical, Literary, and Theological Survey*. Baker Academic, 2009. Pp. 397–413.   M.A.P.

Timothy, Second Letter of Paul to,

one of thirteen NT letters attributed to Paul and one of three that are collectively known as the Pastoral Letters (cf. 1 Tim.; Titus). Many scholars regard these letters as pseudepigraphical, though 2 Tim. is generally viewed as having a greater claim to authenticity than the other two.

Contents: The letter opens with a salutation and greeting (1:1–2). The author (identified as Paul) gives thanks for the faith of Timothy (1:3–5) and offers words of encouragement for his continued zeal (1:6–7). Timothy is told not to be ashamed of Paul's gospel or of the suffering it brings (1:8–14). Paul's status as a prisoner has caused many to turn away, but Timothy should follow the positive examples of Paul and a certain Onesiphorus (1:15–18). Indeed, Timothy is charged with seeing that Paul's teaching gets passed on (2:1–2). He is urged to faithfulness with analogies from daily life (a soldier, an athlete, a farmer) and with lines quoted from a Christian confession or hymn (2:3–13). Timothy is to avoid those things that have been the downfall of false teachers, and he is to strive for the qualities that will allow God to use him as a favored vessel (2:14–26). He is warned about distressing times to come and false teachers who will take advantage of others during those times (3:1–9). As things go from bad to worse, he must remember Paul's life and ministry and commit himself wholeheartedly to learning and teaching the scriptures (3:10–17). The need for Timothy's diligence and persistence in such faithful ministry is made more urgent by the certainty of God's judgment (4:1–5) and by the fact that Paul's days on earth are coming to an end (4:6–8). As the letter winds to a close, it offers some personal instructions and provides updated information on various individuals and circumstances (4:9–18). It concludes with greetings and a benediction (4:19–22).

Authorship: Many scholars believe that the three Pastoral Letters have a common origin (probably written by the same person) and that, when considered together, they must be regarded as pseudepigraphical. The reasons offered in support of this conclusion—and the counterarguments of those who oppose it—are provided in the section on authorship in the entry "Timothy, First Letter of Paul to." Most scholars, however, grant that the arguments for pseudepigraphy carry more force with regard to 1 Timothy and Titus than they do with regard to 2 Timothy. Still, logic deems that 2 Timothy must be pseudepigraphical if the other two Pastoral Letters are so regarded and 2 Timothy is thought to have been written by the same person who wrote those two letters. A mediating position held by some scholars suggests that 2 Timothy was written by Paul (as his only extant letter to Timothy) and then, years later, an unknown author used 2 Timothy as a template for constructing the superficially similar pseudepigraphical letters that are now known as 1 Timothy and Titus.

Historical Setting: If Paul is regarded as the author of 2 Timothy (regardless of whether he wrote 1 Timothy and Titus), then the letter will be dated to the final years of his life, shortly before his execution ca. 62–64 CE. Scholars who think Paul was released from his first imprisonment for a few more years of ministry before being arrested again might date the letter ca. 65–67 CE. The majority of scholars, however, continue to regard 2 Timothy as pseudepigraphical and regard the "letter from prison" scenario as a literary fiction. The actual composition of the letter is then deemed to be later, some years after Paul's death (80–100 CE or even in the early second century).

Major Themes: Although 2 Timothy is less concerned with the appointment of church leaders than the other two Pastoral Letters, it does evince the same concern for sound doctrine expressed in those writings (4:3); significant attention is given to knowledge of the truth (2:25; 3:7), preservation of orthodox ideas (1:13), and the correction of false teaching (2:14, 16–18, 25–26; 3:6–9; 4:3–4). In addition, 2 Timothy calls for fortitude in the face of suffering and shame. Paul's humiliation of being "chained like a criminal" (2:9) is presented as an example of the sort of disgrace that causes some believers to turn away (4:10, 16), but Paul (1:12; 3:10–11) and Onesiphorus (1:16) provide

positive examples of those who recognize the inevitability of persecution (3:12) and accept the invitation to suffer "for the gospel" (1:8). **See also** church; letter; Paul; pseudepigraphy; pseudonym; Timothy; Timothy, First Letter of Paul to; Titus, Letter of Paul to.

Bibliography

Collins, Raymond F. *1 and 2 Timothy and Titus: A Commentary.* Westminster John Knox, 2002.

OUTLINE OF CONTENTS

2 Timothy

I. Introduction (1:1–7)
  A. Prescript (1:1–2)
  B. Thankful remembrance for Christian heritage of Paul and Timothy (1:3–7)
II. Exhortations (1:8–4:5)
  A. Experience of suffering as authentication of elect (1:8–2:26)
  B. Presence of heresy as authentication of prophecy; great value of tradition (3:1–4:5)
III. Conclusion (4:6–22)
  A. Personal notes concerning Paul's situation; final instructions (4:6–18)
  B. Greetings (4:19–21)
  C. Grace, offered on behalf of church (4:22).
  W.W.

PROPOSED HISTORICAL SITUATIONS FOR THE PASTORAL LETTERS

	Titus	1 Timothy	2 Timothy
If there are gaps in our record of Paul's career	by Paul from Ephesus? to Titus in Crete ca. 52–56 CE	by Paul from Macedonia to Timothy in Ephesus ca. 52–56 CE	by Paul from prison in Rome to Timothy ca. 60–62 CE
If Paul had a "second career"	same as above, but ca. 63–66 CE	same as above, but ca. 63–66 CE	same as above, but ca. 65–67 CE
If all three letters are by the same pseudonymous author	by an unknown admirer of Paul from an unknown location to Christians in general late first or early second century		
If expansions of Pauline notes	brief personal references in all three letters: same as "if there are gaps in our record of Paul's career" bulk of all three letters: same as "if all three letters are by the same pseudonymous author"		
If 2 Timothy was written first and by a different author	by admirer of Paul with copy of 2 Timothy from an unknown location to Christians in general late first or early second century		same as "if there are gaps in our record of Paul's career"—or written by Pauline admirer shortly after Paul's death

From Mark Allan Powell, *Introducing the New Testament* (courtesy, Baker Academic)

Harding, Mark. *What Are They Saying About the Pastoral Epistles?* Paulist, 2001.

Johnson, Luke Timothy. *The First and Second Letters to Timothy.* Doubleday, 2000.

Knight, George W., III. *The Pastoral Epistles: A Commentary on the Greek Text.* Eerdmans, 1992.

Marshall, I. Howard. *A Critical and Exegetical Commentary on the Pastoral Epistles.* Clark, 1999.

Mounce, William D. *Pastoral Epistles.* Thomas Nelson, 2000.

Powell, Mark Allan. *Introducing the New Testament: A Historical, Literary, and Theological Survey.* Baker Academic, 2009. Pp. 397–413.   M.A.P.

Tiphsah (tif'suh).

1 A city that marked a northern extremity of Solomon's kingdom (1 Kings 4:24). It is probably modern Dibseh, on the west bank of the Euphrates River where it turns east after coming south from Carchemish. It was called Thapsacus by the fifth- and fourth-century BCE Greek historian Xenophon (1.4.11) and was known as Amphipolis in the third century BCE.

2 The site of a brutal destruction by Menahem (2 Kings 15:16). It is to be identified with modern Sheikh Abu Zarad, about eight miles northwest of Shiloh.

Tiras (ti'ruhs), a son of Japheth who was the ancestor of a family group (Gen. 10:2; 1 Chron. 1:5). His name may be akin to Egyptian (Turusa) and Greek (Tyrsenoi) terms for a group of Aegean sea raiders sometimes called the Sea Peoples. *See also* Sea Peoples.

Tirhakah (tuhr-hay'kuh; Taharka in the Egyptian records), a pharaoh of Egypt's Twenty-Fifth ("Ethiopian") Dynasty who reigned ca. 690–664 BCE. According to 2 Kings 19:9 (Isa. 37:9), Sennacherib received a report that King Tirhakah of Ethiopia was marching out against him. At that moment the Assyrian army was engaged in a military campaign against Judah and was attacking Libnah in the Judean Shephelah (lowlands). According to the Assyrian annals Sennacherib met and defeated the Egyptian force in the Plain of Eltekeh (perhaps modern Tell esh-Shallaf). *See also* Egypt.   D.A.D.

Tirzah (tihr'zuh; Heb., "pleasantness").

1 One of the five daughters of Zelophehad, descendants through Hepher of Manasseh, who appealed to Moses for adjustment of the inheritance custom. This incident gives a glimpse of Israelite attention to issues of justice and land tenure (Num. 26:33; 27:1–11; 36:5–12; cf. Josh. 17:3–6). *See also* law; Mahlah; Zelophehad.

2 The region belonging to the family group of Tirzah, considered to be descendants of **1**. That the names of Zelophehad's five daughters designated territories has been suggested by Samaria ostraca ca. 775–750 BCE. Tirzah is not named on these ostraca, but Noah and Hoglah, the names of two other daughters of Zelophehad, are. Taking all the evidence together, the general region of Tirzah would have been north and east of Samaria.

3 A city in Israel about seven miles northeast of Shechem. It is first listed as a city whose king was defeated by Joshua (Josh. 12:24), so in the thirteenth century BCE Tirzah was probably a Canaanite city-state. Three hundred years later, it emerged as Jeroboam's capital of the northern kingdom. The name of the city, however, is not initially given in the account of Jeroboam. When he first becomes king, he rebuilds Shechem and Penuel, presumably because one of these would serve as his capital city (1 Kings 12:25). In 1 Kings 14, however, a story is related concerning the illness of Jeroboam's son Abijah. His wife takes the boy to Shiloh and is told by the prophet Ahijah that when she crosses the threshold of her home, the child will die (14:12). Jeroboam's wife then returns home to Tirzah (which has not been mentioned previously) and the boy dies (14:17). Thus, Jeroboam has apparently made his home in Tirzah. Later, Baasha, who usurps control from Jeroboam's family, is explicitly said to reign over Israel from Tirzah (15:21, 33; 16:6). When Zimri displaces Baasha's family, the coup occurs at Tirzah (16:8–9). Then Omri lays siege to Zimri at Tirzah and Zimri burns the city's citadel and palace down upon himself. Omri consolidates his reign at Tirzah, but then moves the capital of the northern kingdom to Samaria (16:15–23). All of this takes place within a half century (ca. 922–870 BCE), but Tirzah's brief life as Israel's capital was sufficient for it to be paired with Jerusalem in Song of Sol. 6:4. Around 745 BCE Tirzah reappeared as the base of operations for Menahem, still another usurper of the throne (2 Kings 15:14, 16).

The extensive mound today called Tell el-Far'ah, seven miles northeast of Shechem, is almost certainly the site of Tirzah. It oversees the head of the Wadi Far'ah, a direct route to the Jordan. Travelers going east to west in the central hills would come north-northeast from the Shechem pass around Mount Ebal and turn southeast below Tell el-Far'ah. Excavations reveal that the city was at its largest dimensions in Early Bronze I–II (ca. 3150–2600 BCE); its fortifications on the western, unprotected side became the foundations for all subsequent defenses, though succeeding towns were smaller in extent eastward and northward. Occupation resumed in Middle Bronze II (ca. 1900–1550 BCE), continuing into Late Bronze until roughly 1300 BCE. Evidence of destruction ending this period of the city's life is skimpy and of inconclusive date; correlation with a presumed destruction by Joshua is far from certain.

Correlation with biblical information is much firmer for the period 1000–600 BCE. There are four phases: the tenth century, ending with a destruction, probably that of Zimri; a partial rebuild, early ninth century; the eighth century, ending with destruction, probably by the Assyrians in 724–721 BCE; and a recovery, down to 600 BCE. Sturdy, roomy tenth-century housing of a uniform character is spread throughout a well-planned city layout. By contrast, the eighth-century town had excellently constructed, spacious houses in one sector, but makeshift homes in another, across a dividing wall. It suggests increasing social and economic stratification (cf. Amos 5:11). In the phase between these two well-preserved towns, walls of unfinished buildings were set into the destruction debris of the tenth century. This interim phase may have represented Omri's short stay at Tirzah. Basins and a memorial stone, along with other evidence, suggest that there was a gateside sanctuary in continual use from Middle Bronze to the site's final destruction, perhaps attesting Israelite adoption of Canaanite religious equipment and practices.

The uppermost stratum reflects recovery after the Assyrian destruction. Distinctive Assyrian-style pottery indicates strong influence, perhaps even the presence of an Assyrian garrison. *See also* Baasha; Jeroboam I; Menahem; Omri; Samaria, city of; Samaria, district of; Zimri.

Bibliography

De Vaux, Roland. "Tirzah." In *Archaeology and Old Testament Study*. Oxford University Press: 1967. Pp. 371–83.

———. "El-far'a, Tel, North." In *Encyclopedia of Archaeological Excavations in the Holy Land*. Prentice-Hall, 1976. Pp. 395–404.   E.F.C.

Tishbe (tish′bee), **Tishbite** (tish′bit), the place of origin for the prophet Elijah and the adjective indicating this. Elijah is called a Tishbite six times in the Bible (1 Kings 17:1; 21:17, 28; 2 Kings 1:3, 8; 9:36). The LXX translators understood this as a geographical reference and translated an uncertain Hebrew word in 1 Kings 17:1 as meaning "of Tishbe in Gilead." This reading is followed by the NRSV, although no town by that name is otherwise known to have existed. Alternative proposals have suggested that the Hebrew may have originally identified Elijah as "a Jabeshite from Jabesh-gilead" or as "a settler of Gilead." The dominant theory, however, seems to be that Tishbe was a small and otherwise insignificant village that would never have been mentioned at all, if it had not been the hometown of Elijah. *See also* Elijah.   M.A.S.

Tishri (tish′ree), the postexilic name for the seventh Hebrew month, also called Ethanim (1 Kings 8:2), a thirty-day period from mid-September to mid-October. It marked the beginning of the religious year with the New Year Festival (Heb. *rosh hashanah*) celebrated on the first day of the month (originally on the tenth day; Lev. 23:23–25; Num. 29:1–6) followed by the Day of Atonement (Heb. *yom kippur*) on the tenth day (Lev. 16; 23:26–32; Num. 29:7–11) and the eight-day Festival of Tabernacles (or Booths; Heb. *sukkot*) beginning on the fifteenth day of Tishri (Lev. 23:33–44). *See also* Atonement, Day of; calendar; festivals, feasts, and fasts; New Year Festival; Tabernacles, Festival of.   D.R.B.

'tithe, a tenth part of one's income set aside for special purposes. Tithing was very common throughout the ancient Near East, either for the support of a sanctuary or for nonsacral purposes. Fourteenth-century BCE tablets from Ugarit portray the tithe as a royal tax the king collected and distributed to his officials. The Seleucid kings of Syria likewise viewed the tithe as a source for royal income (1 Macc. 10:31; 11:35), whereas Jews at that time viewed it as a religious tax to be offered in support of the temple (3:49).

Nature and Function: Reconstructing a clear picture of the nature and function of tithing in biblical times is extremely difficult due to the conflicting accounts in the biblical traditions and the problems in identifying the dates and provenance of the texts. Apparently, tithing was understood and practiced differently at different times and localities throughout the biblical period. Most biblical texts concerning the tithe agree that it served some religious purpose and presuppose that it was mandatory, but they differ with regard to how it was expended and by whom.

In the time of Ezra and Nehemiah, the tithe was a tax collected at the temple to support the priests and Levites (Neh. 10:37–38; 12:44; 13:5, 12). Paying the tithe was clearly an expectation, but if it was a legal requirement, then it does not appear to have always been observed or enforced (Mal. 3:8, 10).

Pentateuchal regulations likewise present tithing as a sacral and presumably mandatory practice. Lev. 27:30–33 states that all the tithe of the land, whether of the seed of the land or of the fruit of the trees, belongs to God and that one-tenth of all that passes under the shepherd's staff is also included. Num. 18:21–32 assigns the tithe offerings of the people as the inheritance of the Levites, and they in turn must give one-tenth of what they receive to the priests. Deut. 14:22–29 states that the people shall tithe their grain, wine, and oil together with the firstlings of their herds and flocks and that they shall eat their tithe in the temple. But every third year, the tithe shall go to the Levites, sojourners, orphans, and widows, as these people have little means of support. In the case of the Levites, their poverty was due to Deuteronomy's requirement that all sanctuaries but one be closed, leaving the Levites who served in those sanctuaries unemployed (cf. Deut. 12). If one lived far from the temple so that transporting the actual tithe was impractical, then it could be converted to cash and replacement food could be bought for consumption at the temple, but the requirement to eat the tithe in the temple still stood. Lev. 27:31 states, however, that those who redeemed their tithe with cash should add one-fifth of the actual cash value of the tithe.

Tax or Offering: Other texts raise questions about the sacral or obligatory nature of the tithe. When the prophet Samuel warns the people about the dangers of appointing a king, he mentions that the king will exact a tithe from their grain, vineyards, and flocks to give to his officers and servants

(1 Sam. 8:15, 17). Here, the tithe is a mandatory royal tax, without any mention of religious use. A blending of religious and royal functions may also be observed in that kings had responsibility for maintaining the temple (Ezek. 45:17) and, so, controlled its treasury. According to 2 Chron. 31:5, 6, 12, King Hezekiah collected and stored offerings for the temple, including the tithe.

The traditions of Israel's ancestors record narratives in which a tithe is freely given at the site of a sanctuary. Abraham gives a tenth of his war booty to Melchizedek, the priest-king of Salem (i.e., Jerusalem) after receiving his blessing (Gen. 14:20; cf. Heb. 7:1–10). Jacob vows to offer a tithe of all his income to God at Bethel after his dream of the ladder to heaven (Gen. 28:22). An interesting attempt to reconcile the conception of the tithe as a royal tax with that of a sacral offering notes that both Jerusalem and Bethel were the sites of royal sanctuaries founded by kings (2 Sam. 6; 1 Kings 6–8, 12:25–33; Amos 7:13). In this view, the ancestral stories may be read as etiological narratives justifying the later practice of channeling tithes for the sanctuary through the king.

In the NT, Jesus mentions tithing in two contexts that presume the righteousness of the practice while critiquing those who perform it. In his parable of the Pharisee and the Tax Collector, he depicts the Pharisee as a self-righteous man who brags to God that he gives a tenth of his income (Luke 18:12); the tithing itself would be commendable but, Jesus notes, "all who exalt themselves will be humbled" (8:14). Also, he notes with irony that some devoutly religious people are scrupulous about tithing (paying a tithe not only on their crops, but also on spices that they grow in small amounts) and yet neglect the "weightier matters" of Torah—things like justice, mercy, and faith (Matt. 23:23; cf. Luke 11:42, "justice and the love of God"). Jesus does not, however, condemn the practice of tithing as such, but indeed indicates it is something one should do.

Paul never mentions tithing, even in sections of his letters devoted to the topic of financial giving (2 Cor. 8–9). Although the data is not sufficient to warrant a certain conclusion, it seems likely that he would have regarded mandatory tithing as one of the "works of the law" from which believers had been set free in Christ (Gal. 3:23–26). Paul does speak of proportionate giving (2 Cor. 8:3, 12–13), but he seems inclined to let the percentage be determined by the giver (9:7). He also says that giving should be voluntary and insists that "if the eagerness is there, the gift is acceptable according to what one has" (8:12). These comments, however, are made with regard to a special offering he is collecting for Jerusalem and would not necessarily represent his comprehensive view on giving to support the local congregation. Overall, Paul emphasizes cheerful giving (9:7) and generosity (Rom. 12:8; 2 Cor. 8:2, 6–7, 19–20; 9:11, 13), which is a fruit of the Holy Spirit (Gal. 5:22). Sirach, however, does the same within a context that assumes tithing: "Be generous when you worship the Lord, and do not stint the first fruits of your hands. With every gift show a cheerful face, and dedicate your tithe with gladness" (35:10–11). *See also* Levites; temple, the; worship in the Hebrew Bible; worship in the New Testament.

Bibliography

De Vaux, Roland. *Ancient Israel.* McGraw-Hill, 1965. Pp. 140–41, 380–82, 403–5.

Kaufman, Yehezkel. *The Religion of Israel.* University of Chicago Press, 1960. Pp. 189–93.

Weinfeld, Moshe. "Tithe." *Encyclopedia Judaica.* Vol. 14. Macmillan, 1971. Cols. 1156–62.

M.A.S./M.A.P.

Titius Justus. *See* Justus.

Titus (ti′tuhs).

1 Titus Flavius Sabinus Vespasianus (39–81 CE), the son of Vespasian, and Roman emperor from 79 to 81 CE. After serving in the army in Germany and Britain, he became the commander of a legion under his father in the Jewish war (66–70 CE). When Vespasian was proclaimed emperor, Titus led the forces that captured Jerusalem and destroyed the temple. The Arch of Titus, which still stands at the Roman Forum, commemorates this victory and displays treasures taken from the temple. Titus shared Vespasian's rule until his father's death, whereupon Titus was declared emperor. The aid he provided to victims of the eruption of Mount Vesuvius (79) and of a fire and plague that devastated part of Rome (80) contributed to his popularity. His long-standing affair with the Jewish princess Bernice (mentioned in Acts 25:13) was unpopular in Rome. Upon his death the Senate immediately deified him. *See also* Caesar; emperor; Roman Empire. D.R.E.

2 A Gentile "partner and co-worker" with Paul (2 Cor. 8:23) and the named addressee of a short letter in the NT. Titus is never mentioned in the book of Acts. Information concerning him is drawn principally from Paul's letters, Galatians and 2 Corinthians. References from the Pastoral Letters (including the letter ostensibly addressed to Titus) are often used to supplement this information, though some scholars think these letters are pseudepigraphical, using the literary fiction of a letter from Paul to Titus as a rhetorical device for a work composed some time after Paul's death.

According to Galatians, Paul was accompanied by Barnabas and a Greek named Titus when he visited Jerusalem for the second time after his call to be an apostle to the Gentiles (1:15–18; 2:1–10). Some Jewish Christians insisted that Titus be circumcised, but Paul objected and met in private with acknowledged leaders of the church (Peter, James, and probably other apostles). They agreed with Paul that Titus should not be compelled to be circumcised. Thus, Titus is presented as having provided a sort of test case for the church regarding the controversial question of whether circumcision would be required of Gentile converts to Christianity. In essence, the dispute seems to have concerned the question of whether Christianity was to be viewed as a subset of Judaism. According to one view, Jesus was the Jewish Messiah and the Savior of Israel; Gentiles could participate in the salvation he brought provided they first became Jews. Paul cited the decision regarding Titus as setting a definitive precedent for another understanding; Jesus was Lord and Savior of all, and through faith in him people could be put right with God apart from circumcision or other works of the law (Gal. 2:16).

Titus also figured prominently as a representative of Paul in his dealings with the troubled Corinthian church. At this point, Paul was in Ephesus, and it seems likely that Titus was his associate there. He may have been the one who delivered the letter known as 1 Corinthians to the church for, in 2 Cor. 8:6, Paul notes that Titus is resuming work that he began at Corinth, namely, the collection for the saints in Jerusalem (cf. 1 Cor. 16: 1–4). In any case, Titus delivered another letter to the Corinthians, the "severe letter" or "tearful letter" that Paul wrote to the church in anger (cf. 2 Cor. 2:3–9). Personal attacks against Paul had threatened his leadership in the community and, wishing to avoid "another painful visit" (2 Cor. 2:1), Paul essentially placed his fate in the hands of Titus. Paul indicates that he experienced great anxiety while waiting to hear back. He traveled from Ephesus to Troas, where he says his mind could not rest, because he could not find Titus there (indicating, apparently, that a planned connection was missed). He then went on to Macedonia and there, at last, Titus caught up with him, bringing incredibly good news—the Corinthians were repentant and desired reconciliation with Paul (2 Cor. 2:13; 7:5–16). Taking advantage of the improved situation, Paul sent Titus back to Corinth, along with two unnamed companions (8:6, 16–24). Later in the same letter, Paul expresses his confidence that Titus will take no advantage of the Corinthians—like Paul, he has their best interests at heart (12:17–18).

The Letter to Titus assumes a scenario unrelated to anything mentioned above. According to this letter, Paul and Titus had been ministering together on the island of Crete, and Paul had left, entrusting Titus to continue the work (Titus 1:5). Paul is writing back to Titus from some undisclosed location (perhaps Ephesus), and he indicates that he hopes to see Titus soon in Nicopolis (3:12). Another one of the Pastoral Letters indicates that ca. 62–64 CE (the time of Paul's Roman imprisonment) Titus went to Dalmatia to minister there (2 Tim. 4:10). *See also* circumcision; Titus, Letter of Paul to.   J.L.P.

Titus, Letter of Paul to, one of thirteen NT letters attributed to Paul and one of three that are collectively known as the Pastoral Letters (cf. 1 Tim.; 2 Tim.). Many scholars regard these letters as pseudepigraphical.

Contents: The letter opens with an unusually expansive salutation, which identifies the writer as Paul (1:1–4). The author indicates that Titus

is to appoint elders in the towns of Crete and lists the qualifications for the office of bishop (1:5–9). These instructions segue into a description of the corrupt persons whom the bishops will need to refute (1:10–16), followed by specific advice regarding what Titus is to say to older men, older women, younger men, and slaves (2:1–10). The letter then provides a summary of the gospel and its consequences for human behavior (2:11–14). Titus is exhorted to declare these things in a manner that is both authoritative and tactful (2:15–3:2). This leads to a second summary of the gospel message, one that provides personal testimony to the salvation Paul and Titus share in Christ (3:3–7). Titus is to insist on this message and avoid "stupid controversies" and things that cause divisions (3:8–10). The letter concludes with some discussion of future plans, final greetings, and a benediction (3:12–15).

Authorship: Many scholars believe that the three Pastoral Letters have a common origin (probably written by the same person) and that, when considered together, they must be regarded as pseudepigraphical. The reasons offered in support of this conclusion—and the counterarguments used by those who oppose it—are provided in the section on authorship in the entry "Timothy, First Letter of Paul to." One point specific to the Letter of Titus may be noted here. The presumed situation for this letter is that Paul and Titus have been ministering together on the island of Crete, but that Paul has left, entrusting Titus to continue the work (1:5). Scholars who believe the letter is pseudepigraphical (the majority view) point out that no other NT document ever mentions a Pauline mission in Crete; such a mission does not fit easily into any reconstruction of Paul's biography, so the reference to it must be regarded as anachronistic, reflecting post-Pauline spread of the gospel to new lands. Scholars who think the letter to Titus is authentic (a growing minority) may be more open to allowing a Cretan mission to fit into gaps in Pauline biographies, or they may resolve the problem by moving Paul's presumed date of execution forward several years. If Paul was released from Roman imprisonment (as *1 Clem.* 5:6–7 is said to imply), then he might have ministered in any number of unknown locales for a few years before he was again arrested and put to death.

Historical Setting: Scholars who think that Paul was the author of this letter take the historical situation presumed by the letter's contents at face value. Paul is writing to Titus, who is now in charge of a mission in Crete that Paul initiated, advising him on the appointment of church leaders and the containment of unorthodox teaching. According to such a scenario, Paul might be presumed to have written the letter sometime around 52–56 CE, albeit under circumstances that are unattested elsewhere. More often, those who take the letter to be an authentic Pauline compositon usually assume that Paul wrote it from Ephesus in the mid-60s CE, after the traditional date for his execution. Scholars who believe the letter is pseudepigraphical (the majority view) think that Titus, 1 Timothy, and (possibly) 2 Timothy were all written by some unknown person decades after Paul's death to ensure that the Pauline tradition would be carried forward in the face of competing ideas. Most of these interpreters would date the letter to the last part of the first century (80–100 CE), though some would place it even later (100–125 CE). *See* the chart "Proposed Historical Situations for the Pastoral Letters," accompanying the entry for Timothy, First Letter of Paul to.

Major Themes: The Letter of Titus is primarily concerned with the appointment of church leaders, though in this letter (unlike 1 Tim.) terms such as "bishop" and "elder" seem to be used interchangeably for the same generic position. There is little attention to spelling out the responsibilities of such leaders, apart from teaching and preaching (1:9). Still, a bishop is to be regarded as "God's steward" (1:7) who attends to various matters on God's behalf. Greater emphasis is placed on explicating qualifications for leadership (1:5–9); moral responsibility and social respectability are given priority. The Letter of Titus is also eminently concerned with stemming the tide of false teaching in the church (1:11, 13; 2:15). *See also* bishop; church; Crete; elders; letter; Paul; pseudepigraphy; pseudonym; Timothy, First Letter of Paul to; Timothy, Second Letter of Paul to; Titus.

Bibliography

Collins, Raymond F. *1 and 2 Timothy and Titus: A Commentary.* Westminster John Knox, 2002.

Harding, Mark. *What Are They Saying About the Pastoral Epistles?* Paulist, 2001.

Johnson, Luke Timothy. *The First and Second Letters to Timothy.* Doubleday, 2000.

Knight, George W., III. *The Pastoral Epistles: A Commentary on the Greek Text.* Eerdmans, 1992.

Marshall, I. Howard. *A Critical and Exegetical Commentary on the Pastoral Epistles.* Clark, 1999.

Mounce, William D. *Pastoral Epistles.* Thomas Nelson, 2000.

Powell, Mark Allan. *Introducing the New Testament: A Historical, Literary, and Theological Survey.* Baker Academic, 2009. Pp. 397–413. M.A.P.

Tob (tohb), an Aramean city in the territory of Hauran. Jephthah fled to the land of Tob when his half brothers sought to kill him. He then collected outlaws from the region to join him in raiding parties. The elders of Gilead eventually came to Tob to recruit Jephthah as a commander in their war against the Ammonites (Judg. 11:3–5). Later, the town supplied mercenaries to the Ammonites in their wars with David (2 Sam. 10:6–13). Jews who had settled there were rescued from neighbors' attacks by Judas Maccabeus (1 Macc. 5:13; 2 Macc. 12:17). The location is probably modern et-Taiyibeh, about twelve miles east and slightly north of Ramoth-gilead.

Tobiah (toh-bi′uh; Heb., "the LORD is good").

1 The head of a family who returned to Judah with Zerubbabel, but who were excluded from the priesthood, because their names were not found in the appropriate genealogical records (Ezra 2:60–62; Neh. 7:62).

2 An opponent of Nehemiah, with Sanballat and Geshem (Neh. 2:10, 19; 4:3, 7; 6:1–19; 13:4–8). Tobiah is described as "the Ammonite official" (2:10, 19). The word "Ammonite" could indicate his origin or be a nickname; more probably it indicates his responsibility for that area, placing him alongside Sanballat, who was governor of Samaria, and Geshem, who could have been the Arabic ruler of Qedar. All three would then occupy important positions under Persian authority. They appear together (2:19; 4:7) and show general opposition to the restoration of Jerusalem in the late sixth and early fifth centuries BCE (2:10–20; 4:19). Tobiah and Sanballat are associated with an attempt to get Nehemiah to act sacrilegiously (6:10–14); Tobiah had considerable influence among leading men in Jerusalem who were bound to him by marriage relationships (6:15–19). During Nehemiah's absence in Babylon, Eliashib the priest gave Tobiah a special room in the temple, from which Nehemiah later ejected him (13:4–9). This Tobiah is probably to be regarded as the ancestor of the later Tobiads, who were prominent in the second century BCE (cf. 2 Macc. 5:10–13). *See also* Ezra and Nehemiah, books of; Sanballat. P.R.A.

Tobias (toh-bi′uhs; Heb., "the LORD is good"), a major character in the book of Tobit. Tobias is the son of Tobit and Anna. He is guided by the angel Raphael to heal his father of a serious eye problem and to exorcize the demon Asmodeus from his bride, Sarah. *See also* Sarah; Tobit; Tobit, book of.

Tobijah (toh-bi′juh; Heb., "the LORD is good").

1 A Levite sent by the pious and prosperous Judean king Jehoshaphat (873–849 BCE) to teach the people of Judah from the "book of the law of the LORD" (2 Chron. 17:8–9).

2 One of the men who was memorialized for bringing back gifts of gold from Babylon to Jerusalem (Zech. 6:10, 14).

Tobit (toh′bit), a Naphtalite, the son of Tobiel, and the protagonist of the book of Tobit. He is married to Anna, and they have a son named Tobias. The story told in the book of Tobit is set in the eighth century BCE during the time when Israelites were deported from their homeland by the Assyrian Empire. Tobit has been exiled to Nineveh from his home in Thisbe of Galilee. He is more faithful and righteous than his compatriots, many of whom continue in the apostasy modeled by Jeroboam (Tob. 1:3–9). He rises to a position of prominence in Shalmaneser's court, but is then persecuted for performing acts of charity (1:10–20). Although his fortunes are temporarily restored (1:21–22), he contracts a serious eye problem after sparrow droppings fall in his eyes while he is tending to the burial of murdered Israelites (2:1–10). Reduced to poverty, he has an argument with his wife, which leads him to pray for death (2:11–3:6). In response to Tobit's prayer, God sends the angel Raphael (3:16–17), who aids Tobit's son Tobias in a number of endeavors. Tobit offers testamentary instruction to his son (4:1–19) and sends him to recover money that has been left in trust (4:20–5:3). Eventually, the money is recovered (9:1–6) and Raphael helps Tobias to heal Tobit's eyesight. The story of Tobit is interwoven with the tale of Sarah, a woman whom Tobias marries. *See also* Sarah; Tobit, book of.   M.A.P.

Tobit, book of, a Hellenistic writing produced during the Second Temple period and included among the Apocrypha/deuterocanonical literature. The book of Tobit presents a tale of the tribulation and hope intended for Jews who live outside their homeland in the Dispersion. The story is set in the city of Nineveh in the eighth century BCE, when Israelite exiles were deported to that pagan location following the Assyrian destruction of the northern kingdom, Israel. It revolves around Tobit, an exile of the tribe of Naphtali, his wife, Anna, their son, Tobias, and an unfortunate woman named Sarah.

In the first part of the story, Tobit is blinded and reduced to poverty as a consequence of his efforts to bury Jews killed by the oppressive Assyrian king. Sarah, meanwhile, is plagued by the demon Asmodeus, who has killed her previous seven grooms on their wedding nights before the marriages could be consummated. Both pray to God for death, but God responds by sending the angel Raphael (disguised as Tobit's relative

Azarias) to help. Raphael accompanies Tobias on the way to Rages in Media to recover funds Tobit has left in trust. In Ecbatana, they lodge with Sarah's family, and Tobias meets Sarah. The two marry and defeat the demon with Raphael's aid and return to Tobit and Anna in Nineveh, where the angel helps Tobias restore his father's sight.

In addition to a good bit of sound moral instruction derived from the wisdom tradition, the tale advocates the marriage of relatives to preserve Jewish identity in the Dispersion, and it anticipates the end of the Dispersion and the restoration of the full Israelite community in Jerusalem. The book also contains liturgical materials, including prayers offered by both Tobit (3:1–6) and Sarah (3:11–15).

OUTLINE OF CONTENTS

Tobit

   I. Tobit loses his eyesight in his concern for the burial of Jewish victims of Assyrian oppression (1:1–3:6).

  II. The story of Sarah and the demon-lover (3:7–17).

 III. Tobit's moral instruction to his son, Tobias (4:1–21).

 IV. Tobias and Raphael prepare to set out on a journey to recover Tobit's funds (5:1–22).

  V. The journey: Tobias catches a fish whose liver, heart, and gall will be used to help Sarah and heal Tobit (6:1–18).

 VI. The wedding (7:1–16).

 VII. The defeat of the demon (8:1–21).

VIII. Raphael recovers the funds (9:1–6).

 IX. The anxiety of Tobit and Anna, and the departure of the young couple from Sarah's home (10:1–13).

  X. The return and restoration of Tobit's sight (11:1–18).

 XI. Raphael's true identity revealed (12:1–22).

 XII. Tobit's prayer (13:1–17).

XIII. The testament of Tobit (14:1–15).

The book of Tobit may be contemporary with the stories in Dan. 1–6, which are also concerned with the problems of maintaining Jewish identity and integrity in the Dispersion. Prior to the discovery of the Dead Sea Scrolls it was known only in the Greek version included in the LXX and was assumed to have been written in Greek during the Second Temple period. However, both Aramaic and Hebrew versions of the book were found among the scrolls at Qumran. Thus, the LXX version of Tobit is now regarded as a translation of a Hebrew or Aramaic original.

Protestants include the book of Tobit among the Apocrypha, while Roman Catholic and Eastern Orthodox Christians classify it as one of the deuterocanonical books. *See also* angel; Apocrypha/

deuterocanonical literature; demon; Dispersion; Sarah; Tobit.   D.W.S.

Togarmah (toh-gahr´muh), the third son of Gomer and the brother of Ashkenaz and Riphath (Gen. 10:3; 1 Chron. 1:6). His descendants may be associated with a city named Beth-togarmah (Heb., "house of Togarmah") mentioned in Ezek. 27:14. *See also* Beth-togarmah.

Toi, the king of Hamath who negotiated with David after his defeat of the Ammonites and their allies, some of whom had been enemies of Toi (2 Sam. 8:9–10; 1 Chron. 18:9–10, "Tou").

Tola (toh´luh; Heb., "crimson worm").
   1 The first of the four sons of Issachar (Gen. 46:13; Num. 26:23; 1 Chron. 7:1–2; *Jub.* 44:16) and the ancestral head of the people known as Tolaites. Nothing further is known of the six sons of Tola listed in 1 Chron. 7:2.
   2 A judge (Judg. 10:1) described as a son of Puah, from the tribe of Issachar. He lived in the town of Shamir in the Ephraimite hill country and was a judge in Israel for twenty-three years.

tomb of Jesus. According to the Gospel accounts, the tomb in which the crucified body of Jesus was placed belonged to Joseph of Arimathea, who is variously identified as a rich man (Matt. 27:57), a respected member of the council (Mark 15:43), and a secret disciple of Jesus (John 19:38). It was a new tomb in which no one had ever been laid, and it was located in a garden in the same vicinity as the place where Jesus was crucified (19:41). The Gospel writers also mention a stone that needed to be rolled away from the opening before one could enter the tomb (Matt. 28:2; Mark 16:3; Luke 24:2; John 20:1). This scenario assumes that the tomb of Jesus was probably carved into a limestone hill with an opening that could be closed with a door that looked like a stone wheel. The wheel would have been placed into a groove or track to keep it in place. When the tomb was opened, the wheel could be rolled up a sloping track and held in place with some object. To close the door, it was necessary only to remove the block and let the wheel roll downhill in front of the opening of the tomb.
   The traditional location of Jesus's tomb is the site on which the Church of the Holy Sepulchre now stands. The identification of this site was made under Constantine in 335 CE, but at that time appeared to be based on ancient tradition (e.g., of Christians worshiping at the spot prior to the war with Rome in 66 CE, and of Hadrian building a temple to Aphrodite on the spot, an indication that some group regarded it as sacred, in 135 CE). There is no way of authenticating the tradition.   G.W.B./P.P.

tombs. *See* architecture; burial; Mareshah; Nabatea, Nabateans; ossuaries; Sidon; Tadmor; tomb of Jesus.

tongue.
   1 The bodily organ of taste and speech. It is the latter function that accounts for most references in the Bible (but see Job 6:30). The tongue can produce words of praise (Pss. 51:14; 119:172), deceit (Pss. 10:7; 78:36; Prov. 21:6; Mic. 6:12; Jer. 9:3, 5, 8), boasting (Ps. 12:3); slander (Ps. 15:3), or mischief (Prov. 17:4). The book of Proverbs speaks of the "tongue of the wise" (12:18; 15:2) and also mentions the "gentle tongue" (15:4), the "perverse tongue" (10:31), the "lying tongue" (6:17; 12:19; 21:6; 26:28), the "soft tongue" (25:15), the "back-biting tongue" (25:23), and the "smooth tongue of the adulteress" (6:24). Prov. 18:21 claims that "death and life are in the power of the tongue." The Letter of James condemns the tongue as unrighteous, untamable, and a fount of evil (3:6–12). An inability to speak is typically attributed to a problem with the tongue (e.g., Ps. 137:6; Ezek. 3:26). Moses complains that he is "slow of speech and slow of tongue," meaning that he is not eloquent and needs his brother Aaron to help him (Exod. 4:10). Zechariah's tongue must be "freed" in order for him to speak (Luke 1:64). Jesus touches the tongue of a man with a speech impediment so that it might be "released," and then the man speaks freely (Mark 7:32–35). Paul looks forward to the day when every tongue will confess that Jesus Christ is Lord (Phil. 2:11).
   2 A language (cf. Isa. 45:23; Phil. 2:11; Rom. 14:11), especially a foreign or incomprehensible language, as in the phrases "alien tongue" (Isa. 28:11; cf. 33:19) and "other tongues" (Acts 2:4).   J.B.T.

tongues, as of fire, a phrase used in Acts 2:3 to designate one of the dramatic events of the first Pentecost after Jesus's death and resurrection. The author says that tongues as of fire appeared and rested on each of the apostles. As a result, the apostles began to speak in other tongues (2:4, 8; NRSV: "languages"). The description brings together the association of fire with divine power and the imagery of tongues as languages. *See also* Pentecost; tongue; tongues, speaking in.

tongues, speaking in (Gk. *glossolalia*), the act of speaking in a language that is either incomprehensible or at least unknown to the speaker. The phenomenon of speaking in tongues played a prominent role in the life of some early Christian communities.
   Acts 2 contains a narrative about the events of the first Pentecost after Jesus's resurrection. On that day, the apostles gathered together, and, after hearing a sound like wind and seeing tongues like fire, they "began to speak in other languages [lit., tongues], as the Spirit gave them ability" (2:4). The author of Acts goes on to list various nationalities of persons who heard the apostles speak, noting that everyone heard them speaking in their native languages.
   The phenomenon of speaking in tongues is mentioned twice more in Acts. After Peter preaches in

the house of Cornelius, the Gentiles there began "speaking in tongues and extolling God" (10:46). This is taken as a sign that the Holy Spirit has been poured out among Gentiles and that they should be baptized. In Acts 19, Paul meets some disciples of Apollos at Ephesus. These disciples, who have been brought "into John's baptism" (19:3), say that they have never heard of the Holy Spirit. Paul instructs them, baptizes them in the name of Jesus, and lays his hands on them. Then the Holy Spirit comes upon them, and they speak in tongues and prophesy (19:6). The author of Acts probably thought of these two incidents as similar to the one described in chap. 2, although in the latter incidents there is no explicit mention of people recognizing the inspired speech as actual languages.

Paul addresses the matter of "speaking in tongues" as a possible problem in the church at Corinth. He acknowledges that the ability to speak in "various kinds of tongues" and the ability to interpret these tongues are "spiritual gifts" (1 Cor. 12:10), but he also advises his readers to seek the "higher gifts" (12:31), such as the ability to prophesy (14:1). In 1 Cor. 13, Paul exalts love as the ultimate aim for all believers and, in 1 Cor. 14, he gives a number of specific directions about speaking in tongues. Speaking in tongues is helpful to the community only when it is used in conjunction with the spiritual gift of "interpretation of tongues" (14:5; cf. 12:10). When the community convenes, no more than three should speak in tongues, each in turn, and there must be an interpretation (12:27). Paul feels that uncontrolled and uninterpreted speaking in tongues does not edify the community and that it gives outsiders the impression that believers are mad (12:23). Yet he allows this activity to take place, so long as it is done in an orderly fashion and is accompanied by interpretation. Paul also encourages the believers to speak in tongues in private; indeed, he claims that he does this himself more than any of them (14:15–18).

Interpreters generally note two differences between the portrayals of the phenomenon of speaking in tongues in Acts and 1 Corinthians. First, the persons who speak in tongues in Acts appear to be miraculously inspired to speak in actual foreign languages that they themselves have never learned. In 1 Corinthians, however, the people speak in incomprehensible languages without any expectation that anyone would recognize their words as an actual language spoken on earth. Indeed, 13:1 suggests that the Corinthians might have identified this incomprehensible speech with the language of angels. The interpretation of tongues demanded a spiritual gift, not mere recognition on the part of one who happened to know the language being spoken. Second, the people who speak in tongues in Acts are reported as doing so only once, on the occasion of being filled with the Holy Spirit; there is no indication that Peter, Cornelius, or anyone else who speaks in tongues on one occasion ever does so again. In 1 Corinthians, however, those who have the gift of speaking in tongues

are able to exercise that gift anytime they choose (14:32). *See also* Acts of the Apostles; Pentecost; tongues, as of fire.

J.B.T./M.A.P.

tools, implements used by humans for crafting something. Use of this generic term in the Bible is sparse; writers prefer to designate specific tools, such as ax, pick, or saw (1 Chron. 20:3). According to Gen. 4:22, Tubal-cain (the son of Lamech and Zillah) was remembered as the first person to make "all kinds of bronze and iron tools." When the Israelites constructed an altar for the worship of God, however, they were forbidden to use any tools on the stones, as this would profane them (Deut. 27:5; cf. Exod. 20:25). The same prohibition applied when Joshua built an altar on Mount Ebal, just north of Shechem (Josh. 8:31). Likewise, when the Jerusalem temple was constructed under Solomon, materials were to be prepared and finished at the quarry site, so that neither "hammer nor ax nor any tool of iron was heard in the temple" (1 Kings 6:7). Sirach indicates, however, that Hezekiah used iron tools to tunnel through rock when he fortified the city and built a tunnel (48:17).

Archaeological evidence shows that tool technology followed the course of improvement in material procurement and processing. Thus from prehistoric stone, bone, and shell tools one moves through the successive developments of copper, bronze, and iron, while earlier materials continued to be used where suited or more cheaply available. Each craft developed specialized tools for its work. Jewelers' drills, farmers' sickles, carpenters' adzes, housewives' saddle querns and hand grinders, stonecutters' hammers and chisels, bronze workers' molds, millers' millstones, scholars' inkwells, priests' incense burners, and butchers' knives are a sampling of tools found from the biblical period.

R.S.B.

Topheth (toh´fith), a location in the Valley of the Son of Hinnom (the Valley of Hinnom) south of Jerusalem. It was known as a site where children were sacrificed to Baal and Molech during the time of Isaiah and Jeremiah (Isa. 30:33; Jer. 7:31, 32; 19:6, 11–14; cf. 32:35). Kings Ahaz and Manasseh of Judah are reported to have offered their sons as sacrifices in the Valley of the Son of Hinnom (2 Chron. 28:3; 33:6; cf. 2 Kings 16:3; 21:6). King Josiah attempted to put a stop to the practice by defiling the altar at Topheth (2 Kings 23:10), but the practice was revived after his death. The word "Topheth" that appears in English Bibles is a simple transliteration of the word that appears in Hebrew Bibles. The consonants of this Hebrew word correspond to those of the word *tephat*, which means "hearth" or "fireplace," and since the Hebrew text of the Bible was originally written in consonants only, the word that was actually used in the earliest biblical manuscripts would have been *t-ph-t*, which all readers would have known stood for *tephat* ("hearth"). However, when the

Masoretes added vowels to the Hebrew text of the Bible (sometime after the fifth century CE), they substituted the vowels for the Hebrew word meaning "shame" for the vowels that would properly be used for this word, transforming *tephat* into a nonexistent word, *tophet*. In short, the original biblical text simply referred to a hearth or fireplace located in the Valley of the Son of Hinnom, but the text as we now possess it calls that hearth by a unique name: Topheth. The intention of the Masoretes was for every mention of that hearth to invoke the shame of what transpired there. *See also* Hinnom, Valley of; Masorah; Masoretic Text; Molech.

M.A.S.

Torah (toh´ruh; Heb., "instruction" or "teaching"), God's instructions to Israel. The Hebrew word *torah* is often translated "law" in English Bibles, following the Greek translation of the word as *nomos* in the LXX. The word *nomos* does have a much stronger legal connotation than *torah,* but even *nomos* in the Hellenistic period (333–63 BCE) was used for divinely revealed precepts and ideas that transcended specifically legal contexts. The NRSV is inconsistent in how it translates *torah*—unless otherwise noted, in the biblical passages here the NRSV renders the word "law," "teaching," or "instruction."

In the Hebrew Bible: In different sections and contexts of the Hebrew Bible, the word *torah* is used with different connotations. In Exodus and Genesis, the word refers to God's instruction (Exod. 13:9; 16:4) and is employed in a manner parallel to "commandment" and "statute" (Gen. 26:5; Exod. 18:16). In Leviticus and Numbers, however, *torah* defines instructions for worship and other cultic matters (e.g., Num. 5:29–30). The NRSV often translates *torah* as "ritual" in these contexts (Lev. 6:14; 7:1, 37; 14:2, 54). The phrase "this is the statute of the Torah" emphasizes the reference to such cultic instruction (Num. 19:2; 31:21; cf. 35:29). In Lev. 10:11 the causal form of the verbal root *yrh* ("to instruct," "to teach") is used to define the main priestly duties, "to teach the people of Israel all the statutes which the Lord has spoken to them by Moses." This teaching includes sacrificial laws, ethical behavior, holidays, and regulations concerning purity and impurity (10:10; 14:57; cf. 4–7, 11–15, 23). In Deuteronomy, the priestly teaching function of Torah is also underscored: "If a judicial decision is too difficult for you to make . . . you shall consult with the levitical priests and the judge. . . . You must carry out fully the *torah* [NRSV: "law"] that they interpret for you" (17:8–9, 11; cf. 33:8–10). In many occurrences in Deuteronomy, however, the expression "this *torah*" refers to the composite literary elements of the book—speeches, laws, blessings and curses, etc. (1:5; 4:44; 27:3, 26; 28:58; also "This book of the *torah*," 28:61; 29:20; 30:10; 31:26). Torah in Deuteronomy is thus perceived as basic to Israel's cultural and national identity (4:5, 6, 8).

The Former Prophets (Joshua–2 Kings), which are perceived by modern scholarship as having undergone a systematic editing by adherents to the school of Deuteronomy, follow the predominant usage of *torah* in Deuteronomy, using the word to refer to the comprehensive nature of that book (Josh. 1:7–8; 8:31–34; 22:5; 23:6; 1 Kings 2:3; 2 Kings 10:31; 14:6; 17:13, 34; 21:8). It appears that the book of *torah* found in the temple (2 Kings 22:8; 23:25) was a version of Deuteronomy.

In the Latter Prophets (Hosea, Amos, Isaiah son of Amoz, and Micah; eighth century BCE), *torah* is used in a variety of contexts. The word is used in the sense of cultic rules (Hos. 4:6), as parallel to covenant (8:1), and as written divine instructions known to the northern tribes (8:12). Amos and Isaiah see Torah as including God's moral commands (Amos 2:4, 6–12; Isa. 5:24; 30:9). Isaiah also gives the sense of divine teachings through the prophet (1:10; 8:16). Further, both Isa. 2:3 and Mic. 4:2 indicate that the Torah will be taught by God to all nations in the final times. Hab. 1:4 uses *torah* in the context of ethics. Criticism of the teaching of the Torah by the priests appears in Mic. 3:11, Zeph. 3:4, Ezek. 22:26; and Mal. 2:6–9. Jeremiah uses *torah* in a comprehensive sense similar to Deuteronomy's (6:19; 9:12; 16:11; 26:4). In the New Covenant to be given at the time of redemption (31:33), the Torah's content remains intact (only the method of transmission changes), and all will be naturally obedient to it. Ezekiel shows the influence of the Priestly sections of the Pentateuch in his use of *torah* (43:11; 44:23–24), and he uses the word eschatologically in reference to the temple (43:12). In sum, the prophets use the word *torah* in a broad sense. Even the priestly instruction was not limited to cultic issues, as was illustrated by the example of a request for priestly *torah* given in Hag. 2:11–13.

In the book of Psalms, there is a tendency to praise the Torah and the righteous who cleave to it, so that it is viewed as the purpose and motivation of existence (1:2; 19:8; 37:31; 40:9; 94:12; 112:1; 119:97). These psalms seem to be influenced by the wisdom traditions, perhaps in conjunction with Deuteronomy (see also Ps. 78). Deuteronomistic influence may also be found in Ps. 89:31–33 (cf. 2 Sam. 7:14), while Ps. 105:45 may reflect Priestly writings (which elevate the Sinai covenant above that of Abraham).

Proverbs uses the word *torah* for the advice given by a parent (1:8; 3:1) or a sage (13:14); *torah* is also paralleled to reproof (1:8), command (3:1), and a good lesson (4:2). Although many of the occurrences of *torah* here are in the sense of general wisdom, the specific use of *torah* as religious instruction appears as well (28:9; 29:18).

The Chronicler depicts the kings as subservient to God's Torah (1 Chron. 16:40; 22:12–13; 2 Chron. 14:3; 23:18; 30:16; 31:3–4, 21; 34:14–15, 19), which is perceived as a specific book (2 Chron. 12:1; 25:4; 33:2–9; but cf. the Priestly rule mentioned in 2 Chron. 15:3). In Ezra (3:2; 7:6, 10) and Nehemiah (8:1, 8, 18; 9:3; 10:30; 13:1, 3), a fixed written Torah is assumed.

Conclusions: The vast majority of the occurrences of the word *torah* in the Bible refer to

God's instructions to Moses at Sinai that were transmitted to Israel. These instructions or commandments (in a narrower or wider sense) became Israelite law and the stipulations of the covenant. They were all-important, since they were the specific manifestations of God's will. Since they were God-given, they were obviously good, and obedience would result in long life, prosperity, health, and happiness. Disobedience would be punished with harm, barrenness, exile, destruction, and death. The Torah is the great democratizing influence on Israelite society—all had to obey, especially kings (Deut. 17:18–20). This teaching was permanent, even if the covenant were broken (Jer. 31:33). The teaching of the Torah was an essential priestly function, but the greatest joy was to have God answer one's prayers and teach it directly to the individual (Pss. 94:12; 119:33–34, 72–73).

Proverbs, which uses *torah* in the sense of parental guidance for a child, may provide the reason why this term was used in the religious sphere. The Israelites are frequently portrayed as God's children in the Bible (Exod. 4:22; Deut. 14:1; 32:10–12; Hos. 11:1; Jer. 31:9, 20; Isa. 66:13). Thus, *torah* in the religious sense may have originally connoted the teachings imparted by God the parent to Israel the child. *See also* covenant; Pentateuch.

Bibliography

Crüsemann, Frank. *The Torah: Theology and Social History of Old Testament Law.* Fortress, 1996.

J.U.

An archer shooting from a tower; engraving on an eighth-century BCE quiver.

Tou (too). *See* Toi.

tower. Towers constructed for military purposes included freestanding outposts that were located in strategic positions (2 Chron. 20:24; 26:10; 2 Kings 17:9; 18:8) and projecting bastions that were part of a city's defense system (2 Chron. 14:7; 26:9; 32:5; Neh. 3:25–27). The dimensions of towers varied in accord with their purpose and the available building materials. Towers provided elevated positions for sentries or soldiers repelling enemy attacks (2 Chron. 26:15); some towers were so massively built that they provided refuge for the population in time of attack (Judg. 9:46–52). Reference to the destruction of a city's towers symbolized its fall (Ezek. 26:4, 9), and Isaiah depicted Babylon's demise by predicting that hyenas would inhabit its towers (13:22; cf. 32:14). Siege towers were often used in attacks on cities (Isa. 23:13; 29:3; Ezek. 21:22).

In addition to the military function of towers, farmers built small watchtowers in fields and vineyards (Isa. 5:2; Matt. 21:33). These towers provided elevated positions from which fields could be guarded; the ground floor of such structures served as living quarters for fieldworkers or guards, since ripening crops had to be guarded day and night.

The Bible mentions a number of Jerusalem's towers by name: the Tower of the Hundred (Neh. 3:1; 12:39), the Tower of Hananel (Neh. 3:1; 12:39; Jer. 31:38; Zech. 14:10), the Tower of the Ovens (Neh. 3:11; 12:38), and the Tower of David (Song of Sol. 4:4). The biblical writers also referred to other famous towers: the Tower of Babel (Gen. 11:4–5), the Tower of Eder (Gen. 35:21), the Tower of Penuel (Judg. 8:17), the Tower of Shechem (Judg. 9:46), a tower in Thebez (Judg. 9:50–51), the tower of the flock (Mic. 4:8), and a tower in Siloam (Luke 13:4).

Towers sometimes symbolized security (Pss. 48:12; 61:3; 122:7; Prov. 18:10), but the towers of God's enemies could not protect them from judgment (Isa. 2:15; 30:25; cf. Prov. 12:12). In the Song of Solomon, the young woman's neck is compared to the Tower of David (4:4) and to an ivory tower (7:4); her breasts are also compared to towers (8:10). *See also* fort, fortress; Migdal; watchtower.

G.L.M.

town clerk, an official in the Greco-Roman world who had significant authority and responsibility under the Roman system of government. These officials were responsible for the proper form and wording for decrees that were presented to assemblies of the people, and they appear to have been responsible for keeping order and preventing illegal assemblies. Such a person was one of the chief characters in an account of a riot at Ephesus in which Paul was involved (Acts 19:35–41). The Greek word translated "town clerk" in this passage is *grammateus,* the same term that is regularly translated "scribe" everywhere else in the NT. *See also* cities; Ephesus; scribe.

towns, settlements of small but indeterminate size. They could be walled with gates, as a city (1 Sam. 23:7; Prov. 8:3), but they are also spoken of in terms parallel with villages (Matt. 10:11). In the NT, the NRSV translates the Greek word *polis* as either "city" or "town" and it translates the Greek word *kōmē* as either "village" or "town." Thus, the word "town" seems to be the default mid-level term for a settlement that is regarded as either a relatively small city or a relatively large town. The same is true with comparable Hebrew terms in the Bible. Named towns include Tappuah (Josh. 17:8), Bethlehem (Judg. 17:8), Arimathea (Luke 23:51), and Ephraim (John 11:54). Cities were frequently identified as being surrounded by towns and villages (note Ashdod and Gaza, Josh. 15:47; and numerous references in 1 Chron. 7:28). The public ministry of Jesus was carried out in towns and villages (Luke 13:22) without recourse to the larger cities of Galilee (Caesarea, Sepphoris, and Tiberias).   R.S.B.

Trachonitis (trak'uh-ni'tis), a Greek name in the NT for a 370-square-mile rocky, yet potentially fertile, lava plateau located between Galilee and Damascus. It is referred to in the Hebrew Bible as the land of Bashan. Originally a part of Herod's kingdom, Trachonitis became the territory of Philip (Luke 3:1) and later was governed by Herod Agrippa I. Two NT cities in the region were Caesarea Philippi and Bethsaida. *See also* Bashan; Herod; Philip.

trade, the movement and exchange of goods and services that make up commerce. Commercial trading, both foreign and domestic, is viewed as a normal part of domestic activity by citizens in pursuit of prosperity (Gen. 34:10, 21) Likewise, it is a normal pursuit of visitors to a land not formally their own (cf. 42:34, where Joseph invites his family to Egypt, and trading is encouraged). Trade could be a means of survival for desperate prisoners or refugees (Lam. 1:11). Successful trade brought wealth (Ezek. 28:5), but it could also breed violence and corruption (28:16) leading to destruction (28:18). In John's Gospel, Jesus objects that business conducted in the temple courts (e.g., the selling of animals for sacrifice) has transformed the temple into a "marketplace" (2:16; see also Zech. 14:21). Trade could be planned in advance (James 4:13), but merchants could use dishonest devices for excessive profit (Hos. 12:7), and trade could also be conducted without satisfaction (Job. 20:18). Nevertheless, trade was ignored only at one's peril (Luke 19:20–26).

Trade was an international matter, and biblical references mention a variety of trading partners for Israel in the biblical world, including Midianites (Gen. 37:28), Arabians (1 Kings 10:15), Tyre (Isa. 23:8), Chaldea (Babylon, Ezek. 1:29), Ophir (1 Kings 10:11), and the following places listed in Ezek. 27: Sheba, Raamah, Haran, Canneh, Eden, Asshur, Chilmad, Javan, Tarshish, Tubal, Meshech, Beth-togarmah, Rhodes, Edom, Judah, Israel, Damascus, Helbon, Uzal, Dedan, Arabia, Kedar, Cyprus, and Elishah. In addition, 1 Kings 10:28–29 mentions Egypt, Kue, Syria, and the Hittite royal house. At times trading was a royal enterprise for official purposes of diplomacy (10:1–13) or for profit (10:14–29), a matter in which Solomon was the traditional model for success (2 Chron. 1:16; 9:14). In the NT, the ship that was to carry Paul as a prisoner to Rome is also said to have had a cargo of wheat (Acts 27:38). This would be quite normal inasmuch as it was an Alexandrian ship (27:6) and Egypt served as the breadbasket for Rome.

Goods and Services Exchanged: Any sort of necessary good was subject to trade in circumstances where others were deprived of it, but had means of exchange. Furthermore, as any society becomes prosperous, it begins to look on certain goods as desirable, even if they are not necessary in the strict sense, and that society will develop means of acquiring such goods through trade if they are not easily accessible through some other means. This scenario is vividly evident both in the story of Solomon's dealings for construction goods, services, and luxury materials (1 Kings 5–10) and in a vignette on trade in Ezekiel's oracles against Tyre (27–28). Tyre is described as "merchant of the peoples on many coastlands" (27:3). In Tyre one found: fir from Senir; cedar from Lebanon; oaks from Bashan; pine from Cyprus; ivory; linen from Egypt; blue and purple cloth from Elishah; rowers from Sidon and Arvad; pilots from Zemer; caulkers from Gebal (Byblos); soldiers from Persia, Lud, Put, Arvad, Helech, and Gamad; silver, tin, iron, and lead from Tarshish; bronze vessels and slaves from Javan, Tubal, and Meshech; horses, warhorses (perhaps specially trained), and mules from Beth-togarmah; ivory tusks and ebony from Rhodes and other ports; emeralds, purple, embroidered work, fine linen, coral, and agate from Edom; wheat, olives, figs, honey, oil, and balm from Israel and Judah; unspecified goods from Damascus; wine from Helbon; white wool and wine from Uzal along with wrought iron, cassia, and calamus; saddlecloths from Dedan; lambs, goats, and rams from Arabia and Kedar; spices, precious stones, and gold from Sheba and Raamah; and choice garments, clothes of blue and embroidered work, and colored carpets from Haran, Canneh, Eden, Asshur, and Chilmad. Among the precious stones specified are carnelian, topaz, jasper, chrysolite, beryl, onyx, sapphire (probably lapis lazuli), carbuncle and emeralds, with worked gold settings.

Marketing: The steps from early individual bartering to the development of formal markets are not clear. What is obvious is that in the earliest city-states of Sumer in Mesopotamia the temple served as a major gathering point for goods, if not services. The huge ziggurat and temple constructions, to say nothing of the walls, palaces, canals, and dikes that marked these cities, required extensive acquisition of construction materials and workers. The democratic nature of earliest Sumerian society suggests that such arrangements required elaborate negotiations and records.

For most of the biblical period, marketing was done through small shops where each specialty product was available from the producer or processor. Even in NT times this style of marketing is reflected in rows of shops lining the edges of the more public Greek agora (as at Corinth) or streets (as at Ephesus). The arrangement of market shops was frequently by product; hence there were gold quarters and carpentry rows; shoe shops, bedding shops, metalsmiths, and others with identical or similar products were in close proximity to each other on a particular street or byway. This seems to have been a matter of convenience for producers; it gave them proximity to the competition and thus the capacity to adjust prices according to market changes as well as mutual assistance in production crises, e.g., quick access to borrow a replacement for a broken tool or the quickest access to a supply of materials in case one unexpectedly ran out of an item. It also served as a convenience for shoppers by putting all the competitors producing a given product within easy reach for comparison shopping.

In local markets, the "producers" were often the "sellers." The manufacture of the goods proceeded as the basic occupation, while selling the product, taking special orders, and repairing previously sold items were all conducted by the shopkeeper as integrated parts of the production business. No neat lines separated producer, supplier, and seller in such situations.

Traveling merchants were also common in antiquity. Biblical references reinforce the cottage industry mode of marketing in such cases as Jeremiah's visit to the house of the potter (Jer. 18:3) or the recruitment of a scribe by Paul to write his letters (1 Cor. 16:21).

Records: Most records of trade that have survived from antiquity have been parts of royal or temple archives. Thus, for instance, economic texts predominated in the finds at Ugarit, Mari, and Ebla; the Dead Sea Scrolls are an exception in that, at Qumran, ritual, theological, and other religious interests superseded attention to economic records. The vast spectrum of economic texts discovered throughout the ancient Near East includes orders and receipts for goods; records of shipments made and received; payment of levies and taxes; inventories of goods received and stored; records of goods required, procured, and consumed; and quantities or weights of materials received. That societies took such matters seriously is indicated by the fact that they were recorded on tablets fired for durability and stored in quarters considered secure. There seem not to have been major banking institutions outside the temple precincts or royal houses, but money changing and lending was a readily available

street business. Trade agreements were a major component of diplomatic negotiations, whether in tribal or settled city or national life. The obligation of conquered people to supply both goods, quarters, and services was also assumed. Records concerning trade in humans included bills and receipts of slave purchases as well as manifests of freedom for slaves.

Means of Exchange: The frequent discovery of small ceramic disks, sometimes punctured in the center to allow stringing or hanging on a spindle of some sort, has led some archaeologists to suggest their probable use as local tokens of exchange, a sort of voucher system. The introduction of coinage, traditionally regarded as a sixth-century BCE invention of the Lydians, was made official government practice by the Persians. Coins were usually a government monopoly, with mints sometimes scattered throughout political holdings. Control of the metal value, coin size, design and decoration, and varieties of coins used were thus a means of both economic and political control. The propaganda value of coins should not be underrated. Greeks and Romans brought the art to a high state, and coins, when they are recovered in legible condition, are among the most helpful archaeological articles for dating sites. *See also* money; transportation, travel; weights and measures.   R.S.B.

transfiguration (trans-fig′yuh-ray′shuhn), the title given to an event in Jesus's life in which his physical appearance is temporarily changed as he is "transfigured" (Gk. *metamorphoō*) before three of his disciples on a mountaintop. The story is reported in all three of the Synoptic Gospels (Matt. 17:1–8; Mark 9:2–8; Luke 9:28–36). Jesus takes Peter, James, and John with him to the summit of an unnamed mountain. There his face begins shining like the sun and his clothing becomes dazzling white. Then, suddenly, Moses and Elijah appear with him. Peter offers to build three booths or dwellings for them, and then a voice speaks from heaven, saying "This is my Son, the Beloved; listen to him!" (Mark 9:7; cf. Matt. 17:5; Luke 9:35). The transfiguration has been understood as an instance of Jesus's true form as the Son of God breaking through his humanity (cf. John 1:14) or as a proleptic glimpse of the glory of the Son of God that will be revealed at the Parousia (cf. 2 Pet. 1:16–18).   R.H.S.

transgression. *See* sin.

Transjordan (trans-jor′duhn), strictly speaking the area directly east of the Jordan River, but a term normally used today for the high plateau area from the Yarmuq River in the north to the head of the Gulf of Aqabah in the south. The present Kingdom of Jordan represents the first time in history that the area has formed a single united and independent state. Previously it was always either a group of separate states or part of a foreign empire.

The edge of the plateau, overlooking the north–south rift valley of the Ghor, is everywhere higher than its counterpart in the west and consequently receives heavier winter rainfall, which decreases rapidly as the plateau slopes downward toward the Wadi Sirhan and the great basalt barrier in the east. Throughout history, from the Pre-Pottery Neolithic period (ca. 7000 BCE) to the present, Transjordan has provided a relatively easy north–south route from Syria to the Red Sea and Midian in northwest Arabia, and vice versa. There have been two roads, the King's Highway on the plateau edge and the Pilgrim Route along the edge of the desert. The first has the problem of crossing deep and steep-sided valleys, while the second is more level but less well supplied with food and water. Four major valleys cleave the plateau edge: the Yarmuq in the north, the Zerqa (biblical Jabbok), the Mojjib (Arnon), and the Hesa (Zered). These have often served as administrative boundaries, but only the Hesa is a true cultural division.

Culturally—as well as politically in the period prior to the Assyrian conquests (ninth–eighth centuries BCE)—the main areas of the Transjordan were as follows:

1. Havvoth-jair (Num. 32:41; Deut. 3:14; 1 Kings 4:13), an extension of the Bashan plateau (Josh. 13:30), and a disputed zone between Aram and Israel. In NT times it was part of the Decapolis, including Gadara (Umm Qeis) and Abila (Tell Abil).

2. Gilead, the uplifted highland region of Ajlun, divided by the Zerqa. This area was incorporated into the tribal lands of Manasseh, being the only area east of the Jordan where the three Israelite crops of grain (wheat or barley), grapes, and olives could be cultivated together. A medicinal balm from this region was proverbial (Jer. 8:22; 46:11) and was exported to Phoenicia (Ezek. 27:17) and to Egypt (Gen. 37:25). The plateau to the east, merging rapidly into semidesert, was Ammonite territory, centering on the upper Jabbok, which rises at Amman (Rabboth Ammon). Gerasa (Jerash) in Gilead and Philadelphia (Amman) were the southernmost Decapolis cities.

3. Moab, east of the Dead Sea. This area is divided into two parts by the canyon of the Mojjib. The level tableland of the Mishor to the north (Deut. 3:10; Josh. 13:9) was traditionally the territory of Reuben and Gad (Judg. 5:16; 1 Sam. 13:7). It was famous for its sheep and was essentially Moabite. The Moabite heartland between the Mojjib and Hesa is increasingly pastoral and rises steadily southward; this area was controlled from the great stronghold of Kir-hareseth (Kerak) on the King's Highway (2 Kings 3:21–27).

4. Edom, the high plateau rim south of the Hesa, everywhere well above 4,000 feet and touching 5,704 feet a little north of Petra. Cultivation is confined to a narrow strip along the plateau edge, and the chief source of wealth was trade with Arabia, perhaps as early as 6000 BCE, and with Anatolia as early as 7000. The region reached its zenith under the Nabateans.

5. The Dissected Plateau in the extreme south, a complicated network of hills and gorges. As the entry to the Red Sea and to Midian and Arabia, this may have been the Teman of the Hebrew Bible, though the name (lit., "south") may perhaps signify either southern Edom or northwestern Arabia.

See also Ammonites; Arabia; Arnon River; cities; Gadara, Gadarenes; Gilead; Jabbok; Midian, Midianites; Moab; Zered, Wadi.   D.B.

transportation, travel.
References to travelers and travel are found throughout the Bible, in addition to mention of devices used for moving people or goods. Travel could occur either by day or night (Exod. 13:21), and there were advantages to each. Daytime travel over land reduced the dangers of being waylaid by bandits, but subjected one to the worst heat in summer. Night travel over land needed moonlight for the safest progress, but eliminated the heat problem both for humans and animals. Sea travel was limited to daytime voyaging within sight of land until use of celestial navigation allowed direct crossings. In the biblical period sea traffic consisted predominantly of coastal routes, and safe havens at intervals of a day's sail were a hallmark of the Phoenician sea travel development. Land travel used what roads were available (Job 21:29), and the word of travelers was a major link in communications (21:29). In times of stress roads might be avoided, and travelers would take to roundabout routes for safety, while commercial transport might suspend operations (Judg. 5:6). International travel was commonplace, but was judiciously watched for danger (Job 6:19). Its nature could be trade (Ezek. 27:25), legal business (Acts 9:1–7), casual encounter (2 Sam. 12:4), a deliberate group activity (Acts 19:29; 2 Cor. 8:19), or the result of a crisis (Acts 11:19). For a person or place to be forgotten by travelers was a distinctive form of oblivion (Job. 28:4) and could symbolize an extreme form of future desolation (Ezek. 39:11) .

Rivers: There is little doubt that early settlement patterns reflect transportation by river craft in both Egypt and Mesopotamia. The central role of the Nile was its proximity to all cultivatable land, aided by a dominant northwest wind, which allowed early sailing craft to maneuver upstream as easily as the current allowed raft and barge traffic to move northward downstream. The long stretch below the cataract at Aswan gave an untrammeled waterway to the Mediterranean Sea that served the entire population of Egypt throughout antiquity.

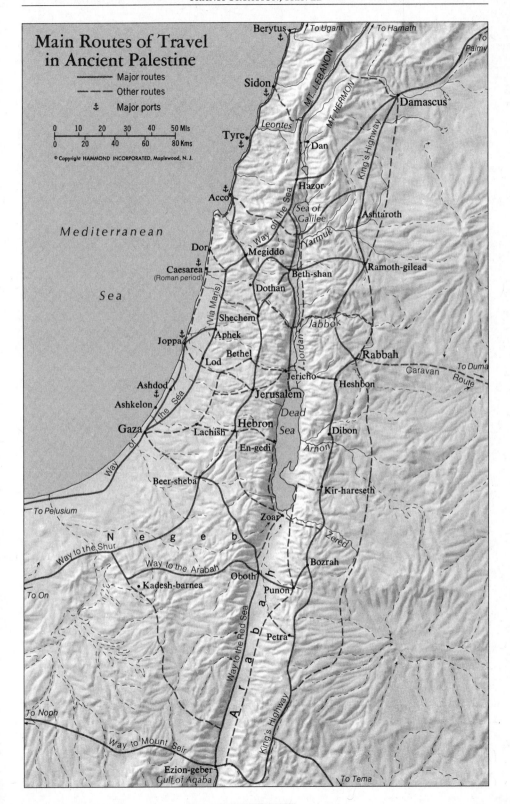

Main Routes of Travel
in Ancient Palestine

——— Major routes
- - - - Other routes
⚓ Major ports

0   10   20   30   40   50 Mls
0   20   40   60   80 Kms

© Copyright HAMMOND INCORPORATED, Maplewood, N. J.

Mediterranean

Sea

Berytus
To Ugarit
To Hamath
To Palmy

Sidon

MT. LEBANON
MT. HERMON

Damascus

Leontes

Tyre
Dan

King's Highway

Acco
Hazor

Sea of
Galilee
Ashtaroth

Dor
Megiddo
Way of the Sea

Caesarea
(Roman period)
Beth-shan
Yarmuk
Ramoth-gilead

Dothan

Via Maris

Shechem
Jabbok

Aphek
Joppa
Bethel
Jordan

Lod
Rabbah
To Duma

Jericho
Caravan Route

Ashdod
Jerusalem
Heshbon

Ashkelon

Gaza
Hebron
Dead
Sea
Dibon

Lachish

En-gedi
Arnon

Beer-sheba
Kir-hareseth

To Pelusium
Zoar
Zered

N e g e b
Bozrah

Way to the Shur

Way to the Arabah
Oboth

Kadesh-barnea
Punon

To On

Petra

A r a b a h

Way to the Red Sea

King's Highway

To Noph
Way to Mount Seir

Ezion-geber
Gulf of Aqaba
To Tema

The same importance of rivers is evident in the earliest settlement patterns of Sumer in lower Mesopotamia. The Tigris and Euphrates were far riskier flood hazards than the Nile, but the city-states of Lagash, Kish, Eridu, and Uruk all grew in proximity to river sources both for ease of moving people and goods and for the water available (as in Egypt) for agricultural development. The earliest literary materials from the region reflect a situation where life's survival was dependent on the successful victory of the river's freshwater over the salty demon of the sea (*Enuma Elish*, tablet 1). Travel on rivers required some sort of stable vehicles to move goods, however, and the history of water transport devices indicates developments from crude rafts to sailing vessels with sufficient cargo capacity to handle large quantities of timber, copper, and other heavy freight.

Seas: The use of open saltwater for transportation is documented at least by Old Kingdom times in Egypt (2700–2200 BCE) when transportation and trade were carried out with Byblos on the coast of modern Lebanon. Such travel involved craft called "Byblites" for moving both goods and passengers. The Phoenicians developed maritime trade into substantial proportions, colonizing for their purposes the entire north coast of Africa beyond the Strait of Gibraltar to the western coast of modern Morocco as well as Cyprus, Greece, Italy, Mediterranean islands such as Sardinia and even the Spanish coast, Malta, and Crete. Subsequent great sea powers like Persia, Greece, and Rome first absorbed and then followed and expanded the trading routes developed by Phoenicia's maritime transportation network.

Solomon turned to the experts of Tyre, not only for his construction projects, but for his maritime development (1 Kings 9:26–28). Both shipbuilding and ship handling were new skills for the Israelites of the monarchy. Seaworthy craft allowed travel from the upper reaches of the Gulf of Aqabah (Solomon's port there was Ezion-geber) into the Red Sea and from there either up the Gulf of Suez or down the coast of Arabia round the tip of the Arabian peninsula and across the east coast of Africa; or they could be sailed eastward along the south coast of Arabia to touch points east along the Persian Gulf of the centers of life in India on the Indus River.

Sail power was employable in all of this, although the Greeks and Persians, followed by the Romans, developed human-powered rowing ships that reached their maximum development in triremes (three tiers of rowers on each side of a vessel). Such ships were used by Persia in unsuccessful attempts to subdue Greece (as at the battle of Salamis, 480 BCE). Roman ships dominated the Mediterranean by NT times and also reached as far north as Britain.

It is in such a maritime network that the report of Paul's journey by ship from Caesarea to Italy is set, giving some idea of both the normal routing and the hazards of such transportation. The route taken by the ship of Adramyttium (a port in Mysia,

in what is modern northwest Turkey) was north up the coast to Sidon, then across the south coast of Cyprus to Myra in Lycia (in modern southwest Turkey). There, Paul and his guards transferred to a ship from Alexandria, Egypt, bound for Italy and headed west along the south shore of Crete. Despite seasonal hazards of storms in winter weather, they struck out from Phoenix on the southwest coast of Crete, running into stormy troubles when they hit the open water exposed to western windy seas. Managing only a temporary relief at an island called Cauda (Acts 27:16–17), they took drastic measures with cargo and gear and managed to drift to shore at Malta, remaining there for the duration of the winter. From Malta they set out for Syracuse on Sicily and Rhegium at the toe of Italy's boot and made landfall at Puteoli two-thirds of the way up the Italian west coast, from which point the journey proceeded overland. Acts reports a roster of 276 people aboard that ship with a staff of soldiers under a centurion in charge of the prisoners.

Land Transport: Limited water supplies first prevented land travel across the major stretches of desert in the biblical world, the Sahara and the Arabian desert. The presence of these deserts funneled land travel around the quarter-moon-shaped arc of land from the Mesopotamian valley, across northern Syria south of the major mountain ranges of eastern Turkey, and down the Levant to the eastern Nile Delta in Egypt (the Fertile Crescent).

Foot travel was common in all biblical periods, walking being cheap, convenient, and not dependent on other people's timetables. Walking was made easier with a staff or walking stick, especially when moving through hilly regions. Animals, after they had been domesticated, were used, especially the donkey. Oxen provided good draft strength for pulling carts, but required more water and forage than many of the zones afforded. Horses were faster and more maneuverable and were traded extensively by Solomon (1 Kings 10:28–29), together with chariots, making both civilian and military transport more efficient. Horses had been used for cavalry presumably since the time of the Hyksos, but they also required more extensive forage, water, and care than the ubiquitous donkey. Presumably the expense of purchase as well as maintenance of horses kept the donkey popular. A donkey could be fitted with a carrier saddle, and its capacity for carrying cargo was enormous for its size. Its sure-footedness added to its value when covering rocky terrain, and its capacity to survive on seemingly inedible plant life allowed it to thrive where other beasts could not. Only the domestication of the camel about 1200 BCE brought a serious challenge to the dominant role of the donkey. The capacity of the camel for cargo was also enormous for its size, and its ability to go without water for days opened up new routes of both freight and passenger traffic that had previously been impossible.

The use of wheeled vehicles is attested in lower Mesopotamia in the third millennium BCE. The early models were made with solid wheels rigidly attached to their axles, which were then mounted to turn under the bed of the cart. Such carts provided noisy, rough transport, but with the invention of a lighter wheel with spokes to a rim from a hub that would rotate on the axle, major improvement in load capacity, maneuverability, and consequent range was achieved. Pictorial representations in Egypt indicate that such chariots were used with teams of four horses for sport or military purposes. For efficiency of wheeled traffic, road development from the previous tracks of mounted animals or footpaths was essential.

Certain basic routes were developed prior to roads, some of which were followed when roads were built. In the Levant, there were three major north–south routes as well as commonly used transverse or east–west crossings. Because of the lay of the land and Canaan's location in relation to the great powers of the time (Egypt, the Hittites, Mesopotamia) the north–south routes were used primarily for both commercial and military traffic over the centuries. Of first importance was the coastal route. Coming up from the eastern Nile Delta in Egypt, it followed the curve of the Mediterranean shore, branching inland at the Mount Carmel mountain range to cross the Esdraelon Plain at Megiddo. This "way of the sea" (Isa. 9:1) was fortified by the Egyptians when they had control of the area, thus discouraging the Israelite migrants from using it after the exodus. North of Megiddo the route went along the west side of the Sea of Galilee to Hazor and Damascus, from where connections north through Syria to both the Hittite and Ugaritic centers and, crossing the arc of the crescent, to Mesopotamia were available. From Megiddo there were also transverse connections north of the Carmel ridge to coastal towns like Acco and points north as well as eastward along the plain to Beth-shan and the Jordan Valley, from which routes continued eastward across the Jordan and southward to Jericho.

The other major north–south route ran from the port on the Gulf of Aqabah up the Transjordan hills of Edom, Moab, and Ammon, continuing northward to Damascus. It was part of the great overland route from Damascus to Arabia, but allowed land–sea connections from Damascus to points east as well. An intermediate north–south route serving Israel was in the hills running southward from Jerusalem to Bethlehem, Hebron, and points further south. North of Jerusalem it connected with Shechem and the Esdraelon Plain, allowing both north and transverse connections at Beth-shan.

Additional crossings from east to west were possible through the pass between Mount Ebal and Mount Gerizim at Shechem, the Valley of Achor and Jerusalem down to Jericho, and across the southern reaches of the Shephelah from Beer-sheba to the Edomite heights. This was especially prominent during Edomite domination of southern Judah and during the Nabatean ascendance. In Hellenistic and Roman times, travel

across the eastern Syrian desert used Palmyra as a major center on the way to the Euphrates.

The Persians constructed a major new facility for travel with their development of the route from Susa (in western Persia) to Ephesus (on the southwest coast of Turkey). By means of carefully spaced stations for fresh mounts and overnight rest stops, Persia cut the travel time from Susa to Ephesus from three months to a week. Its couriers on royal business would carry messages day and night on a road that included bridges and ferries for hazardous terrain or river crossings.

It was Roman engineering, however, that would ultimately get the most credit for building enduring roads for public and military use. Rome built its roads straight and to last. Romans also marked their roads with milestones. Stone was the primary construction material in Roman road preparation as well as its paving. The parable of the Good Samaritan (Luke 10:29–37) indicates that travel on roads could be dangerous due to thieves, but also that inns were found on most routes. Some of these facilities were extensive in order to accommodate large caravans, both animals and drivers, or at major intersections, to handle groups of caravans, giving rise to the term *caravanserai* for such installations.   R.S.B

travel. *See* transportation, travel.

treasures, wealth accumulated and kept primarily in palaces and temples in the ancient world. Treasures were acquired by royal conquest (e.g., 1 Kings 14:25–26; 2 Kings 14:13–14), by trade or taxes on trade (1 Kings 10:11, 15, 22; Ezek. 27:12–27; 28:4–5), or as gifts (e.g., 1 Kings 10:10, 13–15; cf. Matt. 2:2, 11) or tribute (10:14–15). A monarch's treasures were used to adorn the palace and purchase military resources (1 Kings 10:16–21, 26–29). Some were dedicated to the deity for the adornment of the temple (Josh. 6:19). A monarch might use palace or temple treasures to buy off an invader (2 Kings 12:17–18; 18:13–16) or to purchase the assistance of a third party to harass an invader (1 Kings 15:17–21; 2 Kings 16:5, 7–9). A wealthy individual might buy special favors from a king by a contribution to his treasury (Esther 3:8–11; 4:7). Legendary wealth was attributed to Solomon (1 Kings 10; cf. Eccles. 2:8) and Hezekiah (2 Chron. 32:27–29); the latter, by showing his treasures to Babylonian envoys (2 Kings 20:13; Isa. 39:2), prompted Isaiah's prophecy that they would be carried off to Babylon (2 Kings 20:17; Isa. 39:6). The regular contributions of worshipers also benefited the temple treasury and might be designated by the monarch for the materials and labor needed to repair and maintain the temple (2 Kings 12:4–14; 22:3–7, 9).

Nah. 2:9 describes the looting of the treasures of Nineveh: "Plunder the silver, plunder the gold! There is no end of treasure! An abundance of every precious thing!" But of much more consequence in the Bible is the despoiling of Jerusalem

(Jer. 20:5). Nebuchadnezzar took the treasures of the Jerusalem temple (2 Kings 25:13–17) and palace (2 Kings 24:13; 2 Chron. 36:18; 1 Esd. 1:54) to Babylon, where he deposited them in his god's temple treasury (Dan. 1:2). Later Cyrus returned them to the Jewish leaders to be taken back to Jerusalem (Ezra 1:8–11), where the leaders volunteered special contributions to fund the rebuilding of the temple (2:68–69). A model for such special contributions appears in the account in Chronicles of the building of the first temple (1 Chron. 29:2–8). Artaxerxes authorized Ezra to charge additional rebuilding expenses to the Persian imperial treasury (Ezra 7:20–21). Later the treasures of the second Jerusalem temple were plundered by Antiochus Epiphanes (1 Macc. 1:21–24).

Moral reflections on wealth are frequent in the Hebrew Bible and in subsequent wisdom literature. Treasures accumulate for the wise (Prov. 21:20) and the righteous (15:6), those who honor their mothers (Sir. 13:4) and those who give alms (Tob. 4:7–9). Wisdom is the source of treasures (Prov. 8:18–21). However, treasures do not last (27:24) and may be troublesome (15:16). Ill-gotten wealth makes one vulnerable (21:6; 10:2; Tob. 12:8–10). Hidden treasure is useless (Sir. 20:30; 41:14), but a treasure trove is better than an income (40:18). Treasure is a metaphor for wisdom (Prov. 2:4; Wis. 7:14), almsgiving (Sir. 29:12), a faithful friend (Sir. 6:14), and immortality (2 Esd. 8:54). Faithfulness and good works may be accumulated as a treasure deposited with God (6:5; 7:77).

In the NT, the magi open their treasures before the infant Jesus and worship him with gifts of gold and frankincense and myrrh (Matt. 2:11). In general, however, the NT recognizes the vanity of earthly treasures, the permanence of heavenly treasure, and the way one's life and values are shaped by what one treasures (6:19–21; Luke 12:33–34, cf. 20–21). James 5:1–5 denounces those who live for earthly treasures, and Heb. 11:26 presents Moses, who preferred suffering to the treasures of Egypt, as a model of faith in God's future reward. In the Gospels, almsgiving is presented as one way to convert earthly into heavenly treasure (Matt. 19:21–22; Mark 10:21–22; Luke 18:22–23). Buried treasure is an image of the kingdom of heaven (Matt. 13:44), and wisdom and knowledge are treasures hidden in Christ (Col. 2:3). Paul reflects on the fragility of the human condition by telling the Corinthians, "We have this treasure [i.e., life] in clay jars" (2 Cor. 4:7).

S.B.P.

tree of life, a well-known image deeply rooted in the traditions of the ancient Near East. Widely depicted on seals, reliefs, and other artistic forms, the sacred tree represented fertility, or ongoing life, as well as immortality, or eternal life (Gen. 3:9, 22, 24; cf. Ezek. 31:8). In the Bible, the phrase "tree of life" appears most prominently in Gen. 3. Proverbs also refers metaphorically to a tree of life (3:18; 11:30; 13:12; 15:4). The NT also takes up the image

(Rev. 2:7; 22:2, 14, 19). It is possible that the form of the seven-branched lampstand (Heb. *menorah*) was modeled after the "tree of life" image. *See also* lampstand.   C.L.M.

trees. In the ancient Near East, scrub forests of oak and terebinth covered portions of the central hill country, Galilee, and Gilead, and solitary specimens or groves dotted the hills and valleys. Willows formed thickets along the Jordan (Jer. 12:5) and flourished by perennial streams. Tamarisks marked the Negev, and palms, the oases. The prized cedars and firs grew only in Lebanon.

Trees were valued for their shade, making them an attractive place to pitch a tent (Gen. 13:18), build a shrine (12:6–7), or judge disputes (Judg. 4:4). The ability of the deep-rooted tree to maintain its green foliage through summer heat and drought made it a symbol of life and endurance (Ps. 1:3; Isa. 65:22). The tree, especially the oak or cedar, was also a symbol of strength and might (Ezek. 31:3; Dan. 4:10–12).

Trees had sacred associations in both Israelite and Canaanite religion, serving as memorial objects (Gen. 21:33) and symbols of the Canaanite fertility goddess Asherah. They marked the high places (open-air sanctuaries) honored by Israel's ancestors (12:6–7), but condemned by the prophets for the illegitimate rites held there (Jer. 3:6).

Trees were especially esteemed for their fruit (including olives). The garden of Eden was stocked with trees for food (Gen. 2:16), and only fruit-bearing trees are mentioned in Gen. 1:11 (cf. 1:29). Jesus taught that "the tree is known by its fruit" (Matt. 12:33; cf. 3:10).

Most trees in the Levant were not suitable for lumber, though they were used for roof beams, furniture, and implements. Large branches also served as gallows or for public display of executed criminals or enemies. Five NT passages use "tree" to designate the cross (Acts 5:30; 10:39; 13:29; Gal. 3:13; 1 Pet. 2:24). *See also* cedar; fig; fir tree; forest; olive; tamarisk; tree of life; willow; wood.

P.A.B.

trials. *See* temptation, testing.

trial of Jesus. All four NT Gospels report that Jesus appeared before the Roman prefect Pontius Pilate for a hearing that resulted in a sentence of death by crucifixion (Matt. 27:11–14; Mark 15:2–5; Luke 23:17–25; John 18:28–38).

Before Pilate: The basic outline of the trial before Pilate suits known Roman procedures for the trial of a noncitizen, although it is evident that the Gospel accounts are not intended to be court records. A private accuser could charge someone with a misdeed, and the Roman prefect then had considerable freedom in deciding how to treat the charge. In accord with this procedure, Jesus is brought before Pilate's tribunal. Matt. 27:19 mentions the "judgment seat" (Gk. *bēma*) on which an official sat when acting in an official capacity as judge. The accusers in this case are said to be members of the chief priests and elders (Matt. 27:12; Mark 15:3; Luke 23:1, 4).

All four Gospels suggest that the fundamental charge against Jesus may have been one of sedition, in that the trial focuses on the allegation that he has claimed to be "king of the Jews" (Matt. 27:15–26; Mark 15:6–15; Luke 23:17–25; John 18:38–19:16). The Synoptic Gospels suggest that Jesus refused to defend himself against this and other accusations. That motif fits well with the early Christian understanding of Jesus as the "suffering servant" of Isa. 53, since the servant in that passage remains silent before his accusers (53:7). In John's account, however, Jesus does challenge his accusers. John 19:12 further suggests that Jesus's accusers threatened to denounce Pilate to Rome under the law of treason (as not being a "friend of Caesar"), if he failed to condemn Jesus to death. Whatever the pressures brought to bear by those who handed Jesus over to Pilate to be tried, the final responsibility for the sentence in such a case belonged to the Roman governor alone.

Before the Council: The Gospels of Matthew and Mark, and to a lesser extent Luke, appear to conceive of Jesus's appearance before a Jewish council as a formal trial, describing that event in parallel fashion to the trial before Pilate. Matt. 26:59–66 and Mark 15:55–64 present a night meeting of the council that culminates in a verdict that he is guilty of blasphemy and, so, deserves death (Matt. 27:1; Mark 14:64). Luke 22:66–71 has accusations against Jesus occurring during a morning meeting of the council (also mentioned in Mark 15:1), which preceded handing Jesus over to Pilate. John 11:45–53 presumes that the decision to have Jesus put to death was made for political reasons during an earlier meeting of the council sometime before Jesus was even arrested. Thus, in John 18:19–24, Jesus is interrogated only by the high priests Annas and Caiaphas after his arrest and prior to being turned over to Pilate.

The council referred to in these texts is probably to be equated with the Jewish body known as the Sanhedrin, but precise information about that entity is unavailable. Aside from what is found in the NT, the earliest sources of information regarding legal requirements of a Jewish trial are from second-century CE material and reflect post–70 CE understandings that may not have been in force at the time of Jesus. Many interpreters think that, before 70 CE, the Pharisees played only a minor role in the Sanhedrin, which was mainly composed of Sadducees and aristocratic elders from Jerusalem (the Gospels, in fact, do not assign a significant role to the Pharisees in council proceedings regarding Jesus; but cf. Acts 23:6).

Before Herod: Luke 23:6–16 contains a notice that Pilate sent Jesus's case to Herod, since Jesus was a Galilean and Herod was the ruler of Galilee. The scene that unfolds there seems modeled on elements of the trial before Pilate, with a parallel mocking of the victim by soldiers. Historically, there would have been no legal justification for such a transfer of jurisdiction; offenders were tried where their crime occurred. Interpreters have tried to come up with explanations for such an occurrence or for Luke's reasons for including such an episode in his narrative. Some scholars suggest that Pilate might have done this as a gesture of courtesy, so as not to offend further the Jewish ruler with whom his relationship was already strained. Others think that Luke's account might have been prompted by memory of a historical idiosyncrasy of Herod mentioned in Josephus, namely, that he had requested and obtained the extraordinary privilege of being allowed to extradite offenders who had fled his realm for other parts of the empire (*Jewish War* 1.24.2). Another explanation is that Luke added the Herod episode, because he wanted to present the trial of Jesus in parallel fashion to his account of the multiple trials of Paul in Acts, where Festus refers Paul's case to Agrippa (25:13–27). In any case, Luke's account does not portray Herod as taking any action against Jesus; he simply interrogates Jesus and then sends him back to Pilate again. *See also* Barabbas; blasphemy; council, the; cross; crucifixion; Herod; Pilate, Pontius.

Bibliography

Bammel, Ernst, ed. *The Trial of Jesus*. SCM, 1970.

Blinzler, Josef. *The Trial of Jesus*. 2 vols. Doubleday, 1994.

Sherwin-White, A. N. *Roman Society and Roman Law in the New Testament*. Oxford University Press, 1963.

Winter, Paul. *On the Trial of Jesus*. 2nd ed. De Gruyter, 1974.   P.P./D.S.

tribes, territorial groups and primary organizational units in Israel's social structure before the establishment of the monarchy (before the late eleventh century BCE). The tribes can be viewed as distributive parts of one larger entity, Israel, whose identity is traced to an eponymous ancestor, Jacob (Israel; Gen. 33:28; 35:10). The tribe was a kind of corporate personality, a grouping of a varying number of protective associations or family groups. Members of such a group typically lived in the same or nearby villages, rural neighborhoods, or sections of a larger settlement, provided mutual aid to all the extended families constituting the group, and provided troop quotas to the tribal levy. The extended family (which in the Bible is called a "father's house") was the primary residential and productive unit in the social structure.

Although each tribe had its own proper name, it was a tribe, properly speaking, only by virtue of the fact that it was one of the tribes of Israel. By being a part of Israel, the individual tribe had a place as one of the primary segments of the whole people and shared in that status equally with all other tribes. Thus, tribes must be understood in terms of their structure and function within the larger whole. The particular identity of a tribe derived from such things as its migration experience, military struggles, and the ways in which it worked out a mixed agricultural and pastoral subsistence strategy dependent upon such things as rainfall, soil fertility, and other natural resources of its tribal territory, which itself was not fixed either in scope or location, but developed over time. A tribe was thus the part of the social structure that dealt with regional needs, provided for its own military self-defense through a tribal militia, and performed religious and legal functions.

The Lists of Tribes: The lists of tribes in the Bible, of which there are more than twenty, differ from one another in several respects, notably in the position of the names of tribes and their number.

The account that became fairly standard is provided in the narrative material of Genesis (29:30–30:24, 35:18), according to which Jacob had twelve sons by four wives (35:23–26). The sons of Jacob and Leah were Reuben, Simeon, Levi, Judah, Issachar, and Zebulun. The sons of Jacob and Rachel were Joseph and Benjamin. The sons of Jacob and Bilhah were Dan and Naphtali. And the sons of Jacob and Zilpah were Gad and Asher. This listing of the tribes corresponds to the one observed most frequently in the Bible (Gen. 35:22–26; Deut. 27:12–13; 1 Chron. 2:1–2; Ezek. 48:1–7). The most typical variance involves two simultaneous moves: the omission of Levi and the substitution of Ephraim and Manasseh for Joseph. The justification for the first move is that the Levites were to be priests and, so, were not to be given allotments of land. The justification for the second move is that Jacob chose to regard Ephraim and Manasseh (the two sons of Joseph) as his own sons rather than as his grandsons—thus the tribe of Joseph could be subdivided into the tribes of Ephraim and Manasseh. Notably, when both of these moves are made together, the number of tribes is retained as twelve. For examples of this twofold variance, see the census lists in Num. 1:20–43; 26:5–50.

The scenario just described, however, provides only an overview of what eventually became standard in Israel. A closer analysis of tribal lists reveals variety throughout eras and contexts. The Song of Deborah (Judg. 5), which is probably the

oldest list (twelfth century BCE), mentions only ten tribes. Judah, Simeon, and Levi are omitted, and Gilead is included (5:17). No reference is made to Joseph, but instead of Ephraim and Manasseh in place of Joseph, it lists Ephraim and Machir (in Gen. 50:23, Machir is identified as the son of Manasseh, hence Joseph's grandson).

The Blessing of Moses (Deut. 33) lists eleven tribes, omitting Simeon, but arrives at the number twelve by listing Ephraim and Manasseh as two separate tribes in addition to Joseph (rather than instead of Joseph, as would become standard). The Blessing of Jacob (Gen. 49) has the "standard list" of the twelve tribes given above. It also indicates, however, that, even though Reuben is to be listed as the firstborn of Jacob, Reuben loses preeminence among the tribes, because of an indiscretion committed with his father's concubine (35:22); the place of preeminence is thus assigned to Judah. The Blessing of Jacob also links Simeon and Levi together in disgrace, because of the incident in connection with their sister Dinah (34).

The Ideal of Twelve: The notion of twelve tribes remained a prominent concept long after the tribal organization disappeared, even into the NT. Ezekiel, in his vision of an ideal state, redistributed the land among twelve tribes. Jesus seems to have intentionally chosen twelve disciples, perhaps to symbolize a renewal of Israel. He is also reported to have promised his disciples that they would judge the twelve tribes of Israel (Matt. 19:28; Luke 22:30), Paul refers to the twelve tribes (Acts 26:7), and the book of James is addressed to the "twelve tribes," a probable reference to Jewish Christians who think of themselves as constituting the true Israel (1:1). Thus the number twelve seems to have been settled upon at some time in Israel's history, probably early in the monarchy, and the tribal nomenclature deriving from the names of Jacob's sons by his two wives, Leah and Rachel, and his two concubines, Zilpah and Bilhah, became a part of Jewish traditions. The tribes understood in this way can be charted according to the accompanying diagram. *See also* family; government.

THE TRIBES OF ISRAEL

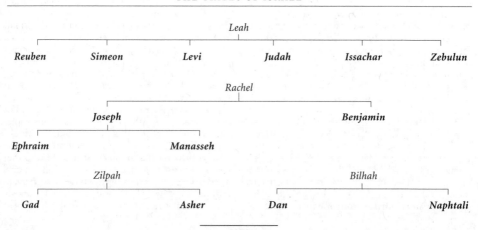

Leah					
Reuben	Simeon	Levi	Judah	Issachar	Zebulun

Rachel	
Joseph	Benjamin

Ephraim	Manasseh

Zilpah		Bilhah	
Gad	Asher	Dan	Naphtali

TRIBAL LISTS IN BIBLICAL TEXTS

Judges 5	Deuteronomy 33	Genesis 49	Numbers 26
Ephraim	Reuben	Reuben	Reuben
Benjamin	Judah	Simeon	Simeon
Machir	Levi	Levi	Gad
Zebulun	Benjamin	Judah	Judah
Issachar	Joseph	Zebulun	Issachar
Reuben	Ephraim	Issachar	Zebulun
Gilead	Manasseh	Dan	Manasseh
Dan	Zebulun	Gad	Ephraim
Asher	Gad	Asher	Benjamin
Naphtali	Dan	Naphtali	Dan
	Naphtali	Joseph	Asher
	Asher	Benjamin	Naphtali

Bibliography

Gottwald, Norman K. *The Tribes of Yahweh.* Orbis Books, 1979.

Mendenhall, George E. *The Tenth Generation.* Johns Hopkins University Press, 1973.

F.S.F./M.A.P.

tribunal, the civil court rostrum or judge's bench in cities of the Roman Empire. According to Acts 18:12–17, Paul was brought before the proconsul Gallio at the tribunal in Corinth. He was accused by Jews of "persuading people to worship God in ways that are contrary to the law" (18:13), but Gallio refused to render any judgment on the matter, since it concerned what he regarded as internal religious disputes rather than anything pertaining to Roman law. In protest, the Jews grabbed Sosthenes, an official of the synagogue (who must have been sympathetic to Paul), and beat him in front of the tribunal.

Excavations at the site of Corinth turned up a large platform in the center of the middle row of shops of the ancient forum or agora. Passages on either side connected the lower and upper areas of the forum. There are benches at the back and sides of the platform, which itself was originally faced with marble. Constructed ca. 44 CE, this was probably the tribunal to which Paul was brought.

According to Acts 25:6–21, Paul was also put on trial before the tribunal in Caesarea after Porcius Festus became governor. The site of that tribunal has not been found.

In Philippi, however, four steps at the north end of the forum have been discovered, which are thought to have led up to the local tribunal, perhaps where Paul and Silas were accused by the owners of a slave girl exorcised by Paul (Acts 16:16–24). Similar steps have been found at Veroia, ancient Beroea.

The Greek term translated "tribunal" in Acts 18 and 25 is *bēma*. That word is also used elsewhere in the NT, but the NRSV translates it as "throne" (Acts 12:21) and as "judgment seat" (Matt. 27:19; John 19:13; Rom. 14:10; 2 Cor. 5:10; cf. also "platform," 1 Esd. 9:42, "public platform," 2 Macc. 13:26). *See also* Corinth; Festus, Porcius; Gallio; judgment seat; Paul; Philippi; throne. C.H.M.

tribute, the payment of money from one nation to a dominating power. Throughout biblical history, people who had been conquered or who were noncitizens of the society in which they lived could be conscripted for purposes of labor (Exod. 5; Matt. 5:41; Josh. 16:10; 2 Chron. 8:7–8). Conquered peoples might also be compelled to pay tribute to the foreign ruler. Royal palaces are regularly decorated with reliefs showing the conquered peoples bringing their tribute to the king (1 Kings 20:1–7; 2 Kings 17:1–6; Neh. 5:4; Esther 10:1).

P.P.

trigon (tri′gon), a small three-cornered, four-stringed musical instrument mentioned only in the book of Daniel (3:5, 7, 10, 15).

triumphal arch, a stone monument constructed to commemorate a signal event or achievement. Their mastery of the arch enabled the Romans to construct large freestanding arches for ceremonial purposes. The triumphal arch was built to honor the emperor, and it carried a dedicatory inscription. It was built with one or three openings and decorated with statuary or bas-reliefs relating the victorious campaigns of the emperor.

The Arch of Titus stands near the entrance to the Forum in the city of Rome. It combines the traditional Italian style of arch with decorative columns of the post-and-lintel Greek style. The arch includes reliefs celebrating Titus's sack of Jerusalem and destruction of its temple in 70 CE, an event that had enormous consequences for both Jews and early Christians.   P.P.

Troas (troh´az), **Alexandria** (al´ig-zan´dree-uh), an important seaport city in Mysia on the northwest coast of Asia Minor. Built in 310 BCE by Antigonus, it was first named Antigonia. The name was later changed to Alexandria Troas by Lysimachus. The latter part of the name was derived from the nearby ancient city of Troy and was intended to distinguish the city from numerous other cities named in honor of Alexander the Great. In the NT, the city is referred to as simply Troas. The city had become a Roman possession in 133 BCE, and Augustus later gave it the status of a Roman colony, probably because of its importance as the nearest seaport for travel to Europe from the northwestern area of the Roman province of Asia. In Troas, during his second missionary journey, Paul had a vision of a man from Macedonia inviting him to come to Europe (Acts 16:8–10). Paul and his companions revisited Troas on their final trip to Jerusalem, and Paul raised or revived Eutychus, who had been "taken up dead" after dozing and falling from a third-story window while Paul was speaking (20:5–12). *See also* Eutychus.   M.K.M.

Trophimus (trof´uh-muhs; Gk., "foster child"), a Christian from Ephesus who, with Tychicus, joined Paul and others for the apostle's final visit to Jerusalem (Acts 20:4–5). Asian Jews mistakenly accused Paul of taking Trophimus, a Gentile, into the temple's court of Israel (21:29), thus provoking a mob disturbance that led to Paul's arrest. Another reference, in 2 Tim. 4:20, indicates that Trophimus (perhaps the same man) had been traveling with Paul, but had to be left behind in Miletus because of illness. *See also* temple, the; Tychicus.

trumpet. Although metal trumpets were known in Israel (cf. Sir. 50:16), the most common word for a trumpet in the Hebrew Bible is *shophar,* which refers to the shofar, or ram's horn. In Exod. 19:16, the revelation at Mount Sinai, it is the loud blast of a shofar that causes the people to tremble in fear. The Israelites were commanded that when they entered the land God would give them, they were to proclaim the jubilee year with a blast of the shofar (Lev. 25:9). In military contexts, the shofar would often signify an important announcement or a call to arms (Judg. 3:27), and it was shofar trumpets that were blown by Joshua and his troops to bring about the collapse of the walls of Jericho (Josh. 6:4–5). The shofar was also used as part of musical ensembles (Ps. 98:6), and it featured in the worship rites of Israel. Num. 29:1 describes the first day of the seventh month as "a day for you to blow the shofar" (NRSV: "trumpets"). Lev. 35:9 says the shofar is to be blown to announce the start of the Day of Atonement. Jewish tradition, based

on Isa. 27:13, maintains that the shofar will be sounded to usher in the final messianic redemption (cf. Rev. 8–9). The shofar also plays a prominent role in the eschatological battle described in the *War Scroll* from Qumran.

The Greek word for trumpet (*salpinx*) can refer to any number of instruments—the shofar, but also any sort of brass horn. In NT eschatology, a trumpet blast is strongly associated with the Parousia, or Second Coming of Christ (1 Thess. 4:16), the resurrection of the saints (1 Cor. 15:52), and the final judgment (Matt. 24:31). The book of Revelation depicts an end-time scenario according to which seven angels blow trumpets, each of which causes disaster to befall the earth and its inhabitants (8–9; 10:7; 11:15). In a very different context, Jesus tells his disciples, "Whenever you give alms, do not sound a trumpet before you, as the hypocrites do in the synagogues and in the streets, so that they may be praised by others" (Matt. 6:2). It is not known whether he was speaking metaphorically or whether trumpets literally were sounded to accompany the presentation of an extravagant gift. *See* music; Trumpets, Festival of.   L.H.S./M.A.P.

Trumpets, Festival of, a celebration on the first day of the seventh month (Tishri) of the Hebrew religious year. Its name comes from its designation as a "day of (horn-)blasts" (Num. 29:1; cf. Lev. 23:24; Num. 10:10). It was a day of rest. An extra set of new-moon offerings was brought (except for one bull as a burnt offering), because it was the foremost of the new-moon celebrations (Num. 29:2–6; cf. 28:11–15). *See also* festivals, feasts, and fasts.

trust. *See* faith.

truth. For Israel, truth (Heb. *'emet*) was moral and relational, not intellectual. God above all is true, because God is reliable (Isa. 65:16; Jer. 10:10); people are to seek God's truth (Pss. 25:5; 51:6; 86:11). People are admonished to judge truly, and the lack of truth is lamented (Zech. 8:16; Isa. 59:14–15). Reports and prophecies may be true or false (1 Kings 10:6–7). In all these instances, the emphasis is upon reliability, something or someone that stands up under testing.

The Greek word for truth (*alētheia*) carries a more intellectual connotation. Truth is something that can be "known," not just trusted or relied upon. The NT authors all employ the Greek word, but they are sufficiently steeped in knowledge of the Jewish scriptures to use the word in a sense heavily influenced by the Hebrew meaning. This is in part because the NT authors knew those scriptures primarily through the form of the LXX, where *alētheia* translates *'emet.* The word "truth" occurs mainly in the Pauline writings and, especially, in the Gospel and Letters of John.

Paul can use the word in the Greek sense (Rom. 1:18), but more often he uses it with the same connotation it has in the Hebrew Bible: truth is something to be obeyed (Rom. 2:8; Gal. 5:7); truth proves reliable (2 Cor. 7:14; 11:10); the opposite of truth is not falsehood, but malice and evil (1 Cor. 5:8). The Greek idea of truth as "correct knowledge" appears most clearly in the Pastoral Letters. Here, one is to know the truth (1 Tim. 4:3; 2 Tim. 2:25) and avoid false beliefs (2 Tim. 2:18; 4:4).

The Gospel of John builds on the Hebrew understanding that God is true or real (3:33; 7:28). Christ reveals God and thus reveals truth (8:26, 40; 18:37). Since Christ shares in God's truth, he is himself full of grace and truth (1:14, 17). Indeed, he is "the way, and the truth, and the life" (14:6); he is the true light and the true vine (1:9; 15:1). Christ sends the Counselor, the Spirit of truth (15:26). In all of these instances, the primary sense is revelation of what proves to have authenticity and integrity, not revelation of things that are merely accurate. The believer is also guided into truth (16:13), to worship God in spirit and truth (4:23–24). Doing Christ's word enables one to know the truth and so be free (8:32). Such freedom, from John's perspective, was not to be achieved through believing propositions that turned out to be correct but, rather, through trusting in something that proves worthy of one's trust.
J.D./M.A.P.

Tryphaena (tri-fee′nuh), a Christian who, with Tryphosa, receives greetings from Paul in Rom. 16:12. Perhaps the two were sisters; the designation "workers in the Lord," however, allows the possibility that Paul associates them because of their common activity in the church. Evidence from inscriptions indicates that both Tryphaena and Tryphosa were common names in that period.

Tryphosa (tri-foh′suh). *See* Tryphaena.

Tubal (too′buhl), one of the sons of Japheth (Gen. 10:2; 1 Chron. 1:5) and the nation that viewed him as their eponymous ancestor. Geographically, the "descendants of Japheth" seem to be linked in the Bible to Asia Minor and adjacent European lands. This location is confirmed by Assyrian records that refer to an area in eastern Asia Minor as Tabal. In biblical references Tubal is often mentioned with Meshech and/or Javan (Isa. 66:19; Ezek. 27:13), and all three of these are associated with their chief, Gog (Ezek. 32:26; 38:2–3; 39:1). *See also* Gog.

Tubal-cain (too′buhl-kayn′), the son of Lamech and Zillah, and the brother of Naamah. Tubal-cain is identified as the first person to make "all kinds of bronze and iron tools" (Gen. 4:22). He was the half brother of the two sons of Lamech and Adah: Jabal, the "ancestor of those who live in tents and have livestock," and Jubal, the "ancestor of all those who play the lyre and pipe" (40:20–21). As descendants of the fugitive-wanderer Cain, Tubal-cain and his relatives—and later the Kenites (Cainites)—typify nomadic traders associated with the rise of urban life and commerce and with

the sin and violence it occasions (4:21–24). Israel will not be descended from this line, but from Adam's third son, Seth, who replaces the slain Abel and in whose era people begin to call upon the name of the Lord (cf. 4:26–). *See also* Cain; Kenites.
J.W.R.

tumors, an affliction, similar to boils, which affected the Philistines while they held the ark of the covenant, which they had captured from Israel in battle. Eventually, the Philistines returned the ark (1 Sam. 5:6–6:17).

tunic, a loose-fitting, knee-length garment worn next to the skin by both men and women (Matt. 10:10; Mark 6:9). Another tunic or garment was worn over the first. *See also* dress.

turban, a cloth draped, wrapped, or wound around the head to give protection or distinctive appearance. The turban functioned as a priestly garment (Exod. 28:4, 37, 39; 29:6; 39:28, 31; Lev. 8:9; 16:4) for Aaron and carried the golden plaque inscribed "Holy to the Lord" (Exod. 28:36–37). Job saw his justice as being "like a robe and turban" (Job 29:14), but Isaiah's indictment of Jerusalem's women included removal of their turbans (3:23). Ezekiel saw the humiliation of Judah in similar terms (defiant Jerusalem doting on Babylonians with flowing turbans, 23:15) or bypassing normal mourning by wearing the turbans as usual (24:17, 23). In his vision of the temple, turbans were part of levitical garb (44:18). Zechariah's vision saw the priestly Joshua fitted with a clean turban in preparation for high-priestly duty (3:5).
R.S.B.

turtledove, a small wild pigeon (*Streptopelia turtur*). This bird migrates through Israel in the spring on the way from its winter quarters in Africa to its breeding areas in Europe. The Hebrew name (*tor*) reflects its typical "tur-tur-tur" call. The turtledove is mentioned in the Bible mainly as a sacrifice (Gen. 15:9; Lev. 1:14; 5:7; cf. Luke 2:24), but Jer. 8:7 alludes to its seasonal appearance (see also Song of Sol. 2:12).

twelve, the, a group chosen by Jesus to accompany him and share his ministry. The twelve are listed in four different places in the NT, but the lists show some variance (Matt. 10:2–4; Mark 3:16–19; Luke 6:13–16; Acts 1:13–14; cf. John 6:70). The most significant difference is that Matthew and Mark both list a disciple named Thaddaeus, who is not listed in Luke or Acts, while Luke and Acts list a disciple named Judas the son (or brother) of James, who is not listed in Matthew or Mark (but cf. John 14:22). Church tradition has resolved this discrepancy by declaring Thaddaeus and Judas to be the same person, offering the not unreasonable suggestion that this disciple went by the name Thaddaeus to avoid confusion with another disciple named Judas who was among the twelve. Modern scholars allow that this could have been the case, but also note the possibility that changes in the personnel of the twelve might have been made at different times. Interpreters also note the slight difference in the order in which the disciples are named, though there is also a high degree of consistency in the various orderings, for example, Peter is always listed first, and Judas Iscariot is always listed last.

John's Gospel, which does mention "the twelve" (6:67, 70–71; 20:24), never provides a list. If one scours the entire book, the names of some of the twelve familiar from the Synoptics do appear: Andrew (1:40), Peter (1:42), Philip (1:44), Judas Iscariot (6:71), another Judas (14:22), Thomas (20:45), and the "sons of Zebedee" (21:22). This, however, accounts for only eight of the twelve. John's Gospel also seems to include someone named Nathanael among the twelve (1:45–49; 21:2). Church tradition declares him to be the same person as Bartholomew, a disciple mentioned in all four lists about whom nothing is known—this would, again, be possible, but strikes many interpreters as a somewhat facetious attempt at harmonization. John's Gospel also mentions an unnamed "disciple whom Jesus loved" (e.g., 19:26), who may or may not have been one of the twelve (though he is traditionally identified with John, the son of Zebedee, a tradition many scholars are inclined to accept).

Whatever the exact names of these disciples might have been, all four Gospels hold that the concept of "the twelve" is significant. This is no doubt because the number recalls the twelve tribes of Israel, so Jesus's designation of a group of followers as "the twelve" was probably intended to symbolize the restoration of Israel that he hoped to effect. Indeed, Jesus is portrayed as promising his disciples that they will judge the twelve tribes of Israel (Matt. 19:28; Luke 22:30). The significance of the number twelve is also evident in the story reported in Acts 1:15–26, where the early church feels a need to replace Judas Iscariot by selecting Matthias to fill out their number. This process does not continue, however; when James the son of Zebedee is killed (12:2), no effort is made to replace him. The apostle Paul knew about "the twelve" and, at least two decades before the Gospels were written, referred to that entity as a group that could authenticate the church's proclamation of Jesus's resurrection (1 Cor. 15:5). *See also* apostle; Beloved Disciple; disciple; Matthias; and entries on all of the individual disciples listed among the twelve. M.A.P.

Twin, the. *See* Didymus; Thomas.

Twin Brothers, in Greek mythology Castor (kas'tuhr) and Pollux (pol'uhks), twin sons of Zeus and Leda. The constellation of Gemini was associated with these two gods and, perhaps because of its usefulness in navigation, the Twin Brothers were of special interest to mariners, who claimed these gods had power over wind and waves. The ship that brought Paul from Malta to Italy (after the first ship had been wrecked, Acts 27) had as its ensign or figurehead an image of the Twin Brothers (28:11). *See also* boats; Zeus.

Tychicus (tik'uh-kuhs; Gk., "fortunate"), a Christian from the Roman province of Asia who, with Trophimus, joined Paul and others on the apostle's final visit to Jerusalem (Acts 20:4–5). Someone named Tychicus (perhaps the same man) is also mentioned in Colossians and Ephesians as the apparent bearer of those letters (Col. 4:7–9; Eph. 6:21–22). The name also comes up in the Pastoral Letters. According to 2 Tim. 4:12, Paul had sent Tychicus to Ephesus, and according to Titus 3:12, Paul planned to send either Tychicus or Artemas to Crete, thus freeing Titus to join Paul at Nicopolis.

NEW TESTAMENT LISTS OF THE TWELVE DISCIPLES

Matthew 10:2–4	Mark 3:16–19	Luke 6:13–16	Acts 1:13–14
Simon Peter	Simon Peter	Simon Peter	Peter
Andrew	James of Zebedee	Andrew	John
James of Zebedee	John of Zebedee	James	James
John of Zebedee	Andrew	John	Andrew
Philip	Philip	Philip	Philip
Bartholomew	Bartholomew	Bartholomew	Thomas
Thomas	Matthew	Matthew	Bartholomew
Matthew	Thomas	Thomas	Matthew
James of Alphaeus	James of Alphaeus	James of Alphaeus	James of Alphaeus
Thaddaeus	Thaddaeus	Simon the Zealot	Simon the Zealot
Simon the Zealot	Simon the Zealot	Judas of James	Judas of James
Judas Iscariot	Judas Iscariot	Judas Iscariot	(Judas Iscariot)
			Matthias, cf. 1:26

Tyrannus (ti-ran'uhs), **hall of,** the place mentioned in Acts 19:9, where it is asserted that Paul gave instruction after he withdrew from the synagogue in Ephesus. It is not clear whether the hall of Tyrannus was a recognized center for moral instruction by philosophers or some sort of local trade union or guild center. *See also* Ephesus; Paul.   A.J.M.

Tyre (tir), the leading city of Phoenicia during much of the first millennium BCE. Tyre is located off the coast of southern Lebanon on a small island that has been connected to the mainland since the construction of a siege ramp to it by Alexander the Great (late fourth century BCE). Of its two harbors the northern (Sidonian) is an excellent natural anchorage, while the southern (Egyptian) was protected by jetties constructed in antiquity. Its mainland settlement, called Ushu by Egyptians and Assyrians, and Old Tyre in classical times, was probably located at Tell Rashidiyeh or Tell Mashouk opposite the island. Fresh water is found in springs on the island, and additional water was ferried to it from the mainland in boats.

Sources for Tyre's history are varied; the most reliable are the biblical and other contemporary Near Eastern records. Detailed information about the kings of Tyre comes in the first century CE from the Jewish historian Josephus, who utilized the lost works of the Hellenistic historians Menander of Ephesus and Dius. They claimed access to Tyrian annals. Excavations have concentrated on the Hellenistic and Roman ruins with a small but important deep sounding of Phoenician layers. The city has been almost continuously occupied from the third millennium BCE until the present, except for a major gap from 2000 to 1600 BCE. From the late Bronze Age there are Egyptian, Ugaritic, and Hittite references to Tyre, particularly during the Amarna age, when the Tyrian king Abi-Milki sent ten letters to Pharaoh Akhenaton requesting supplies and military assistance. A classical tradition states that Tyre was refounded by Sidonians around 1200 BCE, possibly in the wake of disturbances by the Sea Peoples, although archaeology shows there was no gap in the occupation of the city at this time.

Tyre emerges as an important Phoenician city in the tenth century BCE, when King Hiram supplied David with cedars and craftsmen (2 Sam. 5:11; 1 Chron. 14:1; 22:4). Tyre's relations with Israel became much closer when King Solomon turned to Hiram for assistance in building the temple in Jerusalem. In a trade agreement Hiram responded by felling and transporting cedars and pine wood. Solomon, in return, sent wheat and olive oil to Tyre (1 Kings 5; 2 Chron. 2:3–16). Tyrian workers assisted in the construction of the temple (1 Kings 7:13–46; 2 Chron. 2:13–15; 4:11–18).

In Tyre Hiram renovated its temples. He also sent his experienced seafarers to join Solomon's fleet at Ezion-geber on the Gulf of Aqabah, whence they sailed to Ophir (1 Kings 9:26–28; 10:11–12; 2 Chron. 8:17–18; 9:10–11). Elsewhere Solomon's

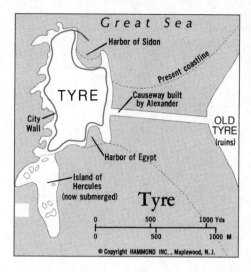

"ships of Tarshish" sailed with Hiram's fleet (1 Kings 10:22; 2 Chron. 9:21–22). Tyre began its sustained program of colonization when it gained control of Kition on Cyprus sometime in the eleventh or tenth century BCE; Hiram may have campaigned there. Ethbaal, a priest of the goddess Astarte, took the throne in the ninth century BCE after a period of unrest. His daughter Jezebel married King Ahab, ruler of the northern kingdom, leading to an increase of Baal worship in Samaria. Tyre's close relations with Samaria, which are also seen in Israel's material culture, continued until Jehu put Jezebel to death (2 Kings 9:30–37).

In North Africa Carthage was founded by Tyre thirty-eight years before the first Olympiad (814 BCE), an event stemming from a rift between King Pygmalion of Tyre and his sister Elissa (Dido) who led colonists there. In another story the ancient Greek historian Herodotus describes how Cadmus of Tyre led Phoenician colonists to Boeotia, where they introduced the alphabet to the Greeks.

Assyrians received tribute from Tyre in the ninth–seventh centuries BCE. In the campaign of 701 BCE, Sennacherib captured most of the cities of the Phoenician mainland, forcing Luli, king of Sidon, to flee Tyre to Cyprus. The Greek poet Menander (342–291 BCE) gives a fuller account of the journey of Elulaeus (Luli), king of Tyre, to Cyprus and an unsuccessful five-year siege of the city by the Assyrians. The title "king of Sidon," or "king of the Sidonians," reflects Tyre's control of Sidon and other Phoenician cities. The Assyrian king Esar-haddon (681–668 BCE) concluded a vassal treaty with King Baal of Tyre stipulating that Tyrian shipwrecks on the coast belonged to Esar-haddon and that an Assyrian official was to advise Baal. In return Esar-haddon granted Tyre trade in most Phoenician ports. The full extent of Tyrian commerce is described in the oracles of the prophets (Ezek. 27; Isa. 23; Amos 1:9–10; Joel 4:4–8; Zech. 9:2–4).

A thirteen-year siege of Tyre (587/6–573 BCE) by the Chaldean (Babylonian) monarch Nebuchadnezzar commenced after his destruction of Jerusalem. The siege failed, but Tyre submitted to Nebuchadnezzar. Later in the Chaldean period (626–539 BCE) judges ruled Tyre briefly. In the Persian period (539–333 BCE) Tyre was surpassed by Sidon as the leading Phoenician city, due to Tyre's loss of its commercial empire in the west to its former colony Carthage and to Persia's preference for Sidon. Tyre's last major act was in 332, BCE when it impeded Alexander's route to Egypt, forcing him to besiege it for seven months. In an epic battle he was the first to conquer the island city.

Although Tyre is mentioned in the NT, it did not play a significant role in the events reported there. The Gospels record that Jesus attracted followers from as far away as Tyre and Sidon (Mark 3:8) and once visited that area (7:24). One saying of Jesus uses Tyre as an example of a Gentile city that will fare better in the Last Judgment than Galilean cities that rejected him (Matt. 11:21–22). According to Acts, Herod (Herod Agrippa I, king of Judea 41–44 CE) was struck dead, because of blasphemous speech after winning a victory over Tyre (12:20–23), and the apostle Paul landed at Tyre on one of his sea voyages (21:3). *See also* Jezebel; Phoenicia; Sidon; Solomon; temple, the.

Bibliography

Bikai, Patricia. *The Pottery of Tyre.* Aris and Phillips, 1979.

Jidejian, Nina. *Tyre Through the Ages.* Dar el-Mashreq, 1969.

Katzenstein, H. Jacob. *The History of Tyre.* Schocken, 1973.   T.L.M.

Tyropoeon   (ti-roh′pee-uhn)   **Valley.** *See* Jerusalem.

Opposite: Casement walls—two parallel walls divided by partitions—were widely used in the Near East beginning in the eleventh century BCE. Buildings, such as this synagogue at Masada (aerial view), could be built directly into the wall; in times of war the partitioned areas in the wall could be filled with rubble for reinforcement. In the Bible, Rahab's house was set in the city wall (Josh. 2:15).

U

Uel (yoo'uhl; Heb., "will of El [God]"), a postexilic member of the family of Bani who divorced his non-Israelite wife in response to Ezra's reforms (Ezra 10:34).

Ugarit (yoo'gahr-it). *See* Ras-Shamra.

Ulai (yoo'li), a river in the Babylonian province of Elam beside which Daniel saw himself in a vision (Dan. 8:2). Of the three streams near Susa (Shushan), the capital city of Babylonia, the Eulaeus is probably the one referred to. It flows near Susa before joining the Chospes River. *See also* Susa.

Ulam (yoo'luhm).
1 A Manassite, the son of Sheresh and a descendant of Maacah and Machir (1 Chron. 7:16, 17).
2 The oldest son of Eshek; he was a Benjaminite descendant of King Saul and head of a family of archers (1 Chron. 8:39–40).

unbeliever, in the NRSV a term used only in Paul's letters, with reference to people who are not part of the Christian community. The word appears a dozen times in Paul's letters to the Corinthians (cf. 1 Cor. 6:6; 7:12–15; 10:27; 14:22–24; 2 Cor. 4:4; 6:14–15) in addition to a single occurrence in 1 Tim. 5:8. The Greek word in all of these instances is *apistos*, meaning "without faith." Paul uses the term to mean "without faith in Jesus Christ," since some of the people he calls "unbelievers" are idol worshipers for whom faith is not nonexistent but, from Paul's perspective, misdirected (cf. 2 Cor. 6:14–15). In 1 Cor. 14:24 an "unbeliever" is the same thing as an "outsider," i.e., a person who is not a part of the Corinthian faith community. In Rom. 15:31, the NRSV translates a completely different word (*apeithountōn*) as "unbelievers," but that word has a stronger sense of "disobedient ones." Outside of Paul's letters, Jesus uses the word *apistos* in John 20:27 with reference to Thomas's refusal to believe in the resurrection without tangible proof; the NRSV translates the word here as "doubt," but a more accurate translation would be "unbelieving" (NJB) or "faithless" (KJV, RSV). The word *apistos* (NRSV: "faithless") is also used in Matt. 17:17; Mark 9:19; Luke 9:41. *See also* faith. M.A.P.

uncle, generally the brother of a person's father. There are various persons in the Bible who are obviously uncles, but the term "uncle" (Heb. *dod*) is used rarely. In Leviticus, the term is used to designate a close relative whose wife is to be considered off-limits sexually (20:20), but who could function as a "redeemer" (Heb. *go'el*) if a family member was forced to sell part of his patrimony (25:49). In the latter instance, the redeemer was allowed to purchase land that would otherwise be lost to a particular family line. Elsewhere the term refers to Aaron's uncle, Uzziel (Lev. 10:4); Saul's uncle, Abner (1 Sam. 10:14–16; 14:50); David's uncle, Jonathan (1 Chron. 27:32); Jehoiachin's uncle, Mattaniah (2 Kings 24:17); Jeremiah's uncle, Shallum (Jer. 32:7–12); and Mordecai's uncle, Abihail (Esther 2:7, 15). F.S.F.

unclean. *See* animals; purity.

unclean spirit. *See* demon.

united kingdom, united monarchy, the period when the twelve tribes of Israel were under one king, usually conceived as the era of David and Solomon. The first king of Israel was actually Saul, but in many ways his rise to power and subsequent reign were similar to those of the judges. He was at least a transitional figure. David first became king over Judah (2 Sam. 2:1–7) and then over Israel (5:1–5), after which he conquered Jerusalem (5:6–12) and initiated what is called the united monarchy (ca. 1000 BCE). This period was short-lived, however, ending with the death of David's son and successor, Solomon, ca. 922 BCE. Despite the strong leadership of David and Solomon, the long-standing traditions of premonarchic tribal alliances continued to influence the monarchic traditions in succeeding centuries. *See also* David; Saul; Solomon. K.H.R.

unknown god, an, a designation referred to in an inscription on an altar seen by Paul in Athens (Acts 17:23), which he then used as the basis for his Areopagus (or Mars Hill) sermon (17:22–31). It was apparently a custom in the ancient world for altars to be dedicated to "unknown gods," lest one be forgotten and thus insulted. Such inscriptions have been found, but only in the plural, "gods." *See also* Areopagus; Athens.

unleavened, an adjective describing something made without yeast, usually bread (Heb. *matsah*). Although unleavened bread could be used for ordinary meals (1 Sam. 28:24–25), the term appears most frequently in religious contexts. The eating of unleavened bread sometimes served as a reminder of the exodus from Egypt, when, according to the narrative tradition, the Israelites could not wait for the dough to rise because of their haste to escape from Egyptian slavery (Exod. 12:14–20, 34–39). This connection was specifically incorporated into traditions associated with the Festival of Unleavened Bread (Lev. 23:5–8; Num. 28:16–25). Furthermore, Lev. 2:4, 11 stipulates that cereal offerings made at the temple must be unleavened. The unleavened bread not consumed on the sacrificial altar was eaten by the priests (Lev. 10:12–13). Perhaps because of the use of unleavened bread in

The baking of unleavened bread illustrated in the fourteenth-century Vogelkopf-Haggada. The artist portrayed humans with birds' heads to comply with the second commandment's prohibition against graven images (Deut. 5:8).

these sacral contexts, leaven became a symbol for corruption (1 Cor. 5:7–8). *See also* leaven; Passover; Unleavened Bread, Festival of.   M.A.S.

Unleavened Bread, Festival of, originally an agricultural festival marking the beginning of harvest; it was celebrated for seven days beginning on the fifteenth day of the month of Nisan (also called Abib; March/April; Exod. 23:15; 34:18–20). The festival was later combined with the Passover (Exod. 12:1–20; Ezek. 45:21–24; Matt. 26:17; Luke 22:1) and was observed as a seven-day celebration that followed the one-day Passover observance (Lev. 23:5–8; Num. 28:16–25; cf. Exod. 23:15; 34:18; Deut. 16:1–8; Ezek. 45:21–25; Matt. 26:17; Mark 14:1; Luke 22:1; Acts 12:3; 20:6). Leavened bread was forbidden during this festival to mark the beginning of the grain harvest, which concluded with the Festival of Weeks (Lev. 23:15–21; Num. 28:26–31; Deut. 16:9–12). The eating of unleavened bread at this festival was also linked to the tradition of Israel's exodus from Egypt when the Israelites' haste in fleeing Pharaoh did not allow them time to wait for dough to rise (Exod. 12:14–20, 34–39). The Festival of Unleavened Bread is also called the Festival of Mazzot," from Heb., *matsah,* "unleavened bread"). *See also* festivals, feasts, and fasts; Passover.

Unni (uhn´i), a levitical musician who was appointed to help celebrate the transfer of the ark of the covenant to Jerusalem (1 Chron. 15:18, 20).

Unno (uhn´oh), a Levite who returned from the Babylonian exile with Zerubbabel (Neh. 12:9).

unpardonable sin. *See* blasphemy of the Holy Spirit.

Uphaz (yoo´faz), an otherwise unknown location where gold was obtained (Jer. 10:9; Dan. 10:5). The Hebrew text, however, is uncertain in both refer-

ences. Some ancient versions (Targums, Syriac, and a few Hebrew manuscripts) read Ophir, a near legendary source of gold (1 Kings 9:28). The LXX does not refer to Uphaz or any other location at this point, but uses an adjective to describe the gold as "pure" or "fine," suggesting to many scholars the Hebrew text available to the LXX translators read *muphaz* (the Hebrew word for "refine"; cf. 1 Kings 10:18; Song of Sol. 5:11) rather than *'uphaz* (a word that occurs nowhere except in these two verses, where the NRSV takes it as a place-name).   D.R.B./M.A.P.

upper room, the room in which Jesus is said to have celebrated his last meal with the disciples (Mark 14:15; Luke 22:12; NRSV: "room upstairs"). According to Acts 1:13, the disciples continued to gather there in the days after the ascension of Jesus until they were filled with the Holy Spirit on the day of Pentecost. The room is described as "large" and "furnished." It may have been a single room built on the flat roof over a fairly large Judean home. Similar rooms are mentioned in Joppa, where Peter raised Dorcas/Tabitha from the dead (9:36–41) and in Troas, where Paul conversed with church members until dawn (20:7–11).   M.A.P.

Ur (oor), one of the oldest cities of southern Mesopotamia. Ur, modern Tell el-Muqayyar, lies ten miles west of the Euphrates, on whose bank it stood in antiquity, before the river changed course. The site is an oval, about a half mile at its greatest extent, dominated by an oblong sacred enclosure.

Modern exploration revealed that Ur was occupied already in the latter phases of the Ubaid period (ca. 5000–4000 BCE), the earliest known period of settlement in southern Mesopotamia. From there, it continued for five thousand years, through all the subsequent periods of Mesopotamian history. So in the Uruk and Jamdat Nasr periods (ca. 4000–2900 BCE), the beginnings of writing and monumental architecture marked the emergence at Ur, as elsewhere in southern Mesopotamia, of complex urban society. In the Early Dynastic period (ca. 2900–2350 BCE), Ur held a key position in what by then had become a thriving network of southern city-states. During the Akkadian period (2350–2154 BCE), Ur and the rest of that network fell under the control of the Sargonic dynasty of Agade, with Ur receiving particular attention for the cult of the moon god, its patron deity. In the Post-Akkadian periods (2154–2004 BCE), Ur resumed its independence and then became the focus of a Mesopotamian empire of its own. Most of that political power was lost in the following Isin-Larsa and Old Babylonian periods (2004–1740 BCE), but Ur managed to retain its importance as a center of international trade and scribal and religious activity.

Devastated in 1740 BCE, Ur entered a millennium of modest existence (1740–ca. 600 BCE), as a relatively unimportant city controlled by a succession of Babylonian and Assyrian overlords. This political subservience remained, but was offset by a major rebuilding program under the Neo-Babylonian/Chaldean Empire (ca. 600–539 BCE). When the Neo-Babylonian Empire fell to Cyrus the Persian (539 BCE), the new construction was maintained and even furthered. By the late fourth century BCE, however, as Persian rule gave way to Greek, Ur was fading fast—its decline due especially, it appears, to the beginning of a shift in the Euphrates River bed, which had been so important for the city's transportation and agriculture. By the following century, the end seems to have come, as all evidence for the city ceases.

The prize discovery of the Early Dynastic period was the royal cemetery (ca. 2600–2450 BCE). Its sixteen large, vaulted shaft tombs yielded a wide array of treasures—a gold dagger and helmet, lyres, he-goat statues, etc.—and the bodies not only of the principal personages, but, in the major tombs, also of male and female attendants and animals, along with wheeled vehicles. The principals

seem to have been Ur's rulers; the animals and other humans were perhaps killed on the rulers' deaths to accompany them to the netherworld. Burial of high persons with retainers is also found contemporaneously at the Mesopotamian city of Kish; whether it is alluded to in any Mesopotamian texts is problematic.

In the Ur III period, the kings sought to make the city as imposing physically as it was politically. Among their achievements were a massive brick city wall; a large complex dubbed the "Mausolea," containing burials of apparently prominent persons; a number of buildings in the sacred enclosure, including the three-storied ziggurat, the giparu-complex, which contained a shrine and rooms for the high priestess of the moon god, and a royal palace. Many of these buildings were enlarged and others added in the Neo-Babylonian/Chaldean revival. For example, a new wall was constructed around the sacred enclosure, the ziggurat was increased from three stories to seven, a new temple and palace were built, the latter (the Palace of Bel-shalti-Nannar) possibly for the Babylonian king or his local governor of Ur. Finally, the private citizen's life at Ur was illuminated by the excavation several private housing quarters, both from the Isin-Larsa/Old Babylonian periods and from the Neo-Babylonian.

In the Bible: As the ancestral home of Abraham, Ur is mentioned four times in the Bible (Gen. 11:28, 31; 15:7; Neh. 9:7); in each instance the Hebrew phrase *'ur kasdim* is used. *Kasdim* here almost certainly indicates the "Chaldeans" (as indicated in the LXX), which suggests that the phrase as a whole refers to the southern Mesopotamian Ur of the period of the Neo-Babylonian/Chaldean Empire. To be sure, this period is much too late for Abraham, and so most modern scholars suppose that the use of the term *kasdim* here is an anachronism of the biblical editors, who would have worked during the Babylonian exile, precisely the heyday of Chaldean Ur. Another suggestion is prompted by the fact that elsewhere in the Bible

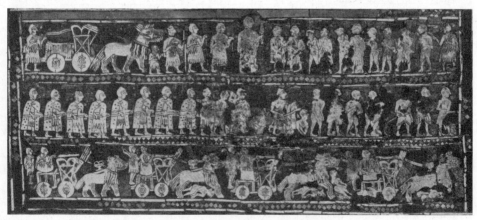

Standard of Ur shows a king at war and triumphant at the defeat of his enemies; Sumerian enameled panel, first half of the third millennium BCE.

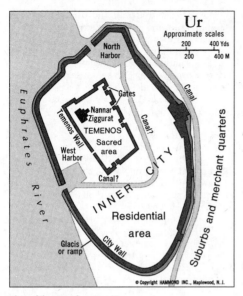

Plan of the site of ancient Ur.

the lineage to which Abraham belongs is located only in northern Syria (e.g., Gen. 24). Thus, 'ur kasdim could refer to an entirely different city, possibly Ura, north-northeast of Harran, or Urfa (Edessa), northwest of Harran. Both of these identifications, however, are largely rejected today in favor of the southern Ur, which better suits the epithet kasdim—the Chaldeans were never centered in northern Syria—and which was by far the best known Ur in antiquity. *See also* Abraham; Babylon; Chaldea; flood, the; Sargon II.   P.B.M.

Uri (yoor′i, a shortened form of Uriah, Heb., "the LORD is my light").

1 A Judahite; the father of Bezalel, the craftsman who supervised the construction of the tabernacle (Exod. 31:2; 2 Chron. 1:5).

2 The father of Geber, a district administrator under King Solomon (1 Kings 4:19).

3 A postexilic levitical gatekeeper who divorced his non-Israelite wife in response to Ezra's reforms (Ezra 10:24).

Uriah (yoo-ri′uh; Heb., "the LORD is light [or fire]").

1 A Hittite who belonged to David's elite group of warriors known as "the Thirty" (2 Sam. 23:39; 1 Chron. 11:41). He was also the husband of Bathsheba, with whom David committed adultery while Uriah was on the battlefield (2 Sam. 11:2–21). His house was in Jerusalem, and David saw Bathsheba bathing on the roof. David sent for her, and as a consequence of their illicit union she became pregnant. When David learned of this, he first conceived a plan to trick Uriah into thinking that the child was his. He called Uriah back from the battlefield on pretense of wanting a report of how the fighting was going and then directed him to spend a night in his home before returning. Uriah, however, thought it inappropriate to seek such comforts while his comrades were sleeping in the open field. David continued to prompt Uriah to go to his home and sleep with his wife and even got him drunk, thinking this might work, but it was all to no avail. Then David had Uriah deliver a private letter to Joab, the army commander, indicating that Joab should place Uriah in an area where the fighting was most fierce and then have the other troops fall back. This was done and Uriah was slain. The prophet Nathan, however, brought a word of judgment against David for doing such a thing: "You have struck down Uriah the Hittite with the sword, and have taken his wife to be your wife. . . . Now therefore the sword shall never depart from your house" (2 Sam. 12:9–10). Although David repented of what he had done, the son born to David and Bathsheba died (12:13–19). Much later, the author of 1 Kings summarized David's career in these terms: "David did what was right in the sight of the LORD, and did not turn aside from anything that (the LORD) commanded him all the days of his life, except in the matter of Uriah the Hittite" (15:5).

2 A chief priest in Jerusalem during the reign of King Ahaz (ca. 735–715 BCE). He built a new altar at the king's request patterned after an Assyrian altar that Ahaz had seen in Damascus. He apparently did not object to other Assyrian-influenced innovations introduced by Ahaz (2 Kings 16:10–18). Isaiah names Uriah as a witness to his prophecy of the Assyrian invasion (8:2).

3 A son of Shemaiah, a prophet of Kiriath-jearim. His rebuke of King Jehoiakim (ca. 608–598 BCE) and his prophecies of destruction, similar to those of Jeremiah, put his life in danger. He fled to Egypt, but was captured and brought back to Jerusalem. There, King Jehoiakim, "struck him down with the sword and threw his dead body into the burial place of the common people" (Jer. 26:20–23). Scholars have suggested that this Uriah may be "the prophet" of the Lachish letters. Lachish Letter IV seems to have been addressed to a person of this name, though it was never received, since the crisis of Babylonian intervention in 598 BCE prevented its being forwarded.

4 A priest, the father of Meremoth, a contemporary of Nehemiah (Ezra 8:33; Neh. 3:4, 21).

5 A priest who stood beside Ezra in Jerusalem when he read the law to the returned exiles (Neh. 8:4).   Y.G.

Uriel (yoor′ee-uhl).

1 A prominent Kohathite Levite who helped bring the ark from the home of Obed-edom to Jerusalem (1 Chron. 6:24; 15:5, 11).

2 A man of Gibeah whose daughter, Micaiah, became the mother of King Abijah of Judah (2 Chron. 13:2).

3 An angel mentioned in certain apocalyptic writings produced during the Second Temple

period (2 Esd. 4:1–11). Uriel served as a guide to Enoch in the upper heavens (*1 Enoch* 19–22) and was one of the four angels of the Presence (cf. *1 Enoch* 9:1).

Urim (yoor'im) **and Thummim** (thum'im), a device consulted by the chief priest (in an unexplained manner) to determine God's response to "yes" or "no" questions asked by the leader of the people (Num. 27:21; 1 Sam. 14:41; 28:6). There is no way of knowing exactly what the Urim and Thummim were, though it is usually presumed that they were some sort of divining stones. They were small enough to be carried in a pouch worn over the priest's heart, on the garment known as the ephod (Exod. 28:30). In the Bible, use of the Urim and Thummim is sometimes indicated by references to the ephod (1 Sam. 23:9–12; 30:7–8); in such passages, it was understood that the person did not consult the ephod itself, but the Urim and Thummim that the ephod contained. Likewise, when Judg. 20:27 says, "The Israelites inquired of the LORD (for the ark of the covenant of God was there in those days)," the point may be that the Urim and Thummim were typically used in the presence of the ark (since the ark itself was not used for divination). Elsewhere people are said to have "inquired of the LORD" when neither the ephod nor the ark is mentioned (1 Sam. 23:2, 4); in such instances, use of the Urim and Thummim may nevertheless be assumed. After the time of David, the Urim and Thummim may have been superseded by prophetic oracles; by postexilic times, use of the Urim and Thummim was regarded as an element of Israel's past (and possible future) that was not presently available (Ezra 2:63; Neh. 7:65). *See also* ephod.   J.U.

usury. *See* loan, loans.

Uthai (yoo'thi).

1 A postexilic inhabitant of Jerusalem, a Judahite from the Perez line (1 Chron. 9:4).

2 A member of the Bigvai group who returned from the Babylonian exile with Ezra (Ezra 8:14). The name may be a variant of Athaiah, which, following an Arabic etymology, would mean "pride of the LORD" or "the LORD is my pride."

Uz (uhz).

1 The son of Aram and grandson of Shem (Gen. 10:23). In 1 Chron. 1:17, Uz is listed as a "son" (probably meaning "descendant") of Shem.

2 The son of Nahor and Milcah and brother of Buz (Gen. 22:21). Nahor was Abraham's brother.

3 The son of Dishan and brother of Aran the Horite (Gen. 36:28; 1 Chron. 1:42).

4 An uncertain location best known in the Bible for being the homeland of Job (Job 1:1). Attempts to locate Uz are frustrated by the fact that scattered bits of information point in different directions. In Jer. 25:20, Uz is linked inexplicably with the land of the Philistines. In Job 1:15 and 1:17, respectively, Uz is said to have been attacked by Sabeans (from Arabia) and Chaldeans (from Mesopotamia), and Job 1:19 describes the land as a desert area. In Lam. 4:21, Uz seems to be virtually equated with Edom. This may be the most promising information, because the geographic identifications provided for Job's counselors—Eliphaz the Temanite, Bildad the Shuhite, and Zophar the Naamathite (Job 2:11)—also point toward Edom. *See also* Edom; Job, book of.   J.M.W.

Uzal (yoo'zuhl).

1 A son of Joktan and a descendant of Shem (Gen. 10:27; 1 Chron. 1:21). As is usually the case, the personal name would also be used as the name of a tribe of people who considered themselves to be his descendants. They probably lived in the region indicated by **2.**

2 A geographical territory mentioned in Ezek. 27:17 as exporting wrought iron, cassia, and sweet cane. The other names and locations listed in this passage suggest an Arabian location, south of Moab. The most likely site would be modern San'a, capital of Yemen.

Uzza (uhz'uh).

1 The burial garden of Manasseh (2 Kings 21:18) and Amon (21:26), kings of Judah. The garden was apparently part of the palace complex.

2 A Benjaminite, the son of Gera and a descendant of Ehud (1 Chron. 8:7).

3 The ancestor of a family of temple servants who returned to Jerusalem from the Babylonian exile with Zerubbabel (Ezra 2:49; Neh. 7:51).

Uzzah (uhz'uh).

1 A son of Abinadab, in whose ·house at Kiriath-jearim the ark of the covenant remained for twenty years. When the ark was moved to Jerusalem, Uzzah and his brother Ahio guided the oxcart that carried it. However, when the oxen stumbled and the ark threatened to tip, Uzzah tried to steady it. Thus, he broke the taboo against touching sacred objects and God struck him dead (2 Sam. 6:3–8; 1 Chron. 13:7–11).

2 A son of Mahli, a Levite belonging to the family of Merari (1 Chron. 6:29).

Uzzen-sheerah (uhz'uhn-shee'uh-ruh; Heb., "ear of Sheerah"), a village built by the Ephraimite daughter Sheerah (1 Chron. 7:24). She also built two other villages, Upper and Lower Beth-horon, which were near the border of Benjamin and the site of considerable military activity. Uzzen-sheerah was presumably in the same general area, but the site remains unidentified. *See also* Beth-horon.

Uzzi (uhz'i; Heb., "strength").

1 An Aaronic priest descended from Eleazar (1 Chron. 6:5–6). He was an ancestor of Ezra (Ezra 7:4).

2 The son of Tola and a family leader from the tribe of Issachar (1 Chron. 7:2–3).

3 A son of Bela of the tribe of Benjamin (1 Chron. 7:7).

4 The father of Elah of the tribe of Benjamin (1 Chron. 9:8).

5 A Levite who was the son of Bani and a descendant of Asaph (Neh. 11:22). He became an overseer of the postexilic Levites in Jerusalem.

6 The head of a priestly family who traced its lineage to Jedaiah at the time of Joiakim (Neh. 12:19).

7 A levitical musician who participated in dedicating the restored walls of Jerusalem (Neh. 12:41).

Uzziah (uh-zi′uh; Heb., "the LORD is strong").

1 The king of Judah ca. 783–742 BCE. He was the son of Amaziah and the father of Jotham, and all three of these men reigned as kings in Jerusalem during the eighth century BCE. Uzziah (called Azariah in 2 Kings 14:21; 15:1–8, 17–27; 1 Chron. 3:12) ascended the throne at age sixteen; his father was driven from office, and the son enjoyed popular support. Uzziah had some military success over local enemies, particularly the Philistines, Ammonites, and Meunites (2 Chron. 26:6–8). During his long reign, he seems to have devoted considerable attention to agriculture. To improve the land's yield, Uzziah built towers in the wilderness and dug wells in the Shephelah and in the plain. On his behalf loyal subjects engaged in viticulture and agriculture. Uzziah also paid close attention to equipping an army, according to 26:11–15. In later life the king was stricken with leprosy. This illness was interpreted as divine punishment for pride, and the occasion for that pride was identified as the king's attempt to usurp priestly prerogatives. Because of this physical defect, Uzziah was forced to abdicate in favor of his son Jotham, who became acting ruler. Uzziah's reign was also remembered as the time of a devastating earthquake (Amos 1:1; Zech. 14:5). At least two prophets, Amos and Hosea, were active in his time, and Isaiah's well-known vision in 6:1–13 occurred in the year of Uzziah's death.

2 A Levite descended from Kohath (1 Chron. 6:24).

3 The father of Jonathan, an official over the royal treasuries in David's time (1 Chron. 27:25).

J.L.C.

Uzziel (uhz′ee-uhl; Heb., "God is strong").

1 The grandson of Levi, son of Kohath, and the founder of the Kohathite levitical guild called the Uzzielites (Exod. 6:18, 22; Lev. 10:4; Num. 3:19, 30; 1 Chron. 6:2, 18; 23:12, 20; 24:24; cf. Num. 3:27). David appointed Uzzielites to assist in bringing the ark to Jerusalem (1 Chron. 15:10) and to serve among the Levites in the temple (23:12, 20; 24:24). Along with other Kohathites, the Uzzielites were given charge of the treasuries (26:23).

2 One of the four Simeonite sons of Ishi who, during the time of Hezekiah, led a successful raid against the Amalekites who had settled at Mount Seir (1 Chron. 4:42). After destroying the Amalekites, Uzziel and the Simeonites settled in Edom.

3 A son of Bela of the tribe of Benjamin (1 Chron. 7:7).

4 One of the descendants of Heman, the founder of a levitical guild of singers appointed for temple service by David (1 Chron. 25:4).

5 A Levite, son of Jeduthun, who helped cleanse the temple under Hezekiah (2 Chron. 29:14).

6 A goldsmith, the son of Harhaiah, who helped rebuild the wall of Jerusalem under Nehemiah (Neh. 3:8)

M.A.S.

V

vale, valley. The Levant features a wide variety of valleys, ravines, and gorges due to the presence of the Carmel and Central mountain ranges. In the north and west there are many wide, fertile valleys or plains, such as the Valley of Jezreel (Josh. 17:16; Judg. 6:33; Hos. 1:5). The territory between the central ridge and the Jordan Valley is marked by numerous narrow gorges or precipitous canyons. The Vale of Succoth (Pss. 60:6; 108:7) was a valley east of the Jordan. Valleys served as the location for military battles (Gen. 14:8), cities (Gen. 19:29), crops (1 Sam. 6:13), springs (1 Kings 18:5), and grazing lands (1 Chron. 27:29). A psalmist uses the expression "valley of the shadow of death" (Ps. 23:4; NRSV: "darkest valley") as an image for distress or suffering.

Animals grazing in the lower Jordan Valley of modern Israel.

vanity, something empty of meaning, purpose, or content. The term occurs thirty-four times in the NRSV, thirty-one of which are in the book of Ecclesiastes, which holds that the search for meaning in life is "vanity" (elusive and without definite substance). The Hebrew word (*hebel*) literally means "a puff of air," "a breath," or "a vapor." In the Bible, the word "vanity" is not used to mean conceit or preoccupation with self.   J.M.E./M.A.P.

Vashni (vash'ni; Heb., "the second"), in some translations (e.g., the KJV), the eldest son of Samuel according to 1 Chron. 6:28. Although the present Hebrew text of this verse reads, "the firstborn [was] Vashni and Abijah," a parallel passage in 1 Sam. 8:2 reads, "the name of his firstborn was Joel and the name of his second, Abijah" (cf. 1 Chron. 6:33). Apparently, in the Chronicles passage the name "Joel" was inadvertently omitted and the Hebrew word meaning "and the second" (Heb. *washeni* or *wehasheni*) was corrupted into a proper name.

Vashti (vash'ti), according to the book of Esther, the queen of the Persian king Ahasuerus (Xerxes I). There are no extrabiblical references to such a person in Persian history, but Vashti is a memorable character in a story related in Esther 1:3–2:4. According to this account, Ahasuerus gave a banquet for his officials and ministers, and Vashti gave a banquet for the women of the palace. On the seventh day of the banquet, the king, who was "merry with wine" (1:10) summoned Vashti to appear before his group wearing her royal crown, so as to show the people and the officials her beauty. Some interpreters take this to mean that she was to wear *only* the crown. In any case, Vashti refused to comply with the king's drunken request; enraged, Ahasuerus consulted his sages to determine what should be done. One of the sages, Memucen, opined that when word of Vashti's noncompliance got out, women would look with contempt upon their husbands and "the noble ladies of Persia and Media" would rebel against the king's officials, and there would be "no end of contempt and wrath" (1:18). Thus, Ahasuerus issued a royal edict depriving Vashti of her royal position, so that all women might "give honor to their husbands, high and low alike" (1:20). A search was held to find a new queen, and that was how Esther, a Jewish woman from Susa, ended up becoming the queen of Persia. Vashti is not mentioned again, so her story is told simply as a prelude to the narrative of Esther. Its attention to male posturing on the part of the king and his officials, who seem threatened by the prospect of women getting the upper hand in the kingdom, provides an ironic setup for the story to follow, in which Esther manages to manipulate Ahasuerus and his officials so as to control all affairs of the kingdom pertinent to the welfare of the Jews. *See also* Ahasuerus; Esther, book of.

Veadar (vay'ah-dahr; Heb., "and Adar," also called *adar sheni*, "the second Adar"), a thirteenth month that was inserted into the Jewish calendar between the months Adar and Nisan; it is added seven times in a cycle of nineteen years to correlate the Jewish lunar-based calendar, composed of twelve lunar months of 29½ days (a 354-day year), with the solar year (365 days). It falls in March/April. *See also* calendar.

vegetables. *See* food.

veil.

1 A piece of fabric worn by a woman to conceal her face or cover her head (Song of Sol. 4:1, 3; 6:7; Isa. 47:2). When Rebekah first saw Isaac, she put on her veil (Gen. 24:65). Tamar apparently put on a veil to disguise herself, so that her father-in-law, Judah (thinking she was a prostitute), would fulfill the levirate duty neglected by his sons (Gen. 38:14, 19). The apostle Paul insisted that women should wear veils when praying or prophesying "as a symbol of authority" (1 Cor. 11:4–16). Paul's point might be that women should be easily identified as

Women covering their faces with veils; first-century CE relief from Palmyra.

under the authority (and protection) of a father or a husband, as opposed to appearing available for sexual encounters. His comment that they should be veiled "because of the angels" (11:10) is mysterious and no satisfactory interpretation has been reached. Is Paul afraid that the angels might lust after earthly women (cf. Gen. 6:4)? Are these good angels or bad angels (demons)? Or human messengers being referred to as angels?

2 A covering that obscures meaning or truth. A veil in this sense can be literal, but in most cases is metaphorical (e.g., "veiled understanding"). The theme is developed by Paul in 2 Cor. 13, where he begins with a literal reference. Moses wore a veil to conceal his face after he received the second set of tablets containing the Ten Commandments at Mount Sinai (Exod. 34:29–35). The ostensive reason was that his face shone as a result of having been in the presence of God, and this made the people afraid. Paul suggests that the real reason was to conceal the temporary nature of the old covenant (i.e., Moses didn't want people to notice that the shine had faded, 2 Cor. 3:13). Then Paul moves to the purely metaphorical. When Jews who do not believe in Jesus as the Messiah read the scriptures, "a veil lies over their minds" and they are unable to see the truth to which the scriptures testify (3:15). For Paul, only christological interpretation of scripture (reading the texts in view of what God has done through Jesus Christ) qualifies as unveiled interpretation.

3 The covering over the entrance to the Holy of Holies in the temple (2 Chron. 3:14), which also hung before the ark in the wilderness tabernacle (Exod. 26:33; 35:12; 39:34; Lev. 24:3). Only Aaron and his sons were permitted to pass beyond the veil (Num. 18:7). At a later time, only the high priest could enter the Holy of Holies and only on the Day of Atonement (Lev. 6:2). Josephus (*Jewish War* 5.212–14) says that this veil was in fact a tapestry woven in Babylon, on which was displayed a portrait of the heavens (probably the starry sky at night); thus, worshipers would associate God's presence in the Holy of Holies (hidden by the veil) with God's presence in the heavens (hidden by the firmament of the sky). According to the Gospels, the veil of the temple tore at Jesus's death (Matt. 27:51; Mark 15:38; Luke 23:45). The meaning of that event is ambiguous and has been debated. For the Gospel of Mark (possibly written before 70 CE) it seems likely that the image was intended to evoke the idea of God removing barriers between God and humanity (cf. 1:10, where the heavens are torn apart at Jesus's baptism). For Matthew and Luke, written after 70 CE (when the temple was destroyed), the ripping of the curtain might be an act of judgment that presages the destruction of the temple and suggests this happened as a consequence of the rejection and crucifixion of Jesus.
M.A.S./M.A.P.

vengeance, punishment in retribution for injury. God appears as a God of vengeance in the Bible, exacting punishment upon Israel for infidelity to the covenant (Lev. 26:25) and upon other nations for their treatment of Israel (Deut. 32:35; Isa. 61:2). The NT speaks of the end times as "days of vengeance" (Luke 21:22), a time when the Lord Jesus will be "revealed from heaven with his mighty angels in flaming fire, inflicting vengeance on those who do not know God and on those who do not obey the gospel" (1 Thess. 1:7–8).

In ancient Israelite society, private vengeance by an "avenger of blood" acting on behalf of an injured family was condoned in cases of injury and death (Num. 35:9–28; cf. Gen. 4:23–24). A tendency to mitigate this practice (cf. Gen. 4:15; 2 Sam. 14:1–24) appears in the institutions of sanctuary (Exod. 21:12–14) and cities of refuge (Num. 35:9–28), which provided some legal protection for one accused of murder. Likewise, the *lex talionis* ("eye for eye, tooth for tooth"; Exod. 21:23–25) limited retribution to the extent of the original injury. Lev. 19:18, however, enjoins the Israelite to "love your neighbor as yourself" rather than to seek revenge (cf. Prov. 25:21). Jesus, in commenting upon the "eye for an eye" tradition, explicitly called for his followers to love even their enemies and to refuse to seek vengeance (Matt. 5:38–42).

Two NT authors quote Deut. 32:35 (in which God claims, "Vengeance is mine!") for different purposes. The author of Hebrews takes the scripture as a threat of judgment, even for Christians; thus, "it is a fearful thing to fall into the hands of the living God" (10:30–31). Paul cites the same passage as a basis for eliminating vengeance as a legitimate motive for human behavior (Rom. 12:19); the logic of his argument seems to be that, since God will avenge wrongs that are done, humans have no need to do so. *See also* avenger; bloodguilt; judgment, day of; retribution.

D.W.S./M.A.P.

vermilion, a bright red pigment consisting of mercuric sulphide and varying in color from crimson to nearly orange. It was the color of Jehoiakim's house, which was condemned by the prophet Jeremiah (Jer. 14:22). Ezekiel refers to Chaldeans painting vermilion images on their walls in the condemned city of Oholibah (i.e., Jerusalem; 23:14). In Wis. 13:14 wooden idols are described as being painted this color (NRSV: "red paint").

Vespasian (ves-pay′zhuhn), a Roman general who began the siege of Jerusalem in the first Jewish war of rebellion against Rome (66–70 CE). In the midst of the siege, he was named Roman emperor, and he ruled from 69 to 79 CE. His son Titus, who took over the siege in Jerusalem and pursued it to its conclusion, also succeeded him as emperor (79–81 CE). *See also* emperor; Roman Empire; Titus.

vestibule. *See* porch.

vial, a small container used to hold oil or perfume. A vial was used by Samuel to anoint Saul as king (1 Sam. 10:1). Most commonly found in archaeological excavations are globular, piriform, or cylindrical vials in the shape of juglets, generally with a single vertical loop handle, an everted rim, and a button or round base.

villages. *See* towns.

vine, a plant whose long trunk grows along the ground or fastens itself to other objects by means of tendrils. In biblical usage a "vine" (Heb. *gephen,* Gk. *ampelos*) is almost always a grapevine (*Vitis vinifera*). Other plants that have vines are referred to by their fruit (melons, Num. 11:5; cucumbers, Isa. 1:8). The "wild vine" of 2 Kings 4:39 was probably a type of gourd. The "choice vine" (Heb. *soreq,* Jer. 2:21) was a particular grape variety producing a rich red wine.

The vine was noted for its luxuriant foliage, intertwining branches, and trailing or climbing shoots (Ps. 80:11; Ezek. 19:10–11). Its fragrant blossoms are recalled in love poetry (Song of Sol. 2:13), but it was its fruit, and especially the wine that was made from that fruit (Isa. 65:8; cf. Matt. 26:29), that gave it a place of honor among plants. Its wood, in contrast, was useless, fit only for burning (Ezek. 15:2–8).

Grapes were eaten fresh (Jer. 31:29) and dried into raisin clusters (1 Sam. 25:18), and the juice was boiled down into a thick syrup. But wine, or "new wine," was the chief product. The climate and terrain of the Near East especially favored viticulture, and its wines were renowned from Egypt to Babylon. Biblical tradition associates vine growing with the beginnings of agriculture and civilization, making Noah the first vinedresser as well as the first drunkard (Gen. 9:20–21).

Terms for vine, vineyard, or wine are commonly paired with terms for fields or grain, representing the two main types of agricultural production (Exod. 22:5; Num. 16:14; Deut. 33:28; cf. plows and pruning hooks, Isa. 2:4; threshing floor and wine vat, Hos. 9:2, 4). Olives or oil extended the basic pair (1 Sam. 8:14; Deut. 6:11), while vine and fig together described the main fruiting plants.

A vine was a common sight in a courtyard, climbing a tree or (in Roman times) a trellis. A peasant ideal of peace and prosperity is expressed in the repeated phrase, everyone "under their

Picking grapes from the vine; tomb of Mennah, Thebes, Egypt, ca. 1400 BCE.

vines and under fig trees" (1 Kings 4:25; cf. Mic. 4:4). Vineyards were commonly planted on hillsides (Isa. 5:1), which were less suitable for grain cultivation, though they were also established in the major valleys and plains. The Hebron area was especially noted for its grapes (Num. 13:22–24; Gen. 49:11–12), as was Sibmah in Transjordan (Isa. 16:8). An annual vintage festival was held at Shiloh (Judg. 21:19–21).

Vineyards required long-term intensive care (Isa. 5:1–7; Mark 12:1). The soil was first dug and cleared of stones and a wall (or hedge) erected to discourage predators (Ps. 80:12–13; Song of Sol. 2:15). A watchtower and wine vat completed the installation, with a booth for lodging during the harvest (Isa. 1:18). Vines required heavy annual pruning (Lev. 25:4; John 15:2), hoeing (Isa. 5:6), thinning and support of fruit clusters, and sometimes irrigation (Isa. 27:3). Intensive labor heightened expectations of the harvest and made loss of the vintage a bitter disappointment (Isa. 5:2; Deut. 28:39). Deuteronomic law exempted from military service the man who had planted a vineyard, but not enjoyed its fruit (Deut. 20:6). Flourishing vineyards meant peacetime; war's devastation was represented by a ravaged vineyard, in which walls were broken, vines choked by thorns, branches trampled by wild beasts (Isa. 5:5–6; Ps. 80:12–13). Restoration would be a time of planting vineyards and drinking their wine (Isa. 65:21), a time when the mountains would "drip sweet wine" (Amos 9:13).

The vine was a rich source of symbolism in ancient Near Eastern literature, ritual, and art. The twining branch signified life, and the grape cluster, or vineyard, fertility (Song of Sol. 7:12). Raisins pressed into cakes were used in the cult of the goddess of love (Hos. 3:1; cf. Song of Sol. 2:5). Wine was the "blood of the grape" (Gen. 49:11; Deut. 32:14), an image recalled in Jesus's words over the cup of the Last Supper (Matt. 26:28). God's judgment of the wicked is like the treading of a wine press (Isa. 63:1–3; Rev. 14:18–20). The Lord's vintage is wine of wrath (Jer. 25:15; Rev. 14:19) and a cup of staggering (Isa. 51:22).

Israel accepted the vine and its fruit as gifts of God (Hos. 2:8–9, 15). Israel itself was likened to a vine, planted and tended by God (Jer. 2:21; Ps. 80:8–9). The NT applies the image to Jesus and the church: "I am the vine, you are the branches. Those who abide in me . . . bear much fruit" (John 15:5). *See also* banquet; drunkenness; raisins; vineyard; wine.   P.A.B.

vine of Sodom, a plant (*Calotropis procera*) whose fruit appears tempting yet is inedible (Deut. 32:32). It grows in the Dead Sea area and bears a greenish-yellow applelike fruit filled with dry white fibers resembling those of the milkweed.

vinegar, sour wine or wine vinegar, a common drink among the poorer classes (Ruth 2:14). It was forbidden to Nazirites (Num. 6:3). The offer of "vinegar" to Jesus on the cross could be under-

stood as a compassionate gesture in Mark 15:36 and Matt. 27:48. However, Ps. 69:21 speaks of "poison and vinegar" given to the suffering righteous by enemies. Both the mocking offer of vinegar in Luke 23:36 and the reference to fulfillment of scripture in John 19:28 suggest this latter context.

vineyard, the plot in which grapes are raised. Vineyards were one of the standard signs of agricultural wealth in biblical times. Although the proper handling of such property was extensively defined in various law codes (Exod. 22:5; 23:11; Lev. 19:10; 25:3, 4; Deut. 20:6; 22:9; 23:24; 24:21; 28:30), breaches of treatment were found even among royalty (1 Kings 21:1–18). Isaiah's "Song of the Vineyard" offers a review of standard viticulture applied to the life of a people (5:1–7). As vineyards were a sign of divine blessing, their absence was a metaphor of divine judgment (Jer. 35:7, 9). The vineyard as a common scene of labor was used in a parable of Jesus found in all three Synoptic Gospels (Matt. 20:1–41; Mark 12:1–9; Luke 20:9–16). *See also* vine.   R.S.B.

viper, a genus of snakes prevalent in the ancient world, some of which were poisonous and some not. Because the bite of the poisonous viper could be fatal, people naturally wanted to avoid any contact with any type of snake. Consequently, the term "viper" came to be used figuratively as a designation for evil (cf. Isa. 30:6; 59:5; Job 20:16) or for people who were evil (cf. Matt. 3:7; 12:34; 23:33; Luke 3:7). Paul's encounter with a viper (Acts 28:3–6) caused people to think of him as a god. *See also* serpent.   J.M.E.

virgin (Heb. *betulah*, lit., "separated"; Gk. *parthenos*). In the Hebrew Bible, a *betulah* is a woman who has not had sexual intercourse with a man. The word is also used metaphorically of Israel in the Hebrew Bible (e.g., Jer. 18:15). A different Hebrew word, *'almah*, means simply "a woman of marriageable age," though that word is also sometimes translated "virgin" in English Bibles. The Greek word *parthenos* is used to translate both Hebrew words in the Greek LXX and, so, apparently carries a range of meanings. In the NT, context must determine whether literal virginity is at issue or whether the reference is simply to unmarried persons (for whom, of course, virginity might sometimes be assumed even if it is not being explicitly indicated). Paul encourages virgins, both male and female, not to marry, but he does permit it (1 Cor. 7:25–38). The book of Acts refers to four virgin daughters of Philip who prophesied (21:9). The word is also used metaphorically of the church (2 Cor. 11:2–3). *See also* Virgin Birth.   W.M./M.A.P.

Virgin Birth, the tradition of Mary's conception of Jesus by the Holy Spirit apart from sexual intercourse, explicitly mentioned in the NT only in the birth stories of Matthew and Luke. In Matt. 1:18–25 it appears as the fulfillment of Isa. 7:14, which indicates that a virgin (Gk. *parthenos,* used in the LXX to translate the Heb. *'almah,* a young woman of marriageable age) would conceive and bear a son. In Luke 1:26–38, this miraculous conception (1:34, 37) is associated with the application of the title Son of God to Jesus (1:32, 35).

Neither Matthew nor Luke displays much interest in how or why this miracle happened. With regard to "how," Matthew and Luke are both content to say that it is the work of the Spirit (Matt. 1:20; Luke 1:35), who, after all, created life out of nothingness at the genesis (the word translated "birth" by the NRSV in Matt. 1:18) of the world (Gen. 1:1; cf. 2:7). As for "why," Matthew and Luke seem to think that it was in accord with God's plan to mark Jesus as unique in this manner. A child being born to a virgin is a miracle that is in line with, but also greater than, miracles of the past in which children were born to women who were infertile or past the age of childbearing (Gen. 21:2; 30:22–24; 1 Sam. 1:19–20). In the same way, Matthew and Luke believed that Jesus would prove to be in line with, but also greater than, all the heroes of Israel's history. Jesus's status as God's Child was unique, distinct from the status of others who could rightly be called children of God (cf. Matt. 5:45; 13:38). There does not appear to be any thought in either of these Gospels that Jesus had to be born of a virgin in order to be free of the effects of inherited sin. Nor is there any evidence that the Gospel writers thought that being born to a virgin would by itself render Jesus more pure than persons conceived through the sexual unions that characterize God's intended order for creation (Gen. 1:28).

It is interesting to scholars that neither Matthew nor Luke ever mentions the Virgin Birth again in their writings—it is recounted in the opening chapters, but nothing that follows assumes such a birth or relies upon it; in both cases, the account of the Virgin Birth could be removed without affecting anything else in the narratives. Thus, in Matthew and Luke—as well as in the rest of the NT—neither the disciples of Jesus, his family members, nor any others ever betray any indication of knowledge of his miraculous birth. Suggested allusions to the tradition elsewhere in the NT (e.g., Matt. 13:55; Mark 6:3; Luke 4:22; John 1:13, 14; Gal. 4:4–5; Heb. 7:3) are generally regarded by scholars as uncertain or implausible. *See also* virgin.   W.M./M.A.P.

vision, an apparition of something normally hidden from human eyes. Visions, dreams, and heavenly journeys are closely related phenomena through which secrets are thought to be revealed. These media of revelation are especially characteristic of apocalyptic literature. Although categories may overlap, visions can typically be distinguished from theophanies and epiphanies. The latter phenomena involve an appearance or manifestation of a heavenly being with an emphasis on the message conveyed by that being. In visions the emphasis is typically on an object that is visualized or a scene or sequence of events that is enacted.

Daniel kneels before the angel Gabriel, who interprets a vision (Dan. 8); woodcut from the Cologne Bible (1478–80).

Accounts of visions have certain typical features. They are usually related in the first person; the visionary describes his or her experience. The setting is often given near the beginning, the date, place, and time at which the vision occurred. Then the content of the vision is recounted, often introduced by the words "I saw." Sometimes the account concludes with remarks about how the visionary reacted to the vision or what he or she did immediately afterward.

Ancient Jewish and Christian visions may be grouped into five types:

1. Visions of the enthroned deity or the divine council (Exod. 24:9–11; 1 Kings 22:19–23; Isa. 6; Ezek. 1:1–3:15; Rev. 4:2–11).

2. Visions of some other heavenly reality or of an earthly reality present, threatened, or to come (1 Kings 22:17; Amos 7:1–3, 4–6; Jer. 4:23–26; Ezek. 8–11; 40–48; Zech. 1:7–17; 3; 6:1–8; 1 Enoch 57, 66; T. Levi 8; 2 Bar. 6–8; 2 Esd. 13; Luke 1:11, 21).

3. Visions based on a play on words or a symbol (Amos 7:7–9; 8:1–3; Jer. 1:11–12, 13–14; Jer. 24; Ezek. 37:1–14; Zech. 2:5–9; 5:1–4; 1 Enoch 61:1–5).

4. Allegorical visions, i.e., visions in which each object, being, or event represents in a figurative or pictorial way a corresponding entity in reality (Zech. 1:18–21; 4; 5:5–11; Dan. 8; 1 Enoch 85–90; 2 Bar. 36–37; 53; Rev. 12, 13, 17; 2 Esd. 9:38–10:59; 11–12).

5. Visions that combine two or more of the above types (Dan. 7; 1 Enoch 14:8–36:4; 40:1–41:7; 43–44; 46; 52; 53:1–54:6; 60:1–6; 71; T. Levi 2:5–5:7; 2 Bar. 22–30).

Vision accounts, especially the symbolic and allegorical types, grasp the imagination and evoke feelings in ways that ordinary language cannot. Like poetry they present an interpretation of reality and invite readers or listeners to share that interpretation. They combine cognitive insight with emotional response. Although they were originally experienced and recorded to address particular historical situations, their symbolic character gives them meaning and application beyond the original contexts. *See also* apocalyptic literature; dreams; theophany; throne.   A.Y.C.

votive offering. *See* sacrifice.

vow, a promise to abstain from something that would not normally be prohibited (e.g., the vow of the Nazirite, Num. 6), or, more commonly, an offer to pay God for help. The first vow mentioned in the Bible is that of Jacob, who promises God worship and tithing in return for protection (Gen. 28:20; 31:13). Similar vows include the vow of Israel to "devote" (i.e., sacrifice) all of Arad to God (Num. 21:1–3), Jephthah's vow of a living being (Judg. 11:30), Hannah's vow of Samuel's service (1 Sam. 1:11), Absalom's vow of worship (2 Sam.

15:7–8), and the unspecified vow of sailors in exchange for safety from shipwreck (Jon. 1:6). Apostate Israel is said to have vowed to offer incense to the queen of heaven (Jer. 44:25).

Animals sacrificed in payment of vows had to be without blemish (Lev. 22:17–25; Mal. 1:14), they could not be firstlings (who already belonged to God; Lev. 27:16–28), and they had to be offered as a communion sacrifice that is eaten within two days (Lev. 7:16–17; see the sacrificial specifications in Num. 15:1–16). Payment could also be made in money with set values for each animal (Lev. 27), with adjustments made for the poor. Payment of vows was ultimately centralized (Deut. 12). Vows did not have to be made (Deut. 23:22), but once they were made, they had to be paid (Num. 30; Deut. 21:21–23). A woman's vow could be cancelled by her husband or, if she lived in her father's house, by her father, if the man acted the same day (Num. 30). Psalms such as 56:12–13 and 66:13–15 mention the offering and payment of vows (cf. 22:26; 61:9; 116:14, 18). In the NT, Acts records that the apostle Paul cut his hair to fulfill a vow (18:18), but no details are offered about the nature or purpose of that vow.

Jesus's prohibition of all vows appears to have been unprecedented within Israel. In the Sermon on the Mount, he expands on the traditional commandment not to swear falsely by saying, "Do not swear at all, either by heaven, for it is the throne of God, or by the earth, for it is his footstool, or by Jerusalem, for it is the city of the great King. And do not swear by your head, for you cannot make one hair white or black. Let your word be 'Yes, Yes' or 'No, No'; anything more than this comes from the evil one" (Matt. 5:34–37). Similar words are offered in James 5:12, which probably relies upon the Jesus tradition without actually attributing the words to Jesus. The logic of this extreme prohibition seems to be that, since some factors in the performance of a vow may be beyond one's control, even the person who fully intends to fulfill the vow might not be able to do so; therefore, the only way to be certain that one does not swear false vows is by avoiding vows altogether.

                                                        T.S.F./M.A.P.

Vulgate, the authorized Latin version of the Bible. In the late fourth century, Pope Damasus commissioned Jerome to bring order to the existing Latin versions. The resulting translation was called the Vulgate ("common text"). In 1546, the Council of Trent decreed that the Latin Vulgate was to be regarded as the authoritative version of scripture, establishing it as the standard Bible of the Roman Catholic church.

vulture, a large carrion-eating bird. All varieties were considered unclean and prohibited as food for the Israelites. In addition to literal references, vultures are referred to figuratively in Hos. 8:1. Jesus also referred to vultures in a proverb, "Wherever the corpse is, there the vultures will gather" (Matt. 24:28; Luke 17:37). Four species occur in Israel: (1) the bearded vulture (*Gypatus barbatus;* Lev. 11:13); (2) the Egyptian eagle (Neophroon *percnopterus*), probably corresponding to the carrion vulture (Lev. 11:18; Deut. 4:17); (3) the black vulture (*Aegypius monachus;* Deut. 4:12); and (4) the griffon vulture (*Gyps fulvus*), for which the NRSV uses the term "eagle" (Deut. 32:11; Ps. 103:5; Prov. 30:17).

wadi (wah'dee), an Arabic word for stream or stream bed. Many streams in the area inhabited by ancient Israel flow only seasonally. During the dry seasons occasional pools of water may collect in the stream beds or the beds may become completely dry. The wadis could be used to advantage in military matters (Josh. 8:10–23; NRSV: "ravine"), but they were also undependable water sources and could symbolize deceit (Jer. 15:18). David took five smooth stones from a wadi to use in his sling when confronting Goliath (1 Sam. 17:40).   M.A.P.

Wadi of Egypt, modern-day Wadi el-Arish, a valley in the Sinai Peninsula of Egypt with a seasonal stream that flows into the Mediterranean (Num. 34:5; Josh. 15:4; 1 Kings 8:65; 2 Kings 24:7; 2 Chron. 7:8; Isa. 27:12). It marked the traditional southwestern border of the land of Canaan (and of the claims of Judah or, in Ezek. 48:28, Gad). Elsewhere, this stream is called the river of Egypt (Gen. 15:18), Shihor (1 Chron. 13:5), and the Wadi Arabah (Amos 6:14). *See also* Arabah; Shihor.
                                                    H.B.H.

wafers, thin cakes, somewhat like tortillas, made of wheat flour (semolina), baked unleavened and spread with oil. Along with other kinds of bread, wafers had to accompany the thank offering of the worshiper, the priests' ordination offering, and the Nazirite's peace offering (cf. Lev. 7:12; Num. 6:15; 8:26). They could also be given independently as a cereal offering.

wages, the compensation paid to a free laborer hired for a fixed period of time or for a specific service. It was apparently common to hire a laborer for a day's work, for the Torah requires payment of wages at the end of the day (Lev. 19:13; Deut. 24:14; Job 14:6; cf. Matt. 20:1–2, 8). However, there are also references to yearly (Lev. 25:53; Isa. 21:16) and triennial hire (Deut. 15:18; Isa. 16:14).

The Bible contains scattered examples of wages paid to individuals: to Jacob as a shepherd, by Laban (Gen. 29:15; 30:32–33; 31:8); to Moses's mother as a nurse, by Pharaoh's daughter (Exod. 2:9); to Tamar for prostitution, by Judah (Gen. 38; cf. Deut. 23:18; Isa. 23:17; Ezek. 16:31; Hos. 9:1; Mic. 1:7); to Balaam for cursing Israel, by Balak (Deut. 23:5; Neh. 13:2); to Shemaiah for prophesying falsely, by Tobiah and Sanballat (Neh. 6:10–13); and to Judas for betraying Jesus, by the chief priests (Matt. 26:14–15). There is also mention of the hiring of mercenaries (Judg. 9:4; 2 Sam. 10:6; Jer. 46:21; 2 Kings 7:6; 2 Chron.

WADIS MENTIONED IN THE BIBLE

Wadi Arabah	Amos 6:14
Wadi Arnon	Deut. 2:24, 36; 3:8, 12, 16; 4:48; Josh. 12:1–2; 13:9, 16; 2 Kings 10:33
Wadi Besor	1 Sam. 30:9, 10, 21
Wadi Cherith	1 Kings 17:3, 5
Wadi Eschol	Num. 13:23–24; 32:9
Wadi Jabbok	Deut. 2:37
Wadi Kanah	Josh. 16:8; 17:9
Wadi Kidron	2 Sam. 15:23; 1 Kings 2:37; 15:13; 2 Kings 23:6, 12; 2 Chron. 15:16; 29:16; 30:14; Jer. 31:40
Wadi Kishon	Judg. 4:7, 13; 1 Kings 18:40; Ps. 83:9
Wadi Mochmur	Jth. 7:18
Wadi Shittim	Joel 3:18
Wadi Zered	Num. 21:12; Deut. 2:13–14
Wadi of Egypt	Num. 34:5; Josh. 15:4; 1 Kings 8:65; 2 Kings 24:7; 2 Chron. 7:8; Isa. 27:12
Wadi of the Willows	Isa. 15:7

24:6); counselors (Ezra 4:5); priests (Judg. 18:4); seers (1 Sam. 9:6–9); goldsmiths (Isa. 46:6), and masons and carpenters (2 Chron. 24:12). Related texts concern the levitical portion (Num. 18:31); wages to be paid to church elders (1 Tim. 5:17–18; cf. Luke 10:7); and wages withheld from mowers (James 5:4).

Specified fixed wages are not mentioned, although occasionally the Bible relates the price in a given situation (Gen. 30:32–33; 1 Sam. 9:8; 2 Chron. 25:6; Matt. 20:1). This indicates that the wage was agreed upon by the employer and employee. Nonetheless, it appears that hired workers were often either not paid or not paid sufficiently, resulting in a poor labor class who come under the concern of the Torah and Prophets (Deut. 24:14–15; Jer. 22:13; Mal. 3:5; cf. Gen. 31:7, 41; 1 Sam. 2:5; Job 7:2–3; James 5:4).

The term "wage" is also used metaphorically to refer to reward given by God for the "labor" of loyalty, suffering, or right action (Gen. 15:1; Ezek. 29:18–19; Isa. 40:10; 61:8; 62:11; 1 Cor. 3:8; of children, Gen. 30:18; Jer. 31:16; Ps. 127:3). Likewise, it may refer to the just recompense for sin (Rom. 6:23; 2 Pet. 2:15). *See also* slavery in the ancient Near East; slavery in the New Testament.

J.U./M.A.P.

wagon. *See* cart.

walls, structures that limit areas, whether in buildings or for defense. This term is used in the Bible to translate a number of Hebrew and Greek words representing various kinds of structures. Ancient literature, art, and archaeological remains provide detailed information on the techniques of wall construction used in the biblical world.

Like their modern counterparts, ancient farmers built low walls around fields and vineyards (Gen.

49:22; Num. 22:24–25; Isa. 5:5). Since these walls were made of unhewn stones, they often needed repair (Prov. 24:31). The stones used in these agricultural walls were sometimes set in mud or mortar, though they were often simply stacked on top of each other. All of these simple structures increased the productivity of arable land by helping to prevent soil erosion, discouraging poachers, and preventing animals from grazing in crops; at the same time, the construction of walls aided in the age-old task of clearing the fields of undesirable stones.

House walls were usually built of unhewn or rough-cut stones or mud-bricks usually set on stone foundations. These walls were sometimes covered with a thin coating of plaster. Naturally, this plaster improved the appearance of walls, but it also played a significant role in the treatment of houses with "leprosy" (Lev. 14:37–45). More important buildings were normally built of large, hammer-dressed stones. Courses of stone or mud-brick were sometimes separated by a course of wooden beams, a technique that was used in the construction of the temple (1 Kings 6:36; 7:12).

City Walls: Throughout most of the biblical period, cities were surrounded by a system of fortifications that consisted of walls, towers, and gates; populations that lived in unwalled settlements were exposed to great risks (Ezek. 38:11; Zech. 2:4). City walls had to be high enough and thick enough and be constructed on such solid foundations that the fortifications and their defenders could deter enemy attacks. There was, in fact, a constant effort made by attackers and defenders to surpass the ingenuity of their opponents; siege warfare was the outgrowth of this competitive effort. The famous bas-reliefs from the Nineveh palace of the Assyrian ruler Sennacherib (705–681 BCE) graphically portray some of the techniques used in attacking and defending a walled

Assyrians lay siege to an unidentified town. A siege machine batters the walls, protected by archers (*right*), while (*left* and *center*) the Assyrians try to break down the foundations with spikes and tunnel underneath; ninth-century BCE reliefs.

city (see Isa. 36:1–2; 37:33). Indeed, the Bible has frequent references to various aspects of siege warfare (Deut. 20:20; 2 Sam. 20:15; Ps. 89:40; Jer. 6:6; Ezek. 4:1–3; 26:7–10; Joel 2:7–9; see also Luke 19:43; 21:20). This list, which is by no means exhaustive, points to the defensive significance of walls and indicates that large amounts of energy and expertise were poured into the task of destroying the barrier (i.e., the city wall) that separated attackers from defenders. Surprisingly, some cities were able to resist besieging forces for a long time (2 Kings 17:5). Perhaps the most efficient way of attacking a city was to trick its defenders into leaving the safety of their walls (Josh. 8:10–17).

Although cities varied in size, the average area enclosed by a city wall in the ancient Near East ranged between five and ten acres. The walls that surrounded these settlements varied in height, width, and design from period to period. The oldest known fortified town in the Levant is Jericho; its earliest walls, which date to ca. 7000 BCE, were made of solid stone and were over 6 feet thick. Between Neolithic Jericho and the next oldest fortifications, there is a gap of about four thousand years, since fortified cities do not appear again until ca. 3000 BCE. The walls of cities like Megiddo and Gezer were erected in this era, and subsequent periods witnessed the modification or rebuilding of the earlier defenses.

From early in the third millennium BCE until the Roman period (beginning in 63 BCE), cities in the Middle East were nearly always surrounded by a stone wall. Some of the earliest city walls were over 15 feet thick and were built of solid stone; other walls had stone facings, but wall cores were filled with rubble. These massive walls were frequently reinforced with earthen buttresses and sloping ramparts. Much attention was given to the construction of deep and wide foundations; this protected the walls from undermining and

breaching operations. Foundation trenches were dug into the rubble of earlier walls, and some walls were built on bedrock. In most instances, only the walls' lower courses were constructed of stone; most of these massive walls had mud-brick superstructures. The stone courses protected the base of the wall from moisture and enemy attack and made the wall far less costly to build. Until well-dressed (i.e., carefully shaped) masonry was introduced in the Solomonic period (tenth century BCE), most of the stone used in city defenses was rough-hewn. The building of fortifications flourished during the second quarter of the second millennium BCE, and many city walls built during the next five centuries were reused remainders from the earlier period.

During the eleventh century BCE, a type of wall known as the casemate began to be used on a regular basis. This construction style consisted of two parallel walls that were separated by 5 or 6 feet of open space; these outer walls were joined by short cross walls at regular intervals, thereby creating a series of small rooms within the wall. These chambers were usually filled with rubble to give added strength. Thus, it was possible to build a wall that possessed great strength and required far less labor than would have been necessary for a solid stone wall of comparable width (about 15 feet). The casemate wall is particularly well known because of its appearance at the Solomonic cities of Hazor, Megiddo, and Gezer (see 1 Kings 9:15), where it was found in association with a sophisticated gate complex. Although the casemate wall did not disappear altogether, the methods of siege warfare that were developed by the Assyrians in the ninth century BCE led to a preference for solid walls with salients and recesses (i.e., offset-inset walls).

During the Hellenistic and Roman periods, sophisticated siege machinery made defense of a city almost futile; city walls and gates were therefore more symbolic and served to control entrance or keep out undesirables. By NT times city walls could no longer impede the Roman legions, as was the case when Jotapata, Gamla, and Jerusalem were overrun during the Jewish revolt.

Importance in the Bible: Because of the cities they protected or because of a particularly memorable event, the walls of some cities became famous: Jericho (Josh. 6:20), Beth-shan (1 Sam. 31:10, 12), Babylon (Jer. 51:44), Damascus (Jer. 49:27), and Tyre (Ezek. 26:4). References to Jerusalem's walls are especially frequent (e.g., 2 Sam. 5:9; 1 Kings 3:1; 2 Chron. 36:19; Neh. 1:3; 2:17).

The preceding survey of ancient city walls places a number of biblical passages in sharper focus. For example, the Bible agrees with the other sources by acknowledging that city walls were wide enough to serve as elevated platforms for defensive activities (2 Sam. 11:20–21, 24; Isa. 36:11–12). Indeed, Josh. 2:15 notes that Rahab helped the Hebrew spies to escape from Jericho by letting "them down by a rope through the window, for her house was built into the city wall, so that she dwelt in the wall." Likewise, the apostle Paul was lowered to safety through a window in the Damascus city wall (Acts 9:25).

Walls were so important in the ancient world that the biblical writers referred to city defenses in some of their most potent figurative expressions. For example, if city walls averaged between 20 and 30 feet in height, David's metaphor in 2 Sam. 22:30 is all the more striking (see Ps. 18:29), and the exaggeration of the Hebrew spies becomes understandable (Num. 13:28; see Deut. 1:28). Other passages that use the imagery of walls to convey their message include Prov. 18:11; 25:28; Isa. 2:15; 22:5; 26:1; 30:13; 60:10, 18; Ezek. 38:20; and Mic. 7:11. Likewise, most of the NT references to walls are figurative. In Acts 23:3, Paul compares Ananias to a "whitewashed wall," while in Eph. 2:14 the hostility between Jew and Gentile is compared to a "dividing wall." The most extensive discussion of walls in the NT is found in Rev. 21:12–19, where the seer describes the walls of the heavenly Jerusalem. *See also* defense, public; house.

Bibliography

Kenyon, Kathleen. *Royal Cities of the Old Testament.* Schocken, 1971.

Paul, Shalom M., and William G. Dever, eds. *Biblical Archaeology.* Quadrangle, 1974.

Yadin, Yigael. *The Art of Warfare in Biblical Lands.* 2 vols. International Publishing, 1963.

G.L.M.

war. War was so common in the biblical period that the Bible makes specific reference to times of peace (Judg. 3:11; 1 Kings 5:4; 2 Chron. 14:1, 5–7). Wars were fought for political, economic, and religious reasons, and Israel's position near the land bridge between Africa and Asia greatly multiplied the number of wars in which the Israelites were involved.

The weapons, strategies, and tactics used for war in the ancient Near East and the Greco-

Roman world were highly diversified, and the methodology of war varied from people to people and from period to period. Nevertheless, some aspects of warfare were universal. For example, battles were fought on land or sea, and land encounters were subdivided into two basic categories: battles in open terrain (1 Sam. 14) and attacks on fortified cities (2 Kings 17:5; 25:1). Only a few ancient peoples developed significant naval forces (e.g., Phoenicians, Greeks, Persians, Romans). Most ancient Near Eastern and Greco-Roman armies included two major divisions, foot soldiers and cavalry, and many armies made effective use of chariots (e.g., the Egyptians and Assyrians). Infantry were divided into various contingents that specialized in the use of particular weapons (e.g., bows and arrows, slings and sling stones). Although some field campaigns were provisioned "off the land," the great imperial armies counted auxiliary troops within their ranks who had the responsibility for provisioning the combat troops; such a system contributed to the success of Alexander the Great.

Since the Hebrew settlement of Canaan was partly accomplished by means of armed conflict with a number of people, Israel's early history (ca. 1225–1025 BCE) is, to some degree, a history of the wars of Israel. After the monarchy was established, it needed to be defended and maintained through warfare (ca. 1025–587/6 BCE). Throughout the entire history of Israel prior to the exile, many of Israel's outstanding leaders were known for their military achievements (e.g., Joshua, Deborah, Gideon, Saul, David, and Uzziah).

Biblical literature does not mention war with nearly as much frequency after the dissolution

Ancient cavalryman carrying a shield and weapon; from a ninth- or tenth-century relief discovered at Tell Halaf (Gozen).

of the monarchy, but warfare between the great empires that dominated the stage forms the background for this long period of Israel's existence under the shadow of Egyptian, Assyrian, Babylonian, Persian, Hellenistic, and Roman conquerors. An exception, of course, must be made for the time of the Maccabean revolt (ca. 167 BCE) and the constant wars involving the Hasmonean dynasty, as related in the first two books of Maccabees.

One of the fundamental images of God in the Bible is that of a warrior (Exod. 15:3; Ps. 24:8; Isa. 42:13). Israel's wars were often sustained through an ideology that understood Israel's enemies as enemies of God (Judg. 5:31; 1 Sam. 30:26), who, consequently, would assist Israel in times of war (Exod. 14:13–14; Josh. 10:11; 24:12; 1 Sam. 17:45). Divinely sanctioned wars are also mentioned quite frequently (Josh. 8:1; Judg. 4:14–15; 1 Sam. 23:4; 2 Kings 3:18).

Although religion was not called upon to explain every war in which Israel engaged, the disastrous defeat that led to the exile in 587/6 BCE was understood as a withdrawal of God's assistance. In fact, the idea that God "used" war to punish an apostate Israel appears again and again in the Bible (Isa. 5:26–28; Jer. 5:15–17; Ezek. 21:1–32; 23:22–28). The belief that God disciplined other nations by means of war was also widespread (Isa. 13; Jer. 46:1–10; Nah. 2:1–9); once again, this theological interpretation of history was common in other parts of the ancient Near East.

Ultimately, the language of war was employed by the biblical writers to depict judgment (Joel 2:1–11; 3:9–12; Zeph. 1:14–18; Rev. 12:7–8; 17: 14; 19:11). Because war was such a well-known phenomenon and such a serious matter, whether in reality or in its literary analogies (Pss. 18:34–42; 55:21; Eccles. 3:8; 9:18), it was also used as an appropriate symbol for the Christian life (2 Cor. 10:3–4; Eph. 6:11–17; 1 Tim. 1:18; 2 Tim. 2:3–4; James 4:1–2; 1 Pet. 2:11). Finally, the book of Revelation and other apocalyptic writings depict the end times as a period of cosmic warfare between the armies of God and Satan (12:7; 17:4; 19:11, 19) as well as a time of unprecedented warfare on the earth (12:17; 13:7; but cf. Mark 13:7–8). *See also* weapons.

Bibliography

Connolly, Peter. *Greece and Rome at War.* Prentice-Hall, 1981.

Warry, John. *Warfare in the Classical World.* St. Martin's, 1980.

Yadin, Yigael. *The Art of Warfare in Biblical Lands.* 2 vols. International Publishing, 1963.

G.L.M.

Wars of the Lord, Book of the,

an otherwise unknown and lost work quoted in Num. 21:14–15. From the context of the quotation, it would seem that the book probably contained poems celebrating the victories of the Israelites over their enemies during the period of the conquest (twelfth century BCE). It is possible that 21:17–18 and 27–30 are also quotations from the book. The title empha-

sizes God's actions in fighting for Israel (cf. 1 Sam. 17:47).

watchman. *See* sentinel.

watchtower, a high fortified tower located either within a town (Judg. 9:51; 2 Chron. 26:9) or elsewhere (2 Chron. 26:10), presumably at a strategic location. The obvious purpose was military: it was either a position to defend or a location from which to assess enemy troop movements. When erected in fortified towns, watchtowers were probably attached to and built into walls of the city and had a separate entrance (Judg. 9:52). In fields, towers could serve both as a lookout and as a fieldhouse for owners of large properties. The upper story or roof was utilized for work or sleeping and the lower portion for storage of agricultural tools.

E.M.M.

water. Rainfall was the primary source of water in Israel, and both crops and springs depended upon rains coming with regularity. Perennial streams were few and located mostly in the highland east of the Jordan, while the wadis (dry stream beds) of western Israel flowed only with the runoff water from winter rains ("freshets that pass away," Job 6:15; cf. Jer. 15:18). Mountainous terrain and lack of dependable streams made irrigation unfeasible in most of the area, though Roman engineers eventually built impressive water systems on the coastal plain and Transjordanian plateau (e.g., the aqueduct at Caesarea). In Egypt, by contrast, rainfall could be scarce, and the primary supply came through the flooding of rivers (fed by rainfall elsewhere) and by way of irrigation canals connected to these rivers. The contrast between Egypt and Canaan is noted poignantly in Deut. 11:11–12, when Moses tells the Israelites, "The land that you are crossing over to occupy is a land . . . watered by rain from the sky, a land that the Lord your God looks after."

Rain determined settlement patterns as well as modes and patterns of cultivation. The earliest towns were established near permanent springs, and elaborate tunnels and conduits were constructed in some cities (Gezer, Jerusalem, Megiddo) to ensure continuous and safe access to the water supply within the city walls. The increased use of plaster-lined cisterns at the beginning of the Iron Age (ca. 1200 BCE) permitted settlement in previously unoccupied areas of the hill country where springs were lacking or inadequate. Fluctuation in the amount and timing of the annual rains affected life in the whole land, but especially in the zone of marginal rainfall between the hill country and the desert. In wet years the area under cultivation might be extended well into the wilderness, but a few successive years of light or erratic rainfall would make agriculture impossible, forcing migration to more fertile areas, such as the Nile Delta (Gen. 41:57), or conversion to pastoral nomadism.

Water was essential to both human and animal life and was especially critical in the wilderness,

Aerial view of the water system at Hazor. It allowed safe access to the water supply even in times of siege; ninth century BCE.

where wells and springs were few and often unreliable (Gen. 21:14–19; Exod. 17:1–7). Migrating groups had to purchase water (Deut. 2:28). A cup of water offered to a guest or stranger was a simple, and expected, sign of hospitality (Job 22:7; Matt. 10:42).

Water was also used for washing and bathing, serving the needs of hygiene, refreshment, and ritual purification. Some Jews of Jesus's time washed their hands before meals in accordance with religious prescription (Mark 7:3), and guests were offered water for foot washing (Luke 7:44)—a service commonly performed by a servant (cf. John 13:5). Biblical laws prescribe ablutions for various types of contaminating conditions, including various skin diseases (Lev. 14:8), bodily emissions (15:1–21), and contact with dead or "unclean" animals (11:1–39). Pilate declared his innocence through a symbolic act of hand washing (Matt. 27:24).

Some waters were thought to have curative properties (John 5:1–7). Others were "bitter" (Exod. 15:23) or "poisoned" (Jer. 8:14), making them undrinkable or likely to cause illness to those who drank them (2 Kings 2:19–21).

Water as Symbol: According to ancient Egyptian and Mesopotamian thought, water was the primary cosmic element from which all life emerged. The Bible reflects something of this view when it speaks of the "deep" (Heb. *tehom*) as the primeval ocean, divided at creation into upper and lower waters (Gen. 1:2, 6–9). The waters above the firmament (i.e., the sky, thought of as a solid dome) are the source of rain, while the waters below form seas, lakes, and underground streams. Babylonian religion deified the power in the sweet and saltwater sources; the subterranean sweet waters were identified with wisdom, fertility, and life, while the restless, raging sea represented chaotic and destructive power. Creation in Mesopotamian and Canaanite myth involved the subduing (or slaying) of the waters of chaos, often personified as a serpent. Elements of this mythic conception persist in poetic images of the Bible, apocalyptic visions, and religious symbolism. God slew the dragon Rahab or Leviathan (Isa. 51:9; Pss. 74:12–14; 89:9–10; cf. the "ancient serpent" identified with Satan in Rev. 12:9), founded the earth upon the seas (Pss. 24:1; 136:6), and sits enthroned over the flood (29:10). God's voice thunders over "many waters," sometimes identified as "many peoples" or hostile nations (Isa. 17:13; cf. Luke 21:25; Rev. 17:15). The power of the sea is reasserted in apocalyptic writings, but in the final day the beast from the sea will be vanquished and the sea itself will be no more (Rev. 21:1).

Water is employed in numerous biblical similes and metaphors describing instability (Gen. 49:4), loss of strength (being "poured out," Job 3:24; Ps. 22:14), and melting away in fear (Josh. 7:5). It vanishes (Ps. 58:7) and cannot be gathered again when spilled (2 Sam. 14:14). But water also conveys ideas of refreshment and power. Good news from afar is "like cold water to a thirsty soul" (Prov. 25:25). God is the "fountain of living [i.e., everflowing] waters" for Israel (Jer. 2:13), and Jesus offers water of eternal life (John 4:10–15). Amos calls for justice to "roll down like (the) waters" of a perennial stream (5:24). A person in distress feels engulfed by waters, submerged in the deep (Ps. 69:1–2; Lam. 3:54). Salvation is experienced as being drawn up from the waters of death (Ps. 18:16).

Baptism recalls this symbolism of salvation as well as cleansing; the baptized are likened to those whom God saved through the flood (1 Pet. 3:20; cf. 1 Cor. 10:1–5). God's cosmic rule was symbolized in Solomon's temple by the great model of the cosmic sea (1 Kings 7:23–26). Ancient Near Eastern tradition located the source of the great rivers of the world, or the life-giving springs, at the mountain or garden of God (cf. Gen. 2:10–14). Ezekiel envisions water flowing from the threshold of the restored temple, bringing life to the whole land (47:1–2), and the author of Revelation depicts the river of the water of life flowing from the throne of God (22:1–2). *See also* baptism; cisterns; Leviathan; Rahab; sea; wadi; well.   P.A.B.

water hen, an unclean fowl, probably an omnivorous water bird (Lev. 11:18; Deut. 14:16). It may refer to a member of the *Rallus* genus, although that is not certain.

water jar. Several types of clay jars were used for water during biblical times. The largest (Heb. *kad*) was used for storage or for carrying a supply of water from the community source; such containers were carried by Rebekah (Gen. 24:14) and Elijah (1 Kings 18:33). The Samaritan woman also carried a water jar (Gk. *hydria*, John 4:28). Stone jars for water are mentioned as being present at the Cana wedding feast (John 2:6, 7). Smaller containers are also mentioned. A pitcher (Heb. *gabia*'; Gk. *keramos*) could hold water or wine (Jer. 35:5). Jesus's disciples searched for a man with a water pitcher (Mark 14:13; Luke 22:10). The jug (Heb. *baqbuq*) that was symbolically smashed by Jeremiah was probably a small decanter (19:1–13). Another word for "water jar" (Heb. *tsappakhat*) refers to a canteen or flask used by soldiers (1 Sam. 26:11) or travelers (1 Kings 19:6). *See also* pottery.   N.L.L.

water of bitterness, a specially prepared potion consisting of holy water and dust from the floor of the tabernacle. It was to be given by a priest to a woman whose husband suspected her of committing adultery, but could offer no adequate proof (Num. 5:11–31). If the woman was guilty, the potion would cause her "uterus to drop" and her "womb to discharge" (5:21–22), which probably means that it would produce a miscarriage as well as rendering her infertile (cf. 5:28). The water of bitterness is also called the "water that brings the curse" (Num. 5:22–24). Notably, the procedure for administering the water of bitterness calls for the woman to take an oath prior to drinking the water in which she calls down the negative consequences upon herself if she is guilty. Presumably, a guilty woman might refuse to take this oath and choose instead to confess her adultery.   J.M.S.

water of purification, the liquid used in an ancient purification ritual to cleanse one from defilement incurred by coming into close contact with human death, either by touching a human bone, grave, or corpse or by entering a tent where someone had died. An unblemished red heifer that had never been put under the yoke was sacrificed and the blood sprinkled toward the sanctuary. The heifer's body was then burned with cedarwood along with hyssop and scarlet (wool?) and the ashes collected and preserved. They were to be mixed with running water and sprinkled upon the defiled person, using a branch of hyssop, on the third and seventh days after the defilement. After bathing and washing the clothes the person would then be considered clean and would be welcomed in the community again. The mixture of water and ashes could also be sprinkled on a tent and its furnishings if a death had occurred within the tent (Num. 19:1–22; 31:21–24). *See also* heifer; hyssop; purity.   D.R.B.

wave offering. *See* sacrifice.

way.

1 A path, road, or journey.

2 A natural pattern of behavior observed in the world. Prov. 30:19 refers to "the way of an eagle in the sky, the way of a snake on a rock, the way of a ship on the high seas, and the way of a man with a girl."

3 God's commandments or expectation of humanity; i.e., the "way of the LORD" (e.g., Gen. 18:19; Judg. 2:22; cf. Ps. 18:30; Isa. 55:8–9). That same phrase can be used, however, to speak of the advent or presence of God; the admonition "prepare the way of the LORD" is spoken in anticipation of a manifestation of God's power (Isa. 40:3; cf. Mark 1:3).

4 A lifestyle or pattern of human behavior. Ps. 1:6 refers to both "the way of the righteous" and "the way of the wicked" (cf. Isa. 26:7).

5 A quality of life defined by one's relationship with God. This meaning is a variation on 4 taken up by NT writers (e.g., Heb. 10:20). Jesus is identified as "the Way," because through him one has access to a spiritually intimate relation with God (John 14:4–6). One of the earliest designations for the emerging Christian community appears to have been followers of "the Way" (Acts 9:2; 19:9, 23; 24:22; cf. Mark 10:52). *See also* Christian.   J.M.E./M.A.P.

wayfarer, a transient person who traveled regularly, either for work or as a mode of life (Judg. 19:17; 2 Sam. 12:4).

wealth. In the Bible, material goods are generally esteemed as gifts of God, received through God's blessing (Deut. 28:1–14). Wealth is attributed to the ancestors (Gen. 13:2), godly kings (2 Chron. 32:27–29), and Job (42:10–17). Solomon was granted great wealth even though he did not ask for it (or perhaps *because* he did not ask for it,

2 Chron. 1:11–12). Wealth may thus be viewed as a sign of God's favor (Ps. 112:1–3), but much of the biblical material deals with problems associated with wealth.

First, Moses warns against the propensity of people to forget that wealth comes from God and to assume that wealth is a credit to their own ingenuity: "When you have eaten your fill and have built fine houses and live in them . . . and all that you have is multiplied, then . . . remember the LORD your God, for it is (God) who gives you power to get wealth" (Deut. 8:12–18). Second, numerous texts address the problem of people trusting in their wealth (Ps. 49:6) or seeking refuge in their riches (52:7).

Third, many biblical writers note a tendency for the wealthy to exploit the poor (Isa. 3:13–26; James 5:1–6) or at least to fail to assist the poor in a manner befitting those who love their neighbors as themselves (cf. Lev. 19:18). According to Moses, the wealthy were expected to exercise generosity in helping to meet the needs of the poor (Deut. 15:10). Job defended his integrity with the claim that he had given to the poor open-handedly (31:16–20). Sodom was condemned for failing to do so (Ezek. 16:49). In all of these texts, the connotation of wealth shifts from mere abundance to excess (cf. Luke 12:15–21). Luxury is described in biting detail and condemned because of the failure of compassion (Amos 6:4–7; Luke 16:19–31).

Fourth, the Bible consistently develops the position that "the love of money is the root of all kinds of evil" (1 Tim. 6:10). Wealth is not to be sought for its own sake (Prov. 28:20, 22), and the desire to be wealthy often involves greed (which is a form of idolatry, Col. 3:5; cf. Luke 12:15; Eph. 5:3) or covetousness (Exod. 20:17). Those who desire to be rich "fall into temptation and are trapped by many senseless and harmful desires that plunge people into ruin and destruction" (1 Tim. 6:9). In Jesus's parable of the Sower, the "lure of wealth" is likened to thorns that choke a young plant, preventing the intended effects of God's word from coming to fruition in people's lives. In the Sermon on the Mount, he describes riches as a distraction or contrary force that draw one's affections away from God and spiritual pursuits (Matt. 6:21; cf. Job 22:23–26). Finally, wealth has the capacity to enslave, so that it becomes one's "master" (Matt. 6:24). The rich man who wants to follow Jesus, but goes away sad because he cannot sell his possessions, seems to exemplify a person caught in such bondage (Mark 10:17–22).

In recognition of such problems, material wealth is often contrasted negatively with spiritual blessings. Silver and gold cannot save (Ezek. 7:19) or heal (Act 3:6), and wealth cannot purchase love (Song of Sol. 8:7). The value of treasure on earth pales in comparison to that of treasure in heaven (Matt. 6:19–20; 19:21; Luke 12:33). Nevertheless, the Bible does speak of wealthy persons who are righteous and who please God. Joseph of Arimathea is a rich man who provides a tomb for Jesus (Matt. 27:57). Zacchaeus is also described as a wealthy man who acts righteously, or at least who pledges to do so after his encounter with Jesus (Luke 19:1–10).

In other texts, a divine preference for the poor is definitely noted. God has chosen the poor to be rich in faith (James 2:5). Some texts also express hostility toward the wealthy. In Luke 6:24, Jesus says, "Woe to you who are rich, for you have received your consolation." Elsewhere, he indicates that it is completely impossible for a rich person to enter the kingdom of God (i.e., it would be easier for a camel to go through the eye of a needle; Mark 10:26). Still, he allows that "with God all things are possible" (10:27).

The Pastoral Letters move away from polemic to offer pragmatic advice for the wealthy. They are "not to be haughty, or to set their hopes on the uncertainty of riches, but rather on God. . . . They are to do good, to be rich in good works, generous, and ready to share (1 Tim. 6:17–18). Overall, the biblical ideal in contrast to poverty or wealth is material sufficiency (Prov. 30:8–9; Eccles. 3:12–13; Matt. 6:11, 25–33; 1 Tim. 6:8) and the cultivation of an attitude of contentment with whatever one has (Phil. 4:11–13). *See also* mammon; ownership; poor, poverty.   S.C.M./M.A.P.

weaning, the practice of training a child to eat food other than mother's milk. In biblical times it was an occasion to celebrate when a child was weaned (Gen. 21:8). It marked Samuel's departure for special training (1 Sam. 1:21–28). A weaned child symbolized the peaceable kingdom of the Messiah (Isa. 11:8) or the helpless result of a delinquent leadership (28:9).

weapons. Weapons used for hunting and fighting were among humankind's earliest inventions. The extant literature, archaeological remains, and artistic representations from the ancient Near East and Greco-Roman world demonstrate that weaponry in the biblical period was highly diversified and sophisticated. Not only was the effective use of certain weapons dependent upon training and skill, but the technical production of such instruments was an art, a science, and an industry. Generally speaking, the evolution of weaponry was driven by competition to obtain an advantage over one's enemy. Changes in the arsenal of one people necessitated alterations in the weapons among neighboring peoples.

As in the modern world, advancements in ancient technology were quickly adapted for use in instruments of war. Naturally, the shape, size, and overall durability of dagger and sword blades and spearheads and arrowheads were affected by improvements in copper, bronze, and iron technology. Another important weapon that improved over time was the chariot, whose speed and maneuverability were increased by changes in design and construction materials, including metals. Other major steps in the development of ancient weaponry included the invention of the composite bow, the piercing battle-ax, the Corinthian helmet, and siege engines.

Although the Bible does not provide detailed description of weapons, 1 Sam. 17:5–7 and Eph. 6:11–17 do list some of the weapons used in different biblical periods (cf. 2 Chron. 26:14–15; Jer.

46:3–4). Moreover, scattered references throughout the Bible make mention of virtually every offensive and defensive instrument of war used in antiquity. Given the geographic location of the biblical lands and the frequency of war in the biblical period, this is to be expected.

Offensive weapons may be divided into categories that correspond to the range at which the weapons were typically used against an enemy (i.e., short-, medium-, and long-range weapons). Short-range weapons were normally used in hand-to-hand combat; this category includes more items than the other two combined. Frequently mentioned in the Bible are the rod and staff (Ps. 2:9; Isa. 10:5, 15), sword or dagger (Judg. 3:16–22; 1 Sam. 17:51), and spear (Num. 25:7–8; 1 Sam. 17:7). The war club (Prov. 25:18) and hammer (Jer. 51:20) were probably akin to the mace, another important weapon in antiquity. The battle-ax was an important short-range weapon in the ancient Near East, though it is not mentioned in the Bible.

Medium-range weapons were designed for throwing at enemies who were a fairly short distance away. Although some spears were light enough to be included in this category (1 Sam. 18:11; 19:10; 20:33), the lighter and shorter javelin was better suited for this purpose (17:6). The NRSV does not always distinguish between the spear and javelin, but uses the word "spear" to translate distinct Hebrew words that refer to these two different weapons. Long-range weapons could be fired at enemies some distance away, such as enemies on a battlefield or on a city's ramparts. The two pri-

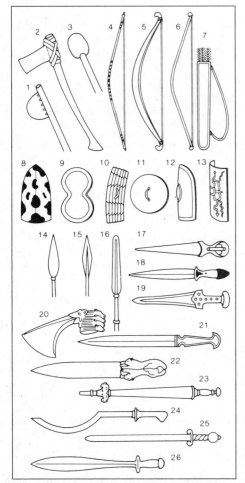

Weapons: **1.** Egyptian poleax (ca. 2700 BCE); **2.** Egyptian ax (1580 BCE); **3.** Type of ancient stone mace; **4.** Type of Egyptian bow (1430 BCE); **5.** Assyrian bow (1200 BCE); **6, 7.** Assyrian bow and quiver with arrows (850 BCE); **8.** Egyptian shield (2000 BCE); **9.** Late Minoan shield (1580–1100 BCE); **10.** Assyrian shield (700 BCE); **11.** Assyrian shield (650 BCE); **12.** Roman shield (100 BCE); **13.** Roman shield (300 BCE); **14.** Assyrian spear; **15.** Syrian spear; **16.** Egyptian spear (1600 BCE); **17.** Egyptian dagger (2000 BCE); **18.** Sumerian dagger; **19.** Late Minoan dagger (1600–1100 BCE); **20.** Weapon with curved blade coming from mouth of animal (ca. 3000 BCE); **21.** Sword of Marduk-shapik-zeri (1250 BCE); **22.** Sword with straight blade, two lions forming hilt (ca. 3000 BCE); **23.** Assyrian sword (900 BCE); **24.** Ancient sickle sword; **25.** Type of Roman sword; **26.** Type of Greek sword.

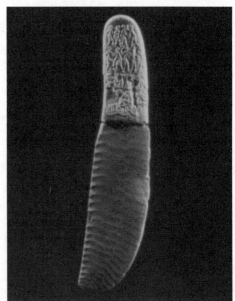

Egyptian knife carved from the tooth of a hippopotamus; the decorated handle shows warriors of different tribes in hand-to-hand combat; fourth millennium BCE.

mary long-range weapons in ancient arsenals were the sling (1 Sam. 17:40, 50; 2 Kings 3:25) and the bow (Isa. 21:17; Jer. 50:14).

Defensive weapons were developed to contend with all of the just mentioned offensive instruments. Included in the Bible's references to pieces of armor are the shield and buckler (1 Chron. 12:24; Ps. 35:2; Eph. 6:16), helmet (1 Sam. 17:38; 2 Chron. 26:14; Eph. 6:17), scale armor and coats of mail (1 Kings 22:34; Neh. 4:16), breastplate (1 Kings 22:34; Eph. 6:14), and greaves (1 Sam. 17:6). The chariot also deserves attention as a mobile fighting platform mentioned frequently by biblical writers (e.g., Exod. 14:17–18; 1 Kings 10:26).

Many of the aforementioned weapons are also referenced in figurative speech. Even the terms "weapon" and "weapons" assumed symbolic meaning in a number of passages (Ps. 7:12–13; Eccles. 9:18; Isa. 54:16–17; 2 Cor. 10:4). *See also* arms, armor; chariots; sling; spear; sword; war.

Bibliography

Gonen, Rivka. *Weapons of the Ancient World.* Cassell, 1975.

Muhly, James D. "How Iron Technology Changed the Ancient World." *Biblical Archaeology Review* (November/December 1982): 40–54.

Yadin, Yigael. *The Art of Warfare in Biblical Lands.* 2 vols. International Publishing, 1963.

G.L.M.

weasel, any small carnivore of the genus *Mustela.* Certain members of this genus were considered unclean (Lev. 11:29).

weather, climatic conditions, which for the Levant (approximately the same latitude as the state of Georgia or southern Spain) are also influenced by the formation of the land and its nearness to the desert and sea. Seasons are described with primary reference to rainfall. The rainy season basically corresponds to winter, with the heaviest rains in December. This is bracketed by the early or "former" rains in October/November (Jer. 5:24) and the "latter" rains in April/May. The dry season corresponds to summer.

The rains come from the sea, watering mainly the western slopes of the central highlands. In general the rain decreases the closer one gets to the Transjordan desert, increasing only on the mountain slopes. Rainfall also tends to decrease as one moves from north (the Lebanon mountains and the hills of Galilee) to south (the Negev and Sinai deserts). Rainfall is about the same in the coastal towns in the west as in Jerusalem in the highlands, i.e., 20–24 inches a year. The western hills of Galilee receive 35–40 inches of rain a year (about the same as New York City), while the deserts of Transjordan, the Negev, and Sinai as well as the Jordan Valley may have 8 inches or less.

Seasonal variations in temperature are relative to the amount of rainfall and to altitude. January is usually the coolest month, with temperatures averaging 45 degrees Fahrenheit in the hills

of Galilee, 48 degrees in Jerusalem, 56 degrees at Acco and Gaza on the coast, and 59 degrees at Jericho in the Jordan Valley. In the summer months, Jerusalem and towns on the central ridge have some of the most pleasant weather, averaging about 74 degrees. In the Jordan Valley, average temperatures are in the upper 80s. *See also* season.

N.L.L.

weaving. *See* spinning and weaving.

wedding. Although marriage is an institution commended and celebrated throughout the Bible, weddings are referred to rarely. It is not certain that public ceremonies or religious services were always held.

The Hebrew Bible contains only two references. Ps. 19:5 describes a sunrise as being like a bridegroom coming out from his "wedding canopy." The Song of Solomon refers to the wedding of King Solomon as "the day of the gladness of his heart" and specifically indicates that on that day his mother gave him a crown (3:11). Both of these references point to what might have been social customs associated with weddings, but neither wedding canopies nor wedding crowns are referred to anywhere else, and it is possible that such appurtenances would only have been associated with weddings of the wealthy or well-to-do.

In the NT, Jesus indicates that it would not be appropriate for guests at a wedding to fast or mourn (Matt. 9:15). He tells a parable about a king who gives a wedding banquet for his son; at this banquet, the guests are expected to be dressed in appropriate wedding robes (22:2–12). In another

The wedding feast at Cana, where Jesus, according to John 2:1–11, turned water into wine; fourteenth-century mosaic at the Kariye Church, Istanbul.

parable, he describes bridesmaids who wait during the night for the bridegroom to come, at which point they will join him in going to a wedding banquet (25:10:1–12; cf. Luke 12:36). Jesus also uses the illustration of a wedding banquet in teaching about humility, noting that one should not immediately seek the seat of honor at such a banquet, but should sit in one of the lower places and wait to be recognized (Luke 14:8–13). The prominence of "wedding banquet" imagery in Jesus's teaching indicates that such events must have been common—or at least well known—among the peasant population of Galilee. It is interesting, however, that the focus of wedding imagery is exclusively on a celebratory banquet, not a religious rite or marriage service. The only actual wedding that is mentioned in the NT is the one in Cana of Galilee at which Jesus turns water into wine (John 2:1–2). Again, however, there is no attention to the marriage service, only to the social event associated with it: the presence of a "steward" is mentioned, though the bridegroom seems to be the one providing for the guests (2:9–10).

The book of Tobit, written during the Second Temple period, refers several times to a "wedding celebration" but, again, never describes a wedding service as such; the celebration was fourteen days long, including a seven-day feast, and many gifts were given to the groom (9:2, 5–6; 10:7; 11:18; 12:1).

One can only speculate as to what an actual wedding would have involved. It seems likely that written contracts were signed, since elsewhere written bills of divorce are mentioned (cf. Deut. 24:1–3; Jer. 3:8; Mark 10:4). A pronouncement of blessings may have been included (Ruth 4:11–12). Ps. 45 is often thought to be a wedding poem, and its existence (along with the Song of Solomon) may indicate that recitation of love poetry was part of a wedding service.

Certain biblical texts indicate that the nuptial celebration may have consisted of a procession from the house of the bride to the bridegroom's home (cf. Matt. 25:6; the latter may have been symbolized by a tent; cf. Num. 25:8; 2 Sam. 16:22; Ps. 19:6; Song of Sol. 1:16). Both parties may have been beautifully dressed and adorned (Isa. 49:18; Jer. 2:32; Ps. 45:14–15). After the procession, a feast may have taken place at the bridegroom's house (Matt. 22:2) or at the bride's house (Gen. 29:27; Judg. 14:10–12). These texts, however, cannot be assumed to reflect practices that were normative for people of all classes or for all time periods. *See also* marriage.

Bibliography
De Vaux, Roland. "Marriage." In *Ancient Israel: Its Life and Institutions.* McGraw-Hill, 1961.

Patai, Raphael. *Sex and the Family in the Bible and the Middle East.* Doubleday, 1959.

W.S.T./M.A.P.

weeds. Weeds are referred to three times in the Hebrew Bible. Job 31:40 refers to "foul weeds" that grow in a field instead of barley. Hos. 10:4

mentions "poisonous weeds" that grow in the furrows of a field; their identification is uncertain. In Jon. 2:5, the weeds that wrap around the prophet's head when he is drowning are no doubt a type of seaweed. In the NT, Jesus tells a parable about weeds being planted among wheat (Matt. 13:24–30). The weeds he had in mind were probably darnel (*Lolium tremulentum*), a somewhat poisonous plant looking very much like wheat during its earliest stages. As a result of the resemblance, early separation from wheat is nearly impossible. This is further complicated by the fact that the roots of the two intertwine, so that when the darnel is pulled up, the wheat is uprooted along with it. These factors figure in the point of the parable (13:29).   R.H.S./M.A.P.

week. *See* time.

Weeks, Festival of. *See* festivals, feasts, and fasts; Pentecost.

weights and measures. The biblical system of weights and measures can be reconstructed, at least tentatively, from three sources: references in the surviving literature of Egypt and Mesopotamia, from which systems used in the Levant were borrowed; scattered references in the Bible to local practices; and archaeological discoveries. In the last case, actual inscribed weights have been found, along with vessels of measurable capacity and items or structures whose dimensions suggest standard modules.

Units for Measuring Weight: All reconstructions of the monetary system in ancient Israel as well as in NT times presuppose the use of balances to weigh out fragments of precious metal, principally silver, in payment. The Hebrew word for the basic unit of currency, the *sheqel* (English "shekel"), comes from the root *shql,* "to weigh," i.e., to pay. Balances, probably consisting simply of two metal pans suspended from a hand-held beam, are mentioned in several passages (Job 6:2; Ps. 62:9; Isa. 40:12; Ezek. 5:1; Dan. 5:27). Accurate or "honest balances" are commended (Lev. 19:36; Job 31:6; Prov. 11:1; 16:11; Ezek. 45:10), but several references to "false balances" show that dishonest manipulation was easy and common (Prov. 11:1; 20:23; Hos. 12:7; Amos 8:5; Mic. 6:11). Archaeologists have found numeous stone weights that would have been used in these balances, and quite a few of them show clear signs of having been chiseled on the bottom so as to correct or otherwise alter their weight—an ancient practice from which may derive use of the modern word "to chisel" in the sense of "to cheat."

The Israelites basically adopted the system of weight used by other Mesopotamian cultures—this, of course, facilitated commerce. The four basic units were the talent, the mina, the shekel, and the gerah. The Israelites, however, appear to have adapted the system to a quinquagesimal system as opposed to the sexagesimal system used elsewhere; in other words, the ratio of the weights

Israelite bronze weights from the
ninth–eighth century BCE.

The only references to weights in the NT are to talents, drachmas, minas, or pounds, which also served as units of money. On these, *see* money.

Units for Measuring Area: There is no special terminology for measures of area in the Bible. A "yoke" (Heb. *tsemed;* 1 Sam. 14:14; Isa. 5:10) is presumably the area a pair of oxen could plow in a day, possibly about an acre. Another Hebrew term for land area is *ma'anah,* translated by the NRSV as "furrow" (Ps. 129:3). Finally, *se'ah* (NRSV: "measure") occurs in the story of Elijah's digging a trench around his altar on Mount Carmel (1 Kings 18:32); it denotes the area that "two measures of seed" would plant, though there is no further information regarding just what that would be.

Units for Measuring Length: As in Mesopotamia and Egypt, the "cubit" (Heb. *'ammah,* "elbow") was the standard unit for linear measure in ancient Israel. Like the subordinate measures, the "span" and the "finger," it derived from a natural, convenient point of reference, the approximate length of a man's forearm. The word occurs in the Hebrew Bible more than a hundred times, in descriptions of distances, buildings, furnishings, and the like. No actual cubit measures have been found by archaeologists, doubtless because they were of perishable wood, but Hezekiah's famous water tunnel in Jerusalem contains an inscription (the Siloam Inscription) that gives its length as "1,200 cubits," which would yield a cubit of about 17.5 inches—very close to the average length of a man's forearm from elbow to fingertips. Solomon's temple would thus have been 90 feet (60 cubits) long, 30 feet (20 cubits) wide, and 45 feet (30 cubits) high (1 Kings 6:2).

There were, however, different versions of a cubit used in ancient Israel, just as there were different versions of the shekel. Ezek. 40:5 makes reference to a "long cubit" that was "a cubit and a handbreadth in length"; this was perhaps the Israelite equivalent of an Egyptian cubit, known to have been about 20.6 inches. A third cubit may be intended by the phrase "common cubit" employed in the description of the bed of Og, king of Bashan (Deut. 3:11); or perhaps that reference simply means a regular cubit as opposed to a "long cubit."

Smaller units of linear measure were the "span". (Heb. *zeret),* or distance between extended fingertips (about ½ a cubit, or 9 inches on the shorter

to one another was based (roughly) on numbers divisible by 5 or 50, rather than by 6 or 60, as in the Assyrian and Babylonian systems.

There are other complicating factors indicating that the Israelite system of weights may not have been consistent at all times and places. First, certain passages refer to a "sanctuary shekel" (Exod. 20:24; 38:25–26), and 2 Sam. 14:26 refers to a "shekel by the king's weight." The suggestion, corroborated by archaeologists, is that Israel knew at least two types of shekels: the "light shekel" for common use (about 11.4 grams or .4 ounce) and a "heavy shekel" (equivalent to the sanctuary or royal shekel), which was slightly larger. Second, the Bible indicates that a shekel was equal to 20 gerahs (Exod. 30:13, Lev. 27:25; Num. 3:47; 18:16; Ezek. 45:12), but archaeological finds suggest that a shekel was normally equivalent to 24 gerahs.

Otherwise, Ezek. 45:12 indicates that the mina was equivalent to 50 shekels. A smaller weight, the pim is referred to only once in the Bible (1 Sam. 13:19–21). Its weight has been determined as about ⅔ that of a shekel (7.8 grams or .27 ounce).

Top view of dome-shaped weights inscribed with their values. Some of the values (*right to left*) are: 18, 8, 4, and 2 shekels.

scale, a little over 10 inches on the longer scale of Ezekiel). A "handbreadth" (Heb. *tephakh*) was equal to the width of the four fingers of a person's hand (about $^1/_6$ of a cubit, or 3 inches). A "finger" (Heb. *'etsba'*) designated a unit equal to the width (not length) of a human finger and, by definition, was equal to $^1/_4$ of a handbreadth, or $^3/_4$ of an inch.

In the NT the word "cubit" (Gk. *pēchys*) seems to be merely a popular estimate of both length and time. Jesus says to his disciples, "Which of you by being anxious can add a cubit to his life?" (Matt. 6:27); and the disciples on the Sea of Galilee started to bring in their boat when they were about "two hundred cubits" offshore (John 21:8). The Greek *stadion* (pl. *stadia;* Luke 24:13; John 6:19; 11:18; Rev. 14:20; 21:16) contained 400 cubits, about 200 yards in either Greek or Roman usage. A "mile" (Matt. 5:41) was probably the standard Roman mile of 1,000 double paces, 5,000 Roman feet, or 1,618 yards.

Units for Measuring Capacity: There are many units of capacity measure in the Bible. They are related mostly to the Assyrian-Babylonian system rather than the Egyptian system, but they were never finally fixed. Still, just as honest balances were demanded by biblical law, so just measures were called for (Lev. 19:36; Ezek. 45:10).

The term "homer" (Heb. *khomer*), a standard dry measure, was derived from the word for "ass" and referred to the load of grain a donkey might normally carry. On the basis of Assyrian texts it would have been about 14 bushels, but some calculations make it more like 6.5 bushels. The homer, equal to the cor, contained 10 baths or ephahs (Ezek. 45:11–14). The cor (Heb. *kor*) was equal to the homer, but it could be used for liquid measure as well (1 Kings 4:22; 5:11, 25; 2 Chron. 2:10; 27:5; Ezek. 45:14), in which case it would have contained about 35 gallons, and possibly up to 60.

The lethech (Heb. *letek*), mentioned only in Hos. 3:2, is about half a homer or cor, or about 2 to 3.25 bushels. Only the NIV uses the word. The RSV and KJV use "half-homer" and the NRSV mis-

translates as "homer." The ephah (Heb. *'ephah*) was equal to $^1/_{10}$ of a homer or cor, thus about 1.5 to 2.5 pecks, or $^3/_8$ to $^2/_3$ of a bushel. The ephah is mentioned numerous times in the Bible, especially with grains and cereals, and must have been the most common dry measure. The bath (Heb. *bat*) was a liquid measure equal to the ephah (Ezek. 45:14). Store jars from the eighth century BCE have been found at Tell Beit Mirsim inscribed "bath" and at Lachish inscribed "royal bath." These jars, when reconstructed, yielded a capacity of about 5.5 gallons, corresponding approximately to the ephah. Quantities of liquid from small to very large were measured with the bath (1 Kings 7:26, 38; 2 Chron. 2:10; 4:5; Isa. 5:10).

The seah (Heb. *se'ah*) was a dry measure of uncertain size. References in Gen. 18:6; 1 Kings 18:32; and 2 Kings 7:1, 16, 18 are rendered by the NRSV as simply "measure," but the LXX suggests 1.5 *modii,* or about $^1/_3$ of a bushel. The hin (Heb. *hin*) is an Egyptian liquid measure that can be shown by actual examples to be 0.46 liter, or about half a quart. But according to calculations based on the writings of the historian Josephus, the Israelite hin was $^1/_6$ of a bath, or a little less than a gallon. Ezek. 4:11 gives a daily ration of water as $^1/_6$ of a hin, or $^2/_3$ of a quart.

The omer (Heb. *'omer*) was $^1/_{10}$ of an ephah (Exod. 10:36), or a little more than 2 dry quarts. According to Exod. 16:16–18, the omer was a day's ration of grain. The issaron (Heb. *'issaron*), mentioned only rarely (Exod. 29:40; Lev. 40:10), is evidently $^1/_{10}$ of some measure, presumably an ephah. The kab (Heb. *qab*) is referred to only in 2 Kings 6:25. In rabbinic sources it is said to have been $^1/_{18}$ of an ephah, or about 1.6 of a dry quart. The smallest unit of capacity, the log (Heb. *log;* only Lev. 14:10, 12, 15, 24), was used for oil. It was apparently $^1/_4$ of a kab, or about $^2/_3$ of a pint.

In the NT, capacity is determined by Greek or Roman measures. The *metrētēs* (KJV: "firkins") of John 2:6 was possibly equal to about 10 gallons; the NRSV translates this reference to "two or three *metrētēs*" as "twenty or thirty gallons." The "bushel basket" (Gk. *modios*) in Matt. 5:15 refers to a container that would hold about $^1/_4$ of an American bushel. The "pound" of costly perfume Mary poured on Jesus's feet (John 12:3) was a *litra,* equal to about 12 ounces. A *choinix* (Rev. 6:6) was about 1 quart.

Bibliography

Barkay, G. "Iron Age Gerah Weights." *Eretz-Israel* 15 (1981): 288–96 (Hebrew; English summary, p. 85).

Dever, William G. "Iron Age Epigraphic Material from the Area of Khirbet el-Kôm." *Hebrew Union College Annual* 40–41 (1969–1970): 139–204.

Scott, R. B. Y. "Weights and Measures of the Bible." *Biblical Archaeologist* 22 (1959): 22–40.

W.G.D.

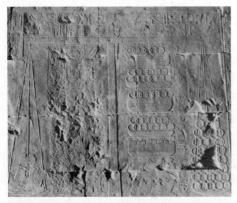

Cattle of Punt (*lower left*) being weighed against gold weights on a balance; fifteenth-century BCE reliefs at Thebes.

well (Heb. *be'er*), a hole or depression dug for the purpose of collecting water. A well was constructed by digging into the ground or by curbing surface springs. Wells, together with cisterns, were the major source of water in the ancient Near East. Digging a well in this semi-arid land was an occasion for rejoicing (Num. 21:17), but could also generate strife (Gen. 21:25–26; 26:15, 18; Exod. 2:16–17). Wells were located in the wilderness (Gen. 16:7, 14), in fields (29:2), and in towns (2 Sam. 23:15), and they supplied both human and animal needs. The city well, which was usually located outside the gate (Neh. 2:13; John 4:6–8), served as a meeting place, especially for women, who had the daily task of drawing water for the household (Gen. 24:11). The well is used figuratively to describe the beloved as a source of pleasure (Prov. 5:15; Song of Sol. 4:15) and to characterize a wicked city that keeps its wickedness as "fresh" as a well keeps its water (Jer. 6:7). *See also* Beer-sheba; cisterns.   P.A.B.

Wheat, as depicted on bas-reliefs at ancient Hermopolis, Egypt.

wheat (genus *Triticum*), one of the principal cereal grasses, along with barley, grown throughout the Near East. After being harvested in the late spring, wheat was prepared for domestic use as flour by threshing, winnowing, parching, and grinding or milling. The finely ground flour was preferred for baking breads and cakes and was therefore a major dietary component (Exod. 29:2; Lev. 2:1).

Wheat is less hardy than barley and is more susceptible to drought, frost, and poor soil conditions. Dependence on wheat as the staff of life often led to famine in times of environmental stress (Gen. 43:1–2). In good years, however, production was so great that it was an item of export. Solomon is said to have sent twenty thousand measures of wheat to Hiram of Tyre in payment for the cedars and cypress sent for the construction of the temple and palace of Jerusalem (1 Kings 5:10–11). *See also* corn; farming; spelt; threshing; winnowing.   P.L.C.

wheels. Early representations of wheels show them to be solid and anchored to the axle so that the whole combination would turn beneath the bed of the vehicle (third millennium BCE). Subsequent developments freed the wheel to turn on the axle, designed spoked wheels with rims for lighter weight and maneuverability, and adapted the device to uses other than transportation (e.g., a potter's wheel for shaping clay, Jer. 18:3; a wheel-and-pulley device for raising water from a cistern, Eccles. 12:6). In addition to carts, wagons, and chariots, biblical writers refer to wheels on the temple court lavers, four on each (1 Kings 7:30–33). Ezekiel's vision of God's throne included wheels with eyes (1:4–28); in Dan. 4:9 and *1 Enoch* 14:18 wheels are part of the throne support. The crushing effect of a wheel is invoked in Prov. 20:26.   R.S.B.

whirlwind, a violent, destructive windstorm, common in Israel during the rainy season. True whirlwinds, i.e., swirling winds or tornadoes, are unusual, though they sometimes do appear near the coast during the early winter. Whirlwinds and storms usually accompanied a theophany, such as God's appearance to Job (Job 38:1; 40:6) and Ezekiel's vision of God (1:4; cf. Nah. 1:3; Zech. 9:14). According to 2 Kings 2:1, 11, the prophet Elijah did not die, but a whirlwind, accompanied by a chariot and horses of fire, carried him up to heaven. *See also* Elijah; Job, book of.

whore. *See* prostitute.

wickedness. *See* evil; redemption; restitution; sin.

widow. The status of widows in ancient society could be precarious, though Israel's legal corpus did provide some measure of security. If a deceased Israelite had brothers, a levirate marriage could be arranged, but this was not always done (Deut. 25:5–10; cf. Gen. 38). A priest's daughter could return to her father's house (Lev. 22:13). Sometimes, however, widows had no respectable recourse but to rely on public charity.

God's concern for the plight of widows is revealed throughout the Bible (Deut. 14:29; Jer. 49:11; Pss. 68:5; 146:9). It was taught that the neglect or oppression of widows provoked divine wrath (Ps. 94:1–7; Job 22:9–11, 29–30; Isa. 1:16–17, 21–25). In Deuteronomy, God's mercy to the Israelites, who were slaves in Egypt, is linked to Israel's obligation to care for widows and others who are at a disadvantage in society (10:14–19; 24:17–22; 27:19). Stories in the Gospels also reveal Jesus's sensitivity to widows: he restores life to the "only son" of the widow of Nain (Luke 7:11–17); he criticizes religious leaders for exploiting widows (Mark 12:40); and he declares that a poor widow's copper coins exceed large gifts to the temple treasury (12:38–44). Likewise, in the early church, widows were cared for and steps were taken to ensure equal distribution of food (Acts 6:1–6). The Letter of James indicates that "to care for orphans and widows in their distress" is one hallmark of "religion that is pure and undefiled before God" (1:27).

Such references indicate that widows were frequently in need of special compassion and assistance, but one should not assume that this was a necessary characteristic of widowhood. Jewish and Roman law allowed widows to retain their husband's assets and, of course, many women were capable of earning and investing money on their own. Judith was a widow (Jth. 8:4) who seemed to do quite well, financially and otherwise. The mother of John Mark, mentioned in the book of Acts, was apparently a widow (no husband is ever mentioned), and she owned at least one slave and had a house big enough to host gatherings of the disciples in Jerusalem (12:12–13).

A particular arrangement known as the "office of widows" is mentioned in 1 Tim. 5:3–16. The idea behind this was that widows who had no family members to care for them could be supported financially by the church while devoting themselves to prayer and good works. But two problems seem to have arisen. First, some church members tried to take advantage of the program and abdicated their personal responsibility to care for family members (5:4, 8). Second, some younger widows had apparently been taken into the program and then dropped out when they decided to remarry. Thus, Timothy is told to limit enrollment in the program to those who are "real widows," i.e., who have been "left alone" with no one to care for them (5:1, 3, 5, 16). He is also told to limit enrollment in the program to widows over age sixty and to women who have demonstrated a capacity for the life of prayer and good works that are expected of those in the program. The second-century writers Ignatius (*Smyrn.* 13:1) and Polycarp (*Phil.* 4:3) indicate that such an order of ministry still existed in their time. *See also* family; marriage.

Bibliography

Thurston, Bonnie. *The Widows: A Women's Ministry in the Early Church.* Fortress, 1989.

J.L.P./M.A.P.

wife. *See* concubine; family; marriage.

wilderness. The Hebrew word (*midbar*) that is usually translated "wilderness" in the Bible refers both to something that is "desolate and deserted" and something that is "beyond," i.e., beyond the limits of settlement and therefore of government control. Thus, a wilderness was not defined by geographic features so much as by a perception of disorder and danger. A wilderness was usually assumed to be the home of wild beasts and savage wandering tribes. In time of war or repression refugees would flee to the wilderness (Isa. 21:13–15; cf. Rev. 12:6, 14).

The Israelites' primary experience with wilderness involved their wandering in the wilderness for forty years after the exodus, before they entered the land of Canaan. The narratives of that experience testify to God's guidance, provision, and protection of Israel in the wilderness, and yet the Israelites would also recall this period as a dreadful time that finally came to an end (Exod. 15:22–25; 16:3; Pss. 78:40; 95:8). They remembered the trek as being through "a great and terrible wilderness, an arid wasteland with poisonous snakes and scorpions" (Deut. 8:15).

Geographically, land referred to as wilderness (*midbar*) included poor steppe land (e.g., the area surrounding the oasis of Damascus, 1 Kings 19:15), the marginally cultivated land on the Transjordan plateau (Num. 21:13; Deut. 4:43), and the pastureland east of Bethlehem, where Luke reports that shepherds watched their flocks at night (Luke 2:8), as David had done centuries before (1 Sam. 17:28). Wilderness could also comprise tangled thickets and scrub, such as the area near Succoth in the Jordan Valley (Judg. 8:7, 16). Wilderness (*midbar*) in fact merged into wooded areas (Heb. *ya'ar,* normally translated "forest"),

Desert "wilderness" in the Sinai Peninsula near Jebal Musa, a traditional site of Mount Sinai.

since both were perceived by the settled Israelites as dangerous trackless country where one could rapidly become lost or be attacked by wild beasts. The two are equated in Ezek. 34:25 when God promises, "I will make with them a covenant of peace and banish wild beasts from the land, so that they may dwell securely in the wilderness [*midbar*] and sleep in the woods [*ya'ar*]."

NT writers also regarded the wilderness (Gk. *erēmos*) as "waterless places" that were the natural habitat of evil spirits (Luke 11:24; cf. Isa. 34:14). Thus, the Spirit led Jesus out into the wilderness to be tempted by the devil (Matt. 4:1–11; Luke 4:1–13). Jesus's forerunner, John the Baptist, had also appeared in the wilderness with his message of repentance (Mark 1:4), thus reminding Israel of its first days as chosen people in the desert of Sinai. The fact that John performed a baptism indicates that the wilderness in that case was not a waterless area, but a desolate stretch somewhere in the Jordan Valley. *See also* desert; Sinai.   D.B./P.J.A.

willow, any water-loving tree of the genus *Salix* (Ezek. 17:5; Lev. 23:40; Job 40:22; Isa. 44:4). Even when it was a sorrowful symbol of the exile in Babylon, the tree was associated with water (Ps. 137:1–2).

Willows, Wadi of the, a stream crossed by Moabite refugees carrying their belongings (Isa. 15:7). The most likely identification is the Seil el-Qurahi, the lower portion of the Wadi el-Hesa southeast of the Dead Sea. *See also* wadi.

winds. In the ancient Near East, winds were an important determinant of weather. In the rainless summer months moisture-laden winds from the Mediterranean (west or northwest) swept over the land during the daytime, moderating the midday heat and leaving a heavy dew at night. These steady winds enabled threshers to winnow grain (Ps. 1:4). In the winter months the western winds brought thunderstorms (1 Kings 18:45), which were always welcomed for their life-giving rain, despite their sometimes violent effects (e.g., shaking the forest, Isa. 7:2; agitating the sea, Ps. 107:25). Unstable weather between these two main seasons spawned the sirocco, the searing east or south wind that descended sporadically from the desert, blasting vegetation (Gen. 41:6; Ps. 103:16; Jon. 4:8), drying up water sources, and wrecking ships at sea (Ezek. 27:26). Striking in violent gusts (Job 1:19) or in a steady blast, it was often laden with suspended dust. According to the Bible, God used an east wind to dry up the flood (Gen. 8:1) and drive back the waters of the sea (Exod. 14:21). Altogether, the four winds of heaven described the extremities of the universe (Dan. 7:2; Matt. 24:31; Rev. 7:1).

Wind was a mysterious force, moving endlessly from unknown origin to unknown destination (Eccles. 1:6; John 3:8). It could be a symbol of transience (Ps. 78:39), fruitless striving (Eccles. 1:14), or empty talk (Jer. 5:13). It was also suggestive of untamed, irresistible power, whirling and scattering (Jer. 18:17) or tossing to and fro (Eph. 4:14). God alone could command the winds (Mark 4:41), sending them forth from heavenly storehouses (Jer. 10:13), riding upon them in the clouds (Pss. 18:10; 104:3; Ezek. 1:4), and commissioning them to do whatever was required (Exod. 15:10; Ps. 104:4). The Holy Spirit at Pentecost arrived with the sound of a mighty wind (Acts 2:2). *See also* whirlwind.   P.A.B.

wine. In the Bible, wine is considered luxurious and sometimes dangerous food (1 Sam. 1:14; Neh. 5:18; Prov. 20:1; 23:29–35; Isa. 25:6; 1 Tim. 3:18).

Wine ranked with oil as an important commercial crop, and the royal house played a major role in its production and trade. A large cellar was required to maintain the rich consumption of the court (Esther 1:1–9; Neh. 5:18), but wine was also an important commodity of exchange; Solomon paid Hiram of Tyre for timber and artisans with provisions of grain, wine, and oil (2 Chron. 2:10, 15). The king's storehouses and wine press (Zech. 14:10) were supplied from the produce of royal lands (1 Chron. 27:27) and from taxes in kind. Potsherds (Gk. *ostraca*) from Samaria record palace receipts of wine and oil from landowners in the region during the eighth century BCE.

Wine was produced by treading the grapes in a large vat connected to a smaller, lower vat by a channel. Fermentation began in the lower vat, where the juice was collected, and continued in jars or skins (Matt. 9:17). The grape harvest was a time of special joy (Isa. 16:10). Singing and shouting accompanied the work (Jer. 48:33), and dancing and feasting celebrated the vintage (Judg. 21:20–21).

Bread and wine represented the basic elements of food and drink (Judg. 19:19; Lam. 2:12), giving rise to metaphorical and symbolic uses (Prov. 4:17), including the Christian Eucharist (1 Cor. 11:23–26). But wine was especially identified with court dining and celebratory feasts (Esther 1:1–9; Dan. 1:5, 8, 16; 1 Sam. 25:36; John 2:1–10). It was frequently mixed with spices (Song of Sol. 8:2; Prov. 9:5).

Wine was generally viewed as a blessing (Gen. 27:28; Deut. 7:13) given by God to "gladden the human heart" (Ps. 104:15; cf. Eccles. 10:19). Wine suppresses pain and banishes misery in forgetfulness (Prov. 31:6). Its absence on special occasions such as weddings was a misfortune, and on one occasion Jesus remedied such a lack by miraculously changing water into wine (John 2:1–10). Wine was offered to God in Israelite worship (Lev. 23:13; Num. 28:14) and was employed medicinally to administer drugs (Matt. 27:34), to treat wounds (Luke 10:34), and to cure digestive ailments (1 Tim. 5:23).

Nevertheless, a glad heart could mean a dull mind (Hos. 4:11), making one irresponsible (Prov. 31:4), unwary of danger (2 Sam. 13:28), and easily manipulated (Gen. 19:32–35; Esther 5:4–10; 7:2). The drunkard is variously depicted as foolish or mad (Jer. 51:7), reeling and vomiting (Isa. 28:7–8), licentious (Rev. 18:3), or babbling incoherently (Acts 2:13). The wise are counseled to avoid strong drink (Prov. 23:29–31). Kings should abstain lest they pervert justice (31:4–5); bishops and deacons should be temperate (1 Tim. 3:3, 8); priests were prohibited from drinking on duty (Lev. 10:9); and Nazirites pledged abstinence for the duration of their vows (Num. 6:3–4, 20; cf. Luke 1:15). The itinerant Rechabites rejected all fruits of the vine as expressions of sedentary life (Jer. 35:7–9). *See also* vine. P.A.B.

wineskin. *See* bag; bottles; skins.

winnowing, the process by which threshed grain is separated from chaff, the extraneous, inedible stalks and husks (Ruth 3:2). In the ancient Near East, the threshed grain was mounded on a flat open surface or piled on a cloth, a wide but shallow basket, or a sieve. It was then raked or thrown into the air where the brisk afternoon wind removed the lighter chaff (Ps. 1:4). The heavier grain dropped back to the ground and was gathered, ready for sifting and the removing of pebbles by hand. Prevalent north and west winds provided a natural fanning mill for farmers to do their winnowing. The threshed and winnowed grain was then ready for use or for storage in granaries. John the Baptist used the process of winnowing as a metaphor for divine judgment (Matt. 3:12; Luke 3:17; cf. Jer. 15:7). *See also* threshing. P.L.C.

winnowing fork, the handheld device used by farmers to throw grain and straw into the air to let the wind carry the straw and chaff away while the heavier grain fell back to the ground for collection (Isa. 41:16). The winnowing fork needed multiple tines spaced closely together to hold nearly clean grain (30:24). *See also* sledge; winnowing. R.S.B.

wisdom, a term used in the Bible for many things ranging from the technical skill of the artisan (Exod. 36:8) to the art of government (1 Kings 3:12, 28). It also designates simple cleverness (2 Sam. 14:2), especially the practical skill of coping with life (Prov. 1; 5; 11; 14) and the pursuit of a lifestyle of proper ethical conduct (2:9–11). Wisdom is also seen as belonging properly to God (Job 28), associated with creation (Prov. 8:22–31), and identified with the Torah or law (Sir. 24:23). In the NT, wisdom is a prominent concern in Paul's letters to the Corinthians and in the Letter of James. In the former, Paul is concerned that faith rest, not on human wisdom, but on the power of God and the Holy Spirit (1 Cor. 2:5, 13), for "the wisdom of this world is foolishness with God" (3:19; cf. 1:17–25; 2:6–16; 2 Cor. 1:12). The Letter of James likewise tries to contrast the wisdom of this world with "wisdom from above" (3:17; cf. 13–18), i.e., wisdom that must be given by God (1:5). *See also* wisdom literature.

wisdom literature, a genre of literature represented by both biblical and extrabiblical writings. Prime examples of wisdom literature include the books of Proverbs, Job, and Ecclesiastes in addition to the apocryphal/deuterocanonical books of Sirach and Wisdom of Solomon. The extent to which other parts of the Bible can be described as fitting the genre of wisdom literature is disputed, but certain psalms (e.g., Ps. 37) and other passages (e.g., the story of Joseph in Gen. 37–50) certainly betray wisdom influences.

This literature has several characteristic traits. (1) There is an absence of reference to motifs typically associated with salvation, such as the ancestral promises, the exodus, the Sinai covenant, etc. (2) The object of the Hebrew sage is to transmit the lessons of experience, so that one may learn to cope with life. The teaching inculcates certain goals, such as self-control (especially in speech), honesty, and diligence. If one follows the counsels of the sage, wisdom will bring life; its opposite, folly—a practical, not merely intellectual, folly—brings destruction. (3) A characteristic problem to be discussed is retribution, i.e., the way in which the wise or virtuous fare in this life compared to the foolish or wrongdoers. Proverbs upholds a traditional view shared by such books as Deuteronomy, but Job and Ecclesiastes dispute this view. (4) Certain literary forms are cultivated: the discrete, separate saying, which is usually a pithy expression in two parallel lines; the admonition, whether positive or negative, which is often accompanied by a motivational clause; wisdom poems (typified by Prov. 1–9); and reflections (characteristic of Ecclesiastes). The book of Job is dominated by disputation speeches between the protagonist and his counselors (chaps. 3–31).

Solomon was famous in biblical tradition for his wisdom (1 Kings 4:29–34), so Proverbs and Ecclesiastes came to be attributed to him. In broader terms, the origins of the Israelite wisdom tradition are presumed to lie in the insights, oral and written, of family and tribal groups and with the scribes or sages, who would have provided training for courtiers in Jerusalem. The existence of some kind of "school" may be inferred from similar institutions in Mesopotamia and Egypt. Wisdom, in fact, is an international possession, cultivated throughout the ancient Near East, and many parallels to Israelite wisdom traditions have been proposed (e.g., in the teaching of the Egyptian sage Amenemopet and Prov. 22:17–24:22).

An outstanding trait of biblical wisdom is the personification of Wisdom as a divine female entity in Prov. 1; 3; 9 (cf. Job 28; Sir. 24). She is described as originating from God and is associated with creation (Prov. 3:19; 8:22–31). She is, in essence, the self-revelation of creation and the revelation of God in and through creation (Ps. 19:1).

In the NT: The wisdom tradition remains evident in some portions of the NT. Jesus is presented in the Synoptic Gospels as a wise teacher, and many of the sayings attributed to him are cast in the aphoristic style of the sages (e.g., Matt. 6:19–7:27). The wisdom of Jesus is said to be "greater than Solomon" (Luke 11:31; cf. Mark 6:2). In Matt. 11:2–19 and Luke 7:18–35, Jesus is implicitly designated as wisdom in a manner that recalls the personification of Wisdom as a divine (female) figure in Proverbs. Words attributed to the Wisdom of God in Luke 11:49–51 are attributed to Jesus in Matt. 23:34–36. Also, like Wisdom in Prov. 8, Jesus issues an invitation to all to follow him and take up his yoke (Matt. 11:28–30). Likewise, in John's Gospel, the presentation of Jesus as an incarnation of the divine Word (Gk. *logos*, 1:1–18) parallels the personification of Wisdom in books that belong to the genre of wisdom literature (Gk. *sophia*, Prov. 8; Sir. 24; Bar. 3:9–4:4; Wis. 7–9).

The Letter of James is usually named as the NT book that best fits into the genre of wisdom literature. Two features are especially noted. First, James tries to reason with his readers. He uses expressions like, "Come now, you rich people . . ." (5:1) and "Come now, you who say . . ." (4:13). His letter is peppered with words like "because" and "for," which introduce reasons for the points that he is making (1:3–4, 20, 23; 2:10–11, 13, 26; 3:1–2, 16; 4:14), and "therefore" and "so," which introduce conclusions to be derived from what he has said (1:21; 2:17, 23; 4:12, 17; 5:7, 16). Sometimes, James asks his readers to consider the benefit or profit of their actions: "What good is it?" (2:14); "What is the good of that?" (2:16; see also 1:16, 20, 26; 2:20, 26; 4:5). Second, James uses secular images drawn from the world at large: the billowing sea (1:6); the scorching sun (1:11); a reflection in a mirror (1:23–24); a horse's bridle (3:3); a ship's rudder (3:4); a forest fire (3:5); domestication of animals (3:7); a freshwater spring (3:11); a fig tree (3:12); a grapevine (3:12); saltwater (3:13); a vanishing mist (4:14); and the rainy seasons for crops (5:7). In both of these ways, James presents his teaching as "common sense"—he is advocating the wisest course of action, as should be obvious from logical reasoning and observation of nature. *See also* Ecclesiastes, book of; Job, book of; logos; Proverbs, book of; Sirach; Sophia; Wisdom of Solomon.

Bibliography

Murphy, Roland E. *Wisdom Literature*. Eerdmans, 1981.

Von Rad, Gerhard. *Wisdom in Israel*. Abingdon, 1972.

Wilken, Robert L., ed. *Aspects of Wisdom in Judaism and Early Christianity*. University of Notre Dame Press, 1975.　　　　R.E.M./M.A.P.

Wisdom of Jesus Son of Sirach. *See* Sirach.

Wisdom of Solomon, a poetic discourse composed in Greek by a Hellenistic Jew, probably in Alexandria, Egypt. The latest likely occasion for its composition is the persecution of Egyptian Jews under Gaius Caligula in 38–41 CE, although dates as early as the last half of the first century BCE have also been suggested. The writer assumes the identity of Solomon (cf. 7:1–14; 8:17–9:18; 1 Kings 3:6–

9) to speak in praise of wisdom and righteousness and to warn against the folly of oppression and idolatry. Although the wicked may seem to prosper in this life, they are not aware, he claims, that they must face a future judgment (4:20). Righteousness, however, is immortal (1:15). The book has survived as a part of the LXX. It is considered a part of the Apocrypha by Protestant Christians and is regarded as one of the deuterocanonical writings by Roman Catholic and Eastern Orthodox Christians.

OUTLINE OF CONTENTS

The Wisdom of Solomon

I. A discourse on the justice of God (1:1–5:23)

II. In praise of wisdom as a guide for life (6:1–9:18)

III. Wisdom as a key to history, from Adam to Moses (10:1–12:27)

IV. The origins and forms of idolatry (13:1–15:17)

V. A case in point: the Egyptians and the Israelites in the exodus (15:18–19:22)

The initial discourse (chaps. 1–5) proclaims that "Because the Spirit of the Lord has filled the world . . . no one who utters unrighteous things will escape notice" (1:7–8). The ungodly have made a covenant with death, and, assuming this life to be the whole of existence, they live as they please and oppress the righteous. With allusions to the Enoch tradition (4:10–15) as well as to Second Isaiah's "suffering servant" (5:1–8; cf. Isa. 52:13–53:12), the discourse speaks of a righteous one who was persecuted but, to the consternation of his persecutors, will come to be numbered among the heavenly beings at the final judgment (5:5). A parallel account of martyrdom among Egyptian Jewry—perhaps even related to the same occasion if the Wisdom of Solomon is from the time of Caligula—is the account of the death of the righteous Eleazar in 4 Maccabees. The latter goes beyond the Wisdom of Solomon by appropriating the theme of vicarious atonement found in Isa. 52:13–53:12 (see 4 Macc. 6:27–30).

The second section of the Wisdom of Solomon picks up the story of Solomon, the king who chose wisdom over all the gifts that God might give (cf. 1 Kings 3:5–9), and advocates that all rulers should seek Wisdom (personified as a woman, as in Prov. 8:22–31; Sir. 24) in order to rule wisely and justly. The woman Wisdom is defined as God's spirit, intelligent, holy, the fashioner of all things, an emanation of God's glory, a reflection of eternal light, and an image of divine goodness (7:22–26). The passage clearly understands Wisdom in terms of Hellenistic philosophy, in a manner similar to Philo's *logos* or rationality of God, a subordinate agent responsible for creation.

Chaps. 10–12 then use the theme of personified Wisdom as a key for unlocking the secrets of history from Adam to Moses, revealing God's providence through history as well as through creation. Curiously, it pictures Wisdom as protecting Adam and delivering him from his transgression. Cain thus becomes the first to perish through folly (10:1–3). At the end of this section, the book shifts its attention to the idolatry of the Egyptians and Canaanites to demonstrate that people are appropriately punished by means of the very things through which they sin (11:16).

The writer then turns to a discussion of the roots of idolatry that suggests several different theories of its origin (13:1–15:17). One theory is that humanity was led by the beauty of God's creation to worship the natural phenomena and then subsequently assumed that it could fabricate gods in accord with this. Another suggestion is that parents made statues to remember dead children, and kings created images to impose their authority at a distance, so that out of the grief of parents and the vanity of kings the cults and secret mysteries of paganism arose.

The Wisdom of Solomon concludes (15:18–19:22) by turning to the exodus to demonstrate the theory of poetic justice enunciated earlier (cf. 11:16). The ultimate irony is that the Egyptians, who had imprisoned the people of God, are themselves captives of the power of darkness. In developing this idea, the writer explores the Hellenistic idea of the psychological self-punishment of the guilty (chap. 17; cf. Philo Flaccus 162–80). The radical drama of liberation is symbolized through the image of the transformation of nature, so that fire burns in water and yet has no power over human flesh (19:18–21).

The Wisdom of Solomon claims to address alien kings in order to teach them how to rule wisely, but its real audience was probably the Hellenistic Jewish community in Alexandria, and its purpose was to support that community in facing persecution and resisting the dangers of idolatry in a pagan culture. See also Apocrypha/deuterocanonical literature; immortality; Sirach; wisdom literature.   D.W.S.

wise men, sages who appear in the biblical traditions within the context of an international wisdom movement (on Egyptian, Persian, and Babylonian wise men, see Gen. 41:8; Esther 1:13; Dan. 2:12).

Wise men functioned in Israel in at least three settings: the tribe, the court, and the school. In each case, the wisdom shared was generally practical, concerned with knowledge about the principles governing the world and the life of the individual. The usual form of instruction was the proverb. Wisdom was based on reason rather than revelation, but on reason enlightened by piety, for "the fear of the Lord is the beginning of wisdom" (Prov. 9:10). According to Deut. 1:13–15, wise men were selected for the tribes in the days of Moses to provide instruction in the law as well

as from their own understanding and experience. A professional class of wise men developed (Jer. 18:18; Isa. 29:14) along with priests and prophets. Some served at the royal court to guide rulers and preserve, as scribes, the sacred traditions (Jer. 8:8–9; 18:18). Finally, professional wise men provided instruction in schools they established (Sir. 51:23). Proverbs, Job, Ecclesiastes, Sirach, and the Wisdom of Solomon are thought to have been composed by professional sages. The preeminent wise man in Israel's traditions was Solomon, whose "wisdom surpassed the wisdom of all the people of the east" (1 Kings 4:30). Occasionally, the traditions speak of the "wise woman" (2 Sam. 14:2; 20:16).

The NRSV translates the Greek word magoi ("magi") as "wise men" in Matt. 2:1, but the persons referred to in that story were not sages (Gk. sophoi). In 23:34, Jesus speaks of "prophets, sages [sophoi], and scribes." See also magi; wisdom; wisdom literature.   A.J.H.

witness (Heb. 'ed; Gk. martys), in the legal sphere, one who speaks from personal experience about what happened to oneself or another. This may occur at a trial (Deut. 17:6; Prov. 19:28; Mark 14:63) or a legal transaction (Isa. 8:2; Jer. 32:10). It is in this legal sense that two or three witnesses must be called upon to corroborate certain accusations (Matt. 26:60; 2 Cor. 13:1; Heb. 10:28). Bearing false witness is roundly condemned (Exod. 20:16; Prov. 12:17; Acts 6:13) and can bring severe reprisal (Deut. 19:16–21; Prov. 21:28). In a more symbolic sense, a pillar or altar of rocks was sometimes built as a visible "witness" to an action, such as a covenantal agreement (Gen. 31:44; Josh. 22:27, 34; Isa. 19:19–20). God is also called upon as an invisible witness to a person's or nation's conduct (1 Sam. 12:15; Rom. 1:9; Jer. 29:23; Mic. 1:2).

The term takes on several specialized meanings in the NT, where it refers to a person present at the ministry, death, resurrection, and ascension of Jesus (Luke 24:48; Acts 1:22) or to one who attests to the truth about God (John 8:17–18; Rev. 1:5; 11:3). The "cloud of witnesses" in Heb. 12:1 compares the multitude who have suffered but retained their faith to the great crowd of spectators at a Greco-Roman athletic contest, whose presence spurs the contestants to give their best efforts. The English word martyr is derived from a transliteration of the Greek word martyrs, meaning "witness." See also testimony.   D.R.E.

wizard, one who practiced such things as magic, sorcery, divination, or necromancy. The word can refer to either a man or a woman. Israel was forbidden to consult wizards (Lev. 19:31; Isa. 8:19). They were banned as early as the reign of Saul in the late eleventh century BCE (1 Sam. 28:3), although Saul did consult a female diviner to raise up the ghost of Samuel (28:9). King Josiah (640–609 BCE) also banned wizards (2 Kings 23:24) after they had gained a foothold during the reign of Manasseh (687/6–642 BCE; 21:6). *See also* divination; magic.

wolf, a member of the species *Canus lupus,* large members of the dog family. The only literal references to such an animal are found in Isa. 11:6; 65:25; and John 10:12. All other usages are metaphorical references to the wolf's hunger (Gen. 49:7) or to its vicious, fierce, or ravenous conduct toward the innocent (Ezek. 22:27; Hab. 1:8; Zeph. 3:3; Acts 20:29). Jesus told his disciples that he was sending them out "like sheep into the midst of wolves" (Matt. 10:16; cf. Luke 10:3). He also compared false prophets to wolves "in sheep's clothing" (Matt. 7:15).

wonders. *See* miracles; sign.

wood. A highly valued resource in the ancient Near East, wood was used for the manufacture of everything from small everyday household items to the palaces of kings and temples and altars of deities. It was especially important as fuel for domestic hearths and industrial installations such as kilns, metal smelters, and forges. It was also used for sacrificial fires (Gen. 22:7; Num. 19:6). Wood was valuable as an export commodity to countries whose timber resources were limited. Luxury woods such as ebony were imported (Ezek. 27:15). Cedar (from Lebanon) was preferred for the construction of items meant to last, such as buildings and furniture. Pine, oak, cypress, and sycamore were also popular as construction materials. Noah used gopher wood (cypress) to build the ark (Gen. 6:14). Olive wood was used by Solomon for the cherubim in the inner sanctuary that housed the ark of the covenant (1 Kings 6:23), and the tabernacle was made of acacia wood (Heb. *shittah;* Exod. 26:15). Sturdy poplar and oak were favored for implementing hafts and roofing. The very light wood of the palm had a broad range of uses.   P.L.C.

wool, the fleece of a sheep, used in the ancient Near East for clothing (Lev. 13:47–48; Ezek. 34:3). White wool was one of the principal products traded by Damascus to Tyre (Ezek. 27:18). The wool of a hundred thousand rams had to be paid by Mesha, king of Moab, as tribute to Ahab, king of Israel (2 Kings 3:4). The color of undyed wool became a symbol of purity (Isa. 1:18) and whiteness (Dan. 7:9; Rev. 1:14).

word, in the Bible a term (Heb. *dabar,* Gk. *logos*) that almost always refers to something that is spoken, usually an entire message uttered either by a human being or by God. The expressions "word of God" or "word of the LORD" typically denote self-revelation of God's will and purpose. The scriptures themselves are called the Word of God by Jesus (Mark 7:13), but the expression "word of God" in the Bible does not usually refer to the written word.

In the Hebrew Bible, *dabar* is only occasionally used for human speech (Ps. 19:14); more often, it refers to some announcement, proclamation, or commandment of God. God creates the heavens and the earth by speaking (Gen. 1:3, 6, 9, 11, 14, 20, 24, 26). God utters the words of the Decalogue before writing them on tablets (Exod. 20:1; cf. 24:12). Prophets likewise hear and speak what God has spoken to them (Isa. 1:2; 6:8–10), for they are primarily recipients and transmitters of the word of the Lord (Jer. 1:2). God's word carries within itself the power to accomplish that of which it speaks, as God indicates in Isa. 55:11: "So shall my word be that goes out from my mouth; it shall not return to me empty, but it shall accomplish that which I purpose, and succeed in the thing for which I sent it."

In the NT, Jesus preaches the word (Mark 2:2), and the gospel of Jesus Christ proclaimed by his followers is called the word of God (Acts 4:31; 1 Pet. 1:23–25). In an explanation of his parable of the Sower, Jesus indicates how the word is received by different people, who are typified as different types of soil (Mark 4:14–20; cf. 4–9). Eventually, Jesus himself would be identified as God's Word (*logos*) made flesh (John 1:1, 14; cf. Rev. 19:13). The notion of God's word as a dynamic, powerful force evident in Isa. 55:11 (cited above) is also evident in the NT. Heb. 4:12 says, "The word of God is living and active, sharper than any two-edged sword, piercing until it divides soul from spirit, joints from marrow; it is able to judge the thoughts and intentions of the heart." *See also* creation; logos; prophet.   D.M.S./M.A.P.

world, the. In the Hebrew Bible, God is Creator of the heavens and the earth (Gen. 1:1–2:3). There is considerable reflection on the Creator's role in establishing the earth and everything in, above, and under it (Job 38), including humankind (Gen. 1:26–28; 2:7, 15–24; Ps. 8:3–8). The world is therefore God's possession or property: "The earth is the LORD's and all that is in it, the world, and those who live in it" (Ps. 24:1). God's sovereignty over the world is stressed; God rules the world and judges it with righteousness (9:8).

The NT employs two Greek words for world, *kosmos* (transliterated into English as "cosmos"), which generally refers to the physical world, and *oikoumenē*, which generally refers to the inhabited world, or the "people of the world." This distinction does not always bear out, however, and the words can be used as synonyms. A third term, *aiōn* ("eon" or "age"), has temporal connotations and is used in some English Bibles in such phrases as "the world to come."

When Paul says that "in Christ, God was reconciling the world" (2 Cor. 5:19), there is no doubt that, in his view, the world is estranged from God and, so, in need of reconciliation. Thus, in the NT, "the world" can be the arena dominated by sin, which alienates people from God. Indeed, Paul refers to the devil as "the god of this world" (4:4). Nevertheless, because of what God has done in

Christ, "the form of this world is passing away" (1 Cor. 7:31). Thus Paul can urge the Romans not to be conformed to this world (12:2). The book of Revelation likewise says that "the kingdom of the world has become the kingdom of our Lord" (11:15).

In the Gospel of John, the world is the object of God's salvation in Christ (3:16; 12:47). It is God's creation through Christ (1:3, 10). Yet the world apart from Christ stands under judgment (16:8–11), hating Jesus's followers, who have been separated from the world and are not of the world (17:16). The dualism between God, Christ, and the disciples, on the one hand, and the world, on the other, is described in terms of a sharp antinomy. Disciples are urged to have nothing to do with the world, especially to not love it (cf. 1 John 2:15–17). At the same time, Jesus does not pray for disciples to be taken out of the world (John 17:15).

In general, the NT views the world as a mission field. In the Gospel of Matthew, Jesus calls his disciples the "light of the world" (5:14; cf. John 8:18), sends them to make disciples of all nations (28:19), and says that the "good news of the kingdom will be proclaimed throughout the world, as a testimony to all the nations" before the end will come (24:14). In Acts, Jesus informs the disciples that they shall be witnesses to the end of the earth (1:8), and those witnesses are later identified as people who turn the world "upside down" (17:6). *See also* creation.   D.M.S./M.A.P.

worms, the members of the phylum *Annelida* as well as the larvae of numerous insects. Most biblical references to worms are probably to larvae or maggots because of their association with death and decay (Job 7:5; 21:26; Isa. 14:11; Acts 12:23; Mark 9:48). Some sort of a worm assaulted a vine that gave shelter to Jonah (4:7). The worm's appetite for wool serves as a metaphor for the destruction God will send on Israel's enemies (Isa. 51:8).

wormwood, a shrublike plant that belongs to the aster family and has a bitter taste. Numerous species of wormwood are found in the Near East, the most common being *Artemisia herba-alba*. The plant is often used as a metaphor for bitterness and sorrow (Prov. 5:4; Lam. 3:15, 19; Amos 5:7; 6:12). In Jer. 9:15 and 23:15, God's punishment of the people of Israel is described in images of wormwood to eat and poisoned water to drink. Rev. 8:11 describes a star called "Wormwood" falling to earth, turning part of the waters into wormwood and killing many people.

worship in the Hebrew Bible. The Hebrew Bible presents worship as a basic human response to God, a response that acknowledges God's worth, often with praise and adoration. To worship God is to ascribe to God the glory that God's name is due (1 Chron. 16:9). The basic Hebrew term for worship (*khawah*) has a root meaning of "to bow down" or "to prostrate oneself" (the same is actually true of the Greek word *proskyneō*,

used for "worship" in the LXX and NT). Thus, the act of worship always assumes a recognition of the individual or community's particular relationship with God (Ps. 95:6).

The Hebrew Bible presents God as desirous of worship and as actually demanding it (Exod. 23:25). God is also a jealous God and is provoked to anger when the Israelites worship any other god (Exod. 20:5; 34:14). Indeed, the psalmist looks forward to the day when all the families and nations of the earth will worship the God of Israel (Ps. 22:27; cf. 102:22).

The primary institutions for worship in the Hebrew Bible are the tabernacle and the temple, but God could be—and certainly was—worshiped, glorified, and praised in noninstitutional settings as well (e.g., 1 Kings 1:47; cf. Mark 14:26). Worship was typically public, however, and the centralization of public, communal worship in Jerusalem was intended to unify the monarchy and to bring a conformity to worship practices that would subvert idolatrous activities that had come to be associated with worship at high places and other sites that had previously been acceptable (e.g., 1 Sam. 1:3; 2 Sam. 15:8; cf. 1 Kings 12:30).

With regard to content, the actual modes of worship seem to have included acclamations of verbal praise (e.g., shouting, Pss. 81:1; 89:15), clapping hands (47:1), playing musical instruments (150), dancing (149:3), and singing (13:6; Exod. 15:21). The primary mode of worship, however, was sacrifice (Deut. 12:4–6). Although Israelites called their sacrifices "the food of God" (Lev. 21:6), they did not believe that God literally needed their sacrifices for food (Ps. 50:12–13). The sacrifices were offered as gifts to honor God (Prov. 3:9). Likewise, the Israelites believed that God was honored by their obedience to Torah, so

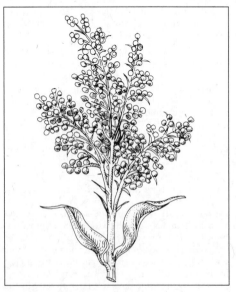

Wormwood (*Artemisia judaica*).

living in a manner that was pleasing to God became a mode of worship.

The Hebrew Bible is also attentive to the spirit in which worship is to be offered. Isaiah bemoans those who worship with their lips but not with their hearts, because their worship is only something "learned by rote" (29:13). The phrase "worship in holy splendor" occurs frequently, indicating a proper reverence for God (1 Chron. 16:29; Pss. 29:2; 96:9). Joy is also a prominent aspect of worship (Ps. 81:1; Isa. 12:6), and Ps. 100:2 commends worshiping "with gladness." *See also* festivals, feasts, and fasts; priests; sacrifice; temple, the.

Bibliography

Brueggemann, Walter. *Worship in Ancient Israel: The Essential Guide.* Abingdon, 2005.   M.A.P.

worship in the New Testament.

In the NT, worship usually refers to expression of praise or thanksgiving (Luke 17:15–16). Sometimes, it implies obeisance as an attitude for supplication (Matt. 8:2). In either case it is the appropriate human response to the magnificent glory of God. Summons and encouragement to worship abound (Col. 4:2; Heb. 13:15), and the centrality of worship is evident in a book such as the Gospel of Luke, which opens and closes with scenes depicting worshipers (1:8; 24:52–53) and contains twenty-one specific references to people glorifying, praising, or giving thanks to God. Likewise, the book of Revelation is inundated with images of worship.

Patterns for public Christian worship seem to have developed through adaptation of synagogue liturgies. Even though Acts portrays the earliest disciples of Jesus continuing to worship in the Jerusalem temple (2:46), the sacrificial cult associated with that institution came to be viewed as obsolete in NT writings (Heb. 9:11–12, 24–26). Synagogue worship, however, was oriented mainly around prayer and teaching, and the NT depicts Christian worship from the first as also involving participation in a sacred meal. Indeed, the Acts text cited above depicts even those believers who continued to worship in the temple as also gathering regularly for "the breaking of bread" (2:46). This meal appears to have had features in common with both Jewish festivals (particularly Passover) and Hellenistic symposia (social banquets). Paul contrasts the Christian celebration with pagan meals in 1 Cor. 10:14–22.

The book of Acts describes Christians gathering to worship daily (2:46), but also notes a preference for the "first day of the week" (20:7; cf. 1 Cor. 16:2). Locations for worship appear to be deemed irrelevant by some NT texts (Matt. 18:20); when locations are designated, the most typical gathering places are homes of community members (Acts 2:46; 1 Cor. 16:19). As for content, the NT never describes a Christian worship service in any detail. Reconstruction of such services or reflection on their general nature employs three sources.

First, the NT writings incorporate materials that were no doubt used in early Christian worship. These include hymns (Luke 1:46–55), doxologies (Rom. 16:25–27), prayers (Matt. 6:1–13), and creedal or confessional statements (1 Cor. 15:3–5). The existence of such materials indicates a fairly high degree of liturgical development.

Second, although no liturgy for Christian worship is ever prescribed, elements of worship are often mentioned. These include characteristic features of the Jewish service: prayer (1 Tim. 2:1–2, 8), singing (Eph. 5:19), teaching (Acts 2:42), preaching (Phil. 1:15–18), collection of offerings (1 Cor. 16:2), and the public reading of scripture (1 Tim. 4:13). The last was transformed early, in that new writings came to be read alongside the scriptures, including works that eventually became part of the NT (1 Thess. 5:27; Rev. 1:3). In some locations, these standard elements of worship were supplemented by the practice of spiritual gifts such as speaking in tongues and prophesying (1 Cor. 14:24–33). Also mentioned frequently are two chief rituals of Christian worship, baptism (Matt. 28:19; Rom. 6:1–11) and the eucharistic meal (Mark 14:16–26; 1 Cor. 11:23–26). Other rituals include foot washing (John 13:3–15), anointing with oil (Mark 6:13; James 5:14), exchanging a kiss of peace (1 Pet. 5:14), and the laying on of hands, which may have been associated with prayer (Acts 28:8), reception of the Spirit (8:17), or ordination (13:3; 1 Tim. 5:22).

Third, more explicit descriptions of worship services are found in writings shortly after the NT period, such as the *Didache* (ca. 100 CE) and the first *Apology* of Justin Martyr (ca. 155 CE). These documents list several of the features mentioned above in what appear to be fixed chronological order. Justin's *Apology* is merely descriptive, but the *Didache* attempts to define or regulate what it regards as normative procedure.

The NT takes over the concern of Hebrew prophets that worship be integrated into the life of faith. Thus, passages that prioritize mercy over sacrifice (Hos. 6:6) or decry worship with lips but not heart (Isa. 29:13) are quoted in new contexts (Matt. 9:13; Mark 7:6–7). Genuine worship is not merely for show (Matt. 6:1–18); it involves surrender of the self to God in faithful obedience (Rom. 12:1).

The most distinctive theological characteristic of NT worship is the centrality of Christ as its rationale, mediator, and ultimate object. First, what Christ has done becomes the principal reason for praising God (1 Cor. 1:4). This perspective colors Luke's narrative of the crucifixion, where the death of Jesus itself becomes an occasion for glorifying God (23:47). At another level, thanks are given to God not only *for* Jesus Christ, but "*through* Jesus Christ" (Rom. 1:8; Heb. 13:15). A common theme in John's Gospel is that the Father is glorified through the Son (17:4). Since God is unseen Spirit, those who would worship in Spirit and in truth must worship the God made known through the Son (1:18; 4:24). Finally, Christ is depicted as one who is himself worthy of receiving worship (Phil. 2:9–11; Rev. 6:11–14). The Gospel of Matthew relates its story of Jesus from this perspective, presenting Jesus as a recipient of worship nine times during his life on earth (e.g., 2:11; 14:33; 28:9). In light of 4:10, such worship is not merely homage or respect, but, in the mind of this evangelist, evidence that Christ is now accorded what is normally the exclusive prerogative of God.

Christ-centered worship is definitively historical and eschatological in orientation. It simultaneously reflects upon the revelation of God in the life and ministry of the earthly Jesus and anticipates the consummation of all things. This dual focus is evident in much of the worship material preserved in NT writings, including hymns (Phil. 2:6–11) and the eucharistic liturgy (1 Cor. 11:23–26).

Bibliography

Hahn, Ferdinand. *The Worship of the Early Church*. Fortress, 1973.

Peterson, David P. *Engaging with God: A Biblical Theology of Worship*. Eerdmans, 1992.   M.A.P.

wrath, when attributed to God, an active response to human sin, particularly idolatry. In the biblical perspective, God is holy and righteous and rejects everything that is not. That rejection manifests itself in such situations as the destruction of Sodom and Gomorrah (Deut. 29:23), the chastisement of Moses for his reluctance to obey God's instructions (Exod. 4:14), and the death of Uzzah for touching the ark of God with his profane hand (2 Sam. 6:7). The wrath of God is thus a divine reaction to human provocation, not a consequence of arbitrary passion or animosity. God is also depicted as "slow to anger" (Ps. 103:8; Joel 2:13). In the NT, the angry reaction of Jesus against those who, in his view, have desecrated the temple (John 2:13–17) bears the characteristics of divine wrath. Wrath is also an essential part of Paul's theology; he often mentions that the wrath of God comes upon human disobedience and transgression (Rom 1:18; 2:5, 8; 5:9; 9:22; Eph. 2:3; 5:6; Col. 3:6;

1 Thess. 1:10). *See also* judgment, day of; mercy.
S.B.

wrestle. The only literal reference to wrestling in the Bible is found in the story of Jacob at Bethel. He wrestled with a messenger of God during the night and emerged triumphant (Gen. 32:24, 25; cf. Hos. 12:5). Even though his hip was put out of joint, he would not let the messenger go until he blessed him. The messenger told him that his name would henceforth be "Israel," because he had striven with God and with humans and prevailed (a possible meaning of the name "Israel" is "one who strives with God"). In a similar but more figurative vein, Rachel named a son "Naphtali," because she said, "With mighty wrestlings, I have wrestled with my sister, and have prevailed" (Gen. 30:8; the name Naphtali is similar to *niphtal*, the Hebrew word for "wrestle"). The figurative wrestling in this case concerned the competition between Rachel and her sister, Leah, to bear sons with their mutual husband, Jacob. Finally, Col. 4:12 refers to Epaphras as a servant of Christ Jesus who is "always wrestling in his prayers" on behalf of the Colossians.   J.L.C.

writing. Writing was invented in the ancient Near East sometime before the beginning of the third millennium BCE. It appeared first in southern Mesopotamia and soon afterward in the Nile Valley. Various systems of writing developed, but all eventually gave way to the alphabet. Alphabetic writing was an important part of the culture of ancient Israel and the early church, and there are numerous references to writing and to written documents in the Bible.

Writing Systems: By the latter centuries of the fourth millennium BCE a pictographic writing system was in use along the lower Euphrates. It evolved into the cuneiform script of the Sumerians, which the Semitic-speaking inhabitants of Mesopotamia inherited. Cuneiform, therefore,

---

CHRISTIAN WORSHIP IN THE SECOND CENTURY

A Christian theologian known as Justin Martyr (110–165 CE) provides the earliest extant description of Christian worship outside the NT itself:

On the day called Sunday, all who live in cities or in the country gather together to one place, and the memoirs of the apostles or the writings of the prophets are read, as long as time permits; then, when the reader has ceased, the president verbally instructs, and exhorts to the imitation of these good things. Then we all rise together and pray, and . . . when our prayer is ended, bread and wine and water are brought, and the president in like manner offers prayers and thanksgivings, according to his ability, and the people assent, saying Amen; and there is a distribution to each, and a participation of that over which thanks have been given, and to those who are absent a portion is sent by the deacons. And they who are well to do, and willing, give what each thinks fit; and what is collected is deposited with the president, who succors the orphans and widows and those who, through sickness or any other cause, are in want, and those who are in bonds and the strangers sojourning among us, and in a word takes care of all who are in need. But Sunday is the day on which we all hold our common assembly, because it is the first day on which God, having wrought a change in the darkness and matter, made the world; and Jesus Christ our Savior on the same day rose from the dead.

Justin Martyr *First Apology* 66

became the writing system of both the Babylonians and Assyrians, and from them it was borrowed and adapted to the languages of several other peoples, including the Hurrians, the Hittites, and the Urartians. Characteristically, cuneiform, or "wedge writing," was impressed on wet clay tablets using a reed stylus with a wedge-shaped tip. The individual signs, composed of combinations of wedges, included both ideograms (signs representing entire words or ideas) and phonograms (signs representing sounds). The phonograms were syllabic, representing combinations of vowels and consonants. The system as a whole was extremely complex and cumbersome in comparison to the alphabetic system that eventually displaced it. A Mesopotamian scribe was obliged to undertake a long and difficult apprenticeship.

Egyptian writing may have emerged under indirect influence from Mesopotamia. In Egypt, however, the pictorial character of the early script was retained. This was true at least of hieroglyphic, the pictographic writing used for monumental inscriptions. As in the case of the cuneiform signs, the individual hieroglyphs included both ideograms and phonograms. In this case, however, the phonograms were alphabetic, representing one or more consonantal sounds, rather than syllabic. There were two cursive derivatives of hieroglyphic, called hieratic and demotic. Hieratic seems to have been developed in very early times, but the oldest demotic documents come from the end of the eighth century BCE. Like his Mesopotamian counterpart, an Egyptian scribe had to study for many years to master the complexities of the writing system.

The alphabet was invented in the Near East in the first half of the second millennium BCE. It was based on a consonantal principle that suggests an initial Egyptian influence. In contrast to Egyptian hieroglyphic, however, the alphabet employed no ideograms, and each of its phonograms represented a single consonantal sound. The signs were pictographic at first, but they soon evolved into abstract, linear shapes. The earliest undisputed examples of alphabetic writing date to the end of the Middle Bronze Age, ca. 1550 BCE. These are the Proto-Sinaitic inscriptions, graffiti scratched on stone by Asiatic laborers in an Egyptian turquoise-mining community at modern Serabit el-Khadem in the southwestern area of the Sinai Peninsula. The alphabet was in general use in the city-states of Syria and Canaan during the Late Bronze Age (ca. 1550–1200 BCE), and in the first millennium specialized national or regional branches developed. Among these was the Hebrew alphabet, which was used in Israel and Judah until the exile (587/6 BCE). Another branch, which developed in the Aramean states of southern and central Syria, was adopted along with the Aramaic language for the official use of the Assyrian, Babylonian, and Persian empires. The Aramaic alphabet eventually replaced most local systems throughout the imperial region. After the sixth century BCE most Jewish literature was written with the Aramaic script.

Cuneiform tablet from Ebla, ca. 2400 BCE.

Sometime before the eighth century BCE the Greeks learned the alphabet from the Phoenicians. By adding vowel signs to the purely consonantal signs of the Phoenicians, they improved the system and produced an alphabet that is the direct ancestor of the one we still use today. Although the alphabet coexisted for centuries with the ancient systems of Mesopotamia and Egypt and several other forms of writing, it eventually triumphed over them all. This was at least in part a consequence of its economy and utility. It was much simpler and more flexible than its competitors, and it made widespread literacy possible for the first time. Given the tenacity with which traditional writing systems are maintained, however, it seems unlikely that the obvious advantages of alphabetic writing would have been enough to displace the older systems in the absence of other factors. Of these the most important was probably its selection as the primary medium of international communication for five empires. The Assyrians adopted the Aramaic alphabet for use in the imperial chancelleries, establishing a convention that the Babylonians and Persians inherited, and in the Hellenistic and Roman worlds the Greek and Latin alphabets held sway.

Writing Materials: Various materials served as writing surfaces. Inscriptions intended to be permanent were most often incised in stone. Thus we have stone stelae and monumental inscriptions in Mesopotamian cuneiform—with wedges engraved in stone to imitate those impressed in clay—and Egyptian hieroglyphic. Many alphabetic texts cut in stone have been found in Syria and Canaan, and there are references in the Bible to stone inscriptions (Josh. 8:32) and their imperishability (Job 19:24). Recent discoveries, however, suggest that during the period of the Israelite and Judean monarchies there was a practice of

SINAITIC SCRIPT	DESCRIPTION OF SIGN	CANAANITE SCRIPT OF 13TH CENT B.C.	CANAANITE SCRIPT OF ca 1000 B.C	SOUTH ARAB SCRIPT OF IRON AGE	MODERN HEBREW SCRIPT	PHONETIC VALUE
	OX-HEAD				א	ʾ
	HOUSE				ב	b
	?				ג	g
	FISH				ד	d
	MAN PRAYING				ה	h
	?				ו	w
	?				ז	z
	?					ḏ
	FENCE?				ח	ḥ
	DOUBLE LOOP					ẖ
	?					ṭ
	?					y
	PALM OF HAND				כ	k
	"OX-GOAD"					l
	WATER				מ	m
	SERPENT				נ	n
	?				ס	s
	EYE					ʿ
	?					ġ
	THROW STICK					p
	?					ṣ
	BLOSSOM					ḏ ẓ
	?					q
	HUMAN HEAD				ר	r
	BOW					ś š
	?					š
	MARK OF CROSS				ת	t

HEBREW NAME	PHOENICIAN SCRIPT OF 8TH CENT B.C. BAAL LEBANON KARATEPE	OLD GREEK SCRIPT OF 8TH CEN B.C	HEBREW CURSIVE OF ca 600 B.C	GREEK NAME	MODERN GREEK SCRIPT	MODERN ROMAN SCRIPT
ALEPH				ALPHA	A	A
BETH				BETA	B	B
GIMEL				GAMMA	Γ	G
DALETH				DELTA	Δ	D
HE				EPSILON	E	E
WAW						V
ZAYIN				ZETA	Z	Z
HETH				ETA	H	H
TETH				THETA	Θ	
YOD				IOTA	I	I
KAPH				KAPPA	K	K
LAMED				LAMBDA	Λ	L
MEM				MU	M	M
NUN				NU	N	N
SAMEKH				XI	Ξ	
AYIN				OMICRON	O	O
PE				PI	Π	P
TSADHE						
QOPH						Q
RESH				RHO	P	R
SHIN				SIGMA	Σ	S
TAW				TAU	T	T

The development of the alphabet, from its origin to modern scripts; from a chart by Frank M. Cross Jr.

preparing stone surfaces with plaster to receive monumental texts written with ink (cf. Deut. 27:2–3). Such texts survived only in exceptional circumstances, and this may be a chief reason that relatively few public documents from this period have been discovered.

The tablets Moses brought down from Mount Sinai were made of stone (Exod. 31:18), but the writing tablets mentioned in Isa. 30:8 and Hab. 2:2 were probably incised sheets of wood (covered with wax; cf. Luke 1:63) or metal. Exactly what the "large tablet" of Isa. 8:1 was is disputed. A silver prayer scroll from the First Temple period (tenth–sixth centuries BCE) has recently come to light in Jerusalem, and the Copper Scroll from Qumran shows that the practice of preserving important documents on sheets of soft metal persisted. Although a chisel was required to execute a stone inscription, metal or waxed wood could be incised with a simple stylus made of iron or tipped with a hard substance like emery (the "point of diamond" of Jer. 17:1). The "iron pen and lead" of Job 19:24 may be a reference to writing on a sheet of lead with an iron stylus or, possibly, to filling letters engraved in stone with molten lead.

The general needs of correspondence and record keeping in ancient Israel were served by specially prepared leather and papyrus, and their use continued into NT times. The deed of sale executed by Jeremiah in prison was probably a sheet of papyrus, folded, sealed, and stored in a ceramic jar (Jer. 32:11–14). There is a reference to the use of "paper [i.e., papyrus] and ink" for letter writing in 2 John 12 (cf. 3 Macc. 3:20; 4 Esd. 15:2), but during the Roman period papyrus was replaced in many of its uses by parchment, a refined type of leather, because of its greater durability. Leather, moreover, seems to have been the preferred material for sacred documents. The Qumran scrolls suggest that this was the case in Hellenistic and Roman times, although portions of the Bible recorded on papyrus have survived from the same period. According to the *Letter of Aristeas* (176 BCE) leather was mandatory for Torah scrolls used in public worship. For both leather and papyrus the writing medium was ink (cf. Jer. 36:18), which was usually black, derived from soot, although both red and yellow ink are also known. The ink was applied with a brush made from a frayed reed and shaped with a penknife, which could also be used to cut leather (cf. 36:23). In imitation of Egyptian practice these materials were kept in a "writing case," a scribal palette equipped with slots for pens and wells for ink and worn at the belt (Ezek. 9:2, 3, 11).

Notes and informal records were written with ink on broken pieces of pottery. Numerous ostraca, as these texts are called, have survived from biblical times, including such well-known collections as the Samaria ostraca of the ninth century BCE, the Lachish letters of the early sixth century, and a group of ostraca from Arad.

Uses of Writing: Writing was put to numerous uses in ancient Israel. One of these was record keeping. There is mention in the Bible of the collection and preservation of various kinds of information (e.g., Josh. 18:8–9). Surviving inscriptions, such as the Samaria ostraca, show that economic transactions were recorded in writing, and there are references in the Bible to the execution of several kinds of legal documents, such as deeds of purchase (Jer. 32:10) or writs of divorce (Deut. 24:1, 3).

Another common use of writing was correspondence. Letters from several periods of Israelite history have been recovered by archaeologists. The Bible makes frequent reference to the official correspondence of the Israelite and Judean courts, mentioning letters sent by David (2 Sam. 11:14), Jezebel (1 Kings 21:8), Jehu (2 Kings 10:1), and Hezekiah (2 Chron. 30:1) in addition to letters received from the king of Syria (2 Kings 5:5), the Assyrian Rabshakeh (2 Kings 19:14; Isa. 37:14), and Sennacherib himself (2 Chron. 32:17). The fortunes of the Jewish community after the return from exile are described largely in terms of correspondence with the Persian court (Ezra 4–7). Many of the NT books are themselves letters, written by Paul and others to distant churches.

In addition to its common uses writing served certain ceremonial functions, both secular and religious. These included the erection of victory stelae (1 Sam. 15:12; 1 Chron. 18:3; cf. 2 Sam. 8:3), which in most cases would have borne inscriptions, and

An ostracon from Arad written on in ink (ca. 600 BCE) mentions the "House of YHWH."

public and personal memorials of various kinds (Exod. 17:14; 2 Sam. 18:18). Here too belongs the commitment of collections of ritual regulations to writing (e.g., Deut. 24:4; Deut. 31:24; Josh. 8:32) and the recording of prophetic sayings for the instruction of later generations (Isa. 8:1, 16; 30:8; Jer. 30:2). Ritual and magical uses of writing are hinted at by passages like Num. 5:23–24 and Jer. 51:59–64 (cf. Ezek. 2:8–3:3).

Literacy: Although it is difficult to estimate how many in the ancient community could read and write, it seems clear that Israel was a literate society from at least the time of the settlement in Canaan (late twelfth century BCE). Thus, the "young man from Succoth" of Judg. 8:14, apparently a common soldier, was able to write the names of seventy-seven men. The existence of some degree of literacy in Israel during the period of the judges is further attested by inscriptional remains, including a scribal practice tablet with a crude abecedarium scratched on it. The Gezer calendar, an inscribed limestone plaque from the tenth century BCE, was probably also used for scribal practice.

Isaiah's allusion to a child's ability to "write down" (the number of) a few trees (Isa. 10:19) also might be taken as a suggestion that literacy had become widespread by the eighth century, but this impression is contradicted by the reference in 29:11, which suggests that "those who can read" were a subset of the general population. In 8:1 Isaiah is commanded to write on a tablet, but this does not necessarily mean that the prophet himself could write. Jeremiah, when commanded to write down his oracles, dictated them to Baruch (Jer. 36:2, 4). Note also that when the scroll produced by Baruch was taken to Jehoiakim, the king had it read to him by a member of his court (36:20). All of these things suggest a pattern of limited literacy in ancient Israel. In a given generation there may have been many who could read and write, but the general population probably relied on a fairly small number of individuals trained in scribal schools or families (cf. 1 Chron. 2:55).

The situation reflected in the NT is much the same. Paul apparently dictated his letters to a companion (e.g., Rom. 16:22; cf. Gal. 6:11), although he may have concluded them with a benediction in his own hand (2 Thess. 3:17). Such letters were intended to be read aloud to the assembled Christians rather than being read individually (e.g., Col. 4:16). *See also* education; ink; letter; papyrus.

Bibliography

Driver, Godfrey R. *Semitic Writing from Pictograph to Alphabet.* 3rd ed. Oxford University Press, 1976.

Gelb, Ignace J. *A Study of Writing.* 2nd ed. University of Chicago Press, 1963.   P.K.M.

Writings, the. *See* Hagiographa.

X Y Z

X

Y

Xerxes (zuhrk´seez), the name of several rulers of the Persian Empire, one, or possibly two, of which are significant for the Bible.

1 Xerxes I, king of Persia 486–465 BCE. He is known from Greek history for his attempts at conquering the Greek mainland. He is probably the ruler referred to in Ezra 4:6 (there called Ahasuerus, from the Persian form of his name) who received a complaint against the Jews who had returned to Jerusalem from the exile. He might also be the ruler indicated in Dan. 9:1, where an Ahasuerus is mentioned as the father of Darius the Mede (but see 2). Finally, the Persian ruler of the book of Esther (e.g., 1:1, there called Ahasuerus) may also be Xerxes I. The Greek translators of the LXX, however, consistently render that person's name as Artaxerxes, a name taken by four Persian rulers, including the son of Xerxes I.

2 Xerxes II, king of Persia 425 BCE. He succeeded Artaxerxes I (the son of Xerxes I), but was assassinated almost immediately. He is probably not referred to in the Bible, but some interpreters think the reference in Dan. 9:1 is to him rather than to Xerxes I.   P.R.A.

Crown Prince Xerxes (who became Xerxes I) standing behind the Persian ruler Darius I, whom he succeeded in 486 BCE; Persepolis relief.

Yahweh (yah´weh), the most important name for God in the Hebrew Bible. The name is formed from the Tetragrammaton, i.e., the consonants YHWH, which occur 6,828 times. Even after the vocalization of the Hebrew text, God's name was traditionally written without vowels to discourage people from speaking it aloud; that practice continues to be followed among many Jews and Christians, although the actual pronunciation of the name has been lost to history, in any case. When vowels are used, the name is typically written as "Yahweh" (e.g., in the JB and NJB). The name occurs in all books of the Hebrew Bible except Ecclesiastes, Esther, and the Song of Solomon. Its shortened forms (e.g., "Yah") occur in many personal names where the letters may be transliterated into English as "jah," "joh," "iah," or a number of other combinations (see, e.g., Jeremiah, Jonathan). An older system of transliteration rendered the Hebrew consonants as JHVH instead; thus, in some older literature the name "Yahweh" is written as "Jahveh," "Yahveh," or "Jahweh." Likewise, the name "Jehovah" is simply an archaic form of "Yahweh" used in the KJV. It was produced by inserting the vowels for the Hebrew word for "Lord" between the consonants JHVH. In many English Bibles, the name Yahweh is simply rendered as "LORD" (with one large and three small capital letters). Gen. 4:26 traces the revelation of the name Yahweh to human beings in the primeval period, while other texts present Moses as the first to receive the knowledge of this name (Exod. 3:14; 6:2–3). In the latter two passages, the deity is specifically identified with the God of the ancestors (3:13, 15; 6:3–4). The meaning of the name probably derives from a form of the Hebrew verb "to be." In 3:14, God responds to Moses with the ambiguous statement, "I am who I will be." *See also* names of God in the Hebrew Bible.   M.A.P.

Yahwist, the name given to the earliest literary source underlying the books of Genesis–Numbers. The siglum given the source is "J," which is derived from the German spelling of the name of God, *Jahveh* (in English usually spelled Yahweh), used throughout this source. The Yahwist source is usually dated around 950 BCE. Among its characteristics are bold anthropomorphisms; positive attitudes toward agricultural civilization, the state, and kingship; a mixture of nationalistic and universalistic concerns; and a style that exudes charm, simplicity, and clarity. The anonymous writer wove together oral and written stories to assist a people in discovering not only the outer history of names and places, but also the inner story of God's work among them. Examples of the Yahwist writing are found in Gen. 2:4b–4:26; 32:22–32; Exod. 1–22; and Num. 24:1–25. *See also* Pentateuch, sources of the.   K.H.R.

year. *See* time.

yoke, a wooden or iron frame for joining two oxen or other draft animals so they can pull a plow, cart, or other heavy load. A yoke generally consisted of a single crossbar with leather or rope nooses or wooden rods that were fastened around the animals' necks (Jer. 27:2). The crossbar was attached to a shaft that pulled the load (Deut. 21:3; 1 Sam. 6:7; 11:5; 1 Kings 19:19). A "yoke of oxen" might refer to a pair of oxen (1 Sam. 11:7; 1 Kings 19:21; Luke 14:19). The NRSV uses the expression "an acre of land" to translate what the Bible literally calls "a yoke of land," i.e., the amount of land a yoke of oxen could plow in one day (1 Sam. 14:14; Isa. 5:10).

The yoke was used figuratively as a symbol of hardship, submission, or servitude. Jeremiah wore a yoke to symbolize his message that Judah should submit to Babylon (Jer. 27–28). When the people of Israel considered whether they would accept Rehoboam as king, they asked him to lighten the heavy yoke, i.e., the hard service, that his father, Solomon, imposed on them (1 Kings 12:1–11); Rehoboam, however, responded by saying, "My father made your yoke heavy, but I will add to your yoke" (12:14). The image of a yoke may also be used to refer to other burdens or responsibilities, such as sin (Lam. 1:14), service to God (Lam. 3:27; Jer. 2:20; 5:5), slavery (Sir. 33:26), obedience to Torah (Acts 15:10), or submission to Christ (Matt. 11:29–30).   M.A.S.

Yom Kippur (yom′ kip′uhr). *See* Atonement, Day of.

Z

Zaanannim (zay′uh-nan′nim), a point on the southern border of Naphtali with Issachar (Josh. 19:33) where Heber the Kenite pitched his tent (Judg. 4:11). It was here that the Canaanite king Sisera was subsequently slain by Jael (4:17–21). The site is probably modern Khan et-Tujjar, some five miles west of the Sea of Galilee.

Zabad (zay′bad; a shortened name, Heb., "[God] has given" or "gift"; cf. the full names Zebadiah, Zabdiel).

1 A descendant of Sheshan in the line of Judah (1 Chron. 2:36–37; cf. v. 31).

2 The son of Tahath, an Ephraimite of the Shuthelah lineage (1 Chron. 7:21).

3 A son of Ahlai, one of David's warriors (1 Chron. 11:41; cf. 2 Sam. 23:24–39).

4 One of the murderers of King Joash according to 2 Chron. 24:26 (Jozacar, 2 Kings 12:21).

5 A descendant of Zattu who, upon returning from the exile, agreed to divorce his non-Israelite wife in compliance with Ezra's reform policies (Ezra 10:27).

6 A descendant of Hattum who, upon returning from the exile, agreed to divorce his non-Israelite wife in compliance with Ezra's reform policies (Ezra 10:33).

7 A descendant of Nebo who, upon returning from the exile, agreed to divorce his non-Israelite wife in compliance with Ezra's reform policies (Ezra 10:43).   P.A.B.

Zabbai (zab′i), a descendant of Bebai, who agreed to divorce his non-Israelite wife in compliance with Ezra's reform policies (Ezra 10:28). He may be the same individual who is mentioned in Neh. 3:20 as the father of the Baruch who helped to rebuild the walls of Jerusalem.

Zabdi (zab′di).

1 The grandfather of Achan of Judah, who violated Joshua's order not to take the devoted spoil from Jericho (Josh. 7:1; Zimri, 1 Chron. 2:6). *See also* Achan.

2 A son of Shimei who belonged to the tribe of Benjamin (1 Chron. 8:19).

3 A Shiphmite who served as an official under David in charge of the "produce of the vineyards for the wine cellars" (1 Chron. 27:27).

4 A Levite in postexilic Jerusalem, the son of Asaph and father of Mica (Neh. 11:17; Zichri, 1 Chron. 9:15).

Zabdiel (zab′dee-uhl).

1 The father of Jashobeam, one of David's military commanders (1 Chron. 27:2).

2 The son of Haggedolim; an overseer of priests in the time of Nehemiah (Neh. 11:14).

3 An Arabian who killed Alexander Balas, a contender for the Syrian throne ca. 150 BCE, and sent the head to the Egyptian king Ptolemy VI Philometor, from whom Alexander had been seeking refuge (1 Macc. 11:17). *See also* Alexander.

Zacchaeus (zuh-kee′uhs; Gk., "pure").

1 An officer in Judas Maccabeus's army (2 Macc. 10:19). *See also* Maccabees.

2 A wealthy tax collector in Jericho (Luke 19:1–10). When Jesus passed through the town, Zacchaeus wanted to see him, but could not on account of the crowd and his short stature. He climbed a tree for a better view. Surprisingly, Jesus summoned him to come down and went to his home, presumably for a meal. This prompted a negative response from the crowd, who grumbled that Jesus had "gone to be the guest of one who is a sinner" (19:7). Zacchaeus offers a comment to Jesus that is somewhat ambiguous; he says, literally, "Half of my possessions, I give to the poor; and if I have defrauded anyone of anything, I pay back four times as much." Some interpreters assume that Zacchaeus is defending himself against the charge that he is a sinner by stating what has always been his normal (and righteous) policy. Others think the context implies a transformation; Zacchaeus is stating what he is going to do from this point on. The NRSV opts for the latter interpretation and translates the present-tense verbs ("I give to the poor"; "I pay back") as future expressions ("I will give to the poor"; "I will pay back").

Zacchaeus in the tree for a better view of Jesus (Luke 19:3–4); pulpit plaque, Ravenna, Italy.

back"). This is grammatically possible since, in Greek, the present tense can be used idiomatically to express inception of future action. The notion that Zacchaeus has undergone a transformation may also be suggested by Jesus's concluding comment, "Today, salvation has come to this house" (19:9), though the rationale stated for that salvation is not that Zacchaeus has repented, but that he "is a son of Abraham." Thus, the story can be read either way. It is, in any case, intended to illustrate Jesus's vocation as one who has come "to seek out and to save the lost" (19:10). The interpretive question is whether Zacchaeus was "lost" because he was a sinner needing repentance, or because he had been mislabeled a sinner and needed to be identified as a true son of Abraham. *See also* tax collectors.   M.A.P.

Zaccur (zak′uhr; Heb., "remembered").

1 A Reubenite, the father of Shammua, one of the twelve spies sent by Moses into Canaan (Num. 13:4).

2 A Simeonite, the son of Hammuel and a descendant of Mishma (1 Chron. 4:26).

3 A Levite belonging to the Merari group (1 Chron. 24:27).

4 A levitical musician belonging to the Asaph group; he was head of the third course of musicians in the time of King David (1 Chron. 25:1, 10). He is probably the same person who is listed as the ancestor of a postexilic musician (Neh. 12:35).

5 The son of Imri who helped repair the walls of Jerusalem under Nehemiah (Neh. 3:2).

6 A Levite who signed Ezra's postexilic covenant to keep the law (Neh. 10:12); he is possibly the same Levite who was the father of Hanan, a temple official in the time of Nehemiah (13:13).

7 A member of the Bigvai family group who returned from the Babylonian exile with Ezra (Ezra 8:14). The Hebrew text reads Zabbud, but with a marginal correction to Zaccur; however, some versions retain Zabbud.   D.R.B.

Zachariah (zak′uh-ri′uh). *See* Zechariah.

Zadok (zay′dok), a priest whose descendants served in the high-priesthood for most of the First and Second Temple periods (tenth century BCE to first century CE). Zadok and Abiathar were priests under David (2 Sam. 20:25) and supported him during Absalom's revolt (15:24–29, 35; 17:15; 19:12). According to biblical genealogies, both were descendants of Aaron, who was a descendant of Levi (1 Chron. 5:24–6:3). In the succession struggle after David's death, however, Zadok supported Solomon (1 Kings 1:8, 32), while Abiathar supported Adonijah (1:7). Zadok therefore anointed Solomon (1:39–45) and became his sole priest.

The genealogy of Zadok is disputed, and many interpreters think that he was not in fact a descendant of Aaron, but the founder of a new priestly line intended to replace the Aaronic line, which was strongly associated with the northern kingdom by virtue of connections to Shiloh and Bethel. The prophecy against the Aaronite Eli and his sons in 1 Sam. 2:27–36 is read as suggestive of such a replacement line. God says, "I will raise up for myself a faithful priest. . . . I will build him a sure house, and he shall go in and out before my anointed one forever" (2:35). According to this view, the genealogies that place Zadok in the line of Aaron represent postexilic attempts at grafting the new priestly line into an orthodox understanding of Israel's singular priestly legacy. Indeed, many scholars have maintained that Zadok's origins might have been non-Israelite, hailing from pre-Israelite Jerusalem or from Hebron, where David had come in contact with him. All of these theories, however, are disputed, and the presentation of Zadok as an Aaronite has been recently defended by some critical scholars.

The descendants of Zadok are listed in 1 Chron. 6:8–15 (cf. 9:11; Ezra 7:1–5; Neh. 11:11), although there are probably gaps in the list. This family controlled the Jerusalem priesthood from the time of Solomon (ca. 965 BCE) until the exile (587/6 BCE). Ezek. 40:46; 43:19; 44:15; and 48:11 specify that only Zadokite priests would minister in the rebuilt temple. The Zadokite line continued to serve in the high-priesthood until 171 BCE, when it passed first to the Hellenizers and then to the Hasmonean house. The Jewish sect at Qumran that preserved the Dead Sea Scrolls was probably founded in the aftermath of the Hasmonean takeover of the high-priesthood. In their scrolls, they repeatedly emphasize the sole legitimacy of the Zadokite priests who appear to have been the early leaders and probably the founders of the sect. One theory for the origin of the word "Sadducee" derives the term from Zadok, in which case the origins of the Sadducees (a powerful Jewish group with strong priestly connections) might also be associated with the Zadokites in some way that is now lost to us. *See also* priests.   L.H.S.

Zair (zay'uhr), a location either in or near Edomite territory where Jehoram, the king of Judah (southern kingdom), fought the Edomites in an attempt to keep them under Israelite control (2 Kings 8:21). The location is unknown, although some scholars connect it with Zoar (Deut. 34:3) or Zior (Josh. 15:54); other scholars think Zair may be a scribal error for Seir, a name for the whole territory of Edom.

Zalmon (zal'muhn).
1 A member of David's elite group of warriors known as "the Thirty" (2 Sam. 23:28; Ilai, 1 Chron. 11:29).
2 A mountain near Shechem from which Abimelech cut branches to burn the temple of El-berith (Judg. 9:48); it is usually identified as a promontory or slope of Mount Gerizim or Mount Ebal, which lie on either side of Shechem.
3 An unknown location mentioned in Ps. 68:14; it could be the same as 2, but probably refers to a

higher elevation east of the Jordan toward Mount Hermon.

Zalmonah (zal-moh'nuh), one of the encampments of the Israelites during the exodus from Egypt (Num. 33:41–42). Although the exact site is not known, it is probably located in the Arabah twenty to thirty miles south of the Dead Sea.

Zalmunna (zal-muhn'uh), a Midianite king who, along with Zebah, was pursued and killed by Gideon (Judg. 8:4–21; Ps. 83:11). *See also* Gideon; Zebah.

Zamzummim (zam-zuhm'mim), the name given by the Ammonites to an ancient race of giants who were the original inhabitants of the area east of the Jordan later occupied by the Ammonites and Moabites; the Israelites called them Rephaim (Deut. 2:20–21). Some scholars identify them with the descendants of Ham, who are elsewhere called Zuzim (Gen. 14:5). *See also* Rephaim.

Zanoah (zuh-noh'uh).
1 A town of Judah in the northern Shephelah (Josh. 15:34; Neh. 11:30), identified with Khirbet Zanu'. After the exile, its inhabitants helped repair the Valley Gate (Neh. 3:13).
2 A town in the hill country of Judah, in the same general area as Maon and Ziph (Josh. 15:56). It is possibly to be identified with Khirbet Beit Amra.
3 The son of Jekuthiel and grandchild of Mered by his Judean wife (1 Chron. 4:18).

Zaphenath-paneah (zaf'uh-nath-puh-nee'uh), the name Pharaoh gave to Joseph when he appointed him as vizier (Gen. 41:45). It was a common practice in Egypt for Semites to take Egyptian names. However, the Egyptian original behind this particular name is uncertain. It has been suggested that it comes from a name meaning "The god speaks and he lives," but that name is not attested in Egypt until considerably later. *See also* Joseph.   J.M.W.

Zaphon (zay'fon), a city east of the Jordan River included in the land given to the tribe of Gad (Josh. 13:27). Formerly it belonged to the kingdom of Sihon. The site is mentioned in the Amarna letters and in the story of Jephthah (Judg. 12:1–7). The site has been identified with Tell es Sa'idiyeh or Tell el Qos in modern Jordan. *See also* Amarna, Tell el-; Sihon.

Zarephath (zair'uh-fath), a port city on the Phoenician coast at modern Sarafand, eight miles south of Sidon and fourteen miles north of Tyre. Phoenician and Hellenistic remains were found at Ras el-Qantara, a promontory overlooking what was a northern harbor and possibly also a southern harbor. Hellenistic, Roman, and later remains cover a wider area along the coast, including a small Roman harbor used from the first to sixth centuries CE. The modern village of Sarafand is centered some distance inland, as are Phoenician rock-cut tombs discovered by villagers.

Occupied from 1600 BCE on, Zarephath was most important during the Phoenician period. In the ninth century BCE the prophet Elijah received the hospitality of a poor widow of Zarephath and miraculously replenished her depleted grain and revived her dying son (1 Kings 17:8–24). Centuries later Jesus referred to Elijah's visit (Luke 4:25–27).

In an Egyptian text of the thirteenth century BCE Zarephath is mentioned along with Byblos, Beirut, Sidon, and Tyre. In his campaign of 701 BCE the Assyrian king Sennacherib included Zarephath in a list of pacified coastal cities, while King Esar-haddon transferred Zarephath to the control of Tyre.

Excavations during 1969–74 by J. Pritchard at Zarephath have provided an archaeological record of Phoenician material culture in its homeland, including a stratigraphic sequence of Phoenician pottery. Continuous occupation at Zarephath from the Late Bronze Age (ca. 1500 BCE) into the Phoenician Iron Age (ca. 1100 BCE) demonstrates that Phoenician culture evolved locally. In an industrial quarter dating to several centuries of the Iron Age, twenty-two bilobate-shaped kilns for pottery were found along with settling basins and heaps of misfired pottery, including red-slip ware, mushroom-lip juglets, and other Phoenician ceramic types.

A small one-room shrine with benches along its walls was discovered in the potters' quarter. Near the front of it a cache of objects was found that included terra-cotta figurines and an ivory plaque with a short dedicatory inscription to Astarte-Tanit. This is the first known syncretism of Astarte, the female deity of the Canaanite Levant, and Tanit, whose center of worship was the western Mediterranean, where child sacrifices were made to her. This demonstrates that the worship of Tanit was not entirely restricted to the western Mediterranean.   T.L.M.

Zarethan (zair'uh-than), a city in the Jordan Valley whose location has not been firmly established. It was beside the clay ground where Solomon's Phoenician smith cast bronze utensils for the temple (1 Kings 7:46; 2 Chron. 4:17). When Joshua led the Israelites across the Jordan River, water backed up near Zarethan (Josh. 3:16). In the period of the judges, Gideon pursued the Midianites toward Zarethan (Judg. 7:22). During the time of Solomon Zarethan was mentioned as belonging to one of the king's new administrative districts (1 Kings 4:12). Several modern sites have been proposed as the location of Zarethan, among them Tell Umm Hamad, Sleihat, and Tell el-Merkbere. The favored suggestion, however, is Tell es-Saʻidiyeh, which has been excavated.

Tell es-Saʻidiyeh consists of twin (upper and lower) mounds and is on the south bank of the Wadi Kufrinjeh, a little more than a mile west of the Jordan River. Iron Age settlement was concentrated on the upper mound. Its water supply was provided in time of siege by a unique semisubterranean stairway cut into the side of the mound; it linked the walled city with springs at the foot of the tell. A mud-brick wall running down the center of the staircase supported a roof that hid the system from attackers.

Excavations at Tell es-Saʻidiyeh, an important Iron Age settlement and one of the sites proposed as the biblical city of Zarethan.

The earliest Iron Age settlement excavated on the upper mound revealed residential houses from the ninth century BCE. They were all made of mud-brick, and one house contained a white-plastered mud platform with associated ashes and incense burners. A later settlement from the eighth century BCE exhibited systematic town planning in which standardized houses were constructed in a residential block that, with its flanking streets, was oriented perpendicularly to the defensive wall protecting the perimeter of the settlement. Houses, built back to back, were of a three-room pillar type. The front room was divided in two by a row of mud-brick pillars. A back room stood on the side opposite the street entrance. This eighth-century settlement was destroyed by a heavy fire, and reoccupation of the area, probably in the seventh century BCE, included scores of circular pits that served as storage facilities for grain. Persian and Hellenistic public buildings were located on the highest point of the upper mound. A large Persian structure was square in shape with a paved central courtyard and a tower built at one of the building's corners.

Early Bronze Age (3000–2000 BCE) potsherds covered the lower mound, but excavation there also revealed a cemetery dating from the Late Bronze Age to the Early Iron Age (ca. 1500–900 BCE). A number of bronze utensils were found in the graves, including a tripod stand, several bowls, and a strainer in the grave of a female. Also found with her were silver jewelry, beads of gold and carnelian, and ivory cosmetic objects. Another grave contained bronze weapons and skeletal remains wrapped in cloth and covered with bitumen.   T.L.M.

Zattu (zat′oo), the head of a family group who returned from the Babylonian exile (Ezra 2:8; Neh. 7:13; 10:14). Some members of this family had married non-Israelite women, whom they agreed to divorce in accord with the reforms of Ezra (Ezra 10:27).

Zealots (zel′uhts), a group who opposed the Roman occupation of Judea, which began in 63 BCE. According to Josephus, the Zealots were a guerilla band of radical anti-Roman Jews who advocated armed rebellion against the Roman forces (*Jewish War* 4.128–584). Their numbers included the *sicarii*, knife-wielding assassins who would mingle in crowds and stab Jews suspected of collaborating with the Romans. Ultimately, the Zealots and their sympathizers were responsible for leading the Jews into a disastrous war against Rome in 66–73 CE. They are probably not mentioned in the NT itself, though one of Jesus's disciples was called "Simon the Zealot" (Luke 6:15; Acts 1:13). That appellation, however, could simply mean "Simon the Zealous One," identifying him as a person devoted to the law or simply "zealous" for God (e.g., Num. 25:13; 2 Kings 10:16; Acts 22:3). The Zealots may not have appeared as an organized force until a few years after the time of Jesus. It is also possible that Josephus's entire construct of the Zealots as revolutionary terrorists is polemically biased (considering that his portrait of anti-Roman Jews as terrorists appears in a work commissioned by the Romans). It is not impossible that many of those called Zealots would have been "radicals" who opposed the Romans in terms similar to what is ascribed to Jesus (who was, after all, crucified as a potential threat to the state) without recourse to the surreptitious violence attributed to Zealots by Josephus.   M.A.P.

Zebadiah (zeb′uh-di′uh; Heb., "the LORD has given a gift"; also Zeraiah).

1 A Benjaminite who was one of nine sons of Beriah (1 Chron. 8:15).

2 A Benjaminite who was one of seven sons of Elpaal (1 Chron. 8:17).

3 A Benjaminite who was a son of Jeroham of Gedor. He fought for David at Ziklag and was distinguished as a warrior, because he could sling stones with either hand (1 Chron. 12:7).

4 The third son of Meshelemiah who served as a temple gatekeeper (1 Chron. 26:2).

5 A son of Asahel who succeeded his father as leader of the labor division for David (1 Chron. 27:7).

6 A Levite who became a teacher of the law during the time of King Jehoshaphat (2 Chron. 17:8).

7 The son of Ishmael and governor of the house of Judah during the time of King Jehoshaphat (2 Chron. 19:11).

8 The son of Michael and head of the descendants of Shephatiah who returned from the exile with Ezra (Ezra 8:8).

9 A descendant of Immer who agreed to divorce his non-Israelite wife in accord with the postexilic reforms of Ezra (Ezra 10:20).   R.S.B.

Zebah (zee′buh; Heb., "sacrifice" or "offering"), a king of Midian who, along with Zalmunna and fifteen thousand survivors of the allied Midianite and Amalekite army, fled from the Israelites led by Gideon. Gideon pursued the kings and the remnant of the army to Karkor, east of the Jordan, where, in a surprise attack, he routed the army and captured Zebah and Zalmunna. After carrying out reprisals against Succoth and Penuel for failing to lend assistance, Gideon killed Zebah and Zalmunna, because he held them responsible for the deaths of his relatives at Tabor (Judg. 8:4–21; Ps. 83:11). *See also* Gideon.

Zebedee (zeb′uh-dee), a fisherman and the father of Jesus's disciples James and John (Matt. 4:21–22; Mark 1:19–20; Luke 5:10). Little is known of him, but his sons became two of the most prominent members of the twelve, and his wife also played a significant role in the Gospel story. Zebedee apparently employed "hired men" (Mark 1:20) and owned a boat, which may mark him as at least a moderately wealthy man. Comparison of Matt. 27:55–56 with Mark 15:40 leads to the plausible suggestion that the wife of Zebedee and mother of James and John was named Salome, one of the women who accompanied Jesus and witnessed his crucifixion. If the reference to her as one who "provided for Jesus" is understood in a financial sense (Matt. 27:56; cf. Luke 8:1–3), it might be conjectured that Zebedee and his wife were patrons of Jesus's ministry. It has also been suggested, however, that his wife and sons may have left him in order to follow Jesus; this would correlate with the biblical tradition that devotion to Jesus sometimes divided families (cf. Matt. 10:34–37). *See also* James; John; Salome.

Zeboiim (zuh-boi'im), a site in the valley near the Dead Sea noted as marking the eastern border of Canaan together with Sodom, Gomorrah, Admah, and Lasha (Gen. 10:19). Ruled by Shemeber, it joined a coalition with neighboring cities (14:2) opposing invaders from the north (14:8). Hosea used both Admah and Zeboiim as symbols of utter destruction (11:8), referring presumably to the legendary destruction of the whole region when Sodom and Gomorrah were destroyed together with "those cities and all the Plain" (19:24–25). Although recent archaeological work has recovered remains of five Early Bronze Age cities southeast of the Dead Sea on the plain below the hill line to the east, no specific identification has been established for Zeboiim to date.
R.S.B.

Zeboim (zuh-boh'im; Heb., "valley of the hyenas").
1 A valley in the tribal territory of Benjamin southeast of Michmash to which the Philistines came for battle with Saul and Jonathan (1 Sam. 13:18).
2 A village occupied by the Benjaminites after the exile (Neh. 11:34).

Zebul (zee'buhl), a city official at Shechem who was loyal to Abimelech, the king. He informed Abimelech of Gaal's plan to lead the Shechemites in a revolt against Israel. After Gaal was defeated, Zebul expelled him and his relatives from Shechem (Judg. 9:28–41).

Zebulun (zeb'yuh-luhn).
1 The sixth son of Jacob and Leah (Gen. 30:19–20). When he was born, his tragically unloved mother (cf. 29:31) is said to have named him Zebulun, because she thought, "Now my husband will honor me, because I have borne him six sons" (30:20). Thus, the name was a pun on the Hebrew word *zabal,* which means "to honor." Zebulun had three sons—Sered, Elon, and Jahlee—and he and his three sons went down to Egypt with the family of Jacob (46:14). Jacob's blessing of Zebulun implies that his descendants would live along or near the Mediterranean coast and maintain close relations with the Phoenicians (49:13).
2 The tribe of Zebulun, whose members identified themselves as descendants of **1**. The territory

allotted to this tribe was in south-central Galilee (Josh. 19:10–16). Their southern boundary corresponded roughly with the southern edge of the hills of Lower Galilee and their northern border reached the Beth Netophah Valley. The land of Zebulun thus extended from just north of Mount Carmel on the west to Mount Tabor on the east. Zebulun was something of a hinterland, almost entirely mountainous, with the exception of the broad valleys on its western and northern edges. Its only towns of note were Hannathon (modern Tell el-Bedeiwiyeh), known from the Tell el-Amarna letters; Shimron, a Canaanite city conquered by Thutmose III and also mentioned in the Tell el-Amarna letters; and Gath-hepher, hometown of Jonah (2 Kings 14:25). But Zebulun was not isolated; some of Canaan's most important highways passed along its boundaries, and the tribe had easy access to the sea (cf. Gen. 49:13; Deut. 33:19). Jesus's hometown, Nazareth, was located in the heart of Zebulun (cf. Isa. 9:1; Matt. 4:15). *See also* tribes.
D.A.D.

Zechariah (zek'uh-ri'uh; Heb., "the LORD remembers").
1 A Benjaminite from Gibeon whose brother Ner was the father of Kish, the father of King Saul (1 Chron. 29:36–39; Zecher, 1 Chron. 8:31).
2 The son Meshelemiah; a Levite who was a gatekeeper for the tent of meeting during the reign of David (1 Chron. 9:21–22; 26:2, 14).
3 A levitical harpist who accompanied the ark of the covenant when it was brought into Jerusalem during the reign of David (1 Chron. 15:18, 20; 16:5).
4 A trumpet-blowing priest who led David's procession accompanying the ark of the covenant into Jerusalem (1 Chron. 15:24).
5 A prophet during the reign of Joash (Jehoash) of Judah (ca. 837–800 BCE). The son of Jehoiada, a priest, he was stoned by the people because of his unpopular preaching (2 Chron. 24:20–23). He may be the Zechariah mentioned by Jesus in Luke 11:51, though a parallel passage in Matt. 23:35 identifies that person as "the son of Berechiah," i.e., the postexilic prophet indicated in **7** below.
6 The son of Jeroboam II, who succeeded his father to the throne of Israel ca. 746/5 BCE. He was the last of the family of Jehu. After reigning only six months, he was assassinated by Shallum, evidence of a period of considerable political unrest (2 Kings 14:29; 15:8–12).
7 The son of Berechiah; he was a prophet who ministered after the exile and is traditionally associated with the canonical book of Zechariah, one of the Minor Prophets. Matt. 23:35 identifies him as one who was "murdered between the sanctuary and the altar," but most scholars think a different Zechariah is intended by Jesus's remark (cf. Luke 11:51; and see **5** above). *See also* Zechariah, book of.
8 The father of John the Baptist. According to Luke 1:5, he was a priest from the line of priests associated with Abijah (cf. 1 Chron. 24:7–19)

and was married to Elizabeth, "of the daughters of Aaron." Described as righteous before the law, the couple was childless and "advanced in years" (reminiscent of the stories of Abraham and Sarah, Gen. 16:1; 17:1–21; 18:9–15; 21:1–8; and of Elkanah and Hannah, 1 Sam. 1:1–20). An angel appeared to Zechariah, announcing that his long desire for a son would be fulfilled, and the son's name was to be John. Asking for a sign, Zechariah was struck mute. It was not until after John's birth that Zechariah, filled with the Holy Spirit, was again able to speak, blessing God and prophesying the fulfillment of Israel's hope for the Messiah (Luke 1:5–25, 57–80). *See also* Elizabeth; John the Baptist.   P.L.S./M.A.P.

Zechariah, book of, the eleventh part of the Book of the Twelve in the Nevi'im, or Prophets section, of the Tanakh (Jewish Bible). In the Christian OT, it is the eleventh of the twelve Minor Prophets. Most scholars believe that, like the book of Isaiah, Zechariah was composed by multiple authors at different time periods. Zech. 1–8 is attributed to the prophet Zechariah, who prophesied between 520 and 518 BCE and is called First Zechariah. Zech. 9–14 is generally thought to have been added later and is attributed to Second (or Deutero-) Zechariah.

Contents: The Book of Zechariah begins with a superscription identifying the author and date of the prophecy (520 BCE). Zechariah then calls the people to return to God, setting the theological framework of the book.

In 1:7–6:15 there are a series of eight "night visions" (probably dreams, but the latter term is avoided, because some did not recognize dreams as vehicles for divine revelation; cf. Deut. 13; Jer. 23:28). The first vision depicts four horsemen patrolling the earth, which anticipates the punishment of foreign nations and the exaltation of Jerusalem. The second vision depicts four horns (representing world powers) and four blacksmiths that come to break them. The third vision is of a man measuring Jerusalem so that its walls can be rebuilt. His measurements of Jerusalem are exceedingly large, and he claims it does not need a wall, because God will be its protecting wall of fire. The fourth vision depicts an unclean Joshua (the high priest) being accused by Satan of being unfit for duty. God comes and confirms Joshua's role as high priest and gives him clean robes. The fifth vision is of two olive trees supplying a golden lampstand that lights the world. Most scholars argue that the two trees are meant to represent Zerubbabel (the governor) and Joshua, while the lampstand points to the menorah, which was a part of the temple furnishings (1 Kings 7:49). The sixth vision depicts a flying scroll containing the covenant laws, which demonstrates that all wrongdoers fall under Torah's judgment. The seventh vision personifies wickedness as a woman who is sitting in a basket and who is flown to Shinar (the ancient name for Babylon). The last vision depicts four horsemen waiting in anticipation of the messianic age.

Zech. 7–8 depict a series of oracles dealing with a question of fasting brought to Jerusalem by the people of Bethel. The concern is over whether they should continue fasting to remember the fall of Jerusalem when the temple is being rebuilt. Most scholars hold this section to be a loose connection of sayings revolving around a discussion of fasting. First, the question of fasting is broached. Instead of answering the question immediately, the discussion moves to God's command for the people to exhibit justice, kindness, and mercy (7:9) and a reminder of their past unfaithfulness to God. God then promises to come and restore the people, being righteous and faithful (8:8). Finally the question of fasting is answered in the negative, because the times that used to be for fasting will be celebrations of God's faithfulness (8:19).

In difficult times, Zechariah was a prophet of comfort. He encouraged the rebuilding of the temple and showed sympathy to the suffering in Israel. Zechariah emphasized God's continuing dedication to Jerusalem and Zion in the midst of their suffering and unfaithfulness. Childs argues that the visions of Zechariah had an independent existence, but were reinterpreted eschatologically and placed within Zechariah. He also argues that chaps. 7–8 were designed to remind the people of Israel that their eschatological concerns do not undermine the ethical concerns of the covenant. Gottwald argues that Zech. 1–8 is a chiastic pattern centering on Zerubbabel and Joshua (it ultimately hides the failed prophecy about Zerubbabel).

Zech. 9–14 (Second Zechariah) is a decidedly apocalyptic text that shares many themes with other prophetic works. It portrays the destruction of foreign nations, the restoration of Israel (9:11–12), the "day of the Lord," and the coming of the messianic king (9:9). Kingship is a theme throughout the section and is found in various manifestations: shepherds (chap. 10), Davidic line (chap. 12), and messianic hope (chap. 9). Zechariah depicts a final eschatological battle between good and evil and predicts the end of prophecy (13:2–6). These oracles may have been originally separate, but their common themes helped tie them to each other and to the book of Zechariah.

Background: Zechariah was a contemporary of Haggai, Zerubbabel, and Joshua, prophesying in Jerusalem between 520 and 518 BCE. Little is definitively known about the prophet other than the identification "son of Berechiah, son of Iddo" (1:1, 7). Baldwin argues that Zechariah may have been a priest from both internal evidence and references elsewhere to Iddo as one of the priests who returned from the exile with Joshua and Zerubbabel (Neh. 12:4). At this time, the Israelites had come back from the exile (538 BCE) and started rebuilding the temple. Yet their efforts waned quickly, and by 520 BCE the temple grounds had remained untouched for years. Zechariah, along with Haggai, called the people to rebuild the temple, which was completed in 516/5 BCE.

The book of Zechariah has deep connections with the prophetic literature. Many of the themes

and images in Zechariah are found elsewhere in the prophetic literature: seventy years of captivity (Jer. 29), a flying scroll (Ezek. 2–3), an "attack on Jerusalem by nations" (Ezek. 38–39; Joel 4), the "end of prophecy" (Neh. 6:10–14), "eschatological transformation of Jerusalem" (Isa. 65:17), the "conversion of nations" (Isa. 56:6), Satan (Job; 1 Chron. 21:1, maybe Num. 22:22), and the expression "my Servant the Branch" (Jer. 23:5; 33:15). In addition, Zechariah affirms the power of God's word spoken through the prophets by claiming that the exile was a result of hardened hearts (a warning to the current generation) and insisting on the certainty of prophetic words concerning the future.

Interpretive Issues: There is very little agreement about the origin or structure of Zech. 9–14. Although most scholars hold that it is not original to Zechariah, there is no overwhelming consensus on the historical origin of these chapters. Dates have ranged from the preexilic period to later than Alexander the Great's invasion (332 BCE). Those who favor a preexilic date find the themes of chaps. 9–14 to be similar to what is found in Jeremiah (a preexilic prophet), whereas those who favor a later date relate Zech. 9:1–8 to Alexander the Great. O'Brien argues for a late date for 9–14 because of its similarities to apocalyptic literature.

There are two definitive superscriptions that divide the text of Second Zechariah (9:1; 12:1). The anonymous character of these superscriptions along with the ambiguous character of the superscription in Malachi has led some scholars to argue that these three sections were anonymous collections added to the end of the Book of the Twelve that were eventually attributed to Zechariah and Malachi.

Interpreters differ on whether Zech. 1–8 and 9–14 ought to be read as separate works or as a single literary work (despite the multiple authors). Some scholars argue that the anonymous oracles in 9–14 were attributed to Zechariah only by virtue of their placement as editorial additions to the Book of the Twelve. Others argue that they were linked as a result of similar themes (i.e., the messiah triumphs in humility, 3:8, 4:6, 9:6). Childs argues that one cannot separate the two sections of the book without destroying its witness: chaps. 1–8 change how one reads chaps. 9–14 and vice versa. Baldwin argues against the unity of the book, because of differences between the sections in the areas of content, style, and vocabulary. Peterson holds that, although chaps. 9–14 could be read as an expansion of the themes of chaps. 1–8, the latter chapters lack any connection to the historical context present throughout the earlier chapters.

Influences: Zechariah was arguably the most influential of the Minor Prophets (or works included in the Book of the Twelve) upon the NT. It is quoted or referenced seventy-one times. The messianic hope within Zechariah is reflected widely throughout the NT. Zech. 9:9, which claims that Israel's king will come riding on a donkey, is explicitly quoted in Matt. 21, where Jesus rides into Jerusalem upon a donkey and a colt (21:2–7).

Bibliography

Baldwin, Joyce. *Haggai, Zechariah, Malachi.* InterVarsity, 1972.

Bandstra, Barry L. *Reading the Old Testament: Introduction to the Hebrew Bible.* 4th ed. Wadsworth, 2009.

Childs, Brevard S. *Introduction to the Old Testament as Scripture.* Fortress, 1979.

Gottwald, Norman K. *The Hebrew Bible: A Socio-Literary Introduction.* Fortress, 1985.

O'Brien, Julia M. *Nahum Habakkuk Zephaniah Haggai Zechariah Malachi.* Abingdon, 2004.

Peterson, David L. *The Prophetic Literature: An Introduction.* Westminster John Knox, 2002.

Sweeney, Marvin A. *The Twelve Prophets.* Vol. 2, *Micah, Nahum, Habakkuk, Zephaniah, Haggai, Zechariah, Malachi.* Liturgical, 2000.   B.B.

Zedekiah (zed´uh-ki´uh; Heb., "the LORD is righteousness").

1 A prophet at the court of Ahab of Israel. He was opposed by Micaiah, son of Imlah (1 Kings 22:11, 24; 2 Chron. 18:10, 23). Zedekiah led four hundred prophets in voicing their support of a military campaign against Aram. Micaiah counseled against that campaign, correctly predicting Israel's defeat at Ramoth-gilead.

2 The son of Hananiah; he was one of the officials of Judah engaged by Micaiah after Jeremiah's scroll was read by Baruch. Zedekiah was alarmed by the scroll and insisted that it be read to the king (Jer. 36:11–19).

3 The last king of Judah, who was placed on the throne as a puppet ruler by Nebuchadnezzar after his first conquest of Jerusalem in 597 BCE (2 Kings 24:17). In spite of repeated warnings provided by the prophet Jeremiah (cf. Jer. 37–39; 52), Zedekiah rebelled against his Babylonian overlords (2 Kings 24:20). As a result, Jerusalem was recaptured and destroyed (587/6 BCE). Zedekiah himself was captured and brought to the king of Babylon at Riblah. There, they slaughtered his sons before his eyes, blinded him, and took him in fetters to Babylon (2 Kings 25:6–7).

4 A prophet among the exiles in Babylon who was opposed by Jeremiah (Jer. 29:21–23). He and a prophet named Ahab were apparently promising the exiles a speedy return to Jerusalem. Jeremiah accused them both of "prophesying a lie" in God's name and of committing adultery with their neighbors' wives. Then he predicted their execution by Nebuchadnezzar, maintaining that their names would henceforth be used in a curse formula, according to which people would say, "The LORD make you like Zedekiah and Ahab, whom the king of Babylon roasted in the fire" (29:22).

5 A priest who signed Ezra's document pledging obedience to the covenant (Neh. 10:2).   W.S.T.

Zeeb (zee´uhb), a Midianite prince whom Gideon captured and killed (Judg. 7:25). *See also* Oreb and Zeeb.

Zelophehad (zuh-loh´fuh-had), a man of Manasseh who died in the wilderness leaving no male heir (Num. 26:33; 27:3; 1 Chron. 7:2). His five daughters, Mahlah, Noah, Hoglah, Milcah, and Tirzah, petitioned Moses and Eleazar, the priest, to recognize the right of female inheritance (Num. 27:1–11; cf. Josh. 17:3–6). The petition was granted with the stipulation that female heirs marry within their own tribe to protect the tribal inheritance (Num. 36:1–12). *See also* law; Mahlah.

Zenas (zee´nuhs), a person identified as a lawyer (to distinguish him from another Zenas?) whom Titus is asked to speed on his way with Apollos, seeing that they lack nothing (Titus 3:13). It is likely that Zenas and Apollos were the bearers of the letter and that they were delivering it on their way to some other location. In the NT, the term "lawyer" usually refers to a scribe who is trained in Torah (the law of God), but in this instance the word might refer to a Gentile who is an expert in Roman law. *See also* Apollos.

Zephaniah (zef´uh-ni´uh; Heb., "the LORD has concealed/preserved").

1 A Kohathite Levite who was an ancestor of the prophet Samuel and the levitical singer Heman (1 Chron. 6:36).

2 The son of Cushi; he was a descendant of King Hezekiah and a prophet during the reign of King Josiah of Judah (640–609 BCE). The book of Zephaniah contains his oracles.

3 The son of Maaseiah; he was a priest who served as an intermediary between King Zedekiah of Judah and the prophet Jeremiah (Jer. 21:1; 37:3; early sixth century BCE). He was taken before the king of Babylon at Riblah and there put to death (Jer. 52:24–27).

4 The father of Josiah; he was living in Jerusalem in the mid-sixth century BCE when Darius decreed the rebuilding of the Jerusalem temple. The prophet Zechariah was directed to take gold and silver brought by the returning exiles to the house of Zephaniah to make a crown for the high priest Joshua (Zech. 6:10–14).   P.J.A.

Zephaniah, book of, the ninth part of the Book of the Twelve in the Nevi'im, or Prophets section, in the Tanakh (Jewish Bible). In the Christian OT, Zephaniah is the ninth of the Minor Prophets. It presents an oracle of judgment followed by promises of salvation.

Structure: Sweeney argues for a two-part structure revolving around the prophet's call for the people to "seek the LORD." He claims that Zeph. 1:2–18 is the announcement of the "day of the LORD" and 2:1–3:20 is the call to "seek the LORD" (and, implicitly, support the reform of Josiah). Most scholars, however, hold that the oracle that follows has three major themes (and one subtheme) that correspond with the three main sections of the book: condemnation of Judah and Jerusalem ("day of the LORD"); condemnation of foreign nations; and, promises of salvation for God's people.

Contents: Zephaniah begins with a superscription identifying the name of the author and his ancestry back three generations. His career is dated to the reign of King Josiah. As the oracle begins, God proclaims a plan to clear the earth of humans, animals, birds, and all wickedness. This account has striking similarities to the reversal of creation that took place during the flood account (Gen. 6–9). Judgment is pronounced upon Judah and Jerusalem. The primary causes for this judgment are religious sins: the people worship Baal and bow down to the hosts of heaven. Judah and Jerusalem swear to the Lord, but also to Milcom (the god of Ammon), which could also be read as *malkam* (Heb., "their king"). Furthermore, those in the royal court are accused of adopting foreign attire (and presumably foreign culture and gods).

As a result of these sins, the people of Judah and Jerusalem will be punished in the coming "day of the LORD." Many scholars argue that this theme comes from the conquest and holy-war tradition of the Lord appearing in victory. But like the prophet Amos, Zephaniah argues that this day will be a sad day for God's people and not a day of victory. The "day of the LORD" will be a time when God's presence brings punishment (cf. Amos 5:18–20).

The next section of Zephaniah is a series of oracles against the foreign nations: Philistia (2:5–7), Moab and Ammon (2:8–11), Ethiopia (2:12), and Assyria (2:13–14). There is a possibility that the choice of nations is intended to point to God's judgment of the whole world by having a nation from each of the cardinal directions: Philistia (west), Moab and Ammon (east), Ethiopia (south), and Assyria (north). In any case, the oracles are followed by a proclamation against Judah (3:1–5), which seems to indicate that Judah stands with all other nations as under God's judgment.

The book ends with an oracle of salvation. That oracle begins with a message of salvation for the nations (3:9–10) and then presents a message of hope to the remnant of Judah (3:11–20).

Background: The introduction of Zephaniah gives a genealogy of the Judean prophet Zephaniah back to the third generation (1:1). One of the members of the genealogy is Cushi, which might imply that Zephaniah was of African descent. Furthermore, the person to whom the genealogy is traced is Hezekiah. Some scholars have claimed that this is King Hezekiah, who ruled Judah at the end of the eighth century BCE, which would make Zephaniah a member of the royal house, even if not necessarily in line for the throne. The support for this claim, however, is only circumstantial.

The author claims to have written during the reign of Josiah (1:1). Most scholars do not doubt this claim (at least for the earlier portions of the book), yet there is much discussion about exactly when Zephaniah would have prophesied during Josiah's long reign (640–609 BCE). Some scholars think that it was during the earlier portion of his reign (640–622), due to the particular practices that Zephaniah condemned, including Baal worship and abusing Torah. Those practices were all outlawed by Josiah in 622 BCE. Other scholars claim that these practices continued after Josiah outlawed them (as mentioned in Ezekiel and Jeremiah), making a later date possible.

Scholars have noted that the book of Zephaniah is strongly rooted within the prophetic tradition of the eighth century BCE. Such themes as the "day of the LORD," the ills of Judean society, and the survival of a righteous remnant were all common motifs for that earlier period.

Interpretive Issues: The major critical issue of Zephaniah concerns the extent of the editing that the book underwent. The majority of scholars believe that the core of the book was compiled during Josiah's reign, with portions (or all) of 3:9–20 being postexilic. Childs, however, argues for an early date for 3:9–20.

Influences: The book of Zephaniah influenced later prophets, including Ezekiel. The metaphor of the Judean leaders as lions and wolves in Zeph. 3:1–5 is developed in Ezek. 22:25–28. Also, Ezek. 22:31 incorporates the metaphor of God's wrath being poured out like fire upon the nations (Zeph. 3:8).

Some scholars have claimed that, not only did Zephaniah prophesy before the Deuteronomic reform of Josiah, but that he actually influenced this reform and was a supporter of it. This conclusion is drawn from the parallels between the critiques of idolatry, infidelity, and social injustice found in both Zephaniah and Deuteronomy.

Bibliography

Bandstra, Barry L. *Reading the Old Testament: Introduction to the Hebrew Bible.* 4th ed. Wadsworth, 2009.

OUTLINE OF CONTENTS

Zephaniah

Childs, Brevard S. *Introduction to the Old Testament as Scripture.* Fortress, 1979.

Gottwald, Norman K. *The Hebrew Bible: A Socio-Literary Introduction.* Fortress, 1985.

O'Brien, Julia M. *Nahum, Habakkuk, Zephaniah, Haggai, Zechariah, Malachi.* Abingdon, 2004.

Peterson, David L. *The Prophetic Literature: An Introduction.* Westminster John Knox, 2002.

Sweeney, Marvin A. *The Twelve Prophets.* Vol. 2, *Micah, Nahum, Habakkuk, Zephaniah, Haggai, Zechariah, Malachi.* Liturgical, 2000.   B.B.

Zerah (zihr′uh).

1 The son of Reul; he was an Edomite, the grandson of Esau and Basemath, the daughter of Ishmael (Gen. 36:13, 17; 1 Chron. 1:37; cf. Gen. 36:1–4).

2 The father of Jobab, an early Edomite king (Gen. 36:33; 1 Chron. 1:44); possibly the same as **1**.

3 A twin son of Judah and Tamar (Gen. 38:30; cf. 46:12; 1 Chron. 2:4, 6). He was the founder of the Zerahites, who were a subgroup of the Judahites (Num. 26:20; cf. 1 Chron. 9:6; Neh. 11:24). Achan, the warrior who took items from Jericho that had been dedicated to God for himself and his family, is identified as a descendant of this Zerah (Josh. 7:1, 18, 24; cf. 1 Chron. 2:6–7). *See also* Zerahites.

4 A son of Simeon who was the founder of Zerahites that were a subgroup of the Simeonites (Num. 26:13; 1 Chron. 4:24). He is called Zohar in Gen. 46:10; Exod. 6:15. *See also* Zerahites.

5 An Ethiopian (Cushite) leader of a large attacking force whom King Asa of Judah defeated at Mareshah (2 Chron. 14:9–15).

Zerahiah (zair′uh-hi′uh; Heb., "the LORD has dawned" or "the LORD has shone forth").

1 A Levite in the priestly line of Aaron who was an ancestor of Ezra (1 Chron. 6:6, 51; Ezra 7:4).

2 A member of the lineage of Pahath-moab whose son Eliehoenai returned from the Babylonian exile with Ezra (Ezra 8:4).

Zerahites (zihr′uh-hīts), the name of two tribal subgroups during the period of the wilderness wanderings, one belonging to the tribe of Simeon (Num. 26:13) and the other to the tribe of Judah (26:20). The association of the Zerahites with both Judah and Simeon probably reflects the fact that after the settlement in the land the tribe of Simeon was absorbed very quickly into the tribe of Judah and lost its identity (see Gen. 49:7; Josh. 19:1). The same practice of dual identification is seen in certain lists in which cities are named as belonging to both Simeon and Judah (cf. Josh. 15:21–63 with 19:1–9). It is therefore likely that there was only one group of Zerahites and that it shows up on two lists. Achan, who precipitated a crisis by keeping some of the spoils of Jericho that were supposed to be dedicated to God, was a Zerahite (Josh. 7:17), as were Sibbecai and Maharai, two of David's military commanders (1 Chron. 27:11, 13). *See also* Simeon; Zerah.   D.R.B.

Zered (zihr′id), **Wadi,** a brook that empties into the Dead Sea at its extreme southeast corner. The crossing of this stream concluded the Israelites' wilderness wanderings (Num. 21:12; Deut. 2:13–14). Probably to be identified with modern Wadi el-Hesa, it cleaves the high eastern plateau to join the southern end of the Dead Sea. It constitutes the frontier between Moab and Edom and is perhaps the "Wadi of the Willows" (Isa. 15:7). *See also* Edom; Moab; wadi.

Zeresh (zihr′ish), the wife of Haman (Esther 5:10, 14; 6:13). Although her husband is clearly the villain of the book of Esther, Zeresh is the one who counsels Haman to build a gallows for Mordecai. Later, when it has been revealed that Haman's adversary Mordecai is "of the Jewish people," Zeresh correctly predicts that Haman will surely fall before him. *See also* Esther, book of; Haman.

Zeruah (zuh-roo′uh), the Ephraimite widow of Nebat, and the mother of King Jeroboam I of Israel (ca. 922–901 BCE; 1 Kings 11:26).

Zerubbabel (zuh-ruhb′uh-buhl; Heb., "shoot of Babylon"), a postexilic figure with whom messianic prophecies came to be associated. He was a descendant of the Davidic family, though the genealogies differ as to whether his father was Shealtiel, the eldest son of Jehoiachin (Hag. 1:1; Ezra 3:2; cf. Matt. 1:12; Luke 3:37), or Pedaiah, a younger son of Jehoiachin (1 Chron. 3:19). Zerubbabel appears with Joshua (Jeshua) the high priest as the recipient of Haggai's message to rebuild the temple (Hag. 1:1; 2:2). The prophet says that God will make him like a "signet ring" as a royal servant of the Lord (2:20–23). In Zechariah, he is named only in 4:6b–10a, inserted in the vision of the golden lampstand; he alone is the initiator and completer of the restored temple, not by human power, but by divine spirit. The "man whose name is Branch" referred to in Zech. 6:12 is also generally believed to be Zerubbabel (cf. Jer. 23:5).

Zerubbabel also appears in Ezra 3:2, 8 and 4:2, 3, usually with Jeshua, as responsible for rebuilding the temple; in 4:1–3 he refuses the help of "adversaries" who claimed to be true worshipers after the Assyrian ruler Esar-haddon brought them to the land. In Ezra 2:2; Neh. 7:7; and Neh. 12:1, 47, Zerubbabel appears as leader of one group of returning exiles. These passages reflect various stages of postexilic life in Judah.

Zerubbabel is called "governor" in Hag. 1:1 and 2:2; the same term appears in *bullae* (seal impressions) of the official responsible for administering the district of Yehud (Judah). He was probably, but not certainly, appointed by Darius I. In 1 Esd. 3:1–5:3 is an apocryphal tale of a contest of wits at the court of Darius; unexpectedly, Zerubbabel is identified as the winner and is granted leave to rebuild Jerusalem and the temple. *See also* Haggai, book of; Zechariah, book of.   P.R.A.

Zeruiah (zuh-roo′yuh), the mother of Joab, Abishai, and Asahel, three of David's warriors. According to 1 Chron. 2:16, Zeruiah was one of David's sisters, though it is possible that, like Abigail, she was his half sister. In 2 Sam. 17:25, Zeruiah is called the sister of Abigail, who is identified there as the daughter of Nahash; David's father was Jesse (1 Sam. 16). It is unusual for Joab, Abishai, and Asahel to be identified by association with their mother ("sons of Zeruiah," e.g., 2 Sam. 2:18) rather than their father (whose name is never given). The sons of Zeruiah are depicted as impetuous and ruthless men, frequently appearing as foils to the milder-tempered king (cf. 2 Sam. 3:39).

Zeus (zoos), the chief deity of the Greek pantheon, often described as the "father of gods and men." Zeus is depicted as the sky god, enthroned on Mount Olympus, wielding the thunder bolt, and responsible for weather and rain. In Hellenistic times (ca. 300 BCE–300 CE), Zeus was identified with the chief deity of any non-Greek religion. Barnabas is taken to be Zeus by the people of Lystra (Acts 14:12).   P.P.

Ziba (zi′buh), a retainer in Saul's household who informs David of a survivor among Saul's people, namely, Jonathan's lame son (and Saul's grandson) Mephibosheth. David restores Saul's estate to Mephibosheth, appointing Ziba as overseer (2 Sam. 9:1–12). When David is forced to flee Jerusalem during Absalom's revolt, Ziba meets him with provisions and a story of Mephibosheth's designs on the crown. For this information Ziba is promised the whole of Mephibosheth's estate (16:1–4). When David returns to Jerusalem, however, Mephibosheth meets him with expressions of loyalty, maintaining that Ziba's claims were false. Unable to know who is telling the truth, David divides the estate between them (19:17–29).   P.A.B.

Zibeon (zib′ee-uhn), the son of Seir the Horite and a chieftain of the Horites (Gen. 36:20, 29). He is identified as the ancestor of Esau's wife (36:2),

which establishes a relationship between the Horites and the Edomites. The reference to Zibeon as a Hivite in 36:2 is regarded as a textual error, since elsewhere Zibeon is always connected with the Horites. *See also* Edomites; Horites.

Zichri (zik′ri).

1 The son of Izhar and the brother of Korah; he was the head of a levitical family in the time of Moses (Exod. 6:21).

2 The son of Joram; he was a Levite appointed by David to oversee the treasury of booty taken in battle that was to be dedicated to the Lord (1 Chron. 26:25).

3 The father of Eliezer, the leader of the Reubenites during David's reign (1 Chron. 27:16).

4 The father of Amasiah, a Judahite general in Jehoshaphat's army (2 Chron. 17:16).

5 The father of Elishaphat, one of Jehoiada's five generals who helped to overthrow Queen Athaliah (2 Chron. 23:1).

6 An Ephraimite warrior in the army of Pekah who slew three of Ahaz's officers, including Maaseiah, the king's son (2 Chron. 28:7).

7 The son of Asaph and grandfather of Mattaniah, a Levite who made the return from exile (1 Chron. 9:15; cf. Zabdi, Neh. 11:17).

8 The father of Joel, a Benjaminite who was one of Nehemiah's overseers in Jerusalem after the return from exile (Neh. 11:9).

9 The head of the priestly family of Abijah in the second generation (the days of Joiakim) after the return from exile (Neh. 12:17).   P.K.M.

ziggurat (zig′uh-rat; from the Akkadian *ziqqurratu*, "temple tower," a noun derived from *zaqaru*, "to build high"), a stepped temple with a rectangular or, later, square base, built mostly in Mesopotamia. Ziggurats usually had a sanctuary on the ground level, which perhaps was matched by a sanctuary on the ziggurat's summit, where the god was thought to appear. Ziggurats were built from the protoliterate period on. They existed at one time or another in most major Mesopotamian

The ziggurat at Ur: a view of the southwest face.

cities, including Babylon, Ashur, Nineveh, Ur, and Eridu, and they honored important gods such as Marduk, Ashur, Shamash, Enlil, Anu, and Ishtar. A ziggurat at Ur, dating from the late third millennium, is well preserved and suggests the great impact that these structures must have had on the ancient Mesopotamians. The first-millennium ziggurat of Marduk in Babylon was called the Etemenanki, "the house that is the foundation of heaven and earth," indicating the important place that ziggurats had in antiquity.

The construction of the Tower of Babel as narrated in Gen. 11:1–9 was probably patterned after the building of a great ziggurat. Indeed, the narrative is set in Mesopotamia (11:2, 9) and even reflects Mesopotamian building techniques and phraseology (11:3). Also, in Gen. 28:12–15, Jacob dreams of angels ascending and descending a staircase (NRSV: "ladder"). Possibly, the staircase in this dream is patterned after a ziggurat, whose stairs led to a summit where the god was manifest (cf. v. 17). *See also* Babel.   M.Z.B.

Ziha (zi´huh).

1 A family group of temple servants (Nethinim) who returned from the Babylonian exile with Zerubbabel (Ezra 2:43; Neh. 7:46).

2 One of the overseers of the temple servants who lived in Ophel after the return from exile (Neh. 11:21).

Ziklag (zik´lag), a city in the Negev, the wilderness area west and south of the Dead Sea; its location cannot be determined with certainty. The city was given to David by the Philistine tyrant of Gath, Achish. It was David's base for military operations for a year and four months (1 Sam. 27:5–12), and it was destroyed by the Amalekites at the time of Saul's last stand against the Philistines (30:1–19). It is listed in the ancestral holdings of both Judah (Josh. 15:31; cf. 1 Sam. 27:6) and Simeon (Josh. 19:5; cf. 1 Chron. 4:30).

Zillah (zil´uh), one of the wives of Lamech and the mother of Tubal-cain and Naamah (Gen. 4:19–23).

Zillethai (zil´uh-thi; Heb., "shadow, protection").

1 A son of Shimei; a Benjaminite who was the leader of a family group in postexilic Jerusalem (1 Chron. 8:20).

2 A member of the tribe of Manasseh who deserted Saul's army to come to the aid of David while he was at Ziklag (1 Chron. 12:20).

Zilpah (zil´puh), the slave of Leah who was given to Jacob as a surrogate mother and who bore Gad and Asher (Gen. 30:9–13). Leah herself had already borne four sons to Jacob, and eventually she would bear two more. Although it was more common for a childless wife to give her slave to her husband as a surrogate mother, Leah apparently gave Zilpah to Jacob because her sister Rachel (who at that point was childless) had given her slave Bilhah

to Jacob and Bilhah had borne two sons, Dan and Naphtali. Gen. 46:18 counts the "children of Zilpah" as sixteen persons (including children and grandchildren of Gad and Asher).   T.S.F.

Zimran (zim´ran), a son of Abraham and Keturah (Gen. 25:2; 1 Chron. 1:32). The name may be connected with a tribe later identified as living in Arabia, possibly at a place along the east shore of the Red Sea west of Mecca.

Zimri (zim´ri; Heb., "[God] is my protection" or "strength").

1 A Simeonite who lived prior to Israel's entry into Canaan (Num. 25:14). He became the paradigmatic example of a problem encountered at Shittim. Israelite men had begun having sexual relations with Moabite women, and these women had invited them to the sacrifices of their gods; thus, "Israel yoked itself with the Baal of Peor" (25:1–3). God sent a plague among the people and, just as Moses was telling the judges that they had to kill all of the chiefs of the people to turn God's fierce anger away, Zimri, the Simeonite chief, came walking up with a Midianite princess named Cozbi, the daughter of Zur, and took her into his tent. Phinehas the priest grabbed a spear, went into the tent, and "pierced the two of them, the Israelite and the woman, through the belly" (25:8). Thus, the plague was stopped.

2 The king of Israel ca. 876 BCE. Zimri had been the commander of half of Israel's chariotry under King Elah. He killed the king in a successful but short-lived coup, ruling in Tirzah for only one week before another officer (Omri) besieged the city and Zimri committed suicide by entering the royal palace he had set afire (1 Kings 16:8–31). Zimri's name would became an epithet for one who kills his master (2 Kings 9:31).

3 The son of Zerah and grandson of Judah and Tamar (1 Chron. 2:6; cf. Zabdi, Jos. 7:1).

4 A descendant of Saul's son Jonathan (1 Chron. 8:36; 9:42).

5 A nation, apparently near southern Mesopotamia (Jer. 25:25). It is not mentioned elsewhere and nothing about it is known.   F.E.G./M.A.P.

Zin, Wilderness of, an area in the southern Levant, including also a place called Zin (Num. 34:3–4; Josh. 15:1–3) within the area of Paran. It included Kadesh-barnea as well as Massah and Meribah (Num. 27:14; Deut. 32:51) and must therefore have been south of the present Israeli border, more or less in the center on an east–west axis. Moses sent spies from here to explore the future homeland (Num. 13:25). It is not the same as the "Wilderness of Sin." *See also* Kadesh; Massah and Meribah; Paran.

Zion (zi´uhn), an ancient name for the temple, Jerusalem, Judah, and the people of God. According to 2 Sam. 5:6–10, David and his men took Jerusalem from the Jebusites, apparently climbing through a water tunnel or shaft and opening the city gate from the inside. The text states that "David took the stronghold of Zion, which is now the city of David" (5:7). Here, the reference seems to be to a pre-Israelite fortress just south of the current Temple Mount complex. Although this city or fortress can be called Zion, the Temple Mount area immediately to the north, which was first constructed under Solomon's reign, also ends up bearing that name. This seems implied from a number of psalms extolling the virtues of Zion and from related themes elsewhere in the Bible: Zion is God's "holy hill" (Ps. 2:6). But in Isa. 33:20, the image is clearly extended to apply to all of Jerusalem: "Look on Zion, the city of our appointed festivals! Your eyes will see Jerusalem." Curiously, Ps. 48:1–2 refers to "Mount Zion in the far north, the city of the great king," which would seem to point to Samaria, not Jerusalem. Then 78:68 applies the image to the nation: God "chose the tribe of Judah, Mount Zion." And in 74:2, Mount Zion is used in a parallel expression that suggests people, not a place: "Remember your congregation, which you acquired long ago, which you redeemed to be the tribe of your heritage. Remember Mount Zion, where you came to dwell."

The descriptive language of Zion is replete with rich imagery. Streams of water come forth from Zion (Ps. 46:4), although in actuality the city of Jerusalem is supplied by two springs, both of which are located off the hill proper. Zion is referred to as God's "holy mountain, beautiful in elevation, the joy of all the earth" (48:1–2). On numerous occasions, the image of Zion is employed as a metaphor for security and protection (e.g., 125). The NT continues this imagery, using the term "heavenly Jerusalem" or Zion metaphorically in reference to the church (Heb. 12:22), the gospel message (1 Pet. 2:6), and the place of God's dwelling (Rev. 14:1). *See also* David; Jerusalem.   J.A.D./M.A.P.

Ziph (zif).

1 A descendant of Caleb (1 Chron. 2:42) and ancestor of the Ziphites, who settled in the city and region of Ziph (cf. **3**).

2 The eldest son of Jehallel; a Judahite member of the Calebite line (1 Chron. 4:16).

3 A city in the hill country of southern Judah (Josh. 15:55). The area between this town and the Dead Sea at En-gedi was called the Wilderness of Ziph (1 Sam. 23:14–15; 24; 26:2). While David was hiding in this area during his flight from Saul, the Ziphites betrayed his location to Saul (1 Sam. 23:19; 26:1). The city was later fortified and provisioned by King Rehoboam as a defensive garrison (2 Chron. 11:8). The city is identified as modern Tell ez-Zif, about three miles southwest of Hebron.

4 A city in the far southern territory of the tribe of Judah (Josh. 15:24). Some scholars identify it as modern Khir-bet ez-Zeifeh, which lies west of the south end of the Dead Sea in the eastern Negev.
                                        D.R.B.

A monumental stepped structure, taller than a five-story building, excavated in the city of David—or Zion—from the tenth century BCE. It continues 22 feet beneath the Israelite houses whose remains are located toward the center of the photo.

Zippor (zip'or; Heb., "bird"), the father of Balak, the king of Moab who hired Balaam to curse Israel (Num. 22:2, 4; Josh. 24:9).

Zipporah (zi-por'uh), the wife of Moses and the mother of Gershom and Eliezer. She was one of the seven daughters of Reuel, priest of Midian (also known as Jethro). Zipporah appears in three narratives. In the first (Exod. 2:16–22), the daughters of Reuel were drawing water for their sheep, when shepherds chased them away. Moses (who had just fled Egypt) came to their defense and watered their flock; upon hearing this, Reuel invited him to his home and gave him Zipporah as his wife.

In a second narrative (Exod. 4:24–26) God inexplicably attacked Moses and tried to kill him, but Zipporah saved his life by doing three things: she circumcised their son Gershom, cutting off his foreskin, touched his feet with the foreskin, and said, "Truly you are a bridegroom of blood to me!" (4:25). For this reason, God left Moses alone, and it was then that Zipporah said, "A bridegroom of blood by circumcision" (4:26). The meaning of this story is not clear. First, the text is ambiguous with regard to whether Zipporah touched the feet of Gershom or the feet of Moses with the severed foreskin (the NRSV opts for the latter). Second, many interpreters note that "feet" is a common euphemism in the Bible for genitals, though the exact import of that point for the story is unclear. Finally, Zipporah's pronouncement has a ritualistic or liturgical ring to it that makes scholars wonder if she is not portrayed here as acting in a priestly capacity. This story is sometimes associated with the origins of circumcision as a practice among the Israelites, although the details of its interpretation have confounded exegetes.

Finally, the Bible reports that Zipporah and her sons stayed with Jethro in Midian when Moses went back to Egypt to lead the exodus; later, Jethro brought them to Moses when he came to meet Israel in the desert (Exod. 18:2–5). *See also* circumcision.   T.S.F./M.A.P.

Ziv. *See* calendar.

Zoan (zoh'uhn; Heb.; Egyptian Djanet; Gk. Tanis), the residence of the kings of Egypt during the Twenty-First and Twenty-Second Dynasties (ca. 1070–715 BCE) and a major commercial and political center down into the Ptolemaic period (ca. 332–30 BCE). Zoan is located at modern San el-Hagar, on the Tanitic branch of the Nile in the northeast Delta, about seventy-three miles northeast of Cairo. The "fields of Zoan," evidently a region around the city, are described in Ps. 78:12, 43 as the scene of the wonders associated with the exodus. According to Num. 13:22, Hebron was built seven years before Zoan. It was still an important city in the days of Isaiah and Ezekiel (Isa. 19:11, 13; 30:4; Ezek. 30:14). Zoan is referred to as Tanis (its Greek name) in Jth. 1:10.

Zoan is one of the largest sites in the Egyptian Delta, and multiple archaeological excavations have been conducted there. The principal feature is an enormous mud-brick enclosure wall, inside of which a second wall surrounds a great temple dedicated to the god Amun. This complex was evidently started by the Twenty-First Dynasty king Psusennes I (1039–991 BCE). Elsewhere within the inner enclosure wall are the subterranean tombs of six kings of the Twenty-First and Twenty-Second Dynasties.   J.M.W.

Zoar (zoh'ahr), one of the five cities of the Plain (along with Sodom, Gomorrah, Admah, and Zeboiim). Four eastern kings led by Chedorlaomer, king of Elam, defeated these five cities in the valley of Siddim (Gen. 14:1–12). God allowed Lot to flee from Sodom to Zoar before he destroyed Sodom and the other three cities with fire and brimstone (19:18–23). Zoar is mentioned later in connection with the destruction of Moab (Isa. 15:5; Jer. 48:34). The exact location of Zoar is uncertain; it may be at the site of es-Safi, located about five miles south of the Dead Sea. *See also* cities.   J.M.W.

Zobah (zoh'buh), or Aram-zobah, one of the independent city-states the Arameans (Syrians) formed at the beginning of the first millennium BCE. Zobah was situated in the Valley of Lebanon, with Hamath to the north and Damascus to the south. The kingdom of Zobah was extensive, controlling eastern Syria from the Hauran to the Euphrates Valley. It was so powerful that it posed a threat, not only to Israel, but even to imperial Assyria. Saul's victory over Zobah is mentioned in 1 Sam. 14:47. Some scholars, however, maintain that the Arameans did not appear on the Israelite stage until the time of David. Aram-zobah was David's archrival for control of Syria and Transjordan. When David was warring with the Ammonites, Hadadezer ben Rehob, the powerful Aramean king of Zobah, intervened in support of the Ammonites (2 Sam. 8:5; 1 Chron. 18:3–9). As a result, David twice defeated Hadadezer and made Zobah subject to Israel.   P.J.K.

Zohar (zoh'hahr).

1 The father of Ephron, the Hittite who sold Abraham the cave of Machpelah in which to bury Sarah (Gen. 23:8; 25:9).

2 A son of Simeon who accompanied Jacob and his family to Egypt (Gen. 46:10) and became the head of a family group there (Exod. 6:15). This is probably the same person who is elsewhere called Zerah (1 Chron. 4:24), the ancestor of the family group called the Zerahites who left Egypt with Moses (Num. 26:13). *See also* Zerah; Zerahites.

3 A descendant of Judah (1 Chron. 4:7), elsewhere called Izhar. *See also* Izhar.   D.R.B.

Zoheleth (zoh'huh-lith; Heb., "serpent"), a stone (called in some English Bibles "the Serpent's

Stone") that was a place of Jebusite worship prior to the capture of that city by David. When David was old and in ill health, his son Adonijah offered sacrifices at the Zoheleth stone prior to having himself crowned king. This prompted Nathan and Bathsheba to intervene with David and ensure that he would name Solomon his successor. This was done, and while Abijah and his companions were still feasting in celebration of the self-coronation, word reached them that Solomon had been made king (1 King 1:9–50). The stone is said to have been beside En-rogel, a site near the confluence of Kidron and Hinnom valleys.

Zophar (zoh'fahr), a Naamathite, one of the three counselors of Job who offered him advice (Job 2:11; 11:1; 20:1). Zophar reproaches Job for claiming innocence (11:2–6) and counsels repentance (11:13–20). In a second speech, he maintains that the wicked always get their just deserts (20:1–29). Eventually, God rebukes Zophar and Job's other counselors for lack of understanding and insight (42:7–9). *See also* Job, book of.

Zorah (zor'uh), a town (modern Sar'ah) located in the Valley of Sorek, three miles northeast of Beth-shemesh and fifteen miles west of Jerusalem. The Danite Manoah, father of Samson, came from Zorah, and Samson was raised there (Judg. 13:2, 25). Both he and his father were buried in the region between Zorah and Eshtaol (Judg. 16:31). The Danites were the first tribe to settle in the Zorah area (Josh. 15:33; 19:31). When the neighboring Philistines encroached upon their territory, the Danites migrated north; they settled at Laish and renamed it Dan (Judg. 18). With the departure of the Danites from Zorah the town became Judahite. To protect Judah from the Egyptians, King Rehoboam fortified Zorah and the surrounding towns in the Shephelah region. Upon return from Babylonian exile Jews settled again in Zorah.   P.J.K.

Zoroaster (zoh'roh-as'tuhr), an east Iranian prophet whose followers worshiped the deity Ahura-Mazda. According to Zoroaster, the history of the world was divided into three ages of three thousand years each. The first was the golden age of Ahura-Mazda. The second was a period of warfare with evil that ended with the coming of Zoroaster. The prophet brought a new force enabling humans to participate in separating truth from falsehood. The final period would extend until the renovation of the world. Some elements of this belief appear to have influenced the development of angelology, dualism, belief in an evil power (Satan), and the dispensational view of history that can be found in apocalyptic Jewish writings of the Second Temple Judaism, including the book of Daniel. *See also* apocalyptic literature; Apocrypha/deuterocanonical literature; Pseudepigrapha; Satan.   P.P.

Zuar (zoo'uhr), father of Nethanel, the leader of the tribe of Issachar during the wandering of the Israelites through Sinai (Num. 1:8; 2:5; 7:18, 23; 10:15).

Zur (zuhr).

1 A Midianite king whose daughter, Cozbi, was killed by Phinehas along with Zimri of Israel as the two were engaged in sexual congress (Num. 25:6–8, 15). Zur himself was slain by the Israelites in the battle in which Moses defeated Sihon, king of the Amorites (Num. 31:8; Josh. 13:21). *See also* Sihon; Zimri.

2 A Gibeonite, the son of Jeiel from the tribe of Benjamin (1 Chron. 8:30; 9:36).

Zurishaddai (zoor'i-shad'i; Heb., "Shaddai is my rock"), the father of Shelumiel, the leader of the tribe of Simeon during the wilderness wandering (Num. 1:6; 2:12; 7:36, 41; 10:19).

Photograph and Illustration Credits

Index to Color Maps

This index lists geographic names found on the color maps at the back of this book. The number(s) of the map(s) on which the name appears is listed first, followed by the key, or grid reference (a letter-figure combination that refers to the letters and figures at the margins of the map). Places whose names have changed over time are identified by a "see also" reference. For example, the entry for Azotus indicates it can be found on Map 11 in location B-5, and on Map 13 in location A-5, and readers are referred to Ashdod, its alternate name.

Physical Map of the Land of Israel and Surrounding Area in Biblical Times

Map 1

0   10   20   30   40 Mls
0   20   40   60 Kms

© Copyright HAMMOND INCORPORATED, Maplewood, N.J.

Elevations are given in feet

The terrain model map here and those on subsequent pages depict the natural vegetation of the Bible world as far as it can be determined. Primary ground cover has undergone changes by time and humans. For example, vast areas of Mediterranean vegetation, originally a maquis-forest type, are now dwarf-shrub with only rare patches of forest. The following sequence of colors applies to maps in the series.

- Mediterranean vegetation
- Grassland — steppe
- Mixed grassland & forest
- Sparse grassland & shrub
- Riverine vegetation & oases
- Snow & ice
- Barren salt flats
- Sandy or salt desert
- Stony desert — hamada
- Barren lava beds

A   B   C   D

Sidon

MT. LEBANON

Damascus

1

MT. HERMON
▲9,232

Pharpar

Leontes

Tyre

P H O E N I C I A

Dan

UPPER
GALILEE

Lake Hula
(L. Semechonitis)
223

2

B A S H A N

Hauran

Acco

▲ Mt. Meron
3,963

L O W E R
GALILEE

-696

Sea of Galilee
(Chinnereth)

Mt. Carmel
1,791

Kishon

Nazareth

Mt. Tabor
▲1,929

Plain
of
Esdrae-
lon

Hill of
Moreh

V. of Jezreel

Yarmuk

Dor.

Megiddo.

Mt. Gilboa
1,640

Beth-shan

3

G I L E A D

Caesarea

Plain of Sharon

Dothan

S A M A R I A

Samaria

Mt. Ebal
▲3,083

Jabbok

(Zerqa)

Mt. Gerizim
2,890

Shechem

Jordan

The Great Sea
(Mediterranean Sea)

Kanah

Farah

Jebel Yusha
▲3,652

A M M O N

4

Joppa

Ajalon

Shiloh

Tell Azur
3,333

Rabbah
(Amman)

Sorek

Bethel

Jericho

Jerusalem.

Mt. of Olives
2,670

Mt. Nebo
▲2,631

Plain of Philistia

Elah

Bethlehem

S H E P H E L A H

J U D E A

Wilderness of Judea

Dead
(Salt)
Sea
-1,296

Plains of
Moab

5

▲3,346

Gaza

Gerar

Hebron

Arnon

M O A B

Besor

Raphia

Beer-sheba

Kir-hareseth

6

I D U M E A

N e g e b

A r a b a h

Zered

Map 2

Caspian Sea

Persian Gulf (Lower Sea)

Dilmun?

F

MEDIA

URARTU

ELAM

E

Cyrus

Araxes

M. Ararat

L. Urmia

L. Van

ZAGROS MOUNTAINS

GUTIUM

Tepe Giyan

Ecbatana

Susa

Diyala

Lagash

Ur

Eridu

The Ancient World
in the Late Bronze Age

Areas of influence of major
powers about 1350 B.C.E.

0   50   100   150   200   250 Mls
0   100   200   300   400 Kms

D

KAISHKA

HURRIANS

Tell Halaf

Tepe Gawra

Arbela

Jarmo

Nuzi

ASSYRIA

Nineveh

Calah

Asshur

MITANNI

Haran

Paddan-aram

Tell Halaf

Nagar

Eshnunna

Agade?

Sippar

Cuthah

Babylon

Nippur

Isin

Erech

Sumer

AKKAD

BABYLONIA

KASSITES

Tigris

Euphrates

Black Sea

HANS

HITTITE EMPIRE (HATTI)

Alaca Huyuk

Ankuwa

Hattusas

Kanish

KIZZUWATNA

Mari

Tadmor

Carchemish

Alalakh

Haleb

Ebla

Hamath

Kadesh

Dumah

C

Sargarius

Hermes

ARZAWA

Maeander

Beycesultan

L. Tuz

Mersin

TAURUS

LUKKA

Ugarit

Arvad

ALASHIYA
KITTIM
(Cyprus)

Gebal

Sidon

Tyre

Damascus

KEDAR

Dor

Hazor

Megiddo

Joppa

Shechem

Jericho

Jerusalem

Gaza

Hebron

Beer-sheba

Kadesh-barnea

TEMA

Dedan

B

Troy

ASSUWA

Xanthus

Rhodes

MINOAN-MYCENAEAN DOMAIN

CAPHTOR (Crete)

Cnossus

Mediterranean Sea
(Great or Upper Sea)

CANAAN

ISRAEL?

MIDIAN

Tema

Red Sea

A

Avaris (Zoan)

Lower Egypt

On

Memphis (Noph)

Heracleopolis

Hermopolis

EGYPT

Akhetaton (Tell el-Amarna)

Nile

Libyan Desert

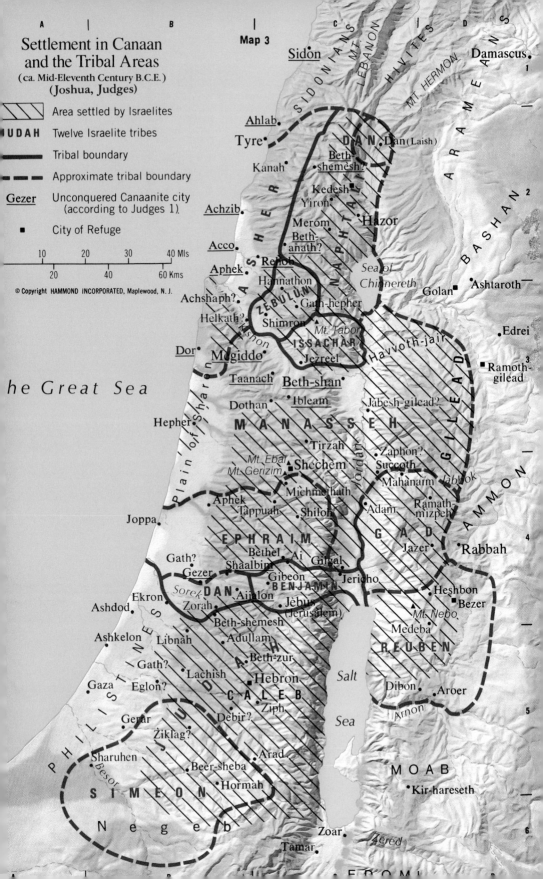

Settlement in Canaan and the Tribal Areas
(ca. Mid-Eleventh Century B.C.E.)
(Joshua, Judges)

Map 3

Area settled by Israelites

JUDAH Twelve Israelite tribes

Tribal boundary

Approximate tribal boundary

Gezer Unconquered Canaanite city (according to Judges 1)

■ City of Refuge

10   20   30   40 Mls
20   40   60 Kms

© Copyright HAMMOND INCORPORATED, Maplewood, N.J.

The Great Sea

A   B   C   D

Sidon
Damascus

SIDONIANS
MT. LEBANON
HIVITES
MT. HERMON
ARAMEANS

Ahlab
Tyre
DAN   Dan (Laish)
Kanah
Beth-shemesh?
Kedesh
Yiron
Merom
Hazor
Achzib
Beth-anath?
Acco
Rehob
Aphek
Hannathon
Achshaph?
ZEBULUN
Gath-hepher
Helkath?
Shimron
Mt. Tabor
ISSACHAR
Dor
Megiddo
Jezreel
Taanach
Beth-shan
Dothan
Ibleam
Jabesh-gilead?
Hepher
MANASSEH
Tirzah
Zaphon?
Succoth
Mt. Ebal
Mt. Gerizim
Shechem
Mahanaim
Joppa
Aphek
Michmethath
Tappuah
Shiloh
Adam
Ramath-mizpeh
EPHRAIM
Bethel
Ai
Gilgal
Jazer
Rabbah
Gath?
Gezer
Shaalbim
Gibeon
Jericho
DAN
Aijalon
BENJAMIN
Ekron
Zorah
Jebus
(Jerusalem)
Heshbon
Ashdod
Beth-shemesh
Bezer
Ashkelon
Libnah
Adullam
Mt. Nebo
Gath?
Beth-zur
Medeba
REUBEN
Gaza
Eglon?
Lachish
Hebron
CALEB
Dibon
Aroer
Debir?
Ziph
Arnon
Gerar
Ziklag?
Arad
Salt Sea
Sharuhen
Beer-sheba
MOAB
Hormah
Kir-hareseth
SIMEON
Negeb
Zoar
Tamar
Zered

ASHER
NAPHTALI
Sea of Chinnereth
Golan
Ashtaroth
BASHAN
Edrei
Ramoth-gilead
Havvoth-jair
GILEAD
Jordan
Jabbok
GAD
AMMON
Plain of Sharon
Kishon
JUDAH
PHILISTINES
Sorek
Besor

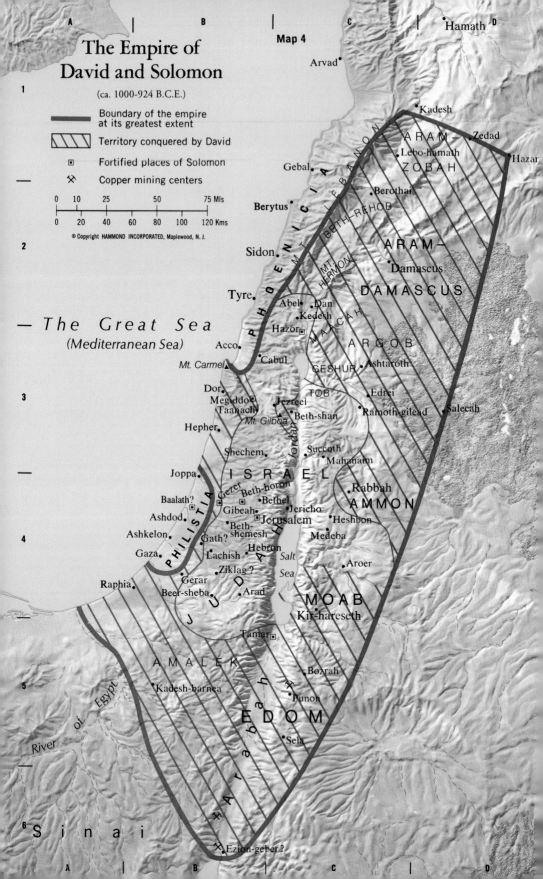

The Empire of David and Solomon

(ca. 1000-924 B.C.E.)

Map 4

Boundary of the empire at its greatest extent

///// Territory conquered by David

▫ Fortified places of Solomon

⚒ Copper mining centers

0 10   25   50   75 Mls
|————————————————————|
0 20 40 60 80 100 120 Kms

® Copyright HAMMOND INCORPORATED, Maplewood, N.J.

The Great Sea
(Mediterranean Sea)

Hamath

Arvad

Kadesh

Zedad

ARAM–
ZOBAH

Lebo-hamath

Hazar

Gebal

Berothai

Berytus

BETH-REHOB

ARAM–
DAMASCUS

Sidon

Damascus

MT. HERMON

MT. LEBANON

PHOENICIA

Tyre

Abel

Dan

Kedesh

MAACAH

ARGOB

Hazor

Acco

Cabul

GESHUR

Ashtaroth

Mt. Carmel

TOB

Edrei

Dor

Megiddo

Jezreel

Ramoth-gilead

Salecah

Taanach

Beth-shan

Mt. Gilboa

Hepher

Succoth

Mahanaim

Shechem

Joppa

ISRAEL

Gezer

Beth-horon

Rabbah

Baalath?

Gibeah

Bethel

AMMON

Ashdod

Jericho

Jerusalem

Heshbon

Beth-shemesh

Ashkelon

Gath?

Medeba

Gaza

Lachish

Hebron

Salt
Sea

Aroer

Raphia

Gerar

Ziklag?

Arad

MOAB

Beer-sheba

JUDAH

Kir-hareseth

Tamar

AMALEK

Bozrah

Kadesh-barnea

Punon

EDOM

Sela

Arabah

River of Egypt

Sinai

Ezion-geber?

The Kingdoms of Israel and Judah

(ca. 924–722 B.C.E.)
(1 and 2 Kings)

Map 5

Approximate frontiers
ISRAEL Hebrew kingdoms
AMMON Foreign kingdoms

10   20   30   40 Mls
20   40   60 Kms

© Copyright HAMMOND INCORPORATED, Maplewood, N.J.

SYRIA (ARAM)
Damascus

PHOENICIA
Sidon
Tyre
Acco
Cabul

MT. HERMON
Leontes
Ijon
Abel-beth-maachah
Dan
Kedesh
Hazor
Merom
Galilee
Chinnereth
Rumah
Hammath
Sea of Chinnereth

Bashan
Karnaim
Ashtaroth
Aphek
Yarmuk
Havvoth-jair
Edrei
Ramoth-gilead

The Great Sea (Mediterranean Sea)

Mt. Carmel
Kishon
Dor
Megiddo
Plain of
Esdraelon
Shunem
Mt. Tabor
Jezreel
Taanach
Mt. Gilboa
Beth-shan
Ibleam
Jabesh-gilead?
Dothan
Abel-meholah?
Tishbe
Plain of Sharon
Socoh
ISRAEL
Tirzah
Samaria
Mt. Ebal
Penuel
Kanah
Mt. Gerizim
Shechem
Succoth
Mahanaim
Aphek
Shiloh
Jordan
Gilead
Jabbok
AMMON
Joppa
Zeredah
Jazer
Rabbah
Lod
Bethel
Zemaraim
Gath?
Mizpah
Gilgal
Jabneel
Gezer
Geba
Ramah
Jericho
Gibbethon
Gibeon
Shittim?
Heshbon
Aijalon
Ekron
Zorah
Jerusalem
Ashdod
Beth-shemesh
Bethlehem
Mt. Nebo
Medeba
Jahaz
Ashkelon
Socoh
Adullam
Etam
Tekoa
Gath?
Mareshah
Beth-zur
Salt
Ataroth
Lachish
JUDAH
Sea
Gaza
Adoraim
Hebron
Ziph
Dibon
Gerar
Debir?
En-gedi
Aroer
Arnon
...aphia
Sharuhen
Ziklag
Wilderness of Judah
Ar?
MOAB
Besor
Great Arad
Beer-sheba
Kir-hareseth
Arad of Beth-yeroham
Ziph
Tamar
Ascent of Akrabbim
Arabah
Zered
EDOM

N e g e b

Map 6

The Assyrian Empire

Assyrian empire — ca. 824 B.C.E.
Assyrian empire — ca. 640 B.C.E.
Greek colonies underlined in red

0 50 100 150 200 250 300 350 Mls

Caspian Sea

F

Ecbatana·

MADAI

ELAM

Lower (Eastern) Sea

L. Sevan
L. Urmia
Cyrus
Araxes

GOMER

CIMMERIANS

URARTU (ARARAT)

Mt. Ararat·

L. Van

·Turushpa

·Susa (Shushan)

PERSIA

·Larsa
·Ur

CHALDEANS

Diyala

ASSYRIA

·Dur-Sharrukin
Nineveh·

·Arbela

BABYLONIA

·Erech
·Nippur

Calah (Nimrud)·
·Asshur

·Sippar
·Cuthah
·Babylon
·Borsippa

Tigris

·Amat

Euphrates

Melitene·

Nisibis·
·Gozan

Haran·

MESHECH

Habor

Carchemish·
·Til Barsib
Arpad·

Tadmor·

ARABS

·Dumah

TUBAL

Samal·

Aleppo·

Qarqar·
Hamath·

SYRIA

ARABIA

·Tema

·Dedan

Kanish·

L. Tuz

PHRYGIA
Gordion·

Ancyra·

TAURUS MTS.

Tarsus·

ARAM

Damascus·

KEDAR

Arvad·

Sidon·
Tyre·

PHOENICIA

AMMON

Samaria·
Eltekeh·

JUDAH

Jerusalem·

Tribe to MOAB
Assyria EDOM

Red Sea

Astacus·
Cyzicus·
Abydos·

Lesbos

MYSIA

Sardis·

LYDIA

Phaselis·

Cyprus

Raphia·

Pelusium·
·Tanis
Bubastis·

Sela·

GREEK

Euboea
Chios

Samos
Miletus

Rhodes

·On

EGYPT

Sais·
·Bubastis

·Memphis

Nile

·Hermopolis

·Thebes

·Siut
·Abydos

Aegean Sea

Athens·

Sparta·
Corinth·

GREEK
CITY STATES

Crete

Upper (Western) Sea

Heracleopolis·

EGYPT
to Assyria 671-651 B.C.E.

·Oasis of Siwa

LIBYANS

Libyan

Desert

Cyrene

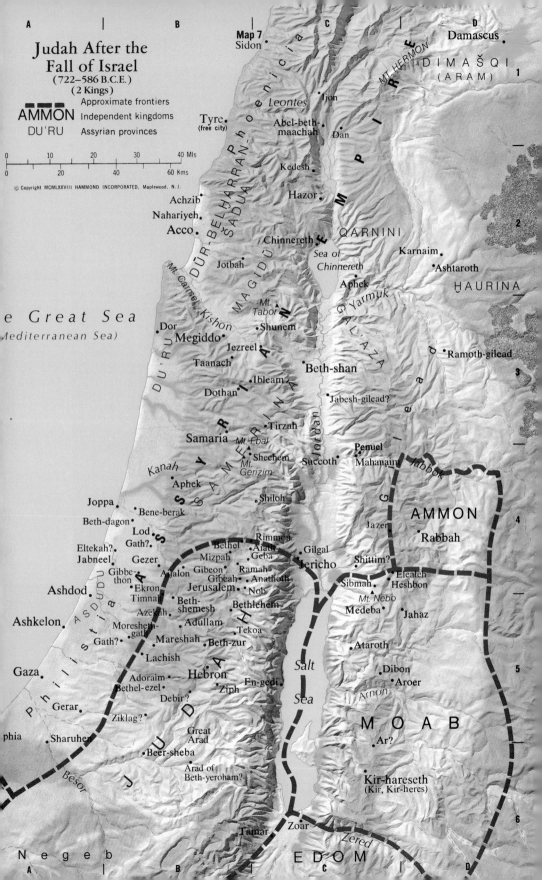

Judah After the Fall of Israel
(722–586 B.C.E.)
(2 Kings)

Approximate frontiers
AMMON Independent kingdoms
DU'RU Assyrian provinces

Map 7

© Copyright MCMLXXVIII HAMMOND INCORPORATED, Maplewood, N.J.

| 0 | 10 | 20 | 30 | 40 Mls |
| 0 | 20 | 40 | 60 Kms |

Sidon

Damascus

D I M A Š Q I
(A R A M)

Leontes

Ijon

Tyre
(free city)

Abel-beth-maachah

Dan

Kedesh

QARNINI

Hazor

Karnaim

Ashtaroth

Achzib

Nahariyeh

Acco

Chinnereth

H A U R I N A

Jotbah

Sea of
Chinnereth

Aphek

The Great Sea
(Mediterranean Sea)

Mt. Tabor

Shunem

Dor

Megiddo

Jezreel

Beth-shan

Ramoth-gilead

Taanach

Kishon

Ibleam

Jabesh-gilead?

Dothan

Tirzah

Samaria

Mt. Ebal

Shechem

Succoth

Penuel

Mahanaim

Mt. Gerizim

Kanah

Aphek

Shiloh

Joppa

Bene-berak

Beth-dagon

Rimmon

Jazer

AMMON

Lod

Gath?

Bethel

Aiath

Geba

Gilgal

Jericho

Shittim?

Rabbah

Eltekah?

Mizpah

Jabneel

Gezer

Gibeon

Ramah

Elealeh

Ajalon

Jerusalem

Anathoth

Sibmah

Heshbon

Gibbethon

Ekron

Timnah

Nob

Mt. Nebo

Ashdod

Beth-shemesh

Bethlehem

Medeba

Jahaz

Azekah

Ashkelon

Moresheth-gath

Adullam

Tekoa

Gath?

Mareshah

Beth-zur

Ataroth

Gaza

Lachish

Dibon

Adoraim

Hebron

En-gedi

Aroer

Gerar

Bethel-ezel

Ziph

Salt
Sea

Arnon

Debir?

M O A B

Ziklag?

Great
Arad

Ar?

Sharuhen

Beer-sheba

Arad of
Beth-yeroham?

Kir-hareseth
(Kir, Kir-heres)

Besor

J U D A H

Tamar

Zoar

Zered

N e g e b

E D O M

Great Empires of the Sixth Century B.C.E.

Map 8

SAKA
Jaxartes
Cyropolis
CHORASMIA
SOGDIANA
Bactra
BACTRIA
MARGUS
Margiana
Oxus
ARIA
ARACHOSIA
Aral Sea
DRANGIANA
CARMANIA
GEDROSIA
MAKA
Pura
Erythraean Sea

Caspian Sea
PARTHIA
HYRCANIA
Zadracarta
Damghan
Rhagae
MEDIAN EMPIRE
(612-550 B.C.E.)
MEDIA
Ecbatana
Behistun
PERSIS
Gabae
Yazd
Pasargadae
Persepolis (Parsa)
ELAM
(SUSIANA)
Susa
Ulai
Gerrha
Persian Gulf

Political boundaries of major powers ca. 560 B.C.E.
Limits of the Persian empire ca. 500 B.C.E.
Persian royal road

500 Mls
0 100 200 300 400
0 200 400 600 800 Kms

Phasis
Trapezus
COLCHIS
Cyrus
SCYTHIANS
MOSCHI
URARTU
Lake Van
Tushpa
Tigris
ASSYRIA
Nineveh
Nisibis
Ashhur
Harran
Carchemish
Euphrates
Opis
Sippar
Babylon
Nippur
BABYLONIA
Erech
Ur
Anat
Tadmor
NEW
BABYLONIAN
EMPIRE
(625-529 B.C.E.)

Sinope
Apollonia
Byzantium
Black Sea
KINGDOM OF
LYDIA
(670-546 B.C.E.)
Gordion
Ancyra
Pteria
Sardis
Halys
LYDIA
LYCIA
Xanthus
CILICIA
Tarsus
Thapsacus
Riblah
Hamath
Arvad
Gebal
Damascus
ARABS
Dumah
Dedan
Tema

THRACE
MACEDONIA
Marathon
GREECE
Athens
Sparta
Ephesus
Miletus
Rhodes
Crete
Ister (Danube)
Chersonesus

Cyprus
trib. to Egypt
569-525 B.C.E.
Mediterranean Sea
Megiddo
Tyre
JUDAH
Jerusalem
Gaza
Elath
Pelusium
Sais
Memphis

Cyrene
LIBYA
KINGDOM OF
EGYPT
(663-525 B.C.E.)
Temple of Amon (Siwa)
Libyan Desert
Thebes
Syene (Elephantine)
Zile
Red Sea
ETHIOPIA
(CUSH)

Map 9

Israel Under Persian Rule (After the Return from Exile)

(539–332 B.C.E.)
(Ezra, Nehemiah)

- ⬢ Satrapy capital   ▣ District capitals
- ◉ Provincial capitals   • Towns

0 5 10 15 20 25 30 35 40 Mls
0 10 20 30 40 50 60 Kms

© Copyright HAMMOND INCORPORATED, Maplewood, N.J.

SIDON

Damascus

D·A·M·A·S·C·U·S

Mt. HERMON

Tyre

TYRE

Kedesh

Achzib
ACHZIB

Hazor

Acco
ACCO

KARNAIM

Karnaim

Lake Gennesaret

Beth-yerah

Yarmuk

HAURAN

Mt. Carmel

Dor

The Great Sea

(Mediterranean Sea)

Strato's Tower

Narbatah

Beth-shan

Pella

GILEAD

Jordan

Gerasa

Samaria

Jabbok

Mt. Ebal
Mt. Gerizim   Shechem

Apollonia

Aphek

SAMARIA

Accrabbah

Joppa

Shiloh

Ono   Neballat   ?

Lod

Hadid

Gittaim

Beeroth   Bethel

Lower   Ai

Beth-horon   Mizpah   Ramah

Jamnia

Gibeon   Geba

Gezer

Anathoth

Kiriath-jearim

Beth-haccherem

Jerusalem

Ashdod

Zanoah

JUDAH
(YAHUD)

Bethlehem

Ashkelon

Azekah

Adullam

Netophah

ASHDOD

Mareshah

Keilah

Tekoa

Lachish

Nebo   Beth-zur

Gaza

Hebron

En-gedi

Rabbah

Beth-gilgal

Jericho

Tyre of Tobiah

AMMON

Heshbon

Medeba

Salt Sea

Arnon

MOAB

Gerar

Ziklag?

En-rimmon

IDUMEA

Jeshua?

Raphia

(E D O M I T E S)

Beer-sheba

Moladah

Beth-pelet?

NABATEAN ARABS

Israel's Boundary Under the Maccabees

- - - - Boundary of Judea before the uprising, 166 B.C.E.

——— Maccabean domain at maximum extent

0 5 10 15 20 25 30 35 Mls
0 10 20 30 40 50 Kms

© Copyright HAMMOND INCORPORATED, Maplewood, N.J.

Map 11

A   B   C   D

The Great Sea
(Mediterranean Sea)

PHOENICIA

Leontes

Tyre

Ladder of Tyre

Cadasa (Kedesh)

Hazor

Ptolemais (Acco)

Mt. HERMON

Paneas

GAULANITIS

Seleucia

Gamala

Arbela

Lake Gennesaret

Hippos

Carnaim

GALILEE

Sepphoris

Dion

Gaba

Philoteria

Abila

Mt. Tabor

Yarmuk

Gadara

Edrei

Dora

Plain of Esdraelon

Mt. Gilboa

Ephron

G I L E A D I T I S

Strato's Tower

Scythopolis (Beth-shan)

Pella

Narbata

Plain of Sharon

SAMARIA

Amathus

Ragaba

Gerasa

Samaria

Jabbok

Apollonia

Capharsaba

Sichem

Pharathon

Mt. Gerizim

Joppa

Alexandrium

Gedor

TOBIADS

Ramathaim

Beth-dagon

Timnah

Adida (Hadid)

Gophna

Apharema

Tyrus

Philadelphia (Rabbah) Free city state

Lydda (Lod)

Modein Bethel

Samaga

Beth-horon

Elasa

Mizpah

Dok

Heshbon

Jamnia (Jabneh)

Caphar-salama

Michmash

Jericho

Gazara (Gezer)

Emmaus

Adasa

Azotus (Ashdod)

Cedron

Jerusalem

Qumran

Ekron

JUDEA

Hyrcania

Medeba

Ascalon Free city state

Beth-zacharias?

Bethbasi

Marisa (Mareshah)

Adullam

Tekoa

Machaerus

Anthedon

Beth-zur

Salt Sea

Gaza

Adora

Hebron

En-gedi

Arnon

PHILISTIA

I D U M E A

Masada

Raphia

Beer-sheba

Arad

N A B A T E A N S

Charachmoba

AKRABATTENE

Zoara

Zered

1

2

3

4

5

6

The Roman World

Map 12

Limits of Roman rule or political influence at the birth of Jesus

---- **Provincial or state boundaries**

SYRIA Roman provinces

<u>LYCIA</u> Client kingdoms or states

0   100   200   300   400   500 Mls

0   200   400   600   800 Kms

© Copyright HAMMOND INCORPORATED, Maplewood, N.J.

Labels on map

Atlantic Ocean

Britannia

Rha (Volga)

Caspian Sea

Sarmatia

Germania Magna

Albis (Elbe)

Lost by Rome in 9 C.E.

Augusta Trevrorum

Rhine

Lutetia

BELGICA

LUGDUNENSIS

Gaul

Lugdunum

AQUITANIA

Burdigala

NARBONENSIS

Narbo

ALPES

RAETIA

NORICUM

PANNONIA

Aquileia

Danube

Dacia

Carpathians

Ister (Danube)

CAUCASUS

Iberia

Albania

Colchis

Artaxata

ARMENIA

PARTHIAN EMPIRE

Ctesiphon

Arabia

Red Sea

BOSPORUS KDM.

Black Sea

Sinope

Trapezus

BITHYNIA & PONTUS

Ancyra

GALATIA

CAPPADOCIA

COMMAGENE

CILICIA

Tarsus

Antioch

SYRIA

NABATEA

KDM. OF HEROD

Jerusalem

Nile

EGYPT

Memphis

Alexandria

Thebes

CYPRUS

LYCIA

PAMPHYLIA

ASIA

Pergamum

Ephesus

THRACE

Byzantium

MACEDONIA

Thessalonica

MOESIA

ILLYRICUM

Salonae

Aegean Sea

ACHAIA

Athens

Corinth

CRETA

Cyrene

CYRENAICA

Leptis Magna

AFRICA

Carthage

SICILIA

Syracuse

Tarentum

I T A L Y

Rome

Rubicon

ALPES

CORSICA AND SARDINIA

Caralis

Mare Internum (Mediterranean Sea)

Sea of Adria

NUMIDIA

Cirta

Caesarea

MAURETANIA

Tingis

BAETICA

Corduba

Hispania

LUSITANIA

Emerita Augusta

TARRACONENSIS

Tarraco

Caesarea Augusta

Map 13

Judea, Samaria, and Surrounding Areas in New Testament Times

— Political boundaries 6-44 C.E.
⊡ Cities of the Decapolis
⋈ Fortresses

0   10   20   30   40 Mls
0   20   40   60 Kms

© Copyright HAMMOND INCORPORATED, Maplewood, N.J.

A   B   C   D

Abila
ABILENE
Iturea
Sidon
MT. LEBANON
MT. HERMON
Damascus   1
Sarepta
SYRIA
Phoenicia
Paneas
Leontes
Caesarea Philippi
(Paneas)
Tyre
Ulatha
Trachonitis
Ladder
of Tyre
Cadasa
Batanea
Ecdippa
Gischala
Gaulanitis
Ptolemais
Chorazin
Bethsaida-Julias
Raphana   2
GALILEE
Capernaum
Cana   Magdala
Asochis   Sea of   Hippos
Mt. Carmel   Tiberias   Galilee   Dion
Nazareth   Sepphoris   Yarmuk   Abila
Plain   Mt.   Gadara   Capitolias
of   Tabor   Nain
Mediterranean   Esdraelon   Agrippina   Arbela   3
Dora   Scythopolis   DECAPOLIS
Crocodilion   Pella
Sea   Caesarea   Narbata   Ginae   Salim
Aenon   Jordan
SAMARIA   Gerasa
Plain of Sharon   Sebaste
(Samaria)   Amathus
Apollonia   Mt. Ebal   Jabbok
Mt. Gerizim   Sychar   4
Antipatris   Alexandrium
Joppa   Arimathea?   Phasaelis   Gadara
Lydda   Gophna   Ephraim   PEREA   Philadelphia
Archelais
Jamnia   Jericho   Betharamphtha
Emmaus?   Emmaus?   Cyprus   (Livias, Julias)
(Nicopolis)   Esbus
Azotus   Jerusalem   Bethany   Qumran   5
Bethlehem   Hyrcania   Medeba
Ascalon   JUDEA   Herodium   Lake
Marisa   Bethsura   Callirhoe
Agrippias   Bethsura   Machaerus
Gaza   Hebron   Asphaltitis
Engaddi   (Dead Sea)   Arnon
Masada   NABATEA
IDUMEA   Areopolis   6
Raphia   Bersabe
Malatha   Charachmoba

A   B   C   D

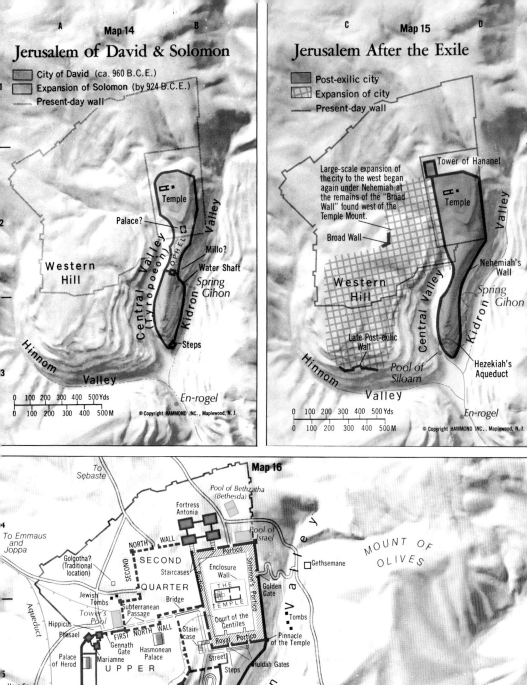

Map 14
Jerusalem of David & Solomon

- ▨ City of David (ca. 960 B.C.E.)
- ☐ Expansion of Solomon (by 924 B.C.E.)
- ⋯ Present-day wall

Temple

Palace?

Western Hill

Central Valley (Tyropoeon)

OPHEL

Millo?

Water Shaft

Spring Gihon

Kidron Valley

Hinnom Valley

Steps

En-rogel

| 0 | 100 | 200 | 300 | 400 | 500 Yds |
| 0 | 100 | 200 | 300 | 400 | 500 M |

© Copyright HAMMOND INC., Maplewood, N.J.

Map 15
Jerusalem After the Exile

- ▨ Post-exilic city
- ▦ Expansion of city
- ⋯ Present-day wall

Large-scale expansion of the city to the west began again under Nehemiah at the remains of the "Broad Wall" found west of the Temple Mount.

Broad Wall

Tower of Hananel

Temple

Western Hill

Central Valley

Nehemiah's Wall

Spring Gihon

Late Post-exilic Wall

Pool of Siloam

Kidron

Hezekiah's Aqueduct

Hinnom Valley

En-rogel

| 0 | 100 | 200 | 300 | 400 | 500 Yds |
| 0 | 100 | 200 | 300 | 400 | 500 M |

© Copyright HAMMOND INC., Maplewood, N.J.

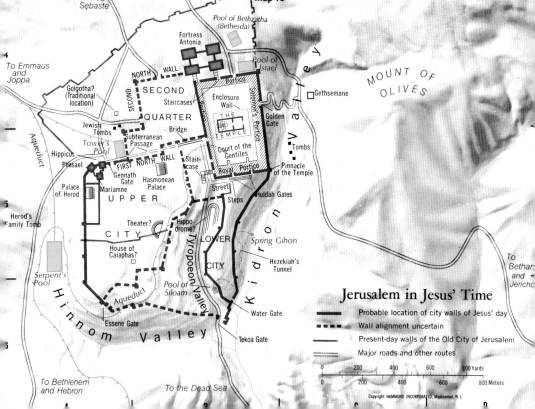

Map 16

To Sebaste

To Emmaus and Joppa

Pool of Bethzatha (Bethesda)

Fortress Antonia

Pool of Israel

Golgotha? (Traditional location)

NORTH WALL

SECOND QUARTER

Staircases

SECOND

Portico

Enclosure Wall

THE TEMPLE

Solomon's Portico

MOUNT OF OLIVES

Gethsemane

Jewish Tombs

Tower's Pool

Subterranean Passage

Bridge

Golden Gate

Court of the Gentiles

Tombs

Hippicus

Phasael

FIRST NORTH WALL

Stair-case

Pinnacle of the Temple

Palace of Herod

Gennath Gate

Mariamne

Hasmonean Palace

Royal Portico

Street

Huldah Gates

UPPER

Theater?

Hippo-drome?

Steps

Herod's Family Tomb

CITY

House of Caiaphas?

LOWER CITY

Spring Gihon

Hezekiah's Tunnel

Tyropoeon Valley

Kidron Valley

To Bethany and Jericho

Serpent's Pool

Aqueduct

Pool of Siloam

Water Gate

Essene Gate

Tekoa Gate

Hinnom Valley

To Bethlehem and Hebron

To the Dead Sea

Jerusalem in Jesus' Time

- ▬ Probable location of city walls of Jesus' day
- ▬ ▬ Wall alignment uncertain
- ▬ Present-day walls of the Old City of Jerusalem
- ≈ Major roads and other routes

| 0 | 200 | 400 | 600 | 800 Yards |
| 0 | 200 | 400 | 600 | 800 Meters |

Copyright HAMMOND INCORPORATED, Maplewood, N.J.

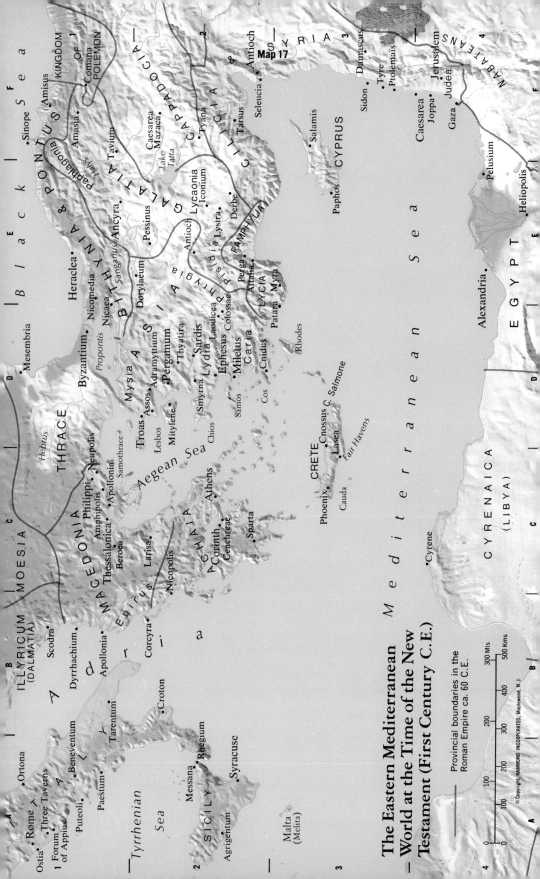

The Eastern Mediterranean World at the Time of the New Testament (First Century C.E.)

Provincial boundaries in the Roman Empire ca. 60 C.E.

© Copyright HAMMOND INCORPORATED, Maplewood, N.J.

Map 17

Archaeological Sites
in Israel and Jordan

■ Principal excavated sites

T, Tel, Tell: city site or mound
Kh, Khirbet: ruin

0   5   10   15   20   25 MIs
0   10   20   30   40 Kms

© Copyright by HAMMOND INC., Maplewood, N.J.

A | B | C | D

Map 18

Sidon
Zarephath
Damascus

Tyre

Dan   Baniyas
             (Caesarea Philippi)
T. Anafa

SYRIA

Achzib   Gush Halab   GOLAN
Kafr Bir'im
Nahariyeh   Hazor
              Meiron   Nabratein   HEIGHTS
Acco   Chorazin   Gamala
              Tabgha   Capernaum
T. Shikmona   Kh. Irbid   Sea of   Kursi
Carmel Caves T. Abu Hawam   Tiberias Galilee
              Sepphoris   Hippos
Atlit   Beth-yerah
                                  Abila
Beth   Nazareth   Umm Qeis
Shearim   (Gadara)
Wadi el-Mughara   Bosra
              Jokneam
Dor   Megiddo   Beth Alpha
                                  Ramoth-gilead
Caesarea   Taanach
              Beth-shan   Pella
T. Zeror   T. el-Hayyat

Dothan

T. el-Far'ah (N)
(Tirzah)   T. es-Saidiyeh   Jerash
                (Zarethan ?)
Samaria   Mt. Ebal
(Sebaste)   T. Deir 'Allā
        Shechem (Succoth ?)
T. Mikhal   Mt. Gerizim
Aphek   Zarethan ?   JORDAN
(Antipatris)
T. el-Qasileh
Izbet Sarta

Joppa   Shiloh

        WEST BANK   Ain Ghazzal

Mezad   Bethel   Ai   Kh. el-Mefjir   Rabbah
Hashavyahu   (Gilgal ?)   Araq el-Emir   Amma
        T. en-Nasbeh
Gezer   (Mizpah ?)   Jericho O.T.
T. Mor Tel Miqne   Gibeon Gibeah   Jericho N.T.   Heshbon
(Ekron)   Teleilat
Ashdod Yam   Timnah   Jerusalem   el-Ghassul   Mt. Nebo
        Ashdod Beth-shemesh   Qumran   Madaba
                'Ain Karim Ramet Rahel 'Ain Feshka
Ashkelon   Bethlehem
        T. es-Safi   Herodium
GAZA   (Gath ?)   Azekah Beth-zur   Kh. Iskander
STRIP   T. el-'Areini Mareshah
        Lachish   Wadi el-Murabba'at
Gaza   Caves   Mamre   Dead   Dibon
T. el-'Ajjul T. el-Hesi   'Aroer
        (Eglon ?) T. 'Aitun (Eglon ?)   Lehun
T. Jemmeh T. en-Nejileh Kh. Rabud En-gedi
        T. Beit Mirsim (Debir ?)
T. esh-Shari'ah T. Halif   Sea

T. el-Far'ah (S)   Masada
(Sharuhen)
T. Abu Matar   Beersheba   Arad-EB   Bab edh-Drah   Lejjun
        Kh. el-Mishash   Arad   Kh. el-Kerak
                                    Numeira   Kh. et-Tannur
Khalasa   Kuraub   Zoar

Mediterranean

Sea

ISRAEL

Jordan

LEBANON

A | B | C | D

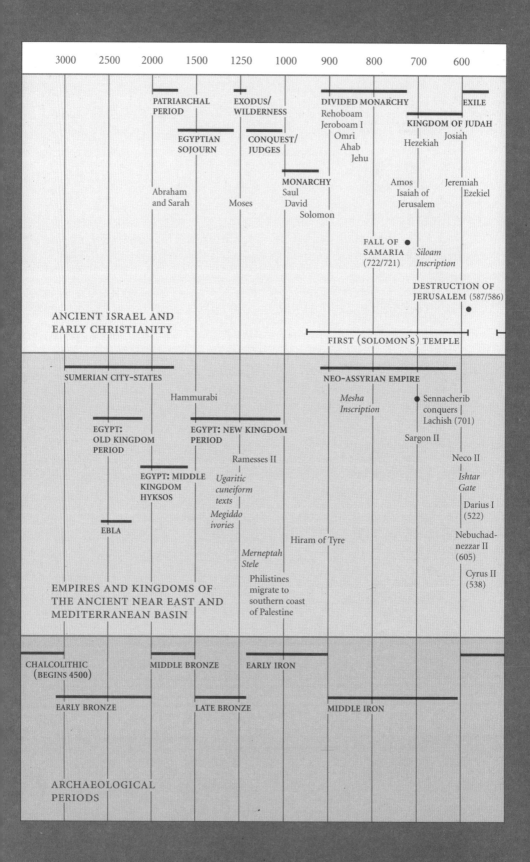

3000	2500	2000	1500	1250	1000	900	800	700	600

**PATRIARCHAL
PERIOD**

**EXODUS/
WILDERNESS**

DIVIDED MONARCHY
Rehoboam
Jeroboam I
Omri
Ahab
Jehu

EXILE

KINGDOM OF JUDAH
Josiah
Hezekiah

**EGYPTIAN
SOJOURN**

**CONQUEST/
JUDGES**

MONARCHY
Saul
David
Solomon

Abraham
and Sarah

Moses

Amos
Isaiah of
Jerusalem

Jeremiah
Ezekiel

FALL OF ●
SAMARIA
(722/721)

*Siloam
Inscription*

DESTRUCTION OF
JERUSALEM (587/586)
●

ANCIENT ISRAEL AND
EARLY CHRISTIANITY

FIRST (SOLOMON'S) TEMPLE

SUMERIAN CITY-STATES

NEO-ASSYRIAN EMPIRE

Hammurabi

*Mesha
Inscription*

● Sennacherib
conquers
Lachish (701)

**EGYPT:
OLD KINGDOM
PERIOD**

**EGYPT: NEW KINGDOM
PERIOD**

Sargon II

Neco II

Ramesses II

*Ishtar
Gate*

**EGYPT: MIDDLE
KINGDOM
HYKSOS**

*Ugaritic
cuneiform
texts*

Darius I
(522)

*Megiddo
ivories*

Nebuchad-
nezzar II
(605)

EBLA

Hiram of Tyre

*Merneptah
Stele*

Cyrus II
(538)

Philistines
migrate to
southern coast
of Palestine

EMPIRES AND KINGDOMS OF
THE ANCIENT NEAR EAST AND
MEDITERRANEAN BASIN

CHALCOLITHIC
(BEGINS 4500)

MIDDLE BRONZE

EARLY IRON

EARLY BRONZE

LATE BRONZE

MIDDLE IRON

ARCHAEOLOGICAL
PERIODS